BUTTER
PROPER
HAND

BUTTERWORTHS PROPERTY LAW HANDBOOK

Eighth edition

CONSULTANT EDITORS

JOANNE WICKS, BA (Oxon) BCL

Barrister, Wilberforce Chambers

JONATHAN DAVEY, MA (Nott), MPhil (Cantab)

Barrister, Wilberforce Chambers

MEMBERS OF THE LEXISNEXIS GROUP WORLDWIDE

United Kingdom	LexisNexis, a Division of Reed Elsevier (UK) Ltd, Halsbury House, 35 Chancery Lane, London, WC2A 1EL, and London House, 20–22 East London Street, Edinburgh EH7 4BQ
Australia	LexisNexis Butterworths, Chatswood, New South Wales
Austria	LexisNexis Verlag ARD Orac GmbH & Co KG, Vienna
Benelux	LexisNexis Benelux, Amsterdam
Canada	LexisNexis Canada, Markham, Ontario
China	LexisNexis China, Beijing and Shanghai
France	LexisNexis SA, Paris
Germany	LexisNexis Deutschland GmbH, Munster
Hong Kong	LexisNexis Hong Kong, Hong Kong
India	LexisNexis India, New Delhi
Italy	Giuffrè Editore, Milan
Japan	LexisNexis Japan, Tokyo
Malaysia	Malayan Law Journal Sdn Bhd, Kuala Lumpur
New Zealand	LexisNexis NZ Ltd, Wellington
Poland	Wydawnictwo Prawnicze LexisNexis Sp, Warsaw
Singapore	LexisNexis Singapore, Singapore
South Africa	LexisNexis Butterworths, Durban
USA	LexisNexis, Dayton, Ohio

Published by LexisNexis
This is a Butterworths title

A CIP Catalogue record for this book is available from the British Library.

ISBN: 978 1 4057 4321 1

Typeset by Columns Design Ltd, Reading, England
Printed in the UK by CPI William Clowes Beccles NR34 7TL
Visit LexisNexis at www.lexisnexis.co.uk

PREFACE

In the preface to the 7th edition we remarked upon the substantial amount of property related legislation which the legislature had seen fit to enact during the preceding two year period. By comparison, the last two years has seen fairly little legislative activity in this area: no doubt the banking crisis has diverted attention away from our field.

Of the primary legislation that has recently been enacted, it is the Housing and Regeneration Act 2008 that is most likely to affect property professionals. As well as establishing the Homes and Communities Agency, which aims to increase levels of social and affordable housing and has wide powers to acquire land, the Act also deals with a number of landlord and tenant related issues, including making changes to the "right to buy" of social tenants and reforming the law on tolerated trespassers. The scope of the Act is wide and we have therefore erred on the side of inclusion: our readers should find those parts of the Act in which they are interested included in this new edition.

In updating the Handbook we have also taken the opportunity to include provisions from a number of older Acts which time and again come into play where property disputes and transactions are concerned. Hence, the Costs of Leases Act 1958 and the Recorded Delivery Service Act 1962 appear in their entirety in this edition. Also included are additional provisions from the Consumer Credit Act 1974, the Charging Orders Act 1979, the Highways Act 1980, the Leasehold Reform, Housing and Urban Development Act 1993 and the Trustee Act 2000.

As regards the ongoing saga of Home Information Packs, the Home Information Pack (No 2) Regulations 2007, SI 2007/1667, remain in force and are printed as amended by various subsequent statutory instruments.

We are keen to ensure that the Handbook remains of relevance to those who practise and study property law and are always pleased to receive suggestions for additional material or amendments. Please feel free to email us at the addresses below.

This edition of the Handbook takes account of material to 21 August 2009, although later changes have been noted where possible.

JOANNE WICKS jwicks@wilberforce.co.uk

JONATHAN DAVEY jdavey@wilberforce.co.uk

Wilberforce Chambers
8 New Square
Lincoln's Inn
London WC2A 3QP
October 2007

CONTENTS

PART II STATUTORY INSTRUMENTS

ALPHABETICAL LIST OF CONTENTS

PART I
STATUTES

LANDLORD AND TENANT ACT 1730

(1730 c 28)

Act for the more effectual preventing Frauds committed by Tenants, and for the more easy Recovery of Rents and Renewal of Leases

1 Persons holding over lands, etc, after expiration of leases, to pay double the yearly value

In case any tenant or tenants for any term for life, lives, or years, or other person or persons who are or shall come into possession of any lands, tenements, or hereditaments by, from, or under, or by collusion with such tenant or tenants, shall wilfully hold over any lands, tenements, or hereditaments after the determination of such term or terms, and after demand made and notice in writing given for delivering the possession thereof by his or their landlords or lessors or the person or persons to whom the remainder or reversion of such lands, tenements, or hereditaments shall belong, his or their agent or agents thereunto lawfully authorized, then and in such case, such person or persons so holding over shall, for and during the time he, she, and they shall so hold over or keep the person or persons entitled out of possession of the said lands, tenements and hereditaments as aforesaid, pay to the person or persons so kept out of possession, their executors, administrators, or assigns, at the rate of double the yearly value of the lands, tenements, and hereditaments so detained, for so long time as the same are detained, to be recovered in any of his Majesty's courts of record by action …

[1]

NOTES

Words omitted repealed by the Statute Law Revision Act 1948.

2–4 (*Repealed by the Statute Law Revision Act 1867.*)

5 Method of recovering seck rents, etc

And whereas the remedy for recovering rents seck, rents of assize, and chief rents are tedious and difficult: … from and after the twenty-fourth day of June, one thousand seven hundred and thirty one, all and every person or persons, bodies politick and corporate, shall and may have the like remedy by distress and by impounding and selling the same, in cases of rents seck, rents of assize, and chief rents, which have been duly answered or paid for the space of three years, within the space of twenty years before the first day of this present session of Parliament, or shall be hereafter created, as in case or rent reserved upon lease, any laws or usage to the contrary notwithstanding.

[2]

NOTES

Repealed by the Tribunals, Courts and Enforcement Act 2007, ss 86, 146, Sch 14, para 3, Sch 23, Pt 4, as from a day to be appointed; words omitted repealed by the Statute Law Revision Act 1948.

6 (*Repealed by the Law of Property Act 1925, s 207, Sch 7.*)

7 Not to extend to Scotland

Provided always, that nothing in this Act contained shall extend to … Scotland.

[3]

NOTES

Words omitted repealed by the Statute Law Revision Act 1948.

FIRES PREVENTION (METROPOLIS) ACT 1774

(1774 c 78)

An Act … for the more effectually preventing Mischiefs by Fire within the Cities of London and Westminster and the Liberties thereof, and other the Parishes, Precincts, and Places within the Weekly Bills of Mortality, the Parishes of Saint Mary-le-bon, Paddington, Saint Pancras and Saint Luke at Chelsea, in the County of Middlesex …

NOTES

Words omitted repealed by the Statute Law Revision Act 1887.

1–82 (*Repealed by the Metropolitan Fire Brigade Act 1865, s 34.*)

83 Money insured on houses burnt how to be applied

And in order to deter and hinder ill-minded persons from wilfully setting their house or houses or other buildings on fire with a view of gaining to themselves the insurance money, whereby the lives and fortunes of many families may be lost or endangered: Be it further enacted by the authority aforesaid, that it shall and may be lawful to and for the respective governors or directors of the several insurance offices for insuring houses or other buildings against loss by fire, and they are hereby authorised and required, upon the request of any person or persons interested in or intitled unto any house or houses or other buildings which may hereafter be burnt down, demolished or damaged by fire, or upon any grounds of suspicion that the owner or owners, occupier or occupiers, or other person or persons who shall have insured such house or houses or other buildings have been guilty of fraud, or of wilfully setting their house or houses or other buildings on fire, to cause the insurance money to be laid out and expended, as far as the same will go, towards rebuilding, reinstating or repairing such house or houses or other buildings so burnt down, demolished or damaged by fire, unless the party or parties claiming such insurance money shall, within sixty days next after his, her or their claim is adjusted, give a sufficient security to the governors or directors of the insurance office where such house or houses or other buildings are insured, that the same insurance money shall be laid out and expended as aforesaid, or unless the said insurance money shall be in that time settled and disposed of to and amongst all the contending parties, to the satisfaction and approbation of such governors or directors of such insurance office respectively.

[4]

84, 85 (*Repealed by the Metropolitan Fire Brigade Act 1865, s 34.*)

86 No action to lie against a person where the fire accidentally begins

And … no action, suit or process whatever shall be had, maintained or prosecuted against any person in whose house, chamber, stable, barn or other building, or on whose estate any fire shall … accidentally begin, nor shall any recompence be made by such person for any damage suffered thereby, any law, usage or custom to the contrary notwithstanding: … provided that no contract or agreement made between landlord and tenant shall be hereby defeated or made void.

[5]

NOTES

First words omitted repealed by the Statute Law Revision Act 1888; second words omitted repealed by the Statute Law Revision Act 1948; final words omitted repealed by the Statute Law Revision Act 1958.

87–102 (*Repealed by the Metropolitan Fire Brigade Act 1865, s 34.*)

PRESCRIPTION ACT 1832

(1832 c 71)

An Act for shortening the Time of Prescription in certain cases

[1 August 1832]

1 Claims to right of common and other profits à prendre, not to be defeated after thirty years enjoyment by merely showing the commencement; after sixty years enjoyment the right to be absolute, unless had by consent or agreement

… No claim which may be lawfully made at the common law, by custom, prescription, or grant, to any right of common or other profit or benefit to be taken and enjoyed from or upon any land of our sovereign lord the King … or any land being parcel of the duchy of Lancaster or the duchy of Cornwall, or of any ecclesiastical or lay person, or body corporate, except such matters and things as are herein specially provided for, and except tithes, rent, and services, shall, where such right, profit, or benefit shall have been actually taken and enjoyed by any person claiming right thereto without interruption for the full period of thirty years, be defeated or destroyed by showing only that such right, profit, or benefit was first taken or enjoyed at any time prior to such period of thirty years, but nevertheless such claim may be defeated in any other way by which the same is now liable to be defeated; and when such right, profit, or benefit shall have been so taken and enjoyed as aforesaid for the full period of sixty years, the right thereto shall be deemed absolute and indefeasible, unless it shall appear that the same was taken and enjoyed by some consent or agreement expressly made or given for that purpose by deed or writing.

[6]

NOTES

Words omitted repealed by the Statute Law Revision Act 1890.

2 In claims of rights of way or other easement the periods to be twenty years and forty years

… No claim which may be lawfully made at the common law, by custom, prescription, or grant, to any way or other easement, or to any watercourse, or the use of any water, to be enjoyed or derived upon, over, or from any land or water of our said lord the King … or being parcel of the duchy of Lancaster or of the duchy of Cornwall, or being the property of any ecclesiastical or lay person, or body corporate, when such way or other matter as herein last before mentioned shall have been actually enjoyed by any person claiming right thereto without interruption for the full period of twenty years, shall be defeated or destroyed by showing only that such way or other matter was first enjoyed at any time prior to such period of twenty years, but nevertheless such claim may be defeated in any other way by which the same is now liable to be defeated; and where such way or other matter as herein last before mentioned shall have been so enjoyed as aforesaid for the full period of forty years, the right thereto shall be deemed absolute and indefeasible, unless it shall appear that the same was enjoyed by some consent or agreement expressly given or made for that purpose by deed or writing.

[7]

NOTES

Words omitted repealed by the Statute Law Revision (No 2) Act 1888 and the Statute Law Revision Act 1890.

3 Right to the use of light enjoyed for twenty years, indefeasible, unless shown to have been by consent

… When the access and use of light to and for any dwelling house, workshop, or other building shall have been actually enjoyed therewith for the full period of twenty years without interruption, the right thereto shall be deemed absolute and indefeasible, any local usage or custom to the contrary notwithstanding, unless it shall appear that the same was enjoyed by some consent or agreement expressly made or given for that purpose by deed or writing.

[8]

NOTES

Words omitted repealed by the Statute Law Revision (No 2) Act 1888.

4 Before mentioned periods to be deemed those next before suits for claiming to which such periods relate—What shall constitute an interruption

… Each of the respective periods of years herein-before mentioned shall be deemed and taken to be the period next before some suit or action wherein the claim or matter to which such period may relate shall have been or shall be brought into question; and … no act or other matter shall be deemed to be an interruption, within the meaning of this statute, unless the same shall have been or shall be submitted to or acquiesced in for one year after the party interrupted shall have had or shall have notice thereof, and of the person making or authorizing the same to be made.

[9]

NOTES

Words omitted repealed by the Statute Law Revision (No 2) Act 1888.

5 In actions on the case the claimant may allege his right generally, as at present. In pleas to trespass and other pleadings, etc, the period mentioned in this Act may be alleged; and exceptions, etc, to be replied to specially

… In all actions upon the case and other pleadings, wherein the party claiming may now by law allege his right generally, without averring the existence of such right from time immemorial, such general allegation shall still be deemed sufficient, and if the same shall be denied, all and every the matters in this Act mentioned and provided, which shall be applicable to the case, shall be admissible in evidence to sustain or rebut such allegation; and … in all pleadings to actions of trespass, and in all other pleadings wherein before the passing of this Act it would have been necessary to allege the right to have existed from time immemorial, it shall be sufficient to allege the enjoyment thereof as of right by the occupiers of the tenement in respect whereof the same is claimed for and during such of the periods mentioned in this Act as may be applicable to the case, and without claiming in the name or right of the owner of the fee, as is now usually done; and if the other party shall intend to rely on any proviso, exception, incapacity, disability, contract, agreement, or other matter herein-before mentioned, or on any cause or matter of fact or of law not inconsistent with the simple fact of enjoyment, the same shall be specially alleged and set forth in answer to the allegation of the party claiming, and shall not be received in evidence on any general traverse or denial of such allegation.

[10]

NOTES

Words omitted repealed by the Statute Law Revision (No 2) Act 1888.

6 Restricting the presumption to be allowed in support of claims herein provided for

... In the several cases mentioned in and provided for by this Act, no presumption shall be allowed or made in favour or support of any claim, upon proof of the exercise or enjoyment of the right or matter claimed for any less period of time or number of years than for such period or number mentioned in this Act as may be applicable to the case and to the nature of the claim.

[11]

NOTES

Words omitted repealed by the Statute Law Revision (No 2) Act 1888.

7 Proviso for infants, etc

Provided also, that the time during which any person otherwise capable of resisting any claim to any of the matters before mentioned shall have been or shall be an infant, idiot, non compos mentis, feme covert, or tenant for life, or during which any action or suit shall have been pending, and which shall have been diligently prosecuted, until abated by the death of any party or parties thereto, shall be excluded in the computation of the periods herein-before mentioned, except only in cases where the right or claim is hereby declared to be absolute and indefeasible.

[12]

NOTES

Amended in relation to Northern Ireland only by the Mental Health (Northern Ireland) Order 1986, SI 1986/595, art 136(1), Sch 5, Pt II.

8 What time to be excluded in computing the term of forty years appointed by this Act

Provided always, ... that when any land or water upon, over or from which any such way or other convenient watercourse or use of water shall have been or shall be enjoyed or derived hath been or shall be held under or by virtue of any term of life, or any term of years exceeding three years from the granting thereof, the time of the enjoyment of any such way or other matter as herein last before mentioned, during the continuance of such term, shall be excluded in the computation of the said period of forty years, in case the claim shall within three years next after the end or sooner determination of such term be resisted by any person entitled to any reversion expectant on the determination thereof.

[13]

NOTES

Words omitted repealed by the Statute Law Revision (No 2) Act 1888.

9 Extent of Act

This Act shall not extend to Scotland ...

[14]

NOTES

Words omitted repealed by the Statute Law Revision Act 1874.

10, 11 (*Repealed by the Statute Law Revision Act 1874.*)

FINES AND RECOVERIES ACT 1833

(1833 c 74)

An Act for the Abolition of Fines and Recoveries and for the Substitution of more simple Modes of Assurance

[28 August 1833]

1–14 (*S 1 outside the scope of this work; ss 2–14 repealed by the Law of Property (Amendment) Act 1924, s 10, Sch 10.*)

15 Power of actual tenants in tail, after 31st December, 1833, to dispose of entailed lands in fee simple or for less estate, saving the rights of certain persons

... After the thirty-first day of December one thousand eight hundred and thirty-three every actual tenant in tail, whether in possession, remainder, contingency or otherwise, shall have full power to dispose of for an estate in fee simple absolute or for any less estate the lands entailed, as against all persons claiming the lands entailed by force of any estate tail which shall be vested in or might be claimed by, or which but for some previous act would have been vested in or might have been claimed by, the person making the disposition at the time of his making the same, and also as against all persons, including the King's most excellent Majesty, whose estates are to take effect after the determination or in defeasance of any such estate tail; saving always the rights of all persons in respect of estates prior to the estate tail in respect of which such disposition shall be made, and the rights of all other persons, except those against whom such disposition is by this Act authorized to be made.

[15]

NOTES

Words omitted repealed by the Statute Law Revision (No 2) Act 1888.

16, 17 (*S 16 repealed by the Law of Property (Amendment) Act 1924, s 10, Sch 10; s 17 repealed by the Statute Law Revision Act 1874.*)

18 The power of disposition not to extend to certain tenants in tail restrained by 34 & 35 Hen 8, c 20, etc

Provided always, … that the power of disposition hereinbefore contained shall not extend to tenants of estates tail who, by an Act passed in the thirty-fourth and thirty-fifth years of the reign of his Majesty King Henry the Eighth, intituled "An Act to embar feigned recovery of lands wherein the King is in reversion", or by any other Act, are restrained from barring their estates tail, or to tenants in tail after possibility of issue extinct.

[16]

NOTES

Words omitted repealed by the Statute Law Revision (No 2) Act 1888.

19 Power after 31st December, 1833, to enlarge base fees; saving the rights of certain persons

… After the thirty-first day of December one thousand eight hundred and thirty-three, in every case in which an estate tail in any lands shall have been barred and converted into a base fee, either before or on or after that day, the person who, if such estate tail had not been barred, would have been actual tenant in tail of the same lands, shall have full power to dispose of such lands as against all persons, including the King's most excellent Majesty, whose estates are to take effect after the determination or in defeasance of the base fee into which the estate tail shall have been converted, so as to enlarge the base fee into a fee simple absolute; saving always the rights of all persons in respect of estates prior to the estate tail which shall have been converted into a base fee, and the rights of all other persons, except those against whom such disposition is by this Act authorized to be made.

[17]

NOTES

Words omitted repealed by the Statute Law Revision (No 2) Act 1888.

20, 21 (*Outside the scope of the work.*)

22 The owner of the first existing estate under a settlement, prior to an estate tail under the same settlement, to be the protector of the settlement

… If, at the time when there shall be a tenant in tail of lands under a settlement, there shall be subsisting in the same lands or any of them, under the same settlement, any estate for years determinable on the dropping of a life or lives, or any greater estate (not being an estate for years), prior to the estate tail, then the person who shall be the owner of the prior estate, or the first of such prior estates if more than one then subsisting under the same settlement, or who would have been so if no absolute disposition thereof had been made, (the first of such prior estates, if more than one, being for all the purposes of this Act deemed the prior estate), shall be the protector of the settlement so far as regards the lands in which such prior estate shall be subsisting, and shall for all the purposes of the Act be deemed the owner of such prior estate, although the same may have been charged or incumbered either by the owner thereof or by the settlor, or otherwise howsoever, and although the whole of the rents and profits be exhausted or required for the payment of the charges and incumbrances on such prior estate, and although such prior estate may have been absolutely disposed of by the owner thereof, or by or in consequence of the bankruptcy or insolvency of such owner, or by any other act or default of such owner; and an estate by the curtesy, in respect of the estate tail, or of any prior estate created by the same settlement, shall be deemed a prior estate under the same settlement within the meaning of this clause; and an estate by way of resulting use or trust to or for the settlor shall be deemed an estate under the same settlement within the meaning of this clause.

[18]

NOTES

Words omitted repealed by the Statute Law Revision (No 2) Act 1888.

23–33 (*Ss 23, 25–28, 32, 33 outside the scope of this work; s 24 repealed by the Law Reform* (*Married Women and Tortfeasors*) *Act 1935, s 5, Sch 2; ss 29–31 repealed by the Law of Property* (*Amendment*) *Act 1924, s 10, Sch 10.*)

34 Where there is a protector, his consent shall be requisite to enable an actual tenant in tail to create a larger estate than a base fee

Provided always, … that if at the time when any person, actual tenant in tail of lands under a settlement, but not entitled to the remainder or reversion in fee immediately expectant on the determination of his estate tail, shall be desirous of making under this Act a disposition of the lands entailed, there shall be a protector of such settlement, then and in every such case the consent of such protector shall be requisite to enable such actual tenant in tail to dispose of the lands entailed to the full extent to which he is herein-before authorized to dispose of the same; but such actual tenant in tail may, without such consent, make a disposition under this Act of the lands entailed, which shall be good against all persons who, by force of any estate tail which shall be vested in or might be claimed by, or which but for some previous act or default would have been vested in or might have been claimed by, the person making the disposition at the time of his making the same, shall claim the lands entailed.

[19]

NOTES

Words omitted repealed by the Statute Law Revision (No 2) Act 1888.

35 Where there is a base fee, and a protector, his consent shall be requisite to the exercise of the power of disposition

Provided always, … that where an estate tail shall have been converted into a base fee, in such case, so long as there shall be a protector of the settlement by which the estate tail was created, the consent of such protector shall be requisite to enable the person who would have been tenant of the estate tail if the same had not been barred to exercise, as to the lands in respect of which there shall be such protector, the power of disposition herein-before contained.

[20]

NOTES

Words omitted repealed by the Statute Law Revision (No 2) Act 1888.

36–38 (*Outside the scope of this work*)

39 Base Fees, when united with the immediate reversions, enlarged, instead of being merged

… If a base fee in any lands, and the remainder or reversion in fee in the same lands, shall at the time of the passing of this Act, or at any time afterwards, be united in the same person, and at any time after the passing of this Act there shall be no intermediate estate between the base fee and the remainder or reversion, then and in such case the base fee shall not merge, but shall be ipso facto enlarged into as large an estate as the tenant in tail, with the consent of the protector, if any, might have created by any disposition under this Act, if such remainder or reversion had been vested in any other person.

[21]

NOTES

Words omitted repealed by the Statute Law Revision (No 2) Act 1888.

40–93 (*Ss 40, 42–45, 47–49, 56–58, 60–65, 67–69, 71, 72, 92 outside the scope of this work; ss 41, 46, 50–54, 59, 66, 73, 74, 76, 79–90 repealed by the Law of Property* (*Amendment*) *Act 1924, s 10, Sch 10; ss 55, 70, 93 repealed by the Statute Law Revision Act 1874; s 75 repealed by the Supreme Court of Judicature* (*Officers*) *Act 1879, s 2, Sch 2; ss 77, 78, 91 repealed by the Statute Law* (*Repeals*) *Act 1969.*)

WILLS ACT 1837

(1837 c 26)

An Act for the amendment of the Laws with respect to Wills

[3 July 1837]

1 Meaning of certain words in this Act

… the words and expressions herein-after mentioned, which in their ordinary signification have a more confined or a different meaning, shall in this Act, except where the nature of the provisions or the context of the Act shall exclude such construction, be interpreted as follows; (that is to say,) the word "will" shall extend to a testament, and to a codicil, and to an appointment by will or by writing in the nature of a will in exercise of a power, [and also to an appointment by will of a guardian of a child], [and also to an appointment by will of a representative under section 4 of the Human Tissue Act 2004,] … and to any other testamentary disposition; and the words "real estate" shall extend to manors, advowsons, messuages, lands, tithes, rents, and hereditaments, … whether corporeal, incorporeal, or personal, … and to any estate, right, or interest (other than a chattel interest) therein; and the words "personal estate" shall extend to leasehold estates and other chattels real, and also to monies, shares of government and other funds, securities for money (not being real estates), debts, choses in action, rights, credits, goods, and all other property whatsoever which by law devolves upon the executor or administrator, and to any share or interest therein; and every word importing the singular number only shall extend and be applied to several persons or things as well as one person or thing; and every word importing the masculine gender only shall extend and be applied to a female as well as a male.

[22]

NOTES

Repealed in part, in relation to Northern Ireland, by the Statute Law Revision (Northern Ireland) Act 1954, the Statute Law Revision (Northern Ireland) Act 1976, and the Wills and Administration Proceedings (NI) Order 1994, SI 1994/1899, art 38, Sch 3.

First words omitted repealed by the Statute Law Revision Act 1893, s 1, Schedule; words in first pair of square brackets substituted by the Children Act 1989, s 108(5), (6), Sch 13, para 1, Sch 14, para 1; words in second pair of square brackets inserted by the Human Tissue Act 2004, s 56, Sch 6, para 1; second and third words omitted repealed by the Statute Law (Repeals) Act 1969, s 1, Schedule, Pt III; final words omitted repealed by the Trusts of Land and Appointment of Trustees 1996, s 25(2), Sch 4, subject to savings in s 25(4), (5) thereof.

2 (*Repealed by the Statute Law Revision Act 1874.*)

3 All property may be disposed of by will

… it shall be lawful for every person to devise, bequeath, or dispose of, by his will executed in manner herein-after required, all real estate and all personal estate which he shall be entitled to, either at law or in equity, at the time of his death, and which, if not so devised, bequeathed, and disposed of, would devolve … upon his executor or administrator; and … the power hereby given shall extend … to all contingent, executory or other future interests in any real or personal estate, whether the testator may or may not be ascertained as the person or one of the persons in whom the same respectively may become vested, and whether he may be entitled thereto under the instrument by which the same respectively were created, or under any disposition thereof by deed or will; and also to all rights of entry for conditions broken, and other rights of entry; and also to such of the same estates, interests, and rights respectively, and other real and personal estate, as the testator may be entitled to at the time of his death, notwithstanding that he may become entitled to the same subsequently to the execution of his will.

[23]

NOTES

Repealed, in relation to Northern Ireland, by the Wills and Administration Proceedings (NI) Order 1994, SI 1994/1899, art 38, Sch 3.

First and third words omitted repealed by the Statute Law Revision (No 2) Act 1888; second and fourth words omitted repealed by the Statute Law (Repeals) Act 1969.

4–6 (*Repealed by the Statute Law* (*Repeals*) *Act 1969.*)

7 No will of a person under age valid

… no will made by any person under the age of [eighteen years] shall be valid.

[24]

NOTES

Repealed, in relation to Northern Ireland, by the Wills and Administration Proceedings (NI) Order 1994, SI 1994/1899, art 38, Sch 3.

Words omitted repealed by the Statute Law Revision (No 2) Act 1888; words in square brackets substituted by the Family Law Reform Act 1969, s 3(1)(a).

8 (*Repealed by the Statute Law* (*Repeals*) *Act 1969.*)

[9 Signing and attestation of wills

No will shall be valid unless—

(a) it is in writing, and signed by the testator, or by some other person in his presence and by his direction; and
(b) it appears that the testator intended by his signature to give effect to the will; and
(c) the signature is made or acknowledged by the testator in the presence of two or more witnesses present at the same time; and
(d) each witness either—
  (i) attests and signs the will; or
  (ii) acknowledges his signature,

in the presence of the testator (but not necessarily in the presence of any other witness),

but no form of attestation shall be necessary.]

[25]

NOTES

Substituted, in relation to England and Wales, by the Administration of Justice Act 1982, s 17.

Repealed, in relation to Northern Ireland, by the Wills and Administration Proceedings (NI) Order 1994, SI 1994/1899, art 38, Sch 3.

10 Appointments by will to be executed like other wills, and to be valid, although other required solemnities are not observed

… no appointment made by will, in exercise of any power, shall be valid, unless the same be executed in manner herein-before required; and every will executed in manner herein-before required shall, so far as respects the execution and attestation thereof, be a valid execution of a power of appointment by will, notwithstanding it shall have been expressly required that a will made in exercise of such power should be executed with some additional or other form of execution or solemnity.

[26]

NOTES

Repealed, in relation to Northern Ireland, by the Wills and Administration Proceedings (NI) Order 1994, SI 1994/1899, art 38, Sch 3.

Words omitted repealed by the Statute Law Revision (No 2) Act 1888.

11 Saving as to wills of soldiers and mariners

Provided always, … that any soldier being in actual military service, or any mariner or seaman being at sea, may dispose of his personal estate as he might have done before the making of this Act.

[27]

NOTES

Words omitted repealed by the Statute Law Revision (No 2) Act 1888.

12 (*Repealed by the Admiralty, &c Acts Repeal Act 1865, s 1.*)

13 Publication of will not requisite

… every will executed in manner herein-before required shall be valid without any other publication thereof.

[28]

NOTES

Repealed, in relation to Northern Ireland, by the Wills and Administration Proceedings (NI) Order 1994, SI 1994/1899, art 38, Sch 3.

Words omitted repealed by the Statute Law Revision (No 2) Act 1888.

14 Will not be void on account of incompetency of attesting witness

… if any person who shall attest the execution of a will shall at the time of the execution thereof or at any time afterwards be incompetent to be admitted a witness to prove the execution thereof, such will shall not on that account be invalid.

[29]

NOTES

Repealed, in relation to Northern Ireland, by the Wills and Administration Proceedings (NI) Order 1994, SI 1994/1899, art 38, Sch 3.

Words omitted repealed by the Statute Law Revision (No 2) Act 1888.

15 Gifts to an attesting witness, or his or her wife or husband, to be void

… if any person shall attest the execution of any will to whom or to whose wife or husband any beneficial devise, legacy, estate, interest, gift, or appointment, of or affecting any real or personal estate (other than and except charges and directions for the payment of any debt or debts), shall be thereby given or made, such devise, legacy, estate, interest, gift, or appointment shall, so far only as concerns such person attesting the execution of such will, or the wife or husband of such person, or any person claiming under such person or wife or husband, be utterly null and void, and such person so attesting shall be admitted as a witness to prove the execution of such will, or to prove the validity or invalidity thereof, notwithstanding such devise, legacy, estate, interest, gift, or appointment mentioned in such will.

[30]

NOTES

Repealed, in relation to Northern Ireland, by the Wills and Administration Proceedings (NI) Order 1994, SI 1994/1899, art 38, Sch 3.

Words omitted repealed by the Statute Law Revision (No 2) Act 1888.

Application: the Civil Partnership Act 2004, s 71, Sch 4, Pt 1, paras 1, 3, 5 provides that this section applies to the attestation of a will by a person to whose civil partner there is given or made any such disposition as it applies in relation to a person to whose spouse there is given or made any such disposition.

16 Creditor attesting a will charging estate with debts shall be admitted a witness

… in case by any will any real or personal estate shall be charged with any debt or debts, and any creditor, or the wife or husband [or civil partner] of any creditor, whose debt is so charged, shall attest the execution of such will, such creditor notwithstanding such charge shall be admitted a witness to prove the execution of such will, or to prove the validity or invalidity thereof.

[31]

NOTES

Repealed, in relation to Northern Ireland, by the Wills and Administration Proceedings (NI) Order 1994, SI 1994/1899, art 38, Sch 3.

Words omitted repealed by the Statute Law Revision (No 2) Act 1888; words in square brackets inserted by the Civil Partnership Act 2004, s 71, Sch 4, Pt 1, paras 1, 4, 5.

17 Executor shall be admitted a witness

… no person shall, on account of his being an executor of a will, be incompetent to be admitted a witness to prove the execution of such will, or a witness to prove the validity or invalidity thereof.

[32]

NOTES

Repealed, in relation to Northern Ireland, by the Wills and Administration Proceedings (NI) Order 1994, SI 1994/1899, art 38, Sch 3.

Words omitted repealed by the Statute Law Revision (No 2) Act 1888.

[18 Will to be revoked by marriage

(1) Subject to subsections (2) to (4) below, a will shall be revoked by the testator's marriage.

(2) A disposition in a will in exercise of a power of appointment shall take effect notwithstanding the testator's subsequent marriage unless the property so appointed would in default of appointment pass to his personal representatives.

(3) Where it appears from a will that at the time it was made the testator was expecting to be married to a particular person and that he intended that the will should not be revoked by the marriage, the will shall not be revoked by his marriage to that person.

(4) Where it appears from a will that at the time it was made the testator was expecting to be married to a particular person and that he intended that a disposition in the will should not be revoked by his marriage to that person,—

(a) that disposition shall take effect notwithstanding the marriage; and

(b) any other disposition in the will shall take effect also, unless it appears from the will that the testator intended the disposition to be revoked by the marriage.]

[33]

NOTES

Substituted, in relation to England and Wales, by the Administration of Justice Act 1982, s 18(1).

Repealed, in relation to Northern Ireland, by the Wills and Administration Proceedings (NI) Order 1994, SI 1994/1899, art 38, Sch 3.

[18A Effect of dissolution or annulment of marriage on wills

(1) Where, after a testator has made a will, *a decree* [an order or decree] of a court [of civil jurisdiction in England and Wales] dissolves or annuls his marriages [or his marriage is dissolved or annulled and the divorce or annulment is entitled to recognition in England and Wales by virtue of Part II of the Family Law Act 1986],—

[(a) provisions of the will appointing executors or trustees or conferring a power of appointment, if they appoint or confer the power on the former spouse, shall take effect as if the former spouse had died on the date on which the marriage is dissolved or annulled, and

(b) any property which, or an interest in which, is devised or bequeathed to the former spouse shall pass as if the former spouse had died on that date,]

except in so far as a contrary intention appears by the will.

(2) Subsection (1)(b) above is without prejudice to any right of the former spouse to apply for financial provision under the Inheritance (Provision for Family and Dependants) Act 1975.

(3) …]

[34]

NOTES

Inserted, in relation to England and Wales, by the Administration of Justice Act 1982, s 18(2).

Sub-s (1): first words in italics substituted by subsequent words in square brackets by the Family Law Act 1996, s 66(1), Sch 8, para 1, subject to savings in s 66(2), Sch 9, para 5 thereof, as from a day to be appointed; second words in square brackets inserted, and third words in square brackets substituted, by the Family Law Act 1986, s 53; paras (a), (b) substituted by the Law Reform (Succession) Act 1995, s 3.

Sub-s (3): repealed by the Law Reform (Succession) Act 1995, s 5, Schedule.

[18B Will to be revoked by civil partnership

(1) Subject to subsections (2) to (6), a will is revoked by the formation of a civil partnership between the testator and another person.

(2) A disposition in a will in exercise of a power of appointment takes effect despite the formation of a subsequent civil partnership between the testator and another person unless the property so appointed would in default of appointment pass to the testator's personal representatives.

(3) If it appears from a will—

(a) that at the time it was made the testator was expecting to form a civil partnership with a particular person, and

(b) that he intended that the will should not be revoked by the formation of the civil partnership,

the will is not revoked by its formation.

(4) Subsections (5) and (6) apply if it appears from a will—

(a) that at the time it was made the testator was expecting to form a civil partnership with a particular person, and

(b) that he intended that a disposition in the will should not be revoked by the formation of the civil partnership.

(5) The disposition takes effect despite the formation of the civil partnership.

(6) Any other disposition in the will also takes effect, unless it appears from the will that the testator intended the disposition to be revoked by the formation of the civil partnership.]

[35]

NOTES

Commencement: 5 December 2005.

Inserted by the Civil Partnership Act 2004, s 71, Sch 4, Pt 1, paras 1, 2, 5.

Disapplication: this section is disapplied to a will made before 5 December 2005 by a person who has registered a recognised overseas relationship under the relevant law before that date, by the Civil Partnership (Treatment of Overseas Relationships No 2) Order 2005, SI 2005/3284, art 2(1).

[18C Effect of dissolution or annulment of civil partnership on wills

(1) This section applies if, after a testator has made a will—

(a) a court of civil jurisdiction in England and Wales dissolves his civil partnership or makes a nullity order in respect of it, or

(b) his civil partnership is dissolved or annulled and the dissolution or annulment is entitled to recognition in England and Wales by virtue of Chapter 3 of Part 5 of the Civil Partnership Act 2004.

(2) Except in so far as a contrary intention appears by the will—

(a) provisions of the will appointing executors or trustees or conferring a power of appointment, if they appoint or confer the power on the former civil partner, take effect as if the former civil partner had died on the date on which the civil partnership is dissolved or annulled, and

(b) any property which, or an interest in which, is devised or bequeathed to the former civil partner shall pass as if the former civil partner had died on that date.

(3) Subsection (2)(b) does not affect any right of the former civil partner to apply for financial provision under the Inheritance (Provision for Family and Dependants) Act 1975.]

[36]

NOTES

Commencement: 5 December 2005.

Inserted by the Civil Partnership Act 2004, s 71, Sch 4, Pt 1, paras 1, 2, 5.

19 No will to be revoked by presumption from altered circumstances

… no will shall be revoked by any presumption of an intention on the ground of an alteration in circumstances.

[37]

NOTES

Repealed, in relation to Northern Ireland, by the Wills and Administration Proceedings (NI) Order 1994, SI 1994/1899, art 38, Sch 3.

Words omitted repealed by the Statute Law Revision (No 2) Act 1888.

20 No will to be revoked otherwise than as aforesaid or by another will or codicil, or by destruction thereof

… no will or codicil, or any part thereof, shall be revoked otherwise than as aforesaid, or by another will or codicil executed in manner herein-before required, or by some writing declaring an intention to revoke the same and executed in the manner in which a will is herein-before required to be executed, or by the burning, tearing, or otherwise destroying the same by the testator, or by some person in his presence and by his direction, with the intention of revoking the same.

[38]

NOTES

Repealed, in relation to Northern Ireland, by the Wills and Administration Proceedings (NI) Order 1994, SI 1994/1899, art 38, Sch 3.

Words omitted repealed by the Statute Law Revision (No 2) Act 1888.

21 No alteration in a will after execution except in certain cases, shall have any effect unless executed as a will

… no obliteration, interlineation, or other alteration made in any will after the execution thereof shall be valid or have any effect, except so far as the words or effect of the will before such alteration shall not be apparent, unless such alteration shall be executed in like manner as herein-before is required for the execution of the will; but the will, with such alteration as part thereof, shall be deemed to be duly executed if the signature of the testator and the subscription of the witnesses be made in the margin or on some other part of the will opposite or near to such alteration, or at the foot or end of or opposite to a memorandum referring to such alteration, and written at the end of some other part of the will.

[39]

NOTES

Repealed, in relation to Northern Ireland, by the Wills and Administration Proceedings (NI) Order 1994, SI 1994/1899, art 38, Sch 3.

Words omitted repealed by the Statute Law Revision (No 2) Act 1888.

22 No revoked will shall be revived otherwise than by re-execution or a codicil, &c

… no will or codicil, or any part thereof, which shall be in any manner revoked, shall be revived otherwise than by the re-execution thereof or by a codicil executed in manner herein-before required and showing an intention to revive the same; and when any will or codicil which shall be partly revoked, and afterwards wholly revoked, shall be revived, such revival shall not extend to so much thereof as shall have been revoked before the revocation of the whole thereof, unless an intention to the contrary shall be shown.

[40]

NOTES

Repealed, in relation to Northern Ireland, by the Wills and Administration Proceedings (NI) Order 1994, SI 1994/1899, art 38, Sch 3.

Words omitted repealed by the Statute Law Revision (No 2) Act 1888.

23 Subsequent conveyance or other act not to prevent operation of will

… no conveyance or other act made or done subsequently to the execution of a will of or relating to any real or personal estate therein comprised, except an act by which such will shall be revoked as aforesaid, shall prevent the operation of the will with respect to such estate or interest in such real or personal estate as the testator shall have power to dispose of by will at the time of his death.

[41]

NOTES

Repealed, in relation to Northern Ireland, by the Wills and Administration Proceedings (NI) Order 1994, SI 1994/1899, art 38, Sch 3.

Words omitted repealed by the Statute Law Revision (No 2) Act 1888.

24 Wills shall be construed, as to the estate comprised, to speak from the death of the testator

… every will shall be construed, with reference to the real estate and personal estate comprised in it, to speak and take effect as if it had been executed immediately before the death of the testator, unless a contrary intention shall appear by the will.

[42]

NOTES

Repealed, in relation to Northern Ireland, by the Wills and Administration Proceedings (NI) Order 1994, SI 1994/1899, art 38, Sch 3.

Words omitted repealed by the Statute Law Revision (No 2) Act 1888.

25 Residuary devises shall include estates comprised in lapsed and void devises

… unless a contrary intention shall appear by the will, such real estate or interest therein as shall be comprised or intended to be comprised in any devise in such will contained, which shall fail or be void by reason of the death of the devisee in the lifetime of the testator, or by reason of such devise being contrary to law or otherwise incapable of taking effect shall be included in the residuary devise (if any) contained in such will.

[43]

NOTES

Repealed, in relation to Northern Ireland, by the Wills and Administration Proceedings (NI) Order 1994, SI 1994/1899, art 38, Sch 3.

Words omitted repealed by the Statute Law Revision (No 2) Act 1888.

26 A general devise of the testator's lands shall include copyhold and leasehold as well as freehold lands, in the absence of a contrary intention

… a devise of the land of the testator, or of the land of the testator in any place or in the occupation of any person mentioned in his will, or otherwise described in a general manner, and any other general devise which would describe a … leasehold estate if the testator had no freehold estate which could be described by it, shall be construed to include the … leasehold estates of the testator, or his … leasehold estates, or any of them, to which such description shall extend, as the case may be, as well as freehold estates, unless a contrary intention shall appear by the will.

[44]

NOTES

Repealed, in relation to Northern Ireland, by the Wills and Administration Proceedings (NI) Order 1994, SI 1994/1899, art 38, Sch 3.

First words omitted repealed by the Statute Law Revision (No 2) Act 1888; other words omitted repealed by the Statute Law (Repeals) Act 1969.

27 A general gift of realty or personalty shall include property over which the testator has a general power of appointment

… a general devise of the real estate of the testator, or of the real estate of the testator in any place or in the occupation of any person mentioned in his will, or otherwise described in a general manner, shall be construed to include any real estate, or any real estate to which such description shall extend (as the case may be), which he may have power to appoint in any manner he may think proper, and shall operate as an execution of such power, unless a contrary intention shall appear by the will; and in like manner a bequest of the personal estate of the testator, or any bequest of personal property described in a general manner, shall be construed to include any personal estate, or any personal estate to which such description shall extend (as the case may be), which he may have power to appoint in any manner he may think proper, and shall operate as an execution of such power, unless a contrary intention shall appear by the will.

[45]

NOTES

Repealed, in relation to Northern Ireland, by the Wills and Administration Proceedings (NI) Order 1994, SI 1994/1899, art 38, Sch 3.

Words omitted repealed by the Statute Law Revision (No 2) Act 1888.

28 A devise of real estate without any words of limitation shall pass the fee, &c

… where any real estate shall be devised to any person without any words of limitation, such devise shall be construed to pass the fee simple, or other the whole estate or interest which the testator had power to dispose of by will in such real estate, unless a contrary intention shall appear by the will.

[46]

NOTES

Repealed, in relation to Northern Ireland, by the Wills and Administration Proceedings (NI) Order 1994, SI 1994/1899, art 38, Sch 3.

Words omitted repealed by the Statute Law Revision (No 2) Act 1888.

29 The words "die without issue," or "die without leaving issue," &c shall mean a want or failure of issue in the lifetime or at the death of the person, except in certain cases

… in any devise or bequest of real or personal estate the words "die without issue" or "die without leaving issue," or "have no issue," or any other words which may import either a want or failure of issue of any person in his lifetime or at the time of his death, or an indefinite failure of his issue, shall be construed to mean a want or failure of issue in the lifetime or at the time of the death of such person, and not an indefinite failure of his issue, unless a contrary intention shall appear by the will, by reason of such person having a prior estate tail, or of a preceding gift, being, without any implication arising from such words, a limitation of an estate tail to such person or issue, or otherwise: Provided, that this Act shall not extend to cases where such words as aforesaid import if no issue described in a preceding gift shall be born, or if there shall be no issue who shall live to attain the age or otherwise answer the description required for obtaining a vested estate by a preceding gift to such issue.

[47]

NOTES

Repealed, in relation to Northern Ireland, by the Wills and Administration Proceedings (NI) Order 1994, SI 1994/1899, art 38, Sch 3.

Words omitted repealed by the Statute Law Revision (No 2) Act 1888.

30 Devise of realty to trustees or executors shall pass the fee, &c, except in certain cases

… where any real estate (other than or not being a presentation to a church) shall be devised to any trustee or executor, such devise shall be construed to pass the fee simple or other the whole estate or interest which the testator had power to dispose of by will in such real estate, unless a definite term of years, absolute or determinable, or an estate of freehold, shall thereby be given to him expressly or by implication.

[48]

NOTES

Repealed, in relation to Northern Ireland, by the Wills and Administration Proceedings (NI) Order 1994, SI 1994/1899, art 38, Sch 3.

Words omitted repealed by the Statute Law Revision (No 2) Act 1888.

31 Trustees under an unlimited devise, where the trust may endure beyond the life of a person beneficially entitled for life, shall take the fee, &c

… where any real estate shall be devised to a trustee, without any express limitation of the estate to be taken by such trustee, and the beneficial interest in such real estate, or in the surplus rents and profits thereof, shall not be given to any person for life, or such beneficial interest shall be given to any person for life, but the purposes of the trust may continue beyond the life of such person, such devise shall be construed to vest in such trustee the fee simple, or other the whole legal estate which the testator had power to dispose of by will in such real estate, and not an estate determinable when the purposes of the trust shall be satisfied.

[49]

NOTES

Repealed, in relation to Northern Ireland, by the Wills and Administration Proceedings (NI) Order 1994, SI 1994/1899, art 38, Sch 3.

Words omitted repealed by the Statute Law Revision (No 2) Act 1888.

32 (*Repealed by the Trusts of Land and Appointment of Trustees Act 1996, s 25(2), Sch 4, subject to savings in s 25(4), (5) thereof; repealed, in relation to Northern Ireland, by the Wills and Administration Proceedings (NI) Order 1994, SI 1994/1899, art 38, Sch 3.*)

[33 Gifts to children or other issue who leave issue living at the testator's death shall not lapse

(1) Where—

(a) a will contains a devise or bequest to a child or remoter descendant of the testator; and

(b) the intended beneficiary dies before the testator, leaving issue; and

(c) issue of the intended beneficiary are living at the testator's death,

then, unless a contrary intention appears by the will, the devise or bequest shall take effect as a devise or bequest to the issue living at the testator's death.

(2) Where—

(a) a will contains a devise or bequest to a class of person consisting of children or remoter descendants of the testator; and

(b) a member of the class dies before the testator, leaving issue, and

(c) issue of that member are living at the testator's death,

then, unless a contrary intention appears by the will, the devise or bequest shall take effect as if the class included the issue of its deceased member living at the testator's death.

(3) Issue shall take under this section through all degrees, according to their stock, in equal shares if more than one, any gift or share which their parent would have taken and so that no issue shall take whose parent is living at the testator's death and that no issue shall take whose parent is living at the testator's death and so capable of taking.

(4) For the purposes of this section—

(a) the illegitimacy of any person is to be disregarded; and

(b) a person conceived before the testator's death and born living thereafter is to be taken to have been living at the testator's death.]

[50]

NOTES

Substituted, in relation to England and Wales, by the Administration of Justice Act 1982, s 19.

Repealed, in relation to Northern Ireland, by the Wills and Administration Proceedings (NI) Order 1994, SI 1994/1899, art 38, Sch 3.

34 Act not to extend to wills made before 1838, nor to estates pur autre vie of persons who die before 1838

… this Act shall not extend to any will made before the first day of January one thousand eight hundred and thirty-eight; and every will re-executed or republished, or revived by any codicil, shall for the purposes of this Act be deemed to have been made at the time at which the same shall be so re-executed, republished or revived; and this Act shall not extend to any estate pur autre vie of any person who shall die before the first day of January one thousand eight hundred and thirty-eight.

[51]

NOTES

Repealed, in relation to Northern Ireland, by the Wills and Administration Proceedings (NI) Order 1994, SI 1994/1899, art 38, Sch 3.

Words omitted repealed by the Statute Law Revision (No 2) Act 1888.

35 Act not to extend to Scotland

… this Act shall not extend to Scotland.

[52]

NOTES

Repealed, in relation to Northern Ireland, by the Wills and Administration Proceedings (NI) Order 1994, SI 1994/1899, art 38, Sch 3.

Words omitted repealed by the Statute Law Repeals (No 2) Act 1888.

36 (*Repealed by the Statute Law Revision Act 1874.*)

SCHOOL SITES ACT 1841

(1841 c 38)

An Act to afford further facilities for the Conveyance and Endowment of Sites for Schools

[21 June 1841]

1 (*Repealed by the Statute Law Revision (No 2) Act 1874.*)

2 Landlords empowered to convey land to be used as sites for schools, etc

… Any person, being seised in fee simple, fee tail, or for life, of and in any manor or lands of freehold, copyhold, or customary tenure, and having the beneficial interest therein, … may grant, convey, or enfranchise by way of gift, sale, or exchange, in fee simple or for a term of years, any quantity not exceeding one acre of such land, as a site for a school for the education of poor persons, or for the residence of the schoolmaster or schoolmistress, or otherwise for the purposes of the education of such poor persons in religious and useful knowledge; provided that no such grant made by any person seised only for life of and in any such manor or lands shall be valid, unless the person next entitled to the same in remainder, in fee simple or fee tail, (if legally competent,) shall be a party to and join in such grant: *Provided also, that where any portion of waste or commonable land shall be gratuitously conveyed by any lord or lady of a manor for any such purposes as aforesaid, the rights and interest of all persons in the said land shall be barred and divested by such conveyance;* Provided also, that upon the said land so granted as aforesaid, or any part thereof, ceasing to be used for the purposes in this Act mentioned, the same shall thereupon immediately revert to and become a portion of the said estate held in fee simple or otherwise, or of any manor or land as aforesaid, as fully to all intents and purposes as if this Act had not been passed, any thing herein contained to the contrary notwithstanding.

[53]

NOTES

First words omitted repealed by the Statute Law Revision (No 2) Act 1888; second words omitted repealed by the Education (Scotland) Act 1945, Sch 5; words in italics repealed, in relation to England and Wales, by the Commons Act 2006, ss 48(2)(b), 53, Sch 6, Pt 3, as from 1 October 2007 (in relation to England) and as from a day to be appointed (in relation to Wales).

3–13 (*Ss 3, 5–11, 13 outside the scope of this work; s 4 repealed by the Statute Law Revision Act 1874 (No 2); s 12 repealed by the Education (Scotland) Act 1945, ss 77, 88, Sch 5.*)

14 Trustees of schools may sell or exchange lands or buildings

… When any land or building shall have been or shall be given or acquired under the provisions of the said first-recited Act or this Act, or shall be held in trust for the purposes aforesaid, and it shall be deemed advisable to sell or exchange the same for any other more convenient or eligible site, it shall be lawful for the trustees in whom the legal estate in the said land or building shall be vested, by the direction or with the consent of the managers and directors of the said school, if any such there be, to sell or exchange the said land or building, or part thereof, for other land or building suitable to the purposes of their trust, and to receive on any exchange any sum of money by way of effecting an equality of exchange, and to apply the money arising from such sale or given on such exchange in the purchase of another site, or in the improvement of other premises used or to be used for the purposes of such trust; provided that where the land shall have been given by any ecclesiastical corporation sole, the consent of the bishop of the diocese shall be required to be given to such sale or exchange before the same shall take place: Provided also, that where a portion of any parliamentary grant shall have been or shall be applied towards the erection of any school, no sale or exchange thereof shall take place [unless the Secretary of State consents].

[54]

NOTES

Words omitted repealed by the Statute Law Revision (No 2) Act 1888; words in square brackets substituted by the Statute Law (Repeals) Act 1978.

Transfer of functions: functions of the Secretary of State, so far as exercisable in relation to Wales, transferred to the National Assembly for Wales, by the National Assembly for Wales (Transfer of Functions) Order 1999, SI 1999/672, art 2, Sch 1.

15–23 (*Ss 17, 20, 21 outside the scope of this work; ss 16, 23 repealed by the Statute Law Revision Act 1874 (No 2); ss 15, 19 repealed by the Statute Law (Repeals) Act 1978; s 18 repealed* *by the Rent Act 1965, s 52, Sch 7, Pt II; s 22 repealed by the Statue Law Revision Act 1874* (*No 2*) *and the Education* (*Scotland*) *Act 1945, ss 77, 88, Sch 5.*)

LANDS CLAUSES CONSOLIDATION ACT 1845

(1845 c 18)

An Act for consolidating in One Act certain Provisions usually inserted in Acts authorizing the taking of Lands for Undertakings of a public Nature

[8 May 1845]

1–67 (*Ss 1–4, 6–9, 11–22, 58, 61–67 outside the scope of this work; s 5 repealed by the Statute Law* (*Repeals*) *Act 1993; s 10 repealed by the Rentcharges Act 1977, s 17*(*2*)*, Sch 2; ss 23–57 repealed by the Compulsory Purchase Act 1965, s 39*(*4*)*, Sch 8, Pt III and the Repeal of Unnecessary Laws Act* (*Northern Ireland*) *1953, ss 1, 2, Schedule, Pt II; ss 54–56 were previously repealed by the Juries Act 1949, ss 18*(*2*)*, 35*(*3*)*, Sch 2, Pt III; ss 59, 60 repealed by the Statute Law* (*Repeals*) *Act 1974.*)

68 Compensation to be settled by arbitration or jury, at the option of the party claiming compensation

If any party shall be entitled to any compensation in respect of any lands, or of any interest therein which shall have been taken for or injuriously affected by the execution of the works, and for which the promoters of the undertaking shall not have made satisfaction under the provisions of this or the special Act, or any Act incorporated therewith, … such party may have the same settled …

[55]

NOTES

Words omitted repealed by the Compulsory Purchase Act 1965, s 39(4), Sch 8, Pt III.

Disapplication: this Act does not apply to the acquisition of land under s 6(1) of the Crossrail Act 2008; see s 6(1), (3), Sch 6, Pt 2, para 1 of that Act.

69–80 (*Outside the scope of this work.*)

Conveyances

81 Form of Conveyances

And with respect to the conveyances of lands, be it enacted as follows:

Conveyances of lands to be purchased under the provisions of this or the special Act, or any Act incorporated therewith, may be according to the forms in the schedules (A) and (B) respectively to this Act annexed, or as near thereto as the circumstances of the case will admit, or by deed in any other form which the promoters of the undertaking may think fit; and all conveyances made according to the forms in the said schedules, or as near thereto as the circumstances of the case will admit, shall be effectual to vest the lands thereby conveyed in the promoters of the undertaking, and shall operate … to bar and to destroy all such estates tail, and all other estates, rights, titles, remainders, reversions, limitations, trusts, and interests whatsoever, of and in the lands comprised in such conveyances, which shall have been purchased or compensated for by the consideration therein mentioned …

[56]

NOTES

Words omitted repealed by the Compulsory Purchase Act 1965, ss 39(4), 40(3), Sch 8, Pt II.

Disapplication: this Act does not apply to the acquisition of land under s 6(1) of the Crossrail Act 2008; see s 6(1), (3), Sch 6, Pt 2, para 1 of that Act.

82–126 (*Ss 82–94, 99–125 outside the scope of this work; ss 95–98 repealed by the Compulsory Purchase Act 1965, s 39*(*4*)*, Sch 8, Pt II and the Statute Law Revision Act* (*Northern Ireland*) *1954; s 126 repealed by the Administration of Justice Act, s 34, Sch 2.*)

Sale of Superfluous Land

127 Lands not wanted to be sold within 10 years after expiration of time limited for completion of works, or in default to vest in owners of adjoining lands

And with respect to lands acquired by the promoters of the undertaking under the provisions of this or the special Act, or any Act incorporated therewith, but which shall not be required for the purposes thereof, be it enacted as follows:

Within the prescribed period, or if no period be prescribed within ten years after the expiration of the time limited by the special Act for the completion of the works, the promoters of the undertaking shall absolutely sell and dispose of all such superfluous lands, and apply the purchase money arising from such sales to the purposes of the special Act; and in default thereof all such superfluous lands remaining unsold at the expiration of such period shall thereupon vest in and become the property of the owners of the lands adjoining thereto, in proportion to the extent of their lands respectively adjoining the same.

[57]

NOTES

Disapplication: this Act does not apply to the acquisition of land under s 6(1) of the Crossrail Act 2008; see s 6(1), (3), Sch 6, Pt 2, para 1 of that Act.

128 Lands not in a town or built upon, etc, to be offered to owner of lands from which they were originally taken, or to adjoining owners

Before the promoters of the undertaking dispose of any such superfluous lands they shall, unless such lands be situate within a town, or be lands built upon or used for building purposes, first offer to sell the same to the person then entitled to the lands (if any) from which the same were originally severed; or if such person refuse to purchase the same, or cannot after diligent inquiry be found, then the like offer shall be made to the person or to the several persons whose lands shall immediately adjoin the lands so proposed to be sold, such persons being capable of entering into a contract for the purchase of such lands; and where more than one such person shall be entitled to such right of pre-emption such offer shall be made to such persons in succession, one after another, in such order as the promoters of the undertaking shall think fit.

[58]

NOTES

Disapplication: this Act does not apply to the acquisition of land under s 6(1) of the Crossrail Act 2008; see s 6(1), (3), Sch 6, Pt 2, para 1 of that Act.

129 Right of pre-emption to be claimed within six weeks from offer—Evidence of refusal, etc, to exercise right

If any such persons be desirous of purchasing such lands, then within six weeks after such offer of sale they shall signify their desire in that behalf to the promoters of the undertaking; or if they decline such offer, or if for six weeks they neglect to signify their desire to purchase such lands, the right of pre-emption of every such person so declining or neglecting in respect of the lands included in such offer shall cease; and a declaration in writing made before a justice by some person not interested in the matter in question, stating that such offer was made, and was refused, or not accepted within six weeks from the time of making the same, or that the person or all the persons entitled to the right of pre-emption were out of the country, or could not after diligent inquiry be found, or were not capable of entering into a contract for the purchase of such lands, shall in all courts be sufficient evidence of the facts therein stated.

[59]

NOTES

Disapplication: this Act does not apply to the acquisition of land under s 6(1) of the Crossrail Act 2008; see s 6(1), (3), Sch 6, Pt 2, para 1 of that Act.

130 Differences as to price to be settled by arbitration

If any person entitled to such pre-emption be desirous of purchasing any such lands, and such person and the promoters of the undertaking do not agree as to the price thereof, then such price shall be ascertained by arbitration, and the costs of such arbitration shall be in the discretion of the arbitrators.

[60]

NOTES

Disapplication: this Act does not apply to the acquisition of land under s 6(1) of the Crossrail Act 2008; see s 6(1), (3), Sch 6, Pt 2, para 1 of that Act.

131 (*Outside the scope of this work*)

132 Effect of the word "grant" in conveyances

In every conveyance of lands to be made by the promoters of the undertaking under this or the special Act the word "grant" shall operate as express covenants by the promoters of the undertaking, for themselves and their successors, or for themselves, their heirs, executors, administrators, and assigns, as the case may be, with the respective grantees therein named, and the successors, heirs, executors, administrators, and assigns of such grantees, according to the quality or nature of such grants, and of the estate or interest therein expressed to be thereby conveyed, as follows, except as the same shall be restrained or limited by express words contained in any such conveyance; (that is to say,)

A covenant that, notwithstanding any act or default done by the promoters of the undertaking, they were at the time of the execution of such conveyance seised or possessed of the lands or premises thereby granted for an indefeasible estate of inheritance in fee simple, free from all incumbrances done or occasioned by them, or otherwise for such estate or interest as therein expressed to be thereby granted, free from incumbrances done or occasioned by them;

A covenant that the grantee of such lands, his heirs, successors, executors, administrators, and assigns (as the case may be,) shall quietly enjoy the same against the promoters of the undertaking, and their successors, and all other persons claiming under them, and be indemnified and saved harmless by the promoters of the undertaking and their successors from all incumbrances created by the promoters of the undertaking:

A covenant for further assurance of such lands, at the expence of such grantee, his heirs, successors, executors, administrators, or assigns, (as the case may be,) by the promoters of the undertaking, or their successors, and all other persons claiming under them:

All and such grantees, and their several successors, heirs, executors, administrators, and assigns respectively, according to their respective quality or nature, and the estate or interest in such conveyance expressed to be conveyed, may in all actions brought by them assign breaches of covenants, as they might do if such covenants were expressly inserted in such conveyances.
[61]

NOTES

Disapplication: this Act does not apply to the acquisition of land under s 6(1) of the Crossrail Act 2008; see s 6(1), (3), Sch 6, Pt 2, para 1 of that Act.

133–153 (*S 133 repealed with savings by the Local Government Finance (Repeals, Savings and Consequential Amendments) Order 1990, SI 1990/776, art 3(1), Sch 1; ss 134, 136, 146, 150–152 outside the scope of this work; ss 135, 140 repealed by the Statute Law (Repeals) Act 1974; s 137 repealed by the Summary Jurisdiction Act 1884, s 4, Schedule and the Statute Law Revision Act 1892; ss 138, 141 repealed by the Statute Law (Repeals) Act 1993; s 139 repealed by the Compulsory Purchase Act 1965, s 39(4), Sch 8, Pt II; ss 142, 144 repealed by the Statute Law Revision Act 1892; ss 143, 145 repealed by the Compulsory Purchase Act 1965, s 39(4), Sch 8, Pts II, III and the Administration of Justice (Northern Ireland) Act 1954, s 29, Sch 7; s 147 repealed by the Compulsory Purchase Act 1965, s 39(4), Sch 8, Pt II and the Statute Law Revision Act (Northern Ireland) 1954; s 148 repealed by the Administration of Justice Act 1964, s 41(8), Sch 5; s 149 repealed by the Perjury Act 1911, s 17, Schedule; s 153 repealed by the Statute Law Revision Act 1875.*)

(*Schs A, B outside the scope of this work; Sch C repealed by the Statute Law Revision Act 1892.*)

COMMON LAW PROCEDURE ACT 1852

(1852 c 76)

An Act to amend the Process, Practice, and Mode of Pleading in the Superior Courts of Common Law at Westminster, and in the Superior Courts of the Counties Palatine of Lancaster and Durham

[30 June 1852]

1–167 (*Ss 1, 10, 24, 26, 92, 100, 104 repealed by the Statute Law Revision Act 1875; ss 2–9, 11–22, 25, 27–91, 93–99, 101–103, 109, 111, 116–125, 128–131, 133–167 repealed by the Statutory Law Revision and Civil Procedure Act 1883, s 3, Schedule; s 23 repealed by the Commissioners for Oaths Act 1889, s 12, Schedule; ss 105–108, 112–115 repealed by the Courts Act 1971, s 56, Sch 11, Pt I; ss 110, 132 repealed by the Statute Law Revision Act 1950; s 126 repealed by the Supreme Court Act 1981, s 152(4), Sch 7; s 127 repealed by the Administration of Justice Act 1965, s 34(1), Sch 2.*)

Ejectment

168–209 (*Ss 168–207 repealed by the Statute Law Revision and Civil Procedure Act 1883, s 3, Schedule; s 208 repealed by the Statute Law Revision Act 1892; s 209 repealed by the Law of Property Act 1925, s 207, Sch 7.*)

210 Proceedings in ejectment by landlord for non-payment of rent

In all cases between landlord and tenant, as often as it shall happen that one half year's rent shall be in arrear, and the landlord or lessor, to whom the same is due, hath right by law to re-enter for the non-payment thereof, such landlord or lessor shall and may, without any formal demand or re-entry, serve a writ in ejectment for the recovery of the demised premises, … which service … shall stand in the place and stead of a demand and re-entry; and in case of judgment against the defendant for nonappearance, if it shall be made appear to the court where the said action is depending, by affidavit, or be proved upon the trial in case the defendant appears, that half a year's rent was due before the said writ was served, *and that no sufficient distress was to be found on the demised premises, countervailing the arrears then due* [and that either of the conditions in section 210A was met in relation to the arrears], and that the lessor had power to re-enter, then and in every such case the lessor shall recover judgment and execution, in the same manner as if the rent in arrear had been legally demanded, and a re-entry made; and in case the lessee or his assignee, or other person claiming or deriving under the said lease, shall permit and suffer judgment to be had and recovered on such trial in ejectment, and execution to be executed thereon, without paying the rent and arrears, together with full costs, and without proceeding for relief in equity within six months after such execution executed, then and in such case the said lessee, his assignee, and all other persons claiming and deriving under the said lease, shall be barred and foreclosed from all relief or remedy in law or equity, other than by bringing error for reversal of such judgment, in case the same shall be erroneous, and the said landlord or lessor shall from thenceforth hold the said demised premises discharged from such lease; … provided that nothing herein contained shall extend to bar the right of any mortgagee of such lease, or any part thereof, who shall not be in possession, so as such mortgagee shall and do, within six months after such judgment obtained and execution executed pay all rent in arrear, and all costs and damages sustained by such lessor or person entitled to the remainder or reversion as aforesaid, and perform all the covenants and agreements which, on the part and behalf of the first lessee, are and ought to be performed.

[62]

NOTES

Words omitted repealed by the Statute Law Revision Act 1892; words in italics substituted by subsequent words in square brackets by the Tribunals, Courts and Enforcement Act 2007, s 86, Sch 14, paras 14, 15, as from a day to be appointed.

[210A Conditions relating to commercial rent arrears recovery

(1) The first condition is that the power under section 72(1) of the Tribunals, Courts and Enforcement Act 2007 (commercial rent arrears recovery) was not exercisable to recover the arrears.

(2) The second condition is that there were not sufficient goods on the premises to recover the arrears by that power.]

[63]

NOTES

Commencement: to be appointed.
Inserted by the Tribunals, Courts and Enforcement Act 2007, s 86, Sch 14, paras 14, 16.

211 Lessee proceeding in equity not to have injunction or relief without payment of rent and costs

In case the said lessee, his assignee, or other person claiming any right, title, or interest, in law or equity, of, in, or to the said lease, shall, within the time aforesaid, proceed for relief in any court of equity, such person shall not have or continue any injunction against the proceedings at law on such ejectment, unless he does or shall, within forty days next after a full and perfect answer shall be made by the claimant in such ejectment, bring into court, and lodge with the proper officer such sum and sums of money as the lessor or landlord shall in his answer swear to be due and in arrear over and above all just allowances, and also the costs taxed in the said suit, there to remain till the hearing of the cause, or to be paid out to the lessor or landlord on good security, subject to the decree of the court; and in case such proceedings for relief in equity shall be taken within the time aforesaid, and after execution is executed, the lessor or landlord shall be accountable only for so much and no more as he shall really and bona fide, without fraud, deceit, or wilful neglect, make of the demised premises from the time of his entering into the actual possession thereof; and if what shall be so made by the lessor or landlord happen to be less than the rent reserved on the said lease, then the said lessee or his assignee, before he shall be restored to his possession, shall pay such lessor or landlord what the money so by him made fell short of the reserved rent for the time such lessor or landlord held the said lands.

[64]

212 Tenant paying all rent, with costs, proceedings to cease

If the tenant or his assignee do or shall, at any time before the trial in such ejectment, pay or tender to the lessor or landlord, his executors or administrators, or his or their attorney in that cause, or pay into the court where the same cause is depending, all the rent and arrears, together with the costs, then and in such case all further proceedings on the said ejectment shall cease and be discontinued; and if such lessee, his executors, administrators, or assigns, shall, upon such proceedings as aforesaid, be relieved in equity, he and they shall have, hold, and enjoy the demised lands, according to the lease thereof made, without any new lease.

[65]

213–234 *(Ss 213 repealed by the Administration of Justice Act 1925, s 34(1), Sch 2; ss 214, 218, 221, 227 outside the scope of this work; ss 215, 216 repealed by the Statute Law Revision Act 1892; s 217 repealed by the Administration of Justice Act 1965, s 43(1), s 34(1), Sch 2; ss 219, 220 repealed by the Administration of Justice Act 1965, s 34(1), Sch 2; s 222 repealed by the Statute Law Revision and Civil Procedure Act 1883, s 3, Schedule; s 223 repealed by the Statute Law Revision Act 1875; ss 224, 225 repealed by the Supreme Court of Judicature (Officers) Act 1879, s 29, Sch 2; s 226 repealed by the Statute Law Revision Act 1892; ss 228–234 repealed by the Statute Law Revision and Civil Procedure Act 1883, s 3, Schedule.)*

235 Short title of Act

In citing this Act in any instrument, document, or proceeding, it shall be sufficient to use the expression "The Common Law Procedure Act 1852."

[66]

236 Act not to extend to Ireland or Scotland

Nothing in this Act shall extend to Ireland or Scotland …

[67]

NOTES

Words omitted repealed by the Statute Law Revision Act 1892.

(Schs (A), (B) repealed by the Statute Law Revision Act 1892.)

APPORTIONMENT ACT 1870

(1870 c 35)

An Act for the better Apportionment of Rents and other periodical Payments

[1 August 1870]

1 Short title

This Act may be cited for all purposes as "The Apportionment Act 1870."

[68]

2 Rents, etc to be apportionable in respect of time

… All rents, annuities, dividends, and other periodical payments in the nature of income (whether reserved or made payable under an instrument in writing or otherwise) shall, like interest on money lent, be considered as accruing from day to day, and shall be apportionable in respect of time accordingly.

[69]

NOTES

Words omitted repealed by the Statute Law Revision (No 2) Act 1893.

3 Apportioned part of rent, etc to be payable when the next entire portion shall have become due

The apportioned part of any such rent, annuity, dividend, or other payment shall be payable or recoverable in the case of a continuing rent, annuity, or other such payment when the entire portion of which such apportioned part shall form part shall become due and payable, and not before, and in the case of a rent, annuity, or other such payment determined by re-entry, death, or otherwise when the next entire portion of the same would have been payable if the same had not so determined, and not before.

[70]

4 Persons shall have the same remedies for recovering apportioned parts as for entire portions—Proviso as to rents reserved in certain cases

All persons and their respective heirs, executors, administrators, and assigns, and also the executors, administrators, and assigns respectively of persons whose interests determine with their own deaths, shall have such or the same remedies at law and in equity for recovering such apportioned parts as aforesaid when payable (allowing proportionate parts of all just allowances) as they respectively would have had for recovering such entire portions as aforesaid if entitled thereto respectively; provided that persons liable to pay rents reserved out of or charged on lands or other hereditaments of any tenure, and the same lands or other hereditaments, shall not be resorted to for any such apportioned part forming part of an entire or continuing rent as aforesaid specifically, but the entire or continuing rent, including such apportioned part, shall be recovered and received by the heir or other person who, if the rent had not been apportionable under this Act, or otherwise, would have been entitled to such entire or continuing rent, and such apportioned part shall be recoverable from such heir or other person by the executors or other parties entitled under this Act to the same by action at law or suit in equity.

[71]

5 Interpretation

In the construction of this Act—

The word "rents" includes rent service, rentcharge, and rent seck, and also tithes and all periodical payments or renderings in lieu of or in the nature of rent or tithe.

The word "annuities" includes salaries and pensions.

The word "dividends" includes (besides dividends strictly so called) all payments made by the name of dividend, bonus, or otherwise out of the revenue of trading or other public companies, divisible between all or any of the members of such respective companies, whether such payments shall be usually made or declared, at any fixed times or otherwise; and all such divisible revenue shall, for the purposes of this Act, be deemed to have accrued by equal daily increment during and within the period for or in respect of which the payment of the same revenue shall be declared or expressed to be made, but the said word "dividend" does not include payments in the nature of a return or reimbursement of capital.

[72]

6 Act not to apply to policies of assurance

Nothing in this Act contained shall render apportionable any annual sums made payable in policies of assurance of any description.

[73]

7 Nor where stipulation made to the contrary

The provisions of this Act shall not extend to any case in which it is or shall be expressly stipulated that no apportionment shall take place.

[74]

PUBLIC HEALTH ACT 1875

(1875 c 55)

An Act for consolidating and amending the Acts relating to Public Health in England

[11 August 1875]

PART I
PRELIMINARY

1 Short title

This Act may be cited as "The Public Health Act 1875."

[75]

2 Extent of Act

This Act shall not extend to Scotland or Ireland …

[76]

NOTES

Words omitted repealed by the London Government Act 1963, s 93(1), Sch 18.

3 (*Repealed by the Statute Law* (*Repeals*) *Act 1989.*)

4 Definitions

In this Act, if not inconsistent with the context, the following words and expressions have the meanings herein-after respectively assigned to them; that is to say,

…

"Person" includes any body of persons, whether corporate or unincorporate:

…

"Lands" and "Premises" include messuages buildings lands easements and hereditaments of any tenure:

"Owner" means the person for the time being receiving the rackrent of the lands or premises in connexion with which the word is used, whether on his own account or as agent or trustee for any other person, or who would so receive the same if such lands or premises were let at a rackrent:

"Rackrent" means rent which is not less than two thirds of the full net annual value of the property out of which the rent arises; and the full net annual value shall be taken to be the rent at which the property might reasonably be expected to let from year to year, free from all usual tenant's rates and taxes, …, and deducting therefrom the probable average annual cost of the repairs, insurance, and other expenses (if any) necessary to maintain the same in a state to command such rent:

"Street" includes any highway …, and any public bridge …, and any road lane footway square court alley or passage whether a thoroughfare or not:

"House" includes schools, also factories and other buildings in which … persons are employed …:

"Drain" means any drain of and used for the drainage of one building only, or premises within the same curtilage, and made merely for the purpose of communicating therefrom with a cesspool or other like receptacle for drainage or with a sewer into which the drainage of two or more buildings or premises occupied by different persons is conveyed:

…

[77]

NOTES

Repealed by the Public Health Act 1936, s 346, Sch 3, Pt I, except in so far as it is material to the construction of the unrepealed provisions of this Act or of any Act directed to be construed with it.

Words omitted repealed by the Factory and Workshop Act 1878, s 107, Sch 6, the Statute Law Revisions (No 2) Act 1893, the Statute Law Revisions Act 1898, the London Government Act 1963, s 93(1), Sch 18, Pt II, the Courts Act 1971, s 56(4), Sch 11, Pt IV, the Local Government Act 1972, s 272(1), Sch 30, the Statute Law (Repeals) Act 1989 and the Statute Law (Repeals) Act 1993.

5–343 ((*Pts II–XI*) *outside the scope of this work.*)

(*Schs 1–5 outside the scope of this work.*)

MARRIED WOMEN'S PROPERTY ACT 1882

(1882 c 75)

An Act to consolidate and amend the Acts relating to the Property of Married Women

[18 August 1882]

1–10 (*Ss 1–5 repealed by the Law Reform* (*Married Women and Tortfeasors*) *Act 1935, ss 5, 8; ss 6–9 repealed by the Statute Law* (*Repeals*) *Act 1969; s 10 outside the scope of this work.*)

11 Moneys payable under policy of assurance not to form part of estate of the insured

A married woman may … effect a policy upon her own life or the life of her husband for her [own benefit]; and the same and all benefit thereof shall enure accordingly.

A policy of assurance effected by any man on his own life, and expressed to be for the benefit of his wife, or of his children, or of his wife and children, or any of them, or by any woman on her own life, and expressed to be for the benefit of her husband, or of her children, or of her husband and children, or any of them, shall create a trust in favour of the objects therein named, and the moneys payable under any such policy shall not, so long as any object of the trust remains unperformed, form part of the estate of the insured, or be subject to his or her debts: Provided, that if it shall be proved that the policy was effected and the premiums paid with intent to defraud the creditors of the insured, they shall be entitled to receive, out of the moneys payable under the policy, a sum equal to the premiums so paid. The insured may by the policy, or by any memorandum under his or her hand, appoint a trustee or trustees of the moneys payable under the policy, and from time to time appoint a new trustee or new trustees thereof, and may make provision for the appointment of a new trustee or new trustees thereof, and for the investment of the moneys payable under such policy. In default of any such appointment of a trustee, such policy, immediately on its being effected, shall vest in the insured and his or her legal personal representatives, in trust for the purposes aforesaid … The receipt of a trustee or trustees duly appointed, or in default of any such appointment, or in default of notice to the insurance office, the receipt of the legal personal representative of the insured shall be a discharge to the office for the sum secured by the policy, or for the value thereof, in whole or in part.

[78]

NOTES

First words omitted repealed and words in square brackets substituted by the Law Reform (Married Women and Tortfeasors) Act 1935, ss 5(1), (2), 8(2), Schs 1, 2; second words omitted repealed by the Statute Law (Repeals) Act 1969.

Application: the Civil Partnership Act 2004, s 70 provides that this section shall apply in relation to a policy of assurance effected by a civil partner on his own life, and expressed to be for the benefit of his civil partner, or of his children, or of his civil partner and children, or any of them, as it applies in relation to a policy of assurance effected by a husband and expressed to be for the benefit of his wife, or of his children, or of his wife and children, or of any of them.

12–16 (*S 12 repealed by the Law Reform* (*Husband and Wife*) *Act 1962, s 3*(*2*), (*5*), *Schedule, and by the Theft Act 1968, ss 33*(*3*), *36*(*3*), *Sch 3, Pt III; s 13 repealed by the Statute Law* (*Repeals*) *Act 1969; ss 14, 15 repealed by the Law Reform* (*Married Women and Tortfeasors*) *Act 1935, ss 5*(*2*), *8*(*2*); *s 16 repealed by the Theft Act 1968, ss 33*(*3*), *36*(*3*), *Sch 3, Pt III.*)

17 Questions between husband and wife as to property to be decided in a summary way

In any question between husband and wife as to the title to or possession of property, either party, … may apply by summons or otherwise in a summary way [to the High Court or such county court as may be prescribed and the court may, on such an application (which may be heard in private), make such order with respect to the property as it thinks fit.

In this section "prescribed" means prescribed by rules of court and rules made for the purposes of this section may confer jurisdiction on county courts whatever the situation or value of the property in dispute.]

[79]

NOTES

Words omitted repealed by the Statute Law (Repeals) Act 1969; words in square brackets substituted by the Matrimonial and Family Proceedings Act 1984, s 43.

18–25 (*Ss 18, 19, 25 repealed by the Statute Law* (*Repeals*) *Act 1969; ss 20, 21 repealed by the Poor Law Act 1927, s 245, Sch 11; s 22 repealed by the Statute Law Revision Act 1898; s 23 repealed by the Law Reform* (*Husband and Wife*) *Act 1962, s 3*(*2*), (*5*), *Schedule; s 24 outside the scope of this work.*)

26 Extent of Act

This Act shall not extend to Scotland.

[80]

27 Short title

This Act may be cited as the Married Women's Property Act 1882.

[81]

WILLS (SOLDIERS AND SAILORS) ACT 1918

(1918 c 58)

An Act to amend the Law with respect to Testamentary Dispositions by Soldiers and Sailors

[6 February 1918]

1 Explanation of s 11 of Wills Act 1837

In order to remove doubts as to the construction of the Wills Act 1837, it is hereby declared and enacted that section eleven of that Act authorises and always has authorised any soldier being in actual military service, or any mariner or seaman being at sea, to dispose of his personal estate as he might have done before the passing of that Act, though under the age of [eighteen years].

[82]

NOTES

Words in square brackets substituted by the Family Law Reform Act 1969, s 3(1)(b).

2 Extension of s 11 of Wills Act 1837

Section eleven of the Wills Act 1837, shall extend to any member of His Majesty's naval or marine forces not only when he is at sea but also when he is so circumstanced that if he were a soldier he would be in actual military service within the meaning of that section.

[83]

3 Validity of testamentary dispositions of real property made by soldiers and sailors

(1) A testamentary disposition of any real estate in England or Ireland made by a person to whom section eleven of the Wills Act 1837, applies, and who dies after the passing of this Act, shall, notwithstanding that the person making the disposition was at the time of making it under [eighteen years] of age or that the disposition has not been made in such manner or form as was at the passing of this Act required by law, be valid in any case where the person making the disposition was of such age and the disposition has been made in such manner and form that if the disposition had been a disposition of personal estate made by such a person domiciled in England or Ireland it would have been valid.

(2) A testamentary disposition of any heritable property in Scotland made after the passing of this Act by a person to whom section eleven of the Wills Act 1837, applies or to whom it would apply if he were domiciled in England, shall not be invalid by reason only of the fact that such person is under twenty-one years of age, provided always that he is of such age that he could, if domiciled in Scotland, have made a valid testamentary disposition of moveable property.

[84]

NOTES

Words in square brackets substituted by the Family Law Reform Act 1969, s 3(1)(b).

4 Power to appoint testamentary guardians

Where any person dies after the passing of this Act having made a will which is, or which, if it had been a disposition of property, would have been rendered valid by section eleven of the Wills Act 1837, any appointment contained in that will of any person as guardian of the infant children of the testator shall be of full force and effect.

[85]

5 Short title and interpretation

(1) This Act may be cited as the Wills (Soldiers and Sailors) Act 1918.

(2) For the purposes of section eleven of the Wills Act 1837, and this Act the expression "soldier" includes a member of the Air Force, and references in this Act to the said section eleven include a reference to that section as explained and extended by this Act.

[86]

LAW OF PROPERTY ACT 1922

(1922 c 16)

An Act to assimilate and amend the law of Real and Personal Estate, to abolish copyhold and other special tenures, to amend the law relating to commonable lands and of intestacy, and to amend the Wills Act 1837, the Settled Land Acts 1882 to 1890, the Conveyancing Acts 1881 to 1911, the Trustee Act 1893, and the Land Transfer Acts 1875 and 1897

[29 June 1922]

1–144A *(Ss 1–3, 5–9, 11, 15, 17–25, 27, 29–34, 72–82, 84, 85, 87, 89–108 repealed by the Law of Property Act 1925, s 207, Sch 7; ss 4, 10, 13, 28 repealed by the Settled Land Act 1925, s 119, Sch 5, and the Law of Property Act 1925, s 207, Sch 7; ss 12, 26, 86 repealed by the Settled Land Act 1925, s 119, Sch 5; ss 14, 16 repealed by the Land Charges Act 1925, s 24, Schedule; ss 35–42, 44–71 repealed by the Settled Land Act 1925, s 119, Sch 5, and the Universities and College Estates Act 1925, s 44, Sch 2; ss 43, 137, 144, 144A outside the scope of this work; ss 83, 113, 123 repealed by the Trustee Act 1925, s 70, Sch 2, and the Law of Property Act 1925, s 207, Sch 7; ss 88, 109, 111, 112, 114–122, 124–127 repealed by the Trustee Act 1925, s 70, Sch 2; s 110 repealed by the Trustee Act 1925, s 70, Sch 2, and the Administration of Estates Act 1925, s 56, Sch 2, Pt II; ss 128–136, 138–143 repealed by the Statute Law (Repeals) Act 1969.)*

PART VII
PROVISIONS RESPECTING LEASEHOLDS

Conversion of Perpetually Renewable Leaseholds into Long Terms

145 Conversion of perpetually renewable leaseholds

For the purpose of converting perpetually renewable leases and underleases (not being an interest in perpetually renewable copyhold land enfranchised by Part V of this Act, but including a perpetually renewable underlease derived out of an interest in perpetually renewable copyhold land) into long terms, for preventing the creation of perpetually renewable leasehold interests and for providing for the interests of the persons affected, the provisions contained in the Fifteenth Schedule to this Act shall have effect.

[87]

146–187 (*Ss 146, 152 repealed by the Law of Property Act 1925, s 207, Sch 7; ss 147–151, 153–155, 157–163 repealed by the Administration of Estates Act 1925, s 56, Sch 2, Pt II; s 156 repealed by the Law of Property Act 1925, s 207, Sch 7, and the Administration of Estates Act 1925, s 56, Sch 2, Pt II; ss 164–187 repealed by the Land Registration Act 1925, s 147, Schedule.*)

PART XI
GENERAL PROVISIONS

188–190 (*Ss 188, 190 outside the scope of this work; s 189 repealed by the Statute Law* (*Repeals*) *Act 1969.*)

191 Short title, commencement and extent

(1) This Act may be cited as the Law of Property Act 1922.

(2) …

(3) This Act (including the repeals therein) shall not extend to Scotland or Ireland.

[88]

NOTES

Sub-s (2): repealed by the Statute Law Revision Act 1950.

(*Schs 1, 3, 9 repealed by the Settled Land Act 1925, s 119, Sch 5, and the Law of Property Act 1925, s 207, Sch 7; Schs 2, 4, 8, 11 repealed by the Law of Property Act 1925, s 207, Sch 7; Sch 5 repealed by the Settled Land Act 1925, s 119, Sch 5; Sch 6 repealed by the Settled Land Act 1925, s 119, Sch 5, The Law of Property Act 1925, s 207, Sch 7, and the Administration of Estates Act 1925, s 56, Sch 2, Pt II; Sch 7 repealed by the Land Charges Act 1925, s 24, Schedule; Sch 10 repealed by the Settled Land Act 1925, s 119, Sch 5, and the Universities and College Estates Act 1925, s 44, Sch 2; Schs 12–14 repealed by the Statute Law* (*Repeals*) *Act 1969.*)

SCHEDULE 15
PROVISIONS RELATING TO PERPETUALLY RENEWABLE LEASES AND UNDERLEASES

Section 145

1 Conversion of perpetually renewable leases into long terms

(1) Land comprised in a perpetually renewable lease which was subsisting at the commencement of this Act shall, by virtue of this Act, vest in the person who at such commencement was entitled to such lease, for a term of two thousand years, to be calculated from the date at which the existing term or interest commenced, at the rent and subject to the lessees' covenants and conditions (if any) which under the lease would have been payable or enforceable during the subsistence of such term or interest.

(2) The rent, covenants and conditions (if any) shall (subject to the express provisions of this Act to the contrary) be payable and enforceable during the subsistence of the term created by this Act; and that term shall take effect in substitution for the term or interest created by the lease, and be subject to the like power of re-entry (if any) and other provisions which affected the term or interest created by the lease, but without any right of renewal.

2 Conversion of perpetually renewable underleases into long terms

(1) Land comprised in any underlease, which at the commencement of this Act was perpetually renewable and was derived out of a head term affected by this Act, shall, be virtue of this Act, vest in the person who at such commencement was entitled to the subterm or interest for a term of two thousand years less one day, to be calculated from the date at which the head term created by this Act commenced, at the rent and subject to the underlessee's covenants and conditions (if any) which under the underlease would have been payable or enforceable during the subsistence of such subterm or interest.

(2) The rent, covenants and conditions (if any) shall (subject to the express provisions of this Act to the contrary) be payable and enforceable during the subsistence of the subterm created by this Act; and that subterm shall take effect in substitution for the subterm or interest created by the underlease, and be subject to the like power of re-entry (if any) and other provisions which affected the subterm or interest created by the underlease, but without any right of renewal.

(3) The foregoing provisions of this section shall also apply to any perpetually renewable subterm or interest which, at the commencement of this Act, was derived out of any other subterm or interest, but so that in every case the subterm created by this Act shall be one day less in duration that the derivative term created by this Act, out of which it takes effect.

3 Incidence of equities, incumbrances, and subterms

(1) Every term or subterm created by this Part of this Act shall be subject to all the same trusts, powers executory limitations over, rights and equities (if any), and to all the same incumbrances and obligations of every kind, as the term, subterm, or other interest which it replaces would have been subject to if this Part of this Act had not been passed, but without prejudice to the provisions of Part I of this Act, and where an infant is entitled, the person, of full age, who by virtue of that part of this Act, becomes entitled to the legal estate of the infant shall be deemed to have been entitled to the said lease, subterm or interest at the commencement of this Act.

(2) Where any subterm or interest, subsisting at the commencement of this Act, was derived out of a lease or underlease affected by this Act, but was not perpetually renewable, the same shall be deemed to take effect out of the term created by this Act or out of any derivative subterm so created, as the case may require.

4 Title acquired and stamps

(1) This Part of this Act shall not operate to confer any better title to any term or subterm hereby created than the title to the perpetually renewable term, subterm, or interest which it replaces.

(2) This Act shall not render any lease or instrument which has been duly stamped according to the law in force at its date, liable to be further stamped, nor shall any stamp duty be payable by reason only of the creation by this Act of any term or subterm.

5 Dispositions purporting to create perpetually renewable leaseholds

[(1)] A grant, after the commencement of this Act, of a term, subterm, or other leasehold interest with a covenant or obligation for perpetual renewal, which would have been valid if this Part of this Act had not been passed, shall (subject to the express provisions of this Act) take effect as a demise for a term of two thousand years or in the case of a subdemise for a term less in duration by one day than the term out of which it is derived, to commence from the date fixed for the commencement of the term, subterm, or other interest, and in every case free from any obligation for renewal or for payment of any fines, fees, costs, or other money in respect of renewal.

[(2) Sub-paragraph (3) applies where a grant—

(a) relates to commonhold land, and

(b) would take effect by virtue of sub-paragraph (1) as a demise for a term of two thousand years or a subdemise for a fixed term.

(3) The grant shall be treated as if it purported to be a grant of the term referred to in sub-paragraph (2)(b) (and sections 17 and 18 of the Commonhold and Leasehold Reform Act 2002 (residential and non-residential leases) shall apply accordingly).]

6 Satisfaction of existing contracts to grant perpetually renewable interests

(1) Any obligation in force at the commencement of this Act for the grant (otherwise than by way of renewal) of a lease, subterm, or other leasehold interest with a covenant or obligation for perpetual renewal shall be deemed to be an obligation for the grant of a lease for a term of two thousand years, or, in the case of an underlease, for a term less in duration by one day than the term out of which it is to be derived, but the amount of the rent to be paid shall, if necessary, be adjusted, having regard to the loss of fines and other payments (if any) which would have been payable on renewal.

(2) In case any dispute arises respecting the adjustment of the rent, the matter shall be submitted to the [Secretary of State] for determination, in the manner provided by this Act.

7 Future contracts for renewal and as to leases for lives

(1) Any contract entered into after the commencement of this Act, for the grant of a lease, subterm, or other leasehold interest with a covenant or obligation for perpetual renewal shall (subject to the express provisions of this Part of this Act) operate as an agreement for a demise for a term of two thousand years, or in the case of a contract for a subdemise, for a term less in duration by one day than the term out of which it is derived, to commence from the date agreed for the commencement of the term, subterm or other interest, and in every case free from the obligation for renewal or for payment of any fines, fees, costs or other money in respect of renewal.

(2) Any contract entered into after such commencement for the renewal of a lease or underlease for a term exceeding sixty years from the termination of the lease or underlease, and whether or not contained in the lease or underlease, shall (subject to the express provisions of this Part of this Act) be void.

(3) …

8 Effect of powers to grant renewable leases

(1) Every power conferred by custom or contained in a statute (except as hereinafter mentioned) or other instrument authorising a tenant for life of full age, statutory owner, trustee, or other person to grant a lease or underlease with a covenant or obligation for perpetual renewal, shall have effect, in regard to any grant made after the commencement of this Act, as if the same authorised the grant of a lease or underlease for a term not exceeding two thousand years at the best rent that can be reasonably obtained, having regard to any fine which may be taken and to all the circumstances of the case, or, if the power authorises a grant at a peppercorn rent or other rent less than the best rent, than at any rent so authorised.

(2) Every power to grant a lease or underlease at a rent or in consideration of a fine for life or lives, or for any term of years determinable with life or lives or on the marriage of any person, shall have effect in regard to any grant made after the commencement of this Act, as if the same authorised the grant of lease or underlease for a term not exceeding ninety years determinable after the death or marriage (as the case may be) of the original lessee or of the survivor of the original lessees by at least one month's notice in writing given to determine the same on one of the usual quarter days, either by the lessor or the persons deriving title under him to the person entitled to the leasehold interest, or by the lessee or other persons in whom the leasehold interest is vested to the lessor or the persons deriving title under him.

9 Saving of rights and powers under 8 Edw 7 c 36

Nothing in this Act shall prejudicially affect any right of renewal conferred by section forty-four of the Small Holdings and Allotments Act 1908, or the power conferred by section forty of that Act, to grant leases for the purposes of that Act, with a similar right of renewal.

10 Powers and covenants implied in leases and underleases affected

(1) Every lease or underlease which, by virtue of this Part of this Act, takes effect for a term of two thousand years or for a derivative term of two thousand years less one or more days (as the case may require) shall be deemed to contain—

(i) A power (exercisable only with the consent of the persons, if any, interested in any derivative interest which might be prejudicially affected) for the lessee or underlessee by giving notice in writing to the lessor at least ten days before the lease or underlease would (but for this Act) have expired if it had not been renewed after the commencement of this Act, to determine the lease or underlease at the date on which (but for this Act) it would have expired if it had not been renewed as aforesaid;

Also a like power (exercisable with the like consent if any) to determine subsequently by notice as aforesaid the lease or underlease at the time at which, if this Act had not been passed and all renewals had in the meantime been made in due course, the lease or underlease would have expired if it had not been further renewed after the date of the notice:

Provided that if any such notice be given all uncommuted additional rent attributable to a fine or other money which, if this Act had not been passed, would have been payable on a renewal made after the date of the notice, shall [cease or] not become payable:

(ii) A covenant by the lessee or underlessee to register every assignment or devolution of the term or subterm, including all probates or letters of administration affecting the same, with the lessor or his solicitor or agent, within six months from the date of the assignment, devolution or grant of probate or letters of administration, and to pay a fee of one guinea (which shall be accepted in satisfaction of all costs) in respect of each registration; and the covenant so deemed to be contained shall be in substitution for any express covenant to register with the lessor or his solicitor or agent, assignments or devolutions of the term or subterm, and to pay fees or costs in respect of such registration:

(iii) A covenant by the lessee or underlessee within one year from the commencement of this Act to produce his lease or underlease or sufficient evidence thereof (including an assignment of part of the land comprised in the lease or underlease) with any particulars required to show that a perpetual right of renewal was subsisting at the commencement of this Act, to the lessor or his solicitor or agent, who shall, subject to the payment of his costs, if the right of renewal is admitted or proved, endorse notice of that fact on the lease, underlease, assignment, or copy thereof, at the expense of the lessee or underlessee; and such endorsement signed by or on behalf of the lessor shall, in favour of a purchaser, be sufficient evidence that the right of renewal was subsisting as aforesaid, either in respect of the whole or part of the land as the case may require:

and the power of re-entry (if any) contained in the lease or underlease shall apply and extend to the breach of every covenant deemed to be contained as aforesaid.

(2) If any dispute arises respecting the date on which a notice is authorised to be served by this section, or whether or not a lease or underlease or assignment or a copy thereof ought to be endorsed as aforesaid, the matter shall be submitted to the [Secretary of State] for determination in the manner provided by this Act.

11 Liability of lessees and underlessees

(1) In the case of every term or subterm created by this Act or under any power conferred by this Part of this Act, each lessee or underlessee, although he may be the original lessee or underlessee, and notwithstanding any stipulation to the contrary, shall be liable only for rent accruing and for breaches of covenants or conditions occurring while he or his personal representatives shall have the term or subterm vested in him or them, and in like manner, as respects an original lessee or underlessee, as if the term or subterm had, immediately after its creation, been assigned to him.

(2) Nothing in this Part of this Act shall affect the liability of any person in respect of rent accruing or the breach of any covenant or condition occurring before the commencement of this Act.

12 Conversion of fines into additional rent

(1) Where, under the lease, underlease, or otherwise, any fine or other money, including a heriot, is payable by the lessee or underlessee on renewal, then and in every such case [an amount to be ascertained as hereinafter provided] shall, save as in this Act provided and unless commuted, become payable to the lessor as additional rent, during the subsistence of the term or subterm created by this Act, by as nearly as may be equal yearly instalments the first instalment to be paid at the end of one year from the commencement of this Act; but no sums payable for costs of examination of the lessee's or underlessee's title or of granting a new lease or underlease or of any other work which is rendered unnecessary by this Act shall be taken into account in ascertaining the additional rent.

[(2) In default of agreement and unless the [Secretary of State], having regard to the practice and other circumstances of the case, otherwise directs, the following provisions shall have effect for the purpose of ascertaining the annual instalments of additional rent:—

(a) the additional rent shall be ascertained on the basis of the fines and other payments which would have been payable on the occasion of the first renewal after the commencement of this Act, if this Act had not been passed;

(b) where the lessee or underlessee has a right to renew at different times, the occasion of the first renewal shall be such date as he may, by notice in writing given to the lessor within one year after the commencement of this Act, select from among the dates at which he would have been entitled to renew his lease or underlease had it remained renewable, or, in default of such notice, the last day on which he would have been entitled to renew, regard being had to the date of the last renewal.]

(3) But where the time at or within which the said fine or other money must be paid is not definitely fixed by or ascertainable from the lease or underlease the same shall, for the purpose of ascertaining the amount of the annual instalments of additional rent, be deemed to have been payable on such date as may, within one year from the commencement of this Act, be agreed between the lessor and the lessee or underlessee [or in default] of such agreement, as may be fixed by the [Secretary of State].

(4) The additional rent shall be deemed part of the rent reserved by the lease or underlease for all purposes, including any covenant for payment of rent or proviso for re-entry contained in the lease or underlease.

(5) Subject to any order by the [Secretary of State] or the court to the contrary, and in default of agreement, the amount of each annual instalment of additional rent shall be ascertained by [an actuary regard being had to the interval or average interval occurring between the dates of renewal and to any circumstances affecting the amount payable on renewal].

(6) If the lessee or underlessee is liable to forfeit his right of renewal if he makes default in payment of a fine or other money or in doing any other act or thing within a time ascertainable by the dropping of a life, but not otherwise, then [such percentage as the [Secretary of State] may generally or in any particular instance with a view to maintaining any existing practice, prescribe] of the annual value of the land (ascertained as provided by this Act in the case of enfranchised land for the extinguishment of manorial incidents) shall be treated as added to the fines and other money payable by the lessee or underlessee on renewal for the purpose of ascertaining the amount of the annual instalment of additional rent, and as compensation to the lessor for loss of his right of re-entry (present or future) which would have accrued by reason of any failure to exercise the right of renewal.

13 Interest on fines

(1) Where, under the lease or underlease, any unpaid fine or other money payable on a renewal carries interest, then any annual instalment of additional rent payable in lieu thereof shall, until paid, carry interest from the date on which the instalment becomes payable, and at the same rate at which such interest would have been payable if this Act had not been passed.

(2) Where the lease or underlease does not provide for payment of such interest, then each annual instalment of additional rent shall, until paid, carry interest at the current rate from the time when demand in writing is made claiming the money.

14 Provisions respecting commutation of additional rent and other matters

(1) The lessor and lessee or underlessee may agree—

(a) For the commutation or discharge of any claims in respect of additional rent [or any part thereof];

(b) The amount (if any) of the annual instalments of additional rent payable;

(c) The dates for payment of additional rent;

(d) The interval or average interval between dates of renewal;

(e) The dates on which the lessee or underlessee has power under this Act to determine the lease or underlease;

(f) The amount of the rent (including the annual instalments of additional rent) to be apportioned in respect of any part of the land comprised in the lease or underlease, and thereupon the lessee's or underlessee's covenants shall be apportioned in regard to the land to which the apportionment relates.

(2) A statement in writing respecting any such agreement, which is endorsed on any such lease or underlease, or the counterpart or assignment, and signed by the lessor and lessee or underlessee, shall be conclusive evidence of the matters stated, and the costs of and incidental to the agreement and any negotiations therefor shall be borne be the lessee or underlessee.

(3) The additional rent may, by such endorsement, be made payable by instalments at the times at which the original rent is made payable or otherwise.

15 Compensation of lessor's agents

Any claims for compensation by any officer, solicitor, or other agent of the lessor in respect of fees or remuneration (not being remuneration attributable to work rendered unnecessary by this Act) which would have been payable by the lessee or underlessee on any renewal, if this Act had not been passed, shall be treated as part of the fines or other money payable to the lessor, and the lessee or underlessee shall not otherwise be concerned therewith.

16 Disputes to be submitted to the [Secretary of State]

(1) If the lessor and lessee or underlessee or the lessor's agent (as the case may require) do not agree, or any dispute arises as to the amount or date for payment of any annual instalment of additional rent, or the amount for which the same ought to be commuted, or the amount at which any rent ought to be adjusted, or apportioned, or the amount of compensation (if any) payable by the lessor to his officer, solicitor or other agent, [or the appointment of or instructions to be given to an actuary under paragraph 12(5) of this Schedule] the question or dispute shall be submitted to the [Secretary of State] for determination, when the parties may be represented by solicitors or counsel, and the award of the [Secretary of State] shall (subject only to such appeal to the court as may be prescribed by rules of court) be final.

(2) The [Secretary of State] may issue regulations in respect of any of the matters aforesaid, and determine by whom and in what proportions the cost of any application to the [Secretary of State] shall be paid.

(3) If a dispute as to the amount for which any annual instalment of additional rent ought to be commuted is submitted to the [Secretary of State], and if the lessor would (under the lease or underlease subsisting at the commencement of this Act, or any lease or underlease which would have been subsisting if this Act had not been passed and the successive renewable leases or underleases had been renewed in the ordinary course) have had a right to refuse renewal by reason of a default in payment of a fine, then the [Secretary of State] shall, in the arbitration, have regard to the value of such right (unless compensation has been given for the loss of the right) in like manner as if a corresponding absolute right to determine the term or subterm created by this Act had, by reason of a corresponding default, been made exercisable by the lessor at the time at which the renewable lease or underlease would have expired if the lessor had lawfully refused to renew it. [For the purposes of this sub-paragraph the compensation to be given for the loss of the said right shall be regulated by the practice (if any) which obtained, before the commencement of this Act, in assessing the value of the said right, unless the [Secretary of State] otherwise directs.]

17 Power to raise and apply capital for commuting additional rent

(1) A power authorising a tenant for life of full age, statutory owner, trustee, or other person to apply or direct the application of or raise any money for or in the discharge of the costs, fines, and

other sums payable on the renewal of any such lease or underlease shall be deemed to authorise the payment, application, or raising of money for the commutation of any additional rent made payable by this Act.

(2) Out of the money so applicable or raiseable, the lessor may discharge any compensation payable to his officer, solicitor, or other agent.

(3) If the reversion is settled land, or [subject to a trust of land], any commutation money shall be treated as capital money or proceeds of sale arising from such land (as the case may require).

(4) If the land comprised in the lease or underlease is settled land or [subject to a trust of land], the commutation money may be paid out of capital money or personal estate (not being chattels real) held on the same trusts as the land.

18 Notices

The provisions of section sixty-seven of the Conveyancing Act 1881, shall apply to any notice required or authorised to be given under this Part of this Act or under any provision implied by this Part of this Act.

19 Registered leases and underleases

Where any lease or underlease to which this Part of this Act applies is registered under the Land Transfer Acts, effect shall be given to the provisions of this Act by making such alterations in the register as may be prescribed under those Acts.

20 Office copies and searches

(1) The original or counterpart of any lease or underlease or assignment to which this Part of this Act applies may be deposited at the Central Office of the *Supreme Court* [Senior Courts].

(2) A separate file of instruments so deposited shall be kept, and any person who furnishes the prescribed evidence to show that he has a sufficient interest in the lease or underlease or reversion expectant thereon may search that file and inspect the lease or underlease or counterpart or assignment, and an office copy thereof shall be delivered to him at his request.

(3) A copy of an instrument so deposited, with any plan or endorsements thereon, may be prescribed at any time at the Central Office, and, if found correct, may be stamped as an office copy, and when so stamped shall become and be an office copy.

(4) An office copy of the instrument so deposited with the plan and endorsements (if any) shall without further proof be sufficient evidence of the contents of the instrument, plan, and endorsements (if any), and of the deposit thereof at the Central Office.

(5) Where an instrument so deposited has perished or become indecipherable, an office copy thereof may be similarly deposited, and office copies thereof may be issued in lieu of office copies of the original, and the provisions of this section shall apply thereto as if office copies so issued were office copies of the original instrument.

(6) General rules may be made for the purposes of this section prescribing the evidence to be furnished before a search is authorised, regulating the practice of the Central Office, and prescribing, with the concurrence of the Treasury, the fees to be taken therein.

[89]

NOTES

Para 5: sub-para (1) numbered as such and sub-paras (2), (3) inserted by the Commonhold and Leasehold Reform Act 2002, s 68, Sch 5, para 1.

Para 6: words in square brackets in sub-para (2) substituted by SI 2002/794, art 5(1), Sch 1, para 1(a).

Para 7: sub-para (3) repealed by the Law of Property Act 1925, s 207, Sch 7.

Para 10: words in square brackets in sub-para (1)(i) proviso inserted by the Law of Property (Amendment) Act 1924, s 2, Sch 2, para 5(1); words in square brackets in sub-para (2) substituted by SI 2002/794, art 5(1), Sch 1, para 1(b).

Para 12: words "Secretary of State" in square brackets in each place they occur substituted by SI 2002/794, art 5(1), Sch 1, para 1(c); other words in square brackets substituted by the Law of Property (Amendment) Act 1924, s 2, Sch 2, para 5(2)–(6).

Para 14: words in square brackets in sub-para (1)(a) inserted by the Law of Property (Amendment) Act 1924, s 2, Sch 2, para 5(7).

Para 16: words "Secretary of State" in square brackets in each place they occur substituted by SI 2002/794, art 5(1), Sch 1, para 1(d); other words in square brackets inserted by the Law of Property (Amendment) Act 1924, s 2, Sch 2, para 5(8), (9).

Para 17: words in square brackets in sub-paras (3), (4) substituted by the Trusts of Land and Appointment of Trustees Act 1996, s 25(1), Sch 2, para 1; for savings in relation to entailed interests created before the commencement of that Act, and savings consequential upon the abolition of the doctrine of conversion, see s 25(4), (5) thereof.

Para 20: words in italics in sub-para (1) substituted by subsequent words in square brackets by the Constitutional Reform Act 2005, s 59(5), Sch 11, Pt 2, para 4(1), (3), as from 1 October 2009.

Modification: References to solicitors etc modified to include references to bodies recognised under the Administration of Justice Act 1985, s 9, by the Solicitors' Incorporated Practices Order 1991, SI 1991/2684, arts 4, 5, Sch 1.

Subordinate Legislation: the Renewable Leaseholds Regulations 1925, SI 1925/857; the Filing of Leases Rules 1925, SI 1925/1128; the Filing of Leases Fee Order 1925, SI 1925/1149.

(*Sch 16 repealed by the Land Registration Act 1925, s 147, Schedule.*)

SETTLED LAND ACT 1925

(1925 c 18)

An Act to consolidate the enactments relating to Settled Land in England and Wales

[9 April 1925]

PART I
GENERAL PRELIMINARY PROVISIONS

Settlements and Settled Land

1 What constitutes a settlement

(1) Any deed, will, agreement for a settlement or other agreement, Act of Parliament, or other instrument, or any number of instruments, whether made or passed before or after, or partly before and partly after, the commencement of this Act, under or by virtue of which instrument or instruments any land, after the commencement of this Act, stands for the time being—

(i) limited in trust for any persons by way of succession; or

(ii) limited in trust for any person in possession—

(a) for an entailed interest whether or not capable of being barred or defeated;

(b) for an estate in fee simple or for a term of years absolute subject to an executory limitation, gift, or disposition over on failure of his issue or in any other event;

(c) for a base or determinable fee [(other than a fee which is a fee simple absolute by virtue of section 7 of the Law of Property Act 1925)] or any corresponding interest in leasehold land;

(d) being an infant, for an estate in fee simple or for a term of years absolute; or

(iii) limited in trust for any person for an estate in fee simple or for a term of years absolute contingently on the happening of any event; or

(iv) …

(v) charged, whether voluntarily or in consideration of marriage or by way of family arrangement, and whether immediately or after an interval, with the payment of any rentcharge for the life of any person, or any less period, or of any capital, annual, or periodical sums for the portions, advancement, maintenance, or otherwise for the benefit of any persons, with or without any term of years for securing or raising the same;

creates or is for the purposes of this Act a settlement and is in this Act referred to as a settlement, or as the settlement, as the case requires;

Provided that, where land is the subject of a compound settlement, references in this Act to the settlement shall be construed as meaning such compound settlement, unless the context otherwise requires.

(2) Where an infant is beneficially entitled to land for an estate in fee simple or for a term of years absolute and by reason of an intestacy or otherwise there is no instrument under which the interest of the infant arises or is acquired, a settlement shall be deemed to have been made by the intestate, or by the person whose interest the infant has acquired.

(3) An infant shall be deemed to be entitled in possession notwithstanding any subsisting right of dower (not assigned by metes and bounds) affecting the land, and such a right of dower shall be deemed to be an interest comprised in the subject of the settlement and coming to the dowress under or by virtue of the settlement.

Where dower has been assigned by metes and bounds, the letters of administration or probate granted in respect of the estate of the husband of the dowress shall be deemed a settlement made by the husband.

(4) An estate or interest not disposed of by a settlement and remaining in or reverting to the settlor, or any person deriving title under him, is for the purposes of this Act an estate or interest comprised in the subject of the settlement and coming to the settlor or such person under or by virtue of the settlement.

(5) Where—

(a) a settlement creates an entailed interest which is incapable of being barred or defeated, or a base or determinable fee, whether or not the reversion or right of reverter is in the Crown, or any corresponding interest in leasehold land; or

(b) the subject of a settlement is an entailed interest, or a base or determinable fee, whether or not the reversion or right of reverter is in the Crown, or any corresponding interest in leasehold land;

the reversion or right of reverter upon the cesser of the interest so created or settled shall be deemed to be an interest comprised in the subject of the settlement, and limited by the settlement.

(6) Subsection (4) and (5) of this section bind the Crown.

[(7) This section does not apply to land held upon trust for sale.]

[90]

NOTES

Sub-s (1): words in square brackets inserted by the Trusts of Land and Appointment of Trustees Act 1996, s 25(1), Sch 3, para 2(2), for savings in relation to entailed interests created before the commencement of that Act, and savings consequential upon the abolition of the doctrine of conversion, see s 25(4), (5) thereof; words omitted repealed by the Married Women (Restraint upon Anticipation) Act 1949, s 1(4), Sch 2.

Sub-s (7): inserted by the Law of Property (Amendment) Act 1926, s 7, Schedule.

2 What is settled land

Land which is or is deemed to be the subject of a settlement is for the purposes of this Act settled land, and is in relation to the settlement referred to in this Act as the settled land.

[91]

3 Duration of settlements

Land [which has been subject to a settlement which is a settlement for the purposes of this Act] shall be deemed for the purposes of this Act to remain and be settled land, and the settlement shall be deemed to be a subsisting settlement for the purposes of this Act so long as—

(a) any limitation, charge, or power of charging under the settlement subsists, or is capable of being exercised; or

(b) the person who, if of full age, would be entitled as beneficial owner to have that land vested in him for a legal estate is an infant.

[92]

NOTES

Words in square brackets substituted by the Trusts of Land and Appointment of Trustees Act 1996, s 25(1), Sch 3, para 2(3); for savings in relation to entailed interests created before the commencement of that Act, and savings consequential upon the abolition of the doctrine of conversion, see s 25(4), (5) thereof.

4 Authorised method of settling land inter vivos

(1) Every settlement of a legal estate in land inter vivos shall, save as in this Act otherwise provided, be effected by two deeds, namely, a vesting deed and a trust instrument and if effected in any other way shall not operate to transfer or create a legal estate.

(2) By the vesting deed the land shall be conveyed to the tenant for life or statutory owner (and if more than one as joint tenants) for the legal estate the subject of the intended settlement:

Provided that, where such legal estate is already vested in the tenant for life or statutory owner, it shall be sufficient, without any other conveyance, if the vesting deed declares that the land is vested in him for that estate.

(3) The trust instrument shall—

(a) declare the trusts affecting the settled land;

(b) appoint or constitute trustees of the settlement:

(c) contain the power, if any, to appoint new trustees of the settlement;

(d) set out, either expressly or by reference, any powers intended to be conferred by the settlement in extension of those conferred by this Act;

(e) bear any ad valorem stamp duty which may be payable (whether by virtue of the vesting deed or otherwise) in respect of the settlement.

[93]

5 Contents of vesting deeds

(1) Every vesting deed for giving effect to a settlement or for conveying settled land to a tenant for life or statutory owner during the subsistence of the settlement (in this Act referred to as a "principal vesting deed") shall contain the following statements and particulars, namely:—

(a) A description, either specific or general, of the settled land;

(b) A statement that the settled land is vested in the person or persons to whom it is conveyed or in whom it is declared to be vested upon the trusts from time to time affecting the settled Land;

(c) The names of the persons who are the trustees of the settlement;

(d) Any additional or larger powers conferred by the trust instrument relating to the settled land which by virtue of this Act operate and are exercisable as if conferred by this Act on a tenant for life;

(e) The name of any person for the time being entitled under the trust instrument to appoint new trustees of the settlement.

(2) The statements or particulars required by this section may be incorporated by reference to an existing vesting instrument, and, where there is a settlement subsisting at the commencement of this Act, by reference to that settlement and to any instrument whereby land has been conveyed to the uses or upon the trusts of that settlement, but not (save as last aforesaid) by reference to a trust instrument nor by reference to a disentailing deed.

(3) A principal vesting deed shall not be invalidated by reason only of any error in any of the statements or particulars by this Act required to be contained therein.

[94]

6 Procedure in the case of settlements by will

Where a settlement is created by the will of an estate owner who dies after the commencement of this Act—

(a) the will is for the purposes of this Act a trust instrument; and

(b) the personal representatives of the testator shall hold the settled land on trust, if and when required so to do, to convey it to the person who, under the will, or by virtue of this Act, is the tenant for life or statutory owner, and, if more than one, as joint tenants.

[95]

7 Procedure on change of ownership

(1) If, on the death of a tenant for life or statutory owner, or of the survivor of two or more tenants for life or statutory owners, in whom the settled land was vested, the land remains settled land, his personal representatives shall hold the settled land on trust, if and when required so to do, to convey it to the person who under the trust instrument or by virtue of this Act becomes the tenant for life or statutory owner and, if more than one, as joint tenants.

(2) If a person by reason of attaining full age becomes a tenant for life for the purposes of this Act of settled land, he shall be entitled to require the trustees of the settlement, personal representatives, or other persons in whom the settled land is vested, to convey the land to him.

(3) If a person who, when of full age, will together with another person or other persons constitute the tenant for life for the purposes of this Act of settled land attains that age, he shall be entitled to require the tenant for life, trustees of the settlement, personal representatives or other persons in whom the settled land is vested to convey the land to him and the other person or persons who together with him constitute the tenant for life as joint tenants.

(4) If by reason of forfeiture, surrender, or otherwise the estate owner of any settled land ceases to have the statutory powers of a tenant for life and the land remains settled land, he shall be bound forthwith to convey the settled land to the person who under the trust instrument, or by virtue of this Act, becomes the tenant for life or statutory owner and, if more than one, as joint tenants.

(5) If any person of full age becomes absolutely entitled to the settled land (whether beneficially, or as personal representative, or as [trustee of land], or otherwise) free from all limitations, powers, and charges taking effect under the settlement, he shall be entitled to require the trustees of the settlement, personal representatives, or other persons in whom the settled land is vested, to convey the land to him, and if more persons than one being of full age become so entitled to the settled land they shall be entitled to require such persons as aforesaid to convey the land to them as joint tenants.

[96]

NOTES

Sub-s (5): words in square brackets substituted by the Trusts of Land and Appointment of Trustees Act 1996, s 25(1), Sch 3, para 2(4); for savings in relation to entailed interests created before the commencement of that Act, and savings consequential upon the abolition of the doctrine of conversion, see s 25(4), (5) thereof.

8 Mode and costs of conveyance, and saving of rights of personal representative and equitable charges

(1) A conveyance by personal representatives under either of the last two preceding sections may be made by an assent in writing signed by them which shall operate as a conveyance.

(2) Every conveyance under either of the last two preceding sections shall be made at the cost of the trust estate.

(3) The obligations to convey settled land imposed by the last two preceding sections are subject and without prejudice—

(a) where the settlement is created by a will, to the rights and powers of the personal representatives for purposes of administration; and

(b) in any case, to the person on whom the obligation is imposed being satisfied that provision has been or will be made for the payment of any unpaid death duties in respect of the land or any interest therein for which he is accountable, and any interest and costs in respect of such duties, or that he is otherwise effectually indemnified against such duties, interest and costs.

(4) Where the land is or remains settled land a conveyance under either of the last two preceding sections shall—

(a) if by deed, be a principal vesting deed; and

(b) if by an assent, be a vesting assent, which shall contain the like statements and particulars as are required by this Act in the case of a principal vesting deed.

(5) Nothing contained in either of the last two preceding sections affects the right of personal representatives to transfer or create such legal estates to take effect in priority to a conveyance under either of those sections as may be required for giving effect to the obligations imposed on them by statute.

(6) A conveyance under either of the last two preceding sections, if made by deed, may contain a reservation to the person conveying of a term of years absolute in the land conveyed, upon trusts for indemnifying him against any unpaid death duties in respect of the land conveyed or any interest therein, and any interest and costs in respect of such duties.

(7) Nothing contained in either of the last two preceding sections affects any right which a person entitled to an equitable charge for securing money actually raised, and affecting the whole estate the subject of the settlement, may have to require effect to be given thereto by a legal mortgage, before the execution of a conveyance under either of those sections.

[97]

9 Procedure in the case of settlement and of instruments deemed to be trust instruments

(1) Each of the following settlements or instruments shall for the purposes of this Act be deemed to be a trust instrument, and any reference to a trust instrument contained in this Act shall apply thereto, namely:—

(i) An instrument executed, or, in case of a will, coming into operation, after the commencement of this Act which by virtue of this Act is deemed to be a settlement;

(ii) A settlement which by virtue of this Act is deemed to have been made by any person after the commencement of this Act;

(iii) An instrument inter vivos intended to create a settlement of a legal estate in land which is executed after the commencement of this Act, and does not comply with the requirements of this Act with respect to the method of effecting such a settlement; and

(iv) A settlement made after the commencement of this Act (including a settlement by the will of a person who dies after such commencement) of any of the following interests—

(a) an equitable interest in land which is capable, when in possession, of subsisting at law; or

(b) an entailed interest; or

(c) a base or determinable fee or any corresponding interest in leasehold land,

but only if and when the interest settled takes effect free from all equitable interests and powers under every prior settlement (if any).

(2) As soon as practicable after a settlement, or an instrument which for the purposes of this Act is deemed to be a trust instrument, takes effect as such, the trustees of the settlement may, and on the request of the tenant for life or statutory owner shall, execute a principal vesting deed, containing the proper statements and particulars, declaring that the legal estate in the settled land shall vest or is vested in the person or persons therein named, being the tenant for life or statutory owner, and including themselves if they are the statutory owners, and such deed shall, unless the legal estate is already so vested, operate to convey or vest the legal estate in the settled land to or in the person or persons aforesaid and, if more than one, as joint tenants.

(3) If there are no trustees of the settlement, then (in default of a person able and willing to appoint such trustees) an application under this Act shall be made to the court for the appointment of such trustees.

(4) The provisions of the last preceding section with reference to a conveyance shall apply, so far as they are applicable, to a principal vesting deed under this section.

[98]

10 Procedure on acquisition of land to be made subject to a settlement

(1) Where after the commencement of this Act land is acquired with capital money arising under this Act or in exchange for settled land, or a rentcharge is reserved on a grant of settled land, the land shall be conveyed to, and the rentcharge shall by virtue of this Act become vested in, the tenant for life or statutory owner, and such conveyance or grant is in this Act referred to as a subsidiary vesting deed:

Provided that, where an instrument is subsisting at the commencement of this Act, or is made or comes into operation after such commencement, by virtue of which any money or securities are liable under this Act, or the Acts which it replaces, or under a trust or direction contained in the instrument, to be invested in the purchase of land to be conveyed so as to become settled land, but at the commencement of this Act, or when such instrument is made or comes into operation after such commencement, as the case may be, there is no land in respect of which a principal vesting deed is capable of being executed, the first deed after the commencement of this Act by which any land is acquired as aforesaid shall be a principal vesting deed and shall be framed accordingly.

(2) A subsidiary vesting deed executed on the acquisition of land to be made subject to a settlement shall contain the following statements and particulars, namely—

(a) particulars of the last or only principal vesting instrument affecting land subject to the settlement;

(b) a statement that the land conveyed is to be held upon and subject to the same trusts and powers as the land comprised in such last or only principal vesting instrument;

(c) the names of the persons who are the trustees of the settlement;

(d) the name of any person for the time being entitled to appoint new trustees of the settlement.

(3) A subsidiary vesting deed reserving a rentcharge on a grant of settled land shall contain the following statements and particulars—

(a) a statement that the rentcharge is vested in the grantor and is subject to the settlement which, immediately before the grant, was subsisting with respect to the land out of which it was reserved;

(b) particulars of the last or only principal vesting instrument affecting such land.

(4) A subsidiary vesting deed shall not be invalidated by reason only of any error in any of the statements or particulars by this Act required to be contained therein.

(5) The acquisition of the land shall not operate to increase or multiply charges or powers of charging.

[99]

11 As to contracts for the settlement of land

(1) A contract made or other liability created or arising after the commencement of this Act for the settlement of land—

(i) by or on the part of an estate owner; or

(ii) by a person entitled to—

(a) an equitable interest which is capable when in possession of subsisting at law; or

(b) an entailed interest; or

(c) a base or determinable fee or any corresponding interest in leasehold land;

shall, but in cases under paragraph (ii) only if and when the interest of the person entitled takes effect free from all equitable interests and powers under every prior settlement, if any, be deemed an estate contract within the meaning of the Land Charges Act 1925, and may be registered as a land charge accordingly, and effect shall be given thereto by a vesting deed and a trust instrument in accordance with this Act.

(2) A contract made or other liability created or arising before the commencement of this Act to make a settlement of land shall be deemed to be sufficiently complied with if effect is given thereto by a vesting deed and a trust instrument in accordance with this Act.

[100]

12 Power to make vesting orders as to settled land

(1) If—

(a) any person who is bound under this Part of this Act to execute a conveyance, vesting deed or vesting assent or in whom settled land is wrongly vested refuses or neglects to execute the requisite conveyance, vesting deed or vesting assent within one month after demand in writing; or

(b) any such person is outside the United Kingdom, or cannot be found, or it is not known whether he is alive or dead; or

(c) for any reason the court is satisfied that the conveyance, vesting deed or vesting assent cannot be executed, or cannot be executed without undue delay or expense;

the court may, on the application of any person interested, make an order vesting the settled land in the tenant for life or statutory owner or person, if any, of full age absolutely entitled (whether beneficially or as personal representative or [trustee of land] or otherwise), and, if the land remains settled land, the provisions of this Act relating to a principal vesting deed or a subsidiary vesting deed, as the case may be, shall apply to any order so made and every such order shall contain the like statements and particulars.

(2) No stamp duty shall be payable in respect of a vesting order made in place of a vesting or other assent.

[101]

NOTES

Sub-s (1): words in square brackets substituted by the Trusts of Land and Appointment of Trustees Act 1996, s 25(1), Sch 3, para 2(5); for savings in relation to entailed interests created before the commencement of that Act, and savings consequential upon the abolition of the doctrine of conversion, see s 25(4), (5) thereof.

13 Dispositions not to take effect until vesting instrument is made

Where a tenant for life or statutory owner has become entitled to have a principal vesting deed or a vesting assent executed in his favour, then until a vesting instrument is executed or made pursuant to this Act in respect of the settled land, any purported disposition thereof inter vivos by any person, other than a personal representative (not being a disposition which he has power to make in right of his equitable interests or powers under a trust instrument), shall not take effect except in favour of a purchaser of a legal estate [without notice of such tenant for life or statutory owner having become so entitled as aforesaid] but, save as aforesaid, shall operate only as a contract for valuable consideration to carry out the transaction after the requisite vesting instrument has been executed or made, and a purchaser of a legal estate shall not be concerned with such disposition unless the contract is registered as a land charge.

[Nothing in this section affects the creation or transfer of a legal estate by virtue of an order of the court or the Minister or other competent authority.]

[102]

NOTES

Amended by the Law of Property (Amendment) Act 1926, ss 6, 7, Schedule.

14 Forfeiture and stamps

(1) Any vesting effected under the powers conferred by this Act in relation to settled land shall not operate as a breach of a covenant or condition against alienation or give rise to a forfeiture.

(2) Nothing in this Act shall operate to impose any stamp duty on a vesting or other assent.

[103]

15 (*Repealed by the Statute Law* (*Repeals*) *Act 2004.*)

Enforcement of Equitable Interests and powers against Estate Owner and discharge on termination of Settlement

16 Enforcement of equitable interests and powers against estate owner

(1) All equitable interests and powers in or over settled land (whether created before or after the date of any vesting instrument affecting the legal estate) shall be enforceable against the estate owner in whom the settled land is vested (but in the case of personal representatives without prejudice to their rights and powers for purposes of administration) in manner following (that is to say):—

(i) The estate owner shall stand possessed of the settled land and the income thereof upon such trusts and subject to such powers and provisions as may be requisite for giving effect to the equitable interests and powers affecting the settled land or income thereof of which he has notice according to their respective priorities;

(ii) Where any person of full age becomes entitled to require a legal estate in the settled land to be vested in him in priority to the settlement, by reason of a right of reverter, statutory or otherwise, or an equitable right of entry taking effect, or on the ground that his interest ought no longer to be capable of being overreached under the powers of this Act, the estate owner shall be bound, if so requested in writing, to transfer or create such legal estate as may be required for giving legal effect to the rights of the person so entitled;

(iii) Where—

(a) any principal sum is required to be raised on the security of the settled land, by virtue of any trust, or by reason of the exercise of an equitable power affecting the settled land, or by any person or persons who under the settlement is or are entitled or together entitled to or has or have a general power of appointment over the settled land, whether subject to any equitable charges or powers of charging subsisting under the settlement or not; or

(b) the settled land is subject to any equitable charge for securing money actually raised and affecting the whole estate the subject of the settlement;

the estate owner shall be bound, if so requested in writing, to create such legal estate or charge by way of legal mortgage as may be required for raising the money or giving legal effect to the equitable charge:

Provided that, so long as the settlement remains subsisting, any legal estate or charge by way of legal mortgage so created shall take effect and shall be expressed to take effect subject to any equitable charges or powers of charging subsisting under the settlement which have priority to the interests or powers of the person or persons by or on behalf of whom the money is required to be raised or legal effect is required to be given to the equitable charge, unless the persons entitled to the prior charges or entitled to exercise the powers consent in writing to the same being postponed, but it shall not be necessary for such consent to be expressed in the instrument creating such legal estate or charge by way of legal mortgage.

(2) Where a mortgage or charge is expressed to be made by an estate owner pursuant to this section, then, in favour of the mortgagee or chargee and persons deriving title under him, the same shall take effect in priority to all the trusts of the settlement and all equitable interests and powers subsisting or to arise under the settlement except those to which it is expressly made subject, and shall so take effect, whether the mortgagee or chargee has notice of any such trusts, interests, or powers, or not, and the mortgagee or chargee shall not be concerned to see that a case had arisen to authorise the mortgage or charge, or that no more money than was wanted was raised.

(3) Nothing contained in paragraph (iii) of subsection (1) of this section affects the power conferred by this Act on a tenant for life of raising money by mortgage or of directing money to be applied in discharge of incumbrances.

(4) Effect may be given by means of a legal mortgage to an agreement for a mortgage, or a charge or lien, whether or not arising by operation of law, if the agreement charge or lien ought to have priority over the settlement.

(5) Save as hereinbefore expressly provided, no legal estate shall, so long as the settlement is subsisting, be transferred or created by the estate owner for giving effect to any equitable interest or power under the settlement.

(6) If a question arises or a doubt is entertained whether any and what legal estate ought to be transferred or created pursuant to this section, an application may be made to the court for directions as hereinafter provided.

(7) If an estate owner refuses or neglects for one month after demand in writing to transfer or create any such legal estate, or if by reason of his being outside the United Kingdom, or being unable to be found, or by reason of the dissolution of a corporation, or for any other reason, the court is satisfied that the transaction cannot otherwise be effected, or cannot be effected without undue delay or expense, the court may, on the application of any person interested, make a vesting order transferring or creating the requisite legal estate.

(8) This section does not affect a purchaser of a legal estate taking free from any equitable interest or power.

[104]

17 Deed of discharge on termination of settlement

(1) Where the estate owner of any settled land holds the land free from all equitable interests and powers under a trust instrument, the persons who in the last or only principal vesting instrument or the last or only endorsement on or annex thereto are declared to be the trustees of the settlement or the survivors of them shall, save as hereinafter mentioned, be bound to execute, at the cost of the trust estate, a deed declaring that they are discharged from the trust so far as regards that land;

Provided that, if the trustees have notice of any derivative settlement, [trust of land] or equitable charge affecting such land, they shall not execute a deed of discharge until—

(a) in the case of a derivative settlement, or [trust of land], a vesting instrument or a conveyance has been executed or made for giving effect thereto; and

(b) in the case of an equitable charge, they are satisfied that the charge is or will be secured by a legal mortgage, or is protected by registration as a land charge, or by deposit of the documents of title, or that the owner thereof consents to the execution of the deed of discharge.

Where the land is affected by a derivative settlement or [trust of land], the deed of discharge shall contain a statement that the land is settled land by virtue of such vesting instrument as aforesaid and the trust instrument therein referred to, or is [subject to a trust of land] by virtue of such conveyance as aforesaid, as the case may require.

(2) If, in the circumstances mentioned in subsection (1) of this section and when the conditions therein mentioned have been complied with, the trustees of a settlement on being requested to execute a deed of discharge—

(a) by the estate owner; or

(b) by a person interested under, or by the trustees of, a derivative settlement; or

(c) by the trustees of [land];

refuse to do so, or if for any reason the discharge cannot be effected without undue delay or expense, the estate owner, person interested, or trustees may apply to the court for an order discharging the first mentioned trustees as respects the whole or any part of the settled land, and the court may make such order as it may think fit.

(3) Where a deed or order of discharge contains no statement to the contrary, a purchaser of a legal estate in the land to which the deed or order relates shall be entitled to assume that the land has ceased to be settled land, and is not subject to [a trust of land].

[105]

NOTES

Sub-ss (1)–(3): words in square brackets substituted by the Trusts of Land and Appointment of Trustees Act 1996, s 25(1), Sch 3, para 2(6); for savings in relation to entailed interests created before the commencement of that Act, and savings consequential upon the abolition of the doctrine of conversion, see s 25(4), (5) thereof.

Restrictions on dispositions of Settled Land where Trustees have not been Discharged

18 Restrictions on dispositions of settled land where trustees have not been discharged

(1) Where land is the subject of a vesting instrument and the trustees of the settlement have not been discharged under this Act, then—

(a) any disposition by the tenant for life or statutory owner of the land, other than a disposition authorised by this Act or any other statute, or made in pursuance of any additional or larger powers mentioned in the vesting instrument, shall be void, except for the purpose of conveying or creating such equitable interests as he has power, in right of his equitable interests and powers under the trust instrument, to convey or create; and

(b) if any capital money is payable in respect of a transaction, a conveyance to a purchaser of the land shall only take effect under this Act if the capital money is paid to or by the direction of the trustees of the settlement or into court; and

(c) notwithstanding anything to the contrary in the vesting instrument, or the trust instrument, capital money shall not, except where the trustee is a trust corporation, be paid to or by the direction of fewer persons than two as trustees of the settlement.

(2) The restrictions imposed by this section do not affect—

(a) the right of a personal representative in whom the settled land may be vested to convey or deal with the land for the purposes of administration;

(b) the right of a person of full age who has become absolutely entitled (whether beneficially or as [trustee of land] or personal representative or otherwise) to the settled land, free from all limitations, powers, and charges taking effect under the trust instrument, to require the land to be conveyed to him;

(c) the power of the tenant for life, statutory owner, or personal representative in whom the settled land is vested to transfer or create such legal estates, to take effect in priority to the settlement, as may be required for giving effect to any obligations imposed on him by statute, but where any capital money is raised or received in respect of the transaction the money shall be paid to or by the direction of the trustees of the settlement or in accordance with an order of the court.

[106]

NOTES

Sub-s (2): words in square brackets substituted by the Trusts of Land and Appointment of Trustees Act 1996, s 25(1), Sch 3, para 2(7); for savings in relation to entailed interests created before the commencement of that Act, and savings consequential upon the abolition of the doctrine of conversion, see s 25(4), (5) thereof.

Tenants for Life and Persons with Powers of Tenant for Life

19 Who is tenant for life

(1) The person of full age who is for the time being beneficially entitled under a settlement to possession of settled land for his life is for the purposes of this Act the tenant for life of that land and the tenant for life under that settlement.

(2) If in any case there are two or more persons of full age so entitled as joint tenants, they together constitute the tenant for life for the purposes of this Act.

(3) If in any case there are two or more persons so entitled as joint tenants and they are not all of full age, such one or more of them as is or are for the time being of full age is or (if more than one) together constitute the tenant for life for the purposes of this Act, but this subsection does not affect the beneficial interests of such of them as are not for the time being of full age.

(4) A person being tenant for life within the foregoing definitions shall be deemed to be such notwithstanding that, under the settlement or otherwise, the settled land, or his estate or interest therein, is incumbered or charged in any manner or to any extent, and notwithstanding any

assignment by operation of law or otherwise of his estate or interest under the settlement, whether before or after it came into possession, other than an assurance which extinguishes that estate or interest.

[107]

20 Other limited owners having powers of tenant for life

(1) Each of the following persons being of full age shall, when his estate or interest is in possession, have the powers of a tenant for life under this Act, (namely):—

(i) A tenant in tail, including a tenant in tail after possibility of issue extinct, and a tenant in tail who is by Act of Parliament restrained from barring or defeating his estate tail, and although the reversion is in the Crown, but not including such a tenant in tail where the land in respect whereof he is so restrained was purchased with money provided by Parliament in consideration of public services;

(ii) A person entitled to land for an estate in fee simple or for a term of years absolute with or subject to, in any of such cases, an executory limitation, gift, or disposition over on failure of his issue or in any other event;

(iii) A person entitled to a base or determinable fee, although the reversion or right of reverter is in the Crown, or to any corresponding interest in leasehold land;

(iv) A tenant for years determinable on life, not holding merely under a lease at a rent;

(v) A tenant for the life of another, not holding merely under a lease at a rent;

(vi) A tenant for his own or any other life, or for years determinable on life, whose estate is liable to cease in any event during that life, whether by expiration of the estate, or by conditional limitation, or otherwise, or to be defeated by an executory limitation, gift, or disposition over, or is subject to a trust for accumulation of income for any purpose;

(vii) A tenant by the curtesy;

(viii) A person entitled to the income of land under a trust or direction for payment thereof to him during his own or any other life, whether or not subject to expenses of management or to a trust for accumulation of income for any purpose, or until sale of the land, or until forfeiture, cesser or determination by any means of his interest therein, unless the land is subject to [a trust of land];

(ix) A person beneficially entitled to land for an estate in fee simple or for a term of years absolute subject to any estates, interests, charges, or powers of charging, subsisting or capable of being exercised under a settlement;

(x) …

(2) In every such case as is mentioned in subsection (1) of this section, the provisions of this Act referring to a tenant for life, either as conferring powers on him or otherwise, shall extend to each of the persons aforesaid, and any reference in this Act to death as regards a tenant for life shall, where necessary, be deemed to refer to the determination by death or otherwise of the estate or interest of the person on whom the powers of a tenant for life are conferred by this section.

(3) For the purposes of this Act the estate or interest of a tenant by the curtesy shall be deemed to be an estate or interest arising under a settlement made by his wife.

(4) Where the reversion of right or reverter or other reversionary right is in the Crown, the exercise by a person on whom the powers of a tenant for life are conferred by this section of his powers under this Act, binds the Crown.

[108]

NOTES

Sub-s (1): words in square brackets in para (viii) substituted by the Trusts of Land and Appointment of Trustees Act 1996, s 25(1), Sch 3, para 2(8), for savings in relation to entailed interests created before the commencement of that Act, and savings consequential upon the abolition of the doctrine of conversion, see s 25(4), (5) thereof; para (x) repealed by the Married Women (Restraint upon Anticipation) Act 1949, s 1(4), Sch 2.

21 Absolute owners subject to certain interests to have the powers of tenant for life

(1) Where a person of full age is beneficially entitled in possession to a legal estate subject to any equitable interests or powers, then, for the purpose of overreaching such interests or powers, he may, notwithstanding any stipulation to the contrary, by deed (which shall have effect as a principal vesting deed within the meaning of this Act) declare that the legal estate is vested in him on trust to give effect to all equitable interests and powers affecting the legal estate, and that deed shall be executed by two or more individuals approved or appointed by the court or a trust corporation, who shall be stated to be the trustees of the settlement for the purposes of this Act.

Thereupon so long as any of the equitable interests and powers are subsisting the following provisions shall have effect:—

(a) The person so entitled as aforesaid and each of his successors in title being an estate owner shall have the powers of a tenant for life and the land shall be deemed to be settled land;

(b) The instrument (if any) under which his estate arises or is acquired, and the instrument (if any) under which the equitable interests or powers are subsisting or capable of taking effect shall be deemed to be the trust instrument:

Provided that where there is no such instrument as last aforesaid then a deed (which shall take effect as a trust instrument) shall be executed contemporaneously with the vesting deed, and shall declare the trusts affecting the land;

(c) The persons stated in the principal vesting deed to be the trustees of the settlement for the purposes of this Act shall also be the trustees of the trust instrument for those purposes; and

(d) Capital money arising on any disposition of the land shall be paid to or by the direction of the trustees of the settlement or into court, and shall be applicable towards discharging or providing for payment in due order of any principal money payable in respect of such interests or charges as are overreached by such disposition, and until so applied shall be invested or applied as capital money under the trust instrument, and the [resultant profits] shall be applied as the income of such capital money, and be liable for keeping down in due order any annual or periodical sum which may be overreached by the disposition.

(2) The following equitable interests and powers are excepted from the operation of subsection (1) of this section namely—

(i) an equitable interest protected by a deposit of documents relating to the legal estate affected;

(ii) the benefit of a covenant or agreement restrictive of the user of land;

(iii) an easement, liberty or privilege over or affecting land and being merely an equitable interest;

(iv) the benefit of a contract to convey or create a legal estate, including a contract conferring either expressly or by statutory implication a valid option of purchase, a right of pre-emption, or any other like right;

(v) any equitable interest protected by registration under the Land Charges Act 1925, other than—

(a) an annuity within the meaning of Part II of that Act;

(b) a limited owner's charge or a general equitable charge within the meaning of that Act.

(3) Subject to the powers conferred by this Act on a tenant for life, nothing contained in this section shall deprive an equitable chargee of any of his rights or of his remedies for enforcing those rights.

[109]

NOTES

Sub-s (1): words in square brackets in para (d) substituted by the Trustee Act 2000, s 40(1), Sch 2, Pt II, para 7.

22 Provisions applicable where interest in settled land is restored

(1) Where by a disentailing assurance settled land is expressed to be limited (whether subject or not to any estates, interests, charges or powers expressly created or conferred thereby) upon the trusts subsisting with respect thereto immediately before the execution of such disentailing assurance, or any of such trusts then, for the purposes of this Act and otherwise, a person entitled to any estate or interest in the settled land under any such previously subsisting trust is entitled thereto after the execution of such disentailing assurance as of his former estate or interest.

(2) Where by a resettlement of settled land any estate or interest therein is expressed to be limited to any person (whether subject or not to any estate, interest, charge or power expressly created or conferred by the resettlement) in restoration or confirmation of his estate or interest under a prior settlement, then, for the purposes of this Act and otherwise, that person is entitled to the estate or interest so restored or confirmed as of his former estate or interest and in addition to the powers exercisable by him in respect of his former estate or interest, he is capable of exercising all such further powers as he could have exercised by virtue of the resettlement, if his estate or interest under the prior settlement had not been so restored or confirmed, but he had been entitled under the resettlement only.

[110]

23 Powers of trustees, etc, when there is no tenant for life

(1) Where under a settlement there is no tenant for life nor, independently of this section, a person having by virtue of this Act the powers of a tenant for life then—

(a) any person of full age on whom such powers are by the settlement expressed to be conferred; and

(b) in any other case the trustees of the settlement;

shall have the powers of a tenant for life under this Act.

(2) This section applies to trustees of settlements of land purchased with money provided by Parliament in consideration of public services where the tenant in tail is restrained from barring or defeating his estate tail, except that, if the tenant in tail is of full age and capacity, the powers shall not be exercised without his consent, but a purchaser shall not be concerned to see or inquire whether such consent has been given.

[111]

24 As to a tenant for life who has parted with his interest

(1) If it is shown to the satisfaction of the court that a tenant for life, who has by reason of bankruptcy, assignment, incumbrance, or otherwise ceased in the opinion of the court to have a substantial interest in his estate or interest in the settled land or any part thereof, has unreasonably refused to exercise any of the powers conferred on him by this Act, or consents to an order under this section, the court may, on the application of any person interested in the settled land or the part thereof affected, make an order authorising the trustees of the settlement, to exercise in the name and on behalf of the tenant for life, any of the powers of a tenant for life under this Act, in relation to the settled land or the part thereof affected, either generally and in such manner and for such period as the court may think fit, or in a particular instance, and the court may by the order direct that any documents of title in the possession of the tenant for life relating to the settled land be delivered to the trustees of the settlement.

(2) While any such order is in force, the tenant for life shall not, in relation to the settled land or the part thereof affected, exercise any of the powers thereby authorised to be exercised in his name and on his behalf, but no person dealing with the tenant for life shall be affected by any such order, unless the order is for the time being registered as an order affecting land.

(3) An order may be made under this section at any time after the estate or interest of the tenant for life under the settlement has taken effect in possession, and notwithstanding that he disposed thereof when it was an estate or interest in remainder or reversion.

[112]

25 Married woman, how to be affected

(1) The foregoing provisions of this Act apply to a married woman of full age, whether or not she is entitled to her estate or interest for her separate use or as her separate property, and she, without her husband, may exercise the powers of a tenant for life under this Act.

(2) …

[113]

NOTES

Sub-s (2): repealed by the Married Women (Restraint upon Anticipation) Act 1949, s 1(4), Sch 2.

26 Infants, how to be affected

(1) Where an infant is beneficially entitled in possession to land for an estate in fee simple or for a term of years absolute or would if of full age be a tenant for life of or have the powers of a tenant for life over settled land, then, during the minority of the infant—

(a) if the settled land is vested in a personal representative, the personal representative, until a principal vesting instrument has been executed pursuant to the provisions of this Act; and

(b) in every other case, the trustees of the settlement;

shall have, in reference to the settled land and capital money, all the powers conferred by this Act and the settlement on a tenant for life, and on the trustees of the settlement.

(2) If the settled land is vested in a personal representative, then, if and when during the minority the infant, if of full age, would have been entitled to have the legal estate in the settled land conveyed to or otherwise vested in him pursuant to the provisions of this Act, a principal vesting instrument shall, if the trustees of the settlement so require, be executed, at the cost of the trust estate, for vesting the legal estate in themselves, and in the meantime the personal representative shall, during the minority, give effect to the directions of the trustees of the settlement, and shall not be concerned with the propriety of any conveyance directed to be made by those trustees if the conveyance appears to be a proper conveyance under the powers conferred by this Act or by the settlement, and the capital money, if any, arising under the conveyance is paid to or by the direction of the trustees of the settlement or into court, but a purchaser dealing with the personal representative and paying the capital money, if any, to him shall not be concerned to see that the money is paid to trustees of the settlement or into court, or to inquire whether the personal representative is liable to give effect to any such directions, or whether any such directions have been given.

(3) Subsection (2) of this section applies whether the infant becomes entitled before or after the commencement of this Act, and has effect during successive minorities until a person of full age becomes entitled to require the settled land to be vested in him.

(4) This section does not apply where an infant is beneficially entitled in possession to land for an estate in fee simple or for a term of years absolute jointly with a person of full age (for which case provision is made in the Law of Property Act 1925), but it applies to two or more infants entitled as aforesaid jointly, until one of them attains full age.

(5) This section does not apply where an infant would, if of full age, constitute the tenant for life or have the powers of a tenant for life together with another person of full age, but it applies to two or more infants who would, if all of them were of full age, together constitute the tenant for life or have the powers of a tenant for life, until one of them attains full age.

(6) Nothing in this section affects prejudicially any beneficial interest of an infant.

[114]

27, 28 (*S 27 repealed by the Trusts of Land and Appointment of Trustees Act 1996, s 25(2), Sch 4; s 28 repealed by the Mental Health Act 1959, s 149(2), Sch 8, Pt I.*)

29 Charitable and public trusts

(1) For the purposes of this section, all land vested or to be vested in trustees on or for charitable, ecclesiastical, or public trusts or purposes shall be deemed to be settled land, and the trustees shall, without constituting them statutory owners, have in reference to the land, all the powers which are by this Act conferred on a tenant for life and on the trustees of a settlement.

In connexion only with the exercise of those powers, and not so as to impose any obligation in respect of or to affect—

(a) the mode of creation or the administration of such trusts; or

(b) the appointment or number of trustees of such trusts;

the statute or other instrument creating the trust or under which it is administered shall be deemed the settlement, and the trustees shall be deemed the trustees of the settlement, and, save where the trust is created by a will coming into operation after the commencement of this Act, a separate instrument shall not be necessary for giving effect to the settlement.

Any conveyance of land held on charitable, ecclesiastical or public trusts shall state that the land is held on such trusts, and, where a purchaser has notice that the land is held on charitable, ecclesiastical, or public trusts, he shall be bound to see that any consents or orders requisite for authorising the transaction have been obtained.

(2) The said powers shall be exercisable subject to such consents or orders, if any, being obtained as would, if this Act had not been passed, have been requisite if the transaction were being effected under an express power conferred by the instrument creating the trust, and where the land is vested in … persons having no powers of management, the said powers shall be exercisable by the managing trustees or committee of management, and the … persons aforesaid shall not be liable for giving effect to directions given by the managing trustees or committee of management:

Provided that where—

(a) a disposition or dealing is to be effected for a nominal price or rent, or for less than the best price or rent that can be reasonably obtained or gratuitously; or

(b) any interest in land is to be acquired;

the like consent or order (if any) shall be required in reference to the disposition, dealing or acquisition, as would have been requisite if the intended transaction were a sale.

(3) Nothing in this section affects the jurisdiction of the court, [Charity Commission], Board of Education, or other competent authority, in regard to the administration of charitable, ecclesiastical, or public trusts.

(4) …

(5) Where any trustees or the majority of any set of trustees have power to transfer or create any legal estate, that estate shall be transferred or created by them in the names and on behalf of the persons … in whom the legal estate is vested.

(6) This section applies (save as otherwise provided) whether the trust was created before or after the commencement of this Act, but does not apply to land to which the Universities and College Estates Act 1925, applies.

[115]

NOTES

Repealed, except in relation to the deed of settlement set out in the Schedule to the Chequers Estate Act 1917 or the trusts instrument set out in the Schedule to the Chevening Estate Act 1959, by the Trusts of Land and Appointment of Trustees Act 1996, s 25(2), Sch 4.

Sub-ss (2), (5): words omitted repealed by the Charities Act 1960, s 48(2), Sch 7, Pt I.

Sub-s (3): words in square brackets substituted by the Charities Act 2006, s 75(1), Sch 8, para 19.

Sub-s (4): repealed by the Charities Act 1960, s 48(2), Sch 7, Pt I.

Trustees of Settlement

30 Who are trustees for purposes of Act

(1) Subject to the provisions of this Act, the following persons are trustees of a settlement for the purposes of this Act, and are in this Act referred to as the "trustees of the settlement" or "trustees of a settlement", namely—

(i) the persons, if any, who are for the time being under the settlement trustees with power of sale of the settled land (subject or not to the consent of any person), or with power of consent to or approval of the exercise of such a power of sale, or if there are no such persons; then

(ii) the persons, if any, for the time being, who are by the settlement declared to be trustees thereof for the purposes of the Settled Land Acts 1882 to 1890, or any of them, or this Act, or if there are no such persons; then

(iii) the persons, if any, who are for the time being under the settlement trustees with [a power or duty to sell] any other land comprised in the settlement and subject to the same limitations as the land to be sold or otherwise dealt with, or with power of consent to or approval of the exercise of such a power of sale, or, if there are no such persons; then

(iv) the persons, if any, who are for the time being under the settlement trustees with [a future power or duty to sell] the settled land, or with power of consent to or approval of the exercise of such a future power of sale, and whether the power [or duty] takes effect in all events or not, or, if there are no such persons; then

(v) the persons, if any, appointed by deed to be trustees of the settlement by all the persons who at the date of the deed were together able, by virtue of their beneficial interests or by the exercise of an equitable power, to dispose of the settled land in equity for the whole estate the subject of the settlement.

(2) Paragraphs (i) (iii) and (iv) of the last preceding subsection take effect in like manner as if the powers therein referred to had not by this Act been made exercisable by the tenant for life or statutory owner.

(3) Where a settlement is created by will, or a settlement has arisen by the effect of an intestacy, and apart from this subsection there would be no trustees for the purposes of this Act of such settlement, then the personal representatives of the deceased shall, until other trustees are appointed, be by virtue of this Act the trustees of the settlement, but where there is a sole personal representative, not being a trust corporation, it shall be obligatory on him to appoint an additional trustee to act with him for the purposes of this Act, and the provisions of the Trustee Act 1925, relating to the appointment of new trustees and the vesting of trust property shall apply accordingly. **[116]**

NOTES

Sub-s (1): words in square brackets substituted by the Trusts of Land and Appointment of Trustees Act 1996, s 25(1), Sch 3, para 2(9); for savings in relation to entailed interests created before the commencement of that Act, and savings consequential upon the abolition of the doctrine of conversion, see s 25(4), (5) thereof.

31 As to trustees of compound settlements

(1) Persons who are for the time being trustees for the purposes of this Act of an instrument which is a settlement, or is deemed to be a subsisting settlement for the purposes of this Act, shall be the trustees for the purposes of this Act of any settlement constituted by that instrument and any instruments subsequent in date or operation.

[Where there are trustees for the purposes of this Act of the instrument under which there is a tenant for life or statutory owner but there are no trustees for those purposes of a prior instrument, being one of the instruments by which a compound settlement is constituted, those trustees shall, unless and until trustees are appointed of the prior instrument or of the compound settlement, be the trustees for the purposes of this Act of the compound settlement.]

(2) This section applies to instruments coming into operation before as well as after the commencement of this Act, but shall have effect without prejudice to any appointment made by the court before such commencement of trustees of a settlement constituted by more than one instrument, and to the power of the court in any case after such commencement to make any such appointment, and where any such appointment has been made before such commencement or is made thereafter this section shall not apply or shall cease to apply to the settlement consisting of the instruments to which the appointment relates.

[117]

NOTES

Sub-s (1): words in square brackets inserted by the Law of Property (Amendment) Act 1926, s 7, Schedule.

32 As to trustees of referential settlements

(1) Where a settlement takes or has taken effect by reference to another settlement, the trustees for the time being of the settlement to which reference is made shall be the trustees of the settlement by reference, but this section does not apply if the settlement by reference contains an appointment of trustees thereof for the purposes of the Settled Land Acts 1882 to 1890, or any of them, or this Act.

(2) This section applies to instruments coming into operation before as well as after the commencement of this Act, but shall have effect without prejudice to any appointment made by the court before such commencement of trustees of a settlement by reference, or of the compound settlement consisting of a settlement and any other settlement or settlements made by reference thereto, and to the power of the court in any case after such commencement to make any such appointment, and where any such appointment has been made before such commencement or is made thereafter this section shall not apply or shall cease to apply.

(3) In this section "a settlement by reference to another settlement" means a settlement of property upon the limitations and subject to the powers and provisions of an existing settlement, with or without variation.

[118]

33 Continuance of trustees in office, and as to certain compound settlements

(1) Where any persons have been appointed or constituted trustees of a settlement, whether by an order of the court or otherwise, or have by reason of [a power or duty to sell], or by reason of a power of consent to, or approval of, the exercise of a power of sale, or by virtue of this Act, or otherwise at any time become trustees of a settlement for the purposes of the Settled Land Acts 1882 to 1890, or this Act, then those persons or their successors in office shall remain and be trustees of the settlement as long as that settlement is subsisting or deemed to be subsisting for the purposes of this Act.

In this subsection "successors in office" means the persons who, by appointment or otherwise, have become trustees for the purposes aforesaid.

(2) Where settled land is or has been expressed to be disposed of under a compound settlement of which trustees were appointed by the court, and the capital money (if any) arising on the disposition is or was paid to the persons who by virtue of the order or any subsequent appointment appear to be or to have been the trustees of that settlement, and where the person by or on whose behalf the disposition is or was made is or was the tenant for life or statutory owner of the land disposed of under an instrument mentioned in the order as constituting part of such compound settlement (in this subsection called "the principal instrument") then the title of the person to whom the disposition is made shall not be impeachable on the ground—

(a) that the instruments mentioned in the order did not constitute a compound settlement; or
(b) that those instruments were not all the instruments at the date of the order or of the disposition constituting the compound settlement of the land disposed of; or
(c) that any of the instruments mentioned in the order did not form part of the settlement of the land disposed of, or had ceased to form part of the settlement at the date of the disposition;

but nothing in this subsection shall prejudice the rights of any person in respect of any estate, interest or charge under any instrument existing at the date of the order and not mentioned therein which would not have been overreached if the disposition had been made by or on behalf of the tenant for life or statutory owner under the principal instrument as such, and there had been trustees of that instrument for the purposes of the Settled Land Acts 1882 to 1890, or this Act, and the capital money, if any, arising on the disposition had been paid to the trustees.

(3) The foregoing provisions of this section operate to confirm all dispositions made before the commencement of this Act, but not so as to render invalid or prejudice any order of the court, or any title or right acquired before the commencement of this Act, and operates without prejudice to any appointment already made by the court of trustees of a settlement, and to the power of the court in any case hereafter to make any such appointment.

[119]

NOTES

Sub-s (1): words in square brackets substituted by the Trusts of Land and Appointment of Trustees Act 1996, s 25(1), Sch 3, para 2(10); for savings in relation to entailed interests created before the commencement of that Act, and savings consequential upon the abolition of the doctrine of conversion, see s 25(4), (5) thereof.

34 Appointment of trustees by court

(1) If at any time there are no trustees of a settlement, or where in any other case it is expedient, for the purposes of this Act, that new trustees of a settlement be appointed, the court may, if it thinks fit, on the application of the tenant for life, statutory owner, or of any other person having, under the

settlement, an estate or interest in the settled land, in possession, remainder or otherwise, or, in the case of an infant, of his testamentary or other guardian or next friend, appoint fit persons to be trustees of the settlement.

(2) The persons so appointed, and the survivors and survivor of them, while continuing to be trustees or trustee, and, until the appointment of new trustees, the personal representatives or representative for the time being of the last surviving or continuing trustee, shall become and be the trustees or trustee of the settlement.

[120]

35 Procedure on appointment of new trustees

(1) Whenever a new trustee for the purposes of this Act is appointed of a trust instrument or a trustee thereof for the purposes aforesaid is discharged from the trust without a new trustee being appointed, a deed shall be executed supplemental to the last or only principal vesting instrument containing a declaration that the persons therein named, being the persons who after such appointment or discharge, as the case may be, are the trustees of the trust instrument for the purposes aforesaid, are the trustees of the settlement for those purposes; and a memorandum shall be endorsed on or annexed to the last or only principal vesting instrument in accordance with the Trustee Act 1925.

(2) Every such deed as aforesaid shall, if the trustee was appointed or discharged by the court be executed by such person as the court may direct, and, in any other case, shall be executed by—

- (i) the person, if any, named in the principal vesting instrument as the person for the time being entitled to appoint new trustees of the settlement, or if no person is so named, or the person is dead or unable or unwilling to act, the persons who if the principal vesting instrument had been the only instrument constituting the settlement would have had power to appoint new trustees thereof;
- (ii) the persons named in the deed of declaration as the trustees of the settlement; and
- (iii) any trustee who is discharged as aforesaid or retires.

(3) A statement contained in any such deed of declaration as is mentioned in this section to the effect that the person named in the principal vesting instrument as the person for the time being entitled to appoint new trustees of the settlement is unable or unwilling to act, or that a trustee has remained outside the United Kingdom for more than twelve months, or refuses or is unfit to act, or is incapable of acting, shall in favour of a purchaser of a legal estate be conclusive evidence of the matter stated.

[121]

Provisions as to Undivided Shares

36 Undivided shares to take effect behind a [trust of land]

(1) If and when, after the commencement of this Act, settled land is held in trust for persons entitled in possession under a trust instrument in undivided shares, the trustees of the settlement (if the settled land is not already vested in them) may require the estate owner in whom the settled land is vested (but in the case of a personal representative subject to his rights and powers for purposes of administration), at the cost of the trust estate, to convey the land to them, or assent to the land vesting in them as joint tenants, and in the meantime the land shall be held on the same trusts as would have been applicable thereto if it had been so conveyed to or vested in the trustees.

(2) If and when the settled land so held in trust in undivided shares is or becomes vested in the trustees of the settlement, the land shall be held by them (subject to any incumbrances affecting the settled land which are secured by a legal mortgage, but freed from any incumbrances affecting the undivided shares or not secured as aforesaid, and from any interests, powers and charges subsisting under the trust instrument which have priority to the trust for the persons entitled to the undivided shares) [in trust for the persons interested in the land].

(3) If the estate owner refuses or neglects for one month after demand in writing to convey the settled land so held in trust in undivided shares in manner aforesaid, or if by reason of his being outside the United Kingdom or being unable to be found, or by reason of the dissolution of a corporation, or for any other reason, the court is satisfied that the conveyance cannot otherwise be made, or cannot be made without undue delay or expense, the court may, on the application of the trustees of the settlement, make an order vesting the settled land in them [in trust for the persons interested in the land].

(4) An undivided share in land shall not be capable of being created except under a trust instrument or under the Law of Property Act 1925, and shall then only take effect behind a [trust of land].

(5) Nothing in this section affects the priority inter se of any incumbrances whether affecting the entirety of the land or an undivided share.

PART I STATUTES

[(6) In subsections (2) and (3) of this section references to the persons interested in the land include persons interested as trustees or personal representatives (as well as persons beneficially interested).]

(7) The provisions of this section bind the Crown.

[122]

NOTES

Section heading, sub-ss (2)–(4): words in square brackets substituted by the Trusts of Land and Appointment of Trustees Act 1996, s 25(1), Sch 3, para 2(11)(a), (b), (d); for savings in relation to entailed interests created before the commencement of that Act, and savings consequential upon the abolition of the doctrine of conversion, see s 25(4), (5) thereof.

Sub-s (6): substituted by the Trusts of Land and Appointment of Trustees Act 1996, s 25(1), Sch 3, para 2(11)(c), subject to savings as noted above.

Transitional Provisions

37 Transitional provisions with respect to existing settlements, etc

The transitional provisions set out in the Second Schedule to this Act shall have effect as regards settlements existing at the commencement of this Act.

[123]

PART II
POWERS OF A TENANT FOR LIFE

Sale and Exchange

38 Powers of sale and exchange

A tenant for life—

(i) May sell the settled land, or any part thereof, or any easement, right or privilege of any kind over or in relation to the land; and

(ii) …

(iii) May make an exchange of the settled land, or any part thereof, or of any easement, right, or privilege of any kind, whether or not newly created, over or in relation to the settled land, or any part thereof, for other land, or for any easement, right or privilege of any kind, whether or not newly created, over or in relation to other land, including an exchange in consideration of money paid for equality of exchange.

[124]

NOTES

Words omitted repealed by the Statute Law (Repeals) Act 1969, s 1, Schedule, Pt III.

39 Regulations respecting sales

(1) Save as hereinafter provided every sale shall be made for the best consideration in money that can reasonably be obtained.

(2) A sale may be made in consideration wholly or partially of a perpetual rent, or a terminable rent consisting of principal and interest combined, payable yearly or half yearly to be secured upon the land sold, or the land to which the easement, right or privilege sold is to be annexed in enjoyment or an adequate part thereof.

In the case of a terminable rent, the conveyance shall distinguish the part attributable to principal and that attributable to interest, and the part attributable to principal shall be capital money arising under this Act:

Provided that, unless the part of the terminable rent attributable to interest varies according to the amount of the principal repaid, the trustees of the settlement shall, during the subsistence of the rent, [accumulate the profits from the capital money by investing them and any resulting profits under the general power of investment in section 3 of the Trustee Act 2000 and shall add the accumulations to capital].

(3) The rent to be reserved on any such sale shall be the best rent that can reasonably be obtained, regard being had to any money paid as part of the consideration, or laid out, or to be laid out, for the benefit of the settled land, and generally to the circumstances of the case, but a peppercorn rent, or a nominal or other rent less than the rent ultimately payable, may be made payable during any period not exceeding five years from the date of the conveyance.

(4) Where a sale is made in consideration of a rent, the following provisions shall have effect:—

(i) The conveyance shall contain a covenant by the purchaser for payment of the rent, and [the statutory powers and remedies for the recovery of the rent shall apply];

(ii) A duplicate of the conveyance shall be executed by the purchaser and delivered to the tenant for life or statutory owner, of which execution and delivery the execution of the conveyance by the tenant for life or statutory owner shall be sufficient evidence;

(iii) A statement, contained in the conveyance or in an indorsement thereon, signed by the tenant for life of statutory owner, respecting any matter of fact or of calculation under this Act in relation to the sale, shall, in favour of the purchaser and of those claiming under him, be sufficient evidence of the matter stated.

(5) The consideration on a sale to any company incorporated by special Act of Parliament or by provisional order confirmed by Parliament or by any other order, scheme or certificate having the force of an Act of Parliament, may, with the consent of the tenant for life, consist, wholly or in part, of fully-paid securities of any description of the company, and such securities shall be vested in the trustees of the settlement and shall be subject to the provisions of this Act relating to securities representing capital money arising under this Act, and may be retained and held by the trustees in like manner as if they had been authorised by this Act for the investment of capital money.

(6) A sale may be made in one lot or in several lots, and either by auction or by private contract, and may be made subject to any stipulations respecting title, or evidence of title, or other things.

(7) On a sale the tenant for life may fix reserve biddings and may buy in at an auction.

[125]

NOTES

Sub-s (2): words in square brackets substituted by the Trustee Act 2000, s 40(1), Sch 2, Pt II, para 8.

Sub-s (4): words in square brackets substituted by the Law of Property (Amendment) Act 1926, s 7, Schedule.

Disapplication: this section is disapplied in relation to the disposal of land by a registered provider: see the Housing and Regeneration Act 2008, s 188 at **[2468]**.

40 Regulations respecting exchanges

(1) Save as in this Part of this Act provided, every exchange shall be made for the best consideration in land or in land and money that can reasonably be obtained.

(2) An exchange may be made subject to any stipulations respecting title, or evidence of title, or other things.

(3) Settled land in England or Wales shall not be given in exchange for land out of England or Wales.

[126]

Leasing Powers

41 Power to lease for ordinary or building or mining or forestry purposes

A tenant for life may lease the settled land, or any part thereof, or any easement, right, or privilege of any kind over or in relation to the land, for any purpose whatever, whether involving waste or not, for any term not exceeding—

(i) In case of a building lease, nine hundred and ninety-nine years;
(ii) In case of a mining lease, one hundred years;
(iii) In case of a forestry lease, nine hundred and ninety-nine years;
(iv) In case of any other lease, fifty years.

[127]

42 Regulations respecting leases generally

(1) Save as hereinafter provided, every lease—

(i) shall be by deed, and be made to take effect in possession not later than twelve months after its date, or in reversion after an existing lease having not more than seven years to run at the date of the new lease;
(ii) shall reserve the best rent that can reasonably be obtained, regard being had to any fine taken, and to any money laid out or to be laid out for the benefit of the settled land, and generally to the circumstances of the case;
(iii) shall contain a covenant by the lessee for payment of the rent, and a condition of re-entry on the rent not being paid within a time therein specified not exceeding thirty days.

(2) A counterpart of every lease shall be executed by the lessee and delivered to the tenant for life or statutory owner, of which execution and delivery the execution of the lease by the tenant for life or statutory owner shall be sufficient evidence.

(3) A statement, contained in a lease or in an indorsement thereon, signed by the tenant for life or statutory owner, respecting any matter of fact or of calculation under this Act in relation to the lease, shall, in favour of the lessee and of those claiming under him, be sufficient evidence of the matter stated.

(4) A fine received on the grant of a lease under any power conferred by this Act shall be deemed to be capital money arising under this Act.

(5) A lease at the best rent that can be reasonably obtained without fine, and whereby the lessee is not exempted from punishment for waste, may be made—

(i) Where the term does not exceed twenty-one years—

(a) without any notice of an intention to make the lease having been given under this Act; and

(b) notwithstanding that there are no trustees of the settlement; and

(ii) Where the term does not extend beyond three years from the date of the writing, by any writing under hand only containing an agreement instead of a covenant by the lessee for payment of rent.

[128]

43 Leasing powers for special objects

The leasing power of a tenant for life extends to the making of—

(i) a lease for giving effect (in such manner and so far as the law permits) to a covenant of renewal, performance whereof could be enforced against the owner for the time being of the settled land; and

(ii) a lease for confirming, as far as may be, a previous lease being void or voidable, but so that every lease, as and when confirmed, shall be such a lease as might at the date of the original lease have been lawfully granted under this Act or otherwise, as the case may require.

[129]

Provisions as to building, mining and forestry leases

44 Regulations respecting building leases

(1) Every building lease shall be made partly in consideration of the lessee, or some person by whose direction the lease is granted, or some other person, having erected or agreeing to erect buildings, new or additional, or having improved or repaired or agreeing to improve or repair buildings, or having executed or agreeing to execute on the land leased, an improvement authorised by this Act for or in connexion with building purposes.

(2) A peppercorn rent or a nominal or other rent less than the rent ultimately payable, may be made payable for the first five years or any less part of the term.

(3) Where the land is contracted to be leased in lots, the entire amount of rent to be ultimately payable may be apportioned among the lots in any manner:

Provided that—

(i) the annual rent reserved by any lease shall not be less than [50p]; and

(ii) the total amount of the rents reserved on all leases for the time being granted shall not be less than the total amount of the rents which, in order that the leases may be in conformity with this Act, ought to be reserved in respect of the whole land for the time being leased; and

(iii) the rent reserved by any lease shall not exceed one-fifth part of the full annual value of the land comprised in that lease with the buildings thereon when completed.

[130]

NOTES

Sub-s (3): sum in square brackets substituted by virtue of the Decimal Currency Act 1969, s 10(1).

45 Regulations respecting mining leases

(1) In a mining lease—

(i) the rent may be made to be ascertainable by or to vary according to the acreage worked, or by or according to the quantities of any mineral or substance gotten, made merchantable, converted, carried away, or disposed of, in or from the settled land, or any other land, or by or according to any facilities given in that behalf; and

(ii) the rent may also be made to vary according to the price of the minerals or substances gotten, or any of them, and such price may be the saleable value, or the price or value appearing in any trade or market or other price list or return from time to time, or may be the marketable value as ascertained in any manner prescribed by the lease (including a reference to arbitration), or may be an average of any such prices of values taken during a specified period; and

(iii) a fixed or minimum rent may be made payable, with or without power for the lessees, in case the rent, according to acreage or quantity or otherwise, in any specified period does not produce an amount equal to the fixed or minimum rent, to make up the deficiency in any subsequent specified period, free of rent other than the fixed or minimum rent.

(2) A lease may be made partly in consideration of the lessee having executed, or agreeing to execute, on the land leased an improvement authorised by this Act, for or in connexion with mining purposes.

[131]

46 Variation of building or mining lease according to circumstances of district

(1) Where it is shown to the court with respect to the district in which any settled land is situate, either—

(i) that it is the custom for land therein to be leased for building or mining purposes for a longer term or on other conditions than the term or conditions specified in that behalf in this Act; or

(ii) that it is difficult to make leases for building or mining purposes of land therein, except for a longer term or on other conditions than the term and conditions specified in that behalf in this Act;

the court may, if it thinks fit, authorise generally the tenant for life or statutory owner to make from time to time leases of or affecting the settled land in that district, or parts thereof for any term or on any conditions as in the order of the court expressed, or may, if it thinks fit, authorise the tenant for life or statutory owner to make any such lease in any particular case.

(2) Thereupon the tenant for life or statutory owner, and, subject to any direction in the order of the court to the contrary, each of his successors in title being a tenant for life or statutory owner, may make in any case, or in the particular case, a lease of the settled land, or part thereof, in conformity with the order.

[132]

47 Capitalisation of part of mining rent

Under a mining lease, whether the mines or minerals leased are already opened or in work or not, unless a contrary intention is expressed in the settlement there shall be from time to time set aside, as capital money arising under this Act, part of the rent as follows, namely—where the tenant for life or statutory owner is impeachable for waste in respect of minerals, three fourth parts of the rent, and otherwise one fourth part thereof, and in every such case the residue of the rent shall go as rents and profits.

[133]

48 Regulations respecting forestry leases

(1) In the case of a forestry lease—

(i) a peppercorn rent or a nominal or other rent less than the rent ultimately payable, may be made payable for the first ten years or any less part of the term;

(ii) the rent may be made to be ascertainable by, or to vary according to the value of the timber on the land comprised in the lease, or the produce thereof, which may during any year be cut, converted carried away, or otherwise disposed of;

(iii) a fixed or minimum rent may be made payable, with or without power for the lessee, in case the rent according to value in any specified period does not produce an amount equal to the fixed or minimum rent, to make up the deficiency in any subsequent specified period, free of rent other than the fixed or minimum rent; and

(iv) any other provisions may be made for the sharing of the proceeds or profits of the user of the land between the reversioner and the Forestry Commissioners.

(2) In this expression "timber" includes all forest products.

[134]

Miscellaneous Powers

49 Power on dispositions to impose restrictions and make reservations and stipulations

(1) On a sale or other disposition or dealing under the powers of this Act—

(a) any easement, right, or privilege of any kind may be reserved or granted over or in relation to the settled land or any part thereof or other land, including the land disposed of, and, in the case of an exchange, the land taken in exchange; and

(b) any restriction with respect to building on or other user of land, or with respect to mines and minerals, or with respect to or for the purpose of the more beneficial working thereof, or with respect to any other thing, may be imposed and made binding, as far as the law permits, by covenant, condition or otherwise, on the tenant for life or statutory owner and the settled land or any part thereof, or on the other party and any land disposed of to him; and

(c) the whole or any part of any capital or annual sum (and in the case of an annual sum whether temporary or perpetual) charged on or payable out of the land disposed of, or any part thereof, and other land subject to the settlement, may as between the tenant for life or statutory owner and his successors in title, and the other party and persons deriving title under or in succession to him (but without prejudice to the rights of the person entitled to such capital or annual sum) be charged exclusively on the land disposed of, or any part thereof, or such other land as aforesaid, or any part thereof, in exoneration of the rest of the land on or out of which such capital or annual sum is charged or payable.

(2) A sale of land may be made subject to a stipulation that all or any of the timber and other trees, pollards, tellers, underwood, saplings and plantations on the land sold (in this section referred to as "timber") or any articles attached to the land (in this section referred to as "fixtures") shall be taken by the purchaser at a valuation and the amount of the valuation shall form part of the price of the land, and shall be capital money accordingly.

(3) Where on a sale the consideration attributable to any timber or fixtures is by mistake paid to a tenant for life or other person not entitled to receive it, then, if such person or the purchaser or the persons deriving title under either of them subsequently pay the aforesaid consideration, with such interest, if any, thereon as the court may direct to the trustees of the settlement or other persons entitled thereto or into court, the court may, on the application of the purchaser or the persons deriving title under him, declare that the disposition is to take effect as if the whole of the consideration had at the date thereof been duly paid to the trustees of the settlement or other persons entitled to receive the same.

The person, not entitled to receive the same, to whom the consideration is paid, and his estate and effects shall remain liable to make good any loss attributable to the mistake.

[135]

50 Separate dealing with surface and minerals with or without wayleaves, etc

A sale, exchange, lease or other authorised disposition, may be made either of land, with or without an exception or reservation of all or any of the mines and minerals therein, or of any mines and minerals, and in any such case with or without a grant or reservation of powers of working, wayleaves or rights of way, rights of water and drainage, and other powers, easements, rights, and privileges for or incident to or connected with mining purposes, in relation to the settled land, or any part thereof, or any other land.

[136]

51 Power to grant options

(1) A tenant for life may at any time, either with or without consideration, grant by writing an option to purchase or take a lease of the settled land, or any part thereof, or any easement, right, or privilege over or in relation to the same at a price or rent fixed at the time of the granting of the option.

(2) Every such option shall be made exercisable within an agreed number of years not exceeding ten.

(3) The price or rent shall be the best which, having regard to all the circumstances, can reasonably be obtained and either—

(a) may be a specified sum of money or rent, or at a specified rate according to the superficial area of the land with respect to which the option is exercised: or the frontage thereof or otherwise; or

(b) in the case of an option to purchase contained in a lease or agreement for a lease, may be a stated number of years' purchase of the highest rent reserved by the lease or agreement; or

(c) if the option is exercisable as regards part of the land comprised in the lease or agreement, may be a proportionate part of such highest rent;

and any aggregate price or rent may be made to be apportionable in any manner, or according to any system, or by reference to arbitration.

(4) An option to take a mining lease may be coupled with the grant of a licence to search for and prove any mines or minerals under the settled land, or any part thereof, pending the exercise of the option.

(5) The consideration for the grant of the option shall be capital money arising under this Act.

[137]

52 Surrenders and regrants

(1) A tenant for life may accept, with or without consideration, a surrender of any lease of settled land, whether made under this Act or not, or a regrant of any land granted in fee simple, whether under this Act or not, in respect of the whole land leased or granted, or any part thereof, with or without an exception of all or any of the mines and minerals therein, or in respect of mines and minerals, or any of them, and with or without an exception of any easement, right or privilege of any kind over or in relation to the land surrendered or regranted.

(2) On a surrender of a lease, or a regrant of land granted in fee simple, in respect of part only of the land or mines and minerals leased or granted, the rent or rentcharge may be apportioned.

(3) On a surrender or regrant, the tenant for life may in relation to the land or mines and minerals surrendered or regranted, or of any part thereof, make a new or other lease, or grant in fee simple, or new or other leases, or grants in fee simple, in lots.

(4) A new or other lease, or grant in fee simple, may comprise additional land or mines and minerals, and may reserve any apportioned or other rent or rentcharge.

(5) On a surrender or regrant, and the making of a new or other lease, whether for the same or for any extended or other term, or of a new or other grant in fee simple, and whether or not subject to the same or to any other covenants, provisions, or conditions, the value of the lessee's or grantee's interests in the lease surrendered, or the land regranted, may be taken into account in the determination of the amount of the rent or rentcharge to be reserved, and of any fine or consideration in money to be taken, and of the nature of the covenants, provisions, and conditions to be inserted in the new or other lease, or grant in fee simple.

(6) Every new or other lease, or grant in fee simple, shall be in conformity with this Act.

(7) All money, not being rent or rentcharge, received on the exercise by the tenant for life of the powers conferred by this section, shall, unless the court, on an application made within six months after the receipt thereof or within such further time as the court may in special circumstances allow, otherwise directs, be capital money arising under this Act.

(8) A regrant shall be made to the tenant for life or statutory owner, and shall be deemed a subsidiary vesting deed, and the statements and particulars required in the case of subsidiary vesting deeds shall be inserted therein.

(9) In this section "land granted in fee simple" means land so granted with or subject to a reservation thereout of a perpetual or terminable rentcharge which is or forms part of the settled land, and "grant in fee simple" has a corresponding meaning.

[138]

53 Acceptance of leases

(1) A tenant for life may accept a lease of any land, or of any mines and minerals or of any easement, right, or privilege, convenient to be held or worked with or annexed in enjoyment to the settled land, or any part thereof, for such period, and upon such terms and conditions, as the tenant for life thinks fit:

Provided that no fine shall be paid out of capital money in respect of such lease.

(2) The lease shall be granted to the tenant for life or statutory owner, and shall be deemed a subsidiary vesting deed, and the statements and particulars required in the case of subsidiary vesting deeds shall either be inserted therein or endorsed thereon.

(3) The lease may contain an option to purchase the reversion expectant on the term thereby granted.

[139]

54 Power to grant water rights to statutory bodies

(1) For the development, improvement, or general benefit of the settled land, or any part thereof, a tenant for life may make a grant in fee simple or absolutely, or a lease for any term of years absolute, for a nominal price or rent, or for less than the best price or rent that can reasonably be obtained, or gratuitously, to any statutory authority, of any water or streams or springs of water in, upon, or under the settled land, and of any rights of taking, using, enjoying and conveying water, and of laying, constructing, maintaining, and repairing mains, pipes, reservoirs, dams, weirs and other works of any kind proper for the supply and distribution of water, and of any part of the settled land required as a site for any of the aforesaid works, and of any easement, right or privilege over or in relation to the settled land or any part thereof in connexion with any of the aforesaid works.

(2) This section does not authorise the creation of any greater rights than could have been created by a person absolutely entitled for his own benefit to the settled land affected.

(3) In this section "statutory authority" means an authority or company for the time being empowered by any Act of Parliament, public general, or local or private, or by any order or certificate having the force of an Act of Parliament, to provide with a supply of water any town, parish or place in which the settled land or any part thereof is situated.

(4) All money, not being rent, received on the exercise of any power conferred by this section shall be capital money arising under this Act.

[140]

55 Power to grant land for public and charitable purposes

(1) For the development, improvement, or general benefit of the settled land, or any part thereof, a tenant for life may make a grant in fee simple, or absolutely, or a lease for any term of years absolute, for a nominal price or rent, or for less than the best price or rent that can reasonably

be obtained, or gratuitously, of any part of the settled land, with or without any easement, right or privilege over or in relation to the settled land or any part thereof, for all or any one or more of the following purposes, namely:—

(i) For the site, or the extension of any existing site, of a place of religious worship, residence for a minister of religion, school house, town hall, market house, public library, public baths, museum, hospital, infirmary, or other public building, literary or scientific institution, drill hall, working-men's club, parish room, reading room or village institute, with or without in any case any yard, garden, or other ground to be held with any such building; or

(ii) For the construction, enlargement, or improvement of any railway, canal, road (public or private), dock, sea-wall, embankment, drain, watercourse, or reservoir; or

(iii) For any other public or charitable purpose in connexion with the settled land, or any part thereof, or tending to the benefit of the persons residing, or for whom dwellings may be erected, on the settled land, or any part thereof.

Not more than one acre shall in any particular case be conveyed for any purpose mentioned in paragraphs (i) and (iii) of this subsection, nor more than five acres for any purpose mentioned in paragraph (ii) of this subsection, unless the full consideration be paid or reserved in respect of the excess.

(2) All money, not being rent, received on the exercise of any power conferred by this section shall be capital money arising under this Act.

[141]

56 Dedication for streets, open spaces, etc

(1) On or after or in connexion with a sale or grant for building purposes, or a building lease, or the development as a building estate of the settled land, or any part thereof, or at any other reasonable time, the tenant for life, for the general benefit of the residents on the settled land, or on any part thereof—

(i) may cause or require any parts of the settled land to be appropriated and laid out for streets, roads, paths, squares, gardens, or other open spaces, for the use, gratuitously or on payment, of the public or of individuals, with sewers, drains, water courses, fences, paving, or other works necessary or proper in connexion therewith; and

(ii) may provide that the parts so appropriated shall be conveyed to or vested in the trustees of the settlement, or other trustees, or any company or public body, on trusts or subject to provisions for securing the continued appropriation thereof to the purposes aforesaid, and the continued repair or maintenance of streets and other places and works aforesaid, with or without provision for appointment of new trustees when required; and

(iii) may execute any general or other deed necessary or proper for giving effect to the provisions of this section (which deed may be inrolled in the Central Office of the *Supreme Court* [Senior Courts]), and thereby declare the mode, terms, and conditions of the appropriation, and the manner in which and the persons by whom the benefit thereof is to be enjoyed, and the nature and extent of the privileges and conveniences granted.

(2) In regard to the dedication of land for the public purposes aforesaid, a tenant for life shall be in the same position as if he were an absolute owner.

(3) A tenant for life shall have power—

(a) to enter into any agreement for the recompense to be made for any part of the settled land which is required for the widening of a highway under [the Highways Act 1980], or otherwise;

(b) to consent to the diversion of any highway over the settled land under [the Highways Act 1980], or otherwise; and

(c) …

and any agreement or consent so made or given shall be valid and effectual, for all purposes, as if made or given by an absolute owner of the settled land.

(4) All money, not being rent, received on the exercise of any power conferred by this section shall be capital money arising under this Act.

[142]

NOTES

Sub-s (1): words in italics in para (iii) substituted by subsequent words in square brackets by the Constitutional Reform Act 2005, s 59(5), Sch 11, Pt 2, para 4(1), (3), as from 1 October 2009.

Sub-s (3): words in square brackets in paras (a), (b) substituted by the Highways Act 1980, s 343(2), Sch 24; para (c) repealed by the Highways Act 1959, s 312(2), Sch 25.

57 Provision of land for small dwellings, small holdings and dwellings for working classes

(1) Where land is sold, or given in exchange or leased—

(a) for the purpose of the erection on such land of small dwellings; or

(b) to the council of a county or county borough for the purposes of small holdings;

the sale, exchange, or lease may, notwithstanding anything contained in this Act, be made for such consideration in money, or land, or in land and money, or may reserve such rent, as having regard to the said purposes and to all the circumstances of the case, is the best that can reasonably be obtained, notwithstanding that a better consideration or rent might have been obtained if the land were sold, exchanged, or leased, for another purpose.

(2) Notwithstanding anything contained in, and in addition to the other powers conferred by this Act, a tenant for life may at any time—

(a) for the purpose of the erection of dwellings for the working classes, or the provision of gardens to be held therewith; or

(b) for the purpose of the Small Holdings and Allotments Acts 1908 to 1919;

make a grant in fee simple or absolutely, or a lease for any term of years absolute of any part of the settled land, with or without any easement, right or privilege of any kind over or in relation to the settled land or any part thereof, for a nominal price or rent, or for less than the best price or rent that can reasonably be obtained or gratuitously:

Provided that, except under an order of the court, not more than two acres in the case of land situate in an urban district, or ten acres in the case of land situate in a rural district, in any one parish shall be granted or leased under the powers conferred by this subsection, unless the full consideration be paid or reserved in respect of the excess.

(3) All money, not being rent, received on the exercise of any power conferred by this section shall be capital money arising under this Act.

[143]

58 Power to compromise claims and release restrictions, etc

(1) A tenant for life may, with the consent in writing of the trustees of the settlement, either with or without giving or taking any consideration in money or otherwise, compromise, compound, abandon, submit to arbitration, or otherwise settle any claim, dispute, or question whatsoever relating to the settled land, or any part thereof, including in particular claims, disputes or questions as to boundaries, the ownership of mines and minerals, rights and powers of working mines and minerals, local laws and customs relative to the working of mines and minerals and other matters … easements, and restrictive covenants, and for any of those purposes may enter into, give, execute, and do such agreements, assurances, releases, and other things as the tenant for life may, with such consent as aforesaid, think proper.

(2) A tenant for life may, with the consent in writing of the trustees of the settlement, at any time, by deed or writing, either with or without consideration in money or otherwise, release, waive, or modify, or agree to release, waive, or modify any covenant, agreement, or restriction imposed on any other land for the benefit of the settled land, or any part thereof, or release, or agree to release, any other land from any easement, right or privilege, including a right of pre-emption, affecting the same for the benefit of the settled land, or any part thereof.

(3) A tenant for life may contract that a transaction effected before or after the commencement of this Act, which (whether subject or not to any variation authorised by this subsection) is affected by section seventy-eight of the Railway Clauses Consolidation Act 1845, or by section twenty-two of the Waterworks Clauses Act 1847 (relating to support by minerals) shall take effect as if some other distance than forty yards or the prescribed distance had been mentioned in such sections or had been otherwise prescribed.

In any case where section seventy-eight aforesaid has effect as amended and re-enacted by Part II of the Mines (Working Facilities and Support) Act 1923, a tenant for life may make any agreement authorised by section eighty-five A of the Railway Clauses Consolidation Act 1845, as enacted in the said Part II.

[144]

NOTES

Sub-s (1): words omitted repealed by the Statute Law (Repeals) Act 1969, s 1, Schedule, Pt III.

59 Power to vary leases and grants and to give licences and consents

(1) A tenant for life may, at any time, by deed, either with or without consideration in money or otherwise, vary, release, waive or modify, either absolutely or otherwise, the terms of any lease whenever made of the settled land or any part thereof, or any covenants or conditions contained in any grant in fee simple whenever made of land with or subject to a reservation thereout of a rent which is or forms part of the settled land, and in either case in respect of the whole or any part of the land comprised in any such lease or grant, but so that every such lease or grant shall, after such variation, release, waiver or modification as aforesaid, be such a lease or grant as might then have been lawfully made under this Act if the lease had been surrendered, or the land comprised in the grant had never been so comprised, or had been regranted.

(2) Where land is or has been disposed of subject to any covenant requiring the licence, consent, or approval of the covenantee or his successors in title as to—

PART I STATUTES

(a) the user of the land in any manner; or
(b) the erection construction or alteration of or addition to buildings or works of any description on the land; or
(c) the plans or elevations of any proposed buildings or other works on the land; or
(d) any other act, matter, or thing relating to the land, or any buildings or works thereon; or
(e) any assignment, under-letting or parting with the possession of all or any part of the property comprised in any lease affecting the settled land;

and the covenant enures for the benefit of settled land (including, where the disposition is a lease, the reversion expectant on the determination thereof), the licence, consent or approval may be given by the tenant for life of the settled land affected.

[145]

60 Power to apportion rents

(1) A tenant for life may, at any time, by deed, either with or without consideration in money or otherwise, agree for the apportionment of any rent reserved or created by any such lease or grant as mentioned in the last preceding section, or any rent being or forming part of the settled land, so that the apportioned parts of such rent shall thenceforth be payable exclusively out of or in respect of such respective portions of the land subject thereto as may be thought proper, and also agree that any covenants, agreements, powers, or remedies for securing such rent and any other covenants or agreements by the lessee or grantee and any conditions shall also be apportioned and made applicable exclusively to the respective portions of the land out of or in respect of which the apportioned parts of such rent shall thenceforth be payable.

(2) Where the settled land, or any part thereof, is held or derived under a lease, or under a grant reserving rent, or subject to covenants, agreements or conditions, whether such lease or grant comprises other land or not, the tenant for life may at any time by deed, with or without giving or taking any consideration in money or otherwise, procure the variation, release, waiver, or modification, either absolutely or otherwise, of the terms, covenants, agreements, or conditions contained in such lease or grant, in respect of the whole or any part of the settled land comprised therein, including the apportionment of any rent, covenants, agreements, conditions, and provisions reserved, or created by, or contained in, such lease or grant.

(3) This section applies to leases or grants made either before or after the commencement of this Act.

[146]

61 Provisions as to consideration

(1) All money, not being rent, payable by the tenant for life in respect of any transaction to which any of the three last preceding sections relates shall be paid out of capital money arising under this Act, and all money, not being rent, received on the exercise by the tenant for life of the powers conferred by any of those sections, shall, unless the court, on an application made within six months after the receipt thereof or within such further time as the court may in special circumstances allow, otherwise directs, be capital money arising under this Act.

(2) For the purpose of the three last preceding sections "consideration in money or otherwise" means—

(a) a capital sum of money or a rent;
(b) land being freehold or leasehold for any term of years whereof not less than sixty years shall be unexpired;
(c) any easement, right or privilege over or in relation to the settled land, or any part thereof, or any other land;
(d) the benefit of any restrictive covenant or condition; and
(e) the release of the settled land, or any part thereof, or any other land, from any easement, right or privilege, including a right of pre-emption, or from the burden of any restrictive covenant or condition affecting the same.

[147]

62 Special provisions as to manorial incidents, etc

(1)–(3) …

(4) In reference to the conversion of a perpetually renewable lease or underlease into a long term, a tenant for life may enter into such agreements and do such acts and things as the lessor or lessee or under lessee, as the case may require, is, by any enactment authorised to enter into or do.

[148]

NOTES

Sub-ss (1)–(3): repealed by the Statute Law (Repeals) Act 1969, s 1, Schedule, Pt III.

63 Power to complete predecessor's contracts

A tenant for life may make any disposition which is necessary or proper for giving effect to a contract entered into by a predecessor in title, and which if made by that predecessor would have been valid as against his successors in title.

[149]

64 General power for the tenant for life to effect any transaction under an order of the court

(1) Any transaction affecting or concerning the settled land, or any part thereof, or any other land (not being a transaction otherwise authorised by this Act, or by the settlement) which in the opinion of the court would be for the benefit of the settled land, or any part thereof, or the persons interested under the settlement, may, under an order of the court, be effected by a tenant for life, if it is one which could have been validly effected by an absolute owner.

(2) In this section "transaction" includes any sale, … exchange, assurance, grant, lease, surrender, reconveyance, release, reservation, or other disposition, and any purchase or other acquisition, and any covenant, contract, or option, and any application of capital money … and any compromise or other dealing, or arrangement … ; and "effected" has the meaning appropriate to the particular transaction; and the references to land include references to restrictions and burdens affecting land.

[150]

NOTES

Sub-s (2): first words omitted repealed by the Statute Law (Repeals) Act 1969, s 1, Schedule, Pt III; other words omitted repealed by the Settled Land and Trustee Acts (Court's General Powers) Act 1943, s 2.

Provisions as to special classes of property

65 Power to dispose of mansion

(1) The powers of disposing of settled land conferred by this Act on a tenant for life may be exercised as respects the principal mansion house, if any, on any settled land, and the pleasure grounds and park and lands, if any, usually occupied therewith:

Provided that those powers shall not be exercised without the consent of the trustees of the settlement or an order of the court—

(a) if the settlement is a settlement made or coming into operation before the commencement of this Act and the settlement does not expressly provide to the contrary; or

(b) if the settlement is a settlement made or coming into operation after the commencement of this Act and the settlement expressly provides that these powers or any of them shall not be exercised without such consent or order.

(2) Where a house is usually occupied as a farmhouse, or where the site of any house and the pleasure grounds and park and lands, if any, usually occupied therewith do not together exceed twenty-five acres in extent, the house is not to be deemed a principal mansion house within the meaning of this section, and may accordingly be disposed of in like manner as any other part of the settled land.

[151]

66 Cutting and sale of timber, and capitalisation of part of proceeds

(1) Where a tenant for life is impeachable for waste in respect of timber, and there is on the settled land timber ripe and fit for cutting, the tenant for life, on obtaining the consent of the trustees of the settlement or an order of the court, may cut and sell that timber, or any part thereof.

(2) Three fourth parts of the net proceeds of the sale shall be set aside as and be capital money arising under this Act, and the other fourth part shall go as rents and profits.

[152]

67 Sale and purchase of heirlooms under order of court

(1) Where personal chattels are settled so as to devolve with settled land, or to devolve therewith as nearly as may be in accordance with the law or practice in force at the date of the settlement, or are settled together with land, or upon trusts declared by reference to the trusts affecting land, a tenant for life of the land may sell the chattels or any of them.

(2) The money arising by the sale shall be capital money arising under this Act, and shall be paid, invested, or applied and otherwise dealt with in like manner in all respects as by this Act directed with respect to other capital money arising under this Act, or may be invested in the purchase of other chattels of the same or any other nature, which, when purchased, shall be settled and held on the same trusts, and shall devolve in the same manner as the chattels sold.

(3) A sale or purchase of chattels under this section shall not be made without an order of the court.

(4) Any reference in any enactment to personal chattels settled as heirlooms shall extend to any chattels to which this section applies.

[153]

Dealings as between tenants for life and the estate

68 Provision enabling dealings with tenant for life

(1) In the manner mentioned and subject to the provisions contained in this section—

(a) a sale, grant, lease, mortgage, charge or other disposition of settled land, or of any easement, right, or privilege over the same may be made to the tenant for life; or

(b) capital money may be advanced on mortgage to him; or

(c) a purchase may be made from him of land to be made subject to the limitations of the settlement; or

(d) an exchange may be made with him of settled land for other land; and

(e) any such disposition, advance, purchase, or exchange as aforesaid may be made to, from, or with any persons of whom the tenant for life is one.

(2) In every such case the trustees of the settlement shall, in addition to their powers as trustees, have all the powers of a tenant for life in reference to negotiating and completing the transaction, and shall have power to enforce any covenants by the tenant for life, or, where the tenant for life is himself one of the trustees, then the other or others of them shall have such power, and the said powers of a tenant for life may be exercised by the trustees of the settlement in the name and on behalf of the tenant for life.

(3) This section applies, notwithstanding that the tenant for life is one of the trustees of the settlement, or that an order has been made authorising the trustees to act on his behalf, or that he is [suffering from mental disorder] but does not apply to dealings with any body of persons which includes a trustee of the settlement, not being the tenant for life, unless the transaction is either previously or subsequently approved by the court.

[154]

NOTES

Sub-s (3): words in square brackets substituted by the Mental Health Act 1959, s 149, Sch 7, Pt I.

Incumbrances

69 Shifting of incumbrances

Where there is an incumbrance affecting any part of the settled land (whether capable of being overreached on the exercise by the tenant for life of his powers under this Act or not), the tenant for life, with the consent of the incumbrancer, may charge that incumbrance on any other part of the settled land, or on all or any part of the capital money or securities representing capital money subject or to become subject to the settlement, whether already charged therewith or not, in exoneration of the first mentioned part, and, by a legal mortgage, or otherwise, make provision accordingly.

[155]

70 Power to vary provisions of an incumbrance and to charge by way of additional security

(1) Where an incumbrance affects any part of the settled land, the tenant for life may, with the consent of the incumbrancer, vary the rate of interest charged and any of the other provisions of the instrument, if any, creating the incumbrance, and with the like consent charge that incumbrance on any part of the settled land, whether already charged therewith or not, or on all or any part of the capital money or securities representing capital money subject or to become subject to the settlement, by way of additional security, or of consolidation of securities, and by a legal mortgage or otherwise, make provision accordingly.

(2) "Incumbrance" in this section includes any annual sum payable during a life or lives or during a term of years absolute or determinable, but in any such case an additional security shall be effected so as only to create a charge or security similar to the original charge or security.

[156]

Raising of Money

71 Power to raise money by mortgage

(1) Where money is required for any of the following purposes namely:—

(i) Discharging an incumbrance on the settled land or part thereof;

(ii) Paying for any improvement authorised by this Act or by the settlement;

(iii) Equality of exchange;

(iv), (v) … ;

(vi) Redeeming a compensation rentcharge in respect of the extinguishment of manorial incidents and affecting the settled land;

(vii) Commuting any additional rent made payable on the conversion of a perpetually renewable leasehold interest into a long term;

(viii) Satisfying any claims for compensation on the conversion of a perpetually renewable leasehold interest into a long term by any officer, solicitor, or other agent of the lessor in respect of fees or remuneration which would have been payable by the lessee or under-lessee on any renewal;

(ix) Payment of the costs of any transaction authorised by this section or either of the two last preceding sections;

the tenant for life may raise the money so required, on the security of the settled land, or of any part thereof, by a legal mortgage, and the money so raised shall be capital money for that purpose, and may be paid or applied accordingly.

(2) "Incumbrance" in this section does not include any annual sum payable only during a life or lives or during a term of years absolute or determinable.

(3) The restrictions imposed by this Part of this Act on the leasing powers of a tenant for life do not apply in relation to a mortgage term created under this Act.

[157]

NOTES

Sub-s (1): words omitted repealed by the Statute Law (Repeals) Act 1969, s 1, Schedule, Pt III.

Modification: in this section and ss 73, 91, 101, references to solicitors etc modified to include references to bodies recognised under the Administration of Justice Act 1985, s 9, by the Solicitors' Incorporated Practices Order 1991, SI 1991/2684, arts 4, 5, Sch 1.

See further: in relation to further purposes for which money may be raised by mortgage: the Coast Protection Act 1949, Pt I, the Landlord and Tenant Act 1954, Pt I, the Leasehold Reform Act 1967, ss 6(2), (3), 17, 18, 23(4), 25, the Mines and Quarries (Tips) Act 1969, s 32, the Town and Country Planning Act 1990, s 328(1), the Leasehold Reform, Housing and Urban Development Act 1993, Chapter II, and the Agricultural Tenancies Act 1995, s 33(1). The purposes authorised by this section as purposes for which moneys may be raised by mortgage include the payment of any expenses incurred by a tenant for life or statutory owner as a member of a RTM company: see the Commonhold and Leasehold Reform Act 2002, s 109(4)(b).

Conveyance

72 Completion of transactions by conveyance

(1) On a sale, exchange, lease, mortgage, charge, or other disposition, the tenant for life may, as regards land sold, given in exchange, leased, mortgaged, charged, or otherwise disposed of, or intended so to be, or as regards easements or other rights or privileges sold, given in exchange, leased, mortgaged, or otherwise disposed of, or intended so to be, effect the transaction by deed to the extent of the estate or interest vested or declared to be vested in him by the last or only vesting instrument affecting the settled land or any less estate or interest, in the manner requisite for giving effect to the sale, exchange, lease, mortgage, charge, or other disposition, but so that a mortgage shall be effected by the creation of a term of years absolute in the settled land or by charge by way of legal mortgage, and not otherwise.

(2) Such a deed, to the extent and in the manner to and in which it is expressed or intended to operate and can operate under this Act, is effectual to pass the land conveyed, or the easements, rights, privileges or other interests created, discharged from all the limitations, powers, and provisions of the settlement, and from all estates, interests, and charges subsisting or to arise thereunder, but subject to and with the exception of—

(i) all legal estates and charges by way of legal mortgage having priority to the settlement; and

(ii) all legal estates and charges by way of legal mortgage which have been conveyed or created for securing money actually raised at the date of the deed; and

(iii) all leases and grants at fee-farm rents or otherwise, and all grants of easements, rights of common, or other rights or privileges which—

(a) were before the date of the deed granted or made for value in money or money's worth, or agreed so to be, by the tenant for life or statutory owner, or by any of his predecessors in title, or any trustees for them, under the settlement, or under any statutory power, or are at that date otherwise binding on the successors in title of the tenant for life or statutory owner; and

(b) are at the date of the deed protected by registration under the Land Charges Act 1925, if capable of registration thereunder.

(3) Notwithstanding registration under the Land Charges Act 1925, of—

(a) an annuity within the meaning of Part II of that Act;

(b) a limited owner's charge or a general equitable charge within the meaning of that Act;

a disposition under this Act operates to overreach such annuity or charge which shall, according to its priority, take effect as if limited by the settlement.

(4) Where a lease is by this Act authorised to be made by writing under hand only, such writing shall have the same operation under this section as if it had been a deed.

[158]

PART III
INVESTMENT OR OTHER APPLICATION OF CAPITAL MONEY

73 Modes of investment or application

(1) Capital money arising under this Act, subject to payment of claims properly payable thereout and to the application thereof for any special authorised object for which the capital money was raised, shall, when received, be invested or otherwise applied wholly in one, or partly in one and partly in another or others, of the following modes (namely):—

[(i) In investment in securities either under the general power of investment in section 3 of the Trustee Act 2000 or under a power to invest conferred on the trustees of the settlement by the settlement;]

(ii) In discharge, purchase, or redemption of incumbrances affecting the whole estate the subject of the settlement, or of … , rentcharge in lieu of tithe, Crown rent, chief rent, or quit rent, charged on or payable out of the settled land, or of any charge in respect of an improvement created on a holding under the [Agricultural Holdings Act 1986], or any similar previous enactment;

(iii) In payment for any improvement authorised by this Act;

(iv) In payment as for an improvement authorised by this Act of any money expended and costs incurred by a landlord under or in pursuance of the [Agricultural Holdings Act 1986], or any similar previous enactment, or under custom or agreement or otherwise, in or about the execution of any improvement comprised in [Schedule 7] to the said Agricultural Holdings Act;

(v) In payment for equality of exchange of settled land;

(vi), (vii) … ;

(viii) In redemption of any compensation rentcharge created in respect of the extinguishment of manorial incidents, and affecting the settled land;

(ix) In commuting any additional rent made payable on the conversion of a perpetually renewable leasehold interest into a long term, and in satisfying any claim for compensation on such conversion by any officer, solicitor, or other agent of the lessor in respect of fees or remuneration which would have been payable by the lessee or under-lessee on any renewal;

(x) In purchase of the freehold reversion in fee of any part of the settled land, being leasehold land held for years;

(xi) In purchase of land in fee simple, or of leasehold land held for sixty years or more unexpired at the time of purchase, subject or not to any exception or reservation of or in respect of mines or minerals therein, or of or in respect of rights or powers relative to the working of mines or minerals therein, or in other land;

(xii) In purchase either in fee simple, or for a term of sixty years or more, of mines and minerals convenient to be held or worked with the settled land, or of any easement, right, or privilege convenient to be held with the settled land for mining or other purposes;

(xiii) In redemption of an improvement rentcharge, that is to say, a rentcharge (temporary or permanent) created, whether before or after the commencement of this Act, in pursuance of any Act of Parliament, with the object of paying off any money advanced for defraying the expenses of an improvement of any kind authorised by Part I of the Third Schedule to this Act;

(xiv) In the purchase, with the leave of the court, of any leasehold interest where the immediate reversion is settled land, so as to merge the leasehold interest (unless the court otherwise directs) in the reversion, and notwithstanding that the leasehold interest may have less than sixty years to run;

(xv) In payment of the costs and expenses of all plans, surveys, and schemes, including schemes under the Town Planning Act 1925, or any similar previous enactment, made with a view to, or in connexion with the improvement or development of the settled land, or any part thereof, or the exercise of any statutory powers, and of all negotiations entered into by the tenant for life with a view to the exercise of any of the said powers, notwithstanding that such negotiations may prove abortive, and in payment of the costs and expenses of opposing any such proposed scheme as aforesaid affecting the settled land, whether or not the scheme is made;

(xvi) …

(xvii) In payment to a local or other authority of such sum as may be agreed in consideration of such authority taking over and becoming liable to repair a private road on the settled land or a road for the maintenance whereof a tenant for life is liable ratione tenurae;

(xviii) In financing any person who may have agreed to take a lease or grant for building purposes of the settled land, or any part thereof, by making advances to him in the usual manner on the security of an equitable mortgage of his building agreement;

(xix) In payment to any person becoming absolutely entitled or empowered to give an absolute discharge;

(xx) In payment of costs, charges, and expenses of or incidental to the exercise of any of the powers, or the execution of any of the provisions of this Act including the costs and expenses incidental to any of the matters referred to in this section;

(xxi) In any other mode authorised by the settlement with respect to money produced by the sale of the settled land.

(2) Notwithstanding anything in this section capital money arising under this Act from settled land in England or Wales shall not be applied in the purchase of land out of England and Wales, unless the settlement expressly authorises the same.

[159]

NOTES

Sub-s (1): para (i) substituted by the Trustee Act 2000, s 40(1), Sch 2, Pt II, para 9; in para (ii) words omitted repealed by the Finance Act 1963, s 73(8)(b), Sch 11, Pt VI; in paras (ii), (iv) words in square brackets substituted by the Agricultural Holdings Act 1986, s 100, Sch 14, para 11; paras (vi), (vii) repealed by the Statute Law Repeals Act 1969, s 1; para (xvi) repealed by the Statute Law (Repeals) Act 1998.

Modification: see the note to s 71 at **[157]**.

See further, in relation to further authorised purposes for the application of capital money: the Coast Protection Act 1949, s 11(2)(a), the Landlord and Tenant Act 1954, s 8(5), Sch 2, the Leasehold Reform Act 1967, ss 6(5), 17(3), 18(5), 23(5), 25(2), Sch 2, the Mines and Quarries (Tips) Act 1969, s 32(2), the Town and Country Planning Act 1990, s 328(2), the Leasehold Reform, Housing and Urban Development Act 1993, ss 9(4), 40(5), Sch 2, the Agricultural Tenancies Act 1995, s 33(1).

The purposes authorised for the application of capital money by this section include the payment of any expenses incurred by a tenant for life or statutory owner as a member of a RTM company: see the Commonhold and Leasehold Reform Act 2002, s 109(4)(a).

74 Power to acquire land subject to certain incumbrances

(1) Land may be acquired on a purchase or exchange to be made subject to a settlement, notwithstanding that the land is subject to any Crown rent, quit rent, chief rent, or other incident of tenure, or to any easement, right or privilege, or to any restrictive covenant, or to any liability to maintain or repair walls, fences, sea-walls, river banks, dykes, roads, streets, sewers, or drains, or to any improvement rentcharge which is capable under this Act of being redeemed out of capital money.

(2) The acquisition on a purchase or exchange before the commencement of this Act of any land subject to any such burden as aforesaid is hereby confirmed.

[160]

75 Regulations respecting investment, devolution, and income of securities, etc

(1) Capital money arising under this Act shall, in order to its being invested or applied as aforesaid, be paid either to the trustees of the settlement or into court at the option of the tenant for life, and shall be invested or applied by the trustees, or under the direction of the court, as the case may be, accordingly.

[(2) Subject to Part IV of the Trustee Act 2000, to section 75A of this Act and to the following provisions of this section—

(a) the investment or other application by the trustees shall be made according to the discretion of the trustees, but subject to any consent required or direction given by the settlement with respect to the investment or other application by the trustees of trust money of the settlement, and]

[(b) any investment shall be in the names or under the control of the trustees.]

(3) The investment or other application under the direction of the court shall be made on the application of the tenant for life, or of the trustees.

[(4) The trustees, in exercising their power to invest or apply capital money, shall—

(a) so far as practicable, consult the tenant for life; and

(b) so far as consistent with the general interest of the settlement, give effect to his wishes.

(4A) Any investment or other application of capital money under the direction of the court shall not during the subsistence of the beneficial interest of the tenant for life be altered without his consent.

(4B) The trustees may not under section 11 of the Trustee Act 2000 authorise a person to exercise their functions with respect to the investment or application of capital money on terms that prevent them from complying with subsection (4) of this section.

(4C) A person who is authorised under section 11 of the Trustee Act 2000 to exercise any of their functions with respect to the investment or application of capital money is not subject to subsection (4) of this section.]

PART I STATUTES

(5) Capital money arising under this Act while remaining uninvested or unapplied, and securities on which an investment of any such capital money is made shall for all purposes of disposition, transmission and devolution be treated as land, and shall be held for and go to the same persons successively, in the same manner and for and on the same estates, interests, and trusts, as the land wherefrom the money arises would, if not disposed of, have been held and have gone under the settlement.

(6) The income of those securities shall be paid or applied as the income of that land, if not disposed of, would have been payable or applicable under the settlement.

(7) Those securities may be converted into money, which shall be capital money arising under this Act.

(8) All or any part of any capital money paid into court may, if the court thinks fit, be at any time paid out to the trustees of the settlement.

[161]

NOTES

Sub-s (2): substituted by the Trustee Act 2000, s 40(1), Sch 2, Pt II, para 10(1); for transitional provisions in relation to directions of the tenant for life given, but not acted upon by the trustees, see para 10(3) thereof.

Sub-ss (4)–(4C): substituted, for original sub-s (4), by the Trustee Act 2000, s 40(1), Sch 2, Pt II, para 10(2), subject to transitional provisions as noted above.

[75A Power to accept charge as security for part payment for land sold

(1) Where—

(a) land subject to the settlement is sold by the tenant for life or statutory owner, for an estate in fee simple or a term having at least five hundred years to run, and

(b) the proceeds of sale are liable to be invested,

the tenant for life or statutory owner may, with the consent of the trustees of the settlement, contract that the payment of any part, not exceeding two-thirds, of the purchase money shall be secured by a charge by way of legal mortgage of the land sold, with or without the security of any other property.

(2) If any buildings are comprised in the property secured by the charge, the charge must contain a covenant by the mortgagor to keep them insured for their full value against loss or damage due to any event.

(3) A person exercising the power under subsection (1) of this section, or giving consent for the purposes of that subsection—

(a) is not required to comply with section 5 of the Trustee Act 2000 before giving his consent, and

(b) is not liable for any loss incurred merely because the security is insufficient at the date of the charge.

(4) The power under subsection (1) of this section is exercisable subject to the consent of any person whose consent to a change of investment is required by the instrument, if any, creating the trust.

(5) Where the sale referred to in subsection (1) of this section is made under the order of the court, the power under that subsection applies only if and as far as the court may by order direct.]

[162]

NOTES

Inserted by the Trustee Act 2000, s 40(1), Sch 2, Pt II, para 11.

76 Application of money in court under Lands Clauses and other Acts

Where, under an Act, or an order or scheme confirmed by or having the force of an Act of Parliament, incorporating or applying, wholly or in part, the Lands Clauses Acts, or under any Act, public general or local or private, money is at the commencement of this Act in court, or is afterwards paid into court, and is liable to be laid out in the purchase of land to be made subject to a settlement, then, in addition to any mode of dealing therewith authorised by the Act under which the money is in court, that money may be invested or applied as capital money arising under this Act, on the like terms, if any, respecting costs and other things, as nearly as circumstances admit, and notwithstanding anything in this Act according to the same procedure, as if the modes of investment or application authorised by this Act were authorised by the Act under which the money is in court.

[163]

77 Application of money in hands of trustees under powers of settlement

Where—

(a) under any instrument coming into operation either before or after the commencement of this Act money is in the hands of trustees, and is liable to be laid out in the purchase of land to be made subject to the trusts declared by that instrument; or

(b) under any instrument coming into operation after the commencement of this Act money or securities or the proceeds of sale of any property is or are held by trustees on trusts creating entailed interests therein;

then, in addition to such powers of dealing therewith as the trustees have independently of this Act, they may, at the option of the tenant for life, invest or apply the money securities or proceeds as if they were capital money arising under this Act.

[164]

78 Provision as to personal estate settled by reference to capital money, or on trusts corresponding with the limitations of land

(1) Where money or securities or the proceeds of sale of any property is or are by any instrument coming into operation either before or after the commencement of this Act directed to be held on trusts declared by reference to capital money arising under this Act from land settled by that instrument or any other instrument, the money securities or proceeds shall be held on the like trusts as if the same had been or represented money which had actually arisen under this Act from the settled land.

[This sub-section operates without prejudice to the rights of any person claiming under a disposition for valuable consideration of any such money securities or proceeds, made before the commencement of this Act].

(2) Where money or securities or the proceeds of sale of any property is or are by any instrument coming into operation after the commencement of this Act directed to be held on the same trusts as, or on trusts corresponding as nearly as may be with the limitations of land settled by that instrument or any other instrument, the money, securities or proceeds shall be held on the like trusts as if the same had been or represented capital money arising under this Act from the settled land.

(3) Such money, securities, or proceeds of sale shall be paid or transferred to or retained by the trustees of the settlement of the settled land, or paid or transferred into court, and invested or applied accordingly.

(4) Where the settled land includes freehold land, the money, securities, or proceeds of sale aforesaid shall be held on the like trusts as if the same had been or represented capital money arising from the freehold land.

(5) This section has effect notwithstanding any direction in the instrument creating the trust that the trust property is not to vest absolutely in any tenant in tail or in tail male or in tail female under the limitations of the settled land who dies under a specified age, or before the happening of a specified event, but, save as aforesaid, has effect with any variations and subject to any contrary intention expressed in the instrument creating the trust.

[165]

NOTES

Sub-s (1): words in square brackets inserted by the Law of Property (Amendment) Act 1926, Schedule.

79 Application of money paid for lease or reversion

Where capital money arising under this Act is purchase-money paid in respect of—

(a) a lease for years; or
(b) any other estate or interest in land less than the fee simple; or
(c) a reversion dependent on any such lease, estate, or interest;

the trustees of the settlement or the court, as the case may be, and in the case of the court on the application of any party interested in that money, may, notwithstanding anything in this Act, require and cause the same to be laid out, invested, accumulated, and paid in such manner as, in the judgment of the trustees or of the court, as the case may be, will give to the parties interested in that money the like benefit therefrom as they might lawfully have had from the lease, estate, interest, or reversion in respect whereof the money was paid, or as near thereto as may be.

[166]

80 As to money received by way of damages for breach of covenant

(1) Money, not being rent, received by way of damages or compensation for breach of any covenant by a lessee or grantee contained in any lease or grant of settled land shall, unless in any case the court on the application of the tenant for life or the trustees of the settlement otherwise directs, be deemed to be capital money arising under this Act, and shall be paid to or retained by the trustees of the settlement, or paid into court, and invested or applied, accordingly.

(2) In addition to the other modes in which capital money may be applied under this Act or the settlement, money so received as aforesaid or any part thereof may, if the circumstances permit, be applied at any time within twelve months after such receipt, or such extended period as the court may allow, in or towards payment of the costs of making good in whole or in part the breach of

covenant in respect of which it was so received, or the consequences thereof, and the trustees of the settlement, if they think fit, may require any money so received or any part thereof to be so applied.

(3) In the application of any such money in or towards payment of the cost of making good any such breach or the consequences of any such breach as aforesaid, the work required to be done for the purpose shall be deemed to be an improvement authorised by Part I of the Third Schedule to this Act.

(4) This section does not apply to money received by way of damages or compensation for the breach of a covenant to repay to the lessor or grantor money laid out or expended by him, or to any case in which if the money received were applied in making good the breach of covenant or the consequences thereof such application would not enure for the benefit of the settled land, or any buildings thereon.

(5) This section does not apply to money received by way of damages or compensation before the commencement of this Act, but it applies whether the lease or grant was made before or after the commencement of this Act, and whether under the powers conferred by the Settled Land Acts 1882 to 1890, or this Act or not.

(6) The provisions of this section apply only if and as far as a contrary intention is not expressed in the settlement, and have effect subject to the terms of the settlement, and to any provisions therein contained, but a contrary intention shall not be deemed to be expressed merely by words negativing impeachment for waste.

[167]

81 As to capital arising otherwise than under the Act

Any money which after the commencement of this Act arises from settled land otherwise than under this Act, as well as any money or securities in the names or under the control of the tenant for life or the trustees of the settlement, being or representing money which had arisen before the commencement of this Act from the settled land otherwise than under the Settled Land Acts 1882 to 1890, and which ought, as between the persons interested in the settled land, to be or to have been treated as capital, shall (without prejudice to any other statutory provisions affecting the same) be deemed to be or to represent capital money arising under this Act, and shall be paid or transferred to or retained by the trustees of the settlement, or paid or transferred into court, and invested or applied, accordingly.

[168]

82 Land acquired may be made a substituted security for released charges

(1) Land acquired by purchase or in exchange or otherwise under the powers of this Act, may be made a substituted security for any charge from which the settled land or any part thereof has theretofore been released on the occasion and in order to the completion of a sale, exchange or other disposition:

Provided that, where a charge does not affect the whole of the settled land, the land acquired shall not be subjected thereto, unless the land is acquired either by purchase with money arising from sale of land which was before the sale subject to the charge, or by an exchange of land which was before the exchange subject to the charge.

(2) On land being so acquired, any person who, by the direction of the tenant for life, so conveys the land as to subject it to any legal estate or charge by way of legal mortgage, is not concerned to inquire whether or not it is proper that the land should be subjected to such legal estate or charge.

[169]

PART IV
IMPROVEMENTS

Improvements with Capital Money

83 Description of improvements authorised by Act

Improvements authorised by this Act are the making or execution on, or in connexion with, and for the benefit of settled land, of any of the works mentioned in the Third Schedule to this Act, or of any works for any of the purposes mentioned in that Schedule, and any operation incident to or necessary or proper in the execution of any of those works, or necessary or proper for carrying into effect any of those purposes, or for securing the full benefit of any of those works or purposes.

[170]

84 Mode of application of capital money

(1) Capital money arising under this Act may be applied in or towards payment for any improvement authorised by this Act or by the settlement, without any scheme for the execution of the improvement being first submitted for approval to, or approved by, the trustees of the settlement or the court.

(2) Where the capital money to be expended is in the hands of the trustees of the settlement, they may apply that money in or towards payment for the whole or any part of any work or operation comprised in the improvement, on—

(i) a certificate to be furnished by a competent engineer or able practical surveyor employed independently of the tenant for life, certifying that the work or operation comprised in the improvement or some specific part thereof, has been properly executed, and what amount is properly payable in respect thereof, which certificate shall be conclusive in favour of the trustees as an authority and discharge for any payment made by them in pursuance thereof; or

(ii) an order of the court directing or authorising the trustees so to apply a specified portion of the capital money:

Provided that—

(a) In the case of improvements not authorised by Part I of the Third Schedule to this Act or by the settlement, the trustees may, if they think fit, and shall if so directed by the court, before they make any such application of capital money require that that money, or any part thereof, shall be repaid to them out of the income of the settled land by not more than fifty half-yearly instalments, the first of such instalments to be paid or to be deemed to have become payable at the expiration of six months from the date when the work or operation, in payment for which the money is to be applied, was completed;

(b) No capital money shall be applied by the trustees in payment for improvements not authorised by Parts I and II of the Third Schedule to this Act, or by the settlement, except subject to provision for the repayment thereof being made in manner mentioned in the preceding paragraph of this proviso.

(3) Where the capital money to be expended is in court, the court may, if it thinks fit, on a report or certificate of the [Secretary of State], or of a competent engineer or able practical surveyor approved by the court, or on such other evidence as the court may think sufficient, make such order and give such directions as it thinks fit for the application of the money, or any part thereof, in or towards payment for the whole or any part of any work or operation comprised in the improvement.

(4) Where the court authorises capital money to be applied in payment for any improvement or intended improvement not authorised by Part I of the Third Schedule to this Act or by the settlement, the court, as a condition of making the order, may in any case require that the capital money or any part thereof, and shall as respects an improvement mentioned in Part III of that Schedule (unless the improvement is authorised by the settlement), require that the whole of the capital money shall be repaid to the trustees of the settlement out of the income of the settled land by a fixed number of periodical instalments to be paid at the times appointed by the court, and may require that any incumbrancer of the estate or interest of the tenant for life shall be served with notice of the proceedings.

(5) All money received by the trustees of the settlement in respect of any instalments under this section shall be held by them as capital money arising from freehold land under the settlement, unless the court otherwise directs.

[171]

NOTES

Sub-s (3): words in square brackets substituted by SI 2002/794, art 5(1), Sch 1, para 2.

85 Creation of rentcharges to discharge instalments

(1) When the tenant for life is required by the trustees to repay by instalments the capital money expended, or any part thereof, the tenant for life is by this section authorised to create out of the settled land, or any part thereof, a yearly rentcharge in favour of the trustees of the settlement sufficient in amount to discharge the said half-yearly instalments.

(2) Where an order is made requiring repayment by instalments, the settled land shall stand charged with the payment to the trustees of the settlement of a yearly rentcharge sufficient in amount to discharge the periodical instalments, and the rentcharge shall accrue from day to day, and be payable at the times appointed for payment of the periodical instalments, and shall have effect as if limited by the settlement prior to the estate of the tenant for life, and the trustees of the settlement shall have all statutory and other powers for recovery thereof.

(3) A rentcharge created by or under this section shall not be redeemed out of capital money, but may be overreached in like manner as if the same were limited by the settlement, and shall cease if and when the land affected by the improvement ceases to be settled or is sold or exchanged, but if part of the land so affected remains subject to the settlement the rentcharge shall remain in force in regard to the settled land.

[172]

Sundry Provisions as to Improvements

86 Concurrence in improvements

The tenant for life may join or concur with any other person interested in executing any improvement authorised by this Act, or in contributing to the cost thereof.

[173]

87 Court may order payment for improvements executed

The court may, in any case where it appears proper, make an order directing or authorising capital money to be applied in or towards payment for any improvement authorised by the Settled Land Acts 1882 to 1890, or this Act, notwithstanding that a scheme was not, before the execution of the improvement, submitted for approval, as required by the Settled Land Act 1882, to the trustees of the settlement or to the court, and notwithstanding that no capital money is immediately available for the purpose.

[174]

88 Obligation on tenant for life and successors to maintain, insure, etc

(1) The tenant for life, and each of his successors in title having under the trust instrument a limited estate or interest only in the settled land, shall, during such period, if any, as the [Secretary of State] by certificate in any case prescribes, maintain and repair, at his own expense, every improvement executed under the foregoing provisions of this Act or the enactments replaced thereby, and where a building or work in its nature insurable against damage by fire is comprised in the improvement, shall at his own expense insure and keep insured the improvement in such amount, if any, as the [Secretary of State] by certificate in any case prescribes.

(2) The tenant for life, or any of his successors as aforesaid, shall not cut down or knowingly permit to be cut down, except in proper thinning, any trees planted as an improvement under the foregoing provisions of this Act, or under the enactments replaced by those provisions.

(3) The tenant for life, and each of his successors as aforesaid, shall from time to time, if required by the [Secretary of State] on or without the application of any person having under the trust instrument any estate or interest in the settled land in possession, remainder, or otherwise, report to the [Secretary of State] the state of every improvement executed under this Act, and the fact and particulars of fire insurance, if any.

(4) The [Secretary of State] may vary any certificate made by him under this section in such manner or to such extent as circumstances appear to him to require, but not so as to increase the liabilities of the tenant for life, or any of his successors as aforesaid.

(5) If the tenant for life, or any of his successors as aforesaid, fails in any respect to comply with the requisitions of this section, or does any act in contravention thereof, any person having, under the trust instrument, any estate or interest in the settled land in possession, remainder, or reversion, shall have a right of action, in respect of that default or act, against the tenant for life; and the estate of the tenant for life, after his death, shall be liable to make good to the persons entitled under the trust instrument any damages occasioned by that default or act.

(6) Where in connexion with any improvement an improvement rentcharge, as hereinbefore defined, has been created, and that rentcharge has been redeemed out of capital money, this section shall apply to the improvement as if it had been an improvement executed under this Act.

[175]

NOTES

Sub-ss (1), (3), (4): words in square brackets substituted by SI 2002/794, art 5(1), Sch 1, para 3.

89 Protection as regards waste in execution and repair of improvements

The tenant for life, and each of his successors in title having, under the trust instrument, a limited estate or interest only in the settled land and all persons employed by or under contract with the tenant for life or any such successor, may from time to time enter on the settled land, and, without impeachment of waste by any remainderman or reversioner, thereon execute any improvement authorised by this Act, or inspect, maintain, and repair the same, and for the purposes thereof do, make, and use on the settled land, all acts, works, and conveniences proper for the execution, maintenance, repair, and use thereof, and get and work freestone, limestone, clay, sand, and other substances, and make tramways and otherways, burn and make bricks, tiles, and other things, and cut down and use timber and other trees not planted or left standing for shelter or ornament.

[176]

PART V
MISCELLANEOUS PROVISIONS

90 Power for tenant for life to enter into contracts

(1) A tenant for life—

(i) may contract to make any sale, exchange, mortgage, charge or other disposition authorised by this Act; and
(ii) may vary or rescind, with or without consideration, the contract in the like cases and manner in which, if he were absolute owner of the settled land, he might lawfully vary or rescind the same, but so that the contract as varied be in conformity with this Act; and
(iii) may contract to make any lease, and in making the lease may vary the terms, with or without consideration, but so that the lease be in conformity with this Act; and
(iv) may accept a surrender of a contract for a lease or a grant in fee simple at a rent, in like manner and on the like terms in and on which he might accept a surrender of a lease or a regrant, and thereupon may make a new or other contract for or relative to a lease or leases, or a grant or grants in fee simple at a rent, in like manner and on the like terms in and on which he might make a new or other lease or grant, or new or other leases or grants, where a lease or a grant in fee simple at a rent had been executed; and
(v) may enter into a contract for or relating to the execution of any improvement authorised by this Act, and may vary or rescind any such contract; and
(vi) may, in any other case, enter into a contract to do any act for carrying into effect any of the purposes of this Act, and may vary or rescind any such contract.

(2) Every contract, including a contract arising by reason of the exercise of an option, shall be binding on and shall enure for the benefit of the settled land, and shall be enforceable against and by every successor in title for the time being of the tenant for life, or statutory owner, and may be carried into effect by any such successor, but so that it may be varied or rescinded by any such successor, in the like case and manner, if any, as if it had been made by himself.

(3) The court may, on the application of the tenant for life, or statutory owner, or of any such successor as aforesaid, or of any person interested in any contract, give directions respecting the enforcing, carrying into effect, varying, or rescinding thereof.

(4) A preliminary contract under this Act for or relating to a lease, and a contract conferring an option, shall not form part of the title or evidence of the title of any person to the lease, or to the benefit thereof, or to the land the subject of the option.

(5) All money, not being rent, received on the exercise by the tenant for life or statutory owner of the powers conferred by subsection (1) of this section, shall, unless the court on an application made within six months after the receipt of the money, or within such further time as the court may in special circumstances allow, otherwise directs, be capital money arising under this Act.

[177]

91 Provisions as to different estates settled upon the same limitations

(1) Where estates are settled by different settlements upon the same limitations, whether by reference or otherwise, the following provisions shall have effect:—

(i) The estates or any two or more of them, as the case may require, may be treated as one aggregate estate, in which case the aggregate estate shall be the settled land for all the purposes of this Act;
(ii) Where the trustees for the purposes of this Act of the two or several settlements are the same persons they shall be the trustees of the settlement of the aggregate estate for all the purposes of this Act, and all or any part of the capital money arising from one of the estates may be applied by the direction of the tenant for life or statutory owner as if the same had arisen from any other of the estates;
(iii) Where the trustees for the purposes of this Act of the settlements or of any two or more of them are not the same persons—
  (a) any notice required to be given by this Act to the trustees of the settlement and to the solicitor of such trustees shall be given to the trustees of every settlement which comprises any part of the land to which such notice relates and to the solicitor of such trustees;
  (b) any capital money arising on any sale, exchange, lease, mortgage, charge, or other disposition of land comprised in more than one settlement, shall be apportioned between the trustees of the different settlements in such manner as the tenant for life or statutory owner may think fit;
  (c) all or any part of the capital money arising from the land comprised in one of the settlements may be paid by the trustees of that settlement, by such direction as aforesaid, to the trustees of any of the other settlements, to be applied by such last-mentioned trustees as if the same had arisen from land comprised in that other settlement:
(iv) For the purposes of this subsection, money liable to be laid out in the purchase of land to be settled upon the same limitations as other land may be applied and dealt with in like manner in all respects as if land had been purchased and settled, and the money were capital money arising therefrom.

(2) Estates shall be deemed to be settled upon the same limitations, notwithstanding that any of them may be subject to incumbrances, charges, or powers of charging to which the other or others of them may not be subject:

Provided that, in any such case as last aforesaid, the powers of this section relating to the payment or application of capital money shall not, unless the settlement under which the capital money is held otherwise provides, be exercisable without an order of the court.

(3) This section has effect without prejudice to any appointment made by the court before the commencement of this Act of trustees of the settlement of an aggregate estate, and to the power of the court in any case after such commencement to make any such appointment, and where any such appointment has been made before such commencement, or is made thereafter, this section has effect as if the trustees so appointed and their successors in office were the trustees for the purposes of this Act of each of the settlements constituting the settlement of the aggregate estate, and there were no other trustees thereof for the purposes of this Act.

(4) In this section "estate" means the land, capital money, and securities representing capital money for the time being subject to a particular settlement.

[178]

NOTES

Modification: see the note to s 71 at **[157]**.

92 Proceedings for protection or recovery of land settled or claimed as settled

The court may, if it thinks fit, approve of any action, defence, petition to Parliament, parliamentary opposition, or other proceeding taken or proposed to be taken for the protection of settled land, or of any action or proceeding taken or proposed to be taken for the recovery of land being or alleged to be subject to a settlement, and may direct that any costs, charges, or expenses incurred or to be incurred in relation thereto, or any part thereof, be paid out of property subject to the settlement.

[179]

93 Reference of questions to court

If a question arises or a doubt is entertained—

(a) respecting the exercise or intended exercise of any of the powers conferred by this Act, or any enactment replaced by this Act, or the settlement, or any matter relating thereto; or

(b) as to the person in whose favour a vesting deed or assent ought to be executed, or as to the contents thereof; or

(c) otherwise in relation to property subject to a settlement;

the tenant for life or statutory owner, or the trustees of the settlement, or any other person interested under the settlement, may apply to the court for its decision or directions thereon, or for the sanction of the court to any conditional contract, and the court may make such order or give such directions respecting the matter as the court thinks fit.

[180]

PART VI
GENERAL PROVISIONS AS TO TRUSTEES

94 Number of trustees to act

(1) Notwithstanding anything in this Act, capital money arising under this Act shall not be paid to fewer than two persons as trustees of a settlement, unless the trustee is a trust corporation.

(2) Subject as aforesaid the provisions of this Act referring to the trustees of a settlement apply to the surviving or continuing trustees or trustee of the settlement for the time being.

[181]

95 Trustees' receipts

The receipt or direction in writing of or by the trustees of the settlement, or where a sole trustee is a trust corporation, of or by that trustee, or of or by the personal representatives of the last surviving or continuing trustee, for or relating to any money or securities, paid or transferred to or by the direction of the trustees, trustee, or representatives, as the case may be, effectually discharges the payer or transferor therefrom, and from being bound to see to the application or being answerable for any loss or misapplication thereof, and, in case of a mortgagee or other person advancing money, from being concerned to see that any money advanced by him is wanted for any purpose of this Act, or that no more than is wanted is raised.

[182]

96 (*Repealed by the Trustee Act 2000, s 40(1), (3), Sch 2, Pt II, para 12, Sch 4, Pt II.*)

97 Protection of trustees generally

The trustees of a settlement, or any of them—

(a) are not liable for giving any consent, or for not making, bringing, taking, or doing any such application, action, proceeding, or thing, as they might make, bring, take, or do; and

(b) in case of a purchase of land with capital money arising under this Act, or of an exchange, lease, or other disposition, are not liable for adopting any contract made by the tenant for life or statutory owner, or bound to inquire as to the propriety of the purchase, exchange, lease, or other disposition, or answerable as regards any price, consideration, or fine; and

(c) are not liable to see to or answerable for the investigation of the title, or answerable for a conveyance of land, if the conveyance purports to convey the land in the proper mode; and

(d) are not liable in respect of purchase-money paid by them by the direction of the tenant for life or statutory owner to any person joining in the conveyance as a conveying party, or as giving a receipt for the purchase-money, or in any other character, or in respect of any other money paid by them by the direction of the tenant for life or statutory owner on the purchase, exchange, lease, or other disposition.

[183]

98 Protection of trustees in particular cases

(1), (2) …

(3) The trustees of the settlements shall not be liable in any way on account of any vesting instrument or other documents of title relating to the settled land, other than securities for capital money, being placed in the possession of the tenant for life or statutory owner:

Provided that where, if the settlement were not disclosed, it would appear that the tenant for life had a general power of appointment over, or was absolutely and beneficially entitled to the settled land, the trustees of the settlement shall, before they deliver the documents to him, require that notice of the last or only principal vesting instrument be written on one of the documents under which the tenant for life acquired his title, and may, if the documents are not in their possession, require such notice to be written as aforesaid, but, in the latter case, they shall not be liable in any way for not requiring the notice to be written.

(4) This section applies to dealings and matters effected before as well as after the commencement of this Act.

[184]

NOTES

Sub-ss (1), (2): repealed by the Trustee Act 2000, s 40(1), (3), Sch 2, Pt II, para 13, Sch 4, Pt II.

99 Indemnities to personal representatives and others

Personal representatives, trustees, or other persons who have in good faith, pursuant to this Act, executed a vesting deed, assent, or other conveyance of the settled land, or a deed of discharge of trustees, shall be absolutely discharged from all liability in respect of the equitable interests and powers taking effect under the settlement, and shall be entitled to be kept indemnified at the cost of the trust estate from all liabilities affecting the settled land, but the person to whom the settled land is conveyed (not being a purchaser taking free therefrom) shall hold the settled land upon the trusts, if any, affecting the same.

[185]

100 *(Repealed by the Trustee Act 2000, s 40(1), (3), Sch 2, Pt II, para 14, Sch 4, Pt II.)*

101 Notice to trustees

(1) Save as otherwise expressly provided by this Act, a tenant for life or statutory owner, when intending to make a sale, exchange, lease, mortgage, or charge or to grant an option—

(a) shall give notice of his intention in that behalf to each of the trustees of the settlement, by posting registered letters, containing the notice, addressed to the trustees severally, each at his usual or last known place of abode in the United Kingdom; and

(b) shall give a like notice to the solicitor for the trustees, if any such solicitor is known to the tenant for life or statutory owner, by posting a registered letter, containing the notice, addressed to the solicitor at his place of business in the United Kingdom;

every letter under this section being posted not less than one month before the making or granting by the tenant for life or statutory owner of the sale, exchange, lease, mortgage, charge, or option, or of a contract for the same:

Provided that a notice under this section shall not be valid unless at the date thereof the trustee is a trust corporation, or the number of trustees is not less than two.

(2) The notice required by this section of intention to make a sale, exchange, or lease, or to grant an option, may be notice of a general intention in that behalf.

(3) The tenant for life or statutory owner is, upon request by a trustee of the settlement, to furnish to him such particulars and information as may reasonably be required by him from time to time with reference to sales, exchanges, or leases effected, or in progress, or immediately intended.

(4) Any trustee, by writing under his hand, may waive notice either in any particular case, or generally, and may accept less than one month's notice.

(5) A person dealing in good faith with the tenant for life is not concerned to inquire respecting the giving of any such notice as is required by this section.

[186]

NOTES

Modification: see the note to s 71 at **[157]**.

102 Management of land during minority or pending contingency

(1) If and as long as any person who is entitled to a beneficial interest in possession affecting land is an infant, the trustees appointed for this purpose by the settlement, or if there are none so appointed, then the trustees of the settlement, unless the settlement or the order of the court whereby they or their predecessors in office were appointed to be such trustees expressly provides to the contrary, or if there are none, then any persons appointed as trustees for this purpose by the court on the application of a guardian or next friend of the infant, may enter into and continue in possession of the land on behalf of the infant, and in every such case the subsequent provisions of this section shall apply.

(2) The trustees shall manage or superintend the management of the land, with full power—

(a) to fell timber or cut underwood from time to time in the usual course for sale, or for repairs or otherwise; and

(b) to erect, pull down, rebuild, and repair houses, and other buildings and erections; and

(c) to continue the working of mines, minerals, and quarries which have usually been worked; and

(d) to drain or otherwise improve the land or any part thereof; and

[(e) to insure against risks of loss or damage due to any event under section 19 of the Trustee Act 1925;]

(f) to make allowances to and arrangements with tenants and others; and

(g) to determine tenancies, and to accept surrenders of leases and tenancies; and

(h) generally to deal with the land in a proper and due course of management;

but so that, where the infant is impeachable for waste, the trustees shall not commit waste, and shall cut timber on the same terms only, and subject to the same restrictions, on and subject to which the infant could, if of full age, cut the same.

(3) The trustees may from time to time, out of the income of the land, including the produce of the sale of timber and underwood, pay the expenses incurred in the management, or in the exercise of any power conferred by this section, or otherwise in relation to the land, and all outgoings not payable by any tenant or other person, and shall keep down any annual sum, and the interest of any principal sum, charged on the land.

(4) This section has effect subject to an express appointment by the settlement, or the court, of trustees for the purposes of this section or of any enactment replaced by this section.

(5) Where any person is contingently entitled to land, this section shall, subject to any prior interests or charges affecting that land, apply until his interest vests, or, if his interest vests during his minority, until he attains [the age of eighteen years].

This subsection applies only where a person becomes contingently entitled under an instrument coming into operation after the commencement of this Act.

(6) This section applies only if and as far as a contrary intention is not expressed in the instrument, if any, under which the interest of the infant or person contingently entitled as aforesaid arises, and has effect subject to the terms of that instrument and to the provisions therein contained.

[187]

NOTES

Sub-s (2): para (e) substituted by the Trustee Act 2000, s 40(1), Sch 2, Pt II, para 15.

Sub-s (5): words in square brackets substituted by the Family Law Reform Act 1969, s 1(3), Sch 1.

PART VII
RESTRICTIONS, SAVINGS AND PROTECTION OF PURCHASERS

103 Legal estate in settled land not to vest in trustee in bankruptcy of estate owner

[For the purposes of determining, where the estate owner of any settled land is bankrupt, whether the legal estate in the settled land is comprised in, or is capable of being claimed for, the bankrupt's estate, the legal estate in the settled land shall be deemed not to vest in the] estate owner unless and until the estate owner becomes absolutely and beneficially entitled to the settled land free from all limitations, powers, and charges taking effect under the settlement.

[188]

NOTES

Words in square brackets substituted by the Insolvency Act 1985, s 235, Sch 8, para 3.

104 Powers not assignable, and contract not to exercise powers void

(1) The powers under this Act of a tenant for life are not capable of assignment or release, and do not pass to a person as being, by operation of law or otherwise, an assignee of a tenant for life, and remain exercisable by the tenant for life after and notwithstanding any assignment, by operation of law or otherwise, of his estate or interest under the settlement.

This subsection applies notwithstanding that the estate or interest of the tenant for life under the settlement was not in possession when the assignment was made or took effect by operation of law.

(2) A contract by a tenant for life not to exercise his powers under this Act or any of them shall be void.

(3) Where an assignment for value of the estate or interest of the tenant for life was made before the commencement of this Act, this section shall operate without prejudice to the rights of the assignee, and in that case the assignee's rights shall not be affected without his consent, except that—

- (a) unless the assignee is actually in possession of the settled land or the part thereof affected, his consent shall not be requisite for the making of leases thereof by the tenant for life or statutory owner, provided the leases are made at the best rent that can reasonably be obtained, without fine, and in other respects are in conformity with this Act; and
- (b) the consent of the assignee shall not be required to an investment of capital money for the time being affected by the assignment in securities …

(4) Where such an assignment for value is made or comes into operation after the commencement of this Act, the consent of the assignee shall not be requisite for the exercise by the tenant for life of any of the powers conferred by this Act:

Provided that—

- (a) the assignee shall be entitled to the same or the like estate or interest in or charge on the land, money, or securities for the time being representing the land, money, or securities comprised in the assignment, as he had by virtue of the assignment in the last-mentioned land, money, or securities; and
- (b) if the assignment so provides, or if it takes effect by operation of the law of bankruptcy, and after notice thereof to the trustees of the settlement, [the consent of the assignee shall be required to an investment of capital money for the time being affected by the assignment in investments other than securities, and to any application of such capital money]; and
- (c) notice of the intended transaction shall, unless the assignment otherwise provides, be given to the assignee, but a purchaser shall not be concerned to see or inquire whether such notice has been given.

(5) Where such an assignment for value was made before the commencement of this Act, then on the exercise by the tenant for life after such commencement of any of the powers conferred by this Act—

- (a) a purchaser shall not be concerned to see or inquire whether the consent of the assignee has been obtained; and
- (b) the provisions of paragraph (a) of the last subsection shall apply for the benefit of the assignee.

(6) A trustee or personal representative who is an assignee for value shall have power to consent to the exercise by the tenant for life of his powers under this Act, or to any such investment or application of capital money as aforesaid, and to bind by such consent all persons interested in the trust estate, or the estate of the testator or intestate.

(7) If by the original assignment, or by any subsequent disposition, the estate or interest assigned or created by the original assignment, or any part thereof, or any derivative interest is settled on persons in succession, whether subject to any prior charge or not, and there is no trustee or personal representative in whom the entirety of the estate or interest so settled is vested, then the

person for the time being entitled in possession under the limitations of that settlement, whether as trustee or beneficiary, or who would, if of full age, be so entitled, and notwithstanding any charge or incumbrance subsisting or to arise under such settlement, shall have power to consent to the exercise by the tenant for life of his powers under this Act, or to any such investment or application of capital money as aforesaid, and to bind by such consent all persons interested or to become interested under such settlement.

(8) Where an assignee for value, or any person who has power to consent as aforesaid under this section, is an infant, the consent may be given on his behalf by his parents or parent or testamentary or other guardian in the order named.

(9) The court shall have power to authorise any person interested under any assignment to consent to the exercise by the tenant for life of his powers under this Act, or to any such investment or application of capital money as aforesaid on behalf of himself and all other persons interested, or who may become interested under such assignment.

(10) An assignment by operation of the law of bankruptcy, where the assignment comes into operation after the commencement of this Act, shall be deemed to be an assignment for value for the purposes of this section.

(11) An instrument whereby a tenant for life, in consideration of marriage or as part or by way of any family arrangement, not being a security for payment of money advanced, makes an assignment of or creates a charge upon his estate or interest under the settlement is to be deemed one of the instruments creating the settlement, and not an assignment for value for the purposes of this section:

Provided that this subsection shall not have effect with respect to any disposition made before the eighteenth day of August, eighteen hundred and ninety, if inconsistent with the nature or terms of the disposition.

(12) This section extends to assignments made or coming into operation before or after the commencement of this Act, and in this section "assignment" includes assignment by way of mortgage, and any partial or qualified assignment, and any charge or incumbrance, "assignee" has a corresponding meaning, and "assignee for value" includes persons deriving title under the original assignee.

[189]

NOTES

Sub-s (3): words omitted repealed by the Trustee Act 2000, s 40(1), (3), Sch 2, Pt II, para 16(1)(a), Sch 4, Pt II, in relation to the determination on or after 1 February 2001 of whether an assignee's consent is required to the investment or application of capital money: see the Trustee Act 2000, s 40(1), Sch 2, Pt II, para 16(2) and SI 2001/49, art 2.

Sub-s (4): words in square brackets substituted by the Trustee Act 2000, s 40(1), Sch 2, Pt II, para 16(1)(b), in relation to the determination on or after 1 February 2001 of whether an assignee's consent is required to the investment or application of capital money: see the Trustee Act 2000, s 40(1), Sch 2, Pt II, para 16(2) and SI 2001/49, art 2.

105 Effect of surrender of life estate to the next remainderman

(1) Where the estate or interest of a tenant for life under the settlement has been or is absolutely assured with intent to extinguish the same, either before or after the commencement of this Act, to the person next entitled in remainder or reversion under the settlement, then, … the statutory powers of the tenant for life under this Act shall, in reference to the property affected by the assurance, and notwithstanding the provisions of the last preceding section, cease to be exercisable by him, and the statutory powers shall thenceforth become exercisable as if he were dead, but without prejudice to any incumbrance affecting the estate or interest assured, and to the rights to which any incumbrancer would have been entitled if those powers had remained exercisable by the tenant for life.

This subsection applies whether or not any term of years or charge intervenes, or the estate of the remainderman or reversioner is liable to be defeated, and whether or not the estate or interest of the tenant for life under the settlement was in possession at the date of the assurance.

This subsection does not prejudice anything done by the tenant for life before the commencement of this Act, in exercise of any power operating under the Settled Land Acts 1882 to 1890, or, unless the assurance provides to the contrary, operate to accelerate any such intervening terms of years or charge as aforesaid.

(2) In this section "assurance" means any surrender, conveyance, assignment or appointment under a power (whether vested in any person solely, or jointly in two or more persons) which operates in equity to extinguish the estate or interest of the tenant for life, and "assured" has a corresponding meaning.

[190]

NOTES

Words omitted repealed by the Law of Property (Amendment) Act 1926, s 7, Schedule.

106 Prohibition or limitation against exercise of powers void, and provision against forfeiture

(1) If in a settlement, will, assurance, or other instrument executed or made before or after, or partly before and partly after, the commencement of this Act a provision is inserted—

(a) purporting or attempting, by way of direction, declaration, or otherwise, to forbid a tenant for life or statutory owner to exercise any power under this Act, or his right to require the settled land to be vested in him; or

(b) attempting, or tending, or intended, by a limitation, gift, or disposition over of settled land, or by a limitation, gift, or disposition of other real or any personal property, or by the imposition of any condition, or by forfeiture, or in any other manner whatever, to prohibit or prevent him from exercising, or to induce him to abstain from exercising, or to put him into a position inconsistent with his exercising any power under this Act, or his right to require the settled land to be vested in him;

that provision, as far as it purports, or attempts, or tends, or is intended to have, or would or might have, the operation aforesaid, shall be deemed to be void.

(2) For the purposes of this section an estate or interest limited to continue so long only as a person abstains from exercising any such power or right as aforesaid shall be and take effect as an estate or interest to continue for the period for which it would continue if that person were to abstain from exercising the power or right, discharged from liability to determination or cesser by or on his exercising the same.

(3) Notwithstanding anything in a settlement, the exercise by the tenant for life or statutory owner of any power under this Act shall not occasion a forfeiture.

[191]

107 Tenant for life trustee for all parties interested

(1) A tenant for life or statutory owner shall, in exercising any power under this Act, have regard to the interests of all parties entitled under the settlement, and shall, in relation to the exercise thereof by him, be deemed to be in the position and to have the duties and liabilities of a trustee for those parties.

[(1A) The following provisions apply to the tenant for life as they apply to the trustees of the settlement—

(a) sections 11, 13 to 15 and 21 to 23 of the Trustee Act 2000 (power to employ agents subject to certain restrictions),

(b) section 32 of that Act (remuneration and expenses of agents etc),

(c) section 19 of the Trustee Act 1925 (power to insure), and

(d) in so far as they relate to the provisions mentioned in paragraphs (a) and (c), Part I of, and Schedule 1 to, the Trustee Act 2000 (the duty of care).]

(2) The provision by a tenant for life or statutory owner, at his own expense, of dwellings available for the working classes on any settled land shall not be deemed to be an injury to any interest in reversion or remainder in that land, but such provision shall not be made by a tenant for life or statutory owner without the previous approval in writing of the trustees of the settlement.

[192]

NOTES

Sub-s (1A): inserted by the Trustee Act 2000, s 40(1), Sch 2, Pt II, para 17.

108 Saving for and exercise of other powers

(1) Nothing in this Act shall take away, abridge, or prejudicially affect any power for the time being subsisting under a settlement, or by statute or otherwise, exercisable by a tenant for life, or (save as hereinafter provided) by trustees with his consent, or on his request, or by his direction, or otherwise, and the powers given by this Act are cumulative.

(2) In case of conflict between the provisions of a settlement and the provisions of this Act, relative to any matter in respect whereof the tenant for life or statutory owner exercises or contracts or intends to exercise any power under this Act, the provisions of this Act shall prevail; and, notwithstanding anything in the settlement, any power (not being merely a power of revocation or appointment) relating to the settled land thereby conferred on the trustees of the settlement or other persons exercisable for any purpose, whether or not provided for in this Act, shall, after the commencement of this Act, be exercisable by the tenant for life or statutory owner as if it were an additional power conferred on the tenant for life within the next following section of this Act and not otherwise.

(3) If a question arises or a doubt is entertained respecting any matter within this section, the tenant for life or statutory owner, or the trustees of the settlement, or any other person interested, under the settlement may apply to the court for its decision thereon, and the court may make such order respecting the matter as the court thinks fit.

[193]

109 Saving for additional or larger powers under settlement

(1) Nothing in this Act precludes a settlor from conferring on the tenant for life, or (save as provided by the last preceding section) on the trustees of the settlement, any powers additional to or larger than those conferred by this Act.

(2) Any additional or larger powers so conferred shall, as far as may be, notwithstanding anything in this Act, operate and be exercisable in the like manner, and with all the like incidents, effects, and consequences, as if they were conferred by this Act, and, if relating to the settled land, as if they were conferred by this Act on a tenant for life.

[194]

110 Protection of purchasers, etc

(1) On a sale, exchange, lease, mortgage, charge, or other disposition, a purchaser dealing in good faith with a tenant for life or statutory owner shall, as against all parties entitled under the settlement, be conclusively taken to have given the best price, consideration, or rent, as the case may require, that could reasonably be obtained by the tenant for life or statutory owner, and to have complied with all the requisitions of this Act.

(2) A purchaser of a legal estate in settled land shall not, except as hereby expressly provided, be bound or entitled to call for the production of the trust instrument or any information concerning that instrument or any ad valorem stamp duty thereon, and whether or not he has notice of its contents he shall, save as hereinafter provided, be bound and entitled if the last or only principal vesting instrument contains the statements and particulars required by this Act to assume that—

- (a) the person in whom the land is by the said instrument vested or declared to be vested is the tenant for life or statutory owner and has all the powers of a tenant for life under this Act, including such additional or larger powers, if any, as are therein mentioned;
- (b) the persons by the said instrument stated to be the trustees of the settlement, or their successors appearing to be duly appointed, are the properly constituted trustees of the settlement;
- (c) the statements and particulars required by this Act and contained (expressly or by reference) in the said instrument were correct at the date thereof;
- (d) the statements contained in any deed executed in accordance with this Act declaring who are the trustees of the settlement for the purposes of this Act are correct;
- (e) the statements contained in any deed of discharge, executed in accordance with this Act, are correct:

Provided that, as regards the first vesting instrument executed for the purpose of giving effect to—

- (a) a settlement subsisting at the commencement of this Act; or
- (b) an instrument which by virtue of this Act is deemed to be a settlement; or
- (c) a settlement which by virtue of this Act is deemed to have been made by any person after the commencement of this Act; or
- (d) an instrument inter vivos intended to create a settlement of a legal estate in land which is executed after the commencement of this Act and does not comply with the requirements of this Act with respect to the method of effecting such a settlement;

a purchaser shall be concerned to see—

- (i) that the land disposed of to him is comprised in such settlement or instrument;
- (ii) that the person in whom the settled land is by such vesting instrument vested, or declared to be vested, is the person in whom it ought to be vested as tenant for life or statutory owner;
- (iii) that the persons thereby stated to be the trustees of the settlement are the properly constituted trustees of the settlement.

(3) A purchaser of a legal estate in settled land from a personal representative shall be entitled to act on the following assumptions:—

- (i) If the capital money, if any, payable in respect of the transaction is paid to the personal representative, that such representative is acting under his statutory or other powers and requires the money for purposes of administration;
- (ii) If such capital money is, by the direction of the personal representative, paid to persons who are stated to be the trustees of a settlement, that such persons are the duly constituted trustees of the settlement for the purposes of this Act, and that the personal representative is acting under his statutory powers during a minority;
- (iii) In any other case, that the personal representative is acting under his statutory or other powers.

(4) Where no capital money arises under a transaction, a disposition by a tenant for life or statutory owner shall, in favour of a purchaser of a legal estate, have effect under this Act notwithstanding that at the date of the transaction there are no trustees of the settlement.

(5) If a conveyance of or an assent relating to land formerly subject to a vesting instrument does not state who are the trustees of the settlement for the purposes of this Act, a purchaser of a legal

estate shall be bound and entitled to act on the assumption that the person in whom the land was thereby vested was entitled to the land free from all limitations, powers, and charges taking effect under that settlement, absolutely and beneficially, or, if so expressed in the conveyance or assent, as personal representative, or [trustee of land] or otherwise, and that every statement of fact in such conveyance or assent is correct.

[195]

NOTES

Sub-s (5): words in square brackets substituted by the Trusts of Land and Appointment of Trustees Act 1996, s 25(1), Sch 3, para 2(12); for savings in relation to entailed interests created before the commencement of that Act, and savings consequential upon the abolition of the doctrine of conversion, see s 25(4), (5) thereof.

111 Purchaser of beneficial interest of tenant for life to have remedies of a legal owner

Where—

(a) at the commencement of this Act the legal beneficial interest of a tenant for life under a settlement is vested in a purchaser; or

(b) after the commencement of this Act a tenant for life conveys or deals with his beneficial interest in possession in favour of a purchaser, and the interest so conveyed or created would, but for the restrictions imposed by statute on the creation of legal estates, have been a legal interest;

the purchaser shall (without prejudice to the powers conferred by this Act on the tenant for life) have and may exercise all the same rights and remedies as he would have had or have been entitled to exercise if the interest had remained or been a legal interest and the reversion, if any, on any leases or tenancies derived out of the settled land had been vested in him:

Provided that, where the conveyance or dealing is effected after the commencement of this Act, the purchaser shall not be entitled to the possession of the documents of title relating to the settled land, but shall have the same rights with respect thereto as if the tenant for life had given to him a statutory acknowledgment of his right to production and delivery of copies thereof, and a statutory undertaking for the safe custody thereof.

The tenant for life shall not deliver any such documents to a purchaser of his beneficial interest, who is not also a purchaser of the whole of the settled land to which such documents relate.

[196]

112 Exercise of powers; limitation of provisions, etc

(1) Where a power of sale, exchange, leasing, mortgaging, charging, or other power is exercised by a tenant for life, or statutory owner or by the trustees of a settlement, he and they may respectively execute, make, and do all deeds, instruments, and things necessary or proper in that behalf.

(2) Where any provision in this Act refers to sale, purchase, exchange, mortgaging, charging, leasing, or other disposition or dealing, or to any power, consent, payment, receipt, deed, assurance, contract, expenses, act, or transaction, it shall (unless the contrary appears) be construed as extending only to sales, purchases, exchanges, mortgages, charges, leases, dispositions, dealings, powers, consents, payments, receipts, deeds, assurances, contracts, expenses, acts, and transactions under this Act.

[197]

PART VIII
COURT, MINISTRY OF AGRICULTURE AND FISHERIES, PROCEDURE

113 Jurisdiction and procedure

(1) All matters within the jurisdiction of the court under this Act shall, subject to the enactments for the time being in force with respect to the procedure of the *Supreme Court of Judicature* [Senior Courts], be assigned to the Chancery Division of the High Court.

(2) …

[(3) The powers of the court may, as regards land not exceeding in capital value the county court limit, or in net annual value for rating the county court limit, and, as regards capital money arising under this Act, and securities in which the same is invested, not exceeding in amount or value the county court limit, and as regards personal chattels settled or to be settled, as in this Act mentioned, not exceeding the county court limit, be exercised by any county court. Section 147(2) and (3) of the County Courts Act 1984 (construction of references to net annual value for rating) shall apply for the purposes of this subsection as it applies for the purposes of that Act.]

[(3A) In the preceding subsection "the county court limit" means the county court limit for the time being specified by an Order in Council under [section 145 of the County Courts Act 1984] as the county court limit for the purposes of that subsection.]

(4) Payment of money into court effectually exonerates therefrom the person making the payment.

(5) Every application to the court under this Act shall, subject to any rules of court to the contrary, be by summons at Chambers.

(6) On an application by the trustees of a settlement notice shall be served in the first instance on the tenant for life.

(7) On any application notice shall be served on such persons, if any, as the court thinks fit.

(8) The court shall have full power and discretion to make such order as it thinks fit respecting the costs, charges, or expenses of all or any of the parties to any application, and may, if it thinks fit, order that all or any of those costs, charges, or expenses be paid out of property subject to the settlement.

(9) The provisions of the Trustee Act 1925, relating to vesting orders and orders appointing a person to convey shall apply to all vesting orders authorised to be made by this Act.

[198]

NOTES

Sub-s (1): words in italics substituted by subsequent words in square brackets by the Constitutional Reform Act 2005, s 59(5), Sch 11, Pt 2, para 4(1), (3), as from 1 October 2009.

Sub-s (2): repealed by the Courts Act 1971, s 56(4), Sch 11, Pt II.

Sub-s (3): substituted by the County Courts Act 1984, s 148(1), Sch 2, para 20.

Sub-s (3A): inserted by the Administration of Justice Act 1982, s 37, Sch 3, Pt II, para 4; amended by the County Courts Act 1984, s 148(1), Sch 2, para 20.

114 Payment of costs out of settled property

Where the court directs that any costs, charges, or expenses be paid out of property subject to a settlement, the same shall, subject and according to the directions of the court, be raised and paid—

(a) out of capital money arising under this Act, or other money liable to be laid out in the purchase of land to be made subject to the settlement; or

(b) out of securities representing such money, or out of income of any such money or securities; or

(c) out of any accumulations of income of land, money, or securities; or

(d) by means of a sale of part of the settled land in respect whereof the costs, charges or expenses are incurred, or of other settled land comprised in the same settlement and subject to the same limitations; or

(e) by means of a legal mortgage of the settled land or any part thereof to be made by such person as the court directs;

or partly in one of those modes and partly in another or others, or in any such other mode as the court thinks fit.

[199]

115 Powers of the [Secretary of State]

(1) The [Secretary of State] shall, by virtue of this Act, have for the purposes of any Act, public general or local or private, making provision for the execution of improvements on settled land, all such powers and authorities as he has for the purposes of the Improvement of Land Act 1864.

(2) The provisions of the last-mentioned Act relating to proceedings and inquiries, and to authentication of instruments, and to declarations, statements, notices, applications, forms, security for expenses, inspections and examinations, shall extend and apply, as far as the nature and circumstances of the case admit, to acts and proceedings done or taken by or in relation to the [Secretary of State] under any Act making provision as last aforesaid.

(3) The provisions of any Act relating … to security for costs to be taken in respect of the business transacted under the Acts administered by the [Secretary of State] as successor of the Land Commissioners for England shall extend and apply to the business transacted by or under the direction of the [Secretary of State] under any Act, public general or local or private, by which any power or duty is conferred or imposed on him as such successor.

[200]

NOTES

Section heading: words in square brackets substituted by virtue of SI 2002/794, art 5(1), Sch 1, para 4.

Sub-ss (1), (2): words in square brackets substituted by SI 2002/794, art 5(1), Sch 1, para 4(1)–(3).

Sub-s (3): words omitted repealed by the Agriculture (Miscellaneous Provisions) Act 1963, s 28, Schedule, Pt II; words in square brackets substituted by SI 2002/794, art 5(1), Sch 1, para 4(1), (4).

116 Filing of certificates, etc at the Ministry of Agriculture

(1) Every certificate and report approved and made by the [Secretary of State] under this Act shall be filed in the office of [the [Secretary of State]].

(2) An office copy of any certificate or report so filed shall be delivered out of such office to any person requiring the same, on payment of the proper fee, and shall be sufficient evidence of the certificate or report whereof it purports to be a copy.

[201]

NOTES

Sub-s (1): words in first and third (inner) pairs of square brackets substituted by SI 2002/794, art 5(1), Sch 1, para 5; words in second (outer) pair of square brackets substituted by the Transfer of Functions (Ministry of Food) Order 1955, SI 1955/554, art 3.

Following the substitution of the words "Secretary of State" as noted above, the reference to the Ministry of Agriculture in the section heading should be construed accordingly.

PART IX SUPPLEMENTARY PROVISIONS

117 Definitions

(1) In this Act, unless the context otherwise requires, the following expressions have the meanings hereby assigned to them respectively, that is to say:—

(i) "Building purposes" include the erecting and the improving of, and the adding to, and the repairing of buildings; and a "building lease" is a lease for any building purposes or purposes connected therewith;

(ii) "Capital money arising under this Act" means capital money arising under the powers and provisions of this Act or the Acts replaced by this Act, and receivable for the trusts and purposes of the settlement and includes securities representing capital money;

(iii) "Death duty" means estate duty … and every other duty leviable or payable on death;

(iv) "Determinable fee" means a fee determinable whether by limitation or condition;

(v) "Disposition" and "conveyance" include a mortgage, charge by way of legal mortgage, lease, assent, vesting declaration, vesting instrument, disclaimer, release and every other assurance of property or of an interest therein by any instrument, except a will, and "dispose of" and "convey" have corresponding meanings;

(vi) "Dower" includes "freebench";

(vii) "Hereditaments" mean real property which on an intestacy might before the commencement of this Act have devolved on an heir;

(viii) "Instrument" does not include a statute unless the statute creates a settlement;

(ix) "Land" includes land of any tenure, and mines and minerals whether or not held apart from the surface, buildings or parts of buildings (whether the division is horizontal, vertical or made in any other way) and other corporeal hereditaments; also a manor, an advowson, and a rent and other incorporeal hereditaments, and an easement, right, privilege, or benefit in, over, or derived from land, and any estate or interest in land[, but does not (except in the phrase "trust of land") include] an undivided share in land;

(x) "Lease" includes an agreement for a lease, and "forestry lease" means a lease to the Forestry Commissioners for any purpose for which they are authorised to acquire land by the Forestry Act 1919;

(xi) "Legal mortgage" means a mortgage by demise or sub-demise or a charge by way of legal mortgage, and "legal mortgagee" has a corresponding meaning; "legal estate" means an estate interest or charge in or over land (subsisting or created at law) which is by statute authorised to subsist or to be created at law; and "equitable interests" mean all other interests and charges in or over land or in the proceeds of sale thereof; an equitable interest "capable of subsisting at law" means such an equitable interest as could validly subsist at law, if clothed with the legal estate; and "estate owner" means the owner of a legal estate;

(xii) "Limitation" includes a trust, and "trust" includes an implied or constructive trust;

(xiii) …

(xiv) "Manor" includes lordship, and reputed manor or lordship; and "manorial incident" has the same meaning as in the Law of Property Act 1922;

(xv) "Mines and minerals" mean mines and minerals whether already opened or in work or not, and include all minerals and substances in, on, or under the land, obtainable by underground or by surface working; and "mining purposes" include the sinking and searching for, winning, working, getting, making merchantable, smelting or otherwise converting or working for the purposes of any manufacture, carrying away, and disposing of mines and minerals, in or under the settled land, or any other land, and the erection of buildings, and the execution of engineering and other works suitable for those purposes; and a "mining lease" is a lease for any mining purposes or purposes connected therewith, and includes a grant or licence for any mining purposes;

(xvi) …

(xvii) "Notice" includes constructive notice;

(xviii) "Personal representative" means the executor, original or by representation, or administrator, for the time being of a deceased person, and where there are special personal representatives for the purposes of settled land means those personal representatives;

(xix) "Possession" includes receipt of rents and profits, or the right to receive the same, if any; and "income" includes rents and profits;

(xx) "Property" includes any thing in action, and any interest in real or personal property;

(xxi) "Purchaser" means a purchaser in good faith for value, and includes a lessee, mortgagee or other person who in good faith acquires an interest in settled land for value; and in reference to a legal estate includes a chargee by way of legal mortgage;

(xxii) "Rent" includes yearly or other rent, and toll, duty, royalty, or other reservation, by the acre, or the ton, or otherwise; and in relation to rent, "payment" includes delivery; and "fine" includes premium or fore-gift, and any payment, consideration, or benefit in the nature of a fine, premium, or fore-gift;

(xxiii) "Securities" include stocks, funds, and shares;

(xxiv) "Settled land" includes land which is deemed to be settled land; "settlement" includes an instrument or instruments which under this Act or the Acts which it replaces is or are deemed to be or which together constitute a settlement, and a settlement which is deemed to have been made by any person or to be subsisting for the purposes of this Act; "a settlement subsisting at the commencement of this Act" includes a settlement created by virtue of this Act immediately on the commencement thereof; and "trustees of the settlement" mean the trustees thereof for the purposes of this Act howsoever appointed or constituted;

(xxv) "Small dwellings" mean dwelling-houses of a rateable value not exceeding one hundred pounds per annum;

(xxvi) "Statutory owner" means the trustees of the settlement or other persons who, during a minority, or at any other time when there is no tenant for life, have the powers of a tenant for life under this Act, but does not include the trustees of the settlement, where by virtue of an order of the court or otherwise the trustees have power to convey the settled land in the name of the tenant for life;

(xxvii) "Steward" includes deputy steward, or other proper officer, of a manor;

(xxviii) "Tenant for life" includes a person (not being a statutory owner) who has the powers of a tenant for life under this Act, and also (where the context requires) one of two or more persons who together constitute the tenant for life, or have the powers of a tenant for life; and "tenant in tail" includes a person entitled to an entailed interest in any property; and "entailed interest" has the same meaning as in the Law of Property Act 1925;

(xxix) A "term of years absolute" means a term of years, taking effect either in possession or in reversion, with or without impeachment for waste, whether at a rent or not and whether subject or not to another legal estate, and whether certain or liable to determination by notice, re-entry, operation of law, or by a provision for cesser on redemption, or in any other event (other than the dropping of a life, or the determination of a determinable life interest), but does not include any term of years determinable with life or lives or with the cesser of a determinable life interest, nor, if created after the commencement of this Act, a term of years which is not expressed to take effect in possession within twenty-one years after the creation thereof where required by statute to take effect within that period; and in this definition the expression "term of years" includes a term for less than a year, or for a year or years and a fraction of a year or from year to year;

(xxx) "Trust corporation" means the Public Trustee or a corporation either appointed by the court in any particular case to be a trustee or entitled by rules made under subsection (3) of section four of the Public Trustee Act 1906, to act as custodian trustee, and "trust for sale" [has the same meaning] as in the Law of Property Act 1925;

(xxxi) In relation to settled land "vesting deed" or "vesting order" means the instrument whereby settled land is conveyed to or vested or declared to be vested in a tenant for life or statutory owner; "vesting assent" means the instrument whereby a personal representative, after the death of a tenant for life or statutory owner, or the survivor of two or more tenants for life or statutory owners, vests settled land in a person entitled as tenant for life or statutory owner; "vesting instrument" means a vesting deed, a vesting assent or, where the land affected remains settled land, a vesting order; "principal vesting instrument" includes any vesting instrument other than a subsidiary vesting deed; and "trust instrument" means the instrument whereby the trusts of the settled land are declared, and includes any two or more such instruments and a settlement or instrument which is deemed to be a trust instrument;

(xxxii) "United Kingdom" means Great Britain and Northern Ireland;

(xxxiii) "Will" includes codicil.

[(1A) Any reference in this Act to money, securities or proceeds of sale being paid or transferred into court shall be construed as referring to the money, securities or proceeds being paid or transferred into the *Supreme Court* [Senior Courts] or any other court that has jurisdiction, and any reference in this Act to the court, in a context referring to the investment or application of money, securities or proceeds of sale paid or transferred into court, shall be construed, in the case of money, securities or proceeds paid or transferred into the *Supreme Court* [Senior Courts], as referring to the High Court, and, in the case of money, securities or proceeds paid or transferred into another court, as referring to that other court.]

(2) Where an equitable interest in or power over property arises by statute or operation of law, references to the "creation" of an interest or power include any interest or power so arising.

(3) References to registration under the Land Charges Act 1925, apply to any registration made under any statute which is by the Land Charges Act 1925, to have effect as if the registration had been made under that Act.

[202]

NOTES

Sub-s (1): words omitted from para (iii) repealed by the Finance Act 1949, s 52, Sch 11, Pt IV; in paras (ix), (xxx) words in square brackets substituted by the Trusts of Land and Appointment of Trustees Act 1996, s 25(1), Sch 3, para 2(13) (for savings in relation to entailed interests created before the commencement of that Act, and savings consequential upon the abolition of the doctrine of conversion, see s 25(4), (5) thereof); para (xiii) repealed by the Mental Health Act 1959, s 149(2), Sch 8, Pt I; para (xvi) repealed by SI 2002/794, art 5(2), Sch 2.

Sub-s (1A): inserted by the Administration of Justice Act 1965, s 17(1), Sch 1; words in italics in both places they appear substituted by subsequent words in square brackets by the Constitutional Reform Act 2005, s 59(5), Sch 11, Pt 2, para 4(1), (3), as from 1 October 2009.

Modification: definition "Trust corporation" modified, in relation to charities, by the Charities Act 1993, s 35.

118 (*Repealed by the Statute Law* (*Repeals*) *Act 2004.*)

119 Repeals, savings, and construction

(1) … without prejudice to the provisions of section thirty-eight of the Interpretation Act 1889—

(a) Nothing in this repeal shall affect the validity or legality of any dealing in land or other transaction completed before the commencement of this Act, or any title or right acquired or appointment made before the commencement of this Act, but, subject as aforesaid, this Act shall, except where otherwise expressly provided, apply to and in respect of settlements and other instruments whether made or coming into operation before or after the commencement of this Act;

(b) Nothing in this repeal shall affect any rules, orders, or other instruments made under any enactment so repealed, but all such rules, orders and instruments shall continue in force as if made under the corresponding enactment in this Act;

(c) References in any document to any enactment repealed by this Act shall be construed as references to this Act or the corresponding enactment in this Act.

(2) References in any statute to the Settled Estates Act 1877, and to any enactment which it replaced shall be construed as references to this Act.

(3) …

[203]

NOTES

Sub-s (1): words omitted repealed by the Statute Law Revision Act 1950.

Sub-s (3): repealed by the Land Registration Act 2002, ss 133, 135, Sch 11, para 1, Sch 13.

120 Short title, commencement and extent

(1) This Act may be cited as the Settled Land Act 1925.

(2) …

(3) This Act extends to England and Wales only.

[204]

NOTES

Sub-s (2): repealed by the Statute Law Revision Act 1950.

(*Sch 1 repealed by the Statute Law* (*Repeals*) *Act 2004.*)

SCHEDULE 2
TRANSITIONAL PROVISIONS AFFECTING EXISTING SETTLEMENTS

Section 37

Paragraph 1
Provisions for vesting legal estate in Tenant for Life or Statutory Owner

1.—(1) A settlement subsisting at the commencement of this Act is for the purposes of this Act, a trust instrument.

(2) As soon as practicable after the commencement of this Act, the trustees for the purposes of this Act of every settlement of land subsisting at the commencement of this Act (whether or not the settled land is already vested in them), may and on the request of the tenant for life or statutory owner, shall at the cost of the trust estate, execute a principal vesting deed (containing the proper statements and particulars) declaring that the legal estate in the settled land shall vest or is vested in the person or persons therein named (being the tenant for life or statutory owner, and including themselves if they are the statutory owners), and such deed shall (unless the legal estate is already so vested) operate to convey or vest the legal estate in the settled land to or in the person or persons aforesaid and, if more than one, as joint tenants.

(3) If there are no trustees of the settlement then (in default of a person able and willing to appoint such trustees), an application shall be made to the court by the tenant for life or statutory owner, or by any other person interested, for the appointment of such trustees.

(4) If default is made in the execution of any such principal vesting deed, the provisions of this Act relating to vesting orders of settled land shall apply in like manner as if the trustees of the settlement were persons in whom the settled land is wrongly vested.

(5) This paragraph does not apply where, at the commencement of this Act, settled land is held at law or in equity in undivided shares vested in possession.

(6) In the case of settlements subsisting at the commencement of this Act, all the estates, interests and powers thereby limited which are not by statute otherwise converted into equitable interests or powers, shall, as from the date of the principal vesting deed or the vesting order, take effect only in equity.

[This sub-paragraph shall not apply to any legal estate or interest vested in a mortgagee or other purchaser for money or money's worth.]

(7) This paragraph does not apply where settled land is vested in personal representatives at the commencement of this Act, or where settled land becomes vested in personal representatives before a principal vesting deed has been executed pursuant to this paragraph.

(8) No ad valorem stamp duty shall be payable in respect of a vesting deed or order made for giving effect to an existing settlement.

Paragraph 2
Provisions where Settled Land is at commencement of Act vested in personal representatives

2.—(1) Where settled land remains at the commencement of this Act vested in the personal representatives of a person who dies before such commencement, or becomes vested in personal representatives before a principal vesting deed has been executed pursuant to the last preceding paragraph, the personal representatives shall hold the settled land on trust, if and when required so to do, to convey the same to the person who, under the trust instrument, or by virtue of this Act, is the tenant for life or statutory owner and, if more than one, as joint tenants.

(2) A conveyance under this paragraph shall be made at the cost of the trust estate and may be made by an assent in writing signed by the personal representatives which shall operate as a conveyance. No stamp duty is payable in respect of a vesting assent.

(3) The obligation to convey settled land imposed on the personal representatives by this paragraph is subject and without prejudice—

(a) to their rights and powers for purposes of administration, and

(b) to their being satisfied that provision has been or will be made for the payment of any unpaid death duties in respect of the land or any interest therein for which they are accountable, and any interest and costs in respect of such duties, or that they are otherwise effectually indemnified against such duties, interest and costs.

(4) A conveyance under this paragraph shall—

(a) if by deed, be a principal vesting deed, and

(b) if by an assent, be a vesting assent, which shall contain the like statements and particulars as are required by this Act in the case of a principal vesting deed.

(5) Nothing contained in this paragraph affects the rights of personal representatives to transfer or create such legal estates to take effect in priority to a conveyance under this paragraph as may be required for giving effect to the obligations imposed on them by statute.

(6) A conveyance by personal representatives under this paragraph, if made by deed, may contain a reservation to themselves of a term of years absolute in the land conveyed upon trusts for indemnifying them against any unpaid death duties in respect of the land conveyed or any interest therein, and any interest and costs in respect of such duties.

(7) Nothing contained in this paragraph affects any right which a person entitled to an equitable charge for securing money actually raised, and affecting the whole estate the subject of the settlement, may have to require effect to be given thereto by a legal mortgage, before the execution of a conveyance under this section.

Paragraph 3
Provisions as to Infants

3.—(1) Where, at the commencement of this Act, an infant is beneficially entitled to land in possession for an estate in fee simple or for a term of years absolute, or would, if of full age, be a tenant for life or have the powers of a tenant for life, the settled land shall, by virtue of this Act, vest in the trustees (if any) of the settlement upon such trusts as may be requisite for giving effect to the rights of the infant and other persons (if any) interested:

Provided that, if there are no such trustees, then—

(i) Pending their appointment, the settled land shall, by virtue of this Act, vest in the Public Trustee upon the trusts aforesaid:

(ii) The Public Trustee shall not be entitled to act in the trust, or charge any fee, or be liable in any manner unless and until requested in writing to act on behalf of the infant by his parents or parent or testamentary or other guardian in the order named:

(iii) After the Public Trustee has been so requested to act, and has accepted the trust, he shall become the trustee of the settlement, and no trustee shall (except by an order of the court) be appointed in his place without his consent:

(iv) If there is no other person able and willing to appoint trustees the parents or parent or testamentary or other guardian of the infant, if respectively able and willing to act, shall (in the order named) have power by deed to appoint trustees of the settlement in place of the Public Trustee in like manner as if the Public Trustee had refused to act in the trust, and to vest the settled land in them on the trusts aforesaid, and the provisions of the Trustee Act 1925, relating to the appointment of new trustees, and the vesting of trust property shall apply as if the persons aforesaid (in the order named) had been nominated by the settlement for the purpose of appointing new trustees thereof; and in default of any such appointment the infant by his next friend, may, at any time during the minority, apply to the court for the appointment of trustees of the settlement, and the court may make such order as it thinks fit, and if thereby trustees of the settlement are appointed, the settled land shall, by virtue of this Act, vest in the trustees as joint tenants upon the trusts aforesaid:

Provided that in favour of a purchaser a statement in the deed of appointment that the father or mother or both are dead or are unable or unwilling to make the appointment shall be conclusive evidence of the fact stated.

(v) If land to which an infant is beneficially entitled in possession for an estate in fee simple or for a term of years absolute vests in the Public Trustee, but the Public Trustee does not become the trustee of the settlement, and trustees of the settlement are not appointed in his place, then, if and when the infant attains the age of twenty-one years, the land shall vest in him.

(2) The provisions of this paragraph shall extend to the legal estate in the settled land, except where such legal estate is, at or immediately after the commencement of this Act, vested in personal representatives, in which case this paragraph shall have effect without prejudice to the provisions of paragraph two of this Schedule.

(3) Where, at the commencement of this Act, any persons appointed under section sixty of the Settled Land Act 1882, have power to act generally or for any specific purpose on behalf of an infant, then those persons shall, by virtue of this Act, become and be the trustees of the settlement.

(4) Notwithstanding that the settled land is by virtue of this paragraph vested in the trustees of the settlement, they shall, at the cost of the trust estate, in accordance with this Act, execute a principal vesting deed declaring that the settled land is vested in them.

(5) This paragraph does not apply where an infant is beneficially entitled in possession to land for an estate in fee simple or for a term of years absolute jointly with a person of full age (for which case provision is made in the Law of Property Act 1925), but it applies to two or more infants entitled as aforesaid jointly.

(6) This paragraph does not apply where an infant would, if of full age, constitute the tenant for life or have the powers of a tenant for life together with another person of full age, but it applies to two or more infants who would, if all of them were of full age, together constitute the tenant for life or have the powers of a tenant for life.

NOTES

Para 1: words in square brackets inserted by the Law of Property (Amendment) Act 1926, s 7, Schedule.

SCHEDULE 3

Section 83

PART I
IMPROVEMENTS, THE COSTS OF WHICH ARE NOT LIABLE TO BE REPLACED BY INSTALMENTS

(i) Drainage, including the straightening, widening, or deepening of drains, streams, and watercourses:

(ii) Bridges:

(iii) Irrigation; warping:

(iv) Drains, pipes, and machinery for supply and distribution of sewage as manure:

(v) Embanking or weiring from a river or lake, or from the sea, or a tidal water:

(vi) Groynes; sea walls; defences against water:

(vii) Inclosing; straightening of fences; re-division of fields:

(viii) Reclamation; dry warping:

(ix) Farm roads; private roads; roads or streets in villages or towns:

(x) Clearing; trenching; planting:

(xi) Cottages for labourers, farm-servants, and artisans, employed on the settled land or not:

(xii) Farmhouses, offices, and outbuildings, and other buildings for farm purposes:

(xiii) Saw-mills, scutch-mills, and other mills, water-wheels, engine-houses, and kilns, which will increase the value of the settled land for agricultural purposes or as woodland or otherwise:

(xiv) Reservoirs, tanks, conduits, watercourses, pipes, wells, ponds, shafts, dams, weirs, sluices, and other works and machinery for supply and distribution of water for agricultural, manufacturing, or other purposes, or for domestic or other consumption:

(xv) Tramways; railways; canals; docks:

(xvi) Jetties, piers, and landing places on rivers, lakes, the sea, or tidal waters, for facilitating transport of persons and of agricultural stock and produce, and of manure and other things required for agricultural purposes, and of minerals, and of things required for mining purposes:

(xvii) Markets and market-places:

(xviii) Streets, roads, paths, squares, gardens, or other open spaces for the use, gratuitously or on payment, of the public or of individuals, or for dedication to the public, the same being necessary or proper in connexion with the conversion of land into building land:

(xix) Sewers, drains, watercourses, pipe-making, fencing, paving, brick-making, tile-making, and other works necessary or proper in connexion with any of the objects aforesaid:

(xx) Trial pits for mines, and other preliminary works necessary or proper in connexion with development of mines:

(xxi) Reconstruction, enlargement, or improvement of any of those works:

(xxii) The provision of small dwellings, either by means of building new buildings or by means of the reconstruction, enlargement, or improvement of existing buildings, if that provision of small dwellings is, in the opinion of the court, not injurious to the settled land or is agreed to by the tenant for life and the trustees of the settlement:

(xxiii) Additions to or alterations in buildings reasonably necessary or proper to enable the same to be let:

(xxiv) Erection of buildings in substitution for buildings within an urban sanitary district taken by a local or other public authority, or for buildings taken under compulsory powers, but so that no more money be expended than the amount received for the buildings taken and the site thereof:

(xxv) The rebuilding of the principal mansion house on the settled land:

Provided that the sum to be applied under this head shall not exceed one-half of the annual rental of the settled land.

[206]

PART II
IMPROVEMENTS, THE COSTS OF WHICH THE TRUSTEES OF THE SETTLEMENT OR THE COURT MAY REQUIRE TO BE REPLACED BY INSTALMENTS

(i) Residential houses for land or mineral agents, managers, clerks, bailiffs, woodmen, gamekeepers and other persons employed on the settled land, or in connexion with the management or development thereof:

(ii) Any offices, workshops and other buildings of a permanent nature required in connexion with the management or development of the settled land or any part thereof:

(iii) The erection and building of dwelling houses, shops, buildings for religious, educational, literary, scientific, or public purposes, market places, market houses, places of amusement and entertainment, gasworks, electric light or power works, or any other works necessary or proper in connexion with the development of the settled land, or any part thereof as a building estate:

(iv) Restoration or reconstruction of buildings damaged or destroyed by dry rot:

(v) Structural additions to or alterations in buildings reasonably required, whether the buildings are intended to be let or not, or are already let:

(vi) Boring for water and other preliminary works in connexion therewith.

[207]

PART III
IMPROVEMENTS, THE COSTS OF WHICH THE TRUSTEES OF THE SETTLEMENT AND THE COURT MUST REQUIRE TO BE REPLACED BY INSTALMENTS

(i) Heating, hydraulic or electric power apparatus for buildings, and engines, pumps, lifts, rams, boilers, flues, and other works required or used in connexion therewith:

(ii) Engine houses, engines, gasometers, dynamos, accumulators, cables, pipes, wiring, switchboards, plant and other works required for the installation of electric, gas, or other artificial light, in connexion with any principal mansion house, or other house or buildings; but not electric lamps, gas fittings, or decorative fittings required in any such house or building:

(iii) Steam rollers, traction engines, motor lorries and moveable machinery for farming or other purposes.

[208]

(*Sch 4 repealed by the Statute Law* (*Repeals*) *Act 2004.*)

TRUSTEE ACT 1925

(1925 c 19)

An Act to consolidate certain enactments relating to trustees in England and Wales

[9 April 1925]

1–11 (*S 1 repealed by the Trustee Investments Act 1961, s 16(2), Sch 5; ss 2–6, 10, 11 repealed by the Trustee Act 2000, s 40(1), (3), Sch 2, Pt II, para 18, Sch 4, Pt II; s 7 repealed by the Trustee Act 2000, s 40, Sch 2, Pt II, para 18, Sch 4, Pt II, subject to transitional provisions contained in Sch 3, para 1 thereto; s 8 repealed by the Trustee Act 2000, s 40, Sch 2, Pt II, para 18, Sch 3, para 2, Sch 4, Pt II, except in relation to loans or investments made before 1 February 2001; s 9 repealed by the Trustee Act 2000, s 40, Sch 2, Pt II, para 18, Sch 3, para 3, Sch 4, Pt II, except in relation to any advance of trust money made before 1 February 2001.*)

PART II
GENERAL POWERS OF TRUSTEES AND PERSONAL REPRESENTATIVES

12 Power of trustees for sale to sell by auction, etc

(1) Where [a trustee has a duty or power to sell property], he may sell or concur with any other person in selling all or any part of the property, either subject to prior charges or not, and either together or in lots, by public auction or by private contract, subject to any such conditions respecting title or evidence of title or other matter as the trustee thinks fit, with power to vary any contract for sale, and to buy in at any auction, or to rescind any contract for sale and to re-sell, without being answerable for any loss.

(2) A [duty] or power to sell or dispose of land includes a [duty] or power to sell or dispose of part thereof, whether the division is horizontal, vertical, or made in any other way.

(3) This section does not enable an express power to sell settled land to be exercised where the power is not vested in the tenant for life or statutory owner.

[209]

NOTES

Sub-ss (1), (2): words in square brackets substituted by the Trusts of Land and Appointment of Trustees Act 1996, s 25(1), Sch 3, para 3(2); for savings in relation to entailed interests created before the commencement of that Act, and savings consequential upon the abolition of the doctrine of conversion, see s 25(4), (5) thereof.

13 Power to sell subject to depreciatory conditions

(1) No sale made by a trustee shall be impeached by any beneficiary upon the ground that any of the conditions subject to which the sale was made may have been unnecessarily depreciatory, unless it also appears that the consideration for the sale was thereby rendered inadequate.

(2) No sale made by a trustee shall, after the execution of the conveyance, be impeached as against the purchaser upon the ground that any of the conditions subject to which the sale was made may have been unnecessarily depreciatory, unless it appears that the purchaser was acting in collusion with the trustee at the time when the contract for sale was made.

(3) No purchaser, upon any sale made by a trustee, shall be at liberty to make any objection against the title upon any of the grounds aforesaid.

(4) This section applies to sales made before or after the commencement of this Act.

[210]

14 Power of trustees to give receipts

(1) The receipt in writing of a trustee for any money, securities, [investments] or other personal property or effects payable, transferable, or deliverable to him under any trust or power shall be a sufficient discharge to the person paying, transferring, or delivering the same and shall effectually exonerate him from seeing to the application or being answerable for any loss or misapplication thereof.

(2) this section does not, except where the trustee is a trust corporation, enable a sole trustee to give a valid receipt for—

[(a) proceeds of sale or other capital money arising under a trust of land;]
(b) capital money arising under the Settled Land Act 1925.

(3) This section applies notwithstanding anything to the contrary in the instrument, if any, creating the trust.

[211]

NOTES

Sub-s (1): word in square brackets inserted by the Trustee Act 2000, s 40(1), Sch 2, Pt II, para 19.

Sub-s (2): para (a) substituted by the Trusts of Land and Appointment of Trustees Act 1996, s 25(1), Sch 3, para 3(3); for savings in relation to entailed interests created before the commencement of that Act, and savings consequential upon the abolition of the doctrine of conversion, see s 25(4), (5) thereof.

15 Power to compound liabilities

A personal representative, or two or more trustees acting together, or, subject to the restrictions imposed in regard to receipts by a sole trustee not being a trust corporation, a sole acting trustee where by the instrument, if any, creating the trust, or by statute, a sole trustee is authorised to execute the trusts and powers reposed in him, may, if and as he or they think fit—

(a) accept any property, real or personal, before the time at which it is made transferable or payable; or
(b) sever and apportion any blended trust funds or property; or
(c) pay or allow any debt or claim on any evidence that he or they think sufficient; or
(d) accept any composition or any security, real or personal, for any debt or for any property, real or personal, claimed; or
(e) allow any time of payment of any debt; or
(f) compromise, compound, abandon, submit to arbitration, or otherwise settle any debt, account, claim, or thing whatever relating to the testator's or intestate's estate or to the trust;

and for any of these purposes may enter into, give, execute, and do such agreements, instruments of composition or arrangement, releases, and other things as to him or them seem expedient, without being responsible for any loss occasioned by any act or thing so done by him or them [if he has or they have discharged the duty of care set out in section 1(1) of the Trustee Act 2000].

[212]

NOTES

Words in square brackets substituted by the Trustee Act 2000, s 40(1), Sch 2, Pt II, para 20.

16 Power to raise money by sale, mortgage, etc.

(1) Where trustees are authorised by the instrument, if any, creating the trust or by law to pay or apply capital money subject to the trust for any purpose or in any manner, they shall have and shall be deemed always to have had power to raise the money required by sale, conversion, calling in, or mortgage of all or any part of the trust property for the time being in possession.

(2) This section applies notwithstanding anything to the contrary contained in the instrument, if any, creating the trust, but does not apply to trustees of property held for charitable purposes, or to trustees of a settlement for the purposes of the Settled Land Act 1925, not being also the statutory owners.

[213]

17 Protection to purchasers and mortgagees dealing with trustees

No purchaser or mortgagee paying or advancing money on a sale or mortgage purporting to be made under any trust or power vested in trustees, shall be concerned to see that such money is wanted; or that no more than is wanted is raised, or otherwise as to the application thereof.

[214]

18 Devolution of powers or trusts

(1) Where a power or trust is given to or imposed on two or more trustees jointly, the same may be exercised or performed by the survivors or survivor of them for the time being.

(2) Until the appointment of new trustees, the personal representatives or representative for the time being of a sole trustee, or, where there were two or more trustees of the last surviving or continuing trustee, shall be capable of exercising or performing any power or trust which was given to, or capable of being exercised by, the sole or last surviving or continuing trustee, or other the trustees or trustee for the time being of the trust.

(3) This section takes effect subject to the restrictions imposed in regard to receipts by a sole trustee, not being a trust corporation.

(4) In this section "personal representative" does not include an executor who has renounced or has not proved.

[215]

[19 Power to insure

(1) A trustee may—
- (a) insure any property which is subject to the trust against risks of loss or damage due to any event, and
- (b) pay the premiums out of the trust funds.

(2) In the case of property held on a bare trust, the power to insure is subject to any direction given by the beneficiary or each of the beneficiaries—
- (a) that any property specified in the direction is not to be insured;
- (b) that any property specified in the direction is not to be insured except on such conditions as may be so specified.

(3) Property is held on a bare trust if it is held on trust for—
- (a) a beneficiary who is of full age and capacity and absolutely entitled to the property subject to the trust, or
- (b) beneficiaries each of whom is of full age and capacity and who (taken together) are absolutely entitled to the property subject to the trust.

(4) If a direction under subsection (2) of this section is given, the power to insure, so far as it is subject to the direction, ceases to be a delegable function for the purposes of section 11 of the Trustee Act 2000 (power to employ agents).

(5) In this section "trust funds" means any income or capital funds of the trust.]

[216]

NOTES

Substituted by the Trustee Act 2000, s 34(1), (3), in relation to trusts created before or after 1 February 2001.

20 Application of insurance money where policy kept up under any trust, power or obligation

(1) Money receivable by trustees or any beneficiary under a policy of insurance against the loss or damage of any property subject to a trust or to a settlement within the meaning of the Settled Land Act 1925 … shall, where the policy has been kept up under any trust in that behalf or under any power statutory or otherwise, or in performance of any covenant or of any obligation statutory or otherwise, or by a tenant for life impeachable for waste, be capital money for the purposes of the trust or settlement, as the case may be.

(2) If any such money is receivable by any person, other than the trustees of the trust or settlement, that person shall use his best endeavours to recover and receive the money, and shall pay the net residue thereof, after discharging any costs of recovering and receiving it, to the trustees of the trust or settlement, or, if there are no trustees capable of giving a discharge therefor, into court.

(3) Any such money—

(a) if it was receivable in respect of settled land within the meaning of the Settled Land Act 1925, or any building or works thereon, shall be deemed to be capital money arising under that Act from the settled land, and shall be invested or applied by the trustees, or, if in court, under the direction of the court, accordingly;

(b) if it was receivable in respect of personal chattels settled as heirlooms within the meaning of the Settled Land Act, 1925, shall be deemed to be capital money arising under that Act; and shall be applicable by the trustees, or, if in court, under the direction of the court, in like manner as provided by that Act with respect to money arising by sale of chattels as heirlooms as aforesaid;

(c) if it was receivable in respect of [land subject to a trust of land or personal property held on trust for sale], shall be held upon the trusts and subject to the powers and provisions applicable to money arising by a sale under such trust;

(d) in any other case, shall be held upon trusts corresponding as nearly as may be with the trusts affecting the property in respect of which it was payable.

(4) Such money, or any part thereof, may also be applied by the trustees, or, if in court, under the direction of the court, in rebuilding, reinstating, replacing, or replacing the property loss or damaged, but any such application by the trustees shall be subject to the consent of any person whose consent is required by the instrument, if any, creating the trust to the investment of money subject to the trust, and, in the case of money which is deemed to be capital money arising under the Settled Land Act 1925, be subject to the provisions of that Act with respect to the application of capital money by the trustees of the settlement.

(5) Nothing contained in this section prejudices or affects the right of any person to require any such money or any part thereof to be applied in rebuilding reinstating, or repairing the property lost or damaged, or the rights of any mortgagee, lessor, or lessee, whether under any statute or otherwise.

(6) This section applies to policies effected either before or after the commencement of this Act, but only to money received after such commencement.

[217]

NOTES

Sub-s (1): words omitted repealed by the Trustee Act 2000, ss 34(2), (3), 40(3), Sch 4, Pt II, in relation to trusts created before or after 1 February 2001.

Sub-s (3): words in square brackets in para (c) substituted by the Trusts of Land and Appointment of Trustees Act 1996, s 25(1), Sch 3, para 3(5); for savings in relation to entailed interests created before the commencement of that Act, and savings consequential upon the abolition of the doctrine of conversion, see s 25(4), (5) thereof.

21 (*Repealed by the Trustee Act 2000, s 40(1), (3), Sch 2, Pt II, para 21, Sch 4, Pt II.*)

22 Reversionary interests, valuations, and audit

(1) Where trust property includes any share or interest in property not vested in the trustees, or the proceeds of the sale of any such property, or any other thing in action, the trustees on the same falling into possession, or becoming payable or transferable may—

(a) agree or ascertain the amount or value thereof or any part thereof in such manner as they may think fit;

(b) accept in or towards satisfaction thereof, at the market or current value, or upon any valuation or estimate of value which they may think fit, any authorised investments;

(c) allow any deductions for duties, costs, charges and expenses which they may think proper or reasonable;

(d) execute any release in respect of the premises so as effectually to discharge all accountable parties from all liability in respect of any matters coming within the scope of such release;

without being responsible in any such case for any loss occasioned by any act or thing so done by them [if they have discharged the duty of care set out in section 1(1) of the Trustee Act 2000].

(2) The trustees shall not be under any obligation and shall not be chargeable with any breach of trust by reason of any omission—

(a) to place any distringas notice or apply for any stop or other like order upon any securities or other property out of or on which such share or interest or other thing in action as aforesaid is derived, payable or charged; or

(b) to take any proceedings on account of any act, default, or neglect on the part of the persons in whom such securities or other property or any of them or any part thereof are for the time being, or had at any time been, vested;

unless and until required in writing so to do by some person, or the guardian of some person, beneficially interested under the trust, and unless also due provision is made to their satisfaction for payment of the costs of any proceedings required to be taken:

Provided that nothing in this subsection shall relieve the trustees of the obligation to get in and obtain payment or transfer of such share or interest or other thing in action on the same falling into possession.

(3) Trustees may, for the purpose of giving effect to the trust, or any of the provisions of the instrument, if any, creating the trust or of any statute, from time to time (by duly qualified agents) ascertain and fix the value of any trust property in such manner as they think proper, and any valuation so made … shall be binding upon all persons interested under the trust [if the trustees have discharged the duty of care set out in section 1(1) of the Trustee Act 2000].

(4) Trustees may, in their absolute discretion, from time to time, but not more than once in every three years unless the nature of the trust or any special dealings with the trust property make a more frequent exercise of the right reasonable, cause the accounts of the trust property to be examined or audited by an independent accountant, and shall, for that purpose, produce such vouchers and give such information to him as he may require; and the costs of such examination or audit, including the fee of the auditor, shall be paid out of the capital or income of the trust property, or partly in one way and partly in the other as the trustees, in their absolute discretion, think fit, but, in default of any direction by the trustees to the contrary in any special case, costs attributable to capital shall be borne by capital and those attributable to income by income.

[218]

NOTES

Sub-s (1): words in square brackets substituted by the Trustee Act 2000, s 40(1), Sch 2, Pt II, para 22(a).

Sub-s (3): words omitted repealed and words in square brackets inserted by the Trustee Act 2000, s 40(1), Sch 2, Pt II, para 22(b).

23 (*Repealed by the Trustee Act 2000, s 40(1), (3), Sch 2, Pt II, para 23, Sch 4, Pt II.*)

24 Power to concur with others

Where an undivided share in [any] property, is subject to a trust, or forms part of the estate of a testator or intestate, the trustees or personal representatives may (without prejudice to the [trust] affecting the entirety of the land and the powers of the [trustees] in reference thereto), execute or exercise any [duty or] power vested in them in relation to such share in conjunction with the persons entitled to or having power in that behalf over the other share or shares, and notwithstanding that any one or more of the trustees or personal representatives may be entitled to or interested in any such other share, either in his or their own right or in a fiduciary capacity.

[219]

NOTES

Words in square brackets substituted by the Trusts of Land and Appointment of Trustees Act 1996, s 25(1), Sch 3, para 3(6); for savings in relation to entailed interests created before the commencement of that Act, and savings consequential upon the abolition of the doctrine of conversion, see s 25(4), (5) thereof.

[25 Delegation of trustee's functions by power of attorney

(1) Notwithstanding any rule of law or equity to the contrary, a trustee may, by power of attorney, delegate the execution or exercise of all or any of the trusts, powers and discretions vested in him as trustee either alone or jointly with any other person or persons.

(2) A delegation under this section—

(a) commences as provided by the instrument creating the power or, if the instrument makes no provision as to the commencement of the delegation, with the date of the execution of the instrument by the donor; and

(b) continues for a period of twelve months or any shorter period provided by the instrument creating the power.

(3) The persons who may be donees of a power of attorney under this section include a trust corporation.

(4) Before or within seven days after giving a power of attorney under this section the donor shall give written notice of it (specifying the date on which the power comes into operation and its duration, the donee of the power, the reason why the power is given and, where some only are delegated, the trusts, powers and discretions delegated) to—

(a) each person (other than himself), if any, who under any instrument creating the trust has power (whether alone or jointly) to appoint a new trustee; and

(b) each of the other trustees, if any;

but failure to comply with this subsection shall not, in favour of a person dealing with the donee of the power, invalidate any act done or instrument executed by the donee.

PART I STATUTES

(5) A power of attorney given under this section by a single donor—
(a) in the form set out in subsection (6) of this section; or
(b) in a form to the like effect but expressed to be made under this subsection,

shall operate to delegate to the person identified in the form as the single donee of the power the execution and exercise of all the trusts, powers and discretions vested in the donor as trustee (either alone or jointly with any other person or persons) under the single trust so identified.

(6) The form referred to in subsection (5) of this section is as follows—

"THIS GENERAL TRUSTEE POWER OF ATTORNEY is made on [date] by [name of one donor] of [address of donor] as trustee of [name or details of one trust].

I appoint [name of one donee] of [address of donee] to be my attorney [if desired, the date on which the delegation commences or the period for which it continues (or both)] in accordance with section 25(5) of the Trustee Act 1925.

[To be executed as a deed]".

(7) The donor of a power of attorney given under this section shall be liable for the acts or defaults of the donee in the same manner as if they were the acts or defaults of the donor.

(8) For the purpose of executing or exercising the trusts or powers delegated to him, the donee may exercise any of the powers conferred on the donor as trustee by statute or by the instrument creating the trust, including power, for the purpose of the transfer of any inscribed stock, himself to delegate to an attorney power to transfer, but not including the power of delegation conferred by this section.

(9) The fact that it appears from any power of attorney given under this section, or from any evidence required for the purposes of any such power of attorney or otherwise, that in dealing with any stock the donee of the power is acting in the execution of a trust shall not be deemed for any purpose to affect any person in whose books the stock is inscribed or registered with any notice of the trust.

(10) This section applies to a personal representative, tenant for life and statutory owner as it applies to a trustee except that subsection (4) shall apply as if it required the notice there mentioned to be given—
(a) in the case of a personal representative, to each of the other personal representatives, if any, except any executor who has renounced probate;
(b) in the case of a tenant for life, to the trustees of the settlement and to each person, if any, who together with the person giving the notice constitutes the tenant for life; and
(c) in the case of a statutory owner, to each of the persons, if any, who together with the person giving the notice constitute the statutory owner and, in the case of a statutory owner by virtue of section 23(1)(a) of the Settled Land Act 1925, to the trustees of the settlement.]

[220]

NOTES

Substituted by the Trustee Delegation Act 1999, s 5(1), (2), in relation to enduring powers created after 1 March 2000.

Indemnities

26 Protection against liability in respect of rents and covenants

(1) Where a personal representative or trustee liable as such for—
(a) any rent, covenant, or agreement reserved by or contained in any lease; or
(b) any rent, covenant or agreement payable under or contained in any grant made in consideration of a rentcharge; or
(c) any indemnity given in respect of any rent, covenant or agreement referred to in either of the foregoing paragraphs;

satisfies all liabilities under the lease or grant [which may have accrued and been claimed] up to the date of the conveyance hereinafter mentioned, and, where necessary, sets apart a sufficient fund to answer any future claim that may be made in respect of any fixed and ascertained sum which the lessee or grantee agreed to lay out on the property demised or granted, although the period for laying out the same may not have arrived, then and in any such case the personal representative or trustee may convey the property demised or granted to a purchaser, legatee, devisee, or other person entitled to call for a conveyance thereof and thereafter—
(i) he may distribute the residuary real and personal estate of the deceased testator or intestate, or, as the case may be, the trust estate (other than the fund, if any, set apart as aforesaid) to or amongst the persons entitled thereto, without appropriating any part, or any further part, as the case may be, of the estate of the deceased or of the trust estate to meet any future liability under the said lease or grant;
(ii) notwithstanding such distribution, he shall not be personally liable in respect of any subsequent claim under the said lease or grant.

[(1A) Where a personal representative or trustee has as such entered into, or may as such be required to enter into, an authorised guarantee agreement with respect to any lease comprised in the estate of a deceased testator or intestate or a trust estate (and, in a case where he has entered into such an agreement, he has satisfied all liabilities under it which may have accrued and been claimed up to the date of distribution)—

(a) he may distribute the residuary real and personal estate of the deceased testator or intestate, or the trust estate, to or amongst the persons entitled thereto—
  (i) without appropriating any part of the estate of the deceased, or the trust estate, to meet any future liability (or, as the case may be, any liability) under any such agreement, and
  (ii) notwithstanding any potential liability of his to enter into any such agreement; and

(b) notwithstanding such distribution, he shall not be personally liable in respect of any subsequent claim (or, as the case may be, any claim) under any such agreement.

In this subsection "authorised guarantee agreement" has the same meaning as in the Landlord and Tenant (Covenants) Act 1995.]

(2) This section operates without prejudice to the right of the lessor or grantor, or the persons deriving title under the lessor or grantor, to follow the assets of the deceased or the trust property into the hands of the persons amongst whom the same may have been respectively distributed, and applies notwithstanding anything to the contrary in the will or other instrument, if any, creating the trust.

(3) In this section "lease" includes an underlease and an agreement for a lease or underlease and any instrument giving any such indemnity as aforesaid or varying the liabilities under the lease; "grant" applies to a grant whether the rent is created by limitation, grant, reservation, or otherwise, and includes an agreement for a grant and any instrument giving any such indemnity as aforesaid or varying the liabilities under the grant; "lessee" and "grantee" include persons respectively deriving title under them.

[221]

NOTES

Sub-s (1): words in square brackets substituted by the Law of Property (Amendment) Act 1926, ss 7, 8(2), Schedule.

Sub-s (1A): inserted by the Landlord and Tenant (Covenants) Act 1995, s 30(1), Sch 1, para 1.

27 Protection by means of advertisements

(1) With a view to the conveyance to or distribution among the persons entitled to any real or personal property, the trustees of a settlement [, trustees of land, trustees for sale of personal property] or personal representatives, may give notice by advertisement in the Gazette, and [in a newspaper circulating in the district in which the land is situated] and such other like notices, including notices elsewhere than in England and Wales, as would, in any special case, have been directed by a court of competent jurisdiction in an action for administration, of their intention to make such conveyance or distribution as aforesaid, and requiring any person interested to send to the trustees or personal representatives within the time, not being less than two months, fixed in the notice or, where more than one notice is given, in the last of the notices, particulars of his claim in respect of the property or any part thereof to which the notice relates.

(2) At the expiration of the time fixed by the notice the trustees or personal representatives may convey or distribute the property or any part thereof to which the notice relates, to or among the persons entitled thereto, having regard only to the claims, whether formal or not, of which the trustees or personal representatives then had notice and shall not, as respects the property so conveyed or distributed, be liable to any person of whose claim the trustees or personal representatives have not had notice at the time of conveyance or distribution; but nothing in this section—

(a) prejudices the right of any person to follow the property, or any property representing the same, into the hands of any person, other than a purchaser, who may have received it; or

(b) frees the trustees or personal representatives from any obligation to make searches or obtain official certificates of search similar to those which an intending purchaser would be advised to make or obtain.

(3) This section applies notwithstanding anything to the contrary in the will or other instrument, if any, creating the trust.

[222]

NOTES

Sub-s (1): first words in square brackets substituted by the Trusts of Land and Appointment of Trustees Act 1996, s 25(1), Sch 3, para 3(7) (for savings in relation to entailed interests created before the commencement of that Act, and savings consequential upon the abolition of the doctrine of conversion, see s 25(4), (5) thereof); second words in square brackets substituted by the Law of Property (Amendment) Act 1926, ss 7, 8(2), Schedule.

28 Protection in regard to notice

A trustee or personal representative acting for the purposes of more than one trust or estate shall not, in the absence of fraud, be affected by notice of any instrument, matter, fact or thing in relation to any particular trust or estate if he has obtained notice thereof merely by reason of his acting or having acted for the purposes of another trust or estate.

[223]

29, 30 *(S 29 repealed by the Powers of Attorney Act 1971, s 11(2), (4), Sch 2; s 30 repealed by the Trustee Act 2000, s 40(1), (3), Sch 2, Pt II, para 24, Sch 4, Pt II.)*

Maintenance Advancement and Protective Trusts

31 Power to apply income for maintenance and to accumulate surplus income during a minority

(1) Where any property is held by trustees in trust for any person for any interest whatsoever, whether vested or contingent, then, subject to any prior interests or charges affecting that property—

(i) during the infancy of any such person, if his interest so long continues, the trustees may, at their sole discretion, pay to his parent or guardian, if any, or otherwise apply for or towards his maintenance, education, or benefit, the whole or such part, if any, of the income of that property as may, in all the circumstances, be reasonable, whether or not there is—

(a) any other fund applicable to the same purpose; or

(b) any person bound by law to provide for his maintenance or education; and

(ii) if such person on attaining the age of [eighteen years] has not a vested interest in such income, the trustees shall thenceforth pay the income of that property and of any accretion thereto under subsection (2) of this section to him, until he either attains a vested interest therein or dies, or until failure of his interest:

Provided that, in deciding whether the whole or any part of the income of the property is during a minority to be paid or applied for the purposes aforesaid, the trustees shall have regard to the age of the infant and his requirements and generally to the circumstances of the case, and in particular to what other income, if any, is applicable for the same purposes; and where trustees have notice that the income of more than one fund is applicable for those purposes, then, so far as practicable, unless the entire income of the funds is paid or applied as aforesaid or the court otherwise directs, a proportionate part only of the income of each fund shall be so paid or applied.

(2) During the infancy of any such person, if his interest so long continues, the trustees shall accumulate all the residue of that income [by investing it, and any profits from so investing it] from time to time in authorised investments, and shall hold those accumulations as follows:—

(i) If any such person—

(a) attains the age of [eighteen years], or marries under that age [or forms a civil partnership under that age], and his interest in such income during his infancy[, or until his marriage or his formation of a civil partnership,] is a vested interest; or

(b) on attaining the age of [eighteen years] or on marriage[, or formation of a civil partnership,] under that age becomes entitled to the property from which such income arose in fee simple, absolute or determinable, or absolutely, or for an entailed interest;

the trustees shall hold the accumulations in trust for such person absolutely, but without prejudice to any provision with respect thereto contained in any settlement by him made under any statutory powers during his infancy, and so that the receipt of such person after marriage [or formation of a civil partnership], and though still an infant, shall be a good discharge; and

(ii) In any other case the trustees shall, notwithstanding that such person had a vested interest in such income, hold the accumulations as an accretion to the capital of the property from which such accumulations arose, and as one fund with such capital for all purposes, and so that, if such property is settled land, such accumulations shall be held upon the same trusts as if the same were capital money arising therefrom;

but the trustees may, at any time during the infancy of such person if his interest so long continues, apply those accumulations, or any part thereof, as if they were income arising in the then current year.

(3) This section applies in the case of a contingent interest only if the limitation or trust carries the intermediate income of the property, but it applies to a future or contingent legacy by the parent of, or a person standing in loco parentis to, the legatee, if and for such period as, under the general law, the legacy carries interest for the maintenance of the legatee, and in any such case as last

aforesaid the rate of interest shall (if the income available is sufficient, and subject to any rules of court to the contrary) be five pounds per centum per annum.

(4) This section applies to a vested annuity in like manner as if the annuity were the income of property held by trustees in trust to pay the income thereof to the annuitant for the same period for which the annuity is payable, save that in any case accumulations made during the infancy of the annuitant shall be held in trust for the annuitant or his personal representatives absolutely.

(5) This section does not apply where the instrument, if any, under which the interest arises came into operation before the commencement of this Act.

[224]

NOTES

Sub-s (1): words in square brackets substituted by the Family Law Reform Act 1969, s 1(3), Sch 1, Pt I.

Sub-s (2): words in first pair of square brackets substituted by the Trustee Act 2000, s 40(1), Sch 2, Pt II, para 25; in para (i)(a), words in first pair of square brackets substituted by the Family Law Reform Act 1969, s 1(3), Sch 1, Pt I, words in second pair of square brackets inserted and words in third pair of square brackets substituted by the Civil Partnership Act 2004, s 261(1), Sch 27, para 5(1), (2); in para (i)(b), words in first pair of square brackets substituted by the Family Law Reform Act 1969, s 1(3), Sch 1, Pt I, words in second and final pairs of square brackets inserted by the Civil Partnership Act 2004, s 261(1), Sch 27, para 5(1), (3), (4).

32 Power of advancement

(1) Trustees may at any time or times pay or apply any capital money subject to a trust, for the advancement or benefit, in such manner as they may, in their absolute discretion, think fit, of any person entitled to the capital of the trust property or of any share thereof, whether absolutely or contingently on his attaining any specified age or on the occurrence of any other event, or subject to a gift over on his death under any specified age or on the occurrence of any other event, and whether in possession or in remainder or reversion, and such payment or application may be made notwithstanding that the interest of such person is liable to be defeated by the exercise of a power of appointment or revocation, or to be diminished by the increase of the class to which he belongs:

Provided that—

(a) the money so paid or applied for the advancement or benefit of any person shall not exceed altogether in amount one-half of the presumptive or vested share or interest of that person in the trust property; and

(b) if that person is or becomes absolutely and indefeasibly entitled to a share in the trust property the money so paid or applied shall be brought into account as part of such share; and

(c) no such payment or application shall be made so as to prejudice any person entitled to any prior life or other interest, whether vested or contingent, in the money paid or applied unless such person is in existence and of full age and consents in writing to such payment or application.

[(2) This section does not apply to capital money arising under the Settled Land Act 1925.]

(3) This section does not apply to trusts constituted or created before the commencement of this Act.

[225]

NOTES

Sub-s (2): substituted by the Trusts of Land and Appointment of Trustees Act 1996, s 25(1), Sch 3, para 3(8); for savings in relation to entailed interests created before the commencement of that Act, and savings consequential upon the abolition of the doctrine of conversion, see s 25(4), (5) thereof.

33 Protective trusts

(1) Where any income, including an annuity or other periodical income payment, is directed to be held on protective trusts for the benefit of any person (in this section called "the principal beneficiary") for the period of his life or for any less period, then, during that period (in this section called the "trust period") the said income shall, without prejudice to any prior interest, be held on the following trusts, namely:—

(i) Upon trust for the principal beneficiary during the trust period or until he, whether before or after the termination of any prior interest, does or attempts to do or suffers any act or thing, or until any event happens, other than an advance under any statutory or express power, whereby, if the said income were payable during the trust period to the principal beneficiary absolutely during that period, he would be deprived of the right to receive the same or any part thereof, in any of which cases, as well as on the termination of the trust period, whichever first happens, this trust of the said income shall fail or determine;

(ii) If the trust aforesaid fails or determines during the subsistence of the trust period, then, during the residue of that period, the said income shall be held upon trust for the application thereof for the maintenance or support, or otherwise for the benefit, of all or any one or more exclusively of the other or others of the following persons (that is to say)—

(a) the principal beneficiary and his or her [spouse or civil partner], if any, and his or her children or more remote issue, if any; or

(b) if there is no [spouse or civil partner] or issue of the principal beneficiary in existence, the principal beneficiary and the persons who would, if he were actually dead, be entitled to the trust property or the income thereof or to the annuity fund, if any, or arrears of the annuity, as the case may be;

as the trustees in their absolute discretion, without being liable to account for the exercise of such discretion, think fit.

(2) This section does not apply to trusts coming into operation before the commencement of this Act, and has effect subject to any variation of the implied trusts aforesaid contained in the instrument creating the trust.

(3) Nothing in this section operates to validate any trust which would, if contained in the instrument creating the trust, be liable to be set aside.

[(4) In relation to the dispositions mentioned in section 19(1) of the Family Law Reform Act 1987, this section shall have effect as if any reference (however expressed) to any relationship between two persons were construed in accordance with section 1 of that Act.]

[226]

NOTES

Sub-s (1): words in square brackets in para (ii) substituted by the Civil Partnership Act 2004, s 261(1), Sch 27, para 6.

Sub-s (4): inserted by the Family Law Reform Act 1987, s 33(1), Sch 2, para 2, Sch 3, para 1.

PART III
APPOINTMENT AND DISCHARGE OF TRUSTEES

34 Limitation of the number of trustees

(1) Where, at the commencement of this Act, there are more than four trustees of a settlement of land, or more than four trustees holding land on trust for sale, no new trustees shall (except where as a result of the appointment the number is reduced to four or less) be capable of being appointed until the number is reduced to less than four, and thereafter the number shall not be increased beyond four.

(2) In the case of settlements and dispositions [creating trusts of land] made or coming into operation after the commencement of this Act—

(a) the number of trustees thereof shall not in any case exceed four, and where more than four persons are named as such trustees, the four first named (who are able and willing to act) shall alone be the trustees, and the other persons named shall not be trustees unless appointed on the occurrence of a vacancy;

(b) the number of the trustees shall not be increased beyond four.

(3) This section only applies to settlements and dispositions of land, and the restrictions imposed on the number of trustees do not apply—

(a) in the case of land vested in trustees for charitable, ecclesiastical, or public purposes; or

(b) where the net proceeds of the sale of the land are held for like purposes; or

(c) to the trustees of a term of years absolute limited by a settlement on trusts for raising money, or of a like term created under the statutory remedies relating to annual sums charged on land.

[227]

NOTES

Sub-s (2): words in square brackets substituted by the Trusts of Land and Appointment of Trustees Act 1996, s 25(1), Sch 3, para 3(9); for savings in relation to entailed interests created before the commencement of that Act, and savings consequential upon the abolition of the doctrine of conversion, see s 25(4), (5) thereof.

35 Appointments of trustees of settlements and [and trustees of land]

[(1) Appointments of new trustees of land and of new trustees of any trust of the proceeds of sale of the land shall, subject to any order of the court, be effected by separate instruments, but in such manner as to secure that the same persons become trustees of land and trustees of the trust of the proceeds of sale.]

(2) Where new trustees of a settlement are appointed, a memorandum of the names and addresses of the persons who are for the time being the trustees thereof for the purposes of the Settled Land Act 1925, shall be endorsed on or annexed to the last or only principal vesting

instrument by or on behalf of the trustees of the settlement, and such vesting instrument shall, for that purpose, be produced by the person having the possession thereof of the trustees of the settlement when so required.

[(3) Where new trustees of land are appointed, a memorandum of the persons who are for the time being the trustees of the land shall be endorsed on or annexed to the conveyance by which the land was vested in trustees of land; and that conveyance shall be produced to the persons who are for the time being the trustees of the land by the person in possession of it in order for that to be done when the trustees require its production.]

(4) This section applies only to settlements and dispositions of land.

[228]

NOTES

Section heading: words in square brackets substituted by the Trusts of Land and Appointment of Trustees Act 1996, s 25(1), Sch 3, para 3(10)(c); for savings in relation to entailed interests created before the commencement of that Act, and savings consequential upon the abolition of the doctrine of conversion, see s 25(4), (5) thereof.

Sub-ss (1), (3): substituted by the Trusts of Land and Appointment of Trustees Act 1996, s 25(1), Sch 3, para 3(10)(a), (b), subject to savings as noted above.

36 Power of appointing new or additional trustees

(1) Where a trustee, either original or substituted, and whether appointed by a court or otherwise, is dead, or remains out of the United Kingdom for more than twelve months, or desires to be discharged from all or any of the trusts or powers reposed in or conferred on him, or refuses or is unfit to act therein, or is incapable of acting therein, or is an infant, then, subject to the restrictions imposed by this Act on the number of trustees,—

(a) the person or persons nominated for the purpose of appointing new trustees by the instrument, if any, creating the trust; or

(b) if there is no such person, or no such person able and willing to act, then the surviving or continuing trustees or trustee for the time being, or the personal representatives of the last surviving or continuing trustee;

may, by writing, appoint one or more other persons (whether or not being the persons exercising the power) to be a trustee or trustees in the place of the trustee so deceased remaining out of the United Kingdom, desiring to be discharged, refusing, or being unfit or being incapable, or being an infant, as aforesaid.

(2) Where a trustee has been removed under a power contained in the instrument creating the trust, a new trustee or new trustees may be appointed in the place of the trustee who is removed, as if he were dead, or, in the case of a corporation, as if the corporation desired to be discharged from the trust, and the provisions of this section shall apply accordingly, but subject to the restrictions imposed by this Act on the number of trustees.

(3) Where a corporation being a trustee is or has been dissolved, either before or after the commencement of this Act, then, for the purposes of this section and of any enactment replaced thereby, the corporation shall be deemed to be and to have been from the date of the dissolution incapable of acting in the trusts or powers reposed in or conferred on the corporation.

(4) The power of appointment given by subsection (1) of this section or any similar previous enactment to the personal representatives of a last surviving or continuing trustee shall be and shall be deemed always to have been exercisable by the executors for the time being (whether original or by representation) of such surviving or continuing trustee who have proved the will of their testator or by the administrators for the time being of such trustee without the concurrence of any executor who has renounced or has not proved.

(5) But a sole or last surviving executor intending to renounce, or all the executors where they all intend to renounce, shall have and shall be deemed always to have had power, at any time before renouncing probate, to exercise the power of appointment given by this section, or by any similar previous enactment, if willing to act for that purpose and without thereby accepting the office of executor.

[(6) Where, in the case of any trust, there are not more than three trustees—]

(a) the person or persons nominated for the purpose of appointing new trustees by the instrument, if any, creating the trust; or

(b) if there is no such person, or no such person able and willing to act, then the trustee or trustees for the time being;

may, by writing appoint another person or other persons to be an additional trustee or additional trustees, but it shall not be obligatory to appoint any additional trustee, unless the instrument, if any, creating the trust, or any statutory enactment provides to the contrary, nor shall the number of trustees be increased beyond four by virtue of any such appointment.

[(6A) A person who is either—

(a) both a trustee and attorney for the other trustee (if one other), or for both of the other trustees (if two others), under a registered power; or

(b) attorney under a registered power for the trustee (if one) or for both or each of the trustees (if two or three),

may, if subsection (6B) of this section is satisfied in relation to him, make an appointment under subsection (6)(b) of this section on behalf of the trustee or trustees.

(6B) This subsection is satisfied in relation to an attorney under a registered power for one or more trustees if (as attorney under the power)—

(a) he intends to exercise any function of the trustee or trustees by virtue of section 1(1) of the Trustee Delegation Act 1999; or

(b) he intends to exercise any function of the trustee or trustees in relation to any land, capital proceeds of a conveyance of land or income from land by virtue of its delegation to him under section 25 of this Act or the instrument (if any) creating the trust.

(6C) In subsections (6A) and (6B) of this section "registered power" means [an enduring power of attorney or lasting power of attorney registered under the Mental Capacity Act 2005].

(6D) Subsection (6A) of this section—

(a) applies only if and so far as a contrary intention is not expressed in the instrument creating the power of attorney (or, where more than one, any of them) or the instrument (if any) creating the trust; and

(b) has effect subject to the terms of those instruments.]

(7) Every new trustee appointed under this section as well before as after all the trust property becomes by law, or by assurance, or otherwise, vested in him, shall have the same powers, authorities, and discretions, and may in all respects act as if he had been originally appointed a trustee by the instrument, if any, creating the trust.

(8) The provisions of this section relating to a trustee who is dead include the case of a person nominated trustee in a will but dying before the testator, and those relative to a continuing trustee include a refusing or retiring trustee, if willing to act in the execution of the provisions of this section.

[(9) Where a trustee [lacks capacity to exercise] his functions as trustee and is also entitled in possession to some beneficial interest in the trust property, no appointment of a new trustee in his place shall be made by virtue of paragraph (b) of subsection (1) of this section unless leave to make the appointment has been given by [the Court of Protection].]

[229]

NOTES

Sub-s (6): words in square brackets substituted by the Trusts of Land and Appointment of Trustees Act 1996, s 25(1), Sch 3, para 3(11); for savings in relation to entailed interests created before the commencement of that Act, and savings consequential upon the abolition of the doctrine of conversion, see s 25(4), (5) thereof.

Sub-ss (6A)–(6D): inserted by the Trustee Delegation Act 1999, s 8, in relation to powers created after 1 March 2000.

Sub-s (6C): words in square brackets substituted by the Mental Capacity Act 2005, s 67(1), Sch 6, para 3(1), (2)(a).

Sub-s (9): substituted by the Mental Health Act 1959, s 149(1), Sch 7, Pt I; words in square brackets substituted by the Mental Capacity Act 2005, s 67(1), Sch 6, para 3(1), (2)(b).

37 Supplemental provisions as to appointment of trustees

(1) On the appointment of a trustee for the whole or any part of trust property—

(a) the number of trustees may, subject to the restrictions imposed by this Act on the number of trustees, be increased; and

(b) a separate set of trustees, not exceeding four, may be appointed for any part of the trust property held on trusts distinct from those relating to any other part or parts of the trust property, notwithstanding that no new trustees or trustee are or is to be appointed for other parts of the trust property, and any existing trustee may be appointed or remain one of such separate set of trustees, or, if only one trustee was originally appointed, then, save as hereinafter provided, one separate trustee may be so appointed; and

(c) it shall not be obligatory, save as hereinafter provided, to appoint more than one new trustee where only one trustee was originally appointed, or to fill up the original number of trustees where more than two trustees were originally appointed, but, except where only one trustee was originally appointed, and a sole trustee when appointed will be able to give valid receipts for all capital money, a trustee shall not be discharged from his trust unless there will be either a trust corporation or at least two [persons] to act as trustees to perform the trust; and

(d) any assurance or thing requisite for vesting the trust property, or any part thereof, in a sole trustee, or jointly in the persons who are the trustees, shall be executed or done.

(2) Nothing in this Act shall authorise the appointment of a sole trustee, not being a trust corporation, where the trustee, when appointed, would not be able to give valid receipts for all capital money arising under the trust.

[230]

NOTES

Sub-s (1): word in square brackets in para (c) substituted by the Trusts of Land and Appointment of Trustees Act 1996, s 25(1), Sch 3, para 3(12); for savings in relation to entailed interests created before the commencement of that Act, and savings consequential upon the abolition of the doctrine of conversion, see s 25(4), (5) thereof.

38 Evidence as to a vacancy in a trust

(1) A statement, contained in any instrument coming into operation after the commencement of this Act by which a new trustee is appointed for any purpose connected with land, to the effect that a trustee has remained out of the United Kingdom for more than twelve months or refuses or is unfit to act, or is incapable of acting, or that he is not entitled to a beneficial interest in the trust property in possession, shall, in favour of a purchaser of a legal estate, be conclusive evidence of the matter stated.

(2) In favour of such purchaser any appointment of a new trustee depending on that statement, and any vesting declaration, express or implied, consequent on the appointment, shall be valid.

[231]

39 Retirement of trustee without a new appointment

(1) Where a trustee is desirous of being discharged from the trust, and after his discharge there will be either a trust corporation or at least two [persons] to act as trustees to perform the trust, then, if such trustee as aforesaid by deed declares that he is desirous of being discharged from the trust, and if his co-trustees and such other person, if any, as is empowered to appoint trustees, by deed consent to the discharge of the trustee, and to the vesting in the co-trustees alone of the trust property, the trustee desirous of being discharged shall be deemed to have retired from the trust, and shall, by the deed, be discharged therefrom under this Act, without any new trustee being appointed in his place.

(2) Any assurance or thing requisite for vesting the trust property in the continuing trustees alone shall be executed or done.

[232]

NOTES

Sub-s (1): word in square brackets substituted by the Trusts of Land and Appointment of Trustees Act 1996, s 25(1), Sch 3, para 3(13); for savings in relation to entailed interests created before the commencement of that Act, and savings consequential upon the abolition of the doctrine of conversion, see s 25(4), (5) thereof.

Modification: modified, in relation to the appointment or discharge of trustees in whom any property is vested in trust for a trade union whose name is entered in the list of trade unions, by the Trade Union and Labour Relations (Consolidation) Act 1992, s 13.

40 Vesting of trust property in new or continuing trustees

(1) Where by a deed a new trustee is appointed to perform any trust, then—

(a) if the deed contains a declaration by the appointor to the effect that any estate or interest in any land subject to the trust, or in any chattel so subject, or right to recover or receive any debt or other thing in action so subject, shall vest in the persons who by virtue of the deed become or are the trustees for performing the trust, the deed shall operate, without any conveyance or assignment, to vest in those persons as joint tenants and for the purposes of the trust the estate interest or right to which the declaration relates; and

(b) if the deed is made after the commencement of this Act and does not contain such a declaration, the deed shall, subject to any express provision to the contrary therein contained, operate as if it had contained such a declaration by the appointor extending to all the estates interests and rights with respect to which a declaration could have been made.

(2) Where by a deed a retiring trustee is discharged under [section 39 of this Act or section 19 of the Trusts of Land and Appointment of Trustees Act 1996] without a new trustee being appointed, then—

(a) if the deed contains such a declaration as aforesaid by the retiring and continuing trustees, and by the other person, if any, empowered to appoint trustees, the deed shall, without any conveyance or assignment, operate to vest in the continuing trustees alone, as joint tenants, and for the purposes of the trust, the estate, interest, or right to which the declaration relates; and

(b) if the deed is made after the commencement of this Act and does not contain such a declaration, the deed shall, subject to any express provision to the contrary therein contained, operate as if it had contained such a declaration by such persons as aforesaid extending to all the estates, interests and rights with respect to which a declaration could have been made.

(3) An express vesting declaration, whether made before or after the commencement of this Act, shall, notwithstanding that the estate, interest or right to be vested is not expressly referred to, and provided that the other statutory requirements were or are complied with, operate and be deemed always to have operated (but without prejudice to any express provision to the contrary contained in the deed of appointment or discharge) to vest in the persons respectively referred to in subsections (1) and (2) of this section, as the case may require, such estates, interests and rights as are capable of being and ought to be vested in those persons.

(4) This section does not extend—

(a) to land conveyed by way of mortgage for securing money subject to the trust, except land conveyed on trust for securing debentures or debenture stock;

(b) to land held under a lease which contains any covenant, condition or agreement against assignment or disposing of the land without licence or consent, unless, prior to the execution of the deed containing expressly or impliedly the vesting declaration, the requisite licence or consent has been obtained, or unless, by virtue of any statute or rule of law, the vesting declaration, express or implied, would not operate as a breach of covenant or give rise to a forfeiture;

(c) to any share, stock, annuity or property which is only transferable in books kept by a company or other body, or in manner directed by or under an Act of Parliament.

In this subsection "lease" includes an underlease and an agreement for a lease or underlease.

(5) For purposes of registration of the deed in any registry, the person or persons making the declaration expressly or impliedly, shall be deemed the conveying party or parties, and the conveyance shall be deemed to be made by him or them under a power conferred by this Act.

(6) This section applies to deeds of appointment or discharge executed on or after the first day of January, eighteen hundred and eighty-two.

[233]

NOTES

Sub-s (2): words in square brackets substituted by the Trusts of Land and Appointment of Trustees Act 1996, s 25(1), Sch 3, para 3(14); for savings in relation to entailed interests created before the commencement of that Act, and savings consequential upon the abolition of the doctrine of conversion, see s 25(4), (5) thereof.

Modification: modified, in relation to the appointment or discharge of trustees in whom any property is vested in trust for a trade union whose name is entered in the list of trade unions, by the Trade Union and Labour Relations (Consolidation) Act 1992, s 13.

PART IV
POWERS OF THE COURT

Appointment of new Trustees

41 Power of court to appoint new trustees

(1) The court may, whenever it is expedient to appoint a new trustee or new trustees, and it is found inexpedient difficult or impracticable so to do without the assistance of the court, make an order appointing a new trustee or new trustees either in substitution for or in addition to any existing trustee or trustees, or although there is no existing trustee.

In particular and without prejudice to the generality of the foregoing provision, the court may make an order appointing a new trustee in substitution for a trustee who … [[lacks capacity to exercise] his functions as trustee], or is a bankrupt, or is a corporation which is in liquidation or has been dissolved.

(2) The power conferred by this section may, in the case of a deed of arrangement within the meaning of the Deeds of Arrangement Act 1914, be exercised either by the High Court or by the court having jurisdiction in bankruptcy in the district in which the debtor resided or carried on business at the date of the execution of the deed.

(3) An order under this section, and any consequential vesting order or conveyance, shall not operate further or otherwise as a discharge to any former or continuing trustee than an appointment of new trustees under any power for that purpose contained in any instrument would have operated.

(4) Nothing in this section gives power to appoint an executor or administrator.

[234]

NOTES

Sub-s (1): words omitted repealed by the Criminal Law Act 1967, s 10, Sch 3, Pt III; words in first (outer) pair of square brackets substituted by the Mental Health Act 1959, s 149(1), Sch 7, Pt I; words in second (inner) pair of square brackets substituted by the Mental Capacity Act 2005, s 67(1), Sch 6, para 3(1), (3).

42 Power to authorise remuneration

Where the court appoints a corporation, other than the Public Trustee, to be a trustee either solely or jointly with another person, the court may authorise the corporation to charge such remuneration for its services as trustee as the court may think fit.

[235]

43 Powers of new trustee appointed by the Court

Every trustee appointed by a court of competent jurisdiction shall, as well before as after the trust property becomes by law, or by assurance, or otherwise, vested in him, have the same powers, authorities, and discretions, and may in all respects act as if he had been originally appointed a trustee by the instrument, if any, creating the trust.

[236]

Vesting Orders

44 Vesting orders of land

In any of the following cases, namely:

(i) Where the court appoints or has appointed a trustee, or where a trustee has been appointed out of court under any statutory or express power;

(ii) Where a trustee entitled to or possessed of any land or interest therein, whether by way of mortgage or otherwise, or entitled to a contingent right therein, either solely or jointly with any other person—

(a) is under disability; or

(b) is out of the jurisdiction of the High Court; or

(c) cannot be found, or, being a corporation, has been dissolved;

(iii) Where it is uncertain who was the survivor of two or more trustees jointly entitled to or possessed of any interest in land;

(iv) Where it is uncertain whether the last trustee known to have been entitled to or possessed of any interest in land is living or dead;

(v) Where there is no personal representative of a deceased trustee who was entitled to or possessed of any interest in land, or where it is uncertain who is the personal representative of a deceased trustee who was entitled to or possessed of any interest in land;

(vi) Where a trustee jointly or solely entitled to or possessed of any interest in land, or entitled to a contingent right therein, has been required, by or on behalf of a person entitled to require a conveyance of the land or interest or a release of the right, to convey the land or interest or to release the right, and has wilfully refused or neglected to convey the land or interest or release the right for twenty-eight days after the date of the requirement;

(vii) Where land or any interest therein is vested in a trustee whether by way of mortgage or otherwise, and it appears to the court to be expedient;

the court may make an order (in this Act called a vesting order) vesting the land or interest therein in any such person in any such manner and for any such estate or interest as the court may direct, or releasing or disposing of the contingent right to such person as the court may direct:

Provided that—

(a) Where the order is consequential on the appointment of a trustee the land or interest therein shall be vested for such estate as the court may direct in the persons who on the appointment are the trustees; and

(b) Where the order relates to a trustee entitled or formerly entitled jointly with another person, and such trustee is under disability or out of the jurisdiction of the High Court or cannot be found, or being a corporation has been dissolved, the land interest or right shall be vested in such other person who remains entitled, either alone or with any other person the court may appoint.

[237]

45 Orders as to contingent rights of unborn persons

Where any interest in land is subject to a contingent right in an unborn person or class of unborn persons who, on coming into existence would, in respect, thereof, become entitled to or possessed of that interest on any trust, the court may make an order releasing the land or interest therein from the contingent right, or may make an order vesting in any person the estate or interest to or of which the unborn person or class of unborn persons would, on coming into existence, be entitled or possessed in the land.

[238]

46 Vesting order in place of conveyance by infant mortgagee

Where any person entitled to or possessed of any interest in land, or entitled to a contingent right in land, by way of security for money, is an infant, the court may make an order vesting or releasing or disposing of the interest in the land or the right in like manner as in the case of a trustee under disability.

[239]

47 Vesting order consequential on order for sale or mortgage of land

Where any court gives a judgment or makes an order directing the sale or mortgage of any land, every person who is entitled to or possessed of any interest in the land, or entitled to a contingent right therein, and is a party to the action or proceeding in which the judgment or order is given or made or is otherwise bound by the judgment or order, shall be deemed to be so entitled or possessed, as the case may be, as a trustee for the purpose of this Act, and the court may, if it thinks expedient, make an order vesting the land or any part thereof for such estate or interest as that court thinks fit in the purchaser or mortgagee or in any other person:

Provided that, in the case of a legal mortgage, the estate to be vested in the mortgagee shall be a term of years absolute.

[240]

48 Vesting order consequential on judgement for specific performance, etc

Where a judgment is given for the specific performance of a contract concerning any interest in land, or for sale or exchange of any interest in land, or generally where any judgment is given for the conveyance of any interest in land either in cases arising out of the doctrine of election or otherwise, the court may declare—

(a) that any of the parties to the action are trustees of any interest in the land or any part thereof within the meaning of this Act; or

(b) that the interests of unborn persons who might claim under any party to the action, or under the will or voluntary settlement of any deceased person who was during his lifetime a party to the contract or transaction concerning which the judgment is given, are the interests of persons who, on coming into existence, would be trustees within the meaning of this Act;

and thereupon the court may make a vesting order relating to the rights of those persons, born and unborn, as if they had been trustees.

[241]

49 Effect of vesting order

A vesting order under any of the foregoing provisions shall in the case of a vesting order consequential on the appointment of a trustee, have the same effect—

(a) as if the persons who before the appointment were the trustees, if any, had duly executed all proper conveyances of the land for such estate or interest as the court directs; or

(b) if there is no such person, or no such person of full capacity, as if such person had existed and been of full capacity and had duly executed all proper conveyances of the land for such estate or interest as the court directs;

and shall in every other case have the same effect as if the trustee or other person or description or class of persons to whose rights or supposed rights the said provisions respectively relate had been an ascertained and existing person of full capacity, and had executed a conveyance or release to the effect intended by the order.

[242]

50 Power to appoint person to convey

In all cases where a vesting order can be made under any of the foregoing provisions, the court may, if it is more convenient, appoint a person to convey the land or any interest therein or release the contingent right, and a conveyance or release by that person in conformity with the order shall have the same effect as an order under the appropriate provision.

[243]

51 Vesting orders as to stock and things in action

(1) In any of the following cases, namely:—

(i) Where the court appoints or has appointed a trustee, or where a trustee has been appointed out of court under any statutory or express power;

(ii) Where a trustee entitled, whether by way of mortgage or otherwise, alone or jointly with another person to stock or to a thing in action—

(a) is under disability; or

(b) is out of the jurisdiction of the High Court; or

(c) cannot be found, or, being a corporation, has been dissolved; or

(d) neglects or refuses to transfer stock or receive the dividends or income thereof, or to sue for or recover a thing in action, according to the direction of the person absolutely entitled thereto for twenty- eight days next after a request in writing has been made to him by the person so entitled; or

(e) neglects or refuses to transfer stock or receive the dividends or income thereof, or to sue for or recover a thing in action for twenty-eight days next after an order of the court for that purpose has been served on him;

(iii) Where it is uncertain whether a trustee entitled alone or jointly with another person to stock or to a thing in action is alive or dead;

(iv) Where stock is standing in the name of a deceased person whose personal representative is under disability;

(v) Where stock or a thing in action is vested in a trustee whether by way of mortgage or otherwise and it appears to the court to be expedient;

the court may make an order vesting the right to transfer or call for a transfer of stock, or to receive the dividends or income thereof, or to sue for or recover the thing in action, in any such person as the court may appoint:

Provided that—

(a) Where the order is consequential on the appointment of a trustee, the right shall be vested in the persons who, on the appointment, are the trustees; and

(b) Where the person whose right is dealt with by the order was entitled jointly with another person, the right shall be vested in that last- mentioned person either alone or jointly with any other person whom the court may appoint.

(2) In all cases where a vesting order can be made under this section, the court may, if it is more convenient, appoint some proper person to make or join in making the transfer:

Provided that the person appointed to make or join in making a transfer of stock shall be some proper officer of the bank, or the company or society whose stock is to be transferred.

(3) The person in whom the right to transfer or call for the transfer of any stock is vested by an order of the court under this Act, may transfer the stock to himself or any other person, according to the order, and the [Registrar of Government Stock and any company] shall obey every order under this section according to its tenor.

(4) After notice in writing of an order under this section it shall not be lawful for the [Registrar of Government Stock or any company] to transfer any stock to which the order relates or to pay any dividends thereon except in accordance with the order.

(5) The court may make declarations and give directions concerning the manner in which the right to transfer any stock or thing in action vested under the provisions of this Act is to be exercised.

(6) The provisions of this Act as to vesting orders shall apply to shares in ships registered under the [Merchant Shipping Act 1995] as if they were stock.

[244]

NOTES

Sub-ss (3), (4): words in square brackets substituted by SI 2004/1662, art 2, Schedule, Pt 2, para 10(1), (2), subject to transitional provisions in art 3 thereof.

Sub-s (6): words in square brackets substituted by the Merchant Shipping Act 1995, s 314(2), Sch 13, para 13.

52 Vesting orders of charity property

The powers conferred by this Act as to vesting orders may be exercised for vesting any interest in land, stock, or thing in action in any trustee of a charity or society over which the court would have jurisdiction upon action duly instituted, whether the appointment of the trustee was made by instrument under a power or by the court under its general or statutory jurisdiction.

[245]

53 Vesting orders in relation to infants' beneficial interests

Where an infant is beneficially entitled to any property the court may, with a view to the application of the capital or income thereof for the maintenance, education, or benefit of the infant, make an order—

(a) appointing a person to convey such property; or

(b) in the case of stock, or a thing in action, vesting in any person the right to transfer or call for a transfer of such stock, or to receive the dividends or income thereof, or to sue for and recover such thing in action, upon such terms as the court may think fit.

[246]

[54 Jurisdiction in regard to mental patients

[(1) Subject to subsection (2), the Court of Protection may not make an order, or give a direction or authority, in relation to a person who lacks capacity to exercise his functions as trustee, if the High Court may make an order to that effect under this Act.]

(2) [Where a person lacks capacity to exercise his functions as a trustee and a deputy is appointed for him by the Court of Protection or an application for the appointment of a deputy] has been made but not determined, then, except as respects a trust which is subject to an order for administration made by the High Court, [the Court of Protection] shall have concurrent jurisdiction with the High Court in relation to—

(a) mortgaged property of which [the person concerned] has become a trustee merely by reason of the mortgage having been paid off;

(b) matters consequent on the making of provision by [the Court of Protection] for the exercise of a power of appointing trustees or retiring from a trust;

(c) matters consequent on the making of provision by [the Court of Protection] for the carrying out of any contract entered into by [the person concerned];

(d) property to some interest in which [the person concerned] is beneficially entitled but which, or some interest in which, is held by [the person concerned] under an express, implied or constructive trust.

[(2A) Rules may be made in accordance with Part 1 of Schedule 1 to the Constitutional Reform Act 2005 with respect to the exercise of the jurisdiction referred to in subsection (2).]

(3) …]

[247]

NOTES

Substituted by the Mental Health Act 1959, s 149(1), Sch 7, Pt I.

Sub-s (1): substituted by the Mental Capacity Act 2005, s 67(1), Sch 6, para 3(1), (4)(a).

Sub-s (2): words in square brackets substituted by the Mental Capacity Act 2005, s 67(1), Sch 6, para 3(1), (4)(b).

Sub-s (2A): substituted for original words following sub-s (2)(d) by the Constitutional Reform Act 2005, s 12(2), Sch 1, Pt 2, para 6.

Sub-s (3): repealed by the Mental Capacity Act 2005, s 67(1), (2), Sch 6, para 3(1), (4)(c), Sch 7.

55 Orders made upon certain allegations to be conclusive evidence

Where a vesting order is made as to any land under this Act or under [sections 15 to 20 of the Mental Capacity Act 2005 or any corresponding provisions having effect in Northern Ireland], founded on an allegation of any of the following matters namely—

[(a) that a trustee or mortgagee lacks capacity in relation to the matter in question;] or

(b) that a trustee or mortgagee or the personal representative of or other person deriving title under a trustee or mortgagee is out of the jurisdiction of the High Court or cannot be found, or being a corporation has been dissolved; or

(c) that it is uncertain which of two or more trustees, or which of two or more persons interested in a mortgage, was the survivor; or

(d) that it is uncertain whether the last trustee or the personal representative of or other person deriving title under a trustee or mortgagee, or the last surviving person interested in a mortgage is living or dead: or

(e) that any trustee or mortgagee has died intestate without leaving a person beneficially interested under the intestacy or has died and it is not known who is his personal representative or the person interested;

the fact that the order has been so made shall be conclusive evidence of the matter so alleged in any court upon any question as to the validity of the order; but this section does not prevent the court from directing a reconveyance or surrender or the payment of costs occasioned by any such order if improperly obtained.

[248]

NOTES

Words in square brackets substituted by the Mental Capacity Act 2005, s 67(1), Sch 6, para 3(1), (5).

56 Application of vesting order to property out of England

The powers of the court to make vesting orders under this Act shall extend to all property in any part of His Majesty's dominions except Scotland.

[249]

Jurisdiction to make other Orders

57 Power of court to authorise dealings with trust property

(1) Where in the management or administration of any property vested in trustees, any sale, lease, mortgage, surrender, release, or other disposition, or any purchase, investment, acquisition, expenditure, or other transaction, is in the opinion of the court expedient, but the same cannot be effected by reason of the absence of any power for that purpose vested in the trustees by the trust instrument, if any, or by law, the court may by order confer upon the trustees, either generally or in any particular instance, the necessary power for the purpose, on such terms, and subject to such

provisions and conditions, if any, as the court may think fit and may direct in what manner any money authorised to be expended, and the costs of any transaction, are to be paid or borne as between capital and income.

(2) The court may, from time to time, rescind or vary any order made under this section, or may make any new or further order.

(3) An application to the court under this section may be made by the trustees, or by any of them, or by any person beneficially interested under the trust.

(4) This section does not apply to trustees of a settlement for the purposes of the Settled Land Act 1925.

[250]

58 Persons entitled to apply for orders

(1) An order under this Act for the appointment of a new trustee or concerning any interest in land, stock, or thing in action subject to a trust, may be made on the application of any person beneficially interested in the land, stock, or thing in action, whether under disability or not, or on the application of any person duly appointed trustee thereof.

(2) An order under this Act concerning any interest in land, stock, or thing in action subject to a mortgage may be made on the application of any person beneficially interested in the equity of redemption, whether under disability or not, or of any person interested in the money secured by the mortgage.

[251]

59 Power to give judgment in absence of a trustee

Where in any action the court is satisfied that diligent search has been made for any person who, in the character of trustee, is made a defendant in any action, to serve him with a process of the court, and that he cannot be found, the court may hear and determine the action and give judgment therein against that person in his character of a trustee as if he had been duly served, or had entered an appearance in the action, and had also appeared by his counsel and solicitor at the hearing, but without prejudice to any interest he may have in the matters in question in the action in any other character.

[252]

NOTES

Modification: references to solicitors etc modified to include references to bodies recognised under the Administration of Justice Act 1985, s 9, by the Solicitors' Incorporated Practices Order 1991, SI 1991/2684, arts 4, 5, Sch 1.

60 Power to charge costs on trust estate

The court may order the costs and expenses of and incident to any application for an order appointing a new trustee, or for a vesting order, or of and incident to any such order, or any conveyance or transfer in pursuance thereof, to be raised and paid out of the property in respect whereof the same is made, or out of the income thereof, or to be borne and paid in such manner and by such persons as to the court may seem just.

[253]

61 Power to relieve trustee from personal liability

If it appears to the court that a trustee, whether appointed by the court or otherwise, is or may be personally liable for any breach of trust, whether the transaction alleged to be a breach of trust occurred before or after the commencement of this Act, but has acted honestly and reasonably, and ought fairly to be excused for the breach of trust and for omitting to obtain the directions of the court in the matter in which he committed such breach, then the court may relieve him either wholly or partly from personal liability for the same.

[254]

62 Power to make beneficiary indemnify for breach of trust

(1) Where a trustee commits a breach of trust at the instigation or request or with the consent in writing of a beneficiary, the court may, if it thinks fit, … make such order as to the court seems just, for impounding all or any part of the interest of the beneficiary in the trust estate by way of indemnity to the trustee or persons claiming through him.

(2) This section applies to breaches of trust committed as well before as after the commencement of this Act.

[255]

NOTES

Sub-s (1): words omitted repealed by the Married Women (Restraint upon Anticipation) Act 1949, s 1(4), Sch 2.

Payment into Court

63 Payment into court by trustees

(1) Trustees, or the majority of trustees, having in their hands or under their control money or securities belonging to a trust, may pay the same into court; …

(2) The receipt or certificate of the proper officer shall be a sufficient discharge to trustees for the money or securities so paid into court.

(3) Where money or securities are vested in any persons as trustees, and the majority are desirous of paying the same into court, but the concurrence of the other or others cannot be obtained, the court may order the payment into court to be made by the majority without the concurrence of the other or others.

(4) Where any such money or securities are deposited with any banker, broker, or other depository, the court may order payment or delivery of the money or securities to the majority of the trustees for the purpose of payment into court.

(5) Every transfer payment and delivery made in pursuance of any such order shall be valid and take effect as if the same had been made on the authority or by the act of all the persons entitled to the money and securities so transferred, paid, or delivered.

[256]

NOTES

Sub-s (1): words omitted repealed by the Administration of Justice Act 1965, s 36(4), Sch 3.

[63A Jurisdiction of County Court

(1) The county court has jurisdiction under the following provisions where the amount or value of the trust estate or fund to be dealt with in the court does not exceed the county court limit—

section 41;
section 42;
section 51;
section 57;
section 60;
section 61;
section 62.

(2) The county court has jurisdiction under the following provisions where the land or the interest or contingent right in land which is to be dealt with in the court forms part of a trust estate which does not exceed in amount or value the county court limit—

section 44;
section 45;
section 46.

(3) The county court has jurisdiction—

(a) under sections 47 and 48 of this Act, where the judgment is given or order is made by the court;

(b) under sections 50 and 56, where a vesting order can be made by the court;

(c) under section 53, where the amount or value of the property to be dealt with in the court does not exceed the county court limit; and

(d) under section 63 (including power to receive payment of money or securities into court) where the money or securities to be paid into court do not exceed in amount or value the county court limit.

(4) Any reference to the court in section 59 of this Act includes a reference to the county court.

(5) In this section, in its application to any enactment, 'the county court limit' means the amount for the time being specified by an Order in Council under section 145 of the County Courts Act 1984 as the county court limit for the purposes of that enactment (or, where no such Order in Council has been made, the corresponding limit specified by Order in Council under section 192 of the County Courts Act 1959).]

[257]

NOTES

Inserted by the County Courts Act 1984, s 148(1), Sch 2, para 1.

PART V
GENERAL PROVISIONS

64 Application of Act to Settled Land Act Trustees

(1) All the powers and provisions contained in this Act with reference to the appointment of new trustees, and the discharge and retirement of trustees, apply to and include trustees for the

purposes of the Settled Land Act 1925, and trustees for the purpose of the management of land during a minority, whether such trustees are appointed by the court or by the settlement, or under provisions contained in any instrument.

(2) Where, either before or after the commencement of this Act, trustees of a settlement have been appointed by the court for the purposes of the Settled Land Acts 1882 to 1890, or of the Settled Land Act 1925, then, after the commencement of this Act—

(a) the person or persons nominated for the purpose of appointing new trustees by the instrument, if any, creating the settlement, though no trustees for the purposes of the said Acts were thereby appointed; or

(b) if there is no such person, or no such person able and willing to act, the surviving or continuing trustees or trustee for the time being for the purposes of the said Acts or the personal representatives of the last surviving or continuing trustee for those purposes,

shall have the powers conferred by this Act to appoint new or additional trustees of the settlement for the purposes of the said Acts.

(3) Appointments of new trustees for the purposes of the said Acts made or expressed to be made before the commencement of this Act by the trustees or trustee or personal representatives referred to in paragraph (b) of the last preceding subsection or by the persons referred to in paragraph (a) of that subsection are, without prejudice to any order of the court made before such commencement, hereby confirmed.

[258]

65 (*Repealed by the Criminal Law Act 1967, s 10, Sch 3, Pt I.*)

66 Indemnity to banks, etc

This Act, and every order purporting to be made under this Act, shall be a complete indemnity to the Bank of England[, the Registrar of Government Stock, any previous Registrar of Government Stock], and to all persons for any acts done pursuant thereto, and it shall not be necessary for the Bank[, the Registrar of Government Stock, any previous Registrar of Government Stock] or for any person to inquire concerning the propriety of the order, or whether the court by which the order was made had jurisdiction to make it.

[259]

NOTES

Words in square brackets inserted by SI 2004/1662, art 2, Schedule, Pt 2, para 10(1), (3), subject to transitional provisions in art 3 thereof.

67 Jurisdiction of the "court"

(1) In this Act "the court" means the High Court … or the county court, where those courts respectively have jurisdiction.

(2) The procedure under this Act in … county courts shall be in accordance with the Acts and rules regulating the procedure of those courts.

[260]

NOTES

Words omitted repealed by the Courts Act 1971, s 56, Sch 11, Pt II.

68 Definitions

[(1)] In this Act, unless the context otherwise requires, the following expressions have the meanings hereby assigned to them respectively, that is to say:—

(1) "Authorised investments" mean investments authorised by the instrument, if any, creating the trust for the investment of money subject to the trust, or by law;

(2) "Contingent right" as applied to land includes a contingent or executory interest, a possibility coupled with an interest, whether the object of the gift or limitation of the interest, or possibility is or is not ascertained, also a right of entry, whether immediate or future, and whether vested or contingent;

(3) "Convey" and "conveyance" as applied to any person include the execution by that person of every necessary or suitable assurance (including an assent) for conveying, assigning, appointing, surrendering, or otherwise transferring or disposing of land whereof he is seised or possessed, or wherein he is entitled to a contingent right, either for his whole estate or for any less estate, together with the performance of all formalities required by law for the validity of the conveyance; "sale" includes an exchange;

(4) "Gazette" means the London Gazette;

(5) "Instrument" includes Act of Parliament;

(6) "Land" includes land of any tenure, and mines and minerals, whether or not severed

from the surface, buildings or parts of buildings, whether the division is horizontal, vertical or made in any other way, and other corporeal hereditaments; also a manor, an advowson, and a rent and other incorporeal hereditaments, and an easement, right, privilege, or benefit in, over, or derived from … ; and in this definition "mines and minerals" include any strata or seam of minerals or substances in or under any land, and powers of working and getting the same … ; and "hereditaments" mean real property which under an intestacy occurring before the commencement of this Act might have devolved on an heir;

(7) "Mortgage" and "mortgagee" include a charge or chargee by way of legal mortgage, and relate to every estate and interest regarded in equity as merely a security for money, and every person deriving title under the original mortgagee;

(8) …

(9) "Personal representative" means the executor, original or by representation, or administrator for the time being of a deceased person;

(10) "Possession" includes receipt of rents and profits or the right to receive the same, if any; "income" includes rents and profits; and "possessed" applies to receipt of income of and to any vested estate less than a life interest in possession or in expectancy in any land;

(11) "Property" includes real and personal property, and any estate share and interest in any property, real or personal, and any debt, and any thing in action, and any other right or interest, whether in possession or not;

(12) "Rights" include estates and interests;

(13) "Securities" include stocks, funds, and shares; … and "securities payable to bearer" include securities transferable by delivery or by delivery and endorsement;

(14) "Stock" includes fully paid up shares, and so far as relates to vesting orders made by the court under this Act, includes any fund, annuity, or security transferable in books kept by any company or society, or by instrument of transfer either alone or accompanied by other formalities, and any share or interest therein;

(15) "Tenant for life," "statutory owner," "settled land," "settlement," "trust instrument," "trustees of the settlement" … "term of years absolute" and "vesting instrument" have the same meanings as in the Settled Land Act 1925, and "entailed interest" has the same meaning as in the Law of Property Act 1925;

(16) "Transfer" in relation to stock or securities, includes the performance and execution of every deed, power of attorney, act, and thing on the part of the transferor to effect and complete the title in the transferee;

(17) "Trust" does not include the duties incident to an estate conveyed by way of mortgage, but with this exception the expressions "trust" and "trustee" extend to implied and constructive trusts, and to cases where the trustee has a beneficial interest in the trust property, and to the duties incident to the office of a personal representative, and "trustee" where the context admits, includes a personal representative, and "new trustee" includes an additional trustee;

(18) "Trust corporation" means the Public Trustee or a corporation either appointed by the court in any particular case to be a trustee, or entitled by rules made under subsection (3) of section four of the Public Trustee Act 1906, to act as custodian trustee;

(19) "Trust for sale" in relation to land means an immediate … trust for sale, whether or not exercisable at the request or with the consent of any person …;

(20) "United Kingdom" means Great Britain and Northern Ireland.

[(2) Any reference in this Act to paying money or securities into court shall be construed as referring to paying the money or transferring or depositing the securities into or in the *Supreme Court* [Senior Courts] or into or in any other court that has jurisdiction, and any reference in this Act to payment of money or securities into court shall be construed—

(a) with reference to an order of the High Court, as referring to payment of the money or transfer or deposit of the securities into or in the *Supreme Court* [Senior Courts]; and

(b) with reference to an order of any other court, as referring to payment of the money or transfer or deposit of the securities into or in that court.]

[(3) Any reference in this Act to a person who lacks capacity in relation to a matter is to a person—

(a) who lacks capacity within the meaning of the Mental Capacity Act 2005 in relation to that matter, or

(b) in respect of whom the powers conferred by section 48 of that Act are exercisable and have been exercised in relation to that matter.]

[261]

NOTES

Sub-s (1): words omitted from paras (6), (19) repealed by the Trusts of Land and Appointment of Trustees Act 1996, s 25(2), Sch 4, for savings in relation to entailed interests created before the commencement of that Act, and savings consequential upon the abolition of the doctrine of conversion, see s 25(4), (5) thereof; para (8) and words omitted from para (13) repealed by the Administration of Justice Act 1965, s 17(1), Sch 1; words omitted from para (15) repealed by the Mental Health Act 1959 s 149(2), Sch 8, Pt I.

Sub-s (2): inserted by the Administration of Justice Act 1965, s 17(1), Sch 1; words in italics substituted by subsequent words in square brackets by the Constitutional Reform Act 2005, s 59(5), Sch 11, Pt 2, para 4(1), (3), as from 1 October 2009.

Sub-s (3): inserted by the Mental Capacity Act 2005, s 67(1), Sch 6, para 3(1), (6).

Modification: definition "Trust corporation" modified in relation to charities, by the Charities Act 1993, s 35.

69 Application of Act

(1) This Act, except where otherwise expressly provided, applies to trusts including, so far as this Act applies thereto, executorships and administratorships constituted or created either before or after the commencement of this Act.

(2) The powers conferred by this Act on trustees are in addition to the powers conferred by the instrument, if any, creating the trust, but those powers, unless otherwise stated, apply if and so far only as a contrary intention is not expressed in the instrument, if any, creating the trust, and have effect subject to the terms of that instrument.

(3) …

[262]

NOTES

Sub-s (3): repealed by the Statute Law (Repeals) Act 1978, s 1, Sch 1, Pt XVII.

70 Enactments repealed

… without prejudice to the provisions of section thirty-eight of the Interpretation Act 1889:

(a) Nothing in this repeal shall affect any vesting order or appointment made or other thing done under any enactment so repealed, and any order or appointment so made may be revoked or varied in like manner as if it has been made under this Act;

(b) References in any document to any enactment repealed by this Act shall be construed as references to this Act or to the corresponding enactment in this Act.

[263]

NOTES

Words omitted repealed by the Statute Law Revision Act 1950.

71 Short title, commencement, extent

(1) This Act may be cited as the Trustee Act, 1925.

(2) …

(3) This Act, except where otherwise expressly provided, extends to England and Wales only.

(4) The provisions of this Act bind the Crown.

[264]

NOTES

Sub-s (2): repealed by the Statute Law Revision Act 1950.

(Sch 1 repealed by the Statute Law (Repeals) Act 1978; Sch 2 repealed by the Statute Law Revision Act 1950.)

LAW OF PROPERTY ACT 1925

(1925 c 20)

An Act to consolidate the enactments relating to Conveyancing and the Law of Property in England and Wales

[9 April 1925]

PART I
GENERAL PRINCIPLES AS TO LEGAL ESTATES, EQUITABLE INTERESTS AND POWERS

1 Legal estates and equitable interests

(1) The only estates in land which are capable of subsisting or of being conveyed or created at law are—

(a) An estate in fee simple absolute in possession;

(b) A term of years absolute.

(2) The only interests or charges in or over land which are capable of subsisting or of being conveyed or created at law are—

(a) An easement, right, or privilege in or over land for an interest equivalent to an estate in fee simple absolute in possession or a term of years absolute;
(b) A rentcharge in possession issuing out of or charged on land being either perpetual or for a term of years absolute;
(c) A charge by way of legal mortgage;
(d) … and any other similar charge on land which is not created by an instrument;
(e) Rights of entry exercisable over or in respect of a legal term of years absolute, or annexed, for any purpose, to a legal rentcharge.

(3) All other estates, interests, and charges in or over land take effect as equitable interests.

(4) The estates, interests, and charges which under this section are authorised to subsist or to be conveyed or created at law are (when subsisting or conveyed or created at law) in this Act referred to as "legal estates", and have the same incidents as legal estates subsisting at the commencement of this Act; and the owner of a legal estate is referred to as "an estate owner" and his legal estate is referred to as his estate.

(5) A legal estate may subsist concurrently with or subject to any other legal estate in the same land in like manner as it could have done before the commencement of this Act.

(6) A legal estate is not capable of subsisting or of being created in an undivided share in land or of being held by an infant.

(7) Every power of appointment over, or power to convey or charge land or any interest therein, whether created by a statute or other instrument or implied by law, and whether created before or after the commencement of this Act (not being a power vested in a legal mortgagee or an estate owner in right of his estate and exercisable by him or by another person in his name and on his behalf), operates only in equity.

(8) Estates, interests, and charges in or over land which are not legal estates are in this Act referred to as "equitable interests", and powers which by this Act are to operate in equity only are in this Act referred to as "equitable powers".

(9) The provisions in any statute or other instrument requiring land to be conveyed to uses shall take effect as directions that the land shall (subject to creating or reserving thereout any legal estate authorised by this Act which may be required) be conveyed to a person of full age upon the requisite trusts.

(10) The repeal of the Statute of Uses (as amended) does not affect the operation thereof in regard to dealings taking effect before the commencement of this Act.

[265]

NOTES

Sub-s (2): words omitted repealed by the Finance Act 1963, s 73(8)(b), Sch 14, Pt IV, and the Tithe Act 1936, s 48(3), Sch 9.

2 Conveyances overreaching certain equitable interests and powers

(1) A conveyance to a purchaser of a legal estate in land shall overreach any equitable interest or power affecting that estate, whether or not he has notice thereof, if—

(i) the conveyance is made under the powers conferred by the Settled Land Act 1925 or any additional powers conferred by a settlement, and the equitable interest or power is capable of being overreached thereby, and the statutory requirements respecting the payment of capital money arising under the settlement are complied with;
(ii) the conveyance is made by [trustees of land] and the equitable interest or power is at the date of the conveyance capable of being overreached by such trustees under the provisions of sub-section (2) of this section or independently of that sub-section, and [the requirements of section 27 of this Act respecting the payment of capital money arising on such a conveyance] are complied with;
(iii) the conveyance is made by a mortgagee or personal representative in the exercise of his paramount powers, and the equitable interest or power is capable of being overreached by such conveyance, and any capital money arising from the transaction is paid to the mortgagee or personal representative;
(iv) the conveyance is made under an order of the court and the equitable interest or power is bound by such order, and any capital money arising from the transaction is paid into, or in accordance with the order of, the court.

[(1A) An equitable interest in land subject to a trust of land which remains in, or is to revert to, the settler shall (subject to any contrary intention) be overreached by the conveyance if it would be so overreached were it an interest under the trust.]

(2) [Where the legal estate affected is subject to [a trust of land], then if at the date of a conveyance made after the commencement of this Act [by the trustees], the trustees (whether original or substituted) are either—]

(a) two or more individuals approved or appointed by the court or the successors in office of the individuals so approved or appointed; or

(b) a trust corporation,

[any equitable interest or power having priority [to the trust]] shall, notwithstanding any stipulation to the contrary, be overreached by the conveyance, and shall, according to its priority, take effect as if created or arising by means of a primary trust affecting the proceeds of sale and the income of the land until sale.

(3) The following equitable interests and powers are excepted from the operation of subsection (2) of this section, namely—

(i) Any equitable interest protected by a deposit of documents relating to the legal estate affected;

(ii) The benefit of any covenant or agreement restrictive of the user of land;

(iii) Any easement, liberty, or privilege over or affecting land and being merely an equitable interest (in this Act referred to as an "equitable easement");

(iv) The benefit of any contract (in this Act referred to as an "estate contract") to convey or create a legal estate, including a contract conferring either expressly or by statutory implication a valid option to purchase, a right of pre-emption, or any other like right;

(v) Any equitable interest protected by registration under the Land Charges Act 1925 other than—

(a) an annuity within the meaning of Part II of that Act;

(b) a limited owner's charge or a general equitable charge within the meaning of that Act.

(4) Subject to the protection afforded by this section to the purchaser of a legal estate, nothing contained in this section shall deprive a person entitled to an equitable charge of any of his rights or remedies for enforcing the same.

(5) So far as regards the following interests, created before the commencement of this Act (which accordingly are not within the provisions of the Land Charges Act 1925), namely—

(a) the benefit of any covenant or agreement restrictive of the user of the land;

(b) any equitable easement;

(c) the interest under a puisne mortgage within the meaning of the Land Charges Act 1925 unless and until acquired under a transfer made after the commencement of this Act;

(d) the benefit of an estate contract, unless and until the same is acquired under a conveyance made after the commencement of this Act;

a purchaser of a legal estate shall only take subject thereto if he has notice thereof, and the same are not overreached under the provisions contained or in the manner referred to in this section.

[266]

NOTES

Sub-s (1): words in square brackets substituted by the Trusts of Land and Appointment of Trustees Act 1996, s 25(1), Sch 3, para 4(2)(a); for savings in relation to entailed interests created before the commencement of that Act, and savings consequential upon the abolition of the doctrine of conversion, see s 25(4), (5) thereof.

Sub-s (1A): inserted by the Trusts of Land and Appointment of Trustees Act 1996, s 25(1), Sch 3, para 4(2)(b), subject to savings as noted to sub-s (1).

Sub-s (2): first and fourth words in square brackets substituted by the Law of Property (Amendment) Act 1926, s 7, Schedule; other words in square brackets substituted by the Trusts of Land and Appointment of Trustees Act 1996, s 25(1), Sch 3, para 4(2)(c), subject to savings as noted to sub-s (1).

3 Manner of giving effect to equitable interests and powers

(1) All equitable interests and powers in or over land shall be enforceable against the estate owner of the legal estate affected in manner following (that is to say):—

(a) Where the legal estate affected is settled land, the tenant for life or statutory owner shall be bound to give effect to the equitable interests and powers in manner provided by the Settled Land Act 1925;

(b) …

(c) [In any other case], the estate owner shall be bound to give effect to the equitable interests and powers affecting his estate of which he has notice according to their respective priorities. This provision does not affect the priority or powers of a legal mortgagee, or the powers of personal representatives for purposes of administration.

(2) …

(3) Where, by reason … of an equitable right of entry taking effect, or for any other reason, a person becomes entitled to require a legal estate to be vested in him, then and in any such case the estate owner whose estate is affected shall be bound to convey or create such legal estate as the case may require.

(4) If any question arises whether any and what legal estate ought to be transferred or created as aforesaid, any person interested may apply to the court for directions in the manner provided by this Act.

(5) If the estate owners refuse or neglect for one month after demand to transfer or create any such legal estate, or if by reason of their being out of the United Kingdom or being unable to be found, or by reason of the dissolution of a corporation, or for any other reason, the court is satisfied that the transaction cannot otherwise be effected, or cannot be effected without undue delay or expense, the court may, on the application of any person interested, make a vesting order transferring or creating a legal estate in the manner provided by this Act.

(6) This section does not affect a purchaser of a legal estate taking free from an equitable interest or power.

[(7) The county court has jurisdiction under this section where the land which is to be dealt with in the court does not exceed [£30,000] in capital value …]

[267]

NOTES

Sub-s (1): para (b) repealed, and words in square brackets in para (c) substituted, by the Trusts of Land and Appointment of Trustees Act 1996, s 25(1), (2), Sch 3, para 4(3), Sch 4; for savings in relation to entailed interests created before the commencement of that Act, and savings consequential upon the abolition of the doctrine of conversion, see s 25(4), (5) thereof.

Sub-s (2): repealed by the Trusts of Land and Appointment of Trustees Act 1996, s 25(2), Sch 4, subject to savings as noted to sub-s (1).

Sub-s (3): words omitted repealed by the Reverter of Sites Act 1987, s 8(2), (3), Schedule.

Sub-s (5): words omitted repealed by the Trusts of Land and Appointment of Trustees Act 1996, s 25(2), Sch 4, subject to savings as noted to sub-s (1).

Sub-s (7): inserted by the County Courts Act 1984, s 148(1), Sch 2, para 2; sum in square brackets substituted and words omitted repealed by SI 1991/724, art 2(3)(a), (8), Schedule, Part I.

4 Creation and disposition of equitable interests

(1) Interests in land validly created or arising after the commencement of this Act, which are not capable of subsisting as legal estates, shall take effect as equitable interests, and, save as otherwise expressly provided by statute, interests in land which under the Statute of Uses or otherwise could before the commencement of this Act have been created as legal interests, shall be capable of being created as equitable interests:

Provided that, after the commencement of this Act (and save as hereinafter expressly enacted), an equitable interest in land shall only be capable of being validly created in any case in which an equivalent equitable interest in property real or personal could have been validly created before such commencement.

(2) All rights and interests in land may be disposed of, including—

(a) a contingent, executory or future equitable interest in any land, or a possibility coupled with an interest in any land, whether or not the object of the gift or limitation of such interest or possibility be ascertained;

(b) a right of entry, into or upon land whether immediate or future, and whether vested or contingent.

(3) All rights of entry affecting a legal estate which are exercisable on condition broken or for any other reason may, after the commencement of this Act, be made exercisable by any person and the persons deriving title under him, but, in regard to an estate in fee simple (not being a rentcharge held for a legal estate) only within the period authorised by the rule relating to perpetuities.

[268]

5 Satisfied terms, whether created out of freehold or leasehold land to cease

(1) Where the purposes of a term of years created or limited at any time out of freehold land, become satisfied either before or after the commencement of this Act (whether or not that term either by express declaration or by construction of law becomes attendant upon the freehold reversion) it shall merge in the reversion expectant thereon and shall cease accordingly.

(2) Where the purposes of a term of years created or limited, at any time, out of leasehold land, become satisfied after the commencement of this Act, that term shall merge in the reversion expectant thereon and shall cease accordingly.

(3) Where the purposes are satisfied only as respects part of the land comprised in a term, this section shall have effect as if a separate term had been created in regard to that part of the land.

[269]

6 Saving of lessors' and lessees' covenants

(1) Nothing in this Part of this Act affects prejudicially the right to enforce any lessor's or lessee's covenants, agreements or conditions (including a valid option to purchase or right of

pre-emption over the reversion), contained in any such instrument as is in this section mentioned, the benefit or burden of which runs with the reversion or the term.

(2) This section applies where the covenant, agreement or condition is contained in any instrument—

(a) creating a term of years absolute, or
(b) varying the rights of the lessor or lessee under the instrument creating the term.

[270]

7 Saving of certain legal estates and statutory powers

(1) A fee simple which, by virtue of the Lands Clauses Acts, … or any similar statute, is liable to be divested, is for the purposes of this Act a fee simple absolute, and remains liable to be divested as if this Act had not been passed, [and a fee simple subject to a legal or equitable right of entry or re-entry is for the purposes of this Act a fee simple absolute].

(2) A fee simple vested in a corporation which is liable to determine by reason of the dissolution of the corporation is, for the purposes of this Act, a fee simple absolute.

(3) The provisions of—

(a) …;
(b) the Friendly Societies Act 1896, in regard to land to which that Act applies;
(c) any other statutes conferring special facilities or prescribing special modes (whether by way of registered memorial or otherwise) for disposing of or acquiring land, or providing for the vesting (by conveyance or otherwise) of the land in trustees or any person, or the holder for the time being of an office or any corporation sole or aggregate (including the Crown);

shall remain in full force.

…

(4) Where any such power for disposing of or creating a legal estate is exercisable by a person who is not the estate owner, the power shall, when practicable, be exercised in the name and on behalf of the estate owner.

[271]

NOTES

Sub-s (1): words omitted repealed by the Reverter of Sites Act 1987, s 8(3), Schedule; words in square brackets inserted by the Law of Property (Amendment) Act 1926, s 7, Schedule.

Sub-s (3): para (a) repealed by the Criminal Justice Act 1948, s 83, Sch 10; final words omitted repealed by the Trusts of Land and Appointment of Trustees Act 1996, s 25(2), Sch 4, for savings in relation to entailed interests created before the commencement of that Act, and savings consequential upon the abolition of the doctrine of conversion, see s 25(4), (5) thereof.

8 Saving of certain legal powers to lease

(1) All leases or tenancies at a rent for a term of years absolute authorised to be granted by a mortgagor or mortgagee or by the Settled Land Act 1925, or any other statute (whether or not extended by any instrument) may be granted in the name and on behalf of the estate owner by the person empowered to grant the same, whether being an estate owner or not, with the same effect and priority as if this Part of this Act had not been passed; but this section does not (except as respects the usual qualified covenant for quiet enjoyment) authorise any person granting a lease in the name of an estate owner to impose any personal liability on him.

(2) Where a rentcharge is held for a legal estate, the owner thereof may under the statutory power or under any corresponding power, create a legal term of years absolute for securing or compelling payment of the same; but in other cases terms created under any such power shall, unless and until the estate owner of the land charged gives legal effect to the transaction, take effect only as equitable interests.

[272]

9 Vesting orders and dispositions of legal estates operating as conveyances by an estate owner

(1) Every such order, declaration, or conveyance as is hereinafter mentioned, namely—

(a) every vesting order made by any court or other competent authority;
(b) every vesting declaration (express or implied) under any statutory power;
(c) every vesting instrument made by the trustees of a settlement or other persons under the provisions of the Settled Land Act 1925;
(d) every conveyance by a person appointed for the purpose under an order of the court or authorised under any statutory power to convey in the name or on behalf of an estate owner;
(e) every conveyance made under any power reserved or conferred by this Act,

which is made or executed for the purpose of vesting, conveying, or creating a legal estate, shall operate to convey or create the legal estate disposed of in like manner as if the same had been a conveyance executed by the estate owner of the legal estate to which the order, declaration, vesting instrument, or conveyance relates.

(2) Where the order, declaration, or conveyance is made in favour of a purchaser, the provisions of this Act relating to a conveyance of a legal estate to a purchaser shall apply thereto.

(3) The provisions of the Trustee Act 1925 relating to vesting orders and orders appointing a person to convey shall apply to all vesting orders authorised to be made by this Part of this Act.

[273]

10 Title to be shown to legal estates

(1) Where title is shown to a legal estate in land, it shall be deemed not necessary or proper to include in the abstract of title an instrument relating only to interests or powers which will be over-reached by the conveyance of the estate to which title is being shown; but nothing in this Part of this Act affects the liability of any person to disclose an equitable interest or power which will not be so over-reached, or to furnish an abstract of any instrument creating or affecting the same.

(2) A solicitor delivering an abstract framed in accordance with this Part of this Act shall not incur any liability on account of an omission to include therein an instrument which, under this section, is to be deemed not necessary or proper to be included, nor shall any liability be implied by reason of the inclusion of any such instrument.

[274]

NOTES

Modifications: modified by the Buildings Societies Act 1986, s 124, Sch 21, paras 9, 12, and the Administration of Justice Act 1985, ss 9, 34(2), Sch 2, para 37. References to solicitors etc modified to include references to bodies recognised under the Administration of Justice Act 1985, s 9, by the Solicitors' Incorporated Practices Order 1991, SI 1991/2684, arts 4, 5, Sch 1.

11 (*Repealed by the Law of Property Act 1969, s 16, Sch 2, Pt I.*)

12 Limitation and Prescription Acts

Nothing in this Part of this Act affects the operation of any statute, or of the general law for the limitation of actions or proceedings relating to land or with reference to the acquisition of easements or rights over or in respect of land.

[275]

13 Effect of possession of documents

This Act shall not prejudicially affect the right or interest of any person arising out of or consequent on the possession by him of any documents relating to a legal estate in land, nor affect any question arising out of or consequent upon any omission to obtain or any other absence of possession by any person of any documents relating to a legal estate in land.

[276]

14 Interests of persons in possession

This Part of this Act shall not prejudicially affect the interest of any person in possession or in actual occupation of land to which he may be entitled in right of such possession or occupation.

[277]

15 Presumption that parties are of full age

The persons expressed to be parties to any conveyance shall, until the contrary is proved, be presumed to be of full age at the date thereof.

[278]

16–18 (*Repealed by the Finance Act 1975, ss 50, 52(2), (3), 59(5), Sch 13, Pt I.*)

Infants and Lunatics

19 (*Repealed by the Trusts of Land and Appointment of Trustees Act 1996, s 25(2), Sch 4.*)

20 Infants not to be appointed trustees

The appointment of an infant to be a trustee in relation to any settlement or trust shall be void, but without prejudice to the power to appoint a new trustee to fill the vacancy.

[279]

21 Receipts by married infants

A married infant shall have power to give valid receipts for all income (including statutory accumulations of income made during the minority) to which the infant may be entitled in like manner as if the infant were of full age.

[280]

[22 Conveyances on behalf of persons suffering from mental disorder and as to land held by them [in trust]

(1) Where a legal estate in land (whether settled or not) is vested[, either solely or jointly with any other person or persons, in a person lacking capacity (within the meaning of the Mental Capacity Act 2005) to convey or create a legal estate, a deputy appointed for him by the Court of Protection or (if no deputy is appointed] for him) any person authorised in that behalf shall, under an order of [the Court of Protection], or of the court, or under any statutory power, make or concur in making all requisite dispositions for conveying or creating a legal estate in his name and on his behalf.

(2) If land [subject to a trust of land] is vested, either solely or jointly with any other person or persons, in a person who [lacks capacity (within the meaning of that Act) to exercise] his functions as trustee, a new trustee shall be appointed in the place of that person, or he shall be otherwise discharged from the trust, before the legal estate is dealt with [by the trustees].

[(3) Subsection (2) of this section does not prevent a legal estate being dealt with without the appointment of a new trustee, or the discharge of the incapable trustee, at a time when the donee of [an enduring power of attorney or lasting power of attorney (within the meaning of the 2005 Act) is entitled to act for the trustee who lacks capacity in relation to the dealing].]]

[281]

NOTES

Substituted by the Mental Health Act 1959, s 149(1), Sch 7, Part I.

Section heading: words in square brackets substituted by the Trusts of Land and Appointment of Trustees Act 1996, s 25(1), Sch 3, para 4(6); for savings in relation to entailed interests created before the commencement of that Act, and savings consequential upon the abolition of the doctrine of conversion, see s 25(4), (5) thereof.

Sub-s (1): words in square brackets substituted by the Mental Capacity Act 2005, s 67(1), Sch 6, para 4(1), (2)(a).

Sub-s (2): words in first and third pairs of square brackets substituted by the Trusts of Land and Appointment of Trustees Act 1996, s 25(1), Sch 3, para 4(6); for savings in relation to entailed interests created before the commencement of that Act, and savings consequential upon the abolition of the doctrine of conversion, see s 25(4), (5) thereof; words in second pair of square brackets substituted by the Mental Capacity Act 2005, s 67(1), Sch 6, para 4(1), (2)(b).

Sub-s (3): inserted by the Trustee Delegation Act 1999, s 9; words in square brackets substituted by the Mental Capacity Act 2005, s 67(1), Sch 6, para 4(1), (2)(c).

[Trusts of land]

NOTES

Cross-heading: substituted by the Trusts of Land and Appointment of Trustees Act 1996, s 25(1), Sch 3, para 4(7).

23 *(Repealed by the Trusts of Land and Appointment of Trustees Act 1996, s 25(2), Sch 4; for savings see ss 3, 18(3), 25(5) thereof.)*

[24 Appointment of trustees of land

(1) The persons having power to appoint new trustees of land shall be bound to appoint the same persons (if any) who are for the time being trustees of any trust of the proceeds of sale of the land.

(2) A purchaser shall not be concerned to see that subsection (1) of this section has been complied with.

(3) This section applies whether the trust of land and the trust of proceeds of sale are created, or arise, before or after the commencement of this Act.]

[282]

NOTES

Substituted by the Trusts of Land and Appointment of Trustees Act 1996, s 25(1), Sch 3, para 4(7); for savings in relation to entailed interests created before the commencement of that Act, and savings consequential upon the abolition of the doctrine of conversion, see s 25(4), (5) thereof.

25, 26 *(Repealed by the Trusts of Land and Appointment of Trustees Act 1996, s 25(2), Sch 4; for savings see ss 3, 18(3), 25(5) thereof.)*

27 Purchaser not to be concerned with the trusts of the proceeds of sale which are to be paid to two or more trustees or to a trust corporation

[(1) A purchaser of a legal estate from trustees of land shall not be concerned with the trusts affecting the land, the net income of the land or the proceeds of sale of the land whether or not those trusts are declared by the same instrument as that by which the trust of land is created.]

[(2) Notwithstanding anything to the contrary in the instrument (if any) creating a [trust] of land or in [any trust affecting the net proceeds of sale of the land if it is sold], the proceeds of sale or other capital money shall not be paid to or applied by the direction of fewer than two persons as [trustees], except where the trustee is a trust corporation, but this subsection does not affect the right of a sole personal representative as such to give valid receipts for, or direct the application of, proceeds of sale or other capital money, nor, except where capital money arises on the transaction, render it necessary to have more than one trustee.]

[283]

NOTES

Sub-s (1): substituted by the Trusts of Land and Appointment of Trustees Act 1996, s 25(1), Sch 3, para 4(8)(a); for savings in relation to entailed interests created before the commencement of that Act, and savings consequential upon the abolition of the doctrine of conversion, see s 25(4), (5) thereof.

Sub-s (2): substituted by the Law of Property (Amendment) Act 1926, s 7, Schedule; words in square brackets substituted by the Trusts of Land and Appointment of Trustees Act 1996, s 25(1), Sch 3, para 4(8)(b), subject to savings as noted to sub-s (1).

28–30 (*Repealed by the Trusts of Land and Appointment of Trustees Act 1996, s 25(2), Sch 4; for savings see ss 3, 18(3), 25(5) thereof.*)

31 [Trust] of mortgaged property where right of redemption is barred

(1) Where any property, vested in trustees by way of security, becomes, by virtue of the statutes of limitation, or of an order for foreclosure or otherwise, discharged from the right of redemption, it shall be held by them [in trust—

(a) to apply the income from the property in the same manner as interest paid on the mortgage debt would have been applicable; and

(b) if the property is sold, to apply the net proceeds of sale, after payment of costs and expenses, in the same manner as repayment of the mortgage debt would have been applicable.]

[(2) Subsection (1) of this section] operates without prejudice to any rule of law relating to the apportionment of capital and income between tenant for life and remainderman.

(3) …

[(4) Where—

(a) the mortgage money is capital money for the purposes of the Settled Land Act 1925;

(b) land other than any forming the whole or part of the property mentioned in subsection (1) of this section is, or is deemed to be, subject to the settlement; and

(c) the tenant for life or statutory owner requires the trustees to execute with respect to land forming the whole or part of that property a vesting deed such as would have been required in relation to the land if it had been acquired on a purchase with capital money,

the trustees shall execute such a vesting deed.]

(5) This section applies whether the right of redemption was discharged before or after the first day of January, nineteen hundred and twelve, but has effect without prejudice to any dealings or arrangements made before that date.

[284]

NOTES

Section heading: words in square brackets substituted by the Trusts of Land and Appointment of Trustees Act 1996, s 5, Sch 2, para 1(6); for savings in relation to entailed interests created before the commencement of that Act, and savings consequential upon the abolition of the doctrine of conversion, see s 25(4), (5) thereof.

Sub-ss (1), (2): words in square brackets substituted by the Trusts of Land and Appointment of Trustees Act 1996, s 5, Sch 2, para 1(2), (3), subject to savings as noted above.

Sub-s (3): repealed by the Trusts of Land and Appointment of Trustees Act 1996, ss 5, 25(2), Sch 2, para 1(4), subject to savings as noted above.

Sub-s (4): substituted by the Trusts of Land and Appointment of Trustees Act 1996, s 5, Sch 2, para 1(5), subject to savings as noted above.

32 (*Repealed by the Trusts of Land and Appointment of Trustees Act 1996, ss 5(1), 25(2), Sch 2, para 2, Sch 4, in relation to land purchased on or after 1 January 1997; for savings see ss 3, 18(3), 25(5) thereof.*)

33 Application of Part I to personal representatives

The provisions of this Part of this Act relating to [trustees of land] apply to personal representatives holding [land in trust], but without prejudice to their rights and powers for purposes of administration.

[285]

NOTES

Words in square brackets substituted by the Trusts of Land and Appointment of Trustees Act 1996, s 25(1), Sch 3, para 4(9); for savings in relation to entailed interests created before the commencement of that Act, and savings consequential upon the abolition of the doctrine of conversion, see s 25(4), (5) thereof.

Undivided Shares and Joint Ownership

34 Effect of future dispositions to tenants in common

(1) An undivided share in land shall not be capable of being created except as provided by the Settled Land Act 1925 or as hereinafter mentioned.

(2) Where, after the commencement of this Act, land is expressed to be conveyed to any persons in undivided shares and those persons are of full age, the conveyance shall (notwithstanding anything to the contrary in this Act) operate as if the land had been expressed to be conveyed to the grantees, or, if there are more than four grantees, to the four first named in the conveyance, as joint tenants [in trust for the persons interested in the land]:

Provided that, where the conveyance is made by way of mortgage the land shall vest in the grantees or such four of them as aforesaid for a term of years absolute (as provided by this Act) as joint tenants subject to cesser on redemption in like manner as if the mortgage money had belonged to them on a joint account, but without prejudice to the beneficial interests in the mortgage money and interest.

(3) A devise bequest or testamentary appointment, coming into operation after the commencement of this Act, of land to two or more persons in undivided shares shall operate as a devise bequest or appointment of the land to the personal representatives of the testator, and (but without prejudice to the rights and powers of the personal representatives for purposes of administration) [in trust for the persons interested in the land].

[(3A) In subsections (2) and (3) of this section references to the persons interested in the land include persons interested as trustees or personal representatives (as well as persons beneficially interested).]

(4) …

[286]

NOTES

Sub-s (2): words in square brackets substituted by the Trusts of Land and Appointment of Trustees Act 1996, s 5, Sch 2, para 3(2); for savings in relation to entailed interests created before the commencement of that Act, and savings consequential upon the abolition of the doctrine of conversion, see s 25(4), (5) thereof.

Sub-s (3): words omitted repealed and words in square brackets substituted by the Trusts of Land and Appointment of Trustees Act 1996, ss 5, 25(2), Sch 2, para 3(3), Sch 4, subject to savings as noted to sub-s (1).

Sub-s (3A): inserted by the Trusts of Land and Appointment of Trustees Act 1996, s 5, Sch 2, para 3(4), subject to savings as noted to sub-s (1).

Sub-s (4): repealed by the Trusts of Land and Appointment of Trustees Act 1996, ss 5, 25(2), Sch 2, para 3(5), Sch 4, subject to savings as noted to sub-s (1).

35 *(Repealed by the Trusts of Land and Appointment of Trustees Act 1996, s 25(2), Sch 4; for savings see ss 3, 18(3), 25(5) thereof.)*

36 Joint tenancies

(1) Where a legal estate (not being settled land) is beneficially limited to or held in trust for any persons as joint tenants, the same shall be held [in trust], in like manner as if the persons beneficially entitled were tenants in common, but not so as to sever their joint tenancy in equity.

(2) No severance of a joint tenancy of a legal estate, so as to create a tenancy in common in land, shall be permissible, whether by operation of law or otherwise, but this subsection does not affect the right of a joint tenant to release his interest to the other joint tenants, or the right to sever a joint tenancy in an equitable interest whether or not the legal estate is vested in the joint tenants:

Provided that, where a legal estate (not being settled land) is vested in joint tenants beneficially, and any tenant desires to sever the joint tenancy in equity, he shall give to the other joint tenants a notice in writing of such desire or do such other acts or things as would, in the case of personal estate, have been effectual to sever the tenancy in equity, and thereupon [the land shall be held in trust on terms] which would have been requisite for giving effect to the beneficial interests if there had been an actual severance.

[Nothing in this Act affects the right of a survivor of joint tenants, who is solely and beneficially interested, to deal with his legal estate as if it were not held [in trust].]

(3) Without prejudice to the right of a joint tenant to release his interest to the other joint tenants no severance of a mortgage term or trust estate, so as to create a tenancy in common, shall be permissible.

[287]

NOTES

Sub-s (1): words in square brackets substituted by the Trusts of Land and Appointment of Trustees Act 1996, s 5, Sch 2, para 4(2); for savings in relation to entailed interests created before the commencement of that Act, and savings consequential upon the abolition of the doctrine of conversion, see s 25(4), (5) thereof.

Sub-s (2): words in first and third (inner) pairs of square brackets substituted by the Trusts of Land and Appointment of Trustees Act 1996, s 5, Sch 2, para 4(3), subject to savings as noted to sub-s (1); words in second (outer) pair of square brackets inserted by the Law of Property (Amendment) Act 1926, s 7, Schedule.

37 Rights of husband and wife

A husband and wife shall, for all purposes of acquisition of any interest in property, under a disposition made or coming into operation after the commencement of this Act, be treated as two persons.

[288]

38 Party structures

(1) Where under a disposition or other arrangement which, if a holding in undivided shares had been permissible, would have created a tenancy in common, a wall or other structure is or is expressed to be made a party wall or structure, that structure shall be and remain severed vertically as between the respective owners, and the owner of each part shall have such rights to support and user over the rest of the structure as may be requisite for conferring rights corresponding to those which would have subsisted if a valid tenancy in common had been created.

(2) Any person interested may, in case of dispute, apply to the court for an order declaring the rights and interests under this section of the persons interested in any such party structure, and the court may make such order as it thinks fit.

[289]

Transitional Provisions

39 Transitional provisions in First Schedule

For the purpose of effecting the transition from the law existing prior to the commencement of the Law of Property Act 1922 to the law enacted by that Act (as amended), the provisions set out in the First Schedule to this Act shall have effect—

(1) for converting existing legal estates, interests and charges not capable under the said Act of taking effect as legal interests into equitable interests;
(2) for discharging, getting in or vesting outstanding legal estates;
(3) for making provision with respect to legal estates vested in infants;
(4) for subjecting land held in undivided shares to [trusts];
(5) for dealing with party structures and open spaces held in common;
(6) …
(7) for converting existing freehold mortgages into mortgages by demise;
(8) for converting existing leasehold mortgages into mortgages by sub-demise.

[290]

NOTES

Para (4): word in square brackets substituted by the Trusts of Land and Appointment of Trustees Act 1996, s 25(1), Sch 3, para 4(10); for savings in relation to entailed interests created before the commencement of that Act, and savings consequential upon the abolition of the doctrine of conversion, see s 25(4), (5) thereof.

Para (6): repealed by the Statute Law (Repeals) Act 2004.

PART II
CONTRACTS, CONVEYANCES AND OTHER INSTRUMENTS

Contracts

40 (*Repealed by the Law of Property (Miscellaneous Provisions) Act 1989, ss 2(8), 4, Sch 2, except in relation to contracts made before 27 September 1989.*)

41 Stipulations not of the essence of a contract

Stipulations in a contract, as to time or otherwise, which according to rules of equity are not deemed to be or to have become of the essence of the contract, are also construed and have effect at law in accordance with the same rules.

[291]

42 Provisions as to contracts

(1) A stipulation that a purchaser of a legal estate in land shall accept a title made with the concurrence of any person entitled to an equitable interest shall be void, if a title can be made discharged from the equitable interest without such concurrence—

(a) under a [trust of land]; or
(b) under this Act, or the Settled Land Act 1925, or any other statute.

(2) A stipulation that a purchaser of a legal estate in land shall pay or contribute towards the costs of or incidental to—

(a) obtaining a vesting order, or the appointment of trustees of a settlement, or the appointment of trustees of [land]; or
(b) the preparation stamping or execution of a conveyance [in trust], or of a vesting instrument for bringing into force the provisions of the Settled Land Act 1925;

shall be void.

(3) A stipulation contained in any contract for the sale or exchange of land made after the commencement of this Act, to the effect that an outstanding legal estate is to be traced or got in by or at the expense of a purchaser or that no objection is to be taken on account of an outstanding legal estate, shall be void.

(4) If the subject matter of any contract for the sale or exchange of land—

(i) is a mortgage term and the vendor has power to convey the fee simple in the land, or, in the case of a mortgage of a term of years absolute, the leasehold reversion affected by the mortgage, the contract shall be deemed to extend to the fee simple in the land or such leasehold reversion;
(ii) is an equitable interest capable of subsisting as a legal estate, and the vendor has power to vest such legal estate in himself or in the purchaser or to require the same to be so vested, the contract shall be deemed to extend to such legal estate;
(iii) is an entailed interest in possession and the vendor has power to vest in himself or in the purchaser the fee simple in the land, (or, if the entailed interest is an interest in a term of years absolute, such term,) or to require the same to be so vested, the contract shall be deemed to extend to the fee simple in the land or the term of years absolute.

(5) This section does not affect the right of a mortgagee of leasehold land to sell his mortgage term only if he is unable to convey or vest the leasehold reversion expectant thereon.

(6) …

(7) Where a purchaser has power to acquire land compulsorily, and a contract, whether by virtue of a notice to treat or otherwise, is subsisting under which title can be made without payment of the compensation money into court, title shall be made in that way unless the purchaser, to avoid expense or delay or for any special reason, considers it expedient that the money should be paid into court.

(8) A vendor shall not have any power to rescind a contract by reason only of the enforcement of any right under this section.

(9) This section only applies in favour of a purchaser for money or money's worth.

[292]

NOTES

Sub-ss (1), (2): words in square brackets substituted by the Trusts of Land and Appointment of Trustees Act 1996, s 25(1), Sch 3, para 4(11); for savings in relation to entailed interests created before the commencement of that Act, and savings consequential upon the abolition of the doctrine of conversion, see s 25(4), (5) thereof.

Sub-s (6): repealed by the Trusts of Land and Appointment of Trustees Act 1996, s 25(2), Sch 4, subject to savings as noted above.

43 Rights protected by registration

(1) Where a purchaser of a legal estate is entitled to acquire the same discharged from an equitable interest which is protected by registration as a pending action, annuity, writ, order, deed of arrangement or land charge, and which will not be overreached by the conveyance to him, he may notwithstanding any stipulation to the contrary, require—

(a) that the registration shall be cancelled; or
(b) that the person entitled to the equitable interest shall concur in the conveyance;

and in either case free of expense to the purchaser.

(2) Where the registration cannot be cancelled or the person entitled to the equitable interest refuses to concur in the conveyance, this section does not affect the right of any person to rescind the contract.

[293]

44 Statutory commencements of title

(1) After the commencement of this Act [fifteen years] shall be substituted for forty years as the period of commencement of title which a purchaser of land may require; nevertheless earlier title than [fifteen years] may be required in cases similar to those in which earlier title than forty years might immediately before the commencement of this Act be required.

(2) Under a contract to grant or assign a term of years, whether derived or to be derived out of freehold or leasehold land, the intended lessee or assign shall not be entitled to call for the title to the freehold.

(3) Under a contract to sell and assign a term of years derived out of a leasehold interest in land, the intended assign shall not have the right to call for the title to the leasehold reversion.

(4) On a contract to grant a lease for a term of years to be derived out of a leasehold interest, with a leasehold reversion, the intended lessee shall not have the right to call for the title to that reversion.

[(4A) Subsections (2) and (4) of this section do not apply to a contract to grant a term of years if the grant will be an event within section 4(1) of the Land Registration Act 2002 (events which trigger compulsory first registration of title).]

(5) Where by reason of any of [subsections (2) to (4) of this section], an intending lessee or assign is not entitled to call for the title to the freehold or to a leasehold reversion, as the case may be, he shall not, where the contract is made after the commencement of this Act, be deemed to be affected with notice of any matter or thing of which, if he had contracted that such title should be furnished, he might have had notice.

(6) Where land of copyhold or customary tenure has been converted into freehold by enfranchisement, then, under a contract to sell and convey the freehold, the purchaser shall not have the right to call for the title to make the enfranchisement.

(7) Where the manorial incidents formerly affecting any land have been extinguished, then, under a contract to sell and convey the freehold, the purchaser shall not have the right to call for the title of the person entering into any compensation agreement or giving a receipt for the compensation money to enter into such agreement or to give such receipt, and shall not be deemed to be affected with notice of any matter or thing of which, if he had contracted that such title should be furnished, he might have had notice.

(8) A purchaser shall not be deemed to be or ever to have been affected with notice of any matter or thing of which, if he had investigated the title or made enquiries in regard to matters prior to the period of commencement of title fixed by this Act, or by any other statute, or by any rule of law, he might have had notice, unless he actually makes such investigation or enquiries.

(9) Where a lease whether made before or after the commencement of this Act, is made under a power contained in a settlement, will, Act of Parliament, or other instrument, any preliminary contract for or relating to the lease shall not, for the purpose of the deduction of title to an intended assign, form part of the title, or evidence of the title, to the lease.

(10) This section, save where otherwise expressly provided, applies to contracts for sale whether made before or after the commencement of this Act, and applies to contracts for exchange in like manner as to contracts for sale, save that it applies only to contracts for exchange made after such commencement.

(11) This section applies only if and so far as a contrary intention is not expressed in the contract.

[(12) Nothing in this section applies in relation to registered land or to a term of years to be derived out of registered land.]

[294]

NOTES

Sub-s (1): words in square brackets substituted by the Law of Property Act 1969, s 23.
Sub-s (4A): inserted by the Land Registration Act 2002, s 133, Sch 11, para 2(1), (2).
Sub-s (5): words in square brackets substituted by the Land Registration Act 2002, s 133, Sch 11, para 2(1), (3).
Sub-s (12): inserted by the Land Registration Act 2002, s 133, Sch 11, para 2(1), (4).

45 Other statutory conditions of sale

(1) A purchaser of any property shall not—

(a) require the production, or any abstract or copy, of any deed, will, or other document, dated or made before the time prescribed by law, or stipulated, for the commencement of the title, even though the same creates a power subsequently exercised by an instrument abstracted in the abstract furnished to the purchaser; or

(b) require any information, or make any requisition, objection, or inquiry, with respect to any such deed, will, or document, or the title prior to that time, notwithstanding that any such deed, will, or other document, or that prior title, is recited, agreed to be produced, or noticed;

and he shall assume, unless the contrary appears, that the recitals, contained in the abstracted instruments, of any deed, will, or other document, forming part of that prior title, are correct, and give all the material contents of the deed, will, or other document so recited, and that every document so recited was duly executed by all necessary parties, and perfected, if and as required, by fine, recovery, acknowledgment, inrolment, or otherwise:

Provided that this subsection shall not deprive a purchaser of the right to require the production, or an abstract or copy of—

(i) any power of attorney under which any abstracted document is executed; or

(ii) any document creating or disposing of an interest, power or obligation which is not shown to have ceased or expired, and subject to which any part of the property is disposed of by an abstracted document; or

(iii) any document creating any limitation or trust by reference to which any part of the property is disposed of by an abstracted document.

(2) Where land sold is held by lease (other than an under-lease), the purchaser shall assume, unless the contrary appears, that the lease was duly granted; and, on production of the receipt for the last payment due for rent under the lease before the date of actual completion of the purchase, he shall assume, unless the contrary appears, that all the covenants and provisions of the lease have been duly performed and observed up to the date of actual completion of the purchase.

(3) Where land sold is held by under-lease, the purchaser shall assume, unless the contrary appears, that the under-lease and every superior lease were duly granted; and, on production of the receipt for the last payment due for rent under the under-lease before the date of actual completion of the purchase, he shall assume, unless the contrary appears, that all the covenants and provisions of the under-lease have been duly performed and observed up to the date of actual completion of the purchase, and further that all rent due under every superior lease, and all the covenants and provisions of every superior lease, have been paid and duly performed and observed up to that date.

(4) On a sale of any property, the following expenses shall be borne by the purchaser where he requires them to be incurred for the purpose of verifying the abstract or any other purpose, that is to say—

(a) the expenses of the production and inspection of all Acts of Parliament, inclosure awards, records, proceedings of courts, court rolls, deeds, wills, probates, letters of administration, and other documents, not in the possession of the vendor or his mortgagee or trustee, and the expenses of all journeys incidental to such production or inspection; and

(b) the expenses of searching for, procuring, making, verifying, and producing all certificates, declarations, evidences, and information not in the possession of the vendor or his mortgagee or trustee, and all attested, stamped, office or other copies or abstracts of, or extracts from, any Acts of Parliament or other documents aforesaid, not in the possession of the vendor or his mortgagee or trustee;

and where the vendor or his mortgagee or trustee retains possession of any document, the expenses of making any copy thereof, attested or unattested, which a purchaser requires to be delivered to him, shall be borne by that purchaser.

(5) On a sale of any property in lots, a purchaser of two or more lots, held wholly or partly under the same title, shall not have a right to more than one abstract of the common title, except at his own expense.

(6) Recitals, statements, and descriptions of facts, matters, and parties contained in deeds, instruments, Acts of Parliament, or statutory declarations, twenty years old at the date of the contract, shall, unless and except so far as they may be proved to be inaccurate, be taken to be sufficient evidence of the truth of such facts, matters, and descriptions.

(7) The inability of a vendor to furnish a purchaser with an acknowledgment of his right to production and delivery of copies of documents of title or with a legal covenant to produce and furnish copies of documents of title shall not be an objection to title in case the purchaser will, on the completion of the contract, have an equitable right to the production of such documents.

(8) Such acknowledgments of the right of production or covenants for production and such undertakings or covenants for safe custody of documents as the purchaser can and does require shall be furnished or made at his expense, and the vendor shall bear the expense of perusal and execution on behalf of and by himself, and on behalf of and by necessary parties other than the purchaser.

(9) A vendor shall be entitled to retain documents of title where—

(a) he retains any part of the land to which the documents relate; or

(b) the document consists of a trust instrument or other instrument creating a trust which is still subsisting, or an instrument relating to the appointment or discharge of a trustee of a subsisting trust.

(10) This section applies to contracts for sale made before or after the commencement of this Act, and applies to contracts for exchange in like manner as to contracts for sale, except that it applies only to contracts for exchange made after such commencement:

Provided that this section shall apply subject to any stipulation or contrary intention expressed in the contract.

(11) Nothing in this section shall be construed as binding a purchaser to complete his purchase in any case where, on a contract made independently of this section, and containing stipulations similar to the provisions of this section, or any of them, specific performance of the contract would not be enforced against him by the court.

[295]

46 Forms of contracts and conditions of sale

The Lord Chancellor may from time to time prescribe and publish forms of contracts and conditions of sale of land, and the forms so prescribed shall, subject to any modification, or any stipulation or intention to the contrary, expressed in the correspondence, apply to contracts by correspondence, and may, but only by express reference thereto, be made to apply to any other cases for which the forms are made available.

[296]

47 Application of insurance money on completion of a sale or exchange

(1) Where after the date of any contract for sale or exchange of property, money becomes payable under any policy of insurance maintained by the vendor in respect of any damage to or destruction of property included in the contract, the money shall, on completion of the contract, be held or receivable by the vendor on behalf of the purchaser and paid by the vendor to the purchaser on completion of the sale or exchange, or so soon thereafter as the same shall be received by the vendor.

(2) This section applies only to contracts made after the commencement of this Act, and has effect subject to—

(a) any stipulation to the contrary contained in the contract,
(b) any requisite consents of the insurers,
(c) the payment by the purchaser of the proportionate part of the premium from the date of the contract.

(3) This section applies to a sale or exchange by an order of the court, as if—

(a) for references to the "vendor" there were substituted references to the "person bound by the order";
(b) for the reference to the completion of the contract there were substituted a reference to the payment of the purchase or equality money (if any) into court;
(c) for the reference to the date of the contract there were substituted a reference to the time when the contract becomes binding.

[297]

48 Stipulations preventing a purchaser, lessee, or underlessee from employing his own solicitor to be void

(1) Any stipulation made on the sale of any interest in land after the commencement of this Act to the effect that the conveyance to, or the registration of the title of, the purchaser shall be prepared or carried out at the expense of the purchaser by a solicitor appointed by or acting for the vendor, and any stipulation which might restrict a purchaser in the selection of a solicitor to act on his behalf in relation to any interest in land agreed to be purchased, shall be void; and, if a sale is effected by demise or subdemise, then, for the purposes of this subsection, the instrument required for giving effect to the transaction shall be deemed to be a conveyance:

Provided that nothing in this subsection shall affect any right reserved to a vendor to furnish a form of conveyance to a purchaser from which the draft can be prepared, or to charge a reasonable fee therefor, or, where a perpetual rentcharge is to be reserved as the only consideration in money or money's worth, the right of a vendor to stipulate that the draft conveyance is to be prepared by his solicitor at the expense of the purchaser.

(2) Any covenant or stipulation contained in, or entered into with reference to any lease or underlease made before or after the commencement of this Act—

(a) whereby the right of preparing, at the expense of a purchaser, any conveyance of the estate or interest of the lessee or underlessee in the demised premises or in any part thereof, or of otherwise carrying out, at the expense of the purchaser, any dealing with such estate or interest, is expressed to be reserved to or vested in the lessor or underlessor or his solicitor; or

(b) which in any way restricts the right of the purchaser to have such conveyance carried out on his behalf by a solicitor appointed by him;

shall be void:

Provided that, where any covenant or stipulation is rendered void by this subsection, there shall be implied in lieu thereof a covenant or stipulation that the lessee or underlessee shall register with the lessor or his solicitor within six months from the date thereof, or as soon after the expiration of that period as may be practicable, all conveyances and devolutions (including probates or letters of administration) affecting the lease or underlease and pay a fee of one guinea in respect of each registration, and the power of entry (if any) on breach of any covenant contained in the lease or underlease shall apply and extend to the breach of any covenant so to be implied.

(3) Save where a sale is effected by demise or subdemise, this section does not affect the law relating to the preparation of a lease or underlease or the draft thereof.

(4) In this section "lease" and "underlease" include any agreement therefor or other tenancy, and "lessee" and "underlessee" and "lessor" and "underlessor" have corresponding meanings.

[298]

NOTES

Modification: modified by the Administration of Justice Act 1985, ss 9, 34(2), Sch 2, para 37, and the Building Societies Act 1986, s 124, Sch 21, paras 9, 12. References to solicitors etc modified to include references to bodies recognised under the Administration of Justice Act 1985, s 9, by the Solicitors' Incorporated Practices Order 1991, SI 1991/2684, arts 4, 5, Sch 1.

49 Applications to the court by vendor and purchaser

(1) A vendor or purchaser of any interest in land, or their representatives respectively, may apply in a summary way to the court, in respect of any requisitions or objections, or any claim for compensation, or any other question arising out of or connected with the contract (not being a question affecting the existence or validity of the contract), and the court may make such order upon the application as to the court may appear just, and may order how and by whom all or any of the costs of and incident to the application are to be borne and paid.

(2) Where the court refuses to grant specific performance of a contract, or in any action for the return of a deposit, the court may, if it thinks fit, order the repayment of any deposit.

(3) This section applies to a contract for the sale or exchange of any interest in land.

[(4) The county court has jurisdiction under this section where the land which is to be dealt with in the court does not exceed [£30,000] in capital value …]

[299]

NOTES

Sub-s (4): inserted by the County Courts Act 1984, s 148(1), Sch 2, para 2; sum in square brackets substituted and words omitted repealed by SI 1991/724, art 2(3)(a), (8), Schedule, Pt I.

50 Discharge of incumbrances by the court on sales or exchanges

(1) Where land subject to any incumbrance, whether immediately realisable or payable or not, is sold or exchanged by the court, or out of court, the court may, if it thinks fit, on the application of any party to the sale or exchange, direct or allow payment into court of such sum as is hereinafter mentioned, that is to say—

(a) in the case of an annual sum charged on the land, or of a capital sum charged on a determinable interest in the land, the sum to be paid into court shall be of such amount as, when invested in Government securities, the court considers will be sufficient, by means of the dividends thereof, to keep down or otherwise provide for that charge; and

(b) in any other case of capital money charged on the land, the sum to be paid into court shall be of an amount sufficient to meet the incumbrance and any interest due thereon;

but in either case there shall also be paid into court such additional amount as the court considers will be sufficient to meet the contingency of further costs, expenses and interests, and any other contingency, except depreciation of investments, not exceeding one-tenth part of the original amount to be paid in, unless the court for special reason thinks fit to require a larger additional amount.

(2) Thereupon, the court may, if it thinks fit, and either after or without any notice to the incumbrancer, as the court thinks fit, declare the land to be freed from the incumbrance, and make any order for conveyance, or vesting order, proper for giving effect to the sale or exchange, and give directions for the retention and investment of the money in court and for the payment or application of the income thereof.

(3) The court may declare all other land, if any, affected by the incumbrance (besides the land sold or exchanged) to be freed from the incumbrance, and this power may be exercised either after

or without notice to the incumbrancer, and notwithstanding that on a previous occasion an order, relating to the same incumbrance, has been made by the court which was confined to the land then sold or exchanged.

(4) On any application under this section the court may, if it thinks fit, as respects any vendor or purchaser, dispense with the service of any notice which would otherwise be required to be served on the vendor or purchaser.

(5) After notice served on the persons interested in or entitled to the money or fund in court, the court may direct payment or transfer thereof to the persons entitled to receive or give a discharge for the same, and generally may give directions respecting the application or distribution of the capital or income thereof.

(6) This section applies to sales or exchanges whether made before or after the commencement of this Act, and to incumbrances whether created by statute or otherwise.

[300]

Conveyances and other Instruments

51 Lands lie in grant only

(1) All lands and all interests therein lie in grant and are incapable of being conveyed by livery or livery and seisin, or by feoffment, or by bargain and sale; and a conveyance of an interest in land may operate to pass the possession or right to possession thereof, without actual entry, but subject to all prior rights thereto.

(2) The use of the word grant is not necessary to convey land or to create any interest therein.

[301]

52 Conveyances to be by deed

(1) All conveyances of land or of any interest therein are void for the purpose of conveying or creating a legal estate unless made by deed.

(2) This section does not apply to—

(a) assents by a personal representative;

(b) disclaimers made in accordance with [sections 178 to 180 or sections 315 to 319 of the Insolvency Act 1986] or not required to be evidenced in writing;

(c) surrenders by operation of law, including surrenders which may, by law, be effected without writing;

(d) leases or tenancies or other assurances not required by law to be made in writing;

(e) receipts [other than those falling within section 115 below];

(f) vesting orders of the court or other competent authority;

(g) conveyances taking effect by operation of law.

[302]

NOTES

Sub-s (2): words in square brackets in para (b) substituted by the Insolvency Act 1986, s 439(2), Sch 14; words in square brackets in para (e) substituted by the Law of Property (Miscellaneous Provisions) Act 1989, s 1, Sch 1, para 2.

53 Instruments required to be in writing

(1) Subject to the provisions hereinafter contained with respect to the creation of interests in land by parol—

(a) no interest in land can be created or disposed of except by writing signed by the person creating or conveying the same, or by his agent thereunto lawfully authorised in writing, or by will, or by operation of law;

(b) a declaration of trust respecting any land or any interest therein must be manifested and proved by some writing signed by some person who is able to declare such trust or by his will;

(c) a disposition of an equitable interest or trust subsisting at the time of the disposition, must be in writing signed by the person disposing of the same, or by his agent thereunto lawfully authorised in writing or by will.

(2) This section does not affect the creation or operation of resulting, implied or constructive trusts.

[303]

NOTES

Disapplication: sub-s (1)(c) does not apply to any transfer of title to uncertificated units of a security by means of a relevant system and any disposition or assignment of an interest in uncertificated units of a security title to which is held by a relevant nominee: see the Uncertificated Securities Regulations 2001, SI 2001/3755, reg 38(5), (6). See also, for the disapplication of sub-s (1)(c) in relation to financial collateral arrangements, the Financial Collateral Arrangements (No 2) Regulations 2003, SI 2003/3226, reg 4(2).

54 Creation of interests in land by parol

(1) All interests in land created by parol and not put in writing and signed by the persons so creating the same, or by their agents thereunto lawfully authorised in writing, have, notwithstanding any consideration having been given for the same, the force and effect of interests at will only.

(2) Nothing in the foregoing provisions of this Part of this Act shall affect the creation by parol of leases taking effect in possession for a term not exceeding three years (whether or not the lessee is given power to extend the term) at the best rent which can be reasonably obtained without taking a fine.

[304]

55 Savings in regard to last two sections

Nothing in the last two foregoing sections shall—

(a) invalidate dispositions by will; or
(b) affect any interest validly created before the commencement of this Act; or
(c) affect the right to acquire an interest in land by virtue of taking possession; or
(d) affect the operation of the law relating to part performance.

[305]

56 Persons taking who are not parties and as to indentures

(1) A person may take an immediate or other interest in land or other property, or the benefit of any condition, right of entry, covenant or agreement over or respecting land or other property, although he may not be named as a party to the conveyance or other instrument.

(2) A deed between parties, to effect its objects, has the effect of an indenture though not indented or expressed to be an indenture.

[306]

57 Description of deeds

Any deed, whether or not being an indenture, may be described (at the commencement thereof or otherwise) as a deed simply, or as a conveyance, deed of exchange, vesting deed, trust instrument, settlement, mortgage, charge, transfer of mortgage, appointment, lease or otherwise according to the nature of the transaction intended to be effected.

[307]

58 Provisions as to supplemental instruments

Any instrument (whether executed before or after the commencement of this Act) expressed to be supplemental to a previous instrument, shall, as far as may be, be read and have effect as if the supplemental instrument contained a full recital of the previous instrument, but this section does not operate to give any right to an abstract or production of any such previous instrument, and a purchaser may accept the same evidence that the previous instrument does not affect the title as if it had merely been mentioned in the supplemental instrument.

[308]

59 Conditions and certain covenants not implied

(1) An exchange or other conveyance of land made by deed after the first day of October, eighteen hundred and forty-five, does not imply any condition in law.

(2) The word "give" or "grant" does not, in a deed made after the date last aforesaid, imply any covenant in law, save where otherwise provided by statute.

[309]

60 Abolition of technicalities in regard to conveyances and deeds

(1) A conveyance of freehold land to any person without words of limitation, or any equivalent expression, shall pass to the grantee the fee simple or other the whole interest which the grantor had power to convey in such land, unless a contrary intention appears in the conveyance.

(2) A conveyance of freehold land to a corporation sole by his corporate designation without the word "successors" shall pass to the corporation the fee simple or other the whole interest which the grantor had power to convey in such land, unless a contrary intention appears in the conveyance.

(3) In a voluntary conveyance a resulting trust for the grantor shall not be implied merely by reason that the property is not expressed to be conveyed for the use or benefit of the grantee.

(4) The foregoing provisions of this section apply only to conveyances and deeds executed after the commencement of this Act:

Provided that in a deed executed after the thirty-first day of December, eighteen hundred and eighty-one, it is sufficient—

(a) In the limitation of an estate in fee simple, to use the words "in fee simple", without the word "heirs";

(b), (c) ...

[310]

NOTES

Sub-s (4): paras (b), (c) repealed by the Trusts of Land and Appointment of Trustees Act 1996, s 25(2), Sch 4; for savings in relation to entailed interests created before the commencement of that Act, and savings consequential upon the abolition of the doctrine of conversion, see s 25(4), (5) thereof.

61 Construction of expressions used in deeds and other instruments

In all deeds, contracts, wills, orders and other instruments executed, made or coming into operation after the commencement of this Act, unless the context otherwise requires—

(a) "Month" means calendar month;
(b) "Person" includes a corporation;
(c) The singular includes the plural and vice versa;
(d) The masculine includes the feminine and vice versa.

[311]

62 General words implied in conveyances

(1) A conveyance of land shall be deemed to include and shall by virtue of this Act operate to convey, with the land, all buildings, erections, fixtures, commons, hedges, ditches, fences, ways, waters, watercourses, liberties, privileges, easements, rights, and advantages whatsoever, appertaining or reputed to appertain to the land, or any part thereof, or, at the time of conveyance, demised, occupied, or enjoyed with or reputed or known as part or parcel of or appurtenant to the land or any part thereof.

(2) A conveyance of land, having houses or other buildings thereon, shall be deemed to include and shall by virtue of this Act operate to convey, with the land, houses, or other buildings, all outhouses, erections, fixtures, cellars, areas, courts, courtyards, cisterns, sewers, gutters, drains, ways, passages, lights, watercourses, liberties, privileges, easements, rights, and advantages whatsoever, appertaining or reputed to appertain to the land, houses, or other buildings conveyed, or any of them, or any part thereof, or, at the time of conveyance, demised, occupied, or enjoyed with, or reputed or known as part or parcel of or appurtenant to, the land, houses, other buildings conveyed, or any of them, or any part thereof.

(3) A conveyance of a manor shall be deemed to include and shall by virtue of this Act operate to convey, with the manor, all pastures, feedings, wastes, warrens, commons, mines, minerals, quarries, furzes, trees, woods, underwoods, coppices, and the ground and soil thereof, fishings, fisheries, fowlings, courts leet, courts baron, and other courts, view of frankpledge and all that to view of frankpledge doth belong, mills, mulctures, customs, tolls, duties, reliefs, heriots, fines, sums of money, amerciaments, waifs, estrays, chief-rents, quitrents, rentscharge, rents seck, rents of assize, fee farm rents, services, royalties, jurisdictions, franchises, liberties, privileges, easements, profits, advantages, rights, emoluments, and hereditaments whatsoever, to the manor appertaining or reputed to appertain, or, at the time of conveyance, demised, occupied, or enjoyed with the same, or reputed or known as part, parcel, or member thereof.

For the purposes of this subsection the right to compensation for manorial incidents on the extinguishment thereof shall be deemed to be a right appertaining to the manor.

(4) This section applies only if and as far as a contrary intention is not expressed in the conveyance, and has effect subject to the terms of the conveyance and to the provisions therein contained.

(5) This section shall not be construed as giving to any person a better title to any property, right, or thing in this section mentioned than the title which the conveyance gives to him to the land or manor expressed to be conveyed, or as conveying to him any property, right, or thing in this section mentioned, further or otherwise than as the same could have been conveyed to him by the conveying parties.

(6) This section applies to conveyances made after the thirty-first day of December, eighteen hundred and eighty-one.

[312]

63 All estate clause implied

(1) .Every conveyance is effectual to pass all the estate, right, title, interest, claim, and demand which the conveying parties respectively have, in, to, or on the property conveyed, or expressed or intended so to be, or which they respectively have power to convey in, to, or on the same.

(2) This section applies only if and as far as a contrary intention is not expressed in the conveyance, and has effect subject to the terms of the conveyance and to the provisions therein contained.

(3) This section applies to conveyances made after the thirty-first day of December, eighteen hundred and eighty-one.

[313]

64 Production and safe custody of documents

(1) Where a person retains possession of documents, and gives to another an acknowledgment in writing of the right of that other to production of those documents, and to delivery of copies thereof (in this section called an acknowledgment), that acknowledgment shall have effect as in this section provided.

(2) An acknowledgment shall bind the documents to which it relates in the possession or under the control of the person who retains them, and in the possession or under the control of every other person having possession or control thereof from time to time, but shall bind each individual possessor or person as long only as he has possession or control thereof; and every person so having possession or control from time to time shall be bound specifically to perform the obligations imposed under this section by an acknowledgment, unless prevented from so doing by fire or other inevitable accident.

(3) The obligations imposed under this section by an acknowledgment are to be performed from time to time at the request in writing of the person to whom an acknowledgment is given, or of any person, not being a lessee at a rent, having or claiming any estate, interest, or right through or under that person, or otherwise becoming through or under that person interested in or affected by the terms of any document to which the acknowledgment relates.

(4) The obligations imposed under this section by an acknowledgment are—

(i) An obligation to produce the documents or any of them at all reasonable times for the purpose of inspection, and of comparison with abstracts or copies thereof, by the person entitled to request production or by any person by him authorised in writing; and

(ii) An obligation to produce the documents or any of them at any trial, hearing, or examination in any court, or in the execution of any commission, or elsewhere in the United Kingdom, on any occasion on which production may properly be required, for proving or supporting the title or claim of the person entitled to request production, or for any other purpose relative to that title or claim; and

(iii) An obligation to deliver to the person entitled to request the same true copies or extracts, attested or unattested, of or from the documents or any of them.

(5) All costs and expenses of or incidental to the specific performance of any obligation imposed under this section by an acknowledgment shall be paid by the person requesting performance.

(6) An acknowledgment shall not confer any right to damages for loss or destruction of, or injury to, the documents to which it relates, from whatever cause arising.

(7) Any person claiming to be entitled to the benefit of an acknowledgment may apply to the court for an order directing the production of the documents to which it relates, or any of them, or the delivery of copies of or extracts from those documents or any of them to him, or some person on his behalf; and the court may, if it thinks fit, order production, or production and delivery, accordingly, and may give directions respecting the time, place, terms, and mode of production or delivery, and may make such order as it thinks fit respecting the costs of the application, or any other matter connected with the application.

(8) An acknowledgment shall by virtue of this Act satisfy any liability to give a covenant for production and delivery of copies of or extracts from documents.

(9) Where a person retains possession of documents and gives to another an undertaking in writing for safe custody thereof, that undertaking shall impose on the person giving it, and on every person having possession or control of the documents from time to time, but on each individual possessor or person as long only as he has possession or control thereof, an obligation to keep the document safe, whole, uncancelled, and undefaced, unless prevented from so doing by fire or other inevitable accident.

(10) Any person claiming to be entitled to the benefit of such an undertaking may apply to the court to assess damages for any loss or destruction of, or injury to, the documents or any of them, and the court may, if it thinks fit, direct an inquiry respecting the amount of damages, and order payment thereof by the person liable, and may make such order as it thinks fit respecting the costs of the application, or any other matter connected with the application.

(11) An undertaking for safe custody of documents shall by virtue of this Act satisfy any liability to give a covenant for safe custody of documents.

(12) The rights conferred by an acknowledgment or an undertaking under this section shall be in addition to all such other rights relative to the production, or inspection, or the obtaining of copies of documents, as are not, by virtue of this Act, satisfied by the giving of the acknowledgment or undertaking, and shall have effect subject to the terms of the acknowledgment or undertaking, and to any provisions therein contained.

(13) This section applies only if and as far as a contrary intention is not expressed in the acknowledgment or undertaking.

(14) This section applies to an acknowledgment or undertaking given, or a liability respecting documents incurred, after the thirty-first day of December, eighteen hundred and eighty-one.

[314]

NOTES

See further: in relation to the transfer of property by scheme, the Water Industry Act 1991, Sch 2, para 3. See also, the Energy Act 2004, s 159(2), Sch 21, para 7(6)(b) which provides that where a person is entitled, in consequence of an energy transfer scheme, to possession of a document relating in part to the title to land or other property in England and Wales, or to the management of such land or other property this section shall have effect accordingly, and on the basis that the acknowledgement did not contain an expression of contrary intention.

65 Reservation of legal estates

(1) A reservation of a legal estate shall operate at law without any execution of the conveyance by the grantee of the legal estate out of which the reservation is made, or any regrant by him, so as to create the legal estate reserved, and so as to vest the same in possession in the person (whether being the grantor or not) for whose benefit the reservation is made.

(2) A conveyance of a legal estate expressed to be made subject to another legal estate not in existence immediately before the date of the conveyance, shall operate as a reservation unless a contrary intention appears.

(3) This section applies only to reservations made after the commencement of this Act.

[315]

66 Confirmation of past transactions

(1) A deed containing a declaration by the estate owner that his estate shall go and devolve in such a manner as may be requisite for confirming any interests intended to affect his estate and capable under this Act of subsisting as legal estates which, at some prior date, were expressed to have been transferred or created, and any dealings therewith which would have been legal if those interests had been legally and validly transferred or created, shall, to the extent of the estate of the estate owner, but without prejudice to the restrictions imposed by this Act in the case of mortgages, operate to give legal effect to the interests so expressed to have been transferred or created and to the subsequent dealings aforesaid.

(2) The powers conferred by this section may be exercised by a tenant for life or statutory owner, [trustee of land] or a personal representative (being in each case an estate owner) as well as by an absolute owner, but if exercised by any person, other than an absolute owner, only with the leave of the court.

(3) This section applies only to deeds containing such a declaration as aforesaid if executed after the commencement of this Act.

[(4) The county court has jurisdiction under this section where the land which is to be dealt with in the court does not exceed [£30,000] in capital value …]

[316]

NOTES

Sub-s (2): words substituted by the Trusts of Land and Appointment of Trustees Act 1996, s 25(1), Sch 3, para 4(12); for savings in relation to entailed interests created before the commencement of that Act, and savings consequential upon the abolition of the doctrine of conversion, see s 25(4), (5) thereof.

Sub-s (4): inserted by the County Courts Act 1984, s 148(1), Sch 2, para 2; sum in square brackets substituted, and words omitted repealed, by SI 1991/724, art 2(3)(a), (8), Schedule, Pt I.

67 Receipt in deed sufficient

(1) A receipt for consideration money or securities in the body of a deed shall be a sufficient discharge for the same to the person paying or delivering the same, without any further receipt for the same being indorsed on the deed.

(2) This section applies to deeds executed after the thirty-first day of December, eighteen hundred and eighty-one.

[317]

68 Receipt in deed or indorsed evidence

(1) A receipt for consideration money or other consideration in the body of a deed or indorsed thereon shall, in favour of a subsequent purchaser, not having notice that the money or other consideration thereby acknowledged to be received was not in fact paid or given, wholly or in part, be sufficient evidence of the payment or giving of the whole amount thereof.

(2) This section applies to deeds executed after the thirty-first day of December, eighteen hundred and eighty-one.

[318]

69 Receipt in deed or indorsed authority for payment to solicitor

(1) Where a solicitor produces a deed, having in the body thereof or indorsed thereon a receipt for consideration money or other consideration, the deed being executed, or the indorsed receipt being signed, by the person entitled to give a receipt for that consideration, the deed shall be a sufficient authority to the person liable to pay or give the same for his paying or giving the same to the solicitor, without the solicitor producing any separate or other direction or authority in that behalf from the person who executed or signed the deed or receipt.

(2) This section applies whether the consideration was paid or given before or after the commencement of this Act.

[319]

NOTES

Modification: references to solicitors etc modified to include references to bodies recognised under the Administration of Justice Act 1985, s 9, by the Solicitors' Incorporated Practices Order 1991, SI 1991/2684, arts 4, 5, Sch 1.

70 Partial release of security from rentcharge

(1) A release from a rentcharge of part of the land charged therewith does not extinguish the whole rentcharge, but operates only to bar the right to recover any part of the rentcharge out of the land released, without prejudice to the rights of any persons interested in the land remaining unreleased, and not concurring in or confirming the release.

(2) This section applies to releases made after the twelfth day of August, eighteen hundred and fifty-nine.

[320]

71 Release of part of land affected from a judgment

(1) A release from a judgment (including any writ or order imposing a charge) of part of any land charged therewith does not affect the validity of the judgment as respects any land not specifically released.

(2) This section operates without prejudice to the rights of any persons interested in the property remaining unreleased and not concurring in or confirming the release.

(3) This section applies to releases made after the twelfth day of August, eighteen hundred and fifty-nine.

[321]

72 Conveyances by a person to himself, etc

(1) In conveyances made after the twelfth day of August, eighteen hundred and fifty-nine, personal property, including chattels real, may be conveyed by a person to himself jointly with another person by the like means by which it might be conveyed by him to another person.

(2) In conveyances made after the thirty-first day of December, eighteen hundred and eighty-one, freehold land, or a thing in action, may be conveyed by a person to himself jointly with another person, by the like means by which it might be conveyed by him to another person; and may, in like manner, be conveyed by a husband to his wife, and by a wife to her husband, alone or jointly with another person.

(3) After the commencement of this Act a person may convey land to or vest land in himself.

(4) Two or more persons (whether or not being trustees or personal representatives) may convey, and shall be deemed always to have been capable of conveying, any property vested in them to any one or more of themselves in like manner as they could have conveyed such property to a third party; provided that if the persons in whose favour the conveyance is made are, by reason of any fiduciary relationship or otherwise, precluded from validly carrying out the transaction, the conveyance shall be liable to be set aside.

73 (*Repealed by the Law of Property* (*Miscellaneous Provisions*) *Act 1989, s 4, Sch 2.*)

74 Execution of instruments by or on behalf of corporations

[(1) In favour of a purchaser an instrument shall be deemed to have been duly executed by a corporation aggregate if a seal purporting to be the corporation's seal purports to be affixed to the instrument in the presence of and attested by—

(a) two members of the board of directors, council or other governing body of the corporation, or

(b) one such member and the clerk, secretary or other permanent officer of the corporation or his deputy.]

[(1A) Subsection (1) of this section applies in the case of an instrument purporting to have been executed by a corporation aggregate in the name or on behalf of another person whether or not that person is also a corporation aggregate.]

[(1B) For the purposes of subsection (1) of this section, a seal purports to be affixed in the presence of and attested by an officer of the corporation, in the case of an officer which is not an individual, if it is affixed in the presence of and attested by an individual authorised by the officer to attest on its behalf.]

(2) The board of directors, council or other governing body of a corporation aggregate may, by resolution or otherwise, appoint an agent either generally or in any particular case, to execute on behalf of the corporation any agreement or other instrument [which is not a deed] in relation to any matter within the powers of the corporation.

(3) Where a person is authorised under a power of attorney or under any statutory or other power to convey any interest in property in the name or on behalf of a corporation sole or aggregate, he may as attorney execute the conveyance by signing the name of the corporation in the presence of at least one witness [who attests the signature], … and such execution shall take effect and be valid in like manner as if the corporation had executed the conveyance.

(4) Where a corporation aggregate is authorised under a power of attorney or under any statutory or other power to convey any interest in property in the name or on behalf of any other person (including another corporation), an officer appointed for that purpose by the board of directors, council or other governing body of the corporation by resolution or otherwise, may execute the [instrument by signing it] in the name of such other person [or, if the instrument is to be a deed, by so signing it in the presence of a witness who attests the signature]; and where an instrument appears to be executed by an officer so appointed, then in favour of a purchaser the instrument shall be deemed to have been executed by an officer duly authorised.

(5) The foregoing provisions of this section apply to transactions wherever effected, but only to deeds and instruments executed after the commencement of this Act, except that, in the case of powers or appointments of an agent or officer, they apply whether the power was conferred or the appointment was made before or after the commencement of this Act or by this Act.

(6) Notwithstanding anything contained in this section, any mode of execution or attestation authorised by law or by practice or by the statute, charter, *memorandum or articles* [articles], deed of settlement or other instrument constituting the corporation or regulating the affairs thereof, shall (in addition to the modes authorised by this section) be as effectual as if this section had not been passed.

[322]

NOTES

Sub-s (1): substituted by SI 2005/1906, art 3, in relation to instruments executed on or after 15 September 2005.

Sub-ss (1A), (1B): inserted by SI 2005/1906, arts 7(1), 10(1), Sch 1, paras 1, 2, in relation to instruments executed on or after 15 September 2005.

Sub-s (2): words in square brackets substituted by the Law of Property (Miscellaneous Provisions) Act 1989, s 1, Sch 1, para 3.

Sub-s (3): words in square brackets inserted by SI 2005/1906, art 10(1), Sch 1, paras 1, 3, in relation to instruments executed on or after 15 September 2005; words omitted repealed by the Law of Property (Miscellaneous Provisions) Act 1989, s 4, Sch 2.

Sub-s (4): words in square brackets substituted by SI 2005/1906, art 10(1), Sch 1, paras 1, 4, in relation to instruments executed on or after 15 September 2005.

Sub-s (6): words in italics substituted for subsequent word in square brackets by SI 2009/1941, art 2(1), Sch 1, para 4, as from 1 October 2009.

[74A Execution of instrument as a deed

(1) An instrument is validly executed by a corporation aggregate as a deed for the purposes of section 1(2)(b) of the Law of Property (Miscellaneous Provisions) Act 1989, if and only if—

(a) it is duly executed by the corporation, and
(b) it is delivered as a deed.

(2) An instrument shall be presumed to be delivered for the purposes of subsection (1)(b) of this section upon its being executed, unless a contrary intention is proved.]

[323]

NOTES

Commencement: 15 September 2005, in relation to instruments executed on or after that date.
Inserted by SI 2005/1906, art 4.

75 Rights of purchaser as to execution

(1) On a sale, the purchaser shall not be entitled to require that the conveyance to him be executed in his presence, or in that of his solicitor, as such; but shall be entitled to have, at his own cost, the execution of the conveyance attested by some person appointed by him, who may, if he thinks fit, be his solicitor.

(2) This section applies to sales made after the thirty-first day of December, eighteen hundred and eighty-one.

[324]

NOTES

See further: the Administration of Justice Act 1985, s 34(1).

Covenants

76 (*Repealed by the Law of Property* (*Miscellaneous Provisions*) *Act 1994, ss 10*(*1*), *21*(*2*), (*3*), *Sch 2, as regards dispositions of property made on or after 1 July 1995.*)

77 Implied covenants in conveyance subject to rents

(1) In addition to the covenants implied under [Part I of the Law of Property (Miscellaneous Provisions) Act 1994], there shall in the several cases in this section mentioned, be deemed to be included and implied, a covenant to the effect in this section stated, by and with such persons as are hereinafter mentioned, that is to say—

(A) In a conveyance for valuable consideration, other than a mortgage, of the entirety of the land affected by a rentcharge, a covenant by the grantee or joint and several covenants by the grantees, if more than one, with the conveying parties and with each of them, if more than one, in the terms set out in Part VII of the Second Schedule to this Act. Where a rentcharge has been apportioned in respect of any land, with the consent of the owner of the rentcharge, the covenants in this paragraph shall be implied in the conveyance of that land in like manner as if the apportioned rentcharge were the rentcharge referred to, and the document creating the rentcharge related solely to that land:

(B) In a conveyance for valuable consideration, other than a mortgage, of part of land affected by a rentcharge, subject to a part of that rentcharge which has been or is by that conveyance apportioned (but in either case without the consent of the owner of the rentcharge) in respect of the land conveyed:—

(i) A covenant by the grantee of the land or joint and several covenants by the grantees, if more than one, with the conveying parties and with each of them, if more than one, in the terms set out in paragraph (i) of Part VIII of the Second Schedule to this Act;

(ii) A covenant by a person who conveys or is expressed to convey as beneficial owner, or joint and several covenants by the persons who so convey or are expressed to so convey, if at the date of the conveyance any part of the land affected by such rentcharge is retained, with the grantees of the land and with each of them (if more than one) in the terms set out in paragraph (ii) of Part VIII of the Second Schedule to this Act:

(C) *In a conveyance for valuable consideration, other than a mortgage, of the entirety of the land comprised in a lease, for the residue of the term or interest created by the lease, a covenant by the assignee or joint and several covenants by the assignees* (*if more than one*) *with the conveying parties and with each of them* (*if more than one*) *in the terms set out in Part IX of the Second Schedule to this Act. Where a rent has been apportioned in respect of any land, with the consent of the lessor, the covenants in this paragraph shall be implied in the conveyance of that land in like manner as if the apportioned rent were the original rent reserved, and the lease related solely to that land:*

(D) *In a conveyance for valuable consideration, other than a mortgage, of part of the land comprised in a lease, for the residue of the term or interest created by the lease, subject to a part of the rent which has been or is by the conveyance apportioned* (*but in either case without the consent of the lessor*) *in respect of the land conveyed:—*

(i) A covenant by the assignee of the land, or joint and several covenants by the assignees, if more than one, with the conveying parties and with each of them, if more than one, in the terms set out in paragraph (*i*) *of Part X of the Second Schedule to this Act;*

(ii) A covenant by a person who conveys or is expressed to convey as beneficial owner, or joint and several covenants by the persons who so convey or are expressed to so convey, if at the date of the conveyance any part of the land comprised in the lease is retained, with the assignees of the land and with each of them (*if more than one*) *in the terms set out in paragraph* (*ii*) *of Part X of the Second Schedule to this Act.*

(2) *Where in a conveyance for valuable consideration, other than a mortgage, part of land affected by a rentcharge, or part of land comprised in a lease is, without the consent of the owner of the rentcharge or of the lessor, as the case may be, expressed to be conveyed—*

(i) *subject to or charged with the entire rent—*

then paragraph (B) (ii) or (D) (i) of the last subsection, as the case may require shall have effect as if the entire rent were the apportioned rent; or

(ii) *discharged or exonerated from the entire rent—*

then paragraph (B) (ii) or (D) (ii) of the last subsection, as the case may require, shall have effect as if the entire rent were the balance of the rent, and the words "other than the covenant to pay the entire rent" had been omitted.

[(2) Where in a conveyance for valuable consideration, other than a mortgage, part of land affected by a rentcharge is, without the consent of the owner of the rentcharge, expressed to be conveyed subject to or charged with the entire rent, paragraph (B)(i) of subsection (1) of this section shall apply as if, in paragraph (i) of Part VIII of the Second Schedule to this Act-

(a) any reference to the apportioned rent were to the entire rent; and

(b) the words "(other than the covenant to pay the entire rent)" were omitted.

(2A) Where in a conveyance for valuable consideration, other than a mortgage, part of land affected by a rentcharge is, without the consent of the owner of the rentcharge, expressed to be conveyed discharged or exonerated from the entire rent, paragraph (B)(ii) of subsection (1) of this section shall apply as if, in paragraph (ii) of Part VIII of the Second Schedule to this Act—

(a) any reference to the balance of the rent were to the entire rent; and

(b) the words ", other than the covenant to pay the entire rent," were omitted.]

(3) In this section "conveyance" does not include a demise by way of lease at a rent.

(4) Any covenant which would be implied under this section by reason of a person conveying or being expressed to convey as beneficial owner may, by express reference to this section, be implied, with or without variation, in a conveyance, whether or not for valuable consideration, by a person who conveys or is expressed to convey as settlor, or as trustee, or as mortgagee, or as personal representative of a deceased person,... or under an order of the court.

(5) The benefit of a covenant implied as aforesaid shall be annexed and incident to, and shall go with, the estate or interest of the implied covenantee, and shall be capable of being enforced by every person in whom that estate or interest is, for the whole or any part thereof, from time to time vested.

(6) A covenant implied as aforesaid may be varied or extended by deed, and, as so varied or extended, shall, as far as may be, operate in the like manner, and with all the like incidents, effects and consequences, as if such variations or extensions were directed in this section to be implied.

(7) In particular any covenant implied under this section may be extended by providing that—

(a) the land conveyed; or

(b) the part of the land affected by the rentcharge which remains vested in the covenantor; *or*

(c) *the part of the land demised which remains vested in the covenantor;*

shall, as the case may require, stand charged with the payment of all money which may become payable under the implied covenant.

(8) This section applies only to conveyances made after the commencement of this Act.

[325]

NOTES

Sub-s (1): words in square brackets substituted by the Law of Property (Miscellaneous Provisions) Act 1994, s 21(1), Sch 1, para 1.

Sub-s (1): paras (C), (D) repealed by the Landlord and Tenant (Covenants) Act 1995, ss 14(a), 30(2), Sch 2, in relation to new tenancies as defined by s 1(3) of the 1995 Act at **[1563]**.

Sub-s (2): text in italics substituted, by subsequent sub-ss (2), (2A) in square brackets, by the Landlord and Tenant (Covenants) Act 1995, s 30(1), (3)(a), Sch 1, para 2, in relation to new tenancies as defined by s 1(3) of the 1995 Act at **[1563]**.

Sub-s (4): words omitted repealed by the Mental Health Act 1959, s 149(2), Sch 8, Pt I.

Sub-s (7): para (c) and the word "or" immediately preceding it repealed by the Landlord and Tenant (Covenants) Act 1995, s 30(2), Sch 2, in relation to new tenancies as defined by s 1(3) of the 1995 Act at **[1563]**.

78 Benefit of covenants relating to land

(1) A covenant relating to any land of the covenantee shall be deemed to be made with the covenantee and his successors in title and the persons deriving title under him or them, and shall have effect as if such successors and other persons were expressed.

For the purposes of this subsection in connexion with covenants restrictive of the user of land "successors in title" shall be deemed to include the owners and occupiers for the time being of the land of the covenantee intended to be benefited.

(2) This section applies to covenants made after the commencement of this Act, but the repeal of section fifty-eight of the Conveyancing Act 1881 does not affect the operation of covenants to which that section applied.

[326]

NOTES

Disapplication: this section does not apply in relation to new tenancies as defined by the Landlord and Tenant (Covenants) Act 1995, ss 1(3), 28(1); see s 30(4) thereof at **[1590]**.

79 Burden of covenants relating to land

(1) A covenant relating to any land of a covenantor or capable of being bound by him, shall, unless a contrary intention is expressed, be deemed to be made by the covenantor on behalf of himself his successors in title and the persons deriving title under him or them, and, subject as aforesaid, shall have effect as if such successors and other persons were expressed.

This subsection extends to a covenant to do some act relating to the land, notwithstanding that the subject-matter may not be in existence when the covenant is made.

(2) For the purposes of this section in connexion with covenants restrictive of the user of land "successors in title" shall be deemed to include the owners and occupiers for the time being of such land.

(3) This section applies only to covenants made after the commencement of this Act.

[327]

NOTES

Disapplication: this section does not apply in relation to new tenancies as defined by the Landlord and Tenant (Covenants) Act 1995, ss 1(3), 28(1); see s 30(4) thereof at **[1590]**.

80 Covenants binding land

(1) A covenant and a bond and an obligation or contract [made under seal after 31st December 1881 but before the coming into force of section 1 of the Law of Property (Miscellaneous Provisions) Act 1989 or executed as a deed in accordance with that section after its coming into force], binds the real estate as well as the personal estate of the person making the same if and so far as a contrary intention is not expressed in the covenant, bond, obligation, or contract.

This subsection extends to a covenant implied by virtue of this Act.

(2) Every covenant running with the land, whether entered into before or after the commencement of this Act, shall take effect in accordance with any statutory enactment affecting the devolution of the land, and accordingly the benefit or burden of every such covenant shall vest in or bind the persons who by virtue of any such enactment or otherwise succeed to the title of the covenantee or the covenantor, as the case may be.

(3) The benefit of a covenant relating to land entered into after the commencement of this Act may be made to run with the land without the use of any technical expression if the covenant is of such a nature that the benefit could have been made to run with the land before the commencement of this Act.

(4) For the purposes of this section, a covenant runs with the land when the benefit or burden of it, whether at law or in equity, passes to the successors in title of the covenantee or the covenantor, as the case may be.

[328]

NOTES

Sub-s (1): words in square brackets substituted by the Law of Property (Miscellaneous Provisions) Act 1989, s 1, Sch 1, para 4.

81 Effect of covenant with two or more jointly

(1) A covenant, and a contract under seal, and a bond or obligation under seal, made with two or more jointly, to pay money or to make a conveyance, or to do any other act, to them or for their benefit, shall be deemed to include, and shall, by virtue of this Act, imply, an obligation to do the act to, or for the benefit of, the survivor or survivors of them, and to, or for the benefit of, any other person to whom the right to sue on the covenant, contract, bond, or obligation devolves, and where made after the commencement of this Act shall be construed as being also made with each of them.

(2) This section extends to a covenant implied by virtue of this Act.

(3) This section applies only if and as far as a contrary intention is not expressed in the covenant, contract, bond, or obligation, and has effect subject to the covenant, contract, bond, or obligation, and to the provisions therein contained.

(4) Except as otherwise expressly provided, this section applies to a covenant, contract, bond, or obligation made or implied after the thirty-first day of December, eighteen hundred and eighty-one.

[(5) In its application to instruments made after the coming into force of section 1 of the Law of Property (Miscellaneous Provisions) Act 1989 subsection (1) above shall have effect as if for the words "under seal, and a bond or obligation under seal," there were substituted the words "bond or obligation executed as a deed in accordance with section 1 of the Law of Property (Miscellaneous Provisions) Act 1989].

[329]

NOTES

Sub-s (5): inserted by the Law of Property (Miscellaneous Provisions) Act 1989, s 1, Sch 1, para 5.

82 Covenants and agreements entered into by a person with himself and another or others

(1) Any covenant, whether express or implied, or agreement entered into by a person with himself and one or more other persons shall be construed and be capable of being enforced in like manner as if the covenant or agreement had been entered into with the other person or persons alone.

(2) This section applies to covenants or agreements entered into before or after the commencement of this Act, and to covenants implied by statute in the case of a person who conveys or is expressed to convey to himself and one or more other persons, but without prejudice to any order of the court made before such commencement.

[330]

83 Construction of implied covenants

In the construction of a covenant or proviso, or other provision, implied in a deed or assent by virtue of this Act, words importing the singular or plural number, or the masculine gender, shall be read as also importing the plural or singular number, or as extending to females, as the case may require.

[331]

84 Power to discharge or modify restrictive covenants affecting land

[(1) The [Upper Tribunal] shall (without prejudice to any concurrent jurisdiction of the court) have power from time to time, on the application of any person interested in any freehold land affected by any restriction arising under covenant or otherwise as to the user thereof or the building thereon, by order wholly or partially to discharge or modify any such restriction on being satisfied—

(a) that by reason of changes in the character of the property or the neighbourhood or other circumstances of the case which the [Upper Tribunal] may deem material, the restriction ought to be deemed obsolete; or

(aa) that (in a case falling within subsection (1A) below) the continued existence thereof would impede some reasonable user of the land for public or private purposes or, as the case may be, would unless modified so impede such user; or

(b) that the persons of full age and capacity for the time being or from time to time entitled to the benefit of the restriction, whether in respect of estates in fee simple or any lesser estates or interests in the property to which the benefit of the restriction is annexed, have agreed, either expressly or by implication, by their acts or omissions, to the same being discharged or modified; or

(c) that the proposed discharge or modification will not injure the persons entitled to the benefit of the restriction;

and an order discharging or modifying a restriction under this subsection may direct the applicant to pay to any person entitled to the benefit of the restriction such sum by way of consideration as the Tribunal may think it just to award under one, but not both, of the following heads, that is to say, either—

(i) a sum to make up for any loss or disadvantage suffered by that person in consequence of the discharge or modification; or

(ii) a sum to make up for any effect which the restriction had, at the time when it was imposed, in reducing the consideration then received for the land affected by it.

(1A) Subsection (1)(aa) above authorises the discharge or modification of a restriction by reference to its impeding some reasonable user of land in any case in which the [Upper Tribunal] is satisfied that the restriction, in impeding that user, either—

(a) does not secure to persons entitled to the benefit of it any practical benefits of substantial value or advantage to them; or

(b) is contrary to the public interest;

and that money will be an adequate compensation for the loss or disadvantage (if any) which any such person will suffer from the discharge or modification.

(1B) In determining whether a case is one falling within subsection (1A) above, and in determining whether (in any such case or otherwise) a restriction ought to be discharged or modified, the [Upper Tribunal] shall take into account the development plan and any declared or ascertainable pattern for the grant or refusal of planning permissions in the relevant areas, as well as the period at which and context in which the restriction was created or imposed and any other material circumstances.

(1C) It is hereby declared that the power conferred by this section to modify a restriction includes power to add such further provisions restricting the user of or the building on the land affected as appear to the [Upper Tribunal] to be reasonable in view of the relaxation of the existing provisions, and as may be accepted by the applicant; and the [Upper Tribunal] may accordingly refuse to modify a restriction without some such addition.

(2) The court shall have power on the application of any person interested—

(a) to declare whether or not in any particular case any freehold land is, or would in any given event be, affected by a restriction imposed by any instrument; or

(b) to declare what, upon the true construction of any instrument purporting to impose a restriction, is the nature and extent of the restriction thereby imposed and whether the same is, or would in any given event be, enforceable and if so by whom.

Neither subsections (7) and (11) of this section nor, unless the contrary is expressed, any later enactment providing for this section not to apply to any restrictions shall affect the operation of this subsection or the operation for purposes of this subsection of any other provisions of this section.

(3) The [Upper Tribunal] shall, before making any order under this section, direct such enquiries, if any, to be made of any government department or local authority, and such notices, if any, whether by way of advertisement or otherwise, to be given to such of the persons who appear to be entitled to the benefit of the restriction intended to be discharged, modified, or dealt with as, having regard to any enquiries, notices or other proceedings previously made, given or taken, the [Upper Tribunal] may think fit.

(3A) On an application to the [Upper Tribunal] under this section the [Upper Tribunal] shall give any necessary directions as to the persons who are or are not to be admitted (as appearing to be entitled to the benefit of the restriction) to oppose the application, and no appeal shall lie against any such direction; but [Tribunal Procedure Rules] shall make provision whereby, in cases in which there arises on such an application (whether or not in connection with the admission of persons to oppose) any such question as is referred to in subsection (2)(a) or (b) of this section, the proceedings on the application can and, if the rules so provide, shall be suspended to enable the decision of the court to be obtained on that question by an application under that subsection, … or otherwise, as may be provided by those rules or by rules of court.

(5) Any order made under this section shall be binding on all persons, whether ascertained or of full age or capacity or not, then entitled or thereafter capable of becoming entitled to the benefit of any restriction, which is thereby discharged, modified or dealt with, and whether such persons are parties to the proceedings or have been served with notice or not.

(6) An order may be made under this section notwithstanding that any instrument which is alleged to impose the restriction intended to be discharged, modified, or dealt with, may not have been produced to the court or the [Upper Tribunal], and the court or the [Upper Tribunal] may act on such evidence of that instrument as it may think sufficient.

(7) This section applies to restrictions whether subsisting at the commencement of this Act or imposed thereafter, but this section does not apply where the restriction was imposed on the occasion of a disposition made gratuitously or for a nominal consideration for public purposes.

(8) This section applies whether the land affected by the restrictions is registered or not …

(9) Where any proceedings by action or otherwise are taken to enforce a restrictive covenant, any person against whom the proceedings are taken, may in such proceedings apply to the court for an order giving leave to apply to the Lands Tribunal under this section, and staying the proceedings in the meantime.

(11) This section does not apply to restrictions imposed by the Commissioners of Works under any statutory power for the protection of any Royal Park or Garden or to restrictions of a like character imposed upon the occasion of any enfranchisement effected before the commencement of this Act in any manor vested in His Majesty in right of the Crown or the Duchy of Lancaster, nor (subject to subsection (11A) below) to restrictions created or imposed—

(a) for naval, military or air force purposes,

[(b) for civil aviation purposes under the powers of the Air Navigation Act 1920, of section 19 or 23 of the Civil Aviation Act 1949 or of section 30 or 41 of the Civil Aviation Act 1982.]

(11A) Subsection (11) of this section—

(a) shall exclude the application of this section to a restriction falling within subsection (11)(a), and not created or imposed in connection with the use of any land as an aerodrome, only so long as the restriction is enforceable by or on behalf of the Crown; and

(b) shall exclude the application of this section to a restriction falling within subsection (11)(b), or created or imposed in connection with the use of any land as an aerodrome, only so long as the restriction is enforceable by or on behalf of the Crown or any public or international authority.

(12) Where a term of more than forty years is created in land (whether before or after the commencement of this Act) this section shall, after the expiration of twenty-five years of the term, apply to restrictions, affecting such leasehold land in like manner as it would have applied had the land been freehold:

Provided that this subsection shall not apply to mining leases.]

[332]

NOTES

Set out as reprinted with amendments in the Law of Property Act 1969, s 28(1), Sch 3.

Sub-ss (1), (1A), (1B), (1C), (3): words in square brackets, in each place they occur, substituted by SI 2009/1307, art 5(1), (2), Sch 1, para 5(a).

Sub-s (3A): words in square brackets substituted, and words omitted repealed, by SI 2009/1307, art 5(1), (2), Sch 1, para 5(b).

Sub-s (6): words in square brackets substituted by SI 2009/1307, art 5(1), (2), Sch 1, para 5(a).

Sub-s (8): words omitted repealed by the Land Registration Act 2002, ss 133, 135, Sch 11, para 2(1), (5), Sch 13.

Sub-s (9): words in square brackets substituted by SI 2009/1307, art 5(1), (2), Sch 1, para 5(a).

Sub-s (11): para (b) substituted by the Civil Aviation Act 1982, s 109, Sch 15, para 1.

Disapplication: this section is disapplied, in relation to Scotland, to an agreement under the Ancient Monuments and Archaeological Areas Act 1979, s 17: see the Ancient Monuments and Archaeological Areas Act 1979, s 17(7) (as substituted by the Title Conditions (Scotland) Act 2003, s 128(1), Sch 14, para 8).

See further: in relation to the exclusion of the power of the Lands Tribunal to discharge or modify restrictions affecting land in the case of land from which the legal effects of consecration are removed, see the Care of Churches and Ecclesiastical Jurisdiction Measure 1991, s 22(7).

PART III
MORTGAGES, RENTCHARGES, AND POWERS OF ATTORNEY

Mortgages

85 Mode of mortgaging freeholds

(1) A mortgage of an estate in fee simple shall only be capable of being effected at law either by a demise for a term of years absolute, subject to a provision for cesser on redemption, or by a charge by deed expressed to be by way of legal mortgage:

Provided that a first mortgagee shall have the same right to the possession of documents as if his security included the fee simple.

(2) Any purported conveyance of an estate in fee simple by way of mortgage made after the commencement of this Act shall (to the extent of the estate of the mortgagor) operate as a demise of the land to the mortgagee for a term of years absolute, without impeachment for waste, but subject to cesser on redemption, in manner following, namely:—

(a) A first or only mortgagee shall take a term of three thousand years from the date of the mortgage:

(b) A second or subsequent mortgagee shall take a term (commencing from the date of the mortgage) one day longer than the term vested in the first or other mortgagee whose security ranks immediately before that of such second or subsequent mortgagee:

and, in this subsection, any such purported conveyance as aforesaid includes an absolute conveyance with a deed of defeasance and any other assurance which, but for this subsection, would operate in effect to vest the fee simple in a mortgagee subject to redemption.

(3) [Subsection (2) does not apply to registered land, but, subject to that, this section applies whether or not the land is registered land and whether or not] the mortgage is expressed to be made by way of trust for sale or otherwise.

(4) Without prejudice to the provisions of this Act respecting legal and equitable powers, every power to mortgage or to lend money on mortgage of an estate in fee simple shall be construed as a power to mortgage the estate for a term of years absolute, without impeachment for waste, or by a charge by way of legal mortgage or to lend on such security.

[333]

NOTES

Sub-s (3): words in square brackets substituted by the Land Registration Act 2002, s 133, Sch 11, para 2(1), (6).

86 Mode of mortgaging leaseholds

(1) A mortgage of a term of years absolute shall only be capable of being effected at law either by a subdemise for a term of years absolute, less by one day at least than the term vested in the mortgagor, and subject to a provision for cesser on redemption, or by a charge by deed expressed to be by way of legal mortgage; and where a licence to subdemise by way of mortgage is required, such licence shall not be unreasonably refused:

Provided that a first mortgagee shall have the same right to the possession of documents as if his security had been effected by assignment.

(2) Any purported assignment of a term of years absolute by way of mortgage made after the commencement of this Act shall (to the extent of the estate of the mortgagor) operate as a subdemise of the leasehold land to the mortgagee for a term of years absolute, but subject to cesser on redemption, in manner following, namely:—

(a) The term to be taken by a first or only mortgagee shall be ten days less than the term expressed to be assigned:

(b) The term to be taken by a second or subsequent mortgagee shall be one day longer than the term vested in the first or other mortgagee whose security ranks immediately before that of the second or subsequent mortgagee, if the length of the last mentioned term permits, and in any case for a term less by one day at least than the term expressed to be assigned:

and, in this subsection, any such purported assignment as aforesaid includes an absolute assignment with a deed of defeasance and any other assurance which, but for this subsection, would operate in effect to vest the term of the mortgagor in a mortgagee subject to redemption.

(3) [Subsection (2) does not apply to registered land, but, subject to that, this section applies whether or not the land is registered land and whether or not] the mortgage is made by way of sub-mortgage of a term of years absolute, or is expressed to be by way of trust for sale or otherwise.

(4) Without prejudice to the provisions of this Act respecting legal and equitable powers, every power to mortgage for or to lend money on mortgage of a term of years absolute by way of assignment shall be construed as a power to mortgage the term by subdemise for a term of years absolute or by a charge by way of legal mortgage, or to lend on such security.

[334]

NOTES

Sub-s (3): words in square brackets substituted by the Land Registration Act 2002, s 133, Sch 11, para 2(1), (7).

87 Charges by way of legal mortgage

(1) Where a legal mortgage of land is created by a charge by deed expressed to be by way of legal mortgage, the mortgagee shall have the same protection, powers and remedies (including the right to take proceedings to obtain possession from the occupiers and the persons in receipt of rents and profits, or any of them) as if—

(a) where the mortgage is a mortgage of an estate in fee simple, a mortgage term for three thousand years without impeachment of waste had been thereby created in favour of the mortgagee; and

(b) where the mortgage is a mortgage of a term of years absolute, a sub-term less by one day than the term vested in the mortgagor had been thereby created in favour of the mortgagee.

(2) Where an estate vested in a mortgagee immediately before the commencement of this Act has by virtue of this Act been converted into a term of years absolute or sub-term, the mortgagee may, by a declaration in writing to that effect signed by him, convert the mortgage into a charge by way of legal mortgage, and in that case the mortgage term shall be extinguished in the inheritance or in the head term as the case may be, and the mortgagee shall have the same protection, powers and remedies (including the right to take proceedings to obtain possession from the occupiers and the persons in receipt of rents and profits or any of them) as if the mortgage term or sub-term had remained subsisting.

The power conferred by this subsection may be exercised by a mortgagee notwithstanding that he is a trustee or personal representative.

(3) Such declaration shall not affect the priority of the mortgagee or his right to retain possession of documents, nor affect his title to or right over any fixtures or chattels personal comprised in the mortgage.

[(4) Subsection (1) of this section shall not be taken to be affected by section 23(1)(a) of the Land Registration Act 2002 (under which owner's powers in relation to a registered estate do not include power to mortgage by demise or sub-demise).]

[335]

NOTES

Sub-s (4): inserted by the Land Registration Act 2002, s 133, Sch 11, para 2(1), (8).

88 Realisation of freehold mortgages

(1) Where an estate in fee simple has been mortgaged by the creation of a term of years absolute limited thereout or by a charge by way of legal mortgage and the mortgagee sells under his statutory or express power of sale—

(a) the conveyance by him shall operate to vest in the purchaser the fee simple in the land conveyed subject to any legal mortgage having priority to the mortgage in right of which the sale is made and to any money thereby secured, and thereupon;

(b) the mortgage term or the charge by way of legal mortgage and any subsequent mortgage term or charges shall merge or be extinguished as respects the land conveyed;

and such conveyance may, as respects the fee simple, be made in the name of the estate owner in whom it is vested.

(2) Where any such mortgagee obtains an order for foreclosure absolute, the order shall operate to vest the fee simple in him (subject to any legal mortgage having priority to the mortgage in right of which the foreclosure is obtained and to any money thereby secured), and thereupon the mortgage term, if any, shall thereby be merged in the fee simple, and any subsequent mortgage term or charge by way of legal mortgage bound by the order shall thereupon be extinguished.

(3) Where any such mortgagee acquires a title under the Limitation Acts, he, or the persons deriving title under him, may enlarge the mortgage term into a fee simple under the statutory power for that purpose discharged from any legal mortgage affected by the title so acquired, or in the case of a chargee by way of legal mortgage may by deed declare that the fee simple is vested in him discharged as aforesaid, and the same shall vest accordingly.

(4) Where the mortgage includes fixtures or chattels personal any statutory power of sale and any right to foreclose or take possession shall extend to the absolute or other interest therein affected by the charge.

(5) In the case of a sub-mortgage by subdemise of a long term (less a nominal period) itself limited out of an estate in fee simple, the foregoing provisions of this section shall operate as if the derivative term, if any, created by the sub-mortgage had been limited out of the fee simple, and so as to enlarge the principal term and extinguish the derivative term created by the sub-mortgage as aforesaid, and to enable the sub-mortgagee to convey the fee simple or acquire it by foreclosure, enlargement, or otherwise as aforesaid.

(6) This section applies to a mortgage whether created before or after the commencement of this Act, and to a mortgage term created by this Act, but does not operate to confer a better title to the fee simple than would have been acquired if the same had been conveyed by the mortgage (being a valid mortgage) and the restrictions imposed by this Act in regard to the effect and creation of mortgages were not in force, and all prior mortgages (if any) not being merely equitable charges had been created by demise or by charge by way of legal mortgage.

[336]

89 Realisation of leasehold mortgages

(1) Where a term of years absolute has been mortgaged by the creation of another term of years absolute limited thereout or by a charge by way of legal mortgage and the mortgagee sells under his statutory or express power of sale,—

(a) the conveyance by him shall operate to convey to the purchaser not only the mortgage term, if any, but also (unless expressly excepted with the leave of the court) the leasehold reversion affected by the mortgage, subject to any legal mortgage having priority to the mortgage in right of which the sale is made and to any money thereby secured, and thereupon

(b) the mortgage term, or the charge by way of legal mortgage and any subsequent mortgage term or charge, shall merge in such leasehold reversion or be extinguished unless excepted as aforesaid;

and such conveyance may, as respects the leasehold reversion, be made in the name of the estate owner in whom it is vested.

Where a licence to assign is required on a sale by a mortgagee, such licence shall not be unreasonably refused.

(2) Where any such mortgagee obtains an order for foreclosure absolute, the order shall, unless it otherwise provides, operate (without giving rise to a forfeiture for want of a licence to assign) to vest the leasehold reversion affected by the mortgage and any subsequent mortgage term in him, subject to any legal mortgage having priority to the mortgage in right of which the foreclosure is obtained and to any money thereby secured, and thereupon the mortgage term and any subsequent

mortgage term or charge by way of legal mortgage bound by the order shall, subject to any express provision to the contrary contained in the order, merge in such leasehold reversion or be extinguished.

(3) Where any such mortgagee acquires a title under the Limitation Acts, he, or the persons deriving title under him, may by deed declare that the leasehold reversion affected by the mortgage and any mortgage term affected by the title so acquired shall vest in him, free from any right of redemption which is barred, and the same shall (without giving rise to a forfeiture for want of a licence to assign) vest accordingly, and thereupon the mortgage term, if any, and any other mortgage term or charge by way of legal mortgage affected by the title so acquired shall, subject to any express provision to the contrary contained in the deed, merge in such leasehold reversion or be extinguished.

(4) Where the mortgage includes fixtures or chattels personal, any statutory power of sale and any right to foreclose or take possession shall extend to the absolute or other interest therein affected by the charge.

(5) In the case of a sub-mortgage by subdemise of a term (less a nominal period) itself limited out of a leasehold reversion, the foregoing provisions of this section shall operate as if the derivative term created by the sub-mortgage had been limited out of the leasehold reversion, and so as (subject as aforesaid) to merge the principal mortgage term therein as well as the derivative term created by the sub-mortgage and to enable the sub-mortgagee to convey the leasehold reversion or acquire it by foreclosure, vesting, or otherwise as aforesaid.

(6) This section takes effect without prejudice to any incumbrance or trust affecting the leasehold reversion which has priority over the mortgage in right of which the sale, foreclosure, or title is made or acquired, and applies to a mortgage whether executed before or after the commencement of this Act, and to a mortgage term created by this Act, but does not apply where the mortgage term does not comprise the whole of the land included in the leasehold reversion unless the rent (if any) payable in respect of that reversion has been apportioned as respects the land affected, or the rent is of no money value or no rent is reserved, and unless the lessee's covenants and conditions (if any) have been apportioned, either expressly or by implication, as respects the land affected.

[In this subsection references to an apportionment include an equitable apportionment made without the consent of the lessor.]

[(7) The county court has jurisdiction under this section where the amount owing in respect of the mortgage or charge at the commencement of the proceedings does not exceed [£30,000].]

[337]

NOTES

Sub-s (6): words in square brackets inserted by the Law of Property (Amendment) Act 1926, s 7, Schedule.

Sub-s (7): inserted by the County Courts Act 1984, s 148(1), Sch 2, para 3; sum in square brackets substituted by SI 1991/724, art 2(4), (8), Schedule, Pt I.

90 Realisation of equitable charges by the court

(1) Where an order for sale is made by the court in reference to an equitable mortgage on land (not secured by a legal term of years absolute or by a charge by way of legal mortgage) the court may, in favour of a purchaser, make a vesting order conveying the land or may appoint a person to convey the land or create and vest in the mortgagee a legal term of years absolute to enable him to carry out the sale, as the case may require, in like manner as if the mortgage had been created by deed by way of legal mortgage pursuant to this Act, but without prejudice to any incumbrance having priority to the equitable mortgage unless the incumbrancer consents to the sale.

(2) This section applies to equitable mortgages made or arising before or after the commencement of this Act, but not to a mortgage which has been over-reached under the powers conferred by this Act or otherwise.

[(3) The county court has jurisdiction under this section where the amount owing in respect of the mortgage or charge at the commencement of the proceedings does not exceed [£30,000].]

[338]

NOTES

Sub-s (3): inserted by the County Courts Act 1984, s 148(1), Sch 2, para 3; sum in square brackets substituted by SI 1991/724, art 2(4), (8), Schedule, Pt I.

91 Sale of mortgaged property in action for redemption or foreclosure

(1) Any person entitled to redeem mortgaged property may have a judgment or order for sale instead of for redemption in an action brought by him either for redemption alone, or for sale alone, or for sale or redemption in the alternative.

(2) In any action, whether for foreclosure, or for redemption, or for sale, or for the raising and payment in any manner of mortgage money, the court, on the request of the mortgagee, or of any person interested either in the mortgage money or in the right of redemption, and, notwithstanding that—

(a) any other person dissents; or

(b) the mortgagee or any person so interested does not appear in the action;

and without allowing any time for redemption or for payment of any mortgage money, may direct a sale of the mortgaged property, on such terms as it thinks fit, including the deposit in court of a reasonable sum fixed by the court to meet the expenses of sale and to secure performance of the terms.

(3) But, in an action brought by a person interested in the right of redemption and seeking a sale, the court may, in the application of any defendant, direct the plaintiff to give such security for costs as the court thinks fit, and may give the conduct of the sale to any defendant, and may give such directions as it thinks fit respecting the costs of the defendants or any of them.

(4) In any case within this section the court may, if it thinks fit, direct a sale without previously determining the priorities of incumbrancers.

(5) This section applies to actions brought either before or after the commencement of this Act.

(6) In this section "mortgaged property" includes the estate or interest which a mortgagee would have had power to convey if the statutory power of sale were applicable.

(7) For the purposes of this section the court may, in favour of a purchaser, make a vesting order conveying the mortgaged property, or appoint a person to do so, subject or not to any incumbrance, as the court may think fit; or, in the case of an equitable mortgage, may create and vest a mortgage term in the mortgagee to enable him to carry out the sale as if the mortgage had been made by deed by way of legal mortgage.

[(8) The county court has jurisdiction under this section where the amount owing in respect of the mortgage or charge at the commencement of the proceedings does not exceed [£30,000].]

[339]

NOTES

Sub-s (8): inserted by the County Courts Act 1984, s 148(1), Sch 2, para 3; sum in square brackets substituted by SI 1991/724, art 2(4), (8), Schedule, Pt I.

92 Power to authorise land and minerals to be dealt with separately

[(1)] Where a mortgagee's power of sale in regard to land has become exercisable but does not extend to the purposes mentioned in this section, the court may, on his application, authorise him and the persons deriving title under him to dispose—

(a) of the land, with an exception or reservation of all or any mines and minerals, and with or without rights and powers of or incidental to the working, getting or carrying away of minerals; or

(b) of all or any mines and minerals, with or without the said rights or powers separately from the land;

and thenceforth the powers so conferred shall have effect as if the same were contained in the mortgage.

[(2) The county court has jurisdiction under this section where the amount owing in respect of the mortgage or charge at the commencement of the proceedings does not exceed [£30,000].]

[340]

NOTES

Sub-s (1): numbered as such by the County Courts Act 1984, s 148(1), Sch 2, para 3.

Sub-s (2): inserted by the County Courts Act 1984, s 148(1), Sch 2, para 3; sum in square brackets substituted by SI 1991/724, art 2(4), (8), Schedule, Pt I.

93 Restriction on consolidation of mortgages

(1) A mortgagor seeking to redeem any one mortgage is entitled to do so without paying any money due under any separate mortgage made by him, or by any person through whom he claims, solely on property other than that comprised in the mortgage which he seeks to redeem.

This subsection applies only if and as far as a contrary intention is not expressed in the mortgage deeds or one of them.

(2) This section does not apply where all the mortgages were made before the first day of January, eighteen hundred and eighty-two.

(3) Save as aforesaid, nothing in this Act, in reference to mortgages, affects any right of consolidation or renders inoperative a stipulation in relation to any mortgage made before or after the commencement of this Act reserving a right to consolidate.

[341]

94 Tacking and further advances

(1) After the commencement of this Act, a prior mortgagee shall have a right to make further advances to rank in priority to subsequent mortgages (whether legal or equitable)—

(a) if an arrangement has been made to that effect with the subsequent mortgagees; or

(b) if he had no notice of such subsequent mortgages at the time when the further advance was made by him; or

(c) whether or not he had such notice as aforesaid, where the mortgage imposes an obligation on him to make such further advances.

This subsection applies whether or not the prior mortgage was made expressly for securing further advances.

(2) In relation to the making of further advances after the commencement of this Act a mortgagee shall not be deemed to have notice of a mortgage merely by reason that it was registered as a land charge … if it was not so registered at the [time when the original mortgage was created] or when the last search (if any) by or on behalf of the mortgagee was made, whichever last happened.

This subsection only applies where the prior mortgage was made expressly for securing a current account or other further advances.

(3) Save in regard to the making of further advances as aforesaid, the right to tack is hereby abolished:

Provided that nothing in this Act shall affect any priority acquired before the commencement of this Act by tacking, or in respect of further advances made without notice of a subsequent incumbrance or by arrangement with the subsequent incumbrancer.

(4) This section applies to mortgages of land made before or after the commencement of this Act, but not to charges [on registered land].

[342]

NOTES

Sub-s (2): words omitted spent for certain purposes, repealed for remaining purposes by the Law of Property Act 1969, s 16, Sch 2, Pt I; words in square brackets substituted by the Law of Property (Amendment) Act 1926, s 7, Schedule.

Sub-s (4): words in square brackets substituted by the Land Registration Act 2002, s 133, Sch 11, para 2(1), (9).

95 Obligation to transfer instead of reconveying, and as to right to take possession

(1) Where a mortgagor is entitled to redeem, then subject to compliance with the terms on compliance with which he would be entitled to require a reconveyance or surrender, he shall be entitled to require the mortgagee, instead of reconveying or surrendering, to assign the mortgage debt and convey the mortgaged property to any third person, as the mortgagor directs; and the mortgagee shall be bound to assign and convey accordingly.

(2) The rights conferred by this section belong to and are capable of being enforced by each incumbrancer, or by the mortgagor, notwithstanding any intermediate incumbrance; but a requisition of an incumbrancer prevails over a requisition of the mortgagor, and, as between incumbrancers, a requisition of a prior incumbrancer prevails over a requisition of a subsequent incumbrancer.

(3) The foregoing provisions of this section do not apply in the case of a mortgagee being or having been in possession.

(4) Nothing in this Act affects prejudicially the right of a mortgagee of land whether or not his charge is secured by a legal term of years absolute to take possession of the land, but the taking of possession by the mortgagee does not convert any legal estate of the mortgagor into an equitable interest.

(5) This section applies to mortgages made either before or after the commencement of this Act, and takes effect notwithstanding any stipulation to the contrary.

[343]

96 Regulations respecting inspection, production and delivery of documents, and priorities

(1) A mortgagor, as long as his right to redeem subsists, shall be entitled from time to time, at reasonable times, on his request, and at his own cost, and on payment of the mortgagee's costs and expenses in this behalf, to inspect and make copies or abstracts of or extracts from the documents of title relating to the mortgaged property in the custody or power of the mortgagee.

This subsection applies to mortgages made after the thirty-first day of December, eighteen hundred and eighty-one, and takes effect notwithstanding any stipulation to the contrary.

(2) A mortgagee, whose mortgage is surrendered or otherwise extinguished, shall not be liable on account of delivering documents of title in his possession to the person not having the best right thereto, unless he has notice of the right or claim of a person having a better right, whether by virtue of a right to require a surrender or reconveyance or otherwise.

[In this subsection notice does not include notice implied by reason of registration under the Land Charges Act 1925 …]

NOTES

Sub-s (2): words in square brackets inserted by the Law of Property (Amendment) Act 1926, s 7, Schedule; words omitted spent for certain purposes, repealed for remaining purposes by the Law of Property Act 1969, s 16, Sch 2, Pt I.

97 Priorities as between puisne mortgages

Every mortgage affecting a legal estate in land made after the commencement of this Act, whether legal or equitable (not being a mortgage protected by the deposit of documents relating to the legal estate affected) shall rank according to its date of registration as a land charge pursuant to the Land Charges Act 1925.

This section does not apply [to mortgages or charges to which the Land Charges Act 1972 does not apply by virtue of section 14(3) of that Act (which excludes certain land charges created by instruments necessitating registration under the [Land Registration Act 2002]), or] to mortgages or charges of registered land …

[344]

NOTES

Words in first (outer) pair of square brackets substituted by the Land Charges Act 1972, s 18(1), Sch 3; words in second (inner) pair of square brackets substituted by the Land Registration Act 2002, s 133, Sch 11, para 2(1), (10); words omitted spent for certain purposes by virtue of the Middlesex Deeds Act 1940, s 1 and repealed for remaining purposes by the Law of Property Act 1969, s 17, Sch 2, Pt II.

98 Actions for possession by mortgagors

(1) A mortgagor for the time being entitled to the possession or receipt of the rents and profits of any land, as to which the mortgagee has not given notice of his intention to take possession or to enter into the receipt of the rents and profits thereof, may sue for such possession, or for the recovery of such rents or profits, or to prevent or recover damages in respect of any trespass or other wrong relative thereto, in his own name only, unless the cause of action arises upon a lease or other contract made by him jointly with any other person.

(2) This section does not prejudice the power of a mortgagor independently of this section to take proceedings in his own name only, either in right of any legal estate vested in him or otherwise.

(3) This section applies whether the mortgage was made before or after the commencement of this Act.

[345]

99 Leasing powers of mortgagor and mortgagee in possession

(1) A mortgagor of land while in possession shall, as against every incumbrancer, have power to make from time to time any such lease of the mortgaged land, or any part thereof, as is by this section authorised.

(2) A mortgagee of land while in possession shall, as against all prior incumbrancers, if any, and as against the mortgagor, have power to make from time to time any such lease as aforesaid.

(3) The leases which this section authorises are—

- (i) agricultural or occupation leases for any term not exceeding twenty-one years, or, in the case of a mortgage made after the commencement of this Act, fifty years; and
- (ii) building leases for any term not exceeding ninety-nine years, or, in the case of a mortgage made after the commencement of this Act, nine hundred and ninety-nine years.

(4) Every person making a lease under this section may execute and do all assurances and things necessary or proper in that behalf.

(5) Every lease shall be made to take effect in possession not later than twelve months after its date.

(6) Every such lease shall reserve the best rent that can reasonably be obtained, regard being had to the circumstances of the case, but without any fine being taken.

(7) Every such lease shall contain a covenant by the lessee for payment of the rent, and a condition of re-entry on the rent not being paid within a time therein specified not exceeding thirty days.

(8) A counterpart of every such lease shall be executed by the lessee and delivered to the lessor, of which execution and delivery the execution of the lease by the lessor shall, in favour of the lessee and all persons deriving title under him, be sufficient evidence.

(9) Every such building lease shall be made in consideration of the lessee, or some person by whose direction the lease is granted, having erected, or agreeing to erect within not more than five years from the date of the lease, buildings, new or additional, or having improved or repaired buildings, or agreeing to improve or repair buildings within that time, or having executed, or agreeing to execute within that time, on the land leased, an improvement for or in connexion with building purposes.

(10) In any such building lease a peppercorn rent, or a nominal or other rent less than the rent ultimately payable, may be made payable for the first five years, or any less part of the term.

(11) In case of a lease by the mortgagor, he shall, within one month after making the lease, deliver to the mortgagee, or, where there are more than one, to the mortgagee first in priority, a counterpart of the lease duly executed by the lessee, but the lessee shall not be concerned to see that this provision is complied with.

(12) A contract to make or accept a lease under this section may be enforced by or against every person on whom the lease if granted would be binding.

(13) [Subject to subsection (13A) below,] this section applies only if and as far as a contrary intention is not expressed by the mortgagor and mortgagee in the mortgage deed, or otherwise in writing, and has effect subject to the terms of the mortgage deed or of any such writing and to the provisions therein contained.

[(13A) Subsection (13) of this section—

(a) shall not enable the application of any provision of this section to be excluded or restricted in relation to any mortgage of agricultural land made after 1st March 1948 but before 1st September 1995, and

(b) shall not enable the power to grant a lease of an agricultural holding to which, by virtue of section 4 of the Agricultural Tenancies Act 1995, the Agricultural Holdings Act 1986 will apply, to be excluded or restricted in relation to any mortgage of agricultural land made on or after 1st September 1995.

(13B) In subsection (13A) of this section—

"agricultural holding" has the same meaning as in the Agricultural Holdings Act 1986; and

"agricultural land" has the same meaning as in the Agriculture Act 1947.]

(14) The mortgagor and mortgagee may, by agreement in writing, whether or not contained in the mortgage deed, reserve to or confer on the mortgagor or the mortgagee, or both, any further or other powers of leasing or having reference to leasing; and any further or other powers so reserved or conferred shall be exercisable, as far as may be, as if they were conferred by this Act, and with all the like incidents, effects, and consequences:

Provided that the powers so reserved or conferred shall not prejudicially affect the rights of any mortgagee interested under any other mortgage subsisting at the date of the agreement, unless that mortgagee joins in or adopts the agreement.

(15) Nothing in this Act shall be construed to enable a mortgagor or mortgagee to make a lease for any longer term or on any other conditions than such as could have been granted or imposed by the mortgagor, with the concurrence of all the incumbrancers, if this Act and the enactments replaced by this section had not been passed:

Provided that, in the case of a mortgage of leasehold land, a lease granted under this section shall reserve a reversion of not less than one day.

(16) Subject as aforesaid, this section applies to any mortgage made after the thirty-first day of December, eighteen hundred and eighty-one, but the provisions thereof, or any of them, may, by agreement in writing made after that date between mortgagor and mortgagee, be applied to a mortgage made before that date, so nevertheless that any such agreement shall not prejudicially affect any right or interest of any mortgagee not joining in or adopting the agreement.

(17) The provisions of this section referring to a lease shall be construed to extend and apply, as far as circumstances admit, to any letting, and to an agreement, whether in writing or not, for leasing or letting.

(18) For the purposes of this section "mortgagor" does not include an incumbrancer deriving title under the original mortgagor.

(19) The powers of leasing conferred by this section shall, after a receiver of the income of the mortgaged property or any part thereof has been appointed by a mortgagee under his statutory power, and so long as the receiver acts, be exercisable by such mortgagee instead of by the

mortgagor, as respects any land affected by the receivership, in like manner as if such mortgagee were in possession of the land, and the mortgagee may, by writing, delegate any of such powers to the receiver.

[346]

NOTES

Sub-s (13): words in square brackets inserted by the Agricultural Tenancies Act 1995, s 31(2).
Sub-ss (13A), (13B): inserted by the Agricultural Tenancies Act 1995, s 31(1), (3).

100 Powers of mortgagor and mortgagee in possession to accept surrenders of leases

(1) For the purpose only of enabling a lease authorised under the last preceding section, or under any agreement made pursuant to that section, or by the mortgage deed (in this section referred to as an authorised lease) to be granted, a mortgagor of land while in possession shall, as against every incumbrancer, have, by virtue of this Act, power to accept from time to time a surrender of any lease of the mortgaged land or any part thereof comprised in the lease, with or without an exception of or in respect of all or any of the mines and minerals therein, and, on a surrender of the lease so far as it comprises part only of the land or mines and minerals leased, the rent may be apportioned.

(2) For the same purpose, a mortgagee of land while in possession shall, as against all prior or other incumbrancers, if any, and as against the mortgagor, have, by virtue of this Act, power to accept from time to time any such surrender as aforesaid.

(3) On a surrender of part only of the land or mines and minerals leased, the original lease may be varied, provided that the lease when varied would have been valid as an authorised lease if granted by the person accepting the surrender; and, on a surrender and the making of a new or other lease, whether for the same or for any extended or other term, and whether subject or not to the same or to any other covenants, provisions, or conditions, the value of the lessee's interest in the lease surrendered may, subject to the provisions of this section, be taken into account in the determination of the amount of the rent to be reserved, and of the nature of the covenants, provisions, and conditions to be inserted in the new or other lease.

(4) Where any consideration for the surrender, other than an agreement to accept an authorised lease, is given by or on behalf of the lessee to or on behalf of the person accepting the surrender, nothing in this section authorises a surrender to a mortgagor without the consent of the incumbrancers, or authorises a surrender to a second or subsequent incumbrancer without the consent of every prior incumbrancer.

(5) No surrender shall, by virtue of this section, be rendered valid unless:—

(a) An authorised lease is granted of the whole of the land or mines and minerals comprised in the surrender to take effect in possession immediately or within one month after the date of the surrender; and

(b) The term certain or other interest granted by the new lease is not less in duration than the unexpired term or interest which would have been subsisting under the original lease if that lease had not been surrendered; and

(c) Where the whole of the land mines and minerals originally leased has been surrendered, the rent reserved by the new lease is not less than the rent which would have been payable under the original lease if it had not been surrendered; or where part only of the land or mines and minerals has been surrendered, the aggregate rents respectively remaining payable or reserved under the original lease and new lease are not less than the rent which would have been payable under the original lease if no partial surrender had been accepted.

(6) A contract to make or accept a surrender under this section may be enforced by or against every person on whom the surrender, if completed, would be binding.

(7) This section applies only if and as far as a contrary intention is not expressed by the mortgagor and mortgagee in the mortgage deed, or otherwise in writing, and shall have effect subject to the terms of the mortgage deed or of any such writing and to the provisions therein contained.

(8) This section applies to a mortgage made after the thirty-first day of December, nineteen hundred and eleven, but the provisions of this section, or any of them, may, by agreement in writing made after that date, between mortgagor and mortgagee, be applied to a mortgage made before that date, so nevertheless that any such agreement shall not prejudicially affect any right or interest of any mortgagee not joining in or adopting the agreement.

(9) The provisions of this section referring to a lease shall be construed to extend and apply, as far as circumstances admit, to any letting, and to an agreement, whether in writing or not, for leasing or letting.

(10) The mortgagor and mortgagee may, by agreement in writing, whether or not contained in the mortgage deed, reserve or confer on the mortgagor or mortgagee, or both, any further or other

powers relating to the surrender of leases; and any further or other powers so conferred or reserved shall be exercisable, as far as may be, as if they were conferred by this Act, and with all the like incidents, effects and consequences:

Provided that the powers so reserved or conferred shall not prejudicially affect the rights of any mortgagee interested under any other mortgage subsisting at the date of the agreement, unless that mortgagee joins in or adopts the agreement.

(11) Nothing in this section operates to enable a mortgagor or mortgagee to accept a surrender which could not have been accepted by the mortgagor with the concurrence of all the incumbrancers if this Act and the enactments replaced by this section had not been passed.

(12) For the purposes of this section "mortgagor" does not include an incumbrancer deriving title under the original mortgagor.

(13) The powers of accepting surrenders conferred by this section shall, after a receiver of the income of the mortgaged property or any part thereof has been appointed by the mortgagee, under the statutory power, and so long as the receiver acts, be exercisable by such mortgagee instead of by the mortgagor, as respects any land affected by the receivership, in like manner as if such mortgagee were in possession of the land; and the mortgagee may, by writing, delegate any of such powers to the receiver.

[347]

101 Powers incident to estate or interest of mortgage

(1) A mortgagee, where the mortgage is made by deed, shall, by virtue of this Act, have the following powers, to the like extent as if they had been in terms conferred by the mortgage deed, but not further (namely)—

(i) A power, when the mortgage money has become due, to sell, or to concur with any other person in selling, the mortgaged property, or any part thereof, either subject to prior charges or not, and either together or in lots, by public auction or by private contract, subject to such conditions respecting title, or evidence of title, or other matter, as the mortgagee thinks fit, with power to vary any contract for sale, and to buy in at an auction, or to rescind any contract for sale, and to re-sell, without being answerable for any loss occasioned thereby; and

(ii) A power, at any time after the date of the mortgage deed, to insure and keep insured against loss or damage by fire any building, or any effects or property of an insurable nature, whether affixed to the freehold or not, being or forming part of the property which or an estate or interest wherein is mortgaged, and the premiums paid for any such insurance shall be a charge on the mortgaged property or estate or interest, in addition to the mortgage money, and with the same priority, and with interest at the same rate, as the mortgage money; and

(iii) A power, when the mortgage money has become due, to appoint a receiver of the income of the mortgaged property, or any part thereof; or, if the mortgaged property consists of an interest in income, or of a rentcharge or an annual or other periodical sum, a receiver of that property or any part thereof; and

(iv) A power, while the mortgagee is in possession, to cut and sell timber and other trees ripe for cutting, and not planted or left standing for shelter or ornament, or to contract for any such cutting and sale, to be completed within any time not exceeding twelve months from the making of the contract.

[(1A) Subsection (1)(i) is subject to section 21 of the Commonhold and Leasehold Reform Act 2002 (no disposition of part-units).]

(2) Where the mortgage deed is executed after the thirty-first day of December, nineteen hundred and eleven, the power of sale aforesaid includes the following powers as incident thereto (namely):—

(i) A power to impose or reserve or make binding, as far as the law permits, by covenant, condition, or otherwise, on the unsold part of the mortgaged property or any part thereof, or on the purchaser and any property sold, any restriction or reservation with respect to building on or other user of land, or with respect to mines and minerals, or for the purpose of the more beneficial working thereof, or with respect to any other thing:

(ii) A power to sell the mortgaged property, or any part thereof, or all or any mines and minerals apart from the surface:—

(a) With or without a grant or reservation of rights of way, rights of water, easements, rights, and privileges for or connected with building or other purposes in relation to the property remaining in mortgage or any part thereof, or to any property sold: and

(b) With or without an exception or reservation of all or any of the mines and minerals in or under the mortgaged property, and with or without a grant or reservation of powers of working, wayleaves, or rights of way, rights of water and drainage and other powers, easements, rights, and privileges for or connected with mining purposes in relation to the property remaining unsold or any part thereof, or to any property sold: and

(c) With or without covenants by the purchaser to expend money on the land sold.

(3) The provisions of this Act relating to the foregoing powers, comprised either in this section, or in any other section regulating the exercise of those powers, may be varied or extended by the mortgage deed, and, as so varied or extended, shall, as far as may be, operate in the like manner and with all the like incidents, effects, and consequences, as if such variations or extensions were contained in this Act.

(4) This section applies only if and as far as a contrary intention is not expressed in the mortgage deed, and has effect subject to the terms of the mortgage deed and to the provisions therein contained.

(5) Save as otherwise provided, this section applies where the mortgage deed is executed after the thirty-first day of December, eighteen hundred and eighty-one.

(6) The power of sale conferred by this section includes such power of selling the estate in fee simple or any leasehold reversion as is conferred by the provisions of this Act relating to the realisation of mortgages.

[348]

NOTES

Sub-s (1A): inserted by the Commonhold and Leasehold Reform Act 2002, s 68, Sch 5, para 2.

102 Provision as to mortgages of undivided shares in land

(1) A person who was before the commencement of this Act a mortgagee of an undivided share in land shall have the same power to sell his [interest under the trust to which the land is subject], as, independently of this Act, he would have had in regard to the share in the land; and shall also have a right to require the [trustees] in whom the land is vested to account to him for the income attributable to that share or to appoint a receiver to receive the same from such trustees corresponding to the right which, independently of this Act, he would have had to take possession or to appoint a receiver of the rents and profits attributable to the same share.

(2) The powers conferred by this section are exercisable by the persons deriving title under such mortgagee.

[349]

NOTES

Sub-s (1): words in square brackets substituted by the Trusts of Land and Appointment of Trustees Act 1996, s 25(1), Sch 3, para 4(13); for savings in relation to entailed interests created before the commencement of that Act, and savings consequential upon the abolition of the doctrine of conversion, see s 25(4), (5) thereof.

103 Regulation of exercise of power of sale

A mortgagee shall not exercise the power of sale conferred by this Act unless and until—

(i) Notice requiring payment of the mortgage money has been served on the mortgagor or one of two or more mortgagors, and default has been made in payment of the mortgage money, or of part thereof, for three months after such service; or

(ii) Some interest under the mortgage is in arrear and unpaid for two months after becoming due; or

(iii) There has been a breach of some provision contained in the mortgage deed or in this Act, or in an enactment replaced by this Act, and on the part of the mortgagor, or of some person concurring in making the mortgage, to be observed or performed, other than and besides a covenant for payment of the mortgage money or interest thereon.

[350]

104 Conveyance on sale

(1) A mortgagee exercising the power of sale conferred by this Act shall have power, by deed, to convey the property sold, for such estate and interest therein as he is by this Act authorised to sell or convey or may be the subject of the mortgage, freed from all estates, interest, and rights to which the mortgage has priority, but subject to all estates, interests, and rights which have priority to the mortgage.

(2) Where a conveyance is made in exercise of the power of sale conferred by this Act, or any enactment replaced by this Act, the title of the purchaser shall not be impeachable on the ground—

(a) that no case had arisen to authorise the sale; or

(b) that due notice was not given; or

(c) where the mortgage is made after the commencement of this Act, that leave of the court, when so required, was not obtained; or

(d) whether the mortgage was made before or after such commencement, that the power was otherwise improperly or irregularly exercised;

and a purchaser is not, either before or on conveyance, concerned to see or inquire whether a case has arisen to authorise the sale, or due notice has been given, or the power is otherwise properly and regularly exercised; but any person damnified by an unauthorised, or improper, or irregular exercise of the power shall have his remedy in damages against the person exercising the power.

(3) A conveyance on sale by a mortgagee, made after the commencement of this Act, shall be deemed to have been made in exercise of the power of sale conferred by this Act unless a contrary intention appears.

[351]

105 Application of proceeds of sale

The money which is received by the mortgagee, arising from the sale, after discharge of prior incumbrances to which the sale is not made subject, if any, or after payment into court under this Act of a sum to meet any prior incumbrance, shall be held by him in trust to be applied by him, first, in payment of all costs, charges, and expenses properly incurred by him as incident to the sale or any attempted sale, or otherwise; and secondly, in discharge of the mortgage money, interest, and costs, and other money, if any, due under the mortgage; and the residue of the money so received shall be paid to the person entitled to the mortgaged property, or authorised to give receipts for the proceeds of the sale thereof.

[352]

106 Provisions as to exercise of power of sale

(1) The power of sale conferred by this Act may be exercised by any person for the time being entitled to receive and give a discharge for the mortgage money.

(2) The power of sale conferred by this Act does not affect the right of foreclosure.

(3) The mortgagee shall not be answerable for any involuntary loss happening in or about the exercise or execution of the power of sale conferred by this Act, or of any trust connected therewith, or, where the mortgage is executed after the thirty-first day of December, nineteen hundred and eleven, of any power or provision contained in the mortgage deed.

(4) At any time after the power of sale conferred by this Act has become exercisable, the person entitled to exercise the power may demand and recover from any person, other than a person having in the mortgaged property an estate, interest, or right in priority to the mortgage, all the deeds and documents relating to the property, or to the title thereto, which a purchaser under the power of sale would be entitled to demand and recover from him.

[353]

107 Mortgagee's receipts, discharges, etc

(1) The receipt in writing of a mortgagee shall be a sufficient discharge for any money arising under the power of sale conferred by this Act, or for any money or securities comprised in his mortgage, or arising thereunder; and a person paying or transferring the same to the mortgagee shall not be concerned to inquire whether any money remains due under the mortgage.

(2) Money received by a mortgagee under his mortgage or from the proceeds of securities comprised in his mortgage shall be applied in like manner as in this Act directed respecting money received by him arising from a sale under the power of sale conferred by this Act, but with this variation, that the costs, charges, and expenses payable shall include the costs, charges, and expenses properly incurred of recovering and receiving the money or securities, and of conversion of securities into money, instead of those incident to sale.

[354]

108 Amount and application of insurance money

(1) The amount of an insurance effected by a mortgagee against loss or damage by fire under the power in that behalf conferred by this Act shall not exceed the amount specified in the mortgage deed, or, if no amount is therein specified two third parts of the amount that would be required, in case of total destruction, to restore the property insured.

(2) An insurance shall not, under the power conferred by this Act, be effected by a mortgagee in any of the following cases (namely)—

(i) Where there is a declaration in the mortgage deed that no insurance is required:

(ii) Where an insurance is kept up by or on behalf of the mortgagor in accordance with the mortgage deed:

(iii) Where the mortgage deed contains no stipulation respecting insurance, and an insurance is kept up by or on behalf of the mortgagor with the consent of the mortgagee to the amount to which the mortgagee is by this Act authorised to insure.

(3) All money received on an insurance of mortgaged property against loss or damage by fire or otherwise effected under this Act, or any enactment replaced by this Act, or on an insurance for the

maintenance of which the mortgagor is liable under the mortgage deed, shall, if the mortgagee so requires, be applied by the mortgagor in making good the loss or damage in respect of which the money is received.

(4) Without prejudice to any obligation to the contrary imposed by law, or by special contract, a mortgagee may require that all money received on an insurance of mortgaged property against loss or damage by fire or otherwise effected under this Act, or any enactment replaced by this Act, or on an insurance for the maintenance of which the mortgagor is liable under the mortgage deed, be applied in or towards the discharge of the mortgage money.

[355]

109 Appointment, powers, remuneration and duties of receiver

(1) A mortgagee entitled to appoint a receiver under the power in that behalf conferred by this Act shall not appoint a receiver until he has become entitled to exercise the power of sale conferred by this Act, but may then, by writing under his hand, appoint such person as he thinks fit to be receiver.

(2) A receiver appointed under the powers conferred by this Act, or any enactment replaced by this Act, shall be deemed to be the agent of the mortgagor; and the mortgagor shall be solely responsible for the receiver's acts or defaults unless the mortgage deed otherwise provides.

(3) The receiver shall have power to demand and recover all the income of which he is appointed receiver, by action, *distress* [or under section 72(1) of the Tribunals, Courts and Enforcement Act 2007 (commercial rent arrears recovery)], or otherwise, in the name either of the mortgagor or of the mortgagee, to the full extent of the estate or interest which the mortgagor could dispose of, and to give effectual receipts accordingly for the same, and to exercise any powers which may have been delegated to him by the mortgagee pursuant to this Act.

(4) A person paying money to the receiver shall not be concerned to inquire whether any case has happened to authorise the receiver to act.

(5) The receiver may be removed, and a new receiver may be appointed, from time to time by the mortgagee by writing under his hand.

(6) The receiver shall be entitled to retain out of any money received by him, for his remuneration, and in satisfaction of all costs, charges, and expenses incurred by him as receiver, a commission at such rate, not exceeding five per centum on the gross amount of all money received, as is specified in his appointment, and if no rate is so specified, then at the rate of five per centum on that gross amount, or at such other rate as the court thinks fit to allow, on application made by him for that purpose.

(7) The receiver shall, if so directed in writing by the mortgagee, insure to the extent, if any, to which the mortgagee might have insured and keep insured against loss or damage by fire, out of the money received by him, any building, effects, or property comprised in the mortgage, whether affixed to the freehold or not, being of an insurable nature.

(8) Subject to the provisions of this Act as to the application of insurance money, the receiver shall apply all money received by him as follows, namely:—

(i) In discharge of all rents, taxes, rates, and outgoings whatever affecting the mortgaged property; and
(ii) In keeping down all annual sums or other payments, and the interest on all principal sums, having priority to the mortgage in right whereof he is receiver; and
(iii) In payment of his commission, and of the premiums on fire, life, or other insurances, if any, properly payable under the mortgage deed or under this Act, and the cost of executing necessary or proper repairs directed in writing by the mortgagee; and
(iv) In payment of the interest accruing due in respect of any principal money due under the mortgage; and
(v) In or towards discharge of the principal money if so directed in writing by the mortgagee;

and shall pay the residue, if any, of the money received by him to the person who, but for the possession of the receiver, would have been entitled to receive the income of which he is appointed receiver, or who is otherwise entitled to the mortgaged property.

[356]

NOTES

Sub-s (3): word in italics substituted by subsequent words in square brackets by the Tribunals, Courts and Enforcement Act 2007, s 86, Sch 14, paras 21, 22, as from a day to be appointed.

110 Effect of bankruptcy of the mortgagor on the power to sell or appoint a receiver

(1) Where the statutory or express power for a mortgagee either to sell or to appoint a receiver is made exercisable by reason of the mortgagor … being adjudged a bankrupt, such power shall not be exercised only on account of the … adjudication, without the leave of the court.

(2) This section applies only where the mortgage deed is executed after the commencement of this Act; …

[357]

NOTES

Sub-ss (1), (2): words omitted repealed by the Insolvency Act 1985, Sch 10, Pt III.

111 Effect of advance on joint account

(1) Where—

(a) in a mortgage, or an obligation for payment of money, or a transfer of a mortgage or of such an obligation, the sum, or any part of the sum, advanced or owing is expressed to be advanced by or owing to more persons than one out of money, or as money, belonging to them on a joint account; or

(b) a mortgage, or such an obligation, or such a transfer is made to more persons than one, jointly;

the mortgage money, or other money or money's worth, for the time being due to those persons on the mortgage or obligation, shall, as between them and the mortgagor or obligor, be deemed to be and remain money or money's worth belonging to those persons on a joint account; and the receipt in writing of the survivors or last survivor of them, or of the personal representative of the last survivor, shall be a complete discharge for all money or money's worth for the time being due, notwithstanding any notice to the payer of a severance of the joint account.

(2) This section applies if and so far as a contrary intention is not expressed in the mortgage, obligation, or transfer, and has effect subject to the terms of the mortgage, obligation, or transfer, and to the provisions therein contained.

(3) This section applies to any mortgage, obligation, or transfer made after the thirty-first day of December, eighteen hundred and eighty-one.

[358]

112 (*Repealed by the Statute Law* (*Repeals*) *Act 2004.*)

113 Notice of trusts affecting mortgage debts

(1) A person dealing in good faith with a mortgagee, or with the mortgagor if the mortgage has been discharged released or postponed as to the whole or any part of the mortgaged property, shall not be concerned with any trust at any time affecting the mortgage money or the income thereof, whether or not he has notice of the trust, and may assume unless the contrary is expressly stated in the instruments relating to the mortgage—

(a) that the mortgagees (if more than one) are or were entitled to the mortgage money on a joint account; and

(b) that the mortgagee has or had power to give valid receipts for the purchase money or mortgage money and the income thereof (including any arrears of interest) and to release or postpone the priority of the mortgage debt or any part thereof or to deal with the same or the mortgaged property or any part thereof;

without investigating the equitable title to the mortgage debt or the appointment or discharge of trustees in reference thereto.

(2) This section applies to mortgages made before or after the commencement of this Act, but only as respects dealings effected after such commencement.

(3) This section does not affect the liability of any person in whom the mortgage debt is vested for the purposes of any trust to give effect to that trust.

[359]

114 Transfers of mortgages

(1) A deed executed by a mortgagee purporting to transfer his mortgage or the benefit thereof shall, unless a contrary intention is therein expressed, and subject to any provisions therein contained, operate to transfer to the transferee—

(a) the right to demand, sue for, recover, and give receipts for, the mortgage money or the unpaid part thereof, and the interest then due, if any, and thenceforth to become due thereon; and

(b) the benefit of all securities for the same, and the benefit of and the right to sue on all covenants with the mortgagee, and the right to exercise all powers of the mortgagee; and

(c) all the estate and interest in the mortgaged property then vested in the mortgagee subject to redemption or cesser, but as to such estate and interest subject to the right of redemption then subsisting.

(2) In this section "transferee" includes his personal representatives and assigns.

(3) A transfer of mortgage may be made in the form contained in the Third Schedule to this Act with such variations and additions, if any, as the circumstances may require.

(4) This section applies, whether the mortgage transferred was made before or after the commencement of this Act, but applies only to transfers made after the commencement of this Act.

(5) This section does not extend to a transfer of a bill of sale of chattels by way of security.

[360]

115 Reconveyances of mortgages by endorsed receipts

(1) A receipt endorsed on, written at the foot of, or annexed to, a mortgage for all money thereby secured, which states the name of the person who pays the money and is executed by the chargee by way of legal mortgage or the person in whom the mortgaged property is vested and who is legally entitled to give a receipt for the mortgage money shall operate, without any reconveyance, surrender, or release—

(a) Where a mortgage takes effect by demise or subdemise, as a surrender of the term, so as to determine the term or merge the same in the reversion immediately expectant thereon;

(b) Where the mortgage does not take effect by demise or subdemise, as a reconveyance thereof to the extent of the interest which is the subject matter of the mortgage, to the person who immediately before the execution of the receipt was entitled to the equity of redemption;

and in either case, as a discharge of the mortgaged property from all principal money and interest secured by, and from all claims under the mortgage, but without prejudice to any term or other interest which is paramount to the estate or interest of the mortgagee or other person in whom the mortgaged property was vested.

(2) Provided that, where by the receipt the money appears to have been paid by a person who is not entitled to the immediate equity of redemption, the receipt shall operate as if the benefit of the mortgage had by deed been transferred to him; unless—

(a) it is otherwise expressly provided; or

(b) the mortgage is paid off out of capital money, or other money in the hands of a personal representative or trustee properly applicable for the discharge of the mortgage, and it is not expressly provided that the receipt is to operate as a transfer.

(3) Nothing in this section confers on a mortgagor a right to keep alive a mortgage paid off by him, so as to affect prejudicially any subsequent incumbrancer; and where there is no right to keep the mortgage alive, the receipt does not operate as a transfer.

(4) This section does not affect the right of any person to require a reassignment, surrender, release, or transfer to be executed in lieu of a receipt.

(5) A receipt may be given in the form contained in the Third Schedule to this Act, with such variations and additions, if any, as may be deemed expedient …

(6) In a receipt given under this section the same covenants shall be implied as if the person who executes the receipt had by deed been expressed to convey the property as mortgagee, subject to any interest which is paramount to the mortgage.

(7) Where the mortgage consists of a mortgage and a further charge or of more than one deed, it shall be sufficient for the purposes of this section, if the receipt refers either to all the deeds whereby the mortgage money is secured or to the aggregate amount of the mortgage money thereby secured and for the time being owing, and is endorsed on, written at the foot of, or annexed to, one of the mortgage deeds.

(8) This section applies to the discharge of a charge by way of legal mortgage, and to the discharge of a mortgage, whether made by way of statutory mortgage or not, executed before or after the commencement of this Act, but only as respects discharges effected after such commencement.

(9) The provisions of this section relating to the operation of a receipt shall (in substitution for the like statutory provisions relating to receipts given by or on behalf of a building … society) apply to the discharge of a mortgage made to any such society, provided that the receipt is executed in the manner required by the statute relating to the society …

(10) This section does not apply to the discharge of a [registered charge (within the meaning of the Land Registration Act 2002)].

(11) In this section "mortgaged property" means the property remaining subject to the mortgage at the date of the receipt.

[361]

NOTES

Sub-s (5): words omitted repealed by the Finance Act 1971, s 69, Sch 14, Part VI.

Sub-s (9): first words omitted repealed by the Friendly Societies Act 1971, s 14(2), Sch 3, and the Industrial and Provident Societies Act 1965, s 77(1), Sch 5; second words omitted repealed by the Finance Act 1971, s 61, Sch 14, Pt VI.

Sub-s (10): words in square brackets substituted by the Land Registration Act 2002, s 133, Sch 11, para 2(1), (11).

116 Cesser of mortgage terms

Without prejudice to the right of a tenant for life or other person having only a limited interest in the equity of redemption to require a mortgage to be kept alive by transfer or otherwise, a mortgage term shall, when the money secured by the mortgage has been discharged, become a satisfied term and shall cease.

[362]

117 Forms of statutory legal charges

(1) As a special form of charge by way of legal mortgage, a mortgage of freehold or leasehold land may be made by a deed expressed to be made by way of statutory mortgage, being in one of the forms (Nos 1 or 4) set out in the Fourth Schedule to this Act, with such variations and additions, if any, as circumstances may require, and if so made the provisions of this section shall apply thereto.

(2) There shall be deemed to be included, and there shall by virtue of this Act be implied, in such a mortgage deed—

First, a covenant with the mortgagee by the person therein expressed to charge as mortgagor to the effect following, namely—

That the mortgagor will, on the stated day, pay to the mortgagee the stated mortgage money, with interest thereon in the meantime at the stated rate, and will thereafter, if and as long as the mortgage money or any part thereof remains unpaid, pay to the mortgagee (as well after as before any judgment is obtained under the mortgage) interest thereon, or on the unpaid part thereof, at the stated rate, by equal half-yearly payments the first thereof to be made at the end of six months from the day stated for payment of the mortgage money:

Secondly, a provision to the following effect (namely)—

That if the mortgagor on the stated day pays to the mortgagee the stated mortgage money, with interest thereon in the meantime at the stated rate, the mortgagee at any time thereafter, at the request and cost of the mortgagor, shall discharge the mortgaged property or transfer the benefit of the mortgage as the mortgagor may direct.

This subsection applies to a mortgage deed made under section twenty-six of the Conveyancing Act 1881 with a substitution of a reference to "the person therein expressed to convey as mortgagor" for the reference in this subsection to "the person therein expressed to charge as mortgagor".

[363]

118 Forms of statutory transfers of legal charges

(1) A transfer of a statutory mortgage may be made by a deed expressed to be made by way of statutory transfer of mortgage, being in such one of the three forms (Nos. 2, 3, or 4) set out in the Fourth Schedule to this Act as may be appropriate to the case with such variations and additions, if any, as circumstances may require, and if so made the provisions of this section shall apply thereto.

(2) In whichever of those three forms the deed of transfer is made, it shall have effect as follows (namely)—

(i) There shall become vested in the person to whom the benefit of the mortgage is expressed to be transferred (who, with his personal representatives and assigns, is in this section designated the transferee), the right to demand, sue for, recover, and give receipts for the mortgage money, or the unpaid part thereof, and the interest then due, if any, and thenceforth to become due thereon, and the benefit of all securities for the same, and the benefit of and the right to sue on all covenants with the mortgagee, and the right to exercise all powers of the mortgagee:

(ii) All the term and interest, if any, subject to redemption, of the mortgagee in the mortgaged land shall vest in the transferee, subject to redemption.

(3) If a covenantor joins in the deed of transfer, there shall also be deemed to be included, and there shall by virtue of this Act be implied therein, a covenant with the transferee by the person expressed to join therein as covenantor to the effect following (namely):—

That the covenantor will, on the next of the days by the mortgage deed fixed for payment of interest pay to the transferee the stated mortgage money, or so much thereof as then remains unpaid, with interest thereon, or on the unpaid part thereof, in the meantime, at the rate stated in the mortgage deed; and will thereafter, as long as the mortgage money or any part thereof remains unpaid, pay to the transferee interest on that sum, or the unpaid part thereof, at the same rate, on the successive days by the mortgage deed fixed for payment of interest

(4) If the deed of transfer is made in the Form No 4, it shall, by virtue of this Act, operate not only as a statutory transfer of mortgage, but also as a statutory mortgage, and the provisions of this section shall have effect in relation thereto accordingly; but it shall not be liable to any increased stamp duty by reason only of it being designated a mortgage.

(5) This section applies to the transfer of a statutory mortgage created under any enactment replaced by this Act.

[364]

119 Implied covenants, joint and several

In a deed of statutory mortgage, or of statutory transfer of mortgage, where more persons than one are expressed to convey or charge as mortgagors, or to join as covenantors, the implied covenant on their part shall be deemed to be a joint and several covenant by them; and where there are more mortgagees or more transferees than one, the implied covenant with them shall be deemed to be a covenant with them jointly, unless the amount secured is expressed to be secured to them in shares or distinct sums, in which latter case the implied covenant with them shall be deemed to be a covenant with each severally in respect of the share or distinct sum secured to him.

[365]

120 Form of discharge of statutory mortgage or charge

A statutory mortgage may be surrendered or discharged by a receipt in the form (No 5) set out in the Fourth Schedule to this Act with such variations and additions, if any, as circumstances may require.

[366]

Rentcharges

121 Remedies for the recovery of annual sums charged on land

(1) Where a person is entitled to receive out of any land, or out of the income of any land, any annual sum, payable half-yearly or otherwise, whether charged on the land or on the income of the land, and whether by way of rentcharge or otherwise, not being rent incident to a reversion, then, subject and without prejudice to all estates, interests, and rights having priority to the annual sum, the person entitled to receive the annual sum shall have such remedies for recovering and compelling payment thereof as are described in this section, as far as those remedies might have been conferred by the instrument under which the annual sum arises, but not further.

(2) *If at any time the annual sum or any part thereof is unpaid for twenty-one days next after the time appointed for any payment in respect thereof, the person entitled to receive the annual sum may enter into and distrain on the land charged or any part thereof, and dispose according to law of any distress found, to the intent that thereby or otherwise the annual sum and all arrears thereof, and all costs and expenses occasioned by non-payment thereof, may be fully paid.*

(3) If at any time the annual sum or any part thereof is unpaid for forty days next after the time appointed for any payment in respect thereof, then, although no legal demand has been made for payment thereof, the person entitled to receive the annual sum may enter into possession of and hold the land charged or any part thereof, and take the income thereof, until thereby or otherwise the annual sum and all arrears thereof due at the time of his entry or afterwards becoming due during his continuance in possession, and all costs and expenses occasioned by nonpayment of the annual sum, are fully paid; and such possession when taken shall be without impeachment of waste.

(4) In the like case the person entitled to the annual sum, whether taking possession or not, may also by deed demise the land charged, or any part thereof, to a trustee for a term of years, with or without impeachment of waste, on trust, by all or any of the means hereinafter mentioned, or by any other reasonable means, to raise and pay the annual sum and all arrears thereof due or to become due, and all costs and expenses occasioned by nonpayment of the annual sum, or incurred in compelling or obtaining payment thereof, or otherwise relating thereto, including the costs of the preparation and execution of the deed of demise, and the costs of the execution of the trusts of that deed:

Provided that this subsection shall not authorise the creation of a legal term of years absolute after the commencement of this Act, save where the annual sum is a rentcharge held for a legal estate.

The surplus, if any, of the money raised, or of the income received, under the trusts of the deed shall be paid to the person for the time being entitled to the land therein comprised in reversion immediately expectant on the term thereby created.

The means by which such annual sum, arrears, costs, and expenses may be raised includes—

(a) the creation of a legal mortgage or a sale (effected by assignment or subdemise) of the term created in the land charged or any part thereof,

(b) the receipt of the income of the land comprised in the term.

(5) This section applies only if and as far as a contrary intention is not expressed in the instrument under which the annual sum arises, and has effect subject to the terms of that instrument and to the provisions therein contained.

(6) The rule of law relating to perpetuities does not apply to any powers or remedies conferred by this section, …

(7) The powers and remedies conferred by this section apply where the instrument creating the annual sum comes into operation after the thirty-first day of December, eighteen hundred and

eighty-one, and whether the instrument conferring the power under which the annual sum was authorised to be created came into operation before or after that date, unless the instrument creating the power or under which the annual sum is created otherwise directs.

[367]

NOTES

Sub-s (2): repealed by the Tribunals, Courts and Enforcement Act 2007, ss 86, 146, Sch 14, paras 21, 23, Sch 23, Pt 4, as from a day to be appointed.

Sub-s (6): words omitted repealed by the Perpetuities and Accumulations Act 1964, s 11(2).

122 Creation of rentcharges charged on another rentcharge and remedies for recovery thereof

(1) A rentcharge or other annual sum (not being rent incident to a reversion) payable half yearly or otherwise may be granted, reserved, charged or created out of or on another rentcharge or annual sum (not being rent incident to a reversion) charged on or payable out of land or on or out of the income of land, in like manner as the same could have been made to issue out of land.

(2) If at any time the annual sum so created or any part thereof is unpaid for twenty-one days next after the time appointed for any payment in respect thereof, the person entitled to receive the annual sum shall (without prejudice to any prior interest or charge) have power to appoint a receiver of the annual sum charged or any part thereof, and the provisions of this Act relating to the appointment, powers, remuneration and duties of a receiver, shall apply in like manner as if such person were a mortgagee entitled to exercise the power of sale conferred by this Act, and the annual sum charged were the mortgaged property and the person entitled thereto were the mortgagor.

(3) The power to appoint a receiver conferred by this section shall (where the annual sum is charged on a rentcharge) take effect in substitution for the remedies conferred, in the case of annual sums charged on land, by the last preceding section, but subsection (6) of that section shall apply and have effect as if herein re-enacted and in terms made applicable to the powers conferred by this section.

(4) This section applies to annual sums expressed to be created before as well as after the commencement of this Act, and, but without prejudice to any order of the court made before the commencement of this Act, operates to confirm any annual sum which would have been validly created if this section had been in force.

[368]

Powers of Attorney

123, 124 (*Repealed by the Powers of Attorney Act 1971, s 11(2), Sch 2.*)

125 Powers of attorney relating to land to be filed

(1) …

(2) Notwithstanding any stipulation to the contrary, a purchaser of any interest in or charge upon land [(not being registered land)] shall be entitled to have any instrument creating a power of attorney which affects his title, or [a copy] thereof or of the material portions thereof delivered to him free of expense.

(3) This section only applies to instruments executed after the commencement of this Act, and no right to rescind a contract shall arise by reason of the enforcement of the provisions of this section.

[369]

NOTES

Sub-s (1): repealed by the Powers of Attorney Act 1971, s 11(2), Sch 2.

Sub-s (2): words in first pair of square brackets substituted by the Land Registration Act 2002, s 133, Sch 11, para 2(1), (12); words in second pair of square brackets substituted by the Law of Property (Amendment) Act 1926, s 7, Schedule.

126–29 (*Repealed by the Powers of Attorney Act 171, ss 8, 11(2), Sch 2.*)

PART IV
EQUITABLE INTERESTS AND THINGS IN ACTION

130 … entailed interests in real and personal property

(1)–(3) …

(4) In default of and subject to the execution of a disentailing assurance or the exercise of the testamentary power conferred by this Act, an entailed interest (to the extent of the property affected) shall devolve as an equitable interest, from time to time, upon the persons who would have been successively entitled thereto as the heirs of the body (either generally or of a particular class) of the

tenant in tail or other person, or as tenant by the curtesy, if the entailed interest had, before the commencement of this Act, been limited in respect of freehold land governed by the general law in force immediately before such commencement, and such law had remained unaffected.

(5) Where personal chattels are settled without reference to settled land on trusts creating entailed interests therein, the trustees, with the consent of the usufructuary for the time being if of full age, may sell the chattels or any of them, and the net proceeds of any such sale shall be held in trust for and shall go to the same persons successively, in the same manner and for the same interests, as the chattels sold would have been held and gone if they had not been sold, and the income of investments representing such proceeds of sale shall be applied accordingly.

(6) …

(7) In this Act where the context so admits "entailed interest" includes an estate tail (now made to take effect as an equitable interest) created before the commencement of this Act.

[370]

NOTES

Section heading: words omitted repealed by the Trusts of Land and Appointment of Trustees Act 1996, s 25(2), Sch 4; for savings in relation to entailed interests created before the commencement of that Act, and savings consequential upon the abolition of the doctrine of conversion, see s 25(4), (5) thereof.

Sub-ss (1)–(3), (6): repealed by the Trusts of Land and Appointment of Trustees Act 1996, s 25(2), Sch 4, subject to savings as noted above.

131 Abolition of the rule in Shelley's case

Where by any instrument coming into operation after the commencement of this Act an interest in any property is expressed to be given to the heir or heirs or issue or any particular heir or any class of the heirs or issue of any person in words which, but for this section [(and paragraph 5 of Schedule 1 to the Trusts of Land and Appointment of Trustees Act 1996)] would, under the rule of law known as the Rule in Shelley's case, have operated to give to that person an interest in fee simple or an entailed interest, such words shall operate in equity as words of purchase and not of limitation, and shall be construed and have effect accordingly, and in the case of an interest in any property expressed to be given to an heir or heirs or any particular heir or class of heirs, the same person or persons shall take as would in the case of freehold land have answered that description under the general law in force before the commencement of this Act.

[371]

NOTES

Words in square brackets inserted by the Trusts of Land and Appointment of Trustees Act 1996, s 25(1), Sch 3, para 4(14); for savings in relation to entailed interests created before the commencement of that Act, and savings consequential upon the abolition of the doctrine of conversion, see s 25(4), (5) thereof.

132 As to heirs taking by purchase

(1) A limitation of real or personal property in favour of the heir, either general or special, of a deceased person which, if limited in respect of freehold land before the commencement of this Act, would have conferred on the heir an estate in the land by purchase, shall operate to confer a corresponding equitable interest in the property on the person who would, if the general law in force immediately before such commencement had remained unaffected, have answered the description of the heir, either general or special, of the deceased in respect of his freehold land, either at the death of the deceased or at the time named in the limitation, as the case may require.

(2) This section applies whether the deceased person dies before or after the commencement of this Act, but only applies to limitations or trusts created by an instrument coming into operation after such commencement.

[372]

133 (*Repealed by the Statute Law* (*Repeals*) *Act 1969, s 1, Schedule, Pt III.*)

134 Restriction on executory limitations

(1) Where there is a person entitled to—

(a) an equitable interest in land for an estate in fee simple or for any less interest not being an entailed interest, or

(b) any interest in other property, not being an entailed interest,

with an executory limitation over on default or failure of all or any of his issue, whether within or at any specified period or time or not, that executory limitation shall be or become void and incapable of taking effect, if and as soon as there is living any issue who has attained the age of [eighteen years] of the class on default or failure whereof the limitation over was to take effect.

(2) This section applies where the executory limitation is contained in an instrument coming into operation after the thirty-first day of December, eighteen hundred and eighty-two, save that, as

regards instruments coming into operation before the commencement of this Act, it only applies to limitations of land for an estate in fee, or for a term of years absolute or determinable on life, or for a term of life.

[373]

NOTES

Sub-s (1): words in square brackets substituted by the Family Law Reform Act 1969, ss 1(3), 28(3), Sch 1.

135 Equitable waste

An equitable interest for life without impeachment of waste does not confer upon the tenant for life any right to commit waste of the description known as equitable waste, unless an intention to confer such right expressly appears by the instrument creating such equitable interest.

[374]

136 Legal assignments of things in action

(1) Any absolute assignment by writing under the hand of the assignor (not purporting to be by way of charge only) of any debt or other legal thing in action, of which express notice in writing has been given to the debtor, trustee or other person from whom the assignor would have been entitled to claim such debt or thing in action, is effectual in law (subject to equities having priority over the right of the assignee) to pass and transfer from the date of such notice—

(a) the legal right to such debt or thing in action;
(b) all legal and other remedies for the same; and
(c) the power to give a good discharge for the same without the concurrence of the assignor:

Provided that, if the debtor, trustee or other person liable in respect of such debt or thing in action has notice—

(a) that the assignment is disputed by the assignor or any person claiming under him; or
(b) of any other opposing or conflicting claims to such debt or thing in action;

he may, if he thinks fit, either call upon the persons making claim thereto to interplead concerning the same, or pay the debt or other thing in action into court under the provisions of the Trustee Act 1925.

(2) This section does not affect the provisions of the Policies of Assurance Act 1867.

[(3) The county court has jurisdiction (including power to receive payment of money or securities into court) under the proviso to subsection (1) of this section where the amount or value of the debt or thing in action does not exceed [£30,000].]

[375]

NOTES

Sub-s (3): inserted by the County Courts Act 1984, s 148(1), Sch 2, para 4; sum in square brackets substituted by SI 1991/724, art 2(5), (8), Schedule, Pt I.

Application: this section applies to an absolute assignment (not purporting to be by way of charge only) of shares by means of electronic communication with the following modifications: (a) the reference in sub-s (1) to writing under the hand of the assignor refers to an electronic communication made by the assignor or by his agent authorised in writing; and (b) the reference in that subsection to express notice in writing refers to express notice by electronic communication to the company; see the Open-Ended Investment Companies Regulations 2001, SI 2001/1228, Sch 4, para 4A (as inserted by SI 2009/553, reg 2(1), (4)(a)).

Disapplication: this section does not apply to any transfer of title to uncertificated units of a security by means of a relevant system and any disposition or assignment of an interest in uncertificated units of a security title to which is held by a relevant nominee; see the Uncertificated Securities Regulations 2001, SI 2001/3755, reg 38(5), (6). See also, as to the disapplication of this section in relation to financial collateral arrangements, the Financial Collateral Arrangements (No 2) Regulations 2003, SI 2003/3226, reg 4(3).

137 Dealings with life interests, reversions and other equitable interests

(1) The law applicable to dealings with equitable things in action which regulates the priority of competing interests therein, shall, as respects dealings with equitable interests in land, capital money, and securities representing capital money effected after the commencement of this Act, apply to and regulate the priority of competing interests therein.

This subsection applies whether or not the money or securities are in court.

(2)

(i) In the case of a dealing with an equitable interest in settled land, capital money or securities representing capital money, the persons to be served with notice of the dealing shall be the trustees of the settlement; and where the equitable interest is created by a derivative or subsidiary settlement, the persons to be served with notice shall be the trustees of that settlement.
(ii) In the case of a dealing with an equitable interest in [land subject to a trust of land, or the proceeds of the sale of such land, the persons to be served with notice shall be the trustees.]

(iii) In any other case the person to be served with notice of a dealing with an equitable interest in land shall be the estate owner of the land affected.

The persons on whom notice is served pursuant to this subsection shall be affected thereby in the same manner as if they had been trustees of personal property out of which the equitable interest was created or arose.

This subsection does not apply where the money or securities are in court.

(3) A notice, otherwise than in writing, given to, or received by, a trustee after the commencement of this Act as respects any dealing with an equitable interest in real or personal property, shall not affect the priority of competing claims of purchasers in that equitable interest.

(4) Where, as respects any dealing with an equitable interest in real or personal property—

(a) the trustees are not persons to whom a valid notice of the dealing can be given; or

(b) there are no trustees to whom a notice can be given; or

(c) for any other reason a valid notice cannot be served, or cannot be served without unreasonable cost or delay;

a purchaser may at his own cost require that—

(i) a memorandum of the dealing be endorsed, written on or permanently annexed to the instrument creating the trust;

(ii) the instrument be produced to him by the person having the possession or custody thereof to prove that a sufficient memorandum has been placed thereon or annexed thereto.

Such memorandum shall, as respects priorities, operate in like manner as if notice in writing of the dealing had been given to trustees duly qualified to receive the notice at the time when the memorandum is placed on or annexed to the instrument creating the trust.

(5) Where the property affected is settled land, the memorandum shall be placed on or annexed to the trust instrument and not the vesting instrument.

Where the property affected is land [subject to a trust of land], the memorandum shall be placed on or annexed to the instrument whereby the equitable interest is created.

(6) Where the trust is created by statute or by operation of law, or in any other case where there is no instrument whereby the trusts are declared, the instrument under which the equitable interest is acquired or which is evidence of the devolution thereof shall, for the purposes of this section, be deemed the instrument creating the trust.

In particular, where the trust arises by reason of an intestacy, the letters of administration or probate in force when the dealing was effected shall be deemed such instrument.

(7) Nothing in this section affects any priority acquired before the commencement of this Act.

(8) Where a notice in writing of a dealing with an equitable interest in real or personal property has been served on a trustee under this section, the trustees from time to time of the property affected shall be entitled to the custody of the notice, and the notice shall be delivered to them by any person who for the time being may have the custody thereof; and subject to the payment of costs, any person interested in the equitable interest may require production of the notice.

(9) The liability of the estate owner of the legal estate affected to produce documents and furnish information to persons entitled to equitable interests therein shall correspond to the liability of a trustee for sale to produce documents and furnish information to persons entitled to equitable interests in the proceeds of sale of the land.

(10) This section does not apply until a trust has been created, and in this section "dealing" includes a disposition by operation of law.

[376]

NOTES

Sub-ss (2), (5): words in square brackets substituted by the Trusts of Land and Appointment of Trustees Act 1996, s 25(1), Sch 3, para 4(15); for savings in relation to entailed interests created before the commencement of that Act, and savings consequential upon the abolition of the doctrine of conversion, see s 25(4), (5) thereof.

138 Power to nominate a trust corporation to receive notices

(1) By any settlement or other instrument creating a trust, a trust corporation may be nominated to whom notices of dealings affecting real or personal property may be given, whether or not under the foregoing section, and in default of such nomination the trustees (if any) of the instrument, or the court on the application of any person interested, may make the nomination.

(2) The person having the possession or custody of any instrument on which notices under that section may be endorsed shall cause the name of the trust corporation to whom notices may be given to be endorsed upon that instrument.

(3) Notice given to any trust corporation whose name is so endorsed shall operate in the same way as a notice or endorsement under the foregoing section.

(4) Where a trust corporation is acting for the purposes of this section a notice given to a trustee of the trust instrument of a dealing relating to the trust property shall forthwith be delivered or sent by post by the trustee to the trust corporation, and until received by the corporation shall not affect any priority.

(5) A trust corporation shall not be nominated for the purposes of this section—

(a) unless that corporation consents to act; or

(b) where that corporation has any beneficial interest in or charge upon the trust property; or

(c) where a trust corporation is acting as the trustee or one of the trustees of the instrument creating the trust.

(6) Where a trust corporation acting for the purposes of this section becomes entitled to any beneficial interest in or charge upon the trust property, another trust corporation shall be nominated in its place and all documents relating to notices affecting the trust shall be delivered to the corporation so nominated.

(7) A trust corporation acting for the purposes of this section shall be bound to keep a separate register of notices of dealings in respect of each equitable interest and shall enter therein—

(a) the date of the notice;

(b) the name of the person giving the notice;

(c) short particulars of the equitable interest intended to be affected; and

(d) short particulars of the effect of the dealing if mentioned in the notice.

(8) The trust corporation may, before making any entry in the register, require the applicant to pay a fee not exceeding the prescribed fee.

(9) Subject to the payment of a fee not exceeding the prescribed fee, the trust corporation shall permit any person who would, if the corporation had been the trustee of the trust investment, have been entitled to inspect notices served on the trustee, to inspect and take copies of the register and any notices held by the corporation.

(10) Subject to the payment by the applicant of a fee not exceeding the prescribed fee, the trust corporation shall reply to all inquiries respecting notices received by the corporation in like manner and in the same circumstances as if the corporation had been the trustee of the trust instrument.

(11) In this section "prescribed fee" means the fee prescribed [by the Lord Chancellor] in cases where the Public Trustee acts as a trust corporation for the purposes of this section.

[377]

NOTES

Sub-s (11): words in square brackets substituted by the Public Trustee (Liability and Fees) Act 2002, s 2(2).

PART V
LEASES AND TENANCIES

139 Effect of extinguishment of reversion

(1) Where a reversion expectant on a lease of land is surrendered or merged, the estate or interest which as against the lessee for the time being confers the next vested right to the land, shall be deemed the reversion for the purpose of preserving the same incidents and obligations as would have affected the original reversion had there been no surrender or merger thereof.

(2) This section applies to surrenders or mergers effected after the first day of October, eighteen hundred and forty-five.

[378]

140 Apportionment of conditions on severance

(1) Notwithstanding the severance by conveyance, surrender, or otherwise of the reversionary estate in any land comprised in a lease, and notwithstanding the avoidance or cesser in any other manner of the term granted by a lease as to part only of the land comprised therein, every condition or right of re-entry, and every other condition contained in the lease, shall be apportioned, and shall remain annexed to the severed parts of the reversionary estate as severed, and shall be in force with respect to the term whereon each severed part is reversionary, or the term in the part of the land as to which the term has not been surrendered, or has not been avoided or has not otherwise ceased, in like manner as if the land comprised in each severed part, or the land as to which the term remains subsisting, as the case may be, had alone originally been comprised in the lease.

(2) In this section "right of re-entry" includes a right to determine the lease by notice to quit or otherwise; but where the notice is served by a person entitled to a severed part of the reversion so that it extends to part only of the land demised, the lessee may within one month determine the lease in regard to the rest of the land by giving to the owner of the reversionary estate therein a counter notice expiring at the same time as the original notice …

(3) This section applies to leases made before or after the commencement of this Act and whether the severance of the reversionary estate or the partial avoidance or cesser of the term was effected before or after such commencement:

Provided that, where the lease was made before the first day of January eighteen hundred and eighty-two nothing in this section shall affect the operation of a severance of the reversionary estate or partial avoidance or cesser of the term which was effected before the commencement of this Act.

[379]

NOTES

Sub-s (2): words omitted repealed by the Agricultural Holdings Act 1948, ss 98, 100(1), Sch 8.

141 Rent and benefit of lessee's covenants to run with the reversion

(1) Rent reserved by a lease, and the benefit of every covenant or provision therein contained, having reference to the subject-matter thereof, and on the lessee's part to be observed or performed, and every condition of re-entry and other condition therein contained, shall be annexed and incident to and shall go with the reversionary estate in the land, or in any part thereof, immediately expectant on the term granted by the lease, notwithstanding severance of that reversionary estate, and without prejudice to any liability affecting a covenantor or his estate.

(2) Any such rent, covenant or provision shall be capable of being recovered, received, enforced, and taken advantage of, by the person from time to time entitled, subject to the term, to the income of the whole or any part, as the case may require, of the land leased.

(3) Where that person becomes entitled by conveyance or otherwise, such rent, covenant or provision may be recovered, received, enforced or taken advantage of by him notwithstanding that he becomes so entitled after the condition of re-entry or forfeiture has become enforceable, but this subsection does not render enforceable any condition of re-entry or other condition waived or released before such person becomes entitled as aforesaid.

(4) This section applies to leases made before or after the commencement of this Act, but does not affect the operation of—

(a) any severance of the reversionary estate; or

(b) any acquisition by conveyance or otherwise of the right to receive or enforce any rent covenant or provision;

effected before the commencement of this Act.

[380]

NOTES

Disapplication: this section does not apply in relation to new tenancies as defined by the Landlord and Tenant (Covenants) Act 1995, ss 1(3), 28(1): see s 30(4) thereof at **[1590]**.

142 Obligation of lessor's covenants to run with reversion

(1) The obligation under a condition or of a covenant entered into by a lessor with reference to the subject-matter of the lease shall, if and as far as the lessor has power to bind the reversionary estate immediately expectant on the term granted by the lease, be annexed and incident to and shall go with that reversionary estate, or the several parts thereof, notwithstanding severance of that reversionary estate, and may be taken advantage of and enforced by the person in whom the term is from time to time vested by conveyance, devolution in law, or otherwise; and, if and as far as the lessor has power to bind the person from time to time entitled to that reversionary estate, the obligation aforesaid may be taken advantage of and entered against any person so entitled.

(2) This section applies to leases made before or after the commencement of this Act, whether the severance of the reversionary estate was effected before or after such commencement:

Provided that, where the lease was made before the first day of January eighteen hundred and eighty-two, nothing in this section shall affect the operation of any severance of the reversionary estate effected before such commencement.

This section takes effect without prejudice to any liability affecting a covenantor or his estate.

[381]

NOTES

Disapplication: this section does not apply in relation to new tenancies as defined by the Landlord and Tenant (Covenants) Act 1995, ss 1(3), 28(1): see s 30(4) thereof at **[1590]**.

143 Effect of licences granted to lessees

(1) Where a licence is granted to a lessee to do any act, the licence, unless otherwise expressed, extends only—

(a) to the permission actually given; or

(b) to the specific breach of any provision or covenant referred to; or

(c) to any other matter thereby specifically authorised to be done;

and the licence does not prevent any proceeding for any subsequent breach unless otherwise specified in the licence.

(2) Notwithstanding any such licence—

(a) All rights under covenants and powers of re-entry contained in the lease remain in full force and are available as against any subsequent breach of covenant, condition or other matter not specifically authorised or waived, in the same manner as if no licence had been granted; and

(b) The condition or right of entry remains in force in all respects as if the licence had not been granted, save in respect of the particular matter authorised to be done.

(3) Where in any lease there is a power or condition of re-entry on the lessee assigning, subletting or doing any other specified act without a licence, and a licence is granted—

(a) to any one of two or more lessees to do any act, or to deal with his equitable share or interest; or

(b) to any lessee, or to any one of two or more lessees to assign or underlet part only of the property, or to do any act in respect of part only of the property;

the licence does not operate to extinguish the right of entry in case of any breach of covenant or condition by the co-lessees of the other shares or interests in the property, or by the lessee or lessees of the rest of the property (as the case may be) in respect of such shares or interests or remaining property, but the right of entry remains in force in respect of the shares, interests or property not the subject of the licence.

This subsection does not authorise the grant after the commencement of this Act of a licence to create an undivided share in a legal estate.

(4) This section applies to licences granted after the thirteenth day of August, eighteen hundred and fifty-nine.

[382]

144 No fine to be exacted for licence to assign

In all leases containing a covenant, condition, or agreement against assigning, underletting, or parting with the possession, or disposing of the land or property leased without licence or consent, such covenant, condition, or agreement shall, unless the lease contains an express provision to the contrary, be deemed to be subject to a proviso to the effect that no fine or sum of money in the nature of a fine shall be payable for or in respect of such licence or consent; but this proviso does not preclude the right to require the payment of a reasonable sum in respect of any legal or other expense incurred in relation to such licence or consent.

[383]

145 Lessee to give notice of ejectment to lessor

Every lessee to whom there is delivered any writ for the recovery of premises demised to or held by him, or to whose knowledge any such writ comes, shall forthwith give notice thereof to his lessor or his bailiff or receiver, and, if he fails so to do, he shall be liable to forfeit to the person of whom he holds the premises an amount equal to the value of three years' improved or rack rent of the premises, to be recovered by action in any court having jurisdiction in respect of claims for such an amount.

[384]

146 Restrictions on and relief against forfeiture of leases and underleases

(1) A right of re-entry or forfeiture under any proviso or stipulation in a lease for a breach of any covenant or condition in the lease shall not be enforceable, by action or otherwise, unless and until the lessor serves on the lessee a notice—

(a) specifying the particular breach complained of; and

(b) if the breach is capable of remedy, requiring the lessee to remedy the breach; and

(c) in any case, requiring the lessee to make compensation in money for the breach;

and the lessee fails, within a reasonable time thereafter, to remedy the breach, if it is capable of remedy, and to make reasonable compensation in money, to the satisfaction of the lessor, for the breach.

(2) Where a lessor is proceeding, by action or otherwise, to enforce such a right of re-entry or forfeiture, the lessee may, in the lessor's action, if any, or in any action brought by himself, apply to the court for relief; and the court may grant or refuse relief, as the court, having regard to the proceedings and conduct of the parties under the foregoing provisions of this section, and to all the other circumstances, thinks fit; and in case of relief may grant it on such terms, if any, as to costs, expenses, damages, compensation, penalty, or otherwise, including the granting of an injunction to restrain any like breach in the future, as the court, in the circumstances of each case, thinks fit.

(3) A lessor shall be entitled to recover as a debt due to him from a lessee, and in addition to damages (if any), all reasonable costs and expenses properly incurred by the lessor in the

employment of a solicitor and surveyor or valuer, or otherwise, in reference to any breach giving rise to a right of re-entry or forfeiture which, at the request of the lessee, is waived by the lessor, or from which the lessee is relieved, under the provisions of this Act.

(4) Where a lessor is proceeding by action or otherwise to enforce a right of re-entry or forfeiture under any covenant, proviso, or stipulation in a lease, or for non-payment of rent, the court may, on application by any person claiming as under-lessee any estate or interest in the property comprised in the lease or any part thereof, either in the lessor's action (if any) or in any action brought by such person for that purpose, make an order vesting, for the whole term of the lease or any less term, the property comprised in the lease or any part thereof in any person entitled as under-lessee to any estate or interest in such property upon such conditions as to execution of any deed or other document, payment of rent, costs, expenses, damages, compensation, giving security, or otherwise, as the court in the circumstances of each case may think fit, but in no case shall any such under-lessee be entitled to require a lease to be granted to him for any longer term than he had under his original sub-lease.

(5) For the purposes of this section—

(a) "Lease" includes an original or derivative under-lease; also an agreement for a lease where the lessee has become entitled to have his lease granted; also a grant at a fee farm rent, or securing a rent by condition;

(b) "Lessee" includes an original or derivative under-lessee, and the persons deriving title under a lessee; also a grantee under any such grant as aforesaid and the persons deriving title under him;

(c) "Lessor" includes an original or derivative under-lessor, and the persons deriving title under a lessor; also a person making such grant as aforesaid and the persons deriving title under him;

(d) "Under-lease" includes an agreement for an underlease where the underlessee has become entitled to have his underlease granted;

(e) "Underlessee" includes any person deriving title under an underlessee.

(6) This section applies although the proviso or stipulation under which the right of re-entry or forfeiture accrues is inserted in the lease in pursuance of the directions of any Act of Parliament.

(7) For the purposes of this section a lease limited to continue as long only as the lessee abstains from committing a breach of covenant shall be and take effect as a lease to continue for any longer term for which it could subsist, but determinable by a proviso for re-entry on such a breach.

(8) This section does not extend—

(i) To a covenant or condition against assigning, underletting, parting with the possession, or disposing of the land leased where the breach occurred before the commencement of this Act; or

(ii) In the case of a mining lease, to a covenant or condition for allowing the lessor to have access to or inspect books, accounts, records, weighing machines or other things, or to enter or inspect the mine or the workings thereof.

(9) This section does not apply to a condition for forfeiture on the bankruptcy of the lessee or on taking in execution of the lessee's interest if contained in a lease of—

(a) Agricultural or pastoral land;

(b) Mines or minerals;

(c) A house used or intended to be used as a public-house or beershop;

(d) A house let as a dwelling-house, with the use of any furniture, books, works of art, or other chattels not being in the nature of fixtures;

(e) Any property with respect to which the personal qualifications of the tenant are of importance for the preservation of the value or character of the property, or on the ground of neighbourhood to the lessor, or to any person holding under him.

(10) Where a condition of forfeiture on the bankruptcy of the lessee or on taking in execution of the lessee's interest is contained in any lease, other than a lease of any of the classes mentioned in the last subsection, then—

(a) if the lessee's interest is sold within one year from the bankruptcy or taking in execution, this section applies to the forfeiture condition aforesaid;

(b) if the lessee's interest is not sold before the expiration of that year, this section only applies to the forfeiture condition aforesaid during the first year from the date of the bankruptcy or taking in execution.

(11) This section does not, save as otherwise mentioned, affect the law relating to re-entry or forfeiture or relief in case of non-payment of rent.

(12) This section has effect notwithstanding any stipulation to the contrary.

[(13) The county court has jurisdiction under this section …]

[385]

NOTES

Sub-s (13): inserted by the County Courts Act 1984, s 148(1), Sch 2, para 5; words omitted repealed by SI 1991/724, art 2(1)(a), (8), Schedule, Pt I.

Modification: references to solicitors etc modified to include references to bodies recognised under the Administration of Justice Act 1985, s 9, by the Solicitors' Incorporated Practices Order 1991, SI 1991/2684, arts 4, 5, Sch 1.

See further: as to exclusion of this section in relation to leases or tenancies granted to contractors in respect of the running of secure training centres, see the Criminal Justice and Public Order Act 1994, s 7(3). As to the exclusion of this section in relation to leases or tenancies granted to contractors in respect of the running of any removal centre or part of a removal centre, see the Immigration and Asylum Act 1999, s 149(3).

147 Relief against notice to effect decorative repairs

(1) After a notice is served on a lessee relating to the internal decorative repairs to a house or other building, he may apply to the court for relief, and if, having regard to all the circumstances of the case (including in particular the length of the lessee's term or interest remaining unexpired), the court is satisfied that the notice is unreasonable, it may, by order, wholly or partially relieve the lessee from liability for such repairs.

(2) This section does not apply:—

(i) where the liability arises under an express covenant or agreement to put the property in a decorative state of repair and the covenant or agreement has never been performed;

(ii) to any matter necessary or proper—

(a) for putting or keeping the property in a sanitary condition, or

(b) for the maintenance or preservation of the structure;

(iii) to any statutory liability to keep a house in all respects reasonably fit for human habitation;

(iv) to any covenant or stipulation to yield up the house or other building in a specified state of repair at the end of the term.

(3) In this section "lease" includes an underlease and an agreement for a lease, and "lessee" has a corresponding meaning and includes any person liable to effect the repairs.

(4) This section applies whether the notice is served before or after the commencement of this Act, and has effect notwithstanding any stipulation to the contrary.

[(5) The county court has jurisdiction under this section …]

[386]

NOTES

Sub-s (5): inserted by the County Courts Act 1984, s 148(1), Sch 2, para 6; words omitted repealed by SI 1991/724, art 2(1)(a), (8), Schedule, Pt I.

148 Waiver of a covenant in a lease

(1) Where any actual waiver by a lessor or the persons deriving title under him of the benefit of any covenant or condition in any lease is proved to have taken place in any particular instance, such waiver shall not be deemed to extend to any instance, or to any breach of covenant or condition save that to which such waiver specially relates, nor operate as a general waiver of the benefit of any such covenant or condition.

(2) This section applies unless a contrary intention appears and extends to waivers effected after the twenty-third day of July, eighteen hundred and sixty.

[387]

149 Abolition of interesse termini, and as to reversionary leases and leases for lives

(1) The doctrine of interesse termini is hereby abolished.

(2) As from the commencement of this Act all terms of years absolute shall, whether the interest is created before or after such commencement, be capable of taking effect at law or in equity, according to the estate interest or powers of the grantor, from the date fixed for commencement of the term, without actual entry.

(3) A term, at a rent or granted in consideration of a fine, limited after the commencement of this Act to take effect more than twenty-one years from the date of the instrument purporting to create it, shall be void, and any contract made after such commencement to create such a term shall likewise be void; but this subsection does not apply to any term taking effect in equity under a settlement, or created out of an equitable interest under a settlement, or under an equitable power for mortgage, indemnity or other like purposes.

(4) Nothing in subsections (1) and (2) of this section prejudicially affects the right of any person to recover any rent or to enforce or take advantage of any covenants or conditions or, as respects terms or interests created before the commencement of this Act, operates to vary any statutory or other obligations imposed in respect of such terms or interests.

(5) Nothing in this Act affects the rule of law that a legal term, whether or not being a mortgage term, may be created to take effect in reversion expectant on a longer term, which rule is hereby confirmed.

(6) Any lease or underlease, at a rent, or in consideration of a fine, for life or lives or for any term of years determinable with life or lives, or on the marriage of the lessee, [or on the formation of a civil partnership between the lessee and another person,] or any contract therefor, made before or after the commencement of this Act, or created by virtue of Part V of the Law of Property Act 1922, shall take effect as a lease, underlease or contract therefor, for a term of ninety years determinable [after (as the case may be) the death or marriage of, or the formation of a civil partnership by, the original lessee or the survivor of the original lessees,] by at least one month's notice in writing given to determine the same on one of the quarter days applicable to the tenancy, either by the lessor or the persons deriving title under him, to the person entitled to the leasehold interest, or if no such person is in existence by affixing the same to the premises, or by the lessee or other persons in whom the leasehold interest is vested to the lessor or the persons deriving title under him:

Provided that—

(a) this subsection shall not apply to any term taking effect in equity under a settlement or created out of an equitable interest under a settlement for mortgage, indemnity, or other like purposes;

(b) the person in whom the leasehold interest is vested by virtue of Part V of the Law of Property Act 1922 shall, for the purposes of this subsection, be deemed an original lessee;

(c) if the lease, underlease, or contract therefor is made determinable on the dropping of the lives of persons other than or besides the lessees, then the notice shall be capable of being served after the death of any person or of the survivor of any persons (whether or not including the lessees) on the cesser of whose life or lives the lease, underlease, or contract is made determinable, instead of after the death of the original lessee or of the survivor of the original lessees;

(d) if there are no quarter days specially applicable to the tenancy, notice may be given to determine the tenancy on one of the usual quarter days.

[(7) Subsection (8) applies where a lease, underlease or contract—

(a) relates to commonhold land, and

(b) would take effect by virtue of subsection (6) as a lease, underlease or contract of the kind mentioned in that subsection.

(8) The lease, underlease or contract shall be treated as if it purported to be a lease, underlease or contract of the kind referred to in subsection (7)(b) (and sections 17 and 18 of the Commonhold and Leasehold Reform Act 2002 (residential and non-residential leases) shall apply accordingly).]

[388]

NOTES

Sub-s (6): words in first pair of square brackets inserted and words in second pair of square brackets substituted by the Civil Partnership Act 2004, s 81, Sch 8, para 1.

Sub-ss (7), (8): inserted by the Commonhold and Leasehold Reform Act 2002, s 68, Sch 5, para 3.

150 Surrender of a lease, without prejudice to underleases with a view to the grant of a new lease

(1) A lease may be surrendered with a view to the acceptance of a new lease in place thereof, without a surrender of any under-lease derived thereout.

(2) A new lease may be granted and accepted, in place of any lease so surrendered, without any such surrender of an under-lease as aforesaid, and the new lease operates as if all under-leases derived out of the surrendered lease had been surrendered before the surrender of that lease was effected.

(3) The lessee under the new lease and any person deriving title under him is entitled to the same rights and remedies in respect of the rent reserved by and the covenants, agreements and conditions contained in any under-lease as if the original lease had not been surrendered but was or remained vested in him.

(4) Each under-lessee and any person deriving title under him is entitled to hold and enjoy the land comprised in his under-lease (subject to the payment of any rent reserved by and to the observance of the covenants agreements and conditions contained in the under-lease) as if the lease out of which the under-lease was derived had not been surrendered.

(5) The lessor granting the new lease and any person deriving title under him is entitled to the same remedies, *by distress or* [under section 72(1) of the Tribunals, Courts and Enforcement Act 2007 (commercial rent arrears recovery) or by] entry in and upon the land comprised in any such under-lease for rent reserved by or for breach of any covenant, agreement or condition contained in the new lease (so far only as the rents reserved by or the covenants, agreements or

conditions contained in the new lease do not exceed or impose greater burdens than those reserved by or contained in the original lease out of which the under-lease is derived) as he would have had—

(a) If the original lease had remained on foot; or

(b) If a new under-lease derived out of the new lease had been granted to the under-lessee or a person deriving title under him;

as the case may require.

(6) This section does not affect the powers of the court to give relief against forfeiture.

[389]

NOTES

Sub-s (5): words in italics substituted by subsequent words in square brackets by the Tribunals, Courts and Enforcement Act 2007, s 86, Sch 14, paras 21, 24, as from a day to be appointed.

151 Provision as to attornments by tenants

(1) Where land is subject to a lease—

(a) the conveyance of a reversion in the land expectant on the determination of the lease; or

(b) the creation or conveyance of a rentcharge to issue or issuing out of the land;

shall be valid without any attornment of the lessee:

Nothing in this subsection—

(i) affects the validity of any payment of rent by the lessee to the person making the conveyance or grant before notice of the conveyance or grant is given to him by the person entitled thereunder; or

(ii) renders the lessee liable for any breach of covenant to pay rent, on account of his failure to pay rent to the person entitled under the conveyance or grant before such notice is given to the lessee.

(2) An attornment by the lessee in respect of any land to a person claiming to be entitled to the interest in the land of the lessor, if made without the consent of the lessor, shall be void.

This subsection does not apply to an attornment—

(a) made pursuant to a judgment of a court of competent jurisdiction; or

(b) to a mortgagee, by a lessee holding under a lease from the mortgagor where the right of redemption is barred; or

(c) to any other person rightfully deriving title under the lessor.

[390]

152 Leases invalidated by reason of non-compliance with terms of powers under which they are granted

(1) Where in the intended exercise of any power of leasing, whether conferred by an Act of Parliament or any other instrument, a lease (in this section referred to as an invalid lease) is granted, which by reason of any failure to comply with the terms of the power is invalid, then—

(a) as against the person entitled after the determination of the interest of the grantor to the reversion; or

(b) as against any other person who, subject to any lease properly granted under the power, would have been entitled to the land comprised in the lease;

the lease, if it was made in good faith, and the lessee has entered thereunder, shall take effect in equity as a contract for the grant, at the request of the lessee, of a valid lease under the power, of like effect as the invalid lease, subject to such variations as may be necessary in order to comply with the terms of the power:

Provided that a lessee under an invalid lease shall not, by virtue of any such implied contract, be entitled to obtain a variation of the lease if the other persons who would have been bound by the contract are willing and able to confirm the lease without variation.

(2) Where a lease granted in the intended exercise of such a power is invalid by reason of the grantor not having power to grant the lease at the date thereof, but the grantor's interest in the land comprised therein continues after the time when he might, in the exercise of the power, have properly granted a lease in the like terms, the lease shall take effect as a valid lease in like manner as if it had been granted at that time.

(3) Where during the continuance of the possession taken under an invalid lease the person for the time being entitled, subject to such possession, to the land comprised therein or to the rents and profits thereof, is able to confirm the lease without variation, the lessee, or other person who would have been bound by the lease had it been valid, shall, at the request of the person so able to confirm the lease, be bound to accept a confirmation thereof, and thereupon the lease shall have effect and be deemed to have had effect as a valid lease from the grant thereof.

Confirmation under this subsection may be by a memorandum in writing signed by or on behalf of the persons respectively confirming and accepting the confirmation of the lease.

(4) Where a receipt or a memorandum in writing confirming an invalid lease is, upon or before the acceptance of rent thereunder, signed by or on behalf of the person accepting the rent, that acceptance shall, as against that person, be deemed to be a confirmation of the lease.

(5) The foregoing provisions of this section do not affect prejudicially—

(a) any right of action or other right or remedy to which, but for those provisions or any enactment replaced by those provisions, the lessee named in an invalid lease would or might have been entitled under any covenant on the part of the grantor for title or quiet enjoyment contained therein or implied thereby; or

(b) any right of re-entry or other right or remedy to which, but for those provisions or any enactment replaced thereby, the grantor or other person for the time being entitled to the reversion expectant on the termination of the lease, would or might have been entitled by reason of any breach of the covenants, conditions or provisions contained in the lease and binding on the lessee.

(6) Where a valid power of leasing is vested in or may be exercised by a person who grants a lease which, by reason of the determination of the interest of the grantor or otherwise, cannot have effect and continuance according to the terms thereof independently of the power, the lease shall for the purposes of this section be deemed to have been granted in the intended exercise of the power although the power is not referred to in the lease.

(7) This section does not apply to a lease of land held on charitable, ecclesiastical or public trusts.

(8) This section takes effect without prejudice to the provision in this Act for the grant of leases in the name and on behalf of the estate owner of the land affected.

[391]

153 Enlargement of residue of long terms into fee simple estates

(1) Where a residue unexpired of not less than two hundred years of a term, which, as originally created, was for not less than three hundred years, is subsisting in land, whether being the whole land originally comprised in the term, or part only thereof,—

(a) without any trust or right of redemption affecting the term in favour of the freeholder, or other person entitled in reversion expectant on the term; and

(b) without any rent, or with merely a peppercorn rent or other rent having no money value, incident to the reversion, or having had a rent, not being merely a peppercorn rent or other rent having no money value, originally so incident, which subsequently has been released or has become barred by lapse of time, or has in any other way ceased to be payable;

the term may be enlarged into a fee simple in the manner, and subject to the restrictions in this section provided.

(2) This section applies to and includes every such term as aforesaid whenever created, whether or not having the freehold as the immediate reversion thereon; but does not apply to—

(i) Any term liable to be determined by re-entry for condition broken; or

(ii) Any term created by subdemise out of a superior term, itself incapable of being enlarged into fee simple.

(3) This section extends to mortgage terms, where the right of redemption is barred.

(4) A rent not exceeding the yearly sum of one pound which has not been collected or paid for a continuous period of twenty years or upwards shall, for the purposes of this section, be deemed to have ceased to be payable:

…

(5) Where a rent incident to a reversion expectant on a term to which this section applies is deemed to have ceased to be payable for the purposes aforesaid, no claim for such rent or for any arrears thereof shall be capable of being enforced.

(6) Each of the following persons, namely—

(i) Any person beneficially entitled in right of the term, whether subject to any incumbrance or not, to possession of any land comprised in the term, and, in the case of a married woman without the concurrence of her husband, whether or not she is entitled for her separate use or as her separate property, … ;

(ii) Any person being in receipt of income as trustee, in right of the term, or having the term vested in him [as a trustee of land], whether subject to any incumbrance or not;

(iii) Any person in whom, as personal representative of any deceased person, the term is vested, whether subject to any incumbrance or not;

shall, so far as regards the land to which he is entitled, or in which he is interested in right of the term, in any such character as aforesaid, have power by deed to declare to the effect that, from and after the execution of the deed, the term shall be enlarged into a fee simple.

(7) Thereupon, by virtue of the deed and of this Act, the term shall become and be enlarged accordingly, and the person in whom the term was previously vested shall acquire and have in the land a fee simple instead of the term.

(8) The estate in fee simple so acquired by enlargement shall be subject to all the same trusts, powers, executory limitations over, rights and equities, and to all the same covenants and provisions relating to user and enjoyment, and to all the same obligations of every kind, as the term would have been subject to if it had not been so enlarged.

(9) But where—

(a) any land so held for the residue of a term has been settled in trust by reference to other land, being freehold land, so as to go along with that other land, or, in the case of settlements coming into operation before the commencement of this Act, so as to go along with that other land as far as the law permits; and

(b) at the time of enlargement, the ultimate beneficial interest in the term, whether subject to any subsisting particular estate or not, has not become absolutely and indefeasibly vested in any person, free from charges or powers of charging created by a settlement;

the estate in fee simple acquired as aforesaid shall, without prejudice to any conveyance for value previously made by a person having a contingent or defeasible interest in the term, be liable to be, and shall be, conveyed by means of a subsidiary vesting instrument and settled in like manner as the other land, being freehold land, aforesaid, and until so conveyed and settled shall devolve beneficially as if it had been so conveyed and settled.

(10) The estate in fee simple so acquired shall, whether the term was originally created without impeachment of waste or not, include the fee simple in all mines and minerals which at the time of enlargement have not been severed in right or in fact, or have not been severed or reserved by an inclosure Act or award.

[392]

NOTES

Sub-s (4): words omitted repealed by the Statute Law (Repeals) Act 2004.

Sub-s (6): words omitted from para (i) repealed by the Married Women (Restraint upon Anticipation) Act 1949, s 1, Sch 2; words in square brackets in para (ii) substituted by the Trusts of Land and Appointment of Trustees Act 1996, s 25(1), Sch 3, para 4(16) (for savings in relation to entailed interests created before the commencement of that Act, and savings consequential upon the abolition of the doctrine of conversion, see s 25(4), (5) thereof).

154 Application of Part V to existing leases

This part of this Act, except where otherwise expressly provided, applies to leases created before or after the commencement of this Act, and "lease" includes an under-lease or other tenancy.

[393]

PART VI
POWERS

155 Release of powers simply collateral

A person to whom any power, whether coupled with an interest or not, is given may by deed release, or contract not to exercise, the power.

[394]

156 Disclaimer of power

(1) A person to whom any power, whether coupled with an interest or not, is given may by deed disclaim the power, and, after disclaimer, shall not be capable of exercising or joining in the exercise of the power.

(2) On such disclaimer, the power may be exercised by the other person or persons or the survivor or survivors of the other persons, to whom the power is given, unless the contrary is expressed in the instrument creating the power.

[395]

157 Protection of purchasers claiming under certain void appointments

(1) An instrument purporting to exercise a power of appointment over property, which, in default of and subject to any appointment, is held in trust for a class or number of persons of whom the appointee is one, shall not (save as hereinafter provided) be void on the ground of fraud on the power as against a purchaser in good faith:

Provided that, if the interest appointed exceeds, in amount or value, the interest in such property to which immediately before the execution of the instrument the appointee was presumptively entitled under the trust in default of appointment, having regard to any advances made in his favour and to any hotchpot provision, the protection afforded by this section to a purchaser shall not extend to such excess.

(2) In this section "a purchaser in good faith" means a person dealing with an appointee of the age of not less than twenty-five years for valuable consideration in money or money's worth, and without notice of the fraud, or of any circumstances from which, if reasonable inquiries had been made, the fraud might have been discovered.

(3) Persons deriving title under any purchaser entitled to the benefit of this section shall be entitled to like benefit.

(4) This section applies only to dealings effected after the commencement of this Act.

[396]

158 Validation of appointments where objects are excluded or take illusory shares

(1) No appointment made in exercise of any power to appoint any property among two or more objects shall be invalid on the ground that—

(a) an unsubstantial, illusory, or nominal share only is appointed to or left unappointed to devolve upon any one or more of the objects of the power; or

(b) any object of the power is thereby altogether excluded;

but every such appointment shall be valid notwithstanding that any one or more of the objects is not thereby, or in default of appointment, to take any share in the property.

(2) This section does not affect any provision in the instrument creating the power which declares the amount of any share from which any object of the power is not to be excluded.

(3) This section applies to appointments made before or after the commencement of this Act.

[397]

159 Execution of powers not testamentary

(1) A deed executed in the presence of and attested by two or more witnesses (in the manner in which deeds are ordinarily executed and attested) is so far as respects the execution and attestation thereof, a valid execution of a power of appointment by deed or by any instrument in writing, not testamentary, notwithstanding that it is expressly required that a deed or instrument in writing, made in exercise of the power, is to be executed or attested with some additional or other form of execution or attestation or solemnity.

(2) This section does not operate to defeat any direction in the instrument creating the power that—

(a) the consent of any particular person is to be necessary to a valid execution;

(b) in order to give validity to any appointment, any act is to be performed having no relation to the mode of executing and attesting the instrument.

(3) This section does not prevent the donee of a power from executing it in accordance with the power by writing, or otherwise than by an instrument executed and attested as a deed; and where a power is so executed this section does not apply.

(4) This section applies to appointments by deed made after the thirteenth day of August, eighteen hundred and fifty-nine.

[398]

160 Application of Part VI to existing powers

This Part of this Act applies to powers created or arising either before or after the commencement of this Act.

[399]

PART VII
PERPETUITIES AND ACCUMULATIONS

Perpetuities

161 Abolition of the double possibility rule

(1) The rule of law prohibiting the limitation, after a life interest to an unborn person, of an interest in land to the unborn child or other issue of an unborn person is hereby abolished, but without prejudice to any other rule relating to perpetuities.

(2) This section only applies to limitations or trusts created by an instrument coming into operation after the commencement of this Act.

[400]

162 Restrictions on the perpetuity rule

(1) For removing doubts, it is hereby declared that the rule of law relating to perpetuities does not apply and shall be deemed never to have applied—

(a) To any power to distrain on or to take possession of land or the income thereof given by way of indemnity against a rent, whether charged upon or payable in respect of any part of that land or not; or

(b) To any rentcharge created only as an indemnity against another rentcharge, although the indemnity rentcharge may only arise or become payable on breach of a condition or stipulation; or

(c) To any power, whether exercisable on breach of a condition or stipulation or not, to retain or withhold payment of any instalment of a rentcharge as an indemnity against another rentcharge; or

(d) To any grant, exception, or reservation of any right of entry on, or user of, the surface of land or of any easements, rights, or privileges over or under land for the purpose of—

(i) winning, working, inspecting, measuring, converting, manufacturing, carrying away, and disposing of mines and minerals;

(ii) inspecting, grubbing up, felling and carrying away timber and other trees, and the tops and lops thereof;

(iii) executing repairs, alterations, or additions to any adjoining land, or the buildings and erections thereon;

(iv) constructing, laying down, altering, repairing, renewing, cleansing, and maintaining sewers, watercourses, cesspools, gutters, drains, water-pipes, gas-pipes, electric wires or cables or other like works.

(2) This section applies to instruments coming into operation before or after the commencement of this Act.

[401]

NOTES

Sub-s (1): para (a) repealed by the Tribunals, Courts and Enforcement Act 2007, ss 86, 146, Sch 14, paras 21, 25, Sch 23, Pt 4, as from a day to be appointed.

163 (*Repealed by the Perpetuities and Accumulations Act 1964, ss 4(6), 15(5).*)

Accumulations

164 General restrictions on accumulation of income

(1) No person may by any instrument or otherwise settle or dispose of any property in such manner that the income thereof shall, save as hereinafter mentioned, be wholly or partially accumulated for any longer period than one of the following, namely:—

(a) the life of the grantor or settlor; or

(b) a term of twenty-one years from the death of the grantor, settlor or testator; or

(c) the duration of the minority or respective minorities of any person or persons living or en ventre sa mere at the death of the grantor, settlor or testator; or

(d) the duration of the minority or respective minorities only of any person or persons who under the limitations of the instrument directing the accumulations would, for the time being, if of full age, be entitled to the income directed to be accumulated.

In every case where any accumulation is directed otherwise than as aforesaid, the direction shall (save as hereinafter mentioned) be void; and the income of the property directed to be accumulated shall, so long as the same is directed to be accumulated contrary to this section, go to and be received by the person or persons who would have been entitled thereto if such accumulation had not been directed.

(2) This section does not extend to any provision—

(i) for payment of the debts of any grantor, settlor, testator or other person;

(ii) for raising portions for—

(a) any child, children or remoter issue of any grantor, settlor or testator; or

(b) any child, children or remoter issue of a person taking any interest under any settlement or other disposition directing the accumulations or to whom any interest is thereby limited;

(iii) respecting the accumulation of the produce of timber or wood;

and accordingly such provisions may be made as if no statutory restrictions on accumulation of income had been imposed.

(3) The restrictions imposed by this section apply to instruments made on or after the twenty-eighth day of July, eighteen hundred, but in the case of wills only where the testator was living and of testamentary capacity after the end of one year from that date.

[402]

165 Qualification of restrictions on accumulation

Where accumulations of surplus income are made during a minority under any statutory power or under the general law, the period for which such accumulations are made is not (whether the trust was created or the accumulations were made before or after the commencement of this Act) to be taken into account in determining the periods for which accumulations are permitted to be made by the last preceding section, and accordingly an express trust for accumulation for any other permitted period shall not be deemed to have been invalidated or become invalid, by reason of accumulations also having been made as aforesaid during such minority.

[403]

166 Restriction on accumulation for the purchase of land

(1) No person may settle or dispose of any property in such manner that the income thereof shall be wholly or partially accumulated for the purchase of land only, for any longer period than the duration of the minority or respective minorities of any person or persons who, under the limitations of the instrument directing the accumulation, would for the time being, if of full age, be entitled to the income so directed to be accumulated.

(2) This section does not, nor do the enactments which it replaces, apply to accumulations to be held as capital money for the purposes of the Settled Land Act 1925 or the enactments replaced by that Act, whether or not the accumulations are primarily liable to be laid out in the purchase of land.

(3) This section applies to settlements and dispositions made after the twenty-seventh day of June eighteen hundred and ninety-two.

[404]

167–171 ((*Pt VIII*) *ss 167–170 repealed by the Statute Law* (*Repeals*) *Act 1969; s 171 repealed by the Mental Health Act 1959, s 149*(*2*), *Sch 8, Pt I.*)

PART IX
VOIDABLE DISPOSITIONS

172 (*Repealed by the Insolvency Act 1985, s 235*(*3*), *Sch 10, Pt IV.*)

173 Voluntary disposition of land how far voidable as against purchasers

(1) Every voluntary disposition of land made with intent to defraud a subsequent purchaser is voidable at the instance of that purchaser.

(2) For the purposes of this section, no voluntary disposition, whenever made, shall be deemed to have been made with intent to defraud by reason only that a subsequent conveyance for valuable consideration was made, if such subsequent conveyance was made after the twenty-eighth day of June, eighteen hundred and ninety-three.

[405]

174 Acquisitions of reversions at an under value

(1) No acquisition made in good faith, without fraud or unfair dealing, of any reversionary interest in real or personal property, for money or money's worth, shall be liable to be opened or set aside merely on the ground of under value.

In this subsection "reversionary interest" includes an expectancy or possibility.

(2) This section does not affect the jurisdiction of the court to set aside or modify unconscionable bargains.

[406]

PART X
WILLS

175 Contingent and future testamentary gifts to carry the intermediate income

(1) A contingent or future specific devise or bequest of property, whether real or personal, and a contingent residuary devise of freehold land, and a specific or residuary devise of freehold land to trustees upon trust for persons whose interests are contingent or executory shall, subject to the statutory provisions relating to accumulations, carry the intermediate income of that property from the death of the testator, except so far as such income, or any part thereof, may be otherwise expressly disposed of.

(2) This section applies only to wills coming into operation after the commencement of this Act.

[407]

176 Power for tenant in tail in possession to dispose of property by specific devise or bequest

(1) A tenant in tail of full age shall have power to dispose by will, by means of a devise or bequest referring specifically either to the property or to the instrument under which it was acquired or to entailed property generally—

(a) of all property of which he is tenant in tail in possession at his death; and

(b) of money (including the proceeds of property directed to be sold) subject to be invested in the purchase of property, of which if it had been so invested he would have been tenant in tail in possession at his death;

in like manner as if, after barring the entail, he had been tenant in fee simple or absolute owner thereof for an equitable interest at his death, but, subject to and in default of any such disposition by will, such property shall devolve in the same manner as if this section had not been passed.

(2) This section applies to entailed interests authorised to be created by this Act as well as to estates tail created before the commencement of this Act, but does not extend to a tenant in tail who is by statute restrained from barring or defeating his estate tail, whether the land or property in respect whereof he is so restrained was purchased with money provided by Parliament in consideration of public services or not, or to a tenant in tail after possibility of issue extinct, and does not render any interest which is not disposed of by the will of the tenant in tail liable for his debts or other liabilities.

(3) In this section "tenant in tail" includes an owner of a base fee in possession who has power to enlarge the base fee into a fee-simple without the concurrence of any other person.

(4) This section only applies to wills executed after the commencement of this Act, or confirmed or republished by codicil executed after such commencement.

[408]

177, 178 (*Repealed by the Statute Law (Repeals) Act 1969, s 1, Schedule, Pt III.*)

179 Prescribed forms for reference in wills

The Lord Chancellor may from time to time prescribe and publish forms to which a testator may refer in his will, and give directions as to the manner in which they may be referred to, but, unless so referred to, such forms shall not be deemed to be incorporated in a will.

[409]

NOTES

Subordinate legislation: the Statutory Will Forms 1925, SI 1925/780.

PART XI
MISCELLANEOUS
Miscellaneous

180 Provisions as to corporations

(1) Where either after or before the commencement of this Act any property or any interest therein is or has been vested in a corporation sole (including the Crown), the same shall, unless and until otherwise disposed of by the corporation, pass and devolve to and vest in and be deemed always to have passed and devolved to or vested in the successors from time to time of such corporation.

(2) Where either after or before the commencement of this Act there is or has been a vacancy in the office of a corporation sole or in the office of the head of a corporation aggregate (in any case in which the vacancy affects the status or powers of the corporation) at the time when, if there had been no vacancy, any interest in or charge on property would have been acquired by the corporation, such interest shall notwithstanding such vacancy vest and be deemed to have vested in the successor to such office on his appointment as a corporation sole, or in the corporation aggregate (as the case may be), but without prejudice to the right of such successor, or of the corporation aggregate after the appointment of its head officer, to disclaim that interest or charge.

(3) Any contract or other transaction expressed or purported to be made with a corporation sole, or any appointment of a corporation sole as a custodian or other trustee or as a personal representative, at a time (either after or before the commencement of this Act) when there was a vacancy in the office, shall on the vacancy being filled take effect and be deemed to have taken effect as if the vacancy had been filled before the contract, transaction or appointment was expressed to be made or was capable of taking effect, and on the appointment of a successor shall be capable of being enforced, accepted, disclaimed, or renounced by him.

[410]

181 Dissolution of a corporation

[(1)] Where, by reason of the dissolution of a corporation either before or after the commencement of this Act, a legal estate in any property has determined, the court may by order create a corresponding estate and vest the same in the person who would have been entitled to the estate which determined had it remained a subsisting estate.

[(2) The county court has jurisdiction under this section where the amount or value of the property or of the interest in the property which is to be dealt with in the court does not exceed [£30,000].]

[411]

NOTES

Sub-s (1): numbered as such by the County Courts Act 1984, s 148(1), Sch 2, para 7.

Sub-s (2): inserted by the County Courts Act 1984, s 148(1), Sch 2, para 7; sum in square brackets substituted by SI 1991/724, art 2(3)(a), (8), Schedule, Pt I.

182 Protection of solicitor and trustees adopting Act

(1) The powers given by this Act to any person, and the covenants, provisions, stipulations, and words which under this Act are to be deemed to be included or implied in any instrument, or are by this Act made applicable to any contract for sale or other transaction, are and shall be deemed in law proper powers, covenants, provisions, stipulations, and words, to be given by or to be contained in any such instrument, or to be adopted in connexion with, or applied to, any such contract or transaction, and a solicitor shall not be deemed guilty of neglect or breach of duty, or become in any way liable, by reason of his omitting, in good faith, in any such instrument, or in connexion with any such contract or transaction, to negative the giving, inclusion, implication, or application of any of those powers, covenants, provisions, stipulations, or words, or to insert or apply any others in place thereof, in any case where the provisions of this Act would allow of his doing so.

(2) But, save as expressly provided by this Act, nothing in this Act shall be taken to imply that the insertion in any such instrument, or the adoption in connexion with, or the application to, any contract or transaction, of any further or other powers, covenants, provisions, stipulations, or words is improper.

(3) Where the solicitor is acting for trustees, executors, or other persons in a fiduciary position, those persons shall also be protected in like manner.

(4) Where such persons are acting without a solicitor, they shall also be protected in like manner.

[412]

NOTES

Modifications: modified by the Building Societies Act 1986, s 124, Sch 21, paras 9, 12, and the Administration of Justice Act 1985, ss 9, 34(2), Sch 2, para 37.

References to solicitors etc modified to include references to bodies recognised under the Administration of Justice Act 1985, s 9, by the Solicitors' Incorporated Practices Order 1991, SI 1991/2684, arts 4, 5, Sch 1.

183 Fraudulent concealment of documents and falsification of pedigrees

(1) Any person disposing of property or any interest therein for money or money's worth to a purchaser, or the solicitor or other agent of such person, who—

(a) conceals from the purchaser any instrument or incumbrance material to the title; or

(b) falsifies any pedigree upon which the title may depend in order to induce the purchaser to accept the title offered or produced;

with intent in any of such cases to defraud, is guilty of a misdemeanour punishable by fine, or by imprisonment for a term not exceeding two years, or by both.

(2) Any such person or his solicitor or agent is also liable to an action for damages by the purchaser or the persons deriving title under him for any loss sustained by reason of—

(a) the concealment of the instrument or incumbrance; or

(b) any claim made by a person under such pedigree whose right was concealed by such falsification as aforesaid.

(3) In estimating damages, where the property or any interest therein is recovered from the purchaser or the persons deriving title under him, regard shall be had to any expenditure by him or them in improvements of any land.

(4) No prosecution for any offence under this section shall be commenced without the leave of the Attorney-General.

(5) Before leave to prosecute is granted there shall be given to the person intended to be prosecuted such notice of the application for leave to prosecute as the Attorney-General may direct.

[413]

NOTES

Modification: references to solicitors etc modified to include references to bodies recognised under the Administration of Justice Act 1985, s 9, by the Solicitors' Incorporated Practices Order 1991, SI 1991/2684, arts 4, 5, Sch 1.

184 Presumption of survivorship in regard to claims to property

In all cases where, after the commencement of this Act, two or more persons have died in circumstances rendering it uncertain which of them survived the other or others, such deaths shall (subject to any order of the court), for all purposes affecting the title of property, be presumed to have occurred in order of seniority, and accordingly the younger shall be deemed to have survived the elder.

[414]

185 Merger

There is no merger by operation of law only of any estate the beneficial interest in which would not be deemed to be merged or extinguished in equity.

[415]

186 Rights of pre-emption capable of release

All statutory and other rights of pre-emption affecting a legal estate shall be and be deemed always to have been capable of release, and unless released shall remain in force as equitable interests only.

[416]

187 Legal easements

(1) Where an easement, right or privilege for a legal estate is created, it shall enure for the benefit of the land to which it is intended to be annexed.

(2) Nothing in this Act affects the right of a person to acquire, hold or exercise an easement, right or privilege over or in relation to land for a legal estate in common with any other person, or the power of creating or conveying such an easement, right or privilege.

[417]

188 Power to direct division of chattels

[(1)] Where any chattels belong to persons in undivided shares, the persons interested in a moiety or upwards may apply to the court for an order for division of the chattels or any of them, according to a valuation or otherwise, and the court may make such order and give any consequential directions as it thinks fit.

[(2) The county court has jurisdiction under this section where the amount or value of the property or of the interest in the property which is to be dealt with in the court does not exceed [£30,000].]

[418]

NOTES

Sub-s (1): numbered as such by the County Courts Act 1984, s 148(1), Sch 2, para 8.

Sub-s (2): inserted by the County Courts Act 1984, s 148(1), Sch 2, para 8; sum in square brackets substituted by SI 1991/724, art 2(3)(a), (8), Schedule, Pt I.

189 Indemnities against rents

(1) A power of distress given by way of indemnity against a rent or any part thereof payable in respect of any land, or against the breach of any covenant or condition in relation to land, is not and shall not be deemed ever to have been a bill of sale, within the meaning of the Bills of Sale Acts 1878 and 1882, as amended by any subsequent enactment.

(2) The benefit of all covenants and powers given by way of indemnity against a rent or any part thereof payable in respect of land, or against the breach of any covenant or condition in relation to land, is and shall be deemed always to have been annexed to the land to which the indemnity is intended to relate, and may be enforced by the estate owner for the time being of the whole or any part of that land, notwithstanding that the benefit may not have been expressly apportioned or assigned to him or to any of his predecessors in title.

[419]

NOTES

Sub-s (1): repealed by the Tribunals, Courts and Enforcement Act 2007, ss 86, 146, Sch 14, paras 21, 26, Sch 23, Pt 4, as from a day to be appointed.

Redemption and Apportionment of Rents, etc

190 Equitable apportionment of rents and remedies for non-payment or breach of covenant

(1) Where in a conveyance for valuable consideration, other than a mortgage, of part of land which is affected by a rentcharge, such rentcharge or a part thereof is, without the consent of the owner thereof, expressed to be—

(a) charged exclusively on the land conveyed or any part thereof in exoneration of the land retained or other land; or

(b) charged exclusively on the land retained or any part thereof in exoneration of the land conveyed or other land; or

(c) apportioned between the land conveyed or any part thereof, and the land retained by the grantor or any part thereof;

then, without prejudice to the rights of the owner of the rentcharge, such charge or apportionment shall be binding as between the grantor and the grantee under the conveyance and their respective successors in title.

(2) Where—

(a) any default is made in payment of the whole or part of a rentcharge by the person who, by reason of such charge or apportionment as aforesaid, is liable to pay the same; or

(b) any breach occurs of any of the covenants (other than in the case of an apportionment the covenant to pay the entire rentcharge) or conditions contained in the deed or other document creating the rentcharge, so far as the same relate to the land retained or conveyed, as the case may be;

the owner for the time being of any other land affected by the entire rentcharge who—

(i) pays or is required to pay the whole or part of the rentcharge which ought to have been paid by the defaulter aforesaid; or

(ii) incurs any costs, damages or expenses by reason of the breach of covenant or condition aforesaid;

may enter into and distrain on the land in respect of which the default or breach is made or occurs, or any part of that land, and dispose according to law of any distress found, and may also take possession of the income of the same land until, by means of such distress and receipt of income or otherwise the whole or part of the rentcharge (charged or apportioned as aforesaid) so unpaid and all costs, damages and expenses incurred by reason of the non-payment thereof or of the breach of the said covenants and conditions, are fully paid or satisfied.

(3) Where in a conveyance for valuable consideration, other than a mortgage, of part of land comprised in a lease, for the residue of the term or interest created by the lease, the rent reserved by such lease or a part thereof is, without the consent of the lessor, expressed to be—

(a) charged exclusively on the land conveyed or any part thereof in exoneration of the land retained by the assignor or other land; or

(b) charged exclusively on the land retained by the assignor or any part thereof in exoneration of the land conveyed or other land; or

(c) apportioned between the land conveyed or any part thereof and the land retained by the assignor or any part thereof;

then, without prejudice to the rights of the lessor, such charge or apportionment shall be binding as between the assignor and the assignee under the conveyance and their respective successors in title.

(4) Where—

(a) any default is made in payment of the whole or part of a rent by the person who, by reason of such charge or apportionment as aforesaid, is liable to pay the same; or

(b) any breach occurs of any of the lessee's covenants (other than in the case of an apportionment the covenant to pay the entire rent) or conditions contained in the lease, so far as the same relate to the land retained or conveyed, as the case may be;

the lessee for the time being of any other land comprised in the lease, in whom, as respects that land, the residue of the term or interest created by the lease is vested, who—

(i) pays or is required to pay the whole or part of the rent which ought to have been paid by the defaulter aforesaid; or

(ii) incurs any costs, damages or expenses by reason of the breach of covenant or condition aforesaid;

may enter into and distrain on the land comprised in the lease in respect of which the default or breach is made or occurs, or any part of that land, and dispose according to law of any distress found, and may also take possession of the income of the same land until (so long as the term or interest created by the lease is subsisting) by means of such distress and receipt of income or otherwise, the whole or part of the rent (charged or apportioned as aforesaid) so unpaid and all costs, damages and expenses incurred by reason of the non-payment thereof or of the breach of the said covenants and conditions, are fully paid or satisfied.

(5) The remedies conferred by this section take effect so far only as they might have been conferred by the conveyance whereby the rent or any part thereof is expressed to be charged or apportioned as aforesaid, but a trustee, personal representative, mortgagee or other person in a fiduciary position has, and shall be deemed always to have had, power to confer the same or like remedies.

[(4) Subsection (5) applies where—

(a) any default is made in payment of the whole or part of a rent by the person ("the defaulter") who, by reason of a charge or apportionment within subsection (3), is liable to pay it, and

(b) the lessee for the time being of any other land comprised in the lease, in whom, as respects that land, the residue of the term or interest created by the lease is vested, ("the paying lessee") pays or is required to pay the whole or part of the rent which ought to have been paid by the defaulter.

(5) Section 72(1) of the Tribunals, Courts and Enforcement Act 2007 (commercial rent arrears recovery) applies, subject to the other provisions of Chapter 2 of Part 3 of that Act, to the recovery by the paying lessee from the defaulter of the rent paid by the paying lessee which ought to have been paid by the defaulter, as if the paying lessee were the landlord, and the defaulter his tenant, under the lease.]

(6) This section applies only if and so far as a contrary intention is not expressed in the conveyance whereby the rent or any part thereof is expressed to be charged or apportioned as aforesaid, and takes effect subject to the terms of that conveyance and to the provisions therein contained.

(7) The remedies conferred by this section apply only where the conveyance whereby the rent or any part thereof is expressed to be charged or apportioned is made after the commencement of this Act, and do not apply where the rent is charged exclusively as aforesaid or legally apportioned with the consent of the *owner or* lessor.

(8) The rule of law relating to perpetuities does not affect the powers or remedies conferred by this section or any like powers or remedies expressly conferred, before or after the commencement of this Act, by an instrument.

[420]

NOTES

Sub-s (2): repealed by the Tribunals, Courts and Enforcement Act 2007, ss 86, 146, Sch 14, paras 21, 27(1), (2), Sch 23, Pt 4, as from a day to be appointed.

Sub-ss (4), (5): substituted by subsequent sub-ss (4), (5) in square brackets by the Tribunals, Courts and Enforcement Act 2007, s 86, Sch 14, paras 21, 27(1), (3), as from a day to be appointed.

Sub-s (7): words in italics repealed by the Tribunals, Courts and Enforcement Act 2007, ss 86, 146, Sch 14, paras 21, 27(1), (4), Sch 23, Pt 4, as from a day to be appointed.

191 (*Repealed by the Rentcharges Act 1977, s 17(2), Sch 2.*)

192 Apportionment of charges payable for redemption of tithe rentcharge

An order of apportionment of a charge on land by way of annuity for redemption of tithe rentcharge may be made by the Minister under sections ten to fourteen (inclusive) of the Inclosure Act 1854 on the application of any person interested, according to the provisions of the Inclosure Acts 1845 to 1882, in the land charged or any part thereof without the concurrence of any other person:

Provided that the Minister may, in any such case, on the application of any person interested in the annuity, require as a condition of making the order that any apportioned part of the annuity which does not exceed the yearly sum of two pounds shall be redeemed forthwith.

[421]

Commons and Waste Lands

193 Rights of the public over commons and waste lands

(1) Members of the public shall, subject as hereinafter provided, have rights of access for air and exercise to any land which is a metropolitan common within the meaning of the Metropolitan Commons Acts, 1866 to 1898, or manorial waste, or a common, which is wholly or partly situated within [an area which immediately before 1st April 1974 was] a borough or urban district, and to any land which at the commencement of this Act is subject to rights of common and to which this section may from time to time be applied in manner hereinafter provided:

Provided that—

(a) such rights of access shall be subject to any Act, scheme, or provisional order for the regulation of the land, and to any byelaw, regulation or order made thereunder or under any other statutory authority; and

(b) the Minister shall, on the application of any person entitled as lord of the manor or otherwise to the soil of the land, or entitled to any commonable rights affecting the land, impose such limitations on and conditions as to the exercise of the rights of access or as to the extent of the land to be affected as, in the opinion of the Minister, are necessary or desirable for preventing any estate, right or interest of a profitable or beneficial nature in, over, or affecting the land from being injuriously affected, [for conserving flora, fauna or geological or physiographical features of the land,] or for protecting any object of historical interest and, where any such limitations or conditions are so imposed, the rights of access shall be subject thereto; and

(c) such rights of access shall not include any right to draw or drive upon the land a carriage, cart, caravan, truck, or other vehicle, or to camp or light any fire thereon; and

(d) the rights of access shall cease to apply—

  (i) to any land over which the commonable rights are extinguished under any statutory provision;

  (ii) to any land over which the commonable rights are otherwise extinguished if the council of the county[, county borough] [or metropolitan district] … in which the land is situated by resolution assent to its exclusion from the operation of this section, and the resolution is approved by the Minister.

(2) *The lord of the manor or other person entitled to the soil of any land subject to rights of common may by deed, revocable or irrevocable, declare that this section shall apply to the land, and upon such deed being deposited with the Minister the land shall, so long as the deed remains operative, be land to which this section applies.*

(3) Where limitations or conditions are imposed by the Minister under this section, they shall be published by such person and in such manner as the Minister may direct.

(4) Any person who, without lawful authority, draws or drives upon any land to which this section applies any carriage, cart, caravan, truck, or other vehicle, or camps or lights any fire thereon, or who fails to observe any limitation or condition imposed by the Minister under this section in respect of any such land, shall be liable on summary conviction to a fine not exceeding [level 1 on the standard scale] for each offence.

(5) Nothing in this section shall prejudice or affect the right of any person to get and remove mines or minerals or to let down the surface of the manorial waste or common.

(6) This section does not apply to any common or manorial waste which is for the time being held for Naval, Military or Air Force purposes and in respect of which rights of common have been extinguished or cannot be exercised.

[422]

NOTES

Sub-s (1): words in first pair of square brackets inserted by the Local Government Act 1972, s 189(4); words in square brackets in para (b) inserted by the Countryside and Rights of Way Act 2000, s 46(3), Sch 4, para 1; in para (d)(ii), words in first pair of square brackets inserted by the Local Government (Wales) Act 1994, s 66(6), Sch 16, para 7(1), words in second pair of square brackets inserted by the Local Government Act 1985, s 16, Sch 8, para 10(5), and words omitted repealed by the Local Government Act 1972, s 272(1), Sch 30.

Sub-s (2): repealed by the Countryside and Rights of Way Act 2000, ss 46(1)(a), 102, Sch 16, Pt I, as from 6 December 2006, in relation to Wales (except in relation to any deed executed under this section which is in force immediately before that date) and as from a day to be appointed, in relation to England.

Sub-s (4): words in square brackets substituted by virtue of the Criminal Justice Act 1982, ss 37, 38, 46.

Transfer of Functions: functions of the Minister, so far as exercisable in relation to Wales, transferred to the National Assembly for Wales, by the National Assembly for Wales (Transfer of Functions) Order 1999, SI 1999/672, art 2, Sch 1.

194 Restrictions on inclosure of commons

(*1*) *The erection of any building or fence, or the construction of any other work, whereby access to land to which this section applies is prevented or impeded, shall not be lawful unless the consent of the Minister thereto is obtained, and in giving or withholding his consent the Minister shall have regard to the same considerations and shall, if necessary, hold the same inquiries as are directed by the Commons Act 1876 to be taken into consideration and held by the Minister before forming an opinion whether an application under the Inclosure Acts 1845 to 1882 shall be acceded to or not.*

(*2*) *Where any building or fence is erected, or any other work constructed without such consent as is required by this section, the county court within whose jurisdiction the land is situated, shall, on an application being made by the council of any county [or county borough] ... or district concerned, or by the lord of the manor or any other person interested in the common, have power to make an order for the removal of the work, and the restoration of the land to the condition in which it was before the work was erected or constructed, but any such order shall be subject to the like appeal as an order made under section thirty of the Commons Act 1876.*

(*3*) *This section applies to any land which at the commencement of this Act is subject to rights of common:*

Provided that this section shall cease to apply—

- (*a*) *to any land over which the rights of common are extinguished under any statutory provision;*
- (*b*) *to any land over which the rights of common are otherwise extinguished, if the council of the county[, county borough] [or metropolitan district] ... in which the land is situated by resolution assent to its exclusion from the operation of this section and the resolution is approved by the Minister.*

(*4*) *This section does not apply to any building or fence erected or work constructed if specially authorised by Act of Parliament, or in pursuance of an Act of Parliament or Order having the force of an Act, or if lawfully erected or constructed in connexion with the taking or working of minerals in or under any land to which the section is otherwise applicable, or to any [electronic communications apparatus installed for the purposes of an electronic communications code network].*

[423]

NOTES

Repealed by the Commons Act 2006, s 53, Sch 6, Pt 2, subject to transitional provisions in s 44(1) of, and Sch 4, paras 6, 7 to, that Act, as from 1 October 2007 (in relation to England) and as from a day to be appointed (in relation to Wales).

Sub-s (2): words in square brackets inserted by the Local Government (Wales) Act 1994, s 66(6), Sch 16, para 7(2); words omitted repealed by the Local Government Act 1972, s 272(1), Sch 30.

Sub-s (3): first words in square brackets inserted by the Local Government (Wales) Act 1994, s 66(6), Sch 16, para 7(2); second words in square brackets inserted by the Local Government Act 1985, s 16, Sch 8, para 10(5); words omitted repealed by the Local Government Act 1972, s 272(1), Sch 30.

Sub-s (4): words in square brackets substituted by the Communications Act 2003, s 406(1), Sch 17, para 3.

Modification: modified, in relation to any registered common which is within any National Park for which a National Park authority is the local planning authority and is not owned by or vested in any other body which is a local authority, by the Environment Act 1995, s 70, Sch 9, para 1.

Transfer of Functions: functions of the Minister, so far as exercisable in relation to Wales, transferred to the National Assembly for Wales, by the National Assembly for Wales (Transfer of Functions) Order 1999, SI 1999/672, art 2, Sch 1.

Judgments, etc affecting Land

195 Equitable charges in right of judgment debt, etc

(1)–(3) …

(4) A recognisance, on behalf of the Crown or otherwise, whether entered into before or after the commencement of this Act, and an inquisition finding a debt due to the Crown, and any obligation or specialty made to or in favour of the Crown, whatever may have been its date, shall not operate as a charge on any interest in land, or on the unpaid purchase money for any land, unless or until a writ or order, for the purpose of enforcing it, is registered in the register of writs and orders at the Land Registry.

(5) …

[424]

NOTES

Sub-ss (1)–(3), (5): repealed by the Administration of Justice Act 1956, ss 34(2), 57(2), Sch 2.

Notices

196 Regulations respecting notices

(1) Any notice required or authorised to be served or given by this Act shall be in writing.

(2) Any notice required or authorised by this Act to be served on a lessee or mortgagor shall be sufficient, although only addressed to the lessee or mortgagor by that designation, without his name, or generally to the persons interested, without any name, and notwithstanding that any person to be affected by the notice is absent, under disability, unborn, or unascertained.

(3) Any notice required or authorised by this Act to be served shall be sufficiently served if it is left at the last-known place of abode or business in the United Kingdom of the lessee, lessor, mortgagee, mortgagor, or other person to be served, or, in case of a notice required or authorised to be served on a lessee or mortgagor, is affixed or left for him on the land or any house or building comprised in the lease or mortgage, or, in case of a mining lease, is left for the lessee at the office or counting-house of the mine.

(4) Any notice required or authorised by this Act to be served shall also be sufficiently served, if it is sent by post in a registered letter addressed to the lessee, lessor, mortgagee, mortgagor, or other person to be served, by name, at the aforesaid place of abode or business, office, or counting-house, and if that letter is not returned [by the postal operator (within the meaning of the Postal Services Act 2000) concerned] undelivered; and that service shall be deemed to be made at the time at which the registered letter would in the ordinary course be delivered.

(5) The provisions of this section shall extend to notices required to be served by any instrument affecting property executed or coming into operation after the commencement of this Act unless a contrary intention appears.

(6) This section does not apply to notices served in proceedings in the court.

[425]

NOTES

Sub-s (4): words in square brackets substituted by SI 2001/1149, art 3(1), Sch 1, para 7.

Modification: modified by the Landlord and Tenant Act 1987, s 49.

197 (*Repealed for certain purposes by the Law of Property Act 1969, s 16, Sch 2, Pt I; spent for remaining purposes by virtue of the Middlesex Deeds Act 1940, s 1.*)

198 Registration under the Land Charges Act 1925 to be notice

(1) The registration of any instrument or matter [in any register kept under the Land Charges Act 1972 or any local land charges register] shall be deemed to constitute actual notice of such instrument or matter, and of the fact of such registration, to all persons and for all purposes connected with the land affected, as from the date of registration or other prescribed date and so long as the registration continues in force.

(2) This section operates without prejudice to the provisions of this Act respecting the making of further advances by a mortgagee, and applies only to instruments and matters required or authorised to be registered [in any such register].

[426]

NOTES

Words in square brackets substituted by the Local Land Charges Act 1975, s 17(2), Sch 1.

199 Restrictions on constructive notice

(1) A purchaser shall not be prejudicially affected by notice of—

(i) any instrument or matter capable of registration under the provisions of the Land Charges Act 1925, or any enactment which it replaces, which is void or not enforceable as against him under that Act or enactment, by reason of the non-registration thereof;

(ii) any other instrument or matter or any fact or thing unless—

(a) it is within his own knowledge, or would have come to his knowledge if such inquiries and inspections had been made as ought reasonably to have been made by him; or

(b) in the same transaction with respect to which a question of notice to the purchaser arises, it has come to the knowledge of his counsel, as such, or of his solicitor or other agent, as such, or would have come to the knowledge of his solicitor or other agent, as such, if such inquiries and inspections had been made as ought reasonably to have been made by the solicitor or other agent.

(2) Paragraph (ii) of the last subsection shall not exempt a purchaser from any liability under, or any obligation to perform or observe, any covenant, condition, provision, or restriction contained in any instrument under which his title is derived, mediately or immediately; and such liability or obligation may be enforced in the same manner and to the same extent as if that paragraph had not been enacted.

(3) A purchaser shall not by reason of anything in this section be affected by notice in any case where he would not have been so affected if this section had not been enacted.

(4) This section applies to purchases made either before or after the commencement of this Act.

[427]

NOTES

Modification: references to solicitors etc modified to include references to bodies recognised under the Administration of Justice Act 1985, s 9, by the Solicitors' Incorporated Practices Order 1991, SI 1991/2684, arts 4, 5, Sch 1.

200 Notice of restrictive covenants and easements

(1) Where land having a common title with other land is disposed of to a purchaser (other than a lessee or a mortgagee) who does not hold or obtain possession of the documents forming the common title, such purchaser, notwithstanding any stipulation to the contrary, may require that a memorandum giving notice of any provision contained in the disposition to him restrictive of user of, or giving rights over, any other land comprised in the common title, shall, where practicable, be written or indorsed on, or, where impracticable, be permanently annexed to some one document selected by the purchaser but retained in the possession or power of the person who makes the disposition, and being or forming part of the common title.

(2) The title of any person omitting to require an indorsement to be made or a memorandum to be annexed shall not, by reason only of this enactment, be prejudiced or affected by the omission.

(3) This section does not apply to dispositions of registered land.

(4) Nothing in this section affects the obligation to register a land charge in respect of—

(a) any restrictive covenant or agreement affecting freehold land; or

(b) any estate contract; or

(c) any equitable easement, liberty or privilege.

[428]

PART XII
CONSTRUCTION, JURISDICTION, AND GENERAL PROVISIONS

201 Provisions of Act to apply to incorporeal hereditaments

(1) The provisions of this Act relating to freehold land apply to manors, reputed manors, lordships, advowsons, … perpetual rentcharges, and other incorporeal hereditaments, subject only to the qualifications necessarily arising by reason of the inherent nature of the hereditament affected.

(2) This Act does not affect the special restrictions imposed on dealings with advowsons by the Benefices Act 1898 or any other statute or measure, nor affect the limitation of, or authorise any disposition to be made of, a title or dignity of honour which in its nature is inalienable.

(3) …

[429]

NOTES

Sub-s (1): words omitted repealed by the Tithe Act 1936, s 48(3), Sch 9.

Sub-s (3): repealed by the Trusts of Land and Appointment of Trustees Act 1996, s 25(2), Sch 4; for savings in relation to entailed interests created before the commencement of that Act, and savings consequential upon the abolition of the doctrine of conversion, see s 25(4), (5) thereof.

202 Provisions as to enfranchisement of copyholds, etc

For giving effect to this Act, the enfranchisement of copyhold land, and the conversion into long terms of perpetually renewable leaseholds, and of leases for lives and of leases for years terminable with life or lives or on marriage, effected by the Law of Property Act 1922 as amended by any subsequent enactment, shall be deemed to have been effected immediately before the commencement of this Act.

[430]

203 Payment into court, jurisdiction and procedure

(1) Payment of money into court effectually exonerates therefrom the person making the payment.

(2) Subject to any rules of court to the contrary—

(a) Every application to the court under this Act shall, save as otherwise expressly provided, be by summons at chambers;

(b) On an application by a purchaser notice shall be served in the first instance on the vendor;

(c) On an application by a vendor notice shall be served in the first instance on the purchaser;

(d) On any application notice shall be served on such person, if any, as the court thinks fit.

(3) In this Act, unless the contrary intention appears, "the court" means the High Court … or the county court, where those courts respectively have jurisdiction.

(4) All matters within the jurisdiction of the High Court under this Act shall, save as otherwise expressly provided, and subject to the enactments for the time being in force with respect to the *Supreme Court of Judicature* [Senior Courts], be assigned to the Chancery Division of the court.

(5) The court shall have full power and discretion to make such order as it thinks fit respecting the costs, charges and expenses of all or any of the parties to any application.

[431]

NOTES

Sub-s (3): words omitted repealed by the Courts Act 1971, s 56(4), Sch 11, Pt II.

Sub-s (4): words in italics substituted by subsequent words in square brackets by the Constitutional Reform Act 2005, s 59(5), Sch 11, Pt 2, para 4(1), (3), as from 1 October 2009.

204 Orders of court conclusive

(1) An order of the court under any statutory or other jurisdiction shall not, as against a purchaser, be invalidated on the ground of want of jurisdiction, or of want of any concurrence, consent, notice, or service, whether the purchaser has notice of any such want or not.

(2) This section has effect with respect to any lease, sale, or other act under the authority of the court, and purporting to be in pursuance of any statutory power notwithstanding any exception in such statute.

(3) This section applies to all orders made before or after the commencement of this Act.

[432]

205 General definitions

(1) In this Act unless the context otherwise requires, the following expressions have the meanings hereby assigned to them respectively, that is to say:—

(i) "Bankruptcy" includes liquidation by arrangement; also in relation to a corporation means the winding up thereof;

(ii) "Conveyance" includes a mortgage, charge, lease, assent, vesting declaration, vesting instrument, disclaimer, release and every other assurance of property or of an interest therein by any instrument, except a will; "convey" has a corresponding meaning; and "disposition" includes a conveyance and also a devise, bequest, or an appointment of property contained in a will; and "dispose of" has a corresponding meaning;

(iii) "Building purposes" include the erecting and improving of, and the adding to, and the repairing of buildings; and a "building lease" is a lease for building purposes or purposes connected therewith;

[(iiiA) …]

(iv) "Death duty" means estate duty, … and every other duty leviable or payable on a death;

(v) "Estate owner" means the owner of a legal estate, but an infant is not capable of being an estate owner;

(vi) "Gazette" means the London Gazette;

(vii) "Incumbrance" includes a legal or equitable mortgage and a trust for securing money, and a lien, and a charge of a portion, annuity, or other capital or annual sum; and "incumbrancer" has a meaning corresponding with that of incumbrance, and includes every person entitled to the benefit of an incumbrance, or to require payment or discharge thereof;

(viii) "Instrument" does not include a statute, unless the statute creates a settlement;

(ix) "Land" includes land of any tenure, and mines and minerals, whether or not held apart from the surface, buildings or parts of buildings (whether the division is horizontal, vertical or made in any other way) and other corporeal hereditaments; also a manor, an advowson, and a rent and other incorporeal hereditaments, and an easement, right, privilege, or benefit in, over, or derived from land; … ; and "mines and minerals" include any strata or seam of minerals or substances in or under any land, and powers of working and getting the same … ; and "manor" includes a lordship, and reputed manor or lordship; and "hereditament" means any real property which on an intestacy occurring before the commencement of this Act might have devolved upon an heir;

(x) "Legal estates" mean the estates, interests and charges, in or over land (subsisting or created at law) which are by this Act authorised to subsist or to be created as legal estates; "equitable interests" mean all the other interests and charges in or over land … ; an equitable interest "capable of subsisting as a legal estate" means such as could validly subsist or be created as a legal estate under this Act;

(xi) "Legal powers" include the powers vested in a chargee by way of legal mortgage or in an estate owner under which a legal estate can be transferred or created; and "equitable powers" mean all the powers in or over land under which equitable interests or powers only can be transferred or created;

(xii) "Limitation Acts" means the Real Property Limitation Acts 1833, 1837 and 1874, and "limitation" includes a trust;

[(xiii) …]

(xiv) a "mining lease" means a lease for mining purposes, that is, the searching for, winning, working, getting, making merchantable, carrying away, or disposing of mines and minerals, or purposes connected therewith, and includes a grant or licence for mining purposes;

(xv) "Minister" means [the Minister of Agriculture, Fisheries and Food];

(xvi) "Mortgage" includes any charge or lien on any property for securing money or money's worth; "legal mortgage" means a mortgage by demise or subdemise or a charge by way of legal mortgage and "legal mortgagee" has a corresponding meaning; "mortgage money" means money or money's worth secured by a mortgage; "mortgagor" includes any person from time to time deriving title under the original mortgagor or entitled to redeem a mortgage according to his estate interest or right in the mortgaged property; "mortgagee" includes a chargee by way of legal mortgage and any person from time to time deriving title under the original mortgagee; and "mortgagee in possession" is, for the purposes of this Act, a mortgagee who, in right of the mortgage, has entered into and is in possession of the mortgaged property; and "right of redemption" includes an option to repurchase only if the option in effect creates a right of redemption;

(xvii) "Notice" includes constructive notice;

(xviii) "Personal representative" means the executor, original or by representation, or administrator for the time being of a deceased person, and as regards any liability for the payment of death duties includes any person who takes possession of or intermeddles with the property of a deceased person without the authority of the personal representatives or the court;

(xix) "Possession" includes receipt of rents and profits or the right to receive the same, if any; and "income" includes rents and profits;

(xx) "Property" includes any thing in action, and any interest in real or personal property;

(xxi) "Purchaser" means a purchaser in good faith for valuable consideration and includes a lessee, mortgagee or other person who for valuable consideration acquires an interest in property except that in Part I of this Act and elsewhere where so expressly provided "purchaser" only means a person who acquires an interest in or charge on property for money or money's worth; and in reference to a legal estate includes a chargee by way of legal mortgage; and where the context so requires "purchaser" includes an intending purchaser; "purchase" has a meaning corresponding with that of "purchaser"; and "valuable consideration" includes marriage[, and formation of a civil partnership,] but does not include a nominal consideration in money;

(xxii) "Registered land" has the same meaning as in the [Land Registration Act 2002;] …

(xxiii) "Rent" includes a rent service or a rentcharge, or other rent, toll, duty, royalty, or annual or periodical payment in money or money's worth, reserved or issuing out of or charged upon land, but does not include mortgage interest; "rentcharge" includes a fee farm rent; "fine" includes a premium or foregift and any payment, consideration, or benefit in the nature of a fine, premium or foregift; "lessor" includes an underlessor and a person deriving title under a lessor or underlessor; and "lessee" includes an underlessee and a person deriving title under a lessee or underlessee, and "lease" includes an underlease or other tenancy;

(xxiv) "Sale" includes an extinguishment of manorial incidents, but in other respects means a sale properly so called;

(xxv) "Securities" include stocks, funds and shares;

(xxvi) "Tenant for life", "statutory owner", "settled land", "settlement", "vesting deed", "subsidiary vesting deed", "vesting order", "vesting instrument", "trust instrument", "capital money" and "trustees of the settlement" have the same meanings as in the Settled Land Act 1925;

(xxvii) "Term of years absolute" means a term of years (taking effect either in possession or in reversion whether or not at a rent) with or without impeachment for waste, subject or not to another legal estate, and either certain or liable to determination by notice, re-entry, operation of law, or by a provision for cesser on redemption, or in any other event (other than the dropping of a life, or the determination of a determinable life interest); but does not include any term of years determinable with life or lives or with the cesser of a determinable life interest, nor, if created after the commencement of this Act, a term of years which is not expressed to take effect in possession within twenty-one years after the creation thereof where required by this Act to take effect within that period; and in this definition the expression "term of years" includes a term for less than a year, or for a year or years and a fraction of a year or from year to year;

(xxviii) "Trust Corporation" means the Public Trustee or a corporation either appointed by the court in any particular case to be a trustee or entitled by rules made under subsection (3) of section four of the Public Trustee Act 1906 to act as custodian trustee;

(xxix) "Trust for sale", in relation to land, means an immediate … trust for sale, whether or not exercisable at the request or with the consent of any person … ; "trustees for sale" mean the persons (including a personal representative) holding land on trust for sale; … ;

(xxx) "United Kingdom" means Great Britain and Northern Ireland;

(xxxi) "Will" includes codicil.

[(1A) Any reference in this Act to money being paid into court shall be construed as referring to the money being paid into the *Supreme Court* [Senior Courts] or any other court that has jurisdiction, and any reference in this Act to the court, in a context referring to the investment or application of money paid into court, shall be construed, in the case of money paid into the *Supreme Court* [Senior Courts], as referring to the High Court, and in the case of money paid into another court, as referring to that other court.]

(2) Where an equitable interest in or power over property arises by statute or operation of law, references to the creation of an interest or power include references to any interest or power so arising.

(3) References to registration under the Land Charges Act 1925 apply to any registration made under any other statute which is by the Land Charges Act 1925 to have effect as if the registration had been made under that Act.

[433]

NOTES

Sub-s (1): para (iiiA) inserted by the County Courts Act 1984, s 148(1), Sch 2, para 15 and repealed by SI 1991/724, art 2(8), Schedule, Pt I; words omitted from para (iv) repealed by the Finance Act 1949, s 52(9), (10), Sch 11, Pt IV; words omitted from paras (ix), (x), (xxix) repealed by the Trusts of Land and Appointment of Trustees Act 1996, s 25(2), Sch 4 (for savings, see s 25(4), (5) thereof); para (xiii) (as previously substituted by the Mental Health Act 1959, s 149(1), Sch 7, Pt I) repealed by the Mental Capacity Act 2005, s 67(1), (2), Sch 6, para 4(1), (3), Sch 7; words in square brackets in para (xv) substituted by SI 1955/554; words in square brackets in para (xxi) inserted by the Civil Partnership Act 2004, s 261(1), Sch 27, para 7; in para (xxii), words in square brackets substituted and words omitted repealed by the Land Registration Act 2002, ss 133, 135, Sch 11, para 2(1), (13), Sch 13.

Sub-s (1A): inserted by the Administration of Justice Act 1965, ss 17, 18, Sch 1; words in italics, in both places they appear, substituted by subsequent words in square brackets by the Constitutional Reform Act 2005, s 59(5), Sch 11, Pt 2, para 4(1), (3), as from 1 October 2009.

Modification: definition "Trust corporation" modified in relation to charities, by the Charities Act 1993, s 35.

206 (*Repealed by the Statute Law* (*Repeals*) *Act 2004*.)

207 Repeals as respects England and Wales

… without prejudice to the provisions of section thirty-eight of the Interpretation Act 1889—

(a) Nothing in this repeal shall affect the validity or legality of any dealing in property or other transaction completed before the commencement of this Act, or any title or right acquired or appointment made before such commencement, but, subject as aforesaid, this Act shall, except where otherwise expressly provided, apply to and in respect of instruments whether made or coming into operation before or after such commencement:

(b) Nothing in this repeal shall affect any rules, orders, or other instruments made under any enactment so repealed, but all such rules, orders and instruments shall continue in force as if made under the corresponding enactment in this Act:

(c) References in any document to any enactment repealed by this Act shall be construed as references to this Act or to the corresponding enactment in this Act.

[434]

NOTES

Words omitted repealed by the Statute Law Revision Act 1950.

208 Application to the Crown

(1) Nothing in this Act shall be construed as rendering any property of the Crown subject to distress, or liable to be taken or disposed of by means of any distress.

(2) This Act shall not in any manner (save as otherwise expressly provided and except so far as it relates to undivided shares, joint ownership, leases for lives or leases for years terminable with life or marriage) affect or alter the descent, devolution or tenure or the nature of the estates and interests of or in any land for the time being vested in His Majesty either in right of the Crown or of the Duchy of Lancaster or of or in any land for the time being belonging to the Duchy of Cornwall and held in right or in respect of the said Duchy, but so nevertheless that after the commencement of this Act, no estates, interests or charges in or over any such lands as aforesaid shall be conveyed or created, except such estates, interests or charges as are capable under this Act of subsisting or of being conveyed or created.

(3) Subject as aforesaid the provisions of this Act bind the Crown.

[435]

209 Short title, commencement, extent

(1) This Act may be cited as the Law of Property Act 1925.

(2) …

(3) This Act extends to England and Wales only.

[436]

NOTES

Sub-s (2): repealed by the Statute Law Revision Act 1950.

SCHEDULE 1
TRANSITIONAL PROVISIONS

Section 39

PART I
CONVERSION OF CERTAIN EXISTING LEGAL ESTATES INTO EQUITABLE INTERESTS

All estates, interests and charges in or over land, including fees determinable whether by limitation or condition, which immediately before the commencement of this Act were estates, interests or charges, subsisting at law, or capable of taking effect as such, but which by virtue of Part I of this Act are not capable of taking effect as legal estates, shall as from the commencement of this Act be converted into equitable interests, and shall not fail by reason of being so converted into equitable interests either in the land or in the proceeds of sale thereof, nor shall the priority of any such estate, charge or interest over other equitable interests be affected.

[437]

PART II
VESTING OF LEGAL ESTATES

1. Where the purposes of a term of years, created or limited out of leasehold land, are satisfied at the commencement of this Act, that term shall merge in the reversion expectant thereon and shall cease accordingly; but where the term was vested in the owner of the reversion, the merger and cesser shall take effect without prejudice to any protection which would have been afforded to the owner for the time being of that reversion had the term remained subsisting.

Where the purposes are satisfied only as respects part of the land comprised in a term, this provision has effect as if a separate term had been created in regard to that part of the land.

2. Where immediately after the commencement of this Act any owner of a legal estate is entitled, subject or not to the payment of the costs of tracing the title and of conveyance, to require any other legal estate in the same land to be surrendered, released or conveyed to him so as to merge or be extinguished, the last-mentioned estate shall by virtue of this Part of this Schedule be extinguished but without prejudice to any protection which would have been afforded to him had that estate remained subsisting.

3. Where immediately after the commencement of this Act any person is entitled, subject or not to the payment of the costs of tracing the title and of conveyance, to require any legal estate (not vested in trustees for sale) to be conveyed to or otherwise vested in him, such legal estate shall, by virtue of this Part of this Schedule, vest in manner hereinafter provided.

[The divesting of a legal estate by virtue of this paragraph shall not, where the person from whom the estate is so divested was a trustee, operate to prevent the legal estate being conveyed, or a legal estate being created, by him in favour of a purchaser for money or money's worth, if the purchaser has no notice of the trust and if the documents of title relating to the estate divested are produced by the trustee or by persons deriving title under him.]

This paragraph shall (without prejudice to any claim, in respect of fines, fees, and other customary payments) apply to a person who, under a surrender or any disposition having the effect of a surrender, or under a covenant to surrender or otherwise, was, immediately before the commencement of this Act, entitled to require a legal customary estate of inheritance to be vested in him, or who, immediately after such commencement becomes entitled to enfranchised land.

4. Any person who, immediately after the commencement of this Act, is entitled to an equitable interest capable of subsisting as a legal estate which has priority over any legal estate in the same land, shall be deemed to be entitled for the foregoing purposes to require a legal estate to be vested in him for an interest of a like nature not exceeding in extent or duration the equitable interest:

Provided that this paragraph shall not—

(a) apply where the equitable interest is capable of being overreached by virtue of a subsisting trust for sale or a settlement;

(b) operate to prevent such person from acquiring any other legal estate under this Part of this Schedule to which he may be entitled.

5. For the purposes of this Part of this Schedule, a tenant for life, statutory owner or personal representative, shall be deemed to be entitled to require to be vested in him any legal estate in settled land (whether or not vested in the Crown) which he is, by the Settled Land Act 1925, given power to convey.

6. Under the provisions of this Part of this Schedule, the legal estate affected (namely, any estate which a person is entitled to require to be vested in him as aforesaid) shall vest as follows—

(a) Where at the commencement of this Act land is subject to a mortgage (not being an equitable charge unsecured by any estate), the legal estate affected shall vest in accordance with the provisions relating to mortgages contained in this Schedule;

(b) Where the land is at the commencement or by virtue of this Act or any Act coming into operation at the same time subject or is by virtue of any statute made subject to a trust for sale, the legal estate affected shall vest in the trustees for sale (including personal representatives holding land on trust for sale) but subject to any mortgage term subsisting or created by this Act;

(c) Where at the commencement of this Act or by virtue of any statute coming into operation at the same time the land is settled land, the legal estate affected shall vest in the tenant for life or statutory owner entitled under the Settled Land Act 1925 to require a vesting deed to be executed in his favour, or in the personal representative, if any, in whom the land may be vested or the Public Trustee, as the case may require but subject to any mortgage term subsisting or created by this Act;

(d) In any case to which the foregoing sub-paragraphs do not apply the legal estate affected shall vest in the person of full age who, immediately after the commencement of this

Act, is entitled (subject or not to the payment of costs and any customary payments) to require the legal estate to be vested in him, but subject to any mortgage term subsisting or created by this Act.

7. Nothing in this Part of this Schedule shall operate—

(a) To vest in a mortgagee of a term of years absolute any nominal leasehold reversion which is held in trust for him subject to redemption; or

(b) To vest in a mortgagee any legal estate except a term of years absolute; or

(c) To vest in a person entitled to a leasehold interest, as respects such interest, any legal estate except a term of years absolute; or

(d) To vest in a person entitled to a rentcharge (either perpetual or held for a term of years absolute) as respects such rentcharge, any legal estate except a legal estate in the rentcharge; or

(e) To vest in a person entitled to an easement, right or privilege with reference thereto, any legal estate except a legal estate in the easement, right or privilege; or

(f) To vest any legal estate in a person for an undivided share; or

(g) To vest any legal estate in an infant; or

(h) To affect prejudicially the priority of any mortgage or other incumbrance or interest subsisting at the commencement of this Act; or

(i) To render invalid any limitation or trust which would have been capable of taking effect as an equitable limitation or trust; or

(j) To vest in a purchaser or his personal representatives any legal estate which he has contracted to acquire and in regard to which a contract, including an agreement to create a legal mortgage, is pending at the commencement of this Act, although the consideration may have been paid or satisfied and the title accepted, or to render unnecessary the conveyance of such estate; or

(k) To vest in the managing trustees or committee of management of a charity any legal estate vested in the Official Trustee of Charity Lands; or

(l) To vest in any person any legal estate which failed to pass to him by reason of his omission to be registered as proprietor under the Land Transfer Acts 1875 and 1897 until brought into operation by virtue of the Land Registration Act 1925.

[(m) To vest in any person any legal estate affected by any rent covenants or conditions if, before any proceedings are commenced in respect of the rent covenants or conditions, and before any conveyance of the legal estate or dealing therewith *inter vivos* is effected, he or his personal representatives disclaim it in writing signed by him or them.]

8. Any legal estate acquired by virtue of this Part of this Schedule shall be held upon the trusts and subject to the powers, provisions, rents, covenants, conditions, rights of redemption (as respects terms of years absolute) and other rights, burdens and obligations, if any, upon or subject to which the estate acquired ought to be held.

9. No stamp duty shall become payable by reason only of any vesting surrender or release effected by this Schedule.

[438]

NOTES

Paras 3, 7: words in square brackets inserted by the Law of Property (Amendment) Act 1926, s 7, Schedule.

PART III

PROVISIONS AS TO LEGAL ESTATE VESTED IN INFANT

1. Where immediately before the commencement of this Act a legal estate in land is vested in one or more infants beneficially, or where immediately after the commencement of this Act a legal estate in land would by virtue of this Act have become vested in one or more infants beneficially if he or they had been of full age, the legal estate shall vest in the manner provided by the Settled Land Act 1925.

2. Where immediately before the commencement of this Act a legal estate in land is vested in an infant jointly with one or more other persons of full age beneficially, the legal estate shall by virtue of this Act vest in that other person or those other persons on the statutory trusts, but not so as to sever any joint tenancy in the net proceeds of sale or in the rents and profits until sale:

Provided that, if by virtue of this paragraph the legal estate becomes vested in one person as trustee, then, if no other person is able and willing to do so, the parents or parent testamentary or other guardian of the infant, if respectively able and willing to act, (in the order named) may, and at the request of any person interested shall (subject to the costs being provided for) by writing appoint an additional trustee and thereupon by virtue of this Act the legal estate shall vest in the additional trustee and existing trustee as joint tenants.

3. Where, immediately before the commencement of this Act, a legal estate in land is vested solely in an infant as a personal representative, or a trustee of a settlement, or on trust for sale or on any other trust, or by way of mortgage, or where immediately after the commencement of this Act a legal estate in land would by virtue of any provision of this Act or otherwise have been so vested if

the infant were of full age, the legal estate and the mortgage debt (if any) and interest thereon shall, by virtue of this Act, vest in the Public Trustee, pending the appointment of trustees as hereinafter provided—

(a) as to the land, upon the trusts, and subject to the equities affecting the same (but in the case of a mortgage estate for a term of years absolute in accordance with this Act); and

(b) as to the mortgage debt and interest, upon such trusts as may be requisite for giving effect to the rights (if any) of the infant or other persons beneficially interested therein:

Provided that—

(i) The Public Trustee shall not be entitled to act in the trust, or charge any fee, or be liable in any manner, unless and until requested in writing to act by or on behalf of the persons interested in the land or the income thereof, or in the mortgage debt or interest thereon (as the case may be), which request may be made on behalf of the infant by his parents or parent, or testamentary or other guardian (in the order named), and those persons may, in the order aforesaid (if no other person is able and willing to do so) appoint new trustees in the place of the Public Trustee, and thereupon by virtue of this Act the land or term and mortgage money shall vest in the trustees so appointed upon the trusts and subject to the equities aforesaid: Provided that the Public Trustee may, before he accepts the trust, but subject to the payment of his costs, convey to a person of full age who becomes entitled;

(ii) After the Public Trustee has been so requested to act, and has accepted the trust, no trustee shall (except by an order of the court) be appointed in his place without his consent;

(iii) Any person interested in the land or the income thereof, or in the mortgage debt or in the interest thereon (as the case may be), may, at the time during the minority, apply to the court for the appointment of trustees of the trust, and the court may make such order as it thinks fit, and if thereby new trustees are appointed the legal estate (but in the case of a mortgage estate only for a term of years absolute as aforesaid) and the mortgage debt (if any) and interest shall, by virtue of this Act, vest in the trustees as joint tenants upon the trusts and subject to the equities aforesaid;

(iv) Neither a purchaser of the land nor a transferee for money or money's worth of the mortgage shall be concerned in any way with the trusts affecting the legal estate or the mortgage debt and interest thereon;

(v) The vesting in the Public Trustee of a legal estate or a mortgage debt by virtue of this Part of this Schedule shall not affect any directions previously given as to the payment of income or of interest on any mortgage money, but such instructions may, until he accepts the trust, continue to be acted on as if no such vesting had been effected.

[3A. The county court has jurisdiction under proviso (iii) to paragraph 3 of this Part where the land which is to be dealt with in the court does not exceed [£30,000] in capital value …]

4. Where, immediately before the commencement of this Act, a legal estate in land is vested in two or more persons jointly as personal representatives, trustees, or mortgagees, and anyone of them is an infant, or where immediately after the commencement of this Act a legal estate in land would, by virtue of this Act, or otherwise have been so vested if the infant were of full age, the legal estate in the land with the mortgage debt (if any) and the interest thereon shall by virtue of this Act, vest in the other person or persons of full age—

(a) as to the legal estate, upon the trusts and subject to the equities affecting the same (but in the case of a mortgage estate only for a term of years absolute as aforesaid); and

(b) as to the mortgage debt and interest, upon such trusts as may be requisite for giving effect to the rights (if any) of the infant or other persons beneficially interested therein;

but neither a purchaser of the land nor a transferee for money or money's worth of the mortgage shall be concerned in any way with the trusts affecting the legal estate or the mortgage debt and interest thereon:

Provided that, if, by virtue of this paragraph, the legal estate and mortgage debt, if any, become vested in a sole trustee, then, if no other person is able and willing to do so, the parents or parent, testamentary or other guardian of the infant (in the order named) may, and at the request of any person interested shall (subject to the costs being provided for) by writing appoint a new trustee in place of the infant, and thereupon by virtue of this Act the legal estate and mortgage money shall vest in the new and continuing trustees upon the trusts and subject to the equities aforesaid.

5. This Part of this Schedule does not affect the estate or powers of an administrator durante minore aetate, nor, where there is a tenant for life or statutory owner of settled land, operate to vest the legal estate therein in the Public Trustee.

[439]

NOTES

Para 3A: inserted by the County Courts Act 1984, s 148(1), Sch 2, para 10; sum in square brackets substituted and words omitted repealed by SI 1991/724, art 2(3)(b), (8), Schedule, Pt I.

PART IV
PROVISIONS SUBJECTING LAND HELD IN UNDIVIDED SHARES TO A TRUST FOR SALE

1. Where, immediately before the commencement of this Act, land is held at law or in equity in undivided shares vested in possession, the following provisions shall have effect—

(1) If the entirety of the land is vested in trustees or personal representatives (whether subject or not to incumbrances affecting the entirety or an undivided share) in trust for persons entitled in undivided shares, then—

(a) if the land is subject to incumbrances affecting undivided shares or to incumbrances affecting the entirety which under this Act or otherwise are not secured by legal terms of years absolute, the entirety of the land shall vest free from such incumbrances in such trustees or personal representatives and be held by them upon the statutory trusts; and

(b) in any other case, the land shall be held by such trustees or personal representatives upon the statutory trusts;

subject in the case of personal representatives, to their rights and powers for the purposes of administration.

(2) If the entirety of the land (not being settled land) is vested absolutely and beneficially in not more than four persons of full age entitled thereto in undivided shares free from incumbrances affecting undivided shares, but subject or not to incumbrances affecting the entirety, it shall, by virtue of this Act, vest in them as joint tenants upon the statutory trusts.

(3) If the entirety of the land is settled land (whether subject or not to incumbrances affecting the entirety or an undivided share) held under one and the same settlement, it shall, by virtue of this Act, vest, free from incumbrances affecting undivided shares, and from incumbrances affecting the entirety, which under this Act or otherwise are not secured by a legal [mortgage, and free from any interests, powers and charges subsisting under the settlement, which have priority to the interests of the persons entitled to the undivided shares], in the trustees (if any) of the settlement as joint tenants upon the statutory trusts.

Provided that if there are no such trustees, then—

(i) pending their appointment, the land shall, by virtue of this Act, vest (free as aforesaid) in the Public Trustee upon the statutory trusts;

(ii) the Public Trustee shall not be entitled to act in the trust, or charge any fee, or be liable in any manner, unless and until requested in writing to act by or on behalf of persons interested in more than an undivided half of the land or the income thereof;

(iii) after the Public Trustee has been so requested to act, and has accepted the trust, no trustee shall (except by an order of the court) be appointed in the place of the Public Trustee without his consent;

(iv) if, before the Public Trustee has accepted the trust, trustees of the settlement are appointed, the land shall, by virtue of this Act, vest (free as aforesaid) in them as joint tenants upon the statutory trusts;

(v) if, before the Public Trustee has accepted the trust, the persons having power to appoint new trustees are unable or unwilling to make an appointment, or if the tenant for life having power to apply to the court for the appointment of trustees of the settlement neglects to make the application for at least three months after being requested by any person interested in writing so to do, or if the tenants for life of the undivided shares are unable to agree, any person interested under the settlement may apply to the court for the appointment of such trustees.

[(3A) The county court has jurisdiction under proviso (v) to sub-paragraph (3) of this paragraph where the land to be dealt with in the court does not exceed [£30,000] in capital value …]

(4) In any case to which the foregoing provisions of this Part of this Schedule do not apply, the entirety of the land shall vest (free as aforesaid) in the Public Trustee upon the statutory trusts:

Provided that—

(i) The Public Trustee shall not be entitled to act in the trust, or charge any fee, or be liable in any manner, unless and until requested in writing to act by or on behalf of the persons interested in more than an undivided half of the land or the income thereof;

(ii) After the Public Trustee has been so requested to act, and has accepted the trust, no trustee shall (except by an order of the court) be appointed in the place of the Public Trustee without his consent;

(iii) Subject as aforesaid, any persons interested in more than an undivided half of the land or the income thereof may appoint new trustees in the place of the Public Trustee with the consent of any incumbrancers of undivided shares (but so that a purchaser shall not be concerned to see whether any such consent has been given) and [thereupon the land shall by virtue of this Act vest] in the persons so appointed (free as aforesaid) upon the statutory trusts; or such persons may (without such consent as aforesaid), at any time, whether or not the Public Trustee has accepted the trust, apply to the court for the appointment of trustees of the land, and the court may make such order as it thinks fit, and if thereby trustees of the land are appointed, the same shall by virtue of this Act, vest (free as aforesaid) in the trustees as joint tenants upon the statutory trusts;

(iv) If the persons interested in more than an undivided half of the land or the income thereof do not either request the Public Trustee to act, or (whether he refuses to act or has not been requested to act) apply to the court for the appointment of trustees in his place, within three months from the time when they have been requested in writing by any person interested so to do, then and in any such case, any person interested may apply to the court for the appointment of trustees in the place of the Public Trustee, and the court may make such order as it thinks fit, and if thereby trustees of the land are appointed the same shall by virtue of this Act vest (free as aforesaid) in the trustees upon the statutory trusts.

[(4A) The county court has jurisdiction under provisos (iii) and (iv) to sub-paragraph (4) of this paragraph where the land which is to be dealt with in the court does not exceed [£30,000] in capital value …]

(5) The vesting in the Public Trustee of land by virtue of this Part of this Schedule shall not affect any directions previously given as to the payment of income or of interest on any mortgage money, but such instructions may, until he accepts the trust, continue to be acted on as if no such vesting had been effected.

(6) The court or the Public Trustee may act on evidence given by affidavit or by statutory declaration as respects the undivided shares without investigating the title to the land.

(7) Where all the undivided shares in the land are vested in the same mortgagees for securing the same mortgage money and the rights of redemption affecting the land are the same as might have been subsisting if the entirety had been mortgaged by an owner before the undivided shares were created, the land shall, by virtue of this Act, vest in the mortgagees as joint tenants for a legal term of years absolute (in accordance with this Act) subject to cesser on redemption by the trustees for sale in whom the right of redemption is vested by this Act, and for the purposes of this Part of this Schedule the mortgage shall be deemed an incumbrance affecting the entirety.

(8) This Part of this Schedule does not (except where otherwise expressly provided) prejudice incumbrancers whose incumbrances affect the entirety of the land at the commencement of this Act, but (if the nature of the incumbrance admits) the land shall vest in them for legal terms of years absolute in accordance with this Act but not so as to affect subsisting priorities.

(9) The trust for sale and powers of management vested in persons who hold the entirety of the land on trust for sale shall, save as hereinafter mentioned, not be exercisable without the consent of any incumbrancer, being of full age, affected whose incumbrance is divested by this Part of this Schedule, but a purchaser shall not be concerned to see or inquire whether any such consent has been given, nor, where the incumbrancer is not in possession, shall any such consent be required if, independently of this Part of this Schedule or any enactment replaced thereby the transaction would have been binding on him, had the same been effected by the mortgagor.

(10) This Part of this Schedule does not apply to land in respect of which a subsisting contract for sale (whether made under an order in a partition action or by or on behalf of all the tenants in common or coparceners) is in force at the commencement of this Act if the contract is completed in due course (in which case title may be made in like manner as if this Act, and any enactment thereby replaced, had not been passed), nor to the land in respect of which a partition action is pending at such commencement if an order for a partition or sale is subsequently made in such action [within eighteen months from the commencement of this Act].

(11) The repeal of the enactments relating to partition shall operate without prejudice to any proceedings thereunder commenced before the commencement of this Act, and to the jurisdiction of the court to make any orders in reference thereto, and subject to the following provisions, namely:—

(i) In any such proceedings, and at any stage thereof, any person or persons interested individually or collectively in [one half or upwards] of the land to which the proceedings relate, may apply to the court for an order staying such proceedings;

(ii) The court may upon such application make an order staying the proceedings as regards the whole or any part, not being an undivided share, of the land;

(iii) As from the date of such order the said enactments shall cease to apply to the land affected by the order and the provisions of this Part of this Schedule shall apply thereto;

(iv) The court may by such order appoint trustees of the land and the same shall by virtue of this Act vest (free as aforesaid) in the trustees as joint tenants upon the statutory trusts;

(v) The court may order that the costs of the proceedings and of the application shall be raised by the trustees, by legal mortgage of the land or any part thereof, and paid either wholly or partially into court or to the trustees;

(vi) The court may act on such evidence as appears to be sufficient, without investigating the title to the land.

(12) In this Part of this Schedule "incumbrance" does not include [a legal rentcharge affecting the entirety,] land tax, tithe rentcharge, or any similar charge on the land not created by an instrument.

2. Where undivided shares in land, created before the commencement of this Act, fall into possession after such commencement, and the land is not settled land when the shares fall into possession, the personal representatives (subject to their rights and powers for purposes of administration) or other estate owners in whom the entirety of the land is vested shall, by an assent or a conveyance, give effect to the foregoing provisions of this Part of this Schedule in like manner as if the shares had fallen into possession immediately before the commencement of this Act, and in the meantime the land shall be held on the statutory trusts.

3. This Part of this Schedule shall not save as hereinafter mentioned apply to party structures and open spaces within the meaning of the next succeeding Part of this Schedule.

[4. Where, immediately before the commencement of this Act, there are two or more tenants for life of full age entitled under the same settlement in undivided shares, and, after the cesser of all their interests in the income of the settled land, the entirety of the land is limited so as to devolve together (not in undivided shares), their interests shall, but without prejudice to any beneficial interest, be converted into a joint tenancy, and the joint tenants and the survivor of them shall, until the said cesser occurs, constitute the tenant for life for the purposes of the Settled Land Act 1925 and this Act.]

[440]

NOTES

Para 1: words in square brackets in sub-paras (3), (4), (11) substituted, and words in sub-paras (10), (12) inserted by the Law of Property (Amendment) Act 1926, s 7, Schedule; sub-paras (3A), (4A) inserted by the County Courts Act 1984, s 148(1), Sch 2, para 10, sums in square brackets therein substituted and words omitted repealed, by SI 1991/724, art 2(3)(c), (d), (8), Schedule, Pt I.

Para 4: inserted by the Law of Property (Amendment) Act 1926, s 7, Schedule.

PART V
PROVISIONS AS TO PARTY STRUCTURES AND OPEN SPACES

1. Where, immediately before the commencement of this Act, a party wall or other party structure is held in undivided shares, the ownership thereof shall be deemed to be severed vertically as between the respective owners, and the owner of each part shall have such rights to support and of user over the rest of the structure as may be requisite for conferring rights corresponding to those subsisting at the commencement of this Act.

2. Where, immediately before the commencement of this Act, an open space of land (with or without any building used in common for the purposes of any adjoining land) is held in undivided shares, in right whereof each owner has rights of access and user over the open space, the ownership thereof shall vest in the Public Trustee on the statutory trusts which shall be executed only with the leave of the court, and, subject to any order of the court to the contrary, each person who would have been a tenant in common shall, until the open space is conveyed to a purchaser, have rights of access and user over the open space corresponding to those which would have subsisted if the tenancy in common had remained subsisting.

3. Any person interested may apply to the court for an order declaring the rights and interests under this Part of this Schedule, of the persons interested in any such party structure or open space, or generally may apply in relation to the provisions of this Part of this Schedule, and the court may make such order as it thinks fit.

[441]

(*Pt VI repealed by the Statute Law* (*Repeals*) *Act 2004.*)

PART VII
CONVERSION OF EXISTING FREEHOLD MORTGAGES INTO MORTGAGES BY DEMISE

1. All land, which immediately before the commencement of this Act, was vested in a first or only mortgagee for an estate in fee simple in possession, whether legal or equitable, shall, from and after the commencement of this Act, vest in the first or only mortgagee for a term of three thousand years from such commencement, without impeachment of waste, but subject to a provision for cesser corresponding to the right of redemption which, at such commencement, was subsisting with respect to the fee simple.

2. All land, which immediately before the commencement of this Act, was vested in a second or subsequent mortgagee for an estate in fee simple in possession, whether legal or equitable, shall, from and after the commencement of this Act, vest in the second or subsequent mortgagee for a term one day longer than the term vested in the first or other mortgagee whose security ranks immediately before that of such second or subsequent mortgagee, without impeachment of waste, but subject to the term or terms vested in such first or other prior mortgagee and subject to a provision for cesser corresponding to the right of redemption which, at such commencement was subsisting with respect to the fee simple.

3. The estate in fee simple which, immediately before the commencement of this Act, was vested in any such mortgagee shall, from and after such commencement vest in the mortgagor or tenant for life, statutory owner, trustee for sale, personal representative, or other person of full age who, if all money owing on the security of the mortgage and all other mortgages or charges (if any) had been discharged at the commencement of this Act, would have been entitled to have the fee simple conveyed to him, but subject to any mortgage term created by this Part of this Schedule or otherwise and to the money secured by any such mortgage or charge.

4. If a sub-mortgage by conveyance of the fee simple is subsisting immediately before the commencement of this Act, the principal mortgagee shall take the principal term created by paragraphs 1 or 2 of this Part of this Schedule (as the case may require) and the sub-mortgagee shall take a derivative term less by one day than the term so created, without impeachment of waste, subject to a provision for cesser corresponding to the right of redemption subsisting under the sub-mortgage.

5. This Part of this Schedule applies to land enfranchised by statute as well as to land which was freehold before the commencement of this Act, and (save where expressly excepted) whether or not the land is registered under the Land Registration Act 1925, or the mortgage is made by way of trust for sale or otherwise.

6. A mortgage affecting a legal estate made before the commencement of this Act which is not protected, either by a deposit of documents of title relating to the legal estate or by registration as a land charge, shall not, as against a purchaser in good faith without notice thereof, obtain any benefit by reason of being converted into a legal mortgage by this Schedule, but shall, in favour of such purchaser, be deemed to remain an equitable interest.

This paragraph does not apply to mortgages or charges registered or protected under the Land Registration Act 1925, or to mortgages or charges registered in a local deeds register.

7. Nothing in this Part of this Schedule shall affect priorities or the right of any mortgagee to retain possession of documents, nor affect his title to or rights over any fixtures or chattels personal comprised in the mortgage.

8. This Part of this Schedule does not apply unless a right of redemption is subsisting immediately before the commencement of this Act.

[442]

PART VIII
CONVERSION OF EXISTING LEASEHOLD MORTGAGES INTO MORTGAGES BY SUBDEMISE

1. All leasehold land, which immediately before the commencement of this Act, was vested in a first or only mortgagee by way of assignment of a term of years absolute shall, from and after the commencement of this Act, vest in the first or only mortgagee for a term equal to the term assigned by the mortgage, less the last ten days thereof, but subject to a provision for cesser corresponding to the right of redemption which at such commencement was subsisting with respect to the term assigned.

2. All leasehold land, which immediately before the commencement of this Act, was vested in a second or subsequent mortgagee by way of assignment of a term of years absolute (whether legal or equitable) shall, from and after the commencement of this Act, vest in the second or subsequent mortgagee for a term one day longer than the term vested in the first or other mortgagee whose security ranks immediately before that of such second or subsequent mortgagee if the length of the last-mentioned term permits, and in any case for a term less by one day at least than the term assigned by the mortgage, but subject to the term or terms vested in such first or other prior mortgagee, and subject to a provision for cesser corresponding to the right of redemption which, at the commencement of this Act, was subsisting with respect to the term assigned by the mortgage.

3. The term of years absolute which was assigned by any such mortgage shall, from and after the commencement of this Act, vest in the mortgagor or tenant for life, statutory owner, trustee for sale, personal representative, or other person of full age who, if all the money owing on the security of the mortgage and all other mortgages or charges, if any, had been discharged at the commencement of this Act, would have been entitled to have the term assigned or surrendered to him, but subject to any derivative mortgage term created by this Part of this Schedule or otherwise and to the money secured by any such mortgage or charge.

4. If a sub-mortgage by assignment of a term is subsisting immediately before the commencement of this Act, the principal mortgagee shall take the principal derivative term created by paragraphs 1 or 2 of this Part of this Schedule or the derivative term created by his mortgage (as the case may require), and the sub-mortgagee shall take a derivative term less by one day than the term so vested in the principal mortgagee, subject to a provision for cesser corresponding to the right of redemption subsisting under the sub-mortgage.

5. A mortgage affecting a legal estate made before the commencement of this Act which is not protected, either by a deposit of documents of title relating to the legal estate or by registration as a

land charge shall not, as against a purchaser in good faith without notice thereof, obtain any benefit by reason of being converted into a legal mortgage by this Schedule, but shall, in favour of such purchaser, be deemed to remain an equitable interest.

This paragraph does not apply to mortgages or charges registered or protected under the Land Registration Act 1925, or to mortgages or charges registered in a local deeds register.

6. This Part of this Schedule applies to perpetually renewable leaseholds, and to leaseholds for lives, which are by statute converted into long terms, with the following variations, namely—

(a) The term to be taken by a first or only mortgagee shall be ten days less than the term created by such statute;

(b) The term to be taken by a second or subsequent mortgagee shall be one day longer than the term vested in the first or other mortgagee whose security ranks immediately before that of the second or subsequent mortgagee, if the length of the last-mentioned term permits, and in any case for a term less by one day at least than the term created by such statute:

(c) The term created by such statute shall, from and after the commencement of this Act, vest in the mortgagor or tenant for life, statutory owner, trustee for sale, personal representative, or other person of full age, who if all the money owing on the security of the mortgage and all other mortgages or charges, if any, had been discharged at the commencement of this Act, would have been entitled to have the term assigned or surrendered to him, but subject to any derivative mortgage term created by this Part of this Schedule or otherwise and to the money secured by any such mortgage or charge.

7. This Part of this Schedule applies (save where expressly excepted) whether or not the leasehold land is registered under the Land Registration Act 1925, or the mortgage is made by way of trust for sale or otherwise.

8. Nothing in this Part of this Schedule shall affect priorities or the right of any mortgagee to retain possession of documents, nor affect his title to or rights over any fixtures or chattels personal comprised in the mortgage, but this Part of this Schedule does not apply unless a right of redemption is subsisting at the commencement of this Act.

[443]

SCHEDULE 2
IMPLIED COVENANTS

Sections 76, 77

(*Pts I–VI repealed by the Law of Property* (*Miscellaneous Provisions*) *Act 1994, ss 10*(*1*), *21*(*2*), *Sch 2, as regards dispositions of property made on or after 1 July 1995.*)

PART VII
COVENANT IMPLIED IN A CONVEYANCE FOR VALUABLE CONSIDERATION, OTHER THAN A MORTGAGE, OF THE ENTIRETY OF LAND AFFECTED BY A RENTCHARGE

That the grantees or the persons deriving title under them will at all times, from the date of the conveyance or other date therein stated, duly pay the said rentcharge and observe and perform all the covenants, agreements and conditions contained in the deed or other document creating the rentcharge, and thenceforth on the part of the owner of the land to be observed and performed:

And also will at all times, from the date aforesaid, save harmless and keep indemnified the conveying parties and their respective estates and effects, from and against all proceedings, costs, claims and expenses on account of any omission to pay the said rentcharge or any part thereof, or any breach of any of the said covenants, agreements and conditions.

[444]

PART VIII
COVENANTS IMPLIED IN A CONVEYANCE FOR VALUABLE CONSIDERATION, OTHER THAN A MORTGAGE, OF PART OF LAND AFFECTED BY A RENTCHARGE, SUBJECT TO A PART (NOT LEGALLY APPORTIONED) OF THAT RENTCHARGE

(i) That the grantees, or the persons deriving title under them, will at all times, from the date of the conveyance or other date therein stated, pay the apportioned rent and observe and perform all the covenants (other than the covenant to pay the entire rent) and conditions contained in the deed or other document creating the rentcharge, so far as the same relate to the land conveyed:

And also will at all times, from the date aforesaid, save harmless and keep indemnified the conveying parties and their respective estates and effects, from and against all proceedings, costs, claims and expenses on account of any omission to pay the said apportioned rent, or any breach of any of the said covenants and conditions, so far as the same relate as aforesaid.

(ii) That the conveying parties, or the persons deriving title under them, will at all times, from the date of the conveyance or other date therein stated, pay the balance of the rentcharge (after deducting the apportioned rent aforesaid, and any other rents similarly apportioned in respect of land not retained), and observe and perform all the covenants, other than the covenant to pay the entire rent, and conditions contained in the deed or other document creating the rentcharge, so far as the same relate to the land not included in the conveyance and remaining vested in the covenantors:

And also will at all times, from the date aforesaid, save harmless and keep indemnified the grantees and their estates and effects, from and against all proceedings, costs, claims and expenses on account of any omission to pay the aforesaid balance of the rentcharge, or any breach of any of the said covenants and conditions so far as they relate aforesaid.

[445]

PART IX
COVENANT IN A CONVEYANCE FOR VALUABLE CONSIDERATION, OTHER THAN A MORTGAGE, OF THE ENTIRETY OF THE LAND COMPRISED IN A LEASE FOR THE RESIDUE OF THE TERM OR INTEREST CREATED BY THE LEASE

That the assignees, or the persons deriving title under them, will at all times, from the date of the conveyance or other date therein stated, duly pay all rent becoming due under the lease creating the term or interest for which the land is conveyed, and observe and perform all the covenants, agreements and conditions therein contained and thenceforth on the part of the lessees to be observed and performed:

And also will at all times, from the date aforesaid, save harmless and keep indemnified the conveying parties and their estates and effects, from and against all proceedings, costs, claims and expenses on account of any omission to pay the said rent or any breach of any of the said covenants, agreements and conditions.

[446]

NOTES

Repealed by the Landlord and Tenant (Covenants) Act 1995, s 30(2), (3)(a), Sch 2, in relation to new tenancies as defined by s 1(3) of the 1995 Act at **[1563]**.

PART X
COVENANTS IMPLIED IN A CONVEYANCE FOR VALUABLE CONSIDERATION, OTHER THAN A MORTGAGE, OF PART OF THE LAND COMPRISED IN A LEASE, FOR THE RESIDUE OF THE TERM OR INTEREST CREATED BY THE LEASE, SUBJECT TO A PART (NOT LEGALLY APPORTIONED) OF THAT RENT

(i) That the assignees, or the persons deriving title under them, will at all times, from the date of the conveyance or other date therein stated, pay the apportioned rent and observe and perform all the covenants, other than the covenant to pay the entire rent, agreements and conditions contained in the lease creating the term or interest for which the land is conveyed, and thenceforth on the part of the lessees to be observed and performed, so far as the same relate to the land conveyed:

And also will at all times from the date aforesaid save harmless and keep indemnified, the conveying parties and their respective estates and effects, from and against all proceedings, costs, claims and expenses on account of any omission to pay the said apportioned rent or any breach of any of the said covenants, agreements and conditions so far as the same relate as aforesaid.

(ii) That the conveying parties, or the persons deriving title under them, will at all times, from the date of the conveyance, or other date therein stated, pay the balance of the rent (after deducting the apportioned rent aforesaid and any other rents similarly apportioned in respect of land not retained) and observe and perform all the covenants, other than the covenant to pay the entire rent, agreements and conditions contained in the lease and on the part of the lessees to be observed and performed so far as the same relate to the land demised (other than the land comprised in the conveyance) and the remaining vested in the covenantors:

And also will at all times, from the date aforesaid, save harmless and keep indemnified, the assignees and their estates and effects, from and against all proceedings, costs, claims and expenses on account of any omission to pay the aforesaid balance of the rent or any breach of any of the said covenants, agreements and conditions so far as they relate as aforesaid.

[447]

NOTES

Repealed by the Landlord and Tenant (Covenants) Act 1995, s 30(2), (3)(a), Sch 2, in relation to new tenancies as defined by s 1(3) of the 1995 Act at **[1563]**.

SCHEDULE 3
FORMS OF TRANSFER AND DISCHARGE OF MORTGAGES

Sections 114, 115

FORM NO 1
FORM OF TRANSFER OF MORTGAGE

This Transfer of Mortgage made the ..... day of ..... 19 ... , between *M.* of (etc) of the one part and *T.* of (etc) of the other part, supplemental to a Mortgage dated (etc), and made between (etc), and to a Further Charge dated (etc), and made between (etc) affecting etc (*here state short particulars of the mortgaged property*).

WITNESSETH that in consideration of the sums of £ ..... and £ ..... (for interest) now paid by *T.* to *M.*, being the respective amounts of the mortgage money and interest owing in respect of the said mortgage and further charge (the receipt of which sums *M.* hereby acknowledges) *M.*, as mortgagee, hereby conveys and transfers to *T.* the benefit of the said mortgage and further charge.

In witness, etc

[448]

FORM NO 2
FORM OF RECEIPT ON DISCHARGE OF A MORTGAGE

I, *A.B., of* (etc.) hereby acknowledge that I have this ..... day of ..... 19 ... , received the sum of £ ..... representing the (aggregate) (balance remaining owing in respect of the) principal money secured by the within (above) written (annexed) mortgage (and by a further charge dated, etc, *or otherwise as required*) together with all interest and costs, the payment having been made by *C.D.* of (etc) and *E.F.* of (etc)

As witness, etc

NOTE.—If the persons paying are not entitled to the equity of redemption state that they are paying the money out of a fund applicable to the discharge of the mortgage.

[449]

SCHEDULE 4
FORMS RELATING TO STATUTORY CHARGES OR MORTGAGES OF FREEHOLD OR LEASEHOLD LAND

Sections 117, 118, 120

NOTES

See further: in relation to covenants implied by virtue of s 76 of this Act, see the Law of Property (Miscellaneous Provisions) Act 1994, s 9 at **[1537]**.

FORM NO 1
STATUTORY CHARGE BY WAY OF LEGAL MORTGAGE

This Legal Charge made by way of Statutory Mortgage the ..... day of ..... 19 ... , between *A.* of (etc) of the one part and *M.* of (etc) of the other part Witnesseth that in consideration of the sum of £ ..... now paid to *A.* by *M.* of which sum *A.* hereby acknowledges the receipt *A.* As Mortgagor and As Beneficial Owner hereby charges by way of legal mortgage All That (etc) with the payment to *M.* on the ..... day of ..... 19 ... , of the principal sum of £ ..... as the mortgage money with interest thereon at the rate of ..... per centum per annum.

In witness etc

NOTE.—Variations in this and the subsequent forms in this Schedule to be made, if required, for leasehold land or for giving effect to special arrangements. *M.* will be in the same position as if the Charge had been effected by a demise of freeholds or a subdemise of leaseholds.

[450]

FORM NO 2
STATUTORY TRANSFER, MORTGAGOR NOT JOINING

This Transfer of Mortgage made by way of statutory transfer the ..... day of ..... 19 ... , between *M.* of (etc) of the one part and *T.* of (etc) of the other part supplemental to a legal charge made by way of statutory mortgage dated (etc) and made (etc) Witnesseth that in consideration of the sum of £ ..... now paid to *M.* by *T.* (being the aggregate amount of £ ..... mortgage money and £ ..... interest due in respect of the said legal charge of which sum *M.* hereby acknowledges the receipt) *M.* as Mortgagee hereby conveys and transfers to *T.* the benefit of the said legal charge.

In witness, etc

NOTE.—This and the next two forms also apply to a transfer of a statutory mortgage made before the commencement of this Act, which will then be referred to as a mortgage instead of a legal charge.

[451]

FORM NO 3
STATUTORY TRANSFER, A COVENANTOR JOINING

This Transfer of Mortgage made by way of statutory transfer the ..... day of ..... 19 ... , between *A.* of (etc) of the first part *B.* of (etc) of the second part and *C.* of (etc) of the third part Supplemental to a Legal Charge made by way of statutory mortgage dated (etc) and made (etc) Witnesseth that in consideration of the sum of £ ..... now paid by *A.* to *C.* (being the mortgage money due in respect of the said Legal Charge no interest being now due or payable thereon of which sum *A.* hereby acknowledges the receipt) *A.* as Mortgagee with the concurrence of *B.* who joins herein as covenantor hereby conveys and transfers to *C.* the benefit of the said Legal Charge.

In witness, etc

[452]

FORM NO 4
STATUTORY TRANSFER AND MORTGAGE COMBINED

This Transfer and Legal Charge is made by way of statutory transfer and mortgage the ..... day of ..... 19 ... , between *A.* of (etc) of the first part *B.* of (etc) of the second part and *C.* of (etc) of the third part Supplemental to a Legal Charge made by way of statutory mortgage dated (etc) and made (etc) Whereas a principal sum of £ ..... only remains due in respect of the said Legal Charge as the mortgage money and no interest is now due thereon And Whereas *B.* is seised in fee simple of the land comprised in the said Legal Charge subject to that Charge.

Now this Deed Witnesseth as follows:—

1. In consideration of the sum of £ ..... now paid to *A.* by *C.* (the receipt and payment of which sum *A.* & *B.* hereby respectively acknowledge) * *A.* as mortgagee hereby conveys and transfers to *C.* the benefit of the said Legal Charge.

2. For the consideration aforesaid *B.* ** as beneficial owner hereby charges by way of legal mortgage. All the premises comprised in the said Legal Charge with the payment to *C.* on the ..... day of ..... 19 ... of *** the sum of £ ..... as the mortgage money with interest thereon at the rate of ..... per centum per annum In Witness etc. (or in the case of a further advance after "acknowledge" at * *insert* "and of the further sum of £ ..... now paid by *C.* to *B.* of which sum *B.* hereby acknowledges the receipt" *also at ** before "as beneficial owner" insert* "as mortgagor and" *as well as where B. is not the original mortgagor. And after* "of" *at *** insert* "the sums of £ ..... and £ ..... making together")

NOTE.—Variations to be made, as required, in case of the deed being by indorsement, or in respect of any other thing.

[453]

FORM NO 5
RECEIPT ON DISCHARGE OF STATUTORY LEGAL CHARGE OR MORTGAGE

I *A.B.* of (etc) hereby acknowledge that I have this ..... day of ..... 19 ... received the sum of £ ..... representing the (aggregate) (balance remaining owing in respect of the) mortgage money secured by the (annexed) within (above) written statutory legal charge (*or* statutory mortgage) (and by the further statutory charge dated etc *or otherwise as required*) together with all interest and costs the payment having been made by *C.D.* of (etc.) and *E.F.* of (etc)

As witness etc

NOTE.—If the persons paying are not entitled to the equity of redemption state that they are paying the money out of a fund applicable to the discharge of the statutory legal charge or mortgage.

[454]

(*Schs 5, 6 repealed by the Statute Law (Repeals) Act 2004; Sch 7 repealed by the Statute Law Revision Act 1950.*)

LAND REGISTRATION ACT 1925

(1925 c 21)

An Act to consolidate the Land Transfer Acts and the statute law relating to registered land

[9 April 1925]

NOTES

This Act is repealed by the Land Registration Act 2002, s 135, Sch 13, as from 13 October 2003, subject to transitional provisions in Sch 12 thereto at **[2026]**. The provisions printed below are reproduced for reference.

1–29 (*Repealed as noted at the beginning of this Act.*)

30 Protection of charges for securing further advances

(*1*) *When a registered charge is made for securing further advances, the registrar shall, before making any entry on the register which would prejudicially affect the priority of any further advance thereunder, give to the proprietor of the charge at his registered address, notice by registered post of the intended entry, and the proprietor of the charge shall not, in respect of any further advance, be affected by such entry, unless the advance is made after the date when the notice ought to have been received in due course of post.*

(2) *If, by reason of any failure on the part of the registrar or the [postal operator (within the meaning of the Postal Services Act 2000)] in reference to the notice, the proprietor of the charge suffers loss in relation to a further advance, he shall be entitled to be indemnified under this Act in like manner as if a mistake had occurred in the register; but if the loss arises by reason of an omission to register or amend the address for service, no indemnity shall be payable under this Act.*

[(3) Where the proprietor of a charge is under an obligation, noted on the register, to make a further advance, a subsequent registered charge shall take effect subject to any further advance made pursuant to the obligation.]

[455]

NOTES

Repealed as noted at the beginning of this Act.
Sub-s (2): words in square brackets substituted by SI 2001/1149, art 3(1), Sch 1, para 8(1), (2).
Sub-s (3): inserted by the Law of Property (Amendment) Act 1926, s 5.

31–52 (*Repealed as noted at the beginning of this Act.*)

53 Cautions against first registration

(*1*) *Any person having or claiming such an interest in land not already registered as entitles him to object to any disposition thereof being made without his consent, may lodge a caution with the registrar to the effect that the cautioner is entitled to notice in the prescribed form, and to be served in the prescribed manner, of any application that may be made for the registration of an interest in the land affecting the right of the cautioner.*

(2) *The caution shall be supported by an affidavit or declaration in the prescribed form, stating the nature of the interest of the cautioner, the land and estate therein to be affected by such caution, and such other matters as may be prescribed.*

(*3*) *After a caution has been lodged in respect of any estate, which has not already been registered, registration shall not be made of such estate until notice has been served on the cautioner to appear and oppose, if he thinks fit, such registration, and the prescribed time has elapsed since the date of the service of such notice, or the cautioner has entered an appearance, whichever may first happen.*

[456]

NOTES

Repealed as noted at the beginning of this Act.

54 Cautions against dealings

(*1*) *Any person interested under any unregistered instrument, or interested as a judgment creditor, or otherwise howsoever, in any land or charge registered in the name of any other person, may lodge a caution with the registrar to the effect that no dealing with such land or charge on the part of the proprietor is to be registered until notice has been served upon the cautioner:*

Provided that a person whose estate, right, interest, or claim has been registered or protected by a notice or restriction shall not be entitled (except with the consent of the registrar) to lodge a caution in respect of such estate, right, interest or claim, …

(2) *A caution lodged under this section shall be supported by such evidence as may be prescribed.*

[457]

NOTES

Repealed as noted at the beginning of this Act.

55 Effect of cautions against dealings

(1) After any such caution against dealings has been lodged in respect of any registered land or charge, the registrar shall not, without the consent of the cautioner, register any dealing or make any entry on the register for protecting the rights acquired under a deposit of a land or charge certificate or other dealing by warning him that his caution will cease to have any effect after the expiration of the prescribed number of days next following the date at which such notice is served; and after the expiration of such time as aforesaid the caution shall cease unless an order to the contrary is made by the registrar, and upon the caution so ceasing the registered land or charge may be dealt with in the same manner as if no caution had been lodged.

(2) If before the expiration of the said period the cautioner, or some person on his behalf, appears before the registrar, and where so required by the registrar gives sufficient security to indemnify every party against any damage that may be sustained by reason of any dealing with the registered land or charge, or the making of any such entry as aforesaid, being delayed, the registrar may thereupon, if he thinks fit to do so, delay registering any dealing with the land or charge or making any such entry for such period as he thinks just.

[458]

NOTES

Repealed as noted at the beginning of this Act.

56 General provisions as to cautions

(1) Any person aggrieved by any act done by the registrar in relation to a caution under this Act may appeal to the court in the prescribed manner.

(2) A caution lodged in pursuance of this Act shall not prejudice the claim or title of any person and shall have no effect whatever except as in this Act mentioned.

(3) If any person lodges a caution with the registrar without reasonable cause, he shall be liable to make to any person who may have sustained damage by the lodging of the caution such compensation as may be just, and such compensation shall be recoverable as a debt by the person who has sustained damage from the person who lodged the caution.

(4) The personal representative of a deceased cautioner may consent or object to registration or a dealing in the same manner as the cautioner.

[459]

NOTES

Repealed as noted at the beginning of this Act.

57–69 *(Repealed as noted at the beginning of this Act.)*

70 Liability of registered land to overriding interests

(1) All registered land shall, unless under the provisions of this Act the contrary is expressed on the register, be deemed to be subject to such of the following overriding interests as may be for the time being subsisting in reference thereto, and such interests shall not be treated as incumbrances within the meaning of this Act, (that is to say)—

(a) *Rights of common, drainage rights, customary rights (until extinguished), public rights, profits à prendre, rights of sheepwalk, rights of way, watercourses, rights of water, and other easements not being equitable easements required to be protected by notice on the register;*

(b)–(h) *(outside the scope of this work.)*

(i) *Rights under local land charges unless and until registered or protected on the register in the prescribed manner;*

(j) *(outside the scope of this work.)*

[(k) *Leases granted for a term not exceeding twenty-one years;]*

(kk)–(m) *(outside the scope of this work.)*

(2)–(4) …

[460]

NOTES

Repealed as noted at the beginning of this Act.

Sub-ss (2)–(4): outside the scope of this work.

71–74 *(Repealed as noted at the beginning of this Act.)*

75 Acquisition of title by possession

(1) The Limitation Acts shall apply to registered land in the same manner and the same extent as those Acts apply to land not registered, except that where, if the land were not registered, the estate of the person registered as proprietor would be extinguished, such estate shall not be extinguished but shall be deemed to be held by the proprietor for the time being in trust for the person who, by virtue of the said Acts, has acquired title against any proprietor, but without prejudice to the estates and interests of any other person interested in the land whose estate or interest is not extinguished by those Acts.

(2)–(5) ...

[461]

NOTES

Repealed as noted at the beginning of this Act.

Sub-s (2)–(5): outside the scope of this work.

76–123 *(Ss 76–84, 86–117, 119, 123 repealed as noted at the beginning of this Act; s 85 repealed by the Land Registration and Land Charges Act 1971, s 14(2)(b), Sch 2, Pt II; s 118 repealed by the Solicitors Act 1932, s 82, Sch 4; s 120 repealed by the Land Registration Act 1997, s 4(2), Sch 2, Pt I; ss 121, 122 repealed by the Land Registration Act 1966, ss 1(1), 2, Schedule.)*

[123A Compulsory registration: effect of requirement to register

(1) This section applies to any disposition which, by virtue of any provision of section 123 of this Act, is one in relation to which the requirement of compulsory registration applies.

(2) Where any such disposition is effected, then—

(a) if it is a disposition falling within section 123(1), the person who under the disposition is entitled to the legal estate transferred or created by it, or

(b) if it is a disposition falling within section 123(2), the estate owner of the legal estate charged by the mortgage, or

(c) (in either case) that person's successor in title or assign,

must before the end of the applicable period apply to the registrar to be registered (or alternatively, where he is not a person in a fiduciary position, to have any nominee registered) as the first proprietor of that estate.

(3) In this section "the applicable period" means in the first instance the period of two months beginning with the date of the disposition, but—

(a) the registrar may, if satisfied on the application of any interested person that there is good reason for doing so, make an order extending or further extending that period; and

(b) if he does so, "the applicable period" means that period as for the time being extended under this subsection.

(4) Pending compliance with subsection (2) above the disposition shall operate to transfer or grant a legal estate, or (as the case may be) create a legal mortgage, in accordance with its terms.

(5) If subsection (2) above is not complied with, the disposition shall at the end of the applicable period become void as regards any such transfer, grant or creation of a legal estate; and—

(a) if it is a disposition purporting to transfer a legal estate, the title to that estate shall thereupon revert to the transferor who shall hold that estate on a bare trust for the transferee;

(b) if it is a disposition purporting to grant a legal estate or create a legal mortgage, the disposition shall thereupon take effect as if it were a contract to grant or create that estate or mortgage made for valuable consideration (whether or not it was so made or satisfies any of the formal requirements of such a contract).

(6) If an order extending the applicable period under subsection (3) above is made at a time when the disposition has become void in accordance with subsection (5) above, then as from the making of the order—

(a) subsection (5) shall cease to apply to the disposition, and

(b) subsection (4) above shall apply to it instead,

and similarly in the case of any further order so made.

(7) If any disposition is subsequently effected by way of replacement for a disposition which has become void in accordance with subsection (5) above, the requirement of compulsory registration shall apply in relation to it under section 123 in the same way as it applied in relation to the void disposition, and the provisions of this section shall have effect accordingly.

(8) Except to the extent to which the parties to any such replacement disposition agree otherwise, the transferee or grantee (as the case may be) shall—

(a) bear all the proper costs of and incidental to that disposition, and

(*b*) *indemnify the transferor or grantor (as the case may be) in respect of any other liability reasonably incurred by him in consequence of the failure to comply with subsection (2) above.*

(9) Where any such replacement disposition is a mortgage falling within section 123(2) of this Act, subsection (8) above shall apply as if the reference to the grantee were a reference to the mortgagor and the reference to the grantor were a reference to the mortgagee.

(10) Rules under this Act may make provision—

(*a*) *applying the provisions of this Act to any dealings which take place between—*

(*i*) *the date of any disposition to which this section applies, and*

(*ii*) *the date of the application for first registration,*

as if the dealings had taken place after the date of the registration, and for the registration to be effective as of the date of the application;

(*b*) *enabling the mortgagee under any mortgage falling within section 123(2) of this Act to require the legal estate charged by the mortgage to be registered whether or not the mortgagor consents.]*

[462]

NOTES

Repealed as noted at the beginning of this Act.

Substituted, together with s 123, for original 123, in relation to dispositions made after 1 April 1998, by the Land Registration Act 1997, ss 1, 5(4).

124–148 *(Ss 124, 126–134, 137–145, 147, 148 repealed as noted at the beginning of this Act; s 125 repealed by the Law of Property Act 1969, s 16(2), Sch 2, Pt I; s 135 repealed for certain purposes by the Law of Property Act 1969, s 16(2), Sch 2, Pt I and spent for remaining purposes by virtue of the Middlesex Deeds Act 1940, s 1; s 136 repealed by the Law of Property Act 1969, s 16(2), Sch 2, Pt I; s 146 repealed by the Solicitors Act 1932, s 82, Sch 4.)*

(Schedule repealed by the Statute Law Revision Act 1950.)

ADMINISTRATION OF ESTATES ACT 1925

(1925 c 23)

An Act to consolidate Enactments relating to the Administration of the Estates of Deceased Persons

[9 April 1925]

PART I
DEVOLUTION OF REAL ESTATE

1 Devolution of real estate on personal representative

(1) Real estate to which a deceased person was entitled for an interest not ceasing on his death shall on his death, and notwithstanding any testamentary disposition thereof, devolve from time to time on the personal representative of the deceased, in like manner as before the commencement of this Act chattels real devolved on the personal representative from time to time of a deceased person.

(2) The personal representatives for the time being of a deceased person are deemed in law his heirs and assigns within the meaning of all trusts and powers.

(3) The personal representatives shall be the representative of the deceased in regard to his real estate to which he was entitled for an interest not ceasing on his death as well as in regard to his personal estate.

[463]

2 Application to real estate of law affecting chattels real

(1) Subject to the provisions of this Act, all enactments and rules of law, and all jurisdiction of any court with respect to the appointment of administrators or to probate or letters of administration, or to dealings before probate in the case of chattels real, and with respect to costs and other matters in the administration of personal estate, in force before the commencement of this Act, and all powers, duties, rights, equities, obligations, and liabilities of a personal representative in force at the commencement of this Act with respect to chattels real, shall apply and attach to the personal representative and shall have effect with respect to real estate vested in him, and in particular all such powers of disposition and dealing as were before the commencement of this Act exercisable as respects chattels real by the survivor or survivors of two or more personal representatives, as well as

by a single personal representative, or by all the personal representatives together, shall be exercisable by the personal representatives or representative of the deceased with respect to his real estate.

(2) Where as respects real estate there are two or more personal representatives, a conveyance of real estate devolving under this Part of this Act [or a contract for such a conveyance] shall not … be made without the concurrence therein of all such representatives or an order of the court, but where probate is granted to one or some of two or more persons named as executors, whether or not power is reserved to the other or others to prove, any conveyance of the real estate [or contract for such a conveyance] may be made by the proving executor or executors for the time being, without an order of the court, and shall be as effectual as if all the persons named as executors had concurred therein.

(3) Without prejudice to the rights and powers of a personal representative, the appointment of a personal representative in regard to real estate shall not, save as hereinafter provided, affect—

- (a) any rule as to marshalling or as to administration of assets;
- (b) the beneficial interest in real estate under any testamentary disposition;
- (c) any mode of dealing with any beneficial interest in real estate, or the proceeds of sale thereof;
- (d) the right of any person claiming to be interested in the real estate to take proceedings for the protection or recovery thereof against any person other than the personal representative.

[464]

NOTES

Sub-s (2): words in square brackets inserted and words omitted repealed, by the Law of Property (Miscellaneous Provisions) Act 1994, ss 16(1), 21(2), Sch 2.

3 Interpretation of Part I

(1) In this Part of this Act "real estate" includes—

- (i) Chattels real, and land in possession, remainder, or reversion, and every interest in or over land to which a deceased person was entitled at the time of his death; and
- (ii) Real estate held on trust (including settled land) or by way of mortgage or security, but not … money secured or charged on land.

(2) A testator shall be deemed to have been entitled at his death to any interest in real estate passing under any gift contained in his will which operates as an appointment under a general power to appoint by will, or operates under the testamentary power conferred by statute to dispose of an entailed interest.

(3) An entailed interest of a deceased person shall (unless disposed of under the testamentary power conferred by statute) be deemed an interest ceasing on his death, but any further or other interest of the deceased in the same property in remainder or reversion which is capable of being disposed of by his will shall not be deemed to be an interest so ceasing.

(4) The interest of a deceased person under a joint tenancy where another tenant survives the deceased is an interest ceasing on his death.

(5) On the death of a corporator sole his interest in the corporation's real and personal estate shall be deemed to be an interest ceasing on his death and shall devolve to his successor.

This subsection applies on the demise of the Crown as respects all property, real and personal, vested in the Crown as a corporation sole.

[465]

NOTES

Sub-s (1): words omitted repealed by the Trusts of Land and Appointment of Trustees Act 1996, s 25(2), Sch 4; for savings in relation to entailed interests created before the commencement of that Act, and savings consequential upon the abolition of the doctrine of conversion, see s 25(4), (5) thereof.

PART II
EXECUTORS AND ADMINISTRATORS

General Provisions

4 (*Repealed by the Supreme Court of Judicature* (*Consolidation*) *Act 1925, s 226, Sch 6.*)

5 Cesser of right of executor to prove

Where a person appointed executor by a will—

- (i) survives the testator but dies without having taken out probate of the will; or
- (ii) is cited to take out probate of the will and does not appear to the citation; or
- (iii) renounces probate of the will;

his rights in respect of the executorship shall wholly cease, and the representation to the testator and the administration of his real and personal estate shall devolve and be committed in like manner as if that person had not been appointed executor.

[466]

6 Withdrawal of renunciation

(1) Where an executor who has renounced probate has been permitted, whether before or after the commencement of this Act, to withdraw the renunciation and prove the will, the probate shall take effect and be deemed always to have taken effect without prejudice to the previous acts and dealings of and notices to any other personal representative who has previously proved the will or taken out letters of administration, and a memorandum of the subsequent probate shall be endorsed on the original probate or letters of administration.

(2) This section applies whether the testator died before or after the commencement of this Act.

[467]

7 Executor of executor represents original testator

(1) An executor of a sole or last surviving executor of a testator is the executor of that testator.

This provision shall not apply to an executor who does not prove the will of his testator, and, in the case of an executor who on his death leaves surviving him some other executor of his testator who afterwards proves the will of that testator, it shall cease to apply on such probate being granted.

(2) So long as the chain of such representation is unbroken, the last executor in the chain is the executor of every preceding testator.

(3) The chain of such representation is broken by—

(a) an intestacy; or

(b) the failure of a testator to appoint an executor; or

(c) the failure to obtain probate of a will;

but is not broken by a temporary grant of administration if probate is subsequently granted.

(4) Every person in the chain of representation to a testator—

(a) has the same rights in respect of the real and personal estate of that testator as the original executor would have had if living; and

(b) is, to the extent to which the estate whether real or personal of that testator has come to his hands, answerable as if he were an original executor.

[468]

8 Right of proving executors to exercise powers

(1) Where probate is granted to one or some of two or more persons named as executors, whether or not power is reserved to the others or other to prove, all the powers which are by law conferred on the personal representative may be exercised by the proving executor or executors for the time being and shall be as effectual as if all the persons named as executors had concurred therein.

(2) This section applies whether the testator died before or after the commencement of this Act.

[469]

[9 Vesting of estate in Public Trustee where intestacy or lack of executors

(1) Where a person dies intestate, his real and personal estate shall vest in the Public Trustee until the grant of administration.

(2) Where a testator dies and—

(a) at the time of his death there is no executor with power to obtain probate of the will, or

(b) at any time before probate of the will is granted there ceases to be any executor with power to obtain probate,

the real and personal estate of which he disposes by the will shall vest in the Public Trustee until the grant of representation.

(3) The vesting of real or personal estate in the Public Trustee by virtue of this section does not confer on him any beneficial interest in, or impose on him any duty, obligation or liability in respect of, the property.]

[470]

NOTES

Substituted by the Law of Property (Miscellaneous Provisions) Act 1994, s 14(1).

10–14 *(Repealed by the Supreme Court of Judicature (Consolidation) Act 1925, s 226, Sch 6.)*

15 Executor not to act while administration is in force

Where administration has been granted in respect of any real or personal estate of a deceased person, no person shall have power to bring any action or otherwise act as executor of the deceased person in respect of the estate comprised in or affected by the grant until the grant has been recalled or revoked.

[471]

16 *Repealed by the Supreme Court of Judicature (Consolidation) Act 1925, s 226, Sch 6.*

17 Continuance of legal proceedings after revocation of temporary administration

[(1)] If, while any legal proceeding is pending in any court by or against an administrator to whom a temporary administration has been granted, that administration is revoked, that court may order that the proceeding be continued by or against the new personal representative in like manner as if the same had been originally commenced by or against him, but subject to such conditions and variations, if any, as that court directs.

[(2) The county court has jurisdiction under this section where the proceedings are pending in that court.]

[472]

NOTES

Sub-s (1): numbered as such by the County Courts Act 1984, s 148(1), Sch 2, Pt III, para 11.
Sub-s (2): inserted by the County Courts Act 1984, s 148(1), Sch 2, Pt III, para 11.

18–20 (*Repealed by the Supreme Court of Judicature (Consolidation) Act 1925, s 226, Sch 6.*)

21 Rights and liabilities of administrator

Every person to whom administration of the real and personal estate of a deceased person is granted, shall, subject to the limitations contained in the grant, have the same rights and liabilities and be accountable in like manner as if he were the executor of the deceased.

[473]

[21A Debtor who becomes creditor's executor by representation or administrator to account for debt to estate

(1) Subject to subsection (2) of this section, where a debtor becomes his deceased creditor's executor by representation or administrator—

(a) his debt shall thereupon be extinguished; but
(b) he shall be accountable for the amount of the debt as part of the creditor's estate in any case where he would be so accountable if he had been appointed as an executor by the creditor's will.

(2) Subsection (1) of this section does not apply where the debtor's authority to act as executor or administrator is limited to part only of the creditor's estate which does not include the debt; and a debtor whose debt is extinguished by virtue of paragraph (a) shall not be accountable for its amount by virtue of paragraph (b) of that subsection in any case where the debt was barred by the Limitation Act 1939 before he became the creditor's executor or administrator.

(3) In this section "debt" includes any liability, and "debtor" and "creditor" shall be construed accordingly.]

[474]

NOTES

Inserted by the Limitation Amendment Act 1980, s 10.

Special Provisions as to Settled Land

22 Special executors as respects settled land

(1) A testator may appoint, and in default of such express appointment shall be deemed to have appointed, as his special executors in regard to settled land, the persons, if any, who are at his death the trustees of the settlement thereof, and probate may be granted to such trustees specially limited to the settled land.

In this subsection "settled land" means land vested in the testator which was settled previously to his death and not by his will.

(2) A testator may appoint other persons either with or without such trustees as aforesaid or any of them to be his general executors in regard to his other property and assets.

[475]

23 Provisions where, as respects settled land, representation is not granted to the trustees of the settlement

(1) Where settled land becomes vested in a personal representative, not being a trustee of the settlement, upon trust to convey the land to or assent to the vesting thereof in the tenant for life or statutory owner in order to give effect to a settlement created before the death of the deceased and not by his will, or would on the grant of representation to him, have become so vested, such representative may—

(a) before representation has been granted, renounce his office in regard only to such settled land without renouncing it in regard to other property;

(b) after representation has been granted, apply to the court for revocation of the grant in regard to the settled land without applying in regard to other property.

(2) Whether such renunciation or revocation is made or not, the trustees of the settlement, or any person beneficially interested thereunder, may apply to the High Court for an order appointing a special or additional personal representative in respect of the settled land, and a special or additional personal representative, if and when appointed under the order, shall be in the same position as if representation had originally been granted to him alone in place of the original personal representative, if any, or to him jointly with the original personal representative, as the case may be, limited to the settled land, but without prejudice to the previous acts and dealings, if any, of the personal representative originally constituted or the effect of notices given to such personal representative.

(3) The court may make such order as aforesaid subject to such security, if any, being given by or on behalf of the special or additional personal representative, as the court may direct, and shall, unless the court considers that special considerations apply, appoint such persons as may be necessary to secure that the persons to act as representatives in respect of the settled land shall, if willing to act, be the same persons as are the trustees of the settlement, and an office copy of the order when made shall be furnished to the [principal registry of the Family Division of the High Court] for entry, and a memorandum of the order shall be endorsed on the probate or administration.

(4) The person applying for the appointment of a special or additional personal representative shall give notice of the application to the [principal registry of the Family Division of the High Court] in the manner prescribed.

(5) Rules of court may be made for prescribing for all matters required for giving effect to the provisions of this section, and in particular—

(a) for notice of any application being given to the proper officer;

(b) for production of orders, probates, and administration to the registry;

(c) for the endorsement on a probate or administration of a memorandum of an order, subject or not to any exceptions;

(d) for the manner in which the costs are to be borne;

(e) for protecting purchasers and trustees and other persons in a fiduciary position, dealing in good faith with or giving notices to a personal representative before notice of any order has been endorsed on the probate or administration or a pending action has been registered in respect of the proceedings.

[476]

NOTES

Sub-ss (3), (4): words in square brackets substituted by the Administration of Justice Act 1970, s 1(6), Sch 2, para 3.

24 Power for special personal representatives to dispose of settled land

(1) The special personal representatives may dispose of the settled land without the concurrence of the general personal representatives, who may likewise dispose of the other property and assets of the deceased without the concurrence of the special personal representatives.

(2) In this section the expression "special personal representatives" means the representatives appointed to act for the purposes of settled land and includes any original personal representative who is to act with an additional personal representative for those purposes.

[477]

Duties, Rights and Obligations

[25 Duty of personal representatives

The personal representative of a deceased person shall be under a duty to—

(a) collect and get in the real and personal estate of the deceased and administer it according to law;

(b) when required to do so by the court, exhibit on oath in the court a full inventory of the estate and when so required render an account of the administration of the estate to the court;

PART I STATUTES

(c) when required to do so by the High Court, deliver up the grant of probate or administration to that court.]

[478]

NOTES

Substituted by the Administration of Estates Act 1971, s 9.

26 Rights of action by and against personal representative

(1), (2) …

(3) A personal representative may distrain for arrears of a rentcharge due or accruing to the deceased in his lifetime on the land affected or charged therewith, so long as the land remains in the possession of the person liable to pay the rentcharge or of the persons deriving title under him, and in like manner as the deceased might have done had he been living.

(4) A personal representative may distrain upon land for arrears of rent due or accruing to the deceased in like manner as the deceased might have done had he been living.

Such arrears may be distrained for after the termination of the lease or tenancy as if the term or interest had not determined, if the distress is made—

(*a*) *within six months after the termination of the lease or tenancy;*
(*b*) *during the continuance of the possession of the lessee or tenant from whom the arrears were due.*

The statutory enactments relating to distress for rent apply to any distress made pursuant to this subsection,

[(4) To recover rent due or accruing to the deceased, a personal representative may exercise any power under section 72(1) (commercial rent arrears recovery) or 81 (right to rent from sub-tenant) of the Tribunals, Courts and Enforcement Act 2007 that would have been exercisable by the deceased if he had still been living.]

(5), (6) …

[479]

NOTES

Sub-ss (1), (2): repealed by the Law Reform (Miscellaneous Provisions) Act 1934, s 1(7).

Sub-s (3): repealed by the Tribunals, Courts and Enforcement Act 2007, ss 86, 146, Sch 14, para 28(1), (2), Sch 23, Pt 4, as from a day to be appointed.

Sub-s (4): substituted by subsequent sub-s (4) in square brackets by the Tribunals, Courts and Enforcement Act 2007, s 86, Sch 14, para 28(1), (3), as from a day to be appointed.

Sub-ss (5), (6): repealed by the Law Reform (Miscellaneous Provisions) Act 1934, s 1(7).

27 Protection of persons on probate or administration

(1) Every person making or permitting to be made any payment or disposition in good faith under a representation shall be indemnified and protected in so doing, notwithstanding any defect or circumstance whatsoever affecting the validity of the representation.

(2) Where a representation is revoked, all payments and dispositions made in good faith to a personal representative under the representation before the revocation thereof are a valid discharge to the person making the same; and the personal representative who acted under the revoked representation may retain and reimburse himself in respect of any payments or dispositions made by him which the person to whom representation is afterwards granted might have properly made.

[480]

28 Liability of person fraudulently obtaining or retaining estate of deceased

If any person, to the defrauding of creditors or without full valuable consideration, obtains, receives or holds any real or personal estate of a deceased person or effects the release of any debt or liability due to the estate of the deceased, he shall be charged as executor in his own wrong to the extent of the real and personal estate received or coming to his hands, or the debt or liability released, after deducting—

(a) any debt for valuable consideration and without fraud due to him from the deceased person at the time of his death; and
(b) any payment made by him which might properly be made by a personal representative.

[481]

29 Liability of estate of personal representative

Where a person as personal representative of a deceased person (including an executor in his own wrong) wastes or converts to his own use any part of the real or personal estate of the deceased, and dies, his personal representative shall to the extent of the available assets of the defaulter be liable and chargeable in respect of such waste or conversion in the same manner as the defaulter would have been if living.

[482]

30 Provisions applicable where administration granted to nominee of the Crown

(1) Where the administration of the real and personal estate of any deceased person is granted to a nominee of the Crown (whether the Treasury Solicitor, or a person nominated by the Treasury Solicitor, or any other person), any legal proceeding by or against that nominee for the recovery of the real or personal estate, or any part or share thereof, shall be of the same character, and be instituted and carried on in the same manner, and be subject to the same rules of law and equity (including, except as otherwise provided by this Act, the rules of limitation under the statutes of limitation or otherwise), in all respects as if the administration had been granted to such nominee as one of the persons interested under this Act in the estate of the deceased.

(2) An information or other proceeding on the part of His Majesty shall not be filed or instituted, and a petition of right shall not be presented, in respect of the real or personal estate of any deceased person or any part or share thereof, or any claim thereon, except … subject to the same rules of law and equity within and subject to which a proceeding for the like purposes might be instituted by or against a subject.

(3) The Treasury Solicitor shall not be required, when applying for or obtaining administration of the estate of a deceased person for the use or benefit of His Majesty, to deliver, nor shall … the High Court or the Commissioners of Inland Revenue be entitled to receive in connexion with any such application or grant of administration, any affidavit, statutory declaration, account, certificate, or other statement verified on oath; but the Treasury Solicitor shall deliver and the said Division and Commissioners respectively shall accept, in lieu thereof, an account or particulars of the estate of the deceased signed by or on behalf of the Treasury Solicitor.

(4) References in sections two, four … and seven of the Treasury Solicitor Act 1876, and in subsection (3) of section three of the Duchy of Lancaster Act, 1920, to "personal estate" shall include real estate.

[483]

NOTES

Sub-s (2): words omitted repealed by the Limitation Act 1939, s 34(4), Schedule.
Sub-s (3): words omitted repealed by the Administration of Justice Act 1970, s 54(3), Sch 11.
Sub-s (4): words omitted repealed by the Statute Law (Repeals) Act 1981.

31 Power to make rules

Provision may be made by rules of court for giving effect to the provisions of this Part of this Act so far as relates to real estate and in particular for adapting the procedure and practice on the grant of letters of administration to the case of real estate.

[484]

PART III
ADMINISTRATION OF ASSETS

32 Real and personal estate of deceased are assets for payment of debts

(1) The real and personal estate, whether legal or equitable, of a deceased person, to the extent of his beneficial interest therein, and the real and personal estate of which a deceased person in pursuance of any general power (including the statutory power to dispose of entailed interests) disposes by his will, are assets for payment of his debts (whether by specialty or simple contract) and liabilities, and any disposition by will inconsistent with this enactment is void as against the creditors, and the court shall if necessary, administer the property for the purpose of the payment of the debts and liabilities.

This subsection takes effect without prejudice to the rights of incumbrancers.

(2) If any person to whom any such beneficial interest devolves, or is given, or in whom any such interest vests, disposes thereof in good faith before an action is brought or process is sued out against him, he shall be personally liable for the value of the interest so disposed of by him, but that interest shall not be liable to be taken in execution in the action or under the process.

[485]

33 Trust for sale

[(1) On the death of a person intestate as to any real or personal estate, that estate shall be held in trust by his personal representatives with the power to sell it.]

(2) [The personal representatives shall pay out of—

(a) the ready money of the deceased (so far as not disposed of by his will, if any); and

(b) any net money arising from disposing of any other part of his estate (after payment of costs),

all] such funeral, testamentary and administration expenses, debts and other liabilities as are properly payable thereout having regard to the rules of administration contained in this Part of this Act, and out of the residue of the said money the personal representative shall set aside a fund sufficient to provide for any pecuniary legacies bequeathed by the will (if any) of the deceased.

(3) During the minority of any beneficiary or the subsistence of any life interest and pending the distribution of the whole or any part of the estate of the deceased, the personal representatives may invest the residue of the said money, or so much thereof as may not have been distributed, [under the Trustee Act 2000].

(4) The residue of the said money and any investments for the time being representing the same, [and any part of the estate of the deceased which remains] unsold and is not required for the administration purposes aforesaid, is in this Act referred to as "the residuary estate of the intestate."

(5) The income (including net rents and profits of real estate and chattels real after payment of rates, taxes, rent, costs of insurance, repairs and other outgoings properly attributable to income) of so much of the real and personal estate of the deceased as may not be disposed of by his will, if any, or may not be required for the administration purposes aforesaid, may, however such estate is invested, as from the death of the deceased, be treated and applied as income, and for that purpose any necessary apportionment may be made between tenant for life and remainderman.

(6) Nothing in this section affects the rights of any creditor of the deceased or the rights of the Crown in respect of death duties.

(7) Where the deceased leaves a will, this section has effect subject to the provisions contained in the will.

[486]

NOTES

Sub-s (1): substituted by the Trusts of Land and Appointment of Trustees Act 1996, s 5, Sch 2, para 5(1), (2); for savings in relation to entailed interests created before the commencement of that Act, and savings consequential upon the abolition of the doctrine of conversion, see s 25(4), (5) thereof.

Sub-s (2): words in square brackets substituted by the Trusts of Land and Appointment of Trustees Act 1996, s 5, Sch 2, para 5(1), (3), subject to savings as noted to sub-s (1).

Sub-s (3): words in square brackets substituted by the Trustee Act 2000, s 40(1), Sch 2, Pt II, para 27.

Sub-s (4): words in square brackets substituted by the Trusts of Land and Appointment of Trustees Act 1996, s 5, Sch 2, para 5(1), (4), subject to savings as noted to sub-s (1).

34 Administration of assets

(1), (2) …

(3) Where the estate of a deceased person is solvent his real and personal estate shall, subject to rules of court and the provisions hereinafter contained as to charges on property of the deceased, and to the provisions, if any, contained in his will, be applicable towards the discharge of the funeral, testamentary and administration expenses, debts and liabilities payable thereout in the order mentioned in Part II of the First Schedule to this Act.

[487]

NOTES

Sub-s (1): repealed by the Insolvency Act 1985, s 235, Sch 10.

Sub-s (2): repealed by the Administration of Estates Act 1971, s 12(2), (4), (6), Sch 2, Pt II.

35 Charges on property of deceased to be paid primarily out of the property charged

(1) Where a person dies possessed of, or entitled to, or, under a general power of appointment (including the statutory power to dispose of entailed interests) by his will disposes of, an interest in property, which at the time of his death is charged with the payment of money, whether by way of legal mortgage, equitable charge or otherwise (including a lien for unpaid purchase money), and the deceased has not by will deed or other document signified a contrary or other intention, the interest so charged, shall as between the different persons claiming through the deceased, be primarily liable for the payment of the charge; and every part of the said interest, according to its value, shall bear a proportionate part of the charge on the whole thereof.

(2) Such contrary or other intention shall not be deemed to be signified—

(a) by a general direction for the payment of debts or of all the debts of the testator out of his personal estate, or his residuary real and personal estate, or his residuary real estate; or

(b) by a charge of debts upon any such estate;

unless such intention is further signified by words expressly or by necessary implication referring to all or some part of the charge.

(3) Nothing in this section affects the right of a person entitled to the charge to obtain payment or satisfaction thereof either out of the other assets of the deceased or otherwise.

[488]

36 Effect of assent or conveyance by personal representative

(1) A personal representative may assent to the vesting, in any person who (whether by devise, bequest, devolution, appropriation or otherwise) may be entitled thereto, either beneficially or as a trustee or personal representative, of any estate or interest in real estate to which the testator or intestate was entitled or over which he exercised a general power of appointment by his will, including the statutory power to dispose of entailed interests, and which devolved upon the personal representative.

(2) The assent shall operate to vest in that person the estate or interest to which the assent relates, and, unless a contrary intention appears, the assent shall relate back to the death of the deceased.

(3) …

(4) An assent to the vesting of a legal estate shall be in writing, signed by the personal representative, and shall name the person in whose favour it is given and shall operate to vest in that person the legal estate to which it relates; and an assent not in writing or not in favour of a named person shall not be effectual to pass a legal estate.

(5) Any person in whose favour an assent or conveyance of a legal estate is made by a personal representative may require that notice of the assent or conveyance be written or endorsed on or permanently annexed to the probate or letters of administration, at the cost of the estate of the deceased, and that the probate or letters of administration be produced, at the like cost, to prove that the notice has been placed thereon or annexed thereto.

(6) A statement in writing by a personal representative that he has not given or made an assent or conveyance in respect of a legal estate, shall, in favour of a purchaser, but without prejudice to any previous disposition made in favour of another purchaser deriving title mediately or immediately under the personal representative, be sufficient evidence that an assent or conveyance has not been given or made in respect of the legal estate to which the statement relates, unless notice of a previous assent or conveyance affecting that estate has been placed on or annexed to the probate or administration.

A conveyance by a personal representative of a legal estate to a purchaser accepted on the faith of such a statement shall (without prejudice as aforesaid and unless notice of a previous assent or conveyance affecting that estate has been placed on or annexed to the probate or administration) operate to transfer or create the legal estate expressed to be conveyed in like manner as if no previous assent or conveyance had been made by the personal representative.

A personal representative making a false statement, in regard to any such matter, shall be liable in like manner as if the statement had been contained in a statutory declaration.

(7) An assent or conveyance by a personal representative in respect of a legal estate shall, in favour of a purchaser, unless notice of a previous assent or conveyance affecting that legal estate has been placed on or annexed to the probate or administration, be taken as sufficient evidence that the person in whose favour the assent or conveyance is given or made is the person entitled to have the legal estate conveyed to him, and upon the proper trusts, if any, but shall not otherwise prejudicially affect the claim of any person rightfully entitled to the estate vested or conveyed or any charge thereon.

(8) A conveyance of a legal estate by a personal representative to a purchaser shall not be invalidated by reason only that the purchaser may have notice that all the debts, liabilities, funeral, and testamentary or administration expenses, duties, and legacies of the deceased have been discharged or provided for.

(9) An assent or conveyance given or made by a personal representative shall not, except in favour of a purchaser of a legal estate, prejudice the right of the personal representative or any other person to recover the estate or interest to which the assent or conveyance relates, or to be indemnified out of such estate or interest against any duties, debts, or liability to which such estate or interest would have been subject if there had not been any assent or conveyance.

(10) A personal representative may, as a condition of giving an assent or making a conveyance, require security for the discharge of any such duties, debt, or liability, but shall not be entitled to postpone the giving of an assent merely by reason of the subsistence of any such duties, debt or liability if reasonable arrangements have been made for discharging the same; and an assent may be given subject to any legal estate or charge by way of legal mortgage.

(11) This section shall not operate to impose any stamp duty in respect of an assent, and in this section "purchaser" means a purchaser for money or money's worth.

(12) This section applies to assents and conveyances made after the commencement of this Act, whether the testator or intestate died before of after such commencement.

[489]

NOTES

Sub-s (3): repealed by the Law of Property (Miscellaneous Provisions) Act 1994, s 21(2), Sch 2.

37 Validity of conveyance not affected by revocation of representation

(1) All conveyances of any interest in real or personal estate made to a purchaser either before or after the commencement of this Act by a person to whom probate or letters of administration have been granted are valid, notwithstanding any subsequent revocation or variation, either before or after the commencement of this Act, of the probate or administration.

(2) This section takes effect without prejudice to any order of the court made before the commencement of this Act, and applies whether the testator or intestate died before or after such commencement.

[490]

38 Right to follow property and powers of the court in relation thereto

(1) An assent or conveyance by a personal representative to a person other than a purchaser does not prejudice the rights of any person to follow the property to which the assent or conveyance relates, or any property representing the same, into the hands of the person in whom it is vested by the assent or conveyance, or of any other person (not being a purchaser) who may have received the same or in whom it may be vested.

(2) Notwithstanding any such assent or conveyance the court may, on the application of any creditor or other person interested,—

- (a) order a sale, exchange, mortgage, charge, lease, payment, transfer or other transaction to be carried out which the court considers requisite for the purpose of giving effect to the rights of the persons interested;
- (b) declare that the person, not being a purchaser, in whom the property is vested is a trustee for those purposes;
- (c) give directions respecting the preparation and execution of any conveyance or other instrument or as to any other matter required for giving effect to the order;
- (d) make any vesting order, or appoint a person to convey in accordance with the provisions of the Trustee Act 1925.

(3) This section does not prejudice the rights of a purchaser or a person deriving title under him, but applies whether the testator or intestate died before or after the commencement of this Act.

[(4) The county court has jurisdiction under this section where the estate in respect of which the application is made does not exceed in amount or value the county court limit.]

[491]

NOTES

Sub-s (4): inserted by the County Courts Act 1984, s 148(1), Sch 2, Pt III, para 12.

39 Powers of management

(1) In dealing with the real and personal estate of the deceased his personal representatives shall, for purposes of administration, or during a minority of any beneficiary or the subsistence of any life interest, or until the period of distribution arrives, have—

- (i) [as respects the personal estate,] the same powers and discretions, including power to raise money by mortgage or charge (whether or not by deposit of documents), as a personal representative had before the commencement of this Act, with respect to personal estate vested in him … ; and
- [(ii) as respects the real estate, all the functions conferred on them by Part I of the Trusts of Land and Appointment of Trustees Act 1996;]
- (iii) all the powers [necessary] so that every contract entered into by a personal representative shall be binding on and be enforceable against and by the personal representative for the time being of the deceased, and may be carried into effect, or be varied or rescinded by him, and, in the case of a contract entered into by a predecessor, as if it had been entered into by himself.

[(1A) Subsection (1) of this section is without prejudice to the powers conferred on personal representatives by the Trustee Act 2000.]

(2) Nothing in this section shall affect the right of any person to require an assent or conveyance to be made.

(3) This section applies whether the testator or intestate died before or after the commencement of this Act.

[492]

NOTES

Sub-s (1): in para (i) words in square brackets inserted and words omitted repealed, para (ii) and word in square brackets in para (iii) substituted by the Trusts of Land and Appointment of Trustees Act 1996, s 25(1), (2), Sch 3, para 6(1), (2), Sch 4; for savings in relation to entailed interests created before the commencement of that Act, and savings consequential upon the abolition of the doctrine of conversion, see s 25(4), (5) thereof.

Sub-s (1A): inserted by the Trustee Act 2000, s 40(1), Sch 2, Pt II, para 28.

40 Powers of personal representative for raising money, etc

(1) For giving effect to beneficial interests the personal representative may limit or demise land for a term of years absolute, with or without impeachment for waste, to trustees on usual trusts for raising or securing any principal sum and the interest thereon for which the land, or any part thereof, is liable, and may limit or grant a rentcharge for giving effect to any annual or periodical sum for which the land or the income thereof or any part thereof is liable.

(2) This section applies whether the testator or intestate died before or after the commencement of this Act.

[493]

41 Powers of personal representative as to appropriation

(1) The personal representative may appropriate any part of the real or personal estate, including things in action, of the deceased in the actual condition or state of investment thereof at the time of appropriation in or towards satisfaction of any legacy bequeathed by the deceased, or of any other interest or share in his property, whether settled or not, as to the personal representative may seem just and reasonable, according to the respective rights of the persons interested in the property of the deceased:

Provided that—

(i) an appropriation shall not be made under this section so as to affect prejudicially any specific devise or bequest;

(ii) an appropriation of property, whether or not being an investment authorised by law or by the will, if any, of the deceased for the investment of money subject to the trust, shall not (save as hereinafter mentioned) be made under this section except with the following consents—

(a) when made for the benefit of a person absolutely and beneficially entitled in possession, the consent of that person;

(b) when made in respect of any settled legacy share or interest, the consent of either the trustee thereof, if any (not being also the personal representative), or the person who may for the time being be entitled to the income:

If the person whose consent is so required as aforesaid is an infant or [lacks capacity (within the meaning of the Mental Capacity Act 2005) to give the consent, it] shall be given on his behalf by his parents or parent, testamentary or other guardian … [or a person appointed as deputy for him by the Court of Protection], or if, in the case of an infant, there is no such parent or guardian, by the court on the application of his next friend;

(iii) no consent (save of such trustee as aforesaid) shall be required on behalf of a person who may come into existence after the time of appropriation, or who cannot be found or ascertained at that time;

(iv) if [no deputy is appointed for a person who lacks capacity to consent] then, if the appropriation is of an investment authorised by law or by the will, if any, of the deceased for the investment of money subject to the trust, no consent shall be required on behalf of the [said person];

(v) if, independently of the personal representative, there is no trustee of a settled legacy share or interest, and no person of full age and capacity entitled to the income thereof, no consent shall be required to an appropriation in respect of such legacy share or interest, provided that the appropriation is of an investment authorised as aforesaid.

[(1A) The county court has jurisdiction under proviso (ii) to subsection (1) of this section where the estate in respect of which the application is made does not exceed in amount or value the county court limit.]

(2) Any property duly appropriated under the powers conferred by this section shall thereafter be treated as an authorised investment, and may be retained or dealt with accordingly.

(3) For the purposes of such appropriation, the personal representative may ascertain and fix the value of the respective parts of the real and personal estate and the liabilities of the deceased as he may think fit, and shall for that purpose employ a duly qualified valuer in any case where such employment may be necessary; and may make any conveyance (including an assent) which may be requisite for giving effect to the appropriation.

(4) An appropriation made pursuant to this section shall bind all persons interested in the property of the deceased whose consent is not hereby made requisite.

(5) The personal representative shall, in making the appropriation, have regard to the rights of any person who may thereafter come into existence, or who cannot be found or ascertained at the time of appropriation, and of any other person whose consent is not required by this section.

(6) This section does not prejudice any other power of appropriation conferred by law or by the will (if any) of the deceased, and takes effect with any extended powers conferred by the will (if any) of the deceased, and where an appropriation is made under this section, in respect of a settled legacy, share or interest, the property appropriated shall remain subject to all [trusts] and powers of leasing, disposition, and management or varying investments which would have been applicable thereto or to the legacy, share or interest in respect of which the appropriation is made, if no such appropriation had been made.

(7) If after any real estate has been appropriated in purported exercise of the powers conferred by this section, the person to whom it was conveyed disposes of it or any interest therein, then, in favour of a purchaser, the appropriation shall be deemed to have been made in accordance with the requirements of this section and after all requisite consents, if any, had been given.

(8) In this section, a settled legacy, share or interest includes any legacy, share or interest to which a person is not absolutely entitled in possession at the date of the appropriation, also an annuity, and "purchaser" means a purchaser for money or money's worth.

(9) This section applies whether the deceased died intestate or not, and whether before or after the commencement of this Act, and extends to property over which a testator exercises a general power of appointment, including the statutory power to dispose of entailed interests, and authorises the setting apart of a fund to answer an annuity by means of the income of that fund or otherwise.

[494]

NOTES

Sub-s (1): in para (ii), words in square brackets substituted by the Mental Capacity Act 2005, s 67(1), Sch 6, para 5(1), (2)(a) and words omitted repealed by the Mental Health Act 1959, s 149(1), Sch 7, Pt I; in para (iv), words in first pair of square brackets substituted by the Mental Capacity Act 2005, s 67(1), Sch 6, para 5(1), (2)(b) and words in second pair of square brackets substituted by the Mental Health Act 1959, s 149(1), Sch 7, Pt I.

Sub-s (1A): inserted by the County Courts Act 1984, s 148(1), Sch 2, Pt III, para 13.

Sub-s (6): word in square brackets substituted by the Trusts of Land and Appointment of Trustees Act 1996, s 25(1), Sch 3, para 6(1), (3); for savings in relation to entailed interests created before the commencement of that Act, and savings consequential upon the abolition of the doctrine of conversion, see s 25(4), (5) thereof.

42 Power to appoint trustees of infants' property

(1) Where an infant is absolutely entitled under the will or on the intestacy of a person dying before or after the commencement of this Act (in this subsection called "the deceased") to a devise or legacy, or to the residue of the estate of the deceased, or any share therein, and such devise, legacy, residue or share is not under the will, if any, of the deceased, devised or bequeathed to trustees for the infant, the personal representatives of the deceased may appoint a trust corporation or two or more individuals not exceeding four (whether or not including the personal representatives or one or more of the personal representatives), to be the trustee or trustees of such devise, legacy, residue or share for the infant, and to be trustees of any land devised or any land being or forming part of such residue or share for the purposes of the Settled Land Act 1925, and of the statutory provisions relating to the management of land during a minority, and may execute or do any assurance or thing requisite for vesting such devise, legacy, residue or share in the trustee or trustees so appointed.

On such appointment the personal representatives, as such, shall be discharged from all further liability in respect of such devise, legacy, residue, or share, and the same may be retained in its existing condition or state of investment, or may be converted into money, and such money may be invested in any authorised investment.

(2) Where a personal representative has before the commencement of this Act retained or sold any such devise, legacy, residue or share, and invested the same or the proceeds thereof in any investments in which he was authorised to invest money subject to the trust, then, subject to any order of the court made before such commencement, he shall not be deemed to have incurred any liability on that account, or by reason of not having paid or transferred the money or property into court.

[495]

43 Obligations of personal representative as to giving possession of land and powers of the court

(1) A personal representative, before giving an assent or making a conveyance in favour of any person entitled, may permit that person to take possession of the land, and such possession shall not prejudicially affect the right of the personal representative to take or resume possession nor his power to convey the land as if he were in possession thereof, but subject to the interest of any lessee, tenant or occupier in possession or in actual occupation of the land.

(2) Any person who as against the personal representative claims possession of real estate, or the appointment of a receiver thereof, or a conveyance thereof, or an assent to the vesting thereof, or to be registered as proprietor thereof under the [Land Registration Act 2002], may apply to the court for directions with reference thereto, and the court may make such vesting or other order as may be deemed proper, and the provisions of the Trustee Act 1925, relating to vesting orders and to the appointment of a person to convey, shall apply.

(3) This section applies whether the testator or intestate died before or after the commencement of this Act.

[(4) The county court has jurisdiction under this section where the estate in respect of which the application is made does not exceed in amount or value the county court limit.]

[496]

NOTES

Sub-s (2): words in square brackets substituted by the Land Registration Act 2002, s 133, Sch 11, para 3.
Sub-s (4): inserted by the County Courts Act 1984, s 148(1), Sch 2, Pt III, para 14.

44 Power to postpone distribution

Subject to the foregoing provisions of this Act, a personal representative is not bound to distribute the estate of the deceased before the expiration of one year from the death.

[497]

PART IV
DISTRIBUTION OF RESIDUARY ESTATE

45 Abolition of descent to heir, curtesy, dower and escheat

(1) With regard to the real estate and personal inheritance of every person dying after the commencement of this Act, there shall be abolished—

(a) All existing modes rules and canons of descent, and of devolution by special occupancy or otherwise, of real estate, or of a personal inheritance, whether operating by the general law or by the custom of gavelkind or borough english or by any other custom of any county, locality, or manor, or otherwise howsoever; and

(b) Tenancy by the curtesy and every other estate and interest of a husband in real estate as to which his wife dies intestate, whether arising under the general law or by custom or otherwise; and

(c) Dower and freebench and every other estate and interest of a wife in real estate as to which her husband dies intestate, whether arising under the general law or by custom or otherwise: Provided that where a right (if any) to freebench or other like right has attached before the commencement of this Act which cannot be barred by a testamentary or other disposition made by the husband, such right shall, unless released, remain in force as an equitable interest; and

(d) Escheat to the Crown or the Duchy of Lancaster or the Duke of Cornwall or to a mesne lord for want of heirs.

(2) Nothing in this section affects the descent or devolution of an entailed interest.

[498]

46 Succession to real and personal estate on intestacy

(1) The residuary estate of an intestate shall be distributed in the manner or be held on the trusts mentioned in this section, namely—

[(i) If the intestate leaves a [spouse or civil partner], then in accordance with the following Table:

If the intestate—

(1) leaves—

(a) no issue, and	
(b) no parent, or brother or sister of the whole blood, or issue of a brother or sister of the whole blood	the residuary estate shall be held in trust for the surviving [spouse or civil partner] absolutely.

(2) leaves issue (whether or not persons mentioned in sub-paragraph (b) above also survive)

the surviving [spouse or civil partner] shall take the personal chattels absolutely and, in addition, the residuary estate of the intestate (other than the personal chattels) shall stand charged with the payment of a [fixed net sum], free of death duties and costs, to the surviving [spouse or civil partner] with interest thereon from the date of the death … [at such rate as the Lord Chancellor may specify by order] until paid or appropriated, and, subject to providing for that sum and the interest thereon, the residuary estate (other than the personal chattels) shall be held—

(a) as to one half upon trust for the surviving [spouse or civil partner] during his or her life, and, subject to such life interest, on the statutory trusts for the issue of the intestate, and

(b) as to the other half, on the statutory trusts for the issue of the intestate.

(3) leaves one or more of the following, that is to say, a parent, a brother or sister of the whole blood, or issue of a brother or sister of the whole blood, but leaves no issue

the surviving [spouse or civil partner] shall take the personal chattels absolutely and, in addition, the residuary estate of the intestate (other than the personal chattels) shall stand charged with the payment of a [fixed net sum], free of death duties and costs, to the surviving [spouse or civil partner] with interest thereon from the date of the death … [at such rate as the Lord Chancellor may specify by order] until paid or appropriated, and, subject to providing for that sum and the interest thereon, the residuary estate (other than the personal chattels) shall be held—

(a) as to one half in trust for the surviving [spouse or civil partner] absolutely, and

(b) as to the other half—

(i) where the intestate leaves one parent or both parents (whether or not brothers or sisters of the intestate or their issue also survive) in trust for the parent absolutely or, as the case may be, for the two parents in equal shares absolutely

(ii) where the intestate leaves no parent, on the statutory trusts for the brothers and sisters of the whole blood of the intestate.]

[The fixed net sums referred to in paragraphs (2) and (3) of this Table shall be of the amounts provided by or under section 1 of the Family Provision Act 1966]

(ii) If the intestate leaves issue but no [spouse or civil partner], the residuary estate of the intestate shall be held on the statutory trusts for the issue of the intestate;

(iii) If the intestate leaves [no [spouse or civil partner] and] no issue but both parents, then … the residuary estate of the intestate shall be held in trust for the father and mother in equal shares absolutely;

(iv) If the intestate leaves [no [spouse or civil partner] and] no issue but one parent, then … the residuary estate of the intestate shall be held in trust for the surviving father or mother absolutely;

(v) If the intestate leaves no [[spouse or civil partner] and no issue and no] parent, then … the residuary estate of the intestate shall be held in trust for the following persons living at the death of the intestate, and in the following order and manner, namely—
First, on the statutory trusts for the brothers and sisters of the whole blood of the intestate; but if no person takes an absolutely vested interest under such trusts; then

Secondly, on the statutory trusts for the brothers and sisters of the half blood of the intestate; but if no person takes an absolutely vested interest under such trusts; then
Thirdly, for the grandparents of the intestate and, if more than one survive the intestate, in equal shares; but if there is no member of this class; then
Fourthly, on the statutory trusts for the uncles and aunts of the intestate (being brothers or sisters of the whole blood of a parent of the intestate); but if no person takes an absolutely vested interest under such trusts; then
Fifthly, on the statutory trusts for the uncles and aunts of the intestate (being brothers or sisters of the half blood of a parent of the intestate) …

(vi) In default of any person taking an absolute interest under the foregoing provisions, the residuary estate of the intestate shall belong to the Crown or to the Duchy of Lancaster or to the Duke of Cornwall for the time being, as the case may be, as bona vacantia, and in lieu of any right to escheat.

The Crown or the said Duchy or the said Duke may (without prejudice to the powers reserved by section nine of the Civil List Act 1910, or any other powers), out of the whole or any part of the property devolving on them respectively, provide, in accordance with the existing practice, for dependents, whether kindred or not, of the intestate, and other persons for whom the intestate might reasonably have been expected to make provision.

[(1A) The power to make orders under subsection (1) above shall be exercisable by statutory instrument subject to annulment in pursuance of a resolution of either House of Parliament; and any such order may be varied or revoked by a subsequent order made under the power.]

(2) A husband and wife shall for all purposes of distribution or division under the foregoing provisions of this section be treated as two persons.

[(2A) Where the intestate's [spouse or civil partner] survived the intestate but died before the end of the period of 28 days beginning with the day on which the intestate died, this section shall have effect as respects the intestate as if the [spouse or civil partner] had not survived the intestate.]

[(3) Where the intestate and the intestate's [spouse or civil partner] have died in circumstances rendering it uncertain which of them survived the other and the intestate's [spouse or civil partner] is by virtue of section one hundred and eighty-four of the Law of Property Act 1925, deemed to have survived the intestate, this section shall, nevertheless, have effect as respects the intestate as if the [spouse or civil partner] had not survived the intestate.

(4) The interest payable on [the fixed net sum] payable to a surviving [spouse or civil partner] shall be primarily payable out of income.]

[499]

NOTES

Sub-s (1): para (i) substituted by the Intestates' Estates Act 1952, s 1; words "spouse or civil partner" in square brackets in each place they appear substituted by the Civil Partnership Act 2004, s 71, Sch 4, Pt 2, para 7; words "fixed net sum" in square brackets substituted by the Family Provision Act 1966, s 1; words omitted repealed by the Statute Law (Repeals) Act 1981; words "at such rate as the Lord Chancellor may specify by order" in square brackets substituted by the Administration of Justice Act 1977, s 28(1)(a); final words in square brackets inserted by the Family Provision Act 1966, s 1.

Sub-s (1): in para (ii), words in square brackets substituted by the Civil Partnership Act 2004, s 71, Sch 4, Pt 2, para 7.

Sub-s (1): in para (iii), words in first (outer) pair of square brackets substituted and words omitted repealed by the Intestates' Estates Act 1952, s 1; words in second (inner) pair of square brackets substituted by the Civil Partnership Act 2004, s 71, Sch 4, Pt 2, para 7.

Sub-s (1): in paras (iv), (v), words in first (outer) pairs of square brackets substituted and words omitted repealed by the Intestates' Estates Act 1952, s 1; words in second (inner) pairs of square brackets substituted by the Civil Partnership Act 2004, s 71, Sch 4, Pt 2, para 7.

Sub-s (1A): inserted by the Administration of Justice Act 1977, s 28(1).

Sub-s (2A): inserted by the Law Reform (Succession) Act 1995, s 1(1), (3); words in square brackets substituted by the Civil Partnership Act 2004, s 71, Sch 4, Pt 2, para 7.

Sub-s (3): inserted by the Intestates' Estates Act 1952, s 1(4); words in square brackets substituted by the Civil Partnership Act 2004, s 71, Sch 4, Pt 2, para 7.

Sub-s (4): inserted by the Intestates' Estates Act 1952, s 1(4); words in first pair of square brackets substituted by the Family Provision Act 1966, s 1; words in second pair of square brackets substituted by the Civil Partnership Act 2004, s 71, Sch 4, Pt 2, para 7.

Order: the Intestate Succession (Interest and Capitalisation) Order 1977, SI 1977/1491, as amended by SI 1983/1374.

47 Statutory trusts in favour of issue and other classes of relatives of intestate

(1) Where under this Part of this Act the residuary estate of an intestate, or any part thereof, is directed to be held on the statutory trusts for the issue of the intestate, the same shall be held upon the following trusts, namely—

(i) In trust, in equal shares if more than one, for all or any the children or child of the intestate, living at the death of the intestate, who attain the age of [eighteen] years or marry under that age [or form a civil partnership under that age], and for all or any of the issue living at the death of the intestate who attain the age of [eighteen] years or marry[, or form a civil partnership,] under that age of any child of the intestate who predeceases the intestate, such issue to take through all degrees, according to their stocks, in equal shares if more than one, the share which their parent would have taken if living at the death of the intestate, and so that no issue shall take whose parent is living at the death of the intestate and so capable of taking;

(ii) The statutory power of advancement, and the statutory provisions which relate to maintenance and accumulation of surplus income, shall apply, but when an infant marries[, or forms a civil partnership,] such infant shall be entitled to give valid receipts for the income of the infant's share or interest;

(iii) …

(iv) The personal representatives may permit any infant contingently interested to have the use and enjoyment of any personal chattels in such manner and subject to such conditions (if any) as the personal representatives may consider reasonable, and without being liable to account for any consequential loss.

(2) If the trusts in favour of the issue of the intestate fail by reason of no child or other issue attaining an absolutely vested interest—

(a) the residuary estate of the intestate and the income thereof and all statutory accumulations, if any, of the income thereof, or so much thereof as may not have been paid or applied under any power affecting the same, shall go, devolve and be held under the provisions of this Part of this Act as if the intestate had died without leaving issue living at the death of the intestate;

(b) references in this Part of this Act to the intestate "leaving no issue" shall be construed as "leaving no issue who attain an absolutely vested interest";

(c) references in this Part of this Act to the intestate "leaving issue" or "leaving a child or other issue" shall be construed as "leaving issue who attain an absolutely vested interest."

(3) Where under this Part of this Act the residuary estate of an intestate or any part thereof is directed to be held on the statutory trusts for any class of relatives of the intestate, other than issue of the intestate, the same shall be held on trusts corresponding to the statutory trusts for the issue of the intestate (other than the provision for bringing any money or property into account) as if such trusts (other than as aforesaid) were repeated with the substitution of references to the members or member of that class for references to the children or child of the intestate.

[(4) References in paragraph (i) of subsection (1) of the last foregoing section to the intestate leaving, or not leaving, a member of the class consisting of brothers or sisters of the whole blood of the intestate and issue of brothers or sisters of the whole blood of the intestate shall be construed as references to the intestate leaving, or not leaving, a member of that class who attains an absolutely vested interest.]

[(5) …]

[500]

NOTES

Sub-s (1): word in first and third pairs of square brackets in para (i) substituted by the Family Law Reform Act 1969, s 3(2); words in second and fourth pairs of square brackets in para (i) and words in square brackets in para (ii) inserted by the Civil Partnership Act 2004, s 71, Sch 4, Pt 2, para 8.

Sub-s (1): para (iii) repealed by the Law Reform (Succession) Act 1995, ss 1(2)(a), (3), 5, Schedule.

Sub-s (4): inserted by the Intestates' Estates Act 1952, s 1(3)(c).

Sub-s (5): inserted by the Intestates' Estates Act 1952, s 1(3)(c); repealed by the Family Provision Act 1966, ss 9, 10, Sch 2.

[47A Right of surviving spouse to have his own life interest redeemed

(1) Where a surviving [spouse or civil partner] is entitled to the interest in part of the residuary estate, and so elects, the personal representative shall purchase or redeem the life interest by paying the capital value thereof to the tenant for life, or the persons deriving title under the tenant for life, and the costs of the transaction; and thereupon the residuary estate of the intestate may be dealt with and distributed free from the life interest.

(2) …

(3) An election under this section shall only be exercisable if at the time of the election the whole of the said part of the residuary estate consists of property in possession, but, for the purposes of this section, a life interest in property partly in possession and partly not in possession shall be treated as consisting of two separate life interests in those respective parts of the property.

[(3A) The capital value shall be reckoned in such manner as the Lord Chancellor may by order direct, and an order under this subsection may include transitional provisions.

(3B) The power to make orders under subsection (3A) above shall be exercisable by statutory instrument subject to annulment in pursuance of a resolution of either House of Parliament; and any such order may be varied or revoked by a subsequent order made under the power.]

(4) …

(5) An election under this section shall be exercisable only within the period of twelve months from the date on which representation with respect to the estate of the intestate is first taken out:

Provided that if the surviving [spouse or civil partner] satisfies the court that the limitation to the said period of twelve months will operate unfairly—

(a) in consequence of the representation first taken out being probate of a will subsequently revoked on the ground that the will was invalid, or

(b) in consequence of a question whether a person had an interest in the estate, or as to the nature of an interest in the estate, not having been determined at the time when representation was first taken out, or

(c) in consequence of some other circumstances affecting the administration or distribution of the estate,

the court may extend the said period.

(6) An election under this section shall be exercisable, except where the tenant for life is the sole personal representative, by notifying the personal representative (or, where there are two or more personal representatives of whom one is the tenant for life, all of them except the tenant for life) in writing; and a notification in writing under this subsection shall not be revocable except with the consent of the personal representative.

(7) Where the tenant for life is the sole personal representative an election under this section shall not be effective unless written notice thereof is given to the [[Senior Registrar] of the Family Division of the High Court] within the period within which it must be made; and provision may be made by probate rules for keeping a record of such notices and making that record available to the public.

In this subsection the expression "probate rules" means rules [of court made under section 127 of the *Supreme Court Act 1981* [Senior Courts Act 1981]].

(8) An election under this section by a tenant for life who is an infant shall be as valid and binding as it would be if the tenant for life were of age; but the personal representative shall, instead of paying the capital value of the life interest to the tenant for life, deal with it in the same manner as with any other part of the residuary estate to which the tenant for life is absolutely entitled.

(9) In considering for the purposes of the foregoing provisions of this section the question when representation was first taken out, a grant limited to settled land or to trust property shall be left out of account and a grant limited to real estate or to personal estate shall be left out of account unless a grant limited to the remainder of the estate has previously been made or is made at the same time.]

[501]

NOTES

Inserted by the Intestates' Estates Act 1952, s 2.

Sub-ss (1), (5): words in square brackets substituted by the Civil Partnership Act 2004, s 71, Sch 4, Pt 2, para 9.

Sub-ss (2), (4): repealed by the Administration of Justice Act 1977, ss 28(2), 32(4), Sch 5, Pt VI.

Sub-ss (3A), (3B): inserted by the Administration of Justice Act 1977, s 28(3).

Sub-s (7): words in first (outer) pair of square brackets substituted by the Administration of Justice Act 1970, s 1(6), Sch 2, para 4; words in second (inner) and third (outer) pairs of square brackets substituted by the Supreme Court Act 1981, s 152(1), Sch 5; words in italics substituted by subsequent words in square brackets by the Constitutional Reform Act 2005, s 59(5), Sch 11, Pt 1, para 1(2), as from 1 October 2009.

Order: the Intestate Succession (Interest and Capitalisation) Order 1977, SI 1977/1491.

48 Powers of personal representative in respect of interests of surviving spouse

(1) …

(2) The personal representatives may raise—

(a) [the fixed net sum] or any part thereof and the interest thereon payable to the surviving [spouse or civil partner] of the intestate on the security of the whole or any part of the residuary estate of the intestate (other than the personal chattels), so far as that estate may be sufficient for the purpose of the said sum and interest may not have been satisfied by an appropriation under the statutory power available in that behalf; and

(b) in like manner the capital sum, if any, required for the purchase or redemption of the life interest of the surviving [spouse or civil partner] of the intestate, or any part thereof not satisfied by the application for that purpose of any part of the residuary estate of the intestate;

and in either case the amount, if any, properly required for the payment of the costs of the transaction.

[502]

NOTES

Sub-s (1): repealed by the Intestates' Estates Act 1952, s 2.

Sub-s (2): words in first pair of square brackets substituted by the Family Provision Act 1966, s 1; words in second and third pairs of square brackets substituted by the Civil Partnership Act 2004, s 71, Sch 4, Pt 2, para 10.

49 Application to cases of partial intestacy

[(1)] Where any person dies leaving a will effectively disposing of part of his property, this Part of this Act shall have effect as respects the part of his property not so disposed of subject to the provisions contained in the will and subject to the following modifications:—

[(aa)], (a) …

(b) The personal representative shall, subject to his rights and powers for the purposes of administration, be a trustee for the persons entitled under this Part of this Act in respect of the part of the estate not expressly disposed of unless it appears by the will that the personal representative is intended to take such part beneficially.

[(2), (3) …

(4) The references in subsection (3) of section forty-seven A of this Act to property are references to property comprised in the residuary estate and, accordingly, where a will of the deceased creates a life interest in property in possession, and the remaining interest in that property forms part of the residuary estate, the said references are references to that remaining interest (which, until the life interest determines, is property not in possession).]

[503]

NOTES

Sub-s (1): para (aa) inserted by the Intestates' Estates Act 1952, s 3, and repealed, together with para (a), by the Law Reform (Succession) Act 1995, ss 1(2)(b), 5, Schedule.

Sub-ss (2), (3): inserted by the Intestates' Estates Act 1952, s 3; repealed by the Law Reform (Succession) Act 1995, ss 1(2)(b), (3), 5, Schedule.

Sub-s (4): inserted by the Intestates' Estates Act 1952, s 3.

50 Construction of documents

(1) References to any Statutes of Distribution in an instrument inter vivos made or in a will coming into operation after the commencement of this Act, shall be construed as references to this Part of this Act; and references in such an instrument or will to statutory next of kin shall be construed, unless the context otherwise requires, as referring to the persons who would take beneficially on an intestacy under the foregoing provisions of this Part of this Act.

(2) Trusts declared in an instrument inter vivos made, or in a will coming into operation, before the commencement of this Act by reference to the Statutes of Distribution, shall, unless the contrary thereby appears, be construed as referring to the enactments (other than the Intestates' Estates Act 1890) relating to the distribution of effects of intestates which were in force immediately before the commencement of this Act.

[(3) In subsection (1) of this section the reference to this Part of this Act, or the foregoing provisions of this Part of this Act, shall in relation to an instrument inter vivos made, or a will or codicil coming into operation, after the coming into force of section 18 of the Family Law Reform Act 1987 (but not in relation to instruments inter vivos made or wills or codicils coming into operation earlier) be construed as including references to that section.]

[504]

NOTES

Sub-s (3): inserted by the Family Law Reform Act 1987, s 33(1), Sch 2, para 3.

51 Savings

(1) Nothing in this Part of this Act affects the right of any person to take beneficially, by purchase, as heir either general or special.

(2) The foregoing provisions of this Part of this Act do not apply to any beneficial interest in real estate (not including chattels real) to which a [person of unsound mind] or defective living and of full age at the commencement of this Act, and unable, by reason of his incapacity, to make a will, who thereafter dies intestate in respect of such interest without having recovered his testamentary capacity, was entitled at his death, and any such beneficial interest (not being an interest ceasing on his death) shall, without prejudice to any will of the deceased, devolve in accordance with the general law in force before the commencement of this Act applicable to freehold land, and that law shall, notwithstanding any repeal, apply to the case.

For the purposes of this subsection, a [person of unsound mind] or defective who dies intestate as respects any beneficial interest in real estate shall not be deemed to have recovered his testamentary capacity unless his … receiver has been discharged.

(3) Where an infant dies after the commencement of this Act without having been married [or having formed a civil partnership,] [and without issue], and independently of this subsection he would, at his death, have been equitably entitled under a [trust or] settlement (including a will) to a vested estate in fee simple or absolute interest in freehold land, or in any property … to devolve therewith or as freehold land, such infant shall be deemed to have had [a life interest], and the [trust or] settlement shall be construed accordingly.

(4) …

[505]

NOTES

Sub-s (2): words in square brackets substituted by the Mental Treatment Act 1930, s 20(5); words omitted repealed by the Mental Health Act 1959, s 149(2), Sch 8.

Sub-s (3): words in first pair of square brackets inserted by the Civil Partnership Act 2004, s 71, Sch 4, Pt 2, para 11; words in second, third and fifth pairs of square brackets inserted, word omitted repealed, and words in fourth pair of square brackets substituted by the Trusts of Land and Appointment of Trustees Act 1996, s 25, Sch 3, para 6(1), (4), Sch 4 (for savings in relation to entailed interests created before the commencement of that Act, and savings consequential upon the abolition of the doctrine of conversion, see s 25(4), (5) thereof).

Sub-s (4): repealed by the Trusts of Land and Appointment of Trustees Act 1996, s 25(2), Sch 4, subject to savings as noted above.

52 Interpretation of Part IV

In this Part of this Act "real and personal estate" means every beneficial interest (including rights of entry and reverter) of the intestate in real and personal estate which (otherwise than in right of a power of appointment or of the testamentary power conferred by statute to dispose of entailed interests) he could, if of full age and capacity, have disposed of by his will [and references (however expressed) to any relationship between two persons shall be construed in accordance with section 1 of the Family Law Reform Act 1987].

[506]

NOTES

Words in square brackets inserted by the Family Law Reform Act 1987, s 33(1), Sch 2, para 4.

PART V
SUPPLEMENTAL

53 General savings

(1) Nothing in this Act shall derogate from the powers of the High Court which exist independently of this Act or alter the distribution of business between the several divisions of the High Court, or operate to transfer any jurisdiction from the High Court to any other court.

(2) Nothing in this Act shall affect any unrepealed enactment in a public general Act dispensing with probate or administration as respects personal estate not including chattels real.

(3) …

[507]

NOTES

Sub-s (3): repealed by the Finance Act 1975, ss 52(2), 59(5), Sch 13, Pt I.

54 Application of Act

Save as otherwise expressly provided, this Act does not apply in any case where the death occurred before the commencement of this Act.

[508]

55 Definitions

In this Act, unless the context otherwise requires, the following expressions have the meanings hereby assigned to them respectively, that is to say:—

(1)

(i) "Administration" means, with reference to the real and personal estate of a deceased person, letters of administration whether general or limited, or with the will annexed or otherwise:

(ii) "Administrator" means a person to whom administration is granted:

(iii) "Conveyance" includes a mortgage, charge by way of legal mortgage, lease, assent, vesting, declaration, vesting instrument, disclaimer, release and every other assurance of property or of an interest therein by any instrument, except a will, and "convey" has a corresponding meaning, and "disposition" includes a "conveyance" also a devise bequest and an appointment of property contained in a will, and "dispose of" has a corresponding meaning:

[(iiiA) "the County Court limit", in relation to any enactment contained in this Act, means the amount for the time being specified by an Order in Council under section 145 of the County Courts Act 1984 as the county court limit for the purposes of that enactment (or, where no such Order in Council has been made, the corresponding limit specified by Order in Council under section 192 of the County Courts Act 1959);]

(iv) "the Court" means the High Court and also the county court, where that court has jurisdiction …

(v) "Income" includes rents and profits:

(vi) "Intestate" includes a person who leaves a will but dies intestate as to some beneficial interest in his real or personal estate:

[(via) "Land" has the same meaning as in the Law of Property Act 1925;]

(vii) "Legal estates" mean the estates charges and interests in or over land (subsisting or created at law) which are by statute authorised to subsist or to be created at law; and "equitable interests" mean all other interests and charges in or over land …

(viii) …

(ix) "Pecuniary legacy" includes an annuity, a general legacy, a demonstrative legacy so far as it is not discharged out of the designated property, and any other general direction by a testator for the payment of money, including all death duties free from which any devise, bequest, or payment is made to take effect:

(x) "Personal chattels" mean carriages, horses, stable furniture and effects (not used for business purposes), motor cars and accessories (not used for business purposes), garden effects, domestic animals, plate, plated articles, linen, china, glass, books, pictures, prints, furniture, jewellery, articles of household or personal use or ornament, musical and scientific instruments and apparatus, wines, liquors and consumable stores, but do not include any chattels used at the death of the intestate for business purposes nor money or securities for money:

(xi) "Personal representative" means the executor, original or by representation, or administrator for the time being of a deceased person, and as regards any liability for the payment of death duties includes any person who takes possession of or intermeddles with the property of a deceased person without the authority of the personal representatives or the court, and "executor" includes a person deemed to be appointed executor as respects settled land:

(xii) "Possession" includes the receipt of rents and profits or the right to receive the same, if any:

(xiii) "Prescribed" means prescribed by rules of court …

(xiv) "Probate" means the probate of a will:

(xv), (xvi) …

(xvii) "Property" includes a thing in action and any interest in real or personal property:

(xviii) "Purchaser" means a lessee, mortgagee, or other person who in good faith acquires an interest in property for valuable consideration, also an intending purchaser and "valuable consideration" includes marriage, [and formation of a civil partnership,] but does not include a nominal consideration in money:

(xix) "Real estate" save as provided in Part IV of this Act means real estate, including chattels real, which by virtue of Part I of this Act devolves on the personal representative of a deceased person:

(xx) "Representation" means the probate of a will and administration, and the expression "taking out representation" refers to the obtaining of the probate of a will or of the grant of administration:

(xxi) "Rent" includes a rent service or a rentcharge, or other rent, toll, duty, or annual or periodical payment in money or money's worth, issuing out of or charged upon land, but does not include mortgage interest; and "rentcharge" includes a fee farm rent:

(xxii) …

(xxiii) "Securities" include stocks, funds, or shares:

(xxiv) "Tenant for life," "statutory owner," … "settled land," "settlement," "trustees of the settlement," "term of years absolute," "death duties," and "legal mortgage," have the same meanings as in the Settled Land Act 1925, and "entailed interest" and "charge by way of legal mortgage" have the same meanings as in the Law of Property Act 1925:

(xxv) "Treasury solicitor" means the solicitor for the affairs of His Majesty's Treasury, and includes the solicitor for the affairs of the Duchy of Lancaster:

(xxvi) "Trust corporation" means the public trustee or a corporation either appointed by the court in any particular case to be a trustee or entitled by rules made under subsection (3) of section four of the Public Trustee Act 1906, to act as custodian trustee:

(xxvii) …

(xxviii) "Will" includes codicil.

(2) References to a child or issue living at the death of any person include child or issue en ventre sa mere at the death.

(3) References to the estate of a deceased person include property over which the deceased exercises a general power of appointment (including the statutory power to dispose of entailed interests) by his will.

[509]

NOTES

Sub-s (1): para (iiiA) inserted by the County Courts Act 1984, s 148(1), Sch 2, Pt III, para 15; words omitted from para (iv) repealed by the Courts Act 1971, s 56(4), Sch 11, Pt II; para (via) inserted, words omitted from paras (vii), (xxiv) repealed, and para (xxvii) repealed by the Trusts of Land and Appointment of Trustees Act 1996, s 25, Sch 3, para 6(1), (5), Sch 4 (for savings in relation to entailed interests created before the commencement of that Act, and savings consequential upon the abolition of the doctrine of conversion, see s 25(4), (5) thereof); para (viii) repealed by the Mental Capacity Act 2005, s 67(1), Sch 6, para 5(1), (3), Sch 7; words omitted from para (xiii) repealed by the Supreme Court Act 1981, s 152(4), Sch 7; para (xv) repealed by the Law of Property (Miscellaneous Provisions) Act 1994, s 21(2), Sch 2; paras (xvi), (xxii) repealed by the Supreme Court Act 1980, s 152(4), Sch 7; in para (xviii) words in square brackets inserted by the Civil Partnership Act 2004, s 71, Sch 4, Pt 2, para 12.

Modification: definition "Trust corporation" modified in relation to charities, by the Charities Act 1993, s 35.

56 (*Spent on the repeal of Sch 2 by the Statute Law Revision Act 1950.*)

57 Application to Crown

(1) The provisions of this Act bind the Crown and the Duchy of Lancaster, and the Duke of Cornwall for the time being as respects the estates of persons dying after the commencement of this Act, but not so as to affect the time within which proceedings for the recovery of real or personal estate vesting in or devolving on His Majesty in right of His Crown, or His Duchy of Lancaster, or on the Duke of Cornwall, may be instituted.

(2) Nothing in this Act in any manner affects or alters the descent or devolution of any property for the time being vested in His Majesty either in right of the Crown or of the Duchy of Lancaster or of any property for the time being belonging to the Duchy of Cornwall.

[510]

58 Short title, commencement and extent

(1) This Act may be cited as the Administration of Estates Act 1925.

(2) …

(3) This Act extends to England and Wales only.

[511]

NOTES

Sub-s (2): repealed by the Statute Law Revision Act 1950.

SCHEDULE 1

(*Pt I repealed by the Insolvency Act 1985, s 253(3), Sch 10, Pt III.*)

PART II
ORDER OF APPLICATION OF ASSETS WHERE THE ESTATE IS SOLVENT

1. Property of the deceased undisposed of by will, subject to the retention thereout of a fund sufficient to meet any pecuniary legacies.

2. Property of the deceased not specifically devised or bequeathed but included (either by a specific or general description) in a residuary gift, subject to the retention out of such property of a fund sufficient to meet any pecuniary legacies, so far as not provided for as aforesaid.

3. Property of the deceased specifically appropriated or devised or bequeathed (either by a specific or general description) for the payment of debts.

4. Property of the deceased charged with, or devised or bequeathed (either by a specific or general description) subject to a charge for the payment of debts.

5. The fund, if any, retained to meet pecuniary legacies.

6. Property specifically devised or bequeathed, rateably according to value,

7. Property appointed by will under a general power, including the statutory power to dispose of entailed interests, rateably according to value.

8. The following provisions shall also apply—

(a) The order of application may be varied by the will of the deceased.

(b) …

[512]

NOTES

Para 8: words omitted repealed by the Finance (No 2) Act 1983, s 16(4), Sch 2, Pt II, in relation to deaths on or after 26 July 1983.

(Sch 2 repealed by the Statute Law Revision Act 1950.)

LAW OF PROPERTY (AMENDMENT) ACT 1926

(1926 c 11)

An Act to amend certain enactments relating to the Law of Property and Trustees

[16 June 1926]

1 Conveyances of legal estates subject to certain interests

(1) Nothing in the Settled Land Act 1925 shall prevent a person on whom the powers of a tenant for life are conferred by paragraph (ix) of subsection (1) of section twenty of that Act from conveying or creating a legal estate subject to a prior interest as if the land had not been settled land.

(2) In any of the following cases, namely—

(a) where a legal estate has been conveyed or created under subsection one of this section, or under section sixteen of the Settled Land Act 1925, subject to any prior interest, or

(b) where before the first day of January, nineteen hundred and twenty-six, land has been conveyed to a purchaser for money or money's worth subject to any prior interest whether or not on the purchase the land was expressed to be exonerated from, or the grantor agreed to indemnify the purchaser against, such prior interest,

the estate owner for the time being of the land subject to such prior interest may, notwithstanding any provision contained in the Settled Land Act 1925, but without prejudice to any power whereby such prior interest is capable of being overreached, convey or create a legal estate subject to such prior interest as if the instrument creating the prior interest was not an instrument or one of the instruments constituting a settlement of the land.

(3) In this section "interest" means an estate, interest, charge or power of charging subsisting, or capable of arising or of being exercised, under a settlement, and, where a prior interest arises under the exercise of a power, "instrument" includes both the instrument conferring the power and the instrument exercising it.

[513]

2 (*Repealed by the Agricultural Holdings Act 1948, ss 98–100, Sch 8.*)

3 Meaning of "trust corporation"

(1) For the purposes of the Law of Property Act 1925, the Settled Land Act 1925, the Trustee Act 1925, the Administration of Estates Act 1925, and the *[Supreme Court Act 1981]* [Senior Courts Act 1981], the expression "Trust Corporation" includes the Treasury Solicitor, the Official Solicitor and any person holding any other official position prescribed by the Lord Chancellor, and, in relation to the property of a bankrupt and property subject to a deed of arrangement, includes the trustee in bankruptcy and the trustee under the deed respectively, and, in relation to charitable ecclesiastical and public trusts, also includes any local or public authority so prescribed, and any other corporation constituted under the laws of the United Kingdom or any part thereof which satisfies the Lord Chancellor that it undertakes the administration of any such trusts without remuneration, or that by its constitution it is required to apply the whole of its net income after payment of outgoings for charitable ecclesiastical or public purposes, and is prohibited from distributing, directly or indirectly, any part thereof by way of profits amongst any of its members, and is authorised by him to act in relation to such trusts as a trust corporation.

(2) For the purposes of this provision, the expression "Treasury Solicitor" means the solicitor for the affairs of His Majesty's Treasury, and includes the solicitor for the affairs of the Duchy of Lancaster.

[514]

NOTES

Sub-s (1): words in italics (as previously substituted by the Supreme Court Act 1981, s 152(1), Sch 5) substituted by subsequent words in square brackets by the Constitutional Reform Act 2005, s 59(5), Sch 11, Pt 1, para 1(2), as from 1 October 2009.

4–7 *(S 4 repealed by the Land Charges Act 1972, s 18, Sch 5; s 5 repealed by the Land Registration Act 2002, s 135, Sch 13; s 6 amends the settled Land Act 1925, s 13; s 7 outside the scope of this work.)*

8 Short title, construction and commencement

(1) This Act may be cited as the Law of Property (Amendment) Act 1926, and so far as it amends any Act shall be construed as one with that Act.

(2) …

[515]

NOTES

Sub-s (2): repealed by the Statute Law Revision Act 1950.

(Schedule, insofar as unrepealed, contains amendments only.)

LANDLORD AND TENANT ACT 1927

(1927 c 36)

An Act to provide for the payment of compensation for improvements and goodwill to tenants of premises used for business purposes, or the grant of a new lease in lieu thereof; and to amend the law of landlord and tenant

[22 December 1927]

PART I
COMPENSATION FOR IMPROVEMENTS AND GOODWILL ON THE TERMINATION OF TENANCIES OF BUSINESS PREMISES

1, 2 *(Outside the scope of this work.)*

3 Landlord's right to object

(1) Where a tenant of a holding to which this Part of this Act applies proposes to make an improvement on his holding, he shall serve on his landlord notice of his intention to make such improvement, together with a specification and plan showing the proposed improvement and the part of the existing premises affected thereby, and if the landlord, within three months after the service of the notice, serves on the tenant notice of objection, the tenant may, in the prescribed manner, apply to the tribunal, and the tribunal may, after ascertaining that notice of such intention has been served upon any superior landlords interested and after giving such persons an opportunity of being heard, if satisfied that the improvement—

(a) is of such a nature as to be calculated to add to the letting value of the holding at the termination of the tenancy; and

(b) is reasonable and suitable to the character thereof; and

(c) will not diminish the value of any other property belonging to the same landlord, or to any superior landlord from whom the immediate landlord of the tenant directly or indirectly holds;

and after making such modifications (if any) in the specification or plan as the tribunal thinks fit, or imposing such other conditions as the tribunal may think reasonable, certify in the prescribed manner that the improvement is a proper improvement:

Provided that, if the landlord proves that he has offered to execute the improvement himself in consideration of a reasonable increase of rent, or of such increase of rent as the tribunal may determine, the tribunal shall not give a certificate under this section unless it is subsequently shown to the satisfaction of the tribunal that the landlord has failed to carry out his undertaking.

(2) In considering whether the improvement is reasonable and suitable to the character of the holding, the tribunal shall have regard to any evidence brought before it by the landlord or any superior landlord (but not any other person) that the improvement is calculated to injure the amenity or convenience of the neighbourhood.

(3) The tenant shall, at the request of any superior landlord or at the request of the tribunal, supply such copies of the plans and specifications of the proposed improvement as may be required.

(4) Where no such notice of objection as aforesaid to a proposed improvement has been served within the time allowed by this section, or where the tribunal has certified an improvement to be a proper improvement, it shall be lawful for the tenant as against the immediate and any superior landlord to execute the improvement according to the plan and specification served on the landlord, or according to such plan and specification as modified by the tribunal or by agreement between the tenant and the landlord or landlords affected, anything in any lease of the premises to the contrary notwithstanding:

Provided that nothing in this subsection shall authorise a tenant to execute an improvement in contravention of any restriction created or imposed—

(a) for naval, military or air force purposes;
(b) for civil aviation purposes under the powers of the Air Navigation Act 1920;
(c) for securing any rights of the public over the foreshore or bed of the sea.

(5) A tenant shall not be entitled to claim compensation under this Part of this Act in respect of any improvement unless he has, or his predecessors in title have, served notice of the proposal to make the improvement under this section, and (in case the landlord has served notice of objection thereto) the improvement has been certified by the tribunal to be a proper improvement and the tenant has complied with the conditions, if any, imposed by the tribunal, nor unless the improvement is completed within such time after the service on the landlord of the notice of the proposed improvement as may be agreed between the tenant and the landlord or may be fixed by the tribunal, and where proceedings have been taken before the tribunal, the tribunal may defer making any order as to costs until the expiration of the time so fixed for the completion of the improvement.

(6) Where a tenant has executed an improvement of which he has served notice in accordance with this section and with respect to which either no notice of objection has been served by the landlord or a certificate that it is a proper improvement has been obtained from the tribunal, the tenant may require the landlord to furnish to him a certificate that the improvement has been duly executed; and if the landlord refuses or fails within one month after the service of the requisition to do so, the tenant may apply to the tribunal who, if satisfied that the improvement has been duly executed, shall give a certificate to that effect.

Where the landlord furnishes such a certificate, the tenant shall be liable to pay any reasonable expenses incurred for the purpose by the landlord, and if any question arises as to the reasonableness of such expenses, it shall be determined by the tribunal.

[516]

4–17 (*Ss 4–7 repealed by the Landlord and Tenant Act 1954, s 45, Sch 7, Pt I; ss 8–17 outside the scope of this work.*)

PART II
GENERAL AMENDMENTS OF THE LAW OF LANDLORD AND TENANT

18 Provisions as to covenants to repair

(1) Damages for a breach of a covenant or agreement to keep or put premises in repair during the currency of a lease, or to leave or put premises in repair at the termination of a lease, whether such covenant or agreement is expressed or implied, and whether general or specific, shall in no case exceed the amount (if any) by which the value of the reversion (whether immediate or not) in the premises is diminished owing to the breach of such covenant or agreement as aforesaid; and in particular no damage shall be recovered for a breach of any such covenant or agreement to leave or put premises in repair at the termination of a lease, if it is shown that the premises, in whatever state of repair they might be, would at or shortly after the termination of the tenancy have been or be pulled down, or such structural alterations made therein as would render valueless the repairs covered by the covenant or agreement.

(2) A right of re-entry or forfeiture for a breach of any such covenant or agreement as aforesaid shall not be enforceable, by action or otherwise, unless the lessor proves that the fact that such a notice as is required by section one hundred and forty-six of the Law of Property Act 1925, had been served on the lessee was known either—

(a) to the lessee; or
(b) to an under-lessee holding under an under-lease which reserved a nominal reversion only to the lessee; or
(c) to the person who last paid the rent due under the lease either on his own behalf or as agent for the lessee or under-lessee;

and that a time reasonably sufficient to enable the repairs to be executed had elapsed since the time when the fact of the service of the notice came to the knowledge of any such person.

Where a notice has been sent by registered post addressed to a person at his last known place of abode in the United Kingdom, then, for the purposes of this subsection, that person shall be deemed, unless the contrary is proved, to have had knowledge of the fact that the notice had been served as from the time at which the letter would have been delivered in the ordinary course of post.

This subsection shall be construed as one with section one hundred and forty-six of the Law of Property Act 1925.

(3) This section applies whether the lease was created before or after the commencement of this Act.

[517]

19 Provisions as to covenants not to assign, etc, without licence or consent

(1) In all leases whether made before or after the commencement of this Act containing a covenant condition or agreement against assigning, under-letting, charging or parting with the possession of demised premises or any part thereof without licence or consent, such covenant condition or agreement shall, notwithstanding any express provision to the contrary, be deemed to be subject—

(a) to a proviso to the effect that such licence or consent is not to be unreasonably withheld, but this proviso does not preclude the right of the landlord to require payment of a reasonable sum in respect of any legal or other expenses incurred in connection with such licence or consent; and

(b) (if the lease is for more than forty years, and is made in consideration wholly or partially of the erection, or the substantial improvement, addition or alteration of buildings, and the lessor is not a Government department or local or public authority, or a statutory or public utility company) to a proviso to the effect that in the case of any assignment, under-letting, charging or parting with the possession (whether by the holders of the lease or any under-tenant whether immediate or not) effected more than seven years before the end of the term no consent or licence shall be required, if notice in writing of the transaction is given to the lessor within six months after the transaction is effected.

[(1A) Where the landlord and the tenant under a qualifying lease have entered into an agreement specifying for the purposes of this subsection—

(a) any circumstances in which the landlord may withhold his licence or consent to an assignment of the demised premises or any part of them, or

(b) any conditions subject to which any such licence or consent may be granted,

then the landlord—

(i) shall not be regarded as unreasonably withholding his licence or consent to any such assignment if he withholds it on the ground (and it is the case) that any such circumstances exist, and

(ii) if he gives any such licence or consent subject to any such conditions, shall not be regarded as giving it subject to unreasonable conditions;

and section 1 of the Landlord and Tenant Act 1988 (qualified duty to consent to assignment etc) shall have effect subject to the provisions of this subsection.

(1B) Subsection (1A) of this section applies to such an agreement as is mentioned in that subsection—

(a) whether it is contained in the lease or not, and

(b) whether it is made at the time when the lease is granted or at any other time falling before the application for the landlord's licence or consent is made.

(1C) Subsection (1A) shall not, however, apply to any such agreement to the extent that any circumstances or conditions specified in it are framed by reference to any matter falling to be determined by the landlord or by any other person for the purposes of the agreement, unless under the terms of the agreement—

(a) that person's power to determine that matter is required to be exercised reasonably, or

(b) the tenant is given an unrestricted right to have any such determination reviewed by a person independent of both landlord and tenant whose identity is ascertainable by reference to the agreement,

and in the latter case the agreement provides for the determination made by any such independent person on the review to be conclusive as to the matter in question.

(1D) In its application to a qualifying lease, subsection (1)(b) of this section shall not have effect in relation to any assignment of the lease.

(1E) In subsections (1A) and (1D) of this section—

(a) "qualifying lease" means any lease which is a new tenancy for the purposes of section 1 of the Landlord and Tenant (Covenants) Act 1995 other than a residential lease, namely a lease by which a building or part of a building is let wholly or mainly as a single private residence; and

(b) references to assignment include parting with possession on assignment.]

(2) In all leases whether made before or after the commencement of this Act containing a covenant condition or agreement against the making of improvements without licence or consent,

such covenant condition or agreement shall be deemed, notwithstanding any express provision to the contrary, to be subject to a proviso that such licence or consent is not to be unreasonably withheld; but this proviso does not preclude the right to require as a condition of such licence or consent the payment of a reasonable sum in respect of any damage to or diminution in the value of the premises or any neighbouring premises belonging to the landlord, and of any legal or other expenses properly incurred in connection with such licence or consent nor, in the case of an improvement which does not add to the letting value of the holding, does it preclude the right to require as a condition of such licence or consent, where such a requirement would be reasonable, an undertaking on the part of the tenant to reinstate the premises in the condition in which they were before the improvement was executed.

(3) In all leases whether made before or after the commencement of this Act containing a covenant condition or agreement against the alteration of the user of the demised premises, without licence or consent, such covenant condition or agreement shall, if the alteration does not involve any structural alteration of the premises, be deemed, notwithstanding any express provision to the contrary, to be subject to a proviso that no fine or sum of money in the nature of a fine, whether by way of increase of rent or otherwise, shall be payable for or in respect of such licence or consent; but this proviso does not preclude the right of the landlord to require payment of a reasonable sum in respect of any damage to or diminution in the value of the premises or any neighbouring premises belonging to him and of any legal or other expenses incurred in connection with such licence or consent.

Where a dispute as to the reasonableness of any such sum has been determined by a court of competent jurisdiction, the landlord shall be bound to grant the licence or consent on payment of the sum so determined to be reasonable.

(4) This section shall not apply to leases of agricultural holdings within the meaning of the [Agricultural Holdings Act 1986] [which are leases in relation to which that Act applies, or to farm business tenancies within the meaning of the Agricultural Tenancies Act 1995], and paragraph (b) of subsection (1), subsection (2) and subsection (3) of this section shall not apply to mining leases. **[518]**

NOTES

Sub-ss (1A)–(1E): inserted by the Landlord and Tenant (Covenants) Act 1995, s 22.

Sub-s (4): first words in square brackets substituted by the Agricultural Holdings Act 1986, s 100, Sch 14, para 15; second words in square brackets inserted by the Agricultural Tenancies Act 1995, s 40, Schedule, para 6.

Modification: sub-ss (1)–(3) are modified, where the RTM company has acquired the right to manage, by the Commonhold and Leasehold Reform Act 2002, s 102, Sch 7, para 1.

See further: as to exclusion of this section in relation to leases or tenancies granted to contractors in respect of the running of secure training centres, see the Criminal Justice and Public Order Act 1994, s 7(3). See also, as to the exclusion of sub-ss (1), (2), (3) in relation to leases or tenancies granted to contractors in respect of the running of any removal centre or part of a removal centre, the Immigration and Asylum Act 1999, s 149(3).

20–22 (*Ss 20, 21 outside the scope of this work; s 22 repealed by the Landlord and Tenant Act 1954, s 68(1), Sch 7, Pt II.*)

23 Service of notices

(1) Any notice, request, demand or other instrument under this Act shall be in writing and may be served on the person on whom it is to be served either personally, or by leaving it for him at his last known place of abode in England or Wales, or by sending it through the post in a registered letter addressed to him there, or, in the case of a local or public authority or a statutory or a public utility company, to the secretary or other proper officer at the principal office of such authority or company, and in the case of a notice to a landlord, the person on whom it is to be served shall include any agent of the landlord duly authorised in that behalf.

(2) Unless or until a tenant of a holding shall have received notice that the person theretofore entitled to the rents and profits of the holding (hereinafter referred to as "the original landlord") has ceased to be so entitled, and also notice of the name and address of the person who has become entitled to such rents and profits, any claim, notice, request, demand, or other instrument, which the tenant shall serve upon or deliver to the original landlord shall be deemed to have been served upon or delivered to the landlord of such holding.

[519]

24, 25 (*Outside the scope of this work.*)

26 Short title, commencement and extent

(1) This Act may be cited as the Landlord and Tenant Act 1927.

(2) …

(3) This Act shall extend to England and Wales only.

[520]

NOTES
Sub-s (2): repealed by the Statute Law Revision Act 1950.

(*Schs 1, 2 outside the scope of this work.*)

AGRICULTURAL CREDITS ACT 1928

(1928 c 43)

An Act to secure, by means of the formation of a company and the assistance thereof out of public funds, the making of loans for agricultural purposes on favourable terms, and to facilitate the borrowing of money on the security of farming stock and other agricultural assets, and for purposes connected therewith

[3 August 1928]

1–4 ((*Pt I*) *ss 1, 2, 4 repealed by the Agriculture and Forestry* (*Financial Provisions*) *Act 1991, s 1*(*1*), (*2*), *Schedule, Pt I; s 3 repealed by the Trustee Investments Act 1961, s 16*(*2*), *Sch 5.*)

PART II
AGRICULTURAL SHORT-TERM CREDITS

5 Agricultural charges on farming stock and assets

(1) It shall be lawful for a farmer as defined by this Act by instrument in writing to create in favour of a bank as so defined a charge (hereinafter referred to as an agricultural charge) on all or any of the farming stock and other agricultural assets belonging to him as security for sums advanced or to be advanced to him or paid or to be paid on his behalf under any guarantee by the bank and interest, commission and charges thereon.

(2) An agricultural charge may be either a fixed charge, or a floating charge, or both a fixed and a floating charge.

(3) The property affected by a fixed charge shall be such property forming part of the farming stock and other agricultural assets belonging to the farmer at the date of the charge as may be specified in the charge, but may include—

(a) in the case of live stock, any progeny thereof which may be born after the date of the charge; and

(b) in the case of agricultural plant, any plant which may whilst the charge is in force be substituted for the plant specified in the charge.

(4) The property affected by a floating charge shall be the farming stock and other agricultural assets from time to time belonging to the farmer, or such part thereof as is mentioned in the charge.

(5) The principal sum secured by an agricultural charge may be either a specified amount, or a fluctuating amount advanced on current account not exceeding at any one time such amount (if any) as may be specified in the charge, and in the latter case the charge shall not be deemed to be redeemed by reason only of the current account having ceased to be in debit.

(6) An agricultural charge may be in such form and made upon such conditions as the parties thereto may agree, and sureties may be made parties thereto.

(7) For the purposes of this Part of this Act—

"Farmer" means any person (not being an incorporated company or society) who, as tenant or owner of an agricultural holding, cultivates the holding for profit; and "agriculture" and "cultivation" shall be deemed to include horticulture, and the use of land for any purpose of husbandry, inclusive of the keeping or breeding of live stock, poultry, or bees, and the growth of fruit, vegetables, and the like;

["Bank" means—

(a) the Bank of England;

(b) a person who has permission under Part 4 of the Financial Services and Markets Act 2000 to accept deposits;

(c) an EEA firm of the kind mentioned in paragraph 5(b) of Schedule 3 to that Act which has permission under paragraph 15 of that Schedule (as a result of qualifying for authorisation under paragraph 12(1) of that Schedule) to accept deposits or other repayable funds from the public;]

"Farming stock" means crops or horticultural produce, whether growing or severed from the land, and after severance whether subjected to any treatment or process of manufacture or not; live stock, including poultry and bees, and the produce and progeny thereof; any other agricultural or horticultural produce whether subjected to any treatment or process of manufacture or not; seeds and manures; agricultural vehicles, machinery, and other plant; agricultural tenant's fixtures and other agricultural fixtures which a tenant is by law authorised to remove;

"Other agricultural assets" means a tenant's right to compensation under the [Agricultural Holdings Act 1986, except under section 60(2)(b) or 62,], for improvements, damage by game, disturbance or otherwise [a tenant's right to compensation under section 16 of the Agricultural Tenancies Act 1995,], and any other tenant right.

[(7A) Paragraphs (b) and (c) of the definition of "Bank" in subsection (7) must be read with—

(a) section 22 of the Financial Services and Markets Act 2000;

(b) any relevant order under that section; and

(c) Schedule 2 to that Act.]

[521]

NOTES

Sub-s (7): definition "Bank" substituted by SI 2001/3649, art 267(1); in definition "Other agricultural assets", words in first pair of square brackets substituted by the Agricultural Holdings Act 1986, s 100, Sch 14, para 16 and words in second pair of square brackets inserted by the Agricultural Tenancies Act 1995, s 40, Schedule, para 7.

Sub-s (7A): inserted by SI 2001/3649, art 267(2).

6 Effect of fixed charge

(1) A fixed charge shall, so long as the charge continues in force, confer on the bank the following rights and impose upon the bank the following obligations, that is to say:—

(a) a right, upon the happening of any event specified in the charge as being an event authorising the seizure of property subject to the charge, to take possession of any property so subject;

(b) where possession of any property has been so taken, a right, after an interval of five clear days or such less time as may be allowed by the charge, to sell the property either by auction or, if the charge so provides, by private treaty, and either for a lump sum payment or payment by instalments;

(c) an obligation, in the event of such power of sale being exercised, to apply the proceeds of sale in or towards the discharge of the moneys and liabilities secured by the charge, and the cost of seizure and sale, and to pay the surplus (if any) of the proceeds to the farmer.

(2) A fixed charge shall, so long as the charge continues in force, impose on the farmer the following obligations—

(a) an obligation whenever he sells any of the property, or receives any money in respect of other agricultural assets comprised in the charge, forthwith to pay to the bank the amount of the proceeds of the sale or the money so received, except to such extent as the charge otherwise provides or the bank otherwise allows; the sums so paid to be applied, except so far as otherwise agreed, by the bank in or towards the discharge of moneys and liabilities secured by the charge;

(b) an obligation in the event of the farmer receiving any money under any policy of insurance on any of the property comprised in the charge, or any money paid by way of compensation under the Diseases of Animals Acts 1894 to 1927 in respect of the destruction of any live stock comprised in the charge, or by way of compensation under the Destructive Insects and Pests Acts 1877 to 1927 in respect of the destruction of any crops comprised in the charge, forthwith to pay the amount of the sums so received to the bank, except to such extent as the charge otherwise provides or the bank otherwise allows; the sums so paid to be applied, except so far as otherwise agreed by the bank, in or towards the discharge of the moneys and liabilities secured by the charge.

(3) Subject to compliance with the obligations so imposed, a fixed charge shall not prevent the farmer selling any of the property subject to the charge, and neither the purchaser, nor, in the case of a sale by auction, the auctioneer, shall be concerned to see that such obligations are complied with notwithstanding that he may be aware of the existence of the charge.

(4) Where any proceeds of sale which in pursuance of such obligation as aforesaid ought to be paid to the bank are paid to some other person, nothing in this Act shall confer on the bank a right to recover such proceeds from that other person unless the bank proves that such other person knew that the proceeds were paid to him in breach of such obligation as aforesaid, but such other person shall not be deemed to have such knowledge by reason only that he has notice of the charge.

[522]

7 Effect of floating charge

(1) An agricultural charge creating a floating charge shall have the like effect as if the charge had been created by a duly registered debenture issued by a company:

Provided that—

(a) the charge shall become a fixed charge upon the property comprised in the charge as existing at the date of its becoming a fixed charge—
  (i) upon [bankruptcy order] being made against the farmer;
  (ii) upon the death of the farmer;
  (iii) upon the dissolution of partnership in the case where the property charged is partnership property;
  (iv) upon notice in writing to that effect being given by the bank on the happening of any event which by virtue of the charge confers on the bank the right to give such a notice;

(b) the farmer, whilst the charge remains a floating charge, shall be subject to the like obligation as in the case of a fixed charge to pay over to the bank the amount received by him by way of proceeds of sale, in respect of other agricultural assets, under policies of insurance, or by way of compensation, and the last foregoing section shall apply accordingly: Provided that it shall not be necessary for a farmer to comply with such obligation if and so far as the amount so received is expended by him in the purchase of farming stock which on purchase becomes subject to the charge.

[523]

NOTES

Words in square brackets substituted by the Insolvency Act 1985, s 235, Sch 8, para 6 and the Insolvency Act 1986, s 437, Sch 11.

8 Supplemental provisions as to agricultural charges

(1) An agricultural charge shall have effect notwithstanding anything in the Bills of Sale Acts 1878 and 1882 and shall not be deemed to be a bill of sale within the meaning of those Acts.

(2) Agricultural charges shall in relation to one another have priority in accordance with the times at which they are respectively registered under this Part of this Act.

(3) Where an agricultural charge creating a floating charge has been made, an agricultural charge purporting to create a fixed charge on, or a bill of sale comprising any of the property comprised in the floating charge shall, as respects the property subject to the floating charge, be void so long as the floating charge remains in force.

(4) …

(5) Where a farmer who is adjudged bankrupt has created in favour of a bank an agricultural charge on any of the farming stock or other agricultural assets belonging to him, and the charge was created within three months of the date of the presentation of the bankruptcy petition and operated to secure any sum owing to the bank immediately prior to the giving of the charge, then, unless it is proved that the farmer immediately after the execution of the charge was solvent, the amount which but for this provision would have been secured by the charge shall be reduced by the amount of the sum so owing to the bank immediately prior to the giving of the charge, but without prejudice to the bank's right to enforce any other security for that sum or to claim payment thereof as an unsecured debt.

(6) Where after the passing of this Act the farmer has mortgaged his interest in the land comprised in the holding, then, if growing crops are included in an agricultural charge, the rights of the bank under the charge in respect of the crops shall have priority to those of the mortgagee, whether in possession or not, and irrespective of the dates of the mortgage and charge.

(7) An agricultural charge shall be no protection in respect of property included in the charge which but for the charge would have been liable to distress for[, or the exercise of a power to use the procedure in Schedule 12 to the Tribunals, Courts and Enforcement Act 2007 (taking control of goods) to recover,] rent, taxes, or rates.

(8) An instrument creating an agricultural charge shall be exempt from stamp duty.

[524]

NOTES

Sub-s (4): repealed by the Insolvency Act 1985, s 235, Sch 10, Pt III and the Insolvency Act 1986, s 437, Sch 11.

Sub-s (7): words in square brackets inserted by the Tribunals, Courts and Enforcement Act 2007, s 62(3), Sch 13, para 23, as from a day to be appointed.

9 Registration of agricultural charges

(1) Every agricultural charge shall be registered under this Act within seven clear days after the execution thereof, and, if not so registered, shall be void as against any person other than the farmer:

Provided that the High Court on proof that omission to register within such time as aforesaid was accidental or due to inadvertence may extend the time for registration on such terms as the Court thinks fit.

(2) The Land Registrar shall keep at the Land Registry a register of agricultural charges in such form and containing such particulars as may be prescribed.

(3) Registration of an agricultural charge shall be effected by sending by post to the Land Registrar at the Land Registry a memorandum of the instrument creating the charge and such particulars of the charge as may be prescribed, together with the prescribed fee; and the Land Registrar shall enter the particulars in the register and shall file the memorandum.

(4) The register kept and the memoranda filed under this section shall at all reasonable times be open to inspection by any person on payment (except where the inspection is made by or on behalf of a bank) of the prescribed fee, and any person inspecting the register or any such filed memorandum on payment (except as aforesaid) of the prescribed fee may make copies or extracts therefrom.

(5) Any person may on payment of the prescribed fee require to be furnished with a copy of any entry in the register or of any filed memorandum or any part thereof certified to be a true copy by the Land Registrar.

(6) Registration of an agricultural charge may be proved by the production of a certified copy of the entry in the register relating to the charge, and a copy of any entry purporting to be certified as a true copy by the Land Registrar shall in all legal proceedings be evidence of the matters stated therein without proof of the signature or authority of the person signing it.

[(7) The Schedule to this Act shall have effect in relation to official searches in the register of agricultural charges.]

(8) Registration of an agricultural charge under this section shall be deemed to constitute actual notice of the charge, and of the fact of such registration, to all persons and for all purposes connected with the property comprised in the charge, as from the date of registration or other prescribed date, and so long as the registration continues in force:

Provided that, where an agricultural charge created in favour of a bank is expressly made for securing a current account or other further advances, the bank, in relation to the making of further advances under the charge, shall not be deemed to have notice of another agricultural charge by reason only that it is so registered if it was not so registered at the time when the first-mentioned charge was created or when the last search (if any) by or on behalf of the bank was made, whichever last happened.

(9) The Lord Chancellor may make regulations prescribing anything which under this section is to be prescribed, subject as respects fees to the approval of the Treasury, and generally as to the keeping of the register and the filing of memoranda, the removal of entries from the register on proof of discharge, and the rectification of the register.

[525]

NOTES

Sub-s (7): substituted by the Land Charges Act 1972, s 18(1), Sch 3, para 7.

Subordinate legislation: the Agricultural Credits Regulations 1928, SI 1928/667; the Agricultural Credits Fees Order 1985, SI 1985/372.

10 Restriction on publication of agricultural charges

(1) It shall not be lawful to print for publication or publish any list of agricultural charges or of the names of farmers who have created agricultural charges.

(2) If any person acts in contravention of this section, he shall in respect of each offence be liable on summary conviction to a fine not exceeding [level 2 on the standard scale]:

Provided that no person other than a proprietor, editor, master printer, or publisher, shall be liable to be convicted under this section.

(3) No prosecution for an offence under this section shall be commenced without the consent of the Attorney-General.

(4) For the purpose of this section, "publication" means the issue of copies to the public, and "publish" has a corresponding meaning, and without prejudice to the generality of the foregoing definition the confidential notification by an association representative of a particular trade to its members trading or carrying on business in the district in which property subject to an agricultural charge is situate of the creation of the charge shall not be deemed to be publication for the purposes of this section.

[526]

NOTES

Sub-s (2): maximum fine increased by the Criminal Law Act 1977, s 31(6), and converted to a level on the standard scale by the Criminal Justice Act 1982, ss 37, 46.

11 Frauds by farmers

(1) If, with intent to defraud, a farmer who has created an agricultural charge—

(a) fails to comply with the obligations imposed by this Act as to the payment over to the bank of any sums received by him by way of proceeds of sale, or in respect of other agricultural assets, or under a policy of insurance or by way of compensation; or

(b) removes or suffers to be removed from his holding any property subject to the charge;

he shall be guilty of a misdemeanour and liable on conviction on indictment to penal servitude for a term not exceeding three years.

(2) …

[527]

NOTES

Sub-s (2): repealed by the Magistrates' Courts Act 1952, s 132, Sch 6.

12 (*Repealed by the Statute Law Revision 1950.*)

13 Rights of tenants

Any farmer being the tenant of an agricultural holding shall have the right to create an agricultural charge notwithstanding any provision in his contract of tenancy to the contrary.

[528]

14 Provisions as to agricultural societies

(1) A debenture issued by a society registered under the Industrial and Provident Societies Acts 1893 to 1928, creating in favour of a bank a floating charge on property which is farming stock within the meaning of this Part of this Act, may be registered in like manner as an agricultural charge, and section nine of this Act shall apply to such a charge in like manner as it applies to an agricultural charge, and the charge if so registered shall as respects such property be valid notwithstanding anything in the Bills of Sale Acts 1878 and 1882, and shall not be deemed to be a bill of sale within the meaning of those Acts:

Provided that, where any such charge is so registered, notice thereof signed by the secretary of the society shall be sent to the central office established under the Friendly Societies Act 1896 and registered there.

(2) Any such debenture may create a floating charge on any farming stock the property in which is vested in the society.

[529]

PART III
GENERAL

15 Short title, commencement and extent

(1) This Act may be cited as the Agricultural Credits Act 1928.

(2) …

(3) This Act shall not (except as otherwise expressly provided) extend to Scotland or Northern Ireland.

[530]

NOTES

Sub-s (2): repealed by the Statute Law Revision Act 1950.

(*Schedule outside the scope of this work.*)

LAW OF PROPERTY (AMENDMENT) ACT 1929

(1929 c 9)

An Act to amend the provisions of the Law of Property Act 1925 relating to relief against forfeiture of under-leases

[5 February 1929]

1 Relief of under-lessees against breach of covenant

Nothing in subsection (8), subsection (9) or subsection (10) of section one hundred and forty-six of the Law of Property Act 1925 (which relates to restrictions on and relief against forfeiture of leases and under-leases), shall affect the provisions of subsection (4) of the said section.

[531]

2 Short title

This Act may be cited as the Law of Property (Amendment) Act 1929, and the Law of Property Act 1925, the Law of Property (Amendment) Act 1926, so far as it amends that Act, and this Act may be cited together as the Law of Property Acts 1925 to 1929.

[532]

LAW OF PROPERTY (ENTAILED INTERESTS) ACT 1932

(1932 c 27)

An Act to prevent the conversion of entailed interests into absolute interests and the destruction of interests expectant thereon by the statutory trusts for sale, and to define the expression "rent charge in possession"

[16 June 1932]

1 (*Repealed by the Trusts of Land and Appointment of Trustees Act 1996, s 25(2), Sch 4, except in relation to any entailed interest created before 1 January 1997.*)

2 Definition of rent charge

For removing doubt it is hereby declared that a rent charge (not being a rent charge limited to take effect in remainder after or expectant on the failure or determination of some other interest) is a rent charge in possession within the meaning of paragraph (b) of subsection (2) of section one of the Law of Property Act 1925, notwithstanding that the payments in respect thereof are limited to commence or accrue at some time subsequent to its creation.

[533]

3 Short title and construction

(1) This Act may be cited as the Law of Property (Entailed Interests) Act 1932, and so far as it amends any Act shall be construed as one with that Act.

(2) The Law of Property Acts 1925 to 1929, and this Act, so far as it amends those Acts, may be cited together as the Law of Property Acts 1925 to 1932.

[534]

PUBLIC HEALTH ACT 1936

(1936 c 49)

An Act to consolidate with amendments certain enactments relating to public health

[31 July 1936]

1–270 ((*Pts I–XI*) *outside the scope of this work.*)

PART XII
GENERAL

271–290 (*Outside the scope of this work.*)

Provisions as to recovery of expenses, etc

291 Certain expenses recoverable from owners to be a charge on the premises: power to order payment by instalments

(1) Where a local authority have incurred expenses for the repayment of which the owner of the premises in respect of which the expenses were incurred is liable, either under this Act or under any enactment repealed thereby, or by agreement with the authority, those expenses, together with interest from the date of service of a demand for the expenses, may be recovered by the authority from the person who is the owner of the premises at the date when the works are completed, or, if he

has ceased to be the owner of the premises before the date when a demand for the expenses is served, either from him or from the person who is the owner at the date when the demand is served, and, as from the date of the completion of the works, the expenses and interest accrued due thereon shall, until recovered, be a charge on the premises and on all estates and interests therein.

(2) A local authority may by order declare any expenses recoverable by them under this section to be payable with interest by instalments within a period not exceeding thirty years, until the whole amount is paid; and any such instalments and interest, or any part thereof, may be recovered from the owner or occupier for the time being of the premises in respect of which the expenses were incurred, and, if recovered from the occupier, may be deducted by him from the rent of the premises:

Provided that an occupier shall not be required to pay at any one time any sum in excess of the amount which was due from him on account of rent at, or has become due from him on account of rent since, the date on which he received a demand from the local authority together with a notice requiring him not to pay rent to his landlord without deducting the sum so demanded.

An order may be made under this subsection at any time with respect to any unpaid balance of expenses and accrued interest so, however, that the period for repayment shall not in any case extend beyond thirty years from the service of the first demand for the expenses.

(3) The rate of interest chargeable under subsection (1) or subsection (2) of this section shall be such [reasonable] rate as the authority may determine:

…

(4) A local authority shall, for the purpose of enforcing a charge under this section, have all the same powers and remedies under the Law of Property Act 1925, and otherwise as if they were mortgagees by deed having powers of sale and lease, of accepting surrenders of leases and of appointing a receiver.

[535]

NOTES

Sub-s (3): words in square brackets inserted and words omitted repealed by the Local Government, Planning and Land Act 1980, ss 1(6), 194, Sch 6, para 4, Sch 34, Pt VI.

292–346 (*Outside the scope of this work.*)

347 Short title, date of commencement, and extent

(1) This Act may be cited as the Public Health Act 1936, …

(2) This Act shall not extend to Scotland nor, except as otherwise expressly provided, to Northern Ireland …

[536]

NOTES

Sub-s (1): words omitted repealed by the Statute Law Revision Act 1950.
Sub-s (2): words omitted repealed by the London Government Act 1963, s 93(1), Sch 18.

(*Schs 1–3 outside the scope of this work.*)

LEASEHOLD PROPERTY (REPAIRS) ACT 1938

(1938 c 34)

An Act to amend the law as to the enforcement by landlords of obligations to repair and similar obligations arising under leases

[23 June 1938]

1 Restriction on enforcement of repairing covenants in long leases of small houses

(1) Where a lessor serves on a lessee under sub-section (1) of section one hundred and forty-six of the Law of Property Act 1925, a notice that relates to a breach of a covenant or agreement to keep or put in repair during the currency of the lease [all or any of the property comprised in the lease], and at the date of the service of the notice [three] years or more of the term of the lease remain unexpired, the lessee may within twenty-eight days from that date serve on the lessor a counter-notice to the effect that he claims the benefit of this Act.

(2) A right to damages for a breach of such a covenant as aforesaid shall not be enforceable by action commenced at any time at which [three] years or more of the term of the lease remain unexpired unless the lessor has served on the lessee not less than one month before the commencement of the action such a notice as is specified in subsection (1) of section one hundred

and forty-six of the Law of Property Act 1925, and where a notice is served under this subsection, the lessee may, within twenty-eight days from the date of the service thereof, serve on the lessor a counter-notice to the effect that he claims the benefit of this Act.

(3) Where a counter-notice is served by a lessee under this section, then, notwithstanding anything in any enactment or rule of law, no proceedings, by action or otherwise, shall be taken by the lessor for the enforcement of any right of re-entry or forfeiture under any proviso or stipulation in the lease for breach of the covenant or agreement in question, or for damages for breach thereof, otherwise than with the leave of the court.

(4) A notice served under subsection (1) of section one hundred and forty-six of the Law of Property Act 1925, in the circumstances specified in subsection (1) of this section, and a notice served under subsection (2) of this section shall not be valid unless it contains a statement, in characters not less conspicuous than those used in any other part of the notice, to the effect that the lessee is entitled under this Act to serve on the lessor a counter-notice claiming the benefit of this Act, and a statement in the like characters specifying the time within which, and the manner in which, under this Act a counter-notice may be served and specifying the name and address for service of the lessor.

(5) Leave for the purposes of this section shall not be given unless the lessor proves—

(a) that the immediate remedying of the breach in question is requisite for preventing substantial diminution in the value of his reversion, or that the value thereof has been substantially diminished by the breach;

(b) that the immediate remedying of the breach is required for giving effect in relation to the [premises] to the purposes of any enactment, or of any byelaw or other provision having effect under an enactment, [or for giving effect to any order of a court or requirement of any authority under any enactment or any such byelaw or other provision as aforesaid];

(c) in a case in which the lessee is not in occupation of the whole of the [premises as respects which the covenant or agreement is proposed to be enforced], that the immediate remedying of the breach is required in the interests of the occupier of [those premises] or of part thereof;

(d) that the breach can be immediately remedied at an expense that is relatively small in comparison with the much greater expense that would probably be occasioned by postponement of the necessary work; or

(e) special circumstances which in the opinion of the court, render it just and equitable that leave should be given.

(6) The court may, in granting or in refusing leave for the purposes of this section, impose such terms and conditions on the lessor or on the lessee as it may think fit.

[537]

NOTES

Sub-ss (1), (2), (5): words in square brackets substituted by the Landlord and Tenant Act 1954, s 5(2), (5).

2 Restriction on right to recover expenses of survey, etc

A lessor on whom a counter-notice is served under the preceding section shall not be entitled to the benefit of subsection (3) of section one hundred and forty-six of the Law of Property Act 1925, (which relates to costs and expenses incurred by a lessor in reference to breaches of covenant), so far as regards any costs or expenses incurred in reference to the breach in question, unless he makes an application for leave for the purposes of the preceding section, and on such an application the court shall have power to direct whether and to what extent the lessor is to be entitled to the benefit thereof.

[538]

3 Saving for obligation to repair on taking possession

This Act shall not apply to a breach of a covenant or agreement in so far as it imposes on the lessee an obligation to put [premises] in repair that is to be performed upon the lessee taking possession of the premises or within a reasonable time thereafter.

[539]

NOTES

Word in square brackets substituted by the Landlord and Tenant Act 1954, s 51(2).

4 (*Repealed by the Landlord and Tenant Act 1954, s 51(2).*)

5 Application to past breaches

This Act applies to leases created, and to breaches occurring, before or after the commencement of this Act.

[540]

6 Court having jurisdiction under this Act

(1) In this Act the expression "the court" means the county court, except in a case in which any proceedings by action for which leave may be given would have to be taken in a court other than the county court, and means in the said excepted case that other court.

(2) …

[541]

NOTES

Sub-s (2): repealed by the County Courts Act 1959, s 204, Sch 3.

7 Application of certain provisions of 15 and 16 Geo 5 c 20

(1) In this Act the expressions "lessor", "lessee" and "lease" have the meanings assigned to them respectively by sections one hundred and forty-six and one hundred and fifty-four of the Law of Property Act 1925, except that they do not include any reference to such a grant as is mentioned in the said section one hundred and forty-six, or to the person making, or to the grantee under such a grant, or to persons deriving title under such a person; and "lease" means a lease for a term of [seven years or more, not being a lease of an agricultural holding within the meaning of the [Agricultural Holdings Act 1986]] [which is a lease in relation to which that Act applies and not being a farm business tenancy within the meaning of the Agricultural Tenancies Act 1995].

(2) The provisions of section one hundred and ninety-six of the said Act (which relate to the service of notices) shall extend to notices and counter-notices required or authorised by this Act.

[542]

NOTES

Sub-s (1): first words in square brackets substituted by the Landlord and Tenant Act 1954, s 51(2), words in square brackets therein substituted by the Agricultural Holdings Act 1986, s 100, Sch 14, para 17; final words in square brackets inserted by the Agricultural Tenancies Act 1995, s 40, Schedule, para 8.

8 Short title and extent

(1) This Act may be cited as the Leasehold Property (Repairs) Act 1938.

(2) This Act shall not extend to Scotland or to Northern Ireland.

[543]

INTESTATES' ESTATES ACT 1952

(1952 c 64)

An Act to amend the law of England and Wales, about the property of persons dying intestate; to amend the Inheritance (Family Provision) Act 1938; and for purposes connected therewith

[30 October 1952]

PART I
AMENDMENTS OF LAW OF INTESTATE SUCCESSION

1–4 (*S 1 repealed in part by the Family Provision Act 1966, s 10(2), Sch 2, remainder amends the Administration of Estates Act 1925, ss 46, 47, 48 at* **[499]**, **[500]**, **[502]**; *s 2 inserts s 47A in the 1925 Act at* **[501]** *and repeals s 48(1) thereof; s 3 amends s 49 of the 1925 Act at* **[503]**; *s 4 outside the scope of this work.*)

5 Rights of surviving spouse [or civil partner] as respects the matrimonial [or civil partnership] home

The Second Schedule to this Act shall have effect for enabling the surviving [spouse or civil partner] of a person dying intestate after the commencement of this Act to acquire the matrimonial [or civil partnership] home.

[544]

NOTES

Section heading: words in square brackets inserted by the Civil Partnership Act 2004, s 71, Sch 4, Pt 2, para 13(1), (4).

Words in first pair of square brackets substituted and words in second pair of square brackets inserted by the Civil Partnership Act 2004, s 71, Sch 4, Pt 2, para 13(1)–(3).

6–8 *(S 6 outside the scope of this work; s 7 repealed by the Inheritance (Provision for Family and Dependants) Act 1975, s 26(2), Schedule; s 8 repealed by the Family Provision Act 1966, s 10(2), Sch 2.)*

9 Short title and commencement

(1) This Act may be cited as the Intestates' Estates Act 1952.

(2) This Act shall come into operation on the first day of January, nineteen hundred and fifty-three.

[545]

(Sch 1 outside the scope of this work.)

SCHEDULE 2
RIGHTS OF SURVIVING SPOUSE [OR CIVIL PARTNER] AS RESPECTS THE MATRIMONIAL [OR CIVIL PARTNERSHIP] HOME

Section 5

NOTES

Schedule heading: words in square brackets inserted by the Civil Partnership Act 2004, s 71, Sch 4, Pt 2, para 13(1), (4).

1.—(1) Subject to the provisions of this Schedule, where the residuary estate of the intestate comprises of interest in a dwelling-house in which the surviving [spouse or civil partner] was resident at the time of the intestate's death, the surviving [spouse or civil partner] may require the personal representative in exercise of the power conferred by section forty-one of the principal Act (and with due regard to the requirements of that section as to valuation) to appropriate the said interest in the dwelling-house in or towards satisfaction of any absolute interest of the surviving [spouse or civil partner] in the real and personal estate of the intestate.

(2) The right conferred by this paragraph shall not be exercisable where the interest is—

(a) a tenancy which at the date of the death of the intestate was a tenancy which would determine within the period of two years from that date; or

(b) a tenancy which the landlord by notice given for that date could determine within the remainder of that period.

(3) Nothing in subsection (5) of section forty-one of the principal Act (which requires the personal representative, in making an appropriation to any person under that section, to have regard to the rights of others) shall prevent the personal representative from giving effect to the right conferred by this paragraph.

(4) The reference in this paragraph to an absolute interest in the real and personal estate of the intestate includes a reference to the capital value of a life interest which the surviving [spouse or civil partner] has under this Act elected to have redeemed.

(5) Where part of a building was, at the date of the death of the intestate, occupied as a separate dwelling, that dwelling shall for the purposes of this Schedule be treated as a dwelling-house.

2. Where—

(a) the dwelling-house forms part of a building and an interest in the whole of the building is comprised in the residuary estate; or

(b) the dwelling-house is held with agricultural land and an interest in the agricultural land is comprised in the residuary estate; or

(c) the whole or part of the dwelling-house was at the time of the intestate's death used as a hotel or lodging house; or

(d) a part of the dwelling-house was at the time of the intestate's death used for purposes other than domestic purposes,

the right conferred by paragraph 1 of this Schedule shall not be exercisable unless the court, on being satisfied that the exercise of that right is not likely to diminish the value of assets in the residuary estate (other than the said interest in the dwelling-house) or make them more difficult to dispose of, so orders.

3.—(1) The right conferred by paragraph 1 of this Schedule.

(a) shall not be exercisable after the expiration of twelve months from the first taking out of representation with respect to the intestate's estate;

(b) shall not be exercisable after the death of the surviving [spouse or civil partner];

(c) shall be exercisable, except where the surviving [spouse or civil partner] is the sole personal representative, by notifying the personal representative (or, where there are two or more personal representatives of whom one is the surviving [spouse or civil partner], all of them except the surviving [spouse or civil partner]) in writing.

(2) A notification in writing under paragraph (c) of the foregoing sub-paragraph shall not be revocable except with the consent of the personal representative; but the surviving [spouse or civil partner] may require the personal representative to have the said interest in the dwelling-house

valued in accordance with section forty-one of the principal Act and to inform him or her of the result of that valuation before he or she decides whether to exercise the right.

(3) Subsection (9) of the section forty-seven A added to the principal Act by section two of this Act shall apply for the purposes of the construction of the reference in this paragraph to the first taking out of representation, and the promise to subsection (5) of that section shall apply for the purpose of enabling the surviving [spouse or civil partner] to apply for an extension of the period of twelve months mentioned in this paragraph.

4.—(1) During the period of twelve months mentioned in paragraph 3 of this Schedule the personal representative shall not without the written consent of the surviving [spouse or civil partner] sell or otherwise dispose of the said interest in the dwelling-house except in the course of administration owing to want of other assets.

(2) An application to the court under paragraph 2 of this Schedule may be made by the personal representative as well as by the surviving [spouse or civil partner], and if, on an application under that paragraph, the court does not order that the right conferred by paragraph 1 of this Schedule shall be exercisable by the surviving [spouse or civil partner], the court may authorise the personal representative to dispose of the said interest in the dwelling-house within the said period of twelve months.

(3) Where the court under sub-paragraph (3) of paragraph 3 of this Schedule extends the said period of twelve months, the court may direct that this paragraph shall apply in relation to the extended period as it applied in relation to the original period of twelve months.

(4) This paragraph shall not apply where the surviving [spouse or civil partner] is the sole personal representative or one of two or more personal representatives.

(5) Nothing in this paragraph shall confer any right on the surviving [spouse or civil partner] as against a purchaser from the personal representative.

5.—(1) Where the surviving [spouse or civil partner] is one of two or more personal representatives, the rule that a trustee may not be a purchaser of trust property shall not prevent the surviving [spouse or civil partner] from purchasing out of the estate of the intestate an interest in a dwelling-house in which the surviving [spouse or civil partner] was resident at the time of the intestate's death.

(2) The power of appropriation under section forty-one of the principal Act shall include power to appropriate an interest in a dwelling-house in which the surviving [spouse or civil partner] was resident at the time of the intestate's death partly in satisfaction of an interest of the surviving [spouse or civil partner] in the real and personal estate of the intestate and partly in return for a payment of money by the surviving [spouse or civil partner] to the personal representative.

6.—[(1) Where the surviving spouse or civil partner lacks capacity (within the meaning of the Mental Capacity Act 2005) to make a requirement or give a consent under this Schedule, the requirement or consent may be made or given by a deputy appointed by the Court of Protection with power in that respect or, if no deputy has that power, by that court.]

(2) A requirement or consent made or given under this Schedule by a surviving [spouse or civil partner] who is an infant shall be as valid and binding as it would be if he or she were of age, and, as respects an appropriation in pursuance of paragraph 1 of this Schedule, the provisions of section forty-one of the principal Act as to obtaining the consent of the infant's parent or guardian, or of the court on behalf of the infant, shall not apply.

7.—(1) Except where the context otherwise requires, references in this Schedule to a dwelling-house include references to any garden or portion of ground attached to and usually occupied with the dwelling-house or otherwise required for the amenity or convenience of the dwelling-house.

(2) This Schedule shall be construed as one with Part IV of the principal Act.

[546]

NOTES

Paras 1, 3–5: words in square brackets substituted by the Civil Partnership Act 2004, s 71, Sch 4, Pt 2, para 13(1), (2).

Para 6: sub-para (1) substituted by the Mental Capacity Act 2005, s 67(1), Sch 6, para 8; words in square brackets in sub-para (2) substituted by the Civil Partnership Act 2004, s 71, Sch 4, Pt 2, para 13(1), (2).

(Sch 3 repealed by the Inheritance (Provision for Family and Dependants) Act 1975, s 26(2), Schedule; Sch 4 repealed by the Family Provision Act 1966, s 10(2), Sch 2.)

LANDLORD AND TENANT ACT 1954

(1954 c 56)

An Act to provide security of tenure for occupying tenants under certain leases of residential property at low rents and for occupying sub-tenants of tenants under such leases; to enable tenants occupying property for business, professional or certain other purposes to obtain new tenancies in certain cases; to amend and extend the Landlord and Tenant Act 1927, the Leasehold Property (Repairs) Act 1938, and section eighty-four of the Law of Property Act 1925; to confer jurisdiction on the County Court in certain disputes between landlords and tenants; to make provision for the termination of tenancies of derelict land; and for purposes connected with the matters aforesaid

[30 July 1954]

NOTES

Transfer of functions: as to the functions of Ministers of the Crown under this Act, so far as exercisable in relation to Wales, being transferred to the National Assembly for Wales, see the National Assembly for Wales (Transfer of Functions) Order 1999, SI 1999/672, art 2, Sch 1.

1–22 ((*Pt I*) *outside the scope of this work.*)

PART II
SECURITY OF TENURE FOR BUSINESS, PROFESSIONAL AND OTHER TENANTS

NOTES

See further: as to exclusion of this Part in relation to tenancies granted to contractors in respect of land in a "designated dockyard", see the Dockyard Services Act 1986, s 3. As to exclusion of this Part in relation to tenancies granted to contractors in respect of land in "designated premises", see the Atomic Weapons Establishment Act 1991, Schedule, para 3. As to exclusion of this Part in relation to leases or tenancies granted to contractors in respect of the running of secure training centres, see the Criminal Justice and Public Order Act 1994, s 7(3). As to the exclusion of this Part in relation to leases or sub-leases granted under the Armed Forces Act 1996, see the Armed Forces Act 1996, s 30(7). As to the exclusion of this Part in relation to leases or tenancies granted to contractors in respect of the running of any removal centre or part of a removal centre, see the Immigration and Asylum Act 1999, s 149(3).

Tenancies to which Part II applies

23 Tenancies to which Part II applies

(1) Subject to the provisions of this Act, this Part of this Act applies to any tenancy where the property comprised in the tenancy is or includes premises which are occupied by the tenant and are so occupied for the purposes of a business carried on by him or for those and other purposes.

[(1A) Occupation or the carrying on of a business—

(a) by a company in which the tenant has a controlling interest; or

(b) where the tenant is a company, by a person with a controlling interest in the company,

shall be treated for the purposes of this section as equivalent to occupation or, as the case may be, the carrying on of a business by the tenant.

(1B) Accordingly references (however expressed) in this Part of this Act to the business of, or to use, occupation or enjoyment by, the tenant shall be construed as including references to the business of, or to use, occupation or enjoyment by, a company falling within subsection (1A)(a) above or a person falling within subsection (1A)(b) above.]

(2) In this Part of this Act the expression "business" includes a trade, profession or employment and includes any activity carried on by a body of persons, whether corporate or unincorporate.

(3) In the following provisions of this Part of this Act the expression "the holding", in relation to a tenancy to which this Part of this Act applies, means the property comprised in the tenancy, there being excluded any part thereof which is occupied neither by the tenant nor by a person employed by the tenant and so employed for the purposes of a business by reason of which the tenancy is one to which this Part of this Act applies.

(4) Where the tenant is carrying on a business, in all or any part of the property comprised in a tenancy, in breach of a prohibition (however expressed) of use for business purposes which subsists under the terms of the tenancy and extends to the whole of that property, this Part of this Act shall not apply to the tenancy unless the immediate landlord or his predecessor in title has consented to the breach or the immediate landlord has acquiesced therein.

In this subsection the reference to a prohibition of use for business purposes does not include a prohibition of use for the purposes of a specified business, or of use for purposes of any but a specified business, but save as aforesaid includes a prohibition of use for the purposes of some one or more only of the classes of business specified in the definition of that expression in subsection (2) of this section.

[547]

NOTES

Sub-ss (1A), (1B): inserted by SI 2003/3096, arts 2, 13.

Continuation and renewal of tenancies

24 Continuation of tenancies to which Part II applies and grant of new tenancies

(1) A tenancy to which this Part of this Act applies shall not come to an end unless terminated in accordance with the provisions of this Part of this Act; and, subject to the [following provisions of this Act either the tenant or the landlord under such a tenancy may apply to the court for an order for the grant of] a new tenancy—

(a) if the landlord has given notice under [section 25 of this Act] to terminate the tenancy, or

(b) if the tenant has made a request for a new tenancy in accordance with section twenty-six of this Act.

(2) The last foregoing subsection shall not prevent the coming to an end of a tenancy by notice to quit given by the tenant, by surrender or forfeiture, or by the forfeiture of a superior tenancy [unless—

(a) in the case of a notice to quit, the notice was given before the tenant had been in occupation in right of the tenancy for one month; …

(b) …]

[(2A) Neither the tenant nor the landlord may make an application under subsection (1) above if the other has made such an application and the application has been served.

(2B) Neither the tenant nor the landlord may make such an application if the landlord has made an application under section 29(2) of this Act and the application has been served.

(2C) The landlord may not withdraw an application under subsection (1) above unless the tenant consents to its withdrawal.]

(3) Notwithstanding anything in subsection (1) of this section,—

(a) where a tenancy to which this Part of this Act applies ceases to be such a tenancy, it shall not come to an end by reason only of the cesser, but if it was granted for a term of years certain and has been continued by subsection (1) of this section then (without prejudice to the termination thereof in accordance with any terms of the tenancy) it may be terminated by not less than three nor more than six months' notice in writing given by the landlord to the tenant;

(b) where, at a time when a tenancy is not one to which this Part of this Act applies, the landlord gives notice to quit, the operation of the notice shall not be affected by reason that the tenancy becomes one to which this Part of this Act applies after the giving of the notice.

[548]

NOTES

Sub-s (1): words in first pair of square brackets substituted by SI 2003/3096, arts 2, 3(1); words in second pair of square brackets substituted by the Law of Property Act 1969, s 3(2).

Sub-s (2): paras (a), (b) and word immediately preceding them inserted by the Law of Property Act 1969, s 4(1); para (b) and word omitted immediately preceding it repealed by SI 2003/3096, art 28(2), Sch 6, subject to transitional provisions in art 29(2) thereof.

Sub-ss (2A)–(2C): inserted by SI 2003/3096, arts 2, 3(2).

[24A Applications for determination of interim rent while tenancy continues

(1) Subject to subsection (2) below, if—

(a) the landlord of a tenancy to which this Part of this Act applies has given notice under section 25 of this Act to terminate the tenancy; or

(b) the tenant of such a tenancy has made a request for a new tenancy in accordance with section 26 of this Act,

either of them may make an application to the court to determine a rent (an "interim rent") which the tenant is to pay while the tenancy ("the relevant tenancy") continues by virtue of section 24 of this Act and the court may order payment of an interim rent in accordance with section 24C or 24D of this Act.

(2) Neither the tenant nor the landlord may make an application under subsection (1) above if the other has made such an application and has not withdrawn it.

(3) No application shall be entertained under subsection (1) above if it is made more than six months after the termination of the relevant tenancy.]

[549]

NOTES

Substituted, together with ss 24B–24D, for s 24A (as inserted by the Law of Property Act 1969, s 3(1)), by SI 2003/3096, arts 2, 18.

[24B Date from which interim rent is payable

(1) The interim rent determined on an application under section 24A(1) of this Act shall be payable from the appropriate date.

(2) If an application under section 24A(1) of this Act is made in a case where the landlord has given a notice under section 25 of this Act, the appropriate date is the earliest date of termination that could have been specified in the landlord's notice.

(3) If an application under section 24A(1) of this Act is made in a case where the tenant has made a request for a new tenancy under section 26 of this Act, the appropriate date is the earliest date that could have been specified in the tenant's request as the date from which the new tenancy is to begin.]

[550]

NOTES

Substituted as noted to s 24A at **[549]**.

[24C Amount of interim rent where new tenancy of whole premises granted and landlord not opposed

(1) This section applies where—

(a) the landlord gave a notice under section 25 of this Act at a time when the tenant was in occupation of the whole of the property comprised in the relevant tenancy for purposes such as are mentioned in section 23(1) of this Act and stated in the notice that he was not opposed to the grant of a new tenancy; or

(b) the tenant made a request for a new tenancy under section 26 of this Act at a time when he was in occupation of the whole of that property for such purposes and the landlord did not give notice under subsection (6) of that section,

and the landlord grants a new tenancy of the whole of the property comprised in the relevant tenancy to the tenant (whether as a result of an order for the grant of a new tenancy or otherwise).

(2) Subject to the following provisions of this section, the rent payable under and at the commencement of the new tenancy shall also be the interim rent.

(3) Subsection (2) above does not apply where—

(a) the landlord or the tenant shows to the satisfaction of the court that the interim rent under that subsection differs substantially from the relevant rent; or

(b) the landlord or the tenant shows to the satisfaction of the court that the terms of the new tenancy differ from the terms of the relevant tenancy to such an extent that the interim rent under that subsection is substantially different from the rent which (in default of such agreement) the court would have determined under section 34 of this Act to be payable under a tenancy which commenced on the same day as the new tenancy and whose other terms were the same as the relevant tenancy.

(4) In this section "the relevant rent" means the rent which (in default of agreement between the landlord and the tenant) the court would have determined under section 34 of this Act to be payable under the new tenancy if the new tenancy had commenced on the appropriate date (within the meaning of section 24B of this Act).

(5) The interim rent in a case where subsection (2) above does not apply by virtue only of subsection (3)(a) above is the relevant rent.

(6) The interim rent in a case where subsection (2) above does not apply by virtue only of subsection (3)(b) above, or by virtue of subsection (3)(a) and (b) above, is the rent which it is reasonable for the tenant to pay while the relevant tenancy continues by virtue of section 24 of this Act.

(7) In determining the interim rent under subsection (6) above the court shall have regard—

(a) to the rent payable under the terms of the relevant tenancy; and

(b) to the rent payable under any sub-tenancy of part of the property comprised in the relevant tenancy,

but otherwise subsections (1) and (2) of section 34 of this Act shall apply to the determination as they would apply to the determination of a rent under that section if a new tenancy of the whole of the property comprised in the relevant tenancy were granted to the tenant by order of the court and the duration of that new tenancy were the same as the duration of the new tenancy which is actually granted to the tenant.

(8) In this section and section 24D of this Act "the relevant tenancy" has the same meaning as in section 24A of this Act.]

[551]

NOTES

Substituted as noted to s 24A at **[549]**.

[24D Amount of interim rent in any other case

(1) The interim rent in a case where section 24C of this Act does not apply is the rent which it is reasonable for the tenant to pay while the relevant tenancy continues by virtue of section 24 of this Act.

(2) In determining the interim rent under subsection (1) above the court shall have regard—

(a) to the rent payable under the terms of the relevant tenancy; and

(b) to the rent payable under any sub-tenancy of part of the property comprised in the relevant tenancy,

but otherwise subsections (1) and (2) of section 34 of this Act shall apply to the determination as they would apply to the determination of a rent under that section if a new tenancy from year to year of the whole of the property comprised in the relevant tenancy were granted to the tenant by order of the court.

(3) If the court—

(a) has made an order for the grant of a new tenancy and has ordered payment of interim rent in accordance with section 24C of this Act, but

(b) either—

(i) it subsequently revokes under section 36(2) of this Act the order for the grant of a new tenancy; or

(ii) the landlord and tenant agree not to act on the order,

the court on the application of the landlord or the tenant shall determine a new interim rent in accordance with subsections (1) and (2) above without a further application under section 24A(1) of this Act.]

[552]

NOTES

Substituted as noted to s 24A at **[549]**.

25 Termination of tenancy by the landlord

(1) The landlord may terminate a tenancy to which this Part of this Act applies by a notice given to the tenant in the prescribed form specifying the date at which the tenancy is to come to an end (hereinafter referred to as "the date of termination"):

Provided that this subsection has effect subject to [the provisions of section 29B(4) of this Act and] the provisions of Part IV of this Act as to the interim continuation of tenancies pending the disposal of applications to the court.

(2) Subject to the provisions of the next following subsection, a notice under this section shall not have effect unless it is given not more than twelve nor less than six months before the date of termination specified therein.

(3) In the case of a tenancy which apart from this Act could have been brought to an end by notice to quit given by the landlord—

(a) the date of termination specified in a notice under this section shall not be earlier than the earliest date on which apart from this Part of this Act the tenancy could have been brought to an end by notice to quit given by the landlord on the date of the giving of the notice under this section; and

(b) where apart from this Part of this Act more than six months' notice to quit would have been required to bring the tenancy to an end, the last foregoing subsection shall have effect with the substitution for twelve months of a period six months longer than the length of notice to quit which would have been required as aforesaid.

(4) In the case of any other tenancy, a notice under this section shall not specify a date of termination earlier than the date on which apart from this Part of this Act the tenancy would have come to an end by effluxion of time.

(5) ...

[(6) A notice under this section shall not have effect unless it states whether the landlord is opposed to the grant of a new tenancy to the tenant.

(7) A notice under this section which states that the landlord is opposed to the grant of a new tenancy to the tenant shall not have effect unless it also specifies one or more of the grounds specified in section 30(1) of this Act as the ground or grounds for his opposition.

(8) A notice under this section which states that the landlord is not opposed to the grant of a new tenancy to the tenant shall not have effect unless it sets out the landlord's proposals as to—

(a) the property to be comprised in the new tenancy (being either the whole or part of the property comprised in the current tenancy);
(b) the rent to be payable under the new tenancy; and
(c) the other terms of the new tenancy.]

[553]

NOTES

Sub-s (1): words in square brackets inserted by SI 2003/3096, arts 2, 11, subject to transitional provisions in art 29(1) thereof.

Sub-s (5): repealed by SI 2003/3096, arts 2, 4(1), 28(2), Sch 6, subject to transitional provisions in art 29(1) thereof.

Sub-ss (6)–(8): substituted, for original sub-s (6), by SI 2003/3096, arts 2, 4(2), subject to transitional provisions in art 29(1) thereof.

26 Tenant's request for a new tenancy

(1) A tenant's request for a new tenancy may be made where the [current tenancy] is a tenancy granted for a term of years certain exceeding one year, whether or not continued by section twenty-four of this Act, or granted for a term of years certain and thereafter from year to year.

(2) A tenant's request for a new tenancy shall be for a tenancy beginning with such date, not more than twelve nor less than six months after the making of the request, as may be specified therein:

Provided that the said date shall not be earlier than the date on which apart from this Act the current tenancy would come to an end by effluxion of time or could be brought to an end by notice to quit given by the tenant.

(3) A tenant's request for a new tenancy shall not have effect unless it is made by notice in the prescribed form given to the landlord and sets out the tenant's proposals as to the property to be comprised in the new tenancy (being either the whole or part of the property comprised in the current tenancy), as to the rent to be payable under the new tenancy and as to the other terms of the new tenancy.

(4) A tenant's request for a new tenancy shall not be made if the landlord has already given notice under the last foregoing section to terminate the current tenancy, or if the tenant has already given notice to quit or notice under the next following section; and no such notice shall be given by the landlord or the tenant after the making by the tenant of a request for a new tenancy.

(5) Where the tenant makes a request for a new tenancy in accordance with the foregoing provisions of this section, the current tenancy shall, subject to the provisions of [sections 29B(4) and 36(2)] of this Act and the provisions of Part IV of this Act as to the interim continuation of tenancies, terminate immediately before the date specified in the request for the beginning of the new tenancy.

(6) Within two months of the making of a tenant's request for a new tenancy the landlord may give notice to the tenant that he will oppose an application to the court for the grant of a new tenancy, and any such notice shall state on which of the grounds mentioned in section thirty of this Act the landlord will oppose the application.

[554]

NOTES

Sub-s (1): words in square brackets substituted by SI 2003/3096, art 28(1), Sch 5, paras 1, 3, subject to transitional provisions in art 29(1) thereof.

Sub-s (5): words in square brackets substituted by SI 2003/3096, arts 2, 12, subject to transitional provisions in art 29(1) thereof.

27 Termination by tenant of tenancy for fixed term

(1) Where the tenant under a tenancy to which this Part of this Act applies, being a tenancy granted for a term of years certain, gives to the immediate landlord, not later than three months before the date on which apart from this Act the tenancy would come to an end by effluxion of time, a notice in writing that the tenant does not desire the tenancy to be continued, section twenty-four of this Act shall not have effect in relation to the tenancy [unless the notice is given before the tenant has been in occupation in right of the tenancy for one month].

[(1A) Section 24 of this Act shall not have effect in relation to a tenancy for a term of years certain where the tenant is not in occupation of the property comprised in the tenancy at the time when, apart from this Act, the tenancy would come to an end by effluxion of time.]

(2) A tenancy granted for a term of years certain which is continuing by virtue of section twenty-four of this Act [shall not come to an end by reason only of the tenant ceasing to occupy the property comprised in the tenancy but] may be brought to an end on any … day by not less than three months' notice in writing given by the tenant to the immediate landlord, whether the notice is given … after the date on which apart from this Act the tenancy would have come to an end [or before that date, but not before the tenant has been in occupation in right of the tenancy for one month].

[(3) Where a tenancy is terminated under subsection (2) above, any rent payable in respect of a period which begins before, and ends after, the tenancy is terminated shall be apportioned, and any rent paid by the tenant in excess of the amount apportioned to the period before termination shall be recoverable by him.]

[555]

NOTES

Sub-s (1): words in square brackets inserted by the Law of Property Act 1969, s 4(2).

Sub-s (1A): inserted by SI 2003/3096, arts 2, 25(1).

Sub-s (2): words in first pair of square brackets inserted and first word omitted repealed by SI 2003/3096, arts 2, 25(2), 28(2), Sch 6, subject to transitional provisions in art 29(2) thereof; second words omitted repealed and words in second pair of square brackets inserted by the Law of Property Act 1969, s 4(2).

Sub-s (3): inserted by SI 2003/3096, arts 2, 25(3).

28 Renewal of tenancies by agreement

Where the landlord and tenant agree for the grant to the tenant of a future tenancy of the holding, or of the holding with other land, on terms and from a date specified in the agreement, the current tenancy shall continue until that date but no longer, and shall not be a tenancy to which this Part of this Act applies.

[556]

[Applications to court

29 Order by court for grant of new tenancy or termination of current tenancy

(1) Subject to the provisions of this Act, on an application under section 24(1) of this Act, the court shall make an order for the grant of a new tenancy and accordingly for the termination of the current tenancy immediately before the commencement of the new tenancy.

(2) Subject to the following provisions of this Act, a landlord may apply to the court for an order for the termination of a tenancy to which this Part of this Act applies without the grant of a new tenancy—

(a) if he has given notice under section 25 of this Act that he is opposed to the grant of a new tenancy to the tenant; or

(b) if the tenant has made a request for a new tenancy in accordance with section 26 of this Act and the landlord has given notice under subsection (6) of that section.

(3) The landlord may not make an application under subsection (2) above if either the tenant or the landlord has made an application under section 24(1) of this Act.

(4) Subject to the provisions of this Act, where the landlord makes an application under subsection (2) above—

(a) if he establishes, to the satisfaction of the court, any of the grounds on which he is entitled to make the application in accordance with section 30 of this Act, the court shall make an order for the termination of the current tenancy in accordance with section 64 of this Act without the grant of a new tenancy; and

(b) if not, it shall make an order for the grant of a new tenancy and accordingly for the termination of the current tenancy immediately before the commencement of the new tenancy.

(5) The court shall dismiss an application by the landlord under section 24(1) of this Act if the tenant informs the court that he does not want a new tenancy.

(6) The landlord may not withdraw an application under subsection (2) above unless the tenant consents to its withdrawal.]

[557]

NOTES

Substituted, together with preceding cross-heading, by SI 2003/3096, arts 2, 5.

[29A Time limits for applications to court

(1) Subject to section 29B of this Act, the court shall not entertain an application—

(a) by the tenant or the landlord under section 24(1) of this Act; or

(b) by the landlord under section 29(2) of this Act,

if it is made after the end of the statutory period.

(2) In this section and section 29B of this Act "the statutory period" means a period ending—

(a) where the landlord gave a notice under section 25 of this Act, on the date specified in his notice; and

(b) where the tenant made a request for a new tenancy under section 26 of this Act, immediately before the date specified in his request.

(3) Where the tenant has made a request for a new tenancy under section 26 of this Act, the court shall not entertain an application under section 24(1) of this Act which is made before the end of the period of two months beginning with the date of the making of the request, unless the application is made after the landlord has given a notice under section 26(6) of this Act.]

[558]

NOTES

Inserted by SI 2003/3096, arts 2, 10.

[29B Agreements extending time limits

(1) After the landlord has given a notice under section 25 of this Act, or the tenant has made a request under section 26 of this Act, but before the end of the statutory period, the landlord and tenant may agree that an application such as is mentioned in section 29A(1) of this Act, may be made before the end of a period specified in the agreement which will expire after the end of the statutory period.

(2) The landlord and tenant may from time to time by agreement further extend the period for making such an application, but any such agreement must be made before the end of the period specified in the current agreement.

(3) Where an agreement is made under this section, the court may entertain an application such as is mentioned in section 29A(1) of this Act if it is made before the end of the period specified in the agreement.

(4) Where an agreement is made under this section, or two or more agreements are made under this section, the landlord's notice under section 25 of this Act or tenant's request under section 26 of this Act shall be treated as terminating the tenancy at the end of the period specified in the agreement or, as the case may be, at the end of the period specified in the last of those agreements.]

[559]

NOTES

Inserted by SI 2003/3096, arts 2, 10.

30 Opposition by landlord to application for a new tenancy

(1) The grounds on which a landlord may oppose an application under [section 24(1) of this Act, or make an application under section 29(2) of this Act,] are such of the following grounds as may be stated in the landlord's notice under section twenty-five of this Act or, as the case may be, under subsection (6) of section twenty-six thereof, that is to say:—

(a) where under the current tenancy the tenant has any obligations as respects the repair and maintenance of the holding, that the tenant ought not to be granted a new tenancy in view of the state of repair of the holding, being a state resulting from the tenant's failure to comply with the said obligations;

(b) that the tenant ought not to be granted a new tenancy in view of his persistent delay in paying rent which has become due;

(c) that the tenant ought not to be granted a new tenancy in view of other substantial breaches by him of his obligations under the current tenancy, or for any other reason connected with the tenant's use or management of the holding;

(d) that the landlord has offered and is willing to provide or secure the provision of alternative accommodation for the tenant, that the terms on which the alternative accommodation is available are reasonable having regard to the terms of the current tenancy and to all other relevant circumstances, and that the accommodation and the time at which it will be available are suitable for the tenant's requirements (including the requirement to preserve goodwill) having regard to the nature and class of his business and to the situation and extent of, and facilities afforded by, the holding;

(e) where the current tenancy was created by the sub-letting of part only of the property comprised in a superior tenancy and the landlord is the owner of an interest in reversion expectant on the termination of that superior tenancy, that the aggregate of the rents reasonably obtainable on separate lettings of the holding and the remainder of that property would be substantially less than the rent reasonably obtainable on a letting of that property as a whole, that on the termination of the current tenancy the landlord requires possession of the holding for the purpose of letting or otherwise disposing of the said property as a whole, and that in view thereof the tenant ought not to be granted a new tenancy;

(f) that on the termination of the current tenancy the landlord intends to demolish or reconstruct the premises comprised in the holding or a substantial part of those premises or to carry out substantial work of construction on the holding or part thereof and that he could not reasonably do so without obtaining possession of the holding;

(g) subject as hereinafter provided, that on the termination of the current tenancy the landlord intends to occupy the holding for the purposes, or partly for the purposes, of a business to be carried on by him therein, or as his residence.

[(1A) Where the landlord has a controlling interest in a company, the reference in subsection (1)(g) above to the landlord shall be construed as a reference to the landlord or that company.

(1B) Subject to subsection (2A) below, where the landlord is a company and a person has a controlling interest in the company, the reference in subsection (1)(g) above to the landlord shall be construed as a reference to the landlord or that person.]

(2) The landlord shall not be entitled to oppose an application [under section 24(1) of this Act, or make an application under section 29(2) of this Act,] on the ground specified in paragraph (g) of the last foregoing subsection if the interest of the landlord, or an interest which has merged in that interest and but for the merger would be the interest of the landlord, was purchased or created after the beginning of the period of five years which ends with the termination of the current tenancy, and at all times since the purchase or creation thereof the holding has been comprised in a tenancy or successive tenancies of the description specified in subsection (1) of section twenty-three of this Act.

[(2A) Subsection (1B) above shall not apply if the controlling interest was acquired after the beginning of the period of five years which ends with the termination of the current tenancy, and at all times since the acquisition of the controlling interest the holding has been comprised in a tenancy or successive tenancies of the description specified in section 23(1) of this Act.]

[(3) …]

[560]

NOTES

Sub-s (1): words in square brackets substituted by SI 2003/3096, arts 2, 6(1).
Sub-ss (1A), (1B): inserted by SI 2003/3096, arts 2, 14(1).
Sub-s (2): words in square brackets inserted by SI 2003/3096, arts 2, 6(2).
Sub-s (2A): inserted by SI 2003/3096, arts 2, 14(2).
Sub-s (3): inserted by the Law of Property Act 1969, s 6; repealed by SI 2003/3096, art 28(2), Sch 6.

31 Dismissal of application for new tenancy where landlord successfully opposes

(1) If the landlord opposes an application under subsection (1) of section twenty-four of this Act on grounds on which he is entitled to oppose it in accordance with the last foregoing section and establishes any of those grounds to the satisfaction of the court, the court shall not make an order for the grant of a new tenancy.

(2) [Where the landlord opposes an application under section 24(1) of this Act, or makes an application under section 29(2) of this Act, on one or more of the grounds specified in section 30(1)(d) to (f) of this Act but establishes none of those grounds, and none of the other grounds specified in section 30(1) of this Act, to the satisfaction of the court, then if the court would have been satisfied on any of the grounds specified in section 30(1)(d) to (f) of this Act] if the date of termination specified in the landlord's notice or, as the case may be, the date specified in the tenant's request for a new tenancy as the date from which the new tenancy is to begin, had been such later date as the court may determine, being a date not more than one year later than the date so specified,—

(a) the court shall make a declaration to that effect, stating of which of the said grounds the court would have been satisfied as aforesaid and specifying the date determined by the court as aforesaid, but shall not make an order for the grant of a new tenancy;

(b) if, within fourteen days after the making of the declaration, the tenant so requires the court shall make an order substituting the said date for the date specified in the said landlord's notice or tenant's request, and thereupon that notice or request shall have effect accordingly.

[561]

NOTES

Sub-s (2): words in square brackets substituted by SI 2003/3096, arts 2, 7.

[31A Grant of new tenancy in some cases where section 30(1)(f) applies

(1) Where the landlord opposes an application under section 24(1) of this Act on the ground specified in paragraph (f) of section 30(1) of this Act[, or makes an application under section 29(2)

of this Act on that ground,] the court shall not hold that the landlord could not reasonably carry out the demolition, reconstruction or work of construction intended without obtaining possession of the holding if—

(a) the tenant agrees to the inclusion in the terms of the new tenancy of terms giving the landlord access and other facilities for carrying out the work intended and, given that access and those facilities, the landlord could reasonably carry out the work without obtaining possession of the holding and without interfering to a substantial extent or for a substantial time with the use of the holding for the purposes of the business carried on by the tenant; or

(b) the tenant is willing to accept a tenancy of an economically separable part of the holding and either paragraph (a) of this section is satisfied with respect to that part or possession of the remainder of the holding would be reasonably sufficient to enable the landlord to carry out the intended work.

(2) For the purposes of subsection (1)(b) of this section a part of a holding shall be deemed to be an economically separable part if, and only if, the aggregate of the rents which, after the completion of the intended work, would be reasonably obtainable on separate lettings of that part and the remainder of the premises affected by or resulting from the work would not be substantially less than the rent which would then be reasonably obtainable on a letting of those premises as a whole.]

[562]

NOTES

Inserted by the Law of Property Act 1969, s 7(1).
Sub-s (1): words in square brackets inserted by SI 2003/3096, arts 2, 8.

32 Property to be comprised in new tenancy

(1) [Subject to the following provisions of this section], an order under section twenty-nine of this Act for the grant of a new tenancy shall be an order for the grant of a new tenancy of the holding; and in the absence of agreement between the landlord and the tenant as to the property which constitutes the holding the court shall in the order designate that property by reference to the circumstances existing at the date of the order.

[(1A) Where the court, by virtue of paragraph (b) of section 31A(1) of this Act, makes an order under section 29 of this Act for the grant of a new tenancy in a case where the tenant is willing to accept a tenancy of part of the holding, the order shall be an order for the grant of a new tenancy of that part only.]

(2) The foregoing provisions of this section shall not apply in a case where the property comprised in the current tenancy includes other property besides the holding and the landlord requires any new tenancy ordered to be granted under section twenty-nine of this Act to be a tenancy of the whole of the property comprised in the current tenancy; but in any such case—

(a) any order under the said section twenty-nine for the grant of a new tenancy shall be an order for the grant of a new tenancy of the whole of the property comprised in the current tenancy, and

(b) references in the following provisions of this Part of this Act to the holding shall be construed as references to the whole of that property.

(3) Where the current tenancy includes rights enjoyed by the tenant in connection with the holding, those rights shall be included in a tenancy ordered to be granted under section twenty-nine of this Act [except as otherwise agreed between the landlord and the tenant or, in default of such agreement, determined by the court].

[563]

NOTES

Sub-ss (1), (3): words in square brackets substituted by the Law of Property Act 1969, ss 7(2), 8.
Sub-s (1A): inserted by the Law of Property Act 1969, ss 7(2), 8.

33 Duration of new tenancy

Where on an application under this Part of this Act the court makes an order for the grant of a new tenancy, the new tenancy shall be such tenancy as may be agreed between the landlord and the tenant, or, in default of such an agreement, shall be such a tenancy as may be determined by the court to be reasonable in all the circumstances, being, if it is a tenancy for a term of years certain, a tenancy for a term not exceeding [fifteen] years, and shall begin on the coming to an end of the current tenancy.

[564]

NOTES

Word in square brackets substituted by SI 2003/3096, arts 2, 26.

34 Rent under new tenancy

[(1)] The rent payable under a tenancy granted by order of the court under this Part of this Act shall be such as may be agreed between the landlord and the tenant or as, in default of such agreement, may be determined by the court to be that at which, having regard to the terms of the tenancy (other than those relating to rent), the holding might reasonably be expected to be let in the open market by a willing lessor, there being disregarded—

(a) any effect on rent of the fact that the tenant has or his predecessors in title have been in occupation of the holding,
(b) any goodwill attached to the holding by reason of the carrying on thereat of the business of the tenant (whether by him or by a predecessor of his in that business),
[(c) any effect on rent of an improvement to which this paragraph applies],
(d) in the case of a holding comprising licensed premises, any addition to its value attributable to the licence, if it appears to the court that having regard to the terms of the current tenancy and any other relevant circumstances the benefit of the licence belongs to the tenant.

[(2) Paragraph (c) of the foregoing subsection applies to any improvement carried out by a person who at the time it was carried out was the tenant, but only if it was carried out otherwise than in pursuance of an obligation to his immediate landlord, and either it was carried out during the current tenancy or the following conditions are satisfied, that is to say,—

(a) that it was completed not more than twenty-one years before the application [to the court] was made; and
(b) that the holding or any part of it affected by the improvement has at all times since the completion of the improvement been comprised in tenancies of the description specified in section 23(1) of this Act; and
(c) that at the termination of each of those tenancies the tenant did not quit.]

[(2A) If this Part of this Act applies by virtue of section 23(1A) of this Act, the reference in subsection (1)(d) above to the tenant shall be construed as including—

(a) a company in which the tenant has a controlling interest, or
(b) where the tenant is a company, a person with a controlling interest in the company.]

[(3) Where the rent is determined by the court the court may, if it thinks fit, further determine that the terms of the tenancy shall include such provision for varying the rent as may be specified in the determination.]

[(4) It is hereby declared that the matters which are to be taken into account by the court in determining the rent include any effect on rent of the operation of the provisions of the Landlord and Tenant (Covenants) Act 1995.]

[565]

NOTES

Sub-s (1): numbered as such, and para (c) substituted, by the Law of Property Act 1969, s 1(1).

Sub-s (2): inserted by the Law of Property Act 1969, ss 1(1), 2; words in square brackets in para (a) substituted by SI 2003/3096, arts 2, 9.

Sub-s (2A): inserted by SI 2003/3096, arts 2, 15.

Sub-s (3): inserted by the Law of Property Act 1969, ss 1(1), 2.

Sub-s (4): inserted by the Landlord and Tenant (Covenants) Act 1995, s 30(1), Sch 1, para 3.

35 Other terms of new tenancy

[(1)] The terms of a tenancy granted by order of the court under this Part of this Act (other than terms as to the duration thereof and as to the rent payable thereunder)[, including, where different persons own interests which fulfil the conditions specified in section 44(1) of this Act in different parts of it, terms as to the apportionment of the rent,] shall be such as may be agreed between the landlord and the tenant or as, in default of such agreement, may be determined by the court; and in determining those terms the court shall have regard to the terms of the current tenancy and to all relevant circumstances.

[(2) In subsection (1) of this section the reference to all relevant circumstances includes (without prejudice to the generality of that reference) a reference to the operation of the provisions of the Landlord and Tenant (Covenants) Act 1995.]

[566]

NOTES

Sub-s (1): numbered as such by the Landlord and Tenant (Covenants) Act 1995, s 30(1), Sch 1, para 4(1); words in square brackets inserted by SI 2003/3096, arts 2, 27(3).

Sub-s (2): inserted by the Landlord and Tenant (Covenants) Act 1995, s 30(1), Sch 1, para 4(2).

36 Carrying out of order for new tenancy

(1) Where under this Part of this Act the court makes an order for the grant of a new tenancy, then, unless the order is revoked under the next following subsection or the landlord and the tenant

agree not to act upon the order, the landlord shall be bound to execute or make in favour of the tenant, and the tenant shall be bound to accept, a lease or agreement for a tenancy of the holding embodying the terms agreed between the landlord and the tenant or determined by the court in accordance with the foregoing provisions of this Part of this Act; and where the landlord executes or makes such a lease or agreement the tenant shall be bound, if so required by the landlord, to execute a counterpart or duplicate thereof.

(2) If the tenant, within fourteen days after the making of an order under this Part of this Act for the grant of a new tenancy, applies to the court for the revocation of the order the court shall revoke the order; and where the order is so revoked, then, if it is so agreed between the landlord and the tenant or determined by the court, the current tenancy shall continue, beyond the date at which it would have come to an end apart from this subsection, for such period as may be so agreed or determined to be necessary to afford to the landlord a reasonable opportunity for reletting or otherwise disposing of the premises which would have been comprised in the new tenancy; and while the current tenancy continues by virtue of this subsection it shall not be a tenancy to which this Part of this Act applies.

(3) Where an order is revoked under the last foregoing subsection any provision thereof as to payment of costs shall not cease to have effect by reason only of the revocation; but the court may, if it thinks fit, revoke or vary any such provision or, where no costs have been awarded in the proceedings for the revoked order, award such costs.

(4) A lease executed or agreement made under this section, in a case where the interest of the lessor is subject to a mortgage, shall be deemed to be one authorised by section ninety-nine of the Law of Property Act 1925 (which confers certain powers of leasing on mortgagors in possession), and subsection (13) of that section (which allows those powers to be restricted or excluded by agreement) shall not have effect in relation to such a lease or agreement.

[567]

37 Compensation where order for new tenancy precluded on certain grounds

[(1) Subject to the provisions of this Act, in a case specified in subsection (1A), (1B) or (1C) below (a "compensation case") the tenant shall be entitled on quitting the holding to recover from the landlord by way of compensation an amount determined in accordance with this section.

(1A) The first compensation case is where on the making of an application by the tenant under section 24(1) of this Act the court is precluded (whether by subsection (1) or subsection (2) of section 31 of this Act) from making an order for the grant of a new tenancy by reason of any of the grounds specified in paragraphs (e), (f) and (g) of section 30(1) of this Act (the "compensation grounds") and not of any grounds specified in any other paragraph of section 30(1).

(1B) The second compensation case is where on the making of an application under section 29(2) of this Act the court is precluded (whether by section 29(4)(a) or section 31(2) of this Act) from making an order for the grant of a new tenancy by reason of any of the compensation grounds and not of any other grounds specified in section 30(1) of this Act.

(1C) The third compensation case is where—

(a) the landlord's notice under section 25 of this Act or, as the case may be, under section 26(6) of this Act, states his opposition to the grant of a new tenancy on any of the compensation grounds and not on any other grounds specified in section 30(1) of this Act; and

(b) either—

(i) no application is made by the tenant under section 24(1) of this Act or by the landlord under section 29(2) of this Act; or

(ii) such an application is made but is subsequently withdrawn.]

(2) [Subject to] [the following provisions of this section, compensation under this section] shall be as follows, that is to say,—

(a) where the conditions specified in the next following subsection are satisfied [in relation to the whole of the holding] it shall be [the product of the appropriate multiplier and] twice the rateable value of the holding,

(b) in any other case it shall be [the product of the appropriate multiplier and] the rateable value of the holding.

(3) The said conditions are—

(a) that, during the whole of the fourteen years immediately preceding the termination of the current tenancy, premises being or comprised in the holding have been occupied for the purposes of a business carried on by the occupier or for those and other purposes;

(b) that, if during those fourteen years there was a change in the occupier of the premises, the person who was the occupier immediately after the change was the successor to the business carried on by the person who was the occupier immediately before the change.

[(3A) If the conditions specified in subsection (3) above are satisfied in relation to part of the holding but not in relation to the other part, the amount of compensation shall be the aggregate of sums calculated separately as compensation in respect of each part, and accordingly, for the purpose of calculating compensation in respect of a part any reference in this section to the holding shall be construed as a reference to that part.

(3B) Where section 44(1A) of this Act applies, the compensation shall be determined separately for each part and compensation determined for any part shall be recoverable only from the person who is the owner of an interest in that part which fulfils the conditions specified in section 44(1) of this Act.]

(4) Where the court is precluded from making an order for the grant of a new tenancy under this Part of this Act in [a compensation case], the court shall on the application of the tenant certify that fact.

(5) For the purposes of subsection (2) of this section the rateable value of the holding shall be determined as follows:—

(a) where in the valuation list in force at the date on which the landlord's notice under section twenty-five or, as the case may be, subsection (6) of section twenty-six of this Act is given a value is then shown as the annual value (as hereinafter defined) of the holding, the rateable value of the holding shall be taken to be that value;

(b) where no such value is so shown with respect to the holding but such a value or such values is or are so shown with respect to premises comprised in or comprising the holding or part of it, the rateable value of the holding shall be taken to be such value as is found by a proper apportionment or aggregation of the value or values so shown;

(c) where the rateable value of the holding cannot be ascertained in accordance with the foregoing paragraphs of this subsection, it shall be taken to be the value which, apart from any exemption from assessment to rates, would on a proper assessment be the value to be entered in the said valuation list as the annual value of the holding;

and any dispute arising, whether in proceedings before the court or otherwise, as to the determination for those purposes of the rateable value of the holding shall be referred to the Commissioners of Inland Revenue for decision by a valuation officer.

An appeal shall lie to the [Upper Tribunal] from any decision of a valuation officer under this subsection, but subject thereto any such decision shall be final.

[(5A) If part of the holding is domestic property, as defined in section 66 of the Local Government Finance Act 1988,—

(a) the domestic property shall be disregarded in determining the rateable value of the holding under subsection (5) of this section; and

(b) if, on the date specified in subsection (5)(a) of this section, the tenant occupied the whole or any part of the domestic property, the amount of compensation to which he is entitled under subsection (1) of this section shall be increased by the addition of a sum equal to his reasonable expenses in removing from the domestic property.

(5B) Any question as to the amount of the sum referred to in paragraph (b) of subsection (5A) of this section shall be determined by agreement between the landlord and the tenant or, in default of agreement, by the court.

(5C) If the whole of the holding is domestic property, as defined in section 66 of the Local Government Finance Act 1988, for the purposes of subsection (2) of this section the rateable value of the holding shall be taken to be an amount equal to the rent at which it is estimated the holding might reasonably be expected to let from year to year if the tenant undertook to pay all usual tenant's rates and taxes and to bear the cost of the repairs and insurance and the other expenses (if any) necessary to maintain the holding in a state to command that rent.

(5D) The following provisions shall have effect as regards a determination of an amount mentioned in subsection (5C) of this section—

(a) the date by reference to which such a determination is to be made is the date on which the landlord's notice under section 25 or, as the case may be, subsection (6) of section 26 of this Act is given;

(b) any dispute arising, whether in proceedings before the court or otherwise, as to such a determination shall be referred to the Commissioners of Inland Revenue for decision by a valuation officer;

(c) an appeal shall lie to the [Upper Tribunal] from such a decision but subject to that, such a decision shall be final.]

[(5E) Any deduction made under paragraph 2A of Schedule 6 to the Local Government Finance Act 1988 (deduction from valuation of hereditaments used for breeding horses etc) shall be disregarded, to the extent that it relates to the holding, in determining the rateable value of the holding under subsection (5) of this section.]

(6) The Commissioners of Inland Revenue may by statutory instrument make rules prescribing the procedure in connection with references under this section.

(7) In this section—

the reference to the termination of the current tenancy is a reference to the date of termination specified in the landlord's notice under section twenty-five of this Act or, as the case may be, the date specified in the tenant's request for a new tenancy as the date from which the new tenancy is to begin;

the expression "annual value" means rateable value except that where the rateable value differs from the net annual value the said expression means net annual value;

the expression "valuation officer" means any officer of the Commissioners of Inland Revenue for the time being authorised by a certificate of the Commissioners to act in relation to a valuation list.

[(8) In subsection (2) of this section "the appropriate multiplier" means such multiplier as the Secretary of State may by order made by statutory instrument prescribe [and different multipliers may be so prescribed in relation to different cases].

(9) A statutory instrument containing an order under subsection (8) of this section shall be subject to annulment in pursuance of a resolution of either House of Parliament.]

[568]

NOTES

Sub-ss (1), (1A)–(1C): substituted, for original sub-s (1), by SI 2003/3096, arts 2, 19(1).

Sub-s (2): words in first pair of square brackets inserted by the Local Government and Housing Act 1989, s 149, Sch 7; words in second and third pairs of square brackets substituted by SI 2003/3096, arts 2, 19(2); words in fourth and fifth pairs of square brackets substituted by the Local Government, Planning and Land Act 1980, s 193, Sch 33.

Sub-ss (3A), (3B): inserted by SI 2003/3096, arts 2, 19(3).

Sub-s (4): words in square brackets substituted by SI 2003/3096, arts 2, 19(4).

Sub-s (5): words in square brackets substituted by SI 2009/1307, art 5(1), (2), Sch 1, para 20.

Sub-ss (5A)–(5C): inserted by the Local Government and Housing Act 1989, s 149, Sch 7.

Sub-s (5D): inserted by the Local Government and Housing Act 1989, s 149, Sch 7; words in square brackets substituted by SI 2009/1307, art 5(1), (2), Sch 1, para 20.

Sub-s (5E): inserted by SI 1990/1285, art 2, Schedule, Pt I, para 4(b).

Sub-s (8): inserted by the Local Government, Planning and Land Act 1980, s 193, Sch 33; words in square brackets inserted by the Local Government and Housing Act 1989, s 149, Sch 7.

Sub-s (9): inserted by the Local Government, Planning and Land Act 1980, s 193, Sch 33.

Modification: modified by the Local Government and Housing Act 1989, s 149, Sch 7, para 4.

Rules: the Landlord and Tenant (Determination of Rateable Value Procedure) Rules 1954, SI 1954/1255.

Order: the Landlord and Tenant Act 1954 (Appropriate Multiplier) Order 1990, SI 1990/363.

[37A Compensation for possession obtained by misrepresentation

(1) Where the court—

(a) makes an order for the termination of the current tenancy but does not make an order for the grant of a new tenancy, or

(b) refuses an order for the grant of a new tenancy,

and it subsequently made to appear to the court that the order was obtained, or the court was induced to refuse the grant, by misrepresentation or the concealment of material facts, the court may order the landlord to pay to the tenant such sum as appears sufficient as compensation for damage or loss sustained by the tenant as the result of the order or refusal.

(2) Where—

(a) the tenant has quit the holding—

  (i) after making but withdrawing an application under section 24(1) of this Act; or

  (ii) without making such an application; and

(b) it is made to appear to the court that he did so by reason of misrepresentation or the concealment of material facts,

the court may order the landlord to pay to the tenant such sum as appears sufficient as compensation for damage or loss sustained by the tenant as the result of quitting the holding.]

[569]

NOTES

Inserted by SI 2003/3096, arts 2, 20, except where the tenant quit the holding before 1 June 2004.

38 Restriction on agreements excluding provisions of Part II

(1) Any agreement relating to a tenancy to which this Part of this Act applies (whether contained in the instrument creating the tenancy or not) shall be void [(except as provided by [section 38A of this Act])] in so far as it purports to preclude the tenant from making an application or request under this Part of this Act or provides for the termination or the surrender of the tenancy in the event of his making such an application or request or for the imposition of any penalty or disability on the tenant in that event.

(2) Where—

(a) during the whole of the five years immediately preceding the date on which the tenant under a tenancy to which this Part of this Act applies is to quit the holding, premises being or comprised in the holding have been occupied for the purposes of a business carried on by the occupier or for those and other purposes, and

(b) if during those five years there was a change in the occupier of the premises, the person who was the occupier immediately after the change was the successor to the business carried on by the person who was the occupier immediately before the change,

any agreement (whether contained in the instrument creating the tenancy or not and whether made before or after the termination of that tenancy) which purports to exclude or reduce compensation under [section 37 of this Act] shall to that extent be void, so however that this subsection shall not affect any agreement as to the amount of any such compensation which is made after the right to compensation has accrued.

(3) In a case not falling within the last foregoing subsection the right to compensation conferred by [section 37 of this Act] may be excluded or modified by agreement.

[(4) …]

[570]

NOTES

Sub-s (1): words in first (outer) pair of square brackets inserted by the Law of Property Act 1969, s 5; words in second (inner) pair of square brackets substituted by SI 2003/3096, arts 2, 21(1).

Sub-ss (2), (3): words in square brackets substituted by SI 2003/3096, art 28(1), Sch 5, paras 1, 4.

Sub-s (4): inserted by the Law of Property Act 1969, s 5; repealed by SI 2003/3096, arts 2, 21(2), 28(2), Sch 6, subject to transitional provisions in art 29(2)–(4) thereof.

[38A Agreements to exclude provisions of Part 2

(1) The persons who will be the landlord and the tenant in relation to a tenancy to be granted for a term of years certain which will be a tenancy to which this Part of this Act applies may agree that the provisions of sections 24 to 28 of this Act shall be excluded in relation to that tenancy.

(2) The persons who are the landlord and the tenant in relation to a tenancy to which this Part of this Act applies may agree that the tenancy shall be surrendered on such date or in such circumstances as may be specified in the agreement and on such terms (if any) as may be so specified.

(3) An agreement under subsection (1) above shall be void unless—

(a) the landlord has served on the tenant a notice in the form, or substantially in the form, set out in Schedule 1 to the Regulatory Reform (Business Tenancies) (England and Wales) Order 2003 ("the 2003 Order"); and

(b) the requirements specified in Schedule 2 to that Order are met.

(4) An agreement under subsection (2) above shall be void unless—

(a) the landlord has served on the tenant a notice in the form, or substantially in the form, set out in Schedule 3 to the 2003 Order; and

(b) the requirements specified in Schedule 4 to that Order are met.]

[571]

NOTES

Inserted by SI 2003/3096, arts 2, 22(1).

General and supplementary provisions

39 Saving for compulsory acquisitions

(1) …

(2) If the amount of the compensation which would have been payable under section thirty-seven of this Act if the tenancy had come to an end in circumstances giving rise to compensation under that section and the date at which the acquiring authority obtained possession had been the termination of the current tenancy exceeds the amount of [the compensation payable under section 121 of the Lands Clauses Consolidation Act 1845 or section 20 of the Compulsory Purchase Act 1965 in the case of a tenancy to which this Part of this Act applies], that compensation shall be increased by the amount of the excess.

(3) Nothing in section twenty-four of this Act shall affect the operation of the said section one hundred and twenty-one.

[572]

NOTES

Sub-s (1): repealed by the Land Compensation Act 1973, ss 47, 86, Sch 3.

Sub-s (2): words in square brackets substituted by the Land Compensation Act 1973, ss 47, 86, Sch 3.

[40 Duties of tenants and landlords of business premises to give information to each other

(1) Where a person who is an owner of an interest in reversion expectant (whether immediately or not) on a tenancy of any business premises has served on the tenant a notice in the prescribed form requiring him to do so, it shall be the duty of the tenant to give the appropriate person in writing the information specified in subsection (2) below.

(2) That information is—

(a) whether the tenant occupies the premises or any part of them wholly or partly for the purposes of a business carried on by him;

(b) whether his tenancy has effect subject to any sub-tenancy on which his tenancy is immediately expectant and, if so—

(i) what premises are comprised in the sub-tenancy;

(ii) for what term it has effect (or, if it is terminable by notice, by what notice it can be terminated);

(iii) what is the rent payable under it;

(iv) who is the sub-tenant;

(v) (to the best of his knowledge and belief) whether the sub-tenant is in occupation of the premises or of part of the premises comprised in the sub-tenancy and, if not, what is the sub-tenant's address;

(vi) whether an agreement is in force excluding in relation to the sub-tenancy the provisions of sections 24 to 28 of this Act; and

(vii) whether a notice has been given under section 25 or 26(6) of this Act, or a request has been made under section 26 of this Act, in relation to the sub-tenancy and, if so, details of the notice or request; and

(c) (to the best of his knowledge and belief) the name and address of any other person who owns an interest in reversion in any part of the premises.

(3) Where the tenant of any business premises who is a tenant under such a tenancy as is mentioned in section 26(1) of this Act has served on a reversioner or a reversioner's mortgagee in possession a notice in the prescribed form requiring him to do so, it shall be the duty of the person on whom the notice is served to give the appropriate person in writing the information specified in subsection (4) below.

(4) That information is—

(a) whether he is the owner of the fee simple in respect of the premises or any part of them or the mortgagee in possession of such an owner,

(b) if he is not, then (to the best of his knowledge and belief)—

(i) the name and address of the person who is his or, as the case may be, his mortgagor's immediate landlord in respect of those premises or of the part in respect of which he or his mortgagor is not the owner in fee simple;

(ii) for what term his or his mortgagor's tenancy has effect and what is the earliest date (if any) at which that tenancy is terminable by notice to quit given by the landlord; and

(iii) whether a notice has been given under section 25 or 26(6) of this Act, or a request has been made under section 26 of this Act, in relation to the tenancy and, if so, details of the notice or request;

(c) (to the best of his knowledge and belief) the name and address of any other person who owns an interest in reversion in any part of the premises; and

(d) if he is a reversioner, whether there is a mortgagee in possession of his interest in the premises and, if so, (to the best of his knowledge and belief) what is the name and address of the mortgagee.

(5) A duty imposed on a person by this section is a duty—

(a) to give the information concerned within the period of one month beginning with the date of service of the notice; and

(b) if within the period of six months beginning with the date of service of the notice that person becomes aware that any information which has been given in pursuance of the notice is not, or is no longer, correct, to give the appropriate person correct information within the period of one month beginning with the date on which he becomes aware.

(6) This section shall not apply to a notice served by or on the tenant more than two years before the date on which apart from this Act his tenancy would come to an end by effluxion of time or could be brought to an end by notice to quit given by the landlord.

(7) Except as provided by section 40A of this Act, the appropriate person for the purposes of this section and section 40A(1) of this Act is the person who served the notice under subsection (1) or (3) above.

(8) In this section—

"business premises" means premises used wholly or partly for the purposes of a business;

"mortgagee in possession" includes a receiver appointed by the mortgagee or by the court who is in receipt of the rents and profits, and "his mortgagor" shall be construed accordingly;

"reversioner" means any person having an interest in the premises, being an interest in reversion expectant (whether immediately or not) on the tenancy;

"reversioner's mortgagee in possession" means any person being a mortgagee in possession in respect of such an interest; and

"sub-tenant" includes a person retaining possession of any premises by virtue of the Rent (Agriculture) Act 1976 or the Rent Act 1977 after the coming to an end of a sub-tenancy, and "sub-tenancy" includes a right so to retain possession.]

[573]

NOTES

Substituted by SI 2003/3096, arts 2, 23, except in relation to a notice served before 1 June 2004.

[40A Duties in transfer cases

(1) If a person on whom a notice under section 40(1) or (3) of this Act has been served has transferred his interest in the premises or any part of them to some other person and gives the appropriate person notice in writing—

(a) of the transfer of his interest; and

(b) of the name and address of the person to whom he transferred it,

on giving the notice he ceases in relation to the premises or (as the case may be) to that part to be under any duty imposed by section 40 of this Act.

(2) If—

(a) the person who served the notice under section 40(1) or (3) of this Act ("the transferor") has transferred his interest in the premises to some other person ("the transferee"); and

(b) the transferor or the transferee has given the person required to give the information notice in writing—

(i) of the transfer; and

(ii) of the transferee's name and address,

the appropriate person for the purposes of section 40 of this Act and subsection (1) above is the transferee.

(3) If—

(a) a transfer such as is mentioned in paragraph (a) of subsection (2) above has taken place; but

(b) neither the transferor nor the transferee has given a notice such as is mentioned in paragraph (b) of that subsection,

any duty imposed by section 40 of this Act may be performed by giving the information either to the transferor or to the transferee.]

[574]

NOTES

Inserted by SI 2003/3096, arts 2, 24, except in relation to a notice served under s 40 before 1 June 2004.

[40B Proceedings for breach of duties to give information

A claim that a person has broken any duty imposed by section 40 of this Act may be made the subject of civil proceedings for breach of statutory duty; and in any such proceedings a court may order that person to comply with that duty and may make an award of damages.]

[575]

NOTES

Inserted by SI 2003/3096, arts 2, 24, except in relation to a notice served under s 40 before 1 June 2004.

41 Trusts

(1) Where a tenancy is held on trust, occupation by all or any of the beneficiaries under the trust, and the carrying on of a business by all or any of the beneficiaries, shall be treated for the purposes of section twenty-three of this Act as equivalent to occupation or the carrying on of a business by the tenant; and in relation to a tenancy to which this Part of this Act applies by virtue of the foregoing provisions of this subsection—

(a) references (however expressed) in this Part of this Act and in the Ninth Schedule to this Act to the business of, or to carrying on of business, use, occupation or enjoyment by, the tenant shall be construed as including references to the business of, or to carrying on of business, use, occupation or enjoyment by, the beneficiaries or beneficiary;

(b) the reference in paragraph (d) of [subsection (1) of] section thirty-four of this Act to the tenant shall be construed as including the beneficiaries or beneficiary; and

(c) a change in the persons of the trustees shall not be treated as a change in the person of the tenant.

(2) Where the landlord's interest is held on trust the references in paragraph (g) of subsection (1) of section thirty of this Act to the landlord shall be construed as including references to the beneficiaries under the trust or any of them; but, except in the case of a trust arising under a will or on the intestacy of any person, the reference in subsection (2) of that section to the creation of the interest therein mentioned shall be construed as including the creation of the trust.

[576]

NOTES

Sub-s (1): words in square brackets substituted by the Law of Property Act 1969, s 1(2).

[41A Partnerships

(1) The following provisions of this section shall apply where—

(a) a tenancy is held jointly by two or more persons (in this section referred to as the joint tenants); and

(b) the property comprised in the tenancy is or includes premises occupied for the purposes of a business; and

(c) the business (or some other business) was at some time during the existence of the tenancy carried on in partnership by all the persons who were then the joint tenants or by those and other persons and the joint tenants' interest in the premises was then partnership property; and

(d) the business is carried on (whether alone or in partnership with other persons) by one or some only of the joint tenants and no part of the property comprised in the tenancy is occupied, in right of the tenancy, for the purposes of a business carried on (whether alone or in partnership with other persons) by the other or others.

(2) In the following provisions of this section those of the joint tenants who for the time being carry on the business are referred to as the business tenants and the others as the other joint tenants.

(3) Any notice given by the business tenants which, had it been given by all the joint tenants, would have been—

(a) a tenant's request for a new tenancy made in accordance with section 26 of this Act; or

(b) a notice under subsection (1) or subsection (2) of section 27 of this Act;

shall be treated as such if it states that it is given by virtue of this section and sets out the facts by virtue of which the persons giving it are the business tenants; and references in those sections and in section 24A of this Act to the tenant shall be construed accordingly.

(4) A notice given by the landlord to the business tenants which, had it been given to all the joint tenants, would have been a notice under section 25 of this Act shall be treated as such a notice, and references in that section to the tenant shall be construed accordingly.

(5) An application under section 24(1) of this Act for a new tenancy may, instead of being made by all the joint tenants, be made by the business tenants alone; and where it is so made—

(a) this Part of this Act shall have effect, in relation to it, as if the references therein to the tenant included references to the business tenants alone; and

(b) the business tenants shall be liable, to the exclusion of the other joint tenants, for the payment of rent and the discharge of any other obligation under the current tenancy for any rental period beginning after the date specified in the landlord's notice under section 25 of this Act or, as the case may be, beginning on or after the date specified in their request for a new tenancy.

(6) Where the court makes an order under [section 29 of this Act for the grant of a new tenancy it may order the grant to be made to the business tenants or to them jointly] with the persons carrying on the business in partnership with them, and may order the grant to be made subject to the satisfaction, within a time specified by the order, of such conditions as to guarantors, sureties or otherwise as appear to the court equitable, having regard to the omission of the other joint tenants from the persons who will be the tenant under the new tenancy.

(7) The business tenants shall be entitled to recover any amount payable by way of compensation under section 37 or section 59 of this Act.]

[577]

NOTES

Inserted by the Law of Property Act 1969, s 9.

Sub-s (6): words in square brackets substituted by SI 2003/3096, art 28(1), Sch 5, paras 1, 5.

42 Groups of companies

(1) For the purposes of this section two bodies corporate shall be taken to be members of a group if and only if one is a subsidiary of the other or both are subsidiaries of a third body corporate [or the same person has a controlling interest in both].

…

(2) Where a tenancy is held by a member of a group, occupation by another member of the group, and the carrying on of a business by another member of the group, shall be treated for the purposes of section twenty-three of this Act as equivalent to occupation or the carrying on of a business by the member of the group holding the tenancy; and in relation to a tenancy to which this Part of this Act applies by virtue of the foregoing provisions of this subsection—

(a) references (however expressed) in this Part of this Act and in the Ninth Schedule to this Act to the business of or to use occupation or enjoyment by the tenant shall be construed as including references to the business of or to use occupation or enjoyment by the said other member;

(b) the reference in paragraph (d) of [subsection (1) of] section thirty-four of this Act to the tenant shall be construed as including the said other member; and

(c) an assignment of the tenancy from one member of the group to another shall not be treated as a change in the person of the tenant.

[(3) Where the landlord's interest is held by a member of a group—

(a) the reference in paragraph (g) of subsection (1) of section 30 of this Act to intended occupation by the landlord for the purposes of a business to be carried on by him shall be construed as including intended occupation by any member of the group for the purposes of a business to be carried on by that member; and

(b) the reference in subsection (2) of that section to the purchase or creation of any interest shall be construed as a reference to a purchase from or creation by a person other than a member of the group.]

[578]

NOTES

Sub-s (1): words in square brackets inserted and words omitted repealed by SI 2003/3096, arts 2, 16, 28(2), Sch 6.

Sub-s (2): words in square brackets in para (b) inserted by the Law of Property Act 1969, s 1(2).

Sub-s (3): inserted by the Law of Property Act 1969, s 10.

43 Tenancies excluded from Part II

(1) This Part of this Act does not apply—

(a) to a tenancy of an agricultural holding [[[which is a tenancy in relation to which the Agricultural Holdings Act 1986 applies or a tenancy which would be a tenancy of an agricultural holding in relation to which that Act applied if subsection (3) of section 2 of that Act] did not have effect or, in a case where approval was given under subsection (1) of that section], if that approval had not been given];

[(aa) to a farm business tenancy;]

(b) to a tenancy created by a mining lease;

(c), (d) …

(2) This Part of this Act does not apply to a tenancy granted by reason that the tenant was the holder of an office, appointment or employment from the grantor thereof and continuing only so long as the tenant holds the office, appointment or employment, or terminable by the grantor on the tenant's ceasing to hold it, or coming to an end at a time fixed by reference to the time at which the tenant ceases to hold it:

Provided that this subsection shall not have effect in relation to a tenancy granted after the commencement of this Act unless the tenancy was granted by an instrument in writing which expressed the purpose for which the tenancy was granted.

(3) This Part of this Act does not apply to a tenancy granted for a term certain not exceeding [six months] unless—

(a) the tenancy contains provision for renewing the term or for extending it beyond [six months] from its beginning; or

(b) the tenant has been in occupation for a period which, together with any period during which any predecessor in the carrying on of the business carried on by the tenant was in occupation, exceeds [twelve months].

[579]

NOTES

Sub-s (1): in para (a) first words in square brackets inserted by the Agriculture Act 1958, s 8(1), Sch 1, Pt I, para 29, first words in square brackets therein substituted by the Agricultural Holdings Act 1986, ss 99, 100, Sch 13, para 3, Sch 14, para 21, second words in square brackets therein substituted by the Agricultural Tenancies Act 1995, s 40, Schedule, para 10(a); para (aa) inserted by the Agricultural Tenancies Act 1995, s 40, Schedule, para 10(b); para (c) repealed by the Housing Act 1980, s 152, Sch 26; para (d) repealed by the Landlord and Tenant (Licensed Premises) Act 1990, ss 1, 2.

Sub-s (3): words in square brackets substituted by the Law of Property Act 1969, s 12.

[43A Jurisdiction of county court to make declaration

Where the rateable value of the holding is such that the jurisdiction conferred on the court by any other provision of this Part of this Act is, by virtue of section 63 of this Act, exercisable by the county court, the county court shall have jurisdiction (but without prejudice to the jurisdiction of the High Court) to make any declaration as to any matter arising under this Part of this Act, whether or not any other relief is sought in the proceedings.]

[580]

NOTES

Inserted by the Law of Property Act 1969, s 13.

44 Meaning of "the landlord" in Part II, and provisions as to mesne landlords, etc

(1) Subject to [subsections (1A) and (2) below,] in this Part of this Act the expression "the landlord", in relation to a tenancy (in this section referred to as "the relevant tenancy"), means the person (whether or not he is the immediate landlord) who is the owner of that interest in the property comprised in the relevant tenancy which for the time being fulfils the following conditions, that is to say—

(a) that it is an interest in reversion expectant (whether immediately or not) on the termination of the relevant tenancy, and

[(b) that it is either the fee simple or a tenancy which will not come to an end within fourteen months by effluxion of time and, if it is such a tenancy, that no notice has been given by virtue of which it will come to an end within fourteen months or any further time by which it may be continued under section 36(2) or section 64 of this Act],

and is not itself in reversion expectant (whether immediately or not) on an interest which fulfils those conditions.

[(1A) The reference in subsection (1) above to a person who is the owner of an interest such as is mentioned in that subsection is to be construed, where different persons own such interests in different parts of the property, as a reference to all those persons collectively.]

(2) References in this Part of this Act to a notice to quit given by the landlord are references to a notice to quit given by the immediate landlord.

(3) The provisions of the Sixth Schedule to this Act shall have effect for the application of this Part of this Act to cases where the immediate landlord of the tenant is not the owner of the fee simple in respect of the holding.

[581]

NOTES

Sub-s (1): first words in square brackets substituted by SI 2003/3096, arts 2, 27(1); para (b) substituted by the Law of Property Act 1969, s 14(1).

Sub-s (1A): inserted by SI 2003/3096, arts 2, 27(2).

45 (*Repealed by the Statute Law (Repeals) Act 1974, s 1, Schedule, Pt XI.*)

46 Interpretation of Part II

[(1)] In this Part of this Act:—

"business" has the meaning assigned to it by subsection (2) of section twenty-three of this Act;

["current tenancy" means the tenancy under which the tenant holds for the time being;]

"date of termination" has the meaning assigned to it by subsection (1) of section twenty-five of this Act;

subject to the provisions of section thirty-two of this Act, "the holding" has the meaning assigned to it by subsection (3) of section twenty-three of this Act;

["interim rent" has the meaning given by section 24A(1) of this Act;]

"mining lease" has the same meaning as in the Landlord and Tenant Act 1927.

[(2) For the purposes of this Part of this Act, a person has a controlling interest in a company, if, had he been a company, the other company would have been its subsidiary; and in this Part—

"company" has the meaning given by *section 735 of the Companies Act 1985* [section 1(1) of the Companies Act 2006]; and

"subsidiary" has the meaning given by *section 736 of that Act* [section 1159 of that Act].]

[582]

NOTES

Sub-s (1): existing provision numbered as such, definition "current tenancy" substituted and definition "interim rent" inserted by SI 2003/3096, arts 2, 17(1), 28(1), Sch 5, paras 1, 6.

Sub-s (2): inserted by SI 2003/3096, arts 2, 17(2); words in italics substituted for subsequent words in square brackets by SI 2009/1941, art 2(1), Sch 1, para 4, as from 1 October 2009

47–50 (*(Pt III) outside the scope of this work.*)

PART IV
MISCELLANEOUS AND SUPPLEMENTARY

51 Extension of Leasehold Property (Repairs) Act 1938

(1) The Leasehold Property (Repairs) Act 1938 (which restricts the enforcement of repairing covenants in long leases of small houses) shall extend to every tenancy (whether of a house or of other property, and without regard to rateable value) where the following conditions are fulfilled, that is to say,—

(a) that the tenancy was granted for a term of years certain of not less than seven years;
(b) that three years or more of the term remain unexpired at the date of the service of the notice of dilapidations or, as the case may be, at the date of commencement of the action for damages; and
[(c) that the tenancy is neither a tenancy of an agricultural holding in relation to which the Agricultural Holdings Act 1986 applies nor a farm business tenancy].

(2) …

(3) The said Act of 1938 shall apply where there is an interest belonging to Her Majesty in right of the Crown or to a Government department, or held on behalf of Her Majesty for the purposes of a Government department, in like manner as if that interest were an interest not so belonging or held.

(4) Subsection (2) of section twenty-three of the Landlord and Tenant Act 1927 (which authorises a tenant to serve documents on the person to whom he has been paying rent) shall apply in relation to any counter-notice to be served under the said Act of 1938.

(5) This section shall apply to tenancies granted, and to breaches occurring, before or after the commencement of this Act, except that it shall not apply where the notice of dilapidations was served, or the action for damages begun, before the commencement of this Act.

(6) In this section the expression "notice of dilapidations" means a notice under subsection (1) of section one hundred and forty-six of the Law of Property Act 1925.

[583]

NOTES

Sub-s (1): para (c) substituted by the Agricultural Tenancies Act 1995, s 40, Schedule, para 11.
Sub-s (2): amends the Leasehold Property (Repairs) Act 1938, ss 1, 3, 7 at **[537]**, **[539]**, **[542]**.

52 (*Outside the scope of this work.*)

53 Jurisdiction of county court where lessor refuses licence or consent

(1) Where a landlord withholds his licence or consent—

(a) to an assignment of the tenancy or a sub-letting, charging or parting with the possession of the demised property or any part thereof, or
(b) to the making of an improvement on the demised property or any part thereof, or
(c) to a change in the use of the demised property or any part thereof, or to the making of a specified use of that property,

and the High Court has jurisdiction to make a declaration that the licence or consent was unreasonably withheld, then without prejudice to the jurisdiction of the High Court the county court shall have [the like jurisdiction whatever the net annual value for rating of the demised property is to be taken to be for the purposes of the County Courts Act 1984] and notwithstanding that the tenant does not seek any relief other than the declaration.

(2) Where on the making of an application to the county court for such a declaration the court is satisfied that the licence or consent was unreasonably withheld, the court shall make a declaration accordingly.

(3) The foregoing provisions of this section shall have effect whether the tenancy in question was created before or after the commencement of this Act and whether the refusal of the licence or consent occurred before or after the commencement of this Act.

(4) Nothing in this section shall be construed as conferring jurisdiction on the county court to grant any relief other than such a declaration as aforesaid.

[584]

NOTES

Sub-s (1): words in square brackets substituted by the County Courts Act 1984, s 148(1), Sch 2, para 23.

54 Determination of tenancies of derelict land

Where a landlord, having power to serve a notice to quit, on an application to the county court satisfies the court—

(a) that he has taken all reasonable steps to communicate with the person last known to him to be the tenant, and has failed to do so,

(b) that during the period of six months ending with the date of the application neither the tenant nor any person claiming under him has been in occupation of the property comprised in the tenancy or any part thereof, and

(c) that during the said period either no rent was payable by the tenant or the rent payable has not been paid,

the court may if it thinks fit by order determine the tenancy as from the date of the order.

[585]

55–62 *(S 55 repealed by SI 2003/3096, art 28(2), Sch 6, subject to transitional provisions in art 29(1), (2) thereof; ss 56–60, 60A outside the scope of this work; s 60B repealed, subject to transitional provisions, by the Government of Wales Act 1998, ss 131, 152, Sch 18, Pt IV; s 61 repealed by the Endowments and Glebe Measure 1976, s 47(4), Sch 8; s 62 repealed by the House of Commons Disqualification Act 1957, s 14(1), Sch 4, Pt I and the Industrial Expansion Act 1968, s 18(2), Sch 4.)*

63 Jurisdiction of court for purposes of Parts I and II and of Part I of Landlord and Tenant Act 1927

(1) Any jurisdiction conferred on the court by any provision of Part I of this Act shall be exercised by the county court.

(2) Any jurisdiction conferred on the court by any provision of Part II of this Act or conferred on the tribunal by Part I of the Landlord and Tenant Act 1927, shall, subject to the provisions of this section, be exercised [by the High Court or a County Court].

(3) …

(4) The following provisions shall have effect as respects transfer of proceedings from or to the High Court or the county court, that is to say—

(a) where an application is made to the one but by virtue of [an Order under section 1 of the Courts and Legal Services Act 1990] cannot be entertained except by the other, the application shall not be treated as improperly made but any proceedings thereon shall be transferred to the other court;

(b) any proceedings under the provisions of Part II of this Act or of Part I of the Landlord and Tenant Act 1927, which are pending before one of those courts may by order of that court made on the application of any person interested be transferred to the other court, if it appears to the court making the order that it is desirable that the proceedings and any proceedings before the other court should both be entertained by the other court.

(5) In any proceedings where in accordance with the foregoing provisions of this section the county court exercises jurisdiction the powers of the judge of summoning one or more assessors under subsection (1) of section eighty-eight of the County Courts Act 1934 may be exercised notwithstanding that no application is made in that behalf by any party to the proceedings.

(6) Where in any such proceedings an assessor is summoned by a judge under the said subsection (1),—

(a) he may, if so directed by the judge, inspect the land to which the proceedings relate without the judge and report to the judge in writing thereon;

(b) the judge may on consideration of the report and any observations of the parties thereon give such judgment or make such order in the proceedings as may be just;

(c) the remuneration of the assessor shall be at such rate as may be determined by the Lord Chancellor with the approval of the Treasury and shall be defrayed out of moneys provided by Parliament.

(7) In this section the expression "the holding"—

(a) in relation to proceedings under Part II of this Act, has the meaning assigned to it by subsection (3) of section twenty-three of this Act,

(b) in relation to proceedings under Part I of the Landlord and Tenant Act 1927, has the same meaning as in the said Part I.

(8) …

(9) Nothing in this section shall prejudice the operation of [section 41 of the County Courts Act 1984] (which relates to the removal into the High Court of proceedings commenced in a county court).

(10) …

[586]

NOTES

Sub-ss (2), (4), (9): words in square brackets substituted by SI 1991/724, art 2(1)(d), (8), Schedule, Pt I.
Sub-ss (3), (8): repealed by SI 1991/724, art 2(1)(d), (8), Schedule, Pt I.
Sub-s (10): substitutes the Landlord and Tenant Act 1927, s 21.

64 Interim continuation of tenancies pending determination by court

(1) In any case where—

(a) a notice to terminate a tenancy has been given under Part I or Part II of this Act or a request for a new tenancy has been made under Part II thereof, and

(b) an application to the court has been made under the said Part I or [under section 24(1) or 29(2) of this Act], as the case may be, and

(c) apart from this section the effect of the notice or request would be to terminate the tenancy before the expiration of the period of three months beginning with the date on which the application is finally disposed of,

the effect of the notice or request shall be to terminate the tenancy at the expiration of the said period of three months and not at any other time.

(2) The reference in paragraph (c) of subsection (1) of this section to the date on which an application is finally disposed of shall be construed as a reference to the earliest date by which the proceedings on the application (including any proceedings on or in consequence of an appeal) have been determined and any time for appealing or further appealing has expired, except that if the application is withdrawn or any appeal is abandoned the reference shall be construed as a reference to the date of the withdrawal or abandonment.

[587]

NOTES

Sub-s (1): words in square brackets in para (b) substituted by SI 2003/3096, art 28(1), Sch 5, paras 1, 9.

65 Provisions as to reversions

(1) Where by virtue of any provision of this Act a tenancy (in this subsection referred to as "the inferior tenancy") is continued for a period such as to extend to or beyond the end of the term of a superior tenancy, the superior tenancy shall, for the purposes of this Act and of any other enactment and of any rule of law, be deemed so long as it subsists to be an interest in reversion expectant upon the termination of the inferior tenancy and, if there is no intermediate tenancy, to be the interest in reversion immediately expectant upon the termination thereof.

(2) In the case of a tenancy continuing by virtue of any provision of this Act after the coming to an end of the interest in reversion immediately expectant upon the termination thereof, subsection (1) of section one hundred and thirty-nine of the Law of Property Act 1925 (which relates to the effect of the extinguishment of a reversion) shall apply as if references in the said subsection (1) to the surrender or merger of the reversion included references to the coming to an end of the reversion for any reason other than surrender or merger.

(3) Where by virtue of any provision of this Act a tenancy (in this subsection referred to as "the continuing tenancy") is continued beyond the beginning of a reversionary tenancy which was granted (whether before or after the commencement of this Act) so as to begin on or after the date on which apart from this Act the continuing tenancy would have come to an end, the reversionary tenancy shall have effect as if it had been granted subject to the continuing tenancy.

(4) Where by virtue of any provision of this Act a tenancy (in this subsection referred to as "the new tenancy") is granted for a period beginning on the same date as a reversionary tenancy or for a period such as to extend beyond the beginning of the term of a reversionary tenancy, whether the reversionary tenancy in question was granted before or after the commencement of this Act, the reversionary tenancy shall have effect as if it had been granted subject to the new tenancy.

[588]

66 Provisions as to notices

(1) Any form of notice required by this Act to be prescribed shall be prescribed by regulations made by [the Secretary of State] by statutory instrument.

(2) Where the form of a notice to be served on persons of any description is to be prescribed for any of the purposes of this Act, the form to be prescribed shall include such an explanation of the relevant provisions of this Act as appears to [the Secretary of State] requisite for informing persons of that description of their rights and obligations under those provisions.

(3) Different forms of notice may be prescribed for the purposes of the operation of any provision of this Act in relation to different cases.

(4) Section twenty-three of the Landlord and Tenant Act 1927 (which relates to the service of notices) shall apply for the purposes of this Act.

(5) Any statutory instrument under this section shall be subject to annulment in pursuance of a resolution of either House of Parliament.

[589]

NOTES

Sub-ss (1), (2): words in square brackets substituted by SI 1974/1896, arts 2, 3(2).

Regulations: the Landlord and Tenant (Notices) Regulations 1957, SI 1957/1157; the Landlord and Tenant Act 1954, Part II (Assured Tenancies) (Notices) Regulations 1986, SI 1986/2181; the Leasehold Reform (Notices) Regulations 1997, SI 1997/640; the Long Residential Tenancies (Supplemental Forms) Regulations 1997, SI 1997/3005; the Landlord and Tenant Act 1954, Part 2 (Notices) Regulations 2004, SI 2004/1005 at **[3421]**.

67 Provisions as to mortgagees in possession

Anything authorised or required by the provisions of this Act, other than subsection … (3) of section forty, to be done at any time by, to or with the landlord, or a landlord of a specified description, shall, if at that time the interest of the landlord in question is subject to a mortgage and the mortgagee is in possession or a receiver appointed by the mortgagee or by the court is in receipt of the rents and profits, be deemed to be authorised or required to be done by, to or with the mortgagee instead of that landlord.

[590]

NOTES

Words omitted repealed by SI 2003/3096, art 28(2), Sch 6, subject to transitional provisions in art 29(6) thereof.

68 (*Outside the scope of this work.*)

69 Interpretation

(1) In this Act the following expressions have the meanings hereby assigned to them respectively, that is to say—

"agricultural holding" has the same meaning as in the [Agricultural Holdings Act 1986];

"development corporation" has the same meaning as in the New Towns Act 1946;

["farm business tenancy" has the same meaning as in the Agricultural Tenancies Act 1995;]

"local authority" [means any local authority within the meaning of the Town and Country Planning Act 1990, any National Park authority, [an authority established for an area in England by an order under section 207 of the Local Government and Public Involvement in Health Act 2007 (joint waste authorities),] the Broads Authority[, the London Fire and Emergency Planning Authority] or] [… a joint authority established by Part IV of the Local Government Act 1985];

"mortgage" includes a charge or lien and "mortgagor" and "mortgagee" shall be construed accordingly;

"notice to quit" means a notice to terminate a tenancy (whether a periodical tenancy or a tenancy for a term of years certain) given in accordance with the provisions (whether express or implied) of that tenancy;

"repairs" includes any work of maintenance, decoration or restoration, and references to repairing, to keeping or yielding up in repair and to state of repair shall be construed accordingly;

"statutory undertakers" has the same meaning as in the Town and Country Planning Act 1947 …;

"tenancy" means a tenancy created either immediately or derivatively out of the freehold, whether by a lease or underlease, by an agreement for a lease or underlease or by a tenancy agreement or in pursuance of any enactment (including this Act), but does not include a mortgage term or any interest arising in favour of a mortgagor by his attorning tenant to his mortgagee, and references to the granting of a tenancy and to demised property shall be construed accordingly;

"terms", in relation to a tenancy, includes conditions.

(2) References in this Act to an agreement between the landlord and the tenant (except in section seventeen and subsections (1) and (2) of section thirty-eight thereof) shall be construed as references to an agreement in writing between them.

(3) References in this Act to an action for any relief shall be construed as including references to a claim for that relief by way of counterclaim in any proceedings.

[591]

NOTES

Sub-s (1): words in square brackets in definition "agricultural holding" substituted by the Agricultural Holdings Act 1986, s 100, Sch 14, para 22; definition "farm business tenancy" inserted by the Agricultural Tenancies Act 1995, s 40, Schedule, para 12; in definition "local authority", words in first (outer) pair of square brackets substituted by the Environment Act 1995, s 78, Sch 10, para 3, words from "an authority established" to "(joint waste authorities)," in second (inner) pair of square brackets inserted by the Local Government and Public Involvement in Health Act 2007, s 209(2), Sch 13, Pt 2, para 25, words in third (inner) pair of square brackets inserted by the Greater London Authority Act 1999, s 328, Sch 29, Pt I, para 1, words in fourth pair of square brackets inserted by the Local Government Act 1985, s 84, Sch 14, Pt II, para 36, and words omitted repealed by the Education Reform Act 1988, s 237(2), Sch 13, Pt I; words omitted from definition "statutory undertakers" repealed by the Coal Industry Act 1994, s 67(1), (8), Sch 9, para 5, Sch 11, Pt II.

Modifications: by virtue of the Waste Regulation and Disposal (Authorities) Order 1985, SI 1985/1884, art 10, Sch 3, the reference to a "joint authority" in the definition "local authority" includes references to a waste regulation or disposal authority established in that Order; the body corporate known as the Residuary Body for Wales is to be treated as a local authority for the purposes of this Act by virtue of the Local Government (Wales) Act 1994, Sch 13, para 20(a); the body corporate known as the Local Government Residuary Body (England) is to be treated as a local authority for the purposes of this Act by virtue of the Local Government Residuary Body (England) Order 1995, SI 1995/401, Schedule, para 2(a).

70 Short title and citation, commencement and extent

(1) This Act may be cited as the Landlord and Tenant Act 1954, and the Landlord and Tenant Act 1927, and this Act may be cited together as the Landlord and Tenant Acts 1927 and 1954.

(2) This Act shall come into operation on the first day of October, nineteen hundred and fifty-four.

(3) This Act shall not extend to Scotland or to Northern Ireland.

[592]

(*Schs 1–5 outside the scope of this work.*)

SCHEDULE 6
PROVISIONS FOR PURPOSES OF PART II WHERE IMMEDIATE LANDLORD IS NOT THE FREEHOLDER

Section 44

Definitions

1. In this Schedule the following expressions have the meanings hereby assigned to them in relation to a tenancy (in this Schedule referred to as "the relevant tenancy"), that is to say:—

"the competent landlord" means the person who in relation to the tenancy is for the time being the landlord (as defined by section forty-four of this Act) for the purposes of Part II of this Act;

"mesne landlord" means a tenant whose interest is intermediate between the relevant tenancy and the interest of the competent landlord; and

"superior landlord" means a person (whether the owner of the fee simple or a tenant) whose interest is superior to the interest of the competent landlord.

Power of court to order reversionary tenancies

2. Where the period for which in accordance with the provisions of Part II of this Act it is agreed or determined by the court that a new tenancy should be granted thereunder will extend beyond the date on which the interest of the immediate landlord will come to an end, the power of the court under Part II of this Act to order such a grant shall include power to order the grant of a new tenancy until the expiration of that interest and also to order the grant of such a reversionary tenancy or reversionary tenancies as may be required to secure that the combined effects of those grants will be equivalent to the grant of a tenancy for that period; and the provisions of Part II of this Act shall, subject to the necessary modifications, apply in relation to the grant of a tenancy together with one or more reversionary tenancies as they apply in relation to the grant of one new tenancy.

Acts of competent landlord binding on other landlords

3.—(1) Any notice given by the competent landlord under Part II of this Act to terminate the relevant tenancy, and any agreement made between that landlord and the tenant as to the granting, duration, or terms of a future tenancy, being an agreement made for the purposes of the said Part II, shall bind the interest of any mesne landlord notwithstanding that he has not consented to the giving of the notice or was not a party to the agreement.

(2) The competent landlord shall have power for the purposes of Part II of this Act to give effect to any agreement with the tenant for the grant of a new tenancy beginning with the coming to an end of the relevant tenancy notwithstanding that the competent landlord will not be the immediate landlord at the commencement of the new tenancy, and any instrument made in the exercise of the power conferred by this sub-paragraph shall have effect as if the mesne landlord had been a party thereto.

(3) Nothing in the foregoing provisions of this paragraph shall prejudice the provisions of the next following paragraph.

Provisions as to consent of mesne landlord to acts of competent landlord

4.—(1) If the competent landlord, not being the immediate landlord, gives any such notice or makes any such agreement as is mentioned in sub-paragraph (1) of the last foregoing paragraph without the consent of every mesne landlord, any mesne landlord whose consent has not been given thereto shall be entitled to compensation from the competent landlord for any loss arising in consequence of the giving of the notice or the making of the agreement.

(2) If the competent landlord applies to any mesne landlord for his consent to such a notice or agreement, that consent shall not be unreasonably withheld, but may be given subject to any conditions which may be reasonable (including conditions as to the modification of the proposed notice or agreement or as to the payment of compensation by the competent landlord).

(3) Any question arising under this paragraph whether consent has been unreasonably withheld or whether any conditions imposed on the giving of consent are unreasonable shall be determined by the court.

Consent of superior landlord required for agreements affecting his interest

5. An agreement between the competent landlord and the tenant made for the purposes of Part II of this Act in a case where—

(a) the competent landlord is himself a tenant, and

(b) the agreement would apart from this paragraph operate as respects any period after the coming to an end of the interest of the competent landlord,

shall not have effect unless every superior landlord who will be the immediate landlord of the tenant during any part of that period is a party to the agreement.

[Withdrawal by competent landlord of notice given by mesne landlord

6. Where the competent landlord has given a notice under section 25 of this Act to terminate the relevant tenancy and, within two months after the giving of the notice, a superior landlord—

(a) becomes the competent landlord; and

(b) gives to the tenant notice in the prescribed form that he withdraws the notice previously given,

the notice under section 25 of this Act shall cease to have effect, but without prejudice to the giving of a further notice under that section by the competent landlord.

Duty to inform superior landlords

7. If the competent landlord's interest in the property comprised in the relevant tenancy is a tenancy which will come or can be brought to an end within sixteen months (or any further time by which it may be continued under section 36(2) or section 64 of this Act) and he gives to the tenant under the relevant tenancy a notice under section 25 of this Act to terminate the tenancy or is given by him a notice under section 26(3) of this Act:—

(a) the competent landlord shall forthwith send a copy of the notice to his immediate landlord; and

(b) any superior landlord whose interest in the property is a tenancy shall forthwith send to his immediate landlord any copy which has been sent to him in pursuance of the preceding sub-paragraph or this sub-paragraph.]

[593]

NOTES

Paras 6, 7: inserted by the Law of Property Act 1969, s 14(2).

(*Sch 7 repealed by the Statute Law (Repeals) Act 1974; Schs 8, 9 outside the scope of this work.*)

OCCUPIERS' LIABILITY ACT 1957

(1957 c 31)

An Act to amend the law of England and Wales as to the liability of occupiers and others for injury or damage resulting to persons or goods lawfully on any land or other property from dangers due to the state of the property or to things done or omitted to be done there, to make provision as to the operation in relation to the Crown of laws made by the Parliament of Northern Ireland for similar purposes or otherwise amending the law of tort, and for purposes connected therewith

[6 June 1957]

Liability in tort

1 Preliminary

(1) The rules enacted by the two next following sections shall have effect, in place of the rules of the common law, to regulate the duty which an occupier of premises owes to his visitors in respect of dangers due to the state of the premises or to things done or omitted to be done on them.

(2) The rules so enacted shall regulate the nature of the duty imposed by law in consequence of a person's occupation or control of premises and of any invitation or permission he gives (or is to be treated as giving) to another to enter or use the premises, but they shall not alter the rules of the common law as to the persons on whom a duty is so imposed or to whom it is owed; and accordingly for the purpose of the rules so enacted the persons who are to be treated as an occupier and as his visitors are the same (subject to subsection (4) of this section) as the persons who would at common law be treated as an occupier and as his invitees or licensees.

(3) The rules so enacted in relation to an occupier of premises and his visitors shall also apply, in like manner and to the like extent as the principles applicable at common law to an occupier of premises and his invitees or licensees would apply, to regulate—

(a) the obligations of a person occupying or having control over any fixed or moveable structure, including any vessel, vehicle or aircraft; and

(b) the obligations of a person occupying or having control over any premises or structure in respect of damage to property, including the property of persons who are not themselves his visitors.

[(4) A person entering any premises in exercise of rights conferred by virtue of—

(a) section 2(1) of the Countryside and Rights of Way Act 2000, or

(b) an access agreement or order under the National Parks and Access to the Countryside Act 1949,

is not, for the purposes of this Act, a visitor of the occupier of the premises.]

[594]

NOTES

Sub-s (4): substituted by the Countryside and Rights of Way Act 2000, s 13(1).

2 Extent of occupier's ordinary duty

(1) An occupier of premises owes the same duty, the "common duty of care", to all his visitors, except in so far as he is free to and does extend, restrict, modify or exclude his duty to any visitor or visitors by agreement or otherwise.

(2) The common duty of care is a duty to take such care as in all the circumstances of the case is reasonable to see that the visitor will be reasonably safe in using the premises for the purposes for which he is invited or permitted by the occupier to be there.

(3) The circumstances relevant for the present purpose include the degree of care, and of want of care, which would ordinarily be looked for in such a visitor, so that (for example) in proper cases—

(a) an occupier must be prepared for children to be less careful than adults; and

(b) an occupier may expect that a person, in the exercise of his calling, will appreciate and guard against any special risks ordinarily incident to it, so far as the occupier leaves him free to do so.

(4) In determining whether the occupier of premises has discharged the common duty of care to a visitor, regard is to be had to all the circumstances, so that (for example)—

(a) where damage is caused to a visitor by a danger of which he had been warned by the occupier, the warning is not to be treated without more as absolving the occupier from liability, unless in all the circumstances it was enough to enable the visitor to be reasonably safe; and

(b) where damage is caused to a visitor by a danger due to the faulty execution of any work of construction, maintenance or repair by an independent contractor employed by the occupier, the occupier is not to be treated without more as answerable for the danger if in all the circumstances he had acted reasonably in entrusting the work to an independent contractor and had taken such steps (if any) as he reasonably ought in order to satisfy himself that the contractor was competent and that the work had been properly done.

(5) The common duty of care does not impose on an occupier any obligation to a visitor in respect of risks willingly accepted as his by the visitor (the question whether a risk was so accepted to be decided on the same principles as in other cases in which one person owes a duty of care to another).

(6) For the purposes of this section, persons who enter premises for any purpose in the exercise of a right conferred by law are to be treated as permitted by the occupier to be there for that purpose, whether they in fact have his permission or not.

[595]

3 Effect of contract on occupier's liability to third party

(1) Where an occupier of premises is bound by contract to permit persons who are strangers to the contract to enter or use the premises, the duty of care which he owes to them as his visitors cannot be restricted or excluded by that contract, but (subject to any provision of the contract to the contrary) shall include the duty to perform his obligations under the contract, whether undertaken for their protection or not, in so far as those obligations go beyond the obligations otherwise involved in that duty.

(2) A contract shall not by virtue of this section have the effect, unless it expressly so provides, of making an occupier who has taken all reasonable care answerable to strangers to the contract for dangers due to the faulty execution of any work of construction, maintenance or repair or other like operation by persons other than himself, his servants and persons acting under his direction and control.

(3) In this section "stranger to the contract" means a person not for the time being entitled to the benefit of the contract as a party to it or as the successor by assignment or otherwise of a party to it or as the successor by assignment or otherwise of a party to it, and accordingly includes a party to the contract who has ceased to be so entitled.

(4) Where by the terms or conditions governing any tenancy (including a statutory tenancy which does not in law amount to a tenancy) either the landlord or the tenant is bound, though not by contract, to permit persons to enter or use premises of which he is the occupier, this section shall apply as if the tenancy were a contract between the landlord and the tenant.

(5) This section, in so far as it prevents the common duty of care from being restricted or excluded, applies to contracts entered into and tenancies created before the commencement of this Act, as well as to those entered into or created after its commencement; but, in so far as it enlarges the duty owed by an occupier beyond the common duty of care, it shall have effect only in relation to obligations which are undertaken after that commencement or which are renewed by agreement (whether express or implied) after that commencement.

[596]

4 (*Repealed by the Defective Premises Act 1972, s 6(4).*)

Liability in contract

5 Implied term in contracts

(1) Where persons enter or use, or bring or send goods to, any premises in exercise of a right conferred by contract with a person occupying or having control of the premises, the duty he owes them in respect of dangers due to the state of the premises or to things done or omitted to be done on them, in so far as the duty depends on a term to be implied in the contract by reason of its conferring that right, shall be the common duty of care.

(2) The foregoing subsection shall apply to fixed and moveable structures as it applies to premises.

(3) This section does not affect the obligations imposed on a person by or by virtue of any contract for the hire of, or for the carriage for reward of persons or goods in, any vehicle, vessel, aircraft or other means of transport, or by or by virtue of any contract of bailment.

(4) This section does not apply to contracts entered into before the commencement of this Act.

[597]

General

6, 7 (*Outside the scope of this work.*)

8 Short title etc

(1) This Act may be cited as the Occupiers' Liability Act 1957.

(2) This Act shall not extend to Scotland, nor to Northern Ireland except in so far as it extends the powers of the Parliament of Northern Ireland.

(3) This Act shall come into force on the first day of January, nineteen hundred and fifty-eight.

[598]

RECREATIONAL CHARITIES ACT 1958

(1958 c 17)

An Act to declare charitable under the law of England and Wales the provision in the interests of social welfare of facilities for recreation or other leisure-time occupation, to make similar provision as to certain trusts heretofore established for carrying out social welfare activities within the meaning of the Miners' Welfare Act 1952, to enable laws for corresponding purposes to be passed by the Parliament of Northern Ireland, and for purposes connected therewith

[13 March 1958]

1 General provision as to recreational and similar trusts, etc

(1) Subject to the provisions of this Act, it shall be and be deemed always to have been charitable to provide, or assist in the provision of, facilities for recreation or other leisure-time occupation, if the facilities are provided in the interests of social welfare:

Provided that nothing in this section shall be taken to derogate from the principle that a trust or institution to be charitable must be for the public benefit.

[(2) The requirement in subsection (1) that the facilities are provided in the interests of social welfare cannot be satisfied if the basic conditions are not met.

(2A) The basic conditions are—

(a) that the facilities are provided with the object of improving the conditions of life for the persons for whom the facilities are primarily intended; and

(b) that either—

(i) those persons have need of the facilities by reason of their youth, age, infirmity or disability, poverty, or social and economic circumstances, or

(ii) the facilities are to be available to members of the public at large or to male, or to female, members of the public at large.]

(3) Subject to the said requirement, subsection (1) of this section applies in particular to the provision of facilities at village halls, community centres and women's institutes, and to the provision and maintenance of grounds and buildings to be used for purposes of recreation or leisure-time occupation, and extends to the provision of facilities for those purposes by the organising of any activity.

[599]

NOTES

Sub-ss (2), (2A): substituted for original sub-s (2) by the Charities Act 2006, s 5(1), (2).

2–5 (*Ss 2, 3, 5 outside the scope of this work; s 4 repealed by the Northern Ireland Constitution Act 1973, s 41(1), Sch 6, Pt I.*)

6 Short title and extent

(1) This Act may be cited as the Recreational Charities Act 1958.

[(2) Section 1 of this Act, as amended by section 5 of the Charities Act 2006, has the same effect in relation to the law of Scotland or Northern Ireland as section 5 of that Act has by virtue of section 80(3) to (6) of that Act.

(3) Sections 1 and 2 of this Act, as in force before the commencement of section 5 of that Act, continue to have effect in relation to the law of Scotland or Northern Ireland so far as they affect the construction of any references to charities or charitable purposes which—

(a) are to be construed in accordance with the law of England and Wales, but

(b) are not contained in enactments relating to matters of the kind mentioned in section 80(4) or (6) of that Act.]

[600]

NOTES

Sub-ss (2), (3): substituted for original sub-s (2) by the Charities Act 2006, s 75(1), Sch 8, para 39.

MATRIMONIAL CAUSES (PROPERTY AND MAINTENANCE) ACT 1958

(1958 c 35)

An Act to enable the power of the court in matrimonial proceedings to order alimony, maintenance or the securing of a sum of money to be exercised at any time after a decree; to provide for the setting aside of dispositions of property made for the purpose of reducing the assets available for satisfying such an order; to enable the court after the death of a party to a marriage which has been dissolved or annulled to make provision out of his estate in favour of the other party; and to extend the powers of the court under section seventeen of the Married Women's Property Act 1882

[7 July 1958]

1–6 (*Repealed by the Matrimonial Causes Act 1965, s 45, Sch 2.*)

7 Extension of s 17 of Married Women's Property Act 1882

(1) Any right of a wife, under section seventeen of the Married Women's Property Act 1882 to apply to a judge of the High Court or of a county court, in any question between husband and wife as to the title to or possession of property, shall include the right to make such an application where it is claimed by the wife that her husband has had in his possession or under his control—

(a) money to which, or to a share of which, she was beneficially entitled (whether by reason that it represented the proceeds of property to which, or to an interest in which, she was beneficially entitled, or for any other reason), or

(b) property (other than money) to which, or to an interest in which, she was beneficially entitled,

and that either that money or other property has ceased to be in his possession or under his control or that she does not know whether it is still in his possession or under his control.

(2) Where, on an application made to a judge of the High Court or of a county court under the said section seventeen, as extended by the preceding subsection, the judge is satisfied—

(a) that the husband has had in his possession or under his control money or other property as mentioned in paragraph (a) or paragraph (b) of the preceding subsection, and

(b) that he has not made to the wife, in respect of that money or other property, such payment or disposition as would have been appropriate in the circumstances,

the power to make orders under that section shall be extended in accordance with the next following subsection.

(3) Where the last preceding subsection applies, the power to make orders under the said section seventeen shall include power for the judge to order the husband to pay to the wife—

(a) in a case falling within paragraph (a) of subsection (1) of this section, such sum in respect of the money to which the application relates, or the wife's share thereof, as the case may be, or

(b) in a case falling within paragraph (b) of the said subsection (1), such sum in respect of the value of the property to which the application relates, or the wife's interest therein, as the case may be,

as the judge may consider appropriate.

(4) Where on an application under the said section seventeen as extended by this section it appears to the judge that there is any property which—

(a) represents the whole or part of the money or property in question, and

(b) is property in respect of which an order could have been made under that section if an application had been made by the wife thereunder in a question as to the title to or possession of that property,

the judge (either in substitution for or in addition to the making of an order in accordance with the last preceding subsection) may make any order under that section in respect of that property which he could have made on such an application as is mentioned in paragraph (b) of this subsection.

(5) The preceding provisions of this section shall have effect in relation to a husband as they have effect in relation to a wife, as if any reference to the husband were a reference to the wife and any reference to the wife were a reference to the husband.

[(6) Any power of a judge which is exercisable on an application under the said section seventeen shall be exercisable in relation to an application made under that section as extended by this section.]

(7) For the avoidance of doubt it is hereby declared that any power conferred by the said section seventeen to make orders with respect to any property includes power to order a sale of the property.

[601]

NOTES

Sub-s (6): substituted by the Matrimonial and Family Proceedings Act 1984, s 46(1), Sch 1.

8 (*Outside the scope of this work.*)

9 Short title, commencement and extent

(1) This Act may be cited as the Matrimonial Causes (Property and Maintenance) Act 1958.

(2) This Act shall come into operation on such day as may be appointed by the Lord Chancellor by an order made by statutory instrument.

(3) This Act shall not extend to Scotland or to Northern Ireland.

[602]

NOTES

Order: the Matrimonial Causes (Property and Maintenance) Act (Commencement) Order 1958, SI 1958/2080.

(*Schedule repealed by the Matrimonial Causes Act 1965, s 45, Sch 2.*)

COSTS OF LEASES ACT 1958

(1958 c 52)

An Act to make provision for the incidence of the costs of leases

[23 July 1958]

1 Costs of leases

Notwithstanding any custom to the contrary, a party to a lease shall, unless the parties thereto agree otherwise in writing, be under no obligation to pay the whole or any part of any other party's solicitor's costs of the lease.

[602A]

NOTES

Modification: references to solicitors etc modified to include references to bodies recognised under the Administration of Justice Act 1985, s 9, by the Solicitors' Incorporated Practices Order 1991, SI 1991/2684, arts 4, 5, Sch 1.

2 Interpretation

In this Act—

(a) "lease" includes an underlease and an agreement for a lease or underlease or for a tenancy or sub-tenancy;

(b) "costs" includes fees, charges, disbursements (including stamp duty), expenses and remuneration.

[602B]

3 Short title

This Act may be cited as the Costs of Leases Act 1958.

[602C]

VARIATION OF TRUSTS ACT 1958

(1958 c 53)

An Act to extend the jurisdiction of courts of law to vary trusts in the interests of beneficiaries and sanction dealings with trust property

[23 July 1958]

1 Jurisdiction of courts to vary trusts

(1) Where property, whether real or personal, is held on trusts arising, whether before or after the passing of this Act, under any will, settlement or other disposition, the court may if it thinks fit by order approve on behalf of—

(a) any person having, directly or indirectly, an interest, whether vested or contingent, under the trusts who by reason of infancy or other incapacity is incapable of assenting, or

(b) any person (whether ascertained or not) who may become entitled, directly or indirectly, to an interest under the trusts as being at a future date or on the happening of a future event a person of any specified description or a member of any specified class of persons, so however that this paragraph shall not include any person who would be of that description, or a member of that class, as the case may be, if the said date had fallen or the said event had happened at the date of the application to the court, or

(c) any person unborn, or

(d) any person in respect of any discretionary interest of his under protective trusts where the interest of the principal beneficiary has not failed or determined,

any arrangement (by whomsoever proposed, and whether or not there is any other person beneficially interested who is capable of assenting thereto) varying or revoking all or any of the trusts, or enlarging the powers of the trustees of managing or administering any of the property subject to the trusts:

Provided that except by virtue of paragraph (d) of this subsection the court shall not approve an arrangement on behalf of any person unless the carrying out thereof would be for the benefit of that person.

(2) In the foregoing subsection "protective trusts" means the trusts specified in paragraphs (i) and (ii) of subsection (1) of section thirty-three of the Trustee Act 1925, or any like trusts, "the principal beneficiary" has the same meaning as in the said subsection (1) and "discretionary interest" means an interest arising under the trust specified in paragraph (ii) of the said subsection (1) or any like trust.

(3) … The jurisdiction conferred by subsection (1) of this section shall be exercisable by the High Court, except that the question whether the carrying out of any arrangement would be for the benefit of a person falling within paragraph (a) of the said subsection (1) [who lacks capacity (within the meaning of the Mental Capacity Act 2005) to give his assent is to be determined by the Court of Protection].

(4) …

(5) Nothing in the foregoing provisions of this section shall apply to trusts affecting property settled by Act of Parliament.

(6) Nothing in this section shall be taken to limit [the powers of the Court of Protection].

[603]

NOTES

Sub-s (3): words omitted repealed by the County Courts Act 1959, s 204, Sch 3; words in square brackets substituted by the Mental Capacity Act 2005, s 67(1), Sch 6, para 9(a).

Sub-s (4): repealed by the County Courts Act 1959, s 204, Sch 3.

Sub-s (6): words in square brackets substituted by the Mental Capacity Act 2005, s 67(1), Sch 6, para 9(b).

2 Extent and provisions as to Northern Ireland

(1) This Act shall not extend to Scotland.

(2) The foregoing section shall not extend to Northern Ireland …

[604]

NOTES

Sub-s (2): words omitted repealed by the Northern Ireland Constitution Act 1973, s 41(1), Sch 6, Pt I.

3 Short title

This Act may be cited as the Variation of Trusts Act 1958.

[605]

RIGHTS OF LIGHT ACT 1959

(1959 c 56)

An Act to amend the law relating to rights of light, and for purposes connected therewith

[16 July 1959]

1 (*Repealed by the Statute Law (Repeals) Act 1974.*)

2 Registration of notice in lieu of obstruction of access of light

(1) For the purpose of preventing the access and use of light from being taken to be enjoyed without interruption, any person who is an owner of land (in this and the next following section referred to as the "servient land") over which light passes to a dwelling-house, workshop or other building (in this and the next following section referred to as "the dominant building") may apply to the local authority in whose area the dominant building is situated for the registration of a notice under this section.

(2) An application for the registration of a notice under this section shall be in the prescribed form and shall—

(a) identify the servient land and the dominant building in the prescribed manner, and

(b) state that the registration of a notice in pursuance of the application is intended to be equivalent to the obstruction of the access of light to the dominant building across the servient land which would be caused by the erection, in such position on the servient land as may be specified in the application, of an opaque structure of such dimensions (including, if the application so states, unlimited height) as may be so specified.

(3) Any such application shall be accompanied by one or other of the following certificates issued by the [Upper Tribunal], that is to say,—

(a) a certificate certifying that adequate notice of the proposed application has been given to all persons who, in the circumstances existing at the time when the certificate is issued, appear to the [Upper Tribunal] to be persons likely to be affected by the registration of a notice in pursuance of the application;

(b) a certificate certifying that, in the opinion of the [Upper Tribunal], the case is one of exceptional urgency, and that accordingly a notice should be registered forthwith as a temporary notice for such period as may be specified in the certificate.

(4) Where application is duly made to a local authority for the registration of a notice under this section, it shall be the duty of [that authority to register the notice in the appropriate local land charges register, and—

(a) any notice so registered under this section shall be a local land charge; but

(b) section 5(1) and (2) and section 10 of the Local Land Charges Act 1975 shall not apply in relation thereto].

(5) Provision [may be made by Tribunal Procedure Rules] with respect to the issue of certificates for the purposes of this section, and, subject to the approval of the Treasury, the fees chargeable in respect of those proceedings; and, without prejudice to the generality of subsection (6) of that section, any such rules made for the purposes of this section shall include provision—

(a) for requiring applicants for certificates under paragraph (a) of subsection (3) of this section to give such notices, whether by way of advertisement or otherwise, and to produce such documents and provide such information, as may be determined by or under the rules;

(b) for determining the period to be specified in a certificate issued under paragraph (b) of subsection (3) of this section; and

(c) in connection with any certificate issued under the said paragraph (b), for enabling a further certificate to be issued in accordance (subject to the necessary modifications) with paragraph (a) of subsection (3) of this section.

[606]

NOTES

Sub-s (3): words in square brackets, in each place they occur, substituted by SI 2009/1307, art 5(1), (2), Sch 1, para 35(a).

Sub-s (4): words in square brackets substituted by the Local Land Charges Act 1975, s 17(2), Sch 1.

Sub-s (5): words in square brackets substituted by SI 2009/1307, art 5(1), (2), Sch 1, para 35(b).

3 Effect of registered notice and proceedings relating thereto

(1) Where, in pursuance of an application made in accordance with the last preceding section, a notice is registered thereunder, then, for the purpose of determining whether any person is entitled (by virtue of the Prescription Act 1832, or otherwise) to a right to the access of light to the dominant building across the servient land, the access of light to that building across that land shall be treated as obstructed to the same extent, and with the like consequences, as if an opaque structure, of the dimensions specified in the application,—

(a) had, on the date of registration of the notice, been erected in the position on the servient land specified in the application, and had been so erected by the person who made the application, and

(b) had remained in that position during the period for which the notice has effect and had been removed at the end of that period.

(2) For the purposes of this section a notice registered under the last preceding section shall be taken to have effect until either—

(a) the registration is cancelled, or

(b) the period of one year beginning with the date of registration of the notice expires, or

(c) in the case of a notice registered in pursuance of an application accompanied by a certificate issued under paragraph (b) of subsection (3) of the last preceding section, the period specified in the certificate expires without such a further certificate as is mentioned in paragraph (c) of subsection (5) of that section having before the end of that period been lodged with the local authority,

and shall cease to have effect on the occurrence of any one of those events.

(3) Subject to the following provisions of this section, any person who, if such a structure as is mentioned in subsection (1) of this section had been erected as therein mentioned, would have had a right of action in any court in respect of that structure, on the grounds that he was entitled to a right to the access of light to the dominant building across the servient land, and that the said right was infringed by that structure, shall have the like right of action in that court in respect of the registration of a notice under the last preceding section:

Provided that an action shall not be begun by virtue of this subsection after the notice in question has ceased to have effect.

(4) Where, at any time during the period for which a notice registered under the last preceding section has effect, the circumstances are such that, if the access of light to the dominant building had been enjoyed continuously from a date one year earlier than the date on which the enjoyment thereof in fact began, a person would have had a right of action in any court by virtue of the last preceding subsection in respect of the registration of the notice, that person shall have the like right of action in that court by virtue of this subsection in respect of the registration of the notice.

(5) The remedies available to the plaintiff in an action brought by virtue of subsection (3) or subsection (4) of this section (apart from any order as to costs) shall be such declaration as the court may consider appropriate in the circumstances, and an order directing the registration of the notice to be cancelled or varied, as the court may determine.

(6) For the purposes of section four of the Prescription Act 1832 (under which a period of enjoyment of any of the rights to which that Act applies is not to be treated as interrupted except by a matter submitted to or acquiesced in for one year after notice thereof)—

(a) as from the date of registration of a notice under the last preceding section, all persons interested in the dominant building or any part thereof shall be deemed to have notice of the registration thereof and of the person on whose application it was registered;

(b) until such time as an action is brought by virtue of subsection (3) or subsection (4) of this section in respect of the registration of a notice under the last preceding section, all persons interested in the dominant building or any part thereof shall be deemed to acquiesce in the obstruction which, in accordance with subsection (1) of this section, is to be treated as resulting from the registration of the notice;

(c) as from the date on which such an action is brought, no person shall be treated as submitting to or acquiescing in that obstruction:

Provided that, if in any such action, the court decides against the claim of the plaintiff, the court may direct that the preceding provisions of this subsection shall apply in relation to the notice as if that action had not been brought.

[607]

4 Application to Crown land

(1) Subject to the next following subsection, this Act shall apply in relation to land in which there is a Crown or Duchy interest as it applies in relation to land in which there is no such interest.

(2) Section three of the Prescription Act 1832, as modified by the preceding provisions of this Act, shall not by virtue of this section be construed as applying to any land to which (by reason that there is a Crown or Duchy interest therein) that section would not apply apart from this Act.

(3) In this section "Crown or Duchy interest" means an interest belonging to Her Majesty in right of the Crown or of the Duchy of Lancaster, or belonging to the Duchy of Cornwall, or belonging to a government department, or held in trust for Her Majesty for the purposes of a government department.

[608]

5 Power to make rules

(1) …

(2) Any rules made [under section 14 of the Local Land Charges Act 1975 for the purposes of section 2 of this Act] shall (without prejudice to the inclusion therein of other provisions as to

cancelling or varying the registration of notices or agreements) include provision for giving effect to any order of the court under subsection (5) of section three of this Act.

[609]

NOTES

Sub-s (1): repealed by the Local Land Charges Act 1975, s 19, Sch 2.

Sub-s (2): words in square brackets substituted by the Local Land Charges Act 1975, s 17(2), Sch 1.

6 (*Repealed by the Northern Ireland Constitution Act 1973, s 41(4), Sch 6, Pt I.*)

7 Interpretation

(1) In this Act, except in so far as the context otherwise requires, the following expressions have the meanings hereby assigned to them respectively, that is to say:—

"action" includes a counterclaim, and any reference to the plaintiff in an action shall be construed accordingly;

["local authority", in relation to land in a district or a London borough, means the council of the district or borough, and, in relation to land in the City of London, means the Common Council of the City;]

"owner", in relation to any land, means a person who is the estate owner in respect of the fee simple thereof, or is entitled to a tenancy thereof (within the meaning of the Landlord and Tenant Act 1954) for a term of years certain of which, at the time in question, not less than seven years remain unexpired, or is a mortgagee in possession (within the meaning of the Law of Property Act 1925) where the interest mortgaged is either the fee simple of the land or such a tenancy thereof;

"prescribed" means prescribed by rules made by virtue of subsection (6) of section fifteen of the Land Charges Act 1925 as applied by section five of this Act.

(2) References in this Act to any enactment shall, except where the context otherwise requires, be construed as references to that enactment as amended by or under any other enactment.

[610]

NOTES

Sub-s (1): definition "local authority" substituted by the Local Land Charges Act 1975, s 17(2), Sch 1.

8 Short title, commencement and extent

(1) This Act may be cited as the Rights of Light Act 1959.

(2) This Act, except sections one and six thereof, shall come into operation at the end of the period of three months beginning with the day on which it is passed.

(3) This Act shall not extend to Scotland.

(4) This Act, … , shall not extend to Northern Ireland.

[611]

NOTES

Sub-s (4): words omitted repealed by the Northern Ireland Constitution Act 1973, s 41(1), Sch 6.

TRUSTEE INVESTMENTS ACT 1961

(1961 c 62)

An Act to make fresh provision with respect to investment by trustees and persons having the investment powers of trustees, and by local authorities, and for purposes connected therewith

[3 August 1961]

1 New powers of investment of trustees

(1) A trustee may invest any property in his hands, whether at the time in a state of investment or not, in any manner specified in Part I or II of the First Schedule to this Act or, subject to the next following section, in any manner specified in Part III of that Schedule, and may also from time to time vary any such investments.

(2) The supplemental provisions contained in Part IV of that Schedule shall have effect for the interpretation and for restricting the operation of the said Parts I to III.

(3) No provision relating to the powers of the trustee contained in any instrument (not being an enactment or an instrument made under an enactment) made before the passing of this Act shall limit the powers conferred by this section, but those powers are exerciseable only in so far as a

contrary intention is not expressed in any Act or instrument made under an enactment, whenever passed or made, and so relating or in any other instrument so relating which is made after the passing of this Act.

For the purposes of this subsection any rule of the law of Scotland whereby a testamentary writing may be deemed to be made on a date other than that on which it was actually executed shall be disregarded.

(4) In this Act "narrower-range investment" means an investment falling within Part I or II of the First Schedule to this Act and "wider-range investment" means an investment falling within Part III of that Schedule.

[612]

NOTES

Repealed, except in so far as this section is applied by or under any other enactment, by the Trustee Act 2000, s 40(1), (3), Sch 2, Pt I, para 1(1), Sch 4, Pt I and by the Charities and Trustee Investment (Scotland) Act 2005, s 95, Sch 3, para 4(1), (2).

2 Restrictions on wider-range investment

(1) A trustee shall not have power by virtue of the foregoing section to make or retain any wider-range investment unless the trust fund has been divided into two parts (hereinafter referred to as the narrower-range part and the wider- range part), the parts being, subject to the provisions of this Act, equal in value at the time of the division; and where such a division has been made no subsequent division of the same fund shall be made for the purposes of this section, and no property shall be transferred from one part of the fund to the other unless either—

- *(a) the transfer is authorised or required by the following provisions of this Act, or*
- *(b) a compensating transfer is made at the same time.*

In this section "compensating transfer", in relation to any transferred property, means a transfer in the opposite direction of property of equal value.

(2) Property belonging to the narrower-range part of a trust fund shall not by virtue of the foregoing section be invested except in narrower-range investments, and any property invested in any other manner which is or becomes comprised in that part of the trust fund shall either be transferred to the wider-range part of the fund, with a compensating transfer, or be reinvested in narrower-range investments as soon as may be.

(3) Where any property accrues to a trust fund after the fund has been divided in pursuance of subsection (1) of this section, then—

- *(a) if the property accrues to the trustee as owner or former owner of property comprised in either part of the fund, it shall be treated as belonging to that part of the fund;*
- *(b) in any other case, the trustee shall secure, by apportionment of the accruing property or the transfer of property from one part of the fund to the other, or both, that the value of each part of the fund is increased by the same amount.*

Where a trustee acquires property in consideration of a money payment the acquisition of the property shall be treated for the purposes of this section as investment and not as the accrual of property to the trust fund, notwithstanding that the amount of the consideration is less than the value of the property acquired; and paragraph (a) of this subsection shall not include the case of a dividend or interest becoming part of a trust fund.

(4) Where in the exercise of any power or duty of a trustee property falls to be taken out of the trust fund, nothing in this section shall restrict his discretion as to the choice of property to be taken out.

[613]

NOTES

Repealed, except in so far as this section is applied by or under any other enactment, by the Trustee Act 2000, s 40(1), (3), Sch 2, Pt I, para 1(1), Sch 4, Pt I and by the Charities and Trustee Investment (Scotland) Act 2005, s 95, Sch 3, para 4(1), (2).

3 Relationship between Act and other powers of investment

(1) The powers conferred by section one of this Act are in addition to and not in derogation from any power conferred otherwise than by this Act of investment or postponing conversion exerciseable by a trustee (hereinafter referred to as a "special power").

(2) Any special power (however expressed) to invest property in any investment for the time being authorised by law for the investment of trust property, being a power conferred on a trustee before the passing of this Act or conferred on him under any enactment passed before the passing of this Act, shall have effect as a power to invest property in like manner and subject to the like provisions as under the foregoing provisions of this Act.

(3) In relation to property, including wider-range but not including narrower-range investments,—

(a) which a trustee is authorised to hold apart from—

(i) the provisions of section one of this Act or any of the provisions of Part I of the Trustee Act 1925, or any of the provisions of the Trusts (Scotland) Act 1921, or

(ii) any such power to invest in authorised investments as is mentioned in the foregoing subsection, or

(b) which became part of a trust fund in consequence of the exercise by the trustee, as owner of property falling within this subsection, of any power conferred by subsection (3) or (4) of section ten of the Trustee Act 1925, or paragraph (o) or (p) of subsection (1) of section four of the Trusts (Scotland) Act 1921,

the foregoing section shall have effect subject to the modifications set out in the Second Schedule to this Act.

(4) The foregoing subsection shall not apply where the powers of the trustee to invest or postpone conversion have been conferred or varied—

(a) by an order of any court made within the period of ten years ending with the passing of this Act, or

(b) by any enactment passed, or instrument having effect under an enactment made, within that period, being an enactment or instrument relating specifically to the trusts in question; or

(c) by an enactment contained in a local Act of the present Session;

but the provisions of the Third Schedule to this Act shall have effect in a case falling within this subsection.

[614]

NOTES

Repealed, except in so far as this section relates to a trustee having a power of investment conferred on him under any enactment which was passed before 3 August 1961 and which is not amended by the Trustee Act 2000, Sch 2 or by the Charities and Trustee Investment (Scotland) Act 2005, Sch 3, by the Trustee Act 2000, s 40(1), (3), Sch 2, Pt I, para 1(2), Sch 4, Pt I and by the Charities and Trustee Investment (Scotland) Act 2005, s 95, Sch 3, para 4(1), (3).

4 Interpretation of references to trust property and trust funds

(1) In this Act "property" includes real or personal property of any description, including money and things in action:

Provided that it does not include an interest in expectancy, but the falling into possession of such an interest, or the receipt of proceeds of the sale thereof, shall be treated for the purposes of this Act as an accrual of property to the trust fund.

(2) So much of the property in the hands of a trustee shall for the purposes of this Act constitute one trust fund as is held on trusts which (as respects the beneficiaries or their respective interests or the purposes of the trust or as respects the powers of the trustee) are not identical with those on which any other property in his hands is held.

(3) Where property is taken out of a trust fund by way of appropriation so as to form a separate fund, and at the time of the appropriation the trust fund had (as to the whole or a part thereof) been divided in pursuance of subsection (1) of section two of this Act, or that subsection as modified by the Second Schedule to this Act, then if the separate fund is so divided the narrower-range and wider-range parts of the separate fund may be constituted so as either to be equal, or to bear to each other the same proportion as the two corresponding parts of the fund out of which it was so appropriated (the values of those parts of those funds being ascertained as at the time of appropriation), or some intermediate proportion.

(4) In the application of this section to Scotland the following subsection shall be substituted for subsection (1) thereof—

"(1) In this Act "property" includes property of any description (whether heritable or moveable, corporeal or incorporeal) which is presently enjoyable, but does not include a future interest, whether vested or contingent.".

[615]

5 Certain valuations to be conclusive for purposes of division of trust fund

(1) If for the purposes of section two or four of this Act or the Second Schedule thereto a trustee obtains, from a person reasonably believed by the trustee to be qualified to make it, a valuation in writing of any property, the valuation shall be conclusive in determining whether the division of the trust fund in pursuance of subsection (1) of the said section two, or any transfer or apportionment of property under that section or the said Second Schedule, has been duly made.

(2) *The foregoing subsection applies to any such valuation notwithstanding that it is made by a person in the course of his employment as an officer or servant.*

[616]

NOTES

Repealed, except in so far as this section is applied by or under any other enactment, by the Trustee Act 2000, s 40(1), (3), Sch 2, Pt I, para 1(1), Sch 4, Pt I and by the Charities and Trustee Investment (Scotland) Act 2005, s 95, Sch 3, para 4(1), (2).

6 Duty of trustees in choosing investments

(*1*) *In the exercise of his powers of investment a trustee shall have regard—*

(*a*) *to the need for diversification of investments of the trust, in so far as is appropriate to the circumstances of the trust;*

(*b*) *to the suitability to the trust of investments of the description of investment proposed and of the investment proposed as an investment of that description.*

(2) *Before exercising any power conferred by section one of this Act to invest a manner specified in Part II or III of the First Schedule to this Act, or before investing in any such manner in the exercise of a power falling within subsection* (2) *of section three of this Act, a trustee shall obtain and consider proper advice on the question whether the investment is satisfactory having regard to the matters mentioned in paragraphs* (a) *and* (b) *of the foregoing subsection.*

(*3*) *A trustee retaining any investment made in the exercise of such a power and in such a manner as aforesaid shall determine at what intervals the circumstances, and in particular the nature of the investment, make it desirable to obtain such advice as aforesaid, and shall obtain and consider such advice accordingly.*

(*4*) *For the purposes of the two foregoing subsections, proper advice is the advice of a person who is reasonably believed by the trustee to be qualified by his ability in and practical experience of financial matters; and such advice may be given by a person notwithstanding that he gives it in the course of his employment as an officer or servant.*

(*5*) *A trustee shall not be treated as having complied with subsection* (2) *or* (3) *of this section unless the advice was given or has been subsequently confirmed in writing.*

(*6*) *Subsections* (2) *and* (3) *of this section shall not apply to one of two or more trustees where he is the person giving the advice required by this section to his co-trustee or co-trustees, and shall not apply where powers of a trustee are lawfully exercised by an officer or servant competent under subsection* (4) *of this section to give proper advice.*

(*7*) *Without prejudice to section eight of the Trustee Act 1925, or section thirty of the Trusts* (*Scotland*) *Act 1921* (*which relate to valuation, and the proportion of the value to be lent, where a trustee lends on the security of property*) *the advice required by this section shall not include, in the case of a loan on the security of freehold or leasehold property in England and Wales or Northern Ireland or on heritable security in Scotland, advice on the suitability of the particular loan.*

[617]

NOTES

Repealed, except in so far as this section is applied by or under any other enactment, by the Trustee Act 2000, s 40(1), (3), Sch 2, Pt I, para 1(1), Sch 4, Pt I and by the Charities and Trustee Investment (Scotland) Act 2005, s 95, Sch 3, para 4(1), (2).

7 Application of ss 1–6 to persons, other than trustees, having trustee investment powers

(1) Where any persons, not being trustees, have a statutory power of making investments which is or includes power—

(a) to make the like investments as are authorised by section one of the Trustee Act 1925, or section ten of the Trusts (Scotland) Act 1921, or

(b) to make the like investments as trustees are for the time being by law authorised to make,

however the power is expressed, the foregoing provisions of this Act shall with the necessary modifications apply in relation to them as if they were trustees:

Provided that property belonging to a Consolidated Loans Fund or any other fund applicable wholly or partly for the redemption of debt shall not by virtue of the foregoing provisions of this Act be invested or held invested in any manner specified in paragraph 6 of Part II of the First Schedule to this Act or in wider-range investments.

(2) Where, in the exercise of powers conferred by any enactment, an authority to which paragraph 9 of Part II of the First Schedule to this Act applies uses money belonging to any fund for a purpose for which the authority has power to borrow, the foregoing provisions of this Act, as applied by the foregoing subsection, shall apply as if there were comprised in the fund (in addition to the actual content thereof) property, being narrower-range investments, having a value equal to so

much of the said money as for the time being has not been repaid to the fund, and accordingly any repayment of such money to the fund shall not be treated for the said purposes as the accrual of property to the fund:

Provided that nothing in this subsection shall be taken to require compliance with any of the provisions of section six of this Act in relation to the exercise of such powers as aforesaid.

(3) In this section "Consolidated Loans Fund" means a fund established under section fifty-five of the Local Government Act 1958, and includes a loans fund established under section two hundred and seventy-five of the Local Government (Scotland) Act 1947, and "statutory power" means a power conferred by an enactment passed before the passing of this Act or by any instrument made under any such enactment.

8–10 *(Ss 8, 9 repealed by the Trustee Act 2000, s 40(1), (3), Sch 2, Pt I, para 1(3)(a), Sch 4, Pt I; s 10 applies to Scotland only.)*

11 Local Authority investment schemes

(1) Without prejudice to powers conferred by or under any other enactment, any authority to which this section applies may invest property held by the authority in accordance with a scheme submitted to the Treasury by any association of local authorities … and approved by the Treasury as enabling investments to be made collectively without in substance extending the scope of powers of investment.

(2) A scheme under this section may apply to a specified authority or to a specified class of authorities, may make different provisions as respects different authorities or different classes of authorities or as respects different descriptions of property or property held for different purposes, and may impose restrictions on the extent to which the power controlled by the foregoing subsection shall be exerciseable.

(3) In approving a scheme under this section, the Treasury may direct that [the [Financial Services and Markets Act 2000]], shall not apply to dealings undertaken or documents issued for the purposes of the scheme, or to such dealings or documents of such descriptions as may be specified in the direction.

(4) The authorities to which this section applies are—

(a) in England and Wales[, the Greater London Authority,] the council of a county, [a county borough,] a … borough … a district or a [parish, the Common] Council of the City of London[, a functional body (within the meaning of the Greater London Authority Act 1999),] [the Broads Authority] [a National Park authority][, a police authority established under [section 3 of the Police Act 1996]][…][, … a joint authority established by Part IV of the Local Government Act 1985][, an authority established for an area in England by an order under section 207 of the Local Government and Public Involvement in Health Act 2007 (joint waste authorities)] … and the Council of the Isles of Scilly;

(b) in Scotland, a local authority within the meaning of the Local Government (Scotland) Act 1947;

(c) in any part of Great Britain, a joint board or joint committee constituted to discharge or advise on the discharge of the functions of any two or more of the authorities mentioned in the foregoing paragraphs (including a joint committee established by [those authorities acting in combination in accordance with regulations made under section 7 of the Superannuation Act 1972];

(d) in Northern Ireland, [a district council established under the Local Government Act (Northern Ireland) 1972] and the Northern Ireland Local Government Officers' Superannuation Committee established under the Local Government (Superannuation) Act (Northern Ireland) 1950;

[(e) …]

[618]

NOTES

Sub-s (1): words omitted repealed by the London Government Act 1963, s 93(1), Sch 8, Pt II and by the Local Government Act 1985, s 102, Sch 17.

Sub-s (3): words in first (outer) pair of square brackets substituted by the Financial Services Act 1986, s 212(2), Sch 16, para 2; words in second (inner) pair of square brackets substituted by SI 2001/3649, art 268.

Sub-s (4): in para (a), words in first and fourth pairs of square brackets inserted by the Greater London Authority Act 1999, s 387(1), (2), words in second pair of square brackets inserted by the Local Government (Wales) Act 1994, s 66(6), Sch 16, para 19(1), first words omitted repealed by the London Government Act 1963, s 93(1), Sch 18, Pt II, second words omitted repealed by the Local Government Act 1972, s 272(1), Sch 30, words in third pair of square brackets substituted by the Water Act 1989, s 190, Sch 25, para 29, words in fifth pair of square brackets inserted by the Norfolk and Suffolk Broads Act 1988, s 21, Sch 6, words in sixth pair of square brackets inserted by the Environment Act 1995, s 78, Sch 10, para 5, words in seventh (outer) pair of square brackets inserted by the Police and Magistrates' Courts Act 1994, s 43, Sch 4, Pt II, para 46, words in eighth (inner) pair of square brackets substituted by the Police Act 1996, s 103, Sch 7, para 1(2)(a), words omitted from ninth pair of square brackets inserted by the Police Act 1997, s 134(1), Sch 9, para 4(a) and repealed by the Serious Organised Crime and Police Act 2005, ss 59, 174(2), Sch 4, paras 7, 8(a), Sch 17, Pt 2, words in tenth pair of square brackets inserted by the Local Government Act 1985, s 84, Sch 14, para 38, fourth words omitted repealed by the Education Reform Act 1988, s 237, Sch 13, Pt I, words in eleventh pair of square brackets inserted by the Local Government and Public Involvement in Health Act 2007, s 209(2), Sch 13, Pt 2, para 26, fifth words omitted repealed by the Local Government Act 1985, s 102, Sch 17; in para (c) words in square brackets substituted by the Superannuation Act 1972, s 29(1), Sch 6, para 40; in para (d) words in square brackets substituted by the Transfer of Functions (Local Government, etc) (Northern Ireland) Order 1973, SR & O 1973/256, art 3, Sch 2; para (e) inserted by the Police Act 1997, s 134(1), Sch 9, para 4(b) and repealed by the Serious Organised Crime and Police Act 2005, ss 59, 174(2), Sch 4, paras 7, 8(b), Sch 17, Pt 2.

Modification: modified by the Waste Regulation and Disposal (Authorities) Order 1985, SI 1985/1884, art 10, Sch 3.

See further: for provision whereby the body corporate known as the Residuary Body for Wales is to be included among the authorities or bodies to which this section applies, see the Local Government (Wales) Act 1994, Sch 13, para 24(a).

12 Power to confer additional powers of investment

(1) Her Majesty may by Order in Council extend the powers of investment conferred by section one of this Act by adding to Part I, Part II or Part III of the First Schedule to this Act any manner of investment specified in the Order.

(2) Any Order under this section shall be subject to annulment in pursuance of a resolution of either House of Parliament.

[619]

NOTES

Repealed, except in so far as this section is applied by or under any other enactment, by the Trustee Act 2000, s 40(1), (3), Sch 2, Pt I, para 1(1), Sch 4, Pt I and by the Charities and Trustee Investment (Scotland) Act 2005, s 95, Sch 3, para 4(1), (2).

Orders: the Trustee Investments (Additional Powers) Order 1962, SI 1962/658; the Trustee Investments (Additional Powers) (No 2) Order 1962, SI 1962/2611; the Trustee Investments (Additional Powers) Order 1964, SI 1964/703; the Trustee Investments (Additional Powers) (No 2) Order 1964, SI 1964/1404; the Trustee Investments (Additional Powers) Order 1966, SI 1966/401; the Trustee Investments (Additional Powers) Order 1968, SI 1968/470; the Trustee Investments (Additional Powers) Order 1972, SI 1972/1818; the Trustee Investments (Additional Powers) Order 1973, SI 1973/1332; the Trustee Investments (Additional Powers) Order 1975, SI 1975/1710; the Trustee Investments (Additional Powers) Order 1977, SI 1977/831; the Trustee Investments (Additional Powers) (No 2) Order 1977, SI 1977/1878; the Trustee Investments (Additional Powers) Order 1982, SI 1982/1086; the Trustee Investments (Additional Powers) Order 1983, SI 1983/772; the Trustee Investments (Additional Powers) (No 2) Order 1983, SI 1983/1525; the Trustee Investments (Additional Powers) Order 1985, SI 1985/1780; the Trustee Investments (Additional Powers) Order 1986, SI 1986/601; the Trustee Investments (Additional Powers) Order 1988, SI 1988/2254; the Trustee Investments (Additional Powers) Order 1991, SI 1991/999; the Trustee Investments (Additional Powers) Order 1992, SI 1992/1738; the Trustee Investments (Additional Powers) Order 1994, SI 1994/265.

13 Power to modify provisions as to division of trust fund

(1) The Treasury may by order made by statutory instrument direct that, subject to subsection (3) of section four of this Act, any division of a trust fund made in pursuance of subsection (1) of section two of this Act during the continuance in force of the order shall be made so that the value of the wider- range part at the time of the division bears to the then value of the narrower- range part such proportion, greater than one but not greater than three to one, as may be prescribed by the order; and in this Act "the prescribed proportion" means the proportion for the time being prescribed under this subsection.

(2) A fund which has been divided in pursuance of subsection (1) of section two of this Act before the coming into operation of an order under the foregoing subsection may notwithstanding anything in that subsection be again divided (once only) in pursuance of the said subsection (1) during the continuance in force of the order.

(3) If an order is made under subsection (1) of this section, then as from the coming into operation of the order—

- *(a) paragraph (b) of subsection (3) of section two of this Act and sub- paragraph (b) of paragraph 3 of the Second Schedule thereto shall have effect with the substitution, for the words from "each" to the end, of the words "the wider-range part of the fund is increased by an amount which bears the prescribed proportion to the amount by which the value of the narrower-range part of the fund is increased";*
- *(b) subsection (3) of section four of this Act shall have effect as if for the words "so as either" to "each other" there were substituted the words "so as to bear to each other either the prescribed proportion or".*

(4) An order under this section may be revoked by a subsequent order thereunder prescribing a greater proportion.

(5) An order under this section shall not have effect unless approved by a resolution of each House of Parliament.

[620]

NOTES

Repealed, except in so far as this section is applied by or under any other enactment, by the Trustee Act 2000, s 40(1), (3), Sch 2, Pt I, para 1(1), Sch 4, Pt I and by the Charities and Trustee Investment (Scotland) Act 2005, s 95, Sch 3, para 4(1), (2).

Order: the Trustee Investments (Division of Trust Fund) Order 1996, SI 1996/845.

14 (*Amends the Trusts (Scotland) Act 1921, s 27.*)

15 Saving for powers of court

The enlargement of the investment powers of trustees by this Act shall not lessen any power of a court to confer wider powers of investment on trustees, or affect the extent to which any such power is to be exercised.

[621]

NOTES

Repealed, except in so far as this section is applied by or under any other enactment, by the Trustee Act 2000, s 40(1), (3), Sch 2, Pt I, para 1(1), Sch 4, Pt I and by the Charities and Trustee Investment (Scotland) Act 2005, s 95, Sch 3, para 4(1), (2).

16 Minor and consequential amendments and repeals

(*1*) *The provisions of the Fourth Schedule to this Act (which contain minor amendments and amendments consequential on the foregoing provisions of this Act) shall have effect.*

(2) …

[622]

NOTES

Sub-s (1): repealed, in so far as it relates to Sch 4, para 1(1), by the Trustee Act 2000, s 40(1), (3), Sch 2, Pt I, para 1(3)(c), Sch 4, Pt I.

Sub-s (2): repealed by the Statute Law (Repeals) Act 1974.

17 Short title, extent and construction

(1) This Act may be cited as the Trustee Investments Act 1961.

[(2) Section 11 of this Act extends to Northern Ireland, but, except as aforesaid and except so far as any other provisions of this Act apply by virtue of Northern Ireland legislation to trusts the execution of which is governed by the law of Northern Ireland, this Act does not apply to such trusts.]

(3) So much of section sixteen of this Act as relates to [the National Savings Bank] … shall extend to the Isle of Man and the Channel Islands.

(4) Except where the context otherwise requires, in this Act, in its application to trusts the execution of which is governed by the law in force in England and Wales, expressions have the same meaning as in the Trustee Act 1925.

(5) Except where the context otherwise requires, in this Act, in its application to trusts the execution of which is governed by the law in force in Scotland, expressions have the same meaning as in the Trusts (Scotland) Act, 1921.

[623]

NOTES

Sub-s (2): substituted by the Trustee Act (Northern Ireland) 2001, s 44(1), Sch 2, para 20.

Sub-s (3): words in square brackets substituted by the Post Office Act 1969, ss 94, 114, Sch 6, Pt III; words omitted repealed by the Trustee Savings Banks Act 1985, ss 4(3), 7(3), Sch 4.

Modification: the Northern Ireland Act 1998 makes new provision for the government of Northern Ireland for the purpose of implementing the Belfast Agreement (the agreement reached at multi-party talks on Northern Ireland and set out in Command Paper 3883). As a consequence of that Act, any reference in this section to the Parliament of Northern Ireland or the Assembly established under the Northern Ireland Assembly Act 1973, s 1, certain office-holders and Ministers, and any legislative act and certain financial dealings thereof, shall, for the period specified, be construed in accordance with Sch 12, paras 1–11 to the 1998 Act.

SCHEDULE 1
MANNER OF INVESTMENT

Section 1

PART I
NARROWER-RANGE INVESTMENTS NOT REQUIRING ADVICE

1. In Defence Bonds, National Savings Certificates Ulster Savings Certificates, [Ulster Development Bonds] [National Development Bonds], [British Savings Bonds], [National Savings

Income Bonds] [National Savings Deposit Bonds] [National Savings Indexed-Income Bonds], [National Savings Capital Bonds] [National Savings FIRST Option Bonds], [National Savings Pensioners Guaranteed Income Bonds].

2. In deposits in [the National Savings Bank], ... and deposits in a bank or department thereof certified under subsection (3) of section nine of the Finance Act 1956.

[624]

NOTES

Repealed, except in so far as this Schedule is applied by or under any other enactment, by virtue of the Trustee Act 2000, s 40(1), (3), Sch 2, Pt I, para 1(1), Sch 4, Pt I.

Words in square brackets inserted by SI 1962/2611, SI 1964/703, SI 1968/470, SI 1982/1086, SI 1983/1525, SI 1985/1780, the Post Office Act 1969, ss 94, 114, Sch 6, Pt III, SI 1988/2254, art 2, SI 1992/1738, art 2 and SI 1994/265, art 2; words omitted repealed by the Trustee Savings Banks Act 1976, s 36(2), Sch 6.

Application: this Part of the Schedule is applied with modifications, in relation to eligible debt securities, by the Uncertificated Securities (Amendment) (Eligible Debt Securities) Regulations 2003, SI 2003/1633, reg 15, Sch 2, para 8(1), (2)(a).

PART II
NARROWER-RANGE OF INVESTMENTS REQUIRING ADVICE

1. In securities issued by Her Majesty's Government in the United Kingdom, the Government of Northern Ireland or the Government of the Isle of Man, not being securities falling within Part I of this Schedule and being fixed-interest securities registered in the United Kingdom or the Isle of Man, Treasury Bills or Tax Reserve Certificates [or any variable interest securities issued by Her Majesty's Government in the United Kingdom and registered in the United Kingdom].

2. In any securities the payment of interest on which is guaranteed by Her Majesty's Government in the United Kingdom or the Government of Northern Ireland.

3. In fixed-interest securities issued in the United Kingdom by any public authority or nationalised industry or undertaking in the United Kingdom.

4. In fixed-interest securities issued in the United Kingdom by the government of any overseas territory within the Commonwealth or by any public or local authority within such a territory, being securities registered in the United Kingdom.

References in this paragraph to an overseas territory or to the government of such a territory shall be construed as if they occurred in the Overseas Service Act, 1958.

[4A. In securities issued in the United Kingdom by the government of an overseas territory within the Commonwealth or by any public or local authority within such a territory, being securities registered in the United Kingdom and in respect of which the rate of interest is variable by reference to one or more of the following:—

(a) the Bank of England's minimum lending rate;
(b) the average rate of discount on allotment on 91-day Treasury bills;
(c) a yield on 91-day Treasury bills;
(d) a London sterling inter-bank offered rate;
(e) a London sterling certificate of deposit rate.

References in this paragraph to an overseas territory or to the government of such a territory shall be construed as if they occurred in the Overseas Service Act 1958.]

5. In fixed-interest securities issued in the United Kingdom by [the African Development Bank, the Asian Development Bank, the Caribbean Development Bank, [the European Bank for Reconstruction and Development,] the International Finance Corporation, the International Monetary Fund or by] the International Bank for Reconstruction and Development, being securities registered in the United Kingdom.

[In fixed-interest securities issued in the United Kingdom by the Inter-American Development Bank],

[In fixed interest securities issued in the United Kingdom by [the European Atomic Energy Community, the European Economic Community,] the European Investment Bank or by the European Coal and Steel Community, being securities registered in the United Kingdom.]

[5A. In securities issued in the United Kingdom by

(i) the International Bank for Reconstruction and Development or by the European Investment Bank or by the European Coal and Steel Community, being securities registered in the United Kingdom or
(ii) the Inter-American Development Bank

being securities in respect of which the rate of interest is variable by reference to one or more of the following:—

(a) the Bank of England's minimum lending rate;
(b) the average rate of discount on allotment on 91-day Treasury bills;
(c) a yield on 91-day Treasury bills;

(d) a London sterling inter-bank offered rate;
(e) a London sterling certificate of deposit rate.]

[5B. In securities issued in the United Kingdom by the African Development Bank, the Asian Development Bank, the Caribbean Development Bank, the European Atomic Energy Community, [the European Bank for Reconstruction and Development,] the European Economic Community, the International Finance Corporation or by the International Monetary Fund, being securities registered in the United Kingdom and in respect of which the rate of interest is variable by reference to one or more of the following:—
(a) The average rate of discount on allotment on 91-day Treasury Bills;
(b) a yield on 91-day Treasury Bills;
(c) a London sterling inter-bank offered rate;
(d) a London sterling certificate of deposit rate.]

6. In debentures issued in the United Kingdom by a company incorporated in the United Kingdom, being debentures registered in the United Kingdom.

7. In stock of the Bank of Ireland.

[In Bank of Ireland 7 per cent. Loan Stock 1968/91].

8. …

9. In loans to any authority to which this paragraph applies charged on all or any of the revenues of the authority or on a fund into which all or any of those revenues are payable, in any fixed-interest securities issued in the United Kingdom by any such authority for the purpose of borrowing money so charged, and in deposits with any such authority by way of temporary loan made on the giving of a receipt for the loan by the treasurer or other similar officer of the authority and on the giving of an undertaking by the authority that, if requested to charge the loan as aforesaid, it will either comply with the request or repay the loan.

This paragraph applies to the following authorities, that is to say—
(a) any local authority in the United Kingdom;
[(aa) the Greater London Authority;
(ab) any functional body, within the meaning of the Greater London Authority Act 1999;]
(b) any authority all the members of which are appointed or elected by one or more local authorities in the United Kingdom;
(c) any authority the majority of the members of which are appointed or elected by one or more local authorities in the United Kingdom, being an authority which by virtue of any enactment has power to issue a precept to a local authority in England and Wales, or a requisition to a local authority in Scotland, or to the expenses of which, by virtue of any enactment, a local authority in the United Kingdom is or can be required to contribute;
(d) … [a police authority established under [section 3 of the Police Act 1996]];
[(da) …]
(e) the Belfast City and District Water Commissioners;
[(f) the Great Ouse Water Authority];
[(g) any district council in Northern Ireland;]
[(h) … ;
(i) any residuary body established by section 57 of the Local Government Act 1985.]

[9A. In any securities issued in the United Kingdom by any authority to which paragraph 9 applies for the purpose of borrowing money charged on all or any of the revenues of the authority or on a fund into which all or any of those revenues are payable and being securities in respect of which the rate of interest is variable by reference to one or more of the following—
(a) the Bank of England's minimum lending rate;
(b) the average rate of discount on allotment on 91-day Treasury bills;
(c) a yield on 91-day Treasury bills;
(d) a London sterling inter-bank offered rate;
(e) a London sterling certificate of deposit rate.]

10. …

[10A. In any units of a gilt unit trust scheme

A gilt unit trust scheme is an authorised unit trust scheme, or a recognised scheme, the objective of which is—
(a) to invest at least 90% of the property of the scheme in loan stock, bonds or other instruments creating indebtedness which—
(i) are transferable; and
(ii) are issued or guaranteed by the government of the United Kingdom or of any other country or territory, by a local authority in the United Kingdom or in a relevant state, or by an international organisation the members of which include the United Kingdom or a relevant state;
(b) to invest the remainder of the property of the scheme in shares, debentures or other instruments creating or acknowledging indebtedness, certificates representing securities or units in a collective investment scheme.

PART I STATUTES

Sub-paragraphs (a) and (b) must be read with—

- *(i) section 22 of the Financial Services and Markets Act 2000;*
- *(ii) any relevant order under that section; and*
- *(iii) Schedule 2 to that Act.]*

11. ...

[12. In deposits with a building society within the meaning of the Building Societies Act 1986.]

13. In mortgages of freehold property in England and Wales or Northern Ireland and of leasehold property in those countries of which the unexpired term at the time of investment is not less than sixty years, and in loans on heritable security in Scotland.

14. In perpetual rent-charges charged on land in England and Wales or Northern Ireland and fee-farm rents (not being rent-charges) issuing out of such land ...

[15. In Certificates of Tax Deposit.]

[16. In fixed-interest or variable interest securities issued by the government of a relevant state.

17. In any securities the payment of interest on which is guaranteed by the government of a relevant state.

18. In fixed-interest securities issued in any relevant state by any public authority or nationalised industry or undertaking in that state.

19. In fixed-interest or variable interest securities issued in a relevant state by the government of any overseas territory within the Commonwealth or by any public or local authority within such a territory.

[For this purpose—

- *(a) "overseas territory" means any territory or country outside the United Kingdom, and*
- *(b) the reference to the government of any overseas territory includes a reference to a government constituted for two or more overseas territories, and to any authority established for the purpose of providing or administering services which are common to, or relate to matters of common interest to, two or more such territories].*

20. In fixed-interest or variable interest securities issued in a relevant state by—

- *(a) the African Development Bank;*
- *(b) the Asian Development Bank;*
- *(c) the Caribbean Development Bank;*
- *(d) the International Finance Corporation;*
- *(e) the International Monetary Fund;*
- *(f) the International Bank for Reconstruction and Development;*
- *(g) the Inter-American Development Bank;*
- *(h) the European Atomic Energy Community;*
- *(i) the European Bank for Reconstruction and Development;*
- *(j) the European Economic Community;*
- *(k) the European Investment Bank; or*
- *(l) the European Coal and Steel Community.*

21. In debentures issued in any relevant state by a company incorporated in that state.

22. In loans to any authority to which this paragraph applies secured on all or any of the revenues of the authority or on a fund into which all or any of those revenues are payable, in fixed-interest or variable interest securities issued in a relevant state by any such authority in that state for the purpose of borrowing money so secured, and in deposits with any authority to which this paragraph applies by way of temporary loan made on the giving of a receipt for the loan by the treasurer or other similar officer of the authority and on the giving of an undertaking by the authority that, if requested to charge the loan as aforesaid, it will either comply with the request or repay the loan.

This paragraph applies to the following authorities, that is to say—

- *(a) any local authority in a relevant state; or*
- *(b) any authority all the members of which are appointed or elected by one or more local authorities in any such state.*

23. In deposits with a mutual investment society whose head office is located in a relevant state.

24. In loans secured on any interest in property in a relevant state which corresponds to an interest in property falling within paragraph 13 of this Part of this Schedule.]

[625]

NOTES

Repealed, except in so far as this Schedule is applied by or under any other enactment, by virtue of the Trustee Act 2000, s 40(1), (3), Sch 2, Pt I, para 1(1), Sch 4, Pt I (for transitional provisions and savings in connection with the repeal of para 14, see s 40(2) of, and Sch 3, para 7 to, the 2000 Act).

Para 1: words in square brackets inserted by SI 1977/831, art 3.

Paras 4A, 5A, 9A: inserted by SI 1977/1878, art 3.

Para 5: first words in square brackets inserted by SI 1983/772, art 2(a), words in square brackets therein inserted by SI 1991/999, art 2; second words in square brackets inserted by SI 1964/1404, art 1; third words in square brackets inserted by SI 1972/1818, art 3, words in square brackets therein inserted by SI 1983/772, art 2(b).

Para 5B: inserted by SI 1983/772, art 2(c); words in square brackets inserted by SI 1991/999, art 2.

Para 7: words in square brackets inserted by SI 1966/401, art 1.

Para 8: repealed by the Agriculture and Forestry (Financial Provisions) Act 1991, s 1, Schedule, Pt IV.

Para 9: sub-paras (aa), (ab) inserted by the Greater London Authority Act 1999, s 387(1), (3)(a); in sub-para (d), words omitted repealed by the Greater London Authority Act 1999, ss 387(1), (3)(b), 423, Sch 34, Pt I, words in first (outer) pair of square brackets substituted by the Police and Magistrates' Courts Act 1994, s 43, Sch 4, Pt II, para 47 and words in second (inner) pair of square brackets substituted by the Police Act 1996, s 103, Sch 7, para 1(2)(a); sub-para (da) inserted by the Police Act 1997, s 134(1), Sch 9, para 5, and repealed by the Serious Organised Crime and Police Act 2005, ss 59, 174(2), Sch 4, paras 7, 9, Sch 17, Pt 2; sub-para (f) inserted by SI 1962/658, art 1; sub-para (g) inserted by SI 1973/1332, art 3; sub-paras (h), (i) inserted by SI 1986/601, art 2; sub-para (h) repealed by the Education Reform Act 1988, s 237, Sch 1, Sch 13, Pt I.

Para 10: repealed by the Water Act 1989, s 190, Sch 25, para 29.

Para 10A: inserted by the Finance Act 1982, s 150 and substituted by SI 2001/3649, art 269(1), (2).

Para 11: repealed by the Trustee Savings Bank Act 1976, s 36(2), Sch 6.

Para 12: substituted by the Building Societies Act 1986, s 120, Sch 18, Pt I, para 4(2).

Para 14: words omitted repealed by the Abolition of Feudal Tenure etc (Scotland) Act 2000, s 76(2), Sch 13, Pt 1.

Para 15: inserted by SI 1975/1710, art 3.

Paras 16–24: inserted by SI 1994/1908, art 2(2).

Para 19: words in square brackets substituted by the International Development Act 2002, s 19(1), Sch 3, para 1.

Application: this Part of the Schedule is applied with modifications, in relation to eligible debt securities, by the Uncertificated Securities (Amendment) (Eligible Debt Securities) Regulations 2003, SI 2003/1633, reg 15, Sch 2, paras 2(b), 8(1), (2)(a).

PART III
WIDER-RANGE INVESTMENTS

1. In any securities issued in the United Kingdom by a company incorporated in the United Kingdom, being securities registered in the United Kingdom and not being securities falling within Part II of this Schedule.

[2. In shares in a building society within the meaning of the Building Societies Act 1986.]

[2A. In any shares in an open-ended investment company within the meaning of the Open-Ended Investment Companies Regulations 2001.]

[3. In any units of an authorised unit trust scheme …]

[4. In any securities issued in any relevant state by a company incorporated in that state or by any unincorporated body constituted under the law of that state, not being (in either case) securities falling within Part II of this Schedule or paragraph 6 of this Part of this Schedule.

5. In shares in a mutual investment society whose head office is located in a relevant state.

[6. In any units of a recognised scheme which does not fall within Part 2 of this Schedule.]]

[626]

NOTES

Repealed, except in so far as this Schedule is applied by or under any other enactment, by virtue of the Trustee Act 2000, s 40(1), (3), Sch 2, Pt I, para 1(1), Sch 4, Pt I.

Para 2: substituted by the Building Societies Act 1986, s 120, Sch 18, Part I, para 4(3).

Para 2A: inserted by SI 1996/2827, reg 75, Sch 8, para 1, and substituted by SI 2001/1228, reg 84, Sch 7, Pt I, para 1.

Para 3: substituted by the Financial Services Act 1986, s 212(2), Sch 16, para 2; words omitted repealed by SI 2001/3649, art 269(1), (3).

Paras 4, 5: inserted by SI 1994/1908, art 2(3).

Para 6: inserted by SI 1994/1908, art 2(3); substituted by SI 2001/3649, art 269(1), (4).

Application: this Part of the Schedule is applied with modifications, in relation to eligible debt securities, by the Uncertificated Securities (Amendment) (Eligible Debt Securities) Regulations 2003, SI 2003/1633, reg 15, Sch 2, paras 2(b), 8(1), (2)(a).

PART IV
SUPPLEMENTAL

1. The securities mentioned in Parts I to III of this Schedule do not include any securities where the holder can be required to accept repayment of the principal, or the payment of any interest, otherwise than in sterling[, in the currency of a relevant state or in the european currency unit (as defined in article 1 of Council Regulation No 3180/78/EEC)].

2. The securities mentioned in paragraphs 1 to 8 of Part II, other than Treasury Bills or Tax Reserve Certificates, securities issued before the passing of this Act by the Government of the Isle of

Man, securities falling within paragraph 4 of the said Part II issued before the passing of this Act or securities falling within paragraph 9 of that Part, and the securities mentioned in paragraph 1 of Part III of this Schedule, do not include—

(*a*) *securities the price of which is not quoted on [a recognised investment exchange ... [or on an investment exchange which constitutes the principal or only market established in a relevant state on which securities admitted to official listing are dealt in or traded]]*

(*b*) *shares or debenture stock not fully paid up (except shares or debenture stock which by the terms of issue are required to be fully paid up within nine months of the date of issue).*

[2A. The securities mentioned in paragraphs 16 to 21 of Part II of this Schedule, other than securities traded on a relevant money market or securities falling within paragraph 22 of Part II of this Schedule, and the securities mentioned in paragraph 4 of Part III of this Schedule do not include—

(*a*) *securities the price for which is not quoted on a recognised investment exchange ... or on an investment exchange which constitutes the principal or only market established in a relevant state on which securities admitted to official listing are dealt in or traded;*

(*b*) *shares or debenture stock not fully paid up (except shares or debenture stock which by the terms of issue are required to be fully paid up within nine months of the date of issue or shares issued with no nominal value).]*

3. The securities mentioned in paragraph 6 [and 21] of Part II and paragraph 1 [or 4] of Part III of this Schedule do not include—

(*a*) *shares or debentures of an incorporated company of which the total issued and paid up share capital is less than one million pounds;*

[(ab) shares or debentures of an incorporated company of which the total issued and paid up share capital at any time on the business day before the investment is made is less than the equivalent of one million pounds in the currency of a relevant state (at the exchange rate prevailing in the United Kingdom at the close of business on the day before the investment is made);]

(*b*) *shares or debentures of an incorporated company which has not in each of the five years immediately preceding the calendar year in which the investment is made paid a dividend on all the shares issued by the company, excluding any shares issued after the dividend was declared and any shares which by their terms of issue did not rank for the dividend for that year.*

For the purposes of sub-paragraph (b) of this paragraph a company formed—

(*i*) *to take over the business of another company or other companies, or*

(*ii*) *to acquire the securities of, or control of, another company or other companies,*

or for either of those purposes and for other purposes shall be deemed to have paid a dividend as mentioned in that sub-paragraph in any year in which such a dividend has been paid by the other company or all the other companies, as the case may be.

[For the purposes of sub-paragraph (b) of this paragraph in relation to investment in shares or debentures of a successor company within the meaning of the Electricity (Northern Ireland) Order 1992 the company shall be deemed to have paid a dividend as mentioned in that sub-paragraph—

(*iii*) *in every year preceding the calendar year in which the transfer date within the meaning of Part III of that Order of 1992 falls ("the first investment year") which is included in the relevant five years; and*

(*iv*) *in the first investment year, if that year is included in the relevant five years and that company does not in fact pay such a dividend in that year; and*

"the relevant five years" means the five years immediately preceding the year in which the investment in question is made or proposed to be made.]

[3A. ...]

4. In this Schedule, unless the context otherwise requires, the following expressions have the meanings hereby respectively assigned to them, that is to say—

"debenture" includes debenture stock and bonds, whether constituting a charge on assets or not, and loan stock or notes;

"enactment" includes an enactment of the Parliament of Northern Ireland;

"fixed-interest securities" means securities which under their terms of issue bear a fixed rate of interest;

"local authority" in relation to the United Kingdom, means any of the following authorities—

(*a*) *in England and Wales, the council of a county, [a county borough,] a ... borough ... an urban or rural district or a parish, the Common Council of the City of London [the Greater London Council] and the Council of the Isles of Scilly;*

(*b*) *in Scotland, a local authority within the meaning of the Local Government (Scotland) Act, 1947;*

(*c*) *...*

["mutual investment society" means a credit institution which operates on mutual principles and which is authorised by the appropriate supervisory authority of a relevant state;

"relevant money market" means a money market which is supervised by the central bank, or a government agency, of a relevant state;

"relevant state" means Austria, Finland, Iceland, [Liechtenstein,] Norway, Sweden or a member state other than the United Kingdom;]

...

"securities" includes shares, debentures [units within paragraph 3 [or 6] of Part III of this Schedule], Treasury Bills and Tax Reserve Certificates;

"shares" includes stock;

"Treasury Bills" includes ... bills issued by Her Majesty's Government in the United Kingdom and Northern Ireland Treasury Bills.

[4A. In this Schedule—

"authorised unit trust scheme" and "recognised scheme" have the meaning given by section 237(3) of the Financial Services and Markets Act 2000; and

"collective investment scheme" has the meaning given by section 235 of that Act; and

"recognised investment exchange" has the meaning given by section 285 of that Act.]

5. It is hereby declared that in this Schedule "mortgage", in relation to freehold or leasehold property in Northern Ireland, includes a registered charge which, by virtue of subsection (4) of section forty of the Local Registration of Title (Ireland) Act, 1891, or any other enactment, operates as a mortgage by deed.

6. [In relation to the United Kingdom,] references in this Schedule to an incorporated company are references to a company incorporated by or under any enactment and include references to a body of persons established for the purpose of trading for profit and incorporated by Royal Charter.]

[6A. ...]

7. ...

[627]

NOTES

Repealed, except in so far as this Schedule is applied by or under any other enactment, by virtue of the Trustee Act 2000, s 40(1), (3), Sch 2, Pt I, para 1(1), Sch 4, Pt I.

Paras 1, 6: words in square brackets inserted by SI 1994/1908, art 3(2), (7).

Para 2: in sub-para (a), words in first (outer) pair of square brackets substituted by the Financial Services Act 1986, s 212(2), Sch 16, para 2, words omitted repealed by SI 2001/3649, art 269(1), (5), and words in second (inner) pair of square brackets inserted by SI 1994/1908, art 3(3).

Para 2A: inserted by SI 1994/1908, art 3(4); words omitted repealed by SI 2001/3649, art 269(1), (5).

Para 3: first and second words in square brackets and sub-para (ab) inserted by SI 1994/1908, art 3(5); final words in square brackets inserted by SI 1992/232, art 4.

Para 3A: inserted by the Housing (Consequential Provisions) Act 1985, s 4, Sch 2, para 5; repealed by the Building Societies Act 1986, s 120, Sch 19, Pt I.

Para 4: in definition "local authority", in sub-para (a) first words in square brackets inserted by the Local Government (Wales) Act 1994, s 66(6), Sch 16, para 19(2), first words omitted repealed by London Government Act 1963, s 93(1), Sch 18 Pt II, final words omitted repealed by the Local Government Act 1972, s 272(1), Sch 30, final words in square brackets inserted by the London Government Act 1963, s 83(1), Sch 17, sub-para (c) repealed by the Statute Law (Repeals) Act 1981; definitions "mutual investment society", "relevant money market", "relevant state" inserted by SI 1994/1908, art 3(6)(a), in definition "relevant state" word in square brackets inserted by SI 1995/768, art 2; definitions "ordinary deposits" and "special investment" repealed by the Trustee Savings Banks Act 1976, s 36(2), Sch 6; in definition "securities" first words in square brackets inserted by the Financial Services Act 1986, s 212(2), Sch 16, para 2, words in square brackets therein inserted by SI 1994/1908, art 3(6)(b); in definition "Treasury Bills" words omitted repealed by the National Loans Act 1968, s 24(2), Sch 6, Pt 1.

Para 4A: inserted by SI 2001/3649, art 269(1), (6).

Para 6A: inserted by SI 1994/1908, art 3(8); repealed by SI 2001/3649, art 269(1), (7).

Para 7: repealed by the Building Societies Act 1986, s 120, Sch 19, Pt I.

Modification: the Northern Ireland Act 1998 makes new provision for the government of Northern Ireland for the purpose of implementing the Belfast Agreement (the agreement reached at multi-party talks on Northern Ireland and set out in Command Paper 3883). As a consequence of that Act, any reference in this Schedule to the Parliament of Northern Ireland or the Assembly established under the Northern Ireland Assembly Act 1973, s 1, certain office-holders and Ministers, and any legislative act and certain financial dealings thereof, shall, for the period specified, be construed in accordance with Sch 12, paras 1–11 to the 1998 Act.

Application: this Part of the Schedule is applied with modifications, in relation to eligible debt securities, by the Uncertificated Securities (Amendment) (Eligible Debt Securities) Regulations 2003, SI 2003/1633, reg 15, Sch 2, paras 2(b), 3(a), 8(1), (2)(a). Para 3(b) was applied to companies nominated by the Secretary of State to succeed the National Research Development Corporation and the National Enterprise Board, by the British Technology Group Act 1991, s 13 (repealed).

SCHEDULE 2
MODIFICATION OF S 2 IN RELATION TO PROPERTY FALLING WITHIN S 3(3)

Section 3

1. In this Schedule "special-range property" means property falling within subsection (3) of section three of this Act.

2.—(1) Where a trust fund includes special-range property, subsection (1) of section two of this Act shall have effect as if references to the trust fund were references to so much thereof as does not consist of special-range property, and the special-range property shall be carried to a separate part of the fund.

(2) Any property which—

(a) being property belonging to the narrower-range or wider-range part of a trust fund, is converted into special-range property, or

(b) being special-range property, accrues to a trust fund after the division of the fund or part thereof in pursuance of subsection (1) of section two of this Act or of that subsection as modified by sub-paragraph (1) of this paragraph,

shall be carried to such a separate part of the fund as aforesaid; and subsections (2) and (3) of the said section two shall have effect subject to this sub-paragraph.

3. Where property carried to such a separate part as aforesaid is converted into property other than special-range property,—

(a) it shall be transferred to the narrower-range part of the fund or the wider-range part of the fund or apportioned between them, and

(b) any transfer of property from one of those parts to the other shall be made which is necessary to secure that the value of each of those parts of the fund is increased by the same amount.

[628]

NOTES

Repealed, except in so far as this Schedule relates to a trustee having a power of investment conferred on him under any enactment which was passed before 3 August 1961 and which is not amended by the Trustee Act 2000, Sch 2 or by the Charities and Trustee Investment (Scotland) Act 2005, Sch 3, by the Trustee Act 2000, s 40(1), (3), Sch 2, Pt I, para 1(2), Sch 4, Pt I and by the Charities and Trustee Investment (Scotland) Act 2005, s 95, Sch 3, para 4(1), (3).

SCHEDULE 3
PROVISIONS SUPPLEMENTARY TO S 3(4)

Section 3

1. Where in a case falling within subsection (4) of section three of this Act, property belonging to the narrower-range part of a trust fund—

(a) is invested otherwise than in a narrower-range investment, or

(b) being so invested, is retained and not transferred or as soon as may be reinvested as mentioned in subsection (2) of section two of this Act.

then, so long as the property continues so invested and comprised in the narrower- range part of the fund, section one of this Act shall not authorise the making or retention of any wider-range investment.

2. Section four of the Trustee Act 1925, or section thirty-three of the Trusts (Scotland) Act, 1921 (which relieve a trustee from liability for retaining an investment which has ceased to be authorised), shall not apply where an investment ceased to be authorised in consequence of the foregoing paragraph.

[629]

NOTES

Repealed, except in so far as this section relates to a trustee having a power of investment conferred on him under any enactment which was passed before 3 August 1961 and which is not amended by the Trustee Act 2000, Sch 2 or by the Charities and Trustee Investment (Scotland) Act 2005, Sch 3, by the Trustee Act 2000, s 40(1), (3), Sch 2, Pt I, para 1(2), Sch 4, Pt I and by the Charities and Trustee Investment (Scotland) Act 2005, s 95, Sch 3, para 4(1), (3).

(Sch 4: para 1(1) repealed by the Trustee Act 2000, s 40(1), (3), Sch 2, Pt I, para 1(3)(b), Sch 4, Pt I; para 1(2) repealed by the Charities and Trustee Investment (Scotland) Act 2005, s 95, Sch 3, para 4(1), (4); paras 2, 3 repealed by the Building Societies Act 1962, s 131, Sch 10, Pt I; paras 4, 5 repealed by the National Savings Bank Act 1971, s 28, Sch 2; para 6 repealed by the Housing (Consequential Provisions) Act 1985, s 3, Sch 1, Pt I. Sch 5 repealed by the Statute Law (Repeals) Act 1974.)

RECORDED DELIVERY SERVICE ACT 1962

(1962 c 27)

An Act to authorise the sending by the recorded delivery service of certain documents and other things required or authorised to be sent by registered post; and for purposes connected therewith

[3 July 1962]

1 Recorded delivery service to be an alternative to registered post

(1) Any enactment which requires or authorises a document or other thing to be sent by registered post (whether or not it makes any other provision in relation thereto) shall have effect as if it required or, as the case may be, authorised that thing to be sent by registered post or the recorded delivery service; and any enactment which makes any other provision in relation to the sending of a document or other thing by registered post or to a thing so sent shall have effect as if it made the like provision in relation to the sending of that thing by the recorded delivery service or, as the case may be, to a thing sent by that service.

(2) The Schedule to this Act shall have effect for the purpose of making consequential adaptations of the enactments therein mentioned.

(3) Subject to the following subsection [the Secretary of State] may by order make such amendments of any enactment contained in a local or private Act (being an enactment to which this Act applies) as appear to him to be necessary or expedient in consequence of subsection (1) of this section.

(4) Before making an order under this section, [the Secretary of State] shall, unless it appears to him to be impracticable to do so, consult with the person who promoted the Bill for the Act to which the order relates, or where it appears to [the Secretary of State] that some other person has succeeded to the promoter's interest in that Act, that other person.

(5) Any order under this section may be varied or revoked by a subsequent order thereunder, and the power to make any such order shall be exercisable by statutory instrument which shall be subject to annulment in pursuance of a resolution of either House of Parliament.

(6) This section shall not be construed as authorising the sending by the recorded delivery service of anything which [by virtue of the Postal Services Act 2000 or the terms and conditions of the service concerned] is not allowed to be sent by that service.

[629A]

NOTES

Sub-ss (3), (4): words in square brackets substituted by virtue of the Post Office Act 1969, s 5, and SI 1974/691, arts 2, 3(3).

Sub-s (6): words in square brackets substituted by SI 2001/1149, art 3(1), Sch 1, para 19.

2 Application and interpretation

(1) Subject to the next following subsection, this Act applies to the following enactments, that is to say,—

(a) the provisions of any Act (whether public general, local or private) passed before or in the same Session as this Act;

(b) the provisions of any Church Assembly Measure so passed;

(c) the provisions of any agricultural marketing scheme made under the Agricultural Marketing Act 1958, before the passing of this Act or having effect as if made under that Act;

and, in the case of a provision which has been applied by or under any other enactment passed, or any instrument made under any enactment passed, before or in the same Session as this Act, applies to that provision as so applied, subject, however, in the case of an instrument made after the passing of this Act to any contrary intention appearing therein; and references in this Act (except this section) to any enactment shall be construed accordingly.

(2) This Act does not apply—

(a) to subsection (2) of section nine of the Crown Proceedings Act 1947 (which enables proceedings to be brought against the Crown for loss of or damage to registered inland postal packets);

(b) to any enactment which, either as originally enacted or as amended by any subsequent enactment, requires or authorises a thing to be sent by the recorded delivery service as an alternative to registered post or makes provision in relation to a thing sent by that service;

(c) to the provisions of any Act of the Parliament of Northern Ireland or of any local or private Act which extends only to Northern Ireland.

(3) In this Act—

references to sending a document or other thing include references to serving, executing, giving or delivering it or doing any similar thing;

references to sending any thing by registered post include references to sending it by or in a registered letter or packet, whether the references are expressed in those terms or terms having the like effect and whether or not there is any mention of the post or prepayment;

references to any thing sent by registered post or the recorded delivery service shall be construed accordingly; and

references to a local Act include references to any Act confirming a provisional order or scheme.

[629B]

NOTES

Modification: the Northern Ireland Act 1998 makes new provision for the government of Northern Ireland for the purpose of implementing the Belfast Agreement (the agreement reached at multi-party talks on Northern Ireland and set out in Command Paper 3883). As a consequence of that Act, any reference in this section to the Parliament of Northern Ireland or the Assembly established under the Northern Ireland Assembly Act 1973, s 1, certain office-holders and Ministers, and any legislative act and certain financial dealings thereof, shall, for the period specified, be construed in accordance with Sch 12, paras 1–11 to the 1998 Act.

3 Extent

(1) It is hereby declared that (subject to subsection (2) of the foregoing section) this Act extends to Northern Ireland.

(2) …

(3) This Act, so far as it amends any enactment which extends to the Isle of Man or to any of the Channel Islands, or which applies in relation to persons of or belonging to any such island, shall extend to that island or, as the case may be, shall apply in like manner in relation to those persons.

[629C]

NOTES

Sub-s (2): repealed by the Northern Ireland Constitution Act 1973, s 41(1), Sch 6, Part I.

4 Short title

This Act may be cited as the Recorded Delivery Service Act 1962.

[629D]

SCHEDULE
ADAPTATION OF ENACTMENTS

Section 1

1. Any reference, however worded,—
   (a) in any enactment the provisions of which apply to, or operate in consequence of the operation of, any enactment amended by section one of this Act; or
   (b) in any enactment relating to the sending of documents or other things otherwise than by registered post or to documents or other things so sent;

to the registered post or to a registered letter or packet, shall be construed as including a reference to the recorded delivery service or to a letter or packet sent by that service; and any reference, however worded, in any such enactment to a Post Office receipt for a registered letter or to an acknowledgment of or certificate of delivery of a registered letter shall be construed accordingly.

2. The foregoing paragraph shall not be taken to prejudice the generality of subsection (1) of section one of this Act.

3. In the Citation Amendment (Scotland) Act 1882, the references in the Second Schedule to the post office charge for registration shall include references to the post office charge for sending by the recorded delivery service.

4. …

5. The requirement imposed by subsection (4) of section nine of the Agricultural Marketing Act 1958 that every scheme under that Act shall be so framed as to secure that the notice mentioned in paragraph (b) of that subsection shall be served by registered post shall have effect as a requirement that that notice shall be served by registered post or by the recorded delivery service.

[629E]

NOTES

Para 4: repealed by the Supreme Court Act 1981, ss 152(4), 153(4)(c), Sch 7.

WILLS ACT 1963

(1963 c 44)

An Act to repeal the Wills Act 1861 and make new provision in lieu thereof; and to provide that certain testamentary instruments shall be probative for the purpose of the conveyance of heritable property in Scotland

[31 July 1963]

1 General rule as to formal validity

A will shall be treated as properly executed if its execution conformed to the internal law in force in the territory where it was executed, or in the territory where, at the time of its execution or of the testator's death, he was domiciled or had his habitual residence, or in a state of which, at either of those times, he was a national.

[630]

2 Additional rules

(1) Without prejudice to the preceding section, the following shall be treated as properly executed—

- (a) a will executed on board a vessel or aircraft of any description, if the execution of the will conformed to the internal law in force in the territory with which, having regard to its registration (if any) and other relevant circumstances, the vessel or aircraft may be taken to have been most closely connected;
- (b) a will so far as it disposes of immovable property, if its execution conformed to the internal law in force in the territory where the property was situated;
- (c) a will so far as it revokes a will which under this Act would be treated as properly executed or revokes a provision which under this Act would be treated as comprised in a properly executed will, if the execution of the later will conformed to any law by reference to which the revoked will or provision would be so treated;
- (d) a will so far as it exercises a power of appointment, if the execution of the will conformed to the law governing the essential validity of the power.

(2) A will so far as it exercises a power of appointment shall not be treated as improperly executed by reason only that its execution was not in accordance with any formal requirements contained in the instrument creating the power.

[631]

3 Certain requirements to be treated as formal

Where (whether in pursuance of this Act or not) a law in force outside the United Kingdom falls to be applied in relation to a will, any requirement of that law whereby special formalities are to be observed by testators answering a particular description, or witnesses to the execution of a will are to possess certain qualifications, shall be treated, notwithstanding any rule of that law to the contrary, as a formal requirement only.

[632]

4 Construction of wills

The construction of a will shall not be altered by reason of any change in the testator's domicile after the execution of the will.

[633]

5 (*Repealed by the Succession* (*Scotland*) *Act 1964, s 34*(*2*), *Sch 3.*)

6 Interpretation

(1) In this Act—

"internal law" in relation to any territory or state means the law which would apply in a case where no question of the law in force in any other territory or state arose;

"state" means a territory or group of territories having its own law of nationality;

"will" includes any testamentary instrument or act, and "testator" shall be construed accordingly.

(2) Where under this Act the internal law in force in any territory or state is to be applied in the case of a will, but there are in force in that territory or state two or more systems of internal law relating to the formal validity of wills, the system to be applied shall be ascertained as follows—

- (a) if there is in force throughout the territory or state a rule indicating which of those systems can properly be applied in the case in question, that rule shall be followed; or
- (b) if there is no such rule, the system shall be that with which the testator was most closely connected at the relevant time, and for this purpose the relevant time is the time of the

testator's death where the matter is to be determined by reference to circumstances prevailing at his death, and the time of execution of the will in any other case.

(3) In determining for the purposes of this Act whether or not the execution of a will conformed to a particular law, regard shall be had to the formal requirements of that law at the time of execution, but this shall not prevent account being taken of an alteration of law affecting wills executed at that time if the alteration enables the will to be treated as properly executed.

[634]

7 Short title, commencement, repeal and extent

(1) This Act may be cited as the Wills Act 1963.

(2) This Act shall come into operation on 1st January 1964.

(3) …

(4) This Act shall not apply to a will of a testator who died before the time of the commencement of this Act and shall apply to a will of a testator who dies after that time whether the will was executed before or after that time, but so that the repeal of the Wills Act 1861 shall not invalidate a will executed before that time.

(5) It is hereby declared that this Act extends to Northern Ireland …

[635]

NOTES

Sub-s (3): repeals the Wills Act 1861.
Sub-s (5): words omitted repealed by the Northern Ireland Constitution Act 1973, Sch 6, Pt I.

PERPETUITIES AND ACCUMULATIONS ACT 1964

(1964 c 55)

An Act to modify the law of England and Wales relating to the avoidance of future interests in property on grounds of remoteness and governing accumulations of income from property

[16 July 1964]

Perpetuities

1 Power to specify perpetuity period

(1) Subject to section 9 (2) of this Act and subsection (2) below, where the instrument by which any disposition is made so provides, the perpetuity period applicable to the disposition under the rule against perpetuities, instead of being of any other duration, shall be of a duration equal to such number of years not exceeding eighty as is specified in that behalf in the instrument.

(2) Subsection (1) above shall not have effect where the disposition is made in exercise of a special power of appointment, but where a period is specified under that subsection in the instrument creating such a power the period shall apply in relation to any disposition under the power as it applies in relation to the power itself.

[636]

2 Presumptions and evidence as to future parenthood

(1) Where in any proceedings there arises on the rule against perpetuities a question which turns on the ability of a person to have a child at some future time, then—

(a) subject to paragraph (b) below, it shall be presumed that a male can have a child at the age of fourteen years or over, but not under that age, and that a female can have a child at the age of twelve years or over, but not under that age or over the age of fifty-five years; but

(b) in the case of a living person evidence may be given to show that he or she will or will not be able to have a child at the time in question.

(2) Where any such question is decided by treating a person as unable to have a child at a particular time, and he or she does so, the High Court may make such order as it thinks fit for placing the persons interested in the property comprised in the disposition, so far as may be just, in the position they would have held if the question had not been so decided.

(3) Subject to subsection (2) above, where any such question is decided in relation to a disposition by treating a person as able or unable to have a child at a particular time, then he or she shall be so treated for the purpose of any question which may arise on the rule against perpetuities in relation to the same disposition in any subsequent proceedings.

(4) In the foregoing provisions of this section references to having a child are references to begetting or giving birth to a child, but those provisions (except subsection (1)(b)) shall apply in

relation to the possibility that a person will at any time have a child by adoption, legitimation or other means as they apply to his or her ability at that time to beget or give birth to a child.

[637]

3 Uncertainty as to remoteness

(1) Where, apart from the provisions of this section and sections 4 and 5 of this Act, a disposition would be void on the ground that the interest disposed of might not become vested until too remote a time, the disposition shall be treated, until such time (if any) as it becomes established that the vesting must occur, if at all, after the end of the perpetuity period, as if the disposition were not subject to the rule against perpetuities; and its becoming so established shall not affect the validity of anything previously done in relation to the interest disposed of by way of advancement, application of intermediate income or otherwise.

(2) Where, apart from the said provisions, a disposition consisting of the conferring of a general power of appointment would be void on the ground that the power might not become exercisable until too remote a time, the disposition shall be treated, until such time (if any) as it becomes established that the power will not be exercisable within the perpetuity period, as if the disposition were not subject to the rule against perpetuities.

(3) Where, apart from the said provisions, a disposition consisting of the conferring of any power, option or other right would be void on the ground that the right might be exercised at too remote a time, the disposition shall be treated as regards any exercise of the right within the perpetuity period as if it were not subject to the rule against perpetuities and, subject to the said provisions, shall be treated as void for remoteness only if, and so far as, the right is not fully exercised within that period.

(4) Where this section applies to a disposition and the duration of the perpetuity period is not determined by virtue of section 1 or 9(2) of this Act, it shall be determined as follows—

(a) where any persons falling within subsection (5) below are individuals in being and ascertainable at the commencement of the perpetuity period the duration of the period shall be determined by reference to their lives and no others, but so that the lives of any description of persons falling within paragraph (b) or (c) of that subsection shall be disregarded if the number of persons of that description is such as to render it impracticable to ascertain the date of death of the survivor;

(b) where there are no lives under paragraph (a) above the period shall be twenty-one years.

(5) The said persons are as follows:—

(a) the person by whom the disposition was made;

(b) a person to whom or in whose favour the disposition was made, that is to say—

(i) in the case of a disposition to a class of persons, any member or potential member of the class;

(ii) in the case of an individual disposition to a person taking only on certain conditions being satisfied, any person as to whom some of the conditions are satisfied and the remainder may in time be satisfied;

(iii) in the case of a special power of appointment exercisable in favour of members of a class, any member or potential member of the class;

(iv) in the case of a special power of appointment exercisable in favour of one person only, that person or, where the object of the power is ascertainable only on certain conditions being satisfied, any person as to whom some of the conditions are satisfied and the remainder may in time be satisfied;

(v) in the case of any power, option or other right, the person on whom the right is conferred;

(c) a person having a child or grandchild within sub-paragraphs (i) to (iv) of paragraph (b) above, or any of whose children or grandchildren, if subsequently born, would by virtue of his or her descent fall within those sub-paragraphs;

(d) any person on the failure or determination of whose prior interest the disposition is limited to take effect.

[638]

4 Reduction of age and exclusion of class members to avoid remoteness

(1) Where a disposition is limited by reference to the attainment by any person or persons of a specified age exceeding twenty-one years, and it is apparent at the time the disposition is made or becomes apparent at a subsequent time—

(a) that the disposition would, apart from this section, be void for remoteness, but

(b) that it would not be so void if the specified age had been twenty-one years,

the disposition shall be treated for all purposes as if, instead of being limited by reference to the age in fact specified, it had been limited by reference to the age nearest to that age which would, if specified instead, have prevented the disposition from being so void.

(2) Where in the case of any disposition different ages exceeding twenty-one years are specified in relation to different persons—

(a) the reference in paragraph (b) of subsection (1) above to the specified age shall be construed as a reference to all the specified ages, and
(b) that subsection shall operate to reduce each such age so far as is necessary to save the disposition from being void for remoteness.

(3) Where the inclusion of any persons, being potential members of a class or unborn persons who at birth would become members or potential members of the class, prevents the foregoing provisions of this section from operating to save a disposition from being void for remoteness, those persons shall thenceforth be deemed for all the purposes of the disposition to be excluded from the class, and the said provisions shall thereupon have effect accordingly.

(4) Where, in the case of a disposition to which subsection (3) above does not apply, it is apparent at the time the disposition is made or becomes apparent at a subsequent time that, apart from this subsection, the inclusion of any persons, being potential members of a class or unborn persons who at birth would become members or potential members of the class, would cause the disposition to be treated as void for remoteness, those persons shall, unless their exclusion would exhaust the class, thenceforth be deemed for all the purposes of the disposition to be excluded from the class.

(5) Where this section has effect in relation to a disposition to which section 3 above applies, the operation of this section shall not affect the validity of anything previously done in relation to the interest disposed of by way of advancement, application of intermediate income or otherwise.

(6) ...

[(7) For the avoidance of doubt it is hereby declared that a question arising under section 3 of this Act or subsection (1)(a) above of whether a disposition would be void apart from this section is to be determined as if subsection (6) above had been a separate section of this Act.]

[639]

NOTES

Sub-s (6): repeals the Law of Property Act 1925, s 163.
Sub-s (7): inserted by the Children Act 1975, s 108(1)(a), Sch 3, para 43.

5 Condition relating to death of surviving spouse

Where a disposition is limited by reference to the time of death of the survivor of a person in being at the commencement of the perpetuity period and any spouse of that person, and that time has not arrived at the end of the perpetuity period, the disposition shall be treated for all purposes, where to do so would save it from being void for remoteness, as if it had instead been limited by reference to the time immediately before the end of that period.

[640]

6 Saving and acceleration of expectant interests

A disposition shall not be treated as void for remoteness by reason only that the interest disposed of is ulterior to and dependent upon an interest under a disposition which is so void, and the vesting of an interest shall not be prevented from being accelerated on the failure of a prior interest by reason only that the failure arises because of remoteness.

[641]

7 Powers of appointment

For the purposes of the rule against perpetuities, a power of appointment shall be treated as a special power unless—

(a) in the instrument creating the power it is expressed to be exercisable by one person only, and
(b) it could, at all times during its currency when that person is of full age and capacity, be exercised by him so as immediately to transfer to himself the whole of the interest governed by the power without the consent of any other person or compliance with any other condition, not being a formal condition relating only to the mode of exercise of the power:

Provided that for the purpose of determining whether a disposition made under a power of appointment exercisable by will only is void for remoteness, the power shall be treated as a general power where it would have fallen to be so treated if exercisable by deed.

[642]

8 Administrative powers of trustees

(1) The rule against perpetuities shall not operate to invalidate a power conferred on trustees or other persons to sell, lease, exchange or otherwise dispose of any property for full consideration, or to do any other act in the administration (as opposed to the distribution) of any property, and shall not prevent the payment to trustees or other persons of reasonable remuneration for their services.

(2) Subsection (1) above shall apply for the purpose of enabling a power to be exercised at any time after the commencement of this Act notwithstanding that the power is conferred by an instrument which took effect before that commencement.

[643]

9 Options relating to land

(1) The rule against perpetuities shall not apply to a disposition consisting of the conferring of an option to acquire for valuable consideration an interest reversionary (whether directly or indirectly) on the term of a lease if—

(a) the option is exercisable only by the lessee or his successors in title, and

(b) it ceases to be exercisable at or before the expiration of one year following the determination of the lease.

This subsection shall apply in relation to an agreement for a lease as it applies in relation to a lease, and "lessee" shall be construed accordingly.

(2) In the case of a disposition consisting of the conferring of an option to acquire for valuable consideration any interest in land, the perpetuity period under the rule against perpetuities shall be twenty-one years, and section 1 of this Act shall not apply:

Provided that this subsection shall not apply to a right of pre-emption conferred on a public or local authority in respect of land used or to be used for religious purposes where the right becomes exercisable only if the land ceases to be used for such purposes.

[644]

10 Avoidance of contractual and other rights in cases of remoteness

Where a disposition inter vivos would fall to be treated as void for remoteness if the rights and duties thereunder were capable of transmission to persons other than the original parties and had been so transmitted, it shall be treated as void as between the person by whom it was made and the person to whom or in whose favour it was made or any successor of his, and no remedy shall lie in contract or otherwise for giving effect to it or making restitution for its lack of effect.

[645]

11 Rights for enforcement of rentcharges

(1) The rule against perpetuities shall not apply to any powers or remedies for recovering or compelling the payment of an annual sum to which section 121 or 122 of the Law of Property Act 1925 applies, or otherwise becoming exercisable or enforceable on the breach of any condition or other requirement relating to that sum.

(2) …

[646]

NOTES

Sub-s (2): amends the Law of Property Act 1925, s 121 at **[367]**.

12 Possibilities of reverter, conditions subsequent, exceptions and reservations

(1) In the case of—

(a) a possibility of reverter on the determination of a determinable fee simple, or

(b) a possibility of a resulting trust on the determination of any other determinable interest in property,

the rule against perpetuities shall apply in relation to the provision causing the interest to be determinable as it would apply if that provision were expressed in the form of a condition subsequent giving rise, on breach thereof, to a right of re-entry or an equivalent right in the case of property other than land, and where the provision falls to be treated as void for remoteness the determinable interest shall become an absolute interest.

(2) Where a disposition is subject to any such provision, or to any such condition subsequent, or to any exception or reservation, the disposition shall be treated for the purposes of this Act as including a separate disposition of any rights arising by virtue of the provision, condition subsequent, exception or reservation.

[647]

Accumulations

13 Amendment of s 164 of Law of Property Act 1925

(1) The periods for which accumulations of income under a settlement or other disposition are permitted by section 164 of the Law of Property Act 1925 shall include—

(a) a term of twenty-one years from the date of the making of the disposition, and

(b) the duration of the minority or respective minorities of any person or persons in being at that date.

(2) It is hereby declared that the restrictions imposed by the said section 164 apply in relation to a power to accumulate income whether or not there is a duty to exercise that power, and that they apply whether or not the power to accumulate extends to income produced by the investment of income previously accumulated.

[648]

14 Right to stop accumulations

Section 2 above shall apply to any question as to the right of beneficiaries to put an end to accumulations of income under any disposition as it applies to questions arising on the rule against perpetuities.

[649]

Supplemental

15 Short title, interpretation and extent

(1) This Act may be cited as the Perpetuities and Accumulations Act 1964.

(2) In this Act—

"disposition" includes the conferring of a power of appointment and any other disposition of an interest in or right over property, and references to the interest disposed of shall be construed accordingly;

"in being" means living or en ventre sa mere;

"power of appointment" includes any discretionary power to transfer a beneficial interest in property without the furnishing of valuable consideration;

"will" includes a codicil;

and for the purposes of this Act a disposition contained in a will shall be deemed to be made at the death of the testator.

(3) For the purposes of this Act a person shall be treated as a member of a class if in his case all the conditions identifying a member of the class are satisfied, and shall be treated as a potential member if in his case some only of those conditions are satisfied but there is a possibility that the remainder will in time be satisfied.

(4) Nothing in this Act shall affect the operation of the rule of law rendering void for remoteness certain dispositions under which property is limited to be applied for purposes other than the benefit of any person or class of persons in cases where the property may be so applied after the end of the perpetuity period.

(5) The foregoing sections of this Act shall apply (except as provided in section 8 (2) above) only in relation to instruments taking effect after the commencement of this Act, and in the case of an instrument made in the exercise of a special power of appointment shall apply only where the instrument creating the power takes effect after that commencement;

Provided that section 7 above shall apply in all cases for construing the foregoing reference to a special power of appointment.

(6) This Act shall apply in relation to a disposition made otherwise than by an instrument as if the disposition had been contained in an instrument taking effect when the disposition was made.

(7) This Act binds the Crown.

(8) Except in so far as the contrary intention appears, any enactment of the Parliament of Northern Ireland passed for purposes similar to the purposes of this Act shall bind the Crown.

(9) This Act shall not extend to Scotland or (apart from subsection (8) above) to Northern Ireland.

[650]

NOTES

Modification: the Northern Ireland Act 1998 makes new provision for the government of Northern Ireland for the purpose of implementing the Belfast Agreement (the agreement reached at multi-party talks on Northern Ireland and set out in Command Paper 3883). As a consequence of that Act, any reference in this section to the Parliament of Northern Ireland or the Assembly established under the Northern Ireland Assembly Act 1973, s 1, certain office-holders and Ministers, and any legislative act and certain financial dealings thereof, shall, for the period specified, be construed in accordance with Sch 12, paras 1–11 to the 1998 Act.

LAW OF PROPERTY (JOINT TENANTS) ACT 1964

(1964 c 63)

An Act to amend the law with respect to land vested in joint tenants

[31 July 1964]

1 Assumptions on sale of land by survivor of joint tenants

(1) For the purposes of section 36(2) of the Law of Property Act 1925, as amended by section 7 of and the Schedule to the Law of Property (Amendment) Act 1926, the survivor of two or more joint tenants shall in favour of a purchaser of the legal estate, be deemed to be solely and beneficially interested if … the conveyance includes a statement that he is so interested.

Provided that the foregoing provisions of this subsection shall not apply if, at any time before the date of the conveyance by the survivor—

(a) a memorandum of severance (that is to say a note or memorandum signed by the joint tenants or one of them and recording that the joint tenancy was severed in equity on a date therein specified) had been endorsed on or annexed to the conveyance by virtue of which the legal estate was vested in the joint tenants; or

(b) [a bankruptcy order] made against any of the joint tenants, or a petition for such an order, had been registered under the Land Charges Act 1925, being an order or petition of which the purchaser has notice, by virtue of the registration, on the date of the conveyance by the survivor.

(2) The foregoing provisions of this section shall apply with the necessary modifications in relation to a conveyance by the personal representatives of the survivor of joint tenants as they apply in relation to a conveyance by such a survivor.

[651]

NOTES

Sub-s (1): words omitted repealed by the Law of Property (Miscellaneous Provisions) Act 1994, s 21(1), (2), Sch 1, para 3, Sch 2; words in square brackets substituted by the Insolvency Act 1985, s 235, Sch 8, para 13 and the Insolvency Act 1986, s 437, Sch 11.

2 Retrospective and transitional provisions

Section 1 of this Act shall be deemed to have come into force on 1st January 1926, and for the purposes of that section in its application to a conveyance executed before the passing of this Act a statement signed by the vendor or by his personal representatives that he was solely and beneficially interested shall be treated as if it had been included in the conveyance.

[652]

3 Exclusion of registered land

This Act shall not apply to [registered land].

[653]

NOTES

Words in square brackets substituted by the Land Registration Act 2002, s 133, Sch 11, para 5.

4 Short title, construction, citation and extent

(1) This Act may be cited as the Law of Property (Joint Tenants) Act 1964, and shall be construed as one with the Law of Property Act 1925.

(2) The Law of Property Acts 1925 to 1932, and this Act, may be cited together as the Law of Property Acts 1925 to 1964.

(3) This Act extends to England and Wales only.

[654]

COMPULSORY PURCHASE ACT 1965

(1965 c 56)

An Act to consolidate the Lands Clauses Acts as applied by Part I of Schedule 2 to the Acquisition of Land (Authorisation Procedure) Act 1946, and by certain other enactments, and to repeal certain provisions in the Lands Clauses Acts and related enactments which have ceased to have any effect

[5 August 1965]

PART I
COMPULSORY PURCHASE UNDER ACQUISITION OF LAND ACT OF 1946

1–9 (*Outside the scope of this work.*)

Further provision as to compensation for injurious affection

10 Further provision as to compensation for injurious affection

(1) If any person claims compensation in respect of any land, or any interest in land, which has been taken for or injuriously affected by the execution of the works, and for which the acquiring authority have not made satisfaction under the provisions of this Act, or of the special Act, any dispute arising in relation to the compensation shall be referred to and determined by the [Upper Tribunal].

(2) This section shall be construed as affording in all cases a right to compensation for injurious affection to land which is the same as the right which section 68 of the Lands Clauses Consolidation Act 1845 has been construed as affording in cases where the amount claimed exceeds fifty pounds.

(3) Where this Part of this Act applies by virtue of [Part IX of the Town and Country Planning Act 1990] references in this section to the acquiring authority shall be construed in accordance with [section 245(4)(b) of that Act].

[655]

NOTES

Sub-s (1): words in square brackets substituted by SI 2009/1307, art 5(1), (2), Sch 1, paras 59, 63.

Sub-s (3): words in square brackets substituted by the Planning (Consequential Provisions) Act 1990, s 4, Sch 2, para 13(2).

11–32 (*Ss 11–23, 25, 26, 28–32 outside the scope of this work; s 24 repealed by the Rentcharges Act 1977, s 17(2), (3), Sch 2; s 27 repealed by SI 1990/776, art 3, Sch 1.*)

PART II
APPLICATION OF PART I TO OTHER CASES AND SUPPLEMENTAL PROVISIONS

33–39 (*Ss 33, 36 repealed by the Water Act 1989, s 190(2), (3), Sch 26, Pt VII, para 41, Sch 27, Pt I; ss 34, 35 repealed by the Housing (Consequential Provisions) Act 1985, s 3, Sch 1, Pt I; ss 37–39 outside the scope of this work.*)

40 Short title, commencement and extent

(1) This Act may be cited as the Compulsory Purchase Act 1965.

(2) Except as otherwise expressly provided, this Act shall come into force on 1st January 1966.

(3) This Act shall not extend to Scotland or Northern Ireland.

[656]

(*Schs 1–8 outside the scope of this work.*)

COMMONS REGISTRATION ACT 1965

(1965 c 64)

An Act to provide for the registration of common land and of town or village greens; to amend the law as to prescriptive claims to rights of common; and for purposes connected therewith

[5 August 1965]

1 Registration of commons and towns or village greens and ownership of and rights over them

(1) There shall be registered, in accordance with the provisions of this Act and subject to the exceptions mentioned therein,—

(*a*) *land in England or Wales which is common land or a town or village green;*
(*b*) *rights of common over such land; and*
(*c*) *persons claiming to be or found to be owners of such land or becoming the owners thereof by virtue of this Act;*

and no rights of common over land which is capable of being registered under this Act shall be registered [in the register of title].

(2) After the end of such period, not being less than three years from the commencement of this Act, as the Minister may by order determine—

(*a*) *no land capable of being registered under this Act shall be deemed to be common land or a town or village green unless it is so registered; and*
(*b*) *no rights of common shall be exercisable over any such land unless they are registered either under this Act or [in the register of title].*

(*3*) *Where any land is registered under this Act but no person is registered as the owner thereof under this Act or [in the register of title], it shall—*

(*a*) *if it is a town or village green, be vested in accordance with the following provisions of this Act; and*

(*b*) *if it is common land, be vested as Parliament may hereafter determine.*

[657]

NOTES

Repealed by the Commons Act 2006, s 53, Sch 6, Pt 1, subject to transitional provisions in s 23 of, Sch 3, para 6 to, that Act at **[2296]**, **[2335]**, as from 1 October 2008 (in England in relation to the pilot areas), and as from a day to be appointed (in England for remaining purposes and in Wales).

Sub-s (1)–(3): words in square brackets substituted by the Land Registration Act 2002, s 133, Sch 11, para 7(1), (2).

Transfer of Functions: functions of the Minister, so far as exercisable in relation to Wales, transferred to the National Assembly for Wales, by the National Assembly for Wales (Transfer of Functions) Order 1999, SI 1999/672, art 2, Sch 1.

Order: the Commons Registration (Time Limits) Order 1966, SI 1966/1470.

2 Registration authorities

(*1*) *The registration authority for the purposes of this Act shall be—*

(*a*) *in relation to any land situated in any county … , the council of that county [or, if the county is a metropolitan county, the council of the metropolitan district in which the land is situated] … ; and*

(*b*) *in relation to any land situated in Greater London, the [council of the London borough in which the land is situated];*

except where an agreement under this section otherwise provides.

(*2*) *Where part of any land is in the area of one registration authority and part in that of another the authorities may by agreement provide for one of them to be the registration authority in relation to the whole of the land.*

[658]

NOTES

Repealed by the Commons Act 2006, s 53, Sch 6, Pt 1, as from 1 October 2008 (in England in relation to the pilot areas), and as from a day to be appointed (in England for remaining purposes and in Wales).

Sub-s (1): in para (a) words omitted repealed by the Local Government Act 1972, s 272(1), Sch 30, words in square brackets inserted by the Local Government Act 1985, s 16, Sch 8, para 10; in para (b) words in square brackets substituted by the Local Government Act 1985, s 16, Sch 8, para 10.

3 The registers

(*1*) *For the purposes of registering such land as is mentioned in section 1(1) of this Act and rights of common over and ownership of such land every registration authority shall maintain—*

(*a*) *a register of common land; and*

(*b*) *a register of town or village greens;*

and regulations under this Act may require or authorise a registration authority to note on those registers such other information as may be prescribed.

(*2*) *Any register maintained under this Act shall be open to inspection by the public at all reasonable times.*

[659]

NOTES

Repealed by the Commons Act 2006, s 53, Sch 6, Pt 1, as from 1 October 2008 (in England in relation to the pilot areas), and as from a day to be appointed (in England for remaining purposes and in Wales).

Regulations: the Commons Registration (General) Regulations 1966, SI 1966/1471; the Commons Registration (Objections and Maps) Regulations 1968, SI 1968/989; the Commons Registration (Disposal of Disputed Registrations) Regulations 1972, SI 1972/437.

4 Provisional registration

(*1*) *Subject to the provisions of this section, a registration authority shall register any land as common land or a town or village green or, as the case may be, any rights of common over or ownership of such land, on application duly made to it and accompanied by such declaration and such other documents (if any) as may be prescribed for the purpose of verification or of proving compliance with any prescribed conditions.*

(*2*) *An application for the registration of any land as common land or as a town or village green may be made by any person, and a registration authority—*

(*a*) *may so register any land notwithstanding that no application for that registration has been made, and* (*b*) *shall so register any land in any case where it registers any rights over it under this section.*

(3) No person shall be registered under this section as the owner of any land which is registered [in the register of title] and no person shall be registered under this section as the owner of any other land unless the land itself is registered under this section.

(4) Where, in pursuance of an application under this section, any land would fall to be registered as common land or as a town or village green, but the land is already so registered, the registration authority shall not register it again but shall note the application in the register.

(5) A registration under this section shall be provisional only until it has become final under the following provisions of this Act.

(6) An application for registration under this section shall not be entertained if made after such date, not less than three years from the commencement of this Act, as the Minister may by order specify; and different dates may be so specified for different classes of applications.

(7) Every local authority shall take such steps as may be prescribed for informing the public of the period within which and the manner in which applications for registration under this section may be made.

[660]

NOTES

Repealed by the Commons Act 2006, s 53, Sch 6, Pt 1, as from 1 October 2008 (in England in relation to the pilot areas), and as from a day to be appointed (in England for remaining purposes and in Wales).

Sub-s (3): words in square brackets substituted by the Land Registration Act 2002, s 133, Sch 11, para 7(1), (2).

Transfer of Functions: see the note to s 1 at **[657]**.

Order: the Commons Registration (Time Limits) Order 1966, SI 1966/1470.

5 Notification of, and objections to, registration

(1) A registration authority shall give such notices and take such other steps as may be prescribed for informing the public of any registration made by it under section 4 of this Act, of the times and places where copies of the relevant entries in the register may be inspected and of the period during which and the manner in which objections to the registration may be made to the authority.

(2) The period during which objections to any registration under section 4 of this Act may be made shall be such period, ending not less than two years after the date of the registration, as may be prescribed.

(3) Where any land or rights over land are registered under section 4 of this Act but no person is so registered as the owner of the land the registration authority may, if it thinks fit, make an objection to the registration notwithstanding that it has no interest in the land.

(4) Where an objection to a registration under section 4 of this Act is made, the registration authority shall note the objection on the register and shall give such notice as may be prescribed to the person (if any) on whose application the registration was made and to any person whose application is noted under section 4(4) of this Act.

(5) Where a person to whom notice has been given under subsection (4) of this section so requests or where the registration was made otherwise than on the application of any person, the registration authority may, if it thinks fit, cancel or modify a registration to which objection is made under this section.

(6) Where such an objection is made, then, unless the objection is withdrawn or the registration cancelled before the end of such period as may be prescribed, the registration authority shall refer the matter to a Commons Commissioner.

(7) An objection to the registration of any land as common land or as a town or village green shall be treated for the purposes of this Act as being also an objection to any registration (whenever made) under section 4 of this Act of any rights over the land.

(8) A registration authority shall take such steps as may be prescribed for informing the public of any objection which they have noted on the register under this section and of the times and places where copies of the relevant entries in the register may be inspected.

(9) Where regulations under this Act require copies of any entries in a register to be sent by the registration authority to another local authority they may require that other authority to make the copies available for inspection in such manner as may be prescribed.

[661]

NOTES

Repealed by the Commons Act 2006, s 53, Sch 6, Pt 1, as from 1 October 2008 (in England in relation to the pilot areas), and as from a day to be appointed (in England for remaining purposes and in Wales).

Regulations: the Commons Commissioners Regulations 1971, SI 1971/1727; the Commons Registration (Second Period References) Regulations 1973, SI 1973/815.

6 Disposal of disputed claims

(1) The Commons Commissioner to whom any matter has been referred under section 5 of this Act shall inquire into it and shall either confirm the registration, with or without modifications, or refuse to confirm it; and the registration shall, if it is confirmed, become final, and, if the confirmation is refused, become void,—

(a) if no appeal is brought against the confirmation or refusal, at the end of the period during which such an appeal could have been brought;

(b) if such an appeal is brought, when it is finally disposed of.

(2) On being informed in the prescribed manner that a registration has become final (with or without modifications) or has become void a registration authority shall indicate that fact in the prescribed manner in the register and, if it has become void, cancel the registration.

(3) Where the registration of any land as common land or as a town or village green is cancelled (whether under this section or under section 5(5) of this Act) the registration authority shall also cancel the registration of any person as the owner thereof.

[662]

NOTES

Repealed by the Commons Act 2006, s 53, Sch 6, Pt 1, as from 1 October 2008 (in England in relation to the pilot areas), and as from a day to be appointed (in England for remaining purposes and in Wales).

Regulations: the Commons Commissioners Regulations 1971, SI 1971/1727; the Commons Registration (Disposal of Disputed Registrations) Regulations 1972, SI 1972/437.

7 Finality of undisputed registrations

(1) If no objection is made to a registration under section 4 of this Act or if all objections made to such a registration are withdrawn the registration shall become final at the end of the period during which such objections could have been made under section 5 of this Act or, if an objection made during that period is withdrawn after the end thereof, at the date of the withdrawal.

(2) Where by virtue of this section a registration has become final the registration authority shall indicate that fact in the prescribed manner in the register.

[663]

NOTES

Repealed by the Commons Act 2006, s 53, Sch 6, Pt 1, as from 1 October 2008 (in England in relation to the pilot areas), and as from a day to be appointed (in England for remaining purposes and in Wales).

Regulations: the Commons Registration (Finality of Undisputed Registrations) Regulations 1970, SI 1970/1371.

8 Vesting of unclaimed land

(1) Where the registration under section 4 of this Act of any land as common land or as a town or village green has become final but no person is registered under that section as the owner of the land, then unless the land is registered [in the register of title], the registration authority shall refer the question of the ownership of the land to a Commons Commissioner.

(2) After the registration authority has given such notices as may be prescribed, the Commons Commissioner shall inquire into the matter and shall, if satisfied that any person is the owner of the land, direct the registration authority to register that person accordingly; and the registration authority shall comply with the direction.

(3) If the Commons Commissioner is not so satisfied and the land is a town or village green he shall direct the registration authority to register as the owner of the land the local authority specified in subsection (5) of this section; and the registration authority shall comply with the direction.

(4) On the registration under this section of a local authority as the owner of any land the land shall vest in that local authority and, if the land is not regulated by a scheme under the Commons Act 1899, sections 10 and 15 of the Open Spaces Act 1906 (power to manage and make byelaws) shall apply in relation to it as if that local authority had acquired the ownership under the said Act of 1906.

[(5) Subject to subsection (6) of this section, the local authority in which any land is to be vested under this section is—

(a) if the land is in a parish or community where there is a parish or community council, that council, but, if the land is regulated by a scheme under the Commons Act 1899, only if the powers of management under Part I of that Act are, in accordance with arrangements under Part VI of the Local Government Act 1972, being exercised by the parish or community council;

PART I STATUTES

(*b*) *if the land is in a London borough, the council of that borough; and*
(*c*) *in any other case, the council of the district in which the land is situated.*

(*6*) *Where—*
(*a*) *any land has been vested in a district council in accordance with subsection* (*5*)(*c*) *of this section, and*
(*b*) *after the land has been so vested a parish or community council comes into being for the parish or community in which the land is situated (whether by the establishment of a new council or by adding that parish or community to a group of parishes or communities for which a council has already been established),*

then, if the circumstances are such that, had the direction under subsection (*3*) *of this section been given at a time after the parish or community council had come into being, the land would in accordance with subsection* (*5*)(*a*) *of this section have been vested in the parish or community council, the district council shall, if requested to do so by the parish or community council, direct the registration authority to register the parish or community council, in place of the district council, as the owner of the land; and the registration authority shall comply with any such direction.*

(*7*) *The council of any district, parish or community affected by any registration made in pursuance of subsection* (*6*) *above shall pay to the other of those councils so affected such sum, if any, as may be agreed between them to be appropriate to take account of any sums received or to be received, or any expenditure incurred or to be incurred, in respect of the land concerned, and, in default of agreement, the question of what sum, if any, is appropriate for that purpose shall be determined by arbitration.]*

[664]

NOTES

Repealed by the Commons Act 2006, s 53, Sch 6, Pt 1, subject to transitional provisions in s 23 of, Sch 3, para 9(1) to, that Act at **[2296]**, **[2335]**, as from 1 October 2006 (in relation to England) (subject to transitional provisions and savings in SI 2006/2504, art 3(2)), and as from 6 September 2007 (in relation to Wales) (subject to transitional provisions and savings in SI 2007/2386, art 4(5).

Sub-s (1): words in square brackets substituted by the Land Registration Act 2002, s 133, Sch 11, para 7(1), (2).

Sub-ss (5)–(7): substituted, for original sub-s (5), by the Local Government Act 1972, s 189(2).

Regulations: the Commons Commissioners Regulations 1971, SI 1971/1727.

9 (*Repealed by the Commons Act 2006, s 53, Sch 6, Pt 1.*)

10 Effect of registration

The registration under this Act of any land as common land or as a town or village green, or of any rights of common over any such land, shall be conclusive evidence of the matters registered, as at the date of registration, except where the registration is provisional only.

[665]

NOTES

Repealed by the Commons Act 2006, s 53, Sch 6, Pt 1, as from 1 October 2008 (in England in relation to the pilot areas), and as from a day to be appointed (in England for remaining purposes and in Wales).

11 Exemption from registration

(*1*) *The foregoing provisions of this Act shall not apply to the New Forest or Epping Forest nor to any land exempted from those provisions by an order of the Minister, and shall not be taken to apply to the Forest of Dean.*

(*2*) *The Minister shall not make an order under this section except on an application made to him before such date as may be prescribed.*

(*3*) *The Minister shall not make an order under this section with respect to any land unless it appears to him—*
(*a*) *that the land is regulated by a scheme under the Commons Act 1899 or the Metropolitan Commons Acts 1866 to 1898 or is regulated under a local Act or under an Act confirming a provisional order made under the Commons Act 1876; and*
(*b*) *that no rights of common have been exercised over the land for at least thirty years and that the owner of the land is known.*

(*4*) *The Minister shall, before dealing with any application under this section, send copies thereof to the registration authority and to such other local authorities as may be prescribed, and shall inform those authorities whether he has granted or refused the application; and those authorities shall take such steps as may be prescribed for informing the public of the application and its grant or refusal.*

(*5*) *If any question arises under this Act whether any land is part of the forests mentioned in subsection* (*1*) *of this section it shall be referred to and decided by the Minister.*

[666]

NOTES

Repealed by the Commons Act 2006, s 53, Sch 6, Pt 1, as from 1 October 2008 (in England in relation to the pilot areas), and as from a day to be appointed (in England for remaining purposes and in Wales).

Transfer of Functions: see the note to s 1 at **[657]**.

Regulations: the Commons Registration (Exempted Land) Regulations 1965, SI 1965/2001.

12 Subsequent registration under Land Registration Acts 1925 and 1936

The following provisions shall have effect with respect to the registration [in the register of title] of any land after the ownership of the land has been registered under this Act, that is to say—

(*a*) ...

(*b*) *if the registration authority is notified by the Chief Land Registrar that the land has been registered [in the register of title] the authority shall delete the registration of the ownership under this Act and indicate in the register in the prescribed manner that it has been registered under those Acts.*

[667]

NOTES

Repealed by the Commons Act 2006, s 53, Sch 6, Pt 1, as from 1 October 2008 (in England in relation to the pilot areas), and as from a day to be appointed (in England for remaining purposes and in Wales).

Words in square brackets in both places they occur substituted by the Land Registration Act 2002, s 133, Sch 11, para 7(1), (4); para (a) repealed by the Land Registration Act 1997, s 4(2), Sch 2, Pt I.

13 Amendment of registers

Regulations under this Act shall provide for the amendment of the registers maintained under this Act where—

(*a*) *any land registered under this Act ceases to be common land or a town or village green; or*

(*b*) *any land becomes common land or a town or village green; or*

(*c*) *any rights registered under this Act are apportioned, extinguished or released, or are varied or transferred in such circumstances as may be prescribed;*

...

[668]

NOTES

Repealed by the Commons Act 2006, s 53, Sch 6, Pt 1, as from 1 October 2006 (in relation to England in so far as relating to para (a), subject to transitional provisions and savings in SI 2006/2504, art 3(3), (4)), as from 6 April 2007 (in relation to England in so far as relating to para (b), subject to transitional provisions and savings in SI 2007/456, art 4(3), (4)), as from 6 September 2007 (in relation to Wales in so far as relating to paras (a), (b), subject to transitional provisions and savings in SI 2007/2386, art 4(2)(b), (3), (6), (7)), as from 1 October 2008 (in England in relation to the pilot areas), and as from a day to be appointed (in England and Wales for remaining purposes).

Words omitted repealed by the Law of Property Act 1969, s 16(2), Sch 2, Pt I.

14 Rectification of registers

The High Court may order a register maintained under this Act to be amended if—

(*a*) *the registration under this Act of any land or rights of common has become final and the court is satisfied that any person was induced by fraud to withdraw an objection to the registration or to refrain from making such an objection; or*

(*b*) *the register has been amended in pursuance of section 13 of this Act and it appears to the court that no amendment or a different amendment ought to have been made and that the error cannot be corrected in pursuance of regulations made under this Act;*

and, in either case, the court deems it just to rectify the register.

[669]

NOTES

Repealed by the Commons Act 2006, s 53, Sch 6, Pt 1, as from 1 October 2008 (in England in relation to the pilot areas), and as from a day to be appointed (in England for remaining purposes and in Wales).

15 Quantification of certain grazing rights

(*1*) *Where a right of common consists of or includes a right, not limited by number, to graze animals or animals of any class, it shall for the purposes of registration under this Act be treated as exercisable in relation to no more animals, or animals of that class, than a definite number.*

(2) Any application for the registration of such a right shall state the number of animals to be entered in the register or, as the case may be, the numbers of animals of different classes to be so entered.

(3) When the registration of such a right has become final the right shall accordingly be exercisable in relation to animals not exceeding the number or numbers registered or such other number or numbers as Parliament may hereafter determine.

[670]

NOTES

Repealed by the Commons Act 2006, s 53, Sch 6, Pt 1, as from 1 October 2008 (in England in relation to the pilot areas), and as from a day to be appointed (in England for remaining purposes and in Wales).

16 Disregard of certain interruptions in prescriptive claims to rights of common

(1) Where during any period a right of common claimed over any land was not exercised, but during the whole or part of that period either—

(a) the land was requisitioned; or

(b) where the right claimed is a right to graze animals, the right could not be or was not exercised for reasons of animal health;

that period or part shall be left out of account, both—

(i) in determining for the purposes of the Prescription Act 1832 whether there was an interruption within the meaning of that Act of the actual enjoyment of the right; and

(ii) in computing the period of thirty or sixty years mentioned in section 1 of that Act.

(2) For the purposes of the said Act any objection under this Act to the registration of a right of common shall be deemed to be such a suit or action as is referred to in section 4 of that Act.

(3) In this section "requisitioned" means in the possession of a Government department in the exercise or purported exercise of powers conferred by regulations made under the Emergency Powers (Defence) Act 1939 or by Part VI of the Requisitioned Land and War Works Act 1945; and in determining in any proceedings any question arising under this section whether any land was requisitioned during any period a document purporting to be a certificate to that effect issued by a Government department shall be admissible in evidence.

(4) Where it is necessary for the purposes of this section to establish that a right to graze animals on any land could not be or was not exercised for reasons of animal health it shall be sufficient to prove either—

(a) that the movement of the animals to that land was prohibited or restricted by or under the Diseases of Animals Act 1950 or any enactment repealed by that Act; or

(b) that the land was not, but some other land was, approved for grazing under any scheme in force under that Act or any such enactment and the animals were registered, or were undergoing tests with a view to registration, under the scheme.

[671]

NOTES

Repealed by the Commons Act 2006, s 53, Sch 6, Pt 1, as from 1 October 2008 (in England in relation to the pilot areas), and as from a day to be appointed (in England for remaining purposes and in Wales).

17 Commons Commissioners and assessors

(1) The Lord Chancellor shall—

(a) appoint to be Commons Commissioners such number of [persons who satisfy the judicial-appointment eligibility condition on a 5-year basis] as he may determine; and

(b) draw up and from time to time revise a panel of assessors to assist the Commons Commissioners in dealing with cases calling for special knowledge;

and shall appoint one of the Commons Commissioners to be Chief Commons Commissioner.

[(1A) A Commons Commissioner shall vacate his office on the day on which he attains the age of seventy years; but this subsection is subject to section 26(4) to (6) of the Judicial Pensions and Retirement Act 1993 (power of Lord Chancellor to authorise continuance in office up to the age of seventy-five years).]

(2) Any matter referred under this Act to a Commons Commissioner shall be dealt with by such one of the Commissioners as the Chief Commons Commissioner may determine, and that Commissioner may sit with an assessor selected by the Chief Commons Commissioner from the panel appointed under this section.

(3) If at any time the Chief Commons Commissioner is for any reason unable to act, the Lord Chancellor may appoint another Commons Commissioner to act in his stead.

(4) A Commons Commissioner may order any party to any proceedings before him to pay to any other party to the proceedings any costs incurred by that party in respect of the proceedings; and any costs so awarded shall be taxed in the county court according to such of the scales

prescribed by county court rules for proceedings in the county court as may be directed by the order, but subject to any modifications specified in the direction, or, if the order gives no direction, by the county court, and shall be recoverable in like manner as costs awarded in the county court.

(*5*) *The Minister shall pay to the Commons Commissioners and assessors appointed under this section such fees and such travelling and other allowances as the Minister may, with the approval of the Treasury, determine, and shall provide the Commons Commissioners with such services and facilities as appear to him required for the discharge of their functions.*

[672]

NOTES

Repealed by the Commons Act 2006, s 53, Sch 6, Pt 1, as from a day to be appointed.

Sub-s (1): words in square brackets substituted by the Tribunals, Courts and Enforcement Act 2007, s 50, Sch 10, Pt 2, paras 45, 49.

Sub-s (1A): inserted by the Judicial Pensions and Retirement Act 1993, s 26, Sch 6, para 26; for savings see s 27, Sch 7 thereof.

Transfer of Functions: see the note to s 1 at **[657]**.

18 Appeals from Commons Commissioners

(*1*) *Any person aggrieved by the decision of a Commons Commissioner as being erroneous in point of law may, within such time as may be limited by rules of court, require the Commissioner to state a case for the decision of the High Court.*

(*2*) *So much of section 63*(*1*) *of the Supreme Court of Judicature* (*Consolidation*) *Act 1925 as requires appeals to the High Court to be heard and determined by a Divisional Court shall not apply to an appeal by way of case stated under this section, but no appeal to the Court of Appeal shall be brought against the decision of the High Court in such a case except with the leave of that Court or the Court of Appeal.*

[673]

NOTES

Repealed by the Commons Act 2006, s 53, Sch 6, Pt 1, as from a day to be appointed.

19 Regulations

(*1*) *The Minister may make regulations—*

(*a*) *for prescribing the form of the registers to be maintained under this Act and of any applications and objections to be made and notices and certificates to be given thereunder;*

(*b*) *for regulating the procedure of registration authorities in dealing with applications for registration and with objections;*

(*c*) *for prescribing the steps to be taken by registration authorities for the information of other local authorities and of the public in cases where registrations are cancelled or modified;*

(*d*) *for requiring registration authorities to supply by post, on payment of such fee as may be prescribed, such information relating to the entries in the registers kept by them as may be prescribed;*

(*e*) *for regulating the procedure of the Commons Commissioners and, in particular, for providing for the summoning of persons to attend and give evidence and produce documents and for authorising the administration of oaths, and for enabling any inquiry or proceedings begun by or before one Commons Commissioner to be continued by or before another;*

(*f*) *for enabling an application for the registration of rights of common attached to any land to be made either by the landlord or by the tenant and for regulating the procedure where such an application is made by both;*

(*g*) *for enabling the Church Commissioners [the Diocesan Board of Finance for the diocese in which the land is situated] to act with respect to any land or rights belonging to an ecclesiastical benefice of the Church of England which is vacant;*

(*h*) *for treating any registration conflicting with another registration as an objection to the other registration;*

(*i*) *for requiring, before applications for registration are entertained, the taking of such steps as may be specified in the regulations for the information of persons having interests in any land affected by the registration;*

(*j*) *for the correction of errors and omissions in the registers;*

(*k*) *for prescribing anything required or authorised to be prescribed by this Act.*

(2) *The regulations may make provision for the preparation of maps to accompany applications for registration and the preparation, as part of the registers, of maps showing any land registered*

therein and any land to which rights of common registered therein are attached, and for requiring registration authorities to deposit copies of such maps with such Government departments and other authorities as may be prescribed.

(*3*) *The regulations may prescribe the payment of a fee not exceeding five pounds on an application made after the end of such period as may be specified in the regulations.*

(*4*) *The regulations may make different provision with respect to different circumstances.*

(*5*) *Regulations under this Act shall be made by statutory instrument which shall be subject to annulment in pursuance of a resolution of either House of Parliament.*

[674]

NOTES

Repealed by the Commons Act 2006, s 53, Sch 6, Pt 1, as from 1 October 2008 (in England in relation to the pilot areas), and as from a day to be appointed (in England for remaining purposes and in Wales).

Sub-s (1): in para (g), words "Church Commissioners" substituted by subsequent words in square brackets by the Church of England (Miscellaneous Provisions) Measure 2006, s 14, Sch 5, para 13, as from a day to be appointed.

Transfer of Functions: see the note to s 1 at **[657]**.

See further: the Common Land (Rectification of Registers) Act 1989, s 2.

Regulations: the Commons Registration (Exempted Land) Regulations 1965, SI 1965/2001; the Commons Registration (Publicity) Regulations 1966, SI 1966/972; the Commons Registration (General) Regulations 1966, SI 1966/1471; the Commons Registration (New Land) Regulations 1969, SI 1969/1843; the Commons Registration (Finality of Undisputed Registrations) Regulations 1970, SI 1970/1371; the Commons Commissioners Regulations 1971, SI 1971/1727; the Commons Registration (Disposal of Disputed Registrations) Regulations 1972, SI 1972/437; the Common Land (Rectification of Registers) Regulations 1990, SI 1990/311.

20 Orders

(*1*) *Any order made by the Minister under any provision of this Act may be varied or revoked by subsequent order made thereunder.*

(2) *Any such order, other than an order made under section 11 of this Act, shall be made by statutory instrument.*

(*3*) *Any statutory instrument made under this section shall be subject to annulment in pursuance of a resolution of either House of Parliament.*

[675]

NOTES

Repealed by the Commons Act 2006, s 53, Sch 6, Pt 1, as from a day to be appointed.

Transfer of Functions: see the note to s 1 at **[657]**.

21 Savings

(*1*) *Section 1(2) of this Act shall not affect the application to any land registered under this Act of section 193 or section 194 of the Law of Property Act 1925 (rights of access to, and restriction on inclosure of, land over which rights of common are exercisable).*

(2) *Section 10 of this Act shall not apply for the purpose of deciding whether any land forms part of a highway.*

[676]

NOTES

Repealed by the Commons Act 2006, s 53, Sch 6, Pt 1, subject to transitional provisions in s 23 of, Sch 3, para 7 to, that Act at **[2296]**, **[2335]**, as from a day to be appointed.

22 Interpretation

(*1*) *In this Act, unless the context otherwise requires,—*

"common land" means—

(*a*) *land subject to rights of common (as defined in this Act) whether those rights are exercisable at all times or only during limited periods;*

(*b*) *waste land of a manor not subject to rights of common;*

but does not include a town or village green or any land which forms part of a highway;

"land" includes land covered with water;

"local authority" means … the council of a county, … London borough or county district, the council of a parish … ;

"the Minister" means the Minister of Land and Natural Resources;

"prescribed" means prescribed by regulations under this Act;

["register of title" means the register kept under section 1 of the Land Registration Act 2002;]

"registration" includes an entry in the register made in pursuance of section 13 of this Act;

"rights of common" includes cattlegates or beastgates (by whatever name known) and rights of sole or several vesture or herbage or of sole or several pasture, but does not include rights held for a term of years or from year to year;

"town or village green" means land which has been allotted by or under any Act for the exercise or recreation of the inhabitants of any locality or on which the inhabitants of any locality have a customary right to indulge in lawful sports and pastimes [or which falls within subsection (1A) of this section].

[(1A) Land falls within this subsection if it is land on which for not less than twenty years a significant number of the inhabitants of any locality, or of any neighbourhood within a locality, have indulged in lawful sports and pastimes as of right, and either—

(a) continue to do so, or

(b) have ceased to do so for not more than such period as may be prescribed, or determined in accordance with prescribed provisions.

(1B) If regulations made for the purposes of paragraph (b) of subsection (1A) of this section provide for the period mentioned in that paragraph to come to an end unless prescribed steps are taken, the regulations may also require registration authorities to make available in accordance with the regulations, on payment of any prescribed fee, information relating to the taking of any such steps.]

(2) References in this Act to the ownership and the owner of any land are references to the ownership of a legal estate in fee simple in any land and to the person holding that estate, and references to land registered [in the register of title] are references to land the fee simple of which is so registered.

[677]

NOTES

Repealed by the Commons Act 2006, s 53, Sch 6, Pt 1, as from a day to be appointed.

Sub-s (1): in definition "local authority" first words omitted repealed by the Local Government Act 1985, s 102(2), Sch 17 and second and final words omitted repealed by the Local Government Act 1972, s 272(1), Sch 30; definition "register of title" inserted by the Land Registration Act 2002, s 133, Sch 11, para 7(1), (5); in definition "town or village green" words in square brackets substituted by the Countryside and Rights of Way Act 2000, s 98(1), (2).

Sub-ss (1A), (1B): inserted by the Countryside and Rights of Way Act 2000, s 98(1), (3).

Sub-s (2): words in square brackets substituted by the Land Registration Act 2002, s 133, Sch 11, para 7(1), (6).

Transfer of Functions: functions of the Minister of Land and Natural Resources transferred to the Secretary of State (as regards England) and the Secretary of State for Wales (as regards Wales), by virtue of the Ministry of Land and Natural Resources (Dissolution) Order 1967, SI 1967/156 and the Secretary of State for the Environment Order 1970, SI 1970/1681. Functions of the Secretary of State for Wales, transferred to the National Assembly for Wales, by the National Assembly for Wales (Transfer of Functions) Order 1999, SI 1999/672, art 2, Sch 1.

23 Application to Crown

(1) This Act shall apply in relation to land in which there is a Crown or Duchy interest as it applies in relation to land in which there is no such interest.

(2) In this section "Crown or Duchy interest" means an interest belonging to Her Majesty in right of the Crown or of the Duchy of Lancaster, or belonging to the Duchy of Cornwall, or belonging to a Government department, or held in trust for Her Majesty for the purposes of a Government department.

[678]

NOTES

Repealed by the Commons Act 2006, s 53, Sch 6, Pt 1, as from a day to be appointed.

24 Expenses

There shall be defrayed out of moneys provided by Parliament any expenses of the Minister under this Act and any increase attributable to this Act in the sums payable under any other Act out of moneys so provided.

[679]

NOTES

Repealed by the Commons Act 2006, s 53, Sch 6, Pt 1, as from a day to be appointed.

Transfer of Functions: see the note to s 1 at **[657]**.

25 Short title, commencement and extent

(1) This Act may be cited as the Commons Registration Act 1965.

(2) *This Act shall come into force on such day as the Minister may by order appoint, and different days may be so appointed for different purposes; and any reference in any provision to the commencement of this Act is a reference to the date on which that provision comes into force.*

(3) *This Act does not extend to Scotland or to Northern Ireland.*

[680]

NOTES

Repealed by the Commons Act 2006, s 53, Sch 6, Pt 1, as from a day to be appointed.
Orders: the Commons Registration Act 1965 (Commencement No 1) Order 1965, SI 1965/2000; the Commons Registration Act 1965 (Commencement No 2) Order 1966, SI 1966/971.

MISREPRESENTATION ACT 1967

(1967 c 7)

An Act to amend the law relating to innocent misrepresentations and to amend sections 11 and 35 of the Sale of Goods Act 1893

[22 March 1967]

1 Removal of certain bars to rescission for innocent misrepresentation

Where a person has entered into a contract after a misrepresentation has been made to him, and—

(a) the misrepresentation has become a term of the contract; or
(b) the contract has been performed;

or both, then, if otherwise he would be entitled to rescind the contract without alleging fraud, he shall be so entitled, subject to the provisions of this Act, notwithstanding the matters mentioned in paragraphs (a) and (b) of this section.

[681]

2 Damages for misrepresentation

(1) Where a person has entered into a contract after a misrepresentation has been made to him by another party thereto and as a result thereof he has suffered loss, then, if the person making the misrepresentation would be liable to damages in respect thereof had the misrepresentation been made fraudulently, that person shall be so liable notwithstanding that the misrepresentation was not made fraudulently, unless he proves that he had reasonable ground to believe and did believe up to the time the contract was made that the facts represented were true.

(2) Where a person has entered into a contract after a misrepresentation has been made to him otherwise than fraudulently, and he would be entitled, by reason of the misrepresentation, to rescind the contract, then, if it is claimed, in any proceedings arising out of the contract, that the contract ought to be or has been rescinded the court or arbitrator may declare the contract subsisting and award damages in lieu of rescission, if of opinion that it would be equitable to do so, having regard to the nature of the misrepresentation and the loss that would be caused by it if the contract were upheld, as well as to the loss that rescission would cause to the other party.

(3) Damages may be awarded against a person under subsection (2) of this section whether or not he is liable to damages under subsection (1) thereof, but where he is so liable any award under the said subsection (2) shall be taken into account in assessing his liability under the said subsection (1).

[682]

[3 Avoidance of provision excluding liability for misrepresentation

If a contract contains a term which would exclude or restrict—

(a) any liability to which a party to a contract may be subject by reason of any misrepresentation made by him before the contract was made; or
(b) any remedy available to another party to the contract by reason of such a misrepresentation,

that term shall be of no effect except in so far as it satisfies the requirement of reasonableness as stated in section 11(1) of the Unfair Contract Terms Act 1977; and it is for those claiming that the term satisfies that requirement to show that it does.]

[683]

NOTES

Substituted by the Unfair Contract Terms Act 1977, s 8(1).

4 (*Repealed by the Sale of Goods Act 1979, s 63(2), Sch 3.*)

5 Saving for past transactions

Nothing in this Act shall apply in relation to any misrepresentation or contract of sale which is made before the commencement of this Act.

[684]

6 Short title, commencement and extent

(1) This Act may be cited as the Misrepresentation Act 1967.

(2) This Act shall come into operation at the expiration of the period of one month beginning with the date on which it is passed.

(3) This Act … does not extend to Scotland.

(4) This Act does not extend to Northern Ireland.

[685]

NOTES

Sub-s (3): words omitted repealed by the Sale of Goods Act 1979, ss 62, 63, Sch 3.

LEASEHOLD REFORM ACT 1967

(1967 c 88)

An Act to enable tenants of houses held on long leases at low rents to acquire the freehold or an extended lease; to apply the Rent Acts to premises held on long leases at a rackrent, and to bring the operation of the Landlord and Tenant Act 1954 into conformity with the Rent Acts as so amended; to make other changes in the law in relation to premises held on long leases, including amendments of the Places of Worship (Enfranchisement) Act 1920; and for purposes connected therewith

[27 October 1967]

PART I
ENFRANCHISEMENT AND EXTENSION OF LONG LEASEHOLDS

1–16 (*Outside the scope of this work.*)

Landlord's overriding rights

17, 18 (*Outside the scope of this work.*)

19 Retention of management powers for general benefit of neighbourhood

(1) Where, in the case of any area which is occupied directly or indirectly under tenancies held from one landlord (apart from property occupied by him or his licensees or for the time being unoccupied), the Minister on an application made within the two years beginning with the commencement of this Part of this Act grants a certificate that, in order to maintain adequate standards of appearance and amenity and regulate redevelopment in the area in the event of tenants acquiring the landlord's interest in their house and premises under this Part of this Act, it is in the Minister's opinion likely to be in the general interest that the landlord should retain powers of management in respect of the house and premises or have rights against the house and premises in respect of the benefits arising from the exercise elsewhere of his powers of management, then the High Court may, on an application made within one year of the giving of the certificate, approve a scheme giving the landlord such powers and rights as are contemplated by this subsection.

For the purposes of this section "the Minister" means as regards areas within Wales and Monmouthshire the Secretary of State, and as regards other areas the Minister of Housing and Local Government.

(2) The Minister shall not give a certificate under this section unless he is satisfied that the applicant has, by advertisement or otherwise as may be required by the Minister, given adequate notice to persons interested, informing them of the application for a certificate and its purpose and inviting them to make representations to the Minister for or against the application within a time which appears to the Minister to be reasonable; and before giving a certificate the Minister shall consider any representations so made within that time, and if from those representations it appears to him that there is among the persons making them substantial opposition to the application, he shall afford to those opposing the application, and on the same occasion to the applicant and such (if any) as the Minister thinks fit of those in favour of the application, an opportunity to appear and be heard by a person appointed by the Minister for the purpose, and shall consider the report of that person.

(3) The Minister in considering whether to grant a certificate authorising a scheme for any area, and the High Court in considering whether to approve a scheme shall have regard primarily to the benefit likely to result from the scheme to the area as a whole (including houses likely to be acquired from the landlord under this Part of this Act), and the extent to which it is reasonable to impose, for the benefit of the area, obligations on tenants so acquiring their freeholds; but regard may also be had to the past development and present character of the area and to architectural or historical considerations, to neighbouring areas and to the circumstances generally.

(4) If, having regard to the matters mentioned in subsection (3) above, to the provision which it is practicable to make by a scheme, and to any change of circumstances since the giving of the certificate under subsection (1), the High Court think it proper so to do, then the High Court may by order—

(a) exclude from the scheme any part of the area certified under that subsection; or
(b) declare that no scheme can be approved for the area;

and before submitting for approval a scheme for an area so certified a person may, if he sees fit, apply to the High Court for general directions as to the matters proper to be included in the scheme and for a decision whether an order should be made under paragraph (a) or (b) above.

(5) Subject to subsections (3) and (4) above, on the submission of a scheme to the High Court, the High Court shall approve the scheme either as originally submitted or with any modifications proposed or agreed to by the applicant for the scheme, if the scheme (with those modifications, if any) appears to the court to be fair and practicable and not to give the landlord a degree of control out of proportion to that previously exercised by him or to that required for the purposes of the scheme; and the High Court shall not dismiss an application for the approval of a scheme, unless either—

(a) the Court makes an order under subsection (4)(b) above; or
(b) in the opinion of the Court the applicant is unwilling to agree to a suitable scheme or is not proceeding in the manner with due despatch.

(6) A scheme under this section may make different provision for different parts of the area, and shall include provision for terminating or varying all or any of the provisions of the scheme, or excluding part of the area, if a change of circumstances makes it appropriate, or for enabling it to be done by or with the approval of the High Court.

(7) Except as provided by the scheme, the operation of a scheme under this section shall not be affected by any disposition or devolution of the landlord's interest in the property within the area or part of that property; but the scheme—

(a) shall include provision for identifying the person who is for the purposes of the scheme to be treated as the landlord for the time being; and
(b) may include provision for transferring, or allowing the landlord for the time being to transfer, all or any of the powers and rights conferred by the scheme on the landlord for the time being to a local authority or other body, including a body constituted for the purpose.

In the following provisions of this section references to the landlord for the time being shall have effect, in relation to powers and rights transferred to a local authority or other body as contemplated by paragraph (b) above, as references to that authority or body.

(8) Without prejudice to any other provision of this section, a scheme under it may provide for all or any of the following matters:—

(a) for regulating the redevelopment, use or appearance of property of which tenants have acquired the landlord's interest under this Part of this Act; and
(b) for empowering the landlord for the time being to carry out work for the maintenance or repair of any such property or carry out work to remedy a failure in respect of any such property to comply with the scheme, or for making the operation of any provisions of the scheme conditional on his doing so or on the provision or maintenance by him of services, facilities or amenities of any description; and
(c) for imposing on persons from time to time occupying or interested in any such property obligations in respect of maintenance or repair of the property or of property used or enjoyed by them in common with others, or in respect of cost incurred by the landlord for the time being on any matter referred to in this paragraph or in paragraph (b) above;
(d) for the inspection from time to time of any such property on behalf of the landlord for the time being, and for the recovery by him of sums due to him under the scheme in respect of any such property by means of a charge on the property;

and the landlord for the time being shall have, for the enforcement of any charge imposed under the scheme, the same powers and remedies under the Law of Property Act 1925 and otherwise as if he were a mortgagee by deed having powers of sale and leasing and of appointing a receiver.

(9) A scheme under this section may extend to property in which the landlord's interest is disposed of otherwise than under this Part of this Act (whether residential property or not), so as to make that property, or allow it to be made, subject to any such provision as is or might be made by the scheme for property in which tenants acquire the landlord's interest under this Part of this Act.

(10) A certificate given or scheme approved under this section [shall (notwithstanding section 2(a) or (b) of the Local Land Charges Act 1975) be a local land charge and for the purposes of that Act the landlord for the area to which it relates shall be treated as the originating authority as respects such charge; and where a scheme is registered in the appropriate local land charges register;]

(a) the provisions of the scheme relating to property of any description shall, so far as they respectively affect the persons from time to time occupying or interested in that property, be enforceable by the landlord for the time being against them, as if each of them had covenanted with the landlord for the time being to be bound by the scheme; and

(b) in relation to a house and premises in the area section 10 above shall have effect subject to the provisions of the scheme, and the price payable under section 9 shall be adjusted accordingly.

[(10A) Section 10 of the Local Land Charges Act 1975 shall not apply in relation to schemes which, by virtue of this section, are local land charges.]

(11) Subject to subsections (12) and (13) below, a certificate shall not be given nor a scheme approved under this section for any area except on the application of the landlord.

(12) Where, on a joint application made by two or more persons as landlords of neighbouring areas, it appears to the Minister—

(a) that a certificate could in accordance with subsection (1) above be given as regards those areas, treated as a unit, if the interests of those persons were held by a single person; and

(b) that the applicants are willing to be bound by any scheme to co-operate in the management of their property in those areas and in the administration of the scheme;

the Minister may give a certificate under this section for those areas as a whole; and where a certificate is given by virtue of this subsection, this section shall apply accordingly, but so that any scheme made by virtue of the certificate shall be made subject to conditions (enforceable in such manner as may be provided by the scheme) for securing that the landlords and their successors co-operate as aforesaid.

(13) Where it appears to the Minister—

(a) that a certificate could be given under this section for any area or areas on the application of the landlord or landlords; and

(b) that any body of persons is so constituted as to be capable of representing for purposes of this section the persons occupying or interested in property in the area or areas (other than the landlord or landlords), or such of them as are or may become entitled to acquire their landlord's interest under this Part of this Act, and is otherwise suitable;

then on an application made by that body either alone or jointly with the landlord or landlords a certificate may be granted accordingly; and where a certificate is so granted, whether to a representative body alone or to a representative body jointly with the landlord or landlords,—

(i) an application for a scheme in pursuance of the certificate may be made by the representative body alone or by the landlord or landlords alone or by both jointly and, by leave of the High Court, may be proceeded with by the representative body or by the landlord or landlords though not the applicant or applicants; and

(ii) without prejudice to subsection (7)(b) above, the scheme may, with the consent of the landlord or landlords or on such terms as to compensation or otherwise as appear to the High Court to be just, confer on the representative body any such rights or powers under the scheme as might be conferred on the landlord or landlords for the time being, or enable the representative body to participate in the administration of the scheme or in the management by the landlord or landlords of his or their property in the area or areas.

(14) Where a certificate under this section has been given for an area, or an application for one is pending, then subject to subsection (15) below if (before or after the making of the application or the giving of the certificate) a tenant of a house in the area gives notice of his desire to have the freehold under this Part of this Act,—

(a) no further proceedings need be taken in relation to the notice beyond those which appear to the landlord to be reasonable in the circumstances; but

(b) the tenant may at any time withdraw the notice by a further notice in writing given to the landlord, and section 9(4) above shall not apply to require him to make any payment to the landlord in respect of costs incurred by reason of the notice withdrawn.

(15) Subsection (14) above shall cease to have effect by virtue of an application for a certificate if the application is withdrawn or the certificate refused, and shall cease to have effect as regards the whole or part of an area to which a certificate relates—

(a) on the approval of a scheme for the area or that part of it; or

(b) on the expiration of one year from the giving of the certificate without an application having been made to the High Court for the approval of a scheme for the area or that part of it, or on the withdrawal of an application so made without a scheme being approved; or

(c) on an order made under subsection (4) above with respect to the area or that part of it, or an order dismissing an application for the approval of a scheme for the area or that part of it, becoming final.

[686]

NOTES

Sub-s (10): words in square brackets substituted by the Local Land Charges Act 1975, s 17(2), Sch 1.

Sub-s (10A): inserted by the Local Land Charges Act 1975, s 17(2), Sch 1.

Transfer of Functions: functions of the Secretary of State, so far as exercisable in relation to Wales, transferred to the National Assembly for Wales, by the National Assembly for Wales (Transfer of Functions) Order 1999, SI 1999/672, art 2, Sch 1.

See further: the Housing Act 1985, s 172–175, and in relation to the certification of the rateable values of certain properties, see the Local Government Finance (Repeals, Savings and Consequential Amendments) Order 1990, SI 1990/776, art 5.

20–37 (*Outside the scope of this work.*)

PART II
AMENDMENTS OF OTHER ACTS

38–40 (*Outside the scope of this work.*)

41 Short title, repeals, extent and commencement

(1) This Act may be cited as the Leasehold Reform Act 1967.

(2) The enactments mentioned in Schedule 7 to this Act are hereby repealed to the extent specified in the third column of that Schedule, but subject to the savings mentioned at the end of Parts I and II of the Schedule.

(3) This Act shall not extend to Scotland or Northern Ireland.

(4) Sections 34 to 36 of this Act shall come into force on the day it is passed; and, … , the other provisions of Part I shall come into force on such day as the Minister of Housing and Local Government and the Secretary of State may appoint by order made by them jointly by statutory instrument, which shall be laid before Parliament after being made.

(5) Part II of this Act shall come into force at the end of one month following the day on which this Act is passed.

[687]

NOTES

Sub-s (4): words omitted repealed by the Statute Law (Repeals) Act 1993.

Order: the Leasehold Reform Act 1967 Commencement Order 1967, SI 1967/1836.

(*Schs 1–7 outside the scope of this work.*)

WILLS ACT 1968

(1968 c 28)

An Act to restrict the operation of section 15 of the Wills Act 1837

[30 May 1968]

1 Restriction of operation of Wills Act 1837, s 15

(1) For the purposes of section 15 of the Wills Act 1837 (avoidance of gifts to attesting witnesses and their spouses) the attestation of a will by a person to whom or to whose spouse there is given or made any such disposition as is described in that section shall be disregarded if the will is duly executed without his attestation and without that of any other such person.

(2) This section applies to the will of any person dying after the passing of this Act, whether executed before or after the passing of this Act.

[688]

NOTES

Application: the Civil Partnership Act 2004, s 71, Sch 4, Pt 1, paras 1, 3, 5 provides that this section applies to the attestation of a will by a person to whose civil partner there is given or made any such disposition (as described in the Wills Act 1837, s 15) as it applies in relation to a person to whose spouse there is given or made any such disposition.

2 Short title and extent

(1) This Act may be cited as the Wills Act 1968.

(2) This Act does not extend to Scotland or Northern Ireland.

[689]

FAMILY LAW REFORM ACT 1969

(1969 c 46)

An Act to amend the law relating to the age of majority, to persons who have not attained that age and to the time when a particular age is attained; to amend the law relating to the property rights of illegitimate children and of other persons whose relationship is traced through an illegitimate link; to make provision for the use of blood tests for the purpose of determining the paternity of any person in civil proceedings; to make provision with respect to the evidence required to rebut a presumption of legitimacy and illegitimacy; to make further provision, in connection with the registration of the birth of an illegitimate child, for entering the name of the father; and for connected purposes

[25 July 1969]

PART I
REDUCTION OF AGE OF MAJORITY AND RELATED PROVISIONS

1 Reduction of age of majority from 21 to 18

(1) As from the date on which this section comes into force a person shall attain full age on attaining the age of eighteen instead of on attaining the age of twenty-one; and a person shall attain full age on that date if he has then already attained the age of eighteen but not the age of twenty-one.

(2) The foregoing subsection applies for the purposes of any rule of law, and, in the absence of a definition or of any indication of a contrary intention, for the construction of "full age", "infant", "infancy", "minor", "minority" and similar expressions in—

(a) any statutory provision, whether passed or made before, on or after the date on which this section comes into force; and

(b) any deed, will or other instrument of whatever nature (not being a statutory provision) made on or after that date.

(3) In the statutory provisions specified in Schedule 1 to this Act for any reference to the age of twenty-one years there shall be substituted a reference to the age of eighteen years; but the amendment by this subsection of the provisions specified in Part II of that Schedule shall be without prejudice to any power of amending or revoking those provisions.

(4) This section does not affect the construction of any such expression as is referred to in subsection (2) of this section in any of the statutory provisions described in Schedule 2 to this Act, and the transitional provisions and savings contained in Schedule 3 to this Act shall have effect in relation to this section.

(5) The Lord Chancellor may by order made by statutory instrument amend any provision in any local enactment passed on or before the date on which this section comes into force (not being a provision described in paragraph 2 of Schedule 2 to this Act) by substituting a reference to the age of eighteen years for any reference therein to the age of twenty-one years; and any statutory instrument containing an order under this subsection shall be subject to annulment in pursuance of a resolution of either House of Parliament.

(6) In this section "statutory provision" means any enactment (including, except where the context otherwise requires, this Act) and any order, rule, regulation, byelaw or other instrument made in the exercise of a power conferred by any enactment.

(7) Notwithstanding any rule of law, a will or codicil executed before the date on which this section comes into force shall not be treated for the purposes of this section as made on or after that date by reason only that the will or codicil is confirmed by a codicil executed on or after that date.

[690]

2 (*Outside the scope of this work.*)

3 Provisions relating to wills and intestacy

(1), (2) …

(3) Any will which—

(a) has been made, whether before or after the coming into force of this section, by a person under the age of eighteen; and

(b) is valid by virtue of the provisions of section 11 of the said Act of 1837 and the said Act of 1918,

may be revoked by that person notwithstanding that he is still under that age whether or not the circumstances are then such that he would be entitled to make a valid will under those provisions.

(4) (*Outside the scope of this work.*)

[691]

NOTES

Sub-s (1): amends the Wills Act 1837, s 7 at **[24]**, and the Wills (Soldiers and Sailors) Act 1918, ss 1, 3 at **[82]**, **[84]**.

Sub-s (2): amends the Administration of Estates Act 1925, s 47.

4–8 (*S 4 repealed by the Guardianship of Minors Act 1971, s 18(2), Sch 2; s 5 repealed by the Matrimonial Proceedings and Property Act 1970, s 42(2), Sch 3, the Inheritance (Provision for Family and Dependants) Act 1975, s 26(2), Schedule and the Domestic Proceedings and Magistrates' Courts Act 1978, s 89(2)(b), Sch 3; s 6 repealed by the Courts and Legal Services Act 1990, s 125(7), Sch 20; s 7 repealed by the Children Act 1989, s 100(1), 108(7), Sch 15; s 8 outside the scope of this work.*)

9 Time at which a person attains a particular age

(1) The time at which a person attains a particular age expressed in years shall be the commencement of the relevant anniversary of the date of his birth.

(2) This section applies only where the relevant anniversary falls on a date after that on which this section comes into force, and, in relation to any enactment, deed, will or other instrument, has effect subject to any provision therein.

[692]

10–25 (*Ss 10–12, 19–25 outside the scope of this work; s 13 repealed by the Northern Ireland Constitution Act 1973, s 41(1), Sch 6, Pt I; ss 14, 15, 17 repealed by the Family Reform Act 1987, ss 20, 33(4), Sch 4; s 16 repealed by the Administration of Justice Act 1982, s 75(1), Sch 9, Pt I; s 18 repealed by the Inheritance (Provision for Family and Dependants) Act 1975, s 26(2), Schedule.*)

PART IV
MISCELLANEOUS AND GENERAL

26, 27 (*S 26 outside the scope of this work; s 27 repealed by the Children Act 1975, s 108(1)(b), Sch 4, Pt VI and the Family Law Reform Act 1987, s 33(4), Sch 4.*)

28 Short title, interpretation, commencement and extent

(1) This Act may be cited as the Family Law Reform Act 1969.

(2) Except where the context otherwise requires, any reference in this Act to any enactment shall be construed as a reference to that enactment as amended, extended or applied by or under any other enactment, including this Act.

(3) This Act shall come into force on such date as the Lord Chancellor may appoint by order made by statutory instrument, and different dates may be appointed for the coming into force of different provisions.

(4) In this Act—

(a) …

(b) section 2, so far as it amends any provision of … the Marriage with Foreigners Act 1906, has the same extent as that provision;

(c) sections … 6(7), so far as they affect Part II of the Maintenance Orders Act 1950, extend to Scotland and Northern Ireland;

(d) section 10, so far as it relates to the Civil List Act 1952, extends to Scotland and Northern Ireland;

(e) section 11, so far as it relates to the Employers and Workmen Act 1875, extends to Scotland;

(f) …

(g) section 19 extends to Scotland;

but, save as aforesaid, this Act shall extend to England and Wales only.

[693]

NOTES

Sub-s (4): para (a) repealed by the British Nationality Act 1981, s 52(8), Sch 9; words omitted from para (b) repealed by the Foreign Marriage (Amendment) Act 1988, s 7(2), Schedule; words omitted from para (c) repealed by the Guardianship of Minors Act 1971, s 18(2), (4), Sch 2; para (f) repealed by the Northern Ireland Constitution Act 1973, s 41(1), Sch 6.

Orders: the Family Law Reform Act 1969 (Commencement No 1) Order 1969, SI 1969/1140; the Family Law Reform Act 1969 (Commencement No 2) Order 1971, SI 1971/1857.

(*Schs 1–3 outside the scope of this work.*)

LAW OF PROPERTY ACT 1969

(1969 c 59)

An Act to amend Part II of the Landlord and Tenant Act 1954; to provide for the closing of the Yorkshire deeds registries; to amend the law relating to dispositions of estates and interests in land and to land charges; to make further provision as to the powers of the Lands Tribunal and court in relation to restrictive covenants affecting land; and for purposes connected with those matters

[22 October 1969]

1–22 ((*Pts I, II*) *outside the scope of this work.*)

PART III
AMENDMENT OF LAW RELATING TO DISPOSITIONS OF ESTATES AND INTERESTS IN LAND AND TO LAND CHARGES

23 Reduction of statutory period of title

Section 44(1) of the Law of Property Act 1925 (under which the period of commencement of title which may be required under a contract expressing no contrary intention is thirty years except in certain cases) shall have effect, in its application to contracts made after the commencement of this Act, as if it specified fifteen years instead of thirty years as the period of commencement of title which may be so required.

[694]

24 Contracts for purchase of land affected by land charge, etc

(1) Where under a contract for the sale or other disposition of any estate or interest in land the title to which is not registered under the [Land Registration Act 2002] or any enactment replaced by it any question arises whether the purchaser had knowledge, at the time of entering into the contract, of a registered land charge, that question shall be determined by reference to his actual knowledge and without regard to the provisions of section 198 of the Law of Property Act 1925 (under which registration under the Land Charges Act 1925 or any enactment replaced by it is deemed to constitute actual notice).

(2) Where any estate or interest with which such a contract is concerned is affected by a registered land charge and the purchaser, at the time of entering into the contract, had not received notice and did not otherwise actually know that the estate or interest was affected by the charge, any provision of the contract shall be void so far as it purports to exclude the operation of subsection (1) above or to exclude or restrict any right or remedy that might otherwise be exercisable by the purchaser on the ground that the estate or interest is affected by the charge.

(3) In this section—

"purchaser" includes a lessee, mortgagee or other person acquiring or intending to acquire an estate or interest in land; and

"registered land charge" means any instrument or matter registered, otherwise than in a register of local land charges, under the Land Charges Act 1925 or any Act replaced by it.

(4) For the purposes of this section any knowledge acquired in the course of a transaction by a person who is acting therein as counsel, or as solicitor or other agent, for another shall be treated as the knowledge of that other.

(5) This section does not apply to contracts made before the commencement of this Act.

[695]

NOTES

Sub-s (1): words in square brackets substituted by the Land Registration Act 2002, s 133, Sch 11, para 9.

Modification: references to solicitors etc modified to include references to bodies recognised under the Administration of Justice Act 1985, s 9, by the Solicitors' Incorporated Practices Order 1991, SI 1991/2684, arts 4, 5, Sch 1.

25 Compensation in certain cases for loss due to undisclosed land charges

(1) Where a purchaser of any estate or interest in land under a disposition to which this section applies has suffered loss by reason that the estate or interest is affected by a registered land charge, then if—

(a) the date of completion was after the commencement of this Act; and
(b) on that date the purchaser had no actual knowledge of the charge; and
(c) the charge was registered against the name of an owner of an estate in the land who was not as owner of any such estate a party to any transaction, or concerned in any event, comprised in the relevant title;

the purchaser shall be entitled to compensation for the loss.

(2) For the purposes of subsection (1)(b) above, the question whether any person had actual knowledge of a charge shall be determined without regard to the provisions of section 198 of the Law of Property Act 1925 (under which registration under the Land Charges Act 1925 or any enactment replaced by it is deemed to constitute actual notice).

(3) Where a transaction comprised in the relevant title was effected or evidenced by a document which expressly provided that it should take effect subject to an interest or obligation capable of registration in any of the relevant registers, the transaction which created that interest or obligation shall be treated for the purposes of subsection (1)(c) above as comprised in the relevant title.

(4) Any compensation for loss under this section shall be paid by the Chief Land Registrar, and where the purchaser of the estate or interest in question has incurred expenditure for the purpose—

(a) of securing that the estate or interest is no longer affected by the registered land charge or is so affected to a less extent; or
(b) of obtaining compensation under this section;

the amount of the compensation shall include the amount of the expenditure (so far as it would not otherwise fall to be treated as compensation for loss) reasonably incurred by the purchaser for that purpose.

(5) In the case of an action to recover compensation under this section, the cause of action shall be deemed for the purposes of [the Limitation Act 1980] to accrue at the time when the registered land charge affecting the estate or interest in question comes to the notice of the purchaser.

(6) Any proceedings for the recovery of compensation under this section shall be commenced in the High Court; and if in such proceedings the High Court dismisses a claim to compensation it shall not order the purchaser to pay the Chief Land Registrar's costs unless it considers that it was unreasonable for the purchaser to commence the proceedings.

(7) …

(8) Where compensation under this section has been paid in a case where the purchaser would have had knowledge of the registered land charge but for the fraud of any person, the Chief Land Registrar, on behalf of the Crown, may recover the amount paid from that person.

(9) This section applies to the following dispositions, that is to say—

(a) any sale or exchange and, subject to the following provisions of this subsection, any mortgage of an estate or interest in land;
(b) any grant of a lease for a term of years derived out of a leasehold interest;
(c) any compulsory purchase, by whatever procedure, of land; and
(d) any conveyance of a fee simple in land under Part I of the Leasehold Reform Act 1967;

but does not apply to the grant of a term of years derived out of the freehold or the mortgage of such a term by the lessee; and references in this section to a purchaser shall be construed accordingly.

(10) In this section—

"date of completion", in relation to land which vests in the Land Commission or another acquiring authority by virtue of a general vesting declaration under the Land Commission Act 1967 or the Town and Country Planning Act 1968, means the date on which it so vests;

"mortgage" includes any charge;

"registered land charge" means any instrument or matter registered, otherwise than in a register of local land charges, under the Land Charges Act 1925 or any Act replaced by it, except that—

(a) in relation to an assignment of a lease or underlease or a mortgage by an assignee under such an assignment, it does not include any instrument or matter affecting the title to the freehold or to any relevant leasehold reversion; and
(b) in relation to the grant of an underlease or the mortgage by the underlessee of the term of years created by an underlease, it does not include any instrument or matter affecting the title to the freehold or to any leasehold reversion superior to the leasehold interest out of which the term of years is derived;

"relevant registers" means the registers kept under section 1 of the Land Charges Act 1925;

"relevant title" means—

(a) in relation to a disposition made under a contract, the title which the purchaser was, apart from any acceptance by him (by agreement or otherwise) of a shorter or an imperfect title, entitled to require; or

(b) in relation to any other disposition, the title which he would have been entitled to require if the disposition had been made under a contract to which section 44(1) of the Law of Property Act 1925 applied and that contract had been made on the date of completion.

(11) For the purposes of this section any knowledge acquired in the course of a transaction by a person who is acting therein as counsel, or as solicitor or other agent, for another shall be treated as the knowledge of that other.

[696]

NOTES

Sub-s (5): words in square brackets substituted by the Limitation Act 1980, s 40(2), Sch 3, para 9.
Sub-s (7): repealed by the Land Charges Act 1972, s 18(3), Sch 5.
Modification: references to solicitors etc modified to include references to bodies recognised under the Administration of Justice Act 1985, s 9, by the Solicitors' Incorporated Practices Order 1991, SI 1991/2684, arts 4, 5, Sch 1.

26–28 (*Ss 26, 27 repealed by the Land Charges Act 1972, s 18(3), Sch 5; s 28 (Pt IV) outside the scope of this work.*)

PART V
SUPPLEMENTARY PROVISIONS

29, 30 (*Outside the scope of this work.*)

31 Short title, commencement and extent

(1) This Act may be cited as the Law of Property Act 1969.

(2) This Act, except section 28(6), shall come into force on 1st January 1970.

(3) This Act does not extend to Scotland or Northern Ireland.

(*Schs 1–3 outside the scope of this work.*)

[696A]

ADMINISTRATION OF JUSTICE ACT 1970

(1970 c 31)

An Act to make further provision about the courts (including assizes), their business, jurisdiction and procedure; to enable a High Court judge to accept appointment as arbitrator or umpire under an arbitration agreement; to amend the law respecting the enforcement of debt and other liabilities; to amend section 106 of the Rent Act 1968; and for miscellaneous purposes connected with the administration of justice

[29 May 1970]

1–35 ((*Pts I–III*) *outside the scope of this work.*)

PART IV
ACTIONS BY MORTGAGEES FOR POSSESSION

36 Additional powers of court in action by mortgagee for possession of dwelling-house

(1) Where the mortgagee under a mortgage of land which consists of or includes a dwelling-house brings an action in which he claims possession of the mortgaged property, not being an action for foreclosure in which a claim for possession of the mortgaged property is also made, the court may exercise any of the powers conferred on it by subsection (2) below if it appears to the court that in the event of its exercising the power the mortgagor is likely to be able within a reasonable period to pay any sums due under the mortgage or to remedy a default consisting of a breach of any other obligation arising under or by virtue of the mortgage.

(2) The court—

(a) may adjourn the proceedings, or

(b) on giving judgment, or making an order, for delivery of possession of the mortgaged property, or at any time before the execution of such judgment or order, may—

(i) stay or suspend execution of the judgment or order, or

(ii) postpone the date for delivery of possession,

for such period or periods as the court thinks reasonable.

(3) Any such adjournment, stay, suspension or postponement as is referred to in subsection (2) above may be made subject to such conditions with regard to payment by the mortgagor of any sum secured by the mortgage or the remedying of any default as the court thinks fit.

(4) The court may from time to time vary or revoke any condition imposed by virtue of this section.

(5) …

(6) In the application of this section to Northern Ireland, "the court" means a judge of the High Court in Northern Ireland, and in subsection (1) the words from "not being" to "made" shall be omitted.

[697]

NOTES

Sub-s (5): repealed by the Statute Law (Repeals) Act 2004.

37–38A (*Ss 37, 38 repealed by the County Courts Act 1984, s 148(3), Sch 4; s 38A outside the scope of this work.*)

39 Interpretation of Part IV

(1) In this Part of this Act—

"dwelling-house" includes any building or part thereof which is used as a dwelling;

"mortgage" includes a charge and "mortgagor" and "mortgagee" shall be construed accordingly;

"mortgagor" and "mortgagee" includes any person deriving title under the original mortgagor or mortgagee.

(2) The fact that part of the premises comprised in a dwelling-house is used as a shop or office or for business, trade or professional purposes shall not prevent the dwelling-house from being a dwelling-house for the purposes of this Part of this Act.

[698]

40–51 (*(Pt V) outside the scope of this work.*)

PART VI
GENERAL

52, 53 (*S 52 outside the scope of this work; s 53 repealed by the Northern Ireland Constitution Act 1973, s 41(1), Sch 6, Pt I.*)

54 Citation, interpretation, repeals, commencement and extent

(1) This Act may be cited as the Administration of Justice Act 1970.

(2) References in this Act to any enactment include references to that enactment as amended or extended by or under any other enactment, including this Act.

(3), (4) …

(5) Except insofar as it amends, or authorises the amendment of, any enactment which extends to Scotland, this Act shall not extend to Scotland.

(6) This section (except subsection (3)) and the following provisions only of this Act extend to Northern Ireland, that is to say—

(a) sections 1(6) … and Schedules 2 … , so far as they relate to any enactment which extends to Northern Ireland … ;

(b) Part III; and

(c) sections 36, [38A], 39 … ;

…

[699]

NOTES

Sub-s (3): outside the scope of this work.

Sub-s (4): repealed by the Statute Law (Repeals) Act 2004.

Sub-s (6): in para (a), first and second words omitted repealed by the Attachment of Earnings Act 1971, s 29(2), Sch 6, and final words omitted repealed by the Statute Law (Repeals) Act 2004; in para (c), figure in square brackets inserted by the Consumer Credit Act 1974, s 192(3)(a), Sch 4, para 31, and words omitted repealed by the Statute Law (Repeals) Act 2004 and the Northern Ireland Constitution Act 1973, s 41, Sch 6, Pt I; final words omitted repealed by the Administration of Estates Act 1971, s 12(1), Sch 2, Pt I.

(*Schs 1–11 outside the scope of this work.*)

LAW REFORM (MISCELLANEOUS PROVISIONS) ACT 1970

(1970 c 33)

An Act to abolish actions for breach of promise of marriage and make provision with respect to the property of, and gifts between, persons who have been engaged to marry; to abolish the right of a husband to claim damages for adultery with his wife; to abolish actions for the enticement or harbouring of a spouse, or for the enticement, seduction or harbouring of a child; to make provision with respect to the maintenance of survivors of void marriages; and for purposes connected with the matters aforesaid

[29 May 1970]

Legal consequences of termination of contract to marry

1 (*Outside the scope of this work.*)

2 Property of engaged couples

(1) Where an agreement to marry is terminated, any rule of law relating to the rights of husbands and wives in relation to property in which either or both has or have a beneficial interest, including any such rule as explained by section 37 of the Matrimonial Proceedings and Property Act 1970, shall apply, in relation to any property in which either or both of the parties to the agreement had a beneficial interest while the agreement was in force, as it applies in relation to property in which a husband or wife has a beneficial interest.

(2) Where an agreement to marry is terminated, section 17 of the Married Women's Property Act 1882 and section 7 of the Matrimonial Causes (Property and Maintenance) Act 1958 (which sections confer power on a judge of the High Court or a county court to settle disputes between husband and wife about property) shall apply, as if the parties were married, to any dispute between, or claim by, one of them in relation to property in which either or both had a beneficial interest while the agreement was in force; but an application made by virtue of this section to the judge under the said section 17, as originally enacted or as extended by the said section 7, shall be made within three years of the termination of the agreement.

[700]

3–6 (*Ss 3, 5 outside the scope of this work; s 4 repealed by the Matrimonial Causes Act 1973, s 54(1), Sch 3; s 6 repealed by the Inheritance (Provision for Family and Dependants) Act 1975, s 26(2), Schedule.*)

7 Citation, repeal, commencement and extent

(1) This Act may be cited as the Law Reform (Miscellaneous Provisions) Act 1970.

(2) The enactments specified in the Schedule to this Act are hereby repealed to the extent specified in the third column of that Schedule, but the repeal of those enactments shall not affect any action commenced or petition presented before this Act comes into force or any claim made in any such action or on any such petition.

(3) This Act shall come into force on 1st January 1971.

(4) This Act does not extend to Scotland or Northern Ireland.

[701]

(*Schedule contains repeals only.*)

MATRIMONIAL PROCEEDINGS AND PROPERTY ACT 1970

(1970 c 45)

An Act to make fresh provision for empowering the court in matrimonial proceedings to make orders ordering either spouse to make financial provision for, or transfer property to, the other spouse or a child of the family, orders for the variation of ante-nuptial and post-nuptial settlements, orders for the custody and education of children and orders varying, discharging or suspending orders made in such proceedings; to make other amendments of the law relating to matrimonial proceedings; to abolish the right to claim restitution of conjugal rights; to declare what interest in property is acquired by a spouse who contributes to its improvement; to make provision as to a spouse's rights of occupation under section 1 of the Matrimonial Homes Act 1967 in certain cases; to extend section 17 of the Married Women's Property Act 1882 and section 7 of the Matrimonial Causes (Property and Maintenance) Act 1958; to amend the law about the property of a person whose marriage is the subject of a decree of judicial separation dying intestate; to

abolish the agency of necessity of a wife; and for purposes connected with the matters aforesaid
[29 May 1970]

1–29 ((*Pt I*) *outside the scope of this work.*)

PART II
MISCELLANEOUS PROVISIONS

30–36 (*S 30 outside the scope of this work; ss 31–33 repealed by the Domestic Proceedings and Magistrates' Courts Act 1978, s 89*(*2*)(*b*), *Sch 3; ss 34, 35 repealed with savings by the Matrimonial Causes Act 1973, ss 53, 54*(*1*), *Schs 1, 3; s 36 repealed by the Inheritance* (*Provision for Family and Dependants*) *Act 1975, s 26*(*2*), *Schedule.*)

Provisions relating to property of married persons

37 Contributions by spouse in money or money's worth to the improvement of property

It is hereby declared that where a husband or wife contributes in money or money's worth to the improvement of real or personal property in which or in the proceeds of sale of which either or both of them has or have a beneficial interest, the husband or wife so contributing shall, if the contribution is of a substantial nature and subject to any agreement between them to the contrary express or implied, be treated as having then acquired by virtue of his or her contribution a share or an enlarged share, as the case may be, in that beneficial interest of such an extent as may have been then agreed or, in default of such agreement, as may seem in all the circumstances just to any court before which the question of the existence or extent of the beneficial interest of the husband or wife arises (whether in proceedings between them or in any other proceedings).

[702]

38 (*Repealed by the Matrimonial Homes Act 1983, s 12, Sch 3.*)

39 Extension of s 17 of Married Women's Property Act 1882

An application may be made to the High Court or a county court under section 17 of the Married Women's Property Act 1882 (powers of the court in disputes between husband and wife about property) (including that section as extended by section 7 of the Matrimonial Causes (Property and Maintenance) Act 1958) by either of the parties to a marriage notwithstanding that their marriage has been dissolved or annulled so long as the application is made within the period of three years beginning with the date on which the marriage was dissolved or annulled; and references in the said section 17 and the said section 7 to a husband or a wife shall be construed accordingly.

[703]

40, 41 (*Repealed with savings by the Matrimonial Causes Act 1973, ss 53, 54*(*1*), *Schs 1, 3.*)

PART III
SUPPLEMENTARY

42 (*Repealed with savings by the Matrimonial Causes Act 1973, ss 53, 54*(*1*), *Schs 1, 3.*)

43 Citation, commencement and extent

(1) This Act may be cited as the Matrimonial Proceedings and Property Act 1970.

(2) …

(3) Any reference in any provision of this Act, or in any enactment amended by a provision of this Act, to the commencement of this Act shall be construed as a reference to the date on which that provision comes into force.

(4) … this Act does not extend to Scotland or Northern Ireland.

[704]

NOTES

Sub-s (2): repealed by the Matrimonial Causes Act 1973, s 54, Sch 3.

Sub-s (4): words omitted repealed by the Matrimonial Causes Act 1973, s 54, Sch 3, and the Statute Law (Repeals) Act 1977.

(*Schs 1–3 repealed with savings by the Matrimonial Causes Act 1983, ss 53, 54*(*1*), *Schs 1, 3.*)

PART I STATUTES

POWERS OF ATTORNEY ACT 1971

(1971 c 27)

An Act to make new provision in relation to powers of attorney and the delegation by trustees of their trusts, powers and discretions

[12 May 1971]

1 Execution of powers of attorney

(1) An instrument creating a power of attorney shall be [executed as a deed by] the donor of the power.

(2) …

(3) This section is without prejudice to any requirement in, or having effect under, any other Act as to the witnessing of instruments creating powers of attorney and does not affect the rules relating to the execution of instruments by bodies corporate.

[705]

NOTES

Sub-s (1): words in square brackets substituted by the Law of Property (Miscellaneous Provisions) Act 1989, s 1, Sch 1, para 6(a).

Sub-s (2): repealed by the Law of Property (Miscellaneous Provisions) Act 1989, ss 1, 4, Sch 1, para 6(b), Sch 2.

2 (*Repealed by the Supreme Court Act 1981, s 152(4), Sch 7.*)

3 Proof of instruments creating powers of attorney

(1) The contents of an instrument creating a power of attorney may be proved by means of a copy which—

(a) is a reproduction of the original made with a photographic or other device for reproducing documents in facsimile; and

(b) contains the following certificate or certificates signed by the donor of the power or by a solicitor *[duly certificated notary public]* [, authorised person] or stockbroker, that is to say—

(i) a certificate at the end to the effect that the copy is a true and complete copy of the original; and

(ii) if the original consists of two or more pages, a certificate at the end of each page of the copy to the effect that it is a true and complete copy of the corresponding page of the original.

(2) Where a copy of an instrument creating a power of attorney has been made which complies with subsection (1) of this section, the contents of the instrument may also be proved by means of a copy of that copy if the further copy itself complies with that subsection, taking references in it to the original as references to the copy from which the further copy is made.

(3) In this section *["duly certificated notary public" has the same meaning as it has in the Solicitors Act 1974 by virtue of section 87(1) of that Act and]* ["authorised person" means a person (other than a solicitor) who, for the purposes of the Legal Services Act 2007, is an authorised person in relation to any activity which constitutes a notarial activity (within the meaning of that Act) and] "stockbroker" means a member of any stock exchange within the meaning of the Stock Transfer Act 1963 or the Stock Transfer Act (Northern Ireland) 1963.

(4) This section is without prejudice to section 4 of the Evidence and Powers of Attorney Act 1940 (proof of deposited instruments by office copy) and to any other method of proof authorised by law.

(5) For the avoidance of doubt, in relation to an instrument made in Scotland the references to a power of attorney in this section and in section 4 of the Evidence and Powers of Attorney Act 1940 include references to a factory and commission.

[706]

NOTES

Sub-ss (1), (3): words in italics (as inserted by the Courts and Legal Services Act 1990, s 125(2), Sch 17, para 4) substituted for subsequent words in square brackets by the Legal Services Act 2007, s 208(1), Sch 21, para 26, as from a day to be appointed.

Modification: references to solicitors etc modified to include references to bodies recognised under the Administration of Justice Act 1985, s 9, by the Solicitors' Incorporated Practices Order 1991, SI 1991/2684, arts 4, 5, Sch 1.

4 Powers of attorney given as security

(1) Where a power of attorney is expressed to be irrevocable and is given to secure—

(a) a proprietary interest of the donee of the power; or

(b) the performance of an obligation owed to the donee,

then, so long as the donee has that interest or the obligation remains undischarged, the power shall not be revoked—

(i) by the donor without the consent of the donee; or

(ii) by the death, incapacity or bankruptcy of the donor or, if the donor is a body corporate, by its winding up or dissolution.

(2) A power of attorney given to secure a proprietary interest may be given to the person entitled to the interest and persons deriving title under him to that interest, and those persons shall be duly constituted donees of the power for all purposes of the power but without prejudice to any right to appoint substitutes given by the power.

(3) This section applies to powers of attorney whenever created.

[707]

5 Protection of donee and third persons where power of attorney is revoked

(1) A donee of a power of attorney who acts in pursuance of the power at a time when it has been revoked shall not, by reason of the revocation, incur any liability (either to the donor or to any other person) if at that time he did not know that the power had been revoked.

(2) Where a power of attorney has been revoked and a person, without knowledge of the revocation, deals with the donee of the power, the transaction between them shall, in favour of that person, be as valid as if the power had then been in existence.

(3) Where the power is expressed in the instrument creating it to be irrevocable and to be given by way of security then, unless the person dealing with the donee knows that it was not in fact given by way of security, he shall be entitled to assume that the power is incapable of revocation except by the donor acting with the consent of the donee and shall accordingly be treated for the purposes of subsection (2) of this section as having knowledge of the revocation only if he knows that it has been revoked in that manner.

(4) Where the interest of a purchaser depends on whether a transaction between the donee of a power of attorney and another person was valid by virtue of subsection (2) of this section, it shall be conclusively presumed in favour of the purchaser that that person did not at the material time know of the revocation of the power if—

(a) the transaction between that person and the donee was completed within twelve months of the date on which the power came into operation; or

(b) that person makes a statutory declaration, before or within three months after the completion of the purchase, that he did not at the material time know of the revocation of the power.

(5) Without prejudice to subsection (3) of this section, for the purposes of this section knowledge of the revocation of a power of attorney includes knowledge of the occurrence of any event (such as the death of the donor) which has the effect of revoking the power.

(6) In this section "purchaser" and "purchase" have the meaning specified in section 205(1) of the Law of Property Act 1925.

(7) This section applies whenever the power of attorney was created but only to acts and transactions after the commencement of this Act.

[708]

NOTES

In the application of this section to a lasting power of attorney made under the Mental Capacity Act 2005, see s 14(5) at **[2197]**.

6 Additional protection for transferees under stock exchange transactions

(1) Without prejudice to section 5 of this Act, where—

(a) the donee of a power of attorney executes, as transferor, an instrument transferring registered securities; and

(b) the instrument is executed for the purposes of a stock exchange transaction,

it shall be conclusively presumed in favour of the transferee that the power had not been revoked at the date of the instrument if a statutory declaration to that effect is made by the donee of the power on or within three months after that date.

(2) In this section "registered securities" and "stock exchange transaction" have the same meanings as in the Stock Transfer Act 1963.

[709]

7 Execution of instruments etc by donee of power of attorney

[(1) If the donee of a power of attorney is an individual, he may, if he thinks fit—

(a) execute any instrument with his own signature, and]

(b) do any other thing in his own name,

by the authority of the donor of the power; and any [instrument executed or thing done in that manner shall, subject to subsection (1A) of this section, be as effective as if executed by the donee in any manner which would constitute due execution of that instrument by the donor or, as the case may be, as if done by the donee in the name of the donor].

[(1A) Where an instrument is executed by the donee as a deed, it shall be as effective as if executed by the donee in a manner which would constitute due execution of it as a deed by the donor only if it is executed in accordance with section 1(3)(a) of the Law of Property (Miscellaneous Provisions) Act 1989.]

(2) For the avoidance of doubt it is hereby declared that an instrument to which subsection (3) … of section 74 of the Law of Property Act 1925 applies may be executed either as provided in [that subsection] or as provided in this section.

(3) …

(4) This section applies whenever the power of attorney was created.

[710]

NOTES

Sub-s (1): words in first pair of square brackets substituted by the Law of Property (Miscellaneous Provisions) Act 1989, s 1, Sch 1, para 7(1); words in second pair of square brackets substituted by SI 2005/1906, art 10(1), Sch 1, paras 5, 6, except in relation to any instrument executed before 15 September 2005.

Sub-s (1A): inserted by SI 2005/1906, art 10(1), Sch 1, paras 5, 7, except in relation to any instrument executed before 15 September 2005.

Sub-s (2): words omitted repealed and words in square brackets substituted by the Law of Property (Miscellaneous Provisions) Act 1989, ss 1, 4, Sch 1, para 7(2), Sch 2.

Sub-s (3): repealed by SI 2005/1906, art 10, Sch 1, paras 5, 8, Sch 2, except in relation to any instrument executed before 15 September 2005.

8, 9 *(S 8 repealed by the Statute Law (Repeals) Act 2004; s 9 repealed by the Trustee Delegation Act 1999, s 12, Schedule.)*

10 Effect of general power of attorney in specified form

(1) Subject to subsection (2) of this section, a general power of attorney in the form set out in Schedule 1 to this Act, or in a form to the like effect but expressed to be made under this Act, shall operate to confer—

(a) on the donee of the power; or

(b) if there is more than one donee, on the donees acting jointly or acting jointly or severally, as the case may be,

authority to do on behalf of the donor anything which he can lawfully do by an attorney.

(2) [Subject to section 1 of the Trustee Delegation Act 1999, this section] does not apply to functions which the donor has as a trustee or personal representative or as a tenant for life or statutory owner within the meaning of the Settled Land Act 1925.

[711]

NOTES

Sub-s (2): words in square brackets substituted by the Trustee Delegation Act 1999, s 3.

11 Short title, repeals, consequential amendments, commencement and extent

(1) This Act may be cited as the Powers of Attorney Act 1971.

(2) The enactments specified in Schedule 2 to this Act are hereby repealed to the extent specified in the third column of that Schedule.

(3), (4) …

(5) Section 3 of this Act extends to Scotland and Northern Ireland but, save as aforesaid, this Act extends to England and Wales only.

[712]

NOTES

Sub-s (3): in part amends the Law of Property Act 1925, s 125 at **[369]**; remainder repealed by the Supreme Court Act 1981, s 152(4), Sch 7.

Sub-s (4): repealed by the Statute Law (Repeals) Act 2004.

SCHEDULE 1
FORM OF GENERAL POWER OF ATTORNEY FOR PURPOSES OF SECTION 10
Section 10

THIS GENERAL POWER OF ATTORNEY is made this ..... day of ..... 19 ... by AB of

I appoint CD of (*or* CD of .... and EF of .... jointly *or* jointly and severally) to be my attorney(s) in accordance with section 10 of the Powers of Attorney Act 1971.
IN WITNESS etc,

[713]

(*Sch 2 contains repeals only.*)

DEFECTIVE PREMISES ACT 1972

(1972 c 35)

An Act to impose duties in connection with the provision of dwellings and otherwise to amend the law of England and Wales as to liability for injury or damage caused to persons through defects in the state of premises

[29 June 1972]

1 Duty to build dwellings properly

(1) A person taking on work for or in connection with the provision of a dwelling (whether the dwelling is provided by the erection or by the conversion or enlargement of a building) owes a duty—

(a) if the dwelling is provided to the order of any person, to that person; and
(b) without prejudice to paragraph (*a*) above, to every person who acquires an interest (whether legal or equitable) in the dwelling;

to see that the work which he takes on is done in a workmanlike or, as the case may be, professional manner, with proper materials and so that as regards that work the dwelling will be fit for habitation when completed.

(2) A person who takes on any such work for another on terms that he is to do it in accordance with instructions given by or on behalf of that other shall, to the extent to which he does it properly in accordance with those instructions, be treated for the purposes of this section as discharging the duty imposed on him by subsection (1) above except where he owes a duty to that other to warn him of any defects in the instructions and fails to discharge that duty.

(3) A person shall not be treated for the purposes of subsection (2) above as having given instructions for the doing of work merely because he has agreed so the work being done in a specified manner, with specified materials or to a specified design.

(4) A person who—

(a) in the course of a business which consists of or includes providing or arranging for the provision of dwellings or installations in dwellings; or
(b) in the exercise of a power of making such provision or arrangements conferred by or by virtue of any enactment;

arranges for another to take on work for or in connection with the provision of a dwelling shall be treated for the purposes of this section as included among the persons who have taken on the work.

(5) Any cause of action in respect of a breach of the duty imposed by this section shall be deemed, for the purposes of the Limitation Act 1939, the Law Reform (Limitation of Actions, &c) Act 1954 and the Limitation Act 1963, to have accrued at the time when the dwelling was completed, but if after that time a person who has done work for or in connection with the provision of the dwelling does further work to rectify the work he has already done, any such cause of action in respect of that further work shall be deemed for those purposes to have accrued at the time when the further work was finished.

[714]

2 Cases excluded from the remedy under section 1

(1) Where—

(a) in connection with the provision of a dwelling or its first sale or letting for habitation any rights in respect of defects in the state of the dwelling are conferred by an approved scheme to which this section applies on a person having or acquiring an interest in the dwelling; and
(b) it is stated in a document of a type approved for the purposes of this section that the requirements as to design or construction imposed by or under the scheme have, or appear to have, been substantially complied with in relation to the dwelling;

no action shall be brought by any person having or acquiring an interest in the dwelling for breach of the duty imposed by section 1 above in relation to the dwelling.

(2) A scheme to which this section applies—

(a) may consist of any number of documents and any number of agreements or other transactions between any number of persons; but

(b) must confer, by virtue of agreements entered into with persons having or acquiring an interest in the dwellings to which the scheme applies, rights on such persons in respect of defects in the state of the dwellings.

(3) In this section "approved" means approved by the Secretary of State, and the power of the Secretary of State to approve a scheme or document for the purposes of this section shall be exercisable by order, except that any requirements as to construction or design imposed under a scheme to which this section applies may be approved by him without making any order or, if he thinks fit, by order.

(4) The Secretary of State—

(a) may approve a scheme or document for the purposes of this section with or without limiting the duration of his approval; and

(b) may by order revoke or vary a previous order under this section or, without such an order, revoke or vary a previous approval under this section given otherwise than by order.

(5) The production of a document purporting to be a copy of an approval given by the Secretary of State otherwise than by order and certified by an officer of the Secretary of State to be a true copy of the approval shall be conclusive evidence of the approval, and without proof of the handwriting or official position of the person purporting to sign the certificate.

(6) The power to make an order under this section shall be exercisable by statutory instrument which shall be subject to annulment in pursuance of a resolution by either House of Parliament.

(7) Where an interest in a dwelling is compulsorily acquired—

(a) no action shall be brought by the acquiring authority for breach of the duty imposed by section 1 above in respect of the dwelling; and

(b) if any work for or in connection with the provision of the dwelling was done otherwise than in the course of a business by the person in occupation of the dwelling at the time of the compulsory acquisition, the acquiring authority and not that person shall be treated as the person who took on the work and accordingly as owing that duty.

[715]

NOTES

Transfer of Functions: functions of the Secretary of State, so far as exercisable in relation to Wales, transferred to the National Assembly for Wales, by the National Assembly for Wales (Transfer of Functions) Order 1999, SI 1999/672, art 2, Sch 1.

3 Duty of care with respect to work done on premises not abated by disposal of premises

(1) Where work of construction, repair, maintenance or demolition or any other work is done on or in relation to premises, any duty of care owed, because of the doing of the work, to persons who might reasonably be expected to be affected by defects in the state of the premises created by the doing of the work shall not be abated by the subsequent disposal of the premises by the person who owed the duty.

(2) This section does not apply—

(a) in the case of premises which are let, where the relevant tenancy of the premises commenced, or the relevant tenancy agreement of the premises was entered into, before the commencement of this Act;

(b) in the case of premises disposed of in any other way, when the disposal of the premises was completed, or a contract for their disposal was entered into, before the commencement of this Act; or

(c) in either case, where the relevant transaction disposing of the premises is entered into in pursuance of an enforceable option by which the consideration for the disposal was fixed before the commencement of this Act.

[716]

4 Landlord's duty of care in virtue of obligation or right to repair premises demised

(1) Where premises are let under a tenancy which puts on the landlord an obligation to the tenant for the maintenance or repair of the premises, the landlord owes to all persons who might reasonably be expected to be affected by defects in the state of the premises a duty to take such care as is reasonable in all the circumstances to see that they are reasonably safe from personal injury or from damage to their property caused by a relevant defect.

(2) The said duty is owed if the landlord knows (whether as the result of being notified by the tenant or otherwise) or if he ought in all the circumstances to have known of the relevant defect.

(3) In this section "relevant defect" means a defect in the state of the premises existing at or after the material time and arising from, or continuing because of, an act or omission by the landlord which constitutes or would if he had had notice of the defect, have constituted a failure by him to carry out his obligation to the tenant for the maintenance or repair of the premises; and for the purposes of the foregoing provision "the material time" means—

(a) where the tenancy commenced before this Act, the commencement of this Act; and
(b) in all other cases, the earliest of the following times, that is to say—
  (i) the time when the tenancy commences;
  (ii) the time when the tenancy agreement is entered into;
  (iii) the time when possession is taken of the premises in contemplation of the letting.

(4) Where premises are let under a tenancy which expressly or impliedly gives the landlord the right to enter the premises to carry out any description of maintenance or repair of the premises, then, as from the time when he first is, or by notice or otherwise can put himself, in a position to exercise the right and so long as he is or can put himself in that position, he shall be treated for the purposes of subsections (1) to (3) above (but for no other purpose) as if he were under an obligation to the tenant for that description of maintenance or repair of the premises; but the landlord shall not owe the tenant any duty by virtue of this subsection in respect of any defect in the state of the premises arising from, or continuing because of, a failure to carry out an obligation expressly imposed on the tenant by the tenancy.

(5) For the purposes of this section obligations imposed or rights given by any enactment in virtue of a tenancy shall be treated as imposed or given by the tenancy.

(6) This section applies to a right of occupation given by contract or any enactment and not amounting to a tenancy as if the right were a tenancy, and "tenancy" and cognate expressions shall be construed accordingly.

[717]

NOTES

Modification: modified, where the RTM company has acquired the right to manage, by the Commonhold and Leasehold Reform Act 2002, s 102, Sch 7, para 2.

5 Application to Crown

This Act shall bind the Crown, but as regards the Crown's liability in tort shall not bind the Crown further than the Crown is made liable in tort by the Crown Proceedings Act 1947.

[718]

6 Supplemental

(1) In this Act—

"disposal", in relation to premises, includes a letting, and an assignment or surrender of a tenancy, of the premises and the creation by contract of any other right to occupy the premises, and "dispose" shall be construed accordingly;

"personal injury" includes any disease and any impairment of a person's physical or mental condition;

"tenancy" means—

(a) a tenancy created either immediately or derivatively out of the freehold, whether by a lease or underlease, by an agreement for a lease or underlease or by a tenancy agreement, but not including a mortgage term or any interest arising in favour of a mortgagor by his attorning tenant to his mortgagee; or
(b) a tenancy at will or a tenancy on sufferance; or
(c) a tenancy, whether or not constituting a tenancy at common law, created by or in pursuance of any enactment;

and cognate expressions shall be construed accordingly.

(2) Any duty imposed by or enforceable by virtue of any provision of this Act is in addition to any duty a person may owe apart from that provision.

(3) Any term of an agreement which purports to exclude or restrict, or has the effect of excluding or restricting, the operation of any of the provisions of this Act, or any liability arising by virtue of any such provision, shall be void.

(4) …

[719]

NOTES

Sub-s (4): repeals the Occupiers' Liability Act 1957, s 4.

7 Short title, commencement and extent

(1) This Act may be cited as the Defective Premises Act 1972.

(2) This Act shall come into force on 1st January 1974.

(3) This Act does not extend to Scotland or Northern Ireland.

[720]

LAND CHARGES ACT 1972

(1972 c 61)

An Act to consolidate certain enactments relating to the registration of land charges and other instruments and matters affecting land

[9 August 1972]

Preliminary

1 The registers and the index

(1) The registrar shall continue to keep at the registry in the prescribed manner the following registers, namely—

(a) a register of land charges;
(b) a register of pending actions;
(c) a register of writs and orders affecting land;
(d) a register of deeds of arrangement affecting land;
(e) a register of annuities,

and shall also continue to keep there an index whereby all entries made in any of those registers can readily be traced.

(2) Every application to register shall be in the prescribed form and shall contain the prescribed particulars.

[(3) Where any charge or other matter is registrable in more than one of the registers kept under this Act, it shall be sufficient if it is registered in one such register, and if it is so registered the person entitled to the benefit of it shall not be prejudicially affected by any provision of this Act as to the effect of non-registration in any other such register.

(3A) Where any charge or other matter is registrable in a register kept under this Act and was also, before the commencement of the Local Land Charges Act 1975, registrable in a local land charges register, then, if before the commencement of the said Act it was registered in the appropriate local land charges register, it shall be treated for the purposes of the provisions of this Act as to the effect of non-registration as if it had been registered in the appropriate register under this Act; and any certificate setting out the result of an official search of the appropriate local land charges register shall, in relation to it, have effect as if it were a certificate setting out the result of an official search under this Act.]

(4) Schedule 1 to this Act shall have effect in relation to the register of annuities.

(5) An office copy of an entry in any register kept under this section shall be admissible in evidence in all proceedings and between all parties to the same extent as the original would be admissible.

(6) Subject to the provisions of this Act, registration may be vacated pursuant to an order of the court.

[(6A) The county courts have jurisdiction under subsection (6) above—

(a) in the case of a land charge of Class C(i), C(ii) or D(i), if the amount does not exceed £30,000;
(b) in the case of a land charge of Class C(iii), if it is for a specified capital sum of money not exceeding £30,000 or, where it is not for a specified capital sum, if the capital value of the land affected does not exceed £30,000;
(c) in the case of a land charge of Class A, Class B, Class C(iv), Class D(ii), Class D(iii) or Class E if the capital value of the land affected does not exceed £30,000;
(d) in the case of a land charge of Class F, if the land affected by it is the subject of an order made by the court under section 1 of the Matrimonial Homes Act 1983 [or section 33 of the Family Law Act 1996] or an application for an order under [either of those sections] relating to that land has been made to the court;
(e) in a case where an application under section 23 of the Deeds of Arrangement Act 1914 could be entertained by the court.]

[(6B) …]

(7) In this section "index" includes any device or combination of devices serving the purpose of an index.

[721]

NOTES

Sub-ss (3), (3A): substituted for original sub-s (3) by the Local Land Charges Act 1975, s 17(1)(a).

Sub-s (6A): inserted by the County Courts Act 1984, s 148(1), Sch 2, para 16; substituted by SI 1991/724, art 2(6), (8), Schedule, Pt I.

Sub-s (6A): in para (d), words in first pair of square brackets inserted and words in second pair of square brackets substituted by the Family Law Act 1996, s 66(1), Sch 8, para 46.

Sub-s (6B): inserted by the County Courts Act 1984, s 148(1), Sch 2, para 16; repealed by SI 1991/724, art 2(6), (8), Schedule, Pt I.

Registration in register of land charges

2 The register of land charges

(1) If a charge on or obligation affecting land falls into one of the classes described in this section, it may be registered in the register of land charges as a land charge of that class.

(2) A Class A land charge is—

(a) a rent or annuity or principal money payable by instalments or otherwise, with or without interest, which is not a charge created by deed but is a charge upon land (other than a rate) created pursuant to the application of some person under the provisions of any Act of Parliament, for securing to any person either the money spent by him or the costs, charges and expenses incurred by him under such Act, or the money advanced by him for repaying the money spent or the costs, charges and expenses incurred by another person under the authority of an Act of Parliament; or

(b) a rent or annuity or principal money payable as mentioned in paragraph (a) above which is not a charge created by deed but is a charge upon land (other than a rate) created pursuant to the application of some person under any of the enactments mentioned in Schedule 2 to this Act.

(3) A Class B land charge is a charge on land (not being a local land charge ...) of any of the kinds described in paragraph (a) of subsection (2) above, created otherwise than pursuant to the application of any person.

(4) A Class C land charge is any of the following [(not being a local land charge)], namely—

(i) a puisne mortgage;

(ii) a limited owner's charge;

(iii) a general equitable charge;

(iv) an estate contract;

and for this purpose—

(i) a puisne mortgage is a legal mortgage which is not protected by a deposit of documents relating to the legal estate affected;

(ii) a limited owner's charge is an equitable charge acquired by a tenant for life or statutory owner under [[the Inheritance Tax Act 1984] or under] any other statute by reason of the discharge by him of any [inheritance tax] or other liabilities and to which special priority is given by the statute;

(iii) a general equitable charge is any equitable charge which—

(a) is not secured by a deposit of documents relating to the legal estate affected; and

(b) does not arise or affect an interest arising under a [trust of land] or a settlement; and

(c) is not a charge given by way of indemnity against rents equitably apportioned or charged exclusively on land in exoneration of other land and against the breach or non-observance of covenants or conditions; and

(d) is not included in any other class of land charge;

(iv) an estate contract is a contract by an estate owner or by a person entitled at the date of the contract to have a legal estate conveyed to him to convey or create a legal estate, including a contract conferring either expressly or by statutory implication a valid option to purchase, a right of pre-emption or any other like right.

(5) A Class D land charge is any of the following [(not being a local land charge)], namely—

(i) an Inland Revenue Charge;

(ii) a restrictive covenant;

(iii) an equitable easement;

and for this purpose—

(i) an Inland Revenue charge is a charge on land, being a charge acquired by the Board under [the Inheritance Tax Act 1984];

(ii) a restrictive covenant is a covenant or agreement (other than a covenant or agreement between a lessor and a lessee) restrictive of the user of land and entered into on or after 1st January 1926;

(iii) an equitable easement is an easement, right or privilege over or affecting land created or arising on or after 1st January 1926, and being merely an equitable interest.

(6) A Class E land charge is an annuity created before 1st January 1926 and not registered in the register of annuities.

(7) A Class F land charge is a charge affecting any land by virtue of the [Part IV of the Family Law Act 1996].

(8) A charge or obligation created before 1st January 1926 can only be registered as a Class B land charge or a Class C land charge if it is acquired under a conveyance made on or after that date.

(9) …

[722]

NOTES

Sub-s (3): words omitted repealed by the Local Land Charges Act 1975, s 19, Sch 2.

Sub-s (4): words in first pair of square brackets inserted by the Local Land Charges Act 1975, s 17(1)(b); in second para (ii), words in first (outer) and third pairs of square brackets substituted by the Finance Act 1975, s 52(1), Sch 12, paras 2, 18(1), (2) and words in second (inner) pair of square brackets substituted by the Inheritance Tax Act 1984, s 276, Sch 8, para 3(1)(a); in second para (iii) words in square brackets substituted by the Trusts of Land and Appointment of Trustees Act 1996, s 25(1), Sch 3, para 12(2) (for savings in relation to entailed interests created before the commencement of that Act, and savings consequential upon the abolition of the doctrine of conversion, see s 25(4), (5) thereof).

Sub-s (5): words in first pair of square brackets inserted by the Local Land Charges Act 1975, s 17(1)(b); words in second pair of square brackets substituted by the Inheritance Tax Act 1984, s 276, Sch 8, para 3(1)(b).

Sub-s (7): words in square brackets substituted by the Family Law Act 1996, s 66(1), Sch 8, para 47.

Sub-s (9): repealed by the Finance Act 1977, s 59, Sch 9.

Inheritance tax: except in relation to a liability to tax arising before 25 July 1986 capital transfer tax shall be known as inheritance tax and the Capital Transfer Tax Act 1984 may be cited as the Inheritance Tax Act 1984, by virtue of the Finance Act 1986, s 100. Accordingly references to capital transfer tax have been changed to references to inheritance tax.

3 Registration of land charges

(1) A land charge shall be registered in the name of the estate owner whose estate is intended to be affected.

[(1A) Where a person has died and a land charge created before his death would apart from his death have been registered in his name, it shall be so registered notwithstanding his death.]

(2) A land charge registered before 1st January 1926 under any enactment replaced by the Land Charges Act 1925 in the name of a person other than the estate owner may remain so registered until it is registered in the name of the estate owner in the prescribed manner.

(3) A puisne mortgage created before 1st January 1926 may be registered as a land charge before any transfer of the mortgage is made.

(4) The expenses incurred by the person entitled to the charge in registering a land charge of Class A, Class B or Class C (other than an estate contract) or by the Board in registering an Inland Revenue charge shall be deemed to form part of the land charge, and shall be recoverable accordingly on the day for payment of any part of the land charge next after such expenses are incurred.

(5) Where a land charge is not created by an instrument, short particulars of the effect of the charge shall be furnished with the application to register the charge.

(6) An application to register an Inland Revenue charge shall state the [tax] in respect of which the charge is claimed and, so far as possible, shall define the land affected, and such particulars shall be entered or referred to in the register.

(7) In the case of a land charge for securing money created by a company before 1st January 1970 or so created at any time as a floating charge, registration under any of the enactments mentioned in subsection (8) below shall be sufficient in place of registration under this Act, and shall have effect as if the land charge had been registered under this Act.

(8) The enactments referred to in subsection (7) above are section 93 of the Companies (Consolidation) Act 1908, section 79 of the Companies Act 1929 … section 95 of the Companies Act 1948 [*and sections 395 to 398 of the Companies Act 1985*] [, sections 395 to 398 of the Companies Act 1985 and Part 25 of the Companies Act 2006 and regulations made under section 1052 of that Act].

[723]

NOTES

Sub-s (1A): inserted by the Law of Property (Miscellaneous Provisions) Act 1994, s 15(2).

Sub-s (6): word in square brackets substituted by the Finance Act 1975, s 52, Sch 12, paras 2, 18(1), (4).

Sub-s (8): word omitted repealed by the Companies Consolidation (Consequential Provisions) Act 1985, s 30, Sch 2; words in italics (as substituted by the Companies Consolidation (Consequential Provisions) Act 1985, s 30, Sch 2) substituted by subsequent words in square brackets by SI 2009/1941, art 2(1), Sch 1, para 24, as from 1 October 2009.

4 Effect of land charges and protection of purchasers

(1) A land charge of Class A (other than a land improvement charge registered after 31st December 1969) or of Class B shall, when registered, take effect as if it had been created by a deed of charge by way of legal mortgage, but without prejudice to the priority of the charge.

(2) A land charge of Class A created after 31st December 1888 shall be void as against a purchaser of the land charged with it or of any interest in such land, unless the land charge is registered in the register of land charges before the completion of the purchase.

(3) After the expiration of one year from the first conveyance occurring on or after 1st January 1889 of a land charge of Class A created before that date the person entitled to the land charge shall not be able to recover the land charge or any part of it as against a purchaser of the land charged with it or of any interest in the land, unless the land charge is registered in the register of land charges before the completion of the purchase.

(4) If a land improvement charge was registered as a land charge of Class A before 1st January 1970, any body corporate which, but for the charge, would have power to advance money on the security of the estate or interest affected by it shall have that power notwithstanding the charge.

(5) A land charge of Class B and a land charge of Class C (other than an estate contract) created or arising on or after 1st January 1926 shall be void as against a purchaser of the land charged with it, or of any interest in such land, unless the land charge is registered in the appropriate register before the completion of the purchase.

(6) An estate contract and a land charge of Class D created or entered into on or after 1st January 1926 shall be void as against a purchaser for money or money's worth [(or, in the case of an Inland Revenue charge, a purchaser within the meaning of [the Inheritance Tax Act 1984)]] of a legal estate in the land charged with it, unless the land charge is registered in the appropriate register before the completion of the purchase.

(7) After the expiration of one year from the first conveyance occurring on or after 1st January 1926 of a land charge of Class B or Class C created before that date the person entitled to the land charge shall not be able to enforce or recover the land charge or any part of it as against a purchaser of the land charged with it, or of any interest in the land, unless the land charge is registered in the appropriate register before the completion of the purchase.

(8) A land charge of Class F shall be void as against a purchaser of the land charged with it, or of any interest in such land, unless the land charge is registered in the appropriate register before the completion of the purchase.

[724]

NOTES

Sub-s (6): first words in square brackets inserted by the Finance Act 1975, s 52, Sch 12, paras 2, 18(1), (5); words in square brackets therein substituted by the Inheritance Tax Act 1984, s 276, Sch 8, para 13.

Inheritance tax: except in relation to a liability to tax arising before 25 July 1986 capital transfer tax shall be known as inheritance tax and the Capital Transfer Tax Act 1984 may be cited as the Inheritance Tax Act 1984, by virtue of the Finance Act 1986, s 100. Accordingly references to capital transfer tax have been changed to references to inheritance tax.

Registration in registers of pending actions, writs and orders and deeds of arrangement

5 The register of pending actions

(1) There may be registered in the register of pending actions—

(a) a pending land action;

(b) a petition in bankruptcy filed on or after 1st January 1926.

(2) Subject to general rules under section 16 of this Act, every application for registration under this section shall contain particulars of the title of the proceedings and the name, address and description of the estate owner or other person whose estate or interest is intended to be affected.

(3) An application for registration shall also state—

(a) if it relates to a pending land action, the court in which and the day on which the action was commenced; and

(b) if it relates to a petition in bankruptcy, the court in which and the day on which the petition was filed.

(4) The registrar shall forthwith enter the particulars in the register, in the name of the estate owner or other person whose estate or interest is intended to be affected.

[(4A) Where a person has died and a pending land action would apart from his death have been registered in his name, it shall be so registered notwithstanding his death.]

(5) An application to register a petition in bankruptcy against a firm shall state the names and addresses of the partners, and the registration shall be effected against each partner as well as against the firm.

(6) No fee shall be charged for the registration of a petition in bankruptcy if the application for registration is made by the registrar of the court in which the petition is filed.

(7) A pending land action shall not bind a purchaser without express notice of it unless it is for the time being registered under this section.

(8) A petition in bankruptcy shall not bind a purchaser of a legal estate in good faith, for money or money's worth, … , unless it is for the time being registered under this section.

(9) …

(10) The court, if it thinks fit, may upon the determination of the proceedings, or during the pendency of the proceedings if satisfied that they are not prosecuted in good faith, make an order vacating a registration under this section, and direct the party on whose behalf it was made to pay all or any of the costs and expenses occasioned by the registration and by its vacation.

[(11) The county court has jurisdiction under subsection (10) of this section where the action was brought or the petition in bankruptcy was filed in that court.]

[725]

NOTES

Sub-s (4A): inserted by the Law of Property (Miscellaneous Provisions) Act 1994, s 15(3).

Sub-s (8): words omitted repealed by the Insolvency Act 1985, s 235, Sch 8, para 21, Sch 10, Pt III.

Sub-s (9): repealed by the Insolvency Act 1985, s 235, Sch 10, Pt III.

Sub-s (11): inserted by the County Courts Act 1984, s 148(1), Sch 2, para 17.

6 The register of writs and orders affecting land

(1) There may be registered in the register of writs and orders affecting land—

(a) any writ or order affecting land issued or made by any court for the purpose of enforcing a judgment or recognisance;

(b) any order appointing a receiver or sequestrator of land;

[(c) any bankruptcy order, whether or not the bankrupt's estate is known to include land.]

[(d) any access order under the Access to Neighbouring Land Act 1992.]

[(1A) No writ or order affecting an interest under a trust of land may be registered under subsection (1) above.]

(2) Every entry made pursuant to this section shall be made in the name of the estate owner or other person whose land, if any, is affected by the writ or order registered.

[(2A) Where a person has died and any such writ or order as is mentioned in subsection (1)(a) or (b) above would apart from his death have been registered in his name, it shall be so registered notwithstanding his death.]

(3) No fee shall be charged for the registration of a [bankruptcy order] if the application for registration is made by an official receiver.

(4) Except as provided by subsection (5) below and by [section 37(5) of the *Supreme Court Act 1981* [Senior Courts Act 1981]] and [section 107(3) of the County Courts Act 1984] (which make special provision as to receiving orders in respect of land of judgment debtors) every such writ and order as is mentioned in subsection (1) above, and every delivery in execution or other proceeding taken pursuant to any such writ or order, or in obedience to any such writ or order, shall be void as against a purchaser of the land unless the writ or order is for the time being registered under this section.

[(5) Subject to subsection (6) below, the title of a trustee in bankruptcy shall be void as against a purchaser of a legal estate in good faith for money or money's worth unless the bankruptcy order is for the time being registered under this section.]

(6) Where a petition in bankruptcy has been registered under section 5 above, the title of the trustee in bankruptcy shall be void as against a purchaser of a legal estate in good faith for money or money's worth … claiming under a conveyance made after the date of registration, unless at the date of the conveyance either the registration of the petition is in force or a receiving order on the petition is registered under this section.

[726]

NOTES

Sub-s (1): para (c) substituted by the Insolvency Act 1985, s 235, Sch 8, para 21; para (d) inserted by the Access to Neighbouring Land Act 1992, s 5(1).

Sub-s (1A): inserted by the Trusts of Land and Appointment of Trustees Act 1996, s 25(1), Sch 3, para 12(3); for savings in relation to entailed interests created before the commencement of that Act, and savings consequential upon the abolition of the doctrine of conversion, see s 25(4), (5) thereof.

Sub-s (2A): inserted by the Law of Property (Miscellaneous Provisions) Act 1994, s 15(4).

Sub-s (3): words in square brackets substituted by the Insolvency Act 1985, s 235, Sch 8, para 21.

Sub-s (4): words in first pair of square brackets substituted by the Supreme Court Act 1981, s 152(1), Sch 5; words in italics substituted by subsequent words in square brackets by the Constitutional Reform Act 2005, s 59(5), Sch 11, Pt 1, para 1(2), as from 1 October 2009; words in third pair of square brackets substituted by the County Courts Act 1984, s 148(1), Sch 2, para 18.

Sub-s (5): substituted by the Insolvency Act 1985, s 235, Sch 8, para 21.

Sub-s (6): words omitted repealed by the Insolvency Act 1985, s 235, Sch 8, para 21, Sch 10, Pt III.

7 The register of deeds of arrangement affecting land

(1) The deed of arrangement affecting land may be registered in the register of deeds of arrangement affecting land, in the name of the debtor, on the application of a trustee of the deed or a creditor assenting to or taking the benefit of the deed.

(2) Every deed of arrangement shall be void as against a purchaser of any land comprised in it or affected by it unless it is for the time being registered under this section.

[727]

8 Expiry and renewal of registrations

A registration under section 5, section 6 or section 7 of this Act shall cease to have effect at the end of the period of five years from the date on which it is made, but may be renewed from time to time and, if so renewed, shall have effect for five years from the date of renewal.

[728]

Searches and official searches

9 Searches

(1) Any person may search in any register kept under this Act on paying the prescribed fee.

(2) Without prejudice to subsection (1) above, the registrar may provide facilities for enabling persons entitled to search in any such register to see photographic or other images or copies of any portion of the register which they may wish to examine.

[729]

10 Official searches

(1) Where any person requires search to be made at the registry for entries of any matters or documents, entries of which are required or allowed to be made in the registry by this Act, he may make a requisition in that behalf to the registrar, which may be either—

(a) a written requisition delivered at or sent by post to the registry; or

(b) a requisition communicated by teleprinter, telephone or other means in such manner as may be prescribed in relation to the means in question, in which case it shall be treated as made to the registrar if, but only if, he accepts it;

and the registrar shall not accept a requisition made in accordance with paragraph (b) above unless it is made by a person maintaining a credit account at the registry, and may at his discretion refuse to accept it notwithstanding that it is made by such a person.

(2) The prescribed fee shall be payable in respect of every requisition made under this section; and that fee—

(a) in the case of a requisition made in accordance with subsection (1)(a) above, shall be paid in such manner as may be prescribed for the purposes of this paragraph unless the requisition is made by a person maintaining a credit account at the registry and the fee is debited to that account;

(b) in the case of a requisition made in accordance with subsection (1)(b) above, shall be debited to the credit account of the person by whom the requisition is made.

(3) Where a requisition is made under subsection (1) above and the fee payable in respect of it is paid or debited in accordance with subsection (2) above, the registrar shall thereupon make the search required and—

(a) shall issue a certificate setting out the result of the search; and

(b) without prejudice to paragraph (a) above, may take such other steps as he considers appropriate to communicate that result to the person by whom the requisition was made.

(4) In favour of a purchaser or an intending purchaser, as against persons interested under or in respect of matters or documents entries of which are required or allowed as aforesaid, the certificate, according to its tenor, shall be conclusive, affirmatively or negatively, as the case may be.

(5) If any officer, clerk or person employed in the registry commits, or is party or privy to, any act of fraud or collusion, or is wilfully negligent, in the making of or otherwise in relation to any certificate under this section, he shall be guilty of an offence and shall be liable on conviction on indictment to imprisonment for a term not exceeding two years, or on summary conviction to imprisonment for a term not exceeding three months or to a fine not exceeding [the prescribed sum], or to both such imprisonment and fine.

(6) Without prejudice to subsection (5) above, no officer, clerk or person employed in the registry shall, in the absence of fraud on his part, be liable for any loss which may be suffered—

(a) by reason of any discrepancy between—
   (i) the particulars which are shown in a certificate under this section as being the particulars in respect of which the search for entries was made, and
   (ii) the particulars in respect of which a search for entries was required by the person who made the requisition; or

(b) by reason of any communication of the result of a search under this section made otherwise than by issuing a certificate under this section.

[730]

NOTES

Sub-s (5): words in square brackets substituted by virtue of the Magistrates' Courts Act 1980, s 32(2).

Miscellaneous and supplementary

11 Date of effective registration and priority notices

(1) Any person intending to make an application for the registration of any contemplated charge, instrument or other matter in pursuance of this Act or any rule made under this Act may give a priority notice in the prescribed form at least the relevant number of days before the registration is to take effect.

(2) Where a notice is given under subsection (1) above, it shall be entered in the register to which the intended application when made will relate.

(3) If the application is presented within the relevant number of days thereafter and refers in the prescribed manner to the notice, the registration shall take effect as if the registration had been made at the time when the charge, instrument or matter was created, entered into, made or arose, and the date at which the registration so takes effect shall be deemed to be the date of registration.

(4) Where—

(a) any two charges, instruments or matters are contemporaneous; and

(b) one of them (whether or not protected by a priority notice) is subject to or dependent on the other; and

(c) the latter is protected by a priority notice,

the subsequent or dependent charge, instrument or matter shall be deemed to have been created, entered into or made, or to have arisen, after the registration of the other.

(5) Where a purchaser has obtained a certificate under section 10 above, any entry which is made in the register after the date of the certificate and before the completion of the purchase, and is not made pursuant to a priority notice entered on the register on or before the date of the certificate, shall not affect the purchaser if the purchase is completed before the expiration of the relevant number of days after the date of the certificate.

(6) The relevant number of days is—

(a) for the purposes of subsections (1) and (5) above, fifteen;

(b) for the purposes of subsection (3) above, thirty;

or such other number as may be prescribed; but in reckoning the relevant number of days for any of the purposes of this section any days when the registry is not open to the public shall be excluded.

[731]

12 Protection of solicitors, trustees, etc

A solicitor, or a trustee, personal representative, agent or other person in a fiduciary position, shall not be answerable—

(a) in respect of any loss occasioned by reliance on an office copy of an entry in any register kept under this Act;

(b) for any loss that may arise from error in a certificate under section 10 above obtained by him.

[732]

NOTES

Modification: modified by the Building Societies Act 1986, s 124, Sch 21, paras 9, 12 and the Administration of Justice Act 1985, ss 9, 34(2), Sch 2.

13 Saving for overreaching powers

(1) The registration of any charge, annuity or other interest under this Act shall not prevent the charge, annuity or interest being overreached under any other Act, except where otherwise provided by that other Act.

(2) The registration as a land charge of a puisne mortgage or charge shall not operate to prevent that mortgage or charge being overreached in favour of a prior mortgagee or a person deriving title under him where, by reason of a sale or foreclosure, or otherwise, the right of the puisne mortgagee or subsequent chargee to redeem is barred.

[733]

14 Exclusion of matters affecting registered land or created by instruments necessitating registration of land

(1) This Act shall not apply to instruments or matters required to be registered or re-registered on or after 1st January 1926, if and so far as they affect registered land, and can be protected under the [Land Registration Act 2002].

(2) Nothing in this Act imposes on the registrar any obligation to ascertain whether or not an instrument or matter affects registered land.

(3) Where an instrument executed on or after 27th July 1971 conveys, grants or assigns an estate in land and creates a land charge affecting that estate, this Act shall not apply to the land charge, so far as it affects that estate, if under [section 7 of the Land Registration Act 2002 (effect of failure to comply with requirement of registration)] the instrument will, unless the necessary application for registration under that Act is made within the time allowed by or under [section 6 of that Act], become void so far as respects the conveyance, grant or assignment of that estate.

[734]

NOTES

Sub-s (1): words in square brackets substituted by the Land Registration Act 2002, s 133, Sch 11, para 10(1), (2).

Sub-s (3): words in square brackets substituted by the Land Registration Act 2002, s 133, Sch 11, para 10(1), (3).

15 Application to the Crown

(1) This Act binds the Crown, but nothing in this Act shall be construed as rendering land owned by or occupied for the purposes of the Crown subject to any charge to which, independently of this Act, it would not be subject.

(2) References in this Act to restrictive covenants include references to any conditions, stipulations or restrictions imposed on or after 1st January 1926, by virtue of section 137 of the Law of Property Act 1922, for the protection of the amenities of royal parks, gardens and palaces.

[735]

16 General rules

(1) The Lord Chancellor may, with the concurrence of the Treasury as to fees, make such general rules as may be required for carrying this Act into effect, and in particular—

(a) as to forms and contents of applications for registration, modes of identifying where practicable the land affected, requisitions for and certificates of official searches, and regulating the practice of the registry in connection therewith;

(b) for providing for the mode of registration of a land charge (and in the case of a puisne mortgage, general equitable charge, estate contract, restrictive covenant or equitable easement by reference to the instrument imposing or creating the charge, interest or restriction, or an extract from that instrument) and for the cancellation without an order of court of the registration of a land charge, on its cesser, or with the consent of the person entitled to it, or on sufficient evidence being furnished that the land charge has been overreached under the provisions of any Act or otherwise;

(c) for determining the date on which applications and notices shall be treated for the purposes of section 11 of this Act as having been made or given;

(d) for determining the times and order at and in which applications and priority notices are to be registered;

(e) for varying the relevant number of days for any of the purposes of section 11 of this Act;

(f) for enabling the registrar to provide credit accounting facilities in respect of fees payable by virtue of this Act;

(g) for treating the debiting of such a fee to a credit account maintained at the registry as being, for such purposes of this Act or of the rules as may be specified in the rules, payment of that fee;

(h) for the termination or general suspension of any credit accounting facilities provided under the rules or for their withdrawal or suspension in particular cases at the discretion of the registrar;

(j) for requiring the registrar to take steps in relation to any instrument or matter in respect of which compensation has been claimed under section 25 of the Law of Property Act 1969 which would be likely to bring that instrument or matter to the notice of any person who subsequently makes a search of the registers kept under section 1 of this Act or requires such a search to be made in relation to the estate or interest affected by the instrument or matter; and

(k) for authorising the use of the index kept under this Act in any manner which will serve that purpose, notwithstanding that its use in that manner is not otherwise authorised by or by virtue of this Act.

(2) The power … to make [rules under section [412 of the Insolvency Act 1986]] shall include power to make rules as respects the registration and re-registration of a petition in bankruptcy under section 5 of this Act and [a bankruptcy order] under section 6 of this Act, as if the registration and re-registration were required [by [Parts VIII to XI] of that Act].

[736]

NOTES

Sub-s (2): words omitted repealed by the Constitutional Reform Act 2005, ss 15(1), 146, Sch 4, Pt 1, para 75, Sch 18, Pt 2; words in first (outer), third and fourth (outer) pairs of square brackets substituted by the Insolvency Act 1985, s 235, Sch 8, para 21; words in second (inner) and fifth (inner) pair of square brackets substituted by the Insolvency Act 1986, s 439(2), Sch 14.

Rules: the Land Charges Rules 1974, SI 1974/1286; the Land Charges Fees Rules 1990, SI 1990/327.

17 Interpretation

(1) In this Act, unless the context otherwise requires,—

"annuity" means a rentcharge or an annuity for a life or lives or for any term of years or greater estate determinable on a life or on lives and created after 25th April 1855 and before 1st January 1926, but does not include an annuity created by a marriage settlement or will;

"the Board" means the Commissioners of Inland Revenue;

"conveyance" includes a mortgage, charge, lease, assent, vesting declaration, vesting instrument, release and every other assurance of property, or of an interest in property, by any instrument except a will, and "convey" has a corresponding meaning;

"court" means the High Court, or the county court in a case where that court has jurisdiction;

"deed of arrangement" has the same meaning as in the Deeds of Arrangement Act 1914;

"estate owner", "legal estate", "equitable interest", … , "charge by way of legal mortgage", [and "will"] have the same meanings as in the Law of Property Act 1925;

"judgment" includes any order or decree having the effect of a judgment;

"land" includes land of any tenure and mines and minerals, whether or not severed from the surface, buildings or parts of buildings (whether the division is horizontal, vertical or made in any other way) and other corporeal hereditaments, also a manor, an advowson and a rent and other incorporeal hereditaments, and an easement, right, privilege or benefit in, over or derived from land, but not an undivided share in land, and "hereditament" means real property which, on an intestacy occurring before 1st January 1926, might have devolved on an heir;

"land improvement charge" means any charge under the Improvement of Land Act 1864 or under any special improvement Act within the meaning of the Improvement of Land Act 1899;

"pending land action" means any action or proceeding pending in court relating to land or any interest in or charge on land;

"prescribed" means prescribed by rules made pursuant to this Act;

"purchaser" means any person (including a mortgagee or lessee) who, for valuable consideration, takes any interest in land or in a charge on land, and "purchase" has a corresponding meaning;

"registrar" means the Chief Land Registrar, "registry" means Her Majesty's Land Registry, and "registered land" has the same meaning as in the [Land Registration Act 2002];

"tenant for life", "statutory owner", "vesting instrument" and "settlement" have the same meanings as in the Settled Land Act 1925.

(2) For the purposes of any provision in this Act requiring or authorising anything to be done at or delivered or sent to the registry, any reference to the registry shall, if the registrar so directs, be read as a reference to such office of the registry (whether in London or elsewhere) as may be specified in the direction.

(3) Any reference in this Act to any enactment is a reference to it as amended by or under any other enactment, including this Act.

[737]

NOTES

Sub-s (1): definition "trust for sale" (omitted) repealed by the Trusts of Land and Appointment of Trustees Act 1996, s 25(2), Sch 4 (for savings in relation to entailed interests created before the commencement of that Act, and savings consequential upon the abolition of the doctrine of conversion, see s 25(4), (5) thereof);

definition "will" and word "and" immediately preceding it substituted by the Finance Act 1975, s 52(1), Sch 12, paras 2, 18(1), (6); in definition "registered land" words in square brackets substituted by the Land Registration Act 2002, s 133, Sch 11, para 10(1), (4).

18 Consequential amendments, repeals, savings, etc

(1) Schedule 3 to this Act, which contains consequential amendments of other Acts, shall have effect.

(2) …

(3) The enactments specified in Schedule 5 to this Act are hereby repealed to the extent specified in the third column of that Schedule.

(4) …

(5) In so far as any entry in a register or instrument made or other thing whatsoever done under any enactment repealed by this Act could have been made or done under a corresponding provision in this Act, it shall have effect as if made or done under that corresponding provision; and for the purposes of this provision any entry in a register which under section 24 of the Land Charges Act 1925 had effect as if made under that Act shall, so far as may be necessary for the continuity of the law, be treated as made under this Act.

(6) Any enactment or other document referring to an enactment repealed by this Act or to an enactment repealed by the Land Charges Act 1925 shall, as far as may be necessary for preserving its effect, be construed as referring, or as including a reference, to the corresponding enactment in this Act.

(7) Nothing in the foregoing provisions of this section shall be taken as prejudicing the operation of section 38 of the Interpretation Act 1889 (which relates to the effect of repeals). **[738]**

NOTES

Sub-s (2): repealed by the Local Land Charges Act 1975, s 19(1), Sch 2.
Sub-s (4): repealed by the Statute Law (Repeals) Act 2004.

19 Short title, commencement and extent

(1) This Act may be cited as the Land Charges Act 1972.

(2) This Act shall come into force on such day as the Lord Chancellor may by order made by statutory instrument appoint; and different days may be so appointed for different purposes.

(3) This Act extends to England and Wales only. **[739]**

NOTES

Order: the Land Charges Act 1972 (Commencement) Order 1972, SI 1972/2058.

SCHEDULE 1
ANNUITIES

Section 1

1. No further entries shall be made in the register of annuities.

2. An entry of an annuity made in the register of annuities before 1st January 1926 may be vacated in the prescribed manner on the prescribed evidence as to satisfaction, cesser or discharge being furnished.

3. The register shall be closed when all the entries in it have been vacated or the prescribed evidence of the satisfaction, cesser or discharge of all the annuities has been furnished.

4. An annuity which before 1st January 1926 was capable of being registered in the register of annuities shall be void as against a creditor or a purchaser of any interest in the land charged with the annuity unless the annuity is for the time being registered in the register of annuities or in the register of land charges. **[740]**

SCHEDULE 2
CLASS A LAND CHARGES

Section 2

1. Charges created pursuant to applications under the enactments mentioned in this Schedule may be registered as land charges of Class A by virtue of paragraph (*b*) of section 2(2) of this Act:—

(a) The Tithe Act 1918 (8 & 9 Geo 5 c 54)	Sections 4(2) and 6(1) (charge of consideration money for redemption of tithe rentcharge).
(b) The Tithe Annuities Apportionment Act 1921 (11 & 12 Geo 5 c 20)	Section 1 (charge of apportioned part of tithe redemption annuity).
(c) The Landlord and Tenant Act 1927 (17 & 18 Geo 5 c 36)	Paragraph (7) of Schedule 1 (charge in respect of improvements to business premises).
(d) [The Land Drainage Act 1991 (c 59)]	[Section 34(2)] (charge in respect of sum paid in commutation of certain obligations to repair banks, water-courses etc).
(e) The Tithe Act 1936 (26 Geo 5 & 1 Edw 8 c 43)	Section 30(1) (charge for redemption of corn rents etc).
(f) …	…
(g) The Agricultural Holdings Act 1948 (11 & 12 Geo 6 c 63)	[Section 74 (charge in respect of sums due to] occupier of agricultural holding).
	…
(h) The Corn Rents Act 1963 (1963 c 14)	Section 1(5) (charge under a scheme for the apportionment or redemption of corn rents or other payments in lieu of tithes).
[(i) The Agricultural Holdings Act 1986	Section 85 (charges in respect of sums due to tenant of agricultural holding).
	Section 86 (charges in favour of landlord of agricultural holding in respect of compensation for or cost of certain improvements).]

2. The following provisions of paragraph 1 above shall cease to have effect upon the coming into operation of the first scheme under the Corn Rents Act 1963, that is to say—
   (a) in sub-paragraph (a), the words "and 6(1)"; and
   (b) sub-paragraph (e).

3. [The reference in paragraph 1(g) above to section 74 of the Agricultural Holdings Act 1948 and the references in paragraph 1(i) above to section 85 and 86 of the Agricultural Holdings Act 1986] include references to any previous similar enactment. **[741]**

NOTES

Para 1: in sub-para (d), words in square brackets substituted by the Water Consolidation (Consequential Provisions) Act 1991, s 2, Sch 1, para 21; sub-para (f) repealed by the Civil Contingencies Act 2004, s 32(2), Sch 3; in sub-para (g), words in square brackets substituted and words omitted repealed by the Agricultural Holdings Act 1986, ss 100, 101, Sch 14, para 51(1), (2), Sch 15, Pt I; sub-para (i) inserted by the Agricultural Holdings Act 1986, s 100, Sch 14, para 51(1), (3).

Para 3: words in square brackets substituted by the Agricultural Holdings Act 1986, s 100, Sch 14, para 51(1), (4).

(Sch 3, para 1 amends the Law of Property Act 1925, s 97 at **[344]***; paras 2–6 repealed by the local Land Charges Act 1975, s 19(1), Sch 2; para 7 substitutes the Agricultural Credits Act 1928, s 9(7) and adds the Schedule thereto; paras 8–12 repealed by the Matrimonial Homes Act 1983, s 12, Sch 3; Sch 4 repealed by the Local Land Charges Act 1975, s 19(1), Sch 2; Sch 5 contains repeals only.)*

LOCAL GOVERNMENT ACT 1972

(1972 c 70)

An Act to make provision with respect to local government and the functions of local authorities in England and Wales; to amend Part II of the Transport Act 1968; to confer rights of appeal in respect of decisions relating to licences under the Home Counties (Music and Dancing) Licensing Act 1926; to make further provision with respect to magistrates' courts committees; to abolish certain inferior courts of record; and for connected purposes

[26 October 1972]

1–110 *((Pts I–VI) outside the scope of this work.)*

PART VII
MISCELLANEOUS POWERS OF LOCAL AUTHORITIES
Subsidiary powers

111 Subsidiary powers of local authorities

(1) Without prejudice to any powers exercisable apart from this section but subject to the provisions of this Act and any other enactment passed before or after this Act, a local authority shall have power to do any thing (whether or not involving the expenditure, borrowing or lending of money or the acquisition or disposal of any property or rights) which is calculated to facilitate, or is conducive or incidental to, the discharge of any of their functions.

(2) For the purposes of this section, transacting the business of a parish or community meeting or any other parish or community business shall be treated as a function of the parish or community council.

(3) A local authority shall not by virtue of this section raise money, whether by means of rates, precepts or borrowing, or lend money except in accordance with the enactments relating to those matters respectively.

(4) In this section "local authority" includes the Common Council.

[742]

NOTES

Application: in relation to the application of this section in respect of charter trustees, see the Charter Trustees Regulations 2009, SI 2009/467, reg 14(1).

See further, in relation to the powers exercisable by a local education authority: the Superannuation Act 1972, s 9(5A).

See further, for provision whereby the body corporate known as the Residuary Body for Wales is to be treated as a local authority for the purposes of subsections (1), (3) above: the Local Government (Wales) Act 1994, Sch 13, para 19(a).

112–119 (*Outside the scope of this work.*)

Land transactions—principal councils

120, 121 (*Outside the scope of this work.*)

122 Appropriation of land by principal councils

(1) Subject to the following provisions of this section, a principal council may appropriate for any purpose for which the council are authorised by this or any other enactment to acquire land by agreement any land which belongs to the council and is no longer required for the purpose for which it is held immediately before the appropriation; but the appropriation of land by a council by virtue of this subsection shall be subject to the rights of other persons in, over or in respect of the land concerned.

(2) A principal council may not appropriate under subsection (1) above any land which they may be authorised to appropriate under [section 229 of the Town and Country Planning Act 1990] (land forming part of a common, etc) unless—

(a) the total of the land appropriated in any particular common, … or fuel or field garden allotment (giving those expressions the same meanings as in [the said section 229]) does not in the aggregate exceed 250 square yards, and

(b) before appropriating the land they cause notice of their intention to do so, specifying the land in question, to be advertised in two consecutive weeks in a newspaper circulating in the area in which the land is situated, and consider any objections to the proposed appropriation which may be made to them, …

[(2A) A principal council may not appropriate under subsection (1) above any land consisting or forming part of an open space unless before appropriating the land they cause notice of their intention to do so, specifying the land in question, to be advertised in two consecutive weeks in a newspaper circulating in the area in which the land is situated, and consider any objections to the proposed appropriation which may be made to them.

(2B) Where land appropriated by virtue of subsection (2A) above is held—

(a) for the purposes of section 164 of the Public Health Act 1875 (pleasure grounds); or

(b) in accordance with section 10 of the Open Spaces Act 1906 (duty of local authority to maintain open spaces and burial grounds),

the land shall by virtue of the appropriation be freed from any trust arising solely by virtue of its being land held in trust for enjoyment by the public in accordance with the said section 164 or, as the case may be, the said section 10.]

(3) …

(4) Where land has been acquired under this Act or any other enactment or any statutory order incorporating the Lands Clauses Acts and is subsequently appropriated under this section, any work executed on the land after the appropriation has been effected shall be treated for the purposes of section 68 of the Lands Clauses Consolidation Act 1845 and section 10 of the Compulsory Purchase Act 1965 as having been authorised by the enactment or statutory order under which the land was acquired.

(5), (6) …

[743]

NOTES

Sub-s (2): words omitted repealed by the Local Government, Planning and Land Act 1980, ss 118, 194, Sch 23, para 12(1), Sch 34, Pt XIII; words in square brackets substituted by the Planning (Consequential Provisions) Act 1990, s 4, Sch 2, para 28(1).

Sub-ss (2A), (2B): inserted by the Local Government, Planning and Land Act 1980, s 118, Sch 23, para 12(2).

Sub-ss (3), (5), (6): repealed by the Local Government, Planning and Land Act 1980, ss 118, 194, Sch 23, para 13, Sch 34, Pt XIII.

Modification: by virtue of the Environment Act 1995, s 65, Sch 8, para 1(1) (and subject to para 1(2) thereto) this section has effect as if a National Park authority were a principal council and the relevant Park were the authority's area.

123 Disposal of land by principal councils

(1) Subject to the following provisions of this section, a principal council may dispose of land held by them in any manner they wish.

(2) Except with the consent of the Secretary of State, a council shall not dispose of land under this section, otherwise than by way of a short tenancy, for a consideration less than the best that can reasonably be obtained.

[(2A) A principal council may not dispose under subsection (1) above of any land consisting or forming part of an open space unless before disposing of the land they cause notice of their intention to do so, specifying the land in question, to be advertised in two consecutive weeks in a newspaper circulating in the area in which the land is situated, and consider any objections to the proposed disposal which may be made to them.

(2B) Where by virtue of subsection (2A) above a council dispose of land which is held—

(a) for the purposes of section 164 of the Public Health Act 1875 (pleasure grounds); or

(b) in accordance with section 10 of the Open Spaces Act 1906 (duty of local authority to maintain open spaces and burial grounds),

the land shall by virtue of the disposal be freed from any trust arising solely by virtue of its being land held in trust for enjoyment by the public in accordance with the said section 164 or, as the case may be, the said section 10.]

(3)–(5) …

(6) …

(7) For the purposes of this section a disposal of land is a disposal by way of a short tenancy if it consists—

(a) of the grant of a term not exceeding seven years, or

(b) of the assignment of a term which at the date of the assignment has not more than seven years to run,

and in this section "public trust land" has the meaning assigned to it by section 122(6) above.

[744]

NOTES

Sub-ss (2A), (2B): inserted by the Local Government, Planning and Land Act 1980, s 118, Sch 23, para 14.

Sub-ss (3)–(5): repealed by the Local Government, Planning and Land Act 1980, ss 118, 194, Sch 23, para 15, Sch 34, Pt XIII.

Sub-s (6): repealed by the Local Government and Housing Act 1989, s 194, Sch 12, Pt I; for effect see SI 2004/533, art 7(3).

Modification: by virtue of the Environment Act 1995, s 65, Sch 8, para 1(1) (and subject to para 1(2) thereto) this section has effect as if a National Park authority were a principal council and the relevant Park were the authority's area.

Transfer of Functions: functions of the Secretary of State, so far as exercisable in relation to Wales, transferred to the National Assembly for Wales, by the National Assembly for Wales (Transfer of Functions) Order 1999, SI 1999/672, art 2, Sch 1.

Disapplication: sub-s (2) is disapplied with respect to the disposal of land to the governing body of a foundation, voluntary or foundation special school, or persons proposing to establish such a school, by the School Standards and Framework Act 1998, s 22, Sch 3, Pt III, para 12.

123A–244 *(S 123A inserted by the Community Land Act 1975, s 42(1), repealed by the Local Government, Planning and Land Act 1980, ss 118, 194, Sch 23, para 16, Sch 34, Pt XIII; ss 124–146A, ss 147–244 (Pts VIII–XI) outside the scope of this work.)*

PART XII
MISCELLANEOUS AND GENERAL

Status, etc

245–269 (*Outside the scope of this work.*)

270 General provisions as to interpretation

(1) In this Act, except where the context otherwise requires, the following expressions have the following meanings respectively, that is to say—

["alternative arrangements" has the same meaning as in Part II of the Local Government Act 2000;]

"appropriate Minister", in relation to the making of an order or regulation or the giving of a direction with respect to any matter, means the Minister in charge of any Government department concerned with that matter; but the validity of any order, regulation or direction purporting to be made or given by any Minister by virtue of a power conferred on the appropriate Minister by this Act shall not be affected by any question as to whether or not that Minister was the appropriate Minister for the purpose;

"bank holiday break" means any bank holiday not included in the Christmas break or the Easter break and the period beginning with the last week day before that bank holiday and ending with the next week day which is not a bank holiday;

["the Broads" has the same meaning as in the Norfolk and Suffolk Broads Act 1988;]

"Christmas break" means the period beginning with the last week day before Christmas Day and ending with the first week day after Christmas Day which is not a bank holiday;

"the City" means the City of London;

…

"Common Council" means the Common Council of the City;

"county" without more, means, in relation to England, a metropolitan county or a non-metropolitan county[, but in the expressions "county council", "council of a county", "county councillor" and "councillor of a county" means, in relation to England, a non-metropolitan county only];

"district", without more, means, in relation to England, a metropolitan district or a non-metropolitan district;

"Easter break" means the period beginning with the Thursday before and ending with the Tuesday after Easter Day;

["elected mayor" has the same meaning as in Part II of the Local Government Act 2000;]

"electoral area" means any area for which councillors are elected to any local authority;

["executive", "executive arrangements" and "executive leader" have the same meaning as in Part II of the Local Government Act 2000;]

…

"existing", in relation to a local government or other area or a local authority or other body, except in sections 1 and 20 above, means that area or body as it existed immediately before the passing of this Act;

"financial year" means the period of twelve months ending with 31st March in any year;

"grouped", in relation to a parish or community, means grouped by or by virtue of any provision of this Act or any previous corresponding enactment under a common parish or community council, and "grouping order" shall be construed accordingly;

["joint authority" means an authority established by Part IV of the Local Government Act 1985;]

["joint waste authority" means an authority established for an area in England by an order under section 207 of the Local Government and Public Involvement in Health Act 2007;]

"land" includes any interest in land and any easement or right in, to or over land;

["leader and cabinet executive" means—

(a) in relation to England: a leader and cabinet executive (England);

(b) in relation to Wales: a leader and cabinet executive (Wales);]

["leader and cabinet executive (England)" has the same meaning as in Part 2 of the Local Government Act 2000;]

["leader and cabinet executive (Wales)" has the same meaning as in Part 2 of the Local Government Act 2000;]

"local authority" means a county council, … a district council, a London borough council or a parish [council but, in relation to Wales, means a county council, county borough council or community council;]

"local government area" means—

(a) in relation to England, a county, Greater London, a district, a London borough or a parish;

[(b) in relation to Wales, a county, county borough or community;]

"local government elector" means a person registered as a local government elector in the register of electors in accordance with the provisions of the Representation of the People Acts;

"local statutory provision" means a provision of a local Act (including an Act confirming a provisional order) or a provision of a public general Act passed with respect only to the whole or part of an existing local government area or a provision of an instrument made under any such local or public general Act or of an instrument in the nature of a local enactment made under any other Act;

["mayor and cabinet executive" and "mayor and council manager executive" have the same meaning as in Part II of the Local Government Act 2000;]

"new", in relation to any area or authority, means an area or authority established by or under this Act [including one established by virtue of any provision of the Local Government (Wales) Act 1994];

"1933 Act" means the Local Government Act 1933;

"1963 Act" means the London Government Act 1963;

["open space" has the meaning assigned to it by [section 336(1) of the Town and Country Planning Act 1990];]

"prescribed" means prescribed by regulations made by the Secretary of State;

["preserved county" means any county created by this Act as a county in Wales, as it stood immediately before the passing of the Local Government (Wales) Act 1994 but subject to any provision of the Act of 1994, or any provision made under this Act, redrawing its boundaries;]

"principal area" means a [non-metropolitan county], a district or a London borough [but, in relation to Wales, means a county or county borough];

"principal council" means a council elected for a principal area;

"public body" includes—

(a) a local authority and a joint board on which, and a joint committee on which, a local authority or parish meeting are represented;

(b) any trustees, commissioners or other persons who, for public purposes and not for their own profit, act under any enactment or instrument for the improvement of any place, for the supply of water to any place, or for providing or maintaining a cemetery or market in any place; and

(c) any other authority having powers of levying or issuing a precept for any rate for public purposes;

and "district" means, in relation to a public body other than a local authority, the area for which the public body acts;

…

"specified papers", in relation to a parish or community, means the public books, writings and papers of the parish or community (including any photographic copies thereof) and all documents directed by law to be kept therewith;

"the Temples" means the Inner Temple and the Middle Temple;

"Welsh Commission" has the meaning assigned to it by section 53 above.

(2) In this Act and in any other enactment, whether passed before, at the same time as, or after this Act, the expression "non-metropolitan county" means any county other than a metropolitan county, and the expression "non-metropolitan district" means any district other than a metropolitan district.

(3) Any reference in this Act to a proper officer and any reference which by virtue of this Act is to be construed as such a reference shall, in relation to any purpose and any local authority or other body or any area, be construed as a reference to an officer appointed for that purpose by that body or for that area, as the case may be.

(4) In any provision of this Act which applies to a London borough, except Schedule 2 to this Act,—

(a) any reference to the chairman of the council or of any class of councils comprising the council or to a member of a local authority shall be construed as or, as the case may be, as including a reference to the mayor of the borough;

(b) any reference to the vice-chairman of the council or any such class of councils shall be construed as a reference to the deputy mayor of the borough; and

(c) any reference to the proper officer of the council or any such class of councils shall be construed as a reference to the proper officer of the borough.

[(4A) Where a London borough council are operating executive arrangements which involve a mayor and cabinet executive …, subsection (4) above shall have effect with the omission of paragraphs (a) and (b).]

(5) In this Act, except where the context otherwise requires, references to any enactment shall be construed as references to that enactment as amended, extended or applied by or under any other enactment, including any enactment contained in this Act.

NOTES

Sub-s (1): definition "alternative arrangements" inserted in relation to England by SI 2001/2237, arts 1(2), 2(a), 9, and in relation to Wales by SI 2002/808, arts 2(a), 9; definition "the Broads" inserted by the Norfolk and Suffolk Broads Act 1988, s 21, Sch 6, para 10(9); definitions omitted repealed by the Local Government act 1992, s 29, Sch 4, Pt II and the Statute Law (Repeals) Act 2004; in definition "county" words in square brackets inserted by the Local Government Act 1985, s 102, Sch 16, para 8; definitions "elected mayor", "executive", "executive arrangements", "executive leader", "mayor and executive cabinet" and "mayor and council manager executive" inserted by the Local Government Act 2000, s 46, Sch 3, para 12; definition "joint authority" inserted by the Local Government Act 1985, s 84, Sch 14, para 34; definition "joint waste authority" inserted by the Local Government and Public Involvement in Health Act 2007, s 209(2), Sch 13, Pt 1, paras 1, 24; definition "leader and cabinet executive" substituted (as inserted by the Local Government Act 2000, s 46, Sch 3, para 12(1), (4)) by the Local Government and Public Involvement in Health Act 2007, s 74(1), Sch 3, paras 1, 10(1), (2); definitions "leader and cabinet executive (England)" and "leader and cabinet executive (Wales)" inserted by the Local Government and Public Involvement in Health Act 2007, s 74(1), Sch 3, paras 1, 10(1), (3); in definition "local authority" words omitted repealed by the Local Government Act 1985, s 102, Sch 16, para 8, Sch 17 and words in square brackets substituted by the Local Government (Wales) Act 1994, s 1(5); in definition "local government area", para (b) substituted by the Local Government (Wales) Act 1994, s 1(6); in definition "new", words in square brackets inserted by the Local Government (Wales) Act 1994, s 66(5), para 57; definition "open space" inserted by the Local Government, Planning and Land Act 1980, s 118, Sch 23 and words in square brackets therein substituted by the Planning (Consequential Provisions) Act 1990, s 4, Sch 2, para 28(3); definition "preserved county" inserted by the Local Government (Wales) Act 1994, s 1(7); in definition "principal area" words in first pair of square brackets substituted by the Local Government Act 1985, s 102, Sch 16, para 8 and words in second pair of square brackets inserted by the Local Government (Wales) Act 1994, s 1(8).

Sub-s (4A): inserted by the Local Government Act 2000, s 46, Sch 3, para 12(1), (6); words omitted repealed by the Local Government and Public Involvement in Health Act 2007, ss 74(1), 241, Sch 3, paras 1, 10(1), (4), Sch 18, Pt 3.

Transfer of Functions: functions of the Secretary of State, the appropriate Minister and the Minister of the Crown, so far as exercisable in relation to Wales, transferred to the National Assembly for Wales, by the National Assembly for Wales (Transfer of Functions) Order 1999, SI 1999/672, art 2, Sch 1.

271–273 (*Outside the scope of this work.*)

274 Short title and extent

(1) This Act may be cited as the Local Government Act 1972.

(2) … This Act shall not extend to Scotland.

(3) … This Act shall not extend to Northern Ireland.

[746]

NOTES

Sub-s (2): words omitted repealed by the Statute Law (Repeals) Act 2004.

Sub-s (3): words omitted repealed by the House of Commons Disqualification Act 1875, s 10(2), Sch 3, and the Northern Ireland Assembly Disqualification Act 1975, s 5(2), Sch 3, Pt I.

(*Schs 1–30 outside the scope of this work.*)

ADMINISTRATION OF JUSTICE ACT 1973

(1973 c 15)

An Act to amend the law relating to justices of the peace and to make further provision with respect to the administration of justice and matters connected therewith

[18 April 1973]

1–5 ((*Pt I*) *outside the scope of this work.*)

PART II
MISCELLANEOUS

6, 7 (*S 6 repealed by the Statute Law (Repeals) Act 2004; s 7 repealed by the County Courts Act 1984, s 148(3), Sch 4.*)

8 Extension of powers of court in action by mortgagee of dwelling-house

(1) Where by a mortgage of land which consists of or includes a dwelling-house, or by any agreement between the mortgagee under such a mortgage and the mortgagor, the mortgagor is

entitled or is to be permitted to pay the principal sum secured by instalments or otherwise to defer payment of it in whole or in part, but provision is also made for earlier payment in the event of any default by the mortgagor or of a demand by the mortgagee or otherwise, then for purposes of section 36 of the Administration of Justice Act 1970 (under which a court has power to delay giving a mortgagee possession of the mortgaged property so as to allow the mortgagor a reasonable time to pay any sums due under the mortgage) a court may treat as due under the mortgage on account of the principal sum secured and of interest on it only such amounts as the mortgagor would have expected to be required to pay if there had been no such provision for earlier payment.

(2) A court shall not exercise by virtue of subsection (1) above the powers conferred by section 36 of the Administration of Justice Act 1970 unless it appears to the court not only that the mortgagor is likely to be able within a reasonable period to pay any amounts regarded (in accordance with subsection (1) above) as due on account of the principal sum secured, together with the interest on those amounts, but also that he is likely to be able by the end of that period to pay any further amounts that he would have expected to be required to pay by then on account of that sum and of interest on it if there had been no such provision as is referred to in subsection (1) above for earlier payment.

(3) Where subsection (1) above would apply to an action in which a mortgagee only claimed possession of the mortgaged property, and the mortgagee brings an action for foreclosure (with or without also claiming possession of the property), then section 36 of the Administration of Justice Act 1970 together with subsections (1) and (2) above shall apply as they would apply if it were an action in which the mortgagee only claimed possession of the mortgaged property, except that—

(a) section 36(2)(b) shall apply only in relation to any claim for possession; and
(b) section 36(5) shall not apply.

(4) For purposes of this section the expressions "dwelling-house", "mortgage", "mortgagee" and "mortgagor" shall be construed in the same way as for the purposes of Part IV of the Administration of Justice Act 1970.

(5) …

(6) In the application of this section to Northern Ireland, subsection (3) shall be omitted.

[747]

NOTES

Sub-s (5): repealed by the Statute Law (Repeals) Act 2004.

9–18 (*Ss 9, 12, 18 outside the scope of this work; ss 10(1)–(7) (except so far as applied by s 10(8), which applies to Northern Ireland only), (9), 11, 13 repealed by the Judicial Pensions Act 1981, s 36(2), Sch 4; s 14(1), (2) amend the Resident Magistrates' Pensions Act (Northern Ireland) 1960, s 22(1), s 14(3) repealed by the Northern Ireland Constitution Act 1973, s 41(1), Sch 6, Pt I; ss 15, 16(1), (7) repealed by the Supreme Court Act 1981, s 152(4), Sch 7; s 16(2)–(6) repealed by the County Courts Act 1984, s 148(3), Sch 4; s 17 repealed by the Prosecution of Offences Act 1985, s 31(6), Sch 2.*)

PART III
SUPPLEMENTARY

19, 20 (*Repealed by the Statute Law (Repeals) Act 1989.*)

21 Short title and extent

(1) This Act may be cited as the Administration of Justice Act 1973.

(2) The foregoing sections of this Act shall not extend to Scotland or to Northern Ireland except to the following extent, that is to say—

(a) sections 9 to 12 of this Act, and the repeals made by Parts IV and V of Schedule 5, shall extend to Scotland or to Northern Ireland in so far as they affect the law of Scotland or of Northern Ireland; and
(b) sections 8, 14 and 18 of this Act (together with so much of section 20(1) as relates to those sections) shall extend to Northern Ireland.

[748]

(*Schs 1–5 outside the scope of this work.*)

MATRIMONIAL CAUSES ACT 1973

(1973 c 18)

An Act to consolidate certain enactments relating to matrimonial proceedings, maintenance agreements, and declarations of legitimacy, validity of marriage and British nationality, with amendments to give effect to recommendations of the Law Commission

[23 May 1973]

PART I
DIVORCE, NULLITY AND OTHER MATRIMONIAL SUITS

1–16 (*Outside the scope of this work.*)

Other matrimonial suits

17 (*Outside the scope of this work.*)

18 Effects of judicial separation

(*1*) *Where the court grants a decree of judicial separation it shall no longer be obligatory for the petitioner to cohabit with the respondent.*

(2) *If while a decree of judicial separation is in force and the separation is continuing either of the parties to the marriage dies intestate as respects all or any of his or her real or personal property, the property as respects which he or she died intestate shall devolve as if the other party to the marriage had then been dead.*

(*3*) *Notwithstanding anything in section 2(1)(a) of the Matrimonial Proceedings (Magistrates' Courts) Act 1960, a provision in force under an order made, or having effect as if made, under that section exempting one party to a marriage from the obligation to cohabit with the other shall not have effect as a decree of judicial separation for the purposes of subsection (2) above.*

[749]

NOTES

Repealed by the Family Law Act 1996, s 66(3), Sch 10, subject to savings in s 66(2) of, Sch 9, para 5 to that Act, as from a day to be appointed.

19, 20 (*Outside the scope of this work.*)

PART II
FINANCIAL RELIEF FOR PARTIES TO MARRIAGE AND CHILDREN OF FAMILY

Financial provision and property adjustment orders

21 Financial provision and property adjustment orders

(*1*) *The financial provision orders for the purposes of this Act are the orders for periodical or lump sum provision available (subject to the provisions of this Act) under section 23 below for the purpose of adjusting the financial position of the parties to a marriage and any children of the family in connection with proceedings for divorce, nullity of marriage or judicial separation and under section 27(6) below on proof of neglect by one party to a marriage to provide, or to make a proper contribution towards, reasonable maintenance for the other or a child of the family, that is to say—*

(*a*) *any order for periodical payments in favour of a party to a marriage under section 23(1)(a) or 27(6)(a) or in favour of a child of the family under section 23(1)(d), (2) or (4) or 27(6)(d);*

(*b*) *any order for secured periodical payments in favour of a party to a marriage under section 23(1)(b) or 27(6)(b) or in favour of a child of the family under section 23(1)(e), (2) or (4) or 27(6)(e); and*

(*c*) *any order for lump sum provision in favour of a party to a marriage under section 23(1)(c) or 27(6)(c) or in favour of a child of the family under section 23(1)(f), (2) or (4) or 27(6)(f);*

and references in this Act (except in paragraphs 17(1) and 23 of Schedule 1 below) to periodical payments orders, secured periodical payments orders, and orders for the payment of a lump sum are references to all or some of the financial provision orders requiring the sort of financial provision in question according as the context of each reference may require.

(2) *The property adjustment orders for the purposes of this Act are the orders dealing with property rights available (subject to the provisions of this Act) under section 24 below for the*

purpose of adjusting the financial position of the parties to a marriage and any children of the family on or after the grant of a decree of divorce, nullity of marriage or judicial separation, that is to say—

(*a*) *any order under subsection (1)(a) of that section for a transfer of property;*

(*b*) *any order under subsection (1)(b) of that section for a settlement of property; and*

(*c*) *any order under subsection (1)(c) or (d) of that section for a variation of settlement.*

[21 Financial provision orders, property adjustment orders and pension sharing orders

(1) For the purposes of this Act, a financial provision order is—

(a) an order that a party must make in favour of another person such periodical payments, for such term, as may be specified (a "periodical payments order");

(b) an order that a party must, to the satisfaction of the court, secure in favour of another person such periodical payments, for such term, as may be specified (a "secured periodical payments order");

(c) an order that a party must make a payment in favour of another person of such lump sum or sums as may be specified (an "order for the payment of a lump sum").

(2) For the purposes of this Act, a property adjustment order is—

(a) an order that a party must transfer such of his or her property as may be specified in favour of the other party or a child of the family;

(b) an order that a settlement of such property of a party as may be specified must be made, to the satisfaction of the court, for the benefit of the other party and of the children of the family, or either or any of them;

(c) an order varying, for the benefit of the parties and of the children of the family, or either or any of them, any marriage settlement, other than one in the form of a pension arrangement (within the meaning of section 25D below);

(d) an order extinguishing or reducing the interest of either of the parties under any marriage settlement, other than one in the form of a pension arrangement (within the meaning of section 25D below).

(3) For the purposes of this Act, a pension sharing order is an order which—

(a) provides that one party's—

(i) shareable rights under a specified pension arrangement, or

(ii) shareable state scheme rights,

be subject to pension sharing for the benefit of the other party, and

(b) specifies the percentage value to be transferred.

(4) Subject to section 40 below, where an order of the court under this Part of this Act requires a party to make or secure a payment in favour of another person or to transfer property in favour of any person, that payment must be made or secured or that property transferred—

(a) if that other person is the other party to the marriage, to that other party; and

(b) if that other person is a child of the family, according to the terms of the order—

(i) to the child; or

(ii) to such other person as may be specified, for the benefit of that child.

(5) References in this section to the property of a party are references to any property to which that party is entitled either in possession or in reversion.

(6) Any power of the court under this Part of this Act to make such an order as is mentioned in subsection (2)(b) to (d) above is exercisable even though there are no children of the family.

(7) In subsection (3)—

(a) the reference to shareable rights under a pension arrangement is to rights in relation to which pension sharing is available under Chapter I of Part IV of the Welfare Reform and Pensions Act 1999, or under corresponding Northern Ireland legislation, and

(b) the reference to shareable state scheme rights is to rights in relation to which pension sharing is available under Chapter II of Part IV of the Welfare Reform and Pensions Act 1999, or under corresponding Northern Ireland legislation.

(8) In this section—

"marriage settlement" means an ante-nuptial or post-nuptial settlement made on the parties (including one made by will or codicil);

"party" means a party to a marriage; and

"specified" means specified in the order in question.]

[750]

NOTES

Substituted, together with section 21A, by new section 21, by the Family Law Act 1996, s 15, Sch 2, para 2 (as amended by the Welfare Reform and Pensions Act 1999, s 84(1), Sch 12, Pt I, paras 64, 65(1)–(8)), subject to savings in s 66(2) of, Sch 9, para 5 to that Act, as from a day to be appointed.

21A–21C (*Outside the scope of this work.*)

Ancillary relief in connection with divorce proceedings, etc.

22 (*Outside the scope of this work.*)

[22A Financial provision orders: divorce and separation

(1) On an application made under this section, the court may at the appropriate time make one or more financial provision orders in favour of—

(a) a party to the marriage to which the application relates; or

(b) any of the children of the family.

(2) The "appropriate time" is any time—

(a) after a statement of marital breakdown has been received by the court and before any application for a divorce order or for a separation order is made to the court by reference to that statement;

(b) when an application for a divorce order or separation order has been made under section 3 of the 1996 Act and has not been withdrawn;

(c) when an application for a divorce order has been made under section 4 of the 1996 Act and has not been withdrawn;

(d) after a divorce order has been made;

(e) when a separation order is in force.

(3) The court may make—

(a) a combined order against the parties on one occasion,

(b) separate orders on different occasions,

(c) different orders in favour of different children,

(d) different orders from time to time in favour of the same child,

but may not make, in favour of the same party, more than one periodical payments order, or more than one order for payment of a lump sum, in relation to any marital proceedings, whether in the course of the proceedings or by reference to a divorce order or separation order made in the proceedings.

(4) If it would not otherwise be in a position to make a financial provision order in favour of a party or child of the family, the court may make an interim periodical payments order, an interim order for the payment of a lump sum or a series of such orders, in favour of that party or child.

(5) Any order for the payment of a lump sum made under this section may—

(a) provide for the payment of the lump sum by instalments of such amounts as may be specified in the order; and

(b) require the payment of the instalments to be secured to the satisfaction of the court.

(6) Nothing in subsection (5) above affects—

(a) the power of the court under this section to make an order for the payment of a lump sum; or

(b) the provisions of this Part of this Act as to the beginning of the term specified in any periodical payments order or secured periodical payments order.

(7) Subsection (8) below applies where the court—

(a) makes an order under this section ("the main order") for the payment of a lump sum; and

(b) directs—

(i) that payment of that sum, or any part of it, is to be deferred; or

(ii) that that sum, or any part of it, is to be paid by instalments.

(8) In such a case, the court may, on or at any time after making the main order, make an order ("the order for interest") for the amount deferred, or the instalments, to carry interest (at such rate as may be specified in the order for interest)—

(a) from such date, not earlier than the date of the main order, as may be so specified;

(b) until the date when the payment is due.

(9) This section is to be read subject to any restrictions imposed by this Act and to section 19 of the 1996 Act.]

[751]

NOTES

Commencement: to be appointed.

Inserted by the Family Law Act 1996, s 15, Sch 2, para 3, subject to savings in s 66(2) of, Sch 9, para 5 to that Act.

22B (*Outside the scope of this work.*)

*23 **Financial provision orders in connection with divorce proceedings, etc***

(1) On granting a decree of divorce, a decree of nullity of marriage or a decree of judicial separation or at any time thereafter (whether, in the case of a decree of divorce or of nullity of marriage, before or after the decree is made absolute), the court may make any one or more of the following orders, that is to say—

(a) an order that either party to the marriage shall make to the other such periodical payments, for such term, as may be specified in the order;

(b) an order that either party to the marriage shall secure to the other to the satisfaction of the court such periodical payments, for such term, as may be so specified;

(c) an order that either party to the marriage shall pay to the other such lump sum or sums as may be so specified;

(d) an order that a party to the marriage shall make to such person as may be specified in the order for the benefit of a child of the family, or to such a child, such periodical payments, for such term, as may be so specified;

(e) an order that a party to the marriage shall secure to such person as may be so specified for the benefit of such a child, or to such a child, to the satisfaction of the court, such periodical payments, for such term, as may be so specified;

(f) an order that a party to the marriage shall pay to such person as may be so specified for the benefit of such a child, or to such a child, such lump sum as may be so specified;

subject, however, in the case of an order under paragraph (d), (e) or (f) above, to the restrictions imposed by section 29(1) and (3) below on the making of financial provision orders in favour of children who have attained the age of eighteen.

(2) The court may also, subject to those restrictions, make any one or more of the orders mentioned in subsection (1)(d), (e) and (f) above—

(a) in any proceedings for divorce, nullity of marriage or judicial separation, before granting a decree; and

(b) where any such proceedings are dismissed after the beginning of the trial, either forthwith or within a reasonable period after the dismissal.

(3) Without prejudice to the generality of subsection (1)(c) or (f) above—

(a) an order under this section that a party to a marriage shall pay a lump sum to the other party may be made for the purpose of enabling that other party to meet any liabilities or expenses reasonably incurred by him or her in maintaining himself or herself or any child of the family before making an application for an order under this section in his or her favour;

(b) an order under this section for the payment of a lump sum to or for the benefit of a child of the family may be made for the purpose of enabling any liabilities or expenses reasonably incurred by or for the benefit of that child before the making of an application for an order under this section in his favour to be met; and

(c) an order under this section for the payment of a lump sum may provide for the payment of that sum by instalments of such amount as may be specified in the order and may require the payment of the instalments to be secured to the satisfaction of the court.

(4) The power of the court under subsection (1) or (2)(a) above to make an order in favour of a child of the family shall be exercisable from time to time; and where the court makes an order in favour of a child under subsection (2)(b) above, it may from time to time, subject to the restrictions mentioned in subsection (1) above, make a further order in his favour of any of the kinds mentioned in subsection (1)(d), (e) or (f) above.

(5) Without prejudice to the power to give a direction under section 30 below for the settlement of an instrument by conveyancing counsel, where an order is made under subsection (1)(a), (b) or (c) above on or after granting a decree of divorce or nullity of marriage, neither the order nor any settlement made in pursuance of the order shall take effect unless the decree has been made absolute.

[(6) Where the court—

(a) makes an order under this section for the payment of a lump of sum; and

(b) directs—

(i) that payment of that sum or any part of it shall be deferred; or

(ii) that that sum or any part of it shall be paid by instalments,

the court may order that the amount deferred or the instalments shall carry interest at such rate as may be specified by the order from such date, not earlier than the date of the order, as may be so specified, until the date when payment of it is due.]

[23 Financial provision orders: nullity

(1) On or after granting a decree of nullity of marriage (whether before or after the decree is made absolute), the court may, on an application made under this section, make one or more financial provision orders in favour of—

(a) either party to the marriage; or

(b) any child of the family.

(2) Before granting a decree in any proceedings for nullity of marriage, the court may make against either or each of the parties to the marriage—

(a) an interim periodical payments order, an interim order for the payment of a lump sum, or a series of such orders, in favour of the other party;

(b) an interim periodical payments order, an interim order for the payment of a lump sum, a series of such orders or any one or more other financial provision orders in favour of each child of the family.

(3) Where any such proceedings are dismissed, the court may (either immediately or within a reasonable period after the dismissal) make any one or more financial provision orders in favour of each child of the family.

(4) An order under this section that a party to a marriage must pay a lump sum to the other party may be made for the purpose of enabling that other party to meet any liabilities or expenses reasonably incurred by him or her in maintaining himself or herself or any child of the family before making an application for an order under this section in his or her favour.

(5) An order under this section for the payment of a lump sum to or for the benefit of a child of the family may be made for the purpose of enabling any liabilities or expenses reasonably incurred by or for the benefit of that child before the making of an application for an order under this section in his favour to be met.

(6) An order under this section for the payment of a lump sum may—

(a) provide for the payment of that sum by instalments of such amount as may be specified in the order; and

(b) require the payment of the instalments to be secured to the satisfaction of the court.

(7) Nothing in subsections (4) to (6) above affects—

(a) the power under subsection (1) above to make an order for the payment of a lump sum; or

(b) the provisions of this Act as to the beginning of the term specified in any periodical payments order or secured periodical payments order.

(8) The powers of the court under this section to make one or more financial provision orders are exercisable against each party to the marriage by the making of—

(a) a combined order on one occasion, or

(b) separate orders on different occasions,

but the court may not make more than one periodical payments order, or more than one order for payment of a lump sum, in favour of the same party.

(9) The powers of the court under this section so far as they consist in power to make one or more orders in favour of the children of the family—

(a) may be exercised differently in favour of different children; and

(b) except in the case of the power conferred by subsection (3) above, may be exercised from time to time in favour of the same child; and

(c) in the case of the power conferred by that subsection, if it is exercised by the making of a financial provision order of any kind in favour of a child, shall include power to make, from time to time, further financial provision orders of that or any other kind in favour of that child.

(10) Where an order is made under subsection (1) above in favour of a party to the marriage on or after the granting of a decree of nullity of marriage, neither the order nor any settlement made in pursuance of the order takes effect unless the decree has been made absolute.

(11) Subsection (10) above does not affect the power to give a direction under section 30 below for the settlement of an instrument by conveyancing counsel.

(12) Where the court—

(a) makes an order under this section ("the main order") for the payment of a lump sum; and

(b) directs—

(i) that payment of that sum or any part of it is to be deferred; or

(ii) that that sum or any part of it is to be paid by instalments,

it may, on or at any time after making the main order, make an order ("the order for interest") for the amount deferred or the instalments to carry interest at such rate as may be specified by the order for interest from such date, not earlier than the date of the main order, as may be so specified, until the date when payment of it is due.

(13) This section is to be read subject to any restrictions imposed by this Act.]

[752]

NOTES

Substituted by the Family Law 1996, s 15, Sch 2, para 4, subject to savings in s 66(2) of, Sch 9, para 5 to that Act, as from a day to be appointed.

Original sub-s (6): inserted by the Administration of Justice Act 1982, s 16.
Modification: in relation to the modification of orders made under this section in pursuance of s 25B(7) hereof, where the Board of the Pension Protection Fund has assumed responsibility for an occupational pension scheme, see the Divorce etc (Pension Protection Fund) Regulations 2006, SI 2006/1932, reg 3.

[23A Property adjustment orders: divorce and separation

(1) On an application made under this section, the court may, at any time mentioned in section 22A(2) above, make one or more property adjustment orders.

(2) If the court makes, in favour of the same party to the marriage, more than one property adjustment order in relation to any marital proceedings, whether in the course of the proceedings or by reference to a divorce order or separation order made in the proceedings, each order must fall within a different paragraph of section 21(2) above.

(3) The court shall exercise its powers under this section, so far as is practicable, by making on one occasion all such provision as can be made by way of one or more property adjustment orders in relation to the marriage as it thinks fit.

(4) Subsection (3) above does not affect section 31 or 31A below.

(5) This section is to be read subject to any restrictions imposed by this Act and to section 19 of the 1996 Act.]

[753]

NOTES

Commencement: to be appointed.
Inserted by the Family Law Act 1996, s 15, Sch 2, para 5, subject to savings in s 66(2) of, Sch 9, para 5 to that Act.

[23B Restrictions affecting section 23A

(1) No property adjustment order may be made under section 23A above so as to take effect before the making of a divorce order or separation order in relation to the marriage unless the court is satisfied—

(a) that the circumstances of the case are exceptional; and
(b) that it would be just and reasonable for the order to be so made.

(2) The court may not make a property adjustment order under section 23A above at any time while the period for reflection and consideration is interrupted under section 7(8) of the 1996 Act.

(3) No property adjustment order may be made under section 23A above by virtue of the making of a statement of marital breakdown if, by virtue of section 5(3) or 7(5) of the 1996 Act (lapse of divorce or separation process), it has ceased to be possible—

(a) for an application to be made by reference to that statement; or
(b) for an order to be made on such an application.

(4) No property adjustment order may be made under section 23A above after a divorce order has been made, or while a separation order is in force, except—

(a) in response to an application made before the divorce order or separation order was made; or
(b) on a subsequent application made with the leave of the court.

(5) In this section, "period for reflection and consideration" means the period fixed by section 7 of the 1996 Act.]

[754]

NOTES

Commencement: to be appointed.
Inserted by the Family Law Act 1996, s 15, Sch 2, para 5, subject to savings in s 66(2) of, Sch 9, para 5 to that Act.

24 *Property adjustment orders in connection with divorce proceedings, etc*

(1) On granting a decree of divorce, a decree of nullity of marriage or a decree of judicial separation or at any time thereafter (whether, in the case of a decree of divorce or of nullity of marriage, before or after the decree is made absolute), the court may make any one or more of the following orders, that is to say—

(a) an order that a party to the marriage shall transfer to the other party, to any child of the family or to such person as may be specified in the order for the benefit of such a child such property as may be so specified, being property to which the first-mentioned party is entitled, either in possession or reversion;

(b) an order that a settlement of such property as may be so specified, being property to which a party to the marriage is so entitled, be made to the satisfaction of the court for the benefit of the other party to the marriage and of the children of the family or either or any of them;

(*c*) *an order varying for the benefit of the parties to the marriage and of the children of the family or either or any of them any ante-nuptial or post-nuptial settlement (including such a settlement made by will or codicil) made on the parties to the marriage [, other than one in the form of a pension arrangement (within the meaning of section 25D below)];*

(*d*) *an order extinguishing or reducing the interest of either of the parties to the marriage under any such settlement [, other than one in the form of a pension arrangement (within the meaning of section 25D below)];*

subject, however, in the case of an order under paragraph (a) above, to the restrictions imposed by section 29(1) and (3) below on the making of orders for a transfer of property in favour of children who have attained the age of eighteen.

(2) *The court may make an order under subsection (1)(c) above notwithstanding that there are no children of the family.*

(3) *Without prejudice to the power to give a direction under section 30 below for the settlement of an instrument by conveyancing counsel, where an order is made under this section on or after granting a decree of divorce or nullity of marriage, neither the order nor any settlement made in pursuance of the order shall take effect unless the decree has been made absolute.*

[24 Property adjustment orders: nullity of marriage

(1) On or after granting a decree of nullity of marriage (whether before or after the decree is made absolute), the court may, on an application made under this section, make one or more property adjustment orders in relation to the marriage.

(2) The court shall exercise its powers under this section, so far as is practicable, by making on one occasion all such provision as can be made by way of one or more property adjustment orders in relation to the marriage as it thinks fit.

(3) Subsection (2) above does not affect section 31 or 31A below.

(4) Where a property adjustment order is made under this section on or after the granting of a decree of nullity of marriage, neither the order nor any settlement made in pursuance of the order is to take effect unless the decree has been made absolute.

(5) That does not affect the power to give a direction under section 30 below for the settlement of an instrument by conveyancing counsel.

(6) This section is to be read subject to any restrictions imposed by this Act.]

[755]

NOTES

Substituted by the Family Law Act 1996, s 15, Sch 2, para 6, subject to savings in s 66(2) of, Sch 9, para 5 to that Act, as from a day to be appointed.

Original sub-s (1): words in square brackets in paras (c), (d) inserted by the Welfare Reform and Pensions Act 1999, s 19, Sch 3, paras 1, 3.

[24A Orders for sale of property

(1) Where the court makes under *section 23 or 24 of this Act* [any of sections 22A to 24 above] a secured periodical payments order, an order for the payment of a lump sum or a property adjustment order, then, on making that order or at any time thereafter, the court may make a further order for the sale of such property as may be specified in the order, being property in which or in the proceeds of sale of which either or both of the parties to the marriage has or have a beneficial interest, either in possession or reversion.

(2) Any order made under subsection (1) above may contain such consequential or supplementary provisions as the court thinks fit and, without prejudice to the generality of the foregoing provision, may include—

(a) provision requiring the making of a payment out of the proceeds of sale of the property to which the order relates, and

(b) provision requiring any such property to be offered for sale to a person, or class of persons, specified in the order.

(3) Where an order is made under subsection (1) above on or after the grant of a decree of *divorce or* nullity of marriage, the order shall not take effect unless the decree has been made absolute.

(4) Where an order is made under subsection (1) above, the court may direct that the order, or such provision thereof as the court may specify, shall not take effect until the occurrence of an event specified by the court or the expiration of a period so specified.

(5) Where an order under subsection (1) above contains a provision requiring the proceeds of sale of the property to which the order relates to be used to secure periodical payments to a party to the marriage, the order shall cease to have effect on the death or re-marriage of[, or formation of a civil partnership by,] that person.

[(6) Where a party to a marriage has a beneficial interest in any property, or in the proceeds of sale thereof, and some other person who is not a party to the marriage also has a beneficial interest in that property or in the proceeds of sale thereof, then, before deciding whether to make an order under this section in relation to that property, it shall be the duty of the court to give that other person an opportunity to make representations with respect to the order; and any representations made by that other person shall be included among the circumstances to which the court is required to have regard under section 25(1) below.]]

[756]

NOTES

Inserted by the Matrimonial Homes and Property Act 1981, s 7.

Sub-s (1): words in italics substituted by subsequent words in square brackets by the Family Law Act 1996, s 66(1), Sch 8, para 8, subject to savings in s 66(2) of, Sch 9, para 5 to that Act, as from a day to be appointed.

Sub-s (3): words in italics repealed by the Family Law Act 1996, s 66(3), Sch 10, subject to savings in s 66(2) of, Sch 9, para 5 to that Act, as from a day to be appointed.

Sub-s (5): words in square brackets inserted by the Civil Partnership Act 2004, s 261(1), Sch 27, para 42.

Sub-s (6): inserted by the Matrimonial and Family Proceedings Act 1984, s 46(1), Sch 1.

24B–24G (*Outside the scope of this work.*)

[25 Matters to which court is to have regard in deciding how to exercise its powers under ss 23, 24 *and 24A*[, 24A, 24B and 24E]]

[(1) It shall be the duty of the court in deciding whether to exercise its powers under *section 23, 24* [*, 24A or 24B* [, 24B or 24E]] [any of sections 22A to 24BB] above and, if so, in what manner, to have regard to all the circumstances of the case, first consideration being given to the welfare while a minor of any child of the family who has not attained the age of eighteen.

(2) As regards the exercise of the powers of the court under *section 23(1)(a), (b) or (c),* [section 22A or 23 above to make a financial provision order in favour of a party to a marriage or the exercise of its powers under section 23A,] 24 [, 24A *or 24B* [*, 24B or 24BB*] [, 24B or 24E]] above in relation to a party to the marriage, the court shall in particular have regard to the following matters—

- (a) the income, earning capacity, property and other financial resources which each of the parties to the marriage has or is likely to have in the foreseeable future, including in the case of earning capacity any increase in that capacity which it would in the opinion of the court be reasonable to expect a party to the marriage to take steps to acquire;
- (b) the financial needs, obligations and responsibilities which each of the parties to the marriage has or is likely to have in the foreseeable future;
- (c) the standard of living enjoyed by the family before the breakdown of the marriage;
- (d) the age of each party to the marriage and the duration of the marriage;
- (e) any physical or mental disability of either of the parties to the marriage;
- (f) the contributions which each of the parties has made or is likely in the foreseeable future to make to the welfare of the family, including any contribution by looking after the home or caring for the family;
- (g) the conduct of each of the parties[, whatever the nature of the conduct and whether it occurred during the marriage or after the separation of the parties or (as the case may be) dissolution or annulment of the marriage], if that conduct is such that it would in the opinion of the court be inequitable to disregard it;
- (h) *in the case of proceedings for divorce or nullity of marriage,* the value to each of the parties to the marriage of any benefit … which, by reason of the dissolution or annulment of the marriage, that party will lose the chance of acquiring.

(3) As regards the exercise of the powers of the court under *section 23(1)(d), (e) or (f), (2) or (4)* [section 22A or 23 above to make a financial provision order in favour of a child of the family or the exercise of its powers under section 23A,] 24 or 24A above in relation to a child of the family, the court shall in particular have regard to the following matters—

- (a) the financial needs of the child;
- (b) the income, earning capacity (if any), property and other financial resources of the child;
- (c) any physical or mental disability of the child;
- (d) the manner in which he was being and in which the parties to the marriage expected him to be educated or trained;
- (e) the considerations mentioned in relation to the parties to the marriage in paragraphs (a), (b), (c) and (e) of subsection (2) above.

(4) As regards the exercise of the powers of the court under *section 23(1)(d), (e) or (f), (2) or (4), 24 or 24A* [any of sections 22A to 24A] above against a party to a marriage in favour of a child of the family who is not the child of that party, the court shall also have regard—

- (a) to whether that party assumed any responsibility for the child's maintenance, and, if so, to the extent to which, and the basis upon which, that party assumed such responsibility and to the length of time for which that party discharged such responsibility;

(b) to whether in assuming and discharging such responsibility that party did so knowing that the child was not his or her own;

(c) to the liability of any other person to maintain the child.

[(5) In relation to any power of the court to make an interim periodical payments order or an interim order for the payment of a lump sum, the preceding provisions of this section, in imposing any obligation on the court with respect to the matters to which it is to have regard, shall not require the court to do anything which would cause such a delay as would, in the opinion of the court, be inappropriate having regard—

(a) to any immediate need for an interim order;

(b) to the matters in relation to which it is practicable for the court to inquire before making an interim order; and

(c) to the ability of the court to have regard to any matter and to make appropriate adjustments when subsequently making a financial provision order which is not interim.]]

[757]

NOTES

Substituted by the Matrimonial and Family Proceedings Act 1984, s 3.

Section heading: words in italics substituted by subsequent words in square brackets by the Pensions Act 2008, s 120, Sch 6, Pt 1, paras 1, 4(1), (2), as from a day to be appointed.

Sub-s (1): words ", 24A or 24B" in square brackets substituted by the Welfare Reform and Pensions Act 1999, s 19, Sch 3, paras 1, 5(a); words "or 24B" in italics substituted by subsequent words in square brackets by the Pensions Act 2008, s 120, Sch 6, Pt 1, paras 1, 4(1), (3), as from a day to be appointed; words "section 23, 24, 24A or 24B" in italics substituted by subsequent words in square brackets by the Family Law Act 1996, s 66(1), Sch 8, Pt I, para 9(2) (as amended by the Welfare Reform and Pensions Act 1999, s 84(1), Sch 12, Pt I, paras 64, 66(1), (2)(a)), subject to savings in s 66(2) of, Sch 9, para 5 to that Act, as from a day to be appointed.

Sub-s (2): first words in italics substituted by subsequent words in square brackets, by the Family Law Act 1996, s 66(1), Sch 8, para 9(3)(a), subject to savings in s 66(2) of, Sch 9, para 5 to that Act, as from a day to be appointed; words ", 24A or 24B" in square brackets substituted by the Welfare Reform and Pensions Act 1999, s 19, Sch 3, paras 1, 5(b); words "or 24B" in italics substituted by subsequent words in square brackets by the Family Law Act 1996, s 66(1), Sch 8, Pt I, para 9(3)(aa) (as inserted by the Welfare Reform and Pensions Act 1999, s 84(1), Sch 12, Pt I, paras 64, 66(1), (2)(b)), subject to savings in s 66(2) of, Sch 9, para 5 to that Act, as from a day to be appointed; words "or 24B" in italics further substituted by subsequent words ", 24B or 24E" in square brackets by the Pensions Act 2008, s 120, Sch 6, Pt 1, paras 1, 4(1), (3), as from a day to be appointed; in para (g), words in square brackets inserted by the Family Law Act 1996, s 66(1), Sch 8, para 9(3)(b), subject to savings in s 66(2) of, Sch 9, para 5 to that Act, as from a day to be appointed; in para (h), first words in italics repealed by the Family Law Act 1996, s 66(1), (3), Sch 8, para 9(3)(c), Sch 10, subject to savings in s 66(2) of, Sch 9, para 5 to that Act, as from a day to be appointed, and words omitted repealed by the Pensions Act 1995, s 166(2), subject to savings in SI 1996/1675, arts 4, 5.

Sub-ss (3), (4): words in italics substituted by subsequent words in square brackets by the Family Law Act 1996, s 66(1), Sch 8, para 9(4), (5), subject to savings in s 66(2) of, Sch 9, para 5 to that Act, as from a day to be appointed.

Sub-s (5): inserted by the Family Law Act 1996, s 66(1), Sch 8, para 9(6), subject to savings in s 66(2) of, Sch 9, para 5 to that Act, as from a day to be appointed.

[25A Exercise of court's powers in favour of party to marriage on decree of divorce or nullity of marriage

(1) *Where on or after the grant of a decree of divorce or nullity of marriage the court decides to exercise its powers under section 23(1)(a), (b) or (c), 24[, 24A or 24B* [, *24B or 24E*]] *above in favour of a party to the marriage*[If the court decides to exercise any of its powers under any of sections 22A to 24BB above in favour of a party to a marriage (other than its power to make an interim periodical payments order or an interim order for the payment of a lump sum)], it shall be the duty of the court to consider whether it would be appropriate so to exercise those powers that the financial obligations of each party towards the other will be terminated as soon after the grant of *the decree* [a divorce order or decree of nullity] as the court considers just and reasonable.

(2) Where the court decides in such a case to make a periodical payments or secured periodical payments order in favour of a party to the marriage, the court shall in particular consider whether it would be appropriate to require those payments to be made or secured only for such term as would in the opinion of the court be sufficient to enable the party in whose favour the order is made to adjust without undue hardship to the termination of his or her financial dependence on the other party.

(3) Where on or after the grant of a decree of divorce or nullity of marriage an application is made by a party to the marriage for a periodical payments or secured periodical payments order in his or her favour, then, if the court considers that no continuing obligation should be imposed on either party to make or secure periodical payments in favour of the other, the court may dismiss the application with a direction that the applicant shall not be entitled to make any future application in relation to that marriage for an order under section 23(1)(a) or (b) above.

[(3) If the court—

(a) would have power under section 22A or 23 above to make a financial provision order in favour of a party to a marriage ("the first party"), but

(b) considers that no continuing obligation should be imposed on the other party to the marriage ("the second party") to make or secure periodical payments in favour of the first party,

it may direct that the first party may not at any time after the direction takes effect, apply to the court for the making against the second party of any periodical payments order or secured periodical payments order and, if the first party has already applied to the court for the making of such an order, it may dismiss the application.

(3A) If the court—

(a) exercises, or has exercised, its power under section 22A at any time before making a divorce order, and

(b) gives a direction under subsection (3) above in respect of a periodical payments order or a secured periodical payments order,

it shall provide for the direction not to take effect until a divorce order is made.]]

[758]

NOTES

Inserted by the Matrimonial and Family Proceedings Act 1984, s 3.

Sub-s (1): words ", 24A or 24B" in square brackets substituted by the Welfare Reform and Pensions Act 1999, s 19, Sch 3, paras 1, 6; words in italics in both places they appear substituted by subsequent words in square brackets by the Family Law Act 1996, s 66(1), Sch 8, Pt I, para 10(2), (3) (as amended by the Welfare Reform and Pensions Act 1999, s 84(1), Sch 12, Pt I, paras 64, 66(1), (3)), subject to savings in s 66(2) of, Sch 9, para 5 to that Act, as from a day to be appointed; words "or 24B" in italics substituted by subsequent words in square brackets by the Pensions Act 2008, s 120, Sch 6, Pt 1, paras 1, 5, as from a day to be appointed.

Sub-ss (3), (3A): substituted, for original sub-s (3), by the Family Law Act 1996, s 66(1), Sch 8, para 10(4), subject to savings in s 66(2) of, Sch 9, para 5 to that Act, as from a day to be appointed.

25B–28 (*Outside the scope of this work.*)

29 Duration of continuing financial provision orders in favour of children, and age limit on making certain orders in their favour

(1) Subject to subsection (3) below, no financial provision order and no order for a transfer of property under *section 24(1)(a)* [such as is mentioned in section 21(2)(a)] above shall be made in favour of a child who has attained the age of eighteen.

[(1A) The term specified in a periodical payments order or secured periodical payments order made in favour of a child shall be such term as the court thinks fit.

(1B) If that term is to begin before the making of the order, it may do so no earlier than—

(a) in the case of an order made by virtue of section 22A(2)(a) or (b) above, except where paragraph (b) below applies, the beginning of the day on which the statement of marital breakdown in question was received by the court;

(b) in the case of an order made by virtue of section 22A(2)(b) above where the application for the divorce order was made following cancellation of an order preventing divorce under section 10 of the 1996 Act, the date of the making of that application;

(c) in the case of an order made by virtue of section 22A(2)(c) above, the date of the making of the application for the divorce order; or

(d) in any other case, the date of the making of the application on which the order is made.]

(2) The term to be specified in a periodical payments or secured periodical payments order in favour of a child *may begin with the date of the making of an application for the order in question or any later date [or a date ascertained in accordance with subsection (5) or (6) below] but*—

(a) shall not in the first instance extend beyond the date of the birthday of the child next following his attaining the upper limit of the compulsory school age [(construed in accordance with section 8 of the Education Act 1996)] [unless the court considers that in the circumstances of the case the welfare of the child requires that it should extend to a later date]; and

(b) shall not in any event, subject to subsection (3) below, extend beyond the date of the child's eighteenth birthday.

(3) Subsection (1) above, and paragraph (b) of subsection (2), shall not apply in the case of a child, if it appears to the court that—

(a) the child is, or will be, or if an order were made without complying with either or both of those provisions would be, receiving instruction at an educational establishment or undergoing training for a trade, profession or vocation, whether or not he is also, or will also be, in gainful employment; or

(b) there are special circumstances which justify the making of an order without complying with either or both of those provisions.

(4) Any periodical payments order in favour of a child shall, notwithstanding anything in the order, cease to have effect on the death of the person liable to make payments under the order, except in relation to any arrears due under the order on the date of the death.

[(5) Where—

(a) a *maintenance assessment* [maintenance calculation] ("the *current assessment* [current calculation]") is in force with respect to a child; and

(b) an application is made under Part II of this Act for a periodical payments or secured periodical payments order in favour of that child—

(i) in accordance with section 8 of the Child Support Act 1991, and

(ii) before the end of the period of 6 months beginning with the making of the *current assessment* [current calculation]

the term to be specified in any such order made on that application may be expressed to begin on, or at any time after, the earliest permitted date.

(6) For the purposes of subsection (5) above, "the earliest permitted date" is whichever is the later of—

(a) the date 6 months before the application is made; or

(b) the date on which the *current assessment* [current calculation] took effect or, where successive *maintenance assessments* [maintenance calculations] have been continuously in force with respect to a child, on which the first of *those assessments* [those calculations] took effect.

(7) Where—

(a) a *maintenance assessment* [maintenance calculation] ceases to have effect *or is cancelled* by or under any provision of the Child Support Act 1991; and

(b) an application is made, before the end of the period of 6 months beginning with the relevant date, for a periodical payments or secured periodical payments order in favour of a child with respect to whom that *maintenance assessment* [maintenance calculation] was in force immediately before it ceased to have effect *or was cancelled*,

the term to be specified in any such order made on that application may begin with the date on which that *maintenance assessment* [maintenance calculation] ceased to have effect *or, as the case may be, the date with effect from which it was cancelled*, or any later date.

(8) In subsection (7)(b) above—

(a) where the *maintenance assessment* [maintenance calculation] ceased to have effect, the relevant date is the date on which it so ceased; *and*

(b) *where the maintenance assessment was cancelled, the relevant date is the later of—*

(i) the date on which the person who cancelled it did so, and

(ii) the date from which the cancellation first had effect.]

[759]

NOTES

Sub-s (1): words in italics substituted by subsequent words in square brackets by the Family Law Act 1996, s 66(1), Sch 8, para 15, subject to savings in s 66(2) of, Sch 9, para 5 to that Act, as from a day to be appointed.

Sub-ss (1A), (1B): inserted by the Family Law Act 1996, s 15, Sch 2, para 7(2), subject to savings in s 66(2) of, Sch 9, para 5 to that Act, as from a day to be appointed.

Sub-s (2): words in italics repealed by the Family Law Act 1996, s 66(3), Sch 10, subject to savings in s 66(2) of, Sch 9, para 5 to that Act, as from a day to be appointed; first words in square brackets inserted by SI 1993/623, art 2, Sch 1, para 1; in para (a), first words in square brackets substituted by the Education Act 1996, s 582(1), Sch 37, para 136, and second words in square brackets inserted by the Matrimonial and Family Proceedings Act 1984, s 5.

Sub-ss (5), (6): inserted by SI 1993/623, art 2, Sch 1, para 2; for the words in italics in each place they appear there are substituted the subsequent words in square brackets by the Child Support, Pensions and Social Security Act 2000, s 26, Sch 3, para 3(1), (2)(a)–(d), partly as from a day to be appointed.

Sub-s (7): inserted by SI 1993/623, art 2, Sch 1, para 2; words "maintenance assessment" in each place they appear in italics substituted by subsequent words in square brackets, and other words in italics repealed by the Child Support, Pensions and Social Security Act 2000, ss 26, 85, Sch 3, para 3(1), (2)(a), Sch 9, Pt I, partly as from a day to be appointed.

Sub-s (8): inserted by SI 1993/623, art 2, Sch 1, para 2; words in italics in para (a) substituted by subsequent words in square brackets, and para (b) and word "and" immediately preceding it repealed by the Child Support, Pensions and Social Security Act 2000, ss 26, 85, Sch 3, para 3(1), (2)(a), Sch 9, Pt I, partly as from a day to be appointed.

30–44 *(Ss 31–41 outside the scope of this work; ss 42–44 repealed with savings by the Children Act 1989, s 108(4), (6), (7), Sch 12, para 32, Sch 14, paras 1, 3, 5–11, 15, 26, Sch 15.)*

PART IV
MISCELLANEOUS AND SUPPLEMENTAL

45–54 *(S 45 repealed with a saving by the Family Law Act 1986, s 68(2), (3)(a), Sch 2; s 46 repealed with savings by the Domicile and Matrimonial Proceedings Act 1973, ss 6, 17(2), Sch 6; ss 47–49, 52–54 outside the scope of this work; ss 50, 51 repealed by the Matrimonial and Family Proceedings Act 1984, s 46(3), Sch 3.)*

55 Citation, commencement and extent

(1) This Act may be cited as the Matrimonial Causes Act 1973.

(2) This Act shall come into force on such day as the Lord Chancellor may appoint by order made by statutory instrument.

(3) Subject to the provisions of paragraphs 3(2) … of Schedule 2 below, this Act does not extend to Scotland or Northern Ireland.

[760]

NOTES

Sub-s (3): words omitted repealed by the Statute Law (Repeals) Act 1977.
Order: the Matrimonial Causes Act 1973 (Commencement) Order 1973, SI 1973/1972.

(*Schs 1–3 outside the scope of this work.*)

CONSUMER CREDIT ACT 1974

(1974 c 39)

An Act to establish for the protection of consumers a new system, administered by the Director General of Fair Trading, of licensing and other control of traders concerned with the provision of credit, or the supply of goods on hire or hire-purchase, and their transactions, in place of the present enactments regulating moneylenders, pawnbrokers and hire-purchase traders and their transactions, and for related matters

[31 July 1974]

1–7 ((*Pt I*) *outside the scope of this work.*)

PART II
CREDIT AGREEMENTS, HIRE AGREEMENTS AND LINKED TRANSACTIONS

8 Consumer credit agreements

(1) A *personal* [consumer] credit agreement is an agreement between an individual ("the debtor") and any other person ("the creditor") by which the creditor provides the debtor with credit of any amount.

(2) …

(3) A consumer credit agreement is a regulated agreement within the meaning of this Act if it is not an agreement (an "exempt agreement") specified in or under section 16[, 16A] [, 16B or 16C].

[761]

NOTES

Sub-s (1): word in italics substituted by subsequent word in square brackets by the Consumer Credit Act 2006, s 2(1)(a), as from a day to be appointed.

Sub-s (2): repealed by the Consumer Credit Act 2006, ss 2(1)(b), 70, Sch 4.

Sub-s (3): first words in square brackets inserted by the Consumer Credit Act 2006, s 5(1); second words in square brackets substituted by SI 2008/2826, art 3(2).

9–14 (*Outside the scope of this work.*)

15 Consumer hire agreements

(1) A consumer hire agreement is an agreement made by a person with an individual (the "hirer") for the bailment or (in Scotland) the hiring of goods to the hirer, being an agreement which—

(a) is not a hire-purchase agreement, and
(b) is capable of subsisting for more than three months, …
(c) …

(2) A consumer hire agreement is a regulated agreement if it is not an exempt agreement. **[762]**

NOTES

Sub-s (1): para (c) and word immediately preceding it repealed by the Consumer Credit Act 2006, ss 2(2), 70, Sch 4.

16 Exempt agreements

(1) This Act does not regulate a consumer credit agreement where the creditor is a local authority … , or a body specified, or of a description specified, in an order made by the Secretary of State, being—

[(a) an insurer,]
(b) a friendly society,
(c) an organisation of employers or organisation of workers,
(d) a charity,
(e) a land improvement company, …
(f) a body corporate named or specifically referred to in any public general Act
[(ff) a body corporate named or specifically referred to in an order made under—
section 156(4), *444*(*1*) or 447(2)(a) of the Housing Act 1985,
[section 156(4) of that Act as it has effect by virtue of section 17 of the Housing Act 1996 (the right to acquire),]
section 2 of the Home Purchase Assistance and Housing Corporation Guarantee Act 1978 or section 31 of the Tenants' Rights, &c (Scotland) Act 1980, or
Article 154(1)(a) or 156AA of the Housing (Northern Ireland) Order 1981 or Article 10(6A) of the Housing (Northern Ireland) Order 1983; or]
[(g) a building society][, or
[(h) a deposit-taker]].

(2) Subsection (1) applies only where the agreement is—

(a) a debtor-creditor-supplier agreement financing—
(i) the purchase of land, or
(ii) the provision of dwellings on any land,
and secured by a land mortgage on that land, or
(b) a debtor-creditor agreement secured by any land mortgage; or
(c) a debtor-creditor-supplier agreement financing a transaction which is a linked transaction in relation to—
(i) an agreement falling within paragraph (a), or
(ii) an agreement falling within paragraph (b) financing—
(aa) the purchase of any land, or
(bb) the provision of dwellings on any land,
and secured by a land mortgage on the land referred to in paragraph (a) or, as the case may be, the land referred to in sub-paragraph (ii).

[(3) Before he makes, varies or revokes an order under subsection (1), the Secretary of State must undertake the necessary consultation.

(3A) The necessary consultation means consultation with the bodies mentioned in the following table in relation to the provision under which the order is to be made, varied or revoked:

Provision of subsection (*1*)	*Consultee*
Paragraph (a) or (b)	The Financial Services Authority
Paragraph (d)	[Charity Commission]
Paragraph (e), (f) or (ff)	Any Minister of the Crown with responsibilities in relation to the body in question
Paragraph (g) or (h)	The Treasury and the Financial Services Authority]

(4) An order under subsection (1) relating to a body may be limited so as to apply only to agreements by that body of a description specified in the order.

(5) The Secretary of State may by order provide that this Act shall not regulate other consumer credit agreements where—

(a) the number of payments to be made by the debtor does not exceed the number specified for that purpose in the order, or
(b) the rate of the total charge for credit does not exceed the rate so specified, or
(c) an agreement has a connection with a country outside the United Kingdom.

(6) The Secretary of State may by order provide that this Act shall not regulate consumer hire agreements of a description specified in the order where—

(a) the owner is a body corporate authorised by or under any enactment to supply electricity, gas or water, and

(b) the subject of the agreement is a meter or metering equipment,

[or where the owner is a [provider of a public electronic communications service who is specified in the order]].

[(6A) This Act does not regulate a consumer credit agreement where the creditor is a housing authority and the agreement is secured by a land mortgage of a dwelling.

(6B) In subsection (6A) "housing authority" means—

(a) as regards England and Wales, [the Housing Corporation … and] an authority or body within section 80(1) of the Housing Act 1985 (the landlord condition for secure tenancies), other than a housing association or a housing trust which is a charity;

(b) as regards Scotland, a development corporation established under an order made, or having effect as if made under the New Towns (Scotland) Act 1968, the Scottish Special Housing Association or the Housing Corporation;

(c) as regards Northern Ireland, the Northern Ireland Housing Executive.]

[[(6C) This Act does not regulate a consumer credit agreement if—

(a) it is secured by a land mortgage and entering into the agreement as lender is a regulated activity for the purposes of the Financial Services and Markets Act 2000; or

(b) it is or forms part of a regulated home purchase plan and entering into the agreement as home purchase provider is a regulated activity for the purposes of that Act.]

(6D) But section 126, and any other provision so far as it relates to section 126, applies to an agreement which would (but for [subsection (6C)(a)]) be a regulated agreement.

(6E) Subsection (6C) must be read with—

(a) section 22 of the Financial Services and Markets Act 2000 (regulated activities: power to specify classes of activity and categories of investment);

(b) any order for the time being in force under that section; and

(c) Schedule 2 to that Act.]

(7) …

[(7A) Nothing in this section affects the application of sections 140A to 140C.]

[(8) In the application of this section to Scotland, subsection (3A) shall have effect as if the reference to the [Charity Commission] were a reference to the Lord Advocate.]

(9) In the application of this section to Northern Ireland [subsection (3A)] shall have effect as if any reference to a Minister of the Crown were a reference to a Northern Ireland department, … and any reference to the [Charity Commission] were a reference to the Department of Finance for Northern Ireland.

[(10) In this section—

(a) "deposit-taker" means—

(i) a person who has permission under Part 4 of the Financial Services and Markets Act 2000 to accept deposits,

(ii) an EEA firm of the kind mentioned in paragraph 5(b) of Schedule 3 to that Act which has permission under paragraph 15 of that Schedule (as a result of qualifying for authorisation under paragraph 12 of that Schedule) to accept deposits,

(iii) any wholly owned subsidiary (within the meaning of *the Companies Act 1985* [the Companies Acts (see section 1159 of the Companies Act 2006)]) of a person mentioned in sub-paragraph (i), or

(iv) any undertaking which, in relation to a person mentioned in sub-paragraph (ii), is a subsidiary undertaking within the meaning of any rule of law in force in the EEA State in question for purposes connected with the implementation of the European Council Seventh Company Law Directive of 13 June 1983 on consolidated accounts (No 83/349/EEC), and which has no members other than that person;

(b) "insurer" means—

(i) a person who has permission under Part 4 of the Financial Services and Markets Act 2000 to effect or carry out contracts of insurance, or

(ii) an EEA firm of the kind mentioned in paragraph 5(d) of Schedule 3 to that Act, which has permission under paragraph 15 of that Schedule (as a result of qualifying for authorisation under paragraph 12 of that Schedule) to effect or carry out contracts of insurance,

but does not include a friendly society or an organisation of workers or of employers.

(11) Subsection (10) must be read with—

(a) section 22 of the Financial Services and Markets Act 2000;
(b) any relevant order under that section; and
(c) Schedule 2 to that Act.]

[763]

NOTES

Sub-s (1): first words omitted repealed by the Building Societies Act 1986, s 120, Sch 18, Pt I, para 10(2), Sch 19, Pt I; para (a) substituted by SI 2001/3649, art 165(1), (2)(a); para (ff) inserted by the Housing and Planning Act 1986, s 22(2), (4) in respect of agreements made after 7 January 1987, number "444(1)" in italics repealed by the Housing Act 1996, s 227, Sch 19, Pt XIV, as from a day to be appointed and words in square brackets inserted by SI 1997/627, art 2, Schedule, para 2; para (g) inserted by the Building Societies Act 1986, s 120, Sch 18, Pt I, para 10(2); para (h) inserted by the Banking Act 1987, s 88 and substituted by SI 2001/3649, art 165(1), (2)(b).

Sub-s (3): substituted, together with sub-s (3A), for original sub-s (3), by SI 2001/3649, art 165(1), (3).

Sub-s (3A): substituted, together with sub-s (3), for original sub-s (3), by SI 2001/3649, art 165(1), (3); words in square brackets substituted by the Charities Act 2006, s 75(1), Sch 8, para 56.

Sub-s (6): words in first (outer) pair of square brackets substituted by the Telecommunications Act 1984, s 109, Sch 4, para 60; words in second (inner) pair of square brackets substituted by the Communications Act 2003, s 406(1), Sch 17, para 47.

Sub-s (6A): inserted with respect to agreements made after 7 January 1987 by the Housing and Planning Act 1986, s 22.

Sub-s (6B): inserted with respect to agreements made after 7 January 1987 by the Housing and Planning Act 1986, s 22; words in square brackets inserted by the Housing Act 1988, s 140, Sch 17, Pt I; words omitted repealed by the Government of Wales Act 1998, s 152, Sch 18, Pt VI.

Sub-s (6C): inserted by SI 2001/544, art 90(1), (2); substituted by SI 2006/2383, art 25(1), (2)(a), subject to transitional provisions in arts 37–39 thereof.

Sub-s (6D): inserted by SI 2001/544, art 90(1), (2); words in square brackets substituted by SI 2006/2383, art 25(1), (2)(b), subject to transitional provisions in arts 37–39 thereof.

Sub-s (6E): inserted by SI 2001/544, art 90(1), (2).

Sub-s (7): repealed by the Consumer Credit Act 2006, s 70, Sch 4, subject to transitional provision and savings in s 69(1) of, Sch 3, paras 1, 15(5)(a), (7) to that Act.

Sub-s (7A): inserted by the Consumer Credit Act 2006, s 22(2).

Sub-s (8): substituted by SI 2001/3649, art 165(1), (4); words in square brackets substituted by the Charities Act 2006, s 75(1), Sch 8, para 56.

Sub-s (9): words in first pair of square brackets substituted and words omitted repealed by SI 2001/3649, art 165(1), (5); words in second pair of square brackets substituted by the Charities Act 2006, s 75(1), Sch 8, para 56.

Sub-ss (10), (11): inserted by SI 2001/3649, art 165(1), (6).

Sub-s (10)(a)(iii): words in italics substituted by subsequent words in square brackets by SI 2009/1941, art 2(1), Sch 1, para 28, as from 1 October 2009.

Modification: in sub-s (6B)(a) the reference to the Housing Corporation shall be treated as if it were a reference to the Regulator of Social Housing: see the Transfer of Housing Corporation Functions (Modifications and Transitional Provisions) Order 2008, SI 2008/2839, arts 1(2), 3, 6, Schedule, para 7.

Order: the Consumer Credit (Exempt Agreements) Order 1989, SI 1989/869.

[16A Exemption relating to high net worth debtors and hirers

(1) The Secretary of State may by order provide that this Act shall not regulate a consumer credit agreement or a consumer hire agreement where—
(a) the debtor or hirer is a natural person;
(b) the agreement includes a declaration made by him to the effect that he agrees to forgo the protection and remedies that would be available to him under this Act if the agreement were a regulated agreement;
(c) a statement of high net worth has been made in relation to him; and
(d) that statement is current in relation to the agreement and a copy of it was provided to the creditor or owner before the agreement was made.

(2) For the purposes of this section a statement of high net worth is a statement to the effect that, in the opinion of the person making it, the natural person in relation to whom it is made—
(a) received during the previous financial year income of a specified description totalling an amount of not less than the specified amount; or
(b) had throughout that year net assets of a specified description with a total value of not less than the specified value.

(3) Such a statement—
(a) may not be made by the person in relation to whom it is made;
(b) must be made by a person of a specified description; and
(c) is current in relation to an agreement if it was made during the period of one year ending with the day on which the agreement is made.

(4) An order under this section may make provision about—
(a) how amounts of income and values of net assets are to be determined for the purposes of subsection (2)(a) and (b);
(b) the form, content and signing of—
(i) statements of high net worth;
(ii) declarations for the purposes of subsection (1)(b).

(5) Where an agreement has two or more debtors or hirers, for the purposes of paragraph (c) of subsection (1) a separate statement of high net worth must have been made in relation to each of them; and paragraph (d) of that subsection shall have effect accordingly.

(6) In this section—

"previous financial year" means, in relation to a statement of high net worth, the financial year immediately preceding the financial year during which the statement is made;

"specified" means specified in an order under this section.

(7) In subsection (6) "financial year" means a period of one year ending with 31st March.

(8) Nothing in this section affects the application of sections 140A to 140C.]

[763A]

NOTES

Commencement: 16 June 2006 (sub-ss (1)–(7)); 6 April 2008 (sub-s (8)).
Inserted by the Consumer Credit Act 2006, s 3.
Orders: the Consumer Credit (Exempt Agreements) Order 2007, SI 2007/1168.

[16B Exemption relating to businesses

(1) This Act does not regulate—

(a) a consumer credit agreement by which the creditor provides the debtor with credit exceeding £25,000, or

(b) a consumer hire agreement that requires the hirer to make payments exceeding £25,000,

if the agreement is entered into by the debtor or hirer wholly or predominantly for the purposes of a business carried on, or intended to be carried on, by him.

(2) If an agreement includes a declaration made by the debtor or hirer to the effect that the agreement is entered into by him wholly or predominantly for the purposes of a business carried on, or intended to be carried on, by him, the agreement shall be presumed to have been entered into by him wholly or predominantly for such purposes.

(3) But that presumption does not apply if, when the agreement is entered into—

(a) the creditor or owner, or

(b) any person who has acted on his behalf in connection with the entering into of the agreement,

knows, or has reasonable cause to suspect, that the agreement is not entered into by the debtor or hirer wholly or predominantly for the purposes of a business carried on, or intended to be carried on, by him.

(4) The Secretary of State may by order make provision about the form, content and signing of declarations for the purposes of subsection (2).

(5) Where an agreement has two or more creditors or owners, in subsection (3) references to the creditor or owner are references to any one or more of them.

(6) Nothing in this section affects the application of sections 140A to 140C]

[763B]

NOTES

Commencement: 16 June 2006 (sub-s (4)); 6 April 2008 (sub-ss (1)–(3), (5), (6)).
Inserted by the Consumer Credit Act 2006, s 4.
Orders: the Consumer Credit (Exempt Agreements) Order 2007, SI 2007/1168.

[16C Exemption relating to investment properties

(1) This Act does not regulate a consumer credit agreement if, at the time the agreement is entered into, any sums due under it are secured by a land mortgage on land where the condition in subsection (2) is satisfied.

(2) The condition is that less than 40% of the land is used, or is intended to be used, as or in connection with a dwelling—

(a) by the debtor or a person connected with the debtor, or

(b) in the case of credit provided to trustees, by an individual who is the beneficiary of the trust or a person connected with such an individual.

(3) For the purposes of subsection (2) the area of any land which comprises a building or other structure containing two or more storeys is to be taken to be the aggregate of the floor areas of each of those storeys.

(4) For the purposes of subsection (2) a person is "connected with" the debtor or an individual who is the beneficiary of a trust if he is—

(a) that person's spouse or civil partner;

(b) a person (whether or not of the opposite sex) whose relationship with that person has the characteristics of the relationship between husband and wife; or

(c) that person's parent, brother, sister, child, grandparent or grandchild.

(5) Section 126 (enforcement of land mortgages) applies to an agreement which would but for this section be a regulated agreement.

(6) Nothing in this section affects the application of sections 140A to 140C.]

[763C]

NOTES

Commencement: 31 October 2008.
Inserted by SI 2008/2826, art 3(1).

17–20 (*Outside the scope of this work.*)

PART III
LICENSING OF CREDIT AND HIRE BUSINESSES

21–33 (*Outside the scope of this work.*)

Miscellaneous

34–39 (*Outside the scope of this work.*)

40 Enforcement of agreements made by unlicensed trader

[(1) A regulated agreement is not enforceable against the debtor or hirer by a person acting in the course of a consumer credit business or a consumer hire business (as the case may be) if that person is not licensed to carry on a consumer credit business or a consumer hire business (as the case may be) of a description which covers the enforcement of the agreement.

(1A) Unless the OFT has made an order under subsection (2) which applies to the agreement, a regulated agreement is not enforceable against the debtor or hirer if—

(a) it was made by the creditor or owner in the course of a consumer credit business or a consumer hire business (as the case may be); and

(b) at the time the agreement was made he was not licensed to carry on a consumer credit business or a consumer hire business (as the case may be) of a description which covered the making of the agreement.

(2) Where—

(a) during any period a person (the 'trader' has made regulated agreements in the course of a consumer credit business or a consumer hire business (as the case may be), and

(b) during that period he was not licensed to carry on a consumer credit business or a consumer hire business (as the case may be) of a description which covered the making of those agreements,

he or his successor in title may apply to the OFT for an order that the agreements are to be treated for the purposes of subsection (1A) as if he had been licensed as required.]

(3) Unless the [OFT] determines to make an order under subsection (2) in accordance with the application, [it] shall, before determining the application, by notice—

(a) inform the applicant, giving [its] reasons, that, as the case may be, [it] is minded to refuse the application, or to grant it in terms different from those applied for, describing them, and

(b) invite the applicant to submit to the [OFT] representations in support of his application in accordance with section 34.

(4) In determining whether or not to make an order under subsection (2) in respect of any period the [OFT] shall consider, in addition to any other relevant factors—

(a) how far, if at all, debtors or hirers under [the regulated agreements in question] were prejudiced by the trader's conduct,

(b) whether or not the [OFT] would have been likely to grant a licence covering [the making of those agreements during] that period on an application by the trader, and

(c) the degree of culpability for the failure to [be licensed as required].

(5) If the [OFT] thinks fit, [it] may in an order under subsection (2)—

(a) limit the order to specified agreements, or agreements of a specified description or made at a specified time;

(b) make the order conditional on the doing of specified acts by the applicant.

[(6) This section [(apart from subsection (1))] does not apply to a regulated agreement, … made by a consumer credit EEA firm unless at the time it was made that firm was precluded from entering into it as a result of

(a) a consumer credit prohibition imposed under section 203 of the Financial Services and Markets Act 2000; or

(b) a restriction imposed on the firm under section 204 of that Act.]

[(7) Subsection (1) does not apply to the enforcement of a regulated agreement by a consumer credit EEA firm unless that firm is precluded from enforcing it as a result of a prohibition or restriction mentioned in subsection (6)(a) or (b).

(8) This section (apart from subsection (1)) does not apply to a regulated agreement made by a person if by virtue of section 21(2) or (3) he was not required to be licensed to make the agreement.

(9) Subsection (1) does not apply to the enforcement of a regulated agreement by a person if by virtue of section 21(2) or (3) he is not required to be licensed to enforce the agreement.]

[764]

NOTES

Sub-ss (1), (1A), (2): substituted, for original sub-ss (1), (2), by the Consumer Credit Act 2006, s 26(1).

Sub-ss (3)–(5): references to "OFT", "it" and "its" in square brackets in each place they appear substituted by the Enterprise Act 2002, s 278(1), Sch 25, para 6(1), (20), subject to transitional provisions and savings in the Enterprise Act 2002, s 276, Sch 24, paras 2–6.

Sub-s (4): words in square brackets in paras (a), (c) substituted, and words in second pair of square brackets in para (b) inserted, by the Consumer Credit Act 2006, s 26(2).

Sub-s (6): inserted by SI 2001/3649, art 170; words in square brackets inserted and words omitted repealed by the Consumer Credit Act 2006, ss 26(3), 70, Sch 4.

Sub-ss (7)–(9): inserted by the Consumer Credit Act 2006, s 26(4).

41–54 ((*Pt IV*) *outside the scope of this work.*)

PART V
ENTRY INTO CREDIT OR HIRE AGREEMENTS

Preliminary matters

55–57 (*Outside the scope of this work.*)

58 Opportunity for withdrawal from prospective land mortgage

(1) Before sending to the debtor or hirer, for his signature, an unexecuted agreement in a case where the prospective regulated agreement is to be secured on land (the "mortgaged land"), the creditor or owner shall give the debtor or hirer a copy of the unexecuted agreement which contains a notice in the prescribed form indicating the right of the debtor or hirer to withdraw from the prospective agreement, and how and when the right is exercisable, together with a copy of any other document referred to in the unexecuted agreement.

(2) Subsection (1) does not apply to—

(a) a restricted-use credit agreement to finance the purchase of the mortgaged land, or

(b) an agreement for a bridging loan in connection with the purchase of the mortgaged land or other land.

[765]

NOTES

Regulations: the Consumer Credit (Cancellation Notices and Copies of Documents) Regulations 1983, SI 1983/1557.

59 (*Outside the scope of this work.*)

Making the agreement

60–64 (*Outside the scope of this work.*)

65 Consequences of improper execution

(1) An improperly-executed regulated agreement is enforceable against the debtor or hirer on an order of the court only.

(2) A retaking of goods or land to which a regulated agreement relates is an enforcement of the agreement.

[766]

66–86 (*Ss 66–74, ss 75–86* (*Pt VI*) *outside the scope of this work.*)

PART VII
DEFAULT AND TERMINATION

86A–86F (*Outside the scope of this work.*)

Default notices

87 Need for default notice

(1) Service of a notice on the debtor or hirer in accordance with section 88 (a "default notice") is necessary before the creditor or owner can become entitled, by reason of any breach by the debtor or hirer of a regulated agreement,—

(a) to terminate the agreement, or
(b) to demand earlier payment of any sum, or
(c) to recover possession of any goods or land, or
(d) to treat any right conferred on the debtor or hirer by the agreement as terminated, restricted or deferred, or
(e) to enforce any security.

(2) Subsection (1) does not prevent the creditor from treating the right to draw upon any credit as restricted or deferred, and taking such steps as may be necessary to make the restriction or deferment effective.

(3) The doing of an act by which a floating charge becomes fixed is not enforcement of a security.

(4) Regulations may provide that subsection (1) is not to apply to agreements described by the regulations.

[767]

88 Contents and effect of default notice

(1) The default notice must be in the prescribed form and specify—
(a) the nature of the alleged breach;
(b) if the breach is capable of remedy, what action is required to remedy it and the date before which that action is to be taken;
(c) if the breach is not capable of remedy, the sum (if any) required to be paid as compensation for the breach, and the date before which it is to be paid.

(2) A date specified under subsection (1) must not be less than [14] days after the date of service of the default notice, and the creditor or owner shall not take action such as is mentioned in section 87(1) before the date so specified or (if no requirement is made under subsection (1)) before those [14] days have elapsed.

(3) The default notice must not treat as a breach failure to comply with a provision of the agreement which becomes operative only on breach of some other provision, but if the breach of that other provision is not duly remedied or compensation demanded under subsection (1) is not duly paid, or (where no requirement is made under subsection (1)) if the [14] days mentioned in subsection (2) have elapsed, the creditor or owner may treat the failure as a breach and section 87(1) shall not apply to it.

(4) The default notice must contain information in the prescribed terms about the consequences of failure to comply with it [and any other prescribed matters relating to the agreement].

[(4A) The default notice must also include a copy of the current default information sheet under section 86A.]

(5) A default notice making a requirement under subsection (1) may include a provision for the taking of action such as is mentioned in section 87(1) at any time after the restriction imposed by subsection (2) will cease, together with a statement that the provision will be ineffective if the breach is duly remedied or the compensation duly paid.

[768]

NOTES

Sub-s (2), (3): reference in square brackets in each place it occurs substituted by the Consumer Credit Act 2006, s 14(1), subject to transitional provisions and savings in s 69(1), of, Sch 3, paras 1, 10, to that Act.

Sub-s (4): words in square brackets inserted by the Consumer Credit Act 2006, s 14(2), subject to transitional provisions and savings in s 69(1), of, Sch 3, paras 1, 10, to that Act.

Sub-s (4A): inserted by the Consumer Credit Act 2006, s 14(3), subject to transitional provisions and savings in s 69(1), of, Sch 3, paras 1, 10, to that Act.

Regulations: Consumer Credit (Enforcement, Default and Termination Notices) Regulations 1983, SI 1983/1561; Consumer Credit (Information Requirements and Duration of Licences and Charges) Regulations 2007, SI 2007/1167.

89 Compliance with default notice

If before the date specified for that purpose in the default notice the debtor or hirer takes the action specified under section 88(1)(b) or (c) the breach shall be treated as not having occurred.

[768A]

Further restriction of remedies for default

90, 91 (*Outside the scope of this work.*)

92 Recovery of possession of goods or land

(1) Except under an order of the court, the creditor or owner shall not be entitled to enter any premises to take possession of goods subject to a regulated hire-purchase agreement, regulated conditional sale agreement or regulated consumer hire agreement.

(2) At any time when the debtor is in breach of a regulated conditional sale agreement relating to land, the creditor is entitled to recover possession of the land from the debtor, or any person claiming under him, on an order of the court only.

(3) An entry in contravention of subsection (1) or (2) is actionable as a breach of statutory duty.

[769]

93–104 (*Ss 93, 94–103 outside the scope of this work; ss 93A, 104 apply to Scotland only.*)

PART VIII SECURITY

105–125 (*Outside the scope of this work.*)

Land mortgages

126 Enforcement of land mortgages

A land mortgage securing a regulated agreement is enforceable (so far as provided in relation to the agreement) on an order of the court only.

[770]

PART IX JUDICIAL CONTROL

Enforcement of certain regulated agreements and securities

127 Enforcement orders in cases of infringement

(1) In the case of an application for an enforcement order under—

(a) section 65(1) (improperly executed agreements), or

(b) section 105(7)(a) or (b) (improperly executed security instruments), or

(c) section 111(2) (failure to serve copy of notice on surety), or

(d) section 124(1) or (2) (taking of negotiable instrument in contravention of section 123),

the court shall dismiss the application if, but … only if, it considers it just to do so having regard to—

(i) prejudice caused to any person by the contravention in question, and the degree of culpability for it; and

(ii) the powers conferred on the court by subsection (2) and sections 135 and 136.

(2) If it appears to the court just to do so, it may in an enforcement order reduce or discharge any sum payable by the debtor or hirer, or any surety, so as to compensate him for prejudice suffered as a result of the contravention in question.

(3)–(5) …

[771]

NOTES

Sub-s (1): words omitted repealed by the Consumer Credit Act 2006, s 70, Sch 4, subject to transitional provision and savings in s 69(1) of, Sch 3, paras 1, 11(a) to, that Act.

Sub-ss (3)–(5): repealed by the Consumer Credit Act 2006, ss 15, 70, Sch 4, subject to transitional provision and savings in s 69(1) of, Sch 3, paras 1, 11(b) to, that Act.

Regulations: the Consumer Credit (Agreements) Regulations 1983, SI 1983/1553.

128–136 (*Outside the scope of this work.*)

Extortionate credit bargains

137 Extortionate credit bargains

(1) If the court finds a credit bargain extortionate it may reopen the credit agreement so as to do justice between the parties.

(2) In this section and sections 138 to 140—

(a) "credit agreement" means any agreement [(other than an agreement which is an exempt agreement as a result of section 16(6C))] between an individual (the "debtor") and any other person (the "creditor") by which the creditor provides the debtor with credit of any amount, and

(b) "credit bargain"—

(i) where no transaction other than the credit agreement is to be taken into account in computing the total charge for credit, means the credit agreement, or

(ii) where one or more other transactions are to be so taken into account, means the credit agreement and those other transactions, taken together.

[771A]

NOTES

Sub-s (2): in para (a) words in square brackets inserted by SI 2001/544, art 90(1), (6).

Repealed by the Consumer Credit Act 2006, ss 22(3), 70, Sch 4, as from 6 April 2007, subject to transitional provision and savings: see the Consumer Credit Act 2006, s 69(1), Sch 3, paras 1, 15, which read as follows:

"1.—(1) Expressions used in the 1974 Act have the same meaning in this Schedule (apart from paragraphs 14 to 16 and 26) as they have in that Act.

(2) For the purposes of this Schedule an agreement becomes a completed agreement once—
(a) there is no sum payable under the agreement; and
(b) there is no sum which will or may become so payable.

15.—(1) The repeal by this Act of sections 137 to 140 of the 1974 Act shall not affect the court's power to reopen an existing agreement under those sections as set out in this paragraph.

(2) The court's power to reopen an existing agreement which—
(a) became a completed agreement before the commencement of section 22(3) of this Act, or
(b) becomes a completed agreement during the transitional period,

is not affected at all.

(3) The court may also reopen an existing agreement—
(a) on an application of the kind mentioned in paragraph (a) of subsection (1) of section 139 made at a time before the end of the transitional period; or
(b) at the instance of the debtor or a surety in any proceedings of the kind mentioned in paragraph (b) or (c) of that subsection which were commenced at such a time.

(4) Nothing in section 16A or 16B of the 1974 Act shall affect the application of sections 137 to 140 (whether by virtue of this paragraph or otherwise).

(5) The repeal or revocation by this Act of the following provisions has no effect in relation to existing agreements so far as they may be reopened as set out in this paragraph—
(a) section 16(7) of the 1974 Act;
(b) in section 143(b) of that Act, the words ", 139(1)(a)";
(c) section 171(7) of that Act;
(d) in subsection (1) of section 181 of that Act, the words "139(5) and (7),";
(e) in subsection (2) of that section, the words "or 139(5) or (7)";
(f) in section 61(6) of the Bankruptcy (Scotland) Act 1985 (c 66), the words from the beginning to "but";
(g) in section 343(6) of the Insolvency Act 1986 (c 45), the words from the beginning to "But";
(h) Article 316(6) of the Insolvency (Northern Ireland) Order 1989 (SI 1989/2405 (NI 19)).

(6) Expressions used in sections 137 to 140 of the 1974 Act have the same meaning in this paragraph as they have in those sections.

(7) In this paragraph—
"existing agreement" means a credit agreement made before the commencement of section 22(3) of this Act;
"the transitional period" means the period of one year beginning with the day of the commencement of section 22(3).

(8) An order under section 69 of this Act may extend, or further extend, the transitional period.".

---

138 When bargains are extortionate

(1) A credit bargain is extortionate if it—
(a) requires the debtor or a relative of his to make payments (whether unconditionally, or on certain contingencies) which are grossly exorbitant, or
(b) otherwise grossly contravenes ordinary principles of fair dealing.

(2) In determining whether a credit bargain is extortionate, regard shall be had to such evidence as is adduced concerning—
(a) interest rates prevailing at the time it was made,
(b) the factors mentioned in subsections (3) to (5), and
(c) any other relevant considerations.

(3) Factors applicable under subsection (2) in relation to the debtor include—
(a) his age, experience, business capacity and state of health; and
(b) the degree to which, at the time of making the credit bargain, he was under financial pressure, and the nature of that pressure.

(4) Factors applicable under subsection (2) in relation to the creditor include—
(a) the degree of risk accepted by him, having regard to the value of any security provided;
(b) his relationship to the debtor; and
(c) whether or not a colourable cash price was quoted for any goods or services included in the credit bargain.

(5) Factors applicable under subsection (2) in relation to a linked transaction include the question how far the transaction was reasonably required for the protection of debtor or creditor, or was in the interest of the debtor.

[771B]

NOTES

Repealed by the Consumer Credit Act 2006, ss 22(3), 70, Sch 4, as from 6 April 2007, subject to transitional provision and savings: see para **[771A]**.

139 Reopening of extortionate agreements

(1) A credit agreement may, if the court thinks just, be reopened on the ground that the credit bargain is extortionate—

(a) on an application for the purpose made by the debtor or any surety to the High Court, county court or sheriff court; or

(b) at the instance of the debtor or a surety in any proceedings to which the debtor and creditor are parties, being proceedings to enforce the agreement, any security relating to it, or any linked transaction; or

(c) at the instance of the debtor or a surety in other proceedings in any court where the amount paid or payable under the credit agreement is relevant.

(2) In reopening the agreement, the court may, for the purpose of relieving the debtor or a surety from payment of any sum in excess of that fairly due and reasonable, by order—

(a) direct accounts to be taken, or (in Scotland) an accounting to be made, between any persons,

(b) set aside the whole or part of any obligation imposed on the debtor or surety by the credit bargain or any related agreement,

(c) require the creditor to repay the whole or part of any sum paid under the credit bargain or any related agreement by the debtor or a surety, whether paid to the creditor or any other person,

(d) direct the return to the surety of any property provided for the purposes of the security, or

(e) alter the terms of the credit agreement or any security instrument.

(3) An order may be made under subsection (2) notwithstanding that its effect is to place a burden on the creditor in respect of an advantage unfairly enjoyed by another person who is a party to a linked transaction.

(4) An order under subsection (2) shall not alter the effect of any judgment.

(5) In England and Wales, an application under subsection (1)(a) shall be brought only in the county court in the case of—

(a) a regulated agreement, or

(b) an agreement (not being a regulated agreement) under which the creditor provides the debtor with fixed-sum credit … or running-account credit …

[(5A) …]

(6) In Scotland an application under subsection (1)(a) may be brought in the sheriff court for the district in which the debtor or surety resides or carries on business.

(7) In Northern Ireland an application under subsection (1)(a) may be brought in the county court in the case of—

(a) a regulated agreement, or

(b) an agreement (not being a regulated agreement) under which the creditor provides the debtor with fixed-sum credit not exceeding [£105,000] or running-account credit on which the credit limit does not exceed [£105,000].

[771C]

NOTES

Repealed by the Consumer Credit Act 2006, ss 22(3), 70, Sch 4, as from 6 April 2007, subject to transitional provision and savings: see para **[771A]**.

Sub-s (5): in para (b) words omitted repealed by SI 1991/724, art 2(1), (8), Schedule, Part I.

Sub-s (5A): inserted by the Administration of Justice Act 1982, s 37, Sch 3, Part II, para 4; repealed by SI 1991/724, art 2(8), Schedule, Part I.

Sub-s (7): sums in square brackets substituted by virtue of the County Courts (Financial Limits) Order (Northern Ireland) 1993, SR 1993/282, art 2, Schedule.

140 Interpretation of sections 137 to 139

Where the credit agreement is not a regulated agreement, expressions used in sections 137 to 139 which, apart from this section, apply only to regulated agreements, shall be construed as nearly as may be as if the credit agreement were a regulated agreement.

[771D]

NOTES

Repealed by the Consumer Credit Act 2006, ss 22(3), 70, Sch 4, as from 6 April 2007, subject to transitional provision and savings: see para **[771A]**.

[Unfair relationships

140A Unfair relationships between creditors and debtors

(1) The court may make an order under section 140B in connection with a credit agreement if it determines that the relationship between the creditor and the debtor arising out of the agreement (or the agreement taken with any related agreement) is unfair to the debtor because of one or more of the following—

(a) any of the terms of the agreement or of any related agreement;

(b) the way in which the creditor has exercised or enforced any of his rights under the agreement or any related agreement;

(c) any other thing done (or not done) by, or on behalf of, the creditor (either before or after the making of the agreement or any related agreement).

(2) In deciding whether to make a determination under this section the court shall have regard to all matters it thinks relevant (including matters relating to the creditor and matters relating to the debtor).

(3) For the purposes of this section the court shall (except to the extent that it is not appropriate to do so) treat anything done (or not done) by, or on behalf of, or in relation to, an associate or a former associate of the creditor as if done (or not done) by, or on behalf of, or in relation to, the creditor.

(4) A determination may be made under this section in relation to a relationship notwithstanding that the relationship may have ended.

(5) An order under section 140B shall not be made in connection with a credit agreement which is an exempt agreement by virtue of section 16(6C).]

[772]

NOTES

Commencement: 6 April 2007.

Inserted, together with preceding cross-heading, by the Consumer Credit Act 2006, s 19, subject to transitional provisions in s 69(1) of, Sch 3, paras 1, 14 to, that Act.

[140B Powers of court in relation to unfair relationships

(1) An order under this section in connection with a credit agreement may do one or more of the following—

(a) require the creditor, or any associate or former associate of his, to repay (in whole or in part) any sum paid by the debtor or by a surety by virtue of the agreement or any related agreement (whether paid to the creditor, the associate or the former associate or to any other person);

(b) require the creditor, or any associate or former associate of his, to do or not to do (or to cease doing) anything specified in the order in connection with the agreement or any related agreement;

(c) reduce or discharge any sum payable by the debtor or by a surety by virtue of the agreement or any related agreement;

(d) direct the return to a surety of any property provided by him for the purposes of a security;

(e) otherwise set aside (in whole or in part) any duty imposed on the debtor or on a surety by virtue of the agreement or any related agreement;

(f) alter the terms of the agreement or of any related agreement;

(g) direct accounts to be taken, or (in Scotland) an accounting to be made, between any persons.

(2) An order under this section may be made in connection with a credit agreement only—

(a) on an application made by the debtor or by a surety;

(b) at the instance of the debtor or a surety in any proceedings in any court to which the debtor and the creditor are parties, being proceedings to enforce the agreement or any related agreement; or

(c) at the instance of the debtor or a surety in any other proceedings in any court where the amount paid or payable under the agreement or any related agreement is relevant.

(3) An order under this section may be made notwithstanding that its effect is to place on the creditor, or any associate or former associate of his, a burden in respect of an advantage enjoyed by another person.

(4) An application under subsection (2)(a) may only be made—

(a) in England and Wales, to the county court;

(b) in Scotland, to the sheriff court;

(c) in Northern Ireland, to the High Court (subject to subsection (6)).

(5) In Scotland such an application may be made in the sheriff court for the district in which the debtor or surety resides or carries on business.

(6) In Northern Ireland such an application may be made to the county court if the credit agreement is an agreement under which the creditor provides the debtor with—

(a) fixed-sum credit not exceeding £15,000; or

(b) running-account credit on which the credit limit does not exceed £15,000.

(7) Without prejudice to any provision which may be made by rules of court made in relation to county courts in Northern Ireland, such rules may provide that an application made by virtue of subsection (6) may be made in the county court for the division in which the debtor or surety resides or carries on business.

(8) A party to any proceedings mentioned in subsection (2) shall be entitled, in accordance with rules of court, to have any person who might be the subject of an order under this section made a party to the proceedings.

(9) If, in any such proceedings, the debtor or a surety alleges that the relationship between the creditor and the debtor is unfair to the debtor, it is for the creditor to prove to the contrary.]

[773]

NOTES

Commencement: 6 April 2007.

Inserted by the Consumer Credit Act 2006, s 20, subject to transitional provisions in s 69(1) of, Sch 3, paras 1, 14, 16 to, that Act.

[140C Interpretation of ss 140A and 140B

(1) In this section and in sections 140A and 140B "credit agreement" means any agreement between an individual (the "debtor") and any other person (the "creditor") by which the creditor provides the debtor with credit of any amount.

(2) References in this section and in sections 140A and 140B to the creditor or to the debtor under a credit agreement include—

(a) references to the person to whom his rights and duties under the agreement have passed by assignment or operation of law;

(b) where two or more persons are the creditor or the debtor, references to any one or more of those persons.

(3) The definition of "court" in section 189(1) does not apply for the purposes of sections 140A and 140B.

(4) References in sections 140A and 140B to an agreement related to a credit agreement (the "main agreement") are references to—

(a) a credit agreement consolidated by the main agreement;

(b) a linked transaction in relation to the main agreement or to a credit agreement within paragraph (a);

(c) a security provided in relation to the main agreement, to a credit agreement within paragraph (a) or to a linked transaction within paragraph (b).

(5) In the case of a credit agreement which is not a regulated consumer credit agreement, for the purposes of subsection (4) a transaction shall be treated as being a linked transaction in relation to that agreement if it would have been such a transaction had that agreement been a regulated consumer credit agreement.

(6) For the purposes of this section and section 140B the definitions of "security" and "surety" in section 189(1) apply (with any appropriate changes) in relation to—

(a) a credit agreement which is not a consumer credit agreement as if it were a consumer credit agreement; and

(b) a transaction which is a linked transaction by virtue of subsection (5).

(7) For the purposes of this section a credit agreement (the "earlier agreement") is consolidated by another credit agreement (the "later agreement") if—

(a) the later agreement is entered into by the debtor (in whole or in part) for purposes connected with debts owed by virtue of the earlier agreement; and

(b) at any time prior to the later agreement being entered into the parties to the earlier agreement included—

(i) the debtor under the later agreement; and

(ii) the creditor under the later agreement or an associate or a former associate of his.

(8) Further, if the later agreement is itself consolidated by another credit agreement (whether by virtue of this subsection or subsection (7)), then the earlier agreement is consolidated by that other agreement as well.]

[774]

NOTES

Commencement: 6 April 2007.

Inserted by the Consumer Credit Act 2006, s 21, subject to transitional provisions in s 69(1) of, Sch 3, paras 1, 16, 17 to, that Act.

[140D Advice and information

The advice and information published by the OFT under section 229 of the Enterprise Act 2002 shall indicate how the OFT expects sections 140A to 140C of this Act to interact with Part 8 of that Act.]

[775]

NOTES

Commencement: 6 April 2007.
Inserted by the Consumer Credit Act 2006, s 22(1).

141–173 (*Ss 141–144, ss 145–173* (*Pts X, XI*) *outside the scope of this work.*)

PART XII
SUPPLEMENTAL

174–183 (*Outside the scope of this work.*)

Interpretation

184–188 (*Outside the scope of this work.*)

189 Definitions

(1) In this Act, unless the context otherwise requires—

"advertisement" includes every form of advertising, whether in a publication, by television or radio, by display of notices, signs, labels, showcards or goods, by distribution of samples, circulars, catalogues, price lists or other material, by exhibition of pictures, models or films, or in any other way, and references to the publishing of advertisements shall be construed accordingly;

"advertiser" in relation to an advertisement, means any person indicated by the advertisement as willing to enter into transactions to which the advertisement relates;

"ancillary credit business" has the meaning given by section 145(1);

"antecedent negotiations" has the meaning given by section 56;

"appeal period" means the period beginning on the first day on which an appeal to the [*Tribunal*] [First-tier Tribunal] may be brought and ending on the last day on which it may be brought or, if it is brought, ending on its final determination, or abandonment;

["appropriate method" means—

(a) post, or

(b) transmission in the form of an electronic communication in accordance with section 176A(1);]

"assignment", in relation to Scotland, means assignation;

"associate" shall be construed in accordance with section 184;

[…]

"bill of sale" has the meaning given by section 4 of the Bills of Sale Act 1878 or, for Northern Ireland, by section 4 of the Bills of Sale (Ireland) Act 1879;

["building society" means a building society within the meaning of the Building Societies Act 1986;]

"business" includes profession or trade, and references to a business apply subject to subsection (2);

"cancellable agreement" means a regulated agreement which, by virtue of section 67, may be cancelled by the debtor or hirer;

"canvass" shall be construed in accordance with sections 48 and 153;

"cash" includes money in any form;

"charity" means as respects England and Wales a charity registered under [the Charities Act 1993] or an exempt charity (within the meaning of that Act), [as respects] Northern Ireland an institution or other organisation established for charitable purposes only ("organisation" including any persons administering a trust and "charitable" being construed in the same way as if it were contained in the Income Tax Acts) [and as respects Scotland a body entered in the Scottish Charity Register];

"conditional sale agreement" means an agreement for the sale of goods or land under which the purchase price or part of it is payable by instalments, and the property in the goods or land is to remain in the seller (notwithstanding that the buyer is to be in possession of the goods or land) until such conditions as to the payment of instalments or otherwise as may be specified in the agreement are fulfilled;

"consumer credit agreement" has the meaning given by section 8, and includes a consumer credit agreement which is cancelled under section 69(1), or becomes subject to section 69(2), so far as the agreement remains in force;

["consumer credit business" means any business being carried on by a person so far as it comprises or relates to—

(a) the provision of credit by him, or

(b) otherwise his being a creditor,
under regulated consumer credit agreements;]

"consumer hire agreement" has the meaning given by section 15;

["consumer hire business" means any business being carried on by a person so far as it comprises or relates to—
(a) the bailment or (in Scotland) the hiring of goods by him, or
(b) otherwise his being an owner,
under regulated consumer hire agreements;]

"controller", in relation to a body corporate, means a person—
(a) in accordance with whose directions or instructions the directors of the body corporate or of another body corporate which is its controller (or any of them) are accustomed to act, or
(b) who, either alone or with any associate or associates, is entitled to exercise or control the exercise of, one third or more of the voting power at any general meeting of the body corporate or of another body corporate which is its controller;

"copy" shall be construed in accordance with section 180;

. . .

"court" means in relation to England and Wales the county court, in relation to Scotland the sheriff court and in relation to Northern Ireland the High Court or the county court;

"credit" shall be construed in accordance with section 9;

"credit-broker" means a person carrying on a business of credit brokerage;

"credit brokerage" has the meaning given by section 145(2);

["credit information services" has the meaning given by section 145(7B);]

"credit limit" has the meaning given by section 10(2);

"creditor" means the person providing credit under a consumer credit agreement or the person to whom his rights and duties under the agreement have passed by assignment or operation of law, and in relation to a prospective consumer credit agreement, includes the prospective creditor;

"credit reference agency" has the meaning given by section 145(8);

"credit-sale agreement" means an agreement for the sale of goods, under which the purchase price or part of it is payable by instalments, but which is not a conditional sale agreement;

"credit-token" has the meaning given by section 14(1);

"credit-token agreement" means a regulated agreement for the provision of credit in connection with the use of a credit-token;

"debt-adjusting" has the meaning given by section 145(5);

["debt administration" has the meaning given by section 145(7A);]

"debt-collecting" has the meaning given by section 145(7);

"debt-counselling" has the meaning given by section 145(6);

"debtor" means the individual receiving credit under a consumer credit agreement or the person to whom his rights and duties under the agreement have passed by assignment or operation of law, and in relation to a prospective consumer credit agreement includes the prospective debtor;

"debtor-creditor agreement" has the meaning given by section 13;

"debtor-creditor-supplier agreement" has the meaning given by section 12;

"default notice" has the meaning given by section 87(1);

["default sum" has the meaning given by section 187A;]

"deposit" means [(except in section 16(10) and 25(1B))] any sum payable by a debtor or hirer by way of deposit or down-payment, or credited or to be credited to him on account of any deposit or down-payment, whether the sum is to be or has been paid to the creditor or owner or any other person, or is to be or has been discharged by a payment of money or a transfer or delivery of goods or by any other means;

. . .

["documents" includes information recorded in any form;]

"electric line" has the meaning given by [the Electricity Act 1989] or, for Northern Ireland, [the Electricity (Northern Ireland) Order 1992];

["electronic communication" means an electronic communication within the meaning of the Electronic Communications Act 2000 (c 7);]

"embodies" and related words shall be construed in accordance with subsection (4);

"enforcement authority" has the meaning given by section 161(1);

"enforcement order" means an order under section 65(1), 105(7)(a) or (b), 111(2) or 124(1) or (2);

"executed agreement" means a document, signed by or on behalf of the parties, embodying the terms of a regulated agreement, or such of them as have been reduced to writing;

"exempt agreement" means an agreement specified in or under section 16[, 16A][, 16B or 16C];

"finance" means to finance wholly or partly and "financed" and "refinanced" shall be construed accordingly;
"file" and "copy of the file" have the meanings given by section 158(5);
"fixed-sum credit" has the meaning given by section 10(1)(b);
"friendly society" means a society registered [or treated as registered under the Friendly Societies Act 1974 or the Friendly Societies Act 1992] … ;
"future arrangements" shall be construed in accordance with section 187;
"general notice" means a notice published by the [OFT] at a time and in a manner appearing to [it] suitable for securing that the notice is seen within a reasonable time by persons likely to be affected by it;
"give", means, deliver or send [by an appropriate method] to;
"goods" has the meaning given by [section 61(1) of the Sale of Goods Act 1979];
"group licence" has the meaning given by section 22(1)(b);
"High Court" means Her Majesty's High Court of Justice, or the Court of Session in Scotland or the High Court of Justice in Northern Ireland;
"hire-purchase agreement" means an agreement, other than a conditional sale agreement, under which—

(a) goods are bailed or (in Scotland) hired in return for periodical payments by the person to whom they are bailed or hired, and
(b) the property in the goods will pass to that person if the terms of the agreement are complied with and one or more of the following occurs—
  (i) the exercise of an option to purchase by that person,
  (ii) the doing of any other specified act by any party to the agreement,
  (iii) the happening of any other specified event;

"hirer" means the individual to whom goods are bailed or (in Scotland) hired under a consumer hire agreement, or the person to whom his rights and duties under the agreement have passed by assignment or operation of law, and in relation to a prospective consumer hire agreement includes the prospective hirer;
["individual" includes—

(a) a partnership consisting of two or three persons not all of whom are bodies corporate; and
(b) an unincorporated body of persons which does not consist entirely of bodies corporate and is not a partnership;]

"installation" means—

(a) the installing of any electric line or any gas or water pipe,
(b) the fixing of goods to the premises where they are to be used, and the alteration of premises to enable goods to be used on them,
(c) where it is reasonably necessary that goods should be constructed or erected on the premises where they are to be used, any work carried out for the purpose of constructing or erecting them on those premises;

…
"judgment" includes an order or decree made by any court;
"land", includes an interest in land, and in relation to Scotland includes heritable subjects of whatever description;
"land improvement company" means an improvement company as defined by section 7 of the Improvement of Land Act 1899;
"land mortgage" includes any security charged on land;
"licence" means a licence under Part III …;
"licensed", in relation to any act, means authorised by a licence to do the act or cause or permit another person to do it;
"licensee", in the case of a group licence, includes any person covered by the licence;
"linked transaction" has the meaning given by section 19(1);
"local authority", in relation to England … , means … a county council, a London borough council, a district council, the Common Council of the City of London, or the Council of Isles of Scilly, [in relation to Wales means a county council or a county borough council,] and in relation to Scotland, means a [council constituted under section 2 of the Local Government etc (Scotland) Act 1994], and, in relation to Northern Ireland, means a district council;
…
"modifying agreement" has the meaning given by section 82(2);
"mortgage", in relation to Scotland, includes any heritable security;
"multiple agreement" has the meaning given by section 18(1);
"negotiator" has the meaning given by section 56(1);
"non-commercial agreement" means a consumer credit agreement or a consumer hire agreement not made by the creditor or owner in the course of a business carried on by him;
"notice" means notice in writing;
"notice of cancellation" has the meaning given by section 69(1);

["OFT" means the Office of Fair Trading;]
"owner" means a person who bails or (in Scotland) hires out goods under a consumer hire agreement or the person to whom his rights and duties under the agreement have passed by assignment or operation of law, and in relation to a prospective consumer hire agreement, includes the prospective bailor or persons from whom the goods are to be hired;
"pawn" means any article subject to a pledge;
"pawn-receipt" has the meaning given by section 114;
"pawnee" and "pawnor" include any person to whom the rights and duties of the original pawnee or the original pawnor, as the case may be, have passed by assignment or operation of law;
"payment" includes tender;
...
"pledge" means the pawnee's rights over an article taken in pawn;
"prescribed" means prescribed by regulations made by the Secretary of State;
"pre-existing arrangements" shall be construed in accordance with section 187;
"principal agreement" has the meaning given by section 19(1);
"protected goods" has the meaning given by section 90(7);
"quotation" has the meaning given by section 52(1)(a);
"redemption period" has the meaning given by section 116(3);
"register" means the register kept by the [OFT] under section 35;
"regulated agreement" means a consumer credit agreement, or consumer hire agreement, other than an exempt agreement, and "regulated" and "unregulated" shall be construed accordingly;
"regulations" means regulations made by the Secretary of State;
"relative", except in section 184, means a person who is an associate by virtue of section 184(1);
"representation" includes any condition or warranty, and any other statement or undertaking, whether oral or in writing;
"restricted-use credit agreement" and "restricted-use credit" have the meanings given by section 11(1);
"rules of court", in relation to Northern Ireland means, in relation to the High Court, rules made under section 7 of the Northern Ireland Act 1962, and, in relation to any other court, rules made by the authority having for the time being power to make rules regulating the practice and procedure in that court;
"running-account credit" shall be construed in accordance with section 10;
"security", in relation to an actual or prospective consumer credit agreement or consumer hire agreement, or any linked transaction, means a mortgage, charge, pledge, bond, debenture, indemnity, guarantee, bill, note or other right provided by the debtor or hirer, or at his request (express or implied), to secure the carrying out of the obligations of the debtor or hirer under the agreement;
"security instrument" has the meaning given by section 105(2);
"serve on" means deliver or send [by an appropriate method] to;
"signed" shall be construed in accordance with subsection (3);
"small agreement" has the meaning given by section 17(1), and "small" in relation to an agreement within any category shall be construed accordingly;
"specified fee" shall be construed in accordance with section 2(4) and (5);
"standard licence" has the meaning given by section 22(1)(a);
"supplier" has the meaning given by section 11(1)(b) or 12(c) or 13(c) or, in relation to an agreement falling within section 11(1)(a), means the creditor, and includes a person to whom the rights and duties of a supplier (as so defined) have passed by assignment or operation of law, or (in relation to a prospective agreement) the prospective supplier;
"surety" means the person by whom any security is provided, or the person to whom his rights and duties in relation to the security have passed by assignment or operation of law;
"technical grounds" shall be construed in accordance with subsection (5);
"time order" has the meaning given by section 129(1);
"total charge for credit" means a sum calculated in accordance with regulations under section 20(1);
"total price" means the total sum payable by the debtor under a hire-purchase agreement or a conditional sale agreement, including any sum payable on the exercise of an option to purchase, but excluding any sum payable as a penalty or as compensation or damages for a breach of the agreement;
[*"the Tribunal" means the Consumer Credit Appeals Tribunal;*]
"unexecuted agreement" means a document embodying the terms of a prospective regulated agreement, or such of them as it is intended to reduce to writing;
"unlicensed" means without a licence but applies only in relation to acts for which a licence is required;

"unrestricted-use credit agreement" and "unrestricted-use credit" have the meanings given by section 11(2);

"working day" means any day other than—

(a) Saturday or Sunday,

(b) Christmas Day or Good Friday,

(c) a bank holiday within the meaning given by section 1 of the Banking and Financial Dealings Act 1971.

[(1A) In sections 36E(3), 70(4), 73(4) and 75(2) *and paragraphs 14 and 15 of Schedule A1* "costs", in relation to proceedings in Scotland, means expenses.]

(2) A person is not to be treated as carrying on a particular type of business merely because occasionally he enters into transactions belonging to a business of that type.

(3) Any provision of this Act requiring a document to be signed is complied with by a body corporate if the document is sealed by that body.

This subsection does not apply to Scotland.

(4) A document embodies a provision if the provision is set out either in the document itself or in another document referred to in it.

(5) An application dismissed by the court or the [OFT] shall, if the court or the [OFT] (as the case may be) so certifies, be taken to be dismissed on technical grounds only.

(6) Except in so far as the context otherwise requires, any reference in this Act to an enactment shall be construed as a reference to that enactment as amended by or under any other enactment, including this Act.

(7) In this Act, except where otherwise indicated—

(a) a reference to a numbered Part, section or Schedule is a reference to the Part or section of, or the Schedule to, this Act so numbered, and

(b) a reference in a section to a numbered subsection is a reference to the subsection of that section so numbered, and

(c) a reference in a section, subsection or Schedule to a numbered paragraph is a reference to the paragraph of that section, subsection or Schedule so numbered.

[776]

NOTES

Sub-s (1): in definition "appeal period" first word in square brackets substituted by the Consumer Credit Act 2006, s 58(4)(a) (subject to transitional provisions and savings in s 69(1), Sch 3, paras 1, 28 thereto) and substituted for second words in square brackets by SI 2009/1835, art 4(1), Sch 1, paras 1, 8(a)(i), as from 1 September 2009.

Sub-s (1): definition "appropriate method" inserted by SI 2004/3236, art 2(1), (8).

Sub-s (1): definition "authorised institution" (omitted) inserted by the Banking Act 1987, s 88 and repealed by SI 2001/3649, art 176(a).

Sub-s (1): definition "building society" substituted by the Building Societies Act 1986, s 120, Sch 18, Pt I, para 10(4).

Sub-s (1): in definition "charity" words in first pair of square brackets substituted by the Charities Act 1993, s 98(1), Sch 6, para 30, words in second pair of square brackets substituted and words in third pair of square brackets inserted by SI 2006/242, art 5, Schedule, Pt 1, para 1.

Sub-s (1): definitions "consumer credit business" and "consumer hire business" substituted by the Consumer Credit Act 2006, s 23.

Sub-s (1): definition "costs" (omitted) repealed by the Consumer Credit Act 2006, s 70, Sch 4.

Sub-s (1): definitions "credit information services", "debt administration", "default sum" inserted by the Consumer Credit Act 2006, ss 18(2), 24(6), 25(5).

Sub-s (1): in definition "deposit" words in square brackets inserted by SI 2001/3649, art 176(b).

Sub-s (1): definition "Director" (omitted) repealed by the Enterprise Act 2002, s 278, Sch 25, para 6(1), (38)(a)(i), Sch 26, subject to transitional and savings in s 276 of, Sch 24, paras 2–6 to, that Act.

Sub-s (1): definition "documents" inserted by the Consumer Credit Act 2006, s 51(6).

Sub-s (1): in definition "electric line" words in first pair of square brackets substituted by the Electricity Act 1989, s 112(1), Sch 16, para 17(1), (3); words in second pair of square brackets substituted by the Electricity (Northern Ireland) Order 1992, SI 1992/231, art 95(1), Sch 12, para 15.

Sub-s (1): definition "electronic communication" inserted by SI 2004/3236, art 2(1), (8).

Sub-s (1): in definition "exempt agreement" first words in square brackets inserted by the Consumer Credit Act 2006, s 5(10); second words in square brackets substituted by SI 2008/2826, art 3(4).

Sub-s (1): in definition "friendly society" words in square brackets substituted by SI 2001/3649, art 176(c) and words omitted repealed by the Friendly Societies Act 1992, s 120, Sch 22, Pt I.

Sub-s (1): in definition "general notice" words in square brackets substituted by the Enterprise Act 2002, s 278(1), Sch 25, para 5(1), (38)(a)(ii), subject to transitional provisions and savings in the s 276 of, Sch 24, paras 2–6 to, that Act.

Sub-s (1): in definition "give" words in square brackets substituted by SI 2004/3236, art 2(1), (9).

Sub-s (1): in definition "goods" words in square brackets substituted by the Sale of Goods Act 1979, s 63, Sch 2, para 18.

Sub-s (1): definition "individual" substituted by the Consumer Credit Act 2006, s 1, subject to transitional provisions and savings in s 69(1), Sch 3, paras 1, 17, 29 thereto, and SI 2007/123, arts 4, 5.

Sub-s (1): definition "insurance company" (omitted) repealed by SI 2001/3649, art 176(a).

Sub-s (1): in definition "licence" words omitted repealed by the Consumer Credit Act 2006, s 70, Sch 4.

Sub-s (1): in definition "local authority" first words omitted repealed and words in first pair of square brackets inserted by the Local Government (Wales) Act 1994, s 66(6), (8), Sch 16, para 45, Sch 18, second words omitted repealed by the Local Government Act 1985, s 102, Sch 17, and words in second pair of square brackets substituted by the Local Government etc (Scotland) Act 1994, s 180(1), Sch 13, para 94.

Sub-s (1): definition "minor" (omitted) repealed by the Age of Legal Capacity (Scotland) Act 1991, s 10, Sch 2.

Sub-s (1): definition "OFT" inserted by the Enterprise Act 2002, s 278(1), Sch 25, para 6(1), (38)(a)(iii), subject to transitional provisions in s 276 of, Sch 24, paras 2–6 to, that Act.

Sub-s (1): definition "personal credit agreement" (omitted) repealed by the Consumer Credit Act 2006, s 70, Sch 4.

Sub-s (1): in definition "register" reference in square brackets substituted by the Enterprise Act 2002, s 278(1), Sch 25, para 6(1), (38)(a)(iv), subject to transitional provisions in s 276 of, Sch 24, paras 2–6 to, that Act.

Sub-s (1): in definition "serve on" words in square brackets substituted by SI 2004/3236, art 2(1), (9).

Sub-s (1): definition "the Tribunal" inserted by the Consumer Credit Act 2006, s 58(4)(b); repealed by SI 2009/1835, art 4(1), Sch 1, paras 1, 8(a)(ii), as from 1 September 2009, subject to transitional provisions and savings in art 4(4), Sch 4 thereto.

Sub-s (1A): inserted by the Consumer Credit Act 2006, s 27(3), words in italics repealed by SI 2009/1835, art 4(1), Sch 1, paras 1, 8(b), as from 1 September 2009, subject to transitional provisions and savings in art 4(4), Sch 4 thereto.

Sub-s (5): references in square brackets substituted by the Enterprise Act 2002, s 278(1), Sch 25, para 6(1), (38)(b), subject to transitional provisions in s 276 of, Sch 24, paras 2–6 to, that Act.

189A, 190–192 (*Outside the scope of this work.*)

193 Short title and extent

(1) This Act may be cited as the Consumer Credit Act 1974.

(2) This Act extends to Northern Ireland.

[777]

(*Schs A1, 1–4 outside the scope of this work.*)

INHERITANCE (PROVISION FOR FAMILY AND DEPENDANTS) ACT 1975

(1975 c 63)

An Act to make fresh provisions for empowering the court to make orders for the making out of the estate of a deceased person of provision for the spouse, former spouse, child, child of the family or dependant of that person; and for matters connected therewith

[12 November 1975]

1 Application for financial provision from deceased's estate

(1) Where after the commencement of this Act a person dies domiciled in England and Wales and is survived by any of the following persons—

[(a) the spouse or civil partner of the deceased;

(b) a former spouse or former civil partner of the deceased, but not one who has formed a subsequent marriage or civil partnership;]

[(ba) any person (not being a person included in paragraph (a) or (b) above) to whom subsection (1A) [or (1B)] below applies;]

(c) a child of the deceased;

(d) any person (not being a child of the deceased) who, in the case of any marriage [or civil partnership] to which the deceased was at any time a party, was treated by the deceased as a child of the family in relation to that marriage [or civil partnership];

(e) any person (not being a person included in the foregoing paragraphs of this subsection) who immediately before the death of the deceased was being maintained, either wholly or partly, by the deceased;

that person may apply to the court for an order under section 2 of this Act on the ground that the disposition of the deceased's estate effected by his will or the law relating to intestacy, or the combination of his will and that law, is not such as to make reasonable financial provision for the applicant.

[(1A) This subsection applies to a person if the deceased died on or after 1st January 1996 and, during the whole of the period of two years ending immediately before the date when the deceased died, the person was living—

(a) in the same household as the deceased, and

(b) as the husband or wife of the deceased.]

[(1B) This subsection applies to a person if for the whole of the period of two years ending immediately before the date when the deceased died the person was living—

(a) in the same household as the deceased, and

(b) as the civil partner of the deceased.]

(2) In this Act "reasonable financial provision"—

(a) in the case of an application made by virtue of subsection (1)(a) above by the husband or wife of the deceased (except where *the marriage with the deceased was the subject of a decree of judicial separation and at the date of death the decree was in force*[, at the date of death, a separation order under the Family Law Act 1996 was in force in relation to the marriage] and the separation was continuing), means such financial provision as it would be reasonable in all the circumstances of the case for a husband or wife to receive, whether or not that provision is required for his or her maintenance;

[(aa) in the case of an application made by virtue of subsection (1)(a) above by the civil partner of the deceased (except where, at the date of death, a separation order under Chapter 2 of Part 2 of the Civil Partnership Act 2004 was in force in relation to the civil partnership and the separation was continuing), means such financial provision as it would be reasonable in all the circumstances of the case for a civil partner to receive, whether or not that provision is required for his or her maintenance;]

(b) in the case of any other application made by virtue of subsection (1) above, means such financial provision as it would be reasonable in all the circumstances of the case for the applicant to receive for his maintenance.

(3) For the purposes of subsection (1)(e) above, a person shall be treated as being maintained by the deceased, either wholly or partly, as the case may be, if the deceased, otherwise than for full valuable consideration, was making a substantial contribution in money or money's worth towards the reasonable needs of that person.

[778]

NOTES

Sub-s (1): paras (a), (b) substituted and words in square brackets in paras (ba), (d) inserted, by the Civil Partnership Act 2004, s 71, Sch 4, Pt 2, para 15(1)–(4); para (ba) inserted by the Law Reform (Succession) Act 1995, s 2(2).

Sub-s (1A): inserted by the Law Reform (Succession) Act 1995, s 2(3).

Sub-s (1B): inserted by the Civil Partnership Act 2004, s 71, Sch 4, Pt 2, para 15(1), (5).

Sub-s (2): in para (a), words in italics substituted by subsequent words in square brackets by the Family Law Act 1996, s 66(1), Sch 8, para 27(2) (for savings see s 66(2), Sch 9, para 5 thereof), as from a day to be appointed; para (aa) inserted by the Civil Partnership Act 2004, s 71, Sch 4, Pt 2, para 15(1), (6).

2 Powers of court to make orders

(1) Subject to the provisions of this Act, where an application is made for an order under this section, the court may, if it is satisfied that the disposition of the deceased's estate effected by his will or the law relating to intestacy, or the combination of his will and that law, is not such as to make reasonable financial provision for the applicant, make any one or more of the following orders—

(a) an order for the making to the applicant out of the net estate of the deceased of such periodical payments and for such term as may be specified in the order;

(b) an order for the payment to the applicant out of that estate of a lump sum of such amount as may be so specified;

(c) an order for the transfer to the applicant of such property comprised in that estate as may be so specified;

(d) an order for the settlement for the benefit of the applicant of such property comprised in that estate as may be so specified;

(e) an order for the acquisition out of property comprised in that estate of such property as may be so specified and for the transfer of the property so acquired to the applicant or for the settlement thereof for his benefit;

(f) an order varying any ante-nuptial or post-nuptial settlement (including such a settlement made by will) made on the parties to a marriage to which the deceased was one of the parties, the variation being for the benefit of the surviving party to that marriage, or any child of that marriage, or any person who was treated by the deceased as a child of the family in relation to that marriage;

[(g) an order varying any settlement made—

(i) during the subsistence of a civil partnership formed by the deceased, or

(ii) in anticipation of the formation of a civil partnership by the deceased,

on the civil partners (including such a settlement made by will), the variation being for the benefit of the surviving civil partner, or any child of both the civil partners, or any person who was treated by the deceased as a child of the family in relation to that civil partnership].

(2) An order under subsection (1)(a) above providing for the making out of the net estate of the deceased of periodical payments may provide for—

(a) payments of such amount as may be specified in the order,

(b) payments equal to the whole of the income of the net estate or of such portion thereof as may be so specified,

(c) payments equal to the whole of the income of such part of the net estate as the court may direct to be set aside or appropriated for the making out of the income thereof of payments under this section,

or may provide for the amount of the payments or any of them to be determined in any other way the court thinks fit.

(3) Where an order under subsection (1)(a) above provides for the making of payments of an amount specified in the order, the order may direct that such part of the net estate as may be so specified shall be set aside or appropriated for the making out of the income thereof of those payments; but no larger part of the net estate shall be so set aside or appropriated than is sufficient, at the date of the order, to produce by the income thereof the amount required for the making of those payments.

(4) An order under this section may contain such consequential and supplemental provisions as the court thinks necessary or expedient for the purpose of giving effect to the order or for the purpose of securing that the order operates fairly as between one beneficiary of the estate of the deceased and another and may, in particular, but without prejudice to the generality of this subsection—

(a) order any person who holds any property which forms part of the net estate of the deceased to make such payment or transfer such property as may be specified in the order;

(b) varying the disposition of the deceased's estate effected by the will or the law relating to intestacy, or by both the will and the law relating to intestacy, in such manner as the court thinks fair and reasonable having regard to the provisions of the order and all the circumstances of the case;

(c) confer on the trustees of any property which is the subject of an order under this section such powers as appear to the court to be necessary or expedient.

[779]

NOTES

Sub-s (1): para (g) inserted by the Civil Partnership Act 2004, s 71, Sch 4, Pt 2, para 16.

3 Matters to which court is to have regard in exercising powers under s 2

(1) Where an application is made for an order under section 2 of this Act, the court shall, in determining whether the disposition of the deceased's estate effected by his will or the law relating to intestacy, or the combination of his will and that law, is such as to make reasonable financial provision for the applicant and, if the court considers that reasonable financial provision has not been made, in determining whether and in what manner it shall exercise its powers under that section, have regard to the following matters, that is to say—

(a) the financial resources and financial needs which the applicant has or is likely to have in the foreseeable future;

(b) the financial resources and financial needs which any other applicant for an order under section 2 of this Act has or is likely to have in the foreseeable future;

(c) the financial resources and financial needs which any beneficiary of the estate of the deceased has or is likely to have in the foreseeable future;

(d) any obligations and responsibilities which the deceased had towards any applicant for an order under the said section 2 or towards any beneficiary of the estate of the deceased;

(e) the size and nature of the net estate of the deceased;

(f) any physical or mental disability of any applicant for an order under the said section 2 or any beneficiary of the estate of the deceased;

(g) any other matter, including the conduct of the applicant or any other person, which in the circumstances of the case the court may consider relevant.

(2) [This subsection applies, without prejudice to the generality of paragraph (g) of subsection (1) above, where an application for an order under section 2 of this Act is made by virtue of section 1(1)(a) or (b) of this Act.]

The court shall, in addition to the matters specifically mentioned in paragraphs (a) to (f) of that subsection, have regard to—

(a) the age of the applicant and the duration of the marriage [or civil partnership];

(b) the contribution made by the applicant to the welfare of the family of the deceased, including any contribution made by looking after the home or caring for the family,

… in the case of an application by the wife or husband of the deceased, the court shall also, unless at the date of death a *decree of judicial separation* [separation order under the Family Law Act 1996] was in force and the separation was continuing, have regard to the provision which the applicant might reasonably have expected to receive if on the day on which the deceased died the marriage, instead of being terminated by death, had been terminated by *a decree of divorce* [a divorce order].

[In the case of an application by the civil partner of the deceased, the court shall also, unless at the date of the death a separation order under Chapter 2 of Part 2 of the Civil Partnership Act 2004 was in force and the separation was continuing, have regard to the provision which the applicant might reasonably have expected to receive if on the day on which the deceased died the civil partnership, instead of being terminated by death, had been terminated by a dissolution order.]

[(2A) Without prejudice to the generality of paragraph (g) of subsection (1) above, where an application for an order under section 2 of this Act is made by virtue of section 1(1)(ba) of this Act, the court shall, in addition to the matters specifically mentioned in paragraphs (a) to (f) of that subsection, have regard to—

(a) the age of the applicant and the length of the period during which the applicant lived as the husband or wife [or civil partner] of the deceased and in the same household as the deceased;

(b) the contribution made by the applicant to the welfare of the family of the deceased, including any contribution made by looking after the home or caring for the family.]

(3) Without prejudice to the generality of paragraph (g) of subsection (1) above, where an application for an order under section 2 of this Act is made by virtue of section 1(1)(c) or 1(1)(d) of this Act, the court shall, in addition to the matters specifically mentioned in paragraphs (a) to (f) of that subsection, have regard to the manner in which the applicant was being or in which he might expect to be educated or trained, and where the application is made by virtue of section 1(1)(d) the court shall also have regard—

(a) to whether the deceased had assumed any responsibility for the applicant's maintenance and, if so, to the extent to which and the basis upon which the deceased assumed that responsibility and to the length of time for which the deceased discharged that responsibility;

(b) to whether in assuming and discharging that responsibility the deceased did so knowing that the applicant was not his own child;

(c) to the liability of any other person to maintain the applicant.

(4) Without prejudice to the generality of paragraph (g) of subsection (1) above, where an application for an order under section 2 of this Act is made by virtue of section 1(1)(e) of this Act, the court shall, in addition to the matters specifically mentioned in paragraphs (a) to (f) of that subsection, have regard to the extent to which and the basis upon which the deceased assumed responsibility for the maintenance of the applicant, and to the length of time for which the deceased discharged that responsibility.

(5) In considering the matters to which the court is required to have regard under this section, the court shall take into account the facts as known to the court at the date of the hearing.

(6) In considering the financial resources of any person for the purposes of this section the court shall take into account his earning capacity and in considering the financial needs of any person for the purposes of this section the court shall take into account his financial obligations and responsibilities.

[780]

NOTES

Sub-s (2): words in first pair of square brackets substituted, words in square brackets in para (a) and words in final pair of square brackets inserted, and word omitted repealed by the Civil Partnership Act 2004, ss 71, 261(4), Sch 4, Pt 2, para 17, Sch 30; words in italics in both places they appear substituted by subsequent words in square brackets by the Family Law Act 1996, s 66(1), Sch 8, para 27(3), as from a day to be appointed (for savings see s 66(2), Sch 9, para 5 thereof).

Sub-s (2A): inserted by the Law Reform (Succession) Act 1995, s 2(4); words in square brackets inserted by the Civil Partnership Act 2004, s 71, Sch 4, Pt 2, para 18.

4 Time-limit for applications

An application for an order under section 2 of this Act shall not, except with the permission of the court, be made after the end of the period of six months from the date on which representation with respect to the estate of the deceased is first taken out.

[781]

5 Interim orders

(1) Where an application for an order under section 3 of this Act it appears to the court-

(a) that the applicant is in immediate need of financial assistance, but it is not yet possible to determine what order (if any) should be made under that section; and

(b) that property forming part of the net estate of the deceased is or can be made available to meet the need of the applicant;

the court may order that, subject to such conditions or restrictions, if any, as the court may impose and to any further order of the court, there shall be paid to the applicant out of the net estate of the deceased such sum or sums and (if more than one) at such intervals as the court thinks reasonable; and the court may order that, subject to the provisions of this Act, such payments are to be made until such date as the court may specify, not being later than the date on which the court either makes an order under the said section 2 or decides not to exercise its powers under that section.

(2) Subsections (2), (3) and (4) of section 2 of this Act shall apply in relation to an order under this section as they apply in relation to an order under that section.

(3) In determining what order, if any, should be made under this section the court shall, so far as the urgency of the case admits, have regard to the same matters as those to which the court is required to have regard under section 3 of this Act.

(4) An order made under section 2 of this Act may provide that any sum paid to the applicant by virtue of this section shall be treated to such an extent and in such manner as may be provided by that order as having been paid on account of any payment provided for by that order.

[782]

6 Variation, discharge, etc of orders for periodical payments

(1) Subject to the provisions of this Act, where the court has made an order under section 2(1)(a) of this Act (in this section referred to as "the original order") for the making of periodical payments to any person (in this section referred to as "the original recipient"), the court, on an application under this section, shall have power by order to vary or discharge the original order or to suspend any provision of it temporarily and to revive the operation of any provision so suspended.

(2) Without prejudice to the generality of subsection (1) above, an order made on an application for the variation of the original order may—

(a) provide for the making out of any relevant property of such periodical payments and for such term as may be specified in the order to any person who has applied, or would but for section 4 of this Act be entitled to apply, for an order under section 2 of this Act (whether or not, in the case of any application, an order was made in favour of the applicant);

(b) provide for the payment out of any relevant property of a lump sum of such amount as may be so specified to the original recipient or to any such person as is mentioned in paragraph (a) above;

(c) provide for the transfer of the relevant property, or such part thereof as may be so specified, to the original recipient or to any such person as is so mentioned.

(3) Where the original order provides that any periodical payments payable thereunder to the original recipient are to cease on the occurrence of an event specified in the order [(other than the formation of a subsequent marriage or civil partnership by a former spouse or former civil partner)] or on the expiration of a period so specified, then, if, before the end of the period of six months from the date of the occurrence of that event or of the expiration of that period, an application is made for an order under this section, the court shall have power to make any order which it would have had power to make if the application had been made before the date (whether in favour of the original recipient or any such person as is mentioned in subsection (2)(a) above and whether having effect from that date or from such later date as the court may specify).

(4) Any reference in this section to the original order shall include a reference to an order made under this section and any reference in this section to the original recipient shall include a reference to any person to whom periodical payments are required to be made by virtue of an order under this section.

(5) An application under this section may be made by any of the following persons, that is to say—

(a) any person who by virtue of section 1(1) of this Act has applied, or would but for section 4 of this Act be entitled to apply, for an order under section 2 of this Act,

(b) the personal representatives of the deceased,

(c) the trustees of any relevant property, and

(d) any beneficiary of the estate of the deceased.

(6) An order under this section may only affect—

(a) property the income of which is at the date of the order applicable wholly or in part for the making of periodical payments to any person who has applied for an order under this Act, or

(b) in the case of an application under subsection (3) above in respect of payments which have ceased to be payable on the occurrence of an event or the expiration of a period, property the income of which was so applicable immediately before the occurrence of that event or the expiration of that period, as the case may be,

and any such property as is mentioned in paragraph (a) or (b) above is in subsections (2) and (5) above referred to as "relevant property".

(7) In exercising the powers conferred by this section the court shall have regard to all circumstances of the case, including any change in any of the matters to which the court was required to have regard when making the order to which the application relates.

(8) Where the court makes an order under this section, it may give such consequential directions as it thinks necessary or expedient having regard to the provisions of the order.

(9) No such order as is mentioned in section 2(1)(d), (e) or (f), 9, 10 or 11 of this Act shall be made on an application under this section.

(10) For the avoidance of doubt it is hereby declared that, in relation to an order which provides for the making of periodical payments which are to cease on the occurrence of an event specified in the order [(other than the formation of a subsequent marriage or civil partnership by a former spouse or former civil partner)] or on the expiration of a period so specified, the power to vary an order includes power to provide for the making of periodical payments after the expiration of that period or the occurrence of that event.

[783]

NOTES

Sub-ss (3), (10): words in square brackets substituted by the Civil Partnership Act 2004, s 71, Sch 4, Pt 2, para 19.

7 Payment of lump sums by instalments

(1) An order under section 2(1)(b) or 6(2)(b) of this Act for the payment of a lump sum may provide for the payment of that sum by instalments of such amount as may be specified in the order.

(2) Where an order is made by virtue of subsection (1) above, the court shall have power, on an application made by the person to whom the lump sum is payable, by the personal representatives of the deceased or by the trustees of the property out of which the lump sum is payable, to vary that order by varying the number of instalments payable, the amount of any instalment and the date on which any instalment becomes payable.

[784]

Property available for financial provision

8 Property treated as part of "net estate"

(1) Where a deceased person has in accordance with the provisions of any enactment nominated any person to receive any sum of money or other property on his death and that nomination is in force at the time of his death, that sum of money, after deducting therefrom any inheritance tax payable in respect thereof, or that other property, to the extent of the value thereof at the date of the death of the deceased after deducting therefrom any inheritance tax so payable, shall be treated for the purposes of this Act as part of the net estate of the deceased; but this subsection shall not render any person liable for having paid that sum or transferred that other property to the person named in the nomination in accordance with the directions given in the nomination.

(2) Where any sum of money or other property is received by any person as a donatio mortis causa made by a deceased person, that sum of money, after deducting therefrom any inheritance tax payable thereon, or that other property, to the extent of the value thereof at the date of the death of the deceased after deducting therefrom any inheritance tax so payable, shall be treated for the purposes of this Act as part of the net estate of the deceased; but this subsection shall not render any person liable for having paid that sum or transferred that other property in order to give effect to that donatio mortis causa.

(3) The amount of inheritance tax to be deducted for the purposes of this section shall not exceed the amount of that tax which has been borne by the person nominated by the deceased or, as the case may be, the person who has received a sum of money or other property as a donatio mortis causa.

[785]

NOTES

Capital Transfer Tax: except in relation to a liability to tax arising before 25 July 1986 capital transfer tax shall be known as inheritance tax and the Capital Transfer Tax Act 1984 may be cited as the Inheritance Tax Act 1984, by virtue of the Finance Act 1986, s 100.

9 Property held on a joint tenancy

(1) Where a deceased person was immediately before his death beneficially entitled to a joint tenancy of any property, then, if, before the end of the period of six months from the date on which representation with respect to the estate of the deceased was first taken out, an application is made for an order under section 2 of this Act, the court for the purpose of facilitating the making of financial provision for the applicant under this Act may order that the deceased's severable share of that property, at the value thereof immediately before his death, shall, to such extent as appears to the court to be just in all the circumstances of the case, be treated for the purposes of this Act as part of the net estate of the deceased.

(2) In determining the extent to which any severable share is to be treated as part of the net estate of the deceased by virtue of an order under subsection (1) above, the court shall have regard to any inheritance tax payable in respect of that severable share.

(3) Where an order is made under subsection (1) above, the provisions of this section shall not render any person liable for anything done by him before the order was made.

(4) For the avoidance of doubt it is hereby declared that for the purposes of this section there may be a joint tenancy of a chose in action.

[786]

NOTES

Capital Transfer Tax: except in relation to a liability to tax arising before 25 July 1986 capital transfer tax shall be known as inheritance tax and the Capital Transfer Tax Act 1984 may be cited as the Inheritance Tax Act 1984, by virtue of the Finance Act 1986, s 100.

Powers of court in relation to transactions intended to defeat applications for financial provision

10 Dispositions intended to defeat applications for financial provision

(1) Where an application is made to the court for an order under section 2 of this Act, the applicant may, in the proceedings on that application, apply to the court for an order under subsection (2) below.

(2) Where on an application under subsection (1) above the court is satisfied—

(a) that, less than six years before the date of the death of the deceased, the deceased with the intention of defeating an application for financial provision under this Act made a disposition, and

(b) that full valuable consideration for that disposition was not given by the person to whom or for the benefit of whom the disposition was made (in this section referred to as "the donee") or by any other person, and

(c) that the exercise of the powers conferred by this section would facilitate the making of financial provision for the applicant under this Act,

then, subject to the provisions of this section and of sections 12 and 13 of this Act, the court may order the donee (whether or not at the date of the order he holds any interest in the property disposed of to him or for his benefit by the deceased) to provide, for the purpose of the making of that financial provision, such sum of money or other property as may be specified in the order.

(3) Where an order is made under subsection (2) above as respects any disposition made by the deceased which consisted of the payment of money to or for the benefit of the donee, the amount of any sum of money or the value of any property ordered to be provided under that subsection shall not exceed the amount of the payment made by the deceased after deducting therefrom any inheritance tax borne by the donee in respect of that payment.

(4) Where an order is made under subsection (2) above as respects any disposition made by the deceased which consisted of the transfer of property (other than a sum of money) to or for the benefit of the donee, the amount of any sum of money or the value of any property ordered to be provided under that subsection shall not exceed the value at the date of the death of the deceased of the property disposed of by him to or for the benefit of the donee (or if that property has been disposed of by the person to whom it was transferred by the deceased, the value at the date of that disposal thereof) after deducting therefrom any inheritance tax borne by the donee in respect of the transfer of that property by the deceased.

(5) Where an application (in this subsection referred to as "the original application") is made for an order under subsection (2) above in relation to any disposition, then, if on an application under this subsection by the donee or by any applicant for an order under section 2 of this Act the court is satisfied—

(a) that, less than six years before the date of the death of the deceased, the deceased with the intention of defeating an application for financial provision under this Act made a disposition other than the disposition which is the subject of the original application, and

(b) that full valuable consideration for that other disposition was not given by the person to whom or for the benefit of whom that other disposition was made or by any other person,

the court may exercise in relation to the person to whom or for the benefit of whom that other disposition was made the powers which the court would have had under subsection (2) above if the original application had been made in respect of that other disposition and the court had been satisfied as to the matters set out in paragraphs (a), (b) and (c) of that subsection; and where any application is made under this subsection, any reference in this section (except in subsection (2)(b)) to the donee shall include a reference to the person to whom or for the benefit of whom that other disposition was made.

(6) In determining whether and in what manner to exercise its powers under this section, the court shall have regard to the circumstances in which any disposition was made and any valuable

consideration which was given therefor, the relationship, if any, of the donee to the deceased, the conduct and financial resources of the donee and all the other circumstances of the case.

(7) In this section "disposition" does not include—

(a) any provision in a will, any such nomination as is mentioned in section 8(1) of this Act or any donatio mortis causa, or

(b) any appointment of property made, otherwise than by will, in the exercise of a special power of appointment,

but, subject to these exceptions, includes any payment of money (including the payment of a premium under a policy of assurance) and any conveyance, assurance, appointment or gift of property of any description, whether made by an instrument or otherwise.

(8) The provisions of this section do not apply to any disposition made before the commencement of this Act.

[787]

NOTES

Capital Transfer Tax: except in relation to a liability to tax arising before 25 July 1986 capital transfer tax shall be known as inheritance tax and the Capital Transfer Tax Act 1984 may be cited as the Inheritance Tax Act 1984, by virtue of the Finance Act 1986, s 100.

11 Contracts to leave property by will

(1) Where an application is made to a court for an order under section 2 of this Act, the applicant may, in the proceedings on that application, apply to the court for an order under this section.

(2) Where on an application under subsection (1) above the court is satisfied—

(a) that the deceased made a contract by which he agreed to leave by his will a sum of money or other property to any person or by which he agreed that a sum of money or other property would be paid or transferred to any person out of his estate, and

(b) that the deceased made that contract with the intention of defeating an application for financial provision under this Act, and

(c) that when the contract was made full valuable consideration for that contract was not given or promised by the person with whom or for the benefit of whom the contract was made (in this section referred to as "the donee") or by any other person, and

(d) that the exercise of the powers conferred by this section would facilitate the making of financial provision for the applicant under this Act,

then, subject to the provisions of this section and of sections 12 and 13 of this Act, the court may make any one or more of the following orders, that is to say—

(i) if any money has been paid or any other property has been transferred to or for the benefit of the donee in accordance with the contract, an order directing the donee to provide, for the purpose of the making of that financial provision, such sum of money or other property as may be specified in the order;

(ii) if the money or all the money has not been paid or the property or all the property has not been transferred in accordance with the contract, an order directing the personal representatives not to make any payment or transfer any property, or not to make any further payment or transfer any further property, as the case may be, in accordance therewith or directing the personal representatives only to make such payment or transfer such property as may be specified in the order.

(3) Notwithstanding anything in subsection (2) above, the court may exercise its powers thereunder in relation to any contract made by the deceased only to the extent that the court considers that the amount of any sum of money paid or to be paid or the value of any property transferred or to be transferred in accordance with the contract exceeds the value of any valuable consideration given or to be given for that contract, and for this purpose the court shall have regard to the value of property at the date of the hearing.

(4) In determining whether and in what manner to exercise its powers under this section, the court shall have regard to the circumstances in which the contract was made, the relationship, if any, of the donee to the deceased, the conduct and financial resources of the donee and all the other circumstances of the case.

(5) Where an order has been made under subsection (2) above in relation to any contract the rights of any person to enforce that contract or to recover damages or to obtain other relief for the breach thereof shall be subject to any adjustment made by the court under section 12(3) of this Act and shall survive to such extent only as is consistent with giving effect to the terms of that order.

(6) The provisions of this section do not apply to a contract made before the commencement of this Act.

[788]

12 Provisions supplementary to ss 10 and 11

(1) Where the exercise of any of the powers conferred by section 10 or 11 of this Act is conditional on the court being satisfied that a disposition or contract was made by a deceased person with the intention of defeating an application for financial provision under this Act, that condition shall be fulfilled if the court is of the opinion that, on a balance of probabilities, the intention of the deceased (though not necessarily his sole intention) in making the disposition or contract was to prevent an order for financial provision being made under this Act or to reduce the amount of the provision which might otherwise be granted by an order thereunder.

(2) Where an application is made under section 11 of this Act with respect to any contract made by the deceased and no valuable consideration was given or promised by any person for that contract then, notwithstanding anything in subsection (1) above, it shall be presumed, unless the contrary is shown, that the deceased made that contract with the intention of defeating an application for financial provision under this Act.

(3) Where the court makes an order under section 10 or 11 of this Act it may give such consequential directions as it thinks fit (including directions requiring the making of any payment or the transfer of any property) for giving effect to the order or for securing a fair adjustment of the rights of the persons affected thereby.

(4) Any power conferred on the court by the said section 10 or 11 to order the donee, in relation to any disposition or contract, to provide any sum of money or other property shall be exercisable in like manner in relation to the personal representative of the donee, and—

(a) any reference in section 10(4) to the disposal of property by the donee shall include a reference to disposal by the personal representative of the donee, and

(b) any reference in section 10(5) to an application by the donee under that subsection shall include a reference to an application by the personal representative of the donee;

but the court shall not have power under the said section 10 or 11 to make an order in respect of any property forming part of the estate of the donee which has been distributed by the personal representative; and the personal representative shall not be liable for having distributed any such property before he has notice of the making of an application under the said section 10 or 11 on the ground that he ought to have taken into account the possibility that such an application would be made.

[789]

13 Provisions as to trustees in relation to ss 10 and 11

(1) Where an application is made for—

(a) an order under section 10 of this Act in respect of a disposition made by the deceased to any person as a trustee, or

(b) an order under section 11 of this Act in respect of any payment made or property transferred, in accordance with a contract made by the deceased, to any person as a trustee,

the powers of the court under the said section 10 or 11 to order that trustee to provide a sum of money or other property shall be subject to the following limitation (in addition, in a case of an application under section 10, to any provision regarding the deduction of inheritance tax) namely, that the amount of any sum of money or the value of any property ordered to be provided—

(i) in the case of an application in respect of a disposition which consisted of the payment of money or an application in respect of the payment of money in accordance with a contract, shall not exceed the aggregate of so much of that money as is at the date of the order in the hands of the trustee and the value at that date of any property which represents that money or is derived therefrom and is at that date in the hands of the trustee;

(ii) in the case of an application in respect of a disposition which consisted of the transfer of property (other than a sum of money) or an application in respect of the transfer of property (other than a sum of money) in accordance with a contract, shall not exceed the aggregate of the value at the date of the order of so much of that property as is at that date in the hands of the trustee and the value at that date of any property which represents the first mentioned property or is derived therefrom and is at that date in the hands of the trustee.

(2) Where any such application is made in respect of a disposition made to any person as a trustee or in respect of any payment made or property transferred in pursuance of a contract to any person as a trustee, the trustee shall not be liable for having distributed any money or other property on the ground that he ought to have taken into account the possibility that such an application would be made.

(3) Where any such application is made in respect of a disposition made to any person as a trustee or in respect of any payment made or property transferred in accordance with a contract to any person as a trustee, any reference in the said section 10 or 11 to the donee shall be construed as

including a reference to the trustee or trustees for the time being of the trust in question and any reference in subsection (1) or (2) above to a trustee shall be construed in the same way.

[790]

NOTES

Capital Transfer Tax: except in relation to a liability to tax arising before 25 July 1986 capital transfer tax shall be known as inheritance tax and the Capital Transfer Tax Act 1984 may be cited as the Inheritance Tax Act 1984, by virtue of the Finance Act 1986, s 100.

Special provisions relating to cases of divorce, separation, etc

14 Provision as to cases where no financial relief was granted in divorce proceedings, etc

(1) Where, within twelve months from the date on which *a decree of divorce or nullity of marriage has been made absolute or a decree of judicial separation has been granted* [a divorce order or separation order has been made under the Family Law Act 1996 in relation to a marriage or a decree of nullity of marriage has been made absolute], a party to the marriage dies and—

(a) an application for a financial provision order under *section 23* [section 22A or 23] of the Matrimonial Causes Act 1973 or a property adjustment order under *section 24* [section 23A or 24] of that Act has not been made by the other party to that marriage, or

(b) such an application has been made but the proceedings thereon have not been determined at the time of the death of the deceased,

then, if an application for an order under section 2 of this Act is made by that other party, the court shall, notwithstanding anything in section 1 or section 3 of this Act, have power, if it thinks it just to do so, to treat that party for the purposes of that application as if *the decree of divorce or nullity of marriage had not been made absolute or the decree of judicial separation had not been granted, as the case may be* [, as the case may be, the divorce order or separation order had not been made or the decree of nullity had not been made absolute].

(2) This section shall not apply in relation to a *decree of judicial separation* [separation order] unless at the date of the death of the deceased *the decree* [the order] was in force and the separation was continuing.

[791]

NOTES

Sub-ss (1), (2): words in italics substituted by subsequent words in square brackets, by the Family Law Act 1996, s 66(1), Sch 8, para 27(4), as from a day to be appointed; for savings see s 66(2), Sch 9, para 5 thereof.

[14A Provision as to cases where no financial relief was granted in proceedings for the dissolution etc of a civil partnership

(1) Subsection (2) below applies where—

(a) a dissolution order, nullity order, separation order or presumption of death order has been made under Chapter 2 of Part 2 of the Civil Partnership Act 2004 in relation to a civil partnership,

(b) one of the civil partners dies within twelve months from the date on which the order is made, and

(c) either—

(i) an application for a financial provision order under Part 1 of Schedule 5 to that Act or a property adjustment order under Part 2 of that Schedule has not been made by the other civil partner, or

(ii) such an application has been made but the proceedings on the application have not been determined at the time of the death of the deceased.

(2) If an application for an order under section 2 of this Act is made by the surviving civil partner, the court shall, notwithstanding anything in section 1 or section 3 of this Act, have power, if it thinks it just to do so, to treat the surviving civil partner as if the order mentioned in subsection (1)(a) above had not been made.

(3) This section shall not apply in relation to a separation order unless at the date of the death of the deceased the separation order was in force and the separation was continuing.]

[792]

NOTES

Commencement: 5 December 2005.

Inserted by the Civil Partnership Act 2004, s 71, Sch 4, Pt 2, para 20.

15 Restriction imposed in divorce proceedings, etc on application under this Act

[(1) *On the grant of a decree of divorce, a decree of nullity of marriage or a decree of judicial separation or at any time thereafter* [At any time when the court—

(a) has jurisdiction under section 23A or 24 of the Matrimonial Causes Act 1973 to make a property adjustment order in relation to a marriage; or

(b) would have such jurisdiction if either the jurisdiction had not already been exercised or an application for such an order were made with the leave of the court,]

the court, if it considers it just to do so, may, on the application of either party to the marriage, order that the other party to the marriage shall not on the death of the applicant be entitled to apply for an order under section 2 of this Act.

In this subsection "the court" means the High Court or, where a county court has jurisdiction by virtue of Part V of the Matrimonial and Family Proceedings Act 1984, a county court.]

(2) *In the case of a decree of divorce or nullity of marriage an order may be made under subsection (1) above before or after the decree is made absolute, but if it is made before the decree is made absolute it shall not take effect unless the decree is made absolute.*

(3) *Where an order made under subsection (1) above on the grant of a decree of divorce or nullity of marriage has come into force with respect to a party to a marriage, then, on the death of the other party to that marriage, the court shall not entertain any application for an order under section 2 of this Act made by the first-mentioned party.*

(4) *Where an order made under subsection (1) above on the grant of a decree of judicial separation has come into force with respect to any party to a marriage, then, if the other party to that marriage dies while the decree is in force and the separation is continuing, the court shall not entertain any application for an order under section 2 of this Act made by the first-mentioned party.*

[(2) An order made under subsection (1) above with respect to any party to a marriage has effect in accordance with subsection (3) below at any time—

(a) after the marriage has been dissolved;
(b) after a decree of nullity has been made absolute in relation to the marriage; and
(c) while a separation order under the Family Law Act 1996 is in force in relation to the marriage and the separation is continuing.

(3) If at any time when an order made under subsection (1) above with respect to any party to a marriage has effect the other party to the marriage dies, the court shall not entertain any application made by the surviving party to the marriage for an order under section 2 of this Act.]

[793]

NOTES

Sub-s (1): substituted by the Matrimonial and Family Proceedings Act 1984, s 8; words in italics substituted by subsequent words in square brackets by the Family Law Act 1996, s 66(1), Sch 8, para 27(5), as from a day to be appointed; for savings see s 66(2), Sch 9, para 5 thereof.

Sub-ss (2)–(4): substituted, by subsequent sub-ss (2), (3) in square brackets, by the Family Law Act 1996, s 66(1), Sch 8, para 27(6), as from a day to be appointed; for savings see s 66(2), Sch 9, para 5 thereof.

[15ZA Restriction imposed in proceedings for the dissolution etc of a civil partnership on application under this Act

(1) On making a dissolution order, nullity order, separation order or presumption of death order under Chapter 2 of Part 2 of the Civil Partnership Act 2004, or at any time after making such an order, the court, if it considers it just to do so, may, on the application of either of the civil partners, order that the other civil partner shall not on the death of the applicant be entitled to apply for an order under section 2 of this Act.

(2) In subsection (1) above "the court" means the High Court or, where a county court has jurisdiction by virtue of Part 5 of the Matrimonial and Family Proceedings Act 1984, a county court.

(3) In the case of a dissolution order, nullity order or presumption of death order ("the main order") an order may be made under subsection (1) above before (as well as after) the main order is made final, but if made before the main order is made final it shall not take effect unless the main order is made final.

(4) Where an order under subsection (1) above made in connection with a dissolution order, nullity order or presumption of death order has come into force with respect to a civil partner, then, on the death of the other civil partner, the court shall not entertain any application for an order under section 2 of this Act made by the surviving civil partner.

(5) Where an order under subsection (1) above made in connection with a separation order has come into force with respect to a civil partner, then, if the other civil partner dies while the separation order is in force and the separation is continuing, the court shall not entertain any application for an order under section 2 of this Act made by the surviving civil partner.]

[794]

NOTES

Commencement: 5 December 2005.

Inserted by the Civil Partnership Act 2004, s 71, Sch 4, Pt 2, para 21.

[15A Restriction imposed in proceedings under Matrimonial and Family Proceedings Act 1984 on application under this Act

(1) On making an order under section 17 of the Matrimonial and Family Proceedings Act 1984 (orders for financial provision and property adjustment following overseas divorces, etc) the court, if it considers it just to do so, may, on the application of either party to the marriage, order that the other party to the marriage shall not on the death of the applicant be entitled to apply for an order under section 2 of this Act.

In this subsection "the court" means the High Court or, where a county court has jurisdiction by virtue of Part V of the Matrimonial and Family Proceedings Act 1984, a county court.

(2) Where an order under subsection (1) above has been made with respect to a party to a marriage which has been dissolved or annulled, then, on the death of the other party to that marriage, the court shall not entertain an application under section 2 of this Act made by the first-mentioned party.

(3) Where an order under subsection (1) above has been made with respect to a party to a marriage the parties to which have been legally separated, then, if the other party to the marriage dies while the legal separation is in force, the court shall not entertain an application under section 2 of this Act made by the first-mentioned party.]

[795]

NOTES

Inserted by the Matrimonial and Family Proceedings Act 1984, s 25.

[15B Restriction imposed in proceedings under Schedule 7 to the Civil Partnership Act 2004 on application under this Act

(1) On making an order under paragraph 9 of Schedule 7 to the Civil Partnership Act 2004 (orders for financial provision, property adjustment and pension-sharing following overseas dissolution etc of civil partnership) the court, if it considers it just to do so, may, on the application of either of the civil partners, order that the other civil partner shall not on the death of the applicant be entitled to apply for an order under section 2 of this Act.

(2) In subsection (1) above "the court" means the High Court or, where a county court has jurisdiction by virtue of Part 5 of the Matrimonial and Family Proceedings Act 1984, a county court.

(3) Where an order under subsection (1) above has been made with respect to one of the civil partners in a case where a civil partnership has been dissolved or annulled, then, on the death of the other civil partner, the court shall not entertain an application under section 2 of this Act made by the surviving civil partner.

(4) Where an order under subsection (1) above has been made with respect to one of the civil partners in a case where civil partners have been legally separated, then, if the other civil partner dies while the legal separation is in force, the court shall not entertain an application under section 2 of this Act made by the surviving civil partner.]

[796]

NOTES

Commencement: 5 December 2005.
Inserted by the Civil Partnership Act 2004, s 71, Sch 4, Pt 2, para 22.

16 Variation and discharge of secured periodical payments orders made under Matrimonial Causes Act 1973

(1) Where an application for an order under section 2 of this Act is made to the court by any person who was at the time of the death of the deceased entitled to payments from the deceased under a secured periodical payments order made under the Matrimonial Causes Act 1973 [or Schedule 5 to the Civil Partnership Act 2004], then, in the proceedings on that application, the court shall have power, if an application is made under this section by that person or by the personal representative of the deceased, to vary or discharge that periodical payments order or to revive the operation of any provision thereof which has been suspended under section 31 of that Act [of 1973 or Part 11 of that Schedule].

(2) In exercising the powers conferred by this section the court shall have regard to all the circumstances of the case, including any order which the court proposes to make under section 2 or section 5 of this Act and any change (whether resulting from the death of the deceased or otherwise) in any of the matters to which the court was required to have regard when making the secured periodical payments order.

(3) The powers exercisable by the court under this section in relation to an order shall be exercisable also in relation to any instrument executed in pursuance of the order.

[797]

NOTES

Sub-s (1): words in square brackets inserted by the Civil Partnership Act 2004, s 71, Sch 4, Pt 2, para 23.

17 Variation and revocation of maintenance agreements

(1) Where an application for an order under section 2 of this Act is made to the court by any person who was at the time of the death of the deceased entitled to payments from the deceased under a maintenance agreement which provided for the continuation of payments under the agreement after the death of the deceased, then, in the proceedings on that application, the court shall have power, if an application is made under this section by that person or by the personal representative of the deceased, to vary or revoke that agreement.

(2) In exercising the powers conferred by this section the court shall have regard to all the circumstances of the case, including any order which the court proposes to make under section 2 or section 5 of this Act and any change (whether resulting from the death of the deceased or otherwise) in any of the circumstances in the light of which the agreement was made.

(3) If a maintenance agreement is varied by the court under this section the like consequences shall ensue as if the variation had been made immediately before the death of the deceased by agreement between the parties and for valuable consideration.

(4) In this section "maintenance agreement", in relation to a deceased person, means any agreement made, whether in writing or not and whether before or after the commencement of this Act, by the deceased with any person with whom he [formed a marriage or civil partnership], being an agreement which contained provisions governing the rights and liabilities towards one another when living separately of the parties to that marriage [or of the civil partners] (whether or not the marriage [or civil partnership] has been dissolved or annulled) in respect of the making or securing of payments or the disposition or use of any property, including such rights and liabilities with respect to the maintenance or education of any child, whether or not a child of the deceased or a person who was treated by the deceased as a child of the family in relation to that marriage [or civil partnership].

[798]

NOTES

Sub-s (4): words in first pair of square brackets substituted and other words in square brackets inserted by the Civil Partnership Act 2004, s 71, Sch 4, Pt 2, para 24.

18 Availability of court's powers under this Act in applications under ss 31 and 36 of the Matrimonial Causes Act 1973

(1) Where—

(a) a person against whom a secured periodical payments order was made under the Matrimonial Causes Act 1973 has died and an application is made under section 31(6) of that Act for the variation or discharge of that order or for the revival of the operation of any provision thereof which has been suspended, or

(b) a party to a maintenance agreement within the meaning of section 34 of that Act has died, the agreement being one which provides for the continuation of payments thereunder after the death of one of the parties, and an application is made under section 36(1) of that Act for the alteration of the agreement under section 35 thereof.

the court shall have power to direct that the application made under the said section 31(6) or 36(1) shall be deemed to have been accompanied by an application for an order under section 2 of this Act.

(2) Where the court gives a direction under subsection (1) above it shall have power, in the proceedings on the application under the said section 31(6) or 36(1), to make any order which the court would have had power to make under the provisions of this Act if the application under the said section 31(6) or 36(1), as the case may be, had been made jointly with an application for an order under the said section 2; and the court shall have power to give such consequential directions as may be necessary for enabling the court to exercise any of the powers available to the court under this Act in the case of an application for an order under section 2.

(3) Where an order made under section 15(1) of this Act is in force with respect to a party to a marriage, the court shall not give a direction under subsection (1) above with respect to any application made under the said section 31(6) or 36(1) by that party on the death of the other party.

[799]

[18A Availability of court's powers under this Act in applications under paragraphs 60 and 73 of Schedule 5 to the Civil Partnership Act 2004

(1) Where—

(a) a person against whom a secured periodical payments order was made under Schedule 5 to the Civil Partnership Act 2004 has died and an application is made under paragraph 60 of that Schedule for the variation or discharge of that order or for the revival of the operation of any suspended provision of the order, or

(b) a party to a maintenance agreement within the meaning of Part 13 of that Schedule has died, the agreement being one which provides for the continuation of payments under the agreement after the death of one of the parties, and an application is made under paragraph 73 of that Schedule for the alteration of the agreement under paragraph 69 of that Schedule, the court shall have power to direct that the application made under paragraph 60 or 73 of that Schedule shall be deemed to have been accompanied by an application for an order under section 2 of this Act.

(2) Where the court gives a direction under subsection (1) above it shall have power, in the proceedings on the application under paragraph 60 or 73 of that Schedule, to make any order which the court would have had power to make under the provisions of this Act if the application under that paragraph had been made jointly with an application for an order under section 2 of this Act; and the court shall have power to give such consequential directions as may be necessary for enabling the court to exercise any of the powers available to the court under this Act in the case of an application for an order under section 2.

(3) Where an order made under section 15ZA(1) of this Act is in force with respect to a civil partner, the court shall not give a direction under subsection (1) above with respect to any application made under paragraph 60 or 73 of that Schedule by that civil partner on the death of the other civil partner.]

[800]

NOTES

Commencement: 5 December 2005.
Inserted by the Civil Partnership Act 2004, s 71, Sch 4, Pt 2, para 25.

Miscellaneous and supplementary provisions

19 Effect, duration and form of orders

(1) Where an order is made under section 2 of this Act then for all purposes, including the purposes of the enactments relating to inheritance tax, the will or the law relating to intestacy, or both the will and the law relating to intestacy, as the case may be, shall have effect and be deemed to have had effect as from the deceased's death subject to the provisions of the order.

(2) Any order made under section 2 or 5 of this Act in favour of—

(a) an applicant who was the [former spouse or former civil partner] of the deceased, or

(b) an applicant who was the husband or wife of the deceased in a case where *the marriage with the deceased was the subject of a decree of judicial separation and at the date of death the decree was in force*[, at the date of death, a separation order under the Family Law Act 1996 was in force in relation to the marriage with the deceased] and the separation was continuing, [or

(c) an applicant who was the civil partner of the deceased in a case where, at the date of death, a separation order under Chapter 2 of Part 2 of the Civil Partnership Act 2004 was in force in relation to their civil partnership and the separation was continuing,]

shall, in so far as it provides for the making of periodical payments, cease to have effect [on the formation by the applicant of a subsequent marriage or civil partnership, except in relation to any arrears due under the order on the date of the formation of the subsequent marriage or civil partnership].

(3) A copy of every order made under this Act [other than an order made under section 15(1) [or 15ZA(1)] of this Act] shall be sent to the principal registry of the Family Division for entry and filing, and a memorandum of the order shall be endorsed on, or permanently annexed to, the probate or letters of administration under which the estate is being administered.

[801]

NOTES

Sub-s (2): words in square brackets in para (a) and words in final pair of square brackets substituted and para (c) and word immediately preceding it inserted by the Civil Partnership Act 2004, s 71, Sch 4, Pt 2, para 26(1)–(4); in para (b), words in italics substituted by subsequent words in square brackets by the Family Law Act 1996, s 66(1), Sch 8, para 27(7), as from a day to be appointed (for savings see s 66(2), Sch 9, para 5 thereof).

Sub-s (3): words in first (outer) pair of square brackets inserted by the Administration of Justice Act 1982, s 52; words in second (inner) pair of square brackets inserted by the Civil Partnership Act 2004, s 71, Sch 4, Pt 2, para 26(1), (5).

Capital Transfer Tax: except in relation to a liability to tax arising before 25 July 1986 capital transfer tax shall be known as inheritance tax and the Capital Transfer Tax Act 1984 may be cited as the Inheritance Tax Act 1984, by virtue of the Finance Act 1986, s 100.

20 Provisions as to personal representatives

(1) The provisions of this Act shall not render the personal representative of a deceased person liable for having distributed any part of the estate of the deceased, after the end of the period of six months from the date on which representation with respect to the estate of the deceased is first taken out, on the ground that he ought to have taken into account the possibility—

(a) that the court might permit the making of an application for an order under section 2 of this Act after the end of that period, or

(b) that, where an order has been made under the said section 2, the court might exercise in relation thereto the powers conferred on it by section 6 of this Act,

but this subsection shall not prejudice any power to recover, by reason of the making of an order under this Act, any part of the estate so distributed.

(2) Where the personal representative of a deceased person pays any sum directed by an order under section 5 of this Act to be paid out of the deceased's net estate, he shall not be under any liability by reason of that estate not being sufficient to make the payment, unless at the time of making the payment he has reasonable cause to believe that the estate is not sufficient.

(3) Where a deceased person entered into a contract by which he agreed to leave by his will any sum of money or other property to any person or by which he agreed that a sum of money or other property would be paid or transferred to any person out of his estate, then, if the personal representative of the deceased has reason to believe that the deceased entered into the contract with the intention of defeating an application for financial provision under this Act, he may, notwithstanding anything in that contract, postpone the payment of that sum of money or the transfer of that property until the expiration of the period of six months from the date on which representation with respect to the estate of the deceased is first taken out or, if during that period an application is made for an order under section 2 of this Act, until the determination of the proceedings on that application.

[802]

21, 22 (*S 21 repealed by the Civil Evidence Act 1995, s 15(2), Sch 2; s 22 repealed by the Administration of Justice Act 1982, s 74, Sch 9, Pt I.*)

23 Determination of date on which representation was first taken out

In considering for the purposes of this Act when representation with respect to the estate of a deceased person was first taken out, a grant limited to settled land or to trust property shall be left out of account, and a grant limited to real estate or to personal estate shall be left out of account unless a grant limited to the remainder of the estate has previously been made or is made at the same time.

[803]

24 Effect of this Act on s 46(1)(vi) of Administration of Estates Act 1925

Section 46(1)(vi) of the Administration of Estates Act 1925, in so far as it provides for the devolution of property on the Crown, the Duchy of Lancaster or the Duke of Cornwall as bona vacantia, shall have effect subject to the provisions of this Act.

[804]

25 Interpretation

(1) In this Act—

"beneficiary", in relation to the estate of a deceased person, means—

(a) a person who under the will of the deceased or under the law relating to intestacy is beneficially interested in the estate or would be so interested if an order had not been made under this Act, and

(b) a person who has received any sum of money or other property which by virtue of section 8(1) or 8(2) of this Act is treated as part of the net estate of the deceased or would have received that sum or other property if an order had not been made under this Act;

"child" includes an illegitimate child and a child en ventre sa mere at the death of the deceased;

"the court" [unless the context otherwise requires] means the High Court, or where a county court has jurisdiction by virtue of section 22 of this Act, a county court;

["former civil partner" means a person whose civil partnership with the deceased was during the lifetime of the deceased either—

(a) dissolved or annulled by an order made under the law of any part of the British Islands, or

(b) dissolved or annulled in any country or territory outside the British Islands by a dissolution or annulment which is entitled to be recognised as valid by the law of England and Wales;]

[["former spouse"] means a person whose marriage with the deceased was during the lifetime of the deceased either—

(a) dissolved or annulled by *a decree* [an order or decree] of divorce or a decree of nullity of marriage granted under the law of any part of the British Islands, or

(b) dissolved or annulled in any country or territory outside the British Islands by a divorce or annulment which is entitled to be recognised as valid by the law of England and Wales;]

"net estate", in relation to a deceased person, means—

(a) all property of which the deceased had power to dispose by his will (otherwise than by virtue of a special power of appointment) less the amount of his funeral, testamentary and administration expenses, debts and liabilities, including any inheritance tax payable out of his estate on his death;

(b) any property in respect of which the deceased held a general power of appointment (not being a power exercisable by will) which has not been exercised;

(c) any sum of money or other property which is treated for the purposes of this Act as part of the net estate of the deceased by virtue of section 8(1) or (2) of this Act;

(d) any property which is treated for the purposes of this Act as part of the net estate of the deceased by virtue of an order made under section 9 of the Act;

(e) any sum of money or other property which is, by reason of a disposition or contract made by the deceased, ordered under section 10 or 11 of this Act to be provided for the purpose of the making of financial provision under this Act;

"property" includes any chose in action;

"reasonable financial provision" has the meaning assigned to it by section 1 of this Act;

"valuable consideration" does not include marriage or a promise of marriage;

"will" includes codicil.

(2) For the purposes of paragraph (a) of the definition of "net estate" in subsection (1) above a person who is not of full age and capacity shall be treated as having power to dispose by will of all property of which he would have had power to dispose by will if he had been of full age and capacity.

(3) Any reference in this Act to provision out of the net estate of a deceased person includes a reference to provision extending to the whole of that estate.

(4) For the purposes of this Act any reference to a [spouse,] wife or husband shall be treated as including a reference to a person who in good faith entered into a void marriage with the deceased unless either—

(a) the marriage of the deceased and that person was dissolved or annulled during the lifetime of the deceased and the dissolution or annulment is recognised by the law of England and Wales, or

(b) that person has during the lifetime of the deceased [formed a subsequent marriage or civil partnership].

[(4A) For the purposes of this Act any reference to a civil partner shall be treated as including a reference to a person who in good faith formed a void civil partnership with the deceased unless either—

(a) the civil partnership between the deceased and that person was dissolved or annulled during the lifetime of the deceased and the dissolution or annulment is recognised by the law of England and Wales, or

(b) that person has during the lifetime of the deceased formed a subsequent civil partnership or marriage.

(5) Any reference in this Act to the formation of, or to a person who has formed, a subsequent marriage or civil partnership includes (as the case may be) a reference to the formation of, or to a person who has formed, a marriage or civil partnership which is by law void or voidable.

(5A) The formation of a marriage or civil partnership shall be treated for the purposes of this Act as the formation of a subsequent marriage or civil partnership, in relation to either of the spouses or civil partners, notwithstanding that the previous marriage or civil partnership of that spouse or civil partner was void or voidable.]

(6) Any reference in this Act to an order or decree made under the Matrimonial Causes Act 1973 or under any section of that Act shall be construed as including a reference to an order or decree which is deemed to have been made under that Act or under that section thereof, as the case may be.

[(6A) Any reference in this Act to an order made under, or under any provision of, the Civil Partnership Act 2004 shall be construed as including a reference to anything which is deemed to be an order made (as the case may be) under that Act or provision.]

(7) Any reference in this Act to any enactment is a reference to that enactment as amended by or under any subsequent enactment.

[805]

NOTES

Sub-s (1): in definition "the court" words in square brackets inserted by the Matrimonial and Family Proceedings Act 1984, s 8; definition "former civil partner" inserted by the Civil Partnership Act 2004, s 71, Sch 4, Pt 2, para 27(1), (3); definition "former spouse" substituted by the Matrimonial and Family Proceedings Act 1984, s 25, words in first pair of square brackets therein substituted by the Civil Partnership Act 2004, s 71, Sch 4, Pt 2, para 27(1), (2) and words in italics in para (a) substituted by subsequent words in square brackets by the Family Law Act 1996, s 66(1), Sch 8, para 27(8), as from a day to be appointed (for savings see s 66(2), Sch 9, para 5 thereof).

Sub-s (4): word in first pair of square brackets inserted and words in square brackets in para (b) substituted by the Civil Partnership Act 2004, s 71, Sch 4, Pt 2, para 27(1), (4).

Sub-ss (4A), (5), (5A): substituted for original sub-s (5) by the Civil Partnership Act 2004, s 71, Sch 4, Pt 2, para 27(1), (5).

Sub-s (6A): inserted by the Civil Partnership Act 2004, s 71, Sch 4, Pt 2, para 27(1), (6).

Capital Transfer Tax: except in relation to a liability to tax arising before 25 July 1986 capital transfer tax shall be known as inheritance tax and the Capital Transfer Tax Act 1984 may be cited as the Inheritance Tax Act 1984, by virtue of the Finance Act 1986, s 100.

26 Consequential amendments, repeals and transitional provisions

(1) …

(2) Subject to the provisions of this section, the enactments specified in the Schedule to this Act are hereby repealed to the extent specified in the third column of the Schedule;…

(3) The repeal of the said enactment shall not affect their operation in relation to any application made thereunder (whether before or after the commencement of this Act) with reference to the death of any person who died before the commencement of this Act.

(4) Without prejudice to the provisions of section 38 of the Interpretation Act 1889 (which relates to the effect of repeals) nothing in any repeal made by this Act shall affect any order made or direction given under any enactment repealed by this Act, and, subject to the provisions of this Act, every such order or direction (other than an order made under section 4A of the Inheritance (Family Provision) Act 1938 or section 28A of the Matrimonial Causes Act 1965) shall, if it is in force at the commencement of this Act or is made by virtue of subsection (2) above, continue in force as if it had been made under section 2(1)(a) of this Act, and for the purposes of section 6(7) of this Act the court in exercising its powers under that section in relation to an order continued in force by this subsection shall be required to have regard to any change in any of the circumstances to which the court would have been required to have regard when making that order if the order had been made with reference to the death of any person who died after the commencement of this Act.

[806]

NOTES

Sub-ss (1), (2): words omitted amend the Matrimonial Causes Act 1973, s 36, Sch 2, para 5(2).

27 Short title, commencement and extent

(1) This Act may be cited as the Inheritance (Provision for Family and Dependants) Act 1975.

(2) This Act does not extend to Scotland or Northern Ireland.

(3) This Act shall come into force on 1st April 1976.

[807]

(*Schedule contains repeals only.*)

SEX DISCRIMINATION ACT 1975

(1975 c 65)

An Act to render unlawful certain kinds of sex discrimination and discrimination on the ground of marriage, and establish a Commission with the function of working towards the elimination of such discrimination and promoting equality of opportunity between men and women generally; and for related purposes

[12 November 1975]

PART I
DISCRIMINATION TO WHICH ACT APPLIES

[1 Direct and indirect discrimination against women

(1) In any circumstances relevant for the purposes of any provision of this Act, other than a provision to which subsection (2) applies, a person discriminates against a woman if—

(a) on the ground of her sex he treats her less favourably than he treats or would treat a man, or

(b) he applies to her a requirement or condition which he applies or would apply equally to a man but—

(i) which is such that the proportion of women who can comply with it is considerably smaller than the proportion of men who can comply with it, and

(ii) which he cannot show to be justifiable irrespective of the sex of the person to whom it is applied, and

(iii) which is to her detriment because she cannot comply with it.

(2) In any circumstances relevant for the purposes of a provision to which this subsection applies, a person discriminates against a woman if—

(a) on the ground of her sex, he treats her less favourably than he treats or would treat a man, or

[(b) he applies to her a provision, criterion or practice which he applies or would apply equally to a man, but—

(i) which puts or would put women at a particular disadvantage when compared with men,

(ii) which puts her at that disadvantage, and

(iii) which he cannot show to be a proportionate means of achieving a legitimate aim].

(3) Subsection (2) applies to—

(a) any provision of Part 2,

[(aa) sections 29 to 31, except in so far as they relate to an excluded matter,]

(b) sections 35A and 35B, and

(c) any other provision of Part 3, so far as it applies to vocational training.

(4) …]

[808]

NOTES

Substituted by SI 2001/2660, reg 3.

Sub-s (2): para (b) substituted by SI 2005/2467, reg 3(1).

Sub-s (3): para (aa) inserted by SI 2008/963, reg 2(1), Sch 1, para 1.

Sub-s (4): repealed by the Civil Partnership Act 2004, ss 251(1), (3), 261(4), Sch 30.

See further: the Employment Act 1989, s 1(3).

Transfer of Functions: functions of the Secretary of State for Trade and Industry transferred to the Secretary of State for Communities and Local Government, by the Secretary of State for Communities and Local Government Order 2006, SI 2006/1926, arts 7(1), (2), (3)(b), 8.

2 Sex discrimination against men

(1) Section 1, and the provisions of Parts II and III relating to sex discrimination against women, are to be read as applying equally to the treatment of men, and for that purpose shall have effect with such modifications as are requisite.

(2) In the application of subsection (1) no account shall be taken of special treatment afforded to women in connection with pregnancy or childbirth.

[809]

NOTES

Transfer of functions: see the note to s 1 at **[808]**.

[2A Discrimination on the grounds of gender reassignment

(1) A person ("A") discriminates against another person ("B") in any circumstances relevant for the purposes of—

(a) any provision of Part II,

[(aa) section 29, 30 or 31, except in so far as it relates to an excluded matter,]

(b) section 35A or 35B, or

(c) any other provision of Part III, so far as it applies to vocational training,

if he treats B less favourably than he treats or would treat other persons, and does so on the ground that B intends to undergo, is undergoing or has undergone gender reassignment.

(2) Subsection (3) applies to arrangements made by any person in relation to another's absence from work or from vocational training.

(3) For the purposes of subsection (1), B is treated less favourably than others under such arrangements if, in the application of the arrangements to any absence due to B undergoing gender reassignment—

(a) he is treated less favourably than he would be if the absence was due to sickness or injury, or

(b) he is treated less favourably than he would be if the absence was due to some other cause and, having regard to the circumstances of the case, it is reasonable for him to be treated no less favourably.

(4) In subsections (2) and (3) "arrangements" includes terms, conditions or arrangements on which employment, a pupillage or tenancy or vocational training is offered.

(5) For the purposes of subsection (1), a provision mentioned in that subsection framed with reference to discrimination against women shall be treated as applying equally to the treatment of men with such modifications as are requisite.]

[810]

NOTES

Inserted by SI 1999/1102, reg 2(1).

Sub-s (1): para (aa) inserted by SI 2008/963, reg 2(1), Sch 1, para 2.

Transfer of functions: see the note to s 1 at **[808]**.

3–21 (*Ss 3–5, ss 6–21* (*Pt II*) *outside the scope of this work.*)

PART III
DISCRIMINATION IN OTHER FIELDS

21A–28 (*Outside the scope of this work.*)

Goods, facilities, services and premises

29 Discrimination in provision of goods, facilities or services

(1) It is unlawful for any person concerned with the provision (for payment or not) of goods, facilities or services to the public or a section of the public to discriminate against a woman who seeks to obtain or use those goods, facilities or services—

(a) by refusing or deliberately omitting to provide her with any of them, or

(b) by refusing or deliberately omitting to provide her with goods, facilities or services of the like quality, in the like manner and on the like terms as are normal in his case in relation to male members of the public or (where she belongs to a section of the public) to male members of that section.

(2) The following are examples of the facilities and services mentioned in subsection (1)—

(a) access to and use of any place which members of the public or a section of the public are permitted to enter;

(b) accommodation in a hotel, boarding house or other similar establishment;

(c) facilities by way of banking or insurance or for grants, loans, credit or finance;

(d) facilities for education;

(e) facilities for entertainment, recreation or refreshment;

(f) facilities for transport or travel;

(g) the services of any profession or trade, or any local or other public authority.

[(2A) It is unlawful in connection with the provision of goods, facilities or services to the public or a section of the public (except in so far as they relate to an excluded matter) for any person to subject to harassment—

(a) a woman who seeks to obtain or use those goods, facilities or services, or

(b) a woman to whom he provides those goods, facilities or services.]

(3) For the avoidance of doubt it is hereby declared that where a particular skill is commonly exercised in a different way for men and for women it does not contravene subsection (1) for a person who does not normally exercise it for women to insist on exercising it for a woman only in accordance with his normal practice or, if he reasonably considers it impracticable to do that in her case, to refuse or deliberately omit to exercise it.

[(4) In its application in relation … to discrimination falling within section 2A, subsection (1)(b) shall have effect as if references to male members of the public, or of a section of the public, were references to members of the public, or of a section of the public, who do not intend to undergo, are not undergoing and have not undergone gender reassignment.]

[811]

NOTES

Sub-s (2A): inserted by SI 2008/963, reg 2(1), Sch 1, para 4(a).

Sub-s (4): inserted by SI 1999/1102, reg 6; words omitted repealed by SI 2008/963, reg 2(1), Sch 1, para 4(b).

See further: the Employment Act 1989, ss 4, 5.

Transfer of functions: see the note to s 1 at **[808]**.

30 Discrimination in disposal or management of premises

(1) It is unlawful for a person, in relation to premises in Great Britain of which he has power to dispose, to discriminate against a women—

(a) in the terms on which he offers her those premises, or

(b) by refusing her application for those premises, or

(c) in his treatment of her in relation to any list of persons in need of premises of that description.

[(1A) It is unlawful for such a person to subject to harassment a woman who applies for the premises.]

(2) It is unlawful for a person, in relation to premises managed by him, to discriminate against a woman occupying the premises—

(a) in the way he affords her access to any benefits or facilities, or by refusing or deliberately omitting to afford her access to them, or
(b) by evicting her, or subjecting her to any other detriment.

[(2A) It is unlawful for such a person to subject to harassment a woman who occupies the premises.]

(3) Subsection (1) does not apply to a person who owns an estate or interest in the premises and wholly occupies them unless he uses the services of an estate agent for the purposes of the disposal of the premises, or publishes or causes to be published an advertisement in connection with the disposal.

[(4) Subsections (1A) and (2A) apply in relation to an application for or occupation of premises except in so far as they relate to an excluded matter.]

[812]

NOTES

Sub-ss (1A), (2A), (4): inserted by SI 2008/963, reg 2(1), Sch 1, para 5.
See further: the Employment Act 1989, ss 4, 5.
Transfer of functions: see the note to s 1 at **[808]**.

31 Discrimination: consent for assignment or sub-letting

(1) Where the licence or consent of the landlord or of any other person is required for the disposal to any person of premises in Great Britain comprised in a tenancy, it is unlawful for the landlord or other person—

[(a) to discriminate against a woman by withholding the licence or consent for disposal of the premises to her, or
(b) in relation to such a licence or consent, to subject to harassment a woman to whom the disposal would be made if the licence or consent were given].

(2) Subsection (1) does not apply if—

(a) the person withholding a licence or consent, or a near relative of his ("the relevant occupier") resides, and intends to continue to reside, on the premises, and
(b) there is on the premises, in addition to the accommodation occupied by the relevant occupier, accommodation (not being storage accommodation or means of access) shared by the relevant occupier with other persons residing on the premises who are not members of his household, and
(c) the premises are small premises as defined in section 32(2).

(3) In this section "tenancy" means a tenancy created by a lease or sub- lease, by an agreement for a lease or sub-lease or by a tenancy agreement or in pursuance of any enactment; and "disposal", in relation to premises comprised in a tenancy, includes assignment or assignation of the tenancy and sub-letting or parting with possession of the premises or any part of the premises.

(4) This section applies to tenancies created before the passing of this Act, as well as to others.

[813]

NOTES

Sub-s (1): paras (a), (b) substituted by SI 2008/963, reg 2(1), Sch 1, para 6
See further: the Employment Act 1989, ss 4, 5.
Transfer of functions: see the note to s 1 at **[808]**.

32 Exception for small dwellings

(1) Sections 29(1) and 30 do not apply to the provision by a person of accommodation in any premises, or the disposal of premises by him, if—

(a) that person or a near relative of his ("the relevant occupier") resides, and intends to continue to reside, on the premises, and
(b) there is on the premises, in addition to the accommodation occupied by the relevant occupier, accommodation (not being storage accommodation or means of access) shared by the relevant occupier with other persons residing on the premises who are not members of his household, and
(c) the premises are small premises.

(2) Premises shall be treated for the purposes of subsection (1) as small premises if—

(a) in the case of premises comprising residential accommodation for one or more households (under separate letting or similar agreements) in addition to the accommodation occupied by the relevant occupier, there is not normally residential accommodation for more than two such households and only the relevant occupier and any member of his household reside in the accommodation occupied by him;
(b) in the case of premises not falling within paragraph (a), there is not normally residential

accommodation on the premises for more than six persons in addition to the relevant occupier and any members of his household.

[814]

NOTES

See further: the Employment Act 1989, ss 4, 5.
Transfer of functions: see the note to s 1 at **[808]**.

33 Exception for political parties

(1) This section applies to a political party if—

(a) it has as its main object, or one of its main objects, the promotion of parliamentary candidatures for the Parliament of the United Kingdom, or

(b) it is an affiliate of, or has as an affiliate, or has similar formal links with, a political party within paragraph (*a*).

(2) Nothing in section 29(1) shall be construed as affecting any special provision for persons of one sex only in the constitution, organisation or administration of the political party.

(3) Nothing in section 29(1) shall render unlawful an act done in order to give effect to such a special provision.

[815]

NOTES

See further: the Employment Act 1989, ss 4, 5.
Transfer of functions: see the note to s 1 at **[808]**.

34 Exception for voluntary bodies

(1) This section applies to a body—

(a) the activities of which are carried on otherwise than for profit, and

(b) which was not set up by any enactment.

(2) Sections 29(1) and 30 shall not be construed as rendering unlawful—

(a) the restriction of membership of any such body to persons of one sex (disregarding any minor exceptions), or

(b) the provision of benefits, facilities or services to members of any such body where the membership is so restricted,

even though membership of the body is open to the public, or to a section of the public.

(3) Nothing in section 29 or 30 shall—

(a) be construed as affecting a provision to which this subsection applies, or

(b) render unlawful an act which is done in order to give effect to such a provision.

(4) Subsection (3) applies to a provision for conferring benefits on persons of one sex only (disregarding any benefits to persons to the opposite sex which are exceptional or are relatively insignificant), being a provision which constitutes the main object of a body within subsection (1).

[(5) Subsections (2) to (4) do not apply to discrimination under section 1 or 2A in its application to sections 29 to 31 unless the treatment mentioned in those subsections is—

(a) a proportionate means of achieving a legitimate aim, or

(b) for the purpose of preventing or compensating for a disadvantage linked to sex.]

[816]

NOTES

Sub-s (5): inserted by SI 2008/963, reg 2(1), Sch 1, para 7.
See further: the Employment Act 1989, ss 4, 5.
Transfer of functions: see the note to s 1 at **[808]**.

35 Further exceptions from ss 29(1) and 30

(1) A person who provides at any place facilities or services restricted to men does not for that reason contravene section 29(1) if [any of the conditions in subsections (1A) to (1C) is satisfied.]

[(1A) The condition is that the place is, or is part of—

(a) a hospital, or

(b) any other establishment for persons requiring special care, supervision or attention.

(1B) The condition is that the place is (permanently or for the time being) occupied or used for the purposes of an organised religion, and the facilities or services are restricted to men so as to comply with the doctrines of that religion or avoid offending the religious susceptibilities of a significant number of its followers.

(1C) The condition is that the facilities or services are provided for, or are likely to be used by, two or more persons at the same time, and—

(a) the facilities or services are such, or those persons are such, that male users are likely to suffer serious embarrassment at the presence of a woman, or
(b) the facilities or services are such that a user is likely to be in a state of undress and a male user might reasonably object to the presence of a female user.]

(2) A person who provides facilities or services restricted to men does not for that reason contravene section 29(1) if the services or facilities are such that physical contact between the user and any other person is likely, and that other person might reasonably object if the user were a woman.

[(2A) In their application to discrimination falling within section 2A, subsections (1A), (1C) and (2) shall apply to the extent that any such discrimination is a proportionate means of achieving a legitimate aim.]

(3) Sections 29(1) and 30 do not apply—
(a) to discrimination [or harassment] which is rendered unlawful by any provision in column 1 of the table below, or
(b) to discrimination [or harassment] which would be so unlawful but for any provision in column 2 of that table, or
(c) to discrimination [or harassment] which contravenes a term modified or included by virtue of an equality clause.

TABLE

Provision creating illegality	*Exception*
Part II	Sections 6(3), 7(1)(b), 15(4), 19 and 20.
	Schedule 4 paragraphs 1 and 2.
Section 22 or 23	[Sections 26 and 27].
	Schedule 4 paragraph 4.

[817]

NOTES

Sub-s (1): words in square brackets substituted by SI 2008/963, reg 2(1), Sch 1, para 8(a).
Sub-ss (1A)–(1C). (2A): inserted by SI 2008/963, reg 2(1), Sch 1, para 8(b) (c).
Sub-s (3): in paras (a)–(c) words in square brackets inserted by SI 2008/963, reg 2(1), Sch 1, para 8(d); in the Table entry relating to "Section 22 or 23" words in square brackets substituted by SI 2005/2467, reg 23(1)(b).
See further: the Employment Act 1989, ss 4, 5.
Transfer of functions: see the note to s 1 at **[808]**.

[35ZA Excluded matters

Each of the following is an excluded matter for the purposes of sections 29 to 31—
(a) education (including vocational training);
(b) the content of media and advertisements;
(c) the provision of goods, facilities or services (not normally provided on a commercial basis) at a place (permanently or for the time being) occupied or used for the purposes of an organised religion.]

[817A]

NOTES

Inserted by SI 2008/963, reg 2(1), Sch 1, para 9(1).

35A–87 (*Ss 35A–36, ss 37–87* (*Pts IV–VIII*) *outside the scope of this work.*)

(*Schs 1–6 outside the scope of this work.*)

LOCAL LAND CHARGES ACT 1975

(1975 c 76)

An Act to make fresh provision for and in connection with the keeping of local land charges registers and the registration of matters therein

[12 November 1975]

Definition of local land charges

1 Local land charges

(1) A charge or other matter affecting land is a local land charge if it falls within any of the following descriptions and is not one of the matters set out in section 2 below:—

(a) any charge acquired either before or after the commencement of this Act by a local authority [or National Park authority], water authority [sewerage undertaker] or new town development corporation under the Public Health Acts 1936 and 1937, ... the Public Health Act 1961 or [the Highways Act 1980 (or any Act repealed by that Act)] [or the Building Act 1984], or any similar charge acquired by a local authority [or National Park authority] under any other Act, whether passed before or after this Act, being a charge that is binding on successive owners of the land affected;

(b) any prohibition of or restriction on the use of land—

(i) imposed by a local authority [or National Park authority] on or after 1st January 1926 (including any prohibition or restriction embodied in any condition attached to a consent, approval or licence granted by a local authority on or after that date), or

(ii) enforceable by a local authority [or National Park authority] under any covenant or agreement made with them on or after that date,

being a prohibition or restriction binding on successive owners of the land affected;

(c) any prohibition of or restriction on the use of land—

(i) imposed by a Minister of the Crown or government department on or after the date of the commencement of this Act (including any prohibition or restriction embodied in any condition attached to a consent, approval or licence granted by such a Minister or department on or after that date), or

(ii) enforceable by such a Minister or department under any covenant or agreement made with him or them on or after that date, being a prohibition or restriction binding on successive owners of the land affected;

(d) any positive obligation affecting land enforceable by a Minister of the Crown, government department or local authority [or National Park authority] under any covenant or agreement made with him or them on or after the date of the commencement of this Act and binding on successive owners of the land affected;

(e) any charge or other matter which is expressly made a local land charge by any statutory provision not contained in this section.

(2) For the purposes of subsection (1)(a) above, any sum which is recoverable from successive owners or occupiers of the land in respect of which the sum is recoverable shall be treated as a charge, whether the sum is expressed to be a charge on the land or not.

[(3) For the purposes of this section and section 2 of this Act, the Broads Authority shall be treated as a local authority [or National Park authority].]

[818]

NOTES

Sub-s (1): words "or National Park authority" wherever they occur inserted by the Environment Act 1995, s 78, Sch 10, para 14; second words in square brackets inserted by the Water Act 1989, s 190, Sch 25, para 52; words omitted repealed and third words in square brackets substituted by the Highways Act 1980, s 343(2), Sch 24, para 26; fourth words in square brackets inserted by the Building Act 1984, s 133(1), Sch 6, para 16.

Sub-s (3): inserted by the Norfolk and Suffolk Broads Act 1988, s 21, Sch 6, para 14; words in square brackets inserted by the Environment Act 1995, s 78, Sch 10, para 14.

See further, in relation to local land charges: the Care of Churches and Ecclesiastical Jurisdiction Measure 1991, s 22(8).

2 Matters which are not local land charges

The following matters are not local land charges—

(a) a prohibition or restriction enforceable under a covenant or agreement made between a lessor and a lessee;

(b) a positive obligation enforceable under a covenant or agreement made between a lessor and a lessee;

(c) a prohibition or restriction enforceable by a Minister of the Crown, government department or local authority [or National Park authority] under any covenant or agreement, being a prohibition or restriction binding on successive owners of the land affected by reason of the fact that the covenant or agreement is made for the benefit of land of the Minister, government department or local authority [or National Park authority];

(d) a prohibition or restriction embodied in any bye-laws;

(e) a condition or limitation subject to which planning permission was granted at any time before the commencement of this Act or was or is (at any time) deemed to be granted under any statutory provision relating to town and country planning, whether by a Minister of the Crown, government department or local authority [or National Park authority];

(f) a prohibition or restriction embodied in a scheme under the Town and Country Planning Act 1932 or any enactment repealed by that Act;

(g) a prohibition or restriction enforceable under a forestry dedication covenant entered into pursuant to section 5 of the Forestry Act 1967;

(h) a prohibition or restriction affecting the whole of any of the following areas—

(i) England, Wales or England and Wales;

(ii) England, or England and Wales, with the exception of, or of any part of, Greater London;

(iii) Greater London.

[819]

NOTES

Words in square brackets inserted by the Environment Act 1995, s 78, Sch 10, para 14.

Disapplication: sub-s (c) is disapplied with respect to prohibitions or restrictions on land use imposed for Crossrail purposes: see the Crossrail Act 2008, s 44(3).

See further, in relation to estate management schemes: the Leasehold Reform, Housing and Urban Development Act 1993, s 70(11).

Local land charges registers, registration and related matters

3 Registering authorities, local land charges registers, and indexes

(1) Each of the following local authorities—

(a) the council of any district;

[(aa) a Welsh county council;

(ab) a county borough council;]

(b) the council of any London borough; and

(c) the Common Council of the City of London,

shall be a registering authority for the purposes of this Act.

(2) There shall continue to be kept for the area of each registering authority—

(a) a local land charges register, and

(b) an index whereby all entries made in that register can readily be traced,

and as from the commencement of this Act the register and index kept for the area of a registering authority shall be kept by that authority.

[(3) Neither a local land charges register nor an index such as is mentioned in subsection (2)(b) above need be kept in documentary form.]

(4) For the purposes of this Act the area of the Common Council of the City of London includes the Inner Temple and the Middle Temple.

[820]

NOTES

Sub-s (1): paras (aa), (ab) inserted by the Local Government (Wales) Act 1994, s 66(6), Sch 16, para 49.

Sub-s (3): substituted by the Local Government (Miscellaneous Provisions) Act 1982, s 34(a).

4 The appropriate local land charges register

In this Act … , unless the context otherwise requires, "the appropriate local land charges register", in relation to any land or to a local land charge, means the local land charges register for the area in which the land or, as the case may be, the land affected by the charge is situated or, if the land in question is situated in two or more areas for which local land charges registers are kept, each of the local land charges registers kept for those areas respectively.

[821]

NOTES

Words omitted repealed by the Interpretation Act 1978, s 25(1), Sch 3.

5 Registration

(1) Subject to subsection (6) below, where the originating authority as respects a local land charge are the registering authority, it shall be their duty to register it in the appropriate local land charges register.

(2) Subject to subsection (6) below, where the originating authority as respects a local land charge are not the registering authority, it shall be the duty of the originating authority to apply to the registering authority for its registration in the appropriate local land charges register and upon any such application being made it shall be the duty of the registering authority to register the charge accordingly.

(3) The registration in a local land charges register of a local land charge, or of any matter which when registered becomes a local land charge, shall be carried out by reference to the land affected or such part of it as is situated in the area for which the register is kept.

(4) In this Act, "the originating authority", as respects a local land charge, means the Minister of the Crown, government department, local authority or other person by whom the charge is brought into existence or by whom, on its coming into existence, the charge is enforceable; and for this purpose—

(a) where a matter that is a local land charge consists of or is embodied in, or is otherwise given effect by, an order, scheme or other instrument made or confirmed by a Minister of the Crown or government department on the application of another authority the charge shall be treated as brought into existence by that other authority; and

(b) a local land charge brought into existence by a Minister of the Crown or government department on an appeal from a decision or determination of another authority or in the exercise of powers ordinarily exercisable by another authority shall be treated as brought into existence by that other authority.

(5) The registration of a local land charge may be cancelled pursuant to an order of the court.

(6) Where a charge or other matter is registrable in a local land charges register and before the commencement of this Act was also registrable in a register kept under the Land Charges Act 1972, then, if before the commencement of this Act it was registered in a register kept under that Act, there shall be no duty to register it, or to apply for its registration, under this Act and section 10 below shall not apply in relation to it.

[822]

6 Local authority's right to register a general charge against land in certain circumstances

(1) Where a local authority have incurred any expenditure in respect of which, when any relevant work is completed and any requisite resolution is passed or order is made, there will arise in their favour a local land charge (in this section referred to as "the specific charge"), the following provisions of this section shall apply.

(2) At any time before the specific charge comes into existence, a general charge against the land, without any amount being specified, may be registered in the appropriate local land charges register by the registering authority if they are the originating authority and, if they are not, shall be registered therein by them if the originating authority make an application for that purpose.

(3) A general charge registered under this section shall be a local land charge, but section 5(1) and (2) above shall not apply in relation to such a charge.

(4) If a general charge is registered under this section pursuant to an application by the originating authority, they shall, when the specific charge comes into existence, notify the registering authority of that fact, and any such notification shall be treated as an application (subject to subsection (5) below) for the cancellation of the general charge and the registration of the specific charge.

(5) Where a general charge is registered under this section its registration shall be cancelled within such period starting with the day on which the specific charge comes into existence, and not being less than 1 year, as may be prescribed, and the specific charge shall not be registered before the general charge is cancelled.

(6) If the registration of the general charge is duly cancelled within the period specified in subsection (5) above and the specific charge is registered forthwith upon the cancellation or was discharged before the cancellation, then, for the purposes of section 10 below, the specific charge shall be treated as having come into existence at the time when the general charge was cancelled.

[823]

7 Effect of registering certain financial charges

A local land charge falling within section 1(1)(a) above shall, when registered, take effect as if it had been created by a deed of charge by way of legal mortgage within the meaning of the Law of Property Act 1925, but without prejudice to the priority of the charge.

[824]

Searches

8 Personal searches

(1) Any person may search in any local land charges register on paying the prescribed fee.

[(1A) If a local land charges register is kept otherwise than in documentary form, the entitlement of a person to search in it is satisfied if the registering authority makes the portion of it which he wishes to examine available for inspection in visible and legible form.]

(2) Without prejudice to [subsections (1) and (1A)] above, a registering authority may provide facilities for enabling persons entitled to search in the authority's local land charges register to see photographic or other images or copies of any portion of the register which they may wish to examine.

[825]

NOTES

Sub-s (1A): inserted by the Local Government (Miscellaneous Provisions) Act 1982, s 34(b).

Sub-s (2): words in square brackets substituted by the Local Government (Miscellaneous Provisions) Act 1982, s 34(c).

9 Official searches

(1) Where any person requires an official search of the appropriate local land charges register to be made in respect of any land, he may make a requisition in that behalf to the registering authority.

(2) *A requisition under this section must be in writing, and* for the purposes of serving any such requisition on the Common Council of the City of London section 231(1) of the Local Government Act 1972 shall apply in relation to that Council as it applies in relation to a local authority within the meaning of that Act.

[(3) In relation to England, the fee (if any) specified by a registering authority under section 13A below shall be payable, in such manner as the authority may specify, in respect of any requisition made under this section to that authority.

(3A) In relation to Wales, the prescribed fee (if any) shall be payable in the prescribed manner in respect of any requisition made under this section.]

(4) Where a requisition is made to a registering authority under this section and the fee [(if any)] payable in respect of it is paid in accordance with subsection (3) [or (3A)] above, the registering authority shall thereupon make the search required and shall issue an official certificate setting out the result of the search.

[826]

NOTES

Sub-s (2): words in italics repealed by the Local Government and Housing Act 1989, ss 158, 194, Sch 12, Pt II, as from a day to be appointed.

Sub-ss (3), (3A): substituted, for original sub-s (3), by the Constitutional Reform Act 2005, s 15(1), Sch 4, Pt 1, paras 82, 84(1), (2).

Sub-s (4): words in square brackets inserted by the Constitutional Reform Act 2005, s 15(1), Sch 4, Pt 1, paras 82, 84(1), (3).

Compensation for non-registration or defective official search certificate

10 Compensation for non-registration or defective official search certificate

(1) Failure to register a local land charge in the appropriate local land charges register shall not affect the enforceability of the charge but where a person has purchased any land affected by a local land charge, then—

(a) in a case where a material personal search of the appropriate local land charges register was made in respect of the land in question before the relevant time, if at the time of the search the charge was in existence but not registered in that register; or

[(aa) in a case where the appropriate local land charges register kept otherwise than in documentary form and a material personal search of that register was made in respect of the land in question before the relevant time, if the entitlement to search in that register conferred by section 8 above was not satisfied as mentioned in subsection (1A) of that section; or]

(b) in a case where a material official search of the appropriate local land charges register was made in respect of the land in question before the relevant time, if the charge was in existence at the time of the search but (whether registered or not) was not shown by the official search certificate as registered in that register,

the purchaser shall (subject to section 11(1) below) be entitled to compensation for any loss suffered by him [in consequence].

(2) At any time when rules made under this Act make provision for local land charges registers to be divided into parts then, for the purposes of subsection (1) above—

(a) a search (whether personal or official) of a part or parts only of any such register shall not constitute a search of that register in relation to any local land charge registrable in a part of the register not searched; and

(b) a charge shall not be taken to be registered in the appropriate local land charges register unless registered in the appropriate part of the register.

(3) For the purposes of this section—

(a) a person purchases land where, for valuable consideration, he acquires any interest in land or the proceeds of sale of land, and this includes cases where he acquires as lessee or mortgagee and shall be treated as including cases where an interest is conveyed or assigned at his direction to another person;

(b) the relevant time—

 (i) where the acquisition of the interest in question was preceded by a contract for its acquisition, other than a qualified liability contract, is the time when that contract was made;

 (ii) in any other case, is the time when the purchaser acquired the interest in question or, if he acquired it under a disposition which took effect only when registered [in the register of title kept under the Land Registration Act 2002], the time when that disposition was made; and for the purposes of sub-paragraph (i) above, a qualified liability contract is a contract containing a term the effect of which is to make the liability of the purchaser dependent upon, or avoidable by reference to, the outcome of a search for local land charges affecting the land to be purchased;

(c) a personal search is material if, but only if—

 (i) it is made after the commencement of this Act, and

 (ii) it is made by or on behalf of the purchaser or, before the relevant time, the purchaser or his agent has knowledge of the result of it;

(d) an official search is material if, but only if—

 (i) it is made after the commencement of this Act, and

 (ii) it is requisitioned by or on behalf of the purchaser or, before the relevant time, the purchaser or his agent has knowledge of the contents of the official search certificate.

(4) Any compensation for loss under this section shall be paid by the registering authority in whose area the land affected is situated; and where the purchaser has incurred expenditure for the purpose of obtaining compensation under this section, the amount of the compensation shall include the amount of the expenditure reasonably incurred by him for that purpose (so far as that expenditure would not otherwise fall to be treated as loss for which he is entitled to compensation under this section).

(5) Where any compensation for loss under this section is paid by a registering authority in respect of a local land charge as respects which they are not the originating authority, then, unless an application for registration of the charge was made to the registering authority by the originating authority in time for it to be practicable for the registering authority to avoid incurring liability to pay that compensation, an amount equal thereto shall be recoverable from the originating authority by the registering authority.

(6) Where any compensation for loss under this section is paid by a registering authority, no part of the amount paid, or of any corresponding amount paid to that authority by the originating authority under subsection (5) above, shall be recoverable by the registering authority or the originating authority from any other person except as provided by subsection (5) above or under a policy of insurance or on grounds of fraud.

(7) In the case of an action to recover compensation under this section the cause of action shall be deemed for the purposes of the Limitation Act 1939 to accrue at the time when the local land charge comes to the notice of the purchaser; and for the purposes of this subsection the question when the charge came to his notice shall be determined without regard to the provisions of section 198 of the Law of Property Act 1925 (under which registration under certain enactments is deemed to constitute actual notice).

[(8) Where the amount claimed by way of compensation under this section does not exceed £5,000, proceedings for the recovery of such compensation may be begun in a county court.]

(9) If in any proceedings for the recovery of compensation under this section the court dismisses a claim to compensation, it shall not order the purchaser to pay the registering authority's costs unless it considers that it was unreasonable for the purchaser to commence the proceedings.
[827]

NOTES

Sub-s (1): para (aa) inserted and other words in square brackets substituted by the Local Government (Miscellaneous Provisions) Act 1982, s 34(d).

Sub-s (3): words in square brackets in para (b)(ii) substituted by the Land Registration Act 2002, s 133, Sch 11, para 13.

Sub-s (8): substituted for existing sub-ss (8), (8A), by SI 1991/724, art 2(2)(a), (8), Schedule, Pt I.

11 Mortgages, trusts for sale and settled land

(1) Where there appear to be grounds for a claim under section 10 above in respect of an interest that is subject to a mortgage—

(a) the claim may be made by any mortgagee of the interest as if he were the person entitled to that interest but without prejudice to the making of a claim by that person;

(b) no compensation shall be payable under that section in respect of the interest of the mortgagee (as distinct from the interest which is subject to the mortgage);

(c) any compensation payable under that section in respect of the interest that is subject to the mortgage shall be paid to the mortgagee or, if there is more than one mortgagee, to the first mortgagee and shall in either case be applied by him as if it were proceeds of sale.

(2) Where an interest is [subject to a trust of land] any compensation payable in respect of it under section 10 above shall be dealt with as if it were proceeds of sale arising under the trust.

(3) Where an interest is settled land for the purposes of the Settled Land Act 1925 any compensation payable in respect of it under section 10 above shall be treated as capital money arising under that Act.

[828]

NOTES

Sub-s (2): words in square brackets substituted by the Trusts of Land and Appointment of Trustees Act 1996, s 25(1), Sch 3, para 14; for savings in relation to entailed interests created before the commencement of that Act, and savings consequential upon the abolition of the doctrine of conversion, see s 25(4), (5) thereof.

Miscellaneous and supplementary

12 Office copies as evidence

An office copy of an entry in any local land charges register shall be admissible in evidence in all proceedings and between all parties to the same extent as the original would be admissible.

[829]

13 Protection of solicitors, trustees etc

A solicitor or a trustee, personal representative, agent or other person in a fiduciary position, shall not be answerable in respect of any loss occasioned by reliance on an erroneous official search certificate or an erroneous office copy of an entry in a local land charges register.

[830]–[831]

NOTES

Modification: modified by the Building Societies Act 1986, s 124, Sch 21, paras 9, 12 and the Administration of Justice Act 1985, ss 9, 34(2), Sch 2, para 37.

13A–15 (*Outside the scope of this work.*)

16 Interpretation

(1) In this Act, except where the context otherwise requires—

"the appropriate local land charges register" has the meaning provided by section 4 above;

"the court" means the High Court, or the county court in a case where the county court has jurisdiction;

"land" includes mines and minerals, whether or not severed from the surface, buildings or parts of buildings (whether the division is horizontal, vertical or made in any other way) and other corporeal hereditaments;

"official search certificate" means a certificate issued pursuant to section 9(4) above;

"the originating authority", as respects a local land charge, has the meaning provided by section 5(4) above;

"personal search" means a search pursuant to section 8 above;

"prescribed" means prescribed by rules made under section 14 above;

"the registering authority", in relation to any land or to a local land charge, means the registering authority in whose area the land or, as the case may be, the land affected by the charge is situated, or, if the land in question is situated in the areas of two or more registering authorities each of those authorities respectively;

"statutory provision" means a provision of this Act or of any other Act or Measure, whenever passed, or a provision of any rules, regulations, order or similar instrument made (whether before or after the passing of this Act) under an Act, whenever passed.

[(1A) Any reference in this Act to an office copy of an entry includes a reference to the reproduction of an entry in a register kept otherwise than in documentary form.]

(2) Except in so far as the context otherwise requires, any reference in this Act to an enactment is a reference to that enactment as amended, extended or applied by or under any other enactment, including this Act.

[832]

NOTES

Sub-s (1A): inserted by the Local Government (Miscellaneous Provisions) Act 1982, s 34(e).

17–19 (*Outside the scope of this work.*)

20 Short title etc

(1) This Act may be cited as the Local Land Charges Act 1975.

(2) This Act binds the Crown, but nothing in this Act shall be taken to render land owned by or occupied for the purposes of the Crown subject to any charge to which, independently of this Act, it would not be subject.

(3) …

(4) This Act extends to England and Wales only.

[833]

NOTES

Sub-s (3): repealed by the Statute Law (Repeals) Act 2004.

Order: the Local Land Charges Act 1975 (Commencement) Order 1977, SI 1977/984.

(*Sch 1 contains consequential amendments; Sch 2 contains repeals.*)

RACE RELATIONS ACT 1976

(1976 c 74)

An Act to make fresh provision with respect to discrimination on racial grounds and relations between people of different racial groups; and to make in the Sex Discrimination Act 1975 amendments for bringing provisions in that Act relating to its administration and enforcement into conformity with the corresponding provisions in this Act

[22 November 1976]

PART I
DISCRIMINATION TO WHICH ACT APPLIES

1 Racial discrimination

(1) A person discriminates against another in any circumstances relevant for the purposes of any provision of this Act if—

(a) on racial grounds he treats that other less favourably than he treats or would treat other persons; or

(b) he applies to that other a requirement or condition which he applies or would apply equally to persons not of the same racial group as that other but—

(i) which is such that the proportion of persons of the same racial group as that other who can comply with it is considerably smaller than the proportion of persons not of that racial group who can comply with it; and

(ii) which he cannot show to be justifiable irrespective of the colour, race, nationality or ethnic or national origins of the person to whom it is applied; and

(iii) which is to the detriment of that other because he cannot comply with it.

[(1A) A person also discriminates against another if, in any circumstances relevant for the purposes of any provision referred to in subsection (1B), he applies to that other a provision, criterion or practice which he applies or would apply equally to persons not of the same race or ethnic or national origins as that other, but—

(a) which puts or would put persons of the same race or ethnic or national origins as that other at a particular disadvantage when compared with other persons,

(b) which puts [or would put] that other at that disadvantage, and

(c) which he cannot show to be a proportionate means of achieving a legitimate aim.

(1B) The provisions mentioned in subsection (1A) are—

(a) Part II;

(b) sections 17 to 18D;

(c) section 19B, so far as relating to—

(i) any form of social security;

(ii) health care;

(iii) any other form of social protection; and

(iv) any form of social advantage;

which does not fall within section 20;

(d) sections 20 to 24;

(e) sections 26A and 26B;

(f) sections 76 and 76ZA; and

(g) Part IV, in its application to the provisions referred to in paragraphs (a) to (f).

(1C) Where, by virtue of subsection (1A), a person discriminates against another, subsection (1)(b) does not apply to him.]

(2) It is hereby declared that, for the purposes of this Act, segregating a person from other persons on racial grounds is treating him less favourably than they are treated.

[834]

NOTES

Sub-ss (1A)–(1C): inserted by SI 2003/1626, reg 3.
Sub-s (1A): in para (b) words in square brackets inserted by SI 2008/3008, reg 2.

2 Discrimination by way of victimisation

(1) A person ("the discriminator") discriminates against another person ("the person victimised") in any circumstances relevant for the purposes of any provision of this Act if he treats the person victimised less favourably than in those circumstances he treats or would treat other persons, and does so by reason that the person victimised has—

(a) brought proceedings against the discriminator or any other person under this Act; or
(b) given evidence or information in connection with proceedings brought by any person against the discriminator or any other person under this Act; or
(c) otherwise done anything under or by reference to this Act in relation to the discriminator or any other person; or
(d) alleged that the discriminator or any other person has committed an act which (whether or not the allegation so states) would amount to a contravention of this Act,

or by reason that the discriminator knows that the person victimised intends to do any of those things, or suspects that the person victimised has done, or intends to do, any of them.

(2) Subsection (1) does not apply to treatment of a person by reason of any allegation made by him if the allegation was false and not made in good faith.

[835]

3 Meaning of "racial grounds", "racial group" etc

(1) In this Act, unless the context otherwise requires—

"racial grounds" means any of the following grounds, namely colour, race nationality or ethnic or national origins;

"racial group" means a group of persons defined by reference to colour, race, nationality or ethnic or national origins, and references to a person's racial group refer to any racial group into which he falls.

(2) The fact that a racial group comprises two or more distinct racial groups does not prevent it from constituting a particular racial group for the purposes of this Act.

(3) In this Act—

(a) references to discrimination refer to any discrimination falling within section 1 or 2; and
(b) references to racial discrimination refer to any discrimination falling within section 1,

and related expressions shall be construed accordingly.

(4) A comparison of the case of a person of a particular racial group with that of a person not of that group under section 1(1) [or (1A)] must be such that the relevant circumstances in the one case are the same, or not materially different, in the other.

[836]

NOTES

Sub-s (4): words in square brackets inserted by SI 2003/1626, reg 4.

[3A Harassment

(1) A person subjects another to harassment in any circumstances relevant for the purposes of any provision referred to in section 1(1B) where, on grounds of race or ethnic or national origins, he engages in unwanted conduct which has the purpose or effect of—

(a) violating that other person's dignity, or
(b) creating an intimidating, hostile, degrading, humiliating or offensive environment for him.

(2) Conduct shall be regarded as having the effect specified in paragraph (a) or (b) of subsection (1) only if, having regard to all the circumstances, including in particular the perception of that other person, it should reasonably be considered as having that effect.]

[837]

NOTES

Inserted by SI 2003/1626, reg 5.

4–16 ((*Pt II*) *outside the scope of this work.*)

PART III
DISCRIMINATION IN OTHER FIELDS

17–19F (*Outside the scope of this work.*)

Goods, facilities, services and premises

20 ... Provision of goods, facilities or services

(1) It is unlawful for any person concerned with the provision (for payment or not) of goods, facilities or services to the public or a section of the public to discriminate against a person who seeks to obtain or use those goods, facilities or services—

(a) by refusing or deliberately omitting to provide him with any of them; or

(b) by refusing or deliberately omitting to provide him with goods, facilities or services of the like quality, in the like manner and on the like terms as are normal in the first-mentioned person's case in relation to other members of the public or (where the person so seeking belongs to a section of the public) to other members of that section.

(2) The following are examples of the facilities and services mentioned in subsection (1)—

(a) access to and use of any place which members of the public are permitted to enter;
(b) accommodation in a hotel, boarding house or other similar establishment;
(c) facilities by way of banking or insurance or for grants, loans, credit or finance;
(d) facilities for education;
(e) facilities for entertainment, recreation or refreshment;
(f) facilities for transport or travel;
(g) the services of any profession or trade, or any local or other public authority.

[(3) It is unlawful for any person concerned with the provision of goods, facilities or services as mentioned in subsection (1), in relation to such provision, to subject to harassment—

(a) a person who seeks to obtain or use those goods, facilities or services, or
(b) a person to whom he provides those goods, facilities or services.]

[838]

NOTES

Section heading: words omitted repealed by SI 2003/1626, reg 22(1).
Sub-s (3): inserted by SI 2003/1626, reg 22(2).

21 ... Disposal or management of premises

(1) It is unlawful for a person, in relation to premises in Great Britain of which he has power to dispose, to discriminate against another—

(a) in the terms on which he offers him those premises; or
(b) by refusing his application for those premises; or
(c) in his treatment of him in relation to any list of persons in need of premises of that description.

(2) It is unlawful for a person, in relation to premises managed by him, to discriminate against a person occupying the premises—

(a) in the way he affords him access to any benefits or facilities, or by refusing or deliberately omitting to afford him access to them; or
(b) by evicting him, or subjecting him to any other detriment.

[(2A) It is unlawful for a person, in relation to such premises as are referred to in subsection (1) or (2), to subject to harassment a person who applies for or, as the case may be, occupies such premises.]

(3) Subsection (1) does not apply to [discrimination, on grounds other than those of race or ethnic or national origins, by] a person who owns an estate or interest in the premises and wholly occupies them unless he uses the services of an estate agent for the purposes of the disposal of the premises, or publishes or causes to be published an advertisement in connection with the disposal.

[839]

NOTES

Section heading: words omitted repealed by SI 2003/1626, reg 23(1).
Sub-s (2A): inserted by SI 2003/1626, reg 23(2)(a).
Sub-s (3): words in square brackets inserted by SI 2003/1626, reg 23(2)(b).

22 Exception from ss 20(1) and 21: small dwellings

(1) Sections 20(1) and 21 do not apply to [discrimination on grounds other than those of race or ethnic or national origins in either] the provision by a person of accommodation in any premises, or the disposal of premises by him, if—

(a) that person or a near relative of his ("the relevant occupier") resides, and intends to continue to reside, on the premises; and
(b) there is on the premises, in addition to the accommodation occupied by the relevant occupier, accommodation (not being storage accommodation or means of access) shared by the relevant occupier with other persons residing on the premises who are not members of his household; and
(c) the premises are small premises.

(2) Premises shall be treated for the purposes of this section as small premises if—
(a) in the case of premises comprising residential accommodation for one or more households (under separate letting or similar agreements) in addition to the accommodation occupied by the relevant occupier, there is not normally residential accommodation for more than two such households and only the relevant occupier and any member of his household reside in the accommodation occupied by him;
(b) in the case of premises not falling within paragraph (a), there is not normally residential accommodation on the premises for more than six persons in addition to the relevant occupier and any members of his household.

[840]

NOTES

Sub-s (1): words in square brackets inserted by SI 2003/1626, reg 24.

23 Further exceptions from [ss 20] and 21

(1) Sections [20] and 21 do not apply—
(a) to discrimination [or harassment] which is rendered unlawful by any provision of Part II or section 17 or 18; or
(b) to discrimination which would be rendered unlawful by any provision of Part II but for any of the following provisions, namely sections 4(3)[, 4A(1)(b)], 5(1)(b), 6, 7(4), 9 and 14(4).

(2) Section 20(1) does not apply to anything done by a person as a participant in arrangements under which he (for reward or not) takes into his home, and treats as if they were members of his family, children, elderly persons, or persons requiring a special degree of care and attention.

[841]

NOTES

Section heading: reference in square brackets substituted by SI 2003/1626, reg 25(1).

Sub-s (1): reference in first pair of square brackets substituted and other words in square brackets inserted by SI 2003/1626, reg 25(2).

24 … Consent for assignment or sub-letting

(1) Where the licence or consent of the landlord or of any other person is required for the disposal to any person of premises in Great Britain comprised in a tenancy, it is unlawful for the landlord or other person—
[(a) to discriminate against a person by withholding the licence or consent for disposal of the premises to him, or
(b) in relation to such a licence or consent, to subject to harassment a person who applies for the licence or consent, or from whom the licence or consent is withheld].

(2) Subsection (1) does not apply [to discrimination on grounds other than those of race or ethnic or national origins] if—
(a) the person withholding a licence or consent, or a near relative of his ("the relevant occupier") resides, and intends to continue to reside, on the premises; and
(b) there is on the premises, in addition to the accommodation occupied by the relevant occupier, accommodation (not being storage accommodation or means of access) shared by the relevant occupier with other persons residing on the premises who are not members of his household; and
(c) the premises are small premises.

(3) Section 22(2) (meaning of "small premises") shall apply for the purposes of this as well as of that section.

(4) In this section "tenancy" means a tenancy created by a lease or sub-lease, by an agreement for a lease or sub-lease or by a tenancy agreement or in pursuance of any enactment; and "disposal", in relation to premises comprised in a tenancy, includes assignment or assignation of the tenancy and sub-letting or parting with possession of the premises or any part of the premises.

(5) This section applies to tenancies created before the passing of this Act, as well as to others.

[842]

PART I STATUTES

NOTES

Section heading: word omitted repealed by SI 2003/1626, reg 26(1).
Sub-s (1): paras (a), (b) substituted by SI 2003/1626, reg 26(2)(a).
Sub-s (2): words in square brackets inserted by SI 2003/1626, reg 26(2)(b).

25–80 *(Ss 25–27, ss 27A–80 (Pts IV–X) outside the scope of this work.)*

(Schs 1–5 outside the scope of this work.)

RENTCHARGES ACT 1977

(1977 c 30)

An Act to prohibit the creation, and provide for the extinguishment, apportionment and redemption, of certain rentcharges

[22 July 1977]

Prohibition and extinguishment

1 Meaning of "rentcharge"

For the purposes of this Act "rentcharge" means any annual or other periodic sum charged on or issuing out of land, except—

(a) rent reserved by a lease or tenancy, or
(b) any sum payable by way of interest.

[843]

2 Creation of rentcharges prohibited

(1) Subject to this section, no rentcharge may be created whether at law or in equity after the coming into force of this section.

(2) Any instrument made after the coming into force of this section shall, to the extent that it purports to create a rentcharge the creation of which is prohibited by this section, be void.

(3) This section does not prohibit the creation of a rentcharge—

[(a) in the case of which paragraph 3 of Schedule 1 to the Trusts of Land and Appointment of Trustees Act 1996 (trust in case of family charge) applies to the land on which the rent is charged;
(b) in the case of which paragraph (a) above would have effect but for the fact that the land on which the rent is charged is settled land or subject to a trust of land;]
(c) which is an estate rentcharge;
(d) under any Act of Parliament providing for the creation of rentcharges in connection with the execution of works on land (whether by way of improvements, repairs or otherwise) or the commutation of any obligation to do any such work; or
(e) by, or in accordance with the requirements of, any order of a court.

(4) For the purposes of this section "estate rentcharge" means (subject to subsection (5) below) a rentcharge created for the purpose—

(a) of making covenants to be performed by the owner of the land affected by the rentcharge enforceable by the rent owner against the owner for the time being of the land; or
(b) of meeting, or contributing towards, the cost of the performance by the rent owner of covenants for the provision of services, the carrying out of maintenance or repairs, the effecting of insurance or the making of any payment by him for the benefit of the land affected by the rentcharge or for the benefit of that and other land.

(5) A rentcharge of more than a nominal amount shall not be treated as an estate rentcharge for the purposes of this section unless it represents a payment for the performance by the rent owner of any such covenant as is mentioned in subsection (4)(b) above which is reasonable in relation to that covenant.

[844]

NOTES

Sub-s (3): paras (a), (b) substituted by the Trusts of Land and Appointment of Trustees Act 1996, s 25(1), Sch 3, para 15(2); for savings in relation to entailed interests created before the commencement of that Act, and savings consequential upon the abolition of the doctrine of conversion, see s 25(4), (5) thereof.

3 Extinguishment of rentcharges

(1) Subject to this section, every rentcharge shall (if it has not then ceased to have effect) be extinguished at the expiry of the period of 60 years beginning—

(a) with the passing of this Act, or
(b) with the date on which the rentcharge first became payable, whichever is the later; and accordingly the land on which it was charged or out of which it issued shall, at the expiration of that period, be discharged and freed from the rentcharge.

(2) The extinguishment of a rentcharge under this section shall not affect the exercise by any person of any right or remedy for the recovery of any rent which accrues before the rentcharge is so extinguished.

(3) This section shall not have the effect of extinguishing any rentcharge—
(a) which is, by virtue of any enactment or agreement or by custom, charged on or otherwise payable in relation to land wholly or partly in lieu of tithes; or
(b) which is of a kind referred to in subsection (3) of section 2 above (disregarding subsection (5) of that section).

(4) Subsection (1) above shall not apply to a variable rentcharge; but where such a rentcharge ceases to be variable, subsection (1) above shall apply as if the date on which the rentcharge first became payable were the date on which it ceased to be variable.

(5) For the purposes of subsection (4) above, a rentcharge shall (at any time) be treated as variable if at any time thereafter the amount of the rentcharge will, or may, vary in accordance with the provisions of the instrument under which it is payable.

[845]

Apportionment

4 Application for apportionment

(1) The owner of any land which is affected by a rentcharge which also affects land which is not in his ownership may, subject to this section, apply to the Secretary of State for an order apportioning the rentcharge between that land and the remaining land affected by the rentcharge.

(2) The owner of any land which is affected by a rentcharge which does not affect land not in his ownership may apply to the Secretary of State for an order apportioning the rentcharge between such parts of his land as may be specified in the application.

(3) No application for apportionment may be made under this section in respect of—
(a) a rentcharge of a kind mentioned in section 2 (3)(d) or 3 (3)(a) above, or
(b) land affected by a rentcharge which also affects other land, if the whole of that other land is exonerated or indemnified from the whole of the rentcharge by means of a charge on the first mentioned land.

(4) Every application—
(a) under subsection (1) above, shall specify the amount (if any) equitably apportioned to the applicant's land, and
(b) under subsection (2) above, shall specify the applicant's proposal for apportioning the rentcharge between the parts of his land specified in the application.

(5) Subject to subsection (4) above, every application under this section shall be in such form and shall contain such information and be accompanied by such documents as may be prescribed by regulations.

(6) In any case where the Secretary of State considers that any additional document or information ought to be furnished by the applicant he may require the applicant—
(a) to deliver to him such documents (including documents of title and, in the case of registered land, an authority to inspect the register), and
(b) to furnish him with such information, as the Secretary of State may specify.

(7) Where an applicant's documents of title are in the custody of a mortgagee the mortgagee shall, if requested to do so by the Secretary of State for the purpose of an application made under this section, deliver those documents to the Secretary of State on such terms as to their custody and return as the mortgagee may reasonably require.

[846]

NOTES

Transfer of Functions: functions of the Secretary of State, so far as exercisable in relation to Wales, transferred to the National Assembly for Wales, by the National Assembly for Wales (Transfer of Functions) Order 1999, SI 1999/672, art 2, Sch 1.

Regulations: the Rentcharges Regulations 1978, SI 1978/16.

5 Apportionment

(1) Where an application for apportionment is made under section 4 above and the Secretary of State is satisfied that he is in a position to do so, he shall prepare a draft order for apportionment of the rentcharge.

(2) If the application is made under section 4 (1) above, the amount specified in the draft order as being that part of the rentcharge apportioned to the applicant's land shall be—

(a) the amount specified in the application as the amount equitably apportioned to that land; or

(b) where no amount has been equitably apportioned to that land, such amount as the Secretary of State considers appropriate.

(3) If the application is made under section 4 (2) above, the amounts specified in the draft order as apportioned between the parts of the applicant's land specified in the application shall be those proposed in the application.

(4) A copy of the draft order shall be served by the Secretary of State on the person appearing to him to be the rent owner or his agent, and, in a case falling within subsection (2)(b) above, on such persons as appear to him to be the owners of the land affected by the rentcharge.

(5) After service of a draft order on the rent owner or his agent under sub-section (4) above, the rent owner may, before the expiry of the period of 21 days beginning with the date on which the draft order is served (or such longer period, not exceeding the period of 42 days beginning with that date, as the Secretary of State may in a particular case allow)—

(a) object to it on the ground that such an apportionment would provide insufficient security for any part of the rentcharge;

(b) make an application to the effect that in the event of the apportionment not exceeding the sum mentioned in section 7 (2) below, a condition should be imposed under that section.

(6) Where a draft order is served under subsection (4) above on a person who is the owner of any land affected by the rentcharge, that person may, before the expiry of the period of 21 days beginning with the date on which the draft order is served (or such longer period, not exceeding the period of 42 days beginning with that date, as the Secretary of State may in a particular case allow), make representations to the Secretary of State concerning the apportionment specified in the draft order.

(7) Any objection, application or representations under subsection (5) or (6) above shall be made in writing.

(8) An objection under subsection (5) above shall state what apportionment (if any) would in the opinion of the rent owner provide sufficient security for the rentcharge or, as the case may be, part of the rentcharge.

(9) The Secretary of State shall consider any objection duly made under subsection (5) above and any representations duly made under subsection (6) above and, if he is satisfied that the draft order should be modified—

(a) in the case of an objection, in order to preserve for the rent owner sufficient security for each apportioned part of the rentcharge, or

(b) to take account of any such representations,

he shall make such modifications in the draft order as appear to him to be appropriate.

(10) Where—

(a) the relevant period has expired without any objection or representation having been duly made, or

(b) an objection has, or any representations have, been duly made and the objection has, or, as the case may be, all the representations have, been considered by the Secretary of State,

the Secretary of State shall, if the applicant has not then withdrawn his application and the Secretary of State is satisfied that it is appropriate to do so, make an order (an "apportionment order") in the form of the draft but incorporating—

(i) any modifications made by the Secretary of State in accordance with subsection (9) above, and

(iii) where appropriate, a condition imposed by virtue of section 7 (2) below.

(11) Immediately after making an apportionment order the Secretary of State shall serve copies of the order on the applicant and on the person appearing to him to be the rent owner or his agent, and, in a case falling within subsection (2)(b) above, on those persons on whom copies of the draft order were served under subsection (4) above.

(12) In a case where modifications have been made in a draft order under subsection (9) above, the Secretary of State shall not make an apportionment order without giving the applicant an opportunity to withdraw his application.

[847]

NOTES

Transfer of Functions: see the note to s 4 at **[846]**.

6 Appeal

(1) Where the applicant or the rent owner or, in a case falling within section 5 (2)(b) above, any other person who is the owner of any land affected by the rentcharge, is aggrieved by the terms of an apportionment order, he may appeal to the [Upper Tribunal].

(2) Where an appeal has been duly made to the [Upper Tribunal] under this section, the Tribunal shall—

(a) confirm the order, or
(b) set it aside, and, subject to section 7(2) below, make such other order apportioning the rentcharge as it thinks fit.

[848]

NOTES

Sub-ss (1), (2): words in square brackets substituted by SI 2009/1307, art 5(1), (2), Sch 1, paras 122, 123, subject to transitional and savings provisions in art 5(6), Sch 5 thereto.

7 Effect of apportionment order

(1) An apportionment order shall, subject to subsection (2) below, have effect—

(a) on the expiry of the period of 28 days beginning with the day on which it is made, or
(b) where an appeal against the order has been duly made under section 6 above, on such day as the [Upper Tribunal] shall specify.

(2) If—

(a) in the case of an application made under section 4 (1) above, the part of the rentcharge apportioned to the applicant's land, or
(b) in the case of an application under section 4 (2) above, any apportioned part of the rentcharge,

does not exceed the annual sum of £5, then, subject to subsection (3) below, it shall, where an application has been duly made under section 5 (5)(b) above, be made a condition of the apportionment order that it shall have effect only for the purpose of the redemption of that part of the rentcharge in accordance with the following provisions of this Act.

(3) The Secretary of State shall not impose a condition under subsection (2) above in any case where he considers that, having regard to all the circumstances, to do so would cause the applicant to suffer financial hardship.

(4) In the case of an application under section 4 (1) above, the effect of an apportionment order shall (subject to subsection (2) above) be to release the applicant's land from any part of the rentcharge not apportioned to it and to release the remaining land affected by the rentcharge from such part (if any) of the rentcharge as is apportioned to the applicant's land.

(5) In the case of an application under section 4 (2) above, the effect of an apportionment order shall (subject to subsection (2) above) be to release each part of the applicant's land from any part of the rentcharge not apportioned to it.

(6) The Secretary of State may by regulations specify, in substitution for the sum mentioned in subsection (2) above, such other annual sum as he considers appropriate.

[849]

NOTES

Sub-s (1): in para (b) words in square brackets substituted by SI 2009/1307, art 5(1), (2), Sch 1, paras 122, 124, subject to transitional and savings provisions in art 5(6), Sch 5 thereto.

Transfer of Functions: see the note to s 4 at **[846]**.

Redemption

8 Application for redemption certificate

(1) The owner of any land affected by a rentcharge may apply to the Secretary of State, in accordance with this section, for a certificate (in this Act referred to as a "redemption certificate") certifying that the rentcharge has been redeemed.

(2) Every application under this section shall be in such form and shall contain such information and be accompanied by such documents as may be prescribed by regulations.

(3) In any case where the Secretary of State considers that any additional document or information ought to be furnished by the applicant he may require the applicant—

(a) to deliver to him such documents (including documents of title and, in the case of registered land, an authority to inspect the register), and
(b) to furnish him with such information.

as the Secretary of State may specify.

(4) No application may be made under this section in respect of a rentcharge of a kind mentioned in section 2 (3) or 3 (3)(a) above.

(5) An application under this section may only be made—

(a) if the period for which the rentcharge concerned would remain payable if it were not redeemed is ascertainable, and

(b) in the case of a rentcharge which has at any time been a variable rentcharge, if it has ceased to be variable at the time of making the application.

For the purposes of this section a rentcharge shall (at any time) be treated as variable if at any time thereafter the amount of the rentcharge will, or may, vary in accordance with the provisions of the instrument under which it is payable.

(6) Where an applicant's documents of title are in the custody of a mortgagee the mortgagee shall, if requested to do so by the Secretary of State for the purpose of an application made under this section, deliver those documents to the Secretary of State on such terms as to their custody and return as the mortgagee may reasonably require.

[850]

NOTES

Transfer of Functions: see the note to s 4 at **[846]**.
Regulations: the Rentcharges Regulations 1978, SI 1978/16.

9 Issue of redemption certificate

(1) Where an application for a redemption certificate has been duly made under section 8 above, the Secretary of State shall serve notice of the application ("notice of application") on the person appearing to him to be the rent owner in relation to the rentcharge to which the application relates or his agent.

(2) A notice of application shall require the person on whom it is served to notify the Secretary of State, before the expiry of the period of 21 days beginning with the date on which the notice of application is served, whether or not he is the rent owner in relation to that rentcharge.

(3) Notification under subsection (2) above shall be given in the form prescribed by regulations and shall contain such information, and be accompanied by such documents, as may be so prescribed.

(4) Where the Secretary of State has been duly notified under subsection (2) above, or the period mentioned in that subsection has expired without his being so notified, he shall serve a notice ("instructions for redemption") on the applicant for the redemption certificate—

(a) specifying the sum required to redeem the rentcharge ('the "redemption price") calculated in accordance with section 10(1) below, and

(b) naming the person (determined in accordance with section 10(2) below), if any, appearing to the Secretary of State to be the person to whom the redemption price should be paid by the applicant.

(5) After service of instructions for redemption, the Secretary of State shall issue the applicant with a redemption certificate on proof—

(a) that the applicant has, before the expiry of the period of 28 days beginning with the date on which the instructions are served—

(i) paid the amount specified as the redemption price to the person named in the instructions as the person to whom payment should be made, or

(ii) where no person is so named, paid that amount into court in accordance with section 10(4) below, or

(b) in a case where the applicant has been authorised to do so under subsection (6) below, that he has paid that amount into court in accordance with section 10(4) below before the expiry of that period (or such longer period as the Secretary of State may allow).

(6) For the purposes of subsection (5)(b) above, the Secretary of State may authorise payment into court in any case where he is satisfied that the applicant is unable to effect payment in accordance with the instructions for redemption or that it would be unreasonable to require him to do so.

[851]

NOTES

Transfer of Functions: see the note to s 4 at **[846]**.
Regulations: the Rentcharges Regulations 1978, SI 1978/16.

10 Provisions supplemental to section 9

(1) For the purposes of section 9 above, the redemption price shall be calculated by applying the formula—

$$P = £\frac{R}{Y} - \frac{R}{Y(1+Y)^n}$$

where:—

P = the redemption price;

R = the annual amount of the rentcharge to be redeemed;

Y = the yield, expressed as a decimal fraction, from 2½ per cent Consolidated Stock; and

N = the period, expressed in years (taking any part of a year as a whole year), for which the rentcharge would remain payable if it were not redeemed.

In calculating the yield from 2 1/2 per cent Consolidated Stock, the price of that stock shall be taken to be the middle market price at the close of business on the last trading day in the week before that in which instructions for redemption are served under section 9(4) above.

(2) For the purposes of section 9(4)(b) above, the person to whom the redemption price should be paid is—

(a) in a case where the rentcharge was subject to a mortgage, the mortgagee or, if there is more than one mortgagee, the first mortgagee;

(b) in a case where the rentcharge was not subject to a mortgage but was settled land or was subject to a [trust of land], the trustees;

(c) in any other case, the rent owner.

(3) Where a redemption certificate has been issued under section 9 above—

(a) it shall have the effect of releasing the applicant's land from the rentcharge concerned, but

(b) it shall not affect the exercise by the rent owner of any right or remedy for the recovery of any rent which accrues before the date on which it was issued.

(4) Where a payment is made into court for the purposes of section 9 above, the sum concerned shall—

(a) if it does not exceed [£5,000], be paid into the county court, and

(b) in any other case, be paid into the High Court.

[(4A) …]

(5) Any person who, in notifying the Secretary of State under section 9 (2) above, makes a statement which he knows to be false in a material particular, or recklessly makes any statement which is so false, shall be guilty of an offence punishable on summary conviction by a fine not exceeding [level 5 on the standard scale].

[852]

NOTES

Sub-s (2): words in square brackets in para (b) substituted by the Trusts of Land and Appointment of Trustees Act 1996, s 25(1), Sch 3, para 15(3); for savings in relation to entailed interests created before the commencement of that Act, and savings consequential upon the abolition of the doctrine of conversion, see s 25(4), (5) thereof.

Sub-s (4): sum in square brackets substituted by SI 1991/724, art 2(2)(b), (8), Schedule, Pt I; for transitional provisions in relation to Crown proceedings, and savings, see arts 11, 12 thereof.

Sub-s (4A): inserted by the County Courts Act 1984, s 148(1), Sch 2, para 63; repealed by SI 1991/724, art 2(2)(b), (8), Schedule, Pt I.

Sub-s (5): maximum fine converted to a level on the standard scale by the Criminal Justice Act 1982, ss 37, 46.

Transfer of Functions: see the note to s 4 at **[846]**.

Miscellaneous and general

11 Implied covenants

(1) Where any land affected by a rentcharge created after the passing of this Act by virtue of section 2(3)(a) or (b) above—

(a) is conveyed for consideration in money or money's worth, and

(b) remains affected by the rentcharge or by any part of it,

the following provisions of this section shall have effect in place of those of section 77 of the Law of Property Act 1925, in respect of the covenants deemed to be included and implied in the conveyance.

(2) In addition to the covenants implied under [Part I of the Law of Property (Miscellaneous Provisions) Act 1994], there shall be deemed to be included and implied in the conveyance covenants by the conveying party or joint and several covenants by the conveying parties (if more than one) with the grantee (or with each of the grantees) in the following terms:—

(a) that the conveying party will at all times from the date of the conveyance duly pay the rentcharge (or part of the rentcharge) and keep the grantee and those deriving title under him and their respective estates and effects indemnified against all claims and demands whatsoever in respect of the rentcharge; and

(b) that the conveying party will (at his expense), in the event of the rentcharge (or part of the rentcharge) ceasing to affect the land conveyed, furnish evidence of that fact to the grantee and those deriving title under him.

(3) The benefit of the covenants deemed to be included and implied in a conveyance, by virtue of subsection (2) above, shall be annexed and incident to and shall go with the estate or interest of the implied covenantee and shall be capable of being enforced by every person in whom the estate or interest is from time to time vested.

(4) Any stipulation which is contained in an agreement and which is inconsistent with, or designed to prevent the operation of, the said covenants (or any part of them) shall be void.

[853]

NOTES

Sub-s (2): words in square brackets substituted by the Law of Property (Miscellaneous Provisions) Act 1994, s 21(1), Sch 1, para 7.

12 Regulations

(1) Regulations under any provision of this Act shall be made by the Secretary of State and shall be contained in a statutory instrument, which shall be subject to annulment in pursuance of a resolution of either House of Parliament.

(2) Regulations under any provision of this Act may contain such incidental and supplemental provisions as the Secretary of State considers appropriate and may make different provisions in relation to different cases or classes of case and in relation to different circumstances.

[854]

NOTES

Transfer of Functions: see the note to s 4 at **[846]**.

13 Interpretation

(1) In this Act—

"apportionment, in relation to a rentcharge, includes an apportionment which provides for the amount apportioned to any part of the land affected by the rentcharge to be nil;

"apportionment order" means an order made under section 5(10) above or, where appropriate, an order made by the [Upper Tribunal] under section 6(2)(b) above;

"conveyance" has the same meaning as in section 205(1) of the Law of Property Act 1925;

"land" has the same meaning as in section 205(1) of the Law of Property Act 1925;

"legal apportionment" and "equitable apportionment" in relation to a rentcharge mean, respectively—

(a) any apportionment of the rentcharge which is binding on the rent owner, and

(b) any apportionment or exoneration of the rentcharge which is not binding on the rent owner;

"owner", in relation to any land, means a person, other than a mortgagee not in possession, who is for the time being entitled to dispose of the fee simple of the land, whether in possession or in reversion, and includes a person holding or entitled to the rents and profits of the land under a lease or agreement;

"redemption certificate" has the meaning given in section 8(1) above;

"rent owner", in relation to a rentcharge, means the person entitled to the rentcharge or empowered to dispose of it absolutely or to give an absolute discharge for the capital value thereof.

(2) The provisions of this Act relating to the redemption and apportionment of rentcharges shall apply equally to the redemption and further apportionment of legally apportioned parts of rentcharges.

(3) Subject to section 3(4) above, a rentcharge shall be treated for the purposes of this Act as becoming payable on the first day of the first period in respect of which it is to be paid.

[855]

NOTES

Sub-s (1): in definition "apportionment order" words in square brackets substituted by SI 2009/1307, art 5(1), (2), Sch 1, paras 122, 125, subject to transitional and savings provisions in art 5(6), Sch 5 thereto.

14 Application to Crown

(1) This Act shall apply in relation to any land in which there subsists a Crown interest as it applies in relation to land in which no such interest subsists.

(2) In this section "Crown interest" means an interest which belongs to Her Majesty in right of the Crown or of the Duchy of Lancaster or to the Duchy of Cornwall or to a government department, or which is held in trust for Her Majesty for the purposes of a government department.

[856]

15 Expenses

(1) Any expenses incurred by the Secretary of State in consequence of this Act shall be paid out of money provided by Parliament.

(2) Subject to any provision made by regulations, any expenses incurred by any person in connection with an application for an apportionment order or for a redemption certificate under this Act shall be borne by that person.

(3) Regulations under subsection (2) above shall, in particular, provide for the reasonable expenses of a mortgagee, incurred in complying with a request under section 4 (7) or 8 (6) above, to be borne by the applicant.

[857]

NOTES

Transfer of Functions: see the note to s 4 at **[846]**.
Regulations: the Rentcharges Regulations 1978, SI 1978/16.

16 Service of notices, etc.

(1) Any document required to be served under this Act may be served on the person to be served either by delivering it to him, or by leaving it at his proper address, or by sending it by post.

(2) Any such document required to be served on a body corporate or a firm shall be duly served if it is served on the secretary or clerk of that body or a partner of that firm.

(3) For the purposes of this section, and of section 26 of the Interpretation Act 1889, in its application to this section, the proper address of a person shall be—

(a) in the case of a secretary or clerk of a body corporate, that of the registered or principal office of that body;
(b) in the case of a partner of a firm, that of the principal office of the firm;
(c) in any other case, the last known address of the person to be served.

[858]

17 (*Outside the scope of this work.*)

18 Short title etc

(1) This Act may be cited as the Rentcharges Act 1977.

(2) …

(3) This Act does not extend to Scotland or Northern Ireland.

[859]

NOTES

Sub-s (2): repealed by the Statute Law (Repeals) Act 2004.
Order: the Rentcharges Act 1977 (Commencement) Order 1978, SI 1978/15.

(*Schs 1, 2 outside the scope of this work.*)

RENT ACT 1977

(1977 c 42)

An Act to consolidate the Rent Act 1968, Parts III, IV and VIII of the Housing Finance Act 1972, the Rent Act 1974, sections 7 to 10 of the Housing Rents and Subsidies Act 1975, and certain related enactments, with amendments to give effect to recommendations of the Law Commission

[29 July 1977]

PART I
PRELIMINARY

Protected and statutory tenancies

1–128 ((*Pts I–IX*) *outside the scope of this work.*)

PART X
MORTGAGES

129, 130 (*Outside the scope of this work.*)

131 Regulated mortgages

(1) Subject to subsection (2) below, a mortgage which falls within section 129(1)(a) of this Act … is a regulated mortgage if—

(a) it is a legal mortgage of land consisting of or including a dwelling-house which is let on or subject to a regulated tenancy; and

(b) the regulated tenancy is binding on the mortgagee.

(2) Notwithstanding that a mortgage falls within subsection (1) above, it is not a regulated mortgage if—

(a) the rateable value on the appropriate day of the dwelling-house which falls within subsection (1)(a) above, or if there is more than one such dwelling-house comprised in the mortgage, the aggregate of the rateable values of those dwelling-houses on the appropriate day is less than one-tenth of the rateable value on the appropriate day of the whole of the land comprised in the mortgage, or

(b) the mortgagor is in breach of covenant, but for this purpose a breach of the covenant for the repayment of the principal money otherwise than by instalments shall be disregarded.

(3) Subsection (2)(a) above shall have effect, in the case of land consisting of or including a dwelling-house which on 22nd March 1973, was subject to a tenancy which became a regulated tenancy by virtue of section 14 of the Counter–Inflation Act 1973, as if for the reference to the appropriate day there were substituted a reference to 7th March 1973.

(4) In this section "legal mortgage" includes a charge by way of legal mortgage.

(5) Any reference in this Part of this Act to a regulated mortgage shall be construed in accordance with this section.

[860]

NOTES

Sub-s (1): words omitted repealed by the Housing Act 1980, s 152, Sch 26.

132 Powers of court to mitigate hardship to mortgagors under regulated mortgages

(1) The powers of the court under this section [become exercisable, in relation to a regulated mortgage] only on an application made by the mortgagor within 21 days, or such longer time as the court may allow, after the occurrence of one of the following events:—

(a) the rate of interest payable in respect of the mortgage is increased; or

(b) a rent for a dwelling-house comprised in the mortgage is registered under Part IV of this Act and the rent so registered is lower than the rent which was payable immediately before the registration; or

(c) the mortgagee, not being a mortgagee who was in possession on the relevant date demands payment of the principal money secured by the mortgage or takes any steps for exercising any right of foreclosure or sale or for otherwise enforcing his security.

Paragraph (b) above shall not apply to a case falling within section 129(2)(b) of this Act.

(2) If the court is satisfied on any such application that, by reason of the event in question and of the operation of this Act, the mortgagor would suffer severe financial hardship unless relief were given under this section, the court may by order make such provision—

(a) limiting the rate of interest,

(b) extending the time for the repayment of the principal money, or

(c) otherwise varying the terms of the mortgage or imposing any limitation or condition on the exercise of any right or remedy in respect thereof,

as it thinks appropriate.

(3) Where the court makes an order under subsection (2) above in relation to a mortgage which comprises other land as well as a dwelling-house or dwelling-houses subject to a regulated tenancy the order may, if the mortgagee so requests, make provision for apportioning the money secured by the mortgage between that other land and the dwelling-house or dwelling-houses.

(4) Where such an apportionment is made, the other provisions of the order made by the court shall not apply in relation to the other land referred to in that subsection and the money secured by the other land, and the mortgage shall have effect for all purposes as two separate mortgages of the apportioned parts.

(5) Where the court has made an order under this section it may vary or revoke it by a subsequent order.

(6) The court for the purposes of this section is a county court, except that where an application under subsection (1) above is made in pursuance of any step taken by the mortgagee in the High Court, it is the High Court.

[861]

NOTES
Sub-s (1): words in square brackets substituted by the Housing Act 1980, s 152, Sch 25, para 49.

133–136 (*Outside the scope of this work.*)

PART XI
GENERAL

137–148 (*Outside the scope of this work.*)

Supplemental

149–155 (*Outside the scope of this work.*)

156 Short title, commencement and extent

(1) This Act may be cited as the Rent Act 1977.

(2) This Act shall come into force on the expiry of the period of one month beginning with the date on which it is passed.

(3) This Act does not extend to Scotland or Northern Ireland. **[862]**

(*Schs 1–25 outside the scope of this work.*)

PROTECTION FROM EVICTION ACT 1977

(1977 c 43)

An Act to consolidate section 16 of the Rent Act 1957 and Part III of the Rent Act 1965, and related enactments

[29 July 1977]

PART I
UNLAWFUL EVICTION AND HARASSMENT

1 Unlawful eviction and harassment of occupier

(1) In this section "residential occupier", in relation to any premises, means a person occupying the premises as a residence, whether under a contract or by virtue of any enactment or rule of law giving him the right to remain in occupation or restricting the right of any other person to recover possession of the premises.

(2) If any person unlawfully deprives the residential occupier of any premises of his occupation of the premises or any part thereof, or attempts to do so, he shall be guilty of an offence unless he proves that he believed, and had reasonable cause to believe, that the residential occupier had ceased to reside in the premises.

(3) If any person with intent to cause the residential occupier of any premises—

(a) to give up the occupation of the premises or any part thereof; or

(b) to refrain from exercising any right or pursuing any remedy in respect of the premises or part thereof;

does acts [likely] to interfere with the peace or comfort of the residential occupier or members of his household, or persistently withdraws or withholds services reasonably required for the occupation of the premises as a residence, he shall be guilty of an offence.

[(3A) Subject to subsection (3B) below, the landlord of a residential occupier or an agent of the landlord shall be guilty of an offence if—

(a) he does acts likely to interfere with the peace or comfort of the residential occupier or members of his household, or

(b) he persistently withdraws or withholds services reasonably required for the occupation of the premises in question as a residence,

and (in either case) he knows, or has reasonable cause to believe, that that conduct is likely to cause the residential occupier to give up the occupation of the whole or part of the premises or to refrain from exercising any right or pursuing any remedy in respect of the whole or part of the premises.

(3B) A person shall not be guilty of an offence under subsection (3A) above if he proves that he had reasonable grounds for doing the acts or withdrawing or withholding the services in question.

(3C) In subsection (3A) above "landlord", in relation to a residential occupier of any premises, means the person who, but for—

(a) the residential occupier's right to remain in occupation of the premises, or

(b) a restriction on the person's right to recover possession of the premises,

would be entitled to occupation of the premises and any superior landlord under whom that person derives title.]

(4) A person guilty of an offence under this section shall be liable—

(a) on summary conviction, to a fine not exceeding [the prescribed sum] or to imprisonment for a term not exceeding 6 months or to both;

(b) on conviction on indictment, to a fine or to imprisonment for a term not exceeding 2 years or to both.

(5) Nothing in this section shall be taken to prejudice any liability or remedy to which a person guilty of an offence thereunder may be subject in civil proceedings.

(6) Where an offence under this section committed by a body corporate is proved to have been committed with the consent or connivance of, or to be attributable to any neglect on the part of, any director, manager or secretary or other similar officer of the body corporate or any person who was purporting to act in any such capacity, he as well as the body corporate shall be guilty of that offence and shall be liable to be proceeded against and punished accordingly.

[863]

NOTES

Sub-s (3): word in square brackets substituted by the Housing Act 1988, s 29(1), with respect to acts done after the commencement of that Act.

Sub-ss (3A)–(3C): inserted by the Housing Act 1988, s 29(2).

Sub-s (4): words in square brackets substituted by the Magistrates' Court Act 1980, s 32(2).

2 Restriction on re-entry without due process of law

Where any premises are let as a dwelling on a lease which is subject to a right of re-entry or forfeiture it shall not be lawful to enforce that right otherwise than by proceedings in the court while any person is lawfully residing in the premises or part of them.

[864]

3 Prohibition of eviction without due process of law

(1) Where any premises have been let as a dwelling under a tenancy which is [neither a statutorily protected tenancy nor an excluded tenancy] and—

(a) the tenancy (in this section referred to as the former tenancy) has come to an end, but

(b) the occupier continues to reside in the premises or part of them,

it shall not be lawful for the owner to enforce against the occupier, otherwise than by proceedings in the court, his right to recover possession of the premises.

(2) In this section "the occupier", in relation to any premises, means any person lawfully residing in the premises or part of them at the termination of the former tenancy.

[(2A) Subsections (1) and (2) above apply in relation to any restricted contract (within the meaning of the Rent Act 1977) which—

(a) creates a licence; and

(b) is entered into after the commencement of section 69 of the Housing Act 1980;

as they apply in relation to a restricted contract which creates a tenancy.]

[(2B) Subsections (1) and (2) above apply in relation to any premises occupied as a dwelling under a licence, other than an excluded licence, as they apply in relation to premises let as a dwelling under a tenancy, and in those subsections the expressions "let" and "tenancy" shall be construed accordingly.

(2C) References in the preceding provisions of this section and section 4(2A) below to an excluded tenancy do not apply to—

(a) a tenancy entered into before the date on which the Housing Act 1988 came into force, or

(b) a tenancy entered into on or after that date but pursuant to a contract made before that date,

but, subject to that, "excluded tenancy" and "excluded licence" shall be construed in accordance with section 3A below.]

(3) This section shall, with the necessary modifications, apply where the owner's right to recover possession arises on the death of the tenant under a statutory tenancy within the meaning of the Rent Act 1977 or the Rent (Agriculture) Act 1976.

[865]

NOTES

Sub-s (1): words in square brackets substituted by the Housing Act 1988, s 30(1).
Sub-s (2A): inserted by the Housing Act 1980, s 69(1).
Sub-ss (2B), (2C): inserted by the Housing Act 1988, s 30(2).

[3A Excluded tenancies and licences

(1) Any reference in this Act to an excluded tenancy or an excluded licence is a reference to a tenancy or licence which is excluded by virtue of any of the following provisions of this section.

(2) A tenancy or licence is excluded if—

(a) under its terms the occupier shares any accommodation with the landlord or licensor; and

(b) immediately before the tenancy or licence was granted and also at the time it comes to an end, the landlord or licensor occupied as his only or principal home premises of which the whole or part of the shared accommodation formed part.

(3) A tenancy or licence is also excluded if—

(a) under its terms the occupier shares any accommodation with a member of the family of the landlord or licensor;

(b) immediately before the tenancy or licence was granted and also at the time it comes to an end, the member of the family of the landlord or licensor occupied as his only or principal home premises of which the whole or part of the shared accommodation formed part; and

(c) immediately before the tenancy or licence was granted and also at the time it comes to an end, the landlord or licensor occupied as his only or principal home premises in the same building as the shared accommodation and that building is not a purpose-built block of flats.

(4) For the purposes of subsections (2) and (3) above, an occupier shares accommodation with another person if he has the use of it in common with that person (whether or not also in common with others) and any reference in those subsections to shared accommodation shall be construed accordingly, and if, in relation to any tenancy or licence, there is at any time more than one person who is the landlord or licensor, any reference in those subsections to the landlord or licensor shall be construed as a reference to any one of those persons.

(5) In subsections (2) to (4) above—

(a) "accommodation" includes neither an area used for storage nor a staircase, passage, corridor or other means of access;

(b) "occupier" means, in relation to a tenancy, the tenant and, in relation to a licence, the licensee; and

(c) "purpose-built block of flats" has the same meaning as in Part III of Schedule 1 to the Housing Act 1988;

and section 113 of the Housing Act 1985 shall apply to determine whether a person is for the purposes of subsection (3) above a member of another's family as it applies for the purposes of Part IV of that Act.

(6) A tenancy or licence is excluded if it was granted as a temporary expedient to a person who entered the premises in question or any other premises as a trespasser (whether or not, before the beginning of that tenancy or licence, another tenancy or licence to occupy the premises or any other premises had been granted to him).

(7) A tenancy or licence is excluded if—

(a) it confers on the tenant or licensee the right to occupy the premises for a holiday only; or

(b) it is granted otherwise than for money or money's worth.

[(7A) A tenancy or licence is excluded if it is granted in order to provide accommodation [under section 4 or Part VI of the Immigration and Asylum Act 1999].]

[(7B) Section 32 of the Nationality, Immigration and Asylum Act 2002 (accommodation centre: tenure) provides for a resident's licence to occupy an accommodation centre to be an excluded licence.]

[(7C) A tenancy or licence is excluded if it is granted in order to provide accommodation under the Displaced Persons (Temporary Protection) Regulations 2005.]

(8) A licence is excluded if it confers rights of occupation in a hostel, within the meaning of the Housing Act 1985, which is provided by—

(a) the council of a county, [county borough,] district or London Borough, the Common Council of the City of London, the Council of the Isle of Scilly, the Inner London Education Authority, [the London Fire and Emergency Planning Authority,] a joint authority within the meaning of the Local Government Act 1985 or a residuary body within the meaning of that Act;

(b) a development corporation within the meaning of the New Towns Act 1981;

(c) the [new towns residuary body];
(d) an urban development corporation established by an order under section 135 of the Local Government, Planning and Land Act 1980;
(e) a housing action trust established under Part III of the Housing Act 1988;
(f) …
(g) the Housing Corporation … ;
[(ga) the Secretary of State under section 89 of the Housing Associations Act 1985;]
[(h) a housing trust (within the meaning of the Housing Associations Act 1985) which is a charity or a registered social landlord (within the meaning of the Housing Act 1985); or]
(i) any other person who is, or who belongs to a class of person which is, specified in an order made by the Secretary of State.

[(8A) In subsection (8)(c) above "new towns residuary body" means—
(a) in relation to England, the Homes and Communities Agency so far as exercising functions in relation to anything transferred (or to be transferred) to it as mentioned in section 52(1)(a) to (d) of the Housing and Regeneration Act 2008; and
(b) in relation to Wales, means the Welsh Ministers so far as exercising functions in relation to anything transferred (or to be transferred) to them as mentioned in section 36(1)(a)(i) to (iii) of the New Towns Act 1981.]

(9) The power to make an order under subsection (8)(i) above shall be exercisable by statutory instrument which shall be subject to annulment in pursuance of a resolution of either House of Parliament.]

[866]

NOTES

Inserted by the Housing Act 1988, s 31.

Sub-s (7A): inserted by the Immigration and Asylum Act 1999, s 169(1), Sch 14, para 73; words in square brackets substituted by the Immigration, Asylum and Nationality Act 2006, s 43(4)(a).

Sub-s (7B): inserted by the Nationality, Immigration and Asylum Act 2002, s 32(5), as from a day to be appointed.

Sub-s (7C): inserted by SI 2005/1379, Schedule, para 1.

Sub-s (8): in para (a), words in first pair of square brackets inserted by the Local Government (Wales) Act 1994, s 22(2), Sch 8, para 4(1) and words in second pair of square brackets inserted by the Greater London Authority Act 1999, s 328, Sch 29, Pt I, para 27; in para (c) words in square brackets substituted by the Housing and Regeneration Act 2008, s 56, Sch 8, para 24(1), (2); para (f) and words omitted from para (g) repealed, and para (ga) inserted by the Government of Wales Act 1998, ss 140, 152, Sch 16, para 2, Sch 18, Pt VI; para (h) substituted by SI 1996/2325, art 5(1), Sch 2, para 7.

Sub-s (8A): inserted by the Housing and Regeneration Act 2008, s 56, Sch 8, para 24(1), (3).

Transfer of Functions: functions of the Secretary of State, so far as exercisable in relation to Wales, transferred to the National Assembly for Wales, by the National Assembly for Wales (Transfer of Functions) Order 1999, SI 1999/672, art 2, Sch 1.

Housing Corporation: in sub-s (8)(g) the reference to the Housing Corporation shall be treated as if it were a reference to the Regulator of Social Housing: see the Transfer of Housing Corporation Functions (Modifications and Transitional Provisions) Order 2008, SI 2008/2839, arts 1(2), 3, 6, Schedule, para 7.

Orders: the Protection from Eviction (Excluded Licences) Order 1991, SI 1991/1943; the Protection from Eviction (Excluded Licences) (The Shaftesbury Society) Order 1999, SI 1999/1758; the Protection from Eviction (Excluded Licences) (Royal British Legion Industries Ltd) (England) Order 2003, SI 2003/2436.

4 Special provisions for agricultural employees

(1) This section shall apply where the tenant under the former tenancy (within the meaning of section 3 of this Act) occupied the premises under the terms of his employment as a person employed in agriculture, as defined in section 1 of the Rent (Agriculture) Act 1976, but is not a statutory tenant as defined in that Act.

(2) In this section "the occupier", in relation to any premises, means—
(a) the tenant under the former tenancy; or
(b) the [surviving spouse or surviving civil partner] of the tenant under the former tenancy residing with him at his death or, if the former tenant leaves no such [surviving spouse or surviving civil partner], any member of his family residing with him at his death.

[(2A) In accordance with section 3(2B) above, any reference in subsections (1) and (2) above to the tenant under the former tenancy includes a reference to the licensee under a licence (other than an excluded licence) which has come to an end (being a licence to occupy premises as a dwelling); and in the following provisions of this section the expressions "tenancy" and "rent" and any other expressions referable to a tenancy shall be construed accordingly.]

(3) Without prejudice to any power of the court apart from this section to postpone the operation or suspend the execution of an order for possession, if in proceedings by the owner against the occupier the court makes an order for the possession of the premises the court may suspend the execution of the order on such terms and conditions, including conditions as to the payment by the occupier of arrears of rent, mesne profits and otherwise as the court thinks reasonable.

(4) Where the order for possession is made within the period of 6 months beginning with the date when the former tenancy came to an end, then, without prejudice to any powers of the court under the preceding provisions of this section or apart from this section to postpone the operation or suspend the execution of the order for a longer period, the court shall suspend the execution of the order for the remainder of the said period of 6 months unless the court—

(a) is satisfied either—

(i) that other suitable accommodation is, or will within that period be made, available to the occupier; or

(ii) that the efficient management of any agricultural land or the efficient carrying on of any agricultural operations would be seriously prejudiced unless the premises are available for occupation by a person employed or to be employed by the owner; or

(iii) that greater hardship (being hardship in respect of matters other than the carrying on of such a business as aforesaid) would be caused by the suspension of the order until the end of that period than by its execution within that period; or

(iv) that the occupier, or any person residing or lodging with the occupier, has been causing damage to the premises or has been guilty of conduct which is a nuisance or annoyance to persons occupying other premises; and

(b) considers that it would be reasonable not to suspend the execution of the order for the remainder of that period.

(5) Where the court suspends the execution of an order for possession under subsection (4) above it shall do so on such terms and conditions, including conditions as to the payment by the occupier of arrears of rent, mesne profits and otherwise as the court thinks reasonable.

(6) A decision of the court not to suspend the execution of the order under subsection (4) above shall not prejudice any other power of the court to postpone the operation or suspend the execution of the order for the whole or part of the period of 6 months mentioned in that subsection.

(7) Where the court has, under the preceding provisions of this section, suspended the execution of an order for possession, it may from time to time vary the period of suspension or terminate it and may vary any terms or conditions imposed by virtue of this section.

(8) In considering whether or how to exercise its powers under subsection (3) above, the court shall have regard to all the circumstances and, in particular, to—

(a) whether other suitable accommodation is or can be made available to the occupier;

(b) whether the efficient management of any agricultural land or the efficient carrying on of any agricultural operations would be seriously prejudiced unless the premises were available for occupation by a person employed or to be employed by the owner; and

(c) whether greater hardship would be caused by the suspension of the execution of the order than by its execution without suspension or further suspension.

(9) Where in proceedings for the recovery of possession of the premises the court makes an order for possession but suspends the execution of the order under this section, it shall make no order for costs, unless it appears to the court, having regard to the conduct of the owner or of the occupier, that there are special reasons for making such an order.

(10) Where, in the case of an order for possession of the premises to which subsection (4) above applies, the execution of the order is not suspended under that subsection or, the execution of the order having been so suspended, the suspension is terminated, then, if it is subsequently made to appear to the court that the failure to suspend the execution of the order or, as the case may be, the termination of the suspension was—

(a) attributable to the provisions of paragraph (a)(ii) of subsection (4), and

(b) due to misrepresentation or concealment of material facts by the owner of the premises,

the court may order the owner to pay to the occupier such sum as appears sufficient as compensation for damage or loss sustained by the occupier as a result of that failure or termination.

[867]

NOTES

Sub-s (2): words in square brackets substituted by the Civil Partnership Act 2004, s 81, Sch 8, para 15.
Sub-s (2A): inserted by the Housing Act 1988, s 30(3).

PART II
NOTICE TO QUIT

5 Validity of notices to quit

(1) [Subject to subsection (1B) below] no notice by a landlord or a tenant to quit any premises let (whether before or after the commencement of this Act) as a dwelling shall be valid unless—

(a) it is in writing and contains such information as may be prescribed, and

(b) it is given not less than 4 weeks before the date on which it is to take effect.

[(1A) Subject to subsection (1B) below, no notice by a licensor or licensee to determine a periodic licence to occupy premises as a dwelling (whether the licence was granted before or after the passing of this Act) shall be valid unless—

(a) it is in writing and contains such information as may be prescribed, and
(b) it is given not less than 4 weeks before the date on which it is to take effect.

(1B) Nothing in subsection (1) or subsection (1A) above applies to—

(a) premises let on an excluded tenancy which is entered into on or after the date on which the Housing Act 1988 came into force unless it is entered into pursuant to a contract made before that date; or
(b) premises occupied under an excluded licence.]

(2) In this section "prescribed" means prescribed by regulations made by the Secretary of State by statutory instrument, and a statutory instrument containing any such regulations shall be subject to annulment in pursuance of a resolution of either House of Parliament.

(3) Regulations under this section may make different provision in relation to different descriptions of lettings and different circumstances.

[868]

NOTES

Sub-s (1): words in square brackets inserted by the Housing Act 1988, s 32(1).
Sub-ss (1A), (1B): inserted by the Housing Act 1988, s 32(2).
Transfer of Functions: functions of the Secretary of State, so far as exercisable in relation to Wales, transferred to the National Assembly for Wales, by the National Assembly for Wales (Transfer of Functions) Order 1999, SI 1999/672, art 2, Sch 1.
Regulations: the Notices to Quit etc (Prescribed Information) Regulations 1988, SI 1988/2201.

PART III
SUPPLEMENTAL PROVISIONS

6, 7 (*Outside the scope of this work.*)

8 Interpretation

(1) In this Act "statutorily protected tenancy" means—

(a) a protected tenancy within the meaning of the Rent Act 1977 or a tenancy to which Part I of the Landlord and Tenant Act 1954 applies;
(b) a protected occupancy or statutory tenancy as defined in the Rent (Agriculture) Act 1976;
(c) a tenancy to which Part II of the Landlord and Tenant Act 1954 applies;
(d) a tenancy of an agricultural holding within the meaning of the [Agricultural Holdings Act 1986] [which is a tenancy in relation to which that Act applies];
[(e) an assured tenancy or assured agricultural occupancy under Part I of the Housing Act 1988];
[(f) a tenancy to which Schedule 10 to the Local Government and Housing Act 1989 applies].
[(g) a farm business tenancy within the meaning of the Agricultural Tenancies Act 1995.]

(2) For the purposes of Part I of this Act a person who, under the terms of his employment, had exclusive possession of any premises other than as a tenant shall be deemed to have been a tenant and the expressions "let" and "tenancy" shall be construed accordingly.

(3) In Part I of this Act "the owner", in relation to any premises, means the person who, as against the occupier, is entitled to possession thereof.

[(4) In this Act "excluded tenancy" and "excluded licence" have the meaning assigned by section 3A of this Act.

(5) If, on or after the date on which the Housing Act 1988 came into force, the terms of an excluded tenancy or excluded licence entered into before that date are varied, then—

(a) if the variation affects the amount of the rent which is payable under the tenancy or licence, the tenancy or licence shall be treated for the purposes of sections 3(2C) and 5(1B) above as a new tenancy or licence entered into at the time of the variation; and
(b) if the variation does not affect the amount of the rent which is so payable, nothing in this Act shall affect the determination of the question whether the variation is such as to give rise to a new tenancy or licence.

(6) Any reference in subsection (5) above to a variation affecting the amount of the rent which is payable under a tenancy or licence does not include a reference to—

(a) a reduction or increase effected under Part III or Part VI of the Rent Act 1977 (rents under regulated tenancies and housing association tenancies), section 78 of that Act (power of rent tribunal in relation to restricted contracts) or sections 11 to 14 of the Rent (Agriculture) Act 1976; or

(b) a variation which is made by the parties and has the effect of making the rent expressed to be payable under the tenancy or licence the same as a rent for the dwelling which is entered in the register under Part IV or section 79 of the Rent Act 1977.]

[869]

NOTES

Sub-s (1): in para (d) first words in square brackets substituted by the Agricultural Holdings Act 1986, s 100, Sch 14, para 61, final words in square brackets inserted by the Agricultural Tenancies Act 1995, s 40, Schedule, para 29(a); para (e) inserted by the Housing Act 1988, s 33(2); para (f) inserted by the Local Government and Housing Act 1989, s 194, Sch 11, para 54; para (g) inserted by the Agricultural Tenancies Act 1995, s 40, Schedule, para 29(b).

Sub-ss (4)–(6): inserted by the Housing Act 1988, s 33(3).

9 The court for purposes of Part I

(1) The court for the purposes of Part I of this Act shall, subject to this section, be—

(a) the county court, in relation to premises with respect to which the county court has for the time being jurisdiction in actions for the recovery of land; and

(b) the High Court, in relation to other premises.

(2) Any powers of a county court in proceedings for the recovery of possession of any premises in the circumstances mentioned in section 3(1) of this Act may be exercised with the leave of the judge by any registrar of the court, except in so far as rules of court otherwise provide.

(3) Nothing in this Act shall affect the jurisdiction of the High Court in proceedings to enforce a lessor's right of re-entry or forfeiture or to enforce a mortgagee's right of possession in a case where the former tenancy was not binding on the mortgagee.

(4) Nothing in this Act shall affect the operation of—

(a) section 59 of the Pluralities Act 1838;
(b) section 19 of the Defence Act 1842;
(c) section 6 of the Lecturers and Parish Clerks Act 1844;
(d) paragraph 3 of Schedule 1 to the Sexual Offences Act 1956; or
(e) section 13 of the Compulsory Purchase Act 1965.

[870]

10–12 (*Outside the scope of this work.*)

13 Short title, etc

(1) This Act may be cited as the Protection from Eviction Act 1977.

(2) This Act shall come into force on the expiry of the period of one month beginning with the date on which it is passed.

(3) This Act does not extend to Scotland or Northern Ireland.

(4) References in this Act to any enactment are references to that enactment as amended, and include references thereto as applied by any other enactment including, except where the context otherwise requires, this Act.

[871]

(*Schs 1–3 outside the scope of this work.*)

CRIMINAL LAW ACT 1977

(1977 c 45)

An Act to amend the law of England and Wales with respect to criminal conspiracy; to make new provision in that law, in place of the provisions of the common law and the Statutes of Forcible Entry, for restricting the use or threat of violence for securing entry into any premises and for penalising unauthorised entry or remaining on premises in certain circumstances; otherwise to amend the criminal law, including the law with respect to the administration of criminal justice; to provide for the alteration of certain pecuniary and other limits; to amend section 9(4) of the Administration of Justice Act 1973, the Legal Aid Act 1974, the Rabies Act 1974 and the Diseases of Animals (Northern Ireland) Order 1975 and the law about juries and coroners' inquests; and for connected purposes

[29 July 1977]

1–5 ((*Pt I*) *outside the scope of this work.*)

PART II
OFFENCES RELATING TO ENTERING AND REMAINING ON PROPERTY

6 Violence for securing entry

(1) Subject to the following provisions of this section, any person who, without lawful authority, uses or threatens violence for the purpose of securing entry into any premises for himself or for any other person is guilty of an offence, provided that—

(a) there is someone present on those premises at the time who is opposed to the entry which the violence is intended to secure; and

(b) the person using or threatening the violence knows that that is the case.

[(1A) Subsection (1) above does not apply to a person who is a displaced residential occupier or a protected intending occupier of the premises in question or who is acting on behalf of such an occupier; and if the accused adduces sufficient evidence that he was, or was acting on behalf of, such an occupier he shall be presumed to be, or to be acting on behalf of, such an occupier unless the contrary is proved by the prosecution.]

(2) [Subject to subsection (1A) above,] the fact that a person has any interest in or right to possession or occupation of any premises shall not for the purposes of subsection (1) above constitute lawful authority for the use or threat of violence by him or anyone else for the purpose of securing his entry into those premises.

(3) …

(4) It is immaterial for the purposes of this section—

(a) whether the violence in question is directed against the person or against property; and

(b) whether the entry which the violence is intended to secure is for the purpose of acquiring possession of the premises in question or for any other purpose.

(5) A person guilty of an offence under this section shall be liable on summary conviction to imprisonment for a term not exceeding six months or to a fine not exceeding [level 5 on the standard scale] or to both.

(6) …

(7) Section 12 below contains provisions which apply for determining when any person is to be regarded for the purposes of this Part of this Act as a displaced residential occupier of any premises or of any access to any premises [and section 12A below contains provisions which apply for determining when any person is to be regarded for the purposes of this Part of this Act as a protected intending occupier of any premises or of any access to any premises.]

[872]

NOTES

Sub-s (1A): inserted by the Criminal Justice and Public Order Act 1994, s 72(2).

Sub-ss (2), (7): words in square brackets inserted by the Criminal Justice and Public Order Act 1994, s 72(3), (5).

Sub-s (3): repealed by the Criminal Justice and Public Order Act 1994, ss 72(4), 168(3), Sch 11.

Sub-s (5): maximum fine converted to a level on the standard scale by virtue of the Criminal Justice Act 1982, ss 37, 38, 46.

Sub-s (6): repealed by the Serious Organised Crime and Police Act 2005, ss 111, 174(2), Sch 7, Pt 1, para 19(1), (2), Sch 17, Pt 2.

7–63 (*Ss 7–13, ss 14–63 (Pts III–V), in so far as unrepealed, outside the scope of this work.*)

PART VI
SUPPLEMENTARY

64 (*Outside the scope of this work.*)

65 Citation, etc

(1) This Act may be cited as the Criminal Law Act 1977.

(2)–(6) (*Outside the scope of this work.*)

(7) This Act shall come into force on such day as the Secretary of State may appoint by order made by statutory instrument, and different days may be so appointed for different purposes.

(8), (9) (*Outside the scope of this work.*)

(10) In this Act—

(a) Part V and, so far as there provided, the provisions mentioned in section 63(2) above extend to Scotland;

(b) the following provisions extend to Northern Ireland namely—
sections 38 to 40,
…

section 52,
…
subsections (1), (3) and (6) to (10) of this section,
Schedule 7,
in Schedule 14, paragraph 5;

(c) section 31 and Schedule 6, so far as they amend any enactment which extends to the Channel Islands or the Isle of Man, extend to the Channel Islands or the Isle of Man, as the case may be;

(d) subsections (4) and (5) above and Schedules 12 and 13, so far as they relate to—

(i) section 45 of the Prison Act 1952 (in its application to persons for the time being in Northern Ireland or in the Channel Islands or the Isle of Man);

(ii) Part III and section 39(1) of the Criminal Justice Act 1961; and

(iii) sections 60 and 63 of the Criminal Justice Act 1967 (in their application to persons for the time being in Northern Ireland or in the Channel Islands or the Isle of Man),

extend to Northern Ireland, the Channel Islands and the Isle of Man (as well as, by virtue of paragraph (a) above, to Scotland);

(e) section 32(3) extends to all places (except Scotland) to which section 2 of the European Communities Act 1972 extends (as well as, by virtue of paragraph (a) above, to Scotland) …

but save as aforesaid, this Act extends to England and Wales only.

[873]

NOTES

Sub-s (2): words in square brackets substituted by the Magistrates' Courts Act 1980, s 154(1), Sch 7, para 153.

Sub-s (10): first words omitted from para (b) repealed by the Criminal Appeal (Northern Ireland) Act 1980, s 51(2), Sch 5, second words omitted from para (b) repealed by the Diseases of Animals (Northern Ireland) Order 1981, SI 1981/1115; words omitted from para (e) repealed by the Magistrates' Courts Act 1980, s 154(3), Sch 9.

Orders: at present, 12 commencement orders have been made under this section. The ones relevant to the provisions of the Act printed in this work are the Criminal Law Act 1977 (Commencement No 1) Order 1977, SI 1977/1365, and the Criminal Law Act 1977 (Commencement No 3) Order 1977, SI 1977/1682.

(*Schs 1–14, in so far as unrepealed, outside the scope of this work.*)

INTERPRETATION ACT 1978

(1978 c 30)

An Act to consolidate the Interpretation Act 1889 and certain other enactments relating to the construction and operation of Acts of Parliament and other instruments, with amendments to give effect to recommendations of the Law Commission and the Scottish Law Commission

[20 July 1978]

1–4 (*Outside the scope of this work.*)

Interpretation and construction

5 Definitions

In any Act, unless the contrary intention appears, words and expressions listed in Schedule 1 to this Act are to be construed according to that Schedule.

[874]

6 (*Outside the scope of this work.*)

7 References to service by post

Where an Act authorises or requires any document to be served by post (whether the expression "serve" or the expression "give" or "send" or any other expression is used) then, unless the contrary intention appears, the service is deemed to be effected by properly addressing, pre-paying and posting a letter containing the document and, unless the contrary is proved, to have been effected at the time at which the letter would be delivered in the ordinary course of post.

[875]

8 (*Outside the scope of this work.*)

9 References to time of day

Subject to section 3 of the Summer Time Act 1972 (construction of references to points of time during the period of summer time), whenever an expression of time occurs in an Act, the time referred to shall, unless it is otherwise specifically stated, be held to be Greenwich mean time.

[876]

10–17 (*Outside the scope of this work.*)

Miscellaneous

18 (*Outside the scope of this work.*)

19 Citation of other Acts

(1) Where an Act cites another Act by year, statute, session or chapter, or a section or other portion of another Act by number or letter, the reference shall, unless the contrary intention appears, be read as referring—

(a) in the case of Acts included in any revised edition of the statutes printed by authority, to that edition;

(b) in the case of Acts not so included but included in the edition prepared under the direction of the Record Commission, to that edition;

(c) in any other case, to the Acts printed by the Queen's Printer, or under the superintendence or authority of Her Majesty's Stationery Office.

(2) (*Outside the scope of this work.*)

[877]

20, 20A (*Outside the scope of this work.*)

Supplementary

21, 22 (*Outside the scope of this work.*)

23 Application to other instruments

(1) The provisions of this Act, except sections 1 to 3 and 4(*b*), apply, so far as applicable and unless the contrary intention appears, to subordinate legislation made after the commencement of this Act and, to the extent specified in Part II of Schedule 2, to subordinate legislation made before the commencement of this Act, as they apply to Acts.

(2) In the application of this Act to Acts passed or subordinate legislation made after the commencement of this Act, all references to an enactment include an enactment comprised in subordinate legislation whenever made, and references to the passing or repeal of an enactment are to be construed accordingly.

(3) Sections 9 and 19(1) also apply to deeds and other instruments and documents as they apply to Acts and subordinate legislation; and in the application of section 17(2)(*a*) to Acts passed or subordinate legislation made after the commencement of this Act, the reference to any other enactment includes any deed or other instrument or document.

(4) Subsections (1) and (2) of this section do not apply to Orders in Council made under section 5 of the Statutory Instruments Act 1946, section 1(3) of the Northern Ireland (Temporary Provisions) Act 1972 or Schedule 1 to the Northern Ireland Act 1974.

[878]

23A–26 (*Outside the scope of this work.*)

27 Short title

This Act may be cited as the Interpretation Act 1978.

[879]

SCHEDULE 1
WORDS AND EXPRESSIONS DEFINED

Section 5

Definitions

...

"Land" includes buildings and other structures, land covered with water, and any estate, interest, easement, servitude or right in or over land.

...

[880]

NOTES

Definitions and other words omitted outside the scope of this work.

(*Schs 2, 3 outside the scope of this work.*)

ESTATE AGENTS ACT 1979

(1979 c 38)

An Act to make provision with respect to the carrying on of and to persons who carry on, certain activities in connection with the disposal and acquisition of interests in land; and for purposes connected therewith

[4 April 1979]

1–11A (*Outside the scope of this work.*)

Clients' money and accounts

12 Meaning of "clients' money" etc

(1) In this Act "clients' money", in relation to a person engaged in estate agency work, means any money received by him in the course of that work which is a contract or pre-contract deposit—

(a) in respect of the acquisition of an interest in land in the United Kingdom, or

(b) in respect of a connected contract,

whether that money is held or received by him as agent, bailee, stakeholder or in any other capacity.

(2) In this Act "contract deposit" means any sum paid by a purchaser—

(a) which in whole or in part is, or is intended to form part of, the consideration for acquiring such an interest as is referred to in subsection (1)(a) above or for a connected contract; and

(b) which is paid by him at or after the time at which he acquires the interest or enters into an enforceable contract to acquire it.

(3) In this Act "pre-contract deposit" means any sum paid by any person—

(a) in whole or in part as an earnest of his intention to acquire such an interest as is referred to in subsection (1)(a) above, or

(b) in whole or in part towards meeting any liability of his in respect of the consideration for the acquisition of such an interest which will arise if he acquires or enters into an enforceable contract to acquire the interest, or

(c) in respect of a connected contract,

and which is paid by him at a time before he either acquires the interest or enters into an enforceable contract to acquire it.

(4) In this Act "connected contract", in relation to the acquisition of an interest in land, means a contract which is conditional upon such an acquisition or upon entering into an enforceable contract for such an acquisition (whether or not it is also conditional on other matters).

[881]

13 Clients' money held on trust or as agent

(1) It is hereby declared that clients' money received by any person in the course of estate agency work in England, Wales or Northern Ireland—

(a) is held by him on trust for the person who is entitled to call for it to be paid over to him or to be paid on his direction or to have it otherwise credited to him, or

(b) if it is received by him as stakeholder, is held by him on trust for the person who may become so entitled on the occurrence of the event against which the money is held.

(2) It is hereby declared that clients' money received by any person in the course of estate agency work in Scotland is held by him as agent for the person who is entitled to call for it to be paid over to him or to be paid on his direction or to have it otherwise credited to him.

(3) The provisions of sections 14 and 15 below as to the investment of clients' money, the keeping of accounts and records and accounting for interest shall have effect in place of the corresponding duties which would be owed by a person holding clients' money as trustee, or in Scotland as agent, under the general law.

(4) Where an order of the [OFT] under section 3 above has the effect of prohibiting a person from holding clients' money the order may contain provision—

(a) appointing another person as trustee, or in Scotland as agent, in place of the person to whom the order relates to hold and deal with clients' money held by that person when the order comes into effect; and

(b) requiring the expenses and such reasonable remuneration of the new trustee or agent as may be specified in the order to be paid by the person to whom the order relates or, if the order so provides, out of the clients' money;

but nothing in this subsection shall affect the power conferred by section 41 of the Trustee Act 1925 or section 40 of the Trustee Act (Northern Ireland) 1958 to appoint a new trustee to hold clients' money.

(5) For the avoidance of doubt it is hereby declared that the fact that any person has or may have a lien on clients' money held by him does not affect the operation of this section and also that nothing in this section shall prevent such a lien from being given effect.

[882]

NOTES

Sub-s (4): reference in square brackets substituted by the Enterprise Act 2002, s 278(1), Sch 25, para 9(1), (9)(b); for transitional provisions and savings see the Enterprise Act 2002, s 276, Sch 24, paras 2–6.

14–27 (*Outside the scope of this work.*)

Supplementary

28–35 (*Ss 28–34 outside the scope of this work; s 35 repealed by the Statute Law* (*Repeals*) *Act 1981.*)

36 Short title, commencement and extent

(1) This Act may be cited as the Estate Agents Act 1979.

(2) This Act shall come into force on such day as the Secretary of State may by order made by statutory instrument appoint and different days may be so appointed for different provisions and for different purposes.

(3) This Act extends to Northern Ireland.

[883]

NOTES

Order: the Estate Agents Act 1979 (Commencement No 1) Order 1981, SI 1981/1517.

(*Schs 1–4 outside the scope of this work.*)

CHARGING ORDERS ACT 1979

(1979 c 53)

An Act to make provision for imposing charges to secure payment of money due, or to become due, under judgments or orders of court; to provide for restraining and prohibiting dealings with, and the making of payments in respect of, certain securities; and for connected purposes

[6 December 1979]

Charging orders

1 Charging orders

(1) Where, under a judgment or order of the High Court or a county court, a person (the "debtor") is required to pay a sum of money to another person (the "creditor") then, for the purpose of enforcing that judgment or order, the appropriate court may make an order in accordance with the provisions of this Act imposing on any such property of the debtor as may be specified in the order a charge for securing the payment of any money due or to become due under the judgment or order.

(2) The appropriate court is—

(a) in a case where the property to be charged is a fund in court, the court in which that fund is lodged;

(b) in a case where paragraph (a) above does not apply and the order to be enforced is a maintenance order of the High Court, the High Court or a county court;

(c) in a case where neither paragraph (a) nor paragraph (b) above applies and the judgment or order to be enforced is a judgment or order of the High Court for a sum exceeding [the county court limit], the High Court [or a county court]; and

(d) in any other case, a county court.

In this section ["county court limit" means the county court limit for the time being specified in an Order in Council under [section 145 of the County Courts Act 1984], as the county court limit for the purposes of this section and] "maintenance order" has the same meaning as in section 2(a) of the Attachment of Earnings Act 1971.

(3) An order under subsection (1) above is referred to in this Act as a "charging order".

(4) Where a person applies to the High Court for a charging order to enforce more than one judgment or order, that court shall be the appropriate court in relation to the application if it would be the appropriate court, apart from this subsection, on an application relating to one or more of the judgments or orders concerned.

(5) In deciding whether to make a charging order the court shall consider all the circumstances of the case and, in particular, any evidence before it as to—

(a) the personal circumstances of the debtor, and

(b) whether any other creditor of the debtor would be likely to be unduly prejudiced by the making of the order.

[(6) Subsections (7) and (8) apply where, under a judgment or order of the High Court or a county court, a debtor is required to pay a sum of money by instalments.

(7) The fact that there has been no default in payment of the instalments does not prevent a charging order from being made in respect of that sum.

(8) But if there has been no default, the court must take that into account when considering the circumstances of the case under subsection (5).]

[884]

NOTES

Sub-s (2): words in square brackets in para (c) substituted or inserted and final words in square brackets substituted by the Administration of Justice Act 1982, ss 34, 37, Sch 3, Pt II, paras 2, 3, 6, words in square brackets therein substituted by the County Courts Act 1984, s 148(1), Sch 2, para 71.

Sub-ss (6)–(8): inserted by the Tribunals, Courts and Enforcement Act 2007, s 93(1), (2), (6), as from a day to be appointed, except in relation to a case where a judgment or order of the High Court or a county court under which a debtor is required to pay a sum of money by instalments was made, or applied for, before this amendment comes into force.

2 Property which may be charged

(1) Subject to subsection (3) below, a charge may be imposed by a charging order only on—

(a) any interest held by the debtor beneficially—

(i) in any asset of a kind mentioned in subsection (2) below, or

(ii) under any trust; or

(b) any interest held by a person as trustee of a trust ("the trust"), if the interest is in such an asset or is an interest under another trust and—

(i) the judgment or order in respect of which a charge is to be imposed was made against that person as trustee of the trust, or

(ii) the whole beneficial interest under the trust is held by the debtor unencumbered and for his own benefit, or

(iii) in a case where there are two or more debtors all of whom are liable to the creditor for the same debt, they together hold the whole beneficial interest under the trust unencumbered and for their own benefit.

(2) The assets referred to in subsection (1) above are—

(a) land,

(b) securities of any of the following kinds—

(i) government stock,

(ii) stock of any body (other than a building society) incorporated within England and Wales,

(iii) stock of any body incorporated outside England and Wales or of any state or territory outside the United Kingdom, being stock registered in a register kept at any place within England and Wales,

(iv) units of any unit trust in respect of which a register of the unit holders is kept at any place within England and Wales, or

(c) funds in court.

(3) In any case where a charge is imposed by a charging order on any interest in an asset of a kind mentioned in paragraph (b) or (c) of subsection (2) above, the court making the order may provide for the charge to extend to any interest or dividend payable in respect of the asset.

[885]

3 Provisions supplementing sections 1 and 2

(1) A charging order may be made either absolutely or subject to conditions as to notifying the debtor or as to the time when the charge is to become enforceable, or as to other matters.

(2) The Land Charges Act 1972 and the [Land Registration Act 2002] shall apply in relation to charging orders as they apply in relation to other orders or writs issued or made for the purpose of enforcing judgments.

(3) …

(4) Subject to the provisions of this Act, a charge imposed by a charging order shall have the like effect and shall be enforceable in the same courts and in the same manner as an equitable charge created by the debtor by writing under his hand.

[(4A) Subsections (4C) to (4E) apply where—

(a) a debtor is required to pay a sum of money in instalments under a judgment or order of the High Court or a county court (an "instalments order"), and

(b) a charge has been imposed by a charging order in respect of that sum.

(4B) In subsections (4C) to (4E) references to the enforcement of a charge are to the making of an order for the enforcement of the charge.

(4C) The charge may not be enforced unless there has been default in payment of an instalment under the instalments order.

(4D) Rules of court may—

(a) provide that, if there has been default in payment of an instalment, the charge may be enforced only in prescribed cases, and

(b) limit the amounts for which, and the times at which, the charge may be enforced.

(4E) Except so far as otherwise provided by rules of court under subsection (4D)—

(a) the charge may be enforced, if there has been default in payment of an instalment, for the whole of the sum of money secured by the charge and the costs then remaining unpaid, or for such part as the court may order, but

(b) the charge may not be enforced unless, at the time of enforcement, the whole or part of an instalment which has become due under the instalments order remains unpaid.]

(5) The court by which a charging order was made may at any time, on the application of the debtor or of any person interested in any property to which the order relates, make an order discharging or varying the charging order.

(6) Where a charging order has been protected by an entry registered under the Land Charges Act 1972 or the [Land Registration Act 2002], an order under subsection (5) above discharging the charging order may direct that the entry be cancelled.

(7) The Lord Chancellor may by order made by statutory instrument amend section 2(2) of this Act by adding to, or removing from, the kinds of asset for the time being referred to there, any asset of a kind which in his opinion ought to be so added or removed.

(8) Any order under subsection (7) above shall be subject to annulment in pursuance of a resolution of either House of Parliament.

[886]

NOTES

Sub-s (2): words in square brackets substituted by the Land Registration Act 2002, s 133, Sch 11, para 15.

Sub-s (3): repealed by the Land Registration Act 2002, s 135, Sch 13.

Sub-ss (4A)–(4E): inserted by the Tribunals, Courts and Enforcement Act 2007, s 93(1), (3), (6), as from a day to be appointed, except in relation to a case where a judgment or order of the High Court or a county court under which a debtor is required to pay a sum of money by instalments was made, or applied for, before this amendment comes into force.

Sub-s (6): words in square brackets substituted by the Land Registration Act 2002, s 133, Sch 11, para 15.

[3A Power to set financial thresholds

(1) The Lord Chancellor may by regulations provide that a charge may not be imposed by a charging order for securing the payment of money of an amount below that determined in accordance with the regulations.

(2) The Lord Chancellor may by regulations provide that a charge imposed by a charging order may not be enforced by way of order for sale to recover money of an amount below that determined in accordance with the regulations.

(3) Regulations under this section may—

(a) make different provision for different cases;

(b) include such transitional provision as the Lord Chancellor thinks fit.

(4) The power to make regulations under this section is exercisable by statutory instrument.

(5) The Lord Chancellor may not make the first regulations under subsection (1) or (2) unless (in each case) a draft of the statutory instrument containing the regulations has been laid before, and approved by a resolution of, each House of Parliament.

(6) A statutory instrument containing any subsequent regulations under those subsections is subject to annulment in pursuance of a resolution of either House of Parliament.]

[886A]

NOTES

Inserted by the Tribunals, Courts and Enforcement Act 2007, s 94, as from a day to be appointed.

4, 5 (*Outside the scope of this work.*)

Supplemental

6 Interpretation

(1) In this Act—

"building society" has the same meaning as in the Building Societies Act [1986];

"charging order" means an order made under section 1(1) of this Act:

"debtor" and "creditor" have the meanings given by section 1(1) of this Act;

"dividend" includes any distribution in respect of any unit of a unit trust;

"government stock" means any stock issued by Her Majesty's government in the United Kingdom or any funds of, or annuity granted by, that government;

"stock" includes shares, debentures and any securities of the body concerned, whether or not constituting a charge on the assets of that body;

"unit trust" means any trust established for the purpose, or having the effect, of providing, for persons having funds available for investment, facilities for the participation by them, as beneficiaries under the trust, in any profits or income arising from the acquisition, holding, management or disposal of any property whatsoever.

(2) For the purposes of *section 1* [sections 1 and 3] of this Act references to a judgment or order of the High Court or a county court shall be taken to include references to a judgment, order, decree or award (however called) of any court or arbitrator (including any foreign court or arbitrator) which is or has become enforceable (whether wholly or to a limited extent) as if it were a judgment or order of the High Court or a county court.

(3) References in section 2 of this Act to any securities include references to any such securities standing in the name of the Accountant General.

[886B]

NOTES

Sub-s (1): date in square brackets substituted by the Building Societies Act 1986, s 120, Sch 18, Part I, para 14.

Sub-s (2): words in italics repealed and subsequent words in square brackets substituted by the Tribunals, Courts and Enforcement Act 2007, s 93(1), (4), (6), as from a day to be appointed, except in relation to a case where a judgment or order of the High Court or a county court under which a debtor is required to pay a sum of money by instalments was made, or applied for, before this amendment comes into force.

7 (*Outside the scope of this work.*)

8 Short title, commencement and extent

(1) This Act may be cited as the Charging Orders Act 1979.

(2) This Act comes into force on such day as the Lord Chancellor may appoint by order made by statutory instrument.

(3) This Act does not extend to Scotland or Northern Ireland.

[887]

NOTES

Order: the Charging Orders Act 1979 (Commencement) Order 1980, SI 1980/627.

HOUSING ACT 1980

(1980 c 51)

An Act to give security of tenure, and the right to buy their homes, to tenants of local authorities and other bodies; to make other provision with respect to those and other tenants; to amend the law about housing finance in the public sector; to make other provision with respect to housing; to restrict the discretion of the court in making orders for possession of land; and for connected purposes

[8 August 1980]

1–85 *(Ss 1–50 (Pt I) repealed by the Housing (Consequential Provisions) Act 1985, s 3, Sch 1, Pt I; ss 51–85 (Pts II, III) in so far as unrepealed outside the scope of this work.)*

PART IV
JURISDICTION AND PROCEDURE

86–88 *(Ss 86, 88 outside the scope of this work; s 87 repealed by the Housing (Consequential Provisions) Act 1985, s 3, Sch 1, Pt I.)*

89 Restriction on discretion of court in making orders for possession of land

(1) Where a court makes an order for the possession of any land in a case not falling within the exceptions mentioned in subsection (2) below, the giving up of possession shall not be postponed (whether by the order or any variation, suspension or stay of execution) to a date later than fourteen days after the making of the order, unless it appears to the court that exceptional hardship would be caused by requiring possession to be given up by that date; and shall not in any event be postponed to a date later than six weeks after the making of the order.

(2) The restrictions in subsection (1) above do not apply if—
- (a) the order is made in an action by a mortgagee for possession; or
- (b) the order is made in an action for forfeiture of a lease; or
- (c) the court had power to make the order only if it considered it reasonable to make it; or
- (d) the order relates to a dwelling-house which is the subject of a restricted contract (within the meaning of section 19 of the 1977 Act); or
- (e) the order is made in proceedings brought as mentioned in section 88(1) above.

[888]

NOTES

1977 Act: Rent Act 1977: section 19 repealed with savings by the Housing Act 140(2), Sch 18.

90–155 *(Ss 90–113, 120–137, 139, 144–147, 149 repealed by the Housing (Consequential Provisions) Act 1985, s 3, Sch 1, Pt I; ss 114–116 repealed by the Finance Act 1982, s 157, Sch 22, Pt V; ss 117–119 repealed by the Social Security and Housing Benefits Act 1982, ss 32(7)(a), 48(6), Sch 5; s 140 repealed, with savings in relation to leases granted before 11 December 1987, by the Housing and Planning Act 1986, s 18, Sch 4, paras 7, 11(2); ss 138, 141–143, 148, 150–155 outside the scope of this work.)*

(Schs 1–26 outside the scope of this work.)

LIMITATION ACT 1980

(1980 c 58)

An Act to consolidate the Limitation Acts 1939 to 1980

[13 November 1980]

PART I
ORDINARY TIME LIMITS FOR DIFFERENT CLASSES OF ACTION

Time limits under Part I subject to extension or exclusion under Part II

1 Time limits under Part I subject to extension or exclusion under Part II

(1) This Part of this Act gives the ordinary time limits for bringing actions of the various classes mentioned in the following provisions of this Part.

(2) The ordinary time limits given in this Part of this Act are subject to extension or exclusion in accordance with the provisions of Part II of this Act.

[889]

Actions founded on tort

2 Time limit for actions founded on tort

An action founded on tort shall not be brought after the expiration of six years from the date on which the cause of action accrued.

[890]

3, 4, 4A (*Outside the scope of this work.*)

Actions founded on simple contract

5 Time limit for actions founded on simple contract

An action founded on simple contract shall not be brought after the expiration of six years from the date on which the cause of action accrued.

[891]

6, 7 (*Outside the scope of this work.*)

General rule for actions on a specialty

8 Time limit for actions on a specialty

(1) An action upon a specialty shall not be brought after the expiration of twelve years from the date on which the cause of action accrued.

(2) Subsection (1) above shall not affect any action for which a shorter period of limitation is prescribed by any other provision of this Act.

[892]

Actions for sums recoverable by statute

9 Time limit for actions for sums recoverable by statute

(1) An action to recover any sum recoverable by virtue of any enactment shall not be brought after the expiration of six years from the date on which the cause of action accrued.

(2) Subsection (1) above shall not affect any action to which section 10 of this Act applies.

[893]

10 Special time limit for claiming contribution

(1) Where under section 1 of the Civil Liability (Contribution) Act 1978 any person becomes entitled to a right to recover contribution in respect of any damage from any other person, no action to recover contribution by virtue of that right shall be brought after the expiration of two years from the date on which that right accrued.

(2) For the purposes of this section the date on which a right to recover contribution in respect of any damage accrues to any person (referred to below in this section as "the relevant date") shall be ascertained as provided in subsections (3) and (4) below.

(3) If the person in question is held liable in respect of that damage—

(a) by a judgment given in any civil proceedings; or
(b) by an award made on any arbitration;

the relevant date shall be the date on which the judgment is given, or the date of the award (as the case may be).

For the purposes of this subsection no account shall be taken of any judgment or award given or made on appeal in so far as it varies the amount of damages awarded against the person in question.

(4) If, in any case not within subsection (3) above, the person in question makes or agrees to make any payment to one or more persons in compensation for that damage (whether he admits any liability in respect of the damage or not), the relevant date shall be the earliest date on which the amount to be paid by him is agreed between him (or his representative) and the person (or each of the persons, as the case may be) to whom the payment is to be made.

(5) An action to recover contribution shall be one to which sections 28, 32 and 35 of this Act apply, but otherwise Parts II and III of this Act (except sections 34, 37 and 38) shall not apply for the purposes of this section.

[894]

11–14 (*Outside the scope of this work.*)

Actions in respect of latent damage not involving personal injuries

[14A Special time limit for negligence actions where facts relevant to cause of action are not known at date of accrual

(1) This section applies to any action for damages for negligence, other than one to which section 11 of this Act applies, where the starting date for reckoning the period of limitation under subsection (4)(b) below falls after the date on which the cause of action accrued.

(2) Section 2 of this Act shall not apply to an action to which this section applies.

(3) An action to which this section applies shall not be brought after the expiration of the period applicable in accordance with subsection (4) below.

(4) That period is either—

(a) six years from the date on which the cause of action accrued; or

(b) three years from the starting date as defined by subsection (5) below, if that period expires later than the period mentioned in paragraph (a) above.

(5) For the purposes of this section, the starting date for reckoning the period of limitation under subsection (4)(b) above is the earliest date on which the plaintiff or any person in whom the cause of action was vested before him first had both the knowledge required for bringing an action for damages in respect of the relevant damage and a right to bring such an action.

(6) In subsection (5) above "the knowledge required for bringing an action for damages in respect of the relevant damage" means knowledge both—

(a) of the material facts about the damage in respect of which damages are claimed; and

(b) of the other facts relevant to the current action mentioned in subsection (8) below.

(7) For the purposes of subsection (6)(a) above, the material facts about the damage are such facts about the damage as would lead a reasonable person who had suffered such damage to consider it sufficiently serious to justify his instituting proceedings for damages against a defendant who did not dispute liability and was able to satisfy a judgment.

(8) The other facts referred to in subsection (6)(b) above are—

(a) that the damage was attributable in whole or in part to the act or omission which is alleged to constitute negligence; and

(b) the identity of the defendant; and

(c) if it is alleged that the act or omission was that of a person other than the defendant, the identity of that person and the additional facts supporting the bringing of an action against the defendant.

(9) Knowledge that any acts or omissions did or did not, as a matter of law, involve negligence is irrelevant for the purposes of subsection (5) above.

(10) For the purposes of this section a person's knowledge includes knowledge which he might reasonably have been expected to acquire—

(a) from facts observable or ascertainable by him; or

(b) from facts ascertainable by him with the help of appropriate expert advice which it is reasonable for him to seek;

but a person shall not be taken by virtue of this subsection to have knowledge of a fact ascertainable only with the help of expert advice so long as he has taken all reasonable steps to obtain (and, where appropriate, to act on) that advice.]

[895]

NOTES

Inserted by the Latent Damage Act 1986, s 1.

[14B Overriding time limit for negligence actions not involving personal injuries

(1) An action for damages for negligence, other than one to which section 11 of this Act applies, shall not be brought after the expiration of fifteen years from the date (or, if more than one, from the last of the dates) on which there occurred any act or omission—

(a) which is alleged to constitute negligence; and

(b) to which the damage in respect of which damages are claimed is alleged to be attributable (in whole or in part).

(2) This section bars the right of action in a case to which subsection (1) above applies notwithstanding that—

(a) the cause of action has not yet accrued; or

(b) where section 14A of this Act applies to the action, the date which is for the purposes of that section the starting date for reckoning the period mentioned in subsection (4)(b) of that section has not yet occurred;

before the end of the period of limitation prescribed by this section.]

[896]

NOTES

Inserted by the Latent Damage Act 1986, s 1.

Actions to recover land and rent

15 Time limit for actions to recover land

(1) No action shall be brought by any person to recover any land after the expiration of twelve years from the date on which the right of action accrued to him or, if it first accrued to some person through whom he claims, to that person.

(2) Subject to the following provisions of this section, where—

(a) the estate or interest claimed was an estate or interest in reversion or remainder or any other future estate or interest and the right of action to recover the land accrued on the date on which the estate or interest fell into possession by the determination of the preceding estate or interest; and

(b) the person entitled to the preceding estate or interest (not being a term of years absolute) was not in possession of the land on that date;

no action shall be brought by the person entitled to the succeeding estate or interest after the expiration of twelve years from the date on which the right of action accrued to the person entitled to the preceding estate or interest or six years from the date on which the right of action accrued to the person entitled to the succeeding estate or interest, whichever period last expires.

(3) Subsection (2) above shall not apply to any estate or interest which falls into possession on the determination of an entailed interest and which might have been barred by the person entitled to the entailed interest.

(4) No person shall bring an action to recover any estate or interest in land under an assurance taking effect after the right of action to recover the land had accrued to the person by whom the assurance was made or some person through whom he claimed or some person entitled to a preceding estate or interest, unless the action is brought within the period during which the person by whom the assurance was made could have brought such an action.

(5) Where any person is entitled to any estate or interest in land in possession and, while so entitled, is also entitled to any future estate or interest in that land, and his right to recover the estate or interest in possession is barred under this Act, no action shall be brought by that person, or by any person claiming through him, in respect of the future estate or interest, unless in the meantime possession of the land has been recovered by a person entitled to an intermediate estate or interest.

(6) Part I of Schedule 1 to this Act contains provisions for determining the date of accrual of rights of action to recover land in the cases there mentioned.

(7) Part II of that Schedule contains provisions modifying the provisions of this section in their application to actions brought by, or by a person claiming through, the Crown or any spiritual or eleemosynary corporation sole.

[897]

NOTES

This section is disapplied as respects any person, other than a chargee, in relation to an estate in land or rentcharge the title to which is registered, by the Land Registration Act 2002, s 96(1) at **[1973]**.

16 Time limit for redemption actions

When a mortgagee of land has been in possession of any of the mortgaged land for a period of twelve years, no action to redeem the land of which the mortgagee has been so in possession shall be brought after the end of that period by the mortgagor or any person claiming through him.

[898]

NOTES

This section is disapplied as respects any person in relation to an estate in land or rentcharge the title to which is registered, by the Land Registration Act 2002, s 96(2) at **[1973]**.

17 Extinction of title to land after expiration of time limit

Subject to—

(a) section 18 of this Act …

(b) …

at the expiration of the period prescribed by this Act for any person to bring an action to recover land (including a redemption action) the title of that person to the land shall be extinguished.

[899]

NOTES

Para (b) and word omitted immediately preceding it repealed by the Land Registration Act 2002, s 135, Sch 13.

This section does not operate to extinguish the title of any person where a period of limitation under ss 15, 16 hereof is disapplied by virtue of the Land Registration Act 2002, s 96(1), (2): see the Land Registration Act 2002, s 96(3) at **[1973]**.

18 Settled land and land held on trust

(1) Subject to section 21(1) and (2) of this Act, the provisions of this Act shall apply to equitable interests in land … as they apply to legal estates.

Accordingly a right of action to recover the land shall, for the purposes of this Act but not otherwise, be treated as accruing to a person entitled in possession to such an equitable interest in the like manner and circumstances, and on the same date, as it would accrue if his interest were a legal estate in the land (and any relevant provision of Part I of Schedule 1 to this Act shall apply in any such case accordingly).

(2) Where the period prescribed by this Act has expired for the bringing of an action to recover land by a tenant for life or a statutory owner of settled land—

(a) his legal estate shall not be extinguished if and so long as the right of action to recover the land of any person entitled to a beneficial interest in the land either has not accrued or has not been barred by this Act; and

(b) the legal estate shall accordingly remain vested in the tenant for life or statutory owner and shall devolve in accordance with the Settled Land Act 1925;

but if and when every such right of action has been barred by this Act, his legal estate shall be extinguished.

(3) Where any land is held upon trust … and the period prescribed by this Act has expired for the bringing of an action to recover the land by the trustees, the estate of the trustees shall not be extinguished if and so long as the right of action to recover the land of any person entitled to a beneficial interest in the land … either has not accrued or has not been barred by this Act; but if and when every such right of action has been so barred the estate of the trustees shall be extinguished.

(4) Where—

(a) any settled land is vested in a statutory owner; or

(b) any land is held upon trust … ;

an action to recover the land may be brought by the statutory owner or trustees on behalf of any person entitled to a beneficial interest in possession in the land … whose right of action has not been barred by this Act, notwithstanding that the right of action of the statutory owner or trustees would apart from this provision have been barred by this Act.

[900]

NOTES

Sub-ss (1), (3), (4): words omitted repealed by the Trusts of Land and Appointment of Trustees Act 1996, s 25(2), Sch 4; for savings in relation to entailed interests created before the commencement of that Act, and savings consequential upon the abolition of the doctrine of conversion, see s 25(4), (5) thereof.

19 Time limit for actions to recover rent

No action shall be brought, *or distress made* [and the power conferred by section 72(1) of the Tribunals, Courts and Enforcement Act 2007 shall not be exercisable], to recover arrears of rent, or damages in respect of arrears of rent, after the expiration of six years from the date on which the arrears became due.

[901]–[902]

NOTES

Words in italics substituted by subsequent words in square brackets by the Tribunals, Courts and Enforcement Act 2007, s 86, Sch 14, paras 35, 36, as from a day to be appointed.

19A (*Outside the scope of this work.*)

Actions to recover money secured by a mortgage or charge or to recover proceeds of the sale of land

20 Time limit for actions to recover money secured by a mortgage or charge or to recover proceeds of the sale of land

(1) No action shall be brought to recover—

(a) any principal sum of money secured by a mortgage or other charge on property (whether real or personal); or

(b) proceeds of the sale of land;

after the expiration of twelve years from the date on which the right to receive the money accrued.

(2) No foreclosure action in respect of mortgaged personal property shall be brought after the expiration of twelve years from the date on which the right to foreclose accrued.

But if the mortgagee was in possession of the mortgaged property after that date, the right to foreclose on the property which was in his possession shall not be treated as having accrued for the purposes of this subsection until the date on which his possession discontinued.

(3) The right to receive any principal sum of money secured by a mortgage or other charge and the right to foreclose on the property subject to the mortgage or charge shall not be treated as accruing so long as that property comprises any future interest or any life insurance policy which has not matured or been determined.

(4) Nothing in this section shall apply to a foreclosure action in respect of mortgaged land, but the provisions of this Act relating to actions to recover land shall apply to such an action.

(5) Subject to subsections (6) and (7) below, no action to recover arrears of interest payable in respect of any sum of money secured by a mortgage or other charge or payable in respect of proceeds of the sale of land, or to recover damages in respect of such arrears shall be brought after the expiration of six years from the date on which the interest became due.

(6) Where—

(a) a prior mortgagee or other incumbrancer has been in possession of the property charged; and

(b) an action is brought within one year of the discontinuance of that possession by the subsequent incumbrancer;

the subsequent incumbrancer may recover by that action all the arrears of interest which fell due during the period of possession by the prior incumbrancer or damages in respect of those arrears, notwithstanding that the period exceeded six years.

(7) Where—

(a) the property subject to the mortgage or charge comprises any future interest or life insurance policy; and

(b) it is a term of the mortgage or charge that arrears of interest shall be treated as part of the principal sum of money secured by the mortgage or charge;

interest shall not be treated as becoming due before the right to recover the principal sum of money has accrued or is treated as having accrued.

[903]

Actions in respect of trust property or the personal estate of deceased persons

21 Time limit for actions in respect of trust property

(1) No period of limitation prescribed by this Act shall apply to an action by a beneficiary under a trust, being an action—

(a) in respect of any fraud or fraudulent breach of trust to which the trustee was a party or privy; or

(b) to recover from the trustee trust property or the proceeds of trust property in the possession of the trustee, or previously received by the trustee and converted to his use.

(2) Where a trustee who is also a beneficiary under the trust receives or retains trust property or its proceeds as his share on a distribution of trust property under the trust, his liability in any action brought by virtue of subsection (1)(b) above to recover that property or its proceeds after the expiration of the period of limitation prescribed by this Act for bringing an action to recover trust property shall be limited to the excess over his proper share.

This subsection only applies if the trustee acted honestly and reasonably in making the distribution.

(3) Subject to the preceding provisions of this section, an action by a beneficiary to recover trust property or in respect of any breach of trust, not being an action for which a period of limitation is prescribed by any other provision of this Act, shall not be brought after the expiration of six years from the date on which the right of action accrued.

For the purposes of this subsection, the right of action shall not be treated as having accrued to any beneficiary entitled to a future interest in the trust property until the interest fell into possession.

(4) No beneficiary as against whom there would be a good defence under this Act shall derive any greater or other benefit from a judgment or order obtained by any other beneficiary than he could have obtained if he had brought the action and this Act had been pleaded in defence.

[904]

22 Time limit for actions claiming personal estate of a deceased person

Subject to section 21(1) and (2) of this Act—

(a) no action in respect of any claim to the personal estate of a deceased person or to any share or interest in any such estate (whether under a will or on intestacy) shall be brought after the expiration of twelve years from the date on which the right to receive the share or interest accrued; and

(b) no action to recover arrears of interest in respect of any legacy, or damages in respect of such arrears, shall be brought after the expiration of six years from the date on which the interest became due.

[905]

Actions for an account

23 Time limit in respect of actions for an account

An action for an account shall not be brought after the expiration of any time limit under this Act which is applicable to the claim which is the basis of the duty to account.

[906]

Miscellaneous and supplemental

24, 25 *(S 24 outside the scope of this work; s 25 repealed by the Patronage (Benefices) Measure 1986, s 4(3).)*

26 Administration to date back to death

For the purposes of the provisions of this Act relating to actions for the recovery of land and advowsons an administrator of the estate of a deceased person shall be treated as claiming as if there had been no interval of time between the death of the deceased person and the grant of the letters of administration.

[907]

27 Cure of defective disentailing assurance

(1) This section applies where—

(a) a person entitled in remainder to an entailed interest in any land makes an assurance of his interest which fails to bar the issue in tail or the estates and interests taking effect on the determination of the entailed interest, or fails to bar those estates and interests only; and

(b) any person takes possession of the land by virtue of the assurance.

(2) If the person taking possession of the land by virtue of the assurance, or any other person whatsoever (other than a person entitled to possession by virtue of the settlement) is in possession of the land for a period of twelve years from the commencement of the time when the assurance could have operated as an effective bar, the assurance shall thereupon operate, and be treated as having always operated, to bar the issue in tail and the estates and interests taking effect on the determination of the entailed interest.

(3) The reference in subsection (2) above to the time when the assurance could have operated as an effective bar is a reference to the time at which the assurance, if it had then been executed by the person entitled to the entailed interest, would have operated, without the consent of any other person, to bar the issue in tail and the estates and interests taking effect on the determination of the entailed interest.

[908]

[27A Actions for recovery of property obtained through unlawful conduct etc

(1) None of the time limits given in the preceding provisions of this Act applies to any proceedings under Chapter 2 of Part 5 of the Proceeds of Crime Act 2002 (civil recovery of proceeds of unlawful conduct).

(2) Proceedings under that Chapter for a recovery order in respect of any recoverable property shall not be brought after the expiration of the period of twelve years from the date on which the [relevant person's] cause of action accrued.

(3) Proceedings under that Chapter are brought when—

(a) a claim form is issued, or

[(aa) an application is made for a property freezing order, or]

(b) an application is made for an interim receiving order,

whichever is the [earliest].

(4) The [relevant person's] cause of action accrues in respect of any recoverable property—

(a) in the case of proceedings for a recovery order in respect of property obtained through unlawful conduct, when the property is so obtained,

(b) in the case of proceedings for a recovery order in respect of any other recoverable property, when the property obtained through unlawful conduct which it represents is so obtained.

(5) If—

(a) a person would (but for the preceding provisions of this Act) have a cause of action in respect of the conversion of a chattel, and

(b) proceedings are started under that Chapter for a recovery order in respect of the chattel,

section 3(2) of this Act does not prevent his asserting on an application under section 281 of that Act that the property belongs to him, or the court making a declaration in his favour under that section.

(6) If the court makes such a declaration, his title to the chattel is to be treated as not having been extinguished by section 3(2) of this Act.

PART I STATUTES

(7) Expressions used in this section and Part 5 of that Act have the same meaning in this section as in that Part.]

[(8) In this section "relevant person" means—

(a) the Serious Organised Crime Agency,
(b) the Director of Public Prosecutions,
(c) the Director of Revenue and Customs Prosecutions, or
(d) the Director of the Serious Fraud Office.]

[909]

NOTES

Inserted by the Proceeds of Crime Act 2002, s 288(1).

Sub-s (2): words in square brackets substituted by the Serious Crime Act 2007, s 74(2)(g), Sch 8, Pt 7, paras 147(1), (2).

Sub-s (3): para (aa) inserted and word in square brackets substituted by the Serious Organised Crime and Police Act 2005, s 109, Sch 6, para 2.

Sub-s (4): words in square brackets substituted by the Serious Crime Act 2007, s 74(2)(g), Sch 8, Pt 7, paras 147(1), (3).

Sub-s (8): inserted by the Serious Crime Act 2007, s 74(2)(g), Sch 8, Pt 7, paras 147(1), (4).

[27B Actions for recovery of property for purposes of an external order

(1) None of the time limits given in the preceding provisions of this Act applies to any proceedings under Chapter 2 of Part 5 of the Proceeds of Crime Act 2002 (External Requests and Orders) Order 2005 (civil proceedings for the realisation of property to give effect to an external order).

(2) Proceedings under that Chapter for a recovery order in respect of any recoverable property shall not be brought after the expiration of the period of twelve years from the date on which the [relevant person's] cause of action accrued.

(3) Proceedings under that Chapter are brought when—

(a) a claim form is issued, or
(b) an application is made for a property freezing order, or
(c) an application is made for an interim receiving order,

whichever is earliest.

(4) The [relevant person's] cause of action accrues in respect of any recoverable property—

(a) in the case of proceedings for a recovery order in respect of property obtained, or believed to have been obtained, as a result of or in connection with criminal conduct, when the property is so obtained,
(b) in the case of proceedings for a recovery order in respect of any other recoverable property, when the property obtained, or believed to have been obtained, as a result of or in connection with criminal conduct which it represents is so obtained.

(5) If—

(a) a person would (but for the preceding provisions of this Act) have a cause of action in respect of the conversion of a chattel, and
(b) proceedings are started under that Chapter for a recovery order in respect of the chattel,

section 3(2) of this Act does not prevent his asserting on an application under article 192 of that Order that the property belongs to him, or the court making a declaration in his favour under that article.

(6) If the court makes such a declaration, his title to the chattel is to be treated as not having been extinguished by section 3(2) of this Act.

(7) In this section—

(a) "criminal conduct" is to be construed in accordance with section 447(8) of the Proceeds of Crime Act 2002, and
(b) expressions used in this section which are also used in Part 5 of the Proceeds of Crime Act 2002 (External Requests and Orders) Order 2005 have the same meaning in this section as in that Part.]

[(8) In this section "relevant person" means—

(a) the Serious Organised Crime Agency,
(b) the Director of Public Prosecutions,
(c) the Director of Revenue and Customs Prosecutions, or
(d) the Director of the Serious Fraud Office.]]

[910]

NOTES

Commencement: 1 January 2006.

Inserted by SI 2005/3181, art 201(1).

Sub-ss (2), (4): words in square brackets substituted by SI 2008/302, art 4(1), (2).

Sub-s (8): inserted by SI 2008/302, art 4(1), (3).

PART II
EXTENSION OR EXCLUSION OF ORDINARY TIME LIMITS

Disability

28 Extension of limitation period in case of disability

(1) Subject to the following provisions of this section, if on the date when any right of action accrued for which a period of limitation is prescribed by this Act, the person to whom it accrued was under a disability, the action may be brought at any time before the expiration of six years from the date when he ceased to be under a disability or died (whichever first occurred) notwithstanding that the period of limitation has expired.

(2) This section shall not affect any case where the right of action first accrued to some person (not under a disability) through whom the person under a disability claims.

(3) When a right of action which has accrued to a person under a disability accrues, on the death of that person while still under a disability, to another person under a disability, no further extension of time shall be allowed by reason of the disability of the second person.

(4) No action to recover land or money charged on land shall be brought by virtue of this section by any person after the expiration of thirty years from the date on which the right of action accrued to that person or some person through whom he claims.

[(4A) If the action is one to which section 4A of this Act applies, subsection (1) above shall have effect—

(a) in the case of an action for libel or slander, as if for the words from "at any time" to "occurred)" there were substituted the words "by him at any time before the expiration of one year from the date on which he ceased to be under a disability"; and

(b) in the case of an action for slander of title, slander of goods or other malicious falsehood, as if for the words "six years" there were substituted the words "one year".]

(5) If the action is one to which section 10 of this Act applies, subsection (1) above shall have effect as if for the words "six years" there were substituted the words "two years".

(6) If the action is one to which section 11 or 12(2) of this Act applies, subsection (1) above shall have effect as if for the words "six years" there were substituted the words "three years".

[(7) If the action is one to which section 11A of this Act applies or one by virtue of section 6(1)(a) of the Consumer Protection Act 1987 (death caused by defective product), subsection (1) above—

(a) shall not apply to the time limit prescribed by subsection (3) of the said section 11A or to that time limit as applied by virtue of section 12(1) of this Act; and

(b) in relation to any other time limit prescribed by this Act shall have effect as if for the word "six years" there were substituted the words "three years".]

[911]

NOTES

Sub-s (4A): inserted by the Administration of Justice Act 1985, ss 57(3), 69(5), Sch 9, para 14; substituted by the Defamation Act 1996, s 5(3), (6).

Sub-s (7): inserted by the Consumer Protection Act 1987, s 6, Sch 1, Pt I, para 4.

[28A Extension for cases where the limitation period is the period under section 14A(4)(b)

(1) Subject to subsection (2) below, if in the case of any action for which a period of limitation is prescribed by section 14A of this Act—

(a) the period applicable in accordance with subsection (4) of that section is the period mentioned in paragraph (b) of that subsection;

(b) on the date which is for the purposes of that section the starting date for reckoning that period the person by reference to whose knowledge that date fell to be determined under subsection (5) of that section was under a disability; and

(c) section 28 of this Act does not apply to the action;

the action may be brought at any time before the expiration of three years from the date when he ceased to be under a disability or died (whichever first occurred) notwithstanding that the period mentioned above has expired.

(2) An action may not be brought by virtue of subsection (1) above after the end of the period of limitation prescribed by section 14B of this Act.]

[912]

NOTES

Inserted by the Latent Damage Act 1986, s 2(1).

Acknowledgment and part payment

29 Fresh accrual of action on acknowledgment or part payment

(1) Subsections (2) and (3) below apply where any right of action (including a foreclosure action) to recover land or an advowson or any right of a mortgagee of personal property to bring a foreclosure action in respect of the property has accrued.

(2) If the person in possession of the land, benefice or personal property in question acknowledges the title of the person to whom the right of action has accrued—

(a) the right shall be treated as having accrued on and not before the date of the acknowledgment; and

(b) in the case of a right of action to recover land which has accrued to a person entitled to an estate or interest taking effect on the determination of an entailed interest against whom time is running under section 27 of this Act, section 27 shall thereupon cease to apply to the land.

(3) In the case of a foreclosure or other action by a mortgagee, if the person in possession of the land, benefice or personal property in question or the person liable for the mortgage debt makes any payment in respect of the debt (whether of principal or interest) the right shall be treated as having accrued on and not before the date of the payment.

(4) Where a mortgagee is by virtue of the mortgage in possession of any mortgaged land and either—

(a) receives any sum in respect of the principal or interest of the mortgage debt; or

(b) acknowledges the title of the mortgagor, or his equity of redemption;

an action to redeem the land in his possession may be brought at any time before the expiration of twelve years from the date of the payment or acknowledgment.

(5) Subject to subsection (6) below, where any right of action has accrued to recover—

(a) any debt or other liquidated pecuniary claim; or

(b) any claim to the personal estate of a deceased person or to any share or interest in any such estate;

and the person liable or accountable for the claim acknowledges the claim or makes any payment in respect of it the right shall be treated as having accrued on and not before the date of the acknowledgment or payment.

(6) A payment of a part of the rent or interest due at any time shall not extend the period for claiming the remainder then due, but any payment of interest shall be treated as a payment in respect of the principal debt.

(7) Subject to subsection (6) above, a current period of limitation may be repeatedly extended under this section by further acknowledgments or payments, but a right of action, once barred by this Act, shall not be revived by any subsequent acknowledgment or payment.

[913]

30 Formal provisions as to acknowledgments and part payments

(1) To be effective for the purposes of section 29 of this Act, an acknowledgment must be in writing and signed by the person making it.

(2) For the purposes of section 29, any acknowledgment or payment—

(a) may be made by the agent of the person by whom it is required to be made under that section; and

(b) shall be made to the person, or to an agent of the person, whose title or claim is being acknowledged or, as the case may be, in respect of whose claim the payment is being made.

[914]

31 Effect of acknowledgment or part payment on persons other than the maker or recipient

(1) An acknowledgment of the title to any land, benefice, or mortgaged personalty by any person in possession of it shall bind all other persons in possession during the ensuing period of limitation.

(2) A payment in respect of a mortgage debt by the mortgagor or any other person liable for the debt, or by any person in possession of the mortgaged property, shall, so far as any right of the mortgagee to foreclose or otherwise to recover the property is concerned, bind all other persons in possession of the mortgaged property during the ensuing period of limitation.

(3) Where two or more mortgagees are by virtue of the mortgage in possession of the mortgaged land, an acknowledgment of the mortgagor's title or of his equity of redemption by one of the mortgagees shall only bind him and his successors and shall not bind any other mortgagee or his successors.

(4) Where in a case within subsection (3) above the mortgagee by whom the acknowledgment is given is entitled to a part of the mortgaged land and not to any ascertained part of the mortgage

debt the mortgagor shall be entitled to redeem that part of the land on payment, with interest, of the part of the mortgage debt which bears the same proportion to the whole of the debt as the value of the part of the land bears to the whole of the mortgaged land.

(5) Where there are two or more mortgagors, and the title or equity of redemption of one of the mortgagors is acknowledged as mentioned above in this section, the acknowledgment shall be treated as having been made to all the mortgagors.

(6) An acknowledgment of any debt or other liquidated pecuniary claim shall bind the acknowledgor and his successors but not any other person.

(7) A payment made in respect of any debt or other liquidated pecuniary claim shall bind all persons liable in respect of the debt or claim.

(8) An acknowledgment by one of several personal representatives of any claim to the personal estate of a deceased person or to any share or interest in any such estate, or a payment by one of several personal representatives in respect of any such claim, shall bind the estate of the deceased person.

(9) In this section "successor", in relation to any mortgagee or person liable in respect of any debt or claim, means his personal representatives and any other person on whom the rights under the mortgage or, as the case may be, the liability in respect of the debt or claim devolve (whether on death or bankruptcy or the disposition of property or the determination of a limited estate or interest in settled property or otherwise).

[915]

Fraud, concealment and mistake

32 Postponement of limitation period in case of fraud, concealment or mistake

(1) Subject to [subsections (3) and (4A)] below, where in the case of any action for which a period of limitation is prescribed by this Act, either—

(a) the action is based upon the fraud of the defendant; or

(b) any fact relevant to the plaintiff's right of action has been deliberately concealed from him by the defendant; or

(c) the action is for relief from the consequences of a mistake;

the period of limitation shall not begin to run until the plaintiff has discovered the fraud, concealment or mistake (as the case may be) or could with reasonable diligence have discovered it. References in this subsection to the defendant include references to the defendant's agent and to any person through whom the defendant claims and his agent.

(2) For the purposes of subsection (1) above, deliberate commission of a breach of duty in circumstances in which it is unlikely to be discovered for some time amounts to deliberate concealment of the facts involved in that breach of duty.

(3) Nothing in this section shall enable any action—

(a) to recover, or recover the value of, any property; or

(b) to enforce any charge against, or set aside any transaction affecting, any property;

to be brought against the purchaser of the property or any person claiming through him in any case where the property has been purchased for valuable consideration by an innocent third party since the fraud or concealment or (as the case may be) the transaction in which the mistake was made took place.

(4) A purchaser is an innocent third party for the purposes of this section—

(a) in the case of fraud or concealment of any fact relevant to the plaintiff's right of action, if he was not a party to the fraud or (as the case may be) to the concealment of that fact and did not at the time of the purchase know or have reason to believe that the fraud or concealment had taken place; and

(b) in the case of mistake, if he did not at the time of the purchase know or have reason to believe that the mistake had been made.

[(4A) Subsection (1) above shall not apply in relation to the time limit prescribed by section 11A(3) of this Act or in relation to that time limit as applied by virtue of section 12(1) of this Act].

[(5) Sections 14A and 14B of this Act shall not apply to any action to which subsection (1)(b) above applies (and accordingly the period of limitation referred to in that subsection, in any case to which either of those sections would otherwise apply, is the period applicable under section 2 of this Act).]

[916]

NOTES

Sub-s (1): words in square brackets substituted by the Consumer Protection Act 1987, s 6, Sch 1, Pt I, para 5.
Sub-s (4A): inserted by the Consumer Protection Act 1987, s 6, Sch 1, Pt I, para 5.
Sub-s (5): inserted by the Latent Damage Act 1986, s 2(2).

Disapplication: sub-s (1)(c) is disapplied with respect to certain actions for mistake of law relating to tax brought before 8 September 2003, by the Finance Act 2007, s 107.

32A (*Outside the scope of this work.*)

Discretionary exclusion of time limit for actions in respect of personal injuries or death

33 Discretionary exclusion of time limit for actions in respect of personal injuries or death

(1) If it appears to the court that it would be equitable to allow an action to proceed having regard to the degree to which—

(a) the provisions of section 11 [or 11A] or 12 of this Act prejudice the plaintiff or any person whom he represents; and

(b) any decision of the court under this subsection would prejudice the defendant or any person whom he represents;

the court may direct that those provisions shall not apply to the action, or shall not apply to any specified cause of action to which the action relates.

[(1A) The court shall not under this section disapply—

(a) subsection (3) of section 11A; or

(b) where the damages claimed by the plaintiff are confined to damages for loss of or damage to any property, any other provision in its application to an action by virtue of Part I of the Consumer Protection Act 1987.]

(2) The court shall not under this section disapply section 12(1) except where the reason why the person injured could no longer maintain an action was because of the time limit in section 11 [or subsection (4) of section 11A].

If, for example, the person injured could at his death no longer maintain an action under the Fatal Accidents Act 1976 because of the time limit in Article 29 in Schedule 1 to the Carriage by Air Act 1961, the court has no power to direct that section 12(1) shall not apply.

(3) In acting under this section the court shall have regard to all the circumstances of the case and in particular to—

(a) the length of, and the reasons for, the delay on the part of the plaintiff;

(b) the extent to which, having regard to the delay, the evidence adduced or likely to be adduced by the plaintiff or the defendant is or is likely to be less cogent than if the action had been brought within the time allowed by section 11 [, by section 11A] or (as the case may be) by section 12;

(c) the conduct of the defendant after the cause of action arose, including the extent (if any) to which he responded to requests reasonably made by the plaintiff for information or inspection for the purpose of ascertaining facts which were or might be relevant to the plaintiff's cause of action against the defendant;

(d) the duration of any disability of the plaintiff arising after the date of the accrual of the cause of action;

(e) the extent to which the plaintiff acted promptly and reasonably once he knew whether or not the act or omission of the defendant, to which the injury was attributable, might be capable at that time of giving rise to an action for damages;

(f) the steps, if any, taken by the plaintiff to obtain medical, legal or other expert advice and the nature of any such advice he may have received.

(4) In a case where the person injured died when, because of section 11 [or subsection (4) of section 11A], he could no longer maintain an action and recover damages in respect of the injury, the court shall have regard in particular to the length of, and the reasons for, the delay on the part of the deceased.

(5) In a case under subsection (4) above, or any other case where the time limit, or one of the time limits, depends on the date of knowledge of a person other than the plaintiff, subsection (3) above shall have effect with appropriate modifications, and shall have effect in particular as if references to the plaintiff included references to any person whose date of knowledge is or was relevant in determining a time limit.

(6) A direction by the court disapplying the provisions of section 12(1) shall operate to disapply the provisions to the same effect in section 1(1) of the Fatal Accidents Act 1976.

(7) In this section "the court" means the court in which the action has been brought.

(8) References in this section to section 11 [or 11A] include references to that section as extended by any of the preceding provisions of this Part of this Act or by any provision of Part III of this Act.

[917]

NOTES

Sub-ss (1), (3), (4), (8): words in square brackets inserted by the Consumer Protection Act 1987, s 6, Sch 1, Pt I, para 6.

Sub-s (1A): inserted by the Consumer Protection Act 1987, s 6, Sch 1, Pt I, para 6.

PART III
MISCELLANEOUS AND GENERAL

34 (*Repealed by the Arbitration Act 1996, s 107(2), Sch 4.*)

35 New claims in pending actions: rules of court

(1) For the purposes of this Act, any new claim made in the course of any action shall be deemed to be a separate action and to have been commenced—

(a) in the case of a new claim made in or by way of third party proceedings, on the date on which those proceedings were commenced; and

(b) in the case of any other new claim, on the same date as the original action.

(2) In this section a new claim means any claim by way of set-off or counterclaim, and any claim involving either—

(a) the addition or substitution of a new cause of action; or

(b) the addition or substitution of a new party;

and "third party proceedings" means any proceedings brought in the course of any action by any party to the action against a person not previously a party to the action, other than proceedings brought by joining any such person as defendant to any claim already made in the original action by the party bringing the proceedings.

(3) Except as provided by section 33 of this Act or by rules of court, neither the High Court nor any county court shall allow a new claim within subsection (1)(b) above, other than an original set-off or counterclaim, to be made in the course of any action after the expiry of any time limit under this Act which would affect a new action to enforce that claim.

For the purposes of this subsection, a claim is an original set-off or an original counterclaim if it is a claim made by way of set-off or (as the case may be) by way of counterclaim by a party who has not previously made any claim in the action.

(4) Rules of court may provide for allowing a new claim to which subsection (3) above applies to be made as there mentioned, but only if the conditions specified in subsection (5) below are satisfied, and subject to any further restrictions the rules may impose.

(5) The conditions referred to in subsection (4) above are the following—

(a) in the case of a claim involving a new cause of action, if the new cause of action arises out of the same facts or substantially the same facts as are already in issue on any claim previously made in the original action; and

(b) in the case of a claim involving a new party, if the addition or substitution of the new party is necessary for the determination of the original action.

(6) The addition or substitution of a new party shall not be regarded for the purposes of subsection (5)(b) above as necessary for the determination of the original action unless either—

(a) the new party is substituted for a party whose name was given in any claim made in the original action in mistake for the new party's name; or

(b) any claim already made in the original action cannot be maintained by or against an existing party unless the new party is joined or substituted as plaintiff or defendant in that action.

(7) Subject to subsection (4) above, rules of court may provide for allowing a party to any action to claim relief in a new capacity in respect of a new cause of action notwithstanding that he had no title to make that claim at the date of the commencement of the action.

This subsection shall not be taken as prejudicing the power of rules of court to provide for allowing a party to claim relief in a new capacity without adding or substituting a new cause of action.

(8) Subsections (3) to (7) above shall apply in relation to a new claim made in the course of third party proceedings as if those proceedings were the original action, and subject to such other modifications as may be prescribed by rules of court in any case or class of case.

(9) . . .

[918]

NOTES

Sub-s (9): repealed by the Supreme Court Act 1981, s 152(4), Sch 7.

36 Equitable jurisdiction and remedies

(1) The following time limits under this Act, that is to say—

(a) the time limit under section 2 for actions founded on tort;

[(aa) the time limit under section 4A for actions for libel or slander, or for slander of title, slander of goods or other malicious falsehood;]

(b) the time limit under section 5 for actions founded on simple contract;
(c) the time limit under section 7 for actions to enforce awards where the submission is not by an instrument under seal;
(d) the time limit under section 8 for actions on a specialty;
(e) the time limit under section 9 for actions to recover a sum recoverable by virtue of any enactment; and
(f) the time limit under section 24 for actions to enforce a judgment;

shall not apply to any claim for specific performance of a contract or for an injunction or for other equitable relief, except in so far as any such time limit may be applied by the court by analogy in like manner as the corresponding time limit under any enactment repealed by the Limitation Act 1939 was applied before 1st July 1940.

(2) Nothing in this Act shall affect any equitable jurisdiction to refuse relief on the ground of acquiescence or otherwise.

[919]

NOTES

Sub-s (1): para (aa) inserted by the Administration of Justice Act 1985, ss 57(5), 69(5), Sch 9, para 14, substituted by the Defamation Act 1996, s 5(5), (6).

37 (*Outside the scope of this work.*)

38 Interpretation

(1) In this Act, unless the context otherwise requires—

"action" includes any proceeding in a court of law, including an ecclesiastical court;

"land" includes corporeal hereditaments, tithes and *rentcharges and* any legal or equitable estate or interest therein … but except as provided above in this definition does not include any incorporeal hereditament;

"personal estate" and "personal property" do not include chattels real;

"personal injuries" includes any disease and any impairment of a person's physical or mental condition, and "injury" and cognate expressions shall be construed accordingly;

"rent" includes a rentcharge and a rentservice; "rentcharge" means any annuity or periodical sum of money charged upon or payable out of land, except a rent service or interest on a mortgage on land;

"settled land", "statutory owner" and "tenant for life" have the same meanings respectively as in the Settled Land Act 1925;

"trust" and "trustee" have the same meanings respectively as in the Trustee Act 1925; and

…

(2) For the purposes of this Act a person shall be treated as under a disability while he is an infant, or [lacks capacity (within the meaning of the Mental Capacity Act 2005) to conduct legal proceedings].

(3), (4) …

(5) Subject to subsection (6) below, a person shall be treated as claiming through another person if he became entitled by, through, under, or by the act of that other person to the right claimed, and any person whose estate or interest might have been barred by a person entitled to an entailed interest in possession shall be treated as claiming through the person so entitled.

(6) A person becoming entitled to any estate or interest by virtue of a special power of appointment shall not be treated as claiming through the appointor.

(7) References in this Act to a right of action to recover land shall include references to a right to enter into possession of the land or, in the case of *rentcharges and* tithes, to distrain for arrears of *rent or* tithe, and references to the bringing of such an action shall include references to the making of such an entry or distress.

(8) References in this Act to the possession of land shall, in the case of tithes and rentcharges, be construed as references to the receipt of the tithe or rent, and references to the date of dispossession or discontinuance of possession of land shall, in the case of rent charges, be construed as references to the date of the last receipt of rent.

(9) References in Part II of this Act to a right of action shall include references to—
(a) a cause of action;
(b) a right to receive money secured by a mortgage or charge on any property;
(c) a right to recover proceeds of the sale of land; and
(d) a right to receive a share or interest in the personal estate of a deceased person.

(10) References in Part II to the date of the accrual of a right of action shall be construed—
(a) in the case of an action upon a judgment, as references to the date on which the judgment became enforceable; and

(b) in the case of an action to recover arrears of rent or interest, or damages in respect of arrears of rent or interest, as references to the date on which the rent or interest became due.

[920]

NOTES

Sub-s (1): in definition "land" words in italics repealed by the Tribunals, Courts and Enforcement Act 2007, ss 86, 146, Sch 14, paras 35, 37, Sch 23, Pt 4, as from a day to be appointed; words omitted from definition "land" repealed, and definition "trust for sale" (omitted) repealed, by the Trusts of Land and Appointment of Trustees Act 1996, s 25(2), Sch 4; for savings in relation to entailed interests created before the commencement of that Act, and savings consequential upon the abolition of the doctrine of conversion, see s 25(4), (5) thereof.

Sub-s (2): words in square brackets substituted by the Mental Capacity Act 2005, s 67(1), Sch 6, para 25(a).

Sub-ss (3), (4): repealed by the Mental Capacity Act 2005, s 67(1), (2), Sch 6, para 25(b), Sch 7.

Sub-s (7): words in italics repealed by the Tribunals, Courts and Enforcement Act 2007, ss 86, 146, Sch 14, paras 35, 37, Sch 23, Pt 4, as from a day to be appointed.

39, 40 (*Outside the scope of this work.*)

41 Short title, commencement and extent

(1) This Act may be cited as the Limitation Act 1980.

(2) This Act, except section 35, shall come into force on 1st May 1981.

(3), (4) …

[921]

NOTES

Sub-ss (3), (4): outside the scope of this work.

Order: the Limitation Act 1980 (Commencement) Order 1981, SI 1981/588.

SCHEDULE 1
PROVISIONS WITH RESPECT TO ACTIONS TO RECOVER LAND

Section 15(6), (7)

PART I
ACCRUAL OF RIGHTS OF ACTION TO RECOVER LAND

Accrual of right of action in case of present interests in land

1. Where the person bringing an action to recover land, or some person through whom he claims, has been in possession of the land, and has while entitled to the land been dispossessed or discontinued his possession, the right of action shall be treated as having accrued on the date of the dispossession or discontinuance.

2. Where any person brings an action to recover any land of a deceased person (whether under a will or on intestacy) and the deceased person—

(a) was on the date of his death in possession of the land or, in the case of a rentcharge created by will or taking effect upon his death, in possession of the land charged; and

(b) was the last person entitled to the land to be in possession of it;

the right of action shall be treated as having accrued on the date of his death.

3. Where any person brings an action to recover land, being an estate or interest in possession assured otherwise than by will to him, or to some person through whom he claims, and—

(a) the person making the assurance was on the date when the assurance took effect in possession of the land or, in the case of a rentcharge created by the assurance, in possession of the land charged; and

(b) no person has been in possession of the land by virtue of the assurance;

the right of action shall be treated as having accrued on the date when the assurance took effect.

Accrual of right of action in case of future interests

4. The right of action to recover any land shall, in a case where—

(a) the estate or interest claimed was an estate or interest in reversion or remainder or any other future estate or interest; and

(b) no person has taken possession of the land by virtue of the estate or interest claimed;

be treated as having accrued on the date on which the estate or interest fell into possession by the determination of the preceding estate or interest.

5.—(1) Subject to sub-paragraph (2) below, a tenancy from year to year or other period, without a lease in writing, shall for the purposes of this Act be treated as being determined at the expiration of the first year or other period; and accordingly the right of action of the person entitled to the land subject to the tenancy shall be treated as having accrued at the date on which in accordance with this sub-paragraph the tenancy is determined.

PART I STATUTES

(2) Where any rent has subsequently been received in respect of the tenancy, the right of action shall be treated as having accrued on the date of the last receipt of rent.

6.—(1) Where—

(a) any person is in possession of land by virtue of a lease in writing by which a rent of not less than ten pounds a year is reserved; and

(b) the rent is received by some person wrongfully claiming to be entitled to the land in reversion immediately expectant on the determination of the lease; and

(c) no rent is subsequently received by the person rightfully so entitled;

the right of action to recover the land of the person rightfully so entitled shall be treated as having accrued on the date when the rent was first received by the person wrongfully claiming to be so entitled and not on the date of the determination of the lease.

(2) Sub-paragraph (1) above shall not apply to any lease granted by the Crown.

Accrual of right of action in case of forfeiture or breach of condition

7.—(1) Subject to sub-paragraph (2) below, a right of action to recover land by virtue of a forfeiture or breach of condition shall be treated as having accrued on the date on which the forfeiture was incurred or the condition broken.

(2) If any such right has accrued to a person entitled to an estate or interest in reversion or remainder and the land was not recovered by virtue of that right, the right of action to recover the land shall not be treated as having accrued to that person until his estate or interest fell into possession, as if no such forfeiture or breach of condition had occurred.

Right of action not to accrue or continue unless there is adverse possession

8.—(1) No right of action to recover land shall be treated as accruing unless the land is in the possession of some person in whose favour the period of limitation can run (referred to below in this paragraph as "adverse possession"); and where under the preceding provisions of this Schedule any such right of action is treated as accruing on a certain date and no person is in adverse possession on that date, the right of action shall not be treated as accruing unless and until adverse possession is taken of the land.

(2) Where a right of action to recover land has accrued and after its accrual, before the right is barred, the land ceases to be in adverse possession, the right of action shall no longer be treated as having accrued and no fresh right of action shall be treated as accruing unless and until the land is again taken into adverse possession.

(3) For the purposes of this paragraph—

(a) possession of any land subject to a rentcharge by a person (other than the person entitled to the rentcharge) who does not pay the rent shall be treated as adverse possession of the rentcharge; and

(b) receipt of rent under a lease by a person wrongfully claiming to be entitled to the land in reversion immediately expectant on the determination of the lease shall be treated as adverse possession of the land.

(4) For the purpose of determining whether a person occupying any land is in adverse possession of the land it shall not be assumed by implication of law that his occupation is by permission of the person entitled to the land merely by virtue of the fact that his occupation is not inconsistent with the latter's present or future enjoyment of the land.

This provision shall not be taken as prejudicing a finding to the effect that a person's occupation of any land is by implied permission of the person entitled to the land in any case where such a finding is justified on the actual facts of the case.

Possession of beneficiary not adverse to others interested in settled land or land held on trust for sale

9. Where any settled land or any land [subject to a trust of land] is in the possession of a person entitled to a beneficial interest in the land … (not being a person solely or absolutely entitled to the land …), no right of action to recover the land shall be treated for the purposes of this Act as accruing during that possession to any person in whom the land is vested as tenant for life, statutory owner or trustee, or to any other person entitled to a beneficial interest in the land …

[922]

NOTES

Para 9: words in square brackets substituted, and words omitted repealed, by the Trusts of Land and Appointment of Trustees Act 1996, s 25(1), (2), Sch 3, para 18, Sch 4; for savings in relation to entailed interests created before the commencement of that Act, and savings consequential upon the abolition of the doctrine of conversion, see s 25(4), (5) thereof.

PART II
MODIFICATIONS OF SECTION 15 WHERE CROWN OR CERTAIN CORPORATIONS SOLE ARE INVOLVED

10. Subject to paragraph 11 below, section 15(1) of this Act shall apply to the bringing of an action to recover any land by the Crown or by any spiritual or eleemosynary corporation sole with the substitution for the reference to twelve years of a reference to thirty years.

11.—(1) An action to recover foreshore may be brought by the Crown at any time before the expiration of sixty years from the date mentioned in section 15(1) of this Act.

(2) Where any right of action to recover land which has ceased to be foreshore but remains in the ownership of the Crown accrued when the land was foreshore, the action may be brought at any time before the expiration of—

(a) sixty years from the date of accrual of the right of action; or
(b) thirty years from the date when the land ceased to be foreshore;

whichever period first expires.

(3) In this paragraph "foreshore" means the shore and bed of the sea and of any tidal water, below the line of the medium high tide between the spring tides and the neap tides.

12. Notwithstanding section 15(1) of this Act, where in the case of any action brought by a person other than the Crown or a spiritual or eleemosynary corporation sole the right of action first accrued to the Crown or any such corporation sole through whom the person in question claims, the action may be brought at any time before the expiration of—

(a) the period during which the action could have been brought by the Crown or the corporation sole; or
(b) twelve years from the date on which the right of action accrued to some person other than the Crown or the corporation sole;

whichever period first expires.

13. Section 15(2) of this Act shall apply in any case where the Crown or a spiritual or eleemosynary corporation sole is entitled to the succeeding estate or interest with the substitution—

(a) for the reference to twelve years of a reference to thirty years; and
(b) for the reference to six years of a reference to twelve years.

[923]

(Schs 2–4 outside the scope of this work.)

HIGHWAYS ACT 1980

(1980 c 66)

An Act to consolidate the Highways Acts 1959 to 1971 and related enactments, with amendments to give effect to recommendations of the Law Commission

[13 November 1980]

1–23 ((*Pts I, II*) *outside the scope of this work.*)

PART III
CREATION OF HIGHWAYS

24 (*Outside the scope of this work.*)

25 Creation of footpath[, bridleway or restricted byway] by agreement

(1) A local authority may enter into an agreement with any person having the necessary power in that behalf for the dedication by that person of a footpath[, bridleway or restricted byway] over land in their area.

An agreement under this section is referred to in this Act as a "public path creation agreement".

(2) For the purposes of this section "local authority"—

(a) in relation to land outside Greater London means a county council, a district council … ; and
(b) in relation to land in Greater London means … a London borough council or the Common Council.

(3) Before entering into an agreement under this section a local authority shall consult any other local authority or authorities in whose area the land concerned is situated.

(4) An agreement under this section shall be on such terms as to payment or otherwise as may be specified in the agreement and may, if it is so agreed, provide for the dedication of the footpath[, bridleway or restricted byway] subject to limitations or conditions affecting the public right of way over it.

(5) Where a public path creation agreement has been made it shall be the duty of the local authority who are a party to it to take all necessary steps for securing that the footpath[, bridleway or restricted byway] is dedicated in accordance with it.

[(6) As soon as may be after the dedication of a footpath[, bridleway or restricted byway] in accordance with a public path creation agreement, the local authority who are party to the agreement shall give notice of the dedication by publication in at least one local newspaper circulating in the area in which the land to which the agreement relates is situated.]

[924]

NOTES

Section heading: words in square brackets substituted by SI 2006/1177, reg 2, Schedule, Pt I.

Sub-ss (1), (4), (5): words in square brackets substituted by SI 2006/1177, reg 2, Schedule, Pt I.

Sub-s (2): words omitted from para (a) repealed by the Environment Act 1995, s 120, Sch 24; words omitted from para (b) repealed by the Local Government Act 1985, s 102, Sch 17.

Sub-s (6): inserted by the Wildlife and Countryside Act 1981, s 64; words in square brackets substituted by SI 2006/1177, reg 2, Schedule, Pt I.

Modification: this section has effect as if references to a local authority or council include references to a National Park authority and as if the relevant Park were the authority's area, by virtue of the Environment Act 1995, s 70, Sch 9, para 11.

26 Compulsory powers for creation of footpaths[, bridleways and restricted byways]

(1) Where it appears to a local authority that there is need for a footpath[, bridleway or restricted byway] over land in their area and they are satisfied that, having regard to—

(a) the extent to which the path or way would add to the convenience or enjoyment of a substantial section of the public, or to the convenience of persons resident in the area, and

(b) the effect which the creation of the path or way would have on the rights of persons interested in the land, account being taken of the provisions as to compensation contained in section 28 below,

it is expedient that the path or way should be created, the authority may by order made by them and submitted to and confirmed by the Secretary of State, or confirmed by them as an unopposed order, create a footpath[, bridleway or restricted byway] over the land.

An order under this section is referred to in this Act as a "public path creation order"; and for the purposes of this section "local authority" has the same meaning as in section 25 above.

(2) Where it appears to the Secretary of State in a particular case that there is need for a footpath[, bridleway or restricted byway] as mentioned in subsection (1) above, and he is satisfied as mentioned in that subsection, he may, after consultation with each body which is a local authority for the purposes of this section in relation to the land concerned, make a public path creation order creating the footpath[, bridleway or restricted byway].

(3) A local authority shall, before exercising any power under this section, consult any other local authority or authorities in whose area the land concerned is situated.

[(3A) The considerations to which—

(a) the Secretary of State is to have regard in determining whether or not to confirm or make a public path creation order, and

(b) a local authority are to have regard in determining whether or not to confirm such an order as an unopposed order,

include any material provision of a rights of way improvement plan prepared by any local highway authority whose area includes land over which the proposed footpath[, bridleway or restricted byway] would be created.]

(4) A right of way created by a public path creation order may be either unconditional or subject to such limitations or conditions as may be specified in the order.

(5) A public path creation order shall be in such form as may be prescribed by regulations made by the Secretary of State, and shall contain a map, on such scale as may be so prescribed, defining the land over which a footpath[, bridleway or restricted byway] is thereby created.

(6) Schedule 6 to this Act shall have effect as to the making, confirmation, validity and date of operation of public path creation orders.

[925]

NOTES

Section heading: words in square brackets substituted by SI 2006/1177, reg 2, Schedule, Pt I.

Sub-ss (1), (2), (5): words in square brackets substituted by SI 2006/1177, reg 2, Schedule, Pt I.

Sub-s (3A): inserted by the Countryside and Rights of Way Act 2000, s 57, Sch 6, Pt I, para 1; words in square brackets substituted by SI 2006/1177, reg 2, Schedule, Pt I.

Modification: see the note to s 25 at **[924]**.

Transfer of Functions: functions of the Secretary of State, so far as exercisable in relation to Wales, transferred to the National Assembly for Wales, by the National Assembly for Wales (Transfer of Functions) Order 1999, SI 1999/672, art 2, Sch 1.

Regulations: the Public Path Orders Regulations 1993, SI 1993/11.

27 Making up of new footpaths[, bridleways and restricted byways]

(1) On the dedication of a footpath[, bridleway or restricted byway] in pursuance of a public path creation agreement, or on the coming into operation of a public path creation order, being—

(a) an agreement or order made by a local authority who are not the highway authority for the path in question, or

(b) an order made by the Secretary of State under section 26(2) above in relation to which he directs that this subsection shall apply,

the highway authority shall survey the path or way and shall certify what work (if any) appears to them to be necessary to bring it into a fit condition for use by the public as a footpath[, bridleway or restricted byway], as the case may be, and shall serve a copy of the certificate on the local authority mentioned in paragraph (a) above or, where paragraph (b) applies, on such local authority as the Secretary of State may direct.

(2) It shall be the duty of the highway authority to carry out any works specified in a certificate under subsection (1) above, and where the authority have carried out the work they may recover from the authority on whom a copy of the certificate was served any expenses reasonably incurred by them in carrying out that work, including any expenses so incurred in the discharge of any liability for compensation in respect of the carrying out thereof.

(3) Notwithstanding anything in the preceding provisions of this section, where an agreement or order is made as mentioned in subsection (1)(a) above, the local authority making the agreement or order may—

(a) with the consent of the highway authority carry out (in place of the highway authority) the duties imposed by that subsection on the highway authority; and

(b) carry out any works which, apart from this subsection, it would be the duty of the highway authority to carry out under subsection (2) above.

(4) Where the Secretary of State makes a public path creation order under section 26(2) above, he may direct that subsection (5) below shall apply.

(5) Where the Secretary of State gives such a direction—

(a) the local authority who, on the coming into force of the order, became the highway authority for the path or way in question shall survey the path or way and shall certify what work (if any) appears to them to be necessary to bring it into a fit condition for use by the public as a footpath[, bridleway or restricted byway], as the case may be, and shall furnish the Secretary of State with a copy of the certificate;

(b) if the Secretary of State is not satisfied with a certificate made under the foregoing paragraph, he shall either cause a local inquiry to be held or shall give to the local authority an opportunity of being heard by a person appointed by him for the purpose and, after considering the report of the person appointed to hold the inquiry or the person so appointed as aforesaid, shall make such order either confirming or varying the certificate as he may think fit; and

(c) subject to the provisions of the last foregoing paragraphs, it shall be the duty of the highway authority to carry out the work specified in a certificate made by them under paragraph (a) above.

(6) In this section "local authority" means any council …

[926]

NOTES

Section heading: words in square brackets substituted by SI 2006/1177, reg 2, Schedule, Pt I.

Sub-ss (1), (5): words in square brackets substituted by SI 2006/1177, reg 2, Schedule, Pt I.

Sub-s (6): words omitted repealed by the Environment Act 1995, s 120, Sch 24.

Modification: see the note to s 25 at **[924]**.

Transfer of Functions: see the note to s 26 at **[925]**.

28 Compensation for loss caused by public path creation order

(1) Subject to the following provisions of this section, if, on a claim made in accordance with this section, it is shown that the value of an interest of a person in land is depreciated, or that a person has suffered damage by being disturbed in his enjoyment of land, in consequence of the coming into operation of a public path creation order, the authority by whom the order was made shall pay to that person compensation equal to the amount of the depreciation or damage.

(2) A claim for compensation under this section shall be made within such time and in such manner as may be prescribed by regulations made by the Secretary of State, and shall be made to the authority by whom the order was made.

(3) For the purposes of the application of this section to an order made by the Secretary of State under section 26(2) above, references in this section to the authority by whom the order was made are to be construed as references to such one of the authorities referred to in that subsection as may be nominated by the Secretary of State for the purposes of this subsection.

(4) Nothing in this section confers on any person, in respect of a footpath[, bridleway or restricted byway] created by a public path creation order, a right to compensation for depreciation of the value of an interest in the land, or for disturbance in his enjoyment of land, not being in either case land over which the path or way was created or land held therewith, unless the creation of the path or way would have been actionable at his suit if it had been effected otherwise than in the exercise of statutory powers.

(5) In this section "interest", in relation to land, includes any estate in land and any right over land, whether the right is exercisable by virtue of the ownership of an interest in land or by virtue of a licence or agreement, and in particular includes sporting rights.

[927]

NOTES

Sub-s (4): words in square brackets substituted by SI 2006/1177, reg 2, Schedule, Pt I.

Modification: see the note to s 25 at **[924]**.

Transfer of Functions: see the note to s 26 at **[925]**.

See further: in relation to interest payable on any award of compensation, the Planning and Compensation Act 1991, s 80, Sch 18, Pt I.

Regulations: the Rail Crossing Extinguishment and Diversion Orders Regulations 1993, SI 1993/9; the Public Path Orders Regulations 1993, SI 1993/11; the Highways, Crime Prevention etc (Special Extinguishment and Special Diversion Orders) Regulations 2003, SI 2003/1479; the Highways (Schools) (Special Extinguishment and Special Diversion Orders) (Wales) Regulations 2005, SI 2005/1809; the Highways (SSSI Diversion Orders) (England) Regulations 2007, SI 2007/1494.

[29 Duty to have regard to agriculture, forestry and nature conservation

(1) In the exercise of their functions under this Part of this Act relating to the making of public path creation agreements and public path creation orders it shall be the duty of councils to have due regard to—

(a) the needs of agriculture and forestry, and

(b) the desirability of conserving flora, fauna and geological and physiographical features.

(2) In this section, "agriculture" includes the breeding or keeping of horses.]

[928]

NOTES

Substituted by the Countryside and Rights of Way Act 2000, s 57, Sch 6, Pt I, para 2.

Modification: see the note to s 25 at **[924]**.

30 Dedication of highway by agreement with parish or community council

(1) The council of a parish or community may enter into an agreement with any person having the necessary power in that behalf for the dedication by that person of a highway over land in the parish or community or an adjoining parish or community in any case where such a dedication would in the opinion of the council be beneficial to the inhabitants of the parish or community or any part thereof.

(2) Where the council of a parish or community have entered into an agreement under subsection (1) above for the dedication of a highway they may carry out any works (including works of maintenance or improvement) incidental to or consequential on the making of the agreement or contribute towards the expense of carrying out such works, and may agree or combine with the council of any other parish or community to carry out such works or to make such a contribution.

[929]

31 Dedication of way as highway presumed after public use for 20 years

(1) Where a way over any land, other than a way of such a character that use of it by the public could not give rise at common law to any presumption of dedication, has been actually enjoyed by the public as of right and without interruption for a full period of 20 years, the way is to be deemed to have been dedicated as a highway unless there is sufficient evidence that there was no intention during that period to dedicate it.

[(1A) Subsection (1)—

(a) is subject to section 66 of the Natural Environment and Rural Communities Act 2006 (dedication by virtue of use for mechanically propelled vehicles no longer possible), but

(b) applies in relation to the dedication of a restricted byway by virtue of use for non-mechanically propelled vehicles as it applies in relation to the dedication of any other description of highway which does not include a public right of way for mechanically propelled vehicles.]

(2) The period of 20 years referred to in subsection (1) above is to be calculated retrospectively from the date when the right of the public to use the way is brought into question, whether by a notice such as is mentioned in subsection (3) below or otherwise.

(3) Where the owner of the land over which any such way as aforesaid passes—

(a) has erected in such manner as to be visible to persons using the way a notice inconsistent with the dedication of the way as a highway, and

(b) has maintained the notice after the 1st January 1934, or any later date on which it was erected,

the notice, in the absence of proof of a contrary intention, is sufficient evidence to negative the intention to dedicate the way as a highway.

(4) In the case of land in the possession of a tenant for a term of years, or from year to year, any person for the time being entitled in reversion to the land shall, notwithstanding the existence of the tenancy, have the right to place and maintain such a notice as is mentioned in subsection (3) above, so, however, that no injury is done thereby to the business or occupation of the tenant.

(5) Where a notice erected as mentioned in subsection (3) above is subsequently torn down or defaced, a notice given by the owner of the land to the appropriate council that the way is not dedicated as a highway is, in the absence of proof of a contrary intention, sufficient evidence to negative the intention of the owner of the land to dedicate the way as a highway.

(6) An owner of land may at any time deposit with the appropriate council—

(a) a map of the land on a scale of not less than 6 inches to 1 mile, and

(b) a statement indicating what ways (if any) over the land he admits to have been dedicated as highways;

and, in any case in which such a deposit has been made, statutory declarations made by that owner or by his successors in title and lodged by him or them with the appropriate council at any time—

(i) within [ten] years from the date of the deposit, or

(ii) within [ten] years from the date on which any previous declaration was last lodged under this section,

to the effect that no additional way (other than any specifically indicated in the declaration) over the land delineated on the said map has been dedicated as a highway since the date of the deposit, or since the date of the lodgment of such previous declaration, as the case may be, are, in the absence of proof of a contrary intention, sufficient evidence to negative the intention of the owner or his successors in title to dedicate any such additional way as a highway.

(7) For the purposes of the foregoing provisions of this section "owner", in relation to any land, means a person who is for the time being entitled to dispose of the fee simple in the land; and for the purposes of subsections (5) and (6) above "the appropriate council" means the council of the county [, metropolitan district] or London borough in which the way (in the case of subsection (5)) or the land (in the case of subsection (6)) is situated or, where the way or land is situated in the City, the Common Council.

[(7A) Subsection (7B) applies where the matter bringing the right of the public to use a way into question is an application under section 53(5) of the Wildlife and Countryside Act 1981 for an order making modifications so as to show the right on the definitive map and statement.

(7B) The date mentioned in subsection (2) is to be treated as being the date on which the application is made in accordance with paragraph 1 of Schedule 14 to the 1981 Act.]

(8) Nothing in this section affects any incapacity of a corporation or other body or person in possession of land for public or statutory purposes to dedicate a way over that land as a highway if the existence of a highway would be incompatible with those purposes.

(9) Nothing in this section operates to prevent the dedication of a way as a highway being presumed on proof of user for any less period than 20 years, or being presumed or proved in any circumstances in which it might have been presumed or proved immediately before the commencement of this Act.

(10) Nothing in this section or section 32 below affects [section 56(1) of the Wildlife and Countryside Act 1981 (which provides that a definitive map and statement] are conclusive evidence as to the existence of the highways shown on the map and as to certain particulars contained in the statement), …

[(10A) Nothing in subsection (1A) affects the obligations of the highway authority, or of any other person, as respects the maintenance of a way.]

(11) For the purposes of this section "land" includes land covered with water.

[(12) For the purposes of subsection (1A) "mechanically propelled vehicle" does not include a vehicle falling within section 189(1)(c) of the Road Traffic Act 1988 (electrically assisted pedal cycle).]

[930]

NOTES

Sub-ss (1A), (10A), (12): inserted by the Natural Environment and Rural Communities Act 2006, s 68.

Sub-s (6): words in square brackets in paras (i), (ii) substituted by the Countryside and Rights of Way Act 2000, s 57, Sch 6, Pt I, para 3, subject to transitional provisions in SI 2005/1314, art 5.

Sub-s (7): words in square brackets inserted by the Local Government Act 1985, s 8, Sch 4, para 7.

Sub-ss (7A), (7B): inserted by the Natural Environment and Rural Communities Act 2006, s 69(1); for effect see s 69(2) thereof.

Sub-s (10): words in square brackets substituted and words omitted repealed by the Wildlife and Countryside Act 1981, ss 72(11), 73, Sch 17, Pt II.

[31A Register of maps, statements and declarations

(1) The appropriate council shall keep, in such manner as may be prescribed, a register containing such information as may be prescribed with respect to maps and statements deposited and declarations lodged with that council under section 31(6) above.

(2) Regulations may make provision for the register to be kept in two or more parts, each part containing such information as may be prescribed with respect to such maps, statements and declarations.

(3) Regulations may make provision as to circumstances in which an entry relating to a map, statement or declaration, or anything relating to it, is to be removed from the register or from any part of it.

(4) Every register kept under this section shall be available for inspection free of charge at all reasonable hours.

(5) In this section—

"appropriate council" has the same meaning as in section 31(6) above;
"prescribed" means prescribed by regulations;
"regulations" means regulations made by the Secretary of State.]

[931]

NOTES

Commencement: 21 November 2005 (in relation to Wales); 1 October 2007 (in relation to England).

Inserted by the Countryside and Rights of Way Act 2000, s 57, Sch 6, Pt I, para 4.

Regulations: the Public Rights of Way (Registers) (Wales) Regulations 2006, SI 2006/42; the Dedicated Highways (Registers under Section 31A of the Highways Act 1980) (England) Regulations 2007, SI 2007/2334.

32 Evidence of dedication of way as highway

A court or other tribunal, before determining whether a way has or has not been dedicated as a highway, or the date on which such dedication, if any, took place, shall take into consideration any map, plan or history of the locality or other relevant document which is tendered in evidence, and shall give such weight thereto as the court or tribunal considers justified by the circumstances, including the antiquity of the tendered document, the status of the person by whom and the purpose for which it was made or compiled, and the custody in which it has been kept and from which it is produced.

[932]

33 Protection of rights of reversioners

The person entitled to the remainder or reversion immediately expectant upon the determination of a tenancy for life, or pour autre vie, in land shall have the like remedies by action for trespass or an injunction to prevent the acquisition by the public of a right of way over that land as if he were in possession thereof.

[933]

34 (*Outside the scope of this work.*)

35 Creation of walkways by agreement

(1) An agreement under this section may be entered into—

(a) by a local highway authority, after consultation with the council of any [non-metropolitan] district in which the land concerned is situated;

(b) by a [non-metropolitan] district council, either alone or jointly with the local highway authority, after consultation with the local highway authority.

(2) An agreement under this section is an agreement with any person having an interest in any land on which a building is, or is proposed to be, situated, being a person who by virtue of that interest has the necessary power in that behalf,—

(a) for the provision of ways over, through or under parts of the building, or the building when constructed, as the case may be, or parts of any structure attached, or to be attached, to the building; and

(b) for the dedication by that person of those ways as footpaths subject to such limitations and conditions, if any, affecting the public right of way thereover as may be specified in the agreement and to any rights reserved by the agreement to that person and any person deriving title to the land under him.

A footpath created in pursuance of an agreement under this section is referred to below as a "walkway".

(3) An agreement under this section may make provision for—

(a) the maintenance, cleansing and drainage of any walkway to which the agreement relates;

(b) the lighting of such walkway and of that part of the building or structure which will be over or above it;

(c) the provision and maintenance of support for such walkway;

(d) entitling the authority entering into the agreement or, where the agreement is entered into jointly by a [non-metropolitan] district council and a local highway authority, either of those authorities to enter on any building or structure in which such walkway will be situated and to execute any works necessary to secure the performance of any obligation which any person is for the time being liable to perform by virtue of the agreement or of subsection (4) below;

(e) the making of payments by the authority entering into the agreement or, where the agreement is entered into jointly by a [non-metropolitan] district council and a local highway authority, either of those authorities to any person having an interest in the land or building affected by the agreement;

(f) the termination, in such manner and subject to such conditions as may be specified in the agreement, of the right of the public to use such walkway;

(g) any incidental and consequential matters.

(4) Any covenant (whether positive or restrictive) contained in an agreement under this section and entered into by a person having an interest in any land affected by the agreement shall be binding upon persons deriving title to the land under the covenantor to the same extent as it is binding upon the covenantor notwithstanding that it would not have been binding upon those persons apart from the provisions of this subsection, and shall be enforceable against those persons by the local highway authority.

(5) A covenant contained in an agreement under this section and entered into by a person having an interest in any land affected by the agreement is a local land charge.

(6) Where an agreement has been entered into under this section the appropriate authority may make byelaws regulating—

(a) the conduct of persons using any walkway to which the agreement relates;

(b) the times at which any such walkway may be closed to the public;

(c) the placing or retention of anything (including any structure or projection) in, on or over any such walkway.

(7) For the purposes of subsection (6) above, "the appropriate authority" means—

(a) where the agreement was entered into by a local highway authority, that authority;

(b) where the agreement was entered into by a [non-metropolitan] district council alone, that council;

(c) where the agreement was entered into by a [non-metropolitan] district council jointly with the local highway authority, the local highway authority;

but in cases falling within paragraph (c) above the local highway authority shall before making any byelaw consult the district council, and in exercising his power of confirmation the Minister shall have regard to any dispute between the local highway authority and the district council.

(8) Not less than 2 months before an authority propose to make byelaws under subsection (6) above they shall display in a conspicuous position on or adjacent to the walkway in question notice of their intention to make such byelaws.

(9) A notice under subsection (8) above shall specify the place where a copy of the proposed byelaws may be inspected and the period, which shall not be less than 6 weeks from the date on which the notice was first displayed as aforesaid, within which representations may be made to the authority, and the authority shall consider any representations made to them within that period.

(10) The Minister of the Crown having power by virtue of section 236 of the Local Government Act 1972 to confirm byelaws made under subsection (6) above may confirm them with or without modifications; and if he proposes to confirm them with modifications he may, before confirming them, direct the authority by whom they were made to give notice of the proposed modifications to such persons and in such manner as may be specified in the direction.

(11) Subject to subsection (12) below, the Minister, after consulting such representative organisations as he thinks fit, may make regulations—

PART I STATUTES

(a) for preventing any enactment or instrument relating to highways or to things done on or in connection with highways from applying to walkways which have been, or are to be, created in pursuance of agreements under this section or to things done on or in connection with such walkways;

(b) for amending, modifying or adapting any such enactment or instrument in its application to such walkways;

(c) without prejudice to the generality of paragraphs (a) and (b) above, for excluding, restricting or regulating the rights of statutory undertakers, … [… and the operators of [electronic communications code networks] to place] and maintain apparatus in, under, over, along or across such walkways;

(d) without prejudice as aforesaid, for defining the circumstances and manner in which such walkways may be closed periodically or temporarily or stopped up and for prescribing the procedure to be followed before such a walkway is stopped up.

(12) Regulations under this section shall not exclude the rights of statutory undertakers, [… and the operators of [electronic communications code networks] to place] and maintain apparatus in, under, along or across any part of a walkway, being a part which is not supported by any structure.

(13) Without prejudice to subsection (11) above, regulations under this section may make different provisions for different classes of walkways and may include such incidental, supplemental and consequential provisions (and, in particular, provisions relating to walkways provided in pursuance of agreements made before the coming into operation of the regulations) as appear to the Minister to be expedient for the purposes of the regulations.

(14) Nothing in this section is to be taken as affecting any other provision of this Act, or any other enactment, by virtue of which highways may be created.

[934]

NOTES

Sub-ss (1), (3), (7): words in square brackets inserted by the Local Government Act 1985, s 8, Sch 4, para 9.

Sub-s (11): in para (c), words omitted repealed by the Water Act 1989, s 190, Sch 27, Pt I, words in first (outer) pair of square brackets substituted by the Telecommunications Act 1984, s 109, Sch 4, para 76, and words in second (inner) pair of square brackets substituted by the Communications Act 2003, s 406(1), Sch 17, para 53.

Sub-s (12): words omitted repealed by the Water Act 1989, s 190, Sch 27, Pt I; words in first (outer) pair of square brackets substituted by the Telecommunications Act 1984, s 109, Sch 4, para 76; words in second (inner) pair of square brackets substituted by the Communications Act 2003, s 406(1), Sch 17, para 53.

Transfer of Functions: see the note to s 26 at **[925]**.

PART IV
MAINTENANCE OF HIGHWAYS

Highways maintainable at public expense

36 Highways maintainable at public expense

(1) All such highways as immediately before the commencement of this Act were highways maintainable at the public expense for the purposes of the Highways Act 1959 continue to be so maintainable (subject to this section and to any order of a magistrates' court under section 47 below) for the purposes of this Act.

(2) Without prejudice to any other enactment (whether contained in this Act or not) whereby a highway may become for the purposes of this Act a highway maintainable at the public expense, and subject to this section and section 232(7) below, and to any order of a magistrates' court under section 47 below, the following highways (not falling within subsection (1) above) shall for the purposes of this Act be highways maintainable at the public expense—

(a) a highway constructed by a highway authority, otherwise than on behalf of some other person who is not a highway authority;

(b) a highway constructed by a council within their own area under [Part II of the Housing Act 1985], other than one in respect of which the local highway authority are satisfied that it has not been properly constructed, and a highway constructed by a council outside their own area under [the said Part II], being, in the latter case, a highway the liability to maintain which is, by virtue of [the said Part II], vested in the council who are the local highway authority for the area in which the highway is situated;

(c) a highway that is a trunk road or a special road; …

(d) a highway, being a footpath[, bridleway or restricted byway], created in consequence of a public path creation order or a public path diversion order or in consequence of an order made by the Minister of Transport or the Secretary of State under [section 247 of the Town and Country Planning Act 1990 or by a competent authority under section 257 of that Act], or dedicated in pursuance of a public path creation agreement;

[(e) a highway, being a footpath [, bridleway or restricted byway], created in consequence of a rail crossing diversion order, or of an order made under section 14 or 16 of the Harbours Act 1964, or of an order made under section 1 or 3 of the Transport and Works Act 1992];

[(f) a highway, being a footpath, a bridleway, a restricted byway or a way over which the public have a right of way for vehicular and all other kinds of traffic, created in consequence of a special diversion order or an SSSI diversion order.]

(3) Paragraph (c) of subsection (2) above is not to be construed as referring to a part of a trunk road or special road consisting of a bridge or other part which a person is liable to maintain under a charter or special enactment, or by reason of tenure, enclosure or prescription.

[(3A) Paragraph (e) of subsection (2) above shall not apply to a footpath[, bridleway or restricted byway], or to any part of a footpath or bridleway, which by virtue of an order of a kind referred to in that subsection is maintainable otherwise than at the public expense.]

(4) Subject to subsection (5) below, where there occurs any event on the occurrence of which, under any rule of law relating to the duty of maintaining a highway by reason of tenure, enclosure or prescription, a highway would, but for the enactment which abrogated the former rule of law under which a duty of maintaining highways fell on the inhabitants at large (section 38(1) of the Highways Act 1959) or any other enactment, become, or cease to be, maintainable by the inhabitants at large of any area, the highway shall become, or cease to be, a highway which for the purposes of this Act is a highway maintainable at the public expense.

(5) A highway shall not by virtue of subsection (4) above become a highway which for the purposes of this Act is a highway maintainable at the public expense unless either—

(a) it was a highway before 31st August 1835; or

(b) it became a highway after that date and has at some time been maintainable by the inhabitants at large of any area or a highway maintainable at the public expense;

and a highway shall not by virtue of that subsection cease to be a highway maintainable at the public expense if it is a highway which under any rule of law would become a highway maintainable by reason of enclosure but is prevented from becoming such a highway by section 51 below.

(6) The council of every county[, metropolitan district] and London borough and the Common Council shall cause to be made, and shall keep corrected up to date, a list of the streets within their area which are highways maintainable at the public expense.

(7) Every list made under subsection (6) above shall be kept deposited at the offices of the council by whom it was made and may be inspected by any person free of charge at all reasonable hours and in the case of a list made by the council of a county [in England], the county council shall supply to the council of each district in the county an up to date list of the streets within the area of the district that are highways maintainable at the public expense, and the list so supplied shall be kept deposited at the office of the district council and may be inspected by any person free of charge at all reasonable hours.

[935]

NOTES

Sub-s (2): in para (b), words in first pair of square brackets substituted by the Housing (Consequential Provisions) Act 1985, s 4(1), Sch 2, para 47(a) and words in second and third pairs of square brackets substituted by the Housing (Consequential Provisions) Act 1985, s 4(1), Sch 2, para 47(b); in para (c), word omitted repealed by the Transport and Works Act 1992, ss 64(1), (2), 68, Sch 4, Pt I; in para (d), words in first pair of square brackets substituted by SI 2006/1177, reg 2, Schedule, Pt I and words in second pair of square brackets substituted by the Planning (Consequential Provisions) Act 1990, s 4, Sch 2, para 45(3); para (e) inserted by the Transport and Works Act 1992, s 64(1), (3), and words in square brackets substituted by SI 2006/1177, reg 2, Schedule, Pt I; para (f) inserted by the Countryside and Rights of Way Act 2000, s 57, Sch 6, Pt I, para 5, partly as from a day to be appointed.

Sub-s (3A): inserted by the Transport and Works Act 1992, s 64(4); words in square brackets substituted by SI 2006/1177, reg 2, Schedule, Pt I.

Sub-s (6): words in square brackets inserted by the Local Government Act 1985, s 8, Sch 4, para 7.

Sub-s (7): words in square brackets inserted by the Local Government (Wales) Act 1994, s 22(1), Sch 7, para 4.

Transfer of Functions: in relation to Wales see the note to s 26 at **[925]**.

Minister of Transport: the functions of the Minister of Transport were transferred to the Secretary of State for Transport by the Transfer of Functions (Transport) Order 1981, SI 1981/238. The functions of the Secretary of State for Transport were transferred to the Secretary of State for the Environment, Transport and the Regions by the Secretary of State for the Environment, Transport and the Regions Order 1997, SI 1997/2971, arts 3–6. The Transfer of Functions (Transport, Local Government and the Regions) Order 2002, SI 2002/2626, art 14, transferred the functions of the Secretary of State for Transport, Local Government and the Regions (the Department of which was created on 8 June 2001 from the Department of the Environment, Transport and the Regions), to the First Secretary of State. Following this, the Transfer of Functions (Miscellaneous) Order 2008, SI 2008/1034, arts 6, 7, 9(b), transferred the functions of the First Secretary of State that were functions of the Secretary of State for Transport immediately before the coming into force of the Secretary of State for the Environment, Transport and the Regions Order 1997, SI 1997/2971, to the Secretary of State.

Methods whereby highways may become maintainable at public expense

37 (*Outside the scope of this work.*)

38 Power of highway authorities to adopt by agreement

(1) Subject to subsection (2) below, where any person is liable under a special enactment or by reason of tenure, enclosure or prescription to maintain a highway, the Minister, in the case of a trunk road, or a local highway authority, in any other case, may agree with that person to undertake the maintenance of that highway; and where an agreement is made under this subsection the highway to which the agreement relates shall, on such date as may be specified in the agreement, become for the purposes of this Act a highway maintainable at the public expense and the liability of that person to maintain the highway shall be extinguished.

(2) A local highway authority shall not have power to make an agreement under subsection (1) above with respect to a highway with respect to which they or any other highway authority have power to make an agreement under Part V or Part XII of this Act.

[(3) A local highway authority may agree with any person to undertake the maintenance of a way—

(a) which that person is willing and has the necessary power to dedicate as a highway, or
(b) which is to be constructed by that person, or by a highway authority on his behalf, and which he proposes to dedicate as a highway;

and where an agreement is made under this subsection the way to which the agreement relates shall, on such date as may be specified in the agreement, become for the purposes of this Act a highway maintainable at the public expense.

(3A) The Minister may agree with any person to undertake the maintenance of a road—

(a) which that person is willing and has the necessary power to dedicate as a highway, or
(b) which is to be constructed by that person, or by a highway authority on his behalf, and which he proposes to dedicate as a highway,

and which the Minister proposes should become a trunk road; and where an agreement is made under this subsection the road shall become for the purposes of this Act a highway maintainable at the public expense on the date on which an order comes into force under section 10 directing that the road become a trunk road or, if later, the date on which the road is opened for the purposes of through traffic.]

(4) Without prejudice to the provisions of subsection (3) above and subject to the following provisions of this section, a local highway authority may, by agreement with railway, canal or tramway undertakers, undertake to maintain as part of a highway maintainable at the public expense a bridge or viaduct which carries the railway, canal or tramway of the undertakers over such a highway or which is intended to carry such a railway, canal or tramway over such a highway and is to be constructed by those undertakers or by the highway authority on their behalf.

(5) …

(6) An agreement under this section may contain such provisions as to the dedication as a highway of any road or way to which the agreement relates, the bearing of the expenses of the construction, maintenance or improvement of any highway, road, bridge or viaduct to which the agreement relates and other relevant matters as the authority making the agreement think fit.

[936]–[937]

NOTES

Sub-ss (3), (3A): substituted for sub-s (3) as originally enacted, by the New Roads and Street Works Act 1991, s 22(1).

Transfer of Functions: see the note to s 26 at **[925]**.

39–61 (*S 39 repealed by the Statute Law (Repeals) Act 1986; ss 40–59, 61 outside the scope of this work; s 60 repealed by the New Roads and Street Works Act 1991, s 168(2), Sch 9.*)

62–115K (*Ss 62–89, 90–105, ss 105A, 106–115, 115A–115K (Pts V, VA–VIIA) outside the scope of this work.*)

PART VIII
STOPPING UP AND DIVERSION OF HIGHWAYS AND STOPPING UP OF MEANS OF ACCESS TO HIGHWAYS

Stopping up and diversion of highways

116, 117 (*Outside the scope of this work.*)

118 Stopping up of footpaths[, bridleways and restricted byways]

(1) Where it appears to a council as respects a footpath[, bridleway or restricted byway] in their area (other than one which is a trunk road or a special road) that it is expedient that the path or way should be stopped up on the ground that it is not needed for public use, the council may by order made by them and submitted to and confirmed by the Secretary of State, or confirmed as an unopposed order, extinguish the public right of way over the path or way.

An order under this section is referred to in this Act as a "public path extinguishment order".

(2) The Secretary of State shall not confirm a public path extinguishment order, and a council shall not confirm such an order as an unopposed order, unless he or, as the case may be, they are satisfied that it is expedient so to do having regard to the extent (if any) to which it appears to him or, as the case may be, them that the path or way would, apart from the order, be likely to be used by the public, and having regard to the effect which the extinguishment of the right of way would have as respects land served by the path or way, account being taken of the provisions as to compensation contained in section 28 above as applied by section 121(2) below.

(3) A public path extinguishment order shall be in such form as may be prescribed by regulations made by the Secretary of State and shall contain a map, on such scale as may be so prescribed, defining the land over which the public right of way is thereby extinguished.

(4) Schedule 6 to this Act has effect as to the making, confirmation, validity and date of operation of public path extinguishment orders.

(5) Where, in accordance with regulations made under paragraph 3 of the said Schedule 6, proceedings preliminary to the confirmation of the public path extinguishment order are taken concurrently with proceedings preliminary to the confirmation of a public path creation order[, public path diversion order or rail crossing diversion order] then, in considering—

(a) under subsection (1) above whether the path or way to which the public path extinguishment order relates is needed for public use, or

(b) under subsection (2) above to what extent (if any) that path or way would apart from the order be likely to be used by the public,

the council or the Secretary of State, as the case may be, may have regard to the extent to which the public path creation order[, public path diversion order or rail crossing diversion order] would provide an alternative path or way.

(6) For the purposes of subsections (1) and (2) above, any temporary circumstances preventing or diminishing the use of a path or way by the public shall be disregarded.

[(6A) The considerations to which—

(a) the Secretary of State is to have regard in determining whether or not to confirm a public path extinguishment order, and

(b) a council are to have regard in determining whether or not to confirm such an order as an unopposed order,

include any material provision of a rights of way improvement plan prepared by any local highway authority whose area includes land over which the order would extinguish a public right of way.]

(7) ...

[938]

NOTES

Section heading: words in square brackets substituted by SI 2006/1177, reg 2, Schedule, Pt I.
Sub-s (1): words in square brackets substituted by SI 2006/1177, reg 2, Schedule, Pt I.
Sub-s (5): words in square brackets substituted by the Transport and Works Act 1992, s 47, Sch 2, para 2(2).
Sub-s (6A): inserted by the Countryside and Rights of Way Act 2000, s 57, Sch 6, Pt I, para 6.
Sub-s (7): repealed by the Environment Act 1995, s 120, Sch 24.
Modification: see the note to s 25 at **[924]**.
Transfer of Functions: see the note to s 26 at **[925]**.
Regulations: the Rail Crossing Extinguishment and Diversion Orders Regulations 1993, SI 1993/9; the Public Path Orders Regulations 1993, SI 1993/11.

118ZA, 118A (*Outside the scope of this work.*)

[118B Stopping up of certain highways for purposes of crime prevention, etc

(1) This section applies where it appears to a council—

(a) that, as respects any relevant highway for which they are the highway authority and which is in an area designated by the Secretary of State by order for the purposes of this section, the conditions in subsection (3) below are satisfied and it is expedient, for the purpose of preventing or reducing crime which would otherwise disrupt the life of the community, that the highway should be stopped up, or

(b) that, as respects any relevant highway for which they are the highway authority and which crosses land occupied for the purposes of a school, it is expedient, for the purpose of protecting the pupils or staff from—

(i) violence or the threat of violence,
(ii) harassment,
(iii) alarm or distress arising from unlawful activity, or
(iv) any other risk to their health or safety arising from such activity,

that the highway should be stopped up.

(2) In subsection (1) above "relevant highway" means—

(a) any footpath, bridleway or restricted byway,
(b) any highway which is shown in a definitive map and statement as a footpath, a bridleway, or a restricted byway, but over which the public have a right of way for vehicular and all other kinds of traffic, or
(c) any highway which is shown in a definitive map and statement as a byway open to all traffic,

but does not include a highway that is a trunk road or a special road.

(3) The conditions referred to in subsection (1)(a) above are—

(a) that premises adjoining or adjacent to the highway are affected by high levels of crime, and
(b) that the existence of the highway is facilitating the persistent commission of criminal offences.

(4) Where this section applies, the council may by order made by them and submitted to and confirmed by the Secretary of State, or confirmed as an unopposed order, extinguish the public right of way over the highway.

(5) An order under subsection (4) above is in this Act referred to as a "special extinguishment order".

(6) Before making a special extinguishment order, the council shall consult the police authority for the area in which the highway lies.

(7) The Secretary of State shall not confirm a special extinguishment order made by virtue of subsection (1)(a) above, and a council shall not confirm such an order as an unopposed order, unless he or, as the case may be, they are satisfied that the conditions in subsection (3) above are satisfied, that the stopping up of the highway is expedient as mentioned in subsection (1)(a) above and that it is expedient to confirm the order having regard to all the circumstances, and in particular to—

(a) whether and, if so, to what extent the order is consistent with any strategy for the reduction of crime and disorder prepared under section 6 of the Crime and Disorder Act 1998,
(b) the availability of a reasonably convenient alternative route or, if no reasonably convenient alternative route is available, whether it would be reasonably practicable to divert the highway under section 119B below rather than stopping it up, and
(c) the effect which the extinguishment of the right of way would have as respects land served by the highway, account being taken of the provisions as to compensation contained in section 28 above as applied by section 121(2) below.

(8) The Secretary of State shall not confirm a special extinguishment order made by virtue of subsection (1)(b) above, and a council shall not confirm such an order as an unopposed order unless he or, as the case may be, they are satisfied that the stopping up of the highway is expedient as mentioned in subsection (1)(b) above and that it is expedient to confirm the order having regard to all the circumstances, and in particular to—

(a) any other measures that have been or could be taken for improving or maintaining the security of the school,
(b) whether it is likely that the coming into operation of the order will result in a substantial improvement in that security,
(c) the availability of a reasonably convenient alternative route or, if no reasonably convenient alternative route is available, whether it would be reasonably practicable to divert the highway under section 119B below rather than stopping it up, and
(d) the effect which the extinguishment of the right of way would have as respects land served by the highway, account being taken of the provisions as to compensation contained in section 28 above as applied by section 121(2) below.

(9) A special extinguishment order shall be in such form as may be prescribed by regulations made by the Secretary of State and shall contain a map, on such scale as may be prescribed, defining the land over which the public right of way is thereby extinguished.

(10) Schedule 6 to this Act has effect as to the making, confirmation, validity and date of operation of special extinguishment orders.]

[939]

NOTES

Commencement: 12 February 2003 (in relation to England); 15 July 2005 (in relation to Wales for certain purposes); to be appointed (in relation to Wales for remaining purposes).

Inserted by the Countryside and Rights of Way Act 2000, s 57, Sch 6, Pt I, para 8.

Regulations: the Highways, Crime Prevention etc (Special Extinguishment and Special Diversion Orders) Regulations 2003, SI 2003/1479; the Highways (Schools) (Special Extinguishment and Special Diversion Orders) (Wales) Regulations 2005, SI 2005/1809.

Orders: the Crime Prevention (Designated Areas) Order 2003, SI 2003/2208; the Crime Prevention (Designated Areas) Order 2004, SI 2004/1239; the Crime Prevention (Designated Areas) Order 2005, SI 2005/829; the Crime Prevention (Designated Areas) (No 2) Order 2005, SI 2005/914; the Crime Prevention (Designated Areas) (No 3) Order 2005, SI 2005/2463; the Crime Prevention (Designated Areas) Order 2006, SI 2006/302; the Crime Prevention (Designated Areas) Order 2007, SI 2007/1829.

118C (*Outside the scope of this work.*)

119 Diversion of footpaths[, bridleways and restricted byways]

(1) [Where it appears to a council as respects a footpath[, bridleway or restricted byway] in their area (other than one that is a trunk road or special road) that, in the interests of the owner, lessee or occupier of land crossed by the path or way or of the public, it is expedient that the line of the path or way, or part of that line, should be diverted (whether on to land of the same or] of another owner, lessee or occupier), the council may, subject to subsection (2) below, by order made by them and submitted to and confirmed by the Secretary of State, or confirmed as an unopposed order,—

(a) create, as from such date as may be specified in the order, any such new footpath[, bridleway or restricted byway] as appears to the council requisite for effecting the diversion, and

(b) extinguish, as from such date as may be [specified in the order or determined] in accordance with the provisions of subsection (3) below, the public right of way over so much of the path or way as appears to the council requisite as aforesaid.

An order under this section is referred to in this Act as a "public path diversion order".

(2) A public path diversion order shall not alter a point of termination of the path or way—

(a) if that point is not on a highway, or

(b) (where it is on a highway) otherwise than to another point which is on the same highway, or a highway connected with it, and which is substantially as convenient to the public.

[(3) Where it appears to the council that work requires to be done to bring the new site of the footpath[, bridleway or restricted byway] into a fit condition for use by the public, the council shall—

(a) specify a date under subsection (1)(a) above, and

(b) provide that so much of the order as extinguishes (in accordance with subsection (1)(b) above) a public right of way is not to come into force until the local highway authority for the new path or way certify that the work has been carried out.]

(4) A right of way created by a public path diversion order may be either unconditional or (whether or not the right of way extinguished by the order was subject to limitations or conditions of any description) subject to such limitations or conditions as may be specified in the order.

(5) Before determining to make a public path diversion order [on an application under section 119ZA below or] [on the representations of an owner, lessee or occupier of land crossed by the path or way, the council may require *him* [the person who made the application or representations]] to enter into an agreement with them to defray, or to make such contribution as may be specified in the agreement towards,—

(a) any compensation which may become payable under section 28 above as applied by section 121(2) below, or

(b) where the council are the highway authority for the path or way in question, any expenses which they may incur in bringing the new site of the path or way into fit condition for use for the public, or

(c) where the council are not the highway authority, any expenses which may become recoverable from them by the highway authority under the provisions of section 27(2) above as applied by subsection (9) below.

(6) The Secretary of State shall not confirm a public path diversion order, and a council shall not confirm such an order as an unopposed order, unless he or, as the case may be, they are satisfied that the diversion to be effected by it is expedient as mentioned in subsection (1) above, and further that the path or way will not be substantially less convenient to the public in consequence of the diversion and that it is expedient to confirm the order having regard to the effect which—

(a) the diversion would have on public enjoyment of the path or way as a whole,

(b) the coming into operation of the order would have as respects other land served by the existing public right of way, and

(c) any new public right of way created by the order would have as respects the land over which the right is so created and any land held with it, so, however, that for the purposes of paragraphs (b) and (c) above the Secretary of State or, as the case may be, the council shall take into account the provisions as to compensation referred to in subsection (5)(a) above.

[(6A) The considerations to which—

(a) the Secretary of State is to have regard in determining whether or not to confirm a public path diversion order, and

(b) a council are to have regard in determining whether or not to confirm such an order as an unopposed order,

include any material provision of a rights of way improvement plan prepared by any local highway authority whose area includes land over which the order would create or extinguish a public right of way.]

(7) A public path diversion order shall be in such form as may be prescribed by regulations made by the Secretary of State and shall contain a map, on such scale as may be so prescribed,—

(a) showing the existing site of so much of the line of the path or way as is to be diverted by the order and the new site to which it is to be diverted,

(b) indicating whether a new right of way is created by the order over the whole of the new site or whether some part of it is already comprised in a footpath[, bridleway or restricted byway], and

(c) where some part of the new site is already so comprised, defining that part.

(8) Schedule 6 to this Act has effect as to the making, confirmation, validity and date of operation of public path diversion orders.

(9) Section 27 above (making up of new footpaths[, bridleways and restricted byways]) applies to a footpath[, bridleway or restricted byway] created by a public path diversion order with the substitution, for references to a public path creation order, of references to a public path diversion order and, for references to section 26(2) above, of references to section 120(3) below.

[940]

NOTES

Section heading: words in square brackets substituted by SI 2006/1177, reg 2, Schedule, Pt I.

Sub-s (1): words in first (outer) pair of square brackets substituted by the Wildlife and Countryside Act 1981, s 63, Sch 16, para 5(1); words in second (inner) and third pairs of square brackets substituted by SI 2006/1177, reg 2, Schedule, Pt I; words in square brackets in para (b) substituted by the Countryside and Rights of Way Act 2000, s 57, Sch 6, Pt I, para 9(1), (2).

Sub-s (3): substituted by the Countryside and Rights of Way Act 2000, s 57, Sch 6, Pt I, para 9(1), (3); words in square brackets substituted by SI 2006/1177, reg 2, Schedule, Pt I.

Sub-s (5): words in first pair of square brackets inserted by the Countryside and Rights of Way Act 2000, s 57, Sch 6, Pt I, para 9(1), (4)(a), as from a day to be appointed; words in second pair of square brackets substituted by the Wildlife and Countryside Act 1981, s 63, Sch 16, para 5(2); word "him" in italics substituted by subsequent words in square brackets by the Countryside and Rights of Way Act 2000, s 57, Sch 6, Pt I, para 9(1), (4)(b), as from a day to be appointed.

Sub-s (6A): inserted by the Countryside and Rights of Way Act 2000, s 57, Sch 6, Pt I, para 9(1), (5).

Sub-ss (7), (9): words in square brackets substituted by SI 2006/1177, reg 2, Schedule, Pt I.

Modification: see the note to s 25 at **[924]**.

Transfer of Functions: see the note to s 26 at **[925]**.

Regulations: the Rail Crossing Extinguishment and Diversion Orders Regulations 1993, SI 1993/9; the Public Path Orders Regulations 1993, SI 1993/11.

[119ZA Application for a public path diversion order

(1) Subject to subsection (2) below, the owner, lessee or occupier of any land used for agriculture, forestry or the breeding or keeping of horses may apply to a council for the area in which the land is situated for the making of a public path diversion order in relation to any footpath or bridleway which crosses the land, on the ground that in his interests it is expedient that the order should be made.

(2) No application may be made under this section for an order which would create a new footpath or bridleway communicating with—

(a) a classified road,

(b) a special road,

(c) a GLA road, or

(d) any highway not falling within paragraph (a) or (b) above for which the Minister is the highway authority,

unless the application is made with the consent of the highway authority for the way falling within paragraph (a), (b), (c) or (d) above.

(3) No application under this section may propose the creation of a new right of way over land covered by works used by any statutory undertakers for the purposes of their undertaking or the curtilage of such land, unless the application is made with the consent of the statutory undertakers; and in this subsection "statutory undertaker" and "statutory undertaking" have the same meaning as in Schedule 6 to this Act.

(4) An application under this section shall be in such form as may be prescribed and shall be accompanied by a map, on such scale as may be prescribed—

(a) showing the existing site of so much of the line of the path or way as it is proposed to divert and the new site to which it is proposed to be diverted,

(b) indicating whether it is proposed to create a new right of way over the whole of the new site or whether some of it is already comprised in a footpath or bridleway, and

(c) where some part of the new site is already so comprised, defining that part,

and by such other information as may be prescribed.

(5) Regulations may provide—

(a) that a prescribed charge is payable on the making of an application under this section, and

(b) that further prescribed charges are payable by the applicant if the council make a public path diversion order on the application.

(6) An application under this section is not to be taken to be received by the council until the requirements of regulations under section 121A below have been satisfied in relation to it.

(7) A council which receives an application under this section shall determine the application as soon as reasonably practicable.

(8) Where—

(a) an application under this section has been made to a council, and

(b) the council have not determined the application within four months of receiving it,

the Secretary of State may, at the request of the applicant and after consulting the council, by direction require the council to determine the application before the end of such period as may be specified in the direction.

(9) As soon as practicable after determining an application under this section, the council shall—

(a) give to the applicant notice in writing of their decision and the reasons for it, and

(b) give a copy of the notice to such other persons as may be prescribed.

(10) The council to whom an application under this section has been made may make a public path diversion order on the application only if—

(a) the land over which the public right of way is to be extinguished by the order, and

(b) the new site to which the path or way is to be diverted,

are those shown for the purposes of subsection (4) above on the map accompanying the application.

(11) Any reference in this Act to the map accompanying an application under this section includes a reference to any revised map submitted by the applicant in prescribed circumstances in substitution for that map.

(12) This section has effect subject to the provisions of sections 121A and 121C below.

(13) In this section—

"prescribed" means prescribed by regulations;

"regulations" means regulations made by the Secretary of State.]

[941]

NOTES

Commencement: to be appointed.

Inserted by the Countryside and Rights of Way Act 2000, s 57, Sch 6, Pt I, para 10.

Modification: see the note to s 25 at **[924]**.

119A (*Outside the scope of this work.*)

[119B Diversion of certain highways for purposes of crime prevention, etc

(1) This section applies where it appears to a council—

(a) that, as respects any relevant highway for which they are the highway authority and which is in an area designated by the Secretary of State by order under section 118B(1)(a) above, the conditions in subsection (3) below are satisfied and it is expedient, for the purpose of preventing or reducing crime which would otherwise disrupt the life of the community, that the line of the highway, or part of that line should be diverted (whether on to land of the same or another owner, lessee or occupier), or

(b) that, as respects any relevant highway for which they are the highway authority and which crosses land occupied for the purposes of a school, it is expedient, for the purpose of protecting the pupils or staff from—

(i) violence or the threat of violence,

(ii) harassment,

(iii) alarm or distress arising from unlawful activity, or

(iv) any other risk to their health or safety arising from such activity, that the line of the highway, or part of that line, should be diverted (whether on to land of the same or another owner, lessee or occupier).

(2) In subsection (1) above "relevant highway" means—

(a) any footpath, bridleway or restricted byway,

(b) any highway which is shown in a definitive map and statement as a footpath, a bridleway, or a restricted byway, but over which the public have a right of way for vehicular and all other kinds of traffic, or

(c) any highway which is shown in a definitive map and statement as a byway open to all traffic,

but does not include a highway that is a trunk road or a special road.

(3) The conditions referred to in subsection (1)(a) above are—

(a) that premises adjoining or adjacent to the highway are affected by high levels of crime, and

(b) that the existence of the highway is facilitating the persistent commission of criminal offences.

(4) Where this section applies, the council may by order made by them and submitted to and confirmed by the Secretary of State, or confirmed as an unopposed order—

(a) create, as from such date as may be specified in the order, any such—

(i) new footpath, bridleway or restricted byway, or

(ii) in a case falling within subsection (2)(b) or (c) above, new highway over which the public have a right of way for vehicular and all other kinds of traffic,

as appears to the council requisite for effecting the diversion, and

(b) extinguish, as from such date as may be specified in the order or determined in accordance with the provisions of subsection (8) below, the public right of way over so much of the highway as appears to the council to be requisite for the purpose mentioned in paragraph (a) or (b) of subsection (1) above.

(5) An order under subsection (4) above is in this Act referred to as a "special diversion order".

(6) Before making a special diversion order, the council shall consult the police authority for the area in which the highway is situated.

(7) A special diversion order shall not alter a point of termination of the highway—

(a) if that point is not on a highway, or

(b) (where it is on a highway) otherwise than to another point which is on the same highway, or a highway connected with it.

(8) Where it appears to the council that work requires to be done to bring the new site of the highway into a fit condition for use by the public, the council shall—

(a) specify a date under subsection (4)(a) above, and

(b) provide that so much of the order as extinguishes (in accordance with subsection (4)(b) above) a public right of way is not to come into force until the local highway authority for the new highway certify that the work has been carried out.

(9) A right of way created by a special diversion order may be either unconditional or (whether or not the right of way extinguished by the order was subject to limitations or conditions of any description) subject to such limitations or conditions as may be specified in the order.

(10) The Secretary of State shall not confirm a special diversion order made by virtue of subsection (1)(a) above, and a council shall not confirm such an order as an unopposed order unless he or, as the case may be, they are satisfied that the conditions in subsection (3) above are satisfied, that the diversion of the highway is expedient as mentioned in subsection (1)(a) above and that it is expedient to confirm the order having regard to all the circumstances, and in particular to—

(a) whether and, if so, to what extent the order is consistent with any strategy for the reduction of crime and disorder prepared under section 6 of the Crime and Disorder Act 1998,

(b) the effect which the coming into operation of the order would have as respects land served by the existing public right of way, and

(c) the effect which any new public right of way created by the order would have as respects the land over which the right is so created and any land held with it,

so, however, that for the purposes of paragraphs (b) and (c) above the Secretary of State or, as the case may be, the council shall take into account the provisions as to compensation contained in section 28 above as applied by section 121(2) below.

(11) The Secretary of State shall not confirm a special diversion order made by virtue of subsection (1)(b) above, and a council shall not confirm such an order as an unopposed order unless he or, as the case may be, they are satisfied that the diversion of the highway is expedient as mentioned in subsection (1)(b) above and that it is expedient to confirm the order having regard to all the circumstances, and in particular to—

(a) any other measures that have been or could be taken for improving or maintaining the security of the school,

(b) whether it is likely that the coming into operation of the order will result in a substantial improvement in that security,

(c) the effect which the coming into operation of the order would have as respects land served by the existing public right of way, and

(d) the effect which any new public right of way created by the order would have as respects the land over which the right is so created and any land held with it,

so, however, that for the purposes of paragraphs (c) and (d) above the Secretary of State or, as the case may be, the council shall take into account the provisions as to compensation contained in section 28 above as applied by section 121(2) below.

(12) A special diversion order shall be in such form as may be prescribed by regulations made by the Secretary of State and shall contain a map, on such scale as may be so prescribed—

(a) showing the existing site of so much of the line of the highway as is to be diverted by the order and the new site to which it is to be diverted,

(b) indicating whether a new right of way is created by the order over the whole of the new site or whether some part of it is already comprised in a highway, and

(c) where some part of the new site is already so comprised, defining that part.

(13) Schedule 6 to this Act has effect as to the making, confirmation, validity and date of operation of special diversion orders.

(14) Section 27 above (making up of new footpaths[, bridleways and restricted byways]) applies to a highway created by a special diversion order with the substitution—

(a) for references to a footpath[, bridleway or restricted byway] of references to a footpath, a bridleway, a restricted byway or a highway over which the public have a right of way for vehicular and all other kinds of traffic,

(b) for references to a public path creation order of references to a special diversion order, and

(c) for references to section 26(2) above of references to section 120(3) below.

(15) Neither section 27 nor section 36 above is to be regarded as obliging a highway authority to provide on any highway created by a special diversion order a metalled carriage-way.]

[941A]

NOTES

Commencement: 12 February 2003 (in relation to England); 15 July 2005 (in relation to Wales for certain purposes); to be appointed (in relation to Wales for remaining purposes).

Inserted by the Countryside and Rights of Way Act 2000, s 57, Sch 6, Pt I, para 12.

Sub-s (14): words in square brackets substituted by SI 2006/1177, reg 2, Schedule, Pt I.

Regulations: Highways, Crime Prevention etc (Special Extinguishment and Special Diversion Orders) Regulations 2003, SI 2003/1479; Highways (Schools) (Special Extinguishment and Special Diversion Orders) (Wales) Regulations 2005, SI 2005/1809.

119C–119E, 120, 121, 121A–121E, 122–129 (*Outside the scope of this work.*)

[PART 8A
RESTRICTION OF RIGHTS OVER HIGHWAY

129A Gating orders

(1) A council may in accordance with this Part make an order under this section in relation to any relevant highway for which they are the highway authority.

(2) An order under this section is to be known as a "gating order".

(3) Before making a gating order in relation to a relevant highway the council must be satisfied that—

(a) premises adjoining or adjacent to the highway are affected by crime or anti-social behaviour;

(b) the existence of the highway is facilitating the persistent commission of criminal offences or anti-social behaviour; and

(c) it is in all the circumstances expedient to make the order for the purposes of reducing crime or anti-social behaviour.

(4) The circumstances referred to in subsection (3)(c) include—

(a) the likely effect of making the order on the occupiers of premises adjoining or adjacent to the highway;

(b) the likely effect of making the order on other persons in the locality; and

(c) in a case where the highway constitutes a through route, the availability of a reasonably convenient alternative route.

(5) In this section "relevant highway" means a highway other than—

(a) a special road;

(b) a trunk road;

(c) a classified or principal road;
(d) a strategic road, within the meaning of sections 60 and 61 of the Traffic Management Act 2004 (strategic roads in London);
(e) a highway of such other description as the appropriate person may by regulations prescribe.]

[942]

NOTES

Commencement: 16 March 2006 (in relation to Wales for certain purposes); 1 April 2006 (in relation to England); 19 February 2007 (in relation to Wales for remaining purposes).

Inserted, together with preceding Part heading and ss 129B–129G, by the Clean Neighbourhoods and Environment Act 2005, s 2.

[129B Effect of gating orders

(1) A gating order restricts, to the extent specified in the order, the public right of way over the highway to which it relates.

(2) A gating order may in particular—
(a) restrict the public right of way at all times, or in respect of such times, days or periods as may be specified in the order;
(b) exclude persons of a description specified in the order from the effect of the restriction.

(3) A gating order may not be made so as to restrict the public right of way over a highway for the occupiers of premises adjoining or adjacent to the highway.

(4) A gating order may not be made so as to restrict the public right of way over a highway which is the only or principal means of access to any dwelling.

(5) In relation to a highway which is the only or principal means of access to any premises used for business or recreational purposes, a gating order may not be made so as to restrict the public right of way over the highway during periods when those premises are normally used for those purposes.

(6) A gating order may authorise the installation, operation and maintenance of a barrier or barriers for the purpose of enforcing the restriction provided for in the order.

(7) A council may install, operate and maintain any barrier authorised under subsection (6).

(8) A highway in relation to which a gating order is made shall not cease to be regarded as a highway by reason of the restriction of the public right of way under the order (or by reason of any barrier authorised under this section).

(9) In subsection (4) "dwelling" means any building or part of a building occupied, or intended to be occupied, as a separate dwelling.]

[943]

NOTES

Commencement: 16 March 2006 (in relation to Wales for certain purposes); 1 April 2006 (in relation to England); 19 February 2007 (in relation to Wales for remaining purposes).

Inserted as noted to s 129A at **[942]**.

[129C Procedure for gating orders

(1) Before making a gating order in relation to a highway a council must notify the occupiers of premises adjacent to or adjoining the highway, in such manner as the appropriate person may by regulations prescribe, of—
(a) the proposed order; and
(b) the period within which they may make representations about it.

(2) The appropriate person must by regulations make provision as to further procedure to be complied with by a council in relation to the making of a gating order.

(3) Regulations under subsection (2) must include provision as to—
(a) the publication of a proposed order;
(b) public availability of copies of a proposed order;
(c) notification of persons (other than those referred to in subsection (1)) likely to be affected by a proposed order;
(d) the making of representations about a proposed order.

(4) Regulations under subsection (2) may include provision—
(a) requiring a council to hold a public inquiry in such circumstances as may be specified in the regulations;
(b) permitting a council to hold a public inquiry at their discretion in such circumstances as may be so specified.

(5) The appropriate person may by regulations specify requirements as to form and content with which a gating order must comply.]

[944]

NOTES

Commencement: 16 March 2006 (in relation to Wales for certain purposes); 1 April 2006 (in relation to England); 19 February 2007 (in relation to Wales for remaining purposes).

Inserted as noted to s 129A at **[942]**.

Regulations: the Highways Act 1980 (Gating Orders) (England) Regulations 2006, SI 2006/537; the Highways Act 1980 (Gating Orders) (Wales) Regulations 2007, SI 2007/306.

[129D Validity of gating orders

(1) A person may apply to the High Court for the purpose of questioning the validity of a gating order on the ground that—

- (a) the council had no power to make it; or
- (b) any requirement under this Part was not complied with in relation to it.

(2) An application under this section must be made within a period of six weeks beginning with the date on which the gating order is made.

(3) On an application under this section the High Court may by order suspend the operation of the gating order, or any of its provisions, until the final determination of the proceedings.

(4) If on an application under this section the High Court is satisfied that—

- (a) the council had no power to make the order, or
- (b) the interests of the applicant have been substantially prejudiced by any failure to comply with a requirement under this Part,

the High Court may quash the order or any of its provisions.

(5) A gating order, or any of its provisions, may be suspended under subsection (3) or quashed under subsection (4)—

- (a) generally; or
- (b) so far as may be necessary for the protection of the interests of the applicant.

(6) Except as provided for by this section, a gating order may not, either before or after it has been made, be questioned in any legal proceedings.]

[945]

NOTES

Commencement: 16 March 2006 (in relation to Wales for certain purposes); 1 April 2006 (in relation to England); 19 February 2007 (in relation to Wales for remaining purposes).

Inserted as noted to s 129A at **[942]**.

[129E Publication and availability of gating orders

(1) The appropriate person may by regulations make provision imposing requirements on councils in relation to—

- (a) the publication of gating orders;
- (b) public availability of copies of gating orders;
- (c) the keeping and inspection of registers of gating orders.

(2) Regulations under subsection (1)(b) may provide that a council need not provide a person with a copy of a gating order otherwise than on payment of a reasonable charge.]

[946]

NOTES

Commencement: 16 March 2006 (in relation to Wales for certain purposes); 1 April 2006 (in relation to England); 19 February 2007 (in relation to Wales for remaining purposes).

Inserted as noted to s 129A at **[942]**.

Regulations: the Highways Act 1980 (Gating Orders) (England) Regulations 2006, SI 2006/537; the Highways Act 1980 (Gating Orders) (Wales) Regulations 2007, SI 2007/306.

[129F Variation and revocation of gating orders

(1) A council may vary a gating order made by them so as further to restrict any public right of way over the highway to which the order relates, if they are satisfied that in all the circumstances it is expedient to do so for the purpose of reducing crime or anti-social behaviour.

(2) A council may vary a gating order made by them so as to reduce the restriction imposed by the order, if and to the extent that they are satisfied that the restriction is no longer expedient in all the circumstances for the purpose of reducing crime or anti-social behaviour.

(3) A council may revoke a gating order made by them, if they are satisfied that the restriction imposed by the order is no longer expedient in all the circumstances for the purpose of reducing crime or anti-social behaviour.

(4) Before varying or revoking a gating order in relation to a highway a council must notify the occupiers of premises adjacent to or adjoining the highway, in such manner as the appropriate person may by regulations prescribe, of—

(a) the proposed variation or revocation; and

(b) the period within which they may make representations about it.

(5) The appropriate person must by regulations make further provision as to the procedure to be followed by a council in relation to the variation or revocation of a gating order.

(6) Regulations under subsection (5) must include provision as to—

(a) publication of any proposed variation or revocation;

(b) notification of persons (other than those referred to in subsection (4)) likely to be affected by a proposed variation or revocation;

(c) the making of representations about a proposed variation or revocation.

(7) Regulations under subsection (5) may include provision—

(a) requiring a council to hold a public inquiry in such circumstances as may be specified in the regulations;

(b) permitting a council to hold a public inquiry at their discretion in such circumstances as may be so specified.]

[947]

NOTES

Commencement: 16 March 2006 (in relation to Wales for certain purposes); 1 April 2006 (in relation to England); 19 February 2007 (in relation to Wales for remaining purposes).

Inserted as noted to s 129A at **[942]**.

Regulations: the Highways Act 1980 (Gating Orders) (England) Regulations 2006, SI 2006/537; the Highways Act 1980 (Gating Orders) (Wales) Regulations 2007, SI 2007/306.

[129G Interpretation

For the purposes of this Part—

"anti-social behaviour" means behaviour by a person which causes or is likely to cause harassment, alarm or distress to one or more other persons not of the same household as himself;

"appropriate person" means—

(a) the Secretary of State, in relation to England;

(b) the National Assembly for Wales, in relation to Wales.]

[948]

NOTES

Commencement: 16 March 2006 (in relation to Wales for certain purposes); 1 April 2006 (in relation to England); 19 February 2007 (in relation to Wales for remaining purposes).

Inserted as noted to s 129A at **[942]**.

Regulations: the Highways Act 1980 (Gating Orders) (England) Regulations 2006, SI 2006/537; the Highways Act 1980 (Gating Orders) (Wales) Regulations 2007, SI 2007/306.

PART IX
LAWFUL AND UNLAWFUL INTERFERENCE WITH HIGHWAYS AND STREETS

130, 130A–130D (*Outside the scope of this work.*)

Damage to highways, streets etc

131, 131A, 132, 133 (*Outside the scope of this work.*)

[134 Ploughing etc of footpath or bridleway

(1) Where in the case of any footpath or bridleway (other than a field-edge path) which passes over a field or enclosure consisting of agricultural land, or land which is being brought into use for agriculture—

(a) the occupier of the field or enclosure desires in accordance with the rules of good husbandry to plough, or otherwise disturb the surface of, all or part of the land comprised in the field or enclosure, and

(b) it is not reasonably convenient in ploughing, or otherwise disturbing the surface of, the land to avoid disturbing the surface of the path or way so as to render it inconvenient for the exercise of the public right of way,

the public right of way shall be subject to the condition that the occupier has the right so to plough or otherwise disturb the surface of the path or way.

(2) Subsection (1) above does not apply in relation to any excavation or any engineering operation.

(3) Where the occupier has disturbed the surface of a footpath or bridleway under the right conferred by subsection (1) above he shall within the relevant period, or within an extension of that period granted under subsection (8) below,—

(a) so make good the surface of the path or way to not less than its minimum width as to make it reasonably convenient for the exercise of the right of way; and

(b) so indicate the line of the path or way on the ground to not less than its minimum width that it is apparent to members of the public wishing to use it.

(4) If the occupier fails to comply with the duty imposed by subsection (3) above he is guilty of an offence and liable to a fine not exceeding level 3 on the standard scale.

(5) …

(6) Without prejudice to section 130 (protection of public rights) above, it is the duty of the highway authority to enforce the provisions of this section.

(7) For the purposes of this section "the relevant period",—

(a) where the disturbance of the surface of the path or way is the first disturbance for the purposes of the sowing of a particular agricultural crop, means fourteen days beginning with the day on which the surface of the path or way was first disturbed for those purposes; or

(b) in any other case, means twenty-four hours beginning with the time when it was disturbed.

(8) On an application made to the highway authority before the disturbance or during the relevant period, the authority may grant an extension of that period for an additional period not exceeding twenty-eight days.

(9) In this section "minimum width", in relation to a highway, has the same meaning as in Schedule 12A to this Act.]

[949]

NOTES

Substituted by the Rights of Way Act 1990, s 1(3).

Sub-s (5): repealed by the Countryside and Rights of Way Act 2000, ss 70(2), 102, Sch 16, Pt II.

[135 Authorisation of other works disturbing footpath[, bridleway or restricted byway]

(1) Where the occupier of any agricultural land, or land which is being brought into use for agriculture, desires to carry out in relation to that land an excavation or engineering operation, and the excavation or operation—

(a) is reasonably necessary for the purposes of agriculture, but

(b) will so disturb the surface of a footpath[, bridleway or restricted byway] which passes over that land as to render it inconvenient for the exercise of the public right of way,

he may apply to the highway authority for an order that the public right of way shall be subject to the condition that he has the right to disturb the surface by that excavation or operation during such period, not exceeding three months, as is specified in the order ("the authorisation period").

(2) The highway authority shall make an order under subsection (1) above if they are satisfied either—

(a) that it is practicable temporarily to divert the path or way in a manner reasonably convenient to users; or

(b) that it is practicable to take adequate steps to ensure that the path or way remains sufficiently convenient, having regard to the need for the excavation or operation, for temporary use while it is being carried out.

(3) An order made by a highway authority under subsection (1) above—

(a) may provide for the temporary diversion of the path or way during the authorisation period, but shall not divert it on to land not occupied by the applicant unless written consent to the making of the order has been given by the occupier of that land, and by any other person whose consent is needed to obtain access to it;

(b) may include such conditions as the authority reasonably think fit for the provision, either by the applicant or by the authority at the expense of the applicant, of facilities for the convenient use of any such diversion, including signposts and other notices, stiles, bridges, and gates;

(c) shall not affect the line of a footpath[, bridleway or restricted byway] on land not occupied by the applicant;

and the authority shall cause notices of any such diversion, together with a plan showing the effect of the diversion and the line of the alternative route provided, to be prominently displayed throughout the authorisation period at each end of the diversion.

(4) An order made by a highway authority under subsection (1) above may include such conditions as the authority reasonably think fit—

PART I STATUTES

(a) for the protection and convenience during the authorisation period of users of the path or way;
(b) for making good the surface of the path or way to not more than its minimum width before the expiration of the authorisation period;
(c) for the recovery from the applicant of expenses incurred by the authority in connection with the order.

(5) An order under this section shall not authorise any interference with the apparatus or works of any statutory undertakers.

(6) If the applicant fails to comply with a condition imposed under subsection (3)(b) or (4)(a) or (b) above he is guilty of an offence and liable to a fine not exceeding level 3 on the standard scale.

(7) Proceedings for an offence under this section in relation to a footpath[, bridleway or restricted byway] shall be brought only by the highway authority or (with the consent of the highway authority) the council of the non-metropolitan district, parish or community in which the offence is committed.

(8) Without prejudice to section 130 (protection of public rights) above, it is the duty of the highway authority to enforce the provisions of this section.

(9) In this section "minimum width", in relation to a highway, has the same meaning as in Schedule 12A to this Act.]

[950]

NOTES

Substituted by the Rights of Way Act 1990, s 1(4).
Section heading: words in square brackets substituted by SI 2006/1177, reg 2, Schedule, Pt I.
Sub-ss (1), (3), (7): words in square brackets substituted by SI 2006/1177, reg 2, Schedule, Pt I.

135A, 135B, 136–202 *(Ss 135A, 135B, 136, 137, 137A, 138–140, 140A, 141–147, 147ZA, 147A, 148–155, 160A, 161, 161A, 162–171, 171A, 172–175, 175A, 176–180, 184, 185 outside the scope of this work; ss 156–160, 181–183 repealed by the New Roads and Street Works Act 1991, s 168(2), Sch 9; ss 157–159 repealed by the Local Government Act 1985, s 102, Sch 17; ss 186–202 (Pt X) repealed with savings by the Planning and Compensation Act 1991, ss 81(1), 84(6), Sch 19, Pt V.)*

PART XI
MAKING UP OF PRIVATE STREETS

203, 204 *(Outside the scope of this work.)*

The private street works code

205 Street works in private streets

(1) Where a private street is not, to the satisfaction of the street works authority, sewered, levelled, paved, metalled, flagged, channelled, made good and lighted, the authority may from time to time resolve with respect to the street to execute street works and, subject to the private street works code, the expenses incurred by the authority in executing those works shall be apportioned between the premises fronting the street.

(2) Where the authority resolve to execute street works with respect to a part only of the street (other than a part extending for the whole of the length of the street), the expenses incurred by them in executing the works shall be apportioned only between the premises fronting the length of the street which constitutes or comprises that part.

(3) Where an authority have passed a resolution under subsection (1) above, the proper officer of the council shall prepare—
(a) a specification of the street works referred to in the resolution, with any necessary plans and sections,
(b) an estimate of the probable expenses of the works, and
(c) a provisional apportionment apportioning the estimated expenses between the premises liable to be charged with them under the private street works code;

and the specification, plans, sections, estimate and provisional apportionment shall comprise the particulars specified in paragraphs 1 to 4 of Schedule 16 to this Act and shall be submitted to the authority, who may by a further resolution (hereafter in the private street works code referred to as "the resolution of approval") approve them with or without modification or addition as they think fit.

(4) If, in the case of a street outside Greater London, the street works referred to in the resolution under subsection (1) above include the sewering of the street, the proper officer of the county council shall, when preparing the specification required by subsection (3) above, consult the council of the district in which the street works are to be carried out.

[(4A) In the case of a street in Wales—

(a) subsection (4) above does not apply; but

(b) if the street works referred to in the resolution under subsection (1) above—

(i) are to be carried out in a part of the street which is treated as being in the area of a street works authority other than the local Welsh council for it; and

(ii) include the sewering of the street,

the proper officer of the council which are the street works authority shall, when preparing the specification required by subsection (3) above, consult the local Welsh council for it.]

(5) After the resolution of approval has been passed, a notice containing the particulars specified in paragraph 5 of Schedule 16 to this Act shall—

(a) be published once in each of 2 successive weeks in a local newspaper circulating in the area of the street works authority, and

(b) be posted in a prominent position in or near to the street to which the resolution relates once at least in each of 3 successive weeks, and

(c) within 7 days from the date of the first publication under paragraph (a) above, be served on the owners of the premises shown in the provisional apportionment as liable to be charged;

and during one month from the said date a copy of the resolution of approval, and the approved documents or copies of them certified by the proper officer of the council, shall be kept deposited and open to inspection free of charge at all reasonable hours at the offices of the street works authority and also[, in the case of a street situated in a non-metropolitan district, at the offices of the council of that district] [and, in the case of any part of a street in Wales which is treated as being in the area of a street works authority which are not the local Welsh council for it, at the offices of the local Welsh council.

(5A) For the purposes of this section, the local Welsh council for a street in Wales are the council of the county or county borough in which it is situated.]

(6) Where a notice is served on an owner of premises under subsection (5)(c) above it shall be accompanied by a statement of the sum apportioned on those premises by the provisional apportionment.

[951]

NOTES

Sub-ss (4A), (5A): inserted by the Local Government (Wales) Act 1994, s 22(1), Sch 7, para 18.

Sub-s (5): first words in square brackets substituted by the Local Government Act 1985, s 8, Sch 4, para 34; final words in square brackets inserted by the Local Government (Wales) Act 1994, s 22(1), Sch 7, para 18.

206 Incidental works

A street works authority may include in street works to be executed under the private street works code with respect to a street any works which they think necessary for bringing the street, as regards sewerage, drainage, level, or other matters, into conformity with any other streets, whether maintainable at the public expense or not, including the provision of separate sewers for the reception of sewage and of surface water respectively.

[952]

207 Provisional apportionment of expenses

(1) In a provisional apportionment of expenses of street works under the private street works code, the apportionment of expenses between the premises liable to be charged with them shall, subject to the provisions of this section, be made according to the frontage of the respective premises.

(2) The street works authority may, if they think just, resolve that in settling the apportionment regard shall be had to the following considerations:—

(a) the greater or less degree of benefit to be derived by any premises from the street works;

(b) the amount and value of any work already done by the owners or occupiers of any premises.

(3) The authority may—

(a) if they think just, include in the apportionment any premises which do not front the street, but have access to it through a court, passage, or otherwise, and which will, in the opinion of the authority, be benefited by the works, and

(b) fix, by reference to the degree of benefit to be derived by those premises, the amount to be apportioned on them.

[953]

208 Objections to proposed works

(1) Within one month from the date of the first publication of a notice under section 205(5)(a) above, an owner of premises shown in a provisional apportionment of expenses as liable to be

charged with any part of the expenses of executing street works with respect to a private street or a part of a private street may, by notice to the street works authority, object to their proposals on any of the following grounds:—

(a) that the alleged private street is not a private street or, as the case may be, that the alleged part of a private street is not a part of a private street;

(b) that there has been some material informality, defect or error in, or in respect of, the resolution, notice, plans, sections or estimate;

(c) that the proposed works are insufficient or unreasonable;

(d) that the estimated expenses of the proposed works are excessive;

(e) that any premises ought to be excluded from or inserted in the provisional apportionment;

(f) that the provisional apportionment is incorrect in respect of some matter of fact to be specified in the objection or, where the provisional apportionment is made with regard to other considerations than frontage, in respect of the degree of benefit to be derived by any premises, or of the amount or value of any work already done by the owner or occupier of premises.

(2) Where premises are owned jointly by 2 or more persons, a notice under subsection (1) above may be given on behalf of those persons by one of their number, if he is authorised in writing by a majority of them to do so.

[954]

209 Hearing and determination of objections

(1) If an objection is made under section 208 above within the period there specified, and is not withdrawn, the street works authority may, after the expiration of that period, apply to a magistrates' court to appoint a time for hearing and determining all objections so made within that period, and shall serve on the objectors notice of the time and place so appointed.

(2) At the hearing the court shall hear and determine the objections in the same manner as nearly as may be as if the authority were proceeding summarily against the objectors to enforce payment of a sum of money summarily recoverable.

The court may quash in whole or in part or may amend the resolution of approval, specification, plans, sections, estimate and provisional apportionment, or any of them, on the application either of an objector or of the authority, and may also, if it thinks fit, adjourn the hearing and direct further notices to be given.

(3) The costs of any proceedings before a magistrates' court in relation to objections under the private street works code are in the discretion of the court, and the court may, if it thinks fit, direct that the whole or a part of any costs ordered to be paid by an objector or objectors are to be paid in the first instance by the authority, and charged as part of the expenses of the works on the premises of the objector, or, as the case may be, on the premises of the objectors in such proportions as may appear just.

[955]

210 Power to amend specification, apportionment, etc

(1) Subject to the provisions of this section, the street works authority may from time to time amend the specification, plans, sections, estimate and provisional apportionment for any street works proposed under section 205 above.

(2) If the street works authority propose to amend the estimate so as to increase the amount of it, then, before the amendment is made, a notice containing the particulars specified in paragraph 6 of Schedule 16 to this Act shall—

(a) be published once in each of 2 successive weeks in a local newspaper circulating in the area of the street works authority, and

(b) be posted in a prominent position in or near to the street to which the resolution of approval relates once at least in each of 3 successive weeks, and

(c) within 7 days from the date of the first publication under paragraph (a) above, be served on the owners of the premises shown in the provisional apportionment as liable to be charged;

and, during one month from the said date, a document certified by the proper officer of the council giving details of the estimate and of the consequential amendment of the provisional apportionment shall be kept deposited and open to inspection free of charge at all reasonable hours at the offices of the street works authority and also[, in the case of a street situated in a non-metropolitan district, at the offices of the council of that district] [and, in the case of any part of a street in Wales, the Welsh council for the county or county borough in which it is situated, if different from the street works authority in whose area it is treated as situated.]

(3) Where a notice is served on an owner of premises under subsection (2)(c) above it shall be accompanied by a statement of the sum apportioned on those premises by the provisional apportionment as proposed to be amended.

(4) Within one month from the date of the first publication of a notice under subsection (2)(a) above, objections may be made and, if made, shall be heard and determined in like manner, and subject to the like provisions with respect to the persons entitled to be heard and otherwise, as objections under section 208 above.

[956]

NOTES

Sub-s (2): first words in square brackets inserted by the Local Government Act 1985, s 8, Sch 4, para 34; final words in square brackets inserted by the Local Government (Wales) Act 1994, s 22(1), Sch 7, para 19.

211 Final apportionment and objections to it

(1) When any street works to be executed under the private street works code have been completed, and the expenses of them ascertained, the proper officer of the council shall make a final apportionment by dividing the expenses in the same proportions as those in which the estimated expenses were divided in the original or amended provisional apportionment, as the case may be, and notice of the final apportionment shall be served on the owners of the premises affected by it.

(2) Within one month from the date on which notice of the final apportionment is served on him, the owner of any premises shown in the apportionment as liable to be charged may, by notice to the authority, object to the apportionment on the following grounds, or any of them:—

(a) that there has been an unreasonable departure from the specification, plans and sections;

(b) that the actual expenses have without sufficient reason exceeded the estimated expenses by more than 15 per cent;

(c) that the apportionment has not been made in accordance with this section

Objections under this section shall be determined in the like manner, and subject to the like provisions with respect to the persons entitled to be heard and otherwise, as objections to the provisional apportionment.

(3) The final apportionment, subject to any amendment made to it by a court on the hearing of objections to it under this section, is conclusive for all purposes.

[957]

212 Recovery of expenses and charge thereof on premises

(1) A street works authority may from time to time recover from the owner for the time being of any premises in respect of which any sum is due for expenses of street works the whole or any portion of that sum together with interest at such reasonable rates as the authority may determine from the date of the final apportionment.

(2) The sum apportioned on any premises by the final apportionment or, as the case may be, by that apportionment as amended by a court, together with interest from the date of the final apportionment is, until recovered, a charge on the premises and on all estates and interests therein.

(3) A street works authority, for the purpose of enforcing a charge under subsection (2) above before it is registered under the Local Land Charges Act 1975, have the same powers and remedies under the Law of Property Act 1925 and otherwise as if they were mortgagees by deed having powers of sale and lease and of appointing a receiver.

(4) A street works authority may by order declare the expenses apportioned on any premises by a final apportionment made by the proper officer of the council or, as the case may be, by that apportionment as amended by a court, to be payable by annual instalments within a period not exceeding 30 years, together with interest from the date of the final apportionment; and any such instalment and interest, or any part thereof, may be recovered from the owner or occupier for the time being of the premises.

Schedule 13 to this Act applies in relation to any sum paid by an occupier of premises under this subsection.

[958]

213 Power for limited owners to borrow for expenses

The owners of any premises, if they are persons who under the Compulsory Purchase Act 1965 are empowered to sell and convey or release lands, may charge those premises with—

(a) such sum as may be necessary to defray the whole or a part of any expenses which the owners of, or any other person in respect of, those premises for the time being are liable to defray under the private street works code, and

(b) the expenses of making such a charge;

and, for securing the repayment of that sum with interest, may mortgage the premises to any person advancing that sum so, however, that the principal due on any such mortgage shall be repaid by equal yearly or half-yearly payments within 20 years.

[959]

214–218 (*Outside the scope of this work.*)

The advance payments code

219 Payments to be made by owners of new buildings in respect of street works

(1) Subject to the provisions of this section, where—

(a) it is proposed to erect a building for which plans are required to be deposited with the local authority in accordance with building regulations, and

(b) the building will have a frontage on a private street in which the street works authority have power under the private street works code to require works to be executed or to execute works,

no work shall be done in or for the purpose of erecting the building unless the owner of the land on which it is to be erected or a previous owner thereof has paid to the street works authority, or secured to the satisfaction of that authority the payment to them of, such sum as may be required under section 220 below in respect of the cost of street works in that street.

(2) If work is done in contravention of subsection (1) above, the owner of the land on which the building is to be erected and, if he is a different person, the person undertaking the erection of the building is guilty of an offence and liable to a fine not exceeding [level 3 on the standard scale], and any further contravention in respect of the same building constitutes a new offence and may be punished accordingly.

Proceedings under this subsection shall not be taken by any person other than the street works authority.

(3) Where the person undertaking the erection of the building is not the owner of the land on which it is to be erected and is charged with an offence under subsection (2) above, it shall be a defence for him to prove that he had reasonable grounds for believing that the sum required under section 220 below had been paid or secured by the owner of the land in accordance with subsection (1) above.

(4) This section does not apply—

(a) where the owner of the land on which the building is to be erected will be exempt, by virtue of a provision in the private street works code, from liability to expenses incurred in respect of street works in the private street in question;

(b) where the building proposed to be erected will be situated in the curtilage of, and be appurtenant to, an existing building;

(c) where the building is proposed to be erected in a parish or community and plans for the building were deposited with the district council or, according to the date of deposit, the rural district council before the date on which the New Streets Act 1951, or the advance payments code (either in this Act or in the Highways Act 1959) was applied in the parish or community or, as the case may require, in the part of the parish or community in which the building is to be erected;

(d) where an agreement has been made by any person with the street works authority under section 38 above providing for the carrying out at the expense of that person of street works in the whole of the street or a part of the street comprising the whole of the part on which the frontage of the building will be, and for securing that the street or the part thereof, on completion of the works, will become a highway maintainable at the public expense;

(e) where the street works authority, being satisfied that the whole of the street or such a part thereof as aforesaid is not, and is not likely within a reasonable time to be, substantially built-up or in so unsatisfactory a condition as to justify the use of powers under the private street works code for securing the carrying out of street works in the street or part thereof, by notice exempt the building from this section;

(f) where the street works authority, being satisfied that the street is not, and is not likely within a reasonable time to become, joined to a highway maintainable at the public expense, by notice exempt the building from this section;

(g) where the whole street, being less than 100 yards in length, or a part of the street not less than 100 yards in length and comprising the whole of the part on which the frontage of the building will be, was on the material date built-up to such an extent that the aggregate length of the frontages of the buildings on both sides of the street or part constituted at least one half of the aggregate length of all the frontages on both sides of the street or part;

(h) where (in a case not falling within paragraph (g) above) the street works authority, being satisfied that the whole of the street was on the material date substantially built-up, by notice exempt the building from this section;

(i) where the building is proposed to be erected on land belonging to, or in the possession of—

(i) the British Railways Board, … , the British Waterways Board, [Transport for London], … any wholly-owned subsidiary (within the meaning of the Transport Act 1968) or joint subsidiary (within the meaning of section 51(5) of that Act) of any of those bodies [other than Transport for London, or any of its subsidiaries (within the meaning of the Greater London Authority Act 1999)];

(ii) the council of a county, district or London borough … or the Common Council;

(iii) the [new towns residuary body] or a new town development corporation;

(j) where the building is to be erected by a company the objects of which include the provision of industrial premises for use by persons other than the company, being a company the constitution of which prohibits the distribution of the profits of the company to its members, and the cost of the building is to be defrayed wholly or mainly by a government department;

(k) where the street works authority, being satisfied—

(i) that more than three-quarters of the aggregate length of all the frontages on both sides of the street, or of a part of the street not less than 100 yards in length and comprising the whole of the part on which the frontage of the building will be, consists, or is at some future time likely to consist, of the frontages of industrial premises, and

(ii) that their powers under the private street works code are not likely to be exercised in relation to the street, or to that part of it, as the case may be, within a reasonable time,

by resolution exempt the street, or that part of it, from this section.

[(4A) In subsection (4)(c) above, "district council" is to be read in relation to plans deposited on or after 1st April 1996 for a building to be erected in Wales as "Welsh council"]

[(4B) In subsection (4)(i)(iii) "new towns residuary body" means—

(a) in relation to England, the Homes and Communities Agency so far as exercising functions in relation to anything transferred (or to be transferred) to it as mentioned in section 52(1)(a) to (d) of the Housing and Regeneration Act 2008; and

(b) in relation to Wales, the Welsh Ministers so far as exercising functions in relation to anything transferred (or to be transferred) to them as mentioned in section 36(1)(a)(i) to (iii) of the New Towns Act 1981.]

(5) Where a sum has been paid or secured under this section by the owner of the land in relation to a building proposed to be erected on it, and thereafter a notice is served under subsection (4) above exempting the building from this section, or a resolution is passed under paragraph (k) of that subsection exempting the street or part of a street on which the building will have a frontage from this section, the street works authority shall refund that sum to the person who is for the time being owner of the land or shall release the security, as the case may be.

Where the said sum was paid, and after the payment but before the service of the said notice or the passing of the said resolution, as the case may be, the land in respect of which it was paid was divided into 2 or more parts each having a frontage on the private street in question, the sum is to be treated for the purposes of this subsection as apportioned between the owners of the land according to their respective frontages.

(6) For the purposes of this section "the material date" is—

(a) in relation to a building proposed to be erected in an area which before 1st April 1974 was a rural district or a contributory place within a rural district, the date on which the New Streets Act 1951 or the advance payments code (either in this Act or in the Highways Act 1959) was applied in that area;

(b) in relation to a building proposed to be erected anywhere else, 1st October 1951.

[960]

NOTES

Sub-s (2): maximum fine increased and converted to a level on the standard scale by the Criminal Justice Act 1982, ss 37, 38, 46.

Sub-s (4): in sub-para (i)(i), words omitted repealed by the Statute Law (Repeals) Act 1989, the Transport Act 1981, ss 14(1), 40(1), Sch 4, para 6, Sch 12, Pt I, and the London Regional Transport Act 1984, s 71(3), Sch 7, words in square brackets substituted by SI 2003/1615, art 2, Sch 1, Pt 1, para 7(1), (6); words omitted from sub-para (i)(ii) repealed by the Local Government Act 1985, s 102, Sch 17; in sub-para (i)(iii) words in square brackets substituted by the Housing and Regeneration Act 2008, s 56, Sch 8, para 32(1), (2), subject to transitional provisions and savings in arts 6–13 thereof.

Sub-s (4A): inserted by the Local Government (Wales) Act 1994, s 22(1), Sch 7, para 20.

Sub-s (4B): inserted by the Housing and Regeneration Act 2008, s 56, Sch 8, para 32(1), (3), subject to transitional provisions and savings in arts 6–13 thereof.

220 Determination of liability for, and amount of, payments

(1) In a case to which section 219 above applies the street works authority shall, within 6 weeks from the passing of any required plans relating to the erection of a building deposited with them or, in a case to which subsection (2) [or (2A)] below applies, with the district council [or Welsh council], serve a notice on the person by or on whose behalf the plans were deposited requiring the payment or the securing under section 219 above of a sum specified in the notice.

In this subsection and [subsections (2) and (2A)] below "required plans" means plans required to be deposited with the local authority in accordance with building regulations.

(2) Where (outside Greater London) the advance payments code is in force in the whole or any part of a [non-metropolitan] district, the district council, in any case to which section 219 above may be applicable, shall within one week from the date of the passing of any required plans deposited with them relating to the erection of a building in an area in which that code is in force inform the street works authority that the plans have been passed.

[(2A) Where any required plans which—

(a) are deposited with a Welsh council; and

(b) relate to the erection of a building in an area—

(i) in which the advance payments code is in force; but

(ii) which is treated as being within the area of a street works authority other than that Welsh council,

are passed, the Welsh council shall, in any case to which section 219 above may be applicable, within one week inform the street works authority of that event.]

(3) Subject to the provisions of this section, the sum to be specified in a notice under subsection (1) above is such sum as, in the opinion of the street works authority, would be recoverable under the private street works code in respect of the frontage of the proposed building on the private street if the authority were then to carry out such street works in the street as they would require under that code before declaring the street to be a highway which for the purposes of this Act is a highway maintainable at the public expense.

In this subsection a reference to a street does not include a reference to a part of a street, except to a part which the street works authority think fit to treat as constituting a separate street for the purposes of this subsection and which comprises the whole of the part on which the frontage of the building will be.

(4) If, at any time after the service of a notice under subsection (1) above, the street works authority—

(a) are of opinion that the sum specified in the notice exceeds such sum as in their opinion would be recoverable as mentioned in subsection (3) above if they were then to carry out such street works as are so mentioned, or

(b) are of opinion that no sum would be so recoverable,

they may, by a further notice, served on the person who is for the time being owner of the land on which the building is to be, or has been, erected, substitute a smaller sum for the sum specified in the notice served under subsection (1) above or, as the case may be, intimate that no sum falls to be paid or secured.

This subsection does not apply where a sum has been paid or secured in compliance with a notice served under subsection (1) above and the case is one in which the authority have power to make a refund or release under section 221(1) below.

(5) Where, under a local Act, the erection of buildings on land having a frontage on a new street is prohibited until works for the construction or sewering of the street have been carried out in accordance with byelaws, the amount of the sum to be specified in a notice served under this section shall be calculated as if those works had been carried out.

(6) Where a notice is served on any person under this section (other than a notice intimating that no sum falls to be paid or secured) that person or, if he is a different person, the owner of the land on which the building is to be, or has been, erected, may, not later than one month from the date of the service of the notice, appeal to the Minister and the Minister may substitute a smaller sum for the sum specified by the street works authority.

On an appeal under this subsection, the Minister shall give the appellant an opportunity of being heard before a person appointed by the Minister.

(7) Where a sum has been paid or secured in compliance with a notice served under subsection (1) above and a notice is subsequently served under subsection (4) above substituting a smaller sum for the sum specified in the first-mentioned notice or intimating that no sum falls to be paid or secured, the street works authority—

(a) if the sum was paid, shall refund the amount of the excess or, as the case may be, the whole sum to the person who is for the time being owner of the land on which the building is to be, or has been, erected;

(b) if the sum was secured and the person whose property is security for the payment of it is for the time being owner of that land, shall release the security to the extent of the excess or, as the case may be, the whole security;

(c) if the sum was secured and the person whose property is security for the payment of it is not for the time being owner of that land, shall pay to that owner an amount equal to the excess or, as the case may be, the whole sum, and are entitled to realise the security for the purpose of recovering the amount so paid.

(8) Where land in respect of which a sum has been paid or secured in compliance with a notice under subsection (1) above is subsequently divided into 2 or more parts so that 2 or more owners would, if street works were carried out, incur liability in respect of it, the sum is to be treated as apportioned between those owners according to their respective frontages and, if the sum was secured and the security is the property of one only of those owners, the street works authority—

- (a) are required under subsection (7)(b) above to release the security only to the extent of the amount apportioned to the owner, and
- (b) are entitled to realise the security for the purpose of recovering the amount or amounts paid to the other owner or owners under subsection (7)(c) above.

(9) Where a security is realised for the purpose of recovering an amount paid by a street works authority under subsection (7)(c) above, and the sum produced by realising the security exceeds the amount so paid, the amount of the excess shall be held by the authority and dealt with under the advance payments code as if it had been an amount paid under section 219 above on the date on which the security was realised.

[961]

NOTES

Sub-s (1): first and second words in square brackets inserted, and final words in square brackets substituted, by the Local Government (Wales) Act 1994, s 22(1), Sch 7, para 21.

Sub-s (2): words in square brackets inserted by the Local Government Act 1985, s 8, Sch 4, para 35.

Sub-s (2A): inserted by the Local Government (Wales) Act 1994, s 22(1), Sch 7, para 21.

Transfer of Functions: see the note to s 26 at **[925]**.

221 Refunds etc where work done otherwise than at expense of street works authority

(1) Where—

- (a) a sum has been paid or secured under section 219 above by the owner of land in respect of the cost of street works to be carried out in the private street on which that land has a frontage, and
- (b) any street works are subsequently carried out in the private street in respect of that frontage to the satisfaction of but otherwise than at the expense of the street works authority,

the authority may refund to the person at whose expense the works are carried out the whole or such proportion of that sum or, as the case may be, release the whole or such part of the security, as in their opinion represents the amount by which the liability of the owner of that land in respect of street works has been reduced as a result of the carrying out of the street works in question.

Where the person at whose expense the works are carried out is not the person who is for the time being owner of that land no refund or release shall be made under this subsection unless the owner has been notified of the proposal to make the refund or release and has been afforded an opportunity of making representations to the street works authority in relation to it.

(2) Where any land which has a frontage on a private street, and in respect of which a sum has been paid or secured under section 219 above, is subsequently divided into 2 or more parts each having a frontage on that private street, the sum is to be treated as apportioned between the owners thereof according to their respective frontages, and subsection (1) above has effect accordingly.

(3) Where—

- (a) a sum has been paid or secured under section 219 above by the owner of land in respect of the cost of street works to be carried out in the private street on which that land has a frontage, and
- (b) thereafter the street works authority enter into an agreement with any person under section 38 above providing for the carrying out at the expense of that person of street works in respect of that frontage,

that agreement may also provide for the refund of the said sum or a part of it either without interest or with interest at such rate as may be specified in the agreement, or for the release of the whole or a part of the security, as the case may be.

[962]

222 Sums paid or secured to be in discharge of further liability for street works

(1) Where a sum has been paid or secured under section 219 above by the owner of land in respect of the cost of street works to be carried out in the private street on which that land has a frontage, the liability of that owner or any subsequent owner of that land in respect of the carrying out of street works in that street under the private street works code ("the street works liability") is, as respects that frontage, to be deemed to be discharged to the extent of the sum so paid or secured.

(2) If, when the street is declared to be a highway which for the purposes of this Act is a highway maintainable at the public expense, the said sum is found to exceed the total street works liability in respect of that frontage or there is no such liability because the street was not made up at the expense of the street works authority, the street works authority—

(a) if the sum was paid, shall refund the amount of the excess or, as the case may be, the whole sum to the person who is for the time being owner of the land;

(b) if the sum was secured and the person whose property is security for the payment of it is for the time being owner of the land, shall release the security to the extent of the excess or, as the case may be, the whole security;

(c) if the sum was secured and the person whose property is security for the payment of it is not for the time being owner of the land, shall pay to that owner an amount equal to the excess or, as the case may be, the whole sum, and are entitled to realise the security for the purpose of recovering the amount so paid.

(3) Where land in respect of which a sum has been paid or secured under section 219 above is subsequently divided into 2 or more parts so that 2 or more owners incur or would incur the street works liability, the sum is to be treated as apportioned between those owners according to their respective frontages, and if the sum was secured and the security is the property of one only of those owners the street works authority—

(a) are required under subsection (2)(b) above to release the security only to the extent to which the amount apportioned to that owner exceeds his street works liability or, as the case may be, to the extent of the whole of that amount, and

(b) are entitled to realise the security for the purpose of recovering the amount or amounts paid to the other owner or owners under subsection (2)(c) above.

(4) Where any refund, release or payment has been made under section 220(7) above, or under section 221 above, the foregoing provisions of this section have effect as if for references therein to a sum paid or secured there were substituted references to any sum remaining paid or secured.

[963]

223 Determination to cease to have effect when plans not proceeded with

(1) Where, on the occasion of the deposit of plans for the erection of a building, the amount to be paid or secured under section 219 above has been determined under section 220 above, and subsequently—

(a) the local authority, under [section 32 of the Building Act 1984], declare the deposit of the plans to be of no effect, or

(b) before any work has been done in or for the purpose of erecting the building the owner gives notice to the local authority of his intention not to proceed with the building,

the said determination and any payment made or security given in accordance with it are, unless there have already been carried out or commenced in the street under the private street works code street works in respect of which the owner of the land on which the building was to be erected is liable, of no effect for the purposes of this Part of this Act.

(2) Where by virtue of subsection (1) above a determination is of no effect and a sum has been paid or security given in accordance with it, the street works authority—

(a) if the sum was paid, shall refund it to the person who is for the time being owner of the land;

(b) if the sum was secured and the person whose property is security for the payment of it is for the time being owner of the land, shall release the security;

(c) if the sum was secured and the person whose property is security for the payment of it is not for the time being owner of the land, shall pay to that owner an amount equal to the said sum, and are entitled to realise the security for the purpose of recovering the amount so paid.

(3) Where land in respect of which a sum has been paid or secured as mentioned in subsection (2) above is subsequently divided into 2 or more parts so that 2 or more owners would, if street works were carried out, incur liability in respect thereof, the sum is to be treated as apportioned between those owners according to their respective frontages and, if the sum was secured and the security is the property of one only of those owners, the street works authority—

(a) are required under subsection (2)(b) above to release the security only to the extent of the amount apportioned to that owner, and

(b) are entitled to realise the security for the purpose of recovering the amount or amounts paid to the other owner or owners under subsection (2)(c) above.

(4) Where any refund, release or payment has been made under section 220(7) above, or under section 221 above, subsections (2) and (3) above have effect as if for references in those subsections to a sum paid and security given there were substituted references to, respectively, any sum remaining paid and any remaining security.

(5) Where—

(a) a person notifies the local authority in accordance with subsection (1)(b) above of his intention not to proceed with the building and by reason thereof a determination is of no effect, and

(b) subsequently notice is given to the local authority by the owner of the land that he intends to proceed with the building in accordance with the plans as originally deposited, the notice to be served under subsection (1) of section 220 above by the street works authority shall, in lieu of being served as required by that subsection, be served on him within one month from the date of the service of the notice of his intention to proceed with the building, and section 220 has effect accordingly.

(6) Where the advance payments code is in force in the whole or any part of a [non-metropolitan] district, the district council, in any case to which this section may be applicable, shall within one week inform the county council of the happening of any of the following events:—

(a) the making of any declaration that the deposit of plans relating to the erection of a building is of no effect,

(b) the giving of any notice by an owner of his intention not to proceed with a building, and

(c) the giving of any notice by an owner of his intention to proceed with the building in accordance with the plans as originally deposited.

[(7) In any case—

(a) to which this section may be applicable; and

(b) which relates to plans for the erection of a building in any part of a street in Wales which is treated as being in the area of a street works authority other than the Welsh council for the county or county borough in which it is situated,

the Welsh council shall within one week inform the street works authority of the happening of any event of a kind described in paragraphs (a) to (c) of subsection (6) above.]

[964]

NOTES

Sub-s (1): words in square brackets substituted by the Building Act 1984, s 133(1), Sch 6, para 21.
Sub-s (6): words in square brackets inserted by the Local Government Act 1985, s 8, Sch 4, para 35.
Sub-s (7): inserted by the Local Government (Wales) Act 1994, s 22(1), Sch 7, para 22.

224 Certain matters to be local land charges

(1) The matters specified in subsection (2) below are local land charges.

(2) The matters referred to in subsection (1) above are:—

(a) notices served by a street works authority under section 220(1) or (4) above;

(b) determinations by the Minister under section 220(6) above;

(c) payments made and securities given under section 219 above;

(d) notices served under subsection (4)(e), (f) or (h) of section 219 above exempting a building from that section;

(e) resolutions passed under subsection (4)(k) of section 219 above exempting a street or a part of a street from that section; and

(f) refunds made and releases of securities granted under section 221, 222 or 223 above.

(3) As respects any matter that is a local land charge by virtue of this section, the street works authority for the street concerned are, notwithstanding anything in section 5(4) of the Local Land Charges Act 1975, to be treated as the originating authority for the purposes of that Act.

[965]

NOTES

Transfer of Functions: see the note to s 26 at **[925]**.

225 Interest on sums paid under advance payments code

(1) Any sum paid by the owner of land to a street works authority under section 219 above, in so far as it continues to be held by the authority, carries simple interest at the appropriate rate from the date of payment until such time as the sum or a part of it remaining so held—

(a) falls to be set off under section 222 above against the liability of the owner of the land in respect of the carrying out of street works; or

(b) falls to be refunded in full under the provisions of the advance payments code;

and the interest shall be held by the authority until that time and dealt with under those provisions as if it formed part of the said sum.

This subsection does not apply to any sum in so far as it is repaid under any such agreement as is referred to in section 221(3) above.

(2) For the purposes of the advance payments code interest on any sum held by a street works authority shall be calculated in respect of each financial year during which it accrues at the appropriate rate prevailing at the commencement of that financial year.

(3) In this section "the appropriate rate" means the rate at the material time determined by the Treasury in respect of local loans for periods of 10 years on the security of local rates (being a determination under section 6(2) of the National Loans Act 1968, and subject to any relevant direction under the said section 6(2)).

General

226, 227 (*Outside the scope of this work.*)

228 Adoption of private street after execution of street works

(1) When any street works have been executed in a private street, the street works authority may, by notice displayed in a prominent position in the street, declare the street to be a highway which for the purposes of this Act is a highway maintainable at the public expense, and on the expiration of one month from the day on which the notice was first so displayed the street shall, subject to subsections (2) to (4) below, become such a highway.

(2) A street shall not become a highway maintainable at the public expense by virtue of subsection (1) above if, within the period there mentioned, the owner of the street or, if more than one, the majority in number of the owners of the street, by notice to the authority object; but within 2 months from the expiration of that period the street works authority may apply to a magistrates' court for an order overruling the objection.

(3) If an order overruling an objection under subsection (2) above is made pursuant to an application under that subsection and no appeal against the order is brought within the time limited for such an appeal, the street or part in question shall become a highway maintainable at the public expense on the expiration of that time.

(4) Where such an order is made or refused and an appeal, or an appeal arising out of that appeal, is brought against or arises out of the order or refusal, then—

(a) if the final determination of the matter is in favour of the authority, or

(b) the appeal is abandoned by the objectors,

the street shall become a highway maintainable at the public expense on that final determination or, as the case may be, on the abandonment of the appeal.

(5) Notwithstanding anything in any other enactment or provision, for the purposes of this section the time for bringing or seeking leave for any appeal (including an application for certiorari) is 2 months from the date of the decision or of the conclusion of the proceedings appealed against, unless apart from this subsection the time is less than that period; and no power, however worded, to enlarge any such time is exercisable for the purposes of this section.

(6) Where street works have been executed in a part only of a street (other than a part extending for the whole of the length of the street), subsections (1) to (4) above have effect as if for references in those subsections to the street there were substituted references to the length of the street which constitutes or comprises that part.

(7) If all street works (whether or not including lighting) have been executed in a private street to the satisfaction of the street works authority, then, on the application of the majority in rateable value of the owners of premises in the street, the street works authority shall, within the period of 3 months from the date of the application, by notice displayed in a prominent position in the street, declare the street to be a highway which for the purposes of this Act is a highway maintainable at the public expense and thereupon the street shall become such a highway.

In this subsection a reference to a street does not include a reference to a part of a street.

[966]

229 Power of majority of frontagers to require adoption where advance payment made

(1) Where a majority in number of the owners of land having a frontage on a built-up private street, or as many of those owners as have between them more than half the aggregate length of all the frontages on both sides of the street, by notice request the street works authority to exercise their powers under the private street works code so as—

(a) to secure the carrying out of such street works in that street as the street works authority require under that code before declaring the street to be a highway which for the purposes of this Act is a highway maintainable at the public expense, and

(b) to declare the street to be such a highway,

the street works authority shall proceed to exercise their powers accordingly.

(2) Subsection (1) above does not apply unless, in at least one case, a payment has been made or security has been given under section 219 above by the owner of land having a frontage on the street and the payment has not been refunded, or the security released or realised, under subsection (5) of that section, or under section 223 above.

(3) For the purposes of this section a street is to be deemed to be built-up if the aggregate length of the frontages of the buildings on both sides of the street constitutes at least one half of the aggregate length of all the frontages on both sides of the street.

(4) This section does not apply in relation to a part of a street unless it is a part not less than 100 yards in length which the owners of land having a frontage on that part of the street elect to treat as constituting a street for the purposes of this section.

[967]

230–234 (*Outside the scope of this work.*)

235 Evasion of private street works expenses by owners

(1) Where a street works authority are empowered by section 212 above to recover any sum from the owner of any premises, and the authority are unable by the exercise of their powers (other than powers conferred by this section) to recover that sum, then if—

(a) the said premises were previously transferred by a person ("the transferor") who at the time of the transfer was the owner of other premises adjoining those premises, and

(b) a magistrates' court is satisfied that the transfer was intended for the purpose of evading the payment of expenses of street works,

the court may make an order under this section.

(2) An order under this section shall provide that, to such extent as the court making the order may determine, the street works authority may recover the said sum, and, where that sum is payable under an order made under section 212(4) above or section 305(2) below, any further sums which may fall due under that order, from the transferor.

(3) In this section "transfer" includes any disposal of land whether by way of sale, lease, exchange, gift or otherwise.

[968]

236 (*Outside the scope of this work.*)

237 Power of street works authority to grant charging order

(1) Where a person has paid, or advanced money for, expenses which by section 212 above a street works authority are empowered to recover, that person may apply to the authority for a charging order, and the authority, on being satisfied as to the amount of the expenditure on private street works, and, in the case of an advance, as to the sum advanced, may make an order accordingly charging on the premises in respect of which the expenses are recoverable, and on all estates and interests therein, an annuity to repay the sum expended or advanced.

(2) The annuity charged shall be such sum as the street works authority may determine in respect of every £100 of the amount of the expenditure and so in proportion in respect of any fraction of that amount, and shall commence from the date of the order and be payable by equal half-yearly payments for a term of 30 years to the person named in the order, his executors, administrators or assigns.

(3) A person aggrieved by an order of a street works authority under subsection (1) above, or by the refusal of the authority to make an order under that subsection, may appeal to a magistrates' court.

(4) Schedule 13 to this Act applies in relation to any sum paid by an occupier of premises in respect of an annuity charged on those premises under this section.

[969]

PART XII
ACQUISITION, VESTING AND TRANSFER OF LAND ETC

238 (*Outside the scope of this work.*)

Acquisition of land generally

239 Acquisition of land for construction, improvement etc of highway: general powers

(1) Subject to section 249 below, the Minister may acquire land required for the construction of a trunk road, and any highway authority may acquire land required for the construction of a highway which is to be a highway maintainable at the public expense, other than a trunk road.

(2) Subject to section 249 below, the Minister may acquire land which in his opinion is required—

(a) for the carrying out of any works authorised by an order relating to a trunk road under section 14 above, or

(b) for the provision of buildings or facilities to be used in connection with the construction or maintenance of a trunk road other than a special road.

(3) Subject to section 249 below, a highway authority may acquire land required for the improvement of a highway, being an improvement which they are authorised by this Act to carry out in relation to the highway.

(4) Subject to section 249 below, a special road authority may acquire land which in the opinion of the authority is required—

(a) for the improvement of a highway which is included in the route of the special road but has not been transferred to the authority by means of an order under section 18 above,

(b) for the purposes of any order made in relation to the special road under section 18 above, or

(c) for the provision of service stations or other buildings or facilities to be used in connection with the construction of the special road or with the use or maintenance of it.

(5) Where a highway authority have acquired, or propose to acquire, in exercise of any of the powers conferred by subsections (1) to (4) above, land forming part of a common, open space, or fuel or field garden allotment, and other land is required for the purpose of being given in exchange for the first-mentioned land, the authority may acquire that other land under the subsection in question as if it were land required for the construction or improvement of a highway, and nothing in section 249 below applies to an acquisition by virtue of this subsection.

(6) A highway authority may acquire land required for the improvement or development of frontages to a highway for which they are the highway authority or of the land adjoining or adjacent to that highway.

[970]

NOTES

Transfer of Functions: see the note to s 26 at **[925]**.
See further: the Town and Country Planning Act 1990, s 170.

240–262 (*Ss 240–258, 260–262 outside the scope of this work; s 259 repealed by the Planning and Compulsory Purchase Act 2004, ss 118(2), 120, Sch 7, para 11(1), (4), Sch 9.*)

Vesting of highways etc

263 Vesting of highways maintainable at public expense

(1) Subject to the provision of this section, every highway maintainable at the public expense, together with the materials and scrapings of it, vests in the authority who are for the time being the highway authority for the highway.

(2) Subsection (1) above does not apply—

(a) to a highway with respect to the vesting of which, on its becoming or ceasing to be a trunk road, provision is made by section 265 below, or

(b) to a part of a trunk road with respect to the vesting of which provision is made by section 266 below, or

(c) to a part of a special road with respect to the vesting of which provision is made by section 267 below.

(3) Where a scheme submitted to the Minister jointly by two or more local highway authorities under section 16 above determines which of those authorities are to be the special road authority for the special road or any part of it ("the designated authority") and the designated authority are not the highway authority for the road or that part of it, the road or that part of it vests in the designated authority.

(4) Where—

(a) the responsibility for the maintenance of a bridge or other part of a highway is transferred to a highway authority by means of an order under section 93 above, but the property in it is not so transferred, or

(b) the responsibility for the maintenance of a part of a highway is transferred to a highway authority in pursuance of an agreement made under section 94 above, but the property in that part is not so transferred,

the part of the highway in question does not by virtue of subsection (1) above vest in that highway authority.

(5) Notwithstanding anything in subsection (1) above, any such material as is referred to in that subsection which is removed from a highway by a [non-metropolitan] district council in exercise of their powers under section 42, 50 or 230(7) above vests in the district council and not in the highway authority.

[971]

NOTES

Sub-s (5): words in square brackets inserted by the Local Government Act 1985, s 8, Sch 4, para 37.
Transfer of Functions: see the note to s 26 at **[925]**.

264–271 (*Ss 264–268, 270, 271 outside the scope of this work; s 269 repealed by the Local Government Act 1985, s 102, Sch 17.*)

PART XIII
FINANCIAL PROVISIONS

272–277 (*Outside the scope of this work.*)

[278 Agreements as to execution of works

(1) A highway authority may, if they are satisfied it will be of benefit to the public, enter into an agreement with any person—

(a) for the execution by the authority of any works which the authority are or may be authorised to execute, or

(b) for the execution by the authority of such works incorporating particular modifications, additions or features, or at a particular time or in a particular manner,

on terms that that person pays the whole or such part of the cost of the works as may be specified in or determined in accordance with the agreement.

(2) Without prejudice to the generality of the reference in subsection (1) to the cost of the works, that reference shall be taken to include—

(a) the whole of the costs incurred by the highway authority in or in connection with—

(i) the making of the agreement,

(ii) the making or confirmation of any scheme or order required for the purposes of the works,

(iii) the granting of any authorisation, permission or consent required for the purposes of the works, and

(iv) the acquisition by the authority of any land required for the purposes of the works; and

(b) all relevant administrative expenses of the highway authority, including an appropriate sum in respect of general staff costs and overheads.

(3) The agreement may also provide for the making to the highway authority of payments in respect of the maintenance of the works to which the agreement relates and may contain such incidental and consequential provisions as appear to the highway authority to be necessary or expedient for the purposes of the agreement.

(4) The fact that works are to be executed in pursuance of an agreement under this section does not affect the power of the authority to acquire land, by agreement or compulsorily, for the purposes of the works.

(5) If any amount due to a highway authority in pursuance of an agreement under this section is not paid in accordance with the agreement, the authority may—

(a) direct that any means of access or other facility afforded by the works to which the agreement relates shall not be used until that amount has been paid,

(b) recover that amount from any person having an estate or interest in any land for the benefit of which any such means of access or other facility is afforded, and

(c) declare that amount to be a charge on any such land (identifying it) and on all estates and interests therein.

(6) If it appears to the highway authority that a direction under subsection (5)(a) is not being complied with, the authority may execute such works as are necessary to stop up the means of access or deny the facility, as the case may be, and may for that purpose enter any land.

(7) Where a highway authority recovers an amount from a person by virtue of subsection (5)(b), he may in turn recover from any other person having an estate or interest in land for the benefit of which the means of access or other facility was afforded such contribution as may be found by the court to be just and equitable.

This does not affect the right of any of those persons to recover from the person liable under the agreement the amount which they are made to pay.

(8) The Local Land Charges Act 1975 applies in relation to a charge under subsection (5)(c) in favour of the Secretary of State as in relation to a charge in favour of a local authority.]

[972]

NOTES

Substituted by the New Roads and Street Works Act 1991, s 23.
Transfer of Functions: see the note to s 26 at **[925]**.

279–281A (*Outside the scope of this work.*)

PART XIV
MISCELLANEOUS AND SUPPLEMENTARY PROVISIONS

Miscellaneous powers etc of highway authorities and local authorities

282–327 (*Ss 282–312, 314–327 outside the scope of this work; s 313 repealed by the Statute Law* (*Repeals*) *Act 1993.*)

328 Meaning of "highway"

(1) In this Act, except where the context otherwise requires, "highway" means the whole or a part of a highway other than a ferry or waterway.

(2) Where a highway passes over a bridge or through a tunnel, that bridge or tunnel is to be taken for the purposes of this Act to be a part of the highway.

(3) In this Act, "highway maintainable at the public expense" and any other expression defined by reference to a highway is to be construed in accordance with the foregoing provisions of this section.

[972A]

329 Further provision as to interpretation

(1) In this Act, except where the context otherwise requires—

…

"Act of 1965" means the Compulsory Purchase Act 1965;

"adjoining" includes abutting on, and "adjoins" is to be construed accordingly;

"advance payments code" has the meaning provided by section 203(1) above;

"agriculture" includes horticulture, fruit growing, seed growing, dairy farming, the breeding and keeping of livestock (including any creature kept for the production of food, wool, skins or fur, or for the purpose of its use in the farming of land), the use of land as grazing land, meadow land, osier land, market gardens and nursery grounds, and the use of land for woodlands where that use is ancillary to the farming of land for other agricultural purposes, and "agricultural" is to be construed accordingly;

"apparatus" includes any structure constructed for the lodging therein of apparatus;

"approach", in relation to a bridge or tunnel, means the highway giving access thereto, that is to say, the surface of that highway together with any embankment, retaining wall or other work or substance supporting or protecting the surface;

"bridge" does not include a culvert, but, save as aforesaid, means a bridge or viaduct which is part of a highway, and includes the abutments and any other part of a bridge but not the highway carried thereby;

"bridleway" means a highway over which the public have the following, but no other, rights of way, that is to say, a right of way on foot and a right of way on horseback or leading a horse, with or without a right to drive animals of any description along the highway;

"by-pass" has the meaning provided by section 82(6) above;

"canal undertakers" means persons authorised by any enactment to carry on a canal undertaking;

"carriageway" means a way constituting or comprised in a highway, being a way (other than a cycle track) over which the public have a right of way for the passage of vehicles;

"cattle-grid" has the meaning provided by section 82(6) above;

"City" means the City of London;

"classified road" means a highway or proposed highway which is a classified road in accordance with section 12 above;

"Common Council" means the Common Council of the City of London;

"contravention" in relation to a condition, restriction or requirement, includes failure to comply with that condition, restriction or requirement, and "contravene" is to be construed accordingly;

"council" means a county council … or a local authority;

"cycle track" means a way constituting or comprised in a highway, being a way over which the public have the following, but no other, rights of way, that is to say, a right of way on pedal cycles [(other than pedal cycles which are motor vehicles within the meaning of [the Road Traffic Act 1988])] with or without a right of way on foot;

["definitive map and statement" has the same meaning as in Part III of the Wildlife and Countryside Act 1981;]

"dock undertakers" means persons authorised by any enactment to carry on a dock undertaking;

"drainage authority" means [the [Environment Agency]] or an internal drainage board;

["driver information system" has the same meaning as in Part II of the Road Traffic (Driver Licensing and Information Systems) Act 1989, and references to an "operator" of a driver information system are references to an operator licensed under that Part of that Act;]

…

"enactment" includes an enactment in a local or private Act of Parliament and a provision of an order, scheme, regulations or other instrument made under or confirmed by a public general, local or private Act of Parliament;

["field-edge path" means a footpath or bridleway that follows the sides or headlands of a field or enclosure;]

"financial year" means a year ending on 31st March;

"footpath" means a highway over which the public have a right of way on foot only, not being a footway;

"footway" means a way comprised in a highway which also comprises a carriageway, being a way over which the public have a right of way on foot only;

"functions" includes powers and duties;

…

["GLA road" shall be construed in accordance with section 14D(1) above;]

"harbour undertakers" means persons authorised by any enactment to carry on a harbour undertaking;

"highway land acquisition powers" has the meaning provided by section 250(1) above;

"highway maintainable at the public expense" means a highway which by virtue of section 36 above or of any other enactment (whether contained in this Act or not) is a highway which for the purposes of this Act is a highway maintainable at the public expense;

"horse" includes pony, ass and mule, and "horseback" is to be construed accordingly;

"hours of darkness" means the time between half an hour after sunset and half an hour before sunrise;

"improvement" means the doing of any act under powers conferred by Part V of this Act and includes the erection, maintenance, alteration and removal of traffic signs, and the freeing of a highway or road-ferry from tolls;

"inland navigation undertakers" means persons authorised by any enactment to carry on an inland navigation undertaking;

"land" includes land covered by water and any interest or right in, over or under land;

"lease" includes an underlease and an agreement for a lease or underlease, but does not include an option to take a lease or mortgage, and "lessee" is to be construed accordingly;

"lighting authority" means a council or other body authorised to provide lighting under section 161 of the Public Health Act 1875 or under section 3 of the Parish Councils Act 1957 or any corresponding local enactment;

"local authority" means the council of a district or London borough or the Common Council [but, in relation to Wales, means a Welsh council];

"local highway authority" means a highway authority other than the Minister;

"local planning authority" has the same meaning as in [the Town and Country Planning Act 1990];

"lorry area" means an area provided under section 115 above;

"made-up carriageway" means a carriageway, or a part thereof, which has been metalled or in any other way provided with a surface suitable for the passage of vehicles;

"maintenance" includes repair, and "maintain" and "maintainable" are to be construed accordingly;

"maintenance compound" means an area of land (with or without buildings) used or to be used in connection with the maintenance of highways, or a particular highway;

…

"the Minister", subject to subsection (5) below, means as respects England, the Minister of Transport and as respects Wales, the Secretary of State; and in section 258 of, and paragraphs 7, 8(1) and (3), 14, 15(1) and (3), 18(2), 19 and 21 of Schedule 1 to, this Act, references to the Minister and the Secretary of State acting jointly are to be construed, as respects Wales, as references to the Secretary of State acting alone;

"navigation authority" means persons authorised by any enactment to work, maintain, conserve, improve or control any canal or other inland navigation, navigable river, estuary, harbour or dock;

"owner", in relation to any premises, means a person, other than a mortgagee not in possession, who, whether in his own right or as trustee or agent for any other person, is entitled to receive the rack rent of the premises or, where the premises are not let at a rack rent, would be so entitled if the premises were so let;

…

"pier undertakers" means persons authorised by any enactment to carry on a pier undertaking;

"premises" includes land and buildings;

"private street works code" has the meaning provided by section 203(1) above;

"proposed highway" means land on which, in accordance with plans made by a highway authority, that authority are for the time being constructing or intending to construct a highway shown in the plans;

["proprietor", in relation to a school, has the same meaning as in the Education Act 1996;]

"public general enactment" means an enactment in an Act treated as a public general Act under the system of division of Acts adopted in the regnal year 38 George 3, other than an Act for confirming a provisional order;

"public path creation agreement" means an agreement under section 25 above;

"public path creation order" means an order under section 26 above;

"public path diversion order" means an order under section 119 above;

"public path extinguishment order" means an order under section 118 above;

"public utility undertakers" means persons authorised by any enactment to carry on any of the following undertakings, that is to say, an undertaking for the supply of … gas, … or hydraulic power;

"rack rent", in relation to any premises, means a rent which is not less than two-thirds of the rent at which the premises might reasonably be expected to let from year to year, free from all usual tenant's rates and taxes … , and deducting therefrom the probable average annual cost of the repairs, insurance and other expenses (if any) necessary to maintain the same in a state to command such rent;

["rail crossing diversion order" means an order under section 119A above;

"rail crossing extinguishment order" means an order under section 118A above;]

"railway" includes a light railway;

"railway undertakers" means persons authorised by any enactment to carry on a railway undertaking;

"reconstruction", in relation to a bridge, includes the construction of a new bridge and approaches thereto in substitution for the existing bridge and the approaches thereto;

["restricted byway" has the same meaning as in Part II of the Countryside and Rights of Way Act 2000;]

"road-ferry" means a ferry connecting the termination of a highway which is, or is to become, a highway maintainable at the public expense with the termination of another highway which is, or is to become, such a highway;

["road hump" has the meaning provided by section 90F(1);]

["school" has the same meaning as in the Education Act 1996;]

"service area" means an area of land adjoining, or in the vicinity of, a special road, being an area in which there are, or are to be, provided service stations or other buildings or facilities to be used in connection with the use of the special road;

…

["special diversion order" means an order under section 119B(4) above;]

"special enactment" means any enactment other than a public general enactment;

["special extinguishment order" means an order under section 118B(4) above;]

"special road" means a highway, or a proposed highway, which is a special road in accordance with section 16 above [or by virtue of an order granting development consent under the Planning Act 2008];

"special road authority" has the meaning provided by section 16(4) above;

["SSSI diversion order" means an order under section 119D above;]

"statutory undertakers" means persons authorised by any enactment to carry on any of the following undertakings—

(a) a railway, tramway, road transport, water transport, canal, inland navigation, dock, harbour, pier or lighthouse undertaking, or

(b) an undertaking for the supply of … , or hydraulic power,

and "statutory undertaking" is to be construed accordingly;

["street" has the same meaning as in Part III of the New Roads and Street Works Act 1991;]

["street works licence" means a licence under section 50 of the New Roads and Street Works Act 1991, and "licensee" in relation to such a licence, has the meaning given by subsection (3) of that section;]

"swing bridge" includes any opening bridge operated by mechanical means;

"traffic" includes pedestrians and animals;

["traffic calming works", in relation to a highway, means works affecting the movement of vehicular or other traffic for the purpose of—

(a) promoting safety (including avoiding or reducing, or reducing the likelihood of, danger connected with terrorism within the meaning of section 1 of the Terrorism Act 2000 (c 11)), or

(b) preserving or improving the environment through which the highway runs;]

"traffic sign" has the same meaning as in [section 64 of the Road Traffic Regulation Act 1984];

"tramway undertakers" means persons authorised by any enactment to carry on a tramway undertaking;

"transport undertakers" means persons authorised by any enactment to carry on any of the following undertakings, that is to say, a railway, canal, inland navigation, dock, harbour or pier undertaking, and "transport undertaking" is to be construed accordingly;

"trunk road" means a highway, or a proposed highway, which is a trunk road by virtue of section 10(1) or section 19 above or by virtue of an order or direction under section 10 above [or an order granting development consent under the Planning Act 2008,] or under any other enactment;

"trunk road picnic area" has the meaning provided by section 112(1) above;

["universal service provider" has the same meaning as in the Postal Services Act 2000; and references to the provision of a universal postal service shall be construed in accordance with that Act;]

["water undertakers" means the [Environment Agency] or a water undertaker;]

["Welsh council" means the council of a Welsh county or county borough].

(2) A highway at the side of a river, canal or other inland navigation is not excluded from the definition in subsection (1) above of ["bridleway", "footpath" or "restricted byway"], by reason only that the public have a right to use the highway for purposes of navigation, if the highway would fall within that definition if the public had no such right thereover.

[(2A) In this Act—

(a) any reference to a county shall be construed in relation to Wales as including a reference to a county borough;

(b) any reference to a county council shall be construed in relation to Wales as including a reference to a county borough council; and

(c) section 17(4) and (5) of the Local Government (Wales) Act 1994 (references to counties and districts to be construed generally in relation to Wales as references to counties and county boroughs) shall not apply.]

(3) In a case where two or more parishes are grouped under a common parish council, references in this Act to a parish are to be construed as references to those parishes.

[(3A) In a case where two or more communities are grouped under a common community council, references in this Act to a community are to be construed as references to those communities.]

(4) Any reference in this Act to property of railway undertakers, canal undertakers, inland navigation undertakers, dock undertakers, harbour undertakers or pier undertakers is, where the undertakers are a body to which this subsection applies, to be taken as a reference to property of that body held or used by them wholly or mainly for the purposes of so much of their undertaking as consists of the carrying on of a railway undertaking or, as the case may be, of a canal undertaking, an inland navigation undertaking, a dock undertaking, a harbour undertaking or a pier undertaking.

This subsection applies to the following bodies, namely, the British Railways Board, the British Transport Docks Board, the British Waterways Board, [Transport for London], … any wholly-owned subsidiary (within the meaning of the Transport Act 1968) or joint subsidiary (within the meaning of section 51(5) of that Act) of any of those bodies [other than Transport for London, or any of its subsidiaries (within the meaning of the Greater London Authority Act 1999)].

[(4A) Any reference in this Act to apparatus belonging to, or used or maintained by the operator of [an electronic communications code network] shall have effect as a reference to [electronic communications apparatus] kept installed for the purposes of that [network].]

(5) In relation to that part of the road constructed by the Minister of Transport along the line described in Schedule 1 to the North of Almondsbury—South of Haysgate Trunk Road Order 1947 and referred to in that Order as "the new road" which lies to the east of the most easterly point before reaching the River Wye at which eastbound traffic of Classes I and II (as specified in Schedule 4 to this Act) can leave that road by another special road, the functions of the Minister under this Act shall be exercisable [by the Secretary of State for Transport].

[973]

NOTES

Sub-s (1): definition "traffic calming works" inserted by the Traffic Calming Act 1992, s 1(3).

Sub-s (1): definition "Act of 1946" (omitted) repealed by the Acquisition of Land Act 1981, s 34, Sch 6.

Sub-s (1): in definition "council" words omitted repealed by the Local Government Act 1985, s 102, Sch 17.

Sub-s (1): in definition "cycle track" words in first (outer) pair of square brackets inserted by the Cycle Tracks Act 1984, s 1; words in second (inner) pair of square brackets substituted by the Road Traffic (Consequential Provisions) Act 1988, s 4, Sch 3, para 21(2).

Sub-s (1): definition "definitive map and statement" inserted by the Countryside and Rights of Way Act 2000, s 57, Sch 6, Pt I, para 20(a).

Sub-s (1): in definition "drainage authority" words in first (outer) pair of square brackets substituted by the Water Act 1989, s 190(1), Sch 25, para 62(12); words in second (inner) pair of square brackets substituted by SI 1996/593, reg 2, Sch 1.

Sub-s (1): definition "driver information system" inserted by the Road Traffic (Driver Licensing and Information Systems) Act 1989, s 13(1), Sch 4, para 3(13).

Sub-s (1): definition "electricity undertakers" (omitted) repealed by the Electricity Act 1989, s 112(4), Sch 18.

Sub-s (1): definition "field-edge path" inserted by the Rights of Way Act 1990, s 2.

Sub-s (1): definition "gas undertakers" (omitted) repealed by the Gas Act 1986, s 67(4), Sch 9, Pt I.

Sub-s (1): definition "GLA road" inserted by the Greater London Authority Act 1999, s 263(6).

PART I STATUTES

Sub-s (1): in definition "local authority" words in square brackets inserted by the Local Government (Wales) Act 1994, s 22(1), Sch 7, para 27(2).

Sub-s (1): in definition "local planning authority" words in square brackets substituted by the Planning (Consequential Provisions) Act 1990, s 4, Sch 2, para 45(17).

Sub-s (1): definition "metropolitan road" (omitted) repealed by the Local Government Act 1985, s 102, Sch 17.

Sub-s (1): definition "petty sessions area" (omitted) repealed by the Access to Justice Act 1999, s 106, Sch 15, Pt V, Table (1).

Sub-s (1): definition "proprietor" inserted by the Countryside and Rights of Way Act 2000, s 57, Sch 6, Pt I, para 20(b).

Sub-s (1): in definition "public utility undertakers" first words omitted repealed by the Electricity Act 1989, s 112(4), Sch 18; second words omitted repealed by the Water Act 1989, s 190(3), Sch 27, Pt I.

Sub-s (1): in definition "rack rent" words omitted repealed by the Statute Law (Repeals) Act 1993.

Sub-s (1): definitions "rail crossing diversion order" and "rail crossing extinguishment order" inserted by the Transport and Works Act 1992, s 47, Sch 2, para 9.

Sub-s (1): definition "restricted byway" inserted by the Countryside and Rights of Way Act 2000, s 51, Sch 5, Pt II, para 16(a).

Sub-s (1): definition "road hump" inserted by the Transport Act 1981, s 32, Sch 10, Pt I, para 1.

Sub-s (1): definition "school" inserted by the Countryside and Rights of Way Act 2000, s 57, Sch 6, Pt I, para 20(c).

Sub-s (1): definition "sewerage authority" (omitted) repealed by the Water Act 1989, s 190(3), Sch 27, Pt I.

Sub-s (1): definitions "special diversion order", "special extinguishment order", "SSSI diversion order" inserted by the Countryside and Rights of Way Act 2000, s 57, Sch 6, Pt I, para 20(d)–(f), partly as from a day to be appointed in relation to Wales.

Sub-s (1): in definition "special road" words in square brackets inserted by the Planning Act 2008, s 36, Sch 2, paras 21, 29(1), (2), as from a day to be appointed.

Sub-s (1): in definition "statutory undertakers" words omitted repealed by the Electricity Act 1989, s 112(4), Sch 18, the Water Act 1989, s 190(3), Sch 27, Pt I, and the Gas Act 1986, s 67(4), Sch 9, Pt I.

Sub-s (1): definition "street" substituted by the New Roads and Street Works Act 1991, s 168(1), Sch 8, Pt I, para 15.

Sub-s (1): definition "street works licence" inserted by the New Roads and Street Works Act 1991, s 168(1), Sch 8, Pt I, para 15.

Sub-s (1): definition "traffic calming works" substituted by the Civil Contingencies Act 2004, s 32(1), Sch 2, Pt 3, para 15(2).

Sub-s (1): in definition "traffic sign" words in square brackets substituted by the Road Traffic Regulation Act 1984, s 146, Sch 13.

Sub-s (1): in definition "trunk road" words in square brackets inserted by the Planning Act 2008, s 36, Sch 2, paras 21, 29(1), (3), as from a day to be appointed.

Sub-s (1): definition "universal service provider" inserted by SI 2001/1149, art 3(1), Sch 1, para 49(1), (10).

Sub-s (1): definition "water undertakers" substituted by the Water Act 1989, s 190(1), Sch 25, para 62(12)(b); words in square brackets substituted by SI 1996/593, reg 2, Sch 1.

Sub-s (1): definition "Welsh council" inserted by the Local Government (Wales) Act 1994, s 22(1), Sch 7, para 27(2).

Sub-s (2): words in square brackets substituted by the Countryside and Rights of Way Act 2000, s 51, Sch 5, Pt II, para 16(b).

Sub-ss (2A), (3A): inserted by the Local Government (Wales) Act 1994, s 22(1), Sch 7, para 27(3), (4).

Sub-s (4): words in square brackets substituted by SI 2003/1615, art 2, Sch 1, Pt 1, para 7(1), (7); words omitted repealed by the Statute Law (Repeals) Act 1989 and the London Regional Transport Act 1984, s 71(3), Sch 7.

Sub-s (4A): inserted by the Telecommunications Act 1984, s 109, Sch 4, para 76.

Sub-s (4A): words in square brackets substituted by the Communications Act 2003, s 406(1), Sch 17, para 56(1)(f), (2)(a), (c), (e).

Sub-s (5): words in square brackets substituted by SI 1981/238, art 3(1).

Transfer of Functions: see the note to s 26 at **[925]**.

Minister of Transport: the functions of the Minister of Transport were transferred to the Secretary of State for Transport by the Transfer of Functions (Transport) Order 1981, SI 1981/238.

Secretary of State for Transport: the functions of the Secretary of State for Transport were transferred to the Secretary of State for the Environment, Transport and the Regions by the Secretary of State for the Environment, Transport and the Regions Order 1997, SI 1997/2971, arts 3–6.

Functions of the First Secretary of State exercisable by virtue of sub-s (5) above, transferred to the Secretary of State, by the Secretary of State for Communities and Local Government Order 2006, SI 2006/1926, arts 4(1)(c), 6, 8.

See further: in relation to definitions of "public utility undertakers" and "statutory undertakers", see the Water Act 1989, s 190(1), Sch 25, para 1(1), (2)(wx), (8), the Electricity Act 1989, s 112(1), Sch 16, para 2(4)(d), (6) and the Gas Act 1995, s 16(1), Sch 4, para 2(1)(xxix).

330–332 (*Outside the scope of this work.*)

Savings etc

333–344 (*Outside the scope of this work.*)

345 Short title, commencement and extent

(1) This Act may be cited as the Highways Act 1980.

(2) This Act shall come into force on 1st January 1981.

(3) This Act (except paragraph 18(c) of Schedule 24) extends to England and Wales only.

[974]

(*Schs 1–25 outside the scope of this work.*)

PART I STATUTES

SUPREME COURT ACT 1981 [SENIOR COURTS ACT 1981]

(1981 c 54)

An Act to consolidate with amendments the Supreme Court of Judicature (Consolidation) Act 1925 and other enactments relating to the Supreme Court in England and Wales and the administration of justice therein; to repeal certain obsolete or unnecessary enactments so relating; to amend Part VIII of the Mental Health Act 1959, the Courts-Martial (Appeals) Act 1968, the Arbitration Act 1979 and the law relating to county courts; and for connected purposes

[28 July 1981]

NOTES

The title of this Act is substituted by the Constitutional Reform Act 2002, s 59(5), Sch 11, Pt 1, para 1, as from 1 October 2009.

1–14 ((*Pt I*) *outside the scope of this work.*)

PART II
JURISDICTION

15–18 (*Outside the scope of this work.*)

THE HIGH COURT

19–31A (*Outside the scope of this work.*)

Powers

32–35 (*Outside the scope of this work.*)

[35A Power of High Court to award interest on debts and damages

(1) Subject to rules of court, in proceedings (whenever instituted) before the High Court for the recovery of a debt or damages there may be included in any sum for which judgment is given simple interest, at such rate as the court thinks fit or as rules of court may provide, on all or any part of the debt or damages in respect of which judgment is given, or payment is made before judgment, for all or any part of the period between the date when the cause of action arose and—

(a) in the case of any sum paid before judgment, the date of the payment; and

(b) in the case of the sum for which judgment is given, the date of the judgment.

(2) In relation to a judgment given for damages for personal injuries or death which exceed £200 subsection (1) shall have effect—

(a) with the substitution of "shall be included" for "may be included"; and

(b) with the addition of "unless the court is satisfied that there are special reasons to the contrary" after "given", where first occurring.

(3) Subject to rules of court, where—

(a) there are proceedings (whenever instituted) before the High Court for the recovery of a debt; and

(b) the defendant pays the whole debt to the plaintiff (otherwise than in pursuance of a judgment in the proceedings),

the defendant shall be liable to pay the plaintiff simple interest at such rate as the court thinks fit or as rules of court may provide on all or any part of the debt for all or any part of the period between the date when the cause of action arose and the date of the payment.

(4) Interest in respect of a debt shall not be awarded under this section for a period during which, for whatever reason, interest on the debt already runs.

(5) Without prejudice to the generality of section 84, rules of court may provide for a rate of interest by reference to the rate specified in section 17 of the Judgments Act 1838 as that section has effect from time to time or by reference to a rate for which any other enactment provides.

(6) Interest under this section may be calculated at different rates in respect of different periods.

(7) In this section "plaintiff" means the person seeking the debt or damages and "defendant" means the person from whom the plaintiff seeks the debt or damages and "personal injuries" includes any disease and any impairment of a person's physical or mental condition.

(8) Nothing in this section affects the damages recoverable for the dishonour of a bill of exchange.]

[975]

NOTES

Inserted by the Administration of Justice Act 1982, s 15(1), Sch 1, Part I.

36 (*Outside the scope of this work.*)

37 Powers of High Court with respect to injunctions and receivers

(1) The High Court may by order (whether interlocutory or final) grant an injunction or appoint a receiver in all cases in which it appears to the court to be just and convenient to do so.

(2) Any such order may be made either unconditionally or on such terms and conditions as the court thinks just.

(3) The power of the High Court under subsection (1) to grant an interlocutory injunction restraining a party to any proceedings from removing from the jurisdiction of the High Court, or otherwise dealing with, assets located within that jurisdiction shall be exercisable in cases where that party is, as well as in cases where he is not, domiciled, resident or present within that jurisdiction.

(4) The power of the High Court to appoint a receiver by way of equitable execution shall operate in relation to all legal estates and interests in land; and that power—

- (a) may be exercised in relation to an estate or interest in land whether or not a charge has been imposed on that land under section 1 of the Charging Orders Act 1979 for the purpose of enforcing the judgment, order or award in question; and
- (b) shall be in addition to, and not in derogation of, any power of any court to appoint a receiver in proceedings for enforcing such a charge.

(5) Where an order under the said section 1 imposing a charge for the purpose of enforcing a judgment, order or award has been, or has effect as if, registered under section 6 of the Land Charges Act 1972, subsection (4) of the said section 6 (effect of non-registration of writs and orders registrable under that section) shall not apply to an order appointing a receiver made either—

- (a) in proceedings for enforcing the charge; or
- (b) by way of equitable execution of the judgment, order or award or, as the case may be, of so much of it as requires payment of moneys secured by the charge.

[976]

38 Relief against forfeiture for non-payment of rent

(1) In any action in the High Court for the forfeiture of a lease for non-payment of rent, the court shall have power to grant relief against forfeiture in a summary manner, and may do so subject to the same terms and conditions as to the payment of rent, costs or otherwise as could have been imposed by it in such an action immediately before the commencement of this Act.

(2) Where the lessee or a person deriving title under him is granted relief under this section, he shall hold the demised premises in accordance with the terms of the lease without the necessity for a new lease.

[977]

39 Execution of instrument by person nominated by High Court

(1) Where the High Court has given or made a judgment or order directing a person to execute any conveyance, contract or other document, or to indorse any negotiable instrument, then, if that person—

- (a) neglects or refuses to comply with the judgment or order; or
- (b) cannot after reasonable inquiry be found, the High Court may, on such terms and conditions, if any, as may be just, order that the conveyance, contract or other document shall be executed, or that the negotiable instrument shall be indorsed, by such person as the court may nominate for that purpose.

(2) A conveyance, contract, document or instrument executed or indorsed in pursuance of an order under this section shall operate, and be for all purposes available, as if it had been executed or indorsed by the person originally directed to execute or indorse it.

[978]

40–48 (*Ss 40–46A, 48 outside the scope of this work; s 47 repealed by the Powers of Criminal Courts (Sentencing) Act 2000, s 165(4), Sch 12, Pt I.*)

GENERAL PROVISIONS

Law and equity

49 Concurrent administration of law and equity

(1) Subject to the provisions of this or any other Act, every court exercising jurisdiction in England or Wales in any civil cause or matter shall continue to administer law and equity on the basis that, wherever there is any conflict or variance between the rules of equity and the rules of the common law with reference to the same matter, the rules of equity shall prevail.

(2) Every such court shall give the same effect as hitherto—

(a) to all equitable estates, titles, rights, reliefs, defences and counterclaims, and to all equitable duties and liabilities; and

(b) subject thereto, to all legal claims and demands and all estates, titles, rights, duties, obligations and liabilities existing by the common law or by any custom or created by any statute,

and, subject to the provisions of this or any other Act, shall so exercise its jurisdiction in every cause or matter before it as to secure that, as far as possible, all matters in dispute between the parties are completely and finally determined, and all multiplicity of legal proceedings with respect to any of those matters is avoided.

(3) Nothing in this Act shall affect the power of the Court of Appeal or the High Court to stay any proceedings before it, where it thinks fit to do so, either of its own motion or on the application of any person, whether or not a party to the proceedings.

[979]

50 Power to award damages as well as, or in substitution for, injunction or specific performance

Where the Court of Appeal or the High Court has jurisdiction to entertain an application for an injunction or specific performance, it may award damages in addition to, or in substitution for, an injunction or specific performance.

[980]

51–104 (*Ss 51, 52, ss 53–104* (*Pts III, IV*) *outside the scope of this work.*)

PART V
PROBATE CAUSES AND MATTERS

105–111 (*Outside the scope of this work.*)

Powers of Court in relation to personal representatives

112 (*Outside the scope of this work.*)

113 Power of court to sever grant

(1) Subject to subsection (2), the High Court may grant probate or administration in respect of any part of the estate of a deceased person, limited in any way the court thinks fit.

(2) Where the estate of a deceased person is known to be insolvent, the grant of representation to it shall not be severed under subsection (1) except as regards a trust estate in which he had no beneficial interest.

[981]

114 Number of personal representatives

(1) Probate or administration shall not be granted by the High Court to more than four persons in respect of the same part of the estate of a deceased person.

(2) Where under a will or intestacy any beneficiary is a minor or a life interest arises, any grant of administration by the High Court shall be made either to a trust corporation (with or without an individual) or to not less than two individuals, unless it appears to the court to be expedient in all the circumstances to appoint an individual as sole administrator.

(3) For the purpose of determining whether a minority or life interest arises in any particular case, the court may act on such evidence as may be prescribed.

(4) If at any time during the minority of a beneficiary or the subsistence of a life interest under a will or intestacy there is only one personal representative (not being a trust corporation), the High Court may, on the application of any person interested or the guardian or receiver of any such person, and in accordance with probate rules, appoint one or more additional personal representatives to act while the minority or life interest subsists and until the estate is fully administered.

(5) An appointment of an additional personal representative under subsection (4) to act with an executor shall not have the effect of including him in any chain of representation.

[982]

115 Grants to trust corporations

(1) The High Court may—

(a) where a trust corporation is named in a will as executor, grant probate to the corporation either solely or jointly with any other person named in the will as executor, as the case may require; or

(b) grant administration to a trust corporation, either solely or jointly with another person;

and the corporation may act accordingly as executor or administrator, as the case may be.

(2) Probate or administration shall not be granted to any person as nominee of a trust corporation.

(3) Any officer authorised for the purpose by a trust corporation or its directors or governing body may, on behalf of the corporation, swear affidavits, give security and do any other act which the court may require with a view to the grant to the corporation of probate or administration; and the acts of an officer so authorised shall be binding on the corporation.

[(4) Subsections (1) to (3) shall also apply in relation to any body which is exempt from the provisions of section 23(1) of the Solicitors Act 1974 (unqualified persons not to prepare papers for probate etc) by virtue of any of paragraphs (e) to (h) of subsection (2) of that section.]

[983]

NOTES

Sub-s (4): inserted by the Courts and Legal Services Act 1990, s 54(2), as from a day to be appointed.

116 Power of court to pass over prior claims to grant

(1) If by reason of any special circumstances it appears to the High Court to be necessary or expedient to appoint as administrator some person other than the person who, but for this section, would in accordance with probate rules have been entitled to the grant, the court may in its discretion appoint as administrator such person as it thinks expedient.

(2) Any grant of administration under this section may be limited in any way the court thinks fit.

[984]

117 Administration pending suit

(1) Where any legal proceedings concerning the validity of the will of a deceased person, or for obtaining, recalling or revoking any grant, are pending, the High Court may grant administration of the estate of the deceased person in question to an administrator pending suit, who shall, subject to subsection (2), have all the rights, duties and powers of a general administrator.

(2) An administrator pending suit shall be subject to the immediate control of the court and act under its direction; and, except in such circumstances as may be prescribed, no distribution of the estate, or any part of the estate, of the deceased person in question shall be made by such an administrator without the leave of the court.

(3) The court may, out of the estate of the deceased, assign an administrator pending suit such reasonable remuneration as it thinks fit.

[985]

118 Effect of appointment of minor as executor

Where a testator by his will appoints a minor to be an executor, the appointment shall not operate to vest in the minor the estate, or any part of the estate, of the testator, or to constitute him a personal representative for any purpose, unless and until probate is granted to him in accordance with probate rules.

[986]

119 Administration with will annexed

(1) Administration with the will annexed shall be granted, subject to and in accordance with probate rules, in every class of case in which the High Court had power to make such a grant immediately before the commencement of this Act.

(2) Where administration with the will annexed is granted, the will of the deceased shall be performed and observed in the same manner as if probate of it had been granted to an executor.

[987]

120 Power to require administrators to produce sureties

(1) As a condition of granting administration to any person the High Court may, subject to the following provisions of this section and subject to and in accordance with probate rules, require one

or more sureties to guarantee that they will make good, within any limit imposed by the court on the total liability of the surety or sureties, any loss which any person interested in the administration of the estate of the deceased may suffer in consequence of a breach by the administrator of his duties as such.

(2) A guarantee given in pursuance of any such requirement shall enure for the benefit of every person interested in the administration of the estate of the deceased as if contained in a contract under seal made by the surety or sureties with every such person and, where there are two or more sureties, as if they had bound themselves jointly and severally.

(3) No action shall be brought on any such guarantee without the leave of the High Court.

(4) Stamp duty shall not be chargeable on any such guarantee.

(5) This section does not apply where administration is granted to the Treasury Solicitor, the Official Solicitor, the Public Trustee, the Solicitor for the affairs of the Duchy of Lancaster or the Duchy of Cornwall or the Crown Solicitor for Northern Ireland, or to the consular officer of a foreign state to which section 1 of the Consular Conventions Act 1949 applies, or in such other cases as may be prescribed.

[988]

Revocation of grants and cancellation of resealing at instance of court

121 Revocation of grants and cancellation of resealing at instance of court

(1) Where it appears to the High Court that a grant either ought not to have been made or contains an error, the court may call in the grant and, if satisfied that it would be revoked at the instance of a party interested, may revoke it.

(2) A grant may be revoked under subsection (1) without being called in, if it cannot be called in.

(3) Where it appears to the High Court that a grant resealed under the Colonial Probates Acts 1892 and 1927 ought not to have been resealed, the court may call in the relevant document and, if satisfied that the resealing would be cancelled at the instance of a party interested, may cancel the resealing.

In this and the following subsection "the relevant document" means the original grant or, where some other document was sealed by the court under those Acts, that document.

(4) A resealing may be cancelled under subsection (3) without the relevant document being called in, if it cannot be called in.

[989]

122–127 (*Outside the scope of this work.*)

Interpretation of Part V and other probate provisions

128 Interpretation of Part V and other probate provisions

In this Part, and in the other provisions of this Act relating to probate causes and matters, unless the context otherwise requires—

"administration" includes all letters of administration of the effects of deceased persons, whether with or without a will annexed, and whether granted for general, special or limited purposes;

"estate" means real and personal estate, and "real estate" includes—

(a) chattels real and land in possession, remainder or reversion and every interest in or over land to which the deceased person was entitled at the time of his death, and

(b) real estate held on trust or by way of mortgage or security, but not … money secured or charged on land;

"grant" means a grant of probate or administration;

"non-contentious or common form probate business" means the business of obtaining probate and administration where there is no contention as to the right thereto, including—

(a) the passing of probates and administrations through the High Court in contentious cases where the contest has been terminated,

(b) all business of a non-contentious nature in matters of testacy and intestacy not being proceedings in any action, and

(c) the business of lodging caveats against the grant of probate or administration;

"Principal Registry" means the Principal Registry of the Family Division;

"probate rules" means rules of court made under section 127;

"trust corporation" means the Public Trustee or a corporation either appointed by the court in any particular case to be a trustee or authorised by rules made under section 4(3) of the Public Trustee Act 1906 to act as a custodian trustee;

"will" includes a nuncupative will and any testamentary document of which probate may be granted.

[990]

NOTES

In definition "real estate" words omitted repealed by the Trusts of Land and Appointment of Trustees Act 1996, s 25(2), Sch 4; for savings in relation to entailed interests created before the commencement of that Act, and savings consequential upon the abolition of the doctrine of conversion, see s 25(4), (5) thereof.

Modification: definition "Trust corporation" modified in relation to charities, by the Charities Act 1993, s 35.

PART VI
MISCELLANEOUS AND SUPPLEMENTARY

Miscellaneous provisions

129–150 (*Outside the scope of this work.*)

Supplementary

151, 152 (*Outside the scope of this work.*)

153 Citation, commencement and extent

(1) This Act may be cited as the *Supreme Court Act 1981* [Senior Courts Act 1981].

(2) This Act, except the provisions mentioned in subsection (3), shall come into force on 1st January 1982; and references to the commencement of this Act shall be construed as references to the beginning of that day.

(3) Sections 72, 143 and 152(2) and this section shall come into force on the passing of this Act.

(4) In this Act—

(a) the following provisions extend to Scotland, namely—
section 80(3);
section 152(4) and Schedule 7, so far as they relate to the Admiralty Court Act 1861;

(b) the following provisions extend to Northern Ireland so far as they relate to the Northern Ireland Assembly Disqualification Act 1975, namely—
section 152(1) and Schedule 5;
section 152(3) and paragraph 3(1) of Schedule 6;

(c) the following provisions extend to Scotland and Northern Ireland, namely—
section 36;
sections 132 and 134(3);
section 152(1) and Schedule 5, so far as they amend—
(i) references to section 49 of the *Supreme Court* [Senior Courts] of Judicature (Consolidation) Act 1925,
(ii) the House of Commons Disqualification Act 1975, and
(iii) section 4 of the Evidence (Proceedings in Other Jurisdictions) Act 1975;
section 152(3) and paragraph 3(1) of Schedule 6, so far as they relate to the House of Commons Disqualification Act 1975;
section 152(4) and Schedule 7, so far as they relate to—
(i) provisions of the *Supreme Court* [Senior Courts] of Judicature (Consolidation) Act 1925 which extend throughout the United Kingdom,
(ii) the Evidence and Powers of Attorney Act 1940, and
(iii) section 57(3)(a) of the Courts Act 1971;

(d) section 145 extends to any place to which the Courts-Martial (Appeals) Act 1968 extends, and section 152(1) and (4) and Schedules 5 and 7, so far as they relate to any of the following enactments, namely—
Army Act 1955,
Air Force Act 1955,
section 9(2) of, and Part II of Schedule 1 to, the Criminal Appeal Act 1966,
Courts-Martial (Appeals) Act 1968,
Hovercraft Act 1968,
…
extend to any place to which that enactment extends;

but, save as aforesaid, the provisions of this Act, other than those mentioned in subsection (5), extend to England and Wales only.

(5) The provisions of this Act whose extent is not restricted by subsection (4) are—
section 27;
section 150;

section 151(1);
section 152(4) and Schedule 7 as far as they relate to the Naval Prize Act 1864, the Prize Courts Act 1915 and section 56 of the Administration of Justice Act 1956;
this section;
paragraph 1 of Schedule 4.

[991]

NOTES

Sub-s (1): words in italics substituted by subsequent words in square brackets by the Constitutional Reform Act 2005, s 59(5), Sch 11, Pt 1, para 1(2), as from 1 October 2009.

Sub-s (4): in para (c), words in italics in both places they appear substituted by subsequent words in square brackets by the Constitutional Reform Act 2005, s 59(5), Sch 11, Pt 4, para 26(1), (2), as from 1 October 2009; words omitted from para (d) repealed by the Merchant Shipping Act 1995, s 314(1), Sch 12.

(*Schs 1–7 outside the scope of this work.*)

WILDLIFE AND COUNTRYSIDE ACT 1981

(1981 c 69)

An Act to repeal and re-enact with amendments the Protection of Birds Acts 1954 to 1967 and the Conservation of Wild Creatures and Wild Plants Act 1975; to prohibit certain methods of killing or taking wild animals; to amend the law relating to protection of certain mammals; to restrict the introduction of certain animals and plants; to amend the Endangered Species (Import and Export) Act 1976; to amend the law relating to nature conservation, the countryside and National Parks and to make provision with respect to the [Countryside Agency]; to amend the law relating to public rights of way; and for connected purposes

[30 October 1981]

NOTES

Words in square brackets substituted by virtue of SI 1999/416, art 3, with effect from 1 April 1999.

1–27 ((*Pt I*) *outside the scope of this work.*)

PART II
NATURE CONSERVATION, COUNTRYSIDE AND NATIONAL PARKS

27A–38 (*Outside the scope of this work.*)

Countryside

39 Management agreements with owners and occupiers of land

(1) A relevant authority may, for the purpose of conserving or enhancing the natural beauty or amenity of any land which is … within their area or promoting its enjoyment by the public, make an agreement (in this section referred to as a "management agreement") with any person having an interest in the land with respect to the management of the land during a specified term or without limitation of the duration of the agreement.

(2) Without prejudice to the generality of subsection (1), a management agreement—

(a) may impose on the person having an interest in the land restrictions as respects the method of cultivating the land, its use for agricultural purposes or the exercise of rights over the land and may impose obligations on that person to carry out works or agricultural or forestry operations or do other things on the land;

(b) may confer on the relevant authority power to carry out works for the purpose of performing their functions under the 1949 Act and the 1968 Act; and

(c) may contain such incidental and consequential provisions (including provisions for the making of payments by either party to the other) as appear to the relevant authority to be necessary or expedient for the purposes of the agreement.

(3) The provisions of a management agreement with any person interested in the land shall, unless the agreement otherwise provides, be binding on persons deriving title under or from that person and be enforceable by the relevant authority against those persons accordingly.

(4) Schedule 2 to the Forestry Act 1967 (power for tenant for life and others to enter into forestry dedication covenants) shall apply to management agreements as it applies to forestry dedication covenants.

(5) In this section "the relevant authority" means—

(a) …
[(aa) as respects land within the Broads, the Broads Authority;]
(b) …
(c) as respects any other land, the local planning authority;
[(d) …
(e) as respects any land in Wales, the Countryside Council for Wales;
(f) as respects land in any area of outstanding natural beauty designated under section 82 of the Countryside and Rights of Way Act 2000 for which a conservation board has been established under section 86 of that Act, that board].

(6) The powers conferred by this section on a relevant authority shall be in addition to and not in derogation of any powers conferred on such an authority by or under any enactment. **[992]**

NOTES

Sub-s (1): words omitted repealed by the Countryside and Rights of Way Act 2000, ss 96(a), 102, Sch 16, Pt VI.

Sub-s (5): para (a) repealed by the Environment Act 1995, s 120, Sch 24; para (aa) inserted by the Norfolk and Suffolk Broads Act 1988, s 2(5), (6), Sch 3, Pt I; para (b) repealed by the Local Government Act 1985, ss 7, 102, Sch 3, para 7, Sch 17; paras (d)–(f) inserted by the Countryside and Rights of Way Act 2000, s 96(b); para (d) repealed by the Natural Environment and Rural Communities Act 2006, s 105, Sch 11, Pt 1, para 87, Sch 12, subject to transitional provisions in SI 2006/2541, art 3, Schedule, para 5.

Modification: as respects any land in any National Park for which a National Park authority is the local planning authority, that authority shall be the relevant authority for the purposes of this section, by virtue of the Environment Act 1995, s 69.

40–52 (*Outside the scope of this work.*)

PART III
PUBLIC RIGHTS OF WAY

Ascertainment of public rights of way

53 Duty to keep definitive map and statement under continuous review

(1) In this Part "definitive map and statement", in relation to any area, means, subject to section 57(3) [and 57A(1)],—
(a) the latest revised map and statement prepared in definitive form for that area under section 33 of the 1949 Act; or
(b) where no such map and statement have been so prepared, the original definitive map and statement prepared for that area under section 32 of that Act; or
(c) where no such map and statement have been so prepared, the map and statement prepared for that area under section 55(3).

(2) As regards every definitive map and statement, the surveying authority shall—
(a) as soon as reasonably practicable after the commencement date, by order make such modifications to the map and statement as appear to them to be requisite in consequence of the occurrence, before that date, of any of the events specified in subsection (3); and
(b) as from that date, keep the map and statement under continuous review and as soon as reasonably practicable after the occurrence, on or after that date, of any of those events, by order make such modifications to the map and statement as appear to them to be requisite in consequence of the occurrence of that event.

(3) The events referred to in subsection (2) are as follows—
(a) the coming into operation of any enactment or instrument, or any other event, whereby—
(i) a highway shown or required to be shown in the map and statement has been authorised to be stopped up, diverted, widened or extended;
(ii) a highway shown or required to be shown in the map and statement as a highway of a particular description has ceased to be a highway of that description; or
(iii) a new right of way has been created over land in the area to which the map relates, being a right of way such that the land over which the right subsists is a public path [or a restricted byway];
(b) the expiration, in relation to any way in the area to which the map relates, of any period such that the enjoyment by the public of the way during that period raises a presumption that the way has been dedicated as a public path [or restricted byway];
(c) the discovery by the authority of evidence which (when considered with all other relevant evidence available to them) shows—
(i) that a right of way which is not shown in the map and statement subsists or is reasonably alleged to subsist over land in the area to which the map relates, being

[a right of way such that the land over which the right subsists is a public path[, a restricted byway] or, subject to section 54A, a byway open to all traffic];

(ii) that a highway shown in the map and statement as a highway of a particular description ought to be there shown as a highway of a different description; or

(iii) that there is no public right of way over land shown in the map and statement as a highway of any description, or any other particulars contained in the map and statement require modification.

(4) The modifications which may be made by an order under subsection (2) shall include the addition to the statement of particulars as to—

(a) the position and width of any public path[, restricted byway] or byway open to all traffic which is or is to be shown on the map; and

(b) any limitations or conditions affecting the public right of way thereover.

[(4A) Subsection (4B) applies to evidence which, when considered with all other relevant evidence available to the surveying authority, shows as respects a way shown in a definitive map and statement as a restricted byway that the public have, and had immediately before the commencement of section 47 of the Countryside and Rights of Way Act 2000, a right of way for vehicular and all other kinds of traffic over that way.

(4B) For the purposes of subsection (3)(c)(ii), such evidence is evidence which, when so considered, shows that the way concerned ought, subject to section 54A, to be shown in the definitive map and statement as a byway open to all traffic.]

(5) Any person may apply to the authority for an order under subsection (2) which makes such modifications as appear to the authority to be requisite in consequence of the occurrence of one or more events falling within paragraph (b) or (c) of subsection (3); and the provisions of Schedule 14 shall have effect as to the making and determination of applications under this subsection.

[(5A) Evidence to which subsection (4B) applies on the commencement of section 47 of the Countryside and Rights of Way Act 2000 shall for the purposes of subsection (5) and any application made under it be treated as not having been discovered by the surveying authority before the commencement of that section.]

(6) Orders under subsection (2) which make only such modifications as appear to the authority to be requisite in consequence of the occurrence of one or more events falling within paragraph (a) of subsection (3) shall take effect on their being made; and the provisions of Schedule 15 shall have effect as to the making, validity and date of coming into operation of other orders under subsection (2).

[993]

NOTES

Sub-s (1): words in square brackets inserted by the Countryside and Rights of Way Act 2000, s 51, Sch 5, Pt I, para 1(1), (2).

Sub-s (3): in para (a)(iii), words in square brackets inserted by the Countryside and Rights of Way Act 2000, s 51, Sch 5, Pt I, para 1(1), (3); in para (b), words in square brackets inserted by the Natural Environment and Rural Communities Act 2006, s 70(1)(a); in para (c)(i), words in first (outer) pair of square brackets substituted by the Countryside and Rights of Way Act 2000, s 51, Sch 5, Pt I, para 1(1), (4); words in second (inner) pair of square brackets inserted by the Natural Environment and Rural Communities Act 2006, s 70(1)(b).

Sub-s (4): words in square brackets in para (a) inserted by the Countryside and Rights of Way Act 2000, s 51, Sch 5, Pt I, para 1(1), (5).

Sub-ss (4A), (4B), (5A): inserted by the Countryside and Rights of Way Act 2000, s 51, Sch 5, Pt I, para 1(1), (6), (7).

[53A Power to include modifications in other orders

(1) This section applies to any order—

(a) which is of a description prescribed by regulations made by the Secretary of State,

(b) whose coming into operation would, as regards any definitive map and statement, be an event within section 53(3)(a),

(c) which is made by the surveying authority, and

(d) which does not affect land outside the authority's area.

(2) The authority may include in the order such provision as it would be required to make under section 53(2)(b) in consequence of the coming into operation of the other provisions of the order.

(3) An authority which has included any provision in an order by virtue of subsection (2)—

(a) may at any time before the order comes into operation, and

(b) shall, if the order becomes subject to special parliamentary procedure,

withdraw the order and substitute for it an order otherwise identical but omitting any provision so included.

(4) Anything done for the purposes of any enactment in relation to an order withdrawn under subsection (3) shall be treated for those purposes as done in relation to the substituted order.

(5) No requirement for the confirmation of an order applies to provisions included in the order by virtue of subsection (2), but any power to modify an order includes power to make consequential modifications to any provision so included.

(6) Provisions included in an order by virtue of subsection (2) shall take effect on the date specified under section 56(3A) as the relevant date.

(7) Where any enactment provides for questioning the validity of an order on any grounds, the validity of any provision included by virtue of subsection (2) may be questioned in the same way on the grounds—

(a) that it is not within the powers of this Part, or

(b) that any requirement of this Part or of regulations made under it has not been complied with.

(8) Subject to subsections (5) to (7), the Secretary of State may by regulations provide that any procedural requirement as to the making or coming into operation of an order to which this section applies shall not apply, or shall apply with modifications prescribed by the regulations, to so much of the order as contains provision included by virtue of subsection (2).

(9) Regulations under this section shall be made by statutory instrument which shall be subject to annulment in pursuance of a resolution of either House of Parliament.]

[994]

NOTES

Commencement: 21 November 2005 (in relation to Wales); 18 February 2008 (in relation to England).
Inserted by the Countryside and Rights of Way Act 2000, s 51, Sch 5, Pt I, para 2.

[53B Register of applications under section 53

(1) Every surveying authority shall keep, in such manner as may be prescribed, a register containing such information as may be prescribed with respect to applications under section 53(5).

(2) The register shall contain such information as may be prescribed with respect to the manner in which such applications have been dealt with.

(3) Regulations may make provision for the register to be kept in two or more parts, each part containing such information relating to applications under section 53(5) as may be prescribed.

(4) Regulations may make provision—

(a) for a specified part of the register to contain copies of applications and of the maps submitted with them, and

(b) for the entry relating to any application, and everything relating to it, to be removed from any part of the register when—

(i) the application (including any appeal to the Secretary of State) has been finally disposed of, and

(ii) if an order is made, a decision has been made to confirm or not to confirm the order,

(without prejudice to the inclusion of any different entry relating to it in another part of the register).

(5) Every register kept under this section shall be available for inspection free of charge at all reasonable hours.

(6) In this section—

"prescribed" means prescribed by regulations;

"regulations" means regulations made by the Secretary of State by statutory instrument;

and a statutory instrument containing regulations under this section shall be subject to annulment in pursuance of a resolution of either House of Parliament.]

[995]

NOTES

Commencement: 27 September 2005 (in relation to England); 21 November 2005 (in relation to Wales).
Inserted by the Countryside and Rights of Way Act 2000, s 51, Sch 5, Pt I, para 2.
Regulations: the Public Rights of Way (Register of Applications under section 53(5) of the Wildlife and Countryside Act 1981) (England) Regulations 2005, SI 2005/2461; the Public Rights of Way (Registers) (Wales) Regulations 2006, SI 2006/42.

54 Duty to reclassify roads used as public paths

(1) As regards every definitive map and statement, the surveying authority shall, as soon as reasonably practicable after the commencement date,—

(a) carry out a review of such of the particulars contained in the map and statement as relate to roads used as public paths; and

(b) by order make such modifications to the map and statement as appear to the authority to be requisite to give effect to subsections (2) and (3);

and the provisions of Schedule 15 shall have effect as to the making, validity and date of coming into operation of orders under this subsection.

(2) A definitive map and statement shall show every road used as a public path by one of the three following descriptions, namely—

(a) a byway open to all traffic;

(b) a bridleway;

(c) a footpath,

and shall not employ the expression "road used as a public path" to describe any way.

(3) A road used as a public path shall be shown in the definitive map and statement as follows—

(a) if a public right of way for vehicular traffic has been shown to exist, as a byway open to all traffic;

(b) if paragraph (a) does not apply and public bridleway rights have not been shown not to exist, as a bridleway; and

(c) if neither paragraph (a) nor paragraph (b) applies, as a footpath.

(4) Each way which, in pursuance of an order under subsection (1), is shown in the map and statement by any of the three descriptions shall, as from the coming into operation of the order, be a highway maintainable at the public expense; and each way which, in pursuance of paragraph 9 of Part III of Schedule 3 to the 1968 Act, is so shown shall continue to be so maintainable.

(5) In this section "road used as a public path" means a way which is shown in the definitive map and statement as a road used as a public path.

(6) In subsections (2)(a) and (5) of section 51 of the 1949 Act (long distance routes) references to roads used as public paths shall include references to any way shown in a definitive map and statement as a byway open to all traffic.

(7) Nothing in this section or section 53 shall limit the operation of traffic orders under the Road Traffic Regulation Act [1984] or oblige a highway authority to provide, on a way shown in a definitive map and statement as a byway open to all traffic, a metalled carriage-way or a carriage-way which is by any other means provided with a surface suitable for the passage of vehicles.

[995A]

NOTES

Sub-s (7): date in square brackets substituted by the Road Traffic Regulation Act 1984, s 146, Sch 13.

Repealed by the Countryside and Rights of Way Act 2000, ss 47(1), 102, Sch 16, Pt II, subject to transitional provisions in SI 2006/1279, art 3 (Wales) and savings in SI 2006/1172, art 3 (England). SI 2006/1172, art 3, reads as follows:

"3 Savings

(1) Nothing in sections 47 or 48 of the Act shall affect the operation of section 53 or 54 of, or Schedule 14 or 15 to, the 1981 Act in relation to—

(a) a relevant order made before the appointed day; or

(b) an application made before the appointed day for a relevant order.

(2) In particular, where, before the appointed day, a surveying authority has made a relevant order under section 54 of the 1981 Act, but that order has not yet come into operation—

(a) the order shall continue to have effect on and after the appointed day, and

(b) the provisions of Schedule 15 to the 1981 Act shall continue to have effect in relation to the order, as if section 54 had not been repealed.".

[54A BOATs not to be added to definitive maps

(1) No order under this Part shall, after the cut-off date, modify a definitive map and statement so as to show as a byway open to all traffic any way not shown in the map and statement as a highway of any description.

(2) In this section "the cut-off date" means, subject to regulations under subsection (3), 1st January 2026.

(3) The Secretary of State may make regulations—

(a) substituting as the cut-off date a date later than the date specified in subsection (2) or for the time being substituted under this paragraph;

(b) containing such transitional provisions or savings as appear to the Secretary of State to be necessary or expedient in connection with the operation of subsection (1), including in particular its operation in relation to—

(i) an order under section 53(2) for which on the cut-off date an application is pending,

(ii) an order under this Part which on that date has been made but not confirmed,

(iii) an order under section 55 made after that date, or

(iv) an order under this Part relating to any way as respects which such an order, or any provision of such an order, has after that date been to any extent quashed.

(4) Regulations under subsection (3)(a)—

(a) may specify different dates for different areas; but

(b) may not specify a date later than 1st January 2031, except as respects an area within subsection (5).

(5) An area is within this subsection if it is in—

(a) the Isles of Scilly, or

(b) an area which, at any time before the repeal by section 73 of this Act of sections 27 to 34 of the 1949 Act—

(i) was excluded from the operation of those sections by virtue of any provision of the 1949 Act, or

(ii) would have been so excluded but for a resolution having effect under section 35(2) of that Act.

(6) Where by virtue of regulations under subsection (3) there are different cut-off dates for areas into which different parts of any way extend, the cut-off date in relation to that way is the later or latest of those dates.

(7) Where it appears to the Secretary of State that any provision of this Part can by virtue of subsection (1) have no further application he may by order make such amendments or repeals in this Part as appear to him to be, in consequence, necessary or expedient.

(8) An order or regulations under this section shall be made by statutory instrument which shall be subject to annulment in pursuance of a resolution of either House of Parliament.]

[996]

NOTES

Commencement: to be appointed.

Inserted by the Countryside and Rights of Way Act 2000, s 51, Sch 5, Pt I, para 4.

55 (*Outside the scope of this work.*)

56 Effect of definitive map and statement

(1) A definitive map and statement shall be conclusive evidence as to the particulars contained therein to the following extent, namely—

(a) where the map shows a footpath, the map shall be conclusive evidence that there was at the relevant date a highway as shown on the map, and that the public had thereover a right of way on foot, so however that this paragraph shall be without prejudice to any question whether the public had at that date any right of way other than that right;

(b) where the map shows a bridleway, the map shall be conclusive evidence that there was at the relevant date a highway as shown on the map, and that the public had thereover at that date a right of way on foot and a right of way on horseback or leading a horse, so however that this paragraph shall be without prejudice to any question whether the public had at that date any right of way other than those rights;

(c) where the map shows a byway open to all traffic, the map shall be conclusive evidence that there was at the relevant date a highway as shown on the map, and that the public had thereover at that date a right of way for vehicular and all other kinds of traffic;

(d) where the map shows a [restricted byway], the map shall[, subject to subsection (2A),] be conclusive evidence that there was at the relevant date a highway as shown on the map, and that the public had thereover at that date a right of way on foot and a right of way on horseback or leading a horse [together with a right of way for vehicles other than mechanically propelled vehicles], so however that this paragraph shall be without prejudice to any question whether the public had at that date any right of way other than those rights; and

(e) where by virtue of the foregoing paragraphs the map is conclusive evidence, as at any date, as to a highway shown thereon, any particulars contained in the statement as to the position or width thereof shall be conclusive evidence as to the position or width thereof at that date, and any particulars so contained as to limitations or conditions affecting the public right of way shall be conclusive evidence that at the said date the said right was subject to those limitations or conditions, but without prejudice to any question whether the right was subject to any other limitations or conditions at that date.

[(1A) In subsection (1)(d) "mechanically propelled vehicle" does not include an electrically assisted pedal cycle of a class prescribed for the purposes of section 189(1)(c) of the Road Traffic Act 1988.]

(2) For the purposes of this section "the relevant date"—

(a) in relation to any way which is shown on the map otherwise than in pursuance of an order under the foregoing provisions of this Part [or an order to which section 53A applies which includes provision made by virtue of subsection (2) of that section], means[, subject to subsection (2A),] the date specified in the statement as the relevant date for the purposes of the map;

(b) in relation to any way which is shown on the map in pursuance of such an order, means the date which, in accordance with subsection (3) [or (3A)], is specified in the order as the relevant date for the purposes of the order.

[(2A) In the case of a map prepared before the date of the coming into force of section 47 of the Countryside and Rights of Way Act 2000—

(a) subsection (1)(d) and (e) have effect subject to the operation of any enactment or instrument, and to any other event, whereby a way shown on the map as a restricted byway has, on or before that date—

(i) been authorised to be stopped up, diverted or widened, or

(ii) become a public path, and

(b) subsection (2)(a) has effect in relation to any way so shown with the substitution of that date for the date mentioned there.]

(3) Every order under the foregoing provisions of this Part shall specify, as the relevant date for the purposes of the order, such date, not being earlier than six months before the making of the order, as the authority may determine.

[(3A) Every order to which section 53A applies which includes provision made by virtue of subsection (2) of that section shall specify, as the relevant date for the purposes of the order, such date as the authority may in accordance with regulations made by the Secretary of State determine.]

(4) A document purporting to be certified on behalf of the surveying authority to be a copy of or of any part of a definitive map or statement as modified in accordance with the provisions of this Part shall be receivable in evidence and shall be deemed, unless the contrary is shown, to be such a copy.

[(4A) Regulations under this section shall be made by statutory instrument which shall be subject to annulment in pursuance of a resolution of either House of Parliament.]

(5) …

[997]

NOTES

Sub-s (1): in para (d), words in first pair of square brackets substituted and words in second and third pairs of square brackets inserted by the Countryside and Rights of Way Act 2000, s 51, Sch 5, Pt I, para 6(1), (2).

Sub-ss (1A), (2A), (3A), (4A): inserted by the Countryside and Rights of Way Act 2000, s 51, Sch 5, Pt I, para 6(1), (3), (5)–(7).

Sub-s (2): words in square brackets inserted by the Countryside and Rights of Way Act 2000, s 51, Sch 5, Pt I, para 6(1), (4).

Sub-s (5): repealed by the Countryside and Rights of Way Act 2000, ss 51, 102, Sch 5, Pt I, para 6(1), (8), Sch 16, Pt II.

Transfer of Functions: functions of the Secretary of State, so far as exercisable in relation to Wales, transferred to the National Assembly for Wales, by the National Assembly for Wales (Transfer of Functions) Order 1999, SI 1999/672, art 2, Sch 1.

Regulations: Public Rights of Way (Combined Orders) (England) Regulations 2008, SI 2008/442.

57, 57A (*Outside the scope of this work.*)

58 Application of ss 53 & 57 to inner London

(1) Subject to subsection (2), the foregoing provisions of this Part shall not apply to any area to which this subsection applies; and this subsection applies to any area which, immediately before 1st April 1965, formed part of the administrative county of London.

(2) A London borough council may be by resolution adopt the said foregoing provisions as respects any part of their area specified in the resolution, being a part to which subsection (1) applies, and those provisions shall thereupon apply accordingly.

(3) Where by virtue of a resolution under subsection (2), the said foregoing provisions apply to any area, those provisions shall have effect in relation thereto as if for references to the commencement date there were substituted references to the date on which the resolution comes into operation.

[998]

Miscellaneous and supplemental

59 Prohibition on keeping bulls on land crossed by public rights of way

(1) If, in a case not falling within subsection (2), the occupier of a field or enclosure crossed by a right of way to which this Part applies [or a restricted byway] permits a bull to be at large in the field or enclosure, he shall be liable on summary conviction to a fine not exceeding [level 3 on the standard scale].

(2) Subsection (1) shall not apply to any bull which—

(a) does not exceed the age of ten months; or

(b) is not of a recognised dairy breed and is at large in any field or enclosure in which cows or heifers are also at large

(3) Nothing in any byelaws, whenever made, shall make unlawful any act which is, or but for subsection (2) would be, made unlawful by subsection (1).

(4) In this section "recognised dairy breed" means one of the following breeds, namely, Ayrshire, British Friesian, British Holstein, Dairy Shorthorn, Guernsey, Jersey and Kerry.

(5) The Secretary of State may by order add any breed to, or remove any breed from, subsection (4); and an order under this subsection shall be made by statutory instrument which shall be subject to annulment in pursuance of a resolution of either House of Parliament.

[999]

NOTES

Sub-s (1): words in first pair of square brackets inserted by SI 2006/1177, reg 2, Schedule, Pt I; words in second pair of square brackets substituted by virtue of the Criminal Justice Act 1982, ss 37, 46.

Transfer of Functions: functions of the Secretary of State, so far as exercisable in relation to Wales, transferred to the National Assembly for Wales, by the National Assembly for Wales (Transfer of Functions) Order 1999, SI 1999/672, art 2, Sch 1.

60–65 (*S 60 repealed by the Road Traffic Regulation Act 1984, s 146, Sch 16; s 61 repealed by the Rights of Way Act 1990, s 6(4); ss 62–65 outside the scope of this work.*)

66 Interpretation of Part III

(1) In this Part—

"bridleway" means a highway over which the public have the following, but no other, rights of way, that is to say, a right of way on foot and a right of way on horseback or leading a horse, with or without a right to drive animals of any description along the highway;

"byway open to all traffic" means a highway over which the public have a right of way for vehicular and all other kinds of traffic, but which is used by the public mainly for the purpose for which footpaths and bridleways are so used;

"definitive map and statement" has the meaning given by section 53(1);

"footpath" means a highway over which the public have a right of way on foot only, other than such a highway at the side of a public road;

"horse" includes a pony, ass and mule, and "horseback" shall be construed accordingly;

"public path" means a highway being either a footpath or a bridleway;

["restricted byway" has the same meaning as in Part II of the Countryside and Rights of Way Act 2000;]

"right of way to which this Part applies" means a right of way such that the land over which the right subsists is a public path or a byway open to all traffic;

["surveying authority", in relation to any area, means the county council, [county borough council,] metropolitan district council or London borough council whose area includes that area.]

(2) A highway at the side of a river, canal or other inland navigation shall not be excluded from any definition contained in subsection (1) by reason only that the public have a right to use the highway for purposes of navigation, if the highway would fall within that definition if the public had no such right thereover.

(3) The provisions of section 30(1) of the 1968 Act (riding of pedal cycles on bridleways) shall not affect the definition of bridleway in subsection (1) and any rights exercisable by virtue of those provisions shall be disregarded for the purposes of this Part.

[1000]

NOTES

Sub-s (1): definition "restricted byway" inserted by the Countryside and Rights of Way Act 2000, s 51, Sch 5, Pt I, para 9; definition "surveying authority" substituted by the Local Government Act 1985, s 7, Sch 3, para 7, and words in square brackets therein inserted by the Local Government (Wales) Act 1994, s 66(6), Sch 16, para 65(8).

PART IV
MISCELLANEOUS AND GENERAL

66A–73 (*Outside the scope of this work.*)

74 Short title, commencement and extent

(1) This Act may be cited as the Wildlife and Countryside Act 1981.

(2) The following provisions of this Act, namely—

Part II, except sections 29 to 32, 41 and 46 to 48 and Schedule 13;
sections 59 to 62 and 65 and 66; and
Part IV, except section 72(4), (6) and (14) and section 73(1) so far as relating to Part II of Schedule 17,

shall come into force on the expiration of the period of one month beginning with the passing of this Act.

(3) The remaining provisions of this Act shall come into force on such day as the Secretary of State may by order made by statutory instrument appoint and different days may be appointed under this subsection for different provisions, different purposes or different areas.

(4) An order under subsection (3) may make such transitional provisions as appears to the Secretary of State to be necessary or expedient in connection with the provisions thereby brought into force.

(5) The following provisions of this Act, namely—

sections 39, 40 and 42 to 49 and Schedule 13; and Part III,

do not extend to Scotland.

[(5A) …]

(6) This Act, except section 15(1) and Schedule 10 and, so far as regards any enactment mentioned in Schedule 17 that so extends, section 73 and that Schedule, does not extend to Northern Ireland.

[1001]

NOTES

Sub-s (5A): inserted by the Countryside and Rights of Way Act 2000, s 76(1), Sch 10, Pt I, para 2; repealed by the Nature Conservation (Scotland) Act 2004, s 57, Sch 7, para 4.

Orders: the Wildlife and Countryside Act 1981 (Commencement No 1) Order 1982, SI 1982/44; the Wildlife and Countryside Act 1981 (Commencement No 2) Order 1982, SI 1982/327; the Wildlife and Countryside Act 1981 (Commencement No 3) Order 1982, SI 1982/990; the Wildlife and Countryside Act 1981 (Commencement No 4) Order 1982, SI 1982/1136; the Wildlife and Countryside Act 1981 (Commencement No 5) Order 1982, SI 1982/1217; the Wildlife and Countryside Act 1981 (Commencement No 6) Order 1983, SI 1983/20; the Wildlife and Countryside Act 1981 (Commencement No 7) Order 1983, SI 1983/87.

(*Schs A1, 1–14 outside the scope of this work.*)

SCHEDULE 15
PROCEDURE IN CONNECTION WITH CERTAIN ORDERS UNDER PART III

Sections 53, 54

Consultation

1. Before making an order, the authority shall consult with every local authority whose area includes the land to which the order relates.

Coming into operation

2. An order shall not take effect until confirmed either by the authority or the Secretary of State under paragraph 6 or by the Secretary of State under paragraph 7.

Publicity for orders

3.—(1) On making an order, the authority shall give notice in the prescribed form—

(a) describing the general effect of the order and stating that it has been made and requires confirmation;
(b) naming a place in the area in which the land to which the order relates is situated where a copy of the order may be inspected free of charge, and copies thereof may be obtained at a reasonable charge, at all reasonable hours; and
(c) specifying the time (not being less than 42 days from the date of the first publication of the notice) within which, and the manner in which, representations or objections with respect to the order[, which must include particulars of the grounds relied on,] may be made.

(2) Subject to sub-paragraph (4), the notice to be given under sub-paragraph (1) shall be given—

(a) by publication in at least one local newspaper circulating in the area in which the land to which the order relates is situated;
(b) by serving a like notice on—
  (i) every owner and occupier of any of that land;

(ii) every local authority whose area includes any of that land;
(iii) every person on whom notice is required to be served in pursuance of sub-paragraph (3); and
(iv) such other persons as may be prescribed in relation to the area in which that land is situated or as the authority may consider appropriate; and

(c) by causing a copy of the notice to be displayed in a prominent position—
(i) at the ends of so much of any way as is affected by the order;
(ii) at council offices in the locality of the land to which the order relates; and
(iii) at such other places as the authority may consider appropriate.

(3) Any person may, on payment of such reasonable charge as the authority may consider appropriate, require an authority to give him notice of all such orders as are made by the authority during a specified period, are of a specified description and relate to land comprised in a specified area; and in this sub-paragraph "specified" means specified in the requirement.

(4) The Secretary of State may, in any particular case, direct that it shall not be necessary to comply with sub-paragraph (2)(b)(i); but if he so directs in the case of any land, then in addition to publication the notice shall be addressed to "The owners and any occupiers" of the land (describing it) and a copy or copies of the notice shall be affixed to some conspicuous object or objects on the land.

(5) Sub-paragraph (2)(b) and (c) and, where applicable, sub-paragraph (4) shall be complied with not less than 42 days before the expiration of the time specified in the notice.

(6) A notice required to be served by sub-paragraph (2)(b) on the owner or occupier of any land, or on a local authority, shall be accompanied by a copy of so much of the order as relates to that land or, as the case may be, the area of that authority; and a notice required to be served by that sub-paragraph on such other persons as may be prescribed or as the authority may consider appropriate shall be accompanied by a copy of the order.

(7) A notice required to be displayed by sub-paragraph (2)(c) at the ends of so much of any way as is affected by the order shall be accompanied by a plan showing the general effect of the order so far as it relates to that way.

(8) At any time after the publication of a notice under this paragraph and before the expiration of the period specified in the notice for the making of representations and objections, any person may require the authority to inform him what documents (if any) were taken into account in preparing the order and—

(a) as respects any such documents in the possession of the authority, to permit him to inspect them and take copies; and
(b) as respects any such documents not in their possession, to give him any information the authority have as to where the documents can be inspected;

and on any requirement being made under this sub-paragraph the authority shall comply therewith within 14 days of the making of the requirement.

(9) Nothing in sub-paragraph [(1)(c) or] (8) shall be construed as limiting [the grounds which may be relied on or] the documentary or other evidence which may be adduced at any local inquiry or hearing held under paragraph 7 or 8.

Representations or objections made with respect to abandoned surveys or reviews

4.—(1) This paragraph applies where a survey begun under sections 27 to 32 of the 1949 Act, or a review begun under section 33 of that Act, is abandoned after a draft map and statement have been prepared.

(2) If an order modifies the definitive map and statement so as—

(a) to show any particulars shown in the draft map and statement but not in the definitive map and statement; or
(b) to omit any particulars shown in the definitive map and statement but not in the draft map and statement,

any representation or objection duly made with respect to the showing in or omission from the draft map and statement of those particulars shall be treated for the purposes of paragraphs 6 and 7 as a representation or objection duly made with respect to the corresponding modification made by the order.

Severance of orders

5.—(1) Where at any time representations or objections duly made and not withdrawn relate to some but not all of the modifications made by an order, the authority may, by notice given to the Secretary of State, elect that, for the purposes of the following provisions of this Schedule, the order shall have effect as two separate orders—

(a) the one comprising the modifications to which the representations or objections relate; and
(b) the other comprising the remaining modifications.

(2) Any reference in sub-paragraph (1) to an order includes a reference to any part of an order which, by virtue of one or more previous elections under that sub-paragraph, has effect as a separate order.

Unopposed orders

6.—(1) If so representations or objections are duly made, or if any so made are withdrawn, the authority may—

(a) confirm the order without modification; or

(b) if they require any modification to be made, submit the order to the Secretary of State for confirmation by him.

(2) Where an order is submitted to the Secretary of State under sub-paragraph (1), the Secretary of State may confirm the order with or without modifications.

Opposed orders

7.—(1) If any representation or objection duly made is not withdrawn the authority shall submit the order to the Secretary of State for confirmation by him.

(2) Where an order is submitted to the Secretary of State under sub-paragraph (1), the Secretary of State shall[, subject to sub-paragraph (2A),] either—

(a) cause a local inquiry to be held; or

(b) afford any person by whom a representation or objection has been duly made and not withdrawn an opportunity of being heard by a person appointed by the Secretary of State for the purpose.

[(2A) The Secretary of State may, but need not, act as mentioned in sub-paragraph (2)(a) or (b) if, in his opinion, no representation or objection which has been duly made and not withdrawn relates to an issue which would be relevant in determining whether or not to confirm the order, either with or without modifications.]

(3) On considering any representations or objections duly made and the report of [any person appointed to hold an inquiry] or hear representations or objections, the Secretary of State may confirm the order with or without modifications.

Restriction on power to confirm orders with modifications

8.—(1) The Secretary of State shall not confirm an order with modifications so as—

(a) to affect land not affected by the order;

(b) not to show any way shown in the order or to show any way not so shown; or

(c) to show as a highway of one description a way which is shown in the order as a highway of another description,

except after complying with the requirements of sub-paragraph (2).

(2) The said requirements are that the Secretary of State shall—

(a) give notice as appears to him requisite of his proposal so to modify the order, specifying the time (which shall not be less than 28 days from the date of the first publication of the notice) within which, and the manner in which, representations or objections with respect to the proposal[, which must include particulars of the grounds relied on,] may be made;

[(b) if any representation or objection duly made is not withdrawn (but subject to sub-paragraph (3)), hold a local inquiry or afford any person by whom any such representation or objection has been made an opportunity of being heard by a person appointed by the Secretary of State for the purpose; and

(c) consider the report of any person appointed to hold an inquiry or to hear representations or objections.

(3) The Secretary of State may, but need not, act as mentioned in sub-paragraph (2)(b) if, in his opinion, no representation or objection which has been duly made and not withdrawn relates to an issue which would be relevant in determining whether or not to confirm the order in accordance with his proposal.

(4) Sub-paragraph (2)(a) shall not be construed as limiting the grounds which may be relied on at any local inquiry or hearing held under this paragraph.]

9. …

Appointment of inspectors etc.

10.—(1) A decision of the Secretary of State under paragraph 6, 7 or 8 shall, except in such classes of case as may for the time being be prescribed or as may be specified in directions given by the Secretary of State, be made by a person appointed by the Secretary of State for the purpose instead of by the Secretary of State; and a decision made by a person so appointed shall be treated as a decision of the Secretary of State.

(2) The Secretary of State may, if he thinks fit, direct that a decision which, by virtue of sub-paragraph (1) and apart from this sub-paragraph, falls to be made by a person appointed by the Secretary of State shall instead be made by the Secretary of State; and a direction under this sub-paragraph shall state the reasons for which it is given and shall be served on the person, if any, so appointed, the authority and any person by whom a representation or objection has been duly made and not withdrawn.

(3) Where the Secretary of State has appointed a person to make a decision under paragraph 6, 7 or 8 the Secretary of State may, at any time before the making of the decision, appoint another person to make it instead of the person first appointed to make it.

(4) Where by virtue of sub-paragraph (2) or (3) a particular decision falls to be made by the Secretary of State or any other person instead of the person first appointed to make it, anything done by or in relation to the latter shall be treated as having been done by or in relation to the former.

(5) Regulations under this paragraph may provide for the giving of publicity to any directions given by the Secretary o State under this paragraph.

[Hearings and local inquiries

10A.—(1) Subject to sub-paragraph (2), subsections (2) to (5) of section 250 of the Local Government Act 1972 (giving of evidence at, and defraying of costs of, inquiries) shall apply in relation to any hearing or local inquiry held under paragraph 7 or 8 as they apply in relation to a local inquiry which a Minister causes to be held under subsection (1) of that section.

(2) In its application to a hearing or inquiry held under paragraph 7 or 8 by a person appointed under paragraph 10(1), subsection (5) of that section shall have effect as if the reference to the Minister causing the inquiry to be held were a reference to the person so appointed or the Secretary of State.

(3) Section 322A of the Town and Country Planning Act 1990 (orders as to costs where no hearing or inquiry takes place) shall apply in relation to a hearing or local inquiry under paragraph 7 or 8 as it applies in relation to a hearing or local inquiry for the purposes referred to in that section.]

Notice of final decisions on orders

11.—(1) As soon as practicable after a decision to confirm an order is made or, in the case of a decision by the Secretary of State, as soon as practicable after receiving notice of his decision, the authority shall give notice—

(a) describing the general effect of the order as confirmed and stating that it has been confirmed (with or without modification) and the date on which it took effect; and

(b) naming a place in the area in which the land to which the order relates is situated where a copy of the order as confirmed may be inspected free of charge, and copies thereof may be obtained at a reasonable charge, at all reasonable hours.

(2) A notice under sub-paragraph (1) shall be given—

(a) by publication in the manner required by paragraph 3(2)(a);

(b) by serving a like notice on any persons on whom notices were required to be served under paragraph 3(2)(b) or (4); and

(c) by causing like notices to be displayed in the like manner as the notices required to be displayed under paragraph 3(2)(c).

(3) A notice required to be served by sub-paragraph (2)(b) on the owner or occupier of any land, or on a local authority, shall be accompanied by a copy of so much of the order as confirmed as relates to that land or, as the case may be, the area of that authority;

and, in the case of an order which has been confirmed with modifications, a notice required to be served by that sub-paragraph on such other persons as may be prescribed or as the authority may consider appropriate shall be accompanied by a copy of the order as confirmed.

(4) As soon as practicable after a decision not to confirm an order or, in the case of a decision by the Secretary of State, as soon as practicable after receiving notice of his decision, the authority shall give notice of the decision by serving a copy of it on any persons on whom notices were required to be served under paragraph 3(2)(b) or (4).

Proceedings for questioning validity of orders

12.—(1) If any person is aggrieved by an order which has taken effect and desires to question its validity on the ground that it is not within the powers of section 53 and 54 or that any of the requirements of this Schedule have not been complied with in relation to it, he may within 42 days from the date of publication of the notice under paragraph 11 make an application to the High Court under this paragraph.

(2) On any such application the High Court may, if satisfied that the order is not within those powers or that the interests of the applicant have been substantially prejudiced by a failure to comply with those requirements, quash the order, or any provision of the order, either generally or in so far as it affects the interests of the applicant.

(3) Except as provided by this paragraph, the validity of an order shall not be questioned in any legal proceedings whatsoever.

Supplemental

13.—(1) The Secretary of State may, subject to the provisions of this Schedule, by regulations make such provision as to the procedure on the making, submission and confirmation of orders as appears to him to be expedient.

(2) In this Schedule—

"council offices" means offices or buildings acquired or provided by the authority or by a local authority;

"local authority" means [a non-metropolitan district council], a parish … council or the parish meeting of a parish not having a separate parish council [but, in relation to Wales, means a community council];

"order" means an order to which the provisions of this Schedule apply;

"prescribed" means prescribed by regulations made by the Secretary of State.

(3) Regulations under this Schedule shall be made by statutory instrument which shall be subject to annulment in pursuance of a resolution of either House of Parliament.

[1002]

NOTES

Para 3: in sub-paras (1)(c), (9), words in square brackets inserted by the Countryside and Rights of Way Act 2000, s 51, Sch 5, Pt I, para 11(1)–(3).

Para 7: words in square brackets in sub-para (2) inserted, sub-para (2A) inserted, and words in square brackets in sub-para (3) substituted by the Countryside and Rights of Way Act 2000, s 51, Sch 5, Pt I, para 11(1), (4)–(6).

Para 8: words in square brackets in sub-para (2)(a) inserted and sub-paras (2)(b), (c), (3), (4) substituted, for original sub-para (2)(b), (c), by the Countryside and Rights of Way Act 2000, s 51, Sch 5, Pt I, para 11(1), (7).

Para 9: repealed by the Countryside and Rights of Way Act 2000, ss 51, 102, Sch 5, Pt I, paras 11(1), (8), Sch 16, Pt II.

Para 10A: inserted by the Countryside and Rights of Way Act 2000, s 51, Sch 5, Pt I, para 11(1), (8).

Para 13: in sub-para (2) in definition "local authority", words in first pair of square brackets substituted by the Local Government Act 1985, s 7, Sch 3, para 7; words omitted repealed and words in second pair of square brackets inserted by the Local Government (Wales) Act 1994, s 66(6), (8), Sch 16, para 65(12), Sch 18.

Regulations: the Wildlife and Countryside (Definitive Maps and Statements) Regulations 1993, SI 1993/12.

(Schs 16, 17 outside the scope of this work.)

LOCAL GOVERNMENT (MISCELLANEOUS PROVISIONS) ACT 1982

(1982 c 30)

An Act to make amendments for England and Wales of provisions of that part of the law relating to local authorities or highways which is commonly amended by local Acts; to make provision for the control of sex establishments; to make further provision for the control of refreshment premises and for consultation between local authorities in England and Wales and fire authorities with regard to fire precautions for buildings and caravan sites; to repeal the Theatrical Employers Registration Acts 1925 and 1928; to make further provision as to the enforcement of section 8 of the Public Utilities Street Works Act 1950 and sections 171 and 174 of the Highways Act 1980; to make provision in connection with the computerisation of local land charges registers; to make further provision in connection with the acquisition of land and rights over land by boards constituted in pursuance of section 1 of the Town and Country Planning Act 1971 or reconstituted in pursuance of Schedule 17 to the Local Government Act 1972; to exclude from the definition of "construction or maintenance work" in section 20 of the Local Government, Planning and Land Act 1980 work undertaken by local authorities and development bodies pursuant to certain agreements with the Manpower Services Commission which specify the work to be undertaken and under which the Commission agrees to pay the whole or part of the cost of the work so specified; to define "year" for the purposes of Part III of the said Act of 1980; to amend section 140 of the Local Government Act 1972 and to provide for the insurance by local authorities of persons voluntarily assisting probation committees; to make provision for controlling nuisance and disturbance on educational premises; to amend section 137 of the Local Government Act 1972; to make further provision as to arrangements made by local authorities under the Employment and Training Act 1973; to extend the duration of certain powers to assist industry or employment conferred by local Acts; to make corrections and minor improvements in certain enactments relating to the local administration of health and planning functions; and for connected purposes

[13 July 1982]

1–32 ((*Pts I–XI*) *outside the scope of this work.*)

PART XII
MISCELLANEOUS

33 Enforceability by local authorities of certain covenants relating to land

(1) The provisions of this section shall apply if a principal council (in the exercise of their powers under section 111 of the Local Government Act 1972 or otherwise) and any other person are parties to an instrument under seal which—

[(a) is executed for the purpose of securing the carrying out of works on land in the council's area in which the other person has an interest, or

(b) is executed for the purpose of regulating the use of or is otherwise connected with land in or outside the council's area in which the other person has an interest,

and which is neither executed for the purpose of facilitating nor connected with the development of the land in question.]

(2) If, in a case where this section applies,—

(a) the instrument contains a covenant on the part of any person having an interest in land, being a covenant to carry out any works or do any other thing on or in relation to that land, and

(b) the instrument defines the land to which the covenant relates, being land in which that person has an interest at the time the instrument is executed, and

(c) the covenant is expressed to be one to which this section or section 126 of the Housing Act 1974 (which is superseded by this section) applies,

the covenant shall be enforceable (without any limit of time) against any person deriving title from the original covenantor in respect of his interest in any of the land defined as mentioned in paragraph (b) above and any person deriving title under him in respect of any lesser interest in that land as if that person had also been an original covenanting party in respect of the interest for the time being held by him.

(3)–(10) …

[1003]

NOTES

Sub-s (1): words in square brackets substituted for original paras (a) to (c), by the Planning and Compensation Act 1991, s 32, Sch 7, para 6.

Sub-ss (3)–(10): outside the scope of this work.

34–46 (*Outside the scope of this work.*)

PART XIII
SUPPLEMENTARY

47, 48 (*Outside the scope of this work.*)

49 Citation and extent

(1) This Act may be cited as the Local Government (Miscellaneous Provisions) Act 1982.

(2) Subject to sections … 38(3) and 47(4) above, and to paragraph 8(2) of Schedule 6 to this Act, this Act extends to England and Wales only.

[1004]

NOTES

Sub-s (2): reference omitted repealed by the Statute Law (Repeals) Act 2004.

(*Schs 1–7 outside the scope of this work.*)

ADMINISTRATION OF JUSTICE ACT 1982

(1982 c 53)

An Act to make further provision with respect to the administration of justice and matters connected therewith; to amend the law relating to actions for damages for personal injuries, including injuries resulting in death, and to abolish certain actions for loss of services; to amend the law relating to wills; to make further provision with respect to funds in court, statutory deposits and schemes for the common investment of such funds and deposits and certain other funds; to amend the law relating to deductions by employers under attachment of earnings orders; to make further provision with regard to penalties that may be awarded by the Solicitors' Disciplinary Tribunal under section 47 of the Solicitors Act 1974; to make further provision for the appointment of justices of the peace in England and Wales and in relation to temporary vacancies in the membership of the Law Commission; to enable the title register kept by the Chief Land Registrar to be kept otherwise than in documentary form; and to authorise the payment of travelling, subsistence and financial loss allowances for justices of the peace in Northern Ireland

[28 October 1982]

1–16 (*(Pts I–III) outside the scope of this work.*)

PART IV WILLS

17–19 (*Ss 17, 19 substitute the Wills Act 1837, ss 9, 33 at* **[25]**, **[50]**; *s 18 substitutes the Wills Act 1837, s 18 at* **[33]** *and inserts s 18A of that Act at* **[34]**.)

Rectification and interpretation of wills

20 Rectification

(1) If a court is satisfied that a will is so expressed that it fails to carry out the testator's intentions, in consequence—

(a) of a clerical error; or

(b) of a failure to understand his instructions,

it may order that the will shall be rectified so as to carry out his intentions.

(2) An application for an order under this section shall not, except with the permission of the court, be made after the end of the period of six months from the date on which representation with respect to the estate of the deceased is first taken out.

(3) The provisions of this section shall not render the personal representatives of a deceased person liable for having distributed any part of the estate of the deceased, after the end of the period of six months from the date on which representation with respect to the estate of the deceased is first taken out, on the ground that they ought to have taken into account the possibility that the court might permit the making of an application for an order under this section after the end of that period; but this subsection shall not prejudice any power to recover, by reason of the making of an order under this section, any part of the estate so distributed.

(4) In considering for the purposes of this section when representation with respect to the estate of a deceased person was first taken out, a grant limited to settled land or to trust property shall be left out of account, and a grant limited to real estate or to personal estate shall be left out of account unless a grant limited to the remainder of the estate has previously been made or is made at the same time.

[1005]

21 Interpretation of wills—general rules as to evidence

(1) This section applies to a will—

(a) in so far as any part of it is meaningless;

(b) in so far as the language used in any part of it is ambiguous on the face of it;

(c) in so far as evidence, other than evidence of the testator's intention, shows that the language used in any part of it is ambiguous in the light of surrounding circumstances.

(2) In so far as this section applies to a will extrinsic evidence, including evidence of the testator's intention, may be admitted to assist in its interpretation.

[1006]

22 Presumption as to effect of gifts to spouses

Except where a contrary intention is shown it shall be presumed that if a testator devises or bequeaths property to his spouse in terms which in themselves would give an absolute interest to the spouse, but by the same instrument purports to give his issue an interest in the same property, the gift to the spouse is absolute notwithstanding the purported gift to the issue.

[1007]

Registration of wills

23 Deposit and registration of wills of living persons

(1) The following, namely—

(a) the Principal Registry of the Family Division of the High Court of Justice;

(b) the Keeper of the Registers of Scotland; and

(c) the Probate and Matrimonial Office of the *Supreme Court* [Court of Judicature] of Northern Ireland,

shall be registering authorities for the purposes of this section.

(2) Each registering authority shall provide and maintain safe and convenient depositories for the custody of the wills of living persons.

(3) Any person may deposit his will in such a depository in accordance with regulations under section 25 below and on payment of the prescribed fee.

(4) It shall be the duty of a registering authority to register in accordance with regulations under section 25 below—

(a) any will deposited in a depository maintained by the authority; and

(b) any other will whose registration is requested under Article 6 of the Registration Convention.

(5) A will deposited in a depository provided—

(a) under section 172 of the Supreme Court of Judicature (Consolidation) Act 1925 or section 126 of the *Supreme Court Act 1981* [Senior Courts Act 1981]; or

(b) under Article 27 of the Administration of Estates (Northern Ireland) Order 1979,

shall be treated for the purposes of this section as if it had been deposited under this section.

(6) In this section "prescribed" means—

(a) in the application of this section to England and Wales, prescribed by an order under [section 92 of the Courts Act 2003];

(b) in its application to Scotland, prescribed by an order under section 26 below; and

(c) in its application to Northern Ireland, prescribed by an order under section 116 of the Judicature (Northern Ireland) Act 1978.

[1008]

NOTES

Sub-s (1): words in italics in para (c) substituted by subsequent words in square brackets by the Constitutional Reform Act 2005, s 59(5), Sch 11, Pt 4, para 27(1), (2)(a), as from 1 October 2009.

Sub-s (5): words in italics in para (a) substituted by subsequent words in square brackets by the Constitutional Reform Act 2005, s 59(5), Sch 11, Pt 1, para 1(2), as from 1 October 2009.

Sub-s (6): words in square brackets in para (a) substituted by the Courts Act 2003, s 109(1), Sch 8, para 270.

24 Designation of Principal Registry as national body under Registration Convention

(1) The Principal Registry of the Family Division of the High Court of Justice shall be the national body for the purposes of the Registration Convention, and shall accordingly have the functions assigned to the national body by the Registration Convention including, without prejudice to the general application of the Convention to the Principal Registry by virtue of this section, the functions—

(a) of arranging for the registration of wills in other Contracting States as provided for in Article 6 of the Convention;

(b) of receiving and answering requests for information arising from the national bodies of other Contracting States.

(2) In this Part of this Act "the Registration Convention" means the Convention on the Establishment of a Scheme of Registration of Wills concluded at Basle on 16th May 1972.

[1009]

NOTES

Commencement: to be appointed.

25 Regulations as to deposit and registration of wills

(1) Regulations may make provision—

(a) as to the conditions for the deposit of a will;

(b) as to the manner of and procedure for—

(i) the deposit and registration of a will; and

(ii) the withdrawal of a will which has been deposited; and

(iii) the cancellation of the registration of a will; and

(c) as to the manner in which the Principal Registry of the Family Division is to perform its functions as the national body under the Registration Convention.

(2) Regulations under this section may contain such incidental or supplementary provisions as the authority making the regulations considers appropriate.

(3) Any such regulations are to be made—

(a) for England and Wales, by the President of the Family Division of the High Court of Justice, with the concurrence of the Lord Chancellor;

(b) for Scotland, by the Secretary of State after consultation with the Lord President of the Court of Session; and

(c) for Northern Ireland, by the Northern Ireland *Supreme Court* [Court of Judicature] Rules Committee, with the concurrence of the Lord Chancellor.

(4) Regulations made by virtue of subsection (1)(c) above shall be made by the Lord Chancellor [after consulting the Lord Chief Justice of England and Wales].

(5) Subject to subsection (6) below, regulations under this section shall be made by statutory instrument and shall be laid before Parliament after being made.

(6) Regulations for Northern Ireland shall be statutory rules for the purposes of the Statutory Rules (Northern Ireland) Order 1979; and any such statutory rule shall be laid before Parliament after being made in like manner as a statutory instrument and section 4 of the Statutory Instruments Act 1946 shall apply accordingly.

(7) The Statutory Instruments Act 1946 shall apply to a statutory instrument containing regulations made in accordance with subsection (3)(a) or (c) above as if the regulations had been made by a Minister of the Crown.

(8) Any regulations made under section 172 of the Supreme Court of Judicature (Consolidation) Act 1925 or section 126 of the *Supreme Court Act 1981* [Senior Courts Act 1981] shall have effect for the purposes of this Part of this Act as they have effect for the purposes of the enactment under which they were made.

[(9) The Lord Chief Justice may nominate a judicial office holder (as defined in section 109(4) of the Constitutional Reform Act 2005) to exercise his functions under subsection (4).]

[1010]

NOTES

Commencement: to be appointed.

Sub-s (3): in para (c) words in italics substituted by subsequent words in square brackets by the Constitutional Reform Act 2005, s 59(5), Sch 11, Pt 4, para 27(1), (2)(b), as from 1 October 2009.

Sub-s (4): words in square brackets inserted by the Constitutional Reform Act 2005, s 15(1), Sch 4, Pt 1, paras 147, 148(1), (2).

Sub-s (8): words in italics substituted by subsequent words in square brackets by the Constitutional Reform Act 2005, s 59(5), Sch 11, Pt 1, para 1(2), as from 1 October 2009.

Sub-s (9): inserted by the Constitutional Reform Act 2005, s 15(1), Sch 4, Pt 1, paras 147, 148(1), (3).

26–72 (*S 26 applies to Scotland only; ss 27, 28, ss 29–72 (Pts V–VIII) outside the scope of this work.*)

PART IX
GENERAL AND SUPPLEMENTARY

73–77 (*Outside the scope of this work.*)

78 Citation

This Act may be cited as the Administration of Justice Act 1982.

[1011]

(*Schs 1–9 outside the scope of this work.*)

MOBILE HOMES ACT 1983

(1983 c 34)

[13 May 1983]

[1 Particulars of agreements

(1) This Act applies to any agreement under which a person ("the occupier") is entitled—

(a) to station a mobile home on land forming part of a protected site; and

(b) to occupy the mobile home as his only or main residence.

(2) Before making an agreement to which this Act applies, the owner of the protected site ("the owner") shall give to the proposed occupier under the agreement a written statement which—

(a) specifies the names and addresses of the parties;

(b) includes particulars of the land on which the proposed occupier is to be entitled to station the mobile home that are sufficient to identify that land;

(c) sets out the express terms to be contained in the agreement;

(d) sets out the terms to be implied by section 2(1) below; and

(e) complies with such other requirements as may be prescribed by regulations made by the appropriate national authority.

(3) The written statement required by subsection (2) above must be given—

(a) not later than 28 days before the date on which any agreement for the sale of the mobile home to the proposed occupier is made, or

(b) (if no such agreement is made before the making of the agreement to which this Act applies) not later than 28 days before the date on which the agreement to which this Act applies is made.

(4) But if the proposed occupier consents in writing to that statement being given to him by a date ("the chosen date") which is less than 28 days before the date mentioned in subsection (3)(a) or (b) above, the statement must be given to him not later than the chosen date.

(5) If any express term—

(a) is contained in an agreement to which this Act applies, but

(b) was not set out in a written statement given to the proposed occupier in accordance with subsections (2) to (4) above,

the term is unenforceable by the owner or any person within section 3(1) below.
This is subject to any order made by the court under section 2(3) below.

(6) If the owner has failed to give the occupier a written statement in accordance with subsections (2) to (4) above, the occupier may, at any time after the making of the agreement, apply to the court for an order requiring the owner—

(a) to give him a written statement which complies with paragraphs (a) to (e) of subsection (2) (read with any modifications necessary to reflect the fact that the agreement has been made), and

(b) to do so not later than such date as is specified in the order.

(7) A statement required to be given to a person under this section may be either delivered to him personally or sent to him by post.

(8) Any reference in this section to the making of an agreement to which this Act applies includes a reference to any variation of an agreement by virtue of which the agreement becomes one to which this Act applies.

(9) Regulations under this section—

(a) shall be made by statutory instrument;

(b) if made by the Secretary of State, shall be subject to annulment in pursuance of a resolution of either House of Parliament; and

(c) may make different provision with respect to different cases or descriptions of case, including different provision for different areas.]

[1012]

NOTES

Commencement: 18 January 2005 (in relation to England and Wales); 28 May 2007 (in relation to Scotland).

Substituted, in relation to England and Wales, by the Housing Act 2004, s 206(1) (for effect see s 206(4), (5) thereof) and in relation to Scotland by the Housing (Scotland) Act 2006, s 167.

Transfer of Functions: functions of the Secretary of State, so far as exercisable in relation to Wales, transferred to the National Assembly for Wales, by the National Assembly for Wales (Transfer of Functions) Order 1999, SI 1999/672, art 2, Sch 1.

Regulations: the Mobile Homes (Written Statement) (England) Regulations 2006, SI 2006/2275; the Mobile Homes (Written Statement) (Wales) Regulations 2007, SI 2007/3164.

2 Terms of agreements

(1) In any agreement to which this Act applies there shall be implied the terms set out in Part I of Schedule 1 to this Act; and this subsection shall have effect notwithstanding any express term of the agreement.

(2) The court may, on the application of either party made [within the relevant period], order that there shall be implied in the agreement terms concerning the matters mentioned in Part II of Schedule 1 to this Act.

[(3) The court may, on the application of either party made within the relevant period, make an order—

(a) varying or deleting any express term of the agreement;
(b) in the case of any express term to which section 1(6) above applies, provide for the term to have full effect or to have such effect subject to any variation specified in the order.

(3A) In subsections (2) and (3) above "the relevant period" means the period beginning with the date on which the agreement is made and ending—
(a) six months after that date, or
(b) where a written statement relating to the agreement is given to the occupier after that date (whether or not in compliance with an order under section 1(6) above), six months after the date on which the statement is given;

and section 1(8) above applies for the purposes of this subsection as it applies for the purposes of section 1.]

(4) On an application under this section, the court shall make such provision as the court considers just and equitable in the circumstances.

[(5) The supplementary provisions in Part 3 of Schedule 1 to this Act have effect for the purposes of paragraphs 8 and 9 of Part 1 of that Schedule.]

[1013]

NOTES

Sub-s (2): words in square brackets substituted, in relation to England and Wales, by the Housing Act 2004, s 206(2)(a), and in relation to Scotland by the Housing (Scotland) Act 2006, s 168(a).

Sub-ss (3), (3A): substituted, for original sub-s (3), in relation to England and Wales, by the Housing Act 2004, s 206(2)(b), and in relation to Scotland by the Housing (Scotland) Act 2006, s 168(b).

Sub-s (5): inserted, in relation to England and Wales, by the Housing Act 2004, s 265(1), Sch 15, para 9.

[2A Power to amend implied terms

(1) The appropriate national authority may by order make such amendments of Part 1 or 2 of Schedule 1 to this Act as the authority considers appropriate.

(2) An order under this section—
(a) shall be made by statutory instrument;
(b) may make different provision with respect to different cases or descriptions of case, including different provision for different areas;
(c) may contain such incidental, supplementary, consequential, transitional or saving provisions as the authority making the order considers appropriate.

(3) Without prejudice to the generality of subsections (1) and (2), an order under this section may—
(a) make provision for or in connection with the determination by the court of such questions, or the making by the court of such orders, as are specified in the order;
(b) make such amendments of any provision of this Act as the authority making the order considers appropriate in consequence of any amendment made by the order in Part 1 or 2 of Schedule 1.

(4) The first order made under this section in relation to England or Wales respectively may provide for all or any of its provisions to apply in relation to agreements to which this Act applies that were made at any time before the day on which the order comes into force (as well as in relation to such agreements made on or after that day).

(5) No order may be made by the appropriate national authority under this section unless the authority has consulted—
(a) such organisations as appear to it to be representative of interests substantially affected by the order; and
(b) such other persons as it considers appropriate.

(6) No order may be made by the Secretary of State under this section unless a draft of the order has been laid before, and approved by a resolution of, each House of Parliament.]

[1014]

NOTES

Commencement: 18 November 2004.

Inserted, in relation to England and Wales, by the Housing Act 2004, s 208(1); for effect see s 208(2) thereof.

Orders: the Mobile Homes Act 1983 (Amendment of Schedule 1) (England) Order 2006, SI 2006/1755; the Mobile Homes Act 1983 (Amendment of Schedule 1) (Wales) Order 2007, SI 2007/3151.

[2B Power to amend implied terms: Scotland

(1) The Scottish Ministers may by order make such amendments of Part 1 or 2 of Schedule 1 to this Act as they consider appropriate.

(2) An order under this section—
(a) shall be made by statutory instrument;

(b) may make different provision with respect to different cases or descriptions of case;
(c) may contain such incidental, supplementary, consequential, transitional or saving provisions as the Scottish Ministers consider appropriate.

(3) Without prejudice to the generality of subsections (1) and (2), an order under this section may—
(a) make provision for or in connection with the determination by the court of such questions, or the making by the court of such orders, as are specified in the order;
(b) make such amendments of any provision of this Act as the Scottish Ministers consider appropriate in consequence of any amendment made by the order in Part 1 or 2 of Schedule 1.

(4) The first order made under this section may provide for all or any of its provisions to apply in relation to agreements to which this Act applies that were made at any time before the day on which the order comes into force (as well as in relation to such agreements made on or after that day).

(5) No order may be made under this section unless the Scottish Ministers have consulted—
(a) such organisations as appear to them to be representative of interests substantially affected by the order; and
(b) such other persons as they consider appropriate.

(6) No order may be made under this section unless a draft of the order has been laid before, and approved by a resolution of, the Scottish Parliament.]

[1015]

NOTES

Commencement: 28 May 2007.
Inserted by the Housing (Scotland) Act 2006, s 170(1).

3 Successors in title

(1) An agreement to which this Act applies shall be binding on and enure for the benefit of any successor in title of the owner and any person claiming through or under the owner or any such successor.

(2) Where an agreement to which this Act applies is lawfully assigned to any person, the agreement shall enure for the benefit of and be binding on that person.

(3) Where a person entitled to the benefit of and bound by an agreement to which this Act applies dies at a time when he is occupying the mobile home as his only or main residence, the agreement shall enure for the benefit of and be binding on—
(a) any person residing with that person ("the deceased") at that time being—
(i) the widow[, widower or surviving civil partner] of the deceased; or
(ii) in default of a widow[, widower or surviving civil partner] so residing, any member of the deceased's family; or
(b) in default of any such person so residing, the person entitled to the mobile home by virtue of the deceased's will or under the law relating to intestacy but subject to subsection (4) below.

(4) An agreement to which this Act applies shall not enure for the benefit of or be binding on a person by virtue of subsection 3(*b*) above in so far as—
(a) it would, but for this subsection, enable or require that person to occupy the mobile home; or
(b) it includes terms implied by virtue of paragraph 5 or 9 of Part I of Schedule 1 to this Act.

[1016]

NOTES

Sub-s (3): words in square brackets substituted by the Civil Partnership Act 2004, s 261(1), Sch 27, para 87.

4 Jurisdiction of the court

The court shall have jurisdiction to determine any question arising under this Act or any agreement to which it applies, and to entertain any proceedings brought under this Act or any such agreement.

[1017]

5 Interpretation

(1) In this Act, unless the context otherwise requires—
["the appropriate national authority" means—
(a) in relation to England, the Secretary of State, and
(b) in relation to Wales, the National Assembly for Wales;]
"the court" means—
(a) in relation to England and Wales, the county court for the district in which the

protected site is situated or, where the parties have agreed in writing to submit any question arising under this Act or, as the case may be, any agreement to which it applies to arbitration, the arbitrator;

(b) in relation to Scotland, the sheriff having jurisdiction where the protected site is situated or, where the parties have so agreed, the arbiter;

"local authority" has the same meaning as in Part I of the Caravan Sites and Control of Development Act 1960;

"mobile home" has the same meaning as "caravan" has in that Part of that Act;

"owner", in relation to a protected site, means the person who, by virtue of an estate or interest held by him, is entitled to possession of the site or would be so entitled but for the rights of any persons to station mobile homes on land forming part of the site;

"planning permission" means permission under [Part III of the Town and Country Planning Act 1990] or [Part III of the Town and Country Planning (Scotland) Act 1997];

"protected site" *does not include any land occupied by a local authority as a caravan site providing accommodation for gipsies or, in Scotland, for persons to whom section 24(8A) of the Caravan Sites and Control of Development Act 1960 applies but, subject to that,* has the same meaning as in Part I of the Caravan Sites Act 1968.

(2) In relation to an agreement to which this Act applies—

(a) any reference in this Act to the owner includes a reference to any person who is bound by and entitled to the benefit of the agreement by virtue of subsection (1) of section 3 above; and

(b) subject to subsection (4) of that section, any reference in this Act to the occupier includes a reference to any person who is entitled to the benefit of and bound by the agreement by virtue of subsection (2) or (3) of that section.

(3) A person is a member of another's family within the meaning of this Act if he is his spouse, [civil partner,] parent, grandparent, child, grandchild, brother, sister, uncle, aunt, nephew or niece; treating—

(a) any relationship by marriage [or civil partnership] as a relationship by blood, any relationship of the half blood as a relationship of the whole blood and the stepchild of any person as his child; and

(b) an illegitimate person as the legitimate child of his mother and reputed father;

or if they live together as husband and wife [or as if they were civil partners].

[(4) In relation to land in Scotland, any reference in this Act to an "estate or interest" shall be construed as a reference to a right in, or to, the land.]

[1018]

NOTES

Sub-s (1): definition "the appropriate national authority" inserted, in relation to England and Wales, by the Housing Act 2004, s 206(3); for effect see s 206(4), (5) thereof; in definition "planning permission" words in first pair of square brackets substituted by the Planning (Consequential Provisions) Act 1990, s 4, Sch 2, para 59 and words in second pair of square brackets substituted by the Planning (Consequential Provisions) (Scotland) Act 1997, s 4, Sch 2, para 36; in definition "protected site" words in italics repealed by the Housing and Regeneration Act 2008, ss 318, 321(1), Sch 16, as from a day to be appointed.

Sub-s (3): words in square brackets inserted by the Civil Partnership Act 2004, s 261(1), Sch 27, para 88.

Sub-s (4): inserted by the Abolition of Feudal Tenure etc (Scotland) Act 2000, s 76(1), Sch 12, para 44.

6 Short title, repeals, commencement and extent

(1) This Act may be cited as the Mobile Homes Act 1983.

(2) The enactments mentioned in Schedule 2 to this Act are hereby repealed to the extent specified in the third column of that Schedule.

(3) This Act shall come into force on the expiry of the period of one week beginning with the day on which it is passed.

(4) This Act does not extend to Northern Ireland.

[1019]

SCHEDULE 1
AGREEMENTS UNDER ACT

Section 2

PART I
TERMS IMPLIED BY ACT

Duration of Agreement

1. Subject to paragraph 2 below, the right to station the mobile home on land forming part of the protected site shall subsist until the agreement is determined under paragraph 3, 4, 5 or 6 below.

2.—(1) If the owner's estate or interest is insufficient to enable him to grant the right for an indefinite period, the period for which the right subsists shall not extend beyond the date when the owner's estate or interest determines.

(2) If planning permission for the use of the protected site as a site for mobile homes has been granted in terms such that it will expire at the end of a specified period, the period for which the right subsists shall not extend beyond the date when the planning permission expires.

(3) If before the end of a period determined by this paragraph there is a change in circumstances which allows a longer period, account shall be taken of that change.

Termination by occupier

3. The occupier shall be entitled to terminate the agreement by notice in writing given to the owner not less than four weeks before the date on which it is to take effect.

4. The owner shall be entitled to terminate the agreement forthwith if, on the application of the owner, the court—

(a) is satisfied that the occupier has breached a term of the agreement and, after service of a notice to remedy the breach, has not complied with the notice within a reasonable time; and

(b) considers it reasonable for the agreement to be terminated.

5. The owner shall be entitled to terminate the agreement forthwith if, on the application of the owner, [the court—

(a) is satisfied that the occupier is not occupying the mobile home as his only or main residence; and

(b) considers it reasonable for the agreement to be terminated].

6.—(1) The owner shall be entitled to terminate the agreement [forthwith] if, on the application of the owner, the court is satisfied that, having regard to its … condition, the mobile home—

(a) is having a detrimental effect on the amenity of the site; *or* [; and]

[(b) the court considers it reasonable for the agreement to be terminated].

(2) …

[(3) Sub-paragraphs (4) and (5) below apply if, on an application under sub-paragraph (1) above—

(a) the court considers that, having regard to the present condition of the mobile home, paragraph (a) … of that sub-paragraph applies to it, but

(b) it also considers that it would be reasonably practicable for particular repairs to be carried out on the mobile home that [would result in sub-paragraph (1)(a) not applying to it], and

(c) the occupier indicates that he intends to carry out those repairs.

(4) In such a case the court may make an order adjourning proceedings on the application for such period specified in the order as the court considers reasonable to allow the repairs to be carried out.

The repairs must be set out in the order.

(5) If the court makes such an order, the application shall not be further proceeded with unless the court is satisfied that the specified period has expired without the repairs having been carried out.]

Recovery of overpayments by occupier

7. Where the agreement is terminated as mentioned in paragraph 3, 4, 5 or 6 above, the occupier shall be entitled to recover from the owner so much of any payment made by him in pursuance of the agreement as is attributable to a period beginning after the termination.

Sale of mobile home

8.—(1) The occupier shall be entitled to sell the mobile home, and to assign the agreement, to a person approved of by the owner, whose approval shall not be unreasonably withheld.

[(1A) The occupier may serve on the owner a request for the owner to approve a person for the purposes of sub-paragraph (1) above.

(1B) Where the owner receives such a request, he must, within the period of 28 days beginning with the date on which he received the request—

(a) approve the person, unless it is reasonable for him not to do so, and

(b) serve on the occupier notice of his decision whether or not to approve the person.

[(1C) The owner may not give his approval subject to conditions.]

[(1D) If the approval is withheld, the notice under sub-paragraph (1B) above must specify the reasons for withholding it.]

(1E) If the owner fails to notify the occupier as required by [sub-paragraph (1B) (and, if applicable, sub-paragraph (1D))] above, the occupier may apply to the court for an order declaring that the person is approved for the purposes of sub-paragraph (1) above; and the court may make such an order if it thinks fit.

(1F) It is for the owner—

(a) if he served a notice as mentioned in [sub-paragraph (1B) (and, if applicable, sub-paragraph (1D)] and the question arises whether he served the notice within the required period of 28 days, to show that he did;

(b) …

(c) if he did not give his approval and the question arises whether it was reasonable for him not to do so, to show that it was reasonable.

(1G) A request or notice under this paragraph—

(a) must be in writing, and

(b) may be served by post.]

(2) Where the occupier sells the mobile home, and assigns the agreement, as mentioned in sub-paragraph (1) above, the owner shall be entitled to receive a commission on the sale at a rate not exceeding such rate as may be specified by an order made by [the appropriate national authority].

[(2A) Except to the extent mentioned in sub-paragraph (2) above, the owner may not require any payment to be made (whether to himself or otherwise) in connection with the sale of the mobile home, and the assignment of the agreement, as mentioned in sub-paragraph (1) above.]

(3) An order under this paragraph—

(a) shall be made by statutory instrument which [(if made by the Secretary of State)] shall be subject to annulment in pursuance of a resolution of either House of Parliament; and

(b) may make different provision for different areas or for sales at different prices.

Gift of mobile home

9.—[(1)] The occupier shall be entitled to give the mobile home, and to assign the agreement, to a member of his family approved by the owner, whose approval shall not be unreasonably withheld.

[(2) Sub-paragraphs (1A) to (1G) of paragraph 8 above shall apply in relation to the approval of a person for the purposes of sub-paragraph (1) above as they apply in relation to the approval of a person for the purposes of sub-paragraph (1) of that paragraph.]

[(3) The owner may not require any payment to be made (whether to himself or otherwise) in connection with the gift of the mobile home, and the assignment of the agreement, as mentioned in sub-paragraph (1) above.]

[Re-siting of mobile home

10.—(1) The owner shall be entitled to require that the occupier's right to station the mobile home is exercisable for any period in relation to another pitch forming part of the protected site ("the other pitch") if (and only if)—

(a) on the application of the owner, the court is satisfied that the other pitch is broadly comparable to the occupier's original pitch and that it is reasonable for the mobile home to be stationed on the other pitch for that period; or

(b) the owner needs to carry out essential repair or emergency works that can only be carried out if the mobile home is moved to the other pitch for that period, and the other pitch is broadly comparable to the occupier's original pitch.

(2) If the owner requires the occupier to station the mobile home on the other pitch so that he can replace, or carry out repairs to, the base on which the mobile home is stationed, he must if the occupier so requires, or the court on the application of the occupier so orders, secure that the mobile home is returned to the original pitch on the completion of the replacement or repairs.

(3) The owner shall pay all the costs and expenses incurred by the occupier in connection with his mobile home being moved to and from the other pitch.

(4) In this paragraph and in paragraph 13 below, "essential repair or emergency works" means—

(a) repairs to the base on which the mobile home is stationed;

(b) works or repairs needed to comply with any relevant legal requirements; or

(c) works or repairs in connection with restoration following flood, landslide or other natural disaster.

Quiet enjoyment of the mobile home

11. The occupier shall be entitled to quiet enjoyment of the mobile home together with the pitch during the continuance of the agreement, subject to paragraphs 10, 12, 13 and 14.

Owner's right of entry to the pitch

12. The owner may enter the pitch without prior notice between the hours of 9 am and 6 pm
- (a) to deliver written communications, including post and notices, to the occupier; and
- (b) to read any meter for gas, electricity, water, sewerage or other services supplied by the owner.

13. The owner may enter the pitch to carry out essential repair or emergency works on giving as much notice to the occupier (whether in writing or otherwise) as is reasonably practicable in the circumstances.

14. Unless the occupier has agreed otherwise, the owner may enter the pitch for a reason other than one specified in paragraph 12 or 13 only if he has given the occupier at least 14 clear days' written notice of the date, time and reason for his visit.

15. The rights conferred by paragraphs 12 to 14 above do not extend to the mobile home.

The pitch fee

16. The pitch fee can only be changed in accordance with paragraph 17, either—
- (a) with the agreement of the occupier, or
- (b) if the court, on the application of the owner or the occupier, considers it reasonable for the pitch fee to be changed and makes an order determining the amount of the new pitch fee.

17.—(1) The pitch fee shall be reviewed annually as at the review date.

(2) At least 28 clear days before the review date the owner shall serve on the occupier a written notice setting out his proposals in respect of the new pitch fee.

(3) If the occupier agrees to the proposed new pitch fee, it shall be payable as from the review date.

(4) If the occupier does not agree to the proposed new pitch fee—
- (a) the owner may apply to the court for an order under paragraph 16(b) determining the amount of the new pitch fee;
- (b) the occupier shall continue to pay the current pitch fee to the owner until such time as the new pitch fee is agreed by the occupier or an order determining the amount of the new pitch fee is made by the court under paragraph 16(b); and
- (c) the new pitch fee shall be payable as from the review date but the occupier shall not be treated as being in arrears until the 28th day after the date on which the new pitch fee is agreed or, as the case may be, the 28th day after the date of the court order determining the amount of the new pitch fee.

(5) An application under sub-paragraph (4)(a) may be made at any time after the end of the period of 28 days beginning with the review date.

(6) Sub-paragraphs (7) to (10) apply if the owner—
- (a) has not served the notice required by sub-paragraph (2) by the time by which it was required to be served, but
- (b) at any time thereafter serves on the occupier a written notice setting out his proposals in respect of a new pitch fee.

(7) If (at any time) the occupier agrees to the proposed pitch fee, it shall be payable as from the 28th day after the date on which the owner serves the notice under sub-paragraph (6)(b).

(8) If the occupier has not agreed to the proposed pitch fee—
- (a) the owner may apply to the court for an order under paragraph 16(b) determining the amount of the new pitch fee;
- (b) the occupier shall continue to pay the current pitch fee to the owner until such time as the new pitch fee is agreed by the occupier or an order determining the amount of the new pitch fee is made by the court under paragraph 16(b); and
- (c) if the court makes such an order, the new pitch fee shall be payable as from the 28th day after the date on which the owner serves the notice under sub-paragraph (6)(b).

(9) An application under sub-paragraph (8) may be made at any time after the end of the period of 56 days beginning with date on which the owner serves the notice under sub-paragraph (6)(b).

(10) The occupier shall not be treated as being in arrears—
- (a) where sub-paragraph (7) applies, until the 28th day after the date on which the new pitch fee is agreed; or
- (b) where sub-paragraph (8)(b) applies, until the 28th day after the date on which the new pitch fee is agreed or, as the case may be, the 28th day after the date of the court order determining the amount of the new pitch fee.

18.—(1) When determining the amount of the new pitch fee particular regard shall be had to—
- (a) any sums expended by the owner since the last review date on improvements—
  - (i) which are for the benefit of the occupiers of mobile homes on the protected site;

(ii) which were the subject of consultation in accordance with paragraph 22(e) and (f) below; and
(iii) to which a majority of the occupiers have not disagreed in writing or which, in the case of such disagreement, the court, on the application of the owner, has ordered should be taken into account when determining the amount of the new pitch fee;
(b) any decrease in the amenity of the protected site since the last review date; and
(c) the effect of any enactment, other than an order made under paragraph 8(2) above, which has come into force since the last review date.

(2) When calculating what constitutes a majority of the occupiers for the purposes of sub-paragraph (1)(b)(iii) each mobile home is to be taken to have only one occupier and, in the event of there being more than one occupier of a mobile home, its occupier is to be taken to be the occupier whose name first appears on the agreement.

(3) In a case where the pitch fee has not been previously reviewed, references in this paragraph to the last review date are to be read as references to the date when the agreement commenced.

19. When determining the amount of the new pitch fee, any costs incurred by the owner in connection with expanding the protected site shall not be taken into account.

20.—(1) There is a presumption that the pitch fee shall increase or decrease by a percentage which is no more than any percentage increase or decrease in the retail prices index since the last review date, unless this would be unreasonable having regard to paragraph 18(1) above.

(2) Paragraph 18(3) above applies for the purposes of this paragraph as it applies for the purposes of paragraph 18.

Occupier's obligations

21. The occupier shall—
(a) pay the pitch fee to the owner;
(b) pay to the owner all sums due under the agreement in respect of gas, electricity, water, sewerage or other services supplied by the owner;
(c) keep the mobile home in a sound state of repair;
(d) maintain—
(i) the outside of the mobile home, and
(ii) the pitch, including all fences and outbuildings belonging to, or enjoyed with, it and the mobile home,
in a clean and tidy condition; and
(e) if requested by the owner, provide him with documentary evidence of any costs or expenses in respect of which the occupier seeks reimbursement.

Owner's obligations

22. The owner shall—
(a) if requested by the occupier, and on payment by the occupier of a charge of not more than £30, provide accurate written details of—
(i) the size of the pitch and the base on which the mobile home is stationed; and
(ii) the location of the pitch and the base within the protected site;
and such details must include measurements between identifiable fixed points on the protected site and the pitch and the base;
(b) if requested by the occupier, provide (free of charge) documentary evidence in support and explanation of—
(i) any new pitch fee;
(ii) any charges for gas, electricity, water, sewerage or other services payable by the occupier to the owner under the agreement; and
(iii) any other charges, costs or expenses payable by the occupier to the owner under the agreement;
(c) be responsible for repairing the base on which the mobile home is stationed and for maintaining any gas, electricity, water, sewerage or other services supplied by the owner to the pitch or to the mobile home;
(d) maintain in a clean and tidy condition those parts of the protected site, including access ways, site boundary fences and trees, which are not the responsibility of any occupier of a mobile home stationed on the protected site;
(e) consult the occupier about improvements to the protected site in general, and in particular about those which the owner wishes to be taken into account when determining the amount of any new pitch fee; and
(f) consult a qualifying residents' association, if there is one, about all matters which relate to the operation and management of, or improvements to, the protected site and may affect the occupiers either directly or indirectly.

23. The owner shall not do or cause to be done anything which may adversely affect the ability of the occupier to perform his obligations under paragraph 21(c) and (d) above.

24. For the purposes of paragraph 22(e) above, to "consult" the occupier means—
 (a) to give the occupier at least 28 clear days' notice in writing of the proposed improvements which—
  (i) describes the proposed improvements and how they will benefit the occupier in the long and short term;
  (ii) details how the pitch fee may be affected when it is next reviewed; and
  (iii) states when and where the occupier can make representations about the proposed improvements; and
 (b) to take into account any representations made by the occupier about the proposed improvements, in accordance with paragraph (a)(iii), before undertaking them.

25. For the purposes of paragraph 22(f) above, to "consult" a qualifying residents' association means—
 (a) to give the association at least 28 clear days' notice in writing of the matters referred to in paragraph 22(f) which—
  (i) describes the matters and how they may affect the occupiers either directly or indirectly in the long and short term; and
  (ii) states when and where the association can make representations about the matters; and
 (b) to take into account any representations made by the association, in accordance with paragraph (a)(ii), before proceeding with the matters.

Owner's name and address

26.—(1) The owner shall by notice inform the occupier and any qualifying residents' association of the address in England or Wales at which notices (including notices of proceedings) may be served on him by the occupier or a qualifying residents' association.

(2) If the owner fails to comply with sub-paragraph (1), then (subject to sub-paragraph (5) below) any amount otherwise due from the occupier to the owner in respect of the pitch fee shall be treated for all purposes as not being due from the occupier to the owner at any time before the owner does so comply.

(3) Where in accordance with the agreement the owner gives any written notice to the occupier or (as the case may be) a qualifying residents' association, the notice must contain the following information—
 (a) the name and address of the owner; and
 (b) if that address is not in England or Wales, an address in England or Wales at which notices (including notices of proceedings) may be served on the owner.

(4) Subject to sub-paragraph (5) below, where—
 (a) the occupier or a qualifying residents' association receives such a notice, but
 (b) it does not contain the information required to be contained in it by virtue of sub-paragraph (3) above,

 the notice shall be treated as not having been given until such time as the owner gives the information to the occupier or (as the case may be) the association in respect of the notice.

(5) An amount or notice within sub-paragraph (2) or (4) (as the case may be) shall not be treated as mentioned in relation to any time when, by virtue of an order of any court or tribunal, there is in force an appointment of a receiver or manager whose functions include receiving from the occupier the pitch fee, payments for services supplied or other charges.

(6) Nothing in sub-paragraphs (3) to (5) applies to any notice containing a demand to which paragraph 27(1) below applies.

27.—(1) Where the owner makes any demand for payment by the occupier of the pitch fee, or in respect of services supplied or other charges, the demand must contain—
 (a) the name and address of the owner; and
 (b) if that address is not in England or Wales, an address in England or Wales at which notices (including notices of proceedings) may be served on the owner.

(2) Subject to sub-paragraph (3) below, where—
 (a) the occupier receives such a demand, but
 (b) it does not contain the information required to be contained in it by virtue of sub-paragraph (1),

the amount demanded shall be treated for all purposes as not being due from the occupier to the owner at any time before the owner gives that information to the occupier in respect of the demand.

(3) The amount demanded shall not be so treated in relation to any time when, by virtue of an order of any court or tribunal, there is in force an appointment of a receiver or manager whose functions include receiving from the occupier the pitch fee, payments for services supplied or other charges.

Qualifying residents' association

28.—(1) A residents' association is a qualifying residents' association in relation to a protected site if—

(a) it is an association representing the occupiers of mobile homes on that site;
(b) at least 50 per cent of the occupiers of the mobile homes on that site are members of the association;
(c) it is independent from the owner, who together with any agent or employee of his is excluded from membership;
(d) subject to paragraph (c) above, membership is open to all occupiers who own a mobile home on that site;
(e) it maintains a list of members which is open to public inspection together with the rules and constitution of the residents' association;
(f) it has a chairman, secretary and treasurer who are elected by and from among the members;
(g) with the exception of administrative decisions taken by the chairman, secretary and treasurer acting in their official capacities, decisions are taken by voting and there is only one vote for each mobile home; and
(h) the owner has acknowledged in writing to the secretary that the association is a qualifying residents' association, or, in default of this, the court has so ordered.

(2) When calculating the percentage of occupiers for the purpose of sub-paragraph (1)(b) above, each mobile home shall be taken to have only one occupier and, in the event of there being more than one occupier of a mobile home, its occupier is to be taken to be the occupier whose name first appears on the agreement.

Interpretation

29. In this Schedule—

"pitch" means the land, forming part of the protected site and including any garden area, on which the occupier is entitled to station the mobile home under the terms of the agreement;

"pitch fee" means the amount which the occupier is required by the agreement to pay to the owner for the right to station the mobile home on the pitch and for use of the common areas of the protected site and their maintenance, but does not include amounts due in respect of gas, electricity, water and sewerage or other services, unless the agreement expressly provides that the pitch fee includes such amounts;

"retail prices index" means the general index (for all items) published by the [Statistics Board] or, if that index is not published for a relevant month, any substituted index or index figures published by [the Board];

"review date" means the date specified in the written statement as the date on which the pitch fee will be reviewed in each year, or if no such date is specified, each anniversary of the date the agreement commenced; and

"written statement" means the written statement that the owner of the protected site is required to give to the occupier by section 1(2) of this Act.]

[1020]

NOTES

Para 5: words in square brackets substituted in relation to England by the Mobile Homes Act 1983 (Amendment of Schedule 1) (England) Order 2006, SI 2006/1755, art 2(1), (2) (subject to transitional provisions and savings). In relation to Wales, the original words read "the court is satisfied that the occupier is not occupying the mobile home as his only or main residence".

Para 6(1): opening para: word in square brackets substituted in relation to England by the Mobile Homes Act 1983 (Amendment of Schedule 1) (England) Order 2006, SI 2006/1755, art 2(1), (3)(a)(i) (subject to transitional provisions and savings), in relation to Wales, the original words read "at the end of a relevant period"; words omitted repealed by the Housing Act 2004, ss 207(1), (2)(a), (6), (7)(a), 266, Sch 16, except in relation to any application made before 18 January 2005 for the purposes of para 6 above.

Para 6(1)(a): word in square brackets substituted in relation to England by the Mobile Homes Act 1983 (Amendment of Schedule 1) (England) Order 2006, SI 2006/1755, art 2(1), (3)(a)(ii) (subject to transitional provisions and savings). In relation to Wales, the original word read "; or".

Para 6(1)(b): substituted in relation to England by the Mobile Homes Act 1983 (Amendment of Schedule 1) (England) Order 2006, SI 2006/1755, art 2(1), (3)(a)(iii) (subject to transitional provisions and savings). In relation to Wales, the original para (b) reads as follows:

"(b) is likely to have such an effect before the end of the next relevant period.".

Para 6(2): repealed in relation to England by the Mobile Homes Act 1983 (Amendment of Schedule 1) (England) Order 2006, SI 2006/1755, art 2(1), (3)(b) (subject to transitional provisions and savings). In relation to Wales, the original para 6(2) reads as follows:

"(2) In sub-paragraph (1) above "relevant period" means the period of five years beginning with the commencement of the agreement and each succeeding period of five years.".

Para 6: sub-paras (3)–(5) inserted, in relation to England and Wales, by the Housing Act 2004, s 207(1), (2)(b) (for effect see s 207(6), (7)(a) thereof), and in relation to Scotland by the Housing (Scotland) Act 2006, s 169(1), (2)(b) (for effect see s 169(5), (6)(a) thereof).

Para 6(3)(a): words omitted repealed in relation to England by the Mobile Homes Act 1983 (Amendment of Schedule 1) (England) Order 2006, SI 2006/1755, art 2(1), (3)(c)(i) (subject to transitional provisions and savings). In relation to Wales, the original words read "or (b)".

Para 6(3)(b): words in square brackets substituted in relation to England by the Mobile Homes Act 1983 (Amendment of Schedule 1) (England) Order 2006, SI 2006/1755, art 2(1), (3)(c)(ii) (subject to transitional provisions and savings). In relation to Wales, original words read "would result in neither of those paragraphs applying to it".

Para 8: sub-paras (1A)–(1G) inserted, in relation to England and Wales, by the Housing Act 2004, s 207(2), (3)(a) (for effect see s 207(6), (7) thereof), and in relation to Scotland by the Housing (Scotland) Act 2006, s 169(1), (3)(a) (for effect see s 169(5), (6)(a) thereof).

Para 8(1C): substituted in relation to England by the Mobile Homes Act 1983 (Amendment of Schedule 1) (England) Order 2006, SI 2006/1755, art 2(1), (4)(a), (subject to transitional provisions and savings). In relation to Wales, the original para 8(1C) reads as follows:

"(1C) A notice under sub-paragraph (1B) above must specify—
(a) if the approval is given subject to conditions, the conditions, and
(b) if the approval is withheld, the reasons for withholding it.".

Para 8(1D): substituted in relation to England by the Mobile Homes Act 1983 (Amendment of Schedule 1) (England) Order 2006, SI 2006/1755, art 2(1), (4)(b) (subject to transitional provisions and savings). In relation to Wales, the original para 8(1D) reads as follows:

"(1D) The giving of approval subject to any condition that is not a reasonable condition does not satisfy the requirement in sub-paragraph (1B)(a) above.".

Para 8(1E): words in square brackets substituted in relation to England by the Mobile Homes Act 1983 (Amendment of Schedule 1) (England) Order 2006, SI 2006/1755, art 2(1), (4)(c) (subject to transitional provisions and savings). In relation to Wales, the original words read "sub-paragraphs (1B) and (1C)".

Para 8(1F)(a): words in square brackets substituted in relation to England by the Mobile Homes Act 1983 (Amendment of Schedule 1) (England) Order 2006, SI 2006/1755, art 2(1), (4)(d)(i) (subject to transitional provisions and savings). In relation to Wales, the original words read "sub-paragraphs (1B) and (1C)".

Para 8(1F)(b): repealed in relation to England by the Mobile Homes Act 1983 (Amendment of Schedule 1) (England) Order 2006, SI 2006/1755, art 2(1), (4)(d)(ii) (subject to transitional provisions and savings). In relation to Wales, the original para 8(1F)(b) reads:

"(b) if he gave his approval subject to any condition and the question arises whether the condition was a reasonable condition, to show that it was;".

Para 8: in sub-para (2) words in square brackets substituted, in relation to England and Wales, by the Housing Act 2004, s 207(1), (3)(b) (for effect see s 207(6), (7) thereof), and in relation to Scotland by the Housing (Scotland) Act 2006, s 169(1), (3)(b) (for effect see s 169(5), (6)(a) thereof).

Para 8(2A): inserted in relation to England by the Mobile Homes Act 1983 (Amendment of Schedule 1) (England) Order 2006, SI 2006/1755, art 2(1), (4)(e) (subject to transitional provisions and savings).

Para 8: in sub-para (3)(a) words in square brackets inserted, in relation to England and Wales, by the Housing Act 2004, s 207(1), (3)(c) (for effect see s 270(6) thereof).

Para 9: sub-para (1) numbered as such and sub-para (2) inserted, in relation to England and Wales, by the Housing Act 2004, s 207(1), (4) (for effect see s 207(6), (7)) thereof) and in relation to Scotland by the Housing (Scotland) Act 2006, s 169(1), (4) (for effect see s 169(5), (6)(a) thereof); sub-para (3) inserted in relation to England by the Mobile Homes Act 1983 (Amendment of Schedule 1) (England) Order 2006, SI 2006/1755, art 2(1), (5) (subject to transitional provisions and savings).

Paras 10–29: substituted (with preceding cross-heading) for para 10 in relation to England by the Mobile Homes Act 1983 (Amendment of Schedule 1) (England) Order 2006, SI 2006/1755, art 2(1), (6) (subject to transitional provisions and savings). In relation to Wales, the original para 10 reads as follows:

"Re-siting of mobile home

10. If the owner is entitled to require that the occupier's right to station the mobile home shall be exercisable for any period in relation to other land forming part of the protected site—
(a) that other land shall be broadly comparable to the land on which the occupier was originally entitled to station the mobile home; and
(b) all costs and expenses incurred in consequence of the requirement shall be paid by the owner.".

Para 29: in definition "retail prices index" words in square brackets substituted by the Statistics and Registration Service Act 2007, s 60(1), Sch 3, para 2.

Order: the Mobile Homes (Commissions) Order 1983, SI 1983/748.

PART II
MATTERS CONCERNING WHICH TERMS MAY BE IMPLIED BY COURT

1. ...

2. The sums payable by the occupier in pursuance of the agreement and the times at which they are to be paid.

3. The review at yearly intervals of the sums so payable.

4. The provision or improvement of services available on the protected site, and the use by the occupier of such services.

5. The preservation of the amenity of the protected site.

6, 7. ...

[1021]

NOTES

Paras 1, 6, 7: repealed by SI 2006/1755, arts 1(2), 3, subject to transitional provisions and savings in arts 1(3), 4 thereof.

Transfer of Functions: functions of the Secretary of State, so far as exercisable in relation to Wales, transferred to the National Assembly for Wales, by the National Assembly for Wales (Transfer of Functions) Order 1999, SI 1999/672, art 2, Sch 1.

[PART III
SUPPLEMENTARY PROVISIONS

Duty to forward requests under paragraph 8 or 9 of Part 1

1.—(1) This paragraph applies to—

(a) a request by the occupier for the owner to approve a person for the purposes of paragraph 8(1) of Part 1 (see paragraph 8(1A)), or

(b) a request by the occupier for the owner to approve a person for the purposes of paragraph 9(1) of Part 1 (see paragraph 8(1A) as applied by paragraph 9(2)).

(2) If a person ("the recipient") receives such a request and he—

(a) though not the owner, has an estate or interest in the protected site, and

(b) believes that another person is the owner (and that the other person has not received such a request),

the recipient owes a duty to the occupier to take such steps as are reasonable to secure that the other person receives the request within the period of 28 days beginning with the date on which the recipient receives it.

(3) In paragraph 8(1B) of Part 1 of this Schedule (as it applies to any request within sub-paragraph (1) above) any reference to the owner receiving such a request includes a reference to his receiving it in accordance with sub-paragraph (2) above.

Action for breach of duty under paragraph 1

2.—(1) A claim that a person has broken the duty under paragraph 1(2) above may be made the subject of civil proceedings in like manner as any other claim in tort for breach of statutory duty.

(2) The right conferred by sub-paragraph (1) is in addition to any right to bring proceedings, in respect of a breach of any implied term having effect by virtue of paragraph 8 or 9 of Part 1 of this Schedule, against a person bound by that term.]

[1022]

NOTES

Commencement: 18 January 2005.

Inserted, in relation to England and Wales, by the Housing Act 2004, s 207(5); for effect see s 207(6), (7)(b) thereof.

(*Sch 2 repeals the Mobile Homes Act 1975, ss 1–6 and repeals in part s 9 thereof.*)

HEALTH AND SOCIAL SERVICES AND SOCIAL SECURITY ADJUDICATIONS ACT 1983

(1983 c 41)

An Act to amend the law relating to the financing of certain social services in England and Wales and Scotland and to children and young persons; to make fresh provision for the Central Council for Education and Training in Social Work and further provision for the remuneration and conditions of service of medical and dental practitioners in the National Health Service and health service officers; to amend the law relating to homes regulated by the Nursing Homes Act 1975, the Child Care Act 1980, the Residential Homes Act 1980 and the Children's Homes Act 1982; to repeal enactments about the designation of health authorities as teaching authorities and membership of authorities so designated; to make further provision for social security adjudication; to make further provision for fees for medical practitioners' certificates relating to notifiable diseases and food poisoning; to abolish certain advisory bodies; to make minor alterations in certain enactments relating to health; and for connected purposes

[13 May 1983]

1–16 ((*Pts I–VI*) *Outside the scope of this work.*)

PART VII
CHARGES FOR LOCAL AUTHORITY SERVICES

17–21 (*Outside the scope of this work.*)

22 Arrears of contributions charged on interest in land in England and Wales

(1) Subject to subsection (2) below, where a person who avails himself of Part III accommodation provided by a local authority in England, Wales or Scotland—

(a) fails to pay any sum assessed as due to be paid by him for the accommodation; and

(b) has a beneficial interest in land in England or Wales,

the local authority may create a charge in their favour on his interest in the land.

(2) In the case of a person who has interests in more than one parcel of land the charge under this section shall be upon his interest in such one of the parcels as the local authority may determine.

[(2A) In determining whether to exercise their power under subsection (1) above and in making any determination under subsection (2) above, the local authority shall comply with any directions given to them by the Secretary of State as to the exercise of those functions.]

(3) …

(4) Subject to subsection (5) below, a charge under this section shall be in respect of any amount assessed as due to be paid which is outstanding from time to time.

(5) The charge on the interest of [an equitable joint tenant in land] shall be in respect of an amount not exceeding the value of the interest that he would enjoy in [the land] if the joint tenancy were severed but the creation of such a charge shall not sever the joint tenancy.

(6) On the death of [an equitable joint tenant in land] whose interest in the [land is] subject to a charge under this section—

(a) if there are surviving joint tenants, their [interests in the land]; and

(b) if the land vests in one person, or one person is entitled to have it vested in him, his interest in it,

shall become subject to a charge for an amount not exceeding the amount of the charge to which the interest of the deceased joint tenant was subject by virtue of subsection (5) above.

(7) A charge under this section shall be created by a declaration in writing made by the local authority.

(8) Any such charge, other than a charge on [the interest of an equitable joint tenant in land], shall in the case of unregistered land be a land charge of Class B within the meaning of section 2 of the Land Charges Act 1972 and in the case of registered land be a registerable charge taking effect as a charge by way of legal mortgage.

[1023]

NOTES

Sub-s (2A): inserted by the National Health Service and Community Care Act 1990, s 45(2).

Sub-s (3): repealed by the Trusts of Land and Appointment of Trustees Act 1996, s 25, Sch 4; for savings in relation to entailed interests created before the commencement of that Act, and savings consequential upon the abolition of the doctrine of conversion, see s 25(4), (5) thereof.

Sub-ss (5), (6), (8): words in square brackets substituted by the Trusts of Land and Appointment of Trustees Act 1996, s 25, Sch 3, para 21; for savings in relation to entailed interests created before the commencement of that Act, and savings consequential upon the abolition of the doctrine of conversion, see s 25(4), (5) thereof.

Transfer of functions: functions of the Secretary of State, so far as exercisable in relation to Wales, transferred to the National Assembly for Wales, by the National Assembly for Wales (Transfer of Functions) Order 1999, SI 1999/672, art 2, Sch 1.

23 (*Outside the scope of this work.*)

24 Interest on sums charged or on secured over interest in land

(1) Any sum charged on or secured over an interest in land under this Part of this Act shall bear interest from the day after than on which the person for whom the local authority provided the accommodation dies.

[(2) The rate of interest shall be such reasonable rate as the Secretary of State may direct or, if no such direction is given, as the local authority may determine.]

[1024]

NOTES

Sub-s (2): substituted by the National Health Service and Community Care Act 1990, s 45(3).

Transfer of functions: functions of the Secretary of State, so far as exercisable in relation to Wales, transferred to the National Assembly for Wales, by the National Assembly for Wales (Transfer of Functions) Order 1999, SI 1999/672, art 2, Sch 1.

25–27 ((*Pt VIII*) *Outside the scope of this work.*)

PART IX
SUPPLEMENTARY

28–32 (*Outside the scope of this work.*)

33 Extent

(1) The following provisions of this Act—
- (a) section 9 and paragraphs 15 and 16 of Schedule 2;
- (b) Part III and Schedule 3;
- (c) section 14(1) (except paragraphs (b) and (c)) and paragraph 1 of Schedule 6;
- (d) section 25(2) and paragraph 31(6) of Schedule 8;
- (e) …

extend to Northern Ireland.

(2) Except where the contrary intention appears, subject to subsection (3) below, where any enactment repealed or amended or instrument revoked by this Act extends to any part of the United Kingdom or to the Channel Islands, the repeal, amendment or revocation extends to that part or those Islands.

(3) Where this Act makes—
- (a) an amendment of an enactment contained in an Act which makes special provision for extending or applying enactments contained in it to the Isles of Scilly; or
- (b) an addition to such an Act,

the provision for extending or applying enactments shall authorise the extension or application of the amended enactment or addition to the Isles.

(4) Subsection (3) above applies to an amended enactment whether or not the enactment was extended or applied to the Isles before it was amended.

(5) Subject to subsections (2) to (4) above, this Act shall, in its application to the Isles, have effect subject to such extensions, adaptations and modifications as the Secretary of State may by order made by statutory instrument prescribe.

(6) Any statutory instrument made in exercise of the power conferred by subsection (5) above shall be subject to annulment in pursuance of a resolution of either House of Parliament.

[1025]

NOTES

Sub-s (1): para (e) repealed by the Statute Law (Repeals) Act 2004.

34 Short title

This Act may be cited as the Health and Social Services and Social Security Adjudications Act 1983.

[1026]

(*Schs 1–10 outside the scope of this work.*)

OCCUPIERS' LIABILITY ACT 1984

(1984 c 3)

An Act to amend the law of England and Wales as to the liability of persons as occupiers of premises for injury suffered by persons other than their visitors; and to amend the Unfair Contract Terms Act 1977, as it applies to England and Wales, in relation to persons obtaining access to premises for recreational or educational purposes

[13 March 1984]

1 Duty of occupier to persons other than his visitors

(1) The rules enacted by this section shall have effect, in place of the rules of the common law, to determine—
- (a) whether any duty is owed by a person as occupier of premises to persons other than his visitors in respect of any risk of their suffering injury on the premises by reason of any danger due to the state of the premises or to things done or omitted to be done on them; and
- (b) if so, what that duty is.

(2) For the purposes of this section, the persons who are to be treated respectively as an occupier of any premises (which, for those purposes, include any fixed or movable structure) and as his visitors are—

(a) any person who owes in relation to the premises the duty referred to in section 2 of the Occupiers' Liability Act 1957 (the common duty of care), and

(b) those who are his visitors for the purposes of that duty.

(3) An occupier of premises owes a duty to another (not being his visitor) in respect of any such risk as is referred to in subsection (1) above if—

(a) he is aware of the danger or has reasonable grounds to believe that it exists;

(b) he knows or has reasonable grounds to believe that the other is in the vicinity of the danger concerned or that he may come into the vicinity of the danger (in either case, whether the other has lawful authority for being in that vicinity or not); and

(c) the risk is one against which, in all the circumstances of the case, he may reasonably be expected to offer the other some protection.

(4) Where, by virtue of this section, an occupier of premises owes a duty to another in respect of such a risk, the duty is to take such care as is reasonable in all the circumstances of the case to see that he does not suffer injury on the premises by reason of the danger concerned.

(5) Any duty owed by virtue of this section in respect of a risk may, in an appropriate case, be discharged by taking such steps as are reasonable in all the circumstances of the case to give warning of the danger concerned or to discourage persons from incurring the risk.

(6) No duty is owed by virtue of this section to any person in respect of risks willingly accepted as his by that person (the question whether a risk was so accepted to be decided on the same principles as in other cases in which one person owes a duty of care to another).

[(6A) At any time when the right conferred by section 2(1) of the Countryside and Rights of Way Act 2000 is exercisable in relation to land which is access land for the purposes of Part I of that Act, an occupier of the land owes (subject to subsection (6C) below) no duty by virtue of this section to any person in respect of—

(a) a risk resulting from the existence of any natural feature of the landscape, or any river, stream, ditch or pond whether or not a natural feature, or

(b) a risk of that person suffering injury when passing over, under or through any wall, fence or gate, except by proper use of the gate or of a stile.

(6B) For the purposes of subsection (6A) above, any plant, shrub or tree, of whatever origin, is to be regarded as a natural feature of the landscape.

(6C) Subsection (6A) does not prevent an occupier from owing a duty by virtue of this section in respect of any risk where the danger concerned is due to anything done by the occupier—

(a) with the intention of creating that risk, or

(b) being reckless as to whether that risk is created.]

(7) No duty is owed by virtue of this section to persons using the highway, and this section does not affect any duty owed to such persons.

(8) Where a person owes a duty by virtue of this section, he does not, by reason of any breach of the duty, incur any liability in respect of any loss of or damage to property.

(9) In this section—

"highway" means any part of a highway other than a ferry or waterway;

"injury" means anything resulting in death or personal injury, including any disease and any impairment of physical or mental condition; and

"movable structure" includes any vessel, vehicle or aircraft.

[1027]

NOTES

Sub-ss (6A)–(6C): inserted by the Countryside and Rights of Way Act 2000, s 13(2).

[1A Special considerations relating to access land

In determining whether any, and if so what, duty is owed by virtue of section 1 by an occupier of land at any time when the right conferred by section 2(1) of the Countryside and Rights of Way Act 2000 is exercisable in relation to the land, regard is to be had, in particular, to—

(a) the fact that the existence of that right ought not to place an undue burden (whether financial or otherwise) on the occupier,

(b) the importance of maintaining the character of the countryside, including features of historic, traditional or archaeological interest, and

(c) any relevant guidance given under section 20 of that Act.]

[1028]

NOTES

Commencement: 19 September 2004 (in relation to England); 28 May 2005 (in relation to Wales).
Inserted by the Countryside and Rights of Way Act 2000, s 13(3).

2 (*Amends the Unfair Contract Terms Act 1977, s 1(3).*)

3 Application to Crown

Section 1 of this Act shall bind the Crown, but as regards the Crown's liability in tort shall not bind the Crown further than the Crown is made liable in tort by the Crown Proceedings Act 1947.
[1029]

4 Short title, commencement and extent

(1) This Act may be cited as the Occupiers' Liability Act 1984.

(2) This Act shall come into force at the end of the period of two months beginning with the day on which it is passed.

(3) This Act extends to England and Wales only.
[1030]

COUNTY COURTS ACT 1984

(1984 c 28)

An Act to consolidate certain enactments relating to county courts

[26 June 1984]

PART I
CONSTITUTION AND ADMINISTRATION

1, 2 (*Outside the scope of this work.*)

Places and times of sittings of courts

3 (*Outside the scope of this work.*)

4 Use of public buildings for courts

(1) Where, in any place in which a county court is held, there is a building, being a town hall, court-house or other public building belonging to any local or other public authority, that building shall, with all necessary rooms, furniture and fittings in it, be used for the purpose of holding the court, without any charge for rent or other payment, except the reasonable and necessary charges for lighting, heating and cleaning the building when used for that purpose.

(2) Where any such building is used for the purpose of holding any court, the sittings of the court shall be so arranged as not to interfere with the business of the local or other public authority usually transacted in the building or with any purpose for which the building may be used by virtue of any local Act.

(3) This section shall not apply to any place in which a building was erected before 1st January 1889 for the purpose of holding and carrying on the business of a county court.
[1031]

5–14 (*Ss 5, 6, 8, 9, 11–14 outside the scope of this work; s 7 repealed by the Judicial Pensions and Retirement Act 1993, s 31(3), (4), Sch 8, para 17(a), Sch 9; s 10 repealed by the Courts and Legal Services Act 1990, s 125(7), Sch 20.*)

PART II
JURISDICTION AND TRANSFER OF PROCEEDINGS

Actions of contract and tort

15 (*Outside the scope of this work.*)

16 Money recoverable by statute

A county court shall have jurisdiction to hear and determine an action for the recovery of a sum recoverable by virtue of any enactment for the time being in force, if—

(a) it is not provided by that or any other enactment that such sums shall only be recoverable in the High Court or shall only be recoverable summarily; …

(b) …

[1032]

NOTES

Words omitted repealed by SI 1991/724, art 2(8), Schedule.

17–20 *(Ss 17, 18 outside the scope of this work; ss 19, 20 repealed by the Courts and Legal Services Act 1990, s 125, Sch 20.)*

Recovery of land and cases where title in question

21 Actions for recovery of land and actions where title is in question

(1) A county court shall have jurisdiction to hear and determine any action for the recovery of land …

(2) A county court shall have jurisdiction to hear and determine any action in which the title to any hereditament comes in question …

(3) Where a mortgage of land consists of or includes a dwelling-house and no part of the land is situated in Greater London then, subject to subsection (4), if a county court has jurisdiction by virtue of this section to hear and determine an action in which the mortgagee under that mortgage claims possession of the mortgaged property, no court other than a county court shall have jurisdiction to hear and determine that action.

(4) Subsection (3) shall not apply to an action for foreclosure or sale in which a claim for possession of the mortgaged property is also made.

(5), (6) …

(7) In this section—

"dwelling-house" includes any building or part of a building which is used as a dwelling;

"mortgage" includes a charge and "mortgagor" and "mortgagee" shall be construed accordingly;

"mortgagor" and "mortgagee" includes any person deriving title under the original mortgagor or mortgagee.

(8) The fact that part of the premises comprised in a dwelling-house is used as a shop or office or for business, trade or professional purposes shall not prevent the dwelling-house from being a dwelling-house for the purposes of this section.

(9) This section does not apply to a mortgage securing an agreement which is a regulated agreement within the meaning of the Consumer Credit Act 1974.

[1033]

NOTES

Sub-ss (1), (2): words omitted repealed by SI 1991/724, art 2(8), Schedule, Pt I.

Sub-ss (5), (6): repealed by SI 1991/724, art 2(8), Schedule, Pt I.

22 *(Repealed by the Courts and Legal Services Act 1990, s 125(7), Sch 20.)*

Equity proceedings

23 Equity jurisdiction

A county court shall have all the jurisdiction of the High Court to hear and determine—

(a) proceedings for the administration of the estate of a deceased person, where the estate does not exceed in amount or value the county court limit;

(b) proceedings—

(i) for the execution of any trust, or

(ii) for a declaration that a trust subsists, or

(iii) under section 1 of the Variation of Trusts Act 1958,

where the estate or fund subject, or alleged to be subject, to the trust does not exceed in amount or value the county court limit;

(c) proceedings for foreclosure or redemption of any mortgage or for enforcing any charge or lien, where the amount owing in respect of the mortgage, charge or lien does not exceed the county court limit;

(d) proceedings for the specific performance, or for the rectification, delivery up or cancellation, of any agreement for the sale, purchase or lease of any property, where, in the case of a sale or purchase, the purchase money, or in the case of a lease, the value of the property, does not exceed the county court limit;

(e) proceedings relating to the maintenance or advancement of a minor, where the property of the minor does not exceed in amount or value the county court limit;
(f) proceedings for the dissolution or winding-up of any partnership (whether or not the existence of the partnership is in dispute), where the whole assets of the partnership do not exceed in amount or value the county court limit;
(g) proceedings for relief against fraud or mistake, where the damage sustained or the estate or fund in respect of which relief is sought does not exceed in amount or value the county court limit.

[1034]

24 Jurisdiction by agreement in certain equity proceedings

(1) If, as respects any proceedings to which this section applies, the parties agree, by a memorandum signed by them or by their respective [legal representatives] or agents, that a county court specified in the memorandum shall have jurisdiction in the proceedings, that court shall, notwithstanding anything in any enactment, have jurisdiction to hear and determine the proceedings accordingly.

(2) Subject to subsection (3), this section applies to any proceedings in which a county court would have jurisdiction by virtue of—
(a) section 113(3) of the Settled Land Act 1925,
(b) section 63A of the Trustee Act 1925,
(c) sections 3(7), … , 49(4), 66(4), 89(7), 90(3), 91(8), 92(2), 136(3), … , 181(2), 188(2) of, and paragraph 3A of Part III and paragraph 1(3A) and (4A) of Part IV of Schedule 1 to, the Law of Property Act 1925,
(d) sections 17(2), 38(4), 41(1A), and 43(4) of the Administration of Estates Act 1925,
(e) section 6(1) of the Leasehold Property (Repairs) Act 1938,
(f) sections 1(6A) and 5(11) of the Land Charges Act 1972, and
(g) sections 23 … of this Act,

but for the limits of the jurisdiction of the court provided in those enactments.

(3) This section does not apply to proceedings under section 1 of the Variation of Trusts Act 1958.

[1035]

NOTES

Sub-s (1): words in square brackets substituted by the Courts and Legal Services Act 1990, s 125(3), Sch 18, para 49.

Sub-s (2): in para (c), figures omitted repealed by SI 1991/724, art 2(8), Schedule; in para (g) words omitted repealed by the Statute Law (Repeals) Act 2004.

Modification: references to solicitors etc modified to include references to bodies recognised under the Administration of Justice Act 1985, s 9, by the Solicitors' Incorporated Practices Order 1991, SI 1991/2684, arts 4, 5, Sch 1.

Family provision proceedings

25 Jurisdiction under Inheritance (Provision for Family and Dependants) Act 1975

A county court shall have jurisdiction to hear and determine any application for an order under section 2 of the Inheritance (Provision for Family and Dependants) Act 1975 (including any application for permission to apply for such an order and any application made, in the proceedings on an application for such an order, for an order under any other provision of that Act) …

[1036]

NOTES

Words omitted repealed by SI 1991/724, art 2(8), Schedule.

26–39 (*Outside the scope of this work.*)

Transfer of proceedings

[40 Transfer of proceedings to county court

(1) Where the High Court is satisfied that any proceedings before it are required by any provision of a kind mentioned in subsection (8) to be in a county court it shall—
(a) order the transfer of the proceedings to a county court; or
(b) if the court is satisfied that the person bringing the proceedings knew, or ought to have known, of that requirement, order that they be struck out.

(2) Subject to any such provision, the High Court may order the transfer of any proceedings before it to a county court.

(3) An order under this section may be made either on the motion of the High Court itself or on the application of any party to the proceedings.

(4) Proceedings transferred under this section shall be transferred to such county court as the High Court considers appropriate, having taken into account the convenience of the parties and that of any other persons likely to be affected and the state of business in the courts concerned.

(5) The transfer of any proceedings under this section shall not affect any right of appeal from the order directing the transfer.

(6) Where proceedings for the enforcement of any judgment or order of the High Court are transferred under this section—

(a) the judgment or order may be enforced as if it were a judgment or order of a county court; and

(b) subject to subsection (7), it shall be treated as a judgment or order of that court for all purposes.

(7) Where proceedings for the enforcement of any judgment or order of the High Court are transferred under this section—

(a) the powers of any court to set aside, correct, vary or quash a judgment or order of the High Court, and the enactments relating to appeals from such a judgment or order, shall continue to apply; and

(b) the powers of any court to set aside, correct, vary or quash a judgment or order of a county court, and the enactments relating to appeals from such a judgment or order, shall not apply.

(8) The provisions referred to in subsection (1) are any made—

(a) under section 1 of the Courts and Legal Services Act 1990; or

(b) by or under any other enactment.

(9) This section does not apply to family proceedings within the meaning of Part V of the Matrimonial and Family Proceedings Act 1984.]

[1037]

NOTES

Substituted by the Courts and Legal Services Act 1990, s 2(1).

41 Transfer to High Court by Order of High Court

(1) If at any stage in proceedings commenced in a county court or transferred to a county court under section 40, the High Court thinks it desirable that the proceedings, or any part of them, should be heard and determined in the High Court, it may order the transfer to the High Court of the proceedings or, as the case may be, of that part of them.

(2) The power conferred by subsection (1) is without prejudice to section 29 of the *Supreme Court Act 1981* [Senior Courts Act 1981] (power of High Court to issue prerogative orders) [but shall be exercised in relation to family proceedings (within the meaning of Part V of the Matrimonial and Family Proceedings Act 1984) in accordance with any directions given under section 37 of that Act (directions as to distribution and transfer of family business and proceedings)].

[(3) The power conferred by subsection (1) shall be exercised subject to any provision made—

(a) under section 1 of the Courts and Legal Services Act 1990; or

(b) by or under any other enactment.]

[1038]

NOTES

Sub-s (2): words in italics substituted by subsequent words in square brackets by the Constitutional Reform Act 2005, s 59(5), Sch 11, Pt 1, para 1(2), as from 1 October 2009; second words in square brackets inserted by the Matrimonial and Family Proceedings Act 1984, s 46(1), Sch 1, para 30.

Sub-s (3): inserted by the Courts and Legal Services Act 1990, s 2(2).

[42 Transfer to High Court by order of a county court

(1) Where a county court is satisfied that any proceedings before it are required by any provision of a kind mentioned in subsection (7) to be in the High Court, it shall—

(a) order the transfer of the proceedings to the High Court; or

(b) if the court is satisfied that the person bringing the proceedings knew, or ought to have known, of that requirement, order that they be struck out.

(2) Subject to any such provision, a county court may order the transfer of any proceedings before it to the High Court.

(3) An order under this section may be made either on the motion of the court itself or on the application of any party to the proceedings.

(4) The transfer of any proceedings under this section shall not affect any right of appeal from the order directing the transfer.

(5) Where proceedings for the enforcement of any judgment or order of a county court are transferred under this section—

(a) the judgment or order may be enforced as if it were a judgment or order of the High Court; and
(b) subject to subsection (6), it shall be treated as a judgment or order of that court for all purposes.

(6) Where proceedings for the enforcement of any judgment or order of a county court are transferred under this section—
(a) the powers of any court to set aside, correct, vary or quash a judgment or order of a county court, and the enactments relating to appeals from such a judgment or order, shall continue to apply; and
(b) the powers of any court to set aside, correct, vary or quash a judgment or order of the High Court, and the enactments relating to appeals from such a judgment or order, shall not apply.

(7) The provisions referred to in subsection (1) are any made—
(a) under section 1 of the Courts and Legal Services Act 1990; or
(b) by or under any other enactment.

(8) This section does not apply to family proceedings within the meaning of Part V of the Matrimonial and Family Proceedings Act 1984.]

[1039]

NOTES

Substituted by the Courts and Legal Services Act 1990, s 2(3).

43–45 (*Outside the scope of this work.*)

PART III
PROCEDURE

46–68 (*Outside the scope of this work.*)

Interest on debts and damages

69 Power to award interest on debts and damages

(1) Subject to [rules of court], in proceedings (whenever instituted) before a county court for the recovery of a debt or damages there may be included in any sum for which judgment is given simple interest, at such rate as the court thinks fit or as may be prescribed, on all or any part of the debt or damages in respect of which judgment is given, or payment is made before judgment, for all or any part of the period between the date when the cause of action arose and—
(a) in the case of any sum paid before judgment, the date of the payment; and
(b) in the case of the sum for which judgment is given, the date of the judgment.

(2) In relation to a judgment given for damages for personal injuries or death which exceed £200 subsection (1) shall have effect—
(a) with the substitution of "shall be included" for "may be included"; and
(b) with the addition of "unless the court is satisfied that there are special reasons to the contrary" after "given", where first occurring.

(3) Subject to [rules of court], where—
(a) there are proceedings (whenever instituted) before a county court for the recovery of a debt; and
(b) the defendant pays the whole debt to the plaintiff (otherwise than in pursuance of a judgment in the proceedings),

the defendant shall be liable to pay the plaintiff simple interest, at such rate as the court thinks fit or as may be prescribed, on all or any part of the debt for all or any part of the period between the date when the cause of action arose and the date of the payment.

(4) Interest in respect of a debt shall not be awarded under this section for a period during which, for whatever reason, interest on the debt already runs.

(5) Interest under this section may be calculated at different rates in respect of different periods.

(6) In this section "plaintiff" means the person seeking the debt or damages and "defendant" means the person from whom the plaintiff seeks the debt or damages and "personal injuries" includes any disease and any impairment of a person's physical or mental condition.

(7) Nothing in this section affects the damages recoverable for the dishonour of a bill of exchange.

[(8) In determining whether the amount of any debt or damages exceeds that prescribed by or under any enactment, no account shall be taken of any interest payable by virtue of this section except where express provision to the contrary is made by or under that or any other enactment.]

[1040]

NOTES

Sub-ss (1), (3): words in square brackets substituted by the Civil Procedure Act 1997, s 10, Sch 2, para 2(2).
Sub-s (8): substituted by the Courts and Legal Services Act 1990, s 125(3), Sch 18, para 46.

70–73A (*Outside the scope of this work.*)

74 Interest on judgment debts etc

(1) The Lord Chancellor may by order made with the concurrence of the Treasury provide that any sums to which this subsection applies shall carry interest at such rate and between such times as may be prescribed by the order.

(2) The sums to which subsection (1) applies are—

(a) sums payable under judgments or orders given or made in a county court, including sums payable by instalments; and

(b) sums which by virtue of any enactment are, if the county court so orders, recoverable as if payable under an order of that court, and in respect of which the county court has so ordered.

(3) The payment of interest due under subsection (1) shall be enforceable as a sum payable under the judgment or order.

(4) The power conferred by subsection (1) includes power—

(a) to specify the descriptions of judgment or order in respect of which interest shall be payable;

(b) to provide that interest shall be payable only on sums exceeding a specified amount;

(c) to make provision for the manner in which and the periods by reference to which the interest is to be calculated and paid;

(d) to provide that any enactment shall or shall not apply in relation to interest payable under subsection (1) or shall apply to it with such modifications as may be specified in the order; and

(e) to make such incidental or supplementary provisions as the Lord Chancellor considers appropriate.

(5) Without prejudice to the generality of subsection (4), an order under subsection (1) may provide that the rate of interest shall be the rate specified in section 17 of the Judgments Act 1838 as that enactment has effect from time to time.

[(5A) The power conferred by subsection (1) includes power to make provision enabling a county court to order that the rate of interest applicable to a sum expressed in a currency other than sterling shall be such rate as the court thinks fit (instead of the rate otherwise applicable).]

(6) The power to make an order under subsection (1) shall be exercisable by statutory instrument subject to annulment in pursuance of a resolution of either House of Parliament.

[1041]

NOTES

Sub-s (5A): inserted by the Private International Law (Miscellaneous Provisions) Act 1995, s 2.
Order: the County Courts (Interest on Judgment Debts) Order 1991, SI 1991/1184.

74A–127 (*Ss 74A–76, ss 77–127 (Pts IV–VIII) outside the scope of this work.*)

PART IX
MISCELLANEOUS AND GENERAL

128–137 (*S 128 repealed by the Courts Act 2003, s 109(1), (3), Sch 8, para 276, Sch 10; s 134 repealed by SI 1998/2940, art 6(f); ss 129–133, 135–137 outside the scope of this work.*)

Forfeiture for non-payment of rent

138 Provisions as to forfeiture for non-payment of rent

(1) This section has effect where a lessor is proceeding by action in a county court (being an action in which the county court has jurisdiction) to enforce against a lessee a right of re-entry or forfeiture in respect of any land for non-payment of rent.

(2) If the lessee pays into court [or to the lessor] not less than 5 clear days before the return day all the rent in arrear and the costs of the action, the action shall cease, and the lessee shall hold the land according to the lease without any new lease.

(3) If—

(a) the action does not cease under subsection (2); and

(b) the court at the trial is satisfied that the lessor is entitled to enforce the right of re-entry or forfeiture,

the court shall order possession of the land to be given to the lessor at the expiration of such period, not being less than 4 weeks from the date of the order, as the court thinks fit, unless within that period the lessee pays into court [or to the lessor] all the rent in arrear and the costs of the action.

(4) The court may extend the period specified under subsection (3) at any time before possession of the land is recovered in pursuance of the order under that subsection.

(5) … if—

(a) within the period specified in the order; or

(b) within that period as extended under subsection (4),

the lessee pays into court [or to the lessor]—

(i) all the rent in arrear; and

(ii) the costs of the action,

he shall hold the land according to the lease without any new lease.

(6) Subsection (2) shall not apply where the lessor is proceeding in the same action to enforce a right of re-entry or forfeiture on any other ground as well as for non-payment of rent, or to enforce any other claim as well as the right of re-entry or forfeiture and the claim for arrears of rent.

(7) If the lessee does not—

(a) within the period specified in the order; or

(b) within that period as extended under subsection (4),

pay into court [or to the lessor]—

(i) all the rent in arrear; and

(ii) the costs of the action,

the order shall be [enforceable] in the prescribed manner and so long as the order remains unreversed the lessee shall[, subject to subsections (8) and (9A),] be barred from all relief.

(8) The extension under subsection (4) of a period fixed by a court shall not be treated as relief from which the lessee is barred by subsection (7) if he fails to pay into court [or to the lessor] all the rent in arrear and the costs of the action within that period.

(9) Where the court extends a period under subsection (4) at a time when—

(a) that period has expired; and

(b) a warrant has been issued for the possession of the land, the court shall suspend the warrant for the extended period; and, if, before the expiration period, the lessee pays into court [or to the lessor] all the rent in arrear and all the costs of the action, the court shall cancel the warrant.

[(9A) Where the lessor recovers possession of the land at any time after the making of the order under subsection (3) (whether as a result of the enforcement of the order or otherwise) the lessee may, at any time within six months from the date on which the lessor recovers possession, apply to the court for relief; and on any such application the court may, if it thinks fit, grant to the lessee such relief, subject to such terms and conditions, as it thinks fit.

(9B) Where the lessee is granted relief on an application under subsection (9A) he shall hold the land according to the lease without any new lease.

(9C) An application under subsection (9A) may be made by a person with an interest under a lease of the land derived (whether immediately or otherwise) from the lessee's interest therein in like manner as if he were the lessee; and on any such application the court may make an order which (subject to such terms and conditions as the court thinks fit) vests the land in such a person, as lessee of the lessor, for the remainder of the term of the lease under which he has any such interest as aforesaid, or for any lesser term.

In this subsection any reference to the land includes a reference to a part of the land.]

(10) Nothing in this section or section 139 shall be taken to affect—

(a) the power of the court to make any order which it would otherwise have power to make as respects a right of re-entry or forfeiture on any ground other than non-payment of rent; or

(b) section 146(4) of the Law of Property Act 1925 (relief against forfeiture).

[1042]

NOTES

Sub-ss (2), (3), (8), (9): words in square brackets inserted by the Courts and Legal Services Act 1990, s 125(2), Sch 17, para 17.

Sub-s (5): words omitted repealed by the Administration of Justice Act 1985, ss 55(2), 67(2), Sch 8, Pt III; words in square brackets inserted by the Courts and Legal Services Act 1990, s 125(2), Sch 17, para 17.

Sub-s (7): first words in square brackets inserted by the Courts and Legal Services Act 1990, s 125(2), Sch 17, para 17; second words in square brackets substituted and final words in square brackets inserted, by the Administration of Justice Act 1985, s 55(3).

Sub-ss (9A)–(9C): inserted by the Administration of Justice Act 1985, s 55(4).

139 Service of summons and re-entry

(1) In a case where section 138 has effect, if—

(a) one-half-year's rent is in arrear at the time of the commencement of the action; and

(b) the lessor has a right to re-enter for non-payment of that rent; and

(*c*) *no sufficient distress is to be found on the premises countervailing the arrears then due,*

[(c) the power under section 72(1) of the Tribunals, Courts and Enforcement Act 2007 (commercial rent arrears recovery) is exercisable to recover the arrears; and

(d) there are not sufficient goods on the premises to recover the arrears by that power,]

the service of the summons in the action in the prescribed manner shall stand in lieu of a demand and re-entry.

(2) Where a lessor has enforced against a lessee, by re-entry without action, a right of re-entry or forfeiture as respects any land for non-payment of rent, the lessee may … at any time within six months from the date on which the lessor re-entered apply to the county court for relief, and on any such application the court may, if it thinks fit, grant to the lessee such relief as the High Court could have granted.

[(3) Subsections (9B) and (9C) of section 138 shall have effect in relation to an application under subsection (2) of this section as they have effect in relation to an application under subsection (9A) of that section.]

[1043]

NOTES

Sub-s (1): para (c) substituted, by subsequent paras (c), (d) in square brackets, by the Tribunals, Courts and Enforcement Act 2007, s 86, Sch 14, paras 38, 40, as from a day to be appointed.

Sub-s (2): words omitted repealed by SI 1991/724, art 2(8), Schedule.

Sub-s (3): inserted by the Administration of Justice Act 1985, s 55.

140 Interpretation of sections 138 and 139

For the purposes of sections 138 and 139—

"lease" includes—

(a) an original or derivative under-lease;

(b) an agreement for a lease where the lessee has become entitled to have his lease granted; and

(c) a grant at a fee farm rent, or under a grant securing a rent by condition;

"lessee" includes—

(a) an original or derivative under-lessee;

(b) the persons deriving title under a lessee;

(c) a grantee under a grant at a fee farm rent, or under a grant securing a rent by condition; and

(d) the persons deriving title under such a grantee;

"lessor" includes—

(a) an original or derivative under-lessor;

(b) the persons deriving title under a lessor;

(c) a person making a grant at a fee farm rent, or a grant securing a rent by condition; and

(d) the persons deriving title under such a grantor;

"under-lease" includes an agreement for an under-lease where the under-lessee has become entitled to have his underlease granted; and

"under-lessee" includes any person deriving title under an under-lessee.

[1044]

141–144 (*S 141 repealed by the Statute Law (Repeals) Act 1986; ss 142–144 outside the scope of this work.*)

Power to raise monetary limits

145 Power to raise monetary limits

(1) If it appears to Her Majesty in Council—

(a) that the county court limit for the purposes of any enactment referring to that limit, or

(b) that the higher limit or the lower limit referred to in section 20 of this Act,

should be increased, Her Majesty may by Order in Council direct that the limit in question shall be such amount as may be specified in the Order.

(2) An Order under subsection (1) may contain such incidental or transitional provisions as Her Majesty considers appropriate.

[(2A) It is for the Lord Chancellor to recommend to Her Majesty the making of an Order under subsection (1).]

(3) No recommendation shall be made to Her Majesty in Council to make an Order under this section unless a draft of the Order has been laid before Parliament and approved by resolution of each House of Parliament.

[1045]

NOTES

Sub-s (2A): inserted by the Constitutional Reform Act 2005, s 15(1), Sch 4, Pt 1, paras 160, 170.
Order: the County Courts Jurisdiction Order 1981, SI 1981/1123.

General

146 (*Outside the scope of this work.*)

147 Interpretation

(1) In this Act, unless the context otherwise requires—

"action" means any proceedings in a county court which may be commenced as prescribed by plaint;

"Admiralty county court" means a county court appointed to have Admiralty jurisdiction by order under this Act;

"Admiralty proceedings" means proceedings in which the claim would not be within the jurisdiction of a county court but for sections 26 and 27;

"bailiff" includes a [district judge];

"the county court limit" means—

(a) in relation to any enactment contained in this Act for which a limit is for the time being specified by an Order under section 145, that limit,

(b) …

(c) in relation to any enactment contained in this Act and not within paragraph (a) … , the county court limit for the time being specified by any other Order in Council or order defining the limit of county court jurisdiction for the purposes of that enactment;

…

"court" and "county court" mean a court held for a district under this Act;

["deposit-taking institution" means a person who may, in the course of his business, lawfully accept deposits in the United Kingdom;]

"district" and "county district" mean a district for which a court is to be held under section 2;

…

"hearing" includes trial, and "hear" and "heard" shall be construed accordingly;

"hereditament" includes both a corporeal and an incorporeal hereditament;

"judge", in relation to a county court, means a judge assigned to the district of that court under subsection (1) of section 5 and any person sitting as a judge for that district under subsection (3) or (4) of that section;

"judgment summons" means a summons issued on the application of a person entitled to enforce a judgment or order under section 5 of the Debtors Act 1869 requiring a person, or, where two or more persons are liable under the judgment or order, requiring any one or more of them, [to attend court];

"landlord", in relation to any land, means the person entitled to the immediate reversion or, if the property therein is held in joint tenancy, any of the persons entitled to the immediate reversion;

["legal representative" means *an authorised advocate or authorised litigator, as defined by section 119(1) of the Courts and Legal Services Act 1990;* [a person who, for the purposes of the Legal Services Act 2007, is an authorised person in relation to an activity which constitutes the exercise of a right of audience or the conduct of litigation (within the meaning of that Act);]]

…

"matter" means every proceeding in a county court which may be commenced as prescribed otherwise than by plaint;

"officer", in relation to a court, means [any district judge or deputy district judge assigned to that court], and any clerk, bailiff, usher or messenger in the service of that court;

"part-time [district judge]" and "part-time [assistant district judge]" have the meaning assigned to them by section 10(3);

"party" includes every person served with notice of, or attending, any proceeding, whether named as a party to that proceeding or not;

"prescribed" means prescribed by [rules of court];

"probate proceedings" means proceedings brought in a county court by virtue of section 32 or transferred to that court under section 40;

"proceedings" includes both actions and matters;

"[district judge]" and "[district judge] of a county court" mean a [district judge] appointed for a district under this Act, or, in a case where two or more [district judges] are appointed jointly, either or any of those [district judges];

"return day" means the day appointed in any summons or proceeding for the appearance of the defendant or any other day fixed for the hearing of any proceedings;

...

"ship" includes any description of vessel used in navigation;

"solicitor" means solicitor of the *Supreme Court* [Senior Courts];

...

...

[(1A) The definition of "deposit-taking institution" in subsection (1) must be read with—

(a) section 22 of the Financial Services and Markets Act 2000;

(b) any relevant order under that section; and

(c) Schedule 2 to that Act.]

(2), (3) ...

[1046]

NOTES

Sub-s (1): definition "bailiff" repealed by the Tribunals, Courts and Enforcement Act 2007, ss 62(3), 146, Sch 13, paras 68, 82, Sch 23, Pt 3, as from a day to be appointed, and words in square brackets therein substituted by virtue of the Courts and Legal Services Act 1990, s 74(1), (3); in definition "the county court limit" words omitted repealed by SI 1991/724, art 2(8), Schedule; definition "county court rules" (omitted) repealed by the Civil Procedure Act 1997, s 10, Sch 2, para 2(9); definition "deposit-taking institution" substituted by SI 2001/3649, art 296(1), (2); definition "fees orders" (omitted) repealed by the Courts Act 2003, s 109(1), (3), Sch 8, para 277, Sch 10; in definition "judgment summons" words in square brackets substituted by SI 2002/439, arts 2, 9; definition "legal representative" inserted by the Courts and Legal Services Act 1990, s 125(3), Sch 18, para 49, and words in italics repealed and subsequent words in square brackets substituted by the Legal Services Act 2007, s 208(1), Sch 21, para 61, as from a day to be appointed; definition "matrimonial cause" (omitted) repealed by the Matrimonial and Family Proceedings Act 1984, s 46(3), Sch 3; in definition "officer" words in square brackets substituted by the Tribunals, Courts and Enforcement Act 2007, s 56, Sch 11, paras 5, 9; in definition "part-time district judge" words in square brackets substituted by virtue of the Courts and Legal Services Act 1990, s 74(1), (3); in definition "prescribed" words in square brackets substituted by the Civil Procedure Act 1997, s 10, Sch 2, para 2(2); in definition "district judge" (definition "registrar" as originally enacted) words in square brackets substituted by virtue of the Courts and Legal Services Act 1990, s 74(1), (3); definition "the rule committee" (omitted) repealed by the Civil Procedure Act 1997, s 10, Sch 2, para 2(9); in definition "solicitor" words in italics substituted by subsequent words in square brackets by the Constitutional Reform Act 2005, s 59(5), Sch 11, Pt 2, para 4(1), (3), as from 1 October 2009; definitions "standard scale" and "statutory minimum" (omitted) repealed by the Statute Law (Repeals) Act 1993.

Sub-s (1A): inserted by SI 2001/3649, art 296(1), (3).

Sub-ss (2), (3): repealed by SI 1990/776, art 3, Sch 1.

Modification: a registered European lawyer may provide professional activities by way of legal advice and assistance or legal aid, and this Act shall be interpreted accordingly: see the European Communities (Lawyer's Practice) Regulations 2000, SI 2000/1119, reg 14.

148–150 (*Outside the scope of this work.*)

151 Short title

This Act may be cited as the County Courts Act 1984.

(*Schs 1–4 outside the scope of this work.*)

MATRIMONIAL AND FAMILY PROCEEDINGS ACT 1984

(1984 c 42)

An Act to amend the Matrimonial Causes Act 1973 so far as it restricts the time within which proceedings for divorce or nullity of marriage can be instituted; to amend that Act, the Domestic Proceedings and Magistrates' Courts Act 1978 and the Magistrates' Courts Act 1980 so far as they relate to the exercise of the jurisdiction of courts in England and Wales to make provision for financial relief or to exercise related powers in matrimonial and certain other family proceedings; to make provision for financial relief to be available where a marriage has been dissolved or annulled, or the parties to a marriage have been legally separated, in a country overseas; to make related amendments in the Maintenance Orders (Reciprocal Enforcement) Act 1972 and the Inheritance (Provision for Family and Dependants) Act 1975; to make provision for the distribution and transfer between the High Court and county courts of, and the exercise in those courts of jurisdiction in, family business and family proceedings and to repeal and re-enact with amendments certain provisions conferring on designated county courts jurisdiction in matrimonial proceedings; to impose a duty to notify changes of address on persons liable to make payments under maintenance orders enforceable under Part II of the Maintenance Orders Act 1950 or Part I of the Maintenance Orders Act 1958; and for connected purposes

[12 July 1984]

1–11 *((Pts I, II) outside the scope of this work.)*

PART III
FINANCIAL RELIEF IN ENGLAND AND WALES AFTER OVERSEAS DIVORCE ETC

12–16 *(Outside the scope of this work.)*

Orders for financial provision and property adjustment

17 Orders for financial provision and property adjustment

[(1) Subject to section 20 below, on an application by a party to a marriage for an order for financial relief under this section, the court may—

(a) *make any one or more of the orders which it could make under Part II of the 1973 Act if a decree of divorce, a decree of nullity of marriage or a decree of judicial separation in respect of the marriage had been granted in England and Wales, that is to say—*

(i) *any order mentioned in section 23(1) of the 1973 Act (financial provision orders); and*

(ii) *any order mentioned in section 24(1) of that Act (property adjustment orders);*

[(a) make one or more orders each of which would, within the meaning of Part II of the 1973 Act, be a financial provision order in favour of a party to the marriage or a child of the family or a property adjustment order in relation to the marriage;] and

(b) if the marriage has been dissolved or annulled, make one or more orders each of which would, within the meaning of that Part of that Act, be a pension sharing order in relation to the marriage.]

[(c) if the marriage has been dissolved or annulled, make an order which would, within the meaning of that Part of that Act, be a pension compensation sharing order in relation to the marriage].]

(2) Subject to section 20 below, where the court makes a secured periodical payments order, an order for the payment of a lump sum or a property adjustment order under subsection (1) above, then, on making that order or at any time thereafter, the court may make any order mentioned in section 24A(1) of the 1973 Act (orders for sale of property) which the court would have power to make if the order under subsection (1) above had been made under Part II of the 1973 Act.

[1047]

NOTES

Sub-s (1): substituted by the Welfare Reform and Pensions Act 1999, s 84(1), Sch 12, Pt I, paras 2, 3; para (a) substituted by the Family Law Act 1996, s 66(1), Sch 8, Pt I, para 32(2) (as amended by the Welfare Reform and Pensions Act 1999, s 84(1), Sch 12, Pt I, paras 64, 66(1), (14)), subject to savings in s 66(2) of, Sch 9, para 5 to, that Act, as from a day to be appointed; para (c) inserted by the Pensions Act 2008, s 120, Sch 6, Pt 2, paras 10, 11, as from a day to be appointed.

18 Matters to which the court is to have regard in exercising its powers under s 17

(1) In deciding whether to exercise its powers under section 17 above and, if so, in what manner the court shall act in accordance with this section.

(2) The court shall have regard to all the circumstances of the case, first consideration being given to the welfare while a minor of any child of the family who has not attained the age of eighteen.

(3) As regards the exercise of those powers in relation to a party to the marriage, the court shall in particular have regard to the matters mentioned in section 25(2)(a) to (h) of the 1973 Act and shall be under duties corresponding with those imposed by section 25A(1) and (2) of the 1973 Act where it decides to exercise under section 17 above powers corresponding with the powers referred to in those subsections.

[(3A) The matters to which the court is to have regard under subsection (3) above—

(a) so far as relating to paragraph (a) of section 25(2) of the 1973 Act, include any benefits under a pension arrangement which a party to the marriage has or is likely to have [and any PPF compensation to which a party to the marriage is or is likely to be entitled,] (whether or not in the foreseeable future), and

(b) so far as relating to paragraph (h) of that provision, include[—

(i)] any benefits under a pension arrangement which, by reason of the dissolution or annulment of the marriage, a party to the marriage will lose the chance of acquiring[,] and

(ii) any PPF compensation which, by reason of the dissolution or annulment of the marriage, a party to the marriage will lose the chance of acquiring entitlement to].

(4) As regards the exercise of those powers in relation to a child of the family, the court shall in particular have regard to the matters mentioned in section 25(3)(a) to (e) of the 1973 Act.

(5) As regards the exercise of those powers against a party to the marriage in favour of a child of the family who is not the child of that party, the court shall also have regard to the matters mentioned in section 25(4)(a) to (c) of the 1973 Act.

(6) Where an order has been made by a court outside England and Wales for the making of payments or the transfer of property by a party to the marriage, the court in considering in accordance with this section the financial resources of the other party to the marriage or a child of the family shall have regard to the extent to which that order has been complied with or is likely to be complied with.

[(7) In this section—

(a) "pension arrangement" has the meaning given by section 25D(3) of the 1973 Act, and

(b) references to benefits under a pension arrangement include any benefits by way of pension, whether under a pension arrangement or not[,] and

(c) *"PPF compensation" means compensation payable under Chapter 3 of Part 2 of the Pensions Act 2004 (pension protection) or any provision in force in Northern Ireland corresponding to that Chapter].*

[(c) "PPF compensation" means compensation payable under—

(i) Chapter 3 of Part 2 of the Pensions Act 2004 (pension protection) or any regulations or order made under it,

(ii) Chapter 1 of Part 3 of the Pensions Act 2008 (pension compensation sharing) or any regulations or order made under it, or

(iii) any provision corresponding to the provisions mentioned in sub-paragraph (i) or (ii) in force in Northern Ireland].

[1048]

NOTES

Sub-s (3A): inserted by the Welfare Reform and Pensions Act 1999, s 22(1), (2); words in square brackets in para (a) inserted, para (b)(i) numbered as such, and para (b)(ii) and word immediately preceding it inserted by the Pensions Act 2004, s 319(1), Sch 12, para 4(1), (2)(a).

Sub-s (7): inserted by the Welfare Reform and Pensions Act 1999, s 22(1), (3); para (c) and word immediately preceding it inserted by the Pensions Act 2004, s 319(1), Sch 12, para 4(1), (2)(b); para (c) substituted by the Pensions Act 2008, s 120, Sch 6, Pt 2, paras 10, 12, as from a day to be appointed.

19 Consent orders for financial provision or property adjustment

(1) Notwithstanding anything in section 18 above, on an application for a consent order for financial relief the court may, unless it has reason to think that there are other circumstances into which it ought to inquire, make an order in the terms agreed on the basis only of the prescribed information furnished with the application.

(2) Subsection (1) above applies to an application for a consent order varying or discharging an order for financial relief as it applies to an application for an order for financial relief.

(3) In this section—

"consent order", in relation to an application for an order, means an order in the terms applied for to which the respondent agrees;

"order for financial relief" means an order under section 17 above; and

"prescribed" means prescribed by rules of court.

[1049]

20 Restriction of powers of court where jurisdiction depends on matrimonial home in England or Wales

(1) Where the court has jurisdiction to entertain an application for an order for financial relief by reason only of the situation in England or Wales of a dwelling-house which was a matrimonial home of the parties, the court may make under section 17 above any one or more of the following orders (but no other)—

(a) an order that either party to the marriage shall pay to the other such lump sum as may be specified in the order;

(b) an order that a party to the marriage shall pay to such person as may be so specified for the benefit of a child of the family, or to such a child, such lump sum as may be so specified;

(c) an order that a party to the marriage shall transfer to the other party, to any child of the family or to such person as may be so specified for the benefit of such a child, the interest of the first-mentioned party in the dwelling-house, or such part of that interest as may be so specified;

(d) an order that a settlement of the interest of a party to the marriage in the dwelling-house, or such part of that interest as may be so specified, be made to the satisfaction of the court for the benefit of the other party to the marriage and of the children of the family or either or any of them;

(e) an order varying for the benefit of the parties to the marriage and of the children of the family or either or any of them any ante-nuptial or post-nuptial settlement (including such a settlement made by will or codicil) made on the parties to the marriage so far as that settlement relates to an interest in the dwelling-house;

(f) an order extinguishing or reducing the interest of either of the parties to the marriage under any such settlement so far as that interest is an interest in the dwelling-house;

(g) an order for the sale of the interest of a party to the marriage in the dwelling-house.

(2) Where, in the circumstances mentioned in subsection (1) above, the court makes an order for the payment of a lump sum by a party to the marriage, the amount of the lump sum shall not exceed, or where more than one such order is made the total amount of the lump sums shall not exceed in aggregate, the following amount, that is to say—

(a) if the interest of that party in the dwelling-house is sold in pursuance of an order made under subsection (1)(g) above, the amount of the proceeds of the sale of that interest after deducting therefrom any costs incurred in the sale thereof;

(b) if the interest of that party is not so sold, the amount which in the opinion of the court represents the value of that interest.

(3) Where the interest of a party to the marriage in the dwelling-house is held jointly or in common with any other person or persons—

(a) the reference in subsection (1)(g) above to the interest of a party to the marriage shall be construed as including a reference to the interest of that other person, or the interest of those other persons, in the dwelling-house, and

(b) the reference in subsection (2)(a) above to the amount of the proceeds of a sale ordered under subsection (1)(g) above shall be construed as a reference to that part of those proceeds which is attributable to the interest of that party to the marriage in the dwelling-house.

[1050]

21 Application to orders under ss 14 and 17 of certain provisions of Part II of Matrimonial Causes Act 1973

[(1)] The following provisions of Part II of the 1973 Act (financial relief for parties to marriage and children of family) shall apply in relation to an order … under section 14 or 17 above as they apply in relation to a like order … under that Part of that Act, that is to say—

(a) section 23(3) (provisions as to lump sums);

[(a) section 22A(5) (provisions about lump sums in relation to divorce or separation);

(aa) section 23(4), (5) and (6) (provisions about lump sums in relation to annulment);]

(b) section 24A(2), (4), (5) and (6) (provisions as to orders for sale);

[(ba) section 24B(3) to (5) (provisions about pension sharing orders in relation to divorce and nullity);

[(ba) sections 24BA(5) to (7) (provisions about pension sharing orders in relation to divorce);

(baa) section 24BC(1) to (3) (provisions about pension sharing orders in relation to nullity);]

(bb) section 24C (duty to stay pension sharing orders);

(bc) section 24D (apportionment of pension sharing charges);]

[(bca) section 24E(3) to (10) (provisions about pension compensation orders in relation to divorce and nullity);

(bcb) section 24F (duty to stay pension compensation sharing orders);

(bcc) section 24G (apportionment of pension compensation sharing charges);]

[(bd) section 25B(3) to (7B) (power, by financial provision order, to attach payments under a pension arrangement, or to require the exercise of a right of commutation under such an arrangement);

(be) section 25C (extension of lump sum powers in relation to death benefits under a pension arrangement);]

[(bf) section 25E(2) to (10) (the Pension Protection Fund);]

[(bg) section 25F (power, by financial provision order, to attach pension compensation payments, or to require the exercise of a right of commutation of pension compensation);]

(c) section 28(1) and (2) (duration of continuing financial provision orders in favour of party to marriage);

(d) section 29 (duration of continuing financial provision orders in favour of children, and age limit on making certain orders in their favour);

(e) section 30 (direction for settlement of instrument for securing payments or effecting property adjustment), except paragraph (b);
(f) section 31 variation, discharge etc of certain orders for financial relief), *except subsection (2)(e) and subsection (4)*;
(g) section 32 (payment of certain arrears unenforceable without the leave of the court);
(h) section 33 (orders for repayment of sums paid under certain orders);
(i) section 38 (orders for repayment of sums paid after cessation of order by reason of remarriage);
(j) section 39 (settlements etc made in compliance with a property adjustment order may be avoided on bankruptcy of settlor); and
(k) section 40 (payments etc under order made in favour of person suffering from mental disorder);
[(l) section 40A (appeals relating to pension sharing orders which have taken effect)];
[(m) section 40B (appeals relating to pension compensation sharing orders which have taken effect)].

[(2) Subsection (1)(bd) *and (be)* [, (be) and (bg)] above shall not apply where the court has jurisdiction to entertain an application for an order for financial relief by reason only of the situation in England or Wales of a dwelling-house which was a matrimonial home of the parties.

(3) Section 25D(1) of the 1973 Act (effect of transfers on orders relating to rights under a pension arrangement) shall apply in relation to an order made under section 17 above by virtue of subsection (1)(bd) or (be) above as it applies in relation to an order made under *section 23* [section 22A or 23] of that Act by virtue of section 25B or 25C of the 1973 Act.

(4) The Lord Chancellor may by regulations make for the purposes of this Part of this Act provision corresponding to any provision which may be made by him under subsections (2) to (2B) of section 25D of the 1973 Act [or under subsections (1) to (3) of section 25G of that Act].

(5) Power to make regulations under this section shall be exercisable by statutory instrument which shall be subject to annulment in pursuance of a resolution of either House of Parliament.]

[1051]

NOTES

Sub-s (1): numbered as such and words omitted repealed by the Welfare Reform and Pensions Act 1999, ss 22(1), (4), 84(1), 88, Sch 12, Pt I, paras 2, 4(a), Sch 13, Pt II; paras (a), (aa) in square brackets substituted, for para (a) as originally enacted, by the Family Law Act 1996, s 66(1), Sch 8, para 32(3), subject to savings in s 66(2) of, Sch 9, para 5 to, that Act, as from a day to be appointed; paras (ba)–(bc), (l) inserted by the Welfare Reform and Pensions Act 1999, s 84(1), Sch 12, Pt I, paras 2, 4(b), (c); para (ba) substituted by subsequent paras (ba), (baa) in square brackets, by the Family Law Act 1996, s 66(1), Sch 8, Pt I, para 32(3A) (as inserted by the Welfare Reform and Pensions Act 1999, s 84(1), Sch 12, Pt I, paras 64, 66(1), (16)), subject to savings in s 66(2) of, Sch 9, para 5 to, that Act, as from a day to be appointed; paras (bca)–(bcc) inserted by the Pensions Act 2008, s 120, Sch 6, Pt 2, paras 10, 13(1), (2), as from a day to be appointed; paras (bd), (be) inserted by the Welfare Reform and Pensions Act 1999, s 22(1), (4); para (bf) inserted by the Pensions Act 2004, s 319(1), Sch 12, para 4(1), (3); para (bg) inserted by the Pensions Act 2008, s 120, Sch 6, Pt 2, paras 10, 13(1), (3), as from a day to be appointed; in para (f) words in italics repealed by the Family Law Act 1996, s 66(3), Sch 10, subject to savings in s 66(2) of, Sch 9, para 5, 8–10 to, that Act, as from a day to be appointed; para (m) inserted by the Pensions Act 2008, s 120, Sch 6, Pt 2, paras 10, 13(1), (4), as from a day to be appointed.

Sub-s (2): inserted by the Welfare Reform and Pensions Act 1999, s 22(1), (5); words in italics repealed and subsequent words in square brackets substituted by the Pensions Act 2008, s 120, Sch 6, Pt 2, paras 10, 13(1), (5), as from a day to be appointed.

Sub-s (3): inserted by the Welfare Reform and Pensions Act 1999, s 22(1), (5); words in italics substituted by subsequent words in square brackets by the Family Law Act 1996, s 66(1), Sch 8, Pt I, para 32(3B) (as inserted by the Welfare Reform and Pensions Act 1999, s 84(1), Sch 12, Pt I, paras 64, 66(1), (16)), subject to savings in s 66(2) of, Sch 9, para 5 to, that Act, as from a day to be appointed.

Sub-s (4): inserted by the Welfare Reform and Pensions Act 1999, s 22(1), (5); words in square brackets inserted by the Pensions Act 2008, s 120, Sch 6, Pt 2, paras 10, 13(1), (6), as from a day to be appointed.

Sub-s (5): inserted by the Welfare Reform and Pensions Act 1999, s 22(1), (5).

Regulations: the Divorce etc (Pensions) Regulations 2000, SI 2000/1123.

22–44 (*Ss 22–24, 27, ss 32–44 (Pt V) outside the scope of this work; s 25 amends the Inheritance (Provision for Family and Dependants) Act 1975, s 25(1) at* **[805]** *and inserts s 15A thereof at* **[795]***; s 26 repealed by the Maintenance Orders (Reciprocal Enforcement) Act 1992, s 2(2), Sch 3; ss 28–31 (Pt IV) apply to Scotland only.*)

PART VI
MISCELLANEOUS AND GENERAL

45–47 (*S 45 repealed by the Children (Northern Ireland) Order 1995, SI 1995/755, art 185(2), Sch 10; ss 46, 47 outside the scope of this work.*)

48 Short title and extent

(1) This Act may be cited as the Matrimonial and Family Proceedings Act 1984.

(2) Parts I to III and V and Schedules 2 and 3 extend to England and Wales only, Part IV extends to Scotland only …

(3) Where any enactment amended by Schedule 1 extends to any part of the United Kingdom, the amendment extends to that part.

[1052]

NOTES

Sub-s (2): words omitted repealed by the Children (Northern Ireland) Order 1995, SI 1995/755, art 185(2), Sch 10.

(*Schs 1–3 outside the scope of this work.*)

INHERITANCE TAX ACT 1984

(1984 c 51)

An Act to consolidate provisions of Part III of the Finance Act 1975 and other enactments relating to inheritance tax

[31 July 1984]

NOTES

Inheritance Tax: except in relation to a liability to tax arising before 25 July 1986 capital transfer tax shall be known as inheritance tax and the Capital Transfer Tax Act 1984 may be cited as the Inheritance Tax Act 1984, by virtue of the Finance Act 1986, s 100. Accordingly references to capital transfer tax have been changed to references to inheritance tax throughout this Act.

1–214 ((*Pts I–VII*) *Outside the scope of this work.*)

PART VIII
ADMINISTRATION AND COLLECTION

215–236 (*Outside the scope of this work.*)

Inland Revenue charge for unpaid tax

237 Imposition of charge

(1) Except as otherwise provided, where any tax charged on the value transferred by a chargeable transfer, or any interest on it, is for the time being unpaid a charge for the amount unpaid (to be known as an Inland Revenue charge) is by virtue of this section imposed in favour of the Board on—

(a) any property to the value of which the value transferred is wholly or partly attributable, and

(b) where the chargeable transfer is made by the making of a settlement or is made under Part III of this Act, any property comprised in the settlement.

(2) References in subsection (1) above to any property include references to any property directly or indirectly representing it.

(3) Where the chargeable transfer is made on death, personal or movable property situated in the United Kingdom which was beneficially owned by the deceased immediately before his death and vests in his personal representatives is not subject to the Inland Revenue charge; and for this purpose ["personal property" does not include leaseholds] *and undivided shares in land held on trust for sale, whether statutory or not,* and the question whether any property was beneficially owned by the deceased shall be determined without regard to section 49(1) above.

[(3A) In the case of a potentially exempt transfer which proves to be a chargeable transfer—

(a) property concerned, or an interest in property concerned, which has been disposed of to a purchaser before the transferor's death is not subject to the Inland Revenue charge, but

(b) property concerned which has been otherwise disposed of before the death and property which at the death represents any property or interest falling within paragraph (a) above shall be subject to the charge;

and in this subsection "property concerned" means property to the value of which the value transferred by the transfer is wholly or partly attributable.]

[(3B) Subsection (3C) below applies to any tax charged—

(a) under section 32, 32A or 79(3) above in respect of any property,

(b) under paragraph 8 of Schedule 4 to this Act in respect of any property, or

(c) under paragraph 1 or 3 of Schedule 5 to this Act with respect to any object or property.

(3C) Where any tax to which this subsection applies, or any interest on it, is for the time being unpaid, a charge for the amount unpaid is also by virtue of this section imposed in favour of the Board—

(a) except where the event giving rise to the charge was a disposal to a purchaser of the property or object in question, on that property or object; and

(b) in the excepted case, on any property for the time being representing that property or object.]

(4) No heritable property situated in Scotland is subject to the Inland Revenue charge, but where such property is disposed of any other property for the time being representing it is subject to the charge to which the first-mentioned property would have been subject but for this subsection.

(5) The Inland Revenue charge imposed on any property shall take effect subject to any incumbrance on it which is allowable as a deduction in valuing that property for the purposes of the tax.

(6) Except as provided by section 238 below, a disposition of property subject to an Inland Revenue charge shall take effect subject to that charge.

[1053]

NOTES

Sub-s (3): words in square brackets substituted by the Finance Act 1999, s 107(1), in relation to deaths occurring on or after 9 March 1999; words in italics repealed, in relation to England and Wales, by the Trusts of Land and Appointment of Trustees Act 1996, s 25(2), Sch 4, for savings in relation to entailed interests created before the commencement of that Act, and savings consequential upon the abolition of the doctrine of conversion, see s 25(4), (5) thereof.

Sub-s (3A): inserted by the Finance Act 1986, s 101, Sch 19, Pt I, para 34, in relation to transfers of value made, and other events occurring, on or after 18 March 1986.

Sub-ss (3B), (3C): inserted by the Finance Act 1999, s 107(2), in relation to tax charged on or after 9 March 1999.

238 Effect of purchases

(1) Where property subject to an Inland Revenue charge, or an interest in such property, is disposed of to a purchaser, then if at the time of the disposition—

(a) in the case of land in England and Wales, the charge was not registered as a land charge or, in the case of registered land, was not protected by notice on the register, or

(b) in the case of land in Northern Ireland the title to which is registered under the Land Registration Act (Northern Ireland) 1970, the charge was not entered as a burden on the appropriate register maintained under that Act or was not protected by a caution or inhibition under that Act or, in the case of other land in Northern Ireland, the purchaser had no notice of the facts giving rise to the charge, or

(c) in the case of personal property situated in the United Kingdom other than such property as is mentioned in paragraph (a) or (b) above, and of any property situated outside the United Kingdom, the purchaser had no notice of the facts giving rise to the charge, or

(d) in the case of any property, a certificate of discharge had been given by the Board under section 239 below and the purchaser had no notice of any fact invalidating the certificate,

the property or interest shall then cease to be subject to the charge but the property for the time being representing it shall be subject to it.

(2) Where property subject to an Inland Revenue charge, or an interest in such property, is disposed of to a purchaser in circumstances where it does not then cease to be subject to the charge, it shall cease to be subject to it at the end of the period of six years beginning with the later of—

(a) the date on which the tax became due, and

(b) the date on which a full and proper account of the property was first delivered to the Board in connection with the chargeable transfer concerned.

(3) In this section "the time of the disposition" means—

[(a) in relation to registered land—

(i) if the disposition is required to be completed by registration, the time of registration, and

(ii) otherwise, the time of completion,] and

(b) in relation to other property, the time of completion.

[1054]

NOTES

Sub-s (3): para (a) substituted by the Land Registration Act 2002, s 133, Sch 11, para 17.

239 Certificates of discharge

(1) Where application is made to the Board by a person liable for any tax on the value transferred by a chargeable transfer which is attributable to the value of property specified in the application, the Board, on being satisfied that the tax so attributable has been or will be paid, may give a certificate to that effect, and shall do so if the chargeable transfer is one made on death or the transferor has died.

(2) Where tax is or may be chargeable on the value transferred by a transfer of value and—

(a) application is made to the Board after the expiration of two years from the transfer (or, if the Board think fit to entertain the application, at an earlier time) by a person who is or might be liable for the whole or part of the tax, and

(b) the applicant delivers to the Board, if the transfer is one made on death, a full statement to the best of his knowledge and belief of all property included in the estate of the deceased immediately before his death and, in any other case, a full and proper account under this Part of this Act,

the Board may, as the case requires, determine the amount of the tax or determine that no tax is chargeable; and subject to the payment of any tax so determined to be chargeable the Board may give a certificate of their determination, and shall do so if the transfer of value is one made on death or the transferor has died.

[(2A) An application under subsection (1) or (2) above with respect to tax which is or may become chargeable on the value transferred by a potentially exempt transfer may not be made before the expiration of two years from the death of the transferor (except where the Board think fit to entertain the application at an earlier time after the death).]

(3) Subject to subsection (4) below,—

(a) a certificate under subsection (1) above shall discharge the property shown in it from the Inland Revenue charge on its acquisition by a purchaser, and

(b) a certificate under subsection (2) above shall discharge all persons from any further claim for the tax on the value transferred by the chargeable transfer concerned and extinguish any Inland Revenue charge for that tax.

(4) A certificate under this section shall not discharge any person from tax in case of fraud or failure to disclose material facts and shall not affect any further tax—

(a) that may afterwards be shown to be payable by virtue of section 93, 142, 143, 144 or 145 above,

[(aa) that may afterwards be shown to be payable by reason of too great an increase having been made under section 8A(3) above,] or

(b) that may be payable if any further property is afterwards shown to have been included in the estate of a deceased person immediately before his death;

but in so far as the certificate shows any tax to be attributable to the value of any property it shall remain valid in favour of a purchaser of that property without notice of any fact invalidating the certificate.

(5) References in this section to a transfer of value, or to the value transferred by a transfer of value, shall be construed as including references to an occasion on which tax is chargeable under Chapter III of Part III of this Act (apart from section 79) or to the amount on which tax is then chargeable.

[1055]

NOTES

Sub-s (2A): inserted by the Finance Act 1986, s 101, Sch 19, Pt I, para 35, in relation to transfers of value made, and other events occurring, on or after 18 March 1986.

Sub-s (4): para (aa) inserted by the Finance Act 2008, s 10, Sch 4, paras 1, 5.

240–278 (*Ss 240–261, ss 262–278 (Pt IX) outside the scope of this work.*)

(*Schs 1–9 outside the scope of this work.*)

COMPANIES ACT 1985

(1985 c 6)

An Act to consolidate the greater part of the Companies Acts

[11 March 1985]

Modification: the Limited Liability Partnerships Act 2000 provides for the creation of Limited Liability Partnerships (LLPs). The Limited Liability Partnerships Regulations 2001, SI 2001/1090 regulate LLPs by applying to them, with modifications, the appropriate provisions of this Act: see SI 2001/1090, reg 4, Sch 2, Pt I.

PART I
FORMATION AND REGISTRATION OF COMPANIES; JURIDICAL STATUS AND MEMBERSHIP

1–34A *((Chs I, II) outside the scope of this work.)*

CHAPTER III
A COMPANY'S CAPACITY; FORMALITIES OF CARRYING ON BUSINESS

[35 A company's capacity not limited by its memorandum

(1) The validity of an act done by a company shall not be called into question on the ground of lack of capacity by reason of anything in the company's memorandum.

(2) A member of a company may bring proceedings to restrain the doing of an act which but for subsection (1) would be beyond the company's capacity; but no such proceedings shall lie in respect of an act to be done in fulfilment of a legal obligation arising from a previous act of the company.

(3) It remains the duty of the directors to observe any limitations on their powers flowing from the company's memorandum; and action by the directors which but for subsection (1) would be beyond the company's capacity may only be ratified by the company by special resolution.

A resolution ratifying such action shall not affect any liability incurred by the directors or any other person; relief from any such liability must be agreed to separately by special resolution.

(4) The operation of this section is restricted by [section 65(1) of the Charities Act 1993] and section 112(3) of the Companies Act 1989 in relation to companies which are charities; and section 322A below (invalidity of certain transactions to which directors or their associates are parties) has effect notwithstanding this section.]

[1056]

NOTES

Substituted, together with ss 35A, 35B, for original s 35, by the Companies Act 1989, s 108(1).

Repealed by the Companies Act 2006, s 1295, Sch 16, as from 1 October 2009, subject to transitional provisions and savings in SI 2008/2860, arts 5, 8, Sch 2.

Sub-s (4): words in square brackets substituted by the Charities Act 1993, s 98(1), Sch 6, para 20(2).

[35A Power of directors to bind the company

(1) In favour of a person dealing with a company in good faith, the power of the board of directors to bind the company, or authorise others to do so, shall be deemed to be free of any limitation under the company's constitution.

(2) For this purpose—

(a) a person "deals with" a company if he is a party to any transaction or other act to which the company is a party;

(b) a person shall not be regarded as acting in bad faith by reason only of his knowing that an act is beyond the powers of the directors under the company's constitution; and

(c) a person shall be presumed to have acted in good faith unless the contrary is proved.

(3) The references above to limitations on the directors' powers under the company's constitution include limitations deriving—

(a) from a resolution of the company in general meeting or a meeting of any class of shareholders, or

(b) from any agreement between the members of the company or of any class of shareholders.

(4) Subsection (1) does not affect any right of a member of the company to bring proceedings to restrain the doing of an act which is beyond the powers of the directors; but no such proceedings shall lie in respect of an act to be done in fulfilment of a legal obligation arising from a previous act of the company.

(5) Nor does that subsection affect any liability incurred by the directors, or any other person, by reason of the directors' exceeding their powers.

(6) The operation of this section is restricted by [section 65(1) of the Charities Act 1993] and section 112(3) of the Companies Act 1989 in relation to companies which are charities; and section 322A below (invalidity of certain transactions to which directors or their associates are parties) has effect notwithstanding this section.]

[1057]

NOTES

Substituted, together with ss 35, 35B, for original s 35, by the Companies Act 1989, s 108.
Repealed by the Companies Act 2006, s 1295, Sch 16, as from 1 October 2009.
Sub-s (6): words in square brackets substituted by the Charities Act 1993, s 98(1), Sch 6, para 20(2).

[35B No duty to enquire as to capacity of company or authority of directors

A party to a transaction with a company is not bound to enquire as to whether it is permitted by the company's memorandum or as to any limitation on the powers of the board of directors to bind the company or authorise others to do so.]

[1058]

NOTES

Substituted, together with ss 35, 35A, for original s 35, by the Companies Act 1989, s 108.
Repealed by the Companies Act 2006, s 1295, Sch 16, as from 1 October 2009.

[36 Company contracts: England and Wales

Under the law of England and Wales a contract may be made—

(*a*) *by a company, by writing under its common seal, or*

(*b*) *on behalf of a company, by any person acting under its authority, express or implied;*

and any formalities required by law in the case of a contract made by an individual also apply, unless a contrary intention appears, to a contract made by or on behalf of a company.]

[1059]

NOTES

Substituted by the Companies Act 1989, s 130(1).
Repealed by the Companies Act 2006, s 1295, Sch 16, as from 1 October 2009.

[36A Execution of documents: England and Wales

(*1*) *Under the law of England and Wales the following provisions have effect with respect to the execution of documents by a company.*

(2) …

(*3*) *A company need not have a common seal, …*

(*4*) …

[(4A) …]

(5)–(*8*) …

[1060]

NOTES

Inserted by the Companies Act 1989, s 130(2).
Repealed by the Companies Act 2006, s 1295, Sch 16, as from 6 April 2008 (in so far as relating to sub-ss (2), (4)–(8), and the words omitted from sub-s (3)), and as from 1 October 2009 (otherwise), subject to transitional provision and savings in SI 2008/2860, arts 5, 8, Sch 2.
Sub-s (4A): inserted by SI 2005/1906, art 10(1), Sch 1, paras 9, 10, except in relation to any instrument executed before 15 September 2005.
Sub-s (5): repealed by SI 2005/1906, art 10(2), Sch 2, except in relation to any instrument executed before 15 September 2005.

[36AA Execution of deeds: England and Wales

(*1*) *A document is validly executed by a company as a deed for the purposes of section 1*(*2*)(*b*) *of the Law of Property* (*Miscellaneous Provisions*) *Act 1989, if and only if—*

(*a*) *it is duly executed by the company, and*

(*b*) *it is delivered as a deed.*

(*2*) *A document shall be presumed to be delivered for the purposes of subsection* (*1*)(*b*) *upon its being executed, unless a contrary intention is proved.]*

[1061]–[1062]

NOTES

Commencement: 15 September 2005.
Inserted by SI 2005/1906, art 6, except in relation to any instrument executed before 15 September 2005.
Repealed by the Companies Act 2006, s 1295, Sch 16, as from 1 October 2009.

36B–116 (*Ss 36B–42, ss 43–116* (*Pts II–IV*) *outside the scope of this work.*)

PART V
SHARE CAPITAL, ITS INCREASE, MAINTENANCE AND REDUCTION

117–181 (*Outside the scope of this work.*)

CHAPTER VIII
MISCELLANEOUS PROVISIONS ABOUT SHARES AND DEBENTURES

182–193 (*ss 182–193 outside the scope of this work; s 193 repealed by the Companies Act 2006, s 1295, Sch 16.*)

194–310 (*Ss 194–197, ss 198–310 (Pts VI–IX) outside the scope of this work.*)

PART X
ENFORCEMENT OF FAIR DEALING BY DIRECTORS

Restrictions on directors taking financial advantage

311–319 (*Outside the scope of this work.*)

320 Substantial property transactions involving directors, etc

(1) With the exceptions provided by the section next following, a company shall not enter into an arrangement—

- *(a) whereby a director of the company or its holding company, or a person connected with such a director, acquires or is to acquire one or more non-cash assets of the requisite value from the company; or*
- *(b) whereby the company acquires or is to acquire one or more non-cash assets of the requisite value from such a director or a person so connected,*

unless the arrangement is first approved by a resolution of the company in general meeting and, if the director or connected person is a director of its holding company or a person connected with such a director, by a resolution in general meeting of the holding company.

(2) For this purpose a non-cash asset is of the requisite value if at the time the arrangement in question is entered into its value is not less than [£2,000] but (subject to that) exceeds [£100,000] or 10 per cent of the company's asset value, that is—

- *(a) except in a case falling within paragraph (b) below, the value of the company's net assets determined by reference to the accounts prepared and laid under Part VII in respect of the last preceding financial year in respect of which such accounts were so laid; and*
- *(b) where no accounts have been so prepared and laid before that time, the amount of the company's called-up share capital.*

(3) For purposes of this section and sections 321 and 322, a shadow director is treated as a director.

[1063]

NOTES

Repealed by the Companies Act 2006, s 1295, Sch 16, except in relation to arrangements or transactions entered into before 1 October 2007.

Sub-s (2): sums in square brackets substituted by SI 1990/1393, art 2.

Disapplication: in relation to the disapplication of this section, in respect of certain specified persons while Northern Rock is wholly owned by the Treasury, see the Northern Rock plc Transfer Order 2008, art 17, Schedule, para 1(c).

See further, in relation to a company which is a charity: the Charities Act 1993, s 66.

---

321 Exceptions from s 320

(1) No approval is required to be given under section 320 by any body corporate unless it is a company within the meaning of this Act or registered under section 680 or, if it is a wholly-owned subsidiary of any body corporate, wherever incorporated.

(2) Section 320(1) does not apply to an arrangement for the acquisition of a non-cash asset—

- *(a) if the asset is to be acquired by a holding company from any of its wholly-owned subsidiaries or from a holding company by any of its wholly-owned subsidiaries, or by one wholly-owned subsidiary of a holding company from another wholly-owned subsidiary of that same holding company, or*
- *(b) if the arrangement is entered into by a company which is being wound up, unless the winding up is a members' voluntary winding up.*

(3) Section 320(1)(a) does not apply to an arrangement whereby a person is to acquire an asset from a company of which he is a member, if the arrangement is made with that person in his character as a member.

[(4) Section 320(1) does not apply to a transaction on a recognised investment exchange which is effected by a director, or a person connected with him, through the agency of a person who in relation to the transaction acts as an independent broker.

For this purpose an "independent broker" means—

(*a*) *in relation to a transaction on behalf of a director, a person who independently of the director selects the person with whom the transaction is to be effected, and*

(*b*) *in relation to a transaction on behalf of a person connected with a director, a person who independently of that person or the director selects the person with whom the transaction is to be effected;*

and "recognised", in relation to an investment exchange, means recognised under the [Financial Services and Markets Act 2000].]

[1064]

NOTES

Repealed by the Companies Act 2006, s 1295, Sch 16, except in relation to arrangements or transactions entered into before 1 October 2007.

Sub-s (4): inserted by the Companies Act 1989, s 145, Sch 19, para 8; words in square brackets substituted by SI 2001/3649, art 19.

322 Liabilities arising from contravention of s 320

(1) An arrangement entered into by a company in contravention of section 320, and any transaction entered into in pursuance of the arrangement (whether by the company or any other person) is voidable at the instance of the company unless one or more of the conditions specified in the next subsection is satisfied.

(2) Those conditions are that—

(*a*) *restitution of any money or other asset which is the subject-matter of the arrangement or transaction is no longer possible or the company has been indemnified in pursuance of this section by any other person for the loss or damage suffered by it; or*

(*b*) *any rights acquired bona fide for value and without actual notice of the contravention by any person who is not a party to the arrangement or transaction would be affected by its avoidance; or*

(*c*) *the arrangement is, within a reasonable period, affirmed by the company in general meeting and, if it is an arrangement for the transfer of an asset to or by a director of its holding company or a person who is connected with such a director, is so affirmed with the approval of the holding company given by a resolution in general meeting.*

(3) If an arrangement is entered into with a company by a director of the company or its holding company or a person connected with him in contravention of section 320, that director and the person so connected, and any other director of the company who authorised the arrangement or any transaction entered into in pursuance of such an arrangement, is liable—

(*a*) *to account to the company for any gain which he has made directly or indirectly by the arrangement or transaction, and*

(*b*) *(jointly and severally with any other person liable under this subsection) to indemnify the company for any loss or damage resulting from the arrangement or transaction.*

(4) Subsection (3) is without prejudice to any liability imposed otherwise than by that subsection, and is subject to the following two subsections; and the liability under subsection (3) arises whether or not the arrangement or transaction entered into has been avoided in pursuance of subsection (1).

(5) If an arrangement is entered into by a company and a person connected with a director of the company or its holding company in contravention of section 320, that director is not liable under subsection (3) if he shows that he took all reasonable steps to secure the company's compliance with that section.

(6) In any case, a person so connected and any such other director as is mentioned in subsection (3) is not so liable if he shows that, at the time the arrangement was entered into, he did not know the relevant circumstances constituting the contravention.

[1065]

NOTES

Repealed by the Companies Act 2006, s 1295, Sch 16, except in relation to arrangements or transactions entered into before 1 October 2007.

322A–394A *(Ss 322A–347, ss 347A–347K (Pt XA), ss 348–394A (Pt XI) outside the scope of this work.)*

PART XII
REGISTRATION OF CHARGES

NOTES

New ss 395–420 (provisions relating to the registration of charges) were prospectively inserted into this Part by the Companies Act 1989 ss 92–104 in place of the then current ss 395–408 (applying to England and Wales), and ss 410–423 (applying to Scotland), as from a day to be appointed. Those substitutions, were never brought into force and the Companies Act 1989, ss 92–104 are repealed by the Companies Act 2006, ss 1180, 1295 and Sch 16, as from 1 October 2009. Consequently, the new ss 395–420 prospectively inserted by Companies Act 1989 ss 92–104 have been omitted from this edition.

CHAPTER I
REGISTRATION OF CHARGES (ENGLAND AND WALES)

395 Certain charges void if not registered

(1) Subject to the provisions of this Chapter, a charge created by a company registered in England and Wales and being a charge to which this section applies is, so far as any security on the company's property or undertaking is conferred by the charge, void against the liquidator [or administrator] and any creditor of the company, unless the prescribed particulars of the charge together with the instrument (if any) by which the charge is created or evidenced, are delivered to or received by the registrar of companies for registration in the manner required by this Chapter within 21 days after the date of the charge's creation.

(2) Subsection (1) is without prejudice to any contract or obligation for repayment of the money secured by the charge; and when a charge becomes void under this section, the money secured by it immediately becomes payable.

[1066]

NOTES

Repealed by the Companies Act 2006, s 1295, Sch 16 as from 1 October 2009, subject to transitional provisions and savings in SI 2008/2860, Sch 2, paras 82–87.

Prospective replacement: see the note preceding this section.

Sub-s (1): words in square brackets inserted by the Insolvency Act 1985, s 109, Sch 6, para 10.

Disapplication: this section is disapplied in relation to a security financial collateral arrangement or any charge created or otherwise arising under a security financial collateral arrangement by the Financial Collateral Arrangements (No 2) Regulations 2003, SI 2003/3226, reg 4(4).

Regulations: the Companies (Forms) Regulations 1985, SI 1985/854; the Limited Liability Partnerships (Forms) Regulations 2001, SI 2001/927.

396 Charges which have to be registered

(1) Section 395 applies to the following charges—

(a) a charge for the purpose of securing any issue of debentures,
(b) a charge on uncalled share capital of the company,
(c) a charge created or evidenced by an instrument which, if executed by an individual, would require registration as a bill of sale,
(d) a charge on land (wherever situated) or any interest in it, but not including a charge for any rent or other periodical sum issuing out of the land,
(e) a charge on book debts of the company,
(f) a floating charge on the Company's undertaking or property,
(g) a charge on calls made but not paid,
(h) a charge on a ship or aircraft, or any share in a ship,
(j) a charge on goodwill, [or on any intellectual property].

(2) Where a negotiable instrument has been given to secure the payment of any book debts of a company, the deposit of the instrument for the purpose of securing an advance to the company is not, for purposes of sections 395, to be treated as a charge on those book debts.

(3) The holding of debentures entitling the holder to a charge on land is not for purposes of this section deemed to be an interest in land.

[(3A) The following are "intellectual property" for the purposes of this section—

(a) any patent, trade mark, ... registered design, copyright or design right;
(b) any licence under or in respect of any such right.]

(4) In this Chapter, "charge" includes mortgage.

[1067]

NOTES

Repealed by the Companies Act 2006, s 1295, Sch 16, as from 1 October 2009, subject to transitional provisions and savings in SI 2008/2860, Sch 2, paras 82–87.

Prospective replacement: see the note preceding s 395.

Sub-s (1): in para (j), words in square brackets substituted by the Copyright, Designs and Patents Act 1988, s 303(1), Sch 7, para 31(2).

Sub-s (3A): inserted by the Copyright, Designs and Patents Act 1988, s 303(1), Sch 7, para 31(2); words omitted repealed by the Trade Marks Act 1994, s 106(2), Sch 5.

Modification: references to trade marks or registered trade marks within the meaning of the Trade Marks Act 1938 shall, unless the context otherwise requires, be construed as references to trade marks or registered trade marks within the meaning of the Trade Marks Act 1994; see the Trade Marks Act 1994, Sch 4, para 1.

397 Formalities of registration (debentures)

(1) Where a series of debentures containing, or giving by reference to another instrument, any charge to the benefit of which the debenture holders of that series are entitled pari passu is created by a company, it is for purposes of section 395 sufficient if there are delivered to or received by the registrar, within 21 days after the execution of the deed containing the charge (or, if there is no such deed, after the execution of any debentures of the series), the following particulars in the prescribed form—

(a) the total amount secured by the whole series, and

(b) the dates of the resolutions authorising the issue of the series and the date of the covering deed (if any) by which the security is created or defined, and

(c) a general description of the property charged, and

(d) the names of the trustees (if any) for the debenture holders,

together with the deed containing the charge or, if there is no such deed, one of the debentures of the series:

Provided that there shall be sent to the registrar of companies, for entry in the register, particulars in the prescribed form of the date and amount of each issue of debentures of the series, but any omission to do this does not affect the validity of any of those debentures.

(2) Where any commission, allowance or discount has been paid or made either directly or indirectly by a company to a person in consideration of his—

(a) subscribing or agreeing to subscribe, whether absolutely or conditionally, for debentures of the company, or

(b) procuring or agreeing to procure subscriptions, whether absolute or conditional, for such debentures,

the particulars required to be sent for registration under section 395 shall include particulars as to the amount or rate per cent of the commission, discount or allowance so paid or made, but omission to do this does not affect the validity of the debentures issued.

(3) The deposit of debentures as security for a debt of the company is not, for the purposes of subsection (2), treated as the issue of the debentures at a discount.

[1068]

NOTES

Repealed by the Companies Act 2006, s 1295, Sch 16, as from 1 October 2009, subject to transitional provisions and savings in SI 2008/2860, Sch 2, paras 82–87.

Prospective replacement: see the note preceding s 395.

Regulations: the Companies (Forms) Regulations 1985, SI 1985/854; the Limited Liability Partnerships (Forms) Regulations 2001, SI 2001/927.

398 Verification of charge on property outside United Kingdom

(1) In the case of a charge created out of the United Kingdom comprising property situated outside the United Kingdom, the delivery to and the receipt by the registrar of companies of a copy (verified in the prescribed manner) of the instrument by which the charge is created or evidenced has the same effect for purposes of sections 395 to 398 as the delivery and receipt of the instrument itself.

(2) In that case, 21 days after the date on which the instrument or copy could, in due course of post (and if despatched with due diligence), have been received in the United Kingdom are substituted for the 21 days mentioned in section 395(2) (or as the case may be, section 397(1)) as the time within which the particulars and instrument or copy are to be delivered to the registrar.

(3) Where a charge is created in the United Kingdom but comprises property outside the United Kingdom, the instrument creating or purporting to create the charge may be sent for registration under section 395 notwithstanding that further proceedings may be necessary to make the charge valid or effectual according to the law of the country in which the property is situated.

(4) Where a charge comprises property situated in Scotland or Northern Ireland and registration in the country where the property is situated is necessary to make the charge valid or effectual according to the law of that country, the delivery to and receipt by the registrar of a copy (verified in the prescribed manner) of the instrument by which the charge is created or evidenced, together with a certificate in the prescribed form stating that the charge was presented for

registration in Scotland or Northern Ireland (as the case may be) on the date on which it was so presented has, for purposes of sections 395 to 398, the same effect as the delivery and receipt of the instrument itself.

[1069]

NOTES

Repealed by the Companies Act 2006, s 1295, Sch 16, as from 1 October 2009, subject to transitional provisions and savings in SI 2008/2860, Sch 2, paras 82–87.

Prospective replacement: see the note preceding s 395.

Regulations: the Companies (Forms) Regulations 1985, SI 1985/854; the Limited Liability Partnerships (Forms) Regulations 2001, SI 2001/927.

399 Company's duty to register charges it creates

(1) It is a company's duty to send to the registrar of companies for registration the particulars of every charge created by the company and of the issues of debentures of a series requiring registration under sections 395 to 398; but registration of any such charge may be effected on the application of any person interested in it.

(2) Where registration is effected on the application of some person other than the company, that person is entitled to recover from the company the amount of any fees properly paid by him to the registrar on the registration.

(3) If a company fails to comply with subsection (1), then, unless the registration has been effected on the application of some other person, the company and every officer of it who is in default is liable to a fine and, for continued contravention, to a daily default fine.

[1070]

NOTES

Repealed by the Companies Act 2006, s 1295, Sch 16, as from 1 October 2009, subject to transitional provisions and savings in SI 2008/2860, Sch 2, paras 82–87.

Prospective replacement: see the note preceding s 395.

400 Charges existing on property acquired

(1) This section applies where a company registered in England and Wales acquires property which is subject to a charge of any such kind as would, if it had been created by the company after the acquisition of the property, have been required to be registered under this Chapter.

(2) The company shall cause the prescribed particulars of the charge, together with a copy (certified in the prescribed manner to be a correct copy) of the instrument (if any) by which the charge was created or is evidenced, to be delivered to the registrar of companies for registration in manner required by this Chapter within 21 days after the date on which the acquisition is completed.

(3) However, if the property is situated and the charge was created outside Great Britain, 21 days after the date on which the copy of the instrument could in due course of post, and if despatched with due diligence, have been received in the United Kingdom is substituted for the 21 days above-mentioned as the time within which the particulars and copy of the instrument are to be delivered to the registrar.

(4) If default is made in complying with this section, the company and every officer of it who is in default is liable to a fine and, for continued contravention, to a daily default fine.

[1071]

NOTES

Repealed by the Companies Act 2006, s 1295, Sch 16, as from 1 October 2009, subject to transitional provisions and savings in SI 2008/2860, Sch 2, paras 82–87.

Prospective replacement: see the note preceding s 395.

Regulations: the Companies (Forms) Regulations 1985, SI 1985/854; the Limited Liability Partnerships (Forms) Regulations 2001, SI 2001/927.

401 Register of charges to be kept by registrar of companies

(1) The registrar of companies shall keep, with respect to each company, a register in the prescribed form of all the charges requiring registration under this Chapter; and he shall enter in the register with respect to such charges the following particulars—

- *(a) in the case of a charge to the benefit of which the holders of a series of debentures are entitled, the particulars specified in section 397(1),*
- *(b) in the case of any other charge—*
  - *(i) if it is a charge created by the company, the date of its creation, and if it is a charge which was existing on property acquired by the company, the date of the acquisition of the property, and*
  - *(ii) the amount secured by the charge, and*

(iii) short particulars of the property charged, and
(iv) the persons entitled to the charge.

(2) *The registrar shall give a certificate of the registration of any charge registered in pursuance of this Chapter, stating the amount secured by the charge.*

The certificate—
(*a*) *shall be either signed by the registrar, or authenticated by his official seal, and*
(*b*) *is conclusive evidence that the requirements of this Chapter as to registration have been satisfied.*

(*3*) *The register kept in pursuance of this section shall be open to inspection by any person.*

[1072]

NOTES

Repealed by the Companies Act 2006, s 1295, Sch 16, as from 1 October 2009, subject to transitional provisions and savings in SI 2008/2860, Sch 2, paras 82–87.

Prospective replacement: see the note preceding s 395.

Regulations: the Companies (Forms) Regulations 1985, SI 1985/854; the Limited Liability Partnerships (Forms) Regulations 2001, SI 2001/927.

402 Endorsement of certificate on debentures

(*1*) *The company shall cause a copy of every certificate of registration given under section 401 to be endorsed on every debenture or certificate of debenture stock which is issued by the company, and the payment of which is secured by the charge so registered.*

(*2*) *But this does not require a company to cause a certificate of registration of any charge so given to be endorsed on any debenture or certificate of debenture stock issued by the company before the charge was created.*

(*3*) *If a person knowingly and wilfully authorises or permits the delivery of a debenture or certificate of debenture stock which under this section is required to have endorsed on it a copy of a certificate of registration, without the copy being so endorsed upon it, he is liable (without prejudice to any other liability) to a fine.*

[1073]

NOTES

Repealed by the Companies Act 2006, s 1295, Sch 16, as from 1 October 2009, subject to transitional provisions and savings in SI 2008/2860, Sch 2, paras 82–87.

Prospective replacement: see the note preceding s 395.

403 Entries of satisfaction and release

(*1*) [*Subject to subsection (1A), the registrar*] *of companies, on receipt of a statutory declaration in the prescribed form verifying, with respect to a registered charge,—*
(*a*) *that the debt for which the charge was given has been paid or satisfied in whole or in part, or*
(*b*) *that part of the property or undertaking charged has been released from the charge or has ceased to form part of the company's property or undertaking,*

may enter on the register a memorandum of satisfaction in whole or in part, or of the fact that part of the property or undertaking has been released from the charge or has ceased to form part of the company's property or undertaking (as the case may be).

[(*1A*) *The registrar of companies may make any such entry as is mentioned in subsection* (*1*) *where, instead of receiving such a statutory declaration as is mentioned in that subsection, he receives a statement by a director, secretary, administrator or administrative receiver of the company which is contained in an electronic communication and that statement—*
(*a*) *verifies the matters set out in paragraph* (*a*) *or* (*b*) *of that subsection,*
(*b*) *contains a description of the charge,*
(*c*) *states the date of creation of the charge and the date of its registration under this Chapter,*
(*d*) *states the name and address of the chargee or, in the case of a debenture, trustee, and*
(*e*) *where paragraph* (*b*) *of subsection* (*1*) *applies, contains short particulars of the property or undertaking which has been released from the charge, or which has ceased to form part of the company's property or undertaking (as the case may be).*]

(*2*) *Where the registrar enters a memorandum of satisfaction in whole, he shall if required furnish the company with a copy of it.*

[(*2A*) *Any person who makes a false statement under subsection (1A) which he knows to be false or does not believe to be true is liable to imprisonment or a fine, or both.*]

[1074]

NOTES

Repealed by the Companies Act 2006, s 1295, Sch 16, as from 1 October 2009, subject to transitional provisions and savings in SI 2008/2860, Sch 2, paras 82–87.

Prospective replacement: see the note preceding s 395.

Sub-s (1): words in square brackets substituted by SI 2000/3373, art 22(1), (2).

Sub-s (1A): inserted by SI 2000/3373, art 22(1), (3).

Sub-s (2A): inserted by SI 2000/3373, art 22(1), (4).

Regulations: the Companies (Forms) Regulations 1985, SI 1985/854; the Limited Liability Partnerships (Forms) Regulations 2001, SI 2001/927.

[Further provisions with respect to voidness of charges]

404 Rectification of register of charges

(1) The following applies if the court is satisfied that the omission to register a charge within the time required by this Chapter or that the omission or mis-statement of any particular with respect to any such charge or in a memorandum of satisfaction was accidental, or due to inadvertence or to some other sufficient cause, or is not of a nature to prejudice the position of creditors or shareholders of the company, or that on other grounds it is just and equitable to grant relief.

(2) The court may, on the application of the company or a person interested, and on such terms and conditions as seem to the court just and expedient, order that the time for registration shall be extended or, as the case may be, that the omission or mis-statement shall be rectified.

[1075]

NOTES

Repealed by the Companies Act 2006, s 1295, Sch 16, as from 1 October 2009, subject to transitional provisions and savings in SI 2008/2860, Sch 2, paras 82–87.

Prospective replacement: see the note preceding s 395.

405 Registration of enforcement of security

(1) If a person obtains an order for the appointment of a receiver or manager of a company's property, or appoints such a receiver or manager under powers contained in an instrument, he shall within 7 days of the order or of the appointment under those powers, give notice of the fact to the registrar of companies; and the registrar shall enter the fact in the register of charges.

(2) Where a person appointed receiver or manager of a company's property under powers contained in an instrument ceases to act as such receiver or manager, he shall, on so ceasing, give the registrar notice to that effect, and the registrar shall enter the fact in the register of charges.

(3) A notice under this section shall be in the prescribed form.

(4) If a person makes default in complying with the requirements of this section, he is liable to a fine and, for continued contravention, to a daily default fine.

[1076]

NOTES

Repealed by the Companies Act 2006, s 1295, Sch 16, as from 1 October 2009, subject to transitional provisions and savings in SI 2008/2860, Sch 2, paras 82–87.

Prospective replacement: see the note preceding s 395.

Regulations: the Companies (Forms) Regulations 1985, SI 1985/854; the Limited Liability Partnerships (Forms) Regulations 2001, SI 2001/927.

406 Companies to keep copies of instruments creating charges

(1) Every company shall cause a copy of every instrument creating a charge requiring registration under this Chapter to be kept at its registered office.

(2) In the case of a series of uniform debentures, a copy of one debenture of the series is sufficient.

[1077]

NOTES

Repealed by the Companies Act 2006, s 1295, Sch 16, as from 1 October 2009, subject to transitional provisions and savings in SI 2008/2860, Sch 2, paras 82–87.

Prospective replacement: see the note preceding s 395.

407 Company's register of charges

(1) Every limited company shall keep at its registered office a register of charges and enter in it all charges specifically affecting property of the company and all floating charges on the company's undertaking or any of its property.

(2) The entry shall in each case give a short description of the property charged, the amount of the charge and, except in the case of securities to bearer, the names of the persons entitled to it.

(3) If an officer of the company knowingly and wilfully authorises or permits the omission of an entry required to be made in pursuance of this section, he is liable to a fine.

[1078]

NOTES

Repealed by the Companies Act 2006, s 1295, Sch 16, as from 1 October 2009, subject to transitional provisions and savings in SI 2008/2860, Sch 2, paras 82–87.

Prospective replacement: see the note preceding s 395.

[Additional information to be registered]

408 Right to inspect instruments which create charges, etc

(1) The copies of instruments creating any charge requiring registration under this Chapter with the registrar of companies, and the register of charges kept in pursuance of section 407, shall be open during business hours (but subject to such reasonable restrictions as the company in general meeting may impose, so that not less than 2 hours in each day be allowed for inspection) to the inspection of any creditor or member of the company without fee.

(2) The register of charges shall also be open to the inspection of any other person on payment of such fee, not exceeding 5 pence, for each inspection, as the company may prescribe.

(3) If inspection of the copies referred to, or of the register, is refused, every officer of the company who is in default is liable to a fine and, for continued contravention, to a daily default fine.

(4) If such a refusal occurs in relation to a company registered in England and Wales, the court may by order compel an immediate inspection of the copies or register.

[1079]

NOTES

Repealed by the Companies Act 2006, s 1295, Sch 16, as from 1 October 2009, subject to transitional provisions and savings in SI 2008/2860, Sch 2, paras 82–87.

Prospective replacement: see the note preceding s 395.

409 Charges on property in England and Wales created by oversea company

(1) This Chapter extends to charges on property in England and Wales which are created, and to charges on property in England and Wales which is acquired, by a company (whether a company within the meaning of this Act or not) incorporated outside Great Britain which has an established place of business in England and Wales.

(2) In relation to such a company, sections 406 and 407 apply with the substitution, for the reference to the company's registered office, of a reference to its principal place of business in England and Wales.

[1080]

NOTES

Repealed by the Companies Act 2006, s 1295, Sch 16, as from 1 October 2009, subject to transitional provisions and savings in SI 2008/2860, Sch 2, paras 82–87.

Prospective replacement: see the note preceding s 395.

Regulations: the Companies (Forms) Regulations 1985, SI 1985/854.

CHAPTER II
REGISTRATION OF CHARGES (SCOTLAND)

410 Charges void unless registered

(1) The following provisions of this Chapter have effect for the purpose of securing the registration in Scotland of charges created by companies.

(2) Every charge created by a company, being a charge to which this section applies, is, so far as any security on the company's property or any part of it is conferred by the charge, void against the liquidator [or administrator] and any creditor of the company unless the prescribed particulars of the charge, together with a copy (certified in the prescribed manner to be a correct copy) of the instrument (if any) by which the charge is created or evidenced, are delivered to or received by the registrar of companies for registration in the manner required by this Chapter within 21 days after the date of the creation of the charge.

(3) Subsection (2) is without prejudice to any contract or obligation for repayment of the money secured by the charge; and when a charge becomes void under this section the money secured by it immediately becomes payable.

(4) This section applies to the following charges—

(*a*) *a charge on land wherever situated, or any interest in such land (not including a charge for any rent … or other periodical sum payable in respect of the land, but including a charge created by a heritable security within the meaning of section 9(8) of the Conveyancing and Feudal Reform (Scotland) Act 1970),*
(*b*) *a security over the uncalled share capital of the company,*
(*c*) *a security over incorporeal moveable property of any of the following categories—*
(*i*) *the book debts of the company,*
(*ii*) *calls made but not paid,*
(*iii*) *goodwill,*
(*iv*) *a patent or a licence under a patent,*
(*v*) *a trade mark,*
(*vi*) *a copyright or a licence under a copyright,*
[(*vii*) *a registered design or a licence in respect of such a design,*
(*viii*) *a design right or a licence under a design right,*]
(*d*) *a security over a ship or aircraft or any share in a ship, and*
(*e*) *a floating charge.*

(*5*) *In this Chapter "company" (except in section 424) means an incorporated company registered in Scotland; "registrar of companies" means the registrar or other officer performing under this Act the duty of registration of companies in Scotland; and references to the date of creation of a charge are—*
(*a*) *in the case of a floating charge, the date on which the instrument creating the floating charge was executed by the company creating the charge, and*
(*b*) *in any other case, the date on which the right of the person entitled to the benefit of the charge was constituted as a real right.*

[1081]

NOTES

Repealed by the Companies Act 2006, s 1295, Sch 16, as from 1 October 2009, subject to transitional provisions and savings in SI 2008/2860, Sch 2, paras 82–87.

Prospective replacement: see the note preceding s 395.

Sub-s (2): words in square brackets inserted by the Insolvency Act 1985, s 109, Sch 6, para 10.

Sub-s (4): in para (a) words omitted repealed by the Abolition of Feudal Tenure etc (Scotland) Act 2000, s 76(1), (2), Sch 12, para 46(1)–(4), Sch 13.

Sub-s (4): sub-paras (c)(vii), (viii) inserted by the Copyright, Designs and Patents Act 1988, s 303(1), Sch 7, para 31(3).

Modification: references to trade marks or registered trade marks within the meaning of the Trade Marks Act 1938 shall, unless the context otherwise requires, be construed as references to trade marks or registered trade marks within the meaning of the Trade Marks Act 1994; see the Trade Marks Act 1994, Sch 4, para 1.

Disapplication: this section is disapplied in relation to a security financial collateral arrangement or any charge created or otherwise arising under a security financial collateral arrangement by the Financial Collateral Arrangements (No 2) Regulations 2003, SI 2003/3226, reg 5.

Regulations: the Companies (Forms) Regulations 1985, SI 1985/854; the Limited Liability Partnerships (Forms) Regulations 2001, SI 2001/927.

[Copies of instruments and register to be kept by company]

411 Charges on property outside United Kingdom

(*1*) *In the case of a charge created out of the United Kingdom comprising property situated outside the United Kingdom, the period of 21 days after the date on which the copy of the instrument creating it could (in due course of post, and if despatched with due diligence) have been received in the United Kingdom is substituted for the period of 21 days after the date of the creation of the charge as the time within which, under section 410(2), the particulars and copy are to be delivered to the registrar.*

(*2*) *Where a charge is created in the United Kingdom but comprises property outside the United Kingdom, the copy of the instrument creating or purporting to create the charge may be sent for registration under section 410 notwithstanding that further proceedings may be necessary to make the charge valid or effectual according to the law of the country in which the property is situated.*

[1082]

NOTES

Repealed by the Companies Act 2006, s 1295, Sch 16, as from 1 October 2009, subject to transitional provisions and savings in SI 2008/2860, Sch 2, paras 82–87.

Prospective replacement: see the note preceding s 395.

412 Negotiable instrument to secure book debts

Where a negotiable instrument has been given to secure the payment of any book debts of a company, the deposit of the instrument for the purpose of securing an advance to the company is not, for purposes of section 410, to be treated as a charge on those book debts.

[1083]

NOTES

Repealed by the Companies Act 2006, s 1295, Sch 16, as from 1 October 2009, subject to transitional provisions and savings in SI 2008/2860, Sch 2, paras 82–87.

Prospective replacement: see the note preceding s 395.

[Supplementary provisions]

413 Charges associated with debentures

(1) The holding of debentures entitling the holder to a charge on land is not, for the purposes of section 410, deemed to be an interest in land.

(2) Where a series of debentures containing, or giving by reference to any other instrument, any charge to the benefit of which the debenture-holders of that series are entitled pari passu, is created by a company, it is sufficient for purposes of section 410 if there are delivered to or received by the registrar of companies within 21 days after the execution of the deed containing the charge or if there is no such deed, after the execution of any debentures of the series, the following particulars in the prescribed form—

- *(a) the total amount secured by the whole series,*
- *(b) the dates of the resolutions authorising the issue of the series and the date of the covering deed (if any) by which the security is created or defined,*
- *(c) a general description of the property charged,*
- *(d) the names of the trustees (if any) for the debenture holders, and*
- *(e) in the case of a floating charge, a statement of any provisions of the charge and of any instrument relating to it which prohibit or restrict or regulate the power of the company to grant further securities ranking in priority to, or pari passu with, the floating charge, or which vary or otherwise regulate the order of ranking of the floating charge in relation to subsisting securities,*

together with a copy of the deed containing the charge or, if there is no such deed, of one of the debentures of the series:

Provided that where more than one issue is made of debentures in the series, there shall be sent to the registrar of companies for entry in the register particulars (in the prescribed form) of the date and amount of each issue of debentures of the series, but any omission to do this does not affect the validity of any of those debentures.

(3) Where any commission, allowance or discount has been paid or made, either directly or indirectly, by a company to any person in consideration of his subscribing or agreeing to subscribe, whether absolutely or conditionally, for any debentures of the company, or procuring or agreeing to procure subscriptions (whether absolute or conditional) for any such debentures, the particulars required to be sent for registration under section 410 include particulars as to the amount or rate per cent of the commission, discount or allowance so paid or made; but any omission to do this does not affect the validity of the debentures issued.

The deposit of any debentures as security for any debt of the company is not, for purposes of this subsection, treated as the issue of the debentures at a discount.

[1084]

NOTES

Repealed by the Companies Act 2006, s 1295, Sch 16, as from 1 October 2009, subject to transitional provisions and savings in SI 2008/2860, Sch 2, paras 82–87.

Prospective replacement: see the note preceding s 395.

Regulations: the Companies (Forms) Regulations 1985, SI 1985/854; the Limited Liability Partnerships (Forms) Regulations 2001, SI 2001/927.

414 Charge by way of ex facie absolute disposition, etc

(1) For the avoidance of doubt, it is hereby declared that, in the case of a charge created by way of an ex facie absolute disposition or assignation qualified by a back letter or other agreement, or by a standard security qualified by an agreement, compliance with section 410(2) does not of itself render the charge unavailable as security for indebtedness incurred after the date of compliance.

(2) Where the amount secured by a charge so created is purported to be increased by a further back letter or agreement, a further charge is held to have been created by the ex facie absolute disposition or assignation or (as the case may be) by the standard security, as qualified by the further back letter or agreement; and the provisions of this Chapter apply to the further charge as if—

- *(a) references in this Chapter (other than in this section) to the charge were references to the further charge, and* (*b*) *references to the date of the creation of the charge were references to the date on which the further back letter or agreement was executed.*

[1085]

NOTES

Repealed by the Companies Act 2006, s 1295, Sch 16, as from 1 October 2009, subject to transitional provisions and savings in SI 2008/2860, Sch 2, paras 82–87.

Prospective replacement: see the note preceding s 395.

415 Company's duty to register charges created by it

(1) It is a company's duty to send to the registrar of companies for registration the particulars of every charge created by the company and of the issues of debentures of a series requiring registration under sections 410 to 414; but registration of any such charge may be effected on the application of any person interested in it.

(2) Where registration is effected on the application of some person other than the company, that person is entitled to recover from the company the amount of any fees properly paid by him to the registrar on the registration.

(3) If a company makes default in sending to the registrar for registration the particulars of any charge created by the company or of the issues of debentures of a series requiring registration as above mentioned, then, unless the registration has been effected on the application of some other person, the company and every officer of it who is in default is liable to a fine and, for continued contravention, to a daily default fine.

[1086]

NOTES

Repealed by the Companies Act 2006, s 1295, Sch 16, as from 1 October 2009, subject to transitional provisions and savings in SI 2008/2860, Sch 2, paras 82–87.

Prospective replacement: see the note preceding s 395.

416 Duty to register charges existing on property acquired

(1) Where a company acquires any property which is subject to a charge of any kind as would, if it had been created by the company after the acquisition of the property, have been required to be registered under this Chapter, the company shall cause the prescribed particulars of the charge, together with a copy (certified in the prescribed manner to be a correct copy) of the instrument (if any) by which the charge was created or is evidenced, to be delivered to the registrar of companies for registration in the manner required by this Chapter within 21 days after the date on which the transaction was settled.

(2) *If, however, the property is situated and the charge was created outside Great Britain, 21 days after the date on which the copy of the instrument could (in due course of post, and if despatched with due diligence) have been received in the United Kingdom are substituted for 21 days after the settlement of the transaction as the time within which the particulars and the copy of the instrument are to be delivered to the registrar.*

(3) If default is made in complying with this section, the company and every officer of it who is in default is liable to a fine and, for continued contravention, to a daily default fine.

[1087]

NOTES

Repealed by the Companies Act 2006, s 1295, Sch 16, as from 1 October 2009, subject to transitional provisions and savings in SI 2008/2860, Sch 2, paras 82–87.

Prospective replacement: see the note preceding s 395.

Regulations: the Companies (Forms) Regulations 1985, SI 1985/854; the Limited Liability Partnerships (Forms) Regulations 2001, SI 2001/927.

417 Register of charges to be kept by registrar of companies

(1) The registrar of companies shall keep, with respect to each company, a register in the prescribed form of all the charges requiring registration under this Chapter, and shall enter in the register with respect to such charges the particulars specified below.

(2) *In the case of a charge to the benefit of which the holders of a series of debentures are entitled, there shall be entered in the register the particulars specified in section 413*(2).

(3) In the case of any other charge there shall be entered—

(*a*) *if it is a charge created by the company, the date of its creation, and if it was a charge existing on property acquired by the company, the date of the acquisition of the property,*

(*b*) *the amount secured by the charge,*

(*c*) *short particulars of the property charged,*

(*d*) *the persons entitled to the charge, and*

(*e*) *in the case of a floating charge, a statement of any of the provisions of the charge and of any instrument relating to it which prohibit or restrict or regulate the company's power to grant further securities ranking in priority to, or pari passu with, the floating charge, or which vary or otherwise regulate the order of ranking of the floating charge in relation to subsisting securities.*

(*4*) *The register kept in pursuance of this section shall be open to inspection by any person.*

[1088]

NOTES

Repealed by the Companies Act 2006, s 1295, Sch 16, as from 1 October 2009, subject to transitional provisions and savings in SI 2008/2860, Sch 2, paras 82–87.

Prospective replacement: see the note preceding s 395.

Regulations: the Companies (Forms) Regulations 1985, SI 1985/854; the Limited Liability Partnerships (Forms) Regulations 2001, SI 2001/927.

418 Certificate of registration to be issued

(*1*) *The registrar of companies shall give a certificate of the registration of any charge registered in pursuance of this Chapter.*

(*2*) *The certificate—*

(*a*) *shall be either signed by the registrar, or authenticated by his official seal,*

(*b*) *shall state the name of the company and the person first-named in the charge among those entitled to the benefit of the charge (or, in the case of a series of debentures, the name of the holder of the first such debenture to be issued) and the amount secured by the charge, and*

(*c*) *is conclusive evidence that the requirements of this Chapter as to registration have been complied with.*

[1089]

NOTES

Repealed by the Companies Act 2006, s 1295, Sch 16, as from 1 October 2009, subject to transitional provisions and savings in SI 2008/2860, Sch 2, paras 82–87.

Prospective replacement: see the note preceding s 395.

419 Entries of satisfaction and relief

(*1*) *[Subject to subsections (1A) and (1B), the registrar] of companies, on application being made to him in the prescribed form, and on receipt of a statutory declaration in the prescribed form verifying, with respect to any registered charge,—*

(*a*) *that the debt for which the charge was given has been paid or satisfied in whole or in part, or*

(*b*) *that part of the property charged has been released from the charge or has ceased to form part of the company's property,*

may enter on the register a memorandum of satisfaction (in whole or in part) regarding that fact.

[(1A) On an application being made to him in the prescribed form, the registrar of companies may make any such entry as is mentioned in subsection (1) where, instead of receiving such a statutory declaration as is mentioned in that subsection, he receives a statement by a director, secretary, liquidator, receiver or administrator of the company which is contained in an electronic communication and that statement—

(*a*) *verifies the matters set out in paragraph (a) or (b) of that subsection,*

(*b*) *contains a description of the charge,*

(*c*) *states the date of creation of the charge and the date of its registration under this Chapter,*

(*d*) *states the name and address of the chargee or, in the case of a debenture, trustee, and*

(*e*) *where paragraph (b) of subsection (1) applies, contains short particulars of the property which has been released from the charge, or which has ceased to form part of the company's property (as the case may be).*

(1B) Where the statement under subsection (1A) concerns the satisfaction of a floating charge, then there shall be delivered to the registrar a further statement which—

(*a*) *is made by the creditor entitled to the benefit of the floating charge or a person authorised to act on his behalf;*

(*b*) *is incorporated into, or logically associated with, the electronic communication containing the statement; and*

(*c*) *certifies that the particulars contained in the statement are correct.]*

(*2*) *Where the registrar enters a memorandum of satisfaction in whole, he shall, if required, furnish the company with a copy of the memorandum.*

(3) Without prejudice to the registrar's duty under this section to require to be satisfied as above mentioned, he shall not be so satisfied unless—

- *(a) the creditor entitled to the benefit of the floating charge, or a person authorised to do so on his behalf, certifies as correct the particulars submitted to the registrar with respect to the entry on the register of a memorandum under this section, or*
- *(b) the court, on being satisfied that such certification cannot readily be obtained, directs him accordingly.*

(4) Nothing in this section requires the company to submit particulars with respect to the entry in the register of a memorandum of satisfaction where the company, having created a floating charge over all or any part of its property, disposes of part of the property subject to the floating charge.

(5) A memorandum or certification required for the purposes of this section shall be in such form as may be prescribed.

[(5A) Any person who makes a false statement under subsection (1A) or (1B) which he knows to be false or does not believe to be true is liable to imprisonment or a fine, or both.]

[1090]

NOTES

Repealed by the Companies Act 2006, s 1295, Sch 16, as from 1 October 2009, subject to transitional provisions and savings in SI 2008/2860, Sch 2, paras 82–87.

Prospective replacement: see the note preceding s 395.

Sub-s (1): words in square brackets substituted by SI 2000/3373, art 23(1), (2).

Sub-ss (1A), (1B): inserted by SI 2000/3373, art 23(1), (3).

Sub-s (5A): inserted by SI 2000/3373, art 23(1), (4).

Regulations: the Companies (Forms) Regulations 1985, SI 1985/854; the Limited Liability Partnerships (Forms) Regulations 2001, SI 2001/927.

420 Rectification of register

The court, on being satisfied that the omission to register a charge within the time required by this Act or that the omission or mis-statement of any particular with respect to any such charge or in a memorandum of satisfaction was accidental, or due to inadvertence or to some other sufficient cause, or is not of a nature to prejudice the position of creditors or shareholders of the company, or that it is on other grounds just and equitable to grant relief, may, on the application of the company or any person interested, and on such terms and conditions as seem to the court just and expedient, order that the time for registration shall be extended or (as the case may be) that the omission or mis-statement shall be rectified.

[1091]

NOTES

Repealed by the Companies Act 2006, s 1295, Sch 16, as from 1 October 2009, subject to transitional provisions and savings in SI 2008/2860, Sch 2, paras 82–87.

Prospective replacement: see the note preceding s 395.

421 Copies of instruments creating charges to be kept by company

(1) Every company shall cause a copy of every instrument creating a charge requiring registration under this Chapter to be kept at the company's registered office.

(2) In the case of a series of uniform debentures, a copy of one debenture of the series is sufficient.

[1092]

NOTES

Repealed by the Companies Act 2006, s 1295, Sch 16, as from 1 October 2009, subject to transitional provisions and savings in SI 2008/2860, Sch 2, paras 82–87.

Prospective replacement: see the note preceding s 395.

422 Company's register of charges

(1) Every company shall keep at its registered office a register of charges and enter in it all charges specifically affecting property of the company, and all floating charges on any property of the company.

(2) There shall be given in each case a short description of the property charged, the amount of the charge and, except in the case of securities to bearer, the names of the persons entitled to it.

(3) If an officer of the company knowingly and wilfully authorises or permits the omission of an entry required to be made in pursuance of this section, he is liable to a fine.

[1093]

NOTES

Repealed by the Companies Act 2006, s 1295, Sch 16, as from 1 October 2009, subject to transitional provisions and savings in SI 2008/2860, Sch 2, paras 82–87.

Prospective replacement: see the note preceding s 395.

423 Right to inspect copies of instruments, and company's register

(*1*) *The copies of instruments creating charges requiring registration under this Chapter with the registrar of companies, and the register of charges kept in pursuance of section 422, shall be open during business hours (but subject to such reasonable restrictions as the company in general meeting may impose, so that not less than 2 hours in each day be allowed for inspection) to the inspection of any creditor or member of the company without fee.*

(*2*) *The register of charges shall be open to the inspection of any other person on payment of such fee, not exceeding 5 pence for each inspection, as the company may prescribe.*

(*3*) *If inspection of the copies or register is refused, every officer of the company who is in default is liable to a fine and, for continued contravention, to a daily default fine.*

(*4*) *If such a refusal occurs in relation to a company, the court may by order compel an immediate inspection of the copies or register.*

[1094]

NOTES

Repealed by the Companies Act 2006, s 1295, Sch 16, as from 1 October 2009, subject to transitional provisions and savings in SI 2008/2860, Sch 2, paras 82–87.

Prospective replacement: see the note preceding s 395.

424 Extension of Chapter II

(*1*) *This Chapter extends to charges on property in Scotland which are created, and to charges on property in Scotland which is acquired, by a company incorporated outside Great Britain which has a place of business in Scotland.*

(*2*) *In relation to such a company, sections 421 and 422 apply with the substitution, for the reference to the company's registered office, of a reference to its principal place of business in Scotland.*

[1095]

NOTES

Repealed by the Companies Act 2006, s 1295, Sch 16, as from 1 October 2009, subject to transitional provisions and savings in SI 2008/2860, Sch 2, paras 82–87.

Prospective replacement: see the note preceding s 395.

425–500 (*Ss 425–487* (*Pts XIII–XVIII*) *outside the scope of this work; ss 488–500* (*Pt XIX*) *repealed by the Insolvency Act 1986, s 438, Sch 12.*)

PART XX
WINDING-UP OF COMPANIES REGISTERED UNDER THIS ACT OR THE FORMER COMPANIES ACTS

501–650 ((*Chs I–V*) *repealed by the Insolvency Act 1986, s 438, Sch 12.*)

CHAPTER VI
MATTERS ARISING SUBSEQUENT TO WINDING UP

651–653 (*Outside the scope of this work.*)

654 Property of dissolved company to be bona vacantia

(*1*) *When a company is dissolved, all property and rights whatsoever vested in or held on trust for the company immediately before its dissolution (including leasehold property, but not including property held by the company on trust for any other person) are deemed to be bona vacantia and—*

(*a*) *accordingly belong to the Crown, or to the Duchy of Lancaster or to the Duke of Cornwall for the time being (as the case may be), and*

(*b*) *vest and may be dealt with in the same manner as other bona vacantia accruing to the Crown, to the Duchy of Lancaster or to the Duke of Cornwall.*

(*2*) *Except as provided by the section next following, the above has effect subject and without prejudice to any order made by the court under section 651 or 653.*

[1096]

NOTES

Repealed by the Companies Act 2006, s 1295, Sch 16, as from 1 October 2009, subject to transitional provisions and savings in SI 2008/2860, Sch 2, para 88.

Modification: modified by the Building Societies Act 1986, s 90, Sch 15, Pt IV, para 57.

See further: the Companies Consolidation (Consequential Provisions) Act 1985, s 22.

655 Effect on s 654 of company's revival after dissolution

(1) The person in whom any property or right is vested by section 654 may dispose of, or of an interest in, that property or right notwithstanding that an order may be made under section 651 or 653.

(2) Where such an order is made—

(a) it does not affect the disposition (but without prejudice to the order so far as it relates to any other property or right previously vested in or held on trust for the company), and

(b) the Crown or, as the case may be, the Duke of Cornwall shall pay to the company an amount equal to—

(i) the amount of any consideration received for the property or right, or interest therein, or

(ii) the value of any such consideration at the time of the disposition,

or, if no consideration was received, an amount equal to the value of the property, right or interest disposed of, as at the date of the disposition.

(3) Where a liability accrues under subsection (2) in respect of any property or right which, before the order under section 651 or 653 was made, had accrued as bona vacantia to the Duchy of Lancaster, the Attorney General of the Duchy shall represent Her Majesty in any proceedings arising in connection with that liability.

(4) Where a liability accrues under subsection (2) in respect of any property or right which, before the order under section 651 or 653 was made, had accrued as bona vacantia to the Duchy of Cornwall, such persons as the Duke of Cornwall (or other possessor for the time being of the Duchy) may appoint shall represent the Duke (or other possessor) in any proceedings arising out of that liability.

(5) This section applies in relation to the disposition of any property, right or interest on or after 22nd December 1981, whether the company concerned was dissolved before, on or after that day.

[1097]

NOTES

Repealed by the Companies Act 2006, s 1295, Sch 16, as from 1 October 2009.

656 Crown disclaimer of property vesting as bona vacantia

(1) Where property vests in the Crown under section 654, the Crown's title to it under that section may be disclaimed by a notice signed by the Crown representative, that is to say the Treasury Solicitor, or, in relation to property in Scotland, the Queen's and Lord Treasurer's Remembrancer.

(2) The right to execute a notice of disclaimer under this section may be waived by or on behalf of the Crown either expressly or by taking possession or other act evincing that intention.

(3) A notice of disclaimer under this section is of no effect unless it is executed—

(a) within 12 months of the date on which the vesting of the property under section 654 came to the notice of the Crown representative, or

(b) if an application in writing is made to the Crown representative by any person interested in the property requiring him to decide whether he will or will not disclaim, within a period of 3 months after the receipt of the application or such further period as may be allowed by the court which would have had jurisdiction to wind up the company if it had not been dissolved.

(4) A statement in a notice of disclaimer of any property under this section that the vesting of it came to the notice of the Crown representative on a specified date, or that no such application as above mentioned was received by him with respect to the property before a specified date, is sufficient evidence of the fact stated, until the contrary is proved.

(5) A notice of disclaimer under this section shall be delivered to the registrar of companies and retained and registered by him; and copies of it shall be published in the Gazette and sent to any persons who have given the Crown representative notice that they claim to be interested in the property.

(6) This section applies to property vested in the Duchy of Lancaster or the Duke of Cornwall under section 654 as if for references to the Crown and the Crown representative there were

respectively substituted references to the Duchy of Lancaster and to the Solicitor to that Duchy, or to the Duke of Cornwall and to the Solicitor to the Duchy of Cornwall, as the case may be.

[1098]–[1111]

NOTES

Repealed by the Companies Act 2006, s 1295, Sch 16, as from 1 October 2009, subject to transitional provisions and savings in SI 2008/2860, Sch 2, para 88.

657–690 (*Ss 657, 658, ss 675–690 (Pt XXII) outside the scope of this work, ss 659–674 (Pt XX, Chapter VII, Pt XXI) repealed by the Insolvency Act 1986, s 438, Sch 12.*)

PART XXIII
OVERSEA COMPANIES

690A–703R ((*Chs I–IV) outside the scope of this work.*)

PART XXIV
THE REGISTRAR OF COMPANIES, HIS FUNCTIONS AND OFFICES

704–711 (*Ss 704–706, 707A–711 outside the scope of this work; s 707 repealed by the Companies Act 1985 (Electronic Communications) Order 2000, SI 2000/3373, art 31(4).*)

711A (*Inserted by the Companies Act 1989, s 142(1), as from a day to be appointed; repealed by the Companies Act 2006, s 1295, Sch 16, as from 1 October 2009.*)

712–734 (*Ss 712, 715 repealed by the Companies Act 1989, ss 127(3), 212, Sch 24; ss 713, 714, 715A, ss 716–734 (Pt XXV) outside the scope of this work.*)

PART XXVI
INTERPRETATION

735–743 (*Outside the scope of this work.*)

744 Expressions used generally in this Act

In this Act, unless the contrary intention appears, the following definitions apply—

"agent" does not include a person's counsel acting as such;

…

"articles" means, in relation to a company, its articles of association, as originally framed or as altered by resolution, including (so far as applicable to the company) regulations contained in or annexed to any enactment relating to companies passed before this Act, as altered by or under any such enactment;

[…]

…

"bank holiday" means a holiday under the Banking and Financial Dealings Act 1971;

[…]

"books and papers" and "books or papers" include accounts, deeds, writings and documents;

["communication" means the same as in the Electronic Communications Act 2000;]

"the Companies Acts" means this Act, the [insider dealing legislation] and the Consequential Provisions Act;

"the Consequential Provisions Act" means the Companies Consolidation (Consequential Provisions) Act 1985;

"the court", in relation to a company, means the court having jurisdiction to wind up the company;

…

"document" includes summons, notice, order, and other legal process, and registers;

[…]

["electronic communication" means the same as in the Electronic Communications Act 2000;]

"equity share capital" means, in relation to a company, its issued share capital excluding any part of that capital which, neither as respects dividends nor as respects capital, carries any right to participate beyond a specified amount in a distribution;

"expert" has the meaning given by section 62;

"floating charge" includes a floating charge within the meaning given by section 462;

"the Gazette" means, as respects companies registered in England and Wales, the London Gazette and, as respects companies registered in Scotland, the Edinburgh Gazette;

…

"hire-purchase agreement" has the same meaning as in the Consumer Credit Act 1974;

["the insider dealing legislation" means Part V of the Criminal Justice Act 1993 (insider dealing).]

[...]

...

"joint stock company" has the meaning given by section 683;

"memorandum", in relation to a company, means its memorandum of association, as originally framed or as altered in pursuance of any enactment;

"number", in relation to shares, includes amount, where the context admits of the reference to shares being construed to include stock;

"officer", in relation to a body corporate, includes a director, manager or secretary;

"official seal", in relation to the registrar of companies, means a seal prepared under section 704(4) for the authentication of documents required for or in connection with the registration of companies;

"oversea company" means—

(*a*) *a company incorporated elsewhere than in Great Britain which, after the commencement of this Act, establishes a place of business in Great Britain, and*

(*b*) *a company so incorporated which has, before that commencement, established a place of business and continues to have an established place of business in Great Britain at that commencement;*

"place of business" includes a share transfer or share registration office;

...

"prospectus" means any prospectus, notice, circular, advertisement, or other invitation, offering to the public for subscription or purchase any shares in or debentures of a company;

"prospectus issued generally" means a prospectus issued to persons who are not existing members of the company or holders of its debentures;

...

["regulated activity" has the meaning given in section 22 of the Financial Services and Markets Act 2000;]

"the registrar of companies" and "the registrar" mean the registrar or other officer performing under this Act the duty of registration of companies in England and Wales or in Scotland, as the case may require;

"share" means share in the share capital of a company, and includes stock (except where a distinction between shares and stock is express or implied); and

...

[1112]

NOTES

Repealed by the Companies Act 2006, s 1295, Sch 16, as from 6 April 2007 (in so far as relating to the definition "EEA State" (omitted)), as from 6 April 2008 (in so far as relating to the definitions "authorised minimum", "debenture", "insurance market activity", "prescribed" and "undistributable reserves" (omitted), and as from 1 October 2009 (otherwise).

Definition "annual return" (omitted) repealed by the Companies Act 1989, s 212, Sch 24.

Definition "authorised institution" (omitted) inserted by the Banking Act 1987, s 108(1), Sch 6, para 18(8) and repealed by the Companies Act 1989, ss 23, 212, Sch 10, Pt I, para 16, Sch 24.

Definitions "authorised minimum", "expert", "floating charge", "joint stock company", "undistributable reserves" repealed by the Companies Act 1989, s 212, Sch 24, as from a day to be appointed.

Definition "banking company" (omitted) inserted by the Companies Act 1989, s 23, Sch 10, Pt I, para 16 and repealed by SI 2001/3649, art 30(a).

Definitions "communication" and "electronic communication" inserted by SI 2000/3373, art 29.

In definition "Companies Acts" words in square brackets substituted by the Criminal Justice Act 1993, s 79(13), Sch 5, para 4.

Definition "EEA State" inserted by SI 1997/2306, reg 4(1); substituted by SI 2007/732, reg 2.

Definition "general rules" (omitted) repealed by the Insolvency Act 1985, s 235(3), Sch 10, Pt II.

Definition "the insider dealing legislation" inserted by the Criminal Justice Act 1993, s 79(13), Sch 5, para 4.

Definitions "insurance market activity", "regulated activity" inserted and definition "insurance company" (omitted) repealed by SI 2001/3649, art 30.

In definition "prescribed" words omitted repealed by the Insolvency Act 1985, s 235(3), Sch 10, Pt II.

Definition "prospectus issued generally" repealed for certain purposes and for remaining purposes as from a day to be appointed by the Financial Services Act 1986, s 212(3), Sch 17, Pt I; for purposes see SI 1988/740, Schedule.

Definition "recognised bank" (omitted) repealed by the Banking Act 1987, s 108, Sch 6, para 18(8), Sch 7, Pt I.

Definition "recognised stock exchange" (omitted) repealed by the Financial Services Act 1986, s 212(3), Sch 17, Pt I.

744A (*Outside the scope of this work.*)

PART XXVII
FINAL PROVISIONS

745, 746 (*Outside the scope of this work.*)

747 Citation

This Act may be cited as the Companies Act 1985.

[1113]–[1134]

(*Schs 1–25 outside the scope of this work.*)

ADMINISTRATION OF JUSTICE ACT 1985

(1985 c 61)

An Act to make further provision with respect to the administration of justice and matters connected therewith; to amend the Solicitors Act 1974; to regulate the provision of solicitors' services in the case of incorporated practices; to regulate the provision of conveyancing services by persons practising as licensed conveyancers; to make further provision with respect to complaints relating to the provision of legal aid services; to amend the law relating to time limits for actions for libel and slander; and to make further provision with respect to arbitrations and proceedings in connection with European patents

[30 October 1985]

1–46 ((*Pts I–III*) *outside the scope of this work.*)

PART IV
THE SUPREME COURT AND COUNTY COURTS

Proceedings relating to estates of deceased persons and trusts

47 Power of High Court to make judgments binding on persons who are not parties

(1) This section applies to actions in the High Court relating to the estates of deceased persons or to trusts and falling within any description specified in rules of court.

(2) Rules of court may make provision for enabling any judgment given in an action to which this section applies to be made binding on persons who—

(a) are or may be affected by the judgment and would not otherwise be bound by it; but
(b) have in accordance with the rules been given notice of the action and of such matters connected with it as the rules may require.

(3) Different provision may be made under this section in relation to actions of different descriptions.

[1135]

48, 49 (*Outside the scope of this work.*)

50 Power of High Court to appoint substitute for, or to remove, personal representative

(1) Where an application relating to the estate of a deceased person is made to the High Court under this subsection by or on behalf of a personal representative of the deceased or a beneficiary of the estate, the court may in its discretion—

(a) appoint a person (in this section called a substituted personal representative) to act as personal representative of the deceased in place of the existing personal representative or representatives of the deceased or any of them; or
(b) if there are two or more existing personal representatives of the deceased, terminate the appointment of one or more, but not all, of those persons.

(2) Where the court appoints a person to act as a substituted personal representative of a deceased person, then—

(a) if that person is appointed to act with an executor or executors the appointment shall (except for the purpose of including him in any chain of representation) constitute him executor of the deceased as from the date of the appointment; and
(b) in any other case the appointment shall constitute that person administrator of the deceased's estate as from the date of the appointment.

(3) The court may authorise a person appointed as a substituted personal representative to charge remuneration for his services as such, on such terms (whether or not involving the submission of bills of charges for taxation by the court) as the court may think fit.

(4) Where an application relating to the estate of a deceased person is made to the court under subsection (1), the court may, if it thinks fit, proceed as if the application were, or included, an application for the appointment under the Judicial Trustees Act 1896 of a judicial trustee in relation to that estate.

(5) In this section "beneficiary", in relation to the estate of a deceased person, means a person who under the will of the deceased or under the law relating to intestacy is beneficially interested in the estate.

(6) …

[1136]

NOTES

Sub-s (6): amends the Judicial Trustees Act 1896, s 1.

51–56 (*Ss 51–53, 55 outside the scope of this work; s 54 repealed by the Courts Act 2003, s 109(3), Sch 10; s 56 amends the County Courts Act 1984, ss 138, 139.*)

PART V
MISCELLANEOUS AND SUPPLEMENTARY

57–65 (*S 57 repealed by the Defamation Act 1996, s 16, Sch 2; s 58 repealed by the Arbitration Act 1996, s 107(2), Sch 4; ss 59, 61, 62, 64 outside the scope of this work; s 60 repealed by the Copyright, Designs and Patents Act 1988, s 303(2), Sch 8; s 63 repealed by the Courts and Legal Services Act 1990, s 125(7), Sch 20; s 65 repealed by the Access to Justice Act 1999, s 106, Sch 15, Pt II.*)

Supplementary

66–68 (*S 66 repealed by the Building Societies Act 1986, s 120(2), Sch 19, Pt I, ss 67, 68 outside the scope of this work.*)

69 Short title, commencement, transitional provisions and savings

(1) This Act may be cited as the Administration of Justice Act 1985.

(2) Subject to subsections (3) and (4), this Act shall come into force on such day as the [Lord Chancellor] may by order made by statutory instrument appoint; and an order under this subsection may appoint different days for different provisions and for different purposes.

(3) The following provisions of this Act shall come into force on the day this Act is passed—
- (a) section 63;
- (b) Part I of Schedule 8 and section 67(2) so far as relating thereto;
- (c) section 68;
- (d) this section and Schedule 9.

(4) The following provisions of this Act shall come into force at the end of the period of two months beginning with the day on which this Act is passed—
- (a) sections 45, 49, 52, 54, 56 to 62 and 64 and 65;
- (b) paragraph 8 of Schedule 7 and section 67(1) so far as relating thereto;
- (c) Part II of Schedule 8 and section 67(2) so far as relating thereto.

(5) The transitional provisions and savings contained in Schedule 9 shall have effect; but nothing in that Schedule shall be taken as prejudicing the operation of sections 16 and 17 of the Interpretation Act 1978 (which relate to repeals).

[1137]

NOTES

Sub-s (2): words in square brackets substituted by the Legal Services Act 2007, s 208(1), Sch 21, paras 65, 67.

Orders: the Administration of Justice Act 1985 (Commencement No 1) Order 1986, SI 1986/364; the Administration of Justice Act 1985 (Commencement No 2) Order 1986, SI 1986/1503; the Administration of Justice Act 1985 (Commencement No 3) Order 1986, SI 1986/2260; the Administration of Justice Act 1985 (Commencement No 4) Order 1987, SI 1987/790; the Administration of Justice Act 1985 (Commencement No 5) Order 1988, SI 1988/1341; the Administration of Justice Act 1985 (Commencement No 6) Order 1989, SI 1989/297; the Administration of Justice Act 1985 (Commencement No 7) Order 1991, SI 1991/2683.

(*Schs 1–9 outside the scope of this work.*)

HOUSING ACT 1985

(1985 c 68)

An Act to consolidate the Housing Acts (except those provisions consolidated in the Housing Associations Act 1985 and the Landlord and Tenant Act 1985), and certain related provisions, with amendments to give effect to recommendations of the Law Commission

[30 October 1985]

NOTES

Transfer of Functions: as to the transfer of functions of Ministers, so far as exercisable in relation to Wales, being transferred to the National Assembly for Wales, see the National Assembly for Wales (Transfer of Functions) Order 1999, SI 1999/672, art 2, Sch 1.

1–78 ((*Pts I–III*) *outside the scope of this work.*)

PART IV
SECURE TENANCIES AND RIGHTS OF SECURE TENANTS

Security of tenure

79 Secure tenancies

(1) A tenancy under which a dwelling-house is let as a separate dwelling is a secure tenancy at any time when the conditions described in sections 80 and 81 as the landlord condition and the tenant condition are satisfied.

(2) Subsection (1) has effect subject to—

(a) the exceptions in Schedule 1 (tenancies which are not secure tenancies),

(b) sections 89(3) and (4) and 90(3) and (4) (tenancies ceasing to be secure after death of tenant), and

(c) sections 91(2) and 93(2) (tenancies ceasing to be secure in consequence of assignment or subletting).

(3) The provisions of this Part apply in relation to a licence to occupy a dwelling-house (whether or not granted for a consideration) as they apply in relation to a tenancy.

(4) Subsection (3) does not apply to a licence granted as a temporary expedient to a person who entered the dwelling-house or any other land as a trespasser (whether or not, before the grant of that licence, another licence to occupy that or another dwelling-house had been granted to him).

[1138]

80 The landlord condition

(1) The landlord condition is that the interest of the landlord belongs to one of the following authorities or bodies—

a local authority,
a [development] corporation,
[a housing action trust]
an urban development corporation, [in the case of a tenancy falling within subsections (2A) to (2E), the Homes and Communities Agency or the Welsh Ministers (as the case may be),]
. . .
the [Relevant Authority]
a housing trust which is a charity, or
a *housing association or* housing co-operative to which this section applies.

(2) *This section applies to—*

(*a*) *a [registered social landlord] other than a co-operative housing association, and*

[(*b*) *a co-operative housing association which is not a registered social landlord].*

[(2A) A tenancy falls within this subsection if the interest of the landlord is transferred to—

(a) the Homes and Communities Agency as mentioned in section 52(1)(a) to (d) of the Housing and Regeneration Act 2008, or

(b) the Welsh Ministers as mentioned in section 36(1)(a)(i) to (iii) of the New Towns Act 1981.

(2B) A tenancy falls within this subsection if it is entered into pursuant to a contract under which the rights and liabilities of the prospective landlord are transferred to the Homes and Communities Agency or the Welsh Ministers as mentioned in subsection (2A)(a) or (b) (as the case may be).

(2C) A tenancy falls within this subsection if it is granted by the Homes and Communities Agency or the Welsh Ministers to a person (alone or jointly with others) who, immediately before it was entered into, was a secure tenant of the Homes and Communities Agency or the Welsh Ministers (as the case may be).

(2D) A tenancy falls within this subsection if—

(a) it is granted by the Homes and Communities Agency or the Welsh Ministers to a person (alone or jointly with others),

(b) before the grant of the tenancy, an order for possession of a dwelling-house let under a secure tenancy was made against the person (alone or jointly with others) and in favour of the Homes and Communities Agency or the Welsh Ministers (as the case may be) on the court being satisfied as mentioned in section 84(2)(b) or (c), and

(c) the tenancy is of the premises which constitute the suitable accommodation as to which the court was so satisfied.

(2E) A tenancy falls within this subsection if it is granted by the Homes and Communities Agency or the Welsh Ministers pursuant to an obligation under section 554(2A).]

(3) If a co-operative housing association ceases to be [a registered social landlord], it shall, within the period of 21 days beginning with the date on which it ceases to be [a registered social landlord], notify each of its tenants who thereby becomes a secure tenant, in writing, that he has become a secure tenant.

[(4) This section applies to a housing co-operative within the meaning of section 27B (agreements under certain superseded provisions) where the dwelling-house is comprised in a housing co-operative agreement within the meaning of that section.]

[(5) In this Act and in any provision made under this Act, or made by or under any other enactment, a reference to—

(a) a person within section 80 or 80(1) of this Act, or

(b) a person who satisfies the landlord condition under this section,

includes a reference to the Homes and Communities Agency or to the Welsh Ministers so far as acting in their capacity as landlord (or, in the case of disposals, former landlord) in respect of a tenancy which falls within subsections (2A) to (2E) above but, subject to this, does not include the Homes and Communities Agency or the Welsh Ministers.

(6) Subsection (5)—

(a) applies whether the person is described as an authority, body or landlord or in any other way and whether the reference is otherwise expressed in a different way, and

(b) is subject to any provision to the contrary.]

[1139]

NOTES

Sub-s (1): word "development" in square brackets substituted, and words from "in the case" to "case may be)," in square brackets inserted, by SI 2008/3002, art 4, Sch 1, paras 2, 10(1), (2), subject to transitional provisions and savings in Sch 2, thereto; words "a housing action trust" in square brackets inserted by the Housing Act 1988, s 83(2); words omitted repealed by the Government of Wales Act 1998, s 152, Sch 18, Pt IV; words in italics repealed with savings by the Housing Act 1988, s 140, Sch 18, subject to savings in s 35 thereof; words "Relevant Authority" in square brackets substituted by the Government of Wales Act 1998, s 140, Sch 16, para 5.

Sub-s (2): repealed with savings by the Housing Act 1988, s 140, Sch 18, subject to savings in s 35 thereof; words in square brackets in para (a), and para (b) substituted by SI 1996/2325, art 5, Sch 2, para 14(8).

Sub-ss (2A)–(2E): inserted by SI 2008/3002, art 4, Sch 1, paras 2, 10(1), (3), subject to transitional provisions and savings in Sch 2, thereto.

Sub-s (3): words in square brackets substituted by SI 1996/2325, art 5, Sch 2, para 14(8).

Sub-s (4): substituted by the Housing and Planning Act 1986, s 24(2), Sch 5, Pt II, para 26.

Sub-ss (5), (6): inserted by SI 2008/3002, art 4, Sch 1, paras 2, 10(1), (4), subject to transitional provisions and savings in Sch 2, thereto.

See further: for provision whereby the body corporate known as the Residuary Body for Wales is to be treated as a local authority for the purposes of this section, see the Local Government (Wales) Act 1994, Sch 13, para 21(c).

81 The tenant condition

The tenant condition is that the tenant is an individual and occupies the dwelling-house as his only or principal home; or, where the tenancy is a joint tenancy, that each of the joint tenants is an individual and at least one of them occupies the dwelling-house as his only or principal home.

[1140]

82–86 (*Outside the scope of this work.*)

Succession on death of tenant

87, 88 (*Outside the scope of this work.*)

89 Succession to periodic tenancy

(1) This section applies where a secure tenant dies and the tenancy is a periodic tenancy.

(2) Where there is a person qualified to succeed the tenant, the tenancy vests by virtue of this section in that person, or if there is more than one such person in the one to be preferred in accordance with the following rules—

(a) the tenant's spouse [or civil partner] is to be preferred to another member of the tenant's family;

(b) of two or more other members of the tenant's family such of them is to be preferred as may be agreed between them or as may, where there is no such agreement, be selected by the landlord.

[(3) Where there is no person qualified to succeed the tenant, the tenancy ceases to be a secure tenancy—

(a) when it is vested or otherwise disposed of in the course of the administration of the tenant's estate, unless the vesting or other disposal is in pursuance of an order made under—

(i) *section 24* [section 23A or 24] of the Matrimonial Causes Act 1973 (property adjustment orders made in connection with matrimonial proceedings),

(ii) section 17(1) of the Matrimonial and Family Proceedings Act 1984 (property adjustment orders after overseas divorce, &c), …

(iii) paragraph 1 of Schedule 1 to the Children Act 1989 (orders for financial relief against parents)[, or

(iv) Part 2 of Schedule 5, or paragraph 9(2) or (3) of Schedule 7, to the Civil Partnership Act 2004 (property adjustment orders in connection with civil partnership proceedings or after overseas dissolution of civil partnership, etc)]; or

(b) when it is known that when the tenancy is so vested or disposed of it will not be in pursuance of such an order.]

(4) A tenancy which ceases to be a secure tenancy by virtue of this section cannot subsequently become a secure tenancy.

[1141]

NOTES

Sub-s (2): words in square brackets inserted by the Civil Partnership Act 2004, s 81, Sch 8, para 22(1), (2).

Sub-s (3): substituted by the Housing Act 1996, s 222, Sch 18, para 10; in para (a)(i), words in italics substituted by subsequent words in square brackets by the Family Law Act 1996, s 66(1), Sch 8, para 34, as from a day to be appointed, subject to savings in Sch 9, para 5 thereto; word omitted from para (a)(ii) repealed and para (a)(iv) and word immediately preceding it inserted by the Civil Partnership Act 2004, ss 81, 261(4), Sch 8, para 22(1), (3), Sch 30.

See further: in relation to a successor, see the Leasehold Reform, Housing and Urban Development Act 1993, Sch 10, para 2.

90 Devolution of term certain

(1) This section applies where a secure tenant dies and the tenancy is a tenancy for a term certain.

(2) The tenancy remain a secure tenancy until—

(a) it is vested or otherwise disposed of in the course of the administration of the tenant's estate, as mentioned in subsection (3), or

(b) it is known that when it is so vested or disposed of it will not be a secure tenancy.

(3) The tenancy ceases to be a secure tenancy on being vested or otherwise disposed of in the course of administration of the tenant's estate, unless—

[(a) the vesting or other disposal is in pursuance of an order made under—

(i) *section 24* [section 23A or 24] of the Matrimonial Causes Act 1973 (property adjustment orders in connection with matrimonial proceedings),

(ii) section 17(1) of the Matrimonial and Family Proceedings Act 1984 (property adjustment orders after overseas divorce, &c), …

(iii) paragraph 1 of Schedule 1 to the Children Act 1989 (orders for financial relief against parents), or

[(iv) Part 2 of Schedule 5, or paragraph 9(2) or (3) of Schedule 7, to the Civil Partnership Act 2004 (property adjustment orders in connection with civil partnership proceedings or after overseas dissolution of civil partnership, etc), or]]

(b) the vesting or other disposal is to a person qualified to succeed the tenant.

(4) A tenancy which ceases to be a secure tenancy by virtue of this section cannot subsequently become a secure tenancy.

[1142]

NOTES

Sub-s (3): para (a) substituted by the Housing Act 1996, s 222, Sch 18, para 11; in para (a)(i), words in italics substituted by subsequent words in square brackets by the Family Law Act 1996, s 66(1), Sch 8, para 34, as from a day to be appointed, subject to savings in Sch 9, para 5 thereto; word omitted from para (a)(ii) repealed and para (a)(iv) inserted by the Civil Partnership Act 2004, ss 81, 261(4), Sch 8, para 23, Sch 30.

See further: in relation to a successor, see the Leasehold Reform, Housing and Urban Development Act 1993, Sch 10, para 2.

91–117 (*Ss 91–106A, 108–110, 111A–117 outside the scope of this work; s 107 repealed by the Local Government and Housing Act 1989, 168(4), 194(4), Sch 12, Pt II; s 111 repealed by the Constitutional Reform Act 2005, ss 15(1), 146, Sch 4, Pt 1, paras 180, 181, Sch 18, Pt 2.*)

PART V
THE RIGHT TO BUY

The right to buy

118 The right to buy

(1) A secure tenant has the right to buy, that is to say, the right, in the circumstances and subject to the conditions and exceptions stated in the following provisions of this Part—

(a) if the dwelling-house is a house and the landlord owns the freehold, to acquire the freehold of the dwelling-house;

(b) if the landlord does not own the freehold or if the dwelling-house is a flat (whether or not the landlord owns the freehold), to be granted a lease of the dwelling-house.

(2) Where a secure tenancy is a joint tenancy then, whether or not each of the joint tenants occupies the dwelling-house as his only or principal home, the right to buy belongs jointly to all of them or to such one or more of them as may be agreed between them; but such an agreement is not valid unless the person or at least one of the persons to whom the right to buy is to belong occupies the dwelling-house as his only or principal home.

[(3) For the purposes of this Part, a dwelling-house which is a commonhold unit (within the meaning of the Commonhold and Leasehold Reform Act 2002) shall be treated as a house and not as a flat.]

[1143]

NOTES

Sub-s (3): inserted by the Commonhold and Leasehold Reform Act 2002, s 68, Sch 5, para 5.

Modification: modified by the Housing (Extension of Right to Buy) Order 1993, SI 1993/2240, art 3, Schedule, para 1, and the Housing (Preservation of Right to Buy) Regulations 1993, SI 1993/2241, reg 2, Sch 1. Modified, in relation to the right of a tenant to acquire a dwelling under the Housing Act 1996, s 16, by the Housing (Right to Acquire) Regulations 1997, SI 1997/619, reg 2, Schs 1, 2.

119–125E (*Outside the scope of this work.*)

Purchase price

126 Purchase price

(1) The price payable for a dwelling-house on a conveyance or grant in pursuance of this Part is—

(a) the amount which under section 127 is to be taken as its value at the relevant time, less

(b) the discount to which the purchaser is entitled under this Part.

(2) References in this Part to the purchase price include references to the consideration for the grant of a lease.

[1144]

NOTES

Modification: modified by the Housing (Extension of Right to Buy) Order 1993, SI 1993/2240, art 3, Schedule, para 13, and the Housing (Preservation of Right to Buy) Regulations 1993, SI 1993/2241, reg 2, Sch 1. Modified, in relation to the right of a tenant to acquire a dwelling under the Housing Act 1996, s 16, by the Housing (Right to Acquire) Regulations 1997, SI 1997/619, reg 2, Schs 1, 2.

127 Value of dwelling-house

(1) The value of a dwelling-house at the relevant time shall be taken to be the price which at that time it would realise if sold on the open market by a willing vendor—

(a) on the assumptions stated for a conveyance in subsection (2) and for a grant in subsection (3), …

(b) disregarding any improvements made by any of the persons specified in subsection (4) and any failure by any of those persons to keep the dwelling-house in good internal repair[, and

(c) on the assumption that any service charges or improvement contributions payable will not be less than the amounts to be expected in accordance with the estimates contained in the landlord's notice under section 125].

(2) For a conveyance the assumptions are—

(a) that the vendor was selling for an estate in fee simple with vacant possession,

(b) that neither the tenant nor a member of his family residing with him wanted to buy, and

(c) that the dwelling-house was to be conveyed with the same rights and subject to the same burdens as it would be in pursuance of this Part.

(3) For the grant of a lease the assumptions are—

(a) that the vendor was granting a lease with vacant possession for the appropriate term defined in paragraph 12 of Schedule 6 (but subject to sub-paragraph (3) of that paragraph),

(b) that neither the tenant nor a member of his family residing with him wanted to take the lease,

(c) that the ground rent would not exceed £10 per annum, and

(d) that the grant was to be made with the same rights and subject to the same burdens as it would be in pursuance of this Part.

(4) The persons referred to in subsection (1)(b) are—

(a) the secure tenant,

(b) any person who under the same tenancy was a secure tenant [or an introductory tenant] before him, and

[(c) any member of his family who, immediately before the secure tenancy was granted (or, where an introductory tenancy has become the secure tenancy, immediately before the introductory tenancy was granted), was a secure tenant or, an introductory tenant of the same dwelling-house under another tenancy,]

but do not include, in a case where the secure tenant's tenancy has at any time been assigned by virtue of section 92 (assignments by way of exchange), a person who under that tenancy was a secure tenant [or an introductory tenant] before the assignment.

[(5) In this section "introductory tenant" and "introductory tenancy" have the same meaning as in Chapter I of Part V of the Housing Act 1996.]

[1145]

NOTES

Sub-s (1): word omitted from para (a) repealed by the Housing and Planning Act 1986, s 24(2), (3), Sch 5, Pt II, para 28, Sch 12, Pt I; para (c) and word immediately preceding it inserted by the Housing and Planning Act 1986, s 4(3), (6).

Sub-s (4): para (c) substituted, and other words in square brackets inserted, by SI 1997/74, art 2, Schedule, para 3(j).

Sub-s (5): inserted by SI 1997/74, art 2, Schedule, para 3(k).

Modification: modified by the Housing (Extension of Right to Buy) Order 1993, SI 1993/2240, art 3, Schedule, para 14, and the Housing (Preservation of Right to Buy) Regulations 1993, SI 1993/2241, reg 2, Sch 1. Modified, in relation to the right of a tenant to acquire a dwelling under the Housing Act 1996, s 16, by the Housing (Right to Acquire) Regulations 1997, SI 1997/619, reg 2, Schs 1, 2.

128–128B (*Outside the scope of this work.*)

129 Discount

[(1) Subject to the following provisions of this Part, a person exercising the right to buy is entitled to a discount of a percentage calculated by reference to the period which is to be taken into account in accordance with Schedule 4 (qualifying period for right to buy and discount).

(2) The discount is, subject to any order under subsection (2A)—

(a) in the case of a house, [35 per cent] plus one per cent for each complete year by which the qualifying period exceeds [five] years, up to a maximum of 60 per cent;

(b) in the case of a flat, [50 per cent] plus two per cent for each complete year by which the qualifying period exceeds [five] years, up to a maximum of 70 per cent.

(2A) The Secretary of State may by order made with the consent of the Treasury provide that, in such cases as may be specified in the order—

(a) the minimum percentage discount,

(b) the percentage increase for each complete year of the qualifying period after the first [five], or

(c) the maximum percentage discount,

shall be such percentage, higher than that specified in subsection (2), as may be specified in the order.

(2B) An order—

(a) may make different provision with respect to different cases or descriptions of case,

(b) may contain such incidental, supplementary or transitional provisions as appear to the Secretary of State to be necessary or expedient, and

(c) shall be made by statutory instrument and shall not be made unless a draft of it has been laid before and approved by resolution of each House of Parliament.]

(3) Where joint tenants exercise the right to buy, Schedule 4 shall be construed as if for the secure tenant there were substituted that one of the joint tenants whose substitution will produce the largest discount.

[1146]

NOTES

Sub-ss (1)–(2B): substituted, for sub-ss (1), (2), as originally enacted, by the Housing and Planning Act 1986, s 2(1), (2).

Sub-ss (2), (2A): words in square brackets substituted by the Housing Act 2004, s 180(2)–(4); for effect see s 180(5), (6) thereof.

Modification: modified by the Housing (Extension of Right to Buy) Order 1993, SI 1993/2240, art 3, Schedule, para 16, and the Housing (Preservation of Right to Buy) Regulations 1993, SI 1993/2241, reg 2, Sch 1. Modified, in relation to the right of a tenant to acquire a dwelling under the Housing Act 1996, s 16, by the Housing (Right to Acquire) Regulations 1997, SI 1997/619, reg 2, Schs 1, 2.

130–154 (*Ss 130, 131, 136–141, 142A–144, 146–154 outside the scope of this work; ss 132–135, 142, 145 repealed by the Leasehold Reform, Housing and Urban Development Act 1993, s 187*(2), *Sch 22, subject to savings in SI 1993/2134, art 4, Sch 1, para 4.*)

Provisions affecting future disposals

155 Repayment of discount on early disposal

(1) A conveyance of the freehold or grant of a lease if pursuance of this Part shall contain (unless, in the case of a conveyance or grant in pursuance of the right to buy, there is no discount) a covenant binding on the secure tenant and his successors in title to the following effect.

[(2) In the case of a conveyance or grant in pursuance of the right to buy, the covenant shall be to pay the landlord such sum (if any) as the landlord may demand in accordance with section 155A on the occasion of the first relevant disposal (other than an exempted disposal) which takes place within the period of five years beginning with the conveyance or grant.

(3) In the case of a conveyance or grant in pursuance of the right to acquire on rent to mortgage terms, the covenant shall be to pay the landlord such sum (if any) as the landlord may demand in accordance with section 155B on the occasion of the first relevant disposal (other than an exempted disposal) which takes place within the period of five years beginning with the making of the initial payment.]

[(3A) Where a secure tenant has served on his landlord an operative notice of delay, as defined in section 153A,—

(a) the [five years] referred to in subsection (2) shall begin from a date which precedes the date of the conveyance of the freehold or grant of the lease by a period equal to the time (or, if there is more than one such notice, the aggregate of the times) during which, by virtue of section 153B, any payment of rent falls to be taken into account in accordance with subsection (3) of that section; and

[(b) any reference in subsection (3) (other than paragraph (a) thereof) to the making of the initial payment shall be construed as a reference to the date which precedes that payment by the period referred to in paragraph (a) of this subsection.]]

[1147]

NOTES

Sub-ss (2), (3): substituted by the Housing Act 2004, s 185(1), (2); for effect see s 185(5)–(8) thereof.

Sub-s (3A): inserted by the Housing Act 1988, s 140, Sch 17, Pt I, para 41; words in square brackets in para (a) substituted by the Housing Act 2004, s 185(1), (3), for effect see sub-ss (5)–(8) thereof; para (b) substituted by the Leasehold Reform, Housing and Urban Development Act 1993, s 120(2).

Modification: modified by the Housing (Extension of Right to Buy) Order 1993, SI 1993/2240, art 3, Schedule, para 41, and the Housing (Preservation of Right to Buy) Regulations 1993, SI 1993/2241, reg 2, Sch 1. Modified, in relation to the right of a tenant to acquire a dwelling under the Housing Act 1996, s 16, by the Housing (Right to Acquire) Regulations 1997, SI 1997/619, reg 2, Schs 1, 2.

[155A Amount of discount which may be demanded by landlord: right to buy

(1) For the purposes of the covenant mentioned in section 155(2), the landlord may demand such sum as he considers appropriate, up to and including the maximum amount specified in this section.

(2) The maximum amount which may be demanded by the landlord is a percentage of the price or premium paid for the first relevant disposal which is equal to the discount to which the secure tenant was entitled, where the discount is expressed as a percentage of the value which under section 127 was taken as the value of the dwelling-house at the relevant time.

(3) But for each complete year which has elapsed after the conveyance or grant and before the disposal the maximum amount which may be demanded by the landlord is reduced by one-fifth.

(4) This section is subject to section 155C.]

[1148]

NOTES

Commencement: 18 January 2005.
Inserted by the Housing Act 2004, s 185(1), (4); for effect see s 185(5)–(8) thereof.

[155B Amount of discount which may be demanded by landlord: right to acquire on rent to mortgage terms

(1) For the purposes of the covenant mentioned in section 155(3), the landlord may demand such sum as he considers appropriate, up to and including the maximum amount specified in this section.

(2) The maximum amount which may be demanded by the landlord is the discount (if any) to which the tenant was entitled on the making of—

(a) the initial payment,
(b) any interim payment made before the disposal, or
(c) the final payment if so made,

reduced, in each case, by one-fifth for each complete year which has elapsed after the making of the initial payment and before the disposal.]

[1149]

NOTES

Commencement: 18 January 2005.
Inserted by the Housing Act 2004, s 185(1), (4); for effect see s 185(5)–(8) thereof.

[155C Increase attributable to home improvements

(1) In calculating the maximum amount which may be demanded by the landlord under section 155A, such amount (if any) of the price or premium paid for the disposal which is attributable to improvements made to the dwelling-house—

(a) by the person by whom the disposal is, or is to be, made, and
(b) after the conveyance or grant and before the disposal,

shall be disregarded.

(2) The amount to be disregarded under this section shall be such amount as may be agreed between the parties or determined by the district valuer.

(3) The district valuer shall not be required by virtue of this section to make a determination for the purposes of this section unless—

(a) it is reasonably practicable for him to do so; and
(b) his reasonable costs in making the determination are paid by the person by whom the disposal is, or is to be, made.

(4) If the district valuer does not make a determination for the purposes of this section (and in default of an agreement), no amount is required to be disregarded under this section.]

[1150]

NOTES

Commencement: 18 January 2005.
Inserted by the Housing Act 2004, s 186(1).

156 Liability to repay is a charge on the premises

(1) The liability that may arise under the covenant required by section 155 is a charge on the dwelling-house, taking effect as if it had been created by deed expressed to be by way of legal mortgage.

[(2) Subject to subsections (2A) and (2B), the charge has priority as follows—

(a) if it secures the liability that may arise under the covenant required by section 155(2), immediately after any legal charge securing an amount advanced to the secure tenant by an approved lending institution for the purpose of enabling him to exercise the right to buy;
(b) if it secures the liability that may arise under the covenant required by section 155(3), immediately after the mortgage—

(i) which is required by section 151B (mortgage for securing redemption of landlord's share), and

(ii) which, by virtue of subsection (2) of that section, has priority immediately after any legal charge securing an amount advanced to the secure tenant by an approved lending institution for the purpose of enabling him to exercise the right to acquire on rent to mortgage terms.

(2A) The following, namely—

(a) any advance which is made otherwise than for the purpose mentioned in paragraph (a) or (b) of subsection (2) and is secured by a legal charge having priority to the charge taking effect by virtue of this section, and

(b) any further advance which is so secured,

shall rank in priority to that charge if, and only if, the landlord by written notice served on the institution concerned gives its consent; and the landlord shall so give its consent if the purpose of the advance or further advance is an approved purpose.

(2B) The landlord may at any time by written notice served on an approved lending institution postpone the charge taking effect by virtue of this section to any advance or further advance which—

(a) is made to the tenant by that institution, and

(b) is secured by a legal charge not having priority to that charge;

and the landlord shall serve such a notice if the purpose of the advance or further advance is an approved purpose.]

(3) …

[(3A) The covenant required by section 155 (covenant for repayment of discount) does not, by virtue of its binding successors in title of the tenant, bind a person exercising rights under a charge having priority over the charge taking effect by virtue of this section, or a person deriving title under him; and a provision of the conveyance or grant, or of a collateral agreement, is void in so far as it purports to authorise a forfeiture, or to impose a penalty or disability, in the event of any such person failing to comply with that covenant.]

(4) The approved lending institutions for the purposes of this section are—

the [Relevant Authority],
[an authorised deposit taker
an authorised insurer],
[an authorised mortgage lender].

[(4A) The approved purposes for the purposes of this section are—

(a) to enable the tenant to make an interim or final payment,

(b) to enable the tenant to defray, or to defray on his behalf, any of the following—

(i) the cost of any works to the dwelling-house,

(ii) any service charge payable in respect of the dwelling-house for works, whether or not to the dwelling-house, and

(iii) any service charge or other amount payable in respect of the dwelling-house for insurance, whether or not of the dwelling-house, and

(c) to enable the tenant to discharge, or to discharge on his behalf, any of the following—

(i) so much as is still outstanding of any advance or further advance which ranks in priority to the charge taking effect by virtue of this section,

(ii) any arrears of interest on such an advance or further advance, and

(iii) any costs and expenses incurred in enforcing payment of any such interest, or repayment (in whole or in part) of any such advance or further advance.

(4B) Where different parts of an advance or further advance are made for different purposes, each of those parts shall be regarded as a separate advance or further advance for the purposes of this section.]

(5), (6) …

[1151]

NOTES

Sub-ss (2)–(2B): substituted, for original sub-s (2), by the Leasehold Reform, Housing and Urban Development Act 1993, s 120(3).

Sub-s (3): repealed by the Land Registration Act 2002, s 135, Sch 13.

Sub-s (3A): inserted, in relation to covenants entered into before or after 7 January 1987, by the Housing and Planning Act 1986, s 24(1), Sch 5, Pt I, para 1.

Sub-s (4): words in first pair of square brackets substituted by the Government of Wales Act 1998, s 140, Sch 16, para 5; words in second pair of square brackets substituted by SI 2001/3649, art 299(1), (4); words in third pair of square brackets substituted by the Housing and Regeneration Act 2008, s 307(1)(a).

Sub-ss (4A), (4B): inserted by the Leasehold Reform, Housing and Urban Development Act 1993, s 120(4).

Sub-ss (5), (6): repealed by the Housing and Regeneration Act 2008, ss 307(1)(b), 321(1), Sch 16.

Modification: modified by the Housing (Extension of Right to Buy) Order 1993, SI 1993/2240, art 3, Schedule, paras 42, 43, and the Housing (Preservation of Right to Buy) Regulations 1993, SI 1993/2241, reg 2,

Sch 1. Modified, in relation to the right of a tenant to acquire a dwelling under the Housing Act 1996, s 16, by the Housing (Right to Acquire) Regulations 1997, SI 1997/619, reg 2, Schs 1, 2.

Orders: the Housing (Right to Buy) (Priority of Charges) Order 1987, SI 1987/1203; the Housing (Right to Buy) (Priority of Charges) (No 2) Order 1987, SI 1987/1810; the Housing (Right to Buy) (Priority of Charges) (No 1) Order 1988, SI 1988/85; the Housing (Right to Buy) (Priority of Charges) (No 2) Order 1988, SI 1988/1726; the Housing (Right to Buy) (Priority of Charges) Order 1989, SI 1989/958; the Housing (Right to Buy) (Priority of Charges) (No 2) Order 1989, SI 1989/2102; the Housing (Right to Buy) (Priority of Charges) (No 3) Order 1989, SI 1989/2329; the Housing (Right to Buy) (Priority of Charges) Order 1990, SI 1990/1388; the Housing (Right to Buy) (Priority of Charges) (No 2) Order 1990, SI 1990/2390; the Housing (Right to Buy) (Priority of Charges) Order 1991, SI 1991/619; the Housing (Right to Buy) (Priority of Charges) (No 2) Order 1991, SI 1991/2052; the Housing (Right to Buy) (Priority of Charges) Order 1992, SI 1992/2317; the Housing (Right to Buy) (Priority of Charges) Order 1993, SI 1993/303; the Housing (Right to Buy) (Priority of Charges) (No 2) Order 1993, SI 1993/2757; the Housing (Right to Buy) (Priority of Charges) Order 1994, SI 1994/1762; the Housing (Right to Buy) (Priority of Charges) Order 1995, SI 1995/211; the Housing (Right to Buy) (Priority of Charges) (No 2) Order 1995, SI 1995/2066; the Housing (Right to Buy) (Priority of Charges) Order 1996, SI 1996/162; the Housing (Right to Buy) (Priority of Charges) Order 1997, SI 1997/945; the Housing (Right to Buy) (Priority of Charges) (No 2) Order 1997, SI 1997/2327; the Housing (Right to Buy) (Priority of Charges) Order 1998, SI 1998/320; the Housing (Right to Buy) (Priority of Charges) (No 2) Order 1998, SI 1998/2015; the Housing (Right to Buy) (Priority of Charges) (England) Order 1999, SI 1999/2919; the Housing (Right to Buy) (Priority of Charges) (Wales) Order 2000, SI 2000/349; the Housing (Right to Buy) (Priority of Charges) (England) Order 2001, SI 2001/205; the Housing (Right to Buy) (Priority of Charges) (Wales) Order 2001, SI 2001/1786; the Housing (Right to Buy) (Priority of Charges) (England) (No 2) Order 2001, SI 2001/3219; the Housing (Right to Buy) (Priority of Charges) (England) (No 3) Order 2001, SI 2001/3874; the Housing (Right to Buy) (Priority of Charges) (Wales) Order 2002, SI 2002/763; the Housing (Right to Buy) (Priority of Charges) (England) Order 2003, SI 2003/1083; the Housing (Right to Buy) (Priority of Charges) (Wales) Order 2003, SI 2003/1853; the Housing (Right to Buy) (Priority of Charges) (England) Order 2004, SI 2004/1071; the Housing (Right to Buy) (Priority of Charges) (Wales) Order 2004, SI 2004/1806; the Housing (Right to Buy) (Priority of Charges) (England) Order 2005, SI 2005/92; the Housing (Right to Buy) (Priority of Charges) (England) (No 2) Order 2005, SI 2005/407; the Housing (Right to Buy) (Priority of Charges) (Wales) Order 2005, SI 2005/1351; the Housing (Right to Buy) (Priority of Charges) (Wales) Order 2006, SI 2006/950; the Housing (Right to Buy) (Priority of Charges) (England) Order 2006, SI 2006/1263; the Housing (Right to Buy) (Priority of Charges) (England) (No 2) Order 2006, SI 2006/2563; the Housing (Right to Buy) (Priority of Charges) (England) (No 3) Order 2006, SI 2006/3242; the Housing (Right to Buy) (Priority of Charges) (Wales) Order 2008, SI 2008/371.

[156A Right of first refusal for landlord etc

(1) A conveyance of the freehold or grant of a lease in pursuance of this Part shall contain the following covenant, which shall be binding on the secure tenant and his successors in title. This is subject to subsection (8).

(2) The covenant shall be to the effect that, until the end of the period of ten years beginning with the conveyance or grant, there will be no relevant disposal which is not an exempted disposal, unless the prescribed conditions have been satisfied in relation to that or a previous such disposal.

(3) In subsection (2) "the prescribed conditions" means such conditions as are prescribed by regulations under this section at the time when the conveyance or grant is made.

(4) The Secretary of State may by regulations prescribe such conditions as he considers appropriate for and in connection with conferring on—

(a) a landlord who has conveyed a freehold or granted a lease to a person ("the former tenant") in pursuance of this Part, or

(b) such other person as is determined in accordance with the regulations,

a right of first refusal to have a disposal within subsection (5) made to him for such consideration as is mentioned in section 158.

(5) The disposals within this subsection are—

(a) a reconveyance or conveyance of the dwelling-house; and

(b) a surrender or assignment of the lease.

(6) Regulations under this section may, in particular, make provision—

(a) for the former tenant to offer to make such a disposal to such person or persons as may be prescribed;

(b) for a prescribed recipient of such an offer to be able either to accept the offer or to nominate some other person as the person by whom the offer may be accepted;

(c) for the person who may be so nominated to be either a person of a prescribed description or a person whom the prescribed recipient considers, having regard to any prescribed matters, to be a more appropriate person to accept the offer;

(d) for a prescribed recipient making such a nomination to give a notification of the nomination to the person nominated, the former tenant and any other prescribed person;

(e) for authorising a nominated person to accept the offer and for determining which acceptance is to be effective where the offer is accepted by more than one person;

(f) for the period within which the offer may be accepted or within which any other prescribed step is to be, or may be, taken;

(g) for the circumstances in which the right of first refusal lapses (whether following the service of a notice to complete or otherwise) with the result that the former tenant is able to make a disposal on the open market;

(h) for the manner in which any offer, acceptance or notification is to be communicated.

(7) In subsection (6) any reference to the former tenant is a reference to the former tenant or his successor in title.

Nothing in that subsection affects the generality of subsection (4).

(8) In a case to which section 157(1) applies—

(a) the conveyance or grant may contain a covenant such as is mentioned in subsections (1) and (2) above instead of a covenant such as is mentioned in section 157(1), but

(b) it may do so only if the Secretary of State or, where the conveyance or grant is executed by a housing association within section 6A(3) or (4), the Relevant Authority consents.

(9) Consent may be given in relation to—

(a) a particular disposal, or

(b) disposals by a particular landlord or disposals by landlords generally,

and may, in any case, be given subject to conditions.

(10) Regulations under this section—

(a) may make different provision with respect to different cases or descriptions of case; and

(b) shall be made by statutory instrument which shall be subject to annulment in pursuance of a resolution of either House of Parliament.

(11) The limitation imposed by a covenant within subsection (2) (whether the covenant is imposed in pursuance of subsection (1) or (8)) is a local land charge.

(12) The Chief Land Registrar must enter in the register of title a restriction reflecting the limitation imposed by any such covenant.]

[1152]

NOTES

Commencement: 18 January 2005.

Inserted by the Housing Act 2004, s 188(1); for effect see s 188(5), (6) thereof.

Regulations: the Housing (Right of First Refusal) (England) Regulations 2005, SI 2005/1917; the Housing (Right of First Refusal) (Wales) Regulations 2005, SI 2005/2680.

157 Restriction on disposal of dwelling-houses in National Parks, etc

(1) Where in pursuance of this Part a conveyance or grant is executed by a local authority … or a housing association ("the landlord") of a dwelling-house situated in—

(a) a National Park,

(b) an area designated under [section 82 of the Countryside and Rights of Way Act 2000] as an area of outstanding natural beauty, or

(c) an area designated by order of the Secretary of State as a rural area,

the conveyance or grant may [(subject to section 156A(8)] contain a covenant limiting the freedom of the tenant (including any successor in title of his and any person deriving title under him or such a successor) to dispose of the dwelling-house in the manner specified below.

(2) The limitation is … that until such time (if any) as may be notified in writing by the landlord to the tenant or a successor in title of his,

[(a)] there will be no relevant disposal which is not an exempted disposal without the written consent of the landlord; but that consent shall not be withheld if the disposal is to a person satisfying the condition stated in subsection (3) [and—

(b) there will be no disposal by way of tenancy or licence without the written consent of the landlord unless the disposal is to a person satisfying that condition or by a person whose only or principal home is and, throughout the duration of the tenancy or licence, remains the dwelling-house].

(3) The condition is that the person to whom the disposal is made (or, if it is made to more than one person, at least one of them) has, throughout the period of three years immediately preceding the application for consent [or, in the case of a disposal by way of tenancy or licence, preceding the disposal]—

(a) had his place of work in a region designated by order of the Secretary of State which, or part of which, is comprised in the National Park or area, or

(b) had his only or principal home in such a region;

or has had the one in part or parts of that period and the other in the remainder; but the region need not have been the same throughout the period.

(4), (5) …

(6) A disposal in breach of such a covenant as is mentioned in subsection (1) is void [and, so far as it relates to disposals by way of tenancy or licence, such a covenant may be enforced by the landlord as if—

(a) the landlord were possessed of land adjacent to the house concerned; and

(b) the covenant were expressed to be made for the benefit of such adjacent land].

[(6A) Any reference in the preceding provisions of this section to a disposal by way of tenancy or licence does not include a reference to a relevant disposal or an exempted disposal.]

(7) Where such a covenant imposes the limitation specified in subsection (2), the limitation is a local land charge and the Chief Land Registrar shall enter [a restriction in the register of title reflecting the limitation].

(8) An order under this section—

(a) may make different provision with respect to different cases or descriptions of case, including different provision for different areas, and

(b) shall be made by statutory instrument which shall be subject to annulment in pursuance of a resolution of either House of Parliament.

[1153]

NOTES

Sub-s (1): words omitted repealed by the Government of Wales Act 1998, s 152, Sch 18, Pt IV; words in square brackets in para (b) substituted by the Countryside and Rights of Way Act 2000, s 93, Sch 15, Pt I, para 9; words in second pair of square brackets inserted by the Housing Act 2004, s 188(2)(a), for effect see s 188(5), (6) thereof.

Sub-s (2): words omitted repealed by the Housing Act 2004, ss 188(2)(b), 266, Sch 16, for effect see s 188(5), (6) thereof; para (a) numbered as such and para (b) added by the Housing Act 1988, s 126, in relation to cases where the conveyance or grant referred to in sub-s (1) above is executed on or after 15 January 1989.

Sub-s (3): words in square brackets inserted by the Housing Act 1988, s 126, in relation to cases where the conveyance or grant referred to in sub-s (1) above is executed on or after 15 January 1989.

Sub-ss (4), (5): repealed by the Housing Act 2004, ss 188(2)(c), 266, Sch 16, for effect see s 188(5), (6) thereof.

Sub-s (6): words in square brackets added by the Housing Act 1988, s 126, in relation to cases where the conveyance or grant referred to in sub-s (1) above is executed on or after 15 January 1989.

Sub-s (6A): inserted by the Housing Act 1988, s 126, in relation to cases where the conveyance or grant referred to in sub-s (1) above is executed on or after 15 January 1989.

Sub-s (7): words in square brackets substituted by the Land Registration Act 2002, s 133, Sch 11, para 18(1), (4).

Modification: modified by the Housing (Extension of Right to Buy) Order 1993, SI 1993/2240, art 3, Schedule, para 44, and the Housing (Preservation of Right to Buy) Regulations 1993, SI 1993/2241, reg 2, Sch 1. Modified, in relation to the right of a tenant to acquire a dwelling under the Housing Act 1996, s 16, by the Housing (Right to Acquire) Regulations 1997, SI 1997/619, reg 2, Schs 1, 2.

Orders: the Housing (Right to Buy) (Designated Rural Areas and Designated Regions) (England) Order 1986, SI 1986/1695; the Housing (Right to Buy) (Designated Rural Areas and Designated Region) (England) Order 1988, SI 1988/2057; the Housing (Right to Buy) (Designated Rural Areas and Designated Regions) (England) Order 1990, SI 1990/1282; the Housing (Right to Buy) (Designated Rural Areas and Designated Regions) (England) Order 2002, SI 2002/1769; the Housing (Right to Acquire and Right to Buy) (Designated Rural Areas and Designated Regions) (Wales) Order 2003, SI 2003/54; the Housing (Right to Buy) (Designated Rural Areas and Designated Region) (England) Order 2003, SI 2003/1105; the Housing (Right to Acquire and Right to Buy) (Designated Rural Areas and Designated Regions) (Amendment) (Wales) Order 2003, SI 2003/1147; the Housing (Right to Buy) (Designated Rural Areas and Designated Regions) (England) Order 2004, SI 2004/418; the Housing (Right to Buy) (Designated Rural Areas and Designated Regions) (England) (No 2) Order 2004, SI 2004/2681; the Housing (Right to Buy) (Designated Rural Areas and Designated Regions) (England) Order 2005, SI 2005/1995; the Housing (Right to Buy) (Designated Rural Areas and Designated Regions) (England) (No 2) Order 2005, SI 2005/2908; the Housing (Right to Buy) (Designated Rural Areas and Designated Region) (England) Order 2006, SI 2006/1948.

Also, by virtue of the Housing (Consequential Provisions) Act 1985, s 2(2), the following orders have effect as if made under this section: the Housing (Right to Buy) (Designated Regions) Order 1980, SI 1980/1345; the Housing (Right to Buy) (Designated Rural Areas and Designated Regions) (Wales) Order 1980, SI 1980/1375; the Housing (Right to Buy) (Designated Rural Areas and Designated Regions) (England) Order 1981, SI 1981/397; the Housing (Right to Buy) (Designated Rural Areas and Designated Regions) (England) (No 2) Order 1981, SI 1981/940; the Housing (Right to Buy) (Designated Rural Areas and Designated Regions) (England) Order 1982, SI 1982/21; and the Housing (Right to Buy) (Designated Rural Areas and Designated Regions) (England) (No 2) Order 1982, SI 1982/187.

158 Consideration for [disposal under section 156A]

[(1) The consideration for such a disposal as is mentioned in section 156A(4) shall be such amount as may be agreed between the parties, or determined by the district valuer, as being the amount which is to be taken to be the value of the dwelling-house at the time when the offer is made (as determined in accordance with regulations under that section).]

(2) That value shall be taken to be the price which, at that time, the interest to be reconveyed[, conveyed, surrendered or assigned] would realise if sold on the open market by a willing vendor, on the assumption that any liability under—

(a) the covenant required by section 155 (repayment of discount on early disposal), and [(aa) any covenant required by paragraph 1 of Schedule 6A (obligation to redeem landlord's share where conveyance or grant executed in pursuance of right to acquire on rent to mortgage terms), and]

(b) any covenant required by paragraph 6 of Schedule 8 (payment for outstanding share on disposal of dwelling-house subject to shared ownership lease),

would be discharged by the vendor.

(3) If [the offer is accepted in accordance with regulations under section 156A,] no payment shall be required in pursuance of any such covenant as is mentioned in subsection (2), but the consideration shall be reduced[, subject to subsection (4),] by such amount (if any) as, on a disposal made at the time the offer was made, being a relevant disposal which is not an exempted disposal, would fall to be paid under that covenant.

[(4) Where there is a charge on the dwelling-house having priority over the charge to secure payment of the sum due under the covenant mentioned in subsection (2), the consideration shall not be reduced under subsection (3) below the amount necessary to discharge the outstanding sum secured by the first-mentioned charge at the date of the offer [(as determined in accordance with regulations under section 156A).]]

[1154]

NOTES

Section heading: words in square brackets substituted by the Housing Act 2004, s 188(3)(a); for effect see s 188(5), (6) thereof.

Sub-s (1): substituted by the Housing Act 2004, s 188(3)(b); for effect see s 188(5), (6) thereof.

Sub-s (2): words in first pair of square brackets substituted by the Housing Act 2004, s 188(3)(c), for effect see s 188(5), (6) thereof; para (aa) inserted by the Leasehold Reform, Housing and Urban Development Act 1993, s 187(1), Sch 21, para 15, subject to savings.

Sub-s (3): words in first pair of square brackets substituted by the Housing Act 2004, s 188(3)(d), for effect see s 188(5), (6) thereof; words in second pair of square brackets inserted by the Housing and Planning Act 1986, s 24(1)(a), Sch 5, Pt I, para 1, in relation to covenants entered into before or after 7 January 1987.

Sub-s (4): added by the Housing and Planning Act 1986, s 24(1)(a), Sch 5, Pt I, para 1, in relation to covenants entered into before or after 7 January 1987; words in square brackets substituted by the Housing Act 2004, s 188(3)(e), for effect see s 188(5), (6) thereof.

Modification: modified by the Housing (Extension of Right to Buy) Order 1993, SI 1993/2240, art 3, Schedule, para 45, and the Housing (Preservation of Right to Buy) Regulations 1993, SI 1993/2241, reg 2, Sch 1. Modified, in relation to the right of a tenant to acquire a dwelling under the Housing Act 1996, s 16, by the Housing (Right to Acquire) Regulations 1997, SI 1997/619, reg 2, Schs 1, 2.

159 Relevant disposals

(1) A disposal, whether of the whole or part of the dwelling-house, is a relevant disposal for the purposes of this Part if it is—

(a) a further conveyance of the freehold or an assignment of the lease, or

(b) the grant of a lease (other than a mortgage term) for a term of more than 21 years otherwise than at a rack rent.

(2) For the purposes of subsection (1)(b) it shall be assumed—

(a) that any option to renew or extend a lease or sub-lease, whether or not forming part of a series of options, is exercised, and

(b) that any option to terminate a lease or sub-lease is not exercised.

[1155]

NOTES

Modification: modified by the Housing (Extension of Right to Buy) Order 1993, SI 1993/2240, art 3, Schedule, para 46, and the Housing (Preservation of Right to Buy) Regulations 1993, SI 1993/2241, reg 2, Sch 1. Modified, in relation to the right of a tenant to acquire a dwelling under the Housing Act 1996, s 16, by the Housing (Right to Acquire) Regulations 1997, SI 1997/619, reg 2, Schs 1, 2.

160 Exempted disposals

(1) A disposal is an exempted disposal for the purposes of this Part if—

(a) it is a disposal of the whole of the dwelling-house and a further conveyance of the freehold or an assignment of the lease and the person or each of the persons to whom it is made is a qualifying person (as defined in subsection (2));

(b) it is a vesting of the whole of the dwelling-house in a person taking under a will or on an intestacy;

[(c) it is a disposal of the whole of the dwelling-house in pursuance of any such order as is mentioned in subsection (3);]

(d) it is a compulsory disposal (as defined in section 161); or

(e) it is a disposal of property consisting of land included in the dwelling-house by virtue of section 184 (land let with or used for the purposes of the dwelling-house).

(2) For the purposes of subsection (1)(a), a person is a qualifying person in relation to a disposal if—

(a) he is the person, or one of the persons, by whom the disposal is made,
(b) he is the spouse or a former spouse[, or the civil partner or a former civil partner,] of that person, or one of those persons, or
(c) he is a member of the family of that person, or one of those persons, and has resided with him throughout the period of twelve months ending with the disposal.

[(3) The orders referred to in subsection (1)(c) are orders under—
(a) *section 24* [section 23A or 24] or 24A of the Matrimonial Causes Act 1973 (property adjustment orders or orders for the sale of property in connection with matrimonial proceedings),
(b) section 2 of the Inheritance (Provision for Family and Dependants) Act 1975 (orders as to financial provision to be made from estate),
(c) section 17 of the Matrimonial and Family Proceedings Act 1984 (property adjustment orders or orders for the sale of property after overseas divorce, &c), …
(d) paragraph 1 of Schedule 1 to the Children Act 1989 (orders for financial relief against parents)[, or
(e) Part 2 or 3 of Schedule 5, or paragraph 9 of Schedule 7, to the Civil Partnership Act 2004 (property adjustment orders, or orders for the sale of property, in connection with civil partnership proceedings or after overseas dissolution of civil partnership, etc)].]

[1156]

NOTES

Sub-s (1): para (c) substituted by the Housing Act 1996, s 222, Sch 18, Pt III, para 15.

Sub-s (2): words in square brackets in para (b) inserted by the Civil Partnership Act 2004, s 81, Sch 8, para 18.

Sub-s (3): added by the Housing Act 1996, s 222, Sch 18, Pt III, para 15; words in italics in para (a) substituted by subsequent words in square brackets by virtue of the Family Law Act 1996, s 66(1), Sch 8, Pt I, para 34, as from a day to be appointed, subject to savings in s 66(2) of, and Sch 9, para 5 to, that Act; word omitted from para (c) repealed and para (e) and word immediately preceding it added by the Civil Partnership Act 2004, ss 81, 261(4), Sch 8, para 30, Sch 30.

It should be noted that the amendment made to sub-s (1)(c) of this section as originally enacted by the Family Law Act 1996, s 66(1), Sch 8, Pt I, para 34, as from a day to be appointed under s 67(3) of that Act, has been superseded by the substitution of that paragraph and the addition of sub-s (3) as noted above.

Modification: modified by the Housing (Preservation of Right to Buy) Regulations 1993, SI 1993/2241, reg 2, Sch 1. Modified, in relation to the right of a tenant to acquire a dwelling under the Housing Act 1996, s 16, by the Housing (Right to Acquire) Regulations 1997, SI 1997/619, reg 2, Schs 1, 2.

161 Meaning of "compulsory disposal"

In this Part a "compulsory disposal" means a disposal of property which is acquired compulsorily, or is acquired by a person who has made or would have made, or for whom another person has made or would have made, a compulsory purchase order authorising its compulsory purchase for the purposes for which it is acquired.

[1157]

NOTES

Modification: modified, in relation to the right of a tenant to acquire a dwelling under the Housing Act 1996, s 16, by the Housing (Right to Acquire) Regulations 1997, SI 1997/619, reg 2, Schs 1, 2.

162 Exempted disposals which end liability under covenants

Where there is a relevant disposal which is an exempted disposal by virtue of section 160(1)(d) or (e) (compulsory disposals or disposals of land let with or used for purposes of dwelling-house)—
(a) the covenant required by section 155 (repayment of discount on early disposal) is not binding on the person to whom the disposal is made or any successor in title of his, and that covenant and the charge taking effect by virtue of section 156 cease to apply in relation to the property disposed of, and
[(aa) the covenant required by section 156A (right of first refusal for landlord etc) is not binding on the person to whom the disposal is made or any successor in title of his, and that covenant ceases to apply in relation to the property disposed of, and]
(b) any such covenant as is mentioned in section 157 (restriction on disposal of dwelling-houses in National Parks, etc) ceases to apply in relation to the property disposed of.

[1158]

NOTES

Para (aa) inserted by the Housing Act 2004, s 188(4); for effect see s 188(5), (6) thereof.

Modification: modified by the Housing (Preservation of Right to Buy) Regulations 1993, SI 1993/2241, reg 2, Sch 1. Modified, in relation to the right of a tenant to acquire a dwelling under the Housing Act 1996, s 16, by the Housing (Right to Acquire) Regulations 1997, SI 1997/619, reg 2, Schs 1, 2.

163 Treatment of options

(1) For the purposes of this Part the grant of an option enabling a person to call for a relevant disposal which is not an exempted disposal shall be treated as such a disposal made to him.

(2) For the purposes of section 157(2) (requirement of consent to disposal of dwelling-house in National Park, etc) a consent to such a grant shall be treated as a consent to a disposal in pursuance of the option.

[1159]

NOTES

Modification: modified by the Housing (Preservation of Right to Buy) Regulations 1993, SI 1993/2241, reg 2, Sch 1. Modified, in relation to the right of a tenant to acquire a dwelling under the Housing Act 1996, s 16, by the Housing (Right to Acquire) Regulations 1997, SI 1997/619, reg 2, Schs 1, 2.

[163A Treatment of deferred resale agreements for purposes of section 155

(1) If a secure tenant or his successor in title enters into an agreement within subsection (3), any liability arising under the covenant required by section 155 shall be determined as if a relevant disposal which is not an exempted disposal had occurred at the appropriate time.

(2) In subsection (1) "the appropriate time" means—

(a) the time when the agreement is entered into, or

(b) if it was made before the beginning of the discount repayment period, immediately after the beginning of that period.

(3) An agreement is within this subsection if it is an agreement between the secure tenant or his successor in title and any other person—

(a) which is made (expressly or impliedly) in contemplation of, or in connection with, the tenant exercising, or having exercised, the right to buy,

(b) which is made before the end of the discount repayment period, and

(c) under which a relevant disposal (other than an exempted disposal) is or may be required to be made to any person after the end of that period.

(4) Such an agreement is within subsection (3)—

(a) whether or not the date on which the disposal is to take place is specified in the agreement, and

(b) whether or not any requirement to make the disposal is or may be made subject to the fulfilment of any condition.

(5) The Secretary of State may by order provide—

(a) for subsection (1) to apply to agreements of any description specified in the order in addition to those within subsection (3);

(b) for subsection (1) not to apply to agreements of any description so specified to which it would otherwise apply.

(6) An order under subsection (5)—

(a) may make different provision with respect to different cases or descriptions of case; and

(b) shall be made by statutory instrument which shall be subject to annulment in pursuance of a resolution of either House of Parliament.

(7) In this section—

"agreement" includes arrangement;

"the discount repayment period" means the period of three or five years that applies for the purposes of section 155(2) or (3) (depending on whether the tenant's notice under section 122 was given before or on or after the date of the coming into force of section 185 of the Housing Act 2004).]

[1160]

NOTES

Commencement: 18 January 2005.

Inserted by the Housing Act 2004, s 187(1), except in relation to any agreement or arrangement made before 18 January 2005.

Powers of Secretary of State

164–167 (*Outside the scope of this work.*)

168 Effect of direction under s 167 on existing covenants and conditions

(1) If a direction under section 167 so provides, the provisions of this section shall apply in relation to a covenant or condition which—

(a) was included in a conveyance or grant executed before the date specified in the direction, and

(b) could not have been so included if the conveyance or grant had been executed on or after that date.

(2) The covenant or condition shall be discharged or (if the direction so provides) modified, as from the specified date, to such extent or in such manner as may be provided by the direction; and the discharge or modification is binding on all persons entitled or capable of becoming entitled to the benefit of the covenant or condition.

(3) The landlord by whom the conveyance or grant was executed shall, within such period as may be specified in the direction—

(a) serve on the person registered as the proprietor of the dwelling-house, and on any person registered as the proprietor of a charge affecting the dwelling-house, a written notice informing him of the discharge or modification, and

(b) on behalf of the person registered as the proprietor of the dwelling-house, apply to the Chief Land Registrar (and pay the appropriate fee) for notice of the discharge or modification to be entered in the register.

(4), (5) …

[1161]

NOTES

Sub-s (4): repealed by the Land Registration Act 1988, s 2, Schedule.

Sub-s (5): repealed by the Land Registration Act 2002, s 135, Sch 13.

Modification: modified by the Housing (Extension of Right to Buy) Order 1993, SI 1993/2240, art 3, Schedule, para 52, and the Housing (Preservation of Right to Buy) Regulations 1993, SI 1993/2241, reg 2, Sch 1. Modified, in relation to the right of a tenant to acquire a dwelling under the Housing Act 1996, s 16, by the Housing (Right to Acquire) Regulations 1997, SI 1997/619, reg 2, Schs 1, 2.

169–171 (*Outside the scope of this work.*)

[Preservation of right to buy on disposal to private sector landlord

171A Cases in which right to buy is preserved

(1) The provisions of this Part continue to apply where a person ceases to be a secure tenant of a dwelling-house by reason of the disposal by the landlord of an interest in the dwelling-house to a person who is not an authority or body within section 80 (the landlord condition for secure tenancies).

(2) In the following provisions of this Part—

(a) references to the preservation of the right to buy and to a person having the preserved right to buy are to the continued application of the provisions of this Part by virtue of this section and to a person in relation to whom those provisions so apply;

(b) "qualifying disposal" means a disposal in relation to which this section applies, and

(c) the "former secure tenant" and the "former landlord" are the persons mentioned in subsection (1).

(3) This section does not apply—

(a) where the former landlord was a person against whom the right to buy could not be exercised by virtue of paragraph 1, 2 or 3 of Schedule 5 (charities and certain housing associations), or

(b) in such other cases as may be excepted from the operation of this section by order of the Secretary of State.

(4) Orders under subsection (3)(b)—

(a) may relate to particular disposals and may make different provision with respect to different cases or descriptions of case, including different provision for different areas, and

(b) shall be made by statutory instrument which shall be subject to annulment in pursuance of a resolution of either House of Parliament.]

[1162]

NOTES

Inserted, together with the preceding cross-heading and ss 171B–171H, in relation to qualifying disposals made on or after 5 April 1989, by the Housing and Planning Act 1986, s 8(1), (3).

Modification: modified by the Housing (Extension of Right to Buy) Order 1993, SI 1993/2240, art 3, Schedule, para 55, and the Housing (Preservation of Right to Buy) Regulations 1993, SI 1993/2241, reg 2, Sch 1. Modified, in relation to the right of a tenant to acquire a dwelling under the Housing Act 1996, s 16, by the Housing (Right to Acquire) Regulations 1997, SI 1997/619, reg 2, Schs 1, 2.

[171B Extent of preserved right: qualifying persons and dwelling-houses

(1) A person to whom this section applies has the preserved right to buy so long as he occupies the relevant dwelling-house as his only or principal home, subject to the following provisions of this Part.

[(1A) A person to whom this section applies ceases to have the preserved right to buy if the tenancy of a relevant dwelling-house becomes a demoted tenancy by virtue of a demotion order under section 6A of the Housing Act 1988.]

(2) References in this Part to a "qualifying person" and "qualifying dwellinghouse", in relation to the preserved right to buy, are to a person who has that right and to a dwelling-house in relation to which a person has that right.

(3) The following are the persons to whom this section applies—

(a) the former secure tenant, or in the case of a joint tenancy, each of them;

(b) a qualifying successor as defined in subsection (4); and

(c) a person to whom a tenancy of a dwelling-house is granted jointly with a person who has the preserved right to buy in relation to that dwelling-house.

(4) The following are qualifying successors for this purpose—

[(a) where the former secure tenancy was not a joint tenancy and, immediately before his death, the former secure tenant was tenant under an assured tenancy of a dwelling-house in relation to which he had the preserved right to buy, a member of the former secure tenant's family who acquired that assured tenancy under the will or intestacy of the former secure tenant [or in whom that assured tenancy vested under section 17 of the Housing Act 1988 (statutory succession to assured tenancy)];

(aa) where the former secure tenancy was not a joint tenancy, a member of the former secure tenant's family to whom the former secure tenant assigned his assured tenancy of a dwelling-house in relation to which, immediately before the assignment, he had the preserved right to buy];

(b) a person who becomes the tenant of a dwelling-house in pursuance of—

(i) a property adjustment order under *section 24* [section 23A or 24] of the Matrimonial Causes Act 1973, or

(ii) an order under Schedule 1 to the Matrimonial Homes Act 1983 [or Schedule 7 to the Family Law Act 1996] transferring the tenancy, [or

(iii) a property adjustment order under section 17(1) of the Matrimonial and Family Proceedings Act 1984 (property adjustment orders after overseas divorce, &c), or

(iv) an order under paragraph 1 of Schedule 1 to the Children Act 1989 (orders for financial relief against parents),] [or

(v) an order under Part 2 of Schedule 5, or a property adjustment order under paragraph 9(2) or (3) of Schedule 7, to the Civil Partnership Act 2004 (property adjustment orders in connection with civil partnership proceedings or after overseas dissolution of civil partnership, etc),]

in place of a person who had the preserved right to buy in relation to that dwelling-house.

(5) The relevant dwelling-house is in the first instance—

(a) in relation to a person within paragraph (a) of subsection (3), the dwelling-house which was the subject of the qualifying disposal;

(b) in relation to a person within paragraph (b) of that subsection, the dwelling-house of which he became the statutory tenant or tenant as mentioned in [subsection (4)];

(c) in relation to a person within paragraph (c) of subsection (3), the dwelling-house of which he became a joint tenant as mentioned in that paragraph.

(6) If a person having the preserved right to buy becomes the tenant of another dwelling-house in place of the relevant dwelling-house (whether the new dwelling-house is entirely different or partly or substantially the same as the previous dwelling-house) and the landlord is the same person as the landlord of the previous dwelling-house or, where that landlord was a company, is a connected company, the new dwelling-house becomes the relevant dwelling-house for the purposes of the preserved right to buy.

For this purpose "connected company" means a subsidiary or holding company within the meaning of section 736 of the Companies Act 1985.]

[1163]

NOTES

Inserted as noted to s 171A at **[1162]**.

Sub-s (1A): inserted by the Anti-social Behaviour Act 2003, s 14(5), Sch 1, para 2(1), (3).

Sub-s (4): paras (a), (aa) substituted, for original para (a), by the Housing Act 1988, s 127(1); words in square brackets in para (a) added (in relation to qualifying disposals made on or after 24 September 1996), and sub-paras (b)(iii), (iv) and the word "or" immediately preceding them added by the Housing Act 1996, s 222, Sch 18, Pt III, para 16, Pt IV, para 26; words in italics in sub-para (b)(i) substituted by subsequent words in square brackets by the Family Law Act 1996, s 66(1), Sch 8, Pt I, para 34, as from a day to be appointed, and words in square brackets in para (b)(ii) inserted by s 66(1) of, and Sch 8, Pt III, para 56 to, that Act (for savings see s 66(2) of that Act, and Sch 9, paras 5, 8–10 thereto); para (b)(v) and the word "or" immediately preceding it added by the Civil Partnership Act 2004, s 81, Sch 8, para 31.

Sub-s (5): words in square brackets substituted by the Housing Act 1996, s 222, Sch 18, Pt IV, para 26.

Modification: modified by the Housing (Extension of Right to Buy) Order 1993, SI 1993/2240, art 3, Schedule, para 55, and the Housing (Preservation of Right to Buy) Regulations 1993, SI 1993/2241, reg 2, Sch 1. Modified, in relation to the right of a tenant to acquire a dwelling under the Housing Act 1996, s 16, by the Housing (Right to Acquire) Regulations 1997, SI 1997/619, reg 2, Schs 1, 2.

[171C Modifications of this Part in relation to preserved right

(1) Where the right to buy is preserved, the provisions of this Part have effect subject to such exceptions, adaptations and other modifications as may be prescribed by regulations made by the Secretary of State.

(2) The regulations may in particular provide—

(a) that paragraphs [1, 3 and] 5 to 11 of Schedule 5 (certain exceptions to the right to buy) do not apply;

(b) …

(c) that the provisions of this Part relating to the [right to acquire on rent to mortgage terms] do not apply; and

(d) that the landlord is not required to but may include a covenant for the repayment of discount, provided its terms are no more onerous than those of the covenant provided for in section 155.

(3) The prescribed exceptions, adaptations and other modifications shall take the form of textual amendments of the provisions of this Part as they apply in cases where the right to buy is preserved; and the first regulations, and any subsequent consolidating regulations, shall set out the provisions of this Part as they so apply.

(4) The regulations—

(a) may make different provision for different cases or descriptions of case, including different provision for different areas,

(b) may contain such incidental, supplementary and transitional provisions as the Secretary of State considers appropriate, and

(c) shall be made by statutory instrument which shall be subject to annulment in pursuance of a resolution of either House of Parliament.

[(5) The disapplication by the regulations of paragraph 1 of Schedule 5 shall not be taken to authorise any action on the part of a charity which would conflict with the trusts of the charity.]]

[1164]

NOTES

Inserted as noted to s 171A at **[1162]**.

Sub-s (2): words in first pair of square brackets inserted by the Housing Act 1988, s 127(2); para (b) repealed and words in second pair of square brackets substituted by the Leasehold Reform, Housing and Urban Development Act 1993, s 187, Sch 21, para 19, Sch 22.

Sub-s (5): added by the Housing Act 1988, s 127(3).

Modification: modified by the Housing (Extension of Right to Buy) Order 1993, SI 1993/2240, art 3, Schedule, para 55, and the Housing (Preservation of Right to Buy) Regulations 1993, SI 1993/2241, reg 2, Sch 1. Modified, in relation to the right of a tenant to acquire a dwelling under the Housing Act 1996, s 16, by the Housing (Right to Acquire) Regulations 1997, SI 1997/619, reg 2, Schs 1, 2.

Regulations: the Housing (Preservation of Right to Buy) Regulations 1993, SI 1993/2241; the Housing (Right of First Refusal) (England) Regulations 2005, SI 2005/1917; the Housing (Right of First Refusal) (Wales) Regulations 2005, SI 2005/2680.

[171D Subsequent dealings: disposal of landlord's interest in qualifying dwelling-house

(1) The disposal by the landlord of an interest in the qualifying dwelling-house, whether his whole interest or a lesser interest, does not affect the preserved right to buy, unless—

(a) as a result of the disposal an authority or body within section 80(1) (the landlord condition for secure tenancies) becomes the landlord of the qualifying person or persons, or

(b) paragraph 6 of Schedule 9A applies (effect of failure to register entry protecting preserved right to buy),

in which case the right to buy ceases to be preserved.

(2) The disposal by the landlord of a qualifying dwelling-house of less than his whole interest as landlord of the dwelling-house, or in part of it, requires the consent of the *Secretary of State* [appropriate authority], unless the disposal is to the qualifying person or persons.

[(2A) "The appropriate authority" means—

(a) in relation to a disposal of land in England by a registered provider of social housing, the Regulator of Social Housing,

(b) in relation to any other disposal of land in England, the Secretary of State, and

(c) in relation to a disposal of land in Wales, the Welsh Ministers.]

(3) Consent may be given in relation to a particular disposal or generally in relation to disposals of a particular description and may, in either case, be given subject to conditions.

(4) A disposal made without the consent required by subsection (2) is void, except in a case where, by reason of a failure to make the entries on the land register or land charges register required by Schedule 9A, the preserved right to buy does not bind the person to whom the disposal is made.]

[1165]

NOTES

Inserted as noted to s 171A at **[1162]**.

Sub-s (2): words in italics repealed and subsequent words in square brackets substituted by the Housing and Regeneration Act 2008, s 191(1)(a), as from a day to be appointed.

Sub-s (2A): inserted by the Housing and Regeneration Act 2008, s 191(1)(b), as from a day to be appointed.

Modification: modified by the Housing (Extension of Right to Buy) Order 1993, SI 1993/2240, art 3, Schedule, para 55. Modified, in relation to the right of a tenant to acquire a dwelling under the Housing Act 1996, s 16, by the Housing (Right to Acquire) Regulations 1997, SI 1997/619, reg 2, Schs 1, 2.

[171E Subsequent dealings: termination of landlord's interest in qualifying dwelling-house

(1) On the termination of the landlord's interest in the qualifying dwelling-house—

(a) on the occurrence of an event determining his estate or interest, or by re-entry on a breach of condition or forfeiture, or

(b) where the interest is a leasehold interest, by notice given by him or a superior landlord, on the expiry or surrender of the term, or otherwise (subject to subsection (2)),

the right to buy ceases to be preserved.

(2) The termination of the landlord's interest by merger on his acquiring a superior interest, or on the acquisition by another person of the landlord's interest together with a superior interest, does not affect the preserved right to buy, unless—

(a) as a result of the acquisition an authority or body within section 80(1) (the landlord condition for secure tenancies) becomes the landlord of the qualifying person or persons, or

(b) paragraph 6 of Schedule 9A applies (effect of failure to register entry protecting preserved right to buy),

in which case the right to buy ceases to be preserved.

(3) Where the termination of the landlord's interest as mentioned in subsection (1) is caused by the act or omission of the landlord, a qualifying person who is thereby deprived of the preserved right to buy is entitled to be compensated by him.]

[1166]

NOTES

Inserted as noted to s 171A at **[1162]**.

Modification: modified by the Housing (Extension of Right to Buy) Order 1993, SI 1993/2240, art 3, Schedule, para 55. Modified, in relation to the right of a tenant to acquire a dwelling under the Housing Act 1996, s 16, by the Housing (Right to Acquire) Regulations 1997, SI 1997/619, reg 2, Schs 1, 2.

[171F Subsequent dealings: transfer of qualifying person to alternative accommodation

The court shall not order a qualifying person to give up possession of the qualifying dwelling-house in pursuance of section 98(1)(a) of the Rent Act 1977 [or on Ground 9 in Schedule 2 to the Housing Act 1988] (suitable alternative accommodation) unless the court is satisfied—

(a) that the preserved right to buy will, by virtue of section 171B(6) (accommodation with same landlord or connected company), continue to be exercisable in relation to the dwelling-house offered by way of alternative accommodation and that the interest of the landlord in the new dwelling-house will be—

  (i) where the new dwelling-house is a house, not less than the interest of the landlord in the existing dwelling-house, or

  (ii) where the new dwelling-house is a flat, not less than the interest of the landlord in the existing dwelling-house or a term of years of which 80 years or more remain unexpired, whichever is the less; or

(b) that the landlord of the new dwelling-house will be an authority or body within section 80(1) (the landlord condition for secure tenancies).]

[1167]

NOTES

Inserted as noted to s 171A at **[1162]**.

Words in square brackets inserted by the Housing Act 1988, s 140(1), Sch 17, Pt I, para 42.

Modification: modified by the Housing (Extension of Right to Buy) Order 1993, SI 1993/2240, art 3, Schedule, para 55. Modified, in relation to the right of a tenant to acquire a dwelling under the Housing Act 1996, s 16, by the Housing (Right to Acquire) Regulations 1997, SI 1997/619, reg 2, Schs 1, 2.

[171G Land registration and related matters

Schedule 9A has effect with respect to registration of title and related matters arising in connection with the preservation of the right to buy.]

[1168]

NOTES

Inserted as noted to s 171A at **[1162]**.

Modification: modified by the Housing (Extension of Right to Buy) Order 1993, SI 1993/2240, art 3, Schedule, para 55. Modified, in relation to the right of a tenant to acquire a dwelling under the Housing Act 1996, s 16, by the Housing (Right to Acquire) Regulations 1997, SI 1997/619, reg 2, Schs 1, 2.

[171H Disposal after notice claiming to exercise right to buy, etc

(1) Where notice has been given in respect of a dwelling-house claiming to exercise the right to buy … and before the completion of the exercise of that right the dwelling-house is the subject of—

(a) a qualifying disposal, or

(b) a disposal to which section 171D(1)(a) or 171E(2)(a) applies (disposal to authority or body satisfying landlord condition for secure tenancies),

all parties shall, subject to subsection (2), be in the same position as if the disponee had become the landlord before the notice was given and had been given that notice and any further notice given by the tenant to the landlord and had taken all steps which the landlord had taken.

(2) If the circumstances after the disposal differ in any material respect, as for example where—

(a) the interest of the disponee in the dwelling-house after the disposal differs from that of the disponor before the disposal, or

(b) …

(c) any of the provisions of Schedule 5 (exceptions to the right to buy) becomes or ceases to be applicable,

all those concerned shall, as soon as practicable after the disposal, take all such steps (whether by way of amending or withdrawing and re-serving any notice or extending any period or otherwise) as may be requisite for the purpose of securing that all parties are, as nearly as may be, in the same position as they would have been if those circumstances had obtained before the disposal.]

[1169]

NOTES

Inserted as noted to s 171A at **[1162]**.

Sub-ss (1), (2): words omitted repealed by the Leasehold Reform, Housing and Urban Development Act 1993, s 187(2), Sch 22.

Modification: modified by the Housing (Extension of Right to Buy) Order 1993, SI 1993/2240, art 3, Schedule, para 55. Modified, in relation to the right of a tenant to acquire a dwelling under the Housing Act 1996, s 16, by the Housing (Right to Acquire) Regulations 1997, SI 1997/619, reg 2, Schs 1, 2.

172–175 (*Ss 172, 174, 175 outside the scope of this work; s 173 repealed by the Statute Law* (*Repeals*) *Act 1998.*)

Supplementary provisions

176–182 (*Outside the scope of this work.*)

183 Meaning of "house", "flat" and "dwelling-house"

(1) The following provisions apply to the interpretation of "house", "flat" and "dwelling-house" when used in this Part.

(2) A dwelling-house is a house if, and only if, it (or so much of it as does not consist of land included by virtue of section 184) is a structure reasonably so called; so that—

(a) where a building is divided horizontally, the flats or other units into which it is divided are not houses;

(b) where a building is divided vertically, the units into which it is divided may be houses;

(c) where a building is not structurally detached, it is not a house if a material part of it lies above or below the remainder of the structure.

(3) A dwelling-house which is not a house is a flat.

[1170]

NOTES

Modification: modified, in relation to the right of a tenant to acquire a dwelling under the Housing Act 1996, s 16, by the Housing (Right to Acquire) Regulations 1997, SI 1997/619, reg 2, Schs 1, 2.

184 Land let with or used for purposes of dwelling-house

(1) For the purpose of this Part land let together with a dwelling-house shall be treated as part of the dwelling-house, unless the land is agricultural land (within the meaning set out in section 26(3)(a) of the General Rate Act 1967) exceeding two acres.

(2) There shall be treated as included in a dwelling-house any land which is not within subsection (1) but is or has been used for the purpose of the dwelling-house if—

(a) the tenant, by a written notice served on the landlord at any time before he exercises the right to buy or the [right to acquire on rent to mortgage terms], requires the land to be included in the dwelling-house, and

(b) it is reasonable in all the circumstances for the land to be so included.

(3) A notice under subsection (2) may be withdrawn by a written notice served on the landlord at any time before the tenant exercises the right to buy or the [right to acquire on rent to mortgage terms].

(4) Where a notice under subsection (2) is served or withdrawn after the service of the notice under section 125 (landlord's notice of purchase price, etc), the parties shall, as soon as practicable after the service or withdrawal, take all such steps (whether by way of amending, withdrawing or re-serving any notice or extending any period or otherwise) as may be requisite for the purpose of securing that all parties are, as nearly as may be, in the same position as they would have been in if the notice under subsection (2) had been served or withdrawn before the service of the notice under section 125.

[1171]

NOTES

Sub-ss (2), (3): words in square brackets substituted by the Leasehold Reform, Housing and Urban Development Act 1993, s 187(1), Sch 21, para 24.

Modification: modified by the Housing (Extension of Right to Buy) Order 1993, SI 1993/2240, art 3, Schedule, para 63, and the Housing (Preservation of Right to Buy) Regulations 1993, SI 1993/2241, reg 2, Sch 1. Modified, in relation to the right of a tenant to acquire a dwelling under the Housing Act 1996, s 16, by the Housing (Right to Acquire) Regulations 1997, SI 1997/619, reg 2, Schs 1, 2.

185 Meaning of "secure tenancy" and "secure tenant"

(1) References in this Part to a secure tenancy or a secure tenant in relation to a time before 26th August 1984 are to a tenancy which would have been a secure tenancy if Chapter II of Part I of the Housing Act 1980 and Part I of the Housing and Building Control Act 1984 had then been in force or to a person who would then have been a secure tenant.

(2) For the purpose of determining whether a person would have been a secure tenant and his tenancy a secure tenancy—

(a) a predecessor of a local authority shall be deemed to have been such an authority, and

(b) a housing association shall be deemed to have been registered if it is or was [a registered social landlord] at any later time.

[1172]

NOTES

Sub-s (2): words in square brackets substituted by SI 1996/2325, art 5, Sch 2, para 14(1), (16).

Modification: modified in relation to the right of a tenant to acquire a dwelling under the Housing Act 1996, s 16, by the Housing (Right to Acquire) Regulations 1997, SI 1997/619, reg 2, Schs 1, 2.

186 Members of a person's family

(1) A person is a member of another's family within the meaning of this Part if—

(a) he is the spouse [or civil partner] of that person, or he and that person live together as husband and wife [or as if they were civil partners], or

(b) he is that person's parent, grandparent, child, grandchild, brother, sister, uncle, aunt, nephew or niece.

(2) For the purposes of subsection (1)(b)—

(a) a relationship by marriage [or civil partnership] shall be treated as a relationship by blood,

(b) a relationship of the half-blood shall be treated as a relationship of the whole blood,

(c) the stepchild of a person shall be treated as his child, and

(d) an illegitimate child shall be treated as the legitimate child of his mother and reputed father.

[1173]–[1174]

NOTES

Words in square brackets inserted by the Civil Partnership Act 2004, s 81, Sch 8, para 27.

Modification: modified in relation to the right of a tenant to acquire a dwelling under the Housing Act 1996, s 16, by the Housing (Right to Acquire) Regulations 1997, SI 1997/619, reg 2, Schs 1, 2.

187, 188 (*Outside the scope of this work.*)

PART VI
REPAIR NOTICES

189, 190, 190A, 191, 191A, 192, 193–199, 198A (*Ss 189, 190, 190A, 191, 191A, 193–198, 198A repealed by the Housing Act 2004, s 266, Sch 16; s 192 repealed by the Local Government and Housing Act 1989, ss 165(1)(a), 194(4), Sch 9, Pt I, para 6, Sch 12, Pt II, except in relation to repair notices served, or orders made thereunder, before 1 April 1990, see the Local Government and Housing Act 1989 (Commencement No 5 and Transitional Provisions) Order 1990, SI 1990/431.*)

Provisions for protection of owner and others

199–203 (*Ss 199–201 repealed by the Housing Act 1988, ss 130(1), (3), 140(2), Sch 15, para 9, Sch 18, except in relation to any repair notice served before 15 January 1989; ss 202, 203 repealed by the Housing Act 2004, s 266, Sch 16.*)

204–603 (*Ss 204, 207, 208 repealed by the Housing Act 2004, s 266, Sch 16; ss 205, 206 repealed by the Local Government and Housing Act 1989, ss 165(1)(a), 194(4), Sch 9, Pt I, paras 10, 11, Sch 12, Pt II, except in relation to repair notices served before 1 April 1990, see the Local Government and Housing Act 1989 (Commencement No 5 and Transitional Provisions) Order 1990, SI 1990/431; ss 209–603 (Pts VII–XVII) in so far as unrepealed, outside the scope of this work.*)

PART XVIII
MISCELLANEOUS AND GENERAL PROVISIONS

604–608 (*Ss 604–606 repealed by the Housing Act 2004, s 266, Sch 16, subject to transitional provisions and savings in SI 2006/1060, SI 2006/1535; ss 607, 608 outside the scope of this work.*)

Enforceability of covenants, etc

609 Enforcement of covenants against owner for the time being

Where—

(a) a local housing authority have disposed of land held by them for any of the purposes of this Act and the person to whom the disposal was made has entered into a covenant with the authority concerning the land, or

(b) an owner of any land has entered into a covenant with the local housing authority concerning the land for the purposes of any of the provisions of this Act,

the authority may enforce the covenant against the persons deriving title under the covenantor, notwithstanding that the authority are not in possession of or interested in any land for the benefit of which the covenant was entered into, in like manner and to the like extent as if they had been possessed of or interested in such land.

[1175]

610–624 (*Outside the scope of this work.*)

Final provisions

625 Short title, commencement and extent

(1) This Act may be cited as the Housing Act 1985.

(2) This Act comes into force on 1st April 1986.

(3) This Act extends to England and Wales only.

[1176]

SCHEDULE 1
TENANCIES WHICH ARE NOT SECURE TENANCIES

Section 79

Long leases

1. A tenancy is not a secure tenancy if it is a long tenancy.

[Introductory tenancies

1A. A tenancy is not a secure tenancy if it is an introductory tenancy or a tenancy which has ceased to be an introductory tenancy—

(a) by virtue of section 133(3) of the Housing Act 1996 (disposal on death to non-qualifying person), or

(b) by virtue of the tenant, or in the case of a joint tenancy every tenant, ceasing to occupy the dwelling-house as his only or principal home.]

[1B. A tenancy is not a secure tenancy if it is a demoted tenancy within the meaning of section 143A of the Housing Act 1996.]

Premises occupied in connection with employment

2.—(1) [Subject to sub-paragraph (4B)] a tenancy is not a secure tenancy if the tenant is an employee of the landlord or of—

a local authority,
a new town corporation,
[a housing action trust]
an urban development corporation,
… , or
the governors of an aided school,

and his contract of employment requires him to occupy the dwelling-house for the better performance of his duties.

(2) [Subject to sub-paragraph (4B)] a tenancy is not a secure tenancy if the tenant is a member of a police force and the dwelling-house is provided for him free of rent and rates in pursuance of regulations made under [section 50 of the Police Act 1996] (general regulations as to government, administration and conditions of service of police forces).

(3) [Subject to sub-paragraph (4B)] a tenancy is not a secure tenancy if the tenant is an employee of a [fire and rescue authority] and—

(a) his contract of employment requires him to live in close proximity to a particular fire station, and

(b) the dwelling-house was let to him by the authority in consequence of that requirement.

(4) [Subject to sub-paragraph (4A) and (4B)] a tenancy is not a secure tenancy if—

(a) within the period of three years immediately preceding the grant the conditions mentioned in sub-paragraph (1), (2) or (3) have been satisfied with respect to a tenancy of the dwelling-house, and

(b) before the grant the landlord notified the tenant in writing of the circumstances in which this exception applies and that in its opinion the proposed tenancy would fall within this exception,

…

[(4A) Except where the landlord is a local housing authority, a tenancy under sub-paragraph (4) shall become a secure tenancy when the periods during which the conditions mentioned in sub-paragraph (1), (2) or (3) are not satisfied with respect to the tenancy amount in aggregate to more than three years.

(4B) Where the landlord is a local housing authority, a tenancy under sub-paragraph (1), (2), (3) or (4) shall become a secure tenancy if the authority notify the tenant that the tenancy is to be regarded as a secure tenancy.]

(5) In this paragraph "contract of employment" means a contract of service or apprenticeship, whether express or implied and (if express) whether oral or in writing.

Land acquired for development

3.—(1) A tenancy is not a secure tenancy if the dwelling-house is on land which has been acquired for development and the dwelling-house is used by the landlord, pending development of the land, as temporary housing accommodation.

(2) In this paragraph "development" has the meaning given by [section 55 of the Town and Country Planning Act 1990] (general definition of development for purposes of that Act).

[Accommodation for homeless persons

4. A tenancy granted in pursuance of any function under Part VII of the Housing Act 1996 (homelessness) is not a secure tenancy unless the local housing authority concerned have notified the tenant that the tenancy is to be regarded as a secure tenancy.]

[Family intervention tenancies

4ZA.—(1) A tenancy is not a secure tenancy if it is a family intervention tenancy.

(2) But a tenancy mentioned in sub-paragraph (1) becomes a secure tenancy if the landlord notifies the tenant that it is to be regarded as a secure tenancy.

(3) In this paragraph "a family intervention tenancy" means, subject to sub-paragraph (4), a tenancy granted by a local housing authority in respect of a dwelling-house—

(a) to a person ("the new tenant") against whom a possession order under section 84 in respect of another dwelling-house—
(i) has been made, in relation to a secure tenancy, on ground 2 or 2A of Part 1 of Schedule 2;
(ii) could, in the opinion of the authority, have been so made in relation to such a tenancy; or
(iii) could, in the opinion of the authority, have been so made if the person had had such a tenancy; and

(b) for the purposes of the provision of behaviour support services.

(4) A tenancy is not a family intervention tenancy for the purposes of this paragraph if the local housing authority has failed to serve a notice under sub-paragraph (5) on the new tenant before the new tenant entered into the tenancy.

(5) A notice under this sub-paragraph is a notice stating—

(a) the reasons for offering the tenancy to the new tenant;
(b) the dwelling-house in respect of which the tenancy is to be granted;
(c) the other main terms of the tenancy (including any requirements on the new tenant in respect of behaviour support services);
(d) the security of tenure available under the tenancy and any loss of security of tenure which is likely to result from the new tenant agreeing to enter into the tenancy;
(e) that the new tenant is not obliged to enter into the tenancy or (unless otherwise required to do so) to surrender any existing tenancy or possession of a dwelling-house;
(f) any likely action by the local housing authority if the new tenant does not enter into the tenancy or surrender any existing tenancy or possession of a dwelling-house.

(6) The appropriate national authority may by regulations made by statutory instrument amend sub-paragraph (5).

(7) A notice under sub-paragraph (5) must contain advice to the new tenant as to how the new tenant may be able to obtain assistance in relation to the notice.

(8) The appropriate national authority may by regulations made by statutory instrument make provision about the type of advice to be provided in such notices.

(9) Regulations under this paragraph may contain such transitional, transitory or saving provision as the appropriate national authority considers appropriate.

(10) A statutory instrument containing (whether alone or with other provision) regulations under this paragraph which amend or repeal any of paragraphs (a) to (f) of sub-paragraph (5) may not be made—

(a) by the Secretary of State unless a draft of the instrument has been laid before, and approved by a resolution of, each House of Parliament; and
(b) by the Welsh Ministers unless a draft of the instrument has been laid before, and approved by a resolution of, the National Assembly for Wales.

(11) Subject to this, a statutory instrument containing regulations made under this paragraph—

(a) by the Secretary of State is subject to annulment in pursuance of a resolution of either House of Parliament; and
(b) by the Welsh Ministers is subject to annulment in pursuance of a resolution of the National Assembly for Wales.

(12) In this paragraph—

"appropriate national authority"—
(a) in relation to England, means the Secretary of State; and
(b) in relation to Wales, means the Welsh Ministers;

"behaviour support agreement" means an agreement in writing about behaviour and the provision of support services made between the new tenant and the local housing authority concerned (or between persons who include those persons);

"behaviour support services" means relevant support services to be provided by any person to—
(a) the new tenant; or
(b) any person who is to reside with the new tenant;
for the purpose of addressing the kind of behaviour which led to the new tenant falling within sub-paragraph (3)(a);

"family intervention tenancy" has the meaning given by sub-paragraph (3);

"the new tenant" has the meaning given by sub-paragraph (3)(a);

"relevant support services" means support services of a kind identified in a behaviour support agreement and designed to meet such needs of the recipient as are identified in the agreement.]

[Accommodation for asylum-seekers

4A.—(1) A tenancy is not a secure tenancy if it is granted in order to provide accommodation [under section 4 or Part VI of the Immigration and Asylum Act 1999].

(2) A tenancy mentioned in sub-paragraph (1) becomes a secure tenancy if the landlord notifies the tenant that it is to be regarded as a secure tenancy.]

[Accommodation for persons with Temporary Protection

4B. A tenancy is not a secure tenancy if it is granted in order to provide accommodation under the Displaced Persons (Temporary Protection) Regulations 2005.]

Temporary accommodation for persons taking up employment

5.—(1) [Subject to sub-paragraphs (1A) and (1B), a tenancy is not a secure tenancy] if—

(a) the person to whom the tenancy was granted was not, immediately before the grant, resident in the district in which the dwelling-house is situated,

(b) before the grant of the tenancy, he obtained employment, or an offer of employment, in the district or its surrounding area,

(c) the tenancy was granted to him for the purpose of meeting his need for temporary accommodation in the district or its surrounding area in order to work there, and of enabling him to find permanent accommodation there, and

(d) the landlord notified him in writing of the circumstances in which this exception applies and that in its opinion the proposed tenancy would fall within this exception;

…

[(1A) Except where the landlord is a local housing authority, a tenancy under sub-paragraph (1) shall become a secure tenancy on the expiry of one year from the grant or on earlier notification by the landlord to the tenant that the tenancy is to be regarded as a secure tenancy.

(1B) Where the landlord is a local housing authority, a tenancy under sub-paragraph (1) shall become a secure tenancy if at any time the authority notify the tenant that the tenancy is to be regarded as a secure tenancy.]

(2) In this paragraph—

"district" means district of a local housing authority; and

"surrounding area", in relation to a district, means the area consisting of each district that adjoins it.

Short-term arrangements

6. A tenancy is not a secure tenancy if—

(a) the dwelling-house has been leased to the landlord with vacant possession for use as temporary housing accommodation,

(b) the terms on which it has been leased include provision for the lessor to obtain vacant possession from the landlord on the expiry of a specified period or when required by the lessor,

(c) the lessor is not a body which is capable of granting secure tenancies, and

(d) the landlord has no interest in the dwelling-house other than under the lease in question or as a mortgagee.

Temporary accommodation during works

7. A tenancy is not a secure tenancy if—

(a) the dwelling-house has been made available for occupation by the tenant (or a predecessor in title of his) while works are carried out on the dwelling-house which he previously occupied as his home, and

(b) the tenant or predecessor was not a secure tenant of that other dwelling-house at the time when he ceased to occupy it as his home.

[Agricultural holdings etc

8.—(1) A tenancy is not a secure tenancy if—

(a) the dwelling-house is comprised in an agricultural holding and is occupied by the person responsible for the control (whether as tenant or as servant or agent of the tenant) of the farming of the holding, or

(b) the dwelling-house is comprised in the holding held under a farm business tenancy and is occupied by the person responsible for the control (whether as tenant or as servant or agent of the tenant) of the management of the holding.

(2) In sub-paragraph (1) above—

(a) "agricultural holding" means any agricultural holding within the meaning of the Agricultural Holdings Act 1986 held under a tenancy in relation to which that Act applies, and

(b) "farm business tenancy", and "holding" in relation to such a tenancy, have the same meaning as in the Agricultural Tenancies Act 1995.]

Licensed premises

9. A tenancy is not a secure tenancy if the dwelling-house consists of or includes [premises which, by virtue of a premises licence under the Licensing Act 2003, may be used for the supply of alcohol (within the meaning of section 14 of that Act)] for consumption on the premises.

Student lettings

10.—(1) [Subject to sub-paragraphs (2A) and (2B), a tenancy of a dwelling-house is not a secure tenancy] if—

(a) it is granted for the purpose of enabling the tenant to attend a designated course at an educational establishment, and

(b) before the grant of the tenancy the landlord notified him in writing of the circumstances in which this exception applies and that in its opinion the proposed tenancy would fall within this exception;

...

(2) A landlord's notice under sub-paragraph (1)(b) shall specify the educational establishment which the person concerned proposes to attend.

[(2A) Except where the landlord is a local housing authority, a tenancy under sub-paragraph (1) shall become a secure tenancy on the expiry of the period specified in sub-paragraph (3) or on earlier notification by the landlord to the tenant that the tenancy is to be regarded as a secure tenancy.

(2B) Where the landlord is a local housing authority, a tenancy under sub-paragraph (1) shall become a secure tenancy if at any time the authority notify the tenant that the tenancy is to be regarded as a secure tenancy.]

(3) The period referred to in [sub-paragraph (2A)] is—

(a) in a case where the tenant attends a designated course at the educational establishment specified in the landlord's notice, the period ending six months after the tenant ceases to attend that (or any other) designated course at that establishment;

(b) in any other case, the period ending six months after the grant of the tenancy.

(4) In this paragraph—

"designated course" means a course of any kind designated by regulations made by the Secretary of State for the purposes of this paragraph;

"educational establishment" means a university or [institution which provides higher education or further education (or both); and for the purposes of this definition "higher education" and "further education" have the same meaning as in [the Education Act 1996]].

(5) Regulations under sub-paragraph (4) shall be made by statutory instrument and may make different provision with respect to different cases or descriptions of case, including different provision for different areas.

1954 Act tenancies

11. A tenancy is not a secure tenancy if it is one to which Part II of the Landlord and Tenant Act 1954 applies (tenancies of premises occupied for business purposes).

Almshouses

[12. A licence to occupy a dwelling-house is not a secure tenancy if—

(a) the dwelling-house is an almshouse, and

(b) the licence was granted by or on behalf of a charity which—

(i) is authorised under its trusts to maintain the dwelling-house as an almshouse, and

(ii) has no power under its trusts to grant a tenancy of the dwelling-house;

and in this paragraph "almshouse" means any premises maintained as an almshouse, whether they are called an almshouse or not; and "trusts", in relation to a charity, means the provisions establishing it as a charity and regulating its purposes and administration, whether those provisions take effect by way of trust or not.]

[1177]

NOTES

Para 1A: inserted by the Housing Act 1996, s 141(1), Sch 14, para 5.

Para 1B: inserted by the Anti-social Behaviour Act 2003, s 14(5), Sch 1, para 2(1), (4).

Para 2: words in first pair of square brackets in sub-paras (1)–(3), words in square brackets in sub-para (4), and the whole of sub-paras (4A), (4B) inserted, and words omitted from sub-para (4) repealed by the Housing Act 1996, ss 173, 227, Sch 16, para 2(1)–(4), Sch 19, Pt VII, except in relation to a tenancy granted before 1 April 1997; words omitted from sub-para (1) repealed by the Government of Wales Act 1998, s 152, Sch 18, Pt IV; words in second pair of square brackets in sub-para (1) inserted by the Housing Act 1988, s 83(1), (6)(a);

words in second pair of square brackets in sub-para (2) substituted by the Police Act 1996, s 103(1), Sch 7, Pt II, para 40; words in second pair of square brackets in sub-para (3) substituted by the Fire and Rescue Services Act 2004, s 53(1), Sch 1, para 62(1), (3).

Para 3: words in square brackets substituted by the Planning (Consequential Provisions) Act 1990, s 4, Sch 2, para 71(6), subject to transitional provisions and savings in s 5 of, and Sch 3 to, that Act.

Para 4: substituted by the Housing Act 1996, s 216(3), Sch 17, para 3, subject to transitional provisions in s 216(2) of that Act.

Para 4ZA: inserted by the Housing and Regeneration Act 2008, s 297(1), subject to transitional provisions and savings: see SI 2008/3068, arts 6, 9, 10.

Para 4A: inserted by the Immigration and Asylum Act 1999, s 169(1), Sch 14, para 81; words in square brackets substituted by the Immigration, Asylum and Nationality Act 2006, s 43(4)(d).

Para 4B: inserted by SI 2005/1379, Schedule, para 4.

Para 5: words in square brackets in sub-para (1) substituted, words omitted from sub-para (1) repealed and sub-paras (1A), (1B) inserted by the Housing Act 1996, ss 173, 227, Sch 16, para 2(1), (5), (6), Sch 19, Pt VII, except in relation to a tenancy granted before 1 April 1997.

Para 8: substituted by the Agricultural Tenancies Act 1995, s 40, Schedule, para 30.

Para 9: words in square brackets substituted by the Licensing Act 2003, Sch 6, paras 102, 104.

Para 10: words in square brackets in sub-paras (1), (3) substituted, words omitted repealed and sub-paras (2A), (2B) inserted by the Housing Act 1996, ss 173, 227, Sch 16, para 2(1), (7)–(9), Sch 19, Pt VII, except in relation to a tenancy granted before 1 April 1997; in sub-para (4) words in first (outer) pair of square brackets substituted by the Education Reform Act 1988, s 237(1), Sch 12, Pt III, para 95, words in second (inner) pair of square brackets substituted by the Education Act 1996, s 582(1), Sch 37, Pt I, para 62.

Para 12: substituted by the Charities Act 1992, s 78(1), Sch 6, para 12.

Regulations: the Secure Tenancies (Designated Courses) Regulations 1980, SI 1980/1407.

(*Sch 2 outside the scope of this work.*)

SCHEDULE 3
GROUNDS FOR WITHHOLDING CONSENT TO ASSIGNMENT BY WAY OF EXCHANGE

Section 92

[Ground 1

The tenant or the proposed assignee is subject to an order of the court for the possession of the dwelling-house of which he is the secure tenant.]

Ground 2

Proceedings have been begun for possession of the dwelling-house of which the tenant or the proposed assignee is the secure tenant on one or more of grounds 1 to 6 in Part I of Schedule 2 (grounds on which possession may be ordered despite absence of suitable alternative accommodation), or there has been served on the tenant or the proposed assignee a notice under section 83 (notice of proceedings for possession) which specifies one or more of those grounds and is still in force.

[Ground 2A

Either—

(a) a relevant order or suspended Ground 2 or 14 possession order is in force, or

(b) an application is pending before any court for a relevant order, a demotion order or a Ground 2 or 14 possession order to be made,

in respect of the tenant or the proposed assignee or a person who is residing with either of them.

A "relevant order" means—

an injunction under section 152 of the Housing Act 1996 (injunctions against anti-social behaviour);

an injunction to which a power of arrest is attached by virtue of section 153 of that Act (other injunctions against anti-social behaviour);

an injunction under section 153A, 153B or 153D of that Act (injunctions against anti-social behaviour on application of certain social landlords);

an anti-social behaviour order under section 1 of the Crime and Disorder Act 1998; or

an injunction to which a power of arrest is attached by virtue of section 91 of the Anti-social Behaviour Act 2003.

A "demotion order" means a demotion order under section 82A of this Act or section 6A of the Housing Act 1988.

A "Ground 2 or 14 possession order" means an order for possession under Ground 2 in Schedule 2 to this Act or Ground 14 in Schedule 2 to the Housing Act 1988.

Where the tenancy of the tenant or the proposed assignee is a joint tenancy, any reference to that person includes (where the context permits) a reference to any of the joint tenants.]

Ground 3

The accommodation afforded by the dwelling-house is substantially more extensive than is reasonably required by the proposed assignee.

Ground 4

The extent of the accommodation afforded by the dwelling-house is not reasonably suitable to the needs of the proposed assignee and his family.

Ground 5

The dwelling-house—

(a) forms part of or is within the curtilage of a building which, or so much of it as is held by the landlord, is held mainly for purposes other than housing purposes and consists mainly of accommodation other than housing accommodation, or is situated in a cemetery, and

(b) was let to the tenant or a predecessor in title of his in consequence of the tenant or predecessor being in the employment of—
the landlord,
a local authority,
a [development] corporation,
[a housing action trust]
…
an urban development corporation, or
the governors of an aided school.

Ground 6

The landlord is a charity and the proposed assignee's occupation of the dwelling-house would conflict with the objects of the charity.

Ground 7

The dwelling-house has features which are substantially different from those of ordinary dwelling-houses and which are designed to make it suitable for occupation by a physically disabled person who requires accommodation of the kind provided by the dwelling-house and if the assignment were made there would no longer be such a person residing in the dwelling-house.

Ground 8

The landlord is a housing association or housing trust which lets dwelling-houses only for occupation (alone or with others) by persons whose circumstances (other than merely financial circumstances) make it especially difficult for them to satisfy their need for housing and if the assignment were made there would no longer be such a person residing in the dwelling-house.

Ground 9

The dwelling-house is one of a group of dwelling-houses which it is the practice of the landlord to let for occupation by persons with special needs and a social service or special facility is provided in close proximity to the group of dwelling-houses in order to assist persons with those special needs and if the assignment were made there would no longer be a person with those special needs residing in the dwelling-house.

[Ground 10

The dwelling-house is the subject of a management agreement under which the manager is a housing association of which at least half the members are tenants of dwelling-houses subject to the agreement, at least half the tenants of the dwelling-houses are members of the association and the proposed assignee is not, and is not willing to become, a member of the association.]

[1178]

NOTES

Ground 1: substituted by the Housing and Regeneration Act 2008, s 299, Sch 11, Pt 1, paras 1, 4, subject to transitional provisions in Sch 11, Pt 1, para 14, thereto.

Ground 2A: inserted by the Housing Act 2004, s 191(1), in relation to applications for consent under section 92 of this Act which are made on or after 6 June 2005 (in relation to England) and 14 July 2005 (in relation to Wales).

Ground 5: first word in square brackets in para (b) substituted by SI 2008/3002, art 4, Sch 1, paras 2, 30, subject to transitional provisions and saving in art 5 thereof, ad Sch 2, thereto; second words in square brackets in para (b) inserted by the Housing Act 1988, s 83(1), (6)(e); words omitted from para (b) repealed by the Government of Wales Act 1998, s 152, Sch 18, Pt IV.

Ground 10: added by the Housing and Planning Act 1986, s 24(1)(g), Sch 5, Pt I, para 7.

(*Schs 3A, 4 outside the scope of this work.*)

SCHEDULE 5
EXCEPTIONS TO THE RIGHT TO BUY

Section 120

Charities

1. The right to buy does not arise if the landlord is a housing trust or a housing association and is a charity.

Certain housing associations

2. The right to buy does not arise if the landlord is a co-operative housing association.

3. The right to buy does not arise if the landlord is a housing association which at no time received a grant under—

any enactment mentioned in paragraph 2 of Schedule 1 to the Housing Associations Act 1985 (grants under enactments superseded by the Housing Act 1974),
section 31 of the Housing Act 1974 (management grants),
section 41 of the Housing Associations Act 1985 (housing association grants),
section 54 of that Act (revenue deficit grants),
section 55 of that Act (hostel deficit grants), …
[section 58] of that Act (grants by local authorities)
[section 50 of the Housing Act 1988 (housing association grants), …
section 51 of that Act (revenue deficit grants)
[section 18 of the Housing Act 1996 (social housing Grants)][, or
section 22 of [that Act] (grants by local authorities for registered social landlords)]][, or
section 19 of the Housing and Regeneration Act 2008 (financial assistance) which was a grant made on condition that the housing association provides social housing (and 'provides social housing' has the same meaning as in Part 1 of that Act)]

Landlord with insufficient interest in the property

4. The right to buy does not arise unless the landlord owns the freehold or has an interest sufficient to grant a lease in pursuance of this Part for—

(a) where the dwelling-house is a house, a term exceeding 21 years, or
(b) where the dwelling-house is a flat, a term of not less than 50 years,

commencing, in either case, with the date on which the tenant's notice claiming to exercise the right to buy is served.

Dwelling-houses let in connection with employment

5.—(1) The right to buy does not arise if the dwelling-house—

(a) forms part of, or is within the curtilage of, a building which, or so much of it as is held by the landlord, is held mainly for purposes other than housing purposes and consists mainly of accommodation other than housing accommodation, or is situated in a cemetery, and
(b) was let to the tenant or a predecessor in title of his in consequence of the tenant or predecessor being in the employment of the landlord or of—
a local authority,
a [development] corporation,
[a housing action trust]
…
an urban development corporation, or
the governors of an aided school.

(2) In sub-paragraph (1)(a) "housing purposes" means the purposes for which dwelling-houses are held by local housing authorities under Part II (provision of housing) or purposes corresponding to those purposes.

Certain dwelling-houses for the disabled

6. …

7. The right to buy does not arise if the dwelling-house has features which are substantially different from those of ordinary dwelling-houses and are designed to make it suitable for occupation by physically disabled persons, and—

(a) it is one of a group of dwelling-houses which it is the practice of the landlord to let for occupation by physically disabled persons, and
(b) a social service or special facilities are provided in close proximity to the group of dwelling-houses wholly or partly for the purpose of assisting those persons.

8. …

9.—(1) The right to buy does not arise if—

(a) the dwelling-house is one of a group of dwelling-houses which it is the practice of the landlord to let for occupation by persons who are suffering or have suffered from a mental disorder, and

(b) a social service or special facilities are provided wholly or partly for the purpose of assisting those persons.

(2) In sub-paragraph (1)(a) "mental disorder" has the same meaning as in the Mental Health Act 1983.

Certain dwelling-houses for persons of pensionable age

10.—(1) The right to buy does not arise if the dwelling-house is one of a group of dwelling-houses—

(a) which are particularly suitable, having regard to their location, size, design, heating systems and other features, for occupation by [elderly persons], and

(b) which it is the practice of the landlord to let for occupation by [persons aged 60 or more], or for occupation by such persons and physically disabled persons,

and special facilities such as are mentioned in sub-paragraph (2) are provided wholly or mainly for the purposes of assisting those persons.

(2) The facilities referred to above are facilities which consist of or include—

(a) the services of a resident warden, or

(b) the services of a non-resident warden, a system for calling him and the use of a common room in close proximity to the group of dwelling-houses.

[11.—(1) The right to buy does not arise if the dwelling-house—

(a) is particularly suitable, having regard to its location, size, design, heating system and other features, for occupation by elderly persons, and

(b) was let to the tenant or a predecessor in title of his for occupation by a person who was aged 60 or more (whether the tenant or predecessor or another person).

(2) In determining whether a dwelling is particularly suitable, no regard shall be had to the presence of any feature provided by the tenant or a predecessor in title of his.

(3) Notwithstanding anything in section 181 (jurisdiction of county court), any question arising under this paragraph shall be determined as follows.

(4) If an application for the purpose is made by the tenant to *the Secretary of State* [the appropriate tribunal or authority] before the end of the period of 56 days beginning with the service of the landlord's notice under section 124, the question shall be determined by *the Secretary of State* [the appropriate tribunal or authority].

(5) If no such application is so made, the question shall be deemed to have been determined in favour of the landlord.

[(5A) In this paragraph "the appropriate tribunal or authority" means—

(a) in relation to England, a residential property tribunal; and

(b) in relation to Wales, the Secretary of State.

(5B) [Section 231(1), (2), (3) and (5)] of the Housing Act 2004 (appeals to [Upper Tribunal]) does not apply to any decision of a residential property tribunal under this paragraph.]

(6) This paragraph does not apply unless the dwelling-house concerned was first let before 1st January 1990.]

Dwelling-houses held on Crown tenancies

12.—(1) The right to buy does not arise if the dwelling-house is held by the landlord on a tenancy from the Crown, unless—

(a) the landlord is entitled to grant a lease in pursuance of this Part without the concurrence of the appropriate authority, or

(b) the appropriate authority notifies the landlord that as regards any Crown interest affected the authority will give its consent to the granting of such a lease.

(2) In this paragraph "tenancy from the Crown" means a tenancy of land in which there is a Crown interest superior to the tenancy, and "Crown interest" and "appropriate authority" mean respectively—

(a) an interest comprised in the Crown Estate, and the Crown Estate Commissioners or other government department having the management of the land in question;

(b) an interest belonging to Her Majesty in right of the Duchy of Lancaster, and the Chancellor of the Duchy;

(c) an interest belonging to the Duchy of Cornwall, and such person as the Duke of Cornwall or the possessor for the time being of the Duchy appoints;

(d) any other interest belonging to a government department or held on behalf of Her Majesty for the purposes of a government department, and that department.

(3) Section 179(1) (which renders ineffective certain provisions restricting the grant of leases under this Part) shall be disregarded for the purposes of sub-paragraph (1)(a).

[Dwelling-house due to be demolished within 24 months

13.—(1) The right to buy does not arise if a final demolition notice is in force in respect of the dwelling-house.

(2) A "final demolition notice" is a notice—
- (a) stating that the landlord intends to demolish the dwelling-house or (as the case may be) the building containing it ("the relevant premises"),
- (b) setting out the reasons why the landlord intends to demolish the relevant premises,
- (c) specifying—
  - (i) the date by which he intends to demolish those premises ("the proposed demolition date"), and
  - (ii) the date when the notice will cease to be in force (unless extended under paragraph 15),
- (d) stating that one of conditions A to C in paragraph 14 is satisfied in relation to the notice (specifying the condition concerned), and
- (e) stating that the right to buy does not arise in respect of the dwelling-house while the notice is in force.

(3) If, at the time when the notice is served, there is an existing claim to exercise the right to buy in respect of the dwelling-house, the notice shall (instead of complying with sub-paragraph (2)(e)) state—
- (a) that that claim ceases to be effective on the notice coming into force, but
- (b) that section 138C confers a right to compensation in respect of certain expenditure,

and the notice shall also give details of that right to compensation and of how it may be exercised.

(4) The proposed demolition date must fall within the period of 24 months beginning with the date of service of the notice on the tenant.

(5) For the purposes of this paragraph a final demolition notice is in force in respect of the dwelling-house concerned during the period of 24 months mentioned in sub-paragraph (4), but this is subject to—
- (a) compliance with the conditions in sub-paragraphs (6) and (7) (in a case to which they apply), …
- (b) the provisions of paragraph 15(1) to [(7A)][, and
- (c) the provisions of paragraph 15A].

(6) If—
- (a) the dwelling-house is contained in a building which contains one or more other dwelling-houses, and
- (b) the landlord intends to demolish the whole of the building,

the landlord must have served a final demolition notice on the occupier of each of the dwelling-houses contained in it (whether addressed to him by name or just as "the occupier").

An accidental omission to serve a final demolition notice on one or more occupiers does not prevent the condition in this sub-paragraph from being satisfied.

(7) A notice stating that the landlord intends to demolish the relevant premises must have appeared—
- (a) in a local or other newspaper circulating in the locality in which those premises are situated (other than one published by the landlord), and
- (b) in any newspaper published by the landlord, and
- (c) on the landlord's website (if he has one).

(8) The notice mentioned in sub-paragraph (7) must contain the following information—
- (a) sufficient information to enable identification of the premises that the landlord intends to demolish;
- (b) the reasons why the landlord intends to demolish those premises;
- (c) the proposed demolition date;
- (d) the date when any final demolition notice or notices relating to those premises will cease to be in force, unless extended or revoked under paragraph 15;
- (e) that the right to buy will not arise in respect of those premises or (as the case may be) in respect of any dwelling-house contained in them;
- (f) that there may be a right to compensation under section 138C in respect of certain expenditure incurred in respect of any existing claim.

(9) In this paragraph and paragraphs 14 and 15 [(other than paragraph 15(7A))] any reference to the landlord, in the context of a reference to an intention or decision on his part to demolish or not to demolish any premises, or of a reference to the acquisition or transfer of any premises, includes a reference to a superior landlord.

14.—(1) A final demolition notice may only be served for the purposes of paragraph 13 if one of conditions A to C is satisfied in relation to the notice.

(2) Condition A is that the proposed demolition of the dwelling-house does not form part of a scheme involving the demolition of other premises.

(3) Condition B is that—

(a) the proposed demolition of the dwelling-house does form part of a scheme involving the demolition of other premises, but

(b) none of those other premises needs to be acquired by the landlord in order for the landlord to be able to demolish them.

(4) Condition C is that—

(a) the proposed demolition of the dwelling-house does form part of a scheme involving the demolition of other premises, and

(b) one or more of those premises need to be acquired by the landlord in order for the landlord to be able to demolish them, but

(c) in each case arrangements for their acquisition are in place.

(5) For the purposes of sub-paragraph (4) arrangements for the acquisition of any premises are in place if—

(a) an agreement under which the landlord is entitled to acquire the premises is in force, or

(b) a notice to treat has been given in respect of the premises under section 5 of the Compulsory Purchase Act 1965, or

(c) a vesting declaration has been made in respect of the premises under section 4 of the Compulsory Purchase (Vesting Declarations) Act 1981.

(6) In this paragraph—

"premises" means premises of any description;

"scheme" includes arrangements of any description.

15.—(1) The Secretary of State may, on an application by the landlord, give a direction extending or further extending the period during which a final demolition notice is in force in respect of a dwelling-house.

(2) A direction under sub-paragraph (1) may provide that any extension of that period is not to have effect unless the landlord complies with such requirements relating to the service of further notices as are specified in the direction.

(3) A direction under sub-paragraph (1) may only be given at a time when the demolition notice is in force (whether by virtue of paragraph 13 or this paragraph).

(4) If, while a final demolition notice is in force, the landlord decides not to demolish the dwelling-house in question, he must, as soon as is reasonably practicable, serve a notice ("a revocation notice") on the tenant which informs him—

(a) of the landlord's decision, and

(b) that the demolition notice is revoked as from the date of service of the revocation notice.

(5) If, while a final demolition notice is in force, it appears to the Secretary of State that the landlord has no intention of demolishing the dwelling-house in question, he may serve a notice ("a revocation notice") on the tenant which informs him—

(a) of the Secretary of State's conclusion, and

(b) that the demolition notice is revoked as from the date of service of the revocation notice.

Section 169 applies in relation to the Secretary of State's power under this sub-paragraph as it applies in relation to his powers under the provisions mentioned in subsection (1) of that section.

(6) But the Secretary of State may not serve a revocation notice unless he has previously served a notice on the landlord which informs him of the Secretary of State's intention to serve the revocation notice.

(7) Where a revocation notice is served under sub-paragraph (4) or (5), the demolition notice ceases to be in force as from the date of service of the revocation notice.

[(7A) Sub-paragraphs (4) to (7) do not apply if the landlord is selling or otherwise transferring his interest as landlord to another person or is offering it for sale or for other transfer.]

(8) Once a final demolition notice [("the earlier notice")] has (for any reason) ceased to be in force in respect of a dwelling-house without it being demolished, no further final demolition [(and no initial demolition notice)] notice may be served in respect of it[, by the landlord who served the earlier notice or any landlord who served a continuation notice in respect of the earlier notice,] during the period of 5 years following the time when the [earlier] notice ceases to be in force, unless—

(a) [the further final demolition notice (or, as the case may be, the initial demolition notice)] is served with the consent of the Secretary of State, and

(b) it states that it is so served.

(9) The Secretary of State's consent under sub-paragraph (8) may be given subject to compliance with such conditions as he may specify.

[(10) In sub-paragraph (8) "initial demolition notice" has the meaning given by paragraph 1 of Schedule 5A (initial demolition notices).]

[15A.—(1) This paragraph applies if—

(a) a final demolition notice is in force in respect of a dwelling-house, and
(b) the landlord transfers his interest as landlord to another person.

(2) The final demolition notice ("the original notice") continues in force but this is subject to—

(a) paragraphs 13(5) and 15, and
(b) the following provisions of this paragraph.

(3) Sub-paragraph (4) applies if the transferee—

(a) intends to demolish the dwelling-house, but
(b) has not—
 (i) served a continuation notice, and
 (ii) complied with the conditions in sub-paragraphs (8) and (10),
within the period of 2 months beginning with the date of transfer.

(4) The transferee must proceed under paragraph 15(4) as if the transferee has decided not to demolish the dwelling-house (and paragraph 15(5) to (7) applies on the same basis).

(5) A continuation notice is a notice—

(a) stating that the transferee—
 (i) has acquired the interest concerned, and
 (ii) intends to demolish the dwelling-house or (as the case may be) the building containing it ("the relevant premises"),
(b) setting out the reasons why the transferee intends to demolish the relevant premises,
(c) stating that one of conditions A to C in paragraph 14 is satisfied in relation to the original notice (specifying the condition concerned),
(d) stating that the original notice is to continue in force, and
(e) explaining the continued effect of the original notice.

(6) A continuation notice may not vary the proposed demolition date in the original notice nor the date when the original notice will cease to be in force.

(7) Sub-paragraph (8) applies if—

(a) the dwelling-house is contained in a building which contains one or more other dwelling-houses, and
(b) the transferee intends to demolish the whole of the building.

(8) The transferee must serve a continuation notice on the occupier of each of the dwelling-houses contained in the building (whether addressed to him by name or just as "the occupier").

(9) An accidental omission to serve a continuation notice on one or more occupiers does not prevent the condition in sub-paragraph (8) from being satisfied.

(10) Paragraph 13(7) and (8) apply in relation to the transferee's intention to demolish so as to impose a condition on the transferee for a notice to appear within the period of 2 months beginning with the date of transfer.

(11) Sub-paragraphs (7) to (10) above apply instead of paragraph 13(6) to (8) in relation to a final demolition notice so far as continued in force under this paragraph.]

16.—(1) Any notice under paragraph 13[, 15 or 15A] may be served on a person—

(a) by delivering it to him, by leaving it at his proper address or by sending it by post to him at that address, or
(b) if the person is a body corporate, by serving it in accordance with paragraph (a) on the secretary of the body.

(2) For the purposes of this section and section 7 of the Interpretation Act 1978 (service of documents by post) the proper address of a person on whom a notice is to be served shall be—

(a) in the case of a body corporate or its secretary, that of the registered or principal office of the body, and
(b) in any other case, the last known address of that person.]

[1179]

NOTES

Para 3: first word omitted repealed and words in second (outer) pair of square brackets added by the Housing Act 1988, s 140, Sch 17, Pt I, para 66, Sch 18; words in first pair of square brackets substituted, second word omitted repealed in relation to England and Wales only and words in fourth (inner) pair of square brackets added by SI 1996/2325, arts 4, 5, Sch 1, Pt I, Sch 2, para 14(1), (33); words in third (inner) pair of square brackets inserted and words in fifth (inner) pair of square brackets substituted by SI 1997/627, art 2, Schedule, para 3(1), (4); sixth words in square brackets inserted by the Housing and Regeneration Act 2008, s 56, Sch 8, para 35, as from a day to be appointed.

Para 5: first words in square brackets substituted by SI 2008/3002, art 4, Sch 1, paras 2, 32, subject to transitional provisions and savings in Sch 2 thereto; second words in square brackets inserted by the Housing Act 1988, s 83(1), (6)(d); words omitted repealed by the Government of Wales Act 1998, s 152, Sch 18, Pt IV.

Paras 6, 8: repealed by the Housing Act 1988, ss 123, 140(2), Sch 18, except in relation to cases where the tenant's notice claiming to exercise his right to buy was served before from 15 January 1989.

Para 10: words in square brackets substituted by the Leasehold Reform, Housing and Urban Development Act 1993, s 106(1), (3), (4).

Para 11: substituted by the Leasehold Reform, Housing and Urban Development Act 1993, s 106(2)–(4); words in italics in sub-para (4) substituted by subsequent words in square brackets and sub-paras (5A), (5B) inserted, by the Housing Act 2004, s 181(1)–(3), as from 4 July 2005 (in relation to England) and as from a day to be appointed (in relation to Wales); for effect see s 181(4)–(6) thereof; first words in square brackets in sub-para (5B) substituted by the Housing and Regeneration Act 2008, s 310(1), subject to transitional savings in s 310(2) thereof; second words in square brackets in sub-para (5B) substituted by SI 2009/1307, art 5(1), (2), Sch 1, paras 171, 176, subject to transitional and savings provisions in art 5(6), Sch 5 thereto.

Paras 13–16: added by the Housing Act 2004, s 182(1), except in relation to any case where the tenant's notice under section 122 of this Act, was served before 18 January 2005.

Para 13: in sub-para (5)(a) word omitted repealed by the Housing and Regeneration Act 2008, ss 305, 321(1), Sch 13, paras 1, 2(1), (2)(a), Sch 16; in sub-para (5)(b) words in square brackets substituted by the Housing and Regeneration Act 2008, s 305, Sch 13, paras 1, 2(1), (2)(b); sub-para (5)(c) and word in square brackets immediately preceding it inserted by the Housing and Regeneration Act 2008, s 305, Sch 13, paras 1, 2(1), (2)(c); in sub-para (9) words in square brackets inserted by the Housing and Regeneration Act 2008, s 305, Sch 13, paras 1, 2(1), (3).

Para 15: sub-para (7A) inserted by the Housing and Regeneration Act 2008, s 305, Sch 13, paras 1, 3(1), (2); in sub-para (8) words in first, second, third and fourth sets of square brackets inserted, and words in fifth set of square brackets substituted by the Housing and Regeneration Act 2008, s 305, Sch 13, paras 1, 3(1), (3); sub-para (10) inserted by the Housing and Regeneration Act 2008, s 305, Sch 13, paras 1, 3(1), (4).

Para 15A: inserted by the Housing and Regeneration Act 2008, s 305, Sch 13, paras 1, 4.

Para 16: in sub-para (1) words in square brackets substituted by the Housing and Regeneration Act 2008, s 305, Sch 13, paras 1, 5.

Modification: modified by the Housing (Extension of Right to Buy) Order 1993, SI 1993/2240, art 3, Schedule, para 66, and the Housing (Preservation of Right to Buy) Regulations 1993, SI 1993/2241, reg 2, Sch 1. Modified, in relation to the right of a tenant to acquire a dwelling under the Housing Act 1996, s 16, by the Housing (Right to Acquire) Regulations 1997, SI 1997/619, reg 2, Schs 1, 2.

(Schs 5A–9, in so far as unrepealed, outside the scope of this work.)

[SCHEDULE 9A
LAND REGISTRATION AND RELATED MATTERS WHERE RIGHT TO BUY PRESERVED

Section 171G

Statement to be contained in instrument effecting qualifying disposal

1. On a qualifying disposal, the disponor shall secure that the instrument effecting the disposal—
   (a) states that the disposal is, so far as it relates to dwelling-houses occupied by secure tenants, a disposal to which section 171A applies (preservation of right to buy on disposal to private landlord), and
   (b) lists, to the best of the disponor's knowledge and belief, the dwelling-houses to which the disposal relates which are occupied by secure tenants.

Registration of title on qualifying disposal

2.—(1) …

(2) [Where on a qualifying disposal the disponor's title to the dwelling-house is not registered, the disponor] shall give the disponee a certificate stating that the disponor is entitled to effect the disposal subject only to such incumbrances, rights and interests as are stated in the instrument effecting the disposal or summarised in the certificate.

(3) Where the disponor's interest in the dwelling-house is a lease, the certificate shall also state particulars of the lease and, with respect to each superior title—
   (a) where it is registered, the title number;
   (b) where it is not registered, whether it was investigated in the usual way on the grant of the disponor's lease.

(4) The certificate shall be—
   (a) in a form approved by the Chief Land Registrar, and
   (b) signed by such officer of the disponor or such other person as may be approved by the Chief Land Registrar,

and the Chief Registrar shall, for the purpose of registration of title, accept the certificate as sufficient evidence of the facts stated in it.

3. …

Entries on register protecting preserved right to buy

[4.—(1) This paragraph applies where the Chief Land Registrar approves an application for registration of—
   (a) a disposition of registered land, or
   (b) the disponee's title under a disposition of unregistered land,

and the instrument effecting the disposition contains the statement required by paragraph 1.

(2) The Chief Land Registrar must enter in the register—

(a) a notice in respect of the rights of qualifying persons under this Part in relation to dwelling-houses comprised in the disposal, and

(b) a restriction reflecting the limitation under section 171D(2) on subsequent disposal.]

Change of qualifying dwelling-house

5.—(1) This paragraph applies where by virtue of section 171B(6) a new dwelling-house becomes the qualifying dwelling-house which—

(a) is entirely different from the previous qualifying dwelling-house, or

(b) includes new land,

and applies to the new dwelling-house or the new land, as the case may be.

[(2) If the landlord's title is registered, the landlord shall apply for the entry in the register of—

(a) a notice in respect of the rights of the qualifying person or persons under the provisions of this Part, and

(b) a restriction reflecting the limitation under section 171D(2) on subsequent disposal.]

(3) …

(4) If the landlord's title is not registered, the rights of the qualifying person or persons under the provisions of this Part are registrable under the Land Charges Act 1972 in the same way as an estate contract and the landlord shall, and a qualifying person may, apply for such registration.

Effect of non-registration

6.—[(1) The rights of a qualifying person under this Part in relation to the qualifying dwelling house shall not be regarded as falling within Schedule 3 to the Land Registration Act 2002 (and so are liable to be postponed under section 29 of that Act, unless protected by means of a notice in the register).]

(2) Where by virtue of paragraph 5(4) the rights of a qualifying person under this Part in relation to the qualifying dwelling-house are registrable under the Land Charges Act 1972 in the same way as an estate contract, section 4(6) of that Act (under which such a contract may be void against a purchaser unless registered) applies accordingly, with the substitution for the reference to the contract being void of a reference to the right to buy ceasing to be preserved.

Statement required on certain disposals on which right to buy ceases to be preserved

7.—(1) A conveyance of the freehold or grant of a lease of the qualifying dwelling-house to a qualifying person in pursuance of the right to buy shall state that it is made in pursuance of the provisions of this Part as they apply by virtue of section 171A (preservation of the right to buy).

(2) Where on a conveyance of the freehold or grant of a lease of the qualifying dwelling-house to a qualifying person otherwise than in pursuance of the right to buy the dwelling-house ceases to be subject to any rights arising under this Part, the conveyance or grant shall contain a statement to that effect.

(3) Where on a disposal of an interest in a qualifying dwelling-house the dwelling-house ceases to be subject to the rights of a qualifying person under this Part by virtue of section 171D(1)(a) or 171E(2)(a) (qualifying person becoming tenant of authority or body satisfying landlord condition for secure tenancies), the instrument by which the disposal is effected shall state that the dwelling-house ceases as a result of the disposal to be subject to any rights arising by virtue of section 171A (preservation of the right to buy).

Removal of entries on land register

8. Where the registered title to land contains an entry made by virtue of this Schedule, the Chief Land Registrar shall, for the purpose of removing or amending the entry, accept as sufficient evidence of the facts stated in it a certificate by the registered proprietor that the whole or a specified part of the land is not subject to any rights of a qualifying person under this Part.

Liability to compensate or indemnify

9.—(1) An action for breach of statutory duty lies where—

(a) the disponor on a qualifying disposal fails to comply with paragraph 1 (duty to secure inclusion of statement in instrument effecting disposal), or

(b) the landlord on a change of the qualifying dwelling-house fails to comply with paragraph 5(2) or (4) (duty to apply for registration protecting preserved right to buy),

and a qualifying person is deprived of the preserved right to buy by reason of the non-registration of the matters which would have been registered if that duty had been complied with.

(2) If the Chief Land Registrar has to meet a claim under the [Land Registration Act 2002] as a result of acting upon—

(a) a certificate given in pursuance of paragraph 2 (certificate of title on first registration),

(b) a statement made in pursuance of paragraph 7 (statements required on disposal on which right to buy ceases to be preserved), or

(c) a certificate given in pursuance of paragraph 8 (certificate that dwelling-house has ceased to be subject to rights under this Part),

the person who gave the certificate or made the statement shall indemnify him.

Meaning of "disposal" and "instrument effecting disposal"

10. References in this Schedule to a disposal or to the instrument effecting a disposal are to the conveyance, transfer, grant or assignment, as the case may be.]

[1180]

NOTES

Inserted by the Housing and Planning Act 1986, s 8(2), (3), Sch 2, in relation to qualifying disposals made on or after 5 April 1989.

Para 2: sub-para (1) repealed and words in square brackets in sub-para (2) substituted by the Land Registration Act 2002, ss 133, 135, Sch 11, para 18(1), (6), Sch 13.

Para 3: repealed by the Land Registration Act 2002, s 135, Sch 13.

Para 4: substituted by the Land Registration Act 2002, s 133, Sch 11, para 18(1), (7).

Para 5: sub-para (2) substituted and sub-para (3) repealed by the Land Registration Act 2002, ss 133, 135, Sch 11, para 18(1), (8), (9), Sch 13.

Para 6: sub-para (1) substituted by the Land Registration Act 2002, s 133, Sch 11, para 18(1), (10).

Para 9: words in square brackets in sub-para (2) substituted by the Land Registration Act 2002, s 133, Sch 11, para 18(1), (11).

Modification: modified by the Housing (Extension of Right to Buy) Order 1993, SI 1993/2240, art 3, Schedule, para 71, and the Housing (Preservation of Right to Buy) Regulations 1993, SI 1993/2241, reg 2, Sch 1.

(*Schs 10–24, in so far as unrepealed, outside the scope of this work.*)

LANDLORD AND TENANT ACT 1985

(1985 c 70)

An Act to consolidate certain provisions of the law of landlord and tenant formerly found in the Housing Acts, together with the Landlord and Tenant Act 1962, with amendments to give effect to recommendations of the Law Commission

[30 October 1985]

1–7 (*Outside the scope of this work.*)

Implied terms as to fitness for human habitation

8 Implied terms as to fitness for human habitation

(1) In a contract to which this section applies for the letting of a house for human habitation there is implied, notwithstanding any stipulation to the contrary—

(a) a condition that the house is fit for human habitation at the commencement of the tenancy, and

(b) an undertaking that the house will be kept by the landlord fit for human habitation during the tenancy.

(2) The landlord, or a person authorised by him in writing, may at reasonable times of the day, on giving 24 hours' notice in writing, to the tenant or occupier, enter premises to which this section applies for the purpose of viewing their state and condition.

(3) This section applies to a contract if—

(a) the rent does not exceed the figure applicable in accordance with subsection (4), and

(b) the letting is not on such terms as to the tenant's responsibility as are mentioned in subsection (5).

(4) The rent limit for the application of this section is shown by the following Table, by reference to the date of making of the contract and the situation of the premises;

TABLE

Date of making of contract	Rent limit
Before 31st July 1923.	In London: £40. Elsewhere: £26 or £16 (see Note 1).
On or after 31st July 1923 and before 6th July 1957.	In London: £40. Elsewhere: £26.
On or after 6th July 1957.	In London: £80. Elsewhere: £52.

Notes

1. The applicable figure for contracts made before 31st July 1923 is £26 in the case of premises situated in a borough or urban district which at the date of the contract had according to the last published census a population of 50,000 or more. In the case of a house situated elsewhere, the figure is £16.

2. The references to "London" are, in relation to contracts made before 1st April 1965, to the administrative county of London and, in relation to contracts made on or after that date, to Greater London exclusive of the outer London boroughs.

(5) This section does not apply where a house is let for a term of three years or more (the lease not being determinable at the option of either party before the expiration of three years) upon terms that the tenant puts the premises into a condition reasonably fit for human habitation.

(6) In this section "house" includes—
- (a) a part of a house, and
- (b) any yard, garden, outhouses and appurtenances belonging to the house or usually enjoyed with it.

[1181]

9 (*Outside the scope of this work.*)

10 Fitness for human habitation

In determining for the purposes of this Act whether a house is unfit for human habitation, regard shall be had to its condition in respect of the following matters—

repair,
stability,
freedom from damp,
internal arrangement,
natural lighting,
ventilation,
water supply,
drainage and sanitary conveniences,
facilities for preparation and cooking of food and for the disposal of waste water;

and the house shall be regarded as unfit for human habitation if, and only if, it is so far defective in one or more of those matters that it is not reasonably suitable for occupation in that condition.

[1182]

Repairing obligations

11 Repairing obligations in short leases

(1) In a lease to which this section applies (as to which, see sections 13 and 14) there is implied a covenant by the lessor—
- (a) to keep in repair the structure and exterior of the dwelling-house (including drains, gutters and external pipes),
- (b) to keep in repair and proper working order the installations in the dwelling-house for the supply of water, gas and electricity and for sanitation (including basins, sinks, baths and sanitary conveniences, but not other fixtures, fittings and appliances for making use of the supply of water, gas or electricity), and
- (c) to keep in repair and proper working order the installations in the dwelling-house for space heating and heating water.

[(1A) If a lease to which this section applies is a lease of a dwelling-house which forms part only of a building, then, subject to subsection (1B), the covenant implied by subsection (1) shall have effect as if—

(a) the reference in paragraph (a) of that subsection to the dwelling-house included a reference to any part of the building in which the lessor has an estate or interest; and
(b) any reference in paragraphs (b) and (c) of that subsection to an installation in the dwelling-house included a reference to an installation which, directly or indirectly, serves the dwelling-house and which either—
(i) forms part of any part of a building in which the lessor has an estate or interest; or
(ii) is owned by the lessor or under his control.

(1B) Nothing in subsection (1A) shall be construed as requiring the lessor to carry out any works or repairs unless the disrepair (or failure to maintain in working order) is such as to affect the lessee's enjoyment of the dwelling-house or of any common parts, as defined in section 60(1) of the Landlord and Tenant Act 1987, which the lessee, as such, is entitled to use.]

(2) The covenant implied by subsection (1) ("the lessor's repairing covenant") shall not be construed as requiring the lessor—
(a) to carry out works or repairs for which the lessee is liable by virtue of his duty to use the premises in a tenant-like manner, or would be so liable but for an express covenant on his part,
(b) to rebuild or reinstate the premises in the case of destruction or damage by fire, or by tempest, flood or other inevitable accident, or
(c) to keep in repair or maintain anything which the lessee is entitled to remove from the dwelling-house.

(3) In determining the standard of repair required by the lessor's repairing covenant, regard shall be had to the age, character and the dwelling-house and the locality in which it is situated.

[(3A) In any case where—
(a) the lessor's repairing covenant has effect as mentioned in subsection (1A), and
(b) in order to comply with the covenant the lessor needs to carry out works or repairs otherwise than in, or to an installation in, the dwelling-house, and
(c) the lessor does not have a sufficient right in the part of the building or the installation concerned to enable him to carry out the required works or repairs,

then, in any proceedings relating to a failure to comply with the lessor's repairing covenant, so far as it requires the lessor to carry out the works or repairs in question, it shall be a defence for the lessor to prove that he used all reasonable endeavours to obtain, but was unable to obtain, such rights as would be adequate to enable him to carry out the works or repairs.]

(4) A covenant by the lessee for the repair of the premises is of no effect so far as it relates to the matters mentioned in subsection (1)(a) to (c), except so far as it imposes on the lessee any of the requirements mentioned in subsection (2)(a) or (c).

(5) The reference in subsection (4) to a covenant by the lessee for the repair of the premises includes a covenant—
(a) to put in repair or deliver up in repair,
(b) to paint, point or render,
(c) to pay money in lieu of repairs by the lessee, or
(d) to pay money on account of repairs by the lessor.

(6) In a case in which the lessor's repairing covenant is implied there is also implied a covenant by the lessee that the lessor, or any person authorised by him in writing, may at reasonable times of the day and on giving 24 hours' notice in writing to the occupier, enter the premises comprised in the lease for the purpose of viewing their condition and state of repair.

[1183]

NOTES

Sub-ss (1A), (1B), (3A): inserted by the Housing Act 1988, s 116, except with respect to a lease entered into before 15 January 1989 or a lease entered into pursuant to a contract made before that date.

Modification: modified, where the RTM company has acquired the right to manage, by the Commonhold and Leasehold Reform Act 2002, s 102, Sch 7, para 3.

12 Restriction on contracting out of s 11

(1) A covenant or agreement, whether contained in a lease to which section 11 applies or in an agreement collateral to such a lease, is void in so far as it purports—
(a) to exclude or limit the obligations of the lessor or the immunities of the lessee under that section, or
(b) to authorise any forfeiture or impose on the lessee any penalty, disability or obligation in the event of his enforcing or relying upon those obligations or immunities,

unless the inclusion of the provision was authorised by the county court.

(2) The county court may, by order made with the consent of the parties, authorise the inclusion in a lease, or in an agreement collateral to a lease, of provisions excluding or modifying in relation to the lease, the provisions of section 11 with respect to the repairing obligations of the parties if it

appears to the court that it is reasonable to do so, having regard to all the circumstances of the case, including the other terms and conditions of the lease.

[1184]

13 Leases to which s 11 applies: general rule

(1) Section 11 (repairing obligations) applies to a lease of a dwelling-house granted on or after 24th October 1961 for a term of less than seven years.

(2) In determining whether a lease is one to which section 11 applies—

(a) any part of the term which falls before the grant shall be left out of account and the lease shall be treated as a lease for a term commencing with the grant,

(b) a lease which is determinable at the option of the lessor before the expiration of seven years from the commencement of the term shall be treated as a lease for a term of less than seven years, and

(c) a lease (other than a lease to which paragraph (b) applies) shall not be treated as a lease for a term of less than seven years if it confers on the lessee an option for renewal for a term which, together with the original term, amounts to seven years or more.

(3) This section has effect subject to—

section 14 (leases to which section 11 applies: exceptions), and

section 32(2) (provisions not applying to tenancies within Part II of the Landlord and Tenant Act 1954).

[1185]

14 Leases to which s 11 applies: exceptions

(1) Section 11 (repairing obligations) does not apply to a new lease granted to an existing tenant, or to a former tenant still in possession, if the previous lease was not a lease to which section 11 applied (and, in the case of a lease granted before 24th October 1961, would not have been if it had been granted on or after that date).

(2) In subsection (1)—

"existing tenant" means a person who is when, or immediately before, the new lease is granted, the lessee under another lease of the dwelling-house;

"former tenant still in possession" means a person who—

(a) was the lessee under another lease of the dwelling-house which terminated at some time before the new lease was granted, and

(b) between the termination of that other lease and the grant of the new lease was continuously in possession of the dwelling-house or of the rents and profits of the dwelling-house; and

"the previous lease" means the other lease referred to in the above definitions.

(3) Section 11 does not apply to a lease of a dwelling-house which is a tenancy of an agricultural holding within the meaning of the [Agricultural Holdings Act 1986] [and in relation to which that Act applies or to a farm business tenancy within the meaning of the Agricultural Tenancies Act 1995.]

(4) Section 11 does not apply to a lease granted on or after 3rd October 1980 to—

a local authority,

[a National Park authority]

a new town corporation,

an urban development corporation,

the Development Board for Rural Wales,

a [registered social landlord],

a co-operative housing association, or

an educational institution or other body specified, or of a class specified, by regulations under section 8 of the Rent Act 1977 [or paragraph 8 of Schedule 1 to the Housing Act 1988] (bodies making student lettings)

[a housing action trust established under Part III of the Housing Act 1988].

(5) Section 11 does not apply to a lease granted on or after 3rd October 1980 to—

(a) Her Majesty in right of the Crown (unless the lease is under the management of the Crown Estate Commissioners), or

(b) a government department or a person holding in trust for Her Majesty for the purposes of a government department.

[1186]

NOTES

Sub-s (3): first words in square brackets substituted by the Agricultural Holdings Act 1986, s 100, Sch 14, para 64; final words in square brackets inserted by the Agricultural Tenancies Act 1995, s 40, Schedule, para 31.

Sub-s (4): first words in square brackets inserted by the Environment Act 1995, s 78, Sch 10, para 25(1); second words in square brackets substituted by SI 1996/2325, art 5, Sch 2, para 16(2); third words in square brackets inserted by the Local Government and Housing Act 1989, s 194, Sch 11, para 89; final words in square brackets inserted by the Housing Act 1988, s 116, except with respect to a lease entered into before 15 January 1989 or a lease entered into in pursuance of a contract made before that date.

See further: for provision whereby the body corporate known as the Residuary Body for Wales is to be treated as a local authority for the purposes of sub-s (4) above, see the Local Government (Wales) Act 1994, Sch 13, para 23(a).

15 Jurisdiction of county court

The county court has jurisdiction to make a declaration that section 11 (repairing obligations) applies, or does not apply, to a lease—

(a) whatever the net annual value of the property in question, and
(b) notwithstanding that no other relief is sought than a declaration.

[1187]

16 Meaning of "lease" and related expressions

In sections 11 to 15 (repairing obligations in short leases)—

(a) "lease" does not include a mortgage term;
(b) "lease of a dwelling-house" means a lease by which a building or part of a building is let wholly or mainly as a private residence, and "dwelling-house" means that building or part of a building;
(c) "lessee" and "lessor" mean, respectively, the person for the time being entitled to the term of a lease and to the reversion expectant on it.

[1188]

17 Specific performance of landlord's repairing obligations

(1) In proceedings in which a tenant of a dwelling alleges a breach on the part of his landlord of a repairing covenant relating to any part of the premises in which the dwelling is comprised, the court may order specific performance of the covenant whether or not the breach relates to a part of the premises let to the tenant and notwithstanding any equitable rule restricting the scope of the remedy, whether on the basis of a lack of mutuality or otherwise.

(2) In this section—

(a) "tenant" includes a statutory tenant,
(b) in relation to a statutory tenant the reference to the premises let to him is to the premises of which he is a statutory tenant,
(c) "landlord", in relation to a tenant, includes any person against whom the tenant has a right to enforce a repairing covenant, and
(d) "repairing covenant" means a covenant to repair, maintain, renew, construct or replace any property.

[1189]

18–39 (*Outside the scope of this work.*)

Final Provisions

40 Short title, commencement and extent

(1) This Act may be cited as the Landlord and Tenant Act 1985.

(2) This Act comes into force on 1st April 1986.

(3) This Act extends to England and Wales.

[1190]

(*Schedule outside the scope of this work.*)

AGRICULTURAL HOLDINGS ACT 1986

(1986 c 5)

An Act to consolidate certain enactments relating to agricultural holdings, with amendments to give effect to recommendations of the Law Commission

[18 March 1986]

PART I
INTRODUCTORY

1 Principal definitions

(1) In this Act "agricultural holding" means the aggregate of the land (whether agricultural land or not) comprised in a contract of tenancy which is a contract for an agricultural tenancy, not being a contract under which the land is let to the tenant during his continuance in any office, appointment or employment held under the landlord.

(2) For the purposes of this section, a contract of tenancy relating to any land is a contract for an agricultural tenancy if, having regard to—

(a) the terms of the tenancy,

(b) the actual or contemplated use of the land at the time of the conclusion of the contract and subsequently, and

(c) any other relevant circumstances,

the whole of the land comprised in the contract, subject to such exceptions only as do not substantially affect the character of the tenancy, is let for use as agricultural land.

(3) A change in user of the land concerned subsequent to the conclusion of a contract of tenancy which involves any breach of the terms of the tenancy shall be disregarded for the purpose of determining whether a contract which was not originally a contract for an agricultural tenancy has subsequently become one unless it is effected with the landlord's permission, consent or acquiescence.

(4) In this Act "agricultural land" means—

(a) land used for agriculture which is so used for the purposes of a trade or business, and

(b) any other land which, by virtue of a designation under section 109(1) of the Agriculture Act 1947, is agricultural land within the meaning of that Act.

(5) In this Act "contract of tenancy" means a letting of land, or agreement for letting land, for a term of years or from year to year; and for the purposes of this definition a letting of land, or an agreement for letting land, which, by virtue of subsection (6) of section 149 of the Law of Property Act 1925, takes effect as such a letting of land or agreement for letting land as is mentioned in that subsection shall be deemed to be a letting of land or, as the case may be, an agreement for letting land, for a term of years.

[1191]

2 Restriction on letting agricultural land for less than from year to year

(1) An agreement to which this section applies shall take effect, with the necessary modifications, as if it were an agreement for the letting of land for a tenancy from year to year unless the agreement was approved by the Minister before it was entered into.

(2) Subject to subsection (3) below, this section applies to an agreement under which—

(a) any land is let to a person for use as agricultural land for an interest less than a tenancy from year to year, or

(b) a person is granted a licence to occupy land for use as agricultural land,

if the circumstances are such that if his interest were a tenancy from year to year he would in respect of that land be the tenant of an agricultural holding.

(3) This section does not apply to an agreement for the letting of land, or the granting of a licence to occupy land—

(a) made (whether or not it expressly so provides) in contemplation of the use of the land only for grazing or mowing (or both) during some specified period of the year, or

(b) by a person whose interest in the land is less than a tenancy from year to year and has not taken effect as such a tenancy by virtue of this section.

(4) Any dispute arising as to the operation of this section in relation to any agreement shall be determined by arbitration under this Act.

[1192]

NOTES

Transfer of Functions: functions of the Minister, so far as exercisable in relation to Wales, transferred to the National Assembly for Wales, by the National Assembly for Wales (Transfer of Functions) Order 1999, SI 1999/672, art 2, Sch 1.

3–82 (*Ss 3–5, ss 6–82 (Pts II–VI) outside the scope of this work.*)

PART VII
MISCELLANEOUS AND SUPPLEMENTAL

83–88 (*Outside the scope of this work.*)

89 Power of limited owners to apply capital for improvements

(1) Where under powers conferred by the Settled Land Act 1925 … capital money is applied in or about the execution of any improvement specified in Schedule 7 to this Act no provision shall be made for requiring the money or any part of it to be replaced out of income, and accordingly any such improvement shall be deemed to be an improvement authorised by Part I of Schedule 3 to the Settled Land Act 1925.

(2) Where under powers conferred by the Universities and College Estates Act 1925 capital money is applied in payment for any improvement specified in Schedule 7 to this Act no provision shall be made for replacing the money out of income unless the Minister requires such provision to be made under section 26(5) of that Act or, in the case of a university or college to which section 2 of the Universities and College Estates Act 1964 applies, it appears to the university or college to be necessary to make such provision under the said section 26(5) as modified by Schedule 1 to the said Act of 1964.

[1193]

NOTES

Sub-s (1): words omitted repealed by the Trusts of Land and Appointment of Trustees Act 1996, s 25(2), Sch 4; for savings in relation to entailed interests created before the commencement of that Act, and savings consequential upon the abolition of the doctrine of conversion, see s 25(4), (5) thereof.

Transfer of Functions: functions of the Minister, so far as exercisable in relation to Wales, transferred to the National Assembly for Wales, by the National Assembly for Wales (Transfer of Functions) Order 1999, SI 1999/672, art 2, Sch 1.

90 Estimation of best rent for purposes of Acts and other instruments

In estimating the best rent or reservation in the nature of rent of an agricultural holding for the purposes of any Act of Parliament, deed or other instrument, authorising a lease to be made provided that the best rent, or reservation in the nature of rent, is reserved, it shall not be necessary to take into account against the tenant any increase in the value of the holding arising from any improvements made or paid for by him.

[1194]

91–101 (*Outside the scope of this work.*)

102 Citation, commencement and extent

(1) This Act may be cited as the Agricultural Holdings Act 1986.

(2) This Act shall come into force at the end of the period of three months beginning with the day on which it is passed.

(3) Subject to subsection (4) below, this Act extends to England and Wales only.

(4) Subject to subsection (5) below and to paragraph 26(6) of Schedule 14 to this Act, the amendment or repeal by this Act of an enactment which extends to Scotland or Northern Ireland shall also extend there.

(5) Subsection (4) above does not apply to the amendment or repeal by this Act of section 9 of the Hill Farming Act 1946, section 48(4) of the Agriculture Act 1967 or an enactment contained in the Agriculture (Miscellaneous Provisions) Act 1968.

[1195]

(*Schs 1–6 outside the scope of this work.*)

SCHEDULE 7
LONG-TERM IMPROVEMENTS BEGUN ON OR AFTER 1ST MARCH 1948 FOR WHICH COMPENSATION IS PAYABLE

Sections 64, 66 etc

PART I
IMPROVEMENTS TO WHICH CONSENT OF LANDLORD REQUIRED

1. Making or planting of osier beds.
2. Making of water meadows.
3. Making of watercress beds.
4. Planting of hops.
5. Planting of orchards or fruit bushes.
6. Warping or weiring of land.
7. Making of gardens.
8. Provision of underground tanks.

[1196]

PART II
IMPROVEMENTS TO WHICH CONSENT OF LANDLORD OR APPROVAL OF TRIBUNAL REQUIRED

9. Erection, alteration or enlargement of buildings, and making or improvement of permanent yards.

10. Carrying out works in compliance with an improvement notice served, or an undertaking accepted, under Part VII of the Housing Act 1985 or Part VIII of the Housing Act 1974.

11. Erection or construction of loading platforms, ramps, hard standings for vehicles or other similar facilities.

12. Construction of silos.

13. Claying of land.

14. Marling of land.

15. Making or improvement of roads or bridges.

16. Making or improvement of water courses, culverts, ponds, wells or reservoirs, or of works for the application of water power for agricultural or domestic purposes or of works for the supply, distribution or use of water for such purposes (including the erection or installation of any structures or equipment which form part of or are to be used for or in connection with operating any such works).

17. Making or removal of permanent fences.

18. Reclaiming of waste land.

19. Making or improvement of embankments or sluices.

20. Erection of wirework for hop gardens.

21. Provision of permanent sheep-dipping accommodation.

22. Removal of bracken, gorse, tree roots, boulders or other like obstructions to cultivation.

23. Land drainage (other than improvements falling within paragraph 1 of Schedule 8 to this Act).

24. Provision or laying-on of electric light or power.

25. Provision of facilities for the storage or disposal of sewage or farm waste.

26. Repairs to fixed equipment, being equipment reasonably required for the proper farming of the holding, other than repairs which the tenant is under an obligation to carry out.

27. The grubbing up of orchards or fruit bushes.

28. Planting trees otherwise than as an orchard and bushes other than fruit bushes.

[1197]

(*Schs 8–15 outside the scope of this work.*)

INSOLVENCY ACT 1986

(1986 c 45)

An Act to consolidate the enactments relating to company insolvency and winding up (including the winding up of companies that are not insolvent, and of unregistered companies); enactments relating to the insolvency and bankruptcy of individuals; and other enactments bearing on those two subject matters, including the functions and qualification of insolvency practitioners, the public administration of insolvency, the penalisation and redress of malpractice and wrongdoing, and the avoidance of certain transactions at an undervalue

[25 July 1986]

1–27 ((*Pts I, II*) *outside the scope of this work.*)

PART III
RECEIVERSHIP

CHAPTER I
RECEIVERS AND MANAGERS (ENGLAND AND WALES)

Preliminary and general provisions

28 (*Outside the scope of this work.*)

29 Definitions

(1) It is hereby declared that, except where the context otherwise requires—

(a) any reference in *the Companies Act or* this Act to a receiver or manager of the property of a company, or to a receiver of it, includes a receiver or manager, or (as the case may be) a receiver of part only of that property and a receiver only of the income arising from the property or from part of it; and

(b) any reference in *the Companies Act or* this Act to the appointment of a receiver or manager under powers contained in an instrument includes an appointment made under powers which, by virtue of any enactment, are implied in and have effect as if contained in an instrument.

(2) In this Chapter "administrative receiver" means—

(a) a receiver or manager of the whole (or substantially the whole) of a company's property appointed by or on behalf of the holders of any debentures of the company secured by a charge which, as created, was a floating charge, or by such a charge and one or more other securities; or

(b) a person who would be such a receiver or manager but for the appointment of some other person as the receiver of part of the company's property.

[1198]

NOTES

Sub-s (1): in paras (a), (b) words in italics repealed by SI 2009/1941, art 2(1), Sch 1, para 74(1), (3), as from 1 October 2009.

30–38 (*Outside the scope of this work.*)

Provisions applicable to every receivership

39 (*Outside the scope of this work.*)

40 Payment of debts out of assets subject to floating charge

(1) The following applies, in the case of a company, where a receiver is appointed on behalf of the holders of any debentures of the company secured by a charge which, as created, was a floating charge.

(2) If the company is not at the time in course of being wound up, its preferential debts (within the meaning given to that expression by section 386 in Part XII) shall be paid out of the assets coming to the hands of the receiver in priority to any claims for principal or interest in respect of the debentures.

(3) Payments made under this section shall be recouped, as far as may be, out of the assets of the company available for payment of general creditors.

[1199]

NOTES

Disapplication: this section is disapplied in relation to regulated covered bonds: see the Regulated Covered Bonds Regulations 2008, SI 2008/346, reg 46, Schedule, Pt 1, para 2(1).

41–72 (*Outside the scope of this work.*)

[CHAPTER IV
PROHIBITION OF APPOINTMENT OF ADMINISTRATIVE RECEIVER

72A Floating charge holder not to appoint administrative receiver

[(1) The holder of a qualifying floating charge in respect of a company's property may not appoint an administrative receiver of the company.

(2) In Scotland, the holder of a qualifying floating charge in respect of a company's property may not appoint or apply to the court for the appointment of a receiver who on appointment would be an administrative receiver of property of the company.

(3) In subsections (1) and (2)—

"holder of a qualifying floating charge in respect of a company's property" has the same meaning as in paragraph 14 of Schedule B1 to this Act, and

"administrative receiver" has the meaning given by section 251.

(4) This section applies—

(a) to a floating charge created on or after a date appointed by the Secretary of State by order made by statutory instrument, and

(b) in spite of any provision of an agreement or instrument which purports to empower a person to appoint an administrative receiver (by whatever name).

(5) An order under subsection (4)(a) may—
(a) make provision which applies generally or only for a specified purpose;
(b) make different provision for different purposes;
(c) make transitional provision.

(6) This section is subject to the exceptions specified in [sections 72B to 72GA].]

[1200]

NOTES

This Chapter (Ch IV (ss 72A–72H)) inserted by the Enterprise Act 2002, s 250(1).
Sub-s (6): words in square brackets substituted by SI 2003/1832, art 2(a).
Date appointed by the Secretary of State: 15 September 2003; see SI 2003/2095.
Order: the Insolvency Act 1986, Section 72A (Appointed Date) Order 2003, SI 2003/2095.

[72B First exception: capital market

(1) Section 72A does not prevent the appointment of an administrative receiver in pursuance of an agreement which is or forms part of a capital market arrangement if—
(a) a party incurs or, when the agreement was entered into was expected to incur, a debt of at least £50 million under the arrangement, and
(b) the arrangement involves the issue of a capital market investment.

(2) In subsection (1)—
"capital market arrangement" means an arrangement of a kind described in paragraph 1 of Schedule 2A, and
"capital market investment" means an investment of a kind described in paragraph 2 or 3 of that Schedule.]

[1201]

NOTES

Inserted as noted to s 72A at **[1200]**.

[72C Second exception: public-private partnership

(1) Section 72A does not prevent the appointment of an administrative receiver of a project company of a project which—
(a) is a public-private partnership project, and
(b) includes step-in rights.

(2) In this section "public-private partnership project" means a project—
(a) the resources for which are provided partly by one or more public bodies and partly by one or more private persons, or
(b) which is designed wholly or mainly for the purpose of assisting a public body to discharge a function.

(3) In this section—
"step-in rights" has the meaning given by paragraph 6 of Schedule 2A, and
"project company" has the meaning given by paragraph 7 of that Schedule.]

[1202]

NOTES

Inserted as noted to s 72A at **[1200]**.

[72D Third exception: utilities

(1) Section 72A does not prevent the appointment of an administrative receiver of a project company of a project which—
(a) is a utility project, and
(b) includes step-in rights.

(2) In this section—
(a) "utility project" means a project designed wholly or mainly for the purpose of a regulated business,
(b) "regulated business" means a business of a kind listed in paragraph 10 of Schedule 2A,
(c) "step-in rights" has the meaning given by paragraph 6 of that Schedule, and
(d) "project company" has the meaning given by paragraph 7 of that Schedule.]

[1203]

NOTES

Inserted as noted to s 72A at **[1200]**.

[72DA Exception in respect of urban regeneration projects

(1) Section 72A does not prevent the appointment of an administrative receiver of a project company of a project which—

(a) is designed wholly or mainly to develop land which at the commencement of the project is wholly or partly in a designated disadvantaged area outside Northern Ireland, and

(b) includes step-in rights.

(2) In subsection (1) "develop" means to carry out—

(a) building operations,

(b) any operation for the removal of substances or waste from land and the levelling of the surface of the land, or

(c) engineering operations in connection with the activities mentioned in paragraph (a) or (b).

(3) In this section—

"building" includes any structure or erection, and any part of a building as so defined, but does not include plant and machinery comprised in a building,

"building operations" includes—

(a) demolition of buildings,

(b) filling in of trenches,

(c) rebuilding,

(d) structural alterations of, or additions to, buildings and

(e) other operations normally undertaken by a person carrying on business as a builder,

"designated disadvantaged area" means an area designated as a disadvantaged area under section 92 of the Finance Act 2001,

"engineering operations" includes the formation and laying out of means of access to highways,

"project company" has the meaning given by paragraph 7 of Schedule 2A,

"step-in rights" has the meaning given by paragraph 6 of that Schedule,

"substance" means any natural or artificial substance whether in solid or liquid form or in the form of a gas or vapour, and

"waste" includes any waste materials, spoil, refuse or other matter deposited on land.]

[1204]

NOTES

Inserted by SI 2003/1832, art 2(b).

[72E Fourth exception: project finance

(1) Section 72A does not prevent the appointment of an administrative receiver of a project company of a project which—

(a) is a financed project, and

(b) includes step-in rights.

(2) In this section—

(a) a project is "financed" if under an agreement relating to the project a project company incurs, or when the agreement is entered into is expected to incur, a debt of at least £50 million for the purposes of carrying out the project,

(b) "project company" has the meaning given by paragraph 7 of Schedule 2A, and

(c) "step-in rights" has the meaning given by paragraph 6 of that Schedule.]

[1205]

NOTES

Inserted as noted to s 72A at **[1200]**.

[72F Fifth exception: financial market

Section 72A does not prevent the appointment of an administrative receiver of a company by virtue of—

(a) a market charge within the meaning of section 173 of the Companies Act 1989 (c 40),

(b) a system-charge within the meaning of the Financial Markets and Insolvency Regulations 1996 (SI 1996/1469),

(c) a collateral security charge within the meaning of the Financial Markets and Insolvency (Settlement Finality) Regulations 1999 (SI 1999/2979).]

[1206]

NOTES

Inserted as noted to s 72A at **[1200]**.

[72G Sixth exception: registered social landlord

Section 72A does not prevent the appointment of an administrative receiver of a company which is registered as a social landlord under Part I of the Housing Act 1996 (c 52) or under Part 3 of the Housing (Scotland) Act 2001 (asp 10).]

[1207]

NOTES

Inserted as noted to s 72A at **[1200]**.

[72GA Exception in relation to protected railway companies etc

Section 72A does not prevent the appointment of an administrative receiver of—

(a) a company holding an appointment under Chapter I of Part II of the Water Industry Act 1991,

(b) a protected railway company within the meaning of section 59 of the Railways Act 1993 (including that section as it has effect by virtue of section 19 of the Channel Tunnel Rail Link Act 1996, or

(c) a licence company within the meaning of section 26 of the Transport Act 2000.]

[1208]

NOTES

Inserted by SI 2003/1832, art 2(c).

[72H Sections 72A to 72G: supplementary

(1) Schedule 2A (which supplements sections 72B to 72G) shall have effect.

(2) The Secretary of State may by order—

(a) insert into this Act provision creating an additional exception to section 72A(1) or (2);

(b) provide for a provision of this Act which creates an exception to section 72A(1) or (2) to cease to have effect;

(c) amend section 72A in consequence of provision made under paragraph (a) or (b);

(d) amend any of sections 72B to 72G;

(e) amend Schedule 2A.

(3) An order under subsection (2) must be made by statutory instrument.

(4) An order under subsection (2) may make—

(a) provision which applies generally or only for a specified purpose;

(b) different provision for different purposes;

(c) consequential or supplementary provision;

(d) transitional provision.

(5) An order under subsection (2)—

(a) in the case of an order under subsection (2)(e), shall be subject to annulment in pursuance of a resolution of either House of Parliament,

(b) in the case of an order under subsection (2)(d) varying the sum specified in section 72B(1)(a) or 72E(2)(a) (whether or not the order also makes consequential or transitional provision), shall be subject to annulment in pursuance of a resolution of either House of Parliament, and

(c) in the case of any other order under subsection (2)(a) to (d), may not be made unless a draft has been laid before and approved by resolution of each House of Parliament.]

[1209]

NOTES

Inserted as noted to s 72A at **[1200]**.

Orders: the Insolvency Act 1986 (Amendment) (Administrative Receivership and Capital Market Arrangements) Order 2003, SI 2003/1468; the Insolvency Act 1986 (Amendment) (Administrative Receivership and Urban Regeneration etc) Order 2003, SI 2003/1832.

PART IV
WINDING UP OF COMPANIES REGISTERED UNDER THE COMPANIES ACTS

73–174 ((*Chs 1–7*) *Outside the scope of this work.*)

CHAPTER VIII
PROVISIONS OF GENERAL APPLICATION IN WINDING UP

Preferential debts

175 Preferential debts (general provision)

(1) In a winding up the company's preferential debts (within the meaning given by section 386 in Part XII) shall be paid in priority to all other debts.

(2) Preferential debts—

(a) rank equally among themselves after the expenses of the winding up and shall be paid in full, unless the assets are insufficient to meet them, in which case they abate in equal proportions; and

(b) so far as the assets of the company available for payment of general creditors are insufficient to meet them, have priority over the claims of holders of debentures secured by, or holders of, any floating charge created by the company, and shall be paid accordingly out of any property comprised in or subject to that charge.

[1210]

NOTES

Application: in relation to the application of this section, with modifications, in respect of bank insolvency, see the Banking Act 2009, s 103(3), (4).

Disapplication: this section is disapplied in relation to regulated covered bonds: see the Regulated Covered Bonds Regulations 2008, SI 2008/346, reg 46, Schedule, Pt 1, para 2(4).

See further: in relation to the partial disapplication of this section in the case of a winding up of a UK insurer, see the Insurers (Reorganisation and Winding Up) Regulations 2004, SI 2004/353, regs 20–27.

176 (*Outside the scope of this work.*)

[Property subject to floating charge]

NOTES

Cross-heading inserted by the Enterprise Act 2002, s 252.

[176ZA Payment of expenses of winding up (England and Wales)

(1) The expenses of winding up in England and Wales, so far as the assets of the company available for payment of general creditors are insufficient to meet them, have priority over any claims to property comprised in or subject to any floating charge created by the company and shall be paid out of any such property accordingly.

(2) In subsection (1)—

(a) the reference to assets of the company available for payment of general creditors does not include any amount made available under section 176A(2)(a);

(b) the reference to claims to property comprised in or subject to a floating charge is to the claims of—

(i) the holders of debentures secured by, or holders of, the floating charge, and

(ii) any preferential creditors entitled to be paid out of that property in priority to them.

(3) Provision may be made by rules restricting the application of subsection (1), in such circumstances as may be prescribed, to expenses authorised or approved—

(a) by the holders of debentures secured by, or holders of, the floating charge and by any preferential creditors entitled to be paid in priority to them, or

(b) by the court.

(4) References in this section to the expenses of the winding up are to all expenses properly incurred in the winding up, including the remuneration of the liquidator.]

[1211]

NOTES

Commencement: 6 April 2008.

Inserted by the Companies Act 2006, s 1282(1).

Application: in relation to the application of this section, with modifications, in respect of bank insolvency, see the Banking Act 2009, s 103(3), (4), Table.

[176A Share of assets for unsecured creditors

(1) This section applies where a floating charge relates to property of a company—

(a) which has gone into liquidation,

(b) which is in administration,

(c) of which there is a provisional liquidator, or

(d) of which there is a receiver.

(2) The liquidator, administrator or receiver—
(a) shall make a prescribed part of the company's net property available for the satisfaction of unsecured debts, and
(b) shall not distribute that part to the proprietor of a floating charge except in so far as it exceeds the amount required for the satisfaction of unsecured debts.

(3) Subsection (2) shall not apply to a company if—
(a) the company's net property is less than the prescribed minimum, and
(b) the liquidator, administrator or receiver thinks that the cost of making a distribution to unsecured creditors would be disproportionate to the benefits.

(4) Subsection (2) shall also not apply to a company if or in so far as it is disapplied by—
(a) a voluntary arrangement in respect of the company, or
(b) a compromise or arrangement agreed under [Part 26 of the Companies Act 2006 (arrangements and reconstructions)].

(5) Subsection (2) shall also not apply to a company if—
(a) the liquidator, administrator or receiver applies to the court for an order under this subsection on the ground that the cost of making a distribution to unsecured creditors would be disproportionate to the benefits, and
(b) the court orders that subsection (2) shall not apply.

(6) In subsections (2) and (3) a company's net property is the amount of its property which would, but for this section, be available for satisfaction of claims of holders of debentures secured by, or holders of, any floating charge created by the company.

(7) An order under subsection (2) prescribing part of a company's net property may, in particular, provide for its calculation—
(a) as a percentage of the company's net property, or
(b) as an aggregate of different percentages of different parts of the company's net property.

(8) An order under this section—
(a) must be made by statutory instrument, and
(b) shall be subject to annulment pursuant to a resolution of either House of Parliament.

(9) In this section—
"floating charge" means a charge which is a floating charge on its creation and which is created after the first order under subsection (2)(a) comes into force, and
"prescribed" means prescribed by order by the Secretary of State.

(10) An order under this section may include transitional or incidental provision.]

[1212]

NOTES

Inserted, together with cross-heading preceding s 176ZA, by the Enterprise Act 2002, s 252.

Sub-s (4): in para (b) words in square brackets substituted by SI 2008/948, arts 3(1)(b), 6, Sch 1, Pt 2, para 103.

Prescribed part; prescribed minimum: see SI 2003/2097.

Application: in relation to the application of this section, with modifications, in respect of bank insolvency, see the Banking Act 2009, s 103(3), (4), Table.

See further: as to the disapplication of this section in relation to any charge created or otherwise arising under a financial collateral arrangement, see the Financial Collateral Arrangements (No 2) Regulations 2003, SI 2003/3226, reg 10(3); see also, as to the disapplication of this section in relation to regulated covered bonds, the Regulated Covered Bonds Regulations 2008, SI 2008/346, reg 46, Schedule, Pt 1, para 2(4).

Order: the Insolvency Act 1986 (Prescribed Part) Order 2003, SI 2003/2097.

177 (*Outside the scope of this work.*)

Disclaimer (*England and Wales only*)

178 Power to disclaim onerous property

(1) This and the next two sections apply to a company that is being wound up in England and Wales.

(2) Subject as follows, the liquidator may, by the giving of the prescribed notice, disclaim any onerous property and may do so notwithstanding that he has taken possession of it, endeavoured to sell it, or otherwise exercised rights of ownership in relation to it.

(3) The following is onerous property for the purposes of this section—
(a) any unprofitable contract, and
(b) any other property of the company which is unsaleable or not readily saleable or is such that it may give rise to a liability to pay money or perform any other onerous act.

(4) A disclaimer under this section—
(a) operates so as to determine, as from the date of the disclaimer, the rights, interests and liabilities of the company in or in respect of the property disclaimed; but

(b) does not, except so far as is necessary for the purpose of releasing the company from any liability, affect the rights or liabilities of any other person.

(5) A notice of disclaimer shall not be given under this section in respect of any property if—

(a) a person interested in the property has applied in writing to the liquidator or one of his predecessors as liquidator requiring the liquidator or that predecessor to decide whether he will disclaim or not, and

(b) the period of 28 days beginning with the day on which that application was made, or such longer period as the court may allow, has expired without a notice of disclaimer having been given under this section in respect of that property.

(6) Any person sustaining loss or damage in consequence of the operation of a disclaimer under this section is deemed a creditor of the company to the extent of the loss or damage and accordingly may prove for the loss or damage in the winding up.

[1213]

NOTES

Application: in relation to the application of this section, with modifications, in respect of bank insolvency, see the Banking Act 2009, s 103(3), (4), Table.

Disapplication in relation to market contracts: see further the Companies Act 1989, s 164(1).

See further: as to the disapplication of this section, or in Scotland any rule of law having the same effect as this section, in relation to any financial collateral arrangement, where the collateral-provider or collateral-taker under the arrangement is being wound-up, see the Financial Collateral Arrangements (No 2) Regulations 2003, SI 2003/3226, reg 10(4).

179–263G (*Ss 179–219, ss 220–263G (Pts V–VIII) outside the scope of this work.*)

PART IX
BANKRUPTCY

CHAPTER I
BANKRUPTCY PETITIONS; BANKRUPTCY ORDERS

264–277 (*Outside the scope of this work.*)

Commencement and duration of bankruptcy; discharge

278 Commencement and continuance

The bankruptcy of an individual against whom a bankruptcy order has been made—

(a) commences with the day on which the order is made, and

(b) continues until the individual is discharged under the following provisions of this Chapter.

[1214]

279–282 (*Outside the scope of this work.*)

CHAPTER II
PROTECTION OF BANKRUPT'S ESTATE AND INVESTIGATION OF HIS AFFAIRS

283 Definition of bankrupt's estate

(1) Subject as follows, a bankrupt's estate for the purposes of any of this Group of Parts comprises—

(a) all property belonging to or vested in the bankrupt at the commencement of the bankruptcy, and

(b) any property which by virtue of any of the following provisions of this Part is comprised in that estate or is treated as falling within the preceding paragraph.

(2) Subsection (1) does not apply to—

(a) such tools, books, vehicles and other items of equipment as are necessary to the bankrupt for use personally by him in his employment, business or vocation;

(b) such clothing, bedding, furniture, household equipment and provisions as are necessary for satisfying the basic domestic needs of the bankrupt and his family.

This subsection is subject to section 308 in Chapter IV (certain excluded property reclaimable by trustee).

(3) Subsection (1) does not apply to—

(a) property held by the bankrupt on trust for any other person, or

(b) the right of nomination to a vacant ecclesiastical benefice.

[(3A) Subject to section 308A in Chapter IV, subsection (1) does not apply to—

(a) a tenancy which is an assured tenancy or an assured agricultural occupancy, within the meaning of Part I of the Housing Act 1988, and the terms of which inhibit an assignment as mentioned in section 127(5) of the Rent Act 1977, or

(b) a protected tenancy, within the meaning of the Rent Act 1977, in respect of which, by virtue of any provision of Part IX of that Act, no premium can lawfully be required as a condition of assignment, or

(c) a tenancy of a dwelling-house by virtue of which the bankrupt is, within the meaning of the Rent (Agriculture) Act 1976, a protected occupier of the dwelling-house, and the terms of which inhibit an assignment as mentioned in section 127(5) of the Rent Act 1977, or

(d) a secure tenancy, within the meaning of Part IV of the Housing Act 1985, which is not capable of being assigned, except in the cases mentioned in section 91(3) of that Act.]

(4) References in any of this Group of Parts to property, in relation to a bankrupt, include references to any power exercisable by him over or in respect of property except in so far as the power is exercisable over or in respect of property not for the time being comprised in the bankrupt's estate and—

(a) is so exercisable at a time after either the official receiver has had his release in respect of that estate under section 299(2) in Chapter III or a meeting summoned by the trustee of that estate under section 331 in Chapter IV has been held, or

(b) cannot be so exercised for the benefit of the bankrupt;

and a power exercisable over or in respect of property is deemed for the purposes of any of this Group of Parts to vest in the person entitled to exercise it at the time of the transaction or event by virtue of which it is exercisable by that person (whether or not it becomes so exercisable at that time).

(5) For the purposes of any such provision in this Group of Parts, property comprised in a bankrupt's estate is so comprised subject to the rights of any person other than the bankrupt (whether as a secured creditor of the bankrupt or otherwise) in relation thereto, but disregarding—

(a) any rights in relation to which a statement such as is required by section 269(1)(a) was made in the petition on which the bankrupt was adjudged bankrupt, and

(b) any rights which have been otherwise given up in accordance with the rules.

(6) This section has effect subject to the provisions of any enactment not contained in this Act under which any property is to be excluded from a bankrupt's estate.

[1215]

NOTES

Sub-s (3A): inserted by the Housing Act 1988, s 117(1).

Property comprising the bankrupt's estate: see further the Criminal Justice Act 1988, s 84 and the Drug Trafficking Act 1994, s 32.

[283A Bankrupt's home ceasing to form part of estate

(1) This section applies where property comprised in the bankrupt's estate consists of an interest in a dwelling-house which at the date of the bankruptcy was the sole or principal residence of—

(a) the bankrupt,

(b) the bankrupt's spouse [or civil partner], or

(c) a former spouse [or former civil partner] of the bankrupt.

(2) At the end of the period of three years beginning with the date of the bankruptcy the interest mentioned in subsection (1) shall—

(a) cease to be comprised in the bankrupt's estate, and

(b) vest in the bankrupt (without conveyance, assignment or transfer).

(3) Subsection (2) shall not apply if during the period mentioned in that subsection—

(a) the trustee realises the interest mentioned in subsection (1),

(b) the trustee applies for an order for sale in respect of the dwelling-house,

(c) the trustee applies for an order for possession of the dwelling-house,

(d) the trustee applies for an order under section 313 in Chapter IV in respect of that interest, or

(e) the trustee and the bankrupt agree that the bankrupt shall incur a specified liability to his estate (with or without the addition of interest from the date of the agreement) in consideration of which the interest mentioned in subsection (1) shall cease to form part of the estate.

(4) Where an application of a kind described in subsection (3)(b) to (d) is made during the period mentioned in subsection (2) and is dismissed, unless the court orders otherwise the interest to which the application relates shall on the dismissal of the application—

(a) cease to be comprised in the bankrupt's estate, and

(b) vest in the bankrupt (without conveyance, assignment or transfer).

(5) If the bankrupt does not inform the trustee or the official receiver of his interest in a property before the end of the period of three months beginning with the date of the bankruptcy, the period of three years mentioned in subsection (2)—

(a) shall not begin with the date of the bankruptcy, but
(b) shall begin with the date on which the trustee or official receiver becomes aware of the bankrupt's interest.

(6) The court may substitute for the period of three years mentioned in subsection (2) a longer period—

(a) in prescribed circumstances, and
(b) in such other circumstances as the court thinks appropriate.

(7) The rules may make provision for this section to have effect with the substitution of a shorter period for the period of three years mentioned in subsection (2) in specified circumstances (which may be described by reference to action to be taken by a trustee in bankruptcy).

(8) The rules may also, in particular, make provision—

(a) requiring or enabling the trustee of a bankrupt's estate to give notice that this section applies or does not apply;
(b) about the effect of a notice under paragraph (a);
(c) requiring the trustee of a bankrupt's estate to make an application to the Chief Land Registrar.

(9) Rules under subsection (8)(b) may, in particular—

(a) disapply this section;
(b) enable a court to disapply this section;
(c) make provision in consequence of a disapplication of this section;
(d) enable a court to make provision in consequence of a disapplication of this section;
(e) make provision (which may include provision conferring jurisdiction on a court or tribunal) about compensation.]

[1216]

NOTES

Inserted by the Enterprise Act 2002, s 261(1), subject to transitional provisions in s 261(7)–(10) thereof.

Sub-s (1): words in square brackets inserted by the Civil Partnership Act 2004, s 261(1), Sch 27, para 113.

284 Restrictions on dispositions of property

(1) Where a person is adjudged bankrupt, any disposition of property made by that person in the period to which this section applies is void except to the extent that it is or was made with the consent of the court, or is or was subsequently ratified by the court.

(2) Subsection (1) applies to a payment (whether in cash or otherwise) as it applies to a disposition of property and, accordingly, where any payment is void by virtue of that subsection, the person paid shall hold the sum paid for the bankrupt as part of his estate.

(3) This section applies to the period beginning with the day of the presentation of the petition for the bankruptcy order and ending with the vesting, under Chapter IV of this Part, of the bankrupt's estate in a trustee.

(4) The preceding provisions of this section do not give a remedy against any person—

(a) in respect of any property or payment which he received before the commencement of the bankruptcy in good faith, for value and without notice that the petition had been presented, or
(b) in respect of any interest in property which derives from an interest in respect of which there is, by virtue of this subsection, no remedy.

(5) Where after the commencement of his bankruptcy the bankrupt has incurred a debt to a banker or other person by reason of the making of a payment which is void under this section, that debt is deemed for the purposes of any of this Group of Parts to have been incurred before the commencement of the bankruptcy unless—

(a) that banker or person had notice of the bankruptcy before the debt was incurred, or
(b) it is not reasonably practicable for the amount of the payment to be recovered from the person to whom it was made.

(6) A disposition of property is void under this section notwithstanding that the property is not or, as the case may be, would not be comprised in the bankrupt's estate; but nothing in this section affects any disposition made by a person of property held by him on trust for any other person.

[1217]

285 Restriction on proceedings and remedies

(1) At any time when proceedings on a bankruptcy petition are pending or an individual has been adjudged bankrupt the court may stay any action, execution or other legal process against the property or person of the debtor or, as the case may be, of the bankrupt.

PART I STATUTES

(2) Any court in which proceedings are pending against any individual may, on proof that a bankruptcy petition has been presented in respect of that individual or that he is an undischarged bankrupt, either stay the proceedings or allow them to continue on such terms as it thinks fit.

(3) After the making of a bankruptcy order no person who is a creditor of the bankrupt in respect of a debt provable in the bankruptcy shall—

(a) have any remedy against the property or person of the bankrupt in respect of that debt, or

(b) before the discharge of the bankrupt, commence any action or other legal proceedings against the bankrupt except with the leave of the court and on such terms as the court may impose.

This is subject to sections 346 (enforcement procedures) and 347 (limited right to distress).

(4) Subject as follows, subsection (3) does not affect the right of a secured creditor of the bankrupt to enforce his security.

(5) Where any goods of an undischarged bankrupt are held by any person by way of pledge, pawn or other security, the official receiver may, after giving notice in writing of his intention to do so, inspect the goods.

Where such a notice has been given to any person, that person is not entitled, without leave of the court, to realise his security unless he has given the trustee of the bankrupt's estate a reasonable opportunity of inspecting the goods and of exercising the bankrupt's right of redemption.

(6) References in this section to the property or goods of the bankrupt are to any of his property or goods, whether or not comprised in his estate.

[1218]

286–304 (*Ss 286–291, ss 292–304 (Ch III) outside the scope of this work.*)

CHAPTER IV
ADMINISTRATION BY TRUSTEE

305 (*Outside the scope of this work.*)

Acquisition, control and realisation of bankrupt's estate

306 Vesting of bankrupt's estate in trustee

(1) The bankrupt's estate shall vest in the trustee immediately on his appointment taking effect or, in the case of the official receiver, on his becoming trustee.

(2) Where any property which is, or is to be, comprised in the bankrupt's estate vests in the trustee (whether under this section or under any other provision of this Part), it shall so vest without any conveyance, assignment or transfer.

[1219]

[306A Property subject to restraint order

(1) This section applies where—

(a) property is excluded from the bankrupt's estate by virtue of section 417(2)(a) of the Proceeds of Crime Act 2002 (property subject to a restraint order),

(b) an order under section 50, … 128 [or 198] of that Act has not been made in respect of the property, and

(c) the restraint order is discharged.

(2) On the discharge of the restraint order the property vests in the trustee as part of the bankrupt's estate.

(3) But subsection (2) does not apply to the proceeds of property realised by a management receiver under section 49(2)(d) or 197(2)(d) of that Act (realisation of property to meet receiver's remuneration and expenses).]

[1220]

NOTES

Inserted, together with ss 306B, 306C, by the Proceeds of Crime Act 2002, s 456, Sch 11, paras 1, 16(1), (3).

Sub-s (1): in para (b) reference omitted repealed, and words in square brackets substituted, by the Serious Crime Act 2007, ss 74(2)(g), 92, Sch 8, Pt 7, para 151(a), (b), Sch 14, subject to transitional provisions and savings in art 3 thereof.

[306B Property in respect of which receivership or administration order made

(1) This section applies where—

(a) property is excluded from the bankrupt's estate by virtue of section 417(2)(b), (c) or (d) of the Proceeds of Crime Act 2002 (property in respect of which an order for the appointment of a receiver or administrator under certain provisions of that Act is in force),

(b) a confiscation order is made under section 6, 92 or 156 of that Act,
(c) the amount payable under the confiscation order is fully paid, and
(d) any of the property remains in the hands of the receiver or administrator (as the case may be).

(2) The property vests in the trustee as part of the bankrupt's estate.]

[1221]

NOTES

Inserted as noted to s 306A at **[1220]**.

[306C Property subject to certain orders where confiscation order discharged or quashed

(1) This section applies where—
(a) property is excluded from the bankrupt's estate by virtue of section 417(2)(a), (b), (c) or (d) of the Proceeds of Crime Act 2002 (property in respect of which a restraint order or an order for the appointment of a receiver or administrator under that Act is in force),
(b) a confiscation order is made under section 6, 92 or 156 of that Act, and
(c) the confiscation order is discharged under section 30, 114 or 180 of that Act (as the case may be) or quashed under that Act or in pursuance of any enactment relating to appeals against conviction or sentence.

(2) Any such property in the hands of a receiver appointed under Part 2 or 4 of that Act or an administrator appointed under Part 3 of that Act vests in the trustee as part of the bankrupt's estate.

(3) But subsection (2) does not apply to the proceeds of property realised by a management receiver under section 49(2)(d) or 197(2)(d) of that Act (realisation of property to meet receiver's remuneration and expenses).]

[1222]

NOTES

Inserted as noted to s 306A at **[1220]**.

307 After-acquired property

(1) Subject to this section and section 309, the trustee may by notice in writing claim for the bankrupt's estate any property which has been acquired by, or has devolved upon, the bankrupt since the commencement of the bankruptcy.

(2) A notice under this section shall not served in respect of—
(a) any property falling within subsection (2) or (3) of section 283 in Chapter II,
[(aa) any property vesting in the bankrupt by virtue of section 283A in Chapter II,]
(b) any property which by virtue of any other enactment is excluded from the bankrupt's estate, or
(c) without prejudice to section 280(2)(c) (order of court on application for discharge), any property which is acquired by or, devolves upon, the bankrupt after his discharge.

(3) Subject to the next subsection, upon the service on the bankrupt of a notice under this section the property to which the notice relates shall vest in the trustee as part of the bankrupt's estate; and the trustee's title to that property has relation back to the time at which the property was acquired by, or devolved upon, the bankrupt.

(4) Where, whether before or after service of a notice under this section—
(a) a person acquires property in good faith, for value and without notice of the bankruptcy, or
(b) a banker enters into a transaction in good faith and without such notice,

the trustee is not in respect of that property or transaction entitled by virtue of this section to any remedy against that person or banker, or any person whose title to any property derives from that person or banker.

(5) References in this section to property do not include any property which, as part of the bankrupt's income, may be the subject of an income payments order under section 310.

[1223]

NOTES

Sub-s (2): para (aa) inserted by the Enterprise Act 2002, s 261(4), subject to transitional provisions in s 261(7)–(10) thereof.

308–312 (*Outside the scope of this work.*)

313 Charge on bankrupt's home

(1) Where any property consisting of an interest in a dwelling house which is occupied by the bankrupt or by his spouse or former spouse [or by his civil partner or former civil partner] is

comprised in the bankrupt's estate and the trustee is, for any reason, unable for the time being to realise that property, the trustee may apply to the court for an order imposing a charge on the property for the benefit of the bankrupt's estate.

(2) If on an application under this section the court imposes a charge on any property, the benefit of that charge shall be comprised in the bankrupt's estate and is enforceable[, up to the charged value from time to time,] for the payment of any amount which is payable otherwise than to the bankrupt out of the estate and of interest on that amount at the prescribed rate.

[(2A) In subsection (2) the charged value means—

(a) the amount specified in the charging order as the value of the bankrupt's interest in the property at the date of the order, plus

(b) interest on that amount from the date of the charging order at the prescribed rate.

(2B) In determining the value of an interest for the purposes of this section the court shall disregard any matter which it is required to disregard by the rules.]

(3) An order under this section made in respect of property vested in the trustee shall provide, in accordance with the rules, for the property to cease to be comprised in the bankrupt's estate and, subject to the charge (and any prior charge), to vest in the bankrupt.

(4) *Subsections (1) and (2) and (4) to (6) of* [Subsection (1), (2), (4), (5) and (6) of] section 3 of the Charging Orders Act 1979 (supplemental provisions with respect to charging orders) have effect in relation to orders under this section as in relation to charging orders under that Act.

[(5) But an order under section 3(5) of that Act may not vary a charged value.]

[1224]

NOTES

Sub-s (1): words in square brackets inserted by the Civil Partnership Act 2004, s 261(1), Sch 27, para 114.

Sub-s (2): words in square brackets substituted for original words "up to the value from time to time of the property secured," by the Enterprise Act 2002, s 261(2)(a), subject to transitional provisions in s 261(7)–(10) of that Act.

Sub-ss (2A), (2B): inserted by the Enterprise Act 2002, s 261(2)(b), subject to transitional provisions in s 261(7)–(10) of that Act.

Sub-s (4): words in italics substituted by subsequent words in square brackets by the Tribunals, Courts and Enforcement Act 2007, s 93(5), subject to savings in s 93(6) thereof, as from a day to be appointed.

Sub-s (5): added by the Enterprise Act 2002, s 261(2)(c), subject to transitional provisions in s 261(7)–(10) of that Act.

[313A Low value home: application for sale, possession or charge

(1) This section applies where—

(a) property comprised in the bankrupt's estate consists of an interest in a dwelling-house which at the date of the bankruptcy was the sole or principal residence of—

(i) the bankrupt,

(ii) the bankrupt's spouse [or civil partner], or

(iii) a former spouse [or former civil partner] of the bankrupt, and

(b) the trustee applies for an order for the sale of the property, for an order for possession of the property or for an order under section 313 in respect of the property.

(2) The court shall dismiss the application if the value of the interest is below the amount prescribed for the purposes of this subsection.

(3) In determining the value of an interest for the purposes of this section the court shall disregard any matter which it is required to disregard by the order which prescribes the amount for the purposes of subsection (2).]

[1225]

NOTES

Inserted by the Enterprise Act 2002, s 261(3), subject to transitional provisions in s 261(7)–(10) thereof.

Sub-s (1): words in square brackets inserted by the Civil Partnership Act 2004, s 261(1), Sch 27, para 115.

See further: the Insolvency Proceedings (Monetary Limits) Order 1986, SI 1986/1996, art 3, Schedule, Pt II which specifies £1,000 as the prescribed amount for the purposes of sub-s (2).

314 Powers of trustee

(1) The trustee may—

(a) with the permission of the creditors' committee or the court, exercise any of the powers specified in Part I of Schedule 5 to this Act, and

(b) without that permission, exercise any of the general powers specified in Part II of that Schedule.

(2) With the permission of the creditors' committee or the court, the trustee may appoint the bankrupt—

(a) to superintend the management of his estate or any part of it,

(b) to carry on his business (if any) for the benefit of his creditors, or
(c) in any other respect to assist in administering the estate in such manner and on such terms as the trustee may direct.

(3) A permission given for the purposes of subsection (1)(a) or (2) shall not be a general permission but shall relate to a particular proposed exercise of the power in question; and a person dealing with the trustee in good faith and for value is not to be concerned to enquire whether any permission required in either case has been given.

(4) Where the trustee has done anything without the permission required by subsection (1)(a) or (2), the court or the creditors' committee may, for the purpose of enabling him to meet his expenses out of the bankrupt's estate, ratify what the trustee has done.

But the committee shall not do so unless it is satisfied that the trustee has acted in a case of urgency and has sought its ratification without undue delay.

(5) Part III of Schedule 5 to this Act has effect with respect to the things which the trustee is able to do for the purposes of, or in connection with, the exercise of any of his powers under any of this Group of Parts.

(6) Where the trustee (not being the official receiver) in exercise of the powers conferred on him by any provision in this Group of Parts—
(a) disposes of any property comprised in the bankrupt's estate to an associate of the bankrupt, or
(b) employs a solicitor,

he shall, if there is for the time being a creditors' committee, give notice to the committee of that exercise of his powers.

(7) Without prejudice to the generality of subsection (5) and Part III of Schedule 5, the trustee may, if he thinks fit, at any time summon a general meeting of the bankrupt's creditors.

Subject to the preceding provisions in this Group of Parts, he shall summon such a meeting if he is requested to do so by a creditor of the bankrupt and the request is made with the concurrence of not less than one-tenth, in value, of the bankrupt's creditors (including the creditor making the request).

(8) Nothing in this Act is to be construed as restricting the capacity of the trustee to exercise any of his powers outside England and Wales.

[1226]

Disclaimer of onerous property

315 Disclaimer (general power)

(1) Subject as follows, the trustee may, by the giving of the prescribed notice, disclaim any onerous property and may do so notwithstanding that he has taken possession of it, endeavoured to sell it or otherwise exercised rights of ownership in relation to it.

(2) The following is onerous property for the purposes of this section, that is to say—
(a) any unprofitable contract, and
(b) any other property comprised in the bankrupt's estate which is unsaleable or not readily saleable, or is such that it may give rise to a liability to pay money or perform any other onerous act.

(3) A disclaimer under this section—
(a) operates so as to determine, as from the date of the disclaimer, the rights, interests and liabilities of the bankrupt and his estate in or in respect of the property disclaimed, and
(b) discharges the trustee from all personal liability in respect of that property as from the commencement of his trusteeship,

but does not, except so far as is necessary for the purpose of releasing the bankrupt, the bankrupt's estate and the trustee from any liability, affect the rights or liabilities of any other person.

(4) A notice of disclaimer shall not be given under this section in respect of any property that has been claimed for the estate under section 307 (after-acquired property) or 308 (personal property of bankrupt exceeding reasonable replacement value) [or 308A], except with the leave of the court.

(5) Any person sustaining loss or damage in consequence of the operation of a disclaimer under this section is deemed to be a creditor of the bankrupt to the extent of the loss or damage and accordingly may prove for the loss or damage as a bankruptcy debt.

[1227]

NOTES

Sub-s (4): words in square brackets inserted by the Housing Act 1988, s 117(4).

316–335 (*Outside the scope of this work.*)

CHAPTER V
EFFECT OF BANKRUPTCY ON CERTAIN RIGHTS, TRANSACTIONS, ETC

[Rights under trusts of land

335A Rights under trusts of land

(1) Any application by a trustee of a bankrupt's estate under section 14 of the Trusts of Land and Appointment of Trustees Act 1996 (powers of court in relation to trusts of land) for an order under that section for the sale of land shall be made to the court having jurisdiction in relation to the bankruptcy.

(2) On such an application the court shall make such order as it thinks just and reasonable having regard to—

- (a) the interests of the bankrupt's creditors;
- (b) where the application is made in respect of land which includes a dwelling house which is or has been the home of the bankrupt or the [bankrupt's spouse or civil partner or former spouse or former civil partner]—
  - (i) the conduct of the [spouse, civil partner, former spouse or former civil partner], so far as contributing to the bankruptcy,
  - (ii) the needs and financial resources of the [spouse, civil partner, former spouse or former civil partner] and
  - (iii) the needs of any children; and
- (c) all the circumstances of the case other than the needs of the bankrupt.

(3) Where such an application is made after the end of the period of one year beginning with the first vesting under Chapter IV of this Part of the bankrupt's estate in a trustee, the court shall assume, unless the circumstances of the case are exceptional, that the interests of the bankrupt's creditors outweigh all other considerations.

(4) The powers conferred on the court by this section are exercisable on an application whether it is made before or after the commencement of this section.]

[1228]

NOTES

Inserted, together with preceding cross-heading, by the Trusts of Land and Appointment of Trustees Act 1996, s 25(1), Sch 3, para 23, subject to savings in s 25(4), (5) thereof.

Sub-s (2): words in square brackets substituted by the Civil Partnership Act 2004, s 261(1), Sch 27, para 118.

Rights of occupation

336 Rights of occupation etc of bankrupt's spouse [or civil partner]

(1) Nothing occurring in the initial period of the bankruptcy (that is to say, the period beginning with the day of the presentation of the petition for the bankruptcy order and ending with the vesting of the bankrupt's estate in a trustee) is to be taken as having given rise to any [[home rights] under Part IV of the Family Law Act 1996] in relation to a dwelling house comprised in the bankrupt's estate.

(2) Where [a spouse's or civil partner's home rights] [under the Act of 1996] are a charge on the estate or interest of the other spouse [or civil partner], or of trustees for the other spouse [or civil partner], and the other spouse [or civil partner] is adjudged bankrupt—

- (a) the charge continues to subsist notwithstanding the bankruptcy and, subject to the provisions of that Act, binds the trustee of the bankrupt's estate and persons deriving title under that trustee, and
- (b) any application for an order [under section 33 of that Act] shall be made to the court having jurisdiction in relation to the bankruptcy.

(3) …

(4) On such an application as is mentioned in subsection (2) … the court shall make such order under [section 33 of the Act of 1996] … as it thinks just and reasonable having regard to—

- (a) the interests of the bankrupt's creditors,
- (b) the conduct of the spouse or former spouse [or civil partner or former civil partner], so far as contributing to the bankruptcy,
- (c) the needs and financial resources of the spouse or former spouse [or civil partner or former civil partner],
- (d) the needs of any children, and
- (e) all the circumstances of the case other than the needs of the bankrupt.

(5) Where such an application is made after the end of the period of one year beginning with the first vesting under Chapter IV of this Part of the bankrupt's estate in a trustee, the court shall assume, unless the circumstances of the case are exceptional, that the interests of the bankrupt's creditors outweigh all other considerations.

[1229]

NOTES

Section heading: words in square brackets inserted by the Civil Partnership Act 2004, s 82, Sch 9, Pt 2, para 21(1), (5), subject to transitional provisions in Sch 9, Pt 3 thereto.

Sub-s (1): words in first (outer) pair of square brackets substituted by the Family Law Act 1996, s 66(1), Sch 8, para 57(2); words in second (inner) pair of square brackets substituted by the Civil Partnership Act 2004, s 82, Sch 9, Pt 2, para 21(1), (2), subject to transitional provisions in Sch 9, Pt 3 thereto.

Sub-s (2): words in first, third, fourth and fifth pairs of square brackets inserted by the Civil Partnership Act 2004, s 82, Sch 9, Pt 2, para 21(1), (3), subject to transitional provisions in Sch 9, Pt 3 thereto; words in second and sixth pairs of square brackets substituted by the Family Law Act 1996, s 66(1), Sch 8, para 57(3).

Sub-s (3): repealed by the Trusts of Land and Appointment of Trustees Act 1996, s 25(2), Sch 4, subject to savings in s 25(4), (5) thereof.

Sub-s (4): words omitted repealed by the Trusts of Land and Appointment of Trustees Act 1996, s 25(2), Sch 4, subject to savings in s 25(4), (5) thereof; words in first pair of square brackets substituted by the Family Law Act 1996, s 66(1), Sch 8, para 57(1), (4); words in second and third pairs of square brackets inserted by the Civil Partnership Act 2004, s 82, Sch 9, Pt 2, para 21(1), (4), subject to transitional provisions in Sch 9, Pt 3 thereto.

337 Rights of occupation of bankrupt

(1) This section applies where—

(a) a person who is entitled to occupy a dwelling house by virtue of a beneficial estate or interest is adjudged bankrupt, and

(b) any persons under the age of 18 with whom that person had at some time occupied that dwelling house had their home with that person at the time when the bankruptcy petition was presented and at the commencement of the bankruptcy.

(2) Whether or not the bankrupt's [spouse or civil partner (if any) has home rights] [under Part IV of the Family Law Act 1996]—

(a) the bankrupt has the following rights as against the trustee of his estate—

(i) if in occupation, a right not to be evicted or excluded from the dwelling house or any part of it, except with the leave of the court,

(ii) if not in occupation, a right with the leave of the court to enter into and occupy the dwelling house, and

(b) the bankrupt's rights are a charge, having the like priority as an equitable interest created immediately before the commencement of the bankruptcy, on so much of his estate or interest in the dwelling house as vests in the trustee.

[(3) The Act of 1996 has effect, with the necessary modifications, as if—

(a) the rights conferred by paragraph (a) of subsection (2) were [home rights] under that Act,

(b) any application for such leave as is mentioned in that paragraph were an application for an order under section 33 of that Act, and

(c) any charge under paragraph (b) of that subsection on the estate or interest of the trustee were a charge under that Act on the estate or interest of a spouse [or civil partner].]

(4) Any application for leave such as is mentioned in subsection (2)(a) or otherwise by virtue of this section for an order under [section 33 of the Act of 1996] shall be made to the court having jurisdiction in relation to the bankruptcy.

(5) On such an application the court shall make such order under [section 33 of the Act of 1996] as it thinks just and reasonable having regard to the interests of the creditors, to the bankrupt's financial resources, to the needs of the children and to all the circumstances of the case other than the needs of the bankrupt.

(6) Where such an application is made after the end of the period of one year beginning with the vesting (under Chapter IV of this Part) of the bankrupt's estate in a trustee, the court shall assume, unless the circumstances of the case are exceptional, that the interests of the bankrupt's creditors outweigh all other considerations.

[1230]

NOTES

Sub-s (2): words if first pair of square brackets substituted by the Civil Partnership Act 2004, s 82, Sch 9, Pt 2, para 22(1), (2), subject to transitional provisions in Sch 9, Pt 3 thereto; words in second pair of square brackets substituted by the Family Law Act 1996, s 66(1), Sch 8, para 58(1), (2).

Sub-s (3): substituted by the Family Law Act 1996, s 66(1), Sch 8, para 58(1), (3); words in square brackets in para (a) substituted, and words in square brackets in para (c) inserted by the Civil Partnership Act 2004, s 82, Sch 9, Pt 2, para 22(1), (3), subject to transitional provisions in Sch 9, Pt 3 thereto.

Sub-ss (4), (5): words in square brackets substituted by the Family Law Act 1996, s 66(1), Sch 8, para 58(1), (4).

338 Payments in respect of premises occupied by bankrupt

Where any premises comprised in a bankrupt's estate are occupied by him (whether by virtue of the preceding section or otherwise) on condition that he makes payments towards satisfying any liability arising under a mortgage of the premises or otherwise towards the outgoings of the premises, the bankrupt does not, by virtue of those payments, acquire any interest in the premises.

[1231]

Adjustment of prior transactions, etc

339 Transactions at an undervalue

(1) Subject as follows in this section and sections 341 and 342, where an individual is adjudged bankrupt and he has at a relevant time (defined in section 341) entered into a transaction with any person at an undervalue, the trustee of the bankrupt's estate may apply to the court for an order under this section.

(2) The court shall, on such an application, make such order as it thinks fit for restoring the position to what it would have been if that individual had not entered into that transaction.

(3) For the purposes of this section and sections 341 and 342, an individual enters into a transaction with a person at an undervalue if—

(a) he makes a gift to that person or he otherwise enters into a transaction with that person on terms that provide for him to receive no consideration,

(b) he enters into a transaction with that person in consideration of marriage [or the formation of a civil partnership], or

(c) he enters into a transaction with that person for a consideration the value of which, in money or money's worth, is significantly less than the value, in money or money's worth, of the consideration provided by the individual.

[1232]

NOTES

Sub-s (3): words in square brackets inserted by the Civil Partnership Act 2004, s 261(1), Sch 27, para 119.

340 Preferences

(1) Subject as follows in this and the next two sections, where an individual is adjudged bankrupt and he has at a relevant time (defined in section 341) given a preference to any person, the trustee of the bankrupt's estate may apply to the court for an order under this section.

(2) The court shall, on such an application, make such order as it thinks fit for restoring the position to what it would have been if that individual had not given that preference.

(3) For the purposes of this and the next two sections, an individual gives a preference to a person if—

(a) that person is one of the individual's creditors or a surety or guarantor for any of his debts or other liabilities, and

(b) the individual does anything or suffers anything to be done which (in either case) has the effect of putting that person into a position which, in the event of the individual's bankruptcy, will be better than the position he would have been in if that thing had not been done.

(4) The court shall not make an order under this section in respect of a preference given to any person unless the individual who gave the preference was influenced in deciding to give it by a desire to produce in relation to that person the effect mentioned in subsection (3)(b) above.

(5) An individual who has given a preference to a person who, at the time the preference was given, was an associate of his (otherwise than by reason only of being his employee) is presumed, unless the contrary is shown, to have been influenced in deciding to give it by such a desire as is mentioned in subsection (4).

(6) The fact that something has been done in pursuance of the order of a court does not, without more, prevent the doing or suffering of that thing from constituting the giving of a preference.

[1233]

341 "Relevant time" under ss 339, 340

(1) Subject as follows, the time at which an individual enters into a transaction at an undervalue or gives a preference is a relevant time if the transaction is entered into or the preference given—

(a) in the case of a transaction at an undervalue, at a time in the period of 5 years ending with the day of the presentation of the bankruptcy petition on which the individual is adjudged bankrupt,

(b) in the case of a preference which is not a transaction at an undervalue and is given to a person who is an associate of the individual (otherwise than by reason only of being his employee), at a time in the period of 2 years ending with that day, and

(c) in any other case of a preference which is not a transaction at an undervalue, at a time in the period of 6 months ending with that day.

(2) Where an individual enters into a transaction at an undervalue or gives a preference at a time mentioned in paragraph (a), (b) or (c) of subsection (1) (not being, in the case of a transaction

at an undervalue, a time less than 2 years before the end of the period mentioned in paragraph (a)), that time is not a relevant time for the purposes of sections 339 and 340 unless the individual—

(a) is insolvent at that time, or
(b) becomes insolvent in consequence of the transaction or preference;

but the requirements of this subsection are presumed to be satisfied, unless the contrary is shown, in relation to any transaction at an undervalue which is entered into by an individual with a person who is an associate of his (otherwise than by reason only of being his employee).

(3) For the purposes of subsection (2), an individual is insolvent if—

(a) he is unable to pay his debts as they fall due, or
(b) the value of his assets is less than the amount of his liabilities, taking into account his contingent and prospective liabilities.

(4) A transaction entered into or preference given by a person who is subsequently adjudged bankrupt on a petition under section 264(1)(d) (criminal bankruptcy) is to be treated as having been entered into or given at a relevant time for the purposes of sections 339 and 340 if it was entered into or given at any time on or after the date specified for the purposes of this subsection in the criminal bankruptcy order on which the petition was based.

(5) No order shall be made under section 339 or 340 by virtue of subsection (4) of this section where an appeal is pending (within the meaning of section 277) against the individual's conviction of any offence by virtue of which the criminal bankruptcy order was made.

[1234]

NOTES

Sub-ss (4), (5): repealed by the Criminal Justice Act 1988, s 170(2), Sch 16, as from a day to be appointed.

342 Orders under ss 339, 340

(1) Without prejudice to the generality of section 339(2) or 340(2), an order under either of those sections with respect to a transaction or preference entered into or given by an individual who is subsequently adjudged bankrupt may (subject as follows)—

(a) require any property transferred as part of the transaction, or in connection with the giving of the preference, to be vested in the trustee of the bankrupt's estate as part of that estate;
(b) require any property to be so vested if it represents in any person's hands the application either of the proceeds of sale of property so transferred or of money so transferred;
(c) release or discharge (in whole or in part) any security given by the individual;
(d) require any person to pay, in respect of benefits received by him from the individual, such sums to the trustee of his estate as the court may direct;
(e) provide for any surety or guarantor whose obligations to any person were released or discharged (in whole or in part) under the transaction or by the giving of the preference to be under such new or revived obligations to that person as the court thinks appropriate;
(f) provide for security to be provided for the discharge of any obligation imposed by or arising under the order, for such an obligation to be charged on any property and for the security or charge to have the same priority as a security or charge released or discharged (in whole or in part) under the transaction or by the giving of the preference; and
(g) provide for the extent to which any person whose property is vested by the order in the trustee of the bankrupt's estate, or on whom obligations are imposed by the order, is to be able to prove in the bankruptcy for debts or other liabilities which arose from, or were released or discharged (in whole or in part) under or by, the transaction or the giving of the preference.

(2) An order under section 339 or 340 may affect the property of, or impose any obligation on, any person whether or not he is the person with whom the individual in question entered into the transaction or, as the case may be, the person to whom the preference was given; but such an order—

(a) shall not prejudice any interest in property which was acquired from a person other than that individual and was acquired [in good faith and for value], or prejudice any interest deriving from such an interest, and
(b) shall not require a person who received a benefit from the transaction or preference [in good faith and for value] to pay a sum to the trustee of the bankrupt's estate, except where he was a party to the transaction or the payment is to be in respect of a preference given to that person at a time when he was a creditor of that individual.

[(2A) Where a person has acquired an interest in property from a person other than the individual in question, or has received a benefit from the transaction or preference, and at the time of that acquisition or receipt—

(a) he had notice of the relevant surrounding circumstances and of the relevant proceedings, or

(b) he was an associate of, or was connected with, either the individual in question or the person with whom that individual entered into the transaction or to whom that individual gave the preference,

then, unless the contrary is shown, it shall be presumed for the purposes of paragraph (a) or (as the case may be) paragraph (b) of subsection (2) that the interest was acquired or the benefit was received otherwise than in good faith.]

(3) Any sums required to be paid to the trustee in accordance with an order under section 339 or 340 shall be comprised in the bankrupt's estate.

[(4) For the purposes of subsection (2A)(a), the relevant surrounding circumstances are (as the case may require)—

(a) the fact that the individual in question entered into the transaction at an undervalue; or

(b) the circumstances which amounted to the giving of the preference by the individual in question.

(5) For the purposes of subsection (2A)(a), a person has notice of the relevant proceedings if he has notice—

(a) of the fact that the petition on which the individual in question is adjudged bankrupt has been presented; or

(b) of the fact that the individual in question has been adjudged bankrupt.

(6) Section 249 in Part VII of this Act shall apply for the purposes of subsection (2A)(b) as it applies for the purposes of the first Group of Parts.]

[1235]

NOTES

Sub-s (2): words in square brackets substituted by the Insolvency (No 2) Act 1994, s 2(1), in relation to interests acquired and benefits received after 26 July 1994.

Sub-s (2A): inserted by the Insolvency (No 2) Act 1994, s 2(2), in relation to interests acquired and benefits received after 26 July 1994.

Sub-ss (4)–(6): substituted for original sub-s (4) by the Insolvency (No 2) Act 1994, s 2(3), in relation to interests acquired and benefits received after 26 July 1994.

[342A Recovery of excessive pension contributions

(1) Where an individual who is adjudged bankrupt—

(a) has rights under an approved pension arrangement, or

(b) has excluded rights under an unapproved pension arrangement,

the trustee of the bankrupt's estate may apply to the court for an order under this section.

(2) If the court is satisfied—

(a) that the rights under the arrangement are to any extent, and whether directly or indirectly, the fruits of relevant contributions, and

(b) that the making of any of the relevant contributions ("the excessive contributions") has unfairly prejudiced the individual's creditors,

the court may make such order as it thinks fit for restoring the position to what it would have been had the excessive contributions not been made.

(3) Subsection (4) applies where the court is satisfied that the value of the rights under the arrangement is, as a result of rights of the individual under the arrangement or any other pension arrangement having at any time become subject to a debit under section 29(1)(a) of the Welfare Reform and Pensions Act 1999 (debits giving effect to pension-sharing), less than it would otherwise have been.

(4) Where this subsection applies—

(a) any relevant contributions which were represented by the rights which became subject to the debit shall, for the purposes of subsection (2), be taken to be contributions of which the rights under the arrangement are the fruits, and

(b) where the relevant contributions represented by the rights under the arrangement (including those so represented by virtue of paragraph (a)) are not all excessive contributions, relevant contributions which are represented by the rights under the arrangement otherwise than by virtue of paragraph (a) shall be treated as excessive contributions before any which are so represented by virtue of that paragraph.

(5) In subsections (2) to (4) "relevant contributions" means contributions to the arrangement or any other pension arrangement—

(a) which the individual has at any time made on his own behalf, or

(b) which have at any time been made on his behalf.

(6) The court shall, in determining whether it is satisfied under subsection (2)(b), consider in particular—

(a) whether any of the contributions were made for the purpose of putting assets beyond the reach of the individual's creditors or any of them, and
(b) whether the total amount of any contributions—
 (i) made by or on behalf of the individual to pension arrangements, and
 (ii) represented (whether directly or indirectly) by rights under approved pension arrangements or excluded rights under unapproved pension arrangements,
is an amount which is excessive in view of the individual's circumstances when those contributions were made.

(7) For the purposes of this section and sections 342B and 342C ("the recovery provisions"), rights of an individual under an unapproved pension arrangement are excluded rights if they are rights which are excluded from his estate by virtue of regulations under section 12 of the Welfare Reform and Pensions Act 1999.

(8) In the recovery provisions—

"approved pension arrangement" has the same meaning as in section 11 of the Welfare Reform and Pensions Act 1999;

"unapproved pension arrangement" has the same meaning as in section 12 of that Act.]

[1236]

NOTES

Substituted (for section as originally inserted by the Pensions Act 1995, s 95(1)) by the Welfare Reform and Pensions Act 1999, s 15.

[342B Orders under section 342A

(1) Without prejudice to the generality of section 342A(2), an order under section 342A may include provision—
(a) requiring the person responsible for the arrangement to pay an amount to the individual's trustee in bankruptcy,
(b) adjusting the liabilities of the arrangement in respect of the individual,
(c) adjusting any liabilities of the arrangement in respect of any other person that derive, directly or indirectly, from rights of the individual under the arrangement,
(d) for the recovery by the person responsible for the arrangement (whether by deduction from any amount which that person is ordered to pay or otherwise) of costs incurred by that person in complying in the bankrupt's case with any requirement under section 342C(1) or in giving effect to the order.

(2) In subsection (1), references to adjusting the liabilities of the arrangement in respect of a person include (in particular) reducing the amount of any benefit or future benefit to which that person is entitled under the arrangement.

(3) In subsection (1)(c), the reference to liabilities of the arrangement does not include liabilities in respect of a person which result from giving effect to an order or provision falling within section 28(1) of the Welfare Reform and Pensions Act 1999 (pension sharing orders and agreements).

(4) The maximum amount which the person responsible for an arrangement may be required to pay by an order under section 342A is the lesser of—
(a) the amount of the excessive contributions, and
(b) the value of the individual's rights under the arrangement (if the arrangement is an approved pension arrangement) or of his excluded rights under the arrangement (if the arrangement is an unapproved pension arrangement).

(5) An order under section 342A which requires the person responsible for an arrangement to pay an amount ("the restoration amount") to the individual's trustee in bankruptcy must provide for the liabilities of the arrangement to be correspondingly reduced.

(6) For the purposes of subsection (5), liabilities are correspondingly reduced if the difference between—
(a) the amount of the liabilities immediately before the reduction, and
(b) the amount of the liabilities immediately after the reduction,
is equal to the restoration amount.

(7) An order under section 342A in respect of an arrangement—
(a) shall be binding on the person responsible for the arrangement, and
(b) overrides provisions of the arrangement to the extent that they conflict with the provisions of the order.]

[1237]

NOTES

Substituted (for section as originally inserted by the Pensions Act 1995, s 95(1)) by the Welfare Reform and Pensions Act 1999, s 15.

[342C Orders under section 342A: supplementary

(1) The person responsible for—

(a) an approved pension arrangement under which a bankrupt has rights,

(b) an unapproved pension arrangement under which a bankrupt has excluded rights, or

(c) a pension arrangement under which a bankrupt has at any time had rights,

shall, on the bankrupt's trustee in bankruptcy making a written request, provide the trustee with such information about the arrangement and rights as the trustee may reasonably require for, or in connection with, the making of applications under section 342A.

(2) Nothing in—

(a) any provision of section 159 of the Pension Schemes Act 1993 or section 91 of the Pensions Act 1995 (which prevent assignment and the making of orders that restrain a person from receiving anything which he is prevented from assigning),

(b) any provision of any enactment (whether passed or made before or after the passing of the Welfare Reform and Pensions Act 1999) corresponding to any of the provisions mentioned in paragraph (a), or

(c) any provision of the arrangement in question corresponding to any of those provisions,

applies to a court exercising its powers under section 342A.

(3) Where any sum is required by an order under section 342A to be paid to the trustee in bankruptcy, that sum shall be comprised in the bankrupt's estate.

(4) Regulations may, for the purposes of the recovery provisions, make provision about the calculation and verification of—

(a) any such value as is mentioned in section 342B(4)(b);

(b) any such amounts as are mentioned in section 342B(6)(a) and (b).

(5) The power conferred by subsection (4) includes power to provide for calculation or verification—

(a) in such manner as may, in the particular case, be approved by a prescribed person; or

[(b) in accordance with guidance from time to time prepared by a prescribed person.]

(6) References in the recovery provisions to the person responsible for a pension arrangement are to—

(a) the trustees, managers or provider of the arrangement, or

(b) the person having functions in relation to the arrangement corresponding to those of a trustee, manager or provider.

(7) In this section and sections 342A and 342B—

"prescribed" means prescribed by regulations;

"the recovery provisions" means this section and sections 342A and 342B;

"regulations" means regulations made by the Secretary of State.

(8) Regulations under the recovery provisions may—

(a) make different provision for different cases;

(b) contain such incidental, supplemental and transitional provisions as appear to the Secretary of State necessary or expedient.

(9) Regulations under the recovery provisions shall be made by statutory instrument subject to annulment in pursuance of a resolution of either House of Parliament.]

[1238]

NOTES

Substituted (for section as originally inserted by the Pensions Act 1995, s 95(1)) by the Welfare Reform and Pensions Act 1999, s 15.

Sub-s (5): para (b) substituted by the Pensions Act 2007, s 17, Sch 5, para 3.

Regulations: the Occupational and Personal Pension Schemes (Bankruptcy) (No 2) Regulations 2002, SI 2002/836.

342D–342F (*Outside the scope of this work.*)

343 Extortionate credit transactions

(1) This section applies where a person is adjudged bankrupt who is or has been a party to a transaction for, or involving, the provision to him of credit.

(2) The court may, on the application of the trustee of the bankrupt's estate, make an order with respect to the transaction if the transaction is or was extortionate and was not entered into more than 3 years before the commencement of the bankruptcy.

(3) For the purposes of this section a transaction is extortionate if, having regard to the risk accepted by the person providing the credit—

(a) the terms of it are or were such as to require grossly exorbitant payments to be made (whether unconditionally or in certain contingencies) in respect of the provision of the credit, or

(b) it otherwise grossly contravened ordinary principles of fair dealing;

and it shall be presumed, unless the contrary is proved, that a transaction with respect to which an application is made under this section is or, as the case may be, was extortionate.

(4) An order under this section with respect to any transaction may contain such one or more of the following as the court thinks fit, that is to say—

(a) provision setting aside the whole or part of any obligation created by the transaction;

(b) provision otherwise varying the terms of the transaction or varying the terms on which any security for the purposes of the transaction is held;

(c) provision requiring any person who is or was party to the transaction to pay to the trustee any sums paid to that person, by virtue of the transaction, by the bankrupt;

(d) provision requiring any person to surrender to the trustee any property held by him as security for the purposes of the transaction;

(e) provision directing accounts to be taken between any persons.

(5) Any sums or property required to be paid or surrendered to the trustee in accordance with an order under this section shall be comprised in the bankrupt's estate.

(6) ... The powers conferred by this section are exercisable in relation to any transaction concurrently with any powers exercisable under this Act in relation to that transaction as a transaction at an undervalue.

[1239]

NOTES

Sub-s (6): words omitted repealed by the Consumer Credit Act 2006, s 70, Sch 4, subject to transitional provisions and savings s 69(1) of, Sch 3, paras 1, 15(5)(g) to that Act.

344, 345 (*Outside the scope of this work.*)

346 Enforcement procedures

(1) Subject to section 285 in Chapter II (restrictions on proceedings and remedies) and to the following provisions of this section, where the creditor of any person who is adjudged bankrupt has, before the commencement of the bankruptcy—

(a) issued execution against the goods or land of that person, or

(b) attached a debt due to that person from another person,

that creditor is not entitled, as against the official receiver or trustee of the bankrupt's estate, to retain the benefit of the execution or attachment, or any sums paid to avoid it, unless the execution or attachment was completed, or the sums were paid, before the commencement of the bankruptcy.

(2) Subject as follows, where any goods of a person have been taken in execution, then, if before the completion of the execution notice is given to the [enforcement officer] or other officer charged with the execution that that person has been adjudged bankrupt—

(a) the [enforcement officer] or other officer shall on request deliver to the official receiver or trustee of the bankrupt's estate the goods and any money seized or recovered in part satisfaction of the execution, but

(b) the costs of the execution are a first charge on the goods or money so delivered and the official receiver or trustee may sell the goods or a sufficient part of them for the purpose of satisfying the charge.

(3) Subject to subsection (6) below, where—

(a) under an execution in respect of a judgment for a sum exceeding such sum as may be prescribed for the purposes of this subsection, the goods of any person are sold or money is paid in order to avoid a sale, and

(b) before the end of the period of 14 days beginning with the day of the sale or payment the [enforcement officer] or other officer charged with the execution is given notice that a bankruptcy petition has been presented in relation to that person, and

(c) a bankruptcy order is or has been made on that petition,

the balance of the proceeds of sale or money paid, after deducting the costs of execution, shall (in priority to the claim of the execution creditor) be comprised in the bankrupt's estate.

(4) Accordingly, in the case of an execution in respect of a judgment for a sum exceeding the sum prescribed for the purposes of subsection (3), the [enforcement officer] or other officer charged with the execution—

(a) shall not dispose of the balance mentioned in subsection (3) at any time within the period of 14 days so mentioned or while there is pending a bankruptcy petition of which he has been given notice under that subsection, and

(b) shall pay that balance, where by virtue of that subsection it is comprised in the bankrupt's estate, to the official receiver or (if there is one) to the trustee of that estate.

(5) For the purposes of this section—

(a) an execution against goods is completed by seizure and sale or by the making of a charging order under section 1 of the Charging Orders Act 1979;

(b) an execution against land is completed by seizure, by the appointment of a receiver or by the making of a charging order under that section;

(c) an attachment of a debt is completed by the receipt of the debt.

(6) The rights conferred by subsections (1) to (3) on the official receiver or the trustee may, to such extent and on such terms as it thinks fit, be set aside by the court in favour of the creditor who has issued the execution or attached the debt.

(7) Nothing in this section entitles the trustee of a bankrupt's estate to claim goods from a person who has acquired them in good faith under a sale by [an enforcement officer] or other officer charged with an execution.

(8) Neither subsection (2) nor subsection (3) applies in relation to any execution against property which has been acquired by or has devolved upon the bankrupt since the commencement of the bankruptcy, unless, at the time the execution is issued or before it is completed—

(a) the property has been or is claimed for the bankrupt's estate under section 307 (after-acquired property), and

(b) a copy of the notice given under that section has been or is served on the [enforcement officer] or other officer charged with the execution.

[(9) In this section "enforcement officer" means an individual who is authorised to act as an enforcement officer under the Courts Act 2003.]

[1240]

NOTES

Sub-ss (2)–(4), (7), (8): words in square brackets substituted by the Courts Act 2003, s 109(1), Sch 8, para 297(1)–(3).

Sub-s (9): added by the Courts Act 2003, s 109(1), Sch 8, para 297(1), (4).

See further: the Insolvency Proceedings (Monetary Limits) Order 1986, SI 1986/1996, art 3, Schedule, Pt II which specifies £1,000 as the prescribed sum.

347–422 (*Ss 347–371, ss 372–422 (Pts X–XV) outside the scope of this work.*)

PART XVI
PROVISIONS AGAINST DEBT AVOIDANCE (ENGLAND AND WALES ONLY)

423 Transactions defrauding creditors

(1) This section relates to transactions entered into at an undervalue; and a person enters into such a transaction with another person if—

(a) he makes a gift to the other person or he otherwise enters into a transaction with the other on terms that provide for him to receive no consideration;

(b) he enters into a transaction with the other in consideration of marriage [or the formation of a civil partnership]; or

(c) he enters into a transaction with the other for a consideration the value of which, in money or money's worth, is significantly less than the value, in money or money's worth, of the consideration provided by himself.

(2) Where a person has entered into such a transaction, the court may, if satisfied under the next subsection, make such order as it thinks fit for—

(a) restoring the position to what it would have been if the transaction had not been entered into, and

(b) protecting the interests of persons who are victims of the transaction.

(3) In the case of a person entering into such a transaction, an order shall only be made if the court is satisfied that it was entered into by him for the purpose—

(a) of putting assets beyond the reach of a person who is making, or may at some time make, a claim against him, or

(b) of otherwise prejudicing the interests of such a person in relation to the claim which he is making or may make.

(4) In this section "the court" means the High Court or—

(a) if the person entering into the transaction is an individual, any other court which would have jurisdiction in relation to a bankruptcy petition relating to him;

(b) if that person is a body capable of being wound up under Part IV or V of this Act, any other court having jurisdiction to wind it up.

(5) In relation to a transaction at an undervalue, references here and below to a victim of the transaction are to a person who is, or is capable of being, prejudiced by it; and in the following two sections the person entering into the transaction is referred to as "the debtor".

[1241]

NOTES

Sub-s (1): words in square brackets inserted by the Civil Partnership Act 2004, s 261(1), Sch 27, para 121.

Application: in relation to the application of this section, with modifications, in respect of bank insolvency, see the Banking Act 2009, s 103(3), (4), Table, 145(3), (4), Table 2.

424 Those who may apply for an order under s 423

(1) An application for an order under section 423 shall not be made in relation to a transaction except—

(a) in a case where the debtor has been adjudged bankrupt or is a body corporate which is being wound up or [is in administration], by the official receiver, by the trustee of the bankrupt's estate or the liquidator or administrator of the body corporate or (with the leave of the court) by a victim of the transaction;

(b) in a case where a victim of the transaction is bound by a voluntary arrangement approved under Part I or Part VIII of this Act, by the supervisor of the voluntary arrangement or by any person who (whether or not so bound) is such a victim; or

(c) in any other case, by a victim of the transaction.

(2) An application made under any of the paragraphs of subsection (1) is to be treated as made on behalf of every victim of the transaction.

[1242]

NOTES

Sub-s (1): in para (a) words in square brackets substituted by the Enterprise Act 2002, s 248(3), Sch 17, paras 9, 36; for transitional provisions and effect see s 249 of, Sch 17, para 1 to, that Act.

Application: in relation to the application of this section, with modifications, in respect of bank insolvency, see the Banking Act 2009, s 103(3), (4), Table, 145(3), (4), Table 2.

425 Provision which may be made by order under s 423

(1) Without prejudice to the generality of section 423, an order made under that section with respect to a transaction may (subject as follows)—

(a) require any property transferred as part of the transaction to be vested in any person, either absolutely or for the benefit of all the persons on whose behalf the application for the order is treated as made;

(b) require any property to be so vested if it represents, in any person's hands, the application either of the proceeds of sale of property so transferred or of money so transferred;

(c) release or discharge (in whole or in part) any security given by the debtor;

(d) require any person to pay to any other person in respect of benefits received from the debtor such sums as the court may direct;

(e) provide for any surety or guarantor whose obligations to any person were released or discharged (in whole or in part) under the transaction to be under such new or revived obligations as the court thinks appropriate;

(f) provide for security to be provided for the discharge of any obligation imposed by or arising under the order, for such an obligation to be charged on any property and for such security or charge to have the same priority as a security or charge released or discharged (in whole or in part) under the transaction.

(2) An order under section 423 may affect the property of, or impose any obligation on, any person whether or not he is the person with whom the debtor entered into the transaction; but such an order—

(a) shall not prejudice any interest in property which was acquired from a person other than the debtor and was acquired in good faith, for value and without notice of the relevant circumstances, or prejudice any interest deriving from such an interest, and

(b) shall not require a person who received a benefit from the transaction in good faith, for value and without notice of the relevant circumstances to pay any sum unless he was a party to the transaction.

(3) For the purposes of this section the relevant circumstances in relation to a transaction are the circumstances by virtue of which an order under section 423 may be made in respect of the transaction.

(4) In this section "security" means any mortgage, charge, lien or other security.

[1243]

NOTES

Application: in relation to the application of this section, with modifications, in respect of bank insolvency, see the Banking Act 2009, s 103(3), (4), Table, 145(3), (4), Table 2.

PART XVII
MISCELLANEOUS AND GENERAL

426 Co-operation between courts exercising jurisdiction in relation to insolvency

(1) An order made by a court in any part of the United Kingdom in the exercise of jurisdiction in relation to insolvency law shall be enforced in any other part of the United Kingdom as if it were made by a court exercising the corresponding jurisdiction in that other part.

(2) However, without prejudice to the following provisions of this section, nothing in subsection (1) requires a court in any part of the United Kingdom to enforce, in relation to property situated in that part, any order made by a court in any other part of the United Kingdom.

(3) The Secretary of State, with the concurrence in relation to property situated in England and Wales of the Lord Chancellor, may by order make provision for securing that a trustee or assignee under the insolvency law of any part of the United Kingdom has, with such modifications as may be specified in the order, the same rights in relation to any property situated in another part of the United Kingdom as he would have in the corresponding circumstances if he were a trustee or assignee under the insolvency law of that other part.

(4) The courts having jurisdiction in relation to insolvency law in any part of the United Kingdom shall assist the courts having the corresponding jurisdiction in any other part of the United Kingdom or any relevant country or territory.

(5) For the purposes of subsection (4) a request made to a court in any part of the United Kingdom by a court in any other part of the United Kingdom or in a relevant country or territory is authority for the court to which the request is made to apply, in relation to any matters specified in the request, the insolvency law which is applicable by either court in relation to comparable matters falling within its jurisdiction.

In exercising its discretion under this subsection, a court shall have regard in particular to the rules of private international law.

(6) Where a person who is a trustee or assignee under the insolvency law of any part of the United Kingdom claims property situated in any other part of the United Kingdom (whether by virtue of an order under subsection (3) or otherwise), the submission of that claim to the court exercising jurisdiction in relation to insolvency law in that other part shall be treated in the same manner as a request made by a court for the purpose of subsection (4).

(7) Section 38 of the Criminal Law Act 1977 (execution of warrant of arrest throughout the United Kingdom) applies to a warrant which, in exercise of any jurisdiction in relation to insolvency law, is issued in any part of the United Kingdom for the arrest of a person as it applies to a warrant issued in that part of the United Kingdom for the arrest of a person charged with an offence.

(8) Without prejudice to any power to make rules of court, any power to make provision by subordinate legislation for the purpose of giving effect in relation to companies or individuals to the insolvency law of any part of the United Kingdom includes power to make provision for the purpose of giving effect in that part to any provision made by or under the preceding provisions of this section.

(9) An order under subsection (3) shall be made by statutory instrument subject to annulment in pursuance of a resolution of either House of Parliament.

(10) In this section "insolvency law" means—

(a) in relation to England and Wales, provision [extending to England and Wales and] made by or under this Act or sections [1A,] 6 to 10, [12 to 15], 19(c) and 20 (with Schedule 1) of the Company Directors Disqualification Act 1986 [and sections 1 to 17 of that Act as they apply for the purposes of those provisions of that Act];

(b) in relation to Scotland, provision extending to Scotland and made by or under this Act, sections [1A,] 6 to 10, [12 to 15], 19(c) and 20 (with Schedule 1) of the Company Directors Disqualification Act 1986 [and sections 1 to 17 of that Act as they apply for the purposes of those provisions of that Act], Part XVIII of the Companies Act or the Bankruptcy (Scotland) Act 1985;

(c) in relation to Northern Ireland, provision made by or under [the Insolvency (Northern Ireland) Order 1989] [*or Part II of the Companies (Northern Ireland) Order 1989*] [or the Company Directors Disqualification (Northern Ireland) Order 2002];

(d) in relation to any relevant country or territory, so much of the law of that country or territory as corresponds to provisions falling within any of the foregoing paragraphs;

and references in this subsection to any enactment include, in relation to any time before the coming into force of that enactment the corresponding enactment in force at that time.

(11) In this section "relevant country or territory" means—

(a) any of the Channel Islands or the Isle of Man, or

(b) any country or territory designated for the purposes of this section by the Secretary of State by order made by statutory instrument.

[(12) In the application of this section to Northern Ireland—

(a) for any reference to the Secretary of State there is substituted a reference to the Department of Economic Development in Northern Ireland;

(b) in subsection (3) for the words "another part of the United Kingdom" and the words "that other part" there are substituted the words "Northern Ireland";

(c) for subsection (9) there is substituted the following subsection—

"(9) An order made under subsection (3) by the Department of Economic Development in Northern Ireland shall be a statutory rule for the purposes of the Statutory Rules (Northern Ireland) Order 1979 and shall be subject to negative resolution within the meaning of section 41(6) of the Interpretation Act (Northern Ireland) 1954.".]

[(13) Section 129 of the Banking Act 2009 provides for provisions of that Act about bank insolvency to be "insolvency law" for the purposes of this section.]

[(14) Section 165 of the Banking Act 2009 provides for provisions of that Act about bank administration to be "insolvency law" for the purposes of this section.]

[1244]

NOTES

Sub-s (10): words in square brackets in paras (a), (b) inserted or substituted by the Insolvency Act 2000, s 8, Sch 4, Pt II, para 16(1), (3); words in first pair of square brackets in para (c) substituted SI 1989/2405 (NI 19), art 381(2), Sch 9, Pt II, para 41(a); words in second pair of square brackets in para (c) added by SI 1989/2404, arts 25(2), 36, Sch 4, Pt I, para 1, and substituted by subsequent words in square brackets by SI 2002/3150 (NI 4), art 26(2), Sch 3, para 2, as from a day to be appointed.

Sub-s (12): added by SI 1989/2405, art 381(2), Sch 9, Pt II, para 41(b).

Sub-s (13): inserted by the Banking Act 2009, s 129.

Sub-s (14): inserted by the Banking Act 2009, s 165.

Orders: the Co-operation of Insolvency Courts (Designation of Relevant Countries and Territories) Order 1986, SI 1986/2123; the Co-operation of Insolvency Courts (Designation of Relevant Countries) Order 1996, SI 1996/253; the Co-operation of Insolvency Courts (Designation of Relevant Country) Order 1998, SI 1998/2766.

426A–436A (*Ss 426A–434, ss 435–436A (Pt XVIII) outside the scope of this work.*)

PART XIX
FINAL PROVISIONS

437–443 (*Outside the scope of this work.*)

444 Citation

This Act may be cited as the Insolvency Act 1986.

[1245]

(*Sch A1 outside the scope of this work.*)

[SCHEDULE B1
ADMINISTRATION

Section 8

1–13. …

APPOINTMENT OF ADMINISTRATOR BY HOLDER OF FLOATING CHARGE

Power to appoint

14.—(1) The holder of a qualifying floating charge in respect of a company's property may appoint an administrator of the company.

(2) For the purposes of sub-paragraph (1) a floating charge qualifies if created by an instrument which—

(a) states that this paragraph applies to the floating charge,

(b) purports to empower the holder of the floating charge to appoint an administrator of the company,

(c) purports to empower the holder of the floating charge to make an appointment which would be the appointment of an administrative receiver within the meaning given by section 29(2), or

(d) purports to empower the holder of a floating charge in Scotland to appoint a receiver who on appointment would be an administrative receiver.

(3) For the purposes of sub-paragraph (1) a person is the holder of a qualifying floating charge in respect of a company's property if he holds one or more debentures of the company secured—

(a) by a qualifying floating charge which relates to the whole or substantially the whole of the company's property,

(b) by a number of qualifying floating charges which together relate to the whole or substantially the whole of the company's property, or

(c) by charges and other forms of security which together relate to the whole or substantially the whole of the company's property and at least one of which is a qualifying floating charge.

Restrictions on power to appoint

15.—(1) A person may not appoint an administrator under paragraph 14 unless—

(a) he has given at least two business days' written notice to the holder of any prior floating charge which satisfies paragraph 14(2), or

(b) the holder of any prior floating charge which satisfies paragraph 14(2) has consented in writing to the making of the appointment.

(2) One floating charge is prior to another for the purposes of this paragraph if—

(a) it was created first, or

(b) it is to be treated as having priority in accordance with an agreement to which the holder of each floating charge was party.

(3) Sub-paragraph (2) shall have effect in relation to Scotland as if the following were substituted for paragraph (a)—

"(a) it has priority of ranking in accordance with section 464(4)(b) of the Companies Act 1985 (c 6),".

16. An administrator may not be appointed under paragraph 14 while a floating charge on which the appointment relies is not enforceable.

17. An administrator of a company may not be appointed under paragraph 14 if—

(a) a provisional liquidator of the company has been appointed under section 135, or

(b) an administrative receiver of the company is in office.

Notice of appointment

18.—(1) A person who appoints an administrator of a company under paragraph 14 shall file with the court—

(a) a notice of appointment, and

(b) such other documents as may be prescribed.

(2) The notice of appointment must include a statutory declaration by or on behalf of the person who makes the appointment—

(a) that the person is the holder of a qualifying floating charge in respect of the company's property,

(b) that each floating charge relied on in making the appointment is (or was) enforceable on the date of the appointment, and

(c) that the appointment is in accordance with this Schedule.

(3) The notice of appointment must identify the administrator and must be accompanied by a statement by the administrator—

(a) that he consents to the appointment,

(b) that in his opinion the purpose of administration is reasonably likely to be achieved, and

(c) giving such other information and opinions as may be prescribed.

(4) For the purpose of a statement under sub-paragraph (3) an administrator may rely on information supplied by directors of the company (unless he has reason to doubt its accuracy).

(5) The notice of appointment and any document accompanying it must be in the prescribed form.

(6) A statutory declaration under sub-paragraph (2) must be made during the prescribed period.

(7) A person commits an offence if in a statutory declaration under sub-paragraph (2) he makes a statement—

(a) which is false, and

(b) which he does not reasonably believe to be true.

Commencement of appointment

19. The appointment of an administrator under paragraph 14 takes effect when the requirements of paragraph 18 are satisfied.

20. A person who appoints an administrator under paragraph 14—

(a) shall notify the administrator and such other persons as may be prescribed as soon as is reasonably practicable after the requirements of paragraph 18 are satisfied, and

(b) commits an offence if he fails without reasonable excuse to comply with paragraph (a).

Invalid appointment: indemnity

21.—(1) This paragraph applies where—

(a) a person purports to appoint an administrator under paragraph 14, and

(b) the appointment is discovered to be invalid.

(2) The court may order the person who purported to make the appointment to indemnify the person appointed against liability which arises solely by reason of the appointment's invalidity.

22–116. …]

[1246]

NOTES

Inserted by the Enterprise Act 2002, s 248(2), Sch 16, subject to transitional provisions and savings in s 249 of the 2002 Act, and SI 2003/2093, art 3.

Paras 1–13, 22–116: outside the scope of this work.

SCHEDULE 1
POWERS OF ADMINISTRATOR OR ADMINISTRATIVE RECEIVER

Sections 14, 42

1. Power to take possession of, collect and get in the property of the company and, for that purpose, to take such proceedings as may seem to him expedient.

2. Power to sell or otherwise dispose of the property of the company by public auction or private contract or, in Scotland, to sell, … hire out or otherwise dispose of the property of the company by public roup or private bargain.

3. Power to raise or borrow money and grant security therefor over the property of the company.

4. Power to appoint a solicitor or accountant or other professionally qualified person to assist him in the performance of his functions.

5. Power to bring or defend any action or other legal proceedings in the name and on behalf of the company.

6. Power to refer to arbitration any question affecting the company.

7. Power to effect and maintain insurances in respect of the business and property of the company.

8. Power to use the company's seal.

9. Power to do all acts and to execute in the name and on behalf of the company any deed, receipt or other document.

10. Power to draw, accept, make and endorse any bill of exchange or promissory note in the name and on behalf of the company.

11. Power to appoint any agent to do any business which he is unable to do himself or which can more conveniently be done by an agent and power to employ and dismiss employees.

12. Power to do all such things (including the carrying out of works) as may be necessary for the realisation of the property of the company.

13. Power to make any payment which is necessary or incidental to the performance of his functions.

14. Power to carry on the business of the company.

15. Power to establish subsidiaries of the company.

16. Power to transfer to subsidiaries of the company the whole or any part of the business and property of the company.

17. Power to grant or accept a surrender of a lease or tenancy of any of the property of the company, and to take a lease or tenancy of any property required or convenient for the business of the company.

18. Power to make any arrangement or compromise on behalf of the company.

19. Power to call up any uncalled capital of the company.

20. Power to rank and claim in the bankruptcy, insolvency, sequestration or liquidation of any person indebted to the company and to receive dividends, and to accede to trust deeds for the creditors of any such person.

21. Power to present or defend a petition for the winding up of the company.

22. Power to change the situation of the company's registered office.

23. Power to do all other things incidental to the exercise of the foregoing powers.

[1247]

NOTES

Para 2: word omitted repealed by the Abolition of Feudal Tenure etc (Scotland) Act 2000, s 76(2), Sch 13, Pt I.

Application: in relation to the application of this section, with modifications, in respect of bank insolvency, see the Banking Act 2009, s 103(3), (4), Table.

(Schs 2–14 outside the scope of this work.)

RECOGNITION OF TRUSTS ACT 1987

(1987 c 14)

An Act to enable the United Kingdom to ratify the Convention on the law applicable to trusts and on their recognition which was signed on behalf of the United Kingdom on 10th January 1986

[9 April 1987]

1 Applicable law and recognition of trusts

(1) The provisions of the Convention set out in the Schedule to this Act shall have the force of law in the United Kingdom.

(2) Those provisions shall, so far as applicable, have effect not only in relation to the trusts described in Articles 2 and 3 of the Convention but also in relation to any other trusts of property arising under the law of any part of the United Kingdom or by virtue of a judicial decision whether in the United Kingdom or elsewhere.

(3) In accordance with Articles 15 and 16 such provisions of the law as are there mentioned shall, to the extent there specified, apply to the exclusion of the other provisions of the Convention.

(4) In Article 17 the reference to a State includes a reference to any country or territory (whether or not a party to the Convention and whether or not forming part of the United Kingdom) which has its own system of law.

(5) Article 22 shall not be construed as affecting the law to be applied in relation to anything done or omitted before the coming into force of this Act.

[1248]

2 Extent

(1) This Act extends to Northern Ireland.

(2) Her Majesty may by Order in Council direct that this Act shall also form part of the law of the Isle of Man, any of the Channel Islands or any colony.

(3) An Order in Council under subsection (2) above may modify this Act in its application to any of the territories there mentioned and may contain such supplementary provisions as Her Majesty considers appropriate.

(4) An Order in Council under subsection (2) above shall be subject to annulment in pursuance of a resolution of either House of Parliament.

[1249]

NOTES

Order: the Recognition of Trusts Act 1987 (Overseas Territories) Order 1989, SI 1989/673.

3 Short title, commencement and application to the Crown

(1) This Act may be cited as the Recognition of Trusts Act 1987.

(2) This Act shall come into force on such date as the Lord Chancellor and the Lord Advocate may appoint by an order made by statutory instrument.

(3) This Act binds the Crown.

[1250]

NOTES

Order: the Recognition of Trusts Act 1987 (Commencement) Order 1987, SI 1987/1177.

SCHEDULE

CONVENTION ON THE LAW APPLICABLE TO TRUSTS AND ON THEIR RECOGNITION

Section 1

CHAPTER I
SCOPE

Article 1

This Convention specifies the law applicable to trusts and governs their recognition.

Article 2

For the purposes of this Convention, the term "trust" refers to the legal relationship created— inter vivos or on death— by a person, the settlor, when assets have been placed under the control of a trustee for the benefit of a beneficiary or for a specified purpose.

A trust has the following characteristics—

(a) the assets constitute a separate fund and are not a part of the trustee's own estate;
(b) title to the trust assets stands in the name of the trustee or in the name of another person on behalf of the trustee;
(c) the trustee has the power and the duty, in respect of which he is accountable, to manage, employ or dispose of the assets in accordance with the terms of the trust and the special duties imposed upon him by law.

The reservation by the settlor of certain rights and powers, and the fact that the trustee may himself have rights as a beneficiary, are not necessarily inconsistent with the existence of a trust.

Article 3

The Convention applies only to trusts created voluntarily and evidenced in writing.

Article 4

The Convention does not apply to preliminary issues relating to the validity of wills or of other acts by virtue of which assets are transferred to the trustee.

Article 5

The Convention does not apply to the extent that the law specified by Chapter II does not provide for trusts or the category of trusts involved.

[1251]

CHAPTER II
APPLICABLE LAW

Article 6

A trust shall be governed by the law chosen by the settlor. The choice must be express or be implied in the terms of the instrument creating or the writing evidencing the trust, interpreted, if necessary, in the light of the circumstances of the case.

Where the law chosen under the previous paragraph does not provide for trusts or the category of trust involved, the choice shall not be effective and the law specified in Article 7 shall apply.

Article 7

Where no applicable law has been chosen, a trust shall be governed by the law with which it is most closely connected.

In ascertaining the law with which a trust is most closely connected reference shall be made in particular to—

(a) the place of administration of the trust designated by the settlor;
(b) the situs of the assets of the trust;
(c) the place of residence or business of the trustee;
(d) the objects of the trust and the places where they are to be fulfilled.

Article 8

The law specified by Article 6 or 7 shall govern the validity of the trust, its construction, its effects and the administration of the trust. In particular that law shall govern—

(a) the appointment, resignation and removal of trustees, the capacity to act as a trustee, and the devolution of the office of trustee;
(b) the rights and duties of trustees among themselves;
(c) the right of trustees to delegate in whole or in part the discharge of their duties or the exercise of their powers;

(d) the power of trustees to administer or to dispose of trust assets, to create security interests in the trust assets, or to acquire new assets;
(e) the powers of investment of trustees;
(f) restrictions upon the duration of the trust, and upon the power to accumulate the income of the trust;
(g) the relationships between the trustees and the beneficiaries including the personal liability of the trustees to the beneficiaries;
(h) the variation or termination of the trust;
(i) the distribution of the trust assets;
(j) the duty of trustees to account for their administration.

Article 9

In applying this Chapter a severable aspect of the trust, particularly matters of administration, may be governed by a different law.

Article 10

The law applicable to the validity of the trust shall determine whether that law or the law governing a severable aspect of the trust may be replaced by another law.

[1252]

CHAPTER III
RECOGNITION

Article 11

A trust created in accordance with the law specified by the preceding Chapter shall be recognised as a trust.

Such recognition shall imply, as a minimum, that the trust property constitutes a separate fund, that the trustee may sue and be sued in his capacity as trustee, and that he may appear or act in this capacity before a notary or any person acting in an official capacity.

In so far as the law applicable to the trust requires or provides, such recognition shall imply in particular—

(a) that personal creditors of the trustee shall have no recourse against the trust assets;
(b) that the trust assets shall not form part of the trustee's estate upon his insolvency or bankruptcy;
(c) that the trust assets shall not form part of the matrimonial property of the trustee or his spouse nor part of the trustee's estate upon his death;
(d) that the trust assets may be recovered when the trustee, in breach of trust, has mingled trust assets with his own property or has alienated trust assets. However, the rights and obligations of any third party holder of the assets shall remain subject to the law determined by the choice of law rules of the forum.

Article 12

Where the trustee desires to register assets, movable or immovable, or documents of title to them, he shall be entitled, in so far as this is not prohibited by or inconsistent with the law of the State where registration is sought, to do so in his capacity as trustee or in such other way that the existence of the trust is disclosed.

Article 14

The Convention shall not prevent the application of rules of law more favourable to the recognition of trusts.

[1253]

CHAPTER IV
GENERAL CLAUSES

Article 15

The Convention does not prevent the application of provisions of the law designated by the conflicts rules of the forum, in so far as those provisions cannot be derogated from by voluntary act, relating in particular to the following matters—

(a) the protection of minors and incapable parties;
(b) the personal and proprietary effects of marriage;
(c) succession rights, testate and intestate, especially the indefeasible shares of spouses and relatives;
(d) the transfer of title property and security interests in property;
(e) the protection of creditors in matters of insolvency;

(f) the protection, in other respects, of third parties acting in good faith.

If recognition of a trust is prevented by application of the preceding paragraph, the court shall try to give effect to the objects of the trust by other means.

Article 16

The Convention does not prevent the application of those provisions of the law of the forum which must be applied even to international situations, irrespective of rules of conflict of laws.

Article 17

In the Convention the word "law" means the rules of law in force in a State other than its rules of conflict of laws.

Article 18

The provisions of the Convention may be disregarded when their application would be manifestly incompatible with public policy.

Article 22

The Convention applies to trusts regardless of the date on which they were created.

[1254]

REVERTER OF SITES ACT 1987

(1987 c 15)

An Act to amend the law with respect to the reverter of sites that have ceased to be used for particular purposes; and for connected purposes

[9 April 1987]

1 Right of reverter replaced by [trust]

(1) Where any relevant enactment provides for land to revert to the ownership of any person at any time, being a time when the land ceases, or has ceased for a specified period, to be used for particular purposes, that enactment shall have effect, and (subject to subsection (4) below) shall be deemed always to have had effect, as if it provided (instead of for the reverter) for the land to be vested after that time, on the trust arising under this section, in the persons in whom it was vested immediately before that time.

(2) Subject to the following provisions of this Act, the trust arising under this section in relation to any land is a trust [for the persons who (but for this Act) would from time to time be entitled to the ownership of the land by virtue of its reverter with a power, without consulting them,] to sell the land and to stand possessed of the net proceeds of sale (after payment of costs and expenses) and of the net rents and profits until sale (after payment of rates, taxes, costs of insurance, repairs and other outgoings) [in trust for those persons; but they shall not be entitled by reason of their interest to occupy the land.]

(3) Where—

(a) a trust in relation to any land has arisen or is treated as having arisen under this section at such a time as is mentioned in subsection (1) above; and

(b) immediately before that time the land was vested in any persons in their capacity as the minister and churchwardens of any parish,

those persons shall be treated as having become [trustees] under this section in that capacity and, accordingly, their interest in the land shall pass and, if the case so requires, be treated as having passed to their successors from time to time.

(4) This section shall not confer any right on any person as a beneficiary—

(a) in relation to any property in respect of which that person's claim was statute-barred before the commencement of this Act, or in relation to any property derived from any such property; or

(b) in relation to any rents or profits received, or breach of trust committed, before the commencement of this Act;

and anything validly done before the commencement of this Act in relation to any land which by virtue of this section is deemed to have been held at the time [in trust] shall, if done by the beneficiaries, be deemed, so far as necessary for preserving its validity, to have been done by the trustees.

(5) Where any property is held by any persons as trustees of a trust which has arisen under this section and, in consequence of subsection (4) above, there are no beneficiaries of that trust, the trustees shall have no power to act in relation to that property except—

(a) for the purposes for which they could have acted in relation to that property if this Act had not been passed; or

(b) for the purpose of securing the establishment of a scheme under section 2 below or the making of an order under [section 554 of the Education Act 1996] (special powers as to trusts for religious education).

(6) In this section—

"churchwardens" includes chapel wardens;

"minister" includes a rector, vicar or perpetual curate; and

"parish" includes a parish of the Church in Wales;

and the reference to a person's claim being statute-barred is a reference to the Limitation Act 1980 providing that no proceedings shall be brought by that person to recover the property in respect of which the claim subsists.

[1255]

NOTES

Section heading: word in square brackets substituted by the Trusts of Land and Appointment of Trustees Act 1996, s 5, Sch 2, para 6(5); for savings in relation to entailed interests created before the commencement of that Act, and savings consequential upon the abolition of the doctrine of conversion, see s 25(4), (5) thereof.

Sub-s (2): first words in square brackets inserted, and second words in square brackets substituted, by the Trusts of Land and Appointment of Trustees Act 1996, s 5, Sch 2, para 6(2), subject to savings as noted above.

Sub-ss (3), (4): words in square brackets substituted by the Trusts of Land and Appointment of Trustees Act 1996, s 5, Sch 2, para 6(3), (4), subject to savings as noted above.

Sub-s (5): words in square brackets substituted by the Education Act 1996, s 582(1), Sch 37, para 67.

2 [Charity Commission's] schemes

(1) Subject to the following provisions of this section and to sections 3 and 4 below, where any persons hold any property as trustees of a trust which has arisen under section 1 above, the [Charity Commission] may, on the application of the trustees, by order establish a scheme which—

(a) extinguishes the rights of beneficiaries under the trust; and

(b) requires the trustees to hold the property on trust for such charitable purposes as may be specified in the order.

(2) Subject to subsections (3) and (4) below, an order made under this section—

(a) may contain any such provision as may be contained in an order made by the High Court for establishing a scheme for the administration of a charity; and

(b) shall have the same effect as an order so made.

[(3) The charitable purposes specified in an order made under this section on an application with respect to any trust shall be such as the Charity Commission consider appropriate, having regard to the matters set out in subsection (3A).

(3A) The matters are—

(a) the desirability of securing that the property is held for charitable purposes ("the new purposes") which are close to the purposes, whether charitable or not, for which the trustees held the relevant land before the cesser of use in consequence of which the trust arose ("the former purposes); and

(b) the need for the new purposes to be capable of having a significant social or economic effect.

(3B) In determining the character of the former purposes, the Commission may, if they think it appropriate to do so, give greater weight to the persons or locality benefited by those purposes than to the nature of the benefit.]

(4) An order made under this section on an application with respect to any trust shall be so framed as to secure that if a person who—

(a) but for the making of the order would have been a beneficiary under the trust; and

(b) has not consented to the establishment of a scheme under this section,

notifies a claim to the trustees within the period of five years after the date of the making of the order, that person shall be paid an amount equal to the value of his rights at the time of their extinguishment.

(5) The [Charity Commission] shall not make any order under this section establishing a scheme unless—

(a) the requirements of section 3 below with respect to the making of the application for the order are satisfied or, by virtue of subsection (4) of that section, do not apply;

(b) one of the conditions specified in subsection (6) below is fulfilled;

(c) public notice of the [Commission's] proposals has been given inviting representations to be made to [it] within a period specified in the notice, being a period ending not less than one month after the date of the giving of the notice; and

(d) that period has ended and the [Commission has] taken into consideration any representations which have been made within that period and not withdrawn.

(6) The conditions mentioned in subsection (5)(b) above are—

(a) that there is no claim by any person to be a beneficiary in respect of rights proposed to be extinguished—

(i) which is outstanding; or

(ii) which has at any time been accepted as valid by the trustees or by persons whose acceptance binds the trustees; or

(iii) which has been upheld in proceedings that have been concluded;

(b) that consent to the establishment of a scheme under this section has been given by every person whose claim to be a beneficiary in respect of those rights is outstanding or has been so accepted or upheld.

(7) The [Charity Commission] shall refuse to consider an application under this section unless it is accompanied by a statutory declaration by the applicants—

(a) that the requirements of section 3 below are satisfied with respect to the making of the application or, if the declaration so declares, do not apply; and

(b) that a condition specified in subsection (6) above and identified in the declaration is fulfilled;

and the declaration shall be conclusive for the purposes of this section of the matters declared therein.

(8) A notice given for the purposes of subsection (5)(c) above shall contain such particulars of the [Commission's] proposals, or such directions for obtaining information about them, and shall be given in such manner, as [it thinks] sufficient and appropriate; and a further such notice shall not be required where the [Commission decides], before proceeding with any proposals of which notice has been so given, to modify them.

[1256]

NOTES

Section heading: words in square brackets substituted by the Charities Act 2006, s 75(1), Sch 8, paras 81, 82(1), (7).

Sub-ss (1), (5), (7), (8): words in square brackets substituted by the Charities Act 2006, s 75(1), Sch 8, paras 81, 82(1), (2), (4)–(6).

Sub-ss (3), (3A), (3B): substituted for original sub-s (3) by the Charities Act 2006, s 75(1), Sch 8, paras 81, 82(1), (3).

3 Applications for schemes

(1) Where an application is made under section 2 above by the trustees of any trust that has arisen under section 1 above, the requirements of this section are satisfied with respect to the making of that application if, before the application is made—

(a) notices under subsection (2) below have been published in two national newspapers and in a local newspaper circulating in the locality where the relevant land is situated;

(b) each of those notices specified a period for the notification to the trustees of claims by beneficiaries, being a period ending not less than three months after the date of publication of the last of those notices to be published;

(c) that period has ended;

(d) for a period of not less than twenty-one days during the first month of that period, a copy of one of those notices was affixed to some object on the relevant land in such a position and manner as, so far as practicable, to make the notice easy for members of the public to see and read without going on to the land; and

(e) the trustees have considered what other steps could be taken to trace the persons who are or may be beneficiaries and to inform those persons of the application to be made under section 2 above and have taken such of the steps considered by them as it was reasonably practicable for them to take.

(2) A notice under this subsection shall—

(a) set out the circumstances that have resulted in a trust having arisen under section 1 above;

(b) state that an application is to be made for the establishment of a scheme with respect to the property subject to the trust; and

(c) contain a warning to every beneficiary that, if he wishes to oppose the extinguishment of his rights, he should notify his claim to the trustees in the manner, and within the period, specified in the notice.

(3) Where at the time when the trustees publish a notice for the purposes of subsection (2) above—

(a) the relevant land is not under their control; and

(b) it is not reasonably practicable for them to arrange for a copy of the notice to be affixed as required by paragraph (d) of subsection (1) above to some object on the land,

that paragraph shall be disregarded for the purposes of this section.

(4) The requirements of this section shall not apply in the case of an application made in respect of any trust if—

(a) the time when that trust is treated as having arisen was before the commencement of this Act; and

(b) more than twelve years have elapsed since that time.

[1257]

4 Provisions supplemental to ss 2 and 3

(1) Where an order is made under section 2 above—

(a) public notice of the order shall be given in such manner as the [Charity Commission thinks] sufficient and appropriate; and

(b) a copy of the order shall, for not less than one month after the date of the giving of the notice, be available for public inspection at all reasonable times at the [Commission's] office and at some convenient place in the locality where the relevant land is situated;

and a notice given for the purposes of paragraph (a) above shall contain such particulars of the order, or such directions for obtaining information about it, as [the Commission thinks] sufficient and appropriate.

[(2) Schedule 1C to the Charities Act 1993 shall apply in relation to an order made under section 2 above as it applies in relation to an order made under section 16(1) of that Act, except that the persons who may bring an appeal against an order made under section 2 above are—

(a) the Attorney General;

(b) the trustees of the trust established under the order;

(c) a beneficiary of, or the trustees of, the trust in respect of which the application for the order had been made;

(d) any person interested in the purposes for which the last-mentioned trustees or any of their predecessors held the relevant land before the cesser of use in consequence of which the trust arose under section 1 above;

(e) any two or more inhabitants of the locality where that land is situated;

(f) any other person who is or may be affected by the order.]

(4) [[Sections 89 and 91] of the Charities Act 1993] (supplemental provisions with respect to orders …) shall apply in relation to … orders under section 2 above as they apply in relation to … orders under that Act.

(5) Trustees of a trust which has arisen under section 1 above may pay or apply capital money for any of the purposes of section 2 or 3 above or of this section.

[1258]

NOTES

Sub-s (1): words in square brackets substituted by the Charities Act 2006, s 75(1), Sch 8, paras 81, 83(1), (2).

Sub-s (2): substituted for sub-s (2), (3) by the Charities Act 2006, s 75(1), Sch 8, paras 81, 83(1), (3), subject to transitional provisions and savings in s 75(3) of, Sch 10, para 18 to, that Act.

Sub-s (4): words in first (outer) pair of square brackets substituted by the Charities Act 1993, s 98(1), Sch 6, para 24; words in second (inner) pair of square brackets substituted and words omitted repealed by the Charities Act 2006, s 75(1), (2), Sch 8, paras 81, 83(1), (4), Sch 9, subject to transitional provisions and savings in s 75(3) of, Sch 10, para 18 to, that Act.

5 Orders under the Education Act 1973

(1) An order made under [section 554 of the Education Act 1996] (special powers as to certain trusts for religious education) with respect to so much of any endowment as consists of—

(a) land in relation to which a trust under section 1 above has arisen or will arise after the land ceased or ceases to be used for particular purposes; or

(b) any other property subject to a trust under that section,

may extinguish any rights to which a person is or may become entitled as a beneficiary under the trust.

(2) The Secretary of State shall not by an order under [section 554 of the 1996 Act] extinguish any such rights unless he is satisfied that all reasonably practicable steps to trace the persons who are or may become entitled to any of those rights have been taken and either—

(a) that there is no claim by any person to be a person who is or may become so entitled—

(i) which is outstanding; or

(ii) which has at any time been accepted as valid by the trustees or by persons whose acceptance binds or will bind the trustees; or

(iii) which has been upheld in proceedings that have been concluded; or

(b) that consent to the making of an order under [section 554 of the 1996 Act] has been given by every person whose claim to be such a person is outstanding or has been so accepted or upheld.

(3) Where applications for the extinguishment of the rights of any beneficiaries are made with respect to the same trust property both to the Secretary of State under [section 554 of the 1996 Act] and to the [Charity Commission] under section 2 above, [the Commission] shall not consider, or further consider, the application made to [it], unless the Secretary of State either—

(a) consents to the application made to the [Charity Commission] being considered before the application made to him; or

(b) disposes of the application made to him without extinguishing the rights of one or more of the beneficiaries.

(4) Trustees of a trust which has arisen under section 1 above may pay or apply capital money for the purposes of any provision of this section or [section 554 of the 1996 Act].

[1259]

NOTES

Sub-ss (1), (2), (4): words in square brackets substituted by the Education Act 1996, s 582(1), Sch 37, para 67.

Sub-s (3): words in first pair of square brackets substituted by the Education Act 1996, s 582(1), Sch 37, para 67; other words in square brackets substituted by the Charities Act 2006, s 75(1), Sch 8, paras 81, 84.

6 Classification of status etc of land before reverter

(1) Nothing in this Act shall require any land which is or has been the subject of any grant, conveyance or other assurance under any relevant enactment to be treated as or as having been settled land.

(2) It is hereby declared—

(a) that the power conferred by section 14 of the School Sites Act 1841 (power of sale etc.) is exercisable at any time in relation to land in relation to which (but for the exercise of the power) a trust might subsequently arise under section 1 above; and

(b) that the exercise of that power in respect of any land prevents any trust from arising under section 1 above in relation to that land or any land representing the proceeds of sale of that land.

[1260]

7 Construction

(1) In this Act—

"relevant enactment" means any enactment contained in—

(a) the School Sites Acts;

(b) the Literary and Scientific Institutions Act 1854; or

(c) the Places of Worship Sites Act 1873;

"relevant land", in relation to a trust which has arisen under section 1 above, means the land which but for this Act would have reverted to the persons who are the first beneficiaries under the trust.

(2) In this Act references to land include references to—

(a) any part of any land which has been the subject of a grant, conveyance or other assurance under any relevant enactment; and

(b) any land an interest in which (including any future or contingent interest arising under any such enactment) belongs to the Crown, the Duchy of Lancaster or the Duchy of Cornwall.

(3) For the purposes of this Act a claim by any person to be a beneficiary under a trust is outstanding if—

(a) it has been notified to the trustees;

(b) it has not been withdrawn; and

(c) proceedings for determining whether it should be upheld have not been commenced or (if commenced) have not been concluded.

(4) For the purposes of this Act proceedings shall not, in relation to any person's claim, be treated as concluded where the time for appealing is unexpired or an appeal is pending unless that person has indicated his intention not to appeal or, as the case may be, not to continue with the appeal.

[1261]

8 Consequential amendments, repeals and saving

(1), (2) …

(3) The enactments mentioned in the Schedule to this Act are hereby repealed to the extent specified in the third column of that Schedule.

(4) The repeals contained in the Schedule to this Act shall not affect the operation at any time after the commencement of this Act of so much of any order made before the commencement of this Act under section 2 of the Education Act 1973 as has excluded the operation of the third proviso to section 2 of the School Sites Act 1841.

[1262]

NOTES

Sub-s (1): repealed by the Education Act 1996, s 582(2), Sch 38, Pt I.
Sub-s (2): amends the Law of Property Act 1925, s 3(3) at **[267]**.

9 Short title, commencement and extent

(1) This Act may be cited as the Reverter of Sites Act 1987.

(2) This Act shall come into force on such day as the Lord Chancellor may by order made by statutory instrument appoint.

(3) This Act shall extend to England and Wales only.

[1263]

NOTES

Order: the Reverter of Sites Act 1987 (Commencement) Order 1987, SI 1987/1260.

(*Schedule contains repeals only.*)

LANDLORD AND TENANT ACT 1987

(1987 c 31)

An Act to confer on tenants of flats rights with respect to the acquisition by them of their landlord's reversion; to make provision for the appointment of a manager at the instance of such tenants and for the variation of long leases held by such tenants; to make further provision with respect to service charges payable by tenants of flats and other dwellings; to make other provision with respect to such tenants; to make further provision with respect to the permissible purposes and objects of registered housing associations as regards the management of leasehold property; and for connected purposes

[15 May 1987]

NOTES

Transfer of functions: as to the functions of Ministers of the Crown under this Act, so far as exercisable in relation to Wales, being transferred to the National Assembly for Wales, see the National Assembly for Wales (Transfer of Functions) Order 1999, SI 1999/672, art 2, Sch 1.

PART I
TENANTS' RIGHTS OF FIRST REFUSAL

Preliminary

1 Qualifying tenants to have rights of first refusal on disposals by landlord

(1) A landlord shall not make a relevant disposal affecting any premises to which at the time of the disposal this Part applies unless—

(a) he has in accordance with section 5 previously served a notice under that section with respect to the disposal on the qualifying tenants of the flats contained in those premises (being a notice by virtue of which rights of first refusal are conferred on those tenants); and

(b) the disposal is made in accordance with the requirements of sections 6 to 10.

(2) Subject to subsections (3) and (4), this Part applies to premises if—

(a) they consist of the whole or part of a building; and

(b) they contain two or more flats held by qualifying tenants; and

(c) the number of flats held by such tenants exceeds 50 per cent of the total number of flats contained in the premises.

(3) This Part does not apply to premises falling within subsection (2) if—

(a) any part or parts of the premises is or are occupied or intended to be occupied otherwise than for residential purposes; and

(b) the internal floor area of that part or those parts (taken together) exceeds 50 per cent of the internal floor area of the premises (taken as a whole);

and for the purposes of this subsection the internal floor area of any common parts shall be disregarded.

(4) This Part also does not apply to any such premises at a time when the interest of the landlord in the premises is held by an exempt landlord or a resident landlord.

(5) The Secretary of State may by order substitute for the percentage for the time being specified in subsection (3)(b) such other percentage as is specified in the order.

[1264]

2 Landlords for the purposes of Part I

(1) Subject to subsection (2) [and section 4(1A)], a person is for the purposes of this Part the landlord in relation to any premises consisting of the whole or part of a building if he is—

(a) the immediate landlord of the qualifying tenants of the flats contained in those premises, or

(b) where any of those tenants is a statutory tenant, the person who, apart from the statutory tenancy, would be entitled to possession of the flat in question.

(2) Where the person who is, in accordance with subsection (1), the landlord in relation to any such premises for the purposes of this Part ("the immediate landlord") is himself a tenant of those premises under a tenancy which is either—

(a) a tenancy for a term of less than seven years, or

(b) a tenancy for a longer term but terminable within the first seven years at the option of the person who is the landlord under that tenancy ("the superior landlord"),

the superior landlord shall also be regarded as the landlord in relation to those premises for the purposes of this Part and, if the superior landlord is himself a tenant of those premises under a tenancy falling within paragraph (a) or (b) above, the person who is the landlord under that tenancy shall also be so regarded (and so on).

[1265]

NOTES

Sub-s (1): words in square brackets inserted by the Housing Act 1988, s 119, Sch 13, para 1, except in relation to a disposal made in pursuance of a contract entered into before 15 January 1989 or where the offer notice was served, or treated as served, under s 5 of this Act, before that date.

3 Qualifying tenants

(1) Subject to the following provisions of this section, a person is for the purposes of this Part a qualifying tenant of a flat if he is the tenant of the flat under a tenancy other than—

(a) a protected shorthold tenancy as defined in section 52 of the Housing Act 1980;

(b) a tenancy to which Part II of the Landlord and Tenant Act 1954 (business tenancies) applies; …

(c) a tenancy terminable on the cessation of his employment [or

(d) an assured tenancy or assured agricultural occupancy within the meaning of Part I of the Housing Act 1988].

(2) A person is not to be regarded as being a qualifying tenant of any flat contained in any particular premises consisting of the whole or part of a building if [by virtue of one or more tenancies none of which falls within paragraphs (a) to (d) of subsection (1), he is the tenant not only of the flat in question but also of at least two other flats contained in those premises].

(3) For the purposes of subsection [(2)] any tenant of a flat contained in the premises in question who is a body corporate shall be treated as the tenant of any other flat so contained and let to an associated company.

(4) A tenant of a flat whose landlord is a qualifying tenant of that flat is not to be regarded as being a qualifying tenant of that flat.

[1266]

NOTES

Sub-s (1): words omitted repealed by the Housing Act 1988, ss 119, 140(2), Sch 13, para 2(1), Sch 18, except in relation to a disposal made in pursuance of a contract entered into before 15 January 1989 or where the offer notice was served, or treated as served, under s 5 of this Act, before that date; words in square brackets added by the Housing Act 1988, s 119, Sch 13, para 2(1).

Sub-s (2): words in square brackets substituted by the Housing Act 1988, s 119, Sch 13, para 2(2), subject to savings as noted above.

Sub-s (3): figure in square brackets substituted by the Housing Act 1988, s 119, Sch 13, para 2(2), subject to savings as noted above.

4 Relevant disposals

(1) In this Part references to a relevant disposal affecting any premises to which this Part applies are references to the disposal by the landlord of any estate or interest (whether legal or equitable) in any such premises, including the disposal of any such estate or interest in any common parts of any such premises but excluding—

(a) the grant of any tenancy under which the demised premises consist of a single flat (whether with or without any appurtenant premises); and

(b) any of the disposals falling within subsection (2).

[(1A) Where an estate or interest of the landlord has been mortgaged, the reference in subsection (1) above to the disposal of an estate or interest by the landlord includes a reference to its disposal by the mortgagee in exercise of a power of sale or leasing, whether or not the disposal is made in the name of the landlord; and, in relation to such a proposed disposal by the mortgagee, any reference in the following provisions of this Part to the landlord shall be construed as a reference to the mortgagee.]

(2) The disposals referred to in subsection (1)(b) are—

(a) a disposal of—

(i) any interest of a beneficiary in settled land within the meaning of the Settled Land Act 1925, [or]

(ii) …

(iii) any incorporeal hereditament;

[(aa) a disposal … by way of security for a loan]

(b) a disposal to a trustee in bankruptcy or to the liquidator of a company;

[(c) a disposal in pursuance of an order made under—

(i) *section 24* of the Matrimonial Causes Act 1973 (property adjustment orders in connection with matrimonial proceedings),

(ii) section 24A of the Matrimonial Causes Act 1973 (orders for the sale of property in connection with matrimonial proceedings) where the order includes provision requiring the property concerned to be offered for sale to a person or class of persons specified in the order,

(iii) section 2 of the Inheritance (Provision for Family and Dependants) Act 1975 (orders as to financial provision to be made from estate),

(iv) section 17(1) of the Matrimonial and Family Proceedings Act 1984 (property adjustment orders after overseas divorce, &c),

(v) section 17(2) of the Matrimonial and Family Proceedings Act 1984 (orders for the sale of property after overseas divorce, &c) where the order includes provision requiring the property concerned to be offered for sale to a person or class of persons specified in the order, …

(vi) paragraph 1 of Schedule 1 to the Children Act 1989 (orders for financial relief against parents);

[(vii) Part 2 of Schedule 5, or paragraph 9(2) or (3) of Schedule 7, to the Civil Partnership Act 2004 (property adjustment orders in connection with civil partnership proceedings or after overseas dissolution of a civil partnership, etc), or

(viii) Part 3 of Schedule 5, or paragraph 9(4) of Schedule 7, to the Civil Partnership Act 2004 (orders for the sale of property in connection with civil partnership proceedings or after overseas dissolution of a civil partnership, etc) where the order includes provision requiring the property concerned to be offered for sale to a person or class of persons specified in the order;]]

(d) a disposal in pursuance of a compulsory purchase order or in pursuance of an agreement entered into in circumstances where, but for the agreement, such an order would have been made or (as the case may be) carried into effect;

[(da) a disposal of any freehold or leasehold interest in pursuance of Chapter I of Part I of the Leasehold Reform, Housing and Urban Development Act 1993;]

(e) a disposal by way of gift to a member of the landlord's family or to a charity;

(f) a disposal by one charity to another of an estate or interest in land which prior to the disposal is functional land of the first-mentioned charity and which is intended to be functional land of the other charity once the disposal is made;

(g) a disposal consisting of the transfer of an estate or interest held on trust for any person where the disposal is made in connection with the appointment of a new trustee or in connection with the discharge of any trustee;

(h) a disposal consisting of a transfer by two or more persons who are members of the same family either—

(i) to fewer of their number, or

(ii) to a different combination of members of the family (but one that includes at least one of the transferors);

[(i) a disposal in pursuance of a contract, option or right of pre-emption binding on the landlord (except as provided by section 8D (application of sections 11 to 17 to disposal in pursuance of option or right of pre-emption));]

(j) a disposal consisting of the surrender of a tenancy in pursuance of any covenant, condition or agreement contained in it;

(k) a disposal to the Crown; and

[(l) a disposal by a body corporate to a company which has been an associated company of that body for at least two years.]

(3) In this Part "disposal" means a disposal whether by the creation or the transfer of an estate or interest and—

(a) includes the surrender of a tenancy and the grant of an option or right of pre-emption, but

(b) excludes a disposal under the terms of a will or under the law relating to intestacy;

and references in this Part to the transferee in connection with a disposal shall be construed accordingly.

(4) In this section "appurtenant premises", in relation to any flat, means any yard, garden, outhouse or appurtenance (not being a common part of the building containing the flat) which belongs to, or is usually enjoyed with, the flat.

(5) A person is a member of another's family for the purposes of this section if—

(a) that person is the spouse [or civil partner] of that other person, or the two of them live together as husband and wife [or as if they were civil partners], or

(b) that person is that other person's parent, grandparent, child, grandchild, brother, sister, uncle, aunt, nephew or niece.

(6) For the purposes of subsection (5)(b)—

(a) a relationship by marriage [or civil partnership] shall be treated as a relationship by blood,

(b) a relationship of the half-blood shall be treated as a relationship of the whole blood,

(c) the stepchild of a person shall be treated as his child, and

(d) the illegitimate child shall be treated as the legitimate child of his mother and reputed father.

[1267]

NOTES

Sub-s (1A): inserted by the Housing Act 1988, s 119, Sch 13, para 3(1), except in relation to a disposal made in pursuance of a contract entered into before 15 January 1989 or where the offer notice was served, or treated as served, under s 5 of this Act, before that date.

Sub-s (2): word in square brackets in para (a)(i) added, para (a)(ii) repealed and para (aa) inserted by the Housing Act 1988, ss 119, 140(2), Sch 13, para 3(2), Sch 18, subject to savings as noted above; words omitted from para (aa) repealed and paras (c), (i) substituted by the Housing Act 1996, ss 89(2), 92(1), 222, 227, Sch 6, Pt IV, para 1, Sch 18, Pt III, para 18, Sch 19, Pt III; for the words in italics in para (c)(i) there are substituted the words "section 23A, 24" by the Family Law Act 1996, s 66(1), Sch 8, Pt I, para 38, as from a day to be appointed, subject to savings in s 66(2) of, and Sch 9, para 5 to, that Act; word omitted from para (c)(v) repealed and para (c)(vii), (viii) inserted by the Civil Partnership Act 2004, ss 81, 261(4), Sch 8, para 40(1), (2), Sch 30; para (da) inserted by the Leasehold Reform, Housing and Urban Development Act 1993, s 187(1), Sch 21, para 26; para (l) substituted by the Housing Act 1996, s 90, except in relation to disposals made in pursuance of an obligation entered into before 1 October 1996.

Sub-ss (5), (6): words in square brackets inserted by the Civil Partnership Act 2004, s 81, Sch 8, para 40(1), (3), (4).

[4A Application of provisions to contracts

(1) The provisions of this Part apply to a contract to create or transfer an estate or interest in land, whether conditional or unconditional and whether or not enforceable by specific performance, as they apply in relation to a disposal consisting of the creation or transfer of such an estate or interest.

As they so apply—

(a) references to a disposal of any description shall be construed as references to a contract to make such a disposal;

(b) references to making a disposal of any description shall be construed as references to entering into a contract to make such a disposal; and

(c) references to the transferee under the disposal shall be construed as references to the other party to the contract and include a reference to any other person to whom an estate or interest is to be granted or transferred in pursuance of the contract.

(2) The provisions of this Part apply to an assignment of rights under such a contract as is mentioned in subsection (1) as they apply in relation to a disposal consisting of the transfer of an estate or interest in land.

As they so apply—

(a) references to a disposal of any description shall be construed as references to an assignment of rights under a contract to make such a disposal;
(b) references to making a disposal of any description shall be construed as references to making an assignment of rights under a contract to make such a disposal;
(c) references to the landlord shall be construed as references to the assignor; and
(d) references to the transferee under the disposal shall be construed as references to the assignee of such rights.

(3) The provisions of this Part apply to a contract to make such an assignment as is mentioned in subsection (2) as they apply (in accordance with subsection (1)) to a contract to create or transfer an estate or interest in land.

(4) Nothing in this section affects the operation of the provisions of this Part relating to options or rights of pre-emption.]

[1268]

NOTES

Inserted by the Housing Act 1996, s 89(1).

[Rights of first refusal

5 Landlord required to serve offer notice on tenants

(1) Where the landlord proposes to make a relevant disposal affecting premises to which this Part applies, he shall serve a notice under this section (an "offer notice") on the qualifying tenants of the flats contained in the premises (the "constituent flats").

(2) An offer notice must comply with the requirements of whichever is applicable of the following sections—

section 5A (requirements in case of contract to be completed by conveyance, &c),
section 5B (requirements in case of sale at auction),
section 5C (requirements in case of grant of option or right of pre-emption),
section 5D (requirements in case of conveyance not preceded by contract, &c);

and in the case of a disposal to which section 5E applies (disposal for non-monetary consideration) shall also comply with the requirements of that section.

(3) Where a landlord proposes to effect a transaction involving the disposal of an estate or interest in more than one building (whether or not involving the same estate or interest), he shall, for the purpose of complying with this section, sever the transaction so as to deal with each building separately.

(4) If, as a result of the offer notice being served on different tenants on different dates, the period specified in the notice as the period for accepting the offer would end on different dates, the notice shall have effect in relation to all the qualifying tenants on whom it is served as if it provided for that period to end with the latest of those dates.

(5) A landlord who has not served an offer notice on all of the qualifying tenants on whom it was required to be served shall nevertheless be treated as having complied with this section—
(a) if he has served an offer notice on not less than 90% of the qualifying tenants on whom such a notice was required to be served, or
(b) where the qualifying tenants on whom it was required to be served number less than ten, if he has served such a notice on all but one of them.]

[1269]

NOTES

Substituted, together with preceding cross-heading and ss 5A–5E, 6–8, 8A–8E, 9A, 9B, 10, for original ss 5–10, by the Housing Act 1996, s 92(1), Sch 6, Pt I.

Modified, where the RTM company has acquired the right to manage, by the Commonhold and Leasehold Reform Act 2002, s 102, Sch 7, para 7.

[5A Offer notice: requirements in case of contract to be completed by conveyance, &c

(1) The following requirements must be met in relation to an offer notice where the disposal consists of entering into a contract to create or transfer an estate or interest in land.

(2) The notice must contain particulars of the principal terms of the disposal proposed by the landlord, including in particular—
(a) the property, and the estate or interest in that property, to which the contract relates,
(b) the principal terms of the contract (including the deposit and consideration required).

(3) The notice must state that the notice constitutes an offer by the landlord to enter into a contract on those terms which may be accepted by the requisite majority of qualifying tenants of the constituent flats.

(4) The notice must specify a period within which that offer may be so accepted, being a period of not less than two months which is to begin with the date of service of the notice.

(5) The notice must specify a further period of not less than two months within which a person or persons may be nominated by the tenants under section 6.

(6) This section does not apply to the grant of an option or right of pre-emption (see section 5C).]

[1270]

NOTES

Substituted as noted to s 5 at **[1269]**.

[5B Offer notice: requirements in case of sale by auction

(1) The following requirements must be met in relation to an offer notice where the landlord proposes to make the disposal by means of a sale at a public auction held in England and Wales.

(2) The notice must contain particulars of the principal terms of the disposal proposed by the landlord, including in particular the property to which it relates and the estate or interest in that property proposed to be disposed of.

(3) The notice must state that the disposal is proposed to be made by means of a sale at a public auction.

(4) The notice must state that the notice constitutes an offer by the landlord, which may be accepted by the requisite majority of qualifying tenants of the constituent flats, for the contract (if any) entered into by the landlord at the auction to have effect as if a person or persons nominated by them, and not the purchaser, had entered into it.

(5) The notice must specify a period within which that offer may be so accepted, being a period of not less than two months beginning with the date of service of the notice.

(6) The notice must specify a further period of not less than 28 days within which a person or persons may be nominated by the tenants under section 6.

(7) The notice must be served not less than four months or more than six months before the date of the auction; and—

- (a) the period specified in the notice as the period within which the offer may be accepted must end not less than two months before the date of the auction, and
- (b) the period specified in the notice as the period within which a person may be nominated under section 6 must end not less than 28 days before the date of the auction.

(8) Unless the time and place of the auction and the name of the auctioneers are stated in the notice, the landlord shall, not less than 28 days before the date of the auction, serve on the requisite majority of qualifying tenants of the constituent flats a further notice stating those particulars.]

[1271]

NOTES

Substituted as noted to s 5 at **[1269]**.

[5C Offer notice: requirements in case of grant or option or right of pre-emption

(1) The following requirements must be met in relation to an offer notice where the disposal consists of the grant of an option or right of pre-emption.

(2) The notice must contain particulars of the principal terms of the disposal proposed by the landlord, including in particular—

- (a) the property, and the estate or interest in that property, to which the option or right of pre-emption relates,
- (b) the consideration required by the landlord for granting the option or right of pre-emption, and
- (c) the principal terms on which the option or right of pre-emption would be exercisable, including the consideration payable on its exercise.

(3) The notice must state that the notice constitutes an offer by the landlord to grant an option or right of pre-emption on those terms which may be accepted by the requisite majority of qualifying tenants of the constituent flats.

(4) The notice must specify a period within which that offer may be so accepted, being a period of not less than two months which is to begin with the date of service of the notice.

(5) The notice must specify a further period of not less than two months within which a person or persons may be nominated by the tenants under section 6.]

[1272]

NOTES

Substituted as noted to s 5 at **[1269]**.

[5D Offer notice: requirements in case of conveyance not preceded by contract, &c

(1) The following requirements must be met in relation to an offer notice where the disposal is not made in pursuance of a contract, option or right of pre-emption binding on the landlord.

(2) The notice must contain particulars of the principal terms of the disposal proposed by the landlord, including in particular—

(a) the property to which it relates and the estate or interest in that property proposed to be disposed of, and

(b) the consideration required by the landlord for making the disposal.

(3) The notice must state that the notice constitutes an offer by the landlord to dispose of the property on those terms which may be accepted by the requisite majority of qualifying tenants of the constituent flats.

(4) The notice must specify a period within which that offer may be so accepted, being a period of not less than two months which is to begin with the date of service of the notice.

(5) The notice must specify a further period of not less than two months within which a person or persons may be nominated by the tenants under section 6.]

[1273]

NOTES

Substituted as noted to s 5 at **[1269]**.

[5E Offer notice: disposal for non-monetary consideration

(1) This section applies where, in any case to which section 5 applies, the consideration required by the landlord for making the disposal does not consist, or does not wholly consist, of money.

(2) The offer notice, in addition to complying with whichever is applicable of sections 5A to 5D, must state—

(a) that an election may be made under section 8C (explaining its effect), and

(b) that, accordingly, the notice also constitutes an offer by the landlord, which may be accepted by the requisite majority of qualifying tenants of the constituent flats, for a person or persons nominated by them to acquire the property in pursuance of sections 11 to 17.

(3) The notice must specify a period within which that offer may be so accepted, being a period of not less than two months which is to begin with the date of service of the notice.]

[1274]

NOTES

Substituted as noted to s 5 at **[1269]**.

[6 Acceptance of landlord's offer: general provisions

(1) Where a landlord has served an offer notice, he shall not during—

(a) the period specified in the notice as the period during which the offer may be accepted, or

(b) such longer period as may be agreed between him and the requisite majority of the qualifying tenants of the constituent flats,

dispose of the protected interest except to a person or persons nominated by the tenants under this section.

(2) Where an acceptance notice is duly served on him, he shall not during the protected period (see subsection (4) below) dispose of the protected interest except to a person duly nominated for the purposes of this section by the requisite majority of qualifying tenants of the constituent flats (a "nominated person").

(3) An "acceptance notice" means a notice served on the landlord by the requisite majority of qualifying tenants of the constituent flats informing him that the persons by whom it is served accept the offer contained in his notice.

An acceptance notice is "duly served" if it is served within—

(a) the period specified in the offer notice as the period within which the offer may be accepted, or

(b) such longer period as may be agreed between the landlord and the requisite majority of qualifying tenants of the constituent flats.

(4) The "protected period" is the period beginning with the date of service of the acceptance notice and ending with—

(a) the end of the period specified in the offer notice as the period for nominating a person under this section, or

(b) such later date as may be agreed between the landlord and the requisite majority of qualifying tenants of constituent flats.

(5) A person is "duly nominated" for the purposes of this section if he is nominated at the same time as the acceptance notice is served or at any time after that notice is served and before the end of—

(a) the period specified in the offer notice as the period for nomination, or

(b) such longer period as may be agreed between the landlord and the requisite majority of qualifying tenants of the constituent flats.

(6) A person nominated for the purposes of this section by the requisite majority of qualifying tenants of the constituent flats may be replaced by another person so nominated if, and only if, he has (for any reason) ceased to be able to act as a nominated person.

(7) Where two or more persons have been nominated and any of them ceases to act without being replaced, the remaining person or persons so nominated may continue to act.]

[1275]

NOTES

Substituted as noted to s 5 at **[1269]**.

[7 Failure to accept landlord's offer or to make nomination

(1) Where a landlord has served an offer notice on the qualifying tenants of the constituent flats and—

(a) no acceptance notice is duly served on the landlord, or

(b) no person is nominated for the purposes of section 6 during the protected period,

the landlord may, during the period of 12 months beginning with the end of that period, dispose of the protected interest to such person as he thinks fit, but subject to the following restrictions.

(2) Where the offer notice was one to which section 5B applied (sale by auction), the restrictions are—

(a) that the disposal is made by means of a sale at a public auction, and

(b) that the other terms correspond to those specified in the offer notice.

(3) In any other case the restrictions are—

(a) that the deposit and consideration required are not less than those specified in the offer notice, and

(b) that the other terms correspond to those specified in the offer notice.

(4) The entitlement of a landlord, by virtue of this section or any other corresponding provision of this Part, to dispose of the protected interest during a specified period of 12 months extends only to a disposal of that interest, and accordingly the requirements of section 1(1) must be satisfied with respect to any other disposal by him during that period of 12 months (unless the disposal is not a relevant disposal affecting any premises to which at the time of the disposal this Part applies).]

[1276]

NOTES

Substituted as noted to s 5 at **[1269]**.

[8 Landlord's obligations in case of acceptance and nomination

(1) This section applies where a landlord serves an offer notice on the qualifying tenants of the constituent flat and—

(a) an acceptance notice is duly served on him, and

(b) a person is duly nominated for the purposes of section 6,

by the requisite majority of qualifying tenants of the constituent flats.

(2) Subject to the following provisions of this Part, the landlord shall not dispose of the protected interest except to the nominated person.

(3) The landlord shall, within the period of one month beginning with the date of service of notice of nomination, either—

(a) serve notice on the nominated person indicating an intention no longer to proceed with the disposal of the protected interest, or

(b) be obliged to proceed in accordance with the following provisions of this Part.

(4) A notice under subsection (3)(a) is a notice of withdrawal for the purposes of section 9B(2) to (4) (consequences of notice of withdrawal by landlord).

(5) Nothing in this section shall be taken as prejudicing the application of the provisions of this Part to any further offer notice served by the landlord on the qualifying tenants of the constituent flats.]

[1277]

NOTES

Substituted as noted to s 5 at **[1269]**.

[8A Landlord's obligation: general provisions

(1) This section applies where the landlord is obliged to proceed and the offer notice was not one to which section 5B applied (sale by auction).

(2) The landlord shall, within the period of one month beginning with the date of service of the notice of nomination, send to the nominated person a form of contract for the acquisition of the protected interest on the terms specified in the landlord's offer notice.

(3) If he fails to do so, the following provisions of this Part apply as if he had given notice under section 9B (notice of withdrawal by landlord) at the end of that period.

(4) If the landlord complies with subsection (2), the nominated person shall, within the period of two months beginning with the date on which it is sent or such longer period beginning with that date as may be agreed between the landlord and that person, either—

(a) serve notice on the landlord indicating an intention no longer to proceed with the acquisition of the protected interest, or

(b) offer an exchange of contracts, that is to say, sign the contract and send it to the landlord, together with the requisite deposit.

In this subsection "the requisite deposit" means a deposit of an amount determined by or under the contract or an amount equal to 10 per cent of the consideration, whichever is the less.

(5) If the nominated person—

(a) serves notice in pursuance of paragraph (a) of subsection (4), or

(b) fails to offer an exchange of contracts within the period specified in that subsection,

the following provisions of this Part apply as if he had given notice under section 9A (withdrawal by nominated person) at the same time as that notice or, as the case may be, at the end of that period.

(6) If the nominated person offers an exchange of contracts within the period specified in subsection (4), but the landlord fails to complete the exchange within the period of seven days beginning with the day on which he received that person's contract, the following provisions of this Part apply as if the landlord had given notice under section 9B (withdrawal by landlord) at the end of that period.]

[1278]

NOTES

Substituted as noted to s 5 at **[1269]**.

[8B Landlord's obligation: election in case of sale at auction

(1) This section applies where the landlord is obliged to proceed and the offer notice was one to which section 5B applied (sale by auction).

(2) The nominated person may, by notice served on the landlord not less than 28 days before the date of the auction, elect that the provisions of this section shall apply.

(3) If a contract for the disposal is entered into at the auction, the landlord shall, within the period of seven days beginning with the date of the auction, send a copy of the contract to the nominated person.

(4) If, within the period of 28 days beginning with the date on which such a copy is so sent, the nominated person—

(a) serves notice on the landlord accepting the terms of the contract, and

(b) fulfils any conditions falling to be fulfilled by the purchaser on entering into the contract,

the contract shall have effect as if the nominated person, and not the purchaser, had entered into the contract.

(5) Unless otherwise agreed, any time limit in the contract as it has effect by virtue of subsection (4) shall start to run again on the service of notice under that subsection; and nothing in the contract as it has effect by virtue of a notice under this section shall require the nominated person to complete the purchase before the end of the period of 28 days beginning with the day on which he is deemed to have entered into the contract.

(6) If the nominated person—

(a) does not serve notice on the landlord under subsection (2) by the time mentioned in that subsection, or

(b) does not satisfy the requirements of subsection (4) within the period mentioned in that subsection,

the following provisions of this Part apply as if he had given notice under section 9A (withdrawal by nominated person) at the end of that period.]

[1279]

NOTES

Substituted as noted to s 5 at **[1269]**.

[8C Election in case of disposal for non-monetary consideration

(1) This section applies where an acceptance notice is duly served on the landlord indicating an intention to accept the offer referred to in section 5E (offer notice: disposal for non-monetary consideration).

(2) The requisite majority of qualifying tenants of the constituent flats may, by notice served on the landlord within—

(a) the period specified in the offer notice for nominating a person or persons for the purposes of section 6, or

(b) such longer period as may be agreed between the landlord and the requisite majority of qualifying tenants of the constituent flats,

elect that the following provisions shall apply.

(3) Where such an election is made and the landlord disposes of the protected interest on terms corresponding to those specified in his offer notice in accordance with section 5A, 5B, 5C or 5D, sections 11 to 17 shall have effect as if—

(a) no notice under section 5 had been served;

(b) in section 11A(3) (period for serving notice requiring information, &c), the reference to four months were a reference to 28 days; and

(c) in section 12A(2) and 12B(3) (period for exercise of tenants' rights against purchaser) each reference to six months were a reference to two months.

(4) For the purposes of sections 11 to 17 as they have effect by virtue of subsection (3) so much of the consideration for the original disposal as did not consist of money shall be treated as such amount in money as was equivalent to its value in the hands of the landlord.

The landlord or the nominated person may apply to have that amount determined by a leasehold valuation tribunal.]

[1280]

NOTES

Substituted as noted to s 5 at **[1269]**.

[8D Disposal in pursuance of option or right of pre-emption

(1) Where—

(a) the original disposal was the grant of an option or right of pre-emption, and

(b) in pursuance of the option or right, the landlord makes another disposal affecting the premises ("the later disposal") before the end of the period specified in subsection (2),

sections 11 to 17 shall have effect as if the later disposal, and not the original disposal, were the relevant disposal.

(2) The period referred to in subsection (1)(b) is the period of four months beginning with the date by which—

(a) notices under section 3A of the Landlord and Tenant Act 1985 (duty of new landlord to inform tenants of rights) relating to the original disposal, or

(b) where that section does not apply, documents of any other description—

(i) indicating that the original disposal has taken place, and

(ii) alerting the tenants to the existence of their rights under this Part and the time within which any such rights must be exercised,

have been served on the requisite majority of qualifying tenants of the constituent flats.]

[1281]

NOTES

Substituted as noted to s 5 at **[1269]**.

[8E Covenant, &c affecting landlord's power to dispose

(1) Where the landlord is obliged to proceed but is precluded by a covenant, condition or other obligation from disposing of the protected interest to the nominated person unless the consent of some other person is obtained—

PART I STATUTES

(a) he shall use his best endeavours to secure that the consent of that person to that disposal is given, and
(b) if it appears to him that that person is obliged not to withhold his consent unreasonably but has nevertheless so withheld it, he shall institute proceedings for a declaration to that effect.

(2) Subsection (1) ceases to apply if a notice of withdrawal is served under section 9A or 9B (withdrawal of either party from transaction) or if notice is served under section 10 (lapse of landlord's offer: premises ceasing to be premises to which this Part applies).

(3) Where the landlord has discharged any duty imposed on him by subsection (1) but any such consent as is there mentioned has been withheld, and no such declaration as is there mentioned has been made, the landlord may serve a notice on the nominated person stating that to be the case.

When such a notice has been served, the landlord may, during the period of 12 months beginning with the date of service of the notice, dispose of the protected interest to such person as he thinks fit, but subject to the following restrictions.

(4) Where the offer notice was one to which section 5B applied (sale by auction), the restrictions are—
(a) that the disposal is made by means of a sale at a public auction, and
(b) that the other terms correspond to those specified in the offer notice.

(5) In any other case the restrictions are—
(a) that the deposit and consideration required are not less than those specified in the offer notice or, if higher, those agreed between the landlord and the nominated person (subject to contract), and
(b) that the other terms correspond to those specified in the offer notice.

(6) Where notice is given under subsection (3), the landlord may recover from the nominated party and the qualifying tenants who served the acceptance notice any costs reasonably incurred by him in connection with the disposal between the end of the first four weeks of the nomination period and the time when that notice is served by him.

Any such liability of the nominated person and those tenants is a joint and several liability.]
[1282]

NOTES
Substituted as noted to s 5 at **[1269]**.

[9A Notice of withdrawal by nominated person

(1) Where the landlord is obliged to proceed, the nominated person may serve notice on the landlord (a "notice of withdrawal") indicating his intention no longer to proceed with the acquisition of the protected interest.

(2) If at any time the nominated person becomes aware that the number of the qualifying tenants of the constituent flats desiring to proceed with the acquisition of the protected interest is less than the requisite majority of qualifying tenants of those flats, he shall forthwith serve a notice of withdrawal.

(3) Where notice of withdrawal is given by the nominated person under this section, the landlord may, during the period of 12 months beginning with the date of service of the notice, dispose of the protected interest to such person as he thinks fit, but subject to the following restrictions.

(4) Where the offer notice was one to which section 5B applied (sale by auction), the restrictions are—
(a) that the disposal is made by means of a sale at a public auction, and
(b) that the other terms correspond to those specified in the offer notice.

(5) In any other case the restrictions are—
(a) that the deposit and consideration required are not less than those specified in the offer notice or, if higher, those agreed between the landlord and the nominated person (subject to contract), and
(b) that the other terms correspond to those specified in the offer notice.

(6) If notice of withdrawal is served under this section before the end of the first four weeks of the nomination period specified in the offer notice, the nominated person and the qualifying tenants who served the acceptance notice are not liable for any costs incurred by the landlord in connection with the disposal.

(7) If notice of withdrawal is served under this section after the end of those four weeks, the landlord may recover from the nominated person and the qualifying tenants who served the acceptance notice any costs reasonably incurred by him in connection with the disposal between the end of those four weeks and the time when the notice of withdrawal was served on him.

Any such liability of the nominated person and those tenants is a joint and several liability.

(8) This section does not apply after a binding contract for the disposal of the protected interest—

(a) has been entered into by the landlord and the nominated person, or

(b) has otherwise come into existence between the landlord and the nominated person by virtue of any provision of this Part.]

[1283]

NOTES

Substituted as noted to s 5 at **[1269]**.

[9B Notice of withdrawal by landlord

(1) Where the landlord is obliged to proceed, he may serve notice on the nominated person (a "notice of withdrawal") indicating his intention no longer to proceed with the disposal of the protected interest.

(2) Where a notice of withdrawal is given by the landlord, he is not entitled to dispose of the protected interest during the period of 12 months beginning with the date of service of the notice.

(3) If a notice of withdrawal is served before the end of the first four weeks of the nomination period specified in the offer notice, the landlord is not liable for any costs incurred in connection with the disposal by the nominated person and the qualifying tenants who served the acceptance notice.

(4) If a notice of withdrawal is served after the end of those four weeks, the nominated person and the qualifying tenants who served the acceptance notice may recover from the landlord any costs reasonably incurred by them in connection with the disposal between the end of those four weeks and the time when the notice of withdrawal was served.

(5) This section does not apply after a binding contract for the disposal of the protected interest—

(a) has been entered into by the landlord and the nominated person, or

(b) has otherwise come into existence between the landlord and the nominated person by virtue of any provision of this Part.]

[1284]

NOTES

Substituted as noted to s 5 at **[1269]**.

[10 Lapse of landlord's offer

(1) If after a landlord has served an offer notice the premises concerned cease to be premises to which this Part applies, the landlord may serve a notice on the qualifying tenants of the constituent flats stating—

(a) that the premises have ceased to be premises to which this Part applies, and

(b) that the offer notice, and anything done in pursuance of it, is to be treated as not having been served or done;

and on the service of such a notice the provisions of this Part cease to have effect in relation to that disposal.

(2) A landlord who has not served such a notice on all of the qualifying tenants of the constituent flats shall nevertheless be treated as having duly served a notice under subsection (1)—

(a) if he has served such a notice on not less than 90% of those tenants, or

(b) where those qualifying tenants number less than ten, if he has served such a notice on all but one of them.

(3) Where the landlord is entitled to serve a notice under subsection (1) but does not do so, this Part shall continue to have effect in relation to the disposal in question as if the premises in question were still premises to which this Part applies.

(4) The above provisions of this section do not apply after a binding contract for the disposal of the protected interest—

(a) has been entered into by the landlord and the nominated person, or

(b) has otherwise come into existence between the landlord and the nominated person by virtue of any provision of this Part.

(5) Where a binding contract for the disposal of the protected interest has been entered into between the landlord and the nominated person but it has been lawfully rescinded by the landlord, the landlord may, during the period of 12 months beginning with the date of the rescission of the contract, dispose of that interest to such person (and on such terms) as he thinks fit.]

[1285]

NOTES
Substituted as noted to s 5 at **[1269]**.

[10A Offence of failure to comply with requirements of Part I

(1) A landlord commits an offence if, without reasonable excuse, he makes a relevant disposal affecting premises to which this Part applies—

(a) without having first complied with the requirements of section 5 as regards the service of notices on the qualifying tenants of flats contained in the premises, or

(b) in contravention of any prohibition or restriction imposed by sections 6 to 10.

(2) A person guilty of an offence under this section is liable on summary conviction to a fine not exceeding level 5 on the standard scale.

(3) Where an offence under this section committed by a body corporate is proved—

(a) to have been committed with the consent or connivance of a director, manager, secretary or other similar officer of the body corporate, or a person purporting to act in such a capacity, or

(b) to be due to any neglect on the part of such an officer or person,

he, as well as the body corporate, is guilty of the offence and liable to be proceeded against and punished accordingly.

Where the affairs of a body corporate are managed by its members, the above provision applies in relation to the acts and defaults of a member in connection with his functions of management as if he were a director of the body corporate.

(4) Proceedings for an offence under this section may be brought by a local housing authority (within the meaning of section 1 of the Housing Act 1985).

(5) Nothing in this section affects the validity of the disposal.]

[1286]

NOTES
Inserted by the Housing Act 1996, s 91, except in relation to disposals made in pursuance of an obligation entered into before 1 October 1996.

[Enforcement by tenants of rights against purchaser

11 Circumstances in which tenants' rights enforceable against purchaser

(1) The following provisions of this Part apply where a landlord has made a relevant disposal affecting premises to which at the time of the disposal this Part applied ("the original disposal"), and either—

(a) no notice was served by the landlord under section 5 with respect to that disposal, or

(b) the disposal was made in contravention of any provision of sections 6 to 10, and the premises are still premises to which this Part applies.

(2) In those circumstances the requisite majority of the qualifying tenants of the flats contained in the premises affected by the relevant disposal (the "constituent flats") have the rights conferred by the following provisions—

section 11A (right to information as to terms of disposal, &c),
section 12A (right of qualifying tenants to take benefit of contract),
section 12B (right of qualifying tenants to compel sale, &c by purchaser), and
section 12C (right of qualifying tenants to compel grant of new tenancy by superior landlord).

(3) In those sections the transferee under the original disposal (or, in the case of the surrender of a tenancy, the superior landlord) is referred to as "the purchaser".

This shall not be read as restricting the operation of those provisions to disposals for consideration.]

[1287]

NOTES
Substituted, together with preceding cross-heading and ss 11A, 12A–12D, 13, 14, for original ss 11–15, by the Housing Act 1996, s 92(1), Sch 6, Pt II.

[11A Right to information as to terms of disposal, &c

(1) The requisite majority of qualifying tenants of the constituent flats may serve a notice on the purchaser requiring him—

(a) to give particulars of the terms on which the original disposal was made (including the deposit and consideration required) and the date on which it was made, and

(b) where the disposal consisted of entering into a contract, to provide a copy of the contract.

(2) The notice must specify the name and address of the person to whom (on behalf of the tenants) the particulars are to be given, or the copy of the contract provided.

(3) Any notice under this section must be served before the end of the period of four months beginning with the date by which—

(a) notices under section 3A of the Landlord and Tenant Act 1985 (duty of new landlord to inform tenants of rights) relating to the original disposal, or

(b) where that section does not apply, documents of any other description—

(i) indicating that the original disposal has taken place, and

(ii) alerting the tenants to the existence of their rights under this Part and the time within which any such rights must be exercised,

have been served on the requisite majority of qualifying tenants of the constituent flats.

(4) A person served with a notice under this section shall comply with it within the period of one month beginning with the date on which it is served on him.]

[1288]

NOTES

Substituted as noted to s 11 at **[1287]**.

[12A Right of qualifying tenants to take benefit of contract

(1) Where the original disposal consisted of entering into a contract, the requisite majority of qualifying tenants of the constituent flats may by notice to the landlord elect that the contract shall have effect as if entered into not with the purchaser but with a person or persons nominated for the purposes of this section by the requisite majority of qualifying tenants of the constituent flats.

(2) Any such notice must be served before the end of the period of six months beginning—

(a) if a notice was served on the purchaser under section 11A (right to information as to terms of disposal, &c), with the date on which the purchaser complied with that notice;

(b) in any other case, with the date by which documents of any description—

(i) indicating that the original disposal has taken place, and

(ii) alerting the tenants to the existence of their rights under this Part and the time within which any such rights must be exercised,

have been served on the requisite majority of qualifying tenants of the constituent flats.

(3) The notice shall not have effect as mentioned in subsection (1) unless the nominated person—

(a) fulfils any requirements as to the deposit required on entering into the contract, and

(b) fulfils any other conditions required to be fulfilled by the purchaser on entering into the contract.

(4) Unless otherwise agreed, any time limit in the contract as it has effect by virtue of a notice under this section shall start to run again on the service of that notice; and nothing in the contract as it has effect by virtue of a notice under this section shall require the nominated person to complete the purchase before the end of the period of 28 days beginning with the day on which he is deemed to have entered into the contract.

(5) Where the original disposal related to other property in addition to premises to which this Part applied at the time of the disposal—

(a) a notice under this section has effect only in relation to the premises to which this Part applied at the time of the original disposal, and

(b) the terms of the contract shall have effect with any necessary modifications.

In such a case the notice under this section may specify the subject-matter of the disposal, and the terms on which the disposal is to be made (whether doing so expressly or by reference to the original disposal), or may provide for that estate or interest, or any such terms, to be determined by a leasehold valuation tribunal.]

[1289]

NOTES

Substituted as noted to s 11 at **[1287]**.

[12B Right of qualifying tenants to compel sale, &c by purchaser

(1) This section applies where—

(a) the original disposal consisted of entering into a contract and no notice has been served under section 12A (right of qualifying tenants to take benefit of contract), or

(b) the original disposal did not consist of entering into a contract.

(2) The requisite majority of qualifying tenants of the constituent flats may serve a notice (a "purchase notice") on the purchaser requiring him to dispose of the estate or interest that was the subject-matter of the original disposal, on the terms on which it was made (including those relating

PART I STATUTES

to the consideration payable), to a person or persons nominated for the purposes of this section by any such majority of qualifying tenants of those flats.

(3) Any such notice must be served before the end of the period of six months beginning—

(a) if a notice was served on the purchaser under section 11A (right to information as to terms of disposal, &c), with the date on which the purchaser complied with that notice;

(b) in any other case, with the date by which—

(i) notices under section 3A of the Landlord and Tenant Act 1985 (duty of new landlord to inform tenants of rights) relating to the original disposal, or

(ii) where that section does not apply, documents of any other description indicating that the original disposal has taken place, and alerting the tenants to the existence of their rights under this Part and the time within which any such rights must be exercised,

have been served on the requisite majority of qualifying tenants of the constituent flats.

(4) A purchase notice shall where the original disposal related to other property in addition to premises to which this Part applied at the time of the disposal—

(a) require the purchaser only to make a disposal relating to those premises, and

(b) require him to do so on the terms referred to in subsection (2) with any necessary modifications.

In such a case the purchase notice may specify the subject-matter of the disposal, and the terms on which the disposal is to be made (whether doing so expressly or by reference to the original disposal), or may provide for those matters to be determined by a leasehold valuation tribunal.

(5) Where the property which the purchaser is required to dispose of in pursuance of the purchase notice has since the original disposal become subject to any charge or other incumbrance, then, unless the court by order directs otherwise—

(a) in the case of a charge to secure the payment of money or the performance of any other obligation by the purchaser or any other person, the instrument by virtue of which the property is disposed of by the purchaser to the person or persons nominated for the purposes of this section shall (subject to the provisions of Part I of Schedule 1) operate to discharge the property from that charge; and

(b) in the case of any other incumbrance, the property shall be so disposed of subject to the incumbrance but with a reduction in the consideration payable to the purchaser corresponding to the amount by which the existence of the incumbrance reduces the value of the property.

(6) Subsection (5)(a) and Part I of Schedule 1 apply, with any necessary modifications, to mortgages and liens as they apply to charges; but nothing in those provisions applies to a rentcharge.

(7) Where the property which the purchaser is required to dispose of in pursuance of the purchase notice has since the original disposal increased in monetary value owing to any change in circumstances (other than a change in the value of money), the amount of the consideration payable to the purchaser for the disposal by him of the property in pursuance of the purchase notice shall be the amount that might reasonably have been obtained on a corresponding disposal made on the open market at the time of the original disposal if the change in circumstances had already taken place.]
[1290]

NOTES

Substituted as noted to s 11 at **[1287]**.

[12C Right of qualifying tenants to compel grant of new tenancy by superior landlord

(1) This section applies where the original disposal consisted of the surrender by the landlord of a tenancy held by him ("the relevant tenancy").

(2) The requisite majority of qualifying tenants of the constituent flats may serve a notice on the purchaser requiring him to grant a new tenancy of the premises which were subject to the relevant tenancy, on the same terms as those of the relevant tenancy and so as to expire on the same date as that tenancy would have expired, to a person or persons nominated for the purposes of this section by any such majority of qualifying tenants of those flats.

(3) Any such notice must be served before the end of the period of six months beginning—

(a) if a notice was served on the purchaser under section 11A (right to information as to terms of disposal, &c), with the date on which the purchaser complied with that notice;

(b) in any other case, with the date by which documents of any description—

(i) indicating that the original disposal has taken place, and

(ii) alerting the tenants to the existence of their rights under this Part and the time within which any such rights must be exercised,

have been served on the requisite majority of qualifying tenants of the constituent flats.

(4) If the purchaser paid any amount to the landlord as consideration for the surrender by him of that tenancy, the nominated person shall pay that amount to the purchaser.

(5) Where the premises subject to the relevant tenancy included premises other than premises to which this Part applied at the time of the disposal, a notice under this section shall—

(a) require the purchaser only to grant a new tenancy relating to the premises to which this Part then applied, and

(b) require him to do so on the terms referred to in subsection (2) subject to any necessary modifications.

(6) The purchase notice may specify the subject-matter of the disposal, and the terms on which the disposal is to be made (whether doing so expressly or by reference to the original disposal), or may provide for those matters to be determined by a leasehold valuation tribunal.]

[1291]

NOTES

Substituted as noted to s 11 at **[1287]**.

[12D Nominated persons: supplementary provisions

(1) The person or persons initially nominated for the purposes of section 12A, 12B or 12C shall be nominated in the notice under that section.

(2) A person nominated for those purposes by the requisite majority of qualifying tenants of the constituent flats may be replaced by another person so nominated if, and only if, he has (for any reason) ceased to be able to act as a nominated person.

(3) Where two or more persons have been nominated and any of them ceases to act without being replaced, the remaining person or persons so nominated may continue to act.

(4) Where, in the exercise of its power to award costs, the court or the [Upper Tribunal] makes, in connection with any proceedings arising under or by virtue of this Part, an award of costs against the person or persons so nominated, the liability for those costs is a joint and several liability of that person or those persons together with the qualifying tenants by whom the relevant notice was served.]

[1292]

NOTES

Substituted as noted to s 11 at **[1287]**.

Sub-s (4): words in square brackets substituted by SI 2009/1307, art 5(1), (2), Sch 1, paras 180, 181, subject to transitional and savings provisions in art 5(6), Sch 5 thereto.

[13 Determination of questions by leasehold valuation tribunal

(1) A leasehold valuation tribunal has jurisdiction to hear and determine—

(a) any question arising in relation to any matters specified in a notice under section 12A, 12B or 12C, and

(b) any question arising for determination as mentioned in section 8C(4), 12A(5) or 12B(4) (matters left for determination by tribunal).

(2) On an application under this section the interests of the persons by whom the notice was served under section 12A, 12B or 12C shall be represented by the nominated person; and accordingly the parties to any such application shall not include those persons.

[1293]

NOTES

Substituted as noted to s 11 at **[1287]**.

[14 Withdrawal of nominated person from transaction under s 12B or 12C

(1) Where notice has been duly served on the landlord under—

section 12B (right of qualifying tenants to compel sale, &c by purchaser), or

section 12C (right of qualifying tenants to compel grant of new tenancy by superior landlord),

the nominated person may at any time before a binding contract is entered into in pursuance of the notice, serve notice under this section on the purchaser (a "notice of withdrawal") indicating an intention no longer to proceed with the disposal.

(2) If at any such time the nominated person becomes aware that the number of qualifying tenants of the constituent flats desiring to proceed with the disposal is less than the requisite majority of those tenants, he shall forthwith serve a notice of withdrawal.

(3) If a notice of withdrawal is served under this section the purchaser may recover from the nominated person any costs reasonably incurred by him in connection with the disposal down to the time when the notice is served on him.

(4) If a notice of withdrawal is served at a time when proceedings arising under or by virtue of this Part are pending before the court or the [Upper Tribunal], the liability of the nominated person

for any costs incurred by the purchaser as mentioned in subsection (3) shall be such as may be determined by the court or (as the case may be) by the Tribunal.

(5) The costs that may be recovered by the purchaser under this section do not include any costs incurred by him in connection with an application to a leasehold valuation tribunal.]

[1294]

NOTES

Substituted as noted to s 11 at **[1287]**.

Sub-s (4): words in square brackets substituted by SI 2009/1307, art 5(1), (2), Sch 1, paras 180, 182, subject to transitional and savings provisions in art 5(6), Sch 5 thereto.

[Enforcement by tenants of rights against subsequent purchasers

16 Rights of qualifying tenants against subsequent purchaser

(1) This section applies where, at the time when a notice is served on the purchaser under section 11A, 12A, 12B or 12C, he no longer holds the estate or interest that was the subject-matter of the original disposal.

(2) In the case of a notice under section 11A (right to information as to terms of disposal, &c) the purchaser shall, within the period for complying with that notice—

(a) serve notice on the person specified in the notice as the person to whom particulars are to be provided of the name and address of the person to whom he has disposed of that estate or interest ("the subsequent purchaser"), and

(b) serve on the subsequent purchaser a copy of the notice under section 11A and of the particulars given by him in response to it.

(3) In the case of a notice under section 12A, 12B or 12C the purchaser shall forthwith—

(a) forward the notice to the subsequent purchaser, and

(b) serve on the nominated person notice of the name and address of the subsequent purchaser.

(4) Once the purchaser serves a notice in accordance with subsection (2)(a) or (3)(b), sections 12A to 14 shall, instead of applying to the purchaser, apply to the subsequent purchaser as if he were the transferee under the original disposal.

(5) Subsections (1) to (4) have effect, with any necessary modifications, in a case where, instead of disposing of the whole of the estate or interest referred to in subsection (1) to another person, the purchaser has disposed of it in part or in parts to one or more other persons.

In such a case, sections 12A to 14—

(a) apply to the purchaser in relation to any part of that estate or interest retained by him, and

(b) in relation to any part of that estate or interest disposed of to any other person, apply to that other person instead as if he were (as respects that part) the transferee under the original disposal.]

[1295]

NOTES

Substituted, together with s 17 and the preceding cross-headings, by the Housing Act 1996, s 92(1), Sch 6, Pt III.

[Termination of rights against purchasers or subsequent purchasers

17 Termination of rights against purchaser or subsequent purchaser

(1) If, at any time after a notice has been served under section 11A, 12A, 12B or 12C, the premises affected by the original disposal cease to be premises to which this Part applies, the purchaser may serve a notice on the qualifying tenants of the constituent flats stating—

(a) that the premises have ceased to be premises to which this Part applies, and

(b) that any such notice served on him, and anything done in pursuance of it, is to be treated as not having been served or done.

(2) A landlord who has not served such a notice on all of the qualifying tenants of the constituent flats shall nevertheless be treated as having duly served a notice under subsection (1)—

(a) if he has served such a notice on not less than 90% of those tenants, or

(b) where those qualifying tenants number less than ten, if he has served such a notice on all but one of them.

(3) Where a period of three months beginning with the date of service of a notice under section 12A, 12B or 12C on the purchaser has expired—

(a) without any binding contract having been entered into between the purchaser and the nominated person, and

(b) without there having been made any application in connection with the notice to the court or to a leasehold valuation tribunal,

the purchaser may serve on the nominated person a notice stating that the notice, and anything done in pursuance of it, is to be treated as not having been served or done.

(4) Where any such application as is mentioned in subsection (3)(b) was made within the period of three months referred to in that subsection, but—

(a) a period of two months beginning with the date of the determination of that application has expired,

(b) no binding contract has been entered into between the purchaser and the nominated person, and

(c) no other such application as is mentioned in subsection (3)(b) is pending,

the purchaser may serve on the nominated person a notice stating that any notice served on him under section 12A, 12B or 12C, and anything done in pursuance of any such notice, is to be treated as not having been served or done.

(5) Where the purchaser serves a notice in accordance with subsection (1), (3) or (4), this Part shall cease to have effect in relation to him in connection with the original disposal.

(6) Where a purchaser is entitled to serve a notice under subsection (1) but does not do so, this Part shall continue to have effect in relation to him in connection with the original disposal as if the premises in question were still premises to which this Part applies.

(7) References in this section to the purchaser include a subsequent purchaser to whom sections 12A to 14 apply by virtue of section 16(4) or (5).]

[1296]

NOTES

Substituted as noted to s 16 at **[1295]**.

Notices served by prospective purchasers

18 Notices served by prospective purchasers to ensure that rights of first refusal do not arise

(1) Where—

(a) any disposal of an estate or interest in any premises consisting of the whole or part of a building is proposed to be made by a landlord, and

(b) it appears to the person who would be the transferee under that disposal ("the purchaser") that any such disposal would, or might, be a relevant disposal affecting premises to which this Part applies,

the purchaser may serve notices under this subsection on the tenants of the flats contained in the premises referred to in paragraph (a) ("the flats affected").

(2) Any notice under subsection (1) shall—

(a) inform the person on whom it is served of the general nature of the principal terms of the proposed disposal, including in particular—

(i) the property to which it would relate and the estate or interest in that property proposed to be disposed of by the landlord, and

(ii) the consideration required by him for making the disposal;

(b) invite that person to serve a notice on the purchaser stating—

(i) whether the landlord has served on him, or on any predecessor in title of his, a notice under section 5 with respect to the disposal, and

(ii) if the landlord has not so served any such notice, whether he is aware of any reason why he is not entitled to be served with any such notice by the landlord, and

(iii) if he is not so aware, whether he would wish to avail himself of the right of first refusal conferred by any such notice if it were served; and

(c) inform that person of the effect of the following provisions of this section.

(3) Where the purchaser has served notices under subsection (1) on at least 80 per cent of the tenants of the flats affected and—

(a) not more than 50 per cent of the tenants on whom those notices have been served by the purchaser have served notices on him in pursuance of subsection (2)(b) by the end of the period of [two months] beginning with the date on which the last of them was served by him with a notice under this section, or

(b) more than 50 per cent of the tenants on whom those notices have been served by the purchaser have served notices on him in pursuance of subsection (2)(b) but the notices in each case indicate that the tenant serving it either—

(i) does not regard himself as being entitled to be served by the landlord with a notice under section 5 with respect to the disposal, or

(ii) would not wish to avail himself of the right of first refusal conferred by such a notice if it were served, the premises affected by the disposal shall, in relation to the disposal, be treated for the purposes of this Part as premises to which this Part does not apply.

(4) For the purposes of subsection (3) each of the flats affected shall be regarded as having one tenant, who shall count towards any of the percentages specified in that subsection whether he is a qualifying tenant of the flat or not.

[1297]

NOTES

Sub-s (3): words in square brackets substituted by SI 1996/2371, in relation to any disposal in a case where the purchaser has served a notice under sub-s (1) above, after 3 October 1996.

Supplementary

[18A The requisite majority of qualifying tenants

(1) In this Part "the requisite majority of qualifying tenants of the constituent flats" means qualifying tenants of constituent flats with more than 50 per cent of the available votes.

(2) The total number of available votes shall be determined as follows—

(a) where an offer notice has been served under section 5, that number is equal to the total number of constituent flats let to qualifying tenants on the date when the period specified in that notice as the period for accepting the offer expires;

(b) where a notice is served under section 11A without a notice having been previously served under section 5, that number is equal to the total number of constituent flats let to qualifying tenants on the date of service of the notice under section 11A;

(c) where a notice is served under section 12A, 12B or 12C without a notice having been previously served under section 5 or section 11A, that number is equal to the total number of constituent flats let to qualifying tenants on the date of service of the notice under section 12A, 12B or 12C, as the case may be.

(3) There is one available vote in respect of each of the flats so let on the date referred to in the relevant paragraph of subsection (2), which shall be attributed to the qualifying tenant to whom it is let.

(4) The persons constituting the requisite majority of qualifying tenants for one purpose may be different from the persons constituting such a majority for another purpose.]

[1298]

NOTES

Inserted by the Housing Act 1996, s 92(1), Sch 6, Pt IV, para 2.

19 Enforcement of obligations under Part I

(1) The court may, on the application of any person interested, make an order requiring any person who has made default in complying with any duty imposed on him by any provision of this Part to make good the default within such time as is specified in the order.

(2) An application shall not be made under subsection (1) unless—

(a) a notice has been previously served on the person in question requiring him to make good the default, and

(b) more than 14 days have elapsed since the date of service of that notice without his having done so.

(3) The restriction imposed by section 1(1) may be enforced by an injunction granted by the court.

[1299]

20 Construction of Part I and power of Secretary of State to prescribe modifications

(1) In this Part—

["acceptance notice" has the meaning given by section 6(3);]

"associated company", in relation to a body corporate, means another body corporate which is (within the meaning of *section 736 of the Companies Act 1985* [section 1159 of the Companies Act 2006]) that body's holding company, a subsidiary of that body or another subsidiary of that body's holding company;

["constituent flat" shall be construed in accordance with section 5(1) or 11(2), as the case may require;]

"disposal" [shall be construed in accordance with section 4(3) and section 4A (application of provisions to contracts)], and references to the acquisition of an estate or interest shall be construed accordingly;

"landlord", in relation to any premises, shall be construed in accordance with section 2;

.....

["the nominated person" means the person or persons for the time being nominated by the requisite majority of the qualifying tenants of the constituent flats for the purposes of section 6, 12A, 12B or 12C, as the case may require;]

"offer notice" means a notice served by a landlord under section 5;

"the original disposal" means the relevant disposal referred to in section 11(1);

["the protected interest" means the estate, interest or other subject-matter of an offer notice;]

["the protected period" has the meaning given by section 6(4);]

["purchase notice" has the meaning given by section 12B(2);]

["purchaser" has the meaning given by section 11(3);]

"qualifying tenant", in relation to a flat, shall be construed in accordance with section 3;

"relevant disposal" shall be construed in accordance with section 4;

"the requisite majority", in relation to qualifying tenants, shall be construed in accordance with [section 18A];

"transferee", in relation to a disposal, shall be construed in accordance with section 4(3).

(2) In this Part—

(a) any reference to an offer … is a reference to an offer … made subject to contract, and

(b) any reference to the acceptance of an offer … is a reference to its acceptance subject to contract.

(3) Any reference in this Part to a tenant of a particular description shall be construed, in relation to any time when the interest under his tenancy has ceased to be vested in him, as a reference to the person who is for the time being the successor in title to that interest.

(4) The Secretary of State may by regulations make such modifications of any of the provisions of sections 5 to 18 as he considers appropriate, and any such regulations may contain such incidental, supplemental or transitional provisions as he considers appropriate in connection with the regulations.

(5) In subsection (4) "modifications" includes additions, omissions and alterations.

[1300]

NOTES

Sub-s (1): definitions "acceptance notice", "constituent flat", "the protected interest" and "purchase notice" substituted, words in square brackets in definitions "disposal" and "the requisite majority" substituted, definitions "the nominated person", "the protected period" and "the purchaser" inserted, and definition "the new landlord" (omitted) repealed by the Housing Act 1996, ss 89(3), 92(1), 227, Sch 6, Pt IV, para 3, Sch 19, Pt III; in definition "associated company" words in italics substituted by subsequent words in square brackets by SI 2009/1941, art 2(1), Sch 1, para 28, as from 1 October 2009.

Sub-s (2): words omitted repealed by the Housing Act 1996, ss 92(1), 227, Sch 6, Pt IV, para 4, Sch 19, Pt III.

21–51 ((*Pts II–VI*) *Outside the scope of this work.*)

PART VII
GENERAL

52–61 (*Outside the scope of this work.*)

62 Short title, commencement and extent

(1) This Act may be cited as the Landlord and Tenant Act 1987.

(2) This Act shall come into force on such day as the Secretary of State may by order appoint.

(3) An order under subsection (2)—

(a) may appoint different days for different provisions or for different purposes; and

(b) may make such transitional, incidental, supplemental or consequential provision or saving as the Secretary of State considers necessary or expedient in connection with the coming into force of any provision of this Act or the operation of any enactment which is repealed or amended by a provision of this Act during any period when the repeal or amendment is not wholly in force.

(4) This Act extends to England and Wales only.

[1301]

NOTES

Orders: the Landlord and Tenant Act 1987 (Commencement No 1) Order 1987, SI 1987/2177; the Landlord and Tenant Act 1987 (Commencement No 2) Order 1988, SI 1988/480; the Landlord and Tenant Act 1987 (Commencement No 3) Order 1988, SI 1988/1283.

SCHEDULE 1
DISCHARGE OF MORTGAGES ETC: SUPPLEMENTARY PROVISIONS

Section 12

PART I
DISCHARGE IN PURSUANCE OF PURCHASE NOTICES

Construction

1. In this Part of this Schedule—

"the consideration payable" means the consideration payable to *the new landlord* [the purchaser] for the disposal by him of the property referred to in *section 12(4)* [section 12B(7)];

["the purchaser"] has the same meaning as in section 12, and accordingly includes any person to whom that section applies by virtue of [section 16(4) or (5)]; and

"the nominated person" means the person or persons nominated as mentioned in [section 12B(2)].

Duty of nominated person to redeem mortgages

2.—(1) Where in accordance with [section 12B(5)(a)] an instrument will operate to discharge any property from a charge to secure the payment of money, it shall be the duty of the nominated person to apply the consideration payable, in the first instance, in or towards the redemption of any such charge (and, if there are more than one, then according to their priorities).

(2) Where sub-paragraph (1) applies to any charge or charges, then if (and only if) the consideration payable is applied by the nominated person in accordance with that sub-paragraph or paid into court by him in accordance with paragraph 4, the instrument in question shall operate as mentioned in sub-paragraph (1) notwithstanding that the consideration payable is insufficient to enable the charge or charges to be redeemed in its or their entirety.

(3) Subject to sub-paragraph (4), sub-paragraph (1) shall not apply to a charge which is a debenture holders' charge, that is to say, a charge (whether a floating charge or not) in favour of the holders of a series of debentures issued by a company or other body of persons, or in favour of trustees for such debenture holders; and any such charge shall be disregarded in determining priorities for the purposes of sub-paragraph (1).

(4) Sub-paragraph (3) above shall not have effect in relation to a charge in favour of trustees for debenture holders which at the date of the instrument by virtue of which the property is disposed of by [the purchaser] is (as regards that property) a specific and not a floating charge.

Determination of amounts due in respect of mortgages

3.—(1) For the purpose of determining the amount payable in respect of any charge under paragraph 2(1), a person entitled to the benefit of a charge to which that provision applies shall not be permitted to exercise any right to consolidate that charge with a separate charge on other property.

(2) For the purpose of discharging any property from a charge to which paragraph 2(1) applies, a person may be required to accept three months or any longer notice of the intention to pay the whole or part of the principal secured by the charge, together with interest to the date of payment, notwithstanding that the terms of the security make other provision or no provision as to the time and manner of payment; but he shall be entitled, if he so requires, to receive such additional payment as is reasonable in the circumstances in respect of the costs of re-investment or other incidental costs and expenses and in respect of any reduction in the rate of interest obtainable on re-investment.

Payments into court

4.—(1) Where under [section 12B(5)(a)] any property is to be discharged from a charge and, in accordance with paragraph 2(1), a person is or may be entitled in respect of the charge to receive the whole or part of the consideration payable, then if—

(a) for any reason difficulty arises in ascertaining how much is payable in respect of the charge, or

(b) for any reason mentioned in sub-paragraph (2) below difficulty arises in making a payment in respect of the charge,

the nominated person may pay into court on account of the consideration payable the amount, if known, of the payment to be made in respect of the charge or, if that amount is not known, the whole of that consideration or such lesser amount as the nominated person thinks right in order to provide for that payment.

(2) Payment may be made into court in accordance with sub-paragraph (1)(a) where the difficulty arises for any of the following reasons, namely—

(a) because a person who is or may be entitled to receive payment cannot be found or ascertained;
(b) because any such person refuses or fails to make out a title, or to accept payment and give a proper discharge, or to take any steps reasonably required of him to enable the sum payable to be ascertained and paid;
(c) because a tender of the sum payable cannot, by reason of complications in the title to it or the want of two or more trustees or for other reasons, be effected, or not without incurring or involving unreasonable cost or delay.

(3) Without prejudice to sub-paragraph (1)(a), the whole or part of the consideration payable shall be paid into court by the nominated person if, before execution of the instrument referred to in paragraph 2(1), notice is given to him—
(a) that [the purchaser] or a person entitled to the benefit of a charge on the property in question requires him to do so for the purpose of protecting the rights of persons so entitled, or for reasons related to the bankruptcy or winding up of [the purchaser], or
(b) that steps have been taken to enforce any charge on [the purchaser's] interest in that property by the bringing of proceedings in any court, or by the appointment of a receiver or otherwise;

and where payment into court is to be made by reason only of a notice under this sub-paragraph, and the notice is given with reference to proceedings in a court specified in the notice other than a county court, payment shall be made into the court so specified.

Savings

5.—(1) Where any property is discharged by [section 12B(5)(a)] from a charge (without the obligations secured by the charge being satisfied by the receipt of the whole or part of the consideration payable), the discharge of that property from the charge shall not prejudice any right or remedy for the enforcement of those obligations against other property comprised in the same or any other security, nor prejudice any personal liability as principal or otherwise of [the purchaser] or any other person.

(2) Nothing in this Schedule shall be construed as preventing a person from joining in the instrument referred to in paragraph 2(1) for the purpose of discharging the property in question from any charge without payment or for a lesser payment than that to which he would otherwise be entitled; and, if he does so, the persons to whom the consideration payable ought to be paid shall be determined accordingly.

[1302]

NOTES

Paras 1, 2, 4, 5: words in square brackets substituted by the Housing Act 1996, s 92(1), Sch 6, Part IV, para 11.

PART II
DISCHARGE IN PURSUANCE OF ACQUISITION ORDERS

Construction

6. In this Part of this Schedule—
"the consideration payable" means the consideration payable for the acquisition of the landlord's interest referred to in section 32(1); and
"the nominated person" means the person or persons nominated for the purposes of Part III by the persons who applied for the acquisition order in question.

Duty of nominated person to redeem mortgages

7.—(1) Where in accordance with section 32(1) an instrument will operate to discharge any premises from a charge to secure the payment of money, it shall be the duty of the nominated person to apply the consideration payable, in the first instance, in or towards the redemption of any such charge (and, if there are more than one, then according to their priorities).

(2) Where sub-paragraph (1) applies to any charge or charges, then if (and only if) the consideration payable is applied by the nominated person in accordance with that sub-paragraph or paid into court by him in accordance with paragraph 9, the instrument in question shall operate as mentioned in sub-paragraph (1) notwithstanding that the consideration payable is insufficient to enable the charge or charges to be redeemed in its or their entirety.

(3) Subject to sub-paragraph (4), sub-paragraph (1) shall not apply to a charge which is a debenture holders' charge within the meaning of paragraph 2(3) in Part I of this Schedule; and any such charge shall be disregarded in determining priorities for the purposes of sub-paragraph (1).

(4) Sub-paragraph (3) above shall not have effect in relation to a charge in favour of trustees for debenture holders which at the date of the instrument by virtue of which the landlord's interest in the premises in question is acquired is (as regards those premises) a specific and not a floating charge.

Determination of amounts due in respect of mortgages

8.—(1) For the purpose of determining the amount payable in respect of any charge under paragraph 7(1), a person entitled to the benefit of a charge to which that provision applies shall not be permitted to exercise any right to consolidate that charge with a separate charge on other property.

(2) For the purpose of discharging any premises from a charge to which paragraph 7(1) applies, a person may be required to accept three months or any longer notice of the intention to pay the whole or part of the principal secured by the charge, together with interest to the date of payment, notwithstanding that the terms of the security make other provision or no provision as to the time and manner of payment; but he shall be entitled, if he so requires, to receive such additional payment as is reasonable in the circumstances in respect of the costs of re-investment or other incidental costs and expenses and in respect of any reduction in the rate of interest obtainable on re-investment.

Payments into court

9.—(1) Where under section 32 any premises are to be discharged from a charge and, in accordance with paragraph 7(1), a person is or may be entitled in respect of the charge to receive the whole or part of the consideration payable., then if—

(a) for any reason difficulty arises in ascertaining how much is payable in respect of the charge, or

(b) for any reason mentioned in sub-paragraph (2) below difficulty arises in making a payment in respect of the charge,

the nominated person may pay into court on account of the consideration payable the amount, if known, of the payment to be made in respect of the charge or, if that amount is not known, the whole of that consideration or such lesser amount as the nominated person thinks right in order to provide for that payment.

(2) Payment may be made into court in accordance with sub-paragraph (k1)(b) where the difficulty arises for any of the following reasons, namely—

(a) because a person who is or may be entitled to receive payment cannot be found or ascertained;

(b) because any such person refuses or fails to make out a title, or to accept payment and give a proper discharge, or to take any steps reasonably required of him to enable the sum payable to be ascertained and paid; or

(c) because a tender of the sum payable cannot, by reason of complications in the title to it or the want of two or more trustees or for other reasons, be effected, or not without incurring or involving unreasonable cost or delay.

(3) Without prejudice to sub-paragraph (1)(a), the whole or part of the consideration payable shall be paid into court by the nominated person if, before execution of the instrument referred to in paragraph 7(1), notice is given to him—

(a) that the landlord or a person entitled to the benefit of a charge on the premises in question requires him to do so for the purpose of protecting the rights of persons so entitled, or for reasons related to the bankruptcy or winding up of the landlord, or

(b) that steps have been taken to enforce any charge on the landlord's interest in those premises by the bringing of proceedings in any court, or by the appointment of a receiver or otherwise;

and where payment into court is to be made by reason only of a notice under this sub-paragraph, and the notice is given with reference to proceedings in a court specified in the notice other than a county court, payment shall be made into the court so specified.

Savings

10.—(1) Where any premises are discharged by section 32 from a charge (without the obligations secured by the charge being satisfied by the receipt of the whole or part of the consideration payable), the discharge of those premises from the charge shall not prejudice any right or remedy for the enforcement of those obligations against other property comprised in the same or any other security, nor prejudice any personal liability as principal or otherwise of the landlord or any other person.

(2) Nothing in this Schedule shall be construed as preventing a person from joining in the instrument referred to in paragraph 7(1) for the purpose of discharging the premises in question from any charge without payment or for a lesser payment than that to which he would otherwise be entitled; and, if he does so, the persons to whom the consideration payable ought to be paid shall be determined accordingly.

[1303]

(*Schs 2–5 outside the scope of this work.*)

FAMILY LAW REFORM ACT 1987

(1987 c 42)

An Act to reform the law relating to the consequences of birth outside marriage; to make further provision with respect to the rights and duties of parents and the determination of parentage; and for connected purposes

[15 May 1987]

PART I
GENERAL PRINCIPLE

1 General principle

(1) In this Act and enactments passed and instruments made after the coming into force of this section, references (however expressed) to any relationship between two persons shall, unless the contrary intention appears, be construed without regard to whether or not the father and mother of either of them, or the father and mother of any person through whom the relationship is deduced, have or had been married to each other at any time.

(2) In this Act and enactments passed after the coming into force of this section, unless the contrary intention appears—

(a) references to a person whose father and mother were married to each other at the time of his birth include; and

(b) references to a person whose father and mother were not married to each other at the time of his birth do not include,

references to any person to whom subsection (3) below applies, and cognate references shall be construed accordingly.

(3) This subsection applies to any person who—

(a) is treated as legitimate by virtue of section 1 of the Legitimacy Act 1976;

(b) is a legitimated person within the meaning of section 10 of that Act;

[(ba) has a parent by virtue of section 42 of the Human Fertilisation and Embryology Act 2008 (which relates to treatment provided to a woman who is at the time of treatment a party to a civil partnership or, in certain circumstances, a void civil partnership);

(bb) has a parent by virtue of section 43 of that Act (which relates to treatment provided to woman who agrees that second woman to be parent) who—

(i) is the civil partner of the child's mother at the time of the child's birth, or

(ii) was the civil partner of the child's mother at any time during the period beginning with the time mentioned in section 43(b) of that Act and ending with the child's birth;]

[(c) is an adopted person within the meaning of Chapter 4 of Part 1 of the Adoption and Children Act 2002]; or

(d) is otherwise treated in law as legitimate.

(4) For the purpose of construing references falling within subsection (2) above, the time of a person's birth shall be taken to include any time during the period beginning with—

(a) the insemination resulting in his birth; or

(b) where there was no such insemination, his conception,

and (in either case) ending with his birth.

[(5) A child whose parents are parties to a void civil partnership shall, subject to subsection (6), be treated as falling within subsection (3)(bb) if at the time when the parties registered as civil partners of each other both or either of the parties reasonably believed that the civil partnership was valid.

(6) Subsection (5) applies only where the woman who is a parent by virtue of section 43 was domiciled in England and Wales at the time of the birth or, if she died before the birth, was so domiciled immediately before her death.

(7) Subsection (5) applies even though the belief that the civil partnership was valid was due to a mistake as to law.

(8) It shall be presumed for the purposes of subsection (5), unless the contrary is shown, that one of the parties to a void civil partnership reasonably believed at the time of the formation of the civil partnership that the civil partnership was valid.]

[1304]

NOTES

Sub-s (3): paras (ba), (bb) inserted by the Human Fertilisation and Embryology Act 2008, s 56, Sch 6, Pt 1, paras 24(1), (2); para (c) substituted by the Adoption and Children Act 2002, s 139(1), Sch 3, paras 50, 51.

Sub-ss (5)–(8): inserted by the Human Fertilisation and Embryology Act 2008, s 56, Sch 6, Pt 1, para 24(3).

2–17 ((*Pt II*) *outside the scope of this work.*)

PART III
PROPERTY RIGHTS

18 Succession on intestacy

(1) In Part IV of the Administration of Estates Act 1925 (which deals with the distribution of the estate of an intestate), references (however expressed) to any relationship between two persons shall be construed in accordance with section 1 above.

(2) For the purposes of subsection (1) above and that Part of that Act, a person whose father and mother were not married to each other at the time of his birth shall be presumed not to have been survived by his father, or by any person related to him only through his father, unless the contrary is shown.

[(2A) In the case of a person who has a parent by virtue of section 43 of the Human Fertilisation and Embryology Act 2008 (treatment provided to woman who agrees that second woman to be parent), the second and third references in subsection (2) to the person's father are to be read as references to the woman who is a parent of the person by virtue of that section.]

(3) In [section 50(1) of the Administration of Estates Act 1925] (which relates to the construction of documents), the reference to Part IV of that Act, or to the foregoing provisions of that Part, shall in relation to an instrument inter vivos made, or a will or codicil coming into operation, after the coming into force of this section (but not in relation to instruments inter vivos made or wills or codicils coming into operation earlier) be construed as including references to this section.

(4) This section does not affect any rights under the intestacy of a person dying before the coming into force of this section.

[1305]

NOTES

Sub-s (2A): inserted by the Human Fertilisation and Embryology Act 2008, s 56, Sch 6, Pt 1, para 25(1), (2).
Sub-s (3): words in square brackets substituted by the Human Fertilisation and Embryology Act 2008, s 56, Sch 6, Pt 1, para 25(1), (3).

19 Dispositions of property

(1) In the following dispositions, namely—

(a) dispositions inter vivos made on or after the date on which this section comes into force; and

(b) dispositions by will or codicil where the will or codicil is made on or after that date,

references (whether express or implied) to any relationship between two persons shall be construed in accordance with section 1 above.

(2) It is hereby declared that the use, without more, of the word "heir" or "heirs" or any expression [purporting to create] an entailed interest in real or personal property does not show a contrary intention for the purposes of section 1 as applied by subsection (1) above.

(3) In relation to the dispositions mentioned in subsection (1) above, section 33 of the Trustee Act 1925 (which specifies the trust implied by a direction that income is to be held on protective trusts for the benefit of any person) shall have effect as if any reference (however expressed) to any relationship between two persons were construed in accordance with section 1 above.

(4) Where under any disposition of real or personal property, any interest in such property is limited (whether subject to any preceding limitation or charge or not) in such a way that it would, apart from this section, devolve (as nearly as the law permits) along with a dignity or title of honour, then—

(a) whether or not the disposition contains an express reference to the dignity or title of honour; and

(b) whether or not the property or some interest in the property may in some event become severed from it,

nothing in this section shall operate to sever the property or any interest in it from the dignity or title, but the property or interest shall devolve in all respects as if this section had not been enacted.

(5) This section is without prejudice to section 42 of the Adoption Act 1976 [or section 69 of the Adoption and Children Act 2002] (construction of dispositions in cases of adoption).

(6) In this section "disposition" means a disposition, including an oral disposition, of real or personal property whether inter vivos or by will or codicil.

(7) Notwithstanding any rule of law, a disposition made by will or codicil executed before the date on which this section comes into force shall not be treated for the purposes of this section as made on or after that date by reason only that the will or codicil is confirmed by a codicil executed on or after that date.

[1306]

NOTES

Sub-s (2): words in square brackets substituted by the Trusts of Land and Appointment of Trustees Act 1996, s 25(1), Sch 3, para 25; for savings in relation to entailed interests created before the commencement of that Act, and savings consequential upon the abolition of the doctrine of conversion, see s 25(4), (5) thereof.

Sub-s (5): words in square brackets inserted by the Adoption and Children Act 2002, s 139(1), Sch 3, paras 50, 52.

20 (*Repeals the Family Law Reform Act 1969, s 17.*)

21 Entitlement to grant of probate etc

(1) For the purpose of determining the person or persons who would in accordance with probate rules be entitled to a grant of probate or administration in respect of the estate of a deceased person, the deceased shall be presumed, unless the contrary is shown, not to have been survived—

(a) by any person related to him whose father and mother were not married to each other at the time of his birth; or

(b) by any person whose relationship with him is deduced through such a person as is mentioned in paragraph (a) above.

(2) In this section "probate rules" means rules of court made under section 127 of the *Supreme Court Act 1981* [Senior Courts Act 1981].

(3) This section does not apply in relation to the estate of a person dying before the coming into force of this section.

[1307]

NOTES

Sub-s (2): words in italics substituted by subsequent words in square brackets by the Constitutional Reform Act 2005, s 59(5), Sch 11, Pt 1, para 1(2), as from 1 October 2009.

22–26 ((*Pts IV, V*) *outside the scope of this work.*)

PART VI
MISCELLANEOUS AND SUPPLEMENTAL

27–29 (*Outside the scope of this work.*)

Supplemental

30–33 (*Outside the scope of this work.*)

34 Short title, commencement and extent

(1) This Act may be cited as the Family Law Reform Act 1987.

(2) This Act shall come into force on such day as the Lord Chancellor may by order made by statutory instrument appoint; and different days may be so appointed for different provisions or different purposes.

(3) Without prejudice to the transitional provisions contained in Schedule 3 to this Act, an order under subsection (2) above may make such further transitional provisions as appear to the Lord Chancellor to be necessary or expedient in connection with the provisions brought into force by the order, including—

(a) such adaptations of the provisions so brought into force; and

(b) such adaptations of any provisions of this Act then in force,

as appear to him necessary or expedient in consequence of the partial operation of this Act.

(4) (*Outside the scope of this work.*)

(5) Subject to subsection (4) above, this Act extends to England and Wales only.

[1308]

NOTES

Orders: the Family Law Reform Act 1987 (Commencement No 1) Order 1988, SI 1988/425; the Family Law Reform Act 1987 (Commencement No 2) Order 1989, SI 1989/382; the Family Law Reform Act 1987 (Commencement No 3) Order 2001, SI 2001/777.

(*Schs 1–4 outside the scope of this work.*)

LANDLORD AND TENANT ACT 1988

(1988 c 26)

An Act to make new provision for imposing statutory duties in connection with covenants in tenancies against assigning, underletting, charging or parting with the possession of premises without consent

[29 July 1988]

NOTES

Exclusions: see further, as to exclusion of this Act in relation to leases or tenancies granted to contractors in respect of the running of secure training centres, see the Criminal Justice and Public Order Act 1994, s 7(3); in relation to leases or tenancies granted to contractors in respect of the running of any prison or part of a prison, see the Criminal Justice Act 1991, s 84(3); in relation to leases or tenancies granted to contractors in respect of the running of any removal centre or part of a removal centre: the Immigration and Asylum Act 1999, s 149(3).

1 Qualified duty to consent to assigning, underletting etc of premises

(1) This section applies in any case where—

(a) a tenancy includes a covenant on the part of the tenant not to enter into one or more of the following transactions, that is—

(i) assigning,
(ii) underletting,
(iii) charging, or
(iv) parting with the possession of,

the premises comprised in the tenancy or any part of the premises without the consent of the landlord or some other person, but

(b) the covenant is subject to the qualification that the consent is not to be unreasonably withheld (whether or not it is also subject to any other qualification).

(2) In this section and section 2 of this Act—

(a) references to a proposed transaction are to any assignment, underletting, charging or parting with possession to which the covenant relates, and

(b) references to the person who may consent to such a transaction are to the person who under the covenant may consent to the tenant entering into the proposed transaction.

(3) Where there is served on the person who may consent to a proposed transaction a written application by the tenant for consent to the transaction, he owes a duty to the tenant within a reasonable time—

(a) to give consent, except in a case where it is reasonable not to give consent,

(b) to serve on the tenant written notice of his decision whether or not to give consent specifying in addition—

(i) if the consent is given subject to conditions, the conditions,
(ii) if the consent is withheld, the reasons for withholding it.

(4) Giving consent subject to any condition that is not a reasonable condition does not satisfy the duty under subsection (3)(a) above.

(5) For the purposes of this Act it is reasonable for a person not to give consent to a proposed transaction only in a case where, if he withheld consent and the tenant completed the transaction, the tenant would be in breach of a covenant.

(6) It is for the person who owed any duty under subsection (3) above—

(a) if he gave consent and the question arises whether he gave it within a reasonable time, to show that he did,

(b) if he gave consent subject to any condition and the question arises whether the condition was a reasonable condition, to show that it was,

(c) if he did not give consent and the question arises whether it was reasonable for him not to do so, to show that it was reasonable,

and, if the question arises whether he served notice under that subsection within a reasonable time, to show that he did.

[1309]

NOTES

Modification: modified, where the RTM company has acquired the right to manage, by the Commonhold and Leasehold Reform Act 2002, s 102, Sch 7, para 13(1), (2).

2 Duty to pass on applications

(1) If, in a case where section 1 of this Act applies, any person receives a written application by the tenant for consent to a proposed transaction and that person—

(a) is a person who may consent to the transaction or (though not such a person) is the landlord, and

(b) believes that another person, other than a person who he believes has received the application or a copy of it, is a person who may consent to the transaction,

he owes a duty to the tenant (whether or not he owes him any duty under section 1 of this Act) to take such steps as are reasonable to secure the receipt within a reasonable time by the other person of a copy of the application.

(2) The reference in section 1(3) of this Act to the service of an application on a person who may consent to a proposed transaction includes a reference to the receipt by him of an application or a copy of an application (whether it is for his consent or that of another).

[1310]

3 Qualified duty to approve consent by another

(1) This section applies in any case where—

(a) a tenancy includes a covenant on the part of the tenant not without the approval of the landlord to consent to the sub-tenant—

(i) assigning,

(ii) underletting,

(iii) charging, or

(iv) parting with the possession of,

the premises comprised in the sub-tenancy or any part of the premises, but

(b) the covenant is subject to the qualification that the approval is not to be unreasonably withheld (whether or not it is also subject to any other qualification).

(2) Where there is served on the landlord a written application by the tenant for approval or a copy of a written application to the tenant by the sub-tenant for consent to a transaction to which the covenant relates the landlord owes a duty to the sub-tenant within a reasonable time—

(a) to give approval, except in a case where it is reasonable not to give approval,

(b) to serve on the tenant and the sub-tenant written notice of his decision whether or not to give approval specifying in addition—

(i) if approval is given subject to conditions, the conditions,

(ii) if approval is withheld, the reasons for withholding it.

(3) Giving approval subject to any condition that is not a reasonable condition does not satisfy the duty under subsection (2)(a) above.

(4) For the purposes of this section it is reasonable for the landlord not to give approval only in a case where, if he withheld approval and the tenant gave his consent, the tenant would be in breach of covenant.

(5) It is for a landlord who owed any duty under subsection (2) above—

(a) if he gave approval and the question arises whether he gave it within a reasonable time, to show that he did,

(b) if he gave approval subject to any condition and the question arises whether the condition was a reasonable condition, to show that it was,

(c) if he did not give approval and the question arises whether it was reasonable for him not to do so, to show that it was reasonable,

and, if the question arises whether he served notice under that subsection within a reasonable time, to show that he did.

[1311]

NOTES

Modification: sub-ss (2), (4), (5) modified, where the RTM company has acquired the right to manage, by the Commonhold and Leasehold Reform Act 2002, s 102, Sch 7, para 13(1), (3).

4 Breach of duty

A claim that a person has broken any duty under this Act may be made the subject of civil proceedings in like manner as any other claim in tort for breach of statutory duty.

[1312]

5 Interpretation

(1) In this Act—

"covenant" includes condition and agreement,

"consent" includes licence,

"landlord" includes any superior landlord from whom the tenant's immediate landlord directly or indirectly holds,

"tenancy", subject to subsection (3) below, means any lease or other tenancy (whether made before or after the coming into force of this Act) and includes—

(a) a sub-tenancy, and

(b) an agreement for a tenancy

and references in this Act to the landlord and to the tenant are to be interpreted accordingly, and

"tenant", where the tenancy is affected by a mortgage (within the meaning of the Law of Property Act 1925) and the mortgagee proposes to exercise his statutory or express power of sale, includes the mortgagee.

(2) An application or notice is to be treated as served for the purposes of this Act if—

(a) served in any manner provided in the tenancy, and

(b) in respect of any matter for which the tenancy makes no provision, served in any manner provided by section 23 of the Landlord and Tenant Act 1927.

(3) This Act does not apply to a secure tenancy (defined in section 79 of the Housing Act 1985) [or to an introductory tenancy (within the meaning of Chapter I of Part V of the Housing Act 1996)].

(4) This Act applies only to applications for consent or approval served after its coming into force.

[1313]

NOTES

Sub-s (3): words in square brackets inserted by SI 1997/74, art 2, Schedule, para 5.

6 Application to Crown

This Act binds the Crown; but as regards the Crown's liability in tort shall not bind the Crown further than the Crown is made liable in tort by the Crown Proceedings Act 1947.

[1314]

7 Short title, commencement and extent

(1) This Act may be cited as the Landlord and Tenant Act 1988.

(2) This Act shall come into force at the end of the period of two months beginning with the day on which it is passed.

(3) This Act extends to England and Wales only.

[1315]

HOUSING ACT 1988

(1988 c 50)

An Act to make further provision with respect to dwelling-houses let on tenancies or occupied under licences; to amend the Rent Act 1977 and the Rent (Agriculture) Act 1976; to establish a body, Housing for Wales, having functions relating to housing associations; to amend the Housing Associations Act 1985 and to repeal and re-enact with amendments certain provisions of Part II of that Act; to make provision for the establishment of housing action trusts for areas designated by the Secretary of State; to confer on persons approved for the purpose the right to acquire from public sector landlords certain dwelling-houses occupied by secure tenants; to make further provision about rent officers, the administration of housing benefit and rent allowance subsidy, the right to buy, repair notices and certain disposals of land and the application of capital money arising thereon; to make provision consequential upon the Housing (Scotland) Act 1988; and for connected purposes

[15 November 1988]

NOTES

Transfer of Functions: functions of the Secretary of State under this Act, so far as exercisable in relation to Wales, are transferred to the National Assembly for Wales, by the National Assembly for Wales (Transfer of Functions) Order 1999, SI 1999/672, art 2, Sch 1.

PART I
RENTED ACCOMMODATION

CHAPTER I
ASSURED TENANCIES

Meaning of assured tenancy etc

1 Assured tenancies

(1) A tenancy under which a dwelling-house is let as a separate dwelling is for the purposes of this Act an assured tenancy if and so long as—

(a) the tenant or, as the case may be, each of the joint tenants is an individual; and

(b) the tenant or, as the case may be, at least one of the joint tenants occupies the dwelling-house as his only or principal home; and

(c) the tenancy is not one which, by virtue of subsection (2) or subsection (6) below, cannot be an assured tenancy.

(2) Subject to subsection (3) below, if and so long as a tenancy falls within any paragraph in Part I of Schedule 1 to this Act, it cannot be an assured tenancy; and in that Schedule—

(a) "tenancy" means a tenancy under which a dwelling-house is let as a separate dwelling;

(b) Part II has effect for determining the rateable value of a dwelling-house for the purposes of Part I; and

(c) Part III has effect for supplementing paragraph 10 in Part I.

[(2A) The Secretary of State may by order replace any amount referred to in paragraphs 2 and 3A of Schedule 1 to this Act by such amount as is specified in the order; and such an order shall be made by statutory instrument which shall be subject to annulment in pursuance of a resolution of either House of Parliament.]

(3) Except as provided in Chapter V below, at the commencement of this Act, a tenancy—

(a) under which a dwelling-house was then let as a separate dwelling, and

(b) which immediately before that commencement was an assured tenancy for the purposes of sections 56 to 58 of the Housing Act 1980 (tenancies granted by approved bodies),

shall become an assured tenancy for the purposes of this Act.

(4) In relation to an assured tenancy falling within subsection (3) above—

(a) Part I of Schedule 1 to this Act shall have effect, subject to subsection (5) below, as if it consisted only of paragraphs 11 and 12; and

(b) sections 56 to 58 of the Housing Act 1980 (and Schedule 5 to that Act) shall not apply after the commencement of this Act.

(5) In any case where—

(a) immediately before the commencement of this Act the landlord under a tenancy is a fully mutual housing association, and

(b) at the commencement of this Act the tenancy becomes an assured tenancy by virtue of subsection (3) above,

then, so long as that association remains the landlord under that tenancy (and under any statutory periodic tenancy which arises on the coming to an end of that tenancy), paragraph 12 of Schedule 1 to this Act shall have effect in relation to that tenancy with the omission of sub-paragraph (1)(h).

(6), (7) …

[1316]

NOTES

Sub-s (2A): inserted by SI 1990/434, reg 2, Schedule, para 27.
Sub-ss (6), (7): repealed by the Housing Act 1996, s 227, Sch 19, Pt VIII.

2 Letting of a dwelling-house together with other land

(1) If, under a tenancy, a dwelling-house is let together with other land, then, for the purposes of this Part of this Act,—

(a) if and so long as the main purpose of the letting is the provision of a home for the tenant or, where there are joint tenants, at least one of them, the other land shall be treated as part of the dwelling-house; and

(b) if and so long as the main purpose of the letting is not as mentioned in paragraph (a) above, the tenancy shall be treated as not being one under which a dwelling-house is let as a separate dwelling.

(2) Nothing in subsection (1) above affects any question whether a tenancy is precluded from being an assured tenancy by virtue of any provision of Schedule 1 to this Act.

[1317]

3 Tenant sharing accommodation with persons other than landlord

(1) Where a tenant has the exclusive occupation of any accommodation (in this section referred to as "the separate accommodation") and—

(a) the terms as between the tenant and his landlord on which he holds the separate accommodation include the use of other accommodation (in this section referred to as "the shared accommodation") in common with another person or other persons, not being or including the landlord, and

(b) by reason only of the circumstances mentioned in paragraph (a) above, the separate accommodation would not, apart from this section, be a dwelling-house let on an assured tenancy,

the separate accommodation shall be deemed to be a dwelling-house let on an assured tenancy and the following provisions of this section shall have effect.

(2) For the avoidance of doubt it is hereby declared that where, for the purpose of determining the rateable value of the separate accommodation, it is necessary to make an apportionment under Part II of Schedule 1 to this Act, regard is to be had to the circumstances mentioned in subsection (1)(a) above.

(3) While the tenant is in possession of the separate accommodation, any term of the tenancy terminating or modifying, or providing for the termination or modification of, his right to the use of any of the shared accommodation which is living accommodation shall be of no effect.

(4) Where the terms of the tenancy are such that, at any time during the tenancy, the persons in common with whom the tenant is entitled to the use of the shared accommodation could be varied or their number could be increased, nothing in subsection (3) above shall prevent those terms from having effect so far as they relate to any such variation or increase.

(5) In this section "living accommodation" means accommodation of such a nature that the fact that it constitutes or is included in the shared accommodation is sufficient, apart from this section, to prevent the tenancy from constituting an assured tenancy of a dwelling-house.

[1318]

4 Certain sublettings not to exclude any part of sub-lessor's premises from assured tenancy

(1) Where the tenant of a dwelling-house has sub-let a part but not the whole of the dwelling-house, then, as against his landlord or any superior landlord, no part of the dwelling-house shall be treated as excluded from being a dwelling-house let on an assured tenancy by reason only that the terms on which any person claiming under the tenant holds any part of the dwelling-house include the use of accommodation in common with other persons.

(2) Nothing in this section affects the rights against, and liabilities to, each other of the tenant and any person claiming under him, or of any two such persons.

[1319]

Security of tenure

5 Security of tenure

[(1) An assured tenancy cannot be brought to an end by the landlord except by—

(a) obtaining—

(i) an order of the court for possession of the dwelling-house under section 7 or 21, and

(ii) the execution of the order,

(b) obtaining an order of the court under section 6A (demotion order), or

(c) in the case of a fixed term tenancy which contains power for the landlord to determine the tenancy in certain circumstances, by the exercise of that power,

and, accordingly, the service by the landlord of a notice to quit is of no effect in relation to a periodic assured tenancy.

(1A) Where an order of the court for possession of the dwelling-house is obtained, the tenancy ends when the order is executed.]

(2) If an assured tenancy which is a fixed term tenancy comes to an end otherwise than by virtue of—

(a) an order of the court [of the kind mentioned in subsection (1)(a) or (b) or any other order of the court], or

(b) a surrender or other action on the part of the tenant,

then, subject to section 7 and Chapter II below, the tenant shall be entitled to remain in possession of the dwelling-house let under that tenancy and, subject to subsection (4) below, his right to possession shall depend upon a periodic tenancy arising by virtue of this section.

(3) The periodic tenancy referred to in subsection (2) above is one—

(a) taking effect in possession immediately on the coming to an end of the fixed term tenancy;

(b) deemed to have been granted by the person who was the landlord under the fixed term tenancy immediately before it came to an end to the person who was then the tenant under that tenancy;

(c) under which the premises which are let are the same dwelling-house as was let under the fixed term tenancy;

(d) under which the periods of the tenancy are the same as those for which rent was last payable under the fixed term tenancy; and

(e) under which, subject to the following provisions of this Part of this Act, the other terms are the same as those of the fixed term tenancy immediately before it came to an end, except that any term which makes provision for determination by the landlord or the tenant shall not have effect while the tenancy remains an assured tenancy.

(4) The periodic tenancy referred to in subsection (2) above shall not arise if, on the coming to an end of the fixed term tenancy, the tenant is entitled, by virtue of the grant of another tenancy, to possession of the same or substantially the same dwelling-house as was let to him under the fixed term tenancy.

(5) If, on or before the date on which a tenancy is entered into or is deemed to have been granted as mentioned in subsection (3)(b) above, the person who is to be the tenant under that tenancy—

(a) enters into an obligation to do any act which (apart from this subsection) will cause the tenancy to come to an end at a time when it is an assured tenancy, or

(b) executes, signs or gives any surrender, notice to quit or other document which (apart from this subsection) has the effect of bringing the tenancy to an end at a time when it is an assured tenancy,

the obligation referred to in paragraph (a) above shall not be enforceable or, as the case may be, the surrender, notice to quit or other document referred to in paragraph (b) above shall be of no effect.

[(5A) Nothing in subsection (5) affects any right of pre-emption—

(a) which is exercisable by the landlord under a tenancy in circumstances where the tenant indicates his intention to dispose of the whole of his interest under the tenancy, and

(b) in pursuance of which the landlord would be required to pay, in respect of the acquisition of that interest, an amount representing its market value.

"Dispose" means dispose by assignment or surrender, and "acquisition" has a corresponding meaning.]

(6) If, by virtue of any provision of this Part of this Act, Part I of Schedule 1 to this Act has effect in relation to a fixed term tenancy as if it consisted only of paragraphs 11 and 12, that Part shall have the like effect in relation to any periodic tenancy which arises by virtue of this section on the coming to an end of the fixed term tenancy.

(7) Any reference in this Part of this Act to a statutory periodic tenancy is a reference to a periodic tenancy arising by virtue of this section.

[1320]

NOTES

Sub-ss (1), (1A): substituted for original sub-s (1) by the Housing and Regeneration Act 2008, s 299, Sch 11, Pt 1, paras 5, 6(1), (2), subject to transitional provisions in Sch 11, Pt 1, para 14 thereto.

Sub-s (2): words in square brackets inserted by the Housing and Regeneration Act 2008, s 299, Sch 11, Pt 1, paras 5, 6(1), (3), subject to transitional provisions in Sch 11, Pt 1, para 14 thereto.

Sub-s (5A): inserted by the Housing Act 2004, s 222(1), (2), except in relation to any right of pre-emption granted before 18 January 2005.

6 Fixing of terms of statutory periodic tenancy

(1) In this section, in relation to a statutory periodic tenancy,—

(a) "the former tenancy" means the fixed term tenancy on the coming to an end of which the statutory periodic tenancy arises; and

(b) "the implied terms" means the terms of the tenancy which have effect by virtue of section 5(3)(e) above, other than terms as to the amount of the rent;

but nothing in the following provisions of this section applies to a statutory periodic tenancy at a time when, by virtue of paragraph 11 or paragraph 12 in Part 1 of Schedule 1 to this Act, it cannot be an assured tenancy.

(2) Not later than the first anniversary of the day on which the former tenancy came to an end, the landlord may serve on the tenant, or the tenant may serve on the landlord, a notice in the prescribed form proposing terms of the statutory periodic tenancy different from the implied terms and, if the landlord or the tenant considers it appropriate, proposing an adjustment of the amount of the rent to take account of the proposed terms.

(3) Where a notice has been served under subsection (2) above,—

(a) within the period of three months beginning on the date on which the notice was served on him, the landlord or the tenant, as the case may be, may, by an application in the prescribed form, refer the notice to a rent assessment committee under subsection (4) below; and

(b) if the notice is not so referred, then, with effect from such date, not falling within the period referred to in paragraph (a) above, as may be specified in the notice, the terms proposed in the notice shall become terms of the tenancy in substitution for any of the implied terms dealing with the same subject matter and the amount of the rent shall be varied in accordance with any adjustment so proposed.

(4) Where a notice under subsection (2) above is referred to a rent assessment committee, the committee shall consider the terms proposed in the notice and shall determine whether those terms, or some other terms (dealing with the same subject matter as the proposed terms), are such as, in the committee's opinion, might reasonably be expected to be found in an assured periodic tenancy of the dwelling-house concerned, being a tenancy—

(a) which begins on the coming to an end of the former tenancy; and

(b) which is granted by a willing landlord on terms which, except in so far as they relate to the subject matter of the proposed terms, are those of the statutory periodic tenancy at the time of the committee's consideration.

(5) Whether or not a notice under subsection (2) above proposes an adjustment of the amount of the rent under the statutory periodic tenancy, where a rent assessment committee determine any terms under subsection (4) above, they shall, if they consider it appropriate, specify such an adjustment to take account of the terms so determined.

(6) In making a determination under subsection (4) above, or specifying an adjustment of an amount of rent under subsection (5) above, there shall be disregarded any effect on the terms or the amount of the rent attributable to the granting of a tenancy to a sitting tenant.

(7) Where a notice under subsection (2) above is referred to a rent assessment committee, then, unless the landlord and the tenant otherwise agree, with effect from such date as the committee may direct—

(a) the terms determined by the committee shall become terms of the statutory periodic tenancy in substitution for any of the implied terms dealing with the same subject matter; and

(b) the amount of the rent under the statutory periodic tenancy shall be altered to accord with any adjustment specified by the committee;

but for the purposes of paragraph (b) above the committee shall not direct a date earlier than the date specified, in accordance with subsection (3)(b) above, in the notice referred to them.

(8) Nothing in this section requires a rent assessment committee to continue with a determination under subsection (4) above if the landlord and tenant give notice in writing that they no longer require such a determination or if the tenancy has come to an end.

[1321]

NOTES

Regulations: the Assured Tenancies and Agricultural Occupancies (Forms) Regulations 1997, SI 1997/194.

[6A Demotion because of anti-social behaviour

(1) This section applies to an assured tenancy if the landlord is a registered social landlord.

(2) The landlord may apply to a county court for a demotion order.

(3) A demotion order has the following effect—

(a) the assured tenancy is terminated with effect from the date specified in the order;

(b) if the tenant remains in occupation of the dwelling-house after that date a demoted tenancy is created with effect from that date;

(c) it is a term of the demoted tenancy that any arrears of rent payable at the termination of the assured tenancy become payable under the demoted tenancy;

(d) it is also a term of the demoted tenancy that any rent paid in advance or overpaid at the termination of the assured tenancy is credited to the tenant's liability to pay rent under the demoted tenancy.

(4) The court must not make a demotion order unless it is satisfied—

(a) that the tenant or a person residing in or visiting the dwelling-house has engaged or has threatened to *engage in conduct to which section 153A or 153B of the Housing Act 1996 (anti-social behaviour or use of premises for unlawful purposes) applies, and* [engage in—

(i) housing-related anti-social conduct, or

(ii) conduct to which section 153B of the Housing Act 1996 (use of premises for unlawful purposes) applies, and]

(b) that it is reasonable to make the order.

(5) The court must not entertain proceedings for a demotion order unless—

(a) the landlord has served on the tenant a notice under subsection (6), or
(b) the court thinks it is just and equitable to dispense with the requirement of the notice.

(6) The notice must—
(a) give particulars of the conduct in respect of which the order is sought;
(b) state that the proceedings will not begin before the date specified in the notice;
(c) state that the proceedings will not begin after the end of the period of twelve months beginning with the date of service of the notice.

(7) The date specified for the purposes of subsection (6)(b) must not be before the end of the period of two weeks beginning with the date of service of the notice.

(8) Each of the following has effect in respect of a demoted tenancy at the time it is created by virtue of an order under this section as it has effect in relation to the assured tenancy at the time it is terminated by virtue of the order—
(a) the parties to the tenancy;
(b) the period of the tenancy;
(c) the amount of the rent;
(d) the dates on which the rent is payable.

(9) Subsection (8)(b) does not apply if the assured tenancy was for a fixed term and in such a case the demoted tenancy is a weekly periodic tenancy.

(10) If the landlord of the demoted tenancy serves on the tenant a statement of any other express terms of the assured tenancy which are to apply to the demoted tenancy such terms are also terms of the demoted tenancy.

[(10A) In subsection (4)(a) "housing-related anti-social conduct" has the same meaning as in section 153A of the Housing Act 1996.]

(11) For the purposes of this section a demoted tenancy is a tenancy to which section 20B of the Housing Act 1988 applies.]

[1322]

NOTES

Commencement: 30 June 2004 (in relation to England); 30 April 2005 (in relation to Wales).
Inserted by the Anti-social Behaviour Act 2003, s 14(4).
Sub-s (4): in para (a), words in italics substituted by subsequent words in square brackets by the Police and Justice Act 2006, s 52, Sch 14, para 15(1), (2), as from a day to be appointed.
Sub-s (10A): inserted by the Police and Justice Act 2006, s 52, Sch 14, para 15(1), (3), as from a day to be appointed.

7 Orders for possession

(1) The court shall not make an order for possession of a dwelling-house let on an assured tenancy except on one or more of the grounds set out in Schedule 2 to this Act; but nothing in this Part of this Act relates to proceedings for possession of such a dwelling-house which are brought by a mortgagee, within the meaning of the Law of Property Act 1925, who has lent money on the security of the assured tenancy.

(2) The following provisions of this section have effect, subject to section 8 below, in relation to proceedings for the recovery of possession of a dwelling-house let on an assured tenancy.

(3) If the court is satisfied that any of the grounds in Part I of Schedule 2 to this Act is established then, subject to [subsections (5A) and (6)] below, the court shall make an order for possession.

(4) If the court is satisfied that any of the grounds in Part II of Schedule 2 to this Act is established, then, subject to [subsections (5A) and (6)] below, the court may make an order for possession if it considers it reasonable to do so.

(5) Part III of Schedule 2 to this Act shall have effect for supplementing Ground 9 in that Schedule and Part IV of that Schedule shall have effect in relation to notices given as mentioned in Grounds 1 to 5 of that Schedule.

[(5A) The court shall not make an order for possession of a dwelling-house let on an assured periodic tenancy arising under Schedule 10 to the Local Government and Housing Act 1989 on any of the following grounds, that is to say,—
(a) Grounds 1, 2 and 5 in Part I of Schedule 2 to this Act;
(b) Ground 16 in Part II of that Schedule; and
(c) if the assured periodic tenancy arose on the termination of a former 1954 Act tenancy, within the meaning of the said Schedule 10, Ground 6 in Part I of Schedule 2 to this Act.]

(6) The court shall not make an order for possession of a dwelling-house to take effect at a time when it is let on an assured fixed term tenancy unless—

(a) the ground for possession is Ground 2 or Ground 8 in Part I of Schedule 2 to this Act or any of the grounds in Part II of that Schedule, other than Ground 9 or Ground 16; and

(b) the terms of the tenancy make provision for it to be brought to an end on the ground in question (whether that provision takes the form of a provision for re-entry, for forfeiture, for determination by notice or otherwise).

(7) Subject to the preceding provisions of this section, the court may make an order for possession of a dwelling-house on grounds relating to a fixed term tenancy which has come to an end; and where an order is made in such circumstances, any statutory periodic tenancy which has arisen on the ending of the fixed term tenancy shall end (without any notice and regardless of the period) on the day on which the order takes effect [in accordance with section 5(1A)].

[1323]

NOTES

Sub-ss (3), (4): words in square brackets substituted by the Local Government and Housing Act 1989, s 194, Sch 11, para 101.

Sub-s (5A): inserted by the Local Government and Housing Act 1989, s 194, Sch 11, para 101.

Sub-s (7): words in square brackets substituted by the Housing and Regeneration Act 2008, s 299, Sch 11, Pt 1, paras 5, 7, subject to transitional provisions in Sch 11, Pt 1, para 14 thereto.

8 Notice of proceedings for possession

(1) The court shall not entertain proceedings for possession of a dwelling-house let on an assured tenancy unless—

(a) the landlord or, in the case of joint landlords, at least one of them has served on the tenant a notice in accordance with this section and the proceedings are begun within the time limits stated in the notice in accordance with [subsections (3) to (4B)] below; or

(b) the court considers it just and equitable to dispense with the requirement of such a notice.

(2) The court shall not make an order for possession on any of the grounds in Schedule 2 to this Act unless that ground and particulars of it are specified in the notice under this section; but the grounds specified in such a notice may be altered or added to with the leave of the court.

(3) A notice under this section is one in the prescribed form informing the tenant that—

(a) the landlord intends to begin proceedings for possession of the dwelling-house on one or more of the grounds specified in the notice; and

(b) those proceedings will not begin earlier than a date specified in the notice [in accordance with subsections (4) to (4B) below]; and

(c) those proceedings will not begin later than twelve months from the date of service of the notice.

[(4) If a notice under this section specifies in accordance with subsection (3)(a) above Ground 14 in Schedule 2 to this Act (whether with or without other grounds), the date specified in the notice as mentioned in subsection (3)(b) above shall not be earlier than the date of the service of the notice.

(4A) If a notice under this section specifies in accordance with subsection (3)(a) above, any of Grounds 1, 2, 5 to 7, 9 and 16 in Schedule 2 to this Act (whether without other grounds or with any ground other than Ground 14), the date specified in the notice as mentioned in subsection (3)(b) above shall not be earlier than—

(a) two months from the date of service of the notice; and

(b) if the tenancy is a periodic tenancy, the earliest date on which, apart from section 5(1) above, the tenancy could be brought to an end by a notice to quit given by the landlord on the same date as the date of service of the notice under this section.

(4B) In any other case, the date specified in the notice as mentioned in subsection (3)(b) above shall not be earlier than the expiry of the period of two weeks from the date of the service of the notice.]

(5) The court may not exercise the power conferred by subsection (1)(b) above if the landlord seeks to recover possession on Ground 8 in Schedule 2 to this Act.

(6) Where a notice under this section—

(a) is served at a time when the dwelling-house is let on a fixed term tenancy, or

(b) is served after a fixed term tenancy has come to an end but relates (in whole or in part) to events occurring during that tenancy,

the notice shall have effect notwithstanding that the tenant becomes or has become tenant under a statutory periodic tenancy arising on the coming to an end of the fixed term tenancy.

[1324]

NOTES

Sub-ss (1), (3): words in square brackets substituted by the Housing Act 1996, s 151(2), (3).

Sub-ss (4)–(4B): substituted, for sub-s (4) as originally enacted, by the Housing Act 1996, s 151(4).

Regulations: the Assured Tenancies and Agricultural Occupancies (Forms) Regulations 1997, SI 1997/194.

[8A Additional notice requirements: ground of domestic violence

(1) Where the ground specified in a notice under section 8 (whether with or without other grounds) is Ground 14A in Schedule 2 to this Act and the partner who has left the dwelling-house as mentioned in that ground is not a tenant of the dwelling-house, the court shall not entertain proceedings for possession of the dwelling-house unless—

(a) the landlord or, in the case of joint landlords, at least one of them has served on the partner who has left a copy of the notice or has taken all reasonable steps to serve a copy of the notice on that partner, or

(b) the court considers it just and equitable to dispense with such requirements as to service.

(2) Where Ground 14A in Schedule 2 to this Act is added to a notice under section 8 with the leave of the court after proceedings for possession are begun and the partner who has left the dwelling-house as mentioned in that ground is not a party to the proceedings, the court shall not continue to entertain the proceedings unless—

(a) the landlord or, in the case of joint landlords, at least one of them has served a notice under subsection (3) below on the partner who has left or has taken all reasonable steps to serve such a notice on that partner, or

(b) the court considers it just and equitable to dispense with the requirement of such a notice.

(3) A notice under this subsection shall—

(a) state that proceedings for the possession of the dwelling-house have begun,

(b) specify the ground or grounds on which possession is being sought, and

(c) give particulars of the ground or grounds.]

[1325]

NOTES

Inserted by the Housing Act 1996, s 150.

9 Extended discretion of court in possession claims

(1) Subject to subsection (6) below, the court may adjourn for such period or periods as it thinks fit proceedings for possession of a dwelling-house let on an assured tenancy.

(2) On the making of an order for possession of a dwelling-house let on an assured tenancy or at any time before the execution of such an order, the court, subject to subsection (6) below, may—

(a) stay or suspend execution of the order, or

(b) postpone the date of possession,

for such period or periods as the court thinks just.

(3) On any such adjournment as is referred to in subsection (1) above or on any such stay, suspension or postponement as is referred to in subsection (2) above, the court, unless it considers that to do so would cause exceptional hardship to the tenant or would otherwise be unreasonable, shall impose conditions with regard to payment by the tenant of arrears of rent (if any) and rent … and may impose such other conditions as it thinks fit.

(4) If any such conditions as are referred to in subsection (3) above are complied with, the court may, if it thinks fit, discharge or rescind any such order as is referred to in subsection (2) above.

[(4) The court may discharge or rescind any such order as is referred to in subsection (2) if it thinks it appropriate to do so having had regard to—

(a) any conditions imposed under subsection (3), and

(b) the conduct of the tenant in connection with those conditions.]

(5), (5A) …

(6) This section does not apply if the court is satisfied that the landlord is entitled to possession of the dwelling-house—

(a) on any of the grounds in Part I of Schedule 2 to this Act; or

(b) by virtue of subsection (1) or subsection (4) of section 21 below.

[1326]

NOTES

Sub-s (3): words omitted repealed by the Housing and Regeneration Act 2008, ss 299, 321(1), Sch 11, Pt 1, paras 5, 8(1), (2), Sch 16, subject to transitional provisions in Sch 11, Pt 1, para 14 thereto.

Para (4): substituted by the Housing and Regeneration Act 2008, s 299, Sch 11, Pt 1, paras 5, 8(1), (3), as from a day to be appointed, subject to transitional provisions in Sch 11, Pt 1, para 14 thereto.

Sub-s (5): repealed by the Housing and Regeneration Act 2008, ss 299, 321(1), Sch 11, Pt 1, paras 5, 8(1), (4), Sch 16, subject to transitional provisions in Sch 11, Pt 1, para 14 thereto.

Sub-s (5A): inserted by the Family Law Act 1996, s 66(1), Sch 8, para 59(3); repealed by the Housing and Regeneration Act 2008, ss 299, 321(1), Sch 11, Pt 1, paras 5, 8(1), (4), Sch 16, subject to transitional provisions in Sch 11, Pt 1, para 14 thereto.

[9A Proceedings for possession: anti-social behaviour

(1) This section applies if the court is considering under section 7(4) whether it is reasonable to make an order for possession on ground 14 set out in Part 2 of Schedule 2 (conduct of tenant or other person).

(2) The court must consider, in particular—

(a) the effect that the nuisance or annoyance has had on persons other than the person against whom the order is sought;

(b) any continuing effect the nuisance or annoyance is likely to have on such persons;

(c) the effect that the nuisance or annoyance would be likely to have on such persons if the conduct is repeated.]

[1327]

NOTES

Commencement: 30 June 2004 (in relation to England, except in relation to any proceedings for the possession of a dwelling-house begun before that date); 30 September 2004 (in relation to Wales, except in relation to any proceeding for possession of a dwelling-house begun before that date.

Inserted by the Anti-social Behaviour Act 2003, s 16(2).

10 Special provisions applicable to shared accommodation

(1) This section applies in a case falling within subsection (1) of section 3 above and expressions used in this section have the same meaning as in that section.

(2) Without prejudice to the enforcement of any order made under subsection (3) below, while the tenant is in possession of the separate accommodation, no order shall be made for possession of any of the shared accommodation, whether on the application of the immediate landlord of the tenant or on the application of any person under whom that landlord derives title, unless a like order has been made, or is made at the same time, in respect of the separate accommodation; and the provisions of section 6 above shall have effect accordingly.

(3) On the application of the landlord, the court may make such order as it thinks just either—

(a) terminating the right of the tenant to use the whole or any part of the shared accommodation other than living accommodation; or

(b) modifying his right to use the whole or any part of the shared accommodation, whether by varying the persons or increasing the number of persons entitled to the use of that accommodation or otherwise.

(4) No order shall be made under subsection (3) above so as to effect any termination or modification of the rights of the tenant which, apart from section 3(3) above, could not be effected by or under the terms of the tenancy.

[1328]

11 Payment of removal expenses in certain cases

(1) Where a court makes an order for possession of a dwelling-house let on an assured tenancy on Ground 6 or Ground 9 in Schedule 2 to this Act (but not on any other ground), the landlord shall pay to the tenant a sum equal to the reasonable expenses likely to be incurred by the tenant in removing from the dwelling-house.

(2) Any question as to the amount of the sum referred to in subsection (1) above shall be determined by agreement between the landlord and the tenant or, in default of agreement, by the court.

(3) Any sum payable to a tenant by virtue of this section shall be recoverable as a civil debt due from the landlord.

[1329]

12 Compensation for misrepresentation or concealment

Where a landlord obtains an order for possession of a dwelling-house let on an assured tenancy on one or more of the grounds in Schedule 2 to this Act and it is subsequently made to appear to the court that the order was obtained by misrepresentation or concealment of material facts, the court may order the landlord to pay to the former tenant such sum as appears sufficient as compensation for damage or loss sustained by that tenant as a result of the order.

[1330]

Rent and other terms

13 Increases of rent under assured periodic tenancies

(1) This section applies to—

(a) a statutory periodic tenancy other than one which, by virtue of paragraph 11 or paragraph 12 in Part I of Schedule 1 to this Act, cannot for the time being be an assured tenancy; and

(b) any other periodic tenancy which is an assured tenancy, other than one in relation to which there is a provision, for the time being binding on the tenant, under which the rent for a particular period of the tenancy will or may be greater than the rent for an earlier period.

(2) For the purpose of securing an increase in the rent under a tenancy to which this section applies, the landlord may serve on the tenant a notice in the prescribed form proposing a new rent to take effect at the beginning of a new period of the tenancy specified in the notice, being a period beginning not earlier than—

(a) the minimum period after the date of the service of the notice; and

(b) except in the case of a statutory periodic [tenancy—

(i) in the case of an assured agricultural occupancy, the first anniversary of the date on which the first period of the tenancy began;

(ii) in any other case, on the date that falls 52 weeks after the date on which the first period of the tenancy began; and]

(c) if the rent under the tenancy has previously been increased by virtue of a notice under this subsection or a determination under section 14 [below—

(i) in the case of an assured agricultural occupancy, the first anniversary of the date on which the increased rent took effect;

(ii) in any other case, the appropriate date].

(3) The minimum period referred to in subsection (2) above is—

(a) in the case of a yearly tenancy, six months;

(b) in the case of a tenancy where the period is less than a month, one month; and

(c) in any other case, a period equal to the period of the tenancy.

[(3A) The appropriate date referred to in subsection (2)(c)(ii) above is—

(a) in a case to which subsection (3B) below applies, the date that falls 53 weeks after the date on which the increased rent took effect;

(b) in any other case, the date that falls 52 weeks after the date on which the increased rent took effect.

(3B) This subsection applies where—

(a) the rent under the tenancy has been increased by virtue of a notice under this section or a determination under section 14 below on at least one occasion after the coming into force of the Regulatory Reform (Assured Periodic Tenancies) (Rent Increases) Order 2003; and

(b) the fifty-third week after the date on which the last such increase took effect begins more than six days before the anniversary of the date on which the first such increase took effect.]

(4) Where a notice is served under subsection (2) above, a new rent specified in the notice shall take effect as mentioned in the notice unless, before the beginning of the new period specified in the notice,—

(a) the tenant by an application in the prescribed form refers the notice to a rent assessment committee; or

(b) the landlord and the tenant agree on a variation of the rent which is different from that proposed in the notice or agree that the rent should not be varied.

(5) Nothing in this section (or in section 14 below) affects the right of the landlord and the tenant under an assured tenancy to vary by agreement any term of the tenancy (including a term relating to rent).

[1331]

NOTES

Sub-s (2): words in square brackets substituted by SI 2003/259, art 2(a), in respect of notices served after 11 February 2003.

Sub-ss (3A), (3B): inserted by SI 2003/259, art 2(b), in respect of notices served after 11 February 2003.

Regulations: the Assured Tenancies and Agricultural Occupancies (Forms) Regulations 1997, SI 1997/194.

14 Determination of rent by rent assessment committee

(1) Where, under subsection (4)(a) of section 13 above, a tenant refers to a rent assessment committee a notice under subsection (2) of that section, the committee shall determine the rent at which, subject to subsections (2) and (4) below, the committee consider that the dwelling-house concerned might reasonably be expected to be let in the open market by a willing landlord under an assured tenancy—

(a) which is a periodic tenancy having the same periods as those of the tenancy to which the notice relates;

(b) which begins at the beginning of the new period specified in the notice;
(c) the terms of which (other than relating to the amount of the rent) are the same as those of the tenancy to which the notice relates; and
(d) in respect of which the same notices, if any, have been given under any of Grounds 1 to 5 of Schedule 2 to this Act, as have been given (or have effect as if given) in relation to the tenancy to which the notice relates.

(2) In making a determination under this section, there shall be disregarded—
(a) any effect on the rent attributable to the granting of a tenancy to a sitting tenant;
(b) any increase in the value of the dwelling-house attributable to a relevant improvement carried out by a person who at the time it was carried out was the tenant, if the improvement—
  (i) was carried out otherwise than in pursuance of an obligation to his immediate landlord, or
  (ii) was carried out pursuant to an obligation to his immediate landlord being an obligation which did not relate to the specific improvement concerned but arose by reference to consent given to the carrying out of that improvement; and
(c) any reduction in the value of the dwelling-house attributable to a failure by the tenant to comply with any terms of the tenancy.

(3) For the purposes of subsection (2)(b) above, in relation to a notice which is referred by a tenant as mentioned in subsection (1) above, an improvement is a relevant improvement if either it was carried out during the tenancy to which the notice relates or the following conditions are satisfied, namely—
(a) that it was carried out not more than twenty-one years before the date of service of the notice; and
(b) that, at all times during the period beginning when the improvement was carried out and ending on the date of service of the notice, the dwelling-house has been let under an assured tenancy; and
(c) that, on the coming to an end of an assured tenancy at any time during that period, the tenant (or, in the case of joint tenants, at least one of them) did not quit.

[(3A) In making a determination under this section in any case where under Part I of the Local Government Finance Act 1992 the landlord or a superior landlord is liable to pay council tax in respect of a hereditament ("the relevant hereditament") of which the dwelling-house forms part, the rent assessment committee shall have regard to the amount of council tax which, as at the date on which the notice under section 13(2) above was served, was set by the billing authority—
(a) for the financial year in which that notice was served, and
(b) for the category of dwellings within which the relevant hereditament fell on that date,

but any discount or other reduction affecting the amount of council tax payable shall be disregarded.

(3B) In subsection (3A) above—
(a) "hereditament" means a dwelling within the meaning of Part I of the Local Government Finance Act 1992,
(b) "billing authority" has the same meaning as in that Part of that Act, and
(c) "category of dwellings" has the same meaning as in section 30(1) and (2) of that Act.]

(4) In this section "rent" does not include any service charge, within the meaning of section 18 of the Landlord and Tenant Act 1985, but, subject to that, includes any sums payable by the tenant to the landlord on account of the use of furniture[, in respect of council tax] or for any of the matters referred to in subsection (1)(a) of that section, whether or not those sums are separate from the sums payable for the occupation of the dwelling-house concerned or are payable under separate agreements.

(5) Where any rates in respect of the dwelling-house concerned are borne by the landlord or a superior landlord, the rent assessment committee shall make their determination under this section as if the rates were not so borne.

(6) In any case where—
(a) a rent assessment committee have before them at the same time the reference of a notice under section 6(2) above relating to a tenancy (in this subsection referred to as "the section 6 reference") and the reference of a notice under section 13(2) above relating to the same tenancy (in this subsection referred to as "the section 13 reference"), and
(b) the date specified in the notice under section 6(2) above is not later than the first day of the new period specified in the notice under section 13(2) above, and
(c) the committee propose to hear the two references together,

the committee shall make a determination in relation to the section 6 reference before making their determination in relation to the section 13 reference and, accordingly, in such a case the reference in subsection (1)(c) above to the terms of the tenancy to which the notice relates shall be construed as a reference to those terms as varied by virtue of the determination made in relation to the section 6 reference.

(7) Where a notice under section 13(2) above has been referred to a rent assessment committee, then, unless the landlord and the tenant otherwise agree, the rent determined by the committee (subject, in a case where subsection (5) above applies, to the addition of the appropriate amount in respect of rates) shall be the rent under the tenancy with effect from the beginning of the new period specified in the notice or, if it appears to the rent assessment committee that that would cause undue hardship to the tenant, with effect from such later date (not being later than the date the rent is determined) as the committee may direct.

(8) Nothing in this section requires a rent assessment committee to continue with their determination of a rent for a dwelling-house if the landlord and tenant give notice in writing that they no longer require such a determination or if the tenancy has come to an end.

[(9) This section shall apply in relation to an assured shorthold tenancy as if in subsection (1) the reference to an assured tenancy were a reference to an assured shorthold tenancy.]

[1332]

NOTES

Sub-ss (3A), (3B): inserted by SI 1993/651, art 2(1), Sch 1, para 17(2).
Sub-s (4): words in square brackets inserted by SI 1993/651, art 2(1), Sch 1, para 17(3).
Sub-s (9): inserted by the Housing Act 1996, s 104, Sch 8, para 2(2).
Modification: modified by the Local Government and Housing Act 1989, s 186, Sch 10, paras 6, 11.

[14A Interim increase before 1st April 1994 of rent under assured periodic tenancies in certain cases where landlord liable for council tax

(1) In any case where—

(a) under Part I of the Local Government Finance Act 1992 the landlord of a dwelling-house let under an assured tenancy to which section 13 above applies or a superior landlord is liable to pay council tax in respect of a dwelling (within the meaning of that Part of that Act) which includes that dwelling-house,
(b) under the terms of the tenancy (or an agreement collateral to the tenancy) the tenant is liable to make payments to the landlord in respect of council tax,
(c) the case falls within subsection (2) or subsection (3) below, and
(d) no previous notice under this subsection has been served in relation to the dwelling-house,

the landlord may serve on the tenant a notice in the prescribed form proposing an increased rent to take account of the tenant's liability to make payments to the landlord in respect of council tax, such increased rent to take effect at the beginning of a new period of the tenancy specified in the notice being a period beginning not earlier than one month after the date on which the notice was served.

(2) The case falls within this subsection if—

(a) the rent under the tenancy has previously been increased by virtue of a notice under section 13(2) above or a determination under section 14 above, and
(b) the first anniversary of the date on which the increased rent took effect has not yet occurred.

(3) The case falls within this subsection if a notice has been served under section 13(2) above before 1st April 1993 but no increased rent has taken effect before that date.

(4) No notice may be served under subsection (1) above after 31st March 1994.

(5) Where a notice is served under subsection (1) above, the new rent specified in the notice shall take effect as mentioned in the notice unless, before the beginning of the new period specified in the notice—

(a) the tenant by an application in the prescribed form refers the notice to a rent assessment committee, or
(b) the landlord and the tenant agree on a variation of the rent which is different from that proposed in the notice or agree that the rent should not be varied.

(6) Nothing in this section (or in section 14B below) affects the right of the landlord and the tenant under an assured tenancy to vary by agreement any term of the tenancy (including a term relating to rent).]

[1333]

NOTES

Inserted by SI 1993/651, art 2(2), Sch 2, para 8.

[14B Interim determination of rent by rent assessment committee

(1) Where, under subsection (5)(a) of section 14A above, a tenant refers to a rent assessment committee a notice under subsection (1) of that section, the committee shall determine the amount by which, having regard to the provisions of section 14(3A) above, the existing rent might reasonably be increased to take account of the tenant's liability to make payments to the landlord in respect of council tax.

(2) Where a notice under section 14A(1) above has been referred to a rent assessment committee, then, unless the landlord and the tenant otherwise agree, the existing rent shall be increased by the amount determined by the committee with effect from the beginning of the new period specified in the notice or, if it appears to the committee that that would cause undue hardship to the tenant, with effect from such later date (not being later than the date the increase is determined) as the committee may direct.

(3) In any case where—

(a) a rent assessment committee have before them at the same time the reference of a notice under section 13(2) above relating to a tenancy (in this subsection referred to as "the section 13 reference") and the reference of a notice under section 14A(1) above relating to the same tenancy (in this subsection referred to as "the section 14A reference"); and

(b) the committee propose to hear the two references together,

the committee shall make a determination in relation to the section 13 reference before making their determination in relation to the section 14A reference, and if in such a case the date specified in the notice under section 13(2) above is later than the date specified in the notice under section 14A(1) above, the rent determined under the section 14A reference shall not take effect until the date specified in the notice under section 13(2).

(4) In this section "rent" has the same meaning as in section 14 above; and section 14(4) above applies to a determination under this section as it applies to a determination under that section.]

[1334]

NOTES

Inserted by SI 1993/651, art 2(2), Sch 2, para 8.

15 Limited prohibition on assignment etc without consent

(1) Subject to subsection (3) below, it shall be an implied term of every assured tenancy which is a periodic tenancy that, except with the consent of the landlord, the tenant shall not—

(a) assign the tenancy (in whole or in part); or

(b) sub-let or part with possession of the whole or any part of the dwelling-house let on the tenancy.

(2) Section 19 of the Landlord and Tenant Act 1927 (consents to assign not to be unreasonably withheld etc) shall not apply to a term which is implied into an assured tenancy by subsection (1) above.

(3) In the case of a periodic tenancy which is not a statutory periodic tenancy [or an assured periodic tenancy arising under Schedule 10 to the Local Government and Housing Act 1989] subsection (1) above does not apply if—

(a) there is a provision (whether contained in the tenancy or not) under which the tenant is prohibited (whether absolutely or conditionally) from assigning or sub-letting or parting with possession or is permitted (whether absolutely or conditionally) to assign, sub-let or part with possession; or

(b) a premium is required to be paid on the grant or renewal of the tenancy.

(4) In subsection (3)(b) above "premium" includes—

(a) any fine or other like sum;

(b) any other pecuniary consideration in addition to rent; and

(c) any sum paid by way of deposit, other than one which does not exceed one-sixth of the annual rent payable under the tenancy immediately after the grant or renewal in question.

[1335]

NOTES

Sub-s (3): words in square brackets inserted by the Local Government and Housing Act 1989, s 194, Sch 11, para 102.

16 Access for repairs

It shall be an implied term of every assured tenancy that the tenant shall afford to the landlord access to the dwelling-house let on the tenancy and all reasonable facilities for executing therein any repairs which the landlord is entitled to execute.

[1336]

Miscellaneous

17 Succession to assured periodic tenancy by spouse

(1) In any case where—

(a) the sole tenant under an assured periodic tenancy dies, and

(b) immediately before the death, the tenant's spouse [or civil partner] was occupying the dwelling-house as his or her only or principal home, and

(c) the tenant was not himself a successor, as defined in subsection (2) or subsection (3) below,

then, on the death, the tenancy vests by virtue of this section in the spouse [or civil partner] (and, accordingly, does not devolve under the tenant's will or intestacy).

(2) For the purposes of this section, a tenant is a successor in relation to a tenancy if—

(a) the tenancy became vested in him either by virtue of this section or under the will or intestacy of a previous tenant; or

(b) at some time before the tenant's death the tenancy was a joint tenancy held by himself and one or more other persons and, prior to his death, he became the sole tenant by survivorship; or

(c) he became entitled to the tenancy as mentioned in section 39(5) below.

(3) For the purposes of this section, a tenant is also a successor in relation to a tenancy (in this subsection referred to as "the new tenancy") which was granted to him (alone or jointly with others) if—

(a) at some time before the grant of the new tenancy, he was, by virtue of subsection (2) above, a successor in relation to an earlier tenancy of the same or substantially the same dwelling-house as is let under the new tenancy; and

(b) at all times since he became such a successor he has been a tenant (alone or jointly with others) of the dwelling-house which is let under the new tenancy or of a dwelling-house which is substantially the same as that dwelling-house.

[(4) For the purposes of this section—

(a) a person who was living with the tenant as his or her wife or husband shall be treated as the tenant's spouse, and

(b) a person who was living with the tenant as if they were civil partners shall be treated as the tenant's civil partner.]

(5) If, on the death of the tenant, there is, by virtue of subsection (4) above, more than one person who fulfils the condition in subsection (1)(b) above, such one of them as may be decided by agreement or, in default of agreement, by the county court [shall for the purposes of this section be treated (according to whether that one of them is of the opposite sex to, or of the same sex as, the tenant) as the tenant's spouse or the tenant's civil partner].

[1337]

NOTES

Sub-s (1): words in square brackets inserted by the Civil Partnership Act 2004, s 81, Sch 8, para 41(1), (2).
Sub-s (4): substituted by the Civil Partnership Act 2004, s 81, Sch 8, para 41(1), (3).
Sub-s (5): words in square brackets substituted by the Civil Partnership Act 2004, s 81, Sch 8, para 41(1), (4).

18 Provisions as to reversions on assured tenancies

(1) If at any time—

(a) a dwelling-house is for the time being lawfully let on an assured tenancy, and

(b) the landlord under the assured tenancy is himself a tenant under a superior tenancy; and

(c) the superior tenancy comes to an end,

then, subject to subsection (2) below, the assured tenancy shall continue in existence as a tenancy held of the person whose interest would, apart from the continuance of the assured tenancy, entitle him to actual possession of the dwelling-house at that time.

(2) Subsection (1) above does not apply to an assured tenancy if the interest which, by virtue of that subsection, would become that of the landlord, is such that, by virtue of Schedule 1 to this Act, the tenancy could not be an assured tenancy.

(3) Where, by virtue of any provision of this Part of this Act, an assured tenancy which is a periodic tenancy (including a statutory periodic tenancy) continues beyond the beginning of a reversionary tenancy which was granted (whether before, on or after the commencement of this Act) so as to begin on or after—

(a) the date on which the previous contractual assured tenancy came to an end, or

(b) a date on which, apart from any provision of this Part, the periodic tenancy could have been brought to an end by the landlord by notice to quit,

the reversionary tenancy shall have effect as if it had been granted subject to the periodic tenancy.

(4) The reference in subsection (3) above to the previous contractual assured tenancy applies only where the periodic tenancy referred to in that subsection is a statutory periodic tenancy and is a reference to the fixed-term tenancy which immediately preceded the statutory periodic tenancy.

[1338]

19 Restriction on levy of distress for rent

(1) Subject to subsection (2) below, no distress for the rent of any dwelling-house let on an assured tenancy shall be levied except with the leave of the county court; and, with respect to any

PART I
STATUTES

application for such leave, the court shall have the same powers with respect to adjournment, stay, suspension, postponement and otherwise as are conferred by section 9 above in relation to proceedings for possession of such a dwelling-house.

(2) *Nothing in subsection (1) above applies to distress levied under section 102 of the County Courts Act 1984.*

[1339]

NOTES

Repealed by the Tribunals, Courts and Enforcement Act 2007, ss 86, 146, Sch 14, para 45, Sch 23, Pt 4, as from a day to be appointed.

CHAPTER II
ASSURED SHORTHOLD TENANCIES

[19A Assured shorthold tenancies: post-Housing Act 1996 tenancies

An assured tenancy which—

(a) is entered into on or after the day on which section 96 of the Housing Act 1996 comes into force (otherwise than pursuant to a contract made before that day), or

(b) comes into being by virtue of section 5 above on the coming to an end of an assured tenancy within paragraph (a) above,

is an assured shorthold tenancy unless it falls within any paragraph in Schedule 2A to this Act.]

[1340]

NOTES

Inserted by the Housing Act 1996, s 96(1).

20 [Assured shorthold tenancies: pre-Housing Act 1996 tenancies]

[(1) Subject to subsection (3) below, an assured tenancy which is not one to which section 19A above applies is an assured shorthold tenancy if—

(a) it is a fixed term tenancy granted for a term certain of not less than six months,

(b) there is no power for the landlord to determine the tenancy at any time earlier than six months from the beginning of the tenancy, and

(c) a notice in respect of it is served as mentioned in subsection (2) below.]

(2) The notice referred to in subsection (1)(c) above is one which—

(a) is in such form as may be prescribed;

(b) is served before the assured tenancy is entered into;

(c) is served by the person who is to be the landlord under the assured tenancy on the person who is to be the tenant under that tenancy; and

(d) states that the assured tenancy to which it relates is to be a shorthold tenancy.

(3) Notwithstanding anything in subsection (1) above, where—

(a) immediately before a tenancy (in this subsection referred to as "the new tenancy") is granted, the person to whom it is granted or, as the case may be, at least one of the persons to whom it is granted was a tenant under an assured tenancy which was not a shorthold tenancy, and

(b) the new tenancy is granted by the person who, immediately before the beginning of the tenancy, was the landlord under the assured tenancy referred to in paragraph (a) above,

the new tenancy cannot be an assured shorthold tenancy.

(4) Subject to subsection (5) below, if, on the coming to an end of an assured shorthold tenancy (including a tenancy which was an assured shorthold but ceased to be assured before it came to an end), a new tenancy of the same or substantially the same premises comes into being under which the landlord and the tenant are the same as at the coming to an end of the earlier tenancy, then, if and so long as the new tenancy is an assured tenancy, it shall be an assured shorthold tenancy, whether or not it fulfils the conditions in paragraphs (a) to (c) of subsection (1) above.

(5) Subsection (4) above does not apply if, before the new tenancy is entered into (or, in the case of a statutory periodic tenancy, takes effect in possession), the landlord serves notice on the tenant that the new tenancy is not to be a shorthold tenancy.

[(5A) Subsections (3) and (4) above do not apply where the new tenancy is one to which section 19A above applies.]

(6) In the case of joint landlords—

(a) the reference in subsection (2)(c) above to the person who is to be the landlord is a reference to at least one of the persons who are to be joint landlords; and

(b) the reference in subsection (5) above to the landlord is a reference to at least one of the joint landlords.

(7) …

[1341]

NOTES

Section heading: substituted by the Housing Act 1996, s 104, Sch 8, para 2(3).
Sub-s (1): substituted by the Housing Act 1996, s 104, Sch 8, para 2(3).
Sub-s (5A): inserted by the Housing Act 1996, s 104, Sch 8, para 2(4).
Sub-s (7): repealed by the Housing Act 1996, s 227, Sch 19, Pt IV.

[20A Post-Housing Act 1996 tenancies: duty of landlord to provide statement as to terms of tenancy

(1) Subject to subsection (3) below, a tenant under an assured shorthold tenancy to which section 19A above applies may, by notice in writing, require the landlord under that tenancy to provide him with a written statement of any term of the tenancy which—

(a) falls within subsection (2) below, and
(b) is not evidenced in writing.

(2) The following terms of a tenancy fall within this subsection, namely—

(a) the date on which the tenancy began or, if it is a statutory periodic tenancy or a tenancy to which section 39(7) below applies, the date on which the tenancy came into being,
(b) the rent payable under the tenancy and the dates on which that rent is payable,
(c) any term providing for a review of the rent payable under the tenancy, and
(d) in the case of a fixed term tenancy, the length of the fixed term.

(3) No notice may be given under subsection (1) above in relation to a term of the tenancy if—

(a) the landlord under the tenancy has provided a statement of that term in response to an earlier notice under that subsection given by the tenant under the tenancy, and
(b) the term has not been varied since the provision of the statement referred to in paragraph (a) above.

(4) A landlord who fails, without reasonable excuse, to comply with a notice under subsection (1) above within the period of 28 days beginning with the date on which he received the notice is liable on summary conviction to a fine not exceeding level 4 on the standard scale.

(5) A statement provided for the purposes of subsection (1) above shall not be regarded as conclusive evidence of what was agreed by the parties to the tenancy in question.

(6) Where—

(a) a term of a statutory periodic tenancy is one which has effect by virtue of section 5(3)(e) above, or
(b) a term of a tenancy to which subsection (7) of section 39 below applies is one which has effect by virtue of subsection (6)(e) of that section,

subsection (1) above shall have effect in relation to it as if paragraph (b) related to the term of the tenancy from which it derives.

(7) In subsections (1) and (3) above—

(a) references to the tenant under the tenancy shall, in the case of joint tenants, be taken to be references to any of the tenants, and
(b) references to the landlord under the tenancy shall, in the case of joint landlords, be taken to be references to any of the landlords.]

[1342]

NOTES

Inserted by the Housing Act 1996, s 97.

[20B Demoted assured shorthold tenancies

(1) An assured tenancy is an assured shorthold tenancy to which this section applies (a demoted assured shorthold tenancy) if—

(a) the tenancy is created by virtue of an order of the court under section 82A of the Housing Act 1985 or section 6A of this Act (a demotion order), and
(b) the landlord is a registered social landlord.

(2) At the end of the period of one year starting with the day when the demotion order takes effect a demoted assured shorthold tenancy ceases to be an assured shorthold tenancy unless subsection (3) applies.

(3) This subsection applies if before the end of the period mentioned in subsection (2) the landlord gives notice of proceedings for possession of the dwelling house.

(4) If subsection (3) applies the tenancy continues to be a demoted assured shorthold tenancy until the end of the period mentioned in subsection (2) or (if later) until one of the following occurs—

(a) the notice of proceedings for possession is withdrawn;
(b) the proceedings are determined in favour of the tenant;
(c) the period of six months beginning with the date on which the notice is given ends and no proceedings for possession have been brought.

(5) Registered social landlord has the same meaning as in Part 1 of the Housing Act 1996.]

[1343]

NOTES

Commencement: 30 June 2004 (in relation to England); 30 April 2005 (in relation to Wales).
Inserted by the Anti-social Behaviour Act 2003, s 15(1).

21 Recovery of possession on expiry or termination of assured shorthold tenancy

(1) Without prejudice to any right of the landlord under an assured shorthold tenancy to recover possession of the dwelling-house let on the tenancy in accordance with Chapter I above, on or after the coming to an end of an assured shorthold tenancy which was a fixed term tenancy, a court shall make an order for possession of the dwelling-house if it is satisfied—

(a) that the assured shorthold tenancy has come to an end and no further assured tenancy (whether shorthold or not) is for the time being in existence, other than [an assured shorthold periodic tenancy (whether statutory or not)]; and
(b) the landlord or, in the case of joint landlords, at least one of them has given to the tenant not less than two months' notice [in writing] stating that he requires possession of the dwelling-house.

(2) A notice under paragraph (b) of subsection (1) above may be given before or on the day on which the tenancy comes to an end; and that subsection shall have effect notwithstanding that on the coming to an end of the fixed term tenancy a statutory periodic tenancy arises.

(3) Where a court makes an order for possession of a dwelling-house by virtue of subsection (1) above, any statutory periodic tenancy which has arisen on the coming to an end of the assured shorthold tenancy shall end (without further notice and regardless of the period) [in accordance with section 5(1A)].

(4) Without prejudice to any such right as is referred to in subsection (1) above, a court shall make an order for possession of a dwelling-house let on an assured shorthold tenancy which is a periodic tenancy if the court is satisfied—

(a) that the landlord or, in the case of joint landlords, at least one of them has given to the tenant a notice [in writing] stating that, after a date specified in the notice, being the last day of a period of the tenancy and not earlier than two months after the date the notice was given, possession of the dwelling-house is required by virtue of this section; and
(b) that the date specified in the notice under paragraph (a) above is not earlier than the earliest day on which, apart from section 5(1) above, the tenancy could be brought to an end by a notice to quit given by the landlord on the same date as the notice under paragraph (a) above.

[(4A) Where a court makes an order for possession of a dwelling-house by virtue of subsection (4) above, the assured shorthold tenancy shall end in accordance with section 5(1A).]

[(5) Where an order for possession under subsection (1) or (4) above is made in relation to a dwelling-house let on a tenancy to which section 19A above applies, the order may not be made so as to take effect earlier than—

(a) in the case of a tenancy which is not a replacement tenancy, six months after the beginning of the tenancy, and
(b) in the case of a replacement tenancy, six months after the beginning of the original tenancy.

[(5A) Subsection (5) above does not apply to an assured shorthold tenancy to which section 20B (demoted assured shorthold tenancies) applies.]

(6) In subsection (5)(b) above, the reference to the original tenancy is—

(a) where the replacement tenancy came into being on the coming to an end of a tenancy which was not a replacement tenancy, to the immediately preceding tenancy, and
(b) where there have been successive replacement tenancies, to the tenancy immediately preceding the first in the succession of replacement tenancies.

(7) For the purposes of this section, a replacement tenancy is a tenancy—

(a) which comes into being on the coming to an end of an assured shorthold tenancy, and
(b) under which, on its coming into being—
    (i) the landlord and tenant are the same as under the earlier tenancy as at its coming to an end, and

(ii) the premises let are the same or substantially the same as those let under the earlier tenancy as at that time.]

[1344]

NOTES

Sub-s (1): in para (a) words in square brackets substituted by the Local Government and Housing Act 1989, s 194, Sch 11, para 103; in para (b) words in square brackets inserted by the Housing Act 1996, s 98(2).

Para (3): words in square brackets substituted by the Housing and Regeneration Act 2008, s 299, Sch 11, Pt 1, paras 5, 9(1), (2), subject to transitional provisions in Sch 11, Pt 1, para 14 thereto.

Sub-s (4): words in square brackets inserted by the Housing Act 1996, s 98(3).

Sub-s (4A): inserted by the Housing and Regeneration Act 2008, s 299, Sch 11, Pt 1, paras 5, 9(1), (3), subject to transitional provisions in Sch 11, Pt 1, para 14 thereto.

Sub-ss (5)–(7): inserted by the Housing Act 1996, s 99.

Sub-s (5A): inserted by the Anti-social Behaviour Act 2003, s 15(2).

22 Reference of excessive rents to rent assessment committee

(1) Subject to section 23 and subsection (2) below, the tenant under an assured shorthold tenancy … may make an application in the prescribed form to a rent assessment committee for a determination of the rent which, in the committee's opinion, the landlord might reasonably be expected to obtain under the assured shorthold tenancy.

(2) No application may be made under this section if—

(a) the rent payable under the tenancy is a rent previously determined under this section; …

[(aa) the tenancy is one to which section 19A above applies and more than six months have elapsed since the beginning of the tenancy or, in the case of a replacement tenancy, since the beginning of the original tenancy; or]

(b) the tenancy is an assured shorthold tenancy falling within subsection (4) of section 20 above (and, accordingly, is one in respect of which notice need not have been served as mentioned in subsection (2) of that section).

(3) Where an application is made to a rent assessment committee under subsection (1) above with respect to the rent under an assured shorthold tenancy, the committee shall not make such a determination as is referred to in that subsection unless they consider—

(a) that there is a sufficient number of similar dwelling-houses in the locality let on assured tenancies (whether shorthold or not); and

(b) that the rent payable under the assured shorthold tenancy in question is significantly higher than the rent which the landlord might reasonably be expected to be able to obtain under the tenancy, having regard to the level of rents payable under the tenancies referred to in paragraph (a) above.

(4) Where, on an application under this section, a rent assessment committee make a determination of a rent for an assured shorthold tenancy—

(a) the determination shall have effect from such date as the committee may direct, not being earlier than the date of the application;

(b) if, at any time on or after the determination takes effect, the rent which, apart from this paragraph, would be payable under the tenancy exceeds the rent so determined, the excess shall be irrecoverable from the tenant; and

(c) no notice may be served under section 13(2) above with respect to a tenancy of the dwelling-house in question until after the first anniversary of the date on which the determination takes effect.

(5) Subsections (4), (5) and (8) of section 14 above apply in relation to a determination of rent under this section as they apply in relation to a determination under that section and, accordingly, where subsection (5) of that section applies, any reference in subsection (4)(b) above to rent is a reference to rent exclusive of the amount attributable to rates.

[(5A) Where—

(a) an assured tenancy ceases to be an assured shorthold tenancy by virtue of falling within paragraph 2 of Schedule 2A to this Act, and

(b) at the time when it so ceases to be an assured shorthold tenancy there is pending before a rent assessment committee an application in relation to it under this section,

the fact that it so ceases to be an assured shorthold tenancy shall, in relation to that application, be disregarded for the purposes of this section.]

[(6) In subsection (2)(aa) above, the references to the original tenancy and to a replacement tenancy shall be construed in accordance with subsections (6) and (7) respectively of section 21 above.]

[1345]

NOTES

Sub-s (1): words omitted repealed by the Housing Act 1996, ss 104, 227, Sch 8, para 2(5), Sch 19, Pt IV.

Sub-s (2): word omitted from para (a) repealed, and para (aa) inserted, by the Housing Act 1996, ss 100(2), 227, Sch 19, Pt IV.

Sub-s (5A): inserted by the Housing Act 1996, s 104, Sch 8, para 2(6).

Sub-s (6): inserted by the Housing Act 1996, s 100(3).

Regulations: the Assured Tenancies and Agricultural Occupancies (Forms) Regulations 1997, SI 1997/194.

23 Termination of rent assessment committee's functions

(1) If the Secretary of State by order made by statutory instrument so provides, section 22 above shall not apply in such cases or to tenancies of dwelling-houses in such areas or in such other circumstances as may be specified in the order.

(2) An order under this section may contain such transitional, incidental and supplementary provisions as appear to the Secretary of State to be desirable.

(3) No order shall be made under this section unless a draft of the order has been laid before, and approved by a resolution of, each House of Parliament.

[1346]

CHAPTER III
ASSURED AGRICULTURAL OCCUPANCIES

24 Assured agricultural occupancies

(1) A tenancy or licence of a dwelling-house is for the purposes of this Part of this Act an "assured agricultural occupancy" if—

(a) it is of a description specified in subsection (2) below; and

(b) by virtue of any provision of Schedule 3 to this Act the agricultural worker condition is for the time being fulfilled with respect to the dwelling-house subject to the tenancy or licence.

(2) The following are the tenancies and licences referred to in subsection (1)(a) above—

(a) an assured tenancy which is not an assured shorthold tenancy;

(b) a tenancy which does not fall within paragraph (a) above by reason only of paragraph 3[, 3A, 3B] or paragraph 7 of Schedule 1 to this Act ([or more than one of those paragraphs]) [and is not an excepted tenancy]; and

(c) a licence under which a person has the exclusive occupation of a dwelling-house as a separate dwelling and which, if it conferred a sufficient interest in land to be a tenancy, would be a tenancy falling within paragraph (a) or paragraph (b) above.

[(2A) For the purposes of subsection (2)(b) above, a tenancy is an excepted tenancy if it is—

(a) a tenancy of an agricultural holding within the meaning of the Agricultural Holdings Act 1986 in relation to which that Act applies, or

(b) a farm business tenancy within the meaning of the Agricultural Tenancies Act 1995.]

(3) For the purposes of Chapter I above and the following provisions of this Chapter, every assured agricultural occupancy which is not an assured tenancy shall be treated as if it were such a tenancy and any reference to a tenant, a landlord or any other expression appropriate to a tenancy shall be construed accordingly; but the provisions of Chapter I above shall have effect in relation to every assured agricultural occupancy subject to the provisions of this Chapter.

(4) Section 14 above shall apply in relation to an assured agricultural occupancy as if in subsection (1) of that section the reference to an assured tenancy were a reference to an assured agricultural occupancy.

[1347]

NOTES

Sub-s (2): in para (b) first and second words in square brackets inserted or substituted by SI 1990/434, reg 2, Schedule, para 28; final words in square brackets inserted by the Housing Act 1996, s 103(2).

Sub-s (2A): inserted by the Housing Act 1996, s 103(3).

25 Security of tenure

(1) If a statutory periodic tenancy arises on the coming to an end of an assured agricultural occupancy—

(a) it shall be an assured agricultural occupancy as long as, by virtue of any provision of Schedule 3 to this Act, the agricultural worker condition is for the time being fulfilled with respect to the dwelling-house in question; and

(b) if no rent was payable under the assured agricultural occupancy which constitutes the fixed term tenancy referred to in subsection (2) of section 5 above, subsection (3)(d) of that section shall apply as if for the words "the same as those for which rent was last payable under" there were substituted "monthly beginning on the day following the coming to an end of".

(2) In its application to an assured agricultural occupancy, Part II of Schedule 2 to this Act shall have effect with the omission of Ground 16.

(3) In its application to an assured agricultural occupancy, Part III of Schedule 2 to this Act shall have effect as if any reference in paragraph 2 to an assured tenancy included a reference to an assured agricultural occupancy.

(4) If the tenant under an assured agricultural occupancy gives notice to terminate his employment then, notwithstanding anything in any agreement or otherwise, that notice shall not constitute a notice to quit as respects the assured agricultural occupancy.

(5) Nothing in subsection (4) above affects the operation of an actual notice to quit given in respect of an assured agricultural occupancy.

[1348]

26 (*Amends the Rent* (*Agriculture*) *Act 1976, s 27.*)

CHAPTER IV
PROTECTION FROM EVICTION

27 Damages for unlawful eviction

(1) This section applies if, at any time after 9th June 1988, a landlord (in this section referred to as "the landlord in default") or any person acting on behalf of the landlord in default unlawfully deprives the residential occupier of any premises of his occupation of the whole or part of the premises.

(2) This section also applies if, at any time after 9th June 1988, a landlord (in this section referred to as "the landlord in default") or any person acting on behalf of the landlord in default—

(a) attempts unlawfully to deprive the residential occupier of any premises of his occupation of the whole or part of the premises, or

(b) knowing or having reasonable cause to believe that the conduct is likely to cause the residential occupier of any premises—

(i) to give up his occupation of the premises or any part thereof, or

(ii) to refrain from exercising any right or pursuing any remedy in respect of the premises or any part thereof,

does acts likely to interfere with the peace or comfort of the residential occupier or members of his household, or persistently withdraws or withholds services reasonably required for the occupation of the premises as a residence,

and, as a result, the residential occupier gives up his occupation of the premises as a residence.

(3) Subject to the following provisions of this section, where this section applies, the landlord in default shall, by virtue of this section, be liable to pay to the former residential occupier, in respect of his loss of the right to occupy the premises in question as his residence, damages assessed on the basis set out in section 28 below.

(4) Any liability arising by virtue of subsection (3) above—

(a) shall be in the nature of a liability in tort; and

(b) subject to subsection (5) below, shall be in addition to any liability arising apart from this section (whether in tort, contract or otherwise).

(5) Nothing in this section affects the right of a residential occupier to enforce any liability which arises apart from this section in respect of his loss of the right to occupy premises as his residence; but damages shall not be awarded both in respect of such a liability and in respect of a liability arising by virtue of this section on account of the same loss.

(6) No liability shall arise by virtue of subsection (3) above if—

(a) before the date on which proceedings to enforce the liability are finally disposed of, the former residential occupier is reinstated in the premises in question in such circumstances that he becomes again the residential occupier of them; or

(b) at the request of the former residential occupier, a court makes an order (whether in the nature of an injunction or otherwise) as a result of which he is reinstated as mentioned in paragraph (a) above;

and, for the purposes of paragraph (a) above, proceedings to enforce a liability are finally disposed of on the earliest date by which the proceedings (including any proceedings on or in consequence of an appeal) have been determined and any time for appealing or further appealing has expired, except that if any appeal is abandoned, the proceedings shall be taken to be disposed of on the date of the abandonment.

(7) If, in proceedings to enforce a liability arising by virtue of subsection (3) above, it appears to the court—

(a) that, prior to the event which gave rise to the liability, the conduct of the former residential occupier or any person living with him in the premises concerned was such that it is reasonable to mitigate the damages for which the landlord in default would otherwise be liable, or

(b) that, before the proceedings were begun, the landlord in default offered to reinstate the former residential occupier in the premises in question and either it was unreasonable of the former residential occupier to refuse that offer or, if he had obtained alternative accommodation before the offer was made, it would have been unreasonable of him to refuse that offer if he had not obtained that accommodation,

the court may reduce the amount of damages which would otherwise be payable to such amount as it thinks appropriate.

(8) In proceedings to enforce a liability arising by virtue of subsection (3) above, it shall be a defence for the defendant to prove that he believed, and had reasonable cause to believe—

(a) that the residential occupier had ceased to reside in the premises in question at the time when he was deprived of occupation as mentioned in subsection (1) above or, as the case may be, when the attempt was made or the acts were done as a result of which he gave up his occupation of those premises; or

(b) that, where the liability would otherwise arise by virtue only of the doing of acts or the withdrawal or withholding of services, he had reasonable grounds for doing the acts or withdrawing or withholding the services in question.

(9) In this section—

(a) "residential occupier", in relation to any premises, has the same meaning as in section 1 of the 1977 Act;

(b) "the right to occupy", in relation to a residential occupier, includes any restriction on the right of another person to recover possession of the premises in question;

(c) "landlord", in relation to a residential occupier, means the person who, but for the occupier's right to occupy, would be entitled to occupation of the premises and any superior landlord under whom that person derives title;

(d) "former residential occupier", in relation to any premises, means the person who was the residential occupier until he was deprived of or gave up his occupation as mentioned in subsection (1) or subsection (2) above (and, in relation to a former residential occupier, "the right to occupy" and "landlord" shall be construed accordingly).

[1349]

28 The measure of damages

(1) The basis for the assessment of damages referred to in section 27(3) above is the difference in value, determined as at the time immediately before the residential occupier ceased to occupy the premises in question as his residence, between—

(a) the value of the interest of the landlord in default determined on the assumption that the residential occupier continues to have the same right to occupy the premises as before that time; and

(b) the value of that interest determined on the assumption that the residential occupier has ceased to have that right.

(2) In relation to any premises, any reference in this section to the interest of the landlord in default is a reference to his interest in the building in which the premises in question are comprised (whether or not that building contains any other premises) together with its curtilage.

(3) For the purposes of the valuations referred to in subsection (1) above, it shall be assumed—

(a) that the landlord in default is selling his interest on the open market to a willing buyer;

(b) that neither the residential occupier nor any member of his family wishes to buy; and

(c) that it is unlawful to carry out any substantial development of any of the land in which the landlord's interest subsists or to demolish the whole or part of any building on that land.

(4) In this section "the landlord in default" has the same meaning as in section 27 above and subsection (9) of that section applies in relation to this section as it applies in relation to that.

(5) Section 113 of the Housing Act 1985 (meaning of "members of a person's family") applies for the purposes of subsection (3)(b) above.

(6) The reference in subsection (3)(c) above to substantial development of any of the land in which the landlord's interest subsists is a reference to any development other than—

(a) development for which planning permission is granted by a general development order for the time being in force and which is carried out so as to comply with any condition or limitation subject to which planning permission is so granted; or

(b) a change of use resulting in the building referred to in subsection (2) above or any part of it being used as, or as part of, one or more dwelling-houses;

and in this subsection "general development order" [has the meaning given in section 56(6) of the Town and Country Planning Act 1990] and other expressions have the same meaning as in that Act. **[1350]**

NOTES

Sub-s (6): words in square brackets substituted by the Planning (Consequential Provisions) Act 1990, s 4, Sch 2, para 79(1).

29–32 (*Amend the Protection from Eviction Act 1977, ss 1, 3–5, and insert s 3A thereof.*)

33 Interpretation of Chapter IV and the 1977 Act

(1) In this Chapter "the 1977 Act" means the Protection from Eviction Act 1977.

(2), (3) …

[1351]

NOTES

Sub-ss (2), (3): amend the Protection from Eviction Act 1977, s 8.

CHAPTER V
PHASING OUT OF RENT ACTS AND OTHER TRANSITIONAL PROVISIONS

34–44 (*Ss 32–42, 44 outside the scope of this work; s 43 amends the Rent Act 1977, s 149.*)

45 Interpretation of Part I

(1) In this Part of this Act, except where the context otherwise requires,—

"dwelling-house" may be a house or part of a house;

"fixed term tenancy" means any tenancy other than a periodic tenancy;

"fully mutual housing association" has the same meaning as in Part I of the Housing Associations Act 1985;

"landlord" includes any person from time to time deriving title under the original landlord and also includes, in relation to a dwelling-house, any person other than a tenant who is, or but for the existence of an assured tenancy would be, entitled to possession of the dwelling-house;

"let" includes "sub-let";

"prescribed" means prescribed by regulations made by the Secretary of State by statutory instrument;

"rates" includes water rates and charges but does not include an owner's drainage rate, as defined in section 63(2)(a) of the Land Drainage Act 1976;

"secure tenancy" has the meaning assigned by section 79 of the Housing Act 1985;

"statutory periodic tenancy" has the meaning assigned by section 5(7) above;

"tenancy" includes a sub-tenancy and an agreement for a tenancy or sub-tenancy; and

"tenant" includes a sub-tenant and any person deriving title under the original tenant or sub-tenant.

(2) Subject to paragraph 11 of Schedule 2 to this Act, any reference in this Part of this Act to the beginning of a tenancy is a reference to the day on which the tenancy is entered into or, if it is later, the day on which, under the terms of any lease, agreement or other document, the tenant is entitled to possession under the tenancy.

(3) Where two or more persons jointly constitute either the landlord or the tenant in relation to a tenancy, then, except where this Part of this Act otherwise provides, any reference to the landlord or to the tenant is a reference to all the persons who jointly constitute the landlord or the tenant, as the case may require.

(4) For the avoidance of doubt, it is hereby declared that any reference in this Part of this Act (however expressed) to a power for a landlord to determine a tenancy does not include a reference to a power of re-entry or forfeiture for breach of any term or condition of the tenancy.

(5) Regulations under subsection (1) above may make different provision with respect to different cases or descriptions of case, including different provision for different areas.

[1352]

46–114 ((*Pts II–IV*) *in so far as unrepealed, outside the scope of this work.*)

PART V
MISCELLANEOUS AND GENERAL

115–137 (*In so far as unrepealed, outside the scope of this work.*)

PART I STATUTES

Supplementary

138–140 (*Outside the scope of this work.*)

141 Short title, commencement and extent

(1) This Act may be cited as the Housing Act 1988.

(2) The provisions of Parts II and IV of this Act and sections 119, 122, 124, 128, 129, 135 and 140 above shall come into force on such day as the Secretary of State may by order made by statutory instrument appoint, and different days may be so appointed for different provisions or for different purposes.

(3) Part I and this Part of this Act, other than sections 119, 122, 124, 128, 129, 132, 133, 134, 135 and 138 onwards, shall come into force at the expiry of the period of two months beginning on the day it is passed; and any reference in those provisions to the commencement of this Act shall be construed accordingly.

(4) An order under subsection (2) above may make such transitional provisions as appear to the Secretary of State necessary or expedient in connection with the provisions brought into force by the order.

(5) Parts I, III and IV of this Act and this Part, except sections 118, 128, 132, 134, 135 and 137 onwards, extend to England and Wales only.

(6) This Act does not extend to Northern Ireland.

[1353]

NOTES

Orders: the Housing Act 1988 (Commencement No 1) Order 1988, SI 1988/2056; the Housing Act 1988 (Commencement No 2) Order 1988, SI 1988/2152; the Housing Act 1988 (Commencement No 3) Order 1989, SI 1989/203; the Housing Act 1988 (Commencement No 4) Order 1989, SI 1989/404; the Housing Act 1988 (Commencement No 5 and Transitional Provisions) Order 1991, SI 1991/954; the Housing Act 1988 (Commencement No 6) Order 1992, SI 1992/324.

SCHEDULE 1
TENANCIES WHICH CANNOT BE ASSURED TENANCIES

Section 1

PART I
THE TENANCIES

Tenancies entered into before commencement

1. A tenancy which is entered into before, or pursuant to a contract made before, the commencement of this Act.

Tenancies of dwelling-houses with high rateable values

[2.—(1) A tenancy—

(a) which is entered into on or after 1st April 1990 (otherwise than, where the dwelling-house had a rateable value on 31st March 1990, in pursuance of a contract made before 1st April 1990), and

(b) under which the rent payable for the time being is payable at a rate exceeding £25,000 a year.

(2) In sub-paragraph (1) "rent" does not include any sum payable by the tenant as is expressed (in whatever terms) to be payable in respect of rates [council tax], services, management, repairs, maintenance or insurance, unless it could not have been regarded by the parties to the tenancy as a sum so payable.

2A. A tenancy—

(a) which was entered into before 1st April 1990, or on or after that date in pursuance of a contract made before that date, and

(b) under which the dwelling-house had a rateable value on 31st March 1990 which, if it is in Greater London, exceeded £1,500 and, if it is elsewhere, exceeded £750.]

Tenancies at a low rent

[3. A tenancy under which for the time being no rent is payable.

3A. A tenancy—

(a) which is entered into on or after 1st April 1990 (otherwise than, where the dwelling-house had a rateable value on 31st March 1990, in pursuance of a contract made before 1st April 1990), and

(b) under which the rent payable for the time being is payable at a rate of, if the dwelling-house is in Greater London, £1,000 or less a year and, if it is elsewhere, £250 or less a year.

3B. A tenancy—

(a) which was entered into before 1st April 1990 or, where the dwelling-house had a rateable value on 31st March 1990, on or after 1st April 1990 in pursuance of a contract made before that date, and

(b) under which the rent for the time being payable is less than two-thirds of the rateable value of the dwelling-house on 31st March 1990.

3C. Paragraph 2(2) above applies for the purposes of paragraphs 3, 3A and 3B as it applies for the purposes of paragraph 2(1).]

Business tenancies

4. A tenancy to which Part II of the Landlord and Tenant Act 1954 applies (business tenancies).

Licensed premises

5. A tenancy under which the dwelling-house consists of or comprises [premises which, by virtue of a premises licence under the Licensing Act 2003, may be used for the supply of alcohol (within the meaning of section 14 of that Act)] for consumption on the premises.

Tenancies of agricultural land

6.—(1) A tenancy under which agricultural land, exceeding two acres, is let together with the dwelling-house.

(2) In this paragraph "agricultural land" has the meaning set out in section 26(3)(a) of the General Rate Act 1967 (exclusion of agricultural land and premises from liability for rating).

[Tenancies of agricultural holdings etc

7.—(1) A tenancy under which the dwelling-house—

(a) is comprised in an agricultural holding, and

(b) is occupied by the person responsible for the control (whether as tenant or as servant or agent of the tenant) of the farming of the holding.

(2) A tenancy under which the dwelling-house—

(a) is comprised in the holding held under a farm business tenancy, and

(b) is occupied by the person responsible for the control (whether as tenant or as servant or agent of the tenant) of the management of the holding.

(3) In this paragraph—

"agricultural holding" means any agricultural holding within the meaning of the Agricultural Holdings Act 1986 held under a tenancy in relation to which that Act applies, and

"farm business tenancy" and "holding", in relation to such a tenancy, have the same meaning as in the Agricultural Tenancies Act 1995.]

Lettings to students

8.—(1) A tenancy which is granted to a person who is pursuing, or intends to pursue, a course of study provided by a specified educational institution and is so granted either by that institution or by another specified institution or body of persons.

(2) In sub-paragraph (1) above "specified" means specified, or of a class specified, for the purposes of this paragraph by regulations made by the Secretary of State by statutory instrument.

(3) A statutory instrument made in the exercise of the power conferred by sub-paragraph (2) above shall be subject to annulment in pursuance of a resolution of either House of Parliament.

Holiday lettings

9. A tenancy the purpose of which is to confer on the tenant the right to occupy the dwelling-house for a holiday.

Resident landlords

10.—(1) A tenancy in respect of which the following conditions are fulfilled—

(a) that the dwelling-house forms part only of a building and, except in a case where the dwelling-house also forms part of a flat, the building is not a purpose-built block of flats; and

(b) that, subject to Part III of this Schedule, the tenancy was granted by an individual who, at the time when the tenancy was granted, occupied as his only or principal home another dwelling-house which,—

(i) in the case mentioned in paragraph (a) above, also forms part of the flat; or

(ii) in any other case, also forms part of the building; and

(c) that, subject to Part III of this Schedule, at all times since the tenancy was granted the interest of the landlord under the tenancy has belonged to an individual who, at the time he owned that interest, occupied as his only or principal home another dwelling-house which,—

(i) in the case mentioned in paragraph (a) above, also formed part of the flat; or

(ii) in any other case, also formed part of the building; and

(d) that the tenancy is not one which is excluded from this sub-paragraph by sub-paragraph (3) below.

(2) If a tenancy was granted by two or more persons jointly, the reference in sub-paragraph (1)(b) above to an individual is a reference to any one of those persons and if the interest of the landlord is for the time being held by two or more persons jointly, the reference in sub-paragraph (1)(c) above to an individual is a reference to any one of those persons.

(3) A tenancy (in this sub-paragraph referred to as "the new tenancy") is excluded from sub-paragraph (1) above if—

(a) it is granted to a person (alone, or jointly with others) who, immediately before it was granted, was a tenant under an assured tenancy (in this sub-paragraph referred to as "the former tenancy") of the same dwelling-house or of another dwelling-house which forms part of the building in question; and

(b) the landlord under the new tenancy and under the former tenancy is the same person or, if either of those tenancies is or was granted by two or more persons jointly, the same person is the landlord or one of the landlords under each tenancy.

Crown tenancies

11.—(1) A tenancy under which the interest of the landlord belongs to Her Majesty in right of the Crown or to a government department or is held in trust for Her Majesty for the purposes of a government department.

(2) The reference in sub-paragraph (1) above to the case where the interest of the landlord belongs to Her Majesty in right of the Crown does not include the case where that interest is under the management of the Crown Estate Commissioners [or it is held by the Secretary of State as the result of the exercise by him of functions under Part III of the Housing Associations Act 1985].

Local authority tenancies etc

12.—(1) A tenancy under which the interest of the landlord belongs to—

(a) a local authority, as defined in sub-paragraph (2) below;

(b) the Commission for the New Towns;

(c) …

(d) an urban development corporation established by an order under section 135 of the Local Government, Planning and Land Act 1980;

(e) a development corporation, within the meaning of the New Towns Act 1981;

(f) an authority established under section 10 of the Local Government Act 1985 (waste disposal authorities);

[(fa) an authority established for an area in England by an order under section 207 of the Local Government and Public Involvement in Health Act 2007 (joint waste authorities);]

(g) a residuary body, within the meaning of the Local Government Act 1985;

[(gg) The Residuary Body for Wales (Corff Gweddilliol Cymru);]

(h) a fully mutual housing association; or

(i) a housing action trust established under Part III of this Act.

(2) The following are local authorities for the purposes of sub-paragraph (1)(a) above—

(a) the council of a county, [county borough,] district or London borough;

(b) the Common Council of the City of London;

(c) the Council of the Isles of Scilly;

(d) the Broads Authority;

[(da) a National Park authority;]

(e) the Inner London Education Authority; and

[(ee) the London Fire and Emergency Planning Authority;]

(f) a joint authority, within the meaning of the Local Government Act 1985 [and

(g) a police authority established under [section 3 of the Police Act 1996] …]

[Family intervention tenancies

12ZA.—(1) A family intervention tenancy.

(2) But a family intervention tenancy becomes an assured tenancy if the landlord notifies the tenant that it is to be regarded as an assured tenancy.

(3) In this paragraph "a family intervention tenancy" means, subject to sub-paragraph (4), a tenancy granted by a registered provider of social housing or a registered social landlord ("the landlord") in respect of a dwelling-house—

(a) to a person ("the new tenant") against whom a possession order under section 7 in respect of another dwelling-house—
(i) has been made, in relation to an assured tenancy, on ground 14 or 14A of Part 2 of Schedule 2;
(ii) could, in the opinion of the landlord, have been so made in relation to such a tenancy; or
(iii) could, in the opinion of the landlord, have been so made if the person had had such a tenancy; and
(b) for the purposes of the provision of behaviour support services.

(4) A tenancy is not a family intervention tenancy for the purposes of this paragraph if the landlord has failed to serve a notice under sub-paragraph (5) on the new tenant before the new tenant entered into the tenancy.

(5) A notice under this sub-paragraph is a notice stating—
(a) the reasons for offering the tenancy to the new tenant;
(b) the dwelling-house in respect of which the tenancy is to be granted;
(c) the other main terms of the tenancy (including any requirements on the new tenant in respect of behaviour support services);
(d) the security of tenure available under the tenancy and any loss of security of tenure which is likely to result from the new tenant agreeing to enter into the tenancy;
(e) that the new tenant is not obliged to enter into the tenancy or (unless otherwise required to do so) to surrender any existing tenancy or possession of a dwelling-house;
(f) any likely action by the landlord if the new tenant does not enter into the tenancy or surrender any existing tenancy or possession of a dwelling-house.

(6) The appropriate national authority may by regulations made by statutory instrument amend sub-paragraph (5).

(7) A notice under sub-paragraph (5) must contain advice to the new tenant as to how the new tenant may be able to obtain assistance in relation to the notice.

(8) The appropriate national authority may by regulations made by statutory instrument make provision about the type of advice to be provided in such notices.

(9) Regulations under this paragraph may contain such transitional, transitory or saving provision as the appropriate national authority considers appropriate.

(10) A statutory instrument containing (whether alone or with other provision) regulations under this paragraph which amend or repeal any of paragraphs (a) to (f) of sub-paragraph (5) may not be made—
(a) by the Secretary of State unless a draft of the instrument has been laid before, and approved by a resolution of, each House of Parliament; and
(b) by the Welsh Ministers unless a draft of the instrument has been laid before, and approved by a resolution of, the National Assembly for Wales.]

[Accommodation for asylum-seekers

12A.—(1) A tenancy granted by a private landlord under arrangements for the provision of support for asylum-seekers or dependants of asylum-seekers made [under section 4 or Part VI of the Immigration and Asylum Act 1999].

(2) "Private landlord" means a landlord who is not within section 80(1) of the Housing Act 1985.]

[Accommodation for persons with Temporary Protection

12B.—(1) A tenancy granted by a private landlord under arrangements for the provision of accommodation for persons with temporary protection made under the Displaced Persons (Temporary Protection) Regulations 2005.

(2) "Private landlord" means a landlord who is not within section 80(1) of the Housing Act 1985.]

Transitional cases

13.—(1) A protected tenancy, within the meaning of the Rent Act 1977.

(2) A housing association tenancy, within the meaning of Part VI of that Act.

(3) A secure tenancy.

(4) Where a person is a protected occupier of a dwelling-house, within the meaning of the Rent (Agriculture) Act 1976, the relevant tenancy, within the meaning of that Act, by virtue of which he occupies the dwelling-house.

[1354]

NOTES

Para 2: substituted, together with para 2A, for original para 2, by SI 1990/434, reg 2, Schedule, para 29; in sub-para (2), words in square brackets inserted by SI 1993/651, art 2(1), Sch 1, para 19.

Para 2A: substituted, together with para 2, for original para 2, by SI 1990/434, reg 2, Schedule, para 29.

Paras 3–3C: substituted, for original para 3, by SI 1990/434, reg 2, Schedule, para 30.

Para 5: words in square brackets substituted by the Licensing Act 2003, s 198(1), Sch 6, para 108.

Para 7: substituted by the Agricultural Tenancies Act 1995, s 40, Schedule, para 34.

Para 11: in sub-para (2), words in square brackets inserted by SI 1999/61, art 2, Schedule, para 3(1), (4).

Para 12: sub-para (1)(c) repealed by the Government of Wales Act 1998, s 152, Sch 18, Pt IV; sub-para (1)(fa) inserted by the Local Government and Public Involvement in Health Act 2007, s 209(2), Sch 13, Pt 2, para 44; sub-para (1)(gg) inserted by the Local Government (Wales) Act 1994, s 39, Sch 13, para 31; in sub-para (2)(a) words in square brackets inserted by the Local Government (Wales) Act 1994, s 22(2), Sch 8, para 9(2); sub-para (2)(da) inserted by the Environment Act 1995, s 78, Sch 10, para 28; sub-para (2)(ee) inserted by the Greater London Authority Act 1999, s 328, Sch 29, Pt I, para 53; sub-para (2)(g) and the word immediately preceding it inserted by the Police and Magistrates' Courts Act 1994, s 43, Sch 4, Pt II, para 62, words in square brackets therein substituted by the Police Act 1996, s 103, Sch 7, para 1(2)(zc), and words omitted repealed by the Police Reform Act 2002, ss 100(2), 107(2), Sch 8.

Para 12ZA: inserted by the Housing and Regeneration Act 2008, s 297(2); for transitional provisions and savings see SI 2008/3068, arts 6, 9, 10.

Para 12A: inserted by the Immigration and Asylum Act 1999, s 169(1), Sch 14, para 88; words in square brackets in sub-para (1) substituted by the Immigration, Asylum and Nationality Act 2006, s 43(4)(f).

Para 12B: inserted by SI 2005/1379, Schedule, para 6.

Regulations: the Assured and Protected Tenancies (Lettings to Students) Regulations 1998, SI 1998/1967.

PART II
RATEABLE VALUES

14.—(1) The rateable value of a dwelling-house at any time shall be ascertained for the purposes of Part I of this Schedule as follows—

(a) if the dwelling-house is a hereditament for which a rateable value is then shown in the valuation list, it shall be that rateable value;

(b) if the dwelling-house forms part only of such a hereditament or consists of or forms part of more than one such hereditament, its rateable value shall be taken to be such value as is found by a proper apportionment or aggregation of the rateable value or values so shown.

(2) Any question arising under this Part of this Schedule as to the proper apportionment or aggregation of any value or values shall be determined by the county court and the decision of that court shall be final.

15. Where, after the time at which the rateable value of a dwelling-house is material for the purposes of any provision of Part I of this Schedule, the valuation list is altered so as to vary the rateable value of the hereditament of which the dwelling-house consists (in whole or in part) or forms part and the alteration has effect from that time or from an earlier time, the rateable value of the dwelling-house at the material time shall be ascertained as if the value shown in the valuation list at the material time had been the value shown in the list as altered.

16. Paragraphs 14 and 15 above apply in relation to any other land which, under section 2 of this Act, is treated as part of a dwelling-house as they apply in relation to the dwelling-house itself.

[1355]

PART III
PROVISIONS FOR DETERMINING APPLICATION OF PARAGRAPH 10 (RESIDENT LANDLORDS)

17.—(1) In determining whether the condition in paragraph 10(1)(c) above is at any time fulfilled with respect to a tenancy, there shall be disregarded—

(a) any period of not more than twenty-eight days, beginning with the date on which the interest of the landlord under the tenancy becomes vested at law and in equity in an individual who, during that period, does not occupy as his only or principal home another dwelling-house which forms part of the building or, as the case may be, flat concerned;

(b) if, within a period falling within paragraph (a) above, the individual concerned notifies the tenant in writing of his intention to occupy as his only or principal home another dwelling-house in the building or, as the case may be, flat concerned, the period beginning with the date on which the interest of the landlord under the tenancy becomes vested in that individual as mentioned in that paragraph and ending—

(i) at the expiry of the period of six months beginning on that date, or

(ii) on the date on which that interest ceases to be so vested, or

(iii) on the date on which that interest becomes again vested in such an individual as is mentioned in paragraph 10(1)(c) or the condition in that paragraph becomes deemed to be fulfilled by virtue of paragraph 18(1) or paragraph 20 below,

whichever is the earlier; and

(c) any period of not more than two years beginning with the date on which the interest of the landlord under the tenancy becomes, and during which it remains, vested—
   (i) in trustees as such; or
   (ii) by virtue of section 9 of the Administration of Estates Act 1925, in [the Probate Judge or the Public Trustee].

(2) Where the interest of the landlord under a tenancy becomes vested at law and in equity in two or more persons jointly, of whom at least one was an individual, sub-paragraph (1) above shall have effect subject to the following modifications—

(a) in paragraph (a) for the words from "an individual" to "occupy" there shall be substituted "the joint landlords if, during that period none of them occupies"; and
(b) in paragraph (b) for the words "the individual concerned" there shall be substituted "any of the joint landlords who is an individual" and for the words "that individual" there shall be substituted "the joint landlords".

18.—(1) During any period when—

(a) the interest of the landlord under the tenancy referred to in paragraph 10 above is vested in trustees as such, and
(b) that interest is … held on trust for any person who or for two or more persons of whom at least one occupies as his only or principal home a dwelling-house which forms part of the building or, as the case may be, flat referred to in paragraph 10(1)(a),

the condition in paragraph 10(1)(c) shall be deemed to be fulfilled and accordingly, no part of that period shall be disregarded by virtue of paragraph 17 above.

(2) If a period during which the condition in paragraph 10(1)(c) is deemed to be fulfilled by virtue of sub-paragraph (1) above comes to an end on the death of a person who was in occupation of a dwelling-house as mentioned in paragraph (b) of that sub-paragraph, then, in determining whether that condition is at any time thereafter fulfilled, there shall be disregarded any period—

(a) which begins on the date of the death;
(b) during which the interest of the landlord remains vested as mentioned in sub-paragraph (1)(a) above; and
(c) which ends at the expiry of the period of two years beginning on the date of the death or on any earlier date on which the condition in paragraph 10(1)(c) becomes again deemed to be fulfilled by virtue of sub-paragraph (1) above.

19. In any case where—

(a) immediately before a tenancy comes to an end the condition in paragraph 10(1)(c) is deemed to be fulfilled by virtue of paragraph 18(1) above, and
(b) on the coming to an end of that tenancy the trustees in whom the interest of the landlord is vested grant a new tenancy of the same or substantially the same dwelling-house to a person (alone or jointly with others) who was the tenant or one of the tenants under the previous tenancy,

the condition in paragraph 10(1)(b) above shall be deemed to be fulfilled with respect to the new tenancy.

20.—(1) The tenancy referred to in paragraph 10 above falls within this paragraph if the interest of the landlord under the tenancy becomes vested in the personal representatives of a deceased person acting in that capacity.

(2) If the tenancy falls within this paragraph, the condition in paragraph 10(1)(c) shall be deemed to be fulfilled for any period, beginning with the date on which the interest becomes vested in the personal representatives and not exceeding two years, during which the interest of the landlord remains so vested.

21. Throughout any period which, by virtue of paragraph 17 or paragraph 18(2) above, falls to be disregarded for the purpose of determining whether the condition in paragraph 10(1)(c) is fulfilled with respect to a tenancy, no order shall be made for possession of the dwelling-house subject to that tenancy, other than an order which might be made if that tenancy were or, as the case may be, had been an assured tenancy.

22. For the purposes of paragraph 10 above, a building is a purpose-built block of flats if as constructed it contained, and it contains, two or more flats; and for this purpose "flat" means a dwelling-house which—

(a) forms part only of a building; and
(b) is separated horizontally from another dwelling-house which forms part of the same building.

[1356]

NOTES

Para 17: in para (1)(c)(ii) words in square brackets substituted by the Law of Property (Miscellaneous Provisions) Act 1994, s 21(1), Sch 1, para 11.

Para 18: words omitted from sub-para (1) repealed by the Trusts of Land and Appointment of Trustees Act 1996, s 25(2), Sch 4; for savings in relation to entailed interests created before the commencement of that Act, and savings consequential upon the abolition of the doctrine of conversion, see s 25(4), (5) thereof.

SCHEDULE 2
GROUNDS FOR POSSESSION OF DWELLING-HOUSES LET ON ASSURED TENANCIES

Section 7

PART I
GROUNDS ON WHICH COURT MUST ORDER POSSESSION

Ground 1

Not later than the beginning of the tenancy the landlord gave notice in writing to the tenant that possession might be recovered on this ground or the court is of the opinion that it is just and equitable to dispense with the requirement of notice and (in either case)—

(a) at some time before the beginning of the tenancy, the landlord who is seeking possession or, in the case of joint landlords seeking possession, at least one of them occupied the dwelling-house as his only or principal home; or

(b) the landlord who is seeking possession or, in the case of joint landlords seeking possession, at least one of them requires the dwelling-house as [his, his spouse's or his civil partner's] only or principal home and neither the landlord (or, in the case of joint landlords, any one of them) nor any other person who, as landlord, derived title under the landlord who gave the notice mentioned above acquired the reversion on the tenancy for money or money's worth.

Ground 2

The dwelling-house is subject to a mortgage granted before the beginning of the tenancy and—

(a) the mortgagee is entitled to exercise a power of sale conferred on him by the mortgage or by section 101 of the Law of Property Act 1925; and

(b) the mortgagee requires possession of the dwelling-house for the purpose of disposing of it with vacant possession in exercise of that power; and

(c) either notice was given as mentioned in Ground 1 above or the court is satisfied that it is just and equitable to dispense with the requirement of notice;

and for the purposes of this ground "mortgage" includes a charge and "mortgagee" shall be construed accordingly.

Ground 3

The tenancy is a fixed term tenancy for a term not exceeding eight months and—

(a) not later than the beginning of the tenancy the landlord gave notice in writing to the tenant that possession might be recovered on this ground; and

(b) at some time within the period of twelve months ending with the beginning of the tenancy, the dwelling-house was occupied under a right to occupy it for a holiday.

Ground 4

The tenancy is a fixed term tenancy for a term not exceeding twelve months and—

(a) not later than the beginning of the tenancy the landlord gave notice in writing to the tenant that possession might be recovered on this ground; and

(b) at some time within the period of twelve months ending with the beginning of the tenancy, the dwelling-house was let on a tenancy falling within paragraph 8 of Schedule 1 to this Act.

Ground 5

The dwelling-house is held for the purpose of being available for occupation by a minister of religion as a residence from which to perform the duties of his office and—

(a) not later than the beginning of the tenancy the landlord gave notice in writing to the tenant that possession might be recovered on this ground; and

(b) the court is satisfied that the dwelling-house is required for occupation by a minister of religion as such a residence.

Ground 6

The landlord who is seeking possession or, if that landlord is a [registered social landlord] or charitable housing trust, a superior landlord intends to demolish or reconstruct the whole or a substantial part of the dwelling-house or to carry out substantial works on the dwelling-house or any part thereof or any building of which it forms part and the following conditions are fulfilled—

(a) the intended work cannot reasonably be carried out without the tenant giving up possession of the dwelling-house because—

(i) the tenant is not willing to agree to such a variation of the terms of the tenancy as would give such access and other facilities as would permit the intended work to be carried out, or

(ii) the nature of the intended work is such that no such variation is practicable, or

(iii) the tenant is not willing to accept an assured tenancy of such part only of the dwelling-house (in this sub-paragraph referred to as "the reduced part") as would leave in the possession of his landlord so much of the dwelling-house as would be reasonable to enable the intended work to be carried out and, where appropriate, as would give such access and other facilities over the reduced part as would permit the intended work to be carried out, or

(iv) the nature of the intended work is such that such a tenancy is not practicable; and

(b) either the landlord seeking possession acquired his interest in the dwelling-house before the grant of the tenancy or that interest was in existence at the time of that grant and neither that landlord (or, in the case of joint landlords, any of them) nor any other person who, alone or jointly with others, has acquired that interest since that time acquired it for money or money's worth; and

(c) the assured tenancy on which the dwelling-house is let did not come into being by virtue of any provision of Schedule 1 to the Rent Act 1977, as amended by Part I of Schedule 4 to this Act or, as the case may be, section 4 of the Rent (Agriculture) Act 1976, as amended by Part II of that Schedule.

For the purposes of this ground, if, immediately before the grant of the tenancy, the tenant to whom it was granted or, if it was granted to joint tenants, any of them was the tenant or one of the joint tenants [of the dwelling-house concerned] under an earlier assured tenancy [or, as the case may be, under a tenancy to which Schedule 10 to the Local Government and Housing Act 1989 applied], any reference in paragraph (b) above to the grant of the tenancy is a reference to the grant of that earlier assured tenancy [or, as the case may be, to the grant of the tenancy to which the said Schedule 10 applied].

For the purposes of this ground ["registered social landlord" has the same meaning as in the Housing Act 1985 (see section 5(4) and (5) of that Act)] and "charitable housing trust" means a housing trust, within the meaning of [the Housing Associations Act 1985], which is a charity, within the meaning of [the Charities Act 1993].

[…]

Ground 7

The tenancy is a periodic tenancy (including a statutory periodic tenancy) which has devolved under the will or intestacy of the former tenant and the proceedings for the recovery of possession are begun not later than twelve months after the death of the former tenant or, if the court so directs, after the date on which, in the opinion of the court, the landlord or, in the case of joint landlords, any one of them became aware of the former tenant's death.

For the purposes of this ground, the acceptance by the landlord of rent from a new tenant after the death of the former tenant shall not be regarded as creating a new periodic tenancy, unless the landlord agrees in writing to a change (as compared with the tenancy before the death) in the amount of the rent, the period of the tenancy, the premises which are let or any other term of the tenancy.

Ground 8

Both at the date of the service of the notice under section 8 of this Act relating to the proceedings for possession and at the date of the hearing—

(a) if rent is payable weekly or fortnightly, at least [eight weeks]' rent is unpaid;

(b) if rent is payable monthly, at least [two months]' rent is unpaid;

(c) if rent is payable quarterly, at least one quarter's rent is more than three months in arrears; and

(d) if rent is payable yearly, at least three months' rent is more than three months in arrears;

and for the purpose of this ground "rent" means rent lawfully due from the tenant.

[1357]

NOTES

Ground 1: words in square brackets in para (b) substituted by the Civil Partnership Act 2004, s 81, Sch 8, para 43(1), (2).

Ground 6: first and third words in square brackets inserted, and second words in square brackets substituted, by the Local Government and Housing Act 1989, s 194, Sch 11, para 108; fourth words in square brackets substituted by the Charities Act 1993, s 98(1), Sch 6, para 30; final words in square brackets inserted by the Local Government and Housing Act 1989, s 194, Sch 11, para 109, and repealed by the Housing Act 1996, s 227, Sch 19, Pt IX.

Ground 8: words in square brackets substituted by the Housing Act 1996, s 101.

PART II
GROUNDS ON WHICH COURT MAY ORDER POSSESSION

Ground 9

Suitable alternative accommodation is available for the tenant or will be available for him when the order for possession takes effect.

Ground 10

Some rent lawfully due from the tenant—

(a) is unpaid on the date on which the proceedings for possession are begun; and
(b) except where subsection (1)(b) of section 8 of this Act applies, was in arrears at the date of the service of the notice under that section relating to those proceedings.

Ground 11

Whether or not any rent is in arrears on the date on which proceedings for possession are begun, the tenant has persistently delayed paying rent which has become lawfully due.

Ground 12

Any obligation of the tenancy (other than one related to the payment of rent) has been broken or not performed.

Ground 13

The condition of the dwelling-house or any of the common parts has deteriorated owing to acts of waste by, or the neglect or default of, the tenant or any other person residing in the dwelling-house and, in the case of an act of waste by, or the neglect or default of, a person lodging with the tenant or a sub-tenant of his, the tenant has not taken such steps as he ought reasonably to have taken for the removal of the lodger or sub-tenant.

For the purposes of this ground, "common parts" means any part of a building comprising the dwelling-house and any other premises which the tenant is entitled under the terms of the tenancy to use in common with the occupiers of other dwelling-houses in which the landlord has an estate or interest.

[Ground 14

The tenant or a person residing in or visiting the dwelling-house—

(a) has been guilty of conduct causing or likely to cause a nuisance or annoyance to a person residing, visiting or otherwise engaging in a lawful activity in the locality, or
(b) has been convicted of—
    (i) using the dwelling-house or allowing it to be used for immoral or illegal purposes, or
    (ii) an [indictable] offence committed in, or in the locality of, the dwelling-house.]

[Ground 14A

The dwelling-house was occupied (whether alone or with others) by [a married couple, a couple who are civil partners of each other,] a couple living together as husband and wife [or a couple living together as if they were civil partners] and—

(a) one or both of the partners is a tenant of the dwelling-house,
(b) the landlord who is seeking possession is a registered social landlord or a charitable housing trust,
(c) one partner has left the dwelling-house because of violence or threats of violence by the other towards—
    (i) that partner, or
    (ii) a member of the family of that partner who was residing with that partner immediately before the partner left, and
(d) the court is satisfied that the partner who has left is unlikely to return.

For the purposes of this ground "registered social landlord" and "member of the family" have the same meaning as in Part I of the Housing Act 1996 and "charitable housing trust" means a housing trust, within the meaning of the Housing Associations Act 1985, which is a charity within the meaning of the Charities Act 1993.]

Ground 15

The condition of any furniture provided for use under the tenancy has, in the opinion of the court, deteriorated owing to ill-treatment by the tenant or any other person residing in the dwelling-house and, in the case of ill-treatment by a person lodging with the tenant or by a sub-tenant of his, the tenant has not taken such steps as he ought reasonably to have taken for the removal of the lodger or sub-tenant.

Ground 16

The dwelling-house was let to the tenant in consequence of his employment by the landlord seeking possession or a previous landlord under the tenancy and the tenant has ceased to be in that employment.

[For the purposes of this ground, at a time when the landlord is or was the Secretary of State, employment by a health service body, as defined in section 60(7) of the National Health Service and Community Care Act 1990, [or by a Local Health Board,] shall be regarded as employment by the Secretary of State.]

[Ground 17

The tenant is the person, or one of the persons, to whom the tenancy was granted and the landlord was induced to grant the tenancy by a false statement made knowingly or recklessly by—

(a) the tenant, or

(b) a person acting at the tenant's instigation.]

[1358]

NOTES

Ground 14: substituted by the Housing Act 1996, s 148; word in square brackets in para (b)(ii) substituted by the Serious Organised Crime and Police Act 2005, s 111, Sch 7, Pt 3, para 46.

Ground 14A: inserted by the Housing Act 1996, s 149; words in first pair of square brackets substituted and words in second pair of square brackets inserted by the Civil Partnership Act 2004, s 81, Sch 8, para 43(1), (3).

Ground 16: proviso inserted by the National Health Service and Community Care Act 1990, s 60(2)(b), Sch 8, Pt II, para 10; words in square brackets therein inserted by the National Health Service Reform and Health Care Professions Act 2002, s 6(2), Sch 5, para 28.

Ground 17: inserted by the Housing Act 1996, s 102.

PART III
SUITABLE ALTERNATIVE ACCOMMODATION

1. For the purposes of Ground 9 above, a certificate of the local housing authority for the district in which the dwelling-house in question is situated, certifying that the authority will provide suitable alternative accommodation for the tenant by a date specified in the certificate, shall be conclusive evidence that suitable alternative accommodation will be available for him by that date.

2. Where no such certificate as is mentioned in paragraph 1 above is produced to the court, accommodation shall be deemed to be suitable for the purposes of Ground 9 above if it consists of either—

(a) premises which are to be let as a separate dwelling such that they will then be let on an assured tenancy, other than—

(i) a tenancy in respect of which notice is given not later than the beginning of the tenancy that possession might be recovered on any of Grounds 1 to 5 above, or

(ii) an assured shorthold tenancy, within the meaning of Chapter II of Part I of this Act, or

(b) premises to be let as a separate dwelling on terms which will, in the opinion of the court, afford to the tenant security of tenure reasonably equivalent to the security afforded by Chapter I of Part I of this Act in the case of an assured tenancy of a kind mentioned in sub-paragraph (a) above,

and, in the opinion of the court, the accommodation fulfils the relevant conditions as defined in paragraph 3 below.

3.—(1) For the purposes of paragraph 2 above, the relevant conditions are that the accommodation is reasonably suitable to the needs of the tenant and his family as regards proximity to place of work, and either—

(a) similar as regards rental and extent to the accommodation afforded by dwelling-houses provided in the neighbourhood by any local housing authority for persons whose needs as regards extent are, in the opinion of the court, similar to those of the tenant and of his family; or

(b) reasonably suitable to the means of the tenant and to the needs of the tenant and his family as regards extent and character; and

that if any furniture was provided for use under the assured tenancy in question, furniture is provided for use in the accommodation which is either similar to that so provided or is reasonably suitable to the needs of the tenant and his family.

(2) For the purposes of sub-paragraph (1)(a) above, a certificate of a local housing authority stating—

(a) the extent of the accommodation afforded by dwelling-houses provided by the authority to meet the needs of tenants with families of such number as may be specified in the certificate, and

(b) the amount of the rent charged by the authority for dwelling-houses affording accommodation of that extent, shall be conclusive evidence of the facts so stated.

4. Accommodation shall not be deemed to be suitable to the needs of the tenant and his family if the result of their occupation of the accommodation would be that it would be an overcrowded dwelling-house for the purposes of Part X of the Housing Act 1985.

5. Any document purporting to be a certificate of a local housing authority named therein issued for the purposes of this Part of this Schedule and to be signed by the proper officer of that authority shall be received in evidence and, unless the contrary is shown, shall be deemed to be such a certificate without further proof.

6. In this Part of this Schedule "local housing authority" and "district", in relation to such an authority, have the same meaning as in the Housing Act 1985.

[1359]

PART IV
NOTICES RELATING TO RECOVERY OF POSSESSION

7. Any reference in Grounds 1 to 5 in Part I of this Schedule or in the following provisions of this Part to the landlord giving a notice in writing to the tenant is, in the case of joint landlords, a reference to at least one of the joint landlords giving such a notice.

8.—(1) If, not later than the beginning of a tenancy (in this paragraph referred to as "the earlier tenancy"), the landlord gives such a notice in writing to the tenant as is mentioned in any of Grounds 1 to 5 in Part I of this Schedule, then, for the purposes of the ground in question and any further application of this paragraph, that notice shall also have effect as if it had been given immediately before the beginning of any later tenancy falling within sub-paragraph (2) below.

(2) Subject to sub-paragraph (3) below, sub-paragraph (1) above applies to a later tenancy—

(a) which takes effect immediately on the coming to an end of the earlier tenancy; and

(b) which is granted (or deemed to be granted) to the person who was the tenant under the earlier tenancy immediately before it came to an end; and

(c) which is of substantially the same dwelling-house as the earlier tenancy.

(3) Sub-paragraph (1) above does not apply in relation to a later tenancy if, not later than the beginning of the tenancy, the landlord gave notice in writing to the tenant that the tenancy is not one in respect of which possession can be recovered on the ground in question.

9. Where paragraph 8(1) above has effect in relation to a notice given as mentioned in Ground 1 in Part I of this Schedule, the reference in paragraph (b) of that ground to the reversion on the tenancy is a reference to the reversion on the earlier tenancy and on any later tenancy falling within paragraph 8(2) above.

10. Where paragraph 8(1) above has effect in relation to a notice given as mentioned in Ground 3 or Ground 4 in Part I of this Schedule, any second or subsequent tenancy in relation to which the notice has effect shall be treated for the purpose of that ground as beginning at the beginning of the tenancy in respect of which the notice was actually given.

11. Any reference in Grounds 1 to 5 in Part I of this Schedule to a notice being given not later than the beginning of the tenancy is a reference to its being given not later than the day on which the tenancy is entered into and, accordingly, section 45(2) of this Act shall not apply to any such reference.

[1360]

[SCHEDULE 2A
ASSURED TENANCIES: NON-SHORTHOLDS

Section 19A

Tenancies excluded by notice

1.—(1) An assured tenancy in respect of which a notice is served as mentioned in sub-paragraph (2) below.

(2) The notice referred to in sub-paragraph (1) above is one which—

(a) is served before the assured tenancy is entered into,

(b) is served by the person who is to be the landlord under the assured tenancy on the person who is to be the tenant under that tenancy, and

(c) states that the assured tenancy to which it relates is not to be an assured shorthold tenancy.

2.—(1) An assured tenancy in respect of which a notice is served as mentioned in sub-paragraph (2) below.

(2) The notice referred to in sub-paragraph (1) above is one which—

(a) is served after the assured tenancy has been entered into,

(b) is served by the landlord under the assured tenancy on the tenant under that tenancy, and

(c) states that the assured tenancy to which it relates is no longer an assured shorthold tenancy.

Tenancies containing exclusionary provision

3. An assured tenancy which contains a provision to the effect that the tenancy is not an assured shorthold tenancy.

Tenancies under section 39

4. An assured tenancy arising by virtue of section 39 above, other than one to which subsection (7) of that section applies.

Former secure tenancies

5. An assured tenancy which became an assured tenancy on ceasing to be a secure tenancy.

[Former demoted tenancies

5A. An assured tenancy which ceases to be an assured shorthold tenancy by virtue of section 20B(2) or (4).]

Tenancies under Schedule 10 to the Local Government and Housing Act 1989

6. An assured tenancy arising by virtue of Schedule 10 to the Local Government and Housing Act 1989 (security of tenure on ending of long residential tenancies).

Tenancies replacing non-shortholds

7.—(1) An assured tenancy which—

(a) is granted to a person (alone or jointly with others) who, immediately before the tenancy was granted, was the tenant (or, in the case of joint tenants, one of the tenants) under an assured tenancy other than a shorthold tenancy ("the old tenancy"),

(b) is granted (alone or jointly with others) by a person who was at that time the landlord (or one of the joint landlords) under the old tenancy, and

(c) is not one in respect of which a notice is served as mentioned in sub-paragraph (2) below.

(2) The notice referred to in sub-paragraph (1)(c) above is one which—

(a) is in such form as may be prescribed,

(b) is served before the assured tenancy is entered into,

(c) is served by the person who is to be the tenant under the assured tenancy on the person who is to be the landlord under that tenancy (or, in the case of joint landlords, on at least one of the persons who are to be joint landlords), and

(d) states that the assured tenancy to which it relates is to be a shorthold tenancy.

8. An assured tenancy which comes into being by virtue of section 5 above on the coming to an end of an assured tenancy which is not a shorthold tenancy.

Assured agricultural occupancies

9.—(1) An assured tenancy—

(a) in the case of which the agricultural worker condition is, by virtue of any provision of Schedule 3 to this Act, for the time being fulfilled with respect to the dwelling-house subject to the tenancy, and

(b) which does not fall within sub-paragraph (2) or (4) below.

(2) An assured tenancy falls within this sub-paragraph if—

(a) before it is entered into, a notice—

(i) in such form as may be prescribed, and

(ii) stating that the tenancy is to be a shorthold tenancy,

is served by the person who is to be the landlord under the tenancy on the person who is to be the tenant under it, and

(b) it is not an excepted tenancy.

(3) For the purposes of sub-paragraph (2)(b) above, an assured tenancy is an excepted tenancy if—

(a) the person to whom it is granted or, as the case may be, at least one of the persons to whom it is granted was, immediately before it is granted, a tenant or licensee under an assured agricultural occupancy, and

(b) the person by whom it is granted or, as the case may be, at least one of the persons by whom it is granted was, immediately before it is granted, a landlord or licensor under the assured agricultural occupancy referred to in paragraph (a) above.

(4) An assured tenancy falls within this sub-paragraph if it comes into being by virtue of section 5 above on the coming to an end of a tenancy falling within sub-paragraph (2) above.]

[1361]

PART I STATUTES

NOTES

Inserted by the Housing Act 1996, s 96(2), Sch 7.
Para 5A: inserted by the Anti-social Behaviour Act 2003, s 15(3).

(*Schs 3–18 outside the scope of this work.*)

ROAD TRAFFIC ACT 1988

(1988 c 52)

An Act to consolidate certain enactments relating to road traffic with amendments to give effect to recommendations of the Law Commission and the Scottish Law Commission

[15 November 1988]

PART I
PRINCIPAL ROAD SAFETY PROVISIONS

1–32 (*Ss 1–19, 20–32 outside the scope of this work; s 19A repealed by the Road Traffic Act 1991, s 83, Sch 8.*)

Use of motor vehicles away from roads

33 (*Outside the scope of this work.*)

[34 Prohibition of driving mechanically propelled vehicles elsewhere than on roads

(1) Subject to the provisions of this section, if without lawful authority a person drives a mechanically propelled vehicle—

(a) on to or upon any common land, moorland or land of any other description, not being land forming part of a road, or

(b) on any road being a footpath, bridleway or restricted byway,

he is guilty of an offence.

(2) For the purposes of subsection (1)(b) above, a way shown in a definitive map and statement as a footpath, bridleway or restricted byway is, without prejudice to section 56(1) of the Wildlife and Countryside Act 1981, to be taken to be a way of the kind shown, unless … the contrary is proved.

[(2A) It is not an offence under this section for a person with an interest in land, or a visitor to any land, to drive a mechanically propelled vehicle on a road if, immediately before the commencement of section 47(2) of the Countryside and Rights of Way Act 2000, the road was—

(a) shown in a definitive map and statement as a road used as a public path, and

(b) in use for obtaining access to the land by the driving of mechanically propelled vehicles by a person with an interest in the land or by visitors to the land.]

(3) It is not an offence under this section to drive a mechanically propelled vehicle on any land within fifteen yards of a road, being a road on which a motor vehicle may lawfully be driven, for the purpose only of parking the vehicle on that land.

(4) A person shall not be convicted of an offence under this section with respect to a vehicle if he proves to the satisfaction of the court that it was driven in contravention of this section for the purpose of saving life or extinguishing fire or meeting any other like emergency.

(5) It is hereby declared that nothing in this section prejudices the operation of—

(a) section 193 of the Law of Property Act 1925 (rights of the public over commons and waste lands), or

(b) any byelaws applying to any land,

or affects the law of trespass to land or any right or remedy to which a person may by law be entitled in respect of any such trespass or in particular confers a right to park a vehicle on any land.

(6) Subsection (2) above [does] not extend to Scotland.

(7) In this section—

"definitive map and statement" has the same meaning as in Part III of the Wildlife and Countryside Act 1981;

["interest", in relation to land, includes any estate in land and any right over land (whether exercisable by virtue of the ownership of an estate or interest in the land or by virtue of a licence or agreement) and, in particular, includes rights of common and sporting rights;]

"mechanically propelled vehicle" does not include a vehicle falling within paragraph (a), (b) or (c) of section 189(1) of this Act; and "restricted byway" means a way over which the public have restricted byway rights within the meaning of Part II of the Countryside and Rights of Way Act 2000, with or without a right to drive animals of any description along the way, but no other rights of way.

[(8) A person—

(a) entering any land in exercise of rights conferred by virtue of section 2(1) of the Countryside and Rights of Way Act 2000, or

(b) entering any land which is treated by section 15(1) of that Act as being accessible to the public apart from that Act,

is not for the purposes of subsection (2A) a visitor to the land.]]

[1362]

NOTES

Substituted by the Countryside and Rights of Way Act 2000, s 67, Sch 7, para 5.

Sub-s (2): words omitted repealed by the Natural Environment and Rural Communities Act 2006, ss 70(2), (3), 105(2), Sch 12.

Sub-s (2A): inserted by the Natural Environment and Rural Communities Act 2006, s 70(2), (4).

Sub-s (6): word in square brackets substituted by the Natural Environment and Rural Communities Act 2006, s 70(2), (5).

Sub-s (7): definition "interest" inserted by the Natural Environment and Rural Communities Act 2006, s 70(2), (6).

Sub-s (8): inserted by the Natural Environment and Rural Communities Act 2006, s 70(2), (7).

[34A Exceptions to presumption in section 34(2)

(1) Where a person is charged with an offence under section 34 of this Act in respect of the driving of any vehicle, it is open to that person to prove under subsection (2) of that section that a way shown in a definitive map and statement as a footpath, bridleway or restricted byway is not a way of the kind shown only—

(a) if he proves to the satisfaction of the court—

(i) that he was a person interested in any land and that the driving of the vehicle by him was reasonably necessary to obtain access to the land,

(ii) that the driving of the vehicle by him was reasonably necessary to obtain access to any land, and was for the purpose of obtaining access to the land as a lawful visitor, or

(iii) that the driving of the vehicle by him was reasonably necessary for the purposes of any business, trade or profession; or

(b) in such circumstances as may be prescribed by regulations made by the Secretary of State (and paragraph (a) above is without prejudice to this paragraph).

(2) In subsection (1) above—

"interest", in relation to land, includes any estate in land and any right over land, whether the right is exercisable by virtue of the ownership of an estate or interest in land or by virtue of a licence or agreement, and in particular includes rights of common and sporting rights, and the reference to a person interested in land shall be construed accordingly;

"lawful visitor", in relation to land, includes any person who enters the land for any purpose in the exercise of a right conferred by law.]

[1363]

NOTES

Commencement: to be appointed.

Inserted by the Countryside and Rights of Way Act 2000, s 67, Sch 7, para 6.

35–162 (*Ss 35–40, ss 40A–162 (Pts II–VI) outside the scope of this work.*)

PART VII
MISCELLANEOUS AND GENERAL

162A–194 (*Outside the scope of this work.*)

Supplementary

195, 196 (*Outside the scope of this work.*)

197 Short title, commencement and extent

(1) This Act may be cited as the Road Traffic Act 1988.

(2) This Act shall come into force, subject to the transitory provisions in Schedule 5 to the Road Traffic (Consequential Provisions) Act 1988, at the end of the period of six months beginning with the day on which it is passed.

(3) This Act, except section 80 and except as provided by section 184, does not extend to Northern Ireland.

[1364]

(*Schs 1–4 outside the scope of this work.*)

LAW OF PROPERTY (MISCELLANEOUS PROVISIONS) ACT 1989

(1989 c 34)

An Act to make new provision with respect to deeds and their execution and contracts for the sale or other disposition of interests in land; and to abolish the rule of law known as the rule in Bain v Fothergill

[27 July 1989]

1 Deeds and their execution

(1) Any rule of law which—

(a) restricts the substances on which a deed may be written;

(b) requires a seal for the valid execution of an instrument as a deed by an individual; or

(c) requires authority by one person to another to deliver an instrument as a deed on his behalf to be given by deed,

is abolished.

(2) An instrument shall not be a deed unless—

(a) it makes it clear on its face that it is intended to be a deed by the person making it or, as the case may be, by the parties to it (whether by describing itself as a deed or expressing itself to be executed or signed as a deed or otherwise); and

(b) it is validly executed as a deed—

[(i) by that person or a person authorised to execute it in the name or on behalf of that person, or

(ii) by one or more of those parties or a person authorised to execute it in the name or on behalf of one or more of those parties].

[(2A) For the purposes of subsection (2)(a) above, an instrument shall not be taken to make it clear on its face that it is intended to be a deed merely because it is executed under seal.]

(3) An instrument is validly executed as a deed by an individual if, and only if—

(a) it is signed—

(i) by him in the presence of a witness who attests the signature; or

(ii) at his direction and in his presence and the presence of two witnesses who each attest the signature; and

(b) it is delivered as a deed …

(4) In subsections (2) and (3) above "sign", in relation to an instrument, includes—

[(a) an individual signing the name of the person or party on whose behalf he executes the instrument; and

(b) making one's mark on the instrument,

and "signature" is to be construed accordingly].

[(4A) Subsection (3) above applies in the case of an instrument executed by an individual in the name or on behalf of another person whether or not that person is also an individual.]

(5) Where *a solicitor[, duly certificated notary public] or licensed conveyancer, or an agent or employee of a solicitor[, duly certificated notary public] or licensed conveyancer* [a relevant lawyer, or an agent or employee of a relevant lawyer], in the course of or in connection with a transaction …, purports to deliver an instrument as a deed on behalf of a party to the instrument, it shall be conclusively presumed in favour of a purchaser that he is authorised so to deliver the instrument.

(6) In subsection (5) above—

["purchaser" has the same meaning] as in the Law of Property Act 1925;

["duly certificated notary public" has the same meaning as it has in the Solicitors Act 1974 by virtue of section 87 of that Act;] …

["relevant lawyer" means a person who, for the purposes of the Legal Services Act 2007, is an authorised person in relation to an activity which constitutes a reserved instrument activity (within the meaning of that Act);]

…

(7) Where an instrument under seal that constitutes a deed is required for the purposes of an Act passed before this section comes into force, this section shall have effect as to signing, sealing or delivery of an instrument by an individual in place of any provision of that Act as to signing, sealing or delivery.

(8) The enactments mentioned in Schedule 1 to this Act (which in consequence of this section require amendments other than those provided by subsection (7) above) shall have effect with the amendments specified in that Schedule.

(9) Nothing in subsection (1)(b), (2), (3), (7) or (8) above applies in relation to deeds required or authorised to be made under—

(a) the seal of the county palatine of Lancaster;
(b) the seal of the Duchy of Lancaster; or
(c) the seal of the Duchy of Cornwall.

(10) The references in this section to the execution of a deed by an individual do not include execution by a corporation sole and the reference in subsection (7) above to signing, sealing or delivery by an individual does not include signing, sealing or delivery by such a corporation.

(11) Nothing in this section applies in relation to instruments delivered as deeds before this section comes into force.

[1365]

NOTES

Sub-s (2): sub-para (b)(i), (ii) substituted by SI 2005/1906, art 7(3), except in relation to any instrument executed before 15 September 2005.

Sub-ss (2A), (4A): inserted by SI 2005/1906, arts 7(4), 8, except in relation to any instrument executed before 15 September 2005.

Sub-s (3): words omitted from para (b) repealed by SI 2005/1906, art 10(2), Sch 2, except in relation to any instrument executed before 15 September 2005.

Sub-s (4): words in square brackets substituted by SI 2005/1906, art 10(1), Sch 1, paras 13, 14, except in relation to any instrument executed before 15 September 2005.

Sub-s (5): words in italics repealed and subsequent words in third pair of square brackets substituted by the Legal Services Act 2007, s 208(1), Sch 21, para 81(a), as from a day to be appointed; words in first and second pairs of square brackets inserted by the Courts and Legal Services Act 1990, s 125(2), Sch 17, para 20; words omitted repealed by SI 2005/1906, arts 9, 10(2), Sch 2, except in relation to any instrument executed before 15 September 2005.

Sub-s (6): in definition "purchaser" words in square brackets substituted, and definition "interest in land" (omitted) repealed by SI 2005/1906, art 10(1), (2), Sch 1, paras 13, 15, Sch 2, except in relation to any instrument executed before 15 September 2005; definition "duly certificated notary public" inserted by the Courts and Legal Services Act 1990, s 125(2), Sch 17, para 20 and word omitted repealed by SI 2005/1906, art 10(2), Sch 2, except in relation to any instrument executed before 15 September 2005; definition "duly certificated notary public" substituted, by subsequent definition "relevant lawyer", by the Legal Services Act 2007, s 208(1), Sch 21, para 81(b), as from a day to be appointed.

2 Contracts for sale etc of land to be made by signed writing

(1) A contract for the sale or other disposition of an interest in land can only be made in writing and only by incorporating all the terms which the parties have expressly agreed in one document or, where contracts are exchanged, in each.

(2) The terms may be incorporated in a document either by being set out in it or by reference to some other document.

(3) The document incorporating the terms or, where contracts are exchanged, one of the documents incorporating them (but not necessarily the same one) must be signed by or on behalf of each party to the contract.

(4) Where a contract for the sale or other disposition of an interest in land satisfies the conditions of this section by reason only of the rectification of one or more documents in pursuance of an order of a court, the contract shall come into being, or be deemed to have come into being, at such time as may be specified in the order.

(5) This section does not apply in relation to—

(a) a contract to grant such a lease as is mentioned in section 54(2) of the Law of Property Act 1925 (short leases);
(b) a contract made in the course of a public auction; or
[(c) a contract regulated under the Financial Services and Markets Act 2000, other than a regulated mortgage contract[, a regulated home reversion plan or a regulated home purchase plan];]

and nothing in this section affects the creation or operation of resulting, implied or constructive trusts.

(6) In this section—

"disposition" has the same meaning as in the Law of Property Act 1925;

"interest in land" means any estate, interest or charge in or over land …

["regulated mortgage contract"[, "regulated home reversion plan" and "regulated home purchase plan"] must be read with—

(a) section 22 of the Financial Services and Markets Act 2000,
(b) any relevant order under that section, and
(c) Schedule 22 to that Act].

(7) Nothing in this section shall apply in relation to contracts made before this section comes into force.

(8) Section 40 of the Law of Property Act 1925 (which is superseded by this section) shall cease to have effect.

[1366]

NOTES

Sub-s (5): para (c) substituted SI 2001/3649, art 317(1), (2); words in square brackets therein inserted by SI 2006/2383, art 27(a), subject to transitional provisions in arts 37–39 thereof.

Sub-s (6): words omitted repealed by the Trusts of Land and Appointment of Trustees Act 1996, s 25(2), Sch 4, subject to savings contained in ss 3, 18(3), 25(5) of that Act; definition "regulated mortgage" inserted by SI 2001/3649, art 317(1), (3); words in square brackets therein inserted by SI 2006/2383, art 27(b), subject to transitional provisions in arts 37–39 thereof.

3 Abolition of rule in Bain v Fothergill

The rule of law known as the rule in Bain v Fothergill is abolished in relation to contracts made after this section comes into force.

[1367]

4 Repeals

The enactments mentioned in Schedule 2 to this Act are repealed to the extent specified in the third column of that Schedule.

[1368]

5 Commencement

(1) The provisions of this Act to which this subsection applies shall come into force on such day as the Lord Chancellor may by order made by statutory instrument appoint.

(2) The provisions to which subsection (1) above applies are—

(a) section 1 above; and

(b) section 4 above, except so far as it relates to section 40 of the Law of Property Act 1925.

(3) The provisions of this Act to which this subsection applies shall come into force at the end of the period of two months beginning with the day on which this Act is passed.

(4) The provisions of this Act to which subsection (3) above applies are—

(a) sections 2 and 3 above; and

(b) section 4 above, so far as it relates to section 40 of the Law of Property Act 1925.

[1369]

NOTES

Order: the Law of Property (Miscellaneous Provisions) Act 1989 (Commencement) Order 1990, SI 1990/1175.

6 Citation

(1) This Act may be cited as the Law of Property (Miscellaneous Provisions) Act 1989.

(2) This Act extends to England and Wales only.

[1370]

(*Schs 1, 2 contain amendments and repeals only.*)

LOCAL GOVERNMENT AND HOUSING ACT 1989

(1989 c 42)

An Act to make provision with respect to the members, officers and other staff and the procedure of local authorities; to amend Part III of the Local Government Act 1974 and Part II of the Local Government (Scotland) Act 1975 and to provide for a national code of local government conduct; to make further provision about the finances and expenditure of local authorities (including provision with respect to housing subsidies) and about companies in which local authorities have interests; to make provision for and in connection with renewal areas, grants towards the cost of improvement and repair of housing accommodation and the carrying out of works of maintenance, repair and improvement; to amend the Housing Act 1985 and Part III of the Local Government Finance Act 1982; to make amendments of and consequential upon Parts I, II and IV of the Housing Act 1988; to amend the Local Government Finance Act 1988 and the Abolition of Domestic Rates Etc (Scotland) Act 1987 and certain enactments relating, as respects Scotland, to rating and valuation, and to provide for the making of grants; to make provision with respect to the imposition of charges by local authorities; to make further provision about certain existing grants and about financial assistance to and planning by local authorities in respect of emergencies; to amend sections 102 and 211 of the Local Government (Scotland) Act 1973; to amend the Local Land Charges Act 1975; to enable local authorities in Wales to be known solely by Welsh language names; to provide for the transfer of new town housing stock; to amend certain of the provisions of the Housing (Scotland) Act 1987 relating to a secure tenant's right to purchase his house; to amend section 47 of the Race Relations Act 1976; to confer certain powers on the Housing Corporation, Housing for Wales and Scottish Homes; to make provision about security of tenure for certain tenants under long tenancies; to provide for the making of grants and giving of guarantees in respect of certain activities carried on in relation to the construction industry; to provide for the repeal of certain enactments relating to improvement notices, town development and education support grants; to make, as respects Scotland, further provision in relation to the phasing of progression to registered rent for houses let by housing associations or Scottish Homes and in relation to the circumstances in which rent increases under assured tenancies may be secured; and for connected purposes

[16 November 1989]

1–138 ((*Pts I–VIII*) *outside the scope of this work.*)

PART IX
MISCELLANEOUS AND GENERAL

139–181 (*Outside the scope of this work.*)

Other provisions

182–185 (*Outside the scope of this work.*)

186 Security of tenure on ending of long residential tenancies

(1) Schedule 10 to this Act shall have effect (in place of Part I of the Landlord and Tenant Act 1954) to confer security of tenure on certain tenants under long tenancies and, in particular, to establish assured periodic tenancies when such long tenancies come to an end.

(2) Schedule 10 to this Act applies, and section 1 of the Landlord and Tenant Act 1954 does not apply, to a tenancy of a dwelling-house—

(a) which is a long tenancy at a low rent, as defined in Schedule 10 to this Act; and
(b) which is entered into on or after the day appointed for the coming into force of this section, otherwise than in pursuance of a contract made before that day.

(3) If a tenancy—

(a) is in existence on 15th January 1999, and
(b) does not fall within subsection (2) above, and
(c) immediately before that date was, or was deemed to be, a long tenancy at a low rent for the purposes of Part I of the Landlord and Tenant Act 1954,

then, on and after that date (and so far as concerns any notice specifying a date of termination on or after that date and any steps taken in consequence thereof), section 1 of that Act shall cease to apply to it and Schedule 10 to this Act shall apply to it unless, before that date, the landlord has served a notice under section 4 of that Act specifying a date of termination which is earlier than that date.

(4) The provisions of Schedule 10 to this Act have effect notwithstanding any agreement to the contrary, but nothing in this subsection or that Schedule shall be construed as preventing the surrender of a tenancy.

(5) Section 18 of the Landlord and Tenant Act 1954 (duty of tenants of residential property to give information to landlords or superior landlords) shall apply in relation to property comprised in a long tenancy at a low rent, within the meaning of Schedule 10 to this Act, as it applies to property comprised in a long tenancy at a low rent within the meaning of Part I of that Act, except that the reference in that section to subsection (1) of section 3 of that Act shall be construed as a reference to sub-paragraph (1) of paragraph 3 of Schedule 10 to this Act.

(6) Where, by virtue of subsection (3) above, Schedule 10 to this Act applies to a tenancy which is not a long tenancy at a low rent as defined in that Schedule, it shall be deemed to be such a tenancy for the purposes of that Schedule.

[1371]

187–195 (*Outside the scope of this work.*)

(*Schs 1–9 outside the scope of this work.*)

SCHEDULE 10
SECURITY OF TENURE ON ENDING OF LONG RESIDENTIAL TENANCIES

Section 186

Preliminary

1.—(1) This Schedule applies to a long tenancy of a dwelling-house at a low rent as respects which for the time being the following condition (in this Schedule referred to as "the qualifying condition") is fulfilled, that is to say, that the circumstances (as respects the property let under the tenancy, the use of that property and all other relevant matters) are such that, if the tenancy were not at a low rent, it would at that time be an assured tenancy within the meaning of Part I of the Housing Act 1988.

(2) For the purpose only of determining whether the qualifying condition is fulfilled with respect to a tenancy, Schedule 1 to the Housing Act 1988 (tenancies which cannot be assured tenancies) shall have effect with the omission of paragraph 1 (which excludes tenancies entered into before, or pursuant to contracts made before, the coming into force of Part I of that Act).

[(2A) For the purpose only of determining whether the qualifying condition is fulfilled with respect to a tenancy which is entered into on or after 1st April 1990 (otherwise than, where the dwelling-house has a rateable value on 31st March 1990, in pursuance of a contract made before 1st April 1990), for paragraph 2(1)(b) and (2) of Schedule 1 to the Housing Act 1988 there shall be substituted—

"(b) where (on the date the contract for the grant of the tenancy was made or, if there was no such contract, on the date the tenancy was entered into) R exceeded £25,000 under the formula—

$$R = \frac{P \times I}{1 - (1 + I)^{-T}}$$

where—

P is the premium payable as a condition of the grant of the tenancy (and includes a payment of money's worth) or, where no premium is so payable, zero,

I is 0·06,

T is the term, expressed in years, granted by the tenancy (disregarding any right to terminate the tenancy before the end of the term or to extend the tenancy).".]

(3) At any time within the period of twelve months ending on the day preceding the term date, application may be made to the court as respects any long tenancy of a dwelling-house at a low rent, not being at the time of the application a tenancy as respects which the qualifying condition is fulfilled, for an order declaring that the tenancy is not to be treated as a tenancy to which this Schedule applies.

(4) Where an application is made under sub-paragraph (3) above—

(a) the court, if satisfied that the tenancy is not likely immediately before the term date to be a tenancy to which this Schedule applies but not otherwise, shall make the order; and

(b) if the court makes the order, then, notwithstanding anything in sub-paragraph (1) above the tenancy shall not thereafter be treated as a tenancy to which this Schedule applies.

(5) A tenancy to which this Schedule applies is hereinafter referred to as a long residential tenancy.

(6) Anything authorised or required to be done under the following provisions of this Schedule in relation to a long residential tenancy shall, if done before the term date in relation to a long tenancy of a dwelling-house at a low rent, not be treated as invalid by reason only that at the time at which it was done the qualifying condition was not fulfilled as respects the tenancy.

(7) In determining for the purposes of any provision of this Schedule whether the property let under a tenancy was let as a separate dwelling, the nature of the property at the time of the creation of the tenancy shall be deemed to have been the same as its nature at the time in relation to which the question arises, and the purpose for which it was let under the tenancy shall be deemed to have been the same as the purpose for which it is or was used at the last-mentioned time.

[(8) The Secretary of State may by order replace the number in the definition of "I" in sub-paragraph (2A) above and any amount referred to in that sub-paragraph and paragraph 2(4)(b) below by such number or amount as is specified in the order; and such an order shall be made by statutory instrument which shall be subject to annulment in pursuance of a resolution of either House of Parliament.]

2.—(1) This paragraph has effect for the interpretation of certain expressions used in this Schedule.

(2) Except where the context otherwise requires, expressions to which a meaning is assigned for the purposes of the 1988 Act or Part I of that Act have the same meaning in this Schedule.

(3) "Long tenancy" means a tenancy granted for a term of years certain exceeding 21 years, whether or not subsequently extended by act of the parties or by any enactment, but excluding any tenancy which is, or may become, terminable before the end of the term by notice given to the tenant.

[(4) A tenancy is "at a low rent" if under the tenancy—

(a) no rent is payable,

(b) where the tenancy is entered into on or after 1st April 1990 (otherwise than, where the dwelling-house had a rateable value on 31st March 1990, in pursuance of a contract made before 1st April 1990), the maximum rent payable at any time is payable at a rate of—

(i) £1,000 or less a year if the dwelling-house is in Greater London and,

(ii) £250 or less a year if the dwelling-house is elsewhere, or,

(c) where the tenancy was entered into before 1st April 1990 or (where the dwelling-house had a rateable value on 31st March 1990) is entered into on or after 1st April 1990 in pursuance of a contract made before that date, and the maximum rent payable at any time under the tenancy is less than two-thirds of the rateable value of the dwelling-house on 31st March 1990.]

(5) [Paragraph 2(2)] of Schedule 1 to the 1988 Act applies to determine whether the rent under a tenancy falls within sub-paragraph (4) above and Part II of that Schedule applies to determine the rateable value of a dwelling-house for the purposes of that sub-paragraph.

(6) "Long residential tenancy" and "qualifying condition" have the meaning assigned by paragraph 1 above and the following expressions shall be construed as follows—

"the 1954 Act" means the Landlord and Tenant Act 1954;

"the 1988 Act" means the Housing Act 1988;

"assured periodic tenancy" shall be construed in accordance with paragraph 9(4) below;

"the date of termination" has the meaning assigned by paragraph 4(4) below;

"disputed terms" shall be construed in accordance with paragraph 11(1)(a) below;

"election by the tenant to retain possession" shall be construed in accordance with paragraph 4(7) below;

"former 1954 Act tenancy" means a tenancy to which, by virtue of section 186(3) of this Act, this Schedule applies on and after 15th January 1999;

"the implied terms" shall be construed in accordance with paragraph 4(5)(a) below;

"landlord" shall be construed in accordance with paragraph 19(1) below;

"landlord's notice" means a notice under sub-paragraph (1) of paragraph 4 below and such a notice is—

(a) a "landlord's notice proposing an assured tenancy" if it contains such proposals as are mentioned in sub-paragraph (5)(a) of that paragraph; and

(b) a "landlord's notice to resume possession" if it contains such proposals as are referred to in sub-paragraph (5)(b) of that paragraph;

"specified date of termination", in relation to a tenancy in respect of which a landlord's notice is served, means the date specified in the notice as mentioned in paragraph 4(1)(a) below;

"tenant's notice" shall be construed in accordance with paragraph 10(1)(a) below;

"term date", in relation to a tenancy granted for a term of years certain, means the date of expiry of that term; and

"the terms of the tenancy specified in the landlord's notice" shall be construed in accordance with paragraph 4(6) below; and

"undisputed terms" shall be construed in accordance with paragraph 11(2) below.

Continuation of long residential tenancies

3.—(1) A tenancy which, immediately before the term date, is a long residential tenancy shall not come to an end on that date except by being terminated under the provisions of this Schedule, and, if not then so terminated, shall subject to those provisions continue until so terminated and, while continuing by virtue of this paragraph, shall be deemed to be a long residential tenancy (notwithstanding any change in circumstances).

(2) Sub-paragraph (1) above does not apply in the case of a former 1954 Act tenancy the term date of which falls before 15th January 1999 but if, in the case of such a tenancy,—

(a) the tenancy is continuing immediately before that date by virtue of section 3 of the 1954 Act, and

(b) on that date the qualifying condition (as defined in paragraph 1(1) above) is fulfilled,

then, subject to the provisions of this Schedule, the tenancy shall continue until terminated under those provisions and, while continuing by virtue of this paragraph, shall be deemed to be a long residential tenancy (notwithstanding any change in circumstances).

(3) Where by virtue of this paragraph a tenancy continues after the term date, the tenancy shall continue at the same rent and in other respects on the same terms as before the term date.

Termination of tenancy by the landlord

4.—(1) Subject to sub-paragraph (2) below and the provisions of this Schedule as to the annulment of notices in certain cases, the landlord may terminate a long residential tenancy by a notice in the prescribed form served on the tenant—

(a) specifying the date at which the tenancy is to come to an end, being either the term date or a later date; and

(b) so served not more than twelve nor less than six months before the date so specified.

(2) In any case where—

(a) a landlord's notice has been served, and

(b) an application has been made to the court or a rent assessment committee under the following provisions of this Schedule other than paragraph 6, and

(c) apart from this paragraph, the effect of the notice would be to terminate the tenancy before the expiry of the period of three months beginning with the date on which the application is finally disposed of,

the effect of the notice shall be to terminate the tenancy at the expiry of the said period of three months and not at any other time.

(3) The reference in sub-paragraph (2)(c) above to the date on which the application is finally disposed of shall be construed as a reference to the earliest date by which the proceedings on the application (including any proceedings on or in consequence of an appeal) have been determined and any time for appealing or further appealing has expired, except that if the application is withdrawn or any appeal is abandoned the reference shall be construed as a reference to the date of withdrawal or abandonment.

(4) In this Schedule "the date of termination", in relation to a tenancy in respect of which a landlord's notice is served, means,—

(a) where the tenancy is continued as mentioned in sub-paragraph (2) above, the last day of the period of three months referred to in that sub-paragraph; and

(b) in any other case, the specified date of termination.

(5) A landlord's notice shall not have effect unless—

(a) it proposes an assured monthly periodic tenancy of the dwelling-house and a rent for that tenancy (such that it would not be a tenancy at a low rent) and, subject to sub-paragraph (6) below, states that the other terms of the tenancy shall be the same as those of the long residential tenancy immediately before it is terminated (in this Schedule referred to as "the implied terms"); or

(b) it gives notice that, if the tenant is not willing to give up possession at the date of termination of the property let under the tenancy, the landlord proposes to apply to the court, on one or more of the grounds specified in paragraph 5(1) below, for the possession of the property let under the tenancy and states the ground or grounds on which he proposes to apply.

(6) In the landlord's notice proposing an assured tenancy the landlord may propose terms of the tenancy referred to in sub-paragraph (5)(a) above different from the implied terms; and any reference in the following provisions of this Schedule to the terms of the tenancy specified in the landlord's notice is a reference to the implied terms or, if the implied terms are varied by virtue of this sub-paragraph, to the implied terms as so varied.

(7) A landlord's notice shall invite the tenant, within the period of two months beginning on the date on which the notice was served, to notify the landlord in writing whether,—

(a) in the case of a landlord's notice proposing an assured tenancy, the tenant wishes to remain in possession; and

(b) in the case of a landlord's notice to resume possession, the tenant is willing to give up possession as mentioned in sub-paragraph (5)(b) above;

and references in this Schedule to an election by the tenant to retain possession are references to his notifying the landlord under this sub-paragraph that he wishes to remain in possession or, as the case may be, that he is not willing to give up possession.

5.—(1) Subject to the following provisions of this paragraph, the grounds mentioned in paragraph 4(5)(b) above are—

(a) Ground 6 in, and those in Part II of, Schedule 2 to the 1988 Act, other than Ground 16;

(b) the ground that, for the purposes of redevelopment after the termination of the tenancy, the landlord proposes to demolish or reconstruct the whole or a substantial part of the premises; and

(c) the ground that the premises or part of them are reasonably required by the landlord for occupation [as a residence for—

(i) himself,

(ii) any son or daughter of his over eighteen years of age,

(iii) his father or mother, or

(iv) the father, or mother, of his spouse or civil partner, and,] if the landlord is not the immediate landlord, that he will be at the specified date of termination.

(2) Ground 6 in Schedule 2 to the 1988 Act may not be specified in a landlord's notice to resume possession if the tenancy is a former 1954 Act tenancy; and in the application of that Ground in accordance with sub-paragraph (1) above in any other case, paragraph (c) shall be omitted.

(3) In its application in accordance with sub-paragraph (1) above, Ground 10 in Schedule 2 to the 1988 Act shall have effect as if, in paragraph (b)—

(a) the words "except where subsection (1)(b) of section 8 of this Act applies" were omitted; and

(b) for the words "notice under that section relating to those proceedings" there were substituted "landlord's notice to resume possession (within the meaning of Schedule 10 to the Local Government and Housing Act 1989)".

(4) The ground mentioned in sub-paragraph (1)(b) above may not be specified in a landlord's notice to resume possession unless the landlord is a body to which section 28 of the Leasehold Reform Act 1967 applies and the premises are required for relevant development within the meaning of that section; and on any application by such a body under paragraph 13 below for possession on that ground, a certificate given by a Minister of the Crown as provided by subsection (1) of that section shall be conclusive evidence that the premises are so required.

(5) The ground mentioned in sub-paragraph (1)(c) above may not be specified in a landlord's notice to resume possession if the interest of the landlord, or an interest which is merged in that interest and but for the merger would be the interest of the landlord, was purchased or created after 18th February 1966.

Interim rent

6.—(1) On the date of service of a landlord's notice proposing an assured tenancy, or at any time between that date and the date of termination, the landlord may serve a notice on the tenant in the prescribed form proposing an interim monthly rent to take effect from a date specified in the notice, being not earlier than the specified date of termination, and to continue while the tenancy is continued by virtue of the preceding provisions of this Schedule.

(2) Where a notice has been served under sub-paragraph (1) above,—

(a) within the period of two months beginning on the date of service, the tenant may refer the interim monthly rent proposed in the notice to a rent assessment committee; and

(b) if the notice is not so referred, then, with effect from the date specified in the notice or, if it is later, the expiry of the period mentioned in paragraph (a) above, the interim monthly rent proposed in the notice shall be the rent under the tenancy.

(3) Where, under sub-paragraph (2) above, the rent specified in a landlord's notice is referred to a rent assessment committee, the committee shall determine the monthly rent at which, subject to sub-paragraph (4) below, the committee consider that the premises let under the tenancy might reasonably be expected to be let on the open market by a willing landlord under a monthly periodic tenancy—

(a) which begins on the day following the specified date of termination;

(b) under which the other terms are the same as those of the existing tenancy at the date on which was given the landlord's notice proposing an assured tenancy; and

(c) which affords the tenant security of tenure equivalent to that afforded by Chapter I of Part I of the 1988 Act in the case of an assured tenancy (other than an assured shorthold tenancy) in respect of which possession may not be recovered under any of Grounds 1 to 5 in Part I of Schedule 2 to that Act.

(4) Subsections (2), [(3A),] (4) and (5) of section 14 of the 1988 Act shall apply in relation to a determination of rent under sub-paragraph (3) above as they apply in relation to a determination under that section subject to the modifications in sub-paragraph (5) below; and in this paragraph "rent" shall be construed in accordance with subsection (4) of that section.

(5) The modifications of section 14 of the 1988 Act referred to in sub-paragraph (4) above are that in subsection (2), the reference in paragraph (b) to a relevant improvement being carried out shall be construed as a reference to an improvement being carried out during the long residential tenancy and the reference in paragraph (c) to a failure to comply with any term of the tenancy shall be construed as a reference to a failure to comply with any term of the long residential tenancy.

(6) Where a reference has been made to a rent assessment committee under sub-paragraph (2) above, then, the rent determined by the committee (subject, in a case where section 14(5) of the 1988 Act applies, to the addition of the appropriate amount in respect of rates) shall be the rent under the tenancy with effect from the date specified in the notice served under sub-paragraph (1) above or, if it is later, the expiry of the period mentioned in paragraph (a) of sub-paragraph (2) above.

7.—(1) Nothing in paragraph 6 above affects the right of the landlord and the tenant to agree the interim monthly rent which is to have effect while the tenancy is continued by virtue of the preceding provisions of this Schedule and the date from which that rent is to take effect; and, in such a case,—

(a) notwithstanding the provisions of paragraph 6 above, that rent shall be the rent under the tenancy with effect from that date; and
(b) no steps or, as the case may be, no further steps may be taken by the landlord or the tenant under the provisions of that paragraph.

(2) Nothing in paragraph 6 above requires a rent assessment committee to continue with a determination under sub-paragraph (3) of that paragraph—
(a) if the tenant gives notice in writing that he no longer requires such a determination; or
(b) if the long residential tenancy has come to an end on or before the specified date of termination.

(3) Notwithstanding that a tenancy in respect of which an interim monthly rent has effect in accordance with paragraph 6 above or this paragraph is no longer at a low rent, it shall continue to be regarded as a tenancy at a low rent and, accordingly, shall continue to be a long residential tenancy.

Termination of tenancy by the tenant

8.—(1) A long residential tenancy may be brought to an end at the term date by not less than one month's notice in writing given by the tenant to his immediate landlord.

(2) A tenancy which is continuing after the term date by virtue of paragraph 3 above may be brought to an end at any time by not less than one month's notice in writing given by the tenant to his immediate landlord, whether the notice is given before or after the term date of the tenancy.

(3) The fact that the landlord has served a landlord's notice or that there has been an election by the tenant to retain possession shall not prevent the tenant from giving notice under this paragraph terminating the tenancy at a date earlier than the specified date of termination.

The assured periodic tenancy

9.—(1) Where a long residential tenancy (in this paragraph referred to as "the former tenancy") is terminated by a landlord's notice proposing an assured tenancy, then, subject to sub-paragraph (3) below, the tenant shall be entitled to remain in possession of the dwelling-house and his right to possession shall depend upon an assured periodic tenancy arising by virtue of this paragraph.

(2) The assured periodic tenancy referred to in sub-paragraph (1) above is one—
(a) taking effect in possession on the day following the date of termination;
(b) deemed to have been granted by the person who was the landlord under the former tenancy on the date of termination to the person who was then the tenant under that tenancy;
(c) under which the premises let are the dwelling-house;
(d) under which the periods of the tenancy, and the intervals at which rent is to be paid, are monthly beginning on the day following the date of termination;
(e) under which the rent is determined in accordance with paragraphs 10 to 12 below; and
(f) under which the other terms are determined in accordance with paragraphs 10 to 12 below.

(3) If, at the end of the period of two months beginning on the date of service of the landlord's notice, the qualifying condition was not fulfilled as respects the tenancy, the tenant shall not be entitled to remain in possession as mentioned in sub-paragraph (1) above unless there has been an election by the tenant to retain possession; and if, at the specified date of termination, the qualifying condition is not fulfilled as respects the tenancy, then, notwithstanding that there has been such an election, the tenant shall not be entitled to remain in possession as mentioned in that sub-paragraph.

(4) Any reference in the following provisions of this Schedule to an assured periodic tenancy is a reference to an assured periodic tenancy arising by virtue of this paragraph.

Initial rent under and terms of assured periodic tenancy

10.—(1) Where a landlord's notice proposing an assured tenancy has been served on the tenant,—
(a) within the period of two months beginning on the date of service of the notice, the tenant may serve on the landlord a notice in the prescribed form proposing either or both of the following, that is to say,—
 (i) a rent for the assured periodic tenancy different from that proposed in the landlord's notice; and
 (ii) terms of the tenancy different from those specified in the landlord's notice, and such a notice is in this Schedule referred to as a "tenant's notice"; and
(b) if a tenant's notice is not so served, then, with effect from the date on which the assured periodic tenancy takes effect in possession,—
 (i) the rent proposed in the landlord's notice shall be the rent under the tenancy; and
 (ii) the terms of the tenancy specified in the landlord's notice shall be terms of the tenancy.

(2) Where a tenant's notice has been served on the landlord under sub-paragraph (1) above—

(a) within the period of two months beginning on the date of service of the notice, the landlord may by an application in the prescribed form refer the notice to a rent assessment committee; and

(b) if the notice is not so referred, then, with effect from the date on which the assured periodic tenancy takes effect in possession,—

(i) the rent (if any) proposed in the tenant's notice, or, if no rent is so proposed, the rent proposed in the landlord's notice, shall be the rent under the tenancy; and

(ii) the other terms of the tenancy (if any) proposed in the tenant's notice and, in so far as they do not conflict with the terms so proposed, the terms specified in the landlord's notice shall be terms of the tenancy.

11.—(1) Where, under sub-paragraph (2) of paragraph 10 above, a tenant's notice is referred to a rent assessment committee, the committee, having regard only to the contents of the landlord's notice and the tenant's notice, shall decide—

(a) whether there is any dispute as to the terms (other than those relating to the amount of the rent) of the assured periodic tenancy (in this Schedule referred to as "disputed terms") and, if so, what the disputed terms are; and

(b) whether there is any dispute as to rent under the tenancy;

and where the committee decide that there are disputed terms and that there is a dispute as to the rent under the tenancy, they shall make a determination under sub-paragraph (3) below before they make a determination under sub-paragraph (5) below.

(2) Where, under paragraph 10(2) above, a tenant's notice is referred to a rent assessment committee, any reference in this Schedule to the undisputed terms is a reference to those terms (if any) which—

(a) are proposed in the landlord's notice or the tenant's notice; and

(b) do not relate to the amount of the rent; and

(c) are not disputed terms.

(3) If the rent assessment committee decide that there are disputed terms, they shall determine whether the terms in the landlord's notice, the terms in the tenant's notice, or some other terms, dealing with the same subject matter as the disputed terms are such as, in the committee's opinion, might reasonably be expected to be found in an assured monthly periodic tenancy of the dwelling-house (not being an assured shorthold tenancy)—

(a) which begins on the day following the date of termination;

(b) which is granted by a willing landlord on terms which, except so far as they relate to the subject matter of the disputed terms, are the undisputed terms; and

(c) in respect of which possession may not be recovered under any of Grounds 1 to 5 in Part I of Schedule 2 to the 1988 Act;

and the committee shall, if they consider it appropriate, specify an adjustment of the undisputed terms to take account of the terms so determined and shall, if they consider it appropriate, specify an adjustment of the rent to take account of the terms so determined and, if applicable, so adjusted.

(4) In making a determination under sub-paragraph (3) above, or specifying an adjustment of the rent or undisputed terms under that sub-paragraph, there shall be disregarded any effect on the terms or the amount of rent attributable to the granting of a tenancy to a sitting tenant.

(5) If the rent assessment committee decide that there is a dispute as to the rent under the assured periodic tenancy, the committee shall determine the monthly rent at which, subject to sub-paragraph (6) below, the committee consider that the dwelling-house might reasonably be expected to be let in the open market by a willing landlord under an assured tenancy (not being an assured shorthold tenancy)—

(a) which is a monthly periodic tenancy;

(b) which begins on the day following the date of termination;

(c) in respect of which possession may not be recovered under any of Grounds 1 to 5 in Part I of Schedule 2 to the 1988 Act; and

(d) the terms of which (other than those relating to the amount of the rent) are the same as—

(i) the undisputed terms; or

(ii) if there has been a determination under sub-paragraph (3) above, the terms determined by the committee under that sub-paragraph and the undisputed terms (as adjusted, if at all, under that sub-paragraph).

(6) Subsections (2), [(3A),] (4) and (5) of section 14 of the 1988 Act shall apply in relation to a determination of rent under sub-paragraph (5) above as they apply in relation to a determination under that section subject to the modifications in sub-paragraph (7) below; and in this paragraph "rent" shall be construed in accordance with subsection (4) of that section.

(7) The modifications of section 14 of the 1988 Act referred to in sub-paragraph (6) above are that in subsection (2), the reference in paragraph (b) to a relevant improvement being carried out shall be construed as a reference to an improvement being carried out during the long residential tenancy and the reference in paragraph (c) to a failure to comply with any term of the tenancy shall be construed as a reference to a failure to comply with any term of the long residential tenancy.

(8) Where a reference has been made to a rent assessment committee under sub-paragraph (2) of paragraph 10 above, then,—

(a) if the committee decide that there are no disputed terms and that there is no dispute as to the rent, paragraph 10(2)(b) above shall apply as if the notice had not been so referred,

(b) where paragraph (a) above does not apply then, so far as concerns the amount of the rent under the tenancy, if there is a dispute as to the rent, the rent determined by the committee (subject, in a case where section 14(5) of the 1988 Act applies, to the addition of the appropriate amount in respect of rates) and, if there is no dispute as to the rent, the rent specified in the landlord's notice or, as the case may be, the tenant's notice (subject to any adjustment under sub-paragraph (3) above) shall be the rent under the tenancy, and

(c) where paragraph (a) above does not apply and there are disputed terms, then, so far as concerns the subject matter of those terms, the terms determined by the committee under sub-paragraph (3) above shall be terms of the tenancy and, so far as concerns any undisputed terms, those terms (subject to any adjustment under sub-paragraph (3) above) shall also be terms of the tenancy,

with effect from the date on which the assured periodic tenancy takes effect in possession.

(9) Nothing in this Schedule affects the right of the landlord and the tenant under the assured periodic tenancy to vary by agreement any term of the tenancy (including a term relating to rent).

12.—(1) Subsections (2) to (4) of section 41 of the 1988 Act (rent assessment committees: information powers) shall apply where there is a reference to a rent assessment committee under the preceding provisions of this Schedule as they apply where a matter is referred to such a committee under Chapter I or Chapter II of Part I of the 1988 Act.

(2) Nothing in paragraph 10 or paragraph 11 above affects the right of the landlord and the tenant to agree any terms of the assured periodic tenancy (including a term relating to the rent) before the tenancy takes effect in possession (in this sub-paragraph referred to as "the expressly agreed terms"); and, in such case,—

(a) the expressly agreed terms shall be terms of the tenancy in substitution for any terms dealing with the same subject matter which would otherwise, by virtue of paragraph 10 or paragraph 11 above, be terms of the tenancy; and

(b) where a reference has already been made to a rent assessment committee under sub-paragraph (2) of paragraph 10 above but there has been no determination by the committee under paragraph 11 above,—

(i) the committee shall have regard to the expressly agreed terms, as notified to them by the landlord and the tenant, in deciding, for the purposes of paragraph 11 above, what the disputed terms are and whether there is any dispute as to the rent; and

(ii) in making any determination under paragraph 11 above the committee shall not make any adjustment of the expressly agreed terms, as so notified.

(3) Nothing in paragraph 11 above requires a rent assessment committee to continue with a determination under that paragraph—

(a) if the long residential tenancy has come to an end; or

(b) if the landlord serves notice in writing on the committee that he no longer requires such a determination;

and, where the landlord serves notice as mentioned in paragraph (b) above, then, for the purposes of sub-paragraph (2) of paragraph 10 above, the landlord shall be treated as not having made a reference under paragraph (a) of that sub-paragraph and, accordingly, paragraph (b) of that sub-paragraph shall, subject to sub-paragraph (2) above, have effect for determining rent and other terms of the assured periodic tenancy.

Landlord's application for possession

13.—(1) Where a landlord's notice to resume possession has been served on the tenant and either—

(a) there is an election by the tenant to retain possession, or

(b) at the end of the period of two months beginning on the date of service of the notice, the qualifying condition is fulfilled as respects the tenancy,

the landlord may apply to the court for an order under this paragraph on such of the grounds mentioned in paragraph 5(1) above as may be specified in the notice.

(2) The court shall not entertain an application under sub-paragraph (1) above unless the application is made—

(a) within the period of two months beginning on the date of the election by the tenant to retain possession; or

(b) if there is no election by the tenant to retain possession, within the period of four months beginning on the date of service of the landlord's notice.

(3) Where the ground or one of the grounds for claiming possession specified in the landlord's notice is Ground 6 in Part I of Schedule 2 to the 1988 Act, then, if on an application made under sub-paragraph (1) above the court is satisfied that the landlord has established that ground, the court shall order that the tenant shall, on the date of termination, give up possession of the property then let under the tenancy.

(4) Subject to sub-paragraph (6) below, where the ground or one of the grounds for claiming possession specified in the landlord's notice is any of Grounds 9 to 15 in Part II of Schedule 2 to the 1988 Act or the ground mentioned in paragraph 5(1)(c) above, then, if on an application made under sub-paragraph (1) above the court is satisfied that the landlord has established that ground and that it is reasonable that the landlord should be granted possession, the court shall order that the tenant shall, on the date of termination, give up possession of the property then let under the tenancy.

(5) Part III of Schedule 2 to the 1988 Act shall have effect for supplementing Ground 9 in that Schedule (as that ground applies in relation to this Schedule) as it has effect for supplementing that ground for the purposes of that Act, subject to the modification that in paragraph 3(1), in the words following paragraph (b) the reference to the assured tenancy in question shall be construed as a reference to the long residential tenancy in question.

(6) Where the ground or one of the grounds for claiming possession specified in the landlord's notice is that mentioned in paragraph 5(1)(c) above, the court shall not make the order mentioned in sub-paragraph (4) above on that ground if it is satisfied that, having regard to all the circumstances of the case, including the question whether other accommodation is available for the landlord or the tenant, greater hardship would be caused by making the order than by refusing to make it.

(7) Where the ground or one of the grounds for claiming possession specified in the landlord's notice is that mentioned in paragraph 5(1)(b) above, then, if on an application made under sub-paragraph (1) above the court is satisfied that the landlord has established that ground and is further satisfied—

- (a) that on that ground possession of those premises will be required by the landlord on the date of termination, and
- (b) that the landlord has made such preparations (including the obtaining or, if that is not reasonably practicable in the circumstances, preparations relating to the obtaining of any requisite permission or consent, whether from any authority whose permission or consent is required under any enactment or from the owner of any interest in any property) for proceeding with the redevelopment as are reasonable in the circumstances,

the court shall order that the tenant shall, on the date of termination, give up possession of the property then let under the tenancy.

14.—(1) Where, in a case falling within sub-paragraph (7) of paragraph 13 above, the court is not satisfied as mentioned in that sub-paragraph but would be satisfied if the date of termination of the tenancy had been such date (in this paragraph referred to as "the postponed date") as the court may determine, being a date later, but not more than one year later, than the specified date of termination, the court shall, if the landlord so requires, make an order as mentioned in sub-paragraph (2) below.

(2) The order referred to in sub-paragraph (1) above is one by which the court specifies the postponed date and orders—

- (a) that the tenancy shall not come to an end on the date of termination but shall continue thereafter, as respects the whole of the property let under the tenancy, at the same rent and in other respects on the same terms as before that date; and
- (b) that, unless the tenancy comes to an end before the postponed date, the tenant shall on that date give up possession of the property then let under the tenancy.

(3) Notwithstanding the provisions of paragraph 13 above and the preceding provisions of this paragraph and notwithstanding that there has been an election by the tenant to retain possession, if the court is satisfied, at the date of the hearing, that the qualifying condition is not fulfilled as respects the tenancy, the court shall order that the tenant shall, on the date of termination, give up possession of the property then let under the tenancy.

(4) Nothing in paragraph 13 above or the preceding provisions of this paragraph shall prejudice any power of the tenant under paragraph 8 above to terminate the tenancy; and sub-paragraph (2) of that paragraph shall apply where the tenancy is continued by an order under sub-paragraph (2) above as it applies where the tenancy is continued by virtue of paragraph 3 above.

Provisions where tenant not ordered to give up possession

15.—(1) The provisions of this paragraph shall have effect where the landlord is entitled to make an application under sub-paragraph (1) of paragraph 13 above but does not obtain an order under that paragraph or paragraph 14 above.

(2) If at the expiration of the period within which an application under paragraph 13(1) above may be made the landlord has not made such an application, the landlord's notice to resume possession, and anything done in pursuance thereof, shall cease to have effect.

(3) If before the expiration of the period mentioned in sub-paragraph (2) above the landlord has made an application under paragraph 13(1) above but the result of the application, at the time when it is finally disposed of, is that no order is made, the landlord's notice to resume possession shall cease to have effect.

(4) In any case where sub-paragraph (3) above applies, then, if within the period of one month beginning on the date that the application to the court is finally disposed of the landlord serves on the tenant a landlord's notice proposing an assured tenancy, the earliest date which may be specified in the notice as the date of termination shall, notwithstanding anything in paragraph 4(1)(b) above, be the day following the last day of the period of four months beginning on the date of service of the subsequent notice.

(5) The reference in sub-paragraphs (3) and (4) above to the time at which an application is finally disposed of shall be construed as a reference to the earliest time at which the proceedings on the application (including any proceedings on or in consequence of an appeal) have been determined and any time for appealing or further appealing has expired, except that if the application is withdrawn or any appeal is abandoned the reference shall be construed as a reference to the time of withdrawal or abandonment.

(6) A landlord's notice to resume possession may be withdrawn at any time by notice in writing served on the tenant (without prejudice, however, to the power of the court to make an order as to costs if the notice is withdrawn after the landlord has made an application under paragraph 13(1) above).

(7) In any case where sub-paragraph (6) above applies, then, if within the period of one month beginning on the date of withdrawal of the landlord's notice to resume possession the landlord serves on the tenant a landlord's notice proposing an assured tenancy, the earliest date which may be specified in the notice as the date of termination shall, notwithstanding anything in paragraph 4(1)(b) above, be the day following the last day of the period of four months beginning on the date of service of the subsequent notice or the day following the last day of the period of six months beginning on the date of service of the withdrawn notice, whichever is the later.

Tenancies granted in continuation of long tenancies

16.—(1) Where on the coming to the end of a tenancy at a low rent the person who was the tenant immediately before the coming to an end thereof becomes (whether by grant or by implication of the law) the tenant under another tenancy at a low rent of a dwelling-house which consists of the whole or any part of the property let under the previous tenancy, then, if the previous tenancy was a long tenancy or is deemed by virtue of this paragraph to have been a long tenancy, the new tenancy shall be deemed for the purposes of this Schedule to be a long tenancy, irrespective of its terms.

(2) In relation to a tenancy from year to year or other tenancy not granted for a term of years certain, being a tenancy which by virtue of sub-paragraph (1) above is deemed for the purposes of this Schedule to be a long tenancy, the preceding provisions of this Schedule shall have effect subject to the modifications set out below.

(3) In sub-paragraph (6) of paragraph 2 above for the expression beginning "term date" there shall be substituted—

> ""term date", in relation to any such tenancy as is mentioned in paragraph 16(2) below, means the first date after the coming into force of this Schedule on which, apart from this Schedule, the tenancy could have been brought to an end by notice to quit given by the landlord".

(4) Notwithstanding anything in sub-paragraph (3) of paragraph 3 above, where by virtue of that paragraph the tenancy is continued after the term date, the provisions of this Schedule as to the termination of a tenancy by notice shall have effect, subject to sub-paragraph (5) below, in substitution for and not in addition to any such provisions included in the terms on which the tenancy had effect before the term date.

(5) The minimum period of notice referred to in paragraph 8(1) above shall be one month or such longer period as the tenant would have been required to give to bring the tenancy to an end at the term date.

(6) Where the tenancy is not terminated under paragraph 4 or paragraph 8 above at the term date, then, whether or not it would have continued after that date apart from the provisions of this Schedule, it shall be treated for the purposes of those provisions as being continued by virtue of paragraph 3 above.

Agreements as to the grant of new tenancies

17. In any case where, prior to the date of termination of a long residential tenancy, the landlord and the tenant agree for the grant to the tenant of a future tenancy of the whole or part of the property let under the tenancy at a rent other than a low rent and on terms and from a date specified

in the agreement, the tenancy shall continue until that date but no longer; and, in such a case, the provisions of this Schedule shall cease to apply in relation to the tenancy with effect from the date of the agreement.

Assumptions on which to determine future questions

18. Where under this Schedule any question falls to be determined by the court or a rent assessment committee by reference to circumstances at a future date, the court or committee shall have regard to all rights, interests and obligations under or relating to the tenancy as they subsist at the time of the determination and to all relevant circumstances as those then subsist and shall assume, except in so far as the contrary is shown, that those rights, interests, obligations and circumstances will continue to subsist unchanged until that future date.

Landlords and mortgagees in possession

19.—(1) Section 21 of the 1954 Act (meaning of "the landlord" and provisions as to mesne landlords) shall apply in relation to this Schedule as it applies in relation to Part I of that Act but subject to the following modifications—

(a) any reference to Part I of that Act shall be construed as a reference to this Schedule; and
(b) subsection (4) (which relates to statutory tenancies arising under that Part) shall be omitted.

(2) Section 67 of the 1954 Act (mortgagees in possession) applies for the purposes of this Schedule except that for the reference to that Act there shall be substituted a reference to this Schedule.

(3) In accordance with sub-paragraph (1) above, Schedule 5 to the 1954 Act shall also apply for the purpose of this Schedule but subject to the following modifications—

(a) any reference to Part I of the 1954 Act shall be construed as a reference to the provisions of this Schedule (other than this sub-paragraph);
(b) any reference to section 21 of the 1954 Act shall be construed as a reference to that section as it applies in relation to this Schedule;
(c) any reference to subsection (1) of section 4 of that Act shall be construed as a reference to sub-paragraph (1) of paragraph 4 above;
(d) any reference to the court includes a reference to a rent assessment committee;
(e) paragraphs 6 to 8 and 11 shall be omitted;
(f) any reference to a particular subsection of section 16 of the 1954 Act shall be construed as a reference to that subsection as it applies in relation to this Schedule;
(g) any reference to a tenancy to which section 1 of the 1954 Act applies shall be construed as a reference to a long residential tenancy; and
(h) expressions to which a meaning is assigned by any provision of this Schedule (other than this sub-paragraph) shall be given that meaning.

Application of other provisions of the 1954 Act

20.—(1) Section 16 of the 1954 Act (relief for tenant where landlord proceeding to enforce covenants) shall apply in relation to this Schedule as it applies in relation to Part I of that Act but subject to the following modifications—

(a) in subsection (1) the reference to a tenancy to which section 1 of the 1954 Act applies shall be construed as a reference to a long residential tenancy;
(b) in subsection (2) the reference to Part I of that Act shall be construed as a reference to this Schedule;
(c) subsection (3) shall have effect as if the words "(without prejudice to section ten of this Act)" were omitted; and
(d) in subsection (7) the reference to subsection (3) of section 2 of the 1954 Act shall be construed as a reference to paragraph 1(6) above.

(2) Section 55 of the 1954 Act (compensation for possession obtained by misrepresentation) shall apply in relation to this Schedule as it applies in relation to Part I of that Act.

(3) Section 63 of the 1954 Act (jurisdiction of court for purposes of Parts I and II of the 1954 Act and of Part I of the Landlord and Tenant Act 1927) shall apply in relation to this Schedule and section 186 of this Act as it applies in relation to Part I of that Act.

(4) Section 65 of the 1954 Act (provisions as to reversions) applies for the purposes of this Schedule except that for any reference to that Act there shall be substituted a reference to this Schedule.

(5) Subsection (4) of section 66 of the 1954 Act (service of notices) shall apply in relation to this Schedule as it applies in relation to that Act.

21.—(1) Where this Schedule has effect in relation to a former 1954 Act tenancy the term date of which falls before 15th January 1999, any reference (however expressed) in the preceding provisions of this Schedule to the dwelling-house (or the property) let under the tenancy shall have effect as a reference to the premises qualifying for protection, within the meaning of the 1954 Act.

(2) Notwithstanding that at any time section 1 of the 1954 Act does not, and this Schedule does, apply to a former 1954 Act tenancy, any question of what are the premises qualifying for protection or (in that context) what is the tenancy shall be determined for the purposes of this Schedule in accordance with Part I of that Act.

Crown application

22.—(1) This Schedule shall apply where—

(a) there is an interest belonging to Her Majesty in right of the Crown and that interest is under the management of the Crown Estate Commissioners, or

(b) there is an interest belonging to Her Majesty in right of the Duchy of Lancaster or belonging to the Duchy of Cornwall,

as if it were an interest not so belonging.

(2) Where an interest belongs to Her Majesty in right of the Duchy of Lancaster, then, for the purposes of this Schedule, the Chancellor of the Duchy of Lancaster shall be deemed to be the owner of the interest.

(3) Where an interest belongs to the Duchy of Cornwall, then, for the purposes of this Schedule, such person as the Duke of Cornwall, or other possessor for the time being of the Duchy of Cornwall, appoints shall be deemed to be the owner of the interest.

[1372]

NOTES

Para 1: sub-paras (2A), (8) inserted by SI 1990/434, reg 2, Schedule, paras 31, 32.

Para 2: sub-para (4) and words in square brackets in sub-para (5) substituted by SI 1990/434, reg 2, Schedule, paras 33, 34.

Para 5: words in square brackets in sub-para (1)(c) substituted by the Civil Partnership Act 2004, s 81, Sch 8, para 46.

Paras 6, 11: figures in square brackets inserted by the Local Government Finance (Housing) (Consequential Amendments) Order 1993, SI 1993/651, art 2(1), Sch 1, para 20.

Transfer of functions: the functions of the Secretary of State and the Treasury, so far as exercisable in relation to Wales, are transferred to the National Assembly for Wales, by the National Assembly for Wales (Transfer of Functions) Order 1999, SI 1999/672, art 2, Sch 1.

Regulations: the Long Residential Tenancies (Principal Forms) Regulations 1997, SI 1997/3008.

(*Sch 11 contains minor and consequential amendments; Sch 12 contains repeals only.*)

TOWN AND COUNTRY PLANNING ACT 1990

(1990 c 8)

An Act to consolidate certain enactments relating to town and country planning (excluding special controls in respect of buildings and areas of special architectural or historic interest and in respect of hazardous substances) with amendments to give effect to recommendations of the Law Commission

[24 May 1990]

1–54A ((*Pts I, II*) *in so far as unrepealed, outside the scope of this work.*)

PART III
CONTROL OVER DEVELOPMENT

Meaning of development

55 Meaning of "development" and "new development"

(1) Subject to the following provisions of this section, in this Act, except where the context otherwise requires, "development," means the carrying out of building, engineering, mining or other operations in, on, over or under land, or the making of any material change in the use of any buildings or other land.

[(1A) For the purposes of this Act "building operations" includes—

(a) demolition of buildings;

(b) rebuilding;

(c) structural alterations of or additions to buildings; and

(d) other operations normally undertaken by a person carrying on business as a builder.]

(2) The following operations or uses of land shall not be taken for the purposes of this Act to involve development of the land—

(a) the carrying out for the maintenance, improvement or other alteration of any building of works which—

(i) affect only the interior of the building, or

(ii) do not materially affect the external appearance of the building,

and are not works for making good war damage or works begun after 5th December 1968 for the alteration of a building by providing additional space in it underground;

(b) the carrying out on land within the boundaries of a road by a … highway authority of any works required for the maintenance or improvement of the road [but, in the case of any such works which are not exclusively for the maintenance of the road, not including any works which may have significant adverse effects on the environment];

(c) the carrying out by a local authority or statutory undertakers of any works for the purpose of inspecting, repairing or renewing any sewers, mains, pipes, cables or other apparatus, including the breaking open of any street or other land for that purpose;

(d) the use of any buildings or other land within the curtilage of a dwellinghouse for any purpose incidental to the enjoyment of the dwellinghouse as such;

(e) the use of any land for the purposes of agriculture or forestry (including afforestation) and the use for any of those purposes of any building occupied together with land so used;

(f) in the case of buildings or other land which are used for a purpose of any class specified in an order made by the Secretary of State under this section, the use of the buildings or other land or, subject to the provisions of the order, of any part of the buildings or the other land, for any other purpose of the same class;

[(g) the demolition of any description of building specified in a direction given by the Secretary of State to local planning authorities generally or to a particular local planning authority.]

[(2A) The Secretary of State may in a development order specify any circumstances or description of circumstances in which subsection (2) does not apply to operations mentioned in paragraph (a) of that subsection which have the effect of increasing the gross floor space of the building by such amount or percentage amount as is so specified.

(2B) The development order may make different provision for different purposes.]

(3) For the avoidance of doubt it is hereby declared that for the purposes of this section—

(a) the use as two or more separate dwellinghouses of any building previously used as a single dwellinghouse involves a material change in the use of the building and of each part of it which is so used;

(b) the deposit of refuse or waste materials on land involves a material change in its use, notwithstanding that the land is comprised in a site already used for that purpose, if—

(i) the superficial area of the deposit is extended, or

(ii) the height of the deposit is extended and exceeds the level of the land adjoining the site.

(4) For the purposes of this Act mining operations include—

(a) the removal of material of any description—

(i) from a mineral-working deposit;

(ii) from a deposit of pulverised fuel ash or other furnace ash or clinker; or

(iii) from a deposit of iron, steel or other metallic slags; and

(b) the extraction of minerals from a disused railway embankment.

[(4A) Where the placing or assembly of any tank in any part of any inland waters for the purpose of fish farming there would not, apart from this subsection, involve development of the land below, this Act shall have effect as if the tank resulted from carrying out engineering operations over that land; and in this subsection—

"fish farming" means the breeding, rearing or keeping of fish or shellfish (which includes any kind of crustacean and mollusc);

"inland waters" means waters which do not form part of the sea or of any creek, bay or estuary or of any river as far as the tide flows; and

"tank" includes any cage and any other structure for use in fish farming.]

(5) Without prejudice to any regulations made under the provisions of this Act relating to the control of advertisements, the use for the display of advertisements of any external part of a building which is not normally used for that purpose shall be treated for the purposes of this section as involving a material change in the use of that part of the building.

(6) …

[1373]

NOTES

Sub-s (1A): inserted by the Planning and Compensation Act 1991, s 13(1).

Sub-s (2): in para (b), word omitted repealed by the Planning and Compulsory Purchase Act 2004, ss 118(1), 120, Sch 6, paras 1, 2, Sch 9, and words in square brackets inserted by SI 1999/293, reg 35(1); para (g) inserted by the Planning and Compensation Act 1991, s 13(2).

Sub-ss (2A), (2B): inserted by the Planning and Compulsory Purchase Act 2004, s 49(1), partly as from a day to be appointed in relation to Wales; for effect see s 49(2)–(4) thereof.

Sub-s (4A): inserted by the Planning and Compensation Act 1991, s 14.

Sub-s (6): repealed by the Planning and Compensation Act 1991, ss 31, 84, Sch 6, para 9, Sch 19, Pts I, II.

Modification: references to waste modified by the Waste Management Licensing Regulations 1994, SI 1994/1056, reg 19, Sch 4, Pt I, para 11, to include "Directive Waste" as defined by reg 1(3), Sch 4, Part II thereof.

Transfer of Functions: functions of the Secretary of State, so far as exercisable in relation to Wales, transferred to the National Assembly for Wales, by the National Assembly for Wales (Transfer of Functions) Order 1999, SI 1999/672, art 2, Sch 1.

Orders: the Town and Country Planning (Application of Subordinate Legislation to the Crown) Order 2006, SI 2006/1282; the Town and Country Planning (Miscellaneous Amendments and Modifications relating to Crown Land) (Wales) Order 2006, SI 2006/1386.

56–101 (*In so far as unrepealed, outside the scope of this work.*)

Other controls over development

102–105 (*Ss 102–104 outside the scope of this work; s 105 repealed by the Environment Act 1995, ss 96(4), 120(3), Sch 24.*)

[106 Planning obligations

(1) Any person interested in land in the area of a local planning authority may, by agreement or otherwise, enter into an obligation (referred to in this section and sections 106A and 106B as "a planning obligation"), enforceable to the extent mentioned in subsection (3)—

- *(a) restricting the development or use of the land in any specified way;*
- *(b) requiring specified operations or activities to be carried out in, on, under or over the land;*
- *(c) requiring the land to be used in any specified way; or*
- *(d) requiring a sum or sums to be paid to the authority [(or, in a case where section 2E applies, to the Greater London Authority)] on a specified date or dates or periodically.*

[(1A) In the case of a development consent obligation, the reference to development in subsection (1)(a) includes anything that constitutes development for the purposes of the Planning Act 2008.]

(2) A planning obligation may—

- *(a) be unconditional or subject to conditions;*
- *(b) impose any restriction or requirement mentioned in subsection (1)(a) to (c) either indefinitely or for such period or periods as may be specified; and*
- *(c) if it requires a sum or sums to be paid, require the payment of a specified amount or an amount determined in accordance with the instrument by which the obligation is entered into and, if it requires the payment of periodical sums, require them to be paid indefinitely or for a specified period.*

(3) Subject to subsection (4) a planning obligation is enforceable by the authority identified in accordance with subsection (9)(d)—

- *(a) against the person entering into the obligation; and*
- *(b) against any person deriving title from that person.*

(4) The instrument by which a planning obligation is entered into may provide that a person shall not be bound by the obligation in respect of any period during which he no longer has an interest in the land.

(5) A restriction or requirement imposed under a planning obligation is enforceable by injunction.

(6) Without prejudice to subsection (5), if there is a breach of a requirement in a planning obligation to carry out any operations in, on, under or over the land to which the obligation relates, the authority by whom the obligation is enforceable may—

- *(a) enter the land and carry out the operations; and*
- *(b) recover from the person or persons against whom the obligation is enforceable any expenses reasonably incurred by them in doing so.*

(7) Before an authority exercise their power under subsection (6)(a) they shall give not less than twenty-one days' notice of their intention to do so to any person against whom the planning obligation is enforceable.

(8) Any person who wilfully obstructs a person acting in the exercise of a power under subsection (6)(a) shall be guilty of an offence and liable on summary conviction to a fine not exceeding level 3 on the standard scale.

(9) A planning obligation may not be entered into except by an instrument executed as a deed which—

(*a*) *states that the obligation is a planning obligation for the purposes of this section;*

[(*aa*) *if the obligation is a development consent obligation, contains a statement to that effect;*]

(*b*) *identifies the land in which the person entering into the obligation is interested;*

(*c*) *identifies the person entering into the obligation and states what his interest in the land is; and*

(*d*) *identifies the local planning authority by whom the obligation is enforceable* [*and, in a case where section 2E applies, identifies the Mayor of London as an authority by whom the obligation is also enforceable*].

(10) A copy of any such instrument shall be given to the [*local planning authority so identified and, in a case where section 2E applies, to the Mayor of London*].

(11) A planning obligation shall be a local land charge and for the purposes of the Local Land Charges Act 1975 the authority by whom the obligation is enforceable shall be treated as the originating authority as respects such a charge.

(12) Regulations may provide for the charging on the land of—

(*a*) *any sum or sums required to be paid under a planning obligation; and*

(*b*) *any expenses recoverable by a local planning authority* [*or the Mayor of London*] *under subsection (6)(b),*

and this section and sections 106A and 106B shall have effect subject to any such regulations.

(13) In this section "specified" means specified in the instrument by which the planning obligation is entered into and in this section and section 106A "land" has the same meaning as in the Local Land Charges Act 1975.]

[*(14) In this section and section 106A "development consent obligation" means a planning obligation entered into in connection with an application (or a proposed application) for an order granting development consent.*]]

[1374]

NOTES

Substituted, together with ss 106A, 106B, for s 106 as originally enacted, by the Planning and Compensation Act 1991, s 12(1).

Repealed by the Planning and Compulsory Purchase Act 2004, ss 118(1), 120, Sch 6, paras 1, 5, Sch 9, as from a day to be appointed.

Sub-s (1): in para (d) words in square brackets inserted by the Greater London Authority Act 2007, s 33(1), (2).

Sub-s (1A): inserted by the Planning Act 2008, s 174(1), (2)(a), as from a day to be appointed.

Sub-s (9): para (aa) inserted by the Planning Act 2008, s 174(1), (2)(b), as from a day to be appointed; in para (d) words in square brackets inserted by the Greater London Authority Act 2007, s 33(1), (3).

Sub-s (10): words in square brackets substituted by the Greater London Authority Act 2007, s 33(1), (4).

Sub-s (12): in para (b) words in square brackets inserted by the Greater London Authority Act 2007, s 33(1), (5).

Sub-s (14): inserted by the Planning Act 2008, s 174(1), (2)(c), as from a day to be appointed.

[106A Modification and discharge of planning obligations

(1) A planning obligation may not be modified or discharged except—

(*a*) *by agreement between* [*the appropriate authority (see subsection (11))*] *and the person or persons against whom the obligation is enforceable; or*

(*b*) *in accordance with this section and section 106B.*

(2) An agreement falling within subsection (1)(a) shall not be entered into except by an instrument executed as a deed.

(3) A person against whom a planning obligation is enforceable may, at any time after the expiry of the relevant period, apply to [*the appropriate authority*] *for the obligation —*

(*a*) *to have effect subject to such modifications as may be specified in the application; or*

(*b*) *to be discharged.*

(4) In subsection (3) "the relevant period" means—

(*a*) *such period as may be prescribed; or*

(*b*) *if no period is prescribed, the period of five years beginning with the date on which the obligation is entered into.*

(5) An application under subsection (3) for the modification of a planning obligation may not specify a modification imposing an obligation on any other person against whom the obligation is enforceable.

(6) Where an application is made to an authority under subsection (3), the authority may determine—

(*a*) *that the planning obligation shall continue to have effect without modification;*

(*b*) *if the obligation no longer serves a useful purpose, that it shall be discharged; or*
(*c*) *if the obligation continues to serve a useful purpose, but would serve that purpose equally well if it had effect subject to the modifications specified in the application, that it shall have effect subject to those modifications.*

(7) The authority shall give notice of their determination to the applicant within such period as may be prescribed.

(8) Where an authority determine that a planning obligation shall have effect subject to modifications specified in the application, the obligation as modified shall be enforceable as if it had been entered into on the date on which notice of the determination was given to the applicant.

(9) Regulations may make provision with respect to—
(*a*) *the form and content of applications under subsection (3);*
(*b*) *the publication of notices of such applications;*
(*c*) *the procedures for considering any representations made with respect to such applications; and*
(*d*) *the notices to be given to applicants of determinations under subsection (6).*

(10) Section 84 of the Law of Property Act 1925 (power to discharge or modify restrictive covenants affecting land) does not apply to a planning obligation.]

[*(11) In this section "the appropriate authority" means—*
(*a*) *the Mayor of London, in the case of any planning obligation enforceable by him;*
[(*aa*) *the Secretary of State, in the case of any development consent obligation where the application in connection with which the obligation was entered into was (or is to be) decided by the Secretary of State;*
(*ab*) *the Infrastructure Planning Commission, in the case of any other development consent obligation;*]
(*b*) *in the case of any other planning obligation, the local planning authority by whom it is enforceable.*

(12) The Mayor of London must consult the local planning authority before exercising any function under this section.]

[1375]

NOTES

Substituted, together with ss 106, 106B, for s 106 as originally enacted, by the Planning and Compensation Act 1991, s 12(1).

Repealed by the Planning and Compulsory Purchase Act 2004, ss 118(1), 120, Sch 6, paras 1, 5, Sch 9, as from a day to be appointed.

Sub-s (1): in para (a) words in square brackets substituted by the Greater London Authority Act 2007, s 34(1), (2).

Sub-s (3): words in square brackets substituted by the Greater London Authority Act 2007, s 34(1), (3).

Sub-ss (11), (12): inserted by the Greater London Authority Act 2007, s 34(1), (4).

Sub-s (11): paras (aa), (ab) inserted by the Planning Act 2008, s 174(1), (3), as from a day to be appointed.

Regulations: the Town and Country Planning (Modification and Discharge of Planning Obligations) Regulations 1992, SI 1992/2832.

[106B Appeals

(1) Where [*an authority*] [(*other than the Secretary of State or the Infrastructure Planning Commission*)]*—*
(*a*) *fail to give notice as mentioned in section 106A(7); or*
(*b*) *determine that a planning obligation shall continue to have effect without modification,*

the applicant may appeal to the Secretary of State.

(2) For the purposes of an appeal under subsection (1)(a), it shall be assumed that the authority have determined that the planning obligation shall continue to have effect without modification.

(3) An appeal under this section shall be made by notice served within such period and in such manner as may be prescribed.

(4) Subsections (6) to (9) of section 106A apply in relation to appeals to the Secretary of State under this section as they apply in relation to applications to authorities under that section.

(5) Before determining the appeal the Secretary of State shall, if either the applicant or the authority so wish, give each of them an opportunity of appearing before and being heard by a person appointed by the Secretary of State for the purpose.

(6) The determination of an appeal by the Secretary of State under this section shall be final.

(7) Schedule 6 applies to appeals under this section.]

[(8) In the application of Schedule 6 to an appeal under this section in a case where the authority mentioned in subsection (1) is the Mayor of London, references in that Schedule to the local planning authority are references to the Mayor of London.]

[1376]

NOTES

Substituted, together with ss 106, 106A, for s 106 as originally enacted, by the Planning and Compensation Act 1991, s 12(1)

Repealed by the Planning and Compulsory Purchase Act 2004, ss 118(1), 120, Sch 6, paras 1, 5, Sch 9, as from a day to be appointed.

Sub-s (1): first words in square brackets substituted by the Greater London Authority Act 2007, s 34(5), (6); second words in square brackets inserted by the Planning Act 2008, s 174(1), (4), as from a day to be appointed.

Sub-s (8): inserted by the Greater London Authority Act 2007, s 34(5), (7).

Transfer of Functions: functions of the Secretary of State, so far as exercisable in relation to Wales, transferred to the National Assembly for Wales, by the National Assembly for Wales (Transfer of Functions) Order 1999, SI 1999/672, art 2, Sch 1.

Regulations: the Town and Country Planning (Modification and Discharge of Planning Obligations) Regulations 1992, SI 1992/2832.

[106C Legal challenges relating to development consent obligations

(1) A court may entertain proceedings for questioning a failure by the Secretary of State or the Infrastructure Planning Commission to give notice as mentioned in section 106A(7) only if—

(a) the proceedings are brought by a claim for judicial review, and

(b) the claim form is filed during the period of 6 weeks beginning with the day on which the period prescribed under section 106A(7) ends.

(2) A court may entertain proceedings for questioning a determination by the Secretary of State or the Infrastructure Planning Commission that a planning obligation shall continue to have effect without modification only if—

(a) the proceedings are brought by a claim for judicial review, and

(b) the claim form is filed during the period of 6 weeks beginning with the day on which notice of the determination is given under section 106A(7).]

[1376A]

NOTES

Commencement: as from a date to be appointed.

Inserted by the Planning Act 2008, s 174(1), (5).

107–171 ((*Pts IV–VI*) *in so far as unrepealed, outside the scope of this work.*)

PART VII
ENFORCEMENT

171A–190 (*Outside the scope of this work.*)

[Certificate of lawful use or development

191 Certificate of lawfulness of existing use or development

(1) If any person wishes to ascertain whether—

(a) any existing use of buildings or other land is lawful;

(b) any operations which have been carried out in, on, over or under land are lawful; or

(c) any other matter constituting a failure to comply with any condition or limitation subject to which planning permission has been granted is lawful,

he may make an application for the purpose to the local planning authority specifying the land and describing the use, operations or other matter.

(2) For the purposes of this Act uses and operations are lawful at any time if—

(a) no enforcement action may then be taken in respect of them (whether because they did not involve development or require planning permission or because the time for enforcement action has expired or for any other reason); and

(b) they do not constitute a contravention of any of the requirements of any enforcement notice then in force.

(3) For the purposes of this Act any matter constituting a failure to comply with any condition or limitation subject to which planning permission has been granted is lawful at any time if—

(a) the time for taking enforcement action in respect of the failure has then expired; and

(b) it does not constitute a contravention of any of the requirements of any enforcement notice or breach of condition notice then in force.

(4) If, on an application under this section, the local planning authority are provided with information satisfying them of the lawfulness at the time of the application of the use, operations or

other matter described in the application, or that description as modified by the local planning authority or a description substituted by them, they shall issue a certificate to that effect; and in any other case they shall refuse the application.

(5) A certificate under this section shall—

(a) specify the land to which it relates;

(b) describe the use, operations or other matter in question (in the case of any use falling within one of the classes specified in an order under section 55(2)(f), identifying it by reference to that class);

(c) give the reasons for determining the use, operations or other matter to be lawful; and

(d) specify the date of the application for the certificate.

(6) The lawfulness of any use, operations or other matter for which a certificate is in force under this section shall be conclusively presumed.

(7) A certificate under this section in respect of any use shall also have effect, for the purposes of the following enactments, as if it were a grant of planning permission—

(a) section 3(3) of the Caravan Sites and Control of Development Act 1960;

(b) section 5(2) of the Control of Pollution Act 1974; and

(c) section 36(2)(a) of the Environmental Protection Act 1990.]

[1377]

NOTES

Substituted, together with preceding cross-heading, by the Planning and Compensation Act 1991, s 10(1).

[192 Certificate of lawfulness of proposed use or development

(1) If any person wishes to ascertain whether—

(a) any proposed use of buildings or other land; or

(b) any operations proposed to be carried out in, on, over or under land,

would be lawful, he may make an application for the purpose to the local planning authority specifying the land and describing the use or operations in question.

(2) If, on an application under this section, the local planning authority are provided with information satisfying them that the use or operations described in the application would be lawful if instituted or begun at the time of the application, they shall issue a certificate to that effect; and in any other case they shall refuse the application.

(3) A certificate under this section shall—

(a) specify the land to which it relates;

(b) describe the use or operations in question (in the case of any use falling within one of the classes specified in an order under section 55(2)(f), identifying it by reference to that class);

(c) give the reasons for determining the use or operations to be lawful; and

(d) specify the date of the application for the certificate.

(4) The lawfulness of any use or operations for which a certificate is in force under this section shall be conclusively presumed unless there is a material change, before the use is instituted or the operations are begun, in any of the matters relevant to determining such lawfulness.]

[1378]

NOTES

Substituted by the Planning and Compensation Act 1991, s 10(1).

193–225 (*Ss 193–196, 196A–196C; ss 197–225 (Pt VIII) outside the scope of this work.*)

PART IX
ACQUISITION AND APPROPRIATION OF LAND FOR PLANNING PURPOSES, ETC

226–235 (*Outside the scope of this work.*)

Extinguishment of certain rights affecting acquired or appropriated land

236 (*Outside the scope of this work.*)

237 Power to override easements and other rights

(1) Subject to subsection (3), the erection, construction or carrying out or maintenance of any building or work on land which has been acquired or appropriated by a local authority for planning purposes (whether done by the local authority or by a person deriving title under them) is authorised by virtue of this section if it is done in accordance with planning permission, notwithstanding that it involves—

(a) interference with an interest or right to which this section applies, or

(b) a breach of a restriction as to the user of land arising by virtue of a contract.

[(1A) Subject to subsection (3), the use of any land in England which has been acquired or appropriated by a local authority for planning purposes (whether the use is by the local authority or by a person deriving title under them) is authorised by virtue of this section if it is in accordance with planning permission even if the use involves—

(a) interference with an interest or right to which this section applies, or
(b) a breach of a restriction as to the user of land arising by virtue of a contract.]

(2) Subject to subsection (3), the interests and rights to which this section applies are any easement, liberty, privilege, right or advantage annexed to land and adversely affecting other land, including any natural right to support.

(3) Nothing in this section shall authorise interference with any right of way or right of laying down, erecting, continuing or maintaining apparatus on, under or over land which is—

(a) a right vested in or belonging to statutory undertakers for the purpose of the carrying on of their undertaking, or
(b) a right conferred by or in accordance with the [electronic communications code] on the operator of [an electronic communications code network].

(4) In respect of any interference or breach in pursuance of subsection (1), [or (1A)], compensation—

(a) shall be payable under section 63 or 68 of the Lands Clauses Consolidation Act 1845 or under section 7 or 10 of the Compulsory Purchase Act 1965, and
(b) shall be assessed in the same manner and subject to the same rules as in the case of other compensation under those sections in respect of injurious affection where—
    (i) the compensation is to be estimated in connection with a purchase under those Acts, or
    (ii) the injury arises from the execution of works on[, or use of,] land acquired under those Acts.

(5) Where a person deriving title under the local authority by whom the land in question was acquired or appropriated—

(a) is liable to pay compensation by virtue of subsection (4), and
(b) fails to discharge that liability,

the liability shall be enforceable against the local authority.

(6) Nothing in subsection (5) shall be construed as affecting any agreement between the local authority and any other person for indemnifying the local authority against any liability under that subsection.

(7) Nothing in this section shall be construed as authorising any act or omission on the part of any person which is actionable at the suit of any person on any grounds other than such an interference or breach as is mentioned in subsection (1) [or (1A)].

[1379]

NOTES

Sub-s (1A): inserted by the Planning Act 2008, s 194(1), Sch 9, para 4(1), (2).

Sub-s (3): in para (b) words in square brackets substituted by the Communications Act 2003, s 406(1), Sch 17, para 103(1)(b), (2).

Sub-ss (4), (7): words in square brackets inserted by the Planning Act 2008, s 194(1), Sch 9, para 4(1), (3), (4).

238–314 (*Ss 238–246, ss 247–314 (Pts X–XV) outside the scope of this work.*)

PART XV
MISCELLANEOUS AND GENERAL PROVISIONS

315–325A (*In so far as unrepealed, outside the scope of this work.*)

Miscellaneous and general provisions

326–336 (*In so far as unrepealed, outside the scope of this work.*)

337 Short title, commencement and extent

(1) This Act may be cited as the Town and Country Planning Act 1990.

(2) Except as provided in Part II and in Schedule 4 to the Planning (Consequential Provisions) Act 1990, this Act shall come into force at the end of the period of three months beginning with the day on which it is passed.

(3) This Act extends to England and Wales only.

[1380]

(*Schs 1–17 outside the scope of this work.*)

COURTS AND LEGAL SERVICES ACT 1990

(1990 c 41)

An Act to make provision with respect to the procedure in, and allocation of business between, the High Court and other courts; to make provision with respect to legal services; to establish a body to be known as the Lord Chancellor's Advisory Committee on Legal Education and Conduct and a body to be known as the Authorised Conveyancing Practitioners Board; to provide for the appointment of a Legal Services Ombudsman; to make provision for the establishment of a Conveyancing Ombudsman Scheme; to provide for the establishment of Conveyancing Appeal Tribunals; to amend the law relating to judicial and related pensions and judicial and other appointments; to make provision with respect to certain officers of the Supreme Court; to amend the Solicitors Act 1974; to amend the Arbitration Act 1950; to make provision with respect to certain loans in respect of residential property; to make provision with respect to the jurisdiction of the Parliamentary Commissioner for Administration in connection with the functions of court staff; to amend the Children Act 1989 and make further provision in connection with that Act; and for connected purposes

[1 November 1990]

PART I
PROCEDURE ETC IN CIVIL COURTS

Allocation and transfer of business

1 Allocation of business between High Court and county courts

(1) The Lord Chancellor may by order make provision—

(a) conferring jurisdiction on the High Court in relation to proceedings in which county courts have jurisdiction;

(b) conferring jurisdiction on county courts in relation to proceedings in which the High Court has jurisdiction;

(c) allocating proceedings to the High Court or to county courts;

(d) specifying proceedings which may be commenced only in the High Court;

(e) specifying proceedings which may be commenced only in a county court;

(f) specifying proceedings which may be taken only in the High Court;

(g) specifying proceedings which may be taken only in a county court.

[(1A) An order under subsection (1)(a) or (b) may be made only with the concurrence of the Lord Chief Justice.]

(2) Without prejudice to the generality of section 120(2), any such order may differentiate between categories of proceedings by reference to such criteria as the Lord Chancellor sees fit to specify in the order.

(3) The criteria so specified may, in particular, relate to—

(a) the value of an action (as defined by the order);

(b) the nature of the proceedings;

(c) the parties to the proceedings;

(d) the degree of complexity likely to be involved in any aspect of the proceedings; and

(e) the importance of any question likely to be raised by, or in the course of, the proceedings.

(4) An order under subsection (1)(b), (e) or (g) may specify one or more particular county courts in relation to the proceedings so specified.

(5) Any jurisdiction exercisable by a county court, under any provision made by virtue of subsection (4), shall be exercisable throughout England and Wales.

(6) Rules of court may provide for a matter—

(a) which is pending in one county court; and

(b) over which that court has jurisdiction under any provision made by virtue of subsection (4),

to be heard and determined wholly or partly in another county court which also has jurisdiction in that matter under any such provision.

(7) Any such order may—

(a) amend or repeal any provision falling within subsection (8) and relating to—

(i) the jurisdiction, practice or procedure of the *Supreme Court* [Senior Courts]; or

(ii) the jurisdiction, practice or procedure of any county court,

so far as the Lord Chancellor considers it to be necessary, or expedient, in consequence of any provision made by the order; or

(b) make such incidental or transitional provision as the Lord Chancellor considers necessary, or expedient, in consequence of any provision made by the order.

(8) A provision falls within this subsection if it is made by any enactment other than this Act or made under any enactment.

(9) Before making any such order the Lord Chancellor shall consult the Lord Chief Justice, the Master of the Rolls, [the President of the Queen's Bench Division, the President of the Family Division, the Chancellor of the High Court] and the Senior Presiding Judge (appointed under section 72).

(10) No such order shall be made so as to confer jurisdiction on any county court to hear any application for judicial review.

(11) For the purposes of this section the commencement of proceedings may include the making of any application in anticipation of any proceedings or in the course of any proceedings.

(12) …

[(13) The Lord Chief Justice may nominate a judicial office holder (as defined in section 109(4) of the Constitutional Reform Act 2005) to exercise his functions under this section.] **[1381]**

NOTES

Sub-s (1A): inserted by the Constitutional Reform Act 2005, s 15(1), Sch 4, Pt 1, paras 211, 212(1), (2).

Sub-s (7): in para (a)(i), words in italics substituted by subsequent words in square brackets by the Constitutional Reform Act 2005, s 59(5), Sch 11, Pt 2, para 4(1), (3), as from 1 October 2009.

Sub-s (9): words in square brackets substituted by the Constitutional Reform Act 2005, s 15(1), Sch 4, Pt 1, paras 211, 212(1), (3).

Sub-s (12): repealed by the Courts Act 2003, s 109(1), (3), Sch 8, para 348, Sch 10.

Sub-s (13): inserted by the Constitutional Reform Act 2005, s 15(1), Sch 4, Pt 1, paras 211, 212(1), (4).

Order: the High Court and County Courts Jurisdiction Order 1991, SI 1991/724 at **[3059]**.

2–125 (*Ss 2–16, ss 17–125* (*Pts II–VI*) *outside the scope of this work.*)

(*Schs 1–20 outside the scope of this work.*)

ENVIRONMENTAL PROTECTION ACT 1990

(1990 c 43)

An Act to make provision for the improved control of pollution arising from certain industrial and other processes; to re-enact the provisions of the Control of Pollution Act 1974 relating to waste on land with modifications as respects the functions of the regulatory and other authorities concerned in the collection and disposal of waste and to make further provision in relation to such waste; to restate the law defining statutory nuisances and improve the summary procedures for dealing with them, to provide for the termination of the existing controls over offensive trades or businesses and to provide for the extension of the Clean Air Acts to prescribed gases; to amend the law relating to litter and make further provision imposing or conferring powers to impose duties to keep public places clear of litter and clean; to make provision conferring powers in relation to trolleys abandoned on land in the open air; to amend the Radioactive Substances Act 1960; to make provision for the control of genetically modified organisms; to make provision for the abolition of the Nature Conservancy Council and for the creation of councils to replace it and discharge the functions of that Council and, as respects Wales, of the Countryside Commission; to make further provision for the control of the importation, exportation, use, supply or storage of prescribed substances and articles and the importation or exportation of prescribed descriptions of waste; to confer powers to obtain information about potentially hazardous substances; to amend the law relating to the control of hazardous substances on, over or under land; to amend section 107(6) of the Water Act 1989 and sections 31(7)(a), 31A(c)(i) and 32(7)(a) of the Control of Pollution Act 1974; to amend the provisions of the Food and Environment Protection Act 1985 as regards the dumping of waste at sea; to make further provision as respects the prevention of oil pollution from ships; to make provision for and in connection with the identification and control of dogs; to confer powers to control the burning of crop residues; to make provision in relation to financial or other assistance for purposes connected with the environment; to make provision as respects superannuation of employees of the Groundwork Foundation and for remunerating the chairman of the Inland Waterways Amenity Advisory Council; and for purposes connected with those purposes

[1 November 1990]

PART I
INTEGRATED POLLUTION CONTROL AND AIR POLLUTION CONTROL BY LOCAL AUTHORITIES

Preliminary

1 Preliminary

(1) The following provisions have effect for the interpretation of this Part.

(2) The "environment" consists of all, or any, of the following media, namely, the air, water and land; and the medium of air includes the air within buildings and the air within other natural or man-made structures above or below ground.

(3) "Pollution of the environment" means pollution of the environment due to the release (into any environmental medium) from any process of substances which are capable of causing harm to man or any other living organisms supported by the environment.

(4) "Harm" means harm to the health of living organisms or other interference with the ecological systems of which they form part and, in the case of man, includes offence caused to any of his senses or harm to his property; and "harmless" has a corresponding meaning.

(5) "Process" means any activities carried on in Great Britain, whether on premises or by means of mobile plant, which are capable of causing pollution of the environment and "prescribed process" means a process prescribed under section 2(1) below.

(6) For the purposes of subsection (5) above—

"activities" means industrial or commercial activities or activities of any other nature whatsoever (including, with or without other activities, the keeping of a substance);

"Great Britain" includes so much of the adjacent territorial sea as is, or is treated as, relevant territorial waters for the purposes of [Part III of the Water Resources Act 1991] or, as respects Scotland, Part II of the Control of Pollution Act 1974; and

"mobile plant" means plant which is designed to move or to be moved whether on roads or otherwise.

(7) The "enforcing authority", in relation to England and Wales, is [the Environment Agency or the local authority by which], under section 4 below, the functions conferred or imposed by this Part otherwise than on the Secretary of State are for the time being exercisable in relation respectively to releases of substances into the environment or into the air; and "local enforcing authority" means any such local authority.

[(8) In relation to Scotland, references to the "enforcing authority" and a local enforcing authority" are references to the Scottish Environment Protection Agency (in this Part referred to as "SEPA").]

(9) "Authorisation" means an authorisation for a process (whether on premises or by means of mobile plant) granted under section 6 below; and a reference to the conditions of an authorisation is a reference to the conditions subject to which at any time the authorisation has effect.

(10) A substance is "released" into any environmental medium whenever it is released directly into that medium whether it is released into it within or outside Great Britain and "release" includes—

(a) in relation to air, any emission of the substance into the air;

(b) in relation to water, any entry (including any discharge) of the substance into water;

(c) in relation to land, any deposit, keeping or disposal of the substance in or on land;

and for this purpose "water" and "land" shall be construed in accordance with subsections (11) and (12) below.

(11) For the purpose of determining into what medium a substance is released—

(a) any release into—

(i) the sea or the surface of the seabed,

(ii) any river, watercourse, lake, loch or pond (whether natural or artificial or above or below ground) or reservoir or the surface of the riverbed or of other land supporting such waters, or

(iii) ground waters,

is a release into water;

(b) any release into—

(i) land covered by water falling outside paragraph (a) above or the water covering such land; or

(ii) the land beneath the surface of the seabed or of other land supporting waters falling within paragraph (a)(ii) above,

is a release into land; and

(c) any release into a sewer (within the meaning of [the Water Industry Act 1991] or, in relation to Scotland, of the Sewerage (Scotland) Act 1968) shall be treated as a release into water;

but a sewer and its contents shall be disregarded in determining whether there is pollution of the environment at any time.

(12) In subsection (11) above "ground waters" means any waters contained in underground strata, or in—

- *(a) a well, borehole or similar work sunk into underground strata, including any adit or passage constructed in connection with the well, borehole or work for facilitating the collection of water in the well, borehole or work; or*
- *(b) any excavation into underground strata where the level of water in the excavation depends wholly or mainly on water entering it from the strata.*

(13) "Substance" shall be treated as including electricity or heat and "prescribed substance" has the meaning given by section 2(7) below.

[(14) In this Part "the appropriate Agency" means—

- *(a) in relation to England and Wales, the Environment Agency; and*
- *(b) in relation to Scotland, SEPA.]*

[1382]

NOTES

Repealed by the Pollution Prevention and Control Act 1999, s 6(2), Sch 3, as from a day to be appointed.

Sub-ss (6), (11): words in square brackets substituted by the Water Consolidation (Consequential Provisions) Act 1991, s 2, Sch 1, para 56(1).

Sub-s (7): words in square brackets substituted by the Environment Act 1995, s 120, Sch 22, para 45(2).

Sub-s (8): substituted by the Environment Act 1995, s 120, Sch 22, para 45(3).

Sub-s (14): inserted by the Environment Act 1995, s 120, Sch 22, para 45(4).

2 Prescribed processes and prescribed substances

(1) The Secretary of State may, by regulations, prescribe any description of process as a process for the carrying on of which after a prescribed date an authorisation is required under section 6 below.

(2) Regulations under subsection (1) above may frame the description of a process by reference to any characteristics of the process or the area or other circumstances in which the process is carried on or the description of person carrying it on.

(3) Regulations under subsection (1) above may prescribe or provide for the determination under the regulations of different dates for different descriptions of persons and may include such transitional provisions as the Secretary of State considers necessary or expedient as respects the making of applications for authorisations and suspending the application of section 6(1) below until the determination of applications made within the period allowed by the regulations.

(4) Regulations under subsection (1) above shall, as respects each description of process, designate it as one for central control or one for local control.

(5) The Secretary of State may, by regulations, prescribe any description of substance as a substance the release of which into the environment is subject to control under sections 6 and 7 below.

(6) Regulations under subsection (5) above may—

- *(a) prescribe separately, for each environmental medium, the substances the release of which into that medium is to be subject to control; and*
- *(b) provide that a description of substance is only prescribed, for any environmental medium, so far as it is released into that medium in such amounts over such periods, in such concentrations or in such other circumstances as may be specified in the regulations;*

and in relation to a substance of a description which is prescribed for releases into the air, the regulations may designate the substance as one for central control or one for local control.

(7) In this Part "prescribed substance" means any substance of a description prescribed in regulations under subsection (5) above or, in the case of a substance of a description prescribed only for releases in circumstances specified under subsection (6)(b) above, means any substance of that description which is released in those circumstances.

[1383]

NOTES

Repealed by the Pollution Prevention and Control Act 1999, s 6(2), Sch 3, as from a day to be appointed.

Transfer of functions: functions of the Secretary of State, so far as exercisable in relation to Wales, transferred to the National Assembly for Wales, by the National Assembly for Wales (Transfer of Functions) Order 1999, SI 1999/672, art 2, Sch 1.

Regulations: the Environmental Protection (Prescribed Processes and Substances) Regulations 1991, SI 1991/472 (revoked in relation to England and Wales).

3 Emission etc limits and quality objectives

(1) The Secretary of State may make regulations under subsection (2) or (4) below establishing standards, objectives or requirements in relation to particular prescribed processes or particular substances.

(2) Regulations under this subsection may—

(a) in relation to releases of any substance from prescribed processes into any environmental medium, prescribe standard limits for—

(i) the concentration, the amount or the amount in any period of that substance which may be so released; and

(ii) any other characteristic of that substance in any circumstances in which it may be so released;

(b) prescribe standard requirements for the measurement or analysis of, or of releases of, substances for which limits have been set under paragraph (a) above; and

(c) in relation to any prescribed process, prescribe standards or requirements as to any aspect of the process.

(3) Regulations under subsection (2) above may make different provision in relation to different cases, including different provision in relation to different processes, descriptions of person, localities or other circumstances.

(4) Regulations under this subsection may establish for any environmental medium (in all areas or in specified areas) quality objectives or quality standards in relation to any substances which may be released into that or any other medium from any process.

(5) The Secretary of State may make plans for—

(a) establishing limits for the total amount, or the total amount in any period, of any substance which may be released into the environment in, or in any area within, the United Kingdom;

(b) allocating quotas as respects the release of substances to persons carrying on processes in respect of which any such limit is established;

(c) establishing limits of the descriptions specified in subsection (2)(a) above so as progressively to reduce pollution of the environment;

(d) the progressive improvement in the quality objectives and quality standards established by regulations under subsection (4) above;

and the Secretary of State may, from time to time, revise any plan so made.

(6) Regulations or plans under this section may be made for any purposes of this Part or for other purposes.

(7) The Secretary of State shall give notice in the London, Edinburgh and Belfast Gazettes of the making and the revision of any plan under subsection (5) above and shall make the documents containing the plan, or the plan as so revised, available for inspection by members of the public at the places specified in the notice.

(8) …

[1384]

NOTES

Repealed by the Pollution Prevention and Control Act 1999, s 6(2), Sch 3, as from a day to be appointed; by virtue of s 7(7) thereof, the repeal of sub-ss (5)–(7) does not extend to Northern Ireland.

Sub-ss (5)–(7): repealed, in relation to Northern Ireland, by SI 2002/3153, art 53(2), Sch 6, Pt I, as from a day to be appointed.

Sub-s (8): repealed by the Northern Ireland Act 1998, s 100(2), Sch 15.

Transfer of functions: see the note to s 2 at **[1383]**.

4 Discharge and scope of functions

(1) This section determines the authority by whom the functions conferred or imposed by this Part otherwise than on the Secretary of State are exercisable and the purposes for which they are exercisable.

(2) Those functions, in their application to prescribed processes designated for central control, shall be functions of [the appropriate Agency], and shall be exercisable for the purpose of preventing or minimising pollution of the environment due to the release of substances into any environmental medium.

(3) Subject to subsection (4) below, those functions, in their application to prescribed processes designated for local control, shall be functions of—

[(a) in the case of a prescribed process carried on (or to be carried on) by means of a mobile plant, where the person carrying on the process has his principal place of business—

(i) in England and Wales, the local authority in whose area that place of business is;

(ii) in Scotland, SEPA;

(b) in any other cases, where the prescribed processes are (or are to be) carried on—

(i) *in England and Wales, the local authority in whose area they are (or are to be) carried on;*

(ii) *in Scotland, SEPA;]*

and the functions applicable to such processes shall be exercisable for the purpose of preventing or minimising pollution of the environment due to the release of substances into the air (but not into any other environmental medium).

(4) The Secretary of State may, as respects the functions under this Part being exercised by a local authority specified in the direction, direct that those functions shall be exercised instead by [the Environment Agency] while the direction remains in force or during a period specified in the direction.

[(4A) In England and Wales, a local authority, in exercising the functions conferred or imposed on it under this Part by virtue of subsection (3) above, shall have regard to the strategy for the time being published pursuant to section 80 of the Environment Act 1995.]

(5) A transfer of functions under subsection (4) above to [the Environment Agency] does not make them exercisable by [that Agency] for the purpose of preventing or minimising pollution of the environment due to releases of substances into any other environmental medium than the air.

(6) A direction under subsection (4) above may transfer those functions as exercisable in relation to all or any description of prescribed processes carried on by all or any description of persons (a "general direction") or in relation to a prescribed process carried on by a specified person (a "specific direction").

(7) A direction under subsection (4) above may include such saving and transitional provisions as the Secretary of State considers necessary or expedient.

(8) The Secretary of State, on giving or withdrawing a direction under subsection (4) above, shall—

(a) *in the case of a general direction—*

(i) *forthwith serve notice of it on [the Environment Agency] and on the local enforcing authorities affected by the direction; and*

(ii) *cause notice of it to be published as soon as practicable in the London Gazette … and in at least one newspaper circulating in the area of each authority affected by the direction;*

(b) *in the case of a specific direction—*

(i) *forthwith serve notice of it on [the Environment Agency], the local enforcing authority and the person carrying on or appearing to the Secretary of State to be carrying on the process affected, and*

(ii) *cause notice of it to be published as soon as practicable in the London Gazette … and in at least one newspaper circulating in the authority's area;*

and any such notice shall specify the date at which the direction is to take (or took) effect and (where appropriate) its duration.

[(8A) The requirements of sub-paragraph (ii) of paragraph (a) or, as the case may be, of paragraph (b) of subsection (8) above shall not apply in any case where, in the opinion of the Secretary of State, the publication of notice in accordance with that sub-paragraph would be contrary to the interests of national security.

(8B) Subsections (4) to (8A) above shall not apply to Scotland.]

[(9) It shall be the duty of local authorities to follow such developments in technology and techniques for preventing or reducing pollution of the environment due to releases of substances from prescribed processes as concern releases into the air of substances from prescribed processes designated for local control.]

(10) It shall be the duty of [the Environment Agency, SEPA] and the local enforcing authorities to give effect to any directions given to them under any provision of this Part.

(11) In this Part "local authority" means, subject to subsection (12) below—

(a) *in Greater London, a London borough council, the Common Council of the City of London, the Sub-Treasurer of the Inner Temple and the Under Treasurer of the Middle Temple;*

(b) *[in England …] outside Greater London, a district council and the Council of the Isles of Scilly;*

[(bb) in Wales, a county council or county borough council;] …

(c) *…*

(12) Where, by an order under section 2 of the Public Health (Control of Disease) Act 1984, a port health authority has been constituted for any port health district, the port health authority shall have by virtue of this subsection, as respects its district, the functions conferred or imposed by this Part and no such order shall be made assigning those functions; and "local authority" and "area" shall be construed accordingly.

[1385]

NOTES

Repealed by the Pollution Prevention and Control Act 1999, s 6(2), Sch 3, as from a day to be appointed.

Sub-s (2): words in square brackets substituted by the Environment Act 1995, s 120, Sch 22, para 46(2).

Sub-s (3): paras (a), (b) substituted by the Environment Act 1995, s 120, Sch 22, para 46(3).

Sub-ss (4), (5), (10): words in square brackets substituted by the Environment Act 1995, s 120, Sch 22, para 46(4), (6), (10).

Sub-s (4A): inserted by the Environment Act 1995, s 120, Sch 22, para 46(5), (8).

Sub-s (8): words in square brackets substituted and words omitted repealed by the Environment Act 1995, s 120, Sch 22, para 46(6)(a), (7), Sch 24.

Sub-ss (8A), (8B): inserted by the Environment Act 1995, s 120, Sch 22, para 46(8).

Sub-s (9): substituted by the Environment Act 1995, s 120, Sch 22, para 46(9).

Sub-s (11): in para (b), words in square brackets inserted and words omitted repealed by the Environment Act 1995, s 120, Sch 22, para 46(11)(a), Sch 24; para (bb) inserted by the Local Government (Wales) Act 1994, s 22(3), Sch 9, para 17(1); para (c) and the word immediately preceding it repealed by the Environment Act 1995, s 120, Sch 22, para 46(11)(b), Sch 24.

Transfer of functions: see the note to s 2 at **[1383]**.

5 (*Repealed by the Environment Act 1995, s 120(1), (3), Sch 22, para 47, Sch 24.*)

Authorisations

6 Authorisations: general provisions

(1) No person shall carry on a prescribed process after the date prescribed or determined for that description of process by or under regulations under section 2(1) above (but subject to any transitional provision made by the regulations) except under an authorisation granted by the enforcing authority and in accordance with the conditions to which it is subject.

(2) An application for an authorisation shall be made to the enforcing authority in accordance with Part I of Schedule 1 to this Act and shall be accompanied by

[(a) in a case where, by virtue of section 41 of the Environment Act 1995, a charge prescribed by a charging scheme under that section is required to be paid to the appropriate Agency in respect of the application, the charge so prescribed; or

(b) in any other case,] the fee prescribed under section 8(2)(a) below.

(3) Where an application is duly made to the enforcing authority, the authority shall either grant the authorisation subject to the conditions required or authorised to be imposed by section 7 below or refuse the application.

(4) An application shall not be granted unless the enforcing authority considers that the applicant will be able to carry on the process so as to comply with the conditions which would be included in the authorisation.

(5) The Secretary of State may, if he thinks fit in relation to any application for an authorisation, give to the enforcing authority directions as to whether or not the authority should grant the authorisation.

(6) [Subject to subsection (6A) below] the enforcing authority shall, as respects each authorisation in respect of which it has functions under this Part, from time to time but not less frequently than once in every period of four years, carry out a review of the conditions of the authorisation.

[(6A) Subsection (6) above shall not require a review of the conditions of an authorisation to be carried out if—

(a) the prescribed process covered by the authorisation is carried on in a new Part A installation or by means of a new Part A mobile plant;

(b) the prescribed process covered by the authorisation is carried on in an existing Part A installation or by means of an existing Part A mobile plant and the review would be carried out within the period of two years ending at the beginning of the relevant period for that installation or mobile plant; or

(c) the prescribed process covered by the authorisation is carried on in an existing Part B installation or by means of an existing Part B mobile plant and the review would be carried out within the period of two years ending on the relevant date for that installation or mobile plant.

(6B) In subsection (6A) above, "new Part A installation", "existing Part A installation", "new Part A mobile plant", "existing Part A mobile plant", "relevant period", "existing Part B installation", "existing Part B mobile plant" and "relevant date" have the meaning given in Schedule 3 to the Pollution Prevention and Control (England and Wales) Regulations 2000.]

(7) The Secretary of State may, by regulations, substitute for the period for the time being specified in subsection (6) above such other period as he thinks fit.

(8) Schedule 1 to this Act (supplementary provisions) shall have effect in relation to authorisations.

[1386]

NOTES

Repealed by the Pollution Prevention and Control Act 1999, s 6(2), Sch 3, as from a day to be appointed.

Sub-s (2): words in square brackets inserted by the Environment Act 1995, s 120, Sch 22, para 48.

Sub-s (6): words in square brackets inserted by SI 2000/1973, reg 39, Sch 10, Pt 1, paras 2, 3(a), and in relation to Scotland by SSI 2000/323, reg 36, Sch 10, Pt 1, para 3(1), (2)(a).

Sub-ss (6A), (6B): inserted by SI 2000/1973, reg 39, Sch 10, Pt 1, paras 2, 3(b), and in relation to Scotland by SSI 2000/323, reg 36, Sch 10, Pt 1, para 3(1), (2)(b).

Transfer of functions: see the note to s 2 at **[1383]**.

7 Conditions of authorisations

(1) There shall be included in an authorisation—

(a) subject to paragraph (b) below, such specific conditions as the enforcing authority considers appropriate, when taken with the general condition implied by subsection (4) below, for achieving the objectives specified in subsection (2) below;

(b) such conditions as are specified in directions given by the Secretary of State under subsection (3) below; and

(c) such other conditions (if any) as appear to the enforcing authority to be appropriate;

but no conditions shall be imposed for the purpose only of securing the health of persons at work (within the meaning of Part I of the Health and Safety at Work etc Act 1974).

(2) Those objectives are—

(a) ensuring that, in carrying on a prescribed process, the best available techniques not entailing excessive cost will be used—

(i) for preventing the release of substances prescribed for any environmental medium into that medium or, where that is not practicable by such means, for reducing the release of such substances to a minimum and for rendering harmless any such substances which are so released; and

(ii) for rendering harmless any other substances which might cause harm if released into any environmental medium;

(b) compliance with any directions by the Secretary of State given for the implementation of any obligations of the United Kingdom under the Community Treaties or international law relating to environmental protection;

(c) compliance with any limits or requirements and achievement of any quality standards or quality objectives prescribed by the Secretary of State under any of the relevant enactments;

(d) compliance with any requirements applicable to the grant of authorisations specified by or under a plan made by the Secretary of State under section 3(5) above.

(3) Except as respects the general condition implied by subsection (4) below, the Secretary of State may give directions to the enforcing authorities as to the conditions which are, or are not, to be included in all authorisations, in authorisations of any specified description or in any particular authorisation.

(4) Subject to subsections (5) and (6) below, there is implied in every authorisation a general condition that, in carrying on the process to which the authorisation applies, the person carrying it on must use the best available techniques not entailing excessive cost—

(a) for preventing the release of substances prescribed for any environmental medium into that medium or, where that is not practicable by such means, for reducing the release of such substances to a minimum and for rendering harmless any such substances which are so released; and

(b) for rendering harmless any other substances which might cause harm if released into any environmental medium.

(5) In the application of subsections (1) to (4) above to authorisations granted by a local enforcing authority references to the release of substances into any environmental medium are to be read as references to the release of substances into the air.

(6) The obligation implied by virtue of subsection (4) above shall not apply in relation to any aspect of the process in question which is regulated by a condition imposed under subsection (1) above.

(7) The objectives referred to in subsection (2) above shall, where the process—

(a) is one designated for central control; and

(b) is likely to involve the release of substances into more than one environmental medium;

include the objective of ensuring that the best available techniques not entailing excessive cost will be used for minimising the pollution which may be caused to the environment taken as a whole by the releases having regard to the best practicable environmental option available as respects the substances which may be released.

(8) An authorisation for carrying on a prescribed process may, without prejudice to the generality of subsection (1) above, include conditions—

- *(a) imposing limits on the amount or composition of any substance produced by or utilised in the process in any period; and*
- *(b) requiring advance notification of any proposed change in the manner of carrying on the process.*

(9) This section has effect subject to section 28 below ...

(10) References to the best available techniques not entailing excessive cost, in relation to a process, include (in addition to references to any technical means and technology) references to the number, qualifications, training and supervision of persons employed in the process and the design, construction, lay-out and maintenance of the buildings in which it is carried on.

(11) It shall be the duty of enforcing authorities to have regard to any guidance issued to them by the Secretary of State for the purposes of the application of subsections (2) and (7) above as to the techniques and environmental options that are appropriate for any description of prescribed process.

(12) In subsection (2) above "the relevant enactments" are any enactments or instruments contained in or made for the time being under—

- *(a) section 2 of the Clean Air Act 1968;*
- *(b) section 2 of the European Communities Act 1972;*
- *(c) Part I of the Health and Safety at Work etc Act 1974;*
- *(d) Parts II, III or IV of the Control of Pollution Act 1974;*
- *[(e) the Water Resources Act 1991; ...]*
- *(f) section 3 of this Act[; ...*
- *(g) section 87 of the Environment Act 1995;][and*
- *(h) Part 1 of the Water Environment and Water Services (Scotland) Act 2003 (asp 3)].*

[1387]

NOTES

Repealed by the Pollution Prevention and Control Act 1999, s 6(2), Sch 3, as from a day to be appointed.

Sub-s (9): words omitted repealed by the Environment Act 1995, s 120, Sch 22, para 49(1), Sch 24.

Sub-s (12): para (e) substituted by the Water Consolidation (Consequential Provisions) Act 1991, s 2, Sch 1, para 56(2); words omitted from paras (e), (f) repealed and para (h) inserted by SSI 2006/181, art 3, Schedule, Pt IV, para 5(1), (2); para (g) inserted by the Environment Act 1995, s 120, Sch 22, para 49(2).

Transfer of functions: see the note to s 2 at **[1383]**.

8 Fees and charges for authorisations

(1) There shall be charged by and paid to the [local enforcing authority] such fees and charges as may be prescribed from time to time by a scheme under subsection (2) below (whether by being specified in or made calculable under the scheme).

(2) The Secretary of State may, with the approval of the Treasury, make, and from time to time revise, a scheme prescribing—

- *(a) fees payable in respect of applications for authorisations;*
- *(b) fees payable by persons holding authorisations in respect of, or of applications for, the variation of authorisations; and*
- *(c) charges payable by such persons in respect of the subsistence of their authorisations.*

(3) The Secretary of State shall, on making or revising a scheme under subsection (2) above, lay a copy of the scheme or of the alterations made in the scheme or, if he considers it more appropriate, the scheme as revised, before each House of Parliament.

(4) ...

(5) A scheme under subsection (2) above may, in particular—

- *(a) make different provision for different cases, including different provision in relation to different persons, circumstances or localities;*
- *(b) allow for reduced fees or charges to be payable in respect of authorisations for a number of prescribed processes carried on by the same person;*
- *(c) provide for the times at which and the manner in which the payments required by the scheme are to be made; and*
- *(d) make such incidental, supplementary and transitional provision as appears to the Secretary of State to be appropriate.*

(6) The Secretary of State, in framing a scheme under subsection (2) above, shall, so far as practicable, secure that the fees and charges payable under the scheme are sufficient, taking one financial year with another, to cover the relevant expenditure attributable to authorisations.

(7) The "relevant expenditure attributable to authorisations" is the expenditure incurred by the [local enforcing authorities] in exercising their functions under this Part in relation to authorisations ... [together with the expenditure incurred by the Environment Agency in exercising, in relation to authorisations granted by local enforcing authorities or the prescribed processes to which such authorisations relate, such of its functions as are specified in the scheme.]

(8) If it appears to the [local enforcing authority] that the holder of an authorisation has failed to pay a charge due in consideration of the subsistence of the authorisation, it may, by notice in writing served on the holder, revoke the authorisation.

(9) ...

[(10) The foregoing provisions of this section shall not apply to Scotland.]

[1388]

NOTES

Repealed by the Pollution Prevention and Control Act 1999, s 6(2), Sch 3, as from a day to be appointed.

Sub-s (1): words in square brackets substituted by the Environment Act 1995, s 120, Sch 22, para 50(2).

Sub-ss (4), (9): repealed by the Environment Act 1995, s 120, Sch 22, para 50(3), (6), Sch 24.

Sub-s (7): words in first pair of square brackets substituted and words omitted repealed by the Environment Act 1995, s 120, Sch 22, para 50(4), Sch 24; words in second pair of square brackets inserted by the Pollution Prevention and Control Act 1999, s 6(1), Sch 2, paras 3, 4, as from a day to be appointed in relation to Scotland.

Sub-s (8): words in square brackets substituted by the Environment Act 1995, s 120, Sch 22, para 50(5).

Sub-s (10): substituted, for sub-ss (10), (11) as originally enacted, by the Environment Act 1995, s 120, Sch 22, para 50(7).

Transfer of functions: see the note to s 2 at **[1383]**.

9 Transfer of authorisations

(1) An authorisation for the carrying on of any prescribed process may be transferred by the holder to a person who proposes to carry on the process in the holder's place.

(2) Where an authorisation is transferred under this section, the person to whom it is transferred shall notify the enforcing authority in writing of that fact not later than the end of the period of twenty-one days beginning with the date of the transfer.

(3) An authorisation which is transferred under this section shall have effect on and after the date of the transfer as if it had been granted to that person under section 6 above, subject to the same conditions as were attached to it immediately before that date.

[1389]

NOTES

Repealed by the Pollution Prevention and Control Act 1999, s 6(2), Sch 3, as from a day to be appointed.

10 Variation of authorisations by enforcing authority

(1) The enforcing authority may at any time, subject to the requirements of section 7 above, and, in cases to which they apply, the requirements of Part II of Schedule 1 to this Act, vary an authorisation and shall do so if it appears to the authority at that time that that section requires conditions to be included which are different from the subsisting conditions.

(2) Where the enforcing authority has decided to vary an authorisation under subsection (1) above the authority shall notify the holder of the authorisation and serve a variation notice on him.

(3) In this Part a "variation notice" is a notice served by the enforcing authority on the holder of an authorisation—

(a) specifying variations of the authorisation which the enforcing authority has decided to make; and

(b) specifying the date or dates on which the variations are to take effect;

and, unless the notice is withdrawn [or is varied under subsection (3A) below], the variations specified in a variation notice shall take effect on the date or dates so specified.

[(3A) An enforcing authority which has served a variation notice may vary that notice by serving on the holder of the authorisation in question a further notice—

(a) specifying the variations which the enforcing authority has decided to make to the variation notice; and

(b) specifying the date or dates on which the variations specified in the variation notice, as varied by the further notice, are to take effect;

and any reference in this Part to a variation notice, or to a variation notice served under subsection (2) above, includes a reference to such a notice as varied by a further notice served under this subsection.]

(4) A variation notice served under subsection (2) above shall also—

(a) require the holder of the authorisation, within such period as may be specified in the notice, to notify the authority what action (if any) he proposes to take to ensure that the process is carried on in accordance with the authorisation as varied by the notice; and

[(b) require the holder to pay, within such period as may be specified in the notice,—

(i) in a case where the enforcing authority is the Environment Agency or SEPA, the charge (if any) prescribed for the purpose by a charging scheme under section 41 of the Environment Act 1995; or

(ii) in any other case, the fee (if any) prescribed by a scheme under section 8 above.]

(5) Where in the opinion of the enforcing authority any action to be taken by the holder of an authorisation in consequence of a variation notice served under subsection (2) above will involve a substantial change in the manner in which the process is being carried on, the enforcing authority shall notify the holder of its opinion.

(6) The Secretary of State may, if he thinks fit in relation to authorisations of any description or particular authorisations, direct the enforcing authorities—

(a) to exercise their powers under this section, or to do so in such circumstances as may be specified in the directions, in such manner as may be so specified; or

(b) not to exercise those powers, or not to do so in such circumstances or such manner as may be so specified;

and the Secretary of State shall have the corresponding power of direction in respect of the powers of the enforcing authorities to vary authorisations under section 11 below.

(7) In this section and section 11 below a "substantial change", in relation to a prescribed process being carried on under an authorisation, means a substantial change in the substances released from the process or in the amount or any other characteristic of any substance so released; and the Secretary of State may give directions to the enforcing authorities as to what does or does not constitute a substantial change in relation to processes generally, any description of process or any particular process.

(8) In this section and section 11 below—

"prescribed" means prescribed in regulations made by the Secretary of State;

"vary"

[(a)] in relation to the subsisting conditions or other provisions of an authorisation, means adding to them or varying or rescinding any of them; [and

(b) in relation to a variation notice, means adding to, or varying or rescinding the notice or any of its contents;]

and "variation" shall be construed accordingly.

[1390]

NOTES

Repealed by the Pollution Prevention and Control Act 1999, s 6(2), Sch 3, as from a day to be appointed.

Sub-s (3): words in square brackets inserted by the Environment Act 1995, s 120, Sch 22, para 51(2).

Sub-s (3A): inserted by the Environment Act 1995, s 120, Sch 22, para 51(3).

Sub-s (4): para (b) substituted by the Environment Act 1995, s 120, Sch 22, para 51(4).

Sub-s (8): in definition "vary" letter "(a)" in square brackets inserted, and para (b) inserted, by the Environment Act 1995, s 120, Sch 22, para 51(5).

Transfer of functions: see the note to s 2 at **[1383]**.

Regulations: the Environmental Protection (Applications, Appeals and Registers) Regulations 1991, SI 1991/507 (revoked in relation to England and Wales).

11 Variation of conditions etc: applications by holders of authorisations

(1) A person carrying on a prescribed process under an authorisation who wishes to make a relevant change in the process may at any time—

(a) notify the enforcing authority in the prescribed form of that fact, and

(b) request the enforcing authority to make a determination, in relation to the proposed change, of the matters mentioned in subsection (2) below;

and a person making a request under paragraph (b) above shall furnish the enforcing authority with such information as may be prescribed or as the authority may by notice require.

(2) On receiving a request under subsection (1) above the enforcing authority shall determine—

(a) whether the proposed change would involve a breach of any condition of the authorisation;

(b) if it would not involve such a breach, whether the authority would be likely to vary the conditions of the authorisation as a result of the change;

(c) if it would involve such a breach, whether the authority would consider varying the conditions of the authorisation so that the change may be made; and

(d) whether the change would involve a substantial change in the manner in which the process is being carried on;

and the enforcing authority shall notify the holder of the authorisation of its determination of those matters.

(3) Where the enforcing authority has determined that the proposed change would not involve a substantial change, but has also determined under paragraph (b) or (c) of subsection (2) above that the change would lead to or require the variation of the conditions of the authorisation, then—

- *(a) the enforcing authority shall (either on notifying its determination under that subsection or on a subsequent occasion) notify the holder of the authorisation of the variations which the authority is likely to consider making; and*
- *(b) the holder may apply in the prescribed form to the enforcing authority for the variation of the conditions of the authorisation so that he may make the proposed change.*

(4) Where the enforcing authority has determined that a proposed change would involve a substantial change that would lead to or require the variation of the conditions of the authorisation, then—

- *(a) the authority shall (either on notifying its determination under subsection (2) above or on a subsequent occasion) notify the holder of the authorisation of the variations which the authority is likely to consider making; and*
- *(b) the holder of the authorisation shall, if he wishes to proceed with the change, apply in the prescribed form to the enforcing authority for the variation of the conditions of the authorisation.*

(5) The holder of an authorisation may at any time, unless he is carrying on a prescribed process under the authorisation and wishes to make a relevant change in the process, apply to the enforcing authority in the prescribed form for the variation of the conditions of the authorisation.

(6) A person carrying on a process under an authorisation who wishes to make a relevant change in the process may, where it appears to him that the change will require the variation of the conditions of the authorisation, apply to the enforcing authority in the prescribed form for the variation of the conditions of the authorisation specified in the application.

(7) A person who makes an application for the variation of the conditions of an authorisation shall furnish the authority with such information as may be prescribed or as the authority may by notice require.

(8) On an application for variation of the conditions of an authorisation under any provision of this section—

- *(a) the enforcing authority may, having fulfilled the requirements of Part II of Schedule 1 to this Act in cases to which they apply, as it thinks fit either refuse the application or, subject to the requirements of section 7 above, vary the conditions or, in the case of an application under subsection (6) above, treat the application as a request for a determination under subsection (2) above; and*
- *(b) if the enforcing authority decides to vary the conditions, it shall serve a variation notice on the holder of the authorisation.*

[(9) Any application to the enforcing authority under this section shall be accompanied—

- *(a) in a case where the enforcing authority is the Environment Agency or SEPA, by the charge (if any) prescribed for the purpose by a charging scheme under section 41 of the Environment Act 1995; or*
- *(b) in any other case, by the fee (if any) prescribed by a scheme under section 8 above.]*

(10) This section applies to any provision other than a condition which is contained in an authorisation as it applies to a condition with the modification that any reference to the breach of a condition shall be read as a reference to acting outside the scope of the authorisation.

(11) For the purposes of this section a relevant change in a prescribed process is a change in the manner of carrying on the process which is capable of altering the substances released from the process or of affecting the amount or any other characteristic of any substance so released.

[1391]

NOTES

Repealed by the Pollution Prevention and Control Act 1999, s 6(2), Sch 3, as from a day to be appointed.
Sub-s (9): substituted by the Environment Act 1995, s 120, Sch 22, para 52.

12 Revocation of authorisation

(1) The enforcing authority may at any time revoke an authorisation by notice in writing to the person holding the authorisation.

(2) Without prejudice to the generality of subsection (1) above, the enforcing authority may revoke an authorisation where it has reason to believe that a prescribed process for which the authorisation is in force has not been carried on or not for a period of twelve months.

(3) The revocation of an authorisation under this section shall have effect from the date specified in the notice; and the period between the date on which the notice is served and the date so specified shall not be less than twenty-eight days.

(4) The enforcing authority may, before the date on which the revocation of an authorisation takes effect, withdraw the notice or vary the date specified in it.

(5) The Secretary of State may, if he thinks fit in relation to an authorisation, give to the enforcing authority directions as to whether the authority should revoke the authorisation under this section.

[1392]

NOTES

Repealed by the Pollution Prevention and Control Act 1999, s 6(2), Sch 3, as from a day to be appointed.
Transfer of functions: see the note to s 2 at **[1383]**.

Enforcement

13 Enforcement notices

(1) If the enforcing authority is of the opinion that the person carrying on a prescribed process under an authorisation is contravening any condition of the authorisation, or is likely to contravene any such condition, the authority may serve on him a notice ("an enforcement notice").

(2) An enforcement notice shall—

- *(a) state that the authority is of the said opinion;*
- *(b) specify the matters constituting the contravention or the matters making it likely that the contravention will arise, as the case may be;*
- *(c) specify the steps that must be taken to remedy the contravention or to remedy the matters making it likely that the contravention will arise, as the case may be; and*
- *(d) specify the period within which those steps must be taken.*

(3) The Secretary of State may, if he thinks fit in relation to the carrying on by any person of a prescribed process, give to the enforcing authority directions as to whether the authority should exercise its powers under this section and as to the steps which are to be required to be taken under this section.

[(4) The enforcing authority may, as respects any enforcement notice it has issued to any person, by notice in writing served on that person, withdraw the notice.]

[1393]

NOTES

Repealed by the Pollution Prevention and Control Act 1999, s 6(2), Sch 3, as from a day to be appointed.
Transfer of functions: see the note to s 2 at **[1383]**.

14 Prohibition notices

(1) If the enforcing authority is of the opinion, as respects the carrying on of a prescribed process under an authorisation, that the continuing to carry it on, or the continuing to carry it on in a particular manner, involves an imminent risk of serious pollution of the environment the authority shall serve a notice (a "prohibition notice") on the person carrying on the process.

(2) A prohibition notice may be served whether or not the manner of carrying on the process in question contravenes a condition of the authorisation and may relate to any aspects of the process, whether regulated by the conditions of the authorisation or not.

(3) A prohibition notice shall—

- *(a) state the authority's opinion;*
- *(b) specify the risk involved in the process;*
- *(c) specify the steps that must be taken to remove it and the period within which they must be taken; and*
- *(d) direct that the authorisation shall, until the notice is withdrawn, wholly or to the extent specified in the notice cease to have effect to authorise the carrying on of the process;*

and where the direction applies to part only of the process it may impose conditions to be observed in carrying on the part which is authorised to be carried on.

(4) The Secretary of State may, if he thinks fit in relation to the carrying on by any person of a prescribed process, give to the enforcing authority directions as to—

- *(a) whether the authority should perform its duties under this section; and*
- *(b) the matters to be specified in any prohibition notice in pursuance of subsection (3) above which the authority is directed to issue.*

(5) The enforcing authority shall, as respects any prohibition notice it has issued to any person, by notice in writing served on that person, withdraw the notice when it is satisfied that the steps required by the notice have been taken.

[1394]

NOTES

Repealed by the Pollution Prevention and Control Act 1999, s 6(2), Sch 3, as from a day to be appointed.
Transfer of functions: see the note to s 2 at **[1383]**.

15 Appeals as respects authorisations and against variation, enforcement and prohibition notices

(1) The following persons, namely—

(a) a person who has been refused the grant of an authorisation under section 6 above;

(b) a person who is aggrieved by the conditions attached, under any provision of this Part, to his authorisation;

(c) a person who has been refused a variation of an authorisation on an application under section 11 above;

(d) a person whose authorisation has been revoked under section 12 above;

may appeal against the decision of the enforcing authority to the Secretary of State (except where the decision implements a direction of his).

(2) A person on whom a variation notice, an enforcement notice or a prohibition notice is served may appeal against the notice to the Secretary of State [(except where the notice implements a direction of his).]

[(3) This section is subject to section 114 of the Environment Act 1995 (delegation or reference of appeals etc).]

(4) An appeal under this section shall, if and to the extent required by regulations under subsection (10) below, be advertised in such manner as may be prescribed by regulations under that subsection.

[(5) Before determining an appeal under this section, the Secretary of State may, if he thinks fit—

(a) cause the appeal to take or continue in the form of a hearing (which may, if the person hearing the appeal so decides, be held, or held to any extent, in private); or

(b) cause a local inquiry to be held;

and the Secretary of State shall act as mentioned in paragraph (a) or (b) above if a request is made by either party to the appeal to be heard with respect to the appeal.]

(6) On determining an appeal against a decision of an enforcing authority under subsection (1) above, the Secretary of State—

(a) may affirm the decision;

(b) where the decision was a refusal to grant an authorisation or a variation of an authorisation, may direct the enforcing authority to grant the authorisation or to vary the authorisation, as the case may be;

(c) where the decision was as to the conditions attached to an authorisation, may quash all or any of the conditions of the authorisation;

(d) where the decision was to revoke an authorisation, may quash the decision;

and where he exercises any of the powers in paragraphs (b), (c) or (d) above, he may give directions as to the conditions to be attached to the authorisation.

(7) On the determination of an appeal under subsection (2) above the Secretary of State may either quash or affirm the notice and, if he affirms it, may do so either in its original form or with such modifications as he may in the circumstances think fit.

(8) Where an appeal is brought under subsection (1) above against the revocation of an authorisation, the revocation shall not take effect pending the final determination or the withdrawal of the appeal.

(9) Where an appeal is brought under subsection (2) above against a notice, the bringing of the appeal shall not have the effect of suspending the operation of the notice.

(10) Provision may be made by the Secretary of State by regulations with respect to appeals under this section and in particular—

(a) as to the period within which and the manner in which appeals are to be brought; and

(b) as to the manner in which appeals are to be considered

[and any such regulations may make different provision for different cases or different circumstances.]

[1395]

NOTES

Repealed by the Pollution Prevention and Control Act 1999, s 6(2), Sch 3, as from a day to be appointed.
Sub-ss (2), (10): words in square brackets inserted by the Environment Act 1995, s 120, Sch 22, para 54(2), (5).
Sub-ss (3), (5): substituted by the Environment Act 1995, s 120, Sch 22, para 54(3), (4).
Transfer of functions: see the note to s 2 at **[1383]**.

Regulations: the Environmental Protection (Applications, Appeals and Registers) Regulations 1991, SI 1991/507 (revoked in relation to England and Wales).

16–22 (*Ss 16–18 repealed by the Environment Act 1995, s 120*(*1*), (*3*), *Sch 22, para 55, Sch 24; ss 19–22 outside the scope of this work.*)

Provisions as to offences

23 Offences

(*1*) *It is an offence for a person—*

(*a*) *to contravene section 6*(*1*) *above;*

(*b*) *to fail to give the notice required by section 9*(*2*) *above;*

(*c*) *to fail to comply with or contravene any requirement or prohibition imposed by an enforcement notice or a prohibition notice;*

(*d*)–(*f*) …

(*g*) *to fail, without reasonable excuse, to comply with any requirement imposed by a notice under section 19*(*2*) *above;*

(*h*) *to make a statement which he knows to be false or misleading in a material particular, or recklessly to make a statement which is false or misleading in a material particular, where the statement is made—*

(*i*) *in purported compliance with a requirement to furnish any information imposed by or under any provision of this Part; or*

(*ii*) *for the purpose of obtaining the grant of an authorisation to himself or any other person or the variation of an authorisation;*

(*i*) *intentionally to make a false entry in any record required to be kept under section 7 above;*

(*j*) *with intent to deceive, to forge or use a document issued or authorised to be issued under section 7 above or required for any purpose thereunder or to make or have in his possession a document so closely resembling any such document as to be likely to deceive;*

(*k*) …

(*l*) *to fail to comply with an order made by a court under section 26 below.*

(*2*) *A person guilty of an offence under paragraph* (*a*), (*c*) *or* (*l*) *of subsection* (*1*) *above shall be liable:*

(*a*) *on summary conviction, to a fine not exceeding [£40,000] [or to imprisonment for a term not exceeding three months, or to both];*

(*b*) *on conviction on indictment, to a fine or to imprisonment for a term not exceeding two years, or to both.*

(*3*) *A person guilty of an offence under paragraph* (*b*), (*g*), (*h*), (*i*) *or* (*j*) *of subsection* (*1*) *above shall be liable—*

(*a*) *on summary conviction, to a fine not exceeding the statutory maximum;*

(*b*) *on conviction on indictment, to a fine or to imprisonment for a term not exceeding two years, or to both.*

(*4*), (*5*) …

[1396]

NOTES

Repealed by the Pollution Prevention and Control Act 1999, s 6(2), Sch 3, as from a day to be appointed.

Sub-s (1): paras (d)–(f), (k) repealed by the Environment Act 1995, s 120, Sch 22, para 59(2), Sch 24.

Sub-s (2): in para (a), sum in square brackets substituted by the Antisocial Behaviour etc (Scotland) Act 2004, s 66, Sch 2, Pt 1, para 4(1), (2) and words in square brackets inserted by the Environment Act 1995, s 59(3).

Sub-ss (4), (5): repealed by the Environment Act 1995, s 120, Sch 22, para 59(4), (5), Sch 24.

24 Enforcement by High Court

If the enforcing authority is of the opinion that proceedings for an offence under section 23(*1*)(*c*) *above would afford an ineffectual remedy against a person who has failed to comply with the requirements of an enforcement notice or a prohibition notice, the authority may take proceedings in the High Court or, in Scotland, in any court of competent jurisdiction for the purpose of securing compliance with the notice.*

[1397]

NOTES

Repealed by the Pollution Prevention and Control Act 1999, s 6(2), Sch 3, as from a day to be appointed.

25 Onus of proof as regards techniques and evidence

(1) In any proceedings for an offence under section 23(1)(a) above consisting in a failure to comply with the general condition implied in every authorisation by section 7(4) above, it shall be for the accused to prove that there was no better available technique not entailing excessive cost than was in fact used to satisfy the condition.

(2) Where—

(a) an entry is required under section 7 above to be made in any record as to the observance of any condition of an authorisation; and

(b) the entry has not been made;

that fact shall be admissible as evidence that that condition has not been observed.

[(3) Subsection (2) above shall not have effect in relation to any entry required to be made in any record by virtue of a condition of a relevant licence, within the meaning of section 111 of the Environment Act 1995 (which makes corresponding provision in relation to such licences).]

[1398]

NOTES

Repealed by the Pollution Prevention and Control Act 1999, s 6(2), Sch 3, as from a day to be appointed.
Sub-s (3): inserted by the Environment Act 1995, s 111(6).

26 Power of court to order cause of offence to be remedied

(1) Where a person is convicted of an offence under section 23(1)(a) or (c) above in respect of any matters which appear to the court to be matters which it is in his power to remedy, the court may, in addition to or instead of imposing any punishment, order him, within such time as may be fixed by the order, to take such steps as may be specified in the order for remedying those matters.

(2) The time fixed by an order under subsection (1) above may be extended or further extended by order of the court on an application made before the end of the time as originally fixed or as extended under this subsection, as the case may be.

(3) Where a person is ordered under subsection (1) above to remedy any matters, that person shall not be liable under section 23 above in respect of those matters in so far as they continue during the time fixed by the order or any further time allowed under subsection (2) above.

[1399]

NOTES

Repealed by the Pollution Prevention and Control Act 1999, s 6(2), Sch 3, as from a day to be appointed.

27 Power of chief inspector to remedy harm

(1) Where the commission of an offence under section 23(1)(a) or (c) above causes any harm which it is possible to remedy, [the appropriate Agency] may, subject to subsection (2) below—

(a) arrange for any reasonable steps to be taken towards remedying the harm; and

(b) recover the cost of taking those steps from any person convicted of that offence.

(2) [The Environment Agency or SEPA, as the case may be, shall not exercise its] powers under this section except with the approval in writing of the Secretary of State and, where any of the steps are to be taken on or will affect land in the occupation of any person other than the person on whose land the prescribed process is being carried on, with the permission of that person.

[1400]

NOTES

Repealed by the Pollution Prevention and Control Act 1999, s 6(2), Sch 3, as from a day to be appointed.
Sub-ss (1), (2): words in square brackets substituted by the Environment Act 1995, s 120, Sch 22, para 60.
Transfer of functions: see the note to s 2 at **[1383]**.

28 (*Outside the scope of this work.*)

PART II
WASTE ON LAND

Preliminary

29 (*Outside the scope of this work.*)

30 Authorities for purposes of this Part

[(1) Any reference in this Part to a waste regulation authority—

(a) in relation to England and Wales, is a reference to the Environment Agency; and

(b) in relation to Scotland, is a reference to the Scottish Environment Protection Agency;

and any reference in this Part to the area of a waste regulation authority shall accordingly be taken as a reference to the area over which the Environment Agency or the Scottish Environment Protection Agency, as the case may be, exercises its functions or, in the case of any particular function, the function in question.]

(2) For the purposes of this Part the following authorities are waste disposal authorities, namely—

(a) for any non-metropolitan county in England, the county council;

(b) in Greater London, the following—

(i) for the area of a London waste disposal authority, the authority constituted as the waste disposal authority for that area;

(ii) for the City of London, the Common Council;

(iii) for any other London borough, the council of the borough;

(c) in the metropolitan county of Greater Manchester, the following—

(i) for the metropolitan district of Wigan, the district council;

(ii) for all other areas in the county, the authority constituted as the Greater Manchester Waste Disposal Authority;

(d) for the metropolitan county of Merseyside, the authority constituted as the Merseyside Waste Disposal Authority;

(e) for any district in any other metropolitan county in England, the council of the district;

[(f) for any county or county borough in Wales, the council of the county or county borough;]

(g) in Scotland, [a council constituted under section 2 of the Local Government etc (Scotland) Act 1994].

(3) For the purposes of this Part the following authorities are waste collection authorities—

(a) for any district in England … not within Greater London, the council of the district;

(b) in Greater London, the following—

(i) for any London borough, the council of the borough;

(ii) for the City of London, the Common Council;

(iii) for the Temples, the Sub-Treasurer of the Inner Temple and the Under Treasurer of the Middle Temple respectively;

[(bb) for any county or county borough in Wales, the council of the county or county borough;]

(c) in Scotland, [a council constituted under section 2 of the Local Government etc (Scotland) Act 1994].

(4) In this section references to particular authorities having been constituted as waste disposal … authorities are references to their having been so constituted by the Waste Regulation and Disposal (Authorities) Order 1985 made by the Secretary of State under section 10 of the Local Government Act 1985 and the reference to London waste disposal authorities is a reference to the authorities named in Parts I, II, III, IV and V of Schedule 1 to that Order and this section has effect subject to any order made under the said section 10 …

(5) *In this Part "waste disposal contractor" means a person who in the course of a business collects, keeps, treats or disposes of waste, being either—*

(*a*) *a company formed for all or any of those purposes by a waste disposal authority whether in pursuance of section 32 below or otherwise; or*

(*b*) *either a company formed for all or any of those purposes by other persons or a partnership or an individual;*

and "company" has the same meaning as in the Companies Act 1985 [means a company as defined in section 1(1) of the Companies Act 2006] and "formed", in relation to a company formed by other persons, includes the alteration of the objects of the company [alteration of the company's articles so as to add, remove or alter a statement of the company's objects].

(6)–(8) …

[1401]

NOTES

Sub-s (1): substituted by the Environment Act 1995, s 120, Sch 22, para 62(2).

Sub-s (2): para (f) substituted by the Local Government (Wales) Act 1994, s 22(3), Sch 9, para 17(2); in para (g) words in square brackets substituted by the Local Government etc (Scotland) Act 1994, s 180(1), Sch 13, para 167(3).

Sub-s (3): in para (a) words omitted repealed, and para (bb) inserted, by the Local Government (Wales) Act 1994, ss 22(3), 66(8), Sch 9, para 17(3), Sch 18; in para (c) words in square brackets substituted by the Local Government etc (Scotland) Act 1994, s 180(1), Sch 13, para 167(3).

Sub-s (4): words omitted repealed by the Environment Act 1995, s 120, Sch 22, para 62(3), Sch 24.

Sub-s (5): repealed, in relation to England and Wales, by the Clean Neighbourhoods and Environment Act 2005, s 107, Sch 5, Pt 4, subject to savings in SI 2005/2896, art 6, and SI 2006/768, art 5; words "has the same meaning as in the Companies Act 1985" and "alteration of the company's objects" substituted by subsequent words in square brackets by SI 2009/1941, art 2(1), Sch 1, para 120, as from 1 October 2009.

Sub-ss (6)–(8): repealed by the Environment Act 1995, s 120, Sch 22, para 62(4), Sch 24.

31–78 (*In so far as unrepealed, outside the scope of this work.*)

[PART IIA
CONTAMINATED LAND

NOTES

Modifications: this Part is modified by the Radioactive Contaminated Land (Enabling Powers) (England) Regulations 2005, SI 2005/3467, the Radioactive Contaminated Land (Modification of Enactments) (England) Regulations 2006, SI 2006/1379, the Radioactive Contaminated Land (Modification of Enactments) (Wales) Regulations 2006, SI 2006/2988, and the Radioactive Contaminated Land (Scotland) Regulations 2007, SSI 2007/179.

78A Preliminary

(1) The following provisions have effect for the interpretation of this Part.

(2) "Contaminated land" is any land which appears to the local authority in whose area it is situated to be in such a condition, by reason of substances in, on or under the land, that–

(a) significant harm is being caused or there is a significant possibility of such harm being caused; or

(*b*) *pollution of controlled waters is being, or is likely to be, caused;*

[(b) significant pollution of controlled waters is being caused or there is a significant possibility of such pollution being caused;]

and, in determining whether any land appears to be such land, a local authority shall, subject to subsection (5) below, act in accordance with guidance issued by the Secretary of State in accordance with section 78YA below with respect to the manner in which that determination is to be made.

(3) A "special site" is any contaminated land–

(a) which has been designated as such a site by virtue of section 78C(7) or 78D(6) below; and

(b) whose designation as such has not been terminated by the appropriate Agency under section 78Q(4) below.

(4) *"Harm"* [Subject to sub section (4A), "harm"] means harm to the health of living organisms or other interference with the ecological systems of which they form part and, in the case of man, includes harm to his property.

[(4A) "Harm", in relation to the water environment has the same meaning as in section 20(6) of the Water Environment and Water Services (Scotland) Act 2003.]

(5) The questions–

(a) what harm [or pollution of controlled waters] is to be regarded as "significant",

(b) whether the possibility of significant harm [or of significant pollution of controlled waters] being caused is "significant",

(c) *whether pollution of controlled waters is being, or is likely to be caused,*

shall be determined in accordance with guidance issued for the purpose by the Secretary of State in accordance with section 78YA below.

(6) Without prejudice to the guidance that may be issued under subsection (5) above, guidance under paragraph (a) of that subsection may make provision for different degrees of importance to be assigned to, or for the disregard of,–

(a) different descriptions of living organisms or ecological systems[, or of poisonous, noxious or polluting matter or solid waste matter];

(b) different descriptions of places [or controlled waters, or different degrees of pollution]; or

(c) different descriptions of harm to health or property, or other interference;

and guidance under paragraph (b) of that subsection may make provision for different degrees of possibility to be regarded as "significant" (or as not being "significant") in relation to different descriptions of significant harm [or of significant pollution].

(7) "Remediation" means–

(a) the doing of anything for the purpose of assessing the condition of–

(i) the contaminated land in question;

(ii) *any controlled waters* [the water environment] affected by that land; or

(iii) any land adjoining or adjacent to that land;

(b) the doing of any works, the carrying out of any operations or the taking of any steps in relation to any such land or *waters* [the water environment] for the purpose—

(i) of preventing or minimising, or remedying or mitigating the effects of, any significant harm, or any [significant] pollution of *controlled waters* [the water environment], by reason of which the contaminated land is such land; or

(ii) of restoring the land or *waters to their* [water environment to its] former state; or

(c) the making of subsequent inspections from time to time for the purpose of keeping under review the condition of the land or *waters* [the water environment];

and cognate expressions shall be construed accordingly.

(8) *Controlled waters are* [The water environment is] "affected by" contaminated land if (and only if) it appears to the enforcing authority that the contaminated land in question is, for the purposes of subsection (2) above, in such a condition, by reason of substances in, on or under the land, that *pollution of those waters is being, or is likely to be caused* [significant pollution of those waters is being caused or there is a significant possibility of such pollution being caused].

(9) The following expressions have the meaning respectively assigned to them–

"the appropriate Agency" means–

(a) in relation to England and Wales, the Environment Agency;

(b) in relation to Scotland, the Scottish Environment Protection Agency;

"appropriate person" means any person who is an appropriate person, determined in accordance with section 78F below, to bear responsibility for any thing which is to be done by way of remediation in any particular case;

"charging notice" has the meaning given by section 78P(3)(b) below;

"controlled waters"–

(*a*) *in relation to England and Wales, has the same meaning as in Part III of the Water Resources Act 1991 [except that "ground waters" does not include waters contained in underground strata but above the saturation zone]; and*

(*b*) *in relation to Scotland, has the same meaning as in section 30A of the Control of Pollution Act 1974;*

"creditor" has the same meaning as in the Conveyancing and Feudal Reform (Scotland) Act 1970;

"enforcing authority" means–

(a) in relation to a special site, the appropriate Agency;

(b) in relation to contaminated land other than a special site, the local authority in whose area the land is situated;

"heritable security" has the same meaning as in the Conveyancing and Feudal Reform (Scotland) Act 1970;

"local authority" in relation to England and Wales means–

(a) any unitary authority;

(b) any district council, so far as it is not a unitary authority;

(c) the Common Council of the City of London and, as respects the Temples, the Sub-Treasurer of the Inner Temple and the Under-Treasurer of the Middle Temple respectively;

and in relation to Scotland means a council for an area constituted under section 2 of the Local Government etc (Scotland) Act 1994;

"notice" means notice in writing;

"notification" means notification in writing;

"owner", in relation to any land in England and Wales, means a person (other than a mortgagee not in possession) who, whether in his own right or as trustee for any other person, is entitled to receive the rack rent of the land, or, where the land is not let at a rack rent, would be so entitled if it were so let;

"owner", in relation to any land in Scotland, means a person (other than a creditor in a heritable security not in possession of the security subjects) for the time being entitled to receive or who would, if the land were let, be entitled to receive, the rents of the land in connection with which the word is used and includes a trustee, factor, guardian or curator and in the case of public or municipal land includes the persons to whom the management of the land is entrusted;

["pollution", in relation to the water environment, means the direct or indirect introduction, as a result of human activity, of substances into the water environment, or any part of it, which may give rise to any harm;]

"pollution of controlled waters" means the entry into controlled waters of any poisonous, noxious or polluting matter or any solid waste matter;

"prescribed" means prescribed by regulations;

"regulations" means regulations made by the Secretary of State;

"remediation declaration" has the meaning given by section 78H(6) below;

"remediation notice" has the meaning given by section 78E(1) below;

"remediation statement" has the meaning given by section 78H(7) below;

"required to be designated as a special site" shall be construed in accordance with section 78C(8) below;

"substance" means any natural or artificial substance, whether in solid or liquid form or in the form of a gas or vapour;

"unitary authority" means–

(a) the council of a county, so far as it is the council of an area for which there are no district councils;
(b) the council of any district comprised in an area for which there is no county council;
(c) the council of a London borough;
(d) the council of a county borough in Wales;

["the water environment" has the same meaning as in section 3 of the Water Environment and Water Services (Scotland) Act 2003].]

[1402]

NOTES

Pt IIA (this section and ss 78B–78YC) inserted by the Environment Act 1995, s 57.

Sub-s (2): para (b) substituted in relation to England and Wales, as from a day to be appointed, by the Water Act 2003, s 86(1), (2)(a), and in relation to Scotland by SSI 2005/658, reg 2(1), (3)(a).

Sub-s (4): word ""Harm"" in italics repealed and subsequent words in square brackets substituted, in relation to Scotland, by SSI 2005/658, reg 2(1), (3)(b).

Sub-s (4A): inserted, in relation to Scotland, by SSI 2005/658, reg 2(1), (3)(c).

Sub-s (5): in paras (a), (b) words in square brackets inserted, and para (c) repealed in relation to England and Wales, as from a day to be appointed, by the Water Act 2003, s 86(1), (2)(b), 101(2), Sch 9, Pt 3, and in relation to Scotland by SSI 2005/658, reg 2(1), (3)(d).

Sub-s (6): words in square brackets inserted in relation to England and Wales, as from a day to be appointed, by the Water Act 2003, s 86(1), (2)(c), and in relation to Scotland by SSI 2005/658, art 2(1), (3)(e).

Sub-s (7): in para (a)(ii) words "any controlled waters" in italics repealed and subsequent words in square bracket substituted, in relation to Scotland, by SSI 2005/658, reg 2(1), (2)(f); in para (b) word "waters" in italics repealed and subsequent words in square brackets substituted, in relation to Scotland, by SSI 2005/658, reg 2(1), (3)(g); in para (b)(i) word "significant" in square brackets inserted in relation to England and Wales, as from a day to be appointed, by the Water Act 2003, s 86(1), (2)(d) and in relation to Scotland by SSI 2005/658, reg 2(1), (3)(g); in para (b)(i) words "controlled waters" in italics repealed and subsequent words in square brackets substituted, in relation to Scotland, by SSI 2005/658, reg 2(1), (2); in para (b)(ii) words "waters to their" in italics repealed and subsequent words in square brackets substituted, in relation to Scotland, by SSI 2005/658, reg 2(1), (3)(i); in para (c) word "waters" in italics repealed and subsequent words in square brackets substituted, in relation to Scotland, by SSI 2005/658, reg 2(1), (3)(j).

Sub-s (8): words "Controlled waters are" in italics repealed and subsequent words in square brackets substituted, in relation to Scotland, by SSI 2005/658, reg 2(1), (3)(k)(i); words "pollution of those waters is being, or is likely to be caused" in italics repealed and subsequent words in square brackets substituted in relation to England and Wales, as from a day to be appointed, by the Water Act 2003, s 86(1), (2)(e), and in relation to Scotland by SSI 2005/658, reg 2(1), (3)(k)(ii).

Sub-s (9): definitions "controlled waters" and "pollution of controlled waters" repealed, definitions "pollution" and "the water environment" inserted in relation to Scotland, by SSI 2005/658, reg 2(1), (3)(l); in definition "controlled waters" in para (a) words in square brackets inserted by the Water Act 2003, s 86(1), (2)(f).

Transfer of functions: see the note to s 2 at **[1383]**.

See further, the application of this section, with modifications, in so far as it applies in relation to and for the purposes of dealing with harm attributable to any radioactivity possessed by any substance, to the Isles of Scilly: the Environmental Protection Act 1990 (Isles of Scilly) Order 2006, SI 2006/1381, art 2.

[78B Identification of contaminated land

(1) Every local authority shall cause its area to be inspected from time to time for the purpose–
(a) of identifying contaminated land; and
(b) of enabling the authority to decide whether any such land is land which is required to be designated as a special site.

(2) In performing its functions under subsection (1) above a local authority shall act in accordance with any guidance issued for the purpose by the Secretary of State in accordance with section 78YA below.

(3) If a local authority identifies any contaminated land in its area, it shall give notice of that fact to–
(a) the appropriate Agency;
(b) the owner of the land;
(c) any person who appears to the authority to be in occupation of the whole or any part of the land; and
(d) each person who appears to the authority to be an appropriate person;

and any notice given under this subsection shall state by virtue of which of paragraphs (a) to (d) above it is given.

(4) If, at any time after a local authority has given any person a notice pursuant to subsection (3)(d) above in respect of any land, it appears to the enforcing authority that another person is an appropriate person, the enforcing authority shall give notice to that other person–
(a) of the fact that the local authority has identified the land in question as contaminated land; and
(b) that he appears to the enforcing authority to be an appropriate person.]

[1403]

NOTES

Inserted as noted to s 78A at **[1402]**.
Transfer of functions: see the note to s 2 at **[1383]**.

[78C Identification and designation of special sites

(1) If at any time it appears to a local authority that any contaminated land in its area might be land which is required to be designated as a special site, the authority–

(a) shall decide whether or not the land is land which is required to be so designated; and

(b) if the authority decides that the land is land which is required to be so designated, shall give notice of that decision to the relevant persons.

(2) For the purposes of this section, "the relevant persons" at any time in the case of any land are the persons who at that time fall within paragraphs (a) to (d) below, that is to say–

(a) the appropriate Agency;

(b) the owner of the land;

(c) any person who appears to the local authority concerned to be in occupation of the whole or any part of the land; and

(d) each person who appears to that authority to be an appropriate person.

(3) Before making a decision under paragraph (a) of subsection (1) above in any particular case, a local authority shall request the advice of the appropriate Agency, and in making its decision shall have regard to any advice given by that Agency in response to the request.

(4) If at any time the appropriate Agency considers that any contaminated land is land which is required to be designated as a special site, that Agency may give notice of that fact to the local authority in whose area the land is situated.

(5) Where notice under subsection (4) above is given to a local authority, the authority shall decide whether the land in question–

(a) is land which is required to be designated as a special site, or

(b) is not land which is required to be so designated,

and shall give notice of that decision to the relevant persons.

(6) Where a local authority makes a decision falling within subsection (1)(b) or (5)(a) above, the decision shall, subject to section 78D below, take effect on the day after whichever of the following events first occurs, that is to say–

(a) the expiration of the period of twenty-one days beginning with the day on which the notice required by virtue of subsection (1)(b) or, as the case may be, (5)(a) above is given to the appropriate Agency; or

(b) if the appropriate Agency gives notification to the local authority in question that it agrees with the decision, the giving of that notification;

and where a decision takes effect by virtue of this subsection, the local authority shall give notice of that fact to the relevant persons.

(7) Where a decision that any land is land which is required to be designated as a special site takes effect in accordance with subsection (6) above, the notice given under subsection (1)(b) or, as the case may be, (5)(a) above shall have effect, as from the time when the decision takes effect, as the designation of that land as such a site.

(8) For the purposes of this Part, land is required to be designated as a special site if, and only if, it is land of a description prescribed for the purposes of this subsection.

(9) Regulations under subsection (8) above may make different provision for different cases or circumstances or different areas or localities and may, in particular, describe land by reference to the area or locality in which it is situated.

(10) Without prejudice to the generality of his power to prescribe any description of land for the purposes of subsection (8) above, the Secretary of State, in deciding whether to prescribe a particular description of contaminated land for those purposes, may, in particular, have regard to–

(a) whether land of the description in question appears to him to be land which is likely to be in such a condition, by reason of substances in, on or under the land that–

(i) serious harm would or might be caused, or

(ii) serious pollution of controlled waters would *be, or would be likely to be, caused* [or might be caused]; or

(b) whether the appropriate Agency is likely to have expertise in dealing with the kind of significant harm, or [significant] pollution of *controlled waters* [the water environment], by reason of which land of the description in question is contaminated land.]

[1404]

NOTES

Inserted as noted to s 78A at **[1402]**.

Sub-s (10): in para (a)(ii), words "be, or would be likely to be, caused" in italics repealed and subsequent words in square brackets substituted in relation to England and Wales, as from a day to be appointed, by the Water Act 2003, s 86(1), (3)(a), and in relation to Scotland by SSI 2005/658, reg 2(1), (4)(a); in para (b) word "significant" in square brackets inserted in relation to England and Wales, as from a day to be appointed, by the Water Act 2003, s 86(1), (3)(b), and in relation to Scotland by SSI 2005/658, art 2(1), (4)(b); in para (b) words "controlled waters" in italics repealed and subsequent words in square brackets substituted, in relation to Scotland, by SSI 2005/658, reg 2(1), (2).

Transfer of functions: see the note to s 2 at **[1383]**.

Regulations: the Contaminated Land (Scotland) Regulations 2000, SSI 2000/178; the Contaminated Land (England) Regulations 2006, SI 2006/1380; the Contaminated Land (Wales) Regulations 2006, SI 2006/2989.

[78D Referral of special site decisions to the Secretary of State

(1) In any case where–

(a) a local authority gives notice of a decision to the appropriate Agency pursuant to subsection (1)(b) or (5)(b) of section 78C above, but

(b) before the expiration of the period of twenty-one days beginning with the day on which that notice is so given, that Agency gives the local authority notice that it disagrees with the decision, together with a statement of its reasons for disagreeing,

the authority shall refer the decision to the Secretary of State and shall send to him a statement of its reasons for reaching the decision.

(2) Where the appropriate Agency gives notice to a local authority under paragraph (b) of subsection (1) above, it shall also send to the Secretary of State a copy of the notice and of the statement given under that paragraph.

(3) Where a local authority refers a decision to the Secretary of State under subsection (1) above, it shall give notice of that fact to the relevant persons.

(4) Where a decision of a local authority is referred to the Secretary of State under subsection (1) above, he–

(a) may confirm or reverse the decision with respect to the whole or any part of the land to which it relates; and

(b) shall give notice of his decision on the referral–

(i) to the relevant persons; and

(ii) to the local authority.

(5) Where a decision of a local authority is referred to the Secretary of State under subsection (1) above, the decision shall not take effect until the day after that on which the Secretary of State gives the notice required by subsection (4) above to the persons there mentioned and shall then take effect as confirmed or reversed by him.

(6) Where a decision which takes effect in accordance with subsection (5) above is to the effect that at least some land is land which is required to be designated as a special site, the notice given under subsection (4)(b) above shall have effect, as from the time when the decision takes effect, as the designation of that land as such a site.

(7) In this section "the relevant persons" has the same meaning as in section 78C above.]

[1405]

NOTES

Inserted as noted to s 78A at **[1402]**.

Transfer of functions: see the note to s 2 at **[1383]**.

[78E Duty of enforcing authority to require remediation of contaminated land etc

(1) In any case where–

(a) any land has been designated as a special site by virtue of section 78C(7) or 78D(6) above, or

(b) a local authority has identified any contaminated land (other than a special site) in its area,

the enforcing authority shall, in accordance with such procedure as may be prescribed and subject to the following provisions of this Part, serve on each person who is an appropriate person a notice (in this Part referred to as a "remediation notice") specifying what that person is to do by way of remediation and the periods within which he is required to do each of the things so specified.

(2) Different remediation notices requiring the doing of different things by way of remediation may be served on different persons in consequence of the presence of different substances in, on or under any land or *waters* [the water environment].

(3) Where two or more persons are appropriate persons in relation to any particular thing which is to be done by way of remediation, the remediation notice served on each of them shall state the proportion, determined under section 78F(7) below, of the cost of doing that thing which each of them respectively is liable to bear.

(4) The only things by way of remediation which the enforcing authority may do, or require to be done, under or by virtue of this Part are things which it considers reasonable, having regard to–

(a) the cost which is likely to be involved; and

(b) the seriousness of the harm, or [of the] pollution of *controlled waters* [the water environment], in question.

(5) In determining for any purpose of this Part–

(a) what is to be done (whether by an appropriate person, the enforcing authority or any other person) by way of remediation in any particular case,

(b) the standard to which any land *is, or waters are* [, or the water environment is], to be remediated pursuant to the notice, or

(c) what is, or is not, to be regarded as reasonable for the purposes of subsection (4) above,

the enforcing authority shall have regard to any guidance issued for the purpose by the Secretary of State.

(6) Regulations may make provision for or in connection with–

(a) the form or content of remediation notices; or

(b) any steps of a procedural nature which are to be taken in connection with, or in consequence of, the service of a remediation notice.]

[1406]

NOTES

Inserted as noted to s 78A at **[1402]**.

Sub-s (2): word "waters" in italics repealed and subsequent words in square brackets substituted, in relation to Scotland, by SSI 2005/658, reg 2(1), (5)(a).

Sub-s (4): in para (b) first words in square brackets inserted in relation to England and Wales, as from a day to be appointed, by the Water Act 2003, s 86(1), (4), and in relation to Scotland by SSI 2005/658, reg 2(1), (5)(b); words "controlled waters" in italics repealed and subsequent words in square brackets substituted, in relation to Scotland, by SSI 2005/658, reg 2(1), (2).

Sub-s (5): in para (b) words "is, or waters are" in italics repealed and subsequent words in square brackets substituted, in relation to Scotland, by SSI 2005/658, reg 2(1), (5)(c).

Transfer of functions: see the note to s 2 at **[1383]**.

Regulations: the Contaminated Land (Scotland) Regulations 2000, SSI 2000/178; the Contaminated Land (England) Regulations 2006, SI 2006/1380; the Contaminated Land (Wales) Regulations 2006, SI 2006/2989.

[78F Determination of the appropriate person to bear responsibility for remediation

(1) This section has effect for the purpose of determining who is the appropriate person to bear responsibility for any particular thing which the enforcing authority determines is to be done by way of remediation in any particular case.

(2) Subject to the following provisions of this section, any person, or any of the persons, who caused or knowingly permitted the substances, or any of the substances, by reason of which the contaminated land in question is such land to be in, on or under that land is an appropriate person.

(3) A person shall only be an appropriate person by virtue of subsection (2) above in relation to things which are to be done by way of remediation which are to any extent referable to substances which he caused or knowingly permitted to be present in, on or under the contaminated land in question.

(4) If no person has, after reasonable inquiry, been found who is by virtue of subsection (2) above an appropriate person to bear responsibility for the things which are to be done by way of remediation, the owner or occupier for the time being of the contaminated land in question is an appropriate person.

(5) If, in consequence of subsection (3) above, there are things which are to be done by way of remediation in relation to which no person has, after reasonable inquiry, been found who is an appropriate person by virtue of subsection (2) above, the owner or occupier for the time being of the contaminated land in question is an appropriate person in relation to those things.

(6) Where two or more persons would, apart from this subsection, be appropriate persons in relation to any particular thing which is to be done by way of remediation, the enforcing authority shall determine in accordance with guidance issued for the purpose by the Secretary of State whether any, and if so which, of them is to be treated as not being an appropriate person in relation to that thing.

(7) Where two or more persons are appropriate persons in relation to any particular thing which is to be done by way of remediation, they shall be liable to bear the cost of doing that thing in proportions determined by the enforcing authority in accordance with guidance issued for the purpose by the Secretary of State.

(8) Any guidance issued for the purposes of subsection (6) or (7) above shall be issued in accordance with section 78YA below.

(9) A person who has caused or knowingly permitted any substance ("substance A") to be in, on or under any land shall also be taken for the purposes of this section to have caused or knowingly

permitted there to be in, on or under that land any substance which is there as a result of a chemical reaction or biological process affecting substance A.

(10) A thing which is to be done by way of remediation may be regarded for the purposes of this Part as referable to the presence of any substance notwithstanding that the thing in question would not have to be done–

(a) in consequence only of the presence of that substance in any quantity; or

(b) in consequence only of the quantity of that substance which any particular person caused or knowingly permitted to be present.]

[1407]

NOTES

Inserted as noted to s 78A at **[1402]**.

Transfer of functions: see the note to s 2 at **[1383]**.

[78G Grant of, and compensation for, rights of entry etc

(1) A remediation notice may require an appropriate person to do things by way of remediation, notwithstanding that he is not entitled to do those things.

(2) Any person whose consent is required before any thing required by a remediation notice may be done shall grant, or join in granting, such rights in relation to any of the relevant land or *waters* [water environment] as will enable the appropriate person to comply with any requirements imposed by the remediation notice.

(3) Before serving a remediation notice, the enforcing authority shall reasonably endeavour to consult every person who appears to the authority–

(a) to be the owner or occupier of any of the relevant land or *waters* [water environment], and

(b) to be a person who might be required by subsection (2) above to grant, or join in granting, any rights,

concerning the rights which that person may be so required to grant.

(4) Subsection (3) above shall not preclude the service of a remediation notice in any case where it appears to the enforcing authority that the contaminated land in question is in such a condition, by reason of substances in, on or under the land, that there is imminent danger of serious harm, or serious pollution of *controlled waters* [the water environment], being caused.

(5) A person who grants, or joins in granting, any rights pursuant to subsection (2) above shall be entitled, on making an application within such period as may be prescribed and in such manner as may be prescribed to such person as may be prescribed, to be paid by the appropriate person compensation of such amount as may be determined in such manner as may be prescribed.

(6) Without prejudice to the generality of the regulations that may be made by virtue of subsection (5) above, regulations by virtue of that subsection may make such provision in relation to compensation under this section as may be made by regulations by virtue of subsection (4) of section 35A above in relation to compensation under that section.

(7) In this section, "relevant land or waters" means–

(a) the contaminated land in question;

(b) any controlled waters affected by that land; or

(c) any land adjoining or adjacent to that land or those waters.

[(7) In this section, "relevant land or water environment" means—

(a) the contaminated land in question;

(b) the water environment affected by that land; or

(c) any land adjoining or adjacent to that land or water environment.]]

[1408]

NOTES

Inserted as noted to s 78A at **[1402]**.

Sub-s (2): word "waters" in italics repealed and subsequent words in square brackets substituted, in relation to Scotland, by SSI 2005/658, reg 2(1), (6)(a).

Sub-s (3): in para (a) word "waters" in italics repealed and subsequent words in square brackets substituted, in relation to Scotland, by SSI 2005/658, reg 2(1), (6)(b).

Sub-s (4): words "controlled waters" in italics repealed and subsequent words in square brackets substituted, in relation to Scotland, by SSI 2005/658, reg 2(1), (2).

Sub-s (7): substituted, in relation to Scotland, by SSI 2005/658, reg 2(1), (6)(c).

Transfer of functions: see the note to s 2 at **[1383]**.

Regulations: the Contaminated Land (Scotland) Regulations 2000, SSI 2000/178; the Contaminated Land (England) Regulations 2006, SI 2006/1380; the Contaminated Land (Wales) Regulations 2006, SI 2006/2989.

[78H Restrictions and prohibitions on serving remediation notices

(1) Before serving a remediation notice, the enforcing authority shall reasonably endeavour to consult–

(a) the person on whom the notice is to be served,

(b) the owner of any land to which the notice relates,

(c) any person who appears to that authority to be in occupation of the whole or any part of the land, and

(d) any person of such other description as may be prescribed,

concerning what is to be done by way of remediation.

(2) Regulations may make provision for, or in connection with, steps to be taken for the purposes of subsection (1) above.

(3) No remediation notice shall be served on any person by reference to any contaminated land during any of the following periods, that is to say–

(a) the period–

(i) beginning with the identification of the contaminated land in question pursuant to section 78B(1) above, and

(ii) ending with the expiration of the period of three months beginning with the day on which the notice required by subsection (3)(d) or, as the case may be, (4) of section 78B above is given to that person in respect of that land;

(b) if a decision falling within paragraph (b) of section 78C(1) above is made in relation to the contaminated land in question, the period beginning with the making of the decision and ending with the expiration of the period of three months beginning with–

(i) in a case where the decision is not referred to the Secretary of State under section 78D above, the day on which the notice required by section 78C(6) above is given, or

(ii) in a case where the decision is referred to the Secretary of State under section 78D above, the day on which he gives the notice required by subsection (4)(b) of that section;

(c) if the appropriate Agency gives a notice under subsection (4) of section 78C above to a local authority in relation to the contaminated land in question, the period beginning with the day on which that notice is given and ending with the expiration of the period of three months beginning with–

(i) in a case where notice is given under subsection (6) of that section, the day on which that notice is given;

(ii) in a case where the authority makes a decision falling within subsection (5)(b) of that section and the appropriate Agency fails to give notice under paragraph (b) of section 78D(1) above, the day following the expiration of the period of twenty-one days mentioned in that paragraph; or

(iii) in a case where the authority makes a decision falling within section 78C(5)(b) above which is referred to the Secretary of State under section 78D above, the day on which the Secretary of State gives the notice required by subsection (4)(b) of that section.

(4) Neither subsection (1) nor subsection (3) above shall preclude the service of a remediation notice in any case where it appears to the enforcing authority that the land in question is in such a condition, by reason of substances in, on or under the land, that there is imminent danger of serious harm, or serious pollution of *controlled waters* [the water environment], being caused.

(5) The enforcing authority shall not serve a remediation notice on a person if and so long as any one or more of the following conditions is for the time being satisfied in the particular case, that is to say–

(a) the authority is satisfied, in consequence of section 78E(4) and (5) above, that there is nothing by way of remediation which could be specified in a remediation notice served on that person;

(b) the authority is satisfied that appropriate things are being, or will be, done by way of remediation without the service of a remediation notice on that person;

(c) it appears to the authority that the person on whom the notice would be served is the authority itself; or

(d) the authority is satisfied that the powers conferred on it by section 78N below to do what is appropriate by way of remediation are exercisable.

(6) Where the enforcing authority is precluded by virtue of section 78E(4) or (5) above from specifying in a remediation notice any particular thing by way of remediation which it would otherwise have specified in such a notice, the authority shall prepare and publish a document (in this Part referred to as a "remediation declaration") which shall record–

(a) the reasons why the authority would have specified that thing; and

(b) the grounds on which the authority is satisfied that it is precluded from specifying that thing in such a notice.

(7) In any case where the enforcing authority is precluded, by virtue of paragraph (b), (c) or (d) of subsection (5) above, from serving a remediation notice, the responsible person shall prepare and publish a document (in this Part referred to as a "remediation statement") which shall record–

(a) the things which are being, have been, or are expected to be, done by way of remediation in the particular case;

(b) the name and address of the person who is doing, has done, or is expected to do, each of those things; and

(c) the periods within which each of those things is being, or is expected to be, done.

(8) For the purposes of subsection (7) above, the "responsible person" is–

(a) in a case where the condition in paragraph (b) of subsection (5) above is satisfied, the person who is doing or has done, or who the enforcing authority is satisfied will do, the things there mentioned; or

(b) in a case where the condition in paragraph (c) or (d) of that subsection is satisfied, the enforcing authority.

(9) If a person who is required by virtue of subsection (8)(a) above to prepare and publish a remediation statement fails to do so within a reasonable time after the date on which a remediation notice specifying the things there mentioned could, apart from subsection (5) above, have been served, the enforcing authority may itself prepare and publish the statement and may recover its reasonable costs of doing so from that person.

(10) Where the enforcing authority has been precluded by virtue only of subsection (5) above from serving a remediation notice on an appropriate person but–

(a) none of the conditions in that subsection is for the time being satisfied in the particular case, and

(b) the authority is not precluded by any other provision of this Part from serving a remediation notice on that appropriate person,

the authority shall serve a remediation notice on that person; and any such notice may be so served without any further endeavours by the authority to consult persons pursuant to subsection (1) above, if and to the extent that that person has bean consulted pursuant to that subsection concerning the things which will be specified in the notice.]

[1409]

NOTES

Inserted as noted to s 78A at **[1402]**.

Sub-s (4): words "controlled waters" in italics repealed and subsequent words in square brackets substituted, in relation to Scotland, by SSI 2005/658, reg 2(1), (2).

Transfer of functions: see the note to s 2 at **[1383]**.

[78J Restrictions on liability relating to the pollution of controlled waters

(1) This section applies where any land is contaminated land by virtue of paragraph (b) of subsection (2) of section 78A above (whether or not the land is also contaminated land by virtue of paragraph (a) of that subsection).

(2) Where this section applies, no remediation notice given in consequence of the land in question being contaminated land shall require a person who is an appropriate person by virtue of section 78F(4) or (5) above to do anything by way of remediation to that or any other land, or *any waters* [the water environment], which he could not have been required to do by such a notice had paragraph (b) of section 78A(2) above (and all other references to pollution of *controlled waters* [the water environment]) been omitted from this Part.

(3) If, in a case where this section applies, a person permits, has permitted, or might permit, water from an abandoned mine or part of a mine–

(a) to enter *any controlled waters* [the water environment], or

(b) to reach a place from which it is or, as the case may be, was likely, in the opinion of the enforcing authority, to enter *such waters* [the water environment],

no remediation notice shall require him in consequence to do anything by way of remediation (whether to the contaminated land in question or to any other land *or waters* [or the water environment]) which he could not have been required to do by such a notice had paragraph (b) of section 78A(2) above (and all other references to pollution of *controlled waters* [the water environment]) been omitted from this Part.

(4) Subsection (3) above shall not apply to the owner or former operator of any mine or part of a mine if the mine or part in question became abandoned after 31st December 1999.

(5) In determining for the purposes of subsection (4) above whether a mine or part of a mine became abandoned before, on or after 31st December 1999 in a case where the mine or part has become abandoned on two or more occasions, of which–

(a) at least one falls on or before that date, and

(b) at least one falls after that date,

the mine or part shall be regarded as becoming abandoned after that date (but without prejudice to the operation of subsection (3) above in relation to that mine or part at, or in relation to, any time before the first of those occasions which falls after that date).

(6) Where, immediately before a part of a mine becomes abandoned, that part is the only part of the mine not falling to be regarded as abandoned for the time being, the abandonment of that part shall not be regarded for the purposes of subsection (4) or (5) above as constituting the abandonment of the mine, but only of that part of it.

(7) Nothing in subsection (2) or (3) above prevents the enforcing authority from doing anything by way of remediation under section 78N below which it could have done apart from that subsection, but the authority shall not be entitled under section 78P below to recover from any person any part of the cost incurred by the authority in doing by way of remediation anything which it is precluded by subsection (2) or (3) above from requiring that person to do.

(8) In this section "mine" has the same meaning as in the Mines and Quarries Act 1954.]

[1410]

NOTES

Inserted as noted to s 78A at **[1402]**.

Sub-ss (2), (3): words in italics repealed and subsequent words in square brackets substituted, in relation to Scotland, by SSI 2005/658, reg 2(1), (2), (7).

[78K Liability in respect of contaminating substances which escape to other land]

[(1) A person who has caused or knowingly permitted any substances to be in, on or under any land shall also be taken for the purposes of this Part to have caused or, as the case may be, knowingly permitted those substances to be in, on or under any other land to which they appear to have escaped.

(2) Subsections (3) and (4) below apply in any case where it appears that any substances are or have been in, on or under any land (in this section referred to as "land A") as a result of their escape, whether directly or indirectly, from other land in, on or under which a person caused or knowingly permitted them to be.

(3) Where this subsection applies, no remediation notice shall require a person–

(a) who is the owner or occupier of land A, and

(b) who has not caused or knowingly permitted the substances in question to be in, on or under that land,

to do anything by way of remediation to any land *or waters* [or the water environment] (other than land *or waters* [or the water environment] of which he is the owner or occupier) in consequence of land A appearing to be in such a condition, by reason of the presence of those substances in, on or under it, that significant harm *is being caused, or there is a significant possibility of such harm being caused, or that pollution of controlled waters is being, or is likely to be caused* [, or significant pollution of controlled waters, is being caused, or there is a significant possibility of such harm or pollution being caused].

(4) Where this subsection applies, no remediation notice shall require a person–

(a) who is the owner or occupier of land A, and

(b) who has not caused or knowingly permitted the substances in question to be in, on or under that land,

to do anything by way of remediation in consequence of any further land in, on or under which those substances or any of them appear to be or to have been present as a result of their escape from land A ("land B") appearing to be in such a condition; by reason of the presence of those substances in, on or under it, that significant harm *is being caused, or there is a significant possibility of such harm being caused, or that pollution of controlled waters is being, or is likely to be caused* [, or significant pollution of controlled waters, is being caused, or there is a significant possibility of such harm or pollution being caused], unless he is also the owner or occupier of land B.

(5) In any case where–

(a) a person ("person A") has caused or knowingly permitted any substances to be in, on, or under any land,

(b) another person ("person B") who has not caused or knowingly permitted those substances to be in, on or under that land becomes the owner or occupier of that land, and

(c) the substances, or any of the substances, mentioned in paragraph (a) above appear to have escaped to other land,

no remediation notice shall require person B to do anything by way of remediation to that other land in consequence of the apparent acts or omissions of person A, except to the extent that person B caused or knowingly permitted the escape.

(6) Nothing in subsection (3), (4) or (5) above prevents the enforcing authority from doing anything by way of remediation under section 78N below which it could have done apart from that

subsection, but the authority shall not be entitled under section 78P below to recover from any person any part of the cost incurred by the authority in doing by way of remediation anything which it is precluded by subsection (3), (4) or (5) above from requiring that person to do.

(7) In this section, "appear" means appear to the enforcing authority, and cognate expressions shall be construed accordingly.]

[1411]

NOTES

Inserted as noted to s 78A at **[1402]**.

Sub-s (3): words "or waters" in italics in both places they occur repealed and subsequent words in square brackets substituted, in relation to Scotland, by SSI 2005/658, reg 2(1), (8)(a)(i).

Sub-ss (3), (4): words from "is being caused" to "to be caused" in italics repealed and subsequent words in square brackets substituted in relation to England and Wales, as from a day to be appointed, by the Water Act 2003, s 86(1), (5), and in relation to Scotland by SSI 2005/658, reg 2(1), (8)(a)(ii), (b).

[78L Appeals against remediation notices

(1) A person on whom a remediation notice is served may, within the period of twenty-one days beginning with the day on which the notice is served, appeal against the notice–

(*a*) *if it was served by a local authority, to a magistrates' court or, in Scotland, to the sheriff by way of summary application; or*

(*b*) *if it was served by the appropriate Agency, to the Secretary of State;*

[(a) if it was served by a local authority in England, or served by the Environment Agency in relation to land in England, to the Secretary of State;

(b) if it was served by a local authority in Wales, or served by the Environment Agency in relation to land in Wales, to the National Assembly for Wales;]

and in the following provisions of this section "the appellate authority" means *the magistrates' court, the sheriff or the Secretary of State, as the case may be* [the Secretary of State or the National Assembly for Wales, as the case may be].

(2) On any appeal under subsection (1) above the appellate authority–

(a) shall quash the notice, if it is satisfied that there is a material defect in the notice; but

(b) subject to that, may confirm the remediation notice, with or without modification, or quash it.

(3) Where an appellate authority confirms a remediation notice, with or without modification, it may extend the period specified in the notice for doing what the notice requires to be done.

(4) Regulations may make provision with respect to–

(a) the grounds on which appeals under subsection (1) above may be made;

(b) *the cases in which, grounds on which, court or tribunal to which, or person at whose instance, an appeal against a decision of a magistrates' court or sheriff court in pursuance of an appeal under subsection (1) above shall lie*; or

(c) the procedure on an appeal under subsection (1) above *or on an appeal by virtue of paragraph (b) above*.

(5) Regulations under subsection (4) above may (among other things)–

(a) include provisions comparable to those in section 290 of the Public Health Act 1936 (appeals against notices requiring the execution of works);

(b) prescribe the cases in which a remediation notice is, or is not, to be suspended until the appeal is decided, or until some other stage in the proceedings;

(c) prescribe the cases in which the decision on an appeal may in some respects be less favourable to the appellant than the remediation notice against which he is appealing;

(d) prescribe the cases in which the appellant may claim that a remediation notice should have been served on some other person and prescribe the procedure to be followed in those cases;

(e) make provision as respects–

(i) the particulars to be included in the notice of appeal;

(ii) the persons on whom notice of appeal is to be served and the particulars, if any, which are to accompany the notice; and

(iii) the abandonment of an appeal;

(f) make different provision for different cases or classes of case.

(6) This section, *so far as relating to appeals to the Secretary of State*, is subject to section 114 of the Environment Act 1995 (delegation or reference of appeals etc).]

[1412]

NOTES

Inserted as noted to s 78A at **[1402]**.

Sub-s (1): paras (a), (b) substituted and words from "the magistrates' court" to the end repealed and subsequent words in square brackets substituted, in relation to England and Wales, by the Clean Neighbourhoods and Environment Act 2005, s 104(1)–(3), (7); for effect see s 104(6) thereof.

Sub-s (4): para (b), and words in italics in para (c) repealed, in relation to England and Wales, by the Clean Neighbourhoods and Environment Act 2005, ss 104(1), (4), (7), 107, Sch 5, Pt 10; for effect see s 104(6) thereof.

Sub-s (6): words in italics repealed, in relation to England and Wales, by the Clean Neighbourhoods and Environment Act 2005, ss 104(1), (5), (7), 107, Sch 5, Pt 10; for effect see s 104(6) thereof.

Transfer of functions: see the note to s 2 at **[1383]**.

Regulations: the Contaminated Land (Scotland) Regulations 2000, SSI 2000/178; the Contaminated Land (England) Regulations 2006, SI 2006/1380; the Contaminated Land (Wales) Regulations 2006, SI 2006/2989.

[78M Offences of not complying with a remediation notice

(1) If a person on whom an enforcing authority serves a remediation notice fails, without reasonable excuse, to comply with any of the requirements of the notice, he shall be guilty of an offence.

(2) Where the remediation notice in question is one which was required by section 78E(3) above to state, in relation to the requirement which has not been complied with, the proportion of the cost involved which the person charged with the offence is liable to bear, it shall be a defence for that person to prove that the only reason why he has not complied with the requirement is that one or more of the other persons who are liable to bear a proportion of that cost refused, or was not able, to comply with the requirement.

(3) Except in a case falling within subsection (4) below, a person who commits an offence under subsection (1) above shall be liable, on summary conviction, to a fine not exceeding level 5 on the standard scale and to a further fine of an amount equal to one-tenth of level 5 on the standard scale for each day on which the failure continues after conviction of the offence and before the enforcing authority has begun to exercise its powers by virtue of section 78N(3)(c) below.

(4) A person who commits an offence under subsection (1) above in a case where the contaminated land to which the remediation notice relates is industrial, trade or business premises shall be liable on summary conviction to a fine not exceeding £20,000 or such greater sum as the Secretary of State may from time to time by order substitute and to a further fine of an amount equal to one-tenth of that sum for each day on which the failure continues after conviction of the offence and before the enforcing authority has begun to exercise its powers by virtue of section 78N(3)(c) below.

(5) If the enforcing authority is of the opinion that proceedings for an offence under this section would afford an ineffectual remedy against a person who has failed to comply with any of the requirements of a remediation notice which that authority has served on him, that authority may take proceedings in the High Court or, in Scotland, in any court of competent jurisdiction, for the purpose of securing compliance with the remediation notice.

(6) In this section, "industrial, trade or business premises" means premises used for any industrial, trade or business purposes or premises not so used on which matter is burnt in connection with any industrial, trade or business process, and premises are used for industrial purposes where they are used for the purposes of any treatment or process as well as where they are used for the purpose of manufacturing.

(7) No order shall be made under subsection (4) above unless a draft of the order has been laid before, and approved by a resolution of, each House of Parliament.]

[1413]

NOTES

Inserted as noted to s 78A at **[1402]**.

Transfer of functions: see the note to s 2 at **[1383]**.

[78N Powers of the enforcing authority to carry out remediation

(1) Where this section applies, the enforcing authority shall itself have power, in a case falling within paragraph (a) or (b) of section 78E(1) above, to do what is appropriate by way of remediation to the relevant land or *waters* [the water environment].

(2) Subsection (1) above shall not confer power on the enforcing authority to do anything by way of remediation if the authority would, in the particular case, be precluded by section 78YB below from serving a remediation notice requiring that thing to be done.

(3) This section applies in each of the following cases, that is to say—

(a) where the enforcing authority considers it necessary to do anything itself by way of remediation for the purpose of preventing the occurrence of any serious harm, or serious pollution of *controlled waters* [the water environment], of which there is imminent danger;

(b) where an appropriate person has entered into a written agreement with the enforcing authority for that authority to do, at the cost of that person, that which he would otherwise be required to do under this Part by way of remediation;

(c) where a person on whom the enforcing authority serves a remediation notice fails to comply with any of the requirements of the notice;

(d) where the enforcing authority is precluded by section 78J or 78K above from including something by way of remediation in a remediation notice;

(e) where the enforcing authority considers that, were it to do some particular thing by way of remediation, it would decide, by virtue of subsection (2) of section 78P below or any guidance issued under that subsection,–

(i) not to seek to recover under subsection (1) of that section any of the reasonable cost incurred by it in doing that thing; or

(ii) to seek so to recover only a portion of that cost;

(f) where no person has, after reasonable inquiry, been found who is an appropriate person in relation to any particular thing.

(4) Subject to section 78E(4) and (5) above, for the purposes of this section, the things which it is appropriate for the enforcing authority to do by way of remediation are–

(a) in a case falling within paragraph (a) of subsection (3) above, anything by way of remediation which the enforcing authority considers necessary for the purpose mentioned in that paragraph;

(b) in a case falling within paragraph (b) of that subsection, anything specified in, or determined under, the agreement mentioned in that paragraph;

(c) in a case falling within paragraph (c) of that subsection, anything which the person mentioned in that paragraph was required to do by virtue of the remediation notice;

(d) in a case falling within paragraph (d) of that subsection, anything by way of remediation which the enforcing authority is precluded by section 78J or 78K above from including in a remediation notice;

(e) in a case falling within paragraph (e) or (f) of that subsection, the particular thing mentioned in the paragraph in question.

(5) In this section "the relevant land or waters" means–

(a) the contaminated land in question;

(b) any controlled waters affected by that land; or

(c) any land adjoining or adjacent to that land or those waters.

[(5) In this section "relevant land or water environment" means—

(a) the contaminated land in question;

(b) the water environment affected by that land; or

(c) any land adjoining or adjacent to that land or that water environment.]]

[1414]

NOTES

Inserted as noted to s 78A at **[1402]**.

Sub-s (1): word "waters" in italics repealed and subsequent words in square brackets substituted, in relation to Scotland, by SSI 2005/658, reg 2(1), (9)(a).

Sub-s (3): in para (a) words "controlled waters" in italics repealed and subsequent words in square brackets substituted, in relation to Scotland, by SSI 2005/658, reg 2(1), (2).

Sub-s (5): substituted, in relation to Scotland, by SSI 2005/658, reg 2(1), (9)(b).

[78P Recovery of, and security for, the cost of remediation by the enforcing authority

(1) Where, by virtue of section 78N(3)(a), (c), (e) or (f) above, the enforcing authority does any particular thing by way of remediation, it shall be entitled, subject to sections 78J(7) and 78K(6) above, to recover the reasonable cost incurred in doing it from the appropriate person or, if there are two or more appropriate persons in relation to the thing in question, from those persons in proportions determined pursuant to section 78F(7) above.

(2) In deciding whether to recover the cost, and, if so, how much of the cost, which it is entitled to recover under subsection (1) above, the enforcing authority shall have regard–

(a) to any hardship which the recovery may cause to the person from whom the cost is recoverable; and

(b) to any guidance issued by the Secretary of State for the purposes of this subsection.

(3) Subsection (4) below shall apply in any case where–

(a) any cost is recoverable under subsection (1) above from a person–

(i) who is the owner of any premises which consist of or include the contaminated land in question; and

(ii) who caused or knowingly permitted the substances, or any of the substances, by reason of which the land is contaminated land to be in, on or under the land; and

(b) the enforcing authority serves a notice under this subsection (in this Part referred to as a "charging notice") on that person.

(4) Where this subsection applies–

(a) the cost shall carry interest, at such reasonable rate as the enforcing authority may determine, from the date of service of the notice until the whole amount is paid; and

(b) subject to the following provisions of this section, the cost and accrued interest shall be a charge on the premises mentioned in subsection (3)(a)(i) above.

(5) A charging notice shall–

(a) specify the amount of the cost which the enforcing authority claims is recoverable;

(b) state the effect of subsection (4) above and the rate of interest determined by the authority under that subsection; and

(c) state the effect of subsections (7) and (8) below.

(6) On the date on which an enforcing authority serves a charging notice on a person, the authority shall also serve a copy of the notice on every other person who, to the knowledge of the authority, has an interest in the premises capable of being affected by the charge.

(7) Subject to any order under subsection (9)(b) or (c) below, the amount of any cost specified in a charging notice and the accrued interest shall be a charge on the premises–

(a) as from the end of the period of twenty-one days beginning with the service of the charging notice, or

(b) where an appeal is brought under subsection (8) below, as from the final determination or (as the case may be) the withdrawal, of the appeal,

until the cost and interest are recovered.

(8) A person served with a charging notice or a copy of a charging notice may appeal against the notice to a county court within the period of twenty-one days beginning with the date of service.

(9) On an appeal under subsection (8) above, the court may–

(a) confirm the notice without modification;

(b) order that the notice is to have effect with the substitution of a different amount for the amount originally specified in it; or

(c) order that the notice is to be of no effect.

(10) Regulations may make provision with respect to–

(a) the grounds on which appeals under this section may be made; or

(b) the procedure on any such appeal.

(11) An enforcing authority shall, for the purpose of enforcing a charge under this section, have all the same powers and remedies under the Law of Property Act 1925, and otherwise, as if it were a mortgagee by deed having powers of sale and lease, of accepting surrenders of leases and of appointing a receiver.

(12) Where any cost is a charge on premises under this section, the enforcing authority may by order declare the cost to be payable with interest by instalments within the specified period until the whole amount is paid.

(13) In subsection (12) above–

"interest" means interest at the rate determined by the enforcing authority under subsection (4) above; and

"the specified period" means such period of thirty years or less from the date of service of the charging notice as is specified in the order.

(14) Subsections (3) to (13) above do not extend to Scotland.]

[1415]

NOTES

Inserted as noted to s 78A at **[1402]**.

Transfer of functions: see the note to s 2 at **[1383]**.

[78Q Special sites

(1) If, in a case where a local authority has served a remediation notice, the contaminated land in question becomes a special site, the appropriate Agency may adopt the remediation notice and, if it does so,–

(a) it shall give notice of its decision to adopt the remediation notice to the appropriate person and to the local authority;

(b) the remediation notice shall have effect, as from the time at which the appropriate Agency decides to adopt it, as a remediation notice given by that Agency; and

(c) the validity of the remediation notice shall not be affected by–

(i) the contaminated land having become a special site;

(ii) the adoption of the remediation notice by the appropriate Agency; or

(iii) anything in paragraph (b) above.

(2) Where a local authority has, by virtue of section 78N above, begun to do any thing, or any series of things, by way of remediation–

(a) the authority may continue doing that thing, or that series of things, by virtue of that section, notwithstanding that the contaminated land in question becomes a special site; and

(b) section 78P above shall apply in relation to the reasonable cost incurred by the authority in doing that thing or those things as if that authority were the enforcing authority.

(3) If and so long as any land is a special site, the appropriate Agency may from time to time inspect that land for the purpose of keeping its condition under review.

(4) If it appears to the appropriate Agency that a special site is no longer land which is required to be designated as such a site, the appropriate Agency may give notice–

(a) to the Secretary of State, and

(b) to the local authority in whose area the site is situated,

terminating the designation of the land in question as a special site as from such date as may be specified in the notice.

(5) A notice under subsection (4) above shall not prevent the land, or any of the land, to which the notice relates being designated as a special site on a subsequent occasion.

(6) In exercising its functions under subsection (3) or (4) above, the appropriate Agency shall act in accordance with any guidance given for the purpose by the Secretary of State.]

[1416]

NOTES

Inserted as noted to s 78A at **[1402]**.

Transfer of functions: see the note to s 2 at **[1383]**.

78R–78W (*Outside the scope of this work.*)

[78X Supplementary provisions

[(1) Where it appears to a local authority that two or more different sites, when considered together, are in such a condition, by reason of substances in, on or under the land, that–

(a) significant harm is being caused or there is a significant possibility of such harm being caused, or

(*b*) *pollution of controlled waters is being, or is likely to be, caused,*

[(b) significant pollution of controlled waters is being caused or there is a significant possibility of such pollution being caused,]

this Part shall apply in relation to each of those sites, whether or not the condition of the land at any of them, when considered alone, appears to the authority to be such that significant harm *is being caused, or there is a significant possibility of such harm being caused, or that pollution of controlled waters is being or is likely to be caused* [, or significant pollution of controlled waters, is being caused, or there is a significant possibility of such harm or pollution being caused].

(2) Where it appears to a local authority that any land outside, but adjoining or adjacent to, its area is in such a condition, by reason of substances in, on or under the land, that significant harm *is being caused, or there is a significant possibility of such harm being caused, or that pollution of controlled waters is being, or is likely to be, caused* [, or significant pollution of controlled waters, is being caused, or there is a significant possibility of such harm or pollution being caused] within its area–

(a) the authority may, in exercising its functions under this Part, treat that land as if it were land situated within its area; and

(b) except in this subsection, any reference–

(i) to land within the area of a local authority, or

(ii) to the local authority in whose area any land is situated,

shall be construed accordingly;

but this subsection is without prejudice to the functions of the local authority in whose area the land is in fact situated.

(3) A person acting in a relevant capacity–

(a) shall not thereby be personally liable, under this Part, to bear the whole or any part of the cost of doing any thing by way of remediation, unless that thing is to any extent referable to substances whose presence in, on or under the contaminated land in question is a result of any act done or omission made by him which it was unreasonable for a person acting in that capacity to do or make; and

(b) shall not thereby be guilty of an offence under or by virtue of section 78M above unless the requirement which has not been complied with is a requirement to do some particular thing for which he is personally liable to bear the whole or any part of the cost.

(4) In subsection (3) above, "person acting in a relevant capacity" means–

(a) a person acting as an insolvency practitioner, within the meaning of section 388 of the Insolvency Act 1986 (including that section as it applies in relation to an insolvent partnership by virtue of any order made under section 421 of that Act);

(b) the official receiver acting in a capacity in which he would be regarded as acting as an insolvency practitioner within the meaning of section 388 of the Insolvency Act 1986 if subsection (5) of that section were disregarded;

(c) the official receiver acting as receiver or manager;

(d) a person acting as a special manager under section 177 or 370 of the Insolvency Act 1986;
(e) the Accountant in Bankruptcy acting as permanent or interim trustee in a sequestration (within the meaning of the Bankruptcy (Scotland) Act 1985);
(f) a person acting as a receiver or receiver and manager–
(i) under or by virtue of any enactment; or
(ii) by virtue of his appointment as such by an order of a court or by any other instrument.

(5) Regulations may make different provision for different cases or circumstances.]

[1417]

NOTES

Inserted as noted to s 78A at **[1402]**.

Sub-s (1): para (b) substituted, and words from "is being caused" to "to be caused" in italics repealed and subsequent words in square brackets substituted in relation to England and Wales, as from a day to be appointed, by the Water Act 2003, s 86(1), (6)(a), and in relation to Scotland by SSI 2005/658, reg 2(1), (10)(a).

Sub-s (2): words from "is being caused" to "to be, caused" in italics repealed and subsequent words in square brackets substituted in relation to England and Wales, as from a day to be appointed, by the Water Act 2003, s 86(1), (6)(b), and in relation to Scotland by SSI 2005/658, reg 2(1), (10)(b).

[78Y Application to the Isles of Scilly

(1) Subject to the provisions of any order under this section, this Part shall not apply in relation to the Isles of Scilly.

(2) The Secretary of State may, after consultation with the Council of the Isles of Scilly, by order provide for the application of any provisions of this Part to the Isles of Scilly; and any such order may provide for the application of those provisions to those Isles with such modifications as may be specified in the order.

(3) An order under this section may–
(a) make different provision for different cases, including different provision in relation to different persons, circumstances or localities; and
(b) contain such supplemental, consequential and transitional provision as the Secretary of State considers appropriate, including provision saving provision repealed by or under any enactment.]

[1418]

NOTES

Inserted as noted to s 78A at **[1402]**.

Order: the Environmental Protection Act 1990 (Isles of Scilly) Order 2006, SI 2006/1381.

78YA (*Outside the scope of this work.*)

[78YB Interaction of this Part with other enactments

[(1) This Part shall not apply if and to the extent that—
(a) any significant harm, or pollution of controlled waters, by reason of which land would otherwise fall to be regarded as contaminated, is attributable to the operation of a regulated facility; and
(b) enforcement action may be taken in relation to that harm or pollution.]

(3) If, in a case falling within subsection (1) or (7) of section 59 above, the land in question is contaminated land, or becomes such land by reason of the deposit of the controlled waste in question, a remediation notice shall not be served in respect of that land by reason of that waste or any consequences of its deposit, if and to the extent that it appears to the enforcing authority that the powers of a waste regulation authority or waste collection authority under that section may be exercised in relation to that waste or the consequences of its deposit.

(4) No remediation notice shall require a person to do anything the effect of which would be to impede or prevent the making of a discharge in pursuance of a consent given under Chapter II of Part III of the Water Resources Act 1991 (pollution offences) or, in relation to Scotland, in pursuance of a consent given under Part II of the Control of Pollution Act 1974.]

[(5) In this section—
"enforcement action" means action under regulation 36, 37 or 42 of the Environmental Permitting (England and Wales) Regulations 2007;
"regulated facility" has the meaning given in regulation 8 of those Regulations.]

[1419]

NOTES

Inserted as noted to s 78A at **[1402]**.

Sub-s (1): substituted for original sub-ss (1), (1A), (2), (2A)–(2C), in relation to England and Wales, by SI 2007/3538, reg 73, Sch 21, Pt 1, paras 2, 18(a); for transitional provisions and savings see regs 69, 72(2), (3), (10) thereof.

Sub-s (5): inserted, in relation to England and Wales, by SI 2007/3538, reg 73, Sch 21, Pt 1, paras 2, 18(b); for transitional provisions and savings see regs 69, 72(2), (3), (10) thereof.

[78YC This Part and radioactivity

Except as provided by regulations, nothing in this Part applies in relation to harm, or pollution of *controlled waters* [the water environment], so far as attributable to any radioactivity possessed by any substance; but regulations may–

(a) provide for prescribed provisions of this Part to have effect with such modifications as the Secretary of State considers appropriate for the purpose of dealing with harm, or pollution of *controlled waters* [the water environment], so far as attributable to any radioactivity possessed by any substances; or

(b) make such modifications of the Radioactive Substances Act 1993 or any other Act as the Secretary of State considers appropriate.]

[1420]

NOTES

Inserted as noted to s 78A at **[1402]**.

Words "controlled waters" in italics in both places they occur repealed and subsequent words in square brackets substituted, in relation to Scotland, by SSI 2005/658, reg 2(1), (2).

Transfer of functions: see the note to s 2 at **[1383]**.

Regulations: the Radioactive Contaminated Land (Enabling Powers) (England) Regulations 2005, SI 2005/3467; the Radioactive Contaminated Land (Modification of Enactments) (England) Regulations 2006, SI 2006/1379; the Radioactive Contaminated Land (Modification of Enactments) (Wales) Regulations 2006, SI 2006/2988; the Radioactive Contaminated Land (Scotland) Regulations 2007, SSI 2007/179.

PART III
STATUTORY NUISANCES AND CLEAN AIR

Statutory nuisances …

NOTES

Words omitted repealed by the Environment Act 1995, s 120, Sch 24.

79 Statutory nuisances and inspections therefor

(1) [Subject to subsections [(1ZA)] to (6A) below], the following matters constitute "statutory nuisances" for the purposes of this Part, that is to say—

(a) any premises in such a state as to be prejudicial to health or a nuisance;
(b) smoke emitted from premises so as to be prejudicial to health or a nuisance;
(c) fumes or gases emitted from premises so as to be prejudicial to health or a nuisance;
(d) any dust, steam, smell or other effluvia arising on industrial, trade or business premises and being prejudicial to health or a nuisance;
(e) any accumulation or deposit which is prejudicial to health or a nuisance;
[(ea) any water covering land or land covered with water which is in such a state as to be prejudicial to health or a nuisance;]
(f) any animal kept in such a place or manner as to be prejudicial to health or a nuisance;
[(fa) any insects emanating from relevant industrial, trade or business premises and being prejudicial to health or a nuisance;]
[(faa) any insects emanating from premises and being prejudicial to health or a nuisance;]
[(fb) artificial light emitted from premises so as to be prejudicial to health or a nuisance;]
[(fba) artificial light emitted from—
(i) premises;
(ii) any stationary object,
so as to be prejudicial to health or a nuisance;]
(g) noise emitted from premises so as to be prejudicial to health or a nuisance;
[(ga) noise that is prejudicial to health or a nuisance and is emitted from or caused by a vehicle, machinery or equipment in a street [or in Scotland, road];]
(h) any other matter declared by any enactment to be a statutory nuisance;

and it shall be the duty of every local authority to cause its area to be inspected from time to time to detect any statutory nuisances which ought to be dealt with under section 80 below [or sections 80 and 80A below] and, where a complaint of a statutory nuisance is made to it by a person living within its area, to take such steps as are reasonably practicable to investigate the complaint.

[(1ZA) The Scottish Ministers may by regulations—
(a) amend this section so as to—

(i) prescribe additional matters which constitute statutory nuisances for the purposes of this Part;

(ii) vary the description of any matter which constitutes a statutory nuisance;

(b) in relation to an amendment under paragraph (a), amend this Act and any other enactment to make such incidental, supplementary, consequential, transitory, transitional or saving provision as the Scottish Ministers consider appropriate.

(1ZB) Before making regulations under subsection (1ZA) above, the Scottish Ministers must consult, in so far as it is reasonably practicable to do so, the persons mentioned in subsection (1ZC) below.

(1ZC) Those persons are—

(a) such associations of local authorities; and

(b) such other persons,

as the Scottish Ministers consider appropriate.]

[(1A) No matter shall constitute a statutory nuisance to the extent that it consists of, or is caused by, any land being in a contaminated state.

(1B) Land is in a "contaminated state" for the purposes of subsection (1A) above if, and only if, it is in such a condition, by reason of substances in, on or under the land, that—

(a) harm is being caused or there is a possibility of harm being caused; or

(b) pollution of controlled waters is being, or is likely to be, caused;

and in this subsection "harm", "pollution of controlled waters" and "substance" have the same meaning as in Part IIA of this Act.]

[(1B) Land is in a "contaminated state" for the purposes of sub section (1A) above if, and only if, it is in such a condition, by reason of substances in, on or under the land, that—

(a) significant harm is being caused or there is a significant possibility of such harm being caused; or

(b) significant pollution of the water environment is being caused or there is a significant possibility of such pollution being caused;

and in this subsection "harm", "pollution" in relation to the water environment, "substance" and "the water environment" have the same meanings as in Part IIA of this Act.]

(2) Subsection (1)(b)[, (fb)][, (fba)] and (g) above do not apply in relation to premises [(or, in respect of paragraph (fba)(ii) above, a stationary object located on premises)]—

(a) occupied on behalf of the Crown for naval, military or air force purposes or for the purposes of the department of the Secretary of State having responsibility for defence, or

(b) occupied by or for the purposes of a visiting force;

and "visiting force" means any such body, contingent or detachment of the forces of any country as is a visiting force for the purposes of any of the provisions of the Visiting Forces Act 1952.

(3) Subsection (1)(b) above does not apply to—

(i) smoke emitted from a chimney of a private dwelling within a smoke control area,

(ii) dark smoke emitted from a chimney of a building or a chimney serving the furnace of a boiler or industrial plant attached to a building or for the time being fixed to or installed on any land,

(iii) smoke emitted from a railway locomotive steam engine, or

(iv) dark smoke emitted otherwise than as mentioned above from industrial or trade premises.

(4) Subsection (1)(c) above does not apply in relation to premises other than private dwellings.

(5) Subsection (1)(d) above does not apply to steam emitted from a railway locomotive engine.

[(5ZA) For the purposes of subsection (1)(ea) above, "land"—

(a) includes structures (other than buildings) in, on or over land;

(b) does not include—

(i) mains or other pipes used for carrying a water supply;

(ii) any part of the public sewerage system;

(iii) any other sewers, drains or other pipes used for carrying sewage;

(iv) the foreshore, that is to say, the land between the high and low water marks of ordinary spring tides;

(v) the seabed.

(5ZB) In subsection (5ZA) above—

"drain", "sewage" and "sewer" have the meanings given by section 59 of the Sewerage (Scotland) Act 1968 (c 47);

"main" has the meaning given by section 109(1) of the Water (Scotland) Act 1980 (c 45);

"pipe" includes a service pipe within the meaning of that section of that Act;

"public sewerage system" has the meaning given by section 29 of the Water Services etc (Scotland) Act 2005 (asp 3).]

[(5A) Subsection (1)(fa) does not apply to insects that are wild animals included in Schedule 5 to the Wildlife and Countryside Act 1981 (animals which are protected), unless they are included in respect of section 9(5) of that Act only.]

[(5AA) Subsection (1)(faa) above does not apply to insects that are wild animals included in Schedule 5 to the Wildlife and Countryside Act 1981 (c 69).

(5AB) For the purposes of subsection (1)(faa) above, "premises" does not include—

(a) a site of special scientific interest (within the meaning of section 3(6) of the Nature Conservation (Scotland) Act 2004 (asp 6));

(b) such other place (or type of place) as may be prescribed in regulations made by the Scottish Ministers.

(5AC) Before making regulations under subsection (5AB)(b) above, the Scottish Ministers must consult, in so far as it is reasonably practicable to do so, the persons mentioned in subsection (5AD) below.

(5AD) Those persons are—

(a) such associations of local authorities; and

(b) such other persons,

as the Scottish Ministers consider appropriate.]

[(5B) Subsection (1)(fb) does not apply to artificial light emitted from—

(a) an airport;

(b) harbour premises;

(c) railway premises, not being relevant separate railway premises;

(d) tramway premises;

(e) a bus station and any associated facilities;

(f) a public service vehicle operating centre;

(g) a goods vehicle operating centre;

(h) a lighthouse;

(i) a prison.]

[(5BA) Subsection (1)(fba) above does not apply to artificial light emitted from a lighthouse (within the meaning of Part 8 of the Merchant Shipping Act 1995 (c 21)).]

(6) Subsection (1)(g) above does not apply to noise caused by aircraft other than model aircraft.

[(6A) Subsection (1)(ga) above does not apply to noise made—

(a) by traffic,

(b) by any naval, military or air force of the Crown or by a visiting force (as defined in subsection (2) above), or

(c) by a political demonstration or a demonstration supporting or opposing a cause or campaign.]

(7) In this Part—

["airport" has the meaning given by section 95 of the Transport Act 2000;]

["appropriate person" means—

(a) in relation to England, the Secretary of State;

(b) in relation to Wales, the National Assembly for Wales;]

["associated facilities", in relation to a bus station, has the meaning given by section 83 of the Transport Act 1985;]

["bus station" has the meaning given by section 83 of the Transport Act 1985;]

"chimney" includes structures and openings of any kind from or through which smoke may be emitted;

"dust" does not include dust emitted from a chimney as an ingredient of smoke;

["equipment" includes a musical instrument;]

"fumes" means any airborne solid matter smaller than dust;

"gas" includes vapour and moisture precipitated from vapour;

["goods vehicle operating centre", in relation to vehicles used under an operator's licence, means a place which is specified in the licence as an operating centre for those vehicles, and for the purposes of this definition "operating centre" and "operator's licence" have the same meaning as in the Goods Vehicles (Licensing of Operators) Act 1995;]

["harbour premises" means premises which form part of a harbour area and which are occupied wholly or mainly for the purposes of harbour operations, and for the purposes of this definition "harbour area" and "harbour operations" have the same meaning as in Part 3 of the Aviation and Maritime Security Act 1990;]

"industrial, trade or business premises" means premises used for any industrial, trade or business purposes or premises not so used on which matter is burnt in connection with any industrial, trade or business process, and premises are used for industrial purposes where they are used for the purposes of any treatment or process as well as where they are used for the purposes of manufacturing;

["lighthouse" has the same meaning as in Part 8 of the Merchant Shipping Act 1995;]

"local authority" means, *subject to subsection (8) below,*—

(a) in Greater London, a London borough council, the Common Council of the City of London and, as respects the Temples, the Sub-Treasurer of the Inner Temple and the Under-Treasurer of the Middle Temple respectively;

(b) [in England] outside Greater London, a district council;

[(bb) in Wales, a county council or county borough council;] …

(c) the Council of the Isles of Scilly; [and

(d) in Scotland, a district or islands council or a council constituted under section 2 of the Local Government etc (Scotland) Act 1994;]

"noise" includes vibration;

["person responsible"—

(a) in relation to a statutory nuisance, means the person to whose act, default or sufferance the nuisance is attributable;

(b) in relation to a vehicle, includes the person in whose name the vehicle is for the time being registered under [the Vehicle Excise and Registration Act 1994] and any other person who is for the time being the driver of the vehicle;

(c) in relation to machinery or equipment, includes any person who is for the time being the operator of the machinery or equipment;]

"prejudicial to health" means injurious, or likely to cause injury, to health;

"premises" includes land [(subject to subsection (5AB) above)] and, subject to subsection (12) [and[, in relation to England and Wales] section 81A(9)] below, any vessel;

["prison" includes a young offender institution;]

"private dwelling" means any building, or part of a building, used or intended to be used, as a dwelling;

["public service vehicle operating centre", in relation to public service vehicles used under a PSV operator's licence, means a place which is an operating centre of those vehicles, and for the purposes of this definition "operating centre", "PSV operator's licence" and "public service vehicle" have the same meaning as in the Public Passenger Vehicles Act 1981;]

["railway premises" means any premises which fall within the definition of "light maintenance depot", "network", "station" or "track" in section 83 of the Railways Act 1993;]

["relevant separate railway premises" has the meaning given by subsection (7A);]

["road" has the same meaning as in Part IV of the New Roads and Street Works Act 1991;]

"smoke" includes soot, ash, grit and gritty particles emitted in smoke;

["street" means a highway and any other road, footway, square or court that is for the time being open to the public;]

["tramway premises" means any premises which, in relation to a tramway, are the equivalent of the premises which, in relation to a railway, fall within the definition of "light maintenance depot", "network", "station" or "track" in section 83 of the Railways Act 1993;]

and any expressions used in this section and in [the Clean Air Act 1993] have the same meaning in this section as in that Act and [section 3 of the Clean Air Act 1993] shall apply for the interpretation of the expression "dark smoke" and the operation of this Part in relation to it.

[(7A) Railway premises are relevant separate railway premises if—

(a) they are situated within—

(i) premises used as a museum or other place of cultural, scientific or historical interest, or

(ii) premises used for the purposes of a funfair or other entertainment, recreation or amusement, and

(b) they are not associated with any other railway premises.

(7B) For the purposes of subsection (7A)—

(a) a network situated as described in subsection (7A)(a) is associated with other railway premises if it is connected to another network (not being a network situated as described in subsection (7A)(a));

(b) track that is situated as described in subsection (7A)(a) but is not part of a network is associated with other railway premises if it is connected to track that forms part of a network (not being a network situated as described in subsection (7A)(a));

(c) a station or light maintenance depot situated as described in subsection (7A)(a) is associated with other railway premises if it is used in connection with the provision of railway services other than services provided wholly within the premises where it is situated.

In this subsection "light maintenance depot", "network", "railway services", "station" and "track" have the same meaning as in Part 1 of the Railways Act 1993.]

[(7C) In this Part "relevant industrial, trade or business premises" means premises that are industrial, trade or business premises as defined in subsection (7), but excluding—

(a) land used as arable, grazing, meadow or pasture land,

(b) land used as osier land, reed beds or woodland,

(c) land used for market gardens, nursery grounds or orchards,

(d) land forming part of an agricultural unit, not being land falling within any of paragraphs (a) to (c), where the land is of a description prescribed by regulations made by the appropriate person, and

(e) land included in a site of special scientific interest (as defined in section 52(1) of the Wildlife and Countryside Act 1981),

and excluding land covered by, and the waters of, any river or watercourse, that is neither a sewer nor a drain, or any lake or pond.

(7D) For the purposes of subsection (7C)—

"agricultural" has the same meaning as in section 109 of the Agriculture Act 1947;

"agricultural unit" means land which is occupied as a unit for agricultural purposes;

"drain" has the same meaning as in the Water Resources Act 1991;

"lake or pond" has the same meaning as in section 104 of that Act;

"sewer" has the same meaning as in that Act.]

(8) Where, by an order under section 2 of the Public Health (Control of Disease) Act 1984, a port health authority has been constituted for any port health district [*or in Scotland where by an order under section 172 of the Public Health (Scotland) Act 1897 a port local authority or a joint port local authority has been constituted for the whole or part of a port,*], the port health authority[, *port local authority or joint port local authority, as the case may be*] shall have by virtue of this subsection, as respects its district, the functions conferred or imposed by this Part in relation to statutory nuisances other than a nuisance falling within paragraph [(fb),] (g) [or (ga)] of subsection (1) above and no such order shall be made assigning those functions; and 'local authority' and 'area' shall be construed accordingly.

(9) In this Part "best practicable means" is to be interpreted by reference to the following provisions—

(a) "practicable" means reasonably practicable having regard among other things to local conditions and circumstances, to the current state of technical knowledge and to the financial implications;

(b) the means to be employed include the design, installation, maintenance and manner and periods of operation of plant and machinery, and the design, construction and maintenance of buildings and structures;

(c) the test is to apply only so far as compatible with any duty imposed by law;

(d) the test is to apply only so far as compatible with safety and safe working conditions, and with the exigencies of any emergency or unforeseeable circumstances;

and, in circumstances where a code of practice under section 71 of the Control of Pollution Act 1974 (noise minimisation) is applicable, regard shall also be had to guidance given in it.

(10) A local authority shall not without the consent of the Secretary of State institute summary proceedings under this Part in respect of a nuisance falling within paragraph (b), (d)[, (e)[, (fb)] or (g)] [and, in relation to Scotland, [paragraph (ga)],] of subsection (1) above if proceedings in respect thereof might be instituted *under Part I* [*or* under regulations under section 2 of the Pollution Prevention and Control Act 1999] …

(11) The area of a local authority which includes part of the seashore shall also include for the purposes of this Part the territorial sea lying seawards from that part of the shore; and subject to subsection (12) [and[, in relation to England and Wales,] section 81A] below, this Part shall have effect, in relation to any area included in the area of a local authority by virtue of this subsection—

(a) as if references to premises and the occupier of premises included respectively a vessel and the master of a vessel; and

(b) with such other modifications, if any, as are prescribed in regulations made by the Secretary of State.

(12) A vessel powered by steam reciprocating machinery is not a vessel to which this Part of this Act applies.

[1421]

NOTES

Sub-s (1): words in first (outer) pair of square brackets substituted by the Environment Act 1995, s 120, Sch 22, para 89(2); reference in second (inner) pair of square brackets substituted, in relation to Scotland only, by the Public Health etc (Scotland) Act 2008, s 112(1), (2)(a); para (ea) inserted, in relation to Scotland only, by the Public Health etc (Scotland) Act 2008, s 111(1), (2); paras (fa), (fb) inserted, in relation to England and Wales, by the Clean Neighbourhoods and Environment Act 2005, s 101(1), (2); para (faa) inserted, in relation to Scotland only, by the Public Health etc (Scotland) Act 2008, s 109(1), (2); para (fba) inserted, in relation to Scotland only, by the Public Health etc (Scotland) Act 2008, s 110(1), (2); para (ga) inserted by the Noise and Statutory Nuisance Act 1993, s 2(1), (2)(b) and words in square brackets inserted by the Environment Act 1995, s 107, Sch 17, para 2(a); final words in square brackets inserted by the Noise and Statutory Nuisance Act 1993, s 2(1), (2)(c).

Sub-ss (1ZA)–(1ZC): inserted, in relation to Scotland only, by the Public Health etc (Scotland) Act 2008, s 112(1), (2)(b).

Sub-s (1A): inserted by the Environment Act 1995, s 120, Sch 22, para 89(3).

Sub-s (1B): inserted by the Environment Act 1995, s 120, Sch 22, para 89(3); substituted in relation to Scotland, by SSI 2005/658, reg 2(1), (12).

Sub-s (2): reference in first pair of square brackets inserted, in relation to England and Wales, by the Clean Neighbourhoods and Environment Act 2005, s 102(1), (3); reference and words in second and third pairs of square brackets inserted, in relation to Scotland only, by the Public Health etc (Scotland) Act 2008, s 110(1), (3).

Sub-ss (5ZA), (5ZB): inserted, in relation to Scotland only, by the Public Health etc (Scotland) Act 2008, s 111(1), (3).

Sub-s (5A): inserted, in relation to England and Wales, by the Clean Neighbourhoods and Environment Act 2005, ss 101(1), (3), 102(1), (4).

Sub-ss (5AA)–(5AD): inserted, in relation to Scotland only, by the Public Health etc (Scotland) Act 2008, s 109(1), (3).

Sub-s (5B): inserted, in relation to England and Wales, by the Clean Neighbourhoods and Environment Act 2005, ss 101(1), (3), 102(1), (4).

Sub-s (5BA): inserted, in relation to Scotland only, by the Public Health etc (Scotland) Act 2008, s 110(1), (4).

Sub-s (6A): inserted by the Noise and Statutory Nuisance Act 1993, s 2(3).

Sub-s (7): definitions "airport", "appropriate person", "associated facilities", "bus station", "harbour premises", "lighthouse", "goods vehicle operating centre", "prison", "public service vehicle operating centre", "railway premises", "relevant separate railway premises", "tramway premises" inserted, in relation to England and Wales, by the Clean Neighbourhoods and Environment Act 2005, s 102(1), (5); definitions "equipment" and "street" inserted, and definition "person responsible" substituted, by the Noise and Statutory Nuisance Act 1993, s 2(4); in definition "local authority" words in italics repealed, in relation to Scotland only, by the Public Health etc (Scotland) Act 2008, s 126(1), Sch 3, Pt 1; words in square brackets in para (b) inserted, and para (bb) inserted, by the Local Government (Wales) Act 1994, s 22(3), Sch 9, para 17(5), para (d) and the word "and" immediately preceding it inserted, and word omitted repealed, by the Environment Act 1995, ss 107, 120, Sch 17, para 2(b)(i), Sch 24; in definition "person responsible" words in square brackets substituted by the Vehicle Excise and Registration Act 1994, s 63, Sch 3, para 27; in definition "premises" first words in square brackets inserted, in relation to Scotland only, by the Public Health etc (Scotland) Act 2008, s 109(1), (4); second (outer) words in square brackets inserted by the Noise and Statutory Nuisance Act 1993, s 10(1), third (inner) words in square brackets inserted by the Environment Act 1995, s 107, Sch 17, para 2(b)(ii); definition "road" inserted by the Environment Act 1995, s 107, Sch 17, para 2(b)(iii); remaining words in square brackets substituted by the Clean Air Act 1993, s 67(1), Sch 4, para 4.

Sub-ss (7A), (7B): inserted, in relation to England and Wales, by the Clean Neighbourhoods and Environment Act 2005, s 102(1), (6).

Sub-ss (7C), (7D): inserted, in relation to England and Wales, by the Clean Neighbourhoods and Environment Act 2005, s 101(1), (5).

Sub-s (8): words italics in first and second pairs of square brackets inserted by the Environment Act 1995, s 107, Sch 17, para 2(c) and repealed, in relation to Scotland only, by the Public Health etc (Scotland) Act 2008, s 126(1), Sch 3, Pt 1; reference in third pair of square brackets inserted, in relation to England and Wales, by the Clean Neighbourhoods and Environment Act 2005, s 102(1), (7); words in fourth pair of square brackets inserted by the Noise and Statutory Nuisance Act 1993, s 2(5).

Sub-s (10): words ", (e) or (g)" in square brackets substituted by SI 2000/1973, reg 39, Sch 10, Pt 1, paras 2, 7; reference to ", (fb)" in square brackets inserted, in relation to England and Wales, by the Clean Neighbourhoods and Environment Act 2005, s 102(1), (8); words in square brackets beginning with the words "and, in relation to Scotland," inserted by the Environment Act 1995, s 107, Sch 17, para 2(d); words "paragraph (ga)" in square brackets substituted in relation to England and Wales by SI 2000/1973, Sch 10, Pt 1, paras 2, 7 and in relation to Scotland by SSI 2000/323, reg 36, Sch 10, Pt 1, para 3(1), (6); words "under Part I or" in italics repealed by the Pollution Prevention and Control Act 1999, s 6(2), Sch 3, as from a day to be appointed; words "or under regulations under section 2 of the Pollution Prevention and Control Act 1999." in square brackets inserted by the Pollution Prevention and Control Act 1999, s 6(1), Sch 2, paras 3, 6; and words omitted repealed by the Environmental Protection Act 1990, s 162, Sch 16, Pt I.

Sub-s (11): first words in square brackets inserted by the Noise and Statutory Nuisance Act 1993, s 10(1), words in square brackets therein inserted by the Environment Act 1995, s 107, Sch 17, para 2(e).

Modification: modified, in relation to London boroughs, by the London Local Authorities Act 1996, s 24(1).

Transfer of functions: see the note to s 2 at **[1383]**.

See further: in relation to provision made regarding radioactivity possessed by any substance or article or by any part of any premises, see the Radioactive Substances Act 1993, s 40.

Miscellaneous: the Environment Act 1995, s 107, Sch 17, para 2(b)(i) adds the words "in England and Wales" immediately before the words "outside Greater London" in para (b) of the definition of "local authority" in sub-s (7) above. In light of the amendment made to that paragraph by the Local Government (Wales) Act 1994, it is understood that the amendment made by the Environment Act 1995 is no longer of any effect.

Regulations: the Statutory Nuisances (Insects) Regulations 2006, SI 2006/770; the Statutory Nuisance (Miscellaneous Provisions) (Wales) Regulations 2007, SI 2007/117.

---

80 Summary proceedings for statutory nuisances

(1) [Subject to subsection (2A)] where a local authority is satisfied that a statutory nuisance exists, or is likely to occur or recur, in the area of the authority, the local authority shall serve a notice ("an abatement notice") imposing all or any of the following requirements—

(a) requiring the abatement of the nuisance or prohibiting or restricting its occurrence or recurrence;

(b) requiring the execution of such works, and the taking of such other steps, as may be necessary for any of those purposes,

and the notice shall specify the time or times within which the requirements of the notice are to be complied with.

(2) [Subject to section 80A(1) below, the abatement notice] shall be served—

(a) except in a case falling within paragraph (b) or (c) below, on the person responsible for the nuisance;
(b) where the nuisance arises from any defect of a structural character, on the owner of the premises;
(c) where the person responsible for the nuisance cannot be found or the nuisance has not yet occurred, on the owner or occupier of the premises.

[(2A) Where a local authority is satisfied that a statutory nuisance falling within paragraph (g) of section 79(1) above exists, or is likely to occur or recur, in the area of the authority, the authority shall—

(a) serve an abatement notice in respect of the nuisance in accordance with subsections (1) and (2) above; or
(b) take such other steps as it thinks appropriate for the purpose of persuading the appropriate person to abate the nuisance or prohibit or restrict its occurrence or recurrence.

(2B) If a local authority has taken steps under subsection (2A)(b) above and either of the conditions in subsection (2C) below is satisfied, the authority shall serve an abatement notice in respect of the nuisance.

(2C) The conditions are—

(a) that the authority is satisfied at any time before the end of the relevant period that the steps taken will not be successful in persuading the appropriate person to abate the nuisance or prohibit or restrict its occurrence or recurrence;
(b) that the authority is satisfied at the end of the relevant period that the nuisance continues to exist, or continues to be likely to occur or recur, in the area of the authority.

(2D) The relevant period is the period of seven days starting with the day on which the authority was first satisfied that the nuisance existed, or was likely to occur or recur.

(2E) The appropriate person is the person on whom the authority would otherwise be required under subsection (2A)(a) above to serve an abatement notice in respect of the nuisance.]

(3) [A person served with an abatement notice] may appeal against the notice to a magistrates' court [or in Scotland, the sheriff] within the period of twenty-one days beginning with the date on which he was served with the notice.

(4) If a person on whom an abatement notice is served, without reasonable excuse, contravenes or fails to comply with any requirement or prohibition imposed by the notice, he shall be guilty of an offence.

[(4A) Where a local authority have reason to believe that a person has committed an offence under subsection (4) above, the local authority may give that person a notice (a "fixed penalty notice") in accordance with section 80ZA offering the person the opportunity of discharging any liability to conviction for that offence by payment of a fixed penalty.]

(5) Except in a case falling within subsection (6) below, a person who commits an offence under subsection (4) above shall be liable on summary conviction to a fine not exceeding level 5 on the standard scale together with a further fine of an amount equal to one-tenth of that level for each day on which the offence continues after the conviction.

(6) A person who commits an offence under subsection (4) above on industrial, trade or business premises shall be liable on summary conviction to a fine not exceeding [£40,000].

(7) Subject to subsection (8) below, in any proceedings for an offence under subsection (4) above in respect of a statutory nuisance it shall be a defence to prove that the best practicable means were used to prevent, or to counteract the effects of, the nuisance.

(8) The defence under subsection (7) above is not available—

(a) in the case of a nuisance falling within paragraph (a), (d), (e), (f)[, (fa)] or (g) of section 79(1) above except where the nuisance arises on industrial, trade or business premises;
[(aza) in the case of a nuisance falling within paragraph (fb) of section 79(1) above except where—
 (i) the artificial light is emitted from industrial, trade or business premises, or
 (ii) the artificial light (not being light to which sub-paragraph (i) applies) is emitted by lights used for the purpose only of illuminating an outdoor relevant sports facility;]
[(aa) in the case of a nuisance falling within paragraph (ga) of section 79(1) above except where the noise is emitted from or caused by a vehicle, machinery or equipment being used for industrial, trade or business purposes;]
(b) in the case of a nuisance falling within paragraph (b) of section 79(1) above except where the smoke is emitted from a chimney; and
(c) in the case of a nuisance falling within paragraph (c) or (h) of section 79(1) above.

PART I STATUTES

[(8A) For the purposes of subsection (8)(aza) a relevant sports facility is an area, with or without structures, that is used when participating in a relevant sport, but does not include such an area comprised in domestic premises.

(8B) For the purposes of subsection (8A) "relevant sport" means a sport that is designated for those purposes by order made by the Secretary of State, in relation to England, or the National Assembly for Wales, in relation to Wales.

A sport may be so designated by reference to its appearing in a list maintained by a body specified in the order.

(8C) In subsection (8A) "domestic premises" means—
- (a) premises used wholly or mainly as a private dwelling, or
- (b) land or other premises belonging to, or enjoyed with, premises so used.]

(9) In proceedings for an offence under subsection (4) above in respect of a statutory nuisance falling within paragraph (g) [or (ga)] of section 79(1) above where the offence consists in contravening requirements imposed by virtue of subsection (1)(a) above it shall be a defence to prove—
- (a) that the alleged offence was covered by a notice served under section 60 or a consent given under section 61 or 65 of the Control of Pollution Act 1974 (construction sites, etc); or
- (b) where the alleged offence was committed at a time when the premises were subject to a notice under section 66 of that Act (noise reduction notice), that the level of noise emitted from the premises at that time was not such as to a constitute a contravention of the notice under that section; or
- (c) where the alleged offence was committed at a time when the premises were not subject to a notice under section 66 of that Act, and when a level fixed under section 67 of that Act (new buildings liable to abatement order) applied to the premises, that the level of noise emitted from the premises at that time did not exceed that level.

(10) Paragraphs (b) and (c) of subsection (9) above apply whether or not the relevant notice was subject to appeal at the time when the offence was alleged to have been committed.

[1422]

NOTES

Sub-s (1): words in square brackets inserted, in relation to England and Wales, by the Clean Neighbourhoods and Environment Act 2005, s 86.

Sub-s (2): words in square brackets substituted by the Noise and Statutory Nuisance Act 1993, s 3(2), (3).

Sub-ss (2A)–(2E): inserted, in relation to England and Wales, by the Clean Neighbourhoods and Environment Act 2005, s 86.

Sub-s (3): first words in square brackets substituted by the Noise and Statutory Nuisance Act 1993, s 3(2), (3); second words in square brackets inserted by the Environment Act 1995, s 107, Sch 17, para 3.

Sub-s (4A): inserted, in relation to Scotland only, by the Public Health etc (Scotland) Act 2008, s 113(1), (2).

Sub-s (6): sum in square brackets substituted by the Antisocial Behaviour etc (Scotland) Act 2004, s 66, Sch 2, Pt 1, para 4(1), (4).

Sub-s (8): reference in square brackets in para (a), and para (aza) inserted, in relation to England and Wales, by the Clean Neighbourhoods and Environment Act 2005, s 103(1), (2); para (aa) inserted by the Noise and Statutory Nuisance Act 1993, s 3(4).

Sub-ss (8A)–(8C): inserted, in relation to England and Wales, by the Clean Neighbourhoods and Environment Act 2005, s 103(1), (3).

Sub-s (9): words in square brackets inserted by the Noise and Statutory Nuisance Act 1993, s 3(5).

See further: in relation to provision made regarding radioactivity possessed by any substance or article or by any part of any premises, see the Radioactive Substances Act 1993, s 40.

Orders: the Statutory Nuisances (Artificial Lighting) (Designation of Relevant Sports) (England) Order 2006, SI 2006/781; the Statutory Nuisances (Miscellaneous Provisions) (Wales) Order 2007, SI 2007/120.

[80ZA Fixed penalty notice: supplemental

(1) This section applies to a fixed penalty notice given under section 80(4A).

(2) A fixed penalty notice must give reasonable particulars of the circumstances alleged to constitute the offence.

(3) A fixed penalty notice must also state—
- (a) the amount of the fixed penalty;
- (b) the period within which it may be paid;
- (c) the—
  - (i) person to whom; and
  - (ii) address at which,

  payment may be made;
- (d) the method or methods by which payment may be made;
- (e) the consequences of not making a payment within the period for payment.

(4) The amount of the fixed penalty under section 80(4A) is—
- (a) in the case of a nuisance relating to industrial, trade or business premises, £400;

(b) in any other case, £150.

(5) The period for payment of the fixed penalty is 14 days beginning with the day after the day on which the notice is given.

(6) The local authority may extend the period for paying the fixed penalty in any particular case if they consider it appropriate to do so by sending notice to the person to whom the fixed penalty notice was given.

(7) No proceedings for an offence under section 80(4) may be commenced before the end of the period for payment of the fixed penalty.

(8) In proceedings for an offence under section 80(4), a certificate which—

(a) purports to be signed by or on behalf of a person having responsibility for the financial affairs of the local authority; and

(b) states that payment of the amount specified in the fixed penalty notice was or was not received by the expiry of the period within which that fixed penalty may be paid,

is sufficient evidence of the facts stated.

(9) Where proceedings for an offence in respect of which a fixed penalty notice has been given are commenced, the notice is to be treated as withdrawn.

(10) Any sum received by a local authority under section 80(4A) accrues to that authority.

(11) The Scottish Ministers may, by regulations—

(a) provide that fixed penalty notices may not be given in such circumstances as may be prescribed;

(b) provide for the form of a fixed penalty notice;

(c) provide for the method or methods by which fixed penalties may be paid;

(d) modify subsection (4)(a) or (b) above so as to substitute a different amount (not exceeding level 2 on the standard scale) for the amount for the time being specified there;

(e) provide for the amount of the fixed penalty to be different in different cases or descriptions of case;

(f) modify subsection (5) above so as to substitute a different period for the period for the time being specified there;

(g) provide for the keeping of accounts, and the preparation and publication of statements of account relating to fixed penalties under section 80(4A).

(12) Before making regulations under subsection (11) above, the Scottish Ministers must consult, in so far as it is reasonably practicable to do so, the persons mentioned in subsection (13) below.

(13) Those persons are—

(a) such associations of local authorities; and

(b) such other persons,

as the Scottish Ministers consider appropriate.]

[1422A]

NOTES

Commencement: 26 January 2009.

Inserted by the Public Health etc (Scotland) Act 2008, s 113(1), (3).

80A–105 (*Ss 80A–85, ss 86–105* (*Pts IV, V*) *outside the scope of this work.*)

PART VI
GENETICALLY MODIFIED ORGANISMS

106–115 (*Outside the scope of this work.*)

Enforcement powers and offences

116–119 (*Outside the scope of this work.*)

120 Power of court to order cause of offence to be remedied

(1) Where a person is convicted of an offence under section 118(1)(a), (b), (c), (d), (e) or (f) above in respect of any matters which appear to the court to be matters which it is in his power to remedy, the court may, in addition to or instead of imposing any punishment, order him, within such time as may be fixed by the order, to take such steps as may be specified in the order for remedying those matters.

(2) The time fixed by an order under subsection (1) above may be extended or further extended by order of the court on an application made before the end of the time as originally fixed or as extended under this subsection, as the case may be.

(3) Where a person is ordered under subsection (1) above to remedy any matters, that person shall not be liable under section 118 above in respect of those matters, in so far as they continue during the time fixed by the order or any further time allowed under subsection (2) above.

[1423]

121–155 (*Ss 121–127, ss 128–155* (*Pts VII, VIII*) *outside the scope of this work.*)

PART IX
GENERAL

156–163A (*Outside the scope of this work.*)

164 Short title, commencement and extent

(1) This Act may be cited as the Environmental Protection Act 1990.

(2) The following provisions of the Act shall come into force at the end of the period of two months beginning with the day on which it is passed, namely—

section 79 to 85;
section 97;
section 99;
section 105 in so far as it relates to paragraphs 7, 13, 14 and 15 of Schedule 5;
section 140;
section 141;
section 142;
section 145;
section 146;
section 148;
section 153;
section 154;
section 155;
section 157;
section 160;
section 161;
section 162(1) in so far as it relates to paragraphs 4, 5, 7, 8, 9, 18, 22, 24 and 31(4)(b) of Schedule 15; but, in the case of paragraph 22, in so far only as that paragraph inserts a paragraph (m) into section 7(4) of the Act of 1984;
section 162(2) in so far as it relates to Part III of Schedule 16 and, in Part IX of that Schedule, the repeal of section 100 of the Control of Pollution Act 1974;
section 162(5);
section 163.

(3) The remainder of this Act (except this section) shall come into force on such day as the Secretary of State may by order appoint and different days may be appointed for different provisions or different purposes.

(4) Only the following provisions of this Act (together with this section) extend to Northern Ireland, namely—

section 3(5) to (8);
section 62(2)(e) in so far as it relates to importation;
Part V;
Part VI in so far as it relates to importation and, without that restriction, section 127(2) in so far as it relates to the continental shelf;
section 140 in so far as it relates to importation;
section 141;
section 142 in so far as it relates to importation;
section 146;
section 147;
section 148;
section 153 except subsection (1)(k) and (m);
section 156 in so far as it relates to Part VI and sections 140, 141 and 142 in so far as they extend to Northern Ireland and in so far as it relates to the Radioactive Substances Act 1960;
section 158 in so far as it relates to Part VI and sections 140, 141 and 142 in so far as they extend to Northern Ireland.

[(4A) Sections 45A, 45B and 47A do not extend to Scotland.]

(5) (*Outside the scope of this work.*)

[1424]

NOTES

Sub-s (4): words in italics repealed by SI 2002/3153, art 53(2), Sch 6, Pt I, as from a day to be appointed.

Sub-s (4A): inserted by the Household Waste Recycling Act 2003, s 4.

Orders: the Environmental Protection Act 1990 (Commencement No 1) Order 1990, SI 1990/2226; the Environmental Protection Act 1990 (Commencement No 2) Order 1990, SI 1990/2243; the Environmental Protection Act 1990 (Commencement No 3) Order 1990, SI 1990/2565 (amended by SI 1990/2635); the Environmental Protection Act 1990 (Commencement No 4) Order 1990, SI 1990/2635; the Environmental Protection Act 1990 (Commencement No 5) Order 1991, SI 1991/96; the Environmental Protection Act 1990 (Commencement No 6 and Appointed Day) Order 1991, SI 1991/685; the Environmental Protection Act 1990 (Commencement No 7) Order 1991, SI 1991/1042; the Environmental Protection Act 1990 (Commencement No 8) Order 1991, SI 1991/1319; the Environmental Protection Act 1990 (Commencement No 9) Order 1991, SI 1991/1577; the Environmental Protection Act 1990 (Commencement No 10) Order 1991, SI 1991/2829; the Environmental Protection Act 1990 (Commencement No 11) Order 1992, SI 1992/266; the Environmental Protection Act 1990 (Commencement No 12) Order 1992, SI 1992/3253; the Environmental Protection Act 1990 (Commencement No 13) Order 1993, SI 1993/274; Environmental Protection Act 1990 (Commencement No 14) Order 1994, SI 1994/780; the Environmental Protection Act 1990 (Commencement No 15) Order 1994, SI 1994/1096 (amended by SI 1994/2487, SI 1994/3234); the Environmental Protection Act 1990 (Commencement No 16) Order 1994, SI 1994/2854; the Environmental Protection Act 1990 (Commencement No 17) Order 1995, SI 1995/2152; the Environmental Protection Act 1990 (Commencement No 18) Order 1996, SI 1996/3056.

(*Schs 1–16 outside the scope of this work.*)

PROPERTY MISDESCRIPTIONS ACT 1991

(1991 c 29)

An Act to prohibit the making of false or misleading statements about property matters in the course of estate agency business and property development business

[27 June 1991]

1 Offence of property misdescription

(1) Where a false or misleading statement about a prescribed matter is made in the course of an estate agency business or a property development business, otherwise than in providing conveyancing services, the person by whom the business is carried on shall be guilty of an offence under this section.

(2) Where the making of the statement is due to the act or default of an employee the employee shall be guilty of an offence under this section; and the employee may be proceeded against and punished whether or not proceedings are also taken against his employer.

(3) A person guilty of an offence under this section shall be liable—

(a) on summary conviction, to a fine not exceeding the statutory maximum, and

(b) on conviction on indictment, to a fine.

(4) No contract shall be void or unenforceable, and no right of action in civil proceedings in respect of any loss shall arise, by reason only of the commission of an offence under this section.

(5) For the purposes of this section—

(a) "false" means false to a material degree,

(b) a statement is misleading if (though not false) what a reasonable person may be expected to infer from it, or from any omission from it, is false,

(c) a statement may be made by pictures or any other method of signifying meaning as well as by words and, if made by words, may be made orally or in writing,

(d) a prescribed matter is any matter relating to land which is specified in an order made by the Secretary of State,

(e) a statement is made in the course of an estate agency business if (but only if) the making of the statement is a thing done as mentioned in subsection (1) of section 1 of the Estate Agents Act 1979 and that Act either applies to it or would apply to it but for subsection (2)(a) of that section (exception for things done in course of profession by practising solicitor or employee),

(f) a statement is made in the course of a property development business if (but only if) it is made—

(i) in the course of a business (including a business in which the person making the statement is employed) concerned wholly or substantially with the development of land, and

(ii) for the purpose of, or with a view to, disposing of an interest in land consisting of or including a building, or a part of a building, constructed or renovated in the course of the business, and

(g) "conveyancing services" means the preparation of any transfer, conveyance, writ, contract or other document in connection with the disposal or acquisition of an interest in land, and services ancillary to that, but does not include anything done as mentioned in section 1(1)(a) of the Estate Agents Act 1979.

(6) For the purposes of this section any reference in this section or section 1 of the Estate Agents Act 1979 to disposing of or acquiring an interest in land—

(a) in England and Wales and Northern Ireland shall be construed in accordance with section 2 of that Act, and

(b) in Scotland is a reference to the transfer or creation of an "interest in land" as defined in section 28(1) of the Land Registration (Scotland) Act 1979.

(7) An order under this section may—

(a) make different provision for different cases, and

(b) include such supplemental, consequential and transitional provisions as the Secretary of State considers appropriate;

and the power to make such an order shall be exercisable by statutory instrument which shall be subject to annulment in pursuance of a resolution of either House of Parliament.

[1425]

NOTES

Order: the Property Misdescriptions (Specified Matters) Order 1992, SI 1992/2834.

2 Due diligence defence

(1) In proceedings against a person for an offence under section 1 above it shall be a defence for him to show that he took all reasonable steps and exercised all due diligence to avoid committing the offence.

(2) A person shall not be entitled to rely on the defence provided by subsection (1) above by reason of his reliance on information given by another unless he shows that it was reasonable in all the circumstances for him to have relied on the information, having regard in particular—

(a) to the steps which he took, and those which might reasonably have been taken, for the purpose of verifying the information, and

(b) to whether he had any reason to disbelieve the information.

(3) Where in any proceedings against a person for an offence under section 1 above the defence provided by subsection (1) above involves an allegation that the commission of the offence was due—

(a) to the act or default of another, or

(b) to reliance on information given by another,

the person shall not, without the leave of the court, be entitled to rely on the defence unless he has served a notice under subsection (4) below on the person bringing the proceedings not less than seven clear days before the hearing of the proceedings or, in Scotland, the diet of trial.

(4) A notice under this subsection shall give such information identifying or assisting in the identification of the person who committed the act or default, or gave the information, as is in the possession of the person serving the notice at the time he serves it.

[1426]

3 Enforcement

The Schedule to this Act (which makes provision about the enforcement of this Act) shall have effect.

[1427]

4 Bodies corporate and Scottish partnerships

(1) Where an offence under this Act committed by a body corporate is proved to have been committed with the consent or connivance of, or to be attributable to neglect on the part of, a director, manager, secretary or other similar officer of the body corporate or a person who was purporting to act in such a capacity, he (as well as the body corporate) is guilty of the offence and liable to be proceeded against and punished accordingly.

(2) Where the affairs of a body corporate are managed by its members, subsection (1) above applies in relation to the acts and defaults of a member in connection with his functions of management as if he were a director of the body corporate.

(3) Where an offence under this Act committed in Scotland by a Scottish partnership is proved to have been committed with the consent or connivance of, or to be attributable to neglect on the part of, a partner, he (as well as the partnership) is guilty of the offence and liable to be proceeded against and punished accordingly.

[1428]

5 Prosecution time limit

(1) No proceedings for an offence under section 1 above or paragraph 5(3), 6 … of the Schedule to this Act shall be commenced after—

(a) the end of the period of three years beginning with the date of the commission of the offence, or

(b) the end of the period of one year beginning with the date of the discovery of the offence by the prosecutor,

whichever is the earlier.

(2) For the purposes of this section a certificate signed by or on behalf of the prosecutor and stating the date on which the offence was discovered by him shall be conclusive evidence of that fact; and a certificate stating that matter and purporting to be so signed shall be treated as so signed unless the contrary is proved.

[1429]

NOTES

Sub-s (1): words omitted repealed by SI 2003/1400, art 7, Sch 5.

6 Financial provision

There shall be paid out of money provided by Parliament any increase attributable to this Act in the sums payable out of such money under any other Act.

[1430]

7 Short title and extent

(1) This Act may be cited as the Property Misdescriptions Act 1991.

(2) This Act extends to Northern Ireland.

[1431]

SCHEDULE
ENFORCEMENT

Section 3

Enforcement authority

1.—(1) Every local weights and measures authority in Great Britain shall be an enforcement authority for the purposes of this Act, and it shall be the duty of each such authority to enforce the provisions of this Act within their area.

(2) The Department of Economic Development in Northern Ireland shall be an enforcement authority for the purposes of this Act, and it shall be the duty of the Department to enforce the provisions of this Act within Northern Ireland.

2. …

Powers of officers of enforcement authority

3.—(1) If a duly authorised officer of an enforcement authority has reasonable grounds for suspecting that an offence under section 1 of this Act has been committed, he may—

(a) require a person carrying on or employed in a business to produce any book or document relating to the business, and take copies of it or any entry in it, or

(b) require such a person to produce in a visible and legible documentary form [or from which it can readily be produced in a visible and legible form] any information so relating which is [stored in any electronic form], and take copies of it,

for the purpose of ascertaining whether such an offence has been committed.

(2) Such an officer may inspect any goods for the purpose of ascertaining whether such an offence has been committed.

(3) If such an officer has reasonable grounds for believing that any documents or goods may be required as evidence in proceedings for such an offence, he may seize and detain them.

(4) An officer seizing any documents or goods in the exercise of his power under sub-paragraph (3) above shall inform the person from whom they are seized.

(5) The powers of an officer under this paragraph may be exercised by him only at a reasonable hour and on production (if required) of his credentials.

(6) Nothing in this paragraph—

(a) requires a person to produce a document if he would be entitled to refuse to produce it in proceedings in a court on the ground that it is the subject of legal professional privilege or, in Scotland, that it contains a confidential communication made by or to an advocate or a solicitor in that capacity, or

(b) authorises the taking possession of a document which is in the possession of a person who would be so entitled.

4.—(1) A duly authorised officer of an enforcement authority may, at a reasonable hour and on production (if required) of his credentials, enter any premises for the purpose of ascertaining whether an offence under section 1 of this Act has been committed.

(2) If a justice of the peace, or in Scotland a justice of the peace or a sheriff, is satisfied—

(a) that any relevant books, documents or goods are on, or that any relevant information contained in a computer is available from, any premises, and that production or inspection is likely to disclose the commission of an offence under section 1 of this Act, or

(b) that such an offence has been, is being or is about to be committed on any premises,

and that any of the conditions specified in sub-paragraph (3) below is met, he may by warrant under his hand authorise an officer of an enforcement authority to enter the premises, if need be by force.

(3) The conditions referred to in sub-paragraph (2) above are—

(a) that admission to the premises has been or is likely to be refused and that notice of intention to apply for a warrant under that sub-paragraph has been given to the occupier,

(b) that an application for admission, or the giving of such a notice, would defeat the object of the entry,

(c) that the premises are unoccupied, and

(d) that the occupier is temporarily absent and it might defeat the object of the entry to await his return.

(4) In sub-paragraph (2) above "relevant", in relation to books, documents, goods or information, means books, documents, goods or information which, under paragraph 3 above, a duly authorised officer may require to be produced or may inspect.

(5) A warrant under sub-paragraph (2) above may be issued only if—

(a) in England and Wales, the justice of the peace is satisfied as required by that sub-paragraph by written information on oath,

(b) in Scotland, the justice of the peace or sheriff is so satisfied by evidence on oath, or

(c) in Northern Ireland, the justice of the peace is so satisfied by complaint on oath.

(6) A warrant under sub-paragraph (2) above shall continue in force for a period of one month.

(7) An officer entering any premises by virtue of this paragraph may take with him such other persons as may appear to him necessary.

(8) On leaving premises which he has entered by virtue of a warrant under sub-paragraph (2) above, an officer shall, if the premises are unoccupied or the occupier is temporarily absent, leave the premises as effectively secured against trespassers as he found them.

(9) In this paragraph "premises" includes any place (including any vehicle, ship or aircraft) except premises used only as a dwelling.

Obstruction of officers

5.—(1) A person who—

(a) intentionally obstructs an officer of an enforcement authority acting in pursuance of this Schedule,

(b) without reasonable excuse fails to comply with a requirement made of him by such an officer under paragraph 3(1)(a) above, or

(c) without reasonable excuse fails to give an officer of an enforcement authority acting in pursuance of this Schedule any other assistance or information which the officer may reasonably require of him for the purpose of the performance of the officer's functions under this Schedule,

shall be guilty of an offence.

(2) A person guilty of an offence under sub-paragraph (1) above shall be liable on summary conviction to a fine not exceeding level 5 on the standard scale.

(3) If a person, in giving any such information as is mentioned in sub-paragraph (1)(c) above,—

(a) makes a statement which he knows is false in a material particular, or

(b) recklessly makes a statement which is false in a material particular,

he shall be guilty of an offence.

(4) A person guilty of an offence under sub-paragraph (3) above shall be liable—

(a) on summary conviction, to a fine not exceeding the statutory maximum, and

(b) on conviction on indictment, to a fine.

Impersonation of officers

6.—(1) If a person who is not a duly authorised officer of an enforcement authority purports to act as such under this Schedule he shall be guilty of an offence.

(2) A person guilty of an offence under sub-paragraph (1) above shall be liable—

(a) on summary conviction, to a fine not exceeding the statutory maximum, and

(b) on conviction on indictment, to a fine.

7. …

Privilege against self-incrimination

8. Nothing in this Schedule requires a person to answer any question or give any information if to do so might incriminate him.

[1432]

NOTES

Para 2: repealed by the Enterprise Act 2002, s 278(2), Sch 26, subject to transitional provisions and savings in s 276 of, Sch 24, paras 2–6 to, that Act.

Para 3: in sub-para (1)(b), words in first pair of square brackets inserted and words in second pair of square brackets substituted by the Criminal Justice and Police Act 2001, s 70, Sch 2, Pt 2, para 20.

Para 7: repealed by the Enterprise Act 2002, ss 247(h), 278(2), Sch 26.

See further: in relation to additional powers of seizure from premises, see the Criminal Justice and Police Act 2001, s 50, Sch 1, Pt 1, para 53.

ACCESS TO NEIGHBOURING LAND ACT 1992

(1992 c 23)

An Act to enable persons who desire to carry out works to any land which are reasonably necessary for the preservation of that land to obtain access to neighbouring land in order to do so; and for purposes connected therewith

[16 March 1992]

1 Access orders

(1) A person—

(a) who, for the purpose of carrying out works to any land (the "dominant land"), desires to enter upon any adjoining or adjacent land (the "servient land"), and

(b) who needs, but does not have, the consent of some other person to that entry,

may make an application to the court for an order under this section ("an access order") against that other person.

(2) On an application under this section, the court shall make an access order if, and only if, it is satisfied—

(a) that the works are reasonably necessary for the preservation of the whole or any part of the dominant land; and

(b) that they cannot be carried out, or would be substantially more difficult to carry out, without entry upon the servient land;

but this subsection is subject to subsection (3) below.

(3) The court shall not make an access order in any case where it is satisfied that, were it to make such an order—

(a) the respondent or any other person would suffer interference with, or disturbance of, his use or enjoyment of the servient land, or

(b) the respondent, or any other person (whether of full age or capacity or not) in occupation of the whole or any part of the servient land, would suffer hardship,

to such a degree by reason of the entry (notwithstanding any requirement of this Act or any term or condition that may be imposed under it) that it would be unreasonable to make the order.

(4) Where the court is satisfied on an application under this section that it is reasonably necessary to carry out any basic preservation works to the dominant land, those works shall be taken for the purposes of this Act to be reasonably necessary for the preservation of the land; and in this subsection "basic preservation works" means any of the following, that is to say—

(a) the maintenance, repair or renewal of any part of a building or other structure comprised in, or situate on, the dominant land;

(b) the clearance, repair or renewal of any drain, sewer, pipe or cable so comprised or situate;

(c) the treatment, cutting back, felling, removal or replacement of any hedge, tree, shrub or other growing thing which is so comprised and which is, or is in danger of becoming, damaged, diseased, dangerous, insecurely rooted or dead;

(d) the filling in, or clearance, of any ditch so comprised;

but this subsection is without prejudice to the generality of the works which may, apart from it, be regarded by the court as reasonably necessary for the preservation of any land.

(5) If the court considers it fair and reasonable in all the circumstances of the case, works may be regarded for the purposes of this Act as being reasonably necessary for the preservation of any land (or, for the purposes of subsection (4) above, as being basic preservation works which it is reasonably necessary to carry out to any land) notwithstanding that the works incidentally involve—

(a) the making of some alteration, adjustment or improvement to the land, or

(b) the demolition of the whole or any part of a building or structure comprised in or situate upon the land.

(6) Where any works are reasonably necessary for the preservation of the whole or any part of the dominant land, the doing to the dominant land of anything which is requisite for, incidental to, or consequential on, the carrying out of those works shall be treated for the purposes of this Act as the carrying out of works which are reasonably necessary for the preservation of that land; and references in this Act to works, or to the carrying out of works, shall be construed accordingly.

(7) Without prejudice to the generality of subsection (6) above, if it is reasonably necessary for a person to inspect the dominant land—

(a) for the purpose of ascertaining whether any works may be reasonably necessary for the preservation of the whole or any part of that land,

(b) for the purpose of making any map or plan, or ascertaining the course of any drain, sewer, pipe or cable, in preparation for, or otherwise in connection with, the carrying out of works which are so reasonably necessary, or

(c) otherwise in connection with the carrying out of any such works,

the making of such an inspection shall be taken for the purposes of this Act to be the carrying out to the dominant land of works which are reasonably necessary for the preservation of that land; and references in this Act to works, or to the carrying out of works, shall be construed accordingly.

[1433]

2 Terms and conditions of access orders

(1) An access order shall specify—

(a) the works to the dominant land that may be carried out by entering upon the servient land in pursuance of the order;

(b) the particular area of servient land that may be entered upon by virtue of the order for the purpose of carrying out those works to the dominant land; and

(c) the date on which, or the period during which, the land may be so entered upon;

and in the following provisions of this Act any reference to the servient land is a reference to the area specified in the order in pursuance of paragraph (b) above.

(2) An access order may impose upon the applicant or the respondent such terms and conditions as appear to the court to be reasonably necessary for the purpose of avoiding or restricting—

(a) any loss, damage, or injury which might otherwise be caused to the respondent or any other person by reason of the entry authorised by the order; or

(b) any inconvenience or loss of privacy that might otherwise be so caused to the respondent or any other person.

(3) Without prejudice to the generality of subsection (2) above, the terms and conditions which may be imposed under that subsection include provisions with respect to—

(a) the manner in which the specified works are to be carried out;

(b) the days on which, and the hours between which, the work involved may be executed;

(c) the persons who may undertake the carrying out of the specified works or enter upon the servient land under or by virtue of the order;

(d) the taking of any such precautions by the applicant as may be specified in the order.

(4) An access order may also impose terms and conditions—

(a) requiring the applicant to pay, or to secure that such person connected with him as may be specified in the order pays, compensation for—

(i) any loss, damage or injury, or

(ii) any substantial loss of privacy or other substantial inconvenience,

which will, or might, be caused to the respondent or any other person by reason of the entry authorised by the order;

(b) requiring the applicant to secure that he, or such person connected with him as may be specified in the order, is insured against any such risks as may be so specified; or

(c) requiring such a record to be made of the condition of the servient land, or of such part of it as may be so specified, as the court may consider expedient with a view to facilitating the determination of any question that may arise concerning damage to that land.

(5) An access order may include provision requiring the applicant to pay the respondent such sum by way of consideration for the privilege of entering the servient land in pursuance of the order as appears to the court to be fair and reasonable having regard to all the circumstances of the case, including, in particular—

(a) the likely financial advantage of the order to the applicant and any persons connected with him; and

(b) the degree of inconvenience likely to be caused to the respondent or any other person by the entry;

but no payment shall be ordered under this subsection if and to the extent that the works which the applicant desires to carry out by means of the entry are works to residential land.

(6) For the purposes of subsection (5)(a) above, the likely financial advantage of an access order to the applicant and any persons connected with him shall in all cases be taken to be a sum of money equal to the greater of the following amounts, that is to say—

(a) the amount (if any) by which so much of any likely increase in the value of any land—

(i) which consists of or includes the dominant land, and

(ii) which is owned or occupied by the same person as the dominant land,

as may reasonably be regarded as attributable to the carrying out of the specified works exceeds the likely cost of carrying out those works with the benefit of the access order; and

(b) the difference (if it would have been possible to carry out the specified works without entering upon the servient land) between—

(i) the likely cost of carrying out those works without entering upon the servient land; and

(ii) the likely cost of carrying them out with the benefit of the access order.

(7) For the purposes of subsection (5) above, "residential land" means so much of any land as consists of—

(a) a dwelling or part of a dwelling;

(b) a garden, yard, private garage or outbuilding which is used and enjoyed wholly or mainly with a dwelling; or

(c) in the case of a building which includes one or more dwellings, any part of the building which is used and enjoyed wholly or mainly with those dwellings or any of them.

(8) The persons who are to be regarded for the purposes of this section as "connected with" the applicant are—

(a) the owner of any estate or interest in, or right over, the whole or any part of the dominant land;

(b) the occupier of the whole or any part of the dominant land; and

(c) any person whom the applicant may authorise under section 3(7) below to exercise the power of entry conferred by the access order.

(9) The court may make provision—

(a) for the reimbursement by the applicant of any expenses reasonably incurred by the respondent in connection with the application which are not otherwise recoverable as costs;

(b) for the giving of security by the applicant for any sum that might become payable to the respondent or any other person by virtue of this section or section 3 below.

[1434]

3 Effect of access order

(1) An access order requires the respondent, so far as he has power to do so, to permit the applicant or any of his associates to do anything which the applicant or associate is authorised or required to do under or by virtue of the order or this section.

(2) Except as otherwise provided by or under this Act, an access order authorises the applicant or any of his associates, without the consent of the respondent,—

(a) to enter upon the servient land for the purpose of carrying out the specified works;

(b) to bring on to that land, leave there during the period permitted by the order and, before the end of that period, remove, such materials, plant and equipment as are reasonably necessary for the carrying out of those works; and

(c) to bring on to that land any waste arising from the carrying out of those works, if it is reasonably necessary to do so in the course of removing it from the dominant land;

but nothing in this Act or in any access order shall authorise the applicant or any of his associates to leave anything in, on or over the servient land (otherwise than in discharge of their duty to make good that land) after their entry for the purpose of carrying out works to the dominant land ceases to be authorised under or by virtue of the order.

(3) An access order requires the applicant—
(a) to secure that any waste arising from the carrying out of the specified works is removed from the servient land forthwith;
(b) to secure that, before the entry ceases to be authorised under or by virtue of the order, the servient land is, so far as reasonably practicable, made good; and
(c) to indemnify the respondent against any damage which may be caused to the servient land or any goods by the applicant or any of his associates which would not have been so caused had the order not been made;

but this subsection is subject to subsections (4) and (5) below.

(4) In making an access order, the court may vary or exclude, in whole or in part,—
(a) any authorisation that would otherwise be conferred by subsection (2)(b) or (c) above; or
(b) any requirement that would otherwise be imposed by subsection (3) above.

(5) Without prejudice to the generality of subsection (4) above, if the court is satisfied that it is reasonably necessary for any such waste as may arise from the carrying out of the specified works to be left on the servient land for some period before removal, the access order may, in place of subsection (3)(a) above, include provision—
(a) authorising the waste to be left on that land for such period as may be permitted by the order; and
(b) requiring the applicant to secure that the waste is removed before the end of that period.

(6) Where the applicant or any of his associates is authorised or required under or by virtue of an access order or this section to enter, or do any other thing, upon the servient land, he shall not (as respects that access order) be taken to be a trespasser from the beginning on account of his, or any other person's, subsequent conduct.

(7) For the purposes of this section, the applicant's "associates" are such number of persons (whether or not servants or agents of his) whom he may reasonably authorise under this subsection to exercise the power of entry conferred by the access order as may be reasonably necessary for carrying out the specified works.

[1435]

4 Persons bound by access order, unidentified persons and bar on contracting out

(1) In addition to the respondent, an access order shall, subject to the provisions of the Land Charges Act 1972 and the [Land Registration Act 2002], be binding on—
(a) any of his successors in title to the servient land; and
(b) any person who has an estate or interest in, or right over, the whole or any part of the servient land which was created after the making of the order and who derives his title to that estate, interest or right under the respondent;

and references to the respondent shall be construed accordingly.

(2) If and to the extent that the court considers it just and equitable to allow him to do so, a person on whom an access order becomes binding by virtue of subsection (1)(a) or (b) above shall be entitled, as respects anything falling to be done after the order becomes binding on him, to enforce the order or any of its terms or conditions as if he were the respondent, and references to the respondent shall be construed accordingly.

(3) Rules of court may—
(a) provide a procedure which may be followed where the applicant does not know, and cannot reasonably ascertain, the name of any person whom he desires to make respondent to the application; and
(b) make provision enabling such an applicant to make such a person respondent by description instead of by name;

and in this subsection "applicant" includes a person who proposes to make an application for an access order.

(4) Any agreement, whenever made, shall be void if and to the extent that it would, apart from this subsection, prevent a person from applying for an access order or restrict his right to do so.

[1436]

NOTES

Sub-s (1): words in square brackets substituted by the Land Registration Act 2002, s 133, Sch 11, para 26(1), (2).

5 Registration of access orders and of applications for such orders

(1)–(3) …

(4) In any case where—
(a) an access order is discharged under section 6(1)(a) below, and
(b) the order has been protected by an entry registered under the Land Charges Act 1972 or by a [notice under the Land Registration Act 2002],

the court may by order direct that the [entry or notice] shall be cancelled.

[(5) The rights conferred on a person by or under an access order shall not be capable of falling within paragraph 2 of Schedule 1 or 3 to the Land Registration Act 2002 (overriding status of interest of person in actual occupation).]

(6) An application for an access order shall be regarded as a pending land action for the purposes of the Land Charges Act 1972 and the [Land Registration Act 2002].

[1437]

NOTES

Sub-s (1): amends the Land Charges Act 1972, s 6(1).

Sub-ss (2), (3): repealed by the Land Registration Act 2002, s 135, Sch 13.

Sub-s (4): words in square brackets substituted by the Land Registration Act 2002, s 133, Sch 11, para 26(1), (3).

Sub-s (5): substituted by the Land Registration Act 2002, s 133, Sch 11, para 26(1), (4).

Sub-s (6): words in square brackets substituted by the Land Registration Act 2002, s 133, Sch 11, para 26(1), (5).

6 Variation of orders and damages for breach

(1) Where an access order or an order under this subsection has been made, the court may, on the application of any party to the proceedings in which the order was made or of any other person on whom the order is binding—

(a) discharge or vary the order or any of its terms or conditions;
(b) suspend any of its terms or conditions; or
(c) revive any term or condition suspended under paragraph (b) above;

and in the application of subsections (1) and (2) of section 4 above in relation to an access order, any order under this subsection which relates to the access order shall be treated for the purposes of those subsections as included in the access order.

(2) If any person contravenes or fails to comply with any requirement, term or condition imposed upon him by or under this Act, the court may, without prejudice to any other remedy available, make an order for the payment of damages by him to any other person affected by the contravention or failure who makes an application for relief under this subsection.

[1438]

7 Jurisdiction over, and allocation of, proceedings

(1) The High Court and the county courts shall both have jurisdiction under this Act.

(2) …

(3) The amendment by subsection (2) above of provisions contained in an order shall not be taken to have prejudiced any power to make further orders revoking or amending those provisions.

[1439]

NOTES

Sub-s (2): amends SI 1991/724, art 4 and inserts art 6A thereof.

8 Interpretation and application

(1) Any reference in this Act to an "entry" upon any servient land includes a reference to the doing on that land of anything necessary for carrying out the works to the dominant land which are reasonably necessary for its preservation; and "enter" shall be construed accordingly.

(2) This Act applies in relation to any obstruction of, or other interference with, a right over, or interest in, any land as it applies in relation to an entry upon that land; and "enter" and "entry" shall be construed accordingly.

(3) In this Act—

"access order" has the meaning given by section 1(1) above;

"applicant" means a person making an application for an access order and, subject to section 4 above, "the respondent" means the respondent, or any of the respondents, to such an application;

"the court" means the High Court or a county court;

"the dominant land" and "the servient land" respectively have the meanings given by section 1(1) above, but subject, in the case of servient land, to section 2(1) above;

"land" does not include a highway;

"the specified works" means the works specified in the access order in pursuance of section 2(1)(a) above.

[1440]

9 Short title, commencement and extent

(1) This Act may be cited as the Access to Neighbouring Land Act 1992.

(2) This Act shall come into force on such day as the Lord Chancellor may by order made by statutory instrument appoint.

(3) This Act extends to England and Wales only.

[1441]

NOTES

Order: the Access to Neighbouring Land Act 1992 (Commencement) Order 1992, SI 1992/3349.

TIMESHARE ACT 1992

(1992 c 35)

An Act to provide for rights to cancel certain agreements about timeshare accommodation

[16 March 1992]

1 Application of Act

(1) In this Act—

(a) "timeshare accommodation" means any living accommodation, in the United Kingdom or elsewhere, used or intended to be used, wholly or partly, for leisure purposes by a class of persons (referred to below in this section as "timeshare users") all of whom have rights to use, or participate in arrangements under which they may use, that accommodation, or accommodation within a pool of accommodation to which that accommodation belongs, for [a specified or ascertainable period of the year], and

(b) "timeshare rights" means rights by virtue of which a person becomes or will become a timeshare user, being rights exercisable during a period of not less than three years.

(2) For the purposes of subsection (1)(a) above—

(a) "accommodation" means accommodation in a building or in a caravan (as defined in section 29(1) of the Caravan Sites and Control of Development Act 1960)…

(b) …

(3) Subsection (1)(b) above does not apply to a person's rights—

…

(b) under a contract of employment ([within the meaning of the Employment Rights Act 1996]) or a policy of insurance, …

…

or to such rights as may be prescribed.

[(3A) For the purposes of sections 1A to 1E, [2(2B) to (2E)], 3(3), 5A, 5B and 6A of this Act, subsection (1) above shall be construed as if in paragraph (b), after "become" there were inserted ", on payment of a global price,".]

(4) In this Act "timeshare agreement" means … an agreement under which timeshare rights are conferred or purport to be conferred on any person and in this Act, in relation to a timeshare agreement—

(a) references to the offeree are to the person on whom timeshare rights are conferred, or purport to be conferred, and

(b) references to the offeror are to the other party to the agreement,

and, in relation to any time before the agreement is entered into, references in this Act to the offeree or the offeror are to the persons who become the offeree and offeror when it is entered into.

[(5) In this Act "timeshare credit agreement" means an agreement, not being a timeshare agreement, under which credit which fully or partly covers the price under a timeshare agreement is granted—

(a) by the offeror, or

(b) by another person, under an arrangement between that person and the offeror;

and a person who grants credit under a timeshare credit agreement is in this Act referred to as "the creditor".]

(6) …

[(6A) No timeshare agreement or timeshare credit agreement to which this Act applies may be cancelled under section 67 of the Consumer Credit Act 1974.]

(7) This Act applies to any timeshare agreement or timeshare credit agreement if—

(a) the agreement is to any extent governed by the law of the United Kingdom or of a part of the United Kingdom, or

(b) when the agreement is entered into, one or both of the parties are in the United Kingdom.

[(7A) This Act also applies to any timeshare agreement if—

(a) the relevant accommodation is situated in the United Kingdom, …

[(ab) the relevant accommodation is situated in another EEA State and the parties to the agreement are to any extent subject to the jurisdiction of any court in the United Kingdom in relation to the agreement, or]

(b) when the agreement is entered into, the offeree is ordinarily resident in the United Kingdom and the relevant accommodation is situated in another EEA State.

(7B) For the purposes of subsection (7A) above, "the relevant accommodation" means—

(a) the accommodation which is the subject of the agreement, or

(b) some or all of the accommodation in the pool of accommodation which is the subject of the agreement,

as the case may be.]

(8) In the application of this section to Northern Ireland—

(a) for the reference in subsection (2)(a) above to section 29(1) of the Caravan Sites and Control of Development Act 1960 there is substituted a reference to section 25(1) of the Caravans Act (Northern Ireland) 1963, and

(b) for the reference in subsection (3)(b) above to [the Employment Rights Act 1996] there is substituted a reference to article 2(2) of the Industrial Relations (Northern Ireland) Order 1976.

[1442]

NOTES

Sub-s (1): words in square brackets substituted by SI 1997/1081, reg 2(2).

Sub-s (2): para (b) and word omitted immediately preceding it repealed by SI 1997/1081, reg 14(1), (2).

Sub-s (3): paras (a), (c) and preceding word, repealed by SI 1997/1081, reg 2(3); in para (b) words in square brackets substituted by the Employment Rights Act 1996, s 240, Sch 1, para 53.

Sub-ss (3A), (6A), (7A), (7B): inserted by SI 1997/1081, reg 2(4), (7), (8).

Sub-s (3A): words in square brackets substituted by SI 2003/1922, reg 2, Schedule, para 1(1), (2).

Sub-s (4): words omitted repealed by SI 1997/1081, reg 14(1), (3).

Sub-s (5): substituted by SI 1997/1081, reg 2(5).

Sub-s (6): repealed by SI 1997/1081, reg 2(6).

Sub-s (7A): word omitted from para (a) repealed and para (ab) inserted by SI 2003/1922, reg 2, Schedule, para 1(1), (3).

Sub-s (8): in para (b) words in square brackets substituted by the Employment Rights Act 1996, s 240, Sch 1, para 53.

[1A Obligations to provide information

(1) A person who proposes in the course of a business to enter into a timeshare agreement to which this Act applies as offeror (an "operator") must provide any person who requests information on the proposed accommodation with a document complying with subsection (2) below.

(2) The document shall provide—

(a) a general description of the proposed accommodation,

(b) information (which may be brief) on the matters referred to in paragraphs (a) to (g) [and (i)] of Schedule 1 to this Act, …

[(ba) information (which may be brief) on the rights under this Act to cancel a timeshare agreement and the effect of cancellation on any related timeshare credit agreement to which this Act applies, and]

(c) information on how further information may be obtained.

[(2A) In subsection (2)(ba) above "related timeshare credit agreement" means a timeshare credit agreement under which credit which fully or partly covers the price under the timeshare agreement is granted.]

(3) Where an operator—

(a) provides a person with a document containing information on the proposed accommodation, and

(b) subsequently enters as offeror into a timeshare agreement to which this Act applies the subject of which is the proposed accommodation,

subsection (4) below applies.

(4) If the offeree under the agreement is an individual who—

(a) is not acting in the course of a business, and

(b) has received the document mentioned in subsection (3) above,

any information contained in that document which was, or would on request have been, required to be provided under section (2)(b) above shall be deemed to be a term of the agreement.

(5) If, in a case where subsection (4) above applies, a change in the information contained in the document is communicated to the offeree in writing before the timeshare agreement is entered into, the change shall be deemed for the purposes of this Act always to have been incorporated in the information contained in the document if—

(a) the change arises from circumstances beyond the offeror's control, or
(b) the offeror and the offeree expressly agree to the change before entering into the timeshare agreement,

and the change is expressly mentioned in the timeshare agreement.

(6) A person who contravenes subsection (1) above is guilty of an offence and liable—
(a) on summary conviction, to a fine not exceeding the statutory maximum, and
(b) on conviction on indictment, to a fine.

(7) In this section "the proposed accommodation" means—
(a) the accommodation which is the subject of the proposed agreement, or
(b) the accommodation in the pool of accommodation which is the subject of the proposed agreement,

as the case may be.

(8) This section only applies if—
(a) the accommodation which is the subject of the proposed agreement or agreement is accommodation in a building, or
(b) some or all of the accommodation in the pool of accommodation which is the subject of the proposed agreement or agreement is accommodation in a building,

as the case may be.]

[1443]

NOTES

Inserted by SI 1997/1081, reg 3(1),

Sub-s (2): in para (b), words in square brackets substituted and word omitted repealed and para (ba) inserted by SI 2003/1922, reg 2, Schedule, para 2(1)–(3).

Sub-s (2A): inserted by SI 2003/1922, reg 2, Schedule, para 2(1), (4).

[1B Advertising of timeshare rights

(1) No person shall advertise timeshare rights in the course of a business unless the advertisement indicates the possibility of obtaining the document referred to in section 1A(1) of this Act and where it may be obtained.

(2) A person who contravenes this section is guilty of an offence and liable—
(a) on summary conviction, to a fine not exceeding the statutory maximum, and
(b) on conviction on indictment, to a fine.

(3) In proceedings against a person for an offence under this section it shall be a defence for that person to show that at the time when he advertised the timeshare rights—
(a) he did not know and had no reasonable cause to suspect that he was advertising timeshare rights, or
(b) he had reasonable cause to believe that the advertisement complied with the requirements of subsection (1) above.

(4) This section only applies if—
(a) the timeshare accommodation concerned is, or appears from the advertisement to be, accommodation in a building, or
(b) some or all of the accommodation in the pool of accommodation concerned is, or appears from the advertisement to be, accommodation in a building,

as the case may be.]

[1444]

NOTES

Inserted by SI 1997/1081, reg 4.

[1C Obligatory terms of timeshare agreement

(1) A person must not in the course of a business enter into a timeshare agreement to which this Act applies as offeror unless the agreement includes, as terms set out in it, the information referred to in Schedule 1 to this Act.

(2) If and to the extent that any information set out in an agreement in accordance with subsection (1) above is inconsistent with any term (the "deemed term") which is deemed to be included in the agreement under section 1A(4) of this Act, the agreement shall be treated for all purposes of this Act as if the deemed term, and not that information, were set out and included in the agreement.

(3) A person who contravenes subsection (1) above is guilty of an offence and liable—
(a) on summary conviction, to a fine not exceeding the statutory maximum, and
(b) on conviction on indictment, to a fine.

(4) This section only applies if the offeree—

(a) is an individual, and
(b) is not acting in the course of a business.

(5) This section only applies if—
(a) the accommodation which is the subject of the agreement is accommodation in a building, or
(b) some or all of the accommodation in the pool of accommodation which is the subject of the agreement is accommodation in a building,

as the case may be.]

[1445]

NOTES

Inserted by SI 1997/1081, reg 5.

[1D Form of agreement and language of brochure and agreement

(1) A person must not in the course of a business enter into a timeshare agreement to which this Act applies as offeror unless the agreement is in writing and complies with subsections (3) to (5) below, so far as applicable.

(2) A person who is required to provide a document under subsection (1) of section 1A of this Act contravenes that subsection if he does not provide a document which complies with subsections (3) and (4) below, so far as applicable.

(3) If the customer is resident in, or a national of, an EEA State, the agreement or document (as the case may be) must be drawn up in a language which is—
(a) the language, or one of the languages, of the EEA State in which he is resident, or
(b) the language, or one of the languages, of the EEA State of which he is a national,

and is an official language of an EEA State.

(4) If, in a case falling within subsection (3) above, there are two or more languages in which the agreement or document may be drawn up in compliance with that subsection and the customer nominates one of those languages, the agreement or document must be drawn up in the language he nominates.

(5) If the offeree is resident in the United Kingdom and the agreement would not, apart from this subsection, be required to be drawn up in English, it must be drawn up in English (in addition to any other language in which it is drawn up).

(6) A person who contravenes subsection (1) above is guilty of an offence and liable—
(a) on summary conviction, to a fine not exceeding the statutory maximum, and
(b) on conviction on indictment, to a fine.

(7) In this section "the customer" means—
(a) for the purposes of subsection (1) above, the offeree, and
(b) for the purposes of subsection (2) above, the person to whom the document is required to be provided.

(8) Subsection (1) above only applies if the offeree—
(a) is an individual, and
(b) is not acting in the course of a business.

(9) Subsection (1) above only applies if—
(a) the accommodation which is the subject of the agreement is accommodation in a building, or
(b) some or all of the accommodation in the pool of accommodation which is the subject of the agreement is accommodation in a building,

as the case may be.]

[1446]

NOTES

Inserted by SI 1997/1081, reg 6.

[1E Translation of agreement

(1) A person must not in the course of a business enter into a timeshare agreement to which this Act applies as offeror unless he complies with subsection (2) below.

(2) If the timeshare accommodation which is the subject of the agreement, or any of the accommodation in the pool of accommodation which is the subject of the agreement, is situated in an EEA State, the offeror must provide the offeree with a certified translation of the agreement in the language, or one of the languages, of that State.

(3) The language of the translation must be an official language of an EEA State.

(4) Subsection (1) above does not apply if the agreement is drawn up in a language in which the translation is required or permitted to be made.

(5) A person who contravenes subsection (1) above is guilty of an offence and liable—

(a) on summary conviction, to a fine not exceeding the statutory maximum, and

(b) on conviction on indictment, to a fine.

(6) In this section "certified translation" means a translation which is certified to be accurate by a person authorised to make or verify translations for the purposes of court proceedings.

(7) This section only applies if the offeree—

(a) is an individual, and

(b) is not acting in the course of a business.

(8) This section only applies if—

(a) the accommodation which is the subject of the agreement is accommodation in a building, or

(b) some or all of the accommodation in the pool of accommodation which is the subject of the agreement is accommodation in a building,

as the case may be.]

[1447]

NOTES

Inserted by SI 1997/1081, reg 7.

2 [Obligation for timeshare agreement to contain information on cancellation rights]

(1) A person must not in the course of a business enter into a timeshare agreement to which this Act applies as offeror unless [the offeree has received the agreement and it complies with the following requirements].

(2) [The agreement] must state—

(a) that the offeree is entitled to give notice of cancellation of the agreement to the offeror at any time on or before the date specified [in the agreement], being a day falling not less than fourteen days after the day on which the agreement is entered into, and

(b) that if the offeree gives such a notice to the offeror on or before that date he will [(subject to section 5(9) of this Act)] have no further rights or obligations under the agreement, but will have the right to recover any sums paid under or in contemplation of the agreement.

[(2A) If the agreement includes provision for providing credit for or in respect of the offeree, it must state that, notwithstanding the giving of notice of cancellation under section 5 or 5A of this Act, so far as the agreement relates to repayment of the credit and payment of interest, it will continue to be enforceable, subject to section 7 of this Act.

(2B) Subsection (2C) below applies if—

(a) the price under the timeshare agreement is covered fully or partly by credit granted under a timeshare credit agreement to which this Act applies,

(b) the offeree is an individual, and

(c) the accommodation which is the subject of the timeshare agreement is accommodation in a building, or some or all of the accommodation in the pool of accommodation which is the subject of the agreement is accommodation in a building.

(2C) The timeshare agreement must state that, if the offeree gives to the offeror a notice as mentioned in subsection (2)(b) above or a notice of cancellation of the agreement under section 5A of this Act which has the effect of cancelling the agreement—

(a) the notice will also have the effect of cancelling the timeshare credit agreement,

(b) so far as the timeshare credit agreement relates to repayment of credit and payment of interest, it shall have effect subject to section 7 of this Act, and

(c) subject to paragraph (b) above, the offeree will have no further rights or obligations under the timeshare credit agreement.

(2D) Subsection (2E) below applies if—

(a) the offeree is an individual, and

(b) the accommodation which is the subject of the timeshare agreement is accommodation in a building, or some or all of the accommodation in the pool of accommodation which is the subject of the agreement is accommodation in a building.

(2E) The agreement must state that the offeree may have, in addition to the rights mentioned in subsection (2) above, further rights under section 5A of this Act to cancel the timeshare agreement.

(2F) The agreement must contain a blank notice of cancellation.]

(3) A person who contravenes this section is guilty of an offence and liable—

(a) on summary conviction, to a fine not exceeding the statutory maximum, and

(b) on conviction on indictment, to a fine.

[(4) …]

[1448]

NOTES

Section heading: substituted by SI 2003/1922, reg 2, Schedule, para 3(1), (6).

Sub-s (1): words in square brackets substituted by SI 2003/1922, reg 2, Schedule, para 3(1), (2).

Sub-s (2): words in first and second pairs of square brackets substituted and words in third pair of square brackets inserted by SI 2003/1922, reg 2, Schedule, para 3(1), (3).

Sub-ss (2A)–(2F): substituted, for sub-ss (2A), (2B) (as inserted by SI 1997/1081, reg 8(1)), by SI 2003/1922, reg 2, Schedule, para 3(1), (4).

Sub-s (4): inserted by SI 1997/1081, reg 8(2); repealed by SI 2003/1922, reg 2, Schedule, para 3(1), (5).

3 [Obligation for timeshare credit agreement to contain information on cancellation rights]

(1) A person must not in the course of a business enter into a timeshare credit agreement to which this Act applies as creditor unless [the offeree has received the agreement and it complies with the following requirements].

(2) [The agreement] must state—

(a) that the offeree is entitled to give notice of cancellation of the agreement to the creditor at any time on or before the date specified [in the agreement], being a day falling not less than fourteen days after the day on which the agreement is entered into, and

(b) that, if the offeree gives such a notice to the creditor on or before that date, then—

(i) so far as the agreement relates to repayment of credit and payment of interest, it shall have effect subject to section 7 of this Act, and

(ii) subject to sub-paragraph (i) above, the offeree will have no further rights or obligations under the agreement.

[(3) [The agreement must state that it] is a timeshare credit agreement for the purposes of this Act.]

[(4) Subsection (5) below applies if—

(a) the offeree is an individual, and

(b) the accommodation which is the subject of the timeshare agreement to which the timeshare credit agreement relates is accommodation in a building, or some or all of the accommodation in the pool of accommodation which is the subject of that timeshare agreement is accommodation in a building.

(5) The timeshare credit agreement must state that, if the offeree gives a notice under section 5 or 5A of this Act of cancellation of the timeshare agreement which has the effect of cancelling it, the notice will also have the effect of cancelling the timeshare credit agreement (with the same consequences as mentioned in subsection (2)(b)(i) and (ii) above).

(6) The agreement must contain a blank notice of cancellation.]

[1449]

NOTES

Section heading: substituted by SI 2003/1922, reg 2, Schedule, para 4(1), (6).

Sub-ss (1), (2): words in square brackets substituted by SI 2003/1922, reg 2, Schedule, para 4(1)–(3).

Sub-s (3): inserted by SI 1997/1081, reg 8(3); words in square brackets substituted by SI 2003/1922, reg 2, Schedule, para 4(1), (4).

Sub-ss (4)–(6): inserted by SI 2003/1922, reg 2, Schedule, para 4(1), (5).

4 Provisions supplementary to sections 2 and 3

(1) Sections 2 and 3 of this Act do not apply where, in entering into the agreement, the offeree is acting in the course of a business.

(2) [A timeshare agreement to which this Act applies and a timeshare credit agreement to which this Act applies must each—]

(a) be in such form as may be prescribed, and

(b) comply with such requirements (whether as to type, size, colour or disposition of lettering, quality or colour of paper, or otherwise) as may be prescribed for securing that [the matters required to be stated or contained in the agreement by virtue of section 2 or 3 are] prominent and easily legible.

(3) An agreement is not invalidated by reason of a contravention of section 2 or 3.

[1450]

NOTES

Sub-s (2): words in square brackets substituted by SI 2003/1922, reg 2, Schedule, para 5(1), (2).

Orders: the Timeshare (Cancellation Notices) Order 1992, SI 1992/1942; the Timeshare (Cancellation Information) Order 2003, SI 2003/2579.

5 Right to cancel timeshare agreement

(1) Where a person—

(a) has entered, or proposes to enter, into a timeshare agreement to which this Act applies as offeree, and

[(b) the agreement complies with the requirements of sections 2 and 4 of this Act,]

the agreement may not be enforced against him on or before the date specified [in the agreement in pursuance of section 2(2)(a) above] and he may give notice of cancellation of the agreement to the offeror at any time on or before that date.

(2) Subject to subsection (3) below, where[—

(a) a person enters into a timeshare agreement to which this Act applies as offeree, but

(b) the agreement does not comply with the requirements of sections 2 and 4 of this Act],

the agreement may not be enforced against him and he may give notice of cancellation of the agreement to the offeror at any time.

(3) If in a case falling within subsection (2) above the offeree affirms the agreement at any time after the expiry of the period of fourteen days beginning with the day on which the agreement is entered into—

(a) subsection (2) above does not prevent the agreement being enforced against him, and

(b) he may not at any subsequent time give notice of cancellation of the agreement to the offeror [under subsection (2) above].

[(3A) Where—

(a) the offeree is an individual, and

(b) the accommodation which is the subject of the agreement is accommodation in a building, or some or all of the accommodation in the pool of accommodation which is the subject of the agreement is accommodation in a building,

subsection (3) above applies as if for "fourteen days" there were substituted "three months and ten days".

(3B) If in a case falling within subsection (3A) above the last day of the period of three months and ten days is a public holiday, the period shall not end until the end of the first working day after the public holiday.]

(4) The offeree's giving, within the time allowed under this section [or section 5A of this Act], notice of cancellation of the agreement to the offeror at a time when the agreement has been entered into shall have the effect of cancelling the agreement.

(5) The offeree's giving notice of cancellation of the agreement [under this section] to the offeror before the agreement has been entered into shall have the effect of withdrawing any offer to enter into the agreement.

(6) Where a timeshare agreement is cancelled under this section [or section 5A of this Act], then, subject to subsection (9) below—

(a) the agreement shall cease to be enforceable, and

(b) subsection (8) below shall apply.

(7) Subsection (8) below shall also apply where giving a notice of cancellation has the effect of withdrawing an offer to enter into a timeshare agreement.

(8) Where this subsection applies—

(a) any sum which the offeree has paid under or in contemplation of the agreement to the offeror, or to any person who is the offeror's agent for the purpose of receiving that sum, shall be recoverable from the offeror by the offeree and shall be due and payable at the time the notice of cancellation is given, but

(b) no sum may be recovered by or on behalf of the offeror from the offeree in respect of the agreement.

(9) Where a timeshare agreement includes provision for providing credit for or in respect of the offeree, then, notwithstanding the giving of notice of cancellation under this section [or section 5A of this Act], so far as the agreement relates to repayment of the credit and payment of interest—

(a) it shall continue to be enforceable, subject to section 7 of this Act, …

(b) …

[1451]

NOTES

Sub-s (1): words in square brackets substituted by SI 2003/1922, reg 2, Schedule, para 6(1), (2).

Sub-s (2): paras (a), (b) substituted by SI 2003/1922, reg 2, Schedule, para 6(1), (3).

Sub-ss (3), (4)–(6): words in square brackets inserted by SI 1997/1081, reg 9(1)–(4).

Sub-ss (3A), (3B): inserted by SI 2003/1922, reg 2, Schedule, para 6(1), (4).

Sub-s (9): words in square brackets inserted by SI 1997/1081, reg 9(1), (5); para (b) and word immediately preceding it repealed by SI 2003/1922, reg 2, Schedule, para 6(1), (5).

[5A Additional right to cancel timeshare agreement

(1) If a timeshare agreement to which this Act applies does not include, as terms set out in it, the information referred to in paragraph (a), (b), (c), (d)(i), (d)(ii), (h), (i), (k) [and (m)] of Schedule 1 to this Act, the agreement may not be enforced against the offeree before the end of the period of three months and ten days beginning with the day on which the agreement was entered into, and the offeree may give notice of cancellation of the agreement to the offeror at any time during that period.

(2) If the information referred to in subsection (1) above is provided to the offeree before the end of the period of three months beginning with the day on which the agreement was entered into—

(a) the offeree may give notice of cancellation of the agreement to the offeror at any time within the period of ten days beginning with the day on which the information is received by the offeree, but

(b) the offeree may not at any subsequent time give notice of cancellation of the agreement to the offeror under subsection (1) above.

(3) If the last day of the period referred to in subsection (1) above or the last day of the period of ten days referred to in subsection (2) above is a public holiday, the period concerned shall not end until the end of the first working day after the public holiday.

(4) The reference in subsection (1) above to a timeshare agreement to which this Act applies includes a reference to a binding preliminary agreement.

(5) This section only applies of the offeree—

(a) is an individual, and

(b) is not acting in the course of a business.

(6) This section only applies if—

(a) the accommodation which is the subject of the agreement is accommodation in a building, or

(b) some or all of the accommodation in the pool of accommodation which is the subject of the agreement is accommodation in a building,

as the case may be.]

[1452]

NOTES

Inserted by SI 1997/1081, reg 9(6).

Sub-s (1): words in square brackets substituted by SI 2003/1922, reg 2, Schedule, para 7.

[5B Advance payments

(1) A person who enters, or proposes to enter, in the course of a business into a timeshare agreement to which this Act applies as offeror must not (either in person or through another person) request or accept from the offeree or proposed offeree any advance payment before the end of the period during which notice of cancellation of the agreement may be given under section 5 or 5A of this Act.

(2) A person who contravenes this section is guilty of an offence and liable—

(a) on summary conviction, to a fine not exceeding the statutory maximum, and

(b) on conviction on indictment, to a fine.

(3) Subsection (1) above only applies if the offeree or proposed offeree—

(a) is an individual, and

(b) is not acting in the course of a business.

(4) Subsection (1) above only applies if—

(a) the accommodation which is the subject of the agreement or proposed agreement is accommodation in a building, or

(b) some or all of the accommodation in the pool of accommodation which is the subject of the agreement or proposed agreement is accommodation in a building,

as the case may be.]

[1453]

NOTES

Inserted by SI 1997/1081, reg 10.

6 [Right to cancel timeshare credit agreement by giving notice]

(1) Where a person—

(a) has entered into a timeshare credit agreement to which this Act applies as offeree, and

[(b) the agreement complies with the requirements of section 3 and 4 of this Act,] he may give notice of cancellation of the agreement to the creditor at any time on or before the date specified [in the agreement in pursuance of section 3(2)(a) above].

(2) Subject to subsection (3) below, where[—

(a) a person enters into a timeshare credit agreement to which this Act applies as offeree, but

(b) the agreement does not comply with the requirements of sections 3 and 4 of this Act,]

he may give notice of cancellation of the agreement to the creditor at any time.

(3) If in a case falling within subsection (2) above the offeree affirms the agreement at any time after the expiry of the period of fourteen days beginning with the day on which the agreement is entered into, he may not at any subsequent time give notice of cancellation of the agreement to the creditor.

(4) The offeree's giving, within the time allowed under this section, notice of cancellation of the agreement to the creditor at a time when the agreement has been entered into shall have the effect of cancelling the agreement.

(5) Where a timeshare credit agreement is cancelled under this section [or section 6A of this Act]—

(a) the agreement shall continue in force, subject to section 7 of this Act, so far as it relates to repayment of the credit and payment of interest, and

(b) subject to paragraph (a) above, the agreement shall cease to be enforceable.

[1454]

NOTES

Section heading: substituted by SI 1997/1081, reg 11(1).
Sub-s (1): words in square brackets substituted by SI 2003/1922, reg 2, Schedule, para 8(1), (2).
Sub-s (2): paras (a), (b) substituted by SI 2003/1922, reg 2, Schedule, para 8(1), (3).
Sub-s (5): words in square brackets inserted by SI 1997/1081, reg 11(2).

[6A Automatic cancellation of timeshare credit agreement

(1) Where—

(a) a notice of cancellation of a timeshare agreement is given under section 5 or 5A of this Act, and

(b) the giving of the notice has the effect of cancelling the agreement,

the notice shall also have the effect of cancelling any related timeshare credit agreement to which this Act applies.

(2) Where a timeshare credit agreement is cancelled as mentioned in subsection (1) above, the offeror shall, if he is not the same person as the creditor under the related timeshare credit agreement, forthwith on receipt of the notice inform the creditor that the notice has been given.

(3) A timeshare credit agreement is related to a timeshare agreement for the purposes of this section if credit under the timeshare credit agreement fully or partly covers the price under the timeshare agreement.

(4) Subsection (1) above only applies if the offeree under the timeshare agreement concerned is an individual.

(5) Subsection (1) above only applies if—

(a) the accommodation which is the subject of the timeshare agreement is accommodation in a building, or

(b) some or all of the accommodation in the pool of accommodation which is the subject of the timeshare agreement is accommodation in a building,

as the case may be.]

[1455]

NOTES

Inserted by SI 1997/1081, reg 11(3).

7 Repayment of credit and interest

(1) This section applies following—

(a) the giving of notice of cancellation of a timeshare agreement in accordance with section 5 of this Act in a case where subsection (9) of that section applies, ...

(b) the giving of notice of cancellation of a timeshare credit agreement in accordance with section 6 of this Act, [or

(c) the cancellation of a timeshare credit agreement by virtue of section 6A of this Act.]

(2) If the offeree repays the whole or a portion of the credit—

(a) before the expiry of one month following the giving of the notice [or the cancellation of the timeshare credit agreement by virtue of section 6A of this Act (as the case may be)], or

(b) in the case of a credit repayable by instalments, before the date on which the first instalment is due,

no interest shall be payable on the amount repaid.

(3) If the whole of a credit repayable by instalments is not repaid on or before the date specified in subsection (2)(b) above, the offeree shall not be liable to repay any of the credit except on receipt of a request in writing in such form as may be prescribed, signed by or on behalf of the offeror or (as the case may be) creditor, stating the amounts of the remaining instalments (recalculated by the offeror or creditor as nearly as may be in accordance with the agreement and without extending the repayment period), but excluding any sum other than principal and interest.

[1456]

NOTES

Sub-s (1): word omitted from para (a) repealed, and para (c) inserted, by SI 1997/1081, reg 14(4), (5).

Sub-s (2): words in square brackets inserted by SI 1997/1081, reg 14(6).

Order: the Timeshare (Repayment of Credit on Cancellation) Order 1992, SI 1992/1943.

8 Defence of due diligence

(1) In proceedings against a person for an offence under section [1A(6), 1B(2), 1C(3), 1D(6), 1E(5), 2(3) or 5B(2)] of this Act it shall be a defence for that person to show that he took all reasonable steps and exercised all due diligence to avoid committing the offence.

(2) Where in proceedings against a person for such an offence the defence provided by subsection (1) above involves an allegation that the commission of the offence was due—

(a) to the act or default of another, or
(b) to reliance on information given by another,

that person shall not, without the leave of the court, be entitled to rely on the defence unless he has served a notice under subsection (3) below on the person bringing the proceedings not less than seven clear days before the hearing of the proceedings or, in Scotland, the diet of trial.

(3) A notice under this subsection shall give such information identifying or assisting in the identification of the person who committed the act or default or gave the information as is in the possession of the person serving the notice at the time when he serves it.

[1457]

NOTES

Sub-s (1): numbers in square brackets substituted by SI 1997/1081, reg 13(1).

9 Liability of person other than principal offender

(1) Where the commission by a person of an offence under section [1A(6), 1B(2), 1C(3), 1D(6), 1E(5), 2(3) or 5B(2)] of this Act is due to the act or default of some other person, that other person is guilty of the offence and may be proceeded against and punished by virtue of this section whether or not proceedings are taken against the first-mentioned person.

(2) Where a body corporate is guilty of an offence under section [1A(6), 1B(2), 1C(3), 1D(6), 1E(5), 2(3) or 5B(2)] of this Act (including where it is so guilty by virtue of subsection (1) above) in respect of an act or default which is shown to have been committed with the consent or connivance of, or to be attributable to neglect on the part of, a director, manager, secretary or other similar officer of the body corporate or a person who was purporting to act in such a capacity, he (as well as the body corporate) is guilty of the offence and liable to be proceeded against and punished accordingly.

(3) Where the affairs of a body corporate are managed by its members, subsection (2) above applies in relation to the acts and defaults of a member in connection with his functions of management as if he were a director of the body corporate.

(4) Where an offence under section [1A(6), 1B(2), 1C(3), 1D(6), 1E(5), 2(3) or 5B(2)] of this Act committed in Scotland by a Scottish partnership is proved to have been committed with the consent or connivance of, or to be attributable to neglect on the part of, a partner, he (as well as the partnership) is guilty of the offence and liable to be proceeded against and punished accordingly.

[1458]

NOTES

Sub-ss (1), (2), (4): words in square brackets substituted by SI 1997/1081, reg 13(2).

10 Enforcement

[Schedule 2] to this Act (which makes provision about enforcement) shall have effect.

[1459]

NOTES

Words in square brackets substituted by SI 1997/1081, reg 14(7).

[10A Civil proceedings

(1) The obligation to comply with subsection (1) of section 1A of this Act shall be a duty owed by the person who proposes to enter into a timeshare agreement to any person whom he is required to provide with a document under that subsection and a contravention of the obligation shall be actionable accordingly.

(2) The obligation to comply with section 1C(1), 1D(1), [1E(1), and 2(1)] of this Act shall in each case be a duty owed by the person who enters into a timeshare agreement as offeror to the offeree and a contravention of the obligation shall be actionable accordingly.

(3) The obligation to comply with section 6A(2) of this Act shall be a duty owed by the offeror under the timeshare agreement to the creditor under the related timeshare credit agreement and a contravention of the obligation shall be actionable accordingly.]

[1460]

NOTES

Inserted by SI 1997/1081, reg 12.

Sub-s (2): words in square brackets substituted by SI 2003/1922, reg 2, Schedule, para 9.

11 Prosecution time limit

(1) No proceedings for an offence under section [1A(6), 1B(2), 1C(3), 1D(6), 1E(5), 2(3) or 5B(2)] of this Act or paragraph 4(3) … to this Act shall be commenced after—

(a) the end of the period of three years beginning with the date of the commission of the offence, or

(b) the end of the period of one year beginning with the date of the discovery of the offence by the prosecutor,

whichever is the earlier.

(2) For the purposes of this section a certificate signed by or on behalf of the prosecutor and stating the date on which the offence was discovered by him shall be conclusive evidence of that fact; and a certificate stating that matter and purporting to be so signed shall be treated as so signed unless the contrary is proved.

(3) In relation to proceedings in Scotland, subsection (3) of [section 136 of the Criminal Procedure (Scotland) Act 1995] (date of commencement of proceedings) shall apply for the purposes of this section as it applies for the purposes of that.

[1461]

NOTES

Sub-s (1): words in square brackets substituted by SI 1997/1081, reg 13(3); words omitted repealed by SI 2003/1400, art 7, Sch 5.

Sub-s (3): words in square brackets substituted by the Criminal Procedure (Consequential Provisions) (Scotland) Act 1995, s 5, Sch 4, para 83.

12 General provisions

(1) For the purposes of this Act, a notice of cancellation of an agreement is a notice (however expressed) showing that the offeree wishes unconditionally to cancel the agreement, whether or not it is in a prescribed form.

(2) The rights conferred and duties imposed by sections [1A] to 7 of this Act are in addition to any rights conferred or duties imposed by or under any other Act.

(3) For the purposes of this Act, if the offeree sends a notice by post in a properly addressed and pre-paid letter the notice is to be treated as given at the time of posting.

(4) This Act shall have effect in relation to any timeshare agreement or timeshare credit agreement notwithstanding any agreement or notice.

(5) …

(6) In this Act—

"credit" includes a cash loan and any other form of financial accommodation,

["EEA State" means a State which is a Contracting Party to the Agreement on the European Economic Area signed at Oporto on 2nd May 1992 as adjusted by the Protocol signed at Brussels on 17th March 1993,]

"notice" means notice in writing,

"order" means an order made by the Secretary of State, and

"prescribed" means prescribed by an order.

(7) An order under this Act may make different provision for different cases or circumstances.

(8) Any power under this Act to make an order shall be exercisable by statutory instrument and a statutory instrument containing an order under this Act (other than an order made for the purposes of section 13(2) of this Act) shall be subject to annulment in pursuance of a resolution of either House of Parliament.

[1462]

NOTES

Sub-s (2): number in square brackets substituted by SI 1997/1081, reg 14(9).
Sub-s (5): repealed by SI 1997/1081, reg 14(10).
Sub-s (6): definition "EEA State" inserted by SI 1997/1081, reg 2(9).
Orders: the Timeshare Act 1992 (Commencement) Order 1992, SI 1992/1941; the Timeshare (Cancellation Notices) Order 1992, SI 1992/1942; the Timeshare (Repayment of Credit on Cancellation) Order 1992, SI 1992/1943.

13 Short title, etc

(1) This Act may be cited as the Timeshare Act 1992.

(2) This Act shall come into force on such day as may be prescribed.

(3) This Act extends to Northern Ireland.

[1463]

NOTES

Order: the Timeshare Act 1992 (Commencement) Order 1992, SI 1992/1941.

[SCHEDULE 1
MINIMUM LIST OF ITEMS TO BE INCLUDED IN A TIMESHARE AGREEMENT TO WHICH SECTION 1C APPLIES

Regulation 3(3)

(a) The identities and domiciles of the parties, including specific information on the offeror's legal status at the time of the conclusion of the agreement and the identity and domicile of the owner.

(b) The exact nature of the right which is the subject of the agreement and, if the accommodation concerned, or any of the accommodation in the pool of accommodation concerned, is situated in the territory of an EEA State, a clause setting out the conditions governing the exercise of that right within the territory of that State and if those conditions have been fulfilled or, if they have not, what conditions remain to be fulfilled.

(c) When the timeshare accommodation has been determined, an accurate description of that accommodation and its location.

(d) Where the timeshare accommodation is under construction—

(i) the state of completion,

(ii) a reasonable estimate of the deadline for completion of the timeshare accommodation,

(iii) where it concerns specific timeshare accommodation, the number of the building permit and the name and full address of the competent authority or authorities,

(iv) the state of completion of the services rendering the timeshare accommodation fully operational (gas, electricity, water and telephone connections),

(v) a guarantee regarding completion of the timeshare accommodation or a guarantee regarding reimbursement of any payment made if the accommodation is not completed and, where appropriate, the conditions governing the operation of those guarantees.

(e) The services (lighting, water, maintenance, refuse collection) to which the offeree has or will have access and on what conditions.

(f) The common facilities, such as swimming pool, sauna, etc, to which the offeree has or may have access, and where appropriate, on what conditions.

(g) The principles on the basis of which the maintenance of and repairs to the timeshare accommodation and its administration and management will be arranged.

(h) The exact period within which the right which is the subject of the agreement may be exercised and, if necessary, its duration; the date on which the offeree may start to exercise that right.

(i) The price to be paid by the offeree to exercise the right under the agreement; an estimate of the amount to be paid by the offeree for the use of common facilities and services; the basis for the calculation of the amount of charges relating to occupation of the timeshare accommodation, the mandatory statutory charges (for example, taxes and fees) and the administrative overheads (for example, management, maintenance and repairs).

(j) A clause stating that acquisitions will not result in costs, charges or obligations other than those specified in the agreement.

(k) Whether or not it is possible to join a scheme for the exchange or resale of the rights under the agreement, and any costs involved should an exchange or resale scheme be organised by the offeror or by a third party designated by him in the agreement.

(l) …

(m) The date and place of each party's signing of the agreement.]

[1464]

NOTES

Inserted by SI 1997/1081, reg 3(3).

Para (l): repealed by SI 2003/1922, reg 2, Schedule, para 10.

SCHEDULE [2]
ENFORCEMENT

Section 10

NOTES

Schedule numbered as such by SI 1997/1081, reg 11(1).

Enforcement authority

1.—(1) Every local weights and measures authority in Great Britain shall be an enforcement authority for the purposes of this Schedule, and it shall be the duty of each such authority to enforce the provisions of this Act within their area.

(2) The Department of Economic Development in Northern Ireland shall be an enforcement authority for the purposes of this Schedule, and it shall be the duty of the Department to enforce the provisions of this Act within Northern Ireland.

Prosecutions

2.—(1) …

(2) Nothing in paragraph 1 above shall authorise a local weights and measures authority to bring proceedings in Scotland for an offence.

Powers of officers of enforcement authority

3.—(1) If a duly authorised officer of an enforcement authority has reasonable grounds for suspecting that an offence under [any of sections 1A to 2 or 5B] of this Act has been committed, he may—

(a) require a person carrying on or employed in a business to produce any book or document relating to the business, and take copies of it or any entry in it, or

(b) require such a person to produce in a visible and legible documentary form [or from which it can readily be produced in a visible and legible form] any information so relating which is [stored in any electronic form], and take copies of it,

for the purposes of ascertaining whether such an offence has been committed.

(2) If such an officer has reasonable grounds for believing that any documents may be required as evidence in proceedings for such an offence, he may seize and detain them and shall, if he does so, inform the person from whom they are seized.

(3) The powers of an officer under this paragraph may be exercised by him only at a reasonable hour and on production (if required) of his credentials.

(4) Nothing in this paragraph requires a person to produce, or authorises the taking from a person of, a document which he could not be compelled to produce in civil proceedings before the High Court or (in Scotland) the Court of Session.

4.—(1) A person who—

(a) intentionally obstructs an officer of an enforcement authority acting in pursuance of this Schedule,

(b) without reasonable excuse fails to comply with a requirement made of him by such an officer under paragraph 3(1) above, or

(c) without reasonable excuse fails to give an officer of an enforcement authority acting in pursuance of this Schedule any other assistance or information which the officer has reasonably required of him for the purpose of the performance of the officer's functions under this Schedule,

is guilty of an offence.

(2) A person guilty of an offence under sub-paragraph (1) above is liable on summary conviction to a fine not exceeding level 5 on the standard scale.

(3) If a person, in giving information to an officer of an enforcement authority who is acting in pursuance of this Schedule—

(a) makes a statement which he knows is false in a material particular, or

(b) recklessly makes a statement which is false in a material particular, he is guilty of an offence.

(4) A person guilty of an offence under sub-paragraph (3) above is liable—

(a) on summary conviction, to a fine not exceeding the statutory maximum, and

(b) on conviction on indictment, to a fine.

5. …

Privilege against self-incrimination

6. Nothing in this Schedule requires a person to answer any question or give any information if to do so might incriminate him.

[1465]

NOTES

Para 2: sub-para (1) repealed by the Enterprise Act 2002, s 278(2), Sch 26, subject to transitional provisions and savings in s 276 of, Sch 24, paras 2–6 to, that Act.

Para 3: words in first pair of square brackets substituted by SI 1997/1081, reg 13(4); words in second pair of square brackets inserted, and words in third pair of square brackets substituted by the Criminal Justice and Police Act 2001, s 70, Sch 2, Pt 2, para 20.

Para 5: repealed by the Enterprise Act 2002, ss 247(i), 278(2), Sch 26.

See further: in relation to additional powers of seizure from premises, see the Criminal Justice and Police Act 2001, s 50, Sch 1, Pt 1, para 56.

LEASEHOLD REFORM, HOUSING AND URBAN DEVELOPMENT ACT 1993

(1993 c 28)

An Act to confer rights to collective enfranchisement and lease renewal on tenants of flats; to make further provision with respect to enfranchisement by tenants of houses; to make provision for auditing the management, by landlords or other persons, of residential property and for the approval of codes of practice relating thereto; to amend Parts III and IV of the Landlord and Tenant Act 1987; to confer jurisdiction on leasehold valuation tribunals as respects Crown land; to make provision for rendering void agreements preventing the occupation of leasehold property by persons with mental disorders; to amend Parts II, IV and V of the Housing Act 1985, Schedule 2 to the Housing Associations Act 1985, Parts I and III and sections 248 and 299 of the Housing (Scotland) Act 1987, Part III of the Housing Act 1988, and Part VI of the Local Government and Housing Act 1989; to make provision with respect to certain disposals requiring consent under Part II of the Housing Act 1985, including provision for the payment of a levy; to alter the basis of certain contributions by the Secretary of State under section 569 of that Act; to establish and confer functions on a body to replace the English Industrial Estates Corporation and to be known as the Urban Regeneration Agency; to provide for the designation of certain urban and other areas and to make provision as to the effect of such designation; to amend section 23 of the Land Compensation Act 1961, section 98 of the Local Government, Planning and Land Act 1980 and section 27 of the Housing and Planning Act 1986; to make further provision with respect to urban development corporations and urban development areas; and for connected purposes

[20 July 1993]

PART I
LANDLORD AND TENANT

1–87 (*Ss 1–87 outside the scope of this work.*)

Jurisdiction of leasehold valuation tribunals in relation to enfranchisement etc of Crown land

88 Jurisdiction of leasehold valuation tribunals in relation to enfranchisement etc of Crown land

(1) This section applies where any tenant under a lease from the Crown is proceeding with a view to acquiring the freehold or an extended lease of a house and premises in circumstances in which, but for the existence of any Crown interest in the land subject to the lease, he would be entitled to acquire the freehold or such an extended lease under Part I of the Leasehold Reform Act 1967.

(2) Where—

(a) this section applies in accordance with subsection (1), and

(b) any question arises in connection with the acquisition of the freehold or an extended lease of the house and premises which is such that, if the tenant were proceeding as mentioned in that subsection in pursuance of a claim made under Part I of that Act, a leasehold valuation tribunal … would have jurisdiction to determine it in proceedings under that Part, and

(c) it is agreed between—

(i) the appropriate authority and the tenant, and

(ii) all other persons (if any) whose interests would fall to be represented in proceedings brought under that Part for the determination of that question by such a tribunal,

that that question should be determined by such a tribunal, a [leasehold valuation tribunal] shall have jurisdiction to determine that question.

(3)–(5) …

(6) For the purposes of this section "lease from the Crown" means a lease of land in which there is, or has during the subsistence of the lease been, a Crown interest superior to the lease; and "Crown interest" and "the appropriate authority" in relation to a Crown interest mean respectively—

(a) an interest comprised in the Crown Estate, and the Crown Estate Commissioners;

(b) an interest belonging to Her Majesty in right of the Duchy of Lancaster, and the Chancellor of the Duchy;

(c) an interest belonging to the Duchy of Cornwall, and such person as the Duke of Cornwall or the possessor for the time being of the Duchy appoints;

(d) any other interest belonging to a government department or held on behalf of Her Majesty for the purposes of a government department, and the Minister in charge of that department.

(7) …

[1466]

NOTES

Sub-s (2): in para (b) words omitted repealed by the Commonhold and Leasehold Reform Act 2002, s 180, Sch 14; words in square brackets substituted by the Commonhold and Leasehold Reform Act 2002, s 176, Sch 13, paras 12, 14.

Sub-s (3)–(5), (7): repealed by the Commonhold and Leasehold Reform Act 2002, s 180, Sch 14.

89–185 (*Ss 89–103,104–157* (*Pt II*), *158–185* (*Pt III*) *outside the scope of this work.*)

PART IV
SUPPLEMENTAL

186, 187 (*Ss 104–157* (*Pt II*), *158–185* (*Pt III*) *outside the scope of this work.*)

188 Short title, commencement and extent

(1) This Act may be cited as the Leasehold Reform, Housing and Urban Development Act 1993.

(2) This Act, except—

(a) this section;

(b) sections 126 and 127, 135 to 140, 149 to 151, 181(1), (2) and (4) and 186; and

(c) the repeal in section 80(1) of the Local Government and Housing Act 1989,

shall come into force on such day as the Secretary of State may by order made by statutory instrument appoint; and different days may be so appointed for different provisions or for different purposes.

(3) An order under subsection (2) may contain such transitional provisions and savings (whether or not involving the modification of any statutory provision) as appear to the Secretary of State necessary or expedient in connection with the provisions thereby brought into force by the order.

(4) The following, namely—

(a) Part I of this Act;

(b) Chapter I of Part II of this Act; and

(c) subject to subsection (6), Part III of this Act,

extend to England and Wales only.

(5) Chapter II of Part II of this Act extends to Scotland only.

(6) In Part III of this Act—

(a) sections … 179 and 180 also extend to Scotland; …

(b) …

(7) This Part, except this section, paragraph 3 of Schedule 21 and the repeals in the House of Commons Disqualification Act 1975 and the Northern Ireland Assembly Disqualification Act 1975, does not extend to Northern Ireland.

[1467]

NOTES

Sub-s (6): in para (a) reference omitted repealed by the Housing Grants, Construction and Regeneration Act 1996, s 147, Sch 3, Pt III; para (b) and word omitted immediately preceding it repealed by the Housing and Regeneration Act 2008, ss 56, 321(1), Sch 8, para 63(1), (3), Sch 16.

Orders: Leasehold Reform, Housing and Urban Development Act 1993 (Commencement and Transitional Provisions No 1) Order 1993, SI 1993/2134; Leasehold Reform, Housing and Urban Development Act 1993 (Commencement No 2) (Scotland) Order 1993, SI 1993/2163; Leasehold Reform, Housing and Urban Development Act 1993 (Commencement and Transitional Provisions No 3) Order 1993, SI 1993/2762; Leasehold Reform, Housing and Urban Development Act 1993 (Commencement No 4) Order 1994, SI 1994/935 (made under sub-ss (2), (3)).

(*Schs 1–22 outside the scope of this work.*)

CHARITIES ACT 1993

(1993 c 10)

An Act to consolidate the Charitable Trustees Incorporation Act 1872 and, except for certain spent or transitional provisions, the Charities Act 1960 and Part I of the Charities Act 1992

[27 May 1993]

PART I
THE [CHARITY COMMISSION] AND THE OFFICIAL CUSTODIAN FOR CHARITIES

NOTES

Words in square brackets substituted by the Charities Act 2006, s 75(1), Sch 8, paras 96, 97.

1 (*Repealed by the Charities Act 2006, ss 6(6), 75(2), Sch 9.*)

[1A The Charity Commission

(1) There shall be a body corporate to be known as the Charity Commission for England and Wales (in this Act referred to as "the Commission").

(2) In Welsh the Commission shall be known as "Comisiwn Elusennau Cymru a Lloegr".

(3) The functions of the Commission shall be performed on behalf of the Crown.

(4) In the exercise of its functions the Commission shall not be subject to the direction or control of any Minister of the Crown or other government department.

(5) But subsection (4) above does not affect—

(a) any provision made by or under any enactment;

(b) any administrative controls exercised over the Commission's expenditure by the Treasury.

(6) The provisions of Schedule 1A to this Act shall have effect with respect to the Commission.]

[1468]

NOTES

Commencement: 27 February 2007.

Inserted by the Charities Act 2006, s 6(1).

[1B The Commission's objectives

(1) The Commission has the objectives set out in subsection (2).

(2) The objectives are—

1 The public confidence objective.
2 The public benefit objective.
3 The compliance objective.
4 The charitable resources objective.
5 The accountability objective.

(3) Those objectives are defined as follows—

1 The public confidence objective is to increase public trust and confidence in charities.

2 The public benefit objective is to promote awareness and understanding of the operation of the public benefit requirement.
3 The compliance objective is to promote compliance by charity trustees with their legal obligations in exercising control and management of the administration of their charities.
4 The charitable resources objective is to promote the effective use of charitable resources.
5 The accountability objective is to enhance the accountability of charities to donors, beneficiaries and the general public.

(4) In this section "the public benefit requirement" means the requirement in section 2(1)(b) of the Charities Act 2006 that a purpose falling within section 2(2) of that Act must be for the public benefit if it is to be a charitable purpose.]

[1469]

NOTES

Commencement: 27 February 2007; for transitional provisions and savings see the Charities Act 2006, ss 4(2), (4)(a), 75(3), Sch 10, para 1.

Inserted by the Charities Act 2006, s 7.

[1C The Commission's general functions

(1) The Commission has the general functions set out in subsection (2).

(2) The general functions are—
1 Determining whether institutions are or are not charities.
2 Encouraging and facilitating the better administration of charities.
3 Identifying and investigating apparent misconduct or mismanagement in the administration of charities and taking remedial or protective action in connection with misconduct or mismanagement therein.
4 Determining whether public collections certificates should be issued, and remain in force, in respect of public charitable collections.
5 Obtaining, evaluating and disseminating information in connection with the performance of any of the Commission's functions or meeting any of its objectives.
6 Giving information or advice, or making proposals, to any Minister of the Crown on matters relating to any of the Commission's functions or meeting any of its objectives.

(3) The Commission's fifth general function includes (among other things) the maintenance of an accurate and up-to-date register of charities under section 3 below.

(4) The Commission's sixth general function includes (among other things) complying, so far as is reasonably practicable, with any request made by a Minister of the Crown for information or advice on any matter relating to any of its functions.

(5) In this section "public charitable collection" and "public collections certificate" have the same meanings as in Chapter 1 of Part 3 of the Charities Act 2006.]

[1470]

NOTES

Commencement: 27 February 2007 (except in so far as relating to sub-s (2), para 4, sub-s (5)); to be appointed (otherwise).

Inserted by the Charities Act 2006, s 7.

[1D The Commission's general duties

(1) The Commission has the general duties set out in subsection (2).

(2) The general duties are—
1 So far as is reasonably practicable the Commission must, in performing its functions, act in a way—
(a) which is compatible with its objectives, and
(b) which it considers most appropriate for the purpose of meeting those objectives.
2 So far as is reasonably practicable the Commission must, in performing its functions, act in a way which is compatible with the encouragement of—
(a) all forms of charitable giving, and
(b) voluntary participation in charity work.
3 In performing its functions the Commission must have regard to the need to use its resources in the most efficient, effective and economic way.
4 In performing its functions the Commission must, so far as relevant, have regard to the principles of best regulatory practice (including the principles under which regulatory activities should be proportionate, accountable, consistent, transparent and targeted only at cases in which action is needed).
5 In performing its functions the Commission must, in appropriate cases, have regard to the desirability of facilitating innovation by or on behalf of charities.

6 In managing its affairs the Commission must have regard to such generally accepted principles of good corporate governance as it is reasonable to regard as applicable to it.]

[1471]

NOTES

Commencement: 27 February 2007.
Inserted by the Charities Act 2006, s 7.

[1E The Commission's incidental powers

(1) The Commission has power to do anything which is calculated to facilitate, or is conducive or incidental to, the performance of any of its functions or general duties.

(2) However, nothing in this Act authorises the Commission—

(a) to exercise functions corresponding to those of a charity trustee in relation to a charity, or

(b) otherwise to be directly involved in the administration of a charity.

(3) Subsection (2) does not affect the operation of section 19A or 19B below (power of Commission to give directions as to action to be taken or as to application of charity property).]

[1472]

NOTES

Commencement: 27 February 2007 (sub-ss (1), (2)); 18 March 2008 (sub-s (3)).
Inserted by the Charities Act 2006, s 7.

2 (*Outside the scope of this work.*)

[PART IA
THE CHARITY TRIBUNAL

[2A The Charity Tribunal

(1) There shall be a tribunal to be known as the Charity Tribunal (in this Act referred to as "the Tribunal").

(2) In Welsh the Tribunal shall be known as "Tribiwnlys Elusennau".

(3) The provisions of Schedule 1B to this Act shall have effect with respect to the constitution of the Tribunal and other matters relating to it.

(4) The Tribunal shall have jurisdiction to hear and determine—

(a) such appeals and applications as may be made to the Tribunal in accordance with Schedule 1C to this Act, or any other enactment, in respect of decisions, orders or directions of the Commission, and

(b) such matters as may be referred to the Tribunal in accordance with Schedule 1D to this Act by the Commission or the Attorney General.

(5) Such appeals, applications and matters shall be heard and determined by the Tribunal in accordance with those Schedules, or any such enactment, taken with section 2B below and rules made under that section.]

[1473]

NOTES

Commencement: 18 March 2008.
Part IA (this section and ss 2B–2D) inserted by the Charities Act 2006, s 8(1).

[2B Practice and procedure

(1) The Lord Chancellor may make rules—

(a) regulating the exercise of rights to appeal or to apply to the Tribunal and matters relating to the making of references to it;

(b) about the practice and procedure to be followed in relation to proceedings before the Tribunal.

(2) Rules under subsection (1)(a) above may, in particular, make provision—

(a) specifying steps which must be taken before appeals, applications or references are made to the Tribunal (and the period within which any such steps must be taken);

(b) specifying the period following the Commission's final decision, direction or order within which such appeals or applications may be made;

(c) requiring the Commission to inform persons of their right to appeal or apply to the Tribunal following a final decision, direction or order of the Commission;

(d) specifying the manner in which appeals, applications or references to the Tribunal are to be made.

PART I
STATUTES

(3) Rules under subsection (1)(b) above may, in particular, make provision—
(a) for the President or a legal member of the Tribunal (see paragraph 1(2)(b) of Schedule 1B to this Act) to determine preliminary, interlocutory or ancillary matters;
(b) for matters to be determined without an oral hearing in specified circumstances;
(c) for the Tribunal to deal with urgent cases expeditiously;
(d) about the disclosure of documents;
(e) about evidence;
(f) about the admission of members of the public to proceedings;
(g) about the representation of parties to proceedings;
(h) about the withdrawal of appeals, applications or references;
(i) about the recording and promulgation of decisions;
(j) about the award of costs.

(4) Rules under subsection (1)(a) or (b) above may confer a discretion on—
(a) the Tribunal,
(b) a member of the Tribunal, or
(c) any other person.

(5) The Tribunal may award costs only in accordance with subsections (6) and (7) below.

(6) If the Tribunal considers that any party to proceedings before it has acted vexatiously, frivolously or unreasonably, the Tribunal may order that party to pay to any other party to the proceedings the whole or part of the costs incurred by that other party in connection with the proceedings.

(7) If the Tribunal considers that a decision, direction or order of the Commission which is the subject of proceedings before it was unreasonable, the Tribunal may order the Commission to pay to any other party to the proceedings the whole or part of the costs incurred by that other party in connection with the proceedings.

(8) Rules of the Lord Chancellor under this section—
(a) shall be made by statutory instrument, and
(b) shall be subject to annulment in pursuance of a resolution of either House of Parliament.

(9) Section 86(3) below applies in relation to rules of the Lord Chancellor under this section as it applies in relation to regulations and orders of the Minister under this Act.]

[1474]

NOTES

Commencement: 27 February 2007 (in so far as relating to sub-ss (1)–(4), (8), (9) for the purposes of exercising the power to make subordinate legislation); 18 March 2008 (otherwise).

Inserted as noted to s 2A at **[1473]**.

Rules: Charity Tribunal Rules 2008, SI 2008/221.

[2C Appeal from Tribunal

(1) A party to proceedings before the Tribunal may appeal to the High Court against a decision of the Tribunal.

(2) Subject to subsection (3) below, an appeal may be brought under this section against a decision of the Tribunal only on a point of law.

(3) In the case of an appeal under this section against a decision of the Tribunal which determines a question referred to it by the Commission or the Attorney General, the High Court—
(a) shall consider afresh the question referred to the Tribunal, and
(b) may take into account evidence which was not available to the Tribunal.

(4) An appeal under this section may be brought only with the permission of—
(a) the Tribunal, or
(b) if the Tribunal refuses permission, the High Court.

(5) For the purposes of subsection (1) above—
(a) the Commission and the Attorney General are to be treated as parties to all proceedings before the Tribunal, and
(b) rules under section 2B(1) above may include provision as to who else is to be treated as being (or not being) a party to proceedings before the Tribunal.]

[1475]

NOTES

Commencement: 27 February 2007 (in so far as relating to sub-s (5)(b) for the purposes of exercising the power to make subordinate legislation); 18 March 2008 (otherwise).

Inserted as noted to s 2A at **[1473]**.

[2D Intervention by Attorney General

(1) This section applies to any proceedings—

(a) before the Tribunal, or
(b) on an appeal from the Tribunal,

to which the Attorney General is not a party.

(2) The Tribunal or, in the case of an appeal from the Tribunal, the court may at any stage of the proceedings direct that all the necessary papers in the proceedings be sent to the Attorney General.

(3) A direction under subsection (2) may be made by the Tribunal or court—
(a) of its own motion, or
(b) on the application of any party to the proceedings.

(4) The Attorney General may—
(a) intervene in the proceedings in such manner as he thinks necessary or expedient, and
(b) argue before the Tribunal or court any question in relation to the proceedings which the Tribunal or court considers it necessary to have fully argued.

(5) Subsection (4) applies whether or not the Tribunal or court has given a direction under subsection (2).]

[1476]

NOTES

Commencement: 18 March 2008.
Inserted as noted to s 2A at **[1473]**.

PART II
REGISTRATION AND NAMES OF CHARITIES
Registration of charities

[3 Register of charities

(1) There shall continue to be a register of charities, which shall be kept by the Commission.

(2) The register shall be kept by the Commission in such manner as it thinks fit.

(3) The register shall contain—
(a) the name of every charity registered in accordance with section 3A below (registration), and
(b) such other particulars of, and such other information relating to, every such charity as the Commission thinks fit.

(4) The Commission shall remove from the register—
(a) any institution which it no longer considers is a charity, and
(b) any charity which has ceased to exist or does not operate.

(5) If the removal of an institution under subsection (4)(a) above is due to any change in its trusts, the removal shall take effect from the date of that change.

(6) A charity which is for the time being registered under section 3A(6) below (voluntary registration) shall be removed from the register if it so requests.

(7) The register (including the entries cancelled when institutions are removed from the register) shall be open to public inspection at all reasonable times.

(8) Where any information contained in the register is not in documentary form, subsection (7) above shall be construed as requiring the information to be available for public inspection in legible form at all reasonable times.

(9) If the Commission so determines, subsection (7) shall not apply to any particular information contained in the register that is specified in the determination.

(10) Copies (or particulars) of the trusts of any registered charity as supplied to the Commission under section 3B below (applications for registration etc) shall, so long as the charity remains on the register—
(a) be kept by the Commission, and
(b) be open to public inspection at all reasonable times.]

[1477]

NOTES

Substituted, together with ss 3A, 3B, for this section as originally enacted, by the Charities Act 2006, s 9.
Regulations: the Charities (Exception from Registration) Regulations 1996, SI 1996/180.

[3A Registration of charities

(1) Every charity must be registered in the register of charities unless subsection (2) below applies to it.

(2) The following are not required to be registered—
[(a) any exempt charity (see Schedule 2 to this Act);

(b) any charity which for the time being—
(i) is permanently or temporarily excepted by order of the Commission, and
(ii) complies with any conditions of the exception,
and whose gross income does not exceed £100,000;
(c) any charity which for the time being—
(i) is, or is of a description, permanently or temporarily excepted by regulations made by the [Minister], and
(ii) complies with any conditions of the exception,
and whose gross income does not exceed £100,000; and]
(d) any charity whose gross income does not exceed £5,000.

(3) For the purposes of subsection (2)(b) above—
(a) any order made or having effect as if made under section 3(5)(b) of this Act (as originally enacted) and in force immediately before the appointed day has effect as from that day as if made under subsection (2)(b) (and may be varied or revoked accordingly); and
(b) no order may be made under subsection (2)(b) so as to except on or after the appointed day any charity that was not excepted immediately before that day.

(4) For the purposes of subsection (2)(c) above—
(a) any regulations made or having effect as if made under section 3(5)(b) of this Act (as originally enacted) and in force immediately before the appointed day have effect as from that day as if made under subsection (2)(c) (and may be varied or revoked accordingly);
(b) such regulations shall be made under subsection (2)(c) as are necessary to secure that all of the formerly specified institutions are excepted under that provision (subject to compliance with any conditions of the exception and the financial limit mentioned in that provision); but
(c) otherwise no regulations may be made under subsection (2)(c) so as to except on or after the appointed day any description of charities that was not excepted immediately before that day.

(5) In subsection (4)(b) above "formerly specified institutions" means—
(a) any institution falling within section 3(5B)(a) or (b) of this Act as in force immediately before the appointed day (certain educational institutions); or
(b) any institution ceasing to be an exempt charity by virtue of section 11 of the Charities Act 2006 or any order made under that section.

(6) A charity within—
(a) subsection (2)(b) or (c) above, or
(b) subsection (2)(d) above,
must, if it so requests, be registered in the register of charities.

(7) The Minister may by order amend—
(a) subsection (2)(b) and (c) above, or
(b) subsection (2)(d) above,
by substituting a different sum for the sum for the time being specified there.

(8) The Minister may only make an order under subsection (7) above—
(a) so far as it amends subsection (2)(b) and (c), if he considers it expedient to so with a view to reducing the scope of the exception provided by those provisions;
(b) so far as it amends subsection (2)(d), if he considers it expedient to do so in consequence of changes in the value of money or with a view to extending the scope of the exception provided by that provision,
and no order may be made by him under subsection (7)(a) unless a copy of a report under section 73 of the Charities Act 2006 (report on operation of that Act) has been laid before Parliament in accordance with that section.

(9) In this section "the appointed day" means the day on which subsections (1) to (5) above come into force by virtue of an order under section 79 of the Charities Act 2006 relating to section 9 of that Act (registration of charities).

(10) In this section any reference to a charity's "gross income" shall be construed, in relation to a particular time—
(a) as a reference to the charity's gross income in its financial year immediately preceding that time, or
(b) if the Commission so determines, as a reference to the amount which the Commission estimates to be the likely amount of the charity's gross income in such financial year of the charity as is specified in the determination.

(11) The following provisions of this section—
(a) subsection (2)(b) and (c),
(b) subsections (3) to (5), and

(c) subsections (6)(a), (7)(a), (8)(a) and (9),

shall cease to have effect on such day as the Minister may by order appoint for the purposes of this subsection.]

[1478]

NOTES

Commencement: 27 February 2007 (in so far as relating to sub-ss (2)(c), (4)(b), (5), for the purposes of exercising the power to make subordinate legislation); 31 January 2009 (in so far as relating to sub-ss (2)(c), (4)(b), (5) for remaining purposes, and in so far as relating to sub-ss (1), (2)(a), (b), (d), (3), (4)(a), (c), (7)–(11)); as from a day to be appointed (in so far as relating to sub-s (6)).

Substituted, together with ss 3, 3B for s 3, as originally enacted, by the Charities Act 2006, s 9.

Sub-s (2): in para (c)(i) word "Minister" in square brackets substituted by SI 2006/2951, art 6, Schedule, para 4(d).

Regulations: the Charities Act 1993 (Exception from Registration) Regulations 2008, SI 2008/3268.

[3B Duties of trustees in connection with registration

[(1) Where a charity required to be registered by virtue of section 3A(1) above is not registered, it is the duty of the charity trustees—

(a) to apply to the Commission for the charity to be registered, and

(b) to supply the Commission with the required documents and information.

(2) The "required documents and information" are—

(a) copies of the charity's trusts or (if they are not set out in any extant document) particulars of them,

(b) such other documents or information as may be prescribed by regulations made by the Minister, and

(c) such other documents or information as the Commission may require for the purposes of the application.

(3) Where an institution is for the time being registered, it is the duty of the charity trustees (or the last charity trustees)—

(a) to notify the Commission if the institution ceases to exist, or if there is any change in its trusts or in the particulars of it entered in the register, and

(b) (so far as appropriate), to supply the Commission with particulars of any such change and copies of any new trusts or alterations of the trusts.

(4) Nothing in subsection (3) above requires a person—

(a) to supply the Commission with copies of schemes for the administration of a charity made otherwise than by the court,

(b) to notify the Commission of any change made with respect to a registered charity by such a scheme, or

(c) if he refers the Commission to a document or copy already in the possession of the Commission, to supply a further copy of the document.

(5) Where a copy of a document relating to a registered charity—

(a) is not required to be supplied to the Commission as the result of subsection (4) above, but

(b) is in the possession of the Commission,

a copy of the document shall be open to inspection under section 3(10) above as if supplied to the Commission under this section.]

[1479]

NOTES

Commencement: 27 February 2007 (in so far as relating to sub-s (2)(b), for the purposes of exercising the power to make subordinate legislation); 31 January 2009 (in so far as relating to sub-s (2)(b) above for remaining purposes, and in so far as relating to sub-ss (1), (2)(a), (c), (3)–(5)).

Substituted, together with ss 3, 3A for s 3, as originally enacted, by the Charities Act 2006, s 9.

4–12 (*Ss 4–7, ss 8–12 (Pt III) outside the scope of this work.*)

PART IV
APPLICATION OF PROPERTY CY-PRÈS AND ASSISTANCE AND SUPERVISION OF CHARITIES BY COURT [AND COMMISSION]

NOTES

Words in square brackets substituted by the Charities Act 2006, s 75(1), Sch 8, paras 96, 106.

Extended powers of court and variation of charters

13 Occasions for applying property cy-près

(1) Subject to subsection (2) below, the circumstances in which the original purposes of a charitable gift can be altered to allow the property given or part of it to be applied cy-près shall be as follows—

(a) where the original purposes, in whole or in part—

(i) have been as far as may be fulfilled; or

(ii) cannot be carried out, or not according to the directions given and to the spirit of the gift; or

(b) where the original purposes provide a use for part only of the property available by virtue of the gift; or

(c) where the property available by virtue of the gift and other property applicable for similar purposes can be more effectively used in conjunction, and to that end can suitably, regard being had to [the appropriate considerations], be made applicable to common purposes; or

(d) where the original purposes were laid down by reference to an area which then was but has since ceased to be a unit for some other purpose, or by reference to a class of persons or to an area which has for any reason since ceased to be suitable, regard being had to [the appropriate considerations], or to be practical in administering the gift; or

(e) where the original purposes, in whole or in part, have, since they were laid down,—

(i) been adequately provided for by other means; or

(ii) ceased, as being useless or harmful to the community or for other reasons, to be in law charitable; or

(iii) ceased in any other way to provide a suitable and effective method of using the property available by virtue of the gift, regard being had to [the appropriate considerations].

[(1A) In subsection (1) above "the appropriate considerations" means—

(a) (on the one hand) the spirit of the gift concerned, and

(b) (on the other) the social and economic circumstances prevailing at the time of the proposed alteration of the original purposes.]

(2) Subsection (1) above shall not affect the conditions which must be satisfied in order that property given for charitable purposes may be applied cy-près except in so far as those conditions require a failure of the original purposes.

(3) References in the foregoing subsections to the original purposes of a gift shall be construed, where the application of the property given has been altered or regulated by a scheme or otherwise, as referring to the purposes for which the property is for the time being applicable.

(4) Without prejudice to the power to make schemes in circumstances falling within subsection (1) above, the court may by scheme made under the court's jurisdiction with respect to charities, in any case where the purposes for which the property is held are laid down by reference to any such area as is mentioned in the first column in Schedule 3 to this Act, provide for enlarging the area to any such area as is mentioned in the second column in the same entry in that Schedule.

(5) It is hereby declared that a trust for charitable purposes places a trustee under a duty, where the case permits and requires the property or some part of it to be applied cy-près, to secure its effective use for charity by taking steps to enable it to be so applied.

[1480]

NOTES

Sub-s (1): in paras (c)–(e) words in in square brackets substituted by the Charities Act 2006, s 15(1), (2).
Sub-s (1A): inserted by the Charities Act 2006, s 15(3).

14 Application cy-près of gifts of donors unknown or disclaiming

(1) Property given for specific charitable purposes which fail shall be applicable cy-près as if given for charitable purposes generally, where it belongs—

(a) to a donor who after—

(i) the prescribed advertisements and inquiries have been published and made, and

(ii) the prescribed period beginning with the publication of those advertisements has expired,

cannot be identified or cannot be found; or

(b) to a donor who has executed a disclaimer in the prescribed form of his right to have the property returned.

(2) Where the prescribed advertisements and inquiries have been published and made by or on behalf of trustees with respect to any such property, the trustees shall not be liable to any person in respect of the property if no claim by him to be interested in it is received by them before the expiry of the period mentioned in subsection (1)(a)(ii) above.

(3) For the purposes of this section property shall be conclusively presumed (without any advertisement or inquiry) to belong to donors who cannot be identified, in so far as it consists—

(a) of the proceeds of cash collections made by means of collecting boxes or by other means not adapted for distinguishing one gift from another; or

(b) of the proceeds of any lottery, competition, entertainment, sale or similar money-raising activity, after allowing for property given to provide prizes or articles for sale or otherwise to enable the activity to be undertaken.

(4) The court [or the Commission] may by order direct that property not falling within subsection (3) above shall for the purposes of this section be treated (without any advertisement or inquiry) as belonging to donors who cannot be identified where it appears to the court [or the Commission] either—

(a) that it would be unreasonable, having regard to the amounts likely to be returned to the donors, to incur expense with a view to returning the property; or

(b) that it would be unreasonable, having regard to the nature, circumstances and amounts of the gifts, and to the lapse of time since the gifts were made, for the donors to expect the property to be returned.

(5) Where property is applied cy-près by virtue of this section, the donor shall be deemed to have parted with all his interest at the time when the gift was made; but where property is so applied as belonging to donors who cannot be identified or cannot be found, and is not so applied by virtue of subsection (3) or (4) above—

(a) the scheme shall specify the total amount of that property; and

(b) the donor of any part of that amount shall be entitled, if he makes a claim not later than six months after the date on which the scheme is made, to recover from the charity for which the property is applied a sum equal to that part, less any expenses properly incurred by the charity trustees after that date in connection with claims relating to his gift; and

(c) the scheme may include directions as to the provision to be made for meeting any such claim.

(6) Where—

(a) any sum is, in accordance with any such directions, set aside for meeting any such claims, but

(b) the aggregate amount of any such claims actually made exceeds the relevant amount,

then, if [the Commission so directs], each of the donors in question shall be entitled only to such proportion of the relevant amount as the amount of his claim bears to the aggregate amount referred to in paragraph (b) above; and for this purpose "the relevant amount" means the amount of the sum so set aside after deduction of any expenses properly incurred by the charity trustees in connection with claims relating to the donors' gifts.

(7) For the purposes of this section, charitable purposes shall be deemed to "fail" where any difficulty in applying property to those purposes makes that property or the part not applicable cy-près available to be returned to the donors.

(8) In this section "prescribed" means prescribed by regulations made by [the Commission]; and such regulations may, as respects the advertisements which are to be published for the purposes of subsection (1)(a) above, make provision as to the form and content of such advertisements as well as the manner in which they are to be published.

(9) Any regulations made by [the Commission] under this section shall be published by [the Commission] in such manner as [it thinks fit].

(10) In this section, except in so far as the context otherwise requires, references to a donor include persons claiming through or under the original donor, and references to property given include the property for the time being representing the property originally given or property derived from it.

(11) This section shall apply to property given for charitable purposes, notwithstanding that it was so given before the commencement of this Act.

[1481]

NOTES

Sub-s (4): words in square brackets inserted by the Charities Act 2006, s 16.

Sub-ss (6), (8), (9): words in square brackets substituted by the Charities Act 2006, s 75(1), Sch 8, paras 96, 107.

[14A Application cy-près of gifts made in response to certain solicitations

(1) This section applies to property given—

(a) for specific charitable purposes, and

(b) in response to a solicitation within subsection (2) below.

(2) A solicitation is within this subsection if—

(a) it is made for specific charitable purposes, and
(b) it is accompanied by a statement to the effect that property given in response to it will, in the event of those purposes failing, be applicable cy-près as if given for charitable purposes generally, unless the donor makes a relevant declaration at the time of making the gift.

(3) A "relevant declaration" is a declaration in writing by the donor to the effect that, in the event of the specific charitable purposes failing, he wishes the trustees holding the property to give him the opportunity to request the return of the property in question (or a sum equal to its value at the time of the making of the gift).

(4) Subsections (5) and (6) below apply if—
(a) a person has given property as mentioned in subsection (1) above,
(b) the specific charitable purposes fail, and
(c) the donor has made a relevant declaration.

(5) The trustees holding the property must take the prescribed steps for the purpose of—
(a) informing the donor of the failure of the purposes,
(b) enquiring whether he wishes to request the return of the property (or a sum equal to its value), and
(c) if within the prescribed period he makes such a request, returning the property (or such a sum) to him.

(6) If those trustees have taken all appropriate prescribed steps but—
(a) they have failed to find the donor, or
(b) the donor does not within the prescribed period request the return of the property (or a sum equal to its value),

section 14(1) above shall apply to the property as if it belonged to a donor within paragraph (b) of that subsection (application of property where donor has disclaimed right to return of property).

(7) If—
(a) a person has given property as mentioned in subsection (1) above,
(b) the specific charitable purposes fail, and
(c) the donor has not made a relevant declaration,

section 14(1) above shall similarly apply to the property as if it belonged to a donor within paragraph (b) of that subsection.

(8) For the purposes of this section—
(a) "solicitation" means a solicitation made in any manner and however communicated to the persons to whom it is addressed,
(b) it is irrelevant whether any consideration is or is to be given in return for the property in question, and
(c) where any appeal consists of both solicitations that are accompanied by statements within subsection (2)(b) and solicitations that are not so accompanied, a person giving property as a result of the appeal is to be taken to have responded to the former solicitations and not the latter, unless he proves otherwise.

(9) In this section "prescribed" means prescribed by regulations made by the Commission, and any such regulations shall be published by the Commission in such manner as it thinks fit.

(10) Subsections (7) and (10) of section 14 shall apply for the purposes of this section as they apply for the purposes of section 14.]

[1482]

NOTES

Commencement: 27 February 2007 (sub-s (9)); 18 March 2008 (otherwise).
Inserted by the Charities Act 2006, s 17.

[14B Cy-près schemes

(1) The power of the court or the Commission to make schemes for the application of property cy-près shall be exercised in accordance with this section.

(2) Where any property given for charitable purposes is applicable cy-près, the court or the Commission may make a scheme providing for the property to be applied—
(a) for such charitable purposes, and
(b) (if the scheme provides for the property to be transferred to another charity) by or on trust for such other charity,

as it considers appropriate, having regard to the matters set out in subsection (3).

(3) The matters are—
(a) the spirit of the original gift,
(b) the desirability of securing that the property is applied for charitable purposes which are close to the original purposes, and

(c) the need for the relevant charity to have purposes which are suitable and effective in the light of current social and economic circumstances.

The "relevant charity" means the charity by or on behalf of which the property is to be applied under the scheme.

(4) If a scheme provides for the property to be transferred to another charity, the scheme may impose on the charity trustees of that charity a duty to secure that the property is applied for purposes which are, so far as is reasonably practicable, similar in character to the original purposes.

(5) In this section references to property given include the property for the time being representing the property originally given or property derived from it.

(6) In this section references to the transfer of property to a charity are references to its transfer—

(a) to the charity, or
(b) to the charity trustees, or
(c) to any trustee for the charity, or
(d) to a person nominated by the charity trustees to hold it in trust for the charity,

as the scheme may provide.]

[1483]

NOTES

Commencement: 18 March 2008.

Inserted by the Charities Act 2006, s 18; for transitional provisions and savings see s 75(3), Sch 10, para 3 thereto.

15 Charities governed by charter, or by or under statute

(1) Where a Royal charter establishing or regulating a body corporate is amendable by the grant and acceptance of a further charter, a scheme relating to the body corporate or to the administration of property held by the body (including a scheme for the cy-près application of any such property) may be made by the court under the court's jurisdiction with respect to charities notwithstanding that the scheme cannot take effect without the alteration of the charter, but shall be so framed that the scheme, or such part of it as cannot take effect without the alteration of the charter, does not purport to come into operation unless or until Her Majesty thinks fit to amend the charter in such manner as will permit the scheme or that part of it to have effect.

(2) Where under the court's jurisdiction with respect to charities or the corresponding jurisdiction of a court in Northern Ireland, or under powers conferred by this Act or by any Northern Ireland legislation relating to charities, a scheme is made with respect to a body corporate, and it appears to Her Majesty expedient, having regard to the scheme, to amend any Royal charter relating to that body, Her Majesty may, on the application of that body, amend the charter accordingly by Order in Council in any way in which the charter could be amended by the grant and acceptance of a further charter; and any such Order in Council may be revoked or varied in like manner as the charter it amends.

(3) The jurisdiction of the court with respect to charities shall not be excluded or restricted in the case of a charity of any description mentioned in Schedule 4 to this Act by the operation of the enactments or instruments there mentioned in relation to that description, and a scheme established for any such charity may modify or supersede in relation to it the provision made by any such enactment or instrument as if made by a scheme of the court, and may also make any such provision as is authorised by that Schedule.

[1484]

NOTES

Orders: the Royal College of Ophthalmologists (Charter Amendment) Order 1998, SI 1998/2252; the Corporation of the Cranleigh and Bramley Schools (Charter Amendments) Order 1999, SI 1999/656; the Royal College of Physicians of London (Charter Amendment) Order 1999, SI 1999/667; the Licensed Victuallers' National Homes (Charter Amendment) Order 2000, SI 2000/1348; the Institution of Chemical Engineers (Charter Amendment) Order 2004, SI 2004/1986.

16–20 (*Outside the scope of this work.*)

Property vested in official custodian

21 Entrusting charity property to official custodian, and termination of trust

(1) The court may by order—

(a) vest in the official custodian any land held by or in trust for a charity;
(b) authorise or require the persons in whom any such land is vested to transfer it to him; or
(c) appoint any person to transfer any such land to him;

but this subsection does not apply to any interest in land by way of mortgage or other security.

(2) Where property is vested in the official custodian in trust for a charity, the court may make an order discharging him from the trusteeship as respects all or any of that property.

(3) Where the official custodian is discharged from his trusteeship of any property, or the trusts on which he holds any property come to an end, the court may make such vesting orders and give such directions as may seem to the court to be necessary or expedient in consequence.

(4) No person shall be liable for any loss occasioned by his acting in conformity with an order under this section or by his giving effect to anything done in pursuance of such an order, or be excused from so doing by reason of the order having been in any respect improperly obtained.

[1485]

22 Supplementary provisions as to property vested in official custodian

(1) Subject to the provisions of this Act, where property is vested in the official custodian in trust for a charity, he shall not exercise any powers of management, but he shall as trustee of any property have all the same powers, duties and liabilities, and be entitled to the same rights and immunities, and be subject to the control and orders of the court, as a corporation appointed custodian trustee under section 4 of the Public Trustee Act 1906 except that he shall have no power to charge fees.

(2) Subject to subsection (3) below, where any land is vested in the official custodian in trust for a charity, the charity trustees shall have power in his name and on his behalf to execute and do all assurances and things which they could properly execute or do in their own name and on their own behalf if the land were vested in them.

(3) If any land is so vested in the official custodian by virtue of an order under section 18 above, the power conferred on the charity trustees by subsection (2) above shall not be exercisable by them in relation to any transaction affecting the land, unless the transaction is authorised by order of the court or of [the Commission].

(4) Where any land is vested in the official custodian in trust for a charity, the charity trustees shall have the like power to make obligations entered into by them binding on the land as if it were vested in them; and any covenant, agreement or condition which is enforceable by or against the custodian by reason of the land being vested in him shall be enforceable by or against the charity trustees as if the land were vested in them.

(5) In relation to a corporate charity, subsections (2), (3) and (4) above shall apply with the substitution of references to the charity for references to the charity trustees.

(6) Subsections (2), (3) and (4) above shall not authorise any charity trustees or charity to impose any personal liability on the official custodian.

(7) Where the official custodian is entitled as trustee for a charity to the custody of securities or documents of title relating to the trust property, he may permit them to be in the possession or under the control of the charity trustees without thereby incurring any liability.

[1486]

NOTES

Sub-s (3): words in square brackets substituted by the Charities Act 2006, s 75(1), Sch 8, paras 96, 114.

23 Divestment in the case of land subject to Reverter of Sites Act 1987

(1) Where—

(a) any land is vested in the official custodian in trust for a charity, and

(b) it appears to [the Commission] that section 1 of the Reverter of Sites Act 1987 (right of reverter replaced by [trust]) will, or is likely to, operate in relation to the land at a particular time or in particular circumstances,

the jurisdiction which, under section 16 above, is exercisable by [the Commission] for the purpose of discharging a trustee for a charity may, at any time before section 1 of that Act ("the 1987 Act") operates in relation to the land, be exercised [by the Commission of its own] motion for the purpose of—

(i) making an order discharging the official custodian from his trusteeship of the land, and

(ii) making such vesting orders and giving such directions as [appear to the Commission] to be necessary or expedient in consequence.

(2) Where—

(a) section 1 of the 1987 Act has operated in relation to any land which, immediately before the time when that section so operated, was vested in the official custodian in trust for a charity, and

(b) the land remains vested in him but on the trust arising under that section,

the court or [the Commission (of its own motion)] may—

(i) make an order discharging the official custodian from his trusteeship of the land, and

(ii) (subject to the following provisions of this section) make such vesting orders and give such directions as appear to it ... to be necessary or expedient in consequence.

(3) Where any order discharging the official custodian from his trusteeship of any land—

(a) is made by the court under section 21(2) above, or by [the Commission] under section 16 above, on the grounds that section 1 of the 1987 Act will, or is likely to, operate in relation to the land, or

(b) is made by the court or [the Commission] under subsection (2) above,

the persons in whom the land is to be vested on the discharge of the official custodian shall be the relevant charity trustees (as defined in subsection (4) below), unless the court or (as the case may be) [the Commission is] satisfied that it would be appropriate for it to be vested in some other persons.

(4) In subsection (3) above "the relevant charity trustees" means—

(a) in relation to an order made as mentioned in paragraph (a) of that subsection, the charity trustees of the charity in trust for which the land is vested in the official custodian immediately before the time when the order takes effect, or

(b) in relation to an order made under subsection (2) above, the charity trustees of the charity in trust for which the land was vested in the official custodian immediately before the time when section 1 of the 1987 Act operated in relation to the land.

(5) Where—

(a) section 1 of the 1987 Act has operated in relation to any such land as is mentioned in subsection (2)(a) above, and

(b) the land remains vested in the official custodian as mentioned in subsection (2)(b) above,

then (subject to subsection (6) below), all the powers, duties and liabilities that would, apart from this section, be those of the official custodian as [trustee] of the land shall instead be those of the charity trustees of the charity concerned; and those trustees shall have power in his name and on his behalf to execute and do all assurances and things which they could properly execute or do in their own name and on their own behalf if the land were vested in them.

(6) Subsection (5) above shall not be taken to require or authorise those trustees to sell the land at a time when it remains vested in the official custodian.

(7) Where—

(a) the official custodian has been discharged from his trusteeship of any land by an order under subsection (2) above, and

(b) the land has, in accordance with subsection (3) above, been vested in the charity trustees concerned or (as the case may be) in any persons other than those trustees,

the land shall be held by those trustees, or (as the case may be) by those persons, as [trustees] on the terms of the trust arising under section 1 of the 1987 Act.

(8) The official custodian shall not be liable to any person in respect of any loss or misapplication of any land vested in him in accordance with that section unless it is occasioned by or through any wilful neglect or default of his or of any person acting for him; but the Consolidated Fund shall be liable to make good to any person any sums for which the official custodian may be liable by reason of any such neglect or default.

(9) In this section any reference to section 1 of the 1987 Act operating in relation to any land is a reference to a [trust] arising in relation to the land under that section.

[1487]

NOTES

Sub-s (1): word "trust" in square brackets substituted by the Trusts of Land and Appointment of Trustees Act 1996, s 25(1), Sch 3, para 26; for savings in relation to entailed interests created before the commencement of that Act, and savings consequential upon the abolition of the doctrine of conversion, see s 25(4), (5) thereof; other words in square brackets substituted by the Charities Act 2006, s 75(1), Sch 8, paras 96, 115(1), (2).

Sub-s (2): words in square brackets substituted and words omitted repealed by the Charities Act 2006, s 75(1), (2), Sch 8, paras 96, 115(1), (3), Sch 9.

Sub-s (3): words in square brackets substituted by the Charities Act 2006, s 75(1), Sch 8, paras 96, 115(1), (4).

Sub-ss (5), (7), (9): words in square brackets substituted by the Trusts of Land and Appointment of Trustees Act 1996, s 25(1), Sch 3, para 26; for savings in relation to entailed interests created before the commencement of that Act, and savings consequential upon the abolition of the doctrine of conversion, see s 25(4), (5) thereof.

Establishment of common investment or deposit funds

24 Schemes to establish common investment funds

(1) The court or [the Commission] may by order make and bring into effect schemes (in this section referred to as "common investment schemes") for the establishment of common investment funds under trusts which provide—

(a) for property transferred to the fund by or on behalf of a charity participating in the scheme to be invested under the control of trustees appointed to manage the fund; and

(b) for the participating charities to be entitled (subject to the provisions of the scheme) to the capital and income of the fund in shares determined by reference to the amount or value of the property transferred to it by or on behalf of each of them and to the value of the fund at the time of the transfers.

PART I STATUTES

(2) The court or [the Commission] may make a common investment scheme on the application of any two or more charities.

(3) A common investment scheme may be made in terms admitting any charity to participate, or the scheme may restrict the right to participate in any manner.

[(3A) A common investment scheme may provide for appropriate bodies to be admitted to participate in the scheme (in addition to the participating charities) to such extent as the trustees appointed to manage the fund may determine.

(3B) In this section "appropriate body" means—

(a) a Scottish recognised body, or

(b) a Northern Ireland charity,

and, in the application of the relevant provisions in relation to a scheme which contains provisions authorised by subsection (3A) above, "charity" includes an appropriate body.

"The relevant provisions" are subsections (1) and (4) to (6) and (in relation only to a charity within paragraph (b)) subsection (7).]

(4) A common investment scheme may make provision for, and for all matters connected with, the establishment, investment, management and winding up of the common investment fund, and may in particular include provision—

(a) for remunerating persons appointed trustees to hold or manage the fund or any part of it, with or without provision authorising a person to receive the remuneration notwithstanding that he is also a charity trustee of or trustee for a participating charity;

(b) for restricting the size of the fund, and for regulating as to time, amount or otherwise the right to transfer property to or withdraw it from the fund, and for enabling sums to be advanced out of the fund by way of loan to a participating charity pending the withdrawal of property from the fund by the charity;

(c) for enabling income to be withheld from distribution with a view to avoiding fluctuations in the amounts distributed, and generally for regulating distributions of income;

(d) for enabling money to be borrowed temporarily for the purpose of meeting payments to be made out of the funds;

(e) for enabling questions arising under the scheme as to the right of a charity to participate, or as to the rights of participating charities, or as to any other matter, to be conclusively determined by the decision of the trustees managing the fund or in any other manner;

(f) for regulating the accounts and information to be supplied to participating charities.

(5) A common investment scheme, in addition to the provision for property to be transferred to the fund on the basis that the charity shall be entitled to a share in the capital and income of the fund, may include provision for enabling sums to be deposited by or on behalf of a charity on the basis that (subject to the provisions of the scheme) the charity shall be entitled to repayment of the sums deposited and to interest thereon at a rate determined by or under the scheme; and where a scheme makes any such provision it shall also provide for excluding from the amount of capital and income to be shared between charities participating otherwise than by way of deposit such amounts (not exceeding the amounts properly attributable to the making of deposits) as are from time to time reasonably required in respect of the liabilities of the fund for the repayment of deposits and for the interest on deposits, including amounts required by way of reserve.

(6) Except in so far as a common investment scheme provides to the contrary, the rights under it of a participating charity shall not be capable of being assigned or charged, nor shall any trustee or other person concerned in the management of the common investment fund be required or entitled to take account of any trust or other equity affecting a participating charity or its property or rights.

(7) The powers of investment of every charity shall include power to participate in common investment schemes unless the power is excluded by a provision specifically referring to common investment schemes in the trusts of the charity.

(8) A common investment fund shall be deemed for all purposes to be a charity*; and if the scheme admits only exempt charities, the fund shall be an exempt charity for the purposes of this Act*.

(9) Subsection (8) above shall apply not only to common investment funds established under the powers of this section, but also to any similar fund established for the exclusive benefit of charities by or under any enactment relating to any particular charities or class of charity.

[1488]

NOTES

Sub-ss (1), (2): words in square brackets substituted by the Charities Act 2006, s 75(1), Sch 8, paras 96, 116.
Sub-ss (3A), (3B): inserted by the Charities Act 2006, s 23(1).
Sub-s (8): words in italics repealed by the Charities Act 2006, s 11(10), as from a day to be appointed.

25 (*Outside the scope of this work.*)

[25A Meaning of "Scottish recognised body" and "Northern Ireland charity" in sections 24 and 25

(1) In sections 24 and 25 above "Scottish recognised body" means a body—

(a) established under the law of Scotland, or

(b) managed or controlled wholly or mainly in or from Scotland,

to which the Commissioners for Her Majesty's Revenue and Customs have given intimation, which has not subsequently been withdrawn, that relief is due under section 505 of the Income and Corporation Taxes Act 1988 [or Part 10 of the Income Tax Act 2007] in respect of income of the body which is applicable and applied to charitable purposes only.

(2) In those sections "Northern Ireland charity" means an institution—

(a) which is a charity under the law of Northern Ireland, and

(b) to which the Commissioners for Her Majesty's Revenue and Customs have given intimation, which has not subsequently been withdrawn, that relief is due under section 505 of the Income and Corporation Taxes Act 1988 [or Part 10 of the Income Tax Act 2007] in respect of income of the institution which is applicable and applied to charitable purposes only.]

[1489]

NOTES

Commencement: 27 February 2007.

Inserted by the Charities Act 2006, s 23(4).

Words in square brackets inserted by the Income Tax Act 2007, s 1027, Sch 1, Pt 2, para 353; for effect see the Income Tax Act 2007, s 1034(1) and for transitional provisions and savings, see s 1030(1), Sch 2 thereto.

[Additional powers of Commission]

NOTES

Substituted by the Charities Act 2006, s 75(1), Sch 8, paras 96, 118.

26 Power to authorise dealings with charity property etc

(1) Subject to the provisions of this section, where it appears to [the Commission] that any action proposed or contemplated in the administration of a charity is expedient in the interests of the charity, [the Commission may] by order sanction that action, whether or not it would otherwise be within the powers exercisable by the charity trustees in the administration of the charity; and anything done under the authority of such an order shall be deemed to be properly done in the exercise of those powers.

(2) An order under this section may be made so as to authorise a particular transaction, compromise or the like, or a particular application of property, or so as to give a more general authority, and (without prejudice to the generality of subsection (1) above) may authorise a charity to use common premises, or employ a common staff, or otherwise combine for any purpose of administration, with any other charity.

(3) An order under this section may give directions as to the manner in which any expenditure is to be borne and as to other matters connected with or arising out of the action thereby authorised; and where anything is done in pursuance of an authority given by any such order, any directions given in connection therewith shall be binding on the charity trustees for the time being as if contained in the trusts of the charity; but any such directions may on the application of the charity be modified or superseded by a further order.

(4) Without prejudice to the generality of subsection (3) above, the directions which may be given by an order under this section shall in particular include directions for meeting any expenditure out of a specified fund, for charging any expenditure to capital or to income, for requiring expenditure charged to capital to be recouped out of income within a specified period, for restricting the costs to be incurred at the expense of the charity, or for the investment of moneys arising from any transaction.

(5) An order under this section may authorise any act notwithstanding that it is prohibited by any of the disabling Acts mentioned in subsection (6) below or that the trusts of the charity provide for the act to be done by or under the authority of the court; but no such order shall authorise the doing of any act expressly prohibited by Act of Parliament other than the disabling Acts or by the trusts of the charity or shall extend or alter the purposes of the charity.

[(5A) In the case of a charity that is a company, an order under this section may authorise an act notwithstanding that it involves the breach of a duty imposed on a director of the company under Chapter 2 of Part 10 of the Companies Act 2006 (general duties of directors).]

(6) The Acts referred to in subsection (5) above as the disabling Acts are the Ecclesiastical Leases Act 1571, the Ecclesiastical Leases Act 1572, the Ecclesiastical Leases Act 1575 and the Ecclesiastical Leases Act 1836.

(7) An order under this section shall not confer any authority in relation to a building which has been consecrated and of which the use or disposal is regulated, and can be further regulated, by a scheme having effect under the Union of Benefices Measures 1923 to 1952, the Reorganisation Areas Measures 1944 and 1954, the Pastoral Measure 1968 or the Pastoral Measure 1983, the reference to a building being taken to include part of a building and any land which under such a scheme is to be used or disposed of with a building to which the scheme applies.

[1490]

NOTES

Sub-s (1): words in square brackets substituted by the Charities Act 2006, s 75(1), Sch 8, paras 96, 119.

Sub-s (5A): inserted by the Companies Act 2006, s 181(4).

27–34 (*Outside the scope of this work.*)

Meaning of "trust corporation"

35 Application of provisions to trust corporations appointed under s 16 or 18

(1) In the definition of "trust corporation" contained in the following provisions—

(a) section 117(xxx) of the Settled Land Act 1925,

(b) section 68(18) of the Trustee Act 1925,

(c) section 205(xxviii) of the Law of Property Act 1925,

(d) section 55(xxvi) of the Administration of Estates Act 1925, and

(e) section 128 of the *Supreme Court Act 1981* [Senior Courts Act 1981],

the reference to a corporation appointed by the court in any particular case to be a trustee includes a reference to a corporation appointed by [the Commission] under this Act to be a trustee.

(2) This section shall be deemed always to have had effect; but the reference to section 128 of the *Supreme Court Act 1981* [Senior Courts Act 1981] shall, in relation to any time before 1st January 1982, be construed as a reference to section 175(1) of the Supreme Court of Judicature (Consolidation) Act 1925.

[1491]

NOTES

Sub-s (1): in para (e) words in italics repealed and subsequent words in square brackets substituted by the Constitutional Reform Act 2005, s 59(5), Sch 11, Pt 1, para 1(2), as from 1 October 2009; words "the Commission" in square brackets substituted by the Charities Act 2006, s 75(1), Sch 8, paras 96, 127.

Sub-s (2): words in italics repealed and subsequent words in square brackets substituted by the Constitutional Reform Act 2005, s 59(5), Sch 11, Pt 1, para 1(2), as from 1 October 2009.

PART V
CHARITY LAND

36 Restrictions on dispositions

(1) Subject to the following provisions of this section and section 40 below, no land held by or in trust for a charity shall be [conveyed, transferred], leased or otherwise disposed of without an order of the court or of [the Commission].

(2) Subsection (1) above shall not apply to a disposition of such land if—

(a) the disposition is made to a person who is not—

(i) a connected person (as defined in Schedule 5 to this Act), or

(ii) a trustee for, or nominee of, a connected person; and

(b) the requirements of subsection (3) or (5) below have been complied with in relation to it.

(3) Except where the proposed disposition is the granting of such a lease as is mentioned in subsection (5) below, [the requirements mentioned in subsection (2)(b) above are that] the charity trustees must, before entering into an agreement for the sale, or (as the case may be) for a lease or other disposition, of the land—

(a) obtain and consider a written report on the proposed disposition from a qualified surveyor instructed by the trustees and acting exclusively for the charity;

(b) advertise the proposed disposition for such period and in such manner as the surveyor has advised in his report (unless he has there advised that it would not be in the best interests of the charity to advertise the proposed disposition); and

(c) decide that they are satisfied, having considered the surveyor's report, that the terms on which the disposition is proposed to be made are the best that can reasonably be obtained for the charity.

(4) For the purposes of subsection (3) above a person is a qualified surveyor if—

(a) he is a fellow or professional associate of the Royal Institution of Chartered Surveyors or of the Incorporated Society of Valuers and Auctioneers or satisfies such other requirement or requirements as may be prescribed by regulations made by the [Minister]; and

(b) he is reasonably believed by the charity trustees to have ability in, and experience of, the valuation of land of the particular kind, and in the particular area, in question;

and any report prepared for the purposes of that subsection shall contain such information, and deal with such matters, as may be prescribed by regulations so made.

(5) Where the proposed disposition is the granting of a lease for a term ending not more than seven years after it is granted (other than one granted wholly or partly in consideration of a fine), [the requirements mentioned in subsection (2)(b) above are that] the charity trustees must, before entering into an agreement for the lease—

(a) obtain and consider the advice on the proposed disposition of a person who is reasonably believed by the trustees to have the requisite ability and practical experience to provide them with competent advice on the proposed disposition; and

(b) decide that they are satisfied, having considered that person's advice, that the terms on which the disposition is proposed to be made are the best that can reasonably be obtained for the charity.

(6) Where—

(a) any land is held by or in trust for a charity, and

(b) the trusts on which it is so held stipulate that it is to be used for the purposes, or any particular purposes, of the charity,

then (subject to subsections (7) and (8) below and without prejudice to the operation of the preceding provisions of this section) the land shall not be [conveyed, transferred], leased or otherwise disposed of unless the charity trustees have [before the relevant time]—

(i) given public notice of the proposed disposition, inviting representations to be made to them within a time specified in the notice, being not less than one month from the date of the notice; and

(ii) taken into consideration any representations made to them within that time about the proposed disposition.

[(6A) In subsection (6) above "the relevant time" means—

(a) where the charity trustees enter into an agreement for the sale, or (as the case may be) for the lease or other disposition, the time when they enter into that agreement, and

(b) in any other case, the time of the disposition.]

(7) Subsection (6) above shall not apply to any such disposition of land as is there mentioned if—

(a) the disposition is to be effected with a view to acquiring by way of replacement other property which is to be held on the trusts referred to in paragraph (b) of that subsection; or

(b) the disposition is the granting of a lease for a term ending not more than two years after it is granted (other than one granted wholly or partly in consideration of a fine).

(8) [The Commission] may direct—

(a) that subsection (6) above shall not apply to dispositions of land held by or in trust for a charity or class of charities (whether generally or only in the case of a specified class of dispositions or land, or otherwise as may be provided in the direction), or

(b) that that subsection shall not apply to a particular disposition of land held by or in trust for a charity,

if, on an application made to them in writing by or on behalf of the charity or charities in question, [the Commission is satisfied] that it would be in the interests of the charity or charities for [the Commission] to give the direction.

(9) The restrictions on disposition imposed by this section apply notwithstanding anything in the trusts of a charity; but nothing in this section applies—

(a) to any disposition for which general or special authority is expressly given (without the authority being made subject to the sanction of an order of the court) by any statutory provision contained in or having effect under an Act of Parliament or by any scheme legally established; or

(b) to any disposition of land held by or in trust for a charity which—

(i) is made to another charity otherwise than for the best price that can reasonably be obtained, and

(ii) is authorised to be so made by the trusts of the first-mentioned charity; or

(c) to the granting, by or on behalf of a charity and in accordance with its trusts, of a lease to any beneficiary under those trusts where the lease—

(i) is granted otherwise than for the best rent that can reasonably be obtained; and

(ii) is intended to enable the demised premises to be occupied for the purposes, or any particular purposes, of the charity.

(10) Nothing in this section applies—

(a) to any disposition of land held by or in trust for an exempt charity;

(b) to any disposition of land by way of mortgage or other security; or

(c) to any disposition of an advowson.

(11) In this section "land" means land in England or Wales.

[1492]

NOTES

Sub-s (1): words in square brackets substituted by the Charities Act 2006, s 75(1), Sch 8, paras 96, 128(1), (2).

Sub-ss (3), (5): words in square brackets inserted by the Charities Act 2006, s 75(1), Sch 8, paras 96, 128(1), (3), (4).

Sub-s (4): word in square brackets in para (a) substituted by SI 2006/2951, art 6, Schedule, para 4(o).

Sub-s (6): words in square brackets substituted by the Charities Act 2006, s 75(1), Sch 8, paras 96, 128(1), (5), subject to savings in SI 2007/309, art 6(1).

Sub-s (6A): inserted by the Charities Act 2006, s 75(1), Sch 8, paras 96, 128(1), (6), subject to savings in SI 2007/309, art 6(1).

Sub-s (8): words in square brackets substituted by the Charities Act 2006, s 75(1), Sch 8, paras 96, 128(1), (7).

37 Supplementary provisions relating to dispositions

(1) Any of the following instruments, namely—

(a) any contract for the sale, or for a lease or other disposition, of land which is held by or in trust for a charity, and

(b) any conveyance, transfer, lease or other instrument effecting a disposition of such land,

shall state—

(i) that the land is held by or in trust for a charity,

(ii) whether the charity is an exempt charity and whether the disposition is one falling within paragraph (a), (b) or (c) of subsection (9) of section 36 above, and

(iii) if it is not an exempt charity and the disposition is not one falling within any of those paragraphs, that the land is land to which the restrictions on disposition imposed by that section apply.

(2) Where any land held by or in trust for a charity is [conveyed, transferred], leased or otherwise disposed of by a disposition to which subsection (1) or (2) of section 36 above applies, the charity trustees shall certify in the instrument by which the disposition is effected—

(a) (where subsection (1) of that section applies) that the disposition has been sanctioned by an order of the court or of [the Commission] (as the case may be), or

(b) (where subsection (2) of that section applies) that the charity trustees have power under the trusts of the charity to effect the disposition, and that they have complied with the provisions of that section so far as applicable to it.

(3) Where subsection (2) above has been complied with in relation to any disposition of land, then in favour of a person who (whether under the disposition or afterwards) acquires an interest in the land for money or money's worth, it shall be conclusively presumed that the facts were as stated in the certificate.

(4) Where—

(a) any land held by or in trust for a charity is [conveyed, transferred], leased or otherwise disposed of by a disposition to which subsection (1) or (2) of section 36 above applies, but

(b) subsection (2) above has not been complied with in relation to the disposition,

then in favour of a person who (whether under the disposition or afterwards) in good faith acquires an interest in the land for money or money's worth, the disposition shall be valid whether or not—

(i) the disposition has been sanctioned by an order of the court or of [the Commission], or

(ii) the charity trustees have power under the trusts of the charity to effect the disposition and have complied with the provisions of that section so far as applicable to it.

(5) Any of the following instruments, namely—

(a) any contract for the sale, or for a lease or other disposition, of land which will, as a result of the disposition, be held by or in trust for a charity, and

(b) any conveyance, transfer, lease or other instrument effecting a disposition of such land,

shall state—

(i) that the land will, as a result of the disposition, be held by or in trust for a charity,

(ii) whether the charity is an exempt charity, and

(iii) if it is not an exempt charity, that the restrictions on disposition imposed by section 36 above will apply to the land (subject to subsection (9) of that section).

(6) ...

[(7) Where the disposition to be effected by any such instrument as is mentioned in subsection (1)(b) or (5)(b) above will be—

(a) a registrable disposition, or

(b) a disposition which triggers the requirement of registration,

the statement which, by virtue of subsection (1) or (5) above, is to be contained in the instrument shall be in such form as may be prescribed by land registration rules.

(8) Where the registrar approves an application for registration of—

(a) a disposition of registered land, or

(b) a person's title under a disposition of unregistered land,

and the instrument effecting the disposition contains a statement complying with subsections (5) and (7) above, he shall enter in the register a restriction reflecting the limitation under section 36 above on subsequent disposal.]

(9) Where—

(a) any such restriction is entered in the register in respect of any land, and

(b) the charity by or in trust for which the land is held becomes an exempt charity,

the charity trustees shall apply to the registrar for [the removal of the entry]; and on receiving any application duly made under this subsection the registrar shall [remove the entry].

(10) Where—

(a) any registered land is held by or in trust for an exempt charity and the charity ceases to be an exempt charity, or

(b) any registered land becomes, as a result of a declaration of trust by the registered proprietor, land held in trust for a charity (other than an exempt charity),

the charity trustees shall apply to the registrar for such a restriction as is mentioned in subsection (8) above to be entered in the register in respect of the land; and on receiving any application duly made under this subsection the registrar shall enter such a restriction in the register in respect of the land.

(11) In this section—

(a) references to a disposition of land do not include references to—

(i) a disposition of land by way of mortgage or other security,

(ii) any disposition of an advowson, or

(iii) any release of a rentcharge failing within section 40(1) below; and

(b) "land" means land in England or Wales;

and subsections (7) to (10) above shall be construed as one with the [Land Registration Act 2002]. **[1493]**

NOTES

Sub-ss (2), (4): in square brackets substituted by the Charities Act 2006, s 75(1), Sch 8, paras 96, 129.

Sub-s (6): repealed by the Trusts of Land and Appointment of Trustees Act 1996, s 25(2), Sch 4; for savings in relation to entailed interests created before the commencement of that Act, and savings consequential upon the abolition of the doctrine of conversion, see s 25(4), (5) thereof.

Sub-ss (7), (8): substituted by the Land Registration Act 2002, s 133, Sch 11, para 29(1), (2).

Sub-s (9): words in square brackets substituted by the Land Registration Act 2002, s 133, Sch 11, para 29(1), (3).

Sub-s (11): words in square brackets substituted by the Land Registration Act 2002, s 133, Sch 11, para 29(1), (4).

Rules: the Land Registration Rules 2003, SI 2003/1417 at **[3067]**.

38 Restrictions on mortgaging

(1) Subject to subsection (2) below, no mortgage of land held by or in trust for a charity shall be granted without an order of the court or of [the Commission].

[(2) Subsection (1) above shall not apply to a mortgage of any such land if the charity trustees have, before executing the mortgage, obtained and considered proper advice, given to them in writing, on the relevant matters or matter mentioned in subsection (3) or (3A) below (as the case may be).

(3) In the case of a mortgage to secure the repayment of a proposed loan or grant, the relevant matters are—

(a) whether the loan or grant is necessary in order for the charity trustees to be able to pursue the particular course of action in connection with which they are seeking the loan or grant;

(b) whether the terms of the loan or grant are reasonable having regard to the status of the charity as the prospective recipient of the loan or grant; and

(c) the ability of the charity to repay on those terms the sum proposed to be paid by way of loan or grant.

(3A) In the case of a mortgage to secure the discharge of any other proposed obligation, the relevant matter is whether it is reasonable for the charity trustees to undertake to discharge the obligation, having regard to the charity's purposes.

(3B) Subsection (3) or (as the case may be) subsection (3A) above applies in relation to such a mortgage as is mentioned in that subsection whether the mortgage—

(a) would only have effect to secure the repayment of the proposed loan or grant or the discharge of the proposed obligation, or
(b) would also have effect to secure the repayment of sums paid by way of loan or grant, or the discharge of other obligations undertaken, after the date of its execution.

(3C) Subsection (3D) below applies where—
(a) the charity trustees of a charity have executed a mortgage of land held by or in trust for a charity in accordance with subsection (2) above, and
(b) the mortgage has effect to secure the repayment of sums paid by way of loan or grant, or the discharge of other obligations undertaken, after the date of its execution.

(3D) In such a case, the charity trustees must not after that date enter into any transaction involving—
(a) the payment of any such sums, or
(b) the undertaking of any such obligations,
unless they have, before entering into the transaction, obtained and considered proper advice, given to them in writing, on the matters or matter mentioned in subsection (3)(a) to (c) or (3A) above (as the case may be).]

(4) For the purposes of [this section] proper advice is the advice of a person—
(a) who is reasonably believed by the charity trustees to be qualified by his ability in and practical experience of financial matters; and
(b) who has no financial interest in [relation to the loan, grant or other transaction in connection with which his advice is given];
and such advice may constitute proper advice for those purposes notwithstanding that the person giving it does so in the course of his employment as an officer or employee of the charity or of the charity trustees.

(5) This section applies notwithstanding anything in the trusts of a charity; but nothing in this section applies to any mortgage for which general or special authority is given as mentioned in section 36(9)(a) above.

(6) In this section—
"land" means land in England or Wales;
"mortgage" includes a charge.

(7) Nothing in this section applies to an exempt charity.

[1494]

NOTES

Sub-s (1): words in square brackets substituted by the Charities Act 2006, s 75(1), Sch 8, paras 96, 130.
Sub-ss (2), (3), (3A)–(3D): substituted, for sub-ss (2), (3) as originally enacted, by the Charities Act 2006, s 27(1), (2).
Sub-s (4): words in square brackets substituted by the Charities Act 2006, s 27(1), (3).

39 Supplementary provisions relating to mortgaging

(1) Any mortgage of land held by or in trust for a charity shall state—
(a) that the land is held by or in trust for a charity,
(b) whether the charity is an exempt charity and whether the mortgage is one falling within subsection (5) of section 38 above, and
(c) if it is not an exempt charity and the mortgage is not one falling within that subsection, that the mortgage is one to which the restrictions imposed by that section apply;
and where the mortgage will be a registered disposition any such statement shall be in such form as may be prescribed [by land registration rules].

[(1A) Where any such mortgage will be one to which section 4(1)(g) of the Land Registration Act 2002 applies—
(a) the statement required by subsection (1) above shall be in such form as may be prescribed by land registration rules; and
(b) if the charity is not an exempt charity, the mortgage shall also contain a statement, in such form as may be prescribed by land registration rules, that the restrictions on disposition imposed by section 36 above apply to the land (subject to subsection (9) of that section).

(1B) Where—
(a) the registrar approves an application for registration of a person's title to land in connection with such a mortgage as is mentioned in subsection (1A) above,
(b) the mortgage contains statements complying with subsections (1) and (1A) above, and
(c) the charity is not an exempt charity,
the registrar shall enter in the register a restriction reflecting the limitation under section 36 above on subsequent disposal.

(1C) Section 37(9) above shall apply in relation to any restriction entered under subsection (1B) as it applies in relation to any restriction entered under section 37(8).]

(2) Where subsection (1) or (2) of section 38 above applies to any mortgage of land held by or in trust for a charity, the charity trustees shall certify in the mortgage—

(a) (where subsection (1) of that section applies) that the mortgage has been sanctioned by an order of the court or of [the Commission] (as the case may be), or

(b) (where subsection (2) of that section applies) that the charity trustees have power under the trusts of the charity to grant the mortgage, and that they have obtained and considered such advice as is mentioned in that subsection.

(3) Where subsection (2) above has been complied with in relation to any mortgage, then in favour of a person who (whether under the mortgage or afterwards) acquires an interest in the land in question for money or money's worth, it shall be conclusively presumed that the facts were as stated in the certificate.

(4) Where—

(a) subsection (1) or (2) of section 38 above applies to any mortgage of land held by or in trust for a charity, but

(b) subsection (2) above has not been complied with in relation to the mortgage,

then in favour of a person who (whether under the mortgage or afterwards) in good faith acquires an interest in the land for money or money's worth, the mortgage shall be valid whether or not—

(i) the mortgage has been sanctioned by an order of the court or of [the Commission], or

(ii) the charity trustees have power under the trusts of the charity to grant the mortgage and have obtained and considered such advice as is mentioned in subsection (2) of that section.

[(4A) Where subsection (3D) of section 38 above applies to any mortgage of land held by or in trust for a charity, the charity trustees shall certify in relation to any transaction falling within that subsection that they have obtained and considered such advice as is mentioned in that subsection.

(4B) Where subsection (4A) above has been complied with in relation to any transaction, then, in favour of a person who (whether under the mortgage or afterwards) has acquired or acquires an interest in the land for money or money's worth, it shall be conclusively presumed that the facts were as stated in the certificate.]

(5) …

(6) In this section—

"mortgage" includes a charge, and "mortgagee" shall be construed accordingly;

"land" means land in England or Wales;

[and subsections (1) to (1B) above shall be construed as one with the Land Registration Act 2002].

[1495]

NOTES

Sub-s (1): words in square brackets inserted by the Land Registration Act 2002, s 133, Sch 11, para 29(1), (5).

Sub-ss (1A)–(1C): substituted, for sub-ss (1A), (1B) (as inserted by the Land Registration Act 1997, s 4(1), Sch 1, para 6(2)), by the Land Registration Act 2002, s 133, Sch 11, para 29(1), (6).

Sub-ss (2), (4): words in square brackets substituted by the Charities Act 2006, s 75(1), Sch 8, paras 96, 131(1), (2).

Sub-ss (4A), (4B): inserted by the Charities Act 2006, s 75(1), Sch 8, paras 96, 131(1), (3).

Sub-s (5): repealed by the Trusts of Land and Appointment of Trustees Act 1996, s 25(2), Sch 4; for savings in relation to entailed interests created before the commencement of that Act, and savings consequential upon the abolition of the doctrine of conversion, see s 25(4), (5) thereof.

Sub-s (6): words in square brackets substituted by the Land Registration Act 2002, s 133, Sch 11, para 29(1), (7).

Rules: the Land Registration Rules 2003, SI 2003/1417 at **[3067]**.

40 Release of charity rentcharges

(1) Section 36(1) above shall not apply to the release by a charity of a rentcharge which it is entitled to receive if the release is given in consideration of the payment of an amount which is not less than ten times the annual amount of the rentcharge.

(2) Where a charity which is entitled to receive a rentcharge releases it in consideration of the payment of an amount not exceeding [£1,000], any costs incurred by the charity in connection with proving its title to the rentcharge shall be recoverable by the charity from the person or persons in whose favour the rentcharge is being released.

(3) Neither section 36(1) nor subsection (2) above applies where a rentcharge which a charity is entitled to receive is redeemed under sections 8 to 10 of the Rentcharges Act 1977.

(4) The [Minister] may by order amend subsection (2) above by substituting a different sum for the sum for the time being specified there.

[1496]

NOTES

Sub-s (2): sum "£1,000" in square brackets substituted by SI 2009/508, arts 7, 8.
Sub-s (4): word in square brackets substituted by SI 2006/2951, art 6, Schedule, para 4(p).
Orders: the Charities Acts 1992 and 1993 (Substitution of Sums) Order 2009, SI 2009/508.

41–69Q ((*Pts VI–VIIIA*) *outside the scope of this work.*)

PART IX
MISCELLANEOUS

70–73F (*Ss 70, 71 repealed by the Trustee Act 2000, s 40(1), (3), Sch 2, Pt I, para 2(1), Sch 4, Pt I; ss 72–73F outside the scope of this work.*)

[Miscellaneous powers of charities]

NOTES

Substituted by the Charities Act 2006, s 75(1), Sch 8, paras 96, 158.

[74 Power to transfer all property of unincorporated charity

[(1) This section applies to a charity if—

(a) its gross income in its last financial year did not exceed £10,000,

(b) it does not hold any designated land, and

(c) it is not a company or other body corporate.

"Designated land" means land held on trusts which stipulate that it is to be used for the purposes, or any particular purposes, of the charity.

(2) The charity trustees of such a charity may resolve for the purposes of this section—

(a) that all the property of the charity should be transferred to another charity specified in the resolution, or

(b) that all the property of the charity should be transferred to two or more charities specified in the resolution in accordance with such division of the property between them as is so specified.

(3) Any charity so specified may be either a registered charity or a charity which is not required to be registered.

(4) But the charity trustees of a charity ("the transferor charity") do not have power to pass a resolution under subsection (2) above unless they are satisfied—

(a) that it is expedient in the interests of furthering the purposes for which the property is held by the transferor charity for the property to be transferred in accordance with the resolution, and

(b) that the purposes (or any of the purposes) of any charity to which property is to be transferred under the resolution are substantially similar to the purposes (or any of the purposes) of the transferor charity.

(5) Any resolution under subsection (2) above must be passed by a majority of not less than two-thirds of the charity trustees who vote on the resolution.

(6) Where charity trustees have passed a resolution under subsection (2), they must send a copy of it to the Commission, together with a statement of their reasons for passing it.

(7) Having received the copy of the resolution, the Commission—

(a) may direct the charity trustees to give public notice of the resolution in such manner as is specified in the direction, and

(b) if it gives such a direction, must take into account any representations made to it by persons appearing to it to be interested in the charity, where those representations are made to it within the period of 28 days beginning with the date when public notice of the resolution is given by the charity trustees.

(8) The Commission may also direct the charity trustees to provide the Commission with additional information or explanations relating to—

(a) the circumstances in and by reference to which they have decided to act under this section, or

(b) their compliance with any obligation imposed on them by or under this section in connection with the resolution.

(9) Subject to the provisions of section 74A below, a resolution under subsection (2) above takes effect at the end of the period of 60 days beginning with the date on which the copy of it was received by the Commission.

(10) Where such a resolution has taken effect, the charity trustees must arrange for all the property of the transferor charity to be transferred in accordance with the resolution, and on terms that any property so transferred—

(a) is to be held by the charity to which it is transferred ("the transferee charity") in accordance with subsection (11) below, but

(b) when so held is nevertheless to be subject to any restrictions on expenditure to which it was subject as property of the transferor charity;

and the charity trustees must arrange for the property to be so transferred by such date after the resolution takes effect as they agree with the charity trustees of the transferee charity or charities concerned.

(11) The charity trustees of any charity to which property is transferred under this section must secure, so far as is reasonably practicable, that the property is applied for such of its purposes as are substantially similar to those of the transferor charity.

But this requirement does not apply if those charity trustees consider that complying with it would not result in a suitable and effective method of applying the property.

(12) For the purpose of enabling any property to be transferred to a charity under this section, the Commission may, at the request of the charity trustees of that charity, make orders vesting any property of the transferor charity—

(a) in the transferee charity, in its charity trustees or in any trustee for that charity, or

(b) in any other person nominated by those charity trustees to hold property in trust for that charity.

(13) The Minister may by order amend subsection (1) above by substituting a different sum for the sum for the time being specified there.

(14) In this section references to the transfer of property to a charity are references to its transfer—

(a) to the charity, or

(b) to the charity trustees, or

(c) to any trustee for the charity, or

(d) to a person nominated by the charity trustees to hold it in trust for the charity,

as the charity trustees may determine.

(15) Where a charity has a permanent endowment, this section has effect in accordance with section 74B.]

[1497]

NOTES

Substituted, together with ss 74A, 74B for s 74 as originally enacted, by the Charities Act 2006, s 40.

Sub-s (11): word in square brackets substituted by SI 2006/2951, art 6, Schedule, para 4(v).

[74A Resolution not to take effect or to take effect at later date

(1) This section deals with circumstances in which a resolution under section 74(2) above either—

(a) does not take effect under section 74(9) above, or

(b) takes effect at a time later than that mentioned in section 74(9).

(2) A resolution does not take effect under section 74(9) above if before the end of—

(a) the period of 60 days mentioned in section 74(9) ("the 60-day period"), or

(b) that period as modified by subsection (3) or (4) below,

the Commission notifies the charity trustees in writing that it objects to the resolution, either on procedural grounds or on the merits of the proposals contained in the resolution.

"On procedural grounds" means on the grounds that any obligation imposed on the charity trustees by or under section 74 above has not been complied with in connection with the resolution.

(3) If under section 74(7) above the Commission directs the charity trustees to give public notice of a resolution, the running of the 60-day period is suspended by virtue of this subsection—

(a) as from the date on which the direction is given to the charity trustees, and

(b) until the end of the period of 42 days beginning with the date on which public notice of the resolution is given by the charity trustees.

(4) If under section 74(8) above the Commission directs the charity trustees to provide any information or explanations, the running of the 60-day period is suspended by virtue of this subsection—

(a) as from the date on which the direction is given to the charity trustees, and

(b) until the date on which the information or explanations is or are provided to the Commission.

(5) Subsection (6) below applies once the period of time, or the total period of time, during which the 60-day period is suspended by virtue of either or both of subsections (3) and (4) above exceeds 120 days.

(6) At that point the resolution (if not previously objected to by the Commission) is to be treated as if it had never been passed.]

[1498]

NOTES

Commencement: 18 March 2008.

Substituted, together with ss 74, 74B for s 74 as originally enacted, by the Charities Act 2006, s 40.

[74B Transfer where charity has permanent endowment

(1) This section provides for the operation of section 74 above where a charity within section 74(1) has a permanent endowment (whether or not the charity's trusts contain provision for the termination of the charity).

(2) In such a case section 74 applies as follows—

(a) if the charity has both a permanent endowment and other property ("unrestricted property")—

(i) a resolution under section 74(2) must relate to both its permanent endowment and its unrestricted property, and

(ii) that section applies in relation to its unrestricted property in accordance with subsection (3) below and in relation to its permanent endowment in accordance with subsections (4) to (11) below;

(b) if all of the property of the charity is comprised in its permanent endowment, that section applies in relation to its permanent endowment in accordance with subsections (4) to (11) below.

(3) Section 74 applies in relation to unrestricted property of the charity as if references in that section to all or any of the property of the charity were references to all or any of its unrestricted property.

(4) Section 74 applies in relation to the permanent endowment of the charity with the following modifications.

(5) References in that section to all or any of the property of the charity are references to all or any of the property comprised in its permanent endowment.

(6) If the property comprised in its permanent endowment is to be transferred to a single charity, the charity trustees must (instead of being satisfied as mentioned in section 74(4)(b)) be satisfied that the proposed transferee charity has purposes which are substantially similar to all of the purposes of the transferor charity.

(7) If the property comprised in its permanent endowment is to be transferred to two or more charities, the charity trustees must (instead of being satisfied as mentioned in section 74(4)(b)) be satisfied—

(a) that the proposed transferee charities, taken together, have purposes which are substantially similar to all of the purposes of the transferor charity, and

(b) that each of the proposed transferee charities has purposes which are substantially similar to one or more of the purposes of the transferor charity.

(8) In the case of a transfer to which subsection (7) above applies, the resolution under section 74(2) must provide for the property comprised in the permanent endowment of the charity to be divided between the transferee charities in such a way as to take account of such guidance as may be given by the Commission for the purposes of this section.

(9) The requirement in section 74(11) shall apply in the case of every such transfer, and in complying with that requirement the charity trustees of a transferee charity must secure that the application of property transferred to the charity takes account of any such guidance.

(10) Any guidance given by the Commission for the purposes of this section may take such form and be given in such manner as the Commission considers appropriate.

(11) For the purposes of sections 74 and 74A above, any reference to any obligation imposed on the charity trustees by or under section 74 includes a reference to any obligation imposed on them by virtue of any of subsections (6) to (8) above.

(12) Section 74(14) applies for the purposes of this section as it applies for the purposes of section 74.]

[1499]

NOTES

Commencement: 18 March 2008.

Substituted, together with ss 74, 74A for s 74 as originally enacted, by the Charities Act 2006, s 40.

[74C Power to replace purposes of unincorporated charity

(1) This section applies to a charity if—

(a) its gross income in its last financial year did not exceed £10,000,

(b) it does not hold any designated land, and

(c) it is not a company or other body corporate.

"Designated land" means land held on trusts which stipulate that it is to be used for the purposes, or any particular purposes, of the charity.

(2) The charity trustees of such a charity may resolve for the purposes of this section that the trusts of the charity should be modified by replacing all or any of the purposes of the charity with other purposes specified in the resolution.

(3) The other purposes so specified must be charitable purposes.

(4) But the charity trustees of a charity do not have power to pass a resolution under subsection (2) above unless they are satisfied—

(a) that it is expedient in the interests of the charity for the purposes in question to be replaced, and

(b) that, so far as is reasonably practicable, the new purposes consist of or include purposes that are similar in character to those that are to be replaced.

(5) Any resolution under subsection (2) above must be passed by a majority of not less than two-thirds of the charity trustees who vote on the resolution.

(6) Where charity trustees have passed a resolution under subsection (2), they must send a copy of it to the Commission, together with a statement of their reasons for passing it.

(7) Having received the copy of the resolution, the Commission—

(a) may direct the charity trustees to give public notice of the resolution in such manner as is specified in the direction, and

(b) if it gives such a direction, must take into account any representations made to it by persons appearing to it to be interested in the charity, where those representations are made to it within the period of 28 days beginning with the date when public notice of the resolution is given by the charity trustees.

(8) The Commission may also direct the charity trustees to provide the Commission with additional information or explanations relating to—

(a) the circumstances in and by reference to which they have decided to act under this section, or

(b) their compliance with any obligation imposed on them by or under this section in connection with the resolution.

(9) Subject to the provisions of section 74A above (as they apply in accordance with subsection (10) below), a resolution under subsection (2) above takes effect at the end of the period of 60 days beginning with the date on which the copy of it was received by the Commission.

(10) Section 74A above applies to a resolution under subsection (2) of this section as it applies to a resolution under subsection (2) of section 74 above, except that any reference to section 74(7), (8) or (9) is to be read as a reference to subsection (7), (8) or (9) above.

(11) As from the time when a resolution takes effect under subsection (9) above, the trusts of the charity concerned are to be taken to have been modified in accordance with the terms of the resolution.

(12) The Minister may by order amend subsection (1) above by substituting a different sum for the sum for the time being specified there.]

[1500]

NOTES

Commencement: 18 March 2008.

Inserted by the Charities Act 2006, s 41.

[74D Power to modify powers or procedures of unincorporated charity

(1) This section applies to any charity which is not a company or other body corporate.

(2) The charity trustees of such a charity may resolve for the purposes of this section that any provision of the trusts of the charity—

(a) relating to any of the powers exercisable by the charity trustees in the administration of the charity, or

(b) regulating the procedure to be followed in any respect in connection with its administration,

should be modified in such manner as is specified in the resolution.

(3) Subsection (4) applies if the charity is an unincorporated association with a body of members distinct from the charity trustees.

(4) Any resolution of the charity trustees under subsection (2) must be approved by a further resolution which is passed at a general meeting of the body either—

(a) by a majority of not less than two-thirds of the members entitled to attend and vote at the meeting who vote on the resolution, or

(b) by a decision taken without a vote and without any expression of dissent in response to the question put to the meeting.

(5) Where—

(a) the charity trustees have passed a resolution under subsection (2), and

(b) (if subsection (4) applies) a further resolution has been passed under that subsection,

the trusts of the charity are to be taken to have been modified in accordance with the terms of the resolution.

(6) The trusts are to be taken to have been so modified as from such date as is specified for this purpose in the resolution under subsection (2), or (if later) the date when any such further resolution was passed under subsection (4).]

[1501]

NOTES

Commencement: 27 February 2007.
Inserted by the Charities Act 2006, s 42.

75–81 (*Outside the scope of this work.*)

Administrative provisions about charities

82 Manner of executing instruments

(1) Charity trustees may, subject to the trusts of the charity, confer on any of their body (not being less than two in number) a general authority, or an authority limited in such manner as the trustees think fit, to execute in the names and on behalf of the trustees assurances or other deeds or instruments for giving effect to transactions to which the trustees are a party; and any deed or instrument executed in pursuance of an authority so given shall be of the same effect as if executed by the whole body.

(2) An authority under subsection (1) above—

(a) shall suffice for any deed or instrument if it is given in writing or by resolution of a meeting of the trustees, notwithstanding the want of any formality that would be required in giving an authority apart from that subsection;

(b) may be given so as to make the powers conferred exercisable by any of the trustees, or may be restricted to named persons or in any other way;

(c) subject to any such restriction, and until it is revoked, shall, notwithstanding any change in the charity trustees, have effect as a continuing authority given by the charity trustees from time to time of the charity and exercisable by such trustees.

(3) In any authority under this section to execute a deed or instrument in the names and on behalf of charity trustees there shall, unless the contrary intention appears, be implied authority also to execute it for them in the name and on behalf of the official custodian or of any other person, in any case in which the charity trustees could do so.

(4) Where a deed or instrument purports to be executed in pursuance of this section, then in favour of a person who (then or afterwards) in good faith acquires for money or money's worth an interest in or charge on property or the benefit of any covenant or agreement expressed to be entered into by the charity trustees, it shall be conclusively presumed to have been duly executed by virtue of this section.

(5) The powers conferred by this section shall be in addition to and not in derogation of any other powers.

[1502]

83 Transfer and evidence of title to property vested in trustees

(1) Where, under the trusts of a charity, trustees of property held for the purposes of the charity may be appointed or discharged by resolution of a meeting of the charity trustees, members or other persons, a memorandum declaring a trustee to have been so appointed or discharged shall be sufficient evidence of that fact if the memorandum is signed either at the meeting by the person presiding or in some other manner directed by the meeting and is attested by two persons present at the meeting.

(2) A memorandum evidencing the appointment or discharge of a trustee under subsection (1) above, if executed as a deed, shall have the like operation under section 40 of the Trustee Act 1925 (which relates to vesting declarations as respects trust property in deeds appointing or discharging trustees) as if the appointment or discharge were effected by the deed.

(3) For the purposes of this section, where a document purports to have been signed and attested as mentioned in subsection (1) above, then on proof (whether by evidence or as a matter of presumption) of the signature the document shall be presumed to have been so signed and attested, unless the contrary is shown.

(4) This section shall apply to a memorandum made at any time, except that subsection (2) shall apply only to those made after the commencement of the Charities Act 1960.

(5) This section shall apply in relation to any institution to which the Literary and Scientific Institutions Act 1854 applies as it applies in relation to a charity.

[1503]

PART X
SUPPLEMENTARY

84–92 (*Outside the scope of this work.*)

93 Miscellaneous provisions as to evidence

(1) Where, in any proceedings to recover or compel payment of any rentcharge or other periodical payment claimed by or on behalf of a charity out of land or of the rents, profits or other income of land, otherwise than as rent incident to a reversion, it is shown that the rentcharge or other periodical payment has at any time been paid for twelve consecutive years to or for the benefit of the charity, that shall be prima facie evidence of the perpetual liability to it of the land or income, and no proof of its origin shall be necessary.

(2) In any proceedings, the following documents, that is to say,—

(a) the printed copies of the reports of the Commissioners for enquiring concerning charities, 1818 to 1837, who were appointed under the Act 58 Geo 3 c 91 and subsequent Acts; and

(b) the printed copies of the reports which were made for various counties and county boroughs to the Charity Commissioners by their assistant commissioners and presented to the House of Commons as returns to orders of various dates beginning with 8th December 1890, and ending with 9th September 1909,

shall be admissible as evidence of the documents and facts stated in them.

[(3) Evidence of any order, certificate or other document issued by the Commission may be given by means of a copy which it retained, or which is taken from a copy so retained, and evidence of an entry in any register kept by it may be given by means of a copy of the entry, if (in each case) the copy is certified in accordance with subsection (4).

(4) The copy shall be certified to be a true copy by any member of the staff of the Commission generally or specially authorised by the Commission to act for that purpose.

(5) A document purporting to be such a copy shall be received in evidence without proof of the official position, authority or handwriting of the person certifying it.

(6) In subsection (3) above "the Commission" includes the Charity Commissioners for England and Wales.]

[1504]

NOTES

Sub-ss (3)–(6): substituted, for sub-s (3) as originally enacted, by the Charities Act 2006, s 75(1), Sch 8, paras 96, 172.

94, 95 (*Outside the scope of this work.*)

96 Construction of references to a "charity" or to particular classes of charity

(1), (2) (*Outside the scope of this work.*)

(3) A charity shall be deemed for the purposes of this Act to have a permanent endowment unless all property held for the purposes of the charity may be expended for those purposes without distinction between capital and income, and in this Act "permanent endowment" means, in relation to any charity, property held subject to a restriction on its being expended for the purposes of the charity.

(4)–(6) (*Outside the scope of this work.*)

[1505]

97 General interpretation

(1) In this Act, except in so far as the context otherwise requires—

"charitable purposes" means purposes which are exclusively [charitable purposes as defined by section 2(1) of the Charities Act 2006];

"charity trustees" means the persons having the general control and management of the administration of a charity;

["CIO" means charitable incorporated organisation;]

["the Commission" means the Charity Commission;]

"company" means a company formed and registered under the Companies Act 1985 or to which the provisions of that Act apply as they apply to such a company; ["company" means a company registered under the Companies Act 2006 in England and Wales or Scotland;]

"the court" means the High Court and, within the limits of its jurisdiction, any other court in England and Wales having a jurisdiction in respect of charities concurrent (within any limit of area or amount) with that of the High Court, and includes any judge or officer of the court exercising the jurisdiction of the court;

"financial year"—

(a) in relation to a charity which is a company, shall be construed in accordance with [section 390 of the Companies Act 2006]; and

(b) in relation to any other charity, shall be construed in accordance with regulations made by virtue of section 42(2) above;

but this definition is subject to the transitional provisions in section 99(4) below and Part II of Schedule 8 to this Act;

"gross income", in relation to charity, means its gross recorded income from all sources including special trusts;

"independent examiner", in relation to a charity, means such a person as is mentioned in section 43(3)(a) above;

"institution" [means an institution whether incorporated or not, and] includes any trust or undertaking;

["members", in relation to a charity with a body of members distinct from the charity trustees, means any of those members;]

["the Minister" means the Minister for the Cabinet Office;]

"the official custodian" means the official custodian for charities;

"permanent endowment" shall be construed in accordance with section 96(3) above;

["principal regulator", in relation to an exempt charity, means the charity's principal regulator within the meaning of section 13 of the Charities Act 2006;]

"the register" means the register of charities kept under section 3 above and "registered" shall be construed accordingly;

"special trust" means property which is held and administered by or on behalf of a charity for any special purposes of the charity, and is so held and administered on separate trusts relating only to that property but a special trust shall not, by itself, constitute a charity for the purposes of Part VI of this Act;

["the Tribunal" means the Charity Tribunal;]

"trusts" in relation to a charity, means the provisions establishing it as a charity and regulating its purposes and administration, whether those provisions take effect by way of trust or not, and in relation to other institutions has a corresponding meaning

(2), (3) (*Outside the scope of this work.*)

[1506]

NOTES

Sub-s (1): in definition "charitable purposes" words in square brackets substituted by the Charities Act 2006, s 75(1), Sch 8, paras 96, 174(a); definition "CIO" inserted by the Charities Act 2006, s 34, Sch 7, Pt 2, paras 3, 7, as from a day to be appointed; definition "the Commission" substituted, for definition "the Commissioners" as originally enacted, by the Charities Act 2006, s 75(1), Sch 8, paras 96, 174(b); definition "company" substituted by SI 2009/1941, art 2(1), Sch 1, para 120, as from 1 October 2009; in definition "financial year" in para (a) words in square brackets substituted by SI 2008/948, arts 3(1)(b), 6, Sch 1, Pt 2, para 192(1), (9); in definition "institution" words in square brackets inserted by the Charities Act 2006, s 75(1), Sch 8, paras 96, 174(c); definitions "members", "the Minister", "principal regulator" and "the Tribunal" inserted by the Charities Act 2006, s 75(1), Sch 8, paras 96, 174(d).

98, 99 (*Outside the scope of this work.*)

100 Short title and extent

(1) This Act may be cited as the Charities Act 1993.

(2) Subject to subsection (3) to (6) below, this Act extends only to England and Wales.

(3) *Section 10* [Sections 10 to 10C] above and this section extend to the whole of the United Kingdom.

(4) Section 15(2) [and sections 24 to 25A extend] also to Northern Ireland.

(5) …

(6) (*Outside the scope of this work.*)

[1507]

NOTES

Sub-s (3): words in italics repealed and subsequent words in square brackets substituted by the Charities Act 2006, s 75(1), Sch 8, paras 96, 176, partly as from a day to be appointed.

Sub-s (4): words in square brackets substituted by the Charities Act 2006, s 23(5).

Sub-s (5): repealed by the Charities and Trustee Investment (Scotland) Act 2005, s 95, Sch 3, para 9.

(*Schs 1–1D outside the scope of this work.*)

SCHEDULE 2
EXEMPT CHARITIES

Sections 3, 96

The following institutions, so far as they are charities, are exempt charities within the meaning of this Act, that is to say—

(a) any institution which, if the Charities Act 1960 had not been passed, would be exempted from the powers and jurisdiction, under the Charitable Trusts Acts 1853 to 1939, of [the Charity Commissioners for England and Wales] or Minister of Education (apart from any power of the Commissioners or Minister to apply those Acts in whole or in part to charities otherwise exempt) by the terms of any enactment not contained in those Acts other than section 9 of the Places of Worship Registration Act 1855 [(*but see Note 1*)];

(b) the universities of Oxford, Cambridge, London, Durham and Newcastle, the colleges and halls in the universities of Oxford, Cambridge, Durham and Newcastle, [and] Queen Mary and Westfield College in the University of London *and the colleges of Winchester and Eton*;

(c) any university, university college, or institution connected with a university or university college, which Her Majesty declares by Order in Council to be an exempt charity for the purposes of this Act;

(d) …

[(da) the Qualifications and Curriculum Authority;]

(e) …

(f) …

(g) …

(h) …

[(h) a higher education corporation;]

(i) a successor company to a higher education corporation (within the meaning of section 129(5) of the Education Reform Act 1988) at a time when an institution conducted by the company is for the time being designated under that section;

(j) …

[(j) a further education corporation;]

(k) the Board of Trustees of the Victoria and Albert Museum;

(l) the Board of Trustees of the Science Museum;

(m) the Board of Trustees of the Armouries;

(n) the Board of Trustees of the Royal Botanic Gardens, Kew;

(o) the Board of Trustees of the National Museums and Galleries on Merseyside;

(p) the trustees of the British Museum and the trustees of the Natural History Museum;

(q) the Board of Trustees of the National Gallery;

(r) the Board of Trustees of the Tate Gallery;

(s) the Board of Trustees of the National Portrait Gallery;

(t) the Board of Trustees of the Wallace Collection;

(u) the Trustees of the Imperial War Museum;

(v) the Trustees of the National Maritime Museum;

(w) any institution which is administered by or on behalf of an institution included above and is established for the general purposes of, or for any special purpose of or in connection with, the last-mentioned institution [(*but see Note 2*)];

(x) the Church Commissioners and any institution which is administered by them;

(y) any registered society within the meaning of the Industrial and Provident Societies Act 1965 *and any registered society or branch within the meaning of the Friendly Societies Act 1974* [and which is also registered in the register of social landlords under Part 1 of the Housing Act 1996];

(z) the Board of Governors of the Museum of London;

(za) the British Library Board;

[(zb) …]

[Notes

1. Paragraph (a) above does not include—

(a) any Investment Fund or Deposit Fund within the meaning of the Church Funds Investment Measure 1958,

(b) any investment fund or deposit fund within the meaning of the Methodist Church Funds Act 1960, or

(c) the representative body of the Welsh Church or property administered by it.

2. Paragraph (w) above does not include any students' union.]

[1508]

NOTES

In para (a), words "the Charity Commissioners for England and Wales" in square brackets substituted by the Charities Act 2006, s 75(1), Sch 8, paras 96, 177, and words "(but see Note 1)" in square brackets inserted by the Charities Act 2006, s 11(1), (2), as from a day to be appointed.

In para (b), word in square brackets inserted and words in italics repealed by the Charities Act 2006, ss 11(1), (3), 75(2), Sch 9, as from a day to be appointed.

Para (d) repealed by the School Standards and Framework Act 1998, s 140(3), Sch 31.

Para (da) inserted by the Education Act 1993, s 307(1), Sch 19, para 175 (repealed) and continued in force by the Education Act 1996, s 582(1), Sch 37, para 120(2); substituted by the Education Act 1997, s 57(1), Sch 7, para 7(a), for savings see SI 1997/1468, Pt II.

Paras (e), (g) repealed by the Education Act 1996, s 582(2), Sch 38, Pt I.

Para (f) repealed by SI 2005/3239, art 9(1), Sch 1, para 4, subject to transitional provisions in art 7(1)–(3) thereof.

First para (h) repealed by the Teaching and Higher Education Act 1998, s 44(2), Sch 4.

Second para (h) inserted by the Charities Act 2006, s 11(1), (4).

First para (j) repealed by the Teaching and Higher Education Act 1998, s 44(2), Sch 4.

Second para (j) inserted by the Charities Act 2006, s 11(1), (5).

In para (w), words "(but see Note 2)" in square brackets inserted by the Charities Act 2006, s 11(1), (6), as from a day to be appointed.

Para (x) repealed by the Charities Act 2006, ss 11(1), (7), 75(2), Sch 9, as from a day to be appointed.

In para (y), words in italics repealed and subsequent words in square brackets substituted by the Charities Act 2006, s 11(1), (8), as from a day to be appointed.

Para (zb) inserted by the National Lottery etc Act 1993, s 37(2), Sch 5, para 12; repealed by the National Lottery Act 2006, s 21, Sch 3.

Notes inserted by the Charities Act 2006, s 11(1), (9), as from a day to be appointed.

Orders: the Exempt Charities Order 1989, SI 1989/2394; the Exempt Charities Order 1993, SI 1993/2359; the Exempt Charities (No 2) Order 1994, SI 1994/2956; the Exempt Charities Order 1995, SI 1995/2998; the Exempt Charities Order 1996, SI 1996/1637; the Exempt Charities (No 2) Order 1996, SI 1996/1932; the Exempt Charities (No 3) Order 1996, SI 1996/1933; the Exempt Charities Order 1999, SI 1999/3139; the Exempt Charities Order 2000, SI 2000/1826; the Exempt Charities Order 2002, SI 2002/1626; the Exempt Charities Order 2003, SI 2003/1881; the Exempt Charities Order 2004, SI 2004/1995; the Exempt Charities Order 2006, SI 2006/1452; the Exempt Charities Order 2007, SI 2007/630; the Exempt Charities (No 2) Order 2007, SI 2007/1364; the Exempt Charities (No 3) Order 2007, SI 2007/2919.

(Schs 3, 4 outside the scope of this work.)

SCHEDULE 5
MEANING OF "CONNECTED PERSON" FOR PURPOSES OF SECTION 36(2)

Section 36(2)

1.—[(1) In section 36(2) of this Act "connected person", in relation to a charity, means any person who falls within sub-paragraph (2)—

(a) at the time of the disposition in question, or

(b) at the time of any contract for the disposition in question.

(2) The persons falling within this sub-paragraph are—]

(a) a charity trustee or trustee for the charity;

(b) a person who is the donor of any land to the charity (whether the gift was made on or after the establishment of the charity);

(c) a child, parent, grandchild, grandparent, brother or sister of any such trustee or donor;

(d) an officer, agent or employee of the charity;

(e) the spouse [or civil partner] of any person falling within any of sub-paragraphs (a) to (d) above;

[(ea) a person carrying on business in partnership with any person falling within any of sub-paragraphs (a) to (e) above;]

(f) an institution which is controlled—

(i) by any person failing within any of sub-paragraphs (a) to [(ea)] above, or

(ii) by two or more such persons taken together; or

(g) a body corporate in which—

(i) any connected person falling within any of sub-paragraphs (a) to (f) above has a substantial interest, or

(ii) two or more such persons, taken together, have a substantial interest.

2.—(1) In paragraph [1(2)(c)] above "child" includes a stepchild and an illegitimate child.

(2) For the purposes of paragraph [1(2)(e)] above a person living with another as that person's husband or wife shall be treated as that person's spouse.

[(3) Where two persons of the same sex are not civil partners but live together as if they were, each of them shall be treated for those purposes as the civil partner of the other.]

3. For the purposes of paragraph [1(2)(f)] above a person controls an institution if he is able to secure that the affairs of the institution are conducted in accordance with his wishes.

4.—(1) For the purposes of paragraph [1(2)(g)] above any such connected person as is there mentioned has a substantial interest in a body corporate if the person or institution in question—

(a) is interested in shares comprised in the equity share capital of that body of a nominal value of more than one-fifth of that share capital, or

(b) is entitled to exercise, or control the exercise of, more than one-fifth of the voting power at any general meeting of that body.

(2) The rules set out in [Schedule 1 to the Companies Act 2006] (rules for interpretation of certain provisions of that Act) shall apply for the purposes of sub-paragraph (1) above as they apply for the purposes of [section 254] of that Act ("connected persons" etc).

(3) In this paragraph "equity share capital" and "share" have the same meaning as in that Act.

[1509]

NOTES

Para 1: first words in square brackets substituted, sub-para (2)(ea) inserted and in sub-para (2)(f)(i) reference in square brackets substituted by the Charities Act 2006, s 75(1), Sch 8, paras 96, 178(1)–(4), subject to savings in SI 2007/309, art 6(2); words in square brackets in sub-para (2)(e) inserted by the Civil Partnership Act 2004, s 261(1), Sch 27, para 147.

Para 2: references in square brackets in sub-paras (1), (2) substituted and sub-para (3) inserted by the Charities Act 2006, s 75(1), Sch 8, paras 96, 178(1), (5).

Para 3: reference in square brackets substituted by the Charities Act 2006, s 75(1), Sch 8, paras 96, 178(1), (6).

Para 4: reference in square brackets in sub-para (1) substituted by the Charities Act 2006, s 75(1), Sch 8, paras 96, 178(1), (7); words in square brackets in sub-para (2) substituted by SI 2007/2194, art 10(1), (2), Sch 4, Pt 3, para 82, subject to savings in art 12 thereof.

(Schs 5A–8 outside the scope of this work.)

CLEAN AIR ACT 1993

(1993 c 11)

An Act to consolidate the Clean Air Acts 1956 and 1968 and certain related enactments, with amendments to give effect to recommendations of the Law Commission and the Scottish Law Commission

[27 May 1993]

PART I
DARK SMOKE

1 Prohibition of dark smoke from chimneys

(1) Dark smoke shall not be emitted from a chimney of any building, and if, on any day, dark smoke is so emitted, the occupier of the building shall be guilty of an offence.

(2) Dark smoke shall not be emitted from a chimney (not being a chimney of a building) which serves the furnace of any fixed boiler or industrial plant, and if, on any day, dark smoke is so emitted, the person having possession of the boiler or plant shall be guilty of an offence.

(3) This section does not apply to emissions of smoke from any chimney, in such classes of case and subject to such limitations as may be prescribed in regulations made by the Secretary of State, lasting for not longer than such periods as may be so prescribed.

(4) In any proceedings for an offence under this section, it shall be a defence to prove—

(a) that the alleged emission was solely due to the lighting up of a furnace which was cold and that all practicable steps had been taken to prevent or minimise the emission of dark smoke;

(b) that the alleged emission was solely due to some failure of a furnace, or of apparatus used in connection with a furnace, and that—

(i) the failure could not reasonably have been foreseen, or, if foreseen, could not reasonably have been provided against; and

(ii) the alleged emission could not reasonably have been prevented by action taken after the failure occurred; or

(c) that the alleged emission was solely due to the use of unsuitable fuel and that—

(i) suitable fuel was unobtainable and the least unsuitable fuel which was available was used; and

(ii) all practicable steps had been taken to prevent or minimise the emission of dark smoke as the result of the use of that fuel;

or that the alleged emission was due to the combination of two or more of the causes specified in paragraphs (a) to (c) and that the other conditions specified in those paragraphs are satisfied in relation to those causes respectively.

(5) A person guilty of an offence under this section shall be liable on summary conviction—

(a) in the case of a contravention of subsection (1) as respects a chimney of a private dwelling, to a fine not exceeding level 3 on the standard scale; and

(b) in any other case, to a fine not exceeding level 5 on the standard scale.

(6) This section has effect subject to section 51 (duty to notify offences to occupier or other person liable).

[1510]

NOTES

Transfer of functions: functions of the Secretary of State, so far as exercisable in relation to Wales, transferred to the National Assembly for Wales, by the National Assembly for Wales (Transfer of Functions) Order 1999, SI 1999/672, art 2, Sch 1.

2 Prohibition of dark smoke from industrial or trade premises

(1) Dark smoke shall not be emitted from any industrial or trade premises and if, on any day, dark smoke is so emitted the occupier of the premises and any person who causes or permits the emission shall be guilty of an offence.

(2) This section does not apply—

(a) to the emission of dark smoke from any chimney to which section 1 above applies; or

(b) to the emission of dark smoke caused by the burning of any matter prescribed in regulations made by the Secretary of State, subject to compliance with such conditions (if any) as may be so prescribed.

(3) In proceedings for an offence under this section, there shall be taken to have been an emission of dark smoke from industrial or trade premises in any case where—

(a) material is burned on those premises; and

(b) the circumstances are such that the burning would be likely to give rise to the emission of dark smoke,

unless the occupier or any person who caused or permitted the burning shows that no dark smoke was emitted.

(4) In proceedings for an offence under this section, it shall be a defence to prove—

(a) that the alleged emission was inadvertent; and

(b) that all practicable steps had been taken to prevent or minimise the emission of dark smoke.

(5) A person guilty of an offence under this section shall be liable on summary conviction to a fine not exceeding [£20,000].

(6) In this section "industrial or trade premises" means—

(a) premises used for any industrial or trade purposes; or

(b) premises not so used on which matter is burnt in connection with any industrial or trade process.

(7) This section has effect subject to section 51 (duty to notify offences to occupier or other person liable).

[1511]

NOTES

Sub-s (5): sum in square brackets substituted by the Environment Act 1995, s 120, Sch 22, para 195.

Transfer of functions: functions of the Secretary of State, so far as exercisable in relation to Wales, transferred to the National Assembly for Wales, by the National Assembly for Wales (Transfer of Functions) Order 1999, SI 1999/672, art 2, Sch 1.

Regulations: the Waste Management (Miscellaneous Provisions) (England and Wales) Regulations 2007, SI 2007/1156 (revoked, subject to savings).

3 Meaning of "dark smoke"

(1) In this Act "dark smoke" means smoke which, if compared in the appropriate manner with a chart of the type known on 5th July 1956 (the date of the passing of the Clean Air Act 1956) as the Ringelmann Chart, would appear to be as dark as or darker than shade 2 on the chart.

(2) For the avoidance of doubt it is hereby declared that in proceedings—

(a) for an offence under section 1 or 2 (prohibition of emissions of dark smoke); …

(b) …

the court may be satisfied that smoke is or is not dark smoke as defined in subsection (1) notwithstanding that there has been no actual comparison of the smoke with a chart of the type mentioned in that subsection.

(3) Without prejudice to the generality of subsections (1) and (2), if the Secretary of State by regulations prescribes any method of ascertaining whether smoke is dark smoke as defined in subsection (1), proof in any such proceedings as are mentioned in subsection (2)—

(a) that that method was properly applied, and

(b) that the smoke was thereby ascertained to be or not to be dark smoke as so defined,

shall be accepted as sufficient.

[1512]

NOTES

Sub-s (2): words omitted repealed by the Environment Act 1995, s 120, Sch 24.

Transfer of functions: functions of the Secretary of State, so far as exercisable in relation to Wales, transferred to the National Assembly for Wales, by the National Assembly for Wales (Transfer of Functions) Order 1999, SI 1999/672, art 2, Sch 1.

4–46 ((*Pts II–VI*) *outside the scope of this work.*)

PART VII
MISCELLANEOUS AND GENERAL

47–62 (*Outside the scope of this work.*)

General

63–67 (*Outside the scope of this work.*)

68 Short title, commencement and extent

(1) This Act may be cited as the Clean Air Act 1993.

(2) …

(3) The following provisions of this Act (apart from this section) extend to Northern Ireland—

(a) section 30;

(b) section 32 so far as it relates to regulations under section 30; and

(c) section 67(3) and Schedule 6, so far as they relate to the repeal of sections 75 and 77 of the Control of Pollution Act 1974;

but otherwise this Act does not extend to Northern Ireland.

[1513]

NOTES

Sub-s (2): repealed by the Statute Law (Repeals) Act 2004.

(*Schs 1–6 outside the scope of this work.*)

CRIMINAL JUSTICE AND PUBLIC ORDER ACT 1994

(1994 c 33)

An Act to make further provision in relation to criminal justice (including employment in the prison service); to amend or extend the criminal law and powers for preventing crime and enforcing that law; to amend the Video Recordings Act 1984; and for purposes connected with those purposes

[3 November 1994]

1–60B ((*Pts I–IV*) *outside the scope of this work.*)

PART V
PUBLIC ORDER: COLLECTIVE TRESPASS OR NUISANCE ON LAND

Powers to remove trespassers on land

61 Power to remove trespassers on land

(1) If the senior police officer present at the scene reasonably believes that two or more persons are trespassing on land and are present there with the common purpose of residing there for any period, that reasonable steps have been taken by or on behalf of the occupier to ask them to leave and—

(a) that any of those persons has caused damage to the land or to property on the land or used threatening, abusive or insulting words or behaviour towards the occupier, a member of his family or an employee or agent of his, or

(b) that those persons have between them six or more vehicles on the land,

he may direct those persons, or any of them, to leave the land and to remove any vehicles or other property they have with them on the land.

(2) Where the persons in question are reasonably believed by the senior police officer to be persons who were not originally trespassers but have become trespassers on the land, the officer must reasonably believe that the other conditions specified in subsection (1) are satisfied after those persons became trespassers before he can exercise the power conferred by that subsection.

(3) A direction under subsection (1) above, if not communicated to the persons referred to in subsection (1) by the police officer giving the direction, may be communicated to them by any constable at the scene.

(4) If a person knowing that a direction under subsection (1) above has been given which applies to him—

(a) fails to leave the land as soon as reasonably practicable, or

(b) having left again enters the land as a trespasser within the period of three months beginning with the day on which the direction was given,

he commits an offence and is liable on summary conviction to imprisonment for a term not exceeding *three months* [51 weeks] or a fine not exceeding level 4 on the standard scale, or both.

[(4A) Where, as respects Scotland, the reason why these persons have become trespassers is that they have ceased to be entitled to exercise access rights by virtue of—

(a) their having formed the common purpose mentioned in subsection (1) above; or

(b) one or more of the conditions specified in paragraphs (a) and (b) of that subsection having been satisfied,

the circumstances constituting that reason shall be treated, for the purposes of subsection (4) above, as having also occurred after these persons became trespassers.

(4B) In subsection (4A) above "access rights" has the meaning given by the Land Reform (Scotland) Act 2003 (asp 2).]

(5) …

(6) In proceedings for an offence under this section it is a defence for the accused to show—

(a) that he was not trespassing on the land, or

(b) that he had a reasonable excuse for failing to leave the land as soon as reasonably practicable or, as the case may be, for again entering the land as a trespasser.

(7) In its application in England and Wales to common land this section has effect as if in the preceding subsections of it—

(a) references to trespassing or trespassers were references to acts and persons doing acts which constitute either a trespass as against the occupier or an infringement of the commoners' rights; and

(b) references to "the occupier" included the commoners or any of them or, in the case of common land to which the public has access, the local authority as well as any commoner.

(8) Subsection (7) above does not—

(a) require action by more than one occupier; or

(b) constitute persons trespassers as against any commoner or the local authority if they are permitted to be there by the other occupier.

(9) In this section—

"common land" means common land as defined in section 22 of the Commons Registration Act 1965;

["common land" means—

(a) land registered as common land in a register of common land kept under Part 1 of the Commons Act 2006; and

(b) land to which Part 1 of that Act does not apply and which is subject to rights of common as defined in that Act;]

"commoner" means a person with rights of common *as defined in section 22 of the Commons Registration Act 1965* [as so defined];

"land" does not include—

(a) buildings other than—

(i) agricultural buildings within the meaning of, in England and Wales, paragraphs 3 to 8 of Schedule 5 to the Local Government Finance Act 1988 or, in Scotland, section 7(2) of the Valuation and Rating (Scotland) Act 1956, or

(ii) scheduled monuments within the meaning of the Ancient Monuments and Archaeological Areas Act 1979;

(b) land forming part of—
  (i) a highway unless [it is a footpath, bridleway or byway open to all traffic within the meaning of Part III of the Wildlife and Countryside Act 1981, is a restricted byway within the meaning of Part II of the Countryside and Rights of Way Act 2000] or is a cycle track under the Highways Act 1980 or the Cycle Tracks Act 1984; or
  (ii) a road within the meaning of the Roads (Scotland) Act 1984 unless it falls within the definitions in section 151(2)(a)(ii) or (b) (footpaths and cycle tracks) of that Act or is a bridleway within the meaning of section 47 of the Countryside (Scotland) Act 1967;

"the local authority", in relation to common land, means any local authority which has powers in relation to the land under *section 9 of the Commons Registration Act 1965* [section 45 of the Commons Act 2006];

"occupier" (and in subsection (8) "the other occupier") means—
  (a) in England and Wales, the person entitled to possession of the land by virtue of an estate or interest held by him; and
  (b) in Scotland, the person lawfully entitled to natural possession of the land;

"property", in relation to damage to property on land, means—
  (a) in England and Wales, property within the meaning of section 10(1) of the Criminal Damage Act 1971; and
  (b) in Scotland, either—
    (i) heritable property other than land; or
    (ii) corporeal moveable property,

and "damage" includes the deposit of any substance capable of polluting the land;

"trespass" means, in the application of this section—
  (a) in England and Wales, subject to the extensions effected by subsection (7) above, trespass as against the occupier of the land;
  (b) in Scotland, entering, or as the case may be remaining on, land without lawful authority and without the occupier's consent; and

"trespassing" and "trespasser" shall be construed accordingly;

"vehicle" includes—
  (a) any vehicle, whether or not it is in a fit state for use on roads, and includes any chassis or body, with or without wheels, appearing to have formed part of such a vehicle, and any load carried by, and anything attached to, such a vehicle; and
  (b) a caravan as defined in section 29(1) of the Caravan Sites and Control of Development Act 1960;

and a person may be regarded for the purposes of this section as having a purpose of residing in a place notwithstanding that he has a home elsewhere.

[1514]

NOTES

Sub-s (4): words in italics repealed and subsequent words in square brackets substituted by the Criminal Justice Act 2003, s 280(2), (3), Sch 26, para 45(1), (4), as from a day to be appointed.

Sub-ss (4A), (4B): inserted by the Land Reform (Scotland) Act 2003, s 99, Sch 2, paras 10, 11.

Sub-s (5): repealed by the Serious Organised Crime and Police Act 2005, ss 111, 174(2), Sch 7, Pt 1, para 31(1), (2), Sch 17, Pt 2.

Sub-s (9): definition "common land" substituted, and in definitions "commoner" and "the local authority" words in italics repealed and subsequent words in square brackets substituted by the Commons Act 2006, s 52, Sch 5, para 5, as from a day to be appointed; in definition "land" words in square brackets substituted by the Countryside and Rights of Way Act 2000, s 51, Sch 5, Pt II, para 17.

62 Supplementary powers of seizure

(1) If a direction has been given under section 61 and a constable reasonably suspects that any person to whom the direction applies has, without reasonable excuse—
  (a) failed to remove any vehicle on the land which appears to the constable to belong to him or to be in his possession or under his control; or
  (b) entered the land as a trespasser with a vehicle within the period of three months beginning with the day on which the direction was given,

the constable may seize and remove that vehicle.

(2) In this section, "trespasser" and "vehicle" have the same meaning as in section 61.

[1515]

[62A Power to remove trespassers: alternative site available

(1) If the senior police officer present at a scene reasonably believes that the conditions in subsection (2) are satisfied in relation to a person and land, he may direct the person—
  (a) to leave the land;
  (b) to remove any vehicle and other property he has with him on the land.

PART I STATUTES

(2) The conditions are—

(a) that the person and one or more others ("the trespassers") are trespassing on the land;

(b) that the trespassers have between them at least one vehicle on the land;

(c) that the trespassers are present on the land with the common purpose of residing there for any period;

(d) if it appears to the officer that the person has one or more caravans in his possession or under his control on the land, that there is a suitable pitch on a relevant caravan site for that caravan or each of those caravans;

(e) that the occupier of the land or a person acting on his behalf has asked the police to remove the trespassers from the land.

(3) A direction under subsection (1) may be communicated to the person to whom it applies by any constable at the scene.

(4) Subsection (5) applies if—

(a) a police officer proposes to give a direction under subsection (1) in relation to a person and land, and

(b) it appears to him that the person has one or more caravans in his possession or under his control on the land.

(5) The officer must consult every local authority within whose area the land is situated as to whether there is a suitable pitch for the caravan or each of the caravans on a relevant caravan site which is situated in the local authority's area.

(6) In this section—

"caravan" and "caravan site" have the same meanings as in Part 1 of the Caravan Sites and Control of Development Act 1960;

"relevant caravan site" means a caravan site which is—

(a) situated in the area of a local authority within whose area the land is situated, and

(b) managed by a relevant site manager;

"relevant site manager" means—

(a) a local authority within whose area the land is situated;

(b) a registered social landlord;

"registered social landlord" means a body registered as a social landlord under Chapter 1 of Part 1 of the Housing Act 1996.

(7) The Secretary of State may by order amend the definition of "relevant site manager" in subsection (6) by adding a person or description of person.

(8) An order under subsection (7) must be made by statutory instrument and is subject to annulment in pursuance of a resolution of either House of Parliament.]

[1516]

NOTES

Inserted, in relation to England and Wales, by the Anti-social Behaviour Act 2003, s 60.

[62B Failure to comply with direction under section 62A: offences

(1) A person commits an offence if he knows that a direction under section 62A(1) has been given which applies to him and—

(a) he fails to leave the relevant land as soon as reasonably practicable, or

(b) he enters any land in the area of the relevant local authority as a trespasser before the end of the relevant period with the intention of residing there.

(2) The relevant period is the period of 3 months starting with the day on which the direction is given.

(3) A person guilty of an offence under this section is liable on summary conviction to imprisonment for a term not exceeding *3 months* [51 weeks] or a fine not exceeding level 4 on the standard scale or both.

(4) …

(5) In proceedings for an offence under this section it is a defence for the accused to show—

(a) that he was not trespassing on the land in respect of which he is alleged to have committed the offence, or

(b) that he had a reasonable excuse—

(i) for failing to leave the relevant land as soon as reasonably practicable, or

(ii) for entering land in the area of the relevant local authority as a trespasser with the intention of residing there, or

(c) that, at the time the direction was given, he was under the age of 18 years and was residing with his parent or guardian.]

[1517]

NOTES

Inserted, in relation to England and Wales, by the Anti-social Behaviour Act 2003, s 61.

Sub-s (3): words in italics repealed and subsequent words in square brackets substituted by the Criminal Justice Act 2003, s 280(2), (3), Sch 26, para 45(1), (5), as from a day to be appointed.

Sub-s (4): repealed by the Serious Organised Crime and Police Act 2005, ss 111, 174(2), Sch 7, Pt 1, para 31(1), (3), Sch 17, Pt 2.

[62C Failure to comply with direction under section 62A: seizure

(1) This section applies if a direction has been given under section 62A(1) and a constable reasonably suspects that a person to whom the direction applies has, without reasonable excuse—

(a) failed to remove any vehicle on the relevant land which appears to the constable to belong to him or to be in his possession or under his control; or

(b) entered any land in the area of the relevant local authority as a trespasser with a vehicle before the end of the relevant period with the intention of residing there.

(2) The relevant period is the period of 3 months starting with the day on which the direction is given.

(3) The constable may seize and remove the vehicle.]

[1518]

NOTES

Inserted, in relation to England and Wales, by the Anti-social Behaviour Act 2003, s 62(1).

[62D Common land: modifications

(1) In their application to common land sections 62A to 62C have effect with these modifications.

(2) References to trespassing and trespassers have effect as if they were references to acts, and persons doing acts, which constitute—

(a) a trespass as against the occupier, or

(b) an infringement of the commoners' rights.

(3) References to the occupier—

(a) in the case of land to which the public has access, include the local authority and any commoner;

(b) in any other case, include the commoners or any of them.

(4) Subsection (1) does not—

(a) require action by more than one occupier, or

(b) constitute persons trespassers as against any commoner or the local authority if they are permitted to be there by the other occupier.

(5) In this section "common land", "commoner" and "the local authority" have the meanings given by section 61.]

[1519]

NOTES

Inserted, in relation to England and Wales, by the Anti-social Behaviour Act 2003, s 63.

[62E Sections 62A to 62D: interpretation

(1) Subsections (2) to (8) apply for the interpretation of sections 62A to 62D and this section.

(2) "Land" does not include buildings other than—

(a) agricultural buildings within the meaning of paragraphs 3 to 8 of Schedule 5 to the Local Government Finance Act 1988, or

(b) scheduled monuments within the meaning of the Ancient Monuments and Archaeological Areas Act 1979.

(3) "Local authority" means—

(a) in Greater London, a London borough or the Common Council of the City of London;

(b) in England outside Greater London, a county council, a district council or the Council of the Isles of Scilly;

(c) in Wales, a county council or a county borough council.

(4) "Occupier", "trespass", "trespassing" and "trespasser" have the meanings given by section 61 in relation to England and Wales.

(5) "The relevant land" means the land in respect of which a direction under section 62A(1) is given.

(6) "The relevant local authority" means—

(a) if the relevant land is situated in the area of more than one local authority (but is not in the Isles of Scilly), the district council or county borough council within whose area the relevant land is situated;

(b) if the relevant land is situated in the Isles of Scilly, the Council of the Isles of Scilly;

(c) in any other case, the local authority within whose area the relevant land is situated.

(7) "Vehicle" has the meaning given by section 61.

(8) A person may be regarded as having a purpose of residing in a place even if he has a home elsewhere.]

[1520]

NOTES

Inserted, in relation to England and Wales, by the Anti-social Behaviour Act 2003, s 64.

63–67 (*Outside the scope of this work.*)

Disruptive trespassers

68 Offence of aggravated trespass

(1) A person commits the offence of aggravated trespass if he trespasses on land … and, in relation to any lawful activity which persons are engaging in or are about to engage in on that or adjoining land … , does there anything which is intended by him to have the effect—

(a) of intimidating those persons or any of them so as to deter them or any of them from engaging in that activity,

(b) of obstructing that activity, or

(c) of disrupting that activity.

[(1A) The reference in subsection (1) above to trespassing includes, in Scotland, the exercise of access rights (within the meaning of the Land Reform (Scotland) Act 2003 (asp 2)) up to the point when they cease to be exercisable by virtue of the commission of the offence under that subsection.]

(2) Activity on any occasion on the part of a person or persons on land is "lawful" for the purposes of this section if he or they may engage in the activity on the land on that occasion without committing an offence or trespassing on the land.

(3) A person guilty of an offence under this section is liable on summary conviction to imprisonment for a term not exceeding *three months* [51 weeks] or a fine not exceeding level 4 on the standard scale, or both.

(4) …

(5) In this section "land" does not include—

(a) the highways and roads excluded from the application of section 61 by paragraph (b) of the definition of "land" in subsection (9) of that section; or

(b) a road within the meaning of the Roads (Northern Ireland) Order 1993.

[1521]

NOTES

Sub-s (1): words omitted repealed by the Anti-social Behaviour Act 2003, ss 59(1), (2), 92, Sch 3.

Sub-s (1A): inserted by the Land Reform (Scotland) Act 2003, s 99, Sch 2, paras 10, 13.

Sub-s (3): words in italics repealed and subsequent words in square brackets substituted by the Criminal Justice Act 2003, s 280(2), (3), Sch 26, para 45(1), (7), as from a day to be appointed.

Sub-s (4): repealed by the Serious Organised Crime and Police Act 2005, ss 111, 174(2), Sch 7, Pt 1, para 31(1), (6), Sch 17, Pt 2.

69 Powers to remove persons committing or participating in aggravated trespass

(1) If the senior police officer present at the scene reasonably believes—

(a) that a person is committing, has committed or intends to commit the offence of aggravated trespass on land … ; or

(b) that two or more persons are trespassing on land … and are present there with the common purpose of intimidating persons so as to deter them from engaging in a lawful activity or of obstructing or disrupting a lawful activity,

he may direct that person or (as the case may be) those persons (or any of them) to leave the land.

(2) A direction under subsection (1) above, if not communicated to the persons referred to in subsection (1) by the police officer giving the direction, may be communicated to them by any constable at the scene.

(3) If a person knowing that a direction under subsection (1) above has been given which applies to him—

(a) fails to leave the land as soon as practicable, or

(b) having left again enters the land as a trespasser within the period of three months beginning with the day on which the direction was given, he commits an offence and is liable on summary conviction to imprisonment for a term not exceeding *three months* [51 weeks] or a fine not exceeding level 4 on the standard scale, or both.

(4) In proceedings for an offence under subsection (3) it is a defence for the accused to show—

(a) that he was not trespassing on the land, or

(b) that he had a reasonable excuse for failing to leave the land as soon as practicable or, as the case may be, for again entering the land as a trespasser.

(5) …

(6) In this section "lawful activity" and "land" have the same meaning as in section 68.

[1522]

NOTES

Sub-s (1): words omitted repealed by the Anti-social Behaviour Act 2003, ss 59(1), (3), 92, Sch 3.

Sub-s (3): words in italics repealed and subsequent words in square brackets substituted by the Criminal Justice Act 2003, s 280(2), (3), Sch 26, para 45(1), (8), as from a day to be appointed.

Sub-s (5): repealed by the Serious Organised Crime and Police Act 2005, ss 111, 174(2), Sch 7, Pt 1, para 31(1), (7), Sch 17, Pt 2.

70–74 (*Outside the scope of this work.*)

75 Interim possession orders: false or misleading statements

(1) A person commits an offence if, for the purpose of obtaining an interim possession order, he—

(a) makes a statement which he knows to be false or misleading in a material particular; or

(b) recklessly makes a statement which is false or misleading in a material particular.

(2) A person commits an offence if, for the purpose of resisting the making of an interim possession order, he—

(a) makes a statement which he knows to be false or misleading in a material particular; or

(b) recklessly makes a statement which is false or misleading in a material particular.

(3) A person guilty of an offence under this section shall be liable—

(a) on conviction on indictment, to imprisonment for a term not exceeding two years or a fine or both;

(b) on summary conviction, to imprisonment for a term not exceeding six months or a fine not exceeding the statutory maximum or both.

(4) In this section—

"interim possession order" means an interim possession order (so entitled) made under rules of court for the bringing of summary proceedings for possession of premises which are occupied by trespassers;

"premises" has the same meaning as in Part II of the Criminal Law Act 1977 (offences relating to entering and remaining on property); and

"statement", in relation to an interim possession order, means any statement, in writing or oral and whether as to fact or belief, made in or for the purposes of the proceedings.

[1523]

76 Interim possession orders: trespassing during currency of order

(1) This section applies where an interim possession order has been made in respect of any premises and served in accordance with rules of court; and references to "the order" and "the premises" shall be construed accordingly.

(2) Subject to subsection (3), a person who is present on the premises as a trespasser at any time during the currency of the order commits an offence.

(3) No offence under subsection (2) is committed by a person if—

(a) he leaves the premises within 24 hours of the time of service of the order and does not return; or

(b) a copy of the order was not fixed to the premises in accordance with rules of court.

(4) A person who was in occupation of the premises at the time of service of the order but leaves them commits an offence if he re-enters the premises as a trespasser or attempts to do so after the expiry of the order but within the period of one year beginning with the day on which it was served.

(5) A person guilty of an offence under this section shall be liable on summary conviction to imprisonment for a term not exceeding six months or a fine not exceeding level 5 on the standard scale or both.

(6) A person who is in occupation of the premises at the time of service of the order shall be treated for the purposes of this section as being present as a trespasser.

(7) …

(8) In this section—

"interim possession order" has the same meaning as in section 75 above and "rules of court" is to be construed accordingly; and

"premises" has the same meaning as in that section, that is to say, the same meaning as in Part II of the Criminal Law Act (offences relating to entering and remaining on property).

[1524]

NOTES

Sub-s (7): repealed by the Serious Organised Crime and Police Act 2005, ss 111, 174(2), Sch 7, Pt 1, para 31(1), (8), Sch 17, Pt 2.

Powers to remove unauthorised campers

77 Power of local authority to direct unauthorised campers to leave land

(1) If it appears to a local authority that persons are for the time being residing in a vehicle or vehicles within that authority's area—

(a) on any land forming part of a highway;

(b) on any other unoccupied land; or

(c) on any occupied land without the consent of the occupier,

the authority may give a direction that those persons and any others with them are to leave the land and remove the vehicle or vehicles and any other property they have with them on the land.

(2) Notice of a direction under subsection (1) must be served on the persons to whom the direction applies, but it shall be sufficient for this purpose for the direction to specify the land and (except where the direction applies to only one person) to be addressed to all occupants of the vehicles on the land, without naming them.

(3) If a person knowing that a direction under subsection (1) above has been given which applies to him—

(a) fails, as soon as practicable, to leave the land or remove from the land any vehicle or other property which is the subject of the direction, or

(b) having removed any such vehicle or property again enters the land with a vehicle within the period of three months beginning with the day on which the direction was given,

he commits an offence and is liable on summary conviction to a fine not exceeding level 3 on the standard scale.

(4) A direction under subsection (1) operates to require persons who re-enter the land within the said period with vehicles or other property to leave and remove the vehicles or other property as it operates in relation to the persons and vehicles or other property on the land when the direction was given.

(5) In proceedings for an offence under this section it is a defence for the accused to show that his failure to leave or to remove the vehicle or other property as soon as practicable or his re-entry with a vehicle was due to illness, mechanical breakdown or other immediate emergency.

(6) In this section—

"land" means land in the open air;

"local authority" means—

(a) in Greater London, a London borough or the Common Council of the City of London;

(b) in England outside Greater London, a county council, a district council or the Council of the Isles of Scilly;

(c) in Wales, a county council or a county borough council;

"occupier" means the person entitled to possession of the land by virtue of an estate or interest held by him;

"vehicle" includes—

(a) any vehicle, whether or not it is in a fit state for use on roads, and includes any body, with or without wheels, appearing to have formed part of such a vehicle, and any load carried by, and anything attached to, such a vehicle; and

(b) a caravan as defined in section 29(1) of the Caravan Sites and Control of Development Act 1960;

and a person may be regarded for the purposes of this section as residing on any land notwithstanding that he has a home elsewhere.

(7) Until 1st April 1996, in this section "local authority" means, in Wales, a county council or a district council.

[1525]

78 Orders for removal of persons and their vehicles unlawfully on land

(1) A magistrates' court may, on a complaint made by a local authority, if satisfied that persons and vehicles in which they are residing are present on land within that authority's area in

contravention of a direction given under section 77, make an order requiring the removal of any vehicle or other property which is so present on the land and any person residing in it.

(2) An order under this section may authorise the local authority to take such steps as are reasonably necessary to ensure that the order is complied with and, in particular, may authorise the authority, by its officers and servants—

(a) to enter upon the land specified in the order; and

(b) to take, in relation to any vehicle or property to be removed in pursuance of the order, such steps for securing entry and rendering it suitable for removal as may be so specified.

(3) The local authority shall not enter upon any occupied land unless they have given to the owner and occupier at least 24 hours notice of their intention to do so, or unless after reasonable inquiries they are unable to ascertain their names and addresses.

(4) A person who wilfully obstructs any person in the exercise of any power conferred on him by an order under this section commits an offence and is liable on summary conviction to a fine not exceeding level 3 on the standard scale.

(5) Where a complaint is made under this section, a summons issued by the court requiring the person or persons to whom it is directed to appear before the court to answer to the complaint may be directed—

(a) to the occupant of a particular vehicle on the land in question; or

(b) to all occupants of vehicles on the land in question, without naming him or them.

(6) Section 55(2) of the Magistrates' Courts Act 1980 (warrant for arrest of defendant failing to appear) does not apply to proceedings on a complaint made under this section.

(7) Section 77(6) of this Act applies also for the interpretation of this section.

[1526]

79 Provisions as to directions under s 77 and orders under s 78

(1) The following provisions apply in relation to the service of notice of a direction under section 77 and of a summons under section 78, referred to in those provisions as a "relevant document".

(2) Where it is impracticable to serve a relevant document on a person named in it, the document shall be treated as duly served on him if a copy of it is fixed in a prominent place to the vehicle concerned; and where a relevant document is directed to the unnamed occupants of vehicles, it shall be treated as duly served on those occupants if a copy of it is fixed in a prominent place to every vehicle on the land in question at the time when service is thus effected.

(3) A local authority shall take such steps as may be reasonably practicable to secure that a copy of any relevant document is displayed on the land in question (otherwise than by being fixed to a vehicle) in a manner designed to ensure that it is likely to be seen by any person camping on the land.

(4) Notice of any relevant document shall be given by the local authority to the owner of the land in question and to any occupier of that land unless, after reasonable inquiries, the authority is unable to ascertain the name and address of the owner or occupier; and the owner of any such land and any occupier of such land shall be entitled to appear and to be heard in the proceedings.

(5) Section 77(6) applies also for the interpretation of this section.

[1527]

80–148 (*S 80, ss 81–148* (*Pts VI–XI*) *outside the scope of this work.*)

PART XII
MISCELLANEOUS AND GENERAL

149–167 (*Outside the scope of this work.*)

General

168–171 (*Outside the scope of this work.*)

172 Short title, commencement and extent

(1) This Act may be cited as the Criminal Justice and Public Order Act 1994.

(2) With the exception of section 82 and subject to subsection (4) below, this Act shall come into force on such day as the Secretary of State or, in the case of sections 52 and 53, the Lord Chancellor may appoint by order made by statutory instrument, and different days may be appointed for different provisions or different purposes.

(3) Any order under subsection (2) above may make such transitional provisions and savings as appear to the authority making the order necessary or expedient in connection with any provision brought into force by the order.

(4) The following provisions and their related amendments, repeals and revocations shall come into force on the passing of this Act, namely sections 5 to 15 (and Schedules 1 and 2), 61, 63, 65, 68 to 71, 77 to 80, 81, 83, 90, Chapters I and IV of Part VIII, sections 142 to 148, 150, 158(1), (3) and (4), 166, 167, 171, paragraph 46 of Schedule 9 and this section.

(5) No order shall be made under subsection (6) of section 166 above unless a draft of the order has been laid before, and approved by a resolution of, each House of Parliament.

(6) For the purposes of subsection (4) above—

(a) the following are the amendments related to the provisions specified in that subsection, namely, in Schedule 10, paragraphs 26, 35, 36, 59, 60 and 63(1), (3), (4) and (5);

(b) the repeals and revocations related to the provisions specified in that subsection are those specified in the Note at the end of Schedule 11.

(7) Except as regards any provisions applied under section 39 and subject to the following provisions, this Act extends to England and Wales only.

(8) Sections 47(3), 49, [60 to 67], 70, 71, 81, 82, 146(4), 157(1), 163, 169 and 170 also extend to Scotland.

(9) ...

(10) This section, sections 68, 69, 83(3) to (5), 88 to 92, 136 to 141, 156, 157(2), (3), (4), (5) and (9), 158, 159, 161, 162, 164, 165, 168, 171 and Chapter IV of Part VIII extend to the United Kingdom and sections 158 and 159 also extend to the Channel Islands and the Isle of Man.

(11)–(16) ...

[1528]

NOTES

Sub-s (8): words in square brackets substituted by the Knives Act 1997, s 8(1), (11).

Sub-ss (9), (11)–(16): outside the scope of this work.

Orders: the Criminal Justice and Public Order Act 1994 (Commencement No 1) Order 1994, SI 1994/2935; the Criminal Justice and Public Order Act 1994 (Commencement No 2) Order 1994, SI 1994/3192; the Criminal Justice and Public Order Act 1994 (Commencement No 3) Order 1994, SI 1994/3258; the Criminal Justice and Public Order Act 1994 (Commencement No 4) Order 1995, SI 1995/24; the Criminal Justice and Public Order Act 1994 (Commencement No 5 and Transitional Provisions) Order 1995, SI 1995/127; the Criminal Justice and Public Order Act 1994 (Commencement No 6) Order 1995, SI 1995/721; the Criminal Justice and Public Order Act 1994 (Commencement No 7) Order 1995, SI 1995/1378; the Criminal Justice and Public Order Act 1994 (Commencement No 8 and Transitional Provision) Order 1995, SI 1995/1957; the Criminal Justice and Public Order Act 1994 (Commencement No 9) Order 1996, SI 1996/625; the Criminal Justice and Public Order Act 1994 (Commencement No 10) Order 1996, SI 1996/1608; the Criminal Justice and Public Order Act 1994 (Commencement No 12 and Transitional Provision) Order 1998, SI 1998/277; the Criminal Justice and Public Order Act 1994 (Commencement No 13) Order 2002, SI 2002/447; the Criminal Justice and Public Order Act 1994 (Commencement No 14) Order 2007, SI 2007/621.

(*Schs 1–11 outside the scope of this work.*)

LAW OF PROPERTY (MISCELLANEOUS PROVISIONS) ACT 1994

(1994 c 36)

An Act to provide for new covenants for title to be implied on dispositions of property; to amend the law with respect to certain matters arising in connection with the death of the owner of property; and for connected purposes

[3 November 1994]

PART I
IMPLIED COVENANTS FOR TITLE

The covenants

1 Covenants to be implied on a disposition of property

(1) In an instrument effecting or purporting to effect a disposition of property there shall be implied on the part of the person making the disposition, whether or not the disposition is for valuable consideration, such of the covenants specified in sections 2 to 5 as are applicable to the disposition.

(2) Of those sections—

(a) sections 2, 3(1) and (2), 4 and 5 apply where dispositions are expressed to be made with full title guarantee; and

(b) sections 2, 3(3), 4 and 5 apply where dispositions are expressed to be made with limited title guarantee.

(3) Sections 2 to 4 have effect subject to section 6 (no liability under covenants in certain cases); and sections 2 to 5 have effect subject to section 8(1) (limitation or extension of covenants by instrument effecting the disposition).

(4) In this Part—

"disposition" includes the creation of a term of years;

"instrument" includes an instrument which is not a deed; and

"property" includes a thing in action, and any interest in real or personal property.

[1529]

2 Right to dispose and further assurance

(1) If the disposition is expressed to be made with full title guarantee or with limited title guarantee there shall be implied the following covenants—

(a) that the person making the disposition has the right (with the concurrence of any other person conveying the property) to dispose of the property as he purports to, and

(b) that that person will at his own cost do all that he reasonably can to give the person to whom he disposes of the property the title he purports to give.

(2) The latter obligation includes—

(a) in relation to a disposition of an interest in land the title to which is registered, doing all that he reasonably can to ensure that the person to whom the disposition is made is entitled to be registered as proprietor with at least the class of title registered immediately before the disposition; and

(b) in relation to a disposition of an interest in land the title to which is required to be registered by virtue of the disposition, giving all reasonable assistance fully to establish to the satisfaction of the Chief Land Registrar the right of the person to whom the disposition is made to registration as proprietor.

(3) In the case of a disposition of an existing legal interest in land, the following presumptions apply, subject to the terms of the instrument, in ascertaining for the purposes of the covenants implied by this section what the person making the disposition purports to dispose of—

(a) where the title to the interest is registered, it shall be presumed that the disposition is of the whole of that interest;

(b) where the title to the interest is not registered, then—

(i) if it appears from the instrument that the interest is a leasehold interest, it shall be presumed that the disposition is of the property for the unexpired portion of the term of years created by the lease; and

(ii) in any other case, it shall be presumed that what is disposed of is the fee simple.

[1530]

3 Charges, incumbrances and third party rights

(1) If the disposition is expressed to be made with full title guarantee there shall be implied a covenant that the person making the disposition is disposing of the property free—

(a) from all charges and incumbrances (whether monetary or not), and

(b) from all other rights exercisable by third parties,

other than any charges, incumbrances or rights which that person does not and could not reasonably be expected to know about.

(2) In its application to charges, incumbrances and other third party rights subsection (1) extends to liabilities imposed and rights conferred by or under any enactment, except to the extent that such liabilities and rights are, by reason of—

(a) being, at the time of the disposition, only potential liabilities and rights in relation to the property, or

(b) being liabilities and rights imposed or conferred in relation to property generally,

not such as to constitute defects in title.

(3) If the disposition is expressed to be made with limited title guarantee there shall be implied a covenant that the person making the disposition has not since the last disposition for value—

(a) charged or incumbered the property by means of any charge or incumbrance which subsists at the time when the disposition is made, or granted third party rights in relation to the property which so subsist, or

(b) suffered the property to be so charged or incumbered or subjected to any such rights,

and that he is not aware that anyone else has done so since the last disposition for value.

[1531]

4 Validity of lease

(1) Where the disposition is of leasehold land and is expressed to be made with full title guarantee or with limited title guarantee, the following covenants shall also be implied—

(a) that the lease is subsisting at the time of the disposition, and

(b) that there is no subsisting breach of a condition or tenant's obligation, and nothing which at that time would render the lease liable to forfeiture.

(2) If the disposition is the grant of an underlease, the references to "the lease" in subsection (1) are references to the lease out of which the underlease is created.

[1532]

5 Discharge of obligations where property subject to rentcharge or leasehold land

(1) Where the disposition is a mortgage of property subject to a rentcharge, [of leasehold land or of a commonhold unit], and is expressed to be made with full title guarantee or with limited title guarantee, the following covenants shall also be implied.

(2) If the property is subject to a rentcharge, there shall be implied a covenant that the mortgagor will fully and promptly observe and perform all the obligations under the instrument creating the rentcharge that are for the time being enforceable with respect to the property by the owner of the rentcharge in his capacity as such.

(3) If the property is leasehold land, there shall be implied a covenant that the mortgagor will fully and promptly observe and perform all the obligations under the lease subject to the mortgage that are for the time being imposed on him in his capacity as tenant under the lease.

[(3A) If the property is a commonhold unit, there shall be implied a covenant that the mortgagor will fully and promptly observe and perform all the obligations under the commonhold community statement that are for the time being imposed on him in his capacity as a unit-holder or as a joint unit-holder.]

[(4) In this section—

(a) "commonhold community statement", "commonhold unit", "joint unit-holder" and "unit-holder" have the same meanings as in the Commonhold and Leasehold Reform Act 2002, and

(b) "mortgage" includes charge, and "mortgagor" shall be construed accordingly.]

[1533]

NOTES

Sub-s (1): words in square brackets substituted by the Commonhold and Leasehold Reform Act 2002, s 68, Sch 5, para 7(1), (2).

Sub-s (3A): inserted by the Commonhold and Leasehold Reform Act 2002, s 68, Sch 5, para 7(1), (3).

Sub-s (4): substituted by the Commonhold and Leasehold Reform Act 2002, s 68, Sch 5, para 7(1), (4).

Effect of covenants

6 No liability under covenants in certain cases

(1) The person making the disposition is not liable under the covenants implied by virtue of—

(a) section 2(1)(a) (right to dispose),

(b) section 3 (charges, incumbrances and third party rights), or

(c) section 4 (validity of lease),

in respect of any particular matter to which the disposition is expressly made subject.

(2) Furthermore that person is not liable under any of those covenants for anything (not falling within subsection (1))—

(a) which at the time of the disposition is within the actual knowledge, or

(b) which is a necessary consequence of facts that are then within the actual knowledge,

of the person to whom the disposition is made.

(3) For this purpose section 198 of the Law of Property Act 1925 (deemed notice by virtue of registration) shall be disregarded.

[(4) Moreover, where the disposition is of an interest the title to which is registered under the Land Registration Act 2002, that person is not liable under any of those covenants for anything (not falling within subsection (1) or (2)) which at the time of the disposition was entered in relation to that interest in the register of title under that Act.]

[1534]

NOTES

Sub-s (4): inserted by the Land Registration Act 2002, s 133, Sch 11, para 31(1), (2).

7 Annexation of benefit of covenants

The benefit of a covenant implied by virtue of this Part shall be annexed and incident to, and shall go with, the estate or interest of the person to whom the disposition is made, and shall be capable of being enforced by every person in whom that estate or interest is (in whole or in part) for the time being vested.

[1535]

8 Supplementary provisions

(1) The operation of any covenant implied in an instrument by virtue of this Part may be limited or extended by a term of that instrument.

(2) Sections 81 and 83 of the Law of Property Act 1925 (effect of covenant with two or more jointly; construction of implied covenants) apply to a covenant implied by virtue of this Part as they apply to a covenant implied by virtue of that Act.

(3) Where in an instrument effecting or purporting to effect a disposition of property a person is expressed to direct the disposition, this Part applies to him as if he were the person making the disposition.

(4) This Part has effect—

(a) where "gyda gwarant teitl llawn" is used instead of "with full title guarantee", and

(b) where "gyda gwarant teitl cyfyngedig" is used instead of "with limited title guarantee",

as it has effect where the English words are used.

[1536]

9 Modifications of statutory forms

(1) Where a form set out in an enactment, or in an instrument made under an enactment, includes words which (in an appropriate case) would have resulted in the implication of a covenant by virtue of section 76 of the Law of Property Act 1925, the form shall be taken to authorise instead the use of the words "with full title guarantee" or "with limited title guarantee" or their Welsh equivalent given in section 8(4).

(2) This applies in particular to the forms set out in … Schedules 4 … to the Law of Property Act 1925.

[1537]

NOTES

Sub-s (2): words omitted repealed by the Statute Law (Repeals) Act 2004.

Transitional provisions

10 General saving for covenants in old form

(1) Except as provided by section 11 below (cases in which covenants in old form implied on disposition after commencement), … as regards dispositions of property made after the commencement of this Part.

(2) The repeal of those provisions by this Act accordingly does not affect the enforcement of a covenant implied by virtue of either of them on a disposition before the commencement of this Part.

[1538]

NOTES

Sub-s (1): words omitted repeal the Law of Property Act 1925, s 76, and the Land Registration Act 1925, s 24(1)(a).

11 Covenants in old form implied in certain cases

(1) Section 76 of the Law of Property Act 1925 applies in relation to a disposition of property made after the commencement of this Part in pursuance of a contract entered into before commencement where—

(a) the contract contains a term providing for a disposition to which that section would have applied if the disposition had been made before commencement, and

(b) the existence of the contract and of that term is apparent on the face of the instrument effecting the disposition,

unless there has been an intervening disposition of the property expressed, in accordance with this Part, to be made with full title guarantee.

(2) Section 24(1)(a) of the Land Registration Act 1925 applies in relation to a disposition of a leasehold interest in land made after the commencement of this Part in pursuance of a contract entered into before commencement where—

(a) the covenant specified in that provision would have been implied on the disposition if it had been made before commencement, and

(b) the existence of the contract is apparent on the face of the instrument effecting the disposition,

unless there has been an intervening disposition of the leasehold interest expressed, in accordance with this Part, to be made with full title guarantee.

(3) In subsections (1) and (2) an "intervening disposition" means a disposition after the commencement of this Part to, or to a predecessor in title of, the person by whom the disposition in question is made.

(4) Where in order for subsection (1) or (2) to apply it is necessary for certain matters to be apparent on the face of the instrument effecting the disposition, the contract shall be deemed to contain an implied term that they should so appear.

[1539]

12 Covenants in new form to be implied in other cases

(1) This section applies to a contract for the disposition of property entered into before the commencement of this Part where the disposition is made after commencement and section 11 (cases in which covenants in old form to be implied) does not apply because there has been an intervening disposition expressed, in accordance with this Part, to be with full title guarantee.

(2) A contract which contains a term that the person making the disposition shall do so as beneficial owner shall be construed as requiring that person to do so by an instrument expressed to be made with full title guarantee.

(3) A contract which contains a term that the person making the disposition shall do so—

(a) as settlor, or

(b) as trustee or mortgagee or personal representative,

shall be construed as requiring that person to do so by an instrument expressed to be made with limited title guarantee.

(4) A contract for the disposition of a leasehold interest in land entered into at a date when the title to the leasehold interest was registered shall be construed as requiring the person making the disposition for which it provides to do so by an instrument expressed to be made with full title guarantee.

(5) Where this section applies and the contract provides that any of the covenants to be implied by virtue of section 76 of the Law of Property Act 1925 or section 24(1)(a) of the Land Registration Act 1925 shall be implied in a modified form, the contract shall be construed as requiring a corresponding modification of the covenants implied by virtue of this Part.

[1540]

13 Application of transitional provisions in relation to options

For the purposes of sections 11 and 12 (transitional provisions, implication of covenants in old form in certain cases and new form in others) as they apply in relation to a disposition of property in accordance with an option granted before the commencement of this Part and exercised after commencement, the contract for the disposition shall be deemed to have been entered into on the grant of the option.

PART II
MATTERS ARISING IN CONNECTION WITH DEATH

14 Vesting of estate in case of intestacy or lack of executors

(1) …

(2) Any real or personal estate of a person dying before the commencement of this section shall, if it is property to which this subsection applies, vest in the Public Trustee on the commencement of this section.

(3) Subsection (2) above applies to any property—

(a) if it was vested in the Probate Judge under section 9 of the Administration of Estates Act 1925 immediately before the commencement of this section, or

(b) if it was not so vested but as at commencement there has been no grant of representation in respect of it and there is no executor with power to obtain such a grant.

(4) Any property vesting in the Public Trustee by virtue of subsection (2) above shall—

(a) if the deceased died intestate, be treated as vesting in the Public Trustee under section 9(1) of the Administration of Estates Act 1925 (as substituted by subsection (1) above); and

(b) otherwise be treated as vesting in the Public Trustee under section 9(2) of that Act (as so substituted).

(5) Anything done by or in relation to the Probate Judge with respect to property vested in him as mentioned in subsection (3)(a) above shall be treated as having been done by or in relation to the Public Trustee.

(6) So far as may be necessary in consequence of the transfer to the Public Trustee of the functions of the Probate Judge under section 9 of the Administration of Estates Act 1925, any reference in an enactment or instrument to the Probate Judge shall be construed as a reference to the Public Trustee.

[1541]

NOTES

Sub-s (1): substitutes the Administration of Estates Act 1925, s 9 at **[470]**.

15 Registration of land charges after death

(1)–(4) …

(5) The amendments made by this section do not apply where the application for registration was made before the commencement of this section, but without prejudice to a person's right to make a new application after commencement.

[1542]

NOTES

Sub-ss (1)–(4): amend the Land Charges Act 1972, ss 3, 5, 6 at **[723]**, **[725]**, **[726]**.

16 Concurrence of personal representatives in dealings with interests in land

(1), (2) …

(3) The amendments made by subsection (1) apply to contracts made after the commencement of this section …

[1543]

NOTES

Sub-s (1): amends the Administration of Estates Act 1925, s 2 at **[464]**.

Sub-s (2): repealed by the Trusts of Land and Appointment of Trustees Act 1996, s 25(2), Sch 4; for savings in relation to entailed interests created before the commencement of that Act, and savings consequential upon the abolition of the doctrine of conversion, see s 25(4), (5) thereof.

Sub-s (3): words omitted repealed by the Trusts of Land and Appointment of Trustees Act 1996, s 25(2), Sch 4; for savings in relation to entailed interests created before the commencement of that Act, and savings consequential upon the abolition of the doctrine of conversion, see s 25(4), (5) thereof.

17 Notices affecting land: absence of knowledge of intended recipient's death

(1) Service of a notice affecting land which would be effective but for the death of the intended recipient is effective despite his death if the person serving the notice has no reason to believe that he has died.

(2) Where the person serving a notice affecting land has no reason to believe that the intended recipient has died, the proper address for the purposes of section 7 of the Interpretation Act 1978 (service of documents by post) shall be what would be the proper address apart from his death.

(3) The above provisions do not apply to a notice authorised or required to be served for the purposes of proceedings before—

(a) any court,

[(b) any tribunal that is (to any extent) a listed tribunal for, or for any of, the purposes of Schedule 7 to the Tribunals, Courts and Enforcement Act 2007 (functions etc of Administrative Justice and Tribunals Council), or]

(c) the Chief Land Registrar or [the Adjudicator to Her Majesty's Land Registry];

but this is without prejudice to the power to make provision in relation to such proceedings by rules of court, procedural rules [within the meaning given by paragraph 28 of Schedule 7 to the Tribunals, Courts and Enforcement Act 2007] or rules under [the Land Registration Act 2002].

[1544]

NOTES

Sub-s (3): para (b) substituted and words in square brackets substituted by the Tribunals, Courts and Enforcement Act 2007, s 48(1), Sch 8, para 33; words in square brackets in para (c) and final words in square brackets substituted by the Land Registration Act 2002, s 133, Sch 11, para 31(1), (3).

18 Notices affecting land: service on personal representatives before filing of grant

(1) A notice affecting land which would have been authorised or required to be served on a person but for his death shall be sufficiently served before a grant of representation has been filed if—

(a) it is addressed to "The Personal Representatives of" the deceased (naming him) and left at or sent by post to his last known place of residence or business in the United Kingdom, and

(b) a copy of it, similarly addressed, is served on the Public Trustee.

(2) The reference in subsection (1) to the filing of a grant of representation is to the filing at the Principal Registry of the Family Division of the High Court of a copy of a grant of representation in respect of the deceased's estate or, as the case may be, the part of his estate which includes the land in question.

(3) The method of service provided for by this section is not available where provision is made—

(a) by or under any enactment, or
(b) by an agreement in writing,

requiring a different method of service, or expressly prohibiting the method of service provided for by this section, in the circumstances.

[1545]

19 Functions of Public Trustee in relation to notices, etc

(1) The Public Trustee may give directions as to the office or offices at which documents may be served on him—

(a) by virtue of section 9 of the Administration of Estates Act 1925 (as substituted by section 14(1) above), or
(b) in pursuance of section 18(1)(b) above (service on Public Trustee of copy of certain notices affecting land);

and he shall publish such directions in such manner as he considers appropriate.

(2) The Lord Chancellor may by regulations make provision with respect to the functions of the Public Trustee in relation to such documents; and the regulations may make different provision in relation to different descriptions of document or different circumstances.

(3) The regulations may, in particular, make provision requiring the Public Trustee—

(a) to keep such documents for a specified period and thereafter to keep a copy or record of their contents in such form as may be specified;
(b) to keep such documents, copies and records available for inspection at such reasonable hours as may be specified; and
(c) to supply copies to any person on request.

In this subsection "specified" means specified by or under the regulations.

(4) Regulations under this section shall be made by statutory instrument which shall be subject to annulment in pursuance of a resolution of either House of Parliament.

(5) The following provisions of the Public Trustee Act 1906, namely—

(a) section 8(5) (payment of expenses out of money provided by Parliament), and
(b) section 9(1) [and (3)] (provisions as to fees),

apply in relation to the functions of the Public Trustee in relation to documents to which this section applies as in relation to his functions under that Act.

[1546]

NOTES

Sub-s (5): words in square brackets in para (b) substituted by the Public Trustee (Liability and Fees) Act 2002, s 2(4).

Regulations: the Public Trustee (Notices Affecting Land) (Title on Death) Regulations 1995, SI 1995/1330.

PART III
GENERAL PROVISIONS

20 Crown application

This Act binds the Crown.

[1547]

21 Consequential amendments and repeals

(1) The enactments specified in Schedule 1 are amended in accordance with that Schedule, the amendments being consequential on the provisions of this Act.

(2) The enactments specified in Schedule 2 are repealed to the extent specified.

(3) In the case of section 76 of the Law of Property Act 1925 and section 24(1)(a) of the Land Registration Act 1925, those provisions are repealed in accordance with section 10(1) above (general saving for covenants in old form).

(4) The amendments consequential on Part I of this Act (namely those in paragraphs 1, 2, 3, 5, 7, 9 and 12 of Schedule 1) shall not have effect in relation to any disposition of property to which, by virtue of section 10(1) or 11 above (transitional provisions), section 76 of the Law of Property Act 1925 or section 24(1)(a) of the Land Registration Act 1925 continues to apply.

[1548]

22 Extent

(1) The provisions of this Act extend to England and Wales.

(2) In addition—

(a) the provisions of Schedules 1 and 2 (consequential amendments and repeals) extend to Scotland so far as they relate to enactments which so extend; and

(b) the provisions of Schedule 1 extend to Northern Ireland so far as they relate to enactments which so extend.

[1549]

23 Commencement

(1) The provisions of this Act come into force on such day as the Lord Chancellor may appoint by order made by statutory instrument.

(2) Different days may be appointed for different provisions and for different purposes.

[1550]

24 Short title

This Act may be cited as the Law of Property (Miscellaneous Provisions) Act 1994.

[1551]

(*Schs 1, 2 contain amendments and repeals only.*)

AGRICULTURAL TENANCIES ACT 1995

(1995 c 8)

An Act to make further provision with respect to tenancies which include agricultural land.

[9 May 1995]

PART I
GENERAL PROVISIONS

Farm business tenancies

1 Meaning of "farm business tenancy"

(1) A tenancy is a "farm business tenancy" for the purposes of this Act if—

(a) it meets the business conditions together with either the agriculture condition or the notice conditions, and

(b) it is not a tenancy which, by virtue of section 2 of this Act, cannot be a farm business tenancy.

(2) The business conditions are—

(a) that all or part of the land comprised in the tenancy is farmed for the purposes of a trade or business, and

(b) that, since the beginning of the tenancy, all or part of the land so comprised has been so farmed.

(3) The agriculture condition is that, having regard to—

(a) the terms of the tenancy,

(b) the use of the land comprised in the tenancy,

(c) the nature of any commercial activities carried on on that land, and

(d) any other relevant circumstances,

the character of the tenancy is primarily or wholly agricultural.

(4) The notice conditions are—

(a) that, on or before the relevant day, the landlord and the tenant each gave the other a written notice—

(i) identifying (by name or otherwise) the land to be comprised in the tenancy or proposed tenancy, and

(ii) containing a statement to the effect that the person giving the notice intends that the tenancy or proposed tenancy is to be, and remain, a farm business tenancy, and

(b) that, at the beginning of the tenancy, having regard to the terms of the tenancy and any other relevant circumstances, the character of the tenancy was primarily or wholly agricultural.

(5) In subsection (4) above "the relevant day" means whichever is the earlier of the following—

(a) the day on which the parties enter into any instrument creating the tenancy, other than an agreement to enter into a tenancy on a future date, or

(b) the beginning of the tenancy.

(6) The written notice referred to in subsection (4) above must not be included in any instrument creating the tenancy.

(7) If in any proceedings—

(a) any question arises as to whether a tenancy was a farm business tenancy at any time, and

(b) it is proved that all or part of the land comprised in the tenancy was farmed for the purposes of a trade or business at that time,

it shall be presumed, unless the contrary is proved, that all or part of the land so comprised has been so farmed since the beginning of the tenancy.

(8) Any use of land in breach of the terms of the tenancy, any commercial activities carried on in breach of those terms, and any cessation of such activities in breach of those terms, shall be disregarded in determining whether at any time the tenancy meets the business conditions or the agriculture condition, unless the landlord or his predecessor in title has consented to the breach or the landlord has acquiesced in the breach.

[1552]

2 Tenancies which cannot be farm business tenancies

(1) A tenancy cannot be a farm business tenancy for the purposes of this Act if—

(a) the tenancy begins before 1st September 1995, or

(b) it is a tenancy of an agricultural holding beginning on or after that date with respect to which, by virtue of section 4 of this Act, the Agricultural Holdings Act 1986 applies.

(2) In this section "agricultural holding" has the same meaning as in the Agricultural Holdings Act 1986.

[1553]

3 Compliance with notice conditions in cases of surrender and re-grant

(1) This section applies where—

(a) a tenancy ("the new tenancy") is granted to a person who, immediately before the grant, was the tenant under a farm business tenancy ("the old tenancy") which met the notice conditions specified in section 1(4) of this Act,

(b) the condition in subsection (2) below or the condition in subsection (3) below is met, and

(c) except as respects the matters mentioned in subsections (2) and (3) below and matters consequential on them, the terms of the new tenancy are substantially the same as the terms of the old tenancy.

(2) The first condition referred to in subsection (1)(b) above is that the land comprised in the new tenancy is the same as the land comprised in the old tenancy, apart from any changes in area which are small in relation to the size of the holding and do not affect the character of the holding.

(3) The second condition referred to in subsection (1)(b) above is that the old tenancy and the new tenancy are both fixed term tenancies, but the term date under the new tenancy is earlier than the term date under the old tenancy.

(4) Where this section applies, the new tenancy shall be taken for the purposes of this Act to meet the notice conditions specified in section 1(4) of this Act.

(5) In subsection (3) above, "the term date", in relation to a fixed term tenancy, means the date fixed for the expiry of the term.

[1554]

Exclusion of Agricultural Holdings Act 1986

4 Agricultural Holdings Act 1986 not to apply in relation to new tenancies except in special cases

(1) The Agricultural Holdings Act 1986 (in this section referred to as "the 1986 Act") shall not apply in relation to any tenancy beginning on or after 1st September 1995 (including any agreement to which section 2 of that Act would otherwise apply beginning on or after that date), except [(subject to subsection (2B) below)] any tenancy of an agricultural holding which—

(a) is granted by a written contract of tenancy entered into before 1st September 1995 and indicating (in whatever terms) that the 1986 Act is to apply in relation to the tenancy,

(b) is obtained by virtue of a direction of an Agricultural Land Tribunal under section 39 or 53 of the 1986 Act,

(c) is granted (following a direction under section 39 of that Act) in circumstances falling within section 45(6) of that Act,

(d) is granted on an agreed succession by a written contract of tenancy indicating (in whatever terms) that Part IV of the 1986 Act is to apply in relation to the tenancy,

(e) is created by the acceptance of a tenant, in accordance with the provisions as to compensation known as the "Evesham custom" and set out in subsections (3) to (5) of section 80 of the 1986 Act, on the terms and conditions of the previous tenancy, …

(f) is granted to a person who, immediately before the grant of the tenancy, was the tenant of the holding, or of any agricultural holding which comprised the whole or a substantial part of the land comprised in the holding, under a tenancy in relation to which the 1986 Act applied[, and is so granted because an agreement between the parties (not being an agreement expressed to take effect as a new tenancy between the parties) has effect as an implied surrender followed by the grant of the tenancy, or]

[(g) is granted to a person who, immediately before the grant of the tenancy, was the tenant of the holding, or of any agricultural holding which comprised the whole or a substantial part of the land comprised in the holding, under a tenancy in relation to which the 1986 Act applied, and is so granted by a written contract of tenancy indicating (in whatever terms) that the 1986 Act is to apply in relation to the tenancy].

(2) For the purposes of subsection (1)(d) above, a tenancy ("the current tenancy") is granted on an agreed succession if, and only if,—

(a) the previous tenancy of the holding or a related holding was a tenancy in relation to which Part IV of the 1986 Act applied, …

[(b) the current tenancy is granted to a person (alone or jointly with other persons) who, if the tenant under that previous tenancy ("the previous tenant") had died immediately before the grant, would have been his close relative, and

(c) either of the conditions in subsection (2A) below is satisfied].

[(2A) The conditions referred to in subsection (2)(c) above are—

(a) the current tenancy is granted to a person (alone or jointly with other persons) who was or had become the sole or sole remaining applicant for a direction of an Agricultural Land Tribunal for a tenancy, and

(b) the current tenancy—

(i) is granted as a result of an agreement between the landlord and the previous tenant, and

(ii) is granted, and begins, before the date of the giving of any retirement notice by the previous tenant, or if no retirement notice is given, before the date of death of the previous tenant.]

[(2B) The 1986 Act shall not apply by virtue of subsection (1)(f) or (g) above in relation to the tenancy of an agricultural holding ("the current holding") where—

(a) the whole or a substantial part of the land comprised in the current holding was comprised in an agricultural holding ("the previous holding") which was subject to a tenancy granted after the commencement of this subsection in relation to which the 1986 Act applied by virtue of subsection (1)(f) or (g) above;

(b) the whole or a substantial part of the land comprised in the previous holding was comprised in an agricultural holding ("the original holding") which was at the commencement of this subsection subject to a tenancy in relation to which the 1986 Act applied; and

(c) the land comprised in the original holding does not, on the date of the grant of the tenancy of the current holding, comprise the whole or a substantial part of the land comprised in the current holding.]

[(2C) The references in subsections (1)(g) and (2B) above to a substantial part of the land comprised in the holding mean a substantial part determined by reference to either area or value.]

(3) In this section—

(a) "agricultural holding" and "contract of tenancy" have the same meaning as in the 1986 Act, …

(b) "close relative" and "related holding" have the meaning given by section 35(2) of that Act[, and

(c) "retirement notice" has the meaning given by section 49(3) of that Act].

[1555]

NOTES

Sub-s (1): words in first pair of square brackets and para (g) inserted, word omitted from para (e) repealed, and words in square brackets in para (f) substituted by SI 2006/2805, arts 11, 12(1)–(5), 18, Sch 2, except in relation to any tenancy granted before 19 October 2006.

Sub-s (2): word omitted from para (a) repealed and paras (b), (c) substituted, for para (b) as originally enacted by SI 2006/2805, arts 11, 12(1), (6), (7), 18, Sch 2, except in relation to any tenancy granted before 19 October 2006.

Sub-ss (2A)–(2C): inserted by SI 2006/2805, arts 11, 12(1), (8)–(10), except in relation to any tenancy granted before 19 October 2006.

Sub-s (3): word omitted from para (a) repealed and para (c) and word immediately preceding it inserted by SI 2006/2805, arts 11, 12(1), (11), 18, Sch 2, except in relation to any tenancy granted before 19 October 2006.

Termination of the tenancy

5 Tenancies for more than two years to continue from year to year unless terminated by notice

(1) A farm business tenancy for a term of more than two years shall, instead of terminating on the term date, continue (as from that date) as a tenancy from year to year, but otherwise on the terms of the original tenancy so far as applicable, unless at least twelve months … before the term date a written notice has been given by either party to the other of his intention to terminate the tenancy.

(2) In subsection (1) above "the term date", in relation to a fixed term tenancy, means the date fixed for the expiry of the term.

(3) For the purposes of section 140 of the Law of Property Act 1925 (apportionment of conditions on severance of reversion), a notice under subsection (1) above shall be taken to be a notice to quit.

(4) This section has effect notwithstanding any agreement to the contrary.

[1556]

NOTES

Sub-s (1): words omitted repealed by SI 2006/2805, arts 11, 13, 18, Sch 2.

6 Length of notice to quit

(1) Where a farm business tenancy is a tenancy from year to year, a notice to quit the holding or part of the holding shall (notwithstanding any provision to the contrary in the tenancy) be invalid unless—

(a) it is in writing,
(b) it is to take effect at the end of a year of the tenancy, and
(c) it is given at least twelve months … before the date on which it is to take effect.

(2) Where, by virtue of section 5(1) of this Act, a farm business tenancy for a term of more than two years is to continue (as from the term date) as a tenancy from year to year, a notice to quit which complies with subsection (1) above and which is to take effect on the first anniversary of the term date shall not be invalid merely because it is given before the term date; and in this subsection "the term date" has the meaning given by section 5(2) of this Act.

(3) Subsection (1) above does not apply in relation to a counter-notice given by the tenant by virtue of subsection (2) of section 140 of the Law of Property Act 1925 (apportionment of conditions on severance of reversion).

[1557]

NOTES

Sub-s (1): words omitted repealed by SI 2006/2805, arts 11, 13, 18, Sch 2.

7 Notice required for exercise of option to terminate tenancy or resume possession of part

(1) Where a farm business tenancy is a tenancy for a term of more than two years, any notice to quit the holding or part of the holding given in pursuance of any provision of the tenancy shall (notwithstanding any provision to the contrary in the tenancy) be invalid unless it is in writing and is given at least twelve months … before the date on which it is to take effect.

(2) Subsection (1) above does not apply in relation to a counter-notice given by the tenant by virtue of subsection (2) of section 140 of the Law of Property Act 1925 (apportionment of conditions on severance of reversion).

(3) Subsection (1) above does not apply to a tenancy which, by virtue of subsection (6) of section 149 of the Law of Property Act 1925 (lease for life or lives or for a term determinable with life or lives or on the marriage of[, or formation of a civil partnership by,] the lessee), takes effect as such a term of years as is mentioned in that subsection.

[1558]

NOTES

Sub-s (1): words omitted repealed by SI 2006/2805, arts 11, 13, 18, Sch 2.
Sub-s (3): words in square brackets inserted by the Civil Partnership Act 2004, s 81, Sch 8, para 49.

Tenant's right to remove fixtures and buildings

8 Tenant's right to remove fixtures and buildings

(1) Subject to the provisions of this section—

(a) any fixture (of whatever description) affixed, whether for the purposes of agriculture or not, to the holding by the tenant under a farm business tenancy, and
(b) any building erected by him on the holding,

may be removed by the tenant at any time during the continuance of the tenancy or at any time after the termination of the tenancy when he remains in possession as tenant (whether or not under a new tenancy), and shall remain his property so long as he may remove it by virtue of this subsection.

(2) Subsection (1) above shall not apply—

(a) to a fixture affixed or a building erected in pursuance of some obligation,

(b) to a fixture affixed or a building erected instead of some fixture or building belonging to the landlord,

(c) to a fixture or building in respect of which the tenant has obtained compensation under section 16 of this Act or otherwise, or

(d) to a fixture or building in respect of which the landlord has given his consent under section 17 of this Act on condition that the tenant agrees not to remove it and which the tenant has agreed not to remove.

(3) In the removal of a fixture or building by virtue of subsection (1) above, the tenant shall not do any avoidable damage to the holding.

(4) Immediately after removing a fixture or building by virtue of subsection (1) above, the tenant shall make good all damage to the holding that is occasioned by the removal.

(5) This section applies to a fixture or building acquired by a tenant as it applies to a fixture or building affixed or erected by him.

(6) Except as provided by subsection (2)(d) above, this section has effect notwithstanding any agreement or custom to the contrary.

(7) No right to remove fixtures that subsists otherwise than by virtue of this section shall be exercisable by the tenant under a farm business tenancy.

[1559]

9–27 ((*Pts II, III*) *outside the scope of this work.*)

PART IV
MISCELLANEOUS AND SUPPLEMENTAL

28–32 (*Outside the scope of this work.*)

33 Power to apply and raise capital money

(1) The purposes authorised by section 73 of the Settled Land Act 1925 … or section 26 of the Universities and College Estates Act 1925 for the application of capital money shall include—

(a) the payment of expenses incurred by a landlord under a farm business tenancy in, or in connection with, the making of any physical improvement on the holding,

(b) the payment of compensation under section 16 of this Act, and

(c) the payment of the costs, charges and expenses incurred by him on a reference to arbitration under section 19 or 22 of this Act.

(2) The purposes authorised by section 71 of the Settled Land Act 1925 … as purposes for which money may be raised by mortgage shall include the payment of compensation under section 16 of this Act.

(3) Where the landlord under a farm business tenancy—

(a) is a tenant for life or in a fiduciary position, and

(b) is liable to pay compensation under section 16 of this Act,

he may require the sum payable as compensation and any costs, charges and expenses incurred by him in connection with the tenant's claim under that section to be paid out of any capital money held on the same trusts as the settled land.

(4) In subsection (3) above—

"capital money" includes any personal estate held on the same trusts as the land; …

[1560]

NOTES

Sub-ss (1), (2), (4): words omitted repealed by the Trusts of Land and Appointment of Trustees Act 1996, s 25(2), Sch 4; for savings in relation to entailed interests created before the commencement of that Act, and savings consequential upon the abolition of the doctrine of conversion, see s 25(4), (5) thereof.

34 Estimation of best rent for purposes of Acts and other instruments

(1) In estimating the best rent or reservation in the nature of rent of land comprised in a farm business tenancy for the purposes of a relevant instrument, it shall not be necessary to take into account against the tenant any increase in the value of that land arising from any tenant's improvements.

(2) In subsection (1) above—

"a relevant instrument" means any Act of Parliament, deed or other instrument which authorises a lease to be made on the condition that the best rent or reservation in the nature of rent is reserved;

"tenant's improvement" has the meaning given by section 15 of this Act.

[1561]

35 (*Outside the scope of this work.*)

Supplemental

36–40 (*Outside the scope of this work.*)

41 Short title, commencement and extent

(1) This Act may be cited as the Agricultural Tenancies Act 1995.

(2) This Act shall come into force on 1st September 1995.

(3) Subject to subsection (4) below, this Act extends to England and Wales only.

(4) The amendment by a provision of the Schedule to this Act of an enactment which extends to Scotland or Northern Ireland also extends there, except that paragraph 9 of the Schedule does not extend to Northern Ireland.

[1562]

(*Schedule outside the scope of this work.*)

LANDLORD AND TENANT (COVENANTS) ACT 1995

(1995 c 30)

An Act to make provision for persons bound by covenants of a tenancy to be released from such covenants on the assignment of the tenancy, and to make other provision with respect to rights and liabilities arising under such covenants; to restrict in certain circumstances the operation of rights of re-entry, forfeiture and disclaimer; and for connected purposes

[19 July 1995]

Preliminary

1 Tenancies to which the Act applies

(1) Sections 3 to 16 and 21 apply only to new tenancies.

(2) Sections 17 to 20 apply to both new and other tenancies.

(3) For the purposes of this section a tenancy is a new tenancy if it is granted on or after the date on which this Act comes into force otherwise than in pursuance of—

(a) an agreement entered into before that date, or

(b) an order of a court made before that date.

(4) Subsection (3) has effect subject to section 20(1) in the case of overriding leases granted under section 19.

(5) Without prejudice to the generality of subsection (3), that subsection applies to the grant of a tenancy where by virtue of any variation of a tenancy there is a deemed surrender and regrant as it applies to any other grant of a tenancy.

(6) Where a tenancy granted on or after the date on which this Act comes into force is so granted in pursuance of an option granted before that date, the tenancy shall be regarded for the purposes of subsection (3) as granted in pursuance of an agreement entered into before that date (and accordingly is not a new tenancy), whether or not the option was exercised before that date.

(7) In subsection (6) "option" includes right of first refusal.

[1563]

2 Covenants to which the Act applies

(1) This Act applies to a landlord covenant or a tenant covenant of a tenancy—

(a) whether or not the covenant has reference to the subject matter of the tenancy, and

(b) whether the covenant is express, implied or imposed by law,

but does not apply to a covenant falling within subsection (2).

(2) Nothing in this Act affects any covenant imposed in pursuance of—

(a) section 35 or 155 of the Housing Act 1985 (covenants for repayment of discount on early disposals);

(b) paragraph 1 of Schedule 6A to that Act (covenants requiring redemption of landlord's share); or

(c) [section 11 or 13 of the Housing Act 1996 or] paragraph 1 or 3 of Schedule 2 to the Housing Associations Act 1985 (covenants for repayment of discount on early disposals or for restricting disposals).

[1564]

NOTES

Sub-s (2): words in square brackets inserted by SI 1996/2325, art 5, Sch 2, para 22.

Transmission of covenants

3 Transmission of benefit and burden of covenants

(1) The benefit and burden of all landlord and tenant covenants of a tenancy—

(a) shall be annexed and incident to the whole, and to each and every part, of the premises demised by the tenancy and of the reversion in them, and

(b) shall in accordance with this section pass on an assignment of the whole or any part of those premises or of the reversion in them.

(2) Where the assignment is by the tenant under the tenancy, then as from the assignment the assignee—

(a) becomes bound by the tenant covenants of the tenancy except to the extent that—

(i) immediately before the assignment they did not bind the assignor, or

(ii) they fall to be complied with in relation to any demised premises not comprised in the assignment; and

(b) becomes entitled to the benefit of the landlord covenants of the tenancy except to the extent that they fall to be complied with in relation to any such premises.

(3) Where the assignment is by the landlord under the tenancy, then as from the assignment the assignee—

(a) becomes bound by the landlord covenants of the tenancy except to the extent that—

(i) immediately before the assignment they did not bind the assignor, or

(ii) they fall to be complied with in relation to any demised premises not comprised in the assignment; and

(b) becomes entitled to the benefit of the tenant covenants of the tenancy except to the extent that they fall to be complied with in relation to any such premises.

(4) In determining for the purposes of subsection (2) or (3) whether any covenant bound the assignor immediately before the assignment, any waiver or release of the covenant which (in whatever terms) is expressed to be personal to the assignor shall be disregarded.

(5) Any landlord or tenant covenant of a tenancy which is restrictive of the user of land shall, as well as being capable of enforcement against an assignee, be capable of being enforced against any other person who is the owner or occupier of any demised premises to which the covenant relates, even though there is no express provision in the tenancy to that effect.

(6) Nothing in this section shall operate—

(a) in the case of a covenant which (in whatever terms) is expressed to be personal to any person, to make the covenant enforceable by or (as the case may be) against any other person; or

(b) to make a covenant enforceable against any person if, apart from this section, it would not be enforceable against him by reason of its not having been registered under the [Land Registration Act 2002] or the Land Charges Act 1972.

(7) To the extent that there remains in force any rule of law by virtue of which the burden of a covenant whose subject matter is not in existence at the time when it is made does not run with the land affected unless the covenantor covenants on behalf of himself and his assigns, that rule of law is hereby abolished in relation to tenancies.

[1565]

NOTES

Sub-s (6): words in square brackets in para (b) substituted by the Land Registration Act 2002, s 133, Sch 11, para 33(1), (2).

4 Transmission of rights of re-entry

The benefit of a landlord's right of re-entry under a tenancy—

(a) shall be annexed and incident to the whole, and to each and every part, of the reversion in the premises demised by the tenancy, and

(b) shall pass on an assignment of the whole or any part of the reversion in those premises.

[1566]

Release of covenants on assignment

5 Tenant released from covenants on assignment of tenancy

(1) This section applies where a tenant assigns premises demised to him under a tenancy.

(2) If the tenant assigns the whole of the premises demised to him, he—

(a) is released from the tenant covenants of the tenancy, and
(b) ceases to be entitled to the benefit of the landlord covenants of the tenancy,

as from the assignment.

(3) If the tenant assigns part only of the premises demised to him, then as from the assignment he—

(a) is released from the tenant covenants of the tenancy, and
(b) ceases to be entitled to the benefit of the landlord covenants of the tenancy,

only to the extent that those covenants fall to be complied with in relation to that part of the demised premises.

(4) This section applies as mentioned in subsection (1) whether or not the tenant is tenant of the whole of the premises comprised in the tenancy.

[1567]

6 Landlord may be released from covenants on assignment of reversion

(1) This section applies where a landlord assigns the reversion in premises of which he is the landlord under a tenancy.

(2) If the landlord assigns the reversion in the whole of the premises of which he is the landlord—

(a) he may apply to be released from the landlord covenants of the tenancy in accordance with section 8; and
(b) if he is so released from all of those covenants, he ceases to be entitled to the benefit of the tenant covenants of the tenancy as from the assignment.

(3) If the landlord assigns the reversion in part only of the premises of which he is the landlord—

(a) he may apply to be so released from the landlord covenants of the tenancy to the extent that they fall to be complied with in relation to that part of those premises; and
(b) if he is, to that extent, so released from all of those covenants, then as from the assignment he ceases to be entitled to the benefit of the tenant covenants only to the extent that they fall to be complied with in relation to that part of those premises.

(4) This section applies as mentioned in subsection (1) whether or not the landlord is landlord of the whole of the premises comprised in the tenancy.

[1568]

7 Former landlord may be released from covenants on assignment of reversion

(1) This section applies where—

(a) a landlord assigns the reversion in premises of which he is the landlord under a tenancy, and
(b) immediately before the assignment a former landlord of the premises remains bound by a landlord covenant of the tenancy ("the relevant covenant").

(2) If immediately before the assignment the former landlord does not remain the landlord of any other premises demised by the tenancy, he may apply to be released from the relevant covenant in accordance with section 8.

(3) In any other case the former landlord may apply to be so released from the relevant covenant to the extent that it falls to be complied with in relation to any premises comprised in the assignment.

(4) If the former landlord is so released from every landlord covenant by which he remained bound immediately before the assignment, he ceases to be entitled to the benefit of the tenant covenants of the tenancy.

(5) If the former landlord is so released from every such landlord covenant to the extent that it falls to be complied with in relation to any premises comprised in the assignment, he ceases to be entitled to the benefit of the tenant covenants of the tenancy to the extent that they fall to be so complied with.

(6) This section applies as mentioned in subsection (1)—

(a) whether or not the landlord making the assignment is landlord of the whole of the premises comprised in the tenancy; and
(b) whether or not the former landlord has previously applied (whether under section 6 or this section) to be released from the relevant covenant.

[1569]

8 Procedure for seeking release from a covenant under section 6 or 7

(1) For the purposes of section 6 or 7 an application for the release of a covenant to any extent is made by serving on the tenant, either before or within the period of four weeks beginning with the date of the assignment in question, a notice informing him of—

(a) the proposed assignment or (as the case may be) the fact that the assignment has taken place, and

(b) the request for the covenant to be released to that extent.

(2) Where an application for the release of a covenant is made in accordance with subsection (1), the covenant is released to the extent mentioned in the notice if—

(a) the tenant does not, within the period of four weeks beginning with the day on which the notice is served, serve on the landlord or former landlord a notice in writing objecting to the release, or

(b) the tenant does so serve such a notice but the court, on the application of the landlord or former landlord, makes a declaration that it is reasonable for the covenant to be so released, or

(c) the tenant serves on the landlord or former landlord a notice in writing consenting to the release and, if he has previously served a notice objecting to it, stating that that notice is withdrawn.

(3) Any release from a covenant in accordance with this section shall be regarded as occurring at the time when the assignment in question takes place.

(4) In this section—

(a) "the tenant" means the tenant of the premises comprised in the assignment in question (or, if different parts of those premises are held under the tenancy by different tenants, each of those tenants);

(b) any reference to the landlord or the former landlord is a reference to the landlord referred to in section 6 or the former landlord referred to in section 7, as the case may be; and

(c) "the court" means a county court.

[1570]

Apportionment of liability between assignor and assignee

9 Apportionment of liability under covenants binding both assignor and assignee of tenancy or reversion

(1) This section applies where—

(a) a tenant assigns part only of the premises demised to him by a tenancy;

(b) after the assignment both the tenant and his assignee are to be bound by a non-attributable tenant covenant of the tenancy; and

(c) the tenant and his assignee agree that as from the assignment liability under the covenant is to be apportioned between them in such manner as is specified in the agreement.

(2) This section also applies where—

(a) a landlord assigns the reversion in part only of the premises of which he is the landlord under a tenancy;

(b) after the assignment both the landlord and his assignee are to be bound by a non-attributable landlord covenant of the tenancy; and

(c) the landlord and his assignee agree that as from the assignment liability under the covenant is to be apportioned between them in such manner as is specified in the agreement.

(3) Any such agreement as is mentioned in subsection (1) or (2) may apportion liability in such a way that a party to the agreement is exonerated from all liability under a covenant.

(4) In any case falling within subsection (1) or (2) the parties to the agreement may apply for the apportionment to become binding on the appropriate person in accordance with section 10.

(5) In any such case the parties to the agreement may also apply for the apportionment to become binding on any person (other than the appropriate person) who is for the time being entitled to enforce the covenant in question; and section 10 shall apply in relation to such an application as it applies in relation to an application made with respect to the appropriate person.

(6) For the purposes of this section a covenant is, in relation to an assignment, a "non-attributable" covenant if it does not fall to be complied with in relation to any premises comprised in the assignment.

(7) In this section "the appropriate person" means either—

(a) the landlord of the entire premises referred to in subsection (1)(a) (or, if different parts of those premises are held under the tenancy by different landlords, each of those landlords), or

(b) the tenant of the entire premises referred to in subsection (2)(a) (or, if different parts of those premises are held under the tenancy by different tenants, each of those tenants),

depending on whether the agreement in question falls within subsection (1) or subsection (2).

[1571]

10 Procedure for making apportionment bind other party to lease

(1) For the purposes of section 9 the parties to an agreement falling within subsection (1) or (2) of that section apply for an apportionment to become binding on the appropriate person if, either before or within the period of four weeks beginning with the date of the assignment in question, they serve on that person a notice informing him of—

(a) the proposed assignment or (as the case may be) the fact that the assignment has taken place;

(b) the prescribed particulars of the agreement; and

(c) their request that the apportionment should become binding on him.

(2) Where an application for an apportionment to become binding has been made in accordance with subsection (1), the apportionment becomes binding on the appropriate person if—

(a) he does not, within the period of four weeks beginning with the day on which the notice is served under subsection (1), serve on the parties to the agreement a notice in writing objecting to the apportionment becoming binding on him, or

(b) he does so serve such a notice but the court, on the application of the parties to the agreement, makes a declaration that it is reasonable for the apportionment to become binding on him, or

(c) he serves on the parties to the agreement a notice in writing consenting to the apportionment becoming binding on him and, if he has previously served a notice objecting thereto, stating that the notice is withdrawn.

(3) Where any apportionment becomes binding in accordance with this section, this shall be regarded as occurring at the time when the assignment in question takes place.

(4) In this section—

"the appropriate person" has the same meaning as in section 9;

"the court" means a county court;

"prescribed" means prescribed by virtue of section 27.

[1572]

Excluded assignments

11 Assignments in breach of covenant or by operation of law

(1) This section provides for the operation of sections 5 to 10 in relation to assignments in breach of a covenant of a tenancy or assignments by operation of law ("excluded assignments").

(2) In the case of an excluded assignment subsection (2) or (3) of section 5—

(a) shall not have the effect mentioned in that subsection in relation to the tenant as from that assignment, but

(b) shall have that effect as from the next assignment (if any) of the premises assigned by him which is not an excluded assignment.

(3) In the case of an excluded assignment subsection (2) or (3) of section 6 or 7—

(a) shall not enable the landlord or former landlord to apply for such a release as is mentioned in that subsection as from that assignment, but

(b) shall apply on the next assignment (if any) of the reversion assigned by the landlord which is not an excluded assignment so as to enable the landlord or former landlord to apply for any such release as from that subsequent assignment.

(4) Where subsection (2) or (3) of section 6 or 7 does so apply—

(a) any reference in that section to the assignment (except where it relates to the time as from which the release takes effect) is a reference to the excluded assignment; but

(b) in that excepted case and in section 8 as it applies in relation to any application under that section made by virtue of subsection (3) above, any reference to the assignment or proposed assignment is a reference to any such subsequent assignment as is mentioned in that subsection.

(5) In the case of an excluded assignment section 9—

(a) shall not enable the tenant or landlord and his assignee to apply for an agreed apportionment to become binding in accordance with section 10 as from that assignment, but

(b) shall apply on the next assignment (if any) of the premises or reversion assigned by the tenant or landlord which is not an excluded assignment so as to enable him and his assignee to apply for such an apportionment to become binding in accordance with section 10 as from that subsequent assignment.

(6) Where section 9 does so apply—

(a) any reference in that section to the assignment or the assignee under it is a reference to the excluded assignment and the assignee under that assignment; but

(b) in section 10 as it applies in relation to any application under section 9 made by virtue of subsection (5) above, any reference to the assignment or proposed assignment is a reference to any such subsequent assignment as is mentioned in that subsection.

(7) If any such subsequent assignment as is mentioned in subsection (2), (3) or (5) above comprises only part of the premises assigned by the tenant or (as the case may be) only part of the premises the reversion in which was assigned by the landlord on the excluded assignment—

(a) the relevant provision or provisions of section 5, 6, 7 or 9 shall only have the effect mentioned in that subsection to the extent that the covenants or covenant in question fall or falls to be complied with in relation to that part of those premises; and

(b) that subsection may accordingly apply on different occasions in relation to different parts of those premises.

[1573]

Third party covenants

12 Covenants with management companies etc

(1) This section applies where—

(a) a person other than the landlord or tenant ("the third party") is under a covenant of a tenancy liable (as principal) to discharge any function with respect to all or any of the demised premises ("the relevant function"); and

(b) that liability is not the liability of a guarantor or any other financial liability referable to the performance or otherwise of a covenant of the tenancy by another party to it.

(2) To the extent that any covenant of the tenancy confers any rights against the third party with respect to the relevant function, then for the purposes of the transmission of the benefit of the covenant in accordance with this Act it shall be treated as if it were—

(a) a tenant covenant of the tenancy to the extent that those rights are exercisable by the landlord; and

(b) a landlord covenant of the tenancy to the extent that those rights are exercisable by the tenant.

(3) To the extent that any covenant of the tenancy confers any rights exercisable by the third party with respect to the relevant function, then for the purposes mentioned in subsection (4), it shall be treated as if it were—

(a) a tenant covenant of the tenancy to the extent that those rights are exercisable against the tenant; and

(b) a landlord covenant of the tenancy to the extent that those rights are exercisable against the landlord.

(4) The purposes mentioned in subsection (3) are—

(a) the transmission of the burden of the covenant in accordance with this Act; and

(b) any release from, or apportionment of liability in respect of, the covenant in accordance with this Act.

(5) In relation to the release of the landlord from any covenant which is to be treated as a landlord covenant by virtue of subsection (3), section 8 shall apply as if any reference to the tenant were a reference to the third party.

[1574]

Joint liability under covenants

13 Covenants binding two or more persons

(1) Where in consequence of this Act two or more persons are bound by the same covenant, they are so bound both jointly and severally.

(2) Subject to section 24(2), where by virtue of this Act—

(a) two or more persons are bound jointly and severally by the same covenant, and

(b) any of the persons so bound is released from the covenant,

the release does not extend to any other of those persons.

(3) For the purpose of providing for contribution between persons who, by virtue of this Act, are bound jointly and severally by a covenant, the Civil Liability (Contribution) Act 1978 shall have effect as if—

(a) liability to a person under a covenant were liability in respect of damage suffered by that person;

(b) references to damage accordingly included a breach of a covenant of a tenancy; and

(c) section 7(2) of that Act were omitted.

[1575]

14 (*Repeals the Law of Property Act 1925, s 77(1)(C), (D) and the Land Registration Act 1925, s 24(1)(b), (2).*)

Enforcement of covenants

15 Enforcement of covenants

(1) Where any tenant covenant of a tenancy, or any right of re-entry contained in a tenancy, is enforceable by the reversioner in respect of any premises demised by the tenancy, it shall also be so enforceable by—

(a) any person (other than the reversioner) who, as the holder of the immediate reversion in those premises, is for the time being entitled to the rents and profits under the tenancy in respect of those premises, or

(b) any mortgagee in possession of the reversion in those premises who is so entitled.

(2) Where any landlord covenant of a tenancy is enforceable against the reversioner in respect of any premises demised by the tenancy, it shall also be so enforceable against any person falling within subsection (1)(a) or (b).

(3) Where any landlord covenant of a tenancy is enforceable by the tenant in respect of any premises demised by the tenancy, it shall also be so enforceable by any mortgagee in possession of those premises under a mortgage granted by the tenant.

(4) Where any tenant covenant of a tenancy, or any right of re-entry contained in a tenancy, is enforceable against the tenant in respect of any premises demised by the tenancy, it shall also be so enforceable against any such mortgagee.

(5) Nothing in this section shall operate—

(a) in the case of a covenant which (in whatever terms) is expressed to be personal to any person, to make the covenant enforceable by or (as the case may be) against any other person; or

(b) to make a covenant enforceable against any person if, apart from this section, it would not be enforceable against him by reason of its not having been registered under the [Land Registration Act 2002] or the Land Charges Act 1972.

(6) In this section—

"mortgagee" and "mortgage" include "chargee" and "charge" respectively;

"the reversioner", in relation to a tenancy, means the holder for the time being of the interest of the landlord under the tenancy.

[1576]

NOTES

Sub-s (5): words in square brackets in para (b) substituted by the Land Registration Act 2002, s 133, Sch 11, para 33(1), (2).

Liability of former tenant etc in respect of covenants

16 Tenant guaranteeing performance of covenant by assignee

(1) Where on an assignment a tenant is to any extent released from a tenant covenant of a tenancy by virtue of this Act ("the relevant covenant"), nothing in this Act (and in particular section 25) shall preclude him from entering into an authorised guarantee agreement with respect to the performance of that covenant by the assignee.

(2) For the purposes of this section an agreement is an authorised guarantee agreement if—

(a) under it the tenant guarantees the performance of the relevant covenant to any extent by the assignee; and

(b) it is entered into in the circumstances set out in subsection (3); and

(c) its provisions conform with subsections (4) and (5).

(3) Those circumstances are as follows—

(a) by virtue of a covenant against assignment (whether absolute or qualified) the assignment cannot be effected without the consent of the landlord under the tenancy or some other person;

(b) any such consent is given subject to a condition (lawfully imposed) that the tenant is to enter into an agreement guaranteeing the performance of the covenant by the assignee; and

(c) the agreement is entered into by the tenant in pursuance of that condition.

(4) An agreement is not an authorised guarantee agreement to the extent that it purports—

(a) to impose on the tenant any requirement to guarantee in any way the performance of the relevant covenant by any person other than the assignee; or

(b) to impose on the tenant any liability, restriction or other requirement (of whatever nature) in relation to any time after the assignee is released from that covenant by virtue of this Act.

(5) Subject to subsection (4), an authorised guarantee agreement may—

(a) impose on the tenant any liability as sole or principal debtor in respect of any obligation owed by the assignee under the relevant covenant;

(b) impose on the tenant liabilities as guarantor in respect of the assignee's performance of that covenant which are no more onerous than those to which he would be subject in the event of his being liable as sole or principal debtor in respect of any obligation owed by the assignee under that covenant;

(c) require the tenant, in the event of the tenancy assigned by him being disclaimed, to enter into a new tenancy of the premises comprised in the assignment—

(i) whose term expires not later than the term of the tenancy assigned by the tenant, and

(ii) whose tenant covenants are no more onerous than those of that tenancy;

(d) make provision incidental or supplementary to any provision made by virtue of any of paragraphs (a) to (c).

(6) Where a person ("the former tenant") is to any extent released from a covenant of a tenancy by virtue of section 11(2) as from an assignment and the assignor under the assignment enters into an authorised guarantee agreement with the landlord with respect to the performance of that covenant by the assignee under the assignment—

(a) the landlord may require the former tenant to enter into an agreement under which he guarantees, on terms corresponding to those of that authorised guarantee agreement, the performance of that covenant by the assignee under the assignment; and

(b) if its provisions conform with subsections (4) and (5), any such agreement shall be an authorised guarantee agreement for the purposes of this section; and

(c) in the application of this section in relation to any such agreement—

(i) subsections (2)(b) and (c) and (3) shall be omitted, and

(ii) any reference to the tenant or to the assignee shall be read as a reference to the former tenant or to the assignee under the assignment.

(7) For the purposes of subsection (1) it is immaterial that—

(a) the tenant has already made an authorised guarantee agreement in respect of a previous assignment by him of the tenancy referred to in that subsection, it having been subsequently revested in him following a disclaimer on behalf of the previous assignee, or

(b) the tenancy referred to in that subsection is a new tenancy entered into by the tenant in pursuance of an authorised guarantee agreement;

and in any such case subsections (2) to (5) shall apply accordingly.

(8) It is hereby declared that the rules of law relating to guarantees (and in particular those relating to the release of sureties) are, subject to its terms, applicable in relation to any authorised guarantee agreement as in relation to any other guarantee agreement.

[1577]

17 Restriction on liability of former tenant or his guarantor for rent or service charge etc

(1) This section applies where a person ("the former tenant") is as a result of an assignment no longer a tenant under a tenancy but—

(a) (in the case of a tenancy which is a new tenancy) he has under an authorised guarantee agreement guaranteed the performance by his assignee of a tenant covenant of the tenancy under which any fixed charge is payable; or

(b) (in the case of any tenancy) he remains bound by such a covenant.

(2) The former tenant shall not be liable under that agreement or (as the case may be) the covenant to pay any amount in respect of any fixed charge payable under the covenant unless, within the period of six months beginning with the date when the charge becomes due, the landlord serves on the former tenant a notice informing him—

(a) that the charge is now due; and

(b) that in respect of the charge the landlord intends to recover from the former tenant such amount as is specified in the notice and (where payable) interest calculated on such basis as is so specified.

(3) Where a person ("the guarantor") has agreed to guarantee the performance by the former tenant of such a covenant as is mentioned in subsection (1), the guarantor shall not be liable under the agreement to pay any amount in respect of any fixed charge payable under the covenant unless, within the period of six months beginning with the date when the charge becomes due, the landlord serves on the guarantor a notice informing him—

(a) that the charge is now due; and

(b) that in respect of the charge the landlord intends to recover from the guarantor such amount as is specified in the notice and (where payable) interest calculated on such basis as is so specified.

(4) Where the landlord has duly served a notice under subsection (2) or (3), the amount (exclusive of interest) which the former tenant or (as the case may be) the guarantor is liable to pay in respect of the fixed charge in question shall not exceed the amount specified in the notice unless—

(a) his liability in respect of the charge is subsequently determined to be for a greater amount,
(b) the notice informed him of the possibility that that liability would be so determined, and
(c) within the period of three months beginning with the date of the determination, the landlord serves on him a further notice informing him that the landlord intends to recover that greater amount from him (plus interest, where payable).

(5) For the purposes of subsection (2) or (3) any fixed charge which has become due before the date on which this Act comes into force shall be treated as becoming due on that date; but neither of those subsections applies to any such charge if before that date proceedings have been instituted by the landlord for the recovery from the former tenant of any amount in respect of it.

(6) In this section—

"fixed charge", in relation to tenancy, means—

(a) rent,
(b) any service charge as defined by section 18 of the Landlord and Tenant Act 1985 (the words "of a dwelling" being disregarded for this purpose), and
(c) any amount payable under a tenant covenant of the tenancy providing for the payment of a liquidated sum in the event of a failure to comply with any such covenant;

"landlord", in relation to a fixed charge, includes any person who has a right to enforce payment of the charge.

[1578]

18 Restriction of liability of former tenant or his guarantor where tenancy subsequently varied

(1) This section applies where a person ("the former tenant") is as a result of an assignment no longer a tenant under a tenancy but—

(a) (in the case of a new tenancy) he has under an authorised guarantee agreement guaranteed the performance by his assignee of any tenant covenant of the tenancy; or
(b) (in the case of any tenancy) he remains bound by such a covenant.

(2) The former tenant shall not be liable under the agreement or (as the case may be) the covenant to pay any amount in respect of the covenant to the extent that the amount is referable to any relevant variation of the tenant covenants of the tenancy effected after the assignment.

(3) Where a person ("the guarantor") has agreed to guarantee the performance by the former tenant of a tenant covenant of the tenancy, the guarantor (where his liability to do so is not wholly discharged by any such variation of the tenant covenants of the tenancy) shall not be liable under the agreement to pay any amount in respect of the covenant to the extent that the amount is referable to any such variation.

(4) For the purposes of this section a variation of the tenant covenants of a tenancy is a "relevant variation" if either—

(a) the landlord has, at the time of the variation, an absolute right to refuse to allow it; or
(b) the landlord would have had such a right if the variation had been sought by the former tenant immediately before the assignment by him but, between the time of that assignment and the time of the variation, the tenant covenants of the tenancy have been so varied as to deprive the landlord of such a right.

(5) In determining whether the landlord has or would have had such a right at any particular time regard shall be had to all the circumstances (including the effect of any provision made by or under any enactment).

(6) Nothing in this section applies to any variation of the tenant covenants of a tenancy effected before the date on which this Act comes into force.

(7) In this section "variation" means a variation whether effected by deed or otherwise.

[1579]

Overriding leases

19 Right of former tenant or his guarantor to overriding lease

(1) Where in respect of any tenancy ("the relevant tenancy") any person ("the claimant") makes full payment of an amount which he has been duly required to pay in accordance with section 17, together with any interest payable, he shall be entitled (subject to and in accordance with this section) to have the landlord under that tenancy grant him an overriding lease of the premises demised by the tenancy.

(2) For the purposes of this section "overriding lease" means a tenancy of the reversion expectant on the relevant tenancy which—

(a) is granted for a term equal to the remainder of the term of the relevant tenancy plus three days or the longest period (less than three days) that will not wholly displace the landlord's reversionary interest expectant on the relevant tenancy, as the case may require; and

(b) (subject to subsections (3) and (4) and to any modifications agreed to by the claimant and the landlord) otherwise contains the same covenants as the relevant tenancy, as they have effect immediately before the grant of the lease.

(3) An overriding lease shall not be required to reproduce any covenant of the relevant tenancy to the extent that the covenant is (in whatever terms) expressed to be a personal covenant between the landlord and the tenant under that tenancy.

(4) If any right, liability or other matter arising under a covenant of the relevant tenancy falls to be determined or otherwise operates (whether expressly or otherwise) by reference to the commencement of that tenancy—

(a) the corresponding covenant of the overriding lease shall be so framed that that right, liability or matter falls to be determined or otherwise operates by reference to the commencement of that tenancy; but

(b) the overriding lease shall not be required to reproduce any covenant of that tenancy to the extent that it has become spent by the time that that lease is granted.

(5) A claim to exercise the right to an overriding lease under this section is made by the claimant making a request for such a lease to the landlord; and any such request—

(a) must be made to the landlord in writing and specify the payment by virtue of which the claimant claims to be entitled to the lease ("the qualifying payment"); and

(b) must be so made at the time of making the qualifying payment or within the period of 12 months beginning with the date of that payment.

(6) Where the claimant duly makes such a request—

(a) the landlord shall (subject to subsection (7)) grant and deliver to the claimant an overriding lease of the demised premises within a reasonable time of the request being received by the landlord; and

(b) the claimant—

(i) shall thereupon deliver to the landlord a counterpart of the lease duly executed by the claimant, and

(ii) shall be liable for the landlord's reasonable costs of and incidental to the grant of the lease.

(7) The landlord shall not be under any obligation to grant an overriding lease of the demised premises under this section at a time when the relevant tenancy has been determined; and a claimant shall not be entitled to the grant of such a lease if at the time when he makes his request—

(a) the landlord has already granted such a lease and that lease remains in force; or

(b) another person has already duly made a request for such a lease to the landlord and that request has been neither withdrawn nor abandoned by that person.

(8) Where two or more requests are duly made on the same day, then for the purposes of subsection (7)—

(a) a request made by a person who was liable for the qualifying payment as a former tenant shall be treated as made before a request made by a person who was so liable as a guarantor; and

(b) a request made by a person whose liability in respect of the covenant in question commenced earlier than any such liability of another person shall be treated as made before a request made by that other person.

(9) Where a claimant who has duly made a request for an overriding lease under this section subsequently withdraws or abandons the request before he is granted such a lease by the landlord, the claimant shall be liable for the landlord's reasonable costs incurred in pursuance of the request down to the time of its withdrawal or abandonment; and for the purposes of this section—

(a) a claimant's request is withdrawn by the claimant notifying the landlord in writing that he is withdrawing his request; and

(b) a claimant is to be regarded as having abandoned his request if—

(i) the landlord has requested the claimant in writing to take, within such reasonable period as is specified in the landlord's request, all or any of the remaining steps required to be taken by the claimant before the lease can be granted, and

(ii) the claimant fails to comply with the landlord's request,

and is accordingly to be regarded as having abandoned it at the time when that period expires.

(10) Any request or notification under this section may be sent by post.

(11) The preceding provisions of this section shall apply where the landlord is the tenant under an overriding lease granted under this section as they apply where no such lease has been granted; and accordingly there may be two or more such leases interposed between the first such lease and the relevant tenancy.

[1580]

20 Overriding leases: supplementary provisions

(1) For the purposes of section 1 an overriding lease shall be a new tenancy only if the relevant tenancy is a new tenancy.

(2) Every overriding lease shall state—

(a) that it is a lease granted under section 19, and

(b) whether it is or is not a new tenancy for the purposes of section 1;

and any such statement shall comply with such requirements as may be prescribed by [land registration rules under the Land Registration Act 2002].

(3) A claim that the landlord has failed to comply with subsection (6)(a) of section 19 may be made the subject of civil proceedings in like manner as any other claim in tort for breach of statutory duty; and if the claimant under that section fails to comply with subsection (6)(b)(i) of that section he shall not be entitled to exercise any of the rights otherwise exercisable by him under the overriding lease.

(4) An overriding lease—

(a) shall be deemed to be authorised as against the persons interested in any mortgage of the landlord's interest (however created or arising); and

(b) shall be binding on any such persons;

and if any such person is by virtue of such a mortgage entitled to possession of the documents of title relating to the landlord's interest—

(i) the landlord shall within one month of the execution of the lease deliver to that person the counterpart executed in pursuance of section 19(6)(b)(i); and

(ii) if he fails to do so, the instrument creating or evidencing the mortgage shall apply as if the obligation to deliver a counterpart were included in the terms of the mortgage as set out in that instrument.

(5) It is hereby declared—

(a) that the fact that an overriding lease takes effect subject to the relevant tenancy shall not constitute a breach of any covenant of the lease against subletting or parting with possession of the premises demised by the lease or any part of them; and

(b) that each of sections 16, 17 and 18 applies where the tenancy referred to in subsection (1) of that section is an overriding lease as it applies in other cases falling within that subsection.

(6) No tenancy shall be registrable under the Land Charges Act 1972 or be taken to be an estate contract within the meaning of that Act by reason of any right or obligation that may arise under section 19, and any right arising from a request made under that section shall not be [capable of falling within paragraph 2 of Schedule 1 or 3 to the Land Registration Act 2002]; but any such request shall be registrable under the Land Charges Act 1972, or may be the subject of a notice [under the Land Registration Act 2002], as if it were an estate contract.

(7) In this section—

(a) "mortgage" includes "charge"; and

(b) any expression which is also used in section 19 has the same meaning as in that section.

[1581]

NOTES

Sub-s (2): words in square brackets substituted by the Land Registration Act 2002, s 133, Sch 11, para 33(1), (3).

Sub-s (6): words in square brackets substituted by the Land Registration Act 2002, s 133, Sch 11, para 33(1), (4).

Forfeiture and disclaimer

21 Forfeiture or disclaimer limited to part only of demised premises

(1) Where—

(a) as a result of one or more assignments a person is the tenant of part only of the premises demised by a tenancy, and

(b) under a proviso or stipulation in the tenancy there is a right of re-entry or forfeiture for a breach of a tenant covenant of the tenancy, and

(c) the right is (apart from this subsection) exercisable in relation to that part and other land demised by the tenancy, the right shall nevertheless, in connection with a breach of any such covenant by that person, be taken to be a right exercisable only in relation to that part.

(2) Where—

(a) a company which is being wound up, or a trustee in bankruptcy, is as a result of one or more assignments the tenant of part only of the premises demised by a tenancy, and

(b) the liquidator of the company exercises his power under section 178 of the Insolvency Act 1986, or the trustee in bankruptcy exercises his power under section 315 of that Act, to disclaim property demised by the tenancy,

the power is exercisable only in relation to the part of the premises referred to in paragraph (a).

[1582]

Landlord's consent to assignments

22 (*Inserts the Landlord and Tenant Act 1927, s 19(1A)–(1E).*)

Supplemental

23 Effects of becoming subject to liability under, or entitled to benefit of, covenant etc

(1) Where as a result of an assignment a person becomes, by virtue of this Act, bound by or entitled to the benefit of a covenant, he shall not by virtue of this Act have any liability or rights under the covenant in relation to any time falling before the assignment.

(2) Subsection (1) does not preclude any such rights being expressly assigned to the person in question.

(3) Where as a result of an assignment a person becomes, by virtue of this Act, entitled to a right of re-entry contained in a tenancy, that right shall be exercisable in relation to any breach of a covenant of the tenancy occurring before the assignment as in relation to one occurring thereafter, unless by reason of any waiver or release it was not so exercisable immediately before the assignment.

[1583]

24 Effects of release from liability under, or loss of benefit of, covenant

(1) Any release of a person from a covenant by virtue of this Act does not affect any liability of his arising from a breach of the covenant occurring before the release.

(2) Where—

(a) by virtue of this Act a tenant is released from a tenant covenant of a tenancy, and

(b) immediately before the release another person is bound by a covenant of the tenancy imposing any liability or penalty in the event of a failure to comply with that tenant covenant,

then, as from the release of the tenant, that other person is released from the covenant mentioned in paragraph (b) to the same extent as the tenant is released from that tenant covenant.

(3) Where a person bound by a landlord or tenant covenant of a tenancy—

(a) assigns the whole or part of his interest in the premises demised by the tenancy, but

(b) is not released by virtue of this Act from the covenant (with the result that subsection (1) does not apply),

the assignment does not affect any liability of his arising from a breach of the covenant occurring before the assignment.

(4) Where by virtue of this Act a person ceases to be entitled to the benefit of a covenant, this does not affect any rights of his arising from a breach of the covenant occurring before he ceases to be so entitled.

[1584]

25 Agreement void if it restricts operation of the Act

(1) Any agreement relating to a tenancy is void to the extent that—

(a) it would apart from this section have effect to exclude, modify or otherwise frustrate the operation of any provision of this Act, or

(b) it provides for—

(i) the termination or surrender of the tenancy, or

(ii) the imposition on the tenant of any penalty, disability or liability,

in the event of the operation of any provision of this Act, or

(c) it provides for any of the matters referred to in paragraph (b)(i) or (ii) and does so (whether expressly or otherwise) in connection with, or in consequence of, the operation of any provision of this Act.

(2) To the extent that an agreement relating to a tenancy constitutes a covenant (whether absolute or qualified) against the assignment, or parting with the possession, of the premises demised by the tenancy or any part of them—

(a) the agreement is not void by virtue of subsection (1) by reason only of the fact that as such the covenant prohibits or restricts any such assignment or parting with possession; but

(b) paragraph (a) above does not otherwise affect the operation of that subsection in relation to the agreement (and in particular does not preclude its application to the agreement to the extent that it purports to regulate the giving of, or the making of any application for, consent to any such assignment or parting with possession).

(3) In accordance with section 16(1) nothing in this section applies to any agreement to the extent that it is an authorised guarantee agreement; but (without prejudice to the generality of subsection (1) above) an agreement is void to the extent that it is one falling within section 16(4)(a) or (b).

(4) This section applies to an agreement relating to a tenancy whether or not the agreement is—

(a) contained in the instrument creating the tenancy; or

(b) made before the creation of the tenancy.

[1585]

26 Miscellaneous savings etc

(1) Nothing in this Act is to be read as preventing—

(a) a party to a tenancy from releasing a person from a landlord covenant or a tenant covenant of the tenancy; or

(b) the parties to a tenancy from agreeing to an apportionment of liability under such a covenant.

(2) Nothing in this Act affects the operation of section 3(3A) of the Landlord and Tenant Act 1985 (preservation of former landlord's liability until tenant notified of new landlord).

(3) No apportionment which has become binding in accordance with section 10 shall be affected by any order or decision made under or by virtue of any enactment not contained in this Act which relates to apportionment.

[1586]

27 Notices for the purposes of the Act

(1) The form of any notice to be served for the purposes of section 8, 10 or 17 shall be prescribed by regulations made by the Lord Chancellor by statutory instrument.

(2) The regulations shall require any notice served for the purposes of section 8(1) or 10(1) ("the initial notice") to include—

(a) an explanation of the significance of the notice and the options available to the person on whom it is served;

(b) a statement that any objections to the proposed release, or (as the case may be) to the proposed binding effect of the apportionment, must be made by notice in writing served on the person or persons by whom the initial notice is served within the period of four weeks beginning with the day on which the initial notice is served; and

(c) an address in England and Wales to which any such objections may be sent.

(3) The regulations shall require any notice served for the purposes of section 17 to include an explanation of the significance of the notice.

(4) If any notice purporting to be served for the purposes of section 8(1), 10(1) or 17 is not in the prescribed form, or in a form substantially to the same effect, the notice shall not be effective for the purposes of section 8, section 10 or section 17 (as the case may be).

(5) Section 23 of the Landlord and Tenant Act 1927 shall apply in relation to the service of notices for the purposes of section 8, 10 or 17.

(6) Any statutory instrument made under this section shall be subject to annulment in pursuance of a resolution of either House of Parliament.

[1587]

NOTES

Regulations: the Landlord and Tenant (Covenants) Act 1995 (Notices) Regulations 1995, SI 1995/2964.

---

28 Interpretation

(1) In this Act (unless the context otherwise requires—

"assignment" includes equitable assignment and in addition (subject to section 11) assignment in breach of a covenant of a tenancy or by operation of law;

"authorised guarantee agreement" means an agreement which is an authorised guarantee agreement for the purposes of section 16;

"collateral agreement", in relation to a tenancy, means any agreement collateral to the tenancy, whether made before or after its creation;

"consent" includes licence;

"covenant" includes term, condition and obligation, and references to a covenant (or any description of covenant) of a tenancy include a covenant (or a covenant of that description) contained in a collateral agreement;

"landlord" and "tenant", in relation to a tenancy, mean the person for the time being entitled to the reversion expectant on the term of the tenancy and the person so entitled to that term respectively;

"landlord covenant", in relation to a tenancy, means a covenant falling to be complied with by the landlord of premises demised by the tenancy;

"new tenancy" means a tenancy which is a new tenancy for the purposes of section 1;

"reversion" means the interest expectant on the termination of a tenancy;

"tenancy" means any lease or other tenancy and includes—

(a) a sub-tenancy, and

(b) an agreement for a tenancy,

but does not include a mortgage term;

"tenant covenant", in relation to a tenancy, means a covenant falling to be complied with by the tenant of premises demised by the tenancy.

(2) For the purposes of any reference in this Act to a covenant falling to be complied with in relation to a particular part of the premises demised by a tenancy, a covenant falls to be so complied with if—

(a) it in terms applies to that part of the premises, or

(b) in its practical application it can be attributed to that part of the premises (whether or not it can also be so attributed to other individual parts of those premises).

(3) Subsection (2) does not apply in relation to covenants to pay money; and, for the purposes of any reference in this Act to a covenant falling to be complied with in relation to a particular part of the premises demised by a tenancy, a covenant of a tenancy which is a covenant to pay money falls to be so complied with if—

(a) the covenant in terms applies to that part; or

(b) the amount of the payment is determinable specifically by reference—

(i) to that part, or

(ii) to anything falling to be done by or for a person as tenant or occupier of that part (if it is a tenant covenant), or

(iii) to anything falling to be done by or for a person as landlord of that part (if it is a landlord covenant).

(4) Where two or more persons jointly constitute either the landlord or the tenant in relation to a tenancy, any reference in this Act to the landlord or the tenant is a reference to both or all of the persons who jointly constitute the landlord or the tenant, as the case may be (and accordingly nothing in section 13 applies in relation to the rights and liabilities of such persons between themselves).

(5) References in this Act to the assignment by a landlord of the reversion in the whole or part of the premises demised by a tenancy are to the assignment by him of the whole of his interest (as owner of the reversion) in the whole or part of those premises.

(6) For the purposes of this Act—

(a) any assignment (however effected) consisting in the transfer of the whole of the landlord's interest (as owner of the reversion) in any premises demised by a tenancy shall be treated as an assignment by the landlord of the reversion in those premises even if it is not effected by him; and

(b) any assignment (however effected) consisting in the transfer of the whole of the tenant's interest in any premises demised by a tenancy shall be treated as an assignment by the tenant of those premises even if it is not effected by him.

[1588]

29 Crown application

This Act binds the Crown.

[1589]

30 Consequential amendments and repeals

(1) The enactments specified in Schedule 1 are amended in accordance with that Schedule, the amendments being consequential on the provisions of this Act.

(2) The enactments specified in Schedule 2 are repealed to the extent specified.

(3) Subsections (1) and (2) do not affect the operation of—

(a) section 77 of, or Part IX or X of Schedule 2 to, the Law of Property Act 1925, or

(b) section 24(1)(b) or (2) of the Land Registration Act 1925,

in relation to tenancies which are not new tenancies.

(4) In consequence of this Act nothing in the following provisions, namely—

(a) sections 78 and 79 of the Law of Property Act 1925 (benefit and burden of covenants relating to land), and
(b) sections 141 and 142 of that Act (running of benefit and burden of covenants with reversion),

shall apply in relation to new tenancies.

(5) The Lord Chancellor may by order made by statutory instrument make, in the case of such enactments as may be specified in the order, such amendments or repeals in, or such modifications of, those enactments as appear to him to be necessary or expedient in consequence of any provision of this Act.

(6) Any statutory instrument made under subsection (5) shall be subject to annulment in pursuance of a resolution of either House of Parliament.

[1590]

31 Commencement

(1) The provisions of this Act come into force on such day as the Lord Chancellor may appoint by order made by statutory instrument.

(2) An order under this section may contain such transitional provisions and savings (whether or not involving the modification of any enactment) as appear to the Lord Chancellor necessary or expedient in connection with the provisions brought into force by the order.

[1591]

NOTES

Order: the Landlord and Tenant (Covenants) Act 1995 (Commencement) Order 1995, SI 1995/2963.

32 Short title and extent

(1) This Act may be cited as the Landlord and Tenant (Covenants) Act 1995.

(2) This Act extends to England and Wales only.

[1592]

(*Sch 1 amends the Trustee Act 1925, s 26, the Law of Property Act 1925, s 77, and the Landlord and Tenant Act 1954, ss 34, 35; Sch 2 contains repeals.*)

LAW REFORM (SUCCESSION) ACT 1995

(1995 c 41)

An Act to amend the law relating to the distribution of the estates of deceased persons and to make provision about the effect of the dissolution or annulment of marriages on wills and appointments of guardians

[8 November 1995]

Distribution of estates

1 Intestacy and partial intestacy

(1), (2) …

(3) Subsections (1) and (2) above have effect as respects an intestate dying on or after 1st January 1996.

(4) In section 50 of the 1925 Act (construction of documents), the references in subsection (1) to Part IV of that Act and to the foregoing provisions of that Part shall, in relation to an instrument inter vivos made or a will or codicil coming into operation on or after 1st January 1996 (but not in relation to instruments inter vivos made or wills or codicils coming into operation earlier), be construed as including references to this section.

(5) In this section "intestate" shall be construed in accordance with section 55(1)(vi) of the 1925 Act.

[1593]

NOTES

Sub-ss (1), (2): insert the Administration of Estates Act 1925, s 46(2A) at **[499]** and repeal ss 47(1)(iii), 49(1)(aa), (a), (2), (3) thereof.

2 (*Amends the Inheritance (Provision for Family and Dependants) Act 1975, ss 1, 3 at* **[778]**, **[780]**.)

Effect of dissolution or annulment of marriage

3 Effect of dissolution or annulment of marriage on will

(1) …

(2) Subsection (1) above has effect as respects a will made by a person dying on or after 1st January 1996 (regardless of the date of the will and the date of the dissolution or annulment).

[1594]

NOTES

Sub-s (1): amends the Wills Act 1837, s 18A at **[34]**.

4 Effect of dissolution or annulment of marriage on appointment of guardian

(1) …

(2) Subsection (1) above has effect as respects an appointment made by a person dying on or after 1st January 1996 (regardless of the date of the appointment and the date of the dissolution or annulment).

[1595]

NOTES

Sub-s (1): inserts the Children Act 1989, s 6(3A).

Supplemental

5 (*Introduces the Schedule to this Act.*)

6 Citation and extent

(1) This Act may be cited as the Law Reform (Succession) Act 1995.

(2) This Act extends to England and Wales only.

[1596]

(*Schedule contains repeals only.*)

DISABILITY DISCRIMINATION ACT 1995

(1995 c 50)

An Act to make it unlawful to discriminate against disabled persons in connection with employment, the provision of goods, facilities and services or the disposal or management of premises; to make provision about the employment of disabled persons; and to establish a National Disability Council

[8 November 1995]

PART I
DISABILITY

1 Meaning of "disability" and "disabled person"

(1) Subject to the provisions of Schedule 1, a person has a disability for the purposes of this Act [and Part III of the 2005 Order] if he has a physical or mental impairment which has a substantial and long-term adverse effect on his ability to carry out normal day-to-day activities.

(2) In this Act [and Part III of the 2005 Order] "disabled person" means a person who has a disability.

[1597]

NOTES

Sub-ss (1), (2): words in square brackets inserted, in relation to Northern Ireland, by the Special Educational Needs and Disability (Northern Ireland) Order 2005, SI 2005/1117, art 48(1), (2).

2 (*Outside the scope of this work.*)

3 Guidance

[(A1) The Secretary of State may issue guidance about matters to be taken into account in determining whether a person is a disabled person.]

(1) [Without prejudice to the generality of subsection (A1),] the Secretary of State may[, in particular,] issue guidance about the matters to be taken into account in determining—

(a) whether an impairment has a substantial adverse effect on a person's ability to carry out normal day-to-day activities; or

(b) whether such an impairment has a long-term effect.

(2) [Without prejudice to the generality of subsection (A1), guidance about the matters mentioned in subsection (1)] may, among other things, give examples of—

(a) effects which it would be reasonable, in relation to particular activities, to regard for purposes of this Act as substantial adverse effects;

(b) effects which it would not be reasonable, in relation to particular activities, to regard for such purposes as substantial adverse effects;

(c) substantial adverse effects which it would be reasonable to regard, for such purposes, as long-term;

(d) substantial adverse effects which it would not be reasonable to regard, for such purposes, as long-term.

(3) [An adjudicating body] determining, for any purpose of this Act [or Part III of the 2005 Order], whether [a person is a disabled person], shall take into account any guidance which appears to it to be relevant.

[(3A) "Adjudicating body" means—

(a) a court;

(b) a tribunal; and

(c) any other person who, or body which, may decide a claim under Part 4.]

(4) In preparing a draft of any guidance, the Secretary of State shall consult such persons as he considers appropriate.

(5) Where the Secretary of State proposes to issue any guidance, he shall publish a draft of it, consider any representations that are made to him about the draft and, if he thinks it appropriate, modify his proposals in the light of any of those representations.

(6) If the Secretary of State decides to proceed with any proposed guidance, he shall lay a draft of it before each House of Parliament.

(7) If, within the 40-day period, either House resolves not to approve the draft, the Secretary of State shall take no further steps in relation to the proposed guidance.

(8) If no such resolution is made within the 40-day period, the Secretary of State shall issue the guidance in the form of his draft.

(9) The guidance shall come into force on such date as the Secretary of State may appoint by order.

(10) Subsection (7) does not prevent a new draft of the proposed guidance from being laid before Parliament.

(11) The Secretary of State may—

(a) from time to time revise the whole or part of any guidance and re-issue it;

(b) by order revoke any guidance.

(12) In this section—

"40-day period", in relation to the draft of any proposed guidance, means—

(a) if the draft is laid before one House on a day later than the day on which it is laid before the other House, the period of 40 days beginning with the later of the two days, and

(b) in any other case, the period of 40 days beginning with the day on which the draft is laid before each House,

no account being taken of any period during which Parliament is dissolved or prorogued or during which both Houses are adjourned for more than 4 days; and

"guidance" means guidance issued by the Secretary of State under this section and includes guidance which has been revised and re-issued.

[1598]

NOTES

Sub-s (A1): inserted by the Disability Discrimination Act 2005, s 19(1), Sch 1, Pt 1, paras 1, 3(1), (2).

Sub-s (1): words in square brackets inserted by the Disability Discrimination Act 2005, s 19(1), Sch 1, Pt 1, paras 1, 3(1), (3).

Sub-s (2): words in square brackets substituted by the Disability Discrimination Act 2005, s 19(1), Sch 1, Pt 1, paras 1, 3(1), (4).

Sub-s (3): words in first pair of square brackets substituted by the Special Educational Needs and Disability Act 2001, s 38(1), (3); words in second pair of square brackets inserted, in relation to Northern Ireland, by the Special Educational Needs and Disability (Northern Ireland) Order 2005, SI 2005/1117, art 48(1), (4); words in third pair of square brackets substituted by the Disability Discrimination Act 2005, s 19(1), Sch 1, Pt 1, paras 1, 3(1), (5).

Sub-s (3A): inserted by the Special Educational Needs and Disability Act 2001, s 38(1), (4).

See further: corresponding amendments to those made to sub-ss (A1), (1)–(3) above by the Disability Discrimination Act 2005 have been made in relation to Northern Ireland: the Disability Discrimination (Northern Ireland) Order 2006, SI 2006/312, art 19(1), Sch 1, paras 1, 3.

Orders: the Disability Discrimination (Guidance on the Definition of Disability) Appointed Day Order 2006, SI 2006/1005; the Disability Discrimination (Guidance on the Definition of Disability) Revocation Order 2006, SI 2006/1007.

3A–18E ((*Pt II*) *Outside the scope of this work.*)

PART III
DISCRIMINATION IN OTHER AREAS

Goods, facilities and services

19 Discrimination in relation to goods, facilities and services

(1) It is unlawful for a provider of services to discriminate against a disabled person—

(a) in refusing to provide, or deliberately not providing, to the disabled person any service which he provides, or is prepared to provide, to members of the public;

(b) in failing to comply with any duty imposed on him by section 21 in circumstances in which the effect of that failure is to make it impossible or unreasonably difficult for the disabled person to make use of any such service;

(c) in the standard of service which he provides to the disabled person or the manner in which he provides it to him; or

(d) in the terms on which he provides a service to the disabled person.

(2) For the purposes of this section and sections 20 [to 21ZA]—

(a) the provision of services includes the provision of any goods or facilities;

(b) a person is "a provider of services" if he is concerned with the provision, in the United Kingdom, of services to the public or to a section of the public; and

(c) it is irrelevant whether a service is provided on payment or without payment.

(3) The following are examples of services to which this section and sections 20 and 21 apply—

(a) access to and use of any place which members of the public are permitted to enter;

(b) access to and use of means of communication;

(c) access to and use of information services;

(d) accommodation in a hotel, boarding house or other similar establishment;

(e) facilities by way of banking or insurance or for grants, loans, credit or finance;

(f) facilities for entertainment, recreation or refreshment;

(g) facilities provided by employment agencies or under section 2 of the Employment and Training Act 1973;

(h) the services of any profession or trade, or any local or other public authority.

(4) In the case of an act which constitutes discrimination by virtue of section 55, this section also applies to discrimination against a person who is not disabled.

[(4A) Subsection (1) does not apply to anything that is governed by Regulation (EC) No 1107/2006 of the European Parliament and of the Council of 5 July 2006 concerning the rights of disabled persons and persons with reduced mobility when travelling by air.]

[(5) Regulations may provide for subsection (1) and section 21(1), (2) and (4) not to apply, or to apply only to a prescribed extent, in relation to a service of a prescribed description.]

[(5A) Nothing in this section or sections 20 to 21A applies to the provision of a service in relation to which discrimination is unlawful under Part 4.]

(6) …

[1599]

NOTES

Sub-s (2): words in square brackets substituted by the Disability Discrimination Act 2005, s 19(1), Sch 1, Pt 1, paras 1, 13(1), (2).

Sub-s (4A): inserted by SI 2007/1895, reg 8.

Sub-s (5): substituted by the Disability Discrimination Act 2005, s 19(1), Sch 1, Pt 1, paras 1, 13(1), (3).

Sub-ss (5), (6): substituted, in relation to Northern Ireland, by the Special Educational Needs and Disability (Northern Ireland) Order 2005, SI 2005/1117, art 48(1), (6).

Sub-s (5A) (as inserted by the Special Educational Needs and Disability Act 2001, s 38(1), (6)): substituted by the Disability Discrimination Act 2005, s 19(1), Sch 1, Pt 1, paras 1, 13(1), (4).

Sub-s (6): repealed by the Special Educational Needs and Disability Act 2001, ss 38(1), (5)(b), 42(6), Sch 9.

See further: corresponding amendments to those made to sub-ss (2), (5), (6) above by the Disability Discrimination Act 2005, have been made in relation to Northern Ireland: the Disability Discrimination (Northern Ireland) Order 2006, SI 2006/312, art 19(1), Sch 1, paras 1, 12.

20 Meaning of "discrimination"

(1) For the purposes of section 19, a provider of services discriminates against a disabled person if—

(a) for a reason which relates to the disabled person's disability, he treats him less favourably than he treats or would treat others to whom that reason does not or would not apply; and

(b) he cannot show that the treatment in question is justified.

(2) For the purposes of section 19, a providers of services also discriminates against a disabled person if—

(a) he fails to comply with a section 21 duty imposed on him in relation to the disabled person; and

(b) he cannot show that his failure to comply with that duty is justified.

(3) For the purposes of this section, treatment is justified only if—

(a) in the opinion of the provider of services, one or more of the conditions mentioned in subsection (4) are satisfied; and

(b) it is reasonable, in all the circumstances of the case, for him to hold that opinion.

(4) The conditions are that—

(a) in any case, the treatment is necessary in order not to endanger the health or safety of any person (which may include that of the disabled person);

(b) in any case, the disabled person is incapable of entering into an enforceable agreement, or of giving an informed consent, and for that reason the treatment is reasonable in that case;

(c) in a case falling within section 19(1)(a), the treatment is necessary because the provider of services would otherwise be unable to provide the service to members of the public;

(d) in a case falling within section 19(1)(c) or (d), the treatment is necessary in order for the provider of services to be able to provide the service to the disabled person or to other members of the public;

(e) in a case falling within section 19(1)(d), the difference in the terms on which the service is provided to the disabled person and those on which it is provided to other members of the public reflects the greater cost to the provider of services in providing the service to the disabled person.

(5) Any increase in the cost of providing a service to a disabled person which results from compliance by a provider of services with a section 21 duty shall be disregarded for the purposes of subsection (4)(e).

(6) Regulations may make provision, for purposes of this section, as to circumstances in which—

(a) it is reasonable for a provider of services to hold the opinion mentioned in subsection (3)(a);

(b) it is not reasonable for a provider of services to hold that opinion.

(7) Regulations may make provision for subsection (4)(b) not to apply in prescribed circumstances where—

(a) a person is acting for a disabled person under a power of attorney;

(b) functions conferred by or under [the Mental Capacity Act 2005] are exercisable in relation to a disabled person's property or affairs; or

[(c) powers are exercisable in relation to a disabled person's property or affairs in consequence of the appointment, under the law of Scotland, of a guardian, tutor or judicial factor].

(8) Regulations may make provision, for purposes of this section, as to circumstances (other than those mentioned in subsection (4)) in which treatment is to be taken to be justified.

(9) In subsections (3), (4) and (8) "treatment" includes failure to comply with a section 21 duty.

[1600]

NOTES

Sub-s (7): words in square brackets in para (b) substituted by the Mental Capacity Act 2005, s 67(1), Sch 6, para 41; para (c) substituted by the Disability Discrimination Act 2005, s 19(1), Sch 1, Pt 1, paras 1, 14.

Regulations: the Disability Discrimination (Service Providers and Public Authorities Carrying Out Functions) Regulations 2005, SI 2005/2901.

21 Duty of providers of services to make adjustments

(1) Where a provider of services has a practice, policy or procedure which makes it impossible or unreasonably difficult for disabled persons to make use of a service which he provides, or is prepared to provide, to other members of the public, it is his duty to take such steps as it is reasonable, in all the circumstances of the case, for him to have to take in order to change that practice, policy or procedure so that it no longer has that effect.

(2) Where a physical feature (for example, one arising from the design or construction of a building or the approach or access to premises) makes it impossible or unreasonably difficult for disabled persons to make use of such a service, it is the duty of the provider of that service to take such steps as it is reasonable, in all the circumstances of the case, for him to have to take in order to—

(a) remove the feature;
(b) alter it so that it no longer has that effect;
(c) provide a reasonable means of avoiding the feature; or
(d) provide a reasonable alternative method of making the service in question available to disabled persons.

(3) Regulations may prescribe—

(a) matters which are to be taken into account in determining whether any provision of a kind mentioned in subsection (2)(c) or (d) is reasonable; and
(b) categories of providers of services to whom subsection (2) does not apply.

(4) Where an auxiliary aid or service (for example, the provision of information on audio tape or of a sign language interpreter) would—

(a) enable disabled persons to make use of a service which a provider of services provides, or is prepared to provide, to members of the public, or
(b) facilitate the use by disabled persons of such a service,

it is the duty of the provider of that service to take such steps as it is reasonable, in all the circumstances of the case, for him to have to take in order to provide that auxiliary aid or service.

(5) Regulations may make provision, for the purposes of this section—

(a) as to circumstances in which it is reasonable for a provider of services to have to take steps of a prescribed description;
(b) as to circumstances in which it is not reasonable for a provider of services to have to take steps of a prescribed description;
(c) as to what is to be included within the meaning of "practice, policy or procedure";
(d) as to what is not to be included within the meaning of that expression;
(e) as to things which are to be treated as physical features;
(f) as to things which are not to be treated as such features;
(g) as to things which are to be treated as auxiliary aids or services;
(h) as to things which are not to be treated as auxiliary aids or services.

(6) Nothing in this section requires a provider of services to take any steps which would fundamentally alter the nature of the service in question or the nature of his trade, profession or business.

(7) Nothing in this section requires a provider of services to take any steps which would cause him to incur expenditure exceeding the prescribed maximum.

(8) Regulations under subsection (7) may provide for the prescribed maximum to be calculated by reference to—

(a) aggregate amounts of expenditure incurred in relation to different cases;
(b) prescribed periods;
(c) services of a prescribed description;
(d) premises of a prescribed description; or
(e) such other criteria as may be prescribed.

(9) Regulations may provide, for the purposes of subsection (7), for expenditure incurred by one provider of services to be treated as incurred by another.

(10) This section imposes duties only for the purpose of determining whether a provider of services has discriminated against a disabled person; and accordingly a breach of any such duty is not actionable as such.

[1601]

NOTES

Regulations: the Disability Discrimination (Providers of Services) (Adjustment of Premises) Regulations 2001, SI 2001/3253; the Disability Discrimination (Service Providers and Public Authorities Carrying Out Functions) Regulations 2005, SI 2005/2901; the Disability Discrimination (Transport Vehicles) Regulations 2005, SI 2005/3190.

[21ZA Application of sections 19 to 21 to transport vehicles

(1) Section 19(1) (a), (c) and (d) do not apply in relation to a case where the service is a transport service and, as provider of that service, the provider of services discriminates against a disabled person—

(a) in not providing, or in providing, him with a vehicle; or
(b) in not providing, or in providing, him with services when he is travelling in a vehicle provided in the course of the transport service.

(2) For the purposes of section 21(1), (2) and (4), it is never reasonable for a provider of services, as a provider of a transport service—

(a) to have to take steps which would involve the alteration or removal of a physical feature of a vehicle used in providing the service;

(b) to have to take steps which would—

(i) affect whether vehicles are provided in the course of the service or what vehicles are so provided, or

(ii) where a vehicle is provided in the course of the service, affect what happens in the vehicle while someone is travelling in it.

(3) Regulations may provide for subsection (1) or (2) not to apply, or to apply only to a prescribed extent, in relation to vehicles of a prescribed description.

(4) In this section—

"transport service" means a service which (to any extent) involves transport of people by vehicle;

"vehicle" means a vehicle for transporting people by land, air or water, and includes (in particular)—

(a) a vehicle not having wheels, and

(b) a vehicle constructed or adapted to carry passengers on a system using a mode of guided transport;

"guided transport" has the same meaning as in the Transport and Works Act 1992.]

[1602]

NOTES

Commencement: 30 June 2005.

Inserted by the Disability Discrimination Act 2005, s 5.

See further: a corresponding amendment has been made in relation to Northern Ireland: the Disability Discrimination (Northern Ireland) Order 2006, SI 2006/312, art 7.

Regulations: the Disability Discrimination (Transport Vehicles) Regulations 2005, SI 2005/3190.

[21A Employment services

(1) In [this Act], "employment services" means—

(a) vocational guidance;

(b) vocational training; or

(c) services to assist a person to obtain or retain employment, or to establish himself as self-employed.

(2) It is unlawful for a provider of employment services, in relation to such services, to subject to harassment a disabled person—

(a) to whom he is providing such services, or

(b) who has requested him to provide such services;

and section 3B (meaning of "harassment") applies for the purposes of this subsection as it applies for the purposes of Part 2.

(3) In their application to employment services, the preceding provisions of this Part have effect as follows.

(4) Section 19 has effect as if—

(a) after subsection (1)(a), there were inserted the following paragraph—

"(aa) in failing to comply with a duty imposed on him by subsection (1) of section 21 in circumstances in which the effect of that failure is to place the disabled person at a substantial disadvantage in comparison with persons who are not disabled in relation to the provision of the service;";

(b) in subsection (1)(b), for "section 21" there were substituted "subsection (2) or (4) of section 21";

[(c) in subsection (2), for "sections 20 to 21ZA" there is substituted "sections 20 to 21A"].

(5) Section 20 has effect as if—

(a) after subsection (1), there were inserted the following subsection—

"(1A) For the purposes of section 19, a provider of services also discriminates against a disabled person if he fails to comply with a duty imposed on him by subsection (1) of section 21 in relation to the disabled person.";

(b) in subsection (2)(a), for "a section 21 duty imposed" there were substituted "a duty imposed by subsection (2) or (4) of section 21";

(c) after subsection (3), there were inserted the following subsection—

"(3A) But treatment of a disabled person cannot be justified under subsection (3) if it amounts to direct discrimination falling within section 3A(5).".

(6) Section 21 has effect as if—

(a) in subsection (1), for "makes it impossible or unreasonably difficult for disabled persons to make use of" there were substituted "places disabled persons at a substantial disadvantage in comparison with persons who are not disabled in relation to the provision of";

(b) after subsection (1), there were inserted the following subsection—

"(1A) In subsection (1), "practice, policy or procedure" includes a provision or criterion.".]

[1603]

NOTES

Commencement 3 July 2003 (for certain purposes); 1 October 2004 (for remaining purposes).

Inserted by SI 2003/1673, regs 3(1), 19(1).

Sub-s (1): words in square brackets substituted by the Disability Discrimination Act 2005, s 19(1), Sch 1, Pt 1, paras 1, 15(1), (2).

Sub-s (4): para (c) substituted by the Disability Discrimination Act 2005, s 19(1), Sch 1, Pt 1, paras 1, 15(1), (3).

See further: corresponding amendments to those made to sub-ss (1), (4) above by the Disability Discrimination Act 2005, have been made in relation to Northern Ireland: the Disability Discrimination (Northern Ireland) Order 2006, SI 2006/312, art 19(1), Sch 1, paras 1, 13.

[Public authorities

21B Discrimination by public authorities

(1) It is unlawful for a public authority to discriminate against a disabled person in carrying out its functions.

(2) In this section, and sections 21D and 21E, "public authority"—

(a) includes any person certain of whose functions are functions of a public nature; but
(b) does not include any person mentioned in subsection (3).

(3) The persons are—

(a) either House of Parliament;
(b) a person exercising functions in connection with proceedings in Parliament;
(c) the Security Service;
(d) the Secret Intelligence Service;
(e) the Government Communications Headquarters; and
(f) a unit, or part of a unit, of any of the naval, military or air forces of the Crown which is for the time being required by the Secretary of State to assist the Government Communications Headquarters in carrying out its functions.

(4) In relation to a particular act, a person is not a public authority by virtue only of subsection (2)(a) if the nature of the act is private.

(5) Regulations may provide for a person of a prescribed description to be treated as not being a public authority for purposes of this section and sections 21D and 21E.

(6) In the case of an act which constitutes discrimination by virtue of section 55, subsection (1) of this section also applies to discrimination against a person who is not disabled.

(7) Subsection (1)—

(a) does not apply to anything which is unlawful under any provision of this Act other than subsection (1); and
(b) does not, subject to subsections (8) and (9), apply to anything which would be unlawful under any such provision but for the operation of any provision in or made under this Act.

(8) Subsection (1) does apply in relation to a public authority's function of appointing a person to, and in relation to a public authority's functions with respect to a person as holder of, an office or post if—

(a) none of the conditions specified in section 4C(3) is satisfied in relation to the office or post; and
(b) sections 4D and 4E would apply in relation to an appointment to the office or post if any of those conditions was satisfied.

(9) Subsection (1) does apply in relation to a public authority's functions with respect to a person as candidate or prospective candidate for election to, and in relation to a public authority's functions with respect to a person as elected holder of, an office or post if—

(a) the office or post is not membership of a House of Parliament, the Scottish Parliament, the National Assembly for Wales or an authority mentioned in section 15A(1);
(b) none of the conditions specified in section 4C(3) is satisfied in relation to the office or post; and
(c) sections 4D and 4E would apply in relation to an appointment to the office or post if—
    (i) any of those conditions was satisfied, and
    (ii) section 4F(1) (but not section 4C(5)) was omitted.

(10) Subsections (8) and (9)—

(a) shall not be taken to prejudice the generality of subsection (1); but

(b) are subject to section 21C(5).]

[1604]

NOTES

Commencement: 4 December 2006.

Inserted, together with preceding cross-heading, by the Disability Discrimination Act 2005, s 2.

See further: a corresponding amendment has been made in relation to Northern Ireland: the Disability Discrimination (Northern Ireland) Order 2006, SI 2006/312, art 4.

[21C Exceptions from section 21B(1)

(1) Section 21B(1) does not apply to—

(a) a judicial act (whether done by a court, tribunal or other person); or

(b) an act done on the instructions, or on behalf, of a person acting in a judicial capacity.

(2) Section 21B(1) does not apply to any act of, or relating to, making, confirming or approving—

(a) an Act, an Act of the Scottish Parliament[, a Measure or Act of the National Assembly for Wales] or an Order in Council; or

(b) an instrument made under an Act, or under an Act of the Scottish Parliament, [or under a Measure or Act of the National Assembly for Wales,] by—

(i) a Minister of the Crown;

(ii) a member of the Scottish Executive; or

(iii) the [Welsh Ministers, the First Minister for Wales or the Counsel General to the Welsh Assembly Government].

(3) Section 21B(1) does not apply to any act of, or relating to, imposing conditions or requirements of a kind falling within section 59(1)(c).

(4) Section 21B(1) does not apply to—

(a) a decision not to institute criminal proceedings;

(b) where such a decision is made, an act done for the purpose of enabling the decision to be made;

(c) a decision not to continue criminal proceedings; or

(d) where such a decision is made—

(i) an act done for the purpose of enabling the decision to be made; or

(ii) an act done for the purpose of securing that the proceedings are not continued.

(5) Section 21B(1) does not apply to an act of a prescribed description.]

[1605]

NOTES

Commencement: 4 December 2006.

Inserted by the Disability Discrimination Act 2005, s 2.

Sub-s (2): words in first and second pairs of square brackets inserted and words in third pair of square brackets substituted by SI 2007/1388, art 3, Sch 1, paras 47, 50.

See further: a corresponding amendment has been made in relation to Northern Ireland: the Disability Discrimination (Northern Ireland) Order 2006, SI 2006/312, art 4.

[21D Meaning of "discrimination" in section 21B

(1) For the purposes of section 21B(1), a public authority discriminates against a disabled person if—

(a) for a reason which relates to the disabled person's disability, it treats him less favourably than it treats or would treat others to whom that reason does not or would not apply; and

(b) it cannot show that the treatment in question is justified under subsection (3), (5) or (7)(c).

(2) For the purposes of section 21B(1), a public authority also discriminates against a disabled person if—

(a) it fails to comply with a duty imposed on it by section 21E in circumstances in which the effect of that failure is to make it—

(i) impossible or unreasonably difficult for the disabled person to receive any benefit that is or may be conferred, or

(ii) unreasonably adverse for the disabled person to experience being subjected to any detriment to which a person is or may be subjected,

by the carrying-out of a function by the authority; and

(b) it cannot show that its failure to comply with that duty is justified under subsection (3), (5) or (7)(c).

(3) Treatment, or a failure to comply with a duty, is justified under this subsection if—

(a) in the opinion of the public authority, one or more of the conditions specified in subsection (4) are satisfied; and

(b) it is reasonable, in all the circumstances of the case, for it to hold that opinion.

(4) The conditions are—

(a) that the treatment, or non-compliance with the duty, is necessary in order not to endanger the health or safety of any person (which may include that of the disabled person);

(b) that the disabled person is incapable of entering into an enforceable agreement, or of giving an informed consent, and for that reason the treatment, or non-compliance with the duty, is reasonable in the particular case;

(c) that, in the case of treatment mentioned in subsection (1), treating the disabled person equally favourably would in the particular case involve substantial extra costs and, having regard to resources, the extra costs in that particular case would be too great;

(d) that the treatment, or non-compliance with the duty, is necessary for the protection of rights and freedoms of other persons.

(5) Treatment, or a failure to comply with a duty, is justified under this subsection if the acts of the public authority which give rise to the treatment or failure are a proportionate means of achieving a legitimate aim.

(6) Regulations may make provision, for purposes of this section, as to circumstances in which it is, or as to circumstances in which it is not, reasonable for a public authority to hold the opinion mentioned in subsection (3)(a).

(7) Regulations may—

(a) amend or omit a condition specified in subsection (4) or make provision for it not to apply in prescribed circumstances;

(b) amend or omit subsection (5) or make provision for it not to apply in prescribed circumstances;

(c) make provision for purposes of this section (in addition to any provision for the time being made by subsections (3) to (5)) as to circumstances in which treatment, or a failure to comply with a duty, is to be taken to be justified.]

[1606]

NOTES

Commencement: 30 June 2005 (for the purpose of exercising any power to make regulations); 4 December 2006 (for remaining purposes).

Inserted by the Disability Discrimination Act 2005, s 2.

See further: a corresponding amendment has been made in relation to Northern Ireland: the Disability Discrimination (Northern Ireland) Order 2006, SI 2006/312, art 4.

Regulations: the Disability Discrimination (Service Providers and Public Authorities Carrying Out Functions) Regulations 2005, SI 2005/2901.

[21E Duties for purposes of section 21D(2) to make adjustments

(1) Subsection (2) applies where a public authority has a practice, policy or procedure which makes it—

(a) impossible or unreasonably difficult for disabled persons to receive any benefit that is or may be conferred, or

(b) unreasonably adverse for disabled persons to experience being subjected to any detriment to which a person is or may be subjected,

by the carrying-out of a function by the authority.

(2) It is the duty of the authority to take such steps as it is reasonable, in all the circumstances of the case, for the authority to have to take in order to change that practice, policy or procedure so that it no longer has that effect.

(3) Subsection (4) applies where a physical feature makes it—

(a) impossible or unreasonably difficult for disabled persons to receive any benefit that is or may be conferred, or

(b) unreasonably adverse for disabled persons to experience being subjected to any detriment to which a person is or may be subjected,

by the carrying-out of a function by a public authority.

(4) It is the duty of the authority to take such steps as it is reasonable, in all the circumstances of the case, for the authority to have to take in order to—

(a) remove the feature;

(b) alter it so that it no longer has that effect;

(c) provide a reasonable means of avoiding the feature; or

(d) adopt a reasonable alternative method of carrying out the function.

(5) Regulations may prescribe—

(a) matters which are to be taken into account in determining whether any provision of a kind mentioned in subsection (4)(c) or (d) is reasonable;
(b) categories of public authorities to whom subsection (4) does not apply.

(6) Subsection (7) applies where an auxiliary aid or service would—
(a) enable disabled persons to receive, or facilitate the receiving by disabled persons of, any benefit that is or may be conferred, or
(b) reduce the extent to which it is adverse for disabled persons to experience being subjected to any detriment to which a person is or may be subjected,

by the carrying-out of a function by a public authority.

(7) It is the duty of the authority to take such steps as it is reasonable, in all the circumstances of the case, for the authority to have to take in order to provide that auxiliary aid or service.

(8) Regulations may make provision, for purposes of this section—
(a) as to circumstances in which it is, or as to circumstances in which it is not, reasonable for a public authority to have to take steps of a prescribed description;
(b) as to steps which it is always, or as to steps which it is never, reasonable for a public authority to have to take;
(c) as to what is, or as to what is not, to be included within the meaning of "practice, policy or procedure";
(d) as to things which are, or as to things which are not, to be treated as physical features;
(e) as to things which are, or as to things which are not, to be treated as auxiliary aids or services.

(9) Nothing in this section requires a public authority to take any steps which, apart from this section, it has no power to take.

(10) This section imposes duties only for the purposes of determining whether a public authority has, for the purposes of section 21B(1), discriminated against a disabled person; and accordingly a breach of any such duty is not actionable as such.]

[1607]

NOTES

Commencement: 30 June 2005 (for the purpose of exercising any power to make regulations); 4 December 2006 (for remaining purposes).

Inserted by the Disability Discrimination Act 2005, s 2.

See further: a corresponding amendment has been made in relation to Northern Ireland: the Disability Discrimination (Northern Ireland) Order 2006, SI 2006/312, art 4.

Regulations: the Disability Discrimination (Service Providers and Public Authorities Carrying Out Functions) Regulations 2005, SI 2005/2901.

[Private clubs etc

21F Discrimination by private clubs etc

(1) This section applies to any association of persons (however described, whether corporate or unincorporate, and whether or not its activities are carried on for profit) if—
(a) it has twenty-five or more members;
(b) admission to membership is regulated by its constitution and is so conducted that the members do not constitute a section of the public within the meaning of section 19(2); and
(c) it is not an organisation to which section 13 applies.

(2) It is unlawful for an association to which this section applies, in the case of a disabled person who is not a member of the association, to discriminate against him—
(a) in the terms on which it is prepared to admit him to membership; or
(b) by refusing or deliberately omitting to accept his application for membership.

(3) It is unlawful for an association to which this section applies, in the case of a disabled person who is a member, or associate, of the association, to discriminate against him—
(a) in the way it affords him access to a benefit, facility or service;
(b) by refusing or deliberately omitting to afford him access to a benefit, facility or service;
(c) in the case of a member—
  (i) by depriving him of membership, or
  (ii) by varying the terms on which he is a member;
(d) in the case of an associate—
  (i) by depriving him of his rights as an associate, or
  (ii) by varying those rights; or
(e) in either case, by subjecting him to any other detriment.

(4) It is unlawful for an association to which this section applies to discriminate against a disabled person—
(a) in the way it affords him access to a benefit, facility or service,

(b) by refusing or deliberately omitting to afford him access to a benefit, facility or service, or

(c) by subjecting him to any other detriment,

in his capacity as a guest of the association.

(5) It is unlawful for an association to which this section applies to discriminate against a disabled person—

(a) in the terms on which it is prepared to invite him, or permit a member or associate to invite him, to be a guest of the association;

(b) by refusing or deliberately omitting to invite him to be a guest of the association; or

(c) by not permitting a member or associate to invite him to be a guest of the association.

(6) It is unlawful for an association to which this section applies to discriminate against a disabled person in failing in prescribed circumstances to comply with a duty imposed on it under section 21H.

(7) In the case of an act which constitutes discrimination by virtue of section 55, this section also applies to discrimination against a person who is not disabled.]

[1608]

NOTES

Commencement: 10 October 2005 (for the purpose of exercising any power to make regulations); 5 December 2005 (for remaining purposes).

Inserted, together with preceding cross-heading, by the Disability Discrimination Act 2005, s 12.

See further: a corresponding amendment has been made in relation to Northern Ireland: the Disability Discrimination (Northern Ireland) Order 2006, SI 2006/312, art 13.

Regulations: the Disability Discrimination (Private Clubs etc) Regulations 2005, SI 2005/3258.

[21G Meaning of "discrimination"

(1) For the purposes of section 21F, an association discriminates against a disabled person if—

(a) for a reason which relates to the disabled person's disability, the association treats him less favourably than it treats or would treat others to whom that reason does not or would not apply; and

(b) it cannot show that the treatment in question is justified.

(2) For the purposes of subsection (1), treatment is justified only if—

(a) in the opinion of the association, one or more of the conditions mentioned in subsection (3) are satisfied; and

(b) it is reasonable, in all the circumstances, for it to hold that opinion.

(3) The conditions are that—

(a) the treatment is necessary in order not to endanger the health or safety of any person (which may include that of the disabled person);

(b) the disabled person is incapable of entering into an enforceable agreement, or giving an informed consent, and for that reason the treatment is reasonable in that case;

(c) in a case falling within section 21F(2)(a), (3)(a), (c)(ii), (d)(ii) or (e), (4)(a) or (c) or (5)(a), the treatment is necessary in order for the association to be able to afford members, associates or guests of the association, or the disabled person, access to a benefit, facility or service;

(d) in a case falling within section 21F(2)(b), (3)(b), (c)(i) or (d)(i), (4)(b) or (5)(b) or (c), the treatment is necessary because the association would otherwise be unable to afford members, associates or guests of the association access to a benefit, facility or service;

(e) in a case falling within section 21F(2)(a), the difference between—

(i) the terms on which membership is offered to the disabled person, and

(ii) those on which it is offered to other persons,

reflects the greater cost to the association of affording the disabled person access to a benefit, facility or service;

(f) in a case falling within section 21F(3)(a), (c)(ii) or (d)(ii) or (4)(a), the difference between—

(i) the association's treatment of the disabled person, and

(ii) its treatment of other members or (as the case may be) other associates or other guests of the association,

reflects the greater cost to the association of affording the disabled person access to a benefit, facility or service;

(g) in a case falling within section 21F(5)(a), the difference between—

(i) the terms on which the disabled person is invited, or permitted to be invited, to be a guest of the association, and

(ii) those on which other persons are invited, or permitted to be invited, to be guests of the association,

reflects the greater cost to the association of affording the disabled person access to a benefit, facility or service.

(4) Any increase in the cost of affording a disabled person access to a benefit, facility or service which results from compliance with a duty under section 21H shall be disregarded for the purposes of subsection (3)(e), (f) and (g).

(5) Regulations may—

(a) make provision, for purposes of this section, as to circumstances in which it is, or as to circumstances in which it is not, reasonable for an association to hold the opinion mentioned in subsection (2)(a);

(b) amend or omit a condition specified in subsection (3) or make provision for it not to apply in prescribed circumstances;

(c) make provision as to circumstances (other than any for the time being mentioned in subsection (3)) in which treatment is to be taken to be justified for the purposes of subsection (1).

(6) For the purposes of section 21F, an association also discriminates against a disabled person if—

(a) it fails to comply with a duty under section 21H imposed on it in relation to the disabled person; and

(b) it cannot show that its failure to comply with that duty is justified.

(7) Regulations may make provision as to circumstances in which failure to comply with a duty under section 21H is to be taken to be justified for the purposes of subsection (6).]

[1609]

NOTES

Commencement: 30 June 2005 (for the purpose of exercising any power to make regulations); 5 December 2005 (for remaining purposes).

Inserted by the Disability Discrimination Act 2005, s 12.

See further: a corresponding amendment has been made in relation to Northern Ireland: the Disability Discrimination (Northern Ireland) Order 2006, SI 2006/312, art 13.

Regulations: the Disability Discrimination (Private Clubs etc) Regulations 2005, SI 2005/3258.

[21H Duty to make adjustments

(1) Regulations may make provision imposing on an association to which section 21F applies—

(a) a duty to take steps for a purpose relating to a policy, practice or procedure of the association, or a physical feature, which adversely affects disabled persons who—

(i) are, or might wish to become, members or associates of the association, or

(ii) are, or are likely to become, guests of the association;

(b) a duty to take steps for the purpose of making an auxiliary aid or service available to any such disabled persons.

(2) Regulations under subsection (1) may (in particular)—

(a) make provision as to the cases in which a duty is imposed;

(b) make provision as to the steps which a duty requires to be taken;

(c) make provision as to the purpose for which a duty requires steps to be taken.

(3) Any duty imposed under this section is imposed only for the purpose of determining whether an association has, for the purposes of section 21F, discriminated against a disabled person; and accordingly a breach of any such duty is not actionable as such.]

[1610]

NOTES

Commencement: 30 June 2005 (for the purpose of exercising any power to make regulations); 5 December 2005 (for remaining purposes).

Inserted by the Disability Discrimination Act 2005, s 12.

See further: a corresponding amendment has been made in relation to Northern Ireland: the Disability Discrimination (Northern Ireland) Order 2006, SI 2006/312, art 13.

Regulations: the Disability Discrimination (Private Clubs etc) Regulations 2005, SI 2005/3258.

[21J "Member", "associate" and "guest"

(1) For the purposes of sections 21F to 21H and this section—

(a) a person is a member of an association to which section 21F applies if he belongs to it by virtue of his admission to any sort of membership provided for by its constitution (and is not merely a person with certain rights under its constitution by virtue of his membership of some other association), and references to membership of an association shall be construed accordingly;

(b) a person is an associate of an association to which section 21F applies if, not being a member of it, he has under its constitution some or all of the rights enjoyed by members (or would have apart from any provision in its constitution authorising the refusal of those rights in particular cases).

(2) References in sections 21F to 21H to a guest of an association include a person who is a guest of the association by virtue of an invitation issued by a member or associate of the association and permitted by the association.

(3) Regulations may make provision, for purposes of sections 21F to 21H, as to circumstances in which a person is to be treated as being, or as to circumstances in which a person is to be treated as not being, a guest of an association.]

[1611]

NOTES

Commencement: 5 December 2005.

Inserted by the Disability Discrimination Act 2005, s 12.

See further: a corresponding amendment has been made in relation to Northern Ireland: the Disability Discrimination (Northern Ireland) Order 2006, SI 2006/312, art 13.

Premises

22 Discrimination in relation to premises

(1) It is unlawful for a person with power to dispose of any premises to discriminate against a disabled person—

- (a) in the terms on which he offers to dispose of those premises to the disabled person;
- (b) by refusing to dispose of those premises to the disabled person; or
- (c) in his treatment of the disabled person in relation to any list of persons in need of premises of that description.

(2) Subsection (1) does not apply to a person who owns an estate or interest in the premises and wholly occupies them unless, for the purpose of disposing of the premises, he—

- (a) uses the services of an estate agent, or
- (b) publishes an advertisement or causes an advertisement to be published.

(3) It is unlawful for a person managing any premises to discriminate against a disabled person occupying those premises—

- (a) in the way he permits the disabled person to make use of any benefits or facilities;
- (b) by refusing or deliberately omitting to permit the disabled person to make use of any benefits or facilities; or
- (c) by evicting the disabled person, or subjecting him to any other detriment.

[(3A) Regulations may make provision, for purposes of subsection (3)—

- (a) as to who is to be treated as being, or as to who is to be treated as not being, a person who manages premises;
- (b) as to who is to be treated as being, or as to who is to be treated as not being, a person occupying premises.]

(4) It is unlawful for any person whose licence or consent is required for the disposal of any premises comprised in, or (in Scotland) the subject of, a tenancy to discriminate against a disabled person by withholding his licence or consent for the disposal of the premises to the disabled person.

(5) Subsection (4) applies to tenancies created before as well as after the passing of this Act.

(6) In this section—

"advertisement" includes every form of advertisement or notice, whether to the public or not;

"dispose", in relation to premises, includes granting a right to occupy the premises, and, in relation to premises comprised in, or (in Scotland) the subject of, a tenancy, includes—

- (a) assigning the tenancy, and
- (b) sub-letting or parting with possession of the premises or any part of the premises;

and "disposal" shall be construed accordingly;

"estate agent" means a person who, by way of profession or trade, provides services for the purpose of finding premises for persons seeking to acquire them or assisting in the disposal of premises; and

"tenancy" means a tenancy created—

- (a) by a lease or sub-lease,
- (b) by an agreement for a lease or sub-lease,
- (c) by a tenancy agreement, or
- (d) in pursuance of any enactment.

(7) In the case of an act which constitutes discrimination by virtue of section 55, this section also applies to discrimination against a person who is not disabled.

(8) This section applies only in relation to premises in the United Kingdom.

[1612]

NOTES

Sub-s (3A): inserted by the Disability Discrimination Act 2005, s 19(1), Sch 1, Pt 1, paras 1, 16.

See further: a corresponding amendment to that made to sub-s (3A) above has been made in relation to Northern Ireland: the Disability Discrimination (Northern Ireland) Order 2006, SI 2006/312, art 19(1), Sch 1, paras 1, 14.

Regulations: the Disability Discrimination (Premises) Regulations 2006, SI 2006/887.

[22A Commonholds

(1) It is unlawful for any person whose licence or consent is required for the disposal of an interest in a commonhold unit by the unit-holder to discriminate against a disabled person by withholding his licence or consent for the disposal of the interest in favour of, or to, the disabled person.

(2) Where it is not possible for an interest in a commonhold unit to be disposed of by the unit-holder unless some other person is a party to the disposal of the interest, it is unlawful for that other person to discriminate against a disabled person by deliberately not being a party to the disposal of the interest in favour of, or to, the disabled person.

(3) Regulations may provide for subsection (1) or (2) not to apply, or to apply only, in cases of a prescribed description.

(4) Regulations may make provision, for purposes of this section—

(a) as to what is, or as to what is not, to be included within the meaning of "dispose" (and "disposal");

(b) as to what is, or as to what is not, to be included within the meaning of "interest in a commonhold unit".

(5) In this section "commonhold unit", and "unit-holder" in relation to such a unit, have the same meaning as in Part 1 of the Commonhold and Leasehold Reform Act 2002.

(6) In the case of an act which constitutes discrimination by virtue of section 55, this section also applies to discrimination against a person who is not disabled.

(7) This section applies only in relation to premises in England and Wales.]

[1613]

NOTES

Commencement: 30 June 2005 (for the purpose of exercising any power to make regulations); 4 December 2006 (for remaining purposes).

Inserted by the Disability Discrimination Act 2005, s 19(1), Sch 1, Pt 1, paras 1, 17.

Regulations: the Disability Discrimination (Premises) Regulations 2006, SI 2006/887.

23 Exemption for small dwellings

(1) Where the conditions mentioned in subsection (2) are satisfied, subsection (1), (3) or (as the case may be) (4) of section 22 does not apply.

(2) The conditions are that—

(a) the relevant occupier resides, and intends to continue to reside, on the premises;

(b) the relevant occupier shares accommodation on the premises with persons who reside on the premises and are not members of his household;

(c) the shared accommodation is not storage accommodation or a means of access; and

(d) the premises are small premises.

(3) For the purposes of this section, premises are "small premises" if they fall within subsection (4) or (5).

(4) Premises fall within this subsection if—

(a) only the relevant occupier and members of his household reside in the accommodation occupied by him;

(b) the premises comprise, in addition to the accommodation occupied by the relevant occupier, residential accommodation for at least one other household;

(c) the residential accommodation for each other household is let, or available for letting, on a separate tenancy or similar agreement; and

(d) there are not normally more than two such other households.

(5) Premises fall within this subsection if there is not normally residential accommodation on the premises for more than six persons in addition to the relevant occupier and any members of his household.

(6) For the purposes of this section "the relevant occupier" means—

(a) in a case falling within section 22(1), the person with power to dispose of the premises, or a near relative of his;

[(aa) in a case falling within section 22(3), the person managing the premises, or a near relative of his;]

(b) in a case falling within section 22(4), the person whose licence or consent is required for the disposal of the premises, or a near relative of his.

(7) For the purposes of this section—

"near relative" means a person's spouse [or civil partner], partner, parent, child, grandparent, grandchild, or brother or sister (whether of full or half blood or [by marriage or civil partnership)]; and

["partner" means the other member of a couple consisting of—

(a) a man and a woman who are not married to each other but are living together as husband and wife, or

(b) two people of the same sex who are not civil partners of each other but are living together as if they were civil partners].

[1614]

NOTES

Sub-s (6): para (aa) inserted by the Disability Discrimination Act 2005, s 19(1), Sch 1, Pt 1, paras 1, 18.

Sub-s (7): in definition "near relative" words in first pair of square brackets inserted and words in second pair of square brackets substituted, and definition "partner" substituted by the Civil Partnership Act 2004, s 261(1), Sch 27, para 150.

See further: a corresponding amendment to that made to sub-s (6) above by the Disability Discrimination Act 2005, has been made in relation to Northern Ireland: the Disability Discrimination (Northern Ireland) Order 2006, SI 2006/312, art 19(1), Sch 1, paras 1, 15.

24 Meaning of "discrimination"

(1) For the purposes of [sections 22 and 22A], a person ("A") discriminates against a disabled person if—

(a) for a reason which relates to the disabled person's disability, he treats him less favourably than he treats or would treat others to whom that reason does not or would not apply; and

(b) he cannot show that the treatment in question is justified.

(2) For the purposes of this section, treatment is justified only if—

(a) in A's opinion, one or more of the conditions mentioned in subsection (3) are satisfied; and

(b) it is reasonable, in all the circumstances of the case, for him to hold that opinion.

(3) The conditions are that—

(a) in any case, the treatment is necessary in order not to endanger the health or safety of any person (which may include that of the disabled person);

(b) in any case, the disabled person is incapable of entering into an enforceable agreement, or of giving an informed consent, and for that reason the treatment is reasonable in that case;

(c) in a case falling within section 22(3)(a), the treatment is necessary in order for the disabled person or the occupiers of other premises forming part of the building to make use of the benefit or facility;

(d) in a case falling within section 22(3)(b), the treatment is necessary in order for the occupiers of other premises forming part of the building to make use of the benefit or facility;

[(e) in a case to which subsection (3A) applies, the terms are less favourable in order to recover costs which—

(i) as a result of the disabled person having a disability, are incurred in connection with the disposal of the premises, and

(ii) are not costs incurred in connection with taking steps to avoid liability under section 24G(1);

(f) in a case to which subsection (3B) applies, the disabled person is subjected to the detriment in order to recover costs which—

(i) as a result of the disabled person having a disability, are incurred in connection with the management of the premises, and

(ii) are not costs incurred in connection with taking steps to avoid liability under section 24A(1) or 24G(1)].

[(3A) This subsection applies to a case if—

(a) the case falls within section 22(1)(a);

(b) the premises are to let;

(c) the person with power to dispose of the premises is a controller of them; and

(d) the proposed disposal of the premises would involve the disabled person becoming a person to whom they are let.

(3B) This subsection applies to a case if—

(a) the case falls within section 22(3)(c);

(b) the detriment is not eviction;

(c) the premises are let premises;

(d) the person managing the premises is a controller of them; and

(e) the disabled person is a person to whom the premises are let or, although not a person to whom they are let, is lawfully under the letting an occupier of them.

(3C) Section 24G(3) and (4) apply for the purposes of subsection (3A) as for those of section 24G; and section 24A(3) and (4) apply for the purposes of subsection (3B) as for those of section 24A.]

(4) Regulations may make provision, for purposes of this section, as to circumstances in which—

(a) it is reasonable for a person to hold the opinion mentioned in subsection 2(a);

(b) it is not reasonable for a person to hold that opinion.

[(4A) Regulations may make provision for the condition specified in subsection (3)(b) not to apply in prescribed circumstances.]

(5) Regulations may make provision, for purposes of this section, as to circumstances (other than those mentioned in subsection (3)) in which treatment is to be taken to be justified.

[1615]

NOTES

Sub-s (1): words in square brackets substituted by the Disability Discrimination Act 2005, s 19(1), Sch 1, Pt 1, paras 1, 19(1), (2).

Sub-s (3): paras (e), (f) inserted by the Disability Discrimination Act 2005, s 19(1), Sch 1, Pt 1, paras 1, 19(1), (3).

Sub-ss (3A)–(3C): inserted by the Disability Discrimination Act 2005, s 19(1), Sch 1, Pt 1, paras 1, 19(1), (4).

Sub-s (4A): inserted by the Disability Discrimination Act 2005, s 19(1), Sch 1, Pt 1, paras 1, 19(1), (5).

See further: corresponding amendments to those made to sub-ss (3), (3A)–(3C), (4A) above by the Disability Discrimination Act 2005, have been made in relation to Northern Ireland: the Disability Discrimination (Northern Ireland) Order 2006, SI 2006/312, art 19(1), Sch 1, paras 1, 16.

See further, in relation to circumstances in which mental incapacity justification does not apply: the Disability Discrimination (Premises) Regulations 2006, SI 2006/887, reg 2.

Regulations: the Disability Discrimination (Premises) Regulations 2006, SI 2006/887.

[24A Let premises: discrimination in failing to comply with duty

(1) It is unlawful for a controller of let premises to discriminate against a disabled person—

(a) who is a person to whom the premises are let; or

(b) who, although not a person to whom the premises are let, is lawfully under the letting an occupier of the premises.

(2) For the purposes of subsection (1), a controller of let premises discriminates against a disabled person if—

(a) he fails to comply with a duty under section 24C or 24D imposed on him by reference to the disabled person; and

(b) he cannot show that failure to comply with the duty is justified (see section 24K).

(3) For the purposes of this section and sections 24B to 24F, a person is a controller of let premises if he is—

(a) a person by whom the premises are let; or

(b) a person who manages the premises.

(4) For the purposes of this section and sections 24B to 24F—

(a) "let" includes sub-let; and

(b) premises shall be treated as let by a person to another where a person has granted another a contractual licence to occupy them.

(5) This section applies only in relation to premises in the United Kingdom.]

[1616]

NOTES

Commencement: 4 December 2006.

Inserted by the Disability Discrimination Act 2005, s 13.

See further: a corresponding amendment has been made in relation to Northern Ireland: the Disability Discrimination (Northern Ireland) Order 2006, SI 2006/312, art 14.

[24B Exceptions to section 24A(1)

(1) Section 24A(1) does not apply if—

(a) the premises are, or have at any time been, the only or principal home of an individual who is a person by whom they are let; and

(b) since entering into the letting—

(i) the individual has not, and

(ii) where he is not the sole person by whom the premises are let, no other person by whom they are let has,

used for the purpose of managing the premises the services of a person who, by profession or trade, manages let premises.

(2) Section 24A(1) does not apply if the premises are of a prescribed description.

(3) Where the conditions mentioned in section 23(2) are satisfied, section 24A(1) does not apply.

(4) For the purposes of section 23 "the relevant occupier" means, in a case falling within section 24A(1), a controller of the let premises, or a near relative of his; and "near relative" has here the same meaning as in section 23.]

[1617]

NOTES

Commencement: 4 December 2006.

Inserted by the Disability Discrimination Act 2005, s 13.

See further: a corresponding amendment has been made in relation to Northern Ireland: the Disability Discrimination (Northern Ireland) Order 2006, SI 2006/312, art 14.

[24C Duty for purposes of section 24A(2) to provide auxiliary aid or service

(1) Subsection (2) applies where—

(a) a controller of let premises receives a request made by or on behalf of a person to whom the premises are let;

(b) it is reasonable to regard the request as a request that the controller take steps in order to provide an auxiliary aid or service; and

(c) either the first condition, or the second condition, is satisfied.

(2) It is the duty of the controller to take such steps as it is reasonable, in all the circumstances of the case, for him to have to take in order to provide the auxiliary aid or service (but see section 24E(1)).

(3) The first condition is that—

(a) the auxiliary aid or service—

(i) would enable a relevant disabled person to enjoy, or facilitate such a person's enjoyment of, the premises, but

(ii) would be of little or no practical use to the relevant disabled person concerned if he were neither a person to whom the premises are let nor an occupier of them; and

(b) it would, were the auxiliary aid or service not to be provided, be impossible or unreasonably difficult for the relevant disabled person concerned to enjoy the premises.

(4) The second condition is that—

(a) the auxiliary aid or service—

(i) would enable a relevant disabled person to make use, or facilitate such a person's making use, of any benefit, or facility, which by reason of the letting is one of which he is entitled to make use, but

(ii) would be of little or no practical use to the relevant disabled person concerned if he were neither a person to whom the premises are let nor an occupier of them; and

(b) it would, were the auxiliary aid or service not to be provided, be impossible or unreasonably difficult for the relevant disabled person concerned to make use of any benefit, or facility, which by reason of the letting is one of which he is entitled to make use.]

[1618]

NOTES

Commencement: 4 December 2006.

Inserted by the Disability Discrimination Act 2005, s 13.

See further: a corresponding amendment has been made in relation to Northern Ireland: the Disability Discrimination (Northern Ireland) Order 2006, SI 2006/312, art 14.

[24D Duty for purposes of section 24A(2) to change practices, terms etc

(1) Subsection (3) applies where—

(a) a controller of let premises has a practice, policy or procedure which has the effect of making it impossible, or unreasonably difficult, for a relevant disabled person—

(i) to enjoy the premises, or

(ii) to make use of any benefit, or facility, which by reason of the letting is one of which he is entitled to make use, or

(b) a term of the letting has that effect,

and (in either case) the conditions specified in subsection (2) are satisfied.

(2) Those conditions are—

(a) that the practice, policy, procedure or term would not have that effect if the relevant disabled person concerned did not have a disability;

(b) that the controller receives a request made by or on behalf of a person to whom the premises are let; and

(c) that it is reasonable to regard the request as a request that the controller take steps in order to change the practice, policy, procedure or term so as to stop it having that effect.

(3) It is the duty of the controller to take such steps as it is reasonable, in all the circumstances of the case, for him to have to take in order to change the practice, policy, procedure or term so as to stop it having that effect (but see section 24E(1)).]

[1619]

NOTES

Commencement: 4 December 2006.

Inserted by the Disability Discrimination Act 2005, s 13.

See further: a corresponding amendment has been made in relation to Northern Ireland: the Disability Discrimination (Northern Ireland) Order 2006, SI 2006/312, art 14.

[24E Sections 24C and 24D: supplementary and interpretation

(1) For the purposes of sections 24C and 24D, it is never reasonable for a controller of let premises to have to take steps consisting of, or including, the removal or alteration of a physical feature.

(2) Sections 24C and 24D impose duties only for the purpose of determining whether a person has, for the purposes of section 24A, discriminated against another; and accordingly a breach of any such duty is not actionable as such.

(3) In sections 24C and 24D "relevant disabled person", in relation to let premises, means a particular disabled person—

(a) who is a person to whom the premises are let; or

(b) who, although not a person to whom the premises are let, is lawfully under the letting an occupier of the premises.

(4) For the purposes of sections 24C and 24D, the terms of a letting of premises include the terms of any agreement which relates to the letting of the premises.]

[1620]

NOTES

Commencement: 4 December 2006.

Inserted by the Disability Discrimination Act 2005, s 13.

See further: a corresponding amendment has been made in relation to Northern Ireland: the Disability Discrimination (Northern Ireland) Order 2006, SI 2006/312, art 14.

[24F Let premises: victimisation of persons to whom premises are let

(1) Where a duty under section 24C or 24D is imposed on a controller of let premises by reference to a person who, although not a person to whom the premises are let, is lawfully under the letting an occupier of the premises, it is unlawful for a controller of the let premises to discriminate against a person to whom the premises are let.

(2) For the purposes of subsection (1), a controller of the let premises discriminates against a person to whom the premises are let if—

(a) the controller treats that person ("T") less favourably than he treats or would treat other persons whose circumstances are the same as T's; and

(b) he does so because of costs incurred in connection with taking steps to avoid liability under section 24A(1) for failure to comply with the duty.

(3) In comparing T's circumstances with those of any other person for the purposes of subsection (2)(a), the following (as well as the costs' having been incurred) shall be disregarded—

(a) the making of the request that gave rise to the imposition of the duty; and

(b) the disability of each person who—

(i) is a disabled person or a person who has had a disability, and

(ii) is a person to whom the premises are let or, although not a person to whom the premises are let, is lawfully under the letting an occupier of the premises.]

[1621]

NOTES

Commencement: 4 December 2006.

Inserted by the Disability Discrimination Act 2005, s 13.

See further: a corresponding amendment has been made in relation to Northern Ireland: the Disability Discrimination (Northern Ireland) Order 2006, SI 2006/312, art 14.

[24G Premises that are to let: discrimination in failing to comply with duty

(1) Where—

(a) a person has premises to let, and
(b) a disabled person is considering taking a letting of the premises,

it is unlawful for a controller of the premises to discriminate against the disabled person.

(2) For the purposes of subsection (1), a controller of premises that are to let discriminates against a disabled person if—
(a) he fails to comply with a duty under section 24J imposed on him by reference to the disabled person; and
(b) he cannot show that failure to comply with the duty is justified (see section 24K).

(3) For the purposes of this section and sections 24H and 24J, a person is a controller of premises that are to let if he is—
(a) a person who has the premises to let; or
(b) a person who manages the premises.

(4) For the purposes of this section and sections 24H and 24J—
(a) "let" includes sub-let;
(b) premises shall be treated as to let by a person to another where a person proposes to grant another a contractual licence to occupy them;

and references to a person considering taking a letting of premises shall be construed accordingly.

(5) This section applies only in relation to premises in the United Kingdom.]

[1622]

NOTES

Commencement: 4 December 2006.

Inserted by the Disability Discrimination Act 2005, s 13.

See further: a corresponding amendment has been made in relation to Northern Ireland: the Disability Discrimination (Northern Ireland) Order 2006, SI 2006/312, art 14.

[24H Exceptions to section 24G(1)

(1) Section 24G(1) does not apply in relation to premises that are to let if the premises are, or have at any time been, the only or principal home of an individual who is a person who has them to let and—
(a) the individual does not use, and
(b) where he is not the sole person who has the premises to let, no other person who has the premises to let uses,

the services of an estate agent (within the meaning given by section 22(6)) for the purposes of letting the premises.

(2) Section 24G(1) does not apply if the premises are of a prescribed description.

(3) Where the conditions mentioned in section 23(2) are satisfied, section 24G(1) does not apply.

(4) For the purposes of section 23 "the relevant occupier" means, in a case falling within section 24G(1), a controller of the premises that are to let, or a near relative of his; and "near relative" has here the same meaning as in section 23.]

[1623]

NOTES

Commencement: 4 December 2006.

Inserted by the Disability Discrimination Act 2005, s 13.

See further: a corresponding amendment has been made in relation to Northern Ireland: the Disability Discrimination (Northern Ireland) Order 2006, SI 2006/312, art 14.

[24J Duties for purposes of section 24G(2)

(1) Subsection (2) applies where—
(a) a controller of premises that are to let receives a request made by or on behalf of a relevant disabled person;
(b) it is reasonable to regard the request as a request that the controller take steps in order to provide an auxiliary aid or service;
(c) the auxiliary aid or service—
  (i) would enable the relevant disabled person to become, or facilitate his becoming, a person to whom the premises are let, but
  (ii) would be of little or no practical use to him if he were not considering taking a letting of the premises; and
(d) it would, were the auxiliary aid or service not to be provided, be impossible or unreasonably difficult for the relevant disabled person to become a person to whom the premises are let.

(2) It is the duty of the controller to take such steps as it is reasonable, in all the circumstances of the case, for the controller to have to take in order to provide the auxiliary aid or service (but see subsection (5)).

(3) Subsection (4) applies where—

(a) a controller of premises that are to let has a practice, policy or procedure which has the effect of making it impossible, or unreasonably difficult, for a relevant disabled person to become a person to whom the premises are let;

(b) the practice, policy or procedure would not have that effect if the relevant disabled person did not have a disability;

(c) the controller receives a request made by or on behalf of the relevant disabled person; and

(d) it is reasonable to regard the request as a request that the controller take steps in order to change the practice, policy or procedure so as to stop it having that effect.

(4) It is the duty of the controller to take such steps as it is reasonable, in all the circumstances of the case, for him to have to take in order to change the practice, policy or procedure so as to stop it having that effect (but see subsection (5)).

(5) For the purposes of this section, it is never reasonable for a controller of premises that are to let to have to take steps consisting of, or including, the removal or alteration of a physical feature.

(6) In this section "relevant disabled person", in relation to premises that are to let, means a particular disabled person who is considering taking a letting of the premises.

(7) This section imposes duties only for the purpose of determining whether a person has, for the purposes of section 24G, discriminated against another; and accordingly a breach of any such duty is not actionable as such.]

[1624]

NOTES

Commencement: 4 December 2006.

Inserted by the Disability Discrimination Act 2005, s 13.

See further: a corresponding amendment has been made in relation to Northern Ireland: the Disability Discrimination (Northern Ireland) Order 2006, SI 2006/312, art 14.

[24K Let premises and premises that are to let: justification

(1) For the purposes of sections 24A(2) and 24G(2), a person's failure to comply with a duty is justified only if—

(a) in his opinion, a condition mentioned in subsection (2) is satisfied; and

(b) it is reasonable, in all the circumstances of the case, for him to hold that opinion.

(2) The conditions are—

(a) that it is necessary to refrain from complying with the duty in order not to endanger the health or safety of any person (which may include that of the disabled person concerned);

(b) that the disabled person concerned is incapable of entering into an enforceable agreement, or of giving informed consent, and for that reason the failure is reasonable.

(3) Regulations may—

(a) make provision, for purposes of this section, as to circumstances in which it is, or as to circumstances in which it is not, reasonable for a person to hold the opinion mentioned in subsection (1)(a);

(b) amend or omit a condition specified in subsection (2) or make provision for it not to apply in prescribed circumstances;

(c) make provision, for purposes of this section, as to circumstances (other than any for the time being mentioned in subsection (2)) in which a failure is to be taken to be justified.]

[1625]

NOTES

Commencement: 30 June 2005 (for the purpose of exercising any power to make regulations); 4 December 2006 (for remaining purposes).

Inserted by the Disability Discrimination Act 2005, s 13.

See further: a corresponding amendment has been made in relation to Northern Ireland: the Disability Discrimination (Northern Ireland) Order 2006, SI 2006/312, art 14.

See further, in relation to circumstances in which mental incapacity justification does not apply: the Disability Discrimination (Premises) Regulations 2006, SI 2006/887, reg 2.

Regulations: the Disability Discrimination (Premises) Regulations 2006, SI 2006/887.

[24L Sections 24 to 24K: power to make supplementary provision

(1) Regulations may make provision, for purposes of sections 24(3A) and (3B) and 24A to 24K—

(a) as to circumstances in which premises are to be treated as let to a person;

(b) as to circumstances in which premises are to be treated as not let to a person;
(c) as to circumstances in which premises are to be treated as being, or as not being, to let;
(d) as to who is to be treated as being, or as to who is to be treated as not being, a person who, although not a person to whom let premises are let, is lawfully under the letting an occupier of the premises;
(e) as to who is to be treated as being, or as to who is to be treated as not being, a person by whom premises are let;
(f) as to who is to be treated as having, or as to who is to be treated as not having, premises to let;
(g) as to who is to be treated as being, or as to who is to be treated as not being, a person who manages premises;
(h) as to things which are, or as to things which are not, to be treated as auxiliary aids or services;
(i) as to what is, or as to what is not, to be included within the meaning of "practice, policy or procedure";
(j) as to circumstances in which it is, or as to circumstances in which it is not, reasonable for a person to have to take steps of a prescribed description;
(k) as to steps which it is always, or as to steps which it is never, reasonable for a person to have to take;
(l) as to circumstances in which it is, or as to circumstances in which it is not, reasonable to regard a request as being of a particular kind;
(m) as to things which are, or as to things which are not, to be treated as physical features;
(n) as to things which are, or as to things which are not, to be treated as alterations of physical features.

(2) Regulations under subsection (1)(a) may (in particular) provide for premises to be treated as let to a person where they are a commonhold unit of which he is a unit-holder; and "commonhold unit", and "unit-holder" in relation to such a unit, have here the same meaning as in Part 1 of the Commonhold and Leasehold Reform Act 2002.

(3) The powers under subsections (1)(j) and (k) are subject to sections 24E(1) and 24J(5).]

[1626]

NOTES

Commencement: 30 June 2005 (for the purpose of exercising any power to make regulations); 4 December 2006 (for remaining purposes).

Inserted by the Disability Discrimination Act 2005, s 13.

See further: a corresponding amendment has been made in relation to Northern Ireland: the Disability Discrimination (Northern Ireland) Order 2006, SI 2006/312, art 14.

Regulations: the Disability Discrimination (Premises) Regulations 2006, SI 2006/887.

[24M Premises provisions do not apply where other provisions operate

(1) Sections 22 to 24L do not apply—
(a) in relation to the provision of premises by a provider of services where he provides the premises in providing services to members of the public;
(b) in relation to the provision, in the course of a Part 2 relationship, of premises by the regulated party to the other party;
(c) in relation to the provision of premises to a student or prospective student—
  (i) by a responsible body within the meaning of Chapter 1 or 2 of Part 4, or
  (ii) by an authority in discharging any functions mentioned in section 28F(1); or
(d) to anything which is unlawful under section 21F or which would be unlawful under that section but for the operation of any provision in or made under this Act.

(2) Subsection (1)(a) has effect subject to any prescribed exceptions.

(3) In subsection (1)(a) "provider of services", and providing services, have the same meaning as in section 19.

(4) For the purposes of subsection (1)(b)—
(a) "Part 2 relationship" means a relationship during the course of which an act of discrimination against, or harassment of, one party to the relationship by the other party to it is unlawful under sections 4 to 15C; and
(b) in relation to a Part 2 relationship, "regulated party" means the party whose acts of discrimination, or harassment, are made unlawful by sections 4 to 15C

(5) In subsection (1)(c) "student" includes pupil.]

[1627]

NOTES

Commencement: 4 December 2006.

Inserted by the Disability Discrimination Act 2005, s 19(1), Sch 1, Pt 1, paras 1, 20.

PART I STATUTES

See further: a corresponding amendment has been made in relation to Northern Ireland: the Disability Discrimination (Northern Ireland) Order 2006, SI 2006/312, art 19(1), Sch 1, paras 1, 17.

Enforcement, etc

25 Enforcement, remedies and procedure

(1) A claim by any person that another person—

(a) has discriminated against him in a way which is unlawful under this Part; or

(b) is by virtue of section 57 or 58 to be treated as having discriminated against him in such a way,

may be made the subject of civil proceedings in the same way as any other claim in tort or (in Scotland) in reparation for breach of statutory duty.

(2) For the avoidance of doubt it is hereby declared that damages in respect of discrimination in a way which is unlawful under this Part may include compensation for injury to feelings whether or not they include compensation under any other head.

(3) Proceedings in England and Wales shall be brought only in a county court.

(4) Proceedings in Scotland shall be brought only in a sheriff court.

(5) The remedies available in such proceedings are those which are available in the High Court or (as the case may be) the Court of Session.

(6) Part II of Schedule 3 makes further provision about the enforcement of this Part and about procedure.

[(6A) Subsection (1) does not apply in relation to a claim by a person that another person—

(a) has discriminated against him in relation to the provision under a group insurance arrangement of facilities by way of insurance; or

(b) is by virtue of section 57 or 58 to be treated as having discriminated against him in relation to the provision under such an arrangement of such facilities.]

[[(7) Subsection (1) does not apply in relation to a claim by a person that another person—

(a) has discriminated against him in relation to the provision of employment services; or

(b) is by virtue of section 57 or 58 to be treated as having discriminated against him in relation to the provision of employment services.

(8) A claim—

(a) of the kind referred to in subsection (6A) or (7), or

(b) by a person that another—

(i) has subjected him to harassment in a way which is unlawful under section 21A(2), or

(ii) is by virtue of section 57 or 58 to be treated as having subjected him to harassment in such a way,

may be presented as a complaint to an employment tribunal.]

(9) Section 17A(1A) to (7) and paragraphs 3 and 4 of Schedule 3 apply in relation to a complaint under subsection (8) as if it were a complaint under section 17A(1) (and paragraphs 6 to 8 of Schedule 3 do not apply in relation to such a complaint).]

[1628]

NOTES

Sub-s (6A): inserted by the Disability Discrimination Act 2005, s 11(2).

Sub-ss (7), (8): inserted by SI 2003/1673, regs 3(1), 19(2); substituted by the Disability Discrimination Act 2005, s 19(1), Sch 1, Pt 1, paras 1, 21.

Sub-s (9): inserted by SI 2003/1673, regs 3(1), 19(2).

See further: corresponding amendments to those made to sub-ss (6A), (7), (8) above by the Disability Discrimination Act 2005, have been made in relation to Northern Ireland: the Disability Discrimination (Northern Ireland) Order 2006, SI 2006/312, arts 12(2), 19(1), Sch 1, paras 1, 18.

26–49 (*Ss 26–28, ss 28A–49F* (*Pts IV, V, VA*) *outside the scope of this work.*)

[PART 5B
IMPROVEMENTS TO DWELLING HOUSES]

NOTES

Inserted by the Disability Discrimination Act 2005, s 16(1).

[49G Improvements to let dwelling houses

(1) This section applies in relation to a lease of a dwelling house if—

(a) the tenancy is not a protected tenancy, a statutory tenancy or a secure tenancy,

(b) the tenant or any other person who lawfully occupies or is intended lawfully to occupy the premises is a disabled person,
(c) the person mentioned in paragraph (b) occupies or is intended to occupy the premises as his only or principal home,
(d) the tenant is entitled under the lease to make improvements to the premises with the consent of the landlord, and
(e) the tenant applies to the landlord for his consent to make a relevant improvement.

(2) If the consent of the landlord is unreasonably withheld it must be taken to have been given.

(3) Where the tenant applies in writing for the consent—
(a) if the landlord refuses to give consent, he must give the tenant a written statement of the reason why the consent was withheld;
(b) if the landlord neither gives nor refuses to give consent within a reasonable time, consent must be taken to have been withheld.

(4) If the landlord gives consent to the making of an improvement subject to a condition which is unreasonable, the consent must be taken to have been unreasonably withheld.

(5) In any question as to whether—
(a) the consent of the landlord was unreasonably withheld, or
(b) a condition imposed by the landlord is unreasonable,

it is for the landlord to show that it was not.

(6) If the tenant fails to comply with a reasonable condition imposed by the landlord on the making of a relevant improvement, the failure is to be treated as a breach by the tenant of an obligation of his tenancy.

(7) An improvement to premises is a relevant improvement if, having regard to the disability which the disabled person mentioned in subsection (1)(b) has, it is likely to facilitate his enjoyment of the premises.

(8) Subsections (2) to (6) apply to a lease only to the extent that provision of a like nature is not made by the lease.

(9) In this section—
"improvement" means any alteration in or addition to premises and includes—
(a) any addition to or alteration in landlord's fittings and fixtures,
(b) any addition or alteration connected with the provision of services to the premises,
(c) the erection of a wireless or television aerial, and
(d) the carrying out of external decoration;
"lease" includes a sub-lease or other tenancy, and "landlord" and "tenant" must be construed accordingly;
"protected tenancy" has the same meaning as in section 1 of the Rent Act 1977;
"statutory tenancy" must be construed in accordance with section 2 of that Act;
"secure tenancy" has the same meaning as in section 79 of the Housing Act 1985.]

[1629]

NOTES

Commencement: 4 December 2006.
Inserted by the Disability Discrimination Act 2005, s 16(1).

49H–59A (*Ss 49H, 49I, ss 50–59A (Pts VI, VII) outside the scope of this work.*)

PART VIII
MISCELLANEOUS

60–67B (*Outside the scope of this work.*)

68 Interpretation

(1) In this Act—
["the 2005 Order" means the Special Educational Needs and Disability (Northern Ireland) Order 2005;]
"accessibility certificate" means a certificate issued under section 41(1)(a);
"act" includes a deliberate omission;
"approval certificate" means a certificate issued under section 42(4);
. . .
"conciliation officer" means a person designated under section 211 of the Trade Union and Labour Relations (Consolidation) Act 1992;
["criminal investigation" has the meaning given in subsection (1A);]
[“criminal proceedings” includes—

(*a*) *proceedings on dealing summarily with a charge under the Army Act 1955 or the Air Force Act 1955 or on summary trial under the Naval Discipline Act 1957;*

(*b*) *proceedings before a summary appeal court constituted under any of those Acts;*

(*c*) *proceedings before a court-martial constituted under any of those Acts or a disciplinary court constituted under section 52G of the Naval Discipline Act 1957;*

(*d*) *proceedings before the Courts-Martial Appeal Court; and*

(*e*) *proceedings before a Standing Civilian Court;]*

["criminal proceedings" includes service law proceedings (as defined by section 324(5) of the Armed Forces Act 2006);]

"employment" means, subject to any prescribed provision, employment under a contract of service or of apprenticeship or a contract personally to do any work, and related expressions are to be construed accordingly;

["employment at an establishment in Great Britain" is to be construed in accordance with subsections (2) to (4A);]

["employment services" has the meaning given in section 21A(1);]

"enactment" includes subordinate legislation and any Order in Council[, and … includes an enactment comprised in, or in an instrument made under, an Act of the Scottish Parliament];

["Great Britain" includes such of the territorial waters of the United Kingdom as are adjacent to Great Britain;]

["group insurance arrangement" means an arrangement between an employer and another for the provision by the other of facilities by way of insurance to the employer's employees or to any class of those employees;]

"licensing authority"[, except in [sections 36, 36A, 37A and 38],] means —

(a) in relation to the area to which the Metropolitan Public Carriage Act 1869 applies, the Secretary of State or the holder of any office for the time being designated by the Secretary of State; or

(b) in relation to any other area in England and Wales, the authority responsible for licensing taxis in that area;

…

["Minister of the Crown" includes the Treasury and the Defence Council;]

"occupational pension scheme" has the same meaning as in the Pension Schemes Act 1993;

"premises" includes land of any description;

"prescribed" means prescribed by regulations[, except in section 28D (where it has the meaning given by section 28D(17))];

"profession" includes any vocation or occupation;

"provider of services" has the meaning given in section 19(2)(b);

["public investigator functions" has the meaning given in subsection (1B);]

"public service vehicle" and "regulated public service vehicle" have the meaning given in section 40;

"PSV accessibility regulations" means regulations made under section 40(1);

"rail vehicle" and "regulated rail vehicle" have the meaning given in section 46;

["rail vehicle accessibility compliance certificate" has the meaning given in section 47A(3);]

"rail vehicle accessibility regulations" means regulations made under section 46(1);

"regulations" means regulations made by the Secretary of State[, except in sections 2(3), 28D, 28L(6), 28Q(7), 33, 49D … and 67 (provisions where the meaning of "regulations" is apparent)];

…

…

"section 21 duty" means any duty imposed by or under section 21;

"subordinate legislation" has the same meaning as in section 21 of the Interpretation Act 1978;

"taxi" and "regulated taxi" have the meaning given in section 32;

"taxi accessibility regulations" means regulations made under section 32(1);

"trade" includes any business;

"trade organisation" has the meaning given in section 13;

"vehicle examiner" means an examiner appointed under section 66A of the Road Traffic Act 1988.

[(1A) In this Act "criminal investigation" means—

(a) any investigation which a person in carrying out functions to which section 21B(1) applies has a duty to conduct with a view to it being ascertained whether a person should be charged with, or in Scotland prosecuted for, an offence, or whether a person charged with or prosecuted for an offence is guilty of it;

(b) any investigation which is conducted by a person in carrying out functions to which section 21B(1) applies and which in the circumstances may lead to a decision by that person to institute criminal proceedings which the person has power to conduct; or

(c) any investigation which is conducted by a person in carrying out functions to which section 21B(1) applies and which in the circumstances may lead to a decision by that person to make a report to the procurator fiscal for the purpose of enabling him to determine whether criminal proceedings should be instituted.

(1B) In this Act "public investigator functions" means functions of conducting criminal investigations or charging offenders.

(1C) In subsections (1A) and (1B)—

"offence" includes *any offence of a kind triable by court-martial under the Army Act 1955, the Air Force Act 1955 or the Naval Discipline Act 1957* [any service offence within the meaning of the Armed Forces Act 2006], and

"offender" is to be construed accordingly.]

[(2) Employment (including employment on board a ship to which subsection (2B) applies or on an aircraft or hovercraft to which subsection (2C) applies) is to be regarded as being employment at an establishment in Great Britain if the employee—

(a) does his work wholly or partly in Great Britain; or

(b) does his work wholly outside Great Britain and subsection (2A) applies.

(2A) This subsection applies if—

(a) the employer has a place of business at an establishment in Great Britain;

(b) the work is for the purposes of the business carried on at the establishment; and

(c) the employee is ordinarily resident in Great Britain—

(i) at the time when he applies for or is offered the employment, or

(ii) at any time during the course of the employment.

(2B) This subsection applies to a ship if—

(a) it is registered at a port of registry in Great Britain; or

(b) it belongs to or is possessed by Her Majesty in right of the Government of the United Kingdom.

(2C) This subsection applies to an aircraft or hovercraft if—

(a) it is—

(i) registered in the United Kingdom, and

(ii) operated by a person who has his principal place of business, or is ordinarily resident, in Great Britain; or

(b) it belongs to or is possessed by Her Majesty in right of the Government of the United Kingdom.

(2D) The following are not to be regarded as being employment at an establishment in Great Britain—

(a) employment on board a ship to which subsection (2B) does not apply;

(b) employment on an aircraft or hovercraft to which subsection (2C) does not apply.]

(4) Employment of a prescribed kind, or in prescribed circumstances, is to be regarded as not being employment at an establishment in Great Britain.

[(4A) For the purposes of determining if employment concerned with the exploration of the sea bed or sub-soil or the exploitation of their natural resources is outside Great Britain, subsections (2)(a) and (b), (2A) and (2C) of this section each have effect as if "Great Britain" had the same meaning as that given to the last reference to Great Britain in section 10(1) of the Sex Discrimination Act 1975 by section 10(5) of that Act read with the Sex Discrimination and Equal Pay (Offshore Employment) Order 1987.]

(5) …

[1630]

NOTES

Sub-s (1): definition "the 2005 Order" inserted, in relation to Northern Ireland, by the Special Educational Needs and Disability (Northern Ireland) Order 2005, SI 2005/1117 art 48(1), (11).

Sub-s (1): definition "benefits" (omitted) repealed by SI 2003/1673, regs 3(1), 27(a)(i).

Sub-s (1): definition "criminal investigation" inserted by the Disability Discrimination Act 2005, s 19(1), Sch 1, Pt 1, paras 1, 34(1), (2).

Sub-s (1): definition "criminal proceedings" inserted by the Disability Discrimination Act 2005, s 19(1), Sch 1, Pt 1, paras 1, 34(1), (2); substituted by the Armed Forces Act 2006, s 378(1), Sch 16, para 134(a), as from 28 March 2009 (for certain purposes) and as from a day to be appointed (for remaining purposes).

Sub-s (1): definition "employment at an establishment in Great Britain" substituted by SI 2003/1673, regs 3(1), 27(a)(ii).

Sub-s (1): definition "employment services" inserted by the Disability Discrimination Act 2005, s 19(1), Sch 1, Pt 1, paras 1, 34(1), (2).

Sub-s (1): in definition "enactment" words in square brackets inserted by SI 2000/2040, art 2(1), Schedule, Pt I, para 18; words omitted repealed by the Disability Discrimination Act 2005, s 19, Sch 1, Pt 1, paras 1, 34(1), (3), Sch 2.

Sub-s (1): definition "Great Britain" inserted by SI 2003/1673, regs 3(1), 27(a)(iii).

Sub-s (1): definition "group insurance arrangement" inserted by the Disability Discrimination Act 2005, s 11(3).

Sub-s (1): in definition "licensing authority" first (outer) words in square brackets inserted by the Private Hire Vehicles (Carriage of Guide Dogs etc) Act 2002, s 5; second (inner) words in square brackets substituted by Local Transport Act 2008, s 56(1), (8).

Sub-s (1): definition "mental impairment (omitted) repealed by SI 2008/2828, art 4.

Sub-s (1): definition "Minister of the Crown" substituted by SI 2003/1673, regs 3(1), 27(a)(iv).

Sub-s (1): in definition "prescribed" words in square brackets inserted by the Disability Discrimination Act 2005, s 19(1), Sch 1, Pt 1, paras 1, 34(1), (5).

Sub-s (1): definition "public investigator functions" inserted by the Disability Discrimination Act 2005, s 19(1), Sch 1, Pt 1, paras 1, 34(1), (2).

Sub-s (1): definition "rail vehicle accessibility compliance certificate" inserted by the Disability Discrimination Act 2005, s 7(3), as from a day to be appointed.

Sub-s (1): in definition "regulations" words in square brackets inserted by the Disability Discrimination Act 2005, s 19(1), Sch 1, Pt 1, paras 1, 34(1), (6); words omitted repealed by the Equality Act 2006, ss 40, 91, Sch 3, paras 41, 54, Sch 4.

Sub-s (1): definitions "section 6 duty", "section 15 duty" (omitted) repealed by SI 2003/1673, regs 3(1), 27(a)(i).

Sub-ss (1A)–(1C): inserted by the Disability Discrimination Act 2005, s 19(1), Sch 1, Pt 1, paras 1, 34(1), (7).

Sub-s (1C): in definition "offence" words in italics substituted by subsequent words in square brackets by the Armed Forces Act 2006, s 378(1), Sch 16, para 134(b), as from 28 March 2009 (for certain purposes) and as from a day to be appointed (for remaining purposes).

Sub-ss (2), (2A)–(2D): substituted, for sub-ss (2), (3) as originally enacted, by SI 2003/1673, regs 3(1), 27(b).

Sub-s (4A): inserted by SI 2003/1673, regs 3(1), 27(c).

Sub-s (5): repealed by SI 2003/1673, regs 3(1), 27(d).

See further: corresponding amendments to those made to sub-ss (1), (1A)–(1C) above have been made in relation to Northern Ireland: the Disability Discrimination (Northern Ireland) Order 2006, SI 2006/312, arts 12(3), 19(1), Sch 1, paras 1, 26.

---

69 (*Outside the scope of this work.*)

70 Short title, commencement, extent etc

(1) This Act may be cited as the Disability Discrimination Act 1995.

(2) This section (apart from subsections (4), (5) and (7)) comes into force on the passing of this Act.

[(2A) The following provisions of this Act—

(a) section 36 so far as it applies to designated vehicles,

(b) section 36A, and

(c) section 38 (which has already been brought in force in England and Wales by an order under subsection (3)) so far as it extends to Scotland,

come into force 2 months after the passing of the Local Transport Act 2008.]

(3) The other provisions of this Act come into force on such day as the Secretary of State may by order appoint and different days may be appointed for different purposes.

(4) Schedule 6 makes consequential amendments.

(5) The repeals set out in Schedule 7 shall have effect.

[(5A) Sections 7A[, [7B and 49G]] extend to England and Wales only.

(5B) Sections 7C and 7D extend to Scotland only.]

(6) [Subject to subsections (5A) and (5B), this Act extends to England and Wales, Scotland and Northern Ireland;] but in their application to Northern Ireland the provisions of this Act mentioned in Schedule 8 shall have effect subject to the modifications set out in that Schedule.

(7) …

(8) Consultations which are required by any provision of this Act to be held by the Secretary of State may be held by him before the coming into force of that provision.

[1631]

NOTES

Sub-s (2A): inserted by the Local Transport Act 2008, s 56(1), (9).

Sub-ss (5A), (5B): inserted by SI 2003/1673, regs 3(1), 28(a).

Sub-s (5A): words in first (outer) pair of square brackets substituted by the Disability Discrimination Act 2005, s 19(1), Sch 1, Pt 1, paras 1, 35; words in second (inner) pair of square brackets substituted by the Equality Act 2006, s 40, Sch 3, paras 41, 55.

Sub-s (6): words in square brackets substituted by SI 2003/1673, regs 3(1), 28(b).

Sub-s (7): amends the House of Commons Disqualification Act 1975, Sch 1, Pt II and the Northern Ireland Assembly Disqualification Act 1975, Sch 1, Pt II; repealed in part by the Disability Rights Commission Act 1999, s 14(2), Sch 5.

Orders: the Disability Discrimination Act 1995 (Commencement No 1) Order 1995, SI 1995/3330; the Disability Discrimination Act 1995 (Commencement No 2) Order 1996, SI 1996/1336; the Disability Discrimination Act 1995 (Commencement No 3 and Saving and Transitional Provisions) Order 1996, SI 1996/1474; the Disability Discrimination Act 1995 (Commencement No 4) Order 1996, SI 1996/3003; the Disability Discrimination Act 1995 (Commencement No 5) Order 1998, SI 1998/1282; the Disability Discrimination Act 1995 (Commencement Order No 6) Order 1999, SI 1999/1190; the Disability Discrimination

Act 1995 (Commencement No 7) Order 2000, SI 2000/1969; the Disability Discrimination Act 1995 (Commencement No 8) Order 2000, SI 2000/2989; the Disability Discrimination Act 1995 (Commencement No 9) Order 2001, SI 2001/2030; the Disability Discrimination Act 1995 (Commencement No 10) (Scotland) Order 2003, SI 2003/215; the Disability Discrimination Act 1995 (Commencement No 11) Order 2005, SI 2005/1122.

SCHEDULE 1
PROVISIONS SUPPLEMENTING SECTION 1

Section 1(1)

1 Impairment

(1) …

(2) Regulations may make provision, for the purposes of this Act—

(a) for conditions of a prescribed description to be treated as amounting to impairments;

(b) for conditions of a prescribed description to be treated as not amounting to impairments.

(3) Regulations made under sub-paragraph (2) may make provision as to the meaning of "condition" for the purposes of those regulations.

2 Long-term effects

(1) The effect of an impairment is a long-term effect if—

(a) it has lasted at least 12 months;

(b) the period for which it lasts is likely to be at least 12 months; or

(c) it is likely to last for the rest of the life of the person affected.

(2) Where an impairment ceases to have a substantial adverse effect on a person's ability to carry out normal day-to-day activities, it is to be treated as continuing to have that effect if that effect is likely to recur.

(3) For the purposes of sub-paragraph (2), the likelihood of an effect recurring shall be disregarded in prescribed circumstances.

(4) Regulations may prescribe circumstances in which, for the purposes of this Act—

(a) an effect which would not otherwise be a long-term effect is to be treated as such an effect; or

(b) an effect which would otherwise be a long-term effect is to be treated as not being such an effect.

3 Severe disfigurement

(1) An impairment which consists of a severe disfigurement is to be treated as having a substantial adverse effect on the ability of the person concerned to carry out normal day-to-day activities.

(2) Regulations may provide that in prescribed circumstances a severe disfigurement is not to be treated as having that effect.

(3) Regulations under sub-paragraph (2) may, in particular, make provision with respect to deliberately acquired disfigurements.

4 Normal day-to-day activities

(1) An impairment is to be taken to affect the ability of the person concerned to carry out normal day-to-day activities only if it affects one of the following—

(a) mobility;

(b) manual dexterity;

(c) physical co-ordination;

(d) continence;

(e) ability to lift, carry or otherwise move everyday objects;

(f) speech, hearing or eyesight;

(g) memory or ability to concentrate, learn or understand; or

(h) perception of the risk of physical danger.

(2) Regulations may prescribe—

(a) circumstances in which an impairment which does not have an effect falling within sub-paragraph (1) is to be taken to affect the ability of the person concerned to carry out normal day-to-day activities;

(b) circumstances in which an impairment which has an effect falling within sub-paragraph (1) is to be taken not to affect the ability of the person concerned to carry out normal day-to-day activities.

5 Substantial adverse effects

Regulations may make provision for the purposes of this Act—

(a) for an effect of a prescribed kind on the ability of a person to carry out normal day-to-day activities to be treated as a substantial adverse effect;

(b) for an effect of a prescribed kind on the ability of a person to carry out normal day-to-day activities to be treated as not being a substantial adverse effect.

6 Effect of medical treatment

(1) An impairment which would be likely to have a substantial adverse effect on the ability of the person concerned to carry out normal day-to-day activities, but for the fact that measures are being taken to treat or correct it, is to be treated as having that effect.

(2) In sub-paragraph (1) "measures" includes, in particular, medical treatment and the use of a prosthesis or other aid.

(3) Sub-paragraph (1) does not apply—

(a) in relation to the impairment of a person's sight, to the extent that the impairment is, in his case, correctable by spectacles or contact lenses or in such other ways as may be prescribed; or

(b) in relation to such other impairments as may be prescribed, in such circumstances as may be prescribed.

[6A.

(1) Subject to sub-paragraph (2), a person who has cancer, HIV infection or multiple sclerosis is to be deemed to have a disability, and hence to be a disabled person.

(2) Regulations may provide for sub-paragraph (1) not to apply in the case of a person who has cancer if he has cancer of a prescribed description.

(3) A description of cancer prescribed under sub-paragraph (2) may (in particular) be framed by reference to consequences for a person of his having it.]

7 Persons deemed to be disabled

(1) Sub-paragraph (2) applies to any person whose name is, both on 12th January 1995 and on the date when this paragraph comes into force, in the register of disabled persons maintained under section 6 of the Disabled Persons (Employment) Act 1944.

(2) That person is to be deemed—

(a) during the initial period, to have a disability, and hence to be a disabled person; and

(b) afterwards, to have had a disability and hence to have been a disabled person during that period.

(3) A certificate of registration shall be conclusive evidence, in relation to the person with respect to whom it was issued, of the matters certified.

(4) Unless the contrary is shown, any document purporting to be a certificate of registration shall be taken to be such a certificate and to have been validly issued.

(5) Regulations may provide for prescribed descriptions of person to be deemed to have disabilities, and hence to be disabled persons, for the purposes of this Act.

[(5A) The generality of sub-paragraph (5) shall not be taken to be prejudiced by the other provisions of this Schedule.]

(6) Regulations may prescribe circumstances in which a person who has been deemed to be a disabled person by the provisions of sub-paragraph (1) or regulations made under sub-paragraph (5) is to be treated as no longer being deemed to be such a person.

(7) In this paragraph—

"certificate of registration" means a certificate issued under regulations made under section 6 of the Act of 1944; and

"initial period" means the period of three years beginning with the date on which this paragraph comes into force.

8 Progressive conditions

(1) Where—

(a) a person has a progressive condition (such as cancer, multiple sclerosis or muscular dystrophy or [HIV infection]),

(b) as a result of that condition, he has an impairment which has (or had) an effect on his ability to carry out normal day-to-day activities, but

(c) that-effect is not (or was not) a substantial adverse effect,

he shall be taken to have an impairment which has such a substantial adverse effect if the condition is likely to result in his having such an impairment.

(2) Regulations may make provision, for the purposes of this paragraph—

(a) for conditions of a prescribed description to be treated as being progressive;

(b) for conditions of a prescribed description to be treated as not being progressive.

[9 Interpretation

In this Schedule "HIV infection" means infection by a virus capable of causing the Acquired Immune Deficiency Syndrome.]

[1632]

NOTES

Para 1: sub-para (1) repealed by the Disability Discrimination Act 2005, ss 18(1), (2), 19(2), Sch 2.

Para 6A: inserted by the Disability Discrimination Act 2005, s 18(1), (3).

Para 7: sub-para (5A) inserted by the Disability Discrimination Act 2005, s 18(1), (4).

Para 8: words in square brackets in sub-para (1)(a) substituted by the Disability Discrimination Act 2005, s 19(1), Sch 1, Pt 1, paras 1, 36.

Para 9: inserted by the Disability Discrimination Act 2005, s 18(1), (5).

See further: corresponding amendments and a repeal to those made to paras 1, 7–9 above by the Disability Discrimination Act 2005, have been made in relation to Northern Ireland: the Disability Discrimination (Northern Ireland) Order 2006, SI 2006/312, arts 18, 19, Sch 1, paras 1, 27, Sch 2.

Regulations: the Disability Discrimination (Meaning of Disability) Regulations 1996, SI 1996/1455; the Disability Discrimination (Blind and Partially Sighted Persons) Regulations 2003, SI 2003/712.

(*Sch 2 outside the scope of this work.*)

SCHEDULE 3
ENFORCEMENT AND PROCEDURE

Sections [17A(8)], 25(6)[, 31ADA]

NOTES

Reference to "17A(8)" in square brackets substituted by SI 2003/1673, regs 3(1), 29(2)(a); reference to ", 31ADA" in square brackets inserted by SI 2007/2405, regs 2(1), 4(1), (2).

PART I
EMPLOYMENT

1. …

2 Restriction on proceedings for breach of Part II

[(1) Except as provided by Part 2, no civil or criminal proceedings may be brought against any person in respect of an act merely because the act is unlawful under that Part.]

(2) Sub-paragraph (1) does not prevent the making of an application for judicial review [or the investigation or determination of any matter in accordance with Part 10 (investigations) of the Pension Schemes Act 1993 by the Pensions Ombudsman].

[(3) Sub-paragraph (1) does not prevent the bringing of proceedings in respect of an offence under section 16B(2B).]

3 Period within which proceedings must be brought

(1) An [employment tribunal] shall not consider a complaint under [section 17A or 25(8)] unless it is presented before the end of the period of three months beginning when the act complained of was done.

(2) A tribunal may consider any such complaint which is out of time if, in all the circumstances of the case, it considers that it is just and equitable to do so.

(3) For the purposes of sub-paragraph (1)—

- (a) where an unlawful act … is attributable to a term in a contract, that act is to be treated as extending throughout the duration of the contract;
- (b) any act extending over a period shall be treated as done at the end of that period; and
- (c) a deliberate omission shall be treated as done when the person in question decided upon it.

(4) In the absence of evidence establishing the contrary, a person shall be taken for the purposes of this paragraph to decide upon an omission—

- (a) when he does an act inconsistent with doing the omitted act; or
- (b) if he has done no such inconsistent act, when the period expires within which he might reasonably have been expected to do the omitted act if it was to be done.

4 Evidence

(1) In any proceedings under [section 17A or 25(8)], a certificate signed by or on behalf of a Minister of the Crown and certifying—

- (a) that any conditions or requirements specified in the certificate were imposed by a Minister of the Crown and were in operation at a time or throughout a time so specified, …
- (b) …

shall be conclusive evidence of the matters certified.

[(1A) In any proceedings under section 17A or 25(8), a certificate signed by or on behalf of the Scottish Ministers and certifying that any conditions or requirements specified in the certificate—

(a) were imposed by a member of the Scottish Executive, and

(b) were in operation at a time or throughout a time so specified,

shall be conclusive evidence of the matters certified.

(1B) In any proceedings under section 17A or 25(8), a certificate signed by or on behalf of the [Welsh Ministers] and certifying that any conditions or requirements specified in the certificate—

(a) were imposed by the [National Assembly for Wales constituted by the Government of Wales Act 1998, the Welsh Ministers, the First Minister for Wales or the Counsel General to the Welsh Assembly Government], and

(b) were in operation at a time or throughout a time so specified,

shall be conclusive evidence of the matters certified.]

(2) A document purporting to be such a certificate [as is mentioned in sub-paragraph (1), (1A) or (1B)] shall be received in evidence and, unless the contrary is proved, be deemed to be such a certificate.

[1633]

NOTES

Para 1: repealed by the Employment Tribunals Act 1996, s 45, Sch 3, Pt I.

Para 2: sub-para (1) substituted by SI 2003/1673, regs 3(1), 29(2)(b); words in square brackets in sub-para (2) inserted by SI 2003/2770, regs 2, 4(5); sub-para (3) inserted by the Disability Discrimination Act 2005, s 19(1), Sch 1, Pt 1, paras 1, 38(1), (2).

Para 3: in sub-para (1), words in first pair of square brackets substituted by the Employment Rights (Dispute Resolution) Act 1998, s 1(2)(a), and words in second pair of square brackets substituted by SI 2003/1673, regs 3(1), 29(2)(c); words omitted from sub-para (3)(a) repealed by SI 2003/1673, regs 3(1), 29(2)(d).

Para 4: in sub-para (1) words in square brackets substituted by SI 2003/1673, regs 3(1), 29(2)(e); word omitted from the end of sub-para (1)(a), and sub-para (1)(b) repealed by the Employment Relations Act 1999, ss 41, 44, Sch 8, para 7, Sch 9, Table 12; sub-paras (1A), (1B) inserted by the Disability Discrimination Act 2005, s 19(1), Sch 1, Pt 1, paras 1, 38(1), (3); words in square brackets in sub-para (1B) substituted by SI 2007/1388, art 3, Sch 1, paras 47, 63(1), (2); words in square brackets in sub-para (2) inserted by the Disability Discrimination Act 2005, s 19(1), Sch 1, Pt 1, paras 1, 38(1), (4).

See further: a corresponding amendment to that made to para 2(3) above by the Disability Discrimination Act 2005, has been made in relation to Northern Ireland: the Disability Discrimination (Northern Ireland) Order 2006, SI 2006/312, art 19(1), Sch 1, paras 1, 29(1), (2).

Note: by virtue of the Employment Rights (Dispute Resolution) Act 1998, s 1(2), the Industrial Tribunals Act 1996 shall be cited as the Employment Tribunals Act 1996; references to the Industrial Tribunals Act 1996 have been changed accordingly.

(*Sch 3, Pts II–V, Sch 3A outside the scope of this work.*)

SCHEDULE 4
PREMISES OCCUPIED UNDER LEASES

Sections [18A(5)], 27(5)[, 31ADB]

NOTES

Reference to "18A(5)" in square brackets substituted by SI 2003/1673, regs 3(1), 29(3)(a); reference to "31ADB" in square brackets inserted by SI 2007/2405, regs 2(1), 6(1), (2) (for effect see regs 8–13 thereof).

PART I
OCCUPATION BY [EMPLOYER ETC]

NOTES

Words in square brackets substituted by SI 2003/1673, regs 3(1), 29(3)(b).

1 Failure to obtain consent to alteration

If any question arises as to whether the occupier has failed to comply with [any duty to make reasonable adjustments], by failing to make a particular alteration to the premises, any constraint attributable to the fact that he occupies the premises under a lease is to be ignored unless he has applied to the lessor in writing for consent to the making of the alteration.

2 Joining lessors in proceedings under [section 17A …]

(1) In any proceedings [on a complaint under section 17A], in a case to which [section 18A] applies, the complainant or the occupier may ask the tribunal hearing the complaint to direct that the lessor be joined or sisted as a party to the proceedings.

(2) The request shall be granted if it is made before the hearing of the complaint begins.

(3) The tribunal may refuse the request if it is made after the hearing of the complaint begins.

(4) The request may not be granted if it is made after the tribunal has determined the complaint.

(5) Where a lessor has been so joined or sisted as a party to the proceedings, the tribunal may determine—

(a) whether the lessor has—
(i) refused consent to the alteration, or
(ii) consented subject to one or more conditions, and
(b) if so, whether the refusal or any of the conditions was unreasonable.

(6) If, under sub-paragraph (5), the tribunal determines that the refusal or any of the conditions was unreasonable it may take one or more of the following steps—

(a) make such declaration as it considers appropriate;
(b) make an order authorising the occupier to make the alteration specified in the order;
(c) order the lessor to pay compensation to the complainant.

(7) An order under sub-paragraph (6)(b) may require the occupier to comply with conditions specified in the order.

(8) Any step taken by the tribunal under sub-paragraph (6) may be in substitution for, or in addition to, any step taken by the tribunal under [section 17A(2)].

(9) If the tribunal orders the lessor to pay compensation it may not make an order under [section 17A(2)] ordering the occupier to do so.

3 Regulations

Regulations may make provision as to circumstances in which—

(a) a lessor is to be taken, for the purposes of [section 18A] and this Part of this Schedule to have—
(i) withheld his consent;
(ii) withheld his consent unreasonably;
(iii) acted reasonably in withholding his consent;
(b) a condition subject to which a lessor has given his consent is to be taken to be reasonable;
(c) a condition subject to which a lessor has given his consent is to be taken to be unreasonable.

4 Sub-leases etc

The Secretary of State may by regulations make provision supplementing, or modifying, the provision made by [section 18A] or any provision made by or under this Part of this Schedule in relation to cases where the occupier occupies premises under a sub-lease or sub-tenancy.

[1634]

NOTES

Para 1: words in square brackets substituted by SI 2003/1673, regs 3(1), 29(3)(c).

Para 2: in the heading, words in square brackets substituted by SI 2003/1673, regs 3(1), 29(3)(d) and words omitted repealed by the Disability Discrimination Act 2005, s 19(1), Sch 1, Pt 1, paras 1, 40(1), (2)(a); in sub-para (1), words in first pair of square brackets substituted by the Disability Discrimination Act 2005, s 19(1), Sch 1, Pt 1, paras 1, 40(1), (2)(b) and words in second pair of square brackets substituted by SI 2003/1673, regs 3(1), 29(3)(e); words in square brackets in sub-paras (8), (9) substituted by SI 2003/1673, regs 3(1), 29(3)(f).

Paras 3, 4: words in square brackets substituted by SI 2003/1673, regs 3(1), 29(3)(g).

Modification: paras 1–3 modified, in relation to cases where the occupier occupies premises under a sub-lease or sub-tenancy, by the Disability Discrimination (Sub-leases and Sub-tenancies) Regulations 1996, SI 1996/1333, reg 4. Para 2 modified, in relation to any case where the occupier occupies premises under a sub-lease or sub-tenancy, by the Disability Discrimination (Employment Field) (Leasehold Premises) Regulations 2004, SI 2004/153, regs 8, 9(c).

See further: a corresponding amendment and repeal to those made to para 2 and the heading preceding it above by the Disability Discrimination Act 2005, have been made in relation to Northern Ireland: the Disability Discrimination (Northern Ireland) Order 2006, SI 2006/312, art 19(1), Sch 1, paras 1, 31(1), (2).

Regulations: the Disability Discrimination (Employment Field) (Leasehold Premises) Regulations 2004, SI 2004/153.

PART II
OCCUPATION BY [PERSONS SUBJECT TO A DUTY UNDER SECTION 21, 21E OR 21H]

NOTES

Words in square brackets substituted by the Disability Discrimination Act 2005, s 19(1), Sch 1, Pt 1, paras 1, 40(1), (3).

5 Failure to obtain consent to alteration

If any question arises as to whether the occupier has failed to comply with the section 21 duty [or a duty imposed under section 21E or 21H], by failing to make a particular alteration to premises, any constraint attributable to the fact that he occupies the premises under a lease is to be ignored unless he has applied to the lessor in writing for consent to the making of the alteration.

6 Reference to court

(1) If the occupier has applied in writing to the lessor for consent to the alteration and—

(a) that consent has been refused, or

(b) the lessor has made his consent subject to one or more conditions,

the occupier or a disabled person who has an interest in the proposed alteration to the premises being made, may refer the matter to a county court or, in Scotland, to the sheriff.

(2) In the following provisions of this Schedule "court" includes "sheriff".

(3) On such a reference the court shall determine whether the lessor's refusal was unreasonable or (as the case may be) whether the condition is, or any of the conditions are, unreasonable.

(4) If the court determines—

(a) that the lessor's refusal was unreasonable, or

(b) that the condition is, or any of the conditions are, unreasonable,

it may make such declaration as it considers appropriate or an order authorising the occupier to make the alteration specified in the order.

(5) An order under sub-paragraph (4) may require the occupier to comply with conditions specified in the order.

7 Joining lessors in proceedings under section 25

(1) In any proceedings on a claim [under section 25 in a case to which section 27 applies, other than a claim presented as a complaint under section 25(8),] the plaintiff, the pursuer or the occupier concerned may ask the court to direct that the lessor be joined or sisted as a party to the proceedings.

(2) The request shall be granted if it is made before the hearing of the claim begins.

(3) The court may refuse the request if it is made after the hearing of the claim begins.

(4) The request may not be granted if it is made after the court has determined the claim.

(5) Where a lessor has been so joined or sisted as a party to the proceedings, the court may determine—

(a) whether the lessor has—

(i) refused consent to the alteration, or

(ii) consented subject to one or more conditions, and

(b) if so, whether the refusal or any of the conditions was unreasonable.

(6) If, under sub-paragraph (5), the court determines that the refusal or any of the conditions was unreasonable it may take one or more of the following steps—

(a) make such declaration as it considers appropriate;

(b) make an order authorising the occupier to make the alteration specified in the order;

(c) order the lessor to pay compensation to the complainant.

(7) An order under sub-paragraph (6)(b) may require the occupier to comply with conditions specified in the order.

(8) If the court orders the lessor to pay compensation it may not order the occupier to do so.

[7A Joining lessors in proceedings relating to group insurance or employment services

(1) In any proceedings on a complaint under section 25(8) in a case to which section 27 applies, the complainant or the occupier may ask the tribunal hearing the complaint to direct that the lessor be joined or sisted as a party to the proceedings.

(2) The request shall be granted if it is made before the hearing of the complaint begins.

(3) The tribunal may refuse the request if it is made after the hearing of the complaint begins.

(4) The request may not be granted if it is made after the tribunal has determined the complaint.

(5) Where a lessor has been so joined or sisted as a party to the proceedings, the tribunal may determine—

(a) whether the lessor has—

(i) refused consent to the alteration, or

(ii) consented subject to one or more conditions; and

(b) if so, whether the refusal or any of the conditions was unreasonable.

(6) If, under sub-paragraph (5), the tribunal determines that the refusal or any of the conditions was unreasonable it may take one or more of the following steps—

(a) make such declaration as it considers appropriate;

(b) make an order authorising the occupier to make the alteration specified in the order;

(c) order the lessor to pay compensation to the complainant.

(7) An order under sub-paragraph (6)(b) may require the occupier to comply with conditions specified in the order.

(8) Any step taken by the tribunal under sub-paragraph (6) may be in substitution for, or in addition to, any step taken by the tribunal under section 17A(2).

(9) If the tribunal orders the lessor to pay compensation it may not make an order under section 17A(2) ordering the occupier to do so.]

8 Regulations

Regulations may make provision as to circumstances in which—

(a) a lessor is to be taken, for the purposes of section 27 and this Part of this Schedule to have—
  (i) withheld his consent;
  (ii) withheld his consent unreasonably;
  (iii) acted reasonably in withholding his consent;
(b) a condition subject to which a lessor has given his consent is to be taken to be reasonable;
(c) a condition subject to which a lessor has given his consent is to be taken to be unreasonable.

9 Sub-leases etc

The Secretary of State may by regulations make provision supplementing, or modifying, the provision made by section 27 or any provision made by or under this Part of this Schedule in relation to cases where the occupier occupies premises under a sub-lease or sub-tenancy.

[1635]–[1639]

NOTES

Para 5: words in square brackets inserted by the Disability Discrimination Act 2005, s 19(1), Sch 1, Pt 1, paras 1, 40(1), (4).

Para 7: words in square brackets in sub-para (1) substituted by the Disability Discrimination Act 2005, s 19(1), Sch 1, Pt 1, paras 1, 40(1), (5).

Para 7A: inserted by the Disability Discrimination Act 2005, s 19(1), Sch 1, Pt 1, paras 1, 40(1), (6).

Modification: the Disability Discrimination (Providers of Services) (Adjustment of Premises) Regulations 2001, reg 9(1), (4)–(7), SI 2001/3253 provides for the modification of this Part in relation to any case where the occupier occupies premises under a sub-lease or sub-tenancy.

See further: a corresponding amendment to that made to paras 5, 7, 7A above by the Disability Discrimination Act 2005, has been made in relation to Northern Ireland: the Disability Discrimination (Northern Ireland) Order 2006, SI 2006/312, art 19(1), Sch 1, paras 1, 31(1), (3)–(6).

Regulations: the Disability Discrimination (Providers of Services) (Adjustment of Premises) Regulations 2001, SI 2001/3253; the Disability Discrimination (Service Providers and Public Authorities Carrying Out Functions) Regulations 2005, SI 2005/2901.

(Sch 4, Pts 3, 4, Schs 4A–8 outside the scope of this work.)

TREASURE ACT 1996

(1996 c 24)

An Act to abolish treasure trove and to make fresh provision in relation to treasure

[4 July 1996]

Meaning of "treasure"

1 Meaning of "treasure"

(1) Treasure is—

(a) any object at least 300 years old when found which—
  (i) is not a coin but has metallic content of which at least 10 per cent by weight is precious metal;
  (ii) when found, is one of at least two coins in the same find which are at least 300 years old at that time and have that percentage of precious metal; or
  (iii) when found, is one of at least ten coins in the same find which are at least 300 years old at that time;
(b) any object at least 200 years old when found which belongs to a class designated under section 2(1);
(c) any object which would have been treasure trove if found before the commencement of section 4;
(d) any object which, when found, is part of the same find as—
  (i) an object within paragraph (a), (b) or (c) found at the same time or earlier; or
  (ii) an object found earlier which would be within paragraph (a) or (b) if it had been found at the same time.

(2) Treasure does not include objects which are—
(a) unworked natural objects, or
(b) minerals as extracted from a natural deposit,
or which belong to a class designated under section 2(2).

[1640]

2 Power to alter meaning

(1) The Secretary of State may by order, for the purposes of section 1(1)(b), designate any class of object which he considers to be of outstanding historical, archaeological or cultural importance.

(2) The Secretary of State may by order, for the purposes of section 1(2), designate any class of object which (apart from the order) would be treasure.

(3) An order under this section shall be made by statutory instrument.

(4) No order is to be made under this section unless a draft of the order has been laid before Parliament and approved by a resolution of each House.

[1641]

NOTES

Order: the Treasure (Designation) Order 2002, SI 2002/2666.

3 Supplementary

(1) This section supplements section 1.

(2) "Coin" includes any metal token which was, or can reasonably be assumed to have been, used or intended for use as or instead of money.

(3) "Precious metal" means gold or silver.

(4) When an object is found, it is part of the same find as another object if—
(a) they are found together,
(b) the other object was found earlier in the same place where they had been left together,
(c) the other object was found earlier in a different place, but they had been left together and had become separated before being found.

(5) If the circumstances in which objects are found can reasonably be taken to indicate that they were together at some time before being found, the objects are to be presumed to have been left together, unless shown not to have been.

(6) An object which can reasonably be taken to be at least a particular age is to be presumed to be at least that age, unless shown not to be.

(7) An object is not treasure if it is wreck within the meaning of Part IX of the Merchant Shipping Act 1995.

[1642]

Ownership of treasure

4 Ownership of treasure which is found

(1) When treasure is found, it vests, subject to prior interests and rights—
(a) in the franchisee, if there is one;
(b) otherwise, in the Crown.

(2) Prior interests and rights are any which, or which derive from any which—
(a) were held when the treasure was left where it was found, or
(b) if the treasure had been moved before being found, were held when it was left where it was before being moved.

(3) If the treasure would have been treasure trove if found before the commencement of this section, neither the Crown nor any franchisee has any interest in it or right over it except in accordance with this Act.

(4) This section applies—
(a) whatever the nature of the place where the treasure was found, and
(b) whatever the circumstances in which it was left (including being lost or being left with no intention of recovery).

[1643]

5 Meaning of "franchisee"

(1) The franchisee for any treasure is the person who—
(a) was, immediately before the commencement of section 4, or
(b) apart from this Act, as successor in title, would have been,
the franchisee of the Crown in right of treasure trove for the place where the treasure was found.

(2) It is as franchisees in right of treasure trove that Her Majesty and the Duke of Cornwall are to be treated as having enjoyed the rights to treasure trove which belonged respectively to the Duchy of Lancaster and the Duchy of Cornwall immediately before the commencement of section 4.

[1644]

6 Treasure vesting in the Crown

(1) Treasure vesting in the Crown under this Act is to be treated as part of the hereditary revenues of the Crown to which section 1 of the Civil List Act 1952 applies (surrender of hereditary revenues to the Exchequer).

(2) Any such treasure may be transferred, or otherwise disposed of, in accordance with directions given by the Secretary of State.

(3) The Crown's title to any such treasure may be disclaimed at any time by the Secretary of State.

(4) If the Crown's title is disclaimed, the treasure—

(a) is deemed not to have vested in the Crown under this Act, and

(b) without prejudice to the interests or rights of others, may be delivered to any person in accordance with the code published under section 11.

[1645]

Coroners' jurisdiction

7 Jurisdiction of coroners

(1) The jurisdiction of coroners which is referred to in section 30 of the Coroners Act 1988 (treasure) is exercisable in relation to anything which is treasure for the purposes of this Act.

(2) That jurisdiction is not exercisable for the purposes of the law relating to treasure trove in relation to anything found after the commencement of section 4.

(3) The Act of 1988 and anything saved by virtue of section 36(5) of that Act (saving for existing law and practice etc) has effect subject to this section.

(4) An inquest held by virtue of this section is to be held without a jury, unless the coroner orders otherwise.

[1646]

8 Duty of finder to notify coroner

(1) A person who finds an object which he believes or has reasonable grounds for believing is treasure must notify the coroner for the district in which the object was found before the end of the notice period.

(2) The notice period is fourteen days beginning with—

(a) the day after the find; or

(b) if later, the day on which the finder first believes or has reason to believe the object is treasure.

(3) Any person who fails to comply with subsection (1) is guilty of an offence and liable on summary conviction to—

(a) imprisonment for a term not exceeding *three months* [51 weeks];

(b) a fine of an amount not exceeding level 5 on the standard scale; or

(c) both.

(4) In proceedings for an offence under this section, it is a defence for the defendant to show that he had, and has continued to have, a reasonable excuse for failing to notify the coroner.

(5) If the office of coroner for a district is vacant, the person acting as coroner for that district is the coroner for the purposes of subsection (1).

[1647]

NOTES

Sub-s (3): in para (a), words in italics substituted by subsequent words in square brackets by the Criminal Justice Act 2003, s 280(2), (3), Sch 26, para 48, as from a day to be appointed.

9 Procedure for inquests

(1) In this section, "inquest" means an inquest held under section 7.

(2) A coroner proposing to conduct an inquest must notify—

(a) the British Museum, if his district is in England; or

(b) the National Museum of Wales, if it is in Wales.

(3) Before conducting the inquest, the coroner must take reasonable steps to notify—

(a) any person who it appears to him may have found the treasure; and

(b) any person who, at the time the treasure was found, occupied land which it appears to him may be where it was found.

(4) During the inquest the coroner must take reasonable steps to notify any such person not already notified.

(5) Before or during the inquest, the coroner must take reasonable steps—

(a) to obtain from any person notified under subsection (3) or (4) the names and addresses of interested persons; and

(b) to notify any interested person whose name and address he obtains.

(6) The coroner must take reasonable steps to give any interested person notified under subsection (3), (4) or (5) an opportunity to examine witnesses at the inquest.

(7) In subsections (5) and (6), "interested person" means a person who appears to the coroner to be likely to be concerned with the inquest—

(a) as the finder of the treasure or otherwise involved in the find;

(b) as the occupier, at the time the treasure was found, of the land where it was found, or

(c) as having had an interest in that land at that time or since.

[1648]

Rewards, codes of practice and report

10 Rewards

(1) This section applies if treasure—

(a) has vested in the Crown under section 4; and

(b) is to be transferred to a museum.

(2) The Secretary of State must determine whether a reward is to be paid by the museum before the transfer.

(3) If the Secretary of State determines that a reward is to be paid, he must also determine, in whatever way he thinks fit—

(a) the treasure's market value;

(b) the amount of the reward;

(c) to whom the reward is to be payable; and

(d) if it is to be payable to more than one person, how much each is to receive.

(4) The total reward must not exceed the treasure's market value.

(5) The reward may be payable to—

(a) the finder or any other person involved in the find;

(b) the occupier of the land at the time of the find;

(c) any person who had an interest in the land at that time, or has had such an interest at any time since then.

(6) Payment of the reward is not enforceable against a museum or the Secretary of State.

(7) In a determination under this section, the Secretary of State must take into account anything relevant in the code of practice issued under section 11.

(8) This section also applies in relation to treasure which has vested in a franchisee under section 4, if the franchisee makes a request to the Secretary of State that it should.

[1649]

11 Codes of practice

(1) The Secretary of State must—

(a) prepare a code of practice relating to treasure;

(b) keep the code under review; and

(c) revise it when appropriate.

(2) The code must, in particular, set out the principles and practice to be followed by the Secretary of State—

(a) when considering to whom treasure should be offered;

(b) when making a determination under section 10; and

(c) where the Crown's title to treasure is disclaimed.

(3) The code may include guidance for—

(a) those who search for or find treasure; and

(b) museums and others who exercise functions in relation to treasure.

(4) Before preparing the code or revising it, the Secretary of State must consult such persons appearing to him to be interested as he thinks appropriate.

(5) A copy of the code and of any proposed revision of the code shall be laid before Parliament.

(6) Neither the code nor any revision shall come into force until approved by a resolution of each House of Parliament.

(7) The Secretary of State must publish the code in whatever way he considers appropriate for bringing it to the attention of those interested.

(8) If the Secretary of State considers that different provision should be made for—

(a) England and Wales, and
(b) Northern Ireland,

or that different provision should otherwise be made for treasure found in different areas, he may prepare two or more separate codes.

[1650]

12 Report on operation of Act

As soon as reasonably practicable after each anniversary of the coming into force of this section, the Secretary of State shall lay before Parliament a report on the operation of this Act in the preceding year.

[1651]

Miscellaneous

13 Application of Act to Northern Ireland

In the application of this Act to Northern Ireland—

(a) in section 7—
 (i) in subsection (1), for "section 30 of the Coroners Act 1988" substitute "section 33 of the Coroners Act (Northern Ireland) 1959";
 (ii) in subsection (3), for the words from "1988" to "practice etc)" substitute "1959";
(b) in section 9(2), for the words from "British Museum" to the end substitute "Department of the Environment for Northern Ireland".

[1652]

14 (*Contains consequential amendments outside the scope of this work.*)

15 Short title, commencement and extent

(1) This Act may be cited as the Treasure Act 1996.

(2) This Act comes into force on such day as the Secretary of State may by order made by statutory instrument appoint; and different days may be appointed for different purposes.

(3) This Act does not extend to Scotland.

[1653]

NOTES

Orders: the Treasure Act 1996 (Commencement No 1) Order 1997, SI 1997/760; the Treasure Act 1996 (Commencement No 2) Order 1997, SI 1997/1977.

FAMILY LAW ACT 1996

(1996 c 27)

An Act to make provision with respect to: divorce and separation; legal aid in connection with mediation in disputes relating to family matters; proceedings in cases where marriages have broken down; rights of occupation of certain domestic premises; prevention of molestation; the inclusion in certain orders under the Children Act 1989 of provisions about the occupation of a dwelling-house; the transfer of tenancies between spouses and persons who have lived together as husband and wife; and for connected purposes

[4 July 1996]

1–29 (*Ss 1–25* (*Pts I, II*) *outside the scope of this work; ss 26–29* (*Pt III*) *repealed by the Access to Justice Act 1999, s 106, Sch 15, Pt I.*)

PART IV
FAMILY HOMES AND DOMESTIC VIOLENCE

Rights to occupy matrimonial [or civil partnership] home

NOTES

Cross-heading: words in square brackets inserted by the Civil Partnership Act 2004, s 82, Sch 9, Pt 1, para 1(1), (11), subject to transitional provisions in s 82, Sch 9, Pt 3 thereof.

30 Rights concerning [home where one spouse or civil partner] has no estate, etc

(1) This section applies if—

(a) one spouse [or civil partner ("A")] is entitled to occupy a dwelling-house by virtue of—

(i) a beneficial estate or interest or contract; or
(ii) any enactment giving [A] the right to remain in occupation; and

(b) the other spouse [or civil partner ("B")] is not so entitled.

(2) Subject to the provisions of this Part, [B] has the following rights [("home rights")]—

(a) if in occupation, a right not to be evicted or excluded from the dwelling-house or any part of it by [A] except with the leave of the court given by an order under section 33;

(b) if not in occupation, a right with the leave of the court so given to enter into and occupy the dwelling-house.

(3) If [B] is entitled under this section to occupy a dwelling-house or any part of a dwelling-house, any payment or tender made or other thing done by [B] in or towards satisfaction of any liability of [A] in respect of rent, mortgage payments or other outgoings affecting the dwelling-house is, whether or not it is made or done in pursuance of an order under section 40, as good as if made or done by [A].

(4) [B's] occupation by virtue of this section—

(a) is to be treated, for the purposes of the Rent (Agriculture) Act 1976 and the Rent Act 1977 (other than Part V and sections 103 to 106 of that Act), as occupation [by A as A's] residence, and

(b) if [B occupies the dwelling-house as B's] only or principal home, is to be treated, for the purposes of the Housing Act 1985[, Part I of the Housing Act 1988 and Chapter I of Part V of the Housing Act 1996], as occupation [by A as A's] only or principal home.

(5) If [B]—

(a) is entitled under this section to occupy a dwelling-house or any part of a dwelling-house, and

(b) makes any payment in or towards satisfaction of any liability of [A] in respect of mortgage payments affecting the dwelling-house,

the person to whom the payment is made may treat it as having been made by [A], but the fact that that person has treated any such payment as having been so made does not affect any claim of [B against A] to an interest in the dwelling-house by virtue of the payment.

(6) If [B] is entitled under this section to occupy a dwelling-house or part of a dwelling-house by reason of an interest of [A] under a trust, all the provisions of subsections (3) to (5) apply in relation to the trustees as they apply in relation to [A].

(7) This section does not apply to a dwelling-house [which—

(a) in the case of spouses, has at no time been, and was at no time intended by them to be, a matrimonial home of theirs; and

(b) in the case of civil partners, has at no time been, and was at no time intended by them to be, a civil partnership home of theirs].

(8) [B's home rights] continue—

(a) only so long as the marriage [or civil partnership] subsists, except to the extent that an order under section 33(5) otherwise provides; and

(b) only so long as [A] is entitled as mentioned in subsection (1) to occupy the dwelling-house, except where provision is made by section 31 for those rights to be a charge on an estate or interest in the dwelling-house.

(9) It is hereby declared that [a person]—

(a) who has an equitable interest in a dwelling-house or in its proceeds of sale, but

(b) is not [a person] in whom there is vested (whether solely or as joint tenant) a legal estate in fee simple or a legal term of years absolute in the dwelling-house,

is to be treated, only for the purpose of determining whether he has [home rights], as not being entitled to occupy the dwelling-house by virtue of that interest.

[1654]

NOTES

Section heading: words in square brackets substituted by the Civil Partnership Act 2004, s 82, Sch 9, Pt 1, para 1(1), (11).

Sub-s (1): words in square brackets inserted and reference in square brackets substituted by the Civil Partnership Act 2004, s 82, Sch 9, Pt 1, para 1(1), (2); for transitional provisions see s 82, Sch 9, Pt 3 thereto.

Sub-ss (2), (3), (5)–(7), (9): words in square brackets substituted by the Civil Partnership Act 2004, s 82, Sch 9, Pt 1, para 1(1), (3), (4), (6)–(8), (10); for transitional provisions see s 82, Sch 9, Pt 3 thereto.

Sub-s (4): in para (b), words ", Part I of the Housing Act 1988 and Chapter I of Part V of the Housing Act 1996" in square brackets substituted by SI 1997/74, art 2, Schedule, para 10(a); other words in square brackets substituted by the Civil Partnership Act 2004, s 82, Sch 9, Pt 1, para 1(1), (5) (for transitional provisions see s 82, Sch 9, Pt 3 thereto).

Sub-s (8): words in first and third pairs of square brackets substituted and words in second pair of square brackets inserted by the Civil Partnership Act 2004, s 82, Sch 9, Pt 1, para 1(1), (9)(a); for transitional provisions see s 82, Sch 9, Pt 3 thereto.

31 Effect of [home rights] as charge on dwelling-house

(1) Subsections (2) and (3) apply if, at any time during a [marriage or civil partnership, A] is entitled to occupy a dwelling-house by virtue of a beneficial estate or interest.

(2) [B's home rights] are a charge on the estate or interest.

(3) The charge created by subsection (2) has the same priority as if it were an equitable interest created at whichever is the latest of the following dates—

(a) the date on which [A] acquires the estate or interest;
(b) the date of the marriage [or of the formation of the civil partnership]; and
(c) 1st January 1968 (the commencement date of the Matrimonial Homes Act 1967).

(4) Subsections (5) and (6) apply if, at any time when [B's home rights] are a charge on an interest of [A] under a trust, there are, apart from [A or B], no persons, living or unborn, who are or could become beneficiaries under the trust.

(5) The rights are a charge also on the estate or interest of the trustees for [A].

(6) The charge created by subsection (5) has the same priority as if it were an equitable interest created (under powers overriding the trusts) on the date when it arises.

(7) In determining for the purposes of subsection (4) whether there are any persons who are not, but could become, beneficiaries under the trust, there is to be disregarded any potential exercise of a general power of appointment exercisable by either or both of [A and B] alone (whether or not the exercise of it requires the consent of another person).

(8) Even though [B's home rights] are a charge on an estate or interest in the dwelling-house, those rights are brought to an end by—

(a) the death of [A], or
(b) the termination (otherwise than by death) of the marriage [or civil partnership],

unless the court directs otherwise by an order made under section 33(5).

(9) If—

(a) [B's home rights] are a charge on an estate or interest in the dwelling-house, and
(b) that estate or interest is surrendered to merge in some other estate or interest expectant on it in such circumstances that, but for the merger, the person taking the estate or interest would be bound by the charge,

the surrender has effect subject to the charge and the persons thereafter entitled to the other estate or interest are, for so long as the estate or interest surrendered would have endured if not so surrendered, to be treated for all purposes of this Part as deriving title to the other estate or interest under [A] or, as the case may be, under the trustees for [A], by virtue of the surrender.

(10) If the title to the legal estate by virtue of which [A] is entitled to occupy a dwelling-house (including any legal estate held by trustees for [A]) is registered under the [Land Registration Act 2002] or any enactment replaced by that Act—

(a) registration of a land charge affecting the dwelling-house by virtue of this Part is to be effected by registering a notice under that Act; and
[(b) [B's home rights] are not to be capable of falling within paragraph 2 of Schedule 1 or 3 to that Act].

(11) …

(12) If—

[(a) B's home rights are a charge on the estate of A or of trustees of A, and]
(b) that estate is the subject of a mortgage,

then if, after the date of the creation of the mortgage ("the first mortgage"), the charge is registered under section 2 of the Land Charges Act 1972, the charge is, for the purposes of section 94 of the Law of Property Act 1925 (which regulates the rights of mortgagees to make further advances ranking in priority to subsequent mortgages), to be deemed to be a mortgage subsequent in date to the first mortgage.

(13) It is hereby declared that a charge under subsection (2) or (5) is not registrable under subsection (10) or under section 2 of the Land Charges Act 1972 unless it is a charge on a legal estate.

[1655]

NOTES

Section heading: words in square brackets substituted by the Civil Partnership Act 2004, s 82, Sch 9, Pt 1, para 2(1), (12).

Sub-ss (1), (2), (4), (5), (7), (9): words in square brackets substituted by the Civil Partnership Act 2004, s 82, Sch 9, Pt 1, para 2(1)–(3), (5)–(7), (9); for transitional provisions see s 82, Sch 9, Pt 3 thereto.

Sub-s (3): reference in square brackets in para (a) substituted and words in square brackets in para (b) inserted by the Civil Partnership Act 2004, s 82, Sch 9, Pt 1, para 2(1), (4)(a); for transitional provisions see s 82, Sch 9, Pt 3 thereto.

Sub-s (8): words in first and second pairs of square brackets substituted and words in third pair of square brackets inserted by the Civil Partnership Act 2004, s 82, Sch 9, Pt 1, para 2(1), (8); for transitional provisions see s 82, Sch 9, Pt 3 thereto.

Sub-s (10): references in square brackets substituted by the Civil Partnership Act 2004, s 82, Sch 9, Pt 1, para 2(1), (10)(a) (for transitional provisions see s 82, Sch 9, Pt 3 thereto); words "Land Registration Act 2002" in square brackets substituted by the Land Registration Act 2002, s 133, Sch 11, para 34(1), (2)(a); para (b) substituted by the Land Registration Act 2002, s 133, Sch 11, para 34(1), (2)(b), and words in square brackets therein substituted by the Civil Partnership Act 2004, s 82, Sch 9, Pt 1, para 2(1), (10)(b) (for transitional provisions see s 82, Sch 9, Pt 3 thereto).

Sub-s (11): repealed by the Land Registration Act 2002, s 135, Sch 13.

Sub-s (12): para (a) substituted by the Civil Partnership Act 2004, s 82, Sch 9, Pt 1, para 2(1), (11); for transitional provisions see s 82, Sch 9, Pt 3 thereto.

[32 Further provisions relating to home rights

Schedule 4 (provisions supplementary to sections 30 and 31) has effect.]

[1656]

NOTES

Commencement: 5 December 2005.

Substituted by the Civil Partnership Act 2004, s 82, Sch 9, Pt 1, para 3; for transitional provisions see s 82, Sch 9, Pt 3 thereto.

Occupation orders

33 Occupation orders where applicant has estate or interest etc or has [home rights]

(1) If—

(a) a person ("the person entitled")—

(i) is entitled to occupy a dwelling-house by virtue of a beneficial estate or interest or contract or by virtue of any enactment giving him the right to remain in occupation, or

(ii) has [home rights] in relation to a dwelling-house, and

(b) the dwelling-house—

(i) is or at any time has been the home of the person entitled and of another person with whom he is associated, or

(ii) was at any time intended by the person entitled and any such other person to be their home,

the person entitled may apply to the court for an order containing any of the provisions specified in subsections (3), (4) and (5).

(2) If an agreement to marry is terminated, no application under this section may be made by virtue of section 62(3)(e) by reference to that agreement after the end of the period of three years beginning with the day on which it is terminated.

[(2A) If a civil partnership agreement (as defined by section 73 of the Civil Partnership Act 2004) is terminated, no application under this section may be made by virtue of section 62(3)(eza) by reference to that agreement after the end of the period of three years beginning with the day on which it is terminated.]

(3) An order under this section may—

(a) enforce the applicant's entitlement to remain in occupation as against the other person ("the respondent");

(b) require the respondent to permit the applicant to enter and remain in the dwelling-house or part of the dwelling-house;

(c) regulate the occupation of the dwelling-house by either or both parties;

(d) if the respondent is entitled as mentioned in subsection (1)(a)(i), prohibit, suspend or restrict the exercise by him of his right to occupy the dwelling-house;

(e) if the respondent has [home rights] in relation to the dwelling-house and the applicant is the other spouse [or civil partner], restrict or terminate those rights;

(f) require the respondent to leave the dwelling-house or part of the dwelling-house; or

(g) exclude the respondent from a defined area in which the dwelling-house is included.

(4) An order under this section may declare that the applicant is entitled as mentioned in subsection (1)(a)(i) or has [home rights].

(5) If the applicant has [home rights] and the respondent is the other spouse [or civil partner], an order under this section made during the marriage [or civil partnership] may provide that those rights are not brought to an end by—

(a) the death of the other spouse [or civil partner]; or

(b) the termination (otherwise than by death) of the marriage [or civil partnership].

(6) In deciding whether to exercise its powers under subsection (3) and (if so) in what manner, the court shall have regard to all the circumstances including—

(a) the housing needs and housing resources of each of the parties and of any relevant child;

(b) the financial resources of each of the parties;

(c) the likely effect of any order, or of any decision by the court not to exercise its powers under subsection (3), on the health, safety or well-being of the parties and of any relevant child; and

(d) the conduct of the parties in relation to each other and otherwise.

(7) If it appears to the court that the applicant or any relevant child is likely to suffer significant harm attributable to conduct of the respondent if an order under this section containing one or more of the provisions mentioned in subsection (3) is not made, the court shall make the order unless it appears to it that—

(a) the respondent or any relevant child is likely to suffer significant harm if the order is made; and

(b) the harm likely to be suffered by the respondent or child in that event is as great as, or greater than, the harm attributable to conduct of the respondent which is likely to be suffered by the applicant or child if the order is not made.

(8) The court may exercise its powers under subsection (5) in any case where it considers that in all the circumstances it is just and reasonable to do so.

(9) An order under this section—

(a) may not be made after the death of either of the parties mentioned in subsection (1); and

(b) except in the case of an order made by virtue of subsection (5)(a), ceases to have effect on the death of either party.

(10) An order under this section may, in so far as it has continuing effect, be made for a specified period, until the occurrence of a specified event or until further order.

[1657]

NOTES

Section heading: words in square brackets substituted by the Civil Partnership Act 2004, s 82, Sch 9, Pt 1, para 4(1), (7); for transitional provisions see s 82, Sch 9, Pt 3 thereto.

Sub-ss (1), (4): words in square brackets substituted by the Civil Partnership Act 2004, s 82, Sch 9, Pt 1, para 4(1), (2), (5); for transitional provisions see s 82, Sch 9, Pt 3 thereto.

Sub-s (2A): inserted by the Civil Partnership Act 2004, s 82, Sch 9, Pt 1, para 4(1), (3); for transitional provisions see s 82, Sch 9, Pt 3 thereto.

Sub-s (3): words in first pair of square brackets substituted and words in second pair of square brackets inserted by the Civil Partnership Act 2004, s 82, Sch 9, Pt 1, para 4(1), (4); for transitional provisions see s 82, Sch 9, Pt 3 thereto.

Sub-s (5): words in first pair of square brackets substituted and words in other pairs of square brackets inserted by the Civil Partnership Act 2004, s 82, Sch 9, Pt 1, para 4(1), (6)(a); for transitional provisions see s 82, Sch 9, Pt 3 thereto.

34 Effect of order under s 33 where rights are charge on dwelling-house

(1) If [B's home rights] are a charge on the estate or interest of [A] or of trustees for [A]—

(a) an order under section 33 against [A] has, except so far as a contrary intention appears, the same effect against persons deriving title under [A] or under the trustees and affected by the charge, and

(b) sections 33(1), (3), (4) and (10) and 30(3) to (6) apply in relation to any person deriving title under [A] or under the trustees and affected by the charge as they apply in relation to [A].

(2) The court may make an order under section 33 by virtue of subsection (1)(b) if it considers that in all the circumstances it is just and reasonable to do so.

[1658]

NOTES

Sub-s (1): words in square brackets substituted by the Civil Partnership Act 2004, s 82, Sch 9, Pt 1, para 5; for transitional provisions see s 82, Sch 9, Pt 3 thereto.

35 One former spouse [or former civil partner] with no existing right to occupy

(1) This section applies if—

(a) one former spouse [or former civil partner] is entitled to occupy a dwelling-house by virtue of a beneficial estate or interest or contract, or by virtue of any enactment giving him the right to remain in occupation;

(b) the other former spouse [or former civil partner] is not so entitled; and

[(c) the dwelling-house—

(i) in the case of former spouses, was at any time their matrimonial home or was at any time intended by them to be their matrimonial home, or

(ii) in the case of former civil partners, was at any time their civil partnership home or was at any time intended by them to be their civil partnership home].

(2) The former spouse [or former civil partner] not so entitled may apply to the court for an order under this section against the other former spouse [or former civil partner] ("the respondent").

(3) If the applicant is in occupation, an order under this section must contain provision—

(a) giving the applicant the right not to be evicted or excluded from the dwelling-house or any part of it by the respondent for the period specified in the order; and

(b) prohibiting the respondent from evicting or excluding the applicant during that period.

(4) If the applicant is not in occupation, an order under this section must contain provision—

(a) giving the applicant the right to enter into and occupy the dwelling-house for the period specified in the order; and

(b) requiring the respondent to permit the exercise of that right.

(5) An order under this section may also—

(a) regulate the occupation of the dwelling-house by either or both of the parties;

(b) prohibit, suspend or restrict the exercise by the respondent of his right to occupy the dwelling-house;

(c) require the respondent to leave the dwelling-house or part of the dwelling-house; or

(d) exclude the respondent from a defined area in which the dwelling-house is included.

(6) In deciding whether to make an order under this section containing provision of the kind mentioned in subsection (3) or (4) and (if so) in what manner, the court shall have regard to all the circumstances including—

(a) the housing needs and housing resources of each of the parties and of any relevant child;

(b) the financial resources of each of the parties;

(c) the likely effect of any order, or of any decision by the court not to exercise its powers under subsection (3) or (4), on the health, safety or well-being of the parties and of any relevant child;

(d) the conduct of the parties in relation to each other and otherwise;

(e) the length of time that has elapsed since the parties ceased to live together;

(f) the length of time that has elapsed since the marriage [or civil partnership] was dissolved or annulled; and

(g) the existence of any pending proceedings between the parties—

(i) for an order under section 23A or 24 of the Matrimonial Causes Act 1973 (property adjustment orders in connection with divorce proceedings etc);

[(ia) for a property adjustment order under Part 2 of Schedule 5 to the Civil Partnership Act 2004;]

(ii) for an order under paragraph 1(2)(d) or (e) of Schedule 1 to the Children Act 1989 (orders for financial relief against parents); or

(iii) relating to the legal or beneficial ownership of the dwelling-house.

(7) In deciding whether to exercise its power to include one or more of the provisions referred to in subsection (5) ("a subsection (5) provision") and (if so) in what manner, the court shall have regard to all the circumstances including the matters mentioned in subsection (6)(a) to (e).

(8) If the court decides to make an order under this section and it appears to it that, if the order does not include a subsection (5) provision, the applicant or any relevant child is likely to suffer significant harm attributable to conduct of the respondent, the court shall include the subsection (5) provision in the order unless it appears to the court that—

(a) the respondent or any relevant child is likely to suffer significant harm if the provision is included in the order; and

(b) the harm likely to be suffered by the respondent or child in that event is as great as or greater than the harm attributable to conduct of the respondent which is likely to be suffered by the applicant or child if the provision is not included.

(9) An order under this section—

(a) may not be made after the death of either of the former spouses [or former civil partners]; and

(b) ceases to have effect on the death of either of them.

(10) An order under this section must be limited so as to have effect for a specified period not exceeding six months, but may be extended on one or more occasions for a further specified period not exceeding six months.

(11) A former spouse [or former civil partner] who has an equitable interest in the dwelling-house or in the proceeds of sale of the dwelling-house but in whom there is not vested (whether solely or as joint tenant) a legal estate in fee simple or a legal term of years absolute in the dwelling-house is to be treated (but only for the purpose of determining whether he is eligible to apply under this section) as not being entitled to occupy the dwelling-house by virtue of that interest.

(12) Subsection (11) does not prejudice any right of such a former spouse [or former civil partner] to apply for an order under section 33.

(13) So long as an order under this section remains in force, subsections (3) to (6) of section 30 apply in relation to the applicant—

[(a) as if he were B (the person entitled to occupy the dwelling-house by virtue of that section); and

(b) as if the respondent were A (the person entitled as mentioned in subsection (1)(a) of that section)].

[1659]

NOTES

Section heading: words in square brackets inserted by the Civil Partnership Act 2004, s 82, Sch 9, Pt 1, para 6(1), (10).

Sub-s (1): words in square brackets in paras (a), (b) inserted and para (c) substituted by the Civil Partnership Act 2004, s 82, Sch 9, Pt 1, para 6(1)–(3); for transitional provisions see s 82, Sch 9, Pt 3 thereto.

Sub-ss (2), (6), (9), (11), (12): words in square brackets inserted by the Civil Partnership Act 2004, s 82, Sch 9, Pt 1, para 6(1), (4)–(8); for transitional provisions see s 82, Sch 9, Pt 3 thereto.

Sub-s (13): paras (a), (b) substituted by the Civil Partnership Act 2004, s 82, Sch 9, Pt 1, para 6(1), (9); for transitional provisions see s 82, Sch 9, Pt 3 thereto.

36 One cohabitant or former cohabitant with no existing right to occupy

(1) This section applies if—

(a) one cohabitant or former cohabitant is entitled to occupy a dwelling-house by virtue of a beneficial estate or interest or contract or by virtue of any enactment giving him the right to remain in occupation;

(b) the other cohabitant or former cohabitant is not so entitled; and

(c) that dwelling-house is the home in which they [cohabit or a home in which they at any time cohabited or intended to cohabit].

(2) The cohabitant or former cohabitant not so entitled may apply to the court for an order under this section against the other cohabitant or former cohabitant ("the respondent").

(3) If the applicant is in occupation, an order under this section must contain provision—

(a) giving the applicant the right not to be evicted or excluded from the dwelling-house or any part of it by the respondent for the period specified in the order; and

(b) prohibiting the respondent from evicting or excluding the applicant during that period.

(4) If the applicant is not in occupation, an order under this section must contain provision—

(a) giving the applicant the right to enter into and occupy the dwelling-house for the period specified in the order; and

(b) requiring the respondent to permit the exercise of that right.

(5) An order under this section may also—

(a) regulate the occupation of the dwelling-house by either or both of the parties;

(b) prohibit, suspend or restrict the exercise by the respondent of his right to occupy the dwelling-house;

(c) require the respondent to leave the dwelling-house or part of the dwelling-house; or

(d) exclude the respondent from a defined area in which the dwelling-house is included.

(6) In deciding whether to make an order under this section containing provision of the kind mentioned in subsection (3) or (4) and (if so) in what manner, the court shall have regard to all the circumstances including—

(a) the housing needs and housing resources of each of the parties and of any relevant child;

(b) the financial resources of each of the parties;

(c) the likely effect of any order, or of any decision by the court not to exercise its powers under subsection (3) or (4), on the health, safety or well-being of the parties and of any relevant child;

(d) the conduct of the parties in relation to each other and otherwise;

(e) the nature of the parties' relationship [and in particular the level of commitment involved in it];

(f) the length of time during which they have [cohabited];

(g) whether there are or have been any children who are children of both parties or for whom both parties have or have had parental responsibility;

(h) the length of time that has elapsed since the parties ceased to live together; and

(i) the existence of any pending proceedings between the parties—

(i) for an order under paragraph 1 (2)(d) or (e) of Schedule to the Children Act 1989 (orders for financial relief against parents); or

(ii) relating to the legal or beneficial ownership of the dwelling-house.

(7) In deciding whether to exercise its powers to include one or more of the provisions referred to in subsection (5) ("a subsection (5) provision") and (if so) in what manner, the court shall have regard to all the circumstances including—

(a) the matters mentioned in subsection (6)(a) to (d); and

(b) the questions mentioned in subsection (8).

(8) The questions are—

(a) whether the applicant or any relevant child is likely to suffer significant harm attributable to conduct of the respondent if the subsection (5) provision is not included in the order; and

(b) whether the harm likely to be suffered by the respondent or child if the provision is included is as great as or greater than the harm attributable to conduct of the respondent which is likely to be suffered by the applicant or child if the provision is not included.

(9) An order under this section—

(a) may not be made after the death of either of the parties; and

(b) ceases to have effect on the death of either of them.

(10) An order under this section must be limited so as to have effect for a specified period not exceeding six months, but may be extended on one occasion for a further specified period not exceeding six months.

(11) A person who has an equitable interest in the dwelling-house or in the proceeds of sale of the dwelling-house but in whom there is not vested (whether solely or as joint tenant) a legal estate in fee simple or a legal term of years absolute in the dwelling-house is to be treated (but only for the purpose of determining whether he is eligible to apply under this section) as not being entitled to occupy the dwelling-house by virtue of that interest.

(12) Subsection (11) does not prejudice any right of such a person to apply for an order under section 33.

(13) So long as the order remains in force, subsections (3) to (6) of section 30 apply in relation to the applicant—

[(a) as if he were B (the person entitled to occupy the dwelling-house by virtue of that section); and

(b) as if the respondent were A (the person entitled as mentioned in subsection (1)(a) of that section)].

[1660]

NOTES

Sub-s (1): words in square brackets in para (c) substituted by the Domestic Violence, Crime and Victims Act 2004, s 58(1), Sch 10, para 34(1), (2).

Sub-s (6): words in square brackets in para (e) inserted and word in square brackets in para (f) substituted by the Domestic Violence, Crime and Victims Act 2004, ss 2(2), 58(1), Sch 10, para 34(1), (3).

Sub-s (13): paras (a), (b) substituted by the Civil Partnership Act 2004, s 82, Sch 9, Pt 1, para 7; for transitional provisions see s 82, Sch 9, Pt 3 thereto.

37 Neither spouse [or civil partner] entitled to occupy

(1) This section applies if—

(a) one spouse or former spouse and the other spouse or former spouse occupy a dwelling-house which is or was the matrimonial home; but

(b) neither of them is entitled to remain in occupation—

(i) by virtue of a beneficial estate or interest or contract; or

(ii) by virtue of any enactment giving him the right to remain in occupation.

[(1A) This section also applies if—

(a) one civil partner or former civil partner and the other civil partner or former civil partner occupy a dwelling-house which is or was the civil partnership home; but

(b) neither of them is entitled to remain in occupation—

(i) by virtue of a beneficial estate or interest or contract; or

(ii) by virtue of any enactment giving him the right to remain in occupation.]

(2) Either of the parties may apply to the court for an order against the other under this section.

(3) An order under this section may—

(a) require the respondent to permit the applicant to enter and remain in the dwelling-house or part of the dwelling-house;

(b) regulate the occupation of the dwelling-house by either or both of the [parties];

(c) require the respondent to leave the dwelling-house or part of the dwelling-house; or

(d) exclude the respondent from a defined area in which the dwelling-house is included.

(4) Subsections (6) and (7) of section 33 apply to the exercise by the court of its powers under this section as they apply to the exercise by the court of its powers under subsection (3) of that section.

(5) An order under this section must be limited so as to have effect for a specified period not exceeding six months, but may be extended on one or more occasions for a further specified period not exceeding six months.

[1661]

NOTES

Section heading: words in square brackets inserted by the Civil Partnership Act 2004, s 82, Sch 9, Pt 1, para 8(1), (4); for transitional provisions see s 82, Sch 9, Pt 3 thereto.

Sub-s (1A): inserted by the Civil Partnership Act 2004, s 82, Sch 9, Pt 1, para 8(1), (2); for transitional provisions see s 82, Sch 9, Pt 3 thereto.

Sub-s (3): word in square brackets in para (b) substituted by the Civil Partnership Act 2004, s 82, Sch 9, Pt 1, para 8(1), (3); for transitional provisions see s 82, Sch 9, Pt 3 thereto.

38 Neither cohabitant or former cohabitant entitled to occupy

(1) This section applies if—

(a) one cohabitant or former cohabitant and the other cohabitant or former cohabitant occupy a dwelling-house which is the home in which they [cohabit or cohabited]; but

(b) neither of them is entitled to remain in occupation—

(i) by virtue of a beneficial estate or interest or contract; or

(ii) by virtue of any enactment giving him the right to remain in occupation.

(2) Either of the parties may apply to the court for an order against the other under this section.

(3) An order under this section may—

(a) require the respondent to permit the applicant to enter and remain in the dwelling-house or part of the dwelling-house;

(b) regulate the occupation of the dwelling-house by either or both of the parties;

(c) require the respondent to leave the dwelling-house or part of the dwelling-house; or

(d) exclude the respondent from a defined area in which the dwelling-house is included.

(4) In deciding whether to exercise its powers to include one or more of the provisions referred to in subsection (3) ("a subsection (3) provision") and (if so) in what manner, the court shall have regard to all the circumstances including—

(a) the housing needs and housing resources of each of the parties and of any relevant child;

(b) the financial resources of each of the parties;

(c) the likely effect of any order, or of any decision by the court not to exercise its powers under subsection (3), on the health, safety or well-being of the parties and of any relevant child;

(d) the conduct of the parties in relation to each other and otherwise; and

(e) the questions mentioned in subsection (5).

(5) The questions are—

(a) whether the applicant or any relevant child is likely to suffer significant harm attributable to conduct of the respondent if the subsection (3) provision is not included in the order; and

(b) whether the harm likely to be suffered by the respondent or child if the provision is included is as great as or greater than the harm attributable to conduct of the respondent which is likely to be suffered by the applicant or child if the provision is not included.

(6) An order under this section shall be limited so as to have effect for a specified period not exceeding six months, but may be extended on one occasion for a further specified period not exceeding six months.

[1662]

NOTES

Sub-s (1): words in square brackets in para (a) substituted by the Domestic Violence, Crime and Victims Act 2004, s 58(1), Sch 10, para 35.

39 Supplementary provisions

(1) In this Part an "occupation order" means an order under section 33, 35, 36, 37 or 38.

(2) An application for an occupation order may be made in other family proceedings or without any other family proceedings being instituted.

(3) If—

(a) an application for an occupation order is made under section 33, 35, 36, 37 or 38, and

(b) the court considers that it has no power to make the order under the section concerned, but that it has power to make an order under one of the other sections,

the court may make an order under that other section.

(4) The fact that a person has applied for an occupation order under sections 35 to 38, or that an occupation order has been made, does not affect the right of any person to claim a legal or equitable interest in any property in any subsequent proceedings (including subsequent proceedings under this Part).

[1663]

40 Additional provisions that may be included in certain occupation orders

(1) The court may on, or at any time after, making an occupation order under section 33, 35 or 36—

(a) impose on either party obligations as to—

(i) the repair and maintenance of the dwelling-house; or

(ii) the discharge of rent, mortgage payments or other outgoings affecting the dwelling-house;

(b) order a party occupying the dwelling-house or any part of it (including a party who is entitled to do so by virtue of a beneficial estate or interest or contract or by virtue of any enactment giving him the right to remain in occupation) to make periodical payments to the other party in respect of the accommodation, if the other party would (but for the order) be entitled to occupy the dwelling-house by virtue of a beneficial estate or interest or contract or by virtue of any such enactment;

(c) grant either party possession or use of furniture or other contents of the dwelling-house;

(d) order either party to take reasonable care of any furniture or other contents of the dwelling-house;

(e) order either party to take reasonable steps to keep the dwelling-house and any furniture or other contents secure.

(2) In deciding whether and, if so, how to exercise its powers under this section, the court shall have regard to all the circumstances of the case including—

(a) the financial needs and financial resources of the parties; and

(b) the financial obligations which they have, or are likely to have in the foreseeable future, including financial obligations to each other and to any relevant child.

(3) An order under this section ceases to have effect when the occupation order to which it relates ceases to have effect.

[1664]

41 (*Repealed by the Domestic Violence, Crime and Victims Act 2004, ss 2(1), 58(2), Sch 11.*)

Non-molestation orders

42–52 (*Outside the scope of this work.*)

Transfer of tenancies

53 Transfer of certain tenancies

Schedule 7 makes provision in relation to the transfer of certain tenancies on divorce etc or on separation of cohabitants.

[1665]

Dwelling-house subject to mortgage

54 Dwelling-house subject to mortgage

(1) In determining for the purposes of this Part whether a person is entitled to occupy a dwelling-house by virtue of an estate or interest, any right to possession of the dwelling-house conferred on a mortgagee of the dwelling-house under or by virtue of his mortgage is to be disregarded.

(2) Subsection (1) applies whether or not the mortgagee is in possession.

(3) Where a person ("A") is entitled to occupy a dwelling-house by virtue of an estate or interest, a connected person does not by virtue of—

(a) any [home rights] conferred by section 30, or

(b) any rights conferred by an order under section 35 or 36,

have any larger right against the mortgagee to occupy the dwelling-house than A has by virtue of his estate or interest and of any contract with the mortgagee.

(4) Subsection (3) does not apply, in the case of [home rights], if under section 31 those rights are a charge, affecting the mortgagee, on the estate or interest mortgaged.

(5) In this section "connected person", in relation to any person, means that person's spouse, former spouse[, civil partner, former civil partner], cohabitant or former cohabitant.

[1666]

NOTES

Sub-ss (3), (4): words in square brackets substituted by the Civil Partnership Act 2004, s 82, Sch 9, Pt 1, para 12(1), (2); for transitional provisions see s 82, Sch 9, Pt 3 thereto.

Sub-s (5): words in square brackets inserted by the Civil Partnership Act 2004, s 82, Sch 9, Pt 1, para 12(1), (3); for transitional provisions see s 82, Sch 9, Pt 3 thereto.

55 Actions by mortgagees: joining connected persons as parties

(1) This section applies if a mortgagee of land which consists of or includes a dwelling-house brings an action in any court for the enforcement of his security.

(2) A connected person who is not already a party to the action is entitled to be made a party in the circumstances mentioned in subsection (3).

(3) The circumstances are that—
- (a) the connected person is enabled by section 30(3) or (6) (or by section 30(3) or (6) as applied by section 35(13) or 36(13)), to meet the mortgagor's liabilities under the mortgage;
- (b) he has applied to the court before the action is finally disposed of in that court; and
- (c) the court sees no special reason against his being made a party to the action and is satisfied—
  - (i) that he may be expected to make such payments or do such other things in or towards satisfaction of the mortgagor's liabilities or obligations as might affect the outcome of the proceedings; or
  - (ii) that the expectation of it should be considered under section 36 of the Administration of Justice Act 1970.

(4) In this section "connected person" has the same meaning as in section 54.

[1667]

56 Actions by mortgagees: service of notice on certain persons

(1) This section applies if a mortgagee of land which consists, or substantially consists, of a dwelling-house brings an action for the enforcement of his security, and at the relevant time there is—
- (a) in the case of unregistered land, a land charge of Class F registered against the person who is the estate owner at the relevant time or any person who, where the estate owner is a trustee, preceded him as trustee during the subsistence of the mortgage; or
- (b) in the case of registered land, a subsisting registration of—
  - (i) a notice under section 31(10);
  - (ii) a notice under section 2(8) of the Matrimonial Homes Act 1983; or
  - (iii) a notice or caution under section 2(7) of the Matrimonial Homes Act 1967.

(2) If the person on whose behalf—
- (a) the land charge is registered, or
- (b) the notice or caution is entered,

is not a party to the action, the mortgagee must serve notice of the action on him.

(3) If—
- (a) an official search has been made on behalf of the mortgagee which would disclose any land charge of Class F, notice or caution within subsection (1)(a) or (b),
- (b) a certificate of the result of the search has been issued, and
- (c) the action is commenced within the priority period,

the relevant time is the date of the certificate.

(4) In any other case the relevant time is the time when the action is commenced.

(5) The priority period is, for both registered and unregistered land, the period for which, in accordance with section 11(5) and (6) of the Land Charges Act 1972, a certificate on an official search operates in favour of a purchaser.

[1668]

Jurisdiction and procedure etc

57 Jurisdiction of courts

(1) For the purposes of this Part "the court" means the High Court, a county court or a magistrates' court.

(2) Subsection (1) is subject to the provision made by or under the following provisions of this section, to section 59 and to any express provision as to the jurisdiction of any court made by any other provision of this Part.

(3) The Lord Chancellor may[, after consulting the Lord Chief Justice,] by order specify proceedings under this Part which may only be commenced in—
- (a) a specified level of court;
- (b) a court which falls within a specified class of court; or
- (c) a particular court determined in accordance with, or specified in, the order.

(4) The Lord Chancellor may[, after consulting the Lord Chief Justice,] by order specify circumstances in which specified proceedings under this Part may only be commenced in—
- (a) a specified level of court;
- (b) a court which falls within a specified class of court; or

(c) a particular court determined in accordance with, or specified in, the order.

(5) The Lord Chancellor may[, after consulting the Lord Chief Justice,] by order provide that in specified circumstances the whole, or any specified part of any specified proceedings under this Part is to be transferred to—

(a) a specified level of court;
(b) a court which falls within a specified class of court; or
(c) a particular court determined in accordance with, or specified in, the order.

(6) An order under subsection (5) may provide for the transfer to be made at any stage, or specified stage, of the proceedings and whether or not the proceedings, or any part of them, have already been transferred.

(7) An order under subsection (5) may make such provision as the Lord Chancellor thinks appropriate[, after consulting the Lord Chief Justice] for excluding specified proceedings from the operation of section 38 or 39 of the Matrimonial and Family Proceedings Act 1984 (transfer of family proceedings) or any other enactment which would otherwise govern the transfer of those proceedings, or any part of them.

(8) For the purposes of subsections (3), (4) and (5), there are three levels of court—

(a) the High Court;
(b) any county court; and
(c) any magistrates' court.

(9) The Lord Chancellor may[, after consulting the Lord Chief Justice,] by order make provision for the principal registry of the Family Division of the High Court to be treated as if it were a county court for specified purposes of this Part, or of any provision made under this Part.

(10) Any order under subsection (9) may make such provision as the Lord Chancellor thinks expedient[, after consulting the Lord Chief Justice,] for the purpose of applying (with or without modifications) provisions which apply in relation to the procedure in county courts to the principal registry when it acts as if it were a county court.

(11) In this section "specified" means specified by an order under this section.

[(12) The Lord Chief Justice may nominate a judicial office holder (as defined in section 109(4) of the Constitutional Reform Act 2005) to exercise his functions under this section.]

[1669]

NOTES

Sub-ss (3)–(5), (7), (9), (10): words in square brackets inserted by the Constitutional Reform Act 2005, s 15(1), Sch 4, Pt 1, paras 252, 253(1)–(5).

Sub-s (12): inserted by the Constitutional Reform Act 2005, s 15(1), Sch 4, Pt 1, paras 252, 253(1), (6).

Orders: the Allocation and Transfer of Proceedings Order 2008, SI 2008/2836.

58–61 (*Outside the scope of this work.*)

General

62 Meaning of "cohabitants", "relevant child" and "associated persons"

(1) For the purposes of this Part—

(a) "cohabitants" are [[two persons who are neither married to each other nor civil partners of each other but are living together as husband and wife or as if they were civil partners;] and]
(b) ["cohabit" and "former cohabitants" are to be read accordingly, but the latter expression] does not include cohabitants who have subsequently married each other [or become civil partners of each other].

(2) In this Part, "relevant child", in relation to any proceedings under this Part, means—

(a) any child who is living with or might reasonably be expected to live with either party to the proceedings;
(b) any child in relation to whom an order under the Adoption Act 1976[, the Adoption and Children Act 2002] or the Children Act 1989 is in question in the proceedings; and
(c) any other child whose interests the court considers relevant.

(3) For the purposes of this Part, a person is associated with another person if—

(a) they are or have been married to each other;
[(aa) they are or have been civil partners of each other;]
(b) they are cohabitants or former cohabitants;
(c) they live or have lived in the same household, otherwise than merely by reason of one of them being the other's employee, tenant, lodger or boarder;
(d) they are relatives;
(e) they have agreed to marry one another (whether or not that agreement has been terminated);

[(eza) they have entered into a civil partnership agreement (as defined by section 73 of the Civil Partnership Act 2004) (whether or not that agreement has been terminated);]
[(ea) they have or have had an intimate personal relationship with each other which is or was of significant duration;]
(f) in relation to any child, they are both persons falling within subsection (4); or
(g) they are parties to the same family proceedings (other than proceedings under this Part).

(4) A person falls within this subsection in relation to a child if—
(a) he is a parent of the child; or
(b) he has or has had parental responsibility for the child.

(5) If a child has been adopted or [falls within subsection (7)], two persons are also associated with each other for the purposes of this Part if—
(a) one is a natural parent of the child or a parent of such a natural parent; and
(b) the other is the child or any person—
(i) who has become a parent of the child by virtue of an adoption order or has applied for an adoption order, or
(ii) with whom the child has at any time been placed for adoption.

(6) A body corporate and another person are not, by virtue of subsection (3)(f) or (g), to be regarded for the purposes of this Part as associated with each other.

[(7) A child falls within this subsection if—
(a) an adoption agency, within the meaning of section 2 of the Adoption and Children Act 2002, has power to place him for adoption under section 19 of that Act (placing children with parental consent) or he has become the subject of an order under section 21 of that Act (placement orders), or
(b) he is freed for adoption by virtue of an order made—
(i) in England and Wales, under section 18 of the Adoption Act 1976,
(ii) in Scotland, under section 18 of the Adoption (Scotland) Act 1978, or
(iii) in Northern Ireland, under Article 17(1) or 18(1) of the Adoption (Northern Ireland) Order 1987.]

[1670]

NOTES

Sub-s (1): words in first (outer) pair of square brackets in para (a) and words in first pair of square brackets in para (b) substituted by the Domestic Violence, Crime and Victims Act 2004, ss 3, 58(1), Sch 10, para 40; words in second (inner) pair of square brackets in para (a) substituted and words in second pair of square brackets in para (b) inserted by the Civil Partnership Act 2004, s 82, Sch 9, Pt 1, para 13(1), (2) (for transitional provisions see s 82, Sch 9, Pt 3 thereto).

Sub-s (2): words in square brackets in para (b) inserted by the Adoption and Children Act 2002, s 139(1), Sch 3, paras 85, 86(a).

Sub-s (3): paras (aa), (eza) inserted by the Civil Partnership Act 2004, s 82, Sch 9, Pt 1, para 13(1), (3), (4) (for transitional provisions see s 82, Sch 9, Pt 3 thereto); para (ea) inserted by the Domestic Violence, Crime and Victims Act 2004, s 4.

Sub-s (5): words in square brackets substituted by the Adoption and Children Act 2002, s 139(1), Sch 3, paras 85, 86(b).

Sub-s (7): inserted by the Adoption and Children Act 2002, s 139(1), Sch 3, paras 85, 87.

63 Interpretation of Part IV

(1) In this Part—

["adoption order" means an adoption order within the meaning of section 72(1) of the Adoption Act 1976 or section 46(1) of the Adoption and Children Act 2002;]

"associated", in relation to a person, is to be read with section 62(3) to (6);

"child" means a person under the age of eighteen years;

["cohabit",] "cohabitant" and "former cohabitant" have the meaning given by section 62(1);

"the court" is to be read with section 57;

"development" means physical, intellectual, emotional, social or behavioural development;

"dwelling-house" includes (subject to subsection (4))—
(a) any building or part of a building which is occupied as a dwelling,
(b) any caravan, house-boat or structure which is occupied as a dwelling,
and any yard, garden, garage or outhouse belonging to it and occupied with it;

"family proceedings" means any proceedings—
(a) under the inherent jurisdiction of the High Court in relation to children; or
(b) under the enactments mentioned in subsection (2);

"harm"—
(a) in relation to a person who has reached the age of eighteen years, means ill-treatment or the impairment of health; and
(b) in relation to a child, means ill-treatment or the impairment of health or development;

"health" includes physical or mental health;

["home rights" has the meaning given by section 30;]

"ill-treatment" includes forms of ill-treatment which are not physical and, in relation to a child, includes sexual abuse;

…

"mortgage", "mortgagor" and "mortgagee" have the same meaning as in the Law of Property Act 1925;

"mortgage payments" includes any payments which, under the terms of the mortgage, the mortgagor is required to make to any person;

"non-molestation order" has the meaning given by section 42(1);

"occupation order" has the meaning given by section 39;

"parental responsibility" has the same meaning as in the Children Act 1989;

"relative", in relation to a person, means—

(a) the father, mother, stepfather, stepmother, son, daughter, stepson, stepdaughter, grandmother, grandfather, grandson or granddaughter of that person or of that person's [spouse, former spouse, civil partner or former civil partner], or

(b) the brother, sister, uncle, aunt, niece[, nephew or first cousin] (whether of the full blood or of the half blood or [by marriage or civil partnership)] of that person or of that person's [spouse, former spouse, civil partner or former civil partner],

and includes, in relation to a person who [is cohabiting or has cohabited with another person], any person who would fall within paragraph (a) or (b) if the parties were married to each other [or were civil partners of each other];

"relevant child", in relation to any proceedings under this Part, has the meaning given by section 62(2);

"the relevant judicial authority", in relation to any order under this Part, means—

(a) where the order was made by the High Court, a judge of that court;

(b) where the order was made by a county court, a judge or district judge of that or any other county court; or

(c) where the order was made by a magistrates' court, any magistrates' court.

(2)–(5) (*Outside the scope of this work.*)

[1671]

NOTES

Sub-s (1): definition "adoption order" substituted by the Adoption and Children Act 2002, s 139(1), Sch 3, paras 85, 88(a).

Sub-s (1): in definition beginning "cohabit", word in square brackets inserted by the Domestic Violence, Crime and Victims Act 2004, s 58(1), Sch 10, para 41(1), (2).

Sub-s (1): definition "home rights" inserted and definition "matrimonial home rights" (omitted) repealed by the Civil Partnership Act 2004, ss 82, 261(4), Sch 9, Pt 1, para 14(1)–(3), Sch 30; for transitional provisions see s 82, Sch 9, Pt 3 thereto.

Sub-s (1): in definition "relative", words in first, third and fourth pairs of square brackets substituted and words in final pair of square brackets inserted by the Civil Partnership Act 2004, s 82, Sch 9, Pt 1, para 14(1), (4); for transitional provisions see s 82, Sch 9, Pt 3 thereto; words in second and fifth pairs of square brackets substituted by the Domestic Violence, Crime and Victims Act 2004, s 58(1), Sch 10, para 41(1), (3).

63A–63S ((*Pt IVA*) *Outside the scope of this work.*)

PART V
SUPPLEMENTAL

64–66 (*Outside the scope of this work.*)

67 Short title, commencement and extent

(1) This Act may be cited as the Family Law Act 1996.

(2) Section 65 and this section come into force on the passing of this Act.

(3) The other provisions of this Act come into force on such day as the Lord Chancellor may by order appoint; and different days may be appointed for different purposes.

(4) This Act, other than section 17, extends only to England and Wales, except that—

(a) in Schedule 8—

(i) the amendments of section 38 of the Family Law Act 1986 extend also to Northern Ireland;

(ii) the amendments of the Judicial Proceedings (Regulation of Reports) Act 1926 extend also to Scotland; and

(iii) the amendments of the Maintenance Orders Act 1950, the Civil Jurisdiction and Judgments Act 1982, the Finance Act 1985 and sections 42 and 51 of the Family Law Act 1986 extend also to both Northern Ireland and Scotland; and

(b) in Schedule 10, the repeal of section 2(1)(b) of the Domestic and Appellate Proceedings (Restriction of Publicity) Act 1968 extends also to Scotland.

[1672]

NOTES

Orders: the Family Law Act 1996 (Commencement No 1) Order 1997, SI 1997/1077; the Family Law Act 1996 (Commencement No 2) Order 1997, SI 1997/1892; the Family Law Act 1996 (Commencement) (No 3) Order 1998, SI 1998/2572.

(*Schs 1–3 outside the scope of this work.*)

SCHEDULE 4
PROVISIONS SUPPLEMENTARY TO SECTIONS 30 AND 31

Section 32

Interpretation

1.—(1) In this Schedule—

(a) any reference to a solicitor includes a reference to a licensed conveyancer or a recognised body, and

(b) any reference to a person's solicitor includes a reference to a licensed conveyancer or recognised body acting for that person.

(2) In sub-paragraph (1)—

"licensed conveyancer" has the meaning given by section 11(2) of the Administration of Justice Act 1985;

"recognised body" means a body corporate for the time being recognised under section 9 (incorporated practices) or section 32 (provision of conveyancing by recognised bodies) of that Act.

[1. In this Schedule "legal representative" means a person who, for the purposes of the Legal Services Act 2007, is an authorised person in relation to an activity which constitutes a reserved instrument activity (within the meaning of that Act).]

Restriction on registration where spouse [or civil partner] entitled to more than one charge

2. Where one spouse [or civil partner] is entitled by virtue of section 31 to a registrable charge in respect of each of two or more dwelling-houses, only one of the charges to which that spouse [or civil partner] is so entitled shall be registered under section 31(10) or under section 2 of the Land Charges Act 1972 at any one time, and if any of those charges is registered under either of those provisions the Chief Land Registrar, on being satisfied that any other of them is so registered, shall cancel the registration of the charge first registered.

Contract for sale of house affected by registered charge to include term requiring cancellation of registration before completion

3.—(1) Where one spouse [or civil partner] is entitled by virtue of section 31 to a charge on an estate in a dwelling-house and the charge is registered under section 31(10) or section 2 of the Land Charges Act 1972, it shall be a term of any contract for the sale of that estate whereby the vendor agrees to give vacant possession of the dwelling-house on completion of the contract that the vendor will before such completion procure the cancellation of the registration of the charge at his expense.

(2) Sub-paragraph (1) shall not apply to any such contract made by a vendor who is entitled to sell the estate in the dwelling-house freed from any such charge.

(3) If, on the completion of such a contract as is referred to in sub-paragraph (1), there is delivered to the purchaser or his *solicitor* [legal representative] an application by the spouse [or civil partner] entitled to the charge for the cancellation of the registration of that charge, the term of the contract for which sub-paragraph (1) provides shall be deemed to have been performed.

(4) This paragraph applies only if and so far as a contrary intention is not expressed in the contract.

(5) This paragraph shall apply to a contract for exchange as it applies to a contract for sale.

(6) This paragraph shall, with the necessary modifications, apply to a contract for the grant of a lease or underlease of a dwelling-house as it applies to a contract for the sale of an estate in a dwelling-house.

Cancellation of registration after termination of marriage [or civil partnership], etc

4.—(1) Where a [spouse's or civil partner's home rights] are a charge on an estate in the dwelling-house and the charge is registered under section 31(10) or under section 2 of the Land Charges Act 1972, the Chief Land Registrar shall, subject to sub-paragraph (2), cancel the registration of the charge if he is satisfied—

[(a) in the case of a marriage—

(i) by the production of a certificate or other sufficient evidence, that either spouse is dead,

(ii) by the production of an official copy of a decree or order of a court, that the marriage has been terminated otherwise than by death, or

(iii) by the production of an order of the court, that the spouse's home rights constituting the charge have been terminated by the order, and

(b) in the case of a civil partnership—

(i) by the production of a certificate or other sufficient evidence, that either civil partner is dead,

(ii) by the production of an official copy of an order or decree of a court, that the civil partnership has been terminated otherwise than by death, or

(iii) by the production of an order of the court, that the civil partner's home rights constituting the charge have been terminated by the order].

(2) Where—

(a) the marriage [or civil partnership] in question has been terminated by the death of the spouse [or civil partner] entitled to an estate in the dwelling-house or otherwise than by death, and

(b) an order affecting the charge of the spouse [or civil partner] not so entitled had been made under section 33(5),

then if, after the making of the order, registration of the charge was renewed or the charge registered in pursuance of sub-paragraph (3), the Chief Land Registrar shall not cancel the registration of the charge in accordance with sub-paragraph (1) unless he is also satisfied that the order has ceased to have effect.

(3) Where such an order has been made, then, for the purposes of sub-paragraph (2), the spouse [or civil partner] entitled to the charge affected by the order may—

(a) if before the date of the order the charge was registered under section 31(10) or under section 2 of the Land Charges Act 1972, renew the registration of the charge, and

(b) if before the said date the charge was not so registered, register the charge under section 31(10) or under section 2 of the Land Charges Act 1972.

(4) Renewal of the registration of a charge in pursuance of sub-paragraph (3) shall be effected in such manner as may be prescribed, and an application for such renewal or for registration of a charge in pursuance of that sub-paragraph shall contain such particulars of any order affecting the charge made under section 33(5) as may be prescribed.

(5) The renewal in pursuance of sub-paragraph (3) of the registration of a charge shall not affect the priority of the charge.

(6) In this paragraph "prescribed" means prescribed by rules made under section 16 of the Land Charges Act 1972 or [by land registration rules under the Land Registration Act 2002], as the circumstances of the case require.

Release of [home rights]

5.—(1) A [spouse or civil partner entitled to home rights] may by a release in writing release those rights or release them as respects part only of the dwelling-house affected by them.

(2) Where a contract is made for the sale of an estate or interest in a dwelling-house, or for the grant of a lease or underlease of a dwelling-house, being (in either case) a dwelling-house affected by a charge registered under section 31(10) or under section 2 of the Land Charges Act 1972, then, without prejudice to sub-paragraph (1), the [home rights] constituting the charge shall be deemed to have been released on the happening of whichever of the following events first occurs—

(a) the delivery to the purchaser or lessee, as the case may be, or his *solicitor* [legal representative] on completion of the contract of an application by the spouse [or civil partner] entitled to the charge for the cancellation of the registration of the charge; or

(b) the lodging of such an application at Her Majesty's Land Registry.

Postponement of priority of charge

6. A spouse [or civil partner] entitled by virtue of section 31 to a charge on an estate or interest may agree in writing that any other charge on, or interest in, that estate or interest shall rank in priority to the charge to which that spouse [or civil partner] is so entitled.

[1673]

NOTES

Para 1: substituted by the Legal Services Act 2007, s 208(1), Sch 21, para 121(a), as from a day to be appointed.

Para 2: words in square brackets inserted by the Civil Partnership Act 2004, s 82, Sch 9, Pt 1, para 15(1)–(3), (12); for transitional provisions see s 82, Sch 9, Pt 3 thereto.

Para 3: in sub-para (1) words in square brackets inserted by the Civil Partnership Act 2004, s 82, Sch 9, Pt 1, para 15(1)–(3), (12) (for transitional provisions see s 82, Sch 9, Pt 3 thereto); in sub-para (3) word in italics substituted by subsequent words in first pair of square brackets by the Legal Services Act 2007, s 208(1), Sch 21, para 121(b), as from a day to be appointed, words in second pair of square brackets inserted by the Civil Partnership Act 2004, s 82, Sch 9, Pt 1, para 15(1)–(3), (12) (for transitional provisions see s 82, Sch 9, Pt 3 thereto).

Para 4: words in first pair of square brackets inserted, words in square brackets in sub-para (1) substituted, and words in square brackets in sub-paras (2), (3) inserted by the Civil Partnership Act 2004, s 82, Sch 9, Pt 1, para 15(1), (4)–(8) (for transitional provisions see s 82, Sch 9, Pt 3 thereto); words in square brackets in sub-para (6) substituted by the Land Registration Act 2002, s 133, Sch 11, para 34(1), (3).

Para 5: words in square brackets in sub-para (1) inserted, and words in square brackets in heading, sub-para (2) and words in second pair of square brackets in sub-para (2)(a) substituted by the Civil Partnership Act 2004, s 82, Sch 9, Pt 1, para 15(1), (9)–(11); for transitional provisions see s 82, Sch 9, Pt 3 thereto; in sub-para (2)(a) word in italics substituted by subsequent words in first pair of square brackets by the Legal Services Act 2007, s 208(1), Sch 21, para 121(c), as from a day to be appointed.

Para 6: words in square brackets inserted by the Civil Partnership Act 2004, s 82, Sch 9, Pt 1, para 15(1)–(3), (12); for transitional provisions see s 82, Sch 9, Pt 3 thereto.

Rules: the Land Registration Rules 2003, SI 2003/1417 at **[3067]**.

(*Schs 5, 6 outside the scope of this work.*)

PART I STATUTES

SCHEDULE 7
TRANSFER OF CERTAIN TENANCIES ON DIVORCE ETC OR ON SEPARATION OF COHABITANTS

Section 53

PART I
GENERAL

Interpretation

1. In this Schedule—

["civil partner", except in paragraph 2, includes (where the context requires) former civil partner;]

"cohabitant", except in paragraph 3, includes (where the context requires) former cohabitant;

"the court" does not include a magistrates' court,

"landlord" includes—

(a) any person from time to time deriving title under the original landlord; and

(b) in relation to any dwelling-house, any person other than the tenant who is, or (but for Part VII of the Rent Act 1977 or Part II of the Rent (Agriculture) Act 1976) would be, entitled to possession of the dwelling-house;

"Part II order" means an order under Part II of this Schedule;

"a relevant tenancy" means—

(a) a protected tenancy or statutory tenancy within the meaning of the Rent Act 1977;

(b) a statutory tenancy within the meaning of the Rent (Agriculture) Act 1976;

(c) a secure tenancy within the meaning of section 79 of the Housing Act 1985; …

(d) an assured tenancy or assured agricultural occupancy within the meaning of Part I of the Housing Act 1988; [or

(e) an introductory tenancy within the meaning of Chapter I of Part V of the Housing Act 1996;]

"spouse", except in paragraph 2, includes (where the context requires) former spouse; and "tenancy" includes sub-tenancy.

Cases in which the court may make an order

2.—(1) This paragraph applies if one spouse [or civil partner] is entitled, either in his own right or jointly with the other spouse [or civil partner], to occupy a dwelling-house by virtue of a relevant tenancy.

[(2) The court may make a Part II order—

(a) on granting a decree of divorce, a decree of nullity of marriage or a decree of judicial separation or at any time thereafter (whether, in the case of a decree of divorce or nullity of marriage, before or after the decree is made absolute), or

(b) at any time when it has power to make a property adjustment order under Part 2 of Schedule 5 to the Civil Partnership Act 2004 with respect to the civil partnership.]

3.—(1) This paragraph applies if one cohabitant is entitled, either in his own right or jointly with the other cohabitant, to occupy a dwelling-house by virtue of a relevant tenancy.

(2) If the cohabitants cease [to cohabit], the court may make a Part II order.

4. The court shall not make a Part II order unless the dwelling-house is or was—

(a) in the case of spouses, a matrimonial home; …

[(aa) in the case of civil partners, a civil partnership home; or]

(b) in the case of cohabitants, a home in which they [cohabited].

Matters to which the court must have regard

5. In determining whether to exercise its powers under Part II of this Schedule and, if so, in what manner, the court shall have regard to all the circumstances of the case including—

(a) the circumstances in which the tenancy was granted to either or both of the spouses[, civil partners] or cohabitants or, as the case requires, the circumstances in which either or both of them became tenant under the tenancy;

(b) the matters mentioned in section 33(6)(a), (b) and (c) and, where the parties are cohabitants and only one of them is entitled to occupy the dwelling-house by virtue of the relevant tenancy, the further matters mentioned in section 36(6)(e), (f), (g) and (h); and

(c) the suitability of the parties as tenants.

[1674]

NOTES

Para 1: definition "civil partner" inserted by the Civil Partnership Act 2004, s 82, Sch 9, Pt 1, para 16(1), (2); for transitional provisions see s 82, Sch 9, Pt 3 thereto; in definition "a relevant tenancy" word omitted from para (c) repealed, and para (e) and word immediately preceding it inserted by SI 1997/74, art 2, Schedule, para 10(b).

Para 2: words in square brackets in sub-para (1) inserted and sub-para (2) substituted by the Civil Partnership Act 2004, s 82, Sch 9, Pt 1, para 16(1), (3), (4); for transitional provisions see s 82, Sch 9, Pt 3 thereto.

Para 3: words in square brackets in sub-para (2) substituted by the Domestic Violence, Crime and Victims Act 2004, s 58(1), Sch 10, para 42(1), (2).

Para 4: word omitted from sub-para (a) repealed and sub-para (aa) inserted by the Civil Partnership Act 2004, ss 82, 261(4), Sch 9, Pt 1, para 16(1), (5), Sch 30; for transitional provisions see s 82, Sch 9, Pt 3 thereto; word in square brackets in sub-para (b) substituted by the Domestic Violence, Crime and Victims Act 2004, s 58(1), Sch 10, para 42(1), (3).

Para 5: words in square brackets in sub-para (a) inserted by the Civil Partnership Act 2004, s 82, Sch 9, Pt 1, para 16(1), (6); for transitional provisions see s 82, Sch 9, Pt 3 thereto.

Modification: para 2(2) temporarily modified by the Family Law Act 1996 (Commencement No 2) Order 1997, SI 1997/1892, art 4(a), until such time as Part II of this Act is brought into force.

PART II
ORDERS THAT MAY BE MADE

References to entitlement to occupy

6. References in this Part of this Schedule to a spouse[, a civil partner] or a cohabitant being entitled to occupy a dwelling-house by virtue of a relevant tenancy apply whether that entitlement is in his own right or jointly with the other spouse[, civil partner] or cohabitant.

Protected, secure or assured tenancy or assured agricultural occupancy

7.—(1) If a spouse[, civil partner] or cohabitant is entitled to occupy the dwelling-house by virtue of a protected tenancy within the meaning of the Rent Act 1977, a secure tenancy within the meaning of the Housing Act 1985[, an assured tenancy] or assured agricultural occupancy within the meaning of Part I of the Housing Act 1988 [or an introductory tenancy within the meaning of Chapter I of Part V of the Housing Act 1996], the court may by order direct that, as from such date as may be specified in the order, there shall, by virtue of the order and without further assurance, be transferred to, and vested in, the other spouse[, civil partner] or cohabitant—

(a) the estate or interest which the spouse[, civil partner] or cohabitant so entitled had in the dwelling-house immediately before that date by virtue of the lease or agreement creating the tenancy and any assignment of that lease or agreement, with all rights, privileges and appurtenances attaching to that estate or interest but subject to all covenants, obligations, liabilities and incumbrances to which it is subject; and

(b) where the spouse[, civil partner] or cohabitant so entitled is an assignee of such lease or agreement, the liability of that spouse[, civil partner] or cohabitant under any covenant of indemnity by the assignee express or implied in the assignment of the lease or agreement to that spouse[, civil partner] or cohabitant.

(2) If an order is made under this paragraph, any liability or obligation to which the spouse[, civil partner] or cohabitant so entitled is subject under any covenant having reference to the dwelling-house in the lease or agreement, being a liability or obligation falling due to be discharged or performed on or after the date so specified, shall not be enforceable against that spouse[, civil partner] or cohabitant.

[(3) If the spouse, civil partner or cohabitant so entitled is a successor within the meaning of Part 4 of the Housing Act 1985—

(a) his former spouse (or, in the case of judicial separation, his spouse),

(b) his former civil partner (or, if a separation order is in force, his civil partner), or

(c) his former cohabitant,

is to be deemed also to be a successor within the meaning of that Part.

(3A) If the spouse, civil partner or cohabitant so entitled is a successor within the meaning of section 132 of the Housing Act 1996—

(a) his former spouse (or, in the case of judicial separation, his spouse),

(b) his former civil partner (or, if a separation order is in force, his civil partner), or

(c) his former cohabitant,

is to be deemed also to be a successor within the meaning of that section.

(4) If the spouse, civil partner or cohabitant so entitled is for the purposes of section 17 of the Housing Act 1988 a successor in relation to the tenancy or occupancy—

(a) his former spouse (or, in the case of judicial separation, his spouse),

(b) his former civil partner (or, if a separation order is in force, his civil partner), or

(c) his former cohabitant,

is to be deemed to be a successor in relation to the tenancy or occupancy for the purposes of that section.]

(5) If the transfer under sub-paragraph (1) is of an assured agricultural occupancy, then, for the purposes of Chapter III of Part I of the Housing Act 1988—

(a) the agricultural worker condition is fulfilled with respect to the dwelling-house while the spouse[, civil partner] or cohabitant to whom the assured agricultural occupancy is transferred continues to be the occupier under that occupancy, and

(b) that condition is to be treated as so fulfilled by virtue of the same paragraph of Schedule 3 to the Housing Act 1988 as was applicable before the transfer.

(6) …

Statutory tenancy within the meaning of the Rent Act 1977

8.—(1) This paragraph applies if the spouse[, civil partner] or cohabitant is entitled to occupy the dwelling-house by virtue of a statutory tenancy within the meaning of the Rent Act 1977.

(2) The court may by order direct that, as from the date specified in the order—

(a) that spouse[, civil partner] or cohabitant is to cease to be entitled to occupy the dwelling-house; and

(b) the other spouse[, civil partner] or cohabitant is to be deemed to be the tenant or, as the case may be, the sole tenant under that statutory tenancy.

(3) The question whether the provisions of paragraphs 1 to 3, or (as the case may be) paragraphs 5 to 7 of Schedule 1 to the Rent Act 1977, as to the succession by the surviving spouse [or surviving civil partner] of a deceased tenant, or by a member of the deceased tenant's family, to the right to retain possession are capable of having effect in the event of the death of the person deemed by an order under this paragraph to be the tenant or sole tenant under the statutory tenancy is to be determined according as those provisions have or have not already had effect in relation to the statutory tenancy.

Statutory tenancy within the meaning of the Rent (Agriculture) Act 1976

9.—(1) This paragraph applies if the spouse[, civil partner] or cohabitant is entitled to occupy the dwelling-house by virtue of a statutory tenancy within the meaning of the Rent (Agriculture) Act 1976.

(2) The court may by order direct that, as from such date as may be specified in the order—

(a) that spouse[, civil partner] or cohabitant is to cease to be entitled to occupy the dwelling-house; and

(b) the other spouse[, civil partner] or cohabitant is to be deemed to be the tenant or, as the case may be, the sole tenant under that statutory tenancy.

(3) A spouse[, civil partner] or cohabitant who is deemed under this paragraph to be the tenant under a statutory tenancy is (within the meaning of that Act) a statutory tenant in his own right, or a statutory tenant by succession, according as the other spouse[, civil partner] or cohabitant was a statutory tenant in his own right or a statutory tenant by succession.

[1675]

NOTES

Paras 6, 8, 9: words in square brackets inserted by the Civil Partnership Act 2004, s 82, Sch 9, Pt 1, para 16(1), (7), (12)–(14); for transitional provisions see s 82, Sch 9, Pt 3 thereto.

Para 7: in sub-paras (1), (2), (5), words ", civil partner" in square brackets in each place they appear inserted, sub-paras (3), (3A) (as inserted by SI 1997/74, art 2, Schedule, para 10(b)(iii)), (4) substituted, and sub-para (6) repealed by the Civil Partnership Act 2004, ss 82, 261(4), Sch 9, Pt 1, para 16(1), (8)–(11), Sch 30 (for transitional provisions see s 82, Sch 9, Pt 3 thereto); in sub-para (1), words in second pair of square brackets substituted and words in third pair of square brackets inserted by SI 1997/74, art 2, Schedule, para 10(b)(ii), (iii).

Modification: para 7(3), (4), (6) temporarily modified by the Family Law Act 1996 (Commencement No 2) Order 1997, SI 1997/1892, art 4(b), (c), until such time as Part II of this Act is brought into force.

PART III
SUPPLEMENTARY PROVISIONS

Compensation

10.—(1) If the court makes a Part II order, it may by the order direct the making of a payment by the spouse[, civil partner] or cohabitant to whom the tenancy is transferred ("the transferee") to the other spouse[, civil partner] or cohabitant ("the transferor").

(2) Without prejudice to that, the court may, on making an order by virtue of sub-paragraph (1) for the payment of a sum—

(a) direct that payment of that sum or any part of it is to be deferred until a specified date or until the occurrence of a specified event, or

(b) direct that that sum or any part of it is to be paid by instalments.

(3) Where an order has been made by virtue of sub-paragraph (1), the court may, on the application of the transferee or the transferor—

(a) exercise its powers under sub-paragraph (2), or

(b) vary any direction previously given under that sub-paragraph,

at any time before the sum whose payment is required by the order is paid in full.

(4) In deciding whether to exercise its powers under this paragraph and, if so, in what manner, the court shall have regard to all the circumstances including—

(a) the financial loss that would otherwise be suffered by the transferor as a result of the order;

(b) the financial needs and financial resources of the parties; and

(c) the financial obligations which the parties have, or are likely to have in the foreseeable future, including financial obligations to each other and to any relevant child.

(5) The court shall not give any direction under sub-paragraph (2) unless it appears to it that immediate payment of the sum required by the order would cause the transferee financial hardship which is greater than any financial hardship that would be caused to the transferor if the direction were given.

Liabilities and obligations in respect of the dwelling-house

11.—(1) If the court makes a Part II order, it may by the order direct that both spouses[, civil partners] or cohabitants are to be jointly and severally liable to discharge or perform any or all of the liabilities and obligations in respect of the dwelling-house (whether arising under the tenancy or otherwise) which—

(a) have at the date of the order fallen due to be discharged or performed by one only of them; or

(b) but for the direction, would before the date specified as the date on which the order is to take effect fall due to be discharged or performed by one only of them.

(2) If the court gives such a direction, it may further direct that either spouse[, civil partner] or cohabitant is to be liable to indemnify the other in whole or in part against any payment made or expenses incurred by the other in discharging or performing any such liability or obligation.

[Date when order made between spouses or civil partners takes effect

12. The date specified in a Part II order as the date on which the order is to take effect must not be earlier than—

(a) in the case of a marriage in respect of which a decree of divorce or nullity has been granted, the date on which the decree is made absolute;

(b) in the case of a civil partnership in respect of which a dissolution or nullity order has been made, the date on which the order is made final.]

[Effect of remarriage or subsequent civil partnership

13.—(1) If after the grant of a decree dissolving or annulling a marriage either spouse remarries or forms a civil partnership, that spouse is not entitled to apply, by reference to the grant of that decree, for a Part II order.

(2) If after the making of a dissolution or nullity order either civil partner forms a subsequent civil partnership or marries, that civil partner is not entitled to apply, by reference to the making of that order, for a Part II order.

(3) In sub-paragraphs (1) and (2)—

(a) the references to remarrying and marrying include references to cases where the marriage is by law void or voidable, and

(b) the references to forming a civil partnership include references to cases where the civil partnership is by law void or voidable.]

Rules of court

14.—(1) Rules of court shall be made requiring the court, before it makes an order under this Schedule, to give the landlord of the dwelling-house to which the order will relate an opportunity of being heard.

(2) Rules of court may provide that an application for a Part II order by reference to an order or decree may not, without the leave of the court by which that order was made or decree was granted, be made after the expiration of such period from the order or grant as may be prescribed by the rules.

Saving for other provisions of Act

15.—(1) If a spouse [or civil partner] is entitled to occupy a dwelling-house by virtue of a tenancy, this Schedule does not affect the operation of sections 30 and 31 in relation to the other [spouse's or civil partner's home rights].

(2) If a spouse[, civil partner] or cohabitant is entitled to occupy a dwelling-house by virtue of a tenancy, the court's powers to make orders under this Schedule are additional to those conferred by sections 33, 35 and 36.

[1676]

NOTES

Paras 10, 11: words in square brackets inserted by the Civil Partnership Act 2004, s 82, Sch 9, Pt 1, para 16(1), (14)–(16); for transitional provisions see s 82, Sch 9, Pt 3 thereto.

Paras 12, 13: substituted by the Civil Partnership Act 2004, s 82, Sch 9, Pt 1, para 16(1), (17), (18); for transitional provisions see s 82, Sch 9, Pt 3 thereto.

Para 15: words in first and third pairs of square brackets inserted, and words in second pair of square brackets substituted by the Civil Partnership Act 2004, s 82, Sch 9, Pt 1, para 16(1), (19), (20); for transitional provisions see s 82, Sch 9, Pt 3 thereto.

Modification: paras 12(1), (2), 13(1) temporarily modified by the Family Law Act 1996 (Commencement No 2) Order 1997, SI 1997/1892, art 4(d), (e), until such time as Part II of this Act is brought into force.

(*Schs 8–10 outside the scope of this work.*)

PARTY WALL ETC ACT 1996

(1996 c 40)

An Act to make provision in respect of party walls, and excavation and construction in proximity to certain buildings or structures; and for connected purposes.

[18 July 1996]

Construction and repair of walls on line of junction

1 New building on line of junction

(1) This section shall have effect where lands of different owners adjoin and—

(a) are not built on at the line of junction; or

(b) are built on at the line of junction only to the extent of a boundary wall (not being a party fence wall or the external wall of a building),

and either owner is about to build on any part of the line of junction.

(2) If a building owner desires to build a party wall or party fence wall on the line of junction he shall, at least one month before he intends the building work to start, serve on any adjoining owner a notice which indicates his desire to build and describes the intended wall.

(3) If, having been served with notice described in subsection (2), an adjoining owner serves on the building owner a notice indicating his consent to the building of a party wall or party fence wall—

(a) the wall shall be built half on the land of each of the two owners or in such other position as may be agreed between the two owners; and

(b) the expense of building the wall shall be from time to time defrayed by the two owners in such proportion as has regard to the use made or to be made of the wall by each of them and to the cost of labour and materials prevailing at the time when that use is made by each owner respectively.

(4) If, having been served with notice described in subsection (2), an adjoining owner does not consent under this subsection to the building of a party wall or party fence wall, the building owner may only build the wall—

(a) at his own expense; and

(b) as an external wall or a fence wall, as the case may be, placed wholly on his own land,

and consent under this subsection is consent by a notice served within the period of fourteen days beginning with the day on which the notice described in subsection (2) is served.

(5) If the building owner desires to build on the line of junction a wall placed wholly on his own land he shall, at least one month before he intends the building work to start, serve on any adjoining owner a notice which indicates his desire to build and describes the intended wall.

(6) Where the building owner builds a wall wholly on his own land in accordance with subsection (4) or (5) he shall have the right, at any time in the period which—

- (a) begins one month after the day on which the notice mentioned in the subsection concerned was served, and
- (b) ends twelve months after that day,

to place below the level of the land of the adjoining owner such projecting footings and foundations as are necessary for the construction of the wall.

(7) Where the building owner builds a wall wholly on his own land in accordance with subsection (4) or (5) he shall do so at his own expense and shall compensate any adjoining owner and any adjoining occupier for any damage to his property occasioned by—

- (a) the building of the wall;
- (b) the placing of any footings or foundations placed in accordance with subsection (6).

(8) Where any dispute arises under this section between the building owner and any adjoining owner or occupier it is to be determined in accordance with section 10.

[1677]

NOTES

See further, in relation to the disapplication of sub-s (6) above for the purposes of the Crossrail Act 2008: the Crossrail Act 2008, s 40, Sch 14, para 17(2).

2 Repair etc of party wall: rights of owner

(1) This section applies where lands of different owners adjoin and at the line of junction the said lands are built on or a boundary wall, being a party fence wall or the external wall of a building, has been erected.

(2) A building owner shall have the following rights—

- (a) to underpin, thicken or raise a party structure, a party fence wall, or an external wall which belongs to the building owner and is built against a party structure or party fence wall;
- (b) to make good, repair, or demolish and rebuild, a party structure or party fence wall in a case where such work is necessary on account of defect or want of repair of the structure or wall;
- (c) to demolish a partition which separates buildings belonging to different owners but does not conform with statutory requirements and to build instead a party wall which does so conform;
- (d) in the case of buildings connected by arches or structures over public ways or over passages belonging to other persons, to demolish the whole or part of such buildings, arches or structures which do not conform with statutory requirements and to rebuild them so that they do so conform;
- (e) to demolish a party structure which is of insufficient strength or height for the purposes of any intended building of the building owner and to rebuild it of sufficient strength or height for the said purposes (including rebuilding to a lesser height or thickness where the rebuilt structure is of sufficient strength and height for the purposes of any adjoining owner);
- (f) to cut into a party structure for any purpose (which may be or include the purpose of inserting a damp proof course);
- (g) to cut away from a party wall, party fence wall, external wall or boundary wall any footing or any projecting chimney breast, jamb or flue, or other projection on or over the land of the building owner in order to erect, raise or underpin any such wall or for any other purpose;
- (h) to cut away or demolish parts of any wall or building of an adjoining owner overhanging the land of the building owner or overhanging a party wall, to the extent that it is necessary to cut away or demolish the parts to enable a vertical wall to be erected or raised against the wall or building of the adjoining owner;
- (j) to cut into the wall of an adjoining owner's building in order to insert a flashing or other weather-proofing of a wall erected against that wall;
- (k) to execute any other necessary works incidental to the connection of a party structure with the premises adjoining it;
- (l) to raise a party fence wall, or to raise such a wall for use as a party wall, and to demolish a party fence wall and rebuild it as a party fence wall or as a party wall;

(m) subject to the provisions of section 11(7), to reduce, or to demolish and rebuild, a party wall or party fence wall to—
   (i) a height of not less than two metres where the wall is not used by an adjoining owner to any greater extent than a boundary wall; or
   (ii) a height currently enclosed upon by the building of an adjoining owner;
(n) to expose a party wall or party structure hitherto enclosed subject to providing adequate weathering.

(3) Where work mentioned in paragraph (a) of subsection (2) is not necessary on account of defect or want of repair of the structure or wall concerned, the right falling within that paragraph is exercisable—
(a) subject to making good all damage occasioned by the work to the adjoining premises or to their internal furnishings and decorations; and
(b) where the work is to a party structure or external wall, subject to carrying any relevant flues and chimney stacks up to such a height and in such materials as may be agreed between the building owner and the adjoining owner concerned or, in the event of dispute, determined in accordance with section 10;

and relevant flues and chimney stacks are those which belong to an adjoining owner and either form part of or rest on or against the party structure or external wall.

(4) The right falling within subsection (2)(e) is exercisable subject to—
(a) making good all damage occasioned by the work to the adjoining premises or to their internal furnishings and decorations; and
(b) carrying any relevant flues and chimney stacks up to such a height and in such materials as may be agreed between the building owner and the adjoining owner concerned or, in the event of dispute, determined in accordance with section 10;

and relevant flues and chimney stacks are those which belong to an adjoining owner and either form part of or rest on or against the party structure.

(5) Any right falling within subsection (2)(f), (g) or (h) is exercisable subject to making good all damage occasioned by the work to the adjoining premises or to their internal furnishings and decorations.

(6) The right falling within subsection (2)(j) is exercisable subject to making good all damage occasioned by the work to the wall of the adjoining owner's building.

(7) The right falling within subsection (2)(m) is exercisable subject to—
(a) reconstructing any parapet or replacing an existing parapet with another one; or
(b) constructing a parapet where one is needed but did not exist before.

(8) For the purposes of this section a building or structure which was erected before the day on which this Act was passed shall be deemed to conform with statutory requirements if it conforms with the statutes regulating buildings or structures on the date on which it was erected.

[1678]

NOTES

See further, in relation to the disapplication of this section for the purposes of the Crossrail Act 2008: the Crossrail Act 2008, s 40, Sch 14, para 17(2).

3 Party structure notices

(1) Before exercising any right conferred on him by section 2 a building owner shall serve on any adjoining owner a notice (in this Act referred to as a "party structure notice") stating—
(a) the name and address of the building owner;
(b) the nature and particulars of the proposed work including, in cases where the building owner proposes to construct special foundations, plans, sections and details of construction of the special foundations together with reasonable particulars of the loads to be carried thereby; and
(c) the date on which the proposed work will begin.

(2) A party structure notice shall—
(a) be served at least two months before the date on which the proposed work will begin;
(b) cease to have effect if the work to which it relates—
   (i) has not begun within the period of twelve months beginning with the day on which the notice is served; and
   (ii) is not prosecuted with due diligence.

(3) Nothing in this section shall—
(a) prevent a building owner from exercising with the consent in writing of the adjoining owners and of the adjoining occupiers any right conferred on him by section 2; or

(b) require a building owner to serve any party structure notice before complying with any notice served under any statutory provisions relating to dangerous or neglected structures.

[1679]

4 Counter notices

(1) An adjoining owner may, having been served with a party structure notice serve on the building owner a notice (in this Act referred to as a "counter notice") setting out—

(a) in respect of a party fence wall or party structure, a requirement that the building owner build in or on the wall or structure to which the notice relates such chimney copings, breasts, jambs or flues, or such piers or recesses or other like works, as may reasonably be required for the convenience of the adjoining owner;

(b) in respect of special foundations to which the adjoining owner consents under section 7(4) below, a requirement that the special foundations—

(i) be placed at a specified greater depth than that proposed by the building owner; or

(ii) be constructed of sufficient strength to bear the load to be carried by columns of any intended building of the adjoining owner,

or both.

(2) A counter notice shall—

(a) specify the works required by the notice to be executed and shall be accompanied by plans, sections and particulars of such works; and

(b) be served within the period of one month beginning with the day on which the party structure notice is served.

(3) A building owner on whom a counter notice has been served shall comply with the requirements of the counter notice unless the execution of the works required by the counter notice would—

(a) be injurious to him;

(b) cause unnecessary inconvenience to him; or

(c) cause unnecessary delay in the execution of the works pursuant to the party structure notice.

[1680]

5 Disputes arising under sections 3 and 4

If an owner on whom a party structure notice or a counter notice has been served does not serve a notice indicating his consent to it within the period of fourteen days beginning with the day on which the party structure notice or counter notice was served, he shall be deemed to have dissented from the notice and a dispute shall be deemed to have arisen between the parties.

[1681]

Adjacent excavation and construction

6 Adjacent excavation and construction

(1) This section applies where—

(a) a building owner proposes to excavate, or excavate for and erect a building or structure, within a distance of three metres measured horizontally from any part of a building or structure of an adjoining owner; and

(b) any part of the proposed excavation, building or structure will within those three metres extend to a lower level than the level of the bottom of the foundations of the building or structure of the adjoining owner.

(2) This section also applies where—

(a) a building owner proposes to excavate, or excavate for and erect a building or structure, within a distance of six metres measured horizontally from any part of a building or structure of an adjoining owner; and

(b) any part of the proposed excavation, building or structure will within those six metres meet a plane drawn downwards in the direction of the excavation, building or structure of the building owner at an angle of forty-five degrees to the horizontal from the line formed by the intersection of the plane of the level of the bottom of the foundations of the building or structure of the adjoining owner with the plane of the external face of the external wall of the building or structure of the adjoining owner.

(3) The building owner may, and if required by the adjoining owner shall, at his own expense underpin or otherwise strengthen or safeguard the foundations of the building or structure of the adjoining owner so far as may be necessary.

(4) Where the buildings or structures of different owners are within the respective distances mentioned in subsections (1) and (2) the owners of those buildings or structures shall be deemed to be adjoining owners for the purposes of this section.

(5) In any case where this section applies the building owner shall, at least one month before beginning to excavate, or excavate for and erect a building or structure, serve on the adjoining owner a notice indicating his proposals and stating whether he proposes to underpin or otherwise strengthen or safeguard the foundations of the building or structure of the adjoining owner.

(6) The notice referred to in subsection (5) shall be accompanied by plans and sections showing—

(a) the site and depth of any excavation the building owner proposes to make;
(b) if he proposes to erect a building or structure, its site.

(7) If an owner on whom a notice referred to in subsection (5) has been served does not serve a notice indicating his consent to it within the period of fourteen days beginning with the day on which the notice referred to in subsection (5) was served, he shall be deemed to have dissented from the notice and a dispute shall be deemed to have arisen between the parties.

(8) The notice referred to in subsection (5) shall cease to have effect if the work to which the notice relates—

(a) has not begun within the period of twelve months beginning with the day on which the notice was served; and
(b) is not prosecuted with due diligence.

(9) On completion of any work executed in pursuance of this section the building owner shall if so requested by the adjoining owner supply him with particulars including plans and sections of the work.

(10) Nothing in this section shall relieve the building owner from any liability to which he would otherwise be subject for injury to any adjoining owner or any adjoining occupier by reason of work executed by him.

[1682]

NOTES

See further, in relation to the disapplication of this section for the purposes of the Crossrail Act 2008: the Crossrail Act 2008, s 40, Sch 14, para 17(2).

Rights etc

7 Compensation etc

(1) A building owner shall not exercise any right conferred on him by this Act in such a manner or at such time as to cause unnecessary inconvenience to any adjoining owner or to any adjoining occupier.

(2) The building owner shall compensate any adjoining owner and any adjoining occupier for any loss or damage which may result to any of them by reason of any work executed in pursuance of this Act.

(3) Where a building owner in exercising any right conferred on him by this Act lays open any part of the adjoining land or building he shall at his own expense make and maintain so long as may be necessary a proper hoarding, shoring or fans or temporary construction for the protection of the adjoining land or building and the security of any adjoining occupier.

(4) Nothing in this Act shall authorise the building owner to place special foundations on land of an adjoining owner without his previous consent in writing.

(5) Any works executed in pursuance of this Act shall—

(a) comply with the provisions of statutory requirements; and
(b) be executed in accordance with such plans, sections and particulars as may be agreed between the owners or in the event of dispute determined in accordance with section 10;

and no deviation shall be made from those plans, sections and particulars except such as may be agreed between the owners (or surveyors acting on their behalf) or in the event of dispute determined in accordance with section 10.

[1683]

8 Rights of entry

(1) A building owner, his servants, agents and workmen may during usual working hours enter and remain on any land or premises for the purpose of executing any work in pursuance of this Act and may remove any furniture or fittings or take any other action necessary for that purpose.

(2) If the premises are closed, the building owner, his agents and workmen may, if accompanied by a constable or other police officer, break open any fences or doors in order to enter the premises.

(3) No land or premises may be entered by any person under subsection (1) unless the building owner serves on the owner and the occupier of the land or premises—

(a) in case of emergency, such notice of the intention to enter as may be reasonably practicable;

(b) in any other case, such notice of the intention to enter as complies with subsection (4).

(4) Notice complies with this subsection if it is served in a period of not less than fourteen days ending with the day of the proposed entry.

(5) A surveyor appointed or selected under section 10 may during usual working hours enter and remain on any land or premises for the purpose of carrying out the object for which he is appointed or selected.

(6) No land or premises may be entered by a surveyor under subsection (5) unless the building owner who is a party to the dispute concerned serves on the owner and the occupier of the land or premises—

(a) in case of emergency, such notice of the intention to enter as may be reasonably practicable;

(b) in any other case, such notice of the intention to enter as complies with subsection (4).

[1684]

9 Easements

Nothing in this Act shall—

(a) authorise any interference with an easement of light or other easements in or relating to a party wall; or

(b) prejudicially affect any right of any person to preserve or restore any right or other thing in or connected with a party wall in case of the party wall being pulled down or rebuilt.

[1685]

Resolution of disputes

10 Resolution of disputes

(1) Where a dispute arises or is deemed to have arisen between a building owner and an adjoining owner in respect of any matter connected with any work to which this Act relates either—

(a) both parties shall concur in the appointment of one surveyor (in this section referred to as an "agreed surveyor"); or

(b) each party shall appoint a surveyor and the two surveyors so appointed shall forthwith select a third surveyor (all of whom are in this section referred to as "the three surveyors").

(2) All appointments and selections made under this section shall be in writing and shall not be rescinded by either party.

(3) If an agreed surveyor—

(a) refuses to act;

(b) neglects to act for a period of ten days beginning with the day on which either party serves a request on him;

(c) dies before the dispute is settled; or

(d) becomes or deems himself incapable of acting,

the proceedings for settling such dispute shall begin *de novo*.

(4) If either party to the dispute—

(a) refuses to appoint a surveyor under subsection (1)(b), or

(b) neglects to appoint a surveyor under subsection (1)(b) for a period of ten days beginning with the day on which the other party serves a request on him,

the other party may make the appointment on his behalf.

(5) If, before the dispute is settled, a surveyor appointed under paragraph (b) of subsection (1) by a party to the dispute dies, or becomes or deems himself incapable of acting, the party who appointed him may appoint another surveyor in his place with the same power and authority.

(6) If a surveyor—

(a) appointed under paragraph (b) of subsection (1) by a party to the dispute; or

(b) appointed under subsection (4) or (5),

refuses to act effectively, the surveyor of the other party may proceed to act *ex parte* and anything so done by him shall be as effectual as if he had been an agreed surveyor.

(7) If a surveyor—

(a) appointed under paragraph (b) of subsection (1) by a party to the dispute; or

(b) appointed under subsection (4) or (5),

neglects to act effectively for a period of ten days beginning with the day on which either party or the surveyor of the other party serves a request on him, the surveyor of the other party may proceed to act *ex parte* in respect of the subject matter of the request and anything so done by him shall be as effectual as if he had been an agreed surveyor.

(8) If either surveyor appointed under subsection (1)(b) by a party to the dispute refuses to select a third surveyor under subsection (1) or (9), or neglects to do so for a period of ten days beginning with the day on which the other surveyor serves a request on him—

(a) the appointing officer; or

(b) in cases where the relevant appointing officer or his employer is a party to the dispute, the Secretary of State,

may on the application of either surveyor select a third surveyor who shall have the same power and authority as if he had been selected under subsection (1) or subsection (9).

(9) If a third surveyor selected under subsection (1)(b)—

(a) refuses to act;

(b) neglects to act for a period of ten days beginning with the day on which either party or the surveyor appointed by either party serves a request on him; or

(c) dies, or becomes or deems himself incapable of acting, before the dispute is settled,

the other two of the three surveyors shall forthwith select another surveyor in his place with the same power and authority.

(10) The agreed surveyor or as the case may be the three surveyors or any two of them shall settle by award any matter—

(a) which is connected with any work to which this Act relates, and

(b) which is in dispute between the building owner and the adjoining owner.

(11) Either of the parties or either of the surveyors appointed by the parties may call upon the third surveyor selected in pursuance of this section to determine the disputed matters and he shall make the necessary award.

(12) An award may determine—

(a) the right to execute any work;

(b) the time and manner of executing any work; and

(c) any other matter arising out of or incidental to the dispute including the costs of making the award;

but any period appointed by the award for executing any work shall not unless otherwise agreed between the building owner and the adjoining owner begin to run until after the expiration of the period prescribed by this Act for service of the notice in respect of which the dispute arises or is deemed to have arisen.

(13) The reasonable costs incurred in—

(a) making or obtaining an award under this section;

(b) reasonable inspections of work to which the award relates; and

(c) any other matter arising out of the dispute,

shall be paid by such of the parties as the surveyor or surveyors making the award determine.

(14) Where the surveyors appointed by the parties make an award the surveyors shall serve it forthwith on the parties.

(15) Where an award is made by the third surveyor—

(a) he shall, after payment of the costs of the award, serve it forthwith on the parties or their appointed surveyors; and

(b) if it is served on their appointed surveyors, they shall serve it forthwith on the parties.

(16) The award shall be conclusive and shall not except as provided by this section be questioned in any court.

(17) Either of the parties to the dispute may, within the period of fourteen days beginning with the day on which an award made under this section is served on him, appeal to the county court against the award and the county court may—

(a) rescind the award or modify it in such manner as the court thinks fit; and

(b) make such order as to costs as the court thinks fit.

[1686]

NOTES

Transfer of Functions: functions of the Secretary of State, so far as exercisable in relation to Wales, are transferred to the National Assembly for Wales, by the National Assembly for Wales (Transfer of Functions) Order 1999, SI 1999/672, art 2, Sch 1.

Expenses

11 Expenses

(1) Except as provided under this section expenses of work under this Act shall be defrayed by the building owner.

(2) Any dispute as to responsibility for expenses shall be settled as provided in section 10.

(3) An expense mentioned in section 1(3)(b) shall be defrayed as there mentioned.

(4) Where work is carried out in exercise of the right mentioned in section 2(2)(a), and the work is necessary on account of defect or want of repair of the structure or wall concerned, the expenses shall be defrayed by the building owner and the adjoining owner in such proportion as has regard to—

(a) the use which the owners respectively make or may make of the structure or wall concerned; and

(b) responsibility for the defect or want of repair concerned, if more than one owner makes use of the structure or wall concerned.

(5) Where work is carried out in exercise of the right mentioned in section 2(2)(b) the expenses shall be defrayed by the building owner and the adjoining owner in such proportion as has regard to—

(a) the use which the owners respectively make or may make of the structure or wall concerned; and

(b) responsibility for the defect or want of repair concerned, if more than one owner makes use of the structure or wall concerned.

(6) Where the adjoining premises are laid open in exercise of the right mentioned in section 2(2)(e) a fair allowance in respect of disturbance and inconvenience shall be paid by the building owner to the adjoining owner or occupier.

(7) Where a building owner proposes to reduce the height of a party wall or party fence wall under section 2(2)(m) the adjoining owner may serve a counter notice under section 4 requiring the building owner to maintain the existing height of the wall, and in such case the adjoining owner shall pay to the building owner a due proportion of the cost of the wall so far as it exceeds—

(a) two metres in height; or

(b) the height currently enclosed upon by the building of the adjoining owner.

(8) Where the building owner is required to make good damage under this Act the adjoining owner has a right to require that the expenses of such making good be determined in accordance with section 10 and paid to him in lieu of the carrying out of work to make the damage good.

(9) Where—

(a) works are carried out, and

(b) some of the works are carried out at the request of the adjoining owner or in pursuance of a requirement made by him,

he shall defray the expenses of carrying out the works requested or required by him.

(10) Where—

(a) consent in writing has been given to the construction of special foundations on land of an adjoining owner; and

(b) the adjoining owner erects any building or structure and its cost is found to be increased by reason of the existence of the said foundations,

the owner of the building to which the said foundations belong shall, on receiving an account with any necessary invoices and other supporting documents within the period of two months beginning with the day of the completion of the work by the adjoining owner, repay to the adjoining owner so much of the cost as is due to the existence of the said foundations.

(11) Where use is subsequently made by the adjoining owner of work carried out solely at the expense of the building owner the adjoining owner shall pay a due proportion of the expenses incurred by the building owner in carrying out that work; and for this purpose he shall be taken to have incurred expenses calculated by reference to what the cost of the work would be if it were carried out at the time when that subsequent use is made.

[1687]

12 Security for expenses

(1) An adjoining owner may serve a notice requiring the building owner before he begins any work in the exercise of the rights conferred by this Act to give such security as may be agreed between the owners or in the event of dispute determined in accordance with section 10.

(2) Where—

(a) in the exercise of the rights conferred by this Act an adjoining owner requires the building owner to carry out any work the expenses of which are to be defrayed in whole or in part by the adjoining owner; or

(b) an adjoining owner serves a notice on the building owner under subsection (1),

the building owner may before beginning the work to which the requirement or notice relates serve a notice on the adjoining owner requiring him to give such security as may be agreed between the owners or in the event of dispute determined in accordance with section 10.

(3) If within the period of one month beginning with—

(a) the day on which a notice is served under subsection (2); or

(b) in the event of dispute, the date of the determination by the surveyor or surveyors, the adjoining owner does not comply with the notice or the determination, the requirement or notice by him to which the building owner's notice under that subsection relates shall cease to have effect.

[1688]

13 Account for work carried out

(1) Within the period of two months beginning with the day of the completion of any work executed by a building owner of which the expenses are to be wholly or partially defrayed by an adjoining owner in accordance with section 11 the building owner shall serve on the adjoining owner an account in writing showing—

(a) particulars and expenses of the work; and
(b) any deductions to which the adjoining owner or any other person is entitled in respect of old materials or otherwise;

and in preparing the account the work shall be estimated and valued at fair average rates and prices according to the nature of the work, the locality and the cost of labour and materials prevailing at the time when the work is executed.

(2) Within the period of one month beginning with the day of service of the said account the adjoining owner may serve on the building owner a notice stating any objection he may have thereto and thereupon a dispute shall be deemed to have arisen between the parties.

(3) If within that period of one month the adjoining owner does not serve notice under subsection (2) he shall be deemed to have no objection to the account.

[1689]

14 Settlement of account

(1) All expenses to be defrayed by an adjoining owner in accordance with an account served under section 13 shall be paid by the adjoining owner.

(2) Until an adjoining owner pays to the building owner such expenses as aforesaid the property in any works executed under this Act to which the expenses relate shall be vested solely in the building owner.

[1690]

Miscellaneous

15 Service of notices etc

(1) A notice or other document required or authorised to be served under this Act may be served on a person—

(a) by delivering it to him in person;
(b) by sending it by post to him at his usual or last-known residence or place of business in the United Kingdom; or
(c) in the case of a body corporate, by delivering it to the secretary or clerk of the body corporate at its registered or principal office or sending it by post to the secretary or clerk of that body corporate at that office.

(2) In the case of a notice or other document required or authorised to be served under this Act on a person as owner of premises, it may alternatively be served by—

(a) addressing it "the owner" of the premises (naming them), and
(b) delivering it to a person on the premises or, if no person to whom it can be delivered is found there, fixing it to a conspicuous part of the premises.

[1691]

16 Offences

(1) If—

(a) an occupier of land or premises refuses to permit a person to do anything which he is entitled to do with regard to the land or premises under section 8(1) or (5); and
(b) the occupier knows or has reasonable cause to believe that the person is so entitled,

the occupier is guilty of an offence.

(2) If—

(a) a person hinders or obstructs a person in attempting to do anything which he is entitled to do with regard to land or premises under section 8(1) or (5); and
(b) the first-mentioned person knows or has reasonable cause to believe that the other person is so entitled,

the first-mentioned person is guilty of an offence.

(3) A person guilty of an offence under subsection (1) or (2) is liable on summary conviction to a fine of an amount not exceeding level 3 on the standard scale.

[1692]

17 Recovery of sums

Any sum payable in pursuance of this Act (otherwise than by way of fine) shall be recoverable summarily as a civil debt.

[1693]

18 Exception in case of Temples etc

(1) This Act shall not apply to land which is situated in inner London and in which there is an interest belonging to—

(a) the Honourable Society of the Inner Temple,
(b) the Honourable Society of the Middle Temple,
(c) the Honourable Society of Lincoln's Inn, or
(d) the Honourable Society of Gray's Inn.

(2) The reference in subsection (1) to inner London is to Greater London other than the outer London boroughs.

[1694]

19 The Crown

(1) This Act shall apply to land in which there is—

(a) an interest belonging to Her Majesty in right of the Crown,
(b) an interest belonging to a government department, or
(c) an interest held in trust for Her Majesty for the purposes of any such department.

(2) This Act shall apply to—

(a) land which is vested in, but not occupied by, Her Majesty in right of the Duchy of Lancaster;
(b) land which is vested in, but not occupied by, the possessor for the time being of the Duchy of Cornwall.

[1695]

20 Interpretation

In this Act, unless the context otherwise requires, the following expressions have the meanings hereby respectively assigned to them—

"adjoining owner" and "adjoining occupier" respectively mean any owner and any occupier of land, buildings, storeys or rooms adjoining those of the building owner and for the purposes only of section 6 within the distances specified in that section;

"appointing officer" means the person appointed under this Act by the local authority to make such appointments as are required under section 10(8);

"building owner" means an owner of land who is desirous of exercising rights under this Act;

"foundation", in relation to a wall, means the solid ground or artificially formed support resting on solid ground on which the wall rests;

"owner" includes—

(a) a person in receipt of, or entitled to receive, the whole or part of the rents or profits of land;
(b) a person in possession of land, otherwise than as a mortgagee or as a tenant from year to year or for a lesser term or as a tenant at will;
(c) a purchaser of an interest in land under a contract for purchase or under an agreement for a lease, otherwise than under an agreement for a tenancy from year to year or for a lesser term;

"party fence wall" means a wall (not being part of a building) which stands on lands of different owners and is used or constructed to be used for separating such adjoining lands, but does not include a wall constructed on the land of one owner the artificially formed support of which projects into the land of another owner;

"party structure" means a party wall and also a floor partition or other structure separating buildings or parts of buildings approached solely by separate staircases or separate entrances;

"party wall" means—

(a) a wall which forms part of a building and stands on lands of different owners to a greater extent than the projection of any artificially formed support on which the wall rests; and
(b) so much of a wall not being a wall referred to in paragraph (a) above as separates buildings belonging to different owners;

"special foundations" means foundations in which an assemblage of beams or rods is employed for the purpose of distributing any load; and

"surveyor" means any person not being a party to the matter appointed or selected under section 10 to determine disputes in accordance with the procedures set out in this Act.

[1696]

21 Other statutory provisions

(1) The Secretary of State may by order amend or repeal any provision of a private or local Act passed before or in the same session as this Act, if it appears to him necessary or expedient to do so in consequence of this Act.

(2) An order under subsection (1) may—

(a) contain such savings or transitional provisions as the Secretary of State thinks fit;
(b) make different provision for different purposes.

(3) The power to make an order under subsection (1) shall be exercisable by statutory instrument subject to annulment in pursuance of a resolution of either House of Parliament.

[1697]

NOTES

Transfer of Functions: functions of the Secretary of State, so far as exercisable in relation to Wales, are transferred to the National Assembly for Wales, by the National Assembly for Wales (Transfer of Functions) Order 1999, SI 1999/672, art 2, Sch 1.

Order: the Party Wall etc Act 1996 (Repeal of Local Enactments) Order 1997, SI 1997/671.

General

22 Short title, commencement and extent

(1) This Act may be cited as the Party Wall etc Act 1996.

(2) This Act shall come into force in accordance with provision made by the Secretary of State by order made by statutory instrument.

(3) An order under subsection (2) may—

(a) contain such savings or transitional provisions as the Secretary of State thinks fit;
(b) make different provision for different purposes.

(4) This Act extends to England and Wales only.

[1698]

NOTES

Order: the Party Wall etc Act 1996 (Commencement) Order 1997, SI 1997/670.

TRUSTS OF LAND AND APPOINTMENT OF TRUSTEES ACT 1996

(1996 c 47)

An Act to make new provision about trusts of land including provision phasing out the Settled Land Act 1925, abolishing the doctrine of conversion and otherwise amending the law about trusts for sale of land; to amend the law about the appointment and retirement of trustees of any trust; and for connected purposes

[24 July 1996]

PART I
TRUSTS OF LAND

Introductory

1 Meaning of "trust of land"

(1) In this Act—

(a) "trust of land" means (subject to subsection (3)) any trust of property which consists of or includes land, and
(b) "trustees of land" means trustees of a trust of land.

(2) The reference in subsection (1)(a) to a trust—

(a) is to any description of trust (whether express, implied, resulting or constructive), including a trust for sale and a bare trust, and
(b) includes a trust created, or arising, before the commencement of this Act.

(3) The reference to land in subsection (1)(a) does not include land which (despite section 2) is settled land or which is land to which the Universities and College Estates Act 1925 applies.

[1699]

Settlements and trusts for sale as trusts of land

2 Trusts in place of settlements

(1) No settlement created after the commencement of this Act is a settlement for the purposes of the Settled Land Act 1925; and no settlement shall be deemed to be made under that Act after that commencement.

(2) Subsection (1) does not apply to a settlement created on the occasion of an alteration in any interest in, or of a person becoming entitled under, a settlement which—

(a) is in existence at the commencement of this Act, or

(b) derives from a settlement within paragraph (a) or this paragraph.

(3) But a settlement created as mentioned in subsection (2) is not a settlement for the purposes of the Settled Land Act 1925 if provision to the effect that it is not is made in the instrument, or any of the instruments, by which it is created.

(4) Where at any time after the commencement of this Act there is in the case of any settlement which is a settlement for the purposes of the Settled Land Act 1925 no relevant property which is, or is deemed to be, subject to the settlement, the settlement permanently ceases at that time to be a settlement for the purposes of that Act.

In this subsection "relevant property" means land and personal chattels to which section 67(1) of the Settled Land Act 1925 (heirlooms) applies.

(5) No land held on charitable, ecclesiastical or public trusts shall be or be deemed to be settled land after the commencement of this Act, even if it was or was deemed to be settled land before that commencement.

(6) Schedule 1 has effect to make provision consequential on this section (including provision to impose a trust in circumstances in which, apart from this section, there would be a settlement for the purposes of the Settled Land Act 1925 (and there would not otherwise be a trust)).

[1700]

3 Abolition of doctrine of conversion

(1) Where land is held by trustees subject to a trust for sale, the land is not to be regarded as personal property; and where personal property is subject to a trust for sale in order that the trustees may acquire land, the personal property is not to be regarded as land.

(2) Subsection (1) does not apply to a trust created by a will if the testator died before the commencement of this Act.

(3) Subject to that, subsection (1) applies to a trust whether it is created, or arises, before or after that commencement.

[1701]

4 Express trusts for sale as trusts of land

(1) In the case of every trust for sale of land created by a disposition there is to be implied, despite any provision to the contrary made by the disposition, a power for the trustees to postpone sale of the land; and the trustees are not liable in any way for postponing sale of the land, in the exercise of their discretion, for an indefinite period.

(2) Subsection (1) applies to a trust whether it is created, or arises, before or after the commencement of this Act.

(3) Subsection (1) does not affect any liability incurred by trustees before that commencement.

[1702]

5 Implied trusts for sale as trusts of land

(1) Schedule 2 has effect in relation to statutory provisions which impose a trust for sale of land in certain circumstances so that in those circumstances there is instead a trust of the land (without a duty to sell).

(2) Section 1 of the Settled Land Act 1925 does not apply to land held on any trust arising by virtue of that Schedule (so that any such land is subject to a trust of land).

[1703]

Functions of trustees of land

6 General powers of trustees

(1) For the purpose of exercising their functions as trustees, the trustees of land have in relation to the land subject to the trust all the powers of an absolute owner.

(2) Where in the case of any land subject to a trust of land each of the beneficiaries interested in the land is a person of full age and capacity who is absolutely entitled to the land, the powers

conferred on the trustees by subsection (1) include the power to convey the land to the beneficiaries even though they have not required the trustees to do so; and where land is conveyed by virtue of this subsection—

(a) the beneficiaries shall do whatever is necessary to secure that it vests in them, and

(b) if they fail to do so, the court may make an order requiring them to do so.

(3) The trustees of land have power to [acquire land under the power conferred by section 8 of the Trustee Act 2000].

(4) …

(5) In exercising the powers conferred by this section trustees shall have regard to the rights of the beneficiaries.

(6) The powers conferred by this section shall not be exercised in contravention of, or of any order made in pursuance of, any other enactment or any rule of law or equity.

(7) The reference in subsection (6) to an order includes an order of any court or of the [Charity Commission].

(8) Where any enactment other than this section confers on trustees authority to act subject to any restriction, limitation or condition, trustees of land may not exercise the powers conferred by this section to do any act which they are prevented from doing under the other enactment by reason of the restriction, limitation or condition.

[(9) The duty of care under section 1 of the Trustee Act 2000 applies to trustees of land when exercising the powers conferred by this section.]

[1704]

NOTES

Sub-s (3): words in square brackets substituted by the Trustee Act 2000, s 40(1), Sch 2, Pt II, para 45(1).
Sub-s (4): repealed by the Trustee Act 2000, s 40(1), (3), Sch 2, Pt II, para 45(2), Sch 4, Pt II.
Sub-s (7): words in square brackets substituted by the Charities Act 2006, s 75(1), Sch 8, para 182.
Sub-s (9): inserted by the Trustee Act 2000, s 40(1), Sch 2, Pt II, para 45(3).

7 Partition by trustees

(1) The trustees of land may, where beneficiaries of full age are absolutely entitled in undivided shares to land subject to the trust, partition the land, or any part of it, and provide (by way of mortgage or otherwise) for the payment of any equality money.

(2) The trustees shall give effect to any such partition by conveying the partitioned land in severalty (whether or not subject to any legal mortgage created for raising equality money), either absolutely or in trust, in accordance with the rights of those beneficiaries.

(3) Before exercising their powers under subsection (2) the trustees shall obtain the consent of each of those beneficiaries.

(4) Where a share in the land is affected by an incumbrance, the trustees may either give effect to it or provide for its discharge from the property allotted to that share as they think fit.

(5) If a share in the land is absolutely vested in a minor, subsections (1) to (4) apply as if he were of full age, except that the trustees may act on his behalf and retain land or other property representing his share in trust for him.

[(6) Subsection (1) is subject to sections 21 (part-unit: interests) and 22 (part-unit: charging) of the Commonhold and Leasehold Reform Act 2002.]

[1705]

NOTES

Sub-s (6): inserted by the Commonhold and Leasehold Reform Act 2002, s 68, Sch 5, para 8.

8 Exclusion and restriction of powers

(1) Sections 6 and 7 do not apply in the case of a trust of land created by a disposition in so far as provision to the effect that they do not apply is made by the disposition.

(2) If the disposition creating such a trust makes provision requiring any consent to be obtained to the exercise of any power conferred by section 6 or 7, the power may not be exercised without that consent.

(3) Subsection (1) does not apply in the case of charitable, ecclesiastical or public trusts.

(4) Subsections (1) and (2) have effect subject to any enactment which prohibits or restricts the effect of provision of the description mentioned in them.

[1706]

PART I STATUTES

9 Delegation by trustees

(1) The trustees of land may, by power of attorney, delegate to any beneficiary or beneficiaries of full age and beneficially entitled to an interest in possession in land subject to the trust any of their functions as trustees which relate to the land.

(2) Where trustees purport to delegate to a person by a power of attorney under subsection (1) functions relating to any land and another person in good faith deals with him in relation to the land, he shall be presumed in favour of that other person to have been a person to whom the functions could be delegated unless that other person has knowledge at the time of the transaction that he was not such a person.

And it shall be conclusively presumed in favour of any purchaser whose interest depends on the validity of that transaction that that other person dealt in good faith and did not have such knowledge if that other person makes a statutory declaration to that effect before or within three months after the completion of the purchase.

(3) A power of attorney under subsection (1) shall be given by all the trustees jointly and (unless expressed to be irrevocable and to be given by way of security) may be revoked by any one or more of them; and such a power is revoked by the appointment as a trustee of a person other than those by whom it is given (though not by any of those persons dying or otherwise ceasing to be a trustee).

(4) Where a beneficiary to whom functions are delegated by a power of attorney under subsection (1) ceases to be a person beneficially entitled to an interest in possession in land subject to the trust—

- (a) if the functions are delegated to him alone, the power is revoked,
- (b) if the functions are delegated to him and to other beneficiaries to be exercised by them jointly (but not separately), the power is revoked if each of the other beneficiaries ceases to be so entitled (but otherwise functions exercisable in accordance with the power are so exercisable by the remaining beneficiary or beneficiaries), and
- (c) if the functions are delegated to him and to other beneficiaries to be exercised by them separately (or either separately or jointly), the power is revoked in so far as it relates to him.

(5) A delegation under subsection (1) may be for any period or indefinite.

(6) A power of attorney under subsection (1) cannot be [an enduring power of attorney or lasting power of attorney within the meaning of the Mental Capacity Act 2005].

(7) Beneficiaries to whom functions have been delegated under subsection (1) are, in relation to the exercise of the functions, in the same position as trustees (with the same duties and liabilities); but such beneficiaries shall not be regarded as trustees for any other purposes (including, in particular, the purposes of any enactment permitting the delegation of functions by trustees or imposing requirements relating to the payment of capital money).

(8) …

(9) Neither this section nor the repeal by this Act of section 29 of the Law of Property Act 1925 (which is superseded by this section) affects the operation after the commencement of this Act of any delegation effected before that commencement.

[1707]

NOTES

Sub-s (6): words in square brackets substituted by the Mental Capacity Act 2005, s 67(1), Sch 6, para 42(1), (2).

Sub-s (8): repealed by the Trustee Act 2000, s 40(1), (3), Sch 2, Pt II, para 46, Sch 4, Pt II.

[9A Duties of trustees in connection with delegation etc

(1) The duty of care under section 1 of the Trustee Act 2000 applies to trustees of land in deciding whether to delegate any of their functions under section 9.

(2) Subsection (3) applies if the trustees of land—

- (a) delegate any of their functions under section 9, and
- (b) the delegation is not irrevocable.

(3) While the delegation continues, the trustees—

- (a) must keep the delegation under review,
- (b) if circumstances make it appropriate to do so, must consider whether there is a need to exercise any power of intervention that they have, and
- (c) if they consider that there is a need to exercise such a power, must do so.

(4) "Power of intervention" includes—

- (a) a power to give directions to the beneficiary;
- (b) a power to revoke the delegation.

(5) The duty of care under section 1 of the 2000 Act applies to trustees in carrying out any duty under subsection (3).

(6) A trustee of land is not liable for any act or default of the beneficiary, or beneficiaries, unless the trustee fails to comply with the duty of care in deciding to delegate any of the trustees' functions under section 9 or in carrying out any duty under subsection (3).

(7) Neither this section nor the repeal of section 9(8) by the Trustee Act 2000 affects the operation after the commencement of this section of any delegation effected before that commencement.]

[1708]

NOTES

Inserted by the Trustee Act 2000, s 40(1), Sch 2, Pt II, para 47.

Consents and consultation

10 Consents

(1) If a disposition creating a trust of land requires the consent of more than two persons to the exercise by the trustees of any function relating to the land, the consent of any two of them to the exercise of the function is sufficient in favour of a purchaser.

(2) Subsection (1) does not apply to the exercise of a function by trustees of land held on charitable, ecclesiastical or public trusts.

(3) Where at any time a person whose consent is expressed by a disposition creating a trust of land to be required to the exercise by the trustees of any function relating to the land is not of full age—

(a) his consent is not, in favour of a purchaser, required to the exercise of the function, but
(b) the trustees shall obtain the consent of a parent who has parental responsibility for him (within the meaning of the Children Act 1989) or of a guardian of his.

[1709]

11 Consultation with beneficiaries

(1) The trustees of land shall in the exercise of any function relating to land subject to the trust—

(a) so far as practicable, consult the beneficiaries of full age and beneficially entitled to an interest in possession in the land, and
(b) so far as consistent with the general interest of the trust, give effect to the wishes of those beneficiaries, or (in case of dispute) of the majority (according to the value of their combined interests).

(2) Subsection (1) does not apply—

(a) in relation to a trust created by a disposition in so far as provision that it does not apply is made by the disposition,
(b) in relation to a trust created or arising under a will made before the commencement of this Act, or
(c) in relation to the exercise of the power mentioned in section 6(2).

(3) Subsection (1) does not apply to a trust created before the commencement of this Act by a disposition, or a trust created after that commencement by reference to such a trust, unless provision to the effect that it is to apply is made by a deed executed—

(a) in a case in which the trust was created by one person and he is of full capacity, by that person, or
(b) in a case in which the trust was created by more than one person, by such of the persons who created the trust as are alive and of full capacity.

(4) A deed executed for the purposes of subsection (3) is irrevocable.

[1710]

Right of beneficiaries to occupy trust land

12 The right to occupy

(1) A beneficiary who is beneficially entitled to an interest in possession in land subject to a trust of land is entitled by reason of his interest to occupy the land at any time if at that time—

(a) the purposes of the trust include making the land available for his occupation (or for the occupation of beneficiaries of a class of which he is a member or of beneficiaries in general), or
(b) the land is held by the trustees so as to be so available.

(2) Subsection (1) does not confer on a beneficiary a right to occupy land if it is either unavailable or unsuitable for occupation by him.

(3) This section is subject to section 13.

[1711]

13 Exclusion and restriction of right to occupy

(1) Where two or more beneficiaries are (or apart from this subsection would be) entitled under section 12 to occupy land, the trustees of land may exclude or restrict the entitlement of any one or more (but not all) of them.

(2) Trustees may not under subsection (1)—

(a) unreasonably exclude any beneficiary's entitlement to occupy land, or
(b) restrict any such entitlement to an unreasonable extent.

(3) The trustees of land may from time to time impose reasonable conditions on any beneficiary in relation to his occupation of land by reason of his entitlement under section 12.

(4) The matters to which trustees are to have regard in exercising the powers conferred by this section include—

(a) the intentions of the person or persons (if any) who created the trust,
(b) the purposes for which the land is held, and
(c) the circumstances and wishes of each of the beneficiaries who is (or apart from any previous exercise by the trustees of those powers would be) entitled to occupy the land under section 12.

(5) The conditions which may be imposed on a beneficiary under subsection (3) include, in particular, conditions requiring him—

(a) to pay any outgoings or expenses in respect of the land, or
(b) to assume any other obligation in relation to the land or to any activity which is or is proposed to be conducted there.

(6) Where the entitlement of any beneficiary to occupy land under section 12 has been excluded or restricted, the conditions which may be imposed on any other beneficiary under subsection (3) include, in particular, conditions requiring him to—

(a) make payments by way of compensation to the beneficiary whose entitlement has been excluded or restricted, or
(b) forgo any payment or other benefit to which he would otherwise be entitled under the trust so as to benefit that beneficiary.

(7) The powers conferred on trustees by this section may not be exercised—

(a) so as prevent any person who is in occupation of land (whether or not by reason of an entitlement under section 12) from continuing to occupy the land, or
(b) in a manner likely to result in any such person ceasing to occupy the land,

unless he consents or the court has given approval.

(8) The matters to which the court is to have regard in determining whether to give approval under subsection (7) include the matters mentioned in subsection (4)(a) to (c).

[1712]

Powers of court

14 Applications for order

(1) Any person who is a trustee of land or has an interest in a property subject to a trust of land may make an application to the court for an order under this section.

(2) On an application for an order under this section the court may make any such order—

(a) relating to the exercise by the trustees of any of their functions (including an order relieving them of any obligation to obtain the consent of, or to consult, any person in connection with the exercise of any of their functions), or
(b) declaring the nature or extent of a person's interest in property subject to the trust,

as the court thinks fit.

(3) The court may not under this section make any order as to the appointment or removal of trustees.

(4) The powers conferred on the court by this section are exercisable on an application whether it is made before or after the commencement of this Act.

[1713]

15 Matters relevant in determining applications

(1) The matters to which the court is to have regard in determining an application for an order under section 14 include—

(a) the intentions of the person or persons (if any) who created the trust,
(b) the purposes for which the property subject to the trust is held,
(c) the welfare of any minor who occupies or might reasonably be expected to occupy any land subject to the trust as his home, and

(d) the interests of any secured creditor of any beneficiary.

(2) In the case of an application relating to the exercise in relation to any land of the powers conferred on the trustees by section 13, the matters to which the court is to have regard also include the circumstances and wishes of each of the beneficiaries who is (or apart from any previous exercise by the trustees of those powers would be) entitled to occupy the land under section 12.

(3) In the case of any other application, other than one relating to the exercise of the power mentioned in section 6(2), the matters to which the court is to have regard also include the circumstances and wishes of any beneficiaries of full age and entitled to an interest in possession in property subject to the trust or (in case of dispute) of the majority (according to the value of their combined interests).

(4) This section does not apply to an application if section 335A of the Insolvency Act 1986 (which is inserted by Schedule 3 and relates to applications by a trustee of a bankrupt) applies to it.

[1714]

Purchaser protection

16 Protection of purchasers

(1) A purchaser of land which is or has been subject to a trust need not be concerned to see that any requirement imposed on the trustees by section 6(5), 7(3) or 11(1) has been complied with.

(2) Where—

(a) trustees of land who convey land which (immediately before it is conveyed) is subject to the trust contravene section 6(6) or (8), but

(b) the purchaser of the land from the trustees has no actual notice of the contravention,

the contravention does not invalidate the conveyance.

(3) Where the powers of trustees of land are limited by virtue of section 8—

(a) the trustees shall take all reasonable steps to bring the limitation to the notice of any purchaser of the land from them, but

(b) the limitation does not invalidate any conveyance by the trustees to a purchaser who has no actual notice of the limitation.

(4) Where trustees of land convey land which (immediately before it is conveyed) is subject to the trust to persons believed by them to be beneficiaries absolutely entitled to the land under the trust and of full age and capacity—

(a) the trustees shall execute a deed declaring that they are discharged from the trust in relation to that land, and

(b) if they fail to do so, the court may make an order requiring them to do so.

(5) A purchaser of land to which a deed under subsection (4) relates is entitled to assume that, as from the date of the deed, the land is not subject to the trust unless he has actual notice that the trustees were mistaken in their belief that the land was conveyed to beneficiaries absolutely entitled to the land under the trust and of full age and capacity.

(6) Subsections (2) and (3) do not apply to land held on charitable, ecclesiastical or public trusts.

(7) This section does not apply to registered land.

[1715]

Supplementary

17 Application of provisions to trusts of proceeds of sale

(1) . . .

(2) Section 14 applies in relation to a trust of proceeds of sale of land and trustees of such a trust as in relation to a trust of land and trustees of land.

(3) In this section "trust of proceeds of sale of land" means (subject to subsection (5)) any trust of property (other than a trust of land) which consists of or includes—

(a) any proceeds of a disposition of land held in trust (including settled land), or

(b) any property representing any such proceeds.

(4) The references in subsection (3) to a trust—

(a) are to any description of trust (whether express, implied, resulting or constructive), including a trust for sale and a bare trust, and

(b) include a trust created, or arising, before the commencement of this Act.

(5) A trust which (despite section 2) is a settlement for the purposes of the Settled Land Act 1925 cannot be a trust of proceeds of sale of land.

(6) In subsection (3)—

(a) "disposition" includes any disposition made, or coming into operation, before the commencement of this Act, and

(b) the reference to settled land includes personal chattels to which section 67(1) of the Settled Land Act 1925 (heirlooms) applies.

[1716]

NOTES

Sub-s (1): repealed by the Trustee Act 2000, s 40(1), (3), Sch 2, Pt II, para 48, Sch 4, Pt II.

18 Application of Part to personal representatives

(1) The provisions of this Part relating to trustees, other than sections 10, 11 and 14, apply to personal representatives, but with appropriate modifications and without prejudice to the functions of personal representatives for the purposes of administration.

(2) The appropriate modifications include—

(a) the substitution of references to persons interested in the due administration of the estate for references to beneficiaries, and

(b) the substitution of references to the will for references to the disposition creating the trust.

(3) Section 3(1) does not apply to personal representatives if the death occurs before the commencement of this Act.

[1717]

PART II
APPOINTMENT AND RETIREMENT OF TRUSTEES

19 Appointment and retirement of trustee at instance of beneficiaries

(1) This section applies in the case of a trust where—

(a) there is no person nominated for the purpose of appointing new trustees by the instrument, if any, creating the trust, and

(b) the beneficiaries under the trust are of full age and capacity and (taken together) are absolutely entitled to the property subject to the trust.

(2) The beneficiaries may give a direction or directions of either or both of the following descriptions—

(a) a written direction to a trustee or trustees to retire from the trust, and

(b) a written direction to the trustees or trustee for the time being (or, if there are none, to the personal representative of the last person who was a trustee) to appoint by writing to be a trustee or trustees the person or persons specified in the direction.

(3) Where—

(a) a trustee has been given a direction under subsection (2)(a),

(b) reasonable arrangements have been made for the protection of any rights of his in connection with the trust,

(c) after he has retired there will be either a trust corporation or at least two persons to act as trustees to perform the trust, and

(d) either another person is to be appointed to be a new trustee on his retirement (whether in compliance with a direction under subsection (2)(b) or otherwise) or the continuing trustees by deed consent to his retirement,

he shall make a deed declaring his retirement and shall be deemed to have retired and be discharged from the trust.

(4) Where a trustee retires under subsection (3) he and the continuing trustees (together with any new trustee) shall (subject to any arrangements for the protection of his rights) do anything necessary to vest the trust property in the continuing trustees (or the continuing and new trustees).

(5) This section has effect subject to the restrictions imposed by the Trustee Act 1925 on the number of trustees.

[1718]

[20 Appointment of substitute for trustee who lacks capacity]

(1) This section applies where—

(a) a trustee [lacks capacity (within the meaning of the Mental Capacity Act 2005) to exercise] his functions as trustee,

(b) there is no person who is both entitled and willing and able to appoint a trustee in place of him under section 36(1) of the Trustee Act 1925, and

(c) the beneficiaries under the trust are of full age and capacity and (taken together) are absolutely entitled to the property subject to the trust.

(2) The beneficiaries may give to—

[(a) a deputy appointed for the trustee by the Court of Protection,]

(b) an attorney acting for him under the authority of [an enduring power of attorney or lasting power of attorney registered under the Mental Capacity Act 2005], or

(c) a person authorised for the purpose by [the Court of Protection],

a written direction to appoint by writing the person or persons specified in the direction to be a trustee or trustees in place of the incapable trustee.

[1719]

NOTES

Section heading: substituted by the Mental Capacity Act 2005, s 67(1), Sch 6, para 42(1), (3).

Sub-s (1): words in square brackets in para (a) substituted by the Mental Capacity Act 2005, s 67(1), Sch 6, para 42(1), (3)(a).

Sub-s (2): para (a), and words in square brackets in paras (b), (c) substituted by the Mental Capacity Act 2005, s 67(1), Sch 6, para 42(1), (3)(b).

21 Supplementary

(1) For the purposes of section 19 or 20 a direction is given by beneficiaries if—

(a) a single direction is jointly given by all of them, or

(b) (subject to subsection (2)) a direction is given by each of them (whether solely or jointly with one or more, but not all, of the others),

and none of them by writing withdraws the direction given by him before it has been complied with.

(2) Where more than one direction is given each must specify for appointment or retirement the same person or persons.

(3) Subsection (7) of section 36 of the Trustee Act 1925 (powers of trustees appointed under that section) applies to a trustee appointed under section 19 or 20 as if he were appointed under that section.

(4) A direction under section 19 or 20 must not specify a person or persons for appointment if the appointment of that person or those persons would be in contravention of section 35(1) of the Trustee Act 1925 or section 24(1) of the Law of Property Act 1925 (requirements as to identity of trustees).

(5) Sections 19 and 20 do not apply in relation to a trust created by a disposition in so far as provision that they do not apply is made by the disposition.

(6) Sections 19 and 20 do not apply in relation to a trust created before the commencement of this Act by a disposition in so far as provision to the effect that they do not apply is made by a deed executed—

(a) in a case in which the trust was created by one person and he is of full capacity, by that person, or

(b) in a case in which the trust was created by more than one person, by such of the persons who created the trust as are alive and of full capacity.

(7) A deed executed for the purposes of subsection (6) is irrevocable.

(8) Where a deed is executed for the purposes of subsection (6)—

(a) it does not affect anything done before its execution to comply with a direction under section 19 or 20, but

(b) a direction under section 19 or 20 which has been given but not complied with before its execution shall cease to have effect.

[1720]

PART III
SUPPLEMENTARY

22 Meaning of "beneficiary"

(1) In this Act "beneficiary", in relation to a trust, means any person who under the trust has an interest in property subject to the trust (including a person who has such an interest as a trustee or a personal representative).

(2) In this Act references to a beneficiary who is beneficially entitled do not include a beneficiary who has an interest in property subject to the trust only by reason of being a trustee or personal representative.

(3) For the purposes of this Act a person who is a beneficiary only by reason of being an annuitant is not to be regarded as entitled to an interest in possession in land subject to the trust.

[1721]

23 Other interpretation provisions

(1) In this Act "purchaser" has the same meaning as in Part I of the Law of Property Act 1925.

(2) Subject to that, where an expression used in this Act is given a meaning by the Law of Property Act 1925 it has the same meaning as in that Act unless the context otherwise requires.

(3) In this Act "the court" means—

(a) the High Court, or

(b) a county court.

[1722]

24 Application to Crown

(1) Subject to subsection (2), this Act binds the Crown.

(2) This Act (except so far as it relates to undivided shares and joint ownership) does not affect or alter the descent, devolution or nature of the estates and interests of or in—

(a) land for the time being vested in Her Majesty in right of the Crown or of the Duchy of Lancaster, or

(b) land for the time being belonging to the Duchy of Cornwall and held in right or respect of the Duchy.

[1723]

25 Amendments, repeals etc

(1) The enactments mentioned in Schedule 3 have effect subject to the amendments specified in that Schedule (which are minor or consequential on other provisions of this Act).

(2) The enactments mentioned in Schedule 4 are repealed to the extent specified in the third column of that Schedule.

(3) Neither section 2(5) nor the repeal by this Act of section 29 of the Settled Land Act 1925 applies in relation to the deed of settlement set out in the Schedule to the Chequers Estate Act 1917 or the trust instrument set out in the Schedule to the Chevening Estate Act 1959.

(4) The amendments and repeals made by this Act do not affect any entailed interest created before the commencement of this Act.

(5) The amendments and repeals made by this Act in consequence of section 3—

(a) do not affect a trust created by a will if the testator died before the commencement of this Act, and

(b) do not affect personal representatives of a person who died before that commencement;

and the repeal of section 22 of the Partnership Act 1890 does not apply in any circumstances involving the personal representatives of a partner who died before that commencement.

[1724]

26 Power to make consequential provision

(1) The Lord Chancellor may by order made by statutory instrument make any such supplementary, transitional or incidental provision as appears to him to be appropriate for any of the purposes of this Act or in consequence of any of the provisions of this Act.

(2) An order under subsection (1) may, in particular, include provision modifying any enactment contained in a public general or local Act which is passed before, or in the same Session as, this Act.

(3) A statutory instrument made in the exercise of the power conferred by this section is subject to annulment in pursuance of a resolution of either House of Parliament.

[1725]

27 Short title, commencement and extent

(1) This Act may be cited as the Trusts of Land and Appointment of Trustees Act 1996.

(2) This Act comes into force on such day as the Lord Chancellor appoints by order made by statutory instrument.

(3) Subject to subsection (4), the provisions of this Act extend only to England and Wales.

(4) The repeal in section 30(2) of the Agriculture Act 1970 extends only to Northern Ireland.

[1726]

NOTES

Order: the Trusts of Land and Appointment of Trustees Act 1996 (Commencement) Order 1996, SI 1996/2974.

SCHEDULE 1
PROVISIONS CONSEQUENTIAL ON SECTION 2

Section 2

Minors

1.—(1) Where after the commencement of this Act a person purports to convey a legal estate in land to a minor, or two or more minors, alone, the conveyance—

(a) is not effective to pass the legal estate, but

(b) operates as a declaration that the land is held in trust for the minor or minors (or if he purports to convey it to the minor or minors in trust for any persons, for those persons).

(2) Where after the commencement of this Act a person purports to convey a legal estate in land to—

(a) a minor or two or more minors, and

(b) another person who is, or other persons who are, of full age,

the conveyance operates to vest the land in the other person or persons in trust for the minor or minors and the other person or persons (or if he purports to convey it to them in trust for any persons, for those persons).

(3) Where immediately before the commencement of this Act a conveyance is operating (by virtue of section 27 of the Settled Land Act 1925) as an agreement to execute a settlement in favour of a minor or minors—

(a) the agreement ceases to have effect on the commencement of this Act, and

(b) the conveyance subsequently operates instead as a declaration that the land is held in trust for the minor or minors.

2. Where after the commencement of this Act a legal estate in land would, by reason of intestacy or in any other circumstances not dealt with in paragraph 1, vest in a person who is a minor if he were a person of full age, the land is held in trust for the minor.

Family charges

3. Where, by virtue of an instrument coming into operation after the commencement of this Act, land becomes charged voluntarily (or in consideration of marriage [or the formation of a civil partnership]) or by way of family arrangement, whether immediately or after an interval, with the payment of—

(a) a rentcharge for the life of a person or a shorter period, or

(b) capital, annual or periodical sums for the benefit of a person,

the instrument operates as a declaration that the land is held in trust for giving effect to the charge.

Charitable, ecclesiastical and public trusts

4.—(1) This paragraph applies in the case of land held on charitable, ecclesiastical or public trusts (other than land to which the Universities and College Estates Act 1925 applies).

(2) Where there is a conveyance of such land—

(a) if neither section 37(1) nor section 39(1) of the Charities Act 1993 applies to the conveyance, it shall state that the land is held on such trusts, and

(b) if neither section 37(2) nor section 39(2) of that Act has been complied with in relation to the conveyance and a purchaser has notice that the land is held on such trusts, he must see that any consents or orders necessary to authorise the transaction have been obtained.

(3) Where any trustees or the majority of any set of trustees have power to transfer or create any legal estate in the land, the estate shall be transferred or created by them in the names and on behalf of the persons in whom it is vested.

Entailed interests

5.—(1) Where a person purports by an instrument coming into operation after the commencement of this Act to grant to another person an entailed interest in real or personal property, the instrument—

(a) is not effective to grant an entailed interest, but

(b) operates instead as a declaration that the property is held in trust absolutely for the person to whom an entailed interest in the property was purportedly granted.

(2) Where a person purports by an instrument coming into operation after the commencement of this Act to declare himself a tenant in tail of real or personal property, the instrument is not effective to create an entailed interest.

Property held on settlement ceasing to exist

6. Where a settlement ceases to be a settlement for the purposes of the Settled Land Act 1925 because no relevant property (within the meaning of section 2(4)) is, or is deemed to be, subject to the settlement, any property which is or later becomes subject to the settlement is held in trust for the persons interested under the settlement.

[1727]

NOTES

Para 3: words in square brackets inserted by the Civil Partnership Act 2004, s 261(1), Sch 27, para 153.

SCHEDULE 2
AMENDMENTS OF STATUTORY PROVISIONS IMPOSING TRUST FOR SALE

Section 5

Mortgaged property held by trustees after redemption barred

1.—(1)–(6) …

(7) The amendments made by this paragraph—

(a) apply whether the right of redemption is discharged before or after the commencement of this Act, but

(b) are without prejudice to any dealings or arrangements made before the commencement of this Act.

Land purchased by trustees of personal property etc

2.—(1) …

(2) The repeal made by this paragraph applies in relation to land purchased after the commencement of this Act whether the trust or will in pursuance of which it is purchased comes into operation before or after the commencement of this Act.

Dispositions to tenants in common

3.—(1)–(5) …

(6) The amendments made by this paragraph apply whether the disposition is made, or comes into operation, before or after the commencement of this Act.

Joint tenancies

4.—(1)–(3) …

(4) The amendments made by this paragraph apply whether the legal estate is limited, or becomes held in trust, before or after the commencement of this Act.

Intestacy

5.—(1)–(4) …

(5) The amendments made by this paragraph apply whether the death occurs before or after the commencement of this Act.

Reverter of sites

6.—(1)–(5) …

(6) The amendments made by this paragraph apply whether the trust arises before or after the commencement of this Act.

Trusts deemed to arise in 1926

7. Where at the commencement of this Act any land is held on trust for sale, or on the statutory trusts, by virtue of Schedule 1 to the Law of Property Act 1925 (transitional provisions), it shall after that commencement be held in trust for the persons interested in the land; and references in that Schedule to trusts for sale or trustees for sale or to the statutory trusts shall be construed accordingly.

[1728]

NOTES

Para 1: sub-paras (1)–(6) amend the Law of Property Act 1925, s 31 at **[284]**.
Para 2: sub-para (1) repeals the Law of Property Act 1925, s 32.
Para 3: sub-paras (1)–(5) amend the Law of Property Act 1925, s 34 at **[286]**.
Para 4: sub-paras (1)–(3) amend the Law of Property Act 1925, s 36 at **[287]**.
Para 5: sub-paras (1)–(4) amend the Administration of Estates Act 1925, s 33 at **[486]**.
Para 6: sub-paras (1)–(5) amend the Reverter of Sites Act 1987, s 1 at **[1255]**.

(Sch 3, in so far as unrepealed, contains minor and consequential amendments; Sch 4 contains repeals.)

HOUSING ACT 1996

(1996 c 52)

An Act to make provision about housing, including provision about the social rented sector, houses in multiple occupation, landlord and tenant matters, the administration of housing benefit, the conduct of tenants, the allocation of housing accommodation by local housing authorities and homelessness; and for connected purposes

[24 July 1996]

NOTES

Transfer of functions: as to the functions of Ministers of the Crown under this Act, so far as exercisable in relation to Wales, being transferred to the National Assembly for Wales, see the National Assembly for Wales (Transfer of Functions) Order 1999, SI 1999/672, art 2, Sch 1.

PART I
SOCIAL RENTED SECTOR [SOCIAL RENTED SECTOR IN WALES]

A1–7 ((*Ch I*) *Outside the scope of this work. Heading substituted by the Housing and Regeneration Act 2008, s 61(1), as from a day to be appointed.*)

CHAPTER II
DISPOSAL OF LAND AND RELATED MATTERS

8–15A (*Outside the scope of this work.*)

Right of tenant to acquire dwelling

16 Right of tenant to acquire dwelling

(*1*) *A tenant of a registered social landlord has the right to acquire the dwelling of which he is a tenant if—*

(*a*) *he is a tenant under an assured tenancy, other than an assured shorthold tenancy or a long tenancy, or under a secure tenancy,*

(*b*) *the dwelling was provided with public money and has remained in the social rented sector, and*

(*c*) *he satisfies any further qualifying conditions applicable under Part V of the Housing Act 1985 (the right to buy) as it applies in relation to the right conferred by this section.*

[(1) The tenant of a dwelling in Wales has a right to acquire the dwelling if—

(a) the landlord is a registered social landlord or a registered provider of social housing,

(b) the tenancy is—

(i) an assured tenancy, other than an assured shorthold tenancy or a long tenancy, or

(ii) a secure tenancy,

(c) the dwelling was provided with public money and has remained in the social rented sector, and

(d) the tenant satisfies any further qualifying conditions applicable under Part V of the Housing Act 1985 (the right to buy) as it applies in relation to the right conferred by this section.]

(2) For this purpose a dwelling shall be regarded as provided with public money if—

(a) it was provided or acquired wholly or in part by means of a grant under section 18 (social housing grant),

(b) it was provided or acquired wholly or in part by applying or appropriating sums standing in the disposal proceeds fund of a registered social landlord (see section 25), or

(c) it was acquired by a registered social landlord [or a registered provider of social housing] after the commencement of this paragraph on a disposal by a public sector landlord at a time when it was capable of being let as a separate dwelling.

(3) A dwelling shall be regarded for the purposes of this section as having remained within the social rented sector if, since it was so provided or acquired—

(a) the person holding the freehold interest in the dwelling has been either a registered social landlord[, a registered provider of social housing] or a public sector landlord; and

(b) any person holding an interest as lessee (otherwise than as mortgagee) in the dwelling has been—

(i) an individual holding otherwise than under a long tenancy; or

(ii) a registered social landlord[, a registered provider of social housing] or a public sector landlord.

[(3A) In subsection (3)(a) the reference to the freehold interest in the dwelling includes a reference to such an interest in the dwelling as is held by the landlord under a lease granted in pursuance of paragraph 3 of Schedule 9 to the Leasehold Reform, Housing and Urban Development Act 1993 (mandatory leaseback to former freeholder on collective enfranchisement).]

(4) A dwelling shall be regarded for the purposes of this section as provided by means of a grant under section 18 (social housing grant) if, and only if, *the* [*Relevant Authority*] [the Welsh Ministers] when making the grant notified the recipient that the dwelling was to be so regarded.

The [*Relevant Authority*] [The Welsh Ministers] shall before making the grant inform the applicant that *it proposes* [they propose] to give such a notice and allow him an opportunity to withdraw his application within a specified time

[(5) But notice must be taken to be given to a registered social landlord under subsection (4) by the Housing Corporation if it is sent using electronic communications to such number or address as the registered social landlord has for the time being notified to the Housing Corporation for that purpose.

(6) The means by which notice is sent by virtue of subsection (5) must be such as to enable the registered social landlord to reproduce the notice by electronic means in a form which is visible and legible.

(7) An electronic communication is a communication transmitted (whether from one person to another, from one device to another, or from a person to a device or vice versa)—

(a) by means of [an electronic communications network]; or
(b) by other means but while in an electronic form.]

[1729]

NOTES

Sub-s (1): substituted by the Housing and Regeneration Act 2008, s 185(1)(a), as from a day to be appointed.

Sub-s (2): in para (c) words in square brackets inserted by the Housing and Regeneration Act 2008, s 185(1)(b), as from a day to be appointed.

Sub-s (3): in paras (a), (b)(ii) words in square brackets inserted by the Housing and Regeneration Act 2008, s 185(1)(c), as from a day to be appointed.

Sub-s (3A): inserted by the Housing Act 2004, s 202(1), (2); for effect see s 202(3) thereof.

Sub-s (4): words in italics substituted by subsequent words in square brackets, by the Housing and Regeneration Act 2008, s 61(1), (7), as from a day to be appointed; words "Relevant Authority" in square brackets in both places they occur previously substituted by the Government of Wales Act 1998, ss 140, 141, Sch 16, paras 81, 82.

Sub-ss (5), (6): inserted in relation to England, by SI 2001/3257, art 2.

Sub-s (7): inserted in relation to England, by SI 2001/3257, art 2; words in square brackets substituted by the Communications Act 2003, s 406(1), Sch 17, para 136.

Functions of the Housing Corporation under this section transferred to the Homes and Communities Agency: see the Transfer of Housing Corporation Functions (Modifications and Transitional Provisions) Order 2008, SI 2008/2839, arts 1(2), 2, 3, 6, Schedule, para 11(2), (3).

[16A Extension of section 16 to dwellings funded by grants under section 27A

(1) Section 16 applies in relation to a dwelling [in Wales] ("a funded dwelling") provided or acquired wholly or in part by means of a grant under section 27A (grants to bodies other than registered social landlords) with the following modifications.

(2) In section 16(1) the reference to a registered social landlord includes a reference to any person to whom a grant has been paid under section 27A.

(3) In section 16(2) and (4) any reference to section 18 includes a reference to section 27A.

(4) For the purposes of section 16 a funded dwelling is to be regarded as having remained within the social rented sector in relation to any relevant time if, since it was acquired or provided as mentioned in subsection (1) above, it was used—

(a) by the recipient of the grant mentioned in that subsection, or
(b) if section 27B applies in relation to the grant, by each person to whom the grant was, or is treated as having been, paid,

exclusively for the purposes for which the grant was made or any other purposes agreed to by *the Relevant Authority* [the Welsh Ministers].

(5) In subsection (4) "relevant time" means a time when the dwelling would not be treated as being within the social rented sector by virtue of section 16(3).]

[1730]

NOTES

Commencement: 17 February 2005 (in relation to England); to be appointed (in relation to Wales).

Inserted by the Housing Act 2004, s 221.

Sub-s (1): words in square brackets inserted by the Housing and Regeneration Act 2008, s 185(2), as from a day to be appointed.

Sub-s (4): words in italics substituted by subsequent words in square brackets by the Housing and Regeneration Act 2008, s 61(1), (7), as from a day to be appointed.

Functions of the Housing Corporation under this section transferred to the Homes and Communities Agency: see the Transfer of Housing Corporation Functions (Modifications and Transitional Provisions) Order 2008, SI 2008/2839, arts 1(2), 2, 3, 6, Schedule, para 11(2), (3).

17 Right of tenant to acquire dwelling: supplementary provisions

(1) The *Secretary of State* [Welsh Ministers] may by order —

(a) specify the amount or rate of discount to be given on the exercise of the right conferred by section 16; and

(b) designate rural areas in relation to dwellings in which the right conferred by that section does not arise.

(2) The provisions of Part V of the Housing Act 1985 apply in relation to the right to acquire under section 16—

(a) subject to any order under subsection (1) above, and

(b) subject to such other exceptions, adaptations and other modifications as may be specified by regulations made by the *Secretary of State* [Welsh Ministers].

(3) The regulations may provide—

(a) that the powers of the Secretary of State under sections 164 to 170 of that Act (powers to intervene, give directions or assist) do not apply,

(b) that paragraphs 1 and 3 (exceptions for charities and certain housing associations), and paragraph 11 (right of appeal to Secretary of State), of Schedule 5 to that Act do not apply,

(c) that the provisions of Part V of that Act relating to the right to acquire on rent to mortgage terms do not apply,

(d) that the provisions of that Part relating to restrictions on disposals in National Parks, &c do not apply, and

(e) that the provisions of that Part relating to the preserved right to buy do not apply.

Nothing in this subsection affects the generality of the power conferred by subsection (2).

(4) The specified exceptions, adaptations and other modifications shall take the form of textual amendments of the provisions of Part V of that Act as they apply in relation to the right to buy under that Part; and the first regulations, and any subsequent consolidating regulations, shall set out the provisions of Part V as they so apply.

(5) An order or regulations under this section—

(a) may make different provision for different cases or classes of case including different areas, and

(b) may contain such incidental, supplementary and transitional provisions as the *Secretary of State considers* [Welsh Ministers consider] appropriate.

(6) Before making an order which would have the effect that an area ceased to be designated under subsection (1)(b), the *Secretary of State* [Welsh Ministers] shall consult —

(a) the local housing authority or authorities in whose district the area or any part of it is situated or, if the order is general in its effect, local housing authorities in general, and

(b) such bodies appearing to *him* [them] to be representative of registered social landlords as *he considers* [they consider] appropriate.

(7) An order or regulations under this section shall be made by statutory instrument which shall be subject to annulment in pursuance of a resolution of *either House of Parliament* [the National Assembly for Wales].

[1731]

NOTES

Sub-ss (1), (2), (5), (6): words in italics substituted by subsequent words in square brackets by the Housing and Regeneration Act 2008, s 62, as from a day to be appointed.

Sub-s (7): words in italics substituted by subsequent words in square brackets by the Housing and Regeneration Act 2008, s 63, as from a day to be appointed.

Orders and regulations: the Housing (Right to Acquire) (Discount) (Wales) Order 1997, SI 1997/569; the Housing (Right to Acquire) Regulations 1997, SI 1997/619; the Leasehold Reform and Housing (Excluded Tenancies) (Designated Rural Areas) (Wales) Order 1997, SI 1997/685; the Housing (Right to Acquire or Enfranchise) (Designated Rural Areas) Order 1999, SI 1999/1307; the Housing (Right to Acquire) (Discount) Order 2002, SI 2002/1091; the Housing (Right to Acquire and Right to Buy) (Designated Rural Areas and Designated Regions) (Wales) Order 2003, SI 2003/54; the Housing (Right of First Refusal) (England) Regulations 2005, SI 2005/1917; the Housing (Right of First Refusal) (Wales) Regulations 2005, SI 2005/2680.

18–80 (*Ss 18–64* (*Chs III–V*), *ss 65–80* (*Pt II*) *in so far as unrepealed, outside the scope of this work.*)

PART III
LANDLORD AND TENANT

CHAPTER I
TENANTS' RIGHTS

Forfeiture

81 Restriction on termination of tenancy for failure to pay service charge

(1) A landlord may not, in relation to premises let as a dwelling, exercise a right of re-entry or forfeiture for failure [by a tenant to pay a service charge or administration charge unless—

(a) it is finally determined by (or on appeal from) a leasehold valuation tribunal or by a court, or by an arbitral tribunal in proceedings pursuant to a post-dispute arbitration agreement, that the amount of the service charge or administration charge is payable by him, or

(b) the tenant has admitted that it is so payable].

[(2) The landlord may not exercise a right of re-entry or forfeiture by virtue of subsection (1)(a) until after the end of the period of 14 days beginning with the day after that on which the final determination is made.]

[(3) For the purposes of this section it is finally determined that the amount of a service charge or administration charge is payable—

(a) if a decision that it is payable is not appealed against or otherwise challenged, at the end of the time for bringing an appeal or other challenge, or

(b) if such a decision is appealed against or otherwise challenged and not set aside in consequence of the appeal or other challenge, at the time specified in subsection (3A).

(3A) The time referred to in subsection (3)(b) is the time when the appeal or other challenge is disposed of—

(a) by the determination of the appeal or other challenge and the expiry of the time for bringing a subsequent appeal (if any), or

(b) by its being abandoned or otherwise ceasing to have effect.]

(4) The reference in subsection (1) to premises let as a dwelling does not include premises let on—

(a) a tenancy to which Part II of the Landlord and Tenant Act 1954 applies (business tenancies),

(b) a tenancy of an agricultural holding within the meaning of the Agricultural Holdings Act 1986 in relation to which that Act applies, or

(c) a farm business tenancy within the meaning of the Agricultural Tenancies Act 1995.

[(4A) References in this section to the exercise of a right of re-entry or forfeiture include the service of a notice under section 146(1) of the Law of Property Act 1925 (restriction on re-entry or forfeiture).]

(5) In this section

[(a) "administration charge" has the meaning given by Part 1 of Schedule 11 to the Commonhold and Leasehold Reform Act 2002,

(b) "arbitration agreement" and "arbitral tribunal" have the same meaning as in Part 1 of the Arbitration Act 1996 (c 23) and "post-dispute arbitration agreement", in relation to any matter, means an arbitration agreement made after a dispute about the matter has arisen,

(c) "dwelling" has the same meaning as in the Landlord and Tenant Act 1985 (c 70), and

(d)] "service charge" means a service charge within the meaning of section 18(1) of the Landlord and Tenant Act 1985, other than one excluded from that section by section 27 of that Act (rent of dwelling registered and not entered as variable).

[(5A) Any order of a court to give effect to a determination of a leasehold valuation tribunal shall be treated as a determination by the court for the purposes of this section.]

(6) Nothing in this section affects the exercise of a right of re-entry or forfeiture on other grounds.

[1732]

NOTES

Sub-s (1): words in square brackets substituted by the Commonhold and Leasehold Reform Act 2002, s 170(1), (2), except in relation to notices served under the Law of Property Act 1925, s 146(1), before 28 February 2005 (in relation to England) or 31 May 2005 (in relation to Wales).

Sub-s (2): substituted by the Commonhold and Leasehold Reform Act 2002, s 170(1), (3), subject to savings as noted above.

Sub-ss (3), (3A): substituted for original sub-s (3) by the Commonhold and Leasehold Reform Act 2002, s 170(1), (4), subject to savings as noted above.

Sub-s (4A): inserted by the Commonhold and Leasehold Reform Act 2002, s 170(1), (5), subject to savings as noted above.

Sub-s (5): paras (a)–(c) inserted and para (d) numbered as such by the Commonhold and Leasehold Reform Act 2002, s 170(1), (6), subject to savings as noted above.

Sub-s (5A): inserted by the Commonhold and Leasehold Reform Act 2002, s 176, Sch 13, para 16, subject to savings as noted above.

82 (*Repealed by the Commonhold and Leasehold Reform Act 2002, s 180, Sch 14.*)

Service charges

83 (*Outside the scope of this work.*)

84 Right to appoint surveyor to advise on matters relating to service charges

(1) A recognised tenants' association may appoint a surveyor for the purposes of this section to advise on any matters relating to, or which may give rise to, service charges payable to a landlord by one or more members of the association.

The provisions of Schedule 4 have effect for conferring on a surveyor so appointed rights of access to documents and premises.

(2) A person shall not be so appointed unless he is a qualified surveyor.

For this purpose "qualified surveyor" has the same meaning as in section 78(4)(a) of the Leasehold Reform, Housing and Urban Development Act 1993 (persons qualified for appointment to carry out management audit).

(3) The appointment shall take effect for the purposes of this section upon notice in writing being given to the landlord by the association stating the name and address of the surveyor, the duration of his appointment and the matters in respect of which he is appointed.

(4) An appointment shall cease to have effect for the purposes of this section if the association gives notice in writing to the landlord to that effect or if the association ceases to exist.

(5) A notice is duly given under this section to a landlord of any tenants if it is given to a person who receives on behalf of the landlord the rent payable by those tenants; and a person to whom such a notice is so given shall forward it as soon as may be to the landlord.

(6) In this section—

"recognised tenants' association" has the same meaning as in the provisions of the Landlord and Tenant Act 1985 relating to service charges (see section 29 of that Act); and

"service charge" means a service charge within the meaning of section 18(1) of that Act, other than one excluded from that section by section 27 of that Act (rent of dwelling registered and not entered as variable).

[1733]

NOTES

Modified, where the RTM company has acquired the right to manage, by the Commonhold and Leasehold Reform Act 2002, s 102, Sch 7, para 15.

85–93 (*Outside the scope of this work.*)

General legal advice

94 Provision of general [advice etc] about residential tenancies

(1) The Secretary of State may give financial assistance to any person in relation to the provision by that person of [information, training or] general advice about[, or a dispute resolution service in connection with]—

(a) any aspect of the law of landlord and tenant, so far as relating to residential tenancies, or

[(aa) any other matter relating to residential tenancies,] or

(b) [any matter relating to] Chapter IV of Part I of the Leasehold Reform, Housing and Urban Development Act 1993 (estate management schemes in connection with enfranchisement).

(2) Financial assistance under this section may be given in such form and on such terms as the Secretary of State considers appropriate.

(3) The terms on which financial assistance under this section may be given may, in particular, include provision as to the circumstances in which the assistance must be repaid or otherwise made good to the Secretary of State and the manner in which that is to be done.

[1734]

NOTES

Heading: words in square brackets substituted by the Housing and Regeneration Act 2008, s 312(2).

Sub-s (1): words in square brackets inserted by the Housing and Regeneration Act 2008, s 312(1)(a), (b); sub-para (aa) inserted by the Housing and Regeneration Act 2008, s 312(1)(c); in sub-para (b) words in square brackets inserted by the Housing and Regeneration Act 2008, s 312(1)(d).

Supplementary

95 Jurisdiction of county courts

(1) Any jurisdiction expressed by a provision to which this section applies to be conferred on the court shall be exercised by a county court.

(2) There shall also be brought in a county court any proceedings for determining any question arising under or by virtue of any provision to which this section applies.

(3) Where, however, other proceedings are properly brought in the High Court, that court has jurisdiction to hear and determine proceedings to which subsection (1) or (2) applies which are joined with those proceedings.

(4) Where proceedings are brought in a county court by virtue of subsection (1) or (2), that court has jurisdiction to hear and determine other proceedings joined with those proceedings despite the fact that they would otherwise be outside its jurisdiction.

(5) The provisions to which this section applies are—

(a) section 81 (restriction on termination of tenancy for failure to pay service charge), and

(b) section 84 (right to appoint surveyor to advise on matters relating to service charges) and Schedule 4 (rights exercisable by surveyor appointed by tenants' association).

[1735]

96–218 (*Ss 96–119, ss 120–218 (Pts IV–VII) outside the scope of this work*)

PART VIII
MISCELLANEOUS AND GENERAL PROVISIONS

218A–222 (*Outside the scope of this work.*)

General

223–228 (*Outside the scope of this work.*)

229 Meaning of "lease" and "tenancy" and related expressions

(1) In this Act "lease" and "tenancy" have the same meaning.

(2) Both expressions include—

(a) a sub-lease or a sub-tenancy, and

(b) an agreement for a lease or tenancy (or sub-lease or sub-tenancy).

(3) The expressions "lessor" and "lessee" and "landlord" and "tenant", and references to letting, to the grant of a lease or to covenants or terms, shall be construed accordingly.

[1736]

230 Minor definitions: general

In this Act—

"assured tenancy", "assured shorthold tenancy" and "assured agricultural occupancy" have the same meaning as in Part I of the Housing Act 1988;

"enactment" includes an enactment comprised in subordinate legislation (within the meaning of the Interpretation Act 1978);

"housing action trust" has the same meaning as in the Housing Act 1988;

"housing association" has the same meaning as in the Housing Associations Act 1985;

"introductory tenancy" and "introductory tenant" have the same meaning as in Chapter I of Part V of this Act;

"local housing authority" has the same meaning as in the Housing Act 1985;

"registered social landlord" has the same meaning as in Part I of this Act;

"secure tenancy" and "secure tenant" have the same meaning as in Part IV of the Housing Act 1985.

[1737]

Final provisions

231 (*Outside the scope of this work.*)

232 Commencement

(1) The following provisions of this Act come into force on Royal Assent—

section 110 (new leases: valuation principles),

section 120 (payment of housing benefit to third parties), and
sections 223 to 226 and 228 to 233 (general provisions).

(2) The following provisions of this Act come into force at the end of the period of two months beginning with the date on which this Act is passed—

sections 81 and 82 (restriction on termination of tenancy for failure to pay service charge),
section 85 (appointment of manager by the court),
section 94 (provision of general legal advice about residential tenancies),
section 95 (jurisdiction of county courts),
section 221 (exercise of compulsory purchase powers in relation to Crown land),
paragraph 24 (powers of local housing authorities to acquire land for housing purposes), paragraph 26 (preserved right to buy) and paragraphs 27 to 29 of Schedule 18 (local authority assistance in connection with mortgages), and
sections 222 and 227, and Schedule 19 (consequential repeals), in so far as they relate to those paragraphs.

(3) The other provisions of this Act come into force on a day appointed by order of the Secretary of State, and different days may be appointed for different areas and different purposes.

(4) An order under subsection (3) shall be made by statutory instrument and may contain such transitional provisions and savings as appear to the Secretary of State to be appropriate.

[1738]

NOTES

Orders: the Housing Act 1996 (Commencement No 1) Order 1996, SI 1996/2048; the Housing Act 1996 (Commencement No 2 and Savings) Order 1996, SI 1996/2212; the Housing Act 1996 (Commencement No 3 and Transitional Provisions) Order 1996, SI 1996/2402; the Housing Act 1996 (Commencement No 4) Order 1996, SI 1996/2658; the Housing Act 1996 (Commencement No 5 and Transitional Provisions) Order 1996, SI 1996/2959; the Housing Act 1996 (Commencement No 6 and Savings) Order 1997, SI 1997/66; the Housing Act 1996 (Commencement No 7 and Savings) Order 1997, SI 1997/225; the Housing Act 1996 (Commencement No 8) Order 1997, SI 1997/350; the Housing Act 1996 (Commencement No 9) Order 1997, SI 1997/596; the Housing Act 1996 (Commencement No 10 and Transitional Provisions) Order 1997, SI 1997/618; the Housing Act 1996 (Commencement No 11 and Savings) Order 1997, SI 1997/1851; the Housing Act 1996 (Commencement No 12 and Transitional Provisions) Order 1998, SI 1998/1768; the Housing Act 1996 (Commencement No 13) Order 2001, SI 2001/3164.

233 Short title

This Act may be cited as the Housing Act 1996.

[1739]

SCHEDULES

(*Schs 1–3 outside the scope of this work.*)

SCHEDULE 4
RIGHTS EXERCISABLE BY SURVEYOR APPOINTED BY TENANTS' ASSOCIATION

Section 84

Introductory

1.—(1) A surveyor appointed for the purposes of section 84 has the rights conferred by this Schedule.

(2) In this Schedule—

(a) "the tenants' association" means the association by whom the surveyor was appointed, and
(b) the surveyor's "functions" are his functions in connection with the matters in respect of which he was appointed.

Appointment of assistants

2.—(1) The surveyor may appoint such persons as he thinks fit to assist him in carrying out his functions.

(2) References in this Schedule to the surveyor in the context of—

(a) being afforded any such facilities as are mentioned in paragraph 3, or
(b) carrying out an inspection under paragraph 4,

include a person so appointed.

Right to inspect documents, &c

3.—(1) The surveyor has a right to require the landlord or any other relevant person—

(a) to afford him reasonable facilities for inspecting any documents sight of which is reasonably required by him for the purposes of his functions, and

(b) to afford him reasonable facilities for taking copies of or extracts from any such documents.

(2) In sub-paragraph (1) "other relevant person" means a person other than the landlord who is or, in relation to a future service charge, will be—

(a) responsible for applying the proceeds of the service charge, or

(b) under an obligation to a tenant who pays the service charge in respect of any matter to which the charge relates.

(3) The rights conferred on the surveyor by this paragraph are extricable by him by notice in writing given by him to the landlord or other person concerned.

Where a notice is given to a person other than the landlord, the surveyor shall give a copy of the notice to the landlord.

(4) The landlord or other person to whom notice is given shall, within the period of one week beginning with the date of the giving of the notice or as soon as reasonably practicable thereafter, either—

(a) afford the surveyor the facilities required by him for inspecting and taking copies or extracts of the documents to which the notice relates, or

(b) give the surveyor a notice stating that he objects to doing so for reasons specified in the notice.

(5) Facilities for the inspection of any documents required under sub-paragraph (1)(a) shall be made available free of charge.

This does not mean that the landlord cannot treat as part of his costs of management any costs incurred by him in connection with making the facilities available.

(6) A reasonable charge may be made for facilities for the taking of copies or extracts required under sub-paragraph (1)(b).

(7) A notice is duly given under this paragraph to the landlord of a tenant if it is given to a person who receives on behalf of the landlord the rent payable by that tenant.

A person to whom such a notice is so given shall forward it as soon as may be to the landlord.

Right to inspect premises

4.—(1) The surveyor also has the right to inspect any common parts comprised in relevant premises or any appurtenant property.

(2) In sub-paragraph (1)—

"common parts", in relation to a building or part of a building, includes the structure and exterior of the building or part and any common facilities within it;

"relevant premises" means so much of—

(i) the building or buildings containing the dwellings let to members of the tenants' association, and

(ii) any other building or buildings,

as constitute premises in relation to which management functions are discharged in respect of the costs of which service charges are payable by members of the association; and

"appurtenant property" means so much of any property not contained in relevant premises as constitutes property in relation to which any such management functions are discharged.

For the purposes of the above definitions "management functions" includes functions with respect to the provision of services, or the repair, maintenance[, improvement] or insurance of property.

(3) On being requested to do so, the landlord shall afford the surveyor reasonable access for the purposes of carrying out an inspection under this paragraph.

(4) Such reasonable access shall be afforded to the surveyor free of charge.

This does not mean that the landlord cannot treat as part of his costs of management any costs incurred by him in connection with affording reasonable access to the surveyor.

(5) A request is duly made under this paragraph to the landlord of a tenant if it is made to a person appointed by the landlord to deal with such requests or, if no such person has been appointed, to a person who receives on behalf of the landlord the rent payable by that tenant.

A person to whom such a request is made shall notify the landlord of the request as soon as may be.

Enforcement of rights by the court

5.—(1) If the landlord or other person to whom notice was given under paragraph 3 has not, by the end of the period of one month beginning with the date on which notice was given, complied with the notice, the court may, on the application of the surveyor, make an order requiring him to do so within such period as is specified in the order.

(2) If the landlord does not, within a reasonable period after the making of a request under paragraph 4, afford the surveyor reasonable access for the purposes of carrying out an inspection under that paragraph, the court may, on the application of the surveyor, make an order requiring the landlord to do so on such date as is specified in the order.

(3) An application for an order under this paragraph must be made before the end of the period of four months beginning with the date on which notice was given under paragraph 3 or the request was made under paragraph 4.

(4) An order under this paragraph may be made in general terms or may require the landlord or other person to do specific things, as the court thinks fit.

Documents held by superior landlord

6.—(1) Where a landlord is required by a notice under paragraph 3 to afford the surveyor facilities for inspection or taking copies or extracts in respect of any document which is in the custody or under the control of a superior landlord—

(a) the landlord shall on receiving the notice inform the surveyor as soon as may be of that fact and of the name and address of the superior landlord, and

(b) the surveyor may then give the superior landlord notice in writing requiring him to afford the facilities in question in respect of the document.

(2) Paragraphs 3 and 5(1) and (3) have effect, with any necessary modifications, in relation to a notice given to a superior landlord under this paragraph.

Effect of disposal by landlord

7.—(1) Where a notice under paragraph 3 has been given or a request under paragraph 4 has been made to a landlord, and at a time when any obligations arising out of the notice or request remain to be discharged by him—

(a) he disposes of the whole or part of his interest as landlord of any member of the tenants' association, and

(b) the person acquiring that interest ("the transferee") is in a position to discharge any of those obligations to any extent,

that person shall be responsible for discharging those obligations to that extent, as if he had been given the notice under paragraph 3 or had received the request under paragraph 4.

(2) If the landlord is, despite the disposal, still in a position to discharge those obligations, he remains responsible for doing so.

Otherwise, the transferee is responsible for discharging them to the exclusion of the landlord.

(3) In connection with the discharge of such obligations by the transferee, paragraphs 3 to 6 apply with the substitution for any reference to the date on which notice was given under paragraph 3 or the request was made under paragraph 4 of a reference to the date of the disposal.

(4) In this paragraph "disposal" means a disposal whether by the creation or transfer of an estate or interest, and includes the surrender of a tenancy; and references to the transferee shall be construed accordingly.

Effect of person ceasing to be a relevant person

8. Where a notice under paragraph 3 has been given to a person other than the landlord and, at a time when any obligations arising out of the notice remain to be discharged by him, he ceases to be such a person as is mentioned in paragraph 3(2), then, if he is still in a position to discharge those obligations to any extent he remains responsible for discharging those obligations, and the provisions of this Schedule continue to apply to him, to that extent.

[1740]

NOTES

Para 4: word in square brackets inserted by the Commonhold and Leasehold Reform Act 2002, s 150, Sch 9, para 12.

Modified, where the RTM company has acquired the right to manage, by the Commonhold and Leasehold Reform Act 2002, s 102, Sch 7, para 15.

(*Schs 5–19 outside the scope of this work.*)

HUMAN RIGHTS ACT 1998

(1998 c 42)

An Act to give further effect to rights and freedoms guaranteed under the European Convention on Human Rights; to make provision with respect to holders of certain judicial offices who become judges of the European Court of Human Rights; and for connected purposes.

[9 November 1998]

Introduction

1 The Convention Rights

(1) In this Act "the Convention rights" means the rights and fundamental freedoms set out in—

(a) Articles 2 to 12 and 14 of the Convention,

(b) Articles 1 to 3 of the First Protocol, and

(c) [Article 1 of the Thirteenth Protocol],

as read with Articles 16 to 18 of the Convention.

(2) Those Articles are to have effect for the purposes of this Act subject to any designated derogation or reservation (as to which see sections 14 and 15).

(3) The Articles are set out in Schedule 1.

(4) The [Secretary of State] may by order make such amendments to this Act as he considers appropriate to reflect the effect, in relation to the United Kingdom, of a protocol.

(5) In subsection (4) "protocol" means a protocol to the Convention—

(a) which the United Kingdom has ratified; or

(b) which the United Kingdom has signed with a view to ratification.

(6) No amendment may be made by an order under subsection (4) so as to come into force before the protocol concerned is in force in relation to the United Kingdom.

[1741]

NOTES

Sub-s (1): words in square brackets in para (c) substituted by SI 2004/1574, art 2(1).
Sub-s (4): words in square brackets substituted by SI 2003/1887, art 9, Sch 2, para 10(1).

2 Interpretation of Convention rights

(1) A court or tribunal determining a question which has arisen in connection with a Convention right must take into account any—

(a) judgment, decision, declaration or advisory opinion of the European Court of Human Rights,

(b) opinion of the Commission given in a report adopted under Article 31 of the Convention,

(c) decision of the Commission in connection with Article 26 or 27(2) of the Convention, or

(d) decision of the Committee of Ministers taken under Article 46 of the Convention,

whenever made or given, so far as, in the opinion of the court or tribunal, it is relevant to the proceedings in which that question has arisen.

(2) Evidence of any judgment, decision, declaration or opinion of which account may have to be taken under this section is to be given in proceedings before any court or tribunal in such manner as may be provided by rules.

(3) In this section "rules" means rules of court or, in the case of proceedings before a tribunal, rules made for the purposes of this section—

(a) by … [the Lord Chancellor or] the Secretary of State, in relation to any proceedings outside Scotland;

(b) by the Secretary of State, in relation to proceedings in Scotland; or

(c) by a Northern Ireland department, in relation to proceedings before a tribunal in Northern Ireland—

(i) which deals with transferred matters; and

(ii) for which no rules made under paragraph (a) are in force.

[1742]

NOTES

Sub-s (3): words omitted repealed by SI 2003/1887, art 9, Sch 2, para 10(2); words in square brackets inserted by SI 2005/3429, art 8, Schedule, para 3.

Legislation

3 Interpretation of legislation

(1) So far as it is possible to do so, primary legislation and subordinate legislation must be read and given effect in a way which is compatible with the Convention rights.

(2) This section—

(a) applies to primary legislation and subordinate legislation whenever enacted;

(b) does not affect the validity, continuing operation or enforcement of any incompatible primary legislation; and

(c) does not affect the validity, continuing operation or enforcement of any incompatible subordinate legislation if (disregarding any possibility of revocation) primary legislation prevents removal of the incompatibility.

[1743]

4, 5 (*Outside the scope of this work.*)

Public authorities

6 Acts of public authorities

(1) It is unlawful for a public authority to act in a way which is incompatible with a Convention right.

(2)–(6) (*Outside the scope of this work.*)

[1744]

7 Proceedings

(1) A person who claims that a public authority has acted (or proposes to act) in a way which is made unlawful by section 6(1) may—

(a) bring proceedings against the authority under this Act in the appropriate court or tribunal, or

(b) rely on the Convention right or rights concerned in any legal proceedings,

but only if he is (or would be) a victim of the unlawful act.

(2) In subsection (1)(a) "appropriate court or tribunal" means such court or tribunal as may be determined in accordance with rules; and proceedings against an authority include a counterclaim or similar proceeding.

(3) If the proceedings are brought on an application for judicial review, the applicant is to be taken to have a sufficient interest in relation to the unlawful act only if he is, or would be, a victim of that act.

(4) If the proceedings are made by way of a petition for judicial review in Scotland, the applicant shall be taken to have title and interest to sue in relation to the unlawful act only if he is, or would be, a victim of that act.

(5) Proceedings under subsection (1)(a) must be brought before the end of—

(a) the period of one year beginning with the date on which the act complained of took place; or

(b) such longer period as the court or tribunal considers equitable having regard to all the circumstances,

but that is subject to any rule imposing a stricter time limit in relation to the procedure in question.

(6) In subsection (1)(b) "legal proceedings" includes—

(a) proceedings brought by or at the instigation of a public authority; and

(b) an appeal against the decision of a court or tribunal.

(7) For the purposes of this section, a person is a victim of an unlawful act only if he would be a victim for the purposes of Article 34 of the Convention if proceedings were brought in the European Court of Human Rights in respect of that act.

(8) Nothing in this Act creates a criminal offence.

(9) In this section "rules" means—

(a) in relation to proceedings before a court or tribunal outside Scotland, rules made by … [the Lord Chancellor or] the Secretary of State for the purposes of this section or rules of court,

(b) in relation to proceedings before a court or tribunal in Scotland, rules made by the Secretary of State for those purposes,

(c) in relation to proceedings before a tribunal in Northern Ireland—

(i) which deals with transferred matters; and

(ii) for which no rules made under paragraph (a) are in force,

rules made by a Northern Ireland department for those purposes,

and includes provision made by order under section 1 of the Courts and Legal Services Act 1990.

(10) In making rules, regard must be had to section 9.

(11) The Minister who has power to make rules in relation to a particular tribunal may, to the extent he considers it necessary to ensure that the tribunal can provide an appropriate remedy in relation to an act (or proposed act) of a public authority which is (or would be) unlawful as a result of section 6(1), by order add to—

(a) the relief or remedies which the tribunal may grant; or

(b) the grounds on which it may grant any of them.

(12) An order made under subsection (11) may contain such incidental, supplemental, consequential or transitional provision as the Minister making it considers appropriate.

(13) "The Minister" includes the Northern Ireland department concerned.

[1745]

NOTES

Sub-s (9): words omitted repealed by SI 2003/1887, art 9, Sch 2, para 10(2); words in square brackets inserted by SI 2005/3429, art 8, Schedule, para 3.

Rules: the Human Rights Act 1998 (Jurisdiction) (Scotland) Rules 2000, SSI 2000/301; the Proscribed Organisations Appeal Commission (Human Rights Act Proceedings) Rules 2006, SI 2006/2290.

8–19 (*Outside the scope of this work.*)

Supplemental

20 (*Outside the scope of this work.*)

21 Interpretation, etc

(1) In this Act—

"amend" includes repeal and apply (with or without modifications);

"the appropriate Minister" means the Minister of the Crown having charge of the appropriate authorised government department (within the meaning of the Crown Proceedings Act 1947);

"the Commission" means the European Commission of Human Rights;

"the Convention" means the Convention for the Protection of Human Rights and Fundamental Freedoms, agreed by the Council of Europe at Rome on 4th November 1950 as it has effect for the time being in relation to the United Kingdom;

"declaration of incompatibility" means a declaration under section 4;

"Minister of the Crown" has the same meaning as in the Ministers of the Crown Act 1975;

"Northern Ireland Minister" includes the First Minister and the deputy First Minister in Northern Ireland;

"primary legislation" means any—

(a) public general Act;
(b) local and personal Act;
(c) private Act;
(d) Measure of the Church Assembly;
(e) Measure of the General Synod of the Church of England;
(f) Order in Council—
  (i) made in exercise of Her Majesty's Royal Prerogative;
  (ii) made under section 38(1)(a) of the Northern Ireland Constitution Act 1973 or the corresponding provision of the Northern Ireland Act 1998; or
  (iii) amending an Act of a kind mentioned in paragraph (a), (b) or (c);

and includes an order or other instrument made under primary legislation (otherwise than by the [Welsh Ministers, the First Minister for Wales, the Counsel General to the Welsh Assembly Government], a member of the Scottish Executive, a Northern Ireland Minister or a Northern Ireland department) to the extent to which it operates to bring one or more provisions of that legislation into force or amends any primary legislation;

"the First Protocol" means the protocol to the Convention agreed at Paris on 20th March 1952;

…

"the Eleventh Protocol" means the protocol to the Convention (restructuring the control machinery established by the Convention) agreed at Strasbourg on 11th May 1994;

["the Thirteenth Protocol" means the protocol to the Convention (concerning the abolition of the death penalty in all circumstances) agreed at Vilnius on 3rd May 2002;]

"remedial order" means an order under section 10;

"subordinate legislation" means any—

(a) Order in Council other than one—
  (i) made in exercise of Her Majesty's Royal Prerogative;
  (ii) made under section 38(1)(a) of the Northern Ireland Constitution Act 1973 or the corresponding provision of the Northern Ireland Act 1998; or
  (iii) amending an Act of a kind mentioned in the definition of primary legislation;
(b) Act of the Scottish Parliament;
[(ba) Measure of the National Assembly for Wales;
(bb) Act of the National Assembly for Wales;]
(c) Act of the Parliament of Northern Ireland;
(d) Measure of the Assembly established under section 1 of the Northern Ireland Assembly Act 1973;

(e) Act of the Northern Ireland Assembly;

(f) order, rules, regulations, scheme, warrant, byelaw or other instrument made under primary legislation (except to the extent to which it operates to bring one or more provisions of that legislation into force or amends any primary legislation);

(g) order, rules, regulations, scheme, warrant, byelaw or other instrument made under legislation mentioned in paragraph (b), (c), (d) or (e) or made under an Order in Council applying only to Northern Ireland;

(h) order, rules, regulations, scheme, warrant, byelaw or other instrument made by a member of the Scottish Executive[, Welsh Ministers, the First Minister for Wales, the Counsel General to the Welsh Assembly Government], a Northern Ireland Minister or a Northern Ireland department in exercise of prerogative or other executive functions of Her Majesty which are exercisable by such a person on behalf of Her Majesty;

"transferred matters" has the same meaning as in the Northern Ireland Act 1998; and

"tribunal" means any tribunal in which legal proceedings may be brought.

(2)–(5) (*Outside the scope of this work.*)

[1746]

NOTES

Sub-s (1): in definition "primary legislation" words in square brackets substituted by the Government of Wales Act 2006, s 160(1), Sch 10, para 56(1), (2); definition "the Sixth Protocol" (omitted) repealed and definition "the Thirteenth Protocol" inserted by SI 2004/1574, art 2(2); in definition "subordinate legislation" paras (ba), (bb), and words in square brackets in para (h) inserted by the Government of Wales Act 2006, s 160(1), Sch 10, para 56(1), (3), (4).

22 Short title, commencement, application and extent

(1) This Act may be cited as the Human Rights Act 1998.

(2) Sections 18, 20 and 21(5) and this section come into force on the passing of this Act.

(3) The other provisions of this Act come into force on such day as the Secretary of State may by order appoint; and different days may be appointed for different purposes.

(4) Paragraph (b) of subsection (1) of section 7 applies to proceedings brought by or at the instigation of a public authority whenever the act in question took place; but otherwise that subsection does not apply to an act taking place before the coming into force of that section.

(5) This Act binds the Crown.

(6) This Act extends to Northern Ireland.

(7) *Section 21(5), so far as it relates to any provision contained in the Army Act 1955, the Air Force Act 1955 or the Naval Discipline Act 1957, extends to any place to which that provision extends.*

[1747]

NOTES

Sub-s (7): repealed by the Armed Forces Act 2006, s 378(2), Sch 17, partly as from 28 March 2009 and fully as from 31 October 2009.

Orders: the Human Rights Act 1998 (Commencement) Order 1998, SI 1998/2882; the Human Rights Act 1998 (Commencement No 2) Order 2000, SI 2000/1851.

SCHEDULE 1
THE ARTICLES

Section 1(3)

PART I
THE CONVENTION RIGHTS AND FREEDOMS

Article 2
Right to life

1. Everyone's right to life shall be protected by law. No one shall be deprived of his life intentionally save in the execution of a sentence of a court following his conviction of a crime for which this penalty is provided by law.

2. Deprivation of life shall not be regarded as inflicted in contravention of this Article when it results from the use of force which is no more than absolutely necessary—

(a) in defence of any person from unlawful violence;

(b) in order to effect a lawful arrest or to prevent the escape of a person lawfully detained;

(c) in action lawfully taken for the purpose of quelling a riot or insurrection.

PART I STATUTES

Article 3
Prohibition of torture

No one shall be subjected to torture or to inhuman or degrading treatment or punishment.

Article 4
Prohibition of slavery and forced labour

1. No one shall be held in slavery or servitude.
2. No one shall be required to perform forced or compulsory labour.
3. For the purpose of this Article the term "forced or compulsory labour" shall not include—
   (a) any work required to be done in the ordinary course of detention imposed according to the provisions of Article 5 of this Convention or during conditional release from such detention;
   (b) any service of a military character or, in case of conscientious objectors in countries where they are recognised, service exacted instead of compulsory military service;
   (c) any service exacted in case of an emergency or calamity threatening the life or well-being of the community;
   (d) any work or service which forms part of normal civic obligations.

Article 5
Right to liberty and security

1. Everyone has the right to liberty and security of person. No one shall be deprived of his liberty save in the following cases and in accordance with a procedure prescribed by law—
   (a) the lawful detention of a person after conviction by a competent court;
   (b) the lawful arrest or detention of a person for non-compliance with the lawful order of a court or in order to secure the fulfilment of any obligation prescribed by law;
   (c) the lawful arrest or detention of a person effected for the purpose of bringing him before the competent legal authority on reasonable suspicion of having committed an offence or when it is reasonably considered necessary to prevent his committing an offence or fleeing after having done so;
   (d) the detention of a minor by lawful order for the purpose of educational supervision or his lawful detention for the purpose of bringing him before the competent legal authority;
   (e) the lawful detention of persons for the prevention of the spreading of infectious diseases, of persons of unsound mind, alcoholics or drug addicts or vagrants;
   (f) the lawful arrest or detention of a person to prevent his effecting an unauthorised entry into the country or of a person against whom action is being taken with a view to deportation or extradition.

2. Everyone who is arrested shall be informed promptly, in a language which he understands, of the reasons for his arrest and of any charge against him.

3. Everyone arrested or detained in accordance with the provisions of paragraph 1(c) of this Article shall be brought promptly before a judge or other officer authorised by law to exercise judicial power and shall be entitled to trial within a reasonable time or to release pending trial. Release may be conditioned by guarantees to appear for trial.

4. Everyone who is deprived of his liberty by arrest or detention shall be entitled to take proceedings by which the lawfulness of his detention shall be decided speedily by a court and his release ordered if the detention is not lawful.

5. Everyone who has been the victim of arrest or detention in contravention of the provisions of this Article shall have an enforceable right to compensation.

Article 6
Right to a fair trial

1. In the determination of his civil rights and obligations or of any criminal charge against him, everyone is entitled to a fair and public hearing within a reasonable time by an independent and impartial tribunal established by law. Judgment shall be pronounced publicly but the press and public may be excluded from all or part of the trial in the interest of morals, public order or national security in a democratic society, where the interests of juveniles or the protection of the private life of the parties so require, or to the extent strictly necessary in the opinion of the court in special circumstances where publicity would prejudice the interests of justice.

2. Everyone charged with a criminal offence shall be presumed innocent until proved guilty according to law.

3. Everyone charged with a criminal offence has the following minimum rights—
   (a) to be informed promptly, in a language which he understands and in detail, of the nature and cause of the accusation against him;
   (b) to have adequate time and facilities for the preparation of his defence;

(c) to defend himself in person or through legal assistance of his own choosing or, if he has not sufficient means to pay for legal assistance, to be given it free when the interests of justice so require;

(d) to examine or have examined witnesses against him and to obtain the attendance and examination of witnesses on his behalf under the same conditions as witnesses against him;

(e) to have the free assistance of an interpreter if he cannot understand or speak the language used in court.

Article 7
No punishment without law

1. No one shall be held guilty of any criminal offence on account of any act or omission which did not constitute a criminal offence under national or international law at the time when it was committed. Nor shall a heavier penalty be imposed than the one that was applicable at the time the criminal offence was committed.

2. This Article shall not prejudice the trial and punishment of any person for any act or omission which, at the time when it was committed, was criminal according to the general principles of law recognised by civilised nations.

Article 8
Right to respect for private and family life

1. Everyone has the right to respect for his private and family life, his home and his correspondence.

2. There shall be no interference by a public authority with the exercise of this right except such as is in accordance with the law and is necessary in a democratic society in the interests of national security, public safety or the economic well-being of the country, for the prevention of disorder or crime, for the protection of health or morals, or for the protection of the rights and freedoms of others.

Article 9
Freedom of thought, conscience and religion

1. Everyone has the right to freedom of thought, conscience and religion; this right includes freedom to change his religion or belief and freedom, either alone or in community with others and in public or private, to manifest his religion or belief, in worship, teaching, practice and observance.

2. Freedom to manifest one's religion or beliefs shall be subject only to such limitations as are prescribed by law and are necessary in a democratic society in the interests of public safety, for the protection of public order, health or morals, or for the protection of the rights and freedoms of others.

Article 10
Freedom of expression

1. Everyone has the right to freedom of expression. This right shall include freedom to hold opinions and to receive and impart information and ideas without interference by public authority and regardless of frontiers. This Article shall not prevent States from requiring the licensing of broadcasting, television or cinema enterprises.

2. The exercise of these freedoms, since it carries with it duties and responsibilities, may be subject to such formalities, conditions, restrictions or penalties as are prescribed by law and are necessary in a democratic society, in the interests of national security, territorial integrity or public safety, for the prevention of disorder or crime, for the protection of health or morals, for the protection of the reputation or rights of others, for preventing the disclosure of information received in confidence, or for maintaining the authority and impartiality of the judiciary.

Article 11
Freedom of assembly and association

1. Everyone has the right to freedom of peaceful assembly and to freedom of association with others, including the right to form and to join trade unions for the protection of his interests.

2. No restrictions shall be placed on the exercise of these rights other than such as are prescribed by law and are necessary in a democratic society in the interests of national security or public safety, for the prevention of disorder or crime, for the protection of health or morals or for the protection of the rights and freedoms of others. This Article shall not prevent the imposition of lawful restrictions on the exercise of these rights by members of the armed forces, of the police or of the administration of the State.

Article 12
Right to marry

Men and women of marriageable age have the right to marry and to found a family, according to the national laws governing the exercise of this right.

Article 14
Prohibition of discrimination

The enjoyment of the rights and freedoms set forth in this Convention shall be secured without discrimination on any ground such as sex, race, colour, language, religion, political or other opinion, national or social origin, association with a national minority, property, birth or other status.

Article 16
Restrictions on political activity of aliens

Nothing in Articles 10, 11 and 14 shall be regarded as preventing the High Contracting Parties from imposing restrictions on the political activity of aliens.

Article 17
Prohibition of abuse of rights

Nothing in this Convention may be interpreted as implying for any State, group or person any right to engage in any activity or perform any act aimed at the destruction of any of the rights and freedoms set forth herein or at their limitation to a greater extent than is provided for in the Convention.

Article 18
Limitation on use of restrictions on rights

The restrictions permitted under this Convention to the said rights and freedoms shall not be applied for any purpose other than those for which they have been prescribed.

[1748]

PART II
THE FIRST PROTOCOL

Article 1
Protection of property

Every natural or legal person is entitled to the peaceful enjoyment of his possessions. No one shall be deprived of his possessions except in the public interest and subject to the conditions provided for by law and by the general principles of international law.

The preceding provisions shall not, however, in any way impair the right of a State to enforce such laws as it deems necessary to control the use of property in accordance with the general interest or to secure the payment of taxes or other contributions or penalties.

Article 2
Right to education

No person shall be denied the right to education. In the exercise of any functions which it assumes in relation to education and to teaching, the State shall respect the right of parents to ensure such education and teaching in conformity with their own religious and philosophical convictions.

Article 3
Right to free elections

The High Contracting Parties undertake to hold free elections at reasonable intervals by secret ballot, under conditions which will ensure the free expression of the opinion of the people in the choice of the legislature.

[1749]

(*Sch 1, Pt III, Schs 2–4 outside the scope of this work.*)

TRUSTEE DELEGATION ACT 1999

(1999 c 15)

An Act to amend the law relating to the delegation of trustee functions by power of attorney and the exercise of such functions by the donee of a power of attorney; and to make provision about the authority of the donee of a power of attorney to act in relation to land.

[15 July 1999]

Attorney of trustee with beneficial interest in land

1 Exercise of trustee functions by attorney

(1) The donee of a power of attorney is not prevented from doing an act in relation to—

(a) land,

(b) capital proceeds of a conveyance of land, or

(c) income from land,

by reason only that the act involves the exercise of a trustee function of the donor if, at the time when the act is done, the donor has a beneficial interest in the land, proceeds or income.

(2) In this section—

(a) "conveyance" has the same meaning as in the Law of Property Act 1925, and

(b) references to a trustee function of the donor are to a function which the donor has as trustee (either alone or jointly with any other person or persons).

(3) Subsection (1) above—

(a) applies only if and so far as a contrary intention is not expressed in the instrument creating the power of attorney, and

(b) has effect subject to the terms of that instrument.

(4) The donor of the power of attorney—

(a) is liable for the acts or defaults of the donee in exercising any function by virtue of subsection (1) above in the same manner as if they were acts or defaults of the donor, but

(b) is not liable by reason only that a function is exercised by the donee by virtue of that subsection.

(5) Subsections (1) and (4) above—

(a) apply only if and so far as a contrary intention is not expressed in the instrument (if any) creating the trust, and

(b) have effect subject to the terms of such an instrument.

(6) The fact that it appears that, in dealing with any shares or stock, the donee of the power of attorney is exercising a function by virtue of subsection (1) above does not affect with any notice of any trust a person in whose books the shares are, or stock is, registered or inscribed.

(7) In any case where (by way of exception to section 3(1) of the Trusts of Land and Appointment of Trustees Act 1996) the doctrine of conversion continues to operate, any person who, by reason of the continuing operation of that doctrine, has a beneficial interest in the proceeds of sale of land shall be treated for the purposes of this section and section 2 below as having a beneficial interest in the land.

(8) The donee of a power of attorney is not to be regarded as exercising a trustee function by virtue of subsection (1) above if he is acting under a trustee delegation power; and for this purpose a trustee delegation power is a power of attorney given under—

(a) a statutory provision, or

(b) a provision of the instrument (if any) creating a trust,

under which the donor of the power is expressly authorised to delegate the exercise of all or any of his trustee functions by power of attorney.

(9) Subject to section 4(6) below, this section applies only to powers of attorney created after the commencement of this Act.

[1750]

2 Evidence of beneficial interest

(1) This section applies where the interest of a purchaser depends on the donee of a power of attorney having power to do an act in relation to any property by virtue of section 1(1) above.

In this subsection "purchaser" has the same meaning as in Part I of the Law of Property Act 1925.

(2) Where this section applies an appropriate statement is, in favour of the purchaser, conclusive evidence of the donor of the power having a beneficial interest in the property at the time of the doing of the act.

(3) In this section "an appropriate statement" means a signed statement made by the donee—

(a) when doing the act in question, or

(b) at any other time within the period of three months beginning with the day on which the act is done,

that the donor has a beneficial interest in the property at the time of the donee doing the act.

(4) If an appropriate statement is false, the donee is liable in the same way as he would be if the statement were contained in a statutory declaration.

[1751]

3–6 (*S 3 amends the Powers of Attorney Act 1971, s 10 at* **[711]**; *ss 4, 6 repealed by the Mental Capacity Act 2005, s 67(2), Sch 7; s 5 substitutes the Trustee Act 1925, s 25 at* **[220]**, *and amends the Pensions Act 1995, s 34.*)

Miscellaneous provisions about attorney acting for trustee

7 Two-trustee rules

(1) A requirement imposed by an enactment—

(a) that capital money be paid to, or dealt with as directed by, at least two trustees or that a valid receipt for capital money be given otherwise than by a sole trustee, or

(b) that, in order for an interest or power to be overreached, a conveyance or deed be executed by at least two trustees,

is not satisfied by money being paid to or dealt with as directed by, or a receipt for money being given by, a relevant attorney or by a conveyance or deed being executed by such an attorney.

(2) In this section "relevant attorney" means a person (other than a trust corporation within the meaning of the Trustee Act 1925) who is acting either—

(a) both as a trustee and as attorney for one or more other trustees, or

(b) as attorney for two or more trustees,

and who is not acting together with any other person or persons.

(3) This section applies whether a relevant attorney is acting under a power created before or after the commencement of this Act (but in the case of such an attorney acting under an enduring power created before that commencement is without prejudice to any continuing application of section 3(3) of the Enduring Powers of Attorney Act 1985 to the enduring power after that commencement …).

[1752]

NOTES

Sub-s (3): words omitted repealed by the Mental Capacity Act 2005, s 67(2), Sch 7.

8, 9 (*S 8 amends the Trustee Act 1925, s 36 at* **[229]**; *s 9 amends the Law of Property Act 1925, s 22 at* **[281]**.)

Authority of attorney to act in relation to land

10 Extent of attorney's authority to act in relation to land

(1) Where the donee of a power of attorney is authorised by the power to do an act of any description in relation to any land, his authority to do an act of that description at any time includes authority to do it with respect to any estate or interest in the land which is held at that time by the donor (whether alone or jointly with any other person or persons).

(2) Subsection (1) above—

(a) applies only if and so far as a contrary intention is not expressed in the instrument creating the power of attorney, and

(b) has effect subject to the terms of that instrument.

(3) This section applies only to powers of attorney created after the commencement of this Act.

[1753]

Supplementary

11 Interpretation

(1) In this Act—

"land" has the same meaning as in the Trustee Act 1925, and

"enduring power" has the same meaning as in the Enduring Powers of Attorney Act 1985.

(2) References in this Act to the creation of a power of attorney are to the execution by the donor of the instrument creating it.

[1754]

12 (*Introduces the Schedule to this Act.*)

13 Commencement, extent and short title

(1) The preceding provisions of this Act shall come into force on such day as the Lord Chancellor may by order made by statutory instrument appoint.

(2) This Act extends to England and Wales only.

(3) This Act may be cited as the Trustee Delegation Act 1999.

[1755]

NOTES

Order: the Trustee Delegation Act 1999 (Commencement) Order 2000, SI 2000/216.

(*Schedule contains repeals only.*)

CONTRACTS (RIGHTS OF THIRD PARTIES) ACT 1999

(1999 c 31)

An Act to make provision for the enforcement of contractual terms by third parties.

[11 November 1999]

1 Right of third party to enforce contractual term

(1) Subject to the provisions of this Act, a person who is not a party to a contract (a "third party") may in his own right enforce a term of the contract if—

(a) the contract expressly provides that he may, or

(b) subject to subsection (2), the term purports to confer a benefit on him.

(2) Subsection (1)(b) does not apply if on a proper construction of the contract it appears that the parties did not intend the term to be enforceable by the third party.

(3) The third party must be expressly identified in the contract by name, as a member of a class or as answering a particular description but need not be in existence when the contract is entered into.

(4) This section does not confer a right on a third party to enforce a term of a contract otherwise than subject to and in accordance with any other relevant terms of the contract.

(5) For the purpose of exercising his right to enforce a term of the contract, there shall be available to the third party any remedy that would have been available to him in an action for breach of contract if he had been a party to the contract (and the rules relating to damages, injunctions, specific performance and other relief shall apply accordingly).

(6) Where a term of a contract excludes or limits liability in relation to any matter references in this Act to the third party enforcing the term shall be construed as references to his availing himself of the exclusion or limitation.

(7) In this Act, in relation to a term of a contract which is enforceable by a third party—

"the promisor" means the party to the contract against whom the term is enforceable by the third party, and

"the promisee" means the party to the contract by whom the term is enforceable against the promisor.

[1756]

2 Variation and rescission of contract

(1) Subject to the provisions of this section, where a third party has a right under section 1 to enforce a term of the contract, the parties to the contract may not, by agreement, rescind the contract, or vary it in such a way as to extinguish or alter his entitlement under that right, without his consent if—

(a) the third party has communicated his assent to the term to the promisor,

(b) the promisor is aware that the third party has relied on the term, or

(c) the promisor can reasonably be expected to have foreseen that the third party would rely on the term and the third party has in fact relied on it.

(2) The assent referred to in subsection (1)(a)—

(a) may be by words or conduct, and

(b) if sent to the promisor by post or other means, shall not be regarded as communicated to the promisor until received by him.

(3) Subsection (1) is subject to any express term of the contract under which—

(a) the parties to the contract may by agreement rescind or vary the contract without the consent of the third party, or

(b) the consent of the third party is required in circumstances specified in the contract instead of those set out in subsection (1)(a) to (c).

(4) Where the consent of a third party is required under subsection (1) or (3), the court or arbitral tribunal may, on the application of the parties to the contract, dispense with his consent if satisfied—

(a) that his consent cannot be obtained because his whereabouts cannot reasonably be ascertained, or

(b) that he is mentally incapable of giving his consent.

(5) The court or arbitral tribunal may, on the application of the parties to a contract, dispense with any consent that may be required under subsection (1)(c) if satisfied that it cannot reasonably be ascertained whether or not the third party has in fact relied on the term.

(6) If the court or arbitral tribunal dispenses with a third party's consent, it may impose such conditions as it thinks fit, including a condition requiring the payment of compensation to the third party.

(7) The jurisdiction conferred on the court by subsections (4) to (6) is exercisable by both the High Court and a county court.

[1757]

3 Defences etc available to promisor

(1) Subsections (2) to (5) apply where, in reliance on section 1, proceedings for the enforcement of a term of a contract are brought by a third party.

(2) The promisor shall have available to him by way of defence or set-off any matter that—
- (a) arises from or in connection with the contract and is relevant to the term, and
- (b) would have been available to him by way of defence or set-off if the proceedings had been brought by the promisee.

(3) The promisor shall also have available to him by way of defence or set-off any matter if—
- (a) an express term of the contract provides for it to be available to him in proceedings brought by the third party, and
- (b) it would have been available to him by way of defence or set-off if the proceedings had been brought by the promisee.

(4) The promisor shall also have available to him—
- (a) by way of defence or set-off any matter, and
- (b) by way of counterclaim any matter not arising from the contract,

that would have been available to him by way of defence or set-off or, as the case may be, by way of counterclaim against the third party if the third party had been a party to the contract.

(5) Subsections (2) and (4) are subject to any express term of the contract as to the matters that are not to be available to the promisor by way of defence, set-off or counterclaim.

(6) Where in any proceedings brought against him a third party seeks in reliance on section 1 to enforce a term of a contract (including, in particular, a term purporting to exclude or limit liability), he may not do so if he could not have done so (whether by reason of any particular circumstances relating to him or otherwise) had he been a party to the contract.

[1758]

4 Enforcement of contract by promisee

Section 1 does not affect any right of the promisee to enforce any term of the contract.

[1759]

5 Protection of party promisor from double liability

Where under section 1 a term of a contract is enforceable by a third party, and the promisee has recovered from the promisor a sum in respect of—
- (a) the third party's loss in respect of the term, or
- (b) the expense to the promisee of making good to the third party the default of the promisor,

then, in any proceedings brought in reliance on that section by the third party, the court or arbitral tribunal shall reduce any award to the third party to such extent as it thinks appropriate to take account of the sum recovered by the promisee.

[1760]

6 Exceptions

(1) Section 1 confers no rights on a third party in the case of a contract on a bill of exchange, promissory note or other negotiable instrument.

(2) Section 1 confers no rights on a third party in the case of any contract binding on a company and its members under *section 14 of the Companies Act 1985* [section 33 of the Companies Act 2006 (effect of company's constitution)].

[(2A) Section 1 confers no rights on a third party in the case of any incorporation document of a limited liability partnership *or any limited liability partnership agreement as defined in the Limited Liability Partnerships Regulations 2001* (*SI No 2001/1090*) [or any agreement (express or implied) between the members of a limited liability partnership, or between a limited liability partnership and its members, that determines the mutual rights and duties of the members and their rights and duties in relation to the limited liability partnership].]

(3) Section 1 confers no right on a third party to enforce—

(a) any term of a contract of employment against an employee,
(b) any term of a worker's contract against a worker (including a home worker), or
(c) any term of a relevant contract against an agency worker.

(4) In subsection (3)—
(a) "contract of employment", "employee", "worker's contract", and "worker" have the meaning given by section 54 of the National Minimum Wage Act 1998,
(b) "home worker" has the meaning given by section 35(2) of that Act,
(c) "agency worker" has the same meaning as in section 34(1) of that Act, and
(d) "relevant contract" means a contract entered into, in a case where section 34 of that Act applies, by the agency worker as respects work falling within subsection (1)(a) of that section.

(5) Section 1 confers no rights on a third party in the case of—
(a) a contract for the carriage of goods by sea, or
(b) a contract for the carriage of goods by rail or road, or for the carriage of cargo by air, which is subject to the rules of the appropriate international transport convention,

except that a third party may in reliance on that section avail himself of an exclusion or limitation of liability in such a contract.

(6) In subsection (5) "contract for the carriage of goods by sea" means a contract of carriage—
(a) contained in or evidenced by a bill of lading, sea waybill or a corresponding electronic transaction, or
(b) under or for the purposes of which there is given an undertaking which is contained in a ship's delivery order or a corresponding electronic transaction.

(7) For the purposes of subsection (6)—
(a) "bill of lading", "sea waybill" and "ship's delivery order" have the same meaning as in the Carriage of Goods by Sea Act 1992, and
(b) a corresponding electronic transaction is a transaction within section 1(5) of that Act which corresponds to the issue, indorsement, delivery or transfer of a bill of lading, sea waybill or ship's delivery order.

(8) In subsection (5) "the appropriate international transport convention" means—
(a) in relation to a contract for the carriage of goods by rail, the Convention which has the force of law in the United Kingdom under [regulation 3 of the Railways (Convention on International Carriage by Rail) Regulations 2005],
(b) in relation to a contract for the carriage of goods by road, the Convention which has the force of law in the United Kingdom under section 1 of the Carriage of Goods by Road Act 1965, and
(c) in relation to a contract for the carriage of cargo by air—
(i) the Convention which has the force of law in the United Kingdom under section 1 of the Carriage by Air Act 1961, or
(ii) the Convention which has the force of law under section 1 of the Carriage by Air (Supplementary Provisions) Act 1962, or
(iii) either of the amended Conventions set out in Part B of Schedule 2 or 3 to the Carriage by Air Acts (Application of Provisions) Order 1967.

[1761]

NOTES

Sub-s (2): words in italics substituted by subsequent words in square brackets by SI 2009/1941, art 2(1), Sch 1, para 179, as from 1 October 2009.

Sub-s (2A): inserted by SI 2001/1090, reg 9(1), Sch 5, para 20; words in italics substituted by subsequent words in square brackets by SI 2009/1941, art 2(1), Sch 1, para 179, as from 1 October 2009.

Sub-s (8): words in square brackets in para (a) substituted by SI 2005/2092, reg 9(2), Sch 3, para 3.

7 Supplementary provisions relating to third party

(1) Section 1 does not affect any right or remedy of a third party that exists or is available apart from this Act.

(2) Section 2(2) of the Unfair Contract Terms Act 1977 (restriction on exclusion etc of liability for negligence) shall not apply where the negligence consists of the breach of an obligation arising from a term of a contract and the person seeking to enforce it is a third party acting in reliance on section 1.

(3) In sections 5 and 8 of the Limitation Act 1980 the references to an action founded on a simple contract and an action upon a specialty shall respectively include references to an action brought in reliance on section 1 relating to a simple contract and an action brought in reliance on that section relating to a specialty.

(4) A third party shall not, by virtue of section 1(5) or 3(4) or (6), be treated as a party to the contract for the purposes of any other Act (or any instrument made under any other Act).

[1762]

8 Arbitration provisions

(1) Where—

(a) a right under section 1 to enforce a term ("the substantive term") is subject to a term providing for the submission of disputes to arbitration ("the arbitration agreement"), and

(b) the arbitration agreement is an agreement in writing for the purposes of Part I of the Arbitration Act 1996,

the third party shall be treated for the purposes of that Act as a party to the arbitration agreement as regards disputes between himself and the promisor relating to the enforcement of the substantive term by the third party.

(2) Where—

(a) a third party has a right under section 1 to enforce a term providing for one or more descriptions of dispute between the third party and the promisor to be submitted to arbitration ("the arbitration agreement"),

(b) the arbitration agreement is an agreement in writing for the purposes of Part I of the Arbitration Act 1996, and

(c) the third party does not fall to be treated under subsection (1) as a party to the arbitration agreement,

the third party shall, if he exercises the right, be treated for the purposes of that Act as a party to the arbitration agreement in relation to the matter with respect to which the right is exercised, and be treated as having been so immediately before the exercise of the right.

[1763]

9 Northern Ireland

(1) In its application to Northern Ireland, this Act has effect with the modifications specified in subsections (2) and (3).

(2) *In section 6(2), for "section 14 of the Companies Act 1985" there is substituted "Article 25 of the Companies (Northern Ireland) Order 1986".*

(3) In section 7, for subsection (3) there is substituted—

"(3) In Articles 4(a) and 15 of the Limitation (Northern Ireland) Order 1989, the references to an action founded on a simple contract and an action upon an instrument under seal shall respectively include references to an action brought in reliance on section 1 relating to a simple contract and an action brought in reliance on that section relating to a contract under seal.".

(4) In the Law Reform (Husband and Wife) (Northern Ireland) Act 1964, the following provisions are hereby repealed—

(a) section 5, and

(b) in section 6, in subsection (1)(a), the words "in the case of section 4" and "and in the case of section 5 the contracting party" and, in subsection (3), the words "or section 5".

[1764]

NOTES

Sub-s (2): repealed by SI 2009/1941, art 2(1), Sch 1, para 179, as from 1 October 2009.

10 Short title, commencement and extent

(1) This Act may be cited as the Contracts (Rights of Third Parties) Act 1999.

(2) This Act comes into force on the day on which it is passed but, subject to subsection (3), does not apply in relation to a contract entered into before the end of the period of six months beginning with that day.

(3) The restriction in subsection (2) does not apply in relation to a contract which—

(a) is entered into on or after the day on which this Act is passed, and

(b) expressly provides for the application of this Act.

(4) This Act extends as follows—

(a) section 9 extends to Northern Ireland only;

(b) the remaining provisions extend to England and Wales and Northern Ireland only.

[1765]

TRUSTEE ACT 2000

(2000 c 29)

An Act to amend the law relating to trustees and persons having the investment powers of trustees; and for connected purposes.

[23 November 2000]

PART I
THE DUTY OF CARE

1 The duty of care

(1) Whenever the duty under this subsection applies to a trustee, he must exercise such care and skill as is reasonable in the circumstances, having regard in particular—

(a) to any special knowledge or experience that he has or holds himself out as having, and
(b) if he acts as trustee in the course of a business or profession, to any special knowledge or experience that it is reasonable to expect of a person acting in the course of that kind of business or profession.

(2) In this Act the duty under subsection (1) is called "the duty of care".

[1766]

2 Application of duty of care

Schedule 1 makes provision about when the duty of care applies to a trustee.

[1767]

PART II
INVESTMENT

3 General power of investment

(1) Subject to the provisions of this Part, a trustee may make any kind of investment that he could make if he were absolutely entitled to the assets of the trust.

(2) In this Act the power under subsection (1) is called "the general power of investment".

(3) The general power of investment does not permit a trustee to make investments in land other than in loans secured on land (but see also section 8).

(4) A person invests in a loan secured on land if he has rights under any contract under which—

(a) one person provides another with credit, and
(b) the obligation of the borrower to repay is secured on land.

(5) "Credit" includes any cash loan or other financial accommodation.

(6) "Cash" includes money in any form.

[1768]

4 Standard investment criteria

(1) In exercising any power of investment, whether arising under this Part or otherwise, a trustee must have regard to the standard investment criteria.

(2) A trustee must from time to time review the investments of the trust and consider whether, having regard to the standard investment criteria, they should be varied.

(3) The standard investment criteria, in relation to a trust, are—

(a) the suitability to the trust of investments of the same kind as any particular investment proposed to be made or retained and of that particular investment as an investment of that kind, and
(b) the need for diversification of investments of the trust, in so far as is appropriate to the circumstances of the trust.

[1769]

5 Advice

(1) Before exercising any power of investment, whether arising under this Part or otherwise, a trustee must (unless the exception applies) obtain and consider proper advice about the way in which, having regard to the standard investment criteria, the power should be exercised.

(2) When reviewing the investments of the trust, a trustee must (unless the exception applies) obtain and consider proper advice about whether, having regard to the standard investment criteria, the investments should be varied.

(3) The exception is that a trustee need not obtain such advice if he reasonably concludes that in all the circumstances it is unnecessary or inappropriate to do so.

(4) Proper advice is the advice of a person who is reasonably believed by the trustee to be qualified to give it by his ability in and practical experience of financial and other matters relating to the proposed investment.

[1770]

6 Restriction or exclusion of this Part etc

(1) The general power of investment is—

(a) in addition to powers conferred on trustees otherwise than by this Act, but
(b) subject to any restriction or exclusion imposed by the trust instrument or by any enactment or any provision of subordinate legislation.

(2) For the purposes of this Act, an enactment or a provision of subordinate legislation is not to be regarded as being, or as being part of, a trust instrument.

(3) In this Act "subordinate legislation" has the same meaning as in the Interpretation Act 1978.

[1771]

7 Existing trusts

(1) This Part applies in relation to trusts whether created before or after its commencement.

(2) No provision relating to the powers of a trustee contained in a trust instrument made before 3rd August 1961 is to be treated (for the purposes of section 6(1)(b)) as restricting or excluding the general power of investment.

(3) A provision contained in a trust instrument made before the commencement of this Part which—
(a) has effect under section 3(2) of the Trustee Investments Act 1961 as a power to invest under that Act, or
(b) confers power to invest under that Act,
is to be treated as conferring the general power of investment on a trustee.

[1772]

PART III
ACQUISITION OF LAND

8 Power to acquire freehold and leasehold land

(1) A trustee may acquire freehold or leasehold land in the United Kingdom—
(a) as an investment,
(b) for occupation by a beneficiary, or
(c) for any other reason.

(2) "Freehold or leasehold land" means—
(a) in relation to England and Wales, a legal estate in land,
(b) in relation to Scotland—
(i) the estate or interest of the proprietor of the dominium utile or, in the case of land not held on feudal tenure, the estate or interest of the owner, or
(ii) a tenancy, and
(c) in relation to Northern Ireland, a legal estate in land, including land held under a fee farm grant.

(3) For the purpose of exercising his functions as a trustee, a trustee who acquires land under this section has all the powers of an absolute owner in relation to the land.

[1773]

9 Restriction or exclusion of this Part etc

The powers conferred by this Part are—
(a) in addition to powers conferred on trustees otherwise than by this Part, but
(b) subject to any restriction or exclusion imposed by the trust instrument or by any enactment or any provision of subordinate legislation.

[1774]

10 Existing trusts

(1) This Part does not apply in relation to—
(a) a trust of property which consists of or includes land which (despite section 2 of the Trusts of Land and Appointment of Trustees Act 1996) is settled land, or
(b) a trust to which the Universities and College Estates Act 1925 applies.

(2) Subject to subsection (1), this Part applies in relation to trusts whether created before or after its commencement.

[1775]

PART IV
AGENTS, NOMINEES AND CUSTODIANS

Agents

11 Power to employ agents

(1) Subject to the provisions of this Part, the trustees of a trust may authorise any person to exercise any or all of their delegable functions as their agent.

(2) In the case of a trust other than a charitable trust, the trustees' delegable functions consist of any function other than—

(a) any function relating to whether or in what way any assets of the trust should be distributed,

(b) any power to decide whether any fees or other payment due to be made out of the trust funds should be made out of income or capital,

(c) any power to appoint a person to be a trustee of the trust, or

(d) any power conferred by any other enactment or the trust instrument which permits the trustees to delegate any of their functions or to appoint a person to act as a nominee or custodian.

(3) In the case of a charitable trust, the trustees' delegable functions are—

(a) any function consisting of carrying out a decision that the trustees have taken;

(b) any function relating to the investment of assets subject to the trust (including, in the case of land held as an investment, managing the land and creating or disposing of an interest in the land);

(c) any function relating to the raising of funds for the trust otherwise than by means of profits of a trade which is an integral part of carrying out the trust's charitable purpose;

(d) any other function prescribed by an order made by the Secretary of State.

(4) For the purposes of subsection (3)(c) a trade is an integral part of carrying out a trust's charitable purpose if, whether carried on in the United Kingdom or elsewhere, the profits are applied solely to the purposes of the trust and either—

(a) the trade is exercised in the course of the actual carrying out of a primary purpose of the trust, or

(b) the work in connection with the trade is mainly carried out by beneficiaries of the trust.

(5) The power to make an order under subsection (3)(d) is exercisable by statutory instrument which shall be subject to annulment in pursuance of a resolution of either House of Parliament.

[1776]

12 Persons who may act as agents

(1) Subject to subsection (2), the persons whom the trustees may under section 11 authorise to exercise functions as their agent include one or more of their number.

(2) The trustees may not authorise two (or more) persons to exercise the same function unless they are to exercise the function jointly.

(3) The trustees may not under section 11 authorise a beneficiary to exercise any function as their agent (even if the beneficiary is also a trustee).

(4) The trustees may under section 11 authorise a person to exercise functions as their agent even though he is also appointed to act as their nominee or custodian (whether under section 16, 17 or 18 or any other power).

[1777]

13 Linked functions etc

(1) Subject to subsections (2) and (5), a person who is authorised under section 11 to exercise a function is (whatever the terms of the agency) subject to any specific duties or restrictions attached to the function.

For example, a person who is authorised under section 11 to exercise the general power of investment is subject to the duties under section 4 in relation to that power.

(2) A person who is authorised under section 11 to exercise a power which is subject to a requirement to obtain advice is not subject to the requirement if he is the kind of person from whom it would have been proper for the trustees, in compliance with the requirement, to obtain advice.

(3) Subsections (4) and (5) apply to a trust to which section 11(1) of the Trusts of Land and Appointment of Trustees Act 1996 (duties to consult beneficiaries and give effect to their wishes) applies.

(4) The trustees may not under section 11 authorise a person to exercise any of their functions on terms that prevent them from complying with section 11(1) of the 1996 Act.

(5) A person who is authorised under section 11 to exercise any function relating to land subject to the trust is not subject to section 11(1) of the 1996 Act.

[1778]

14 Terms of agency

(1) Subject to subsection (2) and sections 15(2) and 29 to 32, the trustees may authorise a person to exercise functions as their agent on such terms as to remuneration and other matters as they may determine.

(2) The trustees may not authorise a person to exercise functions as their agent on any of the terms mentioned in subsection (3) unless it is reasonably necessary for them to do so.

(3) The terms are—

(a) a term permitting the agent to appoint a substitute;

(b) a term restricting the liability of the agent or his substitute to the trustees or any beneficiary;

(c) a term permitting the agent to act in circumstances capable of giving rise to a conflict of interest.

[1779]

15 Asset management: special restrictions

(1) The trustees may not authorise a person to exercise any of their asset management functions as their agent except by an agreement which is in or evidenced in writing.

(2) The trustees may not authorise a person to exercise any of their asset management functions as their agent unless—

(a) they have prepared a statement that gives guidance as to how the functions should be exercised ("a policy statement"), and

(b) the agreement under which the agent is to act includes a term to the effect that he will secure compliance with—

(i) the policy statement, or

(ii) if the policy statement is revised or replaced under section 22, the revised or replacement policy statement.

(3) The trustees must formulate any guidance given in the policy statement with a view to ensuring that the functions will be exercised in the best interests of the trust.

(4) The policy statement must be in or evidenced in writing.

(5) The asset management functions of trustees are their functions relating to—

(a) the investment of assets subject to the trust,

(b) the acquisition of property which is to be subject to the trust, and

(c) managing property which is subject to the trust and disposing of, or creating or disposing of an interest in, such property.

[1780]

Nominees and custodians

16 Power to appoint nominees

(1) Subject to the provisions of this Part, the trustees of a trust may—

(a) appoint a person to act as their nominee in relation to such of the assets of the trust as they determine (other than settled land), and

(b) take such steps as are necessary to secure that those assets are vested in a person so appointed.

(2) An appointment under this section must be in or evidenced in writing.

(3) This section does not apply to any trust having a custodian trustee or in relation to any assets vested in the official custodian for charities.

[1781]

17 Power to appoint custodians

(1) Subject to the provisions of this Part, the trustees of a trust may appoint a person to act as a custodian in relation to such of the assets of the trust as they may determine.

(2) For the purposes of this Act a person is a custodian in relation to assets if he undertakes the safe custody of the assets or of any documents or records concerning the assets.

(3) An appointment under this section must be in or evidenced in writing.

(4) This section does not apply to any trust having a custodian trustee or in relation to any assets vested in the official custodian for charities.

[1782]

18 Investment in bearer securities

(1) If trustees retain or invest in securities payable to bearer, they must appoint a person to act as a custodian of the securities.

(2) Subsection (1) does not apply if the trust instrument or any enactment or provision of subordinate legislation contains provision which (however expressed) permits the trustees to retain or invest in securities payable to bearer without appointing a person to act as a custodian.

(3) An appointment under this section must be in or evidenced in writing.

(4) This section does not apply to any trust having a custodian trustee or in relation to any securities vested in the official custodian for charities.

[1783]

19 Persons who may be appointed as nominees or custodians

(1) A person may not be appointed under section 16, 17 or 18 as a nominee or custodian unless one of the relevant conditions is satisfied.

(2) The relevant conditions are that—

(a) the person carries on a business which consists of or includes acting as a nominee or custodian;

(b) the person is a body corporate which is controlled by the trustees;

(c) the person is a body corporate recognised under section 9 of the Administration of Justice Act 1985.

(3) The question whether a body corporate is controlled by trustees is to be determined in accordance with section 840 of the Income and Corporation Taxes Act 1988.

(4) The trustees of a charitable trust which is not an exempt charity must act in accordance with any guidance given by the [Charity Commission] concerning the selection of a person for appointment as a nominee or custodian under section 16, 17 or 18.

(5) Subject to subsections (1) and (4), the persons whom the trustees may under section 16, 17 or 18 appoint as a nominee or custodian include—

(a) one of their number, if that one is a trust corporation, or

(b) two (or more) of their number, if they are to act as joint nominees or joint custodians.

(6) The trustees may under section 16 appoint a person to act as their nominee even though he is also—

(a) appointed to act as their custodian (whether under section 17 or 18 or any other power), or

(b) authorised to exercise functions as their agent (whether under section 11 or any other power).

(7) Likewise, the trustees may under section 17 or 18 appoint a person to act as their custodian even though he is also—

(a) appointed to act as their nominee (whether under section 16 or any other power), or

(b) authorised to exercise functions as their agent (whether under section 11 or any other power).

[1784]

NOTES

Sub-s (4): words in square brackets substituted by the Charities Act 2006, s 75(1), Sch 8, para 197.

20 Terms of appointment of nominees and custodians

(1) Subject to subsection (2) and sections 29 to 32, the trustees may under section 16, 17 or 18 appoint a person to act as a nominee or custodian on such terms as to remuneration and other matters as they may determine.

(2) The trustees may not under section 16, 17 or 18 appoint a person to act as a nominee or custodian on any of the terms mentioned in subsection (3) unless it is reasonably necessary for them to do so.

(3) The terms are—

(a) a term permitting the nominee or custodian to appoint a substitute;

(b) a term restricting the liability of the nominee or custodian or his substitute to the trustees or to any beneficiary;

(c) a term permitting the nominee or custodian to act in circumstances capable of giving rise to a conflict of interest.

[1785]

Review of and liability for agents, nominees and custodians etc

21 Application of sections 22 and 23

(1) Sections 22 and 23 apply in a case where trustees have, under section 11, 16, 17 or 18—

(a) authorised a person to exercise functions as their agent, or

(b) appointed a person to act as a nominee or custodian.

(2) Subject to subsection (3), sections 22 and 23 also apply in a case where trustees have, under any power conferred on them by the trust instrument or by any enactment or any provision of subordinate legislation—

(a) authorised a person to exercise functions as their agent, or

(b) appointed a person to act as a nominee or custodian.

(3) If the application of section 22 or 23 is inconsistent with the terms of the trust instrument or the enactment or provision of subordinate legislation, the section in question does not apply.

[1786]

22 Review of agents, nominees and custodians etc

(1) While the agent, nominee or custodian continues to act for the trust, the trustees—

(a) must keep under review the arrangements under which the agent, nominee or custodian acts and how those arrangements are being put into effect,

(b) if circumstances make it appropriate to do so, must consider whether there is a need to exercise any power of intervention that they have, and

(c) if they consider that there is a need to exercise such a power, must do so.

(2) If the agent has been authorised to exercise asset management functions, the duty under subsection (1) includes, in particular—

(a) a duty to consider whether there is any need to revise or replace the policy statement made for the purposes of section 15,

(b) if they consider that there is a need to revise or replace the policy statement, a duty to do so, and

(c) a duty to assess whether the policy statement (as it has effect for the time being) is being complied with.

(3) Subsections (3) and (4) of section 15 apply to the revision or replacement of a policy statement under this section as they apply to the making of a policy statement under that section.

(4) "Power of intervention" includes—

(a) a power to give directions to the agent, nominee or custodian;

(b) a power to revoke the authorisation or appointment.

[1787]

23 Liability for agents, nominees and custodians etc

(1) A trustee is not liable for any act or default of the agent, nominee or custodian unless he has failed to comply with the duty of care applicable to him, under paragraph 3 of Schedule 1—

(a) when entering into the arrangements under which the person acts as agent, nominee or custodian, or

(b) when carrying out his duties under section 22.

(2) If a trustee has agreed a term under which the agent, nominee or custodian is permitted to appoint a substitute, the trustee is not liable for any act or default of the substitute unless he has failed to comply with the duty of care applicable to him, under paragraph 3 of Schedule 1—

(a) when agreeing that term, or

(b) when carrying out his duties under section 22 in so far as they relate to the use of the substitute.

[1788]

Supplementary

24 Effect of trustees exceeding their powers

A failure by the trustees to act within the limits of the powers conferred by this Part—

(a) in authorising a person to exercise a function of theirs as an agent, or

(b) in appointing a person to act as a nominee or custodian,

does not invalidate the authorisation or appointment.

[1789]

25 Sole trustees

(1) Subject to subsection (2), this Part applies in relation to a trust having a sole trustee as it applies in relation to other trusts (and references in this Part to trustees—except in sections 12(1) and (3) and 19(5)—are to be read accordingly).

(2) Section 18 does not impose a duty on a sole trustee if that trustee is a trust corporation.

[1790]

26 Restriction or exclusion of this Part etc

The powers conferred by this Part are—

(a) in addition to powers conferred on trustees otherwise than by this Act, but

(b) subject to any restriction or exclusion imposed by the trust instrument or by any enactment or any provision of subordinate legislation.

[1791]

27 Existing trusts

This Part applies in relation to trusts whether created before or after its commencement.

[1792]

PART V
REMUNERATION

28 Trustee's entitlement to payment under trust instrument

(1) Except to the extent (if any) to which the trust instrument makes inconsistent provision, subsections (2) to (4) apply to a trustee if—

(a) there is a provision in the trust instrument entitling him to receive payment out of trust funds in respect of services provided by him to or on behalf of the trust, and

(b) the trustee is a trust corporation or is acting in a professional capacity.

(2) The trustee is to be treated as entitled under the trust instrument to receive payment in respect of services even if they are services which are capable of being provided by a lay trustee.

(3) Subsection (2) applies to a trustee of a charitable trust who is not a trust corporation only—

(a) if he is not a sole trustee, and

(b) to the extent that a majority of the other trustees have agreed that it should apply to him.

(4) Any payments to which the trustee is entitled in respect of services are to be treated as remuneration for services (and not as a gift) for the purposes of—

(a) section 15 of the Wills Act 1837 (gifts to an attesting witness to be void), and

(b) section 34(3) of the Administration of Estates Act 1925 (order in which estate to be paid out).

(5) For the purposes of this Part, a trustee acts in a professional capacity if he acts in the course of a profession or business which consists of or includes the provision of services in connection with—

(a) the management or administration of trusts generally or a particular kind of trust, or

(b) any particular aspect of the management or administration of trusts generally or a particular kind of trust,

and the services he provides to or on behalf of the trust fall within that description.

(6) For the purposes of this Part, a person acts as a lay trustee if he—

(a) is not a trust corporation, and

(b) does not act in a professional capacity.

[1793]

29 Remuneration of certain trustees

(1) Subject to subsection (5), a trustee who—

(a) is a trust corporation, but

(b) is not a trustee of a charitable trust,

is entitled to receive reasonable remuneration out of the trust funds for any services that the trust corporation provides to or on behalf of the trust.

(2) Subject to subsection (5), a trustee who—

(a) acts in a professional capacity, but

(b) is not a trust corporation, a trustee of a charitable trust or a sole trustee,

is entitled to receive reasonable remuneration out of the trust funds for any services that he provides to or on behalf of the trust if each other trustee has agreed in writing that he may be remunerated for the services.

(3) "Reasonable remuneration" means, in relation to the provision of services by a trustee, such remuneration as is reasonable in the circumstances for the provision of those services to or on behalf of that trust by that trustee and for the purposes of subsection (1) includes, in relation to the provision of services by a trustee who is an authorised institution under the Banking Act 1987 and provides the services in that capacity, the institution's reasonable charges for the provision of such services.

(4) A trustee is entitled to remuneration under this section even if the services in question are capable of being provided by a lay trustee.

(5) A trustee is not entitled to remuneration under this section if any provision about his entitlement to remuneration has been made—

(a) by the trust instrument, or

(b) by any enactment or any provision of subordinate legislation.

(6) This section applies to a trustee who has been authorised under a power conferred by Part IV or the trust instrument—

(a) to exercise functions as an agent of the trustees, or

(b) to act as a nominee or custodian,

as it applies to any other trustee.

[1794]

30 Remuneration of trustees of charitable trusts

(1) The Secretary of State may by regulations make provision for the remuneration of trustees of charitable trusts who are trust corporations or act in a professional capacity.

(2) The power under subsection (1) includes power to make provision for the remuneration of a trustee who has been authorised under a power conferred by Part IV or any other enactment or any provision of subordinate legislation, or by the trust instrument—

(a) to exercise functions as an agent of the trustees, or
(b) to act as a nominee or custodian.

(3) Regulations under this section may—

(a) make different provision for different cases;
(b) contain such supplemental, incidental, consequential and transitional provision as the Secretary of State considers appropriate.

(4) The power to make regulations under this section is exercisable by statutory instrument, but no such instrument shall be made unless a draft of it has been laid before Parliament and approved by a resolution of each House of Parliament.

[1795]

31 Trustees' expenses

(1) A trustee—

(a) is entitled to be reimbursed from the trust funds, or
(b) may pay out of the trust funds,

expenses properly incurred by him when acting on behalf of the trust.

(2) This section applies to a trustee who has been authorised under a power conferred by Part IV or any other enactment or any provision of subordinate legislation, or by the trust instrument—

(a) to exercise functions as an agent of the trustees, or
(b) to act as a nominee or custodian,

as it applies to any other trustee.

[1796]

32 Remuneration and expenses of agents, nominees and custodians

(1) This section applies if, under a power conferred by Part IV or any other enactment or any provision of subordinate legislation, or by the trust instrument, a person other than a trustee has been—

(a) authorised to exercise functions as an agent of the trustees, or
(b) appointed to act as a nominee or custodian.

(2) The trustees may remunerate the agent, nominee or custodian out of the trust funds for services if—

(a) he is engaged on terms entitling him to be remunerated for those services, and
(b) the amount does not exceed such remuneration as is reasonable in the circumstances for the provision of those services by him to or on behalf of that trust.

(3) The trustees may reimburse the agent, nominee or custodian out of the trust funds for any expenses properly incurred by him in exercising functions as an agent, nominee or custodian.

[1797]

33 Application

(1) Subject to subsection (2), sections 28, 29, 31 and 32 apply in relation to services provided to or on behalf of, or (as the case may be) expenses incurred on or after their commencement on behalf of, trusts whenever created.

(2) Nothing in section 28 or 29 is to be treated as affecting the operation of—

(a) section 15 of the Wills Act 1837, or
(b) section 34(3) of the Administration of Estates Act 1925,

in relation to any death occurring before the commencement of section 28 or (as the case may be) section 29.

[1798]

PART VI
MISCELLANEOUS AND SUPPLEMENTARY

34 (*Substitutes the Trustee Act 1925, s 19 at* **[216]** *and amends s 20 thereof at* **[217]**.)

35 Personal representatives

(1) Subject to the following provisions of this section, this Act applies in relation to a personal representative administering an estate according to the law as it applies to a trustee carrying out a trust for beneficiaries.

(2) For this purpose this Act is to be read with the appropriate modifications and in particular—

(a) references to the trust instrument are to be read as references to the will,

(b) references to a beneficiary or to beneficiaries, apart from the reference to a beneficiary in section 8(1)(b), are to be read as references to a person or the persons interested in the due administration of the estate, and

(c) the reference to a beneficiary in section 8(1)(b) is to be read as a reference to a person who under the will of the deceased or under the law relating to intestacy is beneficially interested in the estate.

(3) Remuneration to which a personal representative is entitled under section 28 or 29 is to be treated as an administration expense for the purposes of—

(a) section 34(3) of the Administration of Estates Act 1925 (order in which estate to be paid out), and

(b) any provision giving reasonable administration expenses priority over the preferential debts listed in Schedule 6 to the Insolvency Act 1986.

(4) Nothing in subsection (3) is to be treated as affecting the operation of the provisions mentioned in paragraphs (a) and (b) of that subsection in relation to any death occurring before the commencement of this section.

[1799]

36 Pension schemes

(1) In this section "pension scheme" means an occupational pension scheme (within the meaning of the Pension Schemes Act 1993) established under a trust and subject to the law of England and Wales.

(2) Part I does not apply in so far as it imposes a duty of care in relation to—

(a) the functions described in paragraphs 1 and 2 of Schedule 1, or

(b) the functions described in paragraph 3 of that Schedule to the extent that they relate to trustees—

(i) authorising a person to exercise their functions with respect to investment, or

(ii) appointing a person to act as their nominee or custodian.

(3) Nothing in Part II or III applies to the trustees of any pension scheme.

(4) Part IV applies to the trustees of a pension scheme subject to the restrictions in subsections (5) to (8).

(5) The trustees of a pension scheme may not under Part IV authorise any person to exercise any functions relating to investment as their agent.

(6) The trustees of a pension scheme may not under Part IV authorise a person who is—

(a) an employer in relation to the scheme, or

(b) connected with or an associate of such an employer,

to exercise any of their functions as their agent.

(7) For the purposes of subsection (6)—

(a) "employer", in relation to a scheme, has the same meaning as in the Pensions Act 1995;

(b) sections 249 and 435 of the Insolvency Act 1986 apply for the purpose of determining whether a person is connected with or an associate of an employer.

(8) Sections 16 to 20 (powers to appoint nominees and custodians) do not apply to the trustees of a pension scheme.

[1800]

37 Authorised unit trusts

(1) Parts II to IV do not apply to trustees of authorised unit trusts.

(2) "Authorised unit trust" means a unit trust scheme in the case of which an order under section 78 of the Financial Services Act 1986 is in force.

[1801]

38 Common investment schemes for charities etc

Parts II to IV do not apply to—

(a) trustees managing a fund under a common investment scheme made, or having effect as if made, under section 24 of the Charities Act 1993, other than such a fund the trusts of which provide that property is not to be transferred to the fund except by or on behalf of a charity the trustees of which are the trustees appointed to manage the fund, or

(b) trustees managing a fund under a common deposit scheme made, or having effect as if made, under section 25 of that Act.

[1802]

39 Interpretation

(1) In this Act—

"asset" includes any right or interest;

"charitable trust" means a trust under which property is held for charitable purposes and "charitable purposes" has the same meaning as in the Charities Act 1993;
"custodian trustee" has the same meaning as in the Public Trustee Act 1906;
"enactment" includes any provision of a Measure of the Church Assembly or of the General Synod of the Church of England;
"exempt charity" has the same meaning as in the Charities Act 1993;
"functions" includes powers and duties;
"legal mortgage" has the same meaning as in the Law of Property Act 1925;
"personal representative" has the same meaning as in the Trustee Act 1925;
"settled land" has the same meaning as in the Settled Land Act 1925;
"trust corporation" has the same meaning as in the Trustee Act 1925;
"trust funds" means income or capital funds of the trust.

(2) In this Act the expressions listed below are defined or otherwise explained by the provisions indicated—

asset management functions	section 15(5)
custodian	section 17(2)
the duty of care	section 1(2)
the general power of investment	section 3(2)
lay trustee	section 28(6)
power of intervention	section 22(4)
the standard investment criteria	section 4(3)
subordinate legislation	section 6(3)
trustee acting in a professional capacity	section 28(5)
trust instrument	sections 6(2) and 35(2)(a)

[1803]

40 Minor and consequential amendments etc

(1) Schedule 2 (minor and consequential amendments) shall have effect.

(2) Schedule 3 (transitional provisions and savings) shall have effect.

(3) Schedule 4 (repeals) shall have effect.

[1804]

41 Power to amend other Acts

(1) A Minister of the Crown may by order make such amendments of any Act, including an Act extending to places outside England and Wales, as appear to him appropriate in consequence of or in connection with Part II or III.

(2) Before exercising the power under subsection (1) in relation to a local, personal or private Act, the Minister must consult any person who appears to him to be affected by any proposed amendment.

(3) An order under this section may—

(a) contain such transitional provisions and savings as the Minister thinks fit;
(b) make different provision for different purposes.

(4) The power to make an order under this section is exercisable by statutory instrument which shall be subject to annulment in pursuance of a resolution of either House of Parliament.

(5) "Minister of the Crown" has the same meaning as in the Ministers of the Crown Act 1975.

[1805]

42 Commencement and extent

(1) Section 41, this section and section 43 shall come into force on the day on which this Act is passed.

(2) The remaining provisions of this Act shall come into force on such day as the Lord Chancellor may appoint by order made by statutory instrument; and different days may be so appointed for different purposes.

(3) An order under subsection (2) may contain such transitional provisions and savings as the Lord Chancellor considers appropriate in connection with the order.

(4) Subject to section 41(1) and subsection (5), this Act extends to England and Wales only.

(5) An amendment or repeal in Part II or III of Schedule 2 or Part II of Schedule 4 has the same extent as the provision amended or repealed.

[1806]

NOTES

Order: the Trustee Act 2000 (Commencement) Order 2001, SI 2001/49.

43 Short title

This Act may be cited as the Trustee Act 2000.

[1807]

SCHEDULE 1
APPLICATION OF DUTY OF CARE

Section 2

Investment

1. The duty of care applies to a trustee—
   (a) when exercising the general power of investment or any other power of investment, however conferred;
   (b) when carrying out a duty to which he is subject under section 4 or 5 (duties relating to the exercise of a power of investment or to the review of investments).

Acquisition of land

2. The duty of care applies to a trustee—
   (a) when exercising the power under section 8 to acquire land;
   (b) when exercising any other power to acquire land, however conferred;
   (c) when exercising any power in relation to land acquired under a power mentioned in sub-paragraph (a) or (b).

Agents, nominees and custodians

3.—(1) The duty of care applies to a trustee—
   (a) when entering into arrangements under which a person is authorised under section 11 to exercise functions as an agent;
   (b) when entering into arrangements under which a person is appointed under section 16 to act as a nominee;
   (c) when entering into arrangements under which a person is appointed under section 17 or 18 to act as a custodian;
   (d) when entering into arrangements under which, under any other power, however conferred, a person is authorised to exercise functions as an agent or is appointed to act as a nominee or custodian;
   (e) when carrying out his duties under section 22 (review of agent, nominee or custodian, etc).

(2) For the purposes of sub-paragraph (1), entering into arrangements under which a person is authorised to exercise functions or is appointed to act as a nominee or custodian includes, in particular—
   (a) selecting the person who is to act,
   (b) determining any terms on which he is to act, and
   (c) if the person is being authorised to exercise asset management functions, the preparation of a policy statement under section 15.

Compounding of liabilities

4. The duty of care applies to a trustee—
   (a) when exercising the power under section 15 of the Trustee Act 1925 to do any of the things referred to in that section;
   (b) when exercising any corresponding power, however conferred.

Insurance

5. The duty of care applies to a trustee—
   (a) when exercising the power under section 19 of the Trustee Act 1925 to insure property;
   (b) when exercising any corresponding power, however conferred.

Reversionary interests, valuations and audit

6. The duty of care applies to a trustee—
   (a) when exercising the power under section 22(1) or (3) of the Trustee Act 1925 to do any of the things referred to there;
   (b) when exercising any corresponding power, however conferred.

Exclusion of duty of care

7. The duty of care does not apply if or in so far as it appears from the trust instrument that the duty is not meant to apply.

[1808]

(*Sch 2 contains amendments which, in so far as relevant to this work, have been incorporated at the appropriate place.*)

SCHEDULE 3
TRANSITIONAL PROVISIONS AND SAVINGS

Section 40

The Trustee Act 1925 (*c 19*)

1.—(1) Sub-paragraph (2) applies if, immediately before the day on which Part IV of this Act comes into force, a banker or banking company holds any bearer securities deposited with him under section 7(1) of the 1925 Act (investment in bearer securities).

(2) On and after the day on which Part IV comes into force, the banker or banking company shall be treated as if he had been appointed as custodian of the securities under section 18.

2. The repeal of section 8 of the 1925 Act (loans and investments by trustees not chargeable as breaches of trust) does not affect the operation of that section in relation to loans or investments made before the coming into force of that repeal.

3. The repeal of section 9 of the 1925 Act (liability for loss by reason of improper investment) does not affect the operation of that section in relation to any advance of trust money made before the coming into force of that repeal.

4.—(1) Sub-paragraph (2) applies if, immediately before the day on which Part IV of this Act comes into force, a banker or banking company holds any documents deposited with him under section 21 of the 1925 Act (deposit of documents for safe custody).

(2) On and after the day on which Part IV comes into force, the banker or banking company shall be treated as if he had been appointed as custodian of the documents under section 17.

5.—(1) Sub-paragraph (2) applies if, immediately before the day on which Part IV of this Act comes into force, a person has been appointed to act as or be an agent or attorney under section 23(1) or (3) of the 1925 Act (general power to employ agents etc).

(2) On and after the day on which Part IV comes into force, the agent shall be treated as if he had been authorised to exercise functions as an agent under section 11 (and, if appropriate, as if he had also been appointed under that Part to act as a custodian or nominee).

6. The repeal of section 23(2) of the 1925 Act (power to employ agents in respect of property outside the United Kingdom) does not affect the operation after the commencement of the repeal of an appointment made before that commencement.

The Trustee Investments Act 1961 (*c 62*)

7.—(1) A trustee shall not be liable for breach of trust merely because he continues to hold an investment acquired by virtue of paragraph 14 of Part II of Schedule 1 to the 1961 Act (perpetual rent-charges etc).

(2) A person who—

(a) is not a trustee,

(b) before the commencement of Part II of this Act had powers to invest in the investments described in paragraph 14 of Part II of Schedule 1 to the 1961 Act, and

(c) on that commencement acquired the general power of investment,

shall not be treated as exceeding his powers of investment merely because he continues to hold an investment acquired by virtue of that paragraph.

The Cathedrals Measure 1963 (*No 2*)

8. While section 21 of the Cathedrals Measure 1963 (investment powers, etc of capitular bodies) continues to apply in relation to any cathedral, that section shall have effect as if—

(a) in subsection (1), for paragraph (c) and the words from "and the powers" to the end of the subsection there were substituted—

"(c) power to invest in any investments in which trustees may invest under the general power of investment in section 3 of the Trustee Act 2000 (as restricted by sections 4 and 5 of that Act).", and

(b) in subsection (5), for "subsections (2) and (3) of section six of the Trustee Investments Act 1961" there were substituted "section 5 of the Trustee Act 2000".

[1809]

(Sch 4 contains repeals which, in so far as relevant to this work, have been incorporated at the appropriate place.)

COUNTRYSIDE AND RIGHTS OF WAY ACT 2000

(2000 c 37)

An Act to make new provision for public access to the countryside; to amend the law relating to public rights of way; to enable traffic regulation orders to be made for the purpose of conserving an area's natural beauty; to make provision with respect to the driving of mechanically propelled vehicles elsewhere than on roads; to amend the law relating to nature conservation and the protection of wildlife; to make further provision with respect to areas of outstanding natural beauty; and for connected purposes.

[30 November 2000]

PART I
ACCESS TO THE COUNTRYSIDE

CHAPTER I
RIGHT OF ACCESS

General

1 Principal definitions for Part I

(1) In this Part "access land" means any land which—

(a) is shown as open country on a map in conclusive form issued by the appropriate countryside body for the purposes of this Part,

(b) is shown on such a map as registered common land,

(c) is registered common land in any area outside Inner London for which no such map relating to registered common land has been issued,

(d) is situated more than 600 metres above sea level in any area for which no such map relating to open country has been issued, or

(e) is dedicated for the purposes of this Part under section 16,

but does not (in any of those cases) include excepted land or land which is treated by section 15(1) as being accessible to the public apart from this Act.

(2) In this Part—

"access authority"—

(a) in relation to land in a National Park, means the National Park authority, and

(b) in relation to any other land, means the local highway authority in whose area the land is situated;

"the appropriate countryside body" means—

(a) in relation to England, [Natural England], and

(b) in relation to Wales, the Countryside Council for Wales;

"excepted land" means land which is for the time being of any of the descriptions specified in Part I of Schedule 1, those descriptions having effect subject to Part II of that Schedule;

"mountain" includes, subject to the following definition, any land situated more than 600 metres above sea level;

"mountain, moor, heath or down" does not include land which appears to the appropriate countryside body to consist of improved or semi-improved grassland;

"open country" means land which—

(a) appears to the appropriate countryside body to consist wholly or predominantly of mountain, moor, heath or down, and

(b) is not registered common land.

(3) In this Part "registered common land" means—

(a) land which is registered as common land under the Commons Registration Act 1965 (in this section referred to as "the 1965 Act") and whose registration under that Act has become final, or

[(a) land which is registered as common land in a register of common land kept under Part 1 of the Commons Act 2006,]

(b) subject to subsection (4), land which fell within paragraph (a) on the day on which this Act is passed or at any time after that day but has subsequently ceased to be registered as common land under the 1965 Act on the register of common land in which it was included being amended by reason of the land having ceased to be common land within the meaning of that Act.

(4) *Subsection (3)(b) does not apply where—*

(*a*) *the amendment of the register of common land was made in pursuance of an application made before the day on which this Act is passed, or*

(*b*) *the land ceased to be common land by reason of the exercise of—*

(*i*) *any power of compulsory purchase, of appropriation or of sale which is conferred by an enactment,*

(*ii*) *any power so conferred under which land may be made common land within the meaning of the 1965 Act in substitution for other land.*

[1810]

NOTES

Sub-s (2): in definition "the appropriate countryside body" words in square brackets substituted by the Natural Environment and Rural Communities Act 2006, s 105(1), Sch 11, Pt 1, para 154.

Sub-s (3): para (a) substituted and para (b) repealed by the Commons Act 2006, ss 52, 53, Sch 5, para 7(1), (2), Sch 6, Pt 1, as from a day to be appointed.

Sub-s (4): repealed by the Commons Act 2006, ss 52, 53, Sch 5, para 7(1), (3), Sch 6, Pt 1, as from a day to be appointed.

2 Rights of public in relation to access land

(1) Any person is entitled by virtue of this subsection to enter and remain on any access land for the purposes of open-air recreation, if and so long as—

(a) he does so without breaking or damaging any wall, fence, hedge, stile or gate, and

(b) he observes the general restrictions in Schedule 2 and any other restrictions imposed in relation to the land under Chapter II.

(2) Subsection (1) has effect subject to subsections (3) and (4) and to the provisions of Chapter II.

(3) Subsection (1) does not entitle a person to enter or be on any land, or do anything on any land, in contravention of any prohibition contained in or having effect under any enactment, other than an enactment contained in a local or private Act.

(4) If a person becomes a trespasser on any access land by failing to comply with—

(a) subsection (1)(a),

(b) the general restrictions in Schedule 2, or

(c) any other restrictions imposed in relation to the land under Chapter II,

he may not, within 72 hours after leaving that land, exercise his right under subsection (1) to enter that land again or to enter other land in the same ownership.

(5) In this section "owner", in relation to any land which is subject to a farm business tenancy within the meaning of the Agricultural Tenancies Act 1995 or a tenancy to which the Agricultural Holdings Act 1986 applies, means the tenant under that tenancy, and "ownership" shall be construed accordingly.

[1811]

NOTES

Commencement: 19 September 2004 (in relation to England, for certain purposes); 14 December 2004 (in relation to England, for certain purposes); 28 May 2005 (in relation to Wales, and in relation to England, for certain purposes); 28 August 2005 (in relation to England, for certain purposes).

3 Power to extend to coastal land

(1) The Secretary of State (as respects England) or the National Assembly for Wales (as respects Wales) may by order amend the definition of "open country" in section 1(2) so as to include a reference to coastal land or to coastal land of any description.

(2) An order under this section may—

(a) make consequential amendments of other provisions of this Part, and

(b) modify the provisions of this Part in their application to land which is open country merely because it is coastal land.

(3) In this section "coastal land" means—

(a) the foreshore, and

(b) land adjacent to the foreshore (including in particular any cliff, bank, barrier, dune, beach or flat which is adjacent to the foreshore).

[1812]

Maps

4 Duty to prepare maps

(1) It shall be the duty of [Natural England] to prepare, in respect of England outside Inner London, maps which together show—

(a) all registered common land, and

(b) all open country.

(2) It shall be the duty of the Countryside Council for Wales to prepare, in respect of Wales, maps which together show—

(a) all registered common land, and

(b) all open country.

(3) Subsections (1) and (2) have effect subject to the following provisions of this section and to the provisions of sections 5 to 9.

(4) A map prepared under this section must distinguish between open country and registered common land, but need not distinguish between different categories of open country.

(5) In preparing a map under this section, the appropriate countryside body—

(a) may determine not to show as open country areas of open country which are so small that the body consider that their inclusion would serve no useful purpose, and

(b) may determine that any boundary of an area of open country is to be treated as coinciding with a particular physical feature (whether the effect is to include other land as open country or to exclude part of an area of open country).

[1813]

NOTES

Sub-s (1): words in square brackets substituted by the Natural Environment and Rural Communities Act 2006, s 105(1), Sch 11, Pt 1, para 155.

5 Publication of draft maps

The appropriate countryside body shall—

(a) issue in draft form any map prepared by them under section 4,

(b) consider any representations received by them within the prescribed period with respect to the showing of, or the failure to show, any area of land on the map as registered common land or as open country,

(c) confirm the map with or without modifications,

(d) if the map has been confirmed without modifications, issue it in provisional form, and

(e) if the map has been confirmed with modifications, prepare a map incorporating the modifications, and issue that map in provisional form.

[1814]

NOTES

Regulations: the Access to the Countryside (Maps in Draft Form) (England) Regulations 2001, SI 2001/3301.

6 Appeal against map after confirmation

(1) Any person having an interest in any land may appeal—

(a) in the case of land in England, to the Secretary of State, or

(b) in the case of land in Wales, to the National Assembly for Wales,

against the showing of that land on a map in provisional form as registered common land or as open country.

(2) An appeal relating to the showing of any land as registered common land may be brought only on the ground that the land is not registered common land.

(3) An appeal relating to the showing of any land as open country may be brought only on the ground that—

(a) the land does not consist wholly or predominantly of mountain, moor, heath or down, and

(b) to the extent that the appropriate countryside body have exercised their discretion under section 4(5)(b) to treat land which is not open country as forming part of an area of open country, the body ought not to have done so.

(4) On an appeal under this section, the Secretary of State or the National Assembly for Wales may—

(a) approve the whole or part of the map which is the subject of the appeal, with or without modifications, or

(b) require the appropriate countryside body to prepare under section 4 a new map relating to all or part of the area covered by the map which is the subject of the appeal.

[1815]

7 Appeal procedure

(1) Before determining an appeal under section 6, the Secretary of State or the National Assembly for Wales may, if he or it thinks fit—

(a) cause the appeal to take, or continue in, the form of a hearing, or

(b) cause a local inquiry to be held;

and the appeal authority shall act as mentioned in paragraph (a) or (b) if a request is made by either party to the appeal to be heard with respect to the appeal.

(2) Subsections (2) to (5) of section 250 of the Local Government Act 1972 (local inquiries: evidence and costs) apply to a hearing or local inquiry held under this section as they apply to a local inquiry held under that section, but as if—

(a) references in that section to the person appointed to hold the inquiry were references to the Secretary of State or the National Assembly for Wales, and

(b) references in that section to the Minister causing an inquiry to be held were references to the Secretary of State or the Assembly.

(3) Where—

(a) for the purposes of an appeal under section 6, the Secretary of State or the National Assembly for Wales is required by subsection (1)—

(i) to cause the appeal to take, or continue in, the form of a hearing, or

(ii) to cause a local inquiry to be held, and

(b) the inquiry or hearing does not take place, and

(c) if it had taken place, the Secretary of State or the Assembly or a person appointed by the Secretary of State or the Assembly would have had power to make an order under section 250(5) of the Local Government Act 1972 requiring any party to pay the costs of the other party,

the power to make such an order may be exercised, in relation to costs incurred for the purposes of the inquiry or hearing, as if it had taken place.

(4) This section has effect subject to section 8.

[1816]

8 Power of Secretary of State or Assembly to delegate functions relating to appeals

(1) The Secretary of State or the National Assembly for Wales may—

(a) appoint any person to exercise on his or its behalf, with or without payment, the function of determining—

(i) an appeal under section 6, or

(ii) any matter involved in such an appeal, or

(b) refer any matter involved in such an appeal to such person as the Secretary of State or the Assembly may appoint for the purpose, with or without payment.

(2) Schedule 3 has effect with respect to appointments under subsection (1)(a).

[1817]

9 Maps in conclusive form

(1) Where—

(a) the time within which any appeal under section 6 may be brought in relation to a map in provisional form has expired and no appeal has been brought, or

(b) every appeal brought under that section in relation to a map has—

(i) been determined by the map or part of it being approved without modifications, or

(ii) been withdrawn,

the appropriate countryside body shall issue the map (or the part or parts of it that have been approved without modifications) as a map in conclusive form.

(2) Where—

(a) every appeal brought under section 6 in relation to a map in provisional form has been determined or withdrawn, and

(b) on one or more appeals, the map or any part of it has been approved with modifications,

the appropriate countryside body shall prepare a map which covers the area covered by the map in provisional form (or the part or parts of the map in provisional form that have been approved with or without modifications) and incorporates the modifications, and shall issue it as a map in conclusive form.

(3) Where either of the conditions in subsection (1)(a) and (b) is satisfied in relation to any part of a map in provisional form, the Secretary of State (as respects England) or the National Assembly for Wales (as respects Wales) may direct the relevant countryside body to issue that part of the map as a map in conclusive form.

(4) Where on an appeal under section 6 part of a map in provisional form has been approved with modifications but the condition in subsection (2)(a) is not yet satisfied, the Secretary of State (as respects England) or the National Assembly for Wales (as respects Wales) may direct the relevant countryside body to issue a map which covers the area covered by that part of the map in provisional form and incorporates the modifications, and to issue it as a map in conclusive form.

(5) Where a map in conclusive form has been issued in compliance with a direction under subsection (3) or (4), subsections (1) and (2) shall have effect as if any reference to the map in provisional form were a reference to the part not affected by the direction.

(6) A document purporting to be certified on behalf of the appropriate countryside body to be a copy of or of any part of a map in conclusive form issued by that body for the purposes of this Part shall be receivable in evidence and shall be deemed, unless the contrary is shown, to be such a copy.

[1818]

10 Review of maps

(1) Where the appropriate countryside body have issued a map in conclusive form in respect of any area, it shall be the duty of the body from time to time, on a review under this section, to consider—

(a) whether any land shown on that map as open country or registered common land is open country or registered common land at the time of the review, and
(b) whether any land in that area which is not so shown ought to be so shown.

(2) A review under this section must be undertaken—

(a) in the case of the first review, not more than ten years after the issue of the map in conclusive form, and
(b) in the case of subsequent reviews, not more than ten years after the previous review.

(3) Regulations may amend paragraphs (a) and (b) of subsection (2) by substituting for the period for the time being specified in either of those paragraphs such other period as may be specified in the regulations.

[1819]

11 Regulations relating to maps

(1) Regulations may make provision supplementing the provisions of sections 4 to 10.

(2) Regulations under this section may in particular make provision with respect to—

(a) the scale on which maps are to be prepared,
(b) the manner and form in which they are to be prepared and issued,
(c) consultation with access authorities, local access forums and other persons on maps in draft form,
(d) the steps to be taken for informing the public of the issue of maps in draft form, provisional form or conclusive form,
(e) the manner in which maps in draft form, provisional form or conclusive form are to be published or to be made available for inspection,
(f) the period within which and the manner in which representations on a map in draft form may be made to the appropriate countryside body,
(g) the confirmation of a map under section 5(c),
(h) the period within which and manner in which appeals under section 6 are to be brought,
(i) the advertising of such an appeal,
(j) the manner in which such appeals are to be considered,
(k) the procedure to be followed on a review under section 10, including the issue of maps in draft form, provisional form and conclusive form on a review, and
(l) the correction by the appropriate countryside body of minor errors or omissions in maps.

(3) Regulations made by virtue of subsection (2)(b) or (e) may authorise or require a map to be prepared, issued, published or made available for inspection in electronic form, but must require any map in electronic form to be capable of being reproduced in printed form.

(4) Regulations made by virtue of subsection (2)(k) may provide for any of the provisions of this Chapter relating to appeals to apply (with or without modifications) in relation to an appeal against a map issued in provisional form on a review.

[1820]

NOTES

Regulations: the Access to the Countryside (Maps in Draft Form) (England) Regulations 2001, SI 2001/3301; the Countryside Access (Draft Maps) (Wales) Regulations 2001, SI 2001/4001; the Access to the Countryside (Provisional and Conclusive Maps) (England) Regulations 2002, SI 2002/1710; the Countryside Access (Appeals Procedures) (Wales) Regulations 2002, SI 2002/1794; the Countryside Access (Exclusion or Restriction of Access) (Wales) Regulations 2003, SI 2003/142; the Access to the Countryside (Correction of Provisional and Conclusive Maps) (England) Regulations 2003, SI 2003/1591.

Rights and liabilities of owners and occupiers

12 Effect of right of access on rights and liabilities of owners

(1) The operation of section 2(1) in relation to any access land does not increase the liability, under any enactment not contained in this Act or under any rule of law, of a person interested in the access land or any adjoining land in respect of the state of the land or of things done or omitted to be done on the land.

(2) Any restriction arising under a covenant or otherwise as to the use of any access land shall have effect subject to the provisions of this Part, and any liability of a person interested in any access land in respect of such a restriction is limited accordingly.

(3) For the purposes of any enactment or rule of law as to the circumstances in which the dedication of a highway or the grant of an easement may be presumed, or may be established by prescription, the use by the public or by any person of a way across land in the exercise of the right conferred by section 2(1) is to be disregarded.

(4) The use of any land by the inhabitants of any locality for the purposes of open-air recreation in the exercise of the right conferred by section 2(1) is to be disregarded in determining whether the land has become a town or village green.

[1821]

NOTES

Commencement: 19 September 2004 (in relation to England); 28 May 2005 (in relation to Wales).

13 (*Amends the Occupiers' Liability Act 1957, s 1 at* **[594]**, *and the Occupiers' Liability Act 1984, s 1 at* **[1027]** *and inserts s 1A of the 1984 Act at* **[1028]**.)

14 Offence of displaying on access land notices deterring public use

(1) If any person places or maintains—

(a) on or near any access land, or

(b) on or near a way leading to any access land,

a notice containing any false or misleading information likely to deter the public from exercising the right conferred by section 2(1), he is liable on summary conviction to a fine not exceeding level 1 on the standard scale.

(2) The court before whom a person is convicted of an offence under subsection (1) may, in addition to or in substitution for the imposition of a fine, order him to remove the notice in respect of which he is convicted within such period, not being less than four days, as may be specified in the order.

(3) A person who fails to comply with an order under subsection (2) is guilty of a further offence and liable on summary conviction to a fine not exceeding level 3 on the standard scale.

[1822]

NOTES

Commencement: 19 September 2004 (in relation to England); 28 May 2005 (in relation to Wales).

Access under other enactments or by dedication

15 Rights of access under other enactments

(1) For the purposes of section 1(1), land is to be treated as being accessible to the public apart from this Act at any time if, but only if, at that time—

(a) section 193 of the Law of Property Act 1925 (rights of the public over commons and waste lands) applies to it,

(b) by virtue of a local or private Act or a scheme made under Part I of the Commons Act 1899 (as read with subsection (2)), members of the public have a right of access to it at all times for the purposes of open-air recreation (however described),

(c) an access agreement or access order under Part V of the National Parks and Access to the Countryside Act 1949 is in force with respect to it, or

(d) the public have access to it under subsection (1) of section 19 of the Ancient Monuments and Archaeological Areas Act 1979 (public access to monuments under public control) or would have access to it under that subsection but for any provision of subsections (2) to (9) of that section.

(2) Where a local or private Act or a scheme made under Part I of the Commons Act 1899 confers on the inhabitants of a particular district or neighbourhood (however described) a right of access to any land for the purposes of open-air recreation (however described), the right of access exercisable by those inhabitants in relation to that land is by virtue of this subsection exercisable by members of the public generally.

[1823]

16 Dedication of land as access land

(1) Subject to the provisions of this section, a person who, in respect of any land, holds—

(a) the fee simple absolute in possession, or

(b) a legal term of years absolute of which not less than 90 years remain unexpired,

may, by taking such steps as may be prescribed, dedicate the land for the purposes of this Part, whether or not it would be access land apart from this section.

(2) Where any person other than the person making the dedication holds—

(a) any leasehold interest in any of the land to be dedicated, or

(b) such other interest in any of that land as may be prescribed, the dedication must be made jointly with that other person, in such manner as may be prescribed, or with his consent, given in such manner as may be prescribed.

(3) In relation to a dedication under this section by virtue of subsection (1)(b), the reference in subsection (2)(a) to a leasehold interest does not include a reference to a leasehold interest superior to that of the person making the dedication.

(4) A dedication made under this section by virtue of subsection (1)(b) shall have effect only for the remainder of the term held by the person making the dedication.

(5) Schedule 2 to the Forestry Act 1967 (power for tenant for life and others to enter into forestry dedication covenants) applies to dedications under this section as it applies to forestry dedication covenants.

(6) Regulations may—

(a) prescribe the form of any instrument to be used for the purposes of this section,

(b) enable a dedication under this section to include provision removing or relaxing any of the general restrictions in Schedule 2 in relation to any of the land to which the dedication relates,

(c) enable a dedication previously made under this section to be amended by the persons by whom a dedication could be made, so as to remove or relax any of those restrictions in relation to any of the land to which the dedication relates, and

(d) require any dedication under this section, or any amendment of such a dedication by virtue of paragraph (c), to be notified to the appropriate countryside body and to the access authority.

(7) A dedication under this section is irrevocable and, subject to subsection (4), binds successive owners and occupiers of, and other persons interested in, the land to which it relates, but nothing in this section prevents any land from becoming excepted land.

(8) A dedication under this section is a local land charge.

[1824]

NOTES

Regulations: the Countryside Access (Dedication of Land as Access Land) (Wales) Regulations 2003, SI 2003/135; the Access to the Countryside (Dedication of Land) (England) Regulations 2003, SI 2003/2004.

Miscellaneous provisions relating to right of access

17 Byelaws

(1) An access authority may, as respects access land in their area, make byelaws—

(a) for the preservation of order,

(b) for the prevention of damage to the land or anything on or in it, and

(c) for securing that persons exercising the right conferred by section 2(1) so behave themselves as to avoid undue interference with the enjoyment of the land by other persons.

(2) Byelaws under this section may relate to all the access land in the area of the access authority or only to particular land.

(3) Before making byelaws under this section, the access authority shall consult—

(a) the appropriate countryside body, and

(b) any local access forum established for an area to which the byelaws relate.

(4) Byelaws under this section shall not interfere—

(a) with the exercise of any public right of way,

(b) with any authority having under any enactment functions relating to the land to which the byelaws apply, or

[(c) with the provision of an electronic communications code network or the exercise of any right conferred by or in accordance with the electronic communications code on the operator of any such network].

(5) Sections 236 to 238 of the Local Government Act 1972 (which relate to the procedure for making byelaws, authorise byelaws to impose fines not exceeding level 2 on the standard scale, and provide for the proof of byelaws in legal proceedings) apply to all byelaws under this section whether or not the authority making them is a local authority within the meaning of that Act.

(6) The confirming authority in relation to byelaws made under this section is—

(a) as respects England, the Secretary of State, and

(b) as respects Wales, the National Assembly for Wales.

(7) Byelaws under this section relating to any land—

(a) may not be made unless the land is access land or the access authority are satisfied that it is likely to become access land, and

(b) may not be confirmed unless the land is access land.

(8) Any access authority having power under this section to make byelaws also have power to enforce byelaws made by them; and any county council or district or parish council may enforce byelaws made under this section by another authority as respects land in the area of the council.

[1825]

NOTES

Sub-s (4): para (c) substituted by the Communications Act 2003, s 406(1), Sch 17, para 165(1), (2).

18 Wardens

(1) An access authority or a district council may appoint such number of persons as may appear to the authority making the appointment to be necessary or expedient, to act as wardens as respects access land in their area.

(2) As respects access land in an area for which there is a local access forum, an access authority shall, before they first exercise the power under subsection (1) and thereafter from time to time, consult the local access forum about the exercise of that power.

(3) Wardens may be appointed under subsection (1) for the following purposes—

- (a) to secure compliance with byelaws under section 17 and with the general restrictions in Schedule 2 and any other restrictions imposed under Chapter II,
- (b) to enforce any exclusion imposed under Chapter II,
- (c) in relation to the right conferred by section 2(1), to advise and assist the public and persons interested in access land,
- (d) to perform such other duties (if any) in relation to access land as the authority appointing them may determine.

(4) For the purpose of exercising any function conferred on him by or under this section, a warden appointed under subsection (1) may enter upon any access land.

(5) A warden appointed under subsection (1) shall, if so required, produce evidence of his authority before entering any access land in the exercise of the power conferred by subsection (4), and shall also produce evidence of his authority while he remains on the access land, if so required by any person.

(6) Except as provided by subsection (4), this section does not authorise a warden appointed under subsection (1), on land in which any person other than the authority who appointed him has an interest, to do anything which apart from this section would be actionable at that person's suit by virtue of that interest.

[1826]

NOTES

Commencement: 21 June 2004 (in relation to Wales); 19 September 2004 (in relation to England).

19 Notices indicating boundaries, etc

(1) An access authority may erect and maintain—

- (a) notices indicating the boundaries of access land and excepted land, and
- (b) notices informing the public of—
  - (i) the effect of the general restrictions in Schedule 2,
  - (ii) the exclusion or restriction under Chapter II of access by virtue of section 2(1) to any land, and
  - (iii) any other matters relating to access land or to access by virtue of section 2(1) which the access authority consider appropriate.

(2) In subsection (1)(b)(ii), the reference to the exclusion or restriction of access by virtue of section 2(1) is to be interpreted in accordance with section 21(2) and (3).

(3) Before erecting a notice on any land under subsection (1) the access authority shall, if reasonably practicable, consult the owner or occupier of the land.

(4) An access authority may also, as respects any access land in their area, defray or contribute towards, or undertake to defray or contribute towards, expenditure incurred or to be incurred in relation to the land by any person in displaying such notices as are mentioned in subsection (1)(a) and (b).

[1827]

20 Codes of conduct and other information

(1) In relation to England, it shall be the duty of [Natural England] to issue, and from time to time revise, a code of conduct for the guidance of persons exercising the right conferred by section 2(1) and of persons interested in access land, and to take such other steps as appear to them expedient for securing—

- (a) that the public are informed of the situation and extent of, and means of access to, access land, and

(b) that the public and persons interested in access land are informed of their respective rights and obligations—
  (i) under this Part, and
  (ii) with regard to public rights of way on, and nature conservation in relation to, access land.

(2) In relation to Wales, it shall be the duty of the Countryside Council for Wales to issue, and from time to time revise, a code of conduct for the guidance of persons exercising the right conferred by section 2(1) and of persons interested in access land, and to take such other steps as appear to them expedient for securing the results mentioned in paragraphs (a) and (b) of subsection (1).

(3) A code of conduct issued by [Natural England] or the Countryside Council for Wales may include provisions in pursuance of subsection (1) or (2) and in pursuance of section 86(1) of the National Parks and Access to the Countryside Act 1949.

(4) The powers conferred by subsections (1) and (2) include power to contribute towards expenses incurred by other persons.

[1828]

NOTES

Commencement: 21 June 2004 (in relation to Wales); 19 September 2004 (in relation to England).

Sub-ss (1), (3): words in square brackets substituted by the Natural Environment and Rural Communities Act 2006, s 105(1), Sch 11, Pt 1, para 156.

CHAPTER II
EXCLUSION OR RESTRICTION OF ACCESS

21 Interpretation of Chapter II

(1) References in this Chapter to the exclusion or restriction of access to any land by virtue of section 2(1) are to be interpreted in accordance with subsections (2) and (3).

(2) A person excludes access by virtue of subsection (1) of section 2 to any land where he excludes the application of that subsection in relation to that land.

(3) A person restricts access by virtue of subsection (1) of section 2 to any land where he provides that the right conferred by that subsection—
  (a) is exercisable only along specified routes or ways,
  (b) is exercisable only after entering the land at a specified place or places,
  (c) is exercisable only by persons who do not take dogs on the land, or
  (d) is exercisable only by persons who satisfy any other specified conditions.

(4) In this Chapter, except section 23(1), "owner", in relation to land which is subject to a farm business tenancy within the meaning of the Agricultural Tenancies Act 1995 or a tenancy to which the Agricultural Holdings Act 1986 applies, means the tenant under that tenancy.

(5) Subject to subsection (6), in this Chapter "the relevant authority"—
  (a) in relation to any land in a National Park, means the National Park authority, and
  (b) in relation to any other land, means the appropriate countryside body.

(6) Where—
  (a) it appears to the Forestry Commissioners that any land which is dedicated for the purposes of this Part under section 16 consists wholly or predominantly of woodland, and
  (b) the Forestry Commissioners give to the body who are apart from this subsection the relevant authority for the purposes of this Chapter in relation to the land a notice stating that the Forestry Commissioners are to be the relevant authority for those purposes as from a date specified in the notice,

the Forestry Commissioners shall as from that date become the relevant authority in relation to that land for those purposes, but subject to subsection (7).

(7) Where it appears to the Forestry Commissioners that any land in relation to which they are by virtue of subsection (6) the relevant authority for the purposes of this Chapter has ceased to consist wholly or predominantly of woodland, the Forestry Commissioners may, by giving notice to the body who would apart from subsection (6) be the relevant authority, revoke the notice under subsection (6) as from a date specified in the notice under this subsection.

[1829]

22 Exclusion or restriction at discretion of owner and others

(1) Subject to subsections (2) and (6), an entitled person may, by giving notice to the relevant authority in accordance with regulations under section 32(1)(a), exclude or restrict access by virtue of section 2(1) to any land on one or more days specified in the notice.

PART I STATUTES

(2) The number of days on which any entitled person excludes or restricts under this section access by virtue of section 2(1) to any land must not in any calendar year exceed the relevant maximum.

(3) In this section "entitled person", in relation to any land, means—
- (a) the owner of the land, and
- (b) any other person having an interest in the land and falling within a prescribed description.

(4) Subject to subsection (5), in this section "the relevant maximum" means twenty-eight.

(5) If regulations are made under subsection (3)(b), the regulations must provide that, in cases where there are two or more entitled persons having different interests in the land, the relevant maximum in relation to each of them is to be determined in accordance with the regulations, but so that the number of days on which access by virtue of section 2(1) to any land may be excluded or restricted under this section in any calendar year does not exceed twenty-eight.

(6) An entitled person may not under this section exclude or restrict access by virtue of section 2(1) to any land on—
- (a) Christmas Day or Good Friday, or
- (b) any day which is a bank holiday under the Banking and Financial Dealings Act 1971 in England and Wales.

(7) An entitled person may not under this section exclude or restrict access by virtue of section 2(1) to any land—
- (a) on more than four days in any calendar year which are either Saturday or Sunday,
- (b) on any Saturday in the period beginning with 1st June and ending with 11th August in any year,
- (c) on any Sunday in the period beginning with 1st June and ending with 30th September in any year.

(8) Regulations may provide that any exclusion or restriction under subsection (1) of access by virtue of section 2(1) to any land must relate to an area of land the boundaries of which are determined in accordance with the regulations.

[1830]

23 Restrictions on dogs at discretion of owner

(1) The owner of any land consisting of moor managed for the breeding and shooting of grouse may, so far as appears to him to be necessary in connection with the management of the land for that purpose, by taking such steps as may be prescribed, provide that, during a specified period, the right conferred by section 2(1) is exercisable only by persons who do not take dogs on the land.

(2) The owner of any land may, so far as appears to him to be necessary in connection with lambing, by taking such steps as may be prescribed, provide that during a specified period the right conferred by section 2(1) is exercisable only by persons who do not take dogs into any field or enclosure on the land in which there are sheep.

(3) In subsection (2) "field or enclosure" means a field or enclosure of not more than 15 hectares.

(4) As respects any land—
- (a) any period specified under subsection (1) may not be more than five years,
- (b) not more than one period may be specified under subsection (2) in any calendar year, and that period may not be more than six weeks.

(5) A restriction imposed under subsection (1) or (2) does not prevent a blind person from taking with him a trained guide dog, or a deaf person from taking with him a trained hearing dog.

[1831]

NOTES

Regulations: the Access to the Countryside (Exclusions and Restrictions) (England) Regulations 2003, SI 2003/2713.

---

24 Land management

(1) The relevant authority may by direction, on an application made by a person interested in any land, exclude or restrict access to that land by virtue of section 2(1) during a specified period, if the authority are satisfied that the exclusion or restriction under this section of access by virtue of section 2(1) to the extent provided by the direction is necessary for the purposes of the management of the land by the applicant.

(2) The reference in subsection (1) to a specified period includes a reference to—
- (a) a specified period in every calendar year, or
- (b) a period which is to be—
  - (i) determined by the applicant in accordance with the direction, and

(ii) notified by him to the relevant authority in accordance with regulations under section 32(1)(d).

(3) In determining whether to any extent the exclusion or restriction under this section of access by virtue of section 2(1) during any period is necessary for the purposes of land management, the relevant authority shall have regard to—

(a) the existence of the right conferred by section 22,
(b) the extent to which the applicant has exercised or proposes to exercise that right, and
(c) the purposes for which he has exercised or proposes to exercise it.

(4) Where an application under this section relates to land which is not access land at the time when the application is made, the relevant authority shall not give a direction under this section unless they are satisfied that it is likely that the land will be access land during all or part of the period to which the application relates.

[1832]

25 Avoidance of risk of fire or of danger to the public

(1) The relevant authority may by direction exclude or restrict access by virtue of section 2(1) in relation to any land during a specified period if the authority are satisfied—

(a) that, by reason of any exceptional conditions of weather or any exceptional change in the condition of the land, the exclusion or restriction under this section of access to the land by virtue of section 2(1) to the extent provided by the direction is necessary for the purpose of fire prevention, or
(b) that, by reason of anything done, or proposed to be done, on the land or on adjacent land, the exclusion or restriction under this section of access to the land by virtue of section 2(1) to the extent provided by the direction is necessary for the purpose of avoiding danger to the public.

(2) The reference in subsection (1) to a specified period includes a reference to—

(a) a specified period in every calendar year, and
(b) a period which is to be—
 (i) determined by a specified person in accordance with the direction, and
 (ii) notified by him to the relevant authority in accordance with regulations under section 32(1)(d).

(3) The relevant authority may exercise their powers under subsection (1) on the application of any person interested in the land, or without any such application having been made.

(4) In determining on an application made by a person interested in the land whether the condition in subsection (1)(a) or (b) is satisfied, the relevant authority shall have regard to—

(a) the existence of the right conferred by section 22,
(b) the extent to which the applicant has exercised or proposes to exercise that right, and
(c) the purposes for which he has exercised or proposes to exercise it.

(5) Where an application under this section relates to land which is not access land at the time when the application is made, the relevant authority shall not give a direction under this section unless they are satisfied that it is likely that the land will be access land during all or part of the period to which the application relates.

[1833]

26 Nature conservation and heritage preservation

(1) The relevant authority may by direction exclude or restrict access by virtue of section 2(1) to any land during any period if they are satisfied that the exclusion or restriction of access by virtue of section 2(1) to the extent provided by the direction is necessary for either of the purposes specified in subsection (3).

(2) A direction under subsection (1) may be expressed to have effect—

(a) during a period specified in the direction,
(b) during a specified period in every calendar year, or
(c) during a period which is to be—
 (i) determined by a specified person in accordance with the direction, and
 (ii) notified by him to the relevant authority in accordance with regulations under section 32(1)(d), or
(d) indefinitely.

(3) The purposes referred to in subsection (1) are—

(a) the purpose of conserving flora, fauna or geological or physiographical features of the land in question;
(b) the purpose of preserving—
 (i) any scheduled monument as defined by section 1(11) of the Ancient Monuments and Archaeological Areas Act 1979, or
 (ii) any other structure, work, site, garden or area which is of historic, architectural, traditional, artistic or archaeological interest.

(4) In considering whether to give a direction under this section, the relevant authority shall have regard to any advice given to them by the relevant advisory body.

(5) Subsection (4) does not apply where the direction is given by the Countryside Council for Wales for the purpose specified in subsection (3)(a) or revokes a direction given by them for that purpose.

(6) In this section "the relevant advisory body"—

(a) in relation to a direction which is to be given for the purpose specified in subsection (3)(a) or which revokes a direction given for that purpose, means—

(i) in the case of land in England, [in respect of which Natural England is not the relevant authority, Natural England], and

(ii) in the case of land in Wales in respect of which the Countryside Council for Wales are not the relevant authority, the Countryside Council for Wales, and

(b) in relation to a direction which is to be given for the purpose specified in subsection (3)(b) or which revokes a direction given for that purpose, means—

(i) in the case of land in England, the Historic Buildings and Monuments Commission for England, and

(ii) in the case of land in Wales, the National Assembly for Wales.

[1834]

NOTES

Sub-s (6): words in square brackets substituted by the Natural Environment and Rural Communities Act 2006, s 105(1), Sch 11, Pt 1, para 157.

27 Directions by relevant authority: general

(1) Before giving a direction under section 24, 25 or 26 in relation to land in an area for which there is a local access forum so as to exclude or restrict access to the land—

(a) indefinitely, or

(b) during a period which exceeds, or may exceed, six months,

the relevant authority shall consult the local access forum.

(2) Any direction under section 24, 25 or 26 may be revoked or varied by a subsequent direction under that provision.

(3) Where a direction given under section 24, 25 or 26 in relation to any land by the relevant authority excludes or restricts access to the land—

(a) indefinitely,

(b) for part of every year or of each of six or more consecutive calendar years, or

(c) for a specified period of more than five years,

the authority shall review the direction not later than the fifth anniversary of the relevant date.

(4) In subsection (3) "the relevant date", in relation to a direction, means—

(a) the day on which the direction was given, or

(b) where it has already been reviewed, the day on which it was last reviewed.

(5) Before revoking or varying a direction under section 24 or 25 which was given on the application of a person interested in the land to which the direction relates ("the original applicant"), the relevant authority shall—

(a) where the original applicant still holds the interest in the land which he held when he applied for the direction and it is reasonably practicable to consult him, consult the original applicant, and

(b) where the original applicant does not hold that interest, consult any person who holds that interest and with whom consultation is reasonably practicable.

(6) Before revoking or varying a direction under section 26, the relevant authority shall consult the relevant advisory body as defined by section 26(6), unless the direction falls within section 26(5).

[1835]

28 Defence or national security

(1) The Secretary of State may by direction exclude or restrict access by virtue of section 2(1) to any land during any period if he is satisfied that the exclusion or restriction of such access to the extent provided by the direction is necessary for the purposes of defence or national security.

(2) A direction under subsection (1) may be expressed to have effect—

(a) during a period specified in the direction,

(b) during a specified period in every calendar year,

(c) during a period which is to be—

(i) determined in accordance with the direction by a person authorised by the Secretary of State, and

(ii) notified by that person to the relevant authority in accordance with regulations under section 32(1)(c), or

(d) indefinitely.

(3) Any direction given by the Secretary of State under this section may be revoked or varied by a subsequent direction.

(4) Where a direction given under this section in relation to any land excludes or restricts access to the land—

(a) indefinitely,

(b) for part of every year or of each of six or more consecutive calendar years, or

(c) for a specified period of more than five years,

the Secretary of State shall review the direction not later than the fifth anniversary of the relevant date.

(5) In subsection (4) "the relevant date", in relation to a direction, means—

(a) the day on which the direction was given, or

(b) where it has previously been reviewed, the day on which it was last reviewed.

(6) If in any calendar year the Secretary of State reviews a defence direction, he shall—

(a) prepare a report on all reviews of defence directions which he has undertaken during that year, and

(b) lay a copy of the report before each House of Parliament.

(7) In subsection (6) "defence direction" means a direction given under this section for the purposes of defence.

[1836]

29 Reference by relevant advisory body

(1) Subsections (2) and (3) apply where—

(a) the relevant advisory body has given advice under section 26(4) or on being consulted under section 27(6), but

(b) in any respect, the relevant authority decide not to act in accordance with that advice.

(2) The relevant advisory body may refer the decision—

(a) in the case of land in England, to the [Secretary of State], or

(b) in the case of land in Wales, to the National Assembly for Wales.

(3) On a reference under this section the [Secretary of State] or the National Assembly for Wales may, if he or it thinks fit—

(a) cancel any direction given by the relevant authority, or

(b) require the relevant authority to give such direction under section 26 as the [Secretary of State] or, as the case may be, the Assembly, think fit.

(4) Sections 7 and 8 (and Schedule 3) have effect in relation to a reference under this section as they have effect in relation to an appeal under section 6…

(5) In this section—

…

"the relevant advisory body" has the same meaning as in section 26, except that it does not include the National Assembly for Wales.

[1837]

NOTES

Sub-ss (2), (3): words in square brackets substituted by SI 2002/794, art 5(1), Sch 1, para 43.
Sub-s (4): words omitted repealed by SI 2002/794, art 5(2), Sch 2.
Sub-s (5): definition "the appropriate Minister" (omitted) repealed by SI 2002/794, art 5(2), Sch 2.

30 Appeal by person interested in land

(1) Subsections (2) and (3) apply where—

(a) a person interested in any land (in this section referred to as "the applicant")—

(i) has applied for a direction under section 24 or 25, or

(ii) has made representations on being consulted under section 27(5), but

(b) in any respect, the relevant authority decide not to act in accordance with the application or the representations.

(2) The relevant authority shall inform the applicant of their reasons for not acting in accordance with the application or representations.

(3) The applicant may appeal against the decision—

(a) in the case of land in England, to the [Secretary of State], or

(b) in the case of land in Wales, to the National Assembly for Wales.

(4) On appeal under this section the [Secretary of State] or the National Assembly for Wales may, if he or it thinks fit—

(a) cancel any direction given by the relevant authority, or
(b) require the relevant authority to give such direction under section 24 or 25 as the [Secretary of State] or, as the case may be, the Assembly, think fit.

(5) Sections 7 and 8 (and Schedule 3) have effect in relation to an appeal under this section as they have effect in relation to an appeal under section 6…

(6) …

[1838]

NOTES

Sub-ss (3), (4): words in square brackets substituted by SI 2002/794, art 5(1), Sch 1, para 44.
Sub-s (5): words omitted repealed by SI 2002/794, art 5(2), Sch 2.
Sub-s (6): repealed by SI 2002/794, art 5(2), Sch 2.

31 Exclusion or restriction of access in case of emergency

(1) Regulations may make provision enabling the relevant authority, where the authority are satisfied that an emergency has arisen which makes the exclusion or restriction of access by virtue of section 2(1) necessary for any of the purposes specified in section 24(1), 25(1) or 26(3), by direction to exclude or restrict such access in respect of any land for a period not exceeding three months.

(2) Regulations under this section may provide for any of the preceding provisions of this Chapter to apply in relation to a direction given under the regulations with such modifications as may be prescribed.

[1839]

32 Regulations relating to exclusion or restriction of access

(1) Regulations may make provision—
(a) as to the giving of notice under section 22(1),
(b) as to the steps to be taken under section 23(1) and (2),
(c) as to the procedure on any application to the relevant authority under section 24 or 25, including the period within which any such application must be made,
(d) as to the giving of notice for the purposes of section 24(2)(b)(ii), 25(2)(b)(ii), 26(2)(c)(ii) or 28(2)(c)(ii),
(e) prescribing the form of any notice or application referred to in paragraphs (a) to (d),
(f) restricting the cases in which a person who is interested in any land only as the holder of rights of common may make an application under section 24 or 25 in respect of the land,
(g) as to requirements to be met by relevant authorities or the Secretary of State in relation to consultation (whether or not required by the preceding provisions of this Chapter),
(h) as to the giving of directions by relevant authorities or the Secretary of State,
(i) as to notification by relevant authorities or the Secretary of State of decisions under this Chapter,
(j) as to steps to be taken by persons interested in land, by relevant authorities, by the bodies specified in section 26(6) or by the Secretary of State for informing the public about the exclusion or restriction under this Chapter of access by virtue of section 2(1), including the display of notices on or near the land to which the exclusion or restriction relates,
(k) as to the carrying out of reviews by relevant authorities under section 27(3) or by the Secretary of State under section 28(4),
(l) as to the period within which and manner in which appeals under section 30 are to be brought,
(m) as to the advertising of such an appeal, and
(n) as to the manner in which such appeals are to be considered.

(2) Regulations made under subsection (1)(k) may provide for any of the provisions of this Chapter relating to appeals to apply (with or without modifications) on a review under section 27.

[1840]

NOTES

Regulations: the Countryside Access (Appeals Procedures) (Wales) Regulations 2002, SI 2002/1794; the Countryside Access (Exclusion or Restriction of Access) (Wales) Regulations 2003, SI 2003/142; the Access to the Countryside (Exclusions and Restrictions) (England) Regulations 2003, SI 2003/2713; the Countryside Access (Means of Access, Appeals etc) (Wales) Regulations 2005, SI 2005/1270.

33 Guidance by countryside bodies to National Park authorities

(1) Subject to subsection (3), [Natural England] may issue guidance—
(a) to National Park authorities in England with respect to the discharge by National Park authorities of their functions under this Chapter, and

(b) to the Forestry Commissioners with respect to the discharge by the Forestry Commissioners of any functions conferred on them by virtue of section 21(6) in relation to land in England.

(2) Subject to subsection (3), the Countryside Council for Wales may issue guidance—

(a) to National Park authorities in Wales with respect to the discharge by National Park authorities of their functions under this Chapter, and

(b) to the Forestry Commissioners with respect to the discharge by the Forestry Commissioners of any functions conferred on them by virtue of section 21(6) in relation to land in Wales.

(3) [Natural England] or the Countryside Council for Wales may not issue any guidance under this section unless the guidance has been approved—

(a) in the case of [Natural England], by the Secretary of State, and

(b) in the case of the Countryside Council for Wales, by the National Assembly for Wales.

(4) Where [Natural England] or the Countryside Council for Wales issue any guidance under this section, they shall arrange for the guidance to be published in such manner as they consider appropriate.

(5) A National Park authority or the Forestry Commissioners shall have regard to any guidance issued to them under this section.

[1841]

NOTES

Sub-ss (1), (3), (4): words in square brackets substituted by the Natural Environment and Rural Communities Act 2006, s 105(1), Sch 11, Pt 1, para 158.

CHAPTER III
MEANS OF ACCESS

34 Interpretation of Chapter III

In this Chapter—

"access land" does not include any land in relation to which the application of section 2(1) has been excluded under any provision of Chapter II either indefinitely or for a specified period of which at least six months remain unexpired;

"means of access", in relation to land, means—

(a) any opening in a wall, fence or hedge bounding the land (or part of the land), with or without a gate, stile or other works for regulating passage through the opening,

(b) any stairs or steps for enabling persons to enter on the land (or part of the land), or

(c) any bridge, stepping stone or other works for crossing a watercourse, ditch or bog on the land or adjoining the boundary of the land.

[1842]

35 Agreements with respect to means of access

(1) Where, in respect of any access land, it appears to the access authority that—

(a) the opening-up, improvement or repair of any means of access to the land,

(b) the construction of any new means of access to the land,

(c) the maintenance of any means of access to the land, or

(d) the imposition of restrictions—

(i) on the destruction, removal, alteration or stopping-up of any means of access to the land, or

(ii) on the doing of any thing whereby the use of any such means of access to the land by the public would be impeded,

is necessary for giving the public reasonable access to that land in exercise of the right conferred by section 2(1), the access authority may enter into an agreement with the owner or occupier of the land as to the carrying out of the works or the imposition of the restrictions.

(2) An agreement under this section may provide—

(a) for the carrying out of works by the owner or occupier or by the access authority, and

(b) for the making of payments by the access authority—

(i) as a contribution towards, or for the purpose of defraying, costs incurred by the owner or occupier in carrying out any works for which the agreement provides, or

(ii) in consideration of the imposition of any restriction.

[1843]

36 Failure to comply with agreement

(1) If the owner or occupier of any access land fails to carry out within the required time any works which he is required by an agreement under section 35 to carry out, the access authority, after giving not less than twenty-one days' notice of their intention to do so, may take all necessary steps for carrying out those works.

(2) In subsection (1) "the required time" means the time specified in, or determined in accordance with, the agreement as that within which the works must be carried out or, if there is no such time, means a reasonable time.

(3) If the owner or occupier of any access land fails to observe any restriction which he is required by an agreement under section 35 to observe, the access authority may give him a notice requiring him within a specified period of not less than twenty-one days to carry out such works as may be specified in the notice, for the purpose of remedying the failure to observe the restriction.

(4) A notice under subsection (3) must contain particulars of the right of appeal conferred by section 38.

(5) If the person to whom a notice under subsection (3) is given fails to comply with the notice, the access authority may take all necessary steps for carrying out any works specified in the notice.

(6) Where the access authority carry out any works by virtue of subsection (1), the authority may recover the amount of any expenses reasonably incurred by them in carrying out the works, reduced by their contribution under the agreement, from the person by whom under the agreement the cost (apart from the authority's contribution) of carrying out the works would fall to be borne.

(7) Where the access authority carry out any works by virtue of subsection (5), the authority may recover the amount of any expenses reasonably incurred by them in carrying out the works from the person to whom the notice under subsection (3) was given.

[1844]

37 Provision of access by access authority in absence of agreement

(1) Where, in respect of any access land—

(a) it appears to the access authority that—

(i) the opening-up, improvement or repair of any means of access to the land,

(ii) the construction of any new means of access to the land, or

(iii) the maintenance of any means of access to the land,

is necessary for giving the public reasonable access to that land, or to other access land, in pursuance of the right conferred by section 2(1), and

(b) the access authority are satisfied that they are unable to conclude on reasonable terms an agreement under section 35 with the owner or occupier of the land for the carrying out of the works,

the access authority may, subject to subsection (3), give the owner or occupier a notice stating that, after the end of a specified period of not less than twenty-one days, the authority intend to take all necessary steps for carrying out the works specified in the notice for the opening-up, improvement, repair, construction or maintenance of the means of access.

(2) A notice under subsection (1) must contain particulars of the right of appeal conferred by section 38.

(3) Where a notice under subsection (1) is given to any person as the owner or occupier of any land, the access authority shall give a copy of the notice to every other owner or occupier of the land.

(4) An access authority exercising the power conferred by subsection (1) in relation to the provision of a means of access shall have regard to the requirements of efficient management of the land in deciding where the means of access is to be provided.

(5) If, at the end of the period specified in a notice under subsection (1), any of the works specified in the notice have not been carried out, the access authority may take all necessary steps for carrying out those works.

[1845]

38 Appeals relating to notices

(1) Where a notice under section 36(3) or 37(1) has been given to a person in respect of any land, he or any other owner or occupier of the land may appeal against the notice—

(a) in the case of land in England, to the Secretary of State, and

(b) in the case of land in Wales, to the National Assembly for Wales.

(2) An appeal against a notice under section 36(3) may be brought on any of the following grounds—

(a) that the notice requires the carrying out of any works which are not necessary for remedying a breach of the agreement,

(b) that any of the works have already been carried out, and

(c) that the period specified in the notice as that before the end of which the works must be carried out is too short.

(3) An appeal against a notice under section 37(1) may be brought on any of the following grounds—

(a) that the notice requires the carrying out of any works which are not necessary for giving the public reasonable access to the access land in question,

(b) in the case of works to provide a means of access, that the means of access should be provided elsewhere, or that a different means of access should be provided, and
(c) that any of the works have already been carried out.

(4) On an appeal under this section, the Secretary of State or the National Assembly for Wales may—
(a) confirm the notice with or without modifications, or
(b) cancel the notice.

(5) Sections 7 and 8 (and Schedule 3) have effect in relation to an appeal under this section as they have effect in relation to an appeal under section 6.

(6) Regulations may make provision as to—
(a) the period within which and manner in which appeals under this section are to be brought,
(b) the advertising of such an appeal, and
(c) the manner in which such appeals are to be considered.

(7) Where an appeal has been brought under this section against a notice under section 36(3) or 37(1), the access authority may not exercise their powers under section 36(5) or section 37(5) (as the case may be) pending the determination or withdrawal of the appeal.

[1846]

NOTES

Regulations: the Countryside Access (Appeals Procedures) (Wales) Regulations 2002, SI 2002/1794; the Access to the Countryside (Means of Access, Appeals) (England) Regulations 2004, SI 2004/3305; the Countryside Access (Means of Access, Appeals etc) (Wales) Regulations 2005, SI 2005/1270.

39 Order to remove obstruction

(1) Where at any time two or more access notices relating to a means of access have been given to any person within the preceding thirty-six months, a magistrates' court may, on the application of the access authority, order that person—
(a) within such time as may be specified in the order, to take such steps as may be so specified to remove any obstruction of that means of access, and
(b) not to obstruct that means of access at any time when the right conferred by section 2(1) is exercisable.

(2) If a person ("the person in default") fails to comply with an order under this section—
(a) he is liable on summary conviction to a fine not exceeding level 3 on the standard scale, and
(b) the access authority may remove any obstruction of the means of access and recover from the person in default the costs reasonably incurred by them in doing so.

(3) In this section "access notice" means a notice under section 36(3) or 37(1) in respect of which the period specified in the notice has expired, other than a notice in respect of which an appeal is pending or which has been cancelled on appeal.

[1847]

CHAPTER IV
GENERAL

40 Powers of entry for purposes of Part I

(1) A person who is authorised by the appropriate countryside body to do so may enter any land—
(a) for the purpose of surveying it in connection with the preparation of any map under this Part or the review of any map issued under this Part,
(b) for the purpose of determining whether any power conferred on the appropriate countryside body by Chapter II should be exercised in relation to the land,
(c) for the purpose of ascertaining whether members of the public are being permitted to exercise the right conferred by section 2(1),
(d) in connection with an appeal under any provision of this Part, or
(e) for the purpose of determining whether to apply to the Secretary of State or the National Assembly for Wales under section 58.

(2) A person who is authorised by a local highway authority to do so may enter any land—
(a) for the purpose of determining whether the local highway authority should enter into an agreement under section 35, give a notice under section 36(1) or (3) or section 37(1) or carry out works under section 36(1) or (5), section 37(5) or section 39(2)(b),
(b) for the purpose of ascertaining whether an offence under section 14 or 39 has been or is being committed, or
(c) for the purposes of erecting or maintaining notices under section 19(1).

(3) A person who is authorised by a National Park authority to do so may enter any land—

(a) for the purpose of enabling the authority to determine whether to exercise any power under Chapter II of this Act in relation to the land,
(b) for the purpose of determining whether members of the public are being permitted to exercise the right conferred by section 2(1),
(c) in connection with an appeal under any provision of this Part,
(d) for the purpose of determining whether the authority should enter into an agreement under section 35, give a notice under section 36(1) or (3) or section 37(1) or carry out works under section 36(1) or (5), section 37(5) or section 39(2)(b),
(e) for the purpose of ascertaining whether an offence under section 14 or 39 has been or is being committed, or
(f) for the purposes of erecting or maintaining notices under section 19(1).

(4) A person who is authorised by the Forestry Commissioners to do so may enter any land—
(a) for the purpose of determining whether any power conferred on the Forestry Commissioners by Chapter II should be exercised in relation to the land, or
(b) in connection with an appeal under any provision of this Part.

(5) A person acting in the exercise of a power conferred by this section may—
(a) use a vehicle to enter the land;
(b) take a constable with him if he reasonably believes he is likely to be obstructed;
(c) take with him equipment and materials needed for the purpose for which he is exercising the power of entry;
(d) take samples of the land and of anything on it.

(6) If in the exercise of a power conferred by this section a person enters land which is unoccupied or from which the occupier is temporarily absent, he must on his departure leave it as effectively secured against unauthorised entry as he found it.

(7) A person authorised under this section to enter upon any land—
(a) shall, if so required, produce evidence of his authority before entering, and
(b) shall produce such evidence if required to do so at any time while he remains on the land.

(8) A person shall not under this section demand admission as of right to any occupied land, other than access land, unless—
(a) at least twenty-four hours' notice of the intended entry has been given to the occupier, or
(b) it is not reasonably practicable to give such notice, or
(c) the entry is for the purpose specified in subsection (2)(b) and (3)(e).

(9) The rights conferred by this section are not exercisable in relation to a dwelling.

(10) A person who intentionally obstructs a person acting in the exercise of his powers under this section is guilty of an offence and liable on summary conviction to a fine not exceeding level 2 on the standard scale.

[1848]

41 Compensation relating to powers under s 40

(1) It is the duty of a body by which an authorisation may be given under section 40 to compensate any person who has sustained damage as a result of—
(a) the exercise of a power conferred by that section by a person authorised by that body to do so, or
(b) the failure of a person so authorised to perform the duty imposed on him by subsection (6) of that section,

except where the damage is attributable to the fault of the person who sustained it.

(2) Any dispute as to a person's entitlement to compensation under this section or as to its amount shall be referred to an arbitrator to be appointed, in default of agreement—
(a) as respects entry on land in England, by the Secretary of State, and
(b) as respects entry on land in Wales, by the National Assembly for Wales.

[1849]

42 References to public places in existing enactments

(1) This section applies to any enactment which—
(a) is contained in an Act passed before or in the same Session as this Act, and
(b) relates to things done, or omitted to be done, in public places or places to which the public have access.

(2) Regulations may provide that, in determining for the purposes of any specified enactment to which this section applies whether a place is a public place or a place to which the public have access, the right conferred by section 2(1), or access by virtue of that right, is to be disregarded, either generally or in prescribed cases.

[1850]

43 Crown application of Part I

(1) This Part binds the Crown.

(2) No contravention by the Crown of any provision of this Part shall make the Crown criminally liable; but the High Court may declare unlawful any act or omission of the Crown which constitutes such a contravention.

(3) The provisions of this Part apply to persons in the public service of the Crown as they apply to other persons.

[1851]

44 Orders and regulations under Part I

(1) Any power to make an order or regulations which is conferred by this Part on the Secretary of State or the National Assembly for Wales is exercisable by statutory instrument.

(2) Any power to make an order or regulations which is conferred by this Part on the Secretary of State or the National Assembly for Wales includes power—

(a) to make different provision for different cases, and

(b) to make such incidental, supplementary, consequential or transitional provision as the person making the order or regulations considers necessary or expedient.

(3) No order under section 3 or regulations under paragraph 3 of Schedule 2 shall be made by the Secretary of State unless a draft has been laid before, and approved by a resolution of, each House of Parliament.

(4) Any statutory instrument containing regulations made by the Secretary of State under any other provision of this Part shall be subject to annulment in pursuance of a resolution of either House of Parliament.

[1852]

45 Interpretation of Part I

(1) In this Part, unless a contrary intention appears—

"access authority" has the meaning given by section 1(2);

"access land" has the meaning given by section 1(1);

"the appropriate countryside body" has the meaning given by section 1(2);

"excepted land" has the meaning given by section 1(2);

"Inner London" means the area comprising the inner London boroughs, the City of London, the Inner Temple and the Middle Temple;

"interest", in relation to land, includes any estate in land and any right over land, whether the right is exercisable by virtue of the ownership of an estate or interest in land or by virtue of a licence or agreement, and in particular includes rights of common and sporting rights, and references to a person interested in land shall be construed accordingly;

"livestock" means cattle, sheep, goats, swine, horses or poultry, and for the purposes of this definition "cattle" means bulls, cows, oxen, heifers or calves, "horses" include asses and mules, and "poultry" means domestic fowls, turkeys, geese or ducks;

"local highway authority" has the same meaning as in the Highways Act 1980;

"local or private Act" includes an Act confirming a provisional order;

"mountain" has the meaning given by section 1(2);

"open country" has the meaning given by section 1(2);

"owner", in relation to any land, means, subject to subsection (2), any person, other than a mortgagee not in possession, who, whether in his own right or as trustee for another person, is entitled to receive the rack rent of the land, or, where the land is not let at a rack rent, would be so entitled if it were so let;

"prescribed" means prescribed by regulations;

"registered common land" has the meaning given by section 1(3);

"regulations" means regulations made by the Secretary of State (as respects England) or by the National Assembly for Wales (as respects Wales);

"rights of common" has the same meaning as in *the Commons Registration Act 1965* [the Commons Act 2006];

…

(2) In relation to any land which is subject to a farm business tenancy within the meaning of the Agricultural Tenancies Act 1995 or a tenancy to which the Agricultural Holdings Act 1986 applies, the definition of "owner" in subsection (1) does not apply where it is excluded by section 2(5) or 21(4) or by paragraph 7(4) of Schedule 2.

(3) For the purposes of this Part, the Broads are to be treated as a National Park and the Broads Authority as a National Park authority.

(4) In subsection (3) "the Broads" has the same meaning as in the Norfolk and Suffolk Broads Act 1988.

[1853]

NOTES

Sub-s (1): in definition "rights of common", words in italics substituted by subsequent words in square brackets by the Commons Act 2006, s 52, Sch 5, para 7(1), (4), as from a day to be appointed; definition ""telecommunications code" and "telecommunications code system"" (omitted) repealed by the Communications Act 2003, s 406(7), Sch 19(1).

46 Repeal of previous legislation, and amendments relating to Part I

(1) …

(2) No access agreement or access order under Part V of the National Parks and Access to the Countryside Act 1949 (access to open country) may be made after the commencement of this [subsection] in relation to land which is open country or registered common land for the purposes of this Part.

(3) Schedule 4 (which contains minor and consequential amendments relating to access to the countryside) has effect.

[1854]

NOTES

1 April 2001 (sub-s (3) (for certain purposes, in relation to England)); 1 May 2001 (sub-s (3) (for certain purposes, in relation to Wales)); 21 June 2004 (sub-s (1)(a), in relation to Wales); 19 September 2004 (sub-s (3), in relation to England for remaining purposes); 28 May 2005 (sub-s (3), in relation to Wales for remaining purposes); to be appointed (otherwise).

Sub-s (1): repealed by the Commons Act 2006, s 53, Sch 6, Pt 1.

Sub-s (2): word in square brackets substituted by the Commons Act 2006, s 52, Sch 5, para 7(1), (5).

PART II
PUBLIC RIGHTS OF WAY AND ROAD TRAFFIC

Public rights of way and definitive maps and statements

47 Redesignation of roads used as public paths

(1) In the Wildlife and Countryside Act 1981 (in this Act referred to as "the 1981 Act"), section 54 (duty to reclassify roads used as public paths) shall cease to have effect.

(2) Every way which, immediately before the commencement of this section, is shown in any definitive map and statement as a road used as a public path shall be treated instead as shown as a restricted byway; and the expression "road used as a public path" shall not be used in any definitive map and statement to describe any way.

[1855]

NOTES

Commencement: 2 May 2006 (in relation to England, subject to savings in SI 2006/1172, art 3); 11 May 2006 (in relation to Wales, subject to savings in SI 2006/1279, art 3).

48 Restricted byway rights

(1) Subject to subsections (2) and (3), the public shall have restricted byway rights over any way which, immediately before the commencement of section 47, is shown in a definitive map and statement as a road used as a public path.

(2) Subsection (1) has effect subject to the operation of any enactment or instrument (whether coming into operation before or after the commencement of section 47), and to the effect of any event otherwise within section 53(3)(a) of the 1981 Act, whereby a highway—

(a) is authorised to be stopped up, diverted, widened or extended, or
(b) becomes a public path;

and subsection (1) applies accordingly to any way as so diverted, widened or extended.

(3) Subsection (1) does not apply to any way, or part of a way, over which immediately before the commencement of section 47 there was no public right of way.

(4) In this Part—

"restricted byway rights" means—

(a) a right of way on foot,
(b) a right of way on horseback or leading a horse, and
(c) a right of way for vehicles other than mechanically propelled vehicles; and

"restricted byway" means a highway over which the public have restricted byway rights, with or without a right to drive animals of any description along the highway, but no other rights of way.

(5) A highway at the side of a river, canal or other inland navigation is not excluded from the definition of "restricted byway" in subsection (4) merely because the public have a right to use the highway for purposes of navigation, if the highway would fall within that definition if the public had no such right over it.

(6) Subsection (1) is without prejudice to any question whether the public have over any way, in addition to restricted byway rights, a right of way for mechanically propelled vehicles or any other right.

(7) In subsections (4) and (6) "mechanically propelled vehicle" does not include a vehicle falling within paragraph (c) of section 189(1) of the Road Traffic Act 1988.

(8) Every surveying authority shall take such steps as they consider expedient for bringing to the attention of the public the effect of section 47(2) and this section.

(9) The powers conferred by section 103(5) must be so exercised as to secure that nothing in section 47 or this section affects the operation of section 53 or 54 of, or Schedule 14 or 15 to, the 1981 Act in relation to—

- (a) a relevant order made before the commencement of section 47, or
- (b) an application made before that commencement for a relevant order.

(10) In subsection (9) "relevant order" means an order which relates to a way shown in a definitive map and statement as a road used as a public path and which—

- (a) is made under section 53 of the 1981 Act and contains modifications relating to that way by virtue of subsection (3)(c)(ii) of that section, or
- (b) is made under section 54 of the 1981 Act.

(11) Where—

- (a) by virtue of an order under subsection (3) of section 103 ("the commencement order") containing such provision as is mentioned in subsection (5) of that section, an order under Part III of the 1981 Act ("the Part III order") takes effect, after the commencement of section 47, in relation to any way which, immediately before that commencement, was shown in a definitive map and statement as a road used as a public path,
- (b) the commencement order does not prevent subsection (1) from having effect on that commencement in relation to that way, and
- (c) if the Part III order had taken effect before that commencement, that way would not have fallen within subsection (1),

all rights over that way which exist only by virtue of subsection (1) shall be extinguished when the Part III order takes effect.

[1856]

NOTES

Commencement: 2 May 2006 (in relation to England, subject to savings in SI 2006/1172, art 3); 11 May 2006 (in relation to Wales, subject to savings in SI 2006/1279, art 3).

49 Provisions supplementary to ss 47 and 48

(1) Every way over which the public have restricted byway rights by virtue of subsection (1) of section 48 (whether or not they also have a right of way for mechanically propelled vehicles or any other right) shall, as from the commencement of that section, be a highway maintainable at the public expense.

(2) As from the commencement of that section, any liability, under a special enactment (within the meaning of the Highways Act 1980) or by reason of tenure, enclosure or prescription, to maintain, otherwise than as a highway maintainable at the public expense, a restricted byway to which subsection (1) applies is extinguished.

(3) Every way which, in pursuance of—

- (a) paragraph 9 of Part III of Schedule 3 to the Countryside Act 1968, or
- (b) any order made under section 54(1) of the 1981 Act before the coming into force of section 47,

is shown in any definitive map and statement as a byway open to all traffic, a bridleway or a footpath, shall continue to be maintainable at the public expense.

(4) Nothing in subsections (1) and (3) or in section 48(1) obliges a highway authority to provide on any way a metalled carriage-way or a carriage-way which is by any other means provided with a surface suitable for cycles or other vehicles.

(5) Nothing in section 48, or in section 53 of the 1981 Act, limits the operation of orders under the Road Traffic Regulation Act 1984 or the operation of any byelaws.

(6) Section 67 of the 1981 Act (application to the Crown) has effect as if this section and sections 47, 48 and 50 were contained in Part III of that Act.

[1857]

NOTES
Commencement: 2 May 2006 (in relation to England); 11 May 2006 (in relation to Wales).

50 Private rights over restricted byways

(1) Restricted byway rights over any way by virtue of subsection (1) of section 48 are subject to any condition or limitation to which public rights of way over that way were subject immediately before the commencement of that section.

(2) Any owner or lessee of premises adjoining or adjacent to a relevant highway shall, so far as is necessary for the reasonable enjoyment and occupation of the premises, have a right of way for vehicular and all other kinds of traffic over the relevant highway.

(3) In subsection (2), in its application to the owner of any premises, "relevant highway" means so much of any highway maintainable at the public expense by virtue of section 49(1) as was, immediately before it became so maintainable, owned by the person who then owned the premises.

(4) In subsection (2), in its application to the lessee of any premises, "relevant highway" means so much of any highway maintainable at the public expense by virtue of section 49(1) as was, immediately before it became so maintainable, included in the lease on which the premises are held.

(5) In this section—

"lease" and "lessee" have the same meaning as in the 1980 Act;

"owner", in relation to any premises, means a person, other than a mortgagee not in possession, who is for the time being entitled to dispose of the fee simple of the premises, whether in possession or in reversion, and "owned" shall be construed accordingly; and

"premises" has the same meaning as in the 1980 Act.

[1858]

NOTES
Commencement: 2 May 2006 (in relation to England); 11 May 2006 (in relation to Wales).

51 (*Introduces Sch 5 to this Act.*)

52 Restricted byways: power to amend existing legislation

(1) The Secretary of State may by regulations—

(a) provide for any relevant provision which relates—

(i) to highways or highways of a particular description,

(ii) to things done on or in connection with highways or highways of a particular description, or

(iii) to the creation, stopping up or diversion of highways or highways of a particular description,

not to apply, or to apply with or without modification, in relation to restricted byways or to ways shown in a definitive map and statement as restricted byways, and

(b) make in any relevant provision such amendments, repeals or revocations as appear to him appropriate in consequence of the coming into force of sections 47 to 50 or provision made by virtue of paragraph (a) or subsection (6)(a).

(2) In this section—

"relevant provision" means a provision contained—

(a) in an Act passed before or in the same Session as this Act, or

(b) in any subordinate legislation made before the passing of this Act;

"relevant Welsh provision" means a provision contained—

(a) in a local or private Act passed before or in the same Session as this Act and relating only to areas in Wales, or

(b) in any subordinate legislation which was made before the passing of this Act and which the National Assembly for Wales has power to amend or revoke as respects Wales.

(3) In exercising the power to make regulations under subsection (1), the Secretary of State—

(a) may not make provision which has effect in relation to Wales unless he has consulted the National Assembly for Wales, and

(b) may not without the consent of the National Assembly for Wales make any provision which (otherwise than merely by virtue of the amendment or repeal of a provision contained in an Act) amends or revokes subordinate legislation made by the Assembly.

(4) The National Assembly for Wales may submit to the Secretary of State proposals for the exercise by the Secretary of State of the power conferred by subsection (1).

(5) The powers conferred by subsection (1) may be exercised in relation to a relevant provision even though the provision is amended or inserted by this Act.

(6) As respects Wales, the National Assembly for Wales may by regulations—

(a) provide for any relevant Welsh provision which relates—
(i) to highways or highways of a particular description,
(ii) to things done on or in connection with highways or highways of a particular description, or
(iii) to the creation, stopping up or diversion of highways or highways of a particular description,

not to apply, or to apply with or without modification, in relation to restricted byways or to ways shown in a definitive map and statement as restricted byways, and

(b) make in any relevant Welsh provision such amendments, repeals or revocations as appear to the Assembly appropriate in consequence of the coming into force of sections 47 to 50 or provision made by virtue of subsection (1)(a) or paragraph (a).

(7) Regulations under this section shall be made by statutory instrument, but no such regulations shall be made by the Secretary of State unless a draft of the instrument containing them has been laid before, and approved by a resolution of, each House of Parliament.

(8) Where the Secretary of State lays before Parliament the draft of an instrument containing regulations under subsection (1) in respect of which consultation with the National Assembly for Wales is required by subsection (3)(a), he shall also lay before each House of Parliament a document giving details of the consultation and setting out any representations received from the Assembly.

[1859]

NOTES

Regulations: the Restricted Byways (Application and Consequential Amendment of Provisions) Regulations 2006, SI 2006/1177.

53 Extinguishment of unrecorded rights of way

(1) Subsection (2) applies to a highway if—

(a) it was on 1st January 1949 a footpath or a bridleway, is on the cut-off date (in either case) a footpath or a bridleway, and between those dates has not been a highway of any other description,
(b) it is not on the cut-off date shown in a definitive map and statement as a highway of any description, and
(c) it is not on the cut-off date an excepted highway, as defined by section 54(1).

(2) All public rights of way over a highway to which this subsection applies shall be extinguished immediately after the cut-off date.

(3) Where a public right of way created before 1949—

(a) falls within subsection (4) on the cut-off date, and
(b) is not on that date an excepted right of way, as defined by section 54(5),

that right of way shall be extinguished immediately after the cut-off date.

(4) A public right of way falls within this subsection if it is—

(a) a public right of way on horseback, leading a horse or for vehicles over a bridleway, restricted byway or byway open to all traffic which is shown in a definitive map and statement as a footpath;
(b) a right for the public to drive animals of any description along a bridleway, restricted byway or byway open to all traffic which is shown in a definitive map and statement as a footpath;
(c) a public right of way for vehicles over a restricted byway or byway open to all traffic which is shown in a definitive map and statement as a bridleway; or
(d) a public right of way for mechanically propelled vehicles over a byway open to all traffic which is shown in a definitive map and statement as a restricted byway.

(5) Where by virtue of subsection (3) a highway ceases to be a bridleway, the right of way created over it by section 30 of the Countryside Act 1968 (riding of pedal cycles on bridleways) is also extinguished.

(6) In determining—

(a) for the purposes of subsection (1) whether any part of a highway was on 1st January 1949 a footpath or bridleway, or
(b) for the purposes of subsection (3) whether a public right of way over any part of a highway was created before 1st January 1949,

any diversion, widening or extension of the highway on or after that date (and not later than the cut-off date) is to be treated as having occurred before 1st January 1949.

(7) Where a way shown on the cut-off date in a definitive map and statement has at any time been diverted, widened or extended, it is to be treated for the purposes of subsections (1) to (5) as shown as so diverted, widened or extended, whether or not it is so shown.

(8) In this section—

"cut-off date" has the meaning given in section 56, and
"mechanically propelled vehicle" does not include a vehicle falling within paragraph (c) of section 189(1) of the Road Traffic Act 1988.

[1860]

NOTES

Commencement: to be appointed.

54 Excepted highways and rights of way

(1) A footpath or bridleway is an excepted highway for the purposes of section 53(1) if—

(a) it is a footpath or bridleway which satisfies either of the conditions in subsections (2) and (3),

(b) it is, or is part of, a footpath or bridleway any part of which is in an area which, immediately before 1st April 1965, formed part of the administrative county of London,

(c) it is a footpath or bridleway—

(i) at the side of (whether or not contiguous with) a carriageway constituting or comprised in another highway, or

(ii) between two carriageways comprised in the same highway (whether or not the footpath or bridleway is contiguous with either carriageway),

(d) it is a footpath or bridleway of such other description as may be specified in regulations made (as respects England) by the Secretary of State or (as respects Wales) by the National Assembly for Wales, or

(e) it is a footpath or bridleway so specified.

(2) A footpath or bridleway ("the relevant highway") satisfies the first condition if—

(a) it became a footpath or bridleway on or after 1st January 1949 by the diversion, widening or extension of a footpath or, as the case may be, of a bridleway by virtue of an event within section 53(3)(a) of the 1981 Act,

(b) it became a footpath on or after 1st January 1949 by the stopping up of a bridleway,

(c) it was on 1st January 1949 a footpath and is on the cut-off date a bridleway,

(d) it is so much of a footpath or bridleway as on or after 1st January 1949 has been stopped up as respects part only of its width, or

(e) it is so much of a footpath or bridleway as passes over a bridge or through a tunnel,

and it communicates with a retained highway, either directly or by means of one or more footpaths or bridleways each of which forms part of the same highway as the relevant highway and each of which either falls within any of paragraphs (a) to (e) or satisfies the condition in subsection (3).

(3) A footpath or bridleway satisfies the second condition if—

(a) it extends from a footpath or bridleway ("the relevant highway") which—

(i) falls within any of paragraphs (a) to (e) of subsection (2), or

(ii) is an excepted highway by virtue of subsection (1)(c),

to, but not beyond, a retained highway, and

(b) it forms part of the same highway as the relevant highway.

(4) A retained highway for the purposes of subsections (2) and (3) is any highway over which, otherwise than by virtue of subsection (1)(a), section 53(2) does not extinguish rights of way.

(5) A public right of way is an excepted right of way for the purposes of section 53(3) if—

(a) it subsists over land over which there subsists on the cut-off date any public right of way created on or after 1st January 1949 otherwise than by virtue of section 30 of the Countryside Act 1968 (riding of pedal cycles on bridleways),

(b) it subsists over the whole or part of a way any part of which is in an area which, immediately before 1st April 1965, formed part of the administrative county of London,

(c) it is a public right of way of such other description as may be specified in regulations made (as respects England) by the Secretary of State or (as respects Wales) by the National Assembly for Wales, or

(d) it subsists over land so specified.

(6) Regulations under subsection (1)(d) or (e) or (5)(c) or (d) shall be made by statutory instrument, and a statutory instrument containing such regulations made by the Secretary of State shall be subject to annulment in pursuance of a resolution of either House of Parliament.

[1861]

NOTES

Commencement: to be appointed.

55 Bridleway rights over ways shown as bridleways

(1) Subject to subsections (2) and (3), the public shall, as from the day after the cut-off date, have a right of way on horseback or leading a horse over any way which—

(a) was immediately before 1st January 1949 either a footpath or a bridleway, and

(b) is, throughout the period beginning with the commencement of this section and ending with the cut-off date,

a footpath which is shown in a definitive map and statement as a bridleway.

(2) Subsection (1) has effect subject to the operation of any enactment or instrument (whether coming into operation before or after the cut-off date), and to the effect of any event otherwise within section 53(3)(a) of the 1981 Act, whereby a highway is authorised to be stopped up, diverted, widened or extended; and subsection (1) applies accordingly to any way as so diverted, widened or extended.

(3) Subsection (1) does not apply in relation to any way which is, or is part of, a footpath any part of which is in an area which, immediately before 1st April 1965, formed part of the administrative county of London.

(4) Any right of way over a way by virtue of subsection (1) is subject to any condition or limitation to which the public right of way on foot over that way was subject on the cut-off date.

(5) Where—

(a) by virtue of regulations under section 56(2) an order under Part III of the 1981 Act takes effect after the cut-off date in relation to any footpath which, at the cut-off date was shown in a definitive map and statement as a bridleway,

(b) the regulations do not prevent subsection (1) from having effect after the cut-off date in relation to that footpath, and

(c) if the order had taken effect before that date, that footpath would not have fallen within subsection (1),

all rights over that way which exist only by virtue of subsection (1) shall be extinguished when the order takes effect.

(6) In this section "cut-off date" has the meaning given in section 56.

[1862]

NOTES

Commencement: to be appointed.

56 Cut-off date for extinguishment etc

(1) The cut-off date for the purposes of sections 53 and 55 is, subject to regulations under subsection (2), 1st January 2026.

(2) The Secretary of State (as respects England) or the National Assembly for Wales (as respects Wales) may make regulations—

(a) substituting as the cut-off date for the purposes of those sections a date later than the date specified in subsection (1) or for the time being substituted under this paragraph;

(b) containing such transitional provisions or savings as appear to the Secretary of State or the National Assembly for Wales (as the case may be) to be necessary or expedient in connection with the operation of those sections, including in particular their operation in relation to any way as respects which—

(i) on the cut-off date an application for an order under section 53(2) of the 1981 Act is pending,

(ii) on that date an order under Part III of that Act has been made but not confirmed, or

(iii) after that date such an order or any provision of such an order is to any extent quashed.

(3) Regulations under subsection (2)(a)—

(a) may specify different dates for different areas; but

(b) may not specify a date later than 1st January 2031, except as respects an area within subsection (4).

(4) An area is within this subsection if it is in—

(a) the Isles of Scilly, or

(b) an area which, at any time before the repeal by section 73 of the 1981 Act of sections 27 to 34 of the National Parks and Access to the Countryside Act 1949—

(i) was excluded from the operation of those sections by virtue of any provision of the 1949 Act, or

(ii) would have been so excluded but for a resolution having effect under section 35(2) of that Act.

(5) Where by virtue of regulations under subsection (2) there are different cut-off dates for areas into which different parts of any highway extend, the cut-off date in relation to that highway is the later or latest of those dates.

(6) Regulations under this section shall be made by statutory instrument, and a statutory instrument containing such regulations made by the Secretary of State shall be subject to annulment in pursuance of a resolution of either House of Parliament.

[1863]

NOTES

Commencement: to be appointed.

Creation, stopping up and diversion of highways

57 Creation, stopping up and diversion of highways

The Highways Act 1980 (in this Act referred to as "the 1980 Act") has effect subject to the amendments in Part I of Schedule 6 (which relate to the creation, stopping up and diversion of highways); and Part II of that Schedule (which contains consequential amendments of other Acts) has effect.

[1864]

NOTES

Commencement: 30 January 2001 (in relation to England, for certain purposes); 1 May 2001 (in relation to Wales, for certain purposes); 12 February 2003 (in relation to England, for certain purposes); 31 May 2005 (in relation to Wales, for certain purposes); 15 July 2005 (in relation to Wales, for certain purposes); 27 September 2005 (in relation to England, for certain purposes); 21 November 2005 (in relation to Wales, for certain purposes); 11 May 2006 (in relation to Wales, for certain purposes); 6 December 2006 (in relation to Wales, for certain purposes); 21 May 2007 (in relation to England, for certain purposes); 1 October 2007 (in relation to England, for certain purposes); to be appointed (otherwise).

58 Application for path creation order for purposes of Part I

[(1) An application for the making of a public path creation order under section 26(2) of the 1980 Act may be made—

(a) by Natural England to the Secretary of State, or

(b) for the purpose of enabling the public to obtain access to any access land (within the meaning of Part 1) or of facilitating such access, by the Countryside Council for Wales to the National Assembly for Wales.]

(2) Before making a request under subsection (1), the body making the request shall have regard to any rights of way improvement plan prepared by any local highway authority whose area includes land over which the proposed footpath or bridleway would be created.

[1865]

NOTES

Sub-s (1): substituted by the Natural Environment and Rural Communities Act 2006, s 105(1), Sch 11, Pt 1, para 159.

59 Effect of Part I on powers to stop up or divert highways

(1) This section applies to any power to stop up or divert a highway of any description or to make or confirm an order authorising the stopping up or diversion of a highway of any description; and in the following provisions of this section—

(a) "the relevant authority" means the person exercising the power, and

(b) "the existing highway" means the highway to be stopped up or diverted.

(2) Where the relevant authority is required (expressly or by implication) to consider—

(a) whether the existing highway is unnecessary, or is needed for public use,

(b) whether an alternative highway should be provided, or

(c) whether any public right of way should be reserved,

the relevant authority, in considering that question, is not to regard the fact that any land is access land in respect of which the right conferred by section 2(1) is exercisable as reducing the need for the existing highway, for the provision of an alternative highway or for the reservation of a public right of way.

(3) Where—

(a) the existing highway is situated on, or in the vicinity of, any access land, and

(b) the relevant authority is required (expressly or by implication) to consider the extent (if any) to which the existing highway would, apart from the exercise of the power, be likely to be used by the public,

the relevant authority, in considering that question, is to have regard, in particular, to the extent to which the highway would be likely to be used by the public at any time when the right conferred by section 2(1) is not exercisable in relation to the access land.

(4) In this section "access land" has the same meaning as in Part I.

[1866]

Rights of way improvement plans

60 Rights of way improvement plans

(1) Every local highway authority other than an inner London authority shall, within five years after the commencement of this section, prepare and publish a plan, to be known as a rights of way improvement plan, containing—

(a) the authority's assessment of the matters specified in subsection (2),

(b) a statement of the action they propose to take for the management of local rights of way, and for securing an improved network of local rights of way, with particular regard to the matters dealt with in the assessment, and

(c) such other material as the Secretary of State (as respects England) or the National Assembly for Wales (as respects Wales) may direct.

(2) The matters referred to in subsection (1)(a) are—

(a) the extent to which local rights of way meet the present and likely future needs of the public,

(b) the opportunities provided by local rights of way (and in particular by those within paragraph (a) of the definition in subsection (5)) for exercise and other forms of open-air recreation and the enjoyment of the authority's area,

(c) the accessibility of local rights of way to blind or partially sighted persons and others with mobility problems, and

(d) such other matters relating to local rights of way as the Secretary of State (as respects England) or the National Assembly for Wales (as respects Wales) may direct.

(3) An authority by whom a rights of way improvement plan is published shall, not more than ten years after first publishing it and subsequently at intervals of not more than ten years—

(a) make a new assessment of the matters specified in subsection (2), and

(b) review the plan and decide whether to amend it.

(4) On such a review the authority shall—

(a) if they decide to amend the plan, publish it as amended, and

(b) if they decide to make no amendments to it, publish a report of their decision and of their reasons for it.

(5) In this section—

"cycle track"—

(a) means a way over which the public have the following, but no other, rights of way, that is to say, a right of way on pedal cycles (other than pedal cycles which are motor vehicles within the meaning of the Road Traffic Act 1988) with or without a right of way on foot; but

(b) does not include a way in or by the side of a highway consisting of or comprising a made-up carriageway (within the meaning of the 1980 Act);

"inner London authority" means Transport for London, the council of an inner London borough or the Common Council of the City of London;

"local highway authority" has the same meaning as in the 1980 Act;

"local rights of way" in relation to a local highway authority, means—

(a) the footpaths, cycle tracks, bridleways and restricted byways within the authority's area, and

(b) the ways within the authority's area which are shown in a definitive map and statement as restricted byways or byways open to all traffic.

(6) In subsection (5) the definition of "local rights of way" has effect until the commencement of section 47 with the substitution for the references to restricted byways and to ways shown in a definitive map and statement as restricted byways of a reference to ways shown in a definitive map and statement as roads used as public paths.

[1867]

NOTES

Disapplication: this section is disapplied in relation to England, in so far as it relates to local highway authorities which are excellent authorities, by the Local Authorities' Plans and Strategies (Disapplication) (England) Order 2005, SI 2005/157, art 6.

61 Rights of way improvement plans: supplemental

(1) Before preparing or reviewing a rights of way improvement plan, and in particular in making any assessment under section 60(1)(a) or (3)(a), a local highway authority shall consult—

(a) each local highway authority whose area adjoins their area;

(b) each district council, and each parish or community council, whose area is within their area;

(c) the National Park authority for a National Park any part of which is within their area;

(d) where any part of the Broads is within their area, the Broads Authority;

(e) any local access forum established for their area or any part of it;

(f) [Natural England] or the Countryside Council for Wales (as appropriate);
(g) such persons as the Secretary of State (as respects England) or the National Assembly for Wales (as respects Wales) may by regulations prescribe in relation to the local highway authority's area; and
(h) such other persons as the local highway authority may consider appropriate.

(2) In preparing or amending a rights of way improvement plan, a local highway authority shall—

(a) publish a draft of the plan or of the plan as amended,
(b) publish, in two or more local newspapers circulating in their area, notice of how a copy of the draft can be inspected or obtained and how representations on it can be made to them, and
(c) consider any representations made in accordance with the notice.

(3) As regards their rights of way improvement plan, any draft plan on which representations may be made and any report under section 60(4)(b), a local highway authority shall—

(a) keep a copy available for inspection free of charge at all reasonable times at their principal offices, and
(b) supply a copy to any person who requests one, either free of charge or on payment of a reasonable charge determined by the authority.

(4) Local highway authorities shall, in carrying out their functions under section 60 and this section, have regard to such guidance as may from time to time be given to them by the Secretary of State (as respects England) or the National Assembly for Wales (as respects Wales).

(5) A local highway authority may make arrangements with—

(a) any district council whose area is within their area, or
(b) the National Park authority for a National Park any part of which is within their area,

for the functions of the local highway authority under section 60 and this section so far as relating to the area of that council or to the part of the Park within the local highway authority's area, to be discharged jointly by the local highway authority and by that council or National Park authority.

(6) Regulations under subsection (1)(g) shall be made by statutory instrument, and a statutory instrument containing such regulations made by the Secretary of State shall be subject to annulment in pursuance of a resolution of either House of Parliament.

(7) In this section—

"local highway authority" has the same meaning as in the 1980 Act;
"the Broads" has the same meaning as in the Norfolk and Suffolk Broads Act 1988.

[1868]

NOTES

Sub-s (1): words in square brackets in para (f) substituted by the Natural Environment and Rural Communities Act 2006, s 105(1), Sch 11, Pt 1, para 160; for transitional provisions see SI 2006/2541, art 3, Schedule, para 1.

62 Application of ss 60 and 61 to inner London

(1) The council of an inner London borough or the Common Council of the City of London may by resolution adopt sections 60 and 61 as respects their area or any part of it which is specified in the resolution.

(2) On the passing by any authority of a resolution under subsection (1), sections 60 and 61 shall, as respects their area or the part of it specified in the resolution, apply in relation to that authority—

(a) as they apply in relation to a local highway authority other than an inner London authority, but
(b) with the substitution for the reference in subsection (1) of section 60 to the commencement of that section of a reference to the date on which the resolution comes into operation.

[1869]

63–65 *(S 63 inserts the Highways Act 1980, ss 130A–130D, and amends s 317 of that Act; s 64 inserts s 137ZA of the 1980 Act, except in relation to any offence under s 137 of that Act committed before 30 January 2001; s 65 amends s 154 of the 1980 Act.)*

Miscellaneous

66–70 *(S 66 amends the Road Traffic Regulation Act 1984, s 22 and inserts s 22A thereof; s 67 introduces Sch 7 to this Act; s 68 repealed by the Commons Act 2006, ss 51, 53, Sch 6, Pt 5; s 69 inserts the Highways Act 1980, s 147ZA, and amends ss 146, 147, 344; s 70 amends ss 66, 134, 300 of the 1980 Act and the Road Traffic act 1988, s 21.)*

71 Reports on functions relating to rights of way

(1) The Secretary of State (as respects England) or the National Assembly for Wales (as respects Wales) may make regulations requiring local highway authorities of a description specified in the regulations to publish reports on the performance of any of their functions so far as relating to local rights of way (whether or not those functions are conferred on them as highway authorities).

(2) Subsection (1) is without prejudice to section 230 of the Local Government Act 1972 (reports and returns).

(3) Regulations under subsection (1) may prescribe the information to be given in such reports and how and when reports are to be published.

(4) Regulations under subsection (1) shall be made by statutory instrument, and a statutory instrument containing such regulations made by the Secretary of State shall be subject to annulment in pursuance of a resolution of either House of Parliament.

(5) In this section—

"local highway authority" has the same meaning as in the 1980 Act, except that it does not include Transport for London; and

"local rights of way" has the same meaning as in section 60.

[1870]

NOTES

Commencement: to be appointed.

72 Interpretation of Part II

(1) In this Part, unless a contrary intention appears—

(a) "restricted byway" and "restricted byway rights" have the meaning given by section 48(4);

(b) expressions which are defined for the purposes of Part III of the 1981 Act by section 66(1) of that Act have the same meaning as in that Part.

(2) In this Part any reference to a highway includes a reference to part of a highway.

[1871]

73–93 (*(Pts III, IV) outside the scope of this work.*)

PART V
MISCELLANEOUS AND SUPPLEMENTARY

94–98 (*Outside the scope of this work.*)

Supplementary

99 Wales

(1) In Schedule 1 to the National Assembly for Wales (Transfer of Functions) Order 1999—

(a) the reference to the 1980 Act is to be treated as referring to that Act as amended by this Act, and

(b) the reference to the 1981 Act is to be treated as referring to that Act as amended by this Act.

(2) In that Schedule, at the end of the list of Public General Acts there is inserted—

"Countryside and Rights of Way Act 2000 (c 37) Schedule 11.".

(3) Subsection (1), and the amendment made by subsection (2), do not affect the power to make further Orders varying or omitting the references mentioned in subsection (1) or the provision inserted by subsection (2).

[1872]

100 Isles of Scilly

(1) Subject to the provisions of any order under this section, the following provisions of this Act do not apply in relation to the Isles of Scilly—

(a) Part I; and

(b) sections 58 to 61 and 71.

(2) The Secretary of State may by order made by statutory instrument provide for the application of any of the provisions mentioned in subsection (1) in relation to the Isles of Scilly, subject to such modifications as may be specified in the order.

(3) Part IV applies in relation to the Isles of Scilly subject to such modifications as may be specified in an order made by the Secretary of State by statutory instrument.

(4) Before making an order under subsection (2) or (3), the Secretary of State shall consult the Council of the Isles of Scilly.

(5) In section 344 of the 1980 Act (application to the Isles of Scilly)—

(a) in subsection (2)(a) for "121" there is substituted "121E, 130A to 130D", and

(b) before "146" there is inserted "137ZA(4)".

[1873]

101–103 (*Outside the scope of this work.*)

104 Interpretation, short title and extent

(1) (*Outside the scope of this work.*)

(2) Any reference in this Act, or in any enactment amended by this Act, to the commencement of any provision of this Act is, in relation to any area, a reference to the commencement of that provision in relation to that area.

(3) This Act may be cited as the Countryside and Rights of Way Act 2000.

(4) Subject to the following provisions of this section, this Act extends to England and Wales only.

(5)–(7) (*Outside the scope of this work.*)

[1874]

SCHEDULE 1
EXCEPTED LAND FOR PURPOSES OF PART I

Section 1(2)

PART I
EXCEPTED LAND

1. Land on which the soil is being, or has at any time within the previous twelve months been, disturbed by any ploughing or drilling undertaken for the purposes of planting or sowing crops or trees.

2. Land covered by buildings or the curtilage of such land.

3. Land within 20 metres of a dwelling.

4. Land used as a park or garden.

5. Land used for the getting of minerals by surface working (including quarrying).

6. Land used for the purposes of a railway (including a light railway) or tramway.

7. Land used for the purposes of a golf course, racecourse or aerodrome.

8. Land which does not fall within any of the preceding paragraphs and is covered by works used for the purposes of a statutory undertaking or [an electronic communications code network], or the curtilage of any such land.

9. Land as respects which development which will result in the land becoming land falling within any of paragraphs 2 to 8 is in the course of being carried out.

10. Land within 20 metres of a building which is used for housing livestock, not being a temporary or moveable structure.

11. Land covered by pens in use for the temporary reception or detention of livestock.

12. Land habitually used for the training of racehorses.

13. Land the use of which is regulated by byelaws under section 14 of the Military Lands Act 1892 or section 2 of the Military Lands Act 1900.

[1875]

NOTES

Para 8: words in square brackets substituted by the Communications Act 2003, s 406(1), Sch 17, para 165(1), (3).

PART II
SUPPLEMENTARY PROVISIONS

14. In this Schedule—

"building" includes any structure or erection and any part of a building as so defined, but does not include any fence or wall, or anything which is a means of access as defined by section 34; and for this purpose "structure" includes any tent, caravan or other temporary or moveable structure;

"development" and "minerals" have the same meaning as in the Town and Country Planning Act 1990;

"ploughing" and "drilling" include respectively agricultural or forestry operations similar to ploughing and agricultural or forestry operations similar to drilling;

"statutory undertaker" means—

(a) a person authorised by any enactment to carry on any railway, light railway, tramway, road transport, water transport, canal, inland navigation, dock, harbour, pier or lighthouse undertaking or any undertaking for the supply of hydraulic power,
(b) any public gas transporter, within the meaning of Part I of the Gas Act 1986,
(c) any water or sewerage undertaker,
(d) any holder of a licence under section 6(1) of the Electricity Act 1989, or
(e) the Environment Agency, [a universal service provider (within the meaning of the Postal Services Act 2000) in connection with the provision of a universal postal service (within the meaning of that Act)][, the Civil Aviation Authority or a person who holds a licence under Chapter I of Part I of the Transport Act 2000 (to the extent that the person is carrying out activities authorised by the licence)];

"statutory undertaking" means—
(a) the undertaking of a statutory undertaker [(which, in the case of a universal service provider (within the meaning of the Postal Services Act 2000), means his undertaking so far as relating to the provision of a universal postal service (within the meaning of that Act) [and, in the case of a person who holds a licence under Chapter I of Part I of the Transport Act 2000, means that person's undertaking as licence holder])], or
(b) an airport to which Part V of the Airports Act 1986 applies.

15.—(1) Land is not to be treated as excepted land by reason of any development carried out on the land, if the carrying out of the development requires planning permission under Part III of the Town and Country Planning Act 1990 and that permission has not been granted.

(2) Sub-paragraph (1) does not apply where the development is treated by section 191(2) of the Town and Country Planning Act 1990 as being lawful for the purposes of that Act.

16. The land which is excepted land by virtue of paragraph 10 does not include—
(a) any means of access, as defined by section 34, or
(b) any way leading to such a means of access,

if the means of access is necessary for giving the public reasonable access to access land.

17. Land which is habitually used for the training of racehorses is not to be treated by virtue of paragraph 11 as excepted land except—
(a) between dawn and midday on any day, and
(b) at any other time when it is in use for that purpose.

[1876]

NOTES

Para 14: in definition "statutory undertaker" in para (e), words in first pair of square brackets substituted by SI 2001/1149, art 3(1), Sch 1, para 136(1), (2) and words in second pair of square brackets substituted by SI 2001/4050, art 2, Schedule, Pt II, para 9(a); in definition "statutory undertaking" in para (a), words in first (outer) pair of square brackets inserted by SI 2001/1149, art 3(1), Sch 1, para 136(1), (3), and words in second (inner) pair of square brackets inserted by SI 2001/4050, art 2, Schedule, Pt II, para 9(b).

SCHEDULE 2
RESTRICTIONS TO BE OBSERVED BY PERSONS EXERCISING RIGHT OF ACCESS

Section 2

General restrictions

1. Section 2(1) does not entitle a person to be on any land if, in or on that land, he—
(a) drives or rides any vehicle other than an invalid carriage as defined by section 20(2) of the Chronically Sick and Disabled Persons Act 1970,
(b) uses a vessel or sailboard on any non-tidal water,
(c) has with him any animal other than a dog,
(d) commits any criminal offence,
(e) lights or tends a fire or does any act which is likely to cause a fire,
(f) intentionally or recklessly takes, kills, injures or disturbs any animal, bird or fish,
(g) intentionally or recklessly takes, damages or destroys any eggs or nests,
(h) feeds any livestock,
(i) bathes in any non-tidal water,
(j) engages in any operations of or connected with hunting, shooting, fishing, trapping, snaring, taking or destroying of animals, birds or fish or has with him any engine, instrument or apparatus used for hunting, shooting, fishing, trapping, snaring, taking or destroying animals, birds or fish,
(k) uses or has with him any metal detector,
(l) intentionally removes, damages or destroys any plant, shrub, tree or root or any part of a plant, shrub, tree or root,
(m) obstructs the flow of any drain or watercourse, or opens, shuts or otherwise interferes with any sluice-gate or other apparatus,

(n) without reasonable excuse, interferes with any fence, barrier or other device designed to prevent accidents to people or to enclose livestock,
(o) neglects to shut any gate or to fasten it where any means of doing so is provided, except where it is reasonable to assume that a gate is intended to be left open,
(p) affixes or writes any advertisement, bill, placard or notice,
(q) in relation to any lawful activity which persons are engaging in or are about to engage in on that or adjoining land, does anything which is intended by him to have the effect—
 (i) of intimidating those persons so as to deter them or any of them from engaging in that activity,
 (ii) of obstructing that activity, or
 (iii) of disrupting that activity,
(r) without reasonable excuse, does anything which (whether or not intended by him to have the effect mentioned in paragraph (q)) disturbs, annoys or obstructs any persons engaged in a lawful activity on the land,
(s) engages in any organised games, or in camping, hang-gliding or para-gliding, or
(t) engages in any activity which is organised or undertaken (whether by him or another) for any commercial purpose.

2.—(1) In paragraph 1(k), "metal detector" means any device designed or adapted for detecting or locating any metal or mineral in the ground.

(2) For the purposes of paragraph 1(q) and (r), activity on any occasion on the part of a person or persons on land is "lawful" if he or they may engage in the activity on the land on that occasion without committing an offence or trespassing on the land.

3. Regulations may amend paragraphs 1 and 2.

4. During the period beginning with 1st March and ending with 31st July in each year, section 2(1) does not entitle a person to be on any land if he takes, or allows to enter or remain, any dog which is not on a short lead.

5. Whatever the time of year, section 2(1) does not entitle a person to be on any land if he takes, or allows to enter or remain, any dog which is not on a short lead and which is in the vicinity of livestock.

6. In paragraphs 4 and 5, "short lead" means a lead of fixed length and of not more than two metres.

Removal or relaxation of restrictions

7.—(1) The relevant authority may by direction, with the consent of the owner of any land, remove or relax any of the restrictions imposed by paragraphs 1, 4 and 5 in relation to that land, either indefinitely or during a specified period.

(2) In sub-paragraph (1), the reference to a specified period includes references—
(a) to a specified period in every calendar year, or
(b) to a period which is to be determined by the owner of the land in accordance with the direction and notified by him to the relevant authority in accordance with regulations.

(3) Regulations may make provision as to—
(a) the giving or revocation of directions under this paragraph,
(b) the variation of any direction given under this paragraph by a subsequent direction so given,
(c) the giving or revocation of consent for the purposes of sub-paragraph (1), and
(d) the steps to be taken by the relevant authority or the owner for informing the public about any direction under this paragraph or its revocation.

(4) In this paragraph—
"the relevant authority" has the meaning given by section 21;
"owner", in relation to any land which is subject to a farm business tenancy within the meaning of the Agricultural Tenancies Act 1995 or a tenancy to which the Agricultural Holdings Act 1986 applies, means the tenant under that tenancy.

Dedicated land

8. In relation to land to which a dedication under section 16 relates (whether or not it would be access land apart from the dedication), the provisions of this Schedule have effect subject to the terms of the dedication.

[1877]

NOTES

Commencement: 19 September 2004 (in relation to England); 28 May 2005 (in relation to Wales).

(*Schs 3–16 outside the scope of this work.*)

LAND REGISTRATION ACT 2002

(2002 c 9)

An Act to make provision about land registration; and for connected purposes.

[26 February 2002]

PART 1
PRELIMINARY

1 Register of title

(1) There is to continue to be a register of title kept by the registrar.

(2) Rules may make provision about how the register is to be kept and may, in particular, make provision about—

(a) the information to be included in the register,
(b) the form in which information included in the register is to be kept, and
(c) the arrangement of that information.

[1878]

NOTES

Rules: the Land Registration Rules 2003, SI 2003/1417 at **[3067]**; the Land Registration (Electronic Conveyancing) Rules 2008, SI 2008/1750.

2 Scope of title registration

This Act makes provision about the registration of title to—

(a) unregistered legal estates which are interests of any of the following kinds—
(i) an estate in land,
(ii) a rentcharge,
(iii) a franchise,
(iv) a profit a prendre in gross, and
(v) any other interest or charge which subsists for the benefit of, or is a charge on, an interest the title to which is registered; and
(b) interests capable of subsisting at law which are created by a disposition of an interest the title to which is registered.

[1879]

PART 2
FIRST REGISTRATION OF TITLE

CHAPTER 1
FIRST REGISTRATION

Voluntary registration

3 When title may be registered

(1) This section applies to any unregistered legal estate which is an interest of any of the following kinds—

(a) an estate in land,
(b) a rentcharge,
(c) a franchise, and
(d) a profit a prendre in gross.

(2) Subject to the following provisions, a person may apply to the registrar to be registered as the proprietor of an unregistered legal estate to which this section applies if—

(a) the estate is vested in him, or
(b) he is entitled to require the estate to be vested in him.

(3) Subject to subsection (4), an application under subsection (2) in respect of a leasehold estate may only be made if the estate was granted for a term of which more than seven years are unexpired.

(4) In the case of an estate in land, subsection (3) does not apply if the right to possession under the lease is discontinuous.

(5) A person may not make an application under subsection (2)(a) in respect of a leasehold estate vested in him as a mortgagee where there is a subsisting right of redemption.

(6) A person may not make an application under subsection (2)(b) if his entitlement is as a person who has contracted to buy under a contract.

(7) If a person holds in the same right both—
(a) a lease in possession, and
(b) a lease to take effect in possession on, or within a month of, the end of the lease in possession,

then, to the extent that they relate to the same land, they are to be treated for the purposes of this section as creating one continuous term.

[1880]

Compulsory registration

4 When title must be registered

(1) The requirement of registration applies on the occurrence of any of the following events—
(a) the transfer of a qualifying estate—
(i) for valuable or other consideration, by way of gift or in pursuance of an order of any court, ...
(ii) by means of an assent (including a vesting assent); [or
(iii) giving effect to a partition of land subject to a trust of land;]
[(aa) the transfer of a qualifying estate—
(i) by a deed that appoints, or by virtue of section 83 of the Charities Act 1993 has effect as if it appointed, a new trustee or is made in consequence of the appointment of a new trustee, or
(ii) by a vesting order under section 44 of the Trustee Act 1925 that is consequential on the appointment of a new trustee;]
(b) the transfer of an unregistered legal estate in land in circumstances where section 171A of the Housing Act 1985 (c 68) applies (disposal by landlord which leads to a person no longer being a secure tenant);
(c) the grant out of a qualifying estate of an estate in land—
(i) for a term of years absolute of more than seven years from the date of the grant, and
(ii) for valuable or other consideration, by way of gift or in pursuance of an order of any court;
(d) the grant out of a qualifying estate of an estate in land for a term of years absolute to take effect in possession after the end of the period of three months beginning with the date of the grant;
(e) the grant of a lease in pursuance of Part 5 of the Housing Act 1985 (the right to buy) out of an unregistered legal estate in land;
(f) the grant of a lease out of an unregistered legal estate in land in such circumstances as are mentioned in paragraph (b);
(g) the creation of a protected first legal mortgage of a qualifying estate.

(2) For the purposes of subsection (1), a qualifying estate is an unregistered legal estate which is—
(a) a freehold estate in land, or
(b) a leasehold estate in land for a term which, at the time of the transfer, grant or creation, has more than seven years to run.

(3) In subsection (1)(a), the reference to transfer does not include transfer by operation of law.

(4) Subsection (1)(a) does not apply to—
(a) the assignment of a mortgage term, or
(b) the assignment or surrender of a lease to the owner of the immediate reversion where the term is to merge in that reversion.

(5) Subsection (1)(c) does not apply to the grant of an estate to a person as a mortgagee.

(6) For the purposes of subsection (1)(a) and (c), if the estate transferred or granted has a negative value, it is to be regarded as transferred or granted for valuable or other consideration.

(7) In subsection (1)(a) and (c), references to transfer or grant by way of gift include transfer or grant for the purpose of—
(a) constituting a trust under which the settlor does not retain the whole of the beneficial interest, or
(b) uniting the bare legal title and the beneficial interest in property held under a trust under which the settlor did not, on constitution, retain the whole of the beneficial interest.

(8) For the purposes of subsection (1)(g)—
(a) a legal mortgage is protected if it takes effect on its creation as a mortgage to be protected by the deposit of documents relating to the mortgaged estate, and
(b) a first legal mortgage is one which, on its creation, ranks in priority ahead of any other mortgages then affecting the mortgaged estate.

(9) In this section—

"land" does not include mines and minerals held apart from the surface;
"vesting assent" has the same meaning as in the Settled Land Act 1925 (c 18).

[1881]

NOTES

Sub-s (1): in para (a)(i) word "or" (omitted) repealed, and para (a)(iii) and word "or" immediately preceding it inserted, by SI 2008/2872, art 2(1), (2); para (aa) inserted by SI 2008/2872, art 2(1), (3).

5 Power to extend section 4

(1) The Lord Chancellor may by order—

(a) amend section 4 so as to add to the events on the occurrence of which the requirement of registration applies such relevant event as he may specify in the order, and

(b) make such consequential amendments of any provision of, or having effect under, any Act as he thinks appropriate.

(2) For the purposes of subsection (1)(a), a relevant event is an event relating to an unregistered legal estate which is an interest of any of the following kinds—

(a) an estate in land,

(b) a rentcharge,

(c) a franchise, and

(d) a profit a prendre in gross.

(3) The power conferred by subsection (1) may not be exercised so as to require the title to an estate granted to a person as a mortgagee to be registered.

(4) Before making an order under this section the Lord Chancellor must consult such persons as he considers appropriate.

[1882]

NOTES

Orders: Land Registration Act 2002 (Amendment) Order 2008, SI 2008/2872.

6 Duty to apply for registration of title

(1) If the requirement of registration applies, the responsible estate owner, or his successor in title, must, before the end of the period for registration, apply to the registrar to be registered as the proprietor of the registrable estate.

(2) If the requirement of registration applies because of section 4(1)(g)—

(a) the registrable estate is the estate charged by the mortgage, and

(b) the responsible estate owner is the owner of that estate.

(3) If the requirement of registration applies otherwise than because of section 4(1)(g)—

(a) the registrable estate is the estate which is transferred or granted, and

(b) the responsible estate owner is the transferee or grantee of that estate.

(4) The period for registration is 2 months beginning with the date on which the relevant event occurs, or such longer period as the registrar may provide under subsection (5).

(5) If on the application of any interested person the registrar is satisfied that there is good reason for doing so, he may by order provide that the period for registration ends on such later date as he may specify in the order.

(6) Rules may make provision enabling the mortgagee under any mortgage falling within section 4(1)(g) to require the estate charged by the mortgage to be registered whether or not the mortgagor consents.

[1883]

NOTES

Rules: the Land Registration Rules 2003, SI 2003/1417 at **[3067]**.

7 Effect of non-compliance with section 6

(1) If the requirement of registration is not complied with, the transfer, grant or creation becomes void as regards the transfer, grant or creation of a legal estate.

(2) On the application of subsection (1)—

(a) in a case falling within section 4(1)(a) or (b), the title to the legal estate reverts to the transferor who holds it on a bare trust for the transferee, and

[(aa) in a case falling within section 4(1)(aa), the title to the legal estate reverts to the person in whom it was vested immediately before the transfer,] and

(b) in a case falling within section 4(1)(c) to (g), the grant or creation has effect as a contract made for valuable consideration to grant or create the legal estate concerned.

(3) If an order under section 6(5) is made in a case where subsection (1) has already applied, that application of the subsection is to be treated as not having occurred.

(4) The possibility of reverter under subsection (1) is to be disregarded for the purposes of determining whether a fee simple is a fee simple absolute.

[1884]

NOTES

Sub-s (2): para (aa) inserted by SI 2008/2872, art 3.

8 Liability for making good void transfers etc

If a legal estate is retransferred, regranted or recreated because of a failure to comply with the requirement of registration, the transferee, grantee or, as the case may be, the mortgagor—

(a) is liable to the other party for all the proper costs of and incidental to the retransfer, regrant or recreation of the legal estate, and

(b) is liable to indemnify the other party in respect of any other liability reasonably incurred by him because of the failure to comply with the requirement of registration.

[1885]

Classes of title

9 Titles to freehold estates

(1) In the case of an application for registration under this Chapter of a freehold estate, the classes of title with which the applicant may be registered as proprietor are—

(a) absolute title,
(b) qualified title, and
(c) possessory title;

and the following provisions deal with when each of the classes of title is available.

(2) A person may be registered with absolute title if the registrar is of the opinion that the person's title to the estate is such as a willing buyer could properly be advised by a competent professional adviser to accept.

(3) In applying subsection (2), the registrar may disregard the fact that a person's title appears to him to be open to objection if he is of the opinion that the defect will not cause the holding under the title to be disturbed.

(4) A person may be registered with qualified title if the registrar is of the opinion that the person's title to the estate has been established only for a limited period or subject to certain reservations which cannot be disregarded under subsection (3).

(5) A person may be registered with possessory title if the registrar is of the opinion—

(a) that the person is in actual possession of the land, or in receipt of the rents and profits of the land, by virtue of the estate, and

(b) that there is no other class of title with which he may be registered.

[1886]

10 Titles to leasehold estates

(1) In the case of an application for registration under this Chapter of a leasehold estate, the classes of title with which the applicant may be registered as proprietor are—

(a) absolute title,
(b) good leasehold title,
(c) qualified title, and
(d) possessory title;

and the following provisions deal with when each of the classes of title is available.

(2) A person may be registered with absolute title if—

(a) the registrar is of the opinion that the person's title to the estate is such as a willing buyer could properly be advised by a competent professional adviser to accept, and

(b) the registrar approves the lessor's title to grant the lease.

(3) A person may be registered with good leasehold title if the registrar is of the opinion that the person's title to the estate is such as a willing buyer could properly be advised by a competent professional adviser to accept.

(4) In applying subsection (2) or (3), the registrar may disregard the fact that a person's title appears to him to be open to objection if he is of the opinion that the defect will not cause the holding under the title to be disturbed.

(5) A person may be registered with qualified title if the registrar is of the opinion that the person's title to the estate, or the lessor's title to the reversion, has been established only for a limited period or subject to certain reservations which cannot be disregarded under subsection (4).

(6) A person may be registered with possessory title if the registrar is of the opinion—

(a) that the person is in actual possession of the land, or in receipt of the rents and profits of the land, by virtue of the estate, and
(b) that there is no other class of title with which he may be registered.

[1887]

Effect of first registration

11 Freehold estates

(1) This section is concerned with the registration of a person under this Chapter as the proprietor of a freehold estate.

(2) Registration with absolute title has the effect described in subsections (3) to (5).

(3) The estate is vested in the proprietor together with all interests subsisting for the benefit of the estate.

(4) The estate is vested in the proprietor subject only to the following interests affecting the estate at the time of registration—
(a) interests which are the subject of an entry in the register in relation to the estate,
(b) unregistered interests which fall within any of the paragraphs of Schedule 1, and
(c) interests acquired under the Limitation Act 1980 (c 58) of which the proprietor has notice.

(5) If the proprietor is not entitled to the estate for his own benefit, or not entitled solely for his own benefit, then, as between himself and the persons beneficially entitled to the estate, the estate is vested in him subject to such of their interests as he has notice of.

(6) Registration with qualified title has the same effect as registration with absolute title, except that it does not affect the enforcement of any estate, right or interest which appears from the register to be excepted from the effect of registration.

(7) Registration with possessory title has the same effect as registration with absolute title, except that it does not affect the enforcement of any estate, right or interest adverse to, or in derogation of, the proprietor's title subsisting at the time of registration or then capable of arising.

[1888]

12 Leasehold estates

(1) This section is concerned with the registration of a person under this Chapter as the proprietor of a leasehold estate.

(2) Registration with absolute title has the effect described in subsections (3) to (5).

(3) The estate is vested in the proprietor together with all interests subsisting for the benefit of the estate.

(4) The estate is vested subject only to the following interests affecting the estate at the time of registration—
(a) implied and express covenants, obligations and liabilities incident to the estate,
(b) interests which are the subject of an entry in the register in relation to the estate,
(c) unregistered interests which fall within any of the paragraphs of Schedule 1, and
(d) interests acquired under the Limitation Act 1980 (c 58) of which the proprietor has notice.

(5) If the proprietor is not entitled to the estate for his own benefit, or not entitled solely for his own benefit, then, as between himself and the persons beneficially entitled to the estate, the estate is vested in him subject to such of their interests as he has notice of.

(6) Registration with good leasehold title has the same effect as registration with absolute title, except that it does not affect the enforcement of any estate, right or interest affecting, or in derogation of, the title of the lessor to grant the lease.

(7) Registration with qualified title has the same effect as registration with absolute title except that it does not affect the enforcement of any estate, right or interest which appears from the register to be excepted from the effect of registration.

(8) Registration with possessory title has the same effect as registration with absolute title, except that it does not affect the enforcement of any estate, right or interest adverse to, or in derogation of, the proprietor's title subsisting at the time of registration or then capable of arising.

[1889]

Dependent estates

13 Appurtenant rights and charges

Rules may—

(a) make provision for the registration of the proprietor of a registered estate as the proprietor of an unregistered legal estate which subsists for the benefit of the registered estate;
(b) make provision for the registration of a person as the proprietor of an unregistered legal estate which is a charge on a registered estate.

[1890]

NOTES

Rules: the Land Registration Rules 2003, SI 2003/1417 at **[3067]**.

Supplementary

14 Rules about first registration

Rules may—
(a) make provision about the making of applications for registration under this Chapter;
(b) make provision about the functions of the registrar following the making of such an application, including provision about—
  (i) the examination of title, and
  (ii) the entries to be made in the register where such an application is approved;
(c) make provision about the effect of any entry made in the register in pursuance of such an application.

[1891]

NOTES

Rules: the Land Registration Rules 2003, SI 2003/1417 at **[3067]**.

CHAPTER 2
CAUTIONS AGAINST FIRST REGISTRATION

15 Right to lodge

(1) … a person may lodge a caution against the registration of title to an unregistered legal estate if he claims to be—
(a) the owner of a qualifying estate, or
(b) entitled to an interest affecting a qualifying estate.

(2) For the purposes of subsection (1), a qualifying estate is a legal estate which—
(a) relates to land to which the caution relates, and
(b) is an interest of any of the following kinds—
  (i) an estate in land,
  (ii) a rentcharge,
  (iii) a franchise, and
  (iv) a profit a prendre in gross.

(3) …

(4) The right under subsection (1) is exercisable by application to the registrar.

[1892]

NOTES

Sub-s (1): words omitted repealed by s 134(2) of, Sch 12, para 14 to, this Act at **[2011]**, **[2026]**; for effect see Sch 12, para 15 at **[2026]**.

Sub-s (3): repealed by s 134(2) of, Sch 12, para 14 to, this Act at **[2011]**, **[2026]**; for effect see Sch 12, para 15 at **[2026]**.

16 Effect

(1) Where an application for registration under this Part relates to a legal estate which is the subject of a caution against first registration, the registrar must give the cautioner notice of the application and of his right to object to it.

(2) The registrar may not determine an application to which subsection (1) applies before the end of such period as rules may provide, unless the cautioner has exercised his right to object to the application or given the registrar notice that he does not intend to do so.

(3) Except as provided by this section, a caution against first registration has no effect and, in particular, has no effect on the validity or priority of any interest of the cautioner in the legal estate to which the caution relates.

(4) For the purposes of subsection (1), notice given by a person acting on behalf of an applicant for registration under this Part is to be treated as given by the registrar if—
(a) the person is of a description provided by rules, and

(b) notice is given in such circumstances as rules may provide.

[1893]

NOTES

Rules: the Land Registration Rules 2003, SI 2003/1417 at **[3067]**.

17 Withdrawal

The cautioner may withdraw a caution against first registration by application to the registrar.

[1894]

18 Cancellation

(1) A person may apply to the registrar for cancellation of a caution against first registration if he is—

(a) the owner of the legal estate to which the caution relates, or
(b) a person of such other description as rules may provide.

(2) Subject to rules, no application under subsection (1)(a) may be made by a person who—

(a) consented in such manner as rules may provide to the lodging of the caution, or
(b) derives title to the legal estate by operation of law from a person who did so.

(3) Where an application is made under subsection (1), the registrar must give the cautioner notice of the application and of the effect of subsection (4).

(4) If the cautioner does not exercise his right to object to the application before the end of such period as rules may provide, the registrar must cancel the caution.

[1895]

NOTES

Rules: the Land Registration Rules 2003, SI 2003/1417 at **[3067]**.

19 Cautions register

(1) The registrar must keep a register of cautions against first registration.

(2) Rules may make provision about how the cautions register is to be kept and may, in particular, make provision about—

(a) the information to be included in the register,
(b) the form in which information included in the register is to be kept, and
(c) the arrangement of that information.

[1896]

NOTES

Rules: the Land Registration Rules 2003, SI 2003/1417 at **[3067]**.

20 Alteration of register by court

(1) The court may make an order for alteration of the cautions register for the purpose of—

(a) correcting a mistake, or
(b) bringing the register up to date.

(2) An order under subsection (1) has effect when served on the registrar to impose a duty on him to give effect to it.

(3) Rules may make provision about—

(a) the circumstances in which there is a duty to exercise the power under subsection (1),
(b) the form of an order under that subsection, and
(c) service of such an order.

[1897]

NOTES

Rules: the Land Registration Rules 2003, SI 2003/1417 at **[3067]**.

21 Alteration of register by registrar

(1) The registrar may alter the cautions register for the purpose of—

(a) correcting a mistake, or
(b) bringing the register up to date.

(2) Rules may make provision about—

(a) the circumstances in which there is a duty to exercise the power under subsection (1),
(b) how the cautions register is to be altered in exercise of that power,
(c) applications for the exercise of that power, and
(d) procedure in relation to the exercise of that power, whether on application or otherwise.

(3) Where an alteration is made under this section, the registrar may pay such amount as he thinks fit in respect of any costs reasonably incurred by a person in connection with the alteration.

[1898]

NOTES

Rules: the Land Registration Rules 2003, SI 2003/1417 at **[3067]**.

22 Supplementary

In this Chapter, "the cautioner", in relation to a caution against first registration, means the person who lodged the caution, or such other person as rules may provide.

[1899]

NOTES

Rules: the Land Registration Rules 2003, SI 2003/1417 at **[3067]**.

PART 3
DISPOSITIONS OF REGISTERED LAND

Powers of disposition

23 Owner's powers

(1) Owner's powers in relation to a registered estate consist of—

(a) power to make a disposition of any kind permitted by the general law in relation to an interest of that description, other than a mortgage by demise or sub-demise, and

(b) power to charge the estate at law with the payment of money.

(2) Owner's powers in relation to a registered charge consist of—

(a) power to make a disposition of any kind permitted by the general law in relation to an interest of that description, other than a legal sub-mortgage, and

(b) power to charge at law with the payment of money indebtedness secured by the registered charge.

(3) In subsection (2)(a), "legal sub-mortgage" means—

(a) a transfer by way of mortgage,

(b) a sub-mortgage by sub-demise, and

(c) a charge by way of legal mortgage.

[1900]

24 Right to exercise owner's powers

A person is entitled to exercise owner's powers in relation to a registered estate or charge if he is—

(a) the registered proprietor, or

(b) entitled to be registered as the proprietor.

[1901]

25 Mode of exercise

(1) A registrable disposition of a registered estate or charge only has effect if it complies with such requirements as to form and content as rules may provide.

(2) Rules may apply subsection (1) to any other kind of disposition which depends for its effect on registration.

[1902]

NOTES

Rules: the Land Registration Rules 2003, SI 2003/1417 at **[3067]**; the Land Registration (Electronic Conveyancing) Rules 2008, SI 2008/1750.

26 Protection of disponees

(1) Subject to subsection (2), a person's right to exercise owner's powers in relation to a registered estate or charge is to be taken to be free from any limitation affecting the validity of a disposition.

(2) Subsection (1) does not apply to a limitation—

(a) reflected by an entry in the register, or

(b) imposed by, or under, this Act.

(3) This section has effect only for the purpose of preventing the title of a disponee being questioned (and so does not affect the lawfulness of a disposition).

[1903]

Registrable dispositions

27 Dispositions required to be registered

(1) If a disposition of a registered estate or registered charge is required to be completed by registration, it does not operate at law until the relevant registration requirements are met.

(2) In the case of a registered estate, the following are the dispositions which are required to be completed by registration—

- (a) a transfer,
- (b) where the registered estate is an estate in land, the grant of a term of years absolute—
  - (i) for a term of more than seven years from the date of the grant,
  - (ii) to take effect in possession after the end of the period of three months beginning with the date of the grant,
  - (iii) under which the right to possession is discontinuous,
  - (iv) in pursuance of Part 5 of the Housing Act 1985 (c 68) (the right to buy), or
  - (v) in circumstances where section 171A of that Act applies (disposal by landlord which leads to a person no longer being a secure tenant),
- (c) where the registered estate is a franchise or manor, the grant of a lease,
- (d) the express grant or reservation of an interest of a kind falling within section 1(2)(a) of the Law of Property Act 1925 (c 20), other than one which is capable of being registered under *the Commons Registration Act 1965 (c 64)* [Part 1 of the Commons Act 2006],
- (e) the express grant or reservation of an interest of a kind falling within section 1(2)(b) or (e) of the Law of Property Act 1925, and
- (f) the grant of a legal charge.

(3) In the case of a registered charge, the following are the dispositions which are required to be completed by registration—

- (a) a transfer, and
- (b) the grant of a sub-charge.

(4) Schedule 2 to this Act (which deals with the relevant registration requirements) has effect.

(5) This section applies to dispositions by operation of law as it applies to other dispositions, but with the exception of the following—

- (a) a transfer on the death or bankruptcy of an individual proprietor,
- (b) a transfer on the dissolution of a corporate proprietor, and
- (c) the creation of a legal charge which is a local land charge.

(6) Rules may make provision about applications to the registrar for the purpose of meeting registration requirements under this section.

(7) In subsection (2)(d), the reference to express grant does not include grant as a result of the operation of section 62 of the Law of Property Act 1925 (c 20).

[1904]

NOTES

Sub-s (2): in para (d), words in italics substituted by subsequent words in square brackets by the Commons Act 2006, s 52, Sch 5, para 8(1), (2), as from a day to be appointed.

Rules: the Land Registration Rules 2003, SI 2003/1417 at **[3067]**.

Effect of dispositions on priority

28 Basic rule

(1) Except as provided by sections 29 and 30, the priority of an interest affecting a registered estate or charge is not affected by a disposition of the estate or charge.

(2) It makes no difference for the purposes of this section whether the interest or disposition is registered.

[1905]

29 Effect of registered dispositions: estates

(1) If a registrable disposition of a registered estate is made for valuable consideration, completion of the disposition by registration has the effect of postponing to the interest under the disposition any interest affecting the estate immediately before the disposition whose priority is not protected at the time of registration.

(2) For the purposes of subsection (1), the priority of an interest is protected—

- (a) in any case, if the interest—
  - (i) is a registered charge or the subject of a notice in the register,
  - (ii) falls within any of the paragraphs of Schedule 3, or
  - (iii) appears from the register to be excepted from the effect of registration, and
- (b) in the case of a disposition of a leasehold estate, if the burden of the interest is incident to the estate.

(3) Subsection (2)(a)(ii) does not apply to an interest which has been the subject of a notice in the register at any time since the coming into force of this section.

(4) Where the grant of a leasehold estate in land out of a registered estate does not involve a registrable disposition, this section has effect as if—

(a) the grant involved such a disposition, and
(b) the disposition were registered at the time of the grant.

[1906]

30 Effect of registered dispositions: charges

(1) If a registrable disposition of a registered charge is made for valuable consideration, completion of the disposition by registration has the effect of postponing to the interest under the disposition any interest affecting the charge immediately before the disposition whose priority is not protected at the time of registration.

(2) For the purposes of subsection (1), the priority of an interest is protected—

(a) in any case, if the interest—
  (i) is a registered charge or the subject of a notice in the register,
  (ii) falls within any of the paragraphs of Schedule 3, or
  (iii) appears from the register to be excepted from the effect of registration, and
(b) in the case of a disposition of a charge which relates to a leasehold estate, if the burden of the interest is incident to the estate.

(3) Subsection (2)(a)(ii) does not apply to an interest which has been the subject of a notice in the register at any time since the coming into force of this section.

[1907]

31 Inland Revenue charges

The effect of a disposition of a registered estate or charge on a charge under section 237 of the Inheritance Tax Act 1984 (c 51) (charge for unpaid tax) is to be determined, not in accordance with sections 28 to 30 above, but in accordance with sections 237(6) and 238 of that Act (under which a purchaser in good faith for money or money's worth takes free from the charge in the absence of registration).

[1908]

PART 4
NOTICES AND RESTRICTIONS

Notices

32 Nature and effect

(1) A notice is an entry in the register in respect of the burden of an interest affecting a registered estate or charge.

(2) The entry of a notice is to be made in relation to the registered estate or charge affected by the interest concerned.

(3) The fact that an interest is the subject of a notice does not necessarily mean that the interest is valid, but does mean that the priority of the interest, if valid, is protected for the purposes of sections 29 and 30.

[1909]

33 Excluded interests

No notice may be entered in the register in respect of any of the following—

(a) an interest under—
  (i) a trust of land, or
  (ii) a settlement under the Settled Land Act 1925 (c 18),
(b) a leasehold estate in land which—
  (i) is granted for a term of years of three years or less from the date of the grant, and
  (ii) is not required to be registered,
(c) a restrictive covenant made between a lessor and lessee, so far as relating to the demised premises,
(d) an interest which is capable of being registered under *the Commons Registration Act 1965* (*c 64*) [Part 1 of the Commons Act 2006], and
(e) an interest in any coal or coal mine, the rights attached to any such interest and the rights of any person under section 38, 49 or 51 of the Coal Industry Act 1994 (c 21).

[1910]

NOTES

Para (d): words in italics substituted by subsequent words in square brackets by the Commons Act 2006, s 52, Sch 5, para 8(1), (3), as from a day to be appointed.

34 Entry on application

(1) A person who claims to be entitled to the benefit of an interest affecting a registered estate or charge may, if the interest is not excluded by section 33, apply to the registrar for the entry in the register of a notice in respect of the interest.

(2) Subject to rules, an application under this section may be for—
- (a) an agreed notice, or
- (b) a unilateral notice.

(3) The registrar may only approve an application for an agreed notice if—
- (a) the applicant is the relevant registered proprietor, or a person entitled to be registered as such proprietor,
- (b) the relevant registered proprietor, or a person entitled to be registered as such proprietor, consents to the entry of the notice, or
- (c) the registrar is satisfied as to the validity of the applicant's claim.

(4) In subsection (3), references to the relevant registered proprietor are to the proprietor of the registered estate or charge affected by the interest to which the application relates.

[1911]

NOTES

Rules: the Land Registration Rules 2003, SI 2003/1417 at **[3067]**.

35 Unilateral notices

(1) If the registrar enters a notice in the register in pursuance of an application under section 34(2)(b) ("a unilateral notice"), he must give notice of the entry to—
- (a) the proprietor of the registered estate or charge to which it relates, and
- (b) such other persons as rules may provide.

(2) A unilateral notice must—
- (a) indicate that it is such a notice, and
- (b) identify who is the beneficiary of the notice.

(3) The person shown in the register as the beneficiary of a unilateral notice, or such other person as rules may provide, may apply to the registrar for the removal of the notice from the register.

[1912]

NOTES

Rules: the Land Registration Rules 2003, SI 2003/1417 at **[3067]**.

36 Cancellation of unilateral notices

(1) A person may apply to the registrar for the cancellation of a unilateral notice if he is—
- (a) the registered proprietor of the estate or charge to which the notice relates, or
- (b) a person entitled to be registered as the proprietor of that estate or charge.

(2) Where an application is made under subsection (1), the registrar must give the beneficiary of the notice notice of the application and of the effect of subsection (3).

(3) If the beneficiary of the notice does not exercise his right to object to the application before the end of such period as rules may provide, the registrar must cancel the notice.

(4) In this section—

"beneficiary", in relation to a unilateral notice, means the person shown in the register as the beneficiary of the notice, or such other person as rules may provide;

"unilateral notice" means a notice entered in the register in pursuance of an application under section 34(2)(b).

[1913]

NOTES

Rules: the Land Registration Rules 2003, SI 2003/1417 at **[3067]**.

37 Unregistered interests

(1) If it appears to the registrar that a registered estate is subject to an unregistered interest which—
- (a) falls within any of the paragraphs of Schedule 1, and
- (b) is not excluded by section 33,

he may enter a notice in the register in respect of the interest.

(2) The registrar must give notice of an entry under this section to such persons as rules may provide.

[1914]

NOTES

Rules: the Land Registration Rules 2003, SI 2003/1417 at **[3067]**.

38 Registrable dispositions

Where a person is entered in the register as the proprietor of an interest under a disposition falling within section 27(2)(b) to (e), the registrar must also enter a notice in the register in respect of that interest.

[1915]

39 Supplementary

Rules may make provision about the form and content of notices in the register.

[1916]

NOTES

Rules: the Land Registration Rules 2003, SI 2003/1417 at **[3067]**.

Restrictions

40 Nature

(1) A restriction is an entry in the register regulating the circumstances in which a disposition of a registered estate or charge may be the subject of an entry in the register.

(2) A restriction may, in particular—
- (a) prohibit the making of an entry in respect of any disposition, or a disposition of a kind specified in the restriction;
- (b) prohibit the making of an entry—
  - (i) indefinitely,
  - (ii) for a period specified in the restriction, or
  - (iii) until the occurrence of an event so specified.

(3) Without prejudice to the generality of subsection (2)(b)(iii), the events which may be specified include—
- (a) the giving of notice,
- (b) the obtaining of consent, and
- (c) the making of an order by the court or registrar.

(4) The entry of a restriction is to be made in relation to the registered estate or charge to which it relates.

[1917]

41 Effect

(1) Where a restriction is entered in the register, no entry in respect of a disposition to which the restriction applies may be made in the register otherwise than in accordance with the terms of the restriction, subject to any order under subsection (2).

(2) The registrar may by order—
- (a) disapply a restriction in relation to a disposition specified in the order or dispositions of a kind so specified, or
- (b) provide that a restriction has effect, in relation to a disposition specified in the order or dispositions of a kind so specified, with modifications so specified.

(3) The power under subsection (2) is exercisable only on the application of a person who appears to the registrar to have a sufficient interest in the restriction.

[1918]

42 Power of registrar to enter

(1) The registrar may enter a restriction in the register if it appears to him that it is necessary or desirable to do so for the purpose of—
- (a) preventing invalidity or unlawfulness in relation to dispositions of a registered estate or charge,
- (b) securing that interests which are capable of being overreached on a disposition of a registered estate or charge are overreached, or
- (c) protecting a right or claim in relation to a registered estate or charge.

(2) No restriction may be entered under subsection (1)(c) for the purpose of protecting the priority of an interest which is, or could be, the subject of a notice.

(3) The registrar must give notice of any entry made under this section to the proprietor of the registered estate or charge concerned, except where the entry is made in pursuance of an application under section 43.

(4) For the purposes of subsection (1)(c), a person entitled to the benefit of a charging order relating to an interest under a trust shall be treated as having a right or claim in relation to the trust property.

[1919]

43 Applications

(1) A person may apply to the registrar for the entry of a restriction under section 42(1) if—

(a) he is the relevant registered proprietor, or a person entitled to be registered as such proprietor,

(b) the relevant registered proprietor, or a person entitled to be registered as such proprietor, consents to the application, or

(c) he otherwise has a sufficient interest in the making of the entry.

(2) Rules may—

(a) require the making of an application under subsection (1) in such circumstances, and by such person, as the rules may provide;

(b) make provision about the form of consent for the purposes of subsection (1)(b);

(c) provide for classes of person to be regarded as included in subsection (1)(c);

(d) specify standard forms of restriction.

(3) If an application under subsection (1) is made for the entry of a restriction which is not in a form specified under subsection (2)(d), the registrar may only approve the application if it appears to him—

(a) that the terms of the proposed restriction are reasonable, and

(b) that applying the proposed restriction would—

(i) be straightforward, and

(ii) not place an unreasonable burden on him.

(4) In subsection (1), references to the relevant registered proprietor are to the proprietor of the registered estate or charge to which the application relates.

[1920]

NOTES

Rules: the Land Registration Rules 2003, SI 2003/1417 at **[3067]**.

44 Obligatory restrictions

(1) If the registrar enters two or more persons in the register as the proprietor of a registered estate in land, he must also enter in the register such restrictions as rules may provide for the purpose of securing that interests which are capable of being overreached on a disposition of the estate are overreached.

(2) Where under any enactment the registrar is required to enter a restriction without application, the form of the restriction shall be such as rules may provide.

[1921]

NOTES

Rules: the Land Registration Rules 2003, SI 2003/1417 at **[3067]**.

45 Notifiable applications

(1) Where an application under section 43(1) is notifiable, the registrar must give notice of the application, and of the right to object to it, to—

(a) the proprietor of the registered estate or charge to which it relates, and

(b) such other persons as rules may provide.

(2) The registrar may not determine an application to which subsection (1) applies before the end of such period as rules may provide, unless the person, or each of the persons, notified under that subsection has exercised his right to object to the application or given the registrar notice that he does not intend to do so.

(3) For the purposes of this section, an application under section 43(1) is notifiable unless it is—

(a) made by or with the consent of the proprietor of the registered estate or charge to which the application relates, or a person entitled to be registered as such proprietor,

(b) made in pursuance of rules under section 43(2)(a), or

(c) an application for the entry of a restriction reflecting a limitation under an order of the court or registrar, or an undertaking given in place of such an order.

[1922]

NOTES

Rules: the Land Registration Rules 2003, SI 2003/1417 at **[3067]**.

46 Power of court to order entry

(1) If it appears to the court that it is necessary or desirable to do so for the purpose of protecting a right or claim in relation to a registered estate or charge, it may make an order requiring the registrar to enter a restriction in the register.

(2) No order under this section may be made for the purpose of protecting the priority of an interest which is, or could be, the subject of a notice.

(3) The court may include in an order under this section a direction that an entry made in pursuance of the order is to have overriding priority.

(4) If an order under this section includes a direction under subsection (3), the registrar must make such entry in the register as rules may provide.

(5) The court may make the exercise of its power under subsection (3) subject to such terms and conditions as it thinks fit.

[1923]

NOTES

Rules: the Land Registration Rules 2003, SI 2003/1417 at **[3067]**.

47 Withdrawal

A person may apply to the registrar for the withdrawal of a restriction if—

(a) the restriction was entered in such circumstances as rules may provide, and
(b) he is of such a description as rules may provide.

[1924]

NOTES

Rules: the Land Registration Rules 2003, SI 2003/1417 at **[3067]**.

PART 5
CHARGES

Relative priority

48 Registered charges

(1) Registered charges on the same registered estate, or on the same registered charge, are to be taken to rank as between themselves in the order shown in the register.

(2) Rules may make provision about—

(a) how the priority of registered charges as between themselves is to be shown in the register, and
(b) applications for registration of the priority of registered charges as between themselves.

[1925]

NOTES

Rules: the Land Registration Rules 2003, SI 2003/1417 at **[3067]**.

49 Tacking and further advances

(1) The proprietor of a registered charge may make a further advance on the security of the charge ranking in priority to a subsequent charge if he has not received from the subsequent chargee notice of the creation of the subsequent charge.

(2) Notice given for the purposes of subsection (1) shall be treated as received at the time when, in accordance with rules, it ought to have been received.

(3) The proprietor of a registered charge may also make a further advance on the security of the charge ranking in priority to a subsequent charge if—

(a) the advance is made in pursuance of an obligation, and
(b) at the time of the creation of the subsequent charge the obligation was entered in the register in accordance with rules.

(4) The proprietor of a registered charge may also make a further advance on the security of the charge ranking in priority to a subsequent charge if—

(a) the parties to the prior charge have agreed a maximum amount for which the charge is security, and
(b) at the time of the creation of the subsequent charge the agreement was entered in the register in accordance with rules.

(5) Rules may—

(a) disapply subsection (4) in relation to charges of a description specified in the rules, or
(b) provide for the application of that subsection to be subject, in the case of charges of a description so specified, to compliance with such conditions as may be so specified.

(6) Except as provided by this section, tacking in relation to a charge over registered land is only possible with the agreement of the subsequent chargee.

[1926]

NOTES

Rules: the Land Registration Rules 2003, SI 2003/1417 at **[3067]**.

50 Overriding statutory charges: duty of notification

If the registrar enters a person in the register as the proprietor of a charge which—

(a) is created by or under an enactment, and

(b) has effect to postpone a charge which at the time of registration of the statutory charge is—

(i) entered in the register, or

(ii) the basis for an entry in the register,

he must in accordance with rules give notice of the creation of the statutory charge to such person as rules may provide.

[1927]

NOTES

Rules: the Land Registration Rules 2003, SI 2003/1417 at **[3067]**.

Powers as chargee

51 Effect of completion by registration

On completion of the relevant registration requirements, a charge created by means of a registrable disposition of a registered estate has effect, if it would not otherwise do so, as a charge by deed by way of legal mortgage.

[1928]

52 Protection of disponees

(1) Subject to any entry in the register to the contrary, the proprietor of a registered charge is to be taken to have, in relation to the property subject to the charge, the powers of disposition conferred by law on the owner of a legal mortgage.

(2) Subsection (1) has effect only for the purpose of preventing the title of a disponee being questioned (and so does not affect the lawfulness of a disposition).

[1929]

53 Powers as sub-chargee

The registered proprietor of a sub-charge has, in relation to the property subject to the principal charge or any intermediate charge, the same powers as the sub-chargor.

[1930]

Realisation of security

54 Proceeds of sale: chargee's duty

For the purposes of section 105 of the Law of Property Act 1925 (c 20) (mortgagee's duties in relation to application of proceeds of sale), in its application to the proceeds of sale of registered land, a person shall be taken to have notice of anything in the register immediately before the disposition on sale.

[1931]

55 Local land charges

A charge over registered land which is a local land charge may only be realised if the title to the charge is registered.

[1932]

Miscellaneous

56 Receipt in case of joint proprietors

Where a charge is registered in the name of two or more proprietors, a valid receipt for the money secured by the charge may be given by—

(a) the registered proprietors,

(b) the survivors or survivor of the registered proprietors, or

(c) the personal representative of the last survivor of the registered proprietors.

[1933]

57 Entry of right of consolidation

Rules may make provision about entry in the register of a right of consolidation in relation to a registered charge.

[1934]

NOTES

Rules: the Land Registration Rules 2003, SI 2003/1417 at **[3067]**.

PART 6
REGISTRATION: GENERAL

Registration as proprietor

58 Conclusiveness

(1) If, on the entry of a person in the register as the proprietor of a legal estate, the legal estate would not otherwise be vested in him, it shall be deemed to be vested in him as a result of the registration.

(2) Subsection (1) does not apply where the entry is made in pursuance of a registrable disposition in relation to which some other registration requirement remains to be met.

[1935]

59 Dependent estates

(1) The entry of a person in the register as the proprietor of a legal estate which subsists for the benefit of a registered estate must be made in relation to the registered estate.

(2) The entry of a person in the register as the proprietor of a charge on a registered estate must be made in relation to that estate.

(3) The entry of a person in the register as the proprietor of a sub-charge on a registered charge must be made in relation to that charge.

[1936]

Boundaries

60 Boundaries

(1) The boundary of a registered estate as shown for the purposes of the register is a general boundary, unless shown as determined under this section.

(2) A general boundary does not determine the exact line of the boundary.

(3) Rules may make provision enabling or requiring the exact line of the boundary of a registered estate to be determined and may, in particular, make provision about—

(a) the circumstances in which the exact line of a boundary may or must be determined,
(b) how the exact line of a boundary may be determined,
(c) procedure in relation to applications for determination, and
(d) the recording of the fact of determination in the register or the index maintained under section 68.

(4) Rules under this section must provide for applications for determination to be made to the registrar.

[1937]

NOTES

Rules: the Land Registration Rules 2003, SI 2003/1417 at **[3067]**.

61 Accretion and diluvion

(1) The fact that a registered estate in land is shown in the register as having a particular boundary does not affect the operation of accretion or diluvion.

(2) An agreement about the operation of accretion or diluvion in relation to a registered estate in land has effect only if registered in accordance with rules.

[1938]

NOTES

Rules: the Land Registration Rules 2003, SI 2003/1417 at **[3067]**.

Quality of title

62 Power to upgrade title

(1) Where the title to a freehold estate is entered in the register as possessory or qualified, the registrar may enter it as absolute if he is satisfied as to the title to the estate.

(2) Where the title to a leasehold estate is entered in the register as good leasehold, the registrar may enter it as absolute if he is satisfied as to the superior title.

(3) Where the title to a leasehold estate is entered in the register as possessory or qualified the registrar may—

(a) enter it as good leasehold if he is satisfied as to the title to the estate, and

(b) enter it as absolute if he is satisfied both as to the title to the estate and as to the superior title.

(4) Where the title to a freehold estate in land has been entered in the register as possessory for at least twelve years, the registrar may enter it as absolute if he is satisfied that the proprietor is in possession of the land.

(5) Where the title to a leasehold estate in land has been entered in the register as possessory for at least twelve years, the registrar may enter it as good leasehold if he is satisfied that the proprietor is in possession of the land.

(6) None of the powers under subsections (1) to (5) is exercisable if there is outstanding any claim adverse to the title of the registered proprietor which is made by virtue of an estate, right or interest whose enforceability is preserved by virtue of the existing entry about the class of title.

(7) The only persons who may apply to the registrar for the exercise of any of the powers under subsections (1) to (5) are—

(a) the proprietor of the estate to which the application relates,

(b) a person entitled to be registered as the proprietor of that estate,

(c) the proprietor of a registered charge affecting that estate, and

(d) a person interested in a registered estate which derives from that estate.

(8) In determining for the purposes of this section whether he is satisfied as to any title, the registrar is to apply the same standards as those which apply under section 9 or 10 to first registration of title.

(9) The Lord Chancellor may by order amend subsection (4) or (5) by substituting for the number of years for the time being specified in that subsection such number of years as the order may provide.

[1939]

63 Effect of upgrading title

(1) On the title to a registered freehold or leasehold estate being entered under section 62 as absolute, the proprietor ceases to hold the estate subject to any estate, right or interest whose enforceability was preserved by virtue of the previous entry about the class of title.

(2) Subsection (1) also applies on the title to a registered leasehold estate being entered under section 62 as good leasehold, except that the entry does not affect or prejudice the enforcement of any estate, right or interest affecting, or in derogation of, the title of the lessor to grant the lease.

[1940]

64 Use of register to record defects in title

(1) If it appears to the registrar that a right to determine a registered estate in land is exercisable, he may enter the fact in the register.

(2) Rules may make provision about entries under subsection (1) and may, in particular, make provision about—

(a) the circumstances in which there is a duty to exercise the power conferred by that subsection,

(b) how entries under that subsection are to be made, and

(c) the removal of such entries.

[1941]

NOTES

Rules: the Land Registration Rules 2003, SI 2003/1417 at **[3067]**.

Alteration of register

65 Alteration of register

Schedule 4 (which makes provision about alteration of the register) has effect.

[1942]

Information etc

66 Inspection of the registers etc

(1) Any person may inspect and make copies of, or of any part of—

(a) the register of title,

(b) any document kept by the registrar which is referred to in the register of title,

(c) any other document kept by the registrar which relates to an application to him, or
(d) the register of cautions against first registration.

(2) The right under subsection (1) is subject to rules which may, in particular—
(a) provide for exceptions to the right, and
(b) impose conditions on its exercise, including conditions requiring the payment of fees.

[1943]

NOTES

Rules: the Land Registration Rules 2003, SI 2003/1417 at **[3067]**; the Land Registration (Electronic Conveyancing) Rules 2008, SI 2008/1750.

67 Official copies of the registers etc

(1) An official copy of, or of a part of—
(a) the register of title,
(b) any document which is referred to in the register of title and kept by the registrar,
(c) any other document kept by the registrar which relates to an application to him, or
(d) the register of cautions against first registration,
is admissible in evidence to the same extent as the original.

(2) A person who relies on an official copy in which there is a mistake is not liable for loss suffered by another by reason of the mistake.

(3) Rules may make provision for the issue of official copies and may, in particular, make provision about—
(a) the form of official copies,
(b) who may issue official copies,
(c) applications for official copies, and
(d) the conditions to be met by applicants for official copies, including conditions requiring the payment of fees.

[1944]

NOTES

Rules: the Land Registration Rules 2003, SI 2003/1417 at **[3067]**; the Land Registration (Electronic Conveyancing) Rules 2008, SI 2008/1750

68 Index

(1) The registrar must keep an index for the purpose of enabling the following matters to be ascertained in relation to any parcel of land—
(a) whether any registered estate relates to the land,
(b) how any registered estate which relates to the land is identified for the purposes of the register,
(c) whether the land is affected by any, and, if so what, caution against first registration, and
(d) such other matters as rules may provide.

(2) Rules may—
(a) make provision about how the index is to be kept and may, in particular, make provision about—
  (i) the information to be included in the index,
  (ii) the form in which information included in the index is to be kept, and
  (iii) the arrangement of that information;
(b) make provision about official searches of the index.

[1945]

NOTES

Rules: the Land Registration Rules 2003, SI 2003/1417 at **[3067]**.

69 Historical information

(1) The registrar may on application provide information about the history of a registered title.

(2) Rules may make provision about applications for the exercise of the power conferred by subsection (1).

(3) The registrar may—
(a) arrange for the provision of information about the history of registered titles, and
(b) authorise anyone who has the function of providing information under paragraph (a) to have access on such terms as the registrar thinks fit to any relevant information kept by him.

[1946]

NOTES

Rules: the Land Registration Rules 2003, SI 2003/1417 at **[3067]**.

70 Official searches

Rules may make provision for official searches of the register, including searches of pending applications for first registration, and may, in particular, make provision about—

(a) the form of applications for searches,
(b) the manner in which such applications may be made,
(c) the form of official search certificates, and
(d) the manner in which such certificates may be issued.

[1947]

NOTES

Rules: the Land Registration Rules 2003, SI 2003/1417 at **[3067]**.

Applications

71 Duty to disclose unregistered interests

Where rules so provide—

(a) a person applying for registration under Chapter 1 of Part 2 must provide to the registrar such information as the rules may provide about any interest affecting the estate to which the application relates which—
 (i) falls within any of the paragraphs of Schedule 1, and
 (ii) is of a description specified by the rules;
(b) a person applying to register a registrable disposition of a registered estate must provide to the registrar such information as the rules may provide about any unregistered interest affecting the estate which—
 (i) falls within any of the paragraphs of Schedule 3, and
 (ii) is of description specified by the rules.

[1948]

NOTES

Rules: the Land Registration Rules 2003, SI 2003/1417 at **[3067]**; the Land Registration (Electronic Conveyancing) Rules 2008, SI 2008/1750.

72 Priority protection

(1) For the purposes of this section, an application for an entry in the register is protected if—

(a) it is one to which a priority period relates, and
(b) it is made before the end of that period.

(2) Where an application for an entry in the register is protected, any entry made in the register during the priority period relating to the application is postponed to any entry made in pursuance of it.

(3) Subsection (2) does not apply if—

(a) the earlier entry was made in pursuance of a protected application, and
(b) the priority period relating to that application ranks ahead of the one relating to the application for the other entry.

(4) Subsection (2) does not apply if the earlier entry is one to which a direction under section 46(3) applies.

(5) The registrar may defer dealing with an application for an entry in the register if it appears to him that subsection (2) might apply to the entry were he to make it.

(6) Rules may—

(a) make provision for priority periods in connection with—
 (i) official searches of the register, including searches of pending applications for first registration, or
 (ii) the noting in the register of a contract for the making of a registrable disposition of a registered estate or charge;
(b) make provision for the keeping of records in relation to priority periods and the inspection of such records.

(7) Rules under subsection (6)(a) may, in particular, make provision about—

(a) the commencement and length of a priority period,
(b) the applications for registration to which such a period relates,
(c) the order in which competing priority periods rank, and

(d) the application of subsections (2) and (3) in cases where more than one priority period relates to the same application.

[1949]

NOTES

Rules: the Land Registration Rules 2003, SI 2003/1417 at **[3067]**.

73 Objections

(1) Subject to subsections (2) and (3), anyone may object to an application to the registrar.

(2) In the case of an application under section 18, only the person who lodged the caution to which the application relates, or such other person as rules may provide, may object.

(3) In the case of an application under section 36, only the person shown in the register as the beneficiary of the notice to which the application relates, or such other person as rules may provide, may object.

(4) The right to object under this section is subject to rules.

(5) Where an objection is made under this section, the registrar—

(a) must give notice of the objection to the applicant, and
(b) may not determine the application until the objection has been disposed of.

(6) Subsection (5) does not apply if the objection is one which the registrar is satisfied is groundless.

(7) If it is not possible to dispose by agreement of an objection to which subsection (5) applies, the registrar must refer the matter to the adjudicator.

(8) Rules may make provision about references under subsection (7).

[1950]

NOTES

Rules: the Land Registration Rules 2003, SI 2003/1417 at **[3067]**; the Land Registration (Referral to the Adjudicator to HM Land Registry) Rules 2003, SI 2003/2114 at **[3342]**; the Land Registration (Electronic Conveyancing) Rules 2008, SI 2008/1750.

74 Effective date of registration

An entry made in the register in pursuance of—

(a) an application for registration of an unregistered legal estate, or
(b) an application for registration in relation to a disposition required to be completed by registration,

has effect from the time of the making of the application.

[1951]

Proceedings before the registrar

75 Production of documents

(1) The registrar may require a person to produce a document for the purposes of proceedings before him.

(2) The power under subsection (1) is subject to rules.

(3) A requirement under subsection (1) shall be enforceable as an order of the court.

(4) A person aggrieved by a requirement under subsection (1) may appeal to a county court, which may make any order which appears appropriate.

[1952]

NOTES

Rules: the Land Registration Rules 2003, SI 2003/1417 at **[3067]**.

76 Costs

(1) The registrar may make orders about costs in relation to proceedings before him.

(2) The power under subsection (1) is subject to rules which may, in particular, make provision about—

(a) who may be required to pay costs,
(b) whose costs a person may be required to pay,
(c) the kind of costs which a person may be required to pay, and
(d) the assessment of costs.

(3) Without prejudice to the generality of subsection (2), rules under that subsection may include provision about—

(a) costs of the registrar, and

(b) liability for costs thrown away as the result of neglect or delay by a legal representative of a party to proceedings.

(4) An order under subsection (1) shall be enforceable as an order of the court.

(5) A person aggrieved by an order under subsection (1) may appeal to a county court, which may make any order which appears appropriate.

[1953]

NOTES

Rules: the Land Registration Rules 2003, SI 2003/1417 at **[3067]**.

Miscellaneous

77 Duty to act reasonably

(1) A person must not exercise any of the following rights without reasonable cause—

(a) the right to lodge a caution under section 15,
(b) the right to apply for the entry of a notice or restriction, and
(c) the right to object to an application to the registrar.

(2) The duty under this section is owed to any person who suffers damage in consequence of its breach.

[1954]

78 Notice of trust not to affect registrar

The registrar shall not be affected with notice of a trust.

[1955]

PART 7
SPECIAL CASES

The Crown

79 Voluntary registration of demesne land

(1) Her Majesty may grant an estate in fee simple absolute in possession out of demesne land to Herself.

(2) The grant of an estate under subsection (1) is to be regarded as not having been made unless an application under section 3 is made in respect of the estate before the end of the period for registration.

(3) The period for registration is two months beginning with the date of the grant, or such longer period as the registrar may provide under subsection (4).

(4) If on the application of Her Majesty the registrar is satisfied that there is a good reason for doing so, he may by order provide that the period for registration ends on such later date as he may specify in the order.

(5) If an order under subsection (4) is made in a case where subsection (2) has already applied, that application of the subsection is to be treated as not having occurred.

[1956]

80 Compulsory registration of grants out of demesne land

(1) Section 4(1) shall apply as if the following were included among the events listed—

(a) the grant by Her Majesty out of demesne land of an estate in fee simple absolute in possession, otherwise than under section 79;
(b) the grant by Her Majesty out of demesne land of an estate in land—
    (i) for a term of years absolute of more than seven years from the date of the grant, and
    (ii) for valuable or other consideration, by way of gift or in pursuance of an order of any court.

(2) In subsection (1)(b)(ii), the reference to grant by way of gift includes grant for the purpose of constituting a trust under which Her Majesty does not retain the whole of the beneficial interest.

(3) Subsection (1) does not apply to the grant of an estate in mines and minerals held apart from the surface.

(4) The Lord Chancellor may by order—

(a) amend this section so as to add to the events in subsection (1) such events relating to demesne land as he may specify in the order, and
(b) make such consequential amendments of any provision of, or having effect under, any Act as he thinks appropriate.

(5) In its application by virtue of subsection (1), section 7 has effect with the substitution for subsection (2) of—

"(2) On the application of subsection (1), the grant has effect as a contract made for valuable consideration to grant the legal estate concerned".

[1957]

81 Demesne land: cautions against first registration

(1) Section 15 shall apply as if demesne land were held by Her Majesty for an unregistered estate in fee simple absolute in possession.

(2) The provisions of this Act relating to cautions against first registration shall, in relation to cautions lodged by virtue of subsection (1), have effect subject to such modifications as rules may provide.

[1958]

NOTES

Rules: the Land Registration Rules 2003, SI 2003/1417 at **[3067]**.

82 Escheat etc

(1) Rules may make provision about—

(a) the determination of a registered freehold estate in land, and

(b) the registration of an unregistered freehold legal estate in land in respect of land to which a former registered freehold estate in land related.

(2) Rules under this section may, in particular—

(a) make provision for determination to be dependent on the meeting of such registration requirements as the rules may specify;

(b) make provision for entries relating to a freehold estate in land to continue in the register, notwithstanding determination, for such time as the rules may provide;

(c) make provision for the making in the register in relation to a former freehold estate in land of such entries as the rules may provide;

(d) make provision imposing requirements to be met in connection with an application for the registration of such an unregistered estate as is mentioned in subsection (1)(b).

[1959]

NOTES

Rules: the Land Registration Rules 2003, SI 2003/1417 at **[3067]**.

83 Crown and Duchy land: representation

(1) With respect to a Crown or Duchy interest, the appropriate authority—

(a) may represent the owner of the interest for all purposes of this Act,

(b) is entitled to receive such notice as that person is entitled to receive under this Act, and

(c) may make such applications and do such other acts as that person is entitled to make or do under this Act.

(2) In this section—

"the appropriate authority" means—

(a) in relation to an interest belonging to Her Majesty in right of the Crown and forming part of the Crown Estate, the Crown Estate Commissioners;

(b) in relation to any other interest belonging to Her Majesty in right of the Crown, the government department having the management of the interest or, if there is no such department, such person as Her Majesty may appoint in writing under the Royal Sign Manual;

(c) in relation to an interest belonging to Her Majesty in right of the Duchy of Lancaster, the Chancellor of the Duchy;

(d) in relation to an interest belonging to the Duchy of Cornwall, such person as the Duke of Cornwall, or the possessor for the time being of the Duchy of Cornwall, appoints;

(e) in relation to an interest belonging to a government department, or held in trust for Her Majesty for the purposes of a government department, that department;

"Crown interest" means an interest belonging to Her Majesty in right of the Crown, or belonging to a government department, or held in trust for Her Majesty for the purposes of a government department;

"Duchy interest" means an interest belonging to Her Majesty in right of the Duchy of Lancaster, or belonging to the Duchy of Cornwall;

"interest" means any estate, interest or charge in or over land and any right or claim in relation to land.

[1960]

84 Disapplication of requirements relating to Duchy land

Nothing in any enactment relating to the Duchy of Lancaster or the Duchy of Cornwall shall have effect to impose any requirement with respect to formalities or enrolment in relation to a disposition by a registered proprietor.

[1961]

85 Bona vacantia

Rules may make provision about how the passing of a registered estate or charge as bona vacantia is to be dealt with for the purposes of this Act.

[1962]

Pending actions etc

86 Bankruptcy

(1) In this Act, references to an interest affecting an estate or charge do not include a petition in bankruptcy or bankruptcy order.

(2) As soon as practicable after registration of a petition in bankruptcy as a pending action under the Land Charges Act 1972 (c 61), the registrar must enter in the register in relation to any registered estate or charge which appears to him to be affected a notice in respect of the pending action.

(3) Unless cancelled by the registrar in such manner as rules may provide, a notice entered under subsection (2) continues in force until—

- (a) a restriction is entered in the register under subsection (4), or
- (b) the trustee in bankruptcy is registered as proprietor.

(4) As soon as practicable after registration of a bankruptcy order under the Land Charges Act 1972, the registrar must, in relation to any registered estate or charge which appears to him to be affected by the order, enter in the register a restriction reflecting the effect of the Insolvency Act 1986 (c 45).

(5) Where the proprietor of a registered estate or charge is adjudged bankrupt, the title of his trustee in bankruptcy is void as against a person to whom a registrable disposition of the estate or charge is made if—

- (a) the disposition is made for valuable consideration,
- (b) the person to whom the disposition is made acts in good faith, and
- (c) at the time of the disposition—
  - (i) no notice or restriction is entered under this section in relation to the registered estate or charge, and
  - (ii) the person to whom the disposition is made has no notice of the bankruptcy petition or the adjudication.

(6) Subsection (5) only applies if the relevant registration requirements are met in relation to the disposition, but, when they are met, has effect as from the date of the disposition.

(7) Nothing in this section requires a person to whom a registrable disposition is made to make any search under the Land Charges Act 1972.

[1963]

NOTES

Rules: the Land Registration Rules 2003, SI 2003/1417 at **[3067]**.

87 Pending land actions, writs, orders and deeds of arrangement

(1) Subject to the following provisions, references in this Act to an interest affecting an estate or charge include—

- (a) a pending land action within the meaning of the Land Charges Act 1972,
- (b) a writ or order of the kind mentioned in section 6(1)(a) of that Act (writ or order affecting land issued or made by any court for the purposes of enforcing a judgment or recognisance),
- (c) an order appointing a receiver or sequestrator, and
- (d) a deed of arrangement.

(2) No notice may be entered in the register in respect of—

- (a) an order appointing a receiver or sequestrator, or
- (b) a deed of arrangement.

(3) None of the matters mentioned in subsection (1) shall be capable of falling within paragraph 2 of Schedule 1 or 3.

(4) In its application to any of the matters mentioned in subsection (1), this Act shall have effect subject to such modifications as rules may provide.

(5) In this section, "deed of arrangement" has the same meaning as in the Deeds of Arrangement Act 1914 (c 47).

[1964]

NOTES

Rules: the Land Registration Rules 2003, SI 2003/1417 at **[3067]**.

Miscellaneous

88 Incorporeal hereditaments

In its application to—

(a) rentcharges,
(b) franchises,
(c) profits a prendre in gross, or
(d) manors,

this Act shall have effect subject to such modification as rules may provide.

[1965]

89 Settlements

(1) Rules may make provision for the purposes of this Act in relation to the application to registered land of the enactments relating to settlements under the Settled Land Act 1925 (c 18).

(2) Rules under this section may include provision modifying any of those enactments in its application to registered land.

(3) In this section, "registered land" means an interest the title to which is, or is required to be, registered.

[1966]

NOTES

Rules: the Land Registration Rules 2003, SI 2003/1417 at **[3067]**.

90 PPP leases relating to transport in London

(1) No application for registration under section 3 may be made in respect of a leasehold estate in land under a PPP lease.

(2) The requirement of registration does not apply on the grant or transfer of a leasehold estate in land under a PPP lease.

(3) For the purposes of section 27, the following are not dispositions requiring to be completed by registration—

(a) the grant of a term of years absolute under a PPP lease;
(b) the express grant of an interest falling within section 1(2) of the Law of Property Act 1925 (c 20), where the interest is created for the benefit of a leasehold estate in land under a PPP lease.

(4) No notice may be entered in the register in respect of an interest under a PPP lease.

(5) Schedules 1 and 3 have effect as if they included a paragraph referring to a PPP lease.

(6) In this section, "PPP lease" has the meaning given by section 218 of the Greater London Authority Act 1999 (c 29) (which makes provision about leases created for public-private partnerships relating to transport in London).

[1967]

PART 8
ELECTRONIC CONVEYANCING

91 Electronic dispositions: formalities

(1) This section applies to a document in electronic form where—

(a) the document purports to effect a disposition which falls within subsection (2), and
(b) the conditions in subsection (3) are met.

(2) A disposition falls within this subsection if it is—

(a) a disposition of a registered estate or charge,
(b) a disposition of an interest which is the subject of a notice in the register, or
(c) a disposition which triggers the requirement of registration,

which is of a kind specified by rules.

(3) The conditions referred to above are that—

(a) the document makes provision for the time and date when it takes effect,
(b) the document has the electronic signature of each person by whom it purports to be authenticated,

(c) each electronic signature is certified, and
(d) such other conditions as rules may provide are met.

(4) A document to which this section applies is to be regarded as—
(a) in writing, and
(b) signed by each individual, and sealed by each corporation, whose electronic signature it has.

(5) A document to which this section applies is to be regarded for the purposes of any enactment as a deed.

(6) If a document to which this section applies is authenticated by a person as agent, it is to be regarded for the purposes of any enactment as authenticated by him under the written authority of his principal.

(7) If notice of an assignment made by means of a document to which this section applies is given in electronic form in accordance with rules, it is to be regarded for the purposes of any enactment as given in writing.

(8) The right conferred by section 75 of the Law of Property Act 1925 (c 20) (purchaser's right to have the execution of a conveyance attested) does not apply to a document to which this section applies.

[(9) In relation to the execution of a document by a company in accordance with section 44(2) of the Companies Act 2006 (signature on behalf of the company)—
(a) subsection (4) above has effect in relation to paragraph (a) of that provision (signature by two authorised signatories) but not paragraph (b) (signature by director in presence of witness);
(b) the other provisions of section 44 apply accordingly (the references to a document purporting to be signed in accordance with subsection (2) of that section being read as references to its purporting to be authenticated in accordance with this section);
(c) where subsection (4) above has effect in relation to a person signing on behalf of more than one company, the requirement of subsection (6) of that section is treated as met if the document specifies the different capacities in which the person signs.]

[(9A) If subsection (3) of section 29C of the Industrial and Provident Societies Act 1965 (execution of documents) applies to a document because of subsection (4) above, subsection (5) of that section (presumption of due execution) shall have effect in relation to the document with the substitution of "authenticated" for "signed".]

(10) In this section, references to an electronic signature and to the certification of such a signature are to be read in accordance with section 7(2) and (3) of the Electronic Communications Act 2000 (c 7).

[1968]

NOTES

Sub-s (9): substituted by SI 2008/948, arts 3(1)(b), 6, Sch 1, Pt 2, para 224; for transitional provisions and savings see arts 6, 11, 12 thereof.

Sub-s (9A): inserted by the Co-operatives and Community Benefit Societies Act 2003, s 5(8).

Rules: the Land Registration (Electronic Conveyancing) Rules 2008, SI 2008/1750.

92 Land registry network

(1) The registrar may provide, or arrange for the provision of, an electronic communications network for use for such purposes as he thinks fit relating to registration or the carrying on of transactions which—
(a) involve registration, and
(b) are capable of being effected electronically.

(2) Schedule 5 (which makes provision in connection with a network provided under subsection (1) and transactions carried on by means of such a network) has effect.

[1969]

93 Power to require simultaneous registration

(1) This section applies to a disposition of—
(a) a registered estate or charge, or
(b) an interest which is the subject of a notice in the register,

where the disposition is of a description specified by rules.

(2) A disposition to which this section applies, or a contract to make such a disposition, only has effect if it is made by means of a document in electronic form and if, when the document purports to take effect—
(a) it is electronically communicated to the registrar, and
(b) the relevant registration requirements are met.

(3) For the purposes of subsection (2)(b), the relevant registration requirements are—

(a) in the case of a registrable disposition, the requirements under Schedule 2, and
(b) in the case of any other disposition, or a contract, such requirements as rules may provide.

(4) Section 27(1) does not apply to a disposition to which this section applies.

(5) Before making rules under this section the Lord Chancellor must consult such persons as he considers appropriate.

(6) In this section, "disposition", in relation to a registered charge, includes postponement.

[1970]

94 Electronic settlement

The registrar may take such steps as he thinks fit for the purpose of securing the provision of a system of electronic settlement in relation to transactions involving registration.

[1971]

95 Supplementary

Rules may—
(a) make provision about the communication of documents in electronic form to the registrar;
(b) make provision about the electronic storage of documents communicated to the registrar in electronic form.

[1972]

NOTES

Rules: the Land Registration Rules 2003, SI 2003/1417 at **[3067]**; the Land Registration (Electronic Conveyancing) Rules 2008, SI 2008/1750.

PART 9
ADVERSE POSSESSION

96 Disapplication of periods of limitation

(1) No period of limitation under section 15 of the Limitation Act 1980 (c 58) (time limits in relation to recovery of land) shall run against any person, other than a chargee, in relation to an estate in land or rentcharge the title to which is registered.

(2) No period of limitation under section 16 of that Act (time limits in relation to redemption of land) shall run against any person in relation to such an estate in land or rentcharge.

(3) Accordingly, section 17 of that Act (extinction of title on expiry of time limit) does not operate to extinguish the title of any person where, by virtue of this section, a period of limitation does not run against him.

[1973]

97 Registration of adverse possessor

Schedule 6 (which makes provision about the registration of an adverse possessor of an estate in land or rentcharge) has effect.

[1974]

98 Defences

(1) A person has a defence to an action for possession of land if—
(a) on the day immediately preceding that on which the action was brought he was entitled to make an application under paragraph 1 of Schedule 6 to be registered as the proprietor of an estate in the land, and
(b) had he made such an application on that day, the condition in paragraph 5(4) of that Schedule would have been satisfied.

(2) A judgment for possession of land ceases to be enforceable at the end of the period of two years beginning with the date of the judgment if the proceedings in which the judgment is given were commenced against a person who was at that time entitled to make an application under paragraph 1 of Schedule 6.

(3) A person has a defence to an action for possession of land if on the day immediately preceding that on which the action was brought he was entitled to make an application under paragraph 6 of Schedule 6 to be registered as the proprietor of an estate in the land.

(4) A judgment for possession of land ceases to be enforceable at the end of the period of two years beginning with the date of the judgment if, at the end of that period, the person against whom the judgment was given is entitled to make an application under paragraph 6 of Schedule 6 to be registered as the proprietor of an estate in the land.

(5) Where in any proceedings a court determines that—

(a) a person is entitled to a defence under this section, or
(b) a judgment for possession has ceased to be enforceable against a person by virtue of subsection (4),

the court must order the registrar to register him as the proprietor of the estate in relation to which he is entitled to make an application under Schedule 6.

(6) The defences under this section are additional to any other defences a person may have.

(7) Rules may make provision to prohibit the recovery of rent due under a rentcharge from a person who has been in adverse possession of the rentcharge.

[1975]

NOTES

Rules: the Land Registration Rules 2003, SI 2003/1417 at **[3067]**.

PART 10
LAND REGISTRY
Administration

99 The land registry

(1) There is to continue to be an office called Her Majesty's Land Registry which is to deal with the business of registration under this Act.

(2) The land registry is to consist of—
(a) the Chief Land Registrar, who is its head, and
(b) the staff appointed by him;

and references in this Act to a member of the land registry are to be read accordingly.

(3) The Lord Chancellor shall appoint a person to be the Chief Land Registrar.

(4) Schedule 7 (which makes further provision about the land registry) has effect.

[1976]

100 Conduct of business

(1) Any function of the registrar may be carried out by any member of the land registry who is authorised for the purpose by the registrar.

(2) The Lord Chancellor may by regulations make provision about the carrying out of functions during any vacancy in the office of registrar.

(3) The Lord Chancellor may by order designate a particular office of the land registry as the proper office for the receipt of applications or a specified description of application.

(4) The registrar may prepare and publish such forms and directions as he considers necessary or desirable for facilitating the conduct of the business of registration under this Act.

[1977]

NOTES

Orders: the Land Registration (Proper Office) Order 2008, SI 2008/3201; the Land Registration (Proper Office) Order 2009, SI 2009/1393 at **[3710]**.

Regulations: the Land Registration (Acting Chief Land Registrar) Regulations 2003, SI 2003/2281.

101 Annual report

(1) The registrar must make an annual report on the business of the land registry to the Lord Chancellor.

(2) The registrar must publish every report under this section and may do so in such manner as he thinks fit.

(3) The Lord Chancellor must lay copies of every report under this section before Parliament.

[1978]

Fees and indemnities

102 Fee orders

The Lord Chancellor may with the advice and assistance of the body referred to in section 127(2) (the Rule Committee), and the consent of the Treasury, by order—
(a) prescribe fees to be paid in respect of dealings with the land registry, except under section 69(3)(b) or 105;
(b) make provision about the payment of prescribed fees.

[1979]

NOTES

Order: the Land Registration Fee Order 2009, SI 2009/845 at **[3689]**.

103 Indemnities

Schedule 8 (which makes provision for the payment of indemnities by the registrar) has effect.

[1980]

Miscellaneous

104 General information about land

The registrar may publish information about land in England and Wales if it appears to him to be information in which there is legitimate public interest.

[1981]

105 Consultancy and advisory services

(1) The registrar may provide, or arrange for the provision of, consultancy or advisory services about the registration of land in England and Wales or elsewhere.

(2) The terms on which services are provided under this section by the registrar, in particular terms as to payment, shall be such as he thinks fit.

[1982]

106 Incidental powers: companies

(1) If the registrar considers it expedient to do so in connection with his functions under section 69(3)(a), 92(1), 94 or 105(1) or paragraph 10 of Schedule 5, he may—

(a) form, or participate in the formation of, a company, or

(b) purchase, or invest in, a company.

(2) In this section—

"company" means a company *within the meaning of the Companies Act 1985 (c 6)* [as defined in section 1(1) of the Companies Act 2006];

"invest" means invest in any way (whether by acquiring assets, securities or rights or otherwise).

(3) This section is without prejudice to any powers of the registrar exercisable otherwise than by virtue of this section.

[1983]

NOTES

Sub-s (2): words in italics substituted by subsequent words in square brackets by SI 2009/1041, art 2(1), Sch 1, para 193, as from 1 October 2009.

PART 11
ADJUDICATION

107 The adjudicator

(1) The Lord Chancellor shall appoint a person to be the Adjudicator to Her Majesty's Land Registry.

(2) To be qualified for appointment under subsection (1), a person must [satisfy the judicial-appointment eligibility condition on a 7-year basis].

(3) Schedule 9 (which makes further provision about the adjudicator) has effect.

[1984]

NOTES

Sub-s (2): words in square brackets substituted by the Tribunals, Courts and Enforcement Act 2007, s 50, Sch 10, Pt 1, para 35(1), (2); for transitional provisions, see SI 2008/1653, arts 3, 4.

108 Jurisdiction

(1) The adjudicator has the following functions—

(a) determining matters referred to him under section 73(7), and

(b) determining appeals under paragraph 4 of Schedule 5.

(2) Also, the adjudicator may, on application, make any order which the High Court could make for the rectification or setting aside of a document which—

(a) effects a qualifying disposition of a registered estate or charge,

(b) is a contract to make such a disposition, or

(c) effects a transfer of an interest which is the subject of a notice in the register.

(3) For the purposes of subsection (2)(a), a qualifying disposition is—

(a) a registrable disposition, or
(b) a disposition which creates an interest which may be the subject of a notice in the register.

(4) The general law about the effect of an order of the High Court for the rectification or setting aside of a document shall apply to an order under this section.

[1985]

109 Procedure

(1) Hearings before the adjudicator shall be held in public, except where he is satisfied that exclusion of the public is just and reasonable.

(2) Subject to that, rules may regulate the practice and procedure to be followed with respect to proceedings before the adjudicator and matters incidental to or consequential on such proceedings.

(3) Rules under subsection (2) may, in particular, make provision about—
(a) when hearings are to be held,
(b) requiring persons to attend hearings to give evidence or to produce documents,
(c) the form in which any decision of the adjudicator is to be given,
(d) payment of costs of a party to proceedings by another party to the proceedings, and
(e) liability for costs thrown away as the result of neglect or delay by a legal representative of a party to proceedings.

[1986]

NOTES

Rules: the Adjudicator to Her Majesty's Land Registry (Practice and Procedure) Rules 2003, SI 2003/2171 at **[3348]**; the Network Access Appeal Rules 2008, SI 2008/1730.

110 Functions in relation to disputes

(1) In proceedings on a reference under section 73(7), the adjudicator may, instead of deciding a matter himself, direct a party to the proceedings to commence proceedings within a specified time in the court for the purpose of obtaining the court's decision on the matter.

(2) Rules may make provision about the reference under subsection (1) of matters to the court and may, in particular, make provision about—
(a) adjournment of the proceedings before the adjudicator pending the outcome of the proceedings before the court, and
(b) the powers of the adjudicator in the event of failure to comply with a direction under subsection (1).

(3) Rules may make provision about the functions of the adjudicator in consequence of a decision on a reference under section 73(7) and may, in particular, make provision enabling the adjudicator to determine, or give directions about the determination of—
(a) the application to which the reference relates, or
(b) such other present or future application to the registrar as the rules may provide.

(4) If, in the case of a reference under section 73(7) relating to an application under paragraph 1 of Schedule 6, the adjudicator determines that it would be unconscionable because of an equity by estoppel for the registered proprietor to seek to dispossess the applicant, but that the circumstances are not such that the applicant ought to be registered as proprietor, the adjudicator—
(a) must determine how the equity due to the applicant is to be satisfied, and
(b) may for that purpose make any order that the High Court could make in the exercise of its equitable jurisdiction.

[1987]

NOTES

Rules: the Adjudicator to Her Majesty's Land Registry (Practice and Procedure) Rules 2003, SI 2003/2171 at **[3348]**.

111 Appeals

(1) Subject to subsection (2), a person aggrieved by a decision of the adjudicator may appeal to the High Court.

(2) In the case of a decision on an appeal under paragraph 4 of Schedule 5, only appeal on a point of law is possible.

(3) If on an appeal under this section relating to an application under paragraph 1 of Schedule 6 the court determines that it would be unconscionable because of an equity by estoppel for the registered proprietor to seek to dispossess the applicant, but that the circumstances are not such that the applicant ought to be registered as proprietor, the court must determine how the equity due to the applicant is to be satisfied.

[1988]

PART I STATUTES

112 Enforcement of orders etc

A requirement of the adjudicator shall be enforceable as an order of the court.

[1989]

113 Fees

The Lord Chancellor may by order—

(a) prescribe fees to be paid in respect of proceedings before the adjudicator;
(b) make provision about the payment of prescribed fees.

[1990]

114 Supplementary

Power to make rules under this Part is exercisable by the Lord Chancellor.

[1991]

PART 12
MISCELLANEOUS AND GENERAL

Miscellaneous

115 Rights of pre-emption

(1) A right of pre-emption in relation to registered land has effect from the time of creation as an interest capable of binding successors in title (subject to the rules about the effect of dispositions on priority).

(2) This section has effect in relation to rights of pre-emption created on or after the day on which this section comes into force.

[1992]

116 Proprietary estoppel and mere equities

It is hereby declared for the avoidance of doubt that, in relation to registered land, each of the following—

(a) an equity by estoppel, and
(b) a mere equity,

has effect from the time the equity arises as an interest capable of binding successors in title (subject to the rules about the effect of dispositions on priority).

[1993]

117 Reduction in unregistered interests with automatic protection

(1) Paragraphs 10 to 14 of Schedules 1 and 3 shall cease to have effect at the end of the period of ten years beginning with the day on which those Schedules come into force.

(2) If made before the end of the period mentioned in subsection (1), no fee may be charged for—

(a) an application to lodge a caution against first registration by virtue of an interest falling within any of paragraphs 10 to 14 of Schedule 1, or
(b) an application for the entry in the register of a notice in respect of an interest falling within any of paragraphs 10 to 14 of Schedule 3.

[1994]

118 Power to reduce qualifying term

(1) The Lord Chancellor may by order substitute for the term specified in any of the following provisions—

(a) section 3(3),
(b) section 4(1)(c)(i) and (2)(b),
(c) section 15(3)(a)(ii),
(d) section 27(2)(b)(i),
(e) section 80(1)(b)(i),
(f) paragraph 1 of Schedule 1,
(g) paragraphs 4(1), 5(1) and 6(1) of Schedule 2, and
(h) paragraph 1 of Schedule 3,

such shorter term as he thinks fit.

(2) An order under this section may contain such transitional provision as the Lord Chancellor thinks fit.

(3) Before making an order under this section, the Lord Chancellor must consult such persons as he considers appropriate.

[1995]

PART I STATUTES

119 Power to deregister manors

On the application of the proprietor of a registered manor, the registrar may remove the title to the manor from the register.

[1996]

120 Conclusiveness of filed copies etc

(1) This section applies where—

(a) a disposition relates to land to which a registered estate relates, and

(b) an entry in the register relating to the registered estate refers to a document kept by the registrar which is not an original.

(2) As between the parties to the disposition, the document kept by the registrar is to be taken—

(a) to be correct, and

(b) to contain all the material parts of the original document.

(3) No party to the disposition may require production of the original document.

(4) No party to the disposition is to be affected by any provision of the original document which is not contained in the document kept by the registrar.

[1997]

121 Forwarding of applications to registrar of companies

The Lord Chancellor may by rules make provision about the transmission by the registrar to the registrar of companies (within the meaning of the Companies Act 1985 (c 6)) of applications under—

(a) Part 12 of that Act (registration of charges), or

(b) Chapter 3 of Part 23 of that Act (corresponding provision for oversea companies).

[121 Forwarding of applications to registrar of companies

(1) The Lord Chancellor may by rules make provision about the transmission by the registrar to the registrar of companies of applications under—

(a) Part 25 of the Companies Act 2006 (registration of charges over property of companies registered in the United Kingdom), or

(b) regulations under section 1052 of that Act (registration of charges over property in the United Kingdom of overseas companies).

(2) In subsection (1) "the registrar of companies" has the same meaning as in the Companies Acts (see section 1060 of the Companies Act 2006).]

[1998]

NOTES

Substituted by SI 2009/1941, art 2(1), Sch 1, para 193, as from 1 October 2009.

122 Repeal of Land Registry Act 1862

(1) The Land Registry Act 1862 (c 53) shall cease to have effect.

(2) The registrar shall have custody of records of title made under that Act.

(3) The registrar may discharge his duty under subsection (2) by keeping the relevant information in electronic form.

(4) The registrar may on application provide a copy of any information included in a record of title made under that Act.

(5) Rules may make provision about applications for the exercise of the power conferred by subsection (4).

[1999]

Offences etc

123 Suppression of information

(1) A person commits an offence if in the course of proceedings relating to registration under this Act he suppresses information with the intention of—

(a) concealing a person's right or claim, or

(b) substantiating a false claim.

(2) A person guilty of an offence under this section is liable—

(a) on conviction on indictment, to imprisonment for a term not exceeding two years or to a fine;

(b) on summary conviction, to imprisonment for a term not exceeding six months or to a fine not exceeding the statutory maximum, or to both.

[2000]

124 Improper alteration of the registers

(1) A person commits an offence if he dishonestly induces another—
(a) to change the register of title or cautions register, or
(b) to authorise the making of such a change.

(2) A person commits an offence if he intentionally or recklessly makes an unauthorised change in the register of title or cautions register.

(3) A person guilty of an offence under this section is liable—
(a) on conviction on indictment, to imprisonment for a term not exceeding 2 years or to a fine;
(b) on summary conviction, to imprisonment for a term not exceeding six months or to a fine not exceeding the statutory maximum, or to both.

(4) In this section, references to changing the register of title include changing a document referred to in it.

[2001]

125 Privilege against self-incrimination

(1) The privilege against self-incrimination, so far as relating to offences under this Act, shall not entitle a person to refuse to answer any question or produce any document or thing in any legal proceedings other than criminal proceedings.

(2) No evidence obtained under subsection (1) shall be admissible in any criminal proceedings under this Act against the person from whom it was obtained or that person's spouse [or civil partner].

[2002]

NOTES

Sub-s (2): words in square brackets inserted by the Civil Partnership Act 2004, s 261(1), Sch 27, para 167.

Land registration rules

126 Miscellaneous and general powers

Schedule 10 (which contains miscellaneous and general land registration rule-making powers) has effect.

[2003]

127 Exercise of powers

(1) Power to make land registration rules is exercisable by the Lord Chancellor with the advice and assistance of the Rule Committee.

(2) The Rule Committee is a body consisting of—
(a) a judge of the Chancery Division of the High Court nominated by the [Lord Chief Justice, or a judicial office holder (as defined in section 109(4) of the Constitutional Reform Act 2005) nominated by him, after consulting the Lord Chancellor],
(b) the registrar,
(c) a person nominated by the General Council of the Bar,
(d) a person nominated by the Council of the Law Society,
(e) a person nominated by the Council of Mortgage Lenders,
(f) a person nominated by the Council of Licensed Conveyancers,
(g) a person nominated by the Royal Institution of Chartered Surveyors,
(h) a person with experience in, and knowledge of, consumer affairs [nominated by the Lord Chancellor], and
(i) any person nominated under subsection (3).

(3) The Lord Chancellor may nominate to be a member of the Rule Committee any person who appears to him to have qualifications or experience which would be of value to the committee in considering any matter with which it is concerned.

[2004]

NOTES

Sub-s (2): words in square brackets in para (a) substituted and words in square brackets in para (h) inserted by the Constitutional Reform Act 2005, s 15(1), Sch 4, Pt 1, paras 301, 302.

Supplementary

128 Rules, regulations and orders

(1) Any power of the Lord Chancellor to make rules, regulations or orders under this Act includes power to make different provision for different cases.

(2) Any power of the Lord Chancellor to make rules, regulations or orders under this Act is exercisable by statutory instrument.

(3) A statutory instrument containing—
(a) regulations under section 100(2), or
(b) an order under section 100(3), 102 or 113,
is to be laid before Parliament after being made.

(4) A statutory instrument containing—
(a) land registration rules,
(b) rules under Part 11 or section 121,
(c) regulations under paragraph 5 of Schedule 9, or
(d) an order under section 5(1), 62(9), 80(4), 118(1) or 130,
is subject to annulment in pursuance of a resolution of either House of Parliament.

(5) Rules under section 93 or paragraph 1, 2 or 3 of Schedule 5 shall not be made unless a draft of the rules has been laid before and approved by resolution of each House of Parliament. **[2005]**

129 Crown application

This Act binds the Crown.

[2006]

130 Application to internal waters

This Act applies to land covered by internal waters of the United Kingdom which are—
(a) within England or Wales, or
(b) adjacent to England or Wales and specified for the purposes of this section by order made by the Lord Chancellor.

[2007]

131 "Proprietor in possession"

(1) For the purposes of this Act, land is in the possession of the proprietor of a registered estate in land if it is physically in his possession, or in that of a person who is entitled to be registered as the proprietor of the registered estate.

(2) In the case of the following relationships, land which is (or is treated as being) in the possession of the second-mentioned person is to be treated for the purposes of subsection (1) as in the possession of the first-mentioned person—
(a) landlord and tenant;
(b) mortgagor and mortgagee;
(c) licensor and licensee;
(d) trustee and beneficiary.

(3) In subsection (1), the reference to entitlement does not include entitlement under Schedule 6.

[2008]

132 General interpretation

(1) In this Act—

"adjudicator" means the Adjudicator to Her Majesty's Land Registry;

"caution against first registration" means a caution lodged under section 15;

"cautions register" means the register kept under section 19(1);

"charge" means any mortgage, charge or lien for securing money or money's worth;

"demesne land" means land belonging to Her Majesty in right of the Crown which is not held for an estate in fee simple absolute in possession;

"land" includes—
(a) buildings and other structures,
(b) land covered with water, and
(c) mines and minerals, whether or not held with the surface;

"land registration rules" means any rules under this Act, other than rules under section 93, Part 11, section 121 or paragraph 1, 2 or 3 of Schedule 5;

"legal estate" has the same meaning as in the Law of Property Act 1925 (c 20);

"legal mortgage" has the same meaning as in the Law of Property Act 1925;

"mines and minerals" includes any strata or seam of minerals or substances in or under any land, and powers of working and getting any such minerals or substances;

"registrar" means the Chief Land Registrar;

"register" means the register of title, except in the context of cautions against first registration;

"registered" means entered in the register;

"registered charge" means a charge the title to which is entered in the register;

"registered estate" means a legal estate the title to which is entered in the register, other than a registered charge;

"registered land" means a registered estate or registered charge;

"registrable disposition" means a disposition which is required to be completed by registration under section 27;
"requirement of registration" means the requirement of registration under section 4;
"sub-charge" means a charge under section 23(2)(b);
"term of years absolute" has the same meaning as in the Law of Property Act 1925 (c 20);
"valuable consideration" does not include marriage consideration or a nominal consideration in money.

(2) In subsection (1), in the definition of "demesne land", the reference to land belonging to Her Majesty does not include land in relation to which a freehold estate in land has determined, but in relation to which there has been no act of entry or management by the Crown.

(3) In this Act—

(a) references to the court are to the High Court or a county court,
(b) references to an interest affecting an estate or charge are to an adverse right affecting the title to the estate or charge, and
(c) references to the right to object to an application to the registrar are to the right under section 73.

[2009]

Final provisions

133 Minor and consequential amendments

Schedule 11 (which makes minor and consequential amendments) has effect.

[2010]

134 Transition

(1) The Lord Chancellor may by order make such transitional provisions and savings as he thinks fit in connection with the coming into force of any of the provisions of this Act.

(2) Schedule 12 (which makes transitional provisions and savings) has effect.

(3) Nothing in Schedule 12 affects the power to make transitional provisions and savings under subsection (1); and an order under that subsection may modify any provision made by that Schedule.

[2011]

NOTES

Orders: the Land Registration Act 2002 (Transitional Provisions) Order 2003, SI 2003/1953 at **[3308]**; the Land Registration Act 2002 (Transitional Provisions) (No 2) Order 2003, SI 2003/2431 at **[3412]**.

135 Repeals

The enactments specified in Schedule 13 (which include certain provisions which are already spent) are hereby repealed to the extent specified there.

[2012]

136 Short title, commencement and extent

(1) This Act may be cited as the Land Registration Act 2002.

(2) This Act shall come into force on such day as the Lord Chancellor may by order appoint, and different days may be so appointed for different purposes.

(3) Subject to subsection (4), this Act extends to England and Wales only.

(4) Any amendment or repeal by this Act of an existing enactment, other than—

(a) section 37 of the Requisitioned Land and War Works Act 1945 (c 43), and
(b) Schedule 2A to the Building Societies Act 1986 (c 53),

has the same extent as the enactment amended or repealed.

[2013]

NOTES

Orders: the Land Registration Act 2002 (Commencement No 1) Order 2003, SI 2003/935; the Land Registration Act 2002 (Commencement No 2) Order 2003, SI 2003/1028; the Land Registration Act 2002 (Commencement No 3) Order 2003, SI 2003/1612; the Land Registration Act 2002 (Commencement No 4) Order 2003, SI 2003/1725.

SCHEDULE 1
UNREGISTERED INTERESTS WHICH OVERRIDE FIRST REGISTRATION

Sections 11 and 12

Leasehold estates in land

1. A leasehold estate in land granted for a term not exceeding seven years from the date of the grant, except for a lease the grant of which falls within section 4(1) (d), (e) or (f).

Interests of persons in actual occupation

2. An interest belonging to a person in actual occupation, so far as relating to land of which he is in actual occupation, except for an interest under a settlement under the Settled Land Act 1925 (c 18).

Easements and profits a prendre

3. A legal easement or profit a prendre.

Customary and public rights

4. A customary right.

5. A public right.

Local land charges

6. A local land charge.

Mines and minerals

7. An interest in any coal or coal mine, the rights attached to any such interest and the rights of any person under section 38, 49 or 51 of the Coal Industry Act 1994 (c 21).

8. In the case of land to which title was registered before 1898, rights to mines and minerals (and incidental rights) created before 1898.

9. In the case of land to which title was registered between 1898 and 1925 inclusive, rights to mines and minerals (and incidental rights) created before the date of registration of the title.

Miscellaneous

10. A franchise.

11. A manorial right.

12. A right to rent which was reserved to the Crown on the granting of any freehold estate (whether or not the right is still vested in the Crown).

13. A non-statutory right in respect of an embankment or sea or river wall.

14. A right to payment in lieu of tithe.

[15. …]

[16. A right in respect of the repair of a church chancel.]

[2014]

NOTES

Paras 10–14: repealed by s 117(1) at **[1994]**, as from 13 October 2013.

Para 15: inserted by s 134(2), Sch 12, para 7 at **[2011]**, **[2026]**, as from 13 October 2003 (with effect until 13 October 2006). Para 15 read as follows:

"15. A right acquired under the Limitation Act 1980 before the coming into force of this Schedule.".

Para 16: inserted by SI 2003/2431, art 2(1), with effect until 13 October 2013; see SI 2003/1725, art 2(1) and SI 2003/2431, art 2(1).

SCHEDULE 2
REGISTRABLE DISPOSITIONS: REGISTRATION REQUIREMENTS

Section 27

PART 1
REGISTERED ESTATES

Introductory

1. This Part deals with the registration requirements relating to those dispositions of registered estates which are required to be completed by registration.

Transfer

2.—(1) In the case of a transfer of whole or part, the transferee, or his successor in title, must be entered in the register as the proprietor.

(2) In the case of a transfer of part, such details of the transfer as rules may provide must be entered in the register in relation to the registered estate out of which the transfer is made.

Lease of estate in land

3.—(1) This paragraph applies to a disposition consisting of the grant out of an estate in land of a term of years absolute.

(2) In the case of a disposition to which this paragraph applies—
- (a) the grantee, or his successor in title, must be entered in the register as the proprietor of the lease, and
- (b) a notice in respect of the lease must be entered in the register.

Lease of franchise or manor

4.—(1) This paragraph applies to a disposition consisting of the grant out of a franchise or manor of a lease for a term of more than seven years from the date of the grant.

(2) In the case of a disposition to which this paragraph applies—
- (a) the grantee, or his successor in title, must be entered in the register as the proprietor of the lease, and
- (b) a notice in respect of the lease must be entered in the register.

5.—(1) This paragraph applies to a disposition consisting of the grant out of a franchise or manor of a lease for a term not exceeding seven years from the date of the grant.

(2) In the case of a disposition to which this paragraph applies, a notice in respect of the lease must be entered in the register.

Creation of independently registrable legal interest

6.—(1) This paragraph applies to a disposition consisting of the creation of a legal rentcharge or profit a prendre in gross, other than one created for, or for an interest equivalent to, a term of years absolute not exceeding seven years from the date of creation.

(2) In the case of a disposition to which this paragraph applies—
- (a) the grantee, or his successor in title, must be entered in the register as the proprietor of the interest created, and
- (b) a notice in respect of the interest created must be entered in the register.

(3) In sub-paragraph (1), the reference to a legal rentcharge or profit a prendre in gross is to one falling within section 1(2) of the Law of Property Act 1925 (c 20).

Creation of other legal interest

7.—(1) This paragraph applies to a disposition which—
- (a) consists of the creation of an interest of a kind falling within section 1(2)(a), (b) or (e) of the Law of Property Act 1925, and
- (b) is not a disposition to which paragraph 4, 5 or 6 applies.

(2) In the case of a disposition to which this paragraph applies—
- (a) a notice in respect of the interest created must be entered in the register, and
- (b) if the interest is created for the benefit of a registered estate, the proprietor of the registered estate must be entered in the register as its proprietor.

(3) Rules may provide for sub-paragraph (2) to have effect with modifications in relation to a right of entry over or in respect of a term of years absolute.

Creation of legal charge

8. In the case of the creation of a charge, the chargee, or his successor in title, must be entered in the register as the proprietor of the charge.

[2015]

NOTES

Rules: the Land Registration Rules 2003, SI 2003/1417 at **[3067]**.

PART 2
REGISTERED CHARGES

Introductory

9. This Part deals with the registration requirements relating to those dispositions of registered charges which are required to be completed by registration.

Transfer

10. In the case of a transfer, the transferee, or his successor in title, must be entered in the register as the proprietor.

Creation of sub-charge

11. In the case of the creation of a sub-charge, the sub-chargee, or his successor in title, must be entered in the register as the proprietor of the sub-charge.

[2016]

SCHEDULE 3
UNREGISTERED INTERESTS WHICH OVERRIDE REGISTERED DISPOSITIONS

Sections 29 and 30

Leasehold estates in land

1. A leasehold estate in land granted for a term not exceeding seven years from the date of the grant, except for—
   (a) a lease the grant of which falls within section 4(1)(d), (e) or (f);
   (b) a lease the grant of which constitutes a registrable disposition.

Interests of persons in actual occupation

2. An interest belonging at the time of the disposition to a person in actual occupation, so far as relating to land of which he is in actual occupation, except for—
   (a) an interest under a settlement under the Settled Land Act 1925 (c 18);
   (b) an interest of a person of whom inquiry was made before the disposition and who failed to disclose the right when he could reasonably have been expected to do so;
   (c) an interest—
      (i) which belongs to a person whose occupation would not have been obvious on a reasonably careful inspection of the land at the time of the disposition, and
      (ii) of which the person to whom the disposition is made does not have actual knowledge at that time;
   (d) a leasehold estate in land granted to take effect in possession after the end of the period of three months beginning with the date of the grant and which has not taken effect in possession at the time of the disposition.

[2A.—(1) An interest which, immediately before the coming into force of this Schedule, was an overriding interest under section 70(1)(g) of the Land Registration Act 1925 by virtue of a person's receipt of rents and profits, except for an interest of a person of whom inquiry was made before the disposition and who failed to disclose the right when he could reasonably have been expected to do so.

(2) Sub-paragraph (1) does not apply to an interest if at any time since the coming into force of this Schedule it has been an interest which, had the Land Registration Act 1925 (c 21) continued in force, would not have been an overriding interest under section 70(1)(g) of that Act by virtue of a person's receipt of rents and profits.]

Easements and profits a prendre

3.—(1) A legal easement or profit a prendre, except for an easement, or a profit a prendre which is not registered under *the Commons Registration Act 1965 (c 64)* [Part 1 of the Commons Act 2006], which at the time of the disposition—
   (a) is not within the actual knowledge of the person to whom the disposition is made, and
   (b) would not have been obvious on a reasonably careful inspection of the land over which the easement or profit is exercisable.

(2) The exception in sub-paragraph (1) does not apply if the person entitled to the easement or profit proves that it has been exercised in the period of one year ending with the day of the disposition.

Customary and public rights

4. A customary right.

5. A public right.

Local land charges

6. A local land charge.

Mines and minerals

7. An interest in any coal or coal mine, the rights attached to any such interest and the rights of any person under section 38, 49 or 51 of the Coal Industry Act 1994 (c 21).

8. In the case of land to which title was registered before 1898, rights to mines and minerals (and incidental rights) created before 1898.

9. In the case of land to which title was registered between 1898 and 1925 inclusive, rights to mines and minerals (and incidental rights) created before the date of registration of the title.

Miscellaneous

10. A franchise.

11. A manorial right.

12. A right to rent which was reserved to the Crown on the granting of any freehold estate (whether or not the right is still vested in the Crown).

13. A non-statutory right in respect of an embankment or sea or river wall.

14. A right to payment in lieu of tithe.

[15. A right under paragraph 18(1) of Schedule 12.]

[16. A right in respect of the repair of a church chancel.]

[2017]

NOTES

Para 2A: inserted by s 134(2), Sch 12, para 8 at **[2011]**, **[2026]**.

Para 3: in sub-para (1), words in italics substituted by subsequent words in square brackets by the Commons Act 2006, s 52, Sch 5, para 8(1), (4), as from a day to be appointed.

Paras 10–14: repealed by s 117(1) at **[1994]**, as from 13 October 2013.

Para 15: inserted by s 134(2), Sch 12, para 11 at **[2011]**, **[2026]**; for effect see Sch 12, para 11 hereto and SI 2003/1725, art 2(1).

Para 16: inserted by SI 2003/2431, art 2(2), with effect until 13 October 2013: see SI 2003/1725, art 2(1) and SI 2003/2431, art 2(2).

Modification: para 3 modified by s 134(2), Sch 12, para 10 at **[2011]**, **[2026]**;

SCHEDULE 4
ALTERATION OF THE REGISTER

Section 65

Introductory

1. In this Schedule, references to rectification, in relation to alteration of the register, are to alteration which—

(a) involves the correction of a mistake, and

(b) prejudicially affects the title of a registered proprietor.

Alteration pursuant to a court order

2.—(1) The court may make an order for alteration of the register for the purpose of—

(a) correcting a mistake,

(b) bringing the register up to date, or

(c) giving effect to any estate, right or interest excepted from the effect of registration.

(2) An order under this paragraph has effect when served on the registrar to impose a duty on him to give effect to it.

3.—(1) This paragraph applies to the power under paragraph 2, so far as relating to rectification.

(2) If alteration affects the title of the proprietor of a registered estate in land, no order may be made under paragraph 2 without the proprietor's consent in relation to land in his possession unless—

(a) he has by fraud or lack of proper care caused or substantially contributed to the mistake, or

(b) it would for any other reason be unjust for the alteration not to be made.

(3) If in any proceedings the court has power to make an order under paragraph 2, it must do so, unless there are exceptional circumstances which justify its not doing so.

(4) In sub-paragraph (2), the reference to the title of the proprietor of a registered estate in land includes his title to any registered estate which subsists for the benefit of the estate in land.

4. Rules may—

(a) make provision about the circumstances in which there is a duty to exercise the power under paragraph 2, so far as not relating to rectification;
(b) make provision about the form of an order under paragraph 2;
(c) make provision about service of such an order.

Alteration otherwise than pursuant to a court order

5. The registrar may alter the register for the purpose of—
(a) correcting a mistake,
(b) bringing the register up to date,
(c) giving effect to any estate, right or interest excepted from the effect of registration, or
(d) removing a superfluous entry.

6.—(1) This paragraph applies to the power under paragraph 5, so far as relating to rectification.

(2) No alteration affecting the title of the proprietor of a registered estate in land may be made under paragraph 5 without the proprietor's consent in relation to land in his possession unless—
(a) he has by fraud or lack of proper care caused or substantially contributed to the mistake, or
(b) it would for any other reason be unjust for the alteration not to be made.

(3) If on an application for alteration under paragraph 5 the registrar has power to make the alteration, the application must be approved, unless there are exceptional circumstances which justify not making the alteration.

(4) In sub-paragraph (2), the reference to the title of the proprietor of a registered estate in land includes his title to any registered estate which subsists for the benefit of the estate in land.

7. Rules may—
(a) make provision about the circumstances in which there is a duty to exercise the power under paragraph 5, so far as not relating to rectification;
(b) make provision about how the register is to be altered in exercise of that power;
(c) make provision about applications for alteration under that paragraph, including provision requiring the making of such applications;
(d) make provision about procedure in relation to the exercise of that power, whether on application or otherwise.

Rectification and derivative interests

8. The powers under this Schedule to alter the register, so far as relating to rectification, extend to changing for the future the priority of any interest affecting the registered estate or charge concerned.

Costs in non-rectification cases

9.—(1) If the register is altered under this Schedule in a case not involving rectification, the registrar may pay such amount as he thinks fit in respect of any costs or expenses reasonably incurred by a person in connection with the alteration which have been incurred with the consent of the registrar.

(2) The registrar may make a payment under sub-paragraph (1) notwithstanding the absence of consent if—
(a) it appears to him—
(i) that the costs or expenses had to be incurred urgently, and
(ii) that it was not reasonably practicable to apply for his consent, or
(b) he has subsequently approved the incurring of the costs or expenses.

[2018]

NOTES

Rules: the Land Registration Rules 2003, SI 2003/1417 at **[3067]**.

SCHEDULE 5
LAND REGISTRY NETWORK

Section 92

Access to network

1.—(1) A person who is not a member of the land registry may only have access to a land registry network under authority conferred by means of an agreement with the registrar.

(2) An agreement for the purposes of sub-paragraph (1) ("network access agreement") may authorise access for—
(a) the communication, posting or retrieval of information,
(b) the making of changes to the register of title or cautions register,
(c) the issue of official search certificates,

(d) the issue of official copies, or
(e) such other conveyancing purposes as the registrar thinks fit.

(3) Rules may regulate the use of network access agreements to confer authority to carry out functions of the registrar.

(4) The registrar must, on application, enter into a network access agreement with the applicant if the applicant meets such criteria as rules may provide.

Terms of access

2.—(1) The terms on which access to a land registry network is authorised shall be such as the registrar thinks fit, subject to sub-paragraphs (3) and (4), and may, in particular, include charges for access.

(2) The power under sub-paragraph (1) may be used, not only for the purpose of regulating the use of the network, but also for—

(a) securing that the person granted access uses the network to carry on such qualifying transactions as may be specified in, or under, the agreement,
(b) such other purpose relating to the carrying on of qualifying transactions as rules may provide, or
(c) enabling network transactions to be monitored.

(3) It shall be a condition of a network access agreement which enables the person granted access to use the network to carry on qualifying transactions that he must comply with any rules for the time being in force under paragraph 5.

(4) Rules may regulate the terms on which access to a land registry network is authorised.

Termination of access

3.—(1) The person granted access by a network access agreement may terminate the agreement at any time by notice to the registrar.

(2) Rules may make provision about the termination of a network access agreement by the registrar and may, in particular, make provision about—

(a) the grounds of termination,
(b) the procedure to be followed in relation to termination, and
(c) the suspension of termination pending appeal.

(3) Without prejudice to the generality of sub-paragraph (2)(a), rules under that provision may authorise the registrar to terminate a network access agreement if the person granted access—

(a) fails to comply with the terms of the agreement,
(b) ceases to be a person with whom the registrar would be required to enter into a network access agreement conferring the authority which the agreement confers, or
(c) does not meet such conditions as the rules may provide.

Appeals

4.—(1) A person who is aggrieved by a decision of the registrar with respect to entry into, or termination of, a network access agreement may appeal against the decision to the adjudicator.

(2) On determining an appeal under this paragraph, the adjudicator may give such directions as he considers appropriate to give effect to his determination.

(3) Rules may make provision about appeals under this paragraph.

Network transaction rules

5.—(1) Rules may make provision about how to go about network transactions.

(2) Rules under sub-paragraph (1) may, in particular, make provision about dealings with the land registry, including provision about—

(a) the procedure to be followed, and
(b) the supply of information (including information about unregistered interests).

Overriding nature of network access obligations

6. To the extent that an obligation not owed under a network access agreement conflicts with an obligation owed under such an agreement by the person granted access, the obligation not owed under the agreement is discharged.

Do-it-yourself conveyancing

7.—(1) If there is a land registry network, the registrar has a duty to provide such assistance as he thinks appropriate for the purpose of enabling persons engaged in qualifying transactions who wish to do their own conveyancing to do so by means of the network.

(2) The duty under sub-paragraph (1) does not extend to the provision of legal advice.

Presumption of authority

8. Where—
   (a) a person who is authorised under a network access agreement to do so uses the network for the making of a disposition or contract, and
   (b) the document which purports to effect the disposition or to be the contract—
      (i) purports to be authenticated by him as agent, and
      (ii) contains a statement to the effect that he is acting under the authority of his principal,

he shall be deemed, in favour of any other party, to be so acting.

Management of network transactions

9.—(1) The registrar may use monitoring information for the purpose of managing network transactions and may, in particular, disclose such information to persons authorised to use the network, and authorise the further disclosure of information so disclosed, if he considers it is necessary or desirable to do so.

(2) The registrar may delegate his functions under sub-paragraph (1), subject to such conditions as he thinks fit.

(3) In sub-paragraph (1), "monitoring information" means information provided in pursuance of provision in a network access agreement included under paragraph 2(2)(c).

Supplementary

10. The registrar may provide, or arrange for the provision of, education and training in relation to the use of a land registry network.

11.—(1) Power to make rules under paragraph 1, 2 or 3 is exercisable by the Lord Chancellor.

(2) Before making such rules, the Lord Chancellor must consult such persons as he considers appropriate.

(3) In making rules under paragraph 1 or 3(2)(a), the Lord Chancellor must have regard, in particular, to the need to secure—
   (a) the confidentiality of private information kept on the network,
   (b) competence in relation to the use of the network (in particular for the purpose of making changes), and
   (c) the adequate insurance of potential liabilities in connection with use of the network.

12. In this Schedule—

"land registry network" means a network provided under section 92(1);

"network access agreement" has the meaning given by paragraph 1(2);

"network transaction" means a transaction carried on by means of a land registry network;

"qualifying transaction" means a transaction which—
   (a) involves registration, and
   (b) is capable of being effected electronically.

[2019]

NOTES

Rules: the Network Access Appeal Rules 2008, SI 2008/1730; the Land Registration (Network Access) Rules 2008, SI 2008/1748; the Land Registration (Electronic Conveyancing) Rules 2008, SI 2008/1750.

SCHEDULE 6
REGISTRATION OF ADVERSE POSSESSOR

Section 97

Right to apply for registration

1.—(1) A person may apply to the registrar to be registered as the proprietor of a registered estate in land if he has been in adverse possession of the estate for the period of ten years ending on the date of the application.

(2) A person may also apply to the registrar to be registered as the proprietor of a registered estate in land if—
   (a) he has in the period of six months ending on the date of the application ceased to be in adverse possession of the estate because of eviction by the registered proprietor, or a person claiming under the registered proprietor,
   (b) on the day before his eviction he was entitled to make an application under sub-paragraph (1), and
   (c) the eviction was not pursuant to a judgment for possession.

(3) However, a person may not make an application under this paragraph if—
   (a) he is a defendant in proceedings which involve asserting a right to possession of the land, or

(b) judgment for possession of the land has been given against him in the last two years.

(4) For the purposes of sub-paragraph (1), the estate need not have been registered throughout the period of adverse possession.

Notification of application

2.—(1) The registrar must give notice of an application under paragraph 1 to—
(a) the proprietor of the estate to which the application relates,
(b) the proprietor of any registered charge on the estate,
(c) where the estate is leasehold, the proprietor of any superior registered estate,
(d) any person who is registered in accordance with rules as a person to be notified under this paragraph, and
(e) such other persons as rules may provide.

(2) Notice under this paragraph shall include notice of the effect of paragraph 4.

Treatment of application

3.—(1) A person given notice under paragraph 2 may require that the application to which the notice relates be dealt with under paragraph 5.

(2) The right under this paragraph is exercisable by notice to the registrar given before the end of such period as rules may provide.

4. If an application under paragraph 1 is not required to be dealt with under paragraph 5, the applicant is entitled to be entered in the register as the new proprietor of the estate.

5.—(1) If an application under paragraph 1 is required to be dealt with under this paragraph, the applicant is only entitled to be registered as the new proprietor of the estate if any of the following conditions is met.

(2) The first condition is that—
(a) it would be unconscionable because of an equity by estoppel for the registered proprietor to seek to dispossess the applicant, and
(b) the circumstances are such that the applicant ought to be registered as the proprietor.

(3) The second condition is that the applicant is for some other reason entitled to be registered as the proprietor of the estate.

(4) The third condition is that—
(a) the land to which the application relates is adjacent to land belonging to the applicant,
(b) the exact line of the boundary between the two has not been determined under rules under section 60,
(c) for at least ten years of the period of adverse possession ending on the date of the application, the applicant (or any predecessor in title) reasonably believed that the land to which the application relates belonged to him, and
(d) the estate to which the application relates was registered more than one year prior to the date of the application.

(5) In relation to an application under paragraph 1(2), this paragraph has effect as if the reference in sub-paragraph (4)(c) to the date of the application were to the day before the date of the applicant's eviction.

Right to make further application for registration

6.—(1) Where a person's application under paragraph 1 is rejected, he may make a further application to be registered as the proprietor of the estate if he is in adverse possession of the estate from the date of the application until the last day of the period of two years beginning with the date of its rejection.

(2) However, a person may not make an application under this paragraph if—
(a) he is a defendant in proceedings which involve asserting a right to possession of the land,
(b) judgment for possession of the land has been given against him in the last two years, or
(c) he has been evicted from the land pursuant to a judgment for possession.

7. If a person makes an application under paragraph 6, he is entitled to be entered in the register as the new proprietor of the estate.

Restriction on applications

8.—(1) No one may apply under this Schedule to be registered as the proprietor of an estate in land during, or before the end of twelve months after the end of, any period in which the existing registered proprietor is for the purposes of the Limitation (Enemies and War Prisoners) Act 1945 (8 & 9 Geo 6 c 16)—
(a) an enemy, or
(b) detained in enemy territory.

(2) No-one may apply under this Schedule to be registered as the proprietor of an estate in land during any period in which the existing registered proprietor is—

(a) unable because of mental disability to make decisions about issues of the kind to which such an application would give rise, or

(b) unable to communicate such decisions because of mental disability or physical impairment.

(3) For the purposes of sub-paragraph (2), "mental disability" means a disability or disorder of the mind or brain, whether permanent or temporary, which results in an impairment or disturbance of mental functioning.

(4) Where it appears to the registrar that sub-paragraph (1) or (2) applies in relation to an estate in land, he may include a note to that effect in the register.

Effect of registration

9.—(1) Where a person is registered as the proprietor of an estate in land in pursuance of an application under this Schedule, the title by virtue of adverse possession which he had at the time of the application is extinguished.

(2) Subject to sub-paragraph (3), the registration of a person under this Schedule as the proprietor of an estate in land does not affect the priority of any interest affecting the estate.

(3) Subject to sub-paragraph (4), where a person is registered under this Schedule as the proprietor of an estate, the estate is vested in him free of any registered charge affecting the estate immediately before his registration.

(4) Sub-paragraph (3) does not apply where registration as proprietor is in pursuance of an application determined by reference to whether any of the conditions in paragraph 5 applies.

Apportionment and discharge of charges

10.—(1) Where—

(a) a registered estate continues to be subject to a charge notwithstanding the registration of a person under this Schedule as the proprietor, and

(b) the charge affects property other than the estate,

the proprietor of the estate may require the chargee to apportion the amount secured by the charge at that time between the estate and the other property on the basis of their respective values.

(2) The person requiring the apportionment is entitled to a discharge of his estate from the charge on payment of—

(a) the amount apportioned to the estate, and

(b) the costs incurred by the chargee as a result of the apportionment.

(3) On a discharge under this paragraph, the liability of the chargor to the chargee is reduced by the amount apportioned to the estate.

(4) Rules may make provision about apportionment under this paragraph, in particular, provision about—

(a) procedure,

(b) valuation,

(c) calculation of costs payable under sub-paragraph (2)(b), and

(d) payment of the costs of the chargor.

Meaning of "adverse possession"

11.—(1) A person is in adverse possession of an estate in land for the purposes of this Schedule if, but for section 96, a period of limitation under section 15 of the Limitation Act 1980 (c 58) would run in his favour in relation to the estate.

(2) A person is also to be regarded for those purposes as having been in adverse possession of an estate in land—

(a) where he is the successor in title to an estate in the land, during any period of adverse possession by a predecessor in title to that estate, or

(b) during any period of adverse possession by another person which comes between, and is continuous with, periods of adverse possession of his own.

(3) In determining whether for the purposes of this paragraph a period of limitation would run under section 15 of the Limitation Act 1980, there are to be disregarded—

(a) the commencement of any legal proceedings, and

(b) paragraph 6 of Schedule 1 to that Act.

Trusts

12. A person is not to be regarded as being in adverse possession of an estate for the purposes of this Schedule at any time when the estate is subject to a trust, unless the interest of each of the beneficiaries in the estate is an interest in possession.

Crown foreshore

13.—(1) Where—

(a) a person is in adverse possession of an estate in land,

(b) the estate belongs to Her Majesty in right of the Crown or the Duchy of Lancaster or to the Duchy of Cornwall, and

(c) the land consists of foreshore,

paragraph 1(1) is to have effect as if the reference to ten years were to sixty years.

(2) For the purposes of sub-paragraph (1), land is to be treated as foreshore if it has been foreshore at any time in the previous ten years.

(3) In this paragraph, "foreshore" means the shore and bed of the sea and of any tidal water, below the line of the medium high tide between the spring and neap tides.

Rentcharges

14. Rules must make provision to apply the preceding provisions of this Schedule to registered rentcharges, subject to such modifications and exceptions as the rules may provide.

Procedure

15. Rules may make provision about the procedure to be followed pursuant to an application under this Schedule.

[2020]

NOTES

Commencement: 13 October 2003 (paras 1–4, 5(1)–(3), 6–15); 13 October 2004 (para 5(4), (5)).
Rules: the Land Registration Rules 2003, SI 2003/1417 at **[3067]**.

SCHEDULE 7
THE LAND REGISTRY

Section 99

1 Holding of office by Chief Land Registrar

(1) The registrar may at any time resign his office by written notice to the Lord Chancellor.

(2) The Lord Chancellor may remove the registrar from office if he is unable or unfit to discharge the functions of office.

(3) Subject to the above, a person appointed to be the registrar is to hold and vacate office in accordance with the terms of his appointment and, on ceasing to hold office, is eligible for reappointment.

2 Remuneration etc of Chief Land Registrar

(1) The Lord Chancellor shall pay the registrar such remuneration, and such travelling and other allowances, as the Lord Chancellor may determine.

(2) The Lord Chancellor shall—

(a) pay such pension, allowances or gratuities as he may determine to or in respect of a person who is or has been the registrar, or

(b) make such payments as he may determine towards provision for the payment of a pension, allowances or gratuities to or in respect of such a person.

(3) If, when a person ceases to be the registrar, the Lord Chancellor determines that there are special circumstances which make it right that the person should receive compensation, the Lord Chancellor may pay to the person by way of compensation a sum of such amount as he may determine.

3 Staff

(1) The registrar may appoint such staff as he thinks fit.

(2) The terms and conditions of appointments under this paragraph shall be such as the registrar, with the approval of the Minister for the Civil Service, thinks fit.

4 Indemnity for members

No member of the land registry is to be liable in damages for anything done or omitted in the discharge or purported discharge of any function relating to land registration, unless it is shown that the act or omission was in bad faith.

5 Seal

The land registry is to continue to have a seal and any document purporting to be sealed with it is to be admissible in evidence without any further or other proof.

6 Documentary evidence

The Documentary Evidence Act 1868 (c 37) has effect as if—

(a) the registrar were included in the first column of the Schedule to that Act,

(b) the registrar and any person authorised to act on his behalf were mentioned in the second column of that Schedule, and

(c) the regulations referred to in that Act included any form or direction issued by the registrar or by any such person.

7 Parliamentary disqualification

In Part 3 of Schedule 1 to the House of Commons Disqualification Act 1975 (c 24) (other disqualifying offices), there is inserted at the appropriate place—

"Chief Land Registrar.";

and a corresponding amendment is made in Part 3 of Schedule 1 to the Northern Ireland Assembly Disqualification Act 1975 (c 25).

[2021]

SCHEDULE 8
INDEMNITIES

Section 103

Entitlement

1.—(1) A person is entitled to be indemnified by the registrar if he suffers loss by reason of—

(a) rectification of the register,

(b) a mistake whose correction would involve rectification of the register,

(c) a mistake in an official search,

(d) a mistake in an official copy,

(e) a mistake in a document kept by the registrar which is not an original and is referred to in the register,

(f) the loss or destruction of a document lodged at the registry for inspection or safe custody,

(g) a mistake in the cautions register, or

(h) failure by the registrar to perform his duty under section 50.

(2) For the purposes of sub-paragraph (1)(a)—

(a) any person who suffers loss by reason of the change of title under section 62 is to be regarded as having suffered loss by reason of rectification of the register, and

(b) the proprietor of a registered estate or charge claiming in good faith under a forged disposition is, where the register is rectified, to be regarded as having suffered loss by reason of such rectification as if the disposition had not been forged.

(3) No indemnity under sub-paragraph (1)(b) is payable until a decision has been made about whether to alter the register for the purpose of correcting the mistake; and the loss suffered by reason of the mistake is to be determined in the light of that decision.

Mines and minerals

2. No indemnity is payable under this Schedule on account of—

(a) any mines or minerals, or

(b) the existence of any right to work or get mines or minerals,

unless it is noted in the register that the title to the registered estate concerned includes the mines or minerals.

Costs

3.—(1) In respect of loss consisting of costs or expenses incurred by the claimant in relation to the matter, an indemnity under this Schedule is payable only on account of costs or expenses reasonably incurred by the claimant with the consent of the registrar.

(2) The requirement of consent does not apply where—

(a) the costs or expenses must be incurred by the claimant urgently, and

(b) it is not reasonably practicable to apply for the registrar's consent.

(3) If the registrar approves the incurring of costs or expenses after they have been incurred, they shall be treated for the purposes of this paragraph as having been incurred with his consent.

4.—(1) If no indemnity is payable to a claimant under this Schedule, the registrar may pay such amount as he thinks fit in respect of any costs or expenses reasonably incurred by the claimant in connection with the claim which have been incurred with the consent of the registrar.

(2) The registrar may make a payment under sub-paragraph (1) notwithstanding the absence of consent if—

(a) it appears to him—

(i) that the costs or expenses had to be incurred urgently, and
(ii) that it was not reasonably practicable to apply for his consent, or
(b) he has subsequently approved the incurring of the costs or expenses.

Claimant's fraud or lack of care

5.—(1) No indemnity is payable under this Schedule on account of any loss suffered by a claimant—
(a) wholly or partly as a result of his own fraud, or
(b) wholly as a result of his own lack of proper care.

(2) Where any loss is suffered by a claimant partly as a result of his own lack of proper care, any indemnity payable to him is to be reduced to such extent as is fair having regard to his share in the responsibility for the loss.

(3) For the purposes of this paragraph any fraud or lack of care on the part of a person from whom the claimant derives title (otherwise than under a disposition for valuable consideration which is registered or protected by an entry in the register) is to be treated as if it were fraud or lack of care on the part of the claimant.

Valuation of estates etc

6. Where an indemnity is payable in respect of the loss of an estate, interest or charge, the value of the estate, interest or charge for the purposes of the indemnity is to be regarded as not exceeding—
(a) in the case of an indemnity under paragraph 1(1)(a), its value immediately before rectification of the register (but as if there were to be no rectification), and
(b) in the case of an indemnity under paragraph 1(1)(b), its value at the time when the mistake which caused the loss was made.

Determination of indemnity by court

7.—(1) A person may apply to the court for the determination of any question as to—
(a) whether he is entitled to an indemnity under this Schedule, or
(b) the amount of such an indemnity.

(2) Paragraph 3(1) does not apply to the costs of an application to the court under this paragraph or of any legal proceedings arising out of such an application.

Time limits

8. For the purposes of the Limitation Act 1980 (c 58)—
(a) a liability to pay an indemnity under this Schedule is a simple contract debt, and
(b) the cause of action arises at the time when the claimant knows, or but for his own default might have known, of the existence of his claim.

Interest

9. Rules may make provision about the payment of interest on an indemnity under this Schedule, including—
(a) the circumstances in which interest is payable, and
(b) the periods for and rates at which it is payable.

Recovery of indemnity by registrar

10.—(1) Where an indemnity under this Schedule is paid to a claimant in respect of any loss, the registrar is entitled (without prejudice to any other rights he may have)—
(a) to recover the amount paid from any person who caused or substantially contributed to the loss by his fraud, or
(b) for the purpose of recovering the amount paid, to enforce the rights of action referred to in sub-paragraph (2).

(2) Those rights of action are—
(a) any right of action (of whatever nature and however arising) which the claimant would have been entitled to enforce had the indemnity not been paid, and
(b) where the register has been rectified, any right of action (of whatever nature and however arising) which the person in whose favour the register has been rectified would have been entitled to enforce had it not been rectified.

(3) References in this paragraph to an indemnity include interest paid on an indemnity under rules under paragraph 9.

Interpretation

11.—(1) For the purposes of this Schedule, references to a mistake in something include anything mistakenly omitted from it as well as anything mistakenly included in it.

(2) In this Schedule, references to rectification of the register are to alteration of the register which—

(a) involves the correction of a mistake, and

(b) prejudicially affects the title of a registered proprietor.

[2022]

NOTES

Rules: the Land Registration Rules 2003, SI 2003/1417 at **[3067]**.

SCHEDULE 9
THE ADJUDICATOR

Section 107

Holding of office

1.—(1) The adjudicator may at any time resign his office by written notice to the Lord Chancellor.

(2) The Lord Chancellor may[, with the concurrence of the Lord Chief Justice,] remove the adjudicator from office on the ground of incapacity or misbehaviour.

(3) Section 26 of the Judicial Pensions and Retirement Act 1993 (c 8) (compulsory retirement at 70, subject to the possibility of annual extension up to 75) applies to the adjudicator.

(4) Subject to the above, a person appointed to be the adjudicator is to hold and vacate office in accordance with the terms of his appointment and, on ceasing to hold office, is eligible for reappointment.

Remuneration

2.—(1) The Lord Chancellor shall pay the adjudicator such remuneration, and such other allowances, as the Lord Chancellor may determine.

(2) The Lord Chancellor shall—

(a) pay such pension, allowances or gratuities as he may determine to or in respect of a person who is or has been the adjudicator, or

(b) make such payments as he may determine towards provision for the payment of a pension, allowances or gratuities to or in respect of such a person.

(3) Sub-paragraph (2) does not apply if the office of adjudicator is a qualifying judicial office within the meaning of the Judicial Pensions and Retirement Act 1993.

(4) If, when a person ceases to be the adjudicator, the Lord Chancellor determines that there are special circumstances which make it right that the person should receive compensation, the Lord Chancellor may pay to the person by way of compensation a sum of such amount as he may determine.

Staff

3.—(1) The adjudicator may appoint such staff as he thinks fit.

(2) The terms and conditions of appointments under this paragraph shall be such as the adjudicator, with the approval of the Minister for the Civil Service, thinks fit.

Conduct of business

4.—(1) Subject to sub-paragraph (2), any function of the adjudicator may be carried out by any member of his staff who is authorised by him for the purpose.

(2) In the case of functions which are not of an administrative character, sub-paragraph (1) only applies if the member of staff [satisfies the judicial-appointment eligibility condition on a 7-year basis].

5. The Lord Chancellor may by regulations make provision about the carrying out of functions during any vacancy in the office of adjudicator.

Finances

6. The Lord Chancellor shall be liable to reimburse expenditure incurred by the adjudicator in the discharge of his functions.

7. The Lord Chancellor may require the registrar to make payments towards expenses of the Lord Chancellor under this Schedule.

Application of Tribunals and Inquiries Act 1992

8. In Schedule 1 to the Tribunal and Inquiries Act 1992 (c 53) (tribunals under the supervision of the Council on Tribunals), after paragraph 27 there is inserted—

"Land Registration	27B The Adjudicator to Her Majesty's Land Registry."

Parliamentary disqualification

9. In Part 1 of Schedule 1 to the House of Commons Disqualification Act 1975 (c 24) (judicial offices), there is inserted at the end—

"Adjudicator to Her Majesty's Land Registry.";

and a corresponding amendment is made in Part 1 of Schedule 1 to the Northern Ireland Assembly Disqualification Act 1975 (c 25).

[2023]

NOTES

Para 1: in sub-para (2) words in square brackets inserted by the Constitutional Reform Act 2005, s 15(1), Sch 4, Pt 1, paras 301, 303.

Para 4: in sub-para (2) words in square brackets substituted by the Tribunals, Courts and Enforcement Act 2007, s 50, Sch 10, Pt 1, para 35(1), (3); for transitional provisions, see SI 2008/1653, arts 3, 4.

Regulations: the Land Registration (Acting Adjudicator) Regulations 2003, SI 2003/2342 at **[3409]**.

SCHEDULE 10
MISCELLANEOUS AND GENERAL POWERS

Section 126

PART 1
MISCELLANEOUS

1 Dealings with estates subject to compulsory first registration

(1) Rules may make provision—

(a) applying this Act to a pre-registration dealing with a registrable legal estate as if the dealing had taken place after the date of first registration of the estate, and

(b) about the date on which registration of the dealing is effective.

(2) For the purposes of sub-paragraph (1)—

(a) a legal estate is registrable if a person is subject to a duty under section 6 to make an application to be registered as the proprietor of it, and

(b) a pre-registration dealing is one which takes place before the making of such an application.

2 Regulation of title matters between sellers and buyers

(1) Rules may make provision about the obligations with respect to—

(a) proof of title, or

(b) perfection of title,

of the seller under a contract for the transfer, or other disposition, for valuable consideration of a registered estate or charge.

(2) Rules under this paragraph may be expressed to have effect notwithstanding any stipulation to the contrary.

3 Implied covenants

Rules may—

(a) make provision about the form of provisions extending or limiting any covenant implied by virtue of Part 1 of the Law of Property (Miscellaneous Provisions) Act 1994 (c 36) (implied covenants for title) on a registrable disposition;

(b) make provision about the application of section 77 of the Law of Property Act 1925 (c 20) (implied covenants in conveyance subject to rents) to transfers of registered estates;

(c) make provision about reference in the register to implied covenants, including provision for the state of the register to be conclusive in relation to whether covenants have been implied.

4 Land certificates

Rules may make provision about—

(a) when a certificate of registration of title to a legal estate may be issued,

(b) the form and content of such a certificate, and

(c) when such a certificate must be produced or surrendered to the registrar.

[2024]

NOTES

Rules: the Land Registration Rules 2003, SI 2003/1417 at **[3067]**; the Land Registration (Electronic Conveyancing) Rules 2008, SI 2008/1750.

PART 2
GENERAL

5 Notice

(1) Rules may make provision about the form, content and service of notice under this Act.

(2) Rules under this paragraph about the service of notice may, in particular—

(a) make provision requiring the supply of an address for service and about the entry of addresses for service in the register;

(b) make provision about—

(i) the time for service,

(ii) the mode of service, and

(iii) when service is to be regarded as having taken place.

6 Applications

Rules may—

(a) make provision about the form and content of applications under this Act;

(b) make provision requiring applications under this Act to be supported by such evidence as the rules may provide;

(c) make provision about when an application under this Act is to be taken as made;

(d) make provision about the order in which competing applications are to be taken to rank;

(e) make provision for an alteration made by the registrar for the purpose of correcting a mistake in an application or accompanying document to have effect in such circumstances as the rules may provide as if made by the applicant or other interested party or parties.

7 Statutory statements

Rules may make provision about the form of any statement required under an enactment to be included in an instrument effecting a registrable disposition or a disposition which triggers the requirement of registration.

8 Residual power

Rules may make any other provision which it is expedient to make for the purposes of carrying this Act into effect, whether similar or not to any provision which may be made under the other powers to make land registration rules.

[2025]

NOTES

Rules: the Land Registration Rules 2003, SI 2003/1417 at **[3067]**; the Land Registration (Electronic Conveyancing) Rules 2008, SI 2008/1750.

(*Sch 11 contains amendments which, in so far as relevant to this work, have been incorporated at the appropriate place.*)

SCHEDULE 12
TRANSITION

Section 134

Existing entries in the register

1. Nothing in the repeals made by this Act affects the validity of any entry in the register.

2.—(1) This Act applies to notices entered under the Land Registration Act 1925 (c 21) as it applies to notices entered in pursuance of an application under section 34(2)(a).

(2) This Act applies to restrictions and inhibitions entered under the Land Registration Act 1925 as it applies to restrictions entered under this Act.

(3) Notwithstanding their repeal by this Act, sections 55 and 56 of the Land Registration Act 1925 shall continue to have effect so far as relating to cautions against dealings lodged under that Act.

(4) Rules may make provision about cautions against dealings entered under the Land Registration Act 1925.

(5) In this paragraph, references to the Land Registration Act 1925 include a reference to any enactment replaced (directly or indirectly) by that Act.

3. An entry in the register which, immediately before the repeal of section 144(1)(xi) of the Land Registration Act 1925, operated by virtue of rule 239 of the Land Registration Rules (SI 1925/1093) as a caution under section 54 of that Act shall continue to operate as such a caution.

Existing cautions against first registration

4. Notwithstanding the repeal of section 56(3) of the Land Registration Act 1925, that provision shall continue to have effect in relation to cautions against first registration lodged under that Act, or any enactment replaced (directly or indirectly) by that Act.

Pending applications

5. Notwithstanding the repeal of the Land Registration Act 1925, that Act shall continue to have effect in relation to an application for the entry in the register of a notice, restriction, inhibition or caution against dealings which is pending immediately before the repeal of the provision under which the application is made.

6. Notwithstanding the repeal of section 53 of the Land Registration Act 1925, subsections (1) and (2) of that section shall continue to have effect in relation to an application to lodge a caution against first registration which is pending immediately before the repeal of those provisions.

Former overriding interests

7. For the period of three years beginning with the day on which Schedule 1 comes into force, it has effect with the insertion after paragraph 14 of—

> "15. A right acquired under the Limitation Act 1980 before the coming into force of this Schedule."

8. Schedule 3 has effect with the insertion after paragraph 2 of—

> "2A.—(1) An interest which, immediately before the coming into force of this Schedule, was an overriding interest under section 70(1)(g) of the Land Registration Act 1925 by virtue of a person's receipt of rents and profits, except for an interest of a person of whom inquiry was made before the disposition and who failed to disclose the right when he could reasonably have been expected to do so.
>
> (2) Sub-paragraph (1) does not apply to an interest if at any time since the coming into force of this Schedule it has been an interest which, had the Land Registration Act 1925 (c 21) continued in force, would not have been an overriding interest under section 70(1)(g) of that Act by virtue of a person's receipt of rents and profits."

9.—(1) This paragraph applies to an easement or profit a prendre which was an overriding interest in relation to a registered estate immediately before the coming into force of Schedule 3, but which would not fall within paragraph 3 of that Schedule if created after the coming into force of that Schedule.

(2) In relation to an interest to which this paragraph applies, Schedule 3 has effect as if the interest were not excluded from paragraph 3.

10. For the period of three years beginning with the day on which Schedule 3 comes into force, paragraph 3 of the Schedule has effect with the omission of the exception.

11. For the period of three years beginning with the day on which Schedule 3 comes into force, it has effect with the insertion after paragraph 14 of—

> "15. A right under paragraph 18(1) of Schedule 12."

12. Paragraph 1 of each of Schedules 1 and 3 shall be taken to include an interest which immediately before the coming into force of the Schedule was an overriding interest under section 70(1)(k) of the Land Registration Act 1925.

13. Paragraph 6 of each of Schedules 1 and 3 shall be taken to include an interest which immediately before the coming into force of the Schedule was an overriding interest under section 70(1)(i) of the Land Registration Act 1925 and whose status as such was preserved by section 19(3) of the Local Land Charges Act 1975 (c 76) (transitional provision in relation to change in definition of "local land charge").

Cautions against first registration

14.—(1) For the period of two years beginning with the day on which section 15 comes into force, it has effect with the following omissions—

(a) in subsection (1), the words "Subject to subsection (3),", and
(b) subsection (3).

(2) Any caution lodged by virtue of sub-paragraph (1) which is in force immediately before the end of the period mentioned in that sub-paragraph shall cease to have effect at the end of that period, except in relation to applications for registration made before the end of that period.

(3) This paragraph does not apply to section 15 as applied by section 81.

15.—(1) As applied by section 81, section 15 has effect for the period of ten years beginning with the day on which it comes into force, or such longer period as rules may provide, with the omission of subsection (3)(a)(i).

(2) Any caution lodged by virtue of sub-paragraph (1) which is in force immediately before the end of the period mentioned in that sub-paragraph shall cease to have effect at the end of that period, except in relation to applications for registration made before the end of that period.

16. This Act shall apply as if the definition of "caution against first registration" in section 132 included cautions lodged under section 53 of the Land Registration Act 1925 (c 21).

Applications under section 34 or 43 by cautioners

17. Where a caution under section 54 of the Land Registration Act 1925 is lodged in respect of a person's estate, right, interest or claim, he may only make an application under section 34 or 43 above in respect of that estate, right, interest or claim if he also applies to the registrar for the withdrawal of the caution.

Adverse possession

18.—(1) Where a registered estate in land is held in trust for a person by virtue of section 75(1) of the Land Registration Act 1925 immediately before the coming into force of section 97, he is entitled to be registered as the proprietor of the estate.

(2) A person has a defence to any action for the possession of land (in addition to any other defence he may have) if he is entitled under this paragraph to be registered as the proprietor of an estate in the land.

(3) Where in an action for possession of land a court determines that a person is entitled to a defence under this paragraph, the court must order the registrar to register him as the proprietor of the estate in relation to which he is entitled under this paragraph to be registered.

(4) Entitlement under this paragraph shall be disregarded for the purposes of section 131(1).

(5) Rules may make transitional provision for cases where a rentcharge is held in trust under section 75(1) of the Land Registration Act 1925 immediately before the coming into force of section 97.

Indemnities

19.—(1) Schedule 8 applies in relation to claims made before the commencement of that Schedule which have not been settled by agreement or finally determined by that time (as well as to claims for indemnity made after the commencement of that Schedule).

(2) But paragraph 3(1) of that Schedule does not apply in relation to costs and expenses incurred in respect of proceedings, negotiations or other matters begun before 27 April 1997.

Implied indemnity covenants on transfers of pre-1996 leases

20.—(1) On a disposition of a registered leasehold estate by way of transfer, the following covenants are implied in the instrument effecting the disposition, unless the contrary intention is expressed—

(a) in the case of a transfer of the whole of the land comprised in the registered lease, the covenant in sub-paragraph (2), and

(b) in the case of a transfer of part of the land comprised in the lease—

(i) the covenant in sub-paragraph (3), and

(ii) where the transferor continues to hold land under the lease, the covenant in sub-paragraph (4).

(2) The transferee covenants with the transferor that during the residue of the term granted by the registered lease the transferee and the persons deriving title under him will—

(a) pay the rent reserved by the lease,

(b) comply with the covenants and conditions contained in the lease, and

(c) keep the transferor and the persons deriving title under him indemnified against all actions, expenses and claims on account of any failure to comply with paragraphs (a) and (b).

(3) The transferee covenants with the transferor that during the residue of the term granted by the registered lease the transferee and the persons deriving title under him will—

(a) where the rent reserved by the lease is apportioned, pay the rent apportioned to the part transferred,

(b) comply with the covenants and conditions contained in the lease so far as affecting the part transferred, and

(c) keep the transferor and the persons deriving title under him indemnified against all actions, expenses and claims on account of any failure to comply with paragraphs (a) and (b).

(4) The transferor covenants with the transferee that during the residue of the term granted by the registered lease the transferor and the persons deriving title under him will—

(a) where the rent reserved by the lease is apportioned, pay the rent apportioned to the part retained,

(b) comply with the covenants and conditions contained in the lease so far as affecting the part retained, and

(c) keep the transferee and the persons deriving title under him indemnified against all actions, expenses and claims on account of any failure to comply with paragraphs (a) and (b).

(5) This paragraph does not apply to a lease which is a new tenancy for the purposes of section 1 of the Landlord and Tenant (Covenants) Act 1995 (c 30).

[2026]

NOTES

Rules: the Land Registration Rules 2003, SI 2003/1417 at **[3067]**.

See further: in relation to further transitional provisions, the Land Registration Act 2002 (Transitional Provisions) Order 2003, SI 2003/1953 at **[3308]**.

(*Sch 13 contains repeals which, in so far as relevant to this work, have been incorporated at the appropriate place.*)

COMMONHOLD AND LEASEHOLD REFORM ACT 2002

(2002 c 15)

An Act to make provision about commonhold land and to amend the law about leasehold property.

[1 May 2002]

PART 1
COMMONHOLD

Nature of commonhold

1 Commonhold land

(1) Land is commonhold land if—

(a) the freehold estate in the land is registered as a freehold estate in commonhold land,

(b) the land is specified in the *memorandum of association* [articles of association] of a commonhold association as the land in relation to which the association is to exercise functions, and

(c) a commonhold community statement makes provision for rights and duties of the commonhold association and unit-holders (whether or not the statement has come into force).

(2) In this Part a reference to a commonhold is a reference to land in relation to which a commonhold association exercises functions.

(3) In this Part—

"commonhold association" has the meaning given by section 34,
"commonhold community statement" has the meaning given by section 31,
"commonhold unit" has the meaning given by section 11,
"common parts" has the meaning given by section 25, and
"unit-holder" has the meaning given by sections 12 and 13.

(4) Sections 7 and 9 make provision for the vesting in the commonhold association of the fee simple in possession in the common parts of a commonhold.

[2027]

NOTES

Commencement: 27 September 2004.

Sub-s (1): in sub-para (b) words in italics substituted by subsequent words in square brackets SI 2009/1941, art 2(1), Sch 1, para 194(1), (2), as from 1 October 2009.

Registration

2 Application

(1) The Registrar shall register a freehold estate in land as a freehold estate in commonhold land if—

(a) the registered freeholder of the land makes an application under this section, and

(b) no part of the land is already commonhold land.

(2) An application under this section must be accompanied by the documents listed in Schedule 1.

(3) A person is the registered freeholder of land for the purposes of this Part if—

(a) he is registered as the proprietor of a freehold estate in the land with absolute title, or

(b) he has applied, and the Registrar is satisfied that he is entitled, to be registered as mentioned in paragraph (a).

[2028]

NOTES

Commencement: 27 September 2004.

3 Consent

(1) An application under section 2 may not be made in respect of a freehold estate in land without the consent of anyone who—

(a) is the registered proprietor of the freehold estate in the whole or part of the land,

(b) is the registered proprietor of a leasehold estate in the whole or part of the land granted for a term of more than than 21 years,

(c) is the registered proprietor of a charge over the whole or part of the land, or

(d) falls within any other class of person which may be prescribed.

(2) Regulations shall make provision about consent for the purposes of this section; in particular, the regulations may make provision—

(a) prescribing the form of consent;

(b) about the effect and duration of consent (including provision for consent to bind successors);

(c) about withdrawal of consent (including provision preventing withdrawal in specified circumstances);

(d) for consent given for the purpose of one application under section 2 to have effect for the purpose of another application;

(e) for consent to be deemed to have been given in specified circumstances;

(f) enabling a court to dispense with a requirement for consent in specified circumstances.

(3) An order under subsection (2)(f) dispensing with a requirement for consent—

(a) may be absolute or conditional, and

(b) may make such other provision as the court thinks appropriate.

[2029]

NOTES

Commencement: 27 September 2004.

Regulations: the Commonhold Regulations 2004, SI 2004/1829 at **[3432]**.

4 Land which may not be commonhold

Schedule 2 (which provides that an application under section 2 may not relate wholly or partly to land of certain kinds) shall have effect.

[2030]

NOTES

Commencement: 27 September 2004.

5 Registered details

(1) The Registrar shall ensure that in respect of any commonhold land the following are kept in his custody and referred to in the register—

(a) the prescribed details of the commonhold association;

(b) the prescribed details of the registered freeholder of each commonhold unit;

(c) a copy of the commonhold community statement;

(d) a copy of the *memorandum and articles of association* [articles of association] of the commonhold association.

(2) The Registrar may arrange for a document or information to be kept in his custody and referred to in the register in respect of commonhold land if the document or information—

(a) is not mentioned in subsection (1), but

(b) is submitted to the Registrar in accordance with a provision made by or by virtue of this Part.

(3) Subsection (1)(b) shall not apply during a transitional period within the meaning of section 8.

[2031]

NOTES

Commencement: 27 September 2004.

Sub-s (1): in sub-para (d) words in italics substituted by subsequent words in square brackets by SI 2009/1941, art 2(1), Sch 1, para 194(1), (3), as from 1 October 2009.

6 Registration in error

(1) This section applies where a freehold estate in land is registered as a freehold estate in commonhold land and—

(a) the application for registration was not made in accordance with section 2,
(b) the certificate under paragraph 7 of Schedule 1 was inaccurate, or
(c) the registration contravened a provision made by or by virtue of this Part.

(2) The register may not be altered by the Registrar under Schedule 4 to the Land Registration Act 2002 (c 9) (alteration of register).

(3) The court may grant a declaration that the freehold estate should not have been registered as a freehold estate in commonhold land.

(4) A declaration under subsection (3) may be granted only on the application of a person who claims to be adversely affected by the registration.

(5) On granting a declaration under subsection (3) the court may make any order which appears to it to be appropriate.

(6) An order under subsection (5) may, in particular—

(a) provide for the registration to be treated as valid for all purposes;
(b) provide for alteration of the register;
(c) provide for land to cease to be commonhold land;
(d) require a director or other specified officer of a commonhold association to take steps to alter or amend a document;
(e) require a director or other specified officer of a commonhold association to take specified steps;
(f) make an award of compensation (whether or not contingent upon the occurrence or non-occurrence of a specified event) to be paid by one specified person to another;
(g) apply, disapply or modify a provision of Schedule 8 to the Land Registration Act 2002 (c 9) (indemnity).

[2032]

NOTES

Commencement: 27 September 2004.

Effect of registration

7 Registration without unit-holders

(1) This section applies where—

(a) a freehold estate in land is registered as a freehold estate in commonhold land in pursuance of an application under section 2, and
(b) the application is not accompanied by a statement under section 9(1)(b).

(2) On registration—

(a) the applicant shall continue to be registered as the proprietor of the freehold estate in the commonhold land, and
(b) the rights and duties conferred and imposed by the commonhold community statement shall not come into force (subject to section 8(2)(b)).

(3) Where after registration a person other than the applicant becomes entitled to be registered as the proprietor of the freehold estate in one or more, but not all, of the commonhold units—

(a) the commonhold association shall be entitled to be registered as the proprietor of the freehold estate in the common parts,
(b) the Registrar shall register the commonhold association in accordance with paragraph (a) (without an application being made),
(c) the rights and duties conferred and imposed by the commonhold community statement shall come into force, and
(d) any lease of the whole or part of the commonhold land shall be extinguished by virtue of this section.

(4) For the purpose of subsection (3)(d) "lease" means a lease which—
(a) is granted for any term, and
(b) is granted before the commonhold association becomes entitled to be registered as the proprietor of the freehold estate in the common parts.

[2033]

NOTES
Commencement: 27 September 2004.

8 Transitional period

(1) In this Part "transitional period" means the period between registration of the freehold estate in land as a freehold estate in commonhold land and the event mentioned in section 7(3).

(2) Regulations may provide that during a transitional period a relevant provision—
(a) shall not have effect, or
(b) shall have effect with specified modifications.

(3) In subsection (2) "relevant provision" means a provision made—
(a) by or by virtue of this Part,
(b) by a commonhold community statement, or
(c) by the *memorandum or articles* [articles] of the commonhold association.

(4) The Registrar shall arrange for the freehold estate in land to cease to be registered as a freehold estate in commonhold land if the registered proprietor makes an application to the Registrar under this subsection during the transitional period.

(5) The provisions about consent made by or under sections 2 and 3 and Schedule 1 shall apply in relation to an application under subsection (4) as they apply in relation to an application under section 2.

(6) A reference in this Part to a commonhold association exercising functions in relation to commonhold land includes a reference to a case where a commonhold association would exercise functions in relation to commonhold land but for the fact that the time in question falls in a transitional period.

[2034]

NOTES
Commencement: 27 September 2004.
Sub-s (3): in sub-para (c) words in italics substituted by subsequent words in square brackets by SI 2009/1941, art 2(1), Sch 1, para 194(1), (4), as from 1 October 2009.

9 Registration with unit-holders

(1) This section applies in relation to a freehold estate in commonhold land if—
(a) it is registered as a freehold estate in commonhold land in pursuance of an application under section 2, and
(b) the application is accompanied by a statement by the applicant requesting that this section should apply.

(2) A statement under subsection (1)(b) must include a list of the commonhold units giving in relation to each one the prescribed details of the proposed initial unit-holder or joint unit-holders.

(3) On registration—
(a) the commonhold association shall be entitled to be registered as the proprietor of the freehold estate in the common parts,
(b) a person specified by virtue of subsection (2) as the initial unit-holder of a commonhold unit shall be entitled to be registered as the proprietor of the freehold estate in the unit,
(c) a person specified by virtue of subsection (2) as an initial joint unit-holder of a commonhold unit shall be entitled to be registered as one of the proprietors of the freehold estate in the unit,
(d) the Registrar shall make entries in the register to reflect paragraphs (a) to (c) (without applications being made),
(e) the rights and duties conferred and imposed by the commonhold community statement shall come into force, and
(f) any lease of the whole or part of the commonhold land shall be extinguished by virtue of this section.

(4) For the purpose of subsection (3)(f) "lease" means a lease which—
(a) is granted for any term, and
(b) is granted before the commonhold association becomes entitled to be registered as the proprietor of the freehold estate in the common parts.

[2035]

NOTES

Commencement: 27 September 2004.
Regulations: the Commonhold Regulations 2004, SI 2004/1829 at **[3432]**.

10 Extinguished lease: liability

(1) This section applies where—
- (a) a lease is extinguished by virtue of section 7(3)(d) or 9(3)(f), and
- (b) the consent of the holder of that lease was not among the consents required by section 3 in respect of the application under section 2 for the land to become commonhold land.

(2) If the holder of a lease superior to the extinguished lease gave consent under section 3, he shall be liable for loss suffered by the holder of the extinguished lease.

(3) If the holders of a number of leases would be liable under subsection (2), liability shall attach only to the person whose lease was most proximate to the extinguished lease.

(4) If no person is liable under subsection (2), the person who gave consent under section 3 as the holder of the freehold estate out of which the extinguished lease was granted shall be liable for loss suffered by the holder of the extinguished lease.

[2036]

NOTES

Commencement: 27 September 2004.

Commonhold unit

11 Definition

(1) In this Part "commonhold unit" means a commonhold unit specified in a commonhold community statement in accordance with this section.

(2) A commonhold community statement must—
- (a) specify at least two parcels of land as commonhold units, and
- (b) define the extent of each commonhold unit.

(3) In defining the extent of a commonhold unit a commonhold community statement—
- (a) must refer to a plan which is included in the statement and which complies with prescribed requirements,
- (b) may refer to an area subject to the exclusion of specified structures, fittings, apparatus or appurtenances within the area,
- (c) may exclude the structures which delineate an area referred to, and
- (d) may refer to two or more areas (whether or not contiguous).

(4) A commonhold unit need not contain all or any part of a building.

[2037]

NOTES

Commencement: 27 September 2004.
Regulations: the Commonhold Regulations 2004, SI 2004/1829 at **[3432]**.

12 Unit-holder

A person is the unit-holder of a commonhold unit if he is entitled to be registered as the proprietor of the freehold estate in the unit (whether or not he is registered).

[2038]

NOTES

Commencement: 27 September 2004.

13 Joint unit-holders

(1) Two or more persons are joint unit-holders of a commonhold unit if they are entitled to be registered as proprietors of the freehold estate in the unit (whether or not they are registered).

(2) In the application of the following provisions to a unit with joint unit-holders a reference to a unit-holder is a reference to the joint unit-holders together—
- (a) section 14(3),
- (b) section 15(1) and (3),
- (c) section 19(2) and (3),
- (d) section 20(1),
- (e) section 23(1),
- (f) section 35(1)(b),
- (g) section 38(1),

(h) section 39(2), and
(i) section 47(2).

(3) In the application of the following provisions to a unit with joint unit-holders a reference to a unit-holder includes a reference to each joint unit-holder and to the joint unit-holders together—
(a) section 1(1)(c),
(b) section 16,
(c) section 31(1)(b), (3)(b), (5)(j) and (7),
(d) section 32(4)(a) and (c),
(e) section 35(1)(a), (2) and (3),
(f) section 37(2),
(g) section 40(1), and
(h) section 58(3)(a).

(4) Regulations under this Part which refer to a unit-holder shall make provision for the construction of the reference in the case of joint unit-holders.

(5) Regulations may amend subsection (2) or (3).

(6) Regulations may make provision for the construction in the case of joint unit-holders of a reference to a unit-holder in—
(a) an enactment,
(b) a commonhold community statement,
(c) the *memorandum or articles of association* [articles of association] of a commonhold association, or
(d) another document.

[2039]

NOTES

Commencement: 27 September 2004.

Sub-s (6): in sub-para (c) words in italics substituted by subsequent words in square brackets by SI 2009/1941, art 2(1), Sch 1, para 194(1), (5), as from 1 October 2009.

Regulations: the Commonhold Regulations 2004, SI 2004/1829 at **[3432]**.

14 Use and maintenance

(1) A commonhold community statement must make provision regulating the use of commonhold units.

(2) A commonhold community statement must make provision imposing duties in respect of the insurance, repair and maintenance of each commonhold unit.

(3) A duty under subsection (2) may be imposed on the commonhold association or the unit-holder.

[2040]

NOTES

Commencement: 27 September 2004.

15 Transfer

(1) In this Part a reference to the transfer of a commonhold unit is a reference to the transfer of a unit-holder's freehold estate in a unit to another person—
(a) whether or not for consideration,
(b) whether or not subject to any reservation or other terms, and
(c) whether or not by operation of law.

(2) A commonhold community statement may not prevent or restrict the transfer of a commonhold unit.

(3) On the transfer of a commonhold unit the new unit-holder shall notify the commonhold association of the transfer.

(4) Regulations may—
(a) prescribe the form and manner of notice under subsection (3);
(b) prescribe the time within which notice is to be given;
(c) make provision (including provision requiring the payment of money) about the effect of failure to give notice.

[2041]

NOTES

Commencement: 27 September 2004.

16 Transfer: effect

(1) A right or duty conferred or imposed—

(a) by a commonhold community statement, or
(b) in accordance with section 20,

shall affect a new unit-holder in the same way as it affected the former unit-holder.

(2) A former unit-holder shall not incur a liability or acquire a right—
(a) under or by virtue of the commonhold community statement, or
(b) by virtue of anything done in accordance with section 20.

(3) Subsection (2)—
(a) shall not be capable of being disapplied or varied by agreement, and
(b) is without prejudice to any liability or right incurred or acquired before a transfer takes effect.

(4) In this section—

"former unit-holder" means a person from whom a commonhold unit has been transferred (whether or not he has ceased to be the registered proprietor), and

"new unit-holder" means a person to whom a commonhold unit is transferred (whether or not he has yet become the registered proprietor).

[2042]

NOTES

Commencement: 27 September 2004.

17 Leasing: residential

(1) It shall not be possible to create a term of years absolute in a residential commonhold unit unless the term satisfies prescribed conditions.

(2) The conditions may relate to—
(a) length;
(b) the circumstances in which the term is granted;
(c) any other matter.

(3) Subject to subsection (4), an instrument or agreement shall be of no effect to the extent that it purports to create a term of years in contravention of subsection (1).

(4) Where an instrument or agreement purports to create a term of years in contravention of subsection (1) a party to the instrument or agreement may apply to the court for an order—
(a) providing for the instrument or agreement to have effect as if it provided for the creation of a term of years of a specified kind;
(b) providing for the return or payment of money;
(c) making such other provision as the court thinks appropriate.

(5) A commonhold unit is residential if provision made in the commonhold community statement by virtue of section 14(1) requires it to be used only—
(a) for residential purposes, or
(b) for residential and other incidental purposes.

[2043]

NOTES

Commencement: 27 September 2004.
Regulations: the Commonhold Regulations 2004, SI 2004/1829 at **[3432]**.

18 Leasing: non-residential

An instrument or agreement which creates a term of years absolute in a commonhold unit which is not residential (within the meaning of section 17) shall have effect subject to any provision of the commonhold community statement.

[2044]

NOTES

Commencement: 27 September 2004.

19 Leasing: supplementary

(1) Regulations may—
(a) impose obligations on a tenant of a commonhold unit;
(b) enable a commonhold community statement to impose obligations on a tenant of a commonhold unit.

(2) Regulations under subsection (1) may, in particular, require a tenant of a commonhold unit to make payments to the commonhold association or a unit-holder in discharge of payments which—
(a) are due in accordance with the commonhold community statement to be made by the unit-holder, or

(b) are due in accordance with the commonhold community statement to be made by another tenant of the unit.

(3) Regulations under subsection (1) may, in particular, provide—

(a) for the amount of payments under subsection (2) to be set against sums owed by the tenant (whether to the person by whom the payments were due to be made or to some other person);

(b) for the amount of payments under subsection (2) to be recovered from the unit-holder or another tenant of the unit.

(4) Regulations may modify a rule of law about leasehold estates (whether deriving from the common law or from an enactment) in its application to a term of years in a commonhold unit.

(5) Regulations under this section—

(a) may make provision generally or in relation to specified circumstances, and

(b) may make different provision for different descriptions of commonhold land or commonhold unit.

[2045]

NOTES

Commencement: 27 September 2004.

Regulations: the Commonhold Regulations 2004, SI 2004/1829 at **[3432]**.

20 Other transactions

(1) A commonhold community statement may not prevent or restrict the creation, grant or transfer by a unit-holder of—

(a) an interest in the whole or part of his unit, or

(b) a charge over his unit.

(2) Subsection (1) is subject to sections 17 to 19 (which impose restrictions about leases).

(3) It shall not be possible to create an interest of a prescribed kind in a commonhold unit unless the commonhold association—

(a) is a party to the creation of the interest, or

(b) consents in writing to the creation of the interest.

(4) A commonhold association may act as described in subsection (3)(a) or (b) only if—

(a) the association passes a resolution to take the action, and

(b) at least 75 per cent of those who vote on the resolution vote in favour.

(5) An instrument or agreement shall be of no effect to the extent that it purports to create an interest in contravention of subsection (3).

(6) In this section "interest" does not include—

(a) a charge, or

(b) an interest which arises by virtue of a charge.

[2046]

NOTES

Commencement: 27 September 2004.

21 Part-unit: interests

(1) It shall not be possible to create an interest in part only of a commonhold unit.

(2) But subsection (1) shall not prevent—

(a) the creation of a term of years absolute in part only of a residential commonhold unit where the term satisfies prescribed conditions,

(b) the creation of a term of years absolute in part only of a non-residential commonhold unit, or

(c) the transfer of the freehold estate in part only of a commonhold unit where the commonhold association consents in writing to the transfer.

(3) An instrument or agreement shall be of no effect to the extent that it purports to create an interest in contravention of subsection (1).

(4) Subsection (5) applies where—

(a) land becomes commonhold land or is added to a commonhold unit, and

(b) immediately before that event there is an interest in the land which could not be created after that event by reason of subsection (1).

(5) The interest shall be extinguished by virtue of this subsection to the extent that it could not be created by reason of subsection (1).

(6) Section 17(2) and (4) shall apply (with any necessary modifications) in relation to subsection (2)(a) and (b) above.

(7) Where part only of a unit is held under a lease, regulations may modify the application of a provision which—

(a) is made by or by virtue of this Part, and

(b) applies to a unit-holder or a tenant or both.

(8) Section 20(4) shall apply in relation to subsection (2)(c) above.

(9) Where the freehold interest in part only of a commonhold unit is transferred, the part transferred—

(a) becomes a new commonhold unit by virtue of this subsection, or

(b) in a case where the request for consent under subsection (2)(c) states that this paragraph is to apply, becomes part of a commonhold unit specified in the request.

(10) Regulations may make provision, or may require a commonhold community statement to make provision, about—

(a) registration of units created by virtue of subsection (9);

(b) the adaptation of provision made by or by virtue of this Part or by or by virtue of a commonhold community statement to a case where units are created or modified by virtue of subsection (9).

[2047]

NOTES

Commencement: 27 September 2004 (sub-ss (1)–(3), (6)–(10)); to be appointed (otherwise).
Regulations: the Commonhold Regulations 2004, SI 2004/1829 at **[3432]**.

22 Part–unit: charging

(1) It shall not be possible to create a charge over part only of an interest in a commonhold unit.

(2) An instrument or agreement shall be of no effect to the extent that it purports to create a charge in contravention of subsection (1).

(3) Subsection (4) applies where—

(a) land becomes commonhold land or is added to a commonhold unit, and

(b) immediately before that event there is a charge over the land which could not be created after that event by reason of subsection (1).

(4) The charge shall be extinguished by virtue of this subsection to the extent that it could not be created by reason of subsection (1).

[2048]

NOTES

Commencement: 27 September 2004.

23 Changing size

(1) An amendment of a commonhold community statement which redefines the extent of a commonhold unit may not be made unless the unit-holder consents—

(a) in writing, and

(b) before the amendment is made.

(2) But regulations may enable a court to dispense with the requirement for consent on the application of a commonhold association in prescribed circumstances.

[2049]

NOTES

Commencement: 27 September 2004.

24 Changing size: charged unit

(1) This section applies to an amendment of a commonhold community statement which redefines the extent of a commonhold unit over which there is a registered charge.

(2) The amendment may not be made unless the registered proprietor of the charge consents—

(a) in writing, and

(b) before the amendment is made.

(3) But regulations may enable a court to dispense with the requirement for consent on the application of a commonhold association in prescribed circumstances.

(4) If the amendment removes land from the commonhold unit, the charge shall by virtue of this subsection be extinguished to the extent that it relates to the land which is removed.

(5) If the amendment adds land to the unit, the charge shall by virtue of this subsection be extended so as to relate to the land which is added.

(6) Regulations may make provision—

(a) requiring notice to be given to the Registrar in circumstances to which this section applies;
(b) requiring the Registrar to alter the register to reflect the application of subsection (4) or (5).

[2050]

NOTES
Commencement: 27 September 2004.
Regulations: the Commonhold Regulations 2004, SI 2004/1829 at **[3432]**.

Common parts

25 Definition

(1) In this Part "common parts" in relation to a commonhold means every part of the commonhold which is not for the time being a commonhold unit in accordance with the commonhold community statement.

(2) A commonhold community statement may make provision in respect of a specified part of the common parts (a "limited use area") restricting—
(a) the classes of person who may use it;
(b) the kind of use to which it may be put.

(3) A commonhold community statement—
(a) may make provision which has effect only in relation to a limited use area, and
(b) may make different provision for different limited use areas.

[2051]

NOTES
Commencement: 27 September 2004.

26 Use and maintenance

A commonhold community statement must make provision—
(a) regulating the use of the common parts;
(b) requiring the commonhold association to insure the common parts;
(c) requiring the commonhold association to repair and maintain the common parts.

[2052]

NOTES
Commencement: 27 September 2004.

27 Transactions

(1) Nothing in a commonhold community statement shall prevent or restrict—
(a) the transfer by the commonhold association of its freehold estate in any part of the common parts, or
(b) the creation by the commonhold association of an interest in any part of the common parts.

(2) In this section "interest" does not include—
(a) a charge, or
(b) an interest which arises by virtue of a charge.

[2053]

NOTES
Commencement: 27 September 2004.

28 Charges: general prohibition

(1) It shall not be possible to create a charge over common parts.

(2) An instrument or agreement shall be of no effect to the extent that it purports to create a charge over common parts.

(3) Where by virtue of section 7 or 9 a commonhold association is registered as the proprietor of common parts, a charge which relates wholly or partly to the common parts shall be extinguished by virtue of this subsection to the extent that it relates to the common parts.

(4) Where by virtue of section 30 land vests in a commonhold association following an amendment to a commonhold community statement which has the effect of adding land to the common parts, a charge which relates wholly or partly to the land added shall be extinguished by virtue of this subsection to the extent that it relates to that land.

(5) This section is subject to section 29 (which permits certain mortgages).

[2054]

NOTES

Commencement: 27 September 2004.

29 New legal mortgages

(1) Section 28 shall not apply in relation to a legal mortgage if the creation of the mortgage is approved by a resolution of the commonhold association.

(2) A resolution for the purposes of subsection (1) must be passed—
(a) before the mortgage is created, and
(b) unanimously.

(3) In this section "legal mortgage" has the meaning given by section 205(1)(xvi) of the Law of Property Act 1925 (c 20) (interpretation).

[2055]

NOTES

Commencement: 27 September 2004.

30 Additions to common parts

(1) This section applies where an amendment of a commonhold community statement—
(a) specifies land which forms part of a commonhold unit, and
(b) provides for that land (the "added land") to be added to the common parts.

(2) The amendment may not be made unless the registered proprietor of any charge over the added land consents—
(a) in writing, and
(b) before the amendment is made.

(3) But regulations may enable a court to dispense with the requirement for consent on the application of a commonhold association in specified circumstances.

(4) On the filing of the amended statement under section 33—
(a) the commonhold association shall be entitled to be registered as the proprietor of the freehold estate in the added land, and
(b) the Registrar shall register the commonhold association in accordance with paragraph (a) (without an application being made).

[2056]

NOTES

Commencement: 27 September 2004.

Commonhold community statement

31 Form and content: general

(1) A commonhold community statement is a document which makes provision in relation to specified land for—
(a) the rights and duties of the commonhold association, and
(b) the rights and duties of the unit-holders.

(2) A commonhold community statement must be in the prescribed form.

(3) A commonhold community statement may—
(a) impose a duty on the commonhold association;
(b) impose a duty on a unit-holder;
(c) make provision about the taking of decisions in connection with the management of the commonhold or any other matter concerning it.

(4) Subsection (3) is subject to—
(a) any provision made by or by virtue of this Part, and
(b) any provision of the *memorandum or articles* [articles] of the commonhold association.

(5) In subsection (3)(a) and (b) "duty" includes, in particular, a duty—
(a) to pay money;
(b) to undertake works;
(c) to grant access;
(d) to give notice;
(e) to refrain from entering into transactions of a specified kind in relation to a commonhold unit;
(f) to refrain from using the whole or part of a commonhold unit for a specified purpose or for anything other than a specified purpose;

(g) to refrain from undertaking works (including alterations) of a specified kind;
(h) to refrain from causing nuisance or annoyance;
(i) to refrain from specified behaviour;
(j) to indemnify the commonhold association or a unit-holder in respect of costs arising from the breach of a statutory requirement.

(6) Provision in a commonhold community statement imposing a duty to pay money (whether in pursuance of subsection (5)(a) or any other provision made by or by virtue of this Part) may include provision for the payment of interest in the case of late payment.

(7) A duty conferred by a commonhold community statement on a commonhold association or a unit-holder shall not require any other formality.

(8) A commonhold community statement may not provide for the transfer or loss of an interest in land on the occurrence or non-occurrence of a specified event.

(9) Provision made by a commonhold community statement shall be of no effect to the extent that—
(a) it is prohibited by virtue of section 32,
(b) it is inconsistent with any provision made by or by virtue of this Part,
(c) it is inconsistent with anything which is treated as included in the statement by virtue of section 32, or
(d) it is inconsistent with the *memorandum or articles of association* [articles of association] of the commonhold association.

[2057]

NOTES

Commencement: 27 September 2004.

Sub-s (4): words in italics substituted by subsequent words in square brackets by SI 2009/1941, art 2(1), Sch 1, para 194(1), (6)(a), as from 1 October 2009.

Sub-s (9): in sub-para (d) words in italics substituted by subsequent words in square brackets by SI 2009/1941, art 2(1), Sch 1, para 194(1), (6)(b), as from 1 October 2009.

Regulations: the Commonhold Regulations 2004, SI 2004/1829 at **[3432]**.

32 Regulations

(1) Regulations shall make provision about the content of a commonhold community statement.

(2) The regulations may permit, require or prohibit the inclusion in a statement of—
(a) specified provision, or
(b) provision of a specified kind, for a specified purpose or about a specified matter.

(3) The regulations may—
(a) provide for a statement to be treated as including provision prescribed by or determined in accordance with the regulations;
(b) permit a statement to make provision in place of provision which would otherwise be treated as included by virtue of paragraph (a).

(4) The regulations may—
(a) make different provision for different descriptions of commonhold association or unit-holder;
(b) make different provision for different circumstances;
(c) make provision about the extent to which a commonhold community statement may make different provision for different descriptions of unit-holder or common parts.

(5) The matters to which regulations under this section may relate include, but are not limited to—
(a) the matters mentioned in sections 11, 14, 15, 20, 21, 25, 26, 27, 38, 39 and 58, and
(b) any matter for which regulations under section 37 may make provision.

[2058]

NOTES

Commencement: 27 September 2004.

Regulations: the Commonhold Regulations 2004, SI 2004/1829 at **[3432]**.

33 Amendment

(1) Regulations under section 32 shall require a commonhold community statement to make provision about how it can be amended.

(2) The regulations shall, in particular, make provision under section 32(3)(a) (whether or not subject to provision under section 32(3)(b)).

(3) An amendment of a commonhold community statement shall have no effect unless and until the amended statement is registered in accordance with this section.

(4) If the commonhold association makes an application under this subsection the Registrar shall arrange for an amended commonhold community statement to be kept in his custody, and referred to in the register, in place of the unamended statement.

(5) An application under subsection (4) must be accompanied by a certificate given by the directors of the commonhold association that the amended commonhold community statement satisfies the requirements of this Part.

(6) Where an amendment of a commonhold community statement redefines the extent of a commonhold unit, an application under subsection (4) must be accompanied by any consent required by section 23(1) or 24(2) (or an order of a court dispensing with consent).

(7) Where an amendment of a commonhold community statement has the effect of changing the extent of the common parts, an application under subsection (4) must be accompanied by any consent required by section 30(2) (or an order of a court dispensing with consent).

(8) Where the Registrar amends the register on an application under subsection (4) he shall make any consequential amendments to the register which he thinks appropriate.

[2059]

NOTES

Commencement: 27 September 2004.

Commonhold association

34 Constitution

(1) A commonhold association is a private company limited by guarantee the memorandum of which—

- *(a) states that an object of the company is to exercise the functions of a commonhold association in relation to specified commonhold land, and*
- *(b) specifies £1 as the amount required to be specified in pursuance of section 2(4) of the Companies Act 1985 (c 6) (members' guarantee).*

[(1) A commonhold association is a private company limited by guarantee—

- (a) the articles of which state that an object of the company is to exercise the functions of a commonhold association in relation to specified commonhold land, and
- (b) the statement of guarantee of which specifies £1 as the amount of the contribution required from each member in the event of the company being wound up.]

(2) Schedule 3 (which makes provision about the constitution of a commonhold association) shall have effect.

[2060]

NOTES

Commencement: 27 September 2004.
Sub-s (1): substituted by SI 2009/1941, art 2(1), Sch 1, para 194(1), (7), as from 1 October 2009.

35 Duty to manage

(1) The directors of a commonhold association shall exercise their powers so as to permit or facilitate so far as possible—

- (a) the exercise by each unit-holder of his rights, and
- (b) the enjoyment by each unit-holder of the freehold estate in his unit.

(2) The directors of a commonhold association shall, in particular, use any right, power or procedure conferred or created by virtue of section 37 for the purpose of preventing, remedying or curtailing a failure on the part of a unit-holder to comply with a requirement or duty imposed on him by virtue of the commonhold community statement or a provision of this Part.

(3) But in respect of a particular failure on the part of a unit-holder (the "defaulter") the directors of a commonhold association—

- (a) need not take action if they reasonably think that inaction is in the best interests of establishing or maintaining harmonious relationships between all the unit-holders, and that it will not cause any unit-holder (other than the defaulter) significant loss or significant disadvantage, and
- (b) shall have regard to the desirability of using arbitration, mediation or conciliation procedures (including referral under a scheme approved under section 42) instead of legal proceedings wherever possible.

(4) A reference in this section to a unit-holder includes a reference to a tenant of a unit.

[2061]

NOTES

Commencement: 27 September 2004.

36 Voting

(1) This section applies in relation to any provision of this Part (a "voting provision") which refers to the passing of a resolution by a commonhold association.

(2) A voting provision is satisfied only if every member is given an opportunity to vote in accordance with any relevant provision of the *memorandum or articles of association* [articles of association] or the commonhold community statement.

(3) A vote is cast for the purposes of a voting provision whether it is cast in person or in accordance with a provision which—

(a) provides for voting by post, by proxy or in some other manner, and
(b) is contained in the *memorandum or articles of association* [articles of association] or the commonhold community statement.

(4) A resolution is passed unanimously if every member who casts a vote votes in favour.

[2062]

NOTES

Commencement: 27 September 2004.

Sub-ss (2), (3): words in italics substituted by subsequent words in square brackets by SI 2009/1941, art 2(1), Sch 1, para 194(1), (8), as from 1 October 2009.

Operation of commonhold

37 Enforcement and compensation

(1) Regulations may make provision (including provision conferring jurisdiction on a court) about the exercise or enforcement of a right or duty imposed or conferred by or by virtue of—

(a) a commonhold community statement;
(b) the *memorandum or articles* [articles] of a commonhold association;
(c) a provision made by or by virtue of this Part.

(2) The regulations may, in particular, make provision—

(a) requiring compensation to be paid where a right is exercised in specified cases or circumstances;
(b) requiring compensation to be paid where a duty is not complied with;
(c) enabling recovery of costs where work is carried out for the purpose of enforcing a right or duty;
(d) enabling recovery of costs where work is carried out in consequence of the failure to perform a duty;
(e) permitting a unit-holder to enforce a duty imposed on another unit-holder, on a commonhold association or on a tenant;
(f) permitting a commonhold association to enforce a duty imposed on a unit-holder or a tenant;
(g) permitting a tenant to enforce a duty imposed on another tenant, a unit-holder or a commonhold association;
(h) permitting the enforcement of terms or conditions to which a right is subject;
(i) requiring the use of a specified form of arbitration, mediation or conciliation procedure before legal proceedings may be brought.

(3) Provision about compensation made by virtue of this section shall include—

(a) provision (which may include provision conferring jurisdiction on a court) for determining the amount of compensation;
(b) provision for the payment of interest in the case of late payment.

(4) Regulations under this section shall be subject to any provision included in a commonhold community statement in accordance with regulations made by virtue of section 32(5)(b).

[2063]

NOTES

Commencement: 27 September 2004.

Sub-s (1): in sub-para (b) words in italics substituted by subsequent words in square brackets by SI 2009/1941, art 2(1), Sch 1, para 194(1), (9), as from 1 October 2009.

Regulations: the Commonhold Regulations 2004, SI 2004/1829 at **[3432]**.

38 Commonhold assessment

(1) A commonhold community statement must make provision—

(a) requiring the directors of the commonhold association to make an annual estimate of the income required to be raised from unit-holders to meet the expenses of the association,
(b) enabling the directors of the commonhold association to make estimates from time to time of income required to be raised from unit-holders in addition to the annual estimate,
(c) specifying the percentage of any estimate made under paragraph (a) or (b) which is to be allocated to each unit,

(d) requiring each unit-holder to make payments in respect of the percentage of any estimate which is allocated to his unit, and

(e) requiring the directors of the commonhold association to serve notices on unit-holders specifying payments required to be made by them and the date on which each payment is due.

(2) For the purpose of subsection (1)(c)—

(a) the percentages allocated by a commonhold community statement to the commonhold units must amount in aggregate to 100;

(b) a commonhold community statement may specify 0 per cent in relation to a unit.

[2064]

NOTES

Commencement: 27 September 2004.

39 Reserve fund

(1) Regulations under section 32 may, in particular, require a commonhold community statement to make provision—

(a) requiring the directors of the commonhold association to establish and maintain one or more funds to finance the repair and maintenance of common parts;

(b) requiring the directors of the commonhold association to establish and maintain one or more funds to finance the repair and maintenance of commonhold units.

(2) Where a commonhold community statement provides for the establishment and maintenance of a fund in accordance with subsection (1) it must also make provision—

(a) requiring or enabling the directors of the commonhold association to set a levy from time to time,

(b) specifying the percentage of any levy set under paragraph (a) which is to be allocated to each unit,

(c) requiring each unit-holder to make payments in respect of the percentage of any levy set under paragraph (a) which is allocated to his unit, and

(d) requiring the directors of the commonhold association to serve notices on unit-holders specifying payments required to be made by them and the date on which each payment is due.

(3) For the purpose of subsection (2)(b)—

(a) the percentages allocated by a commonhold community statement to the commonhold units must amount in aggregate to 100;

(b) a commonhold community statement may specify 0 per cent in relation to a unit.

(4) The assets of a fund established and maintained by virtue of this section shall not be used for the purpose of enforcement of any debt except a judgment debt referable to a reserve fund activity.

(5) For the purpose of subsection (4)—

(a) "reserve fund activity" means an activity which in accordance with the commonhold community statement can or may be financed from a fund established and maintained by virtue of this section,

(b) assets are used for the purpose of enforcement of a debt if, in particular, they are taken in execution or are made the subject of a charging order under section 1 of the Charging Orders Act 1979 (c 53), and

(c) the reference to a judgment debt includes a reference to any interest payable on a judgment debt.

[2065]

NOTES

Commencement: 27 September 2004.

40 Rectification of documents

(1) A unit-holder may apply to the court for a declaration that—

(a) the *memorandum or articles of association* [articles of association] of the relevant commonhold association do not comply with regulations under paragraph 2(1) of Schedule 3;

(b) the relevant commonhold community statement does not comply with a requirement imposed by or by virtue of this Part.

(2) On granting a declaration under this section the court may make any order which appears to it to be appropriate.

(3) An order under subsection (2) may, in particular—

(a) require a director or other specified officer of a commonhold association to take steps to alter or amend a document;
(b) require a director or other specified officer of a commonhold association to take specified steps;
(c) make an award of compensation (whether or not contingent upon the occurrence or non-occurrence of a specified event) to be paid by the commonhold association to a specified person;
(d) make provision for land to cease to be commonhold land.

(4) An application under subsection (1) must be made—
(a) within the period of three months beginning with the day on which the applicant became a unit-holder,
(b) within three months of the commencement of the alleged failure to comply, or
(c) with the permission of the court.

[2066]

NOTES
Commencement: 27 September 2004.
Sub-s (1): in sub-para (a) words in italics substituted by subsequent words in square brackets by SI 2009/1941, art 2(1), Sch 1, para 194(1), (10), as from 1 October 2009.

41 Enlargement

(1) This section applies to an application under section 2 if the commonhold association for the purposes of the application already exercises functions in relation to commonhold land.

(2) In this section—
(a) the application is referred to as an "application to add land", and
(b) the land to which the application relates is referred to as the "added land".

(3) An application to add land may not be made unless it is approved by a resolution of the commonhold association.

(4) A resolution for the purposes of subsection (3) must be passed—
(a) before the application to add land is made, and
(b) unanimously.

(5) Section 2(2) shall not apply to an application to add land; but the application must be accompanied by—
(a) the documents specified in paragraph 6 of Schedule 1,
(b) an application under section 33 for the registration of an amended commonhold community statement which makes provision for the existing commonhold and the added land, and
(c) a certificate given by the directors of the commonhold association that the application to add land satisfies Schedule 2 and subsection (3).

(6) Where sections 7 and 9 have effect following an application to add land—
(a) the references to "the commonhold land" in sections 7(2)(a) and (3)(d) and 9(3)(f) shall be treated as references to the added land, and
(b) the references in sections 7(2)(b) and (3)(c) and 9(3)(e) to the rights and duties conferred and imposed by the commonhold community statement shall be treated as a reference to rights and duties only in so far as they affect the added land.

(7) In the case of an application to add land where the whole of the added land is to form part of the common parts of a commonhold—
(a) section 7 shall not apply,
(b) on registration the commonhold association shall be entitled to be registered (if it is not already) as the proprietor of the freehold estate in the added land,
(c) the Registrar shall make any registration required by paragraph (b) (without an application being made), and
(d) the rights and duties conferred and imposed by the commonhold community statement shall, in so far as they affect the added land, come into force on registration.

[2067]

NOTES
Commencement: 27 September 2004.

42 Ombudsman

(1) Regulations may provide that a commonhold association shall be a member of an approved ombudsman scheme.

(2) An "approved ombudsman scheme" is a scheme which is approved by the Lord Chancellor and which—

(a) provides for the appointment of one or more persons as ombudsman,
(b) provides for a person to be appointed as ombudsman only if the Lord Chancellor approves the appointment in advance,
(c) enables a unit-holder to refer to the ombudsman a dispute between the unit-holder and a commonhold association which is a member of the scheme,
(d) enables a commonhold association which is a member of the scheme to refer to the ombudsman a dispute between the association and a unit-holder,
(e) requires the ombudsman to investigate and determine a dispute referred to him,
(f) requires a commonhold association which is a member of the scheme to cooperate with the ombudsman in investigating or determining a dispute, and
(g) requires a commonhold association which is a member of the scheme to comply with any decision of the ombudsman (including any decision requiring the payment of money).

(3) In addition to the matters specified in subsection (2) an approved ombudsman scheme—
(a) may contain other provision, and
(b) shall contain such provision, or provision of such a kind, as may be prescribed.

(4) If a commonhold association fails to comply with regulations under subsection (1) a unit-holder may apply to the High Court for an order requiring the directors of the commonhold association to ensure that the association complies with the regulations.

(5) A reference in this section to a unit-holder includes a reference to a tenant of a unit.

[2068]

Termination: voluntary winding-up

43 Winding-up resolution

(1) A winding-up resolution in respect of a commonhold association shall be of no effect unless—
(a) the resolution is preceded by a declaration of solvency,
(b) the commonhold association passes a termination-statement resolution before it passes the winding-up resolution, and
(c) each resolution is passed with at least 80 per cent of the members of the association voting in favour.

(2) In this Part—
"declaration of solvency" means a directors' statutory declaration made in accordance with section 89 of the Insolvency Act 1986 (c 45),
"termination-statement resolution" means a resolution approving the terms of a termination statement (within the meaning of section 47), and
"winding-up resolution" means a resolution for voluntary winding-up within the meaning of section 84 of that Act.

[2069]

NOTES
Commencement: 27 September 2004.

44 100 per cent agreement

(1) This section applies where a commonhold association—
(a) has passed a winding-up resolution and a termination-statement resolution with 100 per cent of the members of the association voting in favour, and
(b) has appointed a liquidator under section 91 of the Insolvency Act 1986 (c 45).

(2) The liquidator shall make a termination application within the period of six months beginning with the day on which the winding-up resolution is passed.

(3) If the liquidator fails to make a termination application within the period specified in subsection (2) a termination application may be made by—
(a) a unit-holder, or
(b) a person falling within a class prescribed for the purposes of this subsection.

[2070]

NOTES
Commencement: 27 September 2004.

45 80 per cent agreement

(1) This section applies where a commonhold association—
(a) has passed a winding-up resolution and a termination-statement resolution with at least 80 per cent of the members of the association voting in favour, and
(b) has appointed a liquidator under section 91 of the Insolvency Act 1986.

(2) The liquidator shall within the prescribed period apply to the court for an order determining—

(a) the terms and conditions on which a termination application may be made, and
(b) the terms of the termination statement to accompany a termination application.

(3) The liquidator shall make a termination application within the period of three months starting with the date on which an order under subsection (2) is made.

(4) If the liquidator fails to make an application under subsection (2) or (3) within the period specified in that subsection an application of the same kind may be made by—

(a) a unit-holder, or
(b) a person falling within a class prescribed for the purposes of this subsection.

[2071]

NOTES

Commencement: 27 September 2004.
Regulations: the Commonhold Regulations 2004, SI 2004/1829 at **[3432]**.

46 Termination application

(1) A "termination application" is an application to the Registrar that all the land in relation to which a particular commonhold association exercises functions should cease to be commonhold land.

(2) A termination application must be accompanied by a termination statement.

(3) On receipt of a termination application the Registrar shall note it in the register.

[2072]

NOTES

Commencement: 27 September 2004.

47 Termination statement

(1) A termination statement must specify—

(a) the commonhold association's proposals for the transfer of the commonhold land following acquisition of the freehold estate in accordance with section 49(3), and
(b) how the assets of the commonhold association will be distributed.

(2) A commonhold community statement may make provision requiring any termination statement to make arrangements—

(a) of a specified kind, or
(b) determined in a specified manner,

about the rights of unit-holders in the event of all the land to which the statement relates ceasing to be commonhold land.

(3) A termination statement must comply with a provision made by the commonhold community statement in reliance on subsection (2).

(4) Subsection (3) may be disapplied by an order of the court—

(a) generally,
(b) in respect of specified matters, or
(c) for a specified purpose.

(5) An application for an order under subsection (4) may be made by any member of the commonhold association.

[2073]

NOTES

Commencement: 27 September 2004.

48 The liquidator

(1) This section applies where a termination application has been made in respect of particular commonhold land.

(2) The liquidator shall notify the Registrar of his appointment.

(3) In the case of a termination application made under section 44 the liquidator shall either—

(a) notify the Registrar that the liquidator is content with the termination statement submitted with the termination application, or
(b) apply to the court under section 112 of the Insolvency Act 1986 (c 45) to determine the terms of the termination statement.

(4) The liquidator shall send to the Registrar a copy of a determination made by virtue of subsection (3)(b).

(5) Subsection (4) is in addition to any requirement under section 112(3) of the Insolvency Act 1986.

(6) A duty imposed on the liquidator by this section is to be performed as soon as possible.

(7) In this section a reference to the liquidator is a reference—

(a) to the person who is appointed as liquidator under section 91 of the Insolvency Act 1986, or

(b) in the case of a members' voluntary winding up which becomes a creditors' voluntary winding up by virtue of sections 95 and 96 of that Act, to the person acting as liquidator in accordance with section 100 of that Act.

[2074]

NOTES

Commencement: 27 September 2004.

49 Termination

(1) This section applies where a termination application is made under section 44 and—

(a) a liquidator notifies the Registrar under section 48(3)(a) that he is content with a termination statement, or

(b) a determination is made under section 112 of the Insolvency Act 1986 (c 45) by virtue of section 48(3)(b).

(2) This section also applies where a termination application is made under section 45.

(3) The commonhold association shall by virtue of this subsection be entitled to be registered as the proprietor of the freehold estate in each commonhold unit.

(4) The Registrar shall take such action as appears to him to be appropriate for the purpose of giving effect to the termination statement.

[2075]

NOTES

Commencement: 27 September 2004.

Termination: winding-up by court

50 Introduction

(1) Section 51 applies where a petition is presented under section 124 of the Insolvency Act 1986 for the winding up of a commonhold association by the court.

(2) For the purposes of this Part—

(a) an "insolvent commonhold association" is one in relation to which a winding-up petition has been presented under section 124 of the Insolvency Act 1986,

(b) a commonhold association is the "successor commonhold association" to an insolvent commonhold association if the land specified for the purpose of section 34(1)(a) is the same for both associations, and

(c) a "winding-up order" is an order under section 125 of the Insolvency Act 1986 for the winding up of a commonhold association.

[2076]

NOTES

Commencement: 27 September 2004.

51 Succession order

(1) At the hearing of the winding-up petition an application may be made to the court for an order under this section (a "succession order") in relation to the insolvent commonhold association.

(2) An application under subsection (1) may be made only by—

(a) the insolvent commonhold association,

(b) one or more members of the insolvent commonhold association, or

(c) a provisional liquidator for the insolvent commonhold association appointed under section 135 of the Insolvency Act 1986.

(3) An application under subsection (1) must be accompanied by—

(a) prescribed evidence of the formation of a successor commonhold association, and

(b) a certificate given by the directors of the successor commonhold association that its *memorandum and articles of association* [articles of association] comply with regulations under paragraph 2(1) of Schedule 3.

(4) The court shall grant an application under subsection (1) unless it thinks that the circumstances of the insolvent commonhold association make a succession order inappropriate.

[2077]

NOTES

Commencement: 27 September 2004.

Sub-s (3): in sub-para (b) words in italics substituted by subsequent words in square brackets by SI 2009/1941, art 2(1), Sch 1, para 194(1), (11), as from 1 October 2009.

Regulations: the Commonhold Regulations 2004, SI 2004/1829 at **[3432]**.

52 Assets and liabilities

(1) Where a succession order is made in relation to an insolvent commonhold association this section applies on the making of a winding-up order in respect of the association.

(2) The successor commonhold association shall be entitled to be registered as the proprietor of the freehold estate in the common parts.

(3) The insolvent commonhold association shall for all purposes cease to be treated as the proprietor of the freehold estate in the common parts.

(4) The succession order—

(a) shall make provision as to the treatment of any charge over all or any part of the common parts;

(b) may require the Registrar to take action of a specified kind;

(c) may enable the liquidator to require the Registrar to take action of a specified kind;

(d) may make supplemental or incidental provision.

[2078]

NOTES

Commencement: 27 September 2004.

53 Transfer of responsibility

(1) Where a succession order is made in relation to an insolvent commonhold association this section applies on the making of a winding-up order in respect of the association.

(2) The successor commonhold association shall be treated as the commonhold association for the commonhold in respect of any matter which relates to a time after the making of the winding-up order.

(3) On the making of the winding-up order the court may make an order requiring the liquidator to make available to the successor commonhold association specified—

(a) records;

(b) copies of records;

(c) information.

(4) An order under subsection (3) may include terms as to—

(a) timing;

(b) payment.

[2079]

NOTES

Commencement: 27 September 2004.

54 Termination of commonhold

(1) This section applies where the court—

(a) makes a winding-up order in respect of a commonhold association, and

(b) has not made a succession order in respect of the commonhold association.

(2) The liquidator of a commonhold association shall as soon as possible notify the Registrar of—

(a) the fact that this section applies,

(b) any directions given under section 168 of the Insolvency Act 1986 (c 45) (liquidator: supplementary powers),

(c) any notice given to the court and the registrar of companies in accordance with section 172(8) of that Act (liquidator vacating office after final meeting),

(d) any notice given to the Secretary of State under section 174(3) of that Act (completion of winding-up),

(e) any application made to the registrar of companies under section 202(2) of that Act (insufficient assets: early dissolution),

(f) any notice given to the registrar of companies under section 205(1)(b) of that Act (completion of winding-up), and

(g) any other matter which in the liquidator's opinion is relevant to the Registrar.

(3) Notification under subsection (2)(b) to (f) must be accompanied by a copy of the directions, notice or application concerned.

(4) The Registrar shall—
- (a) make such arrangements as appear to him to be appropriate for ensuring that the freehold estate in land in respect of which a commonhold association exercises functions ceases to be registered as a freehold estate in commonhold land as soon as is reasonably practicable after he receives notification under subsection (2)(c) to (f), and
- (b) take such action as appears to him to be appropriate for the purpose of giving effect to a determination made by the liquidator in the exercise of his functions.

[2080]

NOTES

Commencement: 27 September 2004.

Termination: miscellaneous

55 Termination by court

(1) This section applies where the court makes an order by virtue of section 6(6)(c) or 40(3)(d) for all the land in relation to which a commonhold association exercises functions to cease to be commonhold land.

(2) The court shall have the powers which it would have if it were making a winding-up order in respect of the commonhold association.

(3) A person appointed as liquidator by virtue of subsection (2) shall have the powers and duties of a liquidator following the making of a winding-up order by the court in respect of a commonhold association.

(4) But the order of the court by virtue of section 6(6)(c) or 40(3)(d) may—
- (a) require the liquidator to exercise his functions in a particular way;
- (b) impose additional rights or duties on the liquidator;
- (c) modify or remove a right or duty of the liquidator.

[2081]

NOTES

Commencement: 27 September 2004.

56 Release of reserve fund

Section 39(4) shall cease to have effect in relation to a commonhold association (in respect of debts and liabilities accruing at any time) if—
- (a) the court makes a winding-up order in respect of the association,
- (b) the association passes a voluntary winding-up resolution, or
- (c) the court makes an order by virtue of section 6(6)(c) or 40(3)(d) for all the land in relation to which the association exercises functions to cease to be commonhold land.

[2082]

NOTES

Commencement: 27 September 2004.

Miscellaneous

57 Multiple site commonholds

(1) A commonhold may include two or more parcels of land, whether or not contiguous.

(2) But section 1(1) of this Act is not satisfied in relation to land specified in the *memorandum of association* [articles of association] of a commonhold association unless a single commonhold community statement makes provision for all the land.

(3) Regulations may make provision about an application under section 2 made jointly by two or more persons, each of whom is the registered freeholder of part of the land to which the application relates.

(4) The regulations may, in particular—
- (a) modify the application of a provision made by or by virtue of this Part;
- (b) disapply the application of a provision made by or by virtue of this Part;
- (c) impose additional requirements.

[2083]

NOTES

Commencement: 27 September 2004.

Sub-s (2): words in italics substituted by subsequent words in square brackets by SI 2009/1941, art 2(1), Sch 1, para 194(1), (12), as from 1 October 2009.

Regulations: the Commonhold Regulations 2004, SI 2004/1829 at **[3432]**.

58 Development rights

(1) In this Part—

"the developer" means a person who makes an application under section 2, and

"development business" has the meaning given by Schedule 4.

(2) A commonhold community statement may confer rights on the developer which are designed—

(a) to permit him to undertake development business, or

(b) to facilitate his undertaking of development business.

(3) Provision made by a commonhold community statement in reliance on subsection (2) may include provision—

(a) requiring the commonhold association or a unit-holder to co-operate with the developer for a specified purpose connected with development business;

(b) making the exercise of a right conferred by virtue of subsection (2) subject to terms and conditions specified in or to be determined in accordance with the commonhold community statement;

(c) making provision about the effect of breach of a requirement by virtue of paragraph (a) or a term or condition imposed by virtue of paragraph (b);

(d) disapplying section 41(2) and (3).

(4) Subsection (2) is subject—

(a) to regulations under section 32, and

(b) in the case of development business of the kind referred to in paragraph 7 of Schedule 4, to the *memorandum and articles of association* [articles of association] of the commonhold association.

(5) Regulations may make provision regulating or restricting the exercise of rights conferred by virtue of subsection (2).

(6) Where a right is conferred on a developer by virtue of subsection (2), if he sends to the Registrar a notice surrendering the right—

(a) the Registrar shall arrange for the notice to be kept in his custody and referred to in the register,

(b) the right shall cease to be exercisable from the time when the notice is registered under paragraph (a), and

(c) the Registrar shall inform the commonhold association as soon as is reasonably practicable.

[2084]

NOTES

Commencement: 27 September 2004.

Sub-s (4): in sub-para (b) words in italics substituted by subsequent words in square brackets by SI 2009/1941, art 2(1), Sch 1, para 194(1), (13), as from 1 October 2009.

Regulations: the Commonhold Regulations 2004, SI 2004/1829 at **[3432]**.

59 Development rights: succession

(1) If during a transitional period the developer transfers to another person the freehold estate in the whole of the commonhold, the successor in title shall be treated as the developer in relation to any matter arising after the transfer.

(2) If during a transitional period the developer transfers to another person the freehold estate in part of the commonhold, the successor in title shall be treated as the developer for the purpose of any matter which—

(a) arises after the transfer, and

(b) affects the estate transferred.

(3) If after a transitional period or in a case where there is no transitional period—

(a) the developer transfers to another person the freehold estate in the whole or part of the commonhold (other than by the transfer of the freehold estate in a single commonhold unit), and

(b) the transfer is expressed to be inclusive of development rights,

the successor in title shall be treated as the developer for the purpose of any matter which arises after the transfer and affects the estate transferred.

(4) Other than during a transitional period, a person shall not be treated as the developer in relation to commonhold land for any purpose unless he—

(a) is, or has been at a particular time, the registered proprietor of the freehold estate in more than one of the commonhold units, and

(b) is the registered proprietor of the freehold estate in at least one of the commonhold units.

[2085]

NOTES
Commencement: 27 September 2004.

60 Compulsory purchase

(1) Where a freehold estate in commonhold land is transferred to a compulsory purchaser the land shall cease to be commonhold land.

(2) But subsection (1) does not apply to a transfer if the Registrar is satisfied that the compulsory purchaser has indicated a desire for the land transferred to continue to be commonhold land.

(3) The requirement of consent under section 21(2)(c) shall not apply to transfer to a compulsory purchaser.

(4) Regulations may make provision about the transfer of a freehold estate in commonhold land to a compulsory purchaser.

(5) The regulations may, in particular—
- (a) make provision about the effect of subsections (1) and (2) (including provision about that part of the commonhold which is not transferred);
- (b) require the service of notice;
- (c) confer power on a court;
- (d) make provision about compensation;
- (e) make provision enabling a commonhold association to require a compulsory purchaser to acquire the freehold estate in the whole, or a particular part, of the commonhold;
- (f) provide for an enactment relating to compulsory purchase not to apply or to apply with modifications.

(6) Provision made by virtue of subsection (5)(a) in respect of land which is not transferred may include provision—
- (a) for some or all of the land to cease to be commonhold land;
- (b) for a provision of this Part to apply with specified modifications.

(7) In this section "compulsory purchaser" means—
- (a) a person acquiring land in respect of which he is authorised to exercise a power of compulsory purchase by virtue of an enactment, and
- (b) a person acquiring land which he is obliged to acquire by virtue of a prescribed enactment or in prescribed circumstances.

[2086]

NOTES
Commencement: 27 September 2004.

61 [Home] rights

In the following provisions of this Part a reference to a tenant includes a reference to a person who has [home rights (within the meaning of section 30(2) of the Family Law Act 1996 (c 27) (rights in respect of matrimonial or civil partnership home))] in respect of a commonhold unit—
- (a) section 19,
- (b) section 35, and
- (c) section 37.

[2087]

NOTES
Commencement: 27 September 2004.
Words in square brackets substituted by the Civil Partnership Act 2004, s 82, Sch 9, Pt 2, para 24; for transitional provisions see s 82, Sch 9, Pt 3 thereto.

62 Advice [etc]

(1) The Lord Chancellor may give financial assistance to a person in relation to the provision by that person of [information, training or] general advice [about, or a dispute resolution service in connection with—
- (a) any] aspect of the law of commonhold land, so far as relating to residential matters[, or
- (b) any other matter relating to commonhold land and residential matters].

(2) Financial assistance under this section may be given in such form and on such terms as the Lord Chancellor thinks appropriate.

(3) The terms may, in particular, require repayment in specified circumstances.

[2088]

NOTES

Commencement: 29 September 2003.

Heading: words in square brackets inserted by the Housing and Regeneration Act 2008, s 319(2).

Sub-s (1): first words in square brackets, and sub-para (b), together with word "or" immediately preceding it, inserted, and second words in square brackets substituted, by Housing and Regeneration Act 2008, s 319(1), (2).

63 The Crown

This Part binds the Crown.

[2089]

NOTES

Commencement: 27 September 2004.

General

64 Orders and regulations

(1) In this Part "prescribed" means prescribed by regulations.

(2) Regulations under this Part shall be made by the Lord Chancellor.

(3) Regulations under this Part—

(a) shall be made by statutory instrument,
(b) may include incidental, supplemental, consequential and transitional provision,
(c) may make provision generally or only in relation to specified cases,
(d) may make different provision for different purposes, and
(e) shall be subject to annulment in pursuance of a resolution of either House of Parliament.

[2090]

65 Registration procedure

(1) The Lord Chancellor may make rules about—

(a) the procedure to be followed on or in respect of commonhold registration documents, and
(b) the registration of freehold estates in commonhold land.

(2) Rules under this section—

(a) shall be made by statutory instrument in the same manner as land registration rules within the meaning of the Land Registration Act 2002 (c 9),
(b) may make provision for any matter for which provision is or may be made by land registration rules, and
(c) may provide for land registration rules to have effect in relation to anything done by virtue of or for the purposes of this Part as they have effect in relation to anything done by virtue of or for the purposes of that Act.

(3) Rules under this section may, in particular, make provision—

(a) about the form and content of a commonhold registration document;
(b) enabling the Registrar to cancel an application by virtue of this Part in specified circumstances;
(c) enabling the Registrar, in particular, to cancel an application by virtue of this Part if he thinks that plans submitted with it (whether as part of a commonhold community statement or otherwise) are insufficiently clear or accurate;
(d) about the order in which commonhold registration documents and general registration documents are to be dealt with by the Registrar;
(e) for registration to take effect (whether or not retrospectively) as from a date or time determined in accordance with the rules.

(4) The rules may also make provision about satisfaction of a requirement for an application by virtue of this Part to be accompanied by a document; in particular the rules may—

(a) permit or require a copy of a document to be submitted in place of or in addition to the original;
(b) require a copy to be certified in a specified manner;
(c) permit or require the submission of a document in electronic form.

(5) A commonhold registration document must be accompanied by such fee (if any) as is specified for that purpose by order under section 102 of the Land Registration Act 2002 (c 9) (fee orders).

(6) In this section—

"commonhold registration document" means an application or other document sent to the Registrar by virtue of this Part, and "general registration document" means a document sent to the Registrar under a provision of the Land Registration Act 2002.

[2091]

NOTES

Rules: the Commonhold (Land Registration) Rules 2004, SI 2004/1830 at **[3451]**.

66 Jurisdiction

(1) In this Part "the court" means the High Court or a county court.

(2) Provision made by or under this Part conferring jurisdiction on a court shall be subject to provision made under section 1 of the Courts and Legal Services Act 1990 (c 41) (allocation of business between High Court and county courts).

(3) A power under this Part to confer jurisdiction on a court includes power to confer jurisdiction on a tribunal established under an enactment.

(4) Rules of court or rules of procedure for a tribunal may make provision about proceedings brought—

(a) under or by virtue of any provision of this Part, or
(b) in relation to commonhold land.

[2092]

67 The register

(1) In this Part—

"the register" means the register of title to freehold and leasehold land kept under section 1 of the Land Registration Act 2002,
"registered" means registered in the register, and
"the Registrar" means the Chief Land Registrar.

(2) Regulations under any provision of this Part may confer functions on the Registrar (including discretionary functions).

(3) The Registrar shall comply with any direction or requirement given to him or imposed on him under or by virtue of this Part.

(4) Where the Registrar thinks it appropriate in consequence of or for the purpose of anything done or proposed to be done in connection with this Part, he may—

(a) make or cancel an entry on the register;
(b) take any other action.

(5) Subsection (4) is subject to section 6(2).

[2093]

68 Amendments

Schedule 5 (consequential amendments) shall have effect.

[2094]

NOTES

Commencement: 27 September 2004.

69 Interpretation

(1) In this Part—

"instrument" includes any document, and
"object" in relation to a commonhold association means an object stated in the association's memorandum of association in accordance with section 2(1)(c) of the Companies Act 1985 (c 6).
["object", in relation to a commonhold association, means an object stated in the association's articles of association (see section 31 of the Companies Act 2006).]

(2) In this Part—

(a) a reference to a duty to insure includes a reference to a duty to use the proceeds of insurance for the purpose of rebuilding or reinstating, and
(b) a reference to maintaining property includes a reference to decorating it and to putting it into sound condition.

(3) A provision of the Law of Property Act 1925 (c 20), *the Companies Act 1985 (c 6)* [the Companies Act 2006] or the Land Registration Act 2002 (c 9) defining an expression shall apply to the use of the expression in this Part unless the contrary intention appears.

[2095]

NOTES

Commencement: 29 September 2003 (in so far as relating to ss 42, 62, 64–67); 27 September 2004 (for remaining purposes).

Sub-s (1): in definition "object" substituted by SI 2009/1941, art 2(1), Sch 1, para 194(1), (13), as from 1 October 2009.

Sub-s (3): words in italics substituted by subsequent words in square brackets by SI 2009/1941, art 2(1), Sch 1, para 194(1), (13), as from 1 October 2009.

70 Index of defined expressions

In this Part the expressions listed below are defined by the provisions specified.

Expression	*Interpretation provision*
Common parts	Section 25
A commonhold	Section 1
Commonhold association	Section 34
Commonhold community statement	Section 31
Commonhold land	Section 1
Commonhold unit	Section 11
Court	Section 66
Declaration of solvency	Section 43
Developer	Section 58
Development business	Section 58
Exercising functions	Section 8
Insolvent commonhold association	Section 50
Instrument	Section 69
Insure	Section 69
Joint unit-holder	Section 13
Liquidator (sections 44 to 49)	Section 44
Maintenance	Section 69
Object	Section 69
Prescribed	Section 64
The register	Section 67
Registered	Section 67
Registered freeholder	Section 2
The Registrar	Section 67
Regulations	Section 64
Residential commonhold unit	Section 17
Succession order	Section 51
Successor commonhold association	Section 50
Termination application	Section 46
Termination-statement resolution	Section 43
Transfer (of unit)	Section 15
Transitional period	Section 8
Unit-holder	Section 12
Winding-up resolution	Section 43

[2096]

NOTES

Commencement: 29 September 2003 (in so far as relating to ss 42, 62, 64–67); 27 September 2004 (for remaining purposes).

PART 2
LEASEHOLD REFORM

71–172 ((*Chs 1–5*) *Outside the scope of this work or contain amendments which in so far as relevant to this work, have been incorporated at the appropriate place.*)

CHAPTER 6
LEASEHOLD VALUATION TRIBUNALS

173 Leasehold valuation tribunals

(1) Any jurisdiction conferred on a leasehold valuation tribunal by or under any enactment is exercisable by a rent assessment committee constituted in accordance with Schedule 10 to the Rent Act 1977 (c 42).

(2) When so constituted for exercising any such jurisdiction a rent assessment committee is known as a leasehold valuation tribunal.

[2097]

174 (*Outside the scope of this work.*)

175 Appeals

(1) A party to proceedings before a leasehold valuation tribunal may appeal to the [Upper Tribunal] from a decision of the leasehold valuation tribunal.

(2) But the appeal may be made only with the permission of—
- (a) the leasehold valuation tribunal, or
- (b) the [Upper Tribunal].

(3) …

(4) On the appeal the [Upper Tribunal] may exercise any power which was available to the leasehold valuation tribunal.

(5) And a decision of the [Upper Tribunal] on the appeal may be enforced in the same way as a decision of the leasehold valuation tribunal.

(6) The [Upper Tribunal] may not order a party to the appeal to pay costs incurred by another party in connection with the appeal unless he has, in the opinion of the [Upper Tribunal], acted frivolously, vexatiously, abusively, disruptively or otherwise unreasonably in connection with the appeal.

(7) In such a case the amount he may be ordered to pay shall not exceed the maximum amount which a party to proceedings before a leasehold valuation tribunal may be ordered to pay in the proceedings under or by virtue of paragraph 10(3) of Schedule 12.

(8) No appeal lies from a decision of a leasehold valuation tribunal to the High Court by virtue of section 11(1) of the Tribunals and Inquiries Act 1992 (c 53).

(9) And no case may be stated for the opinion of the High Court in respect of such a decision by virtue of that provision.

(10) …

[2098]

NOTES

Sub-ss (1), (2), (4)–(6): words in square brackets substituted by SI 2009/1307, art 5(1), (2), Sch 1, para 269(a).
Sub-ss (3), (10): repealed by SI 2009/1307, art 5(1), (2), Sch 1, para 269(b).

176 (*Outside the scope of this work.*)

CHAPTER 7
GENERAL

177 Wales

The references to the 1985 Act, the 1987 Act and the 1993 Act in Schedule 1 to the National Assembly for Wales (Transfer of Functions) Order 1999 (SI 1999/672) are to be treated as referring to those Acts as amended by this Part.

[2099]

178 Orders and regulations

(1) An order or regulations under any provision of this Part—
- (a) may include incidental, supplementary, consequential and transitional provision,
- (b) may make provision generally or only in relation to specified cases, and

(c) may make different provision for different purposes.

(2) Regulations under Schedule 12 may make different provision for different areas.

(3) Any power to make an order or regulations under this Part is exercisable by statutory instrument.

(4) Regulations shall not be made by the Secretary of State under section 167 or 171 or paragraph 9(3)(b) or 10(3)(b) of Schedule 12 unless a draft of the instrument containing them has been laid before and approved by a resolution of each House of Parliament.

(5) A statutory instrument containing an order or regulations made by the Secretary of State under this Part shall, if not so approved, be subject to annulment in pursuance of a resolution of either House of Parliament.

[2100]

179 Interpretation

(1) In this Part "the appropriate national authority" means—

(a) the Secretary of State (as respects England), and
(b) the National Assembly for Wales (as respects Wales).

(2) In this Part—

"the 1967 Act" means the Leasehold Reform Act 1967 (c 88),
"the 1985 Act" means the Landlord and Tenant Act 1985 (c 70),
"the 1987 Act" means the Landlord and Tenant Act 1987 (c 31), and
"the 1993 Act" means the Leasehold Reform, Housing and Urban Development Act 1993 (c 28).

[2101]

PART 3
SUPPLEMENTARY

180 (*Introduces Sch 14 to this Act.*)

181 Commencement etc

(1) Apart from section 104 and sections 177 to 179, the preceding provisions (and the Schedules) come into force in accordance with provision made by order made by the appropriate authority.

(2) The appropriate authority may by order make any transitional provisions or savings in connection with the coming into force of any provision in accordance with an order under subsection (1).

(3) The power to make orders under subsections (1) and (2) is exercisable by statutory instrument.

(4) In this section "the appropriate authority" means—

(a) in relation to any provision of Part 1 or section 180 and Schedule 14 so far as relating to section 104, the Lord Chancellor, and
(b) in relation to any provision of Part 2 or section 180 and Schedule 14 so far as otherwise relating, the Secretary of State (as respects England) and the National Assembly for Wales (as respects Wales).

[2102]

NOTES

Orders: the Commonhold and Leasehold Reform Act 2002 (Commencement No 1, Savings and Transitional Provisions) (Wales) Order 2002, SI 2002/3012; the Commonhold and Leasehold Reform Act 2002 (Commencement No 2 and Savings) (England) Order 2003, SI 2003/1986; the Commonhold and Leasehold Reform Act 2002 (Commencement No 3) Order 2003, SI 2003/2377; the Commonhold and Leasehold Reform Act 2002 (Commencement No 2 and Savings) (Wales) Order 2004, SI 2004/669; the Commonhold and Leasehold Reform Act 2002 (Commencement No 4) Order 2004, SI 2004/1832; the Commonhold and Leasehold Reform Act 2002 (Commencement No 5 and Saving and Transitional Provision) Order 2004, SI 2004/3056; the Commonhold and Leasehold Reform Act 2002 (Commencement No 5 and Saving and Transitional Provision) (Amendment) (England) Order 2005, SI 2005/193; the Commonhold and Leasehold Reform Act 2002 (Commencement No 3 and Saving and Transitional Provision) (Wales) Order 2005, SI 2005/1353; the Commonhold and Leasehold Reform Act 2002 (Commencement No 6) (England) Order 2007, SI 2007/1256; the Commonhold and Leasehold Reform Act 2002 (Commencement No 4) (Wales) Order 2007, SI 2007/3161.

182 Extent

This Act extends to England and Wales only.

[2103]

183 Short title

This Act may be cited as the Commonhold and Leasehold Reform Act 2002.

[2104]

SCHEDULE 1
APPLICATION FOR REGISTRATION: DOCUMENTS

Section 2

Introduction

1. This Schedule lists the documents which are required by section 2 to accompany an application for the registration of a freehold estate as a freehold estate in commonhold land.

Commonhold association documents

2. The commonhold association's *certificate of incorporation under section 13 of the Companies Act 1985* (*c 6*) [certificate of incorporation under section 15 of the Companies Act 2006].

3. Any altered certificate of incorporation issued under *section 28 of that Act* [section 80 of that Act (change of name)].

4. The *memorandum and articles of association* [articles of association] of the commonhold association.

Commonhold community statement

5. The commonhold community statement.

Consent

6.—(1) Where consent is required under or by virtue of section 3—
- (a) the consent,
- (b) an order of a court by virtue of section 3(2)(f) dispensing with the requirement for consent, or
- (c) evidence of deemed consent by virtue of section 3(2)(e).

(2) In the case of a conditional order under section 3(2)(f), the order must be accompanied by evidence that the condition has been complied with.

Certificate

7. A certificate given by the directors of the commonhold association that—
- (a) the *memorandum and articles of association* [articles of association] submitted with the application comply with regulations under paragraph 2(1) of Schedule 3,
- (b) the commonhold community statement submitted with the application satisfies the requirements of this Part,
- (c) the application satisfies Schedule 2,
- (d) the commonhold association has not traded, and
- (e) the commonhold association has not incurred any liability which has not been discharged.

[2105]

NOTES

Commencement: 27 September 2004.

Paras 2, 3, 4, 7: words in italics substituted by subsequent words in square brackets by SI 2009/1941, art 2(1), Sch 1, para 194(1), (20), as from 1 October 2009.

SCHEDULE 2
LAND WHICH MAY NOT BE COMMONHOLD LAND

Section 4

"Flying freehold"

1.—(1) Subject to sub-paragraph (2), an application may not be made under section 2 wholly or partly in relation to land above ground level ("raised land") unless all the land between the ground and the raised land is the subject of the same application.

(2) An application for the addition of land to a commonhold in accordance with section 41 may be made wholly or partly in relation to raised land if all the land between the ground and the raised land forms part of the commonhold to which the raised land is to be added.

Agricultural land

2. An application may not be made under section 2 wholly or partly in relation to land if—
- (a) it is agricultural land within the meaning of the Agriculture Act 1947 (c 48),

(b) it is comprised in a tenancy of an agricultural holding within the meaning of the Agricultural Holdings Act 1986 (c 5), or
(c) it is comprised in a farm business tenancy for the purposes of the Agricultural Tenancies Act 1995 (c 8).

Contingent title

3.—(1) An application may not be made under section 2 if an estate in the whole or part of the land to which the application relates is a contingent estate.

(2) An estate is contingent for the purposes of this paragraph if (and only if)—
(a) it is liable to revert to or vest in a person other than the present registered proprietor on the occurrence or non-occurrence of a particular event, and
(b) the reverter or vesting would occur by operation of law as a result of an enactment listed in sub-paragraph (3).

(3) The enactments are—
(a) the School Sites Act 1841 (c 38) (conveyance for use as school),
(b) the Lands Clauses Acts (compulsory purchase),
(c) the Literary and Scientific Institutions Act 1854 (c 112) (sites for institutions), and
(d) the Places of Worship Sites Act 1873 (c 50) (sites for places of worship).

(4) Regulations may amend sub-paragraph (3) so as to—
(a) add an enactment to the list, or
(b) remove an enactment from the list.

[2106]

NOTES
Commencement: 27 September 2004.

PART I STATUTES

SCHEDULE 3
COMMONHOLD ASSOCIATION

Section 34

PART 1
MEMORANDUM AND ARTICLES OF ASSOCIATION [ARTICLES OF ASSOCIATION]

Introduction

1. In this Schedule—
(a) "memorandum" means the memorandum of association of a commonhold association, and
(b) "articles" means the articles of association of a commonhold association.

[1. In this Schedule "articles" means the articles of association of a commonhold association.]

Form and content

2.—(1) Regulations shall make provision about the form and content of *the memorandum and articles* [the articles].

(2) A commonhold association may adopt provisions of the regulations for its *memorandum or articles* [articles].

(3) The regulations may include provision which is to have effect for a commonhold association whether or not it is adopted under sub-paragraph (2).

(4) A provision of the *memorandum or articles* [articles] shall have no effect to the extent that it is inconsistent with the regulations.

(5) Regulations under this paragraph shall have effect in relation to a *memorandum or articles* [articles]—
(a) irrespective of the date of the *memorandum or articles* [articles], but
(b) subject to any transitional provision of the regulations.

[(6) Section 20 of the Companies Act 2006 (default application of model articles) does not apply to a commonhold association.]

Alteration

3.—(1) *An alteration of the memorandum or articles of association* [Where a commonhold association alters its *memorandum or articles* [articles] at a time when the land *specified in its memorandum* [specified in its articles] is commonhold land, the alteration] shall have no effect until the altered version is registered in accordance with this paragraph.

(2) If the commonhold association makes an application under this sub-paragraph the Registrar shall arrange for *an altered memorandum or altered articles* [altered articles] to be kept in his custody, and referred to in the register, in place of the unaltered version.

(3) An application under sub-paragraph (2) must be accompanied by a certificate given by the directors of the commonhold association that the altered *memorandum or articles* [articles] comply with regulations under paragraph 2(1).

(4) Where the Registrar amends the register on an application under sub-paragraph (2) he shall make any consequential amendments to the register which he thinks appropriate.

Disapplication of Companies Act 1985

4.—(1) The following provisions of the Companies Act 1985 (c 6) shall not apply to a commonhold association—

- *(a) sections 2(7) and 3 (memorandum), and*
- *(b) section 8 (articles of association).*

(2) No application may be made under paragraph 3(2) for the registration of a memorandum altered by special resolution in accordance with section 4(1) of the Companies Act 1985 (objects) unless—

- *(a) the period during which an application for cancellation of the alteration may be made under section 5(1) of that Act has expired without an application being made,*
- *(b) any application made under that section has been withdrawn, or*
- *(c) the alteration has been confirmed by the court under that section.*

[2107]

NOTES

Commencement: 27 September 2004.

Part heading: words in italics substituted by subsequent words in square brackets by SI 2009/1941, art 2(1), Sch 1, para 195(1), (2), as from 1 October 2009.

Para 1: substituted by SI 2009/1941, art 2(1), Sch 1, para 195(1), (3), as from 1 October 2009

Para 2: in sub-paras (1), (2), (4), (5) words in italics substituted by subsequent words in square brackets, and sub-para (6) inserted, by SI 2009/1941, art 2(1), Sch 1, para 195(1), (4), as from 1 October 2009.

Para 3: in sub-para (1), words "An alteration of the memorandum or articles of association" in italics substituted by subsequent words in first (outer) pair of square brackets by the Companies Act 2006, s 1283 as from 1 October 2009 (with effect in relation to amendments made on or after that date): see SI 2008/2860, arts 3(y), 5, Sch 2, para 113; words "memorandum or articles" in italics substituted by subsequent word in second (inner) pair of square brackets, and words "specified in its memorandum" in italics substituted by subsequent words in third (inner) pair of square brackets, by SI 2009/1941, art 2(1), Sch 1, para 195(1), (5)(a), as from 1 October 2009; in sub-paras (2), (3) words in italics substituted by subsequent words in square brackets, by SI 2009/1941, art 2(1), Sch 1, para 195(1), (5)(b), (c), as from 1 October 2009.

Para 4: repealed by SI 2009/1941, art 2(1), Sch 1, para 195(1), (6), as from 1 October 2009

Regulations: the Commonhold Regulations 2004, SI 2004/1829 at **[3432]**.

PART 2
MEMBERSHIP

Pre-commonhold period

5. During the period beginning with incorporation of a commonhold association and ending when *land specified in its memorandum* [land specified in its articles] becomes commonhold land, the subscribers (or subscriber) to *the memorandum* [the association's memorandum of association] shall be the sole members (or member) of the association.

Transitional period

6.—(1) This paragraph applies to a commonhold association during a transitional period.

(2) The subscribers (or subscriber) to *the memorandum* [the association's memorandum of association] shall continue to be members (or the member) of the association.

(3) A person who for the time being is the developer in respect of all or part of the commonhold is entitled to be entered in the register of members of the association.

Unit-holders

7. A person is entitled to be entered in the register of members of a commonhold association if he becomes the unit-holder of a commonhold unit in relation to which the association exercises functions—

- (a) on the unit becoming commonhold land by registration with unit-holders under section 9, or
- (b) on the transfer of the unit.

Joint unit-holders

8.—(1) This paragraph applies where two or more persons become joint unit-holders of a commonhold unit—

(a) on the unit becoming commonhold land by registration with unit-holders under section 9, or

(b) on the transfer of the unit.

(2) If the joint unit-holders nominate one of themselves for the purpose of this sub-paragraph, he is entitled to be entered in the register of members of the commonhold association which exercises functions in relation to the unit.

(3) A nomination under sub-paragraph (2) must—

(a) be made in writing to the commonhold association, and

(b) be received by the association before the end of the prescribed period.

(4) If no nomination is received by the association before the end of the prescribed period the person whose name appears first in the proprietorship register is on the expiry of that period entitled to be entered in the register of members of the association.

(5) On the application of a joint unit-holder the court may order that a joint unit-holder is entitled to be entered in the register of members of a commonhold association in place of a person who is or would be entitled to be registered by virtue of sub-paragraph (4).

(6) If joint unit-holders nominate one of themselves for the purpose of this sub-paragraph, the nominated person is entitled to be entered in the register of members of the commonhold association in place of the person entered by virtue of—

(a) sub-paragraph (2),

(b) sub-paragraph (5), or

(c) this sub-paragraph.

Self-membership

9. A commonhold association may not be a member of itself.

No other members

10. A person may not become a member of a commonhold association otherwise than by virtue of a provision of this Schedule.

Effect of registration

11. A person who is entitled to be entered in the register of members of a commonhold association becomes a member when the company registers him in pursuance of its duty under *section 352 of the Companies Act 1985* (*c 6*) [section 113 of the Companies Act 2006] (duty to maintain register of members).

Termination of membership

12. Where a member of a commonhold association ceases to be a unit-holder or joint unit-holder of a commonhold unit in relation to which the association exercises functions—

(a) he shall cease to be a member of the commonhold association, but

(b) paragraph (a) does not affect any right or liability already acquired or incurred in respect of a matter relating to a time when he was a unit-holder or joint unit-holder.

13. A member of a commonhold association may resign by notice in writing to the association if (and only if) he is a member by virtue of paragraph 5 or 6 of this Schedule (and not also by virtue of any other paragraph).

Register of members

14.—(1) Regulations may make provision about the performance by a commonhold association of its duty under *section 352 of the Companies Act 1985* (*c 6*) [section 113 of the Companies Act 2006] (duty to maintain register of members) where a person—

(a) becomes entitled to be entered in the register by virtue of paragraphs 5 to 8, or

(b) ceases to be a member by virtue of paragraph 12 or on resignation.

(2) The regulations may in particular require entries in the register to be made within a specified period.

(3) A period specified under sub-paragraph (2) may be expressed to begin from—

(a) the date of a notification under section 15(3),

(b) the date on which the directors of the commonhold association first become aware of a specified matter, or

(c) some other time.

(4) A requirement by virtue of this paragraph shall be treated as *a requirement of section 352 for the purposes of section 352(5) (fines)* [a requirement of section 113 for the purposes of section 113(7) and (8) (offences)].

Companies Act 1985

15.—(1) Section 22(1) of the Companies Act 1985 (initial members) shall apply to a commonhold association subject to this Schedule.

(2) Sections 22(2) and 23 of that Act (members: new members and holding company) shall not apply to a commonhold association.

[Supplementary provisions

15.—(1) Section 112(1) of the Companies Act 2006 (initial members of company) applies to a commonhold association subject to the provisions of this Schedule.

(2) The following provisions of that Act do not apply to a commonhold association—
section 112(2) (new members);
section 136 (membership of holding company).]

[2108]

NOTES

Commencement: 27 September 2004.

Paras 5, 6, 11, 14: words in italics substituted by subsequent words in square brackets by SI 2009/1941, art 2(1), Sch 1, para 195(1), (7)–(10), as from 1 October 2009.

Para 15: substituted by SI 2009/1941, art 2(1), Sch 1, para 195(1), (11), as from 1 October 2009.

PART 3
MISCELLANEOUS

Name

16. Regulations may provide—
   (a) that the name by which a commonhold association is registered under the *Companies Act 1985* [Companies Act 2006] must satisfy specified requirements;
   (b) that the name by which a company other than a commonhold association is registered may not include a specified word or expression.

Statutory declaration [Statement of compliance]

17. For the purposes of *section 12 of the Companies Act 1985 (registration: compliance with Act)* [section 13 of the Companies Act 2006 (registration: statement of compliance)] as it applies to a commonhold association, a reference to the requirements of that Act shall be treated as including a reference to a provision of or made under this Schedule.

[2109]

NOTES

Commencement: 27 September 2004.

Para 16: words in italics substituted by subsequent words in square brackets by SI 2009/1941, art 2(1), Sch 1, para 195(1), (12), as from 1 October 2009.

Para 17: cross heading substituted, and words in italics substituted by subsequent words in square brackets, by SI 2009/1941, art 2(1), Sch 1, para 195(1), (13), as from 1 October 2009.

Regulations: the Commonhold Regulations 2004, SI 2004/1829 at **[3432]**.

SCHEDULE 4
DEVELOPMENT RIGHTS

Section 58

Introductory

1. This Schedule sets out the matters which are development business for the purposes of section 58.

Works

2. The completion or execution of works on—
   (a) a commonhold,
   (b) land which is or may be added to a commonhold, or
   (c) land which has been removed from a commonhold.

Marketing

3.—(1) Transactions in commonhold units.

(2) Advertising and other activities designed to promote transactions in commonhold units.

Variation

4. The addition of land to a commonhold.

5. The removal of land from a commonhold.

6. Amendment of a commonhold community statement (including amendment to redefine the extent of a commonhold unit).

Commonhold association

7. Appointment and removal of directors of a commonhold association.

[2110]

NOTES

Commencement: 27 September 2004.

(*Schs 5–14 outside the scope of this work or contain amendments and repeals which, in so far as relevant to this work, have been incorporated at the appropriate place.*)

ANTI-SOCIAL BEHAVIOUR ACT 2003

(2003 c 38)

An Act to make provision in connection with anti-social behaviour.

[20 November 2003]

1–64 ((*Pts 1–7*) *Outside the scope of this work.*)

PART 8
HIGH HEDGES

Introductory

65 Complaints to which this Part applies

(1) This Part applies to a complaint which—

(a) is made for the purposes of this Part by an owner or occupier of a domestic property; and

(b) alleges that his reasonable enjoyment of that property is being adversely affected by the height of a high hedge situated on land owned or occupied by another person.

(2) This Part also applies to a complaint which—

(a) is made for the purposes of this Part by an owner of a domestic property that is for the time being unoccupied, and

(b) alleges that the reasonable enjoyment of that property by a prospective occupier of that property would be adversely affected by the height of a high hedge situated on land owned or occupied by another person,

as it applies to a complaint falling within subsection (1).

(3) In relation to a complaint falling within subsection (2), references in sections 68 and 69 to the effect of the height of a high hedge on the complainant's reasonable enjoyment of a domestic property shall be read as references to the effect that it would have on the reasonable enjoyment of that property by a prospective occupier of the property.

(4) This Part does not apply to complaints about the effect of the roots of a high hedge.

(5) In this Part, in relation to a complaint—

"complainant" means—

(a) a person by whom the complaint is made; or

(b) if every person who made the complaint ceases to be an owner or occupier of the domestic property specified in the complaint, any other person who is for the time being an owner or occupier of that property;

and references to the complainant include references to one or more of the complainants;

"the neighbouring land" means the land on which the high hedge is situated; and

"the relevant authority" means the local authority in whose area that land is situated.

[2111]

NOTES

Commencement: 31 December 2004 (in relation to complaints about hedges situated in Wales); 1 June 2005 (in relation to complaints about hedges situated in England).

66 High hedges

(1) In this Part "high hedge" means so much of a barrier to light or access as—

(a) is formed wholly or predominantly by a line of two or more evergreens; and

(b) rises to a height of more than two metres above ground level.

(2) For the purposes of subsection (1) a line of evergreens is not to be regarded as forming a barrier to light or access if the existence of gaps significantly affects its overall effect as such a barrier at heights of more than two metres above ground level.

(3) In this section "evergreen" means an evergreen tree or shrub or a semi-evergreen tree or shrub.

[2112]

NOTES

Commencement: 31 December 2004 (in relation to complaints about hedges situated in Wales); 1 June 2005 (in relation to complaints about hedges situated in England).

67 Domestic property

(1) In this Part "domestic property" means—

(a) a dwelling; or

(b) a garden or yard which is used and enjoyed wholly or mainly in connection with a dwelling.

(2) In subsection (1) "dwelling" means any building or part of a building occupied, or intended to be occupied, as a separate dwelling.

(3) A reference in this Part to a person's reasonable enjoyment of domestic property includes a reference to his reasonable enjoyment of a part of the property.

[2113]

NOTES

Commencement: 31 December 2004 (in relation to complaints about hedges situated in Wales); 1 June 2005 (in relation to complaints about hedges situated in England).

Complaints procedure

68 Procedure for dealing with complaints

(1) This section has effect where a complaint to which this Part applies—

(a) is made to the relevant authority; and

(b) is accompanied by such fee (if any) as the authority may determine.

(2) If the authority consider—

(a) that the complainant has not taken all reasonable steps to resolve the matters complained of without proceeding by way of such a complaint to the authority, or

(b) that the complaint is frivolous or vexatious,

the authority may decide that the complaint should not be proceeded with.

(3) If the authority do not so decide, they must decide—

(a) whether the height of the high hedge specified in the complaint is adversely affecting the complainant's reasonable enjoyment of the domestic property so specified; and

(b) if so, what action (if any) should be taken in relation to that hedge, in pursuance of a remedial notice under section 69, with a view to remedying the adverse effect or preventing its recurrence.

(4) If the authority decide under subsection (3) that action should be taken as mentioned in paragraph (b) of that subsection, they must as soon as is reasonably practicable—

(a) issue a remedial notice under section 69 implementing their decision;

(b) send a copy of that notice to the following persons, namely—

(i) every complainant; and

(ii) every owner and every occupier of the neighbouring land; and

(c) notify each of those persons of the reasons for their decision.

(5) If the authority—

(a) decide that the complaint should not be proceeded with, or

(b) decide either or both of the issues specified in subsection (3) otherwise than in the complainant's favour, they must as soon as is reasonably practicable notify the appropriate person or persons of any such decision and of their reasons for it.

(6) For the purposes of subsection (5)—

(a) every complainant is an appropriate person in relation to a decision falling within paragraph (a) or (b) of that subsection; and

(b) every owner and every occupier of the neighbouring land is an appropriate person in relation to a decision falling within paragraph (b) of that subsection.

(7) A fee determined under subsection (1)(b) must not exceed the amount prescribed in regulations made—

(a) in relation to complaints relating to hedges situated in England, by the Secretary of State; and

(b) in relation to complaints relating to hedges situated in Wales, by the National Assembly for Wales.

(8) A fee received by a local authority by virtue of subsection (1)(b) may be refunded by them in such circumstances and to such extent as they may determine.

[2114]

NOTES

Commencement: 31 December 2004 (in relation to complaints about hedges situated in Wales); 1 June 2005 (in relation to complaints about hedges situated in England).

Regulations: the High Hedges (Fees) (Wales) Regulations 2004, SI 2004/3241.

69 Remedial notices

(1) For the purposes of this Part a remedial notice is a notice—

(a) issued by the relevant authority in respect of a complaint to which this Part applies; and

(b) stating the matters mentioned in subsection (2).

(2) Those matters are—

(a) that a complaint has been made to the authority under this Part about a high hedge specified in the notice which is situated on land so specified;

(b) that the authority have decided that the height of that hedge is adversely affecting the complainant's reasonable enjoyment of the domestic property specified in the notice;

(c) the initial action that must be taken in relation to that hedge before the end of the compliance period;

(d) any preventative action that they consider must be taken in relation to that hedge at times following the end of that period while the hedge remains on the land; and

(e) the consequences under sections 75 and 77 of a failure to comply with the notice.

(3) The action specified in a remedial notice is not to require or involve—

(a) a reduction in the height of the hedge to less than two metres above ground level; or

(b) the removal of the hedge.

(4) A remedial notice shall take effect on its operative date.

(5) "The operative date" of a remedial notice is such date (falling at least 28 days after that on which the notice is issued) as is specified in the notice as the date on which it is to take effect.

(6) "The compliance period" in the case of a remedial notice is such reasonable period as is specified in the notice for the purposes of subsection (2)(c) as the period within which the action so specified is to be taken; and that period shall begin with the operative date of the notice.

(7) Subsections (4) to (6) have effect in relation to a remedial notice subject to—

(a) the exercise of any power of the relevant authority under section 70; and

(b) the operation of sections 71 to 73 in relation to the notice.

(8) While a remedial notice has effect, the notice—

(a) shall be a local land charge; and

(b) shall be binding on every person who is for the time being an owner or occupier of the land specified in the notice as the land where the hedge in question is situated.

(9) In this Part—

"initial action" means remedial action or preventative action, or both;

"remedial action" means action to remedy the adverse effect of the height of the hedge on the complainant's reasonable enjoyment of the domestic property in respect of which the complaint was made; and

"preventative action" means action to prevent the recurrence of the adverse effect.

[2115]

NOTES

Commencement: 31 December 2004 (in relation to complaints about hedges situated in Wales); 1 June 2005 (in relation to complaints about hedges situated in England).

70 Withdrawal or relaxation of requirements of remedial notices

(1) The relevant authority may—

(a) withdraw a remedial notice issued by them; or

(b) waive or relax a requirement of a remedial notice so issued.

(2) The powers conferred by this section are exercisable both before and after a remedial notice has taken effect.

(3) Where the relevant authority exercise the powers conferred by this section, they must give notice of what they have done to—

(a) every complainant; and

(b) every owner and every occupier of the neighbouring land.

(4) The withdrawal of a remedial notice does not affect the power of the relevant authority to issue a further remedial notice in respect of the same hedge.

[2116]

NOTES

Commencement: 31 December 2004 (in relation to complaints about hedges situated in Wales); 1 June 2005 (in relation to complaints about hedges situated in England).

Appeals

71 Appeals against remedial notices and other decisions of relevant authorities

(1) Where the relevant authority—

(a) issue a remedial notice,

(b) withdraw such a notice, or

(c) waive or relax the requirements of such a notice,

each of the persons falling within subsection (2) may appeal to the appeal authority against the issue or withdrawal of the notice or (as the case may be) the waiver or relaxation of its requirements.

(2) Those persons are—

(a) every person who is a complainant in relation to the complaint by reference to which the notice was given; and

(b) every person who is an owner or occupier of the neighbouring land.

(3) Where the relevant authority decide either or both of the issues specified in section 68(3) otherwise than in the complainant's favour, the complainant may appeal to the appeal authority against the decision.

(4) An appeal under this section must be made before—

(a) the end of the period of 28 days beginning with the relevant date; or

(b) such later time as the appeal authority may allow.

(5) In subsection (4) "the relevant date"—

(a) in the case of an appeal against the issue of a remedial notice, means the date on which the notice was issued; and

(b) in the case of any other appeal under this section, means the date of the notification given by the relevant authority under section 68 or 70 of the decision in question.

(6) Where an appeal is duly made under subsection (1), the notice or (as the case may be) withdrawal, waiver or relaxation in question shall not have effect pending the final determination or withdrawal of the appeal.

(7) In this Part "the appeal authority" means—

(a) in relation to appeals relating to hedges situated in England, the Secretary of State; and

(b) in relation to appeals relating to hedges situated in Wales, the National Assembly for Wales.

[2117]

NOTES

Commencement: 1 October 2004 (sub-s (7), in relation to complaints about hedges situated in England); 31 December 2004 (in relation to complaints about hedges situated in Wales); 1 June 2005 (sub-ss (1)–(6), in relation to complaints about hedges situated in England).

72 Appeals procedure

(1) The appeal authority may by regulations make provision with respect to—

(a) the procedure which is to be followed in connection with appeals to that authority under section 71; and

(b) other matters consequential on or connected with such appeals.

(2) Regulations under this section may, in particular, make provision—

(a) specifying the grounds on which appeals may be made;

(b) prescribing the manner in which appeals are to be made;

(c) requiring persons making appeals to send copies of such documents as may be prescribed to such persons as may be prescribed;
(d) requiring local authorities against whose decisions appeals are made to send to the appeal authority such documents as may be prescribed;
(e) specifying, where a local authority are required by virtue of paragraph (d) to send the appeal authority a statement indicating the submissions which they propose to put forward on the appeal, the matters to be included in such a statement;
(f) prescribing the period within which a requirement imposed by the regulations is to be complied with;
(g) enabling such a period to be extended by the appeal authority;
(h) for a decision on an appeal to be binding on persons falling within section 71(2) in addition to the person by whom the appeal was made;
(i) for incidental or ancillary matters, including the awarding of costs.

(3) Where an appeal is made to the appeal authority under section 71 the appeal authority may appoint a person to hear and determine the appeal on its behalf.

(4) The appeal authority may require such a person to exercise on its behalf any functions which—
(a) are conferred on the appeal authority in connection with such an appeal by section 71 or 73 or by regulations under this section; and
(b) are specified in that person's appointment;

and references to the appeal authority in section 71 or 73 or in any regulations under this section shall be construed accordingly.

(5) The appeal authority may pay a person appointed under subsection (3) such remuneration as it may determine.

(6) Regulations under this section may provide for any provision of Schedule 20 to the Environment Act 1995 (c 25) (delegation of appellate functions) to apply in relation to a person appointed under subsection (3) with such modifications (if any) as may be prescribed.

(7) In this section, "prescribed" means prescribed by regulations made by the appeal authority. **[2118]**

NOTES

Commencement: 1 October 2004 (in relation to complaints about hedges situated in England); 31 December 2004 (in relation to complaints about hedges situated in Wales).

Regulations: the High Hedges (Appeals) (Wales) Regulations 2004, SI 2004/3240; the High Hedges (Appeals) (England) Regulations 2005, SI 2005/711.

73 Determination or withdrawal of appeals

(1) On an appeal under section 71 the appeal authority may allow or dismiss the appeal, either in whole or in part.

(2) Where the appeal authority decides to allow such an appeal to any extent, it may do such of the following as it considers appropriate—
(a) quash a remedial notice or decision to which the appeal relates;
(b) vary the requirements of such a notice; or
(c) in a case where no remedial notice has been issued, issue on behalf of the relevant authority a remedial notice that could have been issued by the relevant authority on the complaint in question.

(3) On an appeal under section 71 relating to a remedial notice, the appeal authority may also correct any defect, error or misdescription in the notice if it is satisfied that the correction will not cause injustice to any person falling within section 71(2).

(4) Once the appeal authority has made its decision on an appeal under section 71, it must, as soon as is reasonably practicable—
(a) give a notification of the decision, and
(b) if the decision is to issue a remedial notice or to vary or correct the requirements of such a notice, send copies of the notice as issued, varied or corrected,

to every person falling within section 71(2) and to the relevant authority.

(5) Where, in consequence of the appeal authority's decision on an appeal, a remedial notice is upheld or varied or corrected, the operative date of the notice shall be—
(a) the date of the appeal authority's decision; or
(b) such later date as may be specified in its decision.

(6) Where the person making an appeal under section 71 against a remedial notice withdraws his appeal, the operative date of the notice shall be the date on which the appeal is withdrawn.

(7) In any case falling within subsection (5) or (6), the compliance period for the notice shall accordingly run from the date which is its operative date by virtue of that subsection (and any period which may have started to run from a date preceding that on which the appeal was made shall accordingly be disregarded).

[2119]

NOTES

Commencement: 31 December 2004 (in relation to complaints about hedges situated in Wales); 1 June 2005 (in relation to complaints about hedges situated in England).

Powers of entry

74 Powers of entry for the purposes of complaints and appeals

(1) Where, under this Part, a complaint has been made or a remedial notice has been issued, a person authorised by the relevant authority may enter the neighbouring land in order to obtain information required by the relevant authority for the purpose of determining—

(a) whether this Part applies to the complaint;
(b) whether to issue or withdraw a remedial notice;
(c) whether to waive or relax a requirement of a remedial notice;
(d) whether a requirement of a remedial notice has been complied with.

(2) Where an appeal has been made under section 71, a person authorised—

(a) by the appeal authority, or
(b) by a person appointed to determine appeals on its behalf,

may enter the neighbouring land in order to obtain information required by the appeal authority, or by the person so appointed, for the purpose of determining an appeal under this Part.

(3) A person shall not enter land in the exercise of a power conferred by this section unless at least 24 hours' notice of the intended entry has been given to every occupier of the land.

(4) A person authorised under this section to enter land—

(a) shall, if so required, produce evidence of his authority before entering; and
(b) shall produce such evidence if required to do so at any time while he remains on the land.

(5) A person who enters land in the exercise of a power conferred by this section may—

(a) take with him such other persons as may be necessary;
(b) take with him equipment and materials needed in order to obtain the information required;
(c) take samples of any trees or shrubs that appear to him to form part of a high hedge.

(6) If, in the exercise of a power conferred by this section, a person enters land which is unoccupied or from which all of the persons occupying the land are temporarily absent, he must on his departure leave it as effectively secured against unauthorised entry as he found it.

(7) A person who intentionally obstructs a person acting in the exercise of the powers under this section is guilty of an offence and shall be liable, on summary conviction, to a fine not exceeding level 3 on the standard scale.

[2120]

NOTES

Commencement: 31 December 2004 (in relation to complaints about hedges situated in Wales); 1 June 2005 (in relation to complaints about hedges situated in England).

Enforcement powers etc

75 Offences

(1) Where—

(a) a remedial notice requires the taking of any action, and
(b) that action is not taken in accordance with that notice within the compliance period or (as the case may be) by the subsequent time by which it is required to be taken,

every person who, at a relevant time, is an owner or occupier of the neighbouring land is guilty of an offence and shall be liable, on summary conviction, to a fine not exceeding level 3 on the standard scale.

(2) In subsection (1) "relevant time"—

(a) in relation to action required to be taken before the end of the compliance period, means a time after the end of that period and before the action is taken; and
(b) in relation to any preventative action which is required to be taken after the end of that period, means a time after that at which the action is required to be taken but before it is taken.

(3) In proceedings against a person for an offence under subsection (1) it shall be a defence for him to show that he did everything he could be expected to do to secure compliance with the notice.

(4) In any such proceedings against a person, it shall also be a defence for him to show, in a case in which he—

(a) is not a person to whom a copy of the remedial notice was sent in accordance with a provision of this Part, and

(b) is not assumed under subsection (5) to have had knowledge of the notice at the time of the alleged offence,

that he was not aware of the existence of the notice at that time.

(5) A person shall be assumed to have had knowledge of a remedial notice at any time if at that time—

(a) he was an owner of the neighbouring land; and

(b) the notice was at that time registered as a local land charge.

(6) Section 198 of the Law of Property Act 1925 (c 20) (constructive notice) shall be disregarded for the purposes of this section.

(7) Where a person is convicted of an offence under subsection (1) and it appears to the court—

(a) that a failure to comply with the remedial notice is continuing, and

(b) that it is within that person's power to secure compliance with the notice,

the court may, in addition to or instead of imposing a punishment, order him to take the steps specified in the order for securing compliance with the notice.

(8) An order under subsection (7) must require those steps to be taken within such reasonable period as may be fixed by the order.

(9) Where a person fails without reasonable excuse to comply with an order under subsection (7) he is guilty of an offence and shall be liable, on summary conviction, to a fine not exceeding level 3 on the standard scale.

(10) Where a person continues after conviction of an offence under subsection (9) (or of an offence under this subsection) to fail, without reasonable excuse, to take steps which he has been ordered to take under subsection (7), he is guilty of a further offence and shall be liable, on summary conviction, to a fine not exceeding one-twentieth of that level for each day on which the failure has so continued.

[2121]

NOTES

Commencement: 31 December 2004 (in relation to complaints about hedges situated in Wales); 1 June 2005 (in relation to complaints about hedges situated in England).

76 Power to require occupier to permit action to be taken by owner

Section 289 of the Public Health Act 1936 (c 49) (power of court to require occupier to permit work to be done by owner) shall apply with any necessary modifications for the purpose of giving an owner of land to which a remedial notice relates the right, as against all other persons interested in the land, to comply with the notice.

[2122]

NOTES

Commencement: 31 December 2004 (in relation to complaints about hedges situated in Wales); 1 June 2005 (in relation to complaints about hedges situated in England).

77 Action by relevant authority

(1) This section applies where—

(a) a remedial notice requires the taking of any action; and

(b) that action is not taken in accordance with that notice within the compliance period or (as the case may be) after the end of that period when it is required to be taken by the notice.

(2) Where this section applies—

(a) a person authorised by the relevant authority may enter the neighbouring land and take the required action; and

(b) the relevant authority may recover any expenses reasonably incurred by that person in doing so from any person who is an owner or occupier of the land.

(3) Expenses recoverable under this section shall be a local land charge and binding on successive owners of the land and on successive occupiers of it.

(4) Where expenses are recoverable under this section from two or more persons, those persons shall be jointly and severally liable for the expenses.

(5) A person shall not enter land in the exercise of a power conferred by this section unless at least 7 days' notice of the intended entry has been given to every occupier of the land.

(6) A person authorised under this section to enter land—

(a) shall, if so required, produce evidence of his authority before entering; and
(b) shall produce such evidence if required to do so at any time while he remains on the land.

(7) A person who enters land in the exercise of a power conferred by this section may—

(a) use a vehicle to enter the land;
(b) take with him such other persons as may be necessary;
(c) take with him equipment and materials needed for the purpose of taking the required action.

(8) If, in the exercise of a power conferred by this section, a person enters land which is unoccupied or from which all of the persons occupying the land are temporarily absent, he must on his departure leave it as effectively secured against unauthorised entry as he found it.

(9) A person who wilfully obstructs a person acting in the exercise of powers under this section to enter land and take action on that land is guilty of an offence and shall be liable, on summary conviction, to a fine not exceeding level 3 on the standard scale.

[2123]

NOTES

Commencement: 31 December 2004 (in relation to complaints about hedges situated in Wales); 1 June 2005 (in relation to complaints about hedges situated in England).

78 Offences committed by bodies corporate

(1) Where an offence under this Part committed by a body corporate is proved to have been committed with the consent or connivance of, or to be attributable to any neglect on the part of—

(a) a director, manager, secretary or other similar officer of the body corporate, or
(b) any person who was purporting to act in any such capacity,

he, as well as the body corporate, shall be guilty of that offence and be liable to be proceeded against and punished accordingly.

(2) Where the affairs of a body corporate are managed by its members, subsection (1) applies in relation to the acts and defaults of a member in connection with his functions of management as if he were a director of the body corporate.

[2124]

NOTES

Commencement: 31 December 2004 (in relation to complaints about hedges situated in Wales); 1 June 2005 (in relation to complaints about hedges situated in England).

Supplementary

79 Service of documents

(1) A notification or other document required to be given or sent to a person by virtue of this Part shall be taken to be duly given or sent to him if served in accordance with the following provisions of this section.

(2) Such a document may be served—

(a) by delivering it to the person in question;
(b) by leaving it at his proper address; or
(c) by sending it by post to him at that address.

(3) Such a document may—

(a) in the case of a body corporate, be served on the secretary or clerk of that body;
(b) in the case of a partnership, be served on a partner or a person having the control or management of the partnership business.

(4) For the purposes of this section and of section 7 of the Interpretation Act 1978 (c 30) (service of documents by post) in its application to this section, a person's proper address shall be his last known address, except that—

(a) in the case of a body corporate or their secretary or clerk, it shall be the address of the registered or principal office of that body; and
(b) in the case of a partnership or person having the control or the management of the partnership business, it shall be the principal office of the partnership.

(5) For the purposes of subsection (4) the principal office of—

(a) a company registered outside the United Kingdom, or
(b) a partnership carrying on business outside the United Kingdom,

shall be their principal office within the United Kingdom.

(6) If a person has specified an address in the United Kingdom other than his proper address within the meaning of subsection (4) as the one at which he or someone on his behalf will accept documents of a particular description, that address shall also be treated for the purposes of this section and section 7 of the Interpretation Act 1978 as his proper address in connection with the service on him of a document of that description.

(7) Where—

(a) by virtue of this Part a document is required to be given or sent to a person who is an owner or occupier of any land, and

(b) the name or address of that person cannot be ascertained after reasonable inquiry,

the document may be served either by leaving it in the hands of a person who is or appears to be resident or employed on the land or by leaving it conspicuously affixed to some building or object on the land.

[2125]

NOTES

Commencement: 31 December 2004 (in relation to complaints about hedges situated in Wales); 1 June 2005 (in relation to complaints about hedges situated in England).

80 Documents in electronic form

(1) A requirement of this Part—

(a) to send a copy of a remedial notice to a person, or

(b) to notify a person under section 68(4) of the reasons for the issue of a remedial notice,

is not capable of being satisfied by transmitting the copy or notification electronically or by making it available on a web-site.

(2) The delivery of any other document to a person (the "recipient") may be effected for the purposes of section 79(2)(a)—

(a) by transmitting it electronically, or

(b) by making it available on a web-site,

but only if it is transmitted or made available in accordance with subsection (3) or (5).

(3) A document is transmitted electronically in accordance with this subsection if—

(a) the recipient has agreed that documents may be delivered to him by being transmitted to an electronic address and in an electronic form specified by him for that purpose; and

(b) the document is a document to which that agreement applies and is transmitted to that address in that form.

(4) A document which is transmitted in accordance with subsection (3) by means of an electronic communications network shall, unless the contrary is proved, be treated as having been delivered at 9 a.m. on the working day immediately following the day on which it is transmitted.

(5) A document is made available on a web-site in accordance with this subsection if—

(a) the recipient has agreed that documents may be delivered to him by being made available on a web-site;

(b) the document is a document to which that agreement applies and is made available on a web-site;

(c) the recipient is notified, in a manner agreed by him, of—

(i) the presence of the document on the web-site;

(ii) the address of the web-site; and

(iii) the place on the web-site where the document may be accessed.

(6) A document made available on a web-site in accordance with subsection (5) shall, unless the contrary is proved, be treated as having been delivered at 9a.m. on the working day immediately following the day on which the recipient is notified in accordance with subsection (5)(c).

(7) In this section—

"electronic address" includes any number or address used for the purposes of receiving electronic communications;

"electronic communication" means an electronic communication within the meaning of the Electronic Communications Act 2000 (c 7) the processing of which on receipt is intended to produce writing;

"electronic communications network" means an electronic communications network within the meaning of the Communications Act 2003 (c 21);

"electronically" means in the form of an electronic communication;

"working day" means a day which is not a Saturday or a Sunday, Christmas Day, Good Friday or a bank holiday in England and Wales under the Banking and Financial Dealings Act 1971 (c 80).

[2126]

NOTES

Commencement: 31 December 2004 (in relation to complaints about hedges situated in Wales); 1 June 2005 (in relation to complaints about hedges situated in England).

81 Power to make further provision about documents in electronic form

(1) Regulations may amend section 80 by modifying the circumstances in which, and the conditions subject to which, the delivery of a document for the purposes of section 79(2)(a) may be effected by—

(a) transmitting the document electronically; or
(b) making the document available on a web-site.

(2) Regulations may also amend section 80 by modifying the day on which and the time at which documents which are transmitted electronically or made available on a web-site in accordance with that section are to be treated as having been delivered.

(3) Regulations under this section may make such consequential amendments of this Part as the person making the regulations considers appropriate.

(4) The power to make such regulations shall be exercisable—

(a) in relation to documents relating to complaints about hedges situated in England, by the Secretary of State; and
(b) in relation to documents relating to complaints about hedges situated in Wales, by the National Assembly for Wales.

(5) In this section "electronically" has the meaning given in section 80.

[2127]

NOTES

Commencement: 31 December 2004 (in relation to complaints about hedges situated in Wales); 1 June 2005 (in relation to complaints about hedges situated in England).

82 Interpretation

In this Part—

"the appeal authority" has the meaning given by section 71(7);
"complaint" shall be construed in accordance with section 65;
"complainant" has the meaning given by section 65(5);
"the compliance period" has the meaning given by section 69(6);
"domestic property" has the meaning given by section 67;
"high hedge" has the meaning given by section 66;
"local authority", in relation to England, means—

(a) a district council;
(b) a county council for a county in which there are no districts;
(c) a London borough council; or
(d) the Common Council of the City of London;

and, in relation to Wales, means a county council or a county borough council;
"the neighbouring land" has the meaning given by section 65(5);
"occupier", in relation to any land, means a person entitled to possession of the land by virtue of an estate or interest in it;
"the operative date" shall be construed in accordance with sections 69(5) and 73(5) and (6);
"owner", in relation to any land, means a person (other than a mortgagee not in possession) who, whether in his own right or as trustee for any person—

(a) is entitled to receive the rack rent of the land, or
(b) where the land is not let at a rack rent, would be so entitled if it were so let;

"preventative action" has the meaning given by section 69(9);
"the relevant authority" has the meaning given by section 65(5);
"remedial notice" shall be construed in accordance with section 69(1);
"remedial action" has the meaning given by section 69(9).

[2128]

NOTES

Commencement: 31 December 2004 (in relation to complaints about hedges situated in Wales); 1 June 2005 (in relation to complaints about hedges situated in England).

83 Power to amend sections 65 and 66

(1) Regulations may do one or both of the following—

(a) amend section 65 for the purpose of extending the scope of complaints relating to high hedges to which this Part applies; and
(b) amend section 66 (definition of "high hedge").

(2) The power to make such regulations shall be exercisable—

(a) in relation to complaints about hedges situated in England, by the Secretary of State; and

(b) in relation to complaints about hedges situated in Wales, by the National Assembly for Wales.

(3) Regulations under this section may make such consequential amendments of this Part as the person making the regulations considers appropriate.

[2129]

NOTES

Commencement: 31 December 2004 (in relation to complaints about hedges situated in Wales); 1 June 2005 (in relation to complaints about hedges situated in England).

84 Crown application

(1) This Part and any provision made under it bind the Crown.

(2) This section does not impose criminal liability on the Crown.

(3) Subsection (2) does not affect the criminal liability of persons in the service of the Crown.

[2130]

NOTES

Commencement: 31 December 2004 (in relation to complaints about hedges situated in Wales); 1 June 2005 (in relation to complaints about hedges situated in England).

85–97 ((*Pts 9, 10*) *Outside the scope of this work.*)

(*Schs 1–3 outside the scope of this work.*)

CIVIL PARTNERSHIP ACT 2004

(2004 c 33)

An Act to make provision for and in connection with civil partnership.

[18 November 2004]

1 ((*Pt 1*) *outside the scope of this work.*)

PART 2
CIVIL PARTNERSHIP: ENGLAND AND WALES

2–64 ((*Chs 1, 2*) *outside the scope of this work.*)

CHAPTER 3
PROPERTY AND FINANCIAL ARRANGEMENTS

65 Contribution by civil partner to property improvement

(1) This section applies if—

(a) a civil partner contributes in money or money's worth to the improvement of real or personal property in which or in the proceeds of sale of which either or both of the civil partners has or have a beneficial interest, and

(b) the contribution is of a substantial nature.

(2) The contributing partner is to be treated as having acquired by virtue of the contribution a share or an enlarged share (as the case may be) in the beneficial interest of such an extent—

(a) as may have been then agreed, or

(b) in default of such agreement, as may seem in all the circumstances just to any court before which the question of the existence or extent of the beneficial interest of either of the civil partners arises (whether in proceedings between them or in any other proceedings).

(3) Subsection (2) is subject to any agreement (express or implied) between the civil partners to the contrary.

[2131]

NOTES

Commencement: 5 December 2005.

See further, in relation to the application of this section, with modifications, to a contribution made by a party to a recognised overseas relationship registered under the relevant law before 5 December 2005: the Civil Partnership (Treatment of Overseas Relationships) Order 2005, SI 2005/3042, art 3(2).

66 Disputes between civil partners about property

(1) In any question between the civil partners in a civil partnership as to title to or possession of property, either civil partner may apply to—

(a) the High Court, or

(b) such county court as may be prescribed by rules of court.

(2) On such an application, the court may make such order with respect to the property as it thinks fit (including an order for the sale of the property).

(3) Rules of court made for the purposes of this section may confer jurisdiction on county courts whatever the situation or value of the property in dispute.

[2132]

NOTES

Commencement: 15 April 2005 (sub-s (1)(b) (for the purpose of making rules of court under s 66(3), sub-s (3)); 5 December 2005 (sub-ss (1)(a), (2), sub-s (1)(b) (for remaining purposes)).

67 Applications under section 66 where property not in possession etc

(1) The right of a civil partner ("A") to make an application under section 66 includes the right to make such an application where A claims that the other civil partner ("B") has had in his possession or under his control—

(a) money to which, or to a share of which, A was beneficially entitled, or

(b) property (other than money) to which, or to an interest in which, A was beneficially entitled,

and that either the money or other property has ceased to be in B's possession or under B's control or that A does not know whether it is still in B's possession or under B's control.

(2) For the purposes of subsection (1)(a) it does not matter whether A is beneficially entitled to the money or share—

(a) because it represents the proceeds of property to which, or to an interest in which, A was beneficially entitled, or

(b) for any other reason.

(3) Subsections (4) and (5) apply if, on such an application being made, the court is satisfied that B—

(a) has had in his possession or under his control money or other property as mentioned in subsection (1)(a) or (b), and

(b) has not made to A, in respect of that money or other property, such payment or disposition as would have been appropriate in the circumstances.

(4) The power of the court to make orders under section 66 includes power to order B to pay to A—

(a) in a case falling within subsection (1)(a), such sum in respect of the money to which the application relates, or A's s share of it, as the court considers appropriate, or

(b) in a case falling within subsection (1)(b), such sum in respect of the value of the property to which the application relates, or A's interest in it, as the court considers appropriate.

(5) If it appears to the court that there is any property which—

(a) represents the whole or part of the money or property, and

(b) is property in respect of which an order could (apart from this section) have been made under section 66,

the court may (either instead of or as well as making an order in accordance with subsection (4)) make any order which it could (apart from this section) have made under section 66.

(6) Any power of the court which is exercisable on an application under section 66 is exercisable in relation to an application made under that section as extended by this section.

[2133]

NOTES

Commencement: 5 December 2005.

68 Applications under section 66 by former civil partners

(1) This section applies where a civil partnership has been dissolved or annulled.

(2) Subject to subsection (3), an application may be made under section 66 (including that section as extended by section 67) by either former civil partner despite the dissolution or annulment (and references in those sections to a civil partner are to be read accordingly).

(3) The application must be made within the period of 3 years beginning with the date of the dissolution or annulment.

[2134]

NOTES

Commencement: 5 December 2005.

69 Actions in tort between civil partners

(1) This section applies if an action in tort is brought by one civil partner against the other during the subsistence of the civil partnership.

(2) The court may stay the proceedings if it appears—

(a) that no substantial benefit would accrue to either civil partner from the continuation of the proceedings, or

(b) that the question or questions in issue could more conveniently be disposed of on an application under section 66.

(3) Without prejudice to subsection (2)(b), the court may in such an action—

(a) exercise any power which could be exercised on an application under section 66, or

(b) give such directions as it thinks fit for the disposal under that section of any question arising in the proceedings.

[2135]

NOTES

Commencement: 5 December 2005.

70 Assurance policy by civil partner for benefit of other civil partner etc

Section 11 of the Married Women's Property Act 1882 (c 75) (money payable under policy of assurance not to form part of the estate of the insured) applies in relation to a policy of assurance—

(a) effected by a civil partner on his own life, and

(b) expressed to be for the benefit of his civil partner, or of his children, or of his civil partner and children, or any of them,

as it applies in relation to a policy of assurance effected by a husband and expressed to be for the benefit of his wife, or of his children, or of his wife and children, or of any of them.

[2136]

NOTES

Commencement: 5 December 2005.

71 Wills, administration of estates and family provision

Schedule 4 amends enactments relating to wills, administration of estates and family provision so that they apply in relation to civil partnerships as they apply in relation to marriage.

[2137]

NOTES

Commencement: 5 December 2005.

72 Financial relief for civil partners and children of family

(1) Schedule 5 makes provision for financial relief in connection with civil partnerships that corresponds to provision made for financial relief in connection with marriages by Part 2 of the Matrimonial Causes Act 1973 (c 18).

(2) Any rule of law under which any provision of Part 2 of the 1973 Act is interpreted as applying to dissolution of a marriage on the ground of presumed death is to be treated as applying (with any necessary modifications) in relation to the corresponding provision of Schedule 5.

(3) Schedule 6 makes provision for financial relief in connection with civil partnerships that corresponds to provision made for financial relief in connection with marriages by the Domestic Proceedings and Magistrates' Courts Act 1978 (c 22).

(4) Schedule 7 makes provision for financial relief in England and Wales after a civil partnership has been dissolved or annulled, or civil partners have been legally separated, in a country outside the British Islands.

[2138]

NOTES

Commencement: 15 April 2005 (sub-ss (1), (3), (4), for certain purposes); 5 December 2005 (sub-ss (1) (for certain purposes), (2), (3) (for remaining purposes), (4) (for certain purposes); 6 April 2006 (sub-ss (1), (4) for remaining purposes).

PART I. STATUTES

CHAPTER 4
CIVIL PARTNERSHIP AGREEMENTS

73 Civil partnership agreements unenforceable

(1) A civil partnership agreement does not under the law of England and Wales have effect as a contract giving rise to legal rights.

(2) No action lies in England and Wales for breach of a civil partnership agreement, whatever the law applicable to the agreement.

(3) In this section and section 74 "civil partnership agreement" means an agreement between two people—

(a) to register as civil partners of each other—

(i) in England and Wales (under this Part),

(ii) in Scotland (under Part 3),

(iii) in Northern Ireland (under Part 4), or

(iv) outside the United Kingdom under an Order in Council made under Chapter 1 of Part 5 (registration at British consulates etc or by armed forces personnel), or

(b) to enter into an overseas relationship.

(4) This section applies in relation to civil partnership agreements whether entered into before or after this section comes into force, but does not affect any action commenced before it comes into force.

[2139]

NOTES

Commencement: 5 December 2005.

74 Property where civil partnership agreement is terminated

(1) This section applies if a civil partnership agreement is terminated.

(2) Section 65 (contributions by civil partner to property improvement) applies, in relation to any property in which either or both of the parties to the agreement had a beneficial interest while the agreement was in force, as it applies in relation to property in which a civil partner has a beneficial interest.

(3) Sections 66 and 67 (disputes between civil partners about property) apply to any dispute between or claim by one of the parties in relation to property in which either or both had a beneficial interest while the agreement was in force, as if the parties were civil partners of each other.

(4) An application made under section 66 or 67 by virtue of subsection (3) must be made within 3 years of the termination of the agreement.

(5) A party to a civil partnership agreement who makes a gift of property to the other party on the condition (express or implied) that it is to be returned if the agreement is terminated is not prevented from recovering the property merely because of his having terminated the agreement.

[2140]

NOTES

Commencement: 5 December 2005.

75–257 (*Ss 75–84* (*Chs V, VI*), *ss 85–257* (*Pts 3–7*) *outside the scope of this work.*)

PART 8
SUPPLEMENTARY

258–261 (*Outside the scope of this work.*)

262 Extent

(1) Part 2 (civil partnership: England and Wales), excluding section 35 but including Schedules 1 to 9, extends to England and Wales only.

(2)–(9) (*Outside the scope of this work.*)

(10) Any amendment, repeal or revocation made by Schedules 24 to 27 and 30 has the same extent as the provision subject to the amendment, repeal or revocation.

[2141]

NOTES

Commencement: 8 November 2004.

263 Commencement

(1) (*Outside the scope of this work.*)

(2) Part 2, including Schedules 1 to 9, comes into force in accordance with provision made by order by the Secretary of State.

(3)–(9) (*Outside the scope of this work.*)

(10) In this Part—

(a) sections 258, 259, 260 and 262, this section and section 264 come into force on the day on which this Act is passed,

(b)–(d) (*outside the scope of this work.*)

(11) The power to make an order under this section is exercisable by statutory instrument.

[2142]

NOTES

Commencement: 8 November 2004.

Orders: the Civil Partnership Act 2004 (Commencement No 1) Order 2005, SI 2005/1112; the Civil Partnership Act 2004 (Commencement No 1) (Northern Ireland) Order 2005, SI 2005/2399; the Civil Partnership Act 2004 (Commencement No 2) (Northern Ireland) Order 2005, SI 2005/3058; the Civil Partnership Act 2004 (Commencement No 2) Order 2005, SI 2005/3175; the Civil Partnership Act 2004 (Commencement No 3) (Northern Ireland) Order 2005, SI 2005/3255; the Civil Partnership Act 2004 (Commencement No 3) Order 2006, SI 2006/639; the Civil Partnership Act 2004 (Commencement No 4) (Northern Ireland) Order 2006, SI 2006/928; the Civil Partnership Act 2004 (Commencement No 1) (Scotland) Order 2005, SSI 2005/428; the Civil Partnership Act 2004 (Commencement No 2) (Scotland) Order 2005, SSI 2005/604.

264 Short title

This Act may be cited as the Civil Partnership Act 2004.

[2143]

NOTES

Commencement: 8 November 2004.

(*Schs 1–3 outside the scope of this work.*)

SCHEDULE 4
WILLS, ADMINISTRATION OF ESTATES AND FAMILY PROVISION

Section 71

PART 1
WILLS

1, 2. …

3. The following provisions—

(a) section 15 of the Wills Act 1837 (c 26) (avoidance of gifts to attesting witnesses and their spouses), and

(b) section 1 of the Wills Act 1968 (c 28) (restriction of operation of section 15),

apply in relation to the attestation of a will by a person to whose civil partner there is given or made any such disposition as is described in section 15 of the 1837 Act as they apply in relation to a person to whose spouse there is given or made any such disposition.

4. …

5. Except where a contrary intention is shown, it is presumed that if a testator—

(a) devises or bequeaths property to his civil partner in terms which in themselves would give an absolute interest to the civil partner, but

(b) by the same instrument purports to give his issue an interest in the same property,

the gift to the civil partner is absolute despite the purported gift to the issue.

[2144]

NOTES

Commencement: 5 December 2005.

Paras 1, 2: insert the Wills Act 1837, ss 18B, 18C at **[35]**, **[36]**.

Para 4: amends the Wills Act 1837, s 16 at **[31]**.

(*Sch 4, Pt 2 outside the scope of this work.*)

SCHEDULE 5
FINANCIAL RELIEF IN THE HIGH COURT OR A COUNTY COURT ETC

Section 72(1)

(*Pt 1 outside the scope of this work.*)

PART 2
PROPERTY ADJUSTMENT ON OR AFTER DISSOLUTION, NULLITY OR SEPARATION

Circumstances in which property adjustment orders may be made

6.—(1) The court may make one or more property adjustment orders—
(a) on making a dissolution, nullity or separation order, or
(b) at any time afterwards.

(2) In this Schedule "property adjustment order" means a property adjustment order under this Part.

Property adjustment orders

7.—(1) The property adjustment orders are—
(a) an order that one of the civil partners must transfer such property as may be specified, being property to which he is entitled—
(i) to the other civil partner,
(ii) to a child of the family, or
(iii) to such person as may be specified for the benefit of a child of the family;
(b) an order that a settlement of such property as may be specified, being property to which one of the civil partners is entitled, be made to the satisfaction of the court for the benefit of—
(i) the other civil partner and the children of the family, or
(ii) either or any of them;
(c) an order varying for the benefit of—
(i) the civil partners and the children of the family, or
(ii) either or any of them,
a relevant settlement;
(d) an order extinguishing or reducing the interest of either of the civil partners under a relevant settlement.

(2) The court may make a property adjustment order under sub-paragraph (1)(c) even though there are no children of the family.

(3) In this paragraph—
"entitled" means entitled in possession or reversion,
"relevant settlement" means, in relation to a civil partnership, a settlement made, during its subsistence or in anticipation of its formation, on the civil partners including one made by will or codicil, but not including one in the form of a pension arrangement (within the meaning of Part 4), and
"specified" means specified in the order.

When property adjustment orders may take effect

8.—(1) If a property adjustment order is made on or after making a dissolution or nullity order, neither the property adjustment order nor any settlement made under it takes effect unless the dissolution or nullity order has been made final.

(2) This paragraph does not affect the power to give a direction under paragraph 76 (settlement of instrument by conveyancing counsel).

Restrictions on making property adjustment orders

9. The power to make a property adjustment order under paragraph 7(1)(a) is subject to paragraph 49(1) and (5) (restrictions on making orders in favour of children who have reached 18).
[2145]

NOTES
Commencement: 5 December 2005.

PART 3
SALE OF PROPERTY ORDERS

Circumstances in which sale of property orders may be made

10.—(1) The court may make a sale of property order—
(a) on making—

(i) under Part 1, a secured periodical payments order or an order for the payment of a lump sum, or
(ii) a property adjustment order, or
(b) at any time afterwards.

(2) In this Schedule "sale of property order" means a sale of property order under this Part.

Sale of property orders

11.—(1) A sale of property order is an order for the sale of such property as may be specified, being property in which, or in the proceeds of sale of which, either or both of the civil partners has or have a beneficial interest, either in possession or reversion.

(2) A sale of property order may contain such consequential or supplementary provisions as the court thinks fit.

(3) A sale of property order may in particular include—
(a) provision requiring the making of a payment out of the proceeds of sale of the property to which the order relates, and
(b) provision requiring any property to which the order relates to be offered for sale to a specified person, or class of persons.

(4) "Specified" means specified in the order.

When sale of property orders may take effect

12.—(1) If a sale of property order is made on or after the making of a dissolution or nullity order, it does not take effect unless the dissolution or nullity order has been made final.

(2) Where a sale of property order is made, the court may direct that—
(a) the order, or
(b) such provision of it as the court may specify,

is not to take effect until the occurrence of an event specified by the court or the end of a period so specified.

When sale of property orders cease to have effect

13. If a sale of property order contains a provision requiring the proceeds of sale of the property to which the order relates to be used to secure periodical payments to a civil partner, the order ceases to have effect—
(a) on the death of the civil partner, or
(b) on the formation of a subsequent civil partnership or marriage by the civil partner.

Protection of third parties

14.—(1) Sub-paragraphs (2) and (3) apply if—
(a) a civil partner has a beneficial interest in any property, or in the proceeds of sale of any property, and
(b) another person ("A") who is not the other civil partner also has a beneficial interest in the property or the proceeds.

(2) Before deciding whether to make a sale of property order in relation to the property, the court must give A an opportunity to make representations with respect to the order.

(3) Any representations made by A are included among the circumstances to which the court is required to have regard under paragraph 20.

[2146]

NOTES

Commencement: 5 December 2005.

(Sch 5, Pts 4–14, Schs 6–30 outside the scope of this work.)

HOUSING ACT 2004

(2004 c 34)

An Act to make provision about housing conditions; to regulate houses in multiple occupation and certain other residential accommodation; to make provision for home information packs in connection with the sale of residential properties; to make provision about secure tenants and the right to buy; to make provision about mobile homes and the accommodation needs of gypsies and travellers; to make other provision about housing; and for connected purposes.

[18 November 2004]

1–147 (*Outside the scope of this work.*)

PART 5
HOME INFORMATION PACKS

Preliminary

148 Meaning of "residential property" and "home information pack"

(1) In this Part—

"residential property" means premises in England and Wales consisting of a single dwelling-house, including any ancillary land; and

"dwelling-house" means a building or part of a building occupied or intended to be occupied as a separate dwelling (and includes one that is being or is to be constructed).

(2) References in this Part to a home information pack, in relation to a residential property, are to a collection of documents relating to the property or the terms on which it is or may become available for sale.

[2147]

NOTES

Commencement: 1 August 2007 (for certain purposes); 10 September 2007 (for certain purposes); 14 December 2007 (for certain purposes); 6 April 2008 (otherwise).

149 Meaning of "on the market" and related expressions

(1) In this Part references to "the market" are to the residential property market in England and Wales.

(2) A residential property is put on the market when the fact that it is or may become available for sale is, with the intention of marketing the property, first made public in England and Wales by or on behalf of the seller.

(3) A residential property which has been put on the market is to be regarded as remaining on the market until it is taken off the market or sold.

(4) A fact is made public when it is advertised or otherwise communicated (in whatever form and by whatever means) to the public or to a section of the public.

[2148]

NOTES

Commencement: 1 August 2007 (for certain purposes); 10 September 2007 (for certain purposes); 14 December 2007 (for certain purposes); 6 April 2008 (otherwise).

150 Acting as estate agent

(1) A person acts as estate agent for the seller of a residential property if he does anything, in the course of a business in England and Wales, in pursuance of marketing instructions from the seller.

(2) For this purpose—

"business in England and Wales" means a business carried on (in whole or in part) from a place in England and Wales; and

"marketing instructions" means instructions to carry out any activities with a view to—

(a) effecting the introduction to the seller of a person wishing to buy the property; or

(b) selling the property by auction or tender.

(3) It is immaterial for the purposes of this section whether or not a person describes himself as an estate agent.

[2149]

NOTES

Commencement: 1 August 2007 (for certain purposes); 10 September 2007 (for certain purposes); 14 December 2007 (for certain purposes); 6 April 2008 (otherwise).

Responsibility for marketing residential properties

151 Responsibility for marketing: general

(1) References in this Part to a responsible person, in relation to a residential property, are to any person who is for the time being responsible for marketing the property.

(2) Sections 152 and 153 identify for the purposes of this Part—

(a) the person or persons who are responsible for marketing a residential property which is on the market ("the property"); and
(b) when the responsibility of any such person arises and ceases.

(3) Only the seller or a person acting as estate agent for the seller may be responsible for marketing the property.

(4) A person may be responsible for marketing the property on more than one occasion.

[2150]

NOTES

Commencement: 1 August 2007 (for certain purposes); 10 September 2007 (for certain purposes); 14 December 2007 (for certain purposes); 6 April 2008 (otherwise).

152 Responsibility of person acting as estate agent

(1) A person acting as estate agent becomes responsible for marketing the property when action taken by him or on his behalf—
(a) puts the property on the market; or
(b) makes public the fact that the property is on the market.

(2) That responsibility ceases when the following conditions are satisfied, namely—
(a) his contract with the seller is terminated (whether by the withdrawal of his instructions or otherwise);
(b) he has ceased to take any action which makes public the fact that the property is on the market; and
(c) any such action being taken on his behalf has ceased.

(3) Any responsibility arising under this section also ceases when the property is taken off the market or sold.

[2151]

NOTES

Commencement: 1 August 2007 (for certain purposes); 10 September 2007 (for certain purposes); 14 December 2007 (for certain purposes); 6 April 2008 (otherwise).

153 Responsibility of the seller

(1) The seller becomes responsible for marketing the property when action taken by him or on his behalf—
(a) puts the property on the market; or
(b) makes public the fact that the property is on the market.

(2) That responsibility ceases when the following conditions are satisfied, namely—
(a) there is at least one person acting as his estate agent who is responsible for marketing the property;
(b) the seller has ceased to take any action which makes public the fact that the property is on the market; and
(c) any such action being taken on the seller's behalf has ceased.

(3) In this section the references to action taken on behalf of the seller exclude action taken by or on behalf of a person acting as his estate agent.

(4) Any responsibility arising under this section also ceases when the property is taken off the market or sold.

[2152]

NOTES

Commencement: 1 August 2007 (for certain purposes); 10 September 2007 (for certain purposes); 14 December 2007 (for certain purposes); 6 April 2008 (otherwise).

Duties of a responsible person where a property is on the market

154 Application of sections 155 to 158

(1) Where a residential property is on the market, a person responsible for marketing the property is subject to the duties relating to home information packs that are imposed by sections 155 to 158 until his responsibility ceases.

(2) Each of those duties is subject to any exception relating to that duty which is provided for in those sections.

(3) The duty under section 156(1) is also subject to any condition imposed under section 157.

[2153]

NOTES

Commencement: 1 August 2007 (for certain purposes); 10 September 2007 (for certain purposes); 14 December 2007 (for certain purposes); 6 April 2008 (otherwise).

155 Duty to have a home information pack

(1) It is the duty of a responsible person to have in his possession or under his control a home information pack for the property which complies with the requirements of any regulations under section 163.

(2) That duty does not apply where the responsible person is the seller at any time when—

(a) there is another person who is responsible for marketing the property under section 152; and

(b) the seller believes on reasonable grounds that the other responsible person has a home information pack for the property in his possession or under his control which complies with the requirements of any regulations under section 163.

[2154]

NOTES

Commencement: 1 August 2007 (for certain purposes); 10 September 2007 (for certain purposes); 14 December 2007 (for certain purposes); 6 April 2008 (otherwise).

Disapplication: as to the disapplication of this section as respects seasonal accommodation, sales mixed with sales of non-residential premises, dwelling houses used for both residential and non-residential purposes, portfolios of residential properties, unsafe properties and properties to be demolished, and also as regards properties marketed before the commencement date: the Home Information Pack (No 2) Regulations 2007, SI 2007/1667, regs 25–34 at **[3606]**–**[3615]**.

156 Duty to provide copy of home information pack on request

(1) Where a potential buyer makes a request to a responsible person for a copy of the home information pack, or of a document (or part of a document) which is or ought to be included in that pack, it is the duty of the responsible person to comply with that request within the permitted period.

(2) The responsible person does not comply with that duty unless—

(a) he provides the potential buyer with a document which is—

(i) a copy of the home information pack for the property as it stands at the time when the document is provided, or

(ii) a copy of a document (or part of a document) which is included in that pack,

as the case may be; and

(b) that pack or document complies with the requirements of any regulations under section 163 at that time.

(3) In subsection (2) "the home information pack" means the home information pack intended by the responsible person to be the one required by section 155.

(4) That duty does not apply if, before the end of the permitted period, the responsible person believes on reasonable grounds that the person making the request—

(a) is unlikely to have sufficient means to buy the property in question;

(b) is not genuinely interested in buying a property of a general description which applies to the property; or

(c) is not a person to whom the seller is likely to be prepared to sell the property.

Nothing in this subsection authorises the doing of anything which constitutes an unlawful act of discrimination.

(5) Subsection (4) does not apply if the responsible person knows or suspects that the person making the request is an officer of an enforcement authority.

(6) That duty does not apply where the responsible person is the seller if, when the request is made, the duty under section 155 does not (by virtue of subsection (2) of that section) apply to him.

(7) But where the duty under this section is excluded by subsection (6), it is the duty of the seller to take reasonable steps to inform the potential buyer that the request should be made to the other person.

(8) The responsible person may charge a sum not exceeding the reasonable cost of making and, if requested, sending a paper copy of the pack or document.

(9) The permitted period for the purposes of this section is (subject to section 157(5)) the period of 14 days beginning with the day on which the request is made.

(10) If the responsible person ceases to be responsible for marketing the property before the end of the permitted period (whether because the property has been taken off the market or sold or for any other reason), he ceases to be under any duty to comply with the request.

(11) A person does not comply with the duty under this section by providing a copy in electronic form unless the potential buyer consents to receiving it in that form.

[2155]

NOTES

Commencement: 1 August 2007 (for certain purposes); 10 September 2007 (for certain purposes); 14 December 2007 (for certain purposes); 6 April 2008 (otherwise).

Disapplication: as to the disapplication of this section as respects seasonal accommodation, sales mixed with sales of non-residential premises, dwelling houses used for both residential and non-residential purposes, portfolios of residential properties, unsafe properties and properties to be demolished, and also as regards properties marketed before the commencement date: the Home Information Pack (No 2) Regulations 2007, SI 2007/1667, regs 25–34 at **[3606]**–**[3615]**.

157 Section 156(1) duty: imposition of conditions

(1) A potential buyer who has made a request to which section 156(1) applies may be required to comply with either or both of the following conditions before any copy is provided.

(2) The potential buyer may be required to pay a charge authorised by section 156(8).

(3) The potential buyer may be required to accept any terms specified in writing which—

(a) are proposed by the seller or in pursuance of his instructions; and

(b) relate to the use or disclosure of the copy (or any information contained in or derived from it).

(4) A condition is only effective if it is notified to the potential buyer before the end of the period of 14 days beginning with the day on which the request is made.

(5) Where the potential buyer has been so notified of either or both of the conditions authorised by this section, the permitted period for the purposes of section 156 is the period of 14 days beginning with—

(a) where one condition is involved, the day on which the potential buyer complies with it by—

(i) making the payment demanded, or

(ii) accepting the terms proposed (or such other terms as may be agreed between the seller and the potential buyer in substitution for those proposed),

as the case may be; or

(b) where both conditions are involved, the day (or the later of the days) on which the potential buyer complies with them by taking the action mentioned in paragraph (a)(i) and (ii).

[2156]

NOTES

Commencement: 1 August 2007 (for certain purposes); 10 September 2007 (for certain purposes); 14 December 2007 (for certain purposes); 6 April 2008 (otherwise).

Disapplication: as to the disapplication of this section as respects seasonal accommodation, sales mixed with sales of non-residential premises, dwelling houses used for both residential and non-residential purposes, portfolios of residential properties, unsafe properties and properties to be demolished, and also as regards properties marketed before the commencement date: the Home Information Pack (No 2) Regulations 2007, SI 2007/1667, regs 25–34 at **[3606]**–**[3615]**.

158 Duty to ensure authenticity of documents in other situations

(1) Where a responsible person provides a potential buyer with, or allows a potential buyer to inspect, any document purporting to be—

(a) a copy of the home information pack for the property, or

(b) a copy of a document (or part of a document) included in that pack,

the responsible person is under a duty to ensure that the document is authentic.

(2) A document is not authentic for the purposes of subsection (1) unless, at the time when it is provided or inspected—

(a) it is a copy of the home information pack for the property or a document (or part of a document) included in that pack, as the case may be; and

(b) that pack or document complies with the requirements of any regulations under section 163.

(3) In subsection (2) "the home information pack" means the pack intended by the responsible person to be the one required by section 155.

(4) The duty under this section does not apply to anything provided in pursuance of the duty under section 156.

[2157]

NOTES

Commencement: 1 August 2007 (for certain purposes); 10 September 2007 (for certain purposes); 14 December 2007 (for certain purposes); 6 April 2008 (otherwise).

Disapplication: as to the disapplication of this section as respects seasonal accommodation, sales mixed with sales of non-residential premises, dwelling houses used for both residential and non-residential purposes, portfolios of residential properties, unsafe properties and properties to be demolished, and also as regards properties marketed before the commencement date: the Home Information Pack (No 2) Regulations 2007, SI 2007/1667, regs 25–34 at **[3606]–[3615]**.

Other duties of person acting as estate agent

159 Other duties of person acting as estate agent

(1) This section applies to a person acting as estate agent for the seller of a residential property where—

(a) the property is not on the market; or

(b) the property is on the market but the person so acting is not a person responsible for marketing the property.

(2) It is the duty of a person to whom this section applies to have in his possession or under his control, when any qualifying action is taken by him or on his behalf, a home information pack for the property which complies with the requirements of any regulations under section 163.

(3) In subsection (2) "qualifying action" means action taken with the intention of marketing the property which—

(a) communicates to any person in England and Wales the fact that the property is or may become available for sale; but

(b) does not put the property on the market or make public the fact that the property is on the market.

(4) Where a person to whom this section applies provides a potential buyer with, or allows a potential buyer to inspect, any document purporting to be—

(a) a copy of the home information pack for the property; or

(b) a copy of a document (or part of a document) included in that pack;

it is his duty to ensure that it is an authentic copy.

(5) A document is not authentic for the purposes of subsection (4) unless, at the time when it is provided or inspected—

(a) it is a copy of the home information pack for the property or a document (or part of a document) included in that pack, as the case may be; and

(b) that pack or document complies with the requirements of any regulations under section 163.

(6) In subsection (5) "the home information pack" means the home information pack intended by the person to whom this section applies to be the one required by subsection (2).

[2158]

NOTES

Commencement: 1 August 2007 (for certain purposes); 10 September 2007 (for certain purposes); 14 December 2007 (for certain purposes); 6 April 2008 (otherwise).

Disapplication: as to the disapplication of this section as respects seasonal accommodation, sales mixed with sales of non-residential premises, dwelling houses used for both residential and non-residential purposes, portfolios of residential properties, unsafe properties and properties to be demolished, and also as regards properties marketed before the commencement date: the Home Information Pack (No 2) Regulations 2007, SI 2007/1667, regs 25–34 at **[3606]–[3615]**.

Exceptions from the duties

160 Residential properties not available with vacant possession

(1) The duties under sections 155 to 159 do not apply in relation to a residential property at any time when it is not available for sale with vacant possession.

(2) But for the purposes of this Part a residential property shall be presumed to be available with vacant possession, at any time when any of those duties would apply in relation to the property if it is so available, unless the contrary appears from the manner in which the property is being marketed at that time.

[2159]

NOTES

Commencement: 1 August 2007 (for certain purposes); 10 September 2007 (for certain purposes); 14 December 2007 (for certain purposes); 6 April 2008 (otherwise).

161 Power to provide for further exceptions

The Secretary of State may by regulations provide for other exceptions from any duty under sections 155 to 159 in such cases and circumstances, and to such extent, as may be specified in the regulations.

[2160]

NOTES

Commencement: 18 November 2004.

Regulations: the Home Information Pack (No 2) Regulations 2007, SI 2007/1667 at **[3582]**.

162 Suspension of duties under sections 155 to 159

(1) The Secretary of State may make an order suspending (or later reviving) the operation of any duty imposed by sections 155 to 159.

(2) An order under this section may provide for the suspension of a duty to take effect only for a period specified in the order.

(3) A duty which is (or is to any extent) revived after being suspended under this section is liable to be suspended again.

[2161]

NOTES

Commencement: 18 November 2004.

Contents of home information packs

163 Contents of home information packs

(1) The Secretary of State may make regulations prescribing—

(a) the documents which are required or authorised to be included in the home information pack for a residential property; and

(b) particular information which is required or authorised to be included in, or which is to be excluded from, any such document.

(2) A document prescribed under subsection (1) must be one that the Secretary of State considers would disclose relevant information.

(3) Any particular information required or authorised to be included in a prescribed document must be information that the Secretary of State considers to be relevant information.

(4) In this section "relevant information" means information about any matter connected with the property (or the sale of the property) that would be of interest to potential buyers.

(5) Without prejudice to the generality of subsection (4), the information which the Secretary of State may consider to be relevant information includes any information about—

(a) the interest which is for sale and the terms on which it is proposed to sell it;

(b) the title to the property;

(c) anything relating to or affecting the property that is contained in—

(i) a register required to be kept by or under any enactment (whenever passed); or

(ii) records kept by a person who can reasonably be expected to give information derived from those records to the seller at his request (on payment, if required, of a reasonable charge);

(d) the physical condition of the property (including any particular characteristics or features of the property);

(e) the energy efficiency of the property;

(f) any warranties or guarantees subsisting in relation to the property;

(g) any taxes, service charges or other charges payable in relation to the property.

(6) The regulations may require or authorise the home information pack to include—

(a) replies the seller proposes to give to prescribed pre-contract enquiries; and

(b) documents or particular information indexing or otherwise explaining the contents of the pack.

(7) The regulations may require a prescribed document—

(a) to be in such form as may be prescribed; and

(b) to be prepared by a person of a prescribed description on such terms (if any) as may be prescribed.

(8) The terms mentioned in subsection (7)(b) may include terms which enable provisions of the contract under which the document is to be prepared to be enforced by—

(a) a potential or actual buyer;

(b) a mortgage lender; or

(c) any other person involved in the sale of the property who is not a party to that contract.

(9) The regulations may—

(a) provide for the time at which any document is to be included in or removed from the home information pack; and

(b) make different provision for different areas, for different descriptions of properties or for other different circumstances (including the manner in which a residential property is marketed).

(10) In this section "prescribed" means prescribed by regulations under this section.

[2162]

NOTES

Commencement: 18 November 2004.

Regulations: the Home Information Pack (No 2) Regulations 2007, SI 2007/1667 at **[3582]**.

164 Home condition reports

(1) Regulations under section 163 may make the provision mentioned in this section in relation to any description of document dealing with matters mentioned in section 163(5)(d) or (e) (reports on physical condition or energy efficiency) which is to be included in the home information pack.

(2) In this section "home condition report" means a document of that description.

(3) The regulations may require a home condition report to be made by an individual who is a member of an approved certification scheme following an inspection carried out by him in accordance with the provisions of the scheme.

(4) The regulations shall, if the provision mentioned in subsection (3) is made, make provision for the approval by the Secretary of State of one or more suitable certification schemes (and for the withdrawal by him of any such approval).

(5) The regulations shall require the Secretary of State to be satisfied, before approving a certification scheme, that the scheme contains appropriate provision—

(a) for ensuring that members of the scheme are fit and proper persons who are qualified (by their education, training and experience) to produce home condition reports;

(b) for ensuring that members of the scheme have in force suitable indemnity insurance;

(c) for facilitating the resolution of complaints against members of the scheme;

(d) for requiring home condition reports made by members of the scheme to be entered on the register mentioned in section 165;

(e) for the keeping of a public register of the members of the scheme; and

(f) for such other purposes as may be specified in the regulations.

(6) Subsection (5)(d) only applies where provision for a register of home condition reports is made under section 165.

(7) The regulations may require or authorise an approved certification scheme to contain provision about any matter relating to the home condition reports with which the scheme is concerned (including the terms on which members of the scheme may undertake to produce a home condition report).

(8) Nothing in this section limits the power under section 163 to make provision about home condition reports in the regulations.

[2163]

NOTES

Commencement: 18 November 2004.

Regulations: the Home Information Pack (No 2) Regulations 2007, SI 2007/1667 at **[3582]**.

Register of home condition reports

165 Register of home condition reports

(1) Where the provision mentioned in section 164(3) is made in relation to an approved certification scheme, regulations under section 163 may make provision for and in connection with a register of the home condition reports made by members of the scheme.

(2) The regulations may provide for the register to be kept—

(a) by (or on behalf of) the Secretary of State; or

(b) by such other person as the regulations may specify.

(3) The regulations may require a person wishing to enter a home condition report onto the register to pay such fee as may be prescribed.

(4) No person may disclose—

(a) the register or any document (or part of a document) contained in it; or

(b) any information contained in, or derived from, the register,

except in accordance with any provision of the regulations which authorises or requires such a disclosure to be made.

(5) The provision which may be made under subsection (1) includes (without prejudice to the generality of that subsection) provision as to circumstances in which or purposes for which a person or a person of a prescribed description—

(a) may (on payment of such fee, if any, as may be prescribed)—

(i) inspect the register or any document (or part of a document) contained in it;

(ii) take or be given copies of the register or any document (or part of a document) contained in it; or

(iii) be given information contained in, or derived from, the register; or

(b) may disclose anything obtained by virtue of provision made under paragraph (a).

(6) The purposes which may be so prescribed may be public purposes or purposes of private undertakings or other persons.

(7) A person who contravenes subsection (4) is guilty of an offence and liable on summary conviction to a fine not exceeding level 5 on the standard scale.

(8) Nothing in this section limits the power to make regulations under section 163.

[2164]

NOTES

Commencement: 18 November 2004 (for the purpose of making orders or regulations); 1 August 2007 (for certain purposes); 10 September 2007 (for certain purposes); 14 December 2007 (for certain purposes); 6 April 2008 (otherwise).

Regulations: the Home Information Pack (No 2) Regulations 2007, SI 2007/1667 at **[3582]**.

Enforcement

166 Enforcement authorities

(1) Every local weights and measures authority is an enforcement authority for the purposes of this Part.

(2) It is the duty of each enforcement authority [to enforce the duties under sections 155 to 159 and 167(4) in their area].

[2165]

NOTES

Commencement: 1 August 2007 (for certain purposes); 10 September 2007 (for certain purposes); 14 December 2007 (for certain purposes); 6 April 2008 (otherwise).

Sub-s (2): words in square brackets substituted by the Consumers, Estate Agents and Redress Act 2007, s 63(1), Sch 7, paras 23(1), (2).

167 Power to require production of home information packs

(1) An authorised officer of an enforcement authority may require a person who appears to him to be or to have been subject to the duty under section 155 or 159(2), in relation to a residential property, to produce for inspection a copy of, or of any document included in, the home information pack for that property.

(2) The power conferred by subsection (1) includes power—

(a) to require the production in a visible and legible documentary form of any document included in the home information pack in question which is held in electronic form; and

(b) to take copies of any document produced for inspection.

(3) A requirement under this section may not be imposed more than six months after the last day on which the person concerned was subject to the duty under section 155 or 159(2) in relation to the property (as the case may be).

(4) Subject to subsection (5), it is the duty of a person subject to such a requirement to comply with it within the period of 7 days beginning with the day after that on which it is imposed.

(5) A person is not required to comply with such a requirement if he has a reasonable excuse for not complying with the requirement.

(6) In this section "the home information pack" means—

(a) where a requirement under this section is imposed on a person at a time when he is subject to the duty under section 155 or 159(2), the home information pack intended by him to be the one he is required to have at that time; or

(b) in any other case, the home information pack intended by the person concerned, when he was last subject to the duty under section 155 or 159(2), to be the one he was required to have at that time.

[2166]

NOTES

Commencement: 1 August 2007 (for certain purposes); 10 September 2007 (for certain purposes); 14 December 2007 (for certain purposes); 6 April 2008 (otherwise).

168 Penalty charge notices

(1) An authorised officer of an enforcement authority may, if he believes that a person has committed [a breach of any duty under sections 155 to 159 and 167(4), give a penalty charge notice to that person].

(2) A penalty charge notice may not be given after the end of the period of six months beginning with the day (or in the case of a continuing breach the last day) on which the breach of duty was committed.

(3) Schedule 8 (which makes further provision about penalty charge notices) has effect.

[2167]

NOTES

Commencement: 18 November 2004 (sub-s (3), for the purpose of making orders or regulations); 1 August 2007 (for certain purposes); 10 September 2007 (for certain purposes); 14 December 2007 (for certain purposes); 6 April 2008 (otherwise).

Sub-s (1): words in square brackets substituted by the Consumers, Estate Agents and Redress Act 2007, s 63(1), Sch 7, para 23(1), (3).

See further, in relation to the disapplication of sub-s (1)(a) above where the content of a pack document fails to comply with the Home Information Pack (No 2) Regulations 2007, SI 2007/1667, but a responsible person believes on reasonable grounds that it does: the Home Information Pack (No 2) Regulations 2007, SI 2007/1667, reg 36 at **[3617]**.

169 Offences relating to enforcement officers

(1) A person who obstructs an officer of an enforcement authority acting in pursuance of section 167 is guilty of an offence.

(2) A person who, not being an authorised officer of an enforcement authority, purports to act as such in pursuance of section 167 or 168 is guilty of an offence.

(3) A person guilty of an offence under this section is liable on summary conviction to a fine not exceeding level 5 on the standard scale.

[2168]

NOTES

Commencement: 1 August 2007 (for certain purposes); 10 September 2007 (for certain purposes); 14 December 2007 (for certain purposes); 6 April 2008 (otherwise).

170 Right of private action

(1) This section applies where a person ("the responsible person") has committed a breach of duty under section 156 by failing to comply with a request from a potential buyer of a residential property for a copy of a prescribed document.

(2) If the potential buyer commissions his own version of the prescribed document at a time when both of the conditions mentioned below are satisfied, he is entitled to recover from the responsible person any reasonable fee paid by him in order to obtain the document.

(3) The first condition is that—

(a) the property is on the market; or

(b) the potential buyer and the seller are attempting to reach an agreement for the sale of the property.

(4) The second condition is that the potential buyer has not been provided with an authentic copy of the prescribed document.

(5) A copy of a prescribed document is not authentic for the purposes of subsection (4) unless—

(a) it is a copy of a document included in the home information pack for the property as it stands at the time the copy is provided to the potential buyer; and

(b) the document so included complies with the requirements of any regulations under section 163 at that time.

(6) In subsection (5) "the home information pack" means the home information pack intended by the responsible person to be the one required by section 155.

(7) In this section "prescribed document" means a document (being one required to be included in the home information pack by regulations under section 163) which is prescribed by regulations made by the Secretary of State for the purposes of this section.

(8) It is immaterial for the purposes of this section that the request in question did not specify the prescribed document but was for a copy of the home information pack or a part of the pack which included (or ought to have included) that document.

[2169]

NOTES

Commencement: 18 November 2004 (for the purpose of making orders or regulations); 1 August 2007 (for certain purposes); 10 September 2007 (for certain purposes); 14 December 2007 (for certain purposes); 6 April 2008 (otherwise).

Supplementary

171 Application of Part to sub-divided buildings

(1) This section applies where—

(a) two or more dwelling-houses in a sub-divided building are marketed for sale (with any ancillary land) as a single property; and

(b) any one or more of those dwelling-houses—

(i) is not available for sale (with any ancillary land) as a separate residential property; but

(ii) is available with vacant possession.

(2) This Part applies to the dwelling-houses mentioned in subsection (1)(a) (with any ancillary land) as if—

(a) they were a residential property, and

(b) section 160 were omitted.

(3) Subsection (2) does not affect the application of this Part to any of those dwelling-houses which is available for sale (with any ancillary land) as a separate residential property.

(4) In this section "sub-divided building" means a building or part of a building originally constructed or adapted for use as a single dwelling which has been divided (on one or more occasions) into separate dwelling-houses.

[2170]–[2170]

NOTES

Commencement: 1 August 2007 (for certain purposes); 10 September 2007 (for certain purposes); 14 December 2007 (for certain purposes); 6 April 2008 (otherwise).

172–174 (*Repealed by the Consumers, Estate Agents and Redress Act 2007, ss 53(3), 64, Sch 8.*)

175 Office of Fair Trading

(1) An enforcement authority may notify the Office of Fair Trading of any breach of duty under this Part appearing to the authority to have been committed by a person acting as estate agent.

(2) An enforcement authority shall notify the Office of Fair Trading of—

(a) any penalty charge notice given by an officer of the authority under section 168;

(b) any notice given by the authority confirming or withdrawing a penalty charge notice; and

(c) the result of any appeal from the confirmation of a penalty charge notice.

(3) The Estate Agents Act 1979 (c 38) applies in relation to a person who has committed a breach of duty under this Part in the course of estate agency work (within the meaning of that Act) as it applies in relation to a person who has engaged in a practice such as is mentioned in section 3(1)(d) of that Act in the course of such work.

[2174]

NOTES

Commencement: 1 August 2007 (for certain purposes); 10 September 2007 (for certain purposes); 14 December 2007 (for certain purposes); 6 April 2008 (otherwise).

176 Grants

(1) The Secretary of State may make grants towards expenditure incurred by any person in connection with—

(a) the development of proposals for any provision to be made by regulations under section 163;

(b) the development of schemes which are intended to be certification schemes for the purposes of any provision made or expected to be made in regulations under section 163 by virtue of section 164; or

(c) the development of a register for the purposes of any provision made or expected to be made in regulations under section 163 by virtue of section 165.

(2) A grant under this section may be made on conditions, which may include (among other things)—

(a) conditions as to the purposes for which the grant or any part of it may be used; and

(b) conditions requiring the repayment of the grant or any part of it in such circumstances as may be specified in the conditions.

[2175]

NOTES

Commencement: 18 November 2004.

177 Interpretation of Part 5

(1) In this Part—

"ancillary land", in relation to a dwelling-house or a sub-divided building, means any land intended to be occupied and enjoyed together with that dwelling-house or building;

"long lease" means—

(a) a lease granted for a term certain exceeding 21 years, whether or not it is (or may become) terminable before the end of that term by notice given by the tenant or by re-entry or forfeiture; or

(b) a lease for a term fixed by law under a grant with a covenant or obligation for perpetual renewal, other than a lease by sub-demise from one which is not a long lease;

and for this purpose "lease" does not include a mortgage term;

"potential buyer" means a person who claims that he is or may become interested in buying a residential property;

"sale", in relation to a residential property, means a disposal, or agreement to dispose, by way of sale of—

(a) the freehold interest;

(b) the interest under a long lease;

(c) an option to acquire the freehold interest or the interest under a long lease;

and "seller" means a person contemplating disposing of such an interest (and related expressions shall be construed accordingly).

(2) Any reference in the definition of "sale" to the disposal of an interest of a kind mentioned in that definition includes a reference to the creation of such an interest.

(3) A document which is not in electronic form is only to be regarded for the purposes of this Part as being under the control of a person while it is in the possession of another if he has the right to take immediate possession of the document on demand (and without payment).

(4) A document held in electronic form is only to be regarded for the purposes of this Part as being in a person's possession or under his control if he is readily able (using equipment available to him)—

(a) to view the document in a form that is visible and legible; and

(b) to produce copies of it in a visible and legible documentary form.

[2176]

NOTES

Commencement: 1 August 2007 (for certain purposes); 10 September 2007 (for certain purposes); 14 December 2007 (for certain purposes); 6 April 2008 (otherwise).

178 Index of defined expressions: Part 5

In this Part, the expressions listed in the left-hand column have the meaning given by, or are to be interpreted in accordance with, the provisions inserted in the right-hand column.

Expression	*Provision of this Act*
Acting as estate agent for the seller	Section 150
Ancillary land	Section 177(1)
Control of documents	Section 177(3) and (4)
Dwelling-house	Section 148(1)
Enforcement authority	Section 166
Home information pack	Section 148(2)
Long lease	Section 177(1)
Make public	Section 149(4)
Possession of electronic documents	Section 177(4)
Potential buyer	Section 177(1)

Expression	*Provision of this Act*
Putting on the market	Section 149(2)
Remaining on the market	Section 149(3)
Residential property	Section 148(1)
Responsible person	Section 151(1)
Sale (and related expressions)	Section 177(1)
Seller (and related expressions)	Section 177(1)
The market	Section 149(1).

[2177]

NOTES

Commencement: 1 August 2007 (for certain purposes); 10 September 2007 (for certain purposes); 14 December 2007 (for certain purposes); 6 April 2008 (otherwise).

PART 6
OTHER PROVISIONS ABOUT HOUSING

CHAPTER 1
SECURE TENANCIES

179–190 (*Outside the scope of this work.*)

Suspension of certain rights in connection with anti-social behaviour

191–193 (*Outside the scope of this work.*)

194 Disclosure of information as to orders etc in respect of anti-social behaviour

(1) Any person may disclose relevant information to a landlord under a secure tenancy if the information is disclosed for the purpose of enabling the landlord—

(a) to decide whether either of the provisions of the Housing Act 1985 (c 68) mentioned in subsection (2) can be invoked in relation to the tenant under the tenancy; or

(b) to take any appropriate action in relation to the tenant in reliance on either of those provisions.

(2) The provisions are—

(a) Ground 2A in Schedule 3 (withholding of consent to mutual exchange where order in force or application pending in connection with anti-social behaviour), and

(b) section 138(2B) (landlord's obligation to complete suspended while application pending in connection with such behaviour).

(3) In this section—

(a) "relevant information" means information relating to any order or application relevant for the purposes of either of the provisions mentioned in subsection (2), including (in particular) information identifying the person in respect of whom any such order or application has been made;

(b) "secure tenancy" has the meaning given by section 79 of the Housing Act 1985; and

(c) any reference to the tenant under a secure tenancy is, in relation to a joint tenancy, a reference to any of the joint tenants.

(4) Regulations under—

(a) section 171C of the Housing Act 1985 (modifications of Part 5 in relation to preserved right to buy), or

(b) section 17 of the Housing Act 1996 (c 52) (application of that Part in relation to right to acquire dwelling),

may make provision corresponding to subsections (1) to (3) of this section so far as those subsections relate to section 138(2B) of the Housing Act 1985.

[2178]

NOTES

Commencement: 6 June 2005 (in relation to England); 25 November 2005 (in relation to Wales).

195–211 ((*Chs 2, 3*) *Outside the scope of this work.*)

CHAPTER 4
TENANCY DEPOSIT SCHEMES

212 Tenancy deposit schemes

(1) The appropriate national authority must make arrangements for securing that one or more tenancy deposit schemes are available for the purpose of safeguarding tenancy deposits paid in connection with shorthold tenancies.

(2) For the purposes of this Chapter a "tenancy deposit scheme" is a scheme which—
- (a) is made for the purpose of safeguarding tenancy deposits paid in connection with shorthold tenancies and facilitating the resolution of disputes arising in connection with such deposits, and
- (b) complies with the requirements of Schedule 10.

(3) Arrangements under subsection (1) must be arrangements made with any body or person under which the body or person ("the scheme administrator") undertakes to establish and maintain a tenancy deposit scheme of a description specified in the arrangements.

(4) The appropriate national authority may—
- (a) give financial assistance to the scheme administrator;
- (b) make payments to the scheme administrator (otherwise than as financial assistance) in pursuance of arrangements under subsection (1).

(5) The appropriate national authority may, in such manner and on such terms as it thinks fit, guarantee the discharge of any financial obligation incurred by the scheme administrator in connection with arrangements under subsection (1).

(6) Arrangements under subsection (1) must require the scheme administrator to give the appropriate national authority, in such manner and at such times as it may specify, such information and facilities for obtaining information as it may specify.

(7) The appropriate national authority may make regulations conferring or imposing—
- (a) on scheme administrators, or
- (b) on scheme administrators of any description specified in the regulations,

such powers or duties in connection with arrangements under subsection (1) as are so specified.

(8) In this Chapter—

"authorised", in relation to a tenancy deposit scheme, means that the scheme is in force in accordance with arrangements under subsection (1);

"custodial scheme" and "insurance scheme" have the meaning given by paragraph 1(2) and (3) of Schedule 10);

"money" means money in the form of cash or otherwise;

"shorthold tenancy" means an assured shorthold tenancy within the meaning of Chapter 2 of Part 1 of the Housing Act 1988 (c 50);

"tenancy deposit", in relation to a shorthold tenancy, means any money intended to be held (by the landlord or otherwise) as security for—
- (a) the performance of any obligations of the tenant, or
- (b) the discharge of any liability of his,

arising under or in connection with the tenancy.

(9) In this Chapter—
- (a) references to a landlord or landlords in relation to any shorthold tenancy or tenancies include references to a person or persons acting on his or their behalf in relation to the tenancy or tenancies, and
- (b) references to a tenancy deposit being held in accordance with a scheme include, in the case of a custodial scheme, references to an amount representing the deposit being held in accordance with the scheme.

[2179]

NOTES

Commencement: 18 November 2004 (for the purpose of making orders or regulations); 6 April 2007 (for remaining purposes).

213 Requirements relating to tenancy deposits

(1) Any tenancy deposit paid to a person in connection with a shorthold tenancy must, as from the time when it is received, be dealt with in accordance with an authorised scheme.

(2) No person may require the payment of a tenancy deposit in connection with a shorthold tenancy which is not to be subject to the requirement in subsection (1).

(3) Where a landlord receives a tenancy deposit in connection with a shorthold tenancy, the initial requirements of an authorised scheme must be complied with by the landlord in relation to the deposit within the period of 14 days beginning with the date on which it is received.

(4) For the purposes of this section "the initial requirements" of an authorised scheme are such requirements imposed by the scheme as fall to be complied with by a landlord on receiving such a tenancy deposit.

(5) A landlord who has received such a tenancy deposit must give the tenant and any relevant person such information relating to—

(a) the authorised scheme applying to the deposit,

(b) compliance by the landlord with the initial requirements of the scheme in relation to the deposit, and

(c) the operation of provisions of this Chapter in relation to the deposit,

as may be prescribed.

(6) The information required by subsection (5) must be given to the tenant and any relevant person—

(a) in the prescribed form or in a form substantially to the same effect, and

(b) within the period of 14 days beginning with the date on which the deposit is received by the landlord.

(7) No person may, in connection with a shorthold tenancy, require a deposit which consists of property other than money.

(8) In subsection (7) "deposit" means a transfer of property intended to be held (by the landlord or otherwise) as security for—

(a) the performance of any obligations of the tenant, or

(b) the discharge of any liability of his,

arising under or in connection with the tenancy.

(9) The provisions of this section apply despite any agreement to the contrary.

(10) In this section—

"prescribed" means prescribed by an order made by the appropriate national authority;

"property" means moveable property;

"relevant person" means any person who, in accordance with arrangements made with the tenant, paid the deposit on behalf of the tenant.

[2180]

NOTES

Commencement: 18 November 2004 (for the purpose of making orders or regulations); 6 April 2007 (for remaining purposes).

Order: the Housing (Tenancy Deposits) (Prescribed Information) Order 2007, SI 2007/797.

214 Proceedings relating to tenancy deposits

(1) Where a tenancy deposit has been paid in connection with a shorthold tenancy, the tenant or any relevant person (as defined by section 213(10)) may make an application to a county court on the grounds—

(a) that the initial requirements of an authorised scheme (see section 213(4)) have not, or section 213(6)(a) has not, been complied with in relation to the deposit; or

(b) that he has been notified by the landlord that a particular authorised scheme applies to the deposit but has been unable to obtain confirmation from the scheme administrator that the deposit is being held in accordance with the scheme.

(2) Subsections (3) and (4) apply if on such an application the court—

(a) is satisfied that those requirements have not, or section 213(6)(a) has not, been complied with in relation to the deposit, or

(b) is not satisfied that the deposit is being held in accordance with an authorised scheme,

as the case may be.

(3) The court must, as it thinks fit, either—

(a) order the person who appears to the court to be holding the deposit to repay it to the applicant, or

(b) order that person to pay the deposit into the designated account held by the scheme administrator under an authorised custodial scheme,

within the period of 14 days beginning with the date of the making of the order.

(4) The court must also order the landlord to pay to the applicant a sum of money equal to three times the amount of the deposit within the period of 14 days beginning with the date of the making of the order.

(5) Where any deposit given in connection with a shorthold tenancy could not be lawfully required as a result of section 213(7), the property in question is recoverable from the person holding it by the person by whom it was given as a deposit.

(6) In subsection (5) "deposit" has the meaning given by section 213(8).

[2181]

NOTES

Commencement: 6 April 2007.

215 Sanctions for non-compliance

(1) If a tenancy deposit has been paid in connection with a shorthold tenancy, no section 21 notice may be given in relation to the tenancy at a time when—

(a) the deposit is not being held in accordance with an authorised scheme, or

(b) the initial requirements of such a scheme (see section 213(4)) have not been complied with in relation to the deposit.

(2) If section 213(6) is not complied with in relation to a deposit given in connection with a shorthold tenancy, no section 21 notice may be given in relation to the tenancy until such time as section 213(6)(a) is complied with.

(3) If any deposit given in connection with a shorthold tenancy could not be lawfully required as a result of section 213(7), no section 21 notice may be given in relation to the tenancy until such time as the property in question is returned to the person by whom it was given as a deposit.

(4) In subsection (3) "deposit" has the meaning given by section 213(8).

(5) In this section a "section 21 notice" means a notice under section 21(1)(b) or (4)(a) of the Housing Act 1988 (recovery of possession on termination of shorthold tenancy).

[2182]

NOTES

Commencement: 6 April 2007.

216–228 ((*Ch 5*) *outside the scope of this work.*)

PART 7
SUPPLEMENTARY AND FINAL PROVISIONS

229–264 (*Outside the scope of this work.*)

Final Provisions

265–269 (*Outside the scope of this work.*)

270 Short title, commencement and extent

(1) This Act may be cited as the Housing Act 2004.

(2) The following provisions come into force on the day on which this Act is passed—

(a) sections 2, 9, 161 to 164, 176, 190, 208, 216, 233, 234, 244, 248, 250, 252, 264, 265(2) to (5), 267 to 269 and this section, and

(b) any other provision of this Act so far as it confers any power to make an order or regulations which is exercisable by the Secretary of State or the National Assembly for Wales.

Subsections (3) to (7) have effect subject to paragraph (b).

(3) (*Outside the scope of this work.*)

(4) The provisions listed in subsection (5) come into force—

(a) where they are to come into force in relation only to Wales, on such day as the National Assembly for Wales may by order appoint, and

(b) otherwise, on such day as the Secretary of State may by order appoint.

(5) The provisions referred to in subsection (4) are—

(a), (b) (*outside the scope of this work.*)

(c) sections 179, 181, 191 to 194, 212 to 215, 220, 221, 223, 225, 226, 227, 229 to 232, 235 to 243, 265(1) and 266,

(d)–(f) (*outside the scope of this work.*)

(6) Part 5 (other than sections 161 to 164 and 176) comes into force on such day as the Secretary of State may by order appoint.

(7) (*Outside the scope of this work.*)

(8) Different days may be appointed for different purposes or different areas under subsection (4), (6) or (7).

(9) The Secretary of State may by order make such provision as he considers necessary or expedient for transitory, transitional or saving purposes in connection with the coming into force of any provision of this Act.

(10) The power conferred by subsection (9) is also exercisable by the National Assembly for Wales in relation to provision dealing with matters with respect to which functions are exercisable by the Assembly

(11) Subject to subsections (12) and (13), this Act extends to England and Wales only.

(12) Any amendment or repeal made by this Act has the same extent as the enactment to which it relates, except that any amendment or repeal in—

the Mobile Homes Act 1983 (c 34), or

the Crime and Disorder Act 1998 (c 37),

extends to England and Wales only.

(13) This section extends to the whole of the United Kingdom.

[2183]

NOTES

Commencement: 18 November 2004.

Orders: the Housing Act 2004 (Commencement No 1) (England) Order 2005, SI 2005/326; the Housing Act 2004 (Commencement No 2) (England) Order 2005, SI 2005/1120; the Housing Act 2004 (Commencement No 3) (England) Order 2005, SI 2005/1451; the Housing Act 2004 (Commencement No 4 and Transitional Provisions) (England) Order 2005, SI 2005/1729; the Housing Act 2004 (Commencement No 1) (Wales) Order 2005, SI 2005/1814; the Housing Act 2004 (Commencement No 2) (Wales) Order 2005, SI 2005/3237; the Housing Act 2004 (Commencement No 5 and Transitional Provisions and Savings) (England) Order 2006, SI 2006/1060; the Housing Act 2004 (Commencement No 3 and Transitional Provisions and Savings) (Wales) Order 2006, SI 2006/1535; the Housing Act 2004 (Commencement No 6) (England) Order 2006, SI 2006/3191; the Housing Act 2004 (Commencement No 4) (Wales) Order 2007, SI 2007/305; the Housing Act 2004 (Commencement No 7) (England) Order 2007, SI 2007/1068; the Housing Act 2004 (Commencement No 9) (England and Wales) Order 2007, SI 2007/2471; the Housing Act 2004 (Commencement No 5) (Wales) Order 2007, SI 2007/3232; the Housing Act 2004 (Commencement No 10) (England and Wales) Order 2007, SI 2007/3308; the Housing Act 2004 (Commencement No 11) (England and Wales) Order 2008, SI 2008/898.

(*Schs 1–16 outside the scope of this work.*)

MENTAL CAPACITY ACT 2005

(2005 c 9)

An Act to make new provision relating to persons who lack capacity; to establish a superior court of record called the Court of Protection in place of the office of the Supreme Court called by that name; to make provision in connection with the Convention on the International Protection of Adults signed at the Hague on 13th January 2000; and for connected purposes.

[7 April 2005]

PART 1
PERSONS WHO LACK CAPACITY

The principles

1 The principles

(1) The following principles apply for the purposes of this Act.

(2) A person must be assumed to have capacity unless it is established that he lacks capacity.

(3) A person is not to be treated as unable to make a decision unless all practicable steps to help him to do so have been taken without success.

(4) A person is not to be treated as unable to make a decision merely because he makes an unwise decision.

(5) An act done, or decision made, under this Act for or on behalf of a person who lacks capacity must be done, or made, in his best interests.

(6) Before the act is done, or the decision is made, regard must be had to whether the purpose for which it is needed can be as effectively achieved in a way that is less restrictive of the person's rights and freedom of action.

[2184]

NOTES

Commencement: 1 April 2007 (for certain purposes); 1 October 2007 (for remaining purposes).

Preliminary

2 People who lack capacity

(1) For the purposes of this Act, a person lacks capacity in relation to a matter if at the material time he is unable to make a decision for himself in relation to the matter because of an impairment of, or a disturbance in the functioning of, the mind or brain.

(2) It does not matter whether the impairment or disturbance is permanent or temporary.

(3) A lack of capacity cannot be established merely by reference to—

(a) a person's age or appearance, or

(b) a condition of his, or an aspect of his behaviour, which might lead others to make unjustified assumptions about his capacity.

(4) In proceedings under this Act or any other enactment, any question whether a person lacks capacity within the meaning of this Act must be decided on the balance of probabilities.

(5) No power which a person ("D") may exercise under this Act—

(a) in relation to a person who lacks capacity, or

(b) where D reasonably thinks that a person lacks capacity,

is exercisable in relation to a person under 16.

(6) Subsection (5) is subject to section 18(3).

[2185]

NOTES

Commencement: 1 April 2007 (for certain purposes); 1 October 2007 (for remaining purposes).

3 Inability to make decisions

(1) For the purposes of section 2, a person is unable to make a decision for himself if he is unable—

(a) to understand the information relevant to the decision,

(b) to retain that information,

(c) to use or weigh that information as part of the process of making the decision, or

(d) to communicate his decision (whether by talking, using sign language or any other means).

(2) A person is not to be regarded as unable to understand the information relevant to a decision if he is able to understand an explanation of it given to him in a way that is appropriate to his circumstances (using simple language, visual aids or any other means).

(3) The fact that a person is able to retain the information relevant to a decision for a short period only does not prevent him from being regarded as able to make the decision.

(4) The information relevant to a decision includes information about the reasonably foreseeable consequences of—

(a) deciding one way or another, or

(b) failing to make the decision.

[2186]

NOTES

Commencement: 1 April 2007 (for certain purposes); 1 October 2007 (for remaining purposes).

4 Best interests

(1) In determining for the purposes of this Act what is in a person's best interests, the person making the determination must not make it merely on the basis of—

(a) the person's age or appearance, or

(b) a condition of his, or an aspect of his behaviour, which might lead others to make unjustified assumptions about what might be in his best interests.

(2) The person making the determination must consider all the relevant circumstances and, in particular, take the following steps.

(3) He must consider—

(a) whether it is likely that the person will at some time have capacity in relation to the matter in question, and

(b) if it appears likely that he will, when that is likely to be.

(4) He must, so far as reasonably practicable, permit and encourage the person to participate, or to improve his ability to participate, as fully as possible in any act done for him and any decision affecting him.

(5) Where the determination relates to life-sustaining treatment he must not, in considering whether the treatment is in the best interests of the person concerned, be motivated by a desire to bring about his death.

(6) He must consider, so far as is reasonably ascertainable—

(a) the person's past and present wishes and feelings (and, in particular, any relevant written statement made by him when he had capacity),

(b) the beliefs and values that would be likely to influence his decision if he had capacity, and

(c) the other factors that he would be likely to consider if he were able to do so.

(7) He must take into account, if it is practicable and appropriate to consult them, the views of—

(a) anyone named by the person as someone to be consulted on the matter in question or on matters of that kind,

(b) anyone engaged in caring for the person or interested in his welfare,

(c) any donee of a lasting power of attorney granted by the person, and

(d) any deputy appointed for the person by the court,

as to what would be in the person's best interests and, in particular, as to the matters mentioned in subsection (6).

(8) The duties imposed by subsections (1) to (7) also apply in relation to the exercise of any powers which—

(a) are exercisable under a lasting power of attorney, or

(b) are exercisable by a person under this Act where he reasonably believes that another person lacks capacity.

(9) In the case of an act done, or a decision made, by a person other than the court, there is sufficient compliance with this section if (having complied with the requirements of subsections (1) to (7)) he reasonably believes that what he does or decides is in the best interests of the person concerned.

(10) "Life-sustaining treatment" means treatment which in the view of a person providing health care for the person concerned is necessary to sustain life.

(11) "Relevant circumstances" are those—

(a) of which the person making the determination is aware, and

(b) which it would be reasonable to regard as relevant.

[2187]

NOTES

Commencement: 1 April 2007 (for certain purposes); 1 October 2007 (for remaining purposes).

4A, 4B (*Outside the scope of this work.*)

5 Acts in connection with care or treatment

(1) If a person ("D") does an act in connection with the care or treatment of another person ("P"), the act is one to which this section applies if—

(a) before doing the act, D takes reasonable steps to establish whether P lacks capacity in relation to the matter in question, and

(b) when doing the act, D reasonably believes—

(i) that P lacks capacity in relation to the matter, and

(ii) that it will be in P's best interests for the act to be done.

(2) D does not incur any liability in relation to the act that he would not have incurred if P—

(a) had had capacity to consent in relation to the matter, and

(b) had consented to D's doing the act.

(3) Nothing in this section excludes a person's civil liability for loss or damage, or his criminal liability, resulting from his negligence in doing the act.

(4) Nothing in this section affects the operation of sections 24 to 26 (advance decisions to refuse treatment).

[2188]

NOTES

Commencement: 1 October 2007.

6 Section 5 acts: limitations

(1) If D does an act that is intended to restrain P, it is not an act to which section 5 applies unless two further conditions are satisfied.

(2) The first condition is that D reasonably believes that it is necessary to do the act in order to prevent harm to P.

(3) The second is that the act is a proportionate response to—

(a) the likelihood of P's suffering harm, and

(b) the seriousness of that harm.

(4) For the purposes of this section D restrains P if he—

(a) uses, or threatens to use, force to secure the doing of an act which P resists, or

(b) restricts P's liberty of movement, whether or not P resists.

(5) …

(6) Section 5 does not authorise a person to do an act which conflicts with a decision made, within the scope of his authority and in accordance with this Part, by—

(a) a donee of a lasting power of attorney granted by P, or

(b) a deputy appointed for P by the court.

(7) But nothing in subsection (6) stops a person—

(a) providing life-sustaining treatment, or

(b) doing any act which he reasonably believes to be necessary to prevent a serious deterioration in P's condition,

while a decision as respects any relevant issue is sought from the court.

[2189]

NOTES

Commencement: 1 October 2007.

Sub-s (5): repealed by the Mental Health Act 2007, ss 50(1), (4)(a), 55, Sch 11, Pt 10; for transitional provisions, see SI 2009/139, art 3, Schedule.

7 Payment for necessary goods and services

(1) If necessary goods or services are supplied to a person who lacks capacity to contract for the supply, he must pay a reasonable price for them.

(2) "Necessary" means suitable to a person's condition in life and to his actual requirements at the time when the goods or services are supplied.

[2190]

NOTES

Commencement: 1 October 2007.

8 Expenditure

(1) If an act to which section 5 applies involves expenditure, it is lawful for D—

(a) to pledge P's credit for the purpose of the expenditure, and

(b) to apply money in P's possession for meeting the expenditure.

(2) If the expenditure is borne for P by D, it is lawful for D—

(a) to reimburse himself out of money in P's possession, or

(b) to be otherwise indemnified by P.

(3) Subsections (1) and (2) do not affect any power under which (apart from those subsections) a person—

(a) has lawful control of P's money or other property, and

(b) has power to spend money for P's benefit.

[2191]

NOTES

Commencement: 1 October 2007.

Lasting powers of attorney

9 Lasting powers of attorney

(1) A lasting power of attorney is a power of attorney under which the donor ("P") confers on the donee (or donees) authority to make decisions about all or any of the following—

(a) P's personal welfare or specified matters concerning P's personal welfare, and

(b) P's property and affairs or specified matters concerning P's property and affairs,

and which includes authority to make such decisions in circumstances where P no longer has capacity.

(2) A lasting power of attorney is not created unless—

(a) section 10 is complied with,

(b) an instrument conferring authority of the kind mentioned in subsection (1) is made and registered in accordance with Schedule 1, and

(c) at the time when P executes the instrument, P has reached 18 and has capacity to execute it.

(3) An instrument which—

(a) purports to create a lasting power of attorney, but

(b) does not comply with this section, section 10 or Schedule 1,

confers no authority.

(4) The authority conferred by a lasting power of attorney is subject to—

(a) the provisions of this Act and, in particular, sections 1 (the principles) and 4 (best interests), and

(b) any conditions or restrictions specified in the instrument.

[2192]

NOTES

Commencement: 1 October 2007.

10 Appointment of donees

(1) A donee of a lasting power of attorney must be—

(a) an individual who has reached 18, or

(b) if the power relates only to P's property and affairs, either such an individual or a trust corporation.

(2) An individual who is bankrupt may not be appointed as donee of a lasting power of attorney in relation to P's property and affairs.

(3) Subsections (4) to (7) apply in relation to an instrument under which two or more persons are to act as donees of a lasting power of attorney.

(4) The instrument may appoint them to act—

(a) jointly,

(b) jointly and severally, or

(c) jointly in respect of some matters and jointly and severally in respect of others.

(5) To the extent to which it does not specify whether they are to act jointly or jointly and severally, the instrument is to be assumed to appoint them to act jointly.

(6) If they are to act jointly, a failure, as respects one of them, to comply with the requirements of subsection (1) or (2) or Part 1 or 2 of Schedule 1 prevents a lasting power of attorney from being created.

(7) If they are to act jointly and severally, a failure, as respects one of them, to comply with the requirements of subsection (1) or (2) or Part 1 or 2 of Schedule 1—

(a) prevents the appointment taking effect in his case, but

(b) does not prevent a lasting power of attorney from being created in the case of the other or others.

(8) An instrument used to create a lasting power of attorney—

(a) cannot give the donee (or, if more than one, any of them) power to appoint a substitute or successor, but

(b) may itself appoint a person to replace the donee (or, if more than one, any of them) on the occurrence of an event mentioned in section 13(6)(a) to (d) which has the effect of terminating the donee's appointment.

[2193]

NOTES

Commencement: 1 October 2007.

11 Lasting powers of attorney: restrictions

(1) A lasting power of attorney does not authorise the donee (or, if more than one, any of them) to do an act that is intended to restrain P, unless three conditions are satisfied.

(2) The first condition is that P lacks, or the donee reasonably believes that P lacks, capacity in relation to the matter in question.

(3) The second is that the donee reasonably believes that it is necessary to do the act in order to prevent harm to P.

(4) The third is that the act is a proportionate response to—

(a) the likelihood of P's suffering harm, and

(b) the seriousness of that harm.

(5) For the purposes of this section, the donee restrains P if he—

(a) uses, or threatens to use, force to secure the doing of an act which P resists, or

(b) restricts P's liberty of movement, whether or not P resists,

or if he authorises another person to do any of those things.

(6) …

(7) Where a lasting power of attorney authorises the donee (or, if more than one, any of them) to make decisions about P's personal welfare, the authority—

(a) does not extend to making such decisions in circumstances other than those where P lacks, or the donee reasonably believes that P lacks, capacity,
(b) is subject to sections 24 to 26 (advance decisions to refuse treatment), and
(c) extends to giving or refusing consent to the carrying out or continuation of a treatment by a person providing health care for P.

(8) But subsection (7)(c)—
(a) does not authorise the giving or refusing of consent to the carrying out or continuation of life-sustaining treatment, unless the instrument contains express provision to that effect, and
(b) is subject to any conditions or restrictions in the instrument.

[2194]

NOTES

Commencement: 1 October 2007.

Sub-s (6): repealed by the Mental Health Act 2007, ss 50(1), (4)(b), 55, Sch 11, Pt 10; for transitional provisions, see SI 2009/139, see art 3, Schedule.

12 Scope of lasting powers of attorney: gifts

(1) Where a lasting power of attorney confers authority to make decisions about P's property and affairs, it does not authorise a donee (or, if more than one, any of them) to dispose of the donor's property by making gifts except to the extent permitted by subsection (2).

(2) The donee may make gifts—
(a) on customary occasions to persons (including himself) who are related to or connected with the donor, or
(b) to any charity to whom the donor made or might have been expected to make gifts,

if the value of each such gift is not unreasonable having regard to all the circumstances and, in particular, the size of the donor's estate.

(3) "Customary occasion" means—
(a) the occasion or anniversary of a birth, a marriage or the formation of a civil partnership, or
(b) any other occasion on which presents are customarily given within families or among friends or associates.

(4) Subsection (2) is subject to any conditions or restrictions in the instrument.

[2195]

NOTES

Commencement: 1 October 2007.

13 Revocation of lasting powers of attorney etc

(1) This section applies if—
(a) P has executed an instrument with a view to creating a lasting power of attorney, or
(b) a lasting power of attorney is registered as having been conferred by P,

and in this section references to revoking the power include revoking the instrument.

(2) P may, at any time when he has capacity to do so, revoke the power.

(3) P's bankruptcy revokes the power so far as it relates to P's property and affairs.

(4) But where P is bankrupt merely because an interim bankruptcy restrictions order has effect in respect of him, the power is suspended, so far as it relates to P's property and affairs, for so long as the order has effect.

(5) The occurrence in relation to a donee of an event mentioned in subsection (6)—
(a) terminates his appointment, and
(b) except in the cases given in subsection (7), revokes the power.

(6) The events are—
(a) the disclaimer of the appointment by the donee in accordance with such requirements as may be prescribed for the purposes of this section in regulations made by the Lord Chancellor,
(b) subject to subsections (8) and (9), the death or bankruptcy of the donee or, if the donee is a trust corporation, its winding-up or dissolution,
(c) subject to subsection (11), the dissolution or annulment of a marriage or civil partnership between the donor and the donee,
(d) the lack of capacity of the donee.

(7) The cases are—
(a) the donee is replaced under the terms of the instrument,

(b) he is one of two or more persons appointed to act as donees jointly and severally in respect of any matter and, after the event, there is at least one remaining donee.

(8) The bankruptcy of a donee does not terminate his appointment, or revoke the power, in so far as his authority relates to P's personal welfare.

(9) Where the donee is bankrupt merely because an interim bankruptcy restrictions order has effect in respect of him, his appointment and the power are suspended, so far as they relate to P's property and affairs, for so long as the order has effect.

(10) Where the donee is one of two or more appointed to act jointly and severally under the power in respect of any matter, the reference in subsection (9) to the suspension of the power is to its suspension in so far as it relates to that donee.

(11) The dissolution or annulment of a marriage or civil partnership does not terminate the appointment of a donee, or revoke the power, if the instrument provided that it was not to do so.

[2196]

NOTES

Commencement: 1 October 2007.

Regulations: the Lasting Powers of Attorney, Enduring Powers of Attorney and Public Guardian Regulations 2007, SI 2007/1253 at **[3521]**.

14 Protection of donee and others if no power created or power revoked

(1) Subsections (2) and (3) apply if—

(a) an instrument has been registered under Schedule 1 as a lasting power of attorney, but

(b) a lasting power of attorney was not created,

whether or not the registration has been cancelled at the time of the act or transaction in question.

(2) A donee who acts in purported exercise of the power does not incur any liability (to P or any other person) because of the non-existence of the power unless at the time of acting he—

(a) knows that a lasting power of attorney was not created, or

(b) is aware of circumstances which, if a lasting power of attorney had been created, would have terminated his authority to act as a donee.

(3) Any transaction between the donee and another person is, in favour of that person, as valid as if the power had been in existence, unless at the time of the transaction that person has knowledge of a matter referred to in subsection (2).

(4) If the interest of a purchaser depends on whether a transaction between the donee and the other person was valid by virtue of subsection (3), it is conclusively presumed in favour of the purchaser that the transaction was valid if—

(a) the transaction was completed within 12 months of the date on which the instrument was registered, or

(b) the other person makes a statutory declaration, before or within 3 months after the completion of the purchase, that he had no reason at the time of the transaction to doubt that the donee had authority to dispose of the property which was the subject of the transaction.

(5) In its application to a lasting power of attorney which relates to matters in addition to P's property and affairs, section 5 of the Powers of Attorney Act 1971 (c 27) (protection where power is revoked) has effect as if references to revocation included the cessation of the power in relation to P's property and affairs.

(6) Where two or more donees are appointed under a lasting power of attorney, this section applies as if references to the donee were to all or any of them.

[2197]

NOTES

Commencement: 1 October 2007.

General powers of the court and appointment of deputies

15 Power to make declarations

(1) The court may make declarations as to—

(a) whether a person has or lacks capacity to make a decision specified in the declaration;

(b) whether a person has or lacks capacity to make decisions on such matters as are described in the declaration;

(c) the lawfulness or otherwise of any act done, or yet to be done, in relation to that person.

(2) "Act" includes an omission and a course of conduct.

[2198]

NOTES

Commencement: 1 October 2007.

16 Powers to make decisions and appoint deputies: general

(1) This section applies if a person ("P") lacks capacity in relation to a matter or matters concerning—

(a) P's personal welfare, or

(b) P's property and affairs.

(2) The court may—

(a) by making an order, make the decision or decisions on P's behalf in relation to the matter or matters, or

(b) appoint a person (a "deputy") to make decisions on P's behalf in relation to the matter or matters.

(3) The powers of the court under this section are subject to the provisions of this Act and, in particular, to sections 1 (the principles) and 4 (best interests).

(4) When deciding whether it is in P's best interests to appoint a deputy, the court must have regard (in addition to the matters mentioned in section 4) to the principles that—

(a) a decision by the court is to be preferred to the appointment of a deputy to make a decision, and

(b) the powers conferred on a deputy should be as limited in scope and duration as is reasonably practicable in the circumstances.

(5) The court may make such further orders or give such directions, and confer on a deputy such powers or impose on him such duties, as it thinks necessary or expedient for giving effect to, or otherwise in connection with, an order or appointment made by it under subsection (2).

(6) Without prejudice to section 4, the court may make the order, give the directions or make the appointment on such terms as it considers are in P's best interests, even though no application is before the court for an order, directions or an appointment on those terms.

(7) An order of the court may be varied or discharged by a subsequent order.

(8) The court may, in particular, revoke the appointment of a deputy or vary the powers conferred on him if it is satisfied that the deputy—

(a) has behaved, or is behaving, in a way that contravenes the authority conferred on him by the court or is not in P's best interests, or

(b) proposes to behave in a way that would contravene that authority or would not be in P's best interests.

[2199]

NOTES

Commencement: 1 October 2007.

16A (*Outside the scope of this work.*)

17 Section 16 powers: personal welfare

(1) The powers under section 16 as respects P's personal welfare extend in particular to—

(a) deciding where P is to live;

(b) deciding what contact, if any, P is to have with any specified persons;

(c) making an order prohibiting a named person from having contact with P;

(d) giving or refusing consent to the carrying out or continuation of a treatment by a person providing health care for P;

(e) giving a direction that a person responsible for P's health care allow a different person to take over that responsibility.

(2) Subsection (1) is subject to section 20 (restrictions on deputies).

[2200]

NOTES

Commencement: 1 October 2007.

18 Section 16 powers: property and affairs

(1) The powers under section 16 as respects P's property and affairs extend in particular to—

(a) the control and management of P's property;

(b) the sale, exchange, charging, gift or other disposition of P's property;

(c) the acquisition of property in P's name or on P's behalf;

(d) the carrying on, on P's behalf, of any profession, trade or business;

(e) the taking of a decision which will have the effect of dissolving a partnership of which P is a member;
(f) the carrying out of any contract entered into by P;
(g) the discharge of P's debts and of any of P's obligations, whether legally enforceable or not;
(h) the settlement of any of P's property, whether for P's benefit or for the benefit of others;
(i) the execution for P of a will;
(j) the exercise of any power (including a power to consent) vested in P whether beneficially or as trustee or otherwise;
(k) the conduct of legal proceedings in P's name or on P's behalf.

(2) No will may be made under subsection (1)(i) at a time when P has not reached 18.

(3) The powers under section 16 as respects any other matter relating to P's property and affairs may be exercised even though P has not reached 16, if the court considers it likely that P will still lack capacity to make decisions in respect of that matter when he reaches 18.

(4) Schedule 2 supplements the provisions of this section.

(5) Section 16(7) (variation and discharge of court orders) is subject to paragraph 6 of Schedule 2.

(6) Subsection (1) is subject to section 20 (restrictions on deputies).

[2201]

NOTES

Commencement: 1 October 2007.

19 Appointment of deputies

(1) A deputy appointed by the court must be—
(a) an individual who has reached 18, or
(b) as respects powers in relation to property and affairs, an individual who has reached 18 or a trust corporation.

(2) The court may appoint an individual by appointing the holder for the time being of a specified office or position.

(3) A person may not be appointed as a deputy without his consent.

(4) The court may appoint two or more deputies to act—
(a) jointly,
(b) jointly and severally, or
(c) jointly in respect of some matters and jointly and severally in respect of others.

(5) When appointing a deputy or deputies, the court may at the same time appoint one or more other persons to succeed the existing deputy or those deputies—
(a) in such circumstances, or on the happening of such events, as may be specified by the court;
(b) for such period as may be so specified.

(6) A deputy is to be treated as P's agent in relation to anything done or decided by him within the scope of his appointment and in accordance with this Part.

(7) The deputy is entitled—
(a) to be reimbursed out of P's property for his reasonable expenses in discharging his functions, and
(b) if the court so directs when appointing him, to remuneration out of P's property for discharging them.

(8) The court may confer on a deputy powers to—
(a) take possession or control of all or any specified part of P's property;
(b) exercise all or any specified powers in respect of it, including such powers of investment as the court may determine.

(9) The court may require a deputy—
(a) to give to the Public Guardian such security as the court thinks fit for the due discharge of his functions, and
(b) to submit to the Public Guardian such reports at such times or at such intervals as the court may direct.

[2202]

NOTES

Commencement: 1 October 2007.

20 Restrictions on deputies

(1) A deputy does not have power to make a decision on behalf of P in relation to a matter if he knows or has reasonable grounds for believing that P has capacity in relation to the matter.

(2) Nothing in section 16(5) or 17 permits a deputy to be given power—

(a) to prohibit a named person from having contact with P;

(b) to direct a person responsible for P's health care to allow a different person to take over that responsibility.

(3) A deputy may not be given powers with respect to—

(a) the settlement of any of P's property, whether for P's benefit or for the benefit of others,

(b) the execution for P of a will, or

(c) the exercise of any power (including a power to consent) vested in P whether beneficially or as trustee or otherwise.

(4) A deputy may not be given power to make a decision on behalf of P which is inconsistent with a decision made, within the scope of his authority and in accordance with this Act, by the donee of a lasting power of attorney granted by P (or, if there is more than one donee, by any of them).

(5) A deputy may not refuse consent to the carrying out or continuation of life-sustaining treatment in relation to P.

(6) The authority conferred on a deputy is subject to the provisions of this Act and, in particular, sections 1 (the principles) and 4 (best interests).

(7) A deputy may not do an act that is intended to restrain P unless four conditions are satisfied.

(8) The first condition is that, in doing the act, the deputy is acting within the scope of an authority expressly conferred on him by the court.

(9) The second is that P lacks, or the deputy reasonably believes that P lacks, capacity in relation to the matter in question.

(10) The third is that the deputy reasonably believes that it is necessary to do the act in order to prevent harm to P.

(11) The fourth is that the act is a proportionate response to—

(a) the likelihood of P's suffering harm, [and]

(b) the seriousness of that harm.

(12) For the purposes of this section, a deputy restrains P if he—

(a) uses, or threatens to use, force to secure the doing of an act which P resists, or

(b) restricts P's liberty of movement, whether or not P resists,

or if he authorises another person to do any of those things.

(13) ...

[2203]

NOTES

Commencement: 1 October 2007.

Sub-s (11): word in square brackets in para (a) substituted by the Mental Health Act 2007, s 51.

Sub-s (13): repealed by the Mental Health Act 2007, ss 50(1), (4)(c), 55, Sch 11, Pt 10.

21 Transfer of proceedings relating to people under 18

[(1)] The [Lord Chief Justice, with the concurrence of the Lord Chancellor,] may by order make provision as to the transfer of proceedings relating to a person under 18, in such circumstances as are specified in the order—

(a) from the Court of Protection to a court having jurisdiction under the Children Act 1989 (c 41), or

(b) from a court having jurisdiction under that Act to the Court of Protection.

[(2) The Lord Chief Justice may nominate any of the following to exercise his functions under this section—

(a) the President of the Court of Protection;

(b) a judicial office holder (as defined in section 109(4) of the Constitutional Reform Act 2005).]

[2204]

NOTES

Commencement: 1 October 2007.

Sub-s (1): numbered as such and words in square brackets substituted by SI 2006/1016, art 2, Sch 1, paras 30, 31(1)–(3).

Sub-s (2): inserted by SI 2006/1016, art 2, Sch 1, paras 30, 31(1), (4).

Order: the Mental Capacity Act 2005 (Transfer Of Proceedings) Order 2007, SI 2007/1899.

21A (*Outside the scope of this work.*)

Powers of the court in relation to lasting powers of attorney

22 Powers of court in relation to validity of lasting powers of attorney

(1) This section and section 23 apply if—

(a) a person ("P") has executed or purported to execute an instrument with a view to creating a lasting power of attorney, or

(b) an instrument has been registered as a lasting power of attorney conferred by P.

(2) The court may determine any question relating to—

(a) whether one or more of the requirements for the creation of a lasting power of attorney have been met;

(b) whether the power has been revoked or has otherwise come to an end.

(3) Subsection (4) applies if the court is satisfied—

(a) that fraud or undue pressure was used to induce P—

(i) to execute an instrument for the purpose of creating a lasting power of attorney, or

(ii) to create a lasting power of attorney, or

(b) that the donee (or, if more than one, any of them) of a lasting power of attorney—

(i) has behaved, or is behaving, in a way that contravenes his authority or is not in P's best interests, or

(ii) proposes to behave in a way that would contravene his authority or would not be in P's best interests.

(4) The court may—

(a) direct that an instrument purporting to create the lasting power of attorney is not to be registered, or

(b) if P lacks capacity to do so, revoke the instrument or the lasting power of attorney.

(5) If there is more than one donee, the court may under subsection (4)(b) revoke the instrument or the lasting power of attorney so far as it relates to any of them.

(6) "Donee" includes an intended donee.

[2205]

NOTES

Commencement: 1 October 2007.

23 Powers of court in relation to operation of lasting powers of attorney

(1) The court may determine any question as to the meaning or effect of a lasting power of attorney or an instrument purporting to create one.

(2) The court may—

(a) give directions with respect to decisions—

(i) which the donee of a lasting power of attorney has authority to make, and

(ii) which P lacks capacity to make;

(b) give any consent or authorisation to act which the donee would have to obtain from P if P had capacity to give it.

(3) The court may, if P lacks capacity to do so—

(a) give directions to the donee with respect to the rendering by him of reports or accounts and the production of records kept by him for that purpose;

(b) require the donee to supply information or produce documents or things in his possession as donee;

(c) give directions with respect to the remuneration or expenses of the donee;

(d) relieve the donee wholly or partly from any liability which he has or may have incurred on account of a breach of his duties as donee.

(4) The court may authorise the making of gifts which are not within section 12(2) (permitted gifts).

(5) Where two or more donees are appointed under a lasting power of attorney, this section applies as if references to the donee were to all or any of them.

[2206]

NOTES

Commencement: 1 October 2007.

24–41 (*Outside the scope of this work.*)

42 Codes of practice

(1) The Lord Chancellor must prepare and issue one or more codes of practice—

(a) for the guidance of persons assessing whether a person has capacity in relation to any matter,

(b) for the guidance of persons acting in connection with the care or treatment of another person (see section 5),

(c) for the guidance of donees of lasting powers of attorney,

(d) for the guidance of deputies appointed by the court,

(e) for the guidance of persons carrying out research in reliance on any provision made by or under this Act (and otherwise with respect to sections 30 to 34),

(f) for the guidance of independent mental capacity advocates,

[(fa) for the guidance of persons exercising functions under Schedule A1,

(fb) for the guidance of representatives appointed under Part 10 of Schedule A1,]

(g) with respect to the provisions of sections 24 to 26 (advance decisions and apparent advance decisions), and

(h) with respect to such other matters concerned with this Act as he thinks fit.

(2) The Lord Chancellor may from time to time revise a code.

(3) The Lord Chancellor may delegate the preparation or revision of the whole or any part of a code so far as he considers expedient.

(4) It is the duty of a person to have regard to any relevant code if he is acting in relation to a person who lacks capacity and is doing so in one or more of the following ways—

(a) as the donee of a lasting power of attorney,

(b) as a deputy appointed by the court,

(c) as a person carrying out research in reliance on any provision made by or under this Act (see sections 30 to 34),

(d) as an independent mental capacity advocate,

[(da) in the exercise of functions under Schedule A1,

(db) as a representative appointed under Part 10 of Schedule A1,]

(e) in a professional capacity,

(f) for remuneration.

(5) If it appears to a court or tribunal conducting any criminal or civil proceedings that—

(a) a provision of a code, or

(b) a failure to comply with a code,

is relevant to a question arising in the proceedings, the provision or failure must be taken into account in deciding the question.

(6) A code under subsection (1)(d) may contain separate guidance for deputies appointed by virtue of paragraph 1(2) of Schedule 5 (functions of deputy conferred on receiver appointed under the Mental Health Act).

(7) In this section and in section 43, "code" means a code prepared or revised under this section.

[2207]

NOTES

Commencement: 1 April 2007 (sub-ss (1)–(3), (4) (for certain purposes), (5) (for certain purposes), (6), (7)); 1 October 2007 (sub-ss (4), (5), for remaining purposes).

Sub-s (1): paras (fa), (fb) inserted by the Mental Health Act 2007, s 50(7), Sch 9, Pt 1, paras 1, 8(1), (2).

Sub-s (4): paras (da), (db) inserted by the Mental Health Act 2007, s 50(7), Sch 9, Pt 1, paras 1, 8(1), (3).

43 Codes of practice: procedure

(1) Before preparing or revising a code, the Lord Chancellor must consult—

(a) the National Assembly for Wales, and

(b) such other persons as he considers appropriate.

(2) The Lord Chancellor may not issue a code unless—

(a) a draft of the code has been laid by him before both Houses of Parliament, and

(b) the 40 day period has elapsed without either House resolving not to approve the draft.

(3) The Lord Chancellor must arrange for any code that he has issued to be published in such a way as he considers appropriate for bringing it to the attention of persons likely to be concerned with its provisions.

(4) "40 day period", in relation to the draft of a proposed code, means—

(a) if the draft is laid before one House on a day later than the day on which it is laid before the other House, the period of 40 days beginning with the later of the two days;

(b) in any other case, the period of 40 days beginning with the day on which it is laid before each House.

(5) In calculating the period of 40 days, no account is to be taken of any period during which Parliament is dissolved or prorogued or during which both Houses are adjourned for more than 4 days.

[2208]

NOTES

Commencement: 1 April 2007.

44 (*Outside the scope of this work.*)

PART 2
THE COURT OF PROTECTION AND THE PUBLIC GUARDIAN

The Court of Protection

45 The Court of Protection

(1) There is to be a superior court of record known as the Court of Protection.

(2) The court is to have an official seal.

(3) The court may sit at any place in England and Wales, on any day and at any time.

(4) The court is to have a central office and registry at a place appointed by the Lord Chancellor[, after consulting the Lord Chief Justice].

(5) The Lord Chancellor may[, after consulting the Lord Chief Justice,] designate as additional registries of the court any district registry of the High Court and any county court office.

[(5A) The Lord Chief Justice may nominate any of the following to exercise his functions under this section—

(a) the President of the Court of Protection;

(b) a judicial office holder (as defined in section 109(4) of the Constitutional Reform Act 2005).]

(6) The office of the Supreme Court called the Court of Protection ceases to exist.

[2209]

NOTES

Commencement: 1 October 2007.

Sub-ss (4), (5): words in square brackets inserted by SI 2006/1016, art 2, Sch 1, paras 30, 32(1)–(3).

Sub-s (5A): inserted by SI 2006/1016, art 2, Sch 1, paras 30, 32(1), (4).

46 (*Outside the scope of this work.*)

Supplementary powers

47 General powers and effect of orders etc

(1) The court has in connection with its jurisdiction the same powers, rights, privileges and authority as the High Court.

(2) Section 204 of the Law of Property Act 1925 (c 20) (orders of High Court conclusive in favour of purchasers) applies in relation to orders and directions of the court as it applies to orders of the High Court.

(3) Office copies of orders made, directions given or other instruments issued by the court and sealed with its official seal are admissible in all legal proceedings as evidence of the originals without any further proof.

[2210]

NOTES

Commencement: 1 October 2007.

48 Interim orders and directions

The court may, pending the determination of an application to it in relation to a person ("P"), make an order or give directions in respect of any matter if—

(a) there is reason to believe that P lacks capacity in relation to the matter,

(b) the matter is one to which its powers under this Act extend, and

(c) it is in P's best interests to make the order, or give the directions, without delay.

[2211]

NOTES
Commencement: 1 October 2007.

49–61 (*Outside the scope of this work.*)

PART 3
MISCELLANEOUS AND GENERAL

62 (*Outside the scope of this work.*)

Private international law

63 International protection of adults

Schedule 3—

(a) gives effect in England and Wales to the Convention on the International Protection of Adults signed at the Hague on 13th January 2000 (Cm 5881) (in so far as this Act does not otherwise do so), and

(b) makes related provision as to the private international law of England and Wales.

[2212]

NOTES
Commencement: 1 October 2007.

General

64 Interpretation

(1) In this Act—

"the 1985 Act" means the Enduring Powers of Attorney Act 1985 (c 29),
"advance decision" has the meaning given in section 24(1),
["authorisation under Schedule A1" means either—
(a) a standard authorisation under that Schedule, or
(b) an urgent authorisation under that Schedule;]
"the court" means the Court of Protection established by section 45,
"Court of Protection Rules" has the meaning given in section 51(1),
"Court of Protection Visitor" has the meaning given in section 61,
"deputy" has the meaning given in section 16(2)(b),
"enactment" includes a provision of subordinate legislation (within the meaning of the Interpretation Act 1978 (c 30)),
"health record" has the meaning given in section 68 of the Data Protection Act 1998 (c 29) (as read with section 69 of that Act),
"the Human Rights Convention" has the same meaning as "the Convention" in the Human Rights Act 1998 (c 42),
"independent mental capacity advocate" has the meaning given in section 35(1),
"lasting power of attorney" has the meaning given in section 9,
"life-sustaining treatment" has the meaning given in section 4(10),
"local authority"[, except in Schedule A1,] means—
(a) the council of a county in England in which there are no district councils,
(b) the council of a district in England,
(c) the council of a county or county borough in Wales,
(d) the council of a London borough,
(e) the Common Council of the City of London, or
(f) the Council of the Isles of Scilly,
"Mental Health Act" means the Mental Health Act 1983 (c 20),
"prescribed", in relation to regulations made under this Act, means prescribed by those regulations,
"property" includes any thing in action and any interest in real or personal property,
"public authority" has the same meaning as in the Human Rights Act 1998,
"Public Guardian" has the meaning given in section 57,
"purchaser" and "purchase" have the meaning given in section 205(1) of the Law of Property Act 1925 (c 20),
"social services function" has the meaning given in section 1A of the Local Authority Social Services Act 1970 (c 42),
"treatment" includes a diagnostic or other procedure,
"trust corporation" has the meaning given in section 68(1) of the Trustee Act 1925 (c 19), and
"will" includes codicil.

(2) In this Act, references to making decisions, in relation to a donee of a lasting power of attorney or a deputy appointed by the court, include, where appropriate, acting on decisions made.

(3) In this Act, references to the bankruptcy of an individual include a case where a bankruptcy restrictions order under the Insolvency Act 1986 (c 45) has effect in respect of him.

(4) "Bankruptcy restrictions order" includes an interim bankruptcy restrictions order.

[(5) In this Act, references to deprivation of a person's liberty have the same meaning as in Article 5(1) of the Human Rights Convention.

(6) For the purposes of such references, it does not matter whether a person is deprived of his liberty by a public authority or not.]

[2213]

NOTES

Commencement: 1 April 2007 (for certain purposes); 1 October 2007 (for remaining purposes).

Sub-s (1): definition "authorisation under Schedule A1" inserted, and words in square brackets in definition "local authority" inserted by the Mental Health Act 2007, s 50(7), Sch 9, Pt 1, paras 1, 10(1)–(3).

Sub-ss (5), (6): inserted by the Mental Health Act 2007, s 50(7), Sch 9, Pt 1, paras 1, 10(1), (4).

65 (*Outside the scope of this work.*)

66 Existing receivers and enduring powers of attorney etc

(1) The following provisions cease to have effect—

(a) Part 7 of the Mental Health Act,

(b) the Enduring Powers of Attorney Act 1985 (c 29).

(2) No enduring power of attorney within the meaning of the 1985 Act is to be created after the commencement of subsection (1)(b).

(3) Schedule 4 has effect in place of the 1985 Act in relation to any enduring power of attorney created before the commencement of subsection (1)(b).

(4) Schedule 5 contains transitional provisions and savings in relation to Part 7 of the Mental Health Act and the 1985 Act.

[2214]

NOTES

Commencement: 1 October 2007.

67 Minor and consequential amendments and repeals

(1) Schedule 6 contains minor and consequential amendments.

(2) Schedule 7 contains repeals.

(3) The Lord Chancellor may by order make supplementary, incidental, consequential, transitional or saving provision for the purposes of, in consequence of, or for giving full effect to a provision of this Act.

(4) An order under subsection (3) may, in particular—

(a) provide for a provision of this Act which comes into force before another provision of this Act has come into force to have effect, until the other provision has come into force, with specified modifications;

(b) amend, repeal or revoke an enactment, other than one contained in an Act or Measure passed in a Session after the one in which this Act is passed.

(5) The amendments that may be made under subsection (4)(b) are in addition to those made by or under any other provision of this Act.

(6) An order under subsection (3) which amends or repeals a provision of an Act or Measure may not be made unless a draft has been laid before and approved by resolution of each House of Parliament.

[2215]

NOTES

Commencement: 1 October 2007.

Order: the Mental Capacity Act 2005 (Transitional and Consequential Provisions) Order 2007, SI 2007/1898.

68 Commencement and extent

(1) This Act, other than sections 30 to 41, comes into force in accordance with provision made by order by the Lord Chancellor.

(2) Sections 30 to 41 come into force in accordance with provision made by order by—

(a) the Secretary of State, in relation to England, and

(b) the National Assembly for Wales, in relation to Wales.

(3) An order under this section may appoint different days for different provisions and different purposes.

(4) Subject to subsections (5) and (6), this Act extends to England and Wales only.

(5) The following provisions extend to the United Kingdom—

(a) paragraph 16(1) of Schedule 1 (evidence of instruments and of registration of lasting powers of attorney),

(b) paragraph 15(3) of Schedule 4 (evidence of instruments and of registration of enduring powers of attorney).

(6) Subject to any provision made in Schedule 6, the amendments and repeals made by Schedules 6 and 7 have the same extent as the enactments to which they relate.

[2216]

NOTES

Commencement: 7 April 2005.

Orders: the Mental Capacity Act 2005 (Commencement No 1) Order 2006, SI 2006/2814, as amended by SI 2006/3473; the Mental Capacity Act 2005 (Commencement No 1) (England and Wales) Order 2007, SI 2007/563; the Mental Capacity Act 2005 (Commencement) (Wales) Order 2007, SI 2007/856; the Mental Capacity Act 2005 (Commencement No 2) Order 2007, SI 2007/1897.

69 Short title

This Act may be cited as the Mental Capacity Act 2005.

[2217]

NOTES

Commencement: 7 April 2005.

(*Sch A1 outside the scope of this work.*)

SCHEDULE 1
LASTING POWERS OF ATTORNEY: FORMALITIES

Section 9

PART 1
MAKING INSTRUMENTS

General requirements as to making instruments

1.—(1) An instrument is not made in accordance with this Schedule unless—

(a) it is in the prescribed form,

(b) it complies with paragraph 2, and

(c) any prescribed requirements in connection with its execution are satisfied.

(2) Regulations may make different provision according to whether—

(a) the instrument relates to personal welfare or to property and affairs (or to both);

(b) only one or more than one donee is to be appointed (and if more than one, whether jointly or jointly and severally).

(3) In this Schedule—

(a) "prescribed" means prescribed by regulations, and

(b) "regulations" means regulations made for the purposes of this Schedule by the Lord Chancellor.

Requirements as to content of instruments

2.—(1) The instrument must include—

(a) the prescribed information about the purpose of the instrument and the effect of a lasting power of attorney,

(b) a statement by the donor to the effect that he—

(i) has read the prescribed information or a prescribed part of it (or has had it read to him), and

(ii) intends the authority conferred under the instrument to include authority to make decisions on his behalf in circumstances where he no longer has capacity,

(c) a statement by the donor—

(i) naming a person or persons whom the donor wishes to be notified of any application for the registration of the instrument, or

(ii) stating that there are no persons whom he wishes to be notified of any such application,

(d) a statement by the donee (or, if more than one, each of them) to the effect that he—

(i) has read the prescribed information or a prescribed part of it (or has had it read to him), and
(ii) understands the duties imposed on a donee of a lasting power of attorney under sections 1 (the principles) and 4 (best interests), and

(e) a certificate by a person of a prescribed description that, in his opinion, at the time when the donor executes the instrument—
(i) the donor understands the purpose of the instrument and the scope of the authority conferred under it,
(ii) no fraud or undue pressure is being used to induce the donor to create a lasting power of attorney, and
(iii) there is nothing else which would prevent a lasting power of attorney from being created by the instrument.

(2) Regulations may—
(a) prescribe a maximum number of named persons;
(b) provide that, where the instrument includes a statement under sub-paragraph (1)(c)(ii), two persons of a prescribed description must each give a certificate under sub-paragraph (1)(e).

(3) The persons who may be named persons do not include a person who is appointed as donee under the instrument.

(4) In this Schedule, "named person" means a person named under sub-paragraph (1)(c).

(5) A certificate under sub-paragraph (1)(e)—
(a) must be made in the prescribed form, and
(b) must include any prescribed information.

(6) The certificate may not be given by a person appointed as donee under the instrument.

Failure to comply with prescribed form

3.—(1) If an instrument differs in an immaterial respect in form or mode of expression from the prescribed form, it is to be treated by the Public Guardian as sufficient in point of form and expression.

(2) The court may declare that an instrument which is not in the prescribed form is to be treated as if it were, if it is satisfied that the persons executing the instrument intended it to create a lasting power of attorney.

[2218]

NOTES

Commencement: 1 October 2007.

PART 2
REGISTRATION

Applications and procedure for registration

4.—(1) An application to the Public Guardian for the registration of an instrument intended to create a lasting power of attorney—
(a) must be made in the prescribed form, and
(b) must include any prescribed information.

(2) The application may be made—
(a) by the donor,
(b) by the donee or donees, or
(c) if the instrument appoints two or more donees to act jointly and severally in respect of any matter, by any of the donees.

(3) The application must be accompanied by—
(a) the instrument, and
(b) any fee provided for under section 58(4)(b).

(4) A person who, in an application for registration, makes a statement which he knows to be false in a material particular is guilty of an offence and is liable—
(a) on summary conviction, to imprisonment for a term not exceeding 12 months or a fine not exceeding the statutory maximum or both;
(b) on conviction on indictment, to imprisonment for a term not exceeding 2 years or a fine or both.

5. Subject to paragraphs 11 to 14, the Public Guardian must register the instrument as a lasting power of attorney at the end of the prescribed period.

Notification requirements

6.—(1) A donor about to make an application under paragraph 4(2)(a) must notify any named persons that he is about to do so.

(2) The donee (or donees) about to make an application under paragraph 4(2)(b) or (c) must notify any named persons that he is (or they are) about to do so.

7. As soon as is practicable after receiving an application by the donor under paragraph 4(2)(a), the Public Guardian must notify the donee (or donees) that the application has been received.

8.—(1) As soon as is practicable after receiving an application by a donee (or donees) under paragraph 4(2)(b), the Public Guardian must notify the donor that the application has been received.

(2) As soon as is practicable after receiving an application by a donee under paragraph 4(2)(c), the Public Guardian must notify—

(a) the donor, and
(b) the donee or donees who did not join in making the application,

that the application has been received.

9.—(1) A notice under paragraph 6 must be made in the prescribed form.

(2) A notice under paragraph 6, 7 or 8 must include such information, if any, as may be prescribed.

Power to dispense with notification requirements

10. The court may—

(a) on the application of the donor, dispense with the requirement to notify under paragraph 6(1), or
(b) on the application of the donee or donees concerned, dispense with the requirement to notify under paragraph 6(2),

if satisfied that no useful purpose would be served by giving the notice.

Instrument not made properly or containing ineffective provision

11.—(1) If it appears to the Public Guardian that an instrument accompanying an application under paragraph 4 is not made in accordance with this Schedule, he must not register the instrument unless the court directs him to do so.

(2) Sub-paragraph (3) applies if it appears to the Public Guardian that the instrument contains a provision which—

(a) would be ineffective as part of a lasting power of attorney, or
(b) would prevent the instrument from operating as a valid lasting power of attorney.

(3) The Public Guardian—

(a) must apply to the court for it to determine the matter under section 23(1), and
(b) pending the determination by the court, must not register the instrument.

(4) Sub-paragraph (5) applies if the court determines under section 23(1) (whether or not on an application by the Public Guardian) that the instrument contains a provision which—

(a) would be ineffective as part of a lasting power of attorney, or
(b) would prevent the instrument from operating as a valid lasting power of attorney.

(5) The court must—

(a) notify the Public Guardian that it has severed the provision, or
(b) direct him not to register the instrument.

(6) Where the court notifies the Public Guardian that it has severed a provision, he must register the instrument with a note to that effect attached to it.

Deputy already appointed

12.—(1) Sub-paragraph (2) applies if it appears to the Public Guardian that—

(a) there is a deputy appointed by the court for the donor, and
(b) the powers conferred on the deputy would, if the instrument were registered, to any extent conflict with the powers conferred on the attorney.

(2) The Public Guardian must not register the instrument unless the court directs him to do so.

Objection by donee or named person

13.—(1) Sub-paragraph (2) applies if a donee or a named person—

(a) receives a notice under paragraph 6, 7 or 8 of an application for the registration of an instrument, and
(b) before the end of the prescribed period, gives notice to the Public Guardian of an objection to the registration on the ground that an event mentioned in section 13(3) or (6)(a) to (d) has occurred which has revoked the instrument.

(2) If the Public Guardian is satisfied that the ground for making the objection is established, he must not register the instrument unless the court, on the application of the person applying for the registration—

(a) is satisfied that the ground is not established, and
(b) directs the Public Guardian to register the instrument.

(3) Sub-paragraph (4) applies if a donee or a named person—

(a) receives a notice under paragraph 6, 7 or 8 of an application for the registration of an instrument, and
(b) before the end of the prescribed period—
  (i) makes an application to the court objecting to the registration on a prescribed ground, and
  (ii) notifies the Public Guardian of the application.

(4) The Public Guardian must not register the instrument unless the court directs him to do so.

Objection by donor

14.—(1) This paragraph applies if the donor—

(a) receives a notice under paragraph 8 of an application for the registration of an instrument, and
(b) before the end of the prescribed period, gives notice to the Public Guardian of an objection to the registration.

(2) The Public Guardian must not register the instrument unless the court, on the application of the donee or, if more than one, any of them—

(a) is satisfied that the donor lacks capacity to object to the registration, and
(b) directs the Public Guardian to register the instrument.

Notification of registration

15. Where an instrument is registered under this Schedule, the Public Guardian must give notice of the fact in the prescribed form to—

(a) the donor, and
(b) the donee or, if more than one, each of them.

Evidence of registration

16.—(1) A document purporting to be an office copy of an instrument registered under this Schedule is, in any part of the United Kingdom, evidence of—

(a) the contents of the instrument, and
(b) the fact that it has been registered.

(2) Sub-paragraph (1) is without prejudice to—

(a) section 3 of the Powers of Attorney Act 1971 (c 27) (proof by certified copy), and
(b) any other method of proof authorised by law.

[2219]

NOTES

Commencement: 1 October 2007.

PART 3
CANCELLATION OF REGISTRATION AND NOTIFICATION OF SEVERANCE

17.—(1) The Public Guardian must cancel the registration of an instrument as a lasting power of attorney on being satisfied that the power has been revoked—

(a) as a result of the donor's bankruptcy, or
(b) on the occurrence of an event mentioned in section 13(6)(a) to (d).

(2) If the Public Guardian cancels the registration of an instrument he must notify—

(a) the donor, and
(b) the donee or, if more than one, each of them.

18. The court must direct the Public Guardian to cancel the registration of an instrument as a lasting power of attorney if it—

(a) determines under section 22(2)(a) that a requirement for creating the power was not met,
(b) determines under section 22(2)(b) that the power has been revoked or has otherwise come to an end, or
(c) revokes the power under section 22(4)(b) (fraud etc).

19.—(1) Sub-paragraph (2) applies if the court determines under section 23(1) that a lasting power of attorney contains a provision which—

(a) is ineffective as part of a lasting power of attorney, or
(b) prevents the instrument from operating as a valid lasting power of attorney.

(2) The court must—

(a) notify the Public Guardian that it has severed the provision, or
(b) direct him to cancel the registration of the instrument as a lasting power of attorney.

20. On the cancellation of the registration of an instrument, the instrument and any office copies of it must be delivered up to the Public Guardian to be cancelled.

[2220]

NOTES

Commencement: 1 October 2007.

PART 4
RECORDS OF ALTERATIONS IN REGISTERED POWERS

Partial revocation or suspension of power as a result of bankruptcy

21. If in the case of a registered instrument it appears to the Public Guardian that under section 13 a lasting power of attorney is revoked, or suspended, in relation to the donor's property and affairs (but not in relation to other matters), the Public Guardian must attach to the instrument a note to that effect.

Termination of appointment of donee which does not revoke power

22. If in the case of a registered instrument it appears to the Public Guardian that an event has occurred—
(a) which has terminated the appointment of the donee, but
(b) which has not revoked the instrument,
the Public Guardian must attach to the instrument a note to that effect.

Replacement of donee

23. If in the case of a registered instrument it appears to the Public Guardian that the donee has been replaced under the terms of the instrument the Public Guardian must attach to the instrument a note to that effect.

Severance of ineffective provisions

24. If in the case of a registered instrument the court notifies the Public Guardian under paragraph 19(2)(a) that it has severed a provision of the instrument, the Public Guardian must attach to it a note to that effect.

Notification of alterations

25. If the Public Guardian attaches a note to an instrument under paragraph 21, 22, 23 or 24 he must give notice of the note to the donee or donees of the power (or, as the case may be, to the other donee or donees of the power).

[2221]

NOTES

Commencement: 1 October 2007.

(*Sch 1A outside the scope of this work.*)

SCHEDULE 2
PROPERTY AND AFFAIRS: SUPPLEMENTARY PROVISIONS

Section 18(4)

Wills: general

1. Paragraphs 2 to 4 apply in relation to the execution of a will, by virtue of section 18, on behalf of P.

Provision that may be made in will

2. The will may make any provision (whether by disposing of property or exercising a power or otherwise) which could be made by a will executed by P if he had capacity to make it.

Wills: requirements relating to execution

3.—(1) Sub-paragraph (2) applies if under section 16 the court makes an order or gives directions requiring or authorising a person ("the authorised person") to execute a will on behalf of P.

(2) Any will executed in pursuance of the order or direction—
(a) must state that it is signed by P acting by the authorised person,

(b) must be signed by the authorised person with the name of P and his own name, in the presence of two or more witnesses present at the same time,
(c) must be attested and subscribed by those witnesses in the presence of the authorised person, and
(d) must be sealed with the official seal of the court.

Wills: effect of execution

4.—(1) This paragraph applies where a will is executed in accordance with paragraph 3.

(2) The Wills Act 1837 (c 26) has effect in relation to the will as if it were signed by P by his own hand, except that—
(a) section 9 of the 1837 Act (requirements as to signing and attestation) does not apply, and
(b) in the subsequent provisions of the 1837 Act any reference to execution in the manner required by the previous provisions is to be read as a reference to execution in accordance with paragraph 3.

(3) The will has the same effect for all purposes as if—
(a) P had had the capacity to make a valid will, and
(b) the will had been executed by him in the manner required by the 1837 Act.

(4) But sub-paragraph (3) does not have effect in relation to the will—
(a) in so far as it disposes of immovable property outside England and Wales, or
(b) in so far as it relates to any other property or matter if, when the will is executed—
(i) P is domiciled outside England and Wales, and
(ii) the condition in sub-paragraph (5) is met.

(5) The condition is that, under the law of P's domicile, any question of his testamentary capacity would fall to be determined in accordance with the law of a place outside England and Wales.

Vesting orders ancillary to settlement etc

5.—(1) If provision is made by virtue of section 18 for—
(a) the settlement of any property of P, or
(b) the exercise of a power vested in him of appointing trustees or retiring from a trust,

the court may also make as respects the property settled or the trust property such consequential vesting or other orders as the case may require.

(2) The power under sub-paragraph (1) includes, in the case of the exercise of such a power, any order which could have been made in such a case under Part 4 of the Trustee Act 1925 (c 19).

Variation of settlements

6.—(1) If a settlement has been made by virtue of section 18, the court may by order vary or revoke the settlement if—
(a) the settlement makes provision for its variation or revocation,
(b) the court is satisfied that a material fact was not disclosed when the settlement was made, or
(c) the court is satisfied that there has been a substantial change of circumstances.

(2) Any such order may give such consequential directions as the court thinks fit.

Vesting of stock in curator appointed outside England and Wales

7.—(1) Sub-paragraph (2) applies if the court is satisfied—
(a) that under the law prevailing in a place outside England and Wales a person ("M") has been appointed to exercise powers in respect of the property or affairs of P on the ground (however formulated) that P lacks capacity to make decisions with respect to the management and administration of his property and affairs, and
(b) that, having regard to the nature of the appointment and to the circumstances of the case, it is expedient that the court should exercise its powers under this paragraph.

(2) The court may direct—
(a) any stocks standing in the name of P, or
(b) the right to receive dividends from the stocks,

to be transferred into M's name or otherwise dealt with as required by M, and may give such directions as the court thinks fit for dealing with accrued dividends from the stocks.

(3) "Stocks" includes—
(a) shares, and
(b) any funds, annuity or security transferable in the books kept by any body corporate or unincorporated company or society or by an instrument of transfer either alone or accompanied by other formalities,

and "dividends" is to be construed accordingly.

Preservation of interests in property disposed of on behalf of person lacking capacity

8.—(1) Sub-paragraphs (2) and (3) apply if—
(a) P's property has been disposed of by virtue of section 18,
(b) under P's will or intestacy, or by a gift perfected or nomination taking effect on his death, any other person would have taken an interest in the property but for the disposal, and
(c) on P's death, any property belonging to P's estate represents the property disposed of.

(2) The person takes the same interest, if and so far as circumstances allow, in the property representing the property disposed of.

(3) If the property disposed of was real property, any property representing it is to be treated, so long as it remains part of P's estate, as if it were real property.

(4) The court may direct that, on a disposal of P's property—
(a) which is made by virtue of section 18, and
(b) which would apart from this paragraph result in the conversion of personal property into real property,

property representing the property disposed of is to be treated, so long as it remains P's property or forms part of P's estate, as if it were personal property.

(5) References in sub-paragraphs (1) to (4) to the disposal of property are to—
(a) the sale, exchange, charging of or other dealing (otherwise than by will) with property other than money;
(b) the removal of property from one place to another;
(c) the application of money in acquiring property;
(d) the transfer of money from one account to another;

and references to property representing property disposed of are to be construed accordingly and as including the result of successive disposals.

(6) The court may give such directions as appear to it necessary or expedient for the purpose of facilitating the operation of sub-paragraphs (1) to (3), including the carrying of money to a separate account and the transfer of property other than money.

9.—(1) Sub-paragraph (2) applies if the court has ordered or directed the expenditure of money—
(a) for carrying out permanent improvements on any of P's property, or
(b) otherwise for the permanent benefit of any of P's property.

(2) The court may order that—
(a) the whole of the money expended or to be expended, or
(b) any part of it,

is to be a charge on the property either without interest or with interest at a specified rate.

(3) An order under sub-paragraph (2) may provide for excluding or restricting the operation of paragraph 8(1) to (3).

(4) A charge under sub-paragraph (2) may be made in favour of such person as may be just and, in particular, where the money charged is paid out of P's general estate, may be made in favour of a person as trustee for P.

(5) No charge under sub-paragraph (2) may confer any right of sale or foreclosure during P's lifetime.

Powers as patron of benefice

10.—(1) Any functions which P has as patron of a benefice may be discharged only by a person ("R") appointed by the court.

(2) R must be an individual capable of appointment under section 8(1)(b) of the 1986 Measure (which provides for an individual able to make a declaration of communicant status, a clerk in Holy Orders, etc to be appointed to discharge a registered patron's functions).

(3) The 1986 Measure applies to R as it applies to an individual appointed by the registered patron of the benefice under section 8(1)(b) or (3) of that Measure to discharge his functions as patron.

(4) "The 1986 Measure" means the Patronage (Benefices) Measure 1986 (No 3).

[2222]

NOTES
Commencement: 1 October 2007.

SCHEDULE 3
INTERNATIONAL PROTECTION OF ADULTS

Section 63

PART 1
PRELIMINARY

Introduction

1. This Part applies for the purposes of this Schedule.

The Convention

2.—(1) "Convention" means the Convention referred to in section 63.

(2) "Convention country" means a country in which the Convention is in force.

(3) A reference to an Article or Chapter is to an Article or Chapter of the Convention.

(4) An expression which appears in this Schedule and in the Convention is to be construed in accordance with the Convention.

Countries, territories and nationals

3.—(1) "Country" includes a territory which has its own system of law.

(2) Where a country has more than one territory with its own system of law, a reference to the country, in relation to one of its nationals, is to the territory with which the national has the closer, or the closest, connection.

Adults with incapacity

4. "Adult" means a person who—
- (a) as a result of an impairment or insufficiency of his personal faculties, cannot protect his interests, and
- (b) has reached 16.

Protective measures

5.—(1) "Protective measure" means a measure directed to the protection of the person or property of an adult; and it may deal in particular with any of the following—
- (a) the determination of incapacity and the institution of a protective regime,
- (b) placing the adult under the protection of an appropriate authority,
- (c) guardianship, curatorship or any corresponding system,
- (d) the designation and functions of a person having charge of the adult's person or property, or representing or otherwise helping him,
- (e) placing the adult in a place where protection can be provided,
- (f) administering, conserving or disposing of the adult's property,
- (g) authorising a specific intervention for the protection of the person or property of the adult.

(2) Where a measure of like effect to a protective measure has been taken in relation to a person before he reaches 16, this Schedule applies to the measure in so far as it has effect in relation to him once he has reached 16.

Central Authority

6.—(1) Any function under the Convention of a Central Authority is exercisable in England and Wales by the Lord Chancellor.

(2) A communication may be sent to the Central Authority in relation to England and Wales by sending it to the Lord Chancellor.

[2223]

NOTES

Commencement: 1 October 2007.

PART 2
JURISDICTION OF COMPETENT AUTHORITY

Scope of jurisdiction

7.—(1) The court may exercise its functions under this Act (in so far as it cannot otherwise do so) in relation to—
- (a) an adult habitually resident in England and Wales,
- (b) an adult's property in England and Wales,

(c) an adult present in England and Wales or who has property there, if the matter is urgent, or

(d) an adult present in England and Wales, if a protective measure which is temporary and limited in its effect to England and Wales is proposed in relation to him.

(2) An adult present in England and Wales is to be treated for the purposes of this paragraph as habitually resident there if—

(a) his habitual residence cannot be ascertained,

(b) he is a refugee, or

(c) he has been displaced as a result of disturbance in the country of his habitual residence.

8.—(1) The court may also exercise its functions under this Act (in so far as it cannot otherwise do so) in relation to an adult if sub-paragraph (2) or (3) applies in relation to him.

(2) This sub-paragraph applies in relation to an adult if—

(a) he is a British citizen,

(b) he has a closer connection with England and Wales than with Scotland or Northern Ireland, and

(c) Article 7 has, in relation to the matter concerned, been complied with.

(3) This sub-paragraph applies in relation to an adult if the Lord Chancellor, having consulted such persons as he considers appropriate, agrees to a request under Article 8 in relation to the adult.

Exercise of jurisdiction

9.—(1) This paragraph applies where jurisdiction is exercisable under this Schedule in connection with a matter which involves a Convention country other than England and Wales.

(2) Any Article on which the jurisdiction is based applies in relation to the matter in so far as it involves the other country (and the court must, accordingly, comply with any duty conferred on it as a result).

(3) Article 12 also applies, so far as its provisions allow, in relation to the matter in so far as it involves the other country.

10. A reference in this Schedule to the exercise of jurisdiction under this Schedule is to the exercise of functions under this Act as a result of this Part of this Schedule.

[2224]

NOTES

Commencement: 1 October 2007.

PART 3
APPLICABLE LAW

Applicable law

11. In exercising jurisdiction under this Schedule, the court may, if it thinks that the matter has a substantial connection with a country other than England and Wales, apply the law of that other country.

12. Where a protective measure is taken in one country but implemented in another, the conditions of implementation are governed by the law of the other country.

Lasting powers of attorney, etc

13.—(1) If the donor of a lasting power is habitually resident in England and Wales at the time of granting the power, the law applicable to the existence, extent, modification or extinction of the power is—

(a) the law of England and Wales, or

(b) if he specifies in writing the law of a connected country for the purpose, that law.

(2) If he is habitually resident in another country at that time, but England and Wales is a connected country, the law applicable in that respect is—

(a) the law of the other country, or

(b) if he specifies in writing the law of England and Wales for the purpose, that law.

(3) A country is connected, in relation to the donor, if it is a country—

(a) of which he is a national,

(b) in which he was habitually resident, or

(c) in which he has property.

(4) Where this paragraph applies as a result of sub-paragraph (3)(c), it applies only in relation to the property which the donor has in the connected country.

(5) The law applicable to the manner of the exercise of a lasting power is the law of the country where it is exercised.

(6) In this Part of this Schedule, "lasting power" means—

(a) a lasting power of attorney (see section 9),
(b) an enduring power of attorney within the meaning of Schedule 4, or
(c) any other power of like effect.

14.—(1) Where a lasting power is not exercised in a manner sufficient to guarantee the protection of the person or property of the donor, the court, in exercising jurisdiction under this Schedule, may disapply or modify the power.

(2) Where, in accordance with this Part of this Schedule, the law applicable to the power is, in one or more respects, that of a country other than England and Wales, the court must, so far as possible, have regard to the law of the other country in that respect (or those respects).

15. Regulations may provide for Schedule 1 (lasting powers of attorney: formalities) to apply with modifications in relation to a lasting power which comes within paragraph 13(6)(c) above.

Protection of third parties

16.—(1) This paragraph applies where a person (a "representative") in purported exercise of an authority to act on behalf of an adult enters into a transaction with a third party.

(2) The validity of the transaction may not be questioned in proceedings, nor may the third party be held liable, merely because—

(a) where the representative and third party are in England and Wales when entering into the transaction, sub-paragraph (3) applies;
(b) where they are in another country at that time, sub-paragraph (4) applies.

(3) This sub-paragraph applies if—

(a) the law applicable to the authority in one or more respects is, as a result of this Schedule, the law of a country other than England and Wales, and
(b) the representative is not entitled to exercise the authority in that respect (or those respects) under the law of that other country.

(4) This sub-paragraph applies if—

(a) the law applicable to the authority in one or more respects is, as a result of this Part of this Schedule, the law of England and Wales, and
(b) the representative is not entitled to exercise the authority in that respect (or those respects) under that law.

(5) This paragraph does not apply if the third party knew or ought to have known that the applicable law was—

(a) in a case within sub-paragraph (3), the law of the other country;
(b) in a case within sub-paragraph (4), the law of England and Wales.

Mandatory rules

17. Where the court is entitled to exercise jurisdiction under this Schedule, the mandatory provisions of the law of England and Wales apply, regardless of any system of law which would otherwise apply in relation to the matter.

Public policy

18. Nothing in this Part of this Schedule requires or enables the application in England and Wales of a provision of the law of another country if its application would be manifestly contrary to public policy.

[2225]

NOTES

Commencement: 1 October 2007.

PART 4
RECOGNITION AND ENFORCEMENT

Recognition

19.—(1) A protective measure taken in relation to an adult under the law of a country other than England and Wales is to be recognised in England and Wales if it was taken on the ground that the adult is habitually resident in the other country.

(2) A protective measure taken in relation to an adult under the law of a Convention country other than England and Wales is to be recognised in England and Wales if it was taken on a ground mentioned in Chapter 2 (jurisdiction).

(3) But the court may disapply this paragraph in relation to a measure if it thinks that—

(a) the case in which the measure was taken was not urgent,
(b) the adult was not given an opportunity to be heard, and

(c) that omission amounted to a breach of natural justice.

(4) It may also disapply this paragraph in relation to a measure if it thinks that—

(a) recognition of the measure would be manifestly contrary to public policy,

(b) the measure would be inconsistent with a mandatory provision of the law of England and Wales, or

(c) the measure is inconsistent with one subsequently taken, or recognised, in England and Wales in relation to the adult.

(5) And the court may disapply this paragraph in relation to a measure taken under the law of a Convention country in a matter to which Article 33 applies, if the court thinks that that Article has not been complied with in connection with that matter.

20.—(1) An interested person may apply to the court for a declaration as to whether a protective measure taken under the law of a country other than England and Wales is to be recognised in England and Wales.

(2) No permission is required for an application to the court under this paragraph.

21. For the purposes of paragraphs 19 and 20, any finding of fact relied on when the measure was taken is conclusive.

Enforcement

22.—(1) An interested person may apply to the court for a declaration as to whether a protective measure taken under the law of, and enforceable in, a country other than England and Wales is enforceable, or to be registered, in England and Wales in accordance with Court of Protection Rules.

(2) The court must make the declaration if—

(a) the measure comes within sub-paragraph (1) or (2) of paragraph 19, and

(b) the paragraph is not disapplied in relation to it as a result of sub-paragraph (3), (4) or (5).

(3) A measure to which a declaration under this paragraph relates is enforceable in England and Wales as if it were a measure of like effect taken by the court.

Measures taken in relation to those aged under 16

23.—(1) This paragraph applies where—

(a) provision giving effect to, or otherwise deriving from, the Convention in a country other than England and Wales applies in relation to a person who has not reached 16, and

(b) a measure is taken in relation to that person in reliance on that provision.

(2) This Part of this Schedule applies in relation to that measure as it applies in relation to a protective measure taken in relation to an adult under the law of a Convention country other than England and Wales.

Supplementary

24. The court may not review the merits of a measure taken outside England and Wales except to establish whether the measure complies with this Schedule in so far as it is, as a result of this Schedule, required to do so.

25. Court of Protection Rules may make provision about an application under paragraph 20 or 22.

[2226]

NOTES

Commencement: 1 October 2007.

PART 5
CO-OPERATION

Proposal for cross-border placement

26.—(1) This paragraph applies where a public authority proposes to place an adult in an establishment in a Convention country other than England and Wales.

(2) The public authority must consult an appropriate authority in that other country about the proposed placement and, for that purpose, must send it—

(a) a report on the adult, and

(b) a statement of its reasons for the proposed placement.

(3) If the appropriate authority in the other country opposes the proposed placement within a reasonable time, the public authority may not proceed with it.

27. A proposal received by a public authority under Article 33 in relation to an adult is to proceed unless the authority opposes it within a reasonable time.

Adult in danger etc

28.—(1) This paragraph applies if a public authority is told that an adult—

(a) who is in serious danger, and

(b) in relation to whom the public authority has taken, or is considering taking, protective measures,

is, or has become resident, in a Convention country other than England and Wales.

(2) The public authority must tell an appropriate authority in that other country about—

(a) the danger, and

(b) the measures taken or under consideration.

29. A public authority may not request from, or send to, an appropriate authority in a Convention country information in accordance with Chapter 5 (co-operation) in relation to an adult if it thinks that doing so—

(a) would be likely to endanger the adult or his property, or

(b) would amount to a serious threat to the liberty or life of a member of the adult's family. **[2227]**

NOTES

Commencement: 1 October 2007.

PART 6
GENERAL

Certificates

30. A certificate given under Article 38 by an authority in a Convention country other than England and Wales is, unless the contrary is shown, proof of the matters contained in it.

Powers to make further provision as to private international law

31. Her Majesty may by Order in Council confer on the Lord Chancellor, the court or another public authority functions for enabling the Convention to be given effect in England and Wales.

32.—(1) Regulations may make provision—

(a) giving further effect to the Convention, or

(b) otherwise about the private international law of England and Wales in relation to the protection of adults.

(2) The regulations may—

(a) confer functions on the court or another public authority;

(b) amend this Schedule;

(c) provide for this Schedule to apply with specified modifications;

(d) make provision about countries other than Convention countries.

Exceptions

33. Nothing in this Schedule applies, and no provision made under paragraph 32 is to apply, to any matter to which the Convention, as a result of Article 4, does not apply.

Regulations and orders

34. A reference in this Schedule to regulations or an order (other than an Order in Council) is to regulations or an order made for the purposes of this Schedule by the Lord Chancellor.

Commencement

35. The following provisions of this Schedule have effect only if the Convention is in force in accordance with Article 57—

(a) paragraph 8,

(b) paragraph 9,

(c) paragraph 19(2) and (5),

(d) Part 5,

(e) paragraph 30.

[2228]

NOTES

Commencement: 1 October 2007.

SCHEDULE 4
PROVISIONS APPLYING TO EXISTING ENDURING POWERS OF ATTORNEY

Section 66(3)

PART 1
ENDURING POWERS OF ATTORNEY

Enduring power of attorney to survive mental incapacity of donor

1.—(1) Where an individual has created a power of attorney which is an enduring power within the meaning of this Schedule—

(a) the power is not revoked by any subsequent mental incapacity of his,

(b) upon such incapacity supervening, the donee of the power may not do anything under the authority of the power except as provided by sub-paragraph (2) unless or until the instrument creating the power is registered under paragraph 13, and

(c) if and so long as paragraph (b) operates to suspend the donee's authority to act under the power, section 5 of the Powers of Attorney Act 1971 (c 27) (protection of donee and third persons), so far as applicable, applies as if the power had been revoked by the donor's mental incapacity,

and, accordingly, section 1 of this Act does not apply.

(2) Despite sub-paragraph (1)(b), where the attorney has made an application for registration of the instrument then, until it is registered, the attorney may take action under the power—

(a) to maintain the donor or prevent loss to his estate, or

(b) to maintain himself or other persons in so far as paragraph 3(2) permits him to do so.

(3) Where the attorney purports to act as provided by sub-paragraph (2) then, in favour of a person who deals with him without knowledge that the attorney is acting otherwise than in accordance with sub-paragraph (2)(a) or (b), the transaction between them is as valid as if the attorney were acting in accordance with sub-paragraph (2)(a) or (b).

Characteristics of an enduring power of attorney

2.—(1) Subject to sub-paragraphs (5) and (6) and paragraph 20, a power of attorney is an enduring power within the meaning of this Schedule if the instrument which creates the power—

(a) is in the prescribed form,

(b) was executed in the prescribed manner by the donor and the attorney, and

(c) incorporated at the time of execution by the donor the prescribed explanatory information.

(2) In this paragraph, "prescribed" means prescribed by such of the following regulations as applied when the instrument was executed—

(a) the Enduring Powers of Attorney (Prescribed Form) Regulations 1986 (SI 1986/126),

(b) the Enduring Powers of Attorney (Prescribed Form) Regulations 1987 (SI 1987/1612),

(c) the Enduring Powers of Attorney (Prescribed Form) Regulations 1990 (SI 1990/1376),

(d) the Enduring Powers of Attorney (Welsh Language Prescribed Form) Regulations 2000 (SI 2000/289).

(3) An instrument in the prescribed form purporting to have been executed in the prescribed manner is to be taken, in the absence of evidence to the contrary, to be a document which incorporated at the time of execution by the donor the prescribed explanatory information.

(4) If an instrument differs in an immaterial respect in form or mode of expression from the prescribed form it is to be treated as sufficient in point of form and expression.

(5) A power of attorney cannot be an enduring power unless, when he executes the instrument creating it, the attorney is—

(a) an individual who has reached 18 and is not bankrupt, or

(b) a trust corporation.

(6) A power of attorney which gives the attorney a right to appoint a substitute or successor cannot be an enduring power.

(7) An enduring power is revoked by the bankruptcy of the donor or attorney.

(8) But where the donor or attorney is bankrupt merely because an interim bankruptcy restrictions order has effect in respect of him, the power is suspended for so long as the order has effect.

(9) An enduring power is revoked if the court—

(a) exercises a power under sections 16 to 20 in relation to the donor, and

(b) directs that the enduring power is to be revoked.

(10) No disclaimer of an enduring power, whether by deed or otherwise, is valid unless and until the attorney gives notice of it to the donor or, where paragraph 4(6) or 15(1) applies, to the Public Guardian.

Scope of authority etc of attorney under enduring power

3.—(1) If the instrument which creates an enduring power of attorney is expressed to confer general authority on the attorney, the instrument operates to confer, subject to—

(a) the restriction imposed by sub-paragraph (3), and
(b) any conditions or restrictions contained in the instrument,

authority to do on behalf of the donor anything which the donor could lawfully do by an attorney at the time when the donor executed the instrument.

(2) Subject to any conditions or restrictions contained in the instrument, an attorney under an enduring power, whether general or limited, may (without obtaining any consent) act under the power so as to benefit himself or other persons than the donor to the following extent but no further—

(a) he may so act in relation to himself or in relation to any other person if the donor might be expected to provide for his or that person's needs respectively, and
(b) he may do whatever the donor might be expected to do to meet those needs.

(3) Without prejudice to sub-paragraph (2) but subject to any conditions or restrictions contained in the instrument, an attorney under an enduring power, whether general or limited, may (without obtaining any consent) dispose of the property of the donor by way of gift to the following extent but no further—

(a) he may make gifts of a seasonal nature or at a time, or on an anniversary, of a birth, a marriage or the formation of a civil partnership, to persons (including himself) who are related to or connected with the donor, and
(b) he may make gifts to any charity to whom the donor made or might be expected to make gifts,

provided that the value of each such gift is not unreasonable having regard to all the circumstances and in particular the size of the donor's estate.

[2229]

NOTES

Commencement: 1 October 2007.

PART 2
ACTION ON ACTUAL OR IMPENDING INCAPACITY OF DONOR

Duties of attorney in event of actual or impending incapacity of donor

4.—(1) Sub-paragraphs (2) to (6) apply if the attorney under an enduring power has reason to believe that the donor is or is becoming mentally incapable.

(2) The attorney must, as soon as practicable, make an application to the Public Guardian for the registration of the instrument creating the power.

(3) Before making an application for registration the attorney must comply with the provisions as to notice set out in Part 3 of this Schedule.

(4) An application for registration—

(a) must be made in the prescribed form, and
(b) must contain such statements as may be prescribed.

(5) The attorney—

(a) may, before making an application for the registration of the instrument, refer to the court for its determination any question as to the validity of the power, and
(b) must comply with any direction given to him by the court on that determination.

(6) No disclaimer of the power is valid unless and until the attorney gives notice of it to the Public Guardian; and the Public Guardian must notify the donor if he receives a notice under this sub-paragraph.

(7) A person who, in an application for registration, makes a statement which he knows to be false in a material particular is guilty of an offence and is liable—

(a) on summary conviction, to imprisonment for a term not exceeding 12 months or a fine not exceeding the statutory maximum or both;
(b) on conviction on indictment, to imprisonment for a term not exceeding 2 years or a fine or both.

(8) In this paragraph, "prescribed" means prescribed by regulations made for the purposes of this Schedule by the Lord Chancellor.

[2230]

NOTES

Commencement: 1 October 2007.

PART 3
NOTIFICATION PRIOR TO REGISTRATION

Duty to give notice to relatives

5. Subject to paragraph 7, before making an application for registration the attorney must give notice of his intention to do so to all those persons (if any) who are entitled to receive notice by virtue of paragraph 6.

6.—(1) Subject to sub-paragraphs (2) to (4), persons of the following classes ("relatives") are entitled to receive notice under paragraph 5—

- (a) the donor's spouse or civil partner,
- (b) the donor's children,
- (c) the donor's parents,
- (d) the donor's brothers and sisters, whether of the whole or half blood,
- (e) the widow, widower or surviving civil partner of a child of the donor,
- (f) the donor's grandchildren,
- (g) the children of the donor's brothers and sisters of the whole blood,
- (h) the children of the donor's brothers and sisters of the half blood,
- (i) the donor's uncles and aunts of the whole blood,
- (j) the children of the donor's uncles and aunts of the whole blood.

(2) A person is not entitled to receive notice under paragraph 5 if—

- (a) his name or address is not known to the attorney and cannot be reasonably ascertained by him, or
- (b) the attorney has reason to believe that he has not reached 18 or is mentally incapable.

(3) Except where sub-paragraph (4) applies—

- (a) no more than 3 persons are entitled to receive notice under paragraph 5, and
- (b) in determining the persons who are so entitled, persons falling within the class in sub-paragraph (1)(a) are to be preferred to persons falling within the class in sub-paragraph (1)(b), those falling within the class in sub-paragraph (1)(b) are to be preferred to those falling within the class in sub-paragraph (1)(c), and so on.

(4) Despite the limit of 3 specified in sub-paragraph (3), where—

- (a) there is more than one person falling within any of classes (a) to (j) of sub-paragraph (1), and
- (b) at least one of those persons would be entitled to receive notice under paragraph 5,

then, subject to sub-paragraph (2), all the persons falling within that class are entitled to receive notice under paragraph 5.

7.—(1) An attorney is not required to give notice under paragraph 5—

- (a) to himself, or
- (b) to any other attorney under the power who is joining in making the application,

even though he or, as the case may be, the other attorney is entitled to receive notice by virtue of paragraph 6.

(2) In the case of any person who is entitled to receive notice by virtue of paragraph 6, the attorney, before applying for registration, may make an application to the court to be dispensed from the requirement to give him notice; and the court must grant the application if it is satisfied—

- (a) that it would be undesirable or impracticable for the attorney to give him notice, or
- (b) that no useful purpose is likely to be served by giving him notice.

Duty to give notice to donor

8.—(1) Subject to sub-paragraph (2), before making an application for registration the attorney must give notice of his intention to do so to the donor.

(2) Paragraph 7(2) applies in relation to the donor as it applies in relation to a person who is entitled to receive notice under paragraph 5.

Contents of notices

9. A notice to relatives under this Part of this Schedule must—

- (a) be in the prescribed form,
- (b) state that the attorney proposes to make an application to the Public Guardian for the registration of the instrument creating the enduring power in question,
- (c) inform the person to whom it is given of his right to object to the registration under paragraph 13(4), and
- (d) specify, as the grounds on which an objection to registration may be made, the grounds set out in paragraph 13(9).

10. A notice to the donor under this Part of this Schedule—

- (a) must be in the prescribed form,
- (b) must contain the statement mentioned in paragraph 9(b), and

(c) must inform the donor that, while the instrument remains registered, any revocation of the power by him will be ineffective unless and until the revocation is confirmed by the court.

Duty to give notice to other attorneys

11.—(1) Subject to sub-paragraph (2), before making an application for registration an attorney under a joint and several power must give notice of his intention to do so to any other attorney under the power who is not joining in making the application; and paragraphs 7(2) and 9 apply in relation to attorneys entitled to receive notice by virtue of this paragraph as they apply in relation to persons entitled to receive notice by virtue of paragraph 6.

(2) An attorney is not entitled to receive notice by virtue of this paragraph if—

(a) his address is not known to the applying attorney and cannot reasonably be ascertained by him, or

(b) the applying attorney has reason to believe that he has not reached 18 or is mentally incapable.

Supplementary

12. Despite section 7 of the Interpretation Act 1978 (c 30) (construction of references to service by post), for the purposes of this Part of this Schedule a notice given by post is to be regarded as given on the date on which it was posted.

[2231]

NOTES

Commencement: 1 October 2007.

PART 4
REGISTRATION

Registration of instrument creating power

13.—(1) If an application is made in accordance with paragraph 4(3) and (4) the Public Guardian must, subject to the provisions of this paragraph, register the instrument to which the application relates.

(2) If it appears to the Public Guardian that—

(a) there is a deputy appointed for the donor of the power created by the instrument, and

(b) the powers conferred on the deputy would, if the instrument were registered, to any extent conflict with the powers conferred on the attorney,

the Public Guardian must not register the instrument except in accordance with the court's directions.

(3) The court may, on the application of the attorney, direct the Public Guardian to register an instrument even though notice has not been given as required by paragraph 4(3) and Part 3 of this Schedule to a person entitled to receive it, if the court is satisfied—

(a) that it was undesirable or impracticable for the attorney to give notice to that person, or

(b) that no useful purpose is likely to be served by giving him notice.

(4) Sub-paragraph (5) applies if, before the end of the period of 5 weeks beginning with the date (or the latest date) on which the attorney gave notice under paragraph 5 of an application for registration, the Public Guardian receives a valid notice of objection to the registration from a person entitled to notice of the application.

(5) The Public Guardian must not register the instrument except in accordance with the court's directions.

(6) Sub-paragraph (7) applies if, in the case of an application for registration—

(a) it appears from the application that there is no one to whom notice has been given under paragraph 5, or

(b) the Public Guardian has reason to believe that appropriate inquiries might bring to light evidence on which he could be satisfied that one of the grounds of objection set out in sub-paragraph (9) was established.

(7) The Public Guardian—

(a) must not register the instrument, and

(b) must undertake such inquiries as he thinks appropriate in all the circumstances.

(8) If, having complied with sub-paragraph (7)(b), the Public Guardian is satisfied that one of the grounds of objection set out in sub-paragraph (9) is established—

(a) the attorney may apply to the court for directions, and

(b) the Public Guardian must not register the instrument except in accordance with the court's directions.

(9) A notice of objection under this paragraph is valid if made on one or more of the following grounds—

(a) that the power purported to have been created by the instrument was not valid as an enduring power of attorney,

(b) that the power created by the instrument no longer subsists,

(c) that the application is premature because the donor is not yet becoming mentally incapable,

(d) that fraud or undue pressure was used to induce the donor to create the power,

(e) that, having regard to all the circumstances and in particular the attorney's relationship to or connection with the donor, the attorney is unsuitable to be the donor's attorney.

(10) If any of those grounds is established to the satisfaction of the court it must direct the Public Guardian not to register the instrument, but if not so satisfied it must direct its registration.

(11) If the court directs the Public Guardian not to register an instrument because it is satisfied that the ground in sub-paragraph (9)(d) or (e) is established, it must by order revoke the power created by the instrument.

(12) If the court directs the Public Guardian not to register an instrument because it is satisfied that any ground in sub-paragraph (9) except that in paragraph (c) is established, the instrument must be delivered up to be cancelled unless the court otherwise directs.

Register of enduring powers

14. The Public Guardian has the function of establishing and maintaining a register of enduring powers for the purposes of this Schedule.

[2232]

NOTES

Commencement: 1 October 2007.

PART 5
LEGAL POSITION AFTER REGISTRATION

Effect and proof of registration

15.—(1) The effect of the registration of an instrument under paragraph 13 is that—

(a) no revocation of the power by the donor is valid unless and until the court confirms the revocation under paragraph 16(3);

(b) no disclaimer of the power is valid unless and until the attorney gives notice of it to the Public Guardian;

(c) the donor may not extend or restrict the scope of the authority conferred by the instrument and no instruction or consent given by him after registration, in the case of a consent, confers any right and, in the case of an instruction, imposes or confers any obligation or right on or creates any liability of the attorney or other persons having notice of the instruction or consent.

(2) Sub-paragraph (1) applies for so long as the instrument is registered under paragraph 13 whether or not the donor is for the time being mentally incapable.

(3) A document purporting to be an office copy of an instrument registered under this Schedule is, in any part of the United Kingdom, evidence of—

(a) the contents of the instrument, and

(b) the fact that it has been so registered.

(4) Sub-paragraph (3) is without prejudice to section 3 of the Powers of Attorney Act 1971 (c 27) (proof by certified copies) and to any other method of proof authorised by law.

Functions of court with regard to registered power

16.—(1) Where an instrument has been registered under paragraph 13, the court has the following functions with respect to the power and the donor of and the attorney appointed to act under the power.

(2) The court may—

(a) determine any question as to the meaning or effect of the instrument;

(b) give directions with respect to—

(i) the management or disposal by the attorney of the property and affairs of the donor;

(ii) the rendering of accounts by the attorney and the production of the records kept by him for the purpose;

(iii) the remuneration or expenses of the attorney whether or not in default of or in accordance with any provision made by the instrument, including directions for the repayment of excessive or the payment of additional remuneration;

(c) require the attorney to supply information or produce documents or things in his possession as attorney;
(d) give any consent or authorisation to act which the attorney would have to obtain from a mentally capable donor;
(e) authorise the attorney to act so as to benefit himself or other persons than the donor otherwise than in accordance with paragraph 3(2) and (3) (but subject to any conditions or restrictions contained in the instrument);
(f) relieve the attorney wholly or partly from any liability which he has or may have incurred on account of a breach of his duties as attorney.

(3) On application made for the purpose by or on behalf of the donor, the court must confirm the revocation of the power if satisfied that the donor—
(a) has done whatever is necessary in law to effect an express revocation of the power, and
(b) was mentally capable of revoking a power of attorney when he did so (whether or not he is so when the court considers the application).

(4) The court must direct the Public Guardian to cancel the registration of an instrument registered under paragraph 13 in any of the following circumstances—
(a) on confirming the revocation of the power under sub-paragraph (3),
(b) on directing under paragraph 2(9)(b) that the power is to be revoked,
(c) on being satisfied that the donor is and is likely to remain mentally capable,
(d) on being satisfied that the power has expired or has been revoked by the mental incapacity of the attorney,
(e) on being satisfied that the power was not a valid and subsisting enduring power when registration was effected,
(f) on being satisfied that fraud or undue pressure was used to induce the donor to create the power,
(g) on being satisfied that, having regard to all the circumstances and in particular the attorney's relationship to or connection with the donor, the attorney is unsuitable to be the donor's attorney.

(5) If the court directs the Public Guardian to cancel the registration of an instrument on being satisfied of the matters specified in sub-paragraph (4)(f) or (g) it must by order revoke the power created by the instrument.

(6) If the court directs the cancellation of the registration of an instrument under sub-paragraph (4) except paragraph (c) the instrument must be delivered up to the Public Guardian to be cancelled, unless the court otherwise directs.

Cancellation of registration by Public Guardian

17. The Public Guardian must cancel the registration of an instrument creating an enduring power of attorney—
(a) on receipt of a disclaimer signed by the attorney;
(b) if satisfied that the power has been revoked by the death or bankruptcy of the donor or attorney or, if the attorney is a body corporate, by its winding up or dissolution;
(c) on receipt of notification from the court that the court has revoked the power;
(d) on confirmation from the court that the donor has revoked the power.

[2233]

NOTES

Commencement: 1 October 2007.

PART 6
PROTECTION OF ATTORNEY AND THIRD PARTIES

Protection of attorney and third persons where power is invalid or revoked

18.—(1) Sub-paragraphs (2) and (3) apply where an instrument which did not create a valid power of attorney has been registered under paragraph 13 (whether or not the registration has been cancelled at the time of the act or transaction in question).

(2) An attorney who acts in pursuance of the power does not incur any liability (either to the donor or to any other person) because of the non-existence of the power unless at the time of acting he knows—
(a) that the instrument did not create a valid enduring power,
(b) that an event has occurred which, if the instrument had created a valid enduring power, would have had the effect of revoking the power, or
(c) that, if the instrument had created a valid enduring power, the power would have expired before that time.

(3) Any transaction between the attorney and another person is, in favour of that person, as valid as if the power had then been in existence, unless at the time of the transaction that person has knowledge of any of the matters mentioned in sub-paragraph (2).

(4) If the interest of a purchaser depends on whether a transaction between the attorney and another person was valid by virtue of sub-paragraph (3), it is conclusively presumed in favour of the purchaser that the transaction was valid if—

(a) the transaction between that person and the attorney was completed within 12 months of the date on which the instrument was registered, or

(b) that person makes a statutory declaration, before or within 3 months after the completion of the purchase, that he had no reason at the time of the transaction to doubt that the attorney had authority to dispose of the property which was the subject of the transaction.

(5) For the purposes of section 5 of the Powers of Attorney Act 1971 (c 27) (protection where power is revoked) in its application to an enduring power the revocation of which by the donor is by virtue of paragraph 15 invalid unless and until confirmed by the court under paragraph 16—

(a) knowledge of the confirmation of the revocation is knowledge of the revocation of the power, but

(b) knowledge of the unconfirmed revocation is not.

Further protection of attorney and third persons

19.—(1) If—

(a) an instrument framed in a form prescribed as mentioned in paragraph 2(2) creates a power which is not a valid enduring power, and

(b) the power is revoked by the mental incapacity of the donor,

sub-paragraphs (2) and (3) apply, whether or not the instrument has been registered.

(2) An attorney who acts in pursuance of the power does not, by reason of the revocation, incur any liability (either to the donor or to any other person) unless at the time of acting he knows—

(a) that the instrument did not create a valid enduring power, and

(b) that the donor has become mentally incapable.

(3) Any transaction between the attorney and another person is, in favour of that person, as valid as if the power had then been in existence, unless at the time of the transaction that person knows—

(a) that the instrument did not create a valid enduring power, and

(b) that the donor has become mentally incapable.

(4) Paragraph 18(4) applies for the purpose of determining whether a transaction was valid by virtue of sub-paragraph (3) as it applies for the purpose or determining whether a transaction was valid by virtue of paragraph 18(3).

[2234]

NOTES

Commencement: 1 October 2007.

PART 7
JOINT AND JOINT AND SEVERAL ATTORNEYS

Application to joint and joint and several attorneys

20.—(1) An instrument which appoints more than one person to be an attorney cannot create an enduring power unless the attorneys are appointed to act—

(a) jointly, or

(b) jointly and severally.

(2) This Schedule, in its application to joint attorneys, applies to them collectively as it applies to a single attorney but subject to the modifications specified in paragraph 21.

(3) This Schedule, in its application to joint and several attorneys, applies with the modifications specified in sub-paragraphs (4) to (7) and in paragraph 22.

(4) A failure, as respects any one attorney, to comply with the requirements for the creation of enduring powers—

(a) prevents the instrument from creating such a power in his case, but

(b) does not affect its efficacy for that purpose as respects the other or others or its efficacy in his case for the purpose of creating a power of attorney which is not an enduring power.

(5) If one or more but not both or all the attorneys makes or joins in making an application for registration of the instrument—

(a) an attorney who is not an applicant as well as one who is may act pending the registration of the instrument as provided in paragraph 1(2),

(b) notice of the application must also be given under Part 3 of this Schedule to the other attorney or attorneys, and

(c) objection may validly be taken to the registration on a ground relating to an attorney or to the power of an attorney who is not an applicant as well as to one or the power of one who is an applicant.

(6) The Public Guardian is not precluded by paragraph 13(5) or (8) from registering an instrument and the court must not direct him not to do so under paragraph 13(10) if an enduring power subsists as respects some attorney who is not affected by the ground or grounds of the objection in question; and where the Public Guardian registers an instrument in that case, he must make against the registration an entry in the prescribed form.

(7) Sub-paragraph (6) does not preclude the court from revoking a power in so far as it confers a power on any other attorney in respect of whom the ground in paragraph 13(9)(d) or (e) is established; and where any ground in paragraph 13(9) affecting any other attorney is established the court must direct the Public Guardian to make against the registration an entry in the prescribed form.

(8) In sub-paragraph (4), "the requirements for the creation of enduring powers" means the provisions of—

(a) paragraph 2 other than sub-paragraphs (8) and (9), and

(b) the regulations mentioned in paragraph 2.

Joint attorneys

21.—(1) In paragraph 2(5), the reference to the time when the attorney executes the instrument is to be read as a reference to the time when the second or last attorney executes the instrument.

(2) In paragraph 2(6) to (8), the reference to the attorney is to be read as a reference to any attorney under the power.

(3) Paragraph 13 has effect as if the ground of objection to the registration of the instrument specified in sub-paragraph (9)(e) applied to any attorney under the power.

(4) In paragraph 16(2), references to the attorney are to be read as including references to any attorney under the power.

(5) In paragraph 16(4), references to the attorney are to be read as including references to any attorney under the power.

(6) In paragraph 17, references to the attorney are to be read as including references to any attorney under the power.

Joint and several attorneys

22.—(1) In paragraph 2(7), the reference to the bankruptcy of the attorney is to be read as a reference to the bankruptcy of the last remaining attorney under the power; and the bankruptcy of any other attorney under the power causes that person to cease to be an attorney under the power.

(2) In paragraph 2(8), the reference to the suspension of the power is to be read as a reference to its suspension in so far as it relates to the attorney in respect of whom the interim bankruptcy restrictions order has effect.

(3) The restriction upon disclaimer imposed by paragraph 4(6) applies only to those attorneys who have reason to believe that the donor is or is becoming mentally incapable.

[2235]

NOTES

Commencement: 1 October 2007.

PART 8
INTERPRETATION

23.—(1) In this Schedule—

"enduring power" is to be construed in accordance with paragraph 2,

"mentally incapable" or "mental incapacity", except where it refers to revocation at common law, means in relation to any person, that he is incapable by reason of mental disorder ... of managing and administering his property and affairs and "mentally capable" and "mental capacity" are to be construed accordingly,

"notice" means notice in writing, and

"prescribed", except for the purposes of paragraph 2, means prescribed by regulations made for the purposes of this Schedule by the Lord Chancellor.

[(1A) In sub-paragraph (1), "mental disorder" has the same meaning as in the Mental Health Act but disregarding the amendments made to that Act by the Mental Health Act 2007.]

(2) Any question arising under or for the purposes of this Schedule as to what the donor of the power might at any time be expected to do is to be determined by assuming that he had full mental capacity at the time but otherwise by reference to the circumstances existing at that time.

[2236]

NOTES

Commencement: 1 October 2007.

Para 23: in sub-para (1), in definition "“mentally incapable” and “mental incapacity”" words omitted repealed, and sub-para (1A) inserted by the Mental Health Act 2007, ss 1(4), 55, Sch 1, Pt 2, para 23, Sch 11, Pt 1; for transitional provisions and savings see s 53, Sch 10, paras 1, 2(1)–(3), (4)(a), (g) thereto.

SCHEDULE 5
TRANSITIONAL PROVISIONS AND SAVINGS

Section 66(4)

PART 1
REPEAL OF PART 7 OF THE MENTAL HEALTH ACT 1983

Existing receivers

1.—(1) This paragraph applies where, immediately before the commencement day, there is a receiver (“R”) for a person (“P”) appointed under section 99 of the Mental Health Act.

(2) On and after that day—

(a) this Act applies as if R were a deputy appointed for P by the court, but with the functions that R had as receiver immediately before that day, and

(b) a reference in any other enactment to a deputy appointed by the court includes a person appointed as a deputy as a result of paragraph (a).

(3) On any application to it by R, the court may end R’s appointment as P’s deputy.

(4) Where, as a result of section 20(1), R may not make a decision on behalf of P in relation to a relevant matter, R must apply to the court.

(5) If, on the application, the court is satisfied that P is capable of managing his property and affairs in relation to the relevant matter—

(a) it must make an order ending R’s appointment as P’s deputy in relation to that matter, but

(b) it may, in relation to any other matter, exercise in relation to P any of the powers which it has under sections 15 to 19.

(6) If it is not satisfied, the court may exercise in relation to P any of the powers which it has under sections 15 to 19.

(7) R’s appointment as P’s deputy ceases to have effect if P dies.

(8) “Relevant matter” means a matter in relation to which, immediately before the commencement day, R was authorised to act as P’s receiver.

(9) In sub-paragraph (1), the reference to a receiver appointed under section 99 of the Mental Health Act includes a reference to a person who by virtue of Schedule 5 to that Act was deemed to be a receiver appointed under that section.

Orders, appointments etc

2.—(1) Any order or appointment made, direction or authority given or other thing done which has, or by virtue of Schedule 5 to the Mental Health Act was deemed to have, effect under Part 7 of the Act immediately before the commencement day is to continue to have effect despite the repeal of Part 7.

(2) In so far as any such order, appointment, direction, authority or thing could have been made, given or done under sections 15 to 20 if those sections had then been in force—

(a) it is to be treated as made, given or done under those sections, and

(b) the powers of variation and discharge conferred by section 16(7) apply accordingly.

(3) Sub-paragraph (1)—

(a) does not apply to nominations under section 93(1) or (4) of the Mental Health Act, and

(b) as respects receivers, has effect subject to paragraph 1.

(4) This Act does not affect the operation of section 109 of the Mental Health Act (effect and proof of orders etc) in relation to orders made and directions given under Part 7 of that Act.

(5) This paragraph is without prejudice to section 16 of the Interpretation Act 1978 (c 30) (general savings on repeal).

Pending proceedings

3.—(1) Any application for the exercise of a power under Part 7 of the Mental Health Act which is pending immediately before the commencement day is to be treated, in so far as a corresponding power is exercisable under sections 16 to 20, as an application for the exercise of that power.

(2) For the purposes of sub-paragraph (1) an application for the appointment of a receiver is to be treated as an application for the appointment of a deputy.

Appeals

4.—(1) Part 7 of the Mental Health Act and the rules made under it are to continue to apply to any appeal brought by virtue of section 105 of that Act which has not been determined before the commencement day.

(2) If in the case of an appeal brought by virtue of section 105(1) (appeal to nominated judge) the judge nominated under section 93 of the Mental Health Act has begun to hear the appeal, he is to continue to do so but otherwise it is to be heard by a puisne judge of the High Court nominated under section 46.

Fees

5. All fees and other payments which, having become due, have not been paid to the former Court of Protection before the commencement day, are to be paid to the new Court of Protection.

Court records

6.—(1) The records of the former Court of Protection are to be treated, on and after the commencement day, as records of the new Court of Protection and are to be dealt with accordingly under the Public Records Act 1958 (c 51).

(2) On and after the commencement day, the Public Guardian is, for the purpose of exercising any of his functions, to be given such access as he may require to such of the records mentioned in sub-paragraph (1) as relate to the appointment of receivers under section 99 of the Mental Health Act.

Existing charges

7. This Act does not affect the operation in relation to a charge created before the commencement day of—

(a) so much of section 101(6) of the Mental Health Act as precludes a charge created under section 101(5) from conferring a right of sale or foreclosure during the lifetime of the patient, or

(b) section 106(6) of the Mental Health Act (charge created by virtue of section 106(5) not to cause interest to fail etc).

Preservation of interests on disposal of property

8. Paragraph 8(1) of Schedule 2 applies in relation to any disposal of property (within the meaning of that provision) by a person living on 1st November 1960, being a disposal effected under the Lunacy Act 1890 (c 5) as it applies in relation to the disposal of property effected under sections 16 to 20.

Accounts

9. Court of Protection Rules may provide that, in a case where paragraph 1 applies, R is to have a duty to render accounts—

(a) while he is receiver;

(b) after he is discharged.

Interpretation

10. In this Part of this Schedule—

(a) "the commencement day" means the day on which section 66(1)(a) (repeal of Part 7 of the Mental Health Act) comes into force,

(b) "the former Court of Protection" means the office abolished by section 45, and

(c) "the new Court of Protection" means the court established by that section.

[2237]

NOTES

Commencement: 1 October 2007.

PART 2
REPEAL OF THE ENDURING POWERS OF ATTORNEY ACT 1985

Orders, determinations, etc

11.—(1) Any order or determination made, or other thing done, under the 1985 Act which has effect immediately before the commencement day continues to have effect despite the repeal of that Act.

(2) In so far as any such order, determination or thing could have been made or done under Schedule 4 if it had then been in force—

(a) it is to be treated as made or done under that Schedule, and
(b) the powers of variation and discharge exercisable by the court apply accordingly.

(3) Any instrument registered under the 1985 Act is to be treated as having been registered by the Public Guardian under Schedule 4.

(4) This paragraph is without prejudice to section 16 of the Interpretation Act 1978 (c 30) (general savings on repeal).

Pending proceedings

12.—(1) An application for the exercise of a power under the 1985 Act which is pending immediately before the commencement day is to be treated, in so far as a corresponding power is exercisable under Schedule 4, as an application for the exercise of that power.

(2) For the purposes of sub-paragraph (1)—

(a) a pending application under section 4(2) of the 1985 Act for the registration of an instrument is to be treated as an application to the Public Guardian under paragraph 4 of Schedule 4 and any notice given in connection with that application under Schedule 1 to the 1985 Act is to be treated as given under Part 3 of Schedule 4,
(b) a notice of objection to the registration of an instrument is to be treated as a notice of objection under paragraph 13 of Schedule 4, and
(c) pending proceedings under section 5 of the 1985 Act are to be treated as proceedings on an application for the exercise by the court of a power which would become exercisable in relation to an instrument under paragraph 16(2) of Schedule 4 on its registration.

Appeals

13.—(1) The 1985 Act and, so far as relevant, the provisions of Part 7 of the Mental Health Act and the rules made under it as applied by section 10 of the 1985 Act are to continue to have effect in relation to any appeal brought by virtue of section 10(1)(c) of the 1985 Act which has not been determined before the commencement day.

(2) If, in the case of an appeal brought by virtue of section 105(1) of the Mental Health Act as applied by section 10(1)(c) of the 1985 Act (appeal to nominated judge), the judge nominated under section 93 of the Mental Health Act has begun to hear the appeal, he is to continue to do so but otherwise the appeal is to be heard by a puisne judge of the High Court nominated under section 46.

Exercise of powers of donor as trustee

14.—(1) Section 2(8) of the 1985 Act (which prevents a power of attorney under section 25 of the Trustee Act 1925 (c 19) as enacted from being an enduring power) is to continue to apply to any enduring power—

(a) created before 1st March 2000, and
(b) having effect immediately before the commencement day.

(2) Section 3(3) of the 1985 Act (which entitles the donee of an enduring power to exercise the donor's powers as trustee) is to continue to apply to any enduring power to which, as a result of the provision mentioned in sub-paragraph (3), it applies immediately before the commencement day.

(3) The provision is section 4(3)(a) of the Trustee Delegation Act 1999 (c 15) (which provides for section 3(3) of the 1985 Act to cease to apply to an enduring power when its registration is cancelled, if it was registered in response to an application made before 1st March 2001).

(4) Even though section 4 of the 1999 Act is repealed by this Act, that section is to continue to apply in relation to an enduring power—

(a) to which section 3(3) of the 1985 Act applies as a result of sub-paragraph (2), or
(b) to which, immediately before the repeal of section 4 of the 1999 Act, section 1 of that Act applies as a result of section 4 of it.

(5) The reference in section 1(9) of the 1999 Act to section 4(6) of that Act is to be read with sub-paragraphs (2) to (4).

Interpretation

15. In this Part of this Schedule, "the commencement day" means the day on which section 66(1)(b) (repeal of the 1985 Act) comes into force.

[2238]

NOTES

Commencement: 1 October 2007.

(*Schs 6, 7 contain consequential amendments and repeals.*)

DISABILITY DISCRIMINATION ACT 2005

(2005 c 13)

An Act to amend the Disability Discrimination Act 1995; and for connected purposes.

[7 April 2005]

1–9 (*Outside the scope of this work.*)

Other matters

10–13 (*Outside the scope of this work.*)

14 Power to modify or end small dwellings exemptions

(1) The Secretary of State may by order made by statutory instrument amend, or repeal provisions of, sections 23, 24B and 24H of the 1995 Act—

(a) for the purpose of adding to the conditions for entitlement to the exemptions conferred by sections 23, 24B(3) and 24H(3);

(b) for the purpose of making any of the conditions for entitlement to those exemptions more onerous;

(c) for the purpose of making the conditions for entitlement to those exemptions more onerous overall;

(d) for the purpose of otherwise restricting the cases in which any of those exemptions is available; or

(e) for the purpose of removing those exemptions.

(2) The power under subsection (1) includes power to make consequential repeals of provisions of enactments (including future enactments) that amend section 23, 24B or 24H of the 1995 Act.

(3) No order under this section shall be made unless a draft of the statutory instrument containing the order (whether alone or with other provisions) has been laid before, and approved by a resolution of, each House of Parliament.

[2239]

NOTES

Commencement: 4 December 2006.

15–18 (*Outside the scope of this work.*)

Supplementary

19 (*Outside the scope of this work.*)

20 Short title, interpretation, commencement and extent

(1) This Act may be cited as the Disability Discrimination Act 2005.

(2) In this Act "the 1995 Act" means the Disability Discrimination Act 1995 (c 50).

(3) This Act, except the blue badge provisions and this section, comes into force on such day as the Secretary of State may by order appoint.

(4) (*Outside the scope of this work.*)

(5) A person who has power under this section to appoint a day for the coming into force of a provision may by order make in connection with the coming into force of that provision such transitional provision or saving as the person considers necessary or expedient.

(6) An order under this section—

(a) shall be made by statutory instrument, and

(b) may make different provision for different purposes.

(7) This Act does not extend to Northern Ireland, subject to subsection (11).

(8)–(11) (*Outside the scope of this work.*)

[2240]

NOTES

Commencement: 7 April 2005.

Orders: the Disability Discrimination Act 2005 (Commencement No 1) Order 2005, SI 2005/1676; the Disability Discrimination Act 2005 (Commencement No 2) Order 2005, SI 2005/2774; the Disability Discrimination Act 2005 (Commencement No 3) Order 2007, SI 2007/1555; the Disability Discrimination Act 2005 (Commencement No 1) (Wales) Order 2007, SI 2007/3285.

(*Schs 1, 2 contain consequential amendments, repeals and revocations.*)

SERIOUS ORGANISED CRIME AND POLICE ACT 2005

(2005 c 15)

An Act to provide for the establishment and functions of the Serious Organised Crime Agency; to make provision about investigations, prosecutions, offenders and witnesses in criminal proceedings and the protection of persons involved in investigations or proceedings; to provide for the implementation of certain international obligations relating to criminal matters; to amend the Proceeds of Crime Act 2002; to make further provision for combatting crime and disorder, including new provision about powers of arrest and search warrants and about parental compensation orders; to make further provision about the police and policing and persons supporting the police; to make provision for protecting certain organisations from interference with their activities; to make provision about criminal records; to provide for the Private Security Industry Act 2001 to extend to Scotland; and for connected purposes.

[7 April 2005]

1–124 ((*Pts 1–3*) *Outside the scope of this work.*)

PART 4
PUBLIC ORDER AND CONDUCT IN PUBLIC PLACES ETC

125–127 (*Outside the scope of this work.*)

Trespass on designated site

128 Offence of trespassing on designated site

(1) A person commits an offence if he enters, or is on, any [protected] site in England and Wales or Northern Ireland as a trespasser.

[(1A) In this section 'protected site' means—

(a) a nuclear site; or

(b) a designated site.

(1B) In this section 'nuclear site' means—

(a) so much of any premises in respect of which a nuclear site licence (within the meaning of the Nuclear Installations Act 1965) is for the time being in force as lies within the outer perimeter of the protection provided for those premises; and

(b) so much of any other premises of which premises falling within paragraph (a) form a part as lies within that outer perimeter.

(1C) For this purpose—

(a) the outer perimeter of the protection provided for any premises is the line of the outermost fences, walls or other obstacles provided or relied on for protecting those premises from intruders; and

(b) that line shall be determined on the assumption that every gate, door or other barrier across a way through a fence, wall or other obstacle is closed.]

(2) A "designated site" means a site—

(a) specified or described (in any way) in an order made by the Secretary of State, and

(b) designated for the purposes of this section by the order.

(3) The Secretary of State may only designate a site for the purposes of this section if—

(a) it is comprised in Crown land; or

(b) it is comprised in land belonging to Her Majesty in Her private capacity or to the immediate heir to the Throne in his private capacity; or

(c) it appears to the Secretary of State that it is appropriate to designate the site in the interests of national security.

(4) It is a defence for a person charged with an offence under this section to prove that he did not know, and had no reasonable cause to suspect, that the site in relation to which the offence is alleged to have been committed was a [protected] site.

(5) A person guilty of an offence under this section is liable on summary conviction—
(a) to imprisonment for a term not exceeding 51 weeks, or
(b) to a fine not exceeding level 5 on the standard scale,
or to both.

(6) No proceedings for an offence under this section may be instituted against any person—
(a) in England and Wales, except by or with the consent of the Attorney General, or
(b) in Northern Ireland, except by or with the consent of the Attorney General for Northern Ireland.

(7) For the purposes of this section a person who is on any [protected] site as a trespasser does not cease to be a trespasser by virtue of being allowed time to leave the site.

(8) In this section—
(a) "site" means the whole or part of any building or buildings, or any land, or both;
(b) "Crown land" means land in which there is a Crown interest or a Duchy interest.

(9) For this purpose—
"Crown interest" means an interest belonging to Her Majesty in right of the Crown, and
"Duchy interest" means an interest belonging to Her Majesty in right of the Duchy of Lancaster or belonging to the Duchy of Cornwall.

(10) In the application of this section to Northern Ireland, the reference to 51 weeks in subsection (5)(a) is to be read as a reference to 6 months.

[2241]

NOTES
Commencement: 1 July 2005.
Sub-ss (1), (4), (7): words in square brackets substituted by the Terrorism Act 2006, s 12(1), (2).
Sub-ss (1A)–(1C): inserted by the Terrorism Act 2006, s 12(1), (3).
Orders: the Serious Organised Crime and Police Act 2005 (Designated Sites) Order 2005, SI 2005/3447; the Serious Organised Crime and Police Act 2005 (Designated Sites under Section 128) Order 2007, SI 2007/930.

129, 130 (*Outside the scope of this work.*)

131 Designated sites: access

(1) The following provisions do not apply to land in respect of which a designation order is in force—
(a) section 2(1) of the Countryside and Rights of Way Act 2000 (c 37) (rights of public in relation to access land),
(b) Part III of the Countryside (Northern Ireland) Order 1983 (SI 1983/1895 (NI 18)) (access to open country), and
(c) section 1 of the Land Reform (Scotland) Act 2003 (asp 2) (access rights).

(2) The Secretary of State may take such steps as he considers appropriate to inform the public of the effect of any designation order, including, in particular, displaying notices on or near the site to which the order relates.

(3) But the Secretary of State may only—
(a) display any such notice, or
(b) take any other steps under subsection (2),
in or on any building or land, if the appropriate person consents.

(4) The "appropriate person" is—
(a) a person appearing to the Secretary of State to have a sufficient interest in the building or land to consent to the notice being displayed or the steps being taken, or
(b) a person acting on behalf of such a person.

(5) In this section a "designation order" means—
(a) in relation to England and Wales or Northern Ireland, an order under section 128, or
(b) in relation to Scotland, an order under section 129.

[2242]

NOTES
Commencement: 1 July 2005.

132–171 (*Ss 132–144, ss 145–171* (*Pt 5*) *outside the scope of this work.*)

PART I STATUTES

PART 6
FINAL PROVISIONS

172–178 (*Outside the scope of this work.*)

179 Short title and extent

(1) This Act may be cited as the Serious Organised Crime and Police Act 2005.

(2) Subject to the following provisions, this Act extends to England and Wales only.

(3) The following extend also to Scotland—

(a)–(c) (*outside the scope of this work.*)
(d) section 131,
(e) (*outside the scope of this work.*)
(f) sections 172, 173, 176 to 178 and this section,
(g) (*outside the scope of this work.*)

(4) (*Outside the scope of this work.*)

(5) The following extend also to Northern Ireland—

(a)–(c) (*outside the scope of this work.*)
(d) sections 128, 131 and 144,
(e) (*outside the scope of this work.*)
(f) sections 172, 173, 176 to 178 and this section,
(g) (*outside the scope of this work.*)

(6)–(8) (*Outside the scope of this work.*)

(9) So far as they relate to any provision of this Act which extends to any place outside the United Kingdom, sections 172, 173, 177, 178 and this section also extend there.

(10) (*Outside the scope of this work.*)

[2243]

NOTES

Commencement: 7 April 2005.

(*Schs 1–17 outside the scope of this work.*)

CLEAN NEIGHBOURHOODS AND ENVIRONMENT ACT 2005

(2005 c 16)

An Act to amend section 6 of the Crime and Disorder Act 1998; to make provision for the gating of certain minor highways; to make provision in relation to vehicles parked on roads that are exposed for sale or being repaired; to make provision in relation to abandoned vehicles and the removal and disposal of vehicles; to make provision relating to litter and refuse, graffiti, fly-posting and the display of advertisements; to make provision relating to the transportation, collection, disposal and management of waste; to make provision relating to the control of dogs and to amend the law relating to stray dogs; to make provision in relation to noise; to provide for the Commission for Architecture and the Built Environment and for the making of grants relating to the quality of the built environment; to amend the law relating to abandoned shopping and luggage trolleys; to amend the law relating to statutory nuisances; to amend section 78L of the Environmental Protection Act 1990; to amend the law relating to offences under Schedule 1 to the Pollution Prevention and Control Act 1999; and for connected purposes.

[7 April 2005]

1–54 ((*Pts 1–5*) *Outside the scope of this work.*)

PART 6
DOGS

CHAPTER 1
CONTROLS ON DOGS

Dog control orders

55 Power to make dog control orders

(1) A primary or secondary authority may in accordance with this Chapter make an order providing for an offence or offences relating to the control of dogs in respect of any land in its area to which this Chapter applies.

(2) An order under subsection (1) is to be known as a "dog control order".

(3) For the purposes of this Chapter an offence relates to the control of dogs if it relates to one of the following matters—

(a) fouling of land by dogs and the removal of dog faeces;
(b) the keeping of dogs on leads;
(c) the exclusion of dogs from land;
(d) the number of dogs which a person may take on to any land.

(4) An offence provided for in a dog control order must be an offence which is prescribed for the purposes of this section by regulations made by the appropriate person.

(5) Regulations under subsection (4) may in particular—

(a) specify all or part of the wording to be used in a dog control order for the purpose of providing for any offence;
(b) permit a dog control order to specify the times at which, or periods during which, an offence is to apply;
(c) provide for an offence to be defined by reference to failure to comply with the directions of a person of a description specified in the regulations.

(6) A dog control order may specify the land in respect of which it applies specifically or by description.

(7) A dog control order may be revoked or amended by the authority which made it; but this Chapter applies in relation to any amendment of a dog control order as if it were the making of a new order.

[2244]

NOTES

Commencement: 14 March 2006 (in relation to England for the purpose of making regulations); 16 March 2006 (in relation to Wales for certain purposes); 6 April 2006 (in relation to England for remaining purposes); 15 March 2007 (in relation to Wales for remaining purposes).

Regulations: the Dog Control Orders (Prescribed Offences and Penalties, etc) Regulations 2006, SI 2006/1059; the Dog Control Orders (Miscellaneous Provisions) (Wales) Regulations 2007, SI 2007/702.

56 Dog control orders: supplementary

(1) The appropriate person must by regulations prescribe the penalties, or maximum penalties, which may be provided for in a dog control order in relation to any offence.

(2) Regulations under subsection (1) may not in any case permit a dog control order to provide for a penalty other than a fine not exceeding level 3 on the standard scale in relation to any offence.

(3) The appropriate person must by regulations prescribe such other requirements relating to the content and form of a dog control order as the appropriate person thinks fit.

(4) The appropriate person must by regulations prescribe the procedure to be followed by a primary or secondary authority before and after making a dog control order.

(5) Regulations under subsection (4) must in particular include provision as to—

(a) consultation to be undertaken before a dog control order is made;
(b) the publicising of a dog control order after it has been made.

[2245]

NOTES

Commencement: 14 March 2006 (in relation to England); 16 March 2006 (in relation to Wales for certain purposes); 27 October 2006 (in relation to Wales for remaining purposes).

Regulations: the Dog Control Orders (Procedures) Regulations 2006, SI 2006/798; the Dog Control Orders (Prescribed Offences and Penalties, etc) Regulations 2006, SI 2006/1059; the Dog Control Orders (Miscellaneous Provisions) (Wales) Regulations 2007, SI 2007/702.

57 Land to which Chapter 1 applies

(1) Subject to this section, this Chapter applies to any land which is open to the air and to which the public are entitled or permitted to have access (with or without payment).

(2) For the purposes of this section, any land which is covered is to be treated as land which is "open to the air" if it is open to the air on at least one side.

(3) The appropriate person may by order designate land as land to which this Chapter does not apply (generally or for such purposes as may be specified in the order).

(4) Land may be designated under subsection (3) specifically or by description.

(5) Where a private Act confers powers on a person other than a primary or secondary authority for the regulation of any land, that person may, by notice in writing given to the primary and secondary authorities in whose area the land is situated, exclude the application of this Chapter to that land.

[2246]

NOTES

Commencement: 14 March 2006 (in relation to England for the purpose of making orders); 16 March 2006 (in relation to Wales for certain purposes); 6 April 2006 (in relation to England for remaining purposes); 15 March 2007 (in relation to Wales for remaining purposes).

Orders: the Controls on Dogs (Non-application to Designated Land) Order 2006, SI 2006/779; the Controls on Dogs (Non-application to Designated Land) (Wales) Order 2007, SI 2007/701.

58 Primary and secondary authorities

(1) Each of the following is a "primary authority" for the purposes of this Chapter—

(a) a district council in England;
(b) a county council in England for an area for which there is no district council;
(c) a London borough council;
(d) the Common Council of the City of London;
(e) the Council of the Isles of Scilly;
(f) a county or county borough council in Wales.

(2) Each of the following is a "secondary authority" for the purposes of this Chapter—

(a) a parish council in England;
(b) a community council in Wales.

(3) The appropriate person may by order designate any person or body exercising functions under an enactment as a secondary authority for the purposes of this Chapter in respect of an area specified in the order.

[2247]

NOTES

Commencement: 16 March 2006 (in relation to Wales for certain purposes); 6 April 2006 (in relation to England); 15 March 2007 (in relation to Wales for remaining purposes).

59–62 (*Outside the scope of this work.*)

Supplementary

63 Overlapping powers

(1) Where a primary authority makes a dog control order providing for an offence relating to a matter specified in any of paragraphs (a) to (d) of section 55(3) as respects any land—

(a) a secondary authority may not make a dog control order providing for any offence which relates to the matter specified in that paragraph as respects that land;
(b) any dog control order previously made by a secondary authority providing for any offence which relates to the matter specified in that paragraph shall, to the extent that it so provides, cease to have effect.

(2) Where the area of an authority designated as a secondary authority under section 58(3) is to any extent the same as that of a parish or community council, subsection (1) applies in relation to orders made by the designated authority and that council as if the council were a primary authority.

[2248]

NOTES

Commencement: 6 April 2006 (in relation to England); 15 March 2007 (in relation to Wales).

64 Byelaws

(1) Where, apart from this subsection, a primary or secondary authority has at any time power to make a byelaw in relation to any matter specified in any of paragraphs (a) to (d) of section 55(3) as respects any land, it may not make such a byelaw if at that time it has power under this Chapter to make a dog control order as respects that land in relation to the matter specified in that paragraph.

(2) Subsection (1) does not affect any byelaw which the authority had power to make at the time it was made.

(3) Where a dog control order is made in relation to any matter specified in any of paragraphs (a) to (d) of section 55(3) as respects any land, any byelaw previously made by a primary or secondary authority which has the effect of making a person guilty of any offence in relation to the matter specified in that paragraph as respects that land shall cease to have that effect.

(4) Where any act or omission would, apart from this subsection, constitute an offence under a dog control order and any byelaw, the act or omission shall not constitute an offence under the byelaw.

[2249]

NOTES

Commencement: 6 April 2006 (in relation to England); 15 March 2007 (in relation to Wales).

65 (*Repeals the Dogs (Fouling of Land) Act 1996.*)

General

66 "Appropriate person"

In this Chapter, "appropriate person" means—

(a) the Secretary of State, in relation to England;

(b) the National Assembly for Wales, in relation to Wales.

[2250]

NOTES

Commencement: 14 March 2006 (in relation to England); 27 October 2006 (in relation to Wales).

67 Regulations and orders

(1) Any power conferred by this Chapter on the Secretary of State or National Assembly for Wales to make regulations or an order includes—

(a) power to make different provision for different purposes (including different provision for different authorities or different descriptions of authority);

(b) power to make consequential, supplementary, incidental and transitional provision and savings.

(2) Any power conferred by this Chapter on the Secretary of State or National Assembly for Wales to make regulations or an order is exercisable by statutory instrument.

(3) The Secretary of State may not make a statutory instrument containing regulations under section 55(4) or 56(1) unless a draft of the instrument has been laid before, and approved by a resolution of, each House of Parliament.

(4) A statutory instrument containing—

(a) regulations made by the Secretary of State under this Chapter to which subsection (3) does not apply, or

(b) an order made by the Secretary of State under this Chapter,

is subject to annulment in pursuance of a resolution of either House of Parliament.

[2251]–[2252]

NOTES

Commencement: 14 March 2006 (in relation to England); 16 March 2006 (in relation to Wales for certain purposes); 27 October 2006 (in relation to Wales for remaining purposes).

68–95 (*S 68 (Ch 2), ss 69–95 (Pts 7, 8) outside the scope of this work.*)

PART 9
MISCELLANEOUS

96–103 (*Outside the scope of this work.*)

104 (*Amends the Environmental Protection Act 1990, s 78L at* **[1412]**.)

105 (*Outside the scope of this work.*)

PART 10
GENERAL

106–109 (*Outside the scope of this work.*)

110 Extent

(1) This Act extends to England and Wales only, subject as follows.

(2), (3) (*Outside the scope of this work.*)

[2253]

NOTES

Commencement: 7 April 2005.

111 Short title

This Act may be cited as the Clean Neighbourhoods and Environment Act 2005.

[2254]

NOTES

Commencement: 7 April 2005.

(Schs 1–3 outside the scope of this work; Schs 4, 5 contain consequential amendments and repeals which, in so far as relevant to this work, have been incorporated at the appropriate place.)

EQUALITY ACT 2006

(2006 c 3)

An Act to make provision for the establishment of the Commission for Equality and Human Rights; to dissolve the Equal Opportunities Commission, the Commission for Racial Equality and the Disability Rights Commission; to make provision about discrimination on grounds of religion or belief; to enable provision to be made about discrimination on grounds of sexual orientation; to impose duties relating to sex discrimination on persons performing public functions; to amend the Disability Discrimination Act 1995; and for connected purposes.

[16 February 2006]

PART 1
THE COMMISSION FOR EQUALITY AND HUMAN RIGHTS

1–32 (*Outside the scope of this work.*)

Interpretation

33, 34 (*Outside the scope of this work.*)

35 General

In this Part—

"act" includes deliberate omission,
"groups" has the meaning given by section 10,
"the Commission" means the Commission for Equality and Human Rights,
"disabled person" has the meaning given by section 8,
"human rights" has the meaning given by section 9,
["the Minister" means the Lord Privy Seal;]
"race" includes colour, nationality, ethnic origin and national origin,
"religion or belief" has the same meaning as in Part 2 (as defined by section 44), and
"sexual orientation" means an individual's sexual orientation towards—

- (a) persons of the same sex as him or her,
- (b) persons of the opposite sex, or
- (c) both.

[2255]

NOTES

Commencement: 18 April 2006.
Definition "the Minister" inserted by SI 2007/2914, art 8, Schedule, para 15(1).

36–43 (*Outside the scope of this work.*)

PART 2
DISCRIMINATION ON GROUNDS OF RELIGION OR BELIEF

Key concepts

44 Religion and belief

In this Part—

- (a) "religion" means any religion,
- (b) "belief" means any religious or philosophical belief,
- (c) a reference to religion includes a reference to lack of religion, and
- (d) a reference to belief includes a reference to lack of belief.

[2256]

NOTES
Commencement: 30 April 2007.

45 Discrimination

(1) A person ("A") discriminates against another ("B") for the purposes of this Part if on grounds of the religion or belief of B or of any other person except A (whether or not it is also A's religion or belief) A treats B less favourably than he treats or would treat others (in cases where there is no material difference in the relevant circumstances).

(2) In subsection (1) a reference to a person's religion or belief includes a reference to a religion or belief to which he is thought to belong or subscribe.

(3) A person ("A") discriminates against another ("B") for the purposes of this Part if A applies to B a provision, criterion or practice—

- (a) which he applies or would apply equally to persons not of B's religion or belief,
- (b) which puts persons of B's religion or belief at a disadvantage compared to some or all others (where there is no material difference in the relevant circumstances),
- (c) which puts B at a disadvantage compared to some or all persons who are not of his religion or belief (where there is no material difference in the relevant circumstances), and
- (d) which A cannot reasonably justify by reference to matters other than B's religion or belief.

(4) A person ("A") discriminates against another ("B") if A treats B less favourably than he treats or would treat another and does so by reason of the fact that, or by reason of A's knowledge or suspicion that, B—

- (a) has brought or intended to bring, or intends to bring, proceedings under this Part,
- (b) has given or intended to give, or intends to give, evidence in proceedings under this Part,
- (c) has provided or intended to provide, or intends to provide, information in connection with proceedings under this Part,
- (d) has done or intended to do, or intends to do, any other thing under or in connection with this Part, or
- (e) has alleged or intended to allege, or intends to allege, that a person contravened this Part.

(5) Subsection (4) does not apply where A's treatment of B relates to B's making or intending to make, not in good faith, a false allegation.

[2257]

NOTES
Commencement: 30 April 2007.

Prohibited discrimination

46 Goods, facilities and services

(1) It is unlawful for a person ("A") concerned with the provision to the public or a section of the public of goods, facilities or services to discriminate against a person ("B") who seeks to obtain or use those goods, facilities or services—

- (a) by refusing to provide B with goods, facilities or services,
- (b) by refusing to provide B with goods, facilities or services of a quality which is the same as or similar to the quality of goods, facilities or services that A normally provides to—
  - (i) the public, or
  - (ii) a section of the public to which B belongs,
- (c) by refusing to provide B with goods, facilities or services in a manner which is the same as or similar to that in which A normally provides goods, facilities or services to—
  - (i) the public, or
  - (ii) a section of the public to which B belongs, or
- (d) by refusing to provide B with goods, facilities or services on terms which are the same as or similar to the terms on which A normally provides goods, facilities or services to—
  - (i) the public, or
  - (ii) a section of the public to which B belongs.

(2) Subsection (1) applies, in particular, to—

- (a) access to and use of a place which the public are permitted to enter,
- (b) accommodation in a hotel, boarding house or similar establishment,
- (c) facilities by way of banking or insurance or for grants, loans, credit or finance,
- (d) facilities for entertainment, recreation or refreshment,
- (e) facilities for transport or travel, and
- (f) the services of a profession or trade.

(3) Where a skill is commonly exercised in different ways in relation to or for the purposes of different religions or beliefs, a person who normally exercises it in relation to or for the purpose of a religion or belief does not contravene subsection (1) by—

(a) insisting on exercising the skill in the way in which he exercises it in relation to or for the purposes of that religion or belief, or

(b) if he reasonably considers it impracticable to exercise the skill in that way in relation to or for the purposes of another religion or belief, refusing to exercise it in relation to or for the purposes of that other religion or belief.

(4) Subsection (1)—

(a) does not apply in relation to the provision of goods, facilities or services by a person exercising a public function, and

(b) does not apply to discrimination in relation to the provision of goods, facilities or services if discrimination in relation to that provision—

(i) is unlawful by virtue of another provision of this Part or by virtue of a provision of the Employment Equality (Religion or Belief) Regulations 2003 (SI 2003/1660), or

(ii) would be unlawful by virtue of another provision of this Part or of those regulations but for an express exception.

(5) For the purposes of subsection (1) it is immaterial whether or not a person charges for the provision of goods, facilities or services.

[2258]

NOTES

Commencement: 30 April 2007.

47 Premises

(1) It is unlawful for a person to discriminate against another—

(a) in the terms on which he offers to dispose of premises to him,

(b) by refusing to dispose of premises to him, or

(c) in connection with a list of persons requiring premises.

(2) It is unlawful for a person managing premises to discriminate against an occupier—

(a) in the manner in which he provides access to a benefit or facility,

(b) by refusing access to a benefit or facility,

(c) by evicting him, or

(d) by subjecting him to another detriment.

(3) It is unlawful for a person to discriminate against another by refusing permission for the disposal of premises to him.

(4) This section applies only to premises in Great Britain.

[2259]

NOTES

Commencement: 30 April 2007.

48 Section 47: exceptions

(1) Section 47 shall not apply to anything done in relation to the disposal or management of part of premises by a person ("the landlord") if—

(a) the landlord or a near relative resides, and intends to continue to reside, in another part of the premises,

(b) the premises include parts (other than storage areas and means of access) shared by residents of the premises, and

(c) the premises are not normally sufficient to accommodate—

(i) in the case of premises to be occupied by households, more than two households in addition to that of the landlord or his near relative, or

(ii) in the case of premises to be occupied by individuals, more than six individuals in addition to the landlord or his near relative.

(2) In subsection (1) "near relative" means—

(a) spouse or civil partner,

(b) parent or grandparent,

(c) child or grandchild (whether or not legitimate),

(d) the spouse or civil partner of a child or grandchild,

(e) brother or sister (whether of full blood or half-blood), and

(f) any of the relationships listed in paragraphs (b) to (e) above that arises through marriage, civil partnership or adoption.

(3) Section 47(1) and (3) shall not apply to the disposal of premises by a person who—

(a) owns an estate or interest in the premises,
(b) occupies the whole of the premises,
(c) does not use the services of an estate agent for the purposes of the disposal, and
(d) does not arrange for the publication of an advertisement for the purposes of the disposal.

[2260]

NOTES

Commencement: 30 April 2007.

49–55 (*Outside the scope of this work.*)

General exceptions

56 Statutory requirements

[(1)] Nothing in this Part shall make it unlawful to do anything which is necessary, or in so far as it is necessary, for the purpose of complying with—

(a) an Act of Parliament,
(b) an Act of the Scottish Parliament,
[(ba) a Measure of the National Assembly for Wales,
(bb) an Act of the National Assembly for Wales,]
(c) legislation made or to be made—
  (i) by a Minister of the Crown,
  (ii) by Order in Council,
  (iii) by the Scottish Ministers or a member of the Scottish Executive,
  (iv) by the National Assembly for Wales [constituted by the Government of Wales Act 1998], …
  [(iva) by the Welsh Ministers, the First Minister for Wales or the Counsel General to the Welsh Assembly Government, or]
  (v) by or by virtue of a Measure of the General Synod of the Church of England, …
(d) a condition or requirement imposed by a Minister of the Crown by virtue of anything listed in [paragraphs (a) to (c), or]
[(e) a condition or requirement imposed after the end of the initial period by the Welsh Ministers, the First Minister for Wales or the Counsel General to the Welsh Assembly Government by virtue of anything listed in paragraphs (a) to (c)].

[(2) In subsection (1)(e) "the initial period" has the same meaning as in the Government of Wales Act 2006 (see section 161(5) of that Act).]

[2261]

NOTES

Commencement: 30 April 2007.

Sub-s (1): numbered as such, paras (ba), (bb), (c)(iva), (e) and words in square brackets in para (c)(iv) inserted, words omitted from para (c)(iv), (v) repealed, and words in square brackets in para (d) substituted by SI 2007/1388, art 3, Sch 1, paras 112, 117(1)–(3).

Sub-s (2): inserted by SI 2007/1388, art 3, Sch 1, paras 112, 117(1), (4).

Functions of the Secretary of State transferred to the Lord Privy Seal, by the Transfer of Functions (Equality) Order 2007, SI 2007/2914, art 3(1), (2)(f).

57 Organisations relating to religion or belief

(1) This section applies to an organisation the purpose of which is—

(a) to practice a religion or belief,
(b) to advance a religion or belief,
(c) to teach the practice or principles of a religion or belief,
(d) to enable persons of a religion or belief to receive any benefit, or to engage in any activity, within the framework of that religion or belief, or
(e) to improve relations, or maintain good relations, between persons of different religions or beliefs.

(2) But this section does not apply to an organisation whose sole or main purpose is commercial.

(3) Nothing in this Part shall make it unlawful for an organisation to which this section applies or anyone acting on behalf of or under the auspices of an organisation to which this section applies—

(a) to restrict membership of the organisation,
(b) to restrict participation in activities undertaken by the organisation or on its behalf or under its auspices,
(c) to restrict the provision of goods, facilities or services in the course of activities undertaken by the organisation or on its behalf or under its auspices, or
(d) to restrict the use or disposal of premises owned or controlled by the organisation.

(4) Nothing in this Part shall make it unlawful for a minister—

(a) to restrict participation in activities carried on in the performance of his functions in connection with or in respect of an organisation to which this section relates, or

(b) to restrict the provision of goods, facilities or services in the course of activities carried on in the performance of his functions in connection with or in respect of an organisation to which this section relates.

(5) But subsections (3) and (4) permit a restriction only if imposed—

(a) by reason of or on the grounds of the purpose of the organisation, or

(b) in order to avoid causing offence, on grounds of the religion or belief to which the organisation relates, to persons of that religion or belief.

(6) In subsection (4) the reference to a minister is a reference to a minister of religion, or other person, who—

(a) performs functions in connection with a religion or belief to which an organisation, to which this section applies, relates, and

(b) holds an office or appointment in, or is accredited, approved or recognised for purposes of, an organisation to which this section applies.

[2262]

NOTES

Commencement: 30 April 2007.

Functions of the Secretary of State transferred to the Lord Privy Seal, by the Transfer of Functions (Equality) Order 2007, SI 2007/2914, art 3(1), (2)(f).

58 Charities relating to religion or belief

(1) Nothing in this Part shall make it unlawful for a person to provide benefits only to persons of a particular religion or belief, if—

(a) he acts in pursuance of a charitable instrument, and

(b) the restriction of benefits to persons of that religion or belief is imposed by reason of or on the grounds of the provisions of the charitable instrument.

(2) Nothing in this Part shall make it unlawful for the [Charity Commission] or the holder of the Office of the Scottish Charity Regulator to exercise a function in relation to a charity in a manner which appears to [the Commission] or to the holder to be expedient in the interests of the charity, having regard to the provisions of the charitable instrument.

(3) In this section "charitable instrument"—

(a) means an instrument establishing or governing a charity, and

(b) includes a charitable instrument made before the commencement of this section.

[2263]

NOTES

Commencement: 30 April 2007.

Sub-s (2): words in square brackets substituted by the Charities Act 2006, s 75(1), Sch 8, paras 212(1), (2).

59 Faith schools, &c

(1) Nothing in this Part shall make it unlawful for an educational institution established or conducted for the purpose of providing education relating to, or within the framework of, a specified religion or belief—

(a) to restrict the provision of goods, facilities or services, or

(b) to restrict the use or disposal of premises.

(2) But subsection (1) permits a restriction only if imposed—

(a) by reason of or on the grounds of the purpose of the institution, or

(b) in order to avoid causing offence, on grounds of the religion or belief to which the institution relates, to persons connected with the institution.

(3) In this Part a reference to the provision of facilities or services shall not, in so far as it applies to an educational institution, include a reference to educational facilities or educational services provided to students of the institution.

[2264]

NOTES

Commencement: 30 April 2007.

60 Membership requirement

(1) Nothing in this Part shall make it unlawful for a charity to require members, or persons wishing to become members, to make a statement which asserts or implies membership or acceptance of a religion or belief.

(2) Subsection (1) shall apply to the imposition of a requirement by a charity only if—

(a) the charity, or an organisation of which the charity is part, first imposed a requirement of the kind specified in subsection (1) before 18th May 2005, and
(b) the charity or organisation has not ceased since that date to impose a requirement of that kind.

[2265]

NOTES
Commencement: 30 April 2007.

61 Education, training and welfare

Nothing in this Part shall make it unlawful to do anything by way of—
(a) meeting special needs for education, training or welfare of persons of a religion or belief, or
(b) providing ancillary benefits in connection with meeting the needs mentioned in paragraph (a).

[2266]

NOTES
Commencement: 30 April 2007.

62 Care within family

Nothing in this Part shall make it unlawful for a person to take into his home, and treat in the same manner as a member of his family, a person who requires a special degree of care and attention (whether by reason of being a child or an elderly person or otherwise).

[2267]

NOTES
Commencement: 30 April 2007.

63 National security

Nothing in this Part shall make unlawful anything which is done for, and justified by, the purpose of safeguarding national security.

[2268]

NOTES
Commencement: 30 April 2007.

64 Amendment of exceptions

(1) The [Minister] may by order amend this Part so as to—
(a) create an exception to the prohibition under section 52(1), or,
(b) vary an exception to a prohibition under this Part.

(2) Before making an order under subsection (1) the [Minister] shall consult the Commission for Equality and Human Rights.

(3) An order under subsection (1)—
(a) may include transitional, incidental or consequential provision (including provision amending an enactment (including an enactment in or under an Act of the Scottish Parliament)),
(b) may make provision generally or only for specified cases or circumstances,
(c) may make different provision for different cases or circumstances,
(d) shall be made by statutory instrument, and
(e) may not be made unless a draft has been laid before and approved by resolution of each House of Parliament.

[2269]

NOTES
Commencement: 30 April 2007.
Sub-ss (1), (2): words in square brackets substituted by SI 2007/2914, art 8, Schedule, para 16(l).
Functions of the Secretary of State transferred to the Lord Privy Seal, by the Transfer of Functions (Equality) Order 2007, SI 2007/2914, art 3(1), (2)(f).

65–80 (*Outside the scope of this work.*)

PART 3
DISCRIMINATION ON GROUNDS OF SEXUAL ORIENTATION

81 Regulations

(1) The [Minister] may by regulations make provision about discrimination or harassment on grounds of sexual orientation.

(2) In subsection (1) "sexual orientation" has the meaning given by section 35.

(3) The regulations may, in particular—
- (a) make provision of a kind similar to Part 2 of this Act;
- (b) define discrimination;
- (c) define harassment;
- (d) make provision for enforcement (which may, in particular, include provision—
  - (i) creating a criminal offence of a kind similar to, and with the same maximum penalties as, an offence created by an enactment relating to discrimination or equality;
  - (ii) about validity and revision of contracts;
  - (iii) about discriminatory advertisements;
  - (iv) about instructing or causing discrimination or harassment);
- (e) provide for exceptions (whether or not of a kind similar to those provided for by Part 2 of this Act or any other enactment relating to discrimination or equality);
- (f) make provision which applies generally or only in specified cases or circumstances;
- (g) make different provision for different cases or circumstances;
- (h) include incidental or consequential provision (which may include provision amending an enactment);
- (i) include transitional provision.

(4) The regulations—
- (a) shall be made by statutory instrument, and
- (b) may not be made unless a draft has been laid before and approved by resolution of each House of Parliament.

(5) In subsection (3)(h) "enactment" includes an enactment in or under an Act of the Scottish Parliament.

[(6) In this section "the Minister" means the Lord Privy Seal.]

[2270]

NOTES

Commencement: 18 April 2006.

Sub-s (1): word in square brackets substituted by SI 2007/2914, art 8, Schedule, para 16(n).

Sub-s (6): inserted by SI 2007/2914, art 8, Schedule, para 15(3).

Functions of the Secretary of State transferred to the Lord Privy Seal, by the Transfer of Functions (Equality) Order 2007, SI 2007/2914, art 3(1), (2)(f).

Regulations: the Equality Act (Sexual Orientation) Regulations 2007, SI 2007/1263.

82–90 (*s 82, ss 83–90* (*Pt 4*) *outside the scope of this work.*)

PART 5
GENERAL

91, 92 (*Outside the scope of this work.*)

93 Commencement

(1) The preceding provisions of this Act, except for sections 41, 42 and 86, shall come into force in accordance with provision made by the Secretary of State by order.

(2) An order under subsection (1)—
- (a) shall be made by statutory instrument,
- (b) may make provision generally or only for a specified purpose,
- (c) may make different provision for different purposes, and
- (d) may include transitional provisions and savings.

[2271]

NOTES

Commencement: 16 February 2006.

Orders: the Equality Act 2006 (Commencement No 1) Order 2006, SI 2006/1082; the Equality Act 2006 (Commencement No 2) Order 2007, SI 2007/1092; the Equality Act 2006 (Commencement No 3 and Savings) Order 2007, SI 2007/2603.

94 Extent

(1) This Act extends only to—
(a) England and Wales, and
(b) Scotland.

(2) But—
(a) section 82 extends only to Northern Ireland, and
(b) except as provided by subsection (3), an amendment of an enactment by this Act shall have the same extent as the enactment amended (or as the relevant part of the enactment amended).

(3) (*Outside the scope of this work.*)

[2272]

NOTES

Commencement: 16 February 2006.

95 Short title

This Act may be cited as the Equality Act 2006.

[2273]

NOTES

Commencement: 16 February 2006.

(*Schs 1, 2 outside the scope of this work; Schs 3, 4 contain consequential amendments and repeals which, in so far as relevant to this work, have been incorporated at the appropriate place.*)

COMMONS ACT 2006

(2006 c 26)

An Act to make provision about common land and town or village greens; and for connected purposes.

[19 July 2006]

PART 1 REGISTRATION

Introductory

1 Registers of common land and greens

Each commons registration authority shall continue to keep—
(a) a register known as a register of common land; and
(b) a register known as a register of town or village greens.

[2274]

NOTES

Commencement: 1 October 2008 (in relation to England in relation to the pilot areas); to be appointed (otherwise).

2 Purpose of registers

(1) The purpose of a register of common land is—
(a) to register land as common land; and
(b) to register rights of common exercisable over land registered as common land.

(2) The purpose of a register of town or village greens is—
(a) to register land as a town or village green; and
(b) to register rights of common exercisable over land registered as a town or village green.

[2275]

NOTES

Commencement: 1 October 2008 (in relation to England in relation to the pilot areas); to be appointed (otherwise).

3 Content of registers

(1) The land registered as common land in a register of common land is, subject to this Part, to be—

(a) the land so registered in it at the commencement of this section; and
(b) such other land as may be so registered in it under this Part.

(2) The land registered as a town or village green in a register of town or village greens is, subject to this Part, to be—
(a) the land so registered in it at the commencement of this section; and
(b) such other land as may be so registered in it under this Part.

(3) The rights of common registered in a register of common land or town or village greens are, subject to this Part, to be—
(a) the rights registered in it at the commencement of this section; and
(b) such other rights as may be so registered in it under this Part.

(4) The following information is to be registered in a register of common land or town or village greens in respect of a right of common registered in it—
(a) the nature of the right;
(b) if the right is attached to any land, the land to which it is attached;
(c) if the right is not so attached, the owner of the right.

(5) Regulations may—
(a) require or permit other information to be included in a register of common land or town or village greens;
(b) make provision as to the form in which any information is to be presented in such a register.

(6) Except as provided under this Part or any other enactment—
(a) no land registered as common land or as a town or village green is to be removed from the register in which it is so registered;
(b) no right of common registered in a register of common land or town or village greens is to be removed from that register.

(7) No right of common over land to which this Part applies is to be registered in the register of title.

[2276]

NOTES

Commencement: 12 August 2007 (sub-s (5), in relation to Wales for certain purposes); 1 October 2008 (in relation to England in relation to the pilot areas); to be appointed (otherwise).

Regulations: the Commons Registration (England) Regulations 2008, SI 2008/1961.

4 Commons registration authorities

(1) The following are commons registration authorities—
(a) a county council in England;
(b) a district council in England for an area without a county council;
(c) a London borough council; and
(d) a county or county borough council in Wales.

(2) For the purposes of this Part, the commons registration authority in relation to any land is the authority in whose area the land is situated.

(3) Where any land falls within the area of two or more commons registration authorities, the authorities may by agreement provide for one of them to be the commons registration authority in relation to the whole of the land.

[2277]

NOTES

Commencement: 6 April 2007 (in relation to England); 6 September 2007 (in relation to Wales).

5 Land to which Part 1 applies

(1) This Part applies to all land in England and Wales, subject as follows.

(2) This Part does not apply to—
(a) the New Forest; or
(b) Epping Forest.

(3) This Part shall not be taken to apply to the Forest of Dean.

(4) If any question arises under this Part whether any land is part of the forests mentioned in this section it is to be referred to and decided by the appropriate national authority.

[2278]

NOTES

Commencement: 6 April 2007 (in relation to England); 6 September 2007 (in relation to Wales).

Registration of rights of common

6 Creation

(1) A right of common cannot at any time after the commencement of this section be created over land to which this Part applies by virtue of prescription.

(2) A right of common cannot at any time after the commencement of this section be created in any other way over land to which this Part applies except—

(a) as specified in subsection (3); or

(b) pursuant to any other enactment.

(3) A right of common may be created over land to which this Part applies by way of express grant if—

(a) the land is not registered as a town or village green; and

(b) the right is attached to land.

(4) The creation of a right of common in accordance with subsection (3) only has effect if it complies with such requirements as to form and content as regulations may provide.

(5) The creation of a right of common in accordance with subsection (3) does not operate at law until on an application under this section—

(a) the right is registered in a register of common land; and

(b) if the right is created over land not registered as common land, the land is registered in a register of common land.

(6) An application under this section to register the creation of a right of common consisting of a right to graze any animal is to be refused if in the opinion of the commons registration authority the land over which it is created would be unable to sustain the exercise of—

(a) that right; and

(b) if the land is already registered as common land, any other rights of common registered as exercisable over the land.

[2279]

NOTES

Commencement: 12 August 2007 (sub-s (4), in relation to Wales for certain purposes); 1 October 2008 (in relation to England in relation to the pilot areas); to be appointed (otherwise).

7 Variation

(1) For the purposes of this section a right of common is varied if by virtue of any disposition—

(a) the right becomes exercisable over new land to which this Part applies instead of all or part of the land over which it was exercisable;

(b) the right becomes exercisable over new land to which this Part applies in addition to the land over which it is already exercisable;

(c) there is any other alteration in what can be done by virtue of the right.

(2) A right of common which is registered in a register of common land or town or village greens cannot at any time after the commencement of this section be varied so as to become exercisable over new land if that land is at the time registered as a town or village green.

(3) A right of common which is registered in a register of town or village greens cannot at any time after the commencement of this section be varied so as to extend what can be done by virtue of the right.

(4) The variation of a right of common which is registered in a register of common land or town or village greens—

(a) only has effect if it complies with such requirements as to form and content as regulations may provide; and

(b) does not operate at law until, on an application under this section, the register is amended so as to record the variation.

(5) An application under this section to record a variation of a right of common consisting of a right to graze any animal is to be refused if in the opinion of the commons registration authority the land over which the right is or is to be exercisable would, in consequence of the variation, be unable to sustain the exercise of—

(a) that right; and

(b) if the land is already registered as common land, any other rights of common registered as exercisable over the land.

[2280]

NOTES

Commencement: 12 August 2007 (sub-s (4), in relation to Wales for certain purposes); 1 October 2008 (in relation to England in relation to the pilot areas); to be appointed (otherwise).

8 Apportionment

(1) Regulations may make provision as to the amendments to be made to a register of common land or town or village greens where a right of common which is registered in a register of common land or town or village greens as attached to any land is apportioned by virtue of any disposition affecting the land.

(2) Regulations under subsection (1) may provide that a register is only to be amended when—

(a) a disposition relating to an apportioned right itself falls to be registered under this Part; or

(b) the register falls to be amended under section 11.

(3) Where at any time—

(a) a right of common which is registered in a register of common land or town or village greens as attached to any land has been apportioned by virtue of any disposition affecting the land, and

(b) no amendments have been made under subsection (1) in respect of the apportionment of that right,

the rights of common subsisting as a result of the apportionment shall be regarded as rights which are registered in that register as attached to the land to which they attach as a result of the apportionment.

[2281]

NOTES

Commencement: 12 August 2007 (sub-ss (1), (2) in relation to Wales for certain purposes); 1 October 2008 (in relation to England in relation to the pilot areas); to be appointed (otherwise).

Regulations: the Commons Registration (England) Regulations 2008, SI 2008/1961.

9 Severance

(1) This section applies to a right of common which—

(a) is registered in a register of common land or town or village greens as attached to any land; and

(b) would, apart from this section, be capable of being severed from that land.

(2) A right of common to which this section applies is not at any time on or after the day on which this section comes into force capable of being severed from the land to which it is attached, except—

(a) where the severance is authorised by or under Schedule 1; or

(b) where the severance is authorised by or under any other Act.

(3) Where any instrument made on or after the day on which this section comes into force would effect a disposition in relation to a right of common to which this section applies in contravention of subsection (2), the instrument is void to the extent that it would effect such a disposition.

(4) Where by virtue of any instrument made on or after the day on which this section comes into force—

(a) a disposition takes effect in relation to land to which a right of common to which this section applies is attached, and

(b) the disposition would have the effect of contravening subsection (2),

the disposition also has effect in relation to the right notwithstanding anything in the instrument to the contrary.

(5) Where by virtue of any instrument made on or after the day on which this section comes into force a right of common to which this section applies falls to be apportioned between different parts of the land to which it is attached, the instrument is void to the extent that it purports to apportion the right otherwise than rateably.

(6) Nothing in this section affects any instrument made before, or made pursuant to a contract made in writing before, the day on which this section comes into force.

(7) This section and Schedule 1 shall be deemed to have come into force on 28 June 2005 (and an order under paragraph 2 of that Schedule may have effect as from that date).

[2282]

NOTES

Commencement: 28 June 2005 (see sub-s (7)).

Orders: the Commons (Severance of Rights) (England) Order 2006, SI 2006/2145; the Commons (Severance of Rights) (Wales) Order 2007, SI 2007/583.

10 Attachment

(1) This section applies to any right of common which is registered in a register of common land or town or village greens but is not registered as attached to any land.

(2) The owner of the right may apply to the commons registration authority for the right to be registered in that register as attached to any land, provided that—

(a) he is entitled to occupy the land; or

(b) the person entitled to occupy the land has consented to the application.

[2283]

NOTES

Commencement: 1 October 2008 (in relation to England in relation to the pilot areas); to be appointed (otherwise).

11 Re-allocation of attached rights

(1) Where—

(a) a right of common is registered in a register of common land or town or village greens as attached to any land, and

(b) subsection (2), (3) or (4) applies in relation to part of the land ("the relevant part"),

the owner of the land may apply to the commons registration authority for the register to be amended so as to secure that the right does not attach to the relevant part.

(2) This subsection applies where the relevant part is not used for agricultural purposes.

(3) This subsection applies where planning permission has been granted for use of the relevant part for purposes which are not agricultural purposes.

(4) This subsection applies where—

(a) an order authorising the compulsory purchase of the relevant part by any authority has been made in accordance with the Acquisition of Land Act 1981 (c 67) (and, if the order requires to be confirmed under Part 2 of that Act, has been so confirmed);

(b) the relevant part has not vested in the authority; and

(c) the relevant part is required for use other than use for agricultural purposes.

(5) Regulations may for the purposes of subsections (2) to (4) make provision as to what is or is not to be regarded as use of land for agricultural purposes.

(6) Regulations may provide that an application under this section is not to be granted without the consent of any person specified in the regulations.

[2284]

NOTES

Commencement: 12 August 2007 (sub-ss (5), (6) in relation to Wales for certain purposes); 1 October 2008 (in relation to England in relation to the pilot areas); to be appointed (otherwise).

Regulations: the Commons Registration (England) Regulations 2008, SI 2008/1961.

12 Transfer of rights in gross

The transfer of a right of common which is registered in a register of common land or town or village greens but is not registered as attached to any land—

(a) only has effect if it complies with such requirements as to form and content as regulations may provide; and

(b) does not operate at law until, on an application under this section, the transferee is registered in the register as the owner of the right.

[2285]

NOTES

Commencement: 12 August 2007 (para (a) in relation to Wales for certain purposes); 1 October 2008 (in relation to England in relation to the pilot areas); to be appointed (otherwise).

13 Surrender and extinguishment

(1) The surrender to any extent of a right of common which is registered in a register of common land or town or village greens—

(a) only has effect if it complies with such requirements as to form and content as regulations may provide; and

(b) does not operate at law until, on an application under this section, the right is removed from the register.

(2) The reference in subsection (1) to a surrender of a right of common does not include a disposition having the effect referred to in section 7(1)(a).

(3) A right of common which is registered in a register of common land or town or village greens cannot be extinguished by operation of common law.

[2286]

NOTES

Commencement: 12 August 2007 (sub-s (1)(a) in relation to Wales for certain purposes); 1 October 2008 (in relation to England in relation to the pilot areas); to be appointed (otherwise).

Registration, deregistration and exchange of land

14 Statutory dispositions

(1) Regulations may make provision as to the amendment of a register of common land or town or village greens where by virtue of any relevant instrument—

(a) a disposition is made in relation to land registered in it as common land or as a town or village green; or

(b) a disposition is made in relation to a right of common registered in it.

(2) Regulations may provide that, where—

(a) by virtue of any relevant instrument a disposition is made in relation to land registered as common land or as a town or village green,

(b) by virtue of regulations under subsection (1) the land ceases to be so registered, and

(c) in connection with the disposition other land is given in exchange,

the land given in exchange is to be registered as common land or as a town or village green.

(3) In this section, "relevant instrument" means—

(a) any order, deed or other instrument made under or pursuant to the Acquisition of Land Act 1981 (c 67);

(b) a conveyance made for the purposes of section 13 of the New Parishes Measure 1943 (No 1);

(c) any other instrument made under or pursuant to any enactment.

(4) Regulations under this section may require the making of an application to a commons registration authority for amendment of a register of common land or town or village greens.

(5) Regulations under this section may provide that a relevant instrument, so far as relating to land registered as common land or as a town or village green or to any right of common, is not to operate at law until any requirement for which they provide is complied with.

[2287]

NOTES

Commencement: 12 August 2007 (in relation to Wales for certain purposes); 1 October 2008 (in relation to England in relation to the pilot areas); to be appointed (otherwise).

Regulations: the Commons Registration (England) Regulations 2008, SI 2008/1961.

15 Registration of greens

(1) Any person may apply to the commons registration authority to register land to which this Part applies as a town or village green in a case where subsection (2), (3) or (4) applies.

(2) This subsection applies where—

(a) a significant number of the inhabitants of any locality, or of any neighbourhood within a locality, have indulged as of right in lawful sports and pastimes on the land for a period of at least 20 years; and

(b) they continue to do so at the time of the application.

(3) This subsection applies where—

(a) a significant number of the inhabitants of any locality, or of any neighbourhood within a locality, indulged as of right in lawful sports and pastimes on the land for a period of at least 20 years;

(b) they ceased to do so before the time of the application but after the commencement of this section; and

(c) the application is made within the period of two years beginning with the cessation referred to in paragraph (b).

(4) This subsection applies (subject to subsection (5)) where—

(a) a significant number of the inhabitants of any locality, or of any neighbourhood within a locality, indulged as of right in lawful sports and pastimes on the land for a period of at least 20 years;

(b) they ceased to do so before the commencement of this section; and

(c) the application is made within the period of five years beginning with the cessation referred to in paragraph (b).

(5) Subsection (4) does not apply in relation to any land where—

(a) planning permission was granted before 23 June 2006 in respect of the land;

(b) construction works were commenced before that date in accordance with that planning permission on the land or any other land in respect of which the permission was granted; and

(c) the land—
   (i) has by reason of any works carried out in accordance with that planning permission become permanently unusable by members of the public for the purposes of lawful sports and pastimes; or
   (ii) will by reason of any works proposed to be carried out in accordance with that planning permission become permanently unusable by members of the public for those purposes.

(6) In determining the period of 20 years referred to in subsections (2)(a), (3)(a) and (4)(a), there is to be disregarded any period during which access to the land was prohibited to members of the public by reason of any enactment.

(7) For the purposes of subsection (2)(b) in a case where the condition in subsection (2)(a) is satisfied—
(a) where persons indulge as of right in lawful sports and pastimes immediately before access to the land is prohibited as specified in subsection (6), those persons are to be regarded as continuing so to indulge; and
(b) where permission is granted in respect of use of the land for the purposes of lawful sports and pastimes, the permission is to be disregarded in determining whether persons continue to indulge in lawful sports and pastimes on the land "as of right".

(8) The owner of any land may apply to the commons registration authority to register the land as a town or village green.

(9) An application under subsection (8) may only be made with the consent of any relevant leaseholder of, and the proprietor of any relevant charge over, the land.

(10) In subsection (9)—
"relevant charge" means—
(a) in relation to land which is registered in the register of title, a registered charge within the meaning of the Land Registration Act 2002 (c 9);
(b) in relation to land which is not so registered—
   (i) a charge registered under the Land Charges Act 1972 (c 61); or
   (ii) a legal mortgage, within the meaning of the Law of Property Act 1925 (c 20), which is not registered under the Land Charges Act 1972;

"relevant leaseholder" means a leaseholder under a lease for a term of more than seven years from the date on which the lease was granted.

[2288]

NOTES

Commencement: 6 April 2007 (in relation to England, subject to transitional provisions in SI 2007/456, art 4(1)); 6 September 2007 (in relation to Wales, subject to transitional provisions in SI 2007/2386, art 4(1)).

16 Deregistration and exchange: applications

(1) The owner of any land registered as common land or as a town or village green may apply to the appropriate national authority for the land ("the release land") to cease to be so registered.

(2) If the release land is more than 200 square metres in area, the application must include a proposal under subsection (3).

(3) A proposal under this subsection is a proposal that land specified in the application ("replacement land") be registered as common land or as a town or village green in place of the release land.

(4) If the release land is not more than 200 square metres in area, the application may include a proposal under subsection (3).

(5) Where the application includes a proposal under subsection (3)—
(a) the replacement land must be land to which this Part applies;
(b) the replacement land must not already be registered as common land or as a town or village green; and
(c) if the owner of the release land does not own the replacement land, the owner of the replacement land must join in the application.

(6) In determining the application, the appropriate national authority shall have regard to—
(a) the interests of persons having rights in relation to, or occupying, the release land (and in particular persons exercising rights of common over it);
(b) the interests of the neighbourhood;
(c) the public interest;
(d) any other matter considered to be relevant.

(7) The appropriate national authority shall in a case where—
(a) the release land is not more than 200 square metres in area, and
(b) the application does not include a proposal under subsection (3),

have particular regard under subsection (6) to the extent to which the absence of such a proposal is prejudicial to the interests specified in paragraphs (a) to (c) of that subsection.

(8) The reference in subsection (6)(c) to the public interest includes the public interest in—

(a) nature conservation;
(b) the conservation of the landscape;
(c) the protection of public rights of access to any area of land; and
(d) the protection of archaeological remains and features of historic interest.

(9) An application under this section may only be made with the consent of any relevant leaseholder of, and the proprietor of any relevant charge over—

(a) the release land;
(b) any replacement land.

(10) In subsection (9) "relevant charge" and "relevant leaseholder" have the meanings given by section 15(10).

[2289]

NOTES

Commencement: 1 October 2007 (in relation to England, subject to transitional provisions and savings in SI 2007/2584, art 3); to be appointed (in relation to Wales).

17 Deregistration and exchange: orders

(1) Where the appropriate national authority grants an application under section 16 it must make an order requiring the commons registration authority to remove the release land from its register of common land or town or village greens.

(2) Where the application included a proposal to register replacement land, the order shall also require the commons registration authority—

(a) to register the replacement land as common land or as a town or village green in place of the release land; and
(b) to register as exercisable over the replacement land any rights of common which, immediately before the relevant date, are registered as exercisable over the release land.

(3) A commons registration authority must take such other steps on receiving an order under this section as regulations may require.

(4) Where immediately before the relevant date any rights of common are registered as exercisable over the release land, those rights are on that date extinguished in relation to that land.

(5) Where immediately before the relevant date any rights are exercisable over the release land by virtue of its being, or being part of, a town or village green—

(a) those rights are extinguished on that date in respect of the release land; and
(b) where any replacement land is registered in its place, those rights shall become exercisable as from that date over the replacement land instead.

(6) Where immediately before the relevant date the release land was registered as common land and any relevant provision applied in relation to it—

(a) the provision shall on that date cease to apply to the release land; and
(b) where any replacement land is registered in its place, the provision shall on that date apply to the replacement land instead.

(7) An order under this section may contain—

(a) provision disapplying the effect of subsection (5)(b) or (6)(b) in relation to any replacement land;
(b) supplementary provision as to the effect in relation to any replacement land of—
    (i) any rights exercisable over the release land by virtue of its being, or being part of, a town or village green;
    (ii) any relevant provision;
(c) supplementary provision as to the effect in relation to the release land or any replacement land of any local or personal Act.

(8) In subsections (6) and (7) "relevant provision" means a provision contained in, or made under—

(a) section 193 of the Law of Property Act 1925 (c 20);
(b) a scheme under the Metropolitan Commons Act 1866 (c 122);
(c) an Act under the Commons Act 1876 (c 56) confirming a provisional order of the Inclosure Commissioners;
(d) a scheme under the Commons Act 1899 (c 30);
(e) section 1 of the Commons Act 1908 (c 44).

(9) In this section, "relevant date" means the date on which the commons registration authority amends its register as required under subsections (1) and (2).

(10) Regulations may make provision for the publication of an order under this section.

[2290]

NOTES

Commencement: 12 August 2007 (sub-ss (3), (10) in relation to Wales for certain purposes); 1 October 2007 (in relation to England, subject to transitional provisions and savings in SI 2007/2584, art 3); to be appointed (in relation to Wales otherwise).

Regulations: the Deregistration and Exchange Orders (Interim Arrangements) (England) Regulations 2007, SI 2007/2585 (revoked for certain purposes); the Deregistration and Exchange of Common Land and Greens (Procedure) (England) Regulations 2007, SI 2007/2589; the Commons Registration (England) Regulations 2008, SI 2008/1961.

Conclusiveness and correction of the registers

18 Conclusiveness

(1) This section applies to land registered as common land, or as a town or village green, which is registered as being subject to a right of common.

(2) If the land would not otherwise have been subject to that right, it shall be deemed to have become subject to that right, as specified in the register, upon its registration.

(3) If the right is registered as attached to any land, the right shall, if it would not otherwise have attached to that land, be deemed to have become so attached upon registration of its attachment.

(4) If the right is not registered as attached to any land, the person registered as the owner of the right shall, if he would not otherwise have been its owner, be deemed to have become its owner upon his registration.

(5) Nothing in subsection (2) affects any constraint on the exercise of a right of common where the constraint does not appear in the register.

(6) It is immaterial whether the registration referred to in subsection (2), (3) or (4) occurred before or after the commencement of this section.

[2291]

NOTES

Commencement: 1 October 2008 (in relation to England in relation to the pilot areas); to be appointed (otherwise).

19 Correction

(1) A commons registration authority may amend its register of common land or town or village greens for any purpose referred to in subsection (2).

(2) Those purposes are—
- (a) correcting a mistake made by the commons registration authority in making or amending an entry in the register;
- (b) correcting any other mistake, where the amendment would not affect—
  - (i) the extent of any land registered as common land or as a town or village green; or
  - (ii) what can be done by virtue of a right of common;
- (c) removing a duplicate entry from the register;
- (d) updating the details of any name or address referred to in an entry;
- (e) updating any entry in the register relating to land registered as common land or as a town or village green to take account of accretion or diluvion.

(3) References in this section to a mistake include—
- (a) a mistaken omission, and
- (b) an unclear or ambiguous description,

and it is immaterial for the purposes of this section whether a mistake was made before or after the commencement of this section.

(4) An amendment may be made by a commons registration authority—
- (a) on its own initiative; or
- (b) on the application of any person.

(5) A mistake in a register may not be corrected under this section if the authority considers that, by reason of reliance reasonably placed on the register by any person or for any other reason, it would in all the circumstances be unfair to do so.

(6) Regulations may make further provision as to the criteria to be applied in determining an application or proposal under this section.

(7) The High Court may order a commons registration authority to amend its register of common land or town or village greens if the High Court is satisfied that—

(a) any entry in the register, or any information in an entry, was at any time included in the register as a result of fraud; and
(b) it would be just to amend the register.

[2292]

NOTES

Commencement: 12 August 2007 (sub-s (6), in relation to Wales for certain purposes); 1 October 2008 (in relation to England in relation to the pilot areas); to be appointed (otherwise).

Information etc

20 Inspection

(1) Any person may inspect and make copies of, or of any part of—
(a) a register of common land or town or village greens;
(b) any document kept by a commons registration authority which is referred to in such a register;
(c) any other document kept by a commons registration authority which relates to an application made at any time in relation to such a register.

(2) The right in subsection (1) is subject to regulations which may, in particular—
(a) provide for exceptions to the right;
(b) impose conditions on its exercise.

(3) Conditions under subsection (2)(b) may include conditions requiring the payment of a fee (which may be a fee determined by a commons registration authority).

[2293]

NOTES

Commencement: 12 August 2007 (sub-ss (2), (3), in relation to Wales for certain purposes); 1 October 2008 (in relation to England in relation to the pilot areas); to be appointed (otherwise).
Regulations: the Commons Registration (England) Regulations 2008, SI 2008/1961.

21 Official copies

(1) An official copy of, or of any part of—
(a) a register of common land or town or village greens,
(b) any document kept by a commons registration authority which is referred to in such a register, or
(c) any other document kept by a commons registration authority which relates to an application made at any time in relation to such a register,

is admissible in evidence to the same extent as the original.

(2) Regulations may make provision for the issue of official copies and may in particular make provision about—
(a) the form of official copies;
(b) who may issue official copies;
(c) applications for official copies;
(d) the conditions to be met by applicants for official copies.

(3) Conditions under subsection (2)(d) may include conditions requiring the payment of a fee (which may be a fee determined by a commons registration authority).

[2294]

NOTES

Commencement: 12 August 2007 (sub-ss (2), (3), in relation to Wales for certain purposes); 1 October 2008 (in relation to England in relation to the pilot areas); to be appointed (otherwise).
Regulations: the Commons Registration (England) Regulations 2008, SI 2008/1961.

Transitory and transitional provision

22 Non-registration or mistaken registration under the 1965 Act

Schedule 2 (non-registration or mistaken registration under the Commons Registration Act 1965 (c 64)) has effect.

[2295]

NOTES

Commencement: 12 August 2007 (in relation to Wales for certain purposes); 1 October 2008 (in relation to England in relation to the pilot areas); to be appointed (otherwise).

23 Transitional

(1) Schedule 3 (transitional provision) has effect.

(2) Nothing in Schedule 3 affects the power to make transitional provision and savings in an order under section 56; and an order under that section may modify any provision made by that Schedule.

[2296]

NOTES

Commencement: 1 October 2006 (in relation to England for certain purposes, subject to transitional provisions and savings in SI 2006/2504, art 3(2)); 12 August 2007 (in relation to Wales for certain purposes); 6 September 2007 (in relation to Wales for certain purposes); 1 October 2008 (in relation to England in relation to the pilot areas); to be appointed (otherwise).

Supplementary

24 Applications etc

(1) Regulations may make provision as to the making and determination of any application for the amendment of a register of common land or town or village greens under or for the purposes of this Part.

(2) Regulations under subsection (1) may in particular make provision as to—

(a) the steps to be taken by a person before making an application;
(b) the form of an application;
(c) the information or evidence to be supplied with an application;
(d) the fee payable on an application (which may be a fee determined by the person to whom the application is made);
(e) the persons to be notified of an application;
(f) the publication of an application;
(g) the making of objections to an application;
(h) the persons who must be consulted, or whose advice must be sought, in relation to an application;
(i) the holding of an inquiry before determination of an application;
(j) the evidence to be taken into account in making a determination and the weight to be given to any evidence;
(k) the persons to be notified of any determination;
(l) the publication of a determination;
(m) the amendments to be made by a commons registration authority to a register of common land or town or village greens pursuant to a determination;
(n) the time at which any such amendments are to be regarded as having been made.

(3) In the case of an application made for the purposes of any of—

(a) sections 6 to 8, 12 and 13,
(b) paragraph 1 or 3 of Schedule 1,
(c) paragraph 2 or 3 of Schedule 2, and
(d) paragraph 2(5)(a) of Schedule 3,

regulations under subsection (1) may make provision as to the persons entitled to make the application.

(4) An application made for the purposes of any of—

(a) sections 6, 7, 10, 11, 12, 13 and 15, and
(b) paragraph 1 or 3 of Schedule 1,

shall, subject to any provision made by or under this Part, be granted.

(5) Regulations under subsection (1) may include provision for the appropriate national authority to appoint a person to discharge any or all of its functions in relation to an application made to it under section 16.

(6) Regulations may make provision as to the making and determination of any proposal by a commons registration authority to amend a register on its own initiative pursuant to section 19, Schedule 2 or paragraph 2(5)(b) of Schedule 3.

(7) Regulations under subsection (6) may in particular make provision as to—

(a) the persons to be notified of a proposal;
(b) the publication of a proposal (and the information or evidence to be published with a proposal);
(c) the making of objections to a proposal;
(d) the persons who must be consulted, or whose advice must be sought, in relation to a proposal;
(e) the holding of an inquiry before determination of a proposal;
(f) the evidence to be taken into account in making a determination and the weight to be given to any evidence;
(g) the persons to be notified of any determination;
(h) the publication of a determination;

(i) the amendments to be made by a commons registration authority to a register of common land or town or village greens pursuant to a determination.

(8) Regulations under this section may include provision for—

(a) the appropriate national authority to appoint persons as eligible to discharge functions of a commons registration authority in relation to applications made to, or proposals made by, the commons registration authority; and

(b) the appointment of one or more of those persons to discharge functions of the commons registration authority in the case of any description of application or proposal.

(9) Regulations under this section may provide for the Church Commissioners to act with respect to any land or rights belonging to an ecclesiastical benefice of the Church of England which is vacant.

[2297]

NOTES

Commencement: 6 April 2007 (in relation to England, subject to transitional provisions in SI 2007/456, art 4(2)); 12 August 2007 (in relation to Wales for certain purposes, subject to transitional provisions in SI 2007/2386, art 4(2)); 6 September 2007 (in relation to Wales for remaining purposes).

Regulations: the Commons (Registration of Town or Village Greens) (Interim Arrangements) (England) Regulations 2007, SI 2007/457 (revoked for certain purposes); the Deregistration and Exchange Orders (Interim Arrangements) (England) Regulations 2007, SI 2007/2585 (revoked for certain purposes); the Deregistration and Exchange of Common Land and Greens (Procedure) (England) Regulations 2007, SI 2007/2589; the Commons Registration (England) Regulations 2008, SI 2008/1961.

25 Electronic registers

(1) Regulations may require or permit the whole or any part of a register kept under this Part to be kept in electronic form.

(2) Regulations under subsection (1) may include provision as to—

(a) requirements to be complied with in relation to the recording of information in electronic form;

(b) the certification of information recorded in electronic form (including the status of print-outs of such information).

(3) Regulations under subsection (1) may also include provision as to the process of converting a register, or part of a register, into electronic form.

(4) The provision referred to in subsection (3) includes in particular provision—

(a) as to the publicity to be given to such a conversion;

(b) requiring a provisional electronic version to be made available for inspection and comment;

(c) as to the holding of an inquiry in relation to any question arising as a result of the conversion.

[2298]

NOTES

Commencement: 12 August 2007 (in relation to Wales for certain purposes); to be appointed (otherwise).

PART 2
MANAGEMENT

Commons councils

26 Establishment

(1) The appropriate national authority may, for any area or areas of land to which this section applies, establish a body corporate to carry out functions conferred under this Part.

(2) This section applies to any land that—

(a) is registered as common land; or

(b) is registered as a town or village green and is subject to rights of common.

(3) A body corporate established under this section is to be known as a "commons council".

(4) A commons council is to be established by order.

(5) An order establishing a commons council must specify—

(a) the name of the council;

(b) the area or areas of land for which the council is established.

[2299]

NOTES

Commencement: to be appointed.

27 Procedure for establishment

(1) This section applies where the appropriate national authority proposes to make an order under section 26 establishing a commons council.

(2) The appropriate national authority must—

(a) publish a draft of the proposed order in such manner as it thinks fit; and
(b) invite representations about it.

(3) The appropriate national authority may cause a local inquiry to be held.

(4) The appropriate national authority may not make the proposed order unless, having regard to—

(a) any representations received pursuant to subsection (2)(b), and
(b) the result of any local inquiry held under subsection (3),

it is satisfied that there is substantial support for the making of the order.

(5) For the purposes of subsection (4) the appropriate national authority must have particular regard to representations received pursuant to subsection (2)(b) from—

(a) persons having rights (other than rights of common) in relation to, or occupying, land specified in the draft order;
(b) persons who are entitled to exercise rights of common (and in particular persons exercising rights of common) over any such land; and
(c) persons with functions under an enactment which relate to the maintenance or management of any such land.

[2300]

NOTES

Commencement: to be appointed.

Status and constitution of commons councils

28 Status

(1) A commons council is not to be regarded as the servant or agent of the Crown or as enjoying any status, immunity or privilege of the Crown.

(2) The property of a commons council is not to be regarded as the property of, or as property held on behalf of, the Crown.

(3) A commons council is not to be regarded as an authority to which section 28G of the Wildlife and Countryside Act 1981 (c 69) applies.

[2301]

NOTES

Commencement: to be appointed.

29 Constitution

(1) The appropriate national authority must by regulations prescribe standard terms as to the constitution and administration of commons councils (in this Part, the "standard constitution").

(2) The terms of the standard constitution apply to every commons council, subject as follows.

(3) An order under section 26 may also make provision as to the constitution and administration of a commons council.

(4) Provision which may be made under subsection (3) includes in particular—

(a) provision supplementary to any term of the standard constitution;
(b) provision disapplying any such term;
(c) provision replacing any such term.

(5) Where in relation to a commons council—

(a) provision is made under subsection (3) that is inconsistent with any term of the standard constitution, and
(b) any such term has not been expressly disapplied under that subsection,

the provision made under subsection (3) prevails, to the extent of the inconsistency, over the term of the standard constitution.

(6) Terms of the standard constitution prescribed by regulations under subsection (1) may be amended by further regulations under that subsection; and this section applies in relation to such terms as amended as it applies in relation to the terms as first prescribed.

[2302]

NOTES

Commencement: 12 August 2007 (sub-ss (1), (6) in relation to Wales for certain purposes); to be appointed (otherwise).

30 Constitution: supplementary

(1) This section applies in relation to terms as to the constitution and administration of a commons council contained in—

(a) the standard constitution; or

(b) an order under section 26.

(2) The terms may in particular include terms as to—

(a) the membership of the council;

(b) participation in the council by persons other than members;

(c) the proceedings of the council;

(d) the keeping and publication of accounts, annual reports and other information relating to the council.

(3) The terms referred to in subsection (2)(a) include in particular terms as to—

(a) the appointment of members (by election or otherwise);

(b) the term for which members are appointed;

(c) co-option of members;

(d) the conduct of members;

(e) resignation and disqualification of members;

(f) termination and renewal of membership;

(g) payment of allowances to members.

(4) The terms referred to in subsection (2)(b) include in particular terms as to—

(a) entitlement to elect members;

(b) entitlement to attend meetings.

(5) The terms referred to in subsection (2)(c) include in particular terms as to—

(a) the frequency of meetings;

(b) voting procedures at meetings;

(c) committees and sub-committees.

(6) The terms referred to in subsection (2)(d) include in particular terms as to—

(a) the appointment of auditors;

(b) the preparation and publication of accounts;

(c) the preparation and publication of annual reports.

(7) Subject to any terms made of the kind referred to in subsection (2)(c), a commons council may regulate its own proceedings.

[2303]

NOTES

Commencement: to be appointed.

Functions of commons councils

31 Functions

(1) An order under section 26 is to confer on a commons council functions relating to any one or more of the following—

(a) the management of agricultural activities on the land for which the council is established;

(b) the management of vegetation on the land;

(c) the management of rights of common on the land.

(2) The functions conferred on a commons council under subsection (1) must be those the appropriate national authority considers appropriate in the case of that council.

(3) The functions which may be conferred on a commons council under subsection (1) include in particular functions of—

(a) making rules relating to agricultural activities, the management of vegetation and the exercise of rights of common on the land for which the council is established;

(b) making rules relating to the leasing or licensing of rights of common;

(c) preparing and maintaining a register of grazing;

(d) establishing and maintaining boundaries;

(e) removing unlawful boundaries and other encroachments;

(f) removing animals unlawfully permitted to graze.

(4) Rules made by virtue of subsection (3)(a) may have the effect of—

(a) limiting or imposing conditions on the exercise of rights of common over, or the exercise of rights to use the surplus of, the land for which the council is established;

(b) requiring the provision of information to the commons council in relation to the exercise of those rights.

(5) In exercising a function conferred under subsection (3)(f), a commons council may—

(a) dispose of any animal it removes; and

(b) recover from the owner of the animal the costs that it may reasonably incur in removing and disposing of it.

(6) A commons council must discharge its functions having regard to—

(a) any guidance given by the appropriate national authority; and
(b) the public interest in relation to the land for which it is established.

(7) The reference in subsection (6)(b) to the public interest includes the public interest in—

(a) nature conservation;
(b) the conservation of the landscape;
(c) the protection of public rights of access to any area of land; and
(d) the protection of archaeological remains and features of historic interest.

[2304]

NOTES

Commencement: 12 August 2007 (sub-s (6)(a), in relation to Wales for certain purposes); to be appointed (otherwise).

32 Ancillary powers

(1) A commons council has the power to do anything which it considers will facilitate, or is conducive or incidental to, the carrying out of its functions.

(2) The power conferred by subsection (1) includes power to—

(a) enter into agreements;
(b) prepare and adopt management plans;
(c) raise money (including by applying for funds from any source);
(d) acquire or dispose of land;
(e) employ staff.

(3) The power of a commons council to raise money as specified in subsection (2)(c) includes power to require the payment of fees in connection with—

(a) the exercise of rights of common over, or the exercise of rights to use the surplus of, the land for which the council is established, and
(b) participation in the council,

and any such fees owed to the council may be recovered as a debt due to it.

[2305]

NOTES

Commencement: to be appointed.

33 Consent

(1) Subject to subsections (2) and (3), nothing in this Part authorises a commons council to do anything on the land for which it is established without the consent of a person with an interest in the land, where that person's consent would otherwise be required.

(2) A commons council does not need the consent of a person who has a right of common over the land for which it is established in order to do anything on the land.

(3) A commons council does not need the consent of any other person with an interest in the land for which it is established in order to do anything on the land where what is proposed to be done could be done without that person's consent by any person who has a right of common over the land.

(4) Where a commons council wishes to obtain the consent of any person with an interest in the land for which the council is established in respect of anything it proposes to do on the land, it may serve a notice on him.

(5) A notice under subsection (4) must specify—

(a) what the commons council proposes to do;
(b) the time within which the person on whom it is served may object (which may not be less than 28 days after service of the notice); and
(c) the manner in which he may object.

(6) If the person on whom a notice under subsection (4) is served does not object within the time and in the manner specified in the notice, he is to be regarded as having given his consent in relation to the proposal specified in the notice.

(7) Where a commons council proposes to serve a notice on a person under subsection (4) but is unable after reasonable enquiry to ascertain his name or proper address—

(a) the council may post the notice on the land; and
(b) the notice is to be treated as having been served on the person at the time the notice is posted.

(8) An order under section 26 may make further provision as to the form and service of notices under subsection (4).

(9) For the purposes of this section, a person with an interest in any land is a person who—
- (a) owns the land; or
- (b) is entitled to exercise any right over the land.

[2306]

NOTES

Commencement: to be appointed.

34 Enforcement of rules

(1) A person who breaches a rule to which subsection (2) applies is guilty of an offence.

(2) This subsection applies to a rule which—
- (a) is made with the consent of the appropriate national authority pursuant to a function of making rules conferred on a commons council under section 31; and
- (b) specifies that a person who contravenes it is guilty of an offence under this section.

(3) A person guilty of an offence under subsection (1) is liable on summary conviction to—
- (a) a fine not exceeding level 4 on the standard scale; and
- (b) in the case of a continuing offence, to a further fine not exceeding one half of level 1 on the standard scale for each day during which the offence continues after conviction.

(4) A commons council may bring proceedings in relation to an offence under subsection (1) in respect of breach of any rule made by it to which subsection (2) applies.

(5) A commons council may apply to a county court for an order to secure compliance with any rule that it has made pursuant to a function of making rules conferred on it under section 31.

(6) But a commons council may only make an application under subsection (5) for the purpose of securing compliance with a rule to which subsection (2) applies if it is of the opinion that proceedings for an offence under subsection (1) would provide an ineffectual remedy against the person who has failed to comply with the rule.

(7) On an application under subsection (5) the court may make such an order as it thinks fit.

[2307]

NOTES

Commencement: to be appointed.

35 Rules: supplementary

(1) Any power to make rules conferred on a commons council under section 31 includes power to vary or revoke the rules made by the council.

(2) An order under section 26 conferring a power to make rules may provide for the procedure to be followed in the exercise of the power (and may in particular require the consent of the appropriate national authority to be obtained before rules are made).

(3) The appropriate national authority may by direction revoke any rule made by a commons council.

(4) A direction under subsection (3) must set out the reason why the rule is being revoked.

(5) Before revoking any rule under subsection (3) the appropriate national authority must consult—
- (a) the commons council; and
- (b) any other person it thinks appropriate.

[2308]

NOTES

Commencement: to be appointed.

Commons councils: supplementary

36 Consequential provision

(1) The appropriate national authority may by order under section 26 make any provision specified in subsection (2) if it appears to the authority desirable to do so in consequence of functions conferred on a commons council in relation to any land.

(2) The provision referred to in subsection (1) is provision to—
- (a) vary or abolish the jurisdiction so far as relating to the land of any court of a description referred to in Part 1 of Schedule 4 to the Administration of Justice Act 1977 (c 38) (certain ancient courts);

(b) vary or revoke any regulations or arrangement made under the Commons Act 1908 (c 44);
(c) vary or revoke any scheme made under the Commons Act 1899 (c 30), or any arrangement arising under such a scheme;
(d) vary or revoke any Act made under the Commons Act 1876 (c 56) confirming a provisional order of the Inclosure Commissioners or any arrangement arising under such an Act;
(e) vary or revoke any local or personal Act, or any scheme or arrangement under such an Act, which relates to the management or maintenance of, or the exercise of rights of common over, the land.

(3) The appropriate national authority may not under subsection (1) make provision specified in subsection (2)(c) to (e) to the extent that to do so would have the effect of abolishing or restricting a right of access of whatever nature exercisable by members of the public generally or by any section of the public.

[2309]

NOTES

Commencement: to be appointed.

37 Variation and revocation of establishment orders

(1) The appropriate national authority may by order under section 26 revoke a previous order under that section establishing a commons council only if it is satisfied that—
(a) the council has ceased to operate;
(b) the council is failing to discharge its functions in an effective manner; or
(c) the council is, in discharging its functions, failing to have sufficient regard to the public interest as required by section 31.

(2) An order under section 26 revoking a previous order under that section may include—
(a) provision for the transfer of rights, property and liabilities of the commons council;
(b) provision amending any enactment previously amended under section 36 in relation to the council.

(3) Section 27 applies to an order under section 26 varying or revoking a previous order under that section as it applies to an order under that section establishing a commons council (but as if the references in section 27 to land specified in the order were to land affected by the variation or revocation).

[2310]

NOTES

Commencement: to be appointed.

PART 3
WORKS

38 Prohibition on works without consent

(1) A person may not, except with the consent of the appropriate national authority, carry out any restricted works on land to which this section applies.

(2) In subsection (1) "restricted works" are—
(a) works which have the effect of preventing or impeding access to or over any land to which this section applies;
(b) works for the resurfacing of land.

(3) The reference to works in subsection (2)(a) includes in particular—
(a) the erection of fencing;
(b) the construction of buildings and other structures;
(c) the digging of ditches and trenches and the building of embankments.

(4) For the purposes of subsection (2)(b) works are for the resurfacing of land if they consist of the laying of concrete, tarmacadam, coated roadstone or similar material on the land (but not if they consist only of the repair of an existing surface of the land made of such material).

(5) This section applies to—
(a) any land registered as common land;
(b) land not so registered which is—
  (i) regulated by an Act made under the Commons Act 1876 (c 56) confirming a provisional order of the Inclosure Commissioners; or
  (ii) subject to a scheme under the Metropolitan Commons Act 1866 (c 122) or the Commons Act 1899 (c 30);
(c) land not falling within paragraph (a) or (b) which is in the New Forest and is subject to rights of common.

(6) The prohibition in subsection (1) does not apply to—

(a) works on any land where those works, or works of a description which includes those works, are carried out under a power conferred in relation to that particular land by or under any enactment;

(b) works on any land where the works are carried out under a power conferred by or under any enactment applying to common land;

(c) works authorised under a scheme under the Metropolitan Commons Act 1866 or the Commons Act 1899 without any requirement for any person to consent to the works;

(d) works for the installation of electronic communications apparatus for the purposes of an electronic communications code network.

(7) In subsection (6)(a) the reference to an enactment does not include Part 2 of this Act.

(8) For the purposes of subsection (6)(b), an enactment applies to common land if it is expressed to apply (generally) to—

(a) registered common land;

(b) common land; or

(c) any common or commons, commonable land, land subject to inclosure under any enactment or other land of a similar description.

(9) Subject to the following provisions of this Part, consent given to works under subsection (1) of this section constitutes consent for the purposes of that subsection only.

[2311]

NOTES

Commencement: 1 October 2007 (in relation to England, subject to transitional provisions and savings in SI 2007/2584, art 3); to be appointed (otherwise).

See further, in relation to the disapplication of this section, in respect of the carrying out on land registered as common land of any works of a specified description and by a specified person for the purposes of the Works on Common Land (Exemptions) (England) Order 2007: the Works on Common Land (Exemptions) (England) Order 2007, SI 2007/2587, arts 2–4, 5(2), Sch 1.

39 Consent: general

(1) In determining an application for consent under subsection (1) of section 38 in relation to works on land to which that section applies, the appropriate national authority shall have regard to—

(a) the interests of persons having rights in relation to, or occupying, the land (and in particular persons exercising rights of common over it);

(b) the interests of the neighbourhood;

(c) the public interest;

(d) any other matter considered to be relevant.

(2) The reference in subsection (1)(c) to the public interest includes the public interest in—

(a) nature conservation;

(b) the conservation of the landscape;

(c) the protection of public rights of access to any area of land; and

(d) the protection of archaeological remains and features of historic interest.

(3) Consent may be given under section 38(1)—

(a) in relation to all or part of the proposed works;

(b) subject to such modifications and conditions relating to the proposed works as the appropriate national authority thinks fit.

(4) In considering the effect in relation to any land of proposed works under this section, the appropriate national authority may consider that effect in conjunction with the effect in relation to that land of any other works for which consent has previously been given under section 38(1) above or section 194 of the Law of Property Act 1925 (c 20).

(5) Where the appropriate national authority imposes any modification or condition in relation to any consent given under section 38(1), it may on the application of any person carrying out or proposing to carry out works in accordance with the consent vary or revoke that modification or condition.

(6) Regulations may specify a time limit for the making of applications under subsection (5).

(7) Consent may be given under section 38(1) in relation to works which have been commenced or completed; and any consent so given has effect from the time of commencement of the works.

[2312]

NOTES

Commencement: 12 August 2007 (sub-s (6) in relation to Wales for certain purposes); 1 October 2007 (in relation to England); to be appointed (otherwise).

Regulations: the Works on Common Land, etc (Procedure) (England) Regulations 2007, SI 2007/2588.

40 Consent: procedure

(1) Regulations may make provision as to the procedure to be followed in the making and determination of applications under sections 38(1) and 39(5).

(2) Regulations under this section may in particular include provision—

(a) as to the steps to be taken by an applicant before submitting an application;
(b) as to the form and content of an application;
(c) as to the procedure to be followed in making an application;
(d) as to the evidence to be supplied in support of an application;
(e) as to the fees payable in relation to an application;
(f) as to the steps to be taken by the appropriate national authority upon receipt of an application;
(g) for the appointment by the appropriate national authority of a person to discharge any (or all) of its functions in relation to the determination of an application;
(h) for the making of representations or objections in relation to an application;
(i) for the holding of a hearing or local inquiry in relation to an application;
(j) for the publication of a determination of an application and the notification of interested persons.

[2313]

NOTES

Commencement: 12 August 2007 (in relation to Wales for certain purposes); 1 October 2007 (in relation to England); to be appointed (otherwise).

Regulations: the Works on Common Land, etc (Procedure) (England) Regulations 2007, SI 2007/2588.

41 Enforcement

(1) Where any works are carried out on land to which section 38 applies in contravention of subsection (1) of that section, any person may apply to the county court in whose area the land is situated.

(2) On an application under this section the court may make an order—

(a) in any case, for removal of the works and restoration of the land to the condition it was in before the works were carried out;
(b) in a case where consent has been given under section 38(1) but the works have not been carried out in accordance with any term of that consent, for the works to be carried out in such manner and subject to such conditions as the order may specify.

[2314]

NOTES

Commencement: 1 October 2007 (in relation to England); to be appointed (otherwise).

42 Schemes

(1) This section applies in relation to works on relevant land where, by virtue of section 38(1), the works may not be carried out without the consent of the appropriate national authority.

(2) In subsection (1) "relevant land" means land which is subject to—

(a) a scheme under the Metropolitan Commons Act 1866 (c 122) which is in force at the commencement of this section; or
(b) a scheme under the Commons Act 1899 (c 30) which is in force at the commencement of this section.

(3) Where—

(a) any provision of the scheme referred to in subsection (2) would also prohibit the carrying out of the works, and
(b) the scheme does not allow for any person to consent to the works to be carried out,

the works do not contravene that provision if they are carried out with (and in accordance with the terms of) the consent of the appropriate national authority under section 38(1) and of any owner of the land (if not the person carrying out the works).

(4) Regulations may make provision as to the procedure to be followed in obtaining the consent of an owner under subsection (3) (and may include provision for the consent of an owner to be regarded as having been given where he has not objected within a period of time specified in the regulations).

(5) Where any provision of the scheme referred to in subsection (2) would also prohibit the carrying out of the works without the consent of the appropriate national authority—

(a) consent given under section 38(1) is to be regarded as consent given under the scheme; and
(b) consent may not be sought separately under the scheme.

[2315]

NOTES

Commencement: 12 August 2007 (sub-s (4), in relation to Wales for certain purposes); 1 October 2007 (in relation to England); to be appointed (otherwise).

43 Power to exempt

(1) The appropriate national authority may by order provide that section 38 is not to apply to—

(a) the carrying out by a specified person of specified works on specified land; or

(b) the carrying out by a specified person, or a person of a specified description, of works of a specified description on—

(i) any land; or

(ii) land of a specified description.

(2) The appropriate national authority may only make an order under subsection (1)(a) if it is satisfied that the works specified in the order are necessary or expedient for any of the purposes in subsection (4).

(3) The appropriate national authority may only make an order under subsection (1)(b) if it is satisfied that works of the description specified in the order are likely to be necessary or expedient on any land, or on land of the description specified in the order, for any of the purposes in subsection (4).

(4) The purposes referred to in subsections (2) and (3) are—

(a) use of land by members of the public for the purposes of open-air recreation pursuant to any right of access;

(b) the exercise of rights of common;

(c) nature conservation;

(d) the protection of archaeological remains or features of historic interest;

(e) the use of the land for sporting or recreational purposes.

(5) Where—

(a) any land was at any time before the commencement of this section land to which section 194 of the Law of Property Act 1925 (c 20) applied, but

(b) at any such time that section ceased to apply to the land by virtue of subsection (3)(a) of that section,

the appropriate national authority may by order provide that section 38 is not to apply to the carrying out of works, or works of a description specified in the order, on that land.

(6) Where any land is the subject of a resolution under section 194(3)(b) of the Law of Property Act 1925 (c 20) immediately before the commencement of this section, the appropriate national authority may by order provide that section 38 is not to apply to the carrying out of works, or works of a description specified in the order, on that land.

(7) An order under this section may provide that section 38 is not to apply only if the works to which the order relates are carried out in accordance with the terms of the order.

(8) In subsection (1) "specified" means specified in an order under that subsection.

[2316]

NOTES

Commencement: 12 August 2007 (in relation to Wales for certain purposes); 1 October 2007 (in relation to England); to be appointed (otherwise).

Order: the Works on Common Land (Exemptions) (England) Order 2007, SI 2007/2587.

44 Supplementary

(1) Schedule 4 (which makes supplementary provision relating to works on common land) has effect.

(2) A national authority may for any purpose specified in subsection (3) by order amend—

(a) any local or personal Act passed before this Act which contains provision for that authority to consent to works on land which is common land; and

(b) any Act made under the Commons Act 1876 (c 56) confirming a provisional order of the Inclosure Commissioners which contains provision for that authority to consent to works on land to which the Act applies.

(3) The purposes referred to in subsection (2) are—

(a) that of securing that sections 39 and 40 apply to an application for the consent referred to in paragraph (a) or (b) of subsection (2) as they apply to an application for consent under section 38(1);

(b) that of securing that section 41 applies in relation to the carrying out of works in contravention of the provision referred to in paragraph (a) or (b) of subsection (2) as it applies to works carried out in contravention of section 38(1).

(4) In subsection (2)—

"national authority" means—

(a) the Secretary of State; and

(b) the National Assembly for Wales;

"common land" means—

(a) any land registered as common land; and

(b) any land not so registered which is subject to a scheme under the Metropolitan Commons Act 1866 (c 122) or the Commons Act 1899 (c 30).

[2317]

NOTES

Commencement: 12 August 2007 (in relation to Wales for certain purposes); 1 October 2006 (sub-s (1), in relation to England for certain purposes); 6 September 2007 (sub-s (1), in relation to Wales for certain purposes); 1 October 2007 (sub-s (1) (in relation to England for remaining purposes), sub-ss (2)–(4) (in relation to England), subject to transitional provisions and savings in SI 2007/2584, art 3); to be appointed (otherwise).

PART 4
MISCELLANEOUS

Intervention powers

45 Powers of local authorities over unclaimed land

(1) This section applies where—

(a) land is registered as common land or a town or village green;

(b) no person is registered in the register of title as the owner of the land; and

(c) it appears to a local authority in whose area the land or any part of it is situated that the owner cannot be identified.

(2) The local authority may—

(a) take any steps to protect the land against unlawful interference that could be taken by an owner in possession of the land; and

(b) institute proceedings against any person for any offence committed in respect of the land (but without prejudice to any power exercisable apart from this section).

(3) In this section "local authority" means—

(a) a county, district or parish council in England;

(b) a London borough council; and

(c) a county, county borough or community council in Wales.

[2318]

NOTES

Commencement: 1 October 2006 (in relation to England, subject to transitional provisions in SI 2006/2504, art 3(1)); 6 September 2007 (in relation to Wales, subject to transitional provisions in SI 2007/2386, art 4(4)).

46 Powers relating to unauthorised agricultural activities

(1) This section applies where it appears to the appropriate national authority that—

(a) a person is carrying out, or causing to be carried out by virtue of any arrangements, an agricultural activity on land which—

(i) is registered as common land; or

(ii) is registered as a town or village green and is subject to rights of common;

(b) the activity is unauthorised; and

(c) the activity is detrimental to—

(i) the interests of persons having rights in relation to, or occupying, the land; or

(ii) the public interest.

(2) The appropriate national authority may, subject to the following provisions of this section, serve a notice on the person requiring him to do any one or more of the following—

(a) within such reasonable period as may be specified in the notice to stop carrying out the activity, or stop causing it to be carried out, to the extent that it is unauthorised;

(b) not to carry out, or cause to be carried out, any other unauthorised agricultural activity on the land which would be detrimental to the matters specified in subsection (1)(c)(i) and (ii);

(c) to supply the authority with such information relating to agricultural activities on the land carried out, or caused to be carried out, by him as it may reasonably require.

(3) Before serving a notice under this section the appropriate national authority must, to the extent that it is appropriate and practicable in all the circumstances to do so—

(a) notify the persons specified in subsection (4) of its intention to serve the notice; and

(b) publicise its intention to do so (in such manner as it thinks fit).

(4) The persons referred to in subsection (3)(a) are—

(a) any commons council for the land;

(b) any other person with functions under any enactment which relate to the maintenance or management of the land; and

(c) any person appearing to the authority to own or occupy the land.

(5) Any notification or publication under subsection (3) may specify a period within which representations about the proposed notice may be made.

(6) In deciding whether to serve a notice under this section the appropriate national authority must have regard to—

(a) any criminal or civil proceedings that have been or may be commenced in relation to the activity; and

(b) any steps taken by a commons council in relation to the activity.

(7) If a person on whom a notice is served under this section fails to comply with it—

(a) the appropriate national authority may apply to a county court for an order requiring him to do so; and

(b) the court may make such an order for the purpose of securing compliance with the notice as it thinks fit.

(8) For the purposes of this section, activity is unauthorised if the person carrying it out or causing it to be carried out—

(a) has no right or entitlement by virtue of his ownership or occupation of the land, or pursuant to any right of common, to do so; or

(b) is not doing so with the authority of the person or persons entitled to give such authority.

(9) The reference in subsection (1)(c)(ii) to the public interest includes the public interest in—

(a) nature conservation;

(b) the conservation of the landscape;

(c) the protection of public rights of access to any area of land; and

(d) the protection of archaeological remains and features of historic interest.

(10) Section 123(1) to (5) of the Environment Act 1995 (c 25) applies in relation to the service of a notice under this section as it applies in relation to the service of a notice under that Act.

[2319]

NOTES

Commencement: 1 October 2008 (in relation to England); to be appointed (otherwise).

Abolition of powers of approvement and inclosure etc

47 Approvement

(1) The Commons Act 1285 (13 Edw 1 c 46) (power of approvement) shall cease to have effect.

(2) Any power of approvement of a common which subsists at common law is abolished.

[2320]

NOTES

Commencement: 1 October 2006 (in relation to England); 6 September 2007 (in relation to Wales).

48–51 (*S 48 repeals the Inclosure Act 1845, s 147 and the Gifts for Churches Act 1811, s 2, and amends the School Sites Act 1841, s 2 at* **[53]** *and the Literary and Scientific Institutions Act 1854, s 1; s 49 repeals the Commons Act 1876, s 31 and amends the Metropolitan Commons Act 1878, s 3; s 50 amends the Commons Act 1899, ss 1, 2, and substitutes ss 9, 10 thereof; s 51 repeals the Countryside and Rights of Way Act 2000, s 68.*)

PART 5
SUPPLEMENTARY AND GENERAL

Amendments and repeals

52 Minor and consequential amendments

Schedule 5 (minor and consequential amendments) has effect.

[2321]

NOTES

Commencement: 1 October 2006 (in relation to England for certain purposes); 20 February 2007 (in relation to England for certain purposes); 6 September 2007 (in relation to Wales for certain purposes); to be appointed (otherwise).

53 Repeals

Schedule 6 (repeals, including consequential repeals and repeals of spent and obsolete enactments) has effect.

[2322]

NOTES

Commencement: 1 October 2006 (in relation to England for certain purposes); 20 February 2007 (in relation to England for certain purposes); 6 April 2007 (in relation to England for certain purposes); 6 September 2007 (in relation to Wales for certain purposes); 1 October 2007 (in relation to England for certain purposes); 1 October 2008 (in relation to England in relation to the pilot areas for certain purposes); to be appointed (otherwise).

54 Power to amend enactments relating to common land or greens

(1) The appropriate national authority may by order amend any relevant Act so as to secure that—

- (a) a provision of that Act applying to common land does not apply to land to which Part 1 applies and which is not registered as common land;
- (b) such a provision applies to either or both of the following—
  - (i) land registered as common land, or particular descriptions or areas of such land;
  - (ii) land to which Part 1 does not apply, or particular descriptions or areas of such land.

(2) The appropriate national authority may by order amend any relevant Act so as to secure that—

- (a) a provision of that Act which is expressed to apply to a town or village green does not apply to land to which Part 1 applies and which is not registered as a town or village green;
- (b) such a provision applies to either or both of the following—
  - (i) land registered as a town or village green, or particular descriptions or areas of such land;
  - (ii) land to which Part 1 does not apply, or particular descriptions or areas of such land.

(3) In this section, "relevant Act" means any public general Act passed before this Act.

(4) For the purposes of subsection (1) a provision applies to common land if it is expressed to apply (generally) to common land, any common or commons, commonable land, land subject to inclosure under any enactment or other land of a similar description.

[2323]

NOTES

Commencement: 19 September 2006.

55 Power to amend enactments conferring functions on national authorities

(1) A national authority may by order amend or repeal any provision of a local or personal Act passed before this Act which applies to common land for any of the following purposes—

- (a) to remove any function of the national authority which relates to the common land;
- (b) to transfer such a function from the national authority to another person;
- (c) to remove a requirement that the national authority be consulted, or that its consent be obtained, in respect of—
  - (i) any act or omission relating to the common land; or
  - (ii) any act or omission of a person concerned with the management of the common land;
- (d) to substitute for a requirement referred to in paragraph (c) a requirement that a person other than the national authority be consulted, or his consent obtained, in relation to the act or omission.

(2) In subsection (1), "common land" means—

- (a) any land registered as common land or as a town or village green;
- (b) any land referred to in section 5(2); and
- (c) any land not falling within paragraph (a) or (b) which is subject to a scheme under the Metropolitan Commons Act 1866 (c 122) or the Commons Act 1899 (c 30).

(3) A national authority may by order amend or repeal any provision of an Act made under the Commons Act 1876 (c 56) confirming a provisional order of the Inclosure Commissioners for any of the following purposes—

- (a) to remove any function of the national authority which relates to land to which the Act applies;
- (b) to transfer such a function from the national authority to another person;

(c) to remove a requirement that the national authority be consulted, or that its consent be obtained, in respect of—
(i) any act or omission relating to land to which the Act applies; or
(ii) any act or omission of a person concerned with the management of such land;
(d) to substitute for a requirement referred to in paragraph (c) a requirement that a person other than the national authority be consulted, or his consent obtained, in relation to the act or omission.

(4) In this section "national authority" means—
(a) the Secretary of State; and
(b) the National Assembly for Wales.

[2324]

NOTES
Commencement: 19 September 2006.

Commencement and transitional provision

56 Commencement

(1) The preceding provisions of this Act, except section 9 and Schedule 1 and sections 54 and 55, come into force in accordance with provision made by order by the appropriate national authority.

(2) Sections 54 and 55 come into force at the end of the period of two months beginning with the day on which this Act is passed.

[2325]

NOTES
Commencement: 19 July 2006.
Orders: the Commons Act 2006 (Commencement No 1, Transitional Provisions and Savings) (England) Order 2006, SI 2006/2504; the Commons Act 2006 (Commencement No 2, Transitional Provisions and Savings) (England) Order 2007, SI 2007/456; the Commons Act 2006 (Commencement No 1, Transitional Provisions and Savings) (Wales) Order 2007, SI 2007/2386; the Commons Act 2006 (Commencement No 3, Transitional Provisions and Savings) (England) Order 2007, SI 2007/2584; the Commons Act 2006 (Commencement No 4 and Savings) (England) Order 2008, SI 2008/1960.

57 Severance: transitional

(1) In relation to any area of England and Wales, the reference in subsection (1) of section 9 to a register of common land or town or village greens shall, during the relevant period in relation to that area, be read as a reference to such a register kept under the Commons Registration Act 1965 (c 64).

(2) Sub-paragraph (6) of paragraph 1 of Schedule 1 shall not have effect in relation to a right of common severed (in accordance with that paragraph) from land in any area of England and Wales during the relevant period in relation to that area.

(3) In this section, the "relevant period", in relation to an area of England and Wales, is the period which—
(a) begins with the coming into force of this section; and
(b) ends with the coming into force of section 1 in relation to that area.

(4) This section is deemed to have come into force on 28 June 2005.

[2326]

NOTES
Commencement: 19 July 2006.

58 Natural England

Any reference in a provision of this Act to Natural England shall, in relation to any time after the coming into force of that provision but before the coming into force of section 1(4) of the Natural Environment and Rural Communities Act 2006, be read as a reference to English Nature.

[2327]

NOTES
Commencement: 19 July 2006.

General

59 Orders and regulations

(1) An order or regulations under this Act may make—
(a) transitional, consequential, incidental and supplemental provision or savings;

(b) different provision for different purposes or areas.

(2) An order or regulations under this Act, other than an order under section 17, must be made by statutory instrument.

(3) A statutory instrument containing regulations under section 29(1) or an order under section 54 or 55 may not be made by the Secretary of State (alone or jointly with the National Assembly for Wales) unless a draft has been laid before and approved by a resolution of each House of Parliament.

(4) Subject to subsection (3), a statutory instrument containing any order or regulations made under this Act by the Secretary of State (alone or jointly with the National Assembly for Wales) other than an order under section 56 shall be subject to annulment in pursuance of a resolution of either House of Parliament.

[2328]

NOTES

Commencement: 19 July 2006.

60 Crown application

(1) This Act (and any provision made under it) binds the Crown.

(2) This section does not impose criminal liability on the Crown in relation to an offence under section 34(1).

(3) Subsection (2) does not affect the criminal liability of persons in the service of the Crown.

[2329]

NOTES

Commencement: 19 July 2006.

61 Interpretation

(1) In this Act—

"appropriate national authority" means—

(a) the Secretary of State, in relation to England; and

(b) the National Assembly for Wales, in relation to Wales;

"commons council" means a commons council established under Part 2;

"land" includes land covered by water;

"nature conservation" means the conservation of flora and fauna and geological and physiographical features;

"regulations" means regulations made by the appropriate national authority;

"register of title" means the register kept under section 1 of the Land Registration Act 2002 (c 9);

"right of common" includes a cattlegate or beastgate (by whatever name known) and a right of sole or several vesture or herbage or of sole or several pasture, but does not include a right held for a term of years or from year to year.

(2) In this Act—

(a) any reference to land registered as common land or a town or village green is to land so registered in a register of common land or town or village greens;

(b) any reference to a register of common land or town or village greens is to such a register kept under Part 1 of this Act.

(3) In this Act—

(a) references to the ownership or the owner of any land are references to the ownership of a legal estate in fee simple in the land or to the person holding that estate;

(b) references to land registered in the register of title are references to land the fee simple of which is so registered.

[2330]

NOTES

Commencement: 19 July 2006.

62 Short title

This Act may be cited as the Commons Act 2006.

[2331]

NOTES

Commencement: 19 July 2006.

63 Extent

This Act extends to England and Wales only.

[2332]

NOTES

Commencement: 19 July 2006.

SCHEDULE 1
AUTHORISED SEVERANCE

Section 9

Severance by transfer to public bodies

1.—(1) A right of common to which section 9 applies may on or after the day on which this Schedule comes into force be severed permanently from the land to which it is attached by being transferred on its own to—

(a) any commons council established for the land over which the right is exercisable;
(b) Natural England (where the land or any part of it is in England); or
(c) the Countryside Council for Wales (where the land or any part of it is in Wales).

(2) Where a person proposes to sever a right of common to which section 9 applies by a transfer under sub-paragraph (1)(b) or (c), Natural England or the Countryside Council for Wales as the case may be must—

(a) give notice of the proposal to the owner of the land over which the right is exercisable unless his name and address cannot reasonably be ascertained;
(b) in a case where there is no commons council established for the land, give notice of the proposal to such persons (if any) as they consider represent the interests of persons exercising rights of common over the land.

(3) A notice under sub-paragraph (2) must be given at least two months before the transfer and must—

(a) specify the name and address of the owner of the land to which the right is attached;
(b) describe the right proposed to be transferred, giving such details as regulations may specify;
(c) state the proposed consideration for the transfer; and
(d) give such other information as regulations may specify.

(4) Where a right of common to which section 9 applies is exercisable over land for which a commons council is established, the right may only be severed by a transfer under sub-paragraph (1)(b) or (c) if that council consents to the transfer.

(5) In a case where there is no commons council established for the land over which a right of common to which section 9 applies is exercisable, the appropriate national authority may by order provide that a person with functions of management conferred by any enactment in relation to that land is to be regarded, for any or all purposes of this paragraph, as a commons council established for the land.

(6) The severance of a right of common by its transfer under sub-paragraph (1)—

(a) only has effect if the transfer complies with such requirements as to form and content as regulations may provide; and
(b) does not operate at law until, on an application under this Schedule, the transferee is registered as the owner of the right in the register of common land or of town or village greens in which the right is registered.

Temporary severance by letting or leasing

2.—(1) A right of common to which section 9 applies may, on or after the day on which this Schedule comes into force, to any extent be severed temporarily from the land to which it is attached by virtue of the right, or all or part of the land, being leased or licensed on its own in accordance with—

(a) provision made by order by the appropriate national authority; or
(b) rules made in relation to the land by a commons council under section 31.

(2) Provision under sub-paragraph (1)(a) and rules referred to in sub-paragraph (1)(b) may be framed by reference to—

(a) particular land or descriptions of land;
(b) descriptions of persons to whom rights of common may be leased or licensed.

(3) Where—

(a) provision under sub-paragraph (1)(a) applies in relation to any land, and
(b) rules referred to in sub-paragraph (1)(b) also apply in relation to that land and are inconsistent with that provision,

the rules prevail over that provision, to the extent of the inconsistency, in relation to that land.

(4) The appropriate national authority may by order provide that the leasing or licensing of a right of common (whether authorised by provision under sub-paragraph (1)(a) or by rules referred to in sub-paragraph (1)(b)) must comply with such requirements as to form and content as the order may provide.

Severance authorised by order

3.—(1) The appropriate national authority may by order make provision authorising rights of common to which section 9 applies to be severed permanently from the land to which they are attached by transfer in accordance with that provision.

(2) Provision under sub-paragraph (1) is to be framed by reference to—

(a) particular land over which the rights of common are exercisable, or
(b) particular descriptions of such land,

and may authorise transfers to particular persons, particular descriptions of persons or any person.

(3) The appropriate national authority must, before making any provision under sub-paragraph (1) in relation to any land, consult such persons (if any) as it considers represent the interests of—

(a) persons who own the land;
(b) persons who exercise rights of common over the land.

(4) Provision under sub-paragraph (1) may include provision securing that the owner of any land over which a right of common is exercisable is to be notified, and his consent obtained, before the right may be transferred.

(5) Provision referred to in sub-paragraph (4) may include—

(a) provision as to the circumstances in which notification may be regarded as having been given; or
(b) provision as to the circumstances in which consent may be regarded as having been obtained.

(6) Provision referred to in sub-paragraph (5)(b) may include—

(a) provision for consent to be regarded as having been obtained if it is withheld unreasonably;
(b) provision for the circumstances in which consent is to be regarded as withheld unreasonably;
(c) provision for the resolution of disputes.

(7) The severance of a right of common by its transfer under provision under sub-paragraph (1)—

(a) only has effect if the transfer complies with such requirements as to form and content as regulations may provide; and
(b) does not operate at law until, on an application under this Schedule, the transferee is registered as the owner of the right in the register of common land or of town or village greens in which the right is registered.

(8) Provision under sub-paragraph (1) may include provision to secure the result that where—

(a) the person to whom the right of common is transferred is the owner of land to which rights of common are attached, and
(b) those rights are exercisable over the same land, or substantially the same land, as the right of common being transferred,

the transferee must, when making an application as specified in sub-paragraph (7)(b), apply to the commons registration authority for the right to be registered as attached to the land referred to in paragraph (a).

[2333]

NOTES

Commencement: 28 June 2005 (see s 9(7) at **[2282]**).

Orders: the Commons (Severance of Rights) (England) Order 2006, SI 2006/2145; the Commons (Severance of Rights) (Wales) Order 2007, SI 2007/583.

SCHEDULE 2
NON-REGISTRATION OR MISTAKEN REGISTRATION UNDER THE 1965 ACT

Section 22

Introductory

1. In this Schedule "the 1965 Act" means the Commons Registration Act 1965 (c 64).

Non-registration of common land

2.—(1) If a commons registration authority is satisfied that any land not registered as common land or as a town or village green is land to which this paragraph applies, the authority shall, subject to this paragraph, register the land as common land in its register of common land.

(2) This paragraph applies to any land which—

(a) was not at any time finally registered as common land or as a town or village green under the 1965 Act;

(b) is land which is—

(i) regulated by an Act made under the Commons Act 1876 (c 56) confirming a provisional order of the Inclosure Commissioners;

(ii) subject to a scheme under Metropolitan Commons Act 1866 (c 122) or the Commons Act 1899 (c 30);

(iii) regulated as common land under a local or personal Act; or

(iv) otherwise recognised or designated as common land by or under an enactment;

(c) is land to which this Part applies; and

(d) satisfies such other conditions as regulations may specify.

(3) A commons registration authority may only register land under sub-paragraph (1) acting on—

(a) the application of any person made before such date as regulations may specify; or

(b) a proposal made and published by the authority before such date as regulations may specify.

Non-registration of town or village green

3.—(1) If a commons registration authority is satisfied that any land not registered as a town or village green or as common land is land to which this paragraph applies, the authority shall, subject to this paragraph, register the land as a town or village green in its register of town or village greens.

(2) This paragraph applies to any land which—

(a) on 31 July 1970 was land allotted by or under any Act for the exercise or recreation of the inhabitants of any locality;

(b) was not at any time finally registered as a town or village green or as common land under the 1965 Act;

(c) continues to be land allotted as specified in paragraph (a);

(d) is land to which this Part applies; and

(e) satisfies such other conditions as regulations may specify.

(3) A commons registration authority may only register land under sub-paragraph (1) acting on—

(a) the application of any person made before such date as regulations may specify; or

(b) a proposal made and published by the authority before such date as regulations may specify.

Waste land of a manor not registered as common land

4.—(1) If a commons registration authority is satisfied that any land not registered as common land or as a town or village green is land to which this paragraph applies, the authority shall, subject to this paragraph, register the land as common land in its register of common land.

(2) This paragraph applies to land which at the time of the application under sub-paragraph (1) is waste land of a manor and where, before the commencement of this paragraph—

(a) the land was provisionally registered as common land under section 4 of the 1965 Act;

(b) an objection was made in relation to the provisional registration; and

(c) the provisional registration was cancelled in the circumstances specified in sub-paragraph (3), (4) or (5).

(3) The circumstances in this sub-paragraph are that—

(a) the provisional registration was referred to a Commons Commissioner under section 5 of the 1965 Act;

(b) the Commissioner determined that, although the land had been waste land of a manor at some earlier time, it was not such land at the time of the determination because it had ceased to be connected with the manor; and

(c) for that reason only the Commissioner refused to confirm the provisional registration.

(4) The circumstances in this sub-paragraph are that—

(a) the provisional registration was referred to a Commons Commissioner under section 5 of the 1965 Act;

(b) the Commissioner determined that the land was not subject to rights of common and for that reason refused to confirm the provisional registration; and

(c) the Commissioner did not consider whether the land was waste land of a manor.

(5) The circumstances in this sub-paragraph are that the person on whose application the provisional registration was made requested or agreed to its cancellation (whether before or after its referral to a Commons Commissioner).

(6) A commons registration authority may only register land under sub-paragraph (1) acting on—

(a) the application of any person made before such date as regulations may specify; or

(b) a proposal made and published by the authority before such date as regulations may specify.

Town or village green wrongly registered as common land

5.—(1) If a commons registration authority is satisfied that any land registered as common land is land to which this paragraph applies, the authority shall, subject to this paragraph, remove the land from its register of common land and register it in its register of town or village greens.

(2) This paragraph applies to land where—

(a) the land was provisionally registered as common land under section 4 of the 1965 Act;

(b) the provisional registration became final; but

(c) immediately before its provisional registration, the land was a town or village green within the meaning of that Act as originally enacted.

(3) A commons registration authority may only remove and register land under sub-paragraph (1) acting on—

(a) the application of any person made before such date as regulations may specify; or

(b) a proposal made and published by the authority before such date as regulations may specify.

Buildings registered as common land

6.—(1) If a commons registration authority is satisfied that any land registered as common land is land to which this paragraph applies, the authority shall, subject to this paragraph, remove that land from its register of common land.

(2) This paragraph applies to land where—

(a) the land was provisionally registered as common land under section 4 of the 1965 Act;

(b) on the date of the provisional registration the land was covered by a building or was within the curtilage of a building;

(c) the provisional registration became final; and

(d) since the date of the provisional registration the land has at all times been, and still is, covered by a building or within the curtilage of a building.

(3) A commons registration authority may only remove land under sub-paragraph (1) acting on—

(a) the application of any person made before such date as regulations may specify; or

(b) a proposal made and published by the authority before such date as regulations may specify.

Other land wrongly registered as common land

7.—(1) If a commons registration authority is satisfied that any land registered as common land is land to which this paragraph applies, the authority shall, subject to this paragraph, remove the land from its register of common land.

(2) This paragraph applies to land where—

(a) the land was provisionally registered as common land under section 4 of the 1965 Act;

(b) the provisional registration of the land as common land was not referred to a Commons Commissioner under section 5 of the 1965 Act;

(c) the provisional registration became final; and

(d) immediately before its provisional registration the land was not any of the following—

(i) land subject to rights of common;

(ii) waste land of a manor;

(iii) a town or village green within the meaning of the 1965 Act as originally enacted; or

(iv) land of a description specified in section 11 of the Inclosure Act 1845 (c 118).

(3) A commons registration authority may only remove land under sub-paragraph (1) acting on—

(a) the application of any person made before such date as regulations may specify; or

(b) a proposal made and published by the authority before such date as regulations may specify.

Buildings registered as town or village green

8.—(1) If a commons registration authority is satisfied that any land registered as a town or village green is land to which this paragraph applies, the authority shall, subject to this paragraph, remove that land from its register of town or village greens.

(2) This paragraph applies to land where—

(a) the land was provisionally registered as a town or village green under section 4 of the 1965 Act;

(b) on the date of the provisional registration the land was covered by a building or was within the curtilage of a building;
(c) the provisional registration became final; and
(d) since the date of the provisional registration the land has at all times been, and still is, covered by a building or within the curtilage of a building.

(3) A commons registration authority may only remove land under sub-paragraph (1) acting on—
(a) the application of any person made before such date as regulations may specify; or
(b) a proposal made and published by the authority before such date as regulations may specify.

Other land wrongly registered as town or village green

9.—(1) If a commons registration authority is satisfied that any land registered as a town or village green is land to which this paragraph applies, the authority shall, subject to this paragraph, remove the land from its register of town or village greens.

(2) This paragraph applies to land where—
(a) the land was provisionally registered as a town or village green under section 4 of the 1965 Act;
(b) the provisional registration of the land as a town or village green was not referred to a Commons Commissioner under section 5 of the 1965 Act;
(c) the provisional registration became final; and
(d) immediately before its provisional registration the land was not—
(i) common land within the meaning of that Act; or
(ii) a town or village green.

(3) For the purposes of sub-paragraph (2)(d)(ii), land is to be taken not to have been a town or village green immediately before its provisional registration if (and only if)—
(a) throughout the period of 20 years preceding the date of its provisional registration the land was, by reason of its physical nature, unusable by members of the public for the purposes of lawful sports and pastimes; and
(b) immediately before its provisional registration the land was not, and at the time of the application under this paragraph still is not, allotted by or under any Act for the exercise or recreation of the inhabitants of any locality.

(4) A commons registration authority may only remove land under sub-paragraph (1) acting on—
(a) the application of any person made before such date as regulations may specify; or
(b) a proposal made and published by the authority before such date as regulations may specify.

Costs

10.—(1) Regulations may make provision as to the payment of costs which pursuant to an application under this Schedule are incurred by the applicant, an objector or the person determining the application.

(2) That provision may in particular include provision—
(a) for the payment of costs by the applicant, an objector or a commons registration authority;
(b) for the person determining an application or the appropriate national authority to determine who is liable to pay costs and how much they are liable to pay.

[2334]

NOTES

Commencement: 12 August 2007 (paras 2(2)(d), (3), 3(2)(e), (3), 4(6), 5(3), 6(3), 7(3), 8(3), 9(4), 10, in relation to Wales for certain purposes); 1 October 2008 (in relation to pilot areas in England); to be appointed (otherwise).

Regulations: the Commons Registration (England) Regulations 2008, SI 2008/1961.

SCHEDULE 3
REGISTRATION: TRANSITIONAL PROVISION

Section 23

Interpretation

1. In this Schedule "the 1965 Act" means the Commons Registration Act 1965 (c 64).

Transitional period for updating registers

2.—(1) Regulations may make provision for commons registration authorities, during a period specified in the regulations ("the transitional period"), to amend their registers of common land and town or village greens in consequence of qualifying events which were not registered under the 1965 Act.

(2) The following are qualifying events for the purposes of this Schedule—

(a) the creation of a right of common (by any means, including prescription), where occurring in relation to land to which this Part applies at any time—

(i) after 2 January 1970; and

(ii) before the commencement of this paragraph;

(b) any relevant disposition in relation to a right of common registered under the 1965 Act, or any extinguishment of such a right, where occurring at any time—

(i) after the date of the registration of the right under that Act; and

(ii) before the commencement of this paragraph;

(c) a disposition occurring before the commencement of this paragraph by virtue of any relevant instrument in relation to land which at the time of the disposition was registered as common land or a town or village green under the 1965 Act;

(d) the giving of land in exchange for any land subject to a disposition referred to in paragraph (c).

(3) In sub-paragraph (2)(b) "relevant disposition" means—

(a) the surrender of a right of common;

(b) the variation of a right of common;

(c) in the case of a right of common attached to land, the apportionment or severance of the right;

(d) in the case of a right not attached to land, the transfer of the right.

(4) In sub-paragraph (2)(c) "relevant instrument" means—

(a) any order, deed or other instrument made under or pursuant to the Acquisition of Land Act 1981 (c 67);

(b) a conveyance made for the purposes of section 13 of the New Parishes Measure 1943 (No 1);

(c) any other instrument made under or pursuant to any enactment.

(5) Regulations under this paragraph may include provision for commons registration authorities to amend their registers as specified in sub-paragraph (1)—

(a) on the application of a person specified in the regulations; or

(b) on their own initiative.

(6) Regulations under sub-paragraph (5)(b) may include provision requiring a commons registration authority to take steps to discover information relating to qualifying events, including in particular requiring an authority to—

(a) carry out a review of information already contained in a register of common land or town or village greens;

(b) publicise the review;

(c) invite persons to supply information for, or to apply for amendment of, the register.

3. At the end of the transitional period, any right of common which—

(a) is not registered in a register of common land or town or village greens, but

(b) was capable of being so registered under paragraph 2,

is by virtue of this paragraph at that time extinguished.

4.—(1) Regulations may make provision for commons registration authorities to amend their registers of common land or town or village greens after the end of the transitional period, in circumstances specified in the regulations, in consequence of qualifying events.

(2) Regulations under this paragraph may provide that paragraph 3 is to be treated as not having applied to any right of common which is registered pursuant to the regulations.

5. Regulations under paragraph 2 or 4 may in particular include provision as to what is or is not to be regarded as severance of a right of common for the purposes of those regulations.

Effect of repeals

6. The repeal by this Act of section 1(2)(b) of the 1965 Act does not affect the extinguishment of rights of common occurring by virtue of that provision.

7. The repeal by this Act of section 21(1) of the 1965 Act does not affect the application of section 193 of the Law of Property Act 1925 (c 20) in relation to any land.

Ownership of common land or town or village green

8.—(1) Where the ownership of any land is registered in any register under the 1965 Act immediately before the commencement of this Schedule the ownership shall, subject to this Part, continue to be registered in that register.

(2) Where the ownership of land continues to be registered in a register of common land or town or village greens pursuant to sub-paragraph (1), if the commons registration authority is notified by the Chief Land Registrar that the land has been registered in the register of title, the authority shall—

(a) remove the registration of ownership; and

(b) indicate in the register in such manner as may be specified in regulations that the land has been registered in the register of title.

(3) Regulations may require commons registration authorities—

(a) to remove registration of ownership of land from their registers of common land and town or village greens;

(b) to keep or otherwise deal with documents received by them in connection with the registration of ownership of land in such manner as the regulations may specify.

Vesting of unclaimed land

9.—(1) The repeal by this Act of section 8 of the 1965 Act does not affect the vesting of land in any local authority (within the meaning of that Act) occurring by virtue of that provision.

(2) Unless land so vesting is regulated by a scheme under the Commons Act 1899 (c 30), sections 10 and 15 of the Open Spaces Act 1906 (c 25) (power to manage and make byelaws) shall continue to apply to it as if the local authority had acquired the ownership under that Act of 1906.

[2335]

NOTES

Commencement: 1 October 2006 (para 9, in relation to England, subject to transitional provisions and savings in SI 2006/2504, art 3(2)); 12 August 2007 (paras 2(1), (5), (6), 4, 5, 8(2), (3), in relation to Wales for certain purposes); 6 September 2007 (para 9, in relation to Wales); 1 October 2008 (paras 1–8, in relation to England in relation to the pilot areas); to be appointed (otherwise).

Regulations: Commons Registration (England) Regulations 2008, SI 2008/1961.

SCHEDULE 4
WORKS: SUPPLEMENTARY

Section 44

1–5. …

Transitional provision

6. In its application to any works carried out on or after 28 June 2005 but before the day on which section 38(1) above comes into force, section 194(2) of the Law of Property Act 1925 (c 20) shall have effect as if the words "interested in the common" were omitted.

7. The prohibition in section 38(1) does not apply to works carried out in connection with the taking or working of minerals if—

(a) the works were granted planning permission under any enactment before the commencement of section 38;

(b) the works are carried out in accordance with that planning permission in the period allowed for the works to be carried out (subject to any extension of time granted before or after the commencement of that section).

[2336]

NOTES

Commencement: 1 October 2006 (para 6, in relation to England); 6 September 2007 (para 6, in relation to Wales); 1 October 2007 (paras 1–5, 7, in relation to England, subject to transitional provisions and savings in SI 2007/2584, art 3); to be appointed (otherwise).

Para 1: amends the Metropolitan Commons Act 1866, s 5.

Para 2: amends the Ministry of Housing and Local Government Provisional Order Confirmation (Greater London Parks and Open Spaces) Act 1967, Schedule.

Para 3: amends the National Trust Act 1907, s 29.

Para 4: amends the National Trust Act 1971, s 23.

Para 5: amends the New Parishes Measure 1943 (No 1), s 15.

(*Schs 5, 6 contain consequential amendments and repeals which, in so far as relevant to this work, have been incorporated at the appropriate place.*)

HEALTH ACT 2006

(2006 c 28)

An Act to make provision for the prohibition of smoking in certain premises, places and vehicles and for amending the minimum age of persons to whom tobacco may be sold; to make provision in relation to the prevention and control of health care associated infections; to make provision in relation to the management and use of controlled drugs; to make provision in relation to the supervision of certain dealings with medicinal products and the running of pharmacy premises, and about orders under the Medicines Act 1968 and orders amending that Act under the Health Act 1999; to make further provision about the National Health Service in England and Wales and about the recovery of National Health Service costs; to make provision for the establishment and functions of the Appointments Commission; to make further provision about the exercise of social care training functions; and for connected purposes.

[19 July 2006]

PART 1
SMOKING

CHAPTER 1
SMOKE-FREE PREMISES, PLACES AND VEHICLES

Introduction

1 Introduction

(1) This Chapter makes provision for the prohibition of smoking in certain premises, places and vehicles which are smoke-free by virtue of this Chapter.

(2) In this Chapter—

(a) "smoking" refers to smoking tobacco or anything which contains tobacco, or smoking any other substance, and

(b) smoking includes being in possession of lit tobacco or of anything lit which contains tobacco, or being in possession of any other lit substance in a form in which it could be smoked.

(3) In this Chapter, "smoke" and other related expressions are to be read in accordance with subsection (2).

[2337]

NOTES

Commencement: 2 April 2007 (in relation to Wales); 1 July 2007 (in relation to England).

See further, the National Assembly for Wales Commission (Crown Status) (No 2) Order 2007, SI 2007/1353, art 7.

Smoke-free premises, etc

2 Smoke-free premises

(1) Premises are smoke-free if they are open to the public.

But unless the premises also fall within subsection (2), they are smoke-free only when open to the public.

(2) Premises are smoke-free if they are used as a place of work—

(a) by more than one person (even if the persons who work there do so at different times, or only intermittently), or

(b) where members of the public might attend for the purpose of seeking or receiving goods or services from the person or persons working there (even if members of the public are not always present).

They are smoke-free all the time.

(3) If only part of the premises is open to the public or (as the case may be) used as a place of work mentioned in subsection (2), the premises are smoke-free only to that extent.

(4) In any case, premises are smoke-free only in those areas which are enclosed or substantially enclosed.

(5) The appropriate national authority may specify in regulations what "enclosed" and "substantially enclosed" mean.

(6) Section 3 provides for some premises, or areas of premises, not to be smoke-free despite this section.

(7) Premises are "open to the public" if the public or a section of the public has access to them, whether by invitation or not, and whether on payment or not.

(8) "Work", in subsection (2), includes voluntary work.

[2338]

NOTES

Commencement: 19 July 2006 (so far as confers power to make regulations); 2 April 2007 (in relation to Wales for remaining purposes); 1 July 2007 (in relation to England for remaining purposes).

See further, the National Assembly for Wales Commission (Crown Status) (No 2) Order 2007, SI 2007/1353, art 7.

Regulations: the Smoke-free (Premises and Enforcement) Regulations 2006, SI 2006/3368; the Smoke-free Premises etc (Wales) Regulations 2007, SI 2007/787.

3 Smoke-free premises: exemptions

(1) The appropriate national authority may make regulations providing for specified descriptions of premises, or specified areas within specified descriptions of premises, not to be smoke-free despite section 2.

(2) Descriptions of premises which may be specified under subsection (1) include, in particular, any premises where a person has his home, or is living whether permanently or temporarily (including hotels, care homes, and prisons and other places where a person may be detained).

(3) The power to make regulations under subsection (1) is not exercisable so as to specify any description of—

- (a) premises in respect of which a premises licence under the Licensing Act 2003 (c 17) authorising the sale by retail of alcohol for consumption on the premises has effect,
- (b) premises in respect of which a club premises certificate (within the meaning of section 60 of that Act) has effect.

(4) But subsection (3) does not prevent the exercise of that power so as to specify any area, within a specified description of premises mentioned in subsection (3), where a person has his home, or is living whether permanently or temporarily.

(5) For the purpose of making provision for those participating as performers in a performance, or in a performance of a specified description, not to be prevented from smoking if the artistic integrity of the performance makes it appropriate for them to smoke—

- (a) the power in subsection (1) also includes power to provide for specified descriptions of premises or specified areas within such premises not to be smoke-free in relation only to such performers, and
- (b) subsection (3) does not prevent the exercise of that power as so extended.

(6) The regulations may provide, in relation to any description of premises or areas of premises specified in the regulations, that the premises or areas are not smoke-free—

- (a) in specified circumstances,
- (b) if specified conditions are satisfied, or
- (c) at specified times,

or any combination of those.

(7) The conditions may include conditions requiring the designation in accordance with the regulations, by the person in charge of the premises, of any rooms in which smoking is to be permitted.

(8) For the purposes of subsection (5), the references to a performance—

- (a) include, for example, the performance of a play, or a performance given in connection with the making of a film or television programme, and
- (b) if the regulations so provide, include a rehearsal.

[2339]

NOTES

Commencement: 19 July 2006 (so far as confers power to make regulations); 2 April 2007 (in relation to Wales for remaining purposes); 1 July 2007 (in relation to England for remaining purposes).

See further, the National Assembly for Wales Commission (Crown Status) (No 2) Order 2007, SI 2007/1353, art 7.

Regulations: the Smoke-free (Exemptions and Vehicles) Regulations 2007, SI 2007/765; the Smoke-free Premises etc (Wales) Regulations 2007, SI 2007/787.

4 Additional smoke-free places

(1) The appropriate national authority may make regulations designating as smoke-free any place or description of place that is not smoke-free under section 2.

(2) The place, or places falling within the description, need not be enclosed or substantially enclosed.

(3) The appropriate national authority may designate a place or description of place under this section only if in the authority's opinion there is a significant risk that, without a designation, persons present there would be exposed to significant quantities of smoke.

(4) The regulations may provide for such places, or places falling within the description, to be smoke-free only—

- (a) in specified circumstances,
- (b) at specified times,
- (c) if specified conditions are satisfied,

(d) in specified areas,

or any combination of those.

[2340]

NOTES

Commencement: 19 July 2006 (so far as confers power to make regulations); 1 July 2007 (in relation to England for remaining purposes); to be appointed (otherwise).

See further, the National Assembly for Wales Commission (Crown Status) (No 2) Order 2007, SI 2007/1353, art 7.

5 (*Outside the scope of this work.*)

No-smoking signs

6 No-smoking signs

(1) It is the duty of any person who occupies or is concerned in the management of smoke-free premises to make sure that no-smoking signs complying with the requirements of this section are displayed in those premises in accordance with the requirements of this section.

(2) Regulations made by the appropriate national authority may provide for a duty corresponding to that mentioned in subsection (1) in relation to—

(a) places which are smoke-free by virtue of section 4,
(b) vehicles which are smoke-free by virtue of section 5.

The duty is to be imposed on persons, or on persons of a description, specified in the regulations.

(3) The signs must be displayed in accordance with any requirements contained in regulations made by the appropriate national authority.

(4) The signs must conform to any requirements specified in regulations made by the appropriate national authority (for example, requirements as to content, size, design, colour, or wording).

(5) A person who fails to comply with the duty in subsection (1), or any corresponding duty in regulations under subsection (2), commits an offence.

(6) It is a defence for a person charged with an offence under subsection (5) to show—

(a) that he did not know, and could not reasonably have been expected to know, that the premises were smoke-free (or, as the case may be, that the place or vehicle was smoke-free), or
(b) that he did not know, and could not reasonably have been expected to know, that no-smoking signs complying with the requirements of this section were not being displayed in accordance with the requirements of this section, or
(c) that on other grounds it was reasonable for him not to comply with the duty.

(7) If a person charged with an offence under subsection (5) relies on a defence in subsection (6), and evidence is adduced which is sufficient to raise an issue with respect to that defence, the court must assume that the defence is satisfied unless the prosecution proves beyond reasonable doubt that it is not.

(8) A person guilty of an offence under subsection (5) is liable on summary conviction to a fine not exceeding a level on the standard scale specified in regulations made by the Secretary of State.

(9) The references in this section, however expressed, to premises, places or vehicles which are smoke-free, are to those premises, places or vehicles so far as they are smoke-free under or by virtue of this Chapter (and references to smoke-free premises include premises which by virtue of regulations under section 3(5) are smoke-free except in relation to performers).

[2341]

NOTES

Commencement: 19 July 2006 (so far as confers power to make regulations); 2 April 2007 (in relation to Wales for remaining purposes); 1 July 2007 (in relation to England for remaining purposes).

See further, the National Assembly for Wales Commission (Crown Status) (No 2) Order 2007, SI 2007/1353, art 7.

Regulations: the Smoke-free (Penalties and Discounted Amounts) Regulations 2007, SI 2007/764; the Smoke-free Premises etc (Wales) Regulations 2007, SI 2007/787; the Smoke-free (Signs) Regulations 2007, SI 2007/923.

Offences relating to smoking in smoke-free premises, etc

7 Offence of smoking in smoke-free place

(1) In this section, a "smoke-free place" means any of the following—

(a) premises, so far as they are smoke-free under or by virtue of sections 2 and 3 (including premises which by virtue of regulations under section 3(5) are smoke-free except in relation to performers),

(b) a place, so far as it is smoke-free by virtue of section 4,
(c) a vehicle, so far as it is smoke-free by virtue of section 5.

(2) A person who smokes in a smoke-free place commits an offence.

(3) But a person who smokes in premises which are not smoke-free in relation to performers by virtue of regulations under section 3(5) does not commit an offence if he is such a performer.

(4) It is a defence for a person charged with an offence under subsection (2) to show that he did not know, and could not reasonably have been expected to know, that it was a smoke-free place.

(5) If a person charged with an offence under this section relies on a defence in subsection (4), and evidence is adduced which is sufficient to raise an issue with respect to that defence, the court must assume that the defence is satisfied unless the prosecution proves beyond reasonable doubt that it is not.

(6) A person guilty of an offence under this section is liable on summary conviction to a fine not exceeding a level on the standard scale specified in regulations made by the Secretary of State.

[2342]

NOTES

Commencement: 19 July 2006 (so far as confers power to make regulations); 2 April 2007 (in relation to Wales for remaining purposes); 1 July 2007 (in relation to England for remaining purposes).

See further, the National Assembly for Wales Commission (Crown Status) (No 2) Order 2007, SI 2007/1353, art 7.

Regulations: the Smoke-free (Penalties and Discounted Amounts) Regulations 2007, SI 2007/764.

8 Offence of failing to prevent smoking in smoke-free place

(1) It is the duty of any person who controls or is concerned in the management of smoke-free premises to cause a person smoking there to stop smoking.

(2) The reference in subsection (1) to a person smoking does not include a performer in relation to whom the premises are not smoke-free by virtue of regulations under section 3(5).

(3) Regulations made by the appropriate national authority may provide for a duty corresponding to that mentioned in subsection (1) in relation to—

(a) places which are smoke-free by virtue of section 4,
(b) vehicles which are smoke-free by virtue of section 5.

The duty is to be imposed on persons, or on persons of a description, specified in the regulations.

(4) A person who fails to comply with the duty in subsection (1), or any corresponding duty in regulations under subsection (3), commits an offence.

(5) It is a defence for a person charged with an offence under subsection (4) to show—

(a) that he took reasonable steps to cause the person in question to stop smoking, or
(b) that he did not know, and could not reasonably have been expected to know, that the person in question was smoking, or
(c) that on other grounds it was reasonable for him not to comply with the duty.

(6) If a person charged with an offence under this section relies on a defence in subsection (5), and evidence is adduced which is sufficient to raise an issue with respect to that defence, the court must assume that the defence is satisfied unless the prosecution proves beyond reasonable doubt that it is not.

(7) A person guilty of an offence under this section is liable on summary conviction to a fine not exceeding a level on the standard scale specified in regulations made by the Secretary of State.

(8) The references in this section, however expressed, to premises, places or vehicles which are smoke-free, are to those premises, places or vehicles so far as they are smoke-free under or by virtue of this Chapter (and references to smoke-free premises include premises which by virtue of regulations under section 3(5) are smoke-free except in relation to performers).

[2343]

NOTES

Commencement: 19 July 2006 (so far as confers power to make regulations); 2 April 2007 (in relation to Wales for remaining purposes); 1 July 2007 (in relation to England for remaining purposes).

See further, the National Assembly for Wales Commission (Crown Status) (No 2) Order 2007, SI 2007/1353, art 7.

Regulations: the Smoke-free (Vehicle Operators and Penalty Notices) Regulations 2007, SI 2007/760; the Smoke-free (Penalties and Discounted Amounts) Regulations 2007, SI 2007/764; the Smoke-free Premises etc (Wales) Regulations 2007, SI 2007/787.

9–11 (*Outside the scope of this work.*)

Interpretation, etc

12 Interpretation and territorial sea

(1) In this Chapter—

"authorised officer" has the meaning given by section 10(5),

"premises" includes a tent, and (if not a ship within the meaning of the Merchant Shipping Act 1995 (c 21)) a moveable structure and an offshore installation (as defined in regulation 3 of the Offshore Installations and Pipeline Works (Management and Administration) Regulations 1995 (SI 1995/738)),

"specified", in relation to regulations, means specified in the regulations,

"vehicle" is to be construed in accordance with section 5(5).

(2) The appropriate national authority may by order provide for the definition of "premises" in subsection (1) to be read as if a reference to another enactment were substituted for the reference to regulation 3 of the Offshore Installations and Pipeline Works (Management and Administration) Regulations 1995.

(3) This Chapter—

(a) has effect in relation to the territorial sea adjacent to England as it has effect in relation to England, and

(b) has effect in relation to the territorial sea adjacent to Wales as it has effect in relation to Wales.

(4) The following have effect for the purposes of subsection (3) if or in so far as expressed to apply for the general or residual purposes of the Act in question or for the purposes of this section—

(a) an Order in Council under section 126(2) of the Scotland Act 1998 (c 46),

(b) an order or Order in Council under or by virtue of section [158(3) and (4) of the Government of Wales Act 2006].

[2344]

NOTES

Commencement: 19 July 2006 (so far as confers power to make regulations); 2 April 2007 (in relation to Wales for remaining purposes); 1 July 2007 (in relation to England for remaining purposes).

Sub-s (4): words in square brackets in para (b) substituted by SI 2007/1388, art 3, Sch 1, para 123.

See further, the National Assembly for Wales Commission (Crown Status) (No 2) Order 2007, SI 2007/1353, art 7.

13–75 (*S 13 (Ch 2), ss 14–75 (Pts 2–6) outside the scope of this work.*)

PART 7
FINAL PROVISIONS

76–78 (*Outside the scope of this work.*)

General

79–83 (*Outside the scope of this work.*)

84 Short title and extent

(1) This Act may be cited as the Health Act 2006.

(2) Subject to subsections (3) and (4), this Act extends to England and Wales only.

(3) The following provisions extend also to Scotland and Northern Ireland—

(a), (b) (*outside the scope of this work.*)

(c) sections 75, 76, 77, 79 to 83 and this section.

(4) Any amendment, repeal or revocation made by this Act has the same extent as the enactment to which it relates.

[2345]

NOTES

Commencement: 19 July 2006.

(*Schs 1–7 outside the scope of this work; Schs 8, 9 contain consequential amendments which, in so far as relevant to this work, have been incorporated at the appropriate place.*)

FRAUD ACT 2006

(2006 c 35)

An Act to make provision for, and in connection with, criminal liability for fraud and obtaining services dishonestly.

[8 November 2006]

Fraud

1 Fraud

(1) A person is guilty of fraud if he is in breach of any of the sections listed in subsection (2) (which provide for different ways of committing the offence).

(2) The sections are—

(a) section 2 (fraud by false representation),
(b) section 3 (fraud by failing to disclose information), and
(c) section 4 (fraud by abuse of position).

(3) A person who is guilty of fraud is liable—

(a) on summary conviction, to imprisonment for a term not exceeding 12 months or to a fine not exceeding the statutory maximum (or to both);
(b) on conviction on indictment, to imprisonment for a term not exceeding 10 years or to a fine (or to both).

(4) Subsection (3)(a) applies in relation to Northern Ireland as if the reference to 12 months were a reference to 6 months.

[2346]

NOTES

Commencement: 15 January 2007.

2 Fraud by false representation

(1) A person is in breach of this section if he—

(a) dishonestly makes a false representation, and
(b) intends, by making the representation—
 (i) to make a gain for himself or another, or
 (ii) to cause loss to another or to expose another to a risk of loss.

(2) A representation is false if—

(a) it is untrue or misleading, and
(b) the person making it knows that it is, or might be, untrue or misleading.

(3) "Representation" means any representation as to fact or law, including a representation as to the state of mind of—

(a) the person making the representation, or
(b) any other person.

(4) A representation may be express or implied.

(5) For the purposes of this section a representation may be regarded as made if it (or anything implying it) is submitted in any form to any system or device designed to receive, convey or respond to communications (with or without human intervention).

[2347]

NOTES

Commencement: 15 January 2007.

3 Fraud by failing to disclose information

A person is in breach of this section if he—

(a) dishonestly fails to disclose to another person information which he is under a legal duty to disclose, and
(b) intends, by failing to disclose the information—
 (i) to make a gain for himself or another, or
 (ii) to cause loss to another or to expose another to a risk of loss.

[2348]

NOTES

Commencement: 15 January 2007.

4 Fraud by abuse of position

(1) A person is in breach of this section if he—

(a) occupies a position in which he is expected to safeguard, or not to act against, the financial interests of another person,

(b) dishonestly abuses that position, and

(c) intends, by means of the abuse of that position—

(i) to make a gain for himself or another, or

(ii) to cause loss to another or to expose another to a risk of loss.

(2) A person may be regarded as having abused his position even though his conduct consisted of an omission rather than an act.

[2349]

NOTES

Commencement: 15 January 2007.

5 "Gain" and "loss"

(1) The references to gain and loss in sections 2 to 4 are to be read in accordance with this section.

(2) "Gain" and "loss"—

(a) extend only to gain or loss in money or other property;

(b) include any such gain or loss whether temporary or permanent;

and "property" means any property whether real or personal (including things in action and other intangible property).

(3) "Gain" includes a gain by keeping what one has, as well as a gain by getting what one does not have.

(4) "Loss" includes a loss by not getting what one might get, as well as a loss by parting with what one has.

[2350]

NOTES

Commencement: 15 January 2007.

6–11 (*Outside the scope of this work.*)

Supplementary

12 Liability of company officers for offences by company

(1) Subsection (2) applies if an offence under this Act is committed by a body corporate.

(2) If the offence is proved to have been committed with the consent or connivance of—

(a) a director, manager, secretary or other similar officer of the body corporate, or

(b) a person who was purporting to act in any such capacity,

he (as well as the body corporate) is guilty of the offence and liable to be proceeded against and punished accordingly.

(3) If the affairs of a body corporate are managed by its members, subsection (2) applies in relation to the acts and defaults of a member in connection with his functions of management as if he were a director of the body corporate.

[2351]

NOTES

Commencement: 15 January 2007.

13 Evidence

(1) A person is not to be excused from—

(a) answering any question put to him in proceedings relating to property, or

(b) complying with any order made in proceedings relating to property,

on the ground that doing so may incriminate him or his spouse or civil partner of an offence under this Act or a related offence.

(2) But, in proceedings for an offence under this Act or a related offence, a statement or admission made by the person in—

(a) answering such a question, or

(b) complying with such an order,

is not admissible in evidence against him or (unless they married or became civil partners after the making of the statement or admission) his spouse or civil partner.

(3) "Proceedings relating to property" means any proceedings for—
(a) the recovery or administration of any property,
(b) the execution of a trust, or
(c) an account of any property or dealings with property,

and "property" means money or other property whether real or personal (including things in action and other intangible property).

(4) "Related offence" means—
(a) conspiracy to defraud;
(b) any other offence involving any form of fraudulent conduct or purpose.

[2352]

NOTES
Commencement: 15 January 2007.

14 (*Outside the scope of this work.*)

15 Commencement and extent

(1) This Act (except this section and section 16) comes into force on such day as the Secretary of State may appoint by an order made by statutory instrument; and different days may be appointed for different purposes.

(2) Subject to subsection (3), sections 1 to 9 and 11 to 13 extend to England and Wales and Northern Ireland only.

(3), (4) (*Outside the scope of this work.*)

[2353]

NOTES
Commencement: 8 November 2006.
Order: the Fraud Act 2006 (Commencement) Order 2006, SI 2006/3200.

16 Short title

This Act may be cited as the Fraud Act 2006.

[2354]

NOTES
Commencement: 8 November 2006.

(*Sch 1 contains consequential amendments; Sch 2 outside the scope of this work; Sch 3 contains repeals and revocations.*)

COMPANIES ACT 2006

(2006 c 46)

An Act to reform company law and restate the greater part of the enactments relating to companies; to make other provision relating to companies and other forms of business organisation; to make provision about directors' disqualification, business names, auditors and actuaries; to amend Part 9 of the Enterprise Act 2002; and for connected purposes.

[8 November 2006]

1–38 ((*Pts 1–3*) *Outside the scope of this work.*)

PART 4
A COMPANY'S CAPACITY AND RELATED MATTERS

Capacity of company and power of directors to bind it

39 A company's capacity

(1) The validity of an act done by a company shall not be called into question on the ground of lack of capacity by reason of anything in the company's constitution.

(2) This section has effect subject to section 42 (companies that are charities).

[2355]

NOTES

Commencement: 1 October 2009; for transitional provisions, see SI 2008/2860, Sch 2, para 15.

40 Power of directors to bind the company

(1) In favour of a person dealing with a company in good faith, the power of the directors to bind the company, or authorise others to do so, is deemed to be free of any limitation under the company's constitution.

(2) For this purpose—

(a) a person "deals with" a company if he is a party to any transaction or other act to which the company is a party,

(b) a person dealing with a company—

(i) is not bound to enquire as to any limitation on the powers of the directors to bind the company or authorise others to do so,

(ii) is presumed to have acted in good faith unless the contrary is proved, and

(iii) is not to be regarded as acting in bad faith by reason only of his knowing that an act is beyond the powers of the directors under the company's constitution.

(3) The references above to limitations on the directors' powers under the company's constitution include limitations deriving—

(a) from a resolution of the company or of any class of shareholders, or

(b) from any agreement between the members of the company or of any class of shareholders.

(4) This section does not affect any right of a member of the company to bring proceedings to restrain the doing of an action that is beyond the powers of the directors.

But no such proceedings lie in respect of an act to be done in fulfilment of a legal obligation arising from a previous act of the company.

(5) This section does not affect any liability incurred by the directors, or any other person, by reason of the directors' exceeding their powers.

(6) This section has effect subject to—

section 41 (transactions with directors or their associates), and
section 42 (companies that are charities).

[2356]

NOTES

Commencement: 1 October 2009.

41 Constitutional limitations: transactions involving directors or their associates

(1) This section applies to a transaction if or to the extent that its validity depends on section 40 (power of directors deemed to be free of limitations under company's constitution in favour of person dealing with company in good faith).

Nothing in this section shall be read as excluding the operation of any other enactment or rule of law by virtue of which the transaction may be called in question or any liability to the company may arise.

(2) Where—

(a) a company enters into such a transaction, and

(b) the parties to the transaction include—

(i) a director of the company or of its holding company, or

(ii) a person connected with any such director,

the transaction is voidable at the instance of the company.

(3) Whether or not it is avoided, any such party to the transaction as is mentioned in subsection (2)(b)(i) or (ii), and any director of the company who authorised the transaction, is liable—

(a) to account to the company for any gain he has made directly or indirectly by the transaction, and

(b) to indemnify the company for any loss or damage resulting from the transaction.

(4) The transaction ceases to be voidable if—

(a) restitution of any money or other asset which was the subject matter of the transaction is no longer possible, or

(b) the company is indemnified for any loss or damage resulting from the transaction, or

(c) rights acquired bona fide for value and without actual notice of the directors' exceeding their powers by a person who is not party to the transaction would be affected by the avoidance, or

(d) the transaction is affirmed by the company.

(5) A person other than a director of the company is not liable under subsection (3) if he shows that at the time the transaction was entered into he did not know that the directors were exceeding their powers.

(6) Nothing in the preceding provisions of this section affects the rights of any party to the transaction not within subsection (2)(b)(i) or (ii).

But the court may, on the application of the company or any such party, make an order affirming, severing or setting aside the transaction on such terms as appear to the court to be just.

(7) In this section—

(a) "transaction" includes any act; and

(b) the reference to a person connected with a director has the same meaning as in Part 10 (company directors).

[2357]

NOTES

Commencement: 1 October 2009.

42 Constitutional limitations: companies that are charities

(1) Sections 39 and 40 (company's capacity and power of directors to bind company) do not apply to the acts of a company that is a charity except in favour of a person who—

(a) does not know at the time the act is done that the company is a charity, or

(b) gives full consideration in money or money's worth in relation to the act in question and does not know (as the case may be)—

(i) that the act is not permitted by the company's constitution, or

(ii) that the act is beyond the powers of the directors.

(2) Where a company that is a charity purports to transfer or grant an interest in property, the fact that (as the case may be)—

(a) the act was not permitted by the company's constitution, or

(b) the directors in connection with the act exceeded any limitation on their powers under the company's constitution,

does not affect the title of a person who subsequently acquires the property or any interest in it for full consideration without actual notice of any such circumstances affecting the validity of the company's act.

(3) In any proceedings arising out of subsection (1) or (2) the burden of proving—

(a) that a person knew that the company was a charity, or

(b) that a person knew that an act was not permitted by the company's constitution or was beyond the powers of the directors,

lies on the person asserting that fact.

(4) In the case of a company that is a charity the affirmation of a transaction to which section 41 applies (transactions with directors or their associates) is ineffective without the prior written consent of—

(a) in England and Wales, the Charity Commission;

(b) in Northern Ireland, the Department for Social Development.

(5) This section does not extend to Scotland (but see section 112 of the Companies Act 1989 (c 40)).

[2358]

NOTES

Commencement: 1 October 2009; for transitional provisions, see SI 2009/1941, art 6.

Formalities of doing business under the law of England and Wales or Northern Ireland

43 Company contracts

(1) Under the law of England and Wales or Northern Ireland a contract may be made—

(a) by a company, by writing under its common seal, or

(b) on behalf of a company, by a person acting under its authority, express or implied.

(2) Any formalities required by law in the case of a contract made by an individual also apply, unless a contrary intention appears, to a contract made by or on behalf of a company.

[2359]

NOTES

Commencement: 1 October 2009.

44 Execution of documents

(1) Under the law of England and Wales or Northern Ireland a document is executed by a company—

(a) by the affixing of its common seal, or
(b) by signature in accordance with the following provisions.

(2) A document is validly executed by a company if it is signed on behalf of the company—

(a) by two authorised signatories, or
(b) by a director of the company in the presence of a witness who attests the signature.

(3) The following are "authorised signatories" for the purposes of subsection (2)—

(a) every director of the company, and
(b) in the case of a private company with a secretary or a public company, the secretary (or any joint secretary) of the company.

(4) A document signed in accordance with subsection (2) and expressed, in whatever words, to be executed by the company has the same effect as if executed under the common seal of the company.

(5) In favour of a purchaser a document is deemed to have been duly executed by a company if it purports to be signed in accordance with subsection (2).

A "purchaser" means a purchaser in good faith for valuable consideration and includes a lessee, mortgagee or other person who for valuable consideration acquires an interest in property.

(6) Where a document is to be signed by a person on behalf of more than one company, it is not duly signed by that person for the purposes of this section unless he signs it separately in each capacity.

(7) References in this section to a document being (or purporting to be) signed by a director or secretary are to be read, in a case where that office is held by a firm, as references to its being (or purporting to be) signed by an individual authorised by the firm to sign on its behalf.

(8) This section applies to a document that is (or purports to be) executed by a company in the name of or on behalf of another person whether or not that person is also a company.

[2360]

NOTES

Commencement: 1 October 2009; for transitional provisions, see SI 2007/3495.

See further in relation to the application of this section, with modifications, in so far as it relates to LLPs: the Limited Liability Partnerships (Application of Companies Act 2006) Regulations 2009, SI 2009/1804, reg 4.

45 Common seal

(1) A company may have a common seal, but need not have one.

(2) A company which has a common seal shall have its name engraved in legible characters on the seal.

(3) If a company fails to comply with subsection (2) an offence is committed by—

(a) the company, and
(b) every officer of the company who is in default.

(4) An officer of a company, or a person acting on behalf of a company, commits an offence if he uses, or authorises the use of, a seal purporting to be a seal of the company on which its name is not engraved as required by subsection (2).

(5) A person guilty of an offence under this section is liable on summary conviction to a fine not exceeding level 3 on the standard scale.

(6) This section does not form part of the law of Scotland.

[2361]

NOTES

Commencement: 1 October 2009.

See further in relation to the application of this section, with modifications, in so far as it relates to LLPs: the Limited Liability Partnerships (Application of Companies Act 2006) Regulations 2009, SI 2009/1804, reg 4.

46 Execution of deeds

(1) A document is validly executed by a company as a deed for the purposes of section 1(2)(b) of the Law of Property (Miscellaneous Provisions) Act 1989 (c 34) and for the purposes of the law of Northern Ireland if, and only if—

(a) it is duly executed by the company, and
(b) it is delivered as a deed.

(2) For the purposes of subsection (1)(b) a document is presumed to be delivered upon its being executed, unless a contrary intention is proved.

[2362]

NOTES

Commencement: 1 October 2009.

See further in relation to the application of this section, with modifications, in so far as it relates to LLPs: the Limited Liability Partnerships (Application of Companies Act 2006) Regulations 2009, SI 2009/1804, reg 4.

47 Execution of deeds or other documents by attorney

(1) Under the law of England and Wales or Northern Ireland a company may, by instrument executed as a deed, empower a person, either generally or in respect of specified matters, as its attorney to execute deeds or other documents on its behalf.

(2) A deed or other document so executed, whether in the United Kingdom or elsewhere, has effect as if executed by the company.

[2363]

NOTES

Commencement: 1 October 2009; for transitional provisions, see SI 2008/2680, Sch 2, para 16.

See further in relation to the application of this section, with modifications, in so far as it relates to LLPs: the Limited Liability Partnerships (Application of Companies Act 2006) Regulations 2009, SI 2009/1804, regs 4, 83, Sch 1, Pt 2, para 2(1).

48 (*Outside the scope of this work.*)

Other matters

49, 50 (*Outside the scope of this work.*)

51 Pre-incorporation contracts, deeds and obligations

(1) A contract that purports to be made by or on behalf of a company at a time when the company has not been formed has effect, subject to any agreement to the contrary, as one made with the person purporting to act for the company or as agent for it, and he is personally liable on the contract accordingly.

(2) Subsection (1) applies—

(a) to the making of a deed under the law of England and Wales or Northern Ireland, and

(b) to the undertaking of an obligation under the law of Scotland,

as it applies to the making of a contract.

[2364]

NOTES

Commencement: 1 October 2009.

See further in relation to the application of this section, with modifications, in so far as it relates to LLPs: the Limited Liability Partnerships (Application of Companies Act 2006) Regulations 2009, SI 2009/1804, reg 7.

52–153 (*S 52, ss 53–153* (*Pts 5–9*) *outside the scope of this work.*)

PART 10
A COMPANY'S DIRECTORS

154–187 ((*Chs 1–3*) *outside the scope of this work.*)

CHAPTER 4
TRANSACTIONS WITH DIRECTORS REQUIRING APPROVAL OF MEMBERS

188, 189 (*Outside the scope of this work.*)

Substantial property transactions

190 Substantial property transactions: requirement of members' approval

(1) A company may not enter into an arrangement under which—

(a) a director of the company or of its holding company, or a person connected with such a director, acquires or is to acquire from the company (directly or indirectly) a substantial non-cash asset, or

(b) the company acquires or is to acquire a substantial non-cash asset (directly or indirectly) from such a director or a person so connected, unless the arrangement has been approved by a resolution of the members of the company or is conditional on such approval being obtained.

For the meaning of "substantial non-cash asset" see section 191.

(2) If the director or connected person is a director of the company's holding company or a person connected with such a director, the arrangement must also have been approved by a resolution of the members of the holding company or be conditional on such approval being obtained.

(3) A company shall not be subject to any liability by reason of a failure to obtain approval required by this section.

(4) No approval is required under this section on the part of the members of a body corporate that—

(a) is not a UK-registered company, or
(b) is a wholly-owned subsidiary of another body corporate.

(5) For the purposes of this section—

(a) an arrangement involving more than one non-cash asset, or
(b) an arrangement that is one of a series involving non-cash assets,

shall be treated as if they involved a non-cash asset of a value equal to the aggregate value of all the non-cash assets involved in the arrangement or, as the case may be, the series.

(6) This section does not apply to a transaction so far as it relates—

(a) to anything to which a director of a company is entitled under his service contract, or
(b) to payment for loss of office as defined in section 215 (payments requiring members' approval).

[2365]

NOTES

Commencement: 1 October 2007; for transitional provisions, see SI 2007/2194, Sch 3, para 7.

See further, in relation to the disapplication of ss 190–196, in respect of certain specified persons while Northern Rock is wholly owned by the Treasury: the Northern Rock plc Transfer Order 2008, SI 2008/432, art 17, Schedule, para 2(h).

See further, in relation to the disapplication of ss 190–196, in respect of certain specified persons while Bradford & Bingley is wholly owned by the Treasury: the Bradford & Bingley plc Transfer of Securities and Property etc Order 2008, SI 2008/2546, art 13(1), Schedule, para 2(h).

See further, in relation to the disapplication of ss 190–196, in respect of certain specified persons while Deposits Management (Heritable) is wholly owned by the Treasury: the Heritable Bank plc Transfer of Certain Rights and Liabilities Order 2008, SI 2008/2644, art 26, Sch 2, para 2(h).

191 Meaning of "substantial"

(1) This section explains what is meant in section 190 (requirement of approval for substantial property transactions) by a "substantial" non-cash asset.

(2) An asset is a substantial asset in relation to a company if its value—

(a) exceeds 10% of the company's asset value and is more than £5,000, or
(b) exceeds £100,000.

(3) For this purpose a company's "asset value" at any time is—

(a) the value of the company's net assets determined by reference to its most recent statutory accounts, or
(b) if no statutory accounts have been prepared, the amount of the company's called-up share capital.

(4) A company's "statutory accounts" means its annual accounts prepared in accordance with Part 15, and its "most recent" statutory accounts means those in relation to which the time for sending them out to members (see section 424) is most recent.

(5) Whether an asset is a substantial asset shall be determined as at the time the arrangement is entered into.

[2366]

NOTES

Commencement: 1 October 2007; for transitional provisions, see SI 2007/2194, Sch 3, para 7.

In relation to Northern Rock, Bradford & Bingley and Heritable Bank, see the note to s 190 at **[2365]**.

192 Exception for transactions with members or other group companies

Approval is not required under section 190 (requirement of members' approval for substantial property transactions)—

(a) for a transaction between a company and a person in his character as a member of that company, or
(b) for a transaction between—
    (i) a holding company and its wholly-owned subsidiary, or

(ii) two wholly-owned subsidiaries of the same holding company.

[2367]

NOTES

Commencement: 1 October 2007; for transitional provisions, see SI 2007/2194, Sch 3, para 7.

In relation to Northern Rock, Bradford & Bingley and Heritable Bank, see the note to s 190 at **[2365]**.

193 Exception in case of company in winding up or administration

(1) This section applies to a company—

(a) that is being wound up (unless the winding up is a members' voluntary winding up), or

(b) that is in administration within the meaning of Schedule B1 to the Insolvency Act 1986 (c 45) or the Insolvency (Northern Ireland) Order 1989 (SI 1989/2405 (NI 19)).

(2) Approval is not required under section 190 (requirement of members' approval for substantial property transactions)—

(a) on the part of the members of a company to which this section applies, or

(b) for an arrangement entered into by a company to which this section applies.

[2368]

NOTES

Commencement: 1 October 2007; for transitional provisions, see SI 2007/2194, Sch 3, para 7.

In relation to Northern Rock, Bradford & Bingley and Heritable Bank, see the note to s 190 at **[2365]**.

194 Exception for transactions on recognised investment exchange

(1) Approval is not required under section 190 (requirement of members' approval for substantial property transactions) for a transaction on a recognised investment exchange effected by a director, or a person connected with him, through the agency of a person who in relation to the transaction acts as an independent broker.

(2) For this purpose—

(a) "independent broker" means a person who, independently of the director or any person connected with him, selects the person with whom the transaction is to be effected; and

(b) "recognised investment exchange" has the same meaning as in Part 18 of the Financial Services and Markets Act 2000 (c 8).

[2369]

NOTES

Commencement: 1 October 2007; for transitional provisions, see SI 2007/2194, Sch 3, para 7.

In relation to Northern Rock, Bradford & Bingley and Heritable Bank, see the note to s 190 at **[2365]**.

195 Property transactions: civil consequences of contravention

(1) This section applies where a company enters into an arrangement in contravention of section 190 (requirement of members' approval for substantial property transactions).

(2) The arrangement, and any transaction entered into in pursuance of the arrangement (whether by the company or any other person), is voidable at the instance of the company, unless—

(a) restitution of any money or other asset that was the subject matter of the arrangement or transaction is no longer possible,

(b) the company has been indemnified in pursuance of this section by any other persons for the loss or damage suffered by it, or

(c) rights acquired in good faith, for value and without actual notice of the contravention by a person who is not a party to the arrangement or transaction would be affected by the avoidance.

(3) Whether or not the arrangement or any such transaction has been avoided, each of the persons specified in subsection (4) is liable—

(a) to account to the company for any gain that he has made directly or indirectly by the arrangement or transaction, and

(b) (jointly and severally with any other person so liable under this section) to indemnify the company for any loss or damage resulting from the arrangement or transaction.

(4) The persons so liable are—

(a) any director of the company or of its holding company with whom the company entered into the arrangement in contravention of section 190,

(b) any person with whom the company entered into the arrangement in contravention of that section who is connected with a director of the company or of its holding company,

(c) the director of the company or of its holding company with whom any such person is connected, and

(d) any other director of the company who authorised the arrangement or any transaction entered into in pursuance of such an arrangement.

(5) Subsections (3) and (4) are subject to the following two subsections.

(6) In the case of an arrangement entered into by a company in contravention of section 190 with a person connected with a director of the company or of its holding company, that director is not liable by virtue of subsection (4)(c) if he shows that he took all reasonable steps to secure the company's compliance with that section.

(7) In any case—

(a) a person so connected is not liable by virtue of subsection (4)(b), and
(b) a director is not liable by virtue of subsection (4)(d),

if he shows that, at the time the arrangement was entered into, he did not know the relevant circumstances constituting the contravention.

(8) Nothing in this section shall be read as excluding the operation of any other enactment or rule of law by virtue of which the arrangement or transaction may be called in question or any liability to the company may arise.

[2370]

NOTES

Commencement: 1 October 2007; for transitional provisions, see SI 2007/2194, Sch 3, para 7.
In relation to Northern Rock, Bradford & Bingley and Heritable Bank, see the note to s 190 at **[2365]**.

196 Property transactions: effect of subsequent affirmation

Where a transaction or arrangement is entered into by a company in contravention of section 190 (requirement of members' approval) but, within a reasonable period, it is affirmed—

(a) in the case of a contravention of subsection (1) of that section, by resolution of the members of the company, and
(b) in the case of a contravention of subsection (2) of that section, by resolution of the members of the holding company,

the transaction or arrangement may no longer be avoided under section 195.

[2371]

NOTES

Commencement: 1 October 2007; for transitional provisions, see SI 2007/2194, Sch 3, para 7.
In relation to Northern Rock, Bradford & Bingley and Heritable Bank, see the note to s 190 at **[2365]**.

197–246 (*Ss 197–226, ss 227–246* (*Chs 5–8*) *outside the scope of this work.*)

CHAPTER 9
SUPPLEMENTARY PROVISIONS

247–249 (*Outside the scope of this work.*)

Meaning of "director" and "shadow director"

250 "Director"

In the Companies Acts "director" includes any person occupying the position of director, by whatever name called.

[2372]

NOTES

Commencement: 1 October 2007.

251 "Shadow director"

(1) In the Companies Acts "shadow director", in relation to a company, means a person in accordance with whose directions or instructions the directors of the company are accustomed to act.

(2) A person is not to be regarded as a shadow director by reason only that the directors act on advice given by him in a professional capacity.

(3) A body corporate is not to be regarded as a shadow director of any of its subsidiary companies for the purposes of—

Chapter 2 (general duties of directors),
Chapter 4 (transactions requiring members' approval), or
Chapter 6 (contract with sole member who is also a director),

by reason only that the directors of the subsidiary are accustomed to act in accordance with its directions or instructions.

[2373]

NOTES

Commencement: 1 October 2007.

Other definitions

252 Persons connected with a director

(1) This section defines what is meant by references in this Part to a person being "connected" with a director of a company (or a director being "connected" with a person).

(2) The following persons (and only those persons) are connected with a director of a company—

(a) members of the director's family (see section 253);
(b) a body corporate with which the director is connected (as defined in section 254);
(c) a person acting in his capacity as trustee of a trust—
 (i) the beneficiaries of which include the director or a person who by virtue of paragraph (a) or (b) is connected with him, or
 (ii) the terms of which confer a power on the trustees that may be exercised for the benefit of the director or any such person,

 other than a trust for the purposes of an employees' share scheme or a pension scheme;
(d) a person acting in his capacity as partner—
 (i) of the director, or
 (ii) of a person who, by virtue of paragraph (a), (b) or (c), is connected with that director;
(e) a firm that is a legal person under the law by which it is governed and in which—
 (i) the director is a partner,
 (ii) a partner is a person who, by virtue of paragraph (a), (b) or (c) is connected with the director, or
 (iii) a partner is a firm in which the director is a partner or in which there is a partner who, by virtue of paragraph (a), (b) or (c), is connected with the director.

(3) References in this Part to a person connected with a director of a company do not include a person who is himself a director of the company.

[2374]

NOTES

Commencement: 1 October 2007.

253 Members of a director's family

(1) This section defines what is meant by references in this Part to members of a director's family.

(2) For the purposes of this Part the members of a director's family are—

(a) the director's spouse or civil partner;
(b) any other person (whether of a different sex or the same sex) with whom the director lives as partner in an enduring family relationship;
(c) the director's children or step-children;
(d) any children or step-children of a person within paragraph (b) (and who are not children or step-children of the director) who live with the director and have not attained the age of 18;
(e) the director's parents.

(3) Subsection (2)(b) does not apply if the other person is the director's grandparent or grandchild, sister, brother, aunt or uncle, or nephew or niece.

[2375]

NOTES

Commencement: 1 October 2007.

254 Director "connected with" a body corporate

(1) This section defines what is meant by references in this Part to a director being "connected with" a body corporate.

(2) A director is connected with a body corporate if, but only if, he and the persons connected with him together—

(a) are interested in shares comprised in the equity share capital of that body corporate of a nominal value equal to at least 20% of that share capital, or
(b) are entitled to exercise or control the exercise of more than 20% of the voting power at any general meeting of that body.

(3) The rules set out in Schedule 1 (references to interest in shares or debentures) apply for the purposes of this section.

(4) References in this section to voting power the exercise of which is controlled by a director include voting power whose exercise is controlled by a body corporate controlled by him.

(5) Shares in a company held as treasury shares, and any voting rights attached to such shares, are disregarded for the purposes of this section.

(6) For the avoidance of circularity in the application of section 252 (meaning of "connected person") —

- (a) a body corporate with which a director is connected is not treated for the purposes of this section as connected with him unless it is also connected with him by virtue of subsection (2)(c) or (d) of that section (connection as trustee or partner); and
- (b) a trustee of a trust the beneficiaries of which include (or may include) a body corporate with which a director is connected is not treated for the purposes of this section as connected with a director by reason only of that fact.

[2376]

NOTES

Commencement: 1 October 2007.

255 Director "controlling" a body corporate

(1) This section defines what is meant by references in this Part to a director "controlling" a body corporate.

(2) A director of a company is taken to control a body corporate if, but only if—

- (a) he or any person connected with him—
  - (i) is interested in any part of the equity share capital of that body, or
  - (ii) is entitled to exercise or control the exercise of any part of the voting power at any general meeting of that body, and
- (b) he, the persons connected with him and the other directors of that company, together—
  - (i) are interested in more than 50% of that share capital, or
  - (ii) are entitled to exercise or control the exercise of more than 50% of that voting power.

(3) The rules set out in Schedule 1 (references to interest in shares or debentures) apply for the purposes of this section.

(4) References in this section to voting power the exercise of which is controlled by a director include voting power whose exercise is controlled by a body corporate controlled by him.

(5) Shares in a company held as treasury shares, and any voting rights attached to such shares, are disregarded for the purposes of this section.

(6) For the avoidance of circularity in the application of section 252 (meaning of "connected person")—

- (a) a body corporate with which a director is connected is not treated for the purposes of this section as connected with him unless it is also connected with him by virtue of subsection (2)(c) or (d) of that section (connection as trustee or partner); and
- (b) a trustee of a trust the beneficiaries of which include (or may include) a body corporate with which a director is connected is not treated for the purposes of this section as connected with a director by reason only of that fact.

[2377]

NOTES

Commencement: 1 October 2007.

256 Associated bodies corporate

For the purposes of this Part—

- (a) bodies corporate are associated if one is a subsidiary of the other or both are subsidiaries of the same body corporate, and
- (b) companies are associated if one is a subsidiary of the other or both are subsidiaries of the same body corporate.

[2378]

NOTES

Commencement: 1 October 2007.

257–737 (*Ss 257–259, ss 260–737* (*Pts 11–18*) *outside the scope of this work.*)

PART 19
DEBENTURES

General provisions

738 Meaning of "debenture"

In the Companies Acts "debenture" includes debenture stock, bonds and any other securities of a company, whether or not constituting a charge on the assets of the company.

[2379]

NOTES

Commencement: 6 April 2008.

739–748 (*Outside the scope of this work.*)

Supplementary provisions

749–753 (*Outside the scope of this work.*)

754 Priorities where debentures secured by floating charge

(1) This section applies where debentures of a company registered in England and Wales or Northern Ireland are secured by a charge that, as created, was a floating charge.

(2) If possession is taken, by or on behalf of the holders of the debentures, of any property comprised in or subject to the charge, and the company is not at that time in the course of being wound up, the company's preferential debts shall be paid out of assets coming to the hands of the persons taking possession in priority to any claims for principal or interest in respect of the debentures.

(3) "Preferential debts" means the categories of debts listed in Schedule 6 to the Insolvency Act 1986 (c 45) or Schedule 4 to the Insolvency (Northern Ireland) Order 1989 (SI 1989/2405 (NI 19)).

For the purposes of those Schedules "the relevant date" is the date of possession being taken as mentioned in subsection (2).

(4) Payments under this section shall be recouped, as far as may be, out of the assets of the company available for payment of general creditors.

[2380]

NOTES

Commencement: 6 April 2008.

See further, in relation to the application of this section, with modifications, in so far as it relates to bank insolvency or administration under the Banking Act 2009, Pts 2, 3: the Banking Act 2009 (Parts 2 and 3 Consequential Amendments) Orders 2009, SI 2009/317, art 3, Schedule.

See further in relation to the application of this section, with modifications, in so far as it relates to LLPs: the Limited Liability Partnerships (Application of Companies Act 2006) Regulations 2009, SI 2009/1804, reg 23.

755–859 ((*Pts 20–24*) *Outside the scope of this work.*)

PART 25
COMPANY CHARGES

CHAPTER 1
COMPANIES REGISTERED IN ENGLAND AND WALES OR IN NORTHERN IRELAND

Requirement to register company charges

860 Charges created by a company

(1) A company that creates a charge to which this section applies must deliver the prescribed particulars of the charge, together with the instrument (if any) by which the charge is created or evidenced, to the registrar for registration before the end of the period allowed for registration.

(2) Registration of a charge to which this section applies may instead be effected on the application of a person interested in it.

(3) Where registration is effected on the application of some person other than the company, that person is entitled to recover from the company the amount of any fees properly paid by him to the registrar on registration.

(4) If a company fails to comply with subsection (1), an offence is committed by—

(a) the company, and

(b) every officer of it who is in default.

(5) A person guilty of an offence under this section is liable—
(a) on conviction on indictment, to a fine;
(b) on summary conviction, to a fine not exceeding the statutory maximum.

(6) Subsection (4) does not apply if registration of the charge has been effected on the application of some other person.

(7) This section applies to the following charges—
(a) a charge on land or any interest in land, other than a charge for any rent or other periodical sum issuing out of land,
(b) a charge created or evidenced by an instrument which, if executed by an individual, would require registration as a bill of sale,
(c) a charge for the purposes of securing any issue of debentures,
(d) a charge on uncalled share capital of the company,
(e) a charge on calls made but not paid,
(f) a charge on book debts of the company,
(g) a floating charge on the company's property or undertaking,
(h) a charge on a ship or aircraft, or any share in a ship,
(i) a charge on goodwill or on any intellectual property.

[2381]

NOTES

Commencement: 20 January 2007 (for the purpose of enabling the exercise of powers to make orders or regulations); 1 October 2009 (otherwise); for transitional provisions, see SI 2008/2860, Sch 2, para 82.

See further, in relation to the disapplication of this Part, to a charge if the person interested in it is the Bank of England, the central bank of a country or territory outside the United Kingdom, or the European Central Bank: the Banking Act 2009, s 252(1).

See further in relation to the application of this section, with modifications, in so far as it relates to LLPs: the Limited Liability Partnerships (Application of Companies Act 2006) Regulations 2009, SI 2009/1804, regs 32, 83, Sch 1, Pt 6, para 16(1).

Regulations: the Companies (Particulars of Company Charges) Regulations 2008, SI 2008/2996.

861 Charges which have to be registered: supplementary

(1) The holding of debentures entitling the holder to a charge on land is not, for the purposes of section 860(7)(a), an interest in the land.

(2) It is immaterial for the purposes of this Chapter where land subject to a charge is situated.

(3) The deposit by way of security of a negotiable instrument given to secure the payment of book debts is not, for the purposes of section 860(7)(f), a charge on those book debts.

(4) For the purposes of section 860(7)(i), "intellectual property" means—
(a) any patent, trade mark, registered design, copyright or design right;
(b) any licence under or in respect of any such right.

(5) In this Chapter—
"charge" includes mortgage, and
"company" means a company registered in England and Wales or in Northern Ireland.

[2382]

NOTES

Commencement: 1 October 2009.

See further in relation to the application of this section, with modifications, in so far as it relates to LLPs: the Limited Liability Partnerships (Application of Companies Act 2006) Regulations 2009, SI 2009/1804, reg 32.

862 Charges existing on property acquired

(1) This section applies where a company acquires property which is subject to a charge of a kind which would, if it had been created by the company after the acquisition of the property, have been required to be registered under this Chapter.

(2) The company must deliver the prescribed particulars of the charge, together with a certified copy of the instrument (if any) by which the charge is created or evidenced, to the registrar for registration.

(3) Subsection (2) must be complied with before the end of the period allowed for registration.

(4) If default is made in complying with this section, an offence is committed by—
(a) the company, and
(b) every officer of it who is in default.

(5) A person guilty of an offence under this section is liable—
(a) on conviction on indictment, to a fine;
(b) on summary conviction, to a fine not exceeding the statutory maximum.

[2383]

NOTES

Commencement: 20 January 2007 (for the purpose of enabling the exercise of powers to make orders or regulations); 1 October 2009 (otherwise); for transitional provisions, see SI 2008/2860, Sch 2, para 83.

See further in relation to the application of this section, with modifications, in so far as it relates to LLPs: the Limited Liability Partnerships (Application of Companies Act 2006) Regulations 2009, SI 2009/1804, regs 32, 83, Sch 1, Pt 6, para 17(1).

Regulations: the Companies (Particulars of Company Charges) Regulations 2008, SI 2008/2996.

Special rules about debentures

863 Charge in series of debentures

(1) Where a series of debentures containing, or giving by reference to another instrument, any charge to the benefit of which debenture holders of that series are entitled pari passu is created by a company, it is for the purposes of section 860(1) sufficient if the required particulars, together with the deed containing the charge (or, if there is no such deed, one of the debentures of the series), are delivered to the registrar before the end of the period allowed for registration.

(2) The following are the required particulars—

(a) the total amount secured by the whole series, and

(b) the dates of the resolutions authorising the issue of the series and the date of the covering deed (if any) by which the series is created or defined, and

(c) a general description of the property charged, and

(d) the names of the trustees (if any) for the debenture holders.

(3) Particulars of the date and amount of each issue of debentures of a series of the kind mentioned in subsection (1) must be sent to the registrar for entry in the register of charges.

(4) Failure to comply with subsection (3) does not affect the validity of the debentures issued.

(5) Subsections (2) to (6) of section 860 apply for the purposes of this section as they apply for the purposes of that section, but as if references to the registration of a charge were references to the registration of a series of debentures.

[2384]

NOTES

Commencement: 1 October 2009; for transitional provisions, see SI 2008/2860, Sch 2, para 84.

See further in relation to the application of this section, with modifications, in so far as it relates to LLPs: the Limited Liability Partnerships (Application of Companies Act 2006) Regulations 2009, SI 2009/1804, regs 33, 83, Sch 1, Pt 6, para 18(1).

864 Additional registration requirement for commission etc in relation to debentures

(1) Where any commission, allowance or discount has been paid or made either directly or indirectly by a company to a person in consideration of his—

(a) subscribing or agreeing to subscribe, whether absolutely or conditionally, for debentures in a company, or

(b) procuring or agreeing to procure subscriptions, whether absolute or conditional, for such debentures,

the particulars required to be sent for registration under section 860 shall include particulars as to the amount or rate per cent. of the commission, discount or allowance so paid or made.

(2) The deposit of debentures as security for a debt of the company is not, for the purposes of this section, treated as the issue of debentures at a discount.

(3) Failure to comply with this section does not affect the validity of the debentures issued.

[2385]

NOTES

Commencement: 1 October 2009.

See further in relation to the application of this section, with modifications, in so far as it relates to LLPs: the Limited Liability Partnerships (Application of Companies Act 2006) Regulations 2009, SI 2009/1804, reg 33.

865 Endorsement of certificate on debentures

(1) The company shall cause a copy of every certificate of registration given under section 869 to be endorsed on every debenture or certificate of debenture stock which is issued by the company, and the payment of which is secured by the charge so registered.

(2) But this does not require a company to cause a certificate of registration of any charge so given to be endorsed on any debenture or certificate of debenture stock issued by the company before the charge was created.

(3) If a person knowingly and wilfully authorises or permits the delivery of a debenture or certificate of debenture stock which under this section is required to have endorsed on it a copy of a certificate of registration, without the copy being so endorsed upon it, he commits an offence.

(4) A person guilty of an offence under this section is liable on summary conviction to a fine not exceeding level 3 on the standard scale.

[2386]

NOTES

Commencement: 1 October 2009.

See further in relation to the application of this section, with modifications, in so far as it relates to LLPs: the Limited Liability Partnerships (Application of Companies Act 2006) Regulations 2009, SI 2009/1804, reg 33.

Charges in other jurisdictions

866 Charges created in, or over property in, jurisdictions outside the United Kingdom

(1) Where a charge is created outside the United Kingdom comprising property situated outside the United Kingdom, the delivery to the registrar of a verified copy of the instrument by which the charge is created or evidenced has the same effect for the purposes of this Chapter as the delivery of the instrument itself.

(2) Where a charge is created in the United Kingdom but comprises property outside the United Kingdom, the instrument creating or purporting to create the charge may be sent for registration under section 860 even if further proceedings may be necessary to make the charge valid or effectual according to the law of the country in which the property is situated.

[2387]

NOTES

Commencement: 1 October 2009.

See further in relation to the application of this section, with modifications, in so far as it relates to LLPs: the Limited Liability Partnerships (Application of Companies Act 2006) Regulations 2009, SI 2009/1804, reg 34.

867 Charges created in, or over property in, another United Kingdom jurisdiction

(1) Subsection (2) applies where—

(a) a charge comprises property situated in a part of the United Kingdom other than the part in which the company is registered, and

(b) registration in that other part is necessary to make the charge valid or effectual under the law of that part of the United Kingdom.

(2) The delivery to the registrar of a verified copy of the instrument by which the charge is created or evidenced, together with a certificate stating that the charge was presented for registration in that other part of the United Kingdom on the date on which it was so presented has, for the purposes of this Chapter, the same effect as the delivery of the instrument itself.

[2388]

NOTES

Commencement: 1 October 2009.

See further in relation to the application of this section, with modifications, in so far as it relates to LLPs: the Limited Liability Partnerships (Application of Companies Act 2006) Regulations 2009, SI 2009/1804, reg 34.

Orders charging land: Northern Ireland

868 Northern Ireland: registration of certain charges etc affecting land

(1) Where a charge imposed by an order under Article 46 of the 1981 Order or notice of such a charge is registered in the Land Registry against registered land or any estate in registered land of a company, the Registrar of Titles shall as soon as may be cause two copies of the order made under Article 46 of that Order or of any notice under Article 48 of that Order to be delivered to the registrar.

(2) Where a charge imposed by an order under Article 46 of the 1981 Order is registered in the Registry of Deeds against any unregistered land or estate in land of a company, the Registrar of Deeds shall as soon as may be cause two copies of the order to be delivered to the registrar.

(3) On delivery of copies under this section, the registrar shall—

(a) register one of them in accordance with section 869, and

(b) not later than 7 days from that date of delivery, cause the other copy together with a certificate of registration under section 869(5) to be sent to the company against which judgment was given.

(4) Where a charge to which subsection (1) or (2) applies is vacated, the Registrar of Titles or, as the case may be, the Registrar of Deeds shall cause a certified copy of the certificate of

satisfaction lodged under Article 132(1) of the 1981 Order to be delivered to the registrar for entry of a memorandum of satisfaction in accordance with section 872.

(5) In this section—

"the 1981 Order" means the Judgments Enforcement (Northern Ireland) Order 1981 (SI 1981/226 (NI 6));

"the Registrar of Deeds" means the registrar appointed under the Registration of Deeds Act (Northern Ireland) 1970 (c 25);

"Registry of Deeds" has the same meaning as in the Registration of Deeds Acts;

"Registration of Deeds Acts" means the Registration of Deeds Act (Northern Ireland) 1970 and every statutory provision for the time being in force amending that Act or otherwise relating to the registry of deeds, or the registration of deeds, orders or other instruments or documents in such registry;

"the Land Registry" and "the Registrar of Titles" are to be construed in accordance with section 1 of the Land Registration Act (Northern Ireland) 1970 (c 18);

"registered land" and "unregistered land" have the same meaning as in Part 3 of the Land Registration Act (Northern Ireland) 1970.

[2389]

NOTES

Commencement: 1 October 2009; for transitional provisions, see SI 2008/2860, Sch 2, para 85.

See further in relation to the application of this section, with modifications, in so far as it relates to LLPs: the Limited Liability Partnerships (Application of Companies Act 2006) Regulations 2009, SI 2009/1804, regs 35, 83, Sch 1, Pt 6, para 19(1).

The register of charges

869 Register of charges to be kept by registrar

(1) The registrar shall keep, with respect to each company, a register of all the charges requiring registration under this Chapter.

(2) In the case of a charge to the benefit of which holders of a series of debentures are entitled, the registrar shall enter in the register the required particulars specified in section 863(2).

(3) In the case of a charge imposed by the Enforcement of Judgments Office under Article 46 of the Judgments Enforcement (Northern Ireland) Order 1981, the registrar shall enter in the register the date on which the charge became effective.

(4) In the case of any other charge, the registrar shall enter in the register the following particulars—

(a) if it is a charge created by a company, the date of its creation and, if it is a charge which was existing on property acquired by the company, the date of the acquisition,
(b) the amount secured by the charge,
(c) short particulars of the property charged, and
(d) the persons entitled to the charge.

(5) The registrar shall give a certificate of the registration of any charge registered in pursuance of this Chapter, stating the amount secured by the charge.

(6) The certificate—

(a) shall be signed by the registrar or authenticated by the registrar's official seal, and
(b) is conclusive evidence that the requirements of this Chapter as to registration have been satisfied.

(7) The register kept in pursuance of this section shall be open to inspection by any person.

[2390]

NOTES

Commencement: 1 October 2009.

See further in relation to the application of this section, with modifications, in so far as it relates to LLPs: the Limited Liability Partnerships (Application of Companies Act 2006) Regulations 2009, SI 2009/1804, reg 36.

870 The period allowed for registration

(1) The period allowed for registration of a charge created by a company is—

(a) 21 days beginning with the day after the day on which the charge is created, or
(b) if the charge is created outside the United Kingdom, 21 days beginning with the day after the day on which the instrument by which the charge is created or evidenced (or a copy of it) could, in due course of post (and if despatched with due diligence) have been received in the United Kingdom.

(2) The period allowed for registration of a charge to which property acquired by a company is subject is—

(a) 21 days beginning with the day after the day on which the acquisition is completed, or

(b) if the property is situated and the charge was created outside the United Kingdom, 21 days beginning with the day after the day on which the instrument by which the charge is created or evidenced (or a copy of it) could, in due course of post (and if despatched with due diligence) have been received in the United Kingdom.

(3) The period allowed for registration of particulars of a series of debentures as a result of section 863 is—

(a) if there is a deed containing the charge mentioned in section 863(1), 21 days beginning with the day after the day on which that deed is executed, or

(b) if there is no such deed, 21 days beginning with the day after the day on which the first debenture of the series is executed.

[2391]

NOTES

Commencement: 1 October 2009.

See further in relation to the application of this section, with modifications, in so far as it relates to LLPs: the Limited Liability Partnerships (Application of Companies Act 2006) Regulations 2009, SI 2009/1804, reg 36.

871 Registration of enforcement of security

(1) If a person obtains an order for the appointment of a receiver or manager of a company's property, or appoints such a receiver or manager under powers contained in an instrument, he shall within 7 days of the order or of the appointment under those powers, give notice of the fact to the registrar.

(2) Where a person appointed receiver or manager of a company's property under powers contained in an instrument ceases to act as such receiver or manager, he shall, on so ceasing, give the registrar notice to that effect.

(3) The registrar must enter a fact of which he is given notice under this section in the register of charges.

(4) A person who makes default in complying with the requirements of this section commits an offence.

(5) A person guilty of an offence under this section is liable on summary conviction to a fine not exceeding level 3 on the standard scale and, for continued contravention, a daily default fine not exceeding one-tenth of level 3 on the standard scale.

[2392]

NOTES

Commencement: 1 October 2009; for transitional provisions, see SI 2008/2860, Sch 2, para 86.

See further in relation to the application of this section, with modifications, in so far as it relates to LLPs: the Limited Liability Partnerships (Application of Companies Act 2006) Regulations 2009, SI 2009/1804, regs 36, 83, Sch 1, Pt 6, para 20(1).

872 Entries of satisfaction and release

(1) Subsection (2) applies if a statement is delivered to the registrar verifying with respect to a registered charge—

(a) that the debt for which the charge was given has been paid or satisfied in whole or in part, or

(b) that part of the property or undertaking charged has been released from the charge or has ceased to form part of the company's property or undertaking.

(2) The registrar may enter on the register a memorandum of satisfaction in whole or in part, or of the fact part of the property or undertaking has been released from the charge or has ceased to form part of the company's property or undertaking (as the case may be).

(3) Where the registrar enters a memorandum of satisfaction in whole, the registrar shall if required send the company a copy of it.

[2393]

NOTES

Commencement: 1 October 2009; for transitional provisions, see SI 2008/2860, Sch 2, para 87.

See further in relation to the application of this section, with modifications, in so far as it relates to LLPs: the Limited Liability Partnerships (Application of Companies Act 2006) Regulations 2009, SI 2009/1804, regs 36, 83, Sch 1, Pt 6, para 21(1).

873 Rectification of register of charges

(1) Subsection (2) applies if the court is satisfied—

(a) that the failure to register a charge before the end of the period allowed for registration, or the omission or mis-statement of any particular with respect to any such charge or in a memorandum of satisfaction—

(i) was accidental or due to inadvertence or to some other sufficient cause, or

(ii) is not of a nature to prejudice the position of creditors or shareholders of the company, or

(b) that on other grounds it is just and equitable to grant relief.

(2) The court may, on the application of the company or a person interested, and on such terms and conditions as seem to the court just and expedient, order that the period allowed for registration shall be extended or, as the case may be, that the omission or mis-statement shall be rectified.

[2394]

NOTES

Commencement: 1 October 2009.

See further in relation to the application of this section, with modifications, in so far as it relates to LLPs: the Limited Liability Partnerships (Application of Companies Act 2006) Regulations 2009, SI 2009/1804, reg 36.

Avoidance of certain charges

874 Consequence of failure to register charges created by a company

(1) If a company creates a charge to which section 860 applies, the charge is void (so far as any security on the company's property or undertaking is conferred by it) against—

(a) a liquidator of the company,

(b) an administrator of the company, and

(c) a creditor of the company,

unless that section is complied with.

(2) Subsection (1) is subject to the provisions of this Chapter.

(3) Subsection (1) is without prejudice to any contract or obligation for repayment of the money secured by the charge; and when a charge becomes void under this section, the money secured by it immediately becomes payable.

[2395]

NOTES

Commencement: 1 October 2009.

See further in relation to the application of this section, with modifications, in so far as it relates to LLPs: the Limited Liability Partnerships (Application of Companies Act 2006) Regulations 2009, SI 2009/1804, reg 37.

Companies' records and registers

875 Companies to keep copies of instruments creating charges

(1) A company must keep available for inspection a copy of every instrument creating a charge requiring registration under this Chapter, including any document delivered to the company under section 868(3)(b) (Northern Ireland: orders imposing charges affecting land).

(2) In the case of a series of uniform debentures, a copy of one of the debentures of the series is sufficient.

[2396]

NOTES

Commencement: 1 October 2009.

See further in relation to the application of this section, with modifications, in so far as it relates to LLPs: the Limited Liability Partnerships (Application of Companies Act 2006) Regulations 2009, SI 2009/1804, reg 38.

876 Company's register of charges

(1) Every limited company shall keep available for inspection a register of charges and enter in it—

(a) all charges specifically affecting property of the company, and

(b) all floating charges on the whole or part of the company's property or undertaking.

(2) The entry shall in each case give a short description of the property charged, the amount of the charge and, except in the cases of securities to bearer, the names of the persons entitled to it.

(3) If an officer of the company knowingly and wilfully authorises or permits the omission of an entry required to be made in pursuance of this section, he commits an offence.

(4) A person guilty of an offence under this section is liable—

(a) on conviction on indictment, to a fine;

(b) on summary conviction, to a fine not exceeding the statutory maximum.

[2397]

NOTES

Commencement: 1 October 2009.

See further in relation to the application of this section, with modifications, in so far as it relates to LLPs: the Limited Liability Partnerships (Application of Companies Act 2006) Regulations 2009, SI 2009/1804, reg 38.

877 Instruments creating charges and register of charges to be available for inspection

(1) This section applies to—

(a) documents required to be kept available for inspection under section 875 (copies of instruments creating charges), and

(b) a company's register of charges kept in pursuance of section 876.

(2) The documents and register must be kept available for inspection—

(a) at the company's registered office, or

(b) at a place specified in regulations under section 1136.

(3) The company must give notice to the registrar—

(a) of the place at which the documents and register are kept available for inspection, and

(b) of any change in that place,

unless they have at all times been kept at the company's registered office.

(4) The documents and register shall be open to the inspection—

(a) of any creditor or member of the company without charge, and

(b) of any other person on payment of such fee as may be prescribed.

(5) If default is made for 14 days in complying with subsection (3) or an inspection required under subsection (4) is refused, an offence is committed by—

(a) the company, and

(b) every officer of the company who is in default.

(6) A person guilty of an offence under this section is liable on summary conviction to a fine not exceeding level 3 on the standard scale and, for continued contravention, a daily default fine not exceeding one-tenth of level 3 on the standard scale.

(7) If an inspection required under subsection (4) is refused the court may by order compel an immediate inspection.

[2398]

NOTES

Commencement: 20 January 2007 (for the purpose of enabling the exercise of powers to make orders or regulations); 1 October 2009 (otherwise).

See further in relation to the application of this section, with modifications, in so far as it relates to LLPs: the Limited Liability Partnerships (Application of Companies Act 2006) Regulations 2009, SI 2009/1804, reg 38.

Regulations: the Companies (Fees for Inspection of Company Records) Regulations 2008, SI 2008/3007.

878–999 (*Ss 878–894* (*Chs 2, 3*), *ss 895–999* (*Pts 26–30*) *outside the scope of this work.*)

PART 31
DISSOLUTION AND RESTORATION TO THE REGISTER

1000–1011 ((*Ch 1*) *Outside the scope of this work.*)

CHAPTER 2
PROPERTY OF DISSOLVED COMPANY

Property vesting as bona vacantia

1012 Property of dissolved company to be bona vacantia

(1) When a company is dissolved, all property and rights whatsoever vested in or held on trust for the company immediately before its dissolution (including leasehold property, but not including property held by the company on trust for another person) are deemed to be bona vacantia and—

(a) accordingly belong to the Crown, or to the Duchy of Lancaster or to the Duke of Cornwall for the time being (as the case may be), and

(b) vest and may be dealt with in the same manner as other *bona vacantia* accruing to the Crown, to the Duchy of Lancaster or to the Duke of Cornwall.

(2) Subsection (1) has effect subject to the possible restoration of the company to the register under Chapter 3 (see section 1034).

[2399]

NOTES

Commencement: 1 October 2009; for transitional provisions, see SI 2008/2860, Sch 2, para 88.

See further in relation to the application of this section, with modifications, in so far as it relates to LLPs: the Limited Liability Partnerships (Application of Companies Act 2006) Regulations 2009, SI 2009/1804, regs 52, 83, Sch 1, Pt 7, para 22(1) (as substituted by SI 2009/2476, reg 3(1), (2)).

1013 Crown disclaimer of property vesting as bona vacantia

(1) Where property vests in the Crown under section 1012, the Crown's title to it under that section may be disclaimed by a notice signed by the Crown representative, that is to say the Treasury Solicitor, or, in relation to property in Scotland, the Queen's and Lord Treasurer's Remembrancer.

(2) The right to execute a notice of disclaimer under this section may be waived by or on behalf of the Crown either expressly or by taking possession.

(3) A notice of disclaimer must be executed within three years after—

(a) the date on which the fact that the property may have vested in the Crown under section 1012 first comes to the notice of the Crown representative, or

(b) if ownership of the property is not established at that date, the end of the period reasonably necessary for the Crown representative to establish the ownership of the property.

(4) If an application in writing is made to the Crown representative by a person interested in the property requiring him to decide whether he will or will not disclaim, any notice of disclaimer must be executed within twelve months after the making of the application or such further period as may be allowed by the court.

(5) A notice of disclaimer under this section is of no effect if it is shown to have been executed after the end of the period specified by subsection (3) or (4).

(6) A notice of disclaimer under this section must be delivered to the registrar and retained and registered by him.

(7) Copies of it must be published in the Gazette and sent to any persons who have given the Crown representative notice that they claim to be interested in the property.

(8) This section applies to property vested in the Duchy of Lancaster or the Duke of Cornwall under section 1012 as if for references to the Crown and the Crown representative there were respectively substituted references to the Duchy of Lancaster and to the Solicitor to that Duchy, or to the Duke of Cornwall and to the Solicitor to the Duchy of Cornwall, as the case may be.

[2400]

NOTES

Commencement: 1 October 2009; for transitional provisions, see SI 2008/2860, Sch 2, para 88.

See further in relation to the application of this section, with modifications, in so far as it relates to LLPs: the Limited Liability Partnerships (Application of Companies Act 2006) Regulations 2009, SI 2009/1804, regs 52, 83, Sch 1, Pt 7, paras 22(1), 22A (as substituted by SI 2009/2476, reg 3(1), (2)).

1014 Effect of Crown disclaimer

(1) Where notice of disclaimer is executed under section 1013 as respects any property, that property is deemed not to have vested in the Crown under section 1012.

(2) The following sections contain provisions as to the effect of the Crown disclaimer—

sections 1015 to 1019 apply in relation to property in England and Wales or Northern Ireland;

sections 1020 to 1022 apply in relation to property in Scotland.

[2401]

NOTES

Commencement: 1 October 2009; for transitional provisions, see SI 2008/2860, Sch 2, para 88.

See further in relation to the application of this section, with modifications, in so far as it relates to LLPs: the Limited Liability Partnerships (Application of Companies Act 2006) Regulations 2009, SI 2009/1804, regs 52, 83, Sch 1, Pt 7, para 22(1) (as substituted by SI 2009/2476, reg 3(1), (2)).

Effect of Crown disclaimer: England and Wales and Northern Ireland

1015 General effect of disclaimer

(1) The Crown's disclaimer operates so as to terminate, as from the date of the disclaimer, the rights, interests and liabilities of the company in or in respect of the property disclaimed.

(2) It does not, except so far as is necessary for the purpose of releasing the company from any liability, affect the rights or liabilities of any other person.

[2402]

NOTES

Commencement: 1 October 2009; for transitional provisions, see SI 2008/2860, Sch 2, para 88.

See further in relation to the application of this section, with modifications, in so far as it relates to LLPs: the Limited Liability Partnerships (Application of Companies Act 2006) Regulations 2009, SI 2009/1804, regs 53, 83, Sch 1, Pt 7, para 22(1) (as substituted by SI 2009/2476, reg 3(1), (2)).

1016 Disclaimer of leaseholds

(1) The disclaimer of any property of a leasehold character does not take effect unless a copy of the disclaimer has been served (so far as the Crown representative is aware of their addresses) on every person claiming under the company as underlessee or mortgagee, and either—

(a) no application under section 1017 (power of court to make vesting order) is made with respect to that property before the end of the period of 14 days beginning with the day on which the last notice under this paragraph was served, or

(b) where such an application has been made, the court directs that the disclaimer shall take effect.

(2) Where the court gives a direction under subsection (1)(b) it may also, instead of or in addition to any order it makes under section 1017, make such order as it thinks fit with respect to fixtures, tenant's improvements and other matters arising out of the lease.

(3) In this section the "Crown representative" means—

(a) in relation to property vested in the Duchy of Lancaster, the Solicitor to that Duchy;

(b) in relation to property vested in the Duke of Cornwall, the Solicitor to the Duchy of Cornwall;

(c) in relation to property in Scotland, the Queen's and Lord Treasurer's Remembrancer;

(d) in relation to other property, the Treasury Solicitor.

[2403]

NOTES

Commencement: 1 October 2009; for transitional provisions, see SI 2008/2860, Sch 2, para 88.

See further in relation to the application of this section, with modifications, in so far as it relates to LLPs: the Limited Liability Partnerships (Application of Companies Act 2006) Regulations 2009, SI 2009/1804, regs 53, 83, Sch 1, Pt 7, para 22(1) (as substituted by SI 2009/2476, reg 3(1), (2)).

1017 Power of court to make vesting order

(1) The court may on application by a person who—

(a) claims an interest in the disclaimed property, or

(b) is under a liability in respect of the disclaimed property that is not discharged by the disclaimer,

make an order under this section in respect of the property.

(2) An order under this section is an order for the vesting of the disclaimed property in, or its delivery to—

(a) a person entitled to it (or a trustee for such a person), or

(b) a person subject to such a liability as is mentioned in subsection (1)(b) (or a trustee for such a person).

(3) An order under subsection (2)(b) may only be made where it appears to the court that it would be just to do so for the purpose of compensating the person subject to the liability in respect of the disclaimer.

(4) An order under this section may be made on such terms as the court thinks fit.

(5) On a vesting order being made under this section, the property comprised in it vests in the person named in that behalf in the order without conveyance, assignment or transfer.

[2404]

NOTES

Commencement: 1 October 2009; for transitional provisions, see SI 2008/2860, Sch 2, para 88.

See further in relation to the application of this section, with modifications, in so far as it relates to LLPs: the Limited Liability Partnerships (Application of Companies Act 2006) Regulations 2009, SI 2009/1804, regs 53, 83, Sch 1, Pt 7, para 22(1) (as substituted by SI 2009/2476, reg 3(1), (2)).

1018 Protection of persons holding under a lease

(1) The court must not make an order under section 1017 vesting property of a leasehold nature in a person claiming under the company as underlessee or mortgagee except on terms making that person—

(a) subject to the same liabilities and obligations as those to which the company was subject under the lease, or

(b) if the court thinks fit, subject to the same liabilities and obligations as if the lease had been assigned to him.

(2) Where the order relates to only part of the property comprised in the lease, subsection (1) applies as if the lease had comprised only the property comprised in the vesting order.

(3) A person claiming under the company as underlessee or mortgagee who declines to accept a vesting order on such terms is excluded from all interest in the property.

(4) If there is no person claiming under the company who is willing to accept an order on such terms, the court has power to vest the company's estate and interest in the property in any person who is liable (whether personally or in a representative character, and whether alone or jointly with the company) to perform the lessee's covenants in the lease.

(5) The court may vest that estate and interest in such a person freed and discharged from all estates, incumbrances and interests created by the company.

[2405]

NOTES

Commencement: 1 October 2009; for transitional provisions, see SI 2008/2860, Sch 2, para 88.

See further in relation to the application of this section, with modifications, in so far as it relates to LLPs: the Limited Liability Partnerships (Application of Companies Act 2006) Regulations 2009, SI 2009/1804, regs 53, 83, Sch 1, Pt 7, para 22(1) (as substituted by SI 2009/2476, reg 3(1), (2)).

1019 Land subject to rentcharge

Where in consequence of the disclaimer land that is subject to a rentcharge vests in any person, neither he nor his successors in title are subject to any personal liability in respect of sums becoming due under the rentcharge, except sums becoming due after he, or some person claiming under or through him, has taken possession or control of the land or has entered into occupation of it.

[2406]

NOTES

Commencement: 1 October 2009; for transitional provisions, see SI 2008/2860, Sch 2, para 88.

See further in relation to the application of this section, with modifications, in so far as it relates to LLPs: the Limited Liability Partnerships (Application of Companies Act 2006) Regulations 2009, SI 2009/1804, regs 53, 83, Sch 1, Pt 7, para 22(1) (as substituted by SI 2009/2476, reg 3(1), (2)).

1020–1022 (*Outside the scope of this work.*)

Supplementary provisions

1023 Liability for rentcharge on company's land after dissolution

(1) This section applies where on the dissolution of a company land in England and Wales or Northern Ireland that is subject to a rentcharge vests by operation of law in the Crown or any other person ("the proprietor").

(2) Neither the proprietor nor his successors in title are subject to any personal liability in respect of sums becoming due under the rentcharge, except sums becoming due after the proprietor, or some person claiming under or through him, has taken possession or control of the land or has entered into occupation of it.

(3) In this section "company" includes any body corporate.

[2407]

NOTES

Commencement: 1 October 2009; for transitional provisions, see SI 2008/2860, Sch 2, para 88.

See further in relation to the application of this section, with modifications, in so far as it relates to LLPs: the Limited Liability Partnerships (Application of Companies Act 2006) Regulations 2009, SI 2009/1804, regs 55, 83, Sch 1, Pt 7, para 22(1) (as substituted by SI 2009/2476, reg 3(1), (2)).

CHAPTER 3
RESTORATION TO THE REGISTER

1024–1032 (*Outside the scope of this work.*)

Supplementary provisions

1033 (*Outside the scope of this work.*)

1034 Effect of restoration to the register where property has vested as bona vacantia

(1) The person in whom any property or right is vested by section 1012 (property of dissolved company to be bona vacantia) may dispose of, or of an interest in, that property or right despite the fact that the company may be restored to the register under this Chapter.

(2) If the company is restored to the register—

(a) the restoration does not affect the disposition (but without prejudice to its effect in relation to any other property or right previously vested in or held on trust for the company), and

(b) the Crown or, as the case may be, the Duke of Cornwall shall pay to the company an amount equal to—

(i) the amount of any consideration received for the property or right or, as the case may be, the interest in it, or

(ii) the value of any such consideration at the time of the disposition,

or, if no consideration was received an amount equal to the value of the property, right or interest disposed of, as at the date of the disposition.

(3) There may be deducted from the amount payable under subsection (2)(b) the reasonable costs of the Crown representative in connection with the disposition (to the extent that they have not been paid as a condition of administrative restoration or pursuant to a court order for restoration).

(4) Where a liability accrues under subsection (2) in respect of any property or right which before the restoration of the company to the register had accrued as bona vacantia to the Duchy of Lancaster, the Attorney General of that Duchy shall represent Her Majesty in any proceedings arising in connection with that liability.

(5) Where a liability accrues under subsection (2) in respect of any property or right which before the restoration of the company to the register had accrued as bona vacantia to the Duchy of Cornwall, such persons as the Duke of Cornwall (or other possessor for the time being of the Duchy) may appoint shall represent the Duke (or other possessor) in any proceedings arising out of that liability.

(6) In this section the "Crown representative" means—

(a) in relation to property vested in the Duchy of Lancaster, the Solicitor to that Duchy;

(b) in relation to property vested in the Duke of Cornwall, the Solicitor to the Duchy of Cornwall;

(c) in relation to property in Scotland, the Queen's and Lord Treasurer's Remembrancer;

(d) in relation to other property, the Treasury Solicitor.

[2408]

NOTES

Commencement: 1 October 2009; for transitional provisions, see SI 2008/2860, Sch 2, para 92.

See further in relation to the application of this section, with modifications, in so far as it relates to LLPs: the Limited Liability Partnerships (Application of Companies Act 2006) Regulations 2009, SI 2009/1804, regs 56, 83, Sch 1, Pt 7, para 26.

1035–1157 ((*Pts 32–37*) *Outside the scope of this work.*)

PART 38
COMPANIES: INTERPRETATION

1158–1162 (*Outside the scope of this work.*)

Other definitions

1163 "Non-cash asset"

(1) In the Companies Acts "non-cash asset" means any property or interest in property, other than cash.

For this purpose "cash" includes foreign currency.

(2) A reference to the transfer or acquisition of a non-cash asset includes—

(a) the creation or extinction of an estate or interest in, or a right over, any property, and

(b) the discharge of a liability of any person, other than a liability for a liquidated sum.

[2409]

NOTES

Commencement: 1 October 2009.

1164–1171 (*Outside the scope of this work.*)

General

1172, 1173 (*Outside the scope of this work.*)

1174 Index of defined expressions

Schedule 8 contains an index of provisions defining or otherwise explaining expressions used in the Companies Acts.

[2410]

NOTES

Commencement: 1 October 2009.

PART I
STATUTES

1175–1297 ((*Pts 39–46*) *Outside the scope of this work.*)

PART 47
FINAL PROVISIONS

1298 Short title

The short title of this Act is the Companies Act 2006.

[2411]

NOTES

Commencement: 8 November 2006.

1299 Extent

Except as otherwise provided (or the context otherwise requires), the provisions of this Act extend to the whole of the United Kingdom.

[2412]

NOTES

Commencement: 8 November 2006.

1300 Commencement

(1) The following provisions come into force on the day this Act is passed—

(a)–(c) …

(d) this Part.

(2) The other provisions of this Act come into force on such day as may be appointed by order of the Secretary of State or the Treasury.

[2413]

NOTES

Commencement: 8 November 2006.

Sub-s (1): paras (a)–(c) outside the scope of this work.

Orders: the Companies Act 2006 (Commencement No 1, Transitional Provisions and Savings) Order 2006, SI 2006/3428; the Companies Act 2006 (Commencement No 2, Consequential Amendments, Transitional Provisions and Savings) Order 2007, SI 2007/1093; the Companies Act 2006 (Commencement No 3, Consequential Amendments, Transitional Provisions and Savings) Order 2007, SI 2007/2194; the Companies Act 2006 (Commencement No 4 and Commencement No 3 (Amendment)) Order 2007, SI 2007/2607; the Companies Act 2006 (Commencement No 5, Transitional Provisions and Savings) Order 2007, SI 2007/3495; the Companies Act 2006 (Commencement No 6, Saving and Commencement Nos 3 and 5 (Amendment)) Order 2008, SI 2008/674; the Companies Act 2006 (Commencement No 7, Transitional Provisions and Savings) Order 2008, SI 2008/1886; the Companies Act 2006 (Commencement No 8, Transitional Provisions and Savings) Order 2008, SI 2008/2860; the Companies Act 2006 (Consequential Amendments, Transitional Provisions and Savings) Order 2009, SI 2009/1941.

(*Schs 1–7 outside the scope of this work.*)

SCHEDULE 8
INDEX OF DEFINED EXPRESSIONS

Section 1174

abbreviated accounts (in Part 15)	sections 444(4) and 445(3)
accounting reference date and accounting reference period	section 391
accounting standards (in Part 15)	section 464
accounts meeting	section 437(3)
acquisition, in relation to a non-cash asset	section 1163(2)
address	
— generally in the Companies Acts	section 1142
— in the company communications provisions	section 1148(1)
affirmative resolution procedure, in relation to regulations and orders	section 1290
allotment (time of)	section 558
allotment of equity securities (in Chapter 3 of Part 17)	section 560(2)

allotted share capital and allotted shares	section 546(1)(b) and (2)
annual accounts (in Part 15)	section 471
annual accounts and reports (in Part 15)	section 471
annual general meeting	section 336
annual return	section 854
appropriate audit authority (in sections 522, 523 and 524)	section 525(1)
appropriate rate of interest	
— in Chapter 5 of Part 17	section 592
— in Chapter 6 of Part 17	section 609
approval after being made, in relation to regulations and orders	section 1291
arrangement	
— in Chapter 7 of Part 17	section 616(1)
— in Part 26	section 895(2)
articles	section 18
associate (in Chapter 3 of Part 28)	section 988
associated bodies corporate and associated company (in Part 10)	section 256
authenticated, in relation to a document or information sent or supplied to a company	section 1146
authorised group, of members of a company (in Part 14)	section 370(3)
authorised insurance company	section 1165(2)
authorised minimum (in relation to share capital of public company)	section 763
available profits (in Chapter 5 of Part 18)	sections 711 and 712
banking company and banking group	section 1164
body corporate	section 1173(1)
called-up share capital	section 547
capital redemption reserve	section 733
capitalisation in relation to a company's profits (in Part 23)	section 853(3)
cash (in relation to paying up or allotting shares)	section 583
cause of action, in relation to derivative proceedings (in Chapter 2 of Part 11)	section 265(7)
certified translation (in Part 35)	section 1107
charge (in Chapter 1 of Part 25)	section 861(5)
circulation date, in relation to a written resolution (in Part 13)	section 290
class of shares	section 629
the Companies Acts	section 2
Companies Act accounts	sections 395(1)(a) and 403(2)(a)
Companies Act group accounts	section 403(2)(a)
Companies Act individual accounts	section 395(1)(a)
companies involved in the division (in Part 27)	section 919(2)
company	
— generally in the Companies Acts	section 1
— in Chapter 7 of Part 17	section 616(1)

PART I STATUTES

— in Chapter 1 of Part 25	section 861(5)
— in Chapter 2 of Part 25	section 879(6)
— in Part 26	section 895(2)
— in Chapter 3 of Part 28	section 991(1)
— in the company communications provisions	section 1148(1)
the company communications provisions	section 1143
the company law provisions of this Act	section 2(2)
company records (in Part 37)	section 1134
connected with, in relation to a director (in Part 10)	sections 252 to 254
constitution, of a company	
— generally in the Companies Acts	section 17
— in Part 10	section 257
[contributory	section 1170B]
controlling, of a body corporate by a director (in Part 10)	section 255
[corporate governance statement and separate corporate governance statement	
— in Part 15	section 472A
— in Part 16	section 538A]
corporation	section 1173(1)
the court	section 1156
credit institution	section 1173(1)
credit transaction (in Chapter 4 of Part 10)	section 202
creditor (in Chapter 1 of Part 31)	section 1011
daily default fine	section 1125
date of the offer (in Chapter 3 of Part 28)	section 991(1)
debenture	section 738
derivative claim (in Chapter 1 of Part 11)	section 260
derivative proceedings (in Chapter 2 of Part 11)	section 265
Directive disclosure requirements	section 1078
director	
— generally in the Companies Acts	section 250
— in Chapter 8 of Part 10	section 240(3)
— in Chapter 1 of Part 11	section 260(5)
— in Chapter 2 of Part 11	section 265(7)
— in Part 14	section 379(1)
directors' remuneration report	section 420
directors' report	section 415
distributable profits	
— in Chapter 2 of Part 18	section 683(1)
— elsewhere in Part 18	section 736
distribution	
— in Chapter 2 of Part 18	section 683(1)
— in Part 23	section 829
division (in Part 27)	section 919
document	
— in Part 35	section 1114(1)

— in the company communications provisions	section 1148(1)
dormant, in relation to a company or other body corporate	section 1169
EEA State and related expressions	section 1170
electronic form, electronic copy, electronic means	
— generally in the Companies Acts	section 1168(3) and (4)
— in relation to communications to a company	Part 3 of Schedule 4
— in relation to communications by a company	Part 3 of Schedule 5
eligible members, in relation to a written resolution	section 289
e-money issuer	
— in Part 15	section 474(1)
— in Part 16	section 539
employees' share scheme	section 1166
employer and employee (in Chapter 1 of Part 18)	section 676
enactment	section 1293
equity securities (in Chapter 3 of Part 17)	section 560(1)
equity share capital	section 548
equity shares (in Chapter 7 of Part 17)	section 616(1)
[establishment of an overseas company (in Part 35)	section 1067(6)]
existing company (in Part 27)	section 902(2)
fellow subsidiary undertakings	section 1161(4)
financial assistance (in Chapter 2 of Part 18)	section 677
financial institution	section 1173(1)
financial year, of a company	section 390
firm	section 1173(1)
fixed assets (in Part 23)	section 853
the former Companies Acts	section 1171
the Gazette	section 1173(1)
group (in Part 15)	section 474(1)
group undertaking	section 1161(5)
hard copy form and hard copy	
— generally in the Companies Acts	section 1168(2)
— in relation to communications to a company	Part 2 of Schedule 4
— in relation to communications by a company	Part 2 of Schedule 5
hire-purchase agreement	section 1173(1)
holder of shares (in Chapter 3 of Part 17)	section 574
holding company	section 1159 (and see section 1160 and Schedule 6)
IAS accounts	sections 395(1)(b) and 403(1) and (2)(b)
IAS group accounts	section 403(1) and (2)(b)
IAS individual accounts	section 395(1)(b)
IAS Regulation (in Part 15)	section 474(1)
included in the consolidation, in relation to group accounts (in Part 15)	section 474(1)
individual accounts	section 394
information rights (in Part 9)	section 146(3)

insurance company	section 1165(3)
insurance group	section 1165(5)
insurance market activity	section 1165(7)
interest in shares (for the purposes of Part 22)	sections 820 to 825
international accounting standards (in Part 15)	section 474(1)
investment company (in Part 23)	section 833
…	…
issued share capital and issued shares	section 546(1)(a) and (2)
the issuing company (in Chapter 7 of Part 17)	section 610(6)
the Joint Stock Companies Acts	section 1171
liabilities (in Part 27)	section 941
liability, references to incurring, reducing or discharging (in Chapter 2 of Part 18)	section 683(2)
limited by guarantee	section 3(3)
limited by shares	section 3(2)
limited company	section 3
the main register (of members) (in Chapter 3 of Part 8)	section 131(1)
major audit (in sections 522 and 525)	section 525(2)
market purchase, by a company of its own shares (in Chapter 4 of Part 18)	section 693(4)
member, of a company	
— generally in the Companies Acts	section 112
— in Chapter 1 of Part 11	section 260(5)
— in Chapter 2 of Part 11	section 265(7)
memorandum of association	section 8
merger (in Part 27)	section 904
merging companies (in Part 27)	section 904(2)
merger by absorption (in Part 27)	section 904(1)(a)
merger by formation of a new company (in Part 27)	section 904(1)(b)
[MiFID investment firm	
— in Part 15	section 474(1)
— in Part 16	section 539]
negative resolution procedure, in relation to regulations and orders	section 1289
net assets (in Part 7)	section 92
new company (in Part 27)	section 902(2)
non-cash asset	section 1163
[non-traded company (in Part 24)	section 855(4)]
non-voting shares (in Chapter 3 of Part 28)	section 991(1)
number, in relation to shares	section 540(4)(b)
off-market purchase, by a company of its own shares (in Chapter 4 of Part 18)	section 693(2)
offer period (in Chapter 2 of Part 28)	section 971(1)
offer to the public (in Chapter 1 of Part 20)	section 756
offeror	
— in Chapter 2 of Part 28	section 971(1)
— in Chapter 3 of Part 28	section 991(1)

officer, in relation to a body corporate	section 1173(1)
officer in default	section 1121
official seal, of registrar	section 1062
opted-in company (in Chapter 2 of Part 28)	section 971(1)
opting-in resolution (in Chapter 2 of Part 28)	section 966(1)
opting-out resolution (in Chapter 2 of Part 28)	section 966(5)
ordinary resolution	section 282
ordinary shares (in Chapter 3 of Part 17)	section 560(1)
organisation (in Part 14)	section 379(1)
other relevant transactions or arrangements (in Chapter 4 of Part 10)	section 210
overseas company	section 1044
overseas branch register	section 129(1)
paid up	section 583
the Panel (in Part 28)	section 942
parent company	section 1173(1)
parent undertaking	section 1162 (and see Schedule 7)
payment for loss of office (in Chapter 4 of Part 10)	section 215
pension scheme (in Chapter 1 of Part 18)	section 675
period for appointing auditors, in relation to a private company	section 485(2)
period for filing, in relation to accounts and reports for a financial year	section 442
permissible capital payment (in Chapter 5 of Part 18)	section 710
political donation (in Part 14)	section 364
political expenditure (in Part 14)	section 365
political organisation (in Part 14)	section 363(2)
prescribed	section 1167
private company	section 4
profit and loss account (in Part 15)	section 474(1) and (2)
profits and losses (in Part 23)	section 853(2)
profits available for distribution (for the purposes of Part 23)	section 830(2)
property (in Part 27)	section 941
protected information (in Chapter 8 of Part 10)	section 240
provision for entrenchment, in relation to a company's articles	section 22
public company	section 4
publication, in relation to accounts and reports (in sections 433 to 435)	section 436
qualified, in relation to an auditor's report etc (in Part 16)	section 539
qualifying shares (in Chapter 6 of Part 18)	section 724(2)
qualifying third party indemnity provision (in Chapter 7 of Part 10)	section 234
qualifying pension scheme indemnity provision (in Chapter 7 of Part 10)	section 235
quasi-loan (in Chapter 4 of Part 10)	section 199
quoted company	

— in Part 13	section 361
— in Part 15	section 385
— in Chapter 5 of Part 16	section 531 (and section 385)
realised profits and losses (in Part 23)	section 853(4)
[receiver or manager (and certain related references)	section 1170A]
redeemable shares	section 684(1)
redenominate	section 622(1)
redenomination reserve	section 628
the register	section 1080
register of charges, kept by registrar	
— in England and Wales and Northern Ireland	section 869
— in Scotland	section 885
register of directors	section 162
register of directors' residential addresses	section 165
register of members	section 113
register of secretaries	section 275
…	…
[registered number, of a company (or an overseas company)	section 1066 (and section 1059A(5))]
[registered number, of a UK establishment of an overseas company	section 1067]
registered office, of a company	section 86
registrar and registrar of companies	section 1060
registrar's index of company names	section 1099
registrar's rules	section 1117
registration in a particular part of the United Kingdom	section 1060(4)
regulated activity	
— generally in the Companies Acts	section 1173(1)
— in Part 15	section 474(1)
regulated market	section 1173(1)
relevant accounts (in Part 23)	section 836(2)
requirements for proper delivery (in Part 35)	section 1072 (and see section 1073)
requirements of this Act	section 1172
[return period (in Part 24)	section 855(4)]
securities (and related expressions)	
— in Chapter 1 of Part 20	section 755(5)
— in Chapter 2 of Part 21	section 783
senior statutory auditor	section 504
sent or supplied, in relation to documents or information (in the company communications provisions)	section 1148(2) and (3)
service address	section 1141
service contract, of a director (in Part 10)	section 227
shadow director	section 251
share	
— generally in the Companies Acts	section 540 (and see section 1161(2))
— in Part 22	section 792

— in section 1162 and Schedule 7	section 1162(7)
share capital, company having a	section 545
share exchange ratio	
— in Chapter 2 of Part 27	section 905(2)
— in Chapter 3 of Part 27	section 920(2)
share premium account	section 610(1)
share warrant	section 779(1)
[small companies exemption (in relation to directors' report)	section 415A]
small companies regime, [(for accounts)]	section 381
solvency statement (in sections 641 to 644)	section 643
special notice, in relation to a resolution	section 312
special resolution	section 283
statutory accounts	section 434(3)
subsidiary	section 1159 (and see section 1160 and Schedule 6)
subsidiary undertaking	section 1162 (and see Schedule 7)
summary financial statement	section 426
takeover bid (in Chapter 2 of Part 28)	section 971(1)
takeover offer (in Chapter 3 of Part 28)	section 974
the Takeovers Directive	
— in Chapter 1 of Part 28	section 943(8)
— in Chapter 2 of Part 28	section 971(1)
[traded company (in Part 13)	section 360C]
[traded company (in Part 24)	section 855(4)]
trading certificate	section 761(1)
transfer, in relation to a non-cash asset	section 1163(2)
treasury shares	section 724(5)
turnover	
— in Part 15	section 474(1)
— in Part 16	section 539
UCITS management company	
— in Part 15	section 474(1)
— in Part 16	section 539
[UK establishment of an overseas company (in Part 35)	section 1067(6)]
UK-registered company	section 1158
uncalled share capital	section 547
unconditional, in relation to a contract to acquire shares (in Chapter 3 of Part 28)	section 991(2)
undistributable reserves	section 831(4)
undertaking	section 1161(1)
unique identifier	section 1082
unlimited company	section 3
unquoted company (in Part 15)	section 385
voting rights	
— in Chapter 2 of Part 28	section 971(1)
— in Chapter 3 of Part 28	section 991(1)

— in section 1159 and Schedule 6	paragraph 2 of Schedule 6
— in section 1162 and Schedule 7	paragraph 2 of Schedule 7
voting shares	
— in Chapter 2 of Part 28	section 971(1)
— in Chapter 3 of Part 28	section 991(1)
website, communication by a company by means of	Part 4 of Schedule 5
Welsh company	section 88
wholly-owned subsidiary	section 1159(2) (and see section 1160 and Schedule 6)
working day, in relation to a company	section 1173(1)
written resolution	section 288

[2414]

NOTES

Commencement: 1 October 2009.

Entries "contributory" and "receiver or manager (and certain related references)" inserted by SI 2009/1941, art 2(1), Sch 1, para 260(1), (9), as from 1 October 2009.

Entry "corporate governance statement and separate corporate governance statement" inserted by SI 2009/1581, reg 9, as from 27 June 2009, in relation to financial years beginning on or after 29 June 2008 which have not ended before 27 June 2009.

Entries "establishment of an overseas company (in Part 35)", "registered number, of a company (or an overseas company)", "registered number, of a UK establishment of an overseas company" and "UK establishment of an overseas company (in Part 35)" inserted, and entries "registered number, of a branch of an overseas company" and "registered number, of a company" (omitted) repealed, by SI 2009/1802, arts 2, 17, as from 1 October 2009.

Entry "ISD investment firm" (omitted) repealed, and entry "MiFID investment firm" inserted, by SI 2007/2932, reg 3(8).

Entries "non-traded company (in Part 24)", "return period (in Part 24)", and "traded company (in Part 24)" inserted by SI 2008/3000, reg 9, as from 1 October 2009 (in relation to annual returns made up to that date or a later date).

Entry "small companies exemption (in relation to directors' report)" inserted by SI 2008/393, reg 6(11), as from 6 April 2008, in relation to financial years beginning on or after that date.

Entry "traded company (in Part 13)" inserted by SI 2009/1632, reg 21(2), as from 3 August 2009, in relation to meetings of which notice is given, or first given, on or after that date.

Words in square brackets in the entry "small companies regime" substituted by SI 2008/393, reg 6(12), as from 6 April 2008, in relation to financial years beginning on or after that date.

(*Schs 9–16 outside the scope of this work.*)

CHARITIES ACT 2006

(2006 c 50)

An Act to provide for the establishment and functions of the Charity Commission for England and Wales and the Charity Tribunal; to make other amendments of the law about charities, including provision about charitable incorporated organisations; to make further provision about public charitable collections and other fund-raising carried on in connection with charities and other institutions; to make other provision about the funding of such institutions; and for connected purposes.

[8 November 2006]

PART 1
MEANING OF "CHARITY" AND "CHARITABLE PURPOSE"

1 Meaning of "charity"

(1) For the purposes of the law of England and Wales, "charity" means an institution which—

(a) is established for charitable purposes only, and

(b) falls to be subject to the control of the High Court in the exercise of its jurisdiction with respect to charities.

(2) The definition of "charity" in subsection (1) does not apply for the purposes of an enactment if a different definition of that term applies for those purposes by virtue of that or any other enactment.

(3) A reference in any enactment or document to a charity within the meaning of the Charitable Uses Act 1601 (c 4) or the preamble to it is to be construed as a reference to a charity as defined by subsection (1).

[2415]

NOTES

Commencement: 1 April 2008: for transitional provisions and savings, see SI 2008/945, arts 4, 5.

2 Meaning of "charitable purpose"

(1) For the purposes of the law of England and Wales, a charitable purpose is a purpose which—

(a) falls within subsection (2), and
(b) is for the public benefit (see section 3).

(2) A purpose falls within this subsection if it falls within any of the following descriptions of purposes—

(a) the prevention or relief of poverty;
(b) the advancement of education;
(c) the advancement of religion;
(d) the advancement of health or the saving of lives;
(e) the advancement of citizenship or community development;
(f) the advancement of the arts, culture, heritage or science;
(g) the advancement of amateur sport;
(h) the advancement of human rights, conflict resolution or reconciliation or the promotion of religious or racial harmony or equality and diversity;
(i) the advancement of environmental protection or improvement;
(j) the relief of those in need by reason of youth, age, ill-health, disability, financial hardship or other disadvantage;
(k) the advancement of animal welfare;
(l) the promotion of the efficiency of the armed forces of the Crown, or of the efficiency of the police, fire and rescue services or ambulance services;
(m) any other purposes within subsection (4).

(3) In subsection (2)—

(a) in paragraph (c) "religion" includes—
 (i) a religion which involves belief in more than one god, and
 (ii) a religion which does not involve belief in a god;
(b) in paragraph (d) "the advancement of health" includes the prevention or relief of sickness, disease or human suffering;
(c) paragraph (e) includes—
 (i) rural or urban regeneration, and
 (ii) the promotion of civic responsibility, volunteering, the voluntary sector or the effectiveness or efficiency of charities;
(d) in paragraph (g) "sport" means sports or games which promote health by involving physical or mental skill or exertion;
(e) paragraph (j) includes relief given by the provision of accommodation or care to the persons mentioned in that paragraph; and
(f) in paragraph (l) "fire and rescue services" means services provided by fire and rescue authorities under Part 2 of the Fire and Rescue Services Act 2004 (c 21).

(4) The purposes within this subsection (see subsection (2)(m)) are—

(a) any purposes not within paragraphs (a) to (l) of subsection (2) but recognised as charitable purposes under existing charity law or by virtue of section 1 of the Recreational Charities Act 1958 (c 17);
(b) any purposes that may reasonably be regarded as analogous to, or within the spirit of, any purposes falling within any of those paragraphs or paragraph (a) above; and
(c) any purposes that may reasonably be regarded as analogous to, or within the spirit of, any purposes which have been recognised under charity law as falling within paragraph (b) above or this paragraph.

(5) Where any of the terms used in any of paragraphs (a) to (l) of subsection (2), or in subsection (3), has a particular meaning under charity law, the term is to be taken as having the same meaning where it appears in that provision.

(6) Any reference in any enactment or document (in whatever terms)—

(a) to charitable purposes, or
(b) to institutions having purposes that are charitable under charity law,

is to be construed in accordance with subsection (1).

(7) Subsection (6)—

(a) applies whether the enactment or document was passed or made before or after the passing of this Act, but
(b) does not apply where the context otherwise requires.

(8) In this section—
"charity law" means the law relating to charities in England and Wales; and
"existing charity law" means charity law as in force immediately before the day on which this section comes into force.

[2416]

NOTES

Commencement: 27 February 2007 (sub-s (1)(b) for certain purposes); 1 April 2008 (otherwise); for transitional provisions and savings, see SI 2008/945, arts 4, 5.

3 The "public benefit" test

(1) This section applies in connection with the requirement in section 2(1)(b) that a purpose falling within section 2(2) must be for the public benefit if it is to be a charitable purpose.

(2) In determining whether that requirement is satisfied in relation to any such purpose, it is not to be presumed that a purpose of a particular description is for the public benefit.

(3) In this Part any reference to the public benefit is a reference to the public benefit as that term is understood for the purposes of the law relating to charities in England and Wales.

(4) Subsection (3) applies subject to subsection (2).

[2417]

NOTES

Commencement: 27 February 2007 (sub-s (1) for certain purposes); 1 April 2008 (otherwise); for transitional provisions and savings, see SI 2008/945, arts 4, 5.

4 Guidance as to operation of public benefit requirement

(1) The Charity Commission for England and Wales (see section 6 of this Act) must issue guidance in pursuance of its public benefit objective.

(2) That objective is to promote awareness and understanding of the operation of the requirement mentioned in section 3(1) (see section 1B(3) and (4) of the Charities Act 1993 (c 10), as inserted by section 7 of this Act).

(3) The Commission may from time to time revise any guidance issued under this section.

(4) The Commission must carry out such public and other consultation as it considers appropriate—
(a) before issuing any guidance under this section, or
(b) (unless it considers that it is unnecessary to do so) before revising any such guidance.

(5) The Commission must publish any guidance issued or revised under this section in such manner as it considers appropriate.

(6) The charity trustees of a charity must have regard to any such guidance when exercising any powers or duties to which the guidance is relevant.

[2418]

NOTES

Commencement: 27 February 2007 (sub-ss (1)–(5)); 1 April 2008 (sub-s (6)); for transitional provisions and savings, see SI 2008/945, arts 4, 5.

5 Special provisions about recreational charities, sports clubs etc

(1)–(3) …

(4) A registered sports club established for charitable purposes is to be treated as not being so established, and accordingly cannot be a charity.

(5) In subsection (4) a "registered sports club" means a club for the time being registered under Schedule 18 to the Finance Act 2002 (c 23) (relief for community amateur sports club).

[2419]

NOTES

Commencement: 1 April 2008 (sub-ss (1) (in so far it relates to sub-s (2)), (2); for transitional provisions and savings, see SI 2008/945, arts 4, 5); 1 April 2009 (sub-ss (4), (5)); 1 April 2010 (sub-ss (1) (for remaining purposes), (3)).

Sub-ss (1)–(3): amend the Recreational Charities Act 1958, s 1 and repeal s 2 thereof.

PART 2
REGULATION OF CHARITIES

6–8 ((*Chs 1, 2*) *Outside the scope of this work.*)

CHAPTER 3
REGISTRATION OF CHARITIES

General

9 (*Outside the scope of this work.*)

10 Interim changes in threshold for registration of small charities

(1) At any time before the appointed day, the Minister may by order amend section 3 of the 1993 Act (the register of charities) so as to—

(a) replace section 3(5)(c) (threshold for registration of small charities) with a provision referring to a charity whose gross income does not exceed such sum as is prescribed in the order, and

(b) define "gross income" for the purposes of that provision.

(2) Subsection (1) does not affect the existing power under section 3(12) of that Act to increase the financial limit specified in section 3(5)(c).

(3) This section ceases to have effect on the appointed day.

(4) In this section "the appointed day" means the day on which section 3A(1) to (5) of the 1993 Act (as substituted by section 9 of this Act) come into force by virtue of an order under section 79 of this Act.

[2420]

NOTES

Commencement: 27 February 2007.

Order: the Charities Act 2006 (Interim changes in threshold for registration of small charities) Order 2007, SI 2007/789.

Exempt charities: registration and regulation

11 Changes in exempt charities

(1)–(10) …

(11) The Minister may by order make such further amendments of Schedule 2 to the 1993 Act as he considers appropriate for securing—

(a) that (so far as they are charities) institutions of a particular description become or (as the case may be) cease to be exempt charities, or

(b) that (so far as it is a charity) a particular institution becomes or (as the case may be) ceases to be an exempt charity,

or for removing from that Schedule an institution that has ceased to exist.

(12) An order under subsection (11) may only be made for the purpose mentioned in paragraph (a) or (b) of that subsection if the Minister is satisfied that the order is desirable in the interests of ensuring appropriate or effective regulation of the charities or charity concerned in connection with compliance by the charity trustees of the charities or charity with their legal obligations in exercising control and management of the administration of the charities or charity.

(13) The Minister may by order make such amendments or other modifications of any enactment as he considers appropriate in connection with—

(a) charities of a particular description becoming, or ceasing to be, exempt charities, or

(b) a particular charity becoming, or ceasing to be, an exempt charity,

by virtue of any provision made by or under this section.

(14) In this section "exempt charity" has the same meaning as in the 1993 Act.

[2421]

NOTES

Commencement: 31 January 2009 (sub-s (1) (for certain purposes), sub-ss (4), (5)); 27 February 2007 (sub-ss (11)–(14)); as from a day to be appoined (otherwise).

Sub-ss (1)–(10): amend the Charities Act 1993, s 24, Sch 2.

12–71 (*Ss 12–14, ss 15–44* (*Chs 4–11*), *ss 45–71* (*Pt 3*) *outside the scope of this work.*)

PART 4
MISCELLANEOUS AND GENERAL

72, 73 (*Outside the scope of this work.*)

General

74–77 (*Outside the scope of this work.*)

78 Interpretation

(1) In this Act—
"the 1992 Act" means the Charities Act 1992 (c 41);
"the 1993 Act" means the Charities Act 1993 (c 10).

(2) In this Act—
(a) "charity" has the meaning given by section 1(1);
(b) "charitable purposes" has (in accordance with section 2(6)) the meaning given by section 2(1); and
(c) "charity trustees" has the same meaning as in the 1993 Act;

but (subject to subsection (3) below) the exclusions contained in section 96(2) of the 1993 Act (ecclesiastical corporations etc) have effect in relation to references to a charity in this Act as they have effect in relation to such references in that Act.

(3) Those exclusions do not have effect in relation to references in section 1 or any reference to the law relating to charities in England and Wales.

(4) In this Act "enactment" includes—
(a) any provision of subordinate legislation (within the meaning of the Interpretation Act 1978 (c 30)),
(b) a provision of a Measure of the Church Assembly or of the General Synod of the Church of England, and
(c) (in the context of section 6(5) or 75(5)) any provision made by or under an Act of the Scottish Parliament or Northern Ireland legislation,

and references to enactments include enactments passed or made after the passing of this Act.

(5) In this Act "institution" means an institution whether incorporated or not, and includes a trust or undertaking.

(6) In this Act "the Minister" means the Minister for the Cabinet Office.

(7) Subsections (2) to (5) apply except where the context otherwise requires.

[2422]

NOTES
Commencement: 8 November 2006.

79 Commencement

(1) The following provisions come into force on the day on which this Act is passed—
(a)–(c) (*outside the scope of this work.*)
(d) section 78,
(e) (*outside the scope of this work.*)
(f) this section and section 80, and
(g) (*outside the scope of this work.*)

(2) Otherwise, this Act comes into force on such day as the Minister may by order appoint.

(3) An order under subsection (2)—
(a) may appoint different days for different purposes or different areas;
(b) make such provision as the Minister considers necessary or expedient for transitory, transitional or saving purposes in connection with the coming into force of any provision of this Act.

[2423]

NOTES
Commencement: 8 November 2006.
Order: the Charities Act 2006 (Commencement No 1, Transitional Provisions and Savings) Order 2007, SI 2007/309; the Charities Act 2006 (Commencement No 2, Transitional Provisions and Savings) Order 2007, SI 2007/3286; the Charities Act 2006 (Commencement No 3, Transitional Provisions and Savings) Order 2008, SI 2008/751; the Charities Act 2006 (Commencement No 4, Transitional Provisions and Savings) Order 2008, SI 2008/945; the Charities Act 2006 (Commencement No 5, Transitional and Transitory Provisions and Savings) Order 2008, SI 2008/3267.

80 Short title and extent

(1) This Act may be cited as the Charities Act 2006.

(2) Subject to subsections (3) to (7), this Act extends to England and Wales only.

(3) The following provisions extend also to Scotland—

(a) sections 1 to 3 and 5,

(b), (c) (*outside the scope of this work.*)

(d) section 75(2) and (3) and Schedules 9 and 10 so far as relating to the Recreational Charities Act 1958 (c 17), and

(e) section 75(4) and (5), sections 76 to 79 and this section.

(4) But the provisions referred to in subsection (3)(a) and (d) affect the law of Scotland only so far as they affect the construction of references to charities or charitable purposes in enactments which relate to matters falling within Section A1 of Part 2 of Schedule 5 to the Scotland Act 1998 (c 46) (reserved matters: fiscal policy etc); and so far as they so affect the law of Scotland—

(a) references in sections 1(1) and 2(1) to the law of England and Wales are to be read as references to the law of Scotland, and

(b) the reference in section 1(1) to the High Court is to be read as a reference to the Court of Session.

(5) The following provisions extend also to Northern Ireland—

(a) sections 1 to 3 and 5,

(b)–(d) (*outside the scope of this work.*)

(e) section 75(2) and (3) and Schedules 9 and 10 so far as relating to the Recreational Charities Act 1958 (c 17), and

(f) section 75(4) and (5), sections 76 to 79 and this section.

(6) But the provisions referred to in subsection (5)(a) and (e) affect the law of Northern Ireland only so far as they affect the construction of references to charities or charitable purposes in enactments which relate to matters falling within paragraph 9 of Schedule 2 to the Northern Ireland Act 1998 (c 47) (excepted matters: taxes and duties); and so far as they so affect the law of Northern Ireland—

(a) references in sections 1(1) and 2(1) to the law of England and Wales are to be read as references to the law of Northern Ireland, and

(b) the reference in section 1(1) to the High Court is to be read as a reference to the High Court in Northern Ireland.

(7) Any amendment, repeal or revocation made by this Act has the same extent as the enactment to which it relates.

(8) But subsection (7) does not apply to any amendment or repeal made in the Recreational Charities Act 1958 by a provision referred to in subsection (3) or (5).

(9) Subsection (7) also does not apply to—

(a) the amendments made by section 32 in the Companies Act 1985 (c 6), or

(b) those made by Schedule 8 in the Police, Factories, &c (Miscellaneous Provisions) Act 1916 (c 31), or

(c) the repeal made in that Act by Schedule 9,

which extend to England and Wales only.

[2424]

NOTES

Commencement: 8 November 2006.

(*Schs 1–9 outside the scope of this work.*)

SCHEDULE 10
TRANSITIONAL PROVISIONS AND SAVINGS

Section 75

Section 4: guidance as to operation of public benefit requirement

1. Any consultation initiated by the Charity Commissioners for England and Wales before the day on which section 4 of this Act comes into force is to be as effective for the purposes of section 4(4)(a) as if it had been initiated by the Commission on or after that day.

Section 5: recreational charities etc

2. Where section 2 of the Recreational Charities Act 1958 (c 17) applies to any trusts immediately before the day on which subsection (3) of section 5 of this Act comes into force, that subsection does not prevent the trusts from continuing to be charitable if they constitute a charity in accordance with section 1(1) of this Act.

Section 18: cy-près schemes

3. The amendment made by section 18 applies to property given for charitable purposes whether before or on or after the day on which that section comes into force.

Section 19: suspension or removal of trustee etc from membership of charity

4. The amendment made by section 19 applies where the misconduct or other relevant conduct on the part of the person suspended or removed from his office or employment took place on or after the day on which section 19 comes into force.

Section 20: specific directions for protection of charity

5. The amendment made by section 20 applies whether the inquiry under section 8 of the 1993 Act was instituted before or on or after the day on which section 20 comes into force.

Section 26: offence of obstructing power of entry

6. In relation to an offence committed before the commencement of section 281(5) of the Criminal Justice Act 2003 (c 44) (alteration of penalties for summary offences), the reference to 51 weeks in section 31A(11) of the 1993 Act (as inserted by section 26 of this Act) is to be read as a reference to 3 months.

Section 28: audit or examination of accounts of charity which is not a company

7. The amendments made by section 28 apply in relation to any financial year of a charity which begins on or after the day on which that section comes into force.

Section 29: auditor etc of charity which is not a company to report matters to Commission

8.—(1) The amendments made by section 29 apply in relation to matters ("pre-commencement matters") of which a person became aware at any time falling—

(a) before the day on which that section comes into force, and

(b) during a financial year ending on or after that day,

as well as in relation to matters of which he becomes aware on or after that day.

(2) Any duty imposed by or by virtue of the new section 44A(2) or 46(2A) of the 1993 Act inserted by section 29 must be complied with in relation to any such pre-commencement matters as soon as practicable after section 29 comes into force.

Section 32: audit or examination of accounts of charitable companies

9. The amendments made by section 32 apply in relation to any financial year of a charity which begins on or after the day on which that section comes into force.

Section 33: auditor etc of charitable company to report matters to Commission

10.—(1) The amendment made by section 33 applies in relation to matters ("pre-commencement matters") of which a person became aware at any time falling—

(a) before the day on which that section comes into force, and

(b) during a financial year ending on or after that day,

as well as in relation to matters of which he becomes aware on or after that day.

(2) Any duty imposed by virtue of the new section 68A(1) of the 1993 Act inserted by section 33 must be complied with in relation to any such pre-commencement matters as soon as practicable after section 33 comes into force.

Section 35: waiver of trustee's disqualification

11. The amendment made by section 35 applies whether the disqualification took effect before, on or after the day on which that section comes into force.

Section 36: remuneration of trustees etc providing services to charity

12. The amendment made by section 36 does not affect the payment of remuneration or provision of services in accordance with an agreement made before the day on which that section comes into force.

Section 38: relief from liability for breach of trust or duty

13. Sections 73D and 73E of the 1993 Act (as inserted by section 38 of this Act) have effect in relation to acts or omissions occurring before the day on which section 38 comes into force as well as in relation to those occurring on or after that day.

Section 44: registration of charity mergers

14. Section 75C of the 1993 Act (as inserted by section 44 of this Act) applies to relevant charity mergers taking place before the day on which section 44 comes into force as well as to ones taking place on or after that day.

Section 67: statements relating to fund-raising

15. The amendments made by section 67 apply in relation to any solicitation or representation to which section 60(1), (2) or (3) of the 1992 Act applies and which is made on or after the day on which section 67 comes into force.

Section 72: Disclosure of information to and by Northern Ireland regulator

16. In relation to an offence committed in England and Wales before the commencement of section 154(1) of the Criminal Justice Act 2003 (c 44) (general limit on magistrates' court's power to impose imprisonment), the reference to 12 months in section 72(6) is to be read as a reference to 6 months.

Schedule 6: group accounts

17. Paragraph 3(2) of the new Schedule 5A inserted in the 1993 Act by Schedule 6 to this Act does not apply in relation to any financial year of a parent charity beginning before the day on which paragraph 3(2) comes into force.

Schedule 8: minor and consequential amendments

18. The following provisions, namely—
  (a) paragraphs 80(6) and (8), 83(3) and (4), 99(3), (4)(a) and (5)(a) and (c), 109(12), 111(7) and 171 of Schedule 8, and
  (b) the corresponding entries in Schedule 9,

do not affect the operation of the Coal Industry Act 1987 (c 3), the Reverter of Sites Act 1987 (c 15) or the 1993 Act in relation to any appeal brought in the High Court before the day on which those provisions come into force.

19. Paragraph 98(2) of Schedule 8 does not affect the validity of any designation made by the Charity Commissioners for England and Wales under section 2(2) of the 1993 Act which is in effect immediately before that paragraph comes into force.

20. In relation to an offence committed in England and Wales before the commencement of section 154(1) of the Criminal Justice Act 2003 (c 44) (general limit on magistrates' court's power to impose imprisonment), the reference to 12 months in section 10A(4) of the 1993 Act (as inserted by paragraph 104 of Schedule 8 to this Act) is to be read as a reference to 6 months.

Schedule 9: savings on repeal of provisions of Charities Act 1960

21.—(1) This paragraph applies where, immediately before the coming into force of the repeal by this Act of section 35(6) of the Charities Act 1960 (c 58) (transfer and evidence of title to property vested in trustees), any relevant provision had effect, in accordance with that provision, as if contained in a conveyance or other document declaring the trusts on which land was held at the commencement of that Act.

(2) In such a case the relevant provision continues to have effect as if so contained despite the repeal of section 35(6) of that Act.

(3) A "relevant provision" means a provision of any of the following Acts providing for the appointment of trustees—
  (a) the Trustee Appointment Act 1850 (c 28),
  (b) the Trustee Appointment Act 1869 (c 26),
  (c) the Trustees Appointment Act 1890 (c 19), or
  (d) the School Sites Act 1852 (c 49) so far as applying any of the above Acts,

as in force at the commencement of the Charities Act 1960.

22. The repeal by this Act of section 39(2) of the Charities Act 1960 (repeal of obsolete enactments) does not affect the continued operation of any trusts which, at the commencement of that Act, were wholly or partly comprised in an enactment specified in Schedule 5 to that Act (enactments repealed as obsolete).

23. The repeal by this Act of section 48(1) of, and Schedule 6 to, the Charities Act 1960 (consequential amendments etc) does not affect the amendments made by Schedule 6 in—
  (a) section 9 of the Places of Worship Registration Act 1855 (c 81),
  (b) section 4(1) of the Open Spaces Act 1906 (c 25),
  (c) section 24(4) of the Landlord and Tenant Act 1927 (c 36), or
  (d) section 14(1) or 31 of the New Parishes Measure 1943.

24. Despite the repeal by this Act of section 48(3) of the Charities Act 1960, section 30(3) to (5) of the 1993 Act continue to apply to documents enrolled by or deposited with the Charity Commissioners under the Charitable Trusts Acts 1853 to 1939.

25. Despite the repeal by this Act of section 48(4) of the Charities Act 1960—

(a) any scheme, order, certificate or other document issued under or for the purposes of the Charitable Trusts Acts 1853 to 1939 and having effect in accordance with section 48(4) immediately before the commencement of that repeal continues to have the same effect (and to be enforceable or liable to be discharged in the same way) as would have been the case if that repeal had not come into force, and

(b) any such document, and any document under the seal of the official trustees of charitable funds, may be proved as if the 1960 Act had not been passed.

26.—(1) Despite the repeal by this Act of section 48(6) of the Charities Act 1960 (c 58), the official custodian for charities is to continue to be treated as the successor for all purposes both of the official trustee of charity lands and of the official trustees of charitable funds as if—

(a) the functions of the official trustee or trustees had been functions of the official custodian, and

(b) as if the official trustee or trustees had been, and had discharged his or their functions as, holder of the office of the official custodian.

(2) Despite the repeal of section 48(6) (and without affecting the generality of sub-paragraph (1))—

(a) any property which immediately before the commencement of that repeal was, by virtue of section 48(6), held by the official custodian as if vested in him under section 21 of the 1993 Act continues to be so held, and

(b) any enactment or document referring to the official trustee or trustees mentioned above continues to have effect, so far as the context permits, as if the official custodian had been mentioned instead.

27. The repeal by this Act of the Charities Act 1960 does not affect any transitional provision or saving contained in that Act which is capable of having continuing effect but whose effect is not preserved by any other provision of this Schedule.

Schedule 9: savings on repeal of provisions of Charities Act 1992

28. The repeal by this Act of section 49 of, and Schedule 5 to, the 1992 Act (amendments relating to redundant churches etc) does not affect the amendments made by that Schedule in the Redundant Churches and Other Religious Buildings Act 1969.

Schedule 9: repeal of certain repeals made by Charities Acts 1960 and 1992

29.—(1) It is hereby declared that (in accordance with sections 15 and 16 of the Interpretation Act 1978 (c 30)) the repeal by this Act of any of the provisions mentioned in sub-paragraph (2) does not revive so much of any enactment or document as ceased to have effect by virtue of that provision.

(2) The provisions are—

(a) section 28(9) of the Charities Act 1960 (repeal of provisions regulating taking of charity proceedings),

(b) section 36 of the 1992 Act (repeal of provisions requiring Charity Commissioners' consent to dealings with charity land), and

(c) section 50 of that Act (repeal of provisions requiring amount of contributions towards maintenance etc of almshouses to be sanctioned by Charity Commissioners).

[2425]

NOTES

Commencement: 27 February 2007 (paras 1, 6, 7, 9, 11, 13, 16, 19, 20); 28 November 2007 (para 14); 18 March 2008 (paras 3–5, 12, 18); 1 April 2008 (para 8, for certain purposes, paras 10, 15, 17, 28, 29(1), (2)(b), (c); for transitional provisions and savings see SI 2008/945, arts 4, 5); 31 January 2009 (paras 21–27, 29(2)(a)); 1 April 2010 (para 2); to be appointed (para 8, for remaining purposes).

HOUSING AND REGENERATION ACT 2008

(2008 c 17)

An Act to establish the Homes and Communities Agency and make provision about it; to abolish the Urban Regeneration Agency and the Commission for the New Towns and make provision in connection with their abolition; to regulate social housing; to enable the abolition of the Housing Corporation; to make provision about sustainability certificates, landlord and tenant matters, building regulations and mobile homes; to make further provision about housing; and for connected purposes

[22 July 2008]

PART 1
THE HOMES AND COMMUNITIES AGENCY

CHAPTER 1
GENERAL

1 Establishment and constitution

(1) There shall be a body corporate known as the Homes and Communities Agency ("the HCA").

(2) Schedule 1 (which makes further provision about the HCA) has effect.

[2426]

NOTES
Commencement: 8 September 2008.

2 Objects

(1) The objects of the HCA are—
- (a) to improve the supply and quality of housing in England,
- (b) to secure the regeneration or development of land or infrastructure in England,
- (c) to support in other ways the creation, regeneration or development of communities in England or their continued well-being, and
- (d) to contribute to the achievement of sustainable development and good design in England,

with a view to meeting the needs of people living in England.

(2) In subsection (1)—
"good design" includes design which has due regard to the needs of elderly persons and disabled persons,
"needs" includes future needs,

and the reference to improving the supply of housing includes a reference to improving the supply of particular kinds of housing.

(3) In this Part—
"building" means a building or other structure (including a house-boat or caravan),
"caravan" has the meaning given by section 29(1) of the Caravan Sites and Control of Development Act 1960 (c 2),
"housing" means a building, or part of a building, occupied or intended to be occupied as a dwelling or as more than one dwelling; and includes a hostel which provides temporary residential accommodation,
"infrastructure" includes—
- (a) water, electricity, gas, telecommunications, sewerage or other services,
- (b) roads or other transport facilities,
- (c) retail or other business facilities,
- (d) health, educational, employment or training facilities,
- (e) social, religious or recreational facilities,
- (f) cremation or burial facilities, and
- (g) community facilities not falling within paragraphs (a) to (f),

"land" includes housing or other buildings (and see also the definition in Schedule 1 to the Interpretation Act 1978 (c 30)),

and references to housing include (where the context permits) any yard, garden, outhouses and appurtenances belonging to, or usually enjoyed with, the building or part of building concerned.

(4) See also sections 19(5) (financial assistance), 44 (local government involvement) and 52 (role of the HCA in relation to certain former functions of the Commission for the New Towns).

[2427]

NOTES
Commencement: 8 September 2008.

3 Principal powers

The HCA may do anything it considers appropriate for the purposes of its objects or for purposes incidental to those purposes.

[2428]

NOTES
Commencement: 8 September 2008.

4 Powers: general

(1) This Part contains various specific powers of the HCA.

(2) The specific powers of the HCA (whether contained in this Part or elsewhere) are to be exercised for the purposes of its objects or for purposes incidental to those purposes.

(3) Each power may be exercised separately or together with, or as part of, another power.

(4) Each power does not limit the scope of another power.

(5) Each power does not limit the scope of the powers conferred by section 3.

(6) But—

(a) subsections (2) and (3) do not apply to the HCA in its capacity as a local planning authority by virtue of sections 13 and 14 or in its exercise of other functions by virtue of those sections, and

(b) the powers conferred by section 3 must not be used to override a restriction imposed on the exercise of a specific power.

[2429]

NOTES

Commencement: 8 September 2008 (in relation to the powers brought into force by SI 2008/2358); 1 December 2008 (in relation to the powers brought into force by SI 2008/3068).

CHAPTER 2
LAND AND INFRASTRUCTURE

General

5 Powers to provide housing or other land

(1) The HCA may provide housing or other land.

(2) The HCA may facilitate the provision of housing or other land.

(3) In this section "provide" includes provide by way of acquisition, construction, conversion, improvement or repair (and "provision" is to be read in the same way).

[2430]

NOTES

Commencement: 1 December 2008.

6 Powers for regeneration, development or effective use of land

(1) The HCA may regenerate or develop land.

(2) The HCA may bring about the more effective use of land.

(3) The HCA may facilitate—

(a) the regeneration or development of land, or

(b) the more effective use of land.

[2431]

NOTES

Commencement: 1 December 2008.

7 Powers in relation to infrastructure

(1) The HCA may provide infrastructure.

(2) The HCA may facilitate the provision of infrastructure.

(3) In this section "provide" includes provide by way of acquisition, construction, conversion, improvement or repair (and "provision" is to be read in the same way).

[2432]

NOTES

Commencement: 1 December 2008.

Powers to deal with land etc

8 Powers to deal with land etc

The HCA may carry out, or facilitate the carrying out of, any of the following activities in relation to land—

(a) acquiring, holding, improving, managing, reclaiming, repairing or disposing of housing,

(b) acquiring, holding, improving, managing, reclaiming, repairing or disposing of other land, plant, machinery, equipment or other property, and

(c) carrying out building and other operations (including converting or demolishing buildings).

[2433]

NOTES

Commencement: 1 December 2008.

9 Acquisition of land

(1) The HCA may acquire land by agreement.

(2) The HCA may acquire land compulsorily if the Secretary of State authorises it to do so.

(3) The power of acquiring land compulsorily under subsection (2) includes power to acquire new rights over land.

(4) Subsection (5) applies where—

(a) land or new rights over land are being acquired compulsorily under subsection (2), and
(b) the land which is being acquired, or over which new rights are being acquired, forms part of a common, open space or allotment.

(5) The power under subsection (2) to acquire land compulsorily includes the power to acquire land compulsorily for giving in exchange for the land or (as the case may be) new rights mentioned in subsection (4)(a).

(6) Schedule 2 (which makes further provision in relation to the acquisition of land by the HCA) has effect.

(7) In this Part—

"allotment" means a fuel or field garden allotment,
"common" has the meaning given by section 19(4) of the Acquisition of Land Act 1981 (c 67),
"open space" means any land which is—
(a) laid out as a public garden,
(b) used for the purposes of public recreation, or
(c) a disused burial ground.

[2434]

NOTES

Commencement: 1 December 2008.

10 Restrictions on disposal of land

(1) The HCA may not dispose of land for less than the best consideration which can reasonably be obtained unless the Secretary of State consents.

(2) Subsection (1) does not apply to a disposal by way of a short tenancy if the disposal consists of—

(a) the grant of a term of not more than 7 years, or
(b) the assignment of a term which, at the date of assignment, has not more than 7 years to run.

(3) The HCA may not dispose of land which has been compulsorily acquired by it under this Part unless the Secretary of State consents.

(4) Subject as above, the HCA may dispose of land held by it in any way it considers appropriate.

[2435]

NOTES

Commencement: 1 December 2008.

Powers in relation to acquired land

11 Main powers in relation to acquired land

Schedule 3 (which makes provision about powers in relation to land of the HCA) has effect.

[2436]

NOTES

Commencement: 1 December 2008.

12 Powers in relation to, and for, statutory undertakers

Schedule 4 (which provides for powers in relation to, and for, statutory undertakers) has effect.

[2437]

NOTES
Commencement: 1 December 2008.

13–16 (*Outside the scope of this work.*)

Other powers etc in relation to land

17 Power to enter and survey land

(1) Any person authorised by the HCA may, at any reasonable time and subject as follows, enter any land for the purpose of surveying it, or estimating its value, in connection with—
(a) any proposal for the HCA to acquire that land or any other land, or
(b) any claim for compensation in respect of any such acquisition.

(2) A person authorised under subsection (1) to enter any land—
(a) must, if required, produce evidence of the authority before entering the land, and
(b) must not demand admission as of right to the land unless the HCA has served notice of the intended entry on every owner or occupier of the land not less than 28 days before the making of the demand.

(3) A notice under subsection (2)(b) must—
(a) state the purpose for which entry is required, and
(b) inform the person to whom it is given of the person's rights under this section and, if applicable, section 18.

(4) A person interested in any land may recover compensation from the HCA in respect of any damage done to the land—
(a) in the exercise of a right of entry under this section, or
(b) in making a survey under this section.

(5) Section 118 of the Town and Country Planning Act 1990 (c 8) (determination of claims for compensation) applies in relation to compensation under subsection (4) as it applies in relation to compensation under Part 4 of that Act.

(6) A person ("A") commits an offence if A intentionally obstructs another person ("B") in the exercise of B's powers under subsection (1) above.

(7) A person who commits an offence under subsection (6) is liable on summary conviction to a fine not exceeding level 2 on the standard scale.

(8) In subsection (2)(b) "owner" has the same meaning as in the Acquisition of Land Act 1981 (c 67).

(9) The references in subsections (4) and (6) to this section or subsection (1) include references to those provisions as extended by section 18.

[2438]

NOTES
Commencement: 1 December 2008.

18 Section 17: supplementary

(1) The power to survey land conferred by section 17(1) includes power to search and bore for the purpose of ascertaining—
(a) the nature of the subsoil, or
(b) the presence of minerals in it.

(2) But this is subject to subsections (3) to (5).

(3) No person may carry out any works authorised by virtue of subsection (1) unless notice of the person's intention to do so was included in the notice required by section 17(2)(b).

(4) The authority of the appropriate Minister is required for the carrying out of any works authorised by virtue of subsection (1) if—
(a) the land concerned is held by statutory undertakers, and
(b) they object to the proposed works on the ground that the execution of the works would be seriously detrimental to carrying on their undertaking.

(5) The references in subsection (4) to the appropriate Minister, statutory undertakers and their undertaking have the same meanings as they have in section 325(9) of the Town and Country Planning Act 1990 (c 8) (supplementary provisions as to rights of entry).

[2439]

NOTES
Commencement: 1 December 2008.

19–45 ((*Chs 3, 4*) *outside the scope of this work.*)

CHAPTER 5
SUPPLEMENTARY

46–48 (*Outside the scope of this work.*)

Abolition of existing bodies

49 Abolition of Urban Regeneration Agency

The Urban Regeneration Agency shall cease to exist on such day as the Secretary of State may by order appoint.

[2440]

NOTES

Commencement: 8 September 2008.

Orders: the Abolition of the Commission for the New Towns and the Urban Regeneration Agency (Appointed Day and Consequential Amendments) Order 2009, SI 2009/801 (appoints 1 April 2009).

50 Abolition of the Commission for the New Towns

(1) The Commission for the New Towns shall cease to exist on such day as the Secretary of State may by order appoint.

(2) Schedule 5 (which transfers Welsh functions of the Commission to the Welsh Ministers and makes other amendments of the New Towns Act 1981 (c 64)) has effect.

[2441]

NOTES

Commencement: 8 September 2008.

Orders: the Abolition of the Commission for the New Towns and the Urban Regeneration Agency (Appointed Day and Consequential Amendments) Order 2009, SI 2009/801 (appoints 1 April 2009).

51 Property etc transfers to the HCA and the Welsh Ministers

(1) The Secretary of State may make one or more schemes for—

(a) the transfer to the HCA of designated property, rights or liabilities of—

(i) the Urban Regeneration Agency,

(ii) the Commission for the New Towns,

(iii) a regional development agency (within the meaning of the Regional Development Agencies Act 1998 (c 45)), or

(iv) a Minister of the Crown, or

(b) the transfer to the Welsh Ministers of designated property, rights or liabilities of—

(i) the Urban Regeneration Agency, or

(ii) the Commission for the New Towns.

(2) On the transfer date, the designated property, rights or liabilities are transferred and vest in accordance with the scheme.

(3) Schedule 6 (which makes further provision about the making of schemes) has effect.

(4) In this section and in Schedule 6—

"designated" in relation to a scheme, means specified in, or determined in accordance with, the scheme,

"Minister of the Crown" has the same meaning as in the Ministers of the Crown Act 1975 (c 26),

"the transfer date" means a date specified by a scheme as the date on which the scheme is to have effect.

(5) Schedule 7 makes provision about the tax implications of schemes under this section (and schemes under section 65).

[2442]

NOTES

Commencement: 8 September 2008.

52 Role of the HCA in relation to former CNT functions

(1) The HCA must, so far as practicable, exercise its powers in relation to—

(a) any property, rights or liabilities of the Commission for the New Towns transferred to it by virtue of section 51 and Schedule 6,

(b) any property, rights or liabilities of a new town development corporation transferred to it by virtue of section 41 of, and Schedule 10 to, the New Towns Act 1981 (c 64),

(c) any undertaking, or part of an undertaking, of an urban development corporation transferred to it by virtue of an agreement under section 165 of the Local Government, Planning and Land Act 1980 (c 65), or
(d) any property, rights or liabilities of an urban development corporation transferred to it by virtue of an order under section 165B of that Act,

for the purposes of the objects mentioned in section 2(1) or for purposes incidental to those purposes.

(2) But subsection (1) does not apply if the HCA does not consider it appropriate to exercise its powers in this way having regard, in particular, to the purposes for which the transferred property was held by the Commission for the New Towns, the new town development corporation or (as the case may be) the urban development corporation.

(3) In such a case, the HCA must exercise its powers in relation to the transferred property in such a way as it considers appropriate having regard, in particular, to—
(a) the objects mentioned in section 2(1), and
(b) the purposes for which the transferred property was held by the body concerned,

and the references in this Part to the objects of the HCA are to be read accordingly.

(4) In this section—
"new town development corporation" means a development corporation established under section 3 of the New Towns Act 1981 (c 64),
"transferred property" means any property, rights or liabilities, or any undertaking or part of an undertaking, falling within paragraphs (a) to (d) of subsection (1) above.

[2443]

NOTES
Commencement: 8 September 2008.

53 Interim arrangements

(1) The Secretary of State may by notice require the Urban Regeneration Agency or the Commission for the New Towns to provide staff, premises, facilities or other assistance on a temporary basis to—
(a) the HCA, or
(b) the Welsh Ministers.

(2) *In paragraph 1(1) of Schedule 17 to the Leasehold Reform, Housing and Urban Development Act 1993 (c 28) (constitution of the Urban Regeneration Agency: number of members), for "six" substitute "two".*

(3) This section is without prejudice to the power of the Secretary of State under section 322(1).

[2444]

NOTES
Commencement: 8 September 2008.
Sub-s (2): repealed by s 321(1), Sch 16, as from a day to be appointed.

Other

54 Validity of transactions

(1) A transaction between a person and the HCA is not invalid merely because of a failure by the HCA to exercise its powers for the purposes mentioned in sections 3 and 4(2).

(2) A transaction between a person and the HCA is not invalid merely because it was carried out in contravention of a direction under section 47.

(3) A transaction between a person and a subsidiary of the HCA is not invalid merely because of a failure by the HCA to comply with section 41(1) or (2).

(4) A person entering into a transaction with the HCA or a subsidiary of the HCA need not be concerned as to whether—
(a) there has been a failure of the kind mentioned in subsection (1) or (3), or
(b) a direction of the kind mentioned in subsection (2) has been given or complied with.

(5) A disposal of land by the HCA is not invalid merely because any consent required by section 10(1) or (3) has not been given.

(6) A person dealing with—
(a) the HCA, or
(b) a person claiming under the HCA,

in relation to any land need not be concerned as to whether any consent required by section 10(1) or (3) has been given.

[2445]

NOTES

Commencement: 8 September 2008.

55 Notices

(1) Any notice required or authorised under this Part to be served on any person may be served by—

(a) delivering it to the person,
(b) leaving it at the person's proper address, or
(c) sending it by post to the person at that address.

(2) Any such notice may—

(a) in the case of a body corporate, be served in accordance with subsection (1) on an officer of the body, and
(b) in the case of a partnership, be served in accordance with subsection (1) on a partner or a person having the control or management of the partnership business.

(3) For the purposes of this section and section 7 of the Interpretation Act 1978 (c 30) (service of documents by post) in its application to this section, the proper address of any person on whom a notice is to be served is the person's last known address except as follows.

(4) For the purposes of this section and section 7 of the Act of 1978 in its application to this section, the proper address is—

(a) in the case of service on a body corporate or an officer of the body, the address of the registered or principal office of the body, and
(b) in the case of service on a partnership, a partner or a person having the control or management of the partnership business, the address of the principal office of the partnership.

(5) For the purposes of subsection (4) the principal office of a company registered outside the United Kingdom or of a partnership carrying on business outside the United Kingdom is its principal office within the United Kingdom.

(6) Subsection (7) applies if a person to be served under this Part with a notice has specified an address within the United Kingdom other than the person's proper address (as decided under subsections (3) and (4)) as the one at which the person, or someone on the person's behalf, will accept documents of the same description as the notice.

(7) The specified address is also to be treated for the purposes of this section and section 7 of the Act of 1978 in its application to this section as the person's proper address.

(8) Subsection (9) applies if the name or address of any owner, lessee or occupier of land on whom a notice is to be served under this Part cannot, after reasonable inquiry, be ascertained.

(9) The notice may be served by—

(a) leaving it in the hands of a person who is, or appears to be, resident or employed on the land, or
(b) leaving it conspicuously affixed to a building or object on the land.

(10) Any notice required or authorised under this Part to be served on any person may be served on the person by transmitting the text of the notice to the person by means of an electronic communications network or by other means but while in electronic form provided the text is received by the person in legible form and is capable of being used for subsequent reference.

(11) In this section—

"body corporate" includes a limited liability partnership,

"director", in relation to a body corporate whose affairs are managed by its members, means a member of the body corporate,

"officer of a body corporate" means any director, manager, secretary or other similar officer of the body corporate,

"partnership" does not include a limited liability partnership,

and references to serving include references to similar expressions (such as giving or sending).

[2446]

NOTES

Commencement: 8 September 2008.

56 Consequential amendments: Part 1

Schedule 8 (which contains amendments of enactments) has effect.

[2447]

NOTES

Commencement: see the note to Sch 8 at **[2496]**.

57 Interpretation: Part 1

(1) In this Part—

"conduit system" has the same meaning as in the electronic communications code; and references to providing a conduit system are to be read in accordance with paragraph 1(3A) of that code,

"develop" (and development), in relation to land or infrastructure, includes redevelop (and redevelopment),

"electronic communications apparatus" has the same meaning as in the electronic communications code,

"the electronic communications code" has the same meaning as in Chapter 1 of Part 2 of the Communications Act 2003 (c 21),

"electronic communications code network" means—

(a) so much of an electronic communications network or conduit system provided by an electronic communications code operator as is not excluded from the application of the electronic communications code by a direction under section 106 of the Act of 2003 (application of the electronic communications code), and

(b) an electronic communications network which the Secretary of State is providing or proposing to provide,

"electronic communications code operator" means a person in whose case the electronic communications code is applied by a direction under section 106 of the Act of 2003,

"electronic communications network" has the same meaning as in the Act of 2003,

"enactment" includes subordinate legislation (within the meaning of the Interpretation Act 1978 (c 30)),

"financial year" means—

(a) the period beginning with the day on which the HCA is established and ending with the next 31 March, and

(b) each subsequent period of 12 months ending with 31 March,

"improve", in relation to housing and other land, includes refurbish, equip and fit out,

"modifications" includes omissions,

"notice" means notice in writing,

"operator", in relation to an electronic communications code network means—

(a) the electronic communications code operator providing that network, or

(b) the Secretary of State, so far as the Secretary of State is providing or proposing to provide that network,

"provide" and related expressions, in relation to an electronic communications network, are to be read in accordance with section 32(4) of the Communications Act 2003 (c 21).

(2) References in this Part to powers of the HCA do not include references to powers contained in duties imposed on the HCA.

[2448]

NOTES

Commencement: 8 September 2008 (so far as required for the interpretation of provisions commenced by SI 2008/2358); 1 December 2008 (so far as required for the interpretation of provisions commenced by SI 2008/3068); to be appointed (for remaining purposes).

58 Index of defined expressions: Part 1

In this Part, the expressions listed in the left-hand column have the meaning given by, or are to be interpreted in accordance with, the provisions listed in the right-hand column.

Expression	*Provision*
Allotment	Section 9(7)
Building	Section 2(3)
Caravan	Section 2(3)
Common	Section 9(7)
Conduit system (and providing such a system)	Section 57(1)
Designated area	Section 13(5)

Expression	*Provision*
Designation order	Section 13(5)
Develop (and development)	Section 57(1)
Electronic communications apparatus	Section 57(1)
Electronic communications code	Section 57(1)
Electronic communications code network	Section 57(1)
Electronic communications code operator	Section 57(1)
Electronic communications network	Section 57(1)
Enactment	Section 57(1)
Financial year	Section 57(1)
Giving directions	Section 47(6)
The HCA	Section 1(1)
Housing	Section 2(3)
Improve	Section 57(1)
Infrastructure	Section 2(3)
Land	Section 2(3) (and Schedule 1 to the Interpretation Act 1978 (c 30))
Local planning authority (in relation to designation orders or proposed designation orders)	Section 13(5)
Modifications	Section 57(1)
Notice	Section 57(1)
Objects of the HCA	Sections 2, 19(5) and 52(3)
Open space	Section 9(7)
Operator (in relation to electronic communications code network)	Section 57(1)
Permitted purposes	Section 13(5)
Powers of the HCA	Section 57(2)
Provide (in relation to an electronic communications network)	Section 57(1)
Registered provider of social housing	Section 80(2)(a)
Regulator of Social Housing	Section 81(2)(a)
Social housing (and its provision)	Section 32(13)
Social housing assistance	Section 32(13)
Subsidiary	Section 23(5)
Urban development corporation	Section 42(7)

[2449]

NOTES

Commencement: 8 September 2008 (so far as required for the interpretation of provisions commenced by SI 2008/2358); 1 December 2008 (so far as required for the interpretation of provisions commenced by SI 2008/3068); 1 April 2009 (so far as required for the interpretation of provisions commenced by SI 2009/803); to be appointed (for remaining purposes).

PART 2
REGULATION OF SOCIAL HOUSING

59–169 ((*Chs 1–4*) *outside the scope of this work.*)

CHAPTER 5
DISPOSAL OF PROPERTY

Introductory

170 Overview

This Chapter makes provision about the disposal of property by registered providers.

[2450]

NOTES

Commencement: to be appointed

171 Power to dispose

(1) A registered provider may dispose of land.

(2) But a non-profit registered provider may dispose of the landlord's interest under a secure tenancy only to another non-profit registered provider.

(3) Subsection (1) is subject to the following provisions of this Chapter (which include provisions requiring the regulator's consent for certain disposals).

[2451]

NOTES

Commencement: to be appointed

Regulator's consent

172 Requirement of consent

(1) Disposal of a dwelling by a registered provider requires the regulator's consent if the dwelling is social housing.

(2) The regulator shall not consent to a disposal by a non-profit registered provider which it thinks is being made with a view to enabling the provider to distribute assets to members.

(3) Consent is not required under this section if the disposal falls within an exception listed in section 173.

[2452]

NOTES

Commencement: to be appointed

173 Exceptions

(1) This section lists exceptions to the requirement of consent in section 172.

(2) Exception 1 is that consent is not required for disposal by a registered provider by way of—

(a) an assured tenancy,

(b) an assured agricultural occupancy,

(c) an arrangement that would be an assured tenancy or an assured agricultural occupancy but for any of paragraphs 4 to 8, 12(1)(h) and 12ZA to 12B of Schedule 1 to the Housing Act 1988 (c 50) (exclusions),

(d) a secure tenancy, or

(e) an arrangement that would be a secure tenancy but for any of paragraphs 2 to 12 of Schedule 1 to the Housing Act 1985 (c 68) (exclusions).

(3) Exception 2 is that consent is not required for a disposal for which consent is required under—

(a) section 81 or 133 of the Housing Act 1988, or

(b) section 173 of the Local Government and Housing Act 1989 (c 42).

(4) Exception 3 is that consent is not required for a disposal under Part V of the Housing Act 1985 (right to buy).

(5) Exception 4 is that consent is not required for a disposal in pursuance of a tenant's right to acquire under—

(a) section 180, or

(b) section 16 of the Housing Act 1996 (c 52) (tenant's right to acquire social housing in Wales).

[2453]

NOTES

Commencement: to be appointed

174 Procedure

(1) Consent may be—

(a) general, or

(b) specific (whether as to particular registered providers, as to particular property, as to particular forms of disposal or in any other way).

(2) Consent may be retrospective.

(3) Consent may be expressed by reference to a policy for disposals submitted by a registered provider.

(4) Consent may be conditional.

(5) Before giving consent the regulator must consult—

(a) the HCA,

(b) one or more bodies appearing to it to represent the interests of registered providers, and

(c) one or more bodies appearing to it to represent the interests of tenants.

(6) Subsection (5) does not apply to specific consent relating only to one or more particular registered providers or properties.

[2454]

NOTES

Commencement: 8 September 2008 (sub-ss (5), (6)); to be appointed (otherwise).

175 Disposal without consent

(1) A purported disposal by a registered provider is void if—

(a) it requires the regulator's consent, and

(b) the regulator has not given consent.

(2) But subsection (1) does not apply to a disposal by a non-profit registered provider to one or more individuals ("the buyer") if—

(a) the disposal is of a single dwelling, and

(b) the registered provider reasonably believes at the time of the disposal that the buyer intends to use the property as the buyer's principal residence.

[2455]

NOTES

Commencement: to be appointed.

176 Notification where disposal consent not required

(1) If a non-profit registered provider disposes of land other than a dwelling which is social housing it shall notify the regulator as soon as is reasonably practicable.

(2) The regulator may give a direction dispensing with the notification requirement.

(3) Section 174(1) and (3) to (6) applies to a direction under this section as it applies to consent under section 172.

Proceeds

[2456]

NOTES

Commencement: to be appointed.

177 Separate accounting

(1) The accounts of a registered provider must show its net disposal proceeds, as a separate "disposal proceeds fund".

(2) The following are net disposal proceeds—

(a) net proceeds of sale to a tenant in pursuance of the right to acquire conferred by section 180,

(b) net proceeds of sale to a tenant in pursuance of the right to acquire conferred by section 16 of the Housing Act 1996 (c 52),

(c) net proceeds of sale of property in respect of which a grant was made under section 21 of that Act,

(d) net proceeds of sale of property in respect of which a grant was made under section 19 of this Act in respect of discounts given by a registered provider on disposals of dwellings to tenants,

(e) grant received under section 20 or 21 of the 1996 Act,

(f) grant received under section 19 of this Act in respect of discounts given by a registered provider on disposals of dwellings to tenants,

(g) repayments of discount in respect of which grant was received under section 20 or 21 of the 1996 Act,
(h) repayments of discount in respect of which grant was received under section 19 of this Act in respect of discounts given by a registered provider on disposals of dwellings to tenants,
(i) other proceeds of sale specified by the regulator, and
(j) other grants specified by the regulator.

(3) The regulator shall determine amounts to be deducted in determining net proceeds of sale.

(4) The method of constituting the disposal proceeds fund and showing it in the accounts shall be in accordance with a direction of the regulator.

(5) Subsections (5) to (7) of section 127 apply to a direction under this section as to a direction under that section.

(6) Sections 141 and 142 apply in relation to a direction under this section as in relation to a direction under section 127.

(7) Interest shall be added to the fund in accordance with a determination made by the regulator.

(8) Where this section applies in relation to the proceeds of sale arising on a disposal, section 32 above, section 27 of the Housing Act 1996 (c 52) and section 52 of the Housing Act 1988 (c 50) do not apply.

[2457]

NOTES
Commencement: to be appointed.

178 Use of proceeds

(1) Sums in a registered provider's disposal proceeds fund may be used or allocated only in accordance with a direction by the regulator.

(2) The regulator may give a direction only with the Secretary of State's approval.

(3) If at the end of a period specified by the regulator the disposal proceeds fund includes sums which have not been allocated in accordance with subsection (1), the regulator may require the registered provider to pay the sums to the HCA.

[2458]

NOTES
Commencement: to be appointed.

Tenants' rights and duties

179 Application of Housing Act 1996

(1) The following provisions of the Housing Act 1996 apply in relation to disposals of social housing by registered providers, with the modifications set out below (and any other necessary modifications).

(2) The provisions are—
(a) sections 11 to 12 (repayment of discount on disposal),
(b) sections 12A and 12B (landlord's right of first refusal),
(c) section 13 (disposal of property in National Park), and
(d) sections 14 and 15 (supplemental).

(3) In those provisions—
(a) references to a registered social landlord shall be treated as references to a registered provider,
(b) references to consent given by the Welsh Ministers under section 9 of the 1996 Act shall be treated as references to consent given by the regulator under section 172 of this Act,
(c) references to the Welsh Ministers in connection with a power to make orders or regulations shall be treated as references to the Secretary of State,
(d) in section 12(5)(b) of the 1996 Act the reference to the Welsh Ministers shall be treated as a reference to the HCA, and
(e) references to a resolution of the National Assembly for Wales shall be treated as references to a resolution of either House of Parliament.

(4) This section does not affect the continued application of the provisions listed in subsection (2) in relation to disposals made before this section comes into force.

[2459]

NOTES

Commencement: to be appointed.

Right to acquire

180 Right to acquire

(1) The tenant of a dwelling in England has a right to acquire the dwelling if—

(a) the landlord is a registered provider or a registered social landlord,

(b) the tenancy is within subsection (2),

(c) the provision of the dwelling was publicly funded,

(d) the dwelling has remained in the social rented sector ever since that provision, and

(e) the tenant satisfies any qualifying conditions applicable under Part V of the Housing Act 1985 (c 68) (as it applies by virtue of section 184).

(2) A tenancy is within this subsection if it is—

(a) an assured tenancy, other than an assured shorthold tenancy or a long tenancy, or

(b) a secure tenancy.

(3) The reference in subsection (1)(a) to a registered provider includes—

(a) a person who provided the dwelling in fulfilment of a condition imposed by the HCA when giving assistance to the person;

(b) a person who provided the dwelling wholly or partly by means of a grant under section 27A of the Housing Act 1996 (c 52).

[2460]

NOTES

Commencement: to be appointed.

181 Interpretation: "publicly funded"

(1) The provision of a dwelling was publicly funded if any of the following conditions is satisfied.

(2) Condition 1 is that—

(a) the dwelling was provided by a person in fulfilment of a condition imposed by the HCA when giving assistance to the person, and

(b) before giving the assistance the HCA notified the person that if it did so the provision of the dwelling would be regarded as publicly funded.

(3) Condition 2 is that the dwelling was provided wholly or partly by using sums in the disposal proceeds fund of—

(a) a registered provider, or

(b) a registered social landlord.

(4) Condition 3 is that—

(a) the dwelling was acquired by a registered provider, or a registered social landlord, on a disposal by a public sector landlord,

(b) the disposal was made on or after 1st April 1997, and

(c) at the time of the disposal the dwelling was capable of being let as a separate dwelling.

(5) Condition 3 is not satisfied if the dwelling was acquired in pursuance of a contract made, or option created, before 1st April 1997.

(6) Condition 4 is that—

(a) the dwelling was provided wholly or partly by means of a grant under section 18 or 27A of the Housing Act 1996 (c 52), and

(b) when the grant was made the recipient was notified under section 16(4) of that Act that the dwelling was to be regarded as funded by means of such a grant.

[2461]

NOTES

Commencement: to be appointed.

182 Interpretation: "remained in the social rented sector"

(1) This section applies for the purposes of determining whether a dwelling has remained in the social rented sector.

(2) A dwelling shall be treated as having remained in the social rented sector for any period during which—

(a) the freeholder was a person within subsection (3), and

(b) each leaseholder was either a person within that subsection or an individual holding otherwise than under a long tenancy.

(3) A person is within this subsection if the person is—

(a) a registered provider,

(b) a registered social landlord, or

(c) a public sector landlord.

(4) A dwelling provided wholly or partly by means of a grant under section 27A of the Housing Act 1996 shall also be treated as having remained in the social rented sector for any period during which it was used exclusively for permitted purposes by—

(a) the recipient of the grant, or

(b) any person treated as the recipient by virtue of section 27B of that Act.

(5) "Permitted purposes" are purposes for which the grant was made and any other purposes agreed by the Housing Corporation or the HCA.

(6) Where a lease of a dwelling has been granted to a former freeholder in pursuance of paragraph 3 of Schedule 9 to the Leasehold Reform, Housing and Urban Development Act 1993 (c 28) (mandatory leaseback to former freeholder on collective enfranchisement) the reference in subsection (1)(a) above to the freeholder shall be construed as a reference to the leaseholder under that lease.

[2462]

NOTES

Commencement: to be appointed.

183 Interpretation: other expressions

(1) The definitions in this section apply to sections 180 to 182.

(2) The HCA gives "assistance" to a person if it—

(a) transfers housing or other land to the person,

(b) provides infrastructure to the person, or

(c) gives financial assistance to the person,

and for this purpose "infrastructure" has the same meaning as in Part 1.

(3) References to a "registered social landlord" are to a body which, at the time to which the reference relates, was a registered social landlord within the meaning of Part 1 of the Housing Act 1996 (c 52) as it then had effect.

(4) "Leaseholder" does not include a mortgagee.

(5) "Long tenancy" has the same meaning as in Part V of the Housing Act 1985 (c 68).

(6) A person provides a dwelling if the person—

(a) acquires, constructs, converts, improves or repairs housing or other land for use as a dwelling, or

(b) ensures such acquisition, construction, conversion, improvement or repair by another.

(7) "Public sector landlord" means anyone falling within section 80(1) of the Housing Act 1985.

[2463]

NOTES

Commencement: to be appointed.

184 Right to acquire: supplemental

(1) Section 17 of the Housing Act 1996 (right to acquire: supplemental) applies in relation to the right to acquire under section 180 of this Act with the modifications set out below.

(2) The modifications are as follows—

(a) references to the right to acquire under section 16 of the 1996 Act shall be treated as references to the right to acquire under section 180 of this Act,

(b) references to the Welsh Ministers shall be treated as references to the Secretary of State,

(c) the reference to registered social landlords shall be treated as a reference to registered providers, and

(d) the reference to a resolution of the National Assembly for Wales shall be treated as a reference to a resolution of either House of Parliament.

[2464]

NOTES

Commencement: to be appointed.

185 Right to acquire: consequential amendments

(1), (2) …

(3) In section 20 (purchase grant where right to acquire exercised)—

(a) in subsection (1) after "landlords" insert "and registered providers of social housing", and
(b) in subsection (4) after "landlord" insert "or registered provider of social housing".

(4) In section 21 (purchase grant in respect of other disposals)—
(a) in subsection (1)—
(i) after "landlords" insert "and registered providers of social housing", and
(ii) after "dwellings" insert "in Wales",
(b) in subsection (2)—
(i) after "section 16" insert "or by section 180 of the Housing and Regeneration Act 2008", and
(ii) for "landlord's" substitute "landlord or provider (as the case may be)", and
(c) in subsection (4) after "landlord" insert "or registered provider of social housing".

[2465]

NOTES
Commencement: to be appointed.
Sub-s (1): amends the Housing Act 1996, s 16 at **[1729]**.
Sub-s (2): amends the Housing Act 1996, s 16A at **[1730]**.
Sub-s (3), (4): amend the Housing Act 1996, ss 20, 21, which are not printed in this work.

Miscellaneous

186 Former registered providers

Where a person ceases to be a registered provider, sections 171 to 175 continue to apply in respect of any property owned by the person at any time when it was registered.

[2466]

NOTES
Commencement: to be appointed.

187 Change of use, etc

(1) Where the regulator's consent is required for the disposal of a dwelling by a registered provider, sections 172 to 175 continue to apply in relation to a disposal of the land by the registered provider even if the land has ceased to be a dwelling.

(2) Sections 172 to 175 also apply in relation to a disposal of land by a registered provider which would fall within Exception 2 or 3 of section 173 but for a change of use of the land by the registered provider.

[2467]

NOTES
Commencement: to be appointed.

188 Trustees

Section 39 of the Settled Land Act 1925 (c 18) (disposal by trustees: best price etc) shall not apply to the disposal of land by a registered provider.

[2468]

NOTES
Commencement: to be appointed.

189 Charities

Nothing in this Chapter authorises a charity to effect a disposal which it would not otherwise have power to effect.

[2469]

NOTES
Commencement: to be appointed.

190, 191 (*Outside the scope of this work.*)

192–269 ((*Chs 6, 7*) *outside the scope of this work.*)

CHAPTER 8
GENERAL

Interpretation

270 Officer

The Table gives the meaning of "officer" in relation to registered providers.

Registered provider	*Meaning of "officer"*
Registered charity which is not a registered company	Trustee, secretary or treasurer
Industrial and provident society	"Officer" within the meaning given by section 74 of the Industrial and Provident Societies Act 1965 (including a person co-opted to serve on the society's committee)
Registered company	"Officer" within the meaning given by section 1173 of the Companies Act 2006
Registered provider	Meaning of "officer"

[2470]

NOTES
Commencement: to be appointed.

271 Subsidiary and associate

(1) A company is a "subsidiary" of a person if any of the following conditions is satisfied.

(2) Condition 1 is that the person—
(a) is a member of the company, and
(b) has power, independent of any other person, to appoint or remove all or a majority of the board of directors.

(3) Condition 2 is that the person holds more than half in nominal value of the company's equity share capital.

(4) Condition 3 is that the company is a subsidiary, within the meaning of the Companies Act 2006 (c 46) or the Friendly and Industrial and Provident Societies Act 1968 (c 55), of a company which is a subsidiary of the person by virtue of Condition 1 or 2.

(5) In relation to a company which is an industrial and provident society a reference to the board of directors is a reference to the committee of management.

(6) "Associate" of a provider means—
(a) a body of which the provider is a subsidiary, and
(b) any other subsidiary of that body.

[2471]

NOTES
Commencement: to be appointed.

272 Family

(1) For the purposes of this Part one person is a member of the family of another if—
(a) they are, or live together as if they were, spouses or civil partners, or
(b) one is the parent, grandparent, child, grandchild, brother, sister, uncle, aunt, nephew or niece of the other.

(2) For those purposes—
(a) a relationship by marriage or civil partnership shall be treated as a relationship by blood (and, in particular, P's stepchild shall be treated as P's child), and
(b) a relationship by half-blood shall be treated as a relationship by whole blood.

[2472]

NOTES
Commencement: to be appointed.

273 Disposal

(1) In this Part a reference to disposing of property is a reference to—
(a) selling it,

(b) leasing it,
(c) mortgaging it,
(d) making it subject to a charge, and
(e) disposing of it, or of any interest in it, in any other way.

(2) Granting an option to require a disposal shall be treated as making a disposal.

[2473]

NOTES

Commencement: to be appointed.

274 Charities that have "received public assistance"

(1) For the purposes of this Part a registered charity has received public assistance if at least one of the following conditions is satisfied.

(2) Condition 1 is that the charity has received financial assistance from the HCA under section 19.

(3) Condition 2 is that the charity has received financial assistance under section 24 of the Local Government Act 1988 (c 9) (assistance for privately let housing accommodation).

(4) Condition 3 is that the charity has had housing transferred to it pursuant to—
(a) a large scale disposal, within the meaning of section 34 of the Housing Act 1985 (c 68), for which consent was required under section 32 or 43 of that Act, or
(b) a qualifying disposal that was made under section 135 of the Leasehold Reform, Housing and Urban Development Act 1993 (c 28).

(5) Condition 4 is that the charity has received a grant or loan under—
(a) section 18 of the Housing Act 1996 (c 52) (social housing grants),
(b) section 22 of that Act (assistance from local authorities),
(c) section 58 of the Housing Associations Act 1985 (c 69) (grants or loans by local authorities),
(d) section 50 of the Housing Act 1988 (c 50), section 41 of the Housing Associations Act 1985 or any enactment replaced by that section (housing association grant),
(e) section 51 of the Housing Act 1988 (c 50) or section 54 or 55 of the Housing Associations Act 1985 (c 69) (revenue deficit grant or hostel deficit grant),
(f) section 79 of the Housing Associations Act 1985 (loans by Housing Corporation),
(g) section 31 of the Housing Act 1974 (c 44) (management grants), or
(h) any enactment mentioned in paragraph 2 or 3 of Schedule 1 to the Housing Associations Act 1985 (pre-1974 grants and certain loans).

[2474]

NOTES

Commencement: to be appointed.

275 General

In this Part, except where the context requires otherwise—

"action" includes inaction, proposed action and decision,

"assured agricultural occupancy" has the same meaning as in Part 1 of the Housing Act 1988,

"assured tenancy" has the same meaning as in that Part,

"the Charity Commission" means the Charity Commission for England and Wales,

"committee", in relation to an industrial and provident society, means the committee of management or other directing body of the society (including any person co-opted to serve on the committee, whether a member of the society or not),

"consent" means written consent,

"constitution" includes rules,

"conveyance" includes grant, assignment and any other instrument,

"district valuer" has the meaning given by section 622 of the Housing Act 1985 (c 68),

"dwelling"—
(a) means a house, flat or other building or part of a building occupied or intended to be occupied as a separate dwelling, and
(b) includes any garden, yard, outhouse or other appurtenance belonging to, or usually enjoyed with, the dwelling,

"the HCA" means the Homes and Communities Agency,

"industrial and provident society" means a society registered under the Industrial and Provident Societies Act 1965 (c 12),

"local authority" has the same meaning as in the Housing Associations Act 1985,

"local housing authority" has the same meaning as in the Housing Act 1985,

"maintenance" includes repair,

"mismanagement", in relation to the affairs of a registered provider, means—

(a) managed in contravention of a provision of this Part or of anything done under this Part, or
(b) otherwise conducted improperly or inappropriately,

"non-registrable charity" means a charity which is not required to be registered, in accordance with section 3A of the Charities Act 1993 (c 10),

"notice" means written notice (and to "notify" means to give written notice),

"preferential creditor" and "preferential debt" have the same meaning as in the Insolvency Act 1986 (c 45),

"price" includes premium,

"registered charity" means a charity registered under the Charities Act 1993 (c 10),

"registered company" means a company within the meaning of the Companies Act 2006 (c 46),

"rent" includes payments under a licence to occupy accommodation,

"representations" means written representations,

"secure tenancy" has the same meaning as in Part 4 of the Housing Act 1985 (c 68),

"secured creditor" means a creditor who holds a mortgage or charge (including a floating charge) over—
(a) land held by a registered provider, or
(b) a present or future interest of a registered provider in rents or other receipts from land,

"tenant" in relation to social housing includes other occupiers, and

"working day" means a day other than—
(a) a Saturday or Sunday,
(b) Christmas Day or Good Friday, or
(c) a day which is a bank holiday in England and Wales under the Banking and Financial Dealings Act 1971 (c 80).

[2475]

NOTES

Commencement: 8 September 2008 (so far as required for the interpretation of provisions commenced by SI 2008/2358); to be appointed (otherwise).

276 Index of defined terms

The Table lists expressions defined in this Part.

Expression	*Section*
Appointed member	Section 82
Associate	Section 271
Assured agricultural occupancy	Section 275
Assured tenancy	Section 275
Charity Commission	Section 275
Committee (industrial and provident society)	Section 275
Compensation notice	Section 240
Consent	Section 275
Constitution	Section 275
Conveyance	Section 275
Disposal	Section 273
District valuer	Section 275
Dwelling	Section 275
Enforcement notice	Sections 219 to 225
Equity percentage arrangements	Section 70(5)
Family	Section 272
Financial year	Section 104
Fundamental objectives	Section 86
The HCA	Section 275
Industrial and provident society	Section 275

Expression	*Section*
Local authority	Section 275
Local housing authority	Section 275
Low cost home ownership accommodation	Section 70
Low cost rental accommodation	Section 69
Maintenance	Section 275
Mismanagement	Section 275
Non-profit organisation	Section 115
Non-registrable charity	Section 275
Notice	Section 275
Officer	Section 270
Penalty notice	Section 228
Pre-compensation warning	Section 242
Pre-penalty warning	Section 230
Preferential creditor	Section 275
Preferential debt	Section 275
Price	Section 275
Profit-making organisation	Section 115
Provider (of social housing)	Section 80
Received public assistance (charities)	Section 274
Registered charity	Section 275
Registered company	Section 275
Registered provider (of social housing)	Section 80
The regulator	Section 81
The Regulator of Social Housing	Section 81
Rent	Section 275
Representations	Section 275
Secure tenancy	Section 275
Secured creditor	Section 275
Shared ownership arrangements	Section 70(4)
Shared ownership trust	Section 70(6)
Social housing	Section 68
Subsidiary	Section 271
Tenant	Section 275
Working day	Section 275

[2476]

NOTES

Commencement: 8 September 2008 (so far as required for the interpretation of provisions commenced by SI 2008/2358); to be appointed (otherwise).

277, 278 (*Outside the scope of this work.*)

PART 3
OTHER PROVISIONS

279–293 ((*Ch 1*) *outside the scope of this work.*)

CHAPTER 2
LANDLORD AND TENANT MATTERS

294–298 (*Outside the scope of this work.*)

Possession orders

299 Possession orders relating to certain tenancies

Schedule 11 (which makes provision about possession orders and their effect on secure tenancies, assured tenancies, introductory tenancies and demoted tenancies including provision about the status of existing occupiers) has effect.

[2477]

NOTES

Commencement: see notes to Sch 11 at **[2497]**, **[2498]**.

300–302 (*Outside the scope of this work.*)

Service charges

303 Service charges: provision of information and designated accounts

Schedule 12 (which relates to the provision of information about service charges and to service charge funds) has effect.

[2478]

NOTES

Commencement: see the note to Sch 12 at **[2499]**.

Right to buy etc: miscellaneous

304 Exclusion of the right to buy: possession orders

(1) For section 121(1) of the Housing Act 1985 (c 68) (circumstances in which the right to buy cannot be exercised) substitute—

"(1) The right to buy cannot be exercised if the tenant is subject to an order of the court for possession of the dwelling-house."

(2) Subsection (1) does not apply where the tenant has served a notice under section 122 of that Act (tenant's notice claiming to exercise right to buy) before the coming into force of subsection (1) above and the notice is not withdrawn.

[2479]

NOTES

Commencement: 22 September 2008.

305 Exclusion of the right to buy: demolition notices

Schedule 13 (which makes provision about demolition notices) has effect.

[2480]

NOTES

Commencement: 22 September 2008.

306–310 (*Outside the scope of this work.*)

Other

311 Disposals of dwelling-houses by local authorities

Schedule 14 (which makes provision about the requirements for consent for disposals of dwelling-houses by local authorities) has effect.

[2481]

NOTES

Commencement: 1 December 2008.

312–319 (*Outside the scope of this work.*)

PART 4
SUPPLEMENTARY AND FINAL PROVISIONS

320–323 (*Outside the scope of this work.*)

324 Extent

(1) Subject as follows, Parts 1 to 3 (including Schedules 1 to 15) and Schedule 16 extend to England and Wales only.

(2) Any amendment, repeal or revocation made by this Act, other than one falling within subsection (3), has the same extent as the provision to which it relates.

(3) The following fall within this subsection—

(a) the repeal in section 5 of the Mobile Homes Act 1983 (c 34),

(b) the repeals of sections 50 and 51 of the Housing Act 1988 (c 50), and

(c) the amendments of sections 52 to 54 and 59 of that Act.

[2482]

NOTES

Commencement: 22 July 2008.

325 Commencement

(1) Subject as follows, this Act comes into force on such day as the Secretary of State may by order appoint; and different days may be appointed for different purposes or different areas.

(2) The following provisions—

(a) sections 294, 304 to 307, 310, 312, 313 and 319 and Schedule 13, and

(b) section 321(1), and Schedule 16, so far as relating to the repeals in sections 125D(2), 128(2) and 136(2) of, and paragraph 13(5) of Schedule 5 to, the Housing Act 1985 (c 68),

come into force at the end of the period of 2 months beginning with the day on which this Act is passed.

(3) Subsection (4) applies to the following provisions—

(a) Chapter 1 of Part 3 (including Schedule 10),

(b) sections 295 to 298, 300 to 303, 308, 309, 315 and 318 and Schedule 12, and

(c) section 321(1), and Schedule 16, so far as relating to repeals and revocations which are connected to the provisions mentioned in paragraph (b) above.

(4) The provisions to which this subsection applies come into force—

(a) in relation to England, on such day as the Secretary of State may by order appoint; and different days may be appointed for different purposes or different areas, and

(b) in relation to Wales, on such day as the Welsh Ministers may by order appoint; and different days may be appointed for different purposes or different areas.

(5) The Secretary of State must consult the Welsh Ministers before making an order under subsection (1) in relation to section 50(2) and Schedule 5 or section 299 and Schedule 11.

(6) Subsection (1) does not apply to sections 320, 321(2) to (4), 322, 323 and 324, this section and section 326.

[2483]

NOTES

Commencement: 22 July 2008.

Orders: the Housing and Regeneration Act 2008 (Commencement No 1 and Transitional Provision) Order 2008, SI 2008/2358; the Housing and Regeneration Act 2008 (Commencement No 2 and Transitional, Saving and Transitory Provisions) Order 2008, SI 2008/2358; the Housing and Regeneration Act 2008 (Commencement No 3) Order 2009, SI 2009/363; the Housing and Regeneration Act 2008 (Commencement No 1 and Saving Provisions) Order 2009, SI 2009/415; the Housing and Regeneration Act 2008 (Commencement No 1) (Wales) Order 2009, SI 2009/773; the Housing and Regeneration Act 2008 (Commencement No 4 and Transitory Provisions) Order 2009, SI 2009/803; the Housing and Regeneration Act 2008 (Commencement No 5) Order 2009, SI 2009/1261; the Housing and Regeneration Act 2008 (Commencement No 6 and Transitional and Savings Provisions) Order 2009, SI 2009/2096.

326 Short title

This Act may be cited as the Housing and Regeneration Act 2008.

[2484]

NOTES

Commencement: 22 July 2008.

(*Schs 1, 2 outside the scope of this work.*)

SCHEDULE 3
MAIN POWERS IN RELATION TO LAND OF THE HCA

Section 11

PART 1
POWERS TO OVERRIDE EASEMENTS ETC

Powers to override easements etc in undertaking works or using land

1.—(1) The HCA or any other person may undertake any construction or maintenance works on land of the HCA even if undertaking the works involves—

(a) interference with a relevant right or interest, or

(b) a breach of a restriction as to the user of land arising by virtue of a contract.

(2) But the construction or maintenance works must still be in accordance with planning permission.

(3) The HCA or any other person may use any land of the HCA even if the use involves—

(a) interference with a relevant right or interest, or

(b) a breach of a restriction as to the user of land arising by virtue of a contract.

(4) But the use of the land must be in accordance with planning permission.

(5) Sub-paragraphs (1) to (4) do not authorise interference with—

(a) any right of way on, under or over land, or

(b) any right of laying down, erecting, continuing or maintaining apparatus on, under or over land,

if the right is a protected right.

(6) In this paragraph—

"construction or maintenance works" means the erection, construction, carrying out or maintenance of any building or work,

"protected right" means—

(a) a right vested in, or belonging to, statutory undertakers for the purpose of carrying on their undertaking, or

(b) a right conferred by, or in accordance with, the electronic communications code on the operator of an electronic communications code network,

"relevant right or interest" means any easement, liberty, privilege, right or advantage annexed to land and adversely affecting other land (including any natural right to support),

"statutory undertakers" means persons who are, or are deemed to be, statutory undertakers for the purposes of any provision of Part 11 of the Town and Country Planning Act 1990 (c 8); and "statutory undertaking" is to be read in accordance with section 262 of that Act (meaning of "statutory undertakers").

Compensation for overridden easements etc

2.—(1) Compensation is payable under section 7 or 10 of the Compulsory Purchase Act 1965 (c 56) in respect of any interference or breach made in pursuance of paragraph 1.

(2) The compensation is to be assessed in the same manner, and subject to the same rules, as in the case of other compensation under those sections in respect of injurious affection where—

(a) the compensation is to be estimated in connection with a purchase by the HCA, or

(b) the injury arises from the execution of works on, or use of, land acquired by the HCA.

(3) Sub-paragraph (4) applies if a person other than the HCA—

(a) is liable to pay compensation by virtue of sub-paragraphs (1) and (2), and

(b) fails to discharge that liability.

(4) The liability is enforceable against the HCA.

(5) But sub-paragraph (4) does not affect any agreement between the HCA and any other person for indemnifying the HCA against any liability under that sub-paragraph.

[2485]

NOTES

Commencement: 1 December 2008.

PART 2
POWERS TO EXTINGUISH PUBLIC RIGHTS OF WAY

Powers of Secretary of State to extinguish public rights of way by order

3. The Secretary of State may by order extinguish any public right of way over land of the HCA if the Secretary of State is satisfied that—

(a) an alternative right of way has been, or will be, provided, or

(b) the provision of an alternative right of way is not required.

Notification of proposal to make order

4.—(1) This paragraph applies if the Secretary of State is proposing to make an order under paragraph 3.

(2) The Secretary of State must—

(a) publish a notice stating—

(i) the effect of the order,

(ii) the time (not less than 28 days starting with the date of publication of the notice) within which objections to the proposal may be made, and

(iii) the manner in which objections to the proposal may be made, and

(b) serve a copy of the notice on—

(i) the local planning authority in whose area the land is situated, and

(ii) the relevant highway authority.

(3) In sub-paragraph (2) "the relevant highway authority" means any authority which is a highway authority in relation to the right of way which is proposed to be extinguished by the order.

(4) Publication under sub-paragraph (2) must be in such manner as the Secretary of State considers appropriate.

Duty to consider objections

5.—(1) The Secretary of State must proceed under paragraph 6 if—

(a) an objection to a proposal to make an order is properly made and not withdrawn, and

(b) the matter is not otherwise dealt with.

(2) For the purposes of sub-paragraph (1) an objection is properly made if (and only if)—

(a) it is made—

(i) within the time, and

(ii) in the manner,

stated in the notice under paragraph 4, and

(b) a written statement of the grounds of the objection is comprised in, or submitted with, the objection.

(3) For the purposes of sub-paragraph (1) the matter is otherwise dealt with if (and only if) the Secretary of State—

(a) decides, irrespective of the objection, not to make the order, or

(b) decides to make a modification to the proposal which is agreed to by the objector as meeting the objection.

6.—(1) The Secretary of State must, before making a final decision, consider the grounds of the objection as set out in the statement comprised in, or submitted with, the objection.

(2) The Secretary of State may require the objector to submit within a particular period a further written statement as to any of the matters to which the objection relates.

Duty to give opportunity to appear

7.—(1) The Secretary of State must, before making a final decision, give the objector an opportunity to appear before, and be heard by, a person appointed for the purpose by the Secretary of State.

(2) Sub-paragraph (3) applies if the objector takes advantage of this opportunity.

(3) The Secretary of State must give an opportunity of appearing and being heard on the same occasion as the objector to—

(a) the HCA, and

(b) any other persons whom the Secretary of State considers ought to be given the opportunity.

(4) Sub-paragraphs (1) to (3) do not apply so far as the Secretary of State has the power to proceed under paragraph 8 or 9.

Power to treat objection as irrelevant

8. The Secretary of State may treat the objection as irrelevant for the purpose of making a final decision—

(a) if the Secretary of State has considered the grounds of the objection as set out in the original statement and in any further statement, and

(b) so far as the Secretary of State is satisfied that the objection relates to a matter which can be dealt with in the assessment of compensation.

Power to curtail decision-making process

9. The Secretary of State may make a final decision without further investigation as to the matters to which the objection relates if—

(a) the Secretary of State—

(i) has considered the grounds of the objection as set out in the original statement and in any further statement, and
(ii) is satisfied that, for the purpose of making a final decision, sufficient information is available as to the matters to which the objection relates, or

(b) a further statement has been required under paragraph 6(2) but is not submitted within the required period.

Power to hold public local inquiry

10.—(1) The Secretary of State must cause a public local inquiry to be held in relation to an objection to a proposal to make an order under paragraph 3 if the Secretary of State considers that the matters to which the objection relates are such as to require investigation by such an inquiry before the Secretary of State makes a final decision.

(2) The duty in sub-paragraph (1) is effective despite any other provisions of paragraphs 4 to 9.

(3) The other provisions of those paragraphs are to be ignored if no effect has been given to them when the Secretary of State decides to cause an inquiry to be held.

Orders relating to electronic communications apparatus: removal or abandonment of apparatus

11. Paragraphs 12 and 13 apply if—

(a) an order under paragraph 3 extinguishing a public right of way is made, and
(b) at the time of the publication of the notice required by paragraph 4 any electronic communications apparatus was kept installed for the purposes of an electronic communications code network under, in, on, over, along or across the land over which the right of way subsisted.

12.—(1) The power of the operator of the network to remove the apparatus is exercisable, despite the order, at any time not later than the end of the period of 3 months beginning with the day on which the right of way is extinguished.

(2) The power of the operator of the network to remove the whole or any part of the apparatus is exercisable after the end of that period if, before the end of the period, the operator has served notice on the HCA of the operator's intention to remove the apparatus or (as the case may be) part.

13.—(1) The operator of the network may abandon the electronic communications apparatus, or any part of it, by serving notice to that effect on the HCA not later than the end of the period of 3 months beginning with the day on which the right of way is extinguished.

(2) In the absence of such a notice, the operator of the network is to be treated at the end of the period of 3 months as having abandoned any part of the apparatus which, at that time, the operator has neither—

(a) removed, nor
(b) served notice of intention to remove.

14.—(1) The operator of the network may recover from the HCA the expense of providing any substitute electronic communications apparatus in such other place as the operator may require.

(2) In sub-paragraph (1) "substitute electronic communications apparatus" means electronic communications apparatus in substitution for—

(a) the electronic communications apparatus removed or abandoned, and
(b) any other electronic communications apparatus connected with the removed or abandoned apparatus which is made useless in consequence of the removal or abandonment.

15. Electronic communications apparatus, or any part of it, abandoned by the operator of an electronic communications code network under paragraph 13—

(a) vests in the HCA, and
(b) is deemed, with its abandonment, to cease to be kept installed for the purposes of an electronic communications code network.

Orders relating to electronic communications apparatus: notice requirements

16.—(1) The Secretary of State must serve notice on the operator of an electronic communications code network of the making of an order under paragraph 3 if the order extinguishes a public right of way in circumstances in which paragraphs 12 and 13 apply in relation to the operator.

(2) The notice must be served as soon as practicable after the making of the order.

Supplementary: Part 2

17. The power of the Secretary of State to make orders under paragraph 3 includes power to—

(a) vary or revoke such orders, and
(b) make supplementary, incidental, consequential, transitional, transitory or saving provision.

18. In this Part of this Schedule, in relation to an order, any reference to making a final decision is a reference to deciding whether to make the order or what modification (if any) ought to be made. **[2486]**

NOTES

Commencement: 1 December 2008.

PART 3
POWERS IN RELATION TO BURIAL GROUNDS AND CONSECRATED LAND ETC

Burial grounds

19.—(1) This paragraph applies in relation to any land of the HCA which consists in, or forms part of, a burial ground.

(2) The HCA may use the land in any way which accords with planning permission despite—
(a) anything in any enactment relating to burial grounds, or
(b) any obligation or restriction imposed under ecclesiastical law or otherwise in respect of burial grounds.

(3) But sub-paragraph (2) does not apply in relation to any land which has been used for the burial of the dead until prescribed requirements about the removal and reinterment of human remains and the disposal of monuments have been complied with in relation to the land.

Consecrated land other than burial grounds

20.—(1) This paragraph applies in relation to any land of the HCA which—
(a) is consecrated land (whether or not including a building), and
(b) does not consist in, or form part of, a burial ground.

(2) The HCA or any other person may use the land in any way which accords with planning permission despite any obligation or restriction imposed under ecclesiastical law or otherwise in respect of consecrated land.

(3) But any such use of the land is subject to—
(a) prescribed requirements about the disposal of monuments, and
(b) prescribed provisions for prohibiting or restricting the use of the land while—
(i) any church or other building used, or formerly used, for religious worship remains on the land, or
(ii) any part of any such church or other building remains on the land.

(4) Prohibitions or restrictions prescribed under sub-paragraph (3)(b) may be absolute or until a prescribed consent is obtained.

Other land connected to religious worship

21.—(1) This paragraph applies in relation to any land of the HCA which—
(a) is neither consecrated land nor land which consists in, or forms part of, a burial ground, and
(b) at the time of acquisition included—
(i) a church or other building used, or formerly used, for religious worship, or
(ii) the site of such a church or other building.

(2) Any use of the land is subject to prescribed requirements about the disposal of monuments.

Regulations: general

22.—(1) Regulations under this Part of this Schedule must secure that any use of land which is subject to compliance with the regulations is (so far as possible) subject to an appropriate level of control.

(2) For the purposes of sub-paragraph (1) an appropriate level of control is the same control—
(a) as imposed by law in relation to a similar use authorised by an enactment not contained in this Part of this Act,
(b) as imposed by a Measure, or
(c) as it would be proper to impose on a disposal of the land concerned otherwise than in pursuance of an enactment or Measure.

(3) Regulations under this Part of this Schedule must impose such requirements in relation to the disposal of the land as the Secretary of State considers appropriate to secure that the requirements and other provisions in the regulations about the use of the land are complied with.

(4) Regulations made for the purposes of paragraphs 19 to 21 may, in particular, include incidental or consequential provision about the closing of registers.

Regulations about human remains and monuments

23.—(1) Regulations under this Part of this Schedule about the removal and reinterment of human remains and the disposal of monuments must require the persons in whom the land is vested to publish notice of their intention to carry out the removal and reinterment of any human remains or the disposal of any monuments.

(2) Regulations under this Part of this Schedule about the removal and reinterment of human remains and the disposal of monuments must make provision for—

(a) enabling the personal representatives or relatives of any deceased person themselves—

(i) to undertake the removal and reinterment of the remains of the deceased, and

(ii) the disposal of any monument commemorating the deceased, and

(b) requiring the persons in whom the land is vested to meet the expenses of such removal, reinterment and disposal provided that they are not more than such amount as may be prescribed.

(3) Regulations under this Part of this Schedule about the removal and reinterment of human remains and the disposal of monuments must require compliance with such reasonable conditions (if any) as may be imposed, in the case of consecrated land, by the bishop of the diocese, in relation to—

(a) the manner of removal of any human remains,

(b) the place and manner of reinterment of any human remains, and

(c) the disposal of any monuments.

(4) Regulations under this Part of this Schedule about the removal and reinterment of human remains must require compliance with any directions given in any case by the Secretary of State in relation to the removal and reinterment of any human remains.

Disapplication of faculties

24.—(1) No faculty is required for—

(a) the removal and reinterment of any human remains, or

(b) the removal or disposal of any monuments,

in accordance with regulations under this Part of this Schedule.

(2) Sub-paragraph (1) is subject to any provision to the contrary made by regulations under this Part of this Schedule.

Disapplication of section 25 of the Burial Act 1857

25. Section 25 of the Burial Act 1857 (c 81) (which prohibits the removal of human remains without the licence of the Secretary of State except in certain cases) does not apply to a removal of human remains carried out in accordance with regulations under this Part of this Schedule.

Interpretation: Part 3

26.—(1) In this Part of this Schedule—

"burial ground" includes any churchyard, cemetery or other ground (whether or not consecrated) which has at any time been set apart for the purposes of interment,

"monument" includes a tombstone or other memorial,

"prescribed" means prescribed by regulations made by the Secretary of State.

(2) Any power conferred by paragraph 19(2) or 20(2) to use land is to be read as a power to use the land, whether or not it involves—

(a) the erection, construction or carrying out of any building or work, or

(b) the maintenance of any building or work.

[2487]

NOTES

Commencement: 1 December 2008.

SCHEDULE 4

POWERS IN RELATION TO, AND FOR, STATUTORY UNDERTAKERS

Section 12

PART 1

EXTINGUISHMENT OR REMOVAL POWERS FOR THE HCA

Notice for extinguishment of rights of undertakers or for removal of their apparatus

1.—(1) Sub-paragraph (2) applies if—

(a) a protected right subsists over land of the HCA and is vested in, or belongs to, statutory undertakers for the purpose of carrying on their undertaking, or

(b) apparatus vested in, or belonging to, statutory undertakers for the purpose of carrying on their undertaking is on, under or over land of the HCA.

(2) The HCA may serve a notice on the statutory undertakers.

(3) The notice may, in the case of a protected right, state that, at the end of the relevant period, the right will be extinguished.

(4) The notice may, in the case of apparatus, require that, before the end of the relevant period, the apparatus must be removed.

(5) In this paragraph—

"protected right" means—

(a) a right of way on, under or over land, or

(b) a right of laying down, erecting, continuing or maintaining apparatus on, under or over land,

"relevant period" means—

(a) the period of 28 days beginning with the date of service of the notice, or

(b) any longer period beginning with that date and specified in the notice.

Counter-notices

2.—(1) Sub-paragraph (2) applies if the HCA serves a notice under paragraph 1 on statutory undertakers.

(2) The statutory undertakers may, before the end of the period of 28 days beginning with the date of the service of the notice, serve a counter-notice on the HCA.

(3) The counter-notice is a notice stating that the statutory undertakers object to all or any provisions of the notice under paragraph 1.

(4) The counter-notice must also specify the grounds of their objection.

Effect of unopposed notice

3.—(1) This paragraph applies if—

(a) a notice is served under paragraph 1, and

(b) no counter-notice is served under paragraph 2.

(2) Any right to which the notice under paragraph 1 relates is extinguished at the end of the period specified for that purpose in the notice.

(3) The HCA may—

(a) remove any apparatus, and

(b) dispose of it as it considers appropriate,

if any requirement of the notice under paragraph 1 as to the removal of the apparatus has not been complied with by the end of the period specified for that purpose in the notice.

Opposed notices and Ministerial orders

4.—(1) This paragraph applies if—

(a) a notice is served under paragraph 1, and

(b) a counter-notice is served under paragraph 2.

(2) The HCA may—

(a) withdraw the notice served under paragraph 1, or

(b) apply to the Secretary of State and the appropriate Minister for an order under sub-paragraph (3).

(3) The Secretary of State and the appropriate Minister may make an order embodying, with or without modifications, the provisions of the notice.

(4) The fact that a notice has been withdrawn under sub-paragraph (2)(a) does not prejudice the service of a further notice.

5.—(1) Before making an order under paragraph 4(3), the Secretary of State and the appropriate Minister must give the statutory undertakers on whom notice was served an opportunity to object to the application for the order.

(2) The Secretary of State and the appropriate Minister—

(a) must consider any objections made by virtue of sub-paragraph (1), and

(b) must give—

(i) the statutory undertakers who made the objections, and

(ii) the HCA,

an opportunity to appear before, and be heard by, a person appointed for this purpose by the Secretary of State and the appropriate Minister.

(3) The Secretary of State and the appropriate Minister may then—

(a) decide not to make an order, or

(b) proceed to make an order in accordance with the application (with or without modifications).

6.—(1) This paragraph applies if an order is made under paragraph 4(3).

(2) Any right to which the order relates is extinguished at the end of the period specified for that purpose in the order.

(3) The HCA may—
(a) remove any apparatus, and
(b) dispose of it as it considers appropriate,

if any requirement of the order as to the removal of the apparatus has not been complied with by the end of the period specified for that purpose in the order.

Compensation

7.—(1) Statutory undertakers are entitled to compensation from the HCA if—
(a) any right vested in, or belonging to, the statutory undertakers is extinguished, or
(b) any requirement is imposed on the statutory undertakers,

by virtue of this Part of this Schedule.

(2) Sections 280 and 282 of the Town and Country Planning Act 1990 (c 8) (measure of compensation to statutory undertakers) apply to compensation under this paragraph as they apply to compensation under section 279(4) of that Act.

Electronic communications

8.—(1) The reference in paragraph 1(1)(a) to a protected right vested in, or belonging to, statutory undertakers for the purpose of carrying on their undertaking includes a reference to a protected right conferred by, or in accordance with, the electronic communications code on the operator of an electronic communications code network.

(2) The reference in paragraph 1(1)(b) to apparatus vested in, or belonging to, statutory undertakers for the purpose of carrying on their undertaking includes a reference to electronic communications apparatus kept installed for the purposes of any such network.

(3) Sub-paragraphs (1) and (2) do not apply where paragraphs 12 and 13 of Part 2 of Schedule 3 apply (orders under paragraph 3 of that Schedule which relate to electronic communications apparatus).

(4) Where paragraph 1 has effect as mentioned in sub-paragraphs (1) and (2) above—
(a) any reference in this Part of this Schedule to statutory undertakers has effect as a reference to the operator of the electronic communications code network, and
(b) any reference in this Part of this Schedule to the appropriate Minister has effect as a reference to the Secretary of State for Business, Enterprise and Regulatory Reform.

[2488]

NOTES

Commencement: 1 December 2008.

PART 2
POWERS FOR UNDERTAKERS TO CARRY OUT WORKS

Notices to carry out works

9.—(1) Sub-paragraph (2) applies if—
(a) apparatus vested in, or belonging to, statutory undertakers is on, under or over land of the HCA, and
(b) the statutory undertakers claim that development to be carried out on the land will require, on technical or other grounds connected with carrying on their undertaking, the removal or re-siting of the apparatus affected by the development.

(2) The statutory undertakers may serve on the HCA a notice claiming the right to—
(a) enter on the land, and
(b) carry out such works for the removal or re-siting of the apparatus or any part of it as may be specified in the notice.

(3) No notice may be served under sub-paragraph (2) more than 21 days after the beginning of the development on the land.

Counter-notices

10.—(1) Sub-paragraph (2) applies if statutory undertakers serve a notice under paragraph 9 on the HCA.

(2) The HCA may, before the end of the period of 28 days beginning with the date of the service of the notice, serve a counter-notice on the statutory undertakers.

(3) The counter-notice is a notice stating that the HCA objects to all or any provisions of the notice under paragraph 9.

(4) The counter-notice must also specify the grounds of the HCA's objection.

Effect of unopposed notice

11.—(1) This paragraph applies if—

(a) a notice is served under paragraph 9,
(b) no counter-notice is served under paragraph 10, and
(c) the period of 28 days beginning with the date of the service of the notice under paragraph 9 has ended.

(2) The statutory undertakers have the rights claimed in their notice under paragraph 9.

Opposed notices and Ministerial orders

12.—(1) This paragraph applies if—

(a) a notice is served under paragraph 9, and
(b) a counter-notice is served under paragraph 10.

(2) The statutory undertakers may—

(a) withdraw the notice served under paragraph 9, or
(b) apply to the Secretary of State and the appropriate Minister for an order under sub-paragraph (3).

(3) The Secretary of State and the appropriate Minister may by order confer on the statutory undertakers—

(a) the rights claimed in the notice under paragraph 9, or
(b) such modified rights as the Secretary of State and the appropriate Minister consider it appropriate to confer on the statutory undertakers.

(4) The fact that a notice has been withdrawn under sub-paragraph (2)(a) does not prejudice the service of a further notice.

Power to arrange for the works to be done by the HCA

13.—(1) Sub-paragraph (2) applies if statutory undertakers have the right to carry out works for the removal or re-siting of apparatus by virtue of this Part of this Schedule.

(2) The statutory undertakers may arrange with the HCA for the works to be carried out by the HCA, under the superintendence of the statutory undertakers, instead of by the statutory undertakers themselves.

Compensation

14.—(1) Statutory undertakers are entitled to compensation from the HCA if works are carried out for the removal or re-siting of their apparatus which they have the right to carry out by virtue of this Part of this Schedule.

(2) Sections 280 and 282 of the Town and Country Planning Act 1990 (c 8) (measure of compensation to statutory undertakers) apply to compensation under this paragraph as they apply to compensation under section 279(4) of that Act.

Electronic communications

15.—(1) The reference in paragraph 9(1)(a) to apparatus vested in, or belonging to, statutory undertakers includes a reference to electronic communications apparatus kept installed for the purposes of an electronic communications code network.

(2) Where paragraph 9(1)(a) has effect as mentioned in sub-paragraph (1) above—

(a) any reference in this Part of this Schedule to statutory undertakers has effect as a reference to the operator of the electronic communications code network, and
(b) any reference in this Part of this Schedule to the appropriate Minister has effect as a reference to the Secretary of State for Business, Enterprise and Regulatory Reform.

[2489]

NOTES

Commencement: 1 December 2008.

PART I STATUTES

PART 3
EXTENSION OR MODIFICATION OF FUNCTIONS OF UNDERTAKERS

Ministerial order following representations by statutory undertakers

16.—(1) The Secretary of State and the appropriate Minister may by order provide for an extension or modification of the functions of particular statutory undertakers if conditions 1 and 2 are met.

(2) Condition 1 is that the statutory undertakers have made representations on the subject to the Secretary of State and the appropriate Minister.

(3) Condition 2 is that the Secretary of State and the appropriate Minister consider it appropriate to extend or modify the functions of the statutory undertakers—
- (a) to secure the provision of services which—
  - (i) would not otherwise be provided, or
  - (ii) would not otherwise be satisfactorily provided,

  in relation to relevant land, or
- (b) to facilitate an adjustment of the carrying on of the undertaking necessitated by any of the acts and events mentioned in sub-paragraph (4).

(4) The acts and events are—
- (a) the acquisition by the HCA under this Part of this Act of any land—
  - (i) in which an interest was held for the purpose of carrying on the undertaking concerned, or
  - (ii) which was used for that purpose, and
- (b) the extinguishment of a right, or the imposition of any requirement, by virtue of Part 1 of this Schedule.

(5) In this Part of this Schedule "relevant land" means land in respect of which any of the functions of the HCA under this Part of this Act are being, or have been, exercised.

Ministerial order following representations by the HCA

17.—(1) The Secretary of State and the appropriate Minister may by order provide for an extension or modification of the functions of particular statutory undertakers if conditions 1 and 2 are met.

(2) Condition 1 is that the HCA has made representations on the subject to the Secretary of State and the appropriate Minister.

(3) Condition 2 is that the Secretary of State and the appropriate Minister consider it appropriate to extend or modify the functions of the statutory undertakers to secure—
- (a) the provision of new services in relation to relevant land, or
- (b) the extension of existing services in relation to such land.

Examples of contents of orders

18.—(1) An order under paragraph 16 or 17 may, in particular—
- (a) give power to statutory undertakers—
  - (i) to acquire (whether compulsorily or by agreement) any land specified in the order, or
  - (ii) to erect or construct any buildings or works specified in the order,
- (b) apply, in relation to the acquisition of any such land or the erection or construction of any such buildings or works, enactments relating to the acquisition of land or the erection or construction of buildings or works.

(2) An order under paragraph 16 which is for the purposes mentioned in sub-paragraph (3)(a) of that paragraph or an order under paragraph 17 may, in particular, give effect to any financial arrangements—
- (a) agreed between the HCA and the statutory undertakers, or
- (b) in the absence of agreement, decided to be equitable in such manner, and by such tribunal, as may be specified in the order.

Notification of proposal to make order

19.—(1) Statutory undertakers must, as soon as possible after making representations of the kind mentioned in paragraph 16(2), publish a notice—
- (a) giving such particulars as the Secretary of State and the appropriate Minister may direct of the matters to which the representations relate,
- (b) specifying the time within which objections to the making of an order as a result of the representations may be made, and
- (c) specifying the manner in which objections to the making of such an order may be made.

(2) The notice must be published in such form and manner as the Secretary of State and the appropriate Minister may direct.

(3) The statutory undertakers must also serve a copy of the notice on such persons, or descriptions of persons, as the Secretary of State and the appropriate Minister may direct if the Secretary of State and the appropriate Minister direct that a copy is to be served.

20.—(1) The HCA must, as soon as possible after making representations of the kind mentioned in paragraph 17(2), publish a notice—
- (a) giving such particulars as the Secretary of State and the appropriate Minister may direct of the matters to which the representations relate,
- (b) specifying the time within which objections to the making of an order as a result of the representations may be made, and
- (c) specifying the manner in which objections to the making of such an order may be made.

(2) The notice must be published in such form and manner as the Secretary of State and the appropriate Minister may direct.

(3) The HCA must also serve a copy of the notice on such persons, or descriptions of persons, as the Secretary of State and the appropriate Minister may direct if the Secretary of State and the appropriate Minister direct that a copy is to be served.

Duty to consider objections

21.—(1) The Secretary of State and the appropriate Minister must proceed under paragraph 22 if—
- (a) an objection to the making of an order under paragraph 16 or 17 is properly made and not withdrawn, and
- (b) the matter is not otherwise dealt with.

(2) For the purposes of sub-paragraph (1) an objection is properly made if (and only if)—
- (a) it is made—
  - (i) within the time, and
  - (ii) in the manner,

  stated in the notice under paragraph 19(1) or (as the case may be) 20(1), and
- (b) a written statement of the grounds of the objection is comprised in, or submitted with, the objection.

(3) For the purposes of sub-paragraph (1) the matter is otherwise dealt with if (and only if) the Secretary of State and the appropriate Minister—
- (a) decide, irrespective of the objection, not to make the order, or
- (b) decide to make a modification which is agreed to by the objector as meeting the objection.

22.—(1) The Secretary of State and the appropriate Minister must, before making a final decision, consider the grounds of the objection as set out in the statement comprised in, or submitted with, the objection.

(2) The Secretary of State and the appropriate Minister may require the objector to submit within a specified period a further written statement as to any of the matters to which the objection relates.

Duty to give opportunity to appear

23.—(1) The Secretary of State and the appropriate Minister must, before making a final decision, give the objector an opportunity to appear before, and be heard by, a person appointed for the purpose by the Secretary of State and the appropriate Minister.

(2) The Secretary of State and the appropriate Minister must give an opportunity of appearing and being heard on the same occasion to—
- (a) the statutory undertakers or (as the case may be) the HCA as a result of whose representations the order is proposed to be made, and
- (b) any other persons whom the Secretary of State and the appropriate Minister consider ought to be given the opportunity,

if the objector takes advantage of the opportunity mentioned in sub-paragraph (1).

(3) Sub-paragraphs (1) and (2) do not apply so far as the Secretary of State and the appropriate Minister have the power to proceed under paragraph 24 or 25.

Power to treat objection as irrelevant

24. The Secretary of State and the appropriate Minister may treat the objection as irrelevant for the purpose of making a final decision—
- (a) if the Secretary of State and the appropriate Minister have considered the grounds of the objection as set out in the original statement and in any further statement, and
- (b) so far as the Secretary of State and the appropriate Minister are satisfied that the objection relates to a matter which can be dealt with in the assessment of compensation.

Power to curtail decision-making process

25. The Secretary of State and the appropriate Minister may make a final decision without further investigation as to the matters to which the objection relates if—

(a) the Secretary of State and the appropriate Minister—

(i) have considered the grounds of the objection as set out in the original statement and in any further statement, and

(ii) are satisfied that, for the purpose of making a final decision, sufficient information is available as to the matters to which the objection relates, or

(b) a further statement has been required under paragraph 22(2) but is not submitted within the specified period.

Power to hold public local inquiry

26.—(1) The Secretary of State and the appropriate Minister must cause a public local inquiry to be held in relation to an objection under this Part of this Schedule if the Secretary of State and the appropriate Minister consider that the matters to which the objection relates are such as to require investigation by such an inquiry before the Secretary of State and the appropriate Minister make a final decision.

(2) The duty in sub-paragraph (1) is effective despite any other provisions of this Part of this Schedule.

(3) The other provisions of this Part of this Schedule are to be ignored if, when the Secretary of State and the appropriate Minister decide to cause an inquiry to be held, effect has not been given to them.

Special parliamentary procedure for orders

27. Orders under paragraph 16 or 17 are subject to special parliamentary procedure.

[2490]

NOTES

Commencement: 1 December 2008.

PART 4
RELIEVING UNDERTAKERS OF OBLIGATIONS

Orders to relieve obligations

28.—(1) The appropriate Minister may by order provide for statutory undertakers to be relieved (whether absolutely or so far as specified in the order) of the need to meet an obligation relating to the carrying on of their undertaking if conditions 1 and 2 are met.

(2) Condition 1 is that the statutory undertakers have made representations on the subject to the appropriate Minister.

(3) Condition 2 is that the appropriate Minister is satisfied that meeting some or all of the obligation has been made impracticable by any of the acts and events mentioned in sub-paragraph (4).

(4) The acts and events are—

(a) the acquisition by the HCA under this Part of this Act of any land—

(i) in which an interest was held for the purpose of carrying on the undertaking concerned, or

(ii) which was used for that purpose, and

(b) the extinguishment of a right, or the imposition of any requirement, by virtue of Part 1 of this Schedule.

Notification of proposal to make order

29.—(1) Statutory undertakers must, as soon as possible after making representations of the kind mentioned in paragraph 28(2), proceed as directed by the appropriate Minister.

(2) The appropriate Minister may direct the statutory undertakers to do either or both of the following—

(a) publish a notice—

(i) giving such particulars as the appropriate Minister may direct of the matters to which the representations relate,

(ii) specifying the time within which objections to the making of an order as a result of the representations may be made, and

(iii) specifying the manner in which objections to the making of such an order may be made, and

(b) serve a corresponding notice on such persons, or descriptions of persons, as the appropriate Minister may direct.

(3) Publication under sub-paragraph (2) must be in such form and manner as the appropriate Minister may direct.

Duty to consider objections

30.—(1) The appropriate Minister must proceed under paragraph 31 if—
(a) an objection to the making of an order is properly made and not withdrawn, and
(b) the matter is not otherwise dealt with.

(2) For the purposes of sub-paragraph (1) an objection is properly made if (and only if)—
(a) it is made—
(i) within the time, and
(ii) in the manner,
stated in the notice under paragraph 29(2), and
(b) a written statement of the grounds of the objection is comprised in, or submitted with, the objection.

(3) For the purposes of sub-paragraph (1) the matter is otherwise dealt with if (and only if) the appropriate Minister—
(a) decides, irrespective of the objection, not to make the order, or
(b) decides to make a modification which is agreed to by the objector as meeting the objection.

31.—(1) The appropriate Minister must, before making a final decision, consider the grounds of the objection as set out in the statement comprised in, or submitted with, the objection.

(2) The appropriate Minister may require the objector to submit within a specified period a further written statement as to any of the matters to which the objection relates.

Duty to give opportunity to appear

32.—(1) The appropriate Minister must, before making a final decision, give the objector an opportunity to appear before, and be heard by, a person appointed for the purpose by the appropriate Minister.

(2) The appropriate Minister must give an opportunity of appearing and being heard on the same occasion to—
(a) the statutory undertakers as a result of whose representations the order is proposed to be made, and
(b) any other persons whom the appropriate Minister considers ought to be given the opportunity,

if the objector takes advantage of the opportunity mentioned in sub-paragraph (1).

(3) Sub-paragraphs (1) and (2) do not apply so far as the appropriate Minister has the power to proceed under paragraph 33 or 34.

Power to treat objection as irrelevant

33. The appropriate Minister may treat the objection as irrelevant for the purpose of making a final decision—
(a) if the appropriate Minister has considered the grounds of the objection as set out in the original statement and in any further statement, and
(b) so far as the appropriate Minister is satisfied that the objection relates to a matter which can be dealt with in the assessment of compensation.

Power to curtail decision-making process

34. The appropriate Minister may make a final decision without further investigation as to the matters to which the objection relates if—
(a) the appropriate Minister—
(i) has considered the grounds of the objection as set out in the original statement and in any further statement, and
(ii) is satisfied that, for the purpose of making a final decision, sufficient information is available as to the matters to which the objection relates, or
(b) a further statement has been required under paragraph 31(2) but is not submitted within the specified period.

Power to hold public local inquiry

35.—(1) The appropriate Minister may cause a public local inquiry to be held in relation to an objection under this Part of this Schedule if the appropriate Minister considers that the matters to which the objection relates are such as to require investigation by such an inquiry before the appropriate Minister makes a final decision.

(2) The power in sub-paragraph (1) is effective despite any other provisions of this Part of this Schedule.

(3) The other provisions of this Part of this Schedule are to be ignored if, when the Secretary of State decides to cause an inquiry to be held, effect has not been given to them.

Notification procedure after the making of an order

36.—(1) The appropriate Minister must, immediately after making an order under paragraph 28, proceed under sub-paragraphs (2) and (3).

(2) The appropriate Minister must publish a notice stating—
(a) that the order has been made, and
(b) a place where a copy of it may be seen at any reasonable hour.

(3) The appropriate Minister must serve a copy of the notice on—
(a) any person who—
(i) duly made an objection to the order, and
(ii) has sent the appropriate Minister a written request for the notice with an address for service, and
(b) any other person whom the appropriate Minister considers appropriate.

Operative date of orders

37. An order under paragraph 28 which is not subject to special parliamentary procedure becomes operative on the date on which the notice required by paragraph 36(2) is first published.

Special parliamentary procedure for orders

38.—(1) An order under paragraph 28 is subject to special parliamentary procedure if any objection to the making of the order is properly made and not withdrawn before the order is made.

(2) Sub-paragraph (2) of paragraph 30 applies for the purposes of sub-paragraph (1) above as it applies for the purposes of sub-paragraph (1) of that paragraph.

Legal challenges to orders

39.—(1) Sub-paragraph (2) applies if a person aggrieved by an order under paragraph 28 wishes to question its validity on the ground that—
(a) it is not within the powers conferred by this Part of this Schedule, or
(b) any requirement of this Part of this Schedule has not been complied with in relation to the order.

(2) The person may, within 6 weeks beginning with the date on which the notice required by paragraph 36(2) is first published, apply to the High Court.

(3) The High Court may, on an application under sub-paragraph (2), make an interim order suspending (whether wholly or in part) the operation of the order under paragraph 28 until the final determination of the proceedings.

(4) The operation of the order may be suspended generally or so far as affecting any property of the applicant.

(5) The High Court may, on an application under sub-paragraph (2), quash (whether wholly or in part) the order under paragraph 28 if satisfied that—
(a) the order is wholly or to any extent outside the powers conferred by this Part of this Schedule, or
(b) the interests of the applicant have been substantially prejudiced by the failure to comply with any requirement of this Part of this Schedule.

(6) The order under paragraph 28 may be quashed generally or so far as affecting any property of the applicant.

[2491]

NOTES
Commencement: 1 December 2008.

PART 5
SUPPLEMENTARY

Orders and directions

40.—(1) The power of—
(a) the Secretary of State and the appropriate Minister,
(b) the Secretary of State and the Secretary of State for Business, Enterprise and Regulatory Reform, or
(c) the appropriate Minister,

to make orders under this Schedule includes power to vary or revoke such orders and to make supplementary, incidental, consequential, transitional, transitory or saving provision.

(2) The power of—

(a) the Secretary of State and the appropriate Minister, or

(b) the appropriate Minister,

to give directions under this Schedule includes power to vary or revoke such directions and to make supplementary, incidental, consequential, transitional, transitory or saving provision.

Interpretation

41.—(1) In this Schedule—

"the appropriate Minister" is to be read as if contained in Part 11 of the Town and Country Planning Act 1990 (c 8),

"the Secretary of State and the appropriate Minister" is to be read as if contained in Part 11 of the Town and Country Planning Act 1990 (and any references to the Secretary of State and the appropriate Minister are, in relation to anything done or to be done by them, to be read as references to them acting jointly),

"statutory undertakers" means persons who are or are deemed to be statutory undertakers for the purposes of any provision of Part 11 of the Town and Country Planning Act 1990; and "statutory undertaking" is to be read in accordance with section 262 of that Act (meaning of "statutory undertaker").

(2) In this Schedule, in relation to an order, any reference to making a final decision is a reference to deciding whether to make the order or what modification (if any) ought to be made. **[2492]**

NOTES

Commencement: 1 December 2008.

SCHEDULE 5
AMENDMENTS OF THE NEW TOWNS ACT 1981

Section 50

1. The New Towns Act 1981 (c 64) is amended as follows.

2. For the heading to Part 2 substitute "Transfers from and dissolution of development corporations etc".

3. For the italic heading before section 35 substitute "Functions of Welsh Ministers in relation to certain transferred property".

4. Omit section 35 (establishment of Commission for the New Towns).

5.—(1) Section 36 (functions of Commission) is amended as follows.

(2) For the heading substitute "Functions of Welsh Ministers".

(3) For subsection (1) substitute—

"(1) The Welsh Ministers may—

(a) take over and, with a view to its eventual disposal, hold, manage and turn to account—

(i) the property of the Commission for the New Towns transferred to them under a scheme made under section 51(1) of the Housing and Regeneration Act 2008;

(ii) the property of development corporations transferred to them under this Act; and

(iii) the property of urban development corporations transferred to them by order under section 165A of the Local Government, Planning and Land Act 1980; and

(b) as soon as they consider it expedient to do so, dispose of property so transferred or any other property arising out of such property.

(1A) In exercising their functions under subsection (1), the Welsh Ministers must have regard to the considerations specified in subsection (2)."

(4) Omit subsections (3) and (3A).

(5) In subsection (4)—

(a) for "Commission", in the first two places where it appears, substitute "Welsh Ministers", and

(b) omit the words from "; nor shall any" to the end.

(6) In subsection (4A)(a) for "Commission by order under section 165B" substitute "Welsh Ministers by order under section 165A".

6. Omit sections 37 (restrictions on functions of Commission) and 38 (local authorities and work for the Commission).

7.—(1) Section 39 (power of development corporations to transfer undertakings) is amended as follows.

(2) In subsection (1) for "Secretary of State" substitute "appropriate national authority".

(3) In subsection (2) for "Secretary of State" substitute "appropriate national authority".

(4) In subsection (2A) for "in relation to Wales" substitute "in the case of a development corporation established by the Welsh Ministers".

(5) In subsection (3) for "Secretary of State" substitute "appropriate national authority".

(6) In subsection (4)—

(a) at the beginning insert "In a case in which the appropriate national authority is the Secretary of State,", and

(b) for "Secretary of State", where it first appears, substitute "appropriate national authority".

(7) In subsection (5)—

(a) for "Secretary of State" substitute "appropriate national authority", and

(b) for "he" substitute "the authority".

(8) For subsection (5A) substitute—

"(5A) No order shall be made under subsection (5) above—

(a) by the Secretary of State unless a draft of the order has been laid before, and approved by a resolution of, the House of Commons;

(b) by the Welsh Ministers unless a draft of the order has been laid before, and approved by a resolution of, the National Assembly for Wales."

8.—(1) Section 41 (transfer of property to Commission and dissolution of corporation) is amended as follows.

(2) In the heading, omit "to Commission".

(3) In subsection (1)—

(a) for "Secretary of State" substitute "appropriate national authority",

(b) for "he" substitute "the authority", and

(c) in paragraph (a), for "Commission" substitute "relevant transferee".

(4) In subsection (1A) for "in relation to Wales" substitute "in the case of a development corporation established by the Welsh Ministers".

(5) In subsection (2)—

(a) for "Commission" substitute "relevant transferee", and

(b) in paragraph (b)—

(i) for "Secretary of State" substitute "appropriate national authority", and

(ii) for "him" substitute "the authority".

(6) In subsection (4) for "Secretary of State" substitute "appropriate national authority".

(7) In subsection (5) for "Commission" substitute "relevant transferee".

9. After section 41 insert—

"41A Part 2: interpretation

In this Part—

"the appropriate national authority"—

(a) in relation to a development corporation established by order made by the Secretary of State, means the Secretary of State; and

(b) in relation to a development corporation established by order made by the Welsh Ministers, means the Welsh Ministers;

"the relevant transferee"—

(a) in relation to an order made under section 41 by the Secretary of State, means the Homes and Communities Agency; and

(b) in relation to an order made under section 41 by the Welsh Ministers, means the Welsh Ministers."

10.—(1) Section 58 (advances to development corporations and Commission) is amended as follows.

(2) In the heading, omit "and Commission".

(3) Omit subsections (5) and (6).

11.—(1) Section 58A (grants to development corporations and Commission) is amended as follows.

(2) In the heading, omit "and Commission".

(3) Omit subsections (4) and (5).

12.—(1) Section 59 (other borrowing powers of development corporations and Commission) is amended as follows.

(2) In the heading, omit "and Commission".

(3) In subsection (1)—

(a) omit "or the Commission", and

(b) for the words from "or the Commission (as the case may be)" to the end substitute "may require for meeting its obligations or performing its functions".

(4) In subsection (2)—

(a) omit "or the Commission", and

(b) for "they may require for enabling them" substitute "it may require for enabling it."

13.—(1) Section 60 (limit on borrowing by development corporations and Commission) is amended as follows.

(2) In the heading, omit "and Commission".

(3) In subsection (1)—

(a) at the end of paragraph (b), insert "and",

(b) omit paragraph (c) and the "and" following it,

(c) in paragraph (d), for "(whether by development corporations or by the Commission)" substitute "by development corporations", and

(d) for "(2) to (4)" substitute "(2) and (3)".

(4) Omit subsection (4).

14.—(1) Section 61 (provisions supplemental to section 58) is amended as follows.

(2) In subsection (1) for from the beginning of paragraph (a) to the end of paragraph (b) substitute "to a development corporation under section 58(1) above".

(3) In subsection (2) omit ", (5) or (6)".

15.—(1) Section 62 (Treasury guarantees) is amended as follows.

(2) In subsection (1) for "or the Commission borrow" substitute "borrows".

(3) In subsection (5) for the words from "or by the Commission" to "(as the case may be)" substitute ", the corporation".

16. Omit section 62B (power to suspend loan obligations of development corporations and Commission).

17.—(1) Section 63 (Secretary of State's general power) is amended as follows.

(2) In subsection (1) omit "or the Commission".

(3) In subsection (2) omit "or the Commission, as the case may be".

18.—(1) Section 65 (disposal of surplus funds) is amended as follows.

(2) In subsection (1) for the words from ", and with the Commission" to the end substitute "and any development corporation, that the corporation has a surplus whether on capital or on revenue account after making allowance by way of transfer to reserve or otherwise for its future requirements".

(3) In subsection (2) for "The Commission or that corporation, as the case may be," substitute "That corporation".

19. In section 66(1) (payments under sections 63 and 65 treated as repayments) for paragraph (a) and the "and" following it substitute—

"(a) as made by way of repayment of such part of the principal of advances under section 58(1) above, and".

20.—(1) Section 67 (accounts of Commission and development corporations) is amended as follows.

(2) In the heading, omit "Commission and".

(3) In subsection (1)—

(a) omit "The Commission and",

(b) in paragraph (b), omit "respectively", and

(c) omit the words from "being, in the Commission's case" in paragraph (b) to the end of the subsection.

(4) Omit subsection (1A).

(5) In subsection (2)—

(a) omit "of the Commission and", and

(b) omit "or the Commission" wherever appearing.

(6) In subsection (3)—

(a) omit "the Commission or", and

(b) in paragraph (a), for "they are" substitute "it is".

21.—(1) Section 68 (audit) is amended as follows.

(2) In subsection (1)—

(a) omit the words from "of the Commission" to "and the accounts", and
(b) omit "Commission or".

(3) Omit subsection (2A).

(4) In subsection (3)—
(a) for "accounts of the Commission or" substitute "accounts of",
(b) for "Commission or corporation, as the case may be," substitute "corporation", and
(c) for "them" substitute "it".

22.—(1) Section 69 (Secretary of State's accounts) is amended as follows.

(2) In subsection (1)—
(a) omit paragraph (a) and the "and" following it, and
(b) omit the words from "and directions under" to the end.

(3) In subsection (2), omit paragraph (a) and the "and" following it.

23.—(1) Section 70 (reports) is amended as follows.

(2) Omit paragraph (a).

(3) Omit "of the Commission or".

24.—(1) Section 71 (information) is amended as follows.

(2) In subsection (1)—
(a) for "the Commission and every development corporation shall respectively" substitute "every development corporation shall", and
(b) for "their" substitute "its".

(3) In subsection (2)—
(a) omit "the Commission and", and
(b) in paragraph (a), for "Commission or corporation, as the case may be" substitute "corporation".

25. In section 72(1)(a) (application and exclusion of certain enactments: section 12 of the Finance Act 1895 (c 16)) omit "or from the Commission".

26. In section 74(3) (local inquiries) for "sections 37, 40 and 41" substitute "sections 40 and 41".

27. In section 77(3) (regulations and orders to be made by statutory instrument) omit "and paragraph 7 of Schedule 9 to this Act".

28. In section 80(1) (general interpretation provisions)—
(a) omit the definition of "the Commission", and
(b) in the definition of "financial year", omit "or the Commission".

29. In section 82 (short title, extent and commencement)—
(a) in subsection (2)(c) for "1, 2 and 12" substitute "1 and 2", and
(b) in subsection (3) omit "paragraph 12 of Schedule 11, and".

30. Omit Schedule 9 (additional provisions as to the Commission).

31.—(1) Schedule 10 (additional provisions as to transfer to Commission of property of development corporation) is amended as follows.

(2) In the heading, omit "to Commission".

(3) In paragraph 1—
(a) for "Commission", wherever appearing, substitute "relevant transferee", and
(b) in sub-paragraph (2)(c), for ", to the member" to the end substitute
"—
(i) in a case where the relevant transferee is the Homes and Communities Agency, to the member or member of staff of the Agency who corresponds as nearly as may be to the member or officer in question of the corporation; and
(ii) in a case where the relevant transferee is the Welsh Ministers, to the member of staff of the Welsh Ministers who corresponds as mentioned in sub-paragraph (i) above."

(4) In paragraph 2—
(a) for "Secretary of State", wherever appearing, substitute "appropriate national authority", and
(b) for "Commission", wherever appearing, substitute "relevant transferee".

(5) In paragraph 3—
(a) in sub-paragraph (1) for "Commission" substitute "relevant transferee",
(b) in sub-paragraph (3)(a) for "Commission" substitute "relevant transferee", and
(c) in sub-paragraph (3)(c)—
(i) for "where the development" substitute "where, in the case of a development corporation established by the Secretary of State, the", and
(ii) for "Commission" substitute "Homes and Communities Agency".

(6) Omit paragraph 4.

(7) In paragraph 5—

(a) omit sub-paragraph (1), and

(b) for sub-paragraph (2) substitute—

"(2) Sub-paragraph (3) applies if, in the case of a development corporation established by the Secretary of State, the liabilities of the corporation for—

(a) the repayment of advances under section 58(1) above; or

(b) the payment of interest on such advances;

are transferred to the Homes and Communities Agency.

(3) The following provisions apply to those advances—

(a) section 61(2); and

(b) section 66(1) but as if the reference to any payment under section 63 or 65 above were a reference to any sum received by the Secretary of State under section 25(2) of the Housing and Regeneration Act 2008."

32.—(1) Schedule 11 (saving and transitional provisions) is amended as follows.

(2) In the italic heading before paragraph 3, omit "to Commission and".

(3) Omit paragraphs 3 and 5.

(4) Omit paragraph 12 and the italic heading before it.

[2493]

NOTES

Commencement: 1 December 2008 (paras 1, 5–9, 25, 26, 29, 31); 1 April 2009 (paras 2–4, 10–24, 27, 28, 30, 32).

SCHEDULE 6
TRANSFER SCHEMES

Sections 51(3) and 65(3)

Creation and apportionment of property, rights and liabilities etc

1. A scheme may—

(a) create for the transferor interests in, or rights over, property transferred by virtue of the scheme,

(b) create for a transferee interests in, or rights over, property retained by the transferor or transferred to another transferee,

(c) create rights or liabilities between the transferor and a transferee or between transferees.

2.—(1) A scheme may provide for the transfer of property, rights or liabilities that would not otherwise be capable of being transferred or assigned.

(2) In particular, it may provide for the transfer to take effect regardless of a contravention, liability or interference with an interest or right that would otherwise exist by reason of a provision having effect in relation to the terms on which the transferor is entitled to the property or right, or subject to the liability, in question.

(3) It does not matter whether the provision referred to in sub-paragraph (2) has effect under an enactment or an agreement or in any other way.

3. A certificate by the Secretary of State that anything specified in the certificate has vested in any person by virtue of a scheme is conclusive evidence for all purposes of that fact.

Employment contracts

4.—(1) This paragraph applies if rights and liabilities under a contract of employment are transferred by virtue of a scheme.

(2) The contract of employment—

(a) is not terminated by the transfer, and

(b) has effect from the transfer date as if made between the employee and the transferee.

(3) The rights, powers, duties and liabilities of the transferor under or in connection with the contract are transferred to the transferee on the transfer date.

(4) Anything done before the transfer date by or in relation to the transferor in respect of the contract or the employee is to be treated from that date as having been done by or in relation to the transferee.

(5) In particular, a period of employment with the transferor is to be treated as a period of employment with the transferee (and the transfer is not to be treated as interrupting the continuity of that employment).

(6) This paragraph is subject to paragraph 5.

5.—(1) Rights and liabilities under a contract of employment are not transferred by virtue of a scheme if the employee objects to the transfer and informs the transferor or transferee of that fact.

(2) If the employee objects to the transfer and informs the transferor or transferee of that fact—

(a) the employee's contract of employment is terminated immediately before the transfer date, but

(b) the employee is not to be treated, for any purpose, as having been dismissed by the transferor.

6. If (apart from the change of employer) a substantial detrimental change is made to a person's working conditions, nothing in this Schedule affects any right the person has to terminate the person's contract of employment.

Civil servants treated as employed under a contract of employment etc

7.—(1) This Schedule applies with the following modifications in relation to employment in the civil service of the Crown on terms which do not constitute a contract of employment.

(2) An individual who holds employment in the civil service of the Crown immediately before the transfer date is to be treated as employed by virtue of a contract of employment.

(3) The terms of the employment in the civil service of the Crown are to be regarded as constituting the terms of the contract of employment.

(4) The reference in paragraph 5 to dismissal by the transferor is to termination of the employment in the civil service of the Crown.

Compensation

8. A scheme may contain provision for the payment of compensation by the Secretary of State to any person whose interests are adversely affected by it.

Continuity

9. A transfer by virtue of a scheme does not affect the validity of anything done by or in relation to the transferor before the transfer takes effect.

10. Anything which—

(a) is done by the transferor for the purposes of, or otherwise in connection with, anything transferred by virtue of a scheme, and

(b) is in effect immediately before the transfer date,

is to be treated as done by the transferee.

11. There may be continued by or in relation to the transferee anything (including legal proceedings)—

(a) which relates to anything transferred by virtue of a scheme, and

(b) which is in the process of being done by or in relation to the transferor immediately before the transfer date.

12.—(1) This paragraph applies to any document—

(a) which relates to anything transferred by virtue of a scheme, and

(b) which is in effect immediately before the transfer date.

(2) Any references in the document to the transferor are to be read as references to the transferee.

Supplementary etc provision

13. A scheme may include supplementary, incidental, transitional and consequential provision.

[2494]

NOTES

Commencement: 8 September 2008.

SCHEDULE 7

TRANSFER SCHEMES: TAX

Sections 51(5), 65(5)

Overview

1. This Schedule makes provision about the fiscal effect of transfers under schemes made under sections 51 and 65.

Key concepts

2.—(1) In this Schedule—

(a) "transfer scheme" means a scheme under section 51 or 65, and

(b) "transfer" means a transfer under a transfer scheme.

(2) In this Schedule "transfer between bodies" means a transfer—

(a) from the Urban Regeneration Agency, the Commission for the New Towns or the Housing Corporation, and

(b) to the HCA or the Regulator of Social Housing.

(3) In this Schedule "transfer to government" means a transfer to—

(a) a Minister of the Crown, or

(b) the Welsh Ministers.

Other definitions

3.—(1) In this Schedule—

(a) ICTA means the Income and Corporation Taxes Act 1988 (c 1),

(b) TCGA means the Taxation of Chargeable Gains Act 1992 (c 12),

(c) FA 1996 means the Finance Act 1996 (c 8),

(d) FA 2002 means the Finance Act 2002 (c 23), and

(e) HMRC means the Commissioners for Her Majesty's Revenue and Customs.

(2) In this Schedule a reference to a trade includes a reference to part of a trade.

Corporation tax: continuity of trade

4.—(1) This paragraph applies if as the result of a transfer scheme—

(a) a transferor ceases a trade, and

(b) a transferee commences it.

(2) In connection with the computation of profits and losses for the purpose of corporation tax in respect of periods wholly or partly after the commencement of the transfer scheme—

(a) the transferee shall be treated as having always carried on the trade, and

(b) the trade shall be considered separately from any other trade of the transferee (with any necessary apportionment being made).

Corporation tax: capital allowances

5.—(1) This paragraph applies in respect of property transferred under a transfer scheme from—

(a) the Urban Regeneration Agency, or

(b) the Commission for the New Towns.

(2) Where the property was used by the transferor, and is to be used by the transferee, in connection with a trade, section 343(2) of ICTA (company reconstructions: capital allowances) shall apply.

6. The following transfers shall be treated as giving rise to neither allowance nor charge for the purposes of capital allowances in respect of a trade (and allowances shall be calculated as if the transferee had always carried on the trade)—

(a) a transfer from the Housing Corporation, and

(b) a transfer to government.

Corporation tax: capital gains

7.—(1) This paragraph applies in respect of property transferred under a transfer scheme from—

(a) the Urban Regeneration Agency,

(b) the Commission for the New Towns, or

(c) the Housing Corporation.

(2) Section 17 of TCGA (disposals and acquisitions treated as at market value) shall not apply.

(3) For the purposes of TCGA the transfer (in relation to the transferor and the transferee) is to be taken as being a disposal for a consideration such that neither gain nor loss accrues.

8. A transfer shall be disregarded for the purposes of section 30 of TCGA (value-shifting: tax-free benefits).

9. …

Corporation tax: intangible assets

10.—(1) This paragraph applies for the purposes of Schedule 29 to FA 2002 (intangible assets).

(2) Expressions used in this paragraph have the same meaning as in that Schedule.

(3) A transfer between bodies of a chargeable intangible asset is a tax-neutral transfer.

(4) An intangible fixed asset which is an existing asset of the transferor at the time of a transfer between bodies is to be treated, on and after the transfer, as an existing asset of the transferee.

(5) A transfer to government of a chargeable intangible asset is to be treated as not involving a realisation of the asset by the transferor.

Corporation tax: loan relationships

11.—(1) If as a result of a transfer the transferee replaces the transferor as a party to a loan relationship, paragraph 12(2) of Schedule 9 to FA 1996 (transfer within group: continuity of treatment) shall apply (whether or not the transferor and transferee are bodies corporate).

(2) Expressions used in this paragraph have the same meaning as in that Schedule.

Stamp duty

12.—(1) Stamp duty shall not be chargeable on a transfer scheme.

(2) Stamp duty shall not be chargeable on a document certified by HMRC as connected with a transfer scheme.

(3) A document which is not chargeable by virtue of this paragraph must be stamped in accordance with section 12 of the Stamp Act 1891 (c 39) with a stamp denoting that it is not chargeable.

[2495]

NOTES

Commencement: 8 September 2008.

Para 9: repealed by the Housing and Regeneration Act 2008 (Consequential Provisions) Order 2008, SI 2008/3002, arts 4–6, Sch 1, paras 55, 59, Schs 2, 3 (subject to transitional and savings provisions).

SCHEDULE 8
AMENDMENTS OF ENACTMENTS: PART 1

Section 56

Public Records Act 1958 (c 51)

1. In Schedule 1 to the Public Records Act 1958 (definition of public records), at the end of paragraph 3, in Part 2 of the Table, insert at the appropriate place—

"The Homes and Communities Agency."

Land Compensation Act 1961 (c 33)

2. In section 23(3) of the Land Compensation Act 1961 (compensation where planning decision made after acquisition: exclusions) for paragraph (d) and the word "or" before it substitute

"or

(d) under Part 1 of the Housing and Regeneration Act 2008 (acquisition by the Homes and Communities Agency)."

Public Health Act 1961 (c 64)

3. In Schedule 4 to the Public Health Act 1961 (attachment of street lighting equipment to certain buildings), in the first column of the Table, for the words from "Commission" to "1959" substitute "Homes and Communities Agency so far as exercising functions in relation to anything transferred (or to be transferred) to it as mentioned in section 52(1)(a) to (d) of the Housing and Regeneration Act 2008".

Parliamentary Commissioner Act 1967 (c 13)

4. In Schedule 2 to the Parliamentary Commissioner Act 1967 (departments etc subject to investigation)—

(a) insert, at the appropriate place, "Homes and Communities Agency",
(b) insert, in the Notes after the paragraph relating to the Treasury—

"Homes and Communities Agency

In the case of the Homes and Communities Agency no investigation is to be conducted in respect of any action in connection with functions in relation to town and country planning.",

(c) omit the entries for the Commission for the New Towns and the Urban Regeneration Agency, and
(d) omit the Notes relating to the Commission for the New Towns and the Urban Regeneration Agency.

Leasehold Reform Act 1967 (c 88)

5. The Leasehold Reform Act 1967 is amended as follows.

6. In section 28(5)(b) (retention or resumption of land required for public purposes) for "Commission for the New Towns" substitute "new towns residuary body".

7.—(1) Section 29 (reservation of future right to develop) is amended as follows.

(2) In subsection (6)—

(a) in paragraph (a) for "Commission for the New Towns" substitute "new towns residuary body", and
(b) for "that Commission" substitute "that residuary body".

(3) In subsection (7) for "Commission for the New Towns" substitute "Welsh new towns residuary body".

8. In section 30(7)(a) (reservation of right of pre-emption in new town or overspill area) for "Commission for the New Towns" substitute "new towns residuary body".

9. In section 33 (Crown land) after subsection (2) insert—

"(2A) For the purposes of this Part of this Act, an interest belonging to the Welsh new towns residuary body in a tenancy of land is to be treated as if it were not an interest belonging to the Crown."

10. In section 37(1) (interpretation of Part 1) after paragraph (b) insert—

"(ba) "new towns residuary body" means—
(i) in relation to England, the Homes and Communities Agency so far as exercising functions in relation to anything transferred (or to be transferred) to it as mentioned in section 52(1)(a) to (d) of the Housing and Regeneration Act 2008; and
(ii) in relation to Wales, means the Welsh Ministers so far as exercising functions in relation to anything transferred (or to be transferred) to them as mentioned in section 36(1)(a)(i) to (iii) of the New Towns Act 1981 (and references to the "Welsh new towns residuary body" shall be construed accordingly);".

11.—(1) Schedule 4 (re-acquisition for development) is amended as follows.

(2) In the heading for Part 2 for "New Towns Commission" substitute "Welsh new towns residuary body".

(3) In paragraph 4—

(a) for "Commission for the New Towns" substitute "Welsh new towns residuary body",
(b) for "the Commission, the Commission" substitute "that body, the body", and
(c) omit the words from "be authorised" to "Government to".

12. In paragraph 2(2)(c) of Schedule 4A (exclusion of certain shared ownership leases) for "Commission for the New Towns" substitute "new towns residuary body".

National Loans Act 1968 (c 13)

13. In Schedule 1 to the National Loans Act 1968 (Government lending and advances) in the entry relating to the New Towns Act 1981 (c 64)—
(a) in column 1 omit "(5)(6)", and
(b) in column 2 omit "and the Commission for the New Towns".

Local Government Act 1972 (c 70)

14. The Local Government Act 1972 is amended as follows.

15.—(1) Section 100J (application of Part 5A of the Act to new authorities, Common Council, etc) is amended as follows.

(2) In subsection (1) after paragraph (f) insert—
"(g) the Homes and Communities Agency so far as it is exercising functions conferred on it in relation to a designated area by virtue of a designation order."

(3) After subsection (2) insert—

"(2A) In its application by virtue of subsection (1)(g) above in relation to the Homes and Communities Agency, a reference in this Part to the offices of the council (however expressed)—

(a) is to be treated as a reference to such premises located within the designated area as the Homes and Communities Agency considers appropriate, and
(b) in the application of section 100A(6)(a) above to a case where the meeting is to be held at premises other than those mentioned in paragraph (a) above, includes a reference to those other premises."

(4) After subsection (3) insert—

"(3ZA) In its application by virtue of subsection (1)(g) above in relation to the Homes and Communities Agency, section 100E above shall have effect as if—

(a) in subsection (2), paragraph (c) was omitted, and
(b) in subsection (3), for paragraphs (a) to (c) there were substituted—
"(a) a committee established under paragraph 6(1) of Schedule 1 to the Housing and

Regeneration Act 2008 for the purpose of exercising functions conferred on the Homes and Communities Agency in relation to a designated area by virtue of a designation order; or

(b) a sub-committee of such a committee established under paragraph 6(2) of that Schedule to that Act for that purpose."

(3ZB) In its application by virtue of subsection (1)(g) above in relation to the Homes and Communities Agency, section 100G(1) above shall have effect as if paragraph (a) was omitted."

(5) After subsection (4A) insert—

"(4B) In this section "designated area" and "designation order" have the same meanings as in Part 1 of the Housing and Regeneration Act 2008."

16. In section 100K (interpretation and application of Part 5A) in the definition of "committee or sub-committee of a principal council" at the end insert "(and see section 100J(3ZA)(b) above)".

Land Compensation Act 1973 (c 26)

17.—(1) Section 39 of the Land Compensation Act 1973 (duty to rehouse residential occupiers) is amended as follows.

(2) In subsection (4)(d) for "Commission for the New Towns" substitute "new towns residuary body".

(3) In subsection (8)—

(a) in paragraph (a) for "Commission for the New Towns" substitute "new towns residuary body", and

(b) in paragraph (c) for "Commission for the New Towns, the Commission" substitute "new towns residuary body, that body".

(4) In subsection (9)—

(a) after "section" insert

"—

(a) ", and

(b) at the end insert—

"(b) "new towns residuary body" means—

(i) in relation to England, the Homes and Communities Agency so far as exercising functions in relation to anything transferred (or to be transferred) to it as mentioned in section 52(1)(a) to (d) of the Housing and Regeneration Act 2008; and

(ii) in relation to Wales, the Welsh Ministers so far as exercising functions in relation to anything transferred (or to be transferred) to them as mentioned in section 36(1)(a)(i) to (iii) of the New Towns Act 1981."

Local Government Act 1974 (c 7)

18.—(1) The Local Government Act 1974 is amended as follows.

(2) In section 25(1) (authorities subject to investigation)—

(a) omit paragraph (ba), and

(b) in paragraph (bf), for "Urban Regeneration" substitute "Homes and Communities".

(3) In section 26(7) (matters subject to investigation)—

(a) omit paragraph (a), and

(b) in paragraph (ba)—

(i) for "Urban Regeneration" substitute "Homes and Communities", and

(ii) for "Part III of the Leasehold Reform, Housing and Urban Development Act 1993" substitute "Part 1 of the Housing and Regeneration Act 2008".

(4) In paragraph 8 of Schedule 5 (matters not subject to investigation) for "Urban Regeneration" substitute "Homes and Communities".

House of Commons Disqualification Act 1975 (c 24)

19.—(1) Part 2 of Schedule 1 to the House of Commons Disqualification Act 1975 (bodies of which all members are disqualified) is amended as follows.

(2) Insert at the appropriate place—

"The Homes and Communities Agency."

(3) Omit the entries relating to—

(a) the Commission for the New Towns, and

(b) the Urban Regeneration Agency.

Northern Ireland Assembly Disqualification Act 1975 (c 25)

20.—(1) Part 2 of Schedule 1 to the Northern Ireland Assembly Disqualification Act 1975 (bodies of which all members are disqualified) is amended as follows.

(2) Insert at the appropriate place—

"The Homes and Communities Agency."

(3) Omit the entry relating to the Urban Regeneration Agency.

Race Relations Act 1976 (c 74)

21.—(1) Schedule 1A to the Race Relations Act 1976 (bodies and other persons subject to general statutory duty) is amended as follows.

(2) In Part 1, after paragraph 52, insert—

"52A.

The Homes and Communities Agency."

(3) In Part 2, omit the entry relating to English Partnerships.

Rent (Agriculture) Act 1976 (c 80)

22.—(1) Section 5 of the Rent (Agriculture) Act 1976 (no statutory tenancy where landlord's interest belongs to certain bodies) is amended as follows.

(2) In subsection (3)(c) for "Commission for the New Towns" substitute "English new towns residuary body".

(3) After subsection (3) insert—

"(3A) In subsection (3)(c) above "English new towns residuary body" means the Homes and Communities Agency so far as exercising functions in relation to anything transferred (or to be transferred) to it as mentioned in section 52(1)(a) to (d) of the Housing and Regeneration Act 2008."

Rent Act 1977 (c 42)

23.—(1) Section 14 of the Rent Act 1977 (landlord's interest belonging to local authority, etc) is amended as follows.

(2) At the beginning insert "(1)".

(3) In paragraph (d) for "Commission for the New Towns" substitute "English new towns residuary body".

(4) At the end insert—

"(2) In subsection (1)(d) "English new towns residuary body" means the Homes and Communities Agency so far as exercising functions in relation to anything transferred (or to be transferred) to it as mentioned in section 52(1)(a) to (d) of the Housing and Regeneration Act 2008."

Protection from Eviction Act 1977 (c 43)

24.—(1) Section 3A of the Protection from Eviction Act 1977 (excluded tenancies and licences) is amended as follows.

(2) In subsection (8)(c) for "Commission for the New Towns" substitute "new towns residuary body".

(3) After subsection (8) insert—

"(8A) In subsection (8)(c) above "new towns residuary body" means—

(a) in relation to England, the Homes and Communities Agency so far as exercising functions in relation to anything transferred (or to be transferred) to it as mentioned in section 52(1)(a) to (d) of the Housing and Regeneration Act 2008; and

(b) in relation to Wales, means the Welsh Ministers so far as exercising functions in relation to anything transferred (or to be transferred) to them as mentioned in section 36(1)(a)(i) to (iii) of the New Towns Act 1981."

Local Government, Planning and Land Act 1980 (c 65)

25. The Local Government, Planning and Land Act 1980 is amended as follows.

26. In section 4(4) (power to direct bodies to publish information) omit paragraph (b).

27. In section 93 (public bodies to whom Part 10 applies) after subsection (1) insert—

"(1A) Sections 95 to 96A also apply to the Homes and Communities Agency so far as it is exercising functions in relation to anything transferred (or to be transferred) to it as mentioned in section 52(1)(a) to (d) of the Housing and Regeneration Act 2008 (and references to a body to which this Part of this Act applies in those sections are to be read accordingly)."

28. In section 99(4)(e) (directions to dispose of land: supplementary) omit "the Commission for the New Towns,".

29. In section 165A(2) (transfer by order of property etc of urban development corporations to the Secretary of State etc)—

(a) in paragraph (a) for the words from "177" to "Agency)" substitute "42 of the Housing and Regeneration Act 2008 (agency arrangements with urban development corporations)", and

(b) in paragraph (b) for "subsection (2)" substitute "subsections (5) and (6)".

30. In section 165B(2) (transfer by order of property etc of urban development corporations to statutory bodies)—

(a) in paragraph (a) for the words from "177" to "Agency)" substitute "42 of the Housing and Regeneration Act 2008 (agency arrangements with urban development corporations)", and

(b) in paragraph (b) for "subsection (2)" substitute "subsections (5) and (6)".

31. In Schedule 16 (bodies to whom Part 10 applies) omit paragraph 6.

32. …

Compulsory Purchase (Vesting Declarations) Act 1981 (c 66)

33.—(1) The Compulsory Purchase (Vesting Declarations) Act 1981 is amended as follows.

(2) In section 15 (application of Act to orders under section 161(1) of the Leasehold Reform, Housing and Urban Development Act 1993) omit the words from "or under subsection (1)" to "similar provision)".

(3) In Schedule 2 (modifications of Act in certain cases)—

(a) in paragraph 1 omit the words from "or under subsection (1)" to "contains similar provision)", and

(b) in paragraph 3 for "the housing action trust or the Urban Regeneration Agency (as the case may be)" substitute "or the housing action trust (as the case may be)".

Local Government (Miscellaneous Provisions) Act 1982 (c 30)

34.—(1) Paragraph 2 of Schedule 4 to the Local Government (Miscellaneous Provisions) Act 1982 (street trading) is amended as follows.

(2) In sub-paragraph (5)(b) for "Commission for the New Towns" substitute "new towns residuary body".

(3) After sub-paragraph (5) insert—

"(5A) In sub-paragraph (5)(b) above "new towns residuary body" means—

(a) in relation to England, the Homes and Communities Agency so far as exercising functions in relation to anything transferred (or to be transferred) to it as mentioned in section 52(1)(a) to (d) of the Housing and Regeneration Act 2008; and

(b) in relation to Wales, the Welsh Ministers so far as exercising functions in relation to anything transferred (or to be transferred) to them as mentioned in section 36(1)(a)(i) to (iii) of the New Towns Act 1981."

35. …

Landlord and Tenant Act 1985 (c 70)

36. In section 38 (minor definitions) of the Landlord and Tenant Act 1985, in the definition of "new town corporation", for paragraph (b) (and the word "or" immediately before it) substitute—

"(b) the Homes and Communities Agency so far as exercising functions in relation to anything transferred (or to be transferred) to it as mentioned in section 52(1)(a) to (d) of the Housing and Regeneration Act 2008, or

(c) the Welsh Ministers so far as exercising functions in relation to anything transferred (or to be transferred) to them as mentioned in section 36(1)(a)(i) to (iii) of the New Towns Act 1981;".

Landlord and Tenant Act 1987 (c 31)

37. The Landlord and Tenant Act 1987 is amended as follows.

38. In section 21(3)(a) (tenant's right to apply to tribunal for appointment of manager)—

(a) after "by" insert

"—

(i) ", and

(b) after "resident landlord," insert
"or
(ii) the Welsh Ministers in their new towns residuary capacity,".

39. In section 29(7)(a) (conditions for making acquisition orders)—

(a) after "by" insert
"—
(i) ", and

(b) after "resident landlord," insert
"or
(ii) the Welsh Ministers in their new towns residuary capacity,".

40. In section 58(1) (exempt landlords and resident landlords)—

(a) in paragraph (b) omit "the Commission for the New Towns or", and
(b) after paragraph (de) insert—
"(df) the Homes and Communities Agency;".

41. In section 60 (general interpretation) after subsection (1) insert—

"(1A) In this Act a reference to the Welsh Ministers in their new towns residuary capacity means the Welsh Ministers so far as exercising functions in relation to anything transferred (or to be transferred) to them as mentioned in section 36(1)(a)(i) to (iii) of the New Towns Act 1981."

Income and Corporation Taxes Act 1988 (c 1)

42. In section 376(4) of the Income and Corporation Taxes Act 1988 (qualifying borrowers and qualifying lenders) for paragraph (j) substitute—

"(j) the Homes and Communities Agency;".

Local Government Act 1988 (c 9)

43. In Schedule 2 to the Local Government Act 1988 (public supply or works contracts: public authorities) for "The Commission for the New Towns." substitute—

"The Homes and Communities Agency so far as exercising functions in relation to anything transferred (or to be transferred) to it as mentioned in section 52(1)(a) to (d) of the Housing and Regeneration Act 2008."

Housing Act 1988 (c 50)

44. The Housing Act 1988 is amended as follows.

45. In the italic heading before section 50 omit ": functions of Relevant Authority".

46. Omit sections 50 (housing association grants) and 51 (revenue deficit grants).

47.—(1) Section 52 (recovery etc of grants) is amended as follows.

(2) For "Relevant Authority", wherever it appears, substitute "appropriate authority".

(3) In subsections (1) and (5)(b) for "housing association which is a registered social landlord" substitute "relevant housing association".

(4) After subsection (9) insert—

"(9A) In this section and sections 53 and 54—

"the appropriate authority"—

(a) in relation to an English relevant housing association, means the Homes and Communities Agency, and
(b) in relation to a Welsh relevant housing association, means the Welsh Ministers,

"relevant housing association" means—

(a) a housing association which is a registered provider of social housing ("an English relevant housing association"), and
(b) a housing association which is a registered social landlord ("a Welsh relevant housing association").

(9B) In this section a reference to registration as a provider of social housing, so far as the context permits, is to be construed as including, in relation to times, circumstances and purposes before the commencement of section 111 of the Housing and Regeneration Act 2008, a reference to registration under—

(a) Part 1 of the Housing Act 1996,
(b) Part 1 of the 1985 Act, or
(c) any corresponding earlier enactment."

48.—(1) Section 53 (determinations under Part 2) is amended as follows.

(2) In subsection (2) for "Housing Corporation" substitute "Homes and Communities Agency".

(3) In subsection (3) for "Relevant Authority", in both places where it appears, substitute "appropriate authority".

(4) In subsection (4) for "any provision of sections 50 to" substitute "section".

49. In section 54(2)(a) (tax relief grants) for "a registered social landlord" substitute "a relevant housing association".

50. In section 59(1A) (interpretation of Part 2 etc) for "50" substitute "52".

Local Government and Housing Act 1989 (c 42)

51. In section 172(8) of the Local Government and Housing Act 1989 (transfers of new town housing stock) in the definition of "new town corporation" omit "the Commission for the New Towns or".

Town and Country Planning Act 1990 (c 8)

52.—(1) Section 8A of the Town and Country Planning Act 1990 (the Urban Regeneration Agency) is amended as follows.

(2) In the heading for "Urban Regeneration" substitute "Homes and Communities".

(3) In subsection (1)—

(a) for "section 170 of the Leasehold Reform, Housing and Urban Development Act 1993" substitute "section 13 of the Housing and Regeneration Act 2008",

(b) for "subsection (1) of section 171" substitute "section 14(2)", and

(c) for "Urban Regeneration" substitute "Homes and Communities".

(4) Omit subsection (2).

Planning (Listed Buildings and Conservation Areas) Act 1990 (c 9)

53. In Schedule 4 to the Planning (Listed Buildings and Conservation Areas) Act 1990 (further provisions as to exercise of functions by different authorities), in paragraph 2, for "and housing action areas" substitute ", housing action areas and areas for which the Homes and Communities Agency is the local planning authority".

Planning (Hazardous Substances) Act 1990 (c 10)

54. In section 3 of the Planning (Hazardous Substances) Act 1990 (hazardous substances authorities: special cases) for subsection (5A) substitute—

"(5A) The power to make a designation order under section 13 of the Housing and Regeneration Act 2008 which contains provision of the kind mentioned in section 14(3) of that Act does not extend to providing for the Homes and Communities Agency to be the hazardous substances authority (whether instead of, or concurrently with, a county council) in relation to land to which subsection (1) above applies.

(5B) Subject to this, section 1 and this section are subject to any provision made by such an order."

Water Industry Act 1991 (c 56)

55. The Water Industry Act 1991 is amended as follows.

56. In section 41(2)(d)(i) (power to require the provision of a water main) for "Commission for the New Towns" substitute "new towns residuary body".

57. In section 97(5) (performance of sewerage undertaker's functions by local authorities etc)—

(a) in the definition of "relevant area" for paragraph (b) substitute—

"(b) in relation to the English new towns residuary body, means any new town in England;

(ba) in relation to the Welsh new towns residuary body, means any new town in Wales;", and

(b) in the definition of "relevant authority" in paragraph (b) for "Commission for the New Towns" substitute "new towns residuary body".

58. In section 98 (power to require the provision of a public sewer etc)—

(a) in subsection (2)(d)(i) for "Commission for the New Towns" substitute "new towns residuary body", and

(b) in subsection (2A)(d)(i) for "Commission for the New Towns" substitute "new towns residuary body".

59. In section 219(1) (general interpretation) after the definition of "navigation authority" insert—

""new towns residuary body" means—

(a) in relation to a new town in England, the Homes and Communities Agency so far as exercising functions in relation to anything transferred (or to be transferred) to it as mentioned in section 52(1)(a) or (b) of the Housing and Regeneration Act 2008 (and references to the "English new towns residuary body" are to be read accordingly); and

(b) in relation to a new town in Wales, the Welsh Ministers so far as exercising functions in relation to anything transferred (or to be transferred) to them as mentioned in section 36(1)(a)(i) or (ii) of the New Towns Act 1981 (and references to the "Welsh new towns residuary body" are to be read accordingly);".

Water Resources Act 1991 (c 57)

60.—(1) Section 72 of the Water Resources Act 1991 (interpretation of Chapter 2 of Part 2) is amended as follows.

(2) In subsection (2)(a)(iii) for "Commission for the New Towns" substitute "new towns residuary body".

(3) After subsection (2) insert—

"(2A) In subsection (2)(a)(iii) "new towns residuary body" means—

(a) in relation to England, the Homes and Communities Agency so far as exercising functions in relation to anything transferred (or to be transferred) to it as mentioned in section 52(1)(a) to (d) of the Housing and Regeneration Act 2008; and

(b) in relation to Wales, the Welsh Ministers so far as exercising functions in relation to anything transferred (or to be transferred) to them as mentioned in section 36(1)(a)(i) to (iii) of the New Towns Act 1981."

Social Security Administration Act 1992 (c 5)

61. In section 191 (interpretation: general), in the definition of "new town corporation", for paragraph (a) (but not the "and" following it) substitute—

"(a) in relation to England—

(i) a development corporation established under the New Towns Act 1981; or

(ii) the Homes and Communities Agency so far as exercising functions in relation to anything transferred (or to be transferred) to it as mentioned in section 52(1)(a) to (d) of the Housing and Regeneration Act 2008;

(ab) in relation to Wales—

(i) a development corporation established under the New Towns Act 1981; and

(ii) the Welsh Ministers so far as exercising functions in relation to anything transferred (or to be transferred) to them as mentioned in section 36(1)(a)(i) to (iii) of that Act;".

Taxation of Chargeable Gains Act 1992 (c 12)

62. In section 219(1) of the Taxation of Chargeable Gains Act 1992 (disposals by Housing Corporation etc)—

(a) in paragraph (a) before "disposes" insert "or the Homes and Communities Agency",

(b) in paragraph (d) at the end insert "or the Homes and Communities Agency", and

(c) in the words after paragraph (d)—

(i) before ", relevant housing" insert ", the Homes and Communities Agency", and

(ii) before "or, as the case" insert ", the Homes and Communities Agency".

Leasehold Reform, Housing and Urban Development Act 1993 (c 28)

63.—(1) The Leasehold Reform, Housing and Urban Development Act 1993 is amended as follows.

(2) Omit—

(a) sections 158 to 173, 175, 177 and 183 to 185, and

(b) Schedules 17 to 20,

(provisions about the Urban Regeneration Agency).

(3) ...

Finance Act 1996 (c 8)

64.—(1) Section 43A of the Finance Act 1996 (landfill tax in relation to contaminated land) is amended as follows.

(2) In subsection (5) omit paragraph (e).

(3) In subsection (6) omit the definition of "English Partnerships".

Housing Act 1996 (c 52)

65.—(1) Section 28 of the Housing Act 1996 (grants under sections 50 to 54 of the Housing Act 1988) is amended as follows.

(2) Omit subsections (1), (2) and (6).

(3) In the heading for "ss 50 to 54" substitute "Part 2".

Regional Development Agencies Act 1998 (c 45)

66. The Regional Development Agencies Act 1998 is amended as follows.

67. Omit section 36 (transfer of property etc of Urban Regeneration Agency) and the italic heading before it.

68. Omit section 37 (powers in relation to the Urban Regeneration Agency).

69. In section 38(10) (corporation tax)—

(a) in the definition of "qualifying transfer" omit paragraph (b), and

(b) in the definition of "transfer scheme" for "any of sections 34 to 37" substitute "section 34 or 35".

70. In section 39(4)(b) (stamp duty) for "any of sections 34 to 37 and" substitute "section 34 or 35 or".

71. Omit Schedule 9 (the Urban Regeneration Agency: transfer schemes).

Greater London Authority Act 1999 (c 29)

72. The Greater London Authority Act 1999 is amended as follows.

73.—(1) Section 333A (the London housing strategy) is amended as follows.

(2) In subsection (3)—

(a) in paragraph (a) for "Housing Corporation for the purpose of making housing grant" substitute "Homes and Communities Agency", and

(b) in paragraph (b)—

(i) for "Housing Corporation", in the first place where it appears, substitute "Homes and Communities Agency",

(ii) for "making housing grant" substitute "giving housing financial assistance", and

(iii) omit the words from "(and see also" to the end of the paragraph.

(3) In subsection (4)—

(a) in paragraph (a)—

(i) for "grant", in both places where it appears, substitute "housing financial assistance",

(ii) for "made" substitute "given", and

(iii) for "payable" substitute "given", and

(b) in paragraph (b) for "grant" substitute "housing financial assistance".

(4) In subsection (8)(a) for "Housing Corporation" substitute "Homes and Communities Agency".

(5) In subsection (10)—

(a) for the definition of "housing grant" substitute—

""housing financial assistance" means financial assistance given under section 19 of the Housing and Regeneration Act 2008 in connection with the provision of housing accommodation;",

(b) after the definition of "local housing authority" insert—

""provide", in relation to houses or housing accommodation, includes—

(a) provide by way of acquisition, construction, conversion, improvement or repair; and

(b) provide indirectly;", and

(c) omit the words from "and the reference" to the end.

74. In section 333D (duty to have regard to the London housing strategy)—

(a) in the heading for "Housing Corporation" substitute "Homes and Communities Agency", and

(b) in subsection (1) for the words from "under" to "Corporation" substitute "relating to Greater London and conferred by or under Part 1 of the Housing and Regeneration Act 2008 (other than any function conferred by virtue of section 13 or 14 of that Act), the Homes and Communities Agency".

75.—(1) Section 408 (transfers of property, rights or liabilities) is amended as follows.

(2) In subsection (3) omit paragraphs (h) and (i).

(3) Omit subsection (6).

76. In section 409 (transfer schemes) omit subsection (5).

Freedom of Information Act 2000 (c 36)

77.—(1) Part 6 of Schedule 1 to the Freedom of Information Act 2000 (public authorities) is amended as follows.

(2) Insert at the appropriate place—

"The Homes and Communities Agency."

(3) Omit the entries relating to—

(a) the Commission for the New Towns, and
(b) the Urban Regeneration Agency.

Finance Act 2003 (c 14)

78. The Finance Act 2003 is amended as follows.

79. In section 71(4) (certain acquisitions by registered social landlord exempt from charge to stamp duty land tax) after paragraph (c) insert—

"(ca) under section 19 of the Housing and Regeneration Act 2008 (financial assistance by the Homes and Communities Agency),".

80.—(1) Schedule 9 (stamp duty land tax: right to buy, shared ownership leases etc) is amended as follows.

(2) In paragraph 1(3)—

(a) after "*and development corporations*" insert "*etc*", and
(b) for "Commission for the New Towns" substitute "Homes and Communities Agency".

(3) In paragraph 5(2) for paragraph (e) substitute—

"(e) the Homes and Communities Agency;".

Planning and Compulsory Purchase Act 2004 (c 5)

81. In section 37 of the Planning and Compulsory Purchase Act 2004 (interpretation of Part 2), after subsection (5), insert—

"(5A) Subsection (4) must also be construed subject to any designation order under section 13 of the Housing and Regeneration Act 2008 (power to make designation orders) providing that the Homes and Communities Agency is to be the local planning authority—

(a) for an area specified in the order, and
(b) for all purposes of this Part or any such purposes so specified.

(5B) Where such an order makes such provision, the Homes and Communities Agency is the local planning authority for the area and the purposes concerned in place of any authority who would otherwise be the local planning authority for that area and those purposes."

Finance Act 2004 (c 12)

82. In section 59(1)(f) of the Finance Act 2004 (contractors) for "Commission for the New Towns" substitute "Homes and Communities Agency".

Local Government and Public Involvement in Health Act 2007 (c 28)

83. In section 104(4) of the Local Government and Public Involvement in Health Act 2007 (partner authorities), after paragraph (e), insert—

"(ea) the Homes and Communities Agency;".

[2496]

NOTES

Commencement: 8 September 2008 (paras 1, 4(a), (b), 19(1), (2), 20(1), (2), 21(1), (2), 77(1), (2)); 1 December 2008 (paras 2, 3, 5–12, 14–18, 22–34, 36–43, 51–62, 63 (except in so far as relates to repeals of the Leasehold Reform, Housing and Urban Development Act 1993, s 158, Schs 17, 18), 64, 66–76, 78–83); 1 April 2009 (paras 4(c), (d), 13, 19(3), 20(3), 21(3), 63 (otherwise), 77(3); to be appointed (otherwise).

Para 32: amends the Highways Act 1980, s 219 at **[960]**.

Para 35: amends the Housing Act 1985, Sch 5 at **[1179]**.

Para 63: sub-para (3) amends the Leashold Reform, Housing and Urban Development Act 1993, s 188 at **[1467]**.

(*Schs 9, 10 outside the scope of this work.*)

SCHEDULE 11
POSSESSION ORDERS RELATING TO CERTAIN TENANCIES

Section 299

PART 1
AMENDMENTS TO THE HOUSING ACTS OF 1985, 1988 AND 1996

Housing Act 1985 (*c 68*)

1. The Housing Act 1985 is amended as follows.

2.—(1) Section 82 (security of tenure: date on which secure tenancy comes to an end as a result of a possession order etc) is amended as follows.

(2) In subsection (1) for "by obtaining an order" substitute "as".

(3) For subsections (1A) and (2) substitute—

"(1A) The tenancy may be brought to an end by the landlord—

(a) obtaining—

(i) an order of the court for the possession of the dwelling-house, and

(ii) the execution of the order,

(b) obtaining an order under subsection (3), or

(c) obtaining a demotion order under section 82A.

(2) In the case mentioned in subsection (1A)(a), the tenancy ends when the order is executed."

3.—(1) Section 85 (extended discretion of court in certain proceedings for possession) is amended as follows.

(2) In subsection (3)(a) omit the words from "or payments" to "profits),".

(3) For subsection (4) substitute—

"(4) The court may discharge or rescind the order for possession if it thinks it appropriate to do so having had regard to—

(a) any conditions imposed under subsection (3), and

(b) the conduct of the tenant in connection with those conditions."

(4) Omit subsections (5) and (5A).

4–9. …

Housing Act 1996 (*c 52*)

10. The Housing Act 1996 is amended as follows.

11.—(1) Section 127 (introductory tenancies: proceedings for possession) is amended as follows.

(2) In subsection (1) for the words from "an order" to the end substitute

"—

(a) an order of the court for the possession of the dwelling-house, and

(b) the execution of the order."

(3) After subsection (1) insert—

"(1A) In such a case, the tenancy ends when the order is executed."

(4) In subsection (2) for "such an order" substitute "an order of the kind mentioned in subsection (1)(a)".

(5) Omit subsection (3).

12.—(1) Section 130 (introductory tenancies: effect of beginning proceedings for possession) is amended as follows.

(2) In subsection (2)(a) for the words from "in pursuance of", where they first appear, to "of the court)" substitute "in accordance with section 127(1A)".

(3) In subsection (3)(b) for "127(2) and (3)" substitute "127(1A) and (2)".

13.—(1) Section 143D (demoted tenancies: proceedings for possession) is amended as follows.

(2) In subsection (1) for the words from "an order" to the end substitute

"—

(a) an order of the court for the possession of the dwelling-house, and

(b) the execution of the order."

(3) After subsection (1) insert—

"(1A) In such a case, the tenancy ends when the order is executed."

(4) Omit subsection (3).

Transitional provisions

14.—(1) Subject as follows, this Part of this Schedule does not apply to any possession order made before the commencement date.

(2) This Part of this Schedule does apply to a possession order made before the commencement date if the order applies to—

(a) a new tenancy by virtue of paragraph 20, or

(b) a tenancy which has not ended pursuant to the order before that date.

(3) Paragraphs 3(3) and 8(3) apply to any possession order regardless of when it was made.

(4) In determining for the purposes of sub-paragraph (2) whether a tenancy has ended, any ending which was temporary because the tenancy was restored in consequence of a court order is to be ignored.

(5) In this paragraph "the commencement date" means the day on which section 299 comes into force for purposes other than the purposes of the Secretary of State or the Welsh Ministers making orders under Part 2 of this Schedule.

[2497]

NOTES

Commencement: 20 May 2009 (except for paras 3(3), 8(3), 14(3)); to be appointed (for paras 3(3), 8(3), 14(3)).

Para 4: amends the Housing Act 1985, Sch 3 at **[1178]**.
Para 6: amends the Housing Act 1988, s 5 at **[1320]**.
Para 7: amends the Housing Act 1988, s 7 at **[1323]**.
Para 8: amends the Housing Act 1988, s 9 at **[1326]**.
Para 9: amends the Housing Act 1988, s 7 at **[1344]**.

PART 2
REPLACEMENT OF CERTAIN TERMINATED TENANCIES

Circumstances in which replacement tenancies arise

15. In this Part of this Schedule "an original tenancy" means any secure tenancy, assured tenancy, introductory tenancy or demoted tenancy—

(a) in respect of which a possession order was made before the commencement date, and

(b) which ended before that date pursuant to the order but not on the execution of the order.

16.—(1) A new tenancy of the dwelling-house which was let under the original tenancy is treated as arising on the commencement date between the ex-landlord and the ex-tenant if—

(a) on that date—

(i) the home condition is met, and

(ii) the ex-landlord is entitled to let the dwelling-house, and

(b) the ex-landlord and the ex-tenant have not entered into another tenancy after the date on which the original tenancy ended but before the commencement date.

(2) The home condition is that the dwelling-house which was let under the original tenancy—

(a) is, on the commencement date, the only or principal home of the ex-tenant, and

(b) has been the only or principal home of the ex-tenant throughout the termination period.

(3) In this Part of this Schedule "the termination period" means the period—

(a) beginning with the end of the original tenancy, and

(b) ending with the commencement date.

(4) For the purposes of sub-paragraph (2)(a) the dwelling-house is the only or principal home of the ex-tenant on the commencement date even though the ex-tenant is then absent from the dwelling-house as a result of having been evicted in pursuance of a warrant if the warrant is subsequently set aside but the possession order under which it was granted remains in force.

(5) In that case, the new tenancy is treated as arising on the first day (if any) on which the ex-tenant resumes occupation of the dwelling-house as that person's only or principal home.

(6) For the purposes of sub-paragraph (2)(b) any period of time within the termination period is to be ignored if—

(a) it is a period in which the ex-tenant was absent from the dwelling-house as a result of having been evicted in pursuance of a warrant which was then set aside although the possession order under which it was granted remained in force, and

(b) the ex-tenant subsequently resumes occupation of the dwelling-house as the ex-tenant's only or principal home.

(7) The appropriate national authority may by order provide for particular cases or descriptions of case, or particular circumstances, where the home condition is met where it would not otherwise be met.

Nature of replacement tenancies

17. The new tenancy is to be—
 (a) a secure tenancy if—
  (i) the original tenancy was a secure tenancy, or
  (ii) the original tenancy was an introductory tenancy but no election by the ex-landlord under section 124 of the Housing Act 1996 (c 52) is in force on the day on which the new tenancy arises,
 (b) an assured shorthold tenancy if the original tenancy was an assured shorthold tenancy,
 (c) an assured tenancy which is not an assured shorthold tenancy if the original tenancy was a tenancy of that kind,
 (d) an introductory tenancy if the original tenancy was an introductory tenancy and an election by the ex-landlord under section 124 of the Housing Act 1996 is in force on the day on which the new tenancy arises,
 (e) a demoted tenancy to which section 20B of the Housing Act 1988 (c 50) applies if the original tenancy was a demoted tenancy of that kind, and
 (f) a demoted tenancy to which section 143A of the Housing Act 1996 applies if the original tenancy was a demoted tenancy of that kind.

18.—(1) The new tenancy is, subject as follows, to have effect on the same terms and conditions as those applicable to the original tenancy immediately before it ended.

(2) The terms and conditions of the new tenancy are to be treated as modified so as to reflect, so far as applicable, any changes made during the termination period to the level of payments for the ex-tenant's occupation of the dwelling-house or to the other terms and conditions of the occupation.

(3) The terms and conditions of the new tenancy are to be treated as modified so that any outstanding liabilities owed by the ex-tenant to the ex-landlord in respect of payments for the ex-tenant's occupation of the dwelling-house during the termination period are liabilities in respect of rent under the new tenancy.

(4) The appropriate national authority may by order provide for other modifications of the terms and conditions of the new tenancy.

(5) Nothing in sub-paragraphs (2) to (4) is to be read as permitting modifications of the new tenancy which would not have been possible if the original tenancy had remained a tenancy throughout the termination period.

(6) The terms and conditions of a new secure tenancy which arises by virtue of paragraph 17(a)(ii) are to be treated as modified so far as necessary to reflect the fact that the new tenancy is a secure tenancy and not an introductory tenancy.

19.—(1) Any provision which is made by or under an enactment and relates to a secure tenancy, assured tenancy, introductory tenancy or demoted tenancy applies, subject as follows, to a new tenancy of a corresponding kind.

(2) Any such provision which relates to an introductory tenancy applies to a new tenancy which is an introductory tenancy as if the trial period mentioned in section 125(2) of the Housing Act 1996 (c 52) were the period of one year beginning with the day on which the new tenancy arises.

(3) Any such provision which relates to a demoted tenancy applies to a new tenancy which is a demoted tenancy as if the demotion period mentioned in section 20B(2) of the Housing Act 1988 (c 50) or section 143B(1) of the Housing Act 1996 were the period of one year beginning with the day on which the new tenancy arises.

(4) The appropriate national authority may by order modify any provision made by or under an enactment in its application to a new tenancy.

Status of possession order and other court orders

20.—(1) The possession order in pursuance of which the original tenancy ended is to be treated, so far as practicable, as if it applies to the new tenancy.

(2) Any court orders made before the commencement date which—
 (a) are in force on that date,
 (b) relate to the occupation of the dwelling-house, and
 (c) were made in contemplation of, in consequence of or otherwise in connection with the possession order,

are to be treated, so far as practicable, as if they apply to the new tenancy.

Continuity of tenancies

21.—(1) The new tenancy and the original tenancy are to be treated for the relevant purposes as—
 (a) the same tenancy, and
 (b) a tenancy which continued uninterrupted throughout the termination period.

(2) The relevant purposes are—
 (a) determining whether the ex-tenant is a successor in relation to the new tenancy,

(b) calculating on or after the commencement date the period qualifying, or the aggregate of such periods, under Schedule 4 to the Housing Act 1985 (c 68) (qualifying period for right to buy and discount),

(c) determining on or after the commencement date whether the condition set out in paragraph (b) of Ground 8 of Schedule 2 to that Act is met, and

(d) any other purposes specified by the appropriate national authority by order.

(3) In proceedings on a relevant claim the court concerned may order that the new tenancy and the original tenancy are to be treated for the purposes of the claim as—

(a) the same tenancy, and

(b) a tenancy which continued uninterrupted throughout the termination period.

(4) The following are relevant claims—

(a) a claim by the ex-tenant or the ex-landlord against the other for breach of a term or condition of the original tenancy—

(i) in respect of which proceedings are brought on or after the commencement date, or

(ii) in respect of which proceedings were brought, but were not finally determined, before that date,

(b) a claim by the ex-tenant against the ex-landlord for breach of statutory duty in respect of which proceedings are or were brought as mentioned in paragraph (a)(i) or (ii), and

(c) any other claim of a description specified by the appropriate national authority by order.

(5) For the purposes of sub-paragraph (4)(a) proceedings must be treated as finally determined if—

(a) they are withdrawn,

(b) any appeal is abandoned, or

(c) the time for appealing has expired without an appeal being brought.

Compliance with consultation requirements

22.—(1) The fact that—

(a) the views of the ex-tenant during the termination period were not sought or taken into account when they should have been sought or taken into account, or

(b) the views of the ex-tenant during that period were sought or taken into account when they should not have been sought or taken into account,

is not to be taken to mean that the consultation requirements were not complied with.

(2) The consultation requirements are—

(a) the requirements under—

(i) section 105(1) of the Housing Act 1985 (c 68),

(ii) paragraphs 3 and 4 of Schedule 3A to that Act,

(iii) regulations made under section 27AB of that Act which relate to arranging for ballots or polls with respect to a proposal to enter into a management agreement, and

(iv) section 137(2) of the Housing Act 1996 (c 52), and

(b) any other requirements specified by the appropriate national authority by order.

Joint tenancies

23.—(1) In the application of this Part of this Schedule in relation to an original tenancy which was a joint tenancy, a reference to the dwelling-house being the only or principal home of the ex-tenant is to be treated as a reference to the dwelling-house being the only or principal home of at least one of the ex-tenants of the joint tenancy.

(2) The appropriate national authority may by order provide for this Part of this Schedule to apply in relation to an original tenancy which was a joint tenancy subject to such additional modifications as may be specified in the order.

Successor landlords

24.—(1) The appropriate national authority may by order provide for this Part of this Schedule to apply, subject to such modifications as may be specified in the order, to successor landlord cases.

(2) For the purposes of sub-paragraph (1) a successor landlord case is a case, in relation to an original tenancy, where the interest of the ex-landlord in the dwelling-house—

(a) has been transferred to another person after the end of the original tenancy and before the commencement date, and

(b) on the commencement date, belongs to the person to whom it has been transferred or a subsequent transferee.

Supplementary

25. In determining for the purposes of this Part of this Schedule whether a tenancy has ended, any ending which was temporary because the tenancy was restored in consequence of a court order is to be ignored.

26.—(1) In this Part of this Schedule—

"appropriate national authority" means—

(a) in relation to a dwelling-house in England, the Secretary of State, and
(b) in relation to a dwelling-house in Wales, the Welsh Ministers,

"assured shorthold tenancy" and "assured tenancy" have the same meanings as in Part 1 of the Housing Act 1988 (c 50) but do not include a demoted tenancy to which section 20B of that Act applies,

"the commencement date" means the day on which section 299 comes into force for purposes other than the purposes of the Secretary of State or the Welsh Ministers making orders under this Part of this Schedule,

"demoted tenancy" means a tenancy to which section 20B of the Act of 1988 or section 143A of the Housing Act 1996 (c 52) applies,

"dwelling-house"—

(a) in relation to an assured tenancy, or a tenancy to which section 20B of the Act of 1988 applies, has the same meaning as in Part 1 of that Act,
(b) in relation to a tenancy to which section 143A of the Act of 1996 applies, has the same meaning as in Chapter 1A of Part 5 of that Act,
(c) in relation to an introductory tenancy, has the meaning given by section 139 of the Act of 1996, and
(d) in relation to a secure tenancy, has the meaning given by section 112 of the Housing Act 1985 (c 68),

"ex-landlord" means the person who was the landlord under an original tenancy,

"ex-tenant" means the person who was the tenant under an original tenancy,

"introductory tenancy" has the same meaning as in Chapter 1 of Part 5 of the Act of 1996,

"modification" includes omission,

"new tenancy" means a tenancy which is treated as arising by virtue of paragraph 16,

"original tenancy" has the meaning given by paragraph 15,

"possession order", in relation to a tenancy, means a court order for the possession of the dwelling-house,

"secure tenancy" has the same meaning as in Part 4 of the Act of 1985,

"successor"—

(a) in relation to a new tenancy which is an assured tenancy or which is a demoted tenancy to which section 20B of the Act of 1988 applies, has the same meaning as in section 17 of that Act,
(b) in relation to a new tenancy which is a demoted tenancy to which section 143A of the Act of 1996 applies, has the meaning given by section 143J of that Act,
(c) in relation to a new tenancy which is an introductory tenancy, has the same meaning as in section 132 of the Act of 1996, and
(d) in relation to a new tenancy which is a secure tenancy, has the same meaning as in section 88 of the Act of 1985.

"termination period" has the meaning given by paragraph 16(3).

(2) For the purposes of the definition of "appropriate national authority" in sub-paragraph (1) a dwelling-house which is partly in England and partly in Wales is to be treated—

(a) as being in England if it is treated as situated in the area of a billing authority in England by virtue of regulations under section 1(3) of the Local Government Finance Act 1992 (c 14) (council tax in respect of dwellings), and
(b) as being in Wales if it is treated as situated in the area of a billing authority in Wales by virtue of regulations under that section.

[2498]

NOTES

Commencement: 1 December 2008 (for the purpose of enabling the appropriate national authority to make orders under this Part of this Schedule); 20 May 2009 (otherwise).

SCHEDULE 12

SERVICE CHARGES: PROVISION OF INFORMATION AND DESIGNATED ACCOUNTS

Section 303

Landlord and Tenant Act 1985 (c 70)

1. The Landlord and Tenant Act 1985 is amended as follows.

2. For section 21 (as substituted by section 152 of the Commonhold and Leasehold Reform Act 2002 (c 15)) (regular statements of account) substitute—

"21 Service charge information

(1) The appropriate national authority may make regulations about the provision, by landlords of dwellings to each tenant by whom service charges are payable, of information about service charges.

(2) The regulations must, subject to any exceptions provided for in the regulations, require the landlord to provide information about—

(a) the service charges of the tenant,
(b) any associated service charges, and
(c) relevant costs relating to service charges falling within paragraph (a) or (b).

(3) The regulations must, subject to any exceptions provided for in the regulations, require the landlord to provide the tenant with a report by a qualified person on information which the landlord is required to provide by virtue of this section.

(4) The regulations may make provision about—

(a) information to be provided by virtue of subsection (2),
(b) other information to be provided (whether in pursuance of a requirement or otherwise),
(c) reports of the kind mentioned in subsection (3),
(d) the period or periods in relation to which information or reports are to be provided,
(e) the times at or by which information or reports are to be provided,
(f) the form and manner in which information or reports are to be provided (including in particular whether information is to be contained in a statement of account),
(g) the descriptions of persons who are to be qualified persons for the purposes of subsection (3).

(5) Subsections (2) to (4) do not limit the scope of the power conferred by subsection (1).

(6) Regulations under this section may—

(a) make different provision for different cases or descriptions of case or for different purposes,
(b) contain such supplementary, incidental, consequential, transitional, transitory or saving provision as the appropriate national authority considers appropriate.

(7) Regulations under this section are to be made by statutory instrument which, subject to subsections (8) and (9)—

(a) in the case of regulations made by the Secretary of State, is to be subject to annulment in pursuance of a resolution of either House of Parliament, and
(b) in the case of regulations made by the Welsh Ministers, is to be subject to annulment in pursuance of a resolution of the National Assembly for Wales.

(8) The Secretary of State may not make a statutory instrument containing the first regulations made by the Secretary of State under this section unless a draft of the instrument has been laid before, and approved by a resolution of, each House of Parliament.

(9) The Welsh Ministers may not make a statutory instrument containing the first regulations made by the Welsh Ministers under this section unless a draft of the instrument has been laid before, and approved by a resolution of, the National Assembly for Wales.

(10) In this section—

"the appropriate national authority"—

(a) in relation to England, means the Secretary of State, and
(b) in relation to Wales, means the Welsh Ministers,

"associated service charges", in relation to a tenant by whom a contribution to relevant costs is payable as a service charge, means service charges of other tenants so far as relating to the same costs."

3.—(1) Section 21A (withholding of service charges) is amended as follows.

(2) For subsection (1) substitute—

"(1) A tenant may withhold payment of a service charge if—

(a) the landlord has not provided him with information or a report—
(i) at the time at which, or
(ii) (as the case may be) by the time by which,
he is required to provide it by virtue of section 21, or
(b) the form or content of information or a report which the landlord has provided him with by virtue of that section (at any time) does not conform exactly or substantially with the requirements prescribed by regulations under that section."

(3) In subsection (2)—

(a) in paragraph (a) for "accounting period to which the document" substitute "period to which the information or report", and
(b) for paragraph (b) substitute—
"(b) amounts standing to the tenant's credit in relation to the service charges at the beginning of that period."

(4) In subsection (3)—

(a) in paragraph (a) for "document concerned has been supplied" substitute "information or report concerned has been provided", and

(b) for paragraph (b) substitute—

"(b) in a case within paragraph (b) of that subsection, after information or a report conforming exactly or substantially with requirements prescribed by regulations under section 21 has been provided to the tenant by the landlord by way of replacement of that previously provided."

4.—(1) Section 22 (as substituted by section 154 of the Commonhold and Leasehold Reform Act 2002 (c 15)) (inspection etc of documents) is amended as follows.

(2) In subsection (1)(a) for the words from "the matters" to "under" substitute "information required to be provided to him by virtue of".

(3) In subsection (3) for "supplied with the statement of account under" substitute "provided with the information concerned by virtue of".

(4) In subsection (4)—

(a) for "statement of account", wherever it appears, substitute "information",

(b) for "supplied", wherever it appears, substitute "provided", and

(c) in paragraph (b) for "21(4)" substitute "21".

5. In section 23(1) (as substituted by paragraph 1 of Schedule 10 to the Commonhold and Leasehold Reform Act 2002 (c 15) (information held by superior landlord))—

(a) for "a statement of account which the landlord is required to supply under" substitute "information which the landlord is required to provide by virtue of", and

(b) after "of the relevant information" insert "which relates to those matters".

6. In section 23A(4) (effect of change of landlord)—

(a) in paragraph (a) after "23" insert "and any regulations under section 21", and

(b) after paragraph (b) insert

"and

(c) any regulations under section 21 apply subject to any modifications contained in the regulations."

7. In section 26(1) (exception: tenants of certain public authorities) for "statements of account" substitute "service charge information, reports on such information".

8. In section 27 (exception: rent registered and not entered as variable) for "statements of account" substitute "service charge information, reports on such information".

9. Omit section 28 (meaning of "qualified accountant").

10. In section 39 (index of defined expressions) omit the entry in the Table for "qualified accountant".

Landlord and Tenant Act 1987 (c 31)

11. The Landlord and Tenant Act 1987 is amended as follows.

12.—(1) Section 42A (service charge contributions to be held in designated account) is amended as follows.

(2) In subsection (2)—

(a) for paragraph (b) substitute—

"(b) any other sums held in the account are sums standing to the credit of one or more other trust funds,", and

(b) for "Secretary of State" substitute "appropriate national authority".

(3) After subsection (2) insert—

"(2A) The appropriate national authority may by regulations ensure that a payee who holds more than one trust fund in the same designated account cannot move any of those funds to another designated account unless conditions specified in the regulations are met."

(4) In subsection (3)(a)—

(a) after "subsection (1) is" insert ", or regulations under subsection (2A) are,", and

(b) for "them" substitute "such documents".

(5) In subsections (5), (6), (7) and (8) for "this section" substitute "subsection (3)".

(6) After subsection (9) insert—

"(9A) Regulations under subsection (2A) may include provision about—

(a) the circumstances in which a contributing tenant who has reasonable grounds for believing that the payee has not complied with a duty imposed on him by the regulations may withhold payment of a service charge,

(b) the period for which payment may be so withheld,

(c) the amount of service charge that may be so withheld;

and the regulations may provide that any provisions of the contributing tenant's tenancy relating to non-payment or late payment of service charge do not have effect in relation to the period for which the payment is so withheld."

(7) In subsection (10)—

(a) after "this section" insert "or in regulations under subsection (2A)", and
(b) for "Secretary of State" substitute "appropriate national authority".

(8) After subsection (10) insert—

"(10A) Regulations under this section may—
(a) make different provision for different cases, including different provision for different areas,
(b) contain such supplementary, incidental, consequential, transitional, transitory or saving provision as the appropriate national authority considers appropriate.

(10B) Regulations under this section are to be made by statutory instrument which—
(a) in the case of regulations made by the Secretary of State, is to be subject to annulment in pursuance of a resolution of either House of Parliament, and
(b) in the case of regulations made by the Welsh Ministers, is to be subject to annulment in pursuance of a resolution of the National Assembly for Wales."

(9) In subsection (11)—

(a) after "section—" insert—
""the appropriate national authority"—
(a) in relation to England, means the Secretary of State, and
(b) in relation to Wales, means the Welsh Ministers,", and
(b) in the definition of "relevant financial institution" for "Secretary of State" substitute "appropriate national authority".

13.—(1) Section 53 (regulations and orders) is amended as follows.

(2) In subsection (2)(b) omit "or 42A".

(3) After subsection (2) insert—

"(3) This section does not apply to any power to make regulations under section 42A."

Leasehold Reform, Housing and Urban Development Act 1993 (c 28)

14. The Leasehold Reform, Housing and Urban Development Act 1993 is amended as follows.

15.—(1) Section 78 (management audits) is amended as follows.

(2) In subsection (4) for paragraphs (a) and (b), and the "and" following paragraph (b), substitute—

"(a) he is—
(i) a member of a body which is a recognised supervisory body for the purposes of Part 42 of the Companies Act 2006;
(ii) a qualified surveyor; or
(iii) where the landlord is a relevant landlord, a member of the Chartered Institute of Public Finance and Accountancy;
(b) he is not any of the following—
(i) an officer, employee or partner of the landlord or, where the landlord is a company, of an associated company;
(ii) a person who is a partner or employee of any such officer or employee;
(iii) an agent of the landlord who is a managing agent for any premises to which the audit in question relates; or
(iv) an employee or partner of any such agent; and".

(3) After subsection (5) insert—

"(5A) For the purposes of subsection (4)(b)(i) above a company is associated with a landlord company if it is the landlord's holding company, a subsidiary of the landlord or another subsidiary of the landlord's holding company.

(5B) Subsection (4)(b)(i) does not apply where the landlord is a relevant landlord.

(5C) For the purposes of subsection (4)(b)(iii) above a person is a managing agent for any premises if he has been appointed to discharge any of the landlord's obligations relating to the management by the landlord of the premises."

(4) After subsection (6) insert—

"(7) In this section—

"holding company" and "subsidiary" have the meanings given by section 1159 of the Companies Act 2006;
"relevant landlord" means—

(a) a local authority (within the meaning of the Landlord and Tenant Act 1985);
(b) a National Park authority; or
(c) a new town corporation (within the meaning of the Act of 1985)."

16. In section 79(2)(a) (rights exercisable in connection with management audits)—

(a) for the words from "the matters" to "supplied" substitute "information required to be provided", and
(b) for "under" substitute "by virtue of".

[2499]

NOTES

Commencement: 1 December 2008 (paras 1–10, for the purpose of enabling the Secretary of State to make regulations under the Landlord and Tenant Act 1985, s 21; paras 11–13, for the purpose of enabling the Secretary of State to make regulations under the Landlord and Tenant Act 1987, s 42A); to be appointed (otherwise).

SCHEDULE 13
DEMOLITION NOTICES

Section 305

Final demolition notices

1–5. …

Initial demolition notices

6. Schedule 5A to the Housing Act 1985 (c 68) (initial demolition notices) is amended as follows.

7. In paragraph 1(4)(b) (initial demolition notices: maximum specified period to carry out demolition) for "five" substitute "seven".

8. In paragraph 2(1) (period of validity of initial demolition notices) for "paragraph 3" substitute "paragraphs 3 and 3A".

9. In paragraph 3(1) (revocation of initial demolition notices: application of paragraph 15(4) to (7) of Schedule 5 to that Act) for "(7)" substitute "(7A)".

10. After paragraph 3 insert—

"Transfer of initial demolition notices

3A.—(1) This paragraph applies if—
(a) an initial demolition notice is in force in respect of a dwelling-house, and
(b) the landlord transfers his interest as landlord to another person.

(2) The initial demolition notice ("the original notice") continues in force but this is subject to—
(a) paragraphs 2 and 3, and
(b) the following provisions of this paragraph.

(3) Sub-paragraph (4) applies if the transferee—
(a) intends to demolish the dwelling-house, but
(b) has not—
(i) served a continuation notice, and
(ii) complied with the conditions in sub-paragraphs (8) and (10),
within the period of 2 months beginning with the date of transfer.

(4) The transferee must proceed under paragraph 15(4) of Schedule 5 as applied by paragraph 3(1) above as if the transferee has decided not to demolish the dwelling-house (and paragraph 15(5) to (7) of that Schedule as so applied applies on the same basis).

(5) A continuation notice is a notice—
(a) stating that the transferee—
(i) has acquired the interest concerned, and
(ii) intends to demolish the dwelling-house or (as the case may be) the building containing it ("the relevant premises"),
(b) setting out the reasons why the transferee intends to demolish the relevant premises,
(c) stating that the original notice is to continue in force, and
(d) explaining the continued effect of the original notice.

(6) A continuation notice may not vary the period specified in the original notice in accordance with paragraph 1(1)(c).

(7) Sub-paragraph (8) applies if—
(a) the dwelling-house is contained in a building which contains one or more other dwelling-houses, and
(b) the transferee intends to demolish the whole of the building.

(8) The transferee must serve a continuation notice on the occupier of each of the dwelling-houses contained in the building (whether addressed to him by name or just as "the occupier").

(9) An accidental omission to serve a continuation notice on one or more occupiers does not prevent the condition in sub-paragraph (8) from being satisfied.

(10) Paragraph 13(7) of Schedule 5 applies in relation to the transferee's intention to demolish so as to impose a condition on the transferee for a notice to appear within the period of 2 months beginning with the date of transfer; and paragraph 2(3) above applies for this purpose.

(11) Sub-paragraphs (7) to (10) above apply instead of paragraph 2(2) and (3) in relation to an initial demolition notice so far as continued in force under this paragraph."

11.—(1) Paragraph 4 (restrictions on service of further notices) is amended as follows.

(2) In sub-paragraph (2) (further initial demolition notices)—

(a) after "dwelling-house" insert ", by the landlord who served the relevant notice or any landlord who served a continuation notice in respect of the relevant notice,", and

(b) in paragraph (a) for "it" substitute "the further notice".

(3) In sub-paragraph (3) (final demolition notices)—

(a) after "dwelling-house" insert ", by the landlord who served the relevant notice or any landlord who served a continuation notice in respect of the relevant notice,", and

(b) in paragraph (a) for "it" substitute "the final demolition notice".

12. In paragraph 5 (notices under Schedule 5A) for "or 15" substitute ", 15 or 15A".

13. In paragraph 6(1) (interpretation) after "Schedule" insert "(other than paragraph 3A)".

Transitional provision

14. This Schedule does not apply to notices served before the coming into force of the Schedule.
[2499A]

NOTES

Commencement: 22 September 2008.
Paras 1–5: amend the Housing Act 1985, Sch 5 at **[1179]**.

SCHEDULE 14
DISPOSALS OF DWELLING-HOUSES BY LOCAL AUTHORITIES

Section 311

Housing Act 1985 (c 68)

1.—(1) The Housing Act 1985 is amended as follows.

(2) In section 34 (consents in relation to disposals of land held for housing purposes)—

(a) in subsection (1) for "Secretary of State's" substitute "appropriate national body's",

(b) in subsection (4A)—

(i) for "Secretary of State" substitute "appropriate national body",

(ii) after "disposal;" at the end of paragraph (c), insert—

"(ca) in the case of a proposed large scale disposal, the appropriate national body's estimate of the exchequer costs of the large scale disposal;", and

(iii) in paragraph (d) for "he" substitute "the appropriate national body", and

(c) after subsection (4A) insert—

"(4AA) The estimate mentioned in subsection (4A)(ca) is to be based on such assumptions (including as to the period during which housing subsidies may be payable) as the appropriate national body may determine, regardless of whether those assumptions are, or are likely to be, borne out by events.

(4AB) In this section—

"appropriate national body"—

(a) in relation to England, means the Secretary of State; and

(b) in relation to Wales, means the Welsh Ministers;

"dwelling-house" has the same meaning as in Part 5 of this Act except that it does not include a hostel or any part of a hostel;

"the exchequer costs", in relation to a large scale disposal, means any increase which is or may be attributable to the disposal in the aggregate of any housing subsidies;

"housing subsidies" means any subsidies payable under—

(a) section 140A of the Social Security Administration Act 1992 (subsidy); or

(b) section 79 of the Local Government and Housing Act 1989 (Housing Revenue Account subsidy);

"large scale disposal" means a disposal of one or more dwelling-houses by a local authority to a person where—

(a) the number of dwelling-houses included in the disposal; and

PART I STATUTES

(b) the number of dwelling-houses which, in the relevant period, have previously been disposed of by the authority to that person, or that person and any of the person's associates taken together,

exceeds 499 or, if the appropriate national body by order so provides, such other number as may be specified in the order;

"long lease" means a lease for a term of years certain exceeding 21 years other than a lease which is terminable before the end of that term by notice given by or to the landlord;

"the relevant period", in relation to a large scale disposal means—

(a) the period of 5 years ending with the date of the disposal; or

(b) if the appropriate national body by order so provides, such other period ending with that date as may be specified in the order;

"subsidiary" has the same meaning as in section 61 of the Housing Act 1996 but as if references in subsection (2) of that section and section 60 of that Act to registered social landlords and landlords were references to housing associations (within the meaning of the Housing Associations Act 1985).

(4AC) For the purposes of this section—

(a) a disposal of any dwelling-house is to be disregarded if at the time of the disposal the local authority's interest in the dwelling-house is or was subject to a long lease;

(b) two persons are associates of each other if—

(i) one of them is a subsidiary of the other;

(ii) they are both subsidiaries of some other person; or

(iii) there exists between them such relationship or other connection as may be specified in a determination made by the appropriate national body; and

(c) a description of an authority may be framed by reference to any circumstances whatever.

(4AD) An order made by the appropriate national body under this section—

(a) is to be made by statutory instrument which—

(i) in the case of an order made by the Secretary of State, is subject to annulment in pursuance of a resolution of either House of Parliament; and

(ii) in the case of an order made by the Welsh Ministers, is subject to annulment in pursuance of a resolution of the National Assembly for Wales;

(b) may make different provision for different cases or descriptions of case, or for different authorities or descriptions of authority; and

(c) may contain such transitional and supplementary provisions as appear to the appropriate national body to be necessary or expedient.

(4AE) A determination under this section—

(a) may make different provision for different cases or descriptions of case, or for different authorities or descriptions of authority; and

(b) may be varied or revoked by a subsequent determination."

(3) In section 43 (consent required for certain disposals not within section 32)—

(a) in subsection (1) for "Secretary of State" substitute "appropriate national body",

(b) in subsection (4A)—

(i) for "Secretary of State" substitute "appropriate national body",

(ii) after "disposal;" at the end of paragraph (c), insert—

"(ca) in the case of a proposed disposal which is part of a proposed large scale disposal, the appropriate national body's estimate of the exchequer costs of the large scale disposal;", and

(iii) in paragraph (d) for "he" substitute "the appropriate national body", and

(c) after subsection (4A) insert—

"(4AA) The estimate mentioned in subsection (4A)(ca) is to be based on such assumptions (including as to the period during which housing subsidies may be payable) as the appropriate national body may determine, regardless of whether those assumptions are, or are likely to be, borne out by events.

(4AB) Subsections (4AB) to (4AE) of section 34 apply for the purposes of this section as they apply for the purposes of that section.", and

(d) in subsection (5A) after "this section" insert "(other than in subsection (4A)(ca) and in subsections (4AB) to (4AE) of section 34 as applied for the purposes of this section)".

Housing Act 1988 (c 50)

2. In section 133(3) of the Housing Act 1988 (consent required for certain subsequent disposals)—

(a) in paragraph (a) for "and (3) to (4A)" substitute ", (3), (4) and (4A)(a) to (c) and (d)",

(b) in paragraph (b) for "and (3) to (4A)" substitute ", (3), (4) and (4A)(a) to (c) and (d)", and

(c) in paragraph (c) for "(4A)" substitute "(4A)(a) to (c) and (d)".

Leasehold Reform, Housing and Urban Development Act 1993 (*c 28*)

3.—(1) The Leasehold Reform, Housing and Urban Development Act 1993 is amended as follows.

(2) Omit section 135 (programmes for disposals of dwelling-houses by local authorities).

(3) In section 136 (levy on disposals) for subsection (14) substitute—

"(14) In this section—

"the 1989 Act" means the Local Government and Housing Act 1989;

"dwelling-house" has the same meaning as in Part 5 of the 1985 Act except that it does not include a hostel (as defined in section 622 of that Act) or any part of a hostel;

"local authority" has the meaning given by section 4 of that Act;

"long lease" means a lease for a term of years certain exceeding 21 years other than a lease which is terminable before the end of that term by notice given by or to the landlord;

"subsidiary" has the same meaning as in section 61 of the Housing Act 1996 but as if references in subsection (2) of that section and section 60 of that Act to registered social landlords and landlords were references to housing associations (within the meaning of the Housing Associations Act 1985).

(15) For the purposes of this section—

(a) a disposal of any dwelling-house is to be disregarded if at the time of the disposal the local authority's interest in the dwelling-house is or was subject to a long lease;

(b) two persons are associates of each other if—

(i) one of them is a subsidiary of the other;

(ii) they are both subsidiaries of some other person; or

(iii) there exists between them such relationship or other connection as may be specified in a determination made by the Secretary of State; and

(c) a description of authority may be framed by reference to any circumstances whatever."

(4) Omit section 137(1) to (3) (disposals: transitional provisions in relation to section 135).

(5) The reference to the Secretary of State in subsection (15) of section 136 of the Act of 1993, as inserted by sub-paragraph (3) above, is to be read in the same way as other references to the Secretary of State in that section of that Act.

Housing Act 1996 (*c 52*)

4.—(1) The Housing Act 1996 is amended as follows.

(2) In section 51(2)(b) (schemes for investigation of complaints) for "a qualifying disposal" substitute

"—

(i) a large scale disposal, within the meaning of section 34 of the Housing Act 1985, for which consent was required under section 32 or 43 of that Act; or

(ii) a qualifying disposal that was made".

(3) In paragraph 5(1)(b) of Part 2 of Schedule 1 (constitution, change of rules, amalgamation and dissolution: restriction on power of removal in case of registered charity) for "a qualifying disposal" substitute

"—

(i) a large scale disposal, within the meaning of section 34 of the Housing Act 1985, for which consent was required under section 32 or 43 of that Act, or

(ii) a qualifying disposal that was made".

(4) In paragraph 28(1)(b) of Part 4 of Schedule 1 (inquiry into affairs of registered social landlords: availability of powers in relation to registered charities) for "a qualifying disposal" substitute

"—

(i) a large scale disposal, within the meaning of section 34 of the Housing Act 1985, for which consent was required under section 32 or 43 of that Act, or

(ii) a qualifying disposal that was made".

[2500]–[3000]

NOTES

Commencement: 1 December 2008.

(*Schs 15, 16 outside the scope of this work.*)

PART II
STATUTORY INSTRUMENTS

LAND CHARGES RULES 1974

(SI 1974/1286)

NOTES

Made: 20 July 1974.
Authority: Land Charges Act 1972, s 16(1).
Commencement: 9 September 1974.

1 Citation, commencement and interpretation

These Rules may be cited as the Land Charges Rules 1974 and shall come into operation on 9th September 1974.

[3001]

2—(1) The Interpretation Act 1889 shall apply to the interpretation of these Rules as it applies to the interpretation of an Act of Parliament.

(2) In these Rules, unless the context otherwise requires—

"the Act" means the Land Charges Act 1972 and "section" means section of the Act;

"application" includes requisition;

"county" includes Greater London;

"credit account" means an account authorised by the registrar for the purpose of providing credit facilities for the payment of fees;

"day" means a day on which the principal office is open to the public;

"index" means the index kept pursuant to section 1;

"principal office" means the office of the Land Charges Department at Burrington Way, Plymouth, Devon, PL5 3LP or such other office as the registrar shall direct to be the principal office;

"register" means a register kept pursuant to section 1;

"relevant particulars" means particulars specified in Schedule 1 to these Rules which have been furnished in an application under these Rules.

(3) A form referred to by number means the form so numbered in Schedule 2 to these Rules.

[3002]

3 The Registers

(1) The registrar shall, in respect of each land charge or other matter for the registration of which an application is made in accordance with these Rules, record in the appropriate register the relevant particulars, the date on which the entry is registered and the date (if any) on which the registration is renewed.

(2) Any person may, upon completion of Form K21 and on payment of the prescribed fee, inspect an entry in the register at the principal office or at such other office as the registrar shall direct.

[3003]

4 Priority notices and applications for registration

A priority notice shall be given in Form K6.

[3004]

5 An application for registration or renewal of registration shall be made in Form K1, K2, K3, K4, K5, K7 or K8, whichever is appropriate.

[3005]

6 An application for registration or rectification (other than an application made by a practising solicitor or relating to a land charge of Class F) shall, unless the registrar otherwise directs, be supported by a statutory declaration in Form K14 by the person on whose behalf the application is made.

[3006]

NOTES

Modification: references to solicitors etc modified to include references to bodies recognised under the Administration of Justice Act 1985, s 9, by the Solicitors' Incorporated Practices Order 1991, SI 1991/2684, arts 4, 5, Sch 1.

PART II STATUTORY INSTRUMENTS

7 Where an application for registration has been duly made pursuant to a priority notice it shall, in order to comply with the requirements of section 11(3), refer to that notice by citing the official reference number allocated thereto.

[3007]

8—(1) Every priority notice and application for registration or renewal of registration or rectification given or made in accordance with these Rules shall, having been received in the principal office between 1500 hours on the next day, be deemed to have been given or made at the same time, namely immediately before 1500 hours on the second of those days.

(2) The date of registration recorded on a register under rule 3(1) above shall be the date on which the application is deemed to have been made, notwithstanding that the entry is made pursuant to a priority notice.

[3008]

9 Cancellation

Where the registrar is satisfied that an application to cancel the whole or part of an entry in the register has been properly made, he shall—

(i) if the application relates to the whole of an entry, cancel that entry and move from the index the reference thereto;

(ii) if the application relates to part only of an entry, note on the register the effect of the cancellation and amend index accordingly.

[3009]

10 An application to cancel an entry (other than the entry of a land charge of Class F) shall be made in Form K11 and shall be accompanied by—

(i) sufficient evidence of the applicant's title to apply for cancellation unless he is the person on whose behalf the registration was made and is entitled to the benefit of the entry; or

(ii) such office copies of orders of the court of the [Upper Tribunal] as shall justify cancellation:

Provided that is the register has first been consulted and is satisfied that the applicant would suffer exceptional hardship or expense by reason of the foregoing provisions of this rule, he may allow the application to be made in Form K12, supported by sufficient evidence that the land charge or other matter has been discharged or overreached or is of no effect.

[3010]

NOTES

Para (ii): words in square brackets substituted by SI 2009/1307, art 5(1), (3), Sch 2, para 17.

11 An application to cancel the registration of a land charge of Class F shall be made in Form K13 and shall, unless it is signed by the person on whose behalf the application for registration was made, be accompanied by—

(i) a written release of the [home rights] to which the charge relates, or

(ii) the evidence referred to in [paragraph 4(1) of Schedule 4 to the Family Law Act 1996] and (if the charge was registered, or the registration of the charge was renewed, pursuant to [paragraph 4(3) of that Schedule] of that Act) evidence to satisfy the registrar that the order referred to in the application for registration or renewal has ceased to have effect.

[3011]

NOTES

Words in square brackets substituted by SI 2005/1981, r 3.

12 An application for a certificate that an entry in the register has been cancelled shall be made in Form K20.

[3012]

13 Registered land

(1) Where an application for registration, or where an entry in a register, relates to an instrument or matter to which by virtue of section 14 the Act does not apply, the registrar may refuse that application or, as the case may be, cancel that entry.

(2) Without prejudice to the provisions of section 14(2), the registrar may, for the purpose of paragraph (1) above, require a person applying for registration or his solicitor to certify that the land the subject of the application is not registered land.

[3013]

NOTES

Modification: references to solicitors etc modified to include references to bodies recognised under the Administration of Justice Act 1985, s 9, by the Solicitors' Incorporated Practices Order 1991, SI 1991/2684, arts 4, 5, Sch 1.

14 Rectification and amendment

(1) Where it appears that an error in an application has led to a corresponding error in the register, application may be made—

(i) in accordance with rule 10 or 11 above for cancellation of the original entry, and, in accordance with rule 5 above, for the registration of a fresh entry; or

(ii) for rectification of the original entry.

(2) Where an application for rectification has been duly made, the register shall rectify the register so as to indicate the original entry and the amendments and shall record on the register the date of rectification.

(3) An application for rectification shall be made in Form K9 and shall be signed by or on behalf of the person on whose behalf the original application was made or, subject to production of sufficient evidence of title, by or on behalf of any successor in title of that person.

(4) No person who has obtained a certificate of the result of an official search in the index or an office copy of the register, dated in either case before the date of rectification, shall, in respect of that search or office copy, be affected by the rectification.

[3014]

15—(1) Where compensation has been claimed under section 25 of the Law of Property Act 1969 in respect of a registered land charge, the registrar shall make such entries in or amendments and additions to the relevant register and the index as he deems necessary in order to bring the charge to the notice of any person who inspects that register, or requires a search to be made in the index, in relation to the estate or interest affected by the charge.

(2) For the purpose of this rule "registered land charge" has the meaning assigned to it by section 25(10) of the Law of Property Act 1969.

[3015]

16 Official searches

(1) A written application for an official search in the index pursuant to section 10(1)(a) shall be made in Form K15 or K16 whichever is appropriate.

(2) An application for an official search in the index made by telephone pursuant to section 10(1)(b) shall provide, in such order as may be requested, the same particulars as are required for an application made in Form K15.

(3) An application for an official search in the index transmitted by teleprinter in accordance with section 10(1)(b) shall be made in the form set out in Part I of Schedule 3.

[(4) An application for an official search in the index may be made by facsimile transmission in accordance with section 10(1)(b) (a requisition communicated by teleprinter, telephone or other means) and if so made shall be made in Form K15 or K16 whichever is appropriate.]

[(5) An application for an official search in the index may be made to the registrar by means of an applicant's remote terminal communicating with the registrar's computer in accordance with section 10(1)(b) (a requisition communicated by teleprinter, telephone or other means) and if so made the applicant shall provide, in such order as may be requested, such of the particulars as are appropriate and are required for an application made in Form K15 or K16.]

[3016]

NOTES

Para (4): inserted by SI 1990/485, r 3.
Para (5): inserted by SI 1994/287, r 3; substituted by SI 1995/1355, r 3.

17—(1) The certificate of the result of a search issued pursuant to section 10(3)(a) shall be in Form K17 or K18, whichever is appropriate, and shall bear a date which shall be the date of the certificate for the purpose of section 11(5).

(2) The date of the certificate shall be the date of the day on which the search is commenced or such earlier day as may be necessary to enable the registrar to comply with paragraph (3) below.

(3) The certificate shall extend to all entries bearing dates of registration up to and including the date of the certificate.

[3017]

18 Official searches

Without prejudice to section 10(3)(a) (issue of certificate), where an applicant for an official search in the index—

(a) makes his application by telephone and requests the result of search to be given to him orally as part of the same telephone call; or

(b) delivers Form K15 in person at the principal office or at such other office as the registrar may direct and requests the result of search to be displayed to him,

the registrar may comply with the request in such manner and on such conditions as he may determine.

[3018]

19 Office copies

(1) A written application for an office copy of an entry in a register shall be made in Form K19.

(2) Where the applicant has a credit account and the prescribed fee is debited by the registrar to that account, an application for an office copy of an entry in a register may also be made by teleprinter in the form set out in Part II of Schedule 3.

(3) Where an application has been made by telephone for an official search in the index and the result has been given orally in accordance with rule 18 above, the applicant may, as part of the same telephone call, request that an office copy of an entry disclosed and identified in the result of search be sent to him whereupon the fee shall be debited to his credit account.

[(4) Where an applicant has a credit account and the prescribed fee is debited by the Registrar to that account, an application for an office copy of an entry in a register may also be made by facsimile transmission in Form K19.]

[(5) Where the applicant has a credit account and the prescribed fee is debited by the registrar to that account, an application for an office copy of an entry in a register may also be made to the registrar by means of the applicant's remote terminal communicating with the registrar's computer and if so made the applicant shall provide, in such order as may be requested, such of the particulars as are appropriate and are required for an application in Form K19.]

[3019]

NOTES

Para (4): inserted by SI 1990/485, r 4.
Para (5): inserted by SI 1994/287, r 4; substituted by SI 1995/1355, r 4.

[19A Registration of land charges after death

(1) Where an application for registration is made by virtue of section 3(1A), section 5(4A) or section 6(2A) of the Act to register a matter in the name of a person who has died, the applicant shall complete the relevant form in Schedule 2 as if—

(i) the reference to particulars of estate owner in the form were to the particulars which the applicant would have given if the person who has died were still living;

(ii) the reference to the estate owner's title were to the title to the estate affected or intended to be affected by the registration.

(2) The reference to the name and address of the estate owner whose land is affected in paragraph 1(iv), 2(iv) and 3(a)(iv) of Schedule 1 is, where the registration is made pursuant to an application to which paragraph (1) applies, to be treated as a reference to the particulars given in accordance with that paragraph.

(3) A reference in a form in Schedule 2 (other than in a form to which paragraph (1) applies or in Form K6) to particulars of estate owner is, where appropriate, to be treated as a reference to particulars entered in the relevant register in accordance with paragraph (2).]

[3020]

NOTES

Inserted by SI 1995/1355, r 5.

20 Applications generally

(1) Every written application shall, unless the registrar otherwise directs, be sent by prepaid post, or delivered by hand, to the principal office.

(2) Every such application shall be accompanied by the prescribed fee, unless that fee is debited by the registrar to a credit account.

(3) An application for an official search pursuant to rule 16(3) above or for an office copy pursuant to rule 19(2) above shall be transmitted by teleprinter to the principal office.

(4) An application for an official search pursuant to rule 16(2) above or for an office copy pursuant to rule 19(3) above shall be made by telephone to the principal office or such other office as the registrar shall direct.

[(5) An application for an official search pursuant to rule 16(4) of these Rules or for an office copy pursuant to rule 19(4) of these Rules shall be made by facsimile transmission to the principal office.]

[3021]

NOTES

Para (5): inserted by SI 1990/485, r 5.

21 No application shall, unless these Rules or the appropriate form so provides, be accompanied or supported by any deed, document or plan.

[3022]

22 Except in the case of an application for cancellation or rectification and without prejudice to the provisions of rule 13 above, the registrar shall not be concerned to inquire into or otherwise verify the accuracy of any matter or thing stated or appearing in any notice given or application made to him.

[3023]

23 Every application for registration, or for renewal, cancellation or rectification of registration and every priority notice shall be acknowledged by the registrar in Form K22.

[3024]

24 Forms

(1) The prescribed forms may be used with such variations as in the opinion of the registrar for the purposes of the Act or these Rules.

(2) Nothing in this rule shall prejudice any powers of the registrar to promulgate additional forms for use under the Act or these Rules.

[3025]

25 Unless the registrar otherwise directs, a separate form of application or priority notice shall be used for each entry in a register and for each full name in respect of which an entry is required to be made, renewed, cancelled or rectified.

[3026]

26 Unless the registrar otherwise directs, no forms except those sold under arrangements made with HM Stationery Office or with such supplier as the registrar may from time to time approve, shall be accepted for the purpose of the Act or these Rules.

[3027]

27 (*Revokes the Land Charges (No 2) Rule 1972, SI 1972/2059.*)

SCHEDULE 1
CONTENTS OF REGISTERS

	REGISTER		*RELEVANT PARTICULARS*
1	REGISTER OF LAND CHARGES	(i)	Name and address of person on whose behalf application is made
		(ii)	Date of and parties to instrument (if any) creating charge or (where charge not created by instrument) particulars sufficient to identify charge
		(iii)	Class and sub-class (if any) into which charge falls under section 2
		(iv)	Name and address of estate owner whose estate is affected
		(v)	County and district in which land charged is situated together with short description identifying land so far as practicable
		(vi)	In the case of a land charge of Class F, details of any order made under [section 33(5) of the Family Law Act 1996]

	REGISTER		*RELEVANT PARTICULARS*
		(vii)	Official reference number of priority notice (if any) pursuant to which application is expressed to be made
2	REGISTER OF PENDING ACTIONS	(*a*)	*Pending land actions—*
		(i)	Name and address of person on whose behalf application is made
		(ii)	Nature of action or proceeding
		(iii)	Court in which and day on which action or proceeding was commenced or filed and title of action or proceeding
		(iv)	Name and address of estate owner whose is intended to be affected
		(v)	County and district in which land affected is situated together with short description identifying land so far as practicable
		(vi)	Official reference number of priority notice (if any) pursuant to which application is expressed to be made
		(*b*)	*Petitions in bankruptcy—*
		(i)	Name and address of petitioner
		(ii)	Court in which and day on which petition was filed
		(iii)	Name, address and description of debtor, and, in case of debtor firm, of each partner
3	REGISTERS OF WRITS AND ORDERS	(*a*)	*Writs and orders other than receiving orders in bankruptcy—*
		(i)	Name and address of person on whose behalf application is made
		(ii)	Nature and date of writ or order
		(iii)	Court by which writ or order was issued or made and title of action or matter
		(iv)	Name and address of estate owner whose land is affected
		(v)	County and district in which land is situated together with short description identifying land so far as practicable
		(vi)	Official reference number of priority notice (if any) pursuant to which application is expressed to be made
		(*b*)	*Receiving orders in bankruptcy—*
		(i)	Name and address of petitioner
		(ii)	Court in which and day on which receiving order was made
		(iii)	Name, address and description of debtor
4	REGISTER OF DEEDS OF ARRANGEMENT	(i)	Name and address of person on whose behalf application is made
		(ii)	Date of deed and names of parties, or, where creditors are numerous, of at least three creditors
		(iii)	Name, address and description of debtor whose land is affected

REGISTER		*RELEVANT PARTICULARS*
	(iv)	Where practicable, county and district in which land is situated together with short description identifying land
	(v)	Official reference number of priority notice (if any) pursuant to which application is expressed to be made

[3028]

NOTES

Para 1: words in square brackets in sub-para (vi) substituted by SI 2005/1981, r 4.

SCHEDULE 2
FORMS

NOTES

The forms are reproduced as they appear on the Land Registry website at www.landregistry.gov.uk.

FORM K1
APPLICATION FOR REGISTRATION OF A LAND CHARGE

Rule 5

Important: Please read the notes overleaf before completing the form	**Form K1** **Land Charges Act 1972** **APPLICATION FOR REGISTRATION OF A LAND CHARGE** Application is hereby made for the registration of a Land Charge in respect of the following particulars	**FEE PANEL** If the fee is to be debited to your credit account put a cross (X) in this box ☐ *(See Note 1 overleaf)*
Enter full Name(s) and Address(es) of Chargee(s) *(See Notes 2 and 3 overleaf)*	**PARTICULARS OF CHARGEE(S)** *(Continue on form K10 if necessary)*	
If land charge is created by an instrument, enter date and full names of the parties here. If it arises (as in Class A or Class B) by statute, enter Act and Section instead. If neither, state short particulars of effect of charge and date on which charge arose.	**PARTICULARS OF CHARGE** Date Parties	
Class and Sub-Class of charge. *(See Note 4 overleaf)*	Class________ Sub-Class________	If application is made pursuant to a Priority Notice please enter here its official reference number ________
(See Note 5 overleaf)	**PARTICULARS OF LAND AFFECTED** County District Short description	
Only one individual or body to be entered. *(See Note 6 overleaf)*	**PARTICULARS OF ESTATE OWNER** Forename(s) **SURNAME** Title, Trade or Profession **Address**	**FOR OFFICIAL USE ONLY**
(See Note 7 overleaf)	**KEY NUMBER**	
Solicitor's name and address (including postcode) If no Solicitor is acting enter applicant's name and address (including postcode) *(See Note 8 overleaf)*	Solicitor's Reference:	

1	2	3
*C		
4	5	6

I/We certify that the estate owner's title is not registered at the Land Registry.

SIGNATURE OF SOLICITOR OR APPLICANT ________________ Date ________

(See Notes 9 and 10 overleaf)

Explanatory Notes

The following notes are supplied for assistance in making the application overleaf. Detailed information for the making of all kinds of applications to the Land Charges Department is contained in a booklet entitled "Computerised Land Charges Department: a practical guide for solicitors" which is obtainable on application at the address shown below.

Fee payable	1.	Fees must be paid by credit account or by cheque or postal order made payable to "HM Land Registry" (see the "Guide" referred to above)
Form completion	2.	The application can be typed or handwritten in **black ink.** If handwritten, **block capitals** should be used. No other document should be enclosed with the application, save that, if the application is not made by a practising solicitor, it must be supported by a statutory declaration on form K14.
Particulars of chargee	3.	Please enter the full name and address of each person entitled to the benefit of the charge and on whose behalf the application is being made.
Classes of land charges	4.	This form is for use in registering anyone of the following classes or sub-classes of land charge, as specified in s.2 of the Land Charges Act 1972: Class A; Class B; Class C(i) - puisne mortgage; Class C(ii) - limited owner's charge; Class C(iii) - general equitable charge; Class C(iv) - estate contract; Class D(i) - inland revenue charge; Class D(ii) - restrictive covenant; Class D(iii) - equitable casement NB. To register a land charge of **Class F** (rights of a spouse to occupy the matrimonial home) use printed form **K2**. To register a **Pending Action** use printed form **K3** and, for a **Writ** or **Order,** printed form **K4**.
Particulars of land affected	5	Enter the names of the administrative county and district in which the land is situated. This must be the appropriate name a set out in Appendix to Land Charges Practice Leaflet No.3. In London, enter 'Greater London' as the county name and the London Borough as that of the district. A short description identifying the location of the land must also be supplied; for urban properties the postal address will usually suffice. In other cases the description should be supplied as given in the instrument. When this does not provide a description which identifies the location of the land, an additional reference may be made to the land as being that defined on a plan to the instrument, but the plan should not accompany the application.
Particulars of estate owner	6.	A **Separate form** is required for each estate owner against whom the land charge is to be registered. Thus, when husband and wife are joint estate owners, two separate forms K1 must be supplied. 'Estate owner" is defined in s.205 of the Law of Property Act 1925. In the case of individuals, forenames must be separated from surname and each entered in the spaces provided. In the case of a corporate body, no such distinction arises and the printed words "Forename(s)" and "Surname" should be deleted before entering in the spaces the corporate name in its ordinary form (eg, "Blankshire County Council", "John Brown and Company Limited").
Key number	7.	If you have been allocated a key number, please take care to enter this in the space provided overleaf, whether or not you are paying fees through your credit account.
Solicitor's reference	8.	Any reference should be limited to 25 characters (including oblique strokes and punctuation).
Signature and certificate	9.	An application will be rejected if it is not signed or if the certificate that it does not affect registered land has been deleted. However, in a case of extreme urgency, where it is not practicable for the applicant first to ascertain whether or not the land is registered, the Department will accept an application with the certificate deleted provided that it is accompanied by a letter to the following effect. The letter must certify that the applicant has applied for an official search of the index map at the appropriate district land registry. It must also contain an undertaking that he will apply to cancel this registration if the result of search shows that the title to the land is registered.
Despatch of form	10.	When completed, this application form should be despatched to the address shown below which is printed in a position to fit within a standard window envelope.

THE SUPERINTENDENT
LAND CHARGES DEPARTMENT
REGISTRATION SECTION
PLUMER HOUSE, TAILYOUR ROAD
CROWNHILL, PLYMOUTH PL6 5HY
DX 8249 PLYMOUTH (3)

[FORM K2
APPLICATION FOR REGISTRATION OF A LAND CHARGE OF CLASS F]

[Rule 5]

Important: Please read the notes overleaf before completing the form.	**Form K2** **Land Charges Act 1972 (Family Law Act 1996)** **Application for registration of a Land Charge of Class F** Application is hereby made for the registration of a Land Charge of Class F in respect of the following particulars	**Fee panel** *Place "X" in the appropriate box. See Note 1 overleaf.* ☐ A cheque or postal order for the correct fee accompanies this application. ☐ Please debit our Credit Account with the appropriate fee payable. ☐ Please debit our Direct Debit under an authorised agreement with Land Registry.
(See Notes 2 and 3 overleaf)	1. Is there any subsisting registration of rights of occupation under the Matrimonial Homes Act 1967 or 1983 or home rights under the Family Law Act 1996 which affects a dwelling-house other than that referred to in this application? **Yes/No** *(delete as applicable).* 2. If "Yes" (a) Give address of such dwelling-house ______ (b) If the subsisting registration is: (i) under the **Land Charges Act** 1925 or 1972 give the official reference number and date of registration. **OR** (ii) under the **Land Registration Act** 2002 give title number under which the dwelling-house is registered. LC ______ Date ______ Title No ______	
	Particulars to be registered	
Enter full name And address. *(See Note 4 overleaf)*	**Person entitled to benefit of the charge**	
Complete if applicable. *(See Note 5 overleaf)*	**Particulars of court order** By an order of the ______ Court dated ______ and made under s.33(5) of the Family Law Act 1996 it was directed that ______	
	F | If application is made pursuant to a Priority Notice please state its official reference number	
(See Note 6 overleaf)	**Particulars of dwelling-house** County District Known as	
Only one individual or body to be entered *(See Note 7 overleaf)*	**Particulars of estate owner** Forename(s) **Surname** Title, Trade or Profession Address	**For official use only**
(See Note 8 overleaf)	**Key number**	
Solicitor's name and address *(See Note 9 overleaf)* If no Solicitor is acting enter applicant's name and address (including postcode) *(See Note 10 overleaf)*	Solicitor's reference	1 | 2 | 3 * C 4 | 5 | 6

I/We certify that the dwelling-house in this application is not registered at Land Registry.

Signature of solicitor or applicant ______ Date ______

(See Notes 11 and 12 overleaf)

Explanatory Notes

The following notes are supplied for assistance in making the application overleaf. Detailed information for the making of all kinds of applications to the Land Charges Department is contained in Practice Guide *63 – Land Charges – Applications for registration, official search, office copy and cancellation* which is obtainable on application at the address shown below.

Fee payable

1. Fees must be paid by credit account, by Direct Debit under an authorised agreement with Land Registry or by cheque or postal order made payable to "Land Registry" (see the Practice Guide referred to above).

Form completion

2. Please complete the form in block letters in writing or typewriting using black ink not liable to smear. No covering letter is required and no plan or other document should be lodged in support of the application.

Particulars of subsisting registration

3. Under s.32 of, and paragraph 2 of Schedule 4 to, the Family Law Act 1996 a charge in respect of home rights under the Act may be registered against one dwellinghouse only at any one time and the Chief Land Registrar will thus be bound to cancel any previous registration.

Person entitled to the benefit of the charge

4. Please give the full name and address of the person whose home rights under s.30(2) of the Family Law Act 1996 it is sought to protect by registration.

Court order

5. Insert details of any direction given by the Court that the Applicant's home rights should not be brought to an end by the death of his/her spouse or civil partner or the termination of the marriage or civil partnership otherwise than by death. Please state the name of the Court making the order and the date of the order.

County

6. Enter as "County" the appropriate name as set out in Practice Guide *63 – Land Charges – Applications for registration, official search, office copy and cancellation.* As stated therein, if the land referred to in the application lies within the Greater London Area, then "Greater London" should be stated as the county name.

Estate owner

7. Please give the full name, address and description of the estate owner as defined in the Law of Property Act 1925 against whom registration is to be effected. Enter forename(s) and surname on separate lines.

Key number

8. If you have been allocated a key number, please take care to enter this in the space provided overleaf, whether or not you are paying fees through your credit account or by Direct Debit.

Name and address

9. The full name and address of the applicant to be inserted.

Solicitor's reference

10. Any reference should be limited to 25 characters (including oblique strokes and punctuation).

Signature and certificate

11. An application will be rejected if it is not signed or if the certificate that it does not affect registered land has been deleted. However, in a case of extreme urgency where it is not practicable for the applicant first to ascertain whether or not the land is registered, the Department will accept an application with the certificate deleted provided that it is accompanied by a letter to the following effect. The letter must certify that the applicant has applied for an official search of the index map at the appropriate Land Registry office. It must also contain an undertaking that he will apply to cancel this registration if he discovers from the result of search that the title to the land is registered.

Despatch of form

12. When completed, this application form should be despatched to the address shown below which is printed in a position to fit within a standard envelope.

The Superintendent
Land Charges Department
Registration Section
Plumer House, Tailyour Road,
Crownhill, PLYMOUTH PL6 5HY
DX 8249 PLYMOUTH (3)

[3030]

NOTES

Commencement: 5 December 2005.
Substituted by SI 2005/1981, r 5, Schedule.

FORM K3
APPLICATION FOR REGISTRATION OF A PENDING ACTION

Rule 5

Important: Please read the notes overleaf before completing the form.

Form K3 **Land Charges Act 1972**

APPLICATION FOR REGISTRATION OF A PENDING ACTION

Application is hereby made for the registration of a Pending Action in respect of the following particulars

FEE PANEL
If the fee is to be debited to your credit account put a cross (X) in the box
(See Note 1 overleaf)

Enter full Name(s) and Address(es) of Chargee(s)
(See Notes 2 and 3 overleaf)

PARTICULARS OF CHARGEE(S)

Continue on form K10 *if necessary)*

PARTICULARS OF ACTION OR PROCEEDING

Nature of action or proceeding

Name of Court and official reference number

Title of action or proceeding

Date commenced or filed

PA

If application is made pursuant to a Priority Notice please state its official reference number

PARTICULARS OF LAND AFFECTED

County

District

Short description

(See Notes 4 and 5 overleaf)

Only one individual or body to be entered.
(See Note 6 overleaf)

PARTICULARS OF ESTATE OWNER

Forename(s)

SURNAME

Title, Trade or Profession

Address

FOR OFFICIAL USE ONLY

1	2	3
*C		
4	5	6

KEY NUMBER

(See Note 7 overleaf)

Solicitor's name and address (including postcode)

If no Solicitor is acting enter applicant's name and address (including postcode)
(See Note 8 overleaf)

Solicitor's Reference:

I/We certify that the estate owner's title is not registered at the Land Registry.

SIGNATURE OF SOLICITOR OR APPLICANT .... Date ....

(See Note 9 overleaf)

EXPLANATORY NOTES

The following notes are supplied to assist you in making the application overleaf. For further information on procedures for making applications to the Land Charges Department, see the booklet "Computerised Land Charges Department: a practical guide for solicitors" obtainable on application at the address shown below.

Fee Payable	1.	Fees must be paid by credit account or by cheque or postal order made payable to "H.M. Land Registry" (see the guide referred to above),
Form completion	2.	Please complete the form in **BLOCK LETTERS** (handwritten or typewritten) using black ink not liable to smear. No covering letter is required and no plan or other document should be lodged in support of the application. If the application is not made by a practising solicitor it must be accompanied by a statutory declaration on form K14.
Chargee's name(s)	3.	Please give the full name(s) and address(es) of the person(s) on whose behalf the application is made.
County and District	4.	Enter as "County" the appropriate name as set out in the Appendix to Land Charge Practice Leaflet No.3. As stated therein, if the land referred to in the application lies within the Greater London area, then "GREATER LONDON" should be stated as the county name.
Short description	5.	A short description, identifying the land as far as may be practicable, should be furnished.
Estate owner	6.	Please give the full name, address and description of the estate owner as defined in the Law of Property Act 1925 against whom registration is to be effected. A separate form is required for each full name. Enter forename(s) and surname on separate lines. The name of a company or other body should commence on the forename line and may continue on the surname line (the words "Forename(s)" and "Surname" should be deleted).
Key number	7.	If you have been allocated a key number, please take care to enter this in the space provided overleaf, whether or not you are paying fees through your credit account.
Solicitor's reference	8.	Any reference should be limited to 25 characters (including oblique strokes and punctuation).
Despatch of form	9.	When completed, this application form should be despatched to the address shown below which is printed in a position to fit within a standard window envelope.

THE SUPERINTENDENT LAND
CHARGES DEPARTMENT
REGISTRATION SECTION
PLUMER HOUSE
TAILYOUR ROAD
CROWNHILL
PLYMOUTH PL6 5HY
DX 8249 PLYMOUTH 3

[3031]

FORM K4
APPLICATION FOR REGISTRATION OF A WRIT OR ORDER

Rule 5

Important: Please read the notes overleaf before completing the form.

Form K4 **Land Charges Act 1972**

APPLICATION FOR REGISTRATION OF A WRIT OR ORDER

Application is hereby made for the registration of a Writ or Order in respect of the following particulars

FEE PANEL
If the fee is to be debited to your credit account put a cross (X) in this box
(See Note 1 overleaf)

Enter full Name(s) and Address(es) of Chargee(s)

PARTICULARS OF CHARGEE(S)

(See Notes 2 and 3 overleaf)

Continue on form K10 (if necessary)

PARTICULARS OF ACTION OR MATTER

Nature of writ or order

Name of court and official reference number

Title of action

Date of writ or order

WO

If application is made pursuant to a Priority Notice please state its official reference number ______

PARTICULARS OF LAND AFFECTED

County

District

Short description

(See Notes 4 and 5 overleaf)

PARTICULARS OF ESTATE OWNER

Only one individual or body to be entered.

Forename(s)

SURNAME

Title, Trade or Profession

Address

(See Note 6 overleaf)

FOR OFFICIAL USE ONLY

KEY NUMBER

(See Note 7 overleaf)

Solicitor's name and address (including postcode)
If no Solicitor is acting enter applicant's name and address (including postcode)

(See Note 8 overleaf)

Solicitor's Reference

1	2	3
*C		
4	5	6

I/We certify that the estate owner's title is not registered at the Land Registry

SIGNATURE OF SOLICITOR OR APPLICANT ______ Date ______

(See Note 9 overleaf)

EXPLANATORY NOTES

The following notes are supplied for assistance in making the application overleaf. Detailed information for the making of all kinds of applications to the Land Charges Department is contained in a booklet entitled "Computerised Land Charges Department: a practical guide for solicitors" which is obtainable on application at the address shown below.

Fee payable	1. Fees must be paid by credit account or by cheque or postal order made payable to "HM Land Registry" (see the guide referred to above).
Form completion	2. Please complete the form in **BLOCK LETTERS** in writing or typewriting using black ink not liable to smear. No covering letter is required and no plan or other document should be lodged with the application. If the application is not made by a practising solicitor it must be accompanied by a statutory declaration on form K14.
Chargee's name(s)	3. Please give the full name(s) and address(es) of the person(s) on whose behalf the application is made.
County	4. Enter as "County" the appropriate name as set out in Part 3 of the Appendix to Land Charges Practice No.3. As stated therein, if the land referred to in the application lies within the Greater London area, then "**GREATER LONDON**" should be stated as the county name.
Short description	5. A short description, identifying the land as far as may be practicable, should be furnished.
Estate owner	6. Please give the full name, address and description of the estate owner as defined in the Law of Property Act 1925 against whom registration is to be effected. A separate form is required for each full name. Enter forename(s) and surname on separate lines. The name of a company or other body should commence on the forename line and may continue on the surname line (the words "Forename(s)" and "Surname" should be deleted).
Key number	7. If you have been allocated a key number, please take care to enter this in the space provided overleaf, whether or not you are paying fees through your credit account.
Solicitor's reference	8. Any reference should be limited to 25 characters (including oblique strokes and punctuation).
Signature and certificate	9. An application will be rejected if it is not signed or if the certificate that it does not affect registered land has been deleted. However, in a case of extreme urgency where it is not practicable for the applicant first to ascertain whether or not the land is registered, the Department will accept an application with the certificate deleted provided that it is accompanied by a letter by the applicant in which he certifies that he has applied for an official search of the index map at the appropriate district land registry and undertakes that he will apply to cancel this registration if he discovers from the result of search that the title to the land is registered.
Despatch of form	10. When completed, this application form should be despatched to the address shown below, which is printed in a position to fit within a standard envelope.

THE SUPERINTENDENT
LAND CHARGES DEPARTMENT
REGISTRATION SECTION
PLUMER HOUSE
TAILYOUR ROAD
CROWNHILL
PLYMOUTH PL6 5HY
DX 8249 PLYMOUTH (3)

FORM K5
APPLICATION FOR REGISTRATION OF A DEED OF ARRANGEMENT

Rule 5

Important: Please read the notes overleaf before completing the form.	**Form K5** **Land Charges Act 1972** **APPLICATION FOR REGISTRATION OF A DEED OF ARRANGEMENT** Application is hereby made for the registration of a Deed of Arrangement in respect of the following particulars	**FEE PANEL** If the fee is to be debited to your credit account put a cross (X) in this box *(See Note 1 overleaf)*
Enter full Name(s) and Address(es) of Chargee(s) *(See Notes 2 and 3 overleaf)*	**PARTICULARS OF CHARGEE(S)** *Continue on form K10 (if necessary)*	
If there are numerous creditors, name first three and add "and others"	**PARTICULARS OF DEED** Date of Deed Parties	
	DA	If application is made pursuant to a Priority Notice please state its official reference number
(See Notes 4 and 5 overleaf)	**PARTICULARS OF LAND AFFECTED** County District Short description	
Only one individual or body to be entered. *(See Note 6 overleaf)*	**PARTICULARS OF DEBTOR** Forename(s) **SURNAME** Title, Trade or Profession Address	**FOR OFFICIAL USE ONLY**
(See Note 7 overleaf)	**KEY NUMBER**	
Solicitor's name and address (including postcode) If no Solicitor is acting enter applicant's name and address (including postcode) *(See Note 8 overleaf)*	Solicitor's Reference:	1 | 2 | 3 *C 4 | 5 | 6

SIGNATURE OF SOLICITOR OR APPLICANT .... **Date** ....

(See Note 9 overleaf)

EXPLANATORY NOTES

Fee payable	1. Fees must be paid by credit account or by cheque or postal order made payable to "HM Land Registry" (see the guide referred to in paragraph 10).
Form completion	2. Please complete the form in **BLOCK LETTERS** in writing or typewriting using black ink not liable to smear. No covering letter is required and no plan or other document should be lodged in support of the application. If the application is not made by a practising solicitor it must be accompanied by a statutory declaration on form K14.
Chargee's name(s)	3. This application may be made on behalf of a trustee of the deed or of a creditor assenting to or taking the benefit of the deed, whose full name and address should be given.
County	4. Enter as "County" the appropriate name as set out in Part 3 of the Appendix to Land Charges Practice Leaflet No.3. As stated therein, if the land referred to in the application lies within the Greater London area, then "**GREATER LONDON**" should be stated as the county name.
Short description	5. Where practicable a short description identifying the land should be furnished.
Debtor	6. Please give the full name, address and description of the debtor. A separate form is required for each full name. Enter forename(s) and surname on separate lines.
Key number	7. If you have been allocated a key number, please take care to enter this in the space provided overleaf, whether or not you are paying fees through your credit account.
Solicitor's reference	8. Any reference should be limited to 25 characters (including oblique strokes and punctuation).
Despatch of form	9. The completed form should be signed and despatched to the address shown below, which is printed in a position to fit within a standard window envelope.
Practical guide	10. For fuller information on making applications to the Land Charges Department, see "Computerised Land Charges Department: a practical guide for solicitors", obtainable on application at the address shown below.

THE SUPERINTENDENT
LAND CHARGES DEPARTMENT
REGISTRATION SECTION
PLUMER HOUSE, TAILYOUR ROAD
CROWNHILL, PLYMOUTH PL6 5HY
DX 8249 PLYMOUTH (3)

FORM K6
APPLICATION FOR REGISTRATION OF A PRIORITY NOTICE

Rule 4

Important: Please read the notes overleaf before completing the form.	**Form K6** **Land Charges Act 1972** **APPLICATION FOR REGISTRATION OF A PRIORITY NOTICE** Application is hereby made for the registration of a Priority Notice in respect of the following particulars	**FEE PANEL** If the fee is to be debited to your credit account put a cross (X) in this box (See Note 1 overleaf)
Enter full Name(s) and Address(es) of Chargee(s) *(See Notes 2 and 3 overleaf)*	**PARTICULARS OF CHARGEE(S)** *Continue on form K10 (if necessary)*	
State register to which intended application for registration will relate If intended registration is a land charge enter class and sub-class *(See Note 4 overleaf)*	**PARTICULARS OF INTENDED REGISTRATION** Land Charges Pending Actions Writs or Orders Deeds of Arrangement *(delete words not applicable)* Class__________ Sub-Class__________	
		PN
(See Notes 5 and 6 overleaf)	**PARTICULARS OF LAND AFFECTED** County District Short description	
Only one individual or body to be entered *(See Note 7 overleaf)*	**PARTICULARS OF ESTATE OWNER** Forename(s) **SURNAME** Title, Trade or Profession Address	**FOR OFFICIAL USE ONLY**
(See Note 8 overleaf)	**KEY NUMBER**	
Solicitor's name and address (including postcode) If no Solicitor is acting enter applicant's name and address (including postcode) *(See Note 9 overleaf)*	Solicitor's Reference:	

1	2	3
*C		
4	5	6

I/We certify that the estate owner's title is not registered at the Land Registry.

SIGNATURE OF SOLICITOR OR APPLICANT ____________________ **Date**____________
(See Note 10 overleaf)

EXPLANATORY NOTES

The following notes are supplied for assistance in making the application overleaf. Detailed information for the making of all kinds of applications to the Land Charges Department is contained in a booklet entitled "Computerised Land Charges Department: a practical guide for solicitors" which is obtainable on application at the address show below.

Fee payable	1. Fees must be paid by credit account or by cheque or postal order made payable to "HM Land Registry" (see the guide referred to above).
Form completion	2. Please complete the form in **BLOCK LETTERS** in writing or typewriting using black ink not liable to smear. No covering letter is required and no plan or other document should be lodged in support of the application.
Chargee's name(s)	3. Please give the full name(s) and address(es) of the person(s) on whose behalf the application is made.
Class and sub-class of charge	4. The following are the relevant classes and sub-classes of land charge (See Land Charges Act 1972, s.2). Class A Class B Class C (i) (puisne mortgage) Class C (ii) (limited owner's charge) Class C (iii) (general equitable charge) Class C (iv) (estate contract) Class D (i) (Inland Revenue charge) Class D (ii) (restrictive covenant) Class D (iii) (equitable easement) Class F
County	5. Enter as "County" the appropriate name as set out in Part 3 of the Appendix to Land Charges Practice Leaflet No.3. As stated therein, if the land referred to in the application lies within the Greater London area then **"GREATER LONDON"** should be stated as the county name.
Short description	6. A short description, identifying the land as far as maybe practicable, should be furnished.
Estate owner	7. Please give the full name and address of the person against whom the intended registration is to be effected. A separate form is required for each full name. Enter forename(s) and surname on separate lines. The name of a company or other body should commence on the forename line and may continue on the surname line (delete the words "Forename(s)" and "Surname").
Key number	8. If you have been allocated a key number, please take care to enter this in the space provided overleaf, whether or not you are paying fees through your credit account.
Solicitor's reference	9. Any reference should be limited to 25 characters (including oblique strokes and punctuation).
Despatch of form	10. When completed, this application form should be despatched to the address shown below, which is printed in a position to fit a standard window envelope.

THE SUPERINTENDENT
LAND CHARGES DEPARTMENT
REGISTRATION SECTION
PLUMER HOUSE, TAILYOUR ROAD
CROWNHILL, PLYMOUTH PL6 5HY
DX 8249 PLYMOUTH (3)

FORM K7
APPLICATION FOR THE RENEWAL OF A REGISTRATION

Rule 5

Important: Please read the notes overleaf before completing the form.	**Form K7** **Land Charges Act 1972** *(Use Form K8 for the renewal of a Class F Land Charge)* **APPLICATION FOR THE RENEWAL OF A REGISTRATION** Application is hereby made for the renewal of a registration in respect of the following particulars	**FEE PANEL** If the fee is to be debited to your credit account put a cross (x) in this box. ☐ *(See Note 1 overleaf)*
Enter full Name(s) and Address(es) of Chargee(s) *(See Notes 2 and 3 overleaf)*	**PARTICULARS OF CHARGEE(S)** *Continue on form* K10 *(if necessary)*	

PARTICULARS OF ENTRY

Pending Action

Writ or Order

Deed of Arrangement
(delete words not applicable)

Insert number and date of the original registration			
Official reference no.	Date of registration *(See Note 4 overleaf)*		
	Day	Month	Year

Only one individual or body to be entered *(See Note 5 overleaf)*	**PARTICULARS OF ESTATE OWNER OR DEBTOR** Forename(s) **SURNAME** Title, Trade or Profession Address	**FOR OFFICIAL USE ONLY**
(See Note 6 overleaf)	**KEY NUMBER**	COUNTY
Solicitor's name and address (Including postcode) If no Solicitor is acting enter applicant's name and address (including postcode) *(See Notes 7 & 8 overleaf)*	Solicitor's reference:	

1	2	3
*C		
4	5	6

SIGNATURE OF SOLICITOR OR APPLICANT .... Date ....
(See Note 8 overleaf)

EXPLANATORY NOTES

The following notes are supplied for assistance in making the application overleaf.
Detailed information for the making of all kinds of applications to the Land Charges Department is contained in a booklet entitled "Computerised Land Charges Department: a practical guide for solicitors", obtainable on application at the address shown below.

Fee payable

1. Fees must be paid by credit account, if you have one, or by cheque or postal order made payable to "HM Land Registry" (see the guide referred to above).

Form Completion

2. Please complete the form in **BLOCK LETTERS** in writing or typewriting using black ink not liable to smear. No covering letter is required and no plan or other document should be lodged in support of the application. Form K8 should be used for a Land Charge of Class F.

Chargee's name(s)

3. Please give the full name(s) and address(es) of the person(s) entitled to the benefit of the charge and on whose behalf the application is made.

Date of original registration

4. Complete all boxes and refer to month by three letters eg:

Day		Month			Year			
0	4	S	E	P	1	9	8	1

Estate owner

5. Please give the full name of the estate owner or debtor as entered on the register. Enter forename(s) and surname on separate lines. The name of a company or other body should commence on the forename line and may continue on the surname line (the words "Forename(s)" and "Surname" should be deleted).

Key number

6. If you have been allocated a key number, please take care to enter this in the space provided overleaf, whether or not you are paying fees through your credit account.

Solicitor's Reference

7. Any reference should be limited to 25 characters (including oblique strokes and punctuation).

Despatch of form

8. When completed, this application form should be despatched to the address shown below which is printed in a position to fit within a standard window envelope.

THE SUPERINTENDENT
LAND CHARGES DEPARTMENT
REGISTRATION SECTION
PLUMER HOUSE, TAILYOUR ROAD
CROWNHILL, PLYMOUTH PL6 5HY
DX 8249 PLYMOUTH (3)

[FORM K8

APPLICATION FOR THE RENEWAL OF A REGISTRATION OF A LAND CHARGE OF CLASS F]

[Rule 5]

Important: Please read the notes overleaf before completing the form.	**Form K8** **Land Charges Act 1972 (Family Law Act 1996)** **Application for the renewal of a registration of a Land Charge of Class F** Application is hereby made for the renewal of the registration of a Land Charge of Class F in respect of the following particulars.	**Fee panel** *Place "X" in the appropriate box. See Note 1 overleaf.* ☐ A cheque or postal order for the correct fee accompanies this application. ☐ Please debit our Credit Account with the appropriate fee payable. ☐ Please debit our Direct Debit under an authorised agreement with Land Registry.

Enter full name(s) and address(es). *(See Notes 2 and 3 above)*	**Persons entitled to benefit of the charge**
(See Note 4 overleaf)	**Particulars of court order** By an order of the ________ Court dated ________ and made under s.33(5) of the Family Law Act 1996 it was directed that

Particulars of the entry to be renewed

Class	Official reference no.	Date of registration (See Note 5 overleaf)		
	Insert number and date of the original registration	Day	Month	Year
F				

Only one individual or body to be entered. *(See Note 6 overleaf)*	**Particulars of estate owner** Forename(s) **Surname**	**For official use only**
(See Note 7 overleaf)	**Key number**	
Solicitor's name and address (including postcode) If no Solicitor is acting enter applicant's name and address (including postcode) *(See Note 8 overleaf)*	Solicitor's reference:	1 2 3 *C 4 5 6

I/We certify that the dwelling-house in this application is not registered at Land Registry.

Signature of solicitor or applicant ____________ Date ________

Explanatory Notes

The following notes are supplied for assistance in making the application overleaf. Detailed information for the making of all kinds of applications to the Land Charges Department is contained in Practice Guide 63 – *Land Charges – Applications for registration, official search, office copy and cancellation*, which is obtainable on application at the address shown below.

Fee payable

1. Fees must be paid by credit account, by Direct Debit under an authorised agreement with Land Registry or by cheque or postal order made payable to "Land Registry" (see the Practice Guide referred to above).

Form completion

2. Please complete the form in **block letters** in writing or typewriting using black ink not liable to smear. No covering letter is required and no plan or other supporting document should be sent with the application.

Person entitled to benefit of the charge

3. Please give the full name and address of the person by whom or on whose behalf the application is made for the renewal of registration pursuant to section 32 of, and paragraph 4(3) of Schedule 4 to, the Family Law Act 1996.

Court Order

4. Give details of any direction given by the court that the applicant's home rights should not be brought to an end by the death of his/her spouse or civil partner or the termination of the marriage or civil partnership otherwise than by death. Please insert name of court making the order and date of order.

Date of original registration

5. Complete all boxes and refer to month by three letters eg:

Day		Month			Year			
0	4	S	E	P	1	9	8	1

Estate owner

6. Please give the full name of the estate owner as already entered on the register.

Key number

7. If you have been allocated a key number, please take care to enter this in the space provided overleaf, whether or not you are paying fees through your credit account or by Direct Debit.

Solicitors reference

8. Any reference should be limited to 25 characters (including oblique strokes and punctuation).

Despatch of form

9. When completed, this application form should be despatched to the address shown below which is printed in a position to fit within a standard window envelope.

The Superintendent
Land Charges Department
Registration Section
Plumer House, Tailyour Road,
Crownhill, PLYMOUTH PL6 5HY
DX 8249 PLYMOUTH (3)

[3036]

NOTES

Commencement: 5 December 2005.
Substituted by SI 2005/1981, r 5, Schedule.

FORM K9
APPLICATION FOR RECTIFICATION OF AN ENTRY IN THE REGISTER

Rule 14(3)

Important. Please read the notes overleaf before completing the form.	**Form K9** **Land Charges Act 1972** **APPLICATION FOR RECTIFICATION OF AN ENTRY IN THE REGISTER**	**FEE PANEL** If the fee is to be debited to your credit account put a cross (X) in this box ☐ *(See Note 1 overleaf)*
Enter Full Name(s) and Address(es) of Applicant(s) *(See Note 2 overleaf)*	**PARTICULARS OF APPLICANT(S)**	
Delete words in *italics* which are not applicable	**CERTIFICATE** I/We *as solicitor(s) acting for* the above-mentioned applicant(s) hereby apply for rectification of an entry in the Register as shown below: I/We certify that: *(a) the applicant is the person entitled to benefit of the entry, and is named as the chargee in the original registration.* *(b) the applicant is the successor in title to the original chargee, and evidence of the applicant's title is enclosed.* *(c) The Estate Owner's title, is not registered at the Land Registry.* Signature (or attested seal of company) Date Address	
	DETAILS OF RECTIFICATION Particulars of the error and of the rectification required: *(Continue on form K10 if necessary)*	

		Insert number and date of the original registration								
Delete words not applicable	**PARTICULARS OF ENTRY** LAND CHARGE (Class______ Sub-Class______) PENDING ACTION WRIT OR ORDER DEED OF ARRANGEMENT	Official reference No.	Date of registration *(See Note 3 overleaf)*							
			Day		Month		Year			

Only one individual or body to be entered *(See Note 4 overleaf)*	**PARTICULARS OF ESTATE OWNER** Forename(s) **SURNAME**	**FOR OFFICIAL USE ONLY**
(See note 5 overleaf)	**KEY NUMBER**	
Solicitor's name and address (including postcode) If no Solicitor is acting enter applicant's name and address (including postcode) *(See Notes 6 and 7 overleaf)*	Solicitor's reference:	

1	2	3
*C		
4	5	6

Explanatory Notes

The following notes are supplied for assistance in making the application overleaf. Detailed information for the making of all kinds of applications to the Land Charges Department is contained in a booklet entitled "Computerised Land Charges Department: a practical guide for solicitors" which is obtainable on application at the address shown below.

Fee payable	1.	Fees may be paid through your credit account, if you have one, or by cheque or postal order made payable to "HM Land Registry" (see the Guide referred to above).
Form completion	2.	Please complete the form in **BLOCK LETTERS** (handwritten or typewritten) using black ink not liable to smear. No covering letter is required and no plan or other supporting document should be sent with the application.
Date of original registration	3.	Complete all boxes and refer to month by three letters, eg:

Day		Month			Year			
0	4	S	E	P	1	9	8	1

Particulars of the estate owner	4.	Please give the full names of the estate owner or debtor as currently entered in the register. Enter forenames and surnames on separate lines. The name of the company or other body should commence on the forename line and may continue on the surname line (the words "Forename(s)" and "Surname" should be deleted).
Key number	5.	If you have been allocated a key number, please take care to enter this in the space provided overleaf, whether or not you are paying fees through your credit account.
Solicitors' reference	6.	Any reference should be limited to 25 characters (including oblique strokes and punctuation).
Despatch of form	7.	When completed, this application form should be despatched to the address shown below which is printed in a position to fit within a standard window envelope.

PART II STATUTORY INSTRUMENTS

THE SUPERINTENDENT
LAND CHARGES DEPARTMENT
REGISTRATION SECTION
PLUMER HOUSE, TAILYOUR ROAD
CROWNHILL, PLYMOUTH PL6 5HY
DX 8249 PLYMOUTH (3)

FORM K10
CONTINUATION OF AN APPLICATION

Form K10 **Land Charges Act 1972**

CONTINUATION OF AN APPLICATION

(1) State type of application and number of form to which this continuation relates (e.g. K1).

(2) State "Land Charge", "Writ or Order", etc. as the case may be.

(3) Give name of the estate owner or debtor.

(1) ....

(2) ....

(3) ....

This margin to be left clear for binding

FORM K11
APPLICATION FOR CANCELLATION OF AN ENTRY IN THE REGISTER

Rule 10

Application to **cancel an entry in the Land Charges Register (other than class F)** (1)(2)

HM Land Registry

Form K11
(Land Charges Act 1972)

(1) For Class F cancellation please use form K13.

(2) **Please complete the appropiate sections of this form in typescript or BLOCK LETTERS using a black ink which will not smear. No covering letter is required.** A separate form K11 must be used for each entry concerned.

(3) Enter full names of the applicant(s).

(4) Please put a cross in the correct box. If the applicant is not that named in the original registration then evidence of title of the new applicant should be enclosed. Any documents lodged should be certified as true copies.

(5) Please put a cross in the correct box.

(6) If the entry is to be cancelled as to part only of the land please describe that part of the land.

(7) Please put a cross in the correct box.

(8) If the entry is a Land Charge please enter the class and sub class here.

(9) An order of the Court directing vacation is necessary to cancel an entry relating to proceedings in bankruptcy or to a deed of arrangement.

(10) Please complete all boxes and refer to month by three letters e.g.

Day		Month			Year			
0	9	O	C	T	1	9	9	5

(11) Please give full name(s) of the estate owner or debtor as entered in the register. Enter forename(s) and surname on separate lines. You may use both lines for the name of a company or other body. (The words forename(s) and surname should then be deleted.)

(12) Please enter your key number even if you are not paying fees through your credit account.

(13) If no solicitor is acting enter full name and address (including postcode) of applicant.

(14) Please limit to 25 characters including oblique strokes and punctuation.

Particulars of applicant(s) entitled to the benefit of the entry. (3)

Fee Panel
Please put a cross in this box if fee is to be paid through your credit account. ☐
(See Note 2 overleaf)

Certificate
I/We as solicitor(s) acting for the above mentioned applicant(s) hereby apply for cancellation in the register as shown below.
I/We certify that: (4)

☐ **a** The applicant(s) is/are the person(s) entitled to the benefit of the entry and is/are named as the chargee(s) in the original registration.

☐ **b** The applicant(s) is/are the successor(s) in title to the original chargee(s) and evidence of the applicant's title is enclosed.

☐ **c** The application is made pursuant to an order of the Court directing vacation of the entry and an office copy of the order is attached.

☐ **d** The restrictive covenants protected by the under-mentioned entry are the covenants discharged by the order of The Lands Tribunal, an office copy of which is attached.

Signature of Solicitor/ Applicants (or attested seal of company) Date

Particulars of the entry
Please cancel the undermentioned entry as to either (5)

☐ the whole
or
☐ the following part

(6)
being part of the land affected by the original registration

(7)
☐ Land Charges
☐ Pending Action (9)
☐ Writ or Order (9)
☐ Deed of Arrangement (9)
☐ Annuity

(8) Class and sub class

Insert the number and date of the original registration below.

Official reference no.	Date of registration (10)		
	Day	Month	Year

Particulars of the estate owner(11)
Forname(s)
Surname

For official use only

Key Number (12)	Solicitor's name and address (including postcode) (13)	Name and address (including postcode) for despatch of acknowledgement (leave blank if it is to be sent to the solicitor/applicant's address). CONTINUATION OF AN APPLICATION

Solicitor's reference (14)		1 *C	2	3	4	5	
For official use only County							

Please see also the Explanatory Notes overleaf

PART II STATUTORY INSTRUMENTS

Explanatory Notes

1 If you need help to fill in this form please write to the address at the foot of this page and ask for the booklet 'Computerised Land Charges Department - a practical guide for solicitors'. A copy will be sent to you free of charge.

2 The fee payable for each application is set out in the current Land Charges Fee Order (which can be bought from any Her Majesty's Stationery Office bookshop or from any law stationer). Fees may be paid either through your credit account, if you have one, or by cheque or postal order made payable to 'HM Land Registry'.

3 When you have completed this form please send it to the address shown below which is printed in a position to fit within a standard window envelope.

THE SUPERINTENDENT
LAND CHARGES DEPARTMENT
CANCELLATION SECTION
PLUMER HOUSE
TAILYOUR ROAD
CROWNHILL
PLYMOUTH PL6 5HY
DX8249 PLYMOUTH (3)

FORM K12
APPLICATION FOR CANCELLATION OF AN ENTRY IN THE REGISTER UNDER SPECIAL DIRECTION OF THE REGISTRAR

Rule 10

Important: Please read the notes overleaf before completing the form.

Form K12 **Land Charges Act 1972**

APPLICATION FOR CANCELLATION OF AN ENTRY IN THE REGISTER UNDER SPECIAL DIRECTIONS OF THE REGISTRAR

IMPORTANT: This form must not be used unless the registrar has first been consulted and has approved its use.

FEE PANEL
If the fee is to be debited to your credit account put a cross (X) in this box ☐

(See Note 1 overleaf)

I/We hereby apply for cancellation in the register of the entry referred to below on behalf of

(See Notes 2 and 3 overleaf) Full Name(s)

Exceptional hardship or expense would be caused if this application were made on form K11 because:

Signature Date

Address

Delete words not applicable

LAND CHARGE (Class______ Sub-Class______)
ANNUITY
PENDING ACTION
WRIT OR ORDER
DEED OF ARRANGEMENT

Insert number and date of the registration			
Official reference no.	Date of registration *(see note 4 overleaf)*		
	Day	Month	Year

Only one individual or body to be entered

PARTICULARS OF ESTATE OWNER

Forename(s)

SURNAME

Address

(See Note 5 overleaf)

FOR OFFICIAL USE ONLY

KEY NUMBER

(See Note 6 overleaf)

COUNTY

1	2	3
*C		
4	5	6

Solicitor's name and address (including postcode)
If no Solicitor is acting enter applicant's name and address (including postcode)
(See Notes 7 and 8 overleaf)

Solicitor's Reference:

PART II STATUTORY INSTRUMENTS

EXPLANATORY NOTES

The following notes are supplied for assistance in making the application overleaf. Detailed information for the making of all kinds of applications to the Land Charges Department is contained in a booklet entitled "Computerised Land Charges Department: a practical guide for solicitors" which is obtainable on application at the address shown below.

Fee payable	1. Fees must be paid through your credit account, if you have one, or by cheque or postal order made payable to "HM Land Registry" (see the guide referred to above).
Use of Form K12	2. This form must not be used unless the Registrar has first been consulted and approved its use.
Form completion	3. Please complete the form in **BLOCK LETTERS** (handwritten or typewritten) using black ink not liable to smear. A separate form is required for each entry to be removed from the register. No covering letter is required.
Date of Registration	4. Complete all boxes and refer to month by three letters, eg:

Day		Month			Year			
0	4	S	E	P	1	9	8	1

Particulars of the estate owner	5. Please give the full name of the estate owner or debtor as entered in the register. Enter forenames and surnames on separate lines. The name of a company or other body should commence on the forename line and may continue on the surname line (the words "Forename(s)" and "Surname" should be deleted).
Key number	6. If you have been allocated a key number, please take care to enter this in the space provided overleaf, whether or not you are paying fees through your credit account.
Solicitors' reference	7. Any reference should be limited to 25 characters (including oblique strokes and punctuation).
Despatch of form	8. When completed, this application form should be despatched to the address shown below which is printed in a position to fit within a standard window envelope.

THE SUPERINTENDENT
LAND CHARGES DEPARTMENT
CANCELLATION SECTION
PLUMER HOUSE, TAILYOUR ROAD,
CROWNHILL, PLYMOUTH PL6 5HY
DX 8249 PLYMOUTH (3)

[3040]

[FORM K13
APPLICATION FOR CANCELLATION OF A LAND CHARGE OF CLASS F]

[Rule 5]

Important: Please read the notes overleaf before completing the form.	**Form K13** **Land Charges Act 1972** **(Family Law Act 1996)** **Application for cancellation of a Land Charge of Class F**	**Fee panel** If the fee is to be debited to your credit account put a cross (X) in this box. ☐ *(See Note 1 overleaf)*
Enter full name(s) and address(es) of applicant(s) *(See Notes 2 and 3 overleaf)*	**Particulars of applicant** I, of hereby apply for cancellation in the register of the entry referred to below. Signature Date	
(See Note 4 overleaf)	**Certificate of solicitor(s)** We hereby certify that we are acting for the applicant and that we are satisfied that our client understands the nature of this application and the effect of the cancellation of the said entry on the register. Signature and address of Solicitors to the above applicant Signature Address	
Delete (a) or (b) as appropriate	**Particulars of entry affected** Please cancel the undermentioned entry as to (a) the whole or (b) the following part	

Class **F**			
	Insert number and date of the registration	Official reference no.	Date of registration *(See Note 5 overleaf)* Day / Month / Year
	Insert, if applicable, the number and date of any renewal of registration	Official reference no.	Date of registration *(See Note 5 overleaf)* Day / Month / Year

Only one individual or body to be entered. *(See Note 6 overleaf)*	**Particulars of estate owner** Forename(s) **Surname** Address	**For official use only**
(See Note 7 overleaf)	**Key number**	
Solicitor's name and address (including postcode) If no Solicitor is acting enter applicant's name and address (including postcode) *(See Notes 8 and 9 overleaf)*	Solicitor's reference:	1 / 2 / 3 *C 4 / 5 / 6

EXPLANATORY NOTES

The following notes are supplied for assistance in making the application overleaf. Detailed information for the making of all kinds of application to the Land Charges Department is contained in a booklet entitled "Computerised Land Charges Department: a practical guide for solicitors" which is obtainable on application at the address shown below.

Fee payable	1.	Fees must be paid by credit account or by cheque or postal order made payable to 'HM Land Registry' (see the guide referred to above).
Form completion	2.	Please complete the form in **BLOCK LETTERS** in writing or typewriting, using black ink not liable to smear. No covering letter is required.
Applicant's name	3.	Please give the name of the person on whose behalf the application is made. If the applicant is not the person on whose behalf the registration was made, the application must be accompanied by:- (a) a release in writing of the matrimonial home rights to which the charge relates, or (b) the evidence referred to in paragraph 4(1)9 of Schedule 4 to the Family Law Act 1996 and, if the charge was registered or the registration of the charge was renewed pursuant to s.33(5) of the said Act, evidence proving to the satisfaction of the Chief Land Registrar that the order referred to in the application for registration or renewal has ceased to have effect.
Certificate of Solicitor(s)	4.	This certificate is only required where the application is signed by the person in whose favour the registration was made and solicitors are acting on his/her behalf.
Date of registration	5.	Complete all boxes and refer to Month by three letters:

Day		Month			Year			
0	4	S	E	P	1	9	8	1

Particulars of the estate owner	6.	Please give the full name of the estate owner as entered on the register. Enter forenames and surnames on separate lines.
Key number	7.	If you have been allocated a key number, please take care to enter this in the space provided overleaf, whether or not you are paying fees through your credit account.
Solicitor's reference	8.	Any reference should be limited to 25 characters (including oblique strokes and punctuation).
Despatch of form	9.	The completed form should be despatched to the address below, which is printed in a position to fit a standard window envelope.

THE SUPERINTENDENT
LAND CHARGES DEPARTMENT
REGISTRATION SECTION
PLUMER HOUSE, TAILYOUR ROAD,
CROWNHILL, PLYMOUTH PL6 5HY
DX 8249 PLYMOUTH (3)

[3041]

NOTES

Commencement: 5 December 2005.
Substituted by SI 2005/1981, r 5, Schedule.

FORM K14
DECLARATION IN SUPPORT OF AN APPLICATION FOR REGISTRATION OR RECTIFICATION

Rule 6

Form K14 **Land Charges Act 1972**

DECLARATION IN SUPPORT OF AN APPLICATION FOR REGISTRATION OR RECTIFICATION

(1) Enter full Name and Address

(2) Description

(3) Description of interest (e.g. agreement for sale, restrictive covenant) which is to be registered or the registration of which is to be rectified.

(4) Land Charge, Pending Action, Writ or Order, or Deed of Arrangement as case may be.

I (1) ....

of ....

....

....

....

(2) ....

solemnly and sincerely declare that I am

entitled to the benefit of (3) ....

which is registrable as a (4) ....

.... and which is the subject of the application made in form ....

and marked 'A' which is now produced and shown to me.

The title to the property affected by this application is not registered at the Land Registry.

I make this solemn declaration, conscientiously believing the same to be true, by virtue of the provisions of the Statutory Declarations Act 1835.

Declared by the said

at

in the county of

this day of , before me

Commissioner for Oaths
Justice of the Peace
Solicitor authorised to administer Oaths
(Delete whichever is not applicable)

FORM K15
APPLICATION FOR AN OFFICIAL SEARCH

Rule 16(1), (2)

FORM K15 **LAND CHARGES ACT 1972**

Payment of fee

Insert a cross (X) in this box if the fee is to be paid through a credit account (see Note 3 overleaf). ☐

APPLICATION FOR AN OFFICIAL SEARCH

NOT APPLICABLE TO REGISTERED LAND

Application is hereby made for an official search in the index to the registers kept pursuant to the Land Charges Act 1972 for any subsisting entries in respect of the undermentioned particulars.

IMPORTANT: **Please read the notes overleaf before completing this form.**

For Official Use Only	NAMES TO BE SEARCHED (Please use block letters and see Note 4 overleaf)		PERIOD OF YEARS (see Note 5 overleaf)	
STX			From	To
	Forename(s)			
	SURNAME			
	Forename(s)			
	SURNAME			
	Forename(s)			
	SURNAME			
	Forename(s)			
	SURNAME			
	Forename(s)			
	SURNAME			
	Forename(s)			
	SURNAME			

COUNTY (see Note 6 overleaf)	
FORMER COUNTY	
DESCRIPTION OF LAND (see Note 7 overleaf)	
FORMER DESCRIPTION	

Particulars of Applicant (see Notes 8, 9 and 10 overleaf)		Name and address (including postcode) for despatch of certificate (Leave blank if certificate is to be returned to applicant's address)
KEY NUMBER	Name and address (including postcode)	

Applicant's reference	Date	**FOR OFFICIAL USE ONLY**

NOTES FOR GUIDANCE OF APPLICANTS

The following notes are supplied for assistance in making the application overleaf. Detailed information for the making of all kinds of applications to the Land Charges Department is contained in a booklet entitled "Computerised Land Charges Department: A practical guide for solicitors" which is obtainable on application at the address shown below.

1. **Effect of search.** The official certificate of the result of this search will have no statutory effect in relation to registered land (see Land Registration Act 1925, s.59 and Land Charges Act 1972, s.14).

2. **Bankruptcy only searches.** Form K16 should be used for Bankruptcy only searches.

3. **Fees** must be paid by credit account or by cheque or postal order made payable to "HM Land Registry" (see the guide referred to above).

4. **Names to be searched.** The forename(s) and surname of each individual must be entered on the appropriate line of the form. The name of a company or other body should commence on the forename line and may continue on the surname line (the words "Forename(s)" and "Surname" should be crossed through). If you are searching more than 6 names, use a second form.

5. **Period of years to be searched.** The inclusive period to be covered by a search should be entered in complete years, e.g. 1968-1975.

6. **County Names.** This must be the appropriate name set out in the Appendix to Land Charges Practice Leaflet No.3. Searches affecting land within the Greater London area should state "GREATER LONDON" as the county name. ANY RELEVANT FORMER COUNTY SHOULD ALWAYS BE STATED (see the Appendix to Land Charges Practice Leaflet No.3 which lists county names).

7. **Land description.** It is not essential to provide a land description but, if one is given, any relevant former description should also be given (see the guide referred to above).

8. **Key number.** If you have been allocated a key number, please take care to enter this in the space provided overleaf, whether or not you are paying fees through your credit account.

9. **Applicant's name and address.** This need not be supplied if the applicant's key number is correctly entered in the space provided overleaf.

10. **Applicant's reference.** Any reference must be limited to 25 characters, including any oblique strokes and punctuation.

11. **Despatch of this form.** When completed, send this application to the address shown below, which is printed in a position so as to fit within a standard window envelope.

THE SUPERINTENDENT
LAND CHARGES DEPARTMENT
SEARCH SECTION
PLUMER HOUSE, TAILYOUR ROAD
CROWNHILL, PLYMOUTH PL6 5HY
DX 8249 PLYMOUTH (3)

(see Note 11 above)

[3043]

FORM K16
APPLICATION FOR AN OFFICIAL SEARCH (BANKRUPTCY ONLY)

Rule 16(1)

Form K16

Land Charges Act 1972

Payment of fee

Insert a cross (X) in this box if the fee is to be paid through a credit account ☐

(see Note 2 overleaf).

APPLICATION FOR AN OFFICIAL SEARCH

(BANKRUPTCY ONLY)

Application is hereby made for an official search in the index to the registers kept pursuant to the Land Charges Act 1972 in respect of the undermentioned names for any subsisting entries of:

(i) petitions in bankruptcy in the register of pending actions
(ii) receiving orders in bankruptcy and bankruptcy orders in the register of writs and orders
(iii) deeds of arrangement in the register of deeds of arrangement

For Official Use Only

#

IMPORTANT: Please read the notes overleaf before completing this form.

NAMES TO BE SEARCHED
(Please use block letters and see Note 3 overleaf)

	Forename(s)	
	Surname	
	Forename(s)	
	Surname	
	Forename(s)	
	Surname	
	Forename(s)	
	Surname	
	Forename(s)	
	Surname	
	Forename(s)	
	Surname	

Particulars of Applicant (see Notes 4, 5 and 6 overleaf)		Name and address (including postcode) for despatch of certificate (Leave blank if certificate is to be returned to applicant's address)
KEY NUMBER	Name and address (including postcode)	

Applicant's reference:	Date	**FOR OFFICIAL USE ONLY**

Notes for Guidance of Applicants

The following notes are supplied for assistance in making the application overleaf. Detailed information for the making of all kinds of applications to the Land Charges Department is contained in a booklet entitled "Computerised Land Charges Department: a practical guide for solicitors" which is obtainable on application at the address shown below.

1. **Effect of search.** The official certificate of the result of this search will have no statutory effect in relation to registered land (see Land Registration Act 1925, s.59 and Land Charges Act 1972, s.14.).

2. **Fees.** A fee is payable for each name searched. Fees must be paid by credit account or by cheque or postal order made payable to "HM Land Registry" (see the guide referred to above).

3. **Names to be searched.** The forename(s) and surname of each individual must be entered on the appropriate lines in the relevant panel overleaf. If you are searching more than 6 names, use a second form.

4. **Key number.** If you have been allocated a key number, please take care to enter this in the space provided overleaf, whether or not you are paying fees through your credit account.

5. **Applicant's name and address.** This need not be supplied if the applicant's key number is correctly entered in the space provided overleaf.

6. **Applicant's reference.** Any reference must be limited to 25 characters, including any oblique strokes and punctuation.

7. **Despatch of this form.** When completed, send this application to the address shown below, which is printed in a position so as to fit within a standard window envelope.

THE SUPERINTENDENT
LAND CHARGES DEPARTMENT
SEARCH SECTION
PLUMER HOUSE
TAILYOUR ROAD
CROWNHILL
PLYMOUTH PL6 5HY
DX 8249 PLYMOUTH (3)

(see Note 7 above)

Rule 17(1)

FORM K17
CERTIFICATE OF THE RESULT OF SEARCH

FORM K17.

LAND CHARGES ACT, 1972.

CERTIFICATE OF THE RESULT OF SEARCH

CERTIFICATE No.	CERTIFICATE DATE	PROTECTION ENDS ON

It is hereby certified that an official search in respect of the undermentioned particulars has been made in the index to the register which are kept pursuant to the Land Charges Act, 1972. The result of the search is that there are NO SUBSISTING ENTRIES.

PARTICULARS SEARCHED			
COUNTY OR COUNTIES			
NAME(S)		PERIOD	Fees £
APPLICANTS REFERENCE	KEY NUMBER		£

Any enquires concerning this certificate to be addressed to:-

The Superintendent,
Land Charges Department,
Burrington Way,
Plymouth PL5 3LP.

IMPORTANT

PLEASE READ THE NOTES OVERLEAF.

NOTES

Effect of search	1. This certificate has no statutory effect with regard to registered land, (see Land Registration Act 1925 s. 59 and Land Charges Act 1972 s.14).
Particulars used for searching	2. The applicant should ensure that the particulars of search which are printed on this certificate (e.g. names, counties) are the exact particulars of the required search, (see s.10(6) of Land Charges Act 1972).
Names	3. Searching against names is conducted in accordance with the arrangements described in the "Practice Guide" (see 7 below). In printing names overleaf the forename(s) of an individual precede the Surname. The surname is contained within asterisks (*) to assist identification. In printing the names of local and certain other authorities, plus signs (+) may be present but these are for official use only.
"Bankruptcy Only" searches	4. If this certificate relates to a search requested on form K16 the words "BANKRUPTCY ONLY" are printed overleaf against the words "COUNTY OR COUNTIES". Any such search is limited to the entries described on form K16.
Protection period	5. The date printed in the box overleaf entitled "CERTIFICATE DATE" is the date of the certificate for the purpose of s.11 of the Land Charges Act 1972. The date printed in the box entitled "PROTECTION ENDS ON" is the latest date for the expiry of the period of protection which is conferred by that section of the Act. The latter date is supplied for the convenience of solicitors.
Fees	6. The fees amount shown on this certificate are provided for information only. Where fees have been debited to an account,a solicitor should await receipt of an invoice before making payment.
Practice Guide	7. For further information on procedures for making applications to the Land Charges Department, see the booklet "Computerised Land Charges Department: a practical guide for solicitors", obtainable on application at the address shown below.
Enquiries	8. Any enquiries regarding this certificate should quote the "CERTIFICATE NUMBER" and the "CERTIFICATE DATE" and should be sent to:- The Superintendent, Land Charges Department, Burrington Way, Plymouth PL5 3LP.

[3045]

FORM K18
CERTIFICATE OF THE RESULT OF SEARCH

Rule 17(1)

LAND CHARGES ACT, 1972.
CERTIFICATE OF THE RESULT OF SEARCH

Form **K18**

CERTIFICATE No.	CERTIFICATE DATE	PROTECTION ENDS ON

It is hereby certified that an official search in respect of the undermentioned particulars has been made in the index to the registers which are kept pursuant to the Land Charges Act, 1972. The result of the search is shown below.

PARTICULARS SEARCHED			
COUNTY OR COUNTIES			
NAME(S) / Particulars of Charge		PERIOD	Fees £

APPLICANT'S REFERENCE		APPLICANT'S KEY NUMBER		£

Any enquiries concerning this certificate to be addressed to:-
The Superintendent
Land Charges Department,
Burrington Way,
Plymouth PL5 3LP.

IMPORTANT
PLEASE READ THE NOTES OVERLEAF.

NOTES

Effect of search	1. This certificate has no statutory effect with regard to registered land, (see Land Registration Act 1925 s.59 and Land Charges Act 1972 s.14).
Particulars used for searching	2. The applicant should ensure that the particulars of search which are printed on this certificate (e.g. names, counties) are the exact particulars of the required search, (see s.10(6) of Land Charges Act 1972).
Use of land description(s)	3. Where a land description taken from the application for search has been used by the Land Charges Department for the purpose of limiting the number of entries revealed, it is produced overleaf with an explanatory note immediately following the charge particulars.
Name	4. Searching against names is conducted in accordance with the arrangements described in the "Practice Guide" (see 9 below). In printing names overleaf the forename(s) of an individual precede the surname. The surname is contained within asterisks (*) to assist identification. Where a search reveals an entry the chargor's name is printed exactly as is recorded in the index. In printing the names of local and certain other authorities, plus signs (+) may be present but these are for official use only.
Charge particulars	5. The information taken from the index is identified overleaf by code numbers, as follows:- Code (1) Type of entry. Official reference number. Date of registration. (2) Short description of the land (3) Parish, place or district (4) County (5) Additional information regarding the entry (e.g. "Priority Notice only" or "Pursuant to Priority Notice No. ...") (6) The title, trade or profession of the chargor (7) Chargor's address.
"Bankruptcy Only" searches	6. If this certificate relates to a search requested on form K16 the words "BANKRUPTCY ONLY" are printed overleaf against the words "COUNTY OR COUNTIES". Any such search is limited to the entries described on form K16.
Protection Period	7. The date printed in the box overleaf entitled "CERTIFICATE DATE" is the date of the certificate for the purposes of s.11 of the Land Charges Act 1972. The date printed on the box entitled "PROTECTION ENDS ON" is the latest date for expiry of the period of protection which is conferred by that section of the Act. This latter date is supplied for the convenience of solicitors.
Fees	8. The fee amounts shown on this certificate are provided for information only. Where fees have been debited to an account, a solicitor should await receipt of an invoice before making payment.
Practice Guide	9. For futher information on procedures for making application to the Land Charges Department, see the booklet "Computerised Land Charges Department: a practical guide for solicitors, "obtainable on application at the address shown below.
Enquiries	10. Any enquiries regarding this certificate should quote the "CERTIFICATE NUMBER" and the "CERTIFICATE DATE" and should be sent to:- The Superintendent, Land Charges Department Burrington Way Plymouth, PL5 3LP.

[3046]

FORM K19
APPLICATION FOR AN OFFICE COPY OF AN ENTRY IN THE REGISTER

Rule 19(1)

Important: Please read the notes overleaf before completing this form.	**Form K19** **Land Charges Act 1972** **APPLICATION FOR AN OFFICE COPY OF AN ENTRY IN THE REGISTER**		**Payment of fee** Insert a cross (X) in this box if the fee is to be paid through a credit account *(See Note 1 overleaf).*
	Application is made for an office copy of the entry described below Is a copy of any plan filed in the register required? Please delete as applicable. YES/NO		
Delete words not applicable.	**PARTICULARS OF ENTRY** LAND CHARGE (Class .... Sub-Class ....) ANNUITY PENDING ACTION WRIT OR ORDER DEED OF ARRANGEMENT	Insert number and date of the registration L/C Registration No.	Date of registration *(See Note 2 overleaf)* Day / Month / Year
Only one individual or body to be entered.	**PARTICULARS OF ESTATE OWNER** Forename(s) **SURNAME**		**FOR OFFICIAL USE ONLY** 1 # 2 OC 3 Ø1 4 5
(See Note 3 overleaf)	**KEY NUMBER**		
Solicitor's name and address (including postcode). If no solicitor is acting enter the applicant's name and address (including postcode). *(See Notes 4 and 5 overleaf)*	Solicitor's reference:		

NAME AND ADDRESS (INCLUDING POSTCODE) TO WHICH COPY IS TO BE SENT (PLEASE USE BLOCK CAPITALS)

☛ THIS SPACE MUST BE COMPLETED BY THE APPLICANT.

Solicitor's reference ....

NOTES FOR GUIDANCE APPLICANTS

The following notes are supplied for assistance in making the application overleaf. Detailed information for the making of all kinds of applications to the Land Charges Department is contained in a booklet entitled "Computerised Land Charges Department: a practical guide for solicitors" which is obtainable on application at the address shown below.

1. **Fees.** These must be paid by credit account or by cheque or postal order made payable to "HM Land Registry" (see the guide referred to above).

2. **Date of completion.** Complete all boxes and refer to month by 3 letters:-

e.g.

Day		Month			Year			
0	4	S	E	P	1	9	8	1

3. **Key number.** If you have been allocated a key number, please take care to enter this in the space provided overleaf, whether or not you are paying fees through your credit account.

4. **Solicitor's reference.** Any references should be limited to 25 characters, including oblique strokes and punctuation.

5. **Despatch of this form.** When completed, send this application form to the address shown below, which is printed in a position so as to fit within a standard window envelope.

THE SUPERINTENDENT
LAND CHARGES DEPARTMENT
OFFICE COPY SECTION
PLUMER HOUSE, TAILYOUR ROAD,
CROWNHILL, PLYMOUTH PL6 5HY
DX 8249 PLYMOUTH (3)

(see Note 5 above)

FORM K20
APPLICATION FOR A CERTIFICATE OF THE CANCELLATION OF AN ENTRY IN THE REGISTER

Rule 12

Important: Please read the notes overleaf before completing this form.

Form K20 **Land Charges Act 1972**

APPLICATION FOR A CERTIFICATE OF THE CANCELLATION OF AN ENTRY IN THE REGISTER

Payment of fee
Insert a cross (X) in this box if the fee is to be paid through a credit account ☐
(See Note 1 overleaf).

Please certify that the entry described below has been cancelled in the register.

(See Note 2 overleaf)

PARTICULARS OF ENTRY

Delete words not applicable.

Land Charge (Class.....................Sub-Class.............)
Annuity
Pending Action
Writ or order
Deed of Arrangement

Insert number and date of the registration			
Official reference no.	Date of registration *(See Note 3 overleaf)*		
	Day	Month	Year

PARTICULARS OF ESTATE OWNER

Only one individual or body to be entered.

Forename(s)
SURNAME
Address

FOR OFFICIAL USE ONLY

1	#
2	CT
3	Ø1
4	
5	

KEY NUMBER

(See Note 4 overleaf)

Solicitor's name and address (including postcode).
If no solicitor is acting enter applicant's name and address (including postcode).
(See Notes 5 and 6 overleaf)

Solicitor's reference

Date ....

CERTIFICATE OF CANCELLATION

It is hereby certified that the entry in the register of ....
under official reference number.. dated ....
was cancelled on .... under official reference number ....

NAME AND ADDRESS INCLUDING POSTCODE, TO WHICH CERTIFICATE IS TO BE SENT (PLEASE USE BLOCK LETTERS)

☛ THIS SPACE MUST BE COMPLETED BY THE APPLICANT.

Official stamp of Land Charges Department

Applicant's Reference ....**NOT APPLICABLE TO REGISTE**..........

NOTES FOR GUIDANCE OF APPLICANTS

The following notes are supplied for assistance in making the application overleaf. Detailed information for the making of all kinds of applications to the Land Charges Department is contained in a booklet entitled "Computerised Land Charges Department: a practical guide for solicitors" which is obtainable on application at the address shown below.

1. **Fees.** These must be paid through your credit account, or by cheque or postal order made payable to "HM Land Registry" (see the guide referred to above).

2. **Form completion.** This form should only be used where a certificate is required that an entry in the register has previously been cancelled. Where it is desired to apply for cancellation of a subsisting entry, form K11 (or, in the case of a land charge of class F, form K13) should be used.

3. **Date of registration.** Complete all boxes and refer to the month by three letters:-

e.g.

Day		Month			Year			
0	4	S	E	P	1	9	8	1

4. **Key number.** If you have been allocated a key number, please take care to enter this in the space provided overleaf, whether or not you are paying fees through your credit account.

5. **Applicant's reference.** Any reference should be limited to 25 characters including any oblique strokes and punctuation.

6. **Despatch of application.** When completed, send this application form to the address shown below, which is printed in a position to fit within a standard window envelope.

THE SUPERINTENDENT
LAND CHARGES DEPARTMENT
CANCELLATION SECTION
PLUMER HOUSE, TAILYOUR ROAD,
CROWNHILL, PLYMOUTH PL6 5HY
DX 8249 PLYMOUTH (3)

[3048]

FORM K21
APPLICATION FOR AN INSPECTION OF THE REGISTER

Rule 3(2)

FEE STAMPS	
Signature	Date

[3049]

FORM K22
ACKNOWLEDGEMENT OF APPLICATION

Rule 23

LAND CHARGES ACT, 1972.

ACKNOWLEDGEMENT OF APPLICATION

Form **K22**

The Chief Land Registrar acknowledges receipt of the undermentioned application to which effect has been given on the date and under the official reference number shown below.

TYPE OF APPLICATION	OFFICIAL REFERENCE NUMBER	DATE OF REGISTRATION

NAME OF THE ESTATE OWNER/CHARGOR Particulars of the entry	**IMPORTANT** PLEASE READ THE NOTES OVERLEAF

APPLICANT'S REFERENCE	KEY NUMBER		£

Please address any enquires to:-

Land Charges Department,
Drakes Hill Court, Burrington Way,
Plymouth PL5 3LP.
DX No. 8249 Plymouth (3)
TEL: 01752 635655 or 635600
FAX: 01752 766666

NOTES

Particulars of the entry	1. Please check the information printed overleaf and notify the Land Charges Department of any apparent inaccuracy.
Authentic acknowledgements	2. All Land Charges acknowledgements are printed on Land Registry watermarked paper.
Name of the Estate owner/Chargor	3. Asterisks (*) are used to identify the surname of an individual.
Code numbers	4. The following is an explanation of the code numbers used to identify information printed overleaf:- (1) Type of Entry. Official Reference Number. Date of Registration. (2) Short description of the land. (3) Parish, place or district. (4) County. (5) Additional information regarding the entry.
Fees	5. The fee amounts shown in this acknowledgement are provided for information only. Where fees have been debited to an account, an applicant should await receipt of an invoice before making payment.
Practice Guide	6. Further information about procedures in the Land Charges Department are contained in "Computerised Land Charges Department - a practical guide for solicitors" obtainable on request from the address shown overleaf.

[3050]

SCHEDULE 3

PART I

FORM OF APPLICATION BY TELEPRINTER FOR AN OFFICIAL SEARCH IN THE INDEX

Each item must be set out on a separate line (with double spacing between lines) thus:—

(Applicant's answer back code and telex number; date in brackets)

SEARCH

(Name to be searched) (1)

PD: (first year to be covered by the search) TO (last year to be covered by the search)

(Repeat preceding two items in respect of each name to be searched)

CO: (name of county) (2)

DES: (short description of land) (3)

KN: (applicant's key number)

REF: (applicant's reference) (4)

(1) For the name of an individual, the forename(s) must precede the surname and be separated from it by an oblique stroke.

(2) The name of any relevant former county or counties must be added and enclosed in brackets.

(3) It is not essential to give this item. If it is given, any relevant former description should be added on a separate line and enclosed in brackets.

(4) This reference must not exceed 10 digits (including punctuation). If it exceeds that number, only the first 10 digits (including punctuation) will be given in the certificate of result of search.

[3051]

PART II

FORM OF APPLICATION BY TELEPRINTER FOR AN OFFICE COPY OF AN ENTRY IN THE REGISTER

Each item must be set out on a separate line (with double spacing between lines), thus:—

(Applicant's answer back code and telex number; date in brackets)

Office Copy

(The register affected) (1)

(Official reference number and date of registration of relevant entry)

(Name against which entry registered)

KN: (applicant's key number)

REF: (applicant's reference) (2)

(Name and address to which office copy to be sent)

(1) State the relevant register: for example, LAND CHARGES or PENDING ACTIONS.

(2) This reference must not exceed 10 digits (including punctuation). If it exceeds that number, only the first 10 digits (including punctuation) will be given when the office copy is issued.

[3052]–[3058]

HIGH COURT AND COUNTY COURTS JURISDICTION ORDER 1991

(SI 1991/724)

NOTES

Made: 19 March 1991.
Authority: Courts and Legal Services Act 1990, ss 1, 120.
Commencement: 1 July 1991.

1 Title and commencement

This Order may be cited as the High Court and County Courts Jurisdiction Order 1991 and shall come into force on 1st July 1991.

[3059]

[1A] [In this Order—

(a) "the EOP Regulation" means Regulation (EC) No 1896/2006 of the European Parliament and of the Council of 12 December 2006 creating a European order for payment procedure; and
(b) "the ESCP Regulation" means Regulation (EC) No 861/2007 of the European Parliament and of the Council of 11 July 2007 establishing a European small claims procedure.]

[3059A]

NOTES

Commencement: 12 December 2008 (in relation to the EOP Regulation), 1 January 2009 (for remaining purposes).
Inserted by SI 2008/2934, art 3

2 Jurisdiction

(1) A county court shall have jurisdiction under—
(a) sections … 146 and 147 of the Law of Property Act 1925,
(b) …
(c) section 26 of the Arbitration Act 1950,
(d) section 63(2) of the Landlord and Tenant Act 1954,
(e) section 28(3) of the Mines and Quarries (Tips) Act 1969,
(f) section 66 of the Taxes Management Act 1970,
(g) section 41 of the Administration of Justice Act 1970,
(h) …
(i) section 13 of the Torts (Interference with Goods) Act 1977,
(j) section 87 of the Magistrates' Courts Act 1980,
[(k) sections 17 and 18 of the Audit Commission Act 1998,]
(l) sections 15, 16, 21, 25 and 139 of the County Courts Act 1984,
(m) section 39(4) of, and paragraph 3(1) of Schedule 3 to, the Legal Aid Act 1988,
(n) sections 99, 102(5), 114, 195, 204, 230, 231 and 235(5) of the Copyright, Designs and Patents Act 1988, …
(o) section 40 of the Housing Act 1988,
[(p) sections 13 and 14 of the Trusts of Land and Appointment of Trustees Act 1996,]
[(q) the EOP Regulation,
(r) the ESCP Regulation,]

whatever the amount involved in the proceedings and whatever the value of any fund or asset connected with the proceedings.

(2) A county court shall have jurisdiction under—
(a) section 10 of the Local Land Charges Act 1975, and
(b) section 10(4) of the Rentcharges Act 1977,

where the sum concerned or amount claimed does not exceed £5,000.

(3) A county court shall have jurisdiction under the following provisions of the Law of Property Act 1925 where the capital value of the land or interest in land which is to be dealt with does not exceed £30,000:
(a) sections 3, 49, 66, 181, and 188;
(b) proviso (iii) to paragraph 3 of Part III of Schedule 1;
(c) proviso (v) to paragraph 1(3) of Part IV of Schedule 1;
(d) provisos (iii) and (iv) to paragraph 1(4) of Part IV of Schedule 1.

(4) A county court shall have jurisdiction under sections 89, 90, 91 and 92 of the Law of Property Act 1925 where the amount owing in respect of the mortgage or charge at the commencement of the proceedings does not exceed £30,000.

(5) A county court shall have jurisdiction under the proviso to section 136(1) of the Law of Property Act 1925 where the amount or value of the debt or thing in action does not exceed £30,000.

(6) A county court shall have jurisdiction under section 1(6) of the Land Charges Act 1972—
(a) in the case of a land charge of Class C(i), C(ii) or D(i), if the amount does not exceed £30,000;
(b) in the case of a land charge of Class C(iii), if it is for a specified capital sum of money not exceeding £30,000 or, where it is not for a specified capital sum, if the capital value of the land affected does not exceed £30,000;
(c) in the case of a land charge of Class A, Class B, Class C(iv), Class D(ii), Class D(iii) or Class E, if the capital value of the land affected does not exceed £30,000;
(d) in the case of a land charge of Class F, if the land affected by it is the subject of an order made by the court under section 1 of the Matrimonial Homes Act 1983 or an application for an order under that section relating to that land has been made to the court;
(e) in a case where an application under section 23 of the Deeds of Arrangement Act 1914 could be entertained by the court.

(7) A county court shall have jurisdiction under sections 69, 70 and 71 of the Solicitors Act 1974 where a bill of costs relates wholly or partly to contentious business done in a county court and the amount of the bill does not exceed £5,000.

[(7A) A patents county court and the county courts listed in paragraph (7B) shall have jurisdiction under the following provisions of the Trade Marks Act 1994—

(a) sections 15, 16, 19, 23(5), 25(4)(b), 30, 31, 46, 47, 64, 73 and 74;
(b) paragraph 12 of Schedule 1; and
(c) paragraph 14 of Schedule 2,

to include jurisdiction to hear and determine any claims or matters ancillary to, or arising from proceedings brought under such provisions.

(7B) For the purposes of paragraph (7A), the county courts at—

(a) Birmingham;
(b) Bristol;
(c) Cardiff;
(d) Leeds;
(e) Liverpool;
(f) Manchester; and
(g) Newcastle upon Tyne,

shall have jurisdiction.]

(8) The enactments and statutory instruments listed in the Schedule to this Order are amended as specified therein, being amendments which are consequential on the provisions of this article.

[3060]

NOTES

Para (1): in sub-para (a) number omitted revoked, in sub-para (n) word omitted revoked, and sub-para (p) inserted by SI 1996/3141, art 2; sub-para (b) revoked by SI 2005/587, art 3(a); sub-para (h) revoked and sub-paras (q), (r) inserted by SI 2008/2934, art 4; sub-para (k) substituted by virtue of the Audit Commission Act 1998, s 54(2), Sch 4, para 4(1).

Paras (7A), (7B): inserted by SI 2005/587, art 3(b).

3 (*Outside the scope of this work.*)

4 Allocation—Commencement of proceedings

Subject to articles [4A,] 5 [, 6[, 6A and 6B]] proceedings in which both the county courts and the High Court have jurisdiction may be commenced either in a county court or in the High Court.

[3061]

NOTES

Reference in first pair of square brackets inserted by SI 1999/1014, art 4; reference in second (outer) pair of square brackets substituted by the Access to Neighbouring Land Act 1992, s 7(2); words in third (inner) pair of square brackets substituted by SI 2008/2934, art 6.

[4A Except for proceedings to which article 5 applies, a claim for money in which the county courts have jurisdiction may only be commenced in the High Court if the value of the claim is more than £25,000.]

[3062]

NOTES

Inserted by SI 1999/1014, art 5; substituted by SI 2009/577, art 2.

5–8A (*Arts 5, 6, 6A, 6B, 8, 8A outside the scope of this work; art 7 revoked by SI 1999/1014, art 7.*)

[8B Enforcement of possession orders against trespassers

(1) A judgment or order of a county court for possession of land made in a possession claim against trespassers may be enforced in the High Court or a county court.

(2) In this article "a possession claim against trespassers" has the same meaning as in Part 55 of the Civil Procedure Rules 1998.]

[3063]

NOTES

Inserted by SI 2001/2685, art 2.

[9 … [Value] of claim]

For the purposes of Articles 4A and 5, the … value of the claim shall be calculated in accordance with rule 16.3(6) of the Civil Procedure Rules 1998.]

[3064]

NOTES

Provision heading: word omitted revoked, and word in square brackets substituted, by SI 2009/577, art 6.
Substituted by SI 1999/1014, art 9; word omitted revoked by SI 2009/577, art 7.

10–12 (*Art 10 revoked by SI 1999/1014, art 10; arts 11, 12 outside the scope of this work.*)

(*Schedule contains repeals and revocations only.*)

FAMILY PROVISION (INTESTATE SUCCESSION) ORDER 1993

(SI 1993/2906)

NOTES

Made: 29 November 1993.
Authority: Family Provision Act 1996, s 1(1)(a), (b).
Commencement: 1 December 1993.

1 This Order may be cited as the Family Provision (Intestate Succession) Order 1993 and shall come into force on 1st December 1993.

[3065]

2 In the case of a person dying after the coming into force of this Order, section 46(1) of the Administration of Estates Act 1925 shall apply as if the net sums charged by paragraph (i) on the residuary estate were—

(a) under paragraph (2) of the Table, the sum of £125,000; and
(b) under paragraph (3) of the Table, the sum of £200,000.

[3066]

LAND REGISTRATION RULES 2003

(SI 2003/1417)

NOTES

Made: 19 May 2003.

Authority: the Land Registration Act 2002, ss 1(2), 6(6), 13(a), (b), 14(a), (b), 16(2), 18(1)(b), (2), (4), 19(2), 20(3)(a)–(c), 21(2)(a)–(d), 22, 25(1), 27(6), 34(2), 35(3), 36(3), (4), 37(2), 39, 43(2)(a)–(d), 44(2), 45(2), 46(4), 47(a), (b), 48(2)(a), (b), 49(2), (3)(b), (4)(b), 50, 57, 60(3), (4), 61(2), 64(2), 66(2), 67(3), 68(1)(d), (2)(a), (b), 69(2), 70, 71(a), (b), 72(6)(a), (b), 73(2)–(4), 75(2), 76(2), 81(2), 82, 86(3), 87(4), 89, 95(a), 98(7), Sch 2, paras 2(2), 7(3), Sch 4, paras 4(a)–(c), 7(a)–(d), Sch 6, paras 2(1)(d), 3(2), 14, 15, Sch 8, para 9, Sch 10, paras 1(1)(a), (b), 3(a)–(c), 5, 6(a)–(e), 7, 8, Sch 12, paras 2(4), 18(5); the Charities Act 1993, ss 37(7), 39(1), (1A); the Leasehold Reform, Housing and Urban Development Act 1993, ss 34(10), (11); the Family Law Act 1996, Sch 4, para 4(4).

Commencement: 13 October 2003 (the day on which the Land Registration Act 2002, s 1 was brought into force by SI 2003/1725).

PRELIMINARY

1 Citation and commencement

These rules may be cited as the Land Registration Rules 2003 and shall come into force on the day that section 1 of the Act comes into force.

[3067]

PART 1
THE REGISTER OF TITLE

2 Form and arrangement of the register of title

(1) The register of title may be kept in electronic or paper form, or partly in one form and partly in the other.

(2) Subject to rule 3, the register of title must include an individual register for each registered estate which is—

(a) an estate in land, or

(b) a rentcharge, franchise, manor or profit a prendre in gross,

vested in a proprietor.

[3068]

3 Individual registers and more than one registered estate, division and amalgamation

(1) The registrar may include more than one registered estate in an individual register if the estates are of the same kind and are vested in the same proprietor.

(2) On first registration of a registered estate, the registrar may open an individual register for each separate area of land affected by the proprietor's registered estate as he designates.

(3) Subsequently, the registrar may open an individual register for part of the registered estate in a registered title and retain the existing individual register for the remainder—

(a) on the application of the proprietor of the registered estate and of any registered charge over it, or

(b) if he considers it desirable for the keeping of the register of title, or

(c) on the registration of a charge of part of the registered estate comprised in the registered title.

(4) The registrar may amalgamate two or more registered titles, or add an estate which is being registered for the first time to an existing registered title, if the estates are of the same kind and are vested in the same proprietor—

(a) on the application of the proprietor of the registered estate and of any registered charge over it, or

(b) if he considers it desirable for the keeping of the register of title.

(5) Where the registrar has divided a registered title under paragraph (3)(b) or amalgamated registered titles or an estate on first registration with a registered title under paragraph (4)(b) he—

(a) must notify the proprietor of the registered estate and any registered charge, unless they have agreed to such action, and

(b) may make a new edition of any individual register or make entries on any individual register to reflect the division or amalgamation.

[3069]

4 Arrangement of individual registers

(1) Each individual register must have a distinguishing number, or series of letters and numbers, known as the title number.

(2) Each individual register must consist of a property register, a proprietorship register and, where necessary, a charges register.

(3) An entry in an individual register may be made by reference to a plan or other document; in which case the registrar must keep the original or a copy of the document.

(4) Whenever the registrar considers it desirable, he may make a new edition of any individual register so that it contains only the subsisting entries, rearrange the entries in the register or alter its title number.

[3070]

5 Contents of the property register

[Except where otherwise permitted, the] property register of a registered estate must contain—

(a) a description of the registered estate which in the case of a registered estate in land, rentcharge or registered franchise which is an affecting franchise must refer to a plan based on the Ordnance Survey map and known as the title plan;

(b) where appropriate, details of—

  (i) the inclusion or exclusion of mines and minerals in or from the registration under rule 32,

  [(ii) easements, rights and privileges benefiting the registered estate and other similar matters,]

  (iii) all exceptions [or reservations] arising on enfranchisement of formerly copyhold land, and

  (iv) any … matter [otherwise] required to be entered in any other part of the register which the registrar considers may more conveniently be entered in the property register, and

(c) such other matters as are required to be entered in the property register by these rules.

[3071]

NOTES

Words in square brackets substituted by SI 2008/1919, r 4(1), Sch 1, para 1(a).

PART II STATUTORY INSTRUMENTS

Para (b): in sub-para (ii) substituted by SI 2008/1919, r 4(1), Sch 1, para 1(b); in sub-para (iii) words in square brackets inserted by SI 2008/1919, r 4(1), Sch 1, para 1(c); in sub-para (iv) word omitted revoked, and word in square brackets inserted, by SI 2008/1919, Sch 1, para 1(d).

6 Property register of a registered leasehold estate

(1) The property register of a registered leasehold estate must also contain sufficient particulars of the registered lease to enable that lease to be identified.

(2) [Subject to rule 72A(3),] if the lease contains a provision that prohibits or restricts dispositions of the leasehold estate, the registrar must make an entry in the property register stating [the lease prohibits or restricts dispositions of the estate].

[3072]

NOTES

Para (2): words in first pair of square brackets inserted by SI 2005/1982, r 4; words in second pair of square brackets substituted by SI 2008/1919, r 4(1), Sch 1, para 2.

7 Property register of a registered estate in a rentcharge, a franchise or a profit a prendre in gross

[Where practicable, the] property register of a registered estate in a rentcharge, franchise or a profit a prendre in gross must, if the estate was created by an instrument, also contain sufficient particulars of the instrument to enable it to be identified.

[3073]

NOTES

Words in square brackets substituted by SI 2008/1919, r 4(1), Sch 1, para 3.

8 Contents of the proprietorship register

(1) The proprietorship register of a registered estate must contain, where appropriate—

- (a) the class of title,
- (b) the name of the proprietor of the registered estate including, where the proprietor is a company registered under the Companies Acts, or a limited liability partnership incorporated under the Limited Liability Partnerships Act 2000, its registered number,
- (c) an address for service of the proprietor of the registered estate in accordance with rule 198,
- (d) restrictions under section 40 of the Act, including one entered under section 86(4) of the Act, in relation to the registered estate,
- (e) notices under section 86(2) of the Act in relation to the registered estate,
- (f) positive covenants by a transferor or transferee and indemnity convenants by a transferee entered under rules 64 or 65,
- (g) details of any modification of the covenants implied by paragraphs 20(2) and (3) of Schedule 12 to the Act entered under rule 66,
- (h) details of any modification of the covenants implied under the Law of Property (Miscellaneous Provisions) Act 1994 entered under rule 67(6),
- (i) …
- (j) such other matters as are required to be entered in the proprietorship register by these rules.

[(2) Where practicable, the registrar must enter in the proprietorship register—

- (a) on first registration of a registered estate,
- (b) following completion by registration of a lease which is a registrable disposition, and
- (c) on a subsequent change of proprietor of a registered estate,

the price paid or value declared for the registered estate.

(3) An entry made under paragraph (2) must remain until there is a change of proprietor, or some other change in the register of title which the registrar considers would result in the entry being misleading.]

[3074]

NOTES

Para (1): sub-para (i) revoked by SI 2008/1919, r 4(1), Sch 1, para 8(a).
Paras (2), (3): substituted for original para (2), by SI 2008/1919, Sch 1, para 4(b).

9 Contents of the charges register

[Except where otherwise permitted, the] charges register of a registered estate must contain, where appropriate—

- (a) details of leases, charges, and any other interests which adversely affect the registered estate subsisting at the time of first registration of the estate or created thereafter,

(b) any dealings with the interests referred to in paragraph (a), or affecting their priority, which are capable of being noted on the register,

(c) sufficient details to enable any registered charge to be identified,

(d) the name of the proprietor of any registered charge including, where the proprietor is a company registered under the Companies Acts, or a limited liability partnership incorporated under the Limited Liability Partnerships Act 2000, its registered number,

(e) an address for service of the proprietor of any registered charge in accordance with rule 198,

(f) restrictions under section 40 of the Act, including one entered under section 86(4) of the Act, in relation to a registered charge,

(g) notices under section 86(2) of the Act in relation to a registered charge, …

(h) such other matters affecting the registered estate or any registered charge as are required to be entered in the charges register by these rules[, and]

[(i) any matter otherwise required to be entered in any other part of the register which the registrar considers may more conveniently be entered in the charges register.]

[3075]

NOTES

Words in square brackets substituted by SI 2008/1919, r 4(1), Sch 1, para 5(a).

Para (g): word omitted revoked by SI 2008/1919, r 4(1), Sch 1, para 5(b).

Para (h): subsequent word in square brackets substituted by SI 2008/1919, r 4(1), Sch 1, para 5(c).

Para (i): inserted by SI 2008/1919, r 4(1), Sch 1, para 5(d).

PART 2
INDICES

10 Index to be kept under section 68 of the Act

(1) The index to be kept under section 68 of the Act must comprise—

(a) an index map from which it is possible to ascertain, in relation to a parcel of land, whether there is—

(i) a pending application for first registration (other than of title to a relating franchise),

(ii) a pending application for a caution against first registration (other than where the subject of the caution is a relating franchise),

(iii) a registered estate in land,

(iv) a registered rentcharge,

(v) a registered profit a prendre in gross,

(vi) a registered affecting franchise, or

(vii) a caution against first registration (other than where the subject of the caution is a relating franchise),

and, if there is such a registered estate or caution, the title number, and

(b) an index of verbal descriptions of—

(i) pending applications for first registration of title to relating franchises,

(ii) pending applications for cautions against first registration where the subject of the caution is a relating franchise,

(iii) registered franchises which are relating franchises,

(iv) registered manors, and

(v) cautions against first registration where the subject of the caution is a relating franchise,

and the title numbers of any such registered estates and cautions, arranged by administrative area.

(2) The information required to be shown in the index to be kept under section 68 is to be entered by the registrar in the index as soon as practicable.

[3076]

11 Index of proprietors' names

(1) Subject to paragraph (2), the registrar must keep an index of proprietors' names, showing for each individual register the name of the proprietor of the registered estate and the proprietor of any registered charge together with the title number.

(2) Until every individual register is held in electronic form, the index need not contain the name of any corporate or joint proprietor of an estate or of a charge registered as proprietor prior to 1st May 1972.

[(3) A person may apply in Form PN1 for a search to be made in the index in respect of—

(a) his own name,

(b) the name of a corporation aggregate, or

(c) the name of some other person in whose property he can satisfy the registrar that he is interested generally (for instance as trustee in bankruptcy or personal representative).]

(4) On receipt of such an application the registrar must make the search and supply the applicant with details of every entry in the index relating to the particulars given in the application.

[3077]

NOTES

Para (3): substituted by SI 2008/1919, r 4(1), Sch 1, para 6.

12 The day list

(1) The registrar must keep a record (known as the day list) showing the date and time at which every pending application under the Act or these rules was made and of every application for an official search with priority under rule 147.

(2) The entry of notice of an application for an official search with priority must remain on the day list until the priority period conferred by the entry has ceased to have effect.

(3) Where the registrar proposes to alter the register without having received an application he must enter his proposal on the day list and, when so entered, the proposal will have the same effect for the purposes of rules 15 and 20 as if it were an application to the registrar made at the date and time of its entry.

(4) In this rule the term "pending application" does not include [an application for a network access agreement under paragraph 1(4) of Schedule 5 to the Act, or] an application within Part 13, other than an application that the registrar designate a document an exempt information document under rule 136.

[3078]

NOTES

Para (4): words in square brackets inserted by SI 2008/1750, r 5, Sch 2, Pt 1, para 1.

PART 3
APPLICATIONS: GENERAL PROVISIONS

13 Form AP1

(1) Any application made under the Act or these rules for which no other application form is prescribed must be made in Form AP1.

(2) Paragraph (1) does not apply to—

(a) an application to remove from the register the name of a deceased joint registered proprietor,

(b) applications made under rule 14, or

(c) outline applications as defined in rule 54.

[3079]

NOTES

Disapplication: in relation to the disapplication of this rule in respect of applications for a network access agreement under the Land Registration Act 2002, Sch 5, para 1(4), see the Land Registration (Electronic Conveyancing) Rules 2008, SI 2008/1750, r 6, Sch 2, Pt 2, para 1.

14 Electronic delivery of applications

Any application to which rule 15 applies (other than an outline application under rule 54) may during the currency of any notice given under Schedule 2, and subject to and in accordance with the limitations contained in that notice, be delivered by electronic means and the applicant shall provide, in such order as may be required by that notice, such of the particulars required for an application of that type as are appropriate in the circumstances and as are required by the notice.

[3080]

NOTES

Disapplication: in relation to the disapplication of this rule in respect of applications for a network access agreement under the Land Registration Act 2002, Sch 5, para 1(4), see the Land Registration (Electronic Conveyancing) Rules 2008, SI 2008/1750, r 6, Sch 2, Pt 2, para 1.

15 Time at which applications are taken to be made

(1) An application received on a business day is to be taken as made at the earlier of—

(a) the time of the day that notice of it is entered in the day list, or

(b)

(i) midnight marking the end of the day it was received if the application was received before 12 noon, or

(ii) midnight marking the end of the next business day after the day it was received if the application was received at or after 12 noon.

(2) An application received on a day which is not a business day is to be taken as made at the earlier of—

(a) the time of [the] business day that notice of it is entered in the day list, or
(b) midnight marking the end of the next business day after the day it was received.

(3) In this rule an application is received when it is delivered—

(a) to the designated proper office in accordance with an order under section 100(3) of the Act, or
(b) to the registrar in accordance with a written arrangement as to delivery made between the registrar and the applicant or between the registrar and the applicant's conveyancer, or
(c) to the registrar under the provisions of any relevant notice given under Schedule 2.

(4) This rule does not apply to applications under Part 13, other than an application that the registrar designate a document an exempt information document under rule 136.

[3081]

NOTES

Para (2): in sub-para (a) word in square brackets substituted by SI 2008/1750, r 5, Sch 2, Pt 1, para 2.

Disapplication: in relation to the disapplication of this rule in respect of applications for a network access agreement under the Land Registration Act 2002, Sch 5, para 1(4), see the Land Registration (Electronic Conveyancing) Rules 2008, SI 2008/1750, r 6, Sch 2, Pt 2, para 1.

16 Applications not in order

(1) If an application is not in order the registrar may raise such requisitions as he considers necessary, specifying a period (being not less than twenty business days) within which the applicant must comply with the requisitions.

(2) If the applicant fails to comply with the requisitions within that period, the registrar may cancel the application or may extend the period when this appears to him to be reasonable in the circumstances.

(3) If an application appears to the registrar to be substantially defective, he may reject it on delivery or he may cancel it at any time thereafter.

(4) Where a fee for an application is paid by means of a cheque and the registrar becomes aware, before that application has been completed, that the cheque has not been honoured, the application may be cancelled.

[3082]

NOTES

Disapplication: in relation to the disapplication of this rule in respect of applications for a network access agreement under the Land Registration Act 2002, Sch 5, para 1(4), see the Land Registration (Electronic Conveyancing) Rules 2008, SI 2008/1750, r 6, Sch 2, Pt 2, para 1.

17 Additional evidence and enquiries

If the registrar at any time considers that the production of any further documents or evidence or the giving of any notice is necessary or desirable, he may refuse to complete or proceed with an application, or to do any act or make any entry, until such documents, evidence or notices have been supplied or given.

[3083]

NOTES

Disapplication: in relation to the disapplication of this rule in respect of applications for a network access agreement under the Land Registration Act 2002, Sch 5, para 1(4), see the Land Registration (Electronic Conveyancing) Rules 2008, SI 2008/1750, r 6, Sch 2, Pt 2, para 1.

18 Continuation of application on a transfer by operation of law

If, before an application has been completed, the whole of the applicant's interest is transferred by operation of law, the application may be continued by the person entitled to that interest in consequence of that transfer.

[3084]

NOTES

Disapplication: in relation to the disapplication of this rule in respect of applications for a network access agreement under the Land Registration Act 2002, Sch 5, para 1(4), see the Land Registration (Electronic Conveyancing) Rules 2008, SI 2008/1750, r 6, Sch 2, Pt 2, para 1.

19 Objections

(1) Subject to paragraph (5), an objection under section 73 of the Act to an application must be made by delivering to the registrar at the appropriate office a written statement signed by the objector or his conveyancer.

(2) The statement must—
- (a) state that the objector objects to the application,
- (b) state the grounds for the objection, and
- (c) give the full name of the objector and an address [for service in accordance with rule 198].

(3) Subject to paragraph (5), the written statement referred to in paragraph (1) must be delivered—
- (a) in paper form, or
- (b) to the electronic address, or
- (c) to the fax number.

(4) In paragraph (3) the reference to the electronic address and the fax number is to the electronic address or fax number for the appropriate office specified in a direction by the registrar under section 100(4) of the Act as that to be used for delivery of objections.

(5) Where a person is objecting to an application in response to a notice given by the registrar, he may alternatively do so in the manner and to the address stated in the notice as provided by rule 197(1)(c).

(6) In this rule the appropriate office is the same office as the proper office, designated under an order under section 100(3) of the Act, for the receipt of an application relating to the land in respect of which the objection is made, but on the assumption that if the order contains exceptions none of the exceptions apply to that application.

[3085]

NOTES

Para (2): in sub-para (c) words in square brackets substituted by SI 2008/1919, r 4(1), Sch 1, para 7.

Disapplication: in relation to the disapplication of this rule in respect of applications for a network access agreement under the Land Registration Act 2002, Sch 5, para 1(4), see the Land Registration (Electronic Conveyancing) Rules 2008, SI 2008/1750, r 6, Sch 2, Pt 2, para 1.

20 Completion of applications

(1) Any entry in, removal of an entry from or alteration of the register pursuant to an application under the Act or these rules has effect from the time of the making of the application.

(2) This rule does not apply to the applications mentioned in section 74 of the Act.

[3086]

NOTES

Disapplication: in relation to the disapplication of this rule in respect of applications for a network access agreement under the Land Registration Act 2002, Sch 5, para 1(4), see the Land Registration (Electronic Conveyancing) Rules 2008, SI 2008/1750, r 6, Sch 2, Pt 2, para 1.

PART 4
FIRST REGISTRATION

21 First registration—application by mortgagee

A mortgagee under a mortgage falling within section 4(1)(g) of the Act may make an application in the name of the mortgagor for the estate charged by the mortgage to be registered whether or not the mortgagor consents.

[3087]

22 Registration of a proprietor of a charge falling within section 4(1)(g) of the Act

(1) This rule applies to an application for first registration made—
- (a) under rule 21, or
- (b) by the owner of an estate that is subject to a legal charge falling within section 4(1)(g) of the Act.

(2) The registrar must enter the mortgagee of the legal charge falling within section 4(1)(g) of the Act as the proprietor of that charge if he is satisfied of that person's entitlement.

[3088]

23 First registration—application form

(1) Subject to paragraph (2), an application for first registration must be made in Form FR1.

(2) Where Her Majesty applies for the first registration of an estate under section 79 of the Act, Form FR1 must be used with such modifications to it as are appropriate and have been approved by the registrar.

[3089]

24 Documents to be delivered with a first registration application

(1) Unless the registrar otherwise directs, every application for first registration must be accompanied by—

(a) sufficient details, by plan or otherwise (subject to rules 25 and 26), so that the land can be identified clearly on the Ordnance Survey map,

(b) in the case of a leasehold estate, the lease, if in the control of the applicant, and a certified copy,

(c) all deeds and documents relating to the title that are in the control of the applicant,

(d) a list in duplicate in Form DL of all the documents delivered.

(2) On an application to register a rentcharge, franchise or profit a prendre in gross, the land to be identified under paragraph (1)(a) is the land affected by that estate or to which it relates.

[3090]

25 First registration of mines and minerals

When applying for first registration of an estate in mines and minerals held apart from the surface, the applicant must provide—

(a) a plan of the surface under which the mines and minerals lie,

(b) any other sufficient details by plan or otherwise so that the mines and minerals can be identified clearly, and

(c) full details of rights incidental to the working of the mines and minerals.

[3091]

26 First registration of cellars, flats, tunnels etc

(1) Subject to paragraph (2), unless all of the land above and below the surface is included in an application for first registration the applicant must provide a plan of the surface on under or over which the land to be registered lies, and sufficient information to define the vertical and horizontal extents of the land.

(2) This rule does not apply where only mines and minerals are excluded from the application.

[3092]

27 First registration application [based on adverse possession or] where title documents are [otherwise] unavailable

[(1)] An application for first registration by a person who is unable to produce a full documentary title must be supported by evidence—

(a) to satisfy the registrar that the applicant is entitled to apply under section 3(2) of the Act or required to apply under section 6(1) of the Act, and

(b) where appropriate, to account for the absence of documentary evidence of title.

[(2) The evidence referred to in paragraph (1) may consist of, or include, a statement of truth, which may be made in Form ST1, ST2 or ST3, as appropriate.]

[3093]

NOTES

Provision heading: words in square brackets inserted by SI 2008/1919, r 4(1), Sch 1, para 8(1).
Para (1): numbered as such by SI 2008/1919, r 4(1), Sch 1, para 8(2).
Para (2): inserted by SI 2008/1919, r 4(1), Sch 1, para 8(3).

28 Duty to disclose unregistered interests that override first registration

(1) Subject to paragraph (2), a person applying for first registration must provide information to the registrar about any of the interests that fall within Schedule 1 to the Act that—

(a) are within the actual knowledge of the applicant, and

(b) affect the estate to which the application relates,

in Form DI.

(2) The applicant is not required to provide information about—

(a) an interest that under section 33 or 90(4) of the Act cannot be protected by notice,

(b) an interest that is apparent from the deeds and documents of title accompanying the application under rule 24,

(c) a public right,

(d) a local land charge,

(e) a leasehold estate in land if—

(i) it is within paragraph 1 of Schedule 1 to the Act, and

(ii) at the time of the application, the term granted by the lease has one year or less to run.

(3) In this rule and in Form FR1, a "disclosable overriding interest" is an interest that the applicant must provide information about under paragraph (1).

(4) Where the applicant provides information about a disclosable overriding interest under this rule, the registrar may enter a notice in the register in respect of that interest.

[3094]

29 First registration—examination of title

In examining the title shown by the documents accompanying an application for first registration the registrar may have regard to any examination of title by a conveyancer prior to the application and to the nature of the property.

[3095]

30 Searches and enquiries by the registrar

In examining title on an application for first registration the registrar may—

(a) make searches and enquiries and give notices to other persons,
(b) direct that searches and enquiries be made by the applicant,
(c) advertise the application.

[3096]

31 First registration—foreshore

(1) Where it appears to the registrar that any land included in an application for first registration comprises foreshore, he must serve a notice of that application on—

(a) the Crown Estate Commissioners in every case,
(b) the Chancellor of the Duchy of Lancaster in the case of land in the county palatine of Lancaster,
(c) the appropriate person in the case of land in the counties of Devon and Cornwall and in the Isles of Scilly and in the case of land within the jurisdiction of the Port of London Authority, and
(d) the Port of London Authority in the case of land within its jurisdiction.

(2) A notice under paragraph (1) must provide a period ending at 12 noon on the twentieth business day after the date of issue of the notice in which to object to the application.

(3) A notice need not be served under paragraph (1) where, if it was served, it would result in it being served on the applicant for first registration.

(4) In this rule—

"the appropriate person" means such person as the Duke of Cornwall, or the possessor for the time being of the Duchy of Cornwall, appoints,

"foreshore" has the meaning given by paragraph 13(3) of Schedule 6 to the Act.

[3097]

32 Mines and minerals—note as to inclusion or exclusion

Where, on first registration of an estate in land which comprises or includes the land beneath the surface, the registrar is satisfied that the mines and minerals are included in or excluded from the applicant's title he must make an appropriate note in the register.

[3098]

33 First registration—entry of beneficial rights

(1) The benefit of an appurtenant right may be entered in the register at the time of first registration if—

(a) on examination of the title, or
(b) on receipt of a written application providing details of the right and evidence of its existence,

the registrar is satisfied that the right subsists as a legal estate and benefits the registered estate.

(2) If the registrar is not satisfied that the right subsists as a legal interest benefiting the registered estate, he may enter details of the right claimed in the property register with such qualification as he considers appropriate.

[(3) The evidence referred to in paragraph (1)(b) may consist of, or include, a statement of truth, which may be made in Form ST4 if appropriate.]

[3099]

NOTES

Para (3): inserted by SI 2008/1919, r 4(1), Sch 1, para 9.

34 First registration—registration of a proprietor of a legal mortgage not within rule 22 or rule 38

(1) The registrar must enter the mortgagee of a legal mortgage to which this rule applies as the proprietor of that charge if on first registration of the legal estate charged by that charge he is satisfied of that person's entitlement.

(2) This rule applies to a legal mortgage—

(a) which is either—

(i) a charge on the legal estate that is being registered, or

(ii) is a charge on such charge, and

(b) which is not a charge falling within rule 22 or rule 38.

[3100]

35 First registration—entry of burdens

(1) On first registration the registrar must enter a notice in the register of the burden of any interest which appears from his examination of the title to affect the registered estate.

(2) This rule does not apply to—

(a) an interest that under section 33 or 90(4) of the Act cannot be protected by notice,

(b) a public right,

(c) a local land charge,

(d) an interest which appears to the registrar to be of a trivial or obvious character, or the entry of a notice in respect of which would be likely to cause confusion or inconvenience.

[3101]

36 First registration—note as to rights of light and air

On first registration, if it appears to the registrar that an agreement prevents the acquisition of rights of light or air for the benefit of the registered estate, he may make an entry in the property register of that estate.

[3102]

37 First registration—notice of lease

[(1) This rule applies where—

(a) an application is made for registration of a leasehold estate under Chapter 1 of Part 2 of the Act,

(b) at the time of the grant of the lease—

(i) the reversion was not registered, or

(ii) the reversion was registered but the grant of the lease was not required to be completed by registration,

(c) the registrar is satisfied that a particular registered estate is the reversion, and

(d) the lease is not noted in the register of the registered reversion.

(2) Before completing registration of the leasehold estate, the registrar must give notice of the application to the proprietor of the registered reversion, unless it is apparent from the application that the proprietor consents to the registration.]

(3) On completing registration of the leasehold estate, the registrar must enter notice of the lease in the register of the registered reversion.

(4) In this rule, "the reversion" refers to the estate that is the immediate reversion to the lease that is the subject of the application referred to in paragraph (1) and "registered reversion" refers to such estate when it is a registered estate.

[3103]

NOTES

Paras (1), (2): substituted by SI 2008/1919, r 4(1), Sch 1, para 10.

38 Application of the Act to dealings prior to first registration

(1) If, while a person is subject to a duty under section 6 of the Act to make an application to be registered as proprietor of a legal estate, there is a dealing with that estate, then the Act applies to that dealing as if the dealing had taken place after the date of first registration of that estate.

(2) The registration of any dealing falling within paragraph (1) that is delivered for registration with the application made pursuant to section 6 has effect from the time of the making of that application.

[3104]

PART 5
CAUTIONS AGAINST FIRST REGISTRATION

39 Definitions

In this Part—

"cautioner" has the same meaning as in section 22 of the Act (read with rule 52),

"cautioner's register" is the register so named in rule 41(2) the contents of which are described in rule 41(5),

"relevant interest" means the interest claimed by the cautioner in the unregistered legal estate to which the caution against first registration relates.

[3105]

40 Form and arrangement of the cautions register

(1) The cautions register may be kept in electronic or paper form, or partly in one form and partly in the other.

(2) Subject to paragraph (3), the cautions register will comprise an individual caution register for each caution against the registration of title to an unregistered estate.

(3) On registration of a caution, the registrar may open an individual caution register for each separate area of land affected by the caution as he designates.

[3106]

41 Arrangement of individual caution registers

(1) Each individual caution register will have a distinguishing number, or series of letters and numbers, known as the caution title number.

(2) Each individual caution register will be in two parts called the caution property register and the cautioner's register.

(3) The caution property register will contain—

(a) a description of the legal estate to which the caution relates, and

(b) a description of the relevant interest.

(4) Where the legal estate to which the caution relates is an estate in land, a rentcharge, or an affecting franchise, the description will refer to a caution plan, which plan will be based on the Ordnance Survey map.

(5) The cautioner's register will contain—

(a) the name of the cautioner including, where the cautioner is a company registered under the Companies Acts, or a limited liability partnership incorporated under the Limited Liability Partnerships Act 2000, its registered number,

(b) an address for service in accordance with rule 198, and

(c) where appropriate, details of any person consenting to the lodging of the caution under rule 47.

[3107]

42 Caution against first registration—application

An application for a caution against first registration must be made in Form CT1 and contain sufficient details, by plan or otherwise, so that the extent of the land to which the caution relates can be identified clearly on the Ordnance Survey map.

[3108]

43 Withdrawal of a caution against first registration—application

An application to withdraw a caution against first registration must be made in Form WCT and, if the application is made in respect of part only of the land to which the individual caution register relates, it must contain sufficient details, by plan or otherwise, so that the extent of that part can be identified clearly on the Ordnance Survey map.

[3109]

44 Cancellation of a caution against first registration—application

(1) Subject to paragraph (5), an application for the cancellation of a caution against first registration must be in Form CCT.

(2) Where the application is made in respect of part only of the land to which the individual caution register relates, it must contain sufficient details, by plan or otherwise, so that the extent of that part can be identified clearly on the Ordnance Survey map.

(3) Where a person applies under section 18(1)(a) of the Act or rule 45(a) or (b)(ii), evidence to satisfy the registrar that he is entitled to apply must accompany the application.

(4) Where the applicant, or a person from whom the applicant derives title to the legal estate by operation of law, has consented to the lodging of the caution, evidence of the facts referred to in rule 46 must accompany the application.

(5) Where an application is made for the cancellation of a caution against first registration by Her Majesty by virtue of rule 45(b)(i), Form CCT must be used with such modifications to it as are appropriate and have been approved by the registrar.

[3110]

45 Other persons who may apply to cancel a caution against first registration

In addition to the owner of the legal estate to which the caution relates—

(a) the owner of a legal estate derived out of that estate, and

(b) where the land to which the caution relates is demesne land,

(i) Her Majesty, or

(ii) the owner of a legal estate affecting the demesne land,

may apply under section 18(1)(b) of the Act for cancellation of a caution against first registration.

[3111]

46 Application for cancellation of a caution against first registration by a person who originally consented

A person to whom section 18(2) of the Act applies may make an application for cancellation of a caution against first registration only if—

(a) the relevant interest has come to an end, or

(b) the consent referred to in section 18(2) was induced by fraud, misrepresentation, mistake or undue influence or given under duress.

[3112]

47 Consent to registration of a caution against first registration

For the purposes of section 18(2) of the Act a person consents to the lodging of a caution against first registration if before the caution is entered in the cautions register—

(a) he has confirmed in writing that he consents to the lodging of the caution, and

(b) that consent is produced to the registrar.

[3113]

48 Alteration of the cautions register by the court

(1) If in any proceedings the court decides that the cautioner does not own the relevant interest, or only owns part, or that such interest either wholly or in part did not exist or has come to an end, the court must make an order for alteration of the cautions register under section 20(1) of the Act.

(2) An order for alteration of the cautions register must state the caution title number of the individual caution register affected, describe the alteration that is to be made, and direct the registrar to make the alteration.

(3) For the purposes of section 20(2) of the Act an order for alteration of the cautions register may only be served on the registrar by making an application for him to give effect to the order.

[3114]

[49 Alteration of the cautions register by the registrar

(1) Subject to paragraph (2), if the registrar is satisfied that the cautioner does not own the relevant interest, or only owns part, or that such interest did not exist or has come to an end wholly or in part, he must on application alter the cautions register under section 21(1) of the Act.

(2) The registrar is not obliged to alter the cautions register under section 21(1) of the Act to substitute another person for the cautioner in the cautioner's register unless the whole of the relevant interest is vested in that other person by operation of law.]

[3115]

NOTES

Substituted by SI 2008/1919, r 4(1), Sch 1, para 11.

50 Applications to the registrar to alter the cautions register and service of notice

(1) A person who wishes the registrar to alter the cautions register under section 21(1) of the Act must request the registrar to do so by an application, which must include—

(a) written details of the alteration required and of the grounds on which the application is made, and

(b) any supporting document.

(2) Before the registrar alters the cautions register under section 21(1) of the Act he must serve a notice on the cautioner giving details of the application, unless the registrar is satisfied that service of the notice is unnecessary.

[3116]

51 Alteration of the cautions register—alteration of cautioner

(1) A person who claims that the whole of the relevant interest described in an individual caution register is vested in him by operation of law as successor to the cautioner may apply for the register to be altered under section 21(1) of the Act [substitute him for the] cautioner in the cautioner's register …

(2) If the registrar does not serve notice under rule 50(2) or if the cautioner does not object within the time specified in the notice, the registrar must give effect to the application.

[3117]

NOTES

Para (1): words in square brackets substituted, and words omitted revoked, by SI 2008/1919, r 4(1), Sch 1, para 12.

[52 Definition of "the cautioner"

(1) The other person referred to in sections 22 and 73(2) of the Act shall be the person for the time being shown as cautioner in the cautioner's register, where that person is not the person who lodged the caution against first registration.

(2) Where the cautioner shown in the cautioner's register comprises more than one person, then each such person has a separate right to object to an application made under section 18 of the Act.]

[3118]

NOTES

Substituted by SI 2008/1919, r 4(1), Sch 1, para 13.

53 The prescribed periods under section 16(2) and section 18(4) of the Act

(1) The period for the purpose of section 16(2) and section 18(4) of the Act is the period ending at 12 noon on the fifteenth business day after the date of issue of the notice under section 16(1) or section 18(3) of the Act, as the case may be, or such longer period as the registrar may allow following a request under paragraph (2), provided that the longer period never exceeds a period ending at 12 noon on the thirtieth business day after the date of issue of the notice.

(2) The request referred to in paragraph (1) is one by the cautioner to the registrar setting out why the longer period referred to in that paragraph should be allowed.

(3) If a request is received under paragraph (2), the registrar may, if he considers it appropriate, seek the views of the person who applied for registration or cancellation, as the case may be, and if, after considering any such views and all other relevant matters, he is satisfied that a longer period should be allowed he may allow such period (not exceeding a period ending at 12 noon on the thirtieth business day after the date of issue of the notice) as he considers appropriate, whether or not the period is the same as any period requested by the cautioner.

(4) A request under paragraph (2) must be made before the period ending at 12 noon on the fifteenth business day after the date of issue of the notice has expired.

[3119]

PART 6
REGISTERED LAND: APPLICATIONS, DISPOSITIONS AND MISCELLANEOUS ENTRIES

Applications

54 Outline applications

(1) An outline application is an application made in accordance with this rule.

(2) Subject to Schedule 2, any application may be made by outline application if it satisfies the following conditions—

(a) the application must not be—

(i) an application which can be protected by an official search with priority within the meaning of rule 147,

(ii) an application for first registration,

(iii) an application for a caution against first registration or in respect of the cautions register,

(iv) an application dealing with part only of the land in a registered title, whether or not also involving any other registered title,

(v) an application under Part 13, and

(b) the right, interest or matter the subject of the application must exist at the time the application is made.

(3) During the currency of any notice given under Schedule 2, and subject to and in accordance with the limitations contained in that notice, an outline application may be made by—

(a) an oral application,

(b) telephone, or
(c) electronic means.

(4) An outline application must contain the following particulars when made—
(a) the title number(s) affected,
(b) if there is only one proprietor or applicant for first registration and that person is an individual, his surname, otherwise the proprietor's or such applicant's full name or the full name of one of the proprietors or such applicants, as appropriate,
(c) the nature of the application,
(d) the name of the applicant,
(e) the name and address of the person or firm lodging the application,
(f) any other particulars specified in any notice made under Schedule 2.

(5) Every outline application must be allocated an official reference number and must be identified on the day list as such and must be marked with the date and time at which the application is taken as made and the registrar must acknowledge receipt of any outline application by notifying the applicant, as soon as practicable, of the official reference number allocated to it.

[(6) Without prejudice to the power of the registrar to cancel an application under rule 16, the outline application must be cancelled by the registrar unless there are delivered together at the appropriate office before the expiry of the reserved period—
(a) the application form prescribed by these rules for the application, the particulars of which have been given in the outline application, duly completed, and
(b) the appropriate documents.]

(7) If the outline application has been cancelled before the [application] form required by paragraph (6)[(a)] is delivered at the appropriate office, the registrar shall accept the form as an application in its own right.

[(8) In this rule the "appropriate office" is—
(a) the proper office, designated under an order under section 100(3) of the Act, for the receipt of an application relating to the land in respect of which the outline application is made, but on the assumption that if the order contains exceptions none of the exceptions apply to the application, or
(b) the office specified in a written arrangement made between the registrar and the applicant or between the registrar and the applicant's conveyancer for the delivery of applications of the nature particularised in the outline application.]

(9) In this rule "reserved period" means the period expiring at 12 noon on the fourth business day following the day that the outline application was taken as made.

[3120]

NOTES

Para (6): substituted by SI 2008/1919, r 4(1), Sch 1, para 14(a).
Para (7): word and reference in square brackets inserted by SI 2008/1919, r 4(1), Sch 1, para 14(b).
Para (8): substituted by SI 2008/1919, r 4(1), Sch 1, para 14(c).

55 Priority of applications

(1) Where two or more applications relating to the same registered title are under the provisions of rule 15 taken as having been made at the same time, the order in which, as between each other, they rank in priority shall be determined in the manner prescribed by this rule.

(2) Where the applications are made by the same applicant, they rank in such order as he may specify.

(3) Where the applications are not made by the same applicant, they rank in such order as the applicants may specify that they have agreed.

(4) Where the applications are not made by the same applicant, and the applicants have not specified the agreed order of priority, the registrar must notify the applicants that their applications are regarded as having been delivered at the same time and request them to agree, within a specified time (being not less than fifteen business days), their order of priority.

(5) Where the parties fail within the time specified by the registrar to indicate the order of priority of their applications the registrar must propose the order of priority and serve notice on the applicants of his proposal.

(6) Any notice served under paragraph (5) must draw attention to the right of any applicant who does not agree with the registrar's proposal to object to another applicant's application under the provisions of section 73 of the Act.

(7) Where one transaction is dependent upon another the registrar must assume (unless the contrary appears) that the applicants have specified that the applications will have priority so as to give effect to the sequence of the documents effecting the transactions.

[3121]

56 Dispositions affecting two or more registered titles

(1) A disposition affecting two or more registered titles may, on the written request of the applicant, be registered as to some or only one of the registered titles.

(2) The applicant may later apply to have the disposition registered as to any of the other registered titles affected by it.

[3122]

57 Duty to disclose unregistered interests that override registered dispositions

(1) Subject to paragraph (2), a person applying to register a registrable disposition of a registered estate must provide information to the registrar about any of the interests that fall within Schedule 3 to the Act that—

(a) are within the actual knowledge of the applicant, and
(b) affect the estate to which the application relates,

in Form DI.

(2) The applicant is not required to provide information about—

(a) an interest that under section 33 or 90(4) of the Act cannot be protected by notice,
(b) a public right,
(c) a local land charge, or
(d) a leasehold estate in land if—
  (i) it is within paragraph 1 of Schedule 3 to the Act, and
  (ii) at the time of the application, the term granted by the lease has one year or less to run.

(3) In this rule and in Form AP1, a "disclosable overriding interest" is an interest that the applicant must provide information about under paragraph (1).

(4) The applicant must produce to the registrar any documentary evidence of the existence of a disclosable overriding interest that is under his control.

(5) Where the applicant provides information about a disclosable overriding interest under this rule, the registrar may enter a notice in the register in respect of that interest.

[3123]

NOTES

Disapplication: in relation to the disapplication of this rule in respect of persons applying to register an electronic legal charge, see the Land Registration (Electronic Conveyancing) Rules 2008, SI 2008/1750, r 6, Sch 2, Pt 2, para 2.

Registrable dispositions—form

58 Form of transfer of registered estates

A transfer of a registered estate must be in Form TP1, TP2, … TR1, TR2, TR5, AS1 or AS3, as appropriate.

[3124]

NOTES

Reference omitted revoked SI 2008/1919, r 4(1), Sch 1, para 15.

[58A Form and content of prescribed clauses leases

(1) Subject to paragraph (3), a prescribed clauses lease must begin with the required wording or that wording must appear immediately after any front sheet.

(2) Subject to paragraph (3), where a person applies for completion of a lease by registration and claims that the lease is not a prescribed clauses lease because the lease falls within (c) or (d) of the definition of prescribed clauses lease in paragraph (4), he must lodge with his application a certificate by a conveyancer to that effect or other evidence to satisfy the registrar as to his claim.

(3) If it appears to the registrar that a lease is not a prescribed clauses lease, then paragraph (1) and, so far as appropriate, paragraph (2) and rule 72A(3) shall not apply to that lease.

(4) In this rule—

"front sheet" means a front cover sheet, or a contents sheet if it is at the lease's beginning, or a front cover sheet and contents sheet where the contents sheet is immediately after the front cover sheet, and a "contents sheet" means a contents sheet or index sheet (in each case, however described) or both,

"prescribed clauses lease" means a lease which—

(a) is within section 27(2)(b) of the Act,
(b) is granted on or after 19 June 2006,
(c) is not granted in a form expressly required—
  (i) by an agreement entered into before 19 June 2006,

(ii) by an order of the court,
(iii) by or under an enactment, or
(iv) by a necessary consent or licence for the grant of the lease given before 19 June 2006, and

(d) is not a lease by virtue of a variation of a lease which is a deemed surrender and re-grant, and

"required wording" means the wording in clauses LR1 to LR14 of Schedule 1A completed in accordance with the instructions in that Schedule and as appropriate for the particular lease.]

[3125]

NOTES

Commencement: 9 January 2006.
Inserted by SI 2005/1982, r 5.

59 Transfers by way of exchange

(1) Where any registered estate is transferred wholly or partly in consideration of a transfer of another estate, the transaction must be effected by a transfer in one of the forms prescribed by rule 58.

(2) A receipt for the equality money (if any) must be given in the receipt panel and the following provision must be included in the additional provisions panel—

"This transfer is in consideration of a transfer (*or* conveyance, *or as appropriate,*) of (*brief description of property exchanged*) dated today [*if applicable*, and of the sum stated above paid for equality of exchange].".

[3126]

60 Transfer of leasehold land, the rent being apportioned or land exonerated

(1) A transfer of a registered leasehold estate in land which contains a legal apportionment of or exoneration from the rent reserved by the lease must include the following statement in the additional provisions panel, with any necessary alterations and additions—

"Liability for the payment of [*if applicable* the previously apportioned rent of (*amount*) being part of] the rent reserved by the registered lease is apportioned between the Transferor and the Transferee as follows—

(*amount*) shall be payable out of the Property and the balance shall be payable out of the land remaining in title number (*title number of retained land*) or

the whole of that rent shall be payable out of the Property and none of it shall be payable out of the land remaining in title number (*title number of retained land*) or

the whole of that rent shall be payable out of the land remaining in title number (*title number of retained land*) and none of it shall be payable out of the Property".

(2) Where in a transfer of part of a registered leasehold estate which is held under an old tenancy that part is, without the consent of the lessor, expressed to be exonerated from the entire rent, and the covenants in paragraph 20(4) of Schedule 12 to the Act are included, that paragraph shall apply as if—

(a) the reference in paragraph 20(4)(a) to the rent apportioned to the part retained were to the entire rent, and

(b) the covenants in paragraphs 20(4)(b) and (c) extended to a covenant to pay the entire rent.

(3) Where in a transfer of part of a registered leasehold estate which is held under an old tenancy that part is, without the consent of the lessor, expressed to be subject to or charged with the entire rent, and the covenants in paragraph 20(3) of Schedule 12 to the Act are included, that paragraph shall apply as if—

(a) the reference in paragraph 20(3)(a) to the rent apportioned to the part transferred were to the entire rent, and

(b) the covenants in paragraphs 20(3)(b) and (c) extended to a covenant to pay the entire rent.

[3127]

Execution by an attorney

61 Documents executed by attorney

(1) If any document executed by an attorney is delivered to the land registry, there must be produced to the registrar—

(a) the instrument creating the power, or

(b) a copy of the power by means of which its contents may be proved under section 3 of the Powers of Attorney Act 1971, or

[(c) a document which under section 4 of the Evidence and Powers of Attorney Act 1940,

paragraph 16 of Part 2 of Schedule 1, or paragraph 15(3) of Part 5 of Schedule 4 to the Mental Capacity Act 2005 (c 9) is sufficient evidence of the contents of the power, or]
(d) a certificate by a conveyancer in Form 1.

[(2) If an order or direction under section 22 or 23 of, or paragraph 16 of Part 5 of Schedule 4 to, the Mental Capacity Act 2005 has been made with respect to a power or the donor of the power or the attorney appointed under it, the order or direction must be produced to the registrar.]

(3) In this rule, "power" means the power of attorney.

[3128]

NOTES

Para (1): sub-para (c) substituted by SI 2007/1898, art 6, Sch 1, para 31(1), (2)(a).
Para (2): substituted by SI 2007/1898, art 6, Sch 1, para 31(1), (2)(b).

62 Evidence of non-revocation of power more than 12 months old

(1) If any transaction between a donee of a power of attorney and the person dealing with him is not completed within 12 months of the date on which the power came into operation, the registrar may require the production of evidence to satisfy him that the power had not been revoked at the time of the transaction.

(2) The evidence that the registrar may require under paragraph (1) may consist of or include a statutory declaration [or statement of truth] by the person who dealt with the attorney or a certificate given by that person's conveyancer in Form 2.

[3129]

NOTES

Para (2): words in square brackets inserted by SI 2008/1919, r 4(1), Sch 1, para 16

63 Evidence in support of power delegating trustees' functions to a beneficiary

(1) If any document executed by an attorney to whom functions have been delegated under section 9 of the Trusts of Land and Appointment of Trustees Act 1996 is delivered to the registrar, the registrar may require the production of evidence to satisfy him that the person who dealt with the attorney—

(a) did so in good faith, and
(b) had no knowledge at the time of the completion of the transaction that the attorney was not a person to whom the functions of the trustees in relation to the land to which the application relates could be delegated under that section.

(2) The evidence that the registrar may require under paragraph (1) may consist of or include a statutory declaration [or statement of truth] by the person who dealt with the attorney or a certificate given by that person's conveyancer either in Form 3 or, where evidence of non-revocation is also required pursuant to rule 62, in Form 2.

[3130]

NOTES

Para (2): words in square brackets inserted by SI 2008/1919, r 4(1), Sch 1, para 17.

Covenants

64 Positive covenants

(1) The registrar may make an appropriate entry in the proprietorship register of any positive covenant that relates to a registered estate given by the proprietor or any previous proprietor of that estate.

(2) Any entry made under paragraph (1) must, where practicable, refer to the instrument that contains the covenant.

(3) If it appears to the registrar that a covenant referred to in an entry made under paragraph (1) does not bind the current proprietor of the registered estate, he must remove the entry.

[3131]

65 Indemnity covenants

(1) The registrar may make an appropriate entry in the proprietorship register of an indemnity covenant given by the proprietor of a registered estate in respect of any restrictive covenant or other matter that affects that estate or in respect of a positive covenant that relates to that estate.

(2) Any entry made under paragraph (1) must, where practicable, refer to the instrument that contains the indemnity covenant.

(3) If it appears to the registrar that a covenant referred to in an entry made under paragraph (1) does not bind the current proprietor of the registered estate, he must remove the entry.

[3132]

66 Modification of implied covenants in transfer of land held under an old tenancy

Where a transfer of a registered leasehold estate which is an old tenancy modifies or negatives any covenants implied by paragraphs 20(2) and (3) of Schedule 12 to the Act, an entry that the covenants have been so modified or negatived must be made in the register.

[3133]

67 Covenants implied under Part I of the Law of Property (Miscellaneous Provisions) Act 1994 and under the Law of Property Act 1925

(1) Subject to paragraph (2), a registrable disposition may be expressed to be made either with full title guarantee or with limited title guarantee and, in the case of a disposition which is effected by an instrument in the Welsh language, the appropriate Welsh expression specified in section 8(4) of the 1994 Act may be used.

(2) In the case of a registrable disposition to which section 76 of the LPA 1925 applies by virtue of section 11(1) of the 1994 Act—

(a) a person may be expressed to execute, transfer or charge as beneficial owner, settlor, trustee, mortgagee, or personal representative of a deceased person or under an order of the court, and the document effecting the disposition may be framed accordingly, and

(b) any covenant implied by virtue of section 76 of the LPA 1925 in such a disposition will take effect as though the disposition was expressly made subject to—

(i) all charges and other interests that are registered at the time of the execution of the disposition and affect the title of the covenantor,

(ii) any of the matters falling within Schedule 3 to the Act of which the purchaser has notice and subject to which it would have taken effect, had the land been unregistered.

(3) The benefit of any covenant implied under sections 76 and 77 of the LPA 1925 or either of them will, on and after the registration of the disposition in which it is implied, be annexed and incident to and will go with the registered proprietorship of the interest for the benefit of which it is given and will be capable of being enforced by the proprietor for the time being of that interest.

(4) The provisions of paragraphs (2)(b) and (3) are in addition to and not in substitution for the other provisions relating to covenants contained in the LPA 1925.

(5) Except as provided in paragraph (6), no reference to any covenant implied by virtue of Part I of the 1994 Act, or by section 76 of the LPA 1925 as applied by section 11(1) of the 1994 Act, shall be made in the register.

(6) A reference may be made in the register where a registrable disposition of leasehold land limits or extends [a covenant implied under section 4(1)(b)] of the 1994 Act.

(7) In this rule "the LPA 1925" means the Law of Property Act 1925 and "the 1994 Act" means the Law of Property (Miscellaneous Provisions) Act 1994.

[3134]

NOTES

Para (6): words in square brackets substituted by SI 2008/1919, r 4(1), Sch 1, para 18.

[68 Additional provision as to implied covenants

A document effecting a registrable disposition of leasehold land which limits or extends a covenant implied under section 4(1)(b) of the Law of Property (Miscellaneous Provisions) Act 1994 must do so by express reference to that section.]

[3135]

NOTES

Substituted by SI 2008/1919, r 4(1), Sch 1, para 19.

69 Transfer of registered estate subject to a rentcharge

(1) Where the covenants set out in Part VII or Part VIII of Schedule 2 to the LPA 1925 are included in a transfer, the references to "the grantees", "the conveyance" and "the conveying parties" shall be treated as references to the transferees, the transfer and the transferors respectively.

(2) Where in a transfer to which section 77(1)(B) of the LPA 1925 does not apply, part of a registered estate affected by a rentcharge is, without the consent of the owner of the rentcharge, expressed to be exonerated from the entire rent, and the covenants in paragraph (ii) of Part VIII of Schedule 2 to the LPA 1925 are included, that paragraph shall apply as if—

(a) any reference to the balance of the rent were to the entire rent, and

(b) the words ", other than the covenant to pay the entire rent," were omitted.

(3) Where in a transfer to which section 77(1)(B) of the LPA 1925 does not apply, part of a registered estate affected by a rentcharge is, without the consent of the owner of the rentcharge,

expressed to be subject to or charged with the entire rent, and the covenants in paragraph (i) of Part VIII of Schedule 2 to the LPA 1925 are included, that paragraph shall apply as if—

(a) any reference to the apportioned rent were to the entire rent, and

(b) the words " (other than the covenant to pay the entire rent)" were omitted.

(4) On a transfer of a registered estate subject to a rentcharge—

(a) any covenant implied by section 77(1)(A) or (B) of the LPA 1925 may be modified or negatived, and

(b) any covenant included in the transfer may be modified,

by adding suitable words to the transfer.

(5) In this rule "the LPA 1925" means the Law of Property Act 1925.

[3136]

Mines or minerals

[70 Description of land where mines or minerals situated

Where the registrar is describing a registered estate in land in the property register by reference to land where mines or minerals are or may be situated, he may make an entry to the effect that the description is an entry made under rule 5(a) and is not a note that the registered estate includes the mines or minerals for the purposes of paragraph 2 of Schedule 8 to the Act.]

[3137]

NOTES

Substituted by SI 2008/1919, r 4(1), Sch 1, para 20.

[71 Note as to inclusion of mines or minerals in the registered estate

(1) An application for a note to be entered that a registered estate includes the mines or minerals, or specified mines or minerals, must be accompanied by evidence to satisfy the registrar that those mines or minerals are included in the registered estate.

(2) If the registrar is satisfied that those mines or minerals are included in the registered estate, he must enter the appropriate note.]

[3138]

NOTES

Substituted by SI 2008/1919, r 4(1), Sch 1, para 21.

Miscellaneous entries

[72 Register entries arising from transfers and charges of part

(1) Subject to paragraphs (2) and (3), on registration of a transfer or charge of part of the registered estate in a registered title the registrar must make an entry in the property register of that registered title referring to the removal of the estate comprised in the transfer or charge.

(2) The registrar may, instead of making the entry referred to in paragraph (1), make a new edition of the registered title out of which the transfer or charge is made and, if the registrar considers it desirable, he may allot a new title number to that registered title.

(3) Paragraph (1) only applies to a charge of part of a registered estate in a registered title if the registrar decides that the charged part will be comprised in a separate registered title from the uncharged part.

(4) Subject to paragraph (5), on registration of a transfer or charge of part of the registered estate in a registered title the registrar must (where appropriate) make entries in the relevant individual registers in respect of any rights, restrictive covenants, provisions and other matters created by the transfer or charge which are capable of being entered in an individual register.

(5) The registrar need make no entries under paragraph (4) in individual registers where the title numbers of those registers in which entries are to be made have not been given in panel 2 of the Form AP1 lodged for the purpose of registering the transfer or charge, unless separate application is made in respect of the rights, restrictive covenants, provisions or other matters.

(6) Unless the Form AP1 contains a specific application, the registrar need not complete under paragraph 6 of Schedule 2 to the Act the registration of an interest of a kind falling within section 1(2)(b) of the Law of Property Act 1925 contained in a transfer or charge of part of the registered estate in a registered title.]

[3139]

NOTES

Substituted by SI 2008/1919, r 4(1), Sch 1, para 22.

[72A Register entries arising in respect of leases within section 27(2)(b) of the Act granted on or after 19 June 2006

(1) This rule applies to leases within section 27(2)(b) of the Act granted on or after 19 June 2006.

(2) Subject to paragraphs (3), (4) and (6), on completion of the lease by registration the registrar must (where appropriate) make entries in the relevant individual register in respect of interests contained in that lease which are of the nature referred to in clauses LR9, LR10, LR11 or LR12.

(3) Subject to rule 58A(3), where the lease is a prescribed clauses lease and contains a prohibition or restriction on disposal of the nature referred to in clause LR8 or contains interests of the nature referred to in clauses LR9, LR10, LR11 or LR12, but the prohibition or restriction or interests are not specified or referred to in those clauses or the lease does not contain the required wording in relation to them, then the registrar need take no action in respect of them unless separate application is made.

(4) The registrar need make no entries in individual registers in respect of interests of the nature referred to in clauses LR9, LR10 or LR11 or a restriction set out in clause LR13 where—

(a) in the case of a prescribed clauses lease, the title numbers of the individual registers have not been given in clause LR2.2, or

(b) in any other case, the title numbers of the individual registers required by clause LR2.2 have not been given in panel 2 of the Form AP1 lodged for the purpose of completing the lease by registration,

unless separate application is made in respect of the interests or restriction.

(5) Where a separate application required by paragraphs (3) or (4) is made in Form AP1 and is in respect of either a prohibition or restriction on disposal of the lease or the grant or reservation of an easement, the Form AP1 must specify the particular clause, schedule or paragraph of a schedule where the prohibition or restriction or easement is contained in the lease.

(6) The requirement under paragraph (2) to make an entry in respect of an interest of the nature referred to in clause LR12 is satisfied by entry (where appropriate) of notice of the interest created.

(7) In this rule—

(a) a reference to a clause with the prefix "LR" followed by a number is to the clause so prefixed and numbered in Schedule 1A, and

(b) "prescribed clauses lease" and "required wording" have the same meanings as in rule 58A(4).]

[3140]

NOTES

Commencement: 9 January 2006.
Inserted by SI 2005/1982, r 6.

[72B Entries in the tenant's registered title in respect of notices in the landlord's registered title

On completion of a lease within section 27(2)(b) or (c) of the Act by registration, the registrar must enter a notice or make another entry, as appropriate, in the individual register of the registered lease in respect of any interest which—

(a) at the time of registration, is the subject of a notice in the individual register of the registered estate out of which the lease is granted, and

(b) the registrar considers may affect the registered lease.]

[3141]

NOTES

Commencement: 10 November 2008.
Inserted by SI 2008/1919, r 4(1), Sch 1, para 23.

[72C Register entries arising from other registrable dispositions

(1) This rule applies to dispositions of registered estates within section 27(2) of the Act, to which rules 72 and 72A do not apply.

(2) Subject to paragraph (3), on registration of a disposition within paragraph (1), the registrar must (where appropriate) make entries in the relevant individual registers in respect of any rights, restrictive covenants, provisions and other matters created by the disposition which are capable of being entered in an individual register.

(3) The registrar need make no entries in individual registers under paragraph (2) where the title numbers of those registers have not been given in panel 2 of the Form AP1 lodged for the purpose of registering the disposition, unless separate application is made in respect of the rights, restrictive covenants, provisions or other matters.

(4) Unless the Form AP1 contains a specific application, the registrar need not complete under paragraph 6 of Schedule 2 to the Act the registration of an interest of a kind falling within section 1(2)(b) of the Law of Property Act 1925 contained in a disposition within paragraph (1).]

[3142]

NOTES

Commencement: 10 November 2008.
Inserted by SI 2008/1919, r 4(1), Sch 1, para 23.

[73A Application for register entries for legal easements and profits a prendre

(1) A proprietor of a registered estate may apply to be registered as the proprietor of a legal easement or profit a prendre which—

(a) has been expressly granted or reserved over an unregistered estate, or
(b) has been acquired otherwise than by express grant or reservation.

(2) The application must be accompanied by evidence to satisfy the registrar that the easement or profit a prendre is a legal estate which subsists for the benefit of the applicant's registered estate.

(3) In paragraph (1)(a) the reference to express grant does not include a grant as a result of the operation of section 62 of the Law of Property Act 1925, but the reference in paragraph (1)(b) to acquisition otherwise than by express grant does include an acquisition as a result of the operation of that section.

(4) The evidence referred to in paragraph (2) may consist of, or include, a statement of truth, which may be made in Form ST4, if appropriate.

(5) Where the registrar is not satisfied that the right claimed is a legal estate which subsists for the benefit of the applicant's registered estate, the registrar may enter details of the right claimed in the property register with such qualification as he considers appropriate.]

[3143]

NOTES

Commencement: 10 November 2008.
Substituted, for rr 73–75 as originally enacted, by SI 2008/1919, r 4(1), Sch 1, para 24.

76 Note as to rights of light or air

If it appears to the registrar that an agreement prevents the acquisition of rights of light or air for the benefit of the registered estate, he may make an entry in the property register of that estate.

[3144]

[77 No entry in the register of a right of entry in certain leases

(1) This rule applies to a right of entry created in a grant of a term of years absolute, the right being exercisable over or in respect of that term of years.

(2) Where the grant is completed by registration, the disposition which consists of the creation of the right of entry is also completed by registration, without any specific entry relating to it being made in the register.]

[3145]–[3146]

NOTES

Substituted by SI 2008/1919, r 4(1), Sch 1, para 25

78 (*Revoked by SI 2008/1919, r 4(1), Sch 1, para 26.*)

79 Determination of registered estates

(1) An application to record in the register the determination of a registered estate must be accompanied by evidence to satisfy the registrar that the estate has determined.

(2) Subject to paragraph (3), if the registrar is satisfied that the estate has determined, he must close the registered title to the estate and cancel any notice in any other registered title relating to it.

(3) Where an entry is made under rule 173 the registrar need not close the registered title to the estate until a freehold legal estate in land in respect of the land in which such former estate subsisted has been registered.

[3147]

[79A Acquisition of the right to manage by a RTM company

(1) This rule applies where a RTM company applies for an entry to be made in an individual register of a registered estate to the effect that the RTM company has acquired the right to manage.

(2) An application for such an entry must be accompanied by evidence to satisfy the registrar that—

(a) the applicant is a RTM company,
(b) the right to manage is in relation to premises comprised in the registered estate,
(c) the registered proprietor of the registered estate is the landlord under a lease of the whole or part of the premises, and
(d) the right to manage the premises has been acquired, and remains exercisable, by the RTM company.

(3) If the registrar is so satisfied, he must make an appropriate entry in the proprietorship register of the registered estate.

(4) In this rule, "right to manage" and "RTM company" have the same meanings as in sections 71 and 73 of the Commonhold and Leasehold Reform Act 2002.]

[3147A]

NOTES

Commencement: 10 November 2008.
Inserted by SI 2008/1919, r 4(1), Sch 1, para 27.

PART 7
NOTICES

80 Certain interests to be protected by agreed notices

A person who applies for the entry of a notice in the register must apply for the entry of an agreed notice where the application is for—

(a) a … home rights notice,
(b) an inheritance tax notice,
(c) a notice in respect of an order under the Access to Neighbouring Land Act 1992,
(d) a notice of any variation of a lease effected by or under an order under section 38 of the Landlord and Tenant Act 1987 (including any variation as modified by an order under section 39(4) of that Act),
(e) a notice in respect of a—
 (i) public right, or
 (ii) customary right.

[3148]

NOTES

Word omitted from para (a) revoked by SI 2005/1982, r 10.

81 Application for an agreed notice

(1) Subject to paragraph (2), an application for the entry in the register of an agreed notice (including an agreed notice in respect of any variation of an interest protected by a notice) must be—

(a) made in Form AN1,
(b) accompanied by the order or instrument (if any) giving rise to the interest claimed or, if there is no such order or instrument, such other details of the interest claimed as satisfy the registrar as to the nature of the applicant's claim, and
(c) accompanied, where appropriate, by—
 (i) the consent referred to in section 34(3)(b) of the Act, and, where appropriate, evidence to satisfy the registrar that the person applying for, or consenting to the entry of, the notice is entitled to be registered as the proprietor of the registered estate or charge affected by the interest to which the application relates, or
 (ii) evidence to satisfy the registrar as to the validity of the applicant's claim.

(2) Paragraph (1) does not apply to an application for the entry of a … home rights notice made under rule 82.

[3149]

NOTES

Para (2): word omitted revoked by SI 2005/1982, r 11.
Disapplication: see further, in relation to the disapplication of para (1)(b) above in respect of an electronic legal charge stored by the registrar, provided that the applicant gives sufficient details of the charge to enable the registrar to identify it, the Land Registration (Electronic Conveyancing) Rules 2008, r 6, Sch 2, Pt 2, para 3.

82 Application for a … home rights notice or its renewal

(1) An application under section 31(10)(a) or section 32 of, and paragraph 4(3)(b) of Schedule 4 to, the Family Law Act 1996 for the entry of an agreed notice in the register must be in [Form HR1].

(2) An application to renew the registration of a … home rights notice or a matrimonial home rights caution under section 32 of, and paragraph 4(3)(a) of Schedule 4 to, the Family Law Act 1996 must be in [Form HR2].

(3) An application in [Form HR1], where the application is made under section 32 of, and paragraph 4(3)(b) of Schedule 4 to, the Family Law Act 1996, or in [Form HR2] must be accompanied by—

(a) an office copy of the section 33(5) order, or

(b) a conveyancer's certificate that he holds an office copy of the section 33(5) order.

[3150]

NOTES

Provision heading: word omitted revoked by SI 2005/1982, r 12(1).

Para (1): words in square brackets substituted by SI 2005/1982, r 12(2), subject to transitional provisions in r 19 thereof.

Para (2): word omitted revoked and words in square brackets substituted, by SI 2005/1982, r 12(3), subject to transitional provisions in r 19 thereof.

Para (3): words in square brackets substituted by SI 2005/1982, r 12(4), subject to transitional provisions in r 19 thereof.

83 Application for entry of a unilateral notice

An application for the entry in the register of a unilateral notice must be in Form UN1.

[3151]

84 Entry of a notice in the register

(1) A notice under section 32 of the Act must be entered in the charges register of the registered title affected.

(2) The entry must identify the registered estate or registered charge affected and, where the interest protected by the notice only affects part of the registered estate in a registered title, it must contain sufficient details, by reference to a plan or otherwise, to identify clearly that part.

(3) In the case of a notice (other than a unilateral notice), the entry must give details of the interest protected.

(4) In the case of a notice (other than a unilateral notice) of a variation of an interest protected by a notice, the entry must give details of the variation.

(5) In the case of a unilateral notice, the entry must give such details of the interest protected as the registrar considers appropriate.

[3152]

85 Removal of a unilateral notice

(1) An application for the removal of a unilateral notice from the register under section 35(3) of the Act must be in Form UN2.

(2) The personal representative or trustee in bankruptcy of the person shown in the register as the beneficiary of a unilateral notice may apply under section 35(3) of the Act; and if he does he must provide evidence to satisfy the registrar as to his appointment as personal representative or trustee in bankruptcy.

(3) If the registrar is satisfied that the application is in order he must remove the notice.

[3153]

86 Cancellation of a unilateral notice

(1) An application to cancel a unilateral notice under section 36 of the Act must be made in Form UN4.

(2) An application made under section 36(1)(b) of the Act must be accompanied by—

(a) evidence to satisfy the registrar of the applicant's entitlement to be registered as the proprietor of the estate or charge to which the unilateral notice the subject of the application relates, or

(b) a conveyancer's certificate that the conveyancer is satisfied that the applicant is entitled to be registered as the proprietor of the estate or charge to which the unilateral notice the subject of the application relates.

(3) The period referred to in section 36(3) of the Act is the period ending at 12 noon on the fifteenth business day after the date of issue of the notice or such longer period as the registrar may allow following a request under paragraph (4), provided that the longer period never exceeds a period ending at 12 noon on the thirtieth business day after the issue of the notice.

(4) The request referred to in paragraph (3) is one by the beneficiary to the registrar setting out why the longer period referred to in that paragraph should be allowed.

(5) If a request is received under paragraph (4) the registrar may, if he considers it appropriate, seek the views of the person who applied for cancellation and if after considering any such views

and all other relevant matters he is satisfied that a longer period should be allowed he may allow such period (not exceeding a period ending at 12 noon on the thirtieth business day after the issue of the notice) as he considers appropriate, whether or not the period is the same as any period requested by the beneficiary.

(6) A request under paragraph (4) must be made before the period ending at 12 noon on the fifteenth business day after the date of issue of the notice under section 36(2) of the Act has expired.

(7) A person entitled to be registered as the beneficiary of a notice under rule 88 may object to an application under section 36(1) of the Act for cancellation of that notice and the reference to the beneficiary in section 36(3) includes such a person.

[(8) Where there are two or more persons—

(a) shown in the register as the beneficiary of the notice, or

(b) to whom paragraph (7) applies,

each such person is a beneficiary of the notice for the purpose of section 36(3) of the Act.]

[3154]

NOTES

Para (8): inserted by SI 2008/1919, r 4(1), Sch 1, para 28.

87 Cancellation of a notice (other than a unilateral notice or a … home rights notice)

(1) An application for the cancellation of a notice (other than a unilateral notice or a … home rights notice) must be in Form CN1 and be accompanied by evidence to satisfy the registrar of the determination of the interest.

(2) Where a person applies for cancellation of a notice in accordance with paragraph (1) and the registrar is satisfied that the interest protected by the notice has come to an end, he must cancel the notice or make an entry in the register that the interest so protected has come to an end.

(3) If the interest protected by the notice has only come to an end in part, the registrar must make an appropriate entry.

[(4) If the registrar is not satisfied that the interest protected by the notice has come to an end, he may enter in the register details of the circumstances in which the applicant claims the interest has determined.]

[3155]

NOTES

Provision heading, para (1): words omitted revoked by SI 2005/1982, r 13.
Para (4): inserted by SI 2008/1919, r 4(1), Sch 1, para 29.

[87A Cancellation of a home rights notice

An application for the cancellation of a home rights notice must be made in Form HR4.]

[3155A]

NOTES

Commencement: 10 November 2008.
Inserted by SI 2008/1919, r 4(1), Sch 1, para 30.

88 Registration of a new or additional beneficiary of a unilateral notice

(1) A person entitled to the benefit of an interest protected by a unilateral notice may apply to be entered in the register in place of, or in addition to, the registered beneficiary.

(2) An application under paragraph (1) must be—

(a) in Form UN3, and

(b) accompanied by evidence to satisfy the registrar of the applicant's title to the interest protected by the unilateral notice.

(3) Subject to paragraph (4), if an application is made in accordance with paragraph (2) and the registrar is satisfied that the interest protected by the unilateral notice is vested—

(a) in the applicant, the registrar must enter the applicant in the register in place of the registered beneficiary, or

(b) in the applicant and the registered beneficiary, the registrar must enter the applicant in addition to the registered beneficiary.

(4) Except where one of the circumstances specified in paragraph (5) applies, the registrar must serve notice of the application on the registered beneficiary before entering the applicant in the register.

(5) The registrar is not obliged to serve notice on the registered beneficiary if—

(a) the registered beneficiary signs Form UN3 or otherwise consents to the application, or

(b) the applicant is the registered beneficiary's personal representative and evidence of his title to act accompanies the application.

(6) In this rule, "registered beneficiary" means the person shown in the register as the beneficiary of the notice at the time an application is made under paragraph (1).

[3156]

89 Notice of unregistered interests

(1) If the registrar enters a notice of an unregistered interest under section 37(1) of the Act, he must give notice—

(a) subject to paragraph (2), to the registered proprietor, and
(b) subject to paragraph (3), to any person who appears to the registrar to be entitled to the interest protected by the notice or whom the registrar otherwise considers appropriate.

(2) The registrar is not obliged to give notice to a registered proprietor under paragraph (1)(a) who applies for entry of the notice or otherwise consents to an application to enter the notice.

(3) The registrar is not obliged to give notice to a person referred to in paragraph (1)(b) if—

(a) that person applied for the entry of the notice or consented to the entry of the notice, or
(b) that person's name and his address for service under rule 198 are not set out in the individual register in which the notice is entered.

[3157]

90 Application for entry of a notice under paragraph 5(2) or, in certain cases, paragraph 7(2)(a) of Part 1 of Schedule 2 to the Act

An application to meet the registration requirements under—

(a) paragraph 5(2) of Part 1 of Schedule 2 to the Act, or
(b) paragraph 7(2)(a) of that Part, where the interest is created for the benefit of an unregistered estate,

must be made in Form AP1.

[3158]

PART 8
RESTRICTIONS

91 Standard forms of restriction

(1) The forms of restriction set out in Schedule 4 [(varied, where appropriate, as permitted by rule 91A)] are standard forms of restriction prescribed under section 43(2)(d) of the Act.

(2) The word "conveyancer", where it appears in any of the standard forms of restriction, has the same meaning as in these rules.

(3) The word "registered", where it appears in any of the standard forms of restriction in relation to a disposition, means completion of the registration of that disposition by meeting the relevant registration requirements under section 27 of the Act.

[3159]

NOTES

Para (1): words in square brackets inserted by SI 2005/1766, r 3.

[91A Completion of standard forms of restriction

(1) Subject to paragraphs (2) and (3), [if] a standard form of restriction is to affect part only of the registered estate, then, where it refers to a disposition, or to a disposition of a specified type, to which it applies, that reference may be followed by the words "of the part of the registered estate" together with a sufficient description, by reference to a plan or otherwise, to identify clearly the part so affected

(2) The words incorporated [under] paragraph (1) shall be in place of the words "of the registered estate" where those latter words appear in a standard form of restriction and are referring to a disposition, or to a disposition of a specified type, to which the restriction applies.

(3) The registrar may alter the words of any restriction affecting part of the registered estate … that he intends to enter in the register so that such part is described by reference to the relevant title plan or in another appropriate way.

[(4) A restriction in Form L, N, S, T, II, NN or OO may commence with—

(a) the words "Until the death of [*name*]",
(b) the words "Until the death of the survivor of [*names of two or more persons*]", or
(c) the word "Until" followed by a calendar date.]

[(5) A restriction in Form M, O, P or PP may commence with the word "Until" followed by a calendar date.

(6) Where a restriction in Form J, K, Q, S, T, BB, DD, FF, HH, JJ, LL or OO relates to a registered charge, which is one of two or more registered charges bearing the same date and affecting the same registered estate, the words "in favour of" followed by the name of the registered proprietor of the charge must be inserted in the restriction after the date of the charge.

(7) Where in a standard form of restriction the word "they" or "their" refers to a person named in the restriction, it may be replaced as appropriate by the word "he", "she", "it", "his", "her" or "its".

(8) Where a standard form of restriction permits a type of disposition to be specified in place of the word "disposition", the types of disposition that may be specified are "transfer", "lease", "charge" or "sub-charge", or any appropriate combination of those types.]]

[3160]

NOTES

Inserted by SI 2005/1766, r 4.
Paras (1), (2); words in square brackets substituted by SI 2008/1919, r 4(1), Sch 1, para 31(a), (b).
Para (3): word omitted revoked by SI 2008/1919, r 4(1), Sch 1, para 31(c).
Para (4): substituted by SI 2008/1919, r 4(1), Sch 1, para 31(d).
Para (5)–(8): inserted by SI 2008/1919, r 4(1), Sch 1, para 31(e).

[91B Where a certificate or consent under a restriction is given by a corporation

(1) Subject to paragraphs (2), (3) and (4), where a certificate or written consent required by the terms of a restriction is given by a corporation aggregate, it must be signed on its behalf by—

(a) its clerk, secretary or other permanent officer,
(b) a member of its board of directors, council or other governing body,
(c) its conveyancer, or
(d) its duly authorised employee or agent.

(2) This rule does not apply where the certificate or written consent is given in a deed executed by the company or in a document to which section 91 of the Act applies.

(3) Paragraph (1) does not apply if a contrary intention appears in the restriction, except where paragraph (4) applies.

(4) Where a restriction requires a certificate or consent to be signed on behalf of a corporation aggregate by its secretary (whether or not it also permits signature by its conveyancer), and the corporation has no secretary, the certificate or consent must be signed on its behalf by a person specified in paragraph (1).

(5) A document signed on behalf of a corporation in accordance with this rule must state the full name of the signatory and the capacity in which the signatory signs.]

[3160A]

NOTES

Commencement: 10 November 2008.
Inserted by SI 2008/1919, r 4(1), Sch 1, para 32.

92 Application for a restriction and the prescribed period under section 45(2) of the Act

(1) Subject to paragraphs (5), (6), (7) and (8) an application for a restriction to be entered in the register must be made in Form RX1.

(2) The application must be accompanied by—

(a) full details of the required restriction,
[(b) where rule 198(2)(d) applies, the address for service of the person named in the restriction,]
(c) if the application is made with the consent of the relevant registered proprietor, or a person entitled to be registered as such proprietor, and that consent is not given in Form RX1, the relevant consent,
(d) if the application is made by or with the consent of a person entitled to be registered as the relevant registered proprietor, evidence to satisfy the registrar of his entitlement, and
(e) if the application is made by a person who claims that he has a sufficient interest in the making of the entry, the statement referred to in paragraph (3) signed by the applicant or his conveyancer.

[(3) The statement required under paragraph (2)(e) must—

(a) give details of the nature of the applicant's interest in the making of the entry of the required restriction, and
(b) give details of how the applicant's interest arose.]

(4) If requested to do so, an applicant within paragraph (2)(e) must supply further evidence to satisfy the registrar that he has a sufficient interest.

PART II STATUTORY INSTRUMENTS

(5) The registrar may accept a certificate given by a conveyancer that the conveyancer is satisfied that the person making or consenting to the application is entitled to be registered as the relevant proprietor, and that either—

(a) the conveyancer holds the originals of the documents that contain evidence of that person's entitlement, or

(b) an application for registration of that person as proprietor is pending at the land registry.

(6) If an application is made with the consent of the relevant registered proprietor, or a person entitled to be registered as such proprietor, the registrar may accept a certificate given by a conveyancer that the conveyancer holds the relevant consent.

[(7) Paragraph (1) of this rule does not apply where a person applies for the entry of a standard form of restriction—

(a) in the additional provisions panel of Form TP1, TP2, TR1, TR2, TR4, TR5, AS1, AS2 or AS3,

(b) in panel 8 of Form CH1 or in an electronic legal charge,

(c) in an approved charge,

(d) in clause LR13 (as set out in Schedule 1A) of a relevant lease, or

(e) in Form A, using Form SEV.]

(8) This rule does not apply to an application to the registrar to give effect to an order of the court made under section 46 of the Act.

(9) The period for the purpose of section 45(2) of the Act is the period ending at 12 noon on the fifteenth business day after the date of issue of the notice under section 45(1) or, if more than one such notice is issued, the date of issue of the latest notice.

[(10) In this rule—

"approved charge" means a charge the form of which (including the application for the restriction) has first been approved by the registrar, and

"relevant lease" means—

(a) a prescribed clauses lease as defined in rule 58A(4), or

(b) any other lease which complies with the requirements as to form and content set out in rule 58A(1) and which either is required to be completed by registration under section 27(2)(b) of the Act or is the subject of an application for first registration of the title to it.]

[3161]

NOTES

Para (2): sub-para (b) substituted by SI 2005/1766, r 5.
Paras (3), (7): substituted by SI 2008/1919, r 4(1), Sch 1, para 33.
Para (10): substituted by SI 2005/1982, r 7(2).

93 Persons regarded as having a sufficient interest to apply for a restriction

The following persons are to be regarded as included in section 43(1)(c) of the Act—

(a) any person who has an interest in a registered estate held under a trust of land where a sole proprietor or a survivor of joint proprietors (unless a trust corporation) will not be able to give a valid receipt for capital money, and who is applying for a restriction in Form A to be entered in the register of that registered estate,

(b) any person who has a sufficient interest in preventing a contravention of section 6(6) or section 6(8) of the Trusts of Land and Appointment of Trustees Act 1996 and who is applying for a restriction in order to prevent such a contravention,

(c) any person who has an interest in a registered estate held under a trust of land where the powers of the trustees are limited by section 8 of the Trusts of Land and Appointment of Trustees Act 1996, and who is applying for a restriction in Form B to be entered in the register of that registered estate,

(d) any person who has an interest in the due administration of the estate of a deceased person, where—

(i) the personal representatives of the deceased hold a registered estate on a trust of land created by the deceased's will and the personal representatives' powers are limited by section 8 of the Trusts of Land and Appointment of Trustees Act 1996, and

(ii) he is applying for a restriction in Form C to be entered in the register of that registered estate,

(e) the donee of a special power of appointment in relation to registered land affected by that power,

(f) the Charity Commissioners in relation to registered land held upon charitable trusts,

(g) the Church Commissioners, the Parsonages Board or the Diocesan Board of Finance if applying for a restriction—

(i) to give effect to any arrangement which is made under any enactment or Measure administered by or relating to the Church Commissioners, the Parsonages Board or the Diocesan Board of Finance, or

(ii) to protect any interest in registered land arising under any such arrangement or statute,

(h) any person with the benefit of a freezing order or an undertaking given in place of a freezing order, who is applying for a restriction in Form AA or BB,

(i) any person who has applied for a freezing order and who is applying for a restriction in Form CC or DD,

[(j) a trustee in bankruptcy in whom a beneficial interest in registered land held under a trust of land has vested, and who is applying for a restriction in Form J to be entered in the register of that land,]

(k) any person with the benefit of a charging order over a beneficial interest in registered land held under a trust of land who is applying for a restriction in Form K to be entered in the register of that land,

(l) a person who has obtained a restraint order under—

(i) paragraph 5(1) or 5(2) of Schedule 4 to the Terrorism Act 2000, or

(ii) section 41 of the Proceeds of Crime Act 2002,

and who is applying for a restriction in Form EE or FF,

(m) a person who has applied for a restraint order under the provisions referred to in paragraph (1) and who is applying for a restriction in Form GG or HH,

(n) a person who has obtained an acquisition order under section 28 of the Landlord and Tenant Act 1987 and who is applying for a restriction in Form L or N,

(o) a person who has applied for an acquisition order under section 28 of the Landlord and Tenant Act 1987 and who is applying for a restriction in Form N,

(p) a person who has obtained a vesting order under section 26(1) or 50(1) of the Leasehold Reform, Housing and Urban Development Act 1993 and who is applying for a restriction in Form L or N,

(q) a person who has applied for a vesting order under section 26(1) or 50(1) of the Leasehold Reform, Housing and Urban Development Act 1993 and who is applying for a restriction in Form N,

(r) the International Criminal Court where it applies for a restriction—

(i) in Form AA or BB to give effect to a freezing order under Schedule 6 to the International Criminal Court Act 2001, or

(ii) in Form CC or DD to protect an application for such a freezing order,

(s) a receiver or a sequestrator appointed by order who applies for a restriction in Form L or N,

(t) a trustee under a deed of arrangement who applies for a restriction in Form L or N,

(u) a person who has obtained an interim receiving order under section 246 of the Proceeds of Crime Act 2002 and who is applying for a restriction in Form EE or FF, …

(v) a person who has applied for an interim receiving order under section 246 of the Proceeds of Crime Act 2002 and who is applying for a restriction in Form GG or HH[, …]

[(w) the Legal Services Commission where it has a statutory charge, created by section 16(6) of the Legal Aid Act 1988 or by section 10(7) of the Access to Justice Act 1999, over a beneficial interest in registered land held under a trust of land and is applying for a restriction in Form JJ to be entered in the register of that land][, and]

[(x) a local authority where it has a statutory charge created under section 22 of the Health and Social Services and Social Security Adjudications Act 1983 on the beneficial interest of an equitable joint tenant in a registered estate and is applying for a restriction in Form MM to be entered in the register of that estate.]

[3162]

NOTES

Para (j) substituted by SI 2008/1919, r 4(1), Sch 1, para 34(a).

Para (u): word omitted revoked by SI 2005/1766, r 6(1), (2).

Para (v): word (as inserted by SI 2005/1766, r 6(1), (3)) omitted revoked by SI 2008/1919, r 4(1), Sch 1, para 34(b).

Para (w): inserted by SI 2005/1766, r 6; word in square brackets substituted by SI 2008/1919, r 4(1), Sch 1, para 34(b).

Para (x): inserted by SI 2008/1919, r 4(1), Sch 1, para 34(d).

94 When an application for a restriction must be made

(1) [Subject to paragraph (9), a proprietor] of a registered estate must apply for a restriction in Form A where—

(a) the estate becomes subject to a trust of land, other than on a registrable disposition, and the proprietor or the survivor of joint proprietors will not be able to give a valid receipt for capital money, or

(b) the estate is held on a trust of land and, as a result of a change in the trusts, the proprietor or the survivor of joint proprietors will not be able to give a valid receipt for capital money.

(2) A sole or last surviving trustee of land held on a trust of land must, when applying to register a disposition of a registered estate in his favour or to be registered as proprietor of an unregistered estate, at the same time apply for a restriction in Form A.

[(2A) Where two or more persons apply to register a disposition of a registered estate in their favour or to be registered as proprietors of an unregistered estate, they must at the same time apply for a restriction in Form A if—

(a) the estate is a rentcharge, profit a prendre in gross, franchise or manor, and
(b) a sole proprietor or the survivor of joint proprietors will not be able to give a valid receipt for capital money.]

(3) Subject to [paragraphs (6) and (10)], a personal representative of a deceased person who holds a registered estate on a trust of land created by the deceased's will, or on a trust of land arising under the laws of intestacy which is subsequently varied, and whose powers have been limited by section 8 of the Trusts of Land and Appointment of Trustees Act 1996, must apply for a restriction in Form C.

(4) Subject to [paragraphs (6), (7) and (9)], a proprietor of a registered estate must apply for a restriction in Form B where—

(a) a declaration of trust of that estate imposes limitations on the powers of the trustees under section 8 of the Trusts of Land and Appointment of Trustees Act 1996, or
(b) a change in the trusts on which that estate is held imposes limitations or changes the limitations on the powers of the trustees under section 8 of the Trusts of Land and Appointment of Trustees Act 1996.

(5) Subject to paragraphs (6) and (7), an applicant for first registration of a legal estate held on a trust of land where the powers of the trustees are limited by section 8 of the Trusts of Land and Appointment of Trustees Act 1996 must at the same time apply for a restriction in Form B.

(6) Paragraphs (3), (4) and (5) do not apply to legal estates held on charitable, ecclesiastical or public trusts.

(7) Paragraphs (4) and (5) apply not only where the legal estate is held by the trustees, but also where it is vested in the personal representatives of a sole or last surviving trustee.

(8) An application for a restriction must be made where required by paragraphs (2) or (3) of rule 176 or paragraph (2) of rule 178.

[(9) Where there are two or more persons entered in the register as the proprietor of a registered estate, an application for the appropriate restriction by one or more of them satisfies the obligation in paragraph (1) or (4).

(10) Where there are two or more personal representatives of a deceased proprietor, an application for a restriction in Form C by one or more of them satisfies the obligation in paragraph (3).]

[3163]

NOTES

Para (1): words in square brackets substituted by SI 2008/1919, r 4(1), Sch 1, para 35(a).
Para (2A): inserted by SI 2008/1919, r 4(1), Sch 1, para 35(b).
Paras (3), (4): words in square brackets substituted by SI 2008/1919, r 4(1), Sch 1, para 35(c), (d).
Paras (9), (10): inserted by SI 2008/1919, r 4(1), Sch 1, para 35(e).

95 Form of obligatory restrictions

(1) The form of any restriction that the registrar is obliged to enter under any enactment shall be—

(a) as specified in these rules,
(b) as required by the relevant enactment, or
(c) in other cases, such form as the registrar may direct having regard to the provisions of the relevant enactment.

(2) The form of the restriction required under—

(a) section 44(1) of the Act is Form A,
(b) section 37(5A) of the Housing Act 1985 is Form U,
(c) section 157(7) of the Housing Act 1985 is Form V,
(d) section 81(10) of the Housing Act 1988 is Form X,
(e) section 133 of the Housing Act 1988 is Form X,
(f) paragraph 4 of Schedule 9A to the Housing Act 1985 is Form W,
(g) section 173(9) of the Local Government and Housing Act 1989 is Form X, and
(h) section 13(5) of the Housing Act 1996 is Form Y.

[3164]

96 Application for an order that a restriction be disapplied or modified

(1) An application to the registrar for an order under section 41(2) of the Act must be made in Form RX2.

(2) The application must—

(a) state whether the application is to disapply or to modify the restriction and, if the latter, give details of the modification requested,
(b) explain why the applicant has a sufficient interest in the restriction to make the application,
(c) give details of the disposition or the kind of dispositions that will be affected by the order, and
(d) state why the applicant considers that the registrar should make the order.

(3) If requested to do so, the applicant must supply further evidence to satisfy the registrar that he should make the order.

(4) The registrar may make such enquiries and serve such notices as he thinks fit in order to determine the application.

(5) A note of the terms of any order made by the registrar under section 41(2) of the Act must[, if appropriate,] be entered in the register.

[3165]

NOTES

Para (5): words in square brackets inserted by SI 2008/1919, r 4(1), Sch 1, para 36.

97 Application to cancel a restriction

(1) An application to cancel a restriction must be made in Form RX3.

(2) The application must be accompanied by evidence to satisfy the registrar that the restriction is no longer required.

(3) If the registrar is satisfied that the restriction is no longer required, he must cancel the restriction.

[3166]

[98 Applications to withdraw a restriction from the register

(1) An application to withdraw a restriction must be made in Form RX4 and be accompanied by the required consent.

(2) The required consent is—

(a) where the restriction requires the consent of a specified person, the consent of that person,
(b) where the restriction requires a certificate to be given by a specified person, the consent of that person,
(c) where the restriction requires notice to be given to a specified person, the consent of that person,
(d) where the restriction requires the consent of a specified person, or alternatively a certificate to be given by a specified person, the consent of all such persons,
(e) in any other case, the consent of all persons who appear to the registrar to have an interest in the restriction.

(3) No application may be made to withdraw a restriction—

(a) that is entered under section 42(1)(a) of the Act and reflects some limitation on the registered proprietor's powers of disposition imposed by statute or the general law,
(b) that is entered in the register following an application under rule 94,
(c) that the registrar is under an obligation to enter in the register,
(d) that reflects a limitation under an order of the court or registrar, or an undertaking given in place of such an order,
(e) that is entered pursuant to a court order under section 46 of the Act.

(4) The registrar may accept a certificate given by a conveyancer that the conveyancer holds a required consent.]

[3167]

NOTES

Substituted by SI 2008/1919, r 4(1), Sch 1, para 37.

99 Cancellation of a restriction relating to a trust

When registering a disposition of a registered estate, the registrar must cancel a restriction entered for the purpose of protecting an interest, right or claim arising under a trust of land if he is satisfied that the registered estate is no longer subject to that trust of land.

[3168]

100 Entry following a direction of the court regarding overriding priority in connection with a restriction

(1) Any entry in the register required under section 46(4) of the Act shall be in such form as the registrar may determine so as to ensure that the priority of the restriction ordered by the court is apparent from the register.

(2) Where the making of the entry is completed by the registrar during the priority period of an official search which was delivered before the making of the application for the entry, he must give notice of the entry to the person who applied for the official search or, if a conveyancer or other agent applied on behalf of that person, to that agent, unless he is satisfied that such notice is unnecessary.

[3169]

PART 9
CHARGES

101 How ranking of registered charges as between themselves to be shown on register

Subject to any entry in the individual register to the contrary, for the purpose of section 48(1) of the Act the order in which registered charges are entered in an individual register shows the order in which the registered charges rank as between themselves.

[3170]

102 Alteration of priority of registered charges

(1) An application to alter the priority of registered charges, as between themselves, must be made by or with the consent of the proprietor or a person entitled to be registered as the proprietor of any registered charge whose priority is adversely affected by the alteration, but no such consent is required from a person who has executed the instrument which alters the priority of the charges.

(2) The registrar may accept a conveyancer's certificate confirming that the conveyancer holds any necessary consents.

(3) The registrar must make an entry in the register in such terms as the registrar considers appropriate to give effect to the application.

[3171]

103 Form of charge of registered estate

A legal charge of a registered estate may be made in Form CH1.

[3172]

104 Application for registration of the title to a local land charge

An application to register the title to a charge over registered land which is a local land charge must be supported by evidence of the charge.

[3173]

105 Overriding statutory charges

(1) An applicant for registration of a statutory charge that has the effect mentioned in section 50 of the Act must lodge Form SC with the application.

(2) If the applicant satisfies the registrar that the statutory charge has the priority specified in that Form SC, the registrar must make an entry showing that priority in the charges register of the affected registered title.

(3) If the applicant does not satisfy the registrar as mentioned in paragraph (2) but the registrar considers that the applicant has an arguable case, the registrar may make an entry in the charges register of the affected registered title that the applicant claims the priority specified in that Form SC.

(4) If the registrar makes an entry under paragraph (3) the registrar must give notice of the entry to the persons mentioned in rule 106(1) (subject to rule 106(2)).

(5) Where an entry has been made under paragraph (3)—

(a) the proprietor of the statutory charge which gave rise to the entry, or

(b) the proprietor of a charge entered in the charges register of the affected registered title which, subject to the effect of the entry, would rank in priority to or have equal priority with that statutory charge under rule 101,

may apply for the entry to be removed or to be replaced by an entry of the kind referred to in paragraph (2).

(6) Paragraph (5)(b) includes the proprietor of a statutory charge entered in the charges register of the affected registered title which has had an entry made in respect of it under paragraph (3) claiming priority over the statutory charge referred to in paragraph (5)(a).

(7) An applicant under paragraph (5) must provide evidence to satisfy the registrar that the registrar should take the action sought by the applicant under that paragraph.

(8) Before taking the action sought by the applicant under paragraph (5), the registrar must give notice of the application to any proprietors within that paragraph (other than the applicant).

[3174]

106 Service of notice of overriding statutory charges

(1) The registrar shall give notice under section 50 of the Act to—

(a) the registered proprietor of a registered charge, and

(b) subject to paragraph (2), any person who appears to the registrar to be entitled to a charge protected by a notice,

entered in the charges register of the affected registered title at the time of registration of the statutory charge.

(2) The registrar shall not be obliged to give notice to a person referred to in paragraph (1)(b) if that person's name and his address for service under rule 198 are not set out in the individual register in which the notice is entered.

[3175]

107 Further advances—notice of creation of subsequent charge

(1) A notice given for the purposes of section 49(1) of the Act by one of the methods mentioned in paragraph (2) ought to have been received at the time shown in the table in paragraph (4).

(2) The methods referred to in paragraph (1) are—

(a) by post, to the postal address, whether or not in the United Kingdom, entered in the register as the prior chargee's address for service, or

(b) by leaving the notice at that address, or

(c) by sending to the box number at the relevant document exchange entered in the register as an additional address for service of the prior chargee, or

(d) by electronic transmission to the electronic address entered in the register as an additional address for service of the prior chargee, or

(e) where paragraph (3) applies, by post, document exchange, fax or electronic transmission to the address, box number or fax number provided.

(3) This paragraph applies where the prior chargee has provided to the subsequent chargee a postal address, document exchange box number, fax number, e-mail or other electronic address, and stated in writing to the subsequent chargee that notices to the prior chargee under section 49(1) of the Act may be sent to that address, box number or fax number.

(4) For the purposes of section 49(2) of the Act a notice sent in accordance with paragraph (2) or (3) ought to have been received at the time shown in the table below—

Method of delivery	*Time of receipt*
Post to an address in the United Kingdom	The second working day after posting
Leaving at a postal address	The working day after it was left
Post to an address outside the United Kingdom	The seventh working day after posting
Document exchange	On the second working day after it was left at the sender's document exchange
Fax	The working day after transmission
Electronic transmission to an electronic address entered in the register as an address for service or e-mail or other electronic means of delivery under paragraph (3)	The second working day after transmission

(5) A notice posted or transmitted after 1700 hours on a working day or posted or transmitted on a day which is not a working day is to be treated as having been posted or transmitted on the next working day.

(6) In this rule—

"post" means pre-paid delivery by a postal service which seeks to deliver documents within the United Kingdom no later than the next working day in all or the majority of cases, and to deliver outside the United Kingdom within such a period as is reasonable in all the circumstances,

"prior chargee" means the proprietor of a registered charge to whom notice is being given under section 49(1) of the Act,

"subsequent chargee" means the chargee giving notice under section 49(1) of the Act,

…

[3176]

PART II STATUTORY INSTRUMENTS

NOTES

Para (6): definition "working day" (omitted) revoked by SI 2008/1919, r 4(1), Sch 1, para 38.

108 Obligations to make further advances

(1) The proprietor of a registered charge or a person applying to be so registered, who is under an obligation to make further advances on the security of that charge, may apply to the registrar for such obligation to be entered in the register for the purposes of section 49(3) of the Act.

(2) Except as provided in paragraph (3), the application must be made in Form CH2.

(3) Form CH2 need not be used if the application is contained in panel [8] of Form CH1 [in an electronic legal charge], or in a charge received for registration where the form of that charge has been approved by the registrar.

(4) The registrar must make an entry in the register in such terms as he considers appropriate to give effect to an application under this rule.

[3177]

NOTES

Para (3): reference in square brackets substituted by SI 2008/1919, r 4(1), Sch 1, para 39; words in square brackets inserted by SI 2008/1750, r 5, Sch 2, Pt 1, para 4.

109 Agreement of maximum amount of security

(1) Where the parties to a legal charge which is a registered charge or which is a registrable disposition have agreed a maximum amount for which the charge is security, the proprietor of the registered charge or a person applying to be registered as proprietor of the registrable disposition may apply to the registrar for such agreement to be entered in the register under section 49(4) of the Act.

(2) The application must be made in Form CH3.

(3) The registrar must make an entry in the register in such terms as he considers appropriate to give effect to an application under this rule.

[3178]

110 Consolidation of registered charges

(1) A chargee who has a right of consolidation in relation to a registered charge may apply to the registrar for an entry to be made in respect of that right in the individual register in which the charge is registered.

(2) The application must be made in Form CC.

(3) The registrar must make an entry in the individual register in such terms as he considers appropriate to give effect to an application under this rule.

[3179]

111 *Certificate of registration of company charges* [Certificate of registration of company charge]

(1) When making an application for the registration of a charge created by a company registered under the Companies Acts, a limited liability partnership incorporated under the Limited Liability Partnerships Act 2000, or a Northern Ireland company, the applicant must produce to the registrar—

- *(a) a certificate issued under section 401 of the 1985 Act that the charge has been registered under section 395 of that Act, or*
- *(b) (in the case of a charge created by a company registered in Scotland) a certificate issued under section 418 of the 1985 Act that the charge has been registered under section 410 of that Act, or*
- *(c) (in the case of a charge created by a Northern Ireland company) a certificate issued under article 409 of the 1986 Order that the charge has been registered under article 403 of that Order.*

(2) If the applicant does not produce the certificate required by paragraph (1) with the application for registration of the charge, the registrar must enter a note in the register that the charge is subject to the provisions of section 395 or section 410 of the 1985 Act, or article 403 of the 1986 Order (as appropriate).

(3) In this rule—

"the 1985 Act" means the Companies Act 1985,

"the 1986 Order" means the Companies (NI) Order 1986,

"Northern Ireland" company means a company formed and registered under the 1986 Order or a company formed and registered, or deemed to have been registered, in Northern Ireland under the former Northern Ireland Companies Acts,

"former Northern Ireland Companies Acts" means the Joint Stock Companies Acts, the Companies Act 1862, the Companies (Consolidation) Act 1908, the Companies Act (Northern Ireland) 1932 and the Companies Acts (Northern Ireland) 1960 to 1983,

"Joint Stock Companies Acts" means the Joint Stock Companies Act 1856, the Joint Stock Companies Act 1857, the Joint Stock Banking Companies Act 1857 and the Act to enable Joint Stock Banking Companies to be formed on the principle of limited liability, or any one or more of those Acts (as the case may require), but does not include the Joint Stock Companies Act 1844.

[(1) When making an application for the registration of a charge created by a company registered under the Companies Acts or a limited liability partnership incorporated under the Limited Liability Partnerships Act 2000 or the Limited Liability Partnership Act (Northern Ireland) 2002 the applicant must produce to the registrar the appropriate certificate issued under section 869 or 885 of the Companies Act 2006 that the charge has been registered under section 860 or 878 of that Act.

(2) If the applicant does not produce the certificate required by paragraph (1) with the application for registration of the charge, the registrar must enter a note in the register stating that no evidence of registration of the charge in accordance with section 860 or 878 of the Companies Act 2006 (as appropriate) has been lodged.]

[3180]

NOTES

Substituted by SI 2008/1919, r 4(1), Sch 1, para 40, as from 1 October 2009.

112 Foreclosure—registration requirements

(1) Subject to paragraph (3), an application by a person who has obtained an order for foreclosure absolute to be entered in the register as proprietor of the registered estate in respect of which the charge is registered must be accompanied by the order.

(2) The registrar must—

(a) cancel the registration of the charge in respect of which the order was made,

(b) cancel all entries in respect of interests over which the charge has priority, and

(c) enter the applicant as proprietor of the registered estate.

(3) The registrar may accept a conveyancer's certificate confirming that the conveyancer holds the order for foreclosure absolute or an office copy of it.

[3181]

[113 Variation of the terms of a registered charge

(1) Subject to paragraph (2), an application to register an instrument varying the terms of a registered charge must be made—

(a) by, or with the consent of, the proprietor of the registered charge and the proprietor of the estate charged,

(b) with the consent of the proprietor, or a person entitled to be registered as proprietor, of every other registered charge of equal or inferior priority that is prejudicially affected by the variation, and

(c) with the consent of the proprietor, or a person entitled to be registered as proprietor, of a registered sub-charge of every registered charge of equal or inferior priority that is prejudicially affected by the variation.

(2) A consent under paragraph (1) is not required if—

(a) the consent of that person is not required by the terms of the registered charge or registered sub-charge of which that person is the proprietor or in respect of which that person is entitled to be registered as proprietor, or

(b) the person from whom a consent would otherwise be required has executed the instrument.

(3) The registrar may accept a conveyancer's certificate confirming that the conveyancer holds any necessary consents.

(4) If the registrar is satisfied that the proprietor of any other registered charge, and of any registered sub-charge of that registered charge, of equal or inferior priority to the varied charge that is prejudicially affected by the variation is bound by it, he shall make a note of the variation in the register.

(5) If the registrar is not so satisfied, he may make an entry in the register that an instrument which is expressed to vary the terms of the registered charge has been entered into.

(6) In this rule a reference to a registered sub-charge includes any registered sub-charge which derives directly or indirectly from the registered charge.]

[3182]

NOTES

Substituted by SI 2008/1919, r 4(1), Sch 1, para 41.

114 Discharges and releases of registered charges

(1) Subject to rule 115, a discharge of a registered charge must be in Form DS1.

(2) Subject to rule 115, a release of part of the registered estate in a registered title from a registered charge must be in Form DS3.

(3) Any discharge or release in Form DS1 or DS3 must be executed as a deed or authenticated in such other manner as the registrar may approve.

(4) Notwithstanding paragraphs (1) and (2) and rule 115, the registrar is entitled to accept and act upon any other proof of satisfaction of a charge that he may regard as sufficient.

(5) An application to register a discharge in Form DS1 must be made in Form AP1 or DS2 and an application to register a release in Form DS3 must be made in Form AP1.

[3183]

115 Discharges and releases of registered charges in electronic form

(1) During the currency of a notice given under Schedule 2 and subject to and in accordance with the limitations contained in such notice, notification of—

(a) the discharge of, or

(b) the release of part of a registered estate in a registered title form, a registered charge may be delivered to the registrar in electronic form.

(2) Notification of discharge or release of part given in accordance with paragraph (1) shall be regarded as having the same effect as a discharge in Form DS1, or a release of part in Form DS3, as appropriate, executed in accordance with rule 114 by or on behalf the person who has delivered it to the registrar.

[3184]

116 Transfer of a registered charge

A transfer of a registered charge must be in Form … TR4 or AS2, as appropriate.

[3185]

NOTES

Reference omitted revoked by SI 2008/1919, r 4(1), Sch 1, para 42.

[116A Information relating to deeds of postponement in respect of registered charges and noted charges

The registrar may, upon application, make an entry in an individual register referring to an agreement which it is claimed relates to priorities between a registered charge and a charge which is the subject of a notice in the same individual register.]

[3185A]

NOTES

Commencement: 10 November 2008.

Inserted by SI 2008/1919, r 4(1), Sch 1, para 43.

PART 10
BOUNDARIES

117 Definition

In this Part, except in rule 121, "boundary" includes part only of a boundary.

[3186]

118 Application for the determination of the exact line of a boundary

(1) A proprietor of a registered estate may apply to the registrar for the exact line of the boundary of that registered estate to be determined.

(2) An application under paragraph (1) must be made in Form DB and be accompanied by—

(a) a plan, or a plan and a verbal description, identifying the exact line of the boundary claimed and showing sufficient surrounding physical features to allow the general position of the boundary to be drawn on the Ordnance Survey map, and

(b) evidence to establish the exact line of the boundary.

[3187]

119 Procedure on an application for the determination of the exact line of a boundary

(1) [Subject to paragraph (2), where] the registrar is satisfied that—

(a) the plan, or plan and verbal description, supplied in accordance with rule 118(2)(a) identifies the exact line of the boundary claimed,

(b) the applicant has shown an arguable case that the exact line of the boundary is in the position shown on the plan, or plan and verbal description, supplied in accordance with rule 118(2)(a), and

(c) he can identify all the owners of the land adjoining the boundary to be determined and has an address at which each owner may be given notice,

he must give the owners of the land adjoining the boundary to be determined (except the applicant) notice of the application … and of the effect of paragraph (6).

[(2) The registrar need not give notice of the application to an owner of the land adjoining the boundary to be determined where the evidence supplied in accordance with rule 118(2)(b) includes—

(a) an agreement in writing with that owner as to the line of the boundary, or

(b) a court order determining the line of the boundary.]

(3) Subject to paragraph (4), the time fixed by the notice to the owner of the land to object to the application shall be the period ending at 12 noon on the twentieth business day after the date of issue of the notice or such longer period as the registrar may decide before the issue of the notice.

(4) The period set for the notice under paragraph (3) may be extended for a particular recipient of the notice by the registrar following a request by that recipient, received by the registrar before that period has expired, setting out why an extension should be allowed.

(5) If a request is received under paragraph (4) the registrar may, if he considers it appropriate, seek the views of the applicant and if, after considering any such views and all other relevant matters, he is satisfied that a longer period should be allowed he may allow such period as he considers appropriate, whether or not the period is the same as any period requested by the recipient of the notice.

(6) Unless any recipient of the notice objects to the application to determine the exact line of the boundary within the time fixed by the notice (as extended under paragraph (5), if applicable), the registrar must complete the application.

(7) Where the registrar is not satisfied as to paragraph (1)(a), (b) and (c), he must cancel the application.

(8) In this rule, the "owner of the land" means—

(a) a person entitled to apply to be registered as the proprietor of an unregistered legal estate in land under section 3 of the Act,

(b) the proprietor of any registered estate or charge affecting the land, [or]

(c) if the land is demesne land, Her Majesty.

[3188]

NOTES

Para (1): words in square brackets substituted, and words omitted revoked, by SI 2008/1919, r 4(1), Sch 1, para 44(a).

Para (2): substituted by SI 2008/1919, r 4(1), Sch 1, para 44(b).

Para (8): in sub-para (b) word in square brackets substituted by SI 2008/1919, r 4(1), Sch 1, para 44(c).

120 Completion of application for the exact line of a boundary to be determined

(1) Where the registrar completes an application under rule 118, he must—

(a) make an entry in the individual register of the applicant's registered title and, if appropriate, in the individual register of any superior or inferior registered title, and any registered title affecting the other land adjoining the determined boundary, stating that the exact line of the boundary is determined under section 60 of the Act, and

(b) subject to paragraph (2), add to the title plan of the applicant's registered title and, if appropriate, to the title plan of any superior or inferior registered title, and any registered title affecting the other land adjoining the determined boundary, such particulars of the exact line of the boundary as he considers appropriate.

(2) Instead of, or as well as, adding particulars of the exact line of the boundary to the title plans mentioned in paragraph (1)(b), the registrar may make an entry in the individual registers mentioned in paragraph (1)(a) referring to any other plan showing the exact line of the boundary.

[3189]

121 Relationship between determined and undetermined parts of a boundary

Where the exact line of part of the boundary of a registered estate has been determined, the ends of that part of the boundary are not to be treated as determined for the purposes of adjoining parts of the boundary the exact line of which has not been determined.

[3190]

PART II STATUTORY INSTRUMENTS

122 Determination of the exact line of a boundary without application

(1) This rule applies where—

(a) there is—

(i) a transfer of part of a registered estate in land, or

(ii) the grant of a term of years absolute which is a registrable disposition of part of a registered estate in land,

(b) there is a common boundary, and

(c) there is sufficient information in the disposition to enable the registrar to determine the exact line of the common boundary.

(2) The registrar may determine the exact line of the common boundary and if he does he must—

(a) make an entry in the individual registers of the affected registered titles stating that the exact line of the common boundary is determined under section 60 of the Act, and

(b) subject to paragraph (3), add to the title plan of the disponor's affected registered title (whether or not the disponor is still the proprietor of that title, or still entitled to be registered as proprietor of that title) and to the title plan of the registered title under which the disposition is being registered, such particulars of the exact line of the common boundary as he considers appropriate.

(3) Instead of, or as well as, adding particulars of the exact line of the common boundary to the title plans mentioned in paragraph (2)(b), the registrar may make an entry in the individual registers of the affected registered titles referring to the description of the common boundary in the disposition.

(4) In this rule—

"common boundary" means any boundary of the land disposed of by a disposition which adjoins land in which the disponor at the date of the disposition had a registered estate in land or of which such disponor was entitled to be registered as proprietor, and

"disposition" means a transfer or grant mentioned in paragraph (1)(a).

[3191]

123 Agreement about accretion or diluvion

(1) An application to register an agreement about the operation of accretion or diluvion in relation to a registered estate in land must be made by, or be accompanied by the consent of, the proprietor of the registered estate and of any registered charge, except that no such consent is required from a person who is party to the agreement.

(2) On registration of such an agreement the registrar must make a note in the property register that the agreement is registered for the purposes of section 61(2) of the Act.

[3192]

PART 11
QUALITY OF TITLE

124 Application to upgrade title under section 62 of the Act

(1) An application for the registrar to upgrade title under section 62 of the Act must be made in Form UT1.

(2) An application referred to in paragraph (1) must, except where made under sections 62(2), (4) or (5) of the Act, be accompanied by such documents as will satisfy the registrar as to the title.

(3) An application under section 62(2) of the Act must be accompanied by—

(a) such documents as will satisfy the registrar as to any superior title which is not registered,

(b) where any superior title is registered with possessory, qualified or good leasehold title, such evidence as will satisfy the registrar that that title qualifies for upgrading to absolute title, and

(c) evidence of any consent to the grant of the lease required from—

(i) any chargee of any superior title, and

(ii) any superior lessor.

(4) An application under section 62(3)(b) of the Act must, in addition to the documents referred to in paragraph (2), be accompanied by the documents listed at paragraph (3)(a) to (c).

(5) An application by a person entitled to be registered as the proprietor of the estate to which the application relates must be accompanied by evidence of that entitlement.

(6) An application by a person interested in a registered estate which derives from the estate to which the application relates must be accompanied by—

(a) details of the interest, and

(b) where the interest is not apparent from the register, evidence to satisfy the registrar of the applicant's interest.

[3193]

125 Use of register to record defects in title

(1) An entry under section 64 of the Act that a right to determine a registered estate in land is exercisable shall be made in the property register.

(2) An application for such an entry must be supported by evidence to satisfy the registrar that the applicant has the right to determine the registered estate and that the right is exercisable.

(3) Subject to paragraph (4), the registrar must make the entry on receipt of an application which relates to a right to determine the registered estate on non-payment of a rentcharge.

(4) Before making an entry under this rule the registrar must give notice of the application to the proprietor of the registered estate to which the application relates and the proprietor of any registered charge on that estate.

(5) A person may apply to the registrar for removal of the entry if he is—

(a) the person entitled to determine the registered estate,
(b) the proprietor of the registered estate to which the entry relates,
(c) a person entitled to be registered as proprietor of that estate, or
(d) any other person whom the registrar is satisfied has an interest in the removal of the entry.

(6) An application for removal of the entry must be supported by evidence to satisfy the registrar that the right to determine the registered estate is not exercisable.

[3194]

PART 12
ALTERATIONS AND CORRECTIONS

126 Alteration under a court order—not rectification

(1) Subject to paragraphs (2) and (3), if in any proceedings the court decides that—

(a) there is a mistake in the register,
(b) the register is not up to date, or
(c) there is an estate, right or interest excepted from the effect of registration that should be given effect to,

it must make an order for alteration of the register under the power given by paragraph 2(1) of Schedule 4 to the Act.

(2) The court is not obliged to make an order if there are exceptional circumstances that justify not doing so.

(3) This rule does not apply to an alteration of the register that amounts to rectification.

[3195]

127 Court order for alteration of the register—form and service

(1) An order for alteration of the register must state the title number of the title affected and the alteration that is to be made, and must direct the registrar to make the alteration.

(2) Service on the registrar of an order for alteration of the register must be made by making an application for the registrar to give effect to the order, accompanied by the order.

[3196]

128 Alteration otherwise than pursuant to a court order—notice and enquiries

(1) Subject to paragraph (5), this rule applies where an application for alteration of the register has been made, or where the registrar is considering altering the register without an application having been made.

(2) The registrar must give notice of the proposed alteration to—

(a) the registered proprietor of any registered estate,
(b) the registered proprietor of any registered charge, and
(c) subject to paragraph (3), any person who appears to the registrar to be entitled to an interest protected by a notice,

where that estate, charge or interest would be affected by the proposed alteration, unless he is satisfied that such notice is unnecessary.

(3) The registrar is not obliged to give notice to a person referred to in paragraph (2)(c) if that person's name and his address for service under rule 198 are not set out in the individual register in which the notice is entered.

(4) The registrar may make such enquiries as he thinks fit.

(5) This rule does not apply to alteration of the register in the specific circumstances covered by any other rule.

[3197]

129 Alteration otherwise than under a court order—evidence

Unless otherwise provided in these rules, an application for alteration of the register (otherwise than under a court order) must be supported by evidence to justify the alteration.

[3198]

130 Correction of mistakes in an application or accompanying document

(1) This rule applies to any alteration made by the registrar for the purpose of correcting a mistake in any application or accompanying document.

(2) The alteration will have effect as if made by the applicant or other interested party or parties—

(a) in the case of a mistake of a clerical or like nature, in all circumstances,

(b) in the case of any other mistake, only if the applicant and every other interested party has requested, or consented to, the alteration.

[3199]

PART 13
INFORMATION ETC

Interpretation of this Part

131 Definitions

In this Part—

"commencement date" means the date of commencement of this Part,

"edited information document" means, where the registrar has designated a document an exempt information document, the edited copy of that document lodged under rule 136(2)(b), [or the document prepared by the registrar under either rule 136(6) or rule 138(4),]

"exempt information document" means the original and copies of a document so designated under rule 136(3),

"prejudicial information" means—

(a) information that relates to an individual who is the applicant under rule 136 and if disclosed to other persons (whether to the public generally or specific persons) would, or would be likely to, cause substantial unwarranted damage or substantial unwarranted distress to the applicant or another, or

(b) information that if disclosed to other persons (whether to the public generally or specific persons) would, or would be likely to, prejudice the commercial interests of the applicant under rule 136,

"priority period" means—

(a) where the application for an official search is entered on the day list before the date referred to in rule 216(3), the period beginning at the time when that application is entered on the day list and ending at midnight marking the end of the thirtieth business day thereafter, and

(b) where the application for an official search is entered on the day list on or after the date referred to in rule 216(3), the period beginning at the time when that application is entered on the day list and ending at midnight marking the end of the thirty sixth business day thereafter,

"protectable disposition" means a registrable disposition (including one by virtue of rule 38) of a registered estate or registered charge made for valuable consideration,

"purchaser" means a person who has entered into or intends to enter into a protectable disposition as disponee,

"registrable estate or charge" means the legal estate and any charge which is sought to be registered as a registered estate or registered charge in an application for first registration,

"search from date" means—

(a) the date stated on an official copy of the individual register of the relevant registered title, as the date on which the entries shown on that official copy were subsisting,

(b) the date stated at the time of an access by remote terminal, where provided for under these rules, to the individual register of the relevant registered title as the date on which the entries accessed were subsisting,

...

[3200]

NOTES

In definition "edited information document" words in square brackets inserted by SI 2008/1919, r 4(1), Sch 1, para 45(a).

Definitions "transitional period" and "transitional period document" (omitted) revoked by SI 2008/1919, r 4(1), Sch 1, para 45(b).

Delivery of applications and issuing of certificates

132 Delivery of applications and issuing of certificates by electronic and other means

(1) During the currency of a relevant notice given under Schedule 2, and subject to and in accordance with the limitations contained in that notice, any application under this Part may be made by delivering the application to the registrar by any means of communication other than post, document exchange or personal delivery, and the applicant must provide, in such order as may be required by that notice, such of the particulars required for an application of that type as are appropriate in the circumstances and as are required by the notice.

(2) During the currency of a relevant notice given under Schedule 2, and subject to and in accordance with the limitations contained in that notice, any certificates and other results of applications and searches under this Part may be issued by any means of communication other than post, document exchange or personal delivery.

(3) Except where otherwise provided in this Part, where information is issued under paragraph (2) it must be to like effect to that which would have been provided had the information been issued in paper form.

[3201]

Inspection and copying

[133 Inspection and copying

(1) This rule applies to the right to inspect and make copies of the registers and documents under section 66(1) of the Act.

(2) Excepted documents are excepted from the right.

(3) Subject to rule 132(1), an application under section 66 of the Act must be in Form PIC

(4) Where inspection and copying under this rule takes place at an office of the land registry it must be undertaken in the presence of a member of the land registry.

(5) In paragraph (2), an "excepted document" is—

(a) an exempt information document,

(b) an edited information document which has been replaced by another edited information document under rule 136(6),

(c) a Form EX1A,

(d) a Form CIT,

(e) any form to which a Form CIT has been attached under rule 140(3) or (4),

(f) any document or copy of any document prepared by the registrar in connection with an application in a form to which Form CIT has been attached under rule 140(3) or (4),

(g) any document relating to an application for a network access agreement under paragraph 1(4) of Schedule 5 to the Act,

(h) an identity document, and

(i) an investigation of crime document.

(6) Subject to paragraph (7), in paragraph (5)(h) an "identity document" means any document within section 66(1)(c) of the Act provided to the registrar as evidence of identity of any person or prepared or obtained by the registrar in connection with such identity.

(7) Forms AP1, DS2 and FR1 are not identity documents.

(8) In paragraph 5(i), an "investigation of crime document" is any document within section 66(1)(c) of the Act (other than an identity document) which relates to the prevention or detection of crime and is not—

(a) a document received by the registrar as part of or in support of an application to the registrar,

(b) a document received by the registrar as part of or in support of an objection made under section 73 of the Act, or

(c) a document to which paragraph (9) applies.

(9) This paragraph applies to a document if—

(a) it is a document prepared by, or at the request of, the registrar as part of the process of considering an application or objection, and

(b) it is not so prepared principally in connection with the prevention or detection of crime.

(10) In paragraph (5), the references to Form EX1A and Form CIT and forms to which Form CIT has been attached include any equivalent information provided under rule 132 and the reference to an application in a form to which Form CIT has been attached includes an equivalent application made by virtue of rule 132.]

[3202]

NOTES

Substituted by SI 2008/1919, r 4(1), Sch 1, para 46.

Official copies

134 Application for official copies of a registered title, the cautions register or for a certificate of inspection of the title plan

(1) A person may apply for—

(a) an official copy of an individual register,

(b) an official copy of any title plan referred to in an individual register,

(c) an official copy of an individual caution register and any caution plan referred to in it, and

(d) a certificate of inspection of any title plan.

(2) Subject to rule 132(1), an application under paragraph (1) must be in Form OC1.

(3) A separate application must be made in respect of each registered title or individual caution register.

(4) Where, notwithstanding paragraph (3), an application is in respect of more than one registered title or individual caution register, but the applicant fails to provide a title number, or the title number provided does not relate to any part of the property in respect of which the application is made, the registrar may—

(a) deal with the application as if it referred only to one of the title numbers relating to the property,

(b) deal with the application as if it referred to all of the title numbers relating to the property, or

(c) cancel the application.

(5) In paragraph (4) the reference to title number includes in the case of an individual caution register a caution title number.

(6) Where the registrar deals with the application under paragraph (4)(b), the applicant is to be treated as having made a separate application in respect of each of the registered titles or each of the individual caution registers.

(7) An official copy of an individual caution register and any caution plan referred to in it must be issued disregarding any application or matter that may affect the subsistence of the caution.

[3203]

[135 Application for official copies of documents referred to in the register of title and other documents kept by the registrar

(1) Subject to paragraph (2), a person may apply for an official copy of—

(a) any document referred to in the register of title and kept by the registrar,

(b) any other document kept by the registrar that relates to an application to the registrar.

(2) Excepted documents are excepted from paragraph (1).

(3) Subject to rule 132(1), an application under paragraph (1) must be made in Form OC2.

(4) In this rule, "excepted document" has the same meaning as in rule 133.]

[3204]

NOTES

Substituted by SI 2008/1919, r 4(1), Sch 1, para 47.

Exempt information documents

136 Application that the registrar designate a document an exempt information document

(1) A person may apply for the registrar to designate a relevant document an exempt information document if he claims that the document contains prejudicial information.

[(2) Subject to rule 132(1), an application under paragraph (1) must be made in Form EX1 and EX1A and include a copy of the relevant document which—

(a) excludes the prejudicial information,

(b) includes the words "excluded information" where the prejudicial information has been excluded, and

(c) is certified as being a true copy of the relevant document, except that it does not include the prejudicial information and includes the words required by sub-paragraph (b).]

(3) Subject to paragraph (4), provided that the registrar is satisfied that the applicant's claim is not groundless he must designate the relevant document an exempt information document.

(4) Where the registrar considers that designating the document an exempt information document could prejudice the keeping of the register, he may cancel the application.

(5) Where a document is an exempt information document, the registrar may make an appropriate entry in the individual register of any affected registered title.

(6) Where a document is an exempt information document and a further application is made under paragraph (1) which would, but for the existing designation, have resulted in its being so designated, the registrar must prepare another edited information document which excludes—

(a) the information excluded from the existing edited information document, and

(b) any further information excluded from the edited information document lodged by the applicant.

(7) In this rule a "relevant document" is a document—

(a) referred to in the register of title, or one that relates to an application to the registrar, the original or a copy of which is kept by the registrar, or

(b) that will be referred to in the register of title as a result of an application (the "accompanying application") made at the same time as an application under this rule, or that relates to the accompanying application, the original or a copy of which will be or is for the time being kept by the registrar.

[3205]

NOTES

Para (2): substituted by SI 2008/1919, r 4(1), Sch 1, para 48.

137 Application for an official copy of an exempt information document

(1) A person may apply for an official copy of an exempt information document.

(2) Subject to rule 132(1), application under paragraph (1) must be made in Form EX2.

(3) The registrar must give notice of an application under paragraph (1) to the person who made the relevant application under rule 136(1) unless he is satisfied that such notice is unnecessary or impracticable.

(4) If the registrar decides that—

(a) none of the information excluded from the edited information document is prejudicial information, or

(b) although all or some of the information excluded is prejudicial information, the public interest in providing an official copy of the exempt information document to the applicant outweighs the public interest in not doing so,

then he must provide an official copy of the exempt information document to the applicant.

(5) Where the registrar has decided an application under paragraph (1) on the basis that none of the information is prejudicial information, he must remove the designation of the document as an exempt information document and any entry made in respect of the document under rule 136(5).

[3206]

138 Application for removal of the designation of a document as an exempt information document

(1) Where a document is an exempt information document, the person who applied for designation under rule 136(1) may apply for the designation to be removed.

(2) Subject to rule 132(1), an application made under paragraph (1) must be in Form EX3.

(3) Subject to paragraph (4), where the registrar is satisfied that the application is in order, he must remove the designation of the document as an exempt information document and remove any entry made in respect of the document under rule 136(5).

(4) Where—

(a) the document has been made an exempt information document under more than one application,

(b) an application under paragraph (1) is made by fewer than all of the applicants under rule 136(1), and

(c) the registrar is satisfied that the application is in order,

the registrar must replace the existing edited information document with one that excludes only the information excluded both from that edited information document and the edited information documents lodged under rule 136(2)(b) by those applicants not applying under paragraph (1).

[3207]–[3208]

139 *(Revoked, together with preceding cross heading, by SI 2008/1919, r 4(1), Sch 1, para 49.)*

Inspection, official copies and searches of the index of proprietors' names in connection with court proceedings, insolvency and tax liability

140 Application in connection with court proceedings, insolvency and tax liability

(1) In this rule, a qualifying applicant is a person referred to in column 1 of Schedule 5 who gives the registrar the appropriate certificate referred to in column 2 of the Schedule or, where rule 132 applies, an equivalent certificate in accordance with a notice given under Schedule 2.

(2) A qualifying applicant may apply—

(a) to inspect or make copies of any document (including a form) within rule 133(2) … ,

(b) for official copies of any document (including a form) within rule 135(2) … , and

(c) for a search in the index of proprietors' names in respect of the name of a person specified in the application.

(3) Subject to rule 132(1), an application under paragraph (2) must be made in Form PIC, OC2 or PN1, as appropriate, with Form CIT attached.

(4) A qualifying applicant who applies—

(a) to inspect and make copies of registers and documents not within paragraph (2)(a) under section 66 of the Act,

(b) for official copies of registers and plans under rule 134(1) and of documents not within paragraph (2)(b) under rule 135,

(c) for an historical edition of a registered title under rule 144,

(d) for an official search of the index map under rule 145, or

(e) for an official search of the index of relating franchises and manors under rule 146,

may attach Form CIT to the Form PIC, OC1, OC2, HC1, SIM or SIF, as appropriate, used in the application.

[(4A) A qualifying applicant who applies for a search in the index of proprietors' names under paragraph (2) may apply at the same time in the Form CIT attached to the Form PN1 for official copies of every individual register referred to in the entries (if any) in the index relating to the particulars given in the search application.]

(5) In Form CIT and Schedule 5, references to tax are references to any of the taxes mentioned in the definition of tax in section 118(1) of the Taxes Management Act 1970.

[3209]

NOTES

Para (2): in sub-paras (a), (b) words omitted revoked by SI 2008/1919, r 4(1), Sch 1, para 50.
Para (4A): inserted by SI 2005/1766, r 7.

Information about the day list, electronic discharges of registered charges and title plans

141 Day list information

(1) In this rule "day list information" means information kept by the registrar under rule 12.

(2) A person may only apply for the day list information relating to a specified title number during the currency of a relevant notice given under Schedule 2, and subject to and in accordance with the limitations contained in the notice.

(3) The registrar must provide the day list information in the manner specified in the relevant notice.

(4) Unless otherwise stated by the registrar, the day list information provided must be based on the entries subsisting in the day list immediately before the information is provided.

(5) The registrar is not required to disclose under this rule details of an application under rule 136.

[3210]

142 Enquiry as to discharge of a charge by electronic means

(1) A person may apply in respect of a specified registered title for confirmation of receipt by the registrar of notification of—

(a) the discharge of a registered charge given by electronic means, or

(b) the release of part of a registered estate from a registered charge given by electronic means.

(2) An application under paragraph (1) may only be made during the currency of a relevant notice given under Schedule 2, and subject to and in accordance with the limitations contained in the notice.

(3) The registrar is not required to disclose under this rule any information concerning a notification once the entries of the registered charge to which it relates have been cancelled from the relevant registered title, or the affected part of it.

[3211]

143 Certificate of inspection of title plan

(1) Where a person has applied under rule 134 for a certificate of inspection of a title plan, on completion of the inspection the registrar must issue a certificate of inspection.

(2) Subject to rule 132(2), the certificate of inspection must be issued by the registrar in Form CI or to like effect.

[3212]

Historical information

144 Application for an historical edition of a registered title kept by the registrar in electronic form

(1) A person may apply for a copy of—
- (a) the last edition for a specified day, or
- (b) every edition for a specified day,

of a registered title, and of a registered title that has been closed, kept by the registrar in electronic form.

(2) Subject to rule 132(1), an application under paragraph (1) must be made in Form HC1.

(3) Subject to paragraph (4), if an application under paragraph (1) is in order and the registrar is keeping in electronic form an edition of the registered title for the day specified in the application, he must issue—
- (a) if the application is under paragraph (1)(a), subject to rule 132(2), a paper copy of the edition of the registered title at the end of that day, or
- (b) if the application is under paragraph (1)(b), subject to rule 132(2), a paper copy of the edition of the registered title at the end of that day and any prior edition kept in electronic form of the registered title for that day.

(4) Where only part of the edition of the registered title requested is kept by the registrar in electronic form he must issue, subject to rule 132(2), a paper copy of that part.

[3213]

Official searches of the index kept under section 68 of the Act

145 Searches of the index map

(1) Any person may apply for an official search of the index map.

(2) Subject to rule 132(1), an application under paragraph (1) must be made in Form SIM.

(3) If the registrar so requires, an applicant must provide a copy of an extract from the Ordnance Survey map on the largest scale published showing the land to which the application relates.

(4) If an application under paragraph (1) is in order, subject to rule 132(2), a paper certificate must be issued including such information specified in Part 1 of Schedule 6 as the case may require.

[3214]

146 Searches of the index of relating franchises and manors

(1) Any person may apply for an official search of the index of relating franchises and manors.

(2) Subject to rule 132(1), an application under paragraph (1) must be made in Form SIF.

(3) If an application under paragraph (1) is in order, subject to rule 132(2), a paper certificate must be issued including such information specified in Part 2 of Schedule 6 as the case may require.

[3215]

Official searches with priority

147 Application for official search with priority by purchaser

(1) A purchaser may apply for an official search with priority of the individual register of a registered title to which the protectable disposition relates.

(2) Where there is a pending application for first registration, the purchaser of a protectable disposition which relates to that pending application may apply for an official search with priority in relation to that pending application.

(3) Subject to rule 132(1), an application for an official search with priority must be made in Form OS1 or Form OS2, as appropriate.

(4) Where the application is made in Form OS2 and an accompanying plan is required, unless the registrar allows otherwise, the plan must be delivered in duplicate.

[3216]

148 Entry on day list of application for official search with priority

(1) An application for an official search with priority is to be taken as having been made on the date and at the time of the day notice of it is entered on the day list.

(2) Paragraph (3) has effect where—
(a) an application for an official search is in order, and
(b) the applicant has not withdrawn the official search.

(3) Subject to paragraph (4), the entry on the day list of notice of an application for an official search with priority confers a priority period on an application for an entry in the register in respect of the protectable disposition to which the official search relates.

(4) Paragraph (3) does not apply if the application for an official search with priority is cancelled subsequently because it is not in order.

[3217]

149 Issue of official search certificate with priority

(1) If an application for an official search with priority is in order an official search certificate with priority must be issued giving the result of the search as at the date and time that the application was entered on the day list.

(2) An official search certificate with priority relating to a registered estate or to a pending application for first registration may, at the registrar's discretion, be issued in one or both of the following ways—
(a) in paper form, or
(b) under rule 132(2).

(3) Subject to paragraph (4), an official search certificate issued under paragraph (2) must include such information as specified in Part 3 or Part 4 of Schedule 6 as the case may require and may be issued by reference to an official copy of the individual register of the relevant registered title.

(4) If an official search certificate is to be, or has been, issued in paper form under paragraph (2)(a), another official search certificate issued under paragraph (2)(b) in respect of the same application need only include the information specified at A, F, G and H of Part 3 and A, H and I of Part 4 of Schedule 6, as the case may require.

[3218]

150 Withdrawal of official search with priority

(1) Subject to paragraph (2), a person who has made an application for an official search with priority of a registered title or in relation to a pending first registration application, may withdraw that official search by application to the registrar.

(2) An application under paragraph (1) cannot be made if an application for an entry in the register in respect of the protectable disposition made pursuant to the official search has been made and completed.

(3) Once an official search has been withdrawn under paragraph (1) rule 148(3) shall cease to apply in relation to it.

[3219]

151 Protection of an application on which a protected application is dependent

(1) Subject to paragraph (4), paragraph (2) has effect where an application for an entry in the register is one on which an official search certificate confers a priority period and there is a prior registrable disposition affecting the same registered land, on which that application is dependent.

(2) An application for an entry in the register in relation to that prior registrable disposition is for the purpose of section 72(1)(a) of the Act an application to which a priority period relates.

(3) The priority period referred to in paragraph (2) is a period expiring at the same time as the priority period conferred by the official search referred to in paragraph (1).

(4) Paragraph (2) does not have effect unless both the application referred to in paragraph (1) and the application referred to in paragraph (2) are—
(a) made before the end of that priority period, and
(b) in due course completed by registration.

[3220]

152 Protection of an application relating to a pending application for first registration on which a protected application is dependent

(1) Subject to paragraphs (4) and (5), paragraph (2) has effect where—
(a) there is a pending application for first registration,
(b) there is a pending application for an entry in the register on which an official search confers a priority period,

(c) there is an application for registration of a prior registrable disposition affecting the same registrable estate or charge as the pending application referred to in sub-paragraph (b),
(d) the pending application referred to in sub-paragraph (b) is dependent on the application referred to in sub-paragraph (c), and
(e) the application referred to in sub-paragraph (c) is subject to the pending application for first registration referred to in sub-paragraph (a).

(2) An application for an entry in the register in relation to the prior registrable disposition referred to in paragraph (1)(c) is for the purpose of section 72(1)(a) of the Act an application to which a priority period relates.

(3) The priority period referred to in paragraph (2) is a period expiring at the same time as the priority period conferred by the official search referred to in paragraph (1)(b).

(4) Paragraph (2) does not have effect unless the pending application for first registration referred to in paragraph (1)(a) is in due course completed by registration of all or any part of the registrable estate.

(5) Paragraph (2) does not have effect unless both the pending application on which an official search confers priority referred to in paragraph (1)(b) and the application relating to the prior registrable disposition referred to in paragraph (1)(c) are—
(a) made before the end of that priority period, and
(b) in due course completed by registration.

[3221]

153 Priority of concurrent applications for official searches with priority and concurrent official search certificates with priority

(1) Where two or more official search certificates with priority relating to the same registrable estate or charge or to the same registered land have been issued and are in operation, the certificates take effect, as far as relates to the priority conferred, in the order of the times at which the applications for official search with priority were entered on the day list, unless the applicants agree otherwise.

(2) Where one transaction is dependent upon another the registrar must assume (unless the contrary appears) that the applicants for official search with priority have agreed that their applications have priority so as to give effect to the sequence of the documents effecting the transactions.

[3222]

154 Applications lodged at the same time as the priority period expires

(1) Where an official search with priority has been made in respect of a registered title and an application relating to that title is taken as having been made at the same time as the expiry of the priority period relating to that search, the time of the making of that application is to be taken as within that priority period.

(2) Where an official search with priority has been made in respect of a pending application for first registration and a subsequent application relating to a registrable estate which is subject to that pending application for first registration, or was so subject before completion of the registration of that registrable estate, is taken as having been made at the same time as the expiry of the priority period relating to that search, the time of the making of that subsequent application is to be taken as within that priority period.

[3223]

Official searches without priority

155 Application for official search without priority

(1) A person may apply for an official search without priority of an individual register of a registered title.

(2) Subject to rule 132(1), an application for an official search without priority must be made in Form OS3.

(3) Where the application is in Form OS3 and an accompanying plan is required, unless the registrar allows otherwise, the plan must be delivered in duplicate.

[3224]

156 Issue of official search certificate without priority

(1) If an application for an official search without priority is in order, an official search certificate without priority must be issued.

(2) An official search certificate without priority may, at the registrar's discretion, be issued in one or both of the following ways—
(a) in paper form, or

(b) under rule 132(2).

(3) Subject to paragraph (4), an official search certificate without priority issued under paragraph (2) must include such information specified in Part 3 of Schedule 6 as the case may require and may be issued by reference to an official copy of the individual register of the relevant registered title.

(4) If an official certificate of search is to be, or has been, issued in paper form under paragraph (2)(a), another official search certificate issued under paragraph (2)(b) in respect of the same application need only include the information specified at A, F, G and H of Part 3 of Schedule 6, as the case may require.

[3225]

Request for information

157 Information requested by telephone, oral or remote terminal application for an official search

(1) If an application under rule 147(3) or rule 155(2) has been made by telephone or orally by virtue of rule 132(1) in respect of a registered title, the registrar may, before or after the official search has been completed, at his discretion, inform the applicant, by telephone or orally, whether or not—

(a) there have been any relevant adverse entries made in the individual register since the search from date given in the application, or

(b) there is any relevant entry subsisting on the day list.

(2) If an application under rule 147(3) has been made by telephone or orally by virtue of rule 132(1) in respect of a legal estate subject to a pending application for first registration, the registrar may, before or after the official search has been completed, at his discretion, inform the applicant, by telephone or orally, whether or not there is any relevant entry subsisting on the day list.

(3) If an application under rule 147(3) or rule 155(2) has been made to the land registry computer system from a remote terminal by virtue of rule 132(1), the registrar may, before or after the official search has been completed, at his discretion, inform the applicant, by a transmission to the remote terminal, whether or not—

(a) in the case of an official search of a registered title, there have been any relevant entries of the kind referred to in paragraph (1)(a) or (b), or

(b) in the case of an official search of a legal estate subject to a pending application for first registration, there have been any relevant entries of the kind referred to in paragraph (2).

(4) Under this rule the registrar need not provide the applicant with details of any relevant entries.

[3226]

Official searches for the purpose of the Family Law Act 1996 and information requests

158 Application for official search for the purpose of the Family Law Act 1996 by a mortgagee

(1) A mortgagee of land comprised in a registered title that consists of or includes all or part of a dwelling-house may apply for an official search certificate of the result of a search of the relevant individual register for the purpose of section 56(3) of the Family Law Act 1996.

(2) Subject to rule 132(1), an application under paragraph (1) must be made in [Form HR3].

[3227]

NOTES

Para (2): words in square brackets substituted by SI 2005/1982, r 14, subject to transitional provision in r 19 thereof.

159 Issue of official search certificate result following an application made by a mortgagee for the purpose of section 56(3) of the Family Law Act 1996

(1) An official search certificate giving the result of a search in respect of an application made under rule 158 may, at the registrar's discretion, be issued in one or both of the following ways—

(a) in paper form, or

(b) under rule 132(2).

(2) Subject to paragraph (3), an official search certificate issued under paragraph (1) must include the information specified in Part 5 of Schedule 6.

(3) If an official search certificate is to be, or has been, issued under paragraph (1)(a), another official search certificate issued under rule 132(2) by virtue of paragraph (1)(b) in respect of the same application need only include the information specified at A, E and F of Part 5 of Schedule 6.

[3228]

160 Information requested by an applicant for an official search for the purpose of the Family Law Act 1996

If an application has been made under rule 158 the registrar may, at his discretion, during the currency of a relevant notice given under Schedule 2, and in accordance with the limitations contained in that notice, before the official search has been completed, inform the applicant, by any means of communication, whether or not—

(a) a … home rights notice or matrimonial home rights caution has been entered in the individual register of the relevant registered title, or

(b) there is a pending application for the entry of a … home rights notice entered on the day list.

[3229]

NOTES

Words omitted revoked by SI 2005/1982, r 15.

PART 14
MISCELLANEOUS AND SPECIAL CASES

Dispositions by operation of law within section 27(5) of the Act

161 Applications to register dispositions by operation of law which are registrable dispositions

(1) Subject to paragraphs (2) and (3), an application to register a disposition by operation of law which is a registrable disposition must be accompanied by sufficient evidence of the disposition.

(2) Where a vesting order has been made, it must accompany the application.

(3) Where there is a vesting declaration to which section 40 of the Trustee Act 1925 applies, the application must be accompanied by the deed of appointment or retirement, and—

(a) a certificate from the conveyancer acting for the persons making the appointment or effecting the retirement that they are entitled to do so, or

(b) such other evidence to satisfy the registrar that the persons making the appointment or effecting the retirement are entitled to do so.

[3230]

Death of proprietor

162 Transfer by a personal representative

[(1) An application to register a transfer by a personal representative, who is not already registered as proprietor, must be accompanied by—

(a) the original grant of probate of the deceased proprietor and, where section 7 of the Administration of Justice Act 1925 applies, the original grant of probate showing the chain of representation, to prove that the transferor is his personal representative,

(b) the original letters of administration of the deceased proprietor showing the transferor as his personal representative,

(c) a court order appointing the transferor as the deceased's personal representative, or

(d) (where a conveyancer is acting for the applicant) a certificate given by a conveyancer that the conveyancer holds the original or a certified or office copy of such grant of probate, letters of administration or court order.]

(2) The registrar shall not be under a duty to investigate the reasons a transfer of registered land by a personal representative of a deceased sole proprietor or last surviving joint proprietor is made nor to consider the contents of the will and, provided the terms of any restriction on the register are complied with, he must assume, whether he knows of the terms of the will or not, that the personal representative is acting correctly and within his powers.

[3231]

NOTES

Para (1): substituted by SI 2008/1919, r 4(1), Sch 1, para 51.

163 Registration of a personal representative

(1) An application by a personal representative to become registered as proprietor of a registered estate or registered charge—

(a) in place of a deceased sole proprietor or the last surviving joint proprietor, or

(b) jointly with another personal representative who is already so registered, or

(c) in place of another personal representative who is already registered as proprietor,

must be accompanied by the evidence specified in paragraph (2).

[(2) Subject to paragraph (3), the evidence that must accompany an application under paragraph (1) is—

(a) the original grant of probate of the deceased proprietor and, where section 7 of the Administration of Justice Act 1925 applies, the original grant of probate showing the chain of representation, to prove that the transferor is his personal representative,

(b) the original letters of administration of the deceased proprietor showing the transferor as his personal representative,

(c) a court order appointing the applicant as the deceased's personal representative, or

(d) (where a conveyancer is acting for the applicant) a certificate given by the conveyancer that he holds the original or an office copy of such grant of probate, letters of administration or court order.]

(3) An application under paragraph (1)(c) must be accompanied by evidence to satisfy the registrar that the appointment of the personal representative whom the applicant is replacing has been terminated.

(4) When registering a personal representative of a deceased proprietor, the registrar must add the following after the personal representative's name—

"executor or executrix (or administrator or administratrix) of [name] deceased".

(5) Before registering another personal representative as a result of an application made under paragraph (1)(b) the registrar must serve notice upon the personal representative who is registered as proprietor.

[3232]

NOTES

Para (2): substituted by SI 2008/1919, r 4(1), Sch 1, para 52.

164 Death of joint proprietor

An application for alteration of the register by the removal from the register of the name of a deceased joint proprietor of a registered estate or registered charge must be accompanied by evidence of his death.

[3233]

Bankruptcy of proprietor

165 Bankruptcy notice

(1) The bankruptcy notice in relation to a registered estate must be entered in the proprietorship register and the bankruptcy notice in relation to a registered charge must be entered in the charges register in the following form—

"BANKRUPTCY NOTICE entered under section 86(2) of the Land Registration Act 2002 in respect of a pending action, as the title of the [proprietor of the registered estate] *or* [the proprietor of the charge dated .... referred to above] appears to be affected by a petition in bankruptcy against [*name of debtor*], presented in the [*name*] Court (Court Reference Number ....) (Land Charges Reference Number PA ....).".

(2) The registrar must give notice of the entry of a bankruptcy notice to the proprietor of the registered estate or registered charge to which it relates.

(3) In this rule, "bankruptcy notice" means the notice which the registrar must enter in the register under section 86(2) of the Act.

[3234]

166 Bankruptcy restriction

(1) The bankruptcy restriction in relation to a registered estate must be entered in the proprietorship register and the bankruptcy restriction in relation to a registered charge must be entered in the charges register in the following form—

"BANKRUPTCY RESTRICTION entered under section 86(4) of the Land Registration Act 2002, as the title of [the proprietor of the registered estate] *or* [the proprietor of the charge dated .... referred to above] appears to be affected by a bankruptcy order made by the [*name*] Court (Court Reference Number ....) against [*name of debtor*] (Land Charges Reference Number WO ....).

[No disposition of the registered estate] *or* [No disposition of the charge] is to be registered until the trustee in bankruptcy of the property of the bankrupt is registered as proprietor of the [registered estate] *or* [charge].".

(2) The registrar must give notice of the entry of a bankruptcy restriction to the proprietor of the registered estate or registered charge to which it relates.

(3) In this rule, "bankruptcy restriction" means the restriction which the registrar must enter in the register under section 86(4) of the Act.

[3235]

167 Action of the registrar in relation to bankruptcy entries

(1) Where the registrar is satisfied that—

(a) the bankruptcy order has been annulled, or

(b) the bankruptcy petition has been dismissed or withdrawn with the court's permission, or

(c) the bankruptcy proceedings do not affect or have ceased to affect the registered estate or registered charge in relation to which a bankruptcy notice or bankruptcy restriction has been entered on the register,

he must as soon as practicable cancel any bankruptcy notice or bankruptcy restriction which relates to that bankruptcy order, to that bankruptcy petition or to those proceedings from the register.

(2) Where it appears to the registrar that there is doubt as to whether the debtor or bankrupt is the same person as the proprietor of the registered estate or registered charge in relation to which a bankruptcy notice or bankruptcy restriction has been entered, he must as soon as practicable take such action as he considers necessary to resolve the doubt.

(3) In this rule—

"bankruptcy notice" means the notice which the registrar must enter in the register under section 86(2) of the Act, and

"bankruptcy restriction" means the restriction which the registrar must enter in the register under section 86(4) of the Act.

[3236]

168 Registration of trustee in bankruptcy

(1) Where—

(a) a proprietor has had a bankruptcy order made against him, or

(b) an insolvency administration order has been made in respect of a deceased proprietor,

and the bankrupt's or deceased's registered estate or registered charge has vested in the trustee in bankruptcy, the trustee may apply for the alteration of the register by registering himself in place of the bankrupt or deceased proprietor.

(2) The application must be supported by, as appropriate—

(a) the bankruptcy order relating to the bankrupt or the insolvency administration order relating to the deceased's estate, and

(b) a certificate signed by the trustee that the registered estate or registered charge is comprised in the bankrupt's estate or deceased's estate, and

(c) where the official receiver is the trustee, a certificate by him to that effect, and, where the trustee is another person, the evidence referred to in paragraph (3).

(3) The evidence referred to at paragraph (2)(c) is—

(a) his certificate of appointment as trustee by the meeting of the bankrupt's or deceased debtor's creditors, or

(b) his certificate of appointment as trustee by the Secretary of State, or

(c) the order of the court appointing him trustee.

(4) In this rule, "insolvency administration order" has the same meaning as in section 385(1) of the Insolvency Act 1986.

[3237]

NOTES

Application: as to the application of this rule, with modifications, in so far as it relates to bank insolvency or administration under the Banking Act 2009, Pts 2, 3, see the Banking Act 2009 (Parts 2 and 3 Consequential Amendments) Order 2009, SI 2009/317, art 3, Schedule.

169 Trustee in bankruptcy vacating office

(1) This rule applies where—

(a) a trustee in bankruptcy, who has been registered as proprietor, vacates his office, and

(b) the official receiver or some other person has been appointed the trustee of the relevant bankrupt's estate, and

(c) the official receiver or that person applies to be registered as proprietor in place of the former trustee.

(2) The application referred to in paragraph (1)(c) must be supported by the evidence required by rule 168(2)(c).

[3238]

170 Description of trustee in register

Where the official receiver or another trustee in bankruptcy is registered as proprietor, the words "Official Receiver and trustee in bankruptcy of [name]" or "Trustee in bankruptcy of [name]" must be added to the register, as appropriate.

[3239]

Overseas insolvency proceedings

171 Proceedings under the EC Regulation on insolvency proceedings

(1) A relevant person may apply for a note of a judgement opening insolvency proceedings to be entered in the register.

(2) An application under paragraph (1) must be accompanied by such evidence as the registrar may reasonably require.

(3) Following an application under paragraph (1) if the registrar is satisfied that the judgement opening insolvency proceedings has been made he may enter a note of the judgement in the register.

(4) In this rule—

"judgement opening insolvency proceedings" means a judgement opening proceedings within the meaning of article 3(1) of the Regulation,

"Regulation" means Council Regulation (EC) No 1346/2000,

"relevant person" means any person or body authorised under the provisions of article 22 of the Regulation to request or require an entry to be made in the register in respect of the judgement opening insolvency proceedings the subject of the application.

[3240]

Pending land actions, writs and orders

172 Benefit of pending land actions, writs and orders

(1) For the purposes of section 34(1) of the Act, a relevant person shall be treated as having the benefit of the pending land action, writ or order, as appropriate.

(2) In determining whether a person has a sufficient interest in the making of an entry of a restriction under section 43(1)(c) of the Act, a relevant person shall be treated as having the benefit of the pending land action, writ or order, as appropriate.

(3) In this rule, "a relevant person" means a person (or his assignee or chargee, if appropriate) who is taking any action or proceedings which are within section 87(1)(a) of the Act, or who has obtained a writ or order within section 87(1)(b) of the Act.

[3241]

The Crown

173 Escheat etc

(1) Where a registered freehold estate in land has determined, the registrar may enter a note of that fact in the property register and in the property register of any inferior affected registered title.

(2) Where the registrar considers that there is doubt as to whether a registered freehold estate in land has determined, the entry under paragraph (1) must be modified by a statement to that effect.

[3242]

Church of England

174 Entry of Incumbent on a transfer to the Church Commissioners

(1) Where by virtue of any Act or Measure a transfer to the Church Commissioners has the effect, subject only to being completed by registration, of vesting any registered land either immediately or at a subsequent time in an incumbent or any other ecclesiastical corporation sole, the registrar must register the incumbent or such other ecclesiastical corporation as proprietor upon receipt of—

(a) an application,
(b) the transfer to the Church Commissioners, and
(c) a certificate by the Church Commissioners in Form 4.

(2) The certificate in Form 4 may be given either in the transfer or in a separate document.

(3) In this rule, "Measure" means a Measure of the National Assembly of the Church of England or of the General Synod of the Church of England.

[3243]

175 Entry of Church Commissioners etc as proprietor

(1) When any registered land is transferred to or (subject only to completion by registration) vested in the Church Commissioners, any ecclesiastical corporation, aggregate or sole, or any other person, by—

(a) a scheme of the Church Commissioners, or
(b) an instrument taking effect on publication in the London Gazette made pursuant to any Act or Measure relating to or administered by the Church Commissioners, or
(c) any transfer authorised by any such Act or Measure,

the registrar must, on application, register the Church Commissioners, such ecclesiastical corporation or such other person as proprietor.

(2) The application must be accompanied by—

(a) a certificate by the Church Commissioners in Form 5, and

[(b) one of the following, as appropriate—

(i) a sealed copy of the scheme of the Church Commissioners,

(ii) a copy of the London Gazette publishing the instrument, or

(iii) the transfer].

(3) The certificate in Form 5 may be given either in the transfer or in a separate document.

(4) In this rule, "Measure" means a Measure of the National Assembly of the Church of England or of the General Synod of the Church of England.

[3244]

NOTES

Para (2): sub-para (b) substituted by SI 2008/1919, r 4(1), Sch 1, para 53

Charities

176 Non-exempt charities—restrictions

(1) The restriction which the registrar is required by section 37(8) or section 39(1B) of the Charities Act 1993 to enter in the register where one of those subsections applies must be the appropriate restriction.

(2) Any of the following applications must, if they relate to a registered or unregistered estate held by or in trust for a non-exempt charity, be accompanied by an application for entry of the appropriate restriction unless, in the case of a registered estate, that restriction is already in the register—

(a) an application for first registration of an unregistered estate unless the disposition which triggers the requirement of registration is effected by an instrument containing the statement set out in rule 179(b) or rule 180(2)(b) or (c),

(b) an application to register a transfer of a registered estate unless the disposition is effected by an instrument containing the statement set out in rule 179(b),

(c) an application under rule 161 to register the vesting of a registered estate in a person other than the proprietor of that estate.

(3) Where a registered estate is held by or in trust for a corporation and the corporation becomes a non-exempt charity, the charity trustees must apply for entry of the appropriate restriction.

(4) In this rule "the appropriate restriction" means a restriction in Form E.

[3245]

177 Registration of trustees incorporated under Part VII of the Charities Act 1993

In any registrable disposition in favour of charity trustees incorporated under Part VII of the Charities Act 1993 they must be described as "a body corporate under Part VII of the Charities Act 1993" and the application to register the disposition must be accompanied by the certificate granted by the Charity Commissioners under section 50 of that Act.

[3246]

178 Registration of official custodian

(1) An application to register the official custodian as proprietor of a registered estate or a registered charge must be accompanied by—

(a) an order of the court made under section 21(1) of the Charities Act 1993, or

(b) an order of the Charity Commissioners made under sections 16 or 18 of the Charities Act 1993.

(2) Where the estate or charge is vested in the official custodian by virtue of an order under section 18 of the Charities Act 1993, an application to register him as proprietor (whether under Chapter 1 of Part 2 of the Act or following a registrable disposition) must be accompanied by an application for the entry of a restriction in Form F.

(3) Where the official custodian is registered as proprietor of a registered estate or a registered charge, except where the estate or charge is vested in him by virtue of an order under section 18 of the Charities Act 1993, the address of the charity trustees or, where the registered estate or registered charge is held on behalf of a charity which is a corporation, the address of the charity, must be entered in the register as his address for service under rule 198.

[3247]

179 Statements to be contained in dispositions in favour of a charity

The statement required by section 37(5) of the Charities Act 1993 must, in an instrument to which section 37(7) of that Act applies, be in one of the following forms—

(a) "The land transferred (*or as the case may be*) will, as a result of this transfer (*or as the case may be*) be held by (or in trust for) (*charity*), an exempt charity."

(b) "The land transferred (*or as the case may be*) will, as a result of this transfer (*or as the case may be*) be held by (*or* in trust for) (*charity*), a non-exempt charity, and the restrictions on disposition imposed by section 36 of the Charities Act 1993 will apply to the land (subject to section 36(9) of that Act).".

[3248]

180 Statements to be contained in dispositions by a charity

(1) The statement required by section 37(1) of the Charities Act 1993 must, in an instrument to which section 37(7) of that Act applies, be in one of the following forms—

(a) "The land transferred (*or as the case may be*) is held by [(*proprietors*) in trust for] (*charity*), an exempt charity."

(b) "The land transferred (*or as the case may be*) is held by [(*proprietors*) in trust for] (*charity*), a non-exempt charity, but this transfer (*or as the case may be*) is one falling within paragraph ((a), (b) or (c) *as the case may be*) of section 36(9) of the Charities Act 1993."

(c) "The land transferred (*or as the case may be*) is held by [(*proprietors*) in trust for] (*charity*), a non-exempt charity, and this transfer (*or as the case may be*) is not one falling within paragraph (a), (b) or (c) of section 36(9) of the Charities Act 1993, so that the restrictions on disposition imposed by section 36 of that Act apply to the land.".

(2) The statement required by section 39(1) of the Charities Act 1993 must, in a mortgage which is a registrable disposition or to which section 4(1)(g) of the Act applies, be in one of the following forms—

(a) "The land charged is held by (*or* in trust for) (*charity*), an exempt charity."

(b) "The land charged is held by (*or* in trust for) (*charity*), a non-exempt charity, but this charge (*or* mortgage) is one falling within section 38(5) of the Charities Act 1993."

(c) "The land charged is held by (*or* in trust for) (*charity*), a non-exempt charity, and this charge (*or* mortgage) is not one falling within section 38(5) of the Charities Act 1993, so that the restrictions imposed by section 38 of that Act apply.".

(3) The statement required by section 39(1A)(b) of the Charities Act 1993 must be in the following form—

"The restrictions on disposition imposed by section 36 of the Charities Act 1993 also apply to the land (subject to section 36(9) of that Act).".

[3249]–[3250]

Companies and other corporations

181 (*Revoked by SI 2008/1919, r 4(1), Sch 1, para 54.*)

182 Registration of trustees of charitable, ecclesiastical or public trust

(1) Subject to paragraph [(2)], where a corporation or body of trustees holding on charitable, ecclesiastical or public trusts applies to be registered as proprietor of a registered estate or registered charge, the application must be accompanied by the document creating the trust.

(2), (3) …

[(2)] Paragraph (1) of this rule does not apply in the case of a registered estate or a registered charge held by or in trust for a non-exempt charity.

[3251]

NOTES

Para (1): reference to in square brackets substituted by SI 2008/1919, r 4(1), Sch 1, para 55(a).
Paras (2), (3): original paras (2), (3) revoked by SI 2008/1919, r 4(1), Sch 1, para 55(b).
Para (4): renumbered as para (2) by SI 2008/1919, r 4(1), Sch 1, para 55(c).

[183 Registration of certain corporations

(1) Where a corporation to which this rule applies makes an application to be registered as proprietor of a registered estate or registered charge the application must also be accompanied by evidence of the extent of its powers to hold and sell, mortgage, lease and otherwise deal with, or to lend money on a mortgage or charge of, land.

(2) The evidence must include—

(a) the charter, statute, rules, memorandum and articles of association or other documents constituting the corporation, or a certificate given either—

(i) in Form 7 by a qualified lawyer practising in the territory of incorporation of the corporation, where the corporation is incorporated outside the United Kingdom, or

(ii) in Form 8 by the applicant's conveyancer, in respect of any other corporation to which this rule applies, and

(b) such further evidence as the registrar may require.

(3) This rule applies to any corporation aggregate which is not—

(a) a company incorporated in any part of the United Kingdom under the Companies Acts,

(b) a limited liability partnership incorporated under the Limited Liability Partnerships Act 2000 or the Limited Liability Partnerships Act (Northern Ireland) 2002, or

(c) a corporation to which rule 182(1) applies.]

[3252]

NOTES

Substituted by SI 2008/1919, r 4(1), Sch 1, para 56.

[183A Registration of registered social landlords and unregistered housing associations

(1) If an applicant for registration as proprietor of a registered estate or a registered charge is, or holds on trust for, a registered social landlord within the meaning of the Housing Act 1996, the application must include a certificate to that effect.

(2) If an applicant for registration as proprietor of a registered estate or a registered charge is, or holds on trust for, an unregistered housing association within the meaning of the Housing Associations Act 1985 and the application relates to grant-aided land as defined in Schedule 1 to that Act, the application must include a certificate to that effect.]

[3252A]

NOTES

Commencement: 10 November 2008.
Inserted by SI 2008/1919, r 4(1), Sch 1, para 57.

184 Administration orders and liquidation of a company

(1) Paragraph (2) applies where a company which is the registered proprietor of a registered estate or registered charge [enters administration] under the Insolvency Act 1986.

(2) Upon the application of the company's administrator, supported by the order [or the notice of appointment], the registrar must make an entry in the individual register of the relevant registered title as to the making of the order [or the notice of appointment] and the appointment of the administrator.

(3) Paragraphs (4) and (5) apply where a company which is the registered proprietor of a registered estate or registered charge is in liquidation.

(4) Upon the application of the company's liquidator, the registrar must make an entry in the individual register of the relevant registered title as to the appointment of the liquidator.

(5) The application under paragraph (4) must be supported by the order, appointment by the Secretary of State or resolution under which the liquidator was appointed and such other evidence as the registrar may require.

[3253]

NOTES

Para (1): words in square brackets substituted by SI 2003/2096, art 5, Schedule, Pt 2, para 80(a), except in relation to any case where a petition for an administration order was presented before 15 September 2003.

Para (2): words in square brackets inserted by SI 2003/2096, art 5, Schedule, Pt 2, para 80(b), except in relation to any case where a petition for an administration order was presented before 15 September 2003.

Application: as to the application of this rule, with modifications, in so far as it relates to bank insolvency or administration under the Banking Act 2009, Pts 2, 3, see the Banking Act 2009 (Parts 2 and 3 Consequential Amendments) Order 2009, SI 2009/317, art 3, Schedule.

185 Note of dissolution of a corporation

Where a corporation shown in an individual register as the proprietor of the registered estate or of a registered charge has been dissolved, the registrar may enter a note of that fact in the proprietorship register or in the charges register, as appropriate.

[3254]

Settlements

186 Settlements

Schedule 7 (which makes provision for the purposes of the Act in relation to the application to registered land of the enactments relating to settlements under the Settled Land Act 1925) has effect.

[3255]

Adverse possession

[187 Interpretation

(1) Where the application is to be registered as proprietor of a registered rentcharge, the references in rules 188, 188A, 189, 190, 192, 193, 194A, 194B, 194C, 194F, and 194G to Schedule 6 to the Act are to Schedule 6 as applied by rule 191.

(2) In rules 194A, 194B and 194F, "post" means pre-paid delivery by a postal service which seeks to deliver documents within the United Kingdom no later than the next working day in all or the majority of cases, and to deliver outside the United Kingdom within such period as is reasonable in all the circumstances.

(3) In rules 194A, 194B, 194C, 194F and 194G, "qualified surveyor" means a fellow or professional associate of the Royal Institution of Chartered Surveyors.]

[3256]

NOTES

Substituted by SI 2008/1919, r 4(1), Sch 1, para 58.

188 Applications for registration—procedure

(1) An application under paragraphs 1 or 6 of Schedule 6 to the Act must be in Form ADV1 and be accompanied by—

(a) a statutory declaration [or statement of truth] made by the applicant not more than one month before the application is taken to have been made, together with any supporting statutory declarations [or statements of truth], to provide evidence of adverse possession of the registered estate in land or rentcharge against which the application is made for a period which if it were to continue from the date of the applicant's statutory declaration [or statement of truth] to the date of the application would be—

(i) where the application is under paragraph 1, of not less than ten years (or sixty years, if paragraph 13 of Schedule 6 to the Act applies) ending on the date of the application, or

(ii) where the application is under paragraph 6, of not less than two years beginning with the date of rejection of the original application under paragraph 1 and ending on the date of the application,

(b) any additional evidence which the applicant considers necessary to support the claim.

(2) The statutory declaration [or statement of truth] by an applicant in support of an application under paragraph 1 of Schedule 6 to the Act must also—

[(a) if the application relates to part only of the land in a registered title, exhibit a plan which enables that part to be identified on the Ordnance Survey map, unless that part is referred to in the statutory declaration or statement of truth by reference to the title plan and this enables that part to be so identified,]

(b) if reliance is placed on paragraph 1(2) of Schedule 6 to the Act, contain the facts relied upon with any appropriate exhibits,

(c) contain confirmation that paragraph 1(3) of Schedule 6 to the Act does not apply,

(d) where the application is to be registered as proprietor of a registered rentcharge, contain confirmation that the proprietor of the registered rentcharge has not re-entered the land out of which the rentcharge issues,

(e) contain confirmation that to the best of his knowledge the restriction on applications in paragraph 8 of Schedule 6 to the Act does not apply,

(f) contain confirmation that to the best of his knowledge the estate or rentcharge is not, and has not been during any of the period of alleged adverse possession, subject to a trust (other than one where the interest of each of the beneficiaries is an interest in possession),

(g) if, should a person given notice under paragraph 2 of Schedule 6 to the Act require the application to be dealt with under paragraph 5 of that Schedule, it is intended to rely on one or more of the conditions set out in paragraph 5 of Schedule 6 to the Act, contain the facts supporting such reliance.

(3) The statutory declaration [or statement of truth] by an applicant in support of an application under paragraph 6 of Schedule 6 to the Act must also—

[(a) if the application relates to part only of the land in a registered title, exhibit a plan which enables that part to be identified clearly on the Ordnance Survey map, unless the previous rejected application related only to that part, or that part is referred to in the statutory declaration or statement of truth by reference to the title plan and this enables that part to be so identified,]

(b) contain full details of the previous rejected application,

(c) contain confirmation that to the best of his knowledge the restriction on applications in paragraph 8 of Schedule 6 to the Act does not apply,

(d) contain confirmation that to the best of his knowledge the estate or rentcharge is not, and has not been during any of the period of alleged adverse possession, subject to a trust (other than one where the interest of each of the beneficiaries is an interest in possession),

(e) contain confirmation that paragraph 6(2) of Schedule 6 to the Act does not apply, and

(f) where the application is to be registered as proprietor of a registered rentcharge, contain confirmation that the proprietor of the registered rentcharge has not re-entered the land out of which the rentcharge issues.

[(4) A statement of truth by an applicant under paragraphs 1 or 6 of Schedule 6 to the Act, and any supporting statements of truth, may be made in Form ST1 or Form ST2, as appropriate.]

[3257]

NOTES

Para (1): in sub-para (a) words in square brackets inserted by SI 2008/1919, r 4(1), Sch 1, para 59(a).

Para (2): words in square brackets inserted, and sub-para (a) substituted by SI 2008/1919, r 4(1), Sch 1, para 59(b).

Para (3): words in square brackets inserted, and sub-para (a) substituted by SI 2008/1919, r 4(1), Sch 1, para 59(b).

Para (4): inserted by SI 2008/1919, r 4(1), Sch 1, para 59(d).

[188A Notification of application where registered proprietor is a dissolved company

(1) This rule applies where an application under paragraph 1 of Schedule 6 to the Act is made.

(2) Where the registrar considers that the proprietor of the estate to which the application relates is, or may be, a company which is dissolved and that its last registered office was, or may have been, situated in the county palatine of Lancaster, the registrar must give notice of the application to the Solicitor for the affairs of the Duchy of Lancaster.

(3) Where the registrar considers that the proprietor of the estate to which the application relates is, or may be, a company which is dissolved and that its last registered office was, or may have been, situated in the county of Cornwall or in the Isles of Scilly, the registrar must give notice of the application to the Duke of Cornwall or the possessor for the time being of the Duchy of Cornwall.

(4) Where the registrar considers that the proprietor of the estate to which the application relates is, or may be, a company which is dissolved and that its last registered office was, or may have been, situated outside the areas referred to in paragraphs (2) and (3), the registrar must give notice of the application to the Treasury Solicitor.

(5) The notice referred to in paragraphs (2) to (4) is notice under paragraph 2 of Schedule 6 to the Act.

(6) In this rule, "company" means a company incorporated in any part of the United Kingdom under the Companies Acts.]

[3257A]

NOTES

Commencement: 10 November 2008.

Inserted by SI 2008/1919, r 4(1), Sch 1, para 60.

189 Time limit for reply to a notice of an application

The period for the purpose of paragraph 3(2) of Schedule 6 to the Act is the period ending at 12 noon on the sixty-fifth business day after the date of issue of the notice.

[3258]

190 Notice under paragraph 3(2) of Schedule 6 to the Act

(1) A notice to the registrar under paragraph 3(2) of Schedule 6 to the Act from a person given a registrar's notice must be—

(a) in Form NAP, and

(b) given to the registrar in the manner and at the address stated in the registrar's notice.

(2) Form NAP must accompany a registrar's notice.

(3) In this rule a "registrar's notice" is a notice given by the registrar under paragraph 2 of Schedule 6 to the Act.

[3259]

191 Adverse possession of rentcharges

Schedule 6 to the Act applies to the registration of an adverse possessor of a registered rentcharge in the modified form set out in Schedule 8.

[3260]

192 Adverse possession of a rentcharge; non-payment of rent

(1) This rule applies where—

(a) a person is entitled to be registered as proprietor of a registered rentcharge under Schedule 6 to the Act, and

(b) if that person were so registered he would not be subject to a registered charge or registered lease or other interest protected in the register, and

(c) that person's adverse possession is based on non-payment of rent due under the registered rentcharge.

(2) Where paragraph (1) applies the registrar must—

(a) close the whole of the registered title of the registered rentcharge, or

(b) cancel the registered rentcharge, if the registered title to it also comprises other rentcharges.

[3261]

193 Prohibition of recovery of rent after adverse possession of a rentcharge

(1) When—

(a) a person has been registered as proprietor of a rentcharge, or

(b) the registered title to a rentcharge has been closed, or

(c) a registered rentcharge has been cancelled, where the registered title also comprises other rentcharges,

following an application made under Schedule 6 to the Act, and, if appropriate, closure or cancellation under rule 192, no previous registered proprietor of the rentcharge may recover any rent due under the rentcharge from a person who has been in adverse possession of the rentcharge.

(2) Paragraph (1) applies whether the adverse possession arose either as a result of non-payment of the rent or by receipt of the rent from the person liable to pay it.

[3262]

194 Registration as a person entitled to be notified of an application for adverse possession

(1) Any person who can satisfy the registrar that he has an interest in a registered estate in land or a registered rentcharge which would be prejudiced by the registration of any other person as proprietor of that estate under Schedule 6 to the Act or as proprietor of a registered rentcharge under that Schedule as applied by rule 191 may apply to be registered as a person to be notified under paragraph 2(1)(d) of Schedule 6.

(2) An application under paragraph (1) must be made in Form ADV2.

(3) The registrar must enter the name of the applicant in the proprietorship register as a person entitled to be notified under paragraph 2 of Schedule 6 to the Act.

[3263]

[194A Arbitration requested by proprietor

(1) This rule applies where a proprietor with the right under paragraph 10(1) of Schedule 6 to the Act to require apportionment has given the chargor notice in accordance with paragraph (2).

(2) The notice referred to in paragraph (1) must—

(a) identify the proprietor and give an address for communications to the proprietor from the chargor,

(b) make proposals as to the values of the registered estate and the other property subject to the charge,

(c) state the proprietor's intention, in the absence of agreement on the respective values of the registered estate and the other property subject to the charge, to request the President of the Royal Institution of Chartered Surveyors to appoint a qualified surveyor to determine these values, and

(d) be served by post to, or by leaving the notice at, any postal address or by electronic transmission to an electronic address (if there is one) entered in the register as an address for service for the chargor.

(3) If the chargor does not provide the proprietor with the chargor's written agreement to the values referred to in paragraph (2)(b), or to any other valuations acceptable to the proprietor, within one month of when the notice was received, the proprietor may make the request referred to in paragraph (2)(c).

(4) Where a qualified surveyor has been appointed pursuant to a request under paragraph (3)—

(a) the proprietor shall be liable for the costs of that appointment,

(b) the qualified surveyor shall act as an arbitrator and the provisions of the Arbitration Act 1996 shall apply,
(c) the proprietor and the chargor shall be parties to the arbitration,
(d) the chargee may elect to be joined as a party to the arbitration, and the qualified surveyor must ascertain whether the chargee so elects, and
(e) the proprietor and the chargor must allow the qualified surveyor access to the land any estate in which is subject to the charge.

(5) In this rule, "an address for communications" means a postal address but if additionally the proprietor provides an e-mail address then that is also an address for communications.]

[3263A]

NOTES
Commencement: 10 November 2008.
Inserted (together with rr 194B–194G) by SI 2008/1919, r 4(1), Sch 1, para 61.

[194B Notice of required apportionment

(1) The right of the proprietor of a registered estate under paragraph 10(1) of Schedule 6 to the Act to require a chargee to apportion the amount secured by a charge is exercisable by notice being given by the proprietor to the chargee.

(2) The notice referred to in paragraph (1) must—
(a) identify the proprietor and give an address for communications to him from the chargee,
(b) state that apportionment is required under paragraph 10 of Schedule 6 to the Act,
(c) identify the chargor and the date of the charge,
(d) state whether the valuations accompanying the notice were by a qualified surveyor appointed pursuant to a request under rule 194A and, if they were, state the effect of rule 194C(1), and
(e) be served by post to, or by leaving the notice at, any postal address or by electronic transmission to an electronic address (if there is one) entered in the register as an address for service for the chargee.

(3) Subject to paragraph (4), the notice referred to in paragraph (1) must be accompanied by—
(a) valuations of the registered estate and of the other property subject to the charge by a qualified surveyor dated no earlier than two months before the notice is sent,
(b) the chargor's written agreement to the valuations,
(c) an official copy of the individual register and title plan of the registered estate, and
(d) a copy of the individual register and title plan, supplied in response to an application under rule 144, in respect of the registered title which immediately before the registration under Schedule 6 to the Act comprised the registered estate, unless such a copy is unavailable.

(4) If the valuations of the registered estate and of the other property subject to the charge are by a qualified surveyor appointed pursuant to a request under rule 194A, the requirements in paragraph (3)(b), (c) and (d) do not apply.

(5) In this rule, "an address for communications" means a postal address but if additionally the proprietor provides an e-mail address then that is also an address for communications.]

[3263B]

NOTES
Commencement: 10 November 2008.
Inserted as noted to s 194A at **[3263A]**.

[194C Apportionment

(1) If the valuations accompanying the notice referred to in rule 194B(1) are by a qualified surveyor appointed pursuant to a request under rule 194A, the chargee must, within two months of when the notice was received, apportion the amount secured by the charge at the time referred to in paragraph 10(1) of Schedule 6 to the Act on the basis of these valuations.

(2) If the valuations accompanying the notice referred to in rule 194B(1) are not by a qualified surveyor pursuant to a request under rule 194A, the chargee must, within two months of when the notice was received, either—
(a) apportion the amount secured by the charge at the time referred to in paragraph 10(1) of Schedule 6 to the Act on the basis of the valuations accompanying the notice, or on the basis of other valuations agreed by the proprietor and the chargor, or
(b) request the President of the Royal Institution of Chartered Surveyors to appoint a qualified surveyor to value the registered estate and the other property subject to the charge.

(3) Where a qualified surveyor has been appointed pursuant to a request under paragraph (2)(b)—

PART II STATUTORY INSTRUMENTS

(a) the chargee shall be liable for the costs of that appointment,
(b) the qualified surveyor shall act as an arbitrator and the provisions of the Arbitration Act 1996 shall apply,
(c) the proprietor and the chargee shall be parties to the arbitration,
(d) the chargor may elect to be joined as a party to the arbitration, and the qualified surveyor must ascertain whether the chargor so elects, and
(e) the proprietor and the chargor must allow the qualified surveyor access to the land any estate in which is subject to the charge.

(4) Where a qualified surveyor has been appointed pursuant to a request under paragraph (2)(b), the chargee must, within two months of when the valuations by the qualified surveyor were received, apportion the amount secured by the charge at the time referred to in paragraph 10(1) of Schedule 6 to the Act on the basis of those valuations.]

[3263C]

NOTES

Commencement: 10 November 2008.
Inserted as noted to s 194A at **[3263A]**.

[194D Basis of valuation

(1) For the purposes of rules 194A, 194B and 194C, where the other property affected by the charge includes an estate in land, the value of the proprietor's registered estate shall be the diminution in value of that other property as determined in accordance with paragraph (2).

(2) The diminution in value of the other property is the difference between—
(a) the value of all the property subject to the charge if the chargor were the proprietor and in possession of the proprietor's registered estate, and
(b) the value of the property subject to the charge without the proprietor's registered estate.]

[3263D]

NOTES

Commencement: 10 November 2008.
Inserted as noted to s 194A at **[3263A]**.

[194E Receipt of notice etc

(1) Notices and valuations shall be treated as received for the purposes of rules 194A(3) and 194C(1), (2) and (4) on—
(a) the second working day after posting, where the notice is posted to an address in the United Kingdom,
(b) the working day after it was left, where the notice is left at a postal address,
(c) the seventh working day after posting, where the notice is posted to an address outside the United Kingdom, and
(d) the second working day after transmission, where the notice is sent by electronic transmission (including email).]

[3263E]

NOTES

Commencement: 10 November 2008.
Inserted as noted to s 194A at **[3263A]**.

[194F Notice of apportionment

(1) Within ten working days of any apportionment under rule 194C, the chargee must issue notice of the apportionment to the proprietor and to the chargor.

(2) The notice referred to in paragraph (1) must state—
(a) the amount secured by the charge at the time referred to in paragraph 10(1) of Schedule 6 to the Act,
(b) the amount apportioned to the registered estate, and
(c) the costs incurred by the chargee as a result of the apportionment and payable under paragraph 10(2)(b) of Schedule 6 to the Act.

(3) The notice referred to in paragraph (1) which is issued to the proprietor must be served by post to, or by leaving the notice at, the postal address or by electronic transmission to any e-mail address given in the notice of required apportionment under rule 194B(1) or at another postal or e-mail address agreed in writing by the chargee and the proprietor.]

[3263F]

NOTES

Commencement: 10 November 2008.
Inserted as noted to s 194A at **[3263A]**.

[194G Costs

(1) Where in the award under rule 194A(4) or rule 194C(3) the qualified surveyor decides that the chargee shall be responsible for payment of the costs incurred by the chargee or any other party to the arbitration, such costs shall be excluded from the costs payable under paragraph 10(2)(b) of Schedule 6 to the Act.

(2) Subject to paragraph (3), the chargor shall be entitled to be paid by the proprietor those costs reasonably incurred by the chargor in the apportionment and, in particular, those in relation to valuations obtained for the purpose of the apportionment.

(3) Where in the award the qualified surveyor decides that the chargor shall be responsible for payment of the costs incurred by the chargor or any other party to the arbitration, such costs shall be excluded from the costs payable under paragraph (2).]

[3263G]

NOTES

Commencement: 10 November 2008.
Inserted as noted to s 194A at **[3263A]**.

Indemnity; interest on

[195 Payment of interest on an indemnity

(1) Subject to paragraph (3), interest is payable in accordance with paragraph (4) on the amount of any indemnity paid under Schedule 8 to the Act—

(a) where paragraph 1(1)(a) of Schedule 8 applies other than in respect of any indemnity on account of costs or expenses, from the date of the rectification to the date of payment,

(b) where any other sub-paragraph of paragraph 1(1) of Schedule 8 applies other than in respect of any indemnity on account of costs or expenses, from the date the loss is suffered by reason of the relevant mistake, loss, destruction or failure to the date of payment,

(c) in respect of an indemnity on account of costs or expenses within paragraph 3 of Schedule 8, from the date when the claimant pays them to the date of payment.

(2) A reference in this rule to a period from a date to the date of payment excludes the former date but includes the latter date.

(3) No interest is payable under paragraph (1) for any period or periods where the registrar or the court is satisfied that the claimant has not taken reasonable steps to pursue with due diligence the claim for indemnity or, where relevant, the application for rectification.

(4) Simple interest is payable—

(a) where the period specified in paragraph (1) starts on or after 10 November 2008, at one percent above the applicable Bank of England base rate or rates, or

(b) where the period specified in paragraph (1) starts before that date,

(i) for the part of the period before that date, at the applicable rate or rates set for court judgment debts, and

(ii) for the part of the period on or after that date, at one percent above the applicable Bank of England base rate or rates.

(5) In this rule "Bank of England base rate" means—

(a) the rate announced from time to time by the Monetary Policy Committee of the Bank of England as the official dealing rate, being the rate at which the Bank is willing to enter into transactions for providing short term liquidity in the money markets, or

(b) where an order under section 19 of the Bank of England Act 1998 is in force, any equivalent rate determined by the Treasury under that section.]

[3264]

NOTES

Substituted by SI 2008/1919, r 4(1), Sch 1, para 62.

Statements under the Leasehold Reform, Housing and Urban Development Act 1993

196 Statements in transfers or conveyances and leases under the Leasehold Reform, Housing and Urban Development Act 1993

(1) The statement required by section 34(10) of the Leasehold Reform, Housing and Urban Development Act 1993 to be contained in a conveyance executed for the purposes of Chapter I of Part I of that Act must be in the following form:

"This conveyance (or transfer) is executed for the purposes of Chapter I of Part I of the Leasehold Reform, Housing and Urban Development Act 1993.".

(2) The statement required by section 57(11) of the Leasehold Reform, Housing and Urban Development Act 1993 to be contained in any new lease granted under section 56 of that Act must be in the following form:

"This lease is granted under section 56 of the Leasehold Reform, Housing and Urban Development Act 1993.".

[3265]

[Modification of Parts 2 and 3 of the Act in their application to incorporeal hereditaments]

[196A Possessory titles to rentcharges

In their application to rentcharges, sections 9(5) and 10(6) of the Act have effect as if for the words "in actual possession of the land, or in receipt of the rents and profits of the land," there were substituted the words "in receipt of the rent".]

[3265A]

NOTES

Commencement: 10 November 2008.
Inserted (together with r 196B) by SI 2008/1919, r 4(1), Sch 1, para 63.

[196B Application of sections 11, 12 and 29 of the Act to franchises

(1) In their application to franchises, sections 11(4) and 12(4) of the Act have effect without prejudice to any right of the Crown to forfeit the franchise.

(2) In its application to franchises, section 29(2)(a) of the Act has effect with the deletion of the word "or" at the end of sub-paragraph (ii) and with the insertion between the words "registration," and "and" at the end of sub-paragraph (iii) of—

"or

(iv) is a right of the Crown to forfeit the franchise,".]

[3265B]

NOTES

Commencement: 10 November 2008.
Inserted as noted to s 196A at **[3265A]**.

PART 15
GENERAL PROVISIONS

Notices and addresses for service

197 Content of notice

(1) Every notice given by the registrar must—

(a) fix the time within which the recipient is to take any action required by the notice,
(b) state what the consequence will be of a failure to take such action as is required by the notice within the time fixed,
(c) state the manner in which any reply to the notice must be given and the address to which it must be sent.

(2) Except where otherwise provided by these rules, the time fixed by the notice will be the period ending at 12 noon on the fifteenth business day after the date of issue of the notice.

[3266]

198 Address for service of notice

(1) A person who is (or will as a result of an application be) a person within paragraph (2) must give the registrar an address for service to which all notices and other communications to him by the registrar may be sent, as provided by paragraph (3).

(2) The persons referred to in paragraph (1) are—

(a) the registered proprietor of a registered estate or registered charge,
(b) the registered beneficiary of a unilateral notice,
(c) a cautioner named in an individual caution register,
[(d) a person named in—
  (i) a standard form of restriction set out in Schedule 4, whose address is required by that restriction, or
  (ii) any other restriction, whose consent or certificate is required, or to whom notice is required to be given by the registrar or another person,

except where the registrar is required to enter the restriction without application,]
(e) a person entitled to be notified of an application for adverse possession under rule 194,

(f) a person who objects to an application under section 73 of the Act,
(g) a person who gives notice to the registrar under paragraph 3(2) of Schedule 6 to the Act, and
(h) any person who while dealing with the registrar in connection with registered land or a caution against first registration is requested by the registrar to give an address for service.

(3) A person within paragraph (1) must give the registrar an address for service which is a postal address, whether or not in the United Kingdom.

(4) A person within paragraph (1) may give the registrar one or two additional addresses for service, provided that he may not have more than three addresses for service, and the address or addresses must be—
(a) a postal address, whether or not in the United Kingdom, or
(b) subject to paragraph (7), a box number at a United Kingdom document exchange, or
(c) an electronic address.

(5) Subject to paragraphs (3) and (4) a person within paragraph (1) may give the registrar a replacement address for service.

(6) A cautioner who is entered in the register of title in respect of a caution against dealings under section 54 of the Land Registration Act 1925 may give the registrar a replacement or additional address for service provided that—
(a) he may not have more than three addresses for service,
(b) one of his addresses for service must be a postal address, whether or not in the United Kingdom, and
(c) all of his addresses for service must be such addresses as are mentioned in paragraph (4).

[(6A) Where a cautioner who is shown in the register of title as having been entered in that register in respect of a caution against dealings under section 54 of the Land Registration Act 1925 has died, his personal representative may apply to the registrar for the entry of a replacement or additional address for service provided that—
(a) there may not be more than three addresses for service,
(b) one of the addresses for service must be a postal address, whether or not in the United Kingdom,
(c) all of the addresses for service must be such addresses as are mentioned in paragraph (4), and
(d) the application must be accompanied by—
(i) the original grant of probate of the deceased proprietor and, where section 7 of the Administration of Justice Act 1925 applies, the original grant of probate showing the chain of representation, to prove that the transferor is his personal representative,
(ii) the original letters of administration of the deceased proprietor showing the transferor as his personal representative,
(iii) a court order appointing the applicant as the deceased's personal representative, or
(iv) (where a conveyancer is acting for the applicant) a certificate given by a conveyancer that he holds the original or a certified office copy of such grant of probate, letters of administration or court order.]

(7) The box number referred to at paragraph (4)(b) must be at a United Kingdom document exchange to which delivery can be made on behalf of the land registry under arrangements already in existence between the land registry and a service provider at the time the box number details are provided to the registrar under this rule.

(8) In this rule an electronic address means—
(a) an e-mail address, or
(b) any other form of electronic address specified in a direction under paragraph (9).

(9) If the registrar is satisfied that a form of electronic address, other than an e-mail address, is a suitable form of address for service he may issue a direction to that effect.

(10) A direction under paragraph (9) may contain such conditions or limitations or both as the registrar considers appropriate.

(11) A person within paragraph (2)(d) shall be treated as having complied with any duty imposed on him under paragraph (1) where rule 92(2)(b) has been complied with.

[3267]

NOTES

Para (2): sub-para (d) substituted by SI 2005/1766, r 8.
Para (6A): inserted by SI 2008/1919, r 4(1), Sch 1, para 64.

199 Service of notice

(1) All notices which the registrar is required to give may be served—

(a) by post, to any postal address in the United Kingdom entered in the register as an address for service,
(b) by post, to any postal address outside the United Kingdom entered in the register as an address for service,
(c) by leaving the notice at any postal address in the United Kingdom entered in the register as an address for service,
(d) by directing the notice to the relevant box number at any document exchange entered in the register as an address for service,
(e) by electronic transmission to the electronic address entered in the register as an address for service,
(f) subject to paragraph (3), by fax, or
(g) by any of the methods of service given in sub-paragraphs (a), (b), (c) and (d) to any other address where the registrar believes the addressee is likely to receive it.

(2) In paragraph (1) references to an address or box number "entered in the register as an address for service" include an address for service given under rule 198(2)(h), whether or not it is entered in the register.

(3) The notice may be served by fax if the recipient has informed the registrar in writing—
(a) that the recipient is willing to accept service of the notice by fax, and
(b) of the fax number to which it should be sent.

(4) Service of a notice which is served in accordance with this rule shall be regarded as having taken place at the time shown in the table below—

Method of service	*Time of service*
Post to an address in the United Kingdom	The second working day after posting
Leaving at a postal address	The working day after it was left
Post to an address outside the United Kingdom	The seventh working day after posting
Document exchange	On the second working day after it was left at the registrar's document exchange
Fax	The working day after transmission
Electronic transmission to an electronic address	The second working day after transmission

(5) In this rule "post" means pre-paid delivery by a postal service which seeks to deliver documents within the United Kingdom no later than the next working day in all or the majority of cases, and to deliver outside the United Kingdom within such a period as is reasonable in all the circumstances.

(6) …

[3268]

NOTES

Para (6): revoked by SI 2008/1919, r 4(1), Sch 1, para 65.

Specialist assistance

200 Use of specialist assistance by the registrar

(1) The registrar may refer to an appropriate specialist—
(a) the examination of the whole or part of any title lodged with an application for first registration, or
(b) any question or other matter which arises in the course of any proceedings before the registrar and which, in his opinion, requires the advice of an appropriate specialist.

(2) The registrar may act upon the advice or opinion of an appropriate specialist to whom he has referred a matter under paragraph (1).

(3) In this rule, "appropriate specialist" means a person who the registrar considers has the appropriate knowledge, experience and expertise to advise on the matter referred to him.

[3269]

Proceedings before the registrar

201 Production of documents

(1) The registrar may only exercise the power conferred on him by section 75(1) of the Act if he receives from a person who is a party to proceedings before him a request that he should require a document holder to produce a document for the purpose of those proceedings.

(2) The request must be made—

(a) in paper form in Form PRD1 delivered to such office of the land registry as the registrar may direct, or

(b) during the currency of a relevant notice given under Schedule 2, and subject to and in accordance with the limitations contained in the notice, by delivering the request to the registrar, by any means of communication, other than as mentioned in sub-paragraph (a).

(3) The registrar must give notice of the request to the document holder.

(4) The address for the document holder provided in Form PRD1 is to be regarded for the purpose of rule 199 as an address for service given under rule 198(2)(h).

(5) The notice must give the document holder a period ending at 12 noon on the twentieth business day after the issue of the notice, or such other period as the registrar thinks appropriate, to deliver a written response to the registrar by the method and to the address stated in the notice.

(6) The response must—

(a) state whether or not the document holder opposes the request,

(b) if he does, state in full the grounds for that opposition,

(c) give an address to which communications may be sent, and

(d) be signed by the document holder or his conveyancer.

(7) The registrar must determine the matter on the basis of the request and any response submitted to him and, subject to paragraph (8), he may make the requirement by sending a notice in Form PRD2 to the document holder if he is satisfied that—

(a) the document is in the control of the document holder, and

(b) the document may be relevant to the proceedings, and

(c) disclosure of the document is necessary in order to dispose fairly of the proceedings or to save costs,

and he is not aware of any valid ground entitling the document holder to withhold the document.

(8) The registrar may, as a condition of making the requirement, provide that the person who has made the request should pay the reasonable costs incurred in complying with the requirement by the document holder.

(9) In this rule, "document holder" means the person who is alleged to have control of a document which is the subject of a request under paragraph (1).

[3270]

202 Costs

(1) A person who has incurred costs in relation to proceedings before the registrar may request the registrar to make an order requiring a party to those proceedings to pay the whole or part of those costs.

(2) The registrar may only order a party to proceedings before him to pay costs where those costs have been occasioned by the unreasonable conduct of that party in relation to the proceedings.

(3) Subject to paragraph (5), a request for the payment of costs must be made by delivering to the registrar a written statement in paper form by 12 noon on the twentieth business day after the completion of the proceedings to which the request relates.

(4) The statement must—

(a) identify the party against whom the order is sought and include an address where notice may be served on that party,

(b) state in full the grounds for the request,

(c) give an address to which communications may be sent, and

(d) be signed by the person making the request or his conveyancer.

(5) During the currency of a relevant notice given under Schedule 2, and subject to and in accordance with the limitations contained in the notice, a request under this rule may also be made by delivering the written statement to the registrar, by any means of communication, other than as mentioned in paragraph (3).

(6) The registrar must give notice of the request to the party against whom the order is sought at the address provided under paragraph (4)(a) and if that party has an address for service in an individual register that relates to the proceedings, at that address.

(7) An address for a party provided under paragraph (4)(a) is to be regarded for the purpose of rule 199 as if it was an address for service given under rule 198(2)(h).

(8) The notice must give the recipient a period ending at 12 noon on the twentieth business day after the issue of the notice, or such other period as the registrar thinks appropriate, to deliver a written response to the registrar by the method and to the address stated in the notice.

(9) The response must—

(a) state whether or not the recipient opposes the request,

(b) if he does, state in full the grounds for that opposition,

(c) give an address to which communications may be sent, and

(d) be signed by the recipient or his conveyancer.

(10) The registrar must determine the matter on the basis of: the written request and any response submitted to him, all the circumstances including the conduct of the parties, and the result of any enquiries he considers it necessary to make.

(11) The registrar must send to all parties his written reasons for any order he makes under paragraph (1).

(12) An order under paragraph (1) may—

(a) require a party against whom it is made to pay to the requesting party the whole or such part as the registrar thinks fit of the costs incurred in the proceedings by the requesting party,

(b) specify the sum to be paid or require the costs to be assessed by the court (if not otherwise agreed), and specify the basis of the assessment to be used by the court.

[3271]

Retention and return of documents

203 Retention of documents on completion of an application

(1) Subject to paragraphs (2) to (5), on completion of any application the registrar may retain all or any of the documents that accompanied the application and must return all other such documents to the applicant or as otherwise specified in the application.

(2) When making an application, an applicant or his conveyancer may request the return of all or any of the documents accompanying the application.

(3) Except on an application for first registration, a person making a request under paragraph (2) must deliver with the application certified copies of the documents which are the subject of the request.

(4) On an application for first registration, a person making a request under paragraph (2) for the return of any statutory declaration, [statement of truth,] subsisting lease, subsisting charge[, a certificate relating to stamp duty land tax as required by section 79 of the Finance Act 2003,] or the latest document of title must deliver with the application certified copies of any such documents as are the subject of the request, but shall not be required to deliver copies of any other documents.

(5) Subject to the delivery of any certified copies required under paragraphs (3) or (4), the registrar must comply with any request made under paragraph (2).

(6) The registrar may destroy any document retained under paragraph (1) if he is satisfied that either—

(a) he has made and retained a sufficient copy of the document, or

(b) further retention of the document is unnecessary.

(7) If the registrar considers that he no longer requires delivery of certified copies of documents, or classes of documents, under this rule he may, in such manner as he thinks appropriate for informing persons who wish to make applications, give notice to that effect and on and after the date specified in such notice—

(a) the requirement under this rule to deliver certified copies of the documents covered by the notice no longer applies, and

(b) the registrar may amend any Schedule 1 form to reflect that fact.

(8) In paragraph (4) the "latest document of title" means the document vesting the estate sought to be registered in the applicant or where the estate vested in the applicant by operation of law the most recent document that vested the estate in a predecessor of the applicant.

[3272]

NOTES

Para (4): words in square brackets inserted by SI 2008/1919, r 4(1), Sch 1, para 66.

See further: the Land Registration (Electronic Conveyancing) Rules 2008, SI 2008/1750, r 6, Sch 2, Pt 2, para 4, which provides that this rule does not apply to an application made using the land registry network where the document delivered with the application is in electronic form but the registrar may retain the document and at any time thereafter delete it if satisfied that further retention is unnecessary.

204 Request for the return of certain documents

(1) This rule applies to all documents on which any entry in the register of title is or was founded and which are kept by the registrar on the relevant date.

(2) During the period of 5 years beginning with the relevant date any person who delivered a document to the registrar may request the return of that document.

(3) Where at the time of the delivery of the document the person delivering the document was the registered proprietor, or was applying to become the registered proprietor, of any registered estate or registered charge in respect of which the entry referred to in paragraph (1) was made, a person who is at the date of the request the registered proprietor of any part of the same registered estate or registered charge may make a request under paragraph (2) for the document to be returned to him.

(4) Subject to paragraph (5), if, at the date of the request under paragraph (2), the document is kept by the registrar he must return it to the person making the request.

(5) If the registrar receives more than one request under paragraph (2) in respect of the same document, he may either retain the document or, in his discretion, return it to one of the persons making a request.

(6) At the end of the period mentioned in paragraph (2) if there is no outstanding request in relation to the document the registrar may destroy any document if he is satisfied that—

(a) he has retained a copy of the document, or
(b) further retention of the document is unnecessary.

(7) Where a request is made for the return of a document after the end of the period mentioned in paragraph (2), the registrar may treat the request as a request under paragraph (2).

(8) The "relevant date" for the purpose of this rule is the date on which these rules come into force.

[3273]

205 Release of documents kept by the registrar

The registrar may release any document retained under rule 203(1) or to which rule 204 applies upon such terms, if any, for its return as he considers appropriate.

[3274]

Forms

206 Use of forms

(1) Subject to paragraph (4) and to rules [207A,] 208 and 209, the Schedule 1 forms must be used where required by these rules and must be prepared in accordance with the requirements of rules 210 and 211.

(2) Subject to paragraph (4) and to rules 208 and 209, except where these rules require the use of a Schedule 1 form, the Schedule 3 forms must be used in all matters to which they refer, or are capable of being applied or adapted, with such alterations and additions as are desired and the registrar allows.

(3) Subject to rule 208(2), the forms of execution in Schedule 9 must be used in the execution of dispositions in the scheduled forms in the cases for which they are provided, or are capable of being applied or adapted, with such alterations and additions, if any, as the registrar may allow.

(4) A requirement in these rules to use a scheduled form is subject, where appropriate, to the provisions in these rules relating to the making of applications and issuing results of applications other than in paper form, during the currency of a notice given under Schedule 2.

[3275]

NOTES

Para (1): reference in square brackets inserted by SI 2008/1919, r 4(1), Sch 1, para 67.

207 (*Revoked by SI 2008/1919, r 4(1), Sch 1, para 68.*)

[207A Amendment of certain Schedule 1 forms to provide for explanatory information to be altered

(1) In order to assist applicants in completing a form or in making an application in relation to a form, the registrar may remove, add to, or alter any explanatory information outside the panels of a Schedule 1 form.

(2) Any amendment under paragraph (1) must not alter the name and description of the form at the top of the first page or instructions as to what must be entered in the form.

(3) Where a form has been amended under paragraph (1) a person may use the form for the purposes of these rules as amended or as unamended.]

[3276]

NOTES

Commencement: 10 November 2008.
Inserted by SI 2008/1919, r 4(1), Sch 1, para 69.

208 Welsh language forms

(1) Where the registrar, in exercise of his powers under section 100(4) of the Act, publishes an instrument as the Welsh language version of a scheduled form, the instrument shall be regarded as being in the scheduled form.

(2) In place of the form of execution provided by Schedule 9, an instrument referred to in paragraph (1) may be executed using a form of execution approved by the registrar as the Welsh language version of the Schedule 9 form.

(3) An instrument containing a statement approved by the registrar as the Welsh language version of a statement prescribed by these rules shall be regarded as containing the prescribed statement.

(4) An instrument containing a provision approved by the registrar as the Welsh language version of a provision prescribed by these rules shall be regarded as containing the prescribed provision.

[3277]

209 Use of non-prescribed forms

(1) This rule applies where—

(a) an application should be accompanied by a scheduled form and a person wishes to make an application relying instead upon an alternative document that is not the relevant scheduled form, and

(b) it is not possible for that person to obtain and lodge the relevant scheduled form (duly executed, if appropriate) at the land registry or it is only possible to do so at unreasonable expense.

(2) Such a person may make a request to the registrar, either before or at the time of making the application which should be accompanied by the relevant scheduled form, that he be permitted to rely upon the alternative document.

(3) The request must contain evidence to satisfy the registrar as mentioned in paragraph (1)(b) and include the original, or, if the request is made before the application, a copy, of the alternative document.

(4) If, after considering the request, the registrar is satisfied as mentioned at paragraph (1)(b) and that neither the rights of any person nor the keeping of the register are likely to be materially prejudiced by allowing the alternative document to be relied upon instead of the relevant scheduled form, he may permit such reliance.

(5) If the registrar allows the request it may be on condition that the person making the request provides other documents or evidence in support of the application.

(6) This rule is without prejudice to any of the registrar's powers under the Act.

[3278]

210 Documents in a Schedule 1 form

(1) Subject to rule 211, any application or document in one of the Schedule 1 forms must—

(a) be printed on durable A4 size paper,

(b) [subject to rule 215A(4) and (5),] be reproduced as set out in the Schedule as to its wording, layout, ruling, font and point size, and

(c) contain all the information required in an easily legible form.

(2) Where on a Schedule 1 form (other than Form DL) any panel is insufficient in size to contain the required insertions, and the method of production of the form does not allow the depth of the panel to be increased, the information to be inserted in the panel must be continued on a continuation sheet in Form CS.

(3) When completing a Schedule 1 form containing an additional provisions panel, any statement, certificate or application required or permitted by these rules to be included in the form for which the form does not otherwise provide and any additional provisions desired by the parties must be inserted in that panel or a continuation of it.

(4) Where the form consists of more than one sheet of paper, or refers to an attached plan or a continuation sheet, all the sheets and any plan must be securely fastened together.

[3279]

NOTES

Para (1): in sub-para (b) words in square brackets inserted by SI 2008/1919, r 4(1), Sch 1, para 70.

211 Electronically produced forms

… Where the method of production of a Schedule 1 form permits—

(a) the depth of a panel may be increased or reduced to fit the material to be comprised in it, and a panel may be divided at a page break,

[(b) the text outside the panels of a Schedule 1 form, other than—

(i) the name and description of the form at the top of the first page, and

(ii) any text after the final panel,

may be omitted,]

(c) inapplicable certificates and statements may be omitted,

(d) the plural may be used instead of the singular and the singular instead of the plural,

(e) panels which would contain only the panel number and the panel heading may be omitted, but such omission must not affect the numbering of subsequent panels,

(f) "X" boxes may be omitted where all inapplicable statements and certificates have been omitted,

(g) the sub-headings in an additional provisions panel may be added to, amended, repositioned or omitted,

(h) "Seller" may be substituted for "Transferor" and "Buyer" for "Transferee" in a transfer on sale,

(i) the vertical lines which define the left and right boundaries of the panel may be omitted.

[3280]

NOTES

Numbering omitted revoked, and para (b) substituted, by SI 2008/1919, r 4(1), Sch 1, para 71.

212 Documents where no form is prescribed

(1) Documents for which no form is prescribed must be in such form as the registrar may direct or allow.

(2) A document prepared under this rule must not bear the number of a Schedule 1 form.

(3) A document affecting a registered title must refer to the title number.

[3281]

Documents accompanying applications

213 Identification of part of the registered title dealt with

(1) Subject to paragraphs (4) and (5) of this rule, a document lodged at the land registry dealing with part of the land in a registered title must have attached to it a plan identifying clearly the land dealt with.

(2) Where the document is a disposition, the disponor must sign the plan.

(3) Where the document is an application, the applicant must sign the plan.

(4) If the land dealt with is identified clearly on the title plan of the registered title, it may instead be described by reference to that title plan.

(5) Where a disposition complies with this rule, the application lodged in respect of it need not.

[3282]

214 Lodging of copy instead of an original document

(1) Subject to paragraphs (2), (3) and (4), where a rule requires that an application be accompanied by an original document (for instance, a grant of representation) the applicant may, instead of lodging the original, lodge a certified or office copy of that document.

(2) This rule does not apply to—

(a) any document required to be lodged under Part 4,

(b) a scheduled form,

(c) a document that is a registrable disposition.

(3) This rule does not apply also where the registrar considers that the circumstances are such that the original of a document should be lodged and the applicant has possession, or the right to possession, of that original document.

(4) Where this rule permits a certified or office copy of a document to be lodged the registrar may permit an uncertified copy of the document to be lodged instead.

[3283]

215 Documents and other evidence in support of an application

(1) This rule applies where—

(a) the lodging of a document (not being a scheduled form) or other evidence in support of an application is required by these rules, and

(b) the document or other evidence is in the particular case unnecessary or the purpose of the lodging of the document or other evidence can be achieved by another document or other evidence.

(2) An applicant may request the registrar to be relieved of the requirement.

(3) The request must contain evidence to satisfy the registrar as mentioned in paragraph (1)(b).

(4) If, after considering the request, the registrar is satisfied as mentioned at paragraph (1)(b) and that neither the rights of any person nor the keeping of the register are likely to be materially prejudiced by relieving the applicant of the requirement, he may so relieve the applicant.

(5) If the registrar allows the request it may be on condition that the applicant provides other documents or evidence in support of the application.

(6) This rule is without prejudice to any of the registrar's powers under the Act.

[3284]

[215A Statements of truth

(1) In these rules, a statement of truth means a statement which—

(a) is made by an individual in writing,

(b) contains a declaration of truth in the following form—

'I believe that the facts and matters contained in this statement are true', and

(c) is signed in accordance with paragraphs (2) to (6).

(2) Subject to paragraph (5), a statement of truth must be signed by the individual making the statement.

(3) The full name of the individual who signs a statement of truth must be printed clearly beneath his signature.

(4) Where a statement of truth is to be signed by an individual who is unable to read, it must—

(a) be signed in the presence of a conveyancer, and

(b) contain a certificate made and signed by that conveyancer in the following form—

'I [*name and address of conveyancer*] certify that I have read over the contents of this statement of truth and explained the nature and effect of any documents referred to in it and the consequences of making a false declaration to the person making this statement who signed it or made [his] *or* [her] mark in my presence having first (a) appeared to me to understand the statement (b) approved its content as accurate and (c) appeared to me to understand the declaration of truth and the consequences of making a false declaration.'.

(5) Where a statement of truth is to be made by an individual who is unable to sign it, it must—

(a) state that individual's full name,

(b) be signed by a conveyancer at the direction and on behalf of that individual, and

(c) contain a certificate made and signed by that conveyancer in the following form—

'I [*name and address of conveyancer*] certify that [the person making this statement of truth has read it in my presence, approved its content as accurate and directed me to sign it on [his] or [her] behalf] or [I have read over the contents of this statement of truth and explained the nature and effect of any documents referred to in it and the consequences of making a false declaration to the person making this statement who directed me to sign it on [his] or [her] behalf] having first (a) appeared to me to understand the statement (b) approved its content as accurate and (c) appeared to me to understand the declaration of truth and the consequences of making a false declaration.'.

(6) Where a statement of truth, or a certificate under paragraph (4) or (5), is signed by a conveyancer—

(a) the conveyancer must sign in their own name and not that of their firm or employer, and

(b) the conveyancer must state the capacity in which they sign and where appropriate the name of their firm or employer.]

[3284A]

NOTES

Commencement: 10 November 2008.
Inserted by SI 2008/1919, r 4(1), Sch 1, para 72.

Land registry—when open to public

216 Days on which the Land Registry is open to the public

[(1) Subject to paragraph (2), the land registry shall be open to the public daily except on—

(a) Saturdays, Sundays, Christmas Day and Good Friday, or

(b) any other day—

(i) specified or declared by proclamation under section 1 of the Banking and Financial Dealings Act 1971,

(ii) appointed by the Lord Chancellor, or
(iii) certified as an interrupted day under paragraph (6).]

(2) If the registrar is satisfied that adequate arrangements have been made or will be in place for opening the land registry to the public on Saturdays, he may, in such manner as he considers appropriate, give notice to that effect.

(3) On and after the date specified in any notice given pursuant to paragraph (2), paragraph (1) shall have effect as though the word "Saturdays" had been omitted.

(4) The date referred to in paragraph (3) must be at least eight weeks after the date of the notice.

(5) On and after the date specified in any notice given pursuant to paragraph (2), the periods in column 3 in the table below are substituted for the periods in column 2 in that table in the rules to which they relate.

(1) Rule	*(2) Prescribed period before any notice given under rule 216(2) takes effect*	*(3) Prescribed period after any notice given under rule 216(2) takes effect*
16(1)	Twenty business days	twenty-four business days
31(2)	the twentieth business day	the twenty-fourth business day
53(1)	the fifteenth business day	the eighteenth business day
53(1)	the thirtieth business day	the thirty-sixth business day
53(3)	the thirtieth business day	the thirty-sixth business day
53(4)	the fifteenth business day	the eighteenth business day
54(9)	the fourth business day	the fourth business day
55(4)	fifteen business days	eighteen business days
86(3)	the fifteenth business day	the eighteenth business day
86(3)	the thirtieth business day	the thirty-sixth business day
86(5)	the thirtieth business day	the thirty-sixth business day
86(6)	the fifteenth business day	the eighteenth business day
92(9)	the fifteenth business day	the eighteenth business day
119(3)	the twentieth business day	the twenty-fourth business day
189	the sixty-fifth business day	the seventy-eighth business day
197(2)	the fifteenth business day	the eighteenth business day
201(5)	the twentieth business day	the twenty-fourth business day
202(3)	the twentieth business day	the twenty-fourth business day
202(8)	the twentieth business day	the twenty-fourth business day
218	the fifteenth business day	the eighteenth business day

[(6) The registrar may certify any day as an interrupted day if he is satisfied that on that day there is likely to be—

(a) a general delay in, or failure of, a communication service in England and Wales, or
(b) any other event or circumstance,

causing a substantial interruption in the normal operation of the land registry.

(7) The registrar must give notice of any certification under paragraph (6) in such manner as he considers appropriate.

(8) Any certification under paragraph (6) must take place before the start of the day being certified.

(9) In this rule, "communication service" means a service by which documents may be sent and delivered and includes a post service, a document exchange service and electronic communications.]

[3285]

NOTES

Para (1): substituted by SI 2008/1919, r 4(1), Sch 1, para 73(a).
Paras (6)–(9): inserted by SI 2008/1919, r 4(1), Sch 1, para 73(b).

Interpretation

217 General Interpretation

(1) In these rules—

"the Act" means the Land Registration Act 2002,

"affecting franchise" means a franchise which relates to a defined area of land and is an adverse right affecting, or capable of affecting, the title to an estate or charge,

"business day" means a day when the land registry is open to the public under rule 216,

"caution plan" has the meaning given by rule 41(4),

"caution title number" has the meaning given by rule 41(1),

"certified copy" means a copy of a document which a conveyancer, or such other person as the registrar may permit, has certified on its face to be a true copy of the original and endorsed with his name and address, and the reference to a conveyancer includes where the document is one referred to in—

(a) rule 168(2)(a) or 168(3), the bankrupt's trustee in bankruptcy or the official receiver,

(b) rule 184(2), the company's administrator,

(c) rule 184(5), the company's liquidator,

"charges register" is the register so named in rule 4 the contents of which are described in rule 9,

"charity" and "charity trustees" have the same meaning as in sections 96 and 97(1) of the Charities Act 1993 respectively,

["Companies Acts" means—

(a) the Companies Act 2006 and any Act amending or replacing that Act,

(b) the provisions of the Companies Act 1985, the Companies Consolidation (Consequential Provisions) Act 1985, Part 2 of the Companies (Audit, Investigations and Community Enterprise) Act 2004 and the Companies (NI) Order 1986 that remain in force, and

(c) any former enactment relating to companies,]

"control" in relation to a document of which a person has control means physical possession, or the right to possession, or right to take copies of the document,

["conveyancer" means—

(a) a solicitor,

(b) a licensed conveyancer within the meaning of section 11(2) of the Administration of Justice Act 1985,

(c) a fellow of the Institute of Legal Executives,

(d) a barrister,

(e) a duly certificated notary public, or

(f) a registered European lawyer within the meaning of the European Communities (Lawyer's Practice) Regulations 2000 who by virtue of regulations 6 and 12 of those Regulations is entitled to prepare for remuneration an instrument creating or transferring an interest in land in England and Wales,]

"day list" has the same meaning given by rule 12,

["electronic legal charge" has the same meaning as in the Land Registration (Electronic Conveyancing) Rules 2008,]

"exempt charity" has the same meaning as in section 96 of the Charities Act 1993 and "non-exempt charity" means a charity which is not an exempt charity,

["home rights notice" means a notice registered under section 31(10)(a) or section 32 of, and paragraph 4(3)(a) or 4(3)(b) of Schedule 4 to, the Family Law Act 1996, or section 2(8) or section 5(3)(b) of the Matrimonial Homes Act 1983, or section 2(7) or section 5(3)(b) of the Matrimonial Homes Act 1967,]

"index map" has the meaning given by rule 10(1)(a),

"index of proprietors' names" has the meaning given by rule 11(1),

"index of relating franchises and manors" is the index described in rule 10(1)(b),

"individual caution register" is the register so named in rule 41(1) the arrangement of which is described in rule 41(2),

"individual register" is the register so named in rule 2 the contents and arrangement of which are described in rules 3 and 4,

"inheritance tax notice" means a notice in respect of an Inland Revenue charge arising under Part III of the Finance Act 1975 or section 237 of the Inheritance Tax Act 1984,

"matrimonial home rights caution" means a caution registered under the Matrimonial Homes Act 1967 before 14 February 1983,

…

"official custodian" means the official custodian for charities,

"old tenancy" means a tenancy as defined in section 28 of the Landlord and Tenant (Covenants) Act 1995 which is not a new tenancy as defined in section 1 of that Act,

"overseas company" means a company incorporated outside [the United Kingdom], "property register" is the register so named in rule 4 the contents of which are described in rules 5, 6 and 7,

"proprietorship register" is the register so named in rule 4 the contents of which are described in rule 8,

"registered title" means an individual register and any title plan referred to in that register,

"relating franchise" means a franchise which is not an affecting franchise,

"Schedule 1 form" means a form in Schedule 1,

"Schedule 3 form" means a form in Schedule 3,

"scheduled form" means a Schedule 1 form or a Schedule 3 form,

"section 33(5) order" means an order made under section 33(5) of the Family Law Act 1996,

["statement of truth" has the meaning given by rule 215A,]

"statutory declaration" includes affidavit,

"title number" has the meaning given by rule 4,

"title plan" has the meaning given by rule 5,

"trust corporation" has the same meaning as in the Settled Land Act 1925,

"trusts" in relation to a charity has the same meaning as in section 97(1) of the Charities Act 1993,

"unregistered company" means a body corporate to which section 718(1) of the Companies Act 1985 applies,

["working day" means any day from Monday to Friday (inclusive) which is not Christmas Day, Good Friday or any other day either specified or declared by proclamation under section 1 of the Banking and Financial Dealings Act 1971 or appointed by the Lord Chancellor].

(2) Subject to paragraph (3), a reference in these rules to a form by letter, or by number, or by a combination of both is to a scheduled form.

(3) A reference in these rules to Forms A to Y and [Forms AA to] [PP] (in each case inclusive) is to the standard form of restriction bearing that letter in Schedule 4.

[3286]

NOTES

Para (1): definitions "Companies Acts" and "conveyancer" substituted by SI 2008/1919, r 4(1), Sch 1, para 74(a), (b); definition "electronic legal charge" inserted by SI 2008/1750, r 5, Sch 2, Pt 1, para 7; definition "home rights notice" inserted and definition "matrimonial home rights notice" (omitted) revoked by SI 2005/1982, r 16; in definition "overseas company" words "the United Kingdom" in square brackets substituted by SI 2008/1919, r 4(1), Sch 1, para 74(c); definitions "statement of truth" and "working day" inserted by SI 2008/1919, r 4(1), Sch 1, para 74(d), (e).

Para (3): words in first pair of square brackets substituted by SI 2005/1766, r 9(2); reference to "PP" in square brackets substituted by SI 2008/1919, r 4(1), Sch 1, para 74(f).

Application: as to the application of this rule, with modifications, in so far as it relates to bank insolvency or administration under the Banking Act 2009, Pts 2, 3, see the Banking Act 2009 (Parts 2 and 3 Consequential Amendments) Order 2009, SI 2009/317, art 3, Schedule.

PART 16
TRANSITIONAL
Cautions against dealings

218 Definitions

In this Part—

"the 1925 Act" means the Land Registration Act 1925,

"caution" means a caution entered in the register of title under section 54 of the 1925 Act,

"cautioner" includes his personal representative,

"the notice period" is the period ending at 12 noon on the fifteenth business day, or ending at 12 noon on such later business day as the registrar may allow, after the date of issue of the notice.

[3287]

219 Consent under a caution

Any consent given under section 55 or 56 of the 1925 Act must be in writing signed by the person giving it or his conveyancer.

[3288]

220 Notice under section 55(1) of the 1925 Act and under rule 223(3)

(1) Rule 199 applies to the method of service of a notice under section 55(1) of the 1925 Act and under rule 223(3).

(2) The notice period applies to a notice served under section 55(1) of the 1925 Act and to one served under rule 223(3).

[3289]

221 Cautioner showing cause

(1) This rule applies where notice is served under section 55(1) of the 1925 Act or rule 223(3).

(2) At any time before expiry of the notice period, the cautioner may show cause why the registrar should not give effect to the application that resulted in the notice being served.

(3) To show cause, the cautioner must—

(a) deliver to the registrar, in the manner and to the address stated in the notice, a written statement signed by the cautioner or his conveyancer setting out the grounds relied upon, and

(b) show that he has a fairly arguable case for the registrar not to give effect to the application that resulted in the notice being served.

(4) If, after reading the written statement, and after making any enquiries he thinks necessary, the registrar is satisfied that cause has been shown, he must order that the caution is to continue until withdrawn or otherwise disposed of under these rules or the Act.

(5) Where the registrar makes an order under paragraph (4)—

(a) the registrar must give notice to the applicant and the cautioner that he has made the order and of the effect of sub-paragraph (b),

(b) the cautioner is to be treated as having objected under section 73 of the Act to the application that resulted in notice being served, and

(c) the notice given by the registrar under sub-paragraph (a) to the applicant is to be treated as notice given under section 73(5)(a) of the Act.

(6) If after service of the notice under section 55(1) of the 1925 Act or rule 223(3) the application that resulted in the notice being served is cancelled, withdrawn or otherwise does not proceed, the registrar must make an order that the caution will continue to have effect, unless he has already done so or the caution has been cancelled.

[3290]

222 Withdrawal of a caution by the cautioner

(1) The cautioner may at any time apply to withdraw his caution in Form WCT.

(2) The form must be signed by the cautioner or his conveyancer.

[3291]

223 Cancellation of a caution—application by the proprietor etc

(1) A person may apply to the registrar for the cancellation of a caution if he is—

(a) the proprietor of the registered estate or a registered charge to which the caution relates, or

[(b) a person who is, or but for the existence of the caution would be, entitled to be registered as the proprietor of that estate or charge].

(2) An application for the cancellation of a caution must be in Form CCD.

(3) Where application is made under this rule, the registrar must give the cautioner notice of the application.

(4) Following the expiry of the notice period, unless the registrar makes an order under rule 221(4), the registrar must cancel the entry of the caution.

[3292]

NOTES

Para (1): sub-para (b) substituted by SI 2008/1919, r 4(1), Sch 1, para 75.

Rentcharges and adverse possession

224 Registered rentcharges held in trust under section 75(1) of the 1925 Act on commencement

Where a rentcharge is held in trust under section 75(1) of the Land Registration Act 1925 immediately before the coming into force of section 97 of the Act, the beneficiary of the trust may apply—

(a) to be registered as proprietor of the rentcharge, or

(b) for the registration of the rentcharge to be cancelled.

[3293]

SCHEDULE 1

SCHEDULE 1 FORMS REFERRED TO IN RULES 206, 207 AND 210

rule 11

NOTES

Substituted by SI 2008/1919, r 4(2), Sch 2. The Forms are not reproduced in this work, but their names and numbers are listed below. The originals can be found at www.landregistry.gov.uk.

Number	*Name*
Form ADV1	Application for registration of a person in adverse possession under Schedule 6 to the Land Registration Act 2002
Form ADV2	Application to be registered as a person to be notified of an application for adverse possession
Form AN1	Application to enter an agreed notice
Form AP1	Application to change the register
Form AS1	Assent of whole of registered title(s) by personal representative(s)
Form AS2	Assent of charge by personal representative(s)
Form AS3	Assent of part of registered title(s) by personal representative(s)
Form CC	Entry of a note of consolidation of charges
Form CCD	Application to cancel a caution against dealings
Form CCT	Application to cancel a caution against first registration
Form CH1	Legal charge of a registered estate
Form CH2	Application to enter an obligation to make further advances
Form CH3	Application to note agreed maximum amount of security
Form CI	Certificate of inspection of title plan
Form CIT	Application in connection with court proceedings, insolvency and tax liability
Form CN1	Application to cancel a notice (other than a unilateral notice)
Form CS	Continuation sheet for use with application and disposition forms
Form CT1	Caution against first registration
Form DB	Application to determine the exact line of a boundary
Form DI	Disclosable overriding interests
Form DL	List of documents
Form DS1	Cancellation of entries relating to a registered charge
Form DS2	Application to cancel entries relating to a registered charge
Form DS3	Release of part of the land from a registered charge
Form EX1	Application for the registrar to designate a document as an exempt information document
Form EX1A	Reasons for exemption in support of an application to designate a document as an exempt information document
Form EX2	Application for official copy of an exempt information document
Form EX3	Application to remove the designation of a document as an exempt information document
Form FR1	Application for first registration
Form HC1	Application for copies of historical edition(s) of the register/title plan held in electronic form
Form HR1	Application for registration of a notice of home rights
Form HR2	Application for renewal of registration in respect of home rights
Form HR3	Application by mortgage for official search in respect of home rights
Form HR4	Cancellation of a home rights notice
Form NAP	Notice to the registrar in respect of an adverse possession application
Form OC1	Application for official copies of register/plan or certificate in Form CI
Form OC2	Application for official copies of documents only
Form OS1	Application by purchaser for official search with priority of the whole of the land in a registered title or a pending first registration application

Form OS2	Application by purchaser for official search with priority of part of the land in a registered title or a pending first registration application
Form OS3	Application for official search without priority of the land in a registered title
Form PIC	Application for a personal inspection under section 66 of the Land Registration Act 2002
Form PN1	Application for a search in the index of proprietors' names
Form PRD1	Request for the production of documents
Form PRD2	Notice to produce a document under section 75 of the Land Registration Act 2002 and rule 201 of the Land Registration Rules 2003
Form RX1	Application to enter a restriction
Form RX2	Application for an order that a restriction be disapplied or modified
Form RX3	Application to cancel a restriction
Form RX4	Application to withdraw a restriction
Form SC	Application for noting the overriding priority of a statutory charge
Form SEV	Application to enter Form A restriction on severance of joint tenancy by agreement or notice
Form SIF	Application for an official search of the index of relating franchises and manors
Form SIM	Application for an official search of the index map
Form ST1	Statement of truth in support of an application for registration based upon adverse possession
Form ST2	Statement of truth in support of an application for registration based upon adverse possession of a rentcharge
Form ST3	Statement of truth in support of an application for registration based upon lost or destroyed title deeds
Form ST3	Statement of truth in support of an application for registration and/or noting of a prescriptive easement
Form TP1	Transfer of part of registered title(s)
Form TP2	Transfer of part of registered title(s) under power of sale
Form TR1	Transfer of whole of registered title(s)
Form TR2	Transfer of whole of registered title(s) under power of sale
Form TR4	Transfer of a portfolio of charges
Form TR5	Transfer of portfolio of whole titles
Form UN1	Application to enter a unilateral notice
Form UN2	Application to remove a unilateral notice
Form UN3	Application to be registered as beneficiary of an existing unilateral notice
Form UN4	Application for the cancellation of a unilateral notice by a person who is (or is entitled to be) the registered proprietor
Form UT1	Application for upgrading of title
Form WCT	Application to withdraw a caution

[3294]

[SCHEDULE 1A

rule 58A

—All words in italicised text and inapplicable alternative wording in a clause may be omitted or deleted.

—Clause LR13 may be omitted or deleted.

—Clause LR14 may be omitted or deleted where the Tenant is one person.

—Otherwise, do not omit or delete any words in bold text unless italicised.

—Side-headings may appear as headings if this is preferred.

—Vertical or horizontal lines, or both, may be omitted.

LR1 Date of lease	
LR2 Title number(s)	LR2.1 Landlord's title number(s) *Title number(s) out of which this lease is granted. Leave blank if not registered.* LR2.2 Other title numbers *Existing title number(s) against which entries of matters referred to in LR9, LR10, LR11 and LR13 are to be made.*
LR3 Parties to this lease *[Give full names and addresses of each of the parties. For UK incorporated companies and limited liability partnerships, also give the registered number including any prefix. For overseas companies, also give the territory of incorporation and, if appropriate, the registered number in England and Wales including any prefix.]*	Landlord Tenant *Other parties* *Specify capacity of each party, for example "management company", "guarantor", etc*
LR4 Property *Insert a full description of the land being leased* *or* *Refer to the clause, schedule or paragraph of a schedule in this lease in which the land being leased is more fully described.* *Where there is a letting of part of a registered title, a plan must be attached to this lease and any floor levels must be specified.*	In the case of a conflict between this clause and the remainder of this lease then, for the purposes of registration, this clause shall prevail.
LR5 Prescribed statements etc *If this lease includes a statement falling within LR5.1, insert under that sub-clause the relevant statement or refer to the clause, schedule or paragraph of a schedule in this lease which contains the statement.* *In LR5.2, omit or delete those Acts which do not apply to this lease.*	*LR5.1 Statements prescribed under rules 179 (dispositions in favour of a charity), 180 (dispositions by a charity) or 196 (leases under the Leasehold Reform, Housing and Urban Development Act 1993) of the Land Registration Rules 2003.* *LR5.2 This lease is made under, or by reference to, provisions of:* *Leasehold Reform Act 1967* *Housing Act 1985* *Housing Act 1988* *Housing Act 1996*
LR6 Term for which the Property is leased *Include only the appropriate statement (duly completed) from the three options.* *NOTE: The information you provide, or refer to, here will be used as part of the particulars to identify the lease under rule 6 of the Land Registration Rules 2003.*	From and including To and including *OR* The term as specified in this lease at clause/schedule/paragraph *OR* The term is as follows:
LR7 Premium *Specify the total premium, inclusive of any VAT where payable.*	
LR8 Prohibitions or restrictions on disposing of this lease *Include whichever of the two statements is appropriate.* *Do not set out here the wording of the provision.*	This lease does not contain a provision that prohibits or restricts dispositions. *OR* This lease contains a provision that prohibits or restricts dispositions.

LR9 Rights of acquisition etc *Insert the relevant provisions in the sub-clauses or refer to the clause, schedule or paragraph of a schedule in this lease which contains the provisions.*	LR9.1 Tenant's contractual rights to renew this lease, to acquire the reversion or another lease of the Property, or to acquire an interest in other land LR9.2 Tenant's covenant to (or offer to) surrender this lease LR9.3 Landlord's contractual rights to acquire this lease
LR10 Restrictive covenants given in this lease by the Landlord in respect of land other than the Property *Insert the relevant provisions or refer to the clause, schedule or paragraph of a schedule in this lease which contains the provisions.*	
LR11 Easements *Refer here only to the clause, schedule or paragraph of a schedule in this lease which sets out the easements.*	LR11.1 Easements granted by this lease for the benefit of the Property LR11.2 Easements granted or reserved by this lease over the Property for the benefit of other property
LR12. Estate rentcharge burdening the Property *Refer here only to the clause, schedule or paragraph of a schedule in this lease which sets out the rentcharge.*	
LR13 Application for standard form of restriction *Set out the full text of the standard form of restriction and the title against which it is to be entered. If you wish to apply for more than one standard form of restriction use this clause to apply for each of them, tell us who is applying against which title and set out the full text of the restriction you are applying for.* *Standard forms of restriction are set out in Schedule 4 to the Land Registration Rules 2003.*	The Parties to this lease apply to enter the following standard form of restriction [against the title of the Property] *or* [against title number]
LR14 Declaration of trust where there is more than one person comprising the Tenant *If the Tenant is one person, omit or delete all the alternative statements.* *If the Tenant is more than one person, complete this clause by omitting or deleting all inapplicable alternative statements.*	The Tenant is more than one person. They are to hold the Property on trust for themselves as joint tenants. *OR* The Tenant is more than one person. They are to hold the Property on trust for themselves as tenants in common in equal shares. *OR* The Tenant is more than one person. They are to hold the Property on trust *Complete as necessary*]

[3295]

NOTES

Inserted by SI 2005/1982, r 8, Sch 1.

In Table in entry relating to "LR3 Parties to this lease" in column 1 words in square brackets substituted by SI 2008/1919, r 4(3).

SCHEDULE 2
NOTICES PUBLICISING ARRANGEMENTS FOR ELECTRONIC AND OTHER MODES OF DELIVERY OF APPLICATIONS AND OTHER MATTERS

rule 14

1. If the registrar is satisfied that adequate arrangements have been made or will be in place for dealing with the applications and other matters specified in paragraph 2 by means other than post, document exchange or personal delivery, he may, in such manner as he thinks appropriate, give notice publicising the arrangements.

2. The applications and other matters referred to in paragraph 1 are—
   (a) an application by electronic means under rule 14,
   (b) an outline application under rule 54,
   (c) a notification of discharge or release of a registered charge under rule 115,
   (d) an application and the result of an application or search under Part 13 to which rule 132 applies,
   (e) information requested by an applicant for an official search for the purpose of the Family Law Act 1996 under rule 160,
   (f) a request to the registrar that he require a person to produce documents under rule 201(2)(b),
   (g) a request for an order requiring a party to proceedings before the registrar to pay costs under rule 202(5).

3. Subject to paragraphs 4, 5 and 6, a notice given under paragraph 1 will be current from the time specified in the notice until the time, if any, specified in the notice or if no expiry date is specified in the notice, indefinitely.

4. A notice given under paragraph 1 may from time to time be varied, suspended, withdrawn, renewed or replaced by a further notice.

5. If and so long as owing [to] the breakdown or other unavailability of facilities or data involved in giving effect to the arrangements made for dealing with applications covered by a notice given under paragraph 1, such arrangements cease, in whole or in part, to be effective, the notice shall cease, to the necessary extent, to be treated as current.

6. Paragraph 5 will apply despite the absence of a variation, suspension or withdrawal of the notice under paragraph 4.

7. The provisions referred to in paragraph 2 will not prevent the registrar, at his discretion, from refusing to accept an application or request made, or to issue a result, under any of those provisions in an individual case.

[3296]

NOTES

Para 5: word in square brackets inserted by SI 2008/1919, r 4(4).

SCHEDULE 3
SCHEDULE 3 FORMS REFERRED TO IN RULE 206

rule 61

Form 1—Certificate as to execution of power of attorney (rule 61)

Date of power of attorney: ....

Donor of power of attorney: ....

Donee of power of attorney: ....

I/We .... of ....

certify that

[—the power of attorney ("the power") is in existence [and is made and, where required, has been registered under (*state statutory provisions under which the power is made and, where required, has been registered, if applicable*)],]

—the power is dated (*insert date*),

—I am/we are satisfied that the power is validly executed as a deed and authorises the attorney to execute the document on behalf of the donor of that power, and

—I/we hold [the instrument creating the power] *or* [a copy of the power by means of which its contents may be proved under section 3 of the Powers of Attorney Act 1971] *or* [a document which under section 4 of the Evidence and Powers of Attorney Act 1940[, paragraph 16 of Part 2 of Schedule 1, or paragraph 15(3) of Part 5 of Schedule 4 to the Mental Capacity Act 2005] is sufficient evidence of the contents of the power].

Signature of
conveyancer .... Date ....

[Form 2—Statutory declaration/certificate/ststement of truth as to non-revocation for powers more than 12 months old at the date of the disposition for which they are used (rule 62)

Date of power of attorney: ....

Donor of power of
attorney: ....

I.. of

....

do [solemnly and sincerely declare] *or* [certify] *or* [state] that at the time of completion of the........................... to me/my client I/my client had no knowledge—

—of a revocation of the power, or

—of the death or bankruptcy of the donor or, if the donor is a corporate body, its winding up or dissolution, or

—of any incapacity of the donor where the power is not a valid lasting or enduring power of attorney, or

Where the power is in the form prescribed for a lasting power of attorney—

—that a lasting power of attorney was not created, or

—of circumstances which, if the lasting power of attorney had been created, would have terminated the attorney's authority to act as an attorney, or

Where the power is in the form prescribed for an enduring power of attorney—

—that the power was not in fact a valid enduring power, or

—of an order or direction of the Court of Protection which revoked the power, or

—of the bankruptcy of the attorney, or

Where the power was given under section 9 of the Trusts of Land and Appointment of Trustees Act 1996—

—of an appointment of another trustee of the land in question, or

—of any other event which would have the effect of revoking the power, or

—of any lack of good faith on the part of the person(s) who dealt with the attorney, or

—that the attorney was not a person to whom the functions of the trustees could be delegated under section 9 of the Trusts of Land and Appointment of Trustees Act 1996, or

Where the power is expressed to be given by way of security—

That the power was not in fact given by way of security, or

of any revocation of the power with the consent of the attorney

of any other event which would have had the effect of revoking the power.

Where a certificate is given—

Signature of
conveyancer .... Date ....

Print name ....

Firm name or employer (if any)...

Capacity (e g acting for …)... ; or

Where a Statutory Declaration is made—

And I make this solemn declaration conscientiously believing the same to be true and by virtue of the provisions of the Statutory Declarations Act 1835.

Signature of
Declarant .... Date ....

DECLARED at .... before me, a person entitled to administer oaths.

Name ....

Address ....

Qualification ....

Signature ....

Where a statement of truth is made—

I believe that the facts and matters contained in this statement are true.

Signature....................................... Date ....

Print name ....

Firm name or employer (if any) of any conveyancer signing..............................

Capacity of any conveyancer signing (e g acting for …)..............................

WARNING

1 If you dishonestly make a statement which you know is, or might be, untrue or misleading, and intend by doing so to make a gain for yourself or another person, or to cause loss or the risk to another person, you may commit the offence of fraud under section 1 of the Fraud Act 2006, the maximum penalty for which is 10 years' imprisonment or an unlimited fine, or both.

2 Failure to complete the form with proper care may result in a loss of protection under the Land Registration Act 2002 if, as a result, a mistake is made in the register.

3 Under section 66 of the Land Registration Act 2002 most documents (including this form) kept by the registrar relating to an application to the registrar or referred to in the register are open to public inspection and copying. If you believe a document contains prejudicial information, you may apply for that part of the document to be made exempt using form EX1, under rule 136 of the Land Registration Rules 2003.]

[Form 3—Statutory declaration/certificate/certificate/statement of truth in support of power delegating trustees' functions to a beneficiary (rule 63)

Date of power of attorney: ....

Donor of power of attorney: ....

I.......................... of

Do [solemnly and sincerely declare] or [certify] or [state] that at the time of completion of the .... to me/my client I/my client had no knowledge—

Of any lack of good faith on the part of the person(s) who dealt with the attorney, or

That the attorney was not a person to whom the functions of the trustees could be delegated under section 9 of the Trusts of Land and Appointment of Trustees Act 1996.

Where a certificate is given—

Signature of conveyancer .... Date .... , or

Print name ....

Firm name or employer (if any)..

Capacity (e g acting for …).. ; or

Where a statutory declaration is made—

And I make this solemn declaration conscientiously believing the same to be true and by virtue of the provisions of the Statutory Declarations Act 1835.

Signature of Declarant.......................... Date ....

DECLARED at .... before me, a person entitled to administer oaths.

Name ....

Address ....

Qualification ....

Signature .... ; or

Where a statement of truth is made—

I believe that the facts and matters contained in this statement are true.

Signature.......................... Date ....

Print name ....

Firm name or employer (if any) of any conveyancer signing..............................

Capacity of any conveyancer signing (e g acting for …)..............................

WARNING

1 If you dishonestly make a statement which you know is, or might be, untrue or misleading, and intend by doing so to make a gain for yourself or another person, or to cause loss or the risk to another person, you may commit the offence of fraud under section 1 of the Fraud Act 2006, the maximum penalty for which is 10 years' imprisonment or an unlimited fine, or both.

2 Failure to complete the form with proper care may result in a loss of protection under the Land Registration Act 2002 if, as a result, a mistake is made in the register.

3 Under section 66 of the Land Registration Act 2002 most documents (including this form) kept by the registrar relating to an application to the registrar or referred to in the register are open

to public inspection and copying. If you believe a document contains prejudicial information, you may apply for that part of the document to be made exempt using form EX1, under rule 136 of the Land Registration Rules 2003.]

Form 4—Certificate as to Vesting in an Incumbent or other Ecclesiastical Corporation (rule 174)

(*Date*). This is to certify that the registered estate (*or* registered charge *or* that part of the registered estate) comprised in a [*describe the transfer*] under the provisions of [*state the Act or Measure*] (if such transfer were a conveyance under such Act or Measure), vests in the incumbent of .... (*or* the bishop of .... *as the case may be*) and his successors immediately (*or as the case may be*) upon the happening of the event following, namely, the [*state event*]

(To be sealed by the Church Commissioners)

Form 5—The Like Certificate under rule 175

(*Date*). This is to certify that the [*describe Scheme, instrument or transfer, &c*] operates to vest immediately (*or* on publication in the "London Gazette", *or at some subsequent period, as the case may be*), the registered estate (*or* registered charge *or* that part of the registered estate [*include description by reference to a plan or to the register if possible*]) in the [*describe the corporation or person*].

(To be sealed by the Church Commissioners)

Form 6—Transfer where the Tenant for Life is already registered as proprietor (rule 186 and paragraph 5 of Schedule 7)

(*Date*). Pursuant to a trust deed of even date herewith, [made between AB (*name of tenant for life*) and CD and EF (*names of trustees of the Settlement*)], I, the said AB, hereby declares as follows—

(a) The land is vested in me upon the trusts from time to time affecting it by virtue of the said trust deed.

[(b) The said CD and EF are the trustees of the Settlement.

(c) The following powers relating to land are expressly conferred by the said trust deed in extension of those conferred by the settled Land Act 1925 (*fill in the powers, if any*).]

(d) I have the power to appoint new trustees of the Settlement.

(To be executed as a deed)

[Form 7—Certificate of powers of overseas corporations (rule 183)

I.. of .... (*insert workplace address, including country*) certify that—

—I give this certificate in respect of... (the corporation)

—I practise law in................................. (*insert territory*) (the territory) and am entitled to do so as a qualified lawyer under the law of the territory,

—I have the requisite knowledge of the law of the territory and of the corporation to give this certificate

—the corporation is incorporated in the territory with own legal personality, and

—the corporation has no limitations on its powers to hold, mortgage, lease and otherwise deal with, or to lend money on a mortgage or charge of, land in England and Wales.

Signature... Date ....

[Form 8—Certificate of powers of corporations other than overseas corporations (rule 183)

I.. of .... (*insert workplace address*) certify that—

—.. (the corporation) has its own legal personality, and

—the corporation has no limitations on its powers to hold, mortgage, lease and otherwise deal with, or to lend money on a mortgage or charge of, land.

Signature of conveyancer....................................... Date ....]

[3297]

NOTES

Form 1: first bullet point and words ", paragraph 16 of Part 2 of Schedule 1, or paragraph 15(3) of Part 5 of Schedule 4 to the Mental Capacity Act 2005" in square brackets in fourth bullet point substituted by SI 2007/1898, art 6, Sch 1, para 31(1), (3)(a).

Forms 2, 3: substituted by SI 2008/1919, r 4(5), Sch 3, para 2, 3.

Forms 7, 8: inserted by SI 2008/1919, r 4(5), Sch 3, para 3.

Application: this Schedule applies, with modifications, in so far as it relates to bank insolvency or administration under the Banking Act 2009, Pts 2, 3: see the Banking Act 2009 (Parts 2 and 3 Consequential Amendments) Order 2009, SI 2009/317, art 3, Schedule.

[SCHEDULE 4
STANDARD FORMS OF RESTRICTION

rule 91

In the forms in this Schedule—

(*a*) *words in [square brackets] in ordinary type are optional parts of the form; the brackets are not to be included in the restriction,*

(*b*) *words in [square brackets] in italic type are instructions for completion of the form, and are not to be included in the restriction,*

(*c*) *where* (*round brackets*) *enclose one or more words, the brackets and all words in ordinary type enclosed in them are part of the form and, unless also enclosed in [square brackets], must be included in the restriction, and*

(*d*) *where a form includes a group of clauses introduced by bullets, only one of the clauses may be used; the bullets are not to be included in the restriction.*

Rule 91A contains other permitted modifications of some forms.

Rule 91B contains provisions as to how a consent or certificate, required by the terms of a restriction to be given by a corporation aggregate, is to be signed on its behalf.

Form A (Restriction on dispositions by sole proprietor)

No disposition by a sole proprietor of the registered estate (except a trust corporation) under which capital money arises is to be registered unless authorised by an order of the court.

Form B (Dispositions by trustees—certificate required)

No [disposition *or specify type of disposition*] by the proprietors of the registered estate is to be registered unless one or more of them makes a statutory declaration or statement of truth, or their conveyancer gives a certificate, that the [disposition *or specify type of disposition*] is in accordance with [*specify the disposition creating the trust*] or some variation thereof referred to in the declaration, statement or certificate.

Form C (Dispositions by personal representatives—certificate required)

No disposition by the personal representative of [*name*] deceased, other than a transfer by way of assent, is to be registered unless such personal representative makes a statutory declaration or statement of truth, or their conveyancer gives a certificate, that the disposition is in accordance with the terms of

[choose whichever bulleted clause is appropriate]

—the will of the deceased [as varied by [specify date of, and parties to, deed of variation or other appropriate details]]

—the law relating to intestacy as varied by [specify date of, and parties to, deed of variation or other appropriate details]

or some [further] variation thereof referred to in the declaration, statement or certificate, or is necessary for the purposes of administration.

Form D (Parsonage, diocesan glebe, church or churchyard land)

No disposition of the registered estate is to be registered unless made in accordance with

[choose whichever bulleted clause is appropriate]

—[in the case of parsonage land] the Parsonages Measure 1938

—[in the case of church or churchyard land] the New Parishes Measure 1943

—[in the case of diocesan glebe land] the Endowments and Glebe Measure 1976,

or some other Measure or authority.

Form E (Non-exempt charity—certificate required)

No disposition by the proprietor of the registered estate to which section 36 or section 38 of the Charities Act 1993 applies is to be registered unless the instrument contains a certificate complying with section 37(2) or section 39(2) of that Act as appropriate.

Form F (Land vested in official custodian on trust for non-exempt charity—authority required)

No disposition executed by the trustees of *[name of charity]* in the name and on behalf of the proprietor is to be registered unless the transaction is authorised by an order of the court or of the Charity Commission, as required by section 22(3) of the Charities Act 1993.

Form G (Tenant for life as registered proprietor of settled land, where there are trustees of the settlement)

No disposition is to be registered unless authorised by the Settled Land Act 1925, or by any extension of those statutory powers in the settlement, and no disposition under which capital money arises is to be registered unless the money is paid to *[name]* of *[address]* and *[name]* of *[address]*, (the trustees of the settlement, who may be a sole trust corporation or, if individuals, must number at least two but not more than four) or into court.

[Note—If applicable under the terms of the settlement, a further provision may be added that no transfer of the mansion house [shown on an attached plan or otherwise adequately described to enable it to be fully identified on the Ordnance Survey map or title plan) is to be registered without the consent of the named trustees or an order of the court.]

Form H (Statutory owners as trustees of the settlement and registered proprietors of settled land)

No disposition is to be registered unless authorised by the Settled Land Act 1925, or by any extension of those statutory powers in the settlement, and, except where the sole proprietor is a trust corporation, no disposition under which capital money arises is to be registered unless the money is paid to at least two proprietors.

[Note—This restriction does not apply where the statutory owners are not the trustees of the settlement.]

Form I (Tenant for life as registered proprietor of settled land—no trustees of the settlement)

No disposition under which capital money arises, or which is not authorised by the Settled Land Act 1925 or by any extension of those statutory powers in the settlement, is to be registered.

Form J (Trustee in bankruptcy and beneficial interest—certificate required)

No disposition of the

[choose whichever bulleted clause is appropriate]

—registered estate, other than a disposition by the proprietor of any registered charge registered before the entry of this restriction,

—registered charge dated *[date]* referred to above, other than a disposition by the proprietor of any registered sub-charge of that charge registered before the entry of this restriction,

is to be registered without a certificate signed by the applicant for registration or their conveyancer that written notice of the disposition was given to *[name of trustee in bankruptcy]* (the trustee in bankruptcy of *[name of bankrupt person]*) at *[address for service]*.

Form K (Charging order affecting beneficial interest—certificate required)

No disposition of the

[choose whichever bulleted clause is appropriate]

—registered estate, other than a disposition by the proprietor of any registered charge registered before the entry of this restriction,

—registered charge dated *[date]* referred to above, other than a disposition by the proprietor of any registered sub-charge of that charge registered before the entry of this restriction,

is to be registered without a certificate signed by the applicant for registration or their conveyancer that written notice of the disposition was given to *[name of person with the benefit of the charging order]* at *[address for service]*, being the person with the benefit of [an interim *or* a final] charging order on the beneficial interest of *[name of judgment debtor]* made by the *[name of court]* on *[date]* (Court reference *[insert reference]*).

Form L (Disposition by registered proprietor of a registered estate or proprietor of chargecertificate required)

No [disposition *or specify type of disposition*] of the registered estate [(other than a charge)] by the proprietor of the registered estate [, or by the proprietor of any registered charge, not being a charge registered before the entry of this restriction,] is to be registered without a certificate signed by

[choose one of the bulleted clauses]

—a conveyancer

—the applicant for registration [or their conveyancer]

—*[name]* of *[address]* [or their personal representatives] [or [their conveyancer *or specify appropriate details*]]

—*[name]* of *[address]* [or their personal representatives] and *[name]* of *[address]* [or their personal representatives] [or [their conveyancer or *specify appropriate details*]]

—*[name]* of *[address]* and *[name]* of *[address]* or the survivor of them [or by the personal representatives of the survivor] [or [their conveyancer *or specify appropriate details*]]

—*[name]* of *[address]* or [after that person's death] by [name] of [address] [or [their conveyancer *or specify appropriate details*]]

that the provisions of *[specify clause, paragraph or other particulars]* of *[specify details]* have been complied with [or that they do not apply to the disposition]

Form M (Disposition by registered proprietor of registered estate or proprietor of charge—of registered proprietor of specified title number required)

No [disposition *or specify type of disposition*] of the registered estate [(other than a charge)] by the proprietor of the registered estate [, or by the proprietor of any registered charge, not being a charge registered before the entry of this restriction,] is to be registered without a certificate signed by the proprietor for the time being of the estate registered under title number [*specify title number*] [or [their conveyancer *or specify appropriate details*]] *that the* provisions of *[specify clause, paragraph or other particulars]* of *[specify details]* have been complied with [or that they do not apply to the disposition].

Form N (Disposition by registered proprietor of registered estate or proprietor of charge—consent required)

No [disposition *or specify type of disposition*] of the registered estate [(other than a charge)] by the proprietor of the registered estate [, or by the proprietor of any registered charge, not being a charge registered before the entry of this restriction,] is to be registered without a written consent signed by *[choose one of the bulleted clauses]*

—*[name]* of *[address]* [or their personal representatives] [or [their conveyancer *or specify appropriate details*]].

—*[name] of [address]* [or their personal representatives] and [name] of [address] [or their personal representatives] [or [their conveyancer *or specify appropriate details*]].

—*[name] of [address]* and *[name]* of *[address]* or the survivor of them [or by the personal representatives of the survivor] [or [their conveyancer *or specify appropriate details*]].

—*[name] of [address]* or [after that person's death] by *[name]* of *[address]* [or [their conveyancer *or specify appropriate details*]].

Form O (Disposition by registered proprietor of registered estate or proprietor of charge—consent of registered proprietor of specified title number or certificate required)

No [disposition *or specify type of disposition]* of the registered estate [(other than a charge)] by the proprietor of the registered estate [, or by the proprietor of any registered charge, not being a charge registered before the entry of this restriction,] is to be registered without a written consent signed by the proprietor for the time being of the estate registered under title number *[specify title number]* [or [their conveyancer *or specify appropriate details]].*

[*The text of the restriction may be continued as follows, to allow for the provision of a certificate as an alternative to the consent.]*

or without a certificate signed by

[choose one of the bulleted clauses]

—a conveyancer

—the applicant for registration [or their conveyancer]

—*[name]* of *[address]* [or [their conveyancer *or specify appropriate details*]]

that the provisions of *[specify clause, paragraph or other particulars]* of *[specify details]* have been complied with *[or that they do not apply to the disposition]*.

Form P (Disposition by registered proprietor of registered estate or proprietor of charge—consent of proprietor of specified charge or certificate required)

No [disposition *or specify type of disposition*] of the registered estate [(other than a charge)] by the proprietor of the registered estate [, or by the proprietor of any registered charge, not being a charge registered before the entry of this restriction,] is to be registered without a written consent signed by the proprietor for the time being of the charge dated *[date]* in favour of *[chargee]* referred to in the charges register [or [their conveyancer *or specify appropriate details*]].

[*The text of the restriction may be continued as follows, to allow for the provision of a certificate as an alternative to the consent.]*

or without a certificate signed by

[choose one of the bulleted clauses]

—a conveyancer

—the applicant for registration [or their conveyancer]

—*[name]* of *[address]* [or] their conveyancer *or specify appropriate details*]]

that the provisions of *[specify clause, paragraph or other particulars]* of *[specify details]* have been complied with [or that they do not apply to the disposition].

Form Q (Disposition by registered proprietor of registered estate or proprietor of charge—consent of personal representatives required)

No [disposition *or specify type of disposition*] of the

[choose whichever bulleted clause is appropriate]

—registered estate by the proprietor of the registered estate

—registered charge dated *[date]* referred to above by the proprietor of that registered charge

is to be registered after the death of *[name of the current proprietor(s) whose personal representatives' consent will be required]* without the written consent of the personal representatives of the deceased.

Form R (Disposition by registered proprietor of registered estate or proprietor of charge—evidence of compliance with club rules required)

No [disposition *or specify type of disposition*] of the registered estate [(other than a charge)] by the proprietor of the registered estate [, or by the proprietor of any registered charge, not being a charge registered before the entry of this restriction,] is to be registered unless authorised by the rules of the *[name of club]* of *[address]* as evidenced by

[choose whichever bulleted clause is appropriate]

—a resolution of its members.
—a certificate signed by its secretary or conveyancer.

[specify appropriate details].

Form S (Disposition by proprietor of charge—certificate of compliance required)

No [disposition *or specify type of disposition*] by the proprietor of the registered charge dated *[date]* referred to above is to be registered without a certificate signed by

[choose one of the bulleted clauses]

—a conveyancer
—the applicant for registration [or their conveyancer]
—*[name]* of *[address]* [or their personal representatives] [or [their conveyancer *or specify appropriate details*]]
—*[name]* of *[address]* [or their personal representatives] and *[name]* of *[address]* [or their personal representatives] [or [their conveyancer *or specify appropriate details*]]
—*[name]* of *[address]* and *[name]* of *[address]* or the survivor of them [or by the personal representatives of the survivor] [or [their conveyancer *or specify appropriate details*]]
—*[name]* of *[address]* or [after that person's death] by *[name]* of *[address]* [or [their conveyancer *or specify appropriate details*]]
—the proprietor for the time being of the sub-charge dated *[date]* in favour of *[sub-chargee]* [or [their conveyancer *or specify appropriate details*]]

that the provisions of *[specify clause, paragraph or other particulars]* of *[specify details]* have been complied with [or that they do not apply to the disposition].

Form T (Disposition by proprietor of charge—consent required)

No [disposition *or specify type of disposition*] by the proprietor of the registered charge dated *[date]* referred to above is to be registered without a written consent signed by

[choose one of the bulleted clauses]

—*[name]* of *[address]* [or their personal representatives] [or [their conveyancer *or specify appropriate details*]].
—*[name]* of *[address]* [or their personal representatives] and *[name]* of *[address]* [or their personal representatives] [or [their conveyancer *or specify appropriate details*]].
—*[name]* of *[address]* and *[name]* of *[address]* or the survivor of them [or by the personal representatives of the survivor] [or [their conveyancer *or specify appropriate details*]].
—*[name]* of *[address]* or [after that person's death] by *[name]* of *[address]* [or [their conveyancer *or specify appropriate details*]].
—the proprietor for the time being of the sub-charge dated *[date]* in favour of *[sub-chargee]* [or [their conveyancer *or specify appropriate details*]].

Form U (Section 37 of the Housing Act 1985)

No transfer or lease by the proprietor of the registered estate or by the proprietor of any registered charge is to be registered unless a certificate by *[specify relevant local authority]* is given that the transfer or lease is made in accordance with section 37 of the Housing Act 1985.

Form V (Section 157 of the Housing Act 1985)

No transfer or lease by the proprietor of the registered estate or by the proprietor of any registered charge is to be registered unless a certificate by *[specify relevant local authority or housing association etc]* is given that the transfer or lease is made in accordance with section 157 of the Housing Act 1985.

Form W (Paragraph 4 of Schedule 9A to the Housing Act 1985)

No disposition (except a transfer) of a qualifying dwellinghouse (except to a qualifying person or persons) is to be registered without the consent of the [Secretary of State *or* Welsh Ministers] given under section 1710(2) of the Housing Act 1985 as it applies by virtue of the Housing (Preservation of Right to Buy) Regulations 1993.

Form X (Section 81 or 133 of the Housing Act 1988 or section 173 of the Local Government and Housing Act 1989)

No disposition by the proprietor of the registered estate or in exercise of the power of sale or leasing in any registered charge (except an exempt disposal as defined by section 81(8) of the Housing Act 1988) is to be registered without the consent of the [Secretary of State *or* Welsh Ministers] to that disposition under the provisions of

[choose whichever bulleted clause is appropriate]

—section 81 of that Act.

—section 133 of that Act.
—section 173 of the Local Government and Housing Act 1989.

Form Y (**Section 13 of the Housing Act 1996**)

No transfer or lease by the proprietor of the registered estate or by the proprietor of any registered charge is to be registered unless a certificate by *[specify relevant registered social landlord]* is given that the transfer or lease is made in accordance with section 13 of the Housing Act 1996.

Form AA (**Freezing order on the registered estate**)

Under an order of the *[name of court]* made on *[date]* (Court reference *[insert reference]*) no disposition by the proprietor of the registered estate is to be registered except with the consent of *[name]* of *[address]* or under a further order of the Court.

Form BB (**Freezing order on charge**)

Under an order of the *[name of court]* made on *[date]* (Court reference *[insert reference]*) no disposition by the proprietor of the registered charge dated *[date]* referred to above is to be registered except with the consent of *[name]* of *[address]* or under a further order of the Court.

Form CC (**Application for freezing order on the registered estate**)

Pursuant to an application made on *[date]* to the *[name of court]* for a freezing order to be made under *[statutory provision]* no disposition by the proprietor of the registered estate is to be registered except with the consent of *[name of the person applying]* of *[address]* or under a further order of the Court.

Form DD (**Application for freezing order on charge**)

Pursuant to an application made on *[date]* to the *[name of court]* for a freezing order to be made under *[statutory provision]* no disposition by the proprietor of the registered charge dated *[date]* referred to above is to be registered except with the consent of *[name of the person applying]* of *[address]* or under a further order of the Court.

Form EE (**Restraint order or interim receiving order on the registered estate**)

Under [a restraint order *or* an interim receiving order] made under *[statutory provision]* on *[date]* (Court reference *[insert reference]*) no disposition by the proprietor of the registered estate is to be registered except with the consent of *[name of prosecutor or other appropriate person]* of *[address]* or under a further order of the Court.

Form FF (**Restraint order or interim receiving order on charge**)

Under [a restraint order *or* an interim receiving order] made under *[statutory provision]* on *[date]* (Court reference *[insert reference]*) no disposition by the proprietor of the registered charge dated *[date]* referred to above is to be registered except with the consent of *[name of prosecutor or other appropriate person]* of *[address]* or under a further order of the Court.

Form GG (**Application for restraint order or interim receiving order on the registered estate**)

Pursuant to an application for [a restraint order *or* an interim receiving order] to be made under *[statutory provision]* and under any order made as a result of that application, no disposition by the proprietor of the registered estate is to be registered except with the consent of *[name of prosecutor or other appropriate person]* of *[address]* or under a further order of the Court.

Form HH (**Application for restraint order or interim receiving order on charge**)

Pursuant to an application for [a restraint order *or* an interim receiving order] to be made under *[statutory provision]* and under any order made as a result of that application no disposition by the proprietor of the registered charge dated *[date]* referred to above is to be registered except with the consent of *[name of prosecutor or other appropriate person]* of *[address]* or under a further order of the Court.

Form II (**Beneficial interest that is a right or claim in relation to a registered estate**)

No disposition of the registered estate, other than a disposition by the proprietor of any registered charge registered before the entry of this restriction, is to be registered without a certificate signed by the applicant for registration or their conveyancer that written notice of the disposition was given to *[name]* at *[address]*.

Form JJ (**Statutory charge of beneficial interest in favour of Legal Services Commission**)

No disposition of the

[choose whichever bulleted clause is appropriate]

—registered estate, other than a disposition by the proprietor of any registered charge registered before the entry of this restriction,
—registered charge dated *[date]* referred to above, other than a disposition by the proprietor of
—any registered sub-charge of that charge registered before the entry of this restriction,

is to be registered without a certificate signed by the applicant for registration or their conveyancer that written notice of the disposition was given to the Legal Services Commission, Land Charge Department, at *[address and Commission's reference number]*.

Form KK (Lease by registered social landlord)

No deed varying the terms of the registered lease is to be registered without the consent of

[choose whichever bulleted clause is appropriate]

—the Housing Corporation

—the Welsh Ministers of *[address]*.

Form LL (Restriction as to evidence of execution)

No disposition of the

[choose whichever bulleted clause is appropriate]

—registered estate by the proprietor of the registered estate

—registered charge dated *[date]* referred to above by the proprietor of that registered charge

is to be registered without a certificate signed by a conveyancer that that conveyancer is satisfied that the person who executed the document submitted for registration as disponor is the same person as the proprietor.

Form MM (Interest in beneficial joint tenancy subject to charge under section 22(1) of the Health and Social Services and Social Security Adjudications Act 1983)

No disposition of the registered estate made after the death of *[specify; the name of the person whose beneficial interest under a beneficial joint tenancy is subject to a charge under section 22(1) of the Health and Social Services and Social Security Adjudications Act 1983]*, or after that person has become the sole proprietor of the registered estate, is to be registered unless-

(1) the disposition is by two or more persons who were registered as proprietors of the legal estate at the time of that person's death,

(2) notice of a charge under section 22(1) or (6) of the Health and Social Services and Social Security Adjudications Act 1983 for the benefit of *[name and address of the local authority]* has been entered in the register or, where appropriate, such charge has been registered, or

(3) it is shown to the registrar's satisfaction that no such charge is subsisting.

Form NN (Disposition by registered proprietor of registered estate or proprietor of charge -consent or certificate required)

No [disposition *or specify type of disposition*] of the registered estate [(other than a charge)] by the proprietor of the registered estate [, or by the proprietor of any registered charge, not being a charge registered before the entry of this restriction,] is to be registered without a written consent signed by

[choose one of the bulleted clauses]

—*[name]* of *[address]* [or their personal representatives] [or [their conveyancer *or specify; appropriate details*]],

—*[name]* of *[address]* [or their personal representatives] and *[name]* of *[address]* [or their personal representatives] [or [their conveyancer *or specify appropriate details*]],

—*[name]* of *[address]* and *[name]* of *[address]* or the survivor of them [or by the personal representatives of the survivor] [or [their conveyancer *or specify appropriate details*]],

—*[name]* of *[address]* or [after that person's death] by *[name]* of *[address]* [or [their conveyancer *or specify appropriate details*]],

or a certificate signed by

[choose one of the bulleted clauses]

—a conveyancer

—the applicant for registration [or their conveyancer]

—*[name]* of *[address]* [or [their conveyancer *or specify; appropriate details*]]

that the provisions of *[specify; clause, paragraph or other particulars]* of *[specify details]* have been complied with [or that they do not apply to the disposition].

Form 00 (Disposition by proprietor of charge—consent or certificate required)

No [disposition *or specify type of disposition*] by the proprietor of the registered charge dated *[date]* referred to above is to be registered without a written consent signed by

[choose one of the bulleted clauses]

—*[name]* of *[address]* [or their personal representatives] [or [their conveyancer *or specify appropriate details*]].

—*[name]* of *[address]* [or their personal representatives] and *[name]* of *[address]* [or their personal representatives] [or [their conveyancer *or specify appropriate details*]].

—*[name]* of *[address]* and *[name]* of *[address]* or the survivor of them [or by the personal representatives of the survivor] [or [their conveyancer *or specify appropriate details*]].

—*[name]* of *[address]* or [after that person's death] by *[name]* of *[address]* [or [their conveyancer *or specify appropriate details*]].

the proprietor for the time being of the sub-charge dated [*date*] in favour of [*sub-chargee*] [or [their conveyancer *or specify appropriate details*]].

or a certificate signed by

[choose one of the bulleted clauses]

—a conveyancer

—the applicant for registration [or their conveyancer]

—*[name]* of *[address]* [or [their conveyancer *or specify appropriate details*]]

that the provisions of *[specify clause, paragraph or other particulars]* of *[specify details]* have been complied with [or that they do not apply to the disposition].

Form PP (Disposition by registered proprietor of registered estate or proprietor of charge -certificate of landlord etc, or of a conveyancer, required)

No [disposition *or specify type of disposition*] of the registered estate [(other than a charge)] by the proprietor of the registered estate [, or by the proprietor of any registered charge, not being a charge registered before the entry of this restriction,] is to be registered without a certificate signed by

[choose one of the bulleted clauses]

—the proprietor for the time being of the registered estate comprising the reversion immediately expectant on the determination of the registered lease,

—the proprietor for the time being of the estate registered under title number *[specify title number]*,

—*[name]* of *[address]* [or by *[name]* of *[address]*],

or by a conveyancer, that the provisions of *[specify clause, paragraph or other particulars]* of *[specify details]* have been complied with [or that they do not apply to the disposition].]

[3298]

NOTES

Substituted by SI 2008/1919, r 4(6), Sch 4.

SCHEDULE 5

APPLICATIONS IN CONNECTION WITH COURT PROCEEDINGS, INSOLVENCY AND TAX LIABILITY—QUALIFYING APPLICANTS AND APPROPRIATE CERTIFICATES

rule 140

Column 1 *Status of applicant*	*Column 2* *Certificate in Form CIT*
[An **accredited financial investigator** falling within section 378(1)(b) of the Proceeds of Crime Act 2002	Certificate H]
[An **accredited financial investigator** falling within section 378(4)(a) of the Proceeds of Crime Act 2002	Certificate N]
An **Administrator** appointed for the purposes of the Insolvency Act 1986	Certificate K
An **Administrator** appointed under section 13 of the Criminal Justice (Scotland) Act 1987	Certificate J
[An **authorised person** within the meaning of section 108(15) of the Environment Act 1995	Certificate P]
A **Chief Officer of Police** or a police officer authorised to apply on behalf of a Chief Officer	Certificate A Certificate B Certificate C Certificate D Certificate E Certificate G
…	…
[A person authorised to apply by the **Commissioners for Her Majesty's Revenue and Customs** and having the consent of [the First-tier Tribunal or, where determined by or under Tribunal Procedure Rules, the Upper Tribunal] to make the application	Certificate L]
…	…
…	…
A **constable**	Certificate H [Certificate N]

PART II STATUTORY INSTRUMENTS

Column 1 *Status of applicant*	*Column 2* *Certificate in Form CIT*
…	…
[**Director of Enforcement at the Financial Services Authority** or a member of the Financial Services Authority authorised to apply on behalf of the Director of Enforcement.	Certificate Q]
The **Director of Public Prosecutions** or a member of the Crown Prosecution Service authorised to apply on behalf of the Director	Certificate A Certificate B Certificate C Certificate D Certificate E [Certificate I]
[The **Director of Revenue and Customs Prosecutions** or a member of the Revenue and Customs Prosecutions Office Authorised to apply on behalf of the Director	Certificate A Certificate B Certificate C Certificate D Certificate E Certificate H [Certificate I]]
The **Director of the Serious Fraud Office** or a member of the Serious Fraud Office authorised to apply on behalf of the Director	Certificate A Certificate B Certificate E [Certificate I]
[**Director General of the Serious Organised Crime Agency** or a member of … staff of the Serious Organised Crime Agency authorised to apply on behalf of the Director General	[Certificate H] [Certificate I] [Certificate M] Certificate O]
[…	…]
[…	…]
The **Director-General of the Security Service** or a member of the Security Service authorised to apply on behalf of the Director-General	Certificate F
A **Liquidator** appointed for the purposes of the Insolvency Act 1986	Certificate K
The **Lord Advocate** or a person conducting a prosecution in Scotland on behalf of the Lord Advocate	Certificate C Certificate D [Certificate H Certificate N]
[An **officer of Revenue and Customs**	Certificate A Certificate B Certificate C Certificate D Certificate E Certificate H Certificate N]
The **Official Assignee** for bankruptcy for Northern Ireland or the **Official Assignee** for company liquidations for Northern Ireland	Certificate K
An **Official Receiver** for the purposes of the Insolvency Act 1986	Certificate K

Column 1 *Status of applicant*	*Column 2* *Certificate in Form CIT*
A **Receiver** appointed under the Criminal Justice Act 1988, the Drug Trafficking Act 1994 or the Proceeds of Crime Act 2002	Certificate J
The **Scottish Ministers** or a person named by them	Certificate I
A person authorised by [the **Secretary of State for Business, Enterprise and Regulatory Reform**]	Certificate A Certificate B Certificate E
A person authorised by the **Secretary of State for Work and Pensions**	Certificate A Certificate B
A **trustee in bankruptcy**, being either a trustee in bankruptcy of a person adjudged bankrupt in England and Wales or Northern Ireland or a permanent or interim trustee in the sequestration of a debtor's estate in Scotland	Certificate K

[3299]

NOTES

Entries relating to "accredited financial investigator" inserted by SI 2005/1766, r 12, Sch 3, para 1.

Entry relating to "authorised person" inserted by SI 2008/1919, r 4(7).

Entry relating to "Commissioners of Customs and Excise" (omitted) revoked by SI 2005/1766, r 12, Sch 3, para 2

Entry relating to "Commissioners for Her Majesty's Revenue and Customs" inserted by SI 2005/1766, r 12, Sch 3, para 1; words from "the First-tier" to "the Upper Tribunal" in square brackets substituted by SI 2009/56, art 3, Sch 2, para 90, for transitional and savings provisions see art 6, Sch 3, paras 1, 6–8, 12, 13 thereto.

Entries relating to "Commissioners of Inland Revenue" (omitted) revoked by SI 2005/1766, r 12, Sch 3, para 2

In entry relating to "constable" in column 2 words "Certificate N" in square brackets inserted by SI 2005/1766, r 12, Sch 3, para 3.

Entry relating to "Director of the Assets Recovery Agency" (omitted) revoked by SI 2008/574, art 2, Schedule, para 6(3)(a).

Entry relating to "Director of Enforcement at the Financial Services Authority" inserted by SI 2008/1919, r 4(7).

In entry relating to "Director of Public Prosecutions" in column 2 words "Certificate I" in square brackets inserted by SI 2008/574, art 2, Schedule, para 6(3)(b).

Entry relating to "Director of Revenue and Customs Prosecutions" inserted by SI 2005/1766, r 12, Sch 3, para 1.

In entry relating to "Director of Revenue and Customs Prosecutions" in column 2 words "Certificate I" in square brackets inserted by SI 2008/574, art 2, Schedule, para 6(3)(c).

In entry relating to "Director of the Serious Fraud Office" in column 2 words "Certificate I" in square brackets inserted by SI 2008/574, art 2, Schedule, para 6(3)(d).

Entry relating to "Director General of the Serious Organised Crime Agency" inserted by SI 2006/594, art 2, Schedule, para 35(1), (3)(b); in column 1 word omitted revoked by SI 2008/574, art 2, Schedule, para 6(3)(e)(i); in column 2 words "Certificate H", "Certificate I", "Certificate M" in square brackets inserted by SI 2008/574, art 2, Schedule, para 6(3)(e)(ii).

Entries relating to "Director General of the National Crime Squad" and "Director General of the National Criminal Intelligence Service" (omitted) inserted by SI 2005/1766, r 12, Sch 3, para 1; revoked by SI 2006/594, art 2, Schedule, para 35(1), (3)(a).

In entry relating to "The Lord Advocate" in column 2 words "Certificate H" and "Certificate N" in square brackets inserted by SI 2005/1766, r 12, Sch 3, para 4.

Entry relating to "officer of Revenue and Customs" inserted by SI 2005/1766, r 12, Sch 3, para 1.

In entry relating to the "Secretary of State for Business, Enterprise and Regulatory Reform" words "the Secretary of State for Business, Enterprise and Regulatory Reform" in square brackets substituted by SI 2007/3224, art 15, Schedule, Pt 2, para 37(1)(b) (entry originally related to the "Secretary of State for the Department of Trade and Industry").

Application: as to the application of this Schedule with modifications, in so far as it relates to bank insolvency or administration under the Banking Act 2009, Pts 2, 3, see the Banking Act 2009 (Parts 2 and 3 Consequential Amendments) Order 2009, SI 2009/317, art 3, Schedule.

SCHEDULE 6
INFORMATION TO BE INCLUDED IN CERTAIN RESULTS OF OFFICIAL SEARCHES

rule 145

PART 1
INFORMATION TO BE INCLUDED IN THE RESULT OF AN OFFICIAL SEARCH OF THE INDEX MAP

A The date and time of the official search certificate

B A description of the land searched

C The reference (if any) of the applicant or the person to whom the search is being sent: limited to 25 characters including spaces

D Whether there is—

(i) a pending application for first registration (other than of title to a relating franchise)
(ii) a pending application for a caution against first registration (other than where the subject of the caution is a relating franchise)
(iii) a registered estate in land
(iv) a registered rentcharge
(v) a registered profit a prendre in gross
(vi) a registered affecting franchise, or
(vii) a caution against first registration (other than where the subject of the caution is a relating franchise)

and, if there is such a registered estate or caution, the title number

[3300]

PART 2
INFORMATION TO BE INCLUDED IN THE RESULT OF AN OFFICIAL SEARCH OF THE INDEX OF RELATING FRANCHISES AND MANORS

A The date and time of the official search certificate

B The administrative area(s) searched

C The reference (if any) of the applicant or the person to whom the search is being sent: limited to 25 characters including spaces

D Whether there is a verbal description of—

(i) a pending application for first registration of title to a relating franchise
(ii) a pending application for a caution against first registration where the subject of the caution is a relating franchise
(iii) a registered franchise which is a relating franchise
(iv) a registered manor, or
(v) a caution against first registration where the subject of the caution is a relating franchise

and the title numbers of any such registered estates and cautions arranged by administrative area

[3301]

PART 3
INFORMATION TO BE INCLUDED IN THE RESULT OF AN OFFICIAL SEARCH OF AN INDIVIDUAL REGISTER OF A REGISTERED TITLE

A The title number

B The date and time of the official search certificate

C If the official search certificate is part of a registered title, a short description of the property or plot number on the approved estate plan

D The applicant's name

E The applicant's, or his agent's, reference (if any): limited to 25 characters including spaces

F Details of any relevant adverse entries made in the individual register since the end of the day specified in the application as the search from date

G Notice of the entry of any relevant pending application [or proposal by the registrar to alter the register] affecting the registered title entered on the day list (other than an application to designate a document as an exempt information document under rule 136)

H Notice of the entry [on the day list] of any relevant official search the priority period of which has not expired

I If the official search is with priority, the date and time at which the priority expires

J If the official search is without priority, a statement that the certificate will not confer on the applicant priority for any registrable disposition

[3302]

NOTES

Paras G, H: words in square brackets inserted by SI 2008/1919, r 4(8), Sch 5, para 1.

PART 4
INFORMATION TO BE INCLUDED IN THE RESULT OF AN OFFICIAL SEARCH WITH PRIORITY IN RELATION TO A PENDING APPLICATION FOR FIRST REGISTRATION

A The title number allotted to the pending application for first registration

B The date and time of the official search certificate

C If the official search is of part, a short description of the property

D The applicant's name

E The applicant's, or his agent's, reference (if any): limited to 25 characters including spaces

F The full name of the person who has applied for first registration

G The date and time at which the pending application for first registration was entered on the day list

H Notice of the entry of any relevant pending application affecting the estate sought to be registered and entered on the day list subsequent to the date and time at which the pending application for first registration was entered on the day list (other than an application to designate a document as an exempt information document under rule 136)

I Notice of the entry [on the day list] of any relevant official search the priority period of which has not expired affecting the pending application for first registration

J The date and time at which priority expires

[3303]

NOTES

Para I: words in square brackets inserted by SI 2008/1919, Sch 5, para 2.

PART 5
INFORMATION TO BE INCLUDED IN THE RESULT OF AN OFFICIAL SEARCH BY A MORTGAGEE FOR THE PURPOSE OF SECTION 56(3) OF THE FAMILY LAW ACT 1996

A The title number

B The date and time of the official search certificate

C The mortgagee's name

D The mortgagee's, or his agent's, reference (if any): limited to 25 characters including spaces

E Whether, at the date [and time] of the official search certificate, a [home rights notice] or matrimonial home rights caution has been registered against the registered title searched and if so the date of registration and the name of the person in whose favour the notice or caution was registered

F Whether [at the date and time of the official search certificate] there is a pending application for the entry of a [home rights notice] entered on the day list

[3304]

NOTES

Paras E, F: words in first pair of square brackets inserted by SI 2008/1919, r 4(8), Sch 5, para 3; words in second pair of square brackets substituted by SI 2005/1982, r 18.

SCHEDULE 7
SETTLEMENTS

rule 186

General

1. Registered land which is settled land must be registered in the name of the tenant for life or the statutory owner.

First registration—restriction required

2. An application for first registration of an unregistered legal estate which is settled land must be accompanied by an application for entry of a restriction in Form G, H, or I, as appropriate.

Standard forms of restriction applicable to settled land

3.—(1) The restrictions in Forms G, H and I apply respectively to the various cases referred to in those forms, and may be modified as the registrar sees fit according to the circumstances.

(2) Where one of the restrictions referred to in sub-paragraph (1) should have been entered in the register and has not been, any person who has an interest in the settled land and who applies for such restriction shall be regarded as included in section 43(1)(c) of the Act.

(3) Subject to paragraphs 8 and 14, the restrictions referred to in sub-paragraph (1) are binding on the proprietor during his life, but do not affect a disposition by his personal representatives.

PART II STATUTORY INSTRUMENTS

Transfer of land into settlement

4.—(1) A transfer of registered land into settlement must include the following provisions, with any necessary alterations and additions—

"The Transferor and the Transferee declare that—

(a) the property is vested in the Transferee upon the trusts declared in a trust deed dated (date) and made between (*parties*),

(b) the trustees of the settlement are (*names of trustees*),

(c) the power of appointment of new trustees is vested in (*name*),

(d) the following powers relating to land are expressly conferred by the trust deed in addition to those conferred by the Settled Land Act 1925: (*insert additional powers*).

or if the tenant for life is a minor and the transferees are the statutory owner—

(a) the property is vested in the Transferee as statutory owner under a trust deed dated (*date*) and made between (*parties*),

(b) the tenant for life is (name), a minor, who was born on (*date*),

(c) the trustees of the settlement are (*names*),

(d) during the minority of the tenant for life the power of appointment of new trustees is vested in the Transferee,

(e) the following powers relating to land are expressly conferred by the trust deed in addition to those conferred by the Settled Land Act 1925: (*insert additional powers*).".

(2) An application for the registration of a transfer of registered land into settlement must be accompanied by an application for entry of a restriction in Form G, H or I, as appropriate.

(3) When the registrar receives the application he must register the transferee named in the transfer as the proprietor of the registered land and enter the appropriate restriction in the register.

Registered land brought into settlement

5. Where registered land has been settled and the existing registered proprietor is the tenant for life under the settlement, the registered proprietor must—

(a) make a declaration in Form 6, and

(b) apply for the entry of a restriction in Form G, modified if appropriate.

Registered land bought with capital money

6.—(1) Where registered land is acquired with capital money the transfer must be in one of the forms prescribed by rule 206 and must include the following provisions, with any necessary alterations and additions—

"The Transferee declares that—

(a) the consideration has been paid out of capital money,

(b) the Property is vested in the Transferee upon the trusts declared in a trust deed dated (*date*) and made between (*parties*),

(c) the trustees of the settlement are (*names of trustees*),

(d) the power of appointment of new trustees is vested in (*name*),

(e) the following powers relating to land are expressly conferred by the trust deed in addition to those conferred by the Settled Land Act 1925: (*set out additional powers*)." .

(2) An application for registration of the transfer must be accompanied by an application for entry of a restriction in Form G, H or I, as appropriate.

Duty to apply for restrictions when registered land is settled

7.—(1) Where registered land is settled land the proprietor, or (if there is no proprietor) the personal representatives of a deceased proprietor, must apply to the registrar for the entry of such restrictions (in addition to a restriction in Form G, H or I) as may be appropriate to the case.

(2) The application must state that the restrictions applied for are required for the protection of the beneficial interests and powers under the settlement.

(3) Subject to section 43(3) of the Act, the registrar must enter such restrictions without inquiry as to the terms of the settlement.

(4) Nothing in this rule affects the rights and powers of personal representatives for purposes of administration.

Proprietor ceasing in his lifetime to be the tenant for life

8. Where a registered proprietor ceases in his lifetime to be a tenant for life and has not become absolutely entitled to the registered land—

(a) he must transfer the land to his successor in tile, or, if the successor is a minor, to the statutory owner, and

(b) on the registration of the successor in title or statutory owner as proprietor, the trustees of the settlement, if the settlement continues, must apply for such alteration in the restrictions as may be required for the protection of the beneficial interests and powers under the settlement.

Tenant for life or statutory owner entitled to have the settled land vested in him

9. Where a tenant for life or statutory owner who, if the registered land were not registered, would be entitled to have the settled land vested in him, is not the registered proprietor, the registered proprietor must at the cost of the trust estate execute such transfers as may be required for giving effect on the register to the rights of such tenant for life or statutory owner.

Registration of statutory owner during a minority otherwise than on death

10.—(1) If a minor becomes entitled in possession (or will become entitled in possession on attaining full age) to registered land otherwise than on a death, the statutory owner during the minority is entitled to require the settled land to be transferred to him and to be registered as proprietor accordingly.

(2) The transfer to the statutory owner—
- (a) must be in Form TR1, and
- (b) must not refer to the settlement.

(3) An application to register the transfer must be accompanied by an application for entry of a restriction in Form H.

Registration of special personal representatives

11.—(1) Where—
- (a) land was settled before the death of the sole or last surviving joint registered proprietor and not by his will, and
- (b) the settlement continues after his death,

the personal representatives in whom the registered land vests under the Administration of Estates Act 1925 may apply to be registered as proprietor in place of the deceased proprietor.

(2) The application must be accompanied by the grant of probate or letters of administration of the deceased proprietor limited to the settled land.

(3) The personal representatives must be registered in place of the deceased proprietor and the following added after his name—

"special executor or executrix (or administrator or administratrix) of [*name*], deceased.".

Transfer on the death of the tenant for life

12.—(1) Where the settlement continues after the death of the proprietor who was the tenant for life—
- (a) an application to register a transfer by the personal representatives to the person next entitled to the registered land which is settled land must be accompanied by—
  - (i) if the personal representatives are not already registered, the grant of probate or letters of administration of the deceased proprietor limited to the settled land,
  - (ii) a transfer in Form AS1 or AS2, as appropriate,
  - (iii) an application for entry of a restriction in Form G or H, as appropriate.
- (b) The transfer must contain the following provisions with any necessary alterations or additions—

"The Personal Representatives and the Transferee declare that—
- a the Property is vested in the Transferee upon the trusts declared in [a trust deed dated (*date*) and made between (*parties*)] or [the will of (*name of deceased*) proved on (*date*)],
- b the trustees of the settlement are (*names of trustees*),
- c the power of appointment of new trustees is vested in (*name*),
- d the following powers relating to land are expressly conferred by the will in addition to those conferred by the Settled Land Act 1925: (*set out additional powers*).".

(2) Where the settlement ends on the death of the proprietor, an application to register a transfer by the personal representatives to the person entitled must be accompanied by—
- (a) if the personal representatives are not already registered, the grant of probate or letters of administration of the deceased proprietor,
- (b) Form RX3 for cancellation of the restriction entered on the register relating to the settlement.

(3) The registrar shall not be under a duty to investigate the reasons any transfer is made by the personal representatives or consider the contents of the will and, provided the terms of any restriction on the register are complied with, he must assume, whether he knows of the terms of the will or not, that the personal representatives are acting correctly and within their powers.

Minority where settlement arises under a will or intestacy

13.—(1) Where a settlement is created or arises under the will or intestacy of a person who died before 1st January 1997—

(a) The personal representatives under the will or intestacy under which the settlement is created or arises must, during a minority, be registered as proprietors and will have all the powers conferred by the Settled Land Act 1925 on the tenant for life and on the trustees of the settlement.

(b) When a minor becomes beneficially entitled to an estate in fee simple or a term of years absolute in the registered land, or would, if he were of full age, be or have the powers of a tenant for life, the personal representatives must (unless they are themselves the statutory owner) during the minority give effect on the register to the directions of the statutory owner.

(c) In particular, the statutory owner shall, after administration is completed as respects the registered land, direct the personal representatives to apply for a restriction in Form H.

(2) The application for the restriction in form H must be made by the personal representatives.

(3) On an application by the personal representatives under sub-paragraph (2), the registrar shall be under no duty to consider or call for any information concerning—

(a) the reason the application is made, or

(b) the terms of the will or the devolution under the intestacy, or

(c) whether the direction by the statutory owner was actually given or not, or its terms,

and whether he has notice of those matters or not, he must assume that the personal representatives are acting according to the directions given and that the directions were given by the statutory owner and were correct.

(4) A disponee dealing with the personal representatives who complies with the restriction entered under sub-paragraph (2) is not concerned to see or enquire whether any directions have been given by the statutory owner with regard to the disposition to him.

(5) Where under subsection (3) of section 19 of the Settled Land Act 1925 there is a tenant for life of full age, he shall be entitled to be registered as proprietor during any minority referred to in that subsection, but subject to the restrictions in Forms G or I, as appropriate.

(6) Nothing in this paragraph shall affect the right of a statutory owner to be registered as proprietor.

Discharge of registered land from beneficial interests and powers under a settlement

14. Where the trustees of a settlement desire to discharge registered land from the beneficial interests and powers under the settlement they may do so by any document sufficient to discharge it.

Discharge from liability in respect of beneficial interests and powers under a settlement

15. Where a proprietor or the personal representatives of a deceased proprietor has or have, in good faith, complied with the requirements of this Schedule in executing a transfer of settled land or discharge of trustees and in applying for the appropriate restrictions that may be required for the protection of the beneficial interests and powers under a settlement—

(a) he is or they are absolutely discharged from all liability in respect of the equitable interests and powers taking effect under the settlement, and

(b) he is or they are entitled to be kept indemnified at the cost of the trust estate from all liabilities affecting the settled land.

Interpretation

16.—(1) In this Schedule—

"capital" money has the same meaning as in the Settled Land Act 1925,

"personal representatives" includes the special personal representatives for the purposes of any settled land where they have been appointed in relation to that land,

"settled land" has the same meaning as in the Settled Land Act 1925,

"settlement" has the same meaning as in the Settled Land Act 1925,

"statutory owner" has the same meaning as in the Settled Land Act 1925,

"tenant for life" has the same meaning as in the Settled Land Act 1925,

"transfer" includes an assent and a vesting assent,

"trustees of the settlement" has the same meaning as in the Settled Land Act 1925,

"vesting assent" has the same meaning as in the Settled Land Act 1925.

(2) References in this Schedule to the "tenant for life" shall, where the context admits, be read as referring to the tenant for life, statutory owner, or personal representatives who is or are entitled to be registered.

(3) Nothing in this Schedule modifies the provisions of section 2 of the Trusts of Land and Appointment of Trustees Act 1996 concerning settlements in relation to their application to registered land (as defined in section 89(3) of the Act).

[3305]

NOTES

See further, in relation to the application of this Schedule, with modifications, in so far as it relates to bank insolvency or administration under the Banking Act 2009, Pts 2, 3: the Banking Act 2009 (Parts 2 and 3 Consequential Amendments) Order 2009, SI 2009/317, art 3, Schedule.

SCHEDULE 8
MODIFIED FORM OF SCHEDULE 6 TO THE ACT APPLICABLE TO REGISTERED RENTCHARGES

rule 191

Schedule 6
REGISTRATION OF ADVERSE POSSESSOR

Right to apply for registration

1.—(1) A person may apply to the registrar to be registered as the proprietor of a registered rentcharge if he has been in adverse possession of the registered rentcharge for the period of ten years ending on the date of the application.

(2) However, a person may not make an application under this paragraph if—

(a) he is a defendant in proceedings by the registered proprietor of the registered rentcharge for recovery of the rent or to enter into possession of the land out of which the registered rentcharge issues,

(b) judgement in favour of the registered proprietor of the registered rentcharge in respect of proceedings of the nature mentioned in sub-paragraph (2)(a) has been given against him in the last two years, or

(c) the registered proprietor of the registered rentcharge of which that person was in adverse possession has entered into possession of the land out of which the registered rentcharge issues.

(3) For the purposes of sub-paragraph (1), the registered rentcharge need not have been registered throughout the period of adverse possession.

Notification of application

2.—(1) The registrar must give notice of an application under paragraph 1 to—

(a) the proprietor of the registered rentcharge to which the application relates,

(b) the proprietor of any registered charge on the registered rentcharge,

(c) where the registered rentcharge is leasehold, the proprietor of any superior registered rentcharge,

(d) any person who is registered in accordance with rules as a person to be notified under this paragraph, and

(e) such other persons as rules may provide.

(2) Notice under this paragraph shall include notice of the effect of paragraph 4.

Treatment of application

3.—(1) A person given notice under paragraph 2 may require that the application to which the notice relates be dealt with under paragraph 5.

(2) The right under this paragraph is exercisable by notice to the registrar given before the end of such period as rules may provide.

4. If an application under paragraph 1 is not required to be dealt with under paragraph 5, the applicant is entitled to be entered in the register as the new proprietor of the registered rentcharge.

5.—(1) If an application under paragraph 1 is required to be dealt with under this paragraph, the applicant is only entitled to be registered as the new proprietor of the registered rentcharge if either of the following conditions is met.

(2) The first condition is that—

(a) it would be unconscionable because of an equity by estoppel for the registered proprietor to seek to assert his title to the registered rentcharge against the applicant, and

(b) the circumstances are such that the applicant ought to be registered as the proprietor.

(3) The second condition is that the applicant is for some other reason entitled to be registered as the proprietor of the registered rentcharge.

Right to make further application for registration

6.—(1) Where a person's application under paragraph 1 is rejected, he may make a further application to be registered as the proprietor of the registered rentcharge if he is in adverse possession of the registered rentcharge from the date of the application until the last day of the period of two years beginning with the date of its rejection.

(2) However, a person may not make an application under this paragraph if—

(a) he is a defendant in proceedings by the registered proprietor of the registered rentcharge for recovery of the rent or to enter into possession of the land out of which the registered rentcharge issues,

(b) judgement in favour of the registered proprietor of the registered rentcharge in respect of proceedings of the nature mentioned in sub-paragraph (2)(a) has been given against him in the last two years, or

(c) the registered proprietor of the registered rentcharge of which that person was in adverse possession has entered into possession of the land out of which the registered rentcharge issues.

7. If a person makes an application under paragraph 6, he is entitled to be entered in the register as the new proprietor of the registered rentcharge.

Restriction on applications

8.—(1) No one may apply under this Schedule to be registered as the proprietor of a registered rentcharge during, or before the end of twelve months after the end of, any period in which the existing registered proprietor is for the purposes of the Limitation (Enemies and War Prisoners) Act 1945 (8 & 9 Geo. 6 c 16)—

(a) an enemy, or

(b) detained in enemy territory.

(2) No-one may apply under this Schedule to be registered as the proprietor of a registered rentcharge during any period in which the existing registered proprietor is—

(a) unable because of mental disability to make decisions about issues of the kind to which such an application would give rise, or

(b) unable to communicate such decisions because of mental disability or physical impairment.

(3) For the purposes of sub-paragraph (2), mental disability means a disability or disorder of the mind or brain, whether permanent or temporary, which results in an impairment or disturbance of mental functioning.

(4) Where it appears to the registrar that sub-paragraph (1) or (2) applies in relation to a registered rentcharge, he may include a note to that effect in the register.

Effect of registration

9.—(1) Where a person is registered as the proprietor of a registered rentcharge in pursuance of an application under this Schedule, the title by virtue of adverse possession which he had at the time of the application is extinguished.

(2) Subject to sub-paragraph (3), the registration of a person under this Schedule as the proprietor of a registered rentcharge does not affect the priority of any interest affecting the registered rentcharge.

(3) Subject to sub-paragraph (4), where a person is registered under this Schedule as the proprietor of a registered rentcharge, the registered rentcharge is vested in him free of any registered charge affecting the registered rentcharge immediately before his registration.

(4) Sub-paragraph (3) does not apply where registration as proprietor is in pursuance of an application determined by reference to whether either of the conditions in paragraph 5 applies.

Apportionment and discharge of charges

10.—(1) Where—

(a) a registered rentcharge continues to be subject to a charge notwithstanding the registration of a person under this Schedule as the proprietor, and

(b) the charge affects property other than the registered rentcharge,

the proprietor of the registered rentcharge may require the chargee to apportion the amount secured by the charge at that time between the registered rentcharge and the other property on the basis of their respective values.

(2) The person requiring the apportionment is entitled to a discharge of his registered rentcharge from the charge on payment of—

(a) the amount apportioned to the registered rentcharge, and

(b) the costs incurred by the chargee as a result of the apportionment.

(3) On a discharge under this paragraph, the liability of the chargor to the chargee is reduced by the amount apportioned to the registered rentcharge.

(4) Rules may make provision about apportionment under this paragraph, in particular, provision about—

- (a) procedure,
- (b) valuation,
- (c) calculation of costs payable under sub-paragraph (2)(b), and
- (d) payment of the costs of the chargor.

Meaning of "adverse possession"

11.—(1) A person is in adverse possession of a registered rentcharge for the purposes of this Schedule if, but for section 96, a period of limitation under section 15 of the Limitation Act 1980 (c 58) would run in his favour in relation to the registered rentcharge.

(2) A person is also to be regarded for those purposes as having been in adverse possession of a registered rentcharge—

- (a) where he is the successor in title to the registered rentcharge, during any period of adverse possession by a predecessor in title to that registered rentcharge, or
- (b) during any period of adverse possession by another person which comes between, and is continuous with, periods of adverse possession of his own.

(3) In determining whether for the purposes of this paragraph a period of limitation would run under section 15 of the Limitation Act 1980, there are to be disregarded—

- (a) the commencement of any legal proceedings, and
- (b) paragraph 6 of Schedule 1 to that Act.

Trusts

12. A person is not to be regarded as being in adverse possession of a registered rentcharge for the purposes of this Schedule at any time when the registered rentcharge is subject to a trust, unless the interest of each of the beneficiaries in the registered rentcharge is an interest in possession.

[3306]

SCHEDULE 9
FORMS OF EXECUTION

rule 206(3)

Note: All dispositions other than assents must be executed as a deed. In the case of an assent the words "as a deed" may be omitted.

A Where the instrument is to be executed personally by an individual—

Signed as a deed by (*full name of individual*) in the presence of:	*Signature*

Signature of witness ....

Name (in BLOCK CAPITALS)

....

Address ....

....

....

B Where the instrument is to be executed by an individual directing another to sign on his behalf—

Signed as a deed by (*full name of person signing*) at the direction and on behalf of (*full name of individual*) in [his][her] presence and in the presence of:	*Sign here the name of the individual and your own name,* *eg:* John Smith by Jane Brown

Signature of first witness ....

Name (in BLOCK CAPITALS)

....

Address ....

....

....

Signature of second witness ....
Name (in BLOCK CAPITALS)
....
Address ....
....
....

[C Where the instrument is to be executed by a company registered under the Companies Acts, or an unregistered company, using its common seal

The common seal of (*name of company*) was affixed in the presence of:	*Common seal of company*

Signature of director..
Signature of [director] [secretary]..]

....
Signature of director

....
Signature of secretary

D[(i)] Where the instrument is to be executed by a company registered under the Companies Acts, or an unregistered company, without using a common seal—

[Executed] as a deed by (*name of company*) acting by [a director and its secretary][two directors]	*Signature* Director *Signature* [Secretary][Director]

[D(ii) Where the instrument is to be executed by a company registered under the Companies Acts, acting by a director—

[Executed] as a deed by (*name of company*) acting by a director in the presence of:

	Signature Director

Signature of witness..
Name (in block capitals)..
Address..
....]

E Where the instrument is to be executed on behalf of an overseas company without using a common seal—

Signed as a deed on behalf of (*name of company*), a company incorporated in (*territory*), by (*full name(s) of person(s) signing*), being [a] person[s] who, in accordance with the laws of that territory, [is][are] acting under the authority of the company.	*Signature* Authorised [signatory][signatories]

Note: In the case of an overseas company having a common seal, the form of execution appropriate to a company registered under the Companies Acts may be used, with such adaptations as may be necessary, in place of execution by a person or persons acting under the authority of the company.

F Where the instrument is to be executed by a limited liability partnership incorporated under the Limited Liability Partnerships Act 2000, without using a common seal—

Signed as a deed by (*name of limited liability partnership*) acting by two members	*Signature* Member *Signature* Member

[3307]

NOTES

Form C: substituted by SI 2008/1919, r 4(9), Sch 6, para 1.
Form D heading: reference to "(i)" in square brackets inserted by SI 2008/1919, r 4(9), Sch 6, para 2(a).
Form D(i): word "Executed" in square brackets substituted by SI 2008/1919, r 4(9), Sch 6, para 2(b).
Form D(ii): inserted by SI 2008/1919, r 4(9), Sch 6, para 2(c).

LAND REGISTRATION ACT 2002 (TRANSITIONAL PROVISIONS) ORDER 2003

(SI 2003/1953)

NOTES

Made: 10 July 2003.
Authority: Land Registration Act 2002, s 134.
Commencement: 13 October 2003.

Preliminary

1 Citation, commencement and interpretation

(1) This Order may be cited as the Land Registration Act 2002 (Transitional Provisions) Order 2003 and shall come into force on the day that section 1 of the Act comes into force.

(2) In this Order—

"the 1925 Act" means the Land Registration Act 1925,
"the 1925 Rules" means the Land Registration Rules 1925,
"the 1972 Rules" means the Land Registration (Souvenir Land) Rules 1972,
"the 1991 Rules" means the Land Registration (Open Register) Rules 1991,
"the 1993 Rules" means the Land Registration (Official Searches) Rules 1993,
"the 2003 Rules" means the Land Registration Rules 2003,
"the Act" means the Land Registration Act 2002,
"commencement" means the day when section 1 of the Act comes into force,
"the Regulations" means the Land Registration (Conduct of Business) Regulations 2000.

[3308]

General and administrative

2 Chief Land Registrar

The person holding the office of Chief Land Registrar immediately before commencement shall continue to be the Chief Land Registrar notwithstanding that he has not been appointed under section 99(3) of the Act.

[3309]

3 Extension of effect of statutory provisions—first registration, dealings, etc

(1) Notwithstanding the repeal of the 1925 Act, that Act shall continue to have effect in relation to any application referred to in paragraph (2) that is pending immediately before commencement.

(2) Paragraph (1) applies to—

(a) an application for the first registration of land,
(b) any other application (whether or not being one within paragraphs 5 or 6 of Schedule 12 to the Act) that, if completed, would result in a change to the register.

(3) Paragraph (1) is subject to articles 5, 7 and 24.

[3310]

PART II STATUTORY INSTRUMENTS

4 Extension of effect of statutory provisions for the purpose of the Order

Notwithstanding the repeal of the 1925 Act, that Act shall continue in force to the extent necessary to enable the remaining provisions of this Order to have effect.

[3311]

5 Notices

(1) The 2003 Rules apply to the giving of—

(a) any notice under this Order, and

(b) any notice under the 1925 Act, as continued under Schedule 12 to the Act or article 3, other than a notice to which paragraph (3) applies.

(2) Section 79 of the 1925 Act does not apply to any notice to which paragraph (1)(b) applies.

(3) Subject to the modification referred to in paragraph (4), sub-sections (1) and (2) of section 30 of the 1925 Act apply to any notice required to be given under sub-section (1) of that section, as continued under article 3.

(4) The modification referred to in paragraph (3) is the omission of the words "by registered post" from section 30(1) of the 1925 Act.

[3312]

Disputes, objections, appeals and proceedings

6 Hearing of existing disputes

(1) This article applies to any pending application in relation to which there is, immediately before commencement, a dispute to which rule 299(1) of the 1925 Rules applies that has not been finally disposed of.

(2) For the purposes of paragraph (1) there is a dispute to which rule 299(1) of the 1925 Rules applies where—

(a) in relation to a caution lodged under section 54 of the 1925 Act or rule 215(2) of the 1925 Rules, an application has been lodged that has resulted in the notice referred to in rule 218 of the 1925 Rules being issued before commencement, provided that (whether before or after commencement) the registrar is satisfied that cause has been shown under rule 219(3) of the 1925 Rules, and

(b) in the case of any other pending application, a person has, before commencement, objected to the application under rule 298(1) of the 1925 Rules, provided that the registrar is satisfied subsequently that the objection cannot be treated as groundless under rule 298(4) of the 1925 Rules.

(3) Neither the objection that has led to the dispute, nor any subsequent objection to the same application, shall constitute an objection for the purpose of section 73 of the Act.

(4) The registrar must deal with or continue to deal with the existing dispute and any dispute resulting from any subsequent objection to the same application, in accordance with rule 299 of the 1925 Rules and, where appropriate, the Land Registration (Hearings Procedure) Rules 2000 until the dispute has been finally disposed of.

(5) Subject to the modifications referred to in paragraph (6), the Regulations shall continue to apply in relation to any dispute referred to in paragraph (1) to enable relevant acts of the registrar to which those regulations relate to be done or continue to be done by a person nominated by the registrar under the Regulations.

(6) The modifications referred to in paragraph (5) are—

(a) substitution of the following sub-paragraph for regulation 2(d) of the Regulations—

"(d) "qualified officer" means a member of staff of the land registry who holds a 10 year general qualification within the meaning of section 71 of the Courts and Legal Services Act 1990; and" ,

(b) substitution of the words "qualified officer" for the words "qualified registrar" where they occur in regulations 3(1), 5(1) and 6(1) of the Regulations,

(c) substitution of the word "person" for the word "registrar" where it occurs in regulations 3(2), 5(2) and 6(2) of the Regulations, and

(d) substitution of the words "qualified officer" for the word "registrar " where it occurs in regulations 5(3) and 6(3) of the Regulations.

[3313]

7 Objection after commencement

(1) This article applies to any application that is pending immediately before commencement in relation to which an objection is made after commencement that is not an objection to which article 6(3) applies.

(2) Notwithstanding paragraph 5 of Schedule 12 to the Act, the objection shall constitute an objection to which section 73 of the Act applies.

[3314]

8 Appeals

Rule 300 of the 1925 Rules (Appeal to the court) shall continue to have effect in relation to—

(a) any decision by the registrar under rule 298(4) of the 1925 Rules that an objection is groundless (whether the decision is made before commencement, or after commencement in relation to an application that is pending immediately before commencement), and

(b) any decision or order by the registrar under rule 299 of the 1925 Rules (whether made before commencement, or after commencement in relation to a dispute to which article 6 applies).

[3315]

9 Legal Proceedings

(1) This article applies to any proceedings which were instituted before commencement but which have not been concluded immediately before commencement.

(2) Any proceedings to which paragraph (1) applies may be continued until concluded, whether by final determination by the court or otherwise, as if the 2002 Act had not been passed.

(3) Where in any proceedings the court gives judgement or makes an order, or has already done so before commencement, and the effect of the judgement or order is to require an entry or cancellation to be made in the register or the register to be rectified or altered, then the proceedings shall not be treated as concluded for the purpose of paragraphs (1) and (2) until the entry or cancellation has been made, or the register rectified or altered, as required by the court.

(4) Paragraphs (2) and (3) have effect without prejudice to the need for any order of the court or alteration of the register made after commencement to comply with rule 127 of the 2003 Rules.

(5) In this article—

"court" has the same meaning as in the 1925 Act, and

"proceedings" means any proceedings within the jurisdiction of the court by virtue of a provision of the 1925 Act.

[3316]

Souvenir land

10 Souvenir land—application of articles and definitions

(1) Articles 11, 12 and 13 apply where—

(a) there is in force in relation to registered land immediately before commencement a declaration by the registrar under rule 3 of the 1972 Rules, and

(b) particulars of the declaration have been entered in the register under rule 6 of those rules.

(2) In articles 11, 12 and 13—

"declaration" means the declaration by the registrar under rule 3 of the 1972 Rules,

"proprietor" in relation to souvenir land means the registered proprietor or, where the registered proprietor has died, been made bankrupt or, being a corporate body, has been dissolved, the person who would be entitled to be registered as proprietor in his place but for any unregistered transaction effected after the declaration was made,

"souvenir land" means the registered land subject to a declaration,

"third party" means a person other than the proprietor.

[3317]

11 Souvenir land—restriction on dispositions

(1) Where any unregistered transaction with souvenir land has been effected after the declaration was made and has resulted in one or more third parties becoming entitled to apply to be registered as proprietor of any part or parts of the land, the proprietor must not dispose of that land otherwise than in a manner that gives effect in the register to the interests of the third parties.

(2) The particulars of a declaration entered in the individual register of any souvenir land shall take effect after commencement as if there were a restriction in the proprietorship register in the following terms—

> "No disposition is to be registered without the consent of the person or persons (if any) entitled to apply to be registered as proprietor of the land disposed of, or any part of it, as the result of any unregistered transaction effected since [*date*] being the date when a declaration made under rule 3 of the Land Registration (Souvenir Land) Rules 1972 was noted in the register.".

(3) The registrar may amend the registered title to any souvenir land so as to substitute for the particulars of the declaration a restriction in the terms set out in paragraph (2).

[3318]

12 Application to cancel entries relating to souvenir land

(1) A proprietor who claims that there has been no unregistered transaction with the souvenir land, or a particular part of the land, after the declaration was made, so that no third party has become entitled to be registered as proprietor of it, may apply in Form RX3 in Schedule 1 to the 2003 Rules in relation to that land to cancel in the register the particulars of the declaration or, where the registrar has registered a restriction in substitution for those particulars under article 11(3), that restriction.

(2) If the registrar is satisfied that there has been no such transaction as is referred to in paragraph (1), he must—

(a) where the application relates to the whole of the land in a registered title, cancel the relevant entry in the register,

(b) where the application relates to part only of the land in a registered title, give effect to the application in the register in such manner as he thinks appropriate.

[3319]

13 Application for registration by a third party

(1) This article applies where, in relation to any souvenir land, a third party is able to satisfy the registrar that one or more unregistered transactions have been effected since the declaration was made and that, as a result of them and any other events that have taken place—

(a) the registered estate is now vested in him, or

(b) a legal estate derived (whether directly or indirectly) out of the land is vested in him, or

(c) a legal estate such as is referred to in sub-paragraph (a) or (b) has been transferred to him (either directly or indirectly) by the person in whom it has become vested.

(2) The third party may apply to be registered as the proprietor of a legal estate if that estate is one to which section 3 of the Act would apply if the estate were an unregistered estate within that section.

(3) Before determining an application under paragraph (2), the registrar must give notice of it to the person named in the proprietorship register as proprietor unless that person has consented to the application.

[3320]

Cautions

14 Cautions against first registration

(1) In relation to a caution against first registration lodged for registration before commencement, Part 5 of the 2003 Rules applies with the modifications set out in paragraph (2).

(2) The modifications referred to in paragraph (1) are—

(a) paragraphs (2) to (5) of rule 41 do not apply,

(b) in rule 51(1) of the 2003 Rules, the omission of the word "cautioner's".

[3321]

15 Cautions against conversion

(1) This article applies where, immediately before commencement, there is an entry in respect of a caution lodged under rule 215(2) of the 1925 Rules in the register of any title.

(2) In the event of an application to upgrade the title under any of subsections (1) to (5) of section 62 of the Act, the registrar shall, before determining the application, give notice of it to the person named in the entry referred to in paragraph (1).

(3) Where the person to whom notice is given, or any person deriving title under that person, responds to the notice by claiming any estate, right or interest in the land in the title, then, to the extent that the estate, right or interest subsists and is otherwise enforceable against the land, the claim is to be treated for the purpose of section 62(6) of the Act as one for an estate right or interest whose enforceability is preserved by virtue of the existing entry about the class of title.

[3322]

16 Mortgage cautions

(1) Subject to this article, mortgage cautions and sub-mortgage cautions entered in the register shall continue to have the same effect after commencement as they had immediately before commencement.

(2) Subject to paragraphs (3) and (4), the registrar must cancel a mortgage caution or a sub-mortgage caution where—

(a) the cautioner, or some other person who can satisfy the registrar that he is entitled to the benefit of the protected mortgage or protected sub-mortgage, makes an application to withdraw it in Form WCT in Schedule 1 to the 2003 Rules, or

(b) evidence is produced that satisfies the registrar, that the protected mortgage or protected sub-mortgage has been discharged, or

(c) an application is made to register the protected mortgage, and any protected sub-mortgage, under section 27 of the Act and the registrar approves the application.

(3) Where there is a sub-mortgage caution entered in the register and application is made to cancel the relevant mortgage caution under sub-paragraph (a) or (b) of paragraph (2), the registrar must give notice of the application to the sub-mortgage cautioner.

(4) An application to register a protected mortgage under section 27(2)(f) of the Act must comply with the 2003 Rules and be accompanied by—

(a) the original deed creating the protected mortgage, and

(b) where title to the protected mortgage is vested in someone other than the cautioner, the documents proving devolution of title to the applicant.

(5) When registering a protected mortgage, the registrar must make an entry showing that it has priority in relation to other entries in the register from the date that the mortgage caution was entered in the register.

(6) Where application is made to register a disposition of the registered estate or registered charge affected by a mortgage caution or sub-mortgage caution, the registrar must—

(a) give notice of the application to the cautioner,

(b) retain the mortgage caution or sub-mortgage caution in the register unless it is to be cancelled in accordance with paragraph (2).

(7) In this article—

"cautioner" means the person named in a mortgage caution or sub-mortgage caution,

"mortgage caution" means a caution entered in the register in a specially prescribed form under section 106 of the 1925 Act as originally enacted,

"protected mortgage" means the mortgage that is protected by a mortgage caution,

"protected sub-mortgage" means the sub-mortgage that is protected by a sub-mortgage caution,

"sub-mortgage caution" means a sub-mortgage caution to which rule 228 of the 1925 Rules applied before commencement.

[3323]

17 Modification of paragraph 2(3) of Schedule 12 to the Act

Paragraph 2(3) of Schedule 12 to the Act shall have the effect as if there were inserted at the end ", but with the substitution for the words in section 55(1) from "prescribed" to "served" of the words "period prescribed under paragraph 2(4) of Schedule 12 to the Land Registration Act 2002".".

[3324]

18 Non-standard restrictions in approved instruments

(1) This article applies where a person applies in an approved instrument to enter a restriction in the register and the registrar considers that there is a standard form of restriction which is to like or similar effect to the restriction applied for (or would be but for the fact that it does not purport to restrict the entry of a notice).

(2) Where this article applies—

(a) the registrar must enter in the register the standard form of restriction referred to in paragraph (1) instead of the restriction applied for,

(b) the application is to be treated as though it was an application for entry in the register of a standard form of restriction, and

(c) rule 92(1) of the 2003 rules does not apply to the application.

(3) In this article—

"approved instrument" means a charge, or transfer—

(a) which contains the application for the restriction applied for (whether in the body of the instrument or, in the case of a charge, in an incorporated document within the meaning of rule 139 of the 1925 Rules),

(b) the form of which (including the application for the restriction) has been approved by the registrar before commencement as capable of being accepted for registration, and

(c) in relation to which the approval referred to in sub-paragraph (b) has not been withdrawn, and

"standard form of restriction" means one referred to in rule 91 of the 2003 Rules.

[3325]

Outline applications

19 Outline applications

(1) This article applies where, immediately before commencement—

(a) there is in force a notice given under rule 83A(9) of the 1925 Rules that allows an outline application to be delivered in respect of any category of application (including, for the avoidance of doubt, a caution to which rule 215 of those rules applies),

(b) an outline application has been validly delivered in relation to such an application,

(c) the reserved period referred to in rule 83A(8) of the 1925 Rules has not expired, and

(d) the form required by rule 83A(6) of the 1925 Rules has not been lodged.

(2) Notwithstanding the repeal of the 1925 Act, the registrar must give effect to the application in the register as of the time at which the outline application was delivered, provided the applicant lodges the appropriate form required by rule 83A(6) of the 1925 Rules at the appropriate office before expiry of the reserved period referred to in rule 83A(8) of those rules and the application otherwise complies with those rules.

(3) In paragraph (2), "appropriate office" means the office of the land registry that, immediately before commencement, would have been the proper office within the meaning of rule 1(5A) of the 1925 Rules.

[3326]

Matrimonial home rights cautions

20 Matrimonial home rights cautions

(1) The registrar shall not be required, on the application of the proprietor of the registered estate affected, to serve the notice referred to in rule 223 of the 2003 Rules in relation to a matrimonial caution except upon production of—

(a) a release in writing of the matrimonial home rights protected by the matrimonial caution, or

(b) a statutory declaration that, as to the whole or any part of the land to which the matrimonial caution relates, no charge under section 2 of the Matrimonial Homes Act 1967, section 2 of the Matrimonial Homes Act 1983 or section 31 of the Family Law Act 1996 has ever arisen or, if such a charge has arisen, it is no longer subsisting.

(2) In this article "matrimonial caution" means a caution registered under section 2(7) of the Matrimonial Homes Act 1967 before 14th February 1983 which remains in the register after commencement.

[3327]

Index of relating franchises and manors

21 Index of relating franchises and manors

(1) As soon as practicable after commencement, the registrar must take such steps as he considers appropriate to create the index of relating franchises and manors from the material parts of the index map maintained by the registrar under rule 8 of the 1925 Rules and other relevant information under his control in such a form that it complies with rule 10(1)(b).

(2) Rule 10(1)(b) shall not have effect until the index of relating franchises and manors has been created so as to comply with it.

(3) Until the index of relating franchises and manors has been created so as to comply with rule 10(1)(b), the registrar must ensure that official certificates of the result of searches of the index of relating franchises and manors issued in accordance with rule 146(3) of the 2003 Rules contain the same information as if the index of relating franchises and manors had been so created.

(4) In this article—

"index of relating franchises and manors" means the index to be kept under rule 10(1)(b), and

"rule 10(1)(b)" means rule 10(1)(b) of the 2003 Rules.

[3328]

Compulsory first registration

22 Dispositions void under section 123A of the 1925 Act

(1) After commencement, a void disposition is to be treated for all purposes as an event to which the requirement of registration applied and as a transfer, grant or creation that has become void as a result of the application of section 7(1) of the Act.

(2) In this article "void disposition" means a disposition of unregistered land that, before commencement, has become void as a result of the application of section 123A(5) of the 1925 Act.

[3329]

23 Other dispositions affected by section 123A of the 1925 Act

(1) Subject to paragraph (2), a relevant disposition is to be treated for all purposes after commencement as an event to which the requirement of registration applies.

(2) For the purposes of section 6(4) of the Act, the period for registration is the period that expires at the end of the applicable period referred to in section 123A(3) of the 1925 Act, or such longer period as the registrar may provide under section 6(5) of the Act.

(3) In this article "relevant disposition" means a disposition of unregistered land where—

(a) before commencement section 123A of the 1925 Act applied to it,

(b) no application to register the relevant legal estate in accordance with section 123A(2) of the 1925 Act had been made before commencement, and

(c) immediately before commencement the applicable period referred to in section 123A(3) of the 1925 Act had not expired.

[3330]

Land and charge certificates

24 Abolition of land and charge certificates

(1) Notwithstanding paragraph 5 of Schedule 12 to the Act, Part V of the 1925 Act shall cease to apply in relation to any application that is pending immediately before commencement.

(2) Rules 203 and 204 of the 2003 Rules do not apply to—

(a) any land certificate or charge certificate held by the registrar immediately before commencement, or

(b) any land certificate or charge certificate lodged in connection with any application, including any application that is pending immediately before commencement, or

(c) any document incorporated in any land certificate or charge certificate.

(3) The registrar may destroy—

(a) any land certificate or charge certificate held by him or which comes into his possession,

(b) any document incorporated in such a land certificate or charge certificate.

(4) Paragraph (3) applies notwithstanding an entry in the register to which paragraph 3 of Schedule 12 to the Act applies but without prejudice to the continuing effect of such an entry.

[3331]

Obligation to make further advances

25 Obligation to make further advances

Where, immediately before commencement, an obligation to make a further advance is noted in the register under section 30(3) of the 1925 Act, the obligation is to be treated after commencement as entered in the register according to rules for the purpose of section 49(3)(b) of the Act.

[3332]

Forms

26 Period of grace for use of old forms

(1) Subject to paragraph (3), an applicant may use in place of any new form the relevant old form—

(a) for the period of 3 months following commencement, and

(b) thereafter, where use of the relevant old form is expressly required by law or under the terms of a valid contract entered into before commencement.

(2) Where the relevant old form is used in accordance with paragraph (1) the 2003 Rules apply to the use of that form as they would apply to the use of the new form.

(3) Where there is an entry in Column 3 in the Schedule, paragraph (1) only applies to the use of the relevant old form—

(a) where the entry limits use of the relevant old form to particular cases, in those cases specified in the entry, and

(b) where the entry places an additional requirement on the applicant, if the applicant complies with that requirement.

(4) In this article—

"new form" means a form prescribed by the 2003 Rules that is referred to in Column 1 in the Schedule, and

"relevant old form" in relation to any particular new form means the form prescribed by the 1925 Rules, the 1991 Rules, the 1993 Rules or the Land Registration (Matrimonial Home Rights) Rules 1997 (as the case may be) that is shown against the new form in Column 2 in the Schedule.

[3333]

27 Exclusion of Forms 112A, 112B and 112C from inspection or copying

Rules 133(2) and 135(2) of the 2003 Rules apply to any Form 112A, Form 112B or Form 112C, as lodged under the 1991 Rules or article 26, as they apply to any Form CIT.

[3334]

Official searches and official copies

28 Priority of unexpired official searches

(1) This article applies to an official search with priority made before commencement under the 1993 Rules whose priority period has not expired at commencement.

(2) Section 72 of the Act and rules 151 to 154 of the 2003 Rules (as appropriate) shall apply to the official search as if it had been made under Part 13 of the 2003 Rules but with the priority period being that which applied to it under the 1993 Rules.

[3335]

29 Office copies issued before commencement

Office copies of and extracts from the register and of and from documents, to which section 113 of the 1925 Act applied before commencement, are to be treated for all purposes after commencement as official copies to which section 67 of the Act applies.

[3336]

SCHEDULE

Article 26

Column 1 *New form*	*Column 2* *Relevant old form*	*Column 3* *Requirements or limitations*
AP1	AP1	***Requirements—*** (1) Where a fee is payable then the applicant must lodge with the form a cheque or postal order for the requisite fee or a request in writing for the fee to be paid by Direct Debit under an authorised agreement with the land registry. (2) The full name of the person applying to change the register must be inserted in the form. (3) Where the application is to register a registrable disposition, but there are no disclosable overriding interests, the form must include a statement to that effect, or be accompanied by such a statement in writing signed by the applicant.
AS1	AS1	
AS2	AS2	
AS3	AS3	
CH1	113	***Requirement—*** Where a fee is payable then the applicant must lodge with the form a cheque or postal order for the requisite fee or a request in writing for the fee to be paid by Direct Debit under an authorised agreement with the land registry.
CI	102	

Column 1 ***New form***	*Column 2* ***Relevant old form***	*Column 3* ***Requirements or limitations***
CIT	112A, or 112B, or 112C	***Limitation—*** The relevant old form may only be used where it is signed by a qualifying applicant (within the meaning of rule 140 of the 2003 Rules) who is able to complete one or more of the certificates contained in the particular form.
CN1	CN1	***Limitation—*** The relevant old form may only be used where application is made to cancel notice of an unregistered lease or rentcharge. ***Requirement—*** Where a fee is payable then the applicant must lodge with the form a cheque or postal order for the requisite fee or a request in writing for the fee to be paid by Direct Debit under an authorised agreement with the land registry.
CT1	CT1	***Limitation—*** The relevant old form may not be used (a) Where the estate affected by the caution is a rentcharge, a franchise or a profit a prendre in gross, or (b) Where the applicant wishes to provide a certificate by a conveyancer as to the cautioner's interest in place of a statutory declaration. ***Requirements—*** (1) The applicant must lodge with the form a cheque or postal order for the fee payable or a request in writing for the fee to be paid by Direct Debit under an authorised agreement with the land registry. (2) Where the estate affected by the caution is a lease, the applicant must add a note as to whether or not the lease is discontinuous.
DL	DL	***Requirement—*** The applicant must leave panels 2 and 3 of the relevant old form blank and use the accompanying application form to provide the relevant information.
DS1	DS1	
DS2	DS2	***Requirement—*** The full name of the applicant must be inserted in the form.
DS3	DS3	

PART II STATUTORY INSTRUMENTS

Column 1 ***New form***	*Column 2* ***Relevant old form***	*Column 3* ***Requirements or limitations***
FR1	FR1	***Requirements—*** (1) The applicant must lodge with the form a cheque or postal order for the fee payable or a request in writing for the fee to be paid by Direct Debit under an authorised agreement with the land registry. (2) The full name of the applicant must be inserted in the form. (3) Where there are no disclosable overriding interests, the form must include a statement to that effect, or be accompanied by such a statement in writing signed by the applicant.
MH1	MH1	***Limitation—*** The relevant old form may not be used where the applicant wishes to provide a certificate by a conveyancer as to the existence of an order made under section 33(5) of the Family Law Act 1996.
MH2	MH2	***Limitation—*** The relevant old form may not be used where the applicant wishes to provide a certificate by a conveyancer as to the existence of an order made under section 33(5) of the Family Law Act 1996.
MH3	MH3	
OC1	109	***Requirements—*** (1) Where a title number is not quoted and the application relates to a caution against first registration, a rentcharge, a franchise, a profit a prendre in gross or a manor, panel 6 of the relevant old form must be amended accordingly. (2) Where the applicant wishes to apply for a certificate of inspection of a title plan, the words "Form 102" in panel 3 of the relevant old form must be amended to read "Form CI".
OC2	110	***Limitation—*** The relevant old form may not be used to apply for an official copy of any document that is not referred to in the register.
OS1	94A	
OS2	94B	
OS3	94C	

Column 1 **New form**	*Column 2* **Relevant old form**	*Column 3* **Requirements or limitations**
PIC		***Limitation—*** The relevant old form may not be used to apply for personal inspection of any document that is not referred to in the register.
PN1	104	
SIM	96	
TP1	TP1	
TP2	TP2	
TP3	TP3	
TR1	TR1	
TR2	TR2	
TR3	TR3	
TR4	TR4	
WCT	WCT	

[3337]–[3341]

LAND REGISTRATION (REFERRAL TO THE ADJUDICATOR TO HM LAND REGISTRY) RULES 2003

(SI 2003/2114)

NOTES

Made: 2 August 2003.
Authority: Land Registration Act 2002, ss 73(8), 127.
Commencement: 13 October 2003.

1 Citation and commencement

These rules may be cited as the Land Registration (Referral to the Adjudicator to HM Land Registry) Rules 2003 and shall come into force on 13 October 2003.

[3342]

2 Interpretation

In these rules—

"the Act" means the Land Registration Act 2002;

"business day" means a day when the land registry is open to the public under rule 216 of the Land Registration Rules 2003;

"disputed application" means an application to the registrar under the Act to which an objection has been made;

"objection" means an objection made under section 73 of the Act;

"the parties" means the person who has made the disputed application and the person who has made an objection to that application.

[3343]

3 Procedure for referral to the adjudicator

(1) When the registrar is obliged to refer a matter to the adjudicator under section 73(7) of the Act, he must as soon as practicable—

(a) prepare a case summary containing the information set out in paragraph (2),
(b) send a copy of the case summary to the parties,
(c) give the parties an opportunity to make comments on the contents of the case summary in the manner, to the address, and within the time specified by him, and
(d) inform the parties in writing that the case summary together with copies of the documents listed in it will be sent to the adjudicator with the notice referred to in rule 5(2).

PART II STATUTORY INSTRUMENTS

(2) The case summary must contain the following information—

(a) the names of the parties,
(b) the addresses of the parties,
(c) details of their legal or other representatives (if any),
(d) a summary of the core facts,
(e) details of the disputed application,
(f) details of the objection to that application,
(g) a list of any documents that will be copied to the adjudicator, and
(h) anything else that the registrar may consider to be appropriate.

(3) The registrar may amend the case summary as he considers appropriate having considered any written comments made to him by the parties under paragraph (1)(c).

[3344]

4 Parties' addresses

(1) If the address of a party set out in the case summary does not comply with paragraph (2), that party must provide the registrar with one that does.

(2) An address complies with this paragraph if it—

(a) is a postal address in England and Wales, and
(b) is either that of the party or of his representative.

[3345]

5 Notice of referral to the adjudicator

(1) This rule applies—

(a) when the registrar has considered any written comments made by the parties under rule 3(1)(c), or
(b) if he has not received any comments from the parties within the time specified under rule 3(1)(c), on the expiry of that period, and
(c) when he has amended the case summary, if appropriate, under rule 3(3).

(2) The registrar must as soon as practicable—

(a) send to the adjudicator a written notice, accompanied by the documents set out in paragraph (3), informing him that the matter is referred to him under section 73(7) of the Act,
(b) inform the parties in writing that the matter has been referred to the adjudicator, and
(c) send the parties a copy of the case summary prepared under rule 3 in the form sent to the adjudicator.

(3) The notice sent to the adjudicator under paragraph (2)(a) must be accompanied by—

(a) the case summary prepared under rule 3 amended, if appropriate, by the registrar under rule 3(3), and
(b) copies of the documents listed in that case summary.

[3346]

6 Specified time periods

(1) For the purposes of rule 3(1)(c), the time specified by the registrar must not end before 12 noon on the fifteenth business day after the date on which the registrar sends the copy of the case summary to the relevant party under rule 3(1)(b) or such earlier time as the parties may agree.

(2) On and after the date specified in any notice given pursuant to rule 216(2) of the Land Registration Rules 2003, paragraph (1) shall have effect with the substitution of the words "eighteenth business day" for the words "fifteenth business day".

[3347]

ADJUDICATOR TO HER MAJESTY'S LAND REGISTRY (PRACTICE AND PROCEDURE) RULES 2003

(SI 2003/2171)

NOTES

Made: 14 August 2003.
Authority: Land Registration Act 2002, ss 109(2), (3), 110(2), (3), 114, 128(1), (2).
Commencement: 13 October 2003.

1 Citation and Commencement

These Rules may be cited as the Adjudicator to Her Majesty's Land Registry (Practice and Procedure) Rules 2003 and shall come into force on 13th October 2003.

[3348]

PART 1
INTRODUCTION

2 Interpretation

(1) In these Rules—

"applicant" means the party whom the adjudicator designates as such under rule 5 or under rule 24, or the party who makes a rectification application;

["document" means anything in which information is recorded in any form, and an obligation in these Rules to provide or allow access to a document or a copy of a document for any purpose means, unless the adjudicator directs otherwise, an obligation to provide access to such document or copy in a legible form or in a form which can be readily made into a legible form;]

"hearing" means a sitting of the adjudicator for the purpose of enabling the adjudicator to reach or announce a substantive decision, but does not include a sitting of the adjudicator solely in the exercise of one or more of the following powers—

(a) to consider an application, representation or objection made in the interim part of the proceedings;

(b) to reach a substantive decision without an oral hearing; or

(c) to consider whether to grant permission to appeal a decision or to stay the implementation of a decision pending the outcome of an appeal;

"matter" means the subject of either a reference or a rectification application;

"office copy" means an official copy of a document held or issued by a public authority;

"original application" means the application originally made to the registrar that resulted in a reference;

"proceedings" means, except in the expression "court proceedings", the proceedings of the matter before the adjudicator but does not include any negotiations, communications or proceedings that occurred prior to the reference or rectification application;

"record of matters" means a record of references, rectification applications and certain other applications and decisions, kept in accordance with these Rules and in particular in accordance with rule 46;

"rectification application" means an application made to rectify or set aside a document under section 108(2) for determination of the matter by the adjudicator;

"reference" means a reference from the registrar to the adjudicator under section 73(7) for determination of the matter by the adjudicator;

"respondent" means the party or parties who the adjudicator designates as such under rule 5 or rule 24, or the party or parties making an objection to a rectification application;

["statement of truth" means—

(a) in the case of a witness statement, a statement signed by the maker of the statement that the maker of the statement believes that the facts stated in the witness statement are true; or

(b) in the case of other documents, a statement that the party by whom or on whose behalf the document is submitted believes the facts stated in the document are true, signed by either—

(i) the party by whom or on whose behalf the document is submitted; or

(ii) that party's authorised representative, in which case the statement of truth must state the name of the representative and the relationship of the representative to the party;]

"substantive decision" means a decision of the adjudicator on the matter or on any substantive issue that arises in it but does not include any direction in interim parts of the proceedings[, any order made under rule 8(4) or 9(4),] or any order as to costs or any order as to costs thrown away;

"substantive order" means an order or direction that records and gives effect to a substantive decision;

"the Act" means the Land Registration Act 2002 and a reference to a section by number alone is a reference to a section of the Act;

"witness statement" means a written statement ... containing the evidence that the witness intends to give [and verified by a statement of truth]; and

"working day" means any day other than a Saturday or Sunday, Christmas Day, Good Friday or any other bank holiday.

(2) [For the purposes of these] Rules a person has a document ... in his possession or control if—

(a) it is in his physical possession;

(b) he has a right to possession of it; or

(c) he has a right to inspect or take copies of it.

[3349]

NOTES

Para (1): definition "document" inserted by SI 2008/1731, rr 4, 5(a)(i); definition "statement of truth" inserted by SI 2008/1731, rr 4, 5(a)(ii); in definition "substantive decision" words in square brackets inserted by SI 2008/1731, rr 4, 5(a)(iii); in definition "witness statement" words omitted revoked, and words in square brackets inserted, by SI 2008/1731, rr 4, 5(a)(iv); for transitional provisions see r 3(1), (2) thereof.

Para (2): words in square brackets substituted, and words omitted revoked, by SI 2008/1731, rr 4, 5(b); for transitional provisions see r 3(1), (2) thereof.

3 The overriding objective

(1) The overriding objective of these Rules is to enable the adjudicator to deal with matters justly.

(2) Dealing with a matter justly includes, so far as is practicable—
- (a) ensuring that the parties are on an equal footing;
- (b) saving expense;
- (c) dealing with the matter in ways that are proportionate—
  - (i) to the value of the land or other interests involved;
  - (ii) to the importance of the matter;
  - (iii) to the complexity of the issues in the matter; and
  - (iv) to the financial position of each party; and
- (d) ensuring that the matter is dealt with expeditiously and fairly.

(3) The adjudicator must seek to give effect to the overriding objective when he—
- (a) exercises any power given to him by these Rules; or
- (b) interprets these Rules.

(4) The parties are required to help the adjudicator to further the overriding objective.

[3350]

NOTES

Commencement: 13 October 2003.

PART 2
REFERENCES TO THE ADJUDICATOR

4 Scope of this Part

The rules in this Part apply to references.

[3351]

5 Notice of receipt by the adjudicator of a reference

Following receipt by the adjudicator of a reference, the adjudicator must—
- (a) enter the particulars of the reference in the record of matters; and
- (b) serve on the parties notice in writing of—
  - (i) the fact that the reference has been received by the adjudicator;
  - (ii) the date when the adjudicator received the reference;
  - (iii) the matter number allocated to the reference;
  - (iv) the name and any known address and address for service of the parties to the proceedings; and
  - (v) which party will be the applicant for the purposes of the proceedings and which party or parties will be the respondent.

[3352]

6 Direction to commence court proceedings under section 110(1)

Where the adjudicator intends to direct a party to commence court proceedings under section 110(1), the parties may make representations or objections but any representations or objections must be concerned with one or more of the following—
- (a) whether the adjudicator should make such a direction;
- (b) which party should be directed to commence court proceedings;
- (c) the time within which court proceedings should commence; and
- (d) the questions the court should determine.

[3353]

7 Notification to the adjudicator of court proceedings following a direction to commence court proceedings under section 110(1)

(1) In this Part—

"the date that the matter before the court is finally disposed of" means the earliest date by which the court proceedings relating to the matter or on the relevant part (including any court proceedings on or in consequence of an appeal) have been determined and any time for appealing or further appealing has expired;

"the relevant part" means the part of the matter in relation to which the adjudicator has directed a party under section 110(1) to commence court proceedings; and

"the final court order" means the order made by the court that records the court's final determination (on appeal or otherwise).

(2) A party who has been directed to commence court proceedings under section 110(1) must serve on the adjudicator—

(a) within 14 days of the commencement of the court proceedings, a written notice stating—

(i) that court proceedings have been issued in accordance with directions given by the adjudicator;

(ii) the date of issue of the court proceedings;

(iii) the names and any known addresses of the parties to the court proceedings;

(iv) the name of the court at which the court proceedings will be heard; and

(v) the case number allocated to the court proceedings;

(b) within 14 days of the date of the court's decision on any application for an extension of time, a copy of that decision; and

(c) within 14 days of the date that the matter before the court is finally disposed of, a copy of the final court order.

[3354]

8 Adjournment of proceedings before the adjudicator following a direction to commence court proceedings on the whole of the matter under section 110(1)

(1) This rule applies where the adjudicator has directed a party under section 110(1) to commence court proceedings for the court's decision on the whole of the matter.

(2) Once he has received notice under rule 7(2)(a) that court proceedings have been issued, the adjudicator must adjourn all of the proceedings before him pending the outcome of the court proceedings.

(3) [Subject to paragraph (4), once the adjudicator] has received a copy of the final court order [in accordance with rule 7(2)(c)] and unless the court directs otherwise, the adjudicator must close the proceedings before him without making a substantive decision.

[(4) Before closing the proceedings in accordance with paragraph (3) the adjudicator may make an order either with or without a hearing and either with or without giving prior notice to the parties if—

(a) such order is necessary, in addition to the final court order, to implement the decision of the court; and

(b) the adjudicator would have had the power to make such order if the adjudicator had made a substantive decision in relation to the proceedings.]

[3355]

NOTES

Para (3): first words in square brackets substituted, and second words in square brackets inserted, by SI 2008/1731, rr 4, 6(a); for transitional provisions see r 3(1), (2) thereof.

Para (4): inserted by SI 2008/1731, rr 4, 6(b); for transitional provisions see r 3(1), (2) thereof.

9 Adjournment of proceedings before the adjudicator following a direction to commence court proceedings on part of the matter under section 110(1)

(1) This rule applies where the adjudicator has directed a party under section 110(1) to commence court proceedings for the court's decision on the relevant part.

[(2) Once the adjudicator has received notice under rule 7(2)(a) that court proceedings have been issued in relation to the relevant part, the adjudicator must adjourn the proceedings brought under these Rules in relation to that part, pending the outcome of the court proceedings.]

(3) [Subject to paragraph (4), once the adjudicator] has received a copy of the final court order on the relevant part [in accordance with rule 7(2)(c)] and unless the court directs otherwise, the adjudicator must close the proceedings before him in relation to the relevant part without making a substantive decision on that relevant part.

[(3A) Before closing the proceedings in relation to the relevant part in accordance with paragraph (3) the adjudicator may make an order either with or without a hearing and either with or without giving prior notice to the parties if—

(a) such order is necessary, in addition to the final court order, to implement the decision of the court; and

(b) the adjudicator would have had the power to make such order if the adjudicator had made a substantive decision in relation to the relevant part.]

(4) The adjudicator may adjourn the proceedings in relation to any other part of the matter before him pending the outcome of the court proceedings.

(5) While the court proceedings are still ongoing, the party directed to commence court proceedings must notify the court of any substantive decision made by the adjudicator within 14 days of service on that party of the substantive decision.

[3356]

NOTES

Para (2): substituted by SI 2008/1731, rr 4, 7(a); for transitional provisions see r 3(1), (2) thereof.

Para (3): first words in square brackets substituted, and second words in square brackets inserted, by SI 2008/1731, rr 4, 7(b); for transitional provisions see r 3(1), (2) thereof.

Para (3A): inserted by SI 2008/1731, rr 4, 7(c); for transitional provisions see r 3(1), (2) thereof.

10 Notification where court proceedings are commenced otherwise than following a direction to commence court proceedings under section 110(1)

Where a party commences or has commenced court proceedings otherwise than following a direction under section 110(1) and those court proceedings concern or relate to the matter before the adjudicator, that party must serve—

(a) on the adjudicator within 14 days of the commencement of the court proceedings or, if later, within 7 days of service on that party of notification of the reference under rule 5(b), a written notice stating—
   (i) that court proceedings have been issued;
   (ii) the way and the extent to which the court proceedings concern or relate to the matter before the adjudicator;
   (iii) the date of issue of the court proceedings;
   (iv) the names and any known addresses of the parties to the court proceedings;
   (v) the name of the court at which the court proceedings will be heard; and
   (vi) the case number allocated to the court proceedings;

(b) on the adjudicator within 14 days of the date that the matter before the court is finally disposed of, a copy of the final court order; and

(c) on the court within 14 days of service on that party of such a decision, a copy of any substantive decision made by the adjudicator on the matter.

[3357]

11 Adjournment of proceedings before the adjudicator where court proceedings are commenced otherwise than following a direction to commence court proceedings under section 110(1)

Where court proceedings are commenced otherwise than following a direction to commence court proceedings under section 110(1), the adjudicator may adjourn the whole or part of the proceedings before him pending the outcome of the court proceedings.

[3358]

12 Applicant's statement of case and documents

Unless otherwise directed by the adjudicator, the applicant must serve on the adjudicator and each of the other parties within 28 days of service of the notification of the reference under rule 5(b)—

(a) his statement of case which must be in accordance with rule 14; and

[(b) copies of any documents in the applicant's possession or control which—
   (i) are central to the applicant's case; or
   (ii) the adjudicator or any other party to the proceedings will require in order properly to understand the applicant's statement of case].

[3359]

NOTES

Para (b): substituted by SI 2008/1731, rr 4, 8; for transitional provisions see r 3(1), (2) thereof.

13 Respondent's statement of case and documents

The respondent must serve on the adjudicator and each of the other parties within 28 days of service of the applicant's statement of case—

(a) his statement of case which must be in accordance with rule 14; and

[(b) copies of any documents in the respondent's possession or control which—
   (i) are central to the respondent's case; or
   (ii) the adjudicator or any other party to the proceedings will require in order properly to understand the respondent's statement of case].

[3360]

NOTES

Para (b): substituted by SI 2008/1731, rr 4, 9; for transitional provisions see r 3(1), (2) thereof.

14 Statement of case

(1) Where under these Rules a party is required to provide a statement of case, that statement of case must be in writing[, be verified by a statement of truth and include]—

(a) the name of the party and confirmation of the party's address for service;
(b) the party's reasons for supporting or objecting to the original application;
(c) the facts on which the party intends to rely in the proceedings; [and]
(d) …
(e) a list of witnesses that the party intends to call to give evidence in support of the party's case.

(2) If in relation to part only of the matter—

(a) a party has been directed to commence or has commenced court proceedings; or
(b) the adjudicator has adjourned proceedings before him,

the adjudicator may direct that the statement of case should contain the information specified in paragraphs (1)(b) to (1)(e) inclusive only in relation to the part of the matter that is not before the court for the court's decision or has not been adjourned before the adjudicator.

[3361]

NOTES

Para (1): words in square brackets substituted by SI 2008/1731, rr 4, 10(a); in sub-para (c) word in square brackets inserted by SI 2008/1731, rr 4, 10(b); sub-para (d) revoked by SI 2008/1731, rr 4, 10(c); for transitional provisions see r 3(1), (2) thereof.

PART 3
RECTIFICATION APPLICATION TO THE ADJUDICATOR TO RECTIFY OR SET ASIDE DOCUMENTS

15 Scope of this Part

The rules in this Part apply to rectification applications.

[3362]

16 Form and contents of a rectification application

(1) A rectification application must—

(a) be made in writing;
(b) be dated and [verified by a statement of truth];
(c) be addressed to the adjudicator;
(d) include the following information—
  (i) the name and address of the person or persons against whom the order is sought;
  (ii) details of the remedy being sought;
  (iii) the grounds on which the rectification application is based;
  (iv) …
  (v) a list of witnesses that the party intends to call to give evidence in support of the rectification application; and
  (vi) the applicant's name and address for service;
(e) include the following copies—
  [(i) copies of any documents in the applicant's possession or control which—
    (aa) are central to the applicant's case; or
    (bb) the adjudicator or any other party to the proceedings will require in order properly to understand the rectification application; and]
  (ii) a copy of the document to which the rectification application relates, or if a copy is not available, details of the document, which must include if available, its nature, its date, the parties to it and any version number or other similar identification number or code that it has; and
(f) be served on the adjudicator.

(2) Following receipt by the adjudicator of a rectification application, the adjudicator must enter the particulars of the rectification application in the record of matters.

(3) If, having considered the rectification application and made any enquiries he thinks necessary, the adjudicator is satisfied that it is groundless, he must reject the rectification application.

[3363]

NOTES

Para (1): in sub-para (b) words in square brackets substituted by SI 2008/1731, rr 4, 11(a); sub-para (d)(iv) revoked by SI 2008/1731, rr 4, 11(b); sub-para (e)(i) substituted by SI 2008/1731, rr 4, 11(c); for transitional provisions see r 3(1), (2) thereof.

17 Notice of a rectification application

(1) This rule does not apply where the adjudicator has rejected a rectification application under rule 16(3).

(2) Where a rectification application has been received by the adjudicator, he must [either serve, or direct the applicant to] serve on the person against whom the order is sought and on any other person who, in the opinion of the adjudicator, should be a party to the proceedings—

(a) written notice of the rectification application; and

(b) a copy of the rectification application.

(3) The … notice under paragraph (2)(a) [must specify] that if a party receiving the notice has any objection to the rectification application and that party wishes to lodge an objection, he must lodge his objection within 28 days of service of the notice under paragraph (2)(a).

[3364]

NOTES

Para (2): words in square brackets inserted by SI 2008/1731, rr 4, 12(a); for transitional provisions see r 3(1), (2) thereof.

Para (3): words omitted revoked, and words in square brackets inserted, by SI 2008/1731, rr 4, 12(b); for transitional provisions see r 3(1), (2) thereof.

18 Objection to a rectification application

A person lodges an objection under rule 17(3) if within 28 days of service of the notice under rule 17(2)(a) he serves—

(a) on the adjudicator—

[(i) a written statement addressed to the adjudicator, dated and verified by a statement of truth, setting out the grounds for the objection;]

(ii) …

[(iii) copies of any documents in the party's possession or control which—

(aa) are central to the party's case; or

(bb) the adjudicator or any other party to the proceedings will require in order properly to understand the party's written statement;]

(iv) a written list of witnesses that the party intends to call to give evidence in support of the objection; and

(v) written confirmation of his name and address for service; and

(b) on the other parties a copy of all the information and documents served on the adjudicator under sub-paragraph (a).

[3365]

NOTES

Para (a)(i) substituted by SI 2008/1731, rr 4, 13(a); for transitional provisions see r 3(1), (2) thereof.

Para (a)(ii) revoked by SI 2008/1731, rr 4, 13(b); for transitional provisions see r 3(1), (2) thereof.

Para (a)(iii) substituted by SI 2008/1731, rr 4, 13(c); for transitional provisions see r 3(1), (2) thereof.

PART 4
PREPARATION FOR DETERMINATION OF REFERENCES AND RECTIFICATION APPLICATIONS

19 Scope of this Part

This Part sets out the procedure for the preparation for the determination of references and rectification applications.

[3366]

[20 Directions

(1) The adjudicator may at any time, on the application of a party or otherwise, give directions to enable the parties to prepare for a hearing, or to assist the adjudicator to conduct the proceedings or determine any question in the proceedings with or without a hearing.

(2) Such directions may include, but are not limited to—

(a) a direction that the parties attend a case management conference or a pre-hearing review; and

(b) such other directions as are provided for in these Rules.]

[3367]

NOTES

Substituted by SI 2008/1731, rr 4, 14; for transitional provisions see r 3(1), (2) thereof.

21 Form of directions

(1) Any direction made by the adjudicator must be—

(a) in writing;
(b) dated; and
(c) except in the case of requirement notices under rule 28, served by him on—
(i) every party to the proceedings;
(ii) where the person who made the application, representation or objection that resulted in the direction was not a party, that person; and
(iii) where the direction requires the registrar to take action, the registrar.

(2) Directions containing a requirement must[, where appropriate,] include a statement of the possible consequences of failure to comply with the requirement within any time limit specified by these Rules, or imposed by the adjudicator.

(3) Directions requiring a party to provide or produce a document ... may require the party to provide or produce it to the adjudicator or to another party or both.

[3368]

NOTES

Para (2): words in square brackets inserted by SI 2008/1731, rr 4, 15(a); for transitional provisions see r 3(1), (2) thereof.

Para (3): words omitted revoked by SI 2008/1731, rr 4, 15(b); for transitional provisions see r 3(1), (2) thereof.

22 Consolidating proceedings

Where a reference or rectification application is related to another reference or rectification application and in the opinion of the adjudicator it is appropriate or practicable to do so, the adjudicator may direct that any or all of those related references or rectification applications be dealt with together.

[3369]

23 Intention to appear

The adjudicator may give directions requiring a party to state whether that party intends to—
(a) attend or be represented at the hearing; and
(b) call witnesses.

[3370]

24 Addition and substitution of parties

(1) The adjudicator may give one or more of the following directions—
(a) that any person be added as a new party to the proceedings, if it appears to the adjudicator desirable for that person to be made a party;
(b) that any person cease to be a party to the proceedings, if it appears to the adjudicator that it is not desirable for that person to remain a party; and
(c) that a new party be substituted for an existing party, if—
(i) the existing party's interest or liability has passed to the new party; and
(ii) it appears to the adjudicator desirable to do this to enable him to resolve the whole or part of the matter or any question of dispute in the proceedings.

(2) If the adjudicator directs that a new party is to be added to the proceedings, the adjudicator must specify—
(a) whether the new party is added as an applicant or a respondent; and
(b) how the new party is to be referred to.

(3) Each new party must be given a single identification that should be in accordance with the order in which they joined the proceedings, for example "second applicant" or "second respondent".

(4) If the adjudicator directs that a new party is to be substituted for an existing party, the adjudicator must specify which party the new party is to substitute, for example "respondent" or "second applicant".

(5) The adjudicator must [either serve, or direct one or more of the existing parties to] serve on each new party a copy of each of the following —
(a) the applicant's statement of case and copy documents served on the adjudicator under rule 12 or the applicant's rectification application served on the adjudicator under rule 16(1); and
(b) the respondent's statement of case and copy documents served on the adjudicator under rule 13 or the documents and information served by the respondent on the adjudicator under rule 18(a).

(6) If the new party is added to or substituted for parties to proceedings on a reference, the new party must serve on the adjudicator and each of the other parties within 28 days of service on him of the documents specified in paragraph (5)—
(a) his statement of case which must be in accordance with rule 14; and
[(b) copies of any documents in the new party's possession or control which—
(i) are central to the new party's case; or

(ii) the adjudicator or any other party to the proceedings will require in order properly to understand the new party's statement of case].

(7) If the new party is added to or substituted for parties to proceedings on a rectification application, the new party must serve on the adjudicator and each of the other parties, within 28 days of service on him of the documents specified in paragraph (5)—

(a) if the new party is added or substituted as an applicant, his rectification application which must be in accordance with rule 16(1); or

(b) if the new party is added or substituted as a respondent, his objection to the rectification application which must be in accordance with rule 18(a).

(8) If a continuing party wishes to respond to the documents specified in paragraph (6) or (7), he may apply to the adjudicator for leave to do so.

(9) If the adjudicator grants the requested leave to respond, the adjudicator must require the party requesting leave to respond to serve a copy of his response on the adjudicator and all other parties.

(10) [When directing] the addition or substitution of parties [or at any time thereafter] and if it is necessary to do so, the adjudicator may give consequential directions, including for —

(a) the preparation and updating of a list of parties;

(b) the delivery and service of documents; and

(c) the waiver of the requirement to supply copies of documents [under paragraph (6)(b)] where copies have already been [served by or on the adjudicator and each of the other parties] in the course of the proceedings.

[3371]

NOTES

Para (5): words in square brackets inserted by SI 2008/1731, rr 4, 16(a); for transitional provisions see r 3(1), (2) thereof.

Para (6): sub-para (b) substituted by SI 2008/1731, rr 4, 16(b); for transitional provisions see r 3(1), (2) thereof.

Para (10): words in first, third and fourth pairs of square brackets substituted and words in second pair of square brackets inserted by SI 2008/1731, rr 4, 16(c); for transitional provisions see r 3(1), (2) thereof.

25 Further information, supplementary statements and further responses to statements of case

The adjudicator may give directions requiring a party to provide one or more of the following—

(a) a statement of the facts in dispute or issues to be decided;

(b) a statement of the facts on which that party intends to rely and the allegations he intends to make;

(c) a summary of the arguments on which that party intends to rely; and

(d) such further information, responses to statements of case or supplementary statements as may reasonably be required for the determination of the whole or part of the matter or any question in dispute in the proceedings.

[3372]

26 Witness statements

The adjudicator may give directions requiring a party to provide a witness statement made by any witness on whose evidence that party intends to rely in the proceedings.

[3373]

27 Disclosure and inspection of documents

(1) Any document … supplied to the adjudicator or to a party under this rule or under rule 28 may only be used for the purpose of the proceedings in which it was disclosed.

[(2) Within 28 days after service of the respondent's statement of case under rule 13 or the lodging of an objection under rule 18, each party must—

(a) serve on the adjudicator and each of the other parties a list, which complies with rule 47, of all documents in that party's possession or control which—

(i) that party intends to rely upon in the proceedings;

(ii) adversely affect that party's own case;

(iii) adversely affect another party's case; or

(iv) support another party's case; and

(b) send to the adjudicator copies of all documents in the list served under sub-paragraph (a).

(3) Paragraph (4) applies to documents—

(a) referred to in a party's—

(i) statement of case;

(ii) rectification application under rule 16(1); or

(iii) written statement under rule 18(a)(i); or

(b) appearing on a list served by a party under paragraph (2).

(4) In addition to any other requirement in these rules to disclose or provide copies of documents, in relation to any document referred to in paragraph (3) each party must—

(a) permit any other party to inspect and take copies on reasonable notice and at a reasonable time and place; and

(b) provide a copy if requested by another party on payment by such other party of reasonable copying costs.

(5) Paragraphs (2), (3) and (4) are subject to any direction of the adjudicator to the contrary.

(6) The adjudicator may at any time give directions requiring a party to state whether that party has any particular document, or class of documents, in its possession or control and, if so, to comply with the requirements of paragraphs (2), (3) and (4) in relation to such documents as if one of the categories at paragraph (2)(a) applied to them.]

[3374]

NOTES

Para (1): words omitted revoked by SI 2008/1731, rr 4, 17(a); for transitional provisions see r 3(1), (2) thereof.

Paras (2)–(6): substituted, for para (2) as originally enacted, by SI 2008/1731, rr 4, 17(b); for transitional provisions see r 3(1), (2) thereof.

28 Requirement notices

(1) The adjudicator may, at any time, require the attendance of any person to give evidence or to produce any document … specified by the adjudicator which is in that person's possession or control.

(2) The adjudicator must make any such requirement in a requirement notice.

(3) The requirement notice must be in the form specified by the adjudicator provided that the requirement notice—

(a) is in writing;

(b) identifies the person who must comply with the requirement;

(c) identifies the matter to which the requirement relates;

(d) states the nature of the requirement being imposed by the adjudicator;

(e) specifies the time and place at which the adjudicator requires the person to attend and, if appropriate, produce any document …; and

(f) includes a statement of the possible consequences of failure to comply with the requirement notice.

(4) The party on whose behalf it is issued must serve the requirement notice.

(5) Subject to paragraph (6) a requirement notice will be binding only if, not less than 7 working days before the time that the person is required to attend—

(a) the requirement notice is served on that person; and

(b) except in the case where that person is a party to the proceedings, the necessary expenses of his attendance are offered and (unless he has refused the offer of payment of his expenses) paid to him.

(6) At any time before the time that the person is required to attend, that person and the party on whose behalf the requirement notice is issued may substitute a shorter period for the period of 7 working days specified in paragraph (5) by—

(a) agreeing in writing such shorter period; and

(b) before the time that the person is required to attend, serving a copy of that agreement on the adjudicator.

(7) Where a requirement has been imposed on a person under paragraph (1), that person may apply to the adjudicator for the requirement to be varied or set aside.

(8) Any application made under paragraph (7) must be made to the adjudicator before the time when the person is to comply with the requirement to which the application under paragraph (7) relates.

[3375]

NOTES

Para (1): words omitted revoked by SI 2008/1731, rr 4, 18; for transitional provisions see r 3(1), (2) thereof.

Para (3): in sub-para (e) words omitted revoked by SI 2008/1731, rr 4, 18; for transitional provisions see r 3(1), (2) thereof.

29 Estimate of length of hearing

The adjudicator may require the parties to provide an estimate of the length of the hearing.

[3376]

30 Site inspections

(1) In this rule—

"the appropriate party" is the party who is in occupation or has ownership or control of the property;

"the property" is the land or premises that the adjudicator wishes to inspect for the purposes of determining the whole or part of the matter; and

"a request for entry" is a written request from the adjudicator to the appropriate party, requesting permission for the adjudicator to enter onto and inspect the property and such a request may include a request to be accompanied by one or more of—

(a) another party;

(b) such number of the adjudicator's officers or staff as he considers necessary; and

(c) if a member of the [Administrative Justice and Tribunals Council] informs the adjudicator that he wishes to attend the inspection, that member.

(2) The adjudicator, at any time for the purpose of determining the whole or part of the matter, may serve a request for entry on an appropriate party.

(3) The request for entry must specify a time for the entry that, unless otherwise agreed in writing by the appropriate party, must be not earlier than 7 days after the date of service of the request for entry.

(4) The adjudicator must serve a copy of the request for entry on any party (other than the appropriate party) and any member of the [Administrative Justice and Tribunals Council] named in the request for entry and, if reasonably practicable to do so in the circumstances, must notify them of any change in the time specified.

(5) If the adjudicator makes a request for entry and the appropriate party withholds or refuses his consent to the whole or part of the request without reasonable excuse, the adjudicator may take such refusal into account when making his substantive decision.

(6) If a request for entry includes a request for a member of the [Administrative Justice and Tribunals Council] to accompany the adjudicator and the appropriate party consents to the presence of that member, then that member shall be entitled to attend the site inspection but must not take an active part in the inspection.

[3377]

NOTES

Para (1): in sub-para (c) words in square brackets substituted by SI 2008/1731, rr 4, 19; for transitional provisions see r 3(1), (2) thereof.

Paras (4), (6): words in square brackets substituted by SI 2008/1731, rr 4, 19; for transitional provisions see r 3(1), (2) thereof.

31 Preliminary issues

(1) At any time and on the application of a party or of his own motion, the adjudicator may dispose of any matter or matters that are in dispute as a preliminary issue.

(2) If in the opinion of the adjudicator the decision on the preliminary issue will dispose of the whole of the matter then the decision on the preliminary issue must be—

(a) made in accordance with the provisions in these Rules on substantive decisions; and

(b) treated as a substantive decision.

[3378]

PART 5
HEARINGS AND SUBSTANTIVE DECISIONS

32 Scope of this Part

This Part sets out the procedure for determination of references and rectification applications, the format of substantive decisions and substantive orders and rules on costs.

[3379]

[32A Summary disposal

(1) The adjudicator may summarily dispose of the proceedings or any particular issue in the proceedings on an application by a party or of its own motion if—

(a) the adjudicator considers that the applicant or respondent has no real prospect of succeeding in the proceedings or on the issue; and

(b) there is no other compelling reason why the proceedings or issue should not be disposed of summarily.

(2) Except with the permission of the adjudicator, an applicant may not apply for summary disposal until the respondent has served a statement of case or lodged an objection (as appropriate), or the respondent's time to do so has expired.

(3) A respondent may apply for summary disposal at any time after the applicant has served a statement of case or rectification application (as appropriate), or (in the case of service of a statement of case) the applicant's time to do so has expired.

(4) Paragraph (5) applies where—

(a) a respondent applies for summary disposal before serving a statement of case or lodging an objection (as appropriate) and before the time to do so has expired; and

(b) that application does not result in the disposal of the entire proceedings.

(5) In the circumstances described in paragraph (4) the respondent's time for serving a statement of case or lodging an objection is extended to—

(a) 28 days after service on the respondent of the adjudicator's decision in relation to the application for summary disposal; or

(b) such other time as the adjudicator directs.

(6) An application for summary disposal must include a witness statement in support of the application. That witness statement must state that the party making the application—

(a) believes that the other party has no real prospect of succeeding on the proceedings or on the issue to which the application relates; and

(b) knows of no other reason why the disposal of the proceedings or issue should not be disposed of summarily.

(7) When serving a notice under rule 51(5) or (7), or directing the party making the application to serve a notice under rule 51(5), and such notice relates in whole or in part to summary disposal, the adjudicator must give directions for the service of evidence by the parties and for the determination of the issue of summary disposal.

(8) When the adjudicator determines the issue of summary disposal the adjudicator may make an order—

(a) disposing of the proceedings or of any issue; or

(b) dismissing the application for or intention to consider summary disposal.

(9) Where an order made under paragraph (8) does not dispose of the entire proceedings, the adjudicator must give case management directions as to the future conduct of the proceedings.]

[3379A]

NOTES

Commencement: 28 July 2008.

Inserted by SI 2008/1781, rr 4, 40; for transitional provisions see r 3(1), (2) thereof.

33 Substantive decision without a hearing

(1) There is a presumption that a substantive decision is made following a hearing.

(2) Subject to paragraph (1), the adjudicator may make a substantive decision without a hearing if—

(a) he is satisfied that there is no important public interest consideration that requires a hearing in public; and

(b) unless paragraph (3) applies, he has served written notice on the parties in accordance with these Rules that he intends to make a substantive decision without a hearing or that he has received an application requesting that the substantive decision be made without a hearing and—

(i) the parties agree to the substantive decision being made without a hearing; or

(ii) the parties fail to object within the specified period for objection to the substantive decision being made without a hearing.

(3) The adjudicator is not required to serve notice under paragraph (2)(b) if all parties have requested the adjudicator to make the substantive decision without a hearing.

[3380]

34 Notice of hearing

(1) Where the adjudicator is to hold a hearing, he must serve written notice of his intention to hear on such parties as he considers necessary.

(2) The adjudicator must specify in the notice under paragraph (1), the date, time and location of the hearing.

(3) The adjudicator must serve the notice under paragraph (1)—

(a) no later than 28 days before the hearing; or

(b) before the expiry of such shorter notice period as agreed by all the parties on whom he intends to serve notice under paragraph (1).

[3381]

35 Representation at the hearing

(1) At the hearing a party may conduct his case himself or, subject to paragraph (2), be represented or assisted by any person, whether or not legally qualified.

(2) If, in any particular case, the adjudicator is satisfied that there is sufficient reason for doing so, he may refuse to permit a particular person to represent or assist a party at the hearing.

[3382]

36 Publication of hearings

The adjudicator must publish details of all listed hearings at the office of the adjudicator and, if different, the venue at which the hearing is to take place.

[3383]–[3384]

37 (*Revoked by SI 2008/1731, rr 4, 21; for transitional provisions see r 3(1), (2) thereof.*)

38 Absence of parties

(1) If any party does not attend and is not represented at any hearing of which notice has been served on him in accordance with these Rules, the adjudicator—

(a) may proceed with the hearing and reach a substantive decision in that party's absence if—

(i) the adjudicator is not satisfied that any reasons given for the absence are justified;

(ii) the absent party consents; or

(iii) it would be unjust to adjourn the hearing; or

(b) must otherwise adjourn the hearing.

(2) Following a decision by the adjudicator under paragraph (1) to proceed with or adjourn the hearing, the adjudicator may make such consequential directions as he sees fit.

[3385]

39 Substantive decision of the adjudicator

(1) Where there is a hearing, the substantive decision of the adjudicator may be given orally at the end of the hearing or reserved.

(2) A substantive decision of the adjudicator, whether made at a hearing or without a hearing, must be recorded in a substantive order.

(3) The adjudicator may not vary or set aside a substantive decision.

[3386]

40 Substantive orders and written reasons

(1) A substantive order must—

(a) be in writing;

(b) be dated;

[(c) be sealed and state the name of the person making the order;]

(d) state the substantive decision that has been reached;

(e) state any steps that must be taken to give effect to that substantive decision; and

(f) [where appropriate,] state the possible consequences of a party's failure to comply with the substantive order within any specified time limits.

(2) The substantive order must be served by the adjudicator on—

(a) every party to the proceedings; and

(b) where the substantive order requires the registrar to take action, the registrar.

(3) A substantive order requiring a party to provide or produce a document … may require the party to provide or produce it to any or all of the adjudicator, the registrar or another party.

(4) Unless the adjudicator directs otherwise, the substantive order must be publicly available.

(5) Where the substantive order is publicly available, the adjudicator may provide copies of it to the public on request.

(6) The adjudicator must give in writing to all parties his reasons for—

(a) his substantive decision; and

(b) any steps that must be taken to give effect to that substantive decision.

(7) The adjudicator's reasons referred to in paragraph (6) need not be given in the substantive order.

[3387]

NOTES

Para (1): sub-para (c) substituted by SI 2008/1731, rr 4, 22(a); for transitional provisions see r 3(1), (2) thereof.

Para (1): in sub-para (f) words in square brackets inserted by SI 2008/1731, rr 4, 22(b); for transitional provisions see r 3(1), (2) thereof.

Para (3): words omitted revoked by SI 2008/1731, rr 4, 22(c); for transitional provisions see r 3(1), (2) thereof.

41 Substantive orders on a reference that include requirements on the registrar

(1) Where the adjudicator has made a substantive decision on a reference, the substantive order giving effect to that substantive decision may include a requirement on the registrar to—

(a) give effect to the original application in whole or in part as if the objection to that original application had not been made; or

(b) cancel the original application in whole or in part.

(2) A requirement on the registrar under this rule may include—

(a) a condition that a specified entry be made on the register of any title affected; or

(b) a requirement to reject any future application of a specified kind by a named party to the proceedings—

(i) unconditionally; or

(ii) unless that party satisfies specified conditions.

[3388]

[41A Orders under rule 8(4) or 9(4)

An order made under rule 8(4) or 9(4) must—

(a) comply with the requirements of rule 40(1)(a), (b), (c) and (f), (2), (3), (4) and (5) as if it were a substantive order;

(b) identify the decision of the court which the order implements; and

(c) state the reasons why the order complies with rule 8(4)(a) or 9(4)(a).]

[3388A]

NOTES

Commencement: 25 July 2008.

Inserted by SI 2008/1731, rr 4, 23; for transitional provisions see r 3(1), (2) thereof.

42 Costs

(1) In this rule—

(a) "all the circumstances" are all the circumstances of the proceedings and include—

[(i) the conduct of the parties—

(aa) in respect of proceedings commenced by a reference, during (but not prior to) the proceedings; or

(bb) in respect of proceedings commenced by a rectification application, before and during the proceedings;]

(ii) whether a party has succeeded on part of his case, even if he has not been wholly successful; and

(iii) any representations made to the adjudicator by the parties; and

(b) the conduct of the parties … includes—

(i) whether it was reasonable for a party to raise, pursue or contest a particular allegation or issue;

(ii) the manner in which a party has pursued or defended his case or a particular allegation or issue; and

(iii) whether a party who has succeeded in his case in whole or in part exaggerated his case.

(2) The adjudicator may, on the application of a party or of his own motion, make an order as to costs.

(3) In deciding what order as to costs (if any) to make, the adjudicator must have regard to all the circumstances.

[(4) An order as to costs may, without limitation—

(a) require a party to pay the whole or a part of the costs of another party and—

(i) specify a fixed sum or proportion to be paid; or

(ii) specify that costs from or until a certain date are to be paid;

(b) if the adjudicator considers it impracticable to make an order in respect of the relevant part of a party's costs under paragraph (a), specify that costs relating to a distinct part of the proceedings are to be paid;

(c) specify an amount to be paid on account before costs are agreed or assessed; or

(d) specify the time within which costs are to be paid.]

[(5) The adjudicator may—

(a) summarily assess the whole or a part of a party's costs; or

(b) specify that, if the parties are unable to reach agreement on an amount to be paid, the whole or a part of a party's costs be assessed in a specified manner.]

(6) [An order as to costs must be recorded in a costs order and] must—

(a) be in writing;

PART II STATUTORY INSTRUMENTS

(b) be dated;
(c) be [sealed and state the name of the person making the order];
(d) state the order as to costs; and
(e) be served by the adjudicator on the parties.

(7) Where the costs are to be assessed by the adjudicator, he may assess the costs—
(a) on the standard basis; or
(b) on the indemnity basis,

but in either case the adjudicator will not allow costs that have been unreasonably incurred or are unreasonable in amount.

(8) The adjudicator must inform the parties of the basis on which he will be assessing the costs.

(9) Where the amount of the costs are to be assessed on the standard basis, the adjudicator must—
(a) only allow costs which are proportionate to the matters in issue; and
(b) resolve any doubt that he may have as to whether costs were reasonably incurred or reasonable and proportionate in favour of the paying party.

(10) In deciding whether costs assessed on the standard basis were either proportionately and reasonably incurred or proportionate and reasonable in amount, the adjudicator must have regard to all the circumstances.

[(11) Where costs are to be assessed on the indemnity basis, the adjudicator must resolve in favour of the receiving party any doubt as to the reasonableness of the incurring or the amount of the costs.]

(12) In deciding whether costs assessed on the indemnity basis were either reasonably incurred or reasonable in amount, the adjudicator must have regard to all the circumstances.

(13) Once the adjudicator has assessed the costs, he must serve on the parties written notice—
(a) of the amount which must be paid;
(b) by whom and to whom the amount must be paid; and
(c) if appropriate, the time by when the amount must be paid.

[3389]

NOTES

Para (1): sub-para (a)(i) substituted by SI 2008/1731, rr 4, 24(a); in sub-para (b) words omitted revoked by SI 2008/1731, rr 4, 24(b); for transitional provisions see r 3(1), (2) thereof.

Paras (4), (5): substituted by SI 2008/1731, rr 4, 24(c), (d); for transitional provisions see r 3(1), (2) thereof.

Para (6): words in square brackets substituted by SI 2008/1731, rr 4, 24(e)(i), (ii); for transitional provisions see r 3(1), (2) thereof.

Para (11): substituted by SI 2008/1731, rr 4, 24(f); for transitional provisions see r 3(1), (2) thereof.

43 Costs thrown away

(1) In this rule—

"costs thrown away" means costs of the proceedings resulting from any neglect or delay of the legal representative during (but not prior to) the proceedings and which—
(a) have been incurred by a party; or
(b) have been—
(i) paid by a party to another party; or
(ii) awarded to a party,
under an order made under rule 42;

"an order as to costs thrown away" means an order requiring the legal representative concerned to meet the whole or part of the costs thrown away; and

"the legal representative" means the legally qualified representative of a party.

(2) The adjudicator may, on the application of a party or otherwise, make an order as to costs thrown away provided the adjudicator is satisfied that—
(a) a party has incurred costs of the proceedings unnecessarily as a result of the neglect or delay of the legal representative; and
(b) it is just in all the circumstances for the legal representative to compensate the party who has incurred or paid the costs thrown away, for the whole or part of those costs.

(3) If the adjudicator has received an application for or proposes to make an order as to costs thrown away, he may give directions to the parties and the legal representative about the procedure to be followed to ensure that the issues are dealt with in a way that is fair and as simple and summary as the circumstances permit.

(4) An order as to costs thrown away may—
(a) specify the amount of costs to be paid by the legal representative; and
(b) if the adjudicator considers it appropriate, specify the time within which the costs are to be paid.

(5) An order as to costs thrown away must be recorded in a costs thrown away order.

(6) A costs thrown away order must—
- (a) be in writing;
- (b) be dated;
- (c) be [sealed and state the name of the person making the order];
- (d) state the order as to costs thrown away; and
- (e) be served by the adjudicator on the parties and the legal representative.

[3390]

NOTES

Para (6): in sub-para (c) words in square brackets substituted by SI 2008/1731, rr 4, 25; for transitional provisions see r 3(1), (2) thereof.

PART 6
APPEALS FROM ADJUDICATOR

44 Scope of this Part

This Part contains provisions in relation to appeals to the High Court of decisions by the adjudicator and includes provisions about the adjudicator staying implementation of his decision pending the outcome of an appeal.

[3391]

45 Appeals to the High Court

(1) Where a party is granted permission to appeal, the adjudicator may, of his own motion or on the application of a party, stay the implementation of the whole or part of his decision pending the outcome of the appeal.

(2) A party who wishes to apply to the adjudicator to stay the implementation of the whole or part of a decision pending the outcome of the appeal must make such an application to the adjudicator at the same time that he applies to the adjudicator for permission to appeal.

(3) Where a party applies under paragraph (2) to the adjudicator to stay implementation of the whole or part of a decision, that party must at the same time provide reasons for the application.

(4) Before reaching a decision as to whether to grant permission to appeal a decision or to stay implementation of a decision, the adjudicator must allow the parties the opportunity to make representations or objections.

(5) The adjudicator must serve written notice on the parties of any decision that he makes as to whether to grant permission to appeal or to stay the implementation of the whole or part of his decision pending the outcome of the appeal.

(6) Where the adjudicator's decision to grant permission to appeal or to stay implementation of a decision relates to a decision contained in a substantive order, the adjudicator must serve on the registrar a copy of the notice under paragraph (5).

(7) The notice under paragraph (5) must—
- (a) be in writing;
- (b) be dated;
- (c) specify the decision made by the adjudicator;
- (d) include the adjudicator's reasons for his decision; and
- (e) be [sealed and state the name of the person making the order].

[3392]

NOTES

Para (7): in sub-para (e) words in square brackets substituted by SI 2008/1731, rr 4, 26; for transitional provisions see r 3(1), (2) thereof.

PART 7
GENERAL

46 Record of matters

(1) The adjudicator must keep at his principal office a record of matters that records the particulars of all—
- (a) references;
- (b) rectification applications;
- (c) substantive decisions; and
- (d) all applications and decisions made under rule 45.

(2) Subject to paragraph (3), the record of matters must be open to the inspection of any person without charge at all reasonable hours on working days.

(3) Where the adjudicator is satisfied that it is just and reasonable to do so, the adjudicator may exclude from inspection any information contained in the record of matters.

(4) Depending on all the circumstances, it may be just and reasonable for the adjudicator to exclude from inspection any information contained in the record of matters if it is in the interest of morals, public order, national security, juveniles or the protection of the private lives of the parties to the proceedings, or where the adjudicator considers that publicity would prejudice the interests of justice.

[3393]

47 List of documents and documents

(1) For the purposes of these Rules, a list of documents must be in writing and[, subject to paragraph (1A),] must contain the following information where available in relation to each document —

(a) a brief description of the nature of the document;
(b) …
(c) whether the document is an original, a copy certified to be a true copy of the original, an office copy or another type of copy;
(d) the date of the document;
(e) the document parties or the original author and recipient of the document; and
(f) the version number or similar identification number or code of the document.

[(1A) If a large number of documents fall into a particular class, that class of documents may be listed in accordance with paragraph (1) as if it were an individual document.

(1B) If a class of documents is listed in accordance with paragraph (1A), the description of the class of documents must be sufficiently clear and precise to enable any party receiving the list to identify—

(a) the nature of the contents of each document included within that class of documents; and
(b) whether any particular document which exists is included within that class of documents.]

(2) Unless the adjudicator otherwise permits, where a document provided for the purposes of the proceedings is or contains a coloured map, plan or drawing, any copy provided of that map, plan or drawing must be in the same colours as the map, plan or drawing of which it is a copy (so for example, where a plan shows the boundary of a property in red, a copy of the plan must also show the boundary in red).

[3394]

NOTES

Para (1): words in square brackets inserted by SI 2008/1731, rr 4, 27(a)(i); sub-para (b) revoked by SI 2008/1731, rr 4, 27(a)(ii); for transitional provisions see r 3(1), (2) thereof.

Paras (1A), (1B): inserted by SI 2008/1731, rr 4, 27(b); for transitional provisions see r 3(1), (2) thereof.

48 Evidence

(1) The adjudicator may require any witness to give evidence on oath or affirmation and for that purpose there may be administered an oath or affirmation in due form.

(2) No person may be compelled to give any evidence or produce any document … that that person could not be compelled to give or produce on a trial of an action in a court of law in England and Wales.

[3395]

NOTES

Para (2): words omitted revoked by SI 2008/1731, rr 4, 28; for transitional provisions see r 3(1), (2) thereof.

49 Expert evidence

No party may call an expert, or submit an expert's report as evidence, without the adjudicator's permission.

[3396]

50 Service of documents

(1) A party's address for service must be a postal address in England and Wales.

(2) The address for service in paragraph (1) must be either that of the party or of the party's representative who has been appointed as his representative for the purposes of the proceedings.

(3) A party's address for service remains that party's address for service for the purposes of these Rules unless and until he serves on the adjudicator and the other parties notice of a different address for service.

(4) Any document to be served on or delivered to any person (other than the adjudicator) under these Rules may only be served—

(a) by first class post to his postal address given as his address for service;
(b) by leaving it at his address for service;
(c) … by document exchange;
(d) subject to paragraph (6), by fax;
(e) subject to paragraph (7), by email; or
(f) where no address for service has been given, by post to or leaving it at his registered office, principal place of business, head or main office or last known address, as appropriate.

(5) …

(6) A document may be served by fax on any person other than the adjudicator, to a fax number at the address for service for that person if, in advance, the recipient has informed the adjudicator and all parties in writing—
(a) that the recipient is willing to accept service by fax; and
(b) of the fax number to which the documents should be sent.

(7) A document may be served by email on any person other than the adjudicator, if, in advance, the recipient has informed the adjudicator and all parties in writing—
(a) that the recipient is willing to accept service by email;
(b) of the email address to which documents should be sent, which shall be deemed to be at the recipient's address for service; and
(c) if the recipient wishes to so specify, the format in which documents must be sent.

(8) Any document addressed to the adjudicator must be sent—
(a) by first class post to an address specified by the adjudicator; or
(b) by such other method as the adjudicator may specify, including document exchange, fax or email.

(9) Where under paragraph (8)(b) the adjudicator specifies another method of service, the adjudicator may—
(a) specify that that method may be used generally or only in relation to a certain document or documents;
(b) specify that the specified method is no longer available or substitute that specified method with another specified method; and
(c) make such directions in relation to the use of the specified method as he deems appropriate.

(10) Any document served on an unincorporated body may be sent to its secretary, manager or similar officer duly authorised to accept such service.

(11) Any document which is served in accordance with this rule shall be regarded as having been served on the day shown in the table below—

Method of service	*Day of service*
First class post to a postal address within England and Wales	The second working day after it was posted.
Leaving it at a postal address within England and Wales	The working day after it was left.
Document exchange within England and Wales	The second working day after it was left at the document exchange.
Fax	The working day after it was transmitted.
Email	The working day after it was transmitted.

(12) The adjudicator may direct that service under these Rules of any document may be dispensed with and in those circumstances may make such consequential directions as he deems appropriate.

[3397]

NOTES

Para (4): in sub-para (c) words omitted revoked by SI 2008/1731, rr 4, 29(a); for transitional provisions see r 3(1), (2) thereof.

Para (5): revoked by SI 2008/1731, rr 4, 29(b); for transitional provisions see r 3(1), (2) thereof.

51 Applications, actions by the adjudicator of his own motion, notification, representations and objections

(1) This rule does not apply to Part 3 and rule 45.

(2) An application to the adjudicator must—
(a) be in writing;

(b) state the name of the person applying or on whose behalf the application is made;
(c) be addressed to the adjudicator;
(d) state the nature of the application;
(e) state the reason or reasons for the application; and
(f) if any of the parties or persons who would be affected by the application consent to it, either—
(i) be signed by all the parties or persons who consent or their duly authorised representatives; or
(ii) have attached to it a copy of their written consent.

(3) The adjudicator may dispense with any or all of the requirements under paragraph (2)—
(a) in relation to an application made to the adjudicator at a time when all persons who would be affected by the application are present before the adjudicator; or
(b) if the adjudicator otherwise considers it appropriate or practicable to do so.

(4) For the purposes of paragraph (2)(f), the written consent referred to in that paragraph may be in the form of a letter, fax or email.

(5) If an application is not consented to by all persons who will be affected by the application then, subject to paragraph (10), the adjudicator must [either serve, or direct the party making the application to] serve written notice on persons who have not consented to the application but who would be affected by it[, and any such direction to the party making the application must include the information to be included in the notice under paragraph (6)(d)].

(6) [The] notice under paragraph (5) … must state —
(a) that the application has been made;
(b) details of the application;
(c) that the person has a right to make written objections to or representations about the application; and
(d) the period within which such objections or representations must be lodged with the adjudicator.

(7) If the adjudicator intends to act of his own motion under these Rules then, subject to paragraph (10), he must serve written notice of his intention on all persons who will be affected by the action.

(8) In the notice under paragraph (7) the adjudicator must state—
(a) that the adjudicator intends to take action of his own motion;
(b) the action the adjudicator intends to take;
(c) that a person has a right to make written objections or representations to the action that the adjudicator intends to take; and
(d) the period within which such objections or representations must be lodged with the adjudicator.

(9) A person lodges an objection or representation if within the specified period he serves—
(a) on the adjudicator a written statement setting out the grounds for his objection or representation; and
(b) on all the other persons who will be affected by the action a copy of the written statement served on the adjudicator under sub-paragraph (a).

(10) The adjudicator shall not be required to [serve, or direct the applicant to] serve notice under paragraphs (5) and (7) if, in the circumstances, he does not consider it appropriate or practicable to do so.

[(11) Paragraph (10) does not apply to notices—
(a) under paragraphs (5) or (7) which relate to a proposal that the adjudicator exercise the power under rule 32A(1); or
(b) required to be served by rule 33.]

[3398]

NOTES

Para (5): words in square brackets inserted by SI 2008/1731, rr 4, 30(a); for transitional provisions see r 3(1), (2) thereof.

Para (6): word in square brackets substituted, and words omitted revoked, by SI 2008/1731, rr 4, 30(b); for transitional provisions see r 3(1), (2) thereof.

Para (10): word in square brackets inserted by SI 2008/1731, rr 4, 30(c); for transitional provisions see r 3(1), (2) thereof.

Para (11): substituted by SI 2008/1731, rr 4, 30(d); for transitional provisions see r 3(1), (2) thereof.

52 Consideration by the adjudicator of applications (including applications for directions), representations and objections

(1) In relation to any application, representation or objection made to the adjudicator, unless—
(a) the adjudicator is satisfied that it is frivolous or vexatious; or

(b) it is received by the adjudicator after the expiry of any time limit specified for making that application, representation or objection,

the adjudicator must consider all applications, representations or objections made to him.

(2) If an application, representation or objection is received by the adjudicator after the expiry of any time limit specified for making it, the adjudicator may consider the application, representation or objection, but he is not bound to do so.

(3) In considering any application, representation or objection, the adjudicator must make all enquiries he thinks necessary and must, if required by these Rules or if he considers it necessary, give the person making the application, representation or objection and the parties or other persons who will be affected by it the opportunity to appear before him or to submit written representations.

(4) The adjudicator may decide to accept or reject an application, representation or objection in whole or in part.

(5) Following his consideration of any applications, representations or objections that are made to him, the adjudicator must notify the person who made the application, representation or objection and the parties and any other persons who will be affected by it, of his decision in accordance with these Rules.

[3399]

53 Adjournment

In addition to the powers and obligations to adjourn proceedings contained in Part 2 and rule 38, the adjudicator may adjourn the whole or part of the proceedings when and to the extent that he feels it reasonable to do so.

[3400]

54 Power to vary or set aside directions

Subject to these Rules, the adjudicator may at any time, on the application of a party or otherwise, vary or set aside directions made under these Rules.

[3401]

55 Failure to comply with a direction

(1) Where a party has failed to comply with a direction given by the adjudicator (including a direction to commence court proceedings under section 110(1)) the adjudicator may impose a sanction on the defaulting party—

(a) on the application of any other party; or
(b) of his own motion.

(2) Where the defaulting party was the person who made (or has been substituted for or added to the party who made) the original application, the sanction may include requiring the registrar to cancel the original application in whole or in part.

(3) Where the defaulting party was a person who objected to (or has been substituted for or added to the party who objected to) the original application, the sanction may include requiring the registrar to give effect to the original application in whole or in part as if the objection had not been made.

(4) A sanction that includes either of the requirements on the registrar under paragraph (2) or (3) shall be treated as the substantive decision on that matter.

(5) If the sanction does not include either of the requirements on the registrar under paragraph (2) or (3), the adjudicator must serve written notice on the parties of his decision as to what if any sanctions are imposed, and he may make consequential directions.

[3402]

56 Errors of procedure

Where, before the adjudicator has made his final substantive order in relation to a matter, there has been an error of procedure such as a failure to comply with a rule—

(a) the error does not invalidate any step taken in the proceedings, unless the adjudicator so orders; and
(b) the adjudicator may make an order or take any other step that he considers appropriate to remedy the error.

[3403]

57 Accidental slips or omissions

The adjudicator may at any time amend an order or direction to correct a clerical error or other accidental slip or omission.

[3404]

58 Time and place

If the adjudicator deems it appropriate to do so, he may alter—

(a) any time limit specified in these Rules;
(b) any time limit set by the adjudicator; or
(c) the date, time or location appointed for a hearing or for any other appearance of the parties before him.

[3405]

59 Calculation of time

(1) Where a period of time for doing an act is specified by these Rules or by a direction of the adjudicator, that period is to be calculated—
(a) excluding the day on which the period begins; and
(b) unless otherwise specified, by reference to calendar days.

(2) Where the time specified by these Rules or by a direction of the adjudicator for doing an act ends on a day which is not a working day, that act is done in time if it is done on the next working day.

[3406]

60 Representation of parties

(1) If a party who was previously unrepresented appoints a representative or, having been represented, appoints a replacement representative, that party must, as soon as reasonably practicable following the appointment, notify the adjudicator and the other parties in writing—
(a) of the fact that he has appointed a representative or replacement representative;
(b) the name and contact details of the representative or replacement representative;
(c) whether the representative or replacement representative has been authorised by the party to accept service of documents; and
(d) if the representative or replacement representative has been authorised to accept service, the address for service.

(2) If a party who was previously represented ceases to be represented, that party must, as soon as reasonably practicable following the ending of his representation, notify the adjudicator and the other parties in writing—
(a) of the fact that he is no longer represented; and
(b) where the party's address for service had previously been the address of the representative, the party's new address for service.

[3407]

61 Independence of adjudicator's staff

When undertaking a non-administrative function of the adjudicator on the adjudicator's authorisation, a member of the adjudicator's staff is not subject to the direction of the Lord Chancellor or any other person or body.

[3408]

LAND REGISTRATION (ACTING ADJUDICATOR) REGULATIONS 2003

(SI 2003/2342)

NOTES

Made: 8 September 2003.
Authority: Land Registration Act 2002, Sch 9, para 5.
Commencement: 13 October 2003.

---

1 Citation and commencement

These Regulations may be cited as the Land Registration (Acting Adjudicator) Regulations 2003 and shall come into force on 13th October 2003.

[3409]

2 Appointment

(1) The [Lord Chief Justice, after consulting the Lord Chancellor] may, in order to facilitate the disposal of the business of the adjudicator, appoint a person to carry out the functions of the adjudicator during any vacancy in that office.

(2) To be qualified for appointment under paragraph (1), a person must hold the office of district judge (as defined in section 74(1) of the Courts and Legal Services Act 1990).

(3) The person appointed shall carry out the functions of the adjudicator during the vacancy, unless within that period, he—
(a) dies; or

(b) resigns by giving notice in writing to the Lord Chancellor; or
(c) is removed by the Lord Chancellor[, with the concurrence of the Lord Chief Justice,] on the grounds of incapacity or misbehaviour.

[(4) The Lord Chief Justice may nominate a judicial office holder (as defined in section 109(4) of the Constitutional Reform Act 2005) to exercise his functions under this regulation.]

[3410]

NOTES

Para (1): words in square brackets substituted by SI 2006/680, art 2, Sch 1, para 64(1), (2).
Para (3): words in square brackets in sub-para (c) inserted by SI 2006/680, art 2, Sch 1, para 64(1), (3).
Para (4): inserted by SI 2006/680, art 2, Sch 1, para 64(1), (4).

3 Functions

Every person appointed, whilst acting under these Regulations, shall have all the jurisdiction and powers of the person appointed to the office of adjudicator pursuant to section 107 of the Land Registration Act 2002.

[3411]

LAND REGISTRATION ACT 2002 (TRANSITIONAL PROVISIONS) (NO 2) ORDER 2003

(SI 2003/2431)

NOTES

Made: 14 September 2003.
Authority: Land Registration Act 2002, s 134.
Commencement: 13 October 2003.

1 Citation, commencement and interpretation

(1) This Order may be cited as the Land Registration Act 2002 (Transitional Provisions) (No 2) Order 2003 and shall come into force on 13th October 2003.

(2) In this Order "the Act" means the Land Registration Act 2002.

[3412]

2 A right in respect of the repair of a church chancel

(1) For the period of ten years beginning with the day on which Schedule 1 to the Act comes into force, it has effect with the insertion at the end of—

"16. A right in respect of the repair of a church chancel."

(2) For the period of ten years beginning with the day on which Schedule 3 to the Act comes into force, it has effect with the insertion at the end of—

"16. A right in respect of the repair of a church chancel."

[3413]

REGULATORY REFORM (BUSINESS TENANCIES) (ENGLAND AND WALES) ORDER 2003

(SI 2003/3096)

NOTES

Made: 1 December 2003.
Authority: Regulatory Reform Act 2001, ss 1, 4.
Commencement: 1 June 2004.

Introduction

1 Citation, commencement and interpretation

(1) This Order may be cited as the Regulatory Reform (Business Tenancies) (England and Wales) Order 2003.

(2) This Order extends to England and Wales only.

(3) This Order shall come into force at the end of the period of 6 months beginning with the day on which it is made.

(4) In this Order, "the Act" means the Landlord and Tenant Act 1954.

[3414]

2–27 (*Amend the Landlord and Tenant Act 1954 at* **[547]** *et seq.*)

Final provisions

28 Consequential amendments, repeals and subordinate provisions

(1) Schedule 5 to this Order, which contains amendments consequential on the provisions of this Order, shall have effect.

(2) The enactments specified in Schedule 6 to this Order are repealed to the extent mentioned in the third column of that Schedule.

(3) Schedules 1 to 4 to this Order are designated as subordinate provisions for the purposes of section 4 of the Regulatory Reform Act 2001.

(4) A subordinate provisions order relating to the subordinate provisions designated by paragraph (3) above shall be subject to annulment in pursuance of a resolution of either House of Parliament.

(5) The power to make a subordinate provisions order relating to those provisions is to be exercisable in relation to Wales by the National Assembly for Wales concurrently with a Minister of the Crown.

(6) Paragraph (4) above does not apply to a subordinate provisions order made by the National Assembly for Wales.

(7) The notices and statutory declarations set out in Schedules 1 to 4 to this Order shall be treated for the purposes of section 26 of the Welsh Language Act 1993 (power to prescribe Welsh forms) as if they were specified by an Act of Parliament; and accordingly the power conferred by section 26(2) of that Act may be exercised in relation to those notices and declarations.

[3415]

29 Transitional provisions

(1) Where, before this Order came into force—

(a) the landlord gave the tenant notice under section 25 of the Act; or

(b) the tenant made a request for a new tenancy in accordance with section 26 of the Act,

nothing in this Order has effect in relation to the notice or request or anything done in consequence of it.

(2) Nothing in this Order has effect in relation—

(a) to an agreement—

(i) for the surrender of a tenancy which was made before this Order came into force and which fell within section 24(2)(b) of the Act; or

(ii) which was authorised by the court under section 38(4) of the Act before this Order came into force; or

(b) to a notice under section 27(2) of the Act which was given by the tenant to the immediate landlord before this Order came into force.

(3) Any provision in a tenancy which requires an order under section 38(4) of the Act to be obtained in respect of any subtenancy shall, so far as is necessary after the coming into force of this Order, be construed as if it required the procedure mentioned in section 38A of the Act to be followed, and any related requirement shall be construed accordingly.

(4) If a person has, before the coming into force of this Order, entered into an agreement to take a tenancy, any provision in that agreement which requires an order under section 38(4) of the Act to be obtained in respect of the tenancy shall continue to be effective, notwithstanding the repeal of that provision by Article 21(2) of this Order, and the court shall retain jurisdiction to make such an order.

(5) Article 20 above does not have effect where the tenant quit the holding before this Order came into force.

(6) Nothing in Articles 23 and 24 above applies to a notice under section 40 of the Act served before this Order came into force.

[3416]

SCHEDULE 1
FORM OF NOTICE THAT SECTIONS 24 TO 28 OF THE LANDLORD AND TENANT ACT 1954 ARE NOT TO APPLY TO A BUSINESS TENANCY

Article 22(2)

To:

....

....

....

[*Name and address of tenant*]

From:

....

....

....

[*Name and address of landlord*]

IMPORTANT NOTICE

You are being offered a lease without security of tenure. Do not commit yourself to the lease unless you have read this message carefully and have discussed it with a professional adviser.

Business tenants normally have security of tenure – the right to stay in their business premises when the lease ends.

If you commit yourself to the lease you will be giving up these important legal rights.

—You will have **no right** to stay in the premises when the lease ends.

—Unless the landlord chooses to offer you another lease, you will need to leave the premises.

—You will be unable to claim compensation for the loss of your business premises, unless the lease specifically gives you this right.

—If the landlord offers you another lease, you will have no right to ask the court to fix the rent.

It is therefore important to get professional advice – from a qualified surveyor, lawyer or accountant – before agreeing to give up these rights.

If you want to ensure that you can stay in the same business premises when the lease ends, you should consult your adviser about another form of lease that does not exclude the protection of the Landlord and Tenant Act 1954.

If you receive this notice at least 14 days before committing yourself to the lease, you will need to sign a simple declaration that you have received this notice and have accepted its consequences, before signing the lease.

But if you do not receive at least 14 days notice, you will need to sign a "statutory" declaration. To do so, you will need to visit an independent solicitor (or someone else empowered to administer oaths).

Unless there is a special reason for committing yourself to the lease sooner, you may want to ask the landlord to let you have 14 days to consider whether you wish to give up your statutory rights. If you then decide to go ahead with the agreement to exclude the protection of the Landlord and Tenant Act 1954, you would only need to make a simple declaration, and so would not need to make a separate visit to an independent solicitor.

[3417]

SCHEDULE 2
REQUIREMENTS FOR A VALID AGREEMENT THAT SECTIONS 24 TO 28 OF THE LANDLORD AND TENANT ACT 1954 ARE NOT TO APPLY TO A BUSINESS TENANCY

Article 22(2)

1. The following are the requirements referred to in section 38A(3)(b) of the Act.

2. Subject to paragraph 4, the notice referred to in section 38A(3)(a) of the Act must be served on the tenant not less than 14 days before the tenant enters into the tenancy to which it applies, or (if earlier) becomes contractually bound to do so.

3. If the requirement in paragraph 2 is met, the tenant, or a person duly authorised by him to do so, must, before the tenant enters into the tenancy to which the notice applies, or (if earlier) becomes contractually bound to do so, make a declaration in the form, or substantially in the form, set out in paragraph 7.

4. If the requirement in paragraph 2 is not met, the notice referred to in section 38A(3)(a) of the Act must be served on the tenant before the tenant enters into the tenancy to which it applies, or (if

earlier) becomes contractually bound to do so, and the tenant, or a person duly authorised by him to do so, must before that time make a statutory declaration in the form, or substantially in the form, set out in paragraph 8.

5. A reference to the notice and, where paragraph 3 applies, the declaration or, where paragraph 4 applies, the statutory declaration must be contained in or endorsed on the instrument creating the tenancy.

6. The agreement under section 38A(1) of the Act, or a reference to the agreement, must be contained in or endorsed upon the instrument creating the tenancy.

7. The form of declaration referred to in paragraph 3 is as follows:—

I................................ (*name of declarant*) of................................ (*address*) declare that—

1 I/................................ (*name of tenant*) propose(s) to enter into a tenancy of premises at................................ (*address of premises*) for a term commencing on................................

2 I/The tenant propose(s) to enter into an agreement with................................ (*name of landlord*) that the provisions of sections 24 to 28 of the Landlord and Tenant Act 1954 (security of tenure) shall be excluded in relation to the tenancy.

3 The landlord has, not less than 14 days before I/the tenant enter(s) into the tenancy, or (if earlier) become(s) contractually bound to do so served on me/the tenant a notice in the form, or substantially in the form, set out in Schedule 1 to the Regulatory Reform (Business Tenancies) (England and Wales) Order 2003. The form of notice set out in that Schedule is reproduced below.

4 I have/The tenant has read the notice referred to in paragraph 3 above and accept(s) the consequences of entering into the agreement referred to in paragraph 2 above.

5 (*as appropriate*) I am duly authorised by the tenant to make this declaration.

DECLARED this................................ day of................................

To:

....

....

....

[*Name and address of tenant*]

From:

....

....

....

[*Name and address of landlord*]

IMPORTANT NOTICE

You are being offered a lease without security of tenure. Do not commit yourself to the lease unless you have read this message carefully and have discussed it with a professional adviser.

Business tenants normally have security of tenure – the right to stay in their business premises when the lease ends.

If you commit yourself to the lease you will be giving up these important legal rights.

—You will have **no right** to stay in the premises when the lease ends.

—Unless the landlord chooses to offer you another lease, you will need to leave the premises.

—You will be unable to claim compensation for the loss of your business premises, unless the lease specifically gives you this right.

—If the landlord offers you another lease, you will have no right to ask the court to fix the rent.

It is therefore important to get professional advice – from a qualified surveyor, lawyer or accountant – before agreeing to give up these rights.

If you want to ensure that you can stay in the same business premises when the lease ends, you should consult your adviser about another form of lease that does not exclude the protection of the Landlord and Tenant Act 1954.

If you receive this notice at least 14 days before committing yourself to the lease, you will need to sign a simple declaration that you have received this notice and have accepted its consequences, before signing the lease.

But if you do not receive at least 14 days notice, you will need to sign a "statutory" declaration. To do so, you will need to visit an independent solicitor (or someone else empowered to administer oaths).

Unless there is a special reason for committing yourself to the lease sooner, you may want to ask the landlord to let you have at least 14 days to consider whether you wish to give up your statutory rights. If you then decide to go ahead with the agreement to exclude the protection of the Landlord and Tenant Act 1954, you would only need to make a simple declaration, and so would not need to make a separate visit to an independent solicitor.

8. The form of statutory declaration referred to in paragraph 4 is as follows:—

I.................................. (*name of declarant*) of.................................. (*address*) do solemnly and sincerely declare that—

1 I.................................. (*name of tenant*) propose(s) to enter into a tenancy of premises at .... (*address of premises*) for a term commencing on..................................

2 I/The tenant propose(s) to enter into an agreement with.................................. (*name of landlord*) that the provisions of sections 24 to 28 of the Landlord and Tenant Act 1954 (security of tenure) shall be excluded in relation to the tenancy.

3 The landlord has served on me/the tenant a notice in the form, or substantially in the form, set out in Schedule 1 to the Regulatory Reform (Business Tenancies) (England and Wales) Order 2003. The form of notice set out in that Schedule is reproduced below.

4 I have/The tenant has read the notice referred to in paragraph 3 above and accept(s) the consequences of entering into the agreement referred to in paragraph 2 above.

5 (*as appropriate*) I am duly authorised by the tenant to make this declaration.

To:

....

....

....

[*Name and address of tenant*]

From:

....

....

....

[*Name and address of landlord*]

IMPORTANT NOTICE

You are being offered a lease without security of tenure. Do not commit yourself to the lease unless you have read this message carefully and have discussed it with a professional adviser.

Business tenants normally have security of tenure – the right to stay in their business premises when the lease ends.

If you commit yourself to the lease you will be giving up these important legal rights.

—You will have **no right** to stay in the premises when the lease ends.

—Unless the landlord chooses to offer you another lease, you will need to leave the premises.

—You will be unable to claim compensation for the loss of your business premises, unless the lease specifically gives you this right.

—If the landlord offers you another lease, you will have no right to ask the court to fix the rent.

It is therefore important to get professional advice – from a qualified surveyor, lawyer or accountant – before agreeing to give up these rights.

If you want to ensure that you can stay in the same business premises when the lease ends, you should consult your adviser about another form of lease that does not exclude the protection of the Landlord and Tenant Act 1954.

If you receive this notice at least 14 days before committing yourself to the lease, you will need to sign a simple declaration that you have received this notice and have accepted its consequences, before signing the lease.

But if you do not receive at least 14 days notice, you will need to sign a "statutory" declaration. To do so, you will need to visit an independent solicitor (or someone else empowered to administer oaths).

Unless there is a special reason for committing yourself to the lease sooner, you may want to ask the landlord to let you have at least 14 days to consider whether you wish to give up your statutory rights. If you then decide to go ahead with the agreement to exclude the protection of the Landlord and Tenant Act 1954, you would only need to make a simple declaration, and so would not need to make a separate visit to an independent solicitor.

AND I make this solemn declaration conscientiously believing the same to be true and by virtue of the Statutory Declaration Act 1835.

DECLARED at......................... this........................... day of............................

Before me

(*signature of person before whom declaration is made*)

A commissioner for oaths *or* A solicitor empowered to administer oaths or (*as appropriate*)

[3418]

SCHEDULE 3
FORM OF NOTICE THAT AN AGREEMENT TO SURRENDER A BUSINESS TENANCY IS TO BE MADE

Article 22(2)

To:

....

....

....

[*Name and address of tenant*]

From:

....

....

....

[*Name and address of landlord*]

IMPORTANT NOTICE FOR TENANT

Do not commit yourself to any agreement to surrender your lease unless you have read this message carefully and discussed it with a professional adviser.

Normally, you have the right to renew your lease when it expires. By committing yourself to an agreement to surrender, **you will be giving up this important statutory right.**

—You will **not** be able to continue occupying the premises beyond the date provided for under the agreement for surrender, **unless** the landlord chooses to offer you a further term (in which case you would lose the right to ask the court to determine the new rent). You will need to leave the premises.

—You will be unable to claim compensation for the loss of your premises, unless the lease or agreement for surrender gives you this right.

A qualified surveyor, lawyer or accountant would be able to offer you professional advice on your options.

You do not have to commit yourself to the agreement to surrender your lease unless you want to.

If you receive this notice at least 14 days before committing yourself to the agreement to surrender, you will need to sign a simple declaration that you have received this notice and have accepted its consequences, before signing the agreement to surrender.

But if you do not receive at least 14 days notice, you will need to sign a "statutory" declaration. To do so, you will need to visit an independent solicitor (or someone else empowered to administer oaths).

Unless there is a special reason for committing yourself to the agreement to surrender sooner, you may want to ask the landlord to let you have at least 14 days to consider whether you wish to give up your statutory rights. If you then decided to go ahead with the agreement to end your lease, you would only need to make a simple declaration, and so you would not need to make a separate visit to an independent solicitor.

[3419]

SCHEDULE 4
REQUIREMENTS FOR A VALID AGREEMENT TO SURRENDER A BUSINESS TENANCY

Article 22(2)

1. The following are the requirements referred to in section 38A(4)(b) of the Act.

2. Subject to paragraph 4, the notice referred to in section 38A(4)(a) of the Act must be served on the tenant not less than 14 days before the tenant enters into the agreement under section 38A(2) of the Act, or (if earlier) becomes contractually bound to do so.

3. If the requirement in paragraph 2 is met, the tenant or a person duly authorised by him to do so, must, before the tenant enters into the agreement under section 38A(2) of the Act, or (if earlier) becomes contractually bound to do so, make a declaration in the form, or substantially in the form, set out in paragraph 6.

4. If the requirement in paragraph 2 is not met, the notice referred to in section 38A(4)(a) of the Act must be served on the tenant before the tenant enters into the agreement under section 38A(2) of the Act, or (if earlier) becomes contractually bound to do so, and the tenant, or a person duly authorised by him to do so, must before that time make a statutory declaration in the form, or substantially in the form, set out in paragraph 7.

5. A reference to the notice and, where paragraph 3 applies, the declaration or, where paragraph 4 applies, the statutory declaration must be contained in or endorsed on the instrument creating the agreement under section 38A(2).

6. The form of declaration referred to in paragraph 3 is as follows:—

I........................ (*name of declarant*) of........................ (*address*) declare that—

1 I have/... (*name of tenant*) has a tenancy of premises at .... (*address of premises*) for a term commencing on ....

2 I/The tenant propose(s) to enter into an agreement with .... (*name of landlord*) to surrender the tenancy on a date or in circumstances specified in the agreement.

3 The landlord has not less than 14 days before I/the tenant enter(s) into the agreement referred to in paragraph 2 above, or (if earlier) become(s) contractually bound to do so, served on me/the tenant a notice in the form, or substantially in the form, set out in Schedule 3 to Regulatory Reform (Business Tenancies) (England and Wales) Order 2003. The form of notice set out in that Schedule is reproduced below.

4 I have/The tenant has read the notice referred to in paragraph 3 above and accept(s) the consequences of entering into the agreement referred to in paragraph 2 above.

5 (*as appropriate*) I am duly authorised by the tenant to make this declaration.

DECLARED this... day of.....................................

To:

....

....

....

[*Name and address of tenant*]

From:

....

....

....

[*Name and address of landlord*]

IMPORTANT NOTICE FOR TENANT

Do not commit yourself to any agreement to surrender your lease unless you have read this message carefully and discussed it with a professional adviser.

Normally, you have the right to renew your lease when it expires. By committing yourself to an agreement to surrender, **you will be giving up this important statutory right.**

—You will **not** be able to continue occupying the premises beyond the date provided for under the agreement for surrender, **unless** the landlord chooses to offer you a further term (in which case you would lose the right to ask the court to determine the new rent). You will need to leave the premises.

—You will be unable to claim compensation for the loss of your premises, unless the lease or agreement for surrender gives you this right.

A qualified surveyor, lawyer or accountant would be able to offer you professional advice on your options.

You do not have to commit yourself to the agreement to surrender your lease unless you want to.

If you receive this notice at least 14 days before committing yourself to the agreement to surrender, you will need to sign a simple declaration that you have received this notice and have accepted its consequences, before signing the agreement to surrender.

But if you do not receive at least 14 days notice, you will need to sign a "statutory" declaration. To do so, you will need to visit an independent solicitor (or someone else empowered to administer oaths).

Unless there is a special reason for committing yourself to the agreement to surrender sooner, you may want to ask the landlord to let you have at least 14 days to consider whether you wish to give up your statutory rights. If you then decided to go ahead with the agreement to end your lease, you would only need to make a simple declaration, and so you would not need to make a separate visit to an independent solicitor.

7. The form of statutory declaration referred to in paragraph 4 is as follows:—

I.................................. (*name of declarant*) of .... (*address*) do solemnly and sincerely declare that—

1 I have/.................................. (*name of tenant*) has a tenancy of premises at .... (*address of premises*) for a term commencing on ....

2 I/The tenant propose(s) to enter into an agreement with.................................. (*name of landlord*) to surrender the tenancy on a date or in circumstances specified in the agreement.

3 The landlord has served on me/the tenant a notice in the form, or substantially in the form, set out in Schedule 3 to the Regulatory Reform (Business Tenancies) (England and Wales) Order 2003. The form of notice set out in that Schedule is reproduced below.

4 I have/The tenant has read the notice referred to in paragraph 3 above and accept(s) the consequences of entering into the agreement referred to in paragraph 2 above.

5 (*as appropriate*) I am duly authorised by the tenant to make this declaration.

To:

....

....

....

[*Name and address of tenant*]

From:

....

....

....

[*Name and address of landlord*]

IMPORTANT NOTICE FOR TENANT

Do not commit yourself to any agreement to surrender your lease unless you have read this message carefully and discussed it with a professional adviser.

Normally, you have the right to renew your lease when it expires. By committing yourself to an agreement to surrender, **you will be giving up this important statutory right.**

—You will **not** be able to continue occupying the premises beyond the date provided for under the agreement for surrender, **unless** the landlord chooses to offer you a further term (in which case you would lose the right to ask the court to determine the new rent). You will need to leave the premises.

—You will be unable to claim compensation for the loss of your premises, unless the lease or agreement for surrender gives you this right.

A qualified surveyor, lawyer or accountant would be able to offer you professional advice on your options.

You do not have to commit yourself to the agreement to surrender your lease unless you want to.

If you receive this notice at least 14 days before committing yourself to the agreement to surrender, you will need to sign a simple declaration that you have received this notice and have accepted its consequences, before signing the agreement to surrender.

But if you do not receive at least 14 days notice, you will need to sign a "statutory" declaration. To do so, you will need to visit an independent solicitor (or someone else empowered to administer oaths).

Unless there is a special reason for committing yourself to the agreement to surrender sooner, you may want to ask the landlord to let you have at least 14 days to consider whether you wish to give up your statutory rights. If you then decided to go ahead with the agreement to end your lease, you would only need to make a simple declaration, and so you would not need to make a separate visit to an independent solicitor.

AND I make this solemn declaration conscientiously believing the same to be true and by virtue of the Statutory Declarations Act 1835

DECLARED a.......................... this.......................... day of..........................

Before me (*signature of person before whom declaration is made*)

A commissioner for oaths or A solicitor empowered to administer oaths *or* (*as appropriate*)

[3420]

(*Schs 5, 6 contain consequential amendments and repeals which, in so far as relevant to this work, have been incorporated at the appropriate place.*)

PART II STATUTORY INSTRUMENTS

LANDLORD AND TENANT ACT 1954, PART 2 (NOTICES) REGULATIONS 2004

(SI 2004/1005)

NOTES

Made: 30 March 2004.
Authority: Landlord and Tenant Act 1954, s 66.
Commencement: 1 June 2004.

1 Citation and commencement

These Regulations may be cited as the Landlord and Tenant Act 1954, Part 2 (Notices) Regulations 2004 and shall come into force on 1st June 2004.

[3421]

2 Interpretation

(1) In these Regulations—
"the Act" means the Landlord and Tenant Act 1954; and
"the 1967 Act" means the Leasehold Reform Act 1967.

(2) Any reference in these Regulations to a numbered form (in whatever terms) is a reference to the form bearing that number in Schedule 2 to these Regulations or a form substantially to the same effect.

[3422]

3 Prescribed forms, and purposes for which they are to be used.

The form with the number shown in column (1) of Schedule 1 to these Regulations is prescribed for use for the purpose shown in the corresponding entry in column (2) of that Schedule.

[3423]

4 (*Revokes the Landlord and Tenant Act 1954, Part II (Notices) Regulations 1983, SI 1983/133 and the Landlord and Tenant Act 1954, Part II (Notices) (Amendment) Regulations 1989, SI 1989/1548.*)

SCHEDULE 1
PRESCRIBED FORMS, AND PURPOSES FOR WHICH THEY ARE TO BE USED

Regulations 2(2) and 3

(*1*) *Form number*	(*2*) *Purpose for which to be used*
1	Ending a tenancy to which Part 2 of the Act applies, where the landlord is not opposed to the grant of a new tenancy (notice under section 25 of the Act).

(1) *Form number*	(2) *Purpose for which to be used*
2	Ending a tenancy to which Part 2 of the Act applies, where— (a) the landlord is opposed to the grant of a new tenancy (notice under section 25 of the Act); and (b) the tenant is not entitled under the 1967 Act to buy the freehold or an extended lease.
3	Tenant's request for a new tenancy of premises where Part 2 of the Act applies (notice under section 26 of the Act).
4	Landlord's notice activating tenant's duty under section 40(1) of the Act to give information as to his or her occupation of the premises and as to any sub-tenancies.
5	Tenant's notice activating duty under section 40(3) of the Act of reversioner or reversioner's mortgagee in possession to give information about his or her interest in the premises.
6	Withdrawal of notice given under section 25 of the Act ending a tenancy to which Part 2 of the Act applies (notice under section 44 of, and paragraph 6 of Schedule 6 to, the Act).
7	Ending a tenancy to which Part 2 of the Act applies, where the landlord is opposed to the grant of a new tenancy but where the tenant may be entitled under the 1967 Act to buy the freehold or an extended lease (notice under section 25 of the Act and paragraph 10 of Schedule 3 to the 1967 Act).
8	Ending a tenancy to which Part 2 of the Act applies, where: (a) the notice under section 25 of the Act contains a copy of a certificate given under section 57 of the Act that the use or occupation of the property or part of it is to be changed by a specified date; (b) the date of termination of the tenancy specified in the notice is not earlier than the date specified in the certificate; and (c) the tenant is not entitled under the 1967 Act to buy the freehold or an extended lease.
9	Ending a tenancy to which Part 2 of the Act applies, where: (a) the notice under section 25 of the Act contains a copy of a certificate given under section 57 of the Act that the use or occupation of the property or part of it is to be changed at a future date; (b) the date of termination of the tenancy specified in the notice is earlier than the date specified in the certificate; (c) the landlord opposes the grant of a new tenancy; and (d) the tenant is not entitled under the 1967 Act to buy the freehold or an extended lease.
10	Ending a tenancy to which Part 2 of the Act applies, where: (a) the notice under section 25 of the Act contains a copy of a certificate given under section 57 of the Act that the use or occupation of the property or part of it is to be changed at a future date; (b) the date of termination of the tenancy specified in the notice is earlier than the date specified in the certificate; (c) the landlord does not oppose the grant of a new tenancy; and (d) the tenant is not entitled under the 1967 Act to buy the freehold or an extended lease.
11	Ending a tenancy to which Part 2 of the Act applies, where the notice under section 25 of the Act contains a copy of a certificate given under section 58 of the Act that for reasons of national security it is necessary that the use or occupation of the property should be discontinued or changed.
12	Ending a tenancy to which Part 2 of the Act applies, where—

(*1*) *Form number*	(2) *Purpose for which to be used*
	(a) the notice under section 25 of the Act contains a copy of a certificate given under section 58 of the Act (as applied by section 60 of the Act) that it is necessary or expedient for achieving the purpose mentioned in section 2(1) of the Local Employment Act 1972 that the use or occupation of the property should be changed; and (b) the tenant is not entitled under the 1967 Act to buy the freehold or an extended lease.
13	Ending a tenancy to which Part 2 of the Act applies, where: (a) the notice under section 25 of the Act contains a copy of a certificate given under section 57 of the Act that the use or occupation of the property or part of it is to be changed by a specified date; and (b) the date of termination of the tenancy specified in the notice is not earlier than the date specified in the certificate; and (c) the tenant may be entitled under the 1967 Act to buy the freehold or an extended lease.
14	Ending a tenancy to which Part 2 of the Act applies, where: (a) the notice under section 25 of the Act contains a copy of a certificate given under section 57 of the Act that the use or occupation of the property or part of it is to be changed at a future date; (b) the date of termination of the tenancy specified in the notice is earlier than the date specified in the certificate; and (c) the tenant may be entitled under the 1967 Act to buy the freehold or an extended lease the landlord opposes the grant of a new tenancy.
15	Ending a tenancy to which Part 2 of the Act applies, where: (a) the notice under section 25 of the Act contains a copy of a certificate given under section 58 of the Act (as applied by section 60 of the Act) that it is necessary or expedient for achieving the purpose mentioned in section 2(1) of the Local Employment Act 1972 that the use or occupation of the property should be changed; and (b) the tenant may be entitled under the 1967 Act to buy the freehold or an extended lease the landlord opposes the grant of a new tenancy.
16	Ending a tenancy of Welsh Development Agency [Act 1975] premises where— (a) the notice under section 25 of the Act contains a copy of a certificate given under section 58 of the Act (as applied by section 60A of the Act) that it is necessary or expedient, for the purposes of providing employment appropriate to the needs of the area in which the premises are situated, that the use or occupation of the property should be changed; and (b) the tenant is not entitled under the 1967 Act to buy the freehold or an extended lease.
17	Ending a tenancy of Welsh Development Agency [Act 1975] premises where: (a) the notice under section 25 of the Act contains a copy of a certificate given under section 58 of the Act (as applied by section 60A of the Act) that it is necessary or expedient, for the purposes of providing employment appropriate to the needs of the area in which the premises are situated, that the use or occupation of the property should be changed; and (b) the tenant may be entitled under the 1967 Act to buy the freehold or an extended lease.

[3424]

NOTES

In entries relating to Forms 16, 17 in column 2 words in square brackets inserted by SI 2005/3226, art 7(1)(b), Sch 2, Pt 1, para 7(1), subject to transitional provisions in art 3 thereof.

SCHEDULE 2
PRESCRIBED FORMS

Regulation 2(2)

FORM 1
LANDLORD'S NOTICE ENDING A BUSINESS TENANCY WITH PROPOSALS FOR A NEW ONE

Section 25 of the Landlord and Tenant Act 1954

IMPORTANT NOTE FOR THE LANDLORD: If you are willing to grant a new tenancy, complete this form and send it to the tenant. If you wish to oppose the grant of a new tenancy, use form 2 in Schedule 2 to the Landlord and Tenant Act 1954, Part 2 (Notices) Regulations 2004 or, where the tenant may be entitled to acquire the freehold or an extended lease, form 7 in that Schedule, instead of this form.

To: (*insert name and address of tenant*)

From: (*insert name and address of landlord*)

1 This notice applies to the following property: (*insert address or description of property*).

2 I am giving you notice under section 25 of the Landlord and Tenant Act 1954 to end your tenancy on (*insert date*).

3 I am not opposed to granting you a new tenancy. You will find my proposals for the new tenancy, which we can discuss, in the Schedule to this notice.

4 If we cannot agree on all the terms of a new tenancy, either you or I may ask the court to order the grant of a new tenancy and settle the terms on which we cannot agree.

5 If you wish to ask the court for a new tenancy you must do so by the date in paragraph 2, unless we agree in writing to a later date and do so before the date in paragraph 2.

6 Please send all correspondence about this notice to:

Name:

Address:

Signed: Date:

*[Landlord] *[On behalf of the landlord] *[Mortgagee] *[On behalf of the mortgagee]

*(*delete if inapplicable*)

SCHEDULE
LANDLORD'S PROPOSALS FOR A NEW TENANCY

(*attach or insert proposed terms of the new tenancy*)

IMPORTANT NOTE FOR THE TENANT

This Notice is intended to bring your tenancy to an end. If you want to continue to occupy your property after the date specified in paragraph 2 you must act quickly. If you are in any doubt about the action that you should take, get advice immediately from a solicitor or a surveyor.

The landlord is prepared to offer you a new tenancy and has set out proposed terms in the Schedule to this notice. You are not bound to accept these terms. They are merely suggestions as a basis for negotiation. In the event of disagreement, ultimately the court would settle the terms of the new tenancy.

It would be wise to seek professional advice before agreeing to accept the landlord's terms or putting forward your own proposals.

NOTES

The sections mentioned below are sections of the Landlord and Tenant Act 1954, as amended, (most recently by the Regulatory Reform (Business Tenancies) (England and Wales) Order 2003).

Ending of tenancy and grant of new tenancy

This notice is intended to bring your tenancy to an end on the date given in paragraph 2. Section 25 contains rules about the date that the landlord can put in that paragraph.

However, your landlord is prepared to offer you a new tenancy and has set out proposals for it in the Schedule to this notice (section 25(8)). You are not obliged to accept these proposals and may put forward your own.

If you and your landlord are unable to agree terms either one of you may apply to the court. You may not apply to the court if your landlord has already done so (section 24(2A)). If you wish to apply to the court you must do so by the date given in paragraph 2 of this notice, unless you and your landlord have agreed in writing to extend the deadline (sections 29A and 29B).

The court will settle the rent and other terms of the new tenancy or those on which you and your landlord cannot agree (sections 34 and 35). If you apply to the court your tenancy will continue after the date shown in paragraph 2 of this notice while your application is being considered (section 24).

If you are in any doubt about what action you should take, get advice immediately from a solicitor or a surveyor.

Negotiating a new tenancy

Most tenancies are renewed by negotiation. You and your landlord may agree in writing to extend the deadline for making an application to the court while negotiations continue. Either you or your landlord can ask the court to fix the rent that you will have to pay while the tenancy continues (sections 24A to 24D).

You may only stay in the property after the date in paragraph 2 (or if we have agreed in writing to a later date, that date), if by then you or the landlord has asked the court to order the grant of a new tenancy.

If you do try to agree a new tenancy with your landlord remember:

- that your present tenancy will not continue after the date in paragraph 2 of this notice without the agreement in writing mentioned above, unless you have applied to the court or your landlord has done so, and
- that you will lose your right to apply to the court once the deadline in paragraph 2 of this notice has passed, unless there is a written agreement extending the deadline.

Validity of this notice

The landlord who has given you this notice may not be the landlord to whom you pay your rent (sections 44 and 67). This does not necessarily mean that the notice is invalid.

If you have any doubts about whether this notice is valid, get advice immediately from a solicitor or a surveyor.

Further information

An explanation of the main points to consider when renewing or ending a business tenancy, "Renewing and Ending Business Leases: a Guide for Tenants and Landlords", can be found at www.odpm.gov.uk. Printed copies of the explanation, but not of this form, are available from 1st June 2004 from Free Literature, PO Box 236, Wetherby, West Yorkshire, LS23 7NB (0870 1226 236).

[3425]

FORM 2
LANDLORD'S NOTICE ENDING A BUSINESS TENANCY AND REASONS FOR REFUSING A NEW ONE

Section 25 of the Landlord and Tenant Act 1954

IMPORTANT NOTE FOR THE LANDLORD: If you wish to oppose the grant of a new tenancy on any of the grounds in section 30(1) of the Landlord and Tenant Act 1954, complete this form and send it to the tenant. If the tenant may be entitled to acquire the freehold or an extended lease, use form 7 in Schedule 2 to the Landlord and Tenant Act 1954, Part 2 (Notices) Regulations 2004 instead of this form.

To: (*insert name and address of tenant*)

From: (*insert name and address of landlord*)

1 This notice relates to the following property: (*insert address or description of property*)

2 I am giving you notice under section 25 of the Landlord and Tenant Act 1954 to end your tenancy on (*insert date*).

3 I am opposed to the grant of a new tenancy.

4 You may ask the court to order the grant of a new tenancy. If you do, I will oppose your application on the ground(s) mentioned in paragraph(s)* of section 30(1) of that Act. I draw your attention to the Table in the Notes below, which sets out all the grounds of opposition.

*(*insert letter(s) of the paragraph(s) relied on*)

5 If you wish to ask the court for a new tenancy you must do so before the date in paragraph 2 unless, before that date, we agree in writing to a later date.

6 I can ask the court to order the ending of your tenancy without granting you a new tenancy. I may have to pay you compensation if I have relied only on one or more of the grounds mentioned in paragraphs (e), (f) and (g) of section 30(1). If I ask the court to end your tenancy, you can challenge my application.

7 Please send all correspondence about this notice to:

Name:

Address:

Signed: Date:

*[Landlord] *[On behalf of the landlord] *[Mortgagee] *[On behalf of the mortgagee]

(*delete if inapplicable*)

IMPORTANT NOTE FOR THE TENANT

This notice is intended to bring your tenancy to an end on the date specified in paragraph 2.

Your landlord is not prepared to offer you a new tenancy. You will not get a new tenancy unless you successfully challenge in court the grounds on which your landlord opposes the grant of a new tenancy.

If you want to continue to occupy your property you must act quickly. The notes below should help you to decide what action you now need to take. If you want to challenge your landlord's refusal to renew your tenancy, get advice immediately from a solicitor or a surveyor.

NOTES

The sections mentioned below are sections of the Landlord and Tenant Act 1954, as amended, (most recently by the Regulatory Reform (Business Tenancies) (England and Wales) Order 2003)

Ending of your tenancy

This notice is intended to bring your tenancy to an end on the date given in paragraph 2. Section 25 contains rules about the date that the landlord can put in that paragraph.

Your landlord is not prepared to offer you a new tenancy. If you want a new tenancy you will need to apply to the court for a new tenancy and successfully challenge the landlord's grounds for opposition (see the section below headed "*Landlord's opposition to new tenancy*"). If you wish to apply to the court you must do so before the date given in paragraph 2 of this notice, unless you and your landlord have agreed in writing, before that date, to extend the deadline (sections 29A and 29B).

If you apply to the court your tenancy will continue after the date given in paragraph 2 of this notice while your application is being considered (section 24). You may not apply to the court if your landlord has already done so (section 24(2A) and (2B)).

You may only stay in the property after the date given in paragraph 2 (or such later date as you and the landlord may have agreed in writing) if before that date you have asked the court to order the grant of a new tenancy or the landlord has asked the court to order the ending of your tenancy without granting you a new one.

If you are in any doubt about what action you should take, get advice immediately from a solicitor or a surveyor.

Landlord's opposition to new tenancy

If you apply to the court for a new tenancy, the landlord can only oppose your application on one or more of the grounds set out in section 30(1). If you match the letter(s) specified in paragraph 4 of this notice with those in the first column in the Table below, you can see from the second column the ground(s) on which the landlord relies.

Paragraph of section 30(1)	*Grounds*
(a)	Where under the current tenancy the tenant has any obligations as respects the repair and maintenance of the holding, that the tenant ought not to be granted a new tenancy in view of the state of repair of the holding, being a state resulting from the tenant's failure to comply with the said obligations.
(b)	That the tenant ought not to be granted a new tenancy in view of his persistent delay in paying rent which has become due.

Paragraph of section 30(1)	*Grounds*
(c)	That the tenant ought not to be granted a new tenancy in view of other substantial breaches by him of his obligations under the current tenancy, or for any other reason connected with the tenant's use or management of the holding.
(d)	That the landlord has offered and is willing to provide or secure the provision of alternative accommodation for the tenant, that the terms on which the alternative accommodation is available are reasonable having regard to the terms of the current tenancy and to all other relevant circumstances, and that the accommodation and the time at which it will be available are suitable for the tenant's requirements (including the requirement to preserve goodwill) having regard to the nature and class of his business and to the situation and extent of, and facilities afforded by, the holding.
(e)	Where the current tenancy was created by the sub-letting of part only of the property comprised in a superior tenancy and the landlord is the owner of an interest in reversion expectant on the termination of that superior tenancy, that the aggregate of the rents reasonably obtainable on separate lettings of the holding and the remainder of that property would be substantially less than the rent reasonably obtainable on a letting of that property as a whole, that on the termination of the current tenancy the landlord requires possession of the holding for the purposes of letting or otherwise disposing of the said property as a whole, and that in view thereof the tenant ought not to be granted a new tenancy.
(f)	That on the termination of the current tenancy the landlord intends to demolish or reconstruct the premises comprised in the holding or a substantial part of those premises or to carry out substantial work of construction on the holding or part thereof and that he could not reasonably do so without obtaining possession of the holding.
(g)	On the termination of the current tenancy the landlord intends to occupy the holding for the purposes, or partly for the purposes, of a business to be carried on by him therein, or as his residence.

In this Table "the holding" means the property that is the subject of the tenancy.

In ground (e), "the landlord is the owner an interest in reversion expectant on the termination of that superior tenancy" means that the landlord has an interest in the property that will entitle him or her, when your immediate landlord's tenancy comes to an end, to exercise certain rights and obligations in relation to the property that are currently exercisable by your immediate landlord.

If the landlord relies on ground (f), the court can sometimes still grant a new tenancy if certain conditions set out in section 31A are met.

If the landlord relies on ground (g), please note that "the landlord" may have an extended meaning. Where a landlord has a controlling interest in a company then either the landlord or the company can rely on ground (g). Where the landlord is a company and a person has a controlling interest in that company then either of them can rely on ground (g) (section 30(1A) and (1B)). A person has a "controlling interest" in a company if, had he been a company, the other company would have been its subsidiary (section 46(2)).

The landlord must normally have been the landlord for at least five years before he or she can rely on ground (g).

Compensation

If you cannot get a new tenancy solely because one or more of grounds (e), (f) and (g) applies, you may be entitled to compensation under section 37. If your landlord has opposed your application on any of the other grounds as well as (e), (f) or (g) you can only get compensation if the court's refusal to grant a new tenancy is based solely on one or more of grounds (e), (f) and (g). In other words, you cannot get compensation under section 37 if the court has refused your tenancy on *other* grounds, even if one or more of grounds (e), (f) and (g) also applies.

If your landlord is an authority possessing compulsory purchase powers (such as a local authority) you may be entitled to a disturbance payment under Part 3 of the Land Compensation Act 1973.

Validity of this notice

The landlord who has given you this notice may not be the landlord to whom you pay your rent (sections 44 and 67). This does not necessarily mean that the notice is invalid.

If you have any doubts about whether this notice is valid, get advice immediately from a solicitor or a surveyor.

Further information

An explanation of the main points to consider when renewing or ending a business tenancy, "Renewing and Ending Business Leases: a Guide for Tenants and Landlords", can be found at www.odpm.gov.uk. Printed copies of the explanation, but not of this form, are available from 1st June 2004 from Free Literature, PO Box 236, Wetherby, West Yorkshire, LS23 7NB (0870 1226 236).

[3426]

FORM 3
TENANT'S REQUEST FOR A NEW BUSINESS TENANCY

Section 26 of The Landlord and Tenant Act 1954

To (*insert name and address of landlord*):

From (*insert name and address of tenant*):

1 This notice relates to the following property: (*insert address or description of property*).

2 I am giving you notice under section 26 of the Landlord and Tenant Act 1954 that I request a new tenancy beginning on (*insert date*).

3 You will find my proposals for the new tenancy, which we can discuss, in the Schedule to this notice.

4 If we cannot agree on all the terms of a new tenancy, either you or I may ask the court to order the grant of a new tenancy and settle the terms on which we cannot agree.

5 If you wish to ask the court to order the grant of a new tenancy you must do so by the date in paragraph 2, unless we agree in writing to a later date and do so before the date in paragraph 2.

6 You may oppose my request for a new tenancy only on one or more of the grounds set out in section 30(1) of the Landlord and Tenant Act 1954. You must tell me what your grounds are within two months of receiving this notice. If you miss this deadline you will not be able to oppose renewal of my tenancy and you will have to grant me a new tenancy.

7 Please send all correspondence about this notice to:

Name:

Address:

Signed: Date:

*[Tenant] *[On behalf of the tenant] (**delete whichever is inapplicable*)

SCHEDULE
TENANT'S PROPOSALS FOR A NEW TENANCY

(*attach or insert proposed terms of the new tenancy*)

IMPORTANT NOTE FOR THE LANDLORD

This notice requests a new tenancy of your property or part of it. If you want to oppose this request you must act quickly.

Read the notice and all the Notes carefully. It would be wise to seek professional advice.

NOTES

The sections mentioned below are sections of the Landlord and Tenant Act 1954, as amended, (most recently by the Regulatory Reform (Business Tenancies) (England and Wales) Order 2003)

Tenant's request for a new tenancy

This request by your tenant for a new tenancy brings his or her current tenancy to an end on the day before the date mentioned in paragraph 2 of this notice. Section 26 contains rules about the date that the tenant can put in paragraph 2 of this notice.

Your tenant can apply to the court under section 24 for a new tenancy. You may apply for a new tenancy yourself, under the same section, but not if your tenant has already served an application. Once an application has been made to the court, your tenant's current tenancy will continue after the date mentioned in paragraph 2 while the application is being considered by the court. Either you or your tenant can ask the court to fix the rent which your tenant will have to pay whilst the tenancy continues (sections 24A to 24D). The court will settle any terms of a new tenancy on which you and your tenant disagree (sections 34 and 35).

Time limit for opposing your tenant's request

If you do not want to grant a new tenancy, you have two months from the making of your tenant's request in which to notify him or her that you will oppose any application made to the court for a new tenancy. You do not need a special form to do this, but the notice must be in writing and it must state on which of the grounds set out in section 30(1) you will oppose the application. If you do not use the same wording of the ground (or grounds), as set out below, your notice may be ineffective.

If there has been any delay in your seeing this notice, you may need to act very quickly. If you are in any doubt about what action you should take, get advice immediately from a solicitor or a surveyor.

Grounds for opposing tenant's application

If you wish to oppose the renewal of the tenancy, you can do so by opposing your tenant's application to the court, or by making your own application to the court for termination without renewal. However, you can only oppose your tenant's application, or apply for termination without renewal, on one or more of the grounds set out in section 30(1). These grounds are set out below. You will only be able to rely on the ground(s) of opposition that you have mentioned in your written notice to your tenant.

In this Table "the holding" means the property that is the subject of the tenancy.

Paragraph of section 30(1)	*Grounds*
(a)	Where under the current tenancy the tenant has any obligations as respects the repair and maintenance of the holding, that the tenant ought not to be granted a new tenancy in view of the state of repair of the holding, being a state resulting from the tenant's failure to comply with the said obligations.
(b)	That the tenant ought not to be granted a new tenancy in view of his persistent delay in paying rent which has become due.
(c)	That the tenant ought not to be granted a new tenancy in view of other substantial breaches by him of his obligations under the current tenancy, or for any other reason connected with the tenant's use or management of the holding.
(d)	That the landlord has offered and is willing to provide or secure the provision of alternative accommodation for the tenant, that the terms on which the alternative accommodation is available are reasonable having regard to the terms of the current tenancy and to all other relevant circumstances, and that the accommodation and the time at which it will be available are suitable for the tenant's requirements (including the requirement to preserve goodwill) having regard to the nature and class of his business and to the situation and extent of, and facilities afforded by, the holding.
(e)	Where the current tenancy was created by the sub-letting of part only of the property comprised in a superior tenancy and the landlord is the owner of an interest in reversion expectant on the termination of that superior tenancy, that the aggregate of the rents reasonably obtainable on separate lettings of the holding and the remainder of that property would be substantially less than the rent reasonably obtainable on a letting of that property as a whole, that on the termination of the current tenancy the landlord requires possession of the holding for the purposes of letting or otherwise disposing of the said property as a whole, and that in view thereof the tenant ought not to be granted a new tenancy.
(f)	That on the termination of the current tenancy the landlord intends to demolish or reconstruct the premises comprised in the holding or a substantial part of those premises or to carry out substantial work of construction on the holding or part thereof and that he could not reasonably do so without obtaining possession of the holding.
(g)	On the termination of the current tenancy the landlord intends to occupy the holding for the purposes, or partly for the purposes, of a business to be carried on by him therein, or as his residence.

Compensation

If your tenant cannot get a new tenancy solely because one or more of grounds (e), (f) and (g) applies, he or she is entitled to compensation under section 37. If you have opposed your tenant's application on any of the other grounds mentioned in section 30(1), as well as on one or more of grounds (e), (f) and (g), your tenant can only get compensation if the court's refusal to grant a new tenancy is based solely on ground (e), (f) or (g). In other words, your tenant cannot get compensation under section 37 if the court has refused the tenancy on other grounds, even if one or more of grounds (e), (f) and (g) also applies.

If you are an authority possessing compulsory purchase powers (such as a local authority), your tenant may be entitled to a disturbance payment under Part 3 of the Land Compensation Act 1973.

Negotiating a new tenancy

Most tenancies are renewed by negotiation and your tenant has set out proposals for the new tenancy in paragraph 3 of this notice. You are not obliged to accept these proposals and may put forward your own. You and your tenant may agree in writing to extend the deadline for making an application to the court while negotiations continue. Your tenant may not apply to the court for a new tenancy until two months have passed from the date of the making of the request contained in this notice, unless you have already given notice opposing your tenant's request as mentioned in paragraph 6 of this notice (section 29A(3)).

If you try to agree a new tenancy with your tenant, remember:

- that one of you will need to apply to the court before the date in paragraph 2 of this notice, unless you both agree to extend the period for making an application.
- that any such agreement must be in writing and must be made before the date in paragraph 2 (sections 29A and 29B).

Validity of this notice

The tenant who has given you this notice may not be the person from whom you receive rent (sections 44 and 67). This does not necessarily mean that the notice is invalid.

If you have any doubts about whether this notice is valid, get advice immediately from a solicitor or a surveyor.

Further information

An explanation of the main points to consider when renewing or ending a business tenancy, "Renewing and Ending Business Leases: a Guide for Tenants and Landlords", can be found at www.odpm.gov.uk. Printed copies of the explanation, but not of this form, are available from 1st June 2004 from Free Literature, PO Box 236, Wetherby, West Yorkshire, LS23 7NB (0870 1226 236).

[3427]

FORM 4
LANDLORD'S REQUEST FOR INFORMATION ABOUT OCCUPATION AND SUB-TENANCIES

Section 40(1) of the Landlord and Tenant Act 1954

To: (*insert name and address of tenant*)

From: (*insert name and address of landlord*)

1 This notice relates to the following premises: (*insert address or description of premises*)

2 I give you notice under section 40(1) of the Landlord and Tenant Act 1954 that I require you to provide information—

(a) by answering questions (1) to (3) in the Table below;

(b) if you answer "yes" to question (2), by giving me the name and address of the person or persons concerned;

(c) if you answer "yes" to question (3), by also answering questions (4) to (10) in the Table below;

(d) if you answer "no" to question (8), by giving me the name and address of the sub-tenant; and

(e) if you answer "yes" to question (10), by giving me details of the notice or request.

TABLE
(1) Do you occupy the premises or any part of them wholly or partly for the purposes of a business that is carried on by you?

(2) To the best of your knowledge and belief, does any other person own an interest in reversion in any part of the premises?
(3) Does your tenancy have effect subject to any sub-tenancy on which your tenancy is immediately expectant?
(4) What premises are comprised in the sub-tenancy?
(5) For what term does it have effect or, if it is terminable by notice, by what notice can it be terminated?
(6) What is the rent payable under it?
(7) Who is the sub-tenant?
(8) To the best of your knowledge and belief, is the sub-tenant in occupation of the premises or of part of the premises comprised in the sub-tenancy?
(9) Is an agreement in force excluding, in relation to the sub-tenancy, the provisions of sections 24 to 28 of the Landlord and Tenant Act 1954?
(10) Has a notice been given under section 25 or 26(6) of that Act, or has a request been made under section 26 of that Act, in relation to the sub-tenancy?

3 You must give the information concerned in writing and within the period of one month beginning with the date of service of this notice.

4 Please send all correspondence about this notice to:

Name:

Address:

Signed: Date:

*[Landlord] *[on behalf of the landlord] **delete whichever is inapplicable*

IMPORTANT NOTE FOR THE TENANT

This notice contains some words and phrases that you may not understand. The Notes below should help you, but it would be wise to seek professional advice, for example, from a solicitor or surveyor, before responding to this notice.

Once you have provided the information required by this notice, you must correct it if you realise that it is not, or is no longer, correct. This obligation lasts for six months from the date of service of this notice, but an exception is explained in the next paragraph. If you need to correct information already given, you must do so within one month of becoming aware that the information is incorrect.

The obligation will cease if, after transferring your tenancy, you notify the landlord of the transfer and of the name and address of the person to whom your tenancy has been transferred.

If you fail to comply with the requirements of this notice, or the obligation mentioned above, you may face civil proceedings for breach of the statutory duty that arises under section 40 of the Landlord and Tenant Act 1954. In any such proceedings a court may order you to comply with that duty and may make an award of damages.

NOTES

The sections mentioned below are sections of the Landlord and Tenant Act 1954, as amended, (most recently by the Regulatory Reform (Business Tenancies) (England and Wales) Order 2003)

Purpose of this notice

Your landlord (or, if he or she is a tenant, possibly your landlord's landlord) has sent you this notice in order to obtain information about your occupation and that of any sub-tenants. This information may be relevant to the taking of steps to end or renew your business tenancy.

Time limit for replying

You must provide the relevant information within one month of the date of service of this notice (section 40(1), (2) and (5)).

Information required

You do not have to give your answers on this form; you may use a separate sheet for this purpose. The notice requires you to provide, in writing, information in the form of answers to questions (1) to (3) in the Table above and, if you answer "yes" to question (3), also to provide information in the form of answers to questions (4) to (10) in that Table. Depending on your answer to question (2) and, if applicable in your case, questions (8) and (10), you must also provide the information referred to in paragraph 2(b), (d) and (e) of this notice. Question (2) refers to a person who owns an interest in reversion. You should answer "yes" to this question if you know or believe that there is a person who receives, or is entitled to receive, rent in respect of any part of the premises (other than the landlord who served this notice).

When you answer questions about sub-tenants, please bear in mind that, for these purposes, a sub-tenant includes a person retaining possession of premises by virtue of the Rent (Agriculture) Act 1976 or the Rent Act 1977 after the coming to an end of a sub-tenancy, and "sub-tenancy" includes a right so to retain possession (section 40(8)).

You should keep a copy of your answers and of any other information provided in response to questions (2), (8) or (10) above.

If, once you have given this information, you realise that it is not, or is no longer, correct, you must give the correct information within one month of becoming aware that the previous information is incorrect. Subject to the next paragraph, your duty to correct any information that you have already given continues for six months after you receive this notice (section 40(5)). You should give the correct information to the landlord who gave you this notice unless you receive notice of the transfer of his or her interest, and of the name and address of the person to whom that interest has been transferred. In that case, the correct information must be given to that person.

If you transfer your tenancy within the period of six months referred to above, your duty to correct information already given will cease if you notify the landlord of the transfer and of the name and address of the person to whom your tenancy has been transferred.

If you do not provide the information requested, or fail to correct information that you have provided earlier, after realising that it is not, or is no longer, correct, proceedings may be taken against you and you may have to pay damages (section 40B).

If you are in any doubt about the information that you should give, get immediate advice from a solicitor or a surveyor.

Validity of this notice

The landlord who has given you this notice may not be the landlord to whom you pay your rent (sections 44 and 67). This does not necessarily mean that the notice is invalid.

If you have any doubts about whether this notice is valid, get advice immediately from a solicitor or a surveyor.

Further information

An explanation of the main points to consider when renewing or ending a business tenancy, "Renewing and Ending Business Leases: a Guide for Tenants and Landlords", can be found at www.odpm.gov.uk. Printed copies of the explanation, but not of this form, are available from 1st June 2004 from Free Literature, PO Box 236, Wetherby, West Yorkshire, LS23 7NB (0870 1226 236).

[3428]

FORM 5
TENANT'S REQUEST FOR INFORMATION FROM LANDLORD OR LANDLORD'S MORTGAGEE ABOUT LANDLORD'S INTEREST

Section 40(3) Of The Landlord And Tenant Act 1954

To: (*insert name and address of reversioner or reversioner's mortgagee in possession [see the first note below]*)

From: (*insert name and address of tenant*)

1 This notice relates to the following premises: (*insert address or description of premises*)

2 In accordance with section 40(3) of the Landlord and Tenant Act 1954 I require you—

(a) to state in writing whether you are the owner of the fee simple in respect of the premises or any part of them or the mortgagee in possession of such an owner,

(b) if you answer "no" to (a), to state in writing, to the best of your knowledge and belief—

(i) the name and address of the person who is your or, as the case may be, your mortgagor's immediate landlord in respect of the premises or of the part in respect of which you are not, or your mortgagor is not, the owner in fee simple;

(ii) for what term your or your mortgagor's tenancy has effect and what is the earliest date (if any) at which that tenancy is terminable by notice to quit given by the landlord; and

(iii) whether a notice has been given under section 25 or 26(6) of the Landlord and Tenant Act 1954, or a request has been made under section 26 of that Act, in relation to the tenancy and, if so, details of the notice or request;

(c) to state in writing, to the best of your knowledge and belief, the name and address of any other person who owns an interest in reversion in any part of the premises;

(d) if you are a reversioner, to state in writing whether there is a mortgagee in possession of your interest in the premises; and

(e) if you answer "yes" to (d), to state in writing, to the best of your knowledge and belief, the name and address of the mortgagee in possession.

3 You must give the information concerned within the period of one month beginning with the date of service of this notice.

4 Please send all correspondence about this notice to:

Name:

Address:

Signed: Date:

*[Tenant] *[on behalf of the tenant] (**delete whichever is inapplicable*)

IMPORTANT NOTE FOR LANDLORD OR LANDLORD'S MORTGAGEE

This notice contains some words and phrases that you may not understand. The Notes below should help you, but it would be wise to seek professional advice, for example, from a solicitor or surveyor, before responding to this notice.

Once you have provided the information required by this notice, you must correct it if you realise that it is not, or is no longer, correct. This obligation lasts for six months from the date of service of this notice, but an exception is explained in the next paragraph. If you need to correct information already given, you must do so within one month of becoming aware that the information is incorrect.

The obligation will cease if, after transferring your interest, you notify the tenant of the transfer and of the name and address of the person to whom your interest has been transferred.

If you fail to comply with the requirements of this notice, or the obligation mentioned above, you may face civil proceedings for breach of the statutory duty that arises under section 40 of the Landlord and Tenant Act 1954. In any such proceedings a court may order you to comply with that duty and may make an award of damages.

NOTES

The sections mentioned below are sections of the Landlord and Tenant Act 1954, as amended, (most recently by the Regulatory Reform (Business Tenancies) (England and Wales) Order 2003)

Terms used in this notice

The following terms, which are used in paragraph 2 of this notice, are defined in section 40(8):

"mortgagee in possession" includes a receiver appointed by the mortgagee or by the court who is in receipt of the rents and profits;

"reversioner" means any person having an interest in the premises, being an interest in reversion expectant (whether immediately or not) on the tenancy; and

"reversioner's mortgagee in possession" means any person being a mortgagee in possession in respect of such an interest.

Section 40(8) requires the reference in paragraph 2(b) of this notice to your mortgagor to be read in the light of the definition of "mortgagee in possession".

A mortgagee (mortgage lender) will be "in possession" if the mortgagor (the person who owes money to the mortgage lender) has failed to comply with the terms of the mortgage. The mortgagee may then be entitled to receive rent that would normally have been paid to the mortgagor.

The term "the owner of the fee simple" means the freehold owner.

The term "reversioner" includes the freehold owner and any intermediate landlord as well as the immediate landlord of the tenant who served this notice.

Purpose of this notice and information required

This notice requires you to provide, in writing, the information requested in paragraph 2(a) and (c) of the notice and, if applicable in your case, in paragraph 2(b), (d) and (e). You do not need to use a special form for this purpose.

If, once you have given this information, you realise that it is not, or is no longer, correct, you must give the correct information within one month of becoming aware that the previous information is incorrect. Subject to the last paragraph in this section of these Notes, your duty to correct any information that you have already given continues for six months after you receive this notice (section 40(5)).

You should give the correct information to the tenant who gave you this notice unless you receive notice of the transfer of his or her interest, and of the name and address of the person to whom that interest has been transferred. In that case, the correct information must be given to that person.

If you do not provide the information requested, or fail to correct information that you have provided earlier, after realising that it is not, or is no longer, correct, proceedings may be taken against you and you may have to pay damages (section 40B).

If you are in any doubt as to the information that you should give, get advice immediately from a solicitor or a surveyor.

If you transfer your interest within the period of six months referred to above, your duty to correct information already given will cease if you notify the tenant of that transfer and of the name and address of the person to whom your interest has been transferred.

Time limit for replying

You must provide the relevant information within one month of the date of service of this notice (section 40(3), (4) and (5)).

Validity of this notice

The tenant who has given you this notice may not be the person from whom you receive rent (sections 44 and 67). This does not necessarily mean that the notice is invalid.

If you have any doubts about the validity of the notice, get advice immediately from a solicitor or a surveyor.

Further information

An explanation of the main points to consider when renewing or ending a business tenancy, "Renewing and Ending Business Leases: a Guide for Tenants and Landlords", can be found at www.odpm.gov.uk. Printed copies of the explanation, but not of this form, are available from 1st June 2004 from Free Literature, PO Box 236, Wetherby, West Yorkshire, LS23 7NB (0870 1226 236).

[3429]

FORM 6

LANDLORD'S WITHDRAWAL OF NOTICE TERMINATING TENANCY

Section 44 of, and Paragraph 6 of Schedule 6 to, the Landlord And Tenant Act 1954

To: (*insert name and address of tenant*)

From: (*insert name and address of landlord*)

1 This notice is given under section 44 of, and paragraph 6 of Schedule 6 to, the Landlord and Tenant Act 1954 ("the 1954 Act").

2 It relates to the following property: (*insert address or description of property*)

3 I have become your landlord for the purposes of the 1954 Act.

4 I withdraw the notice given to you by (*insert name of former landlord*), terminating your tenancy on (*insert date*).

5 Please send any correspondence about this notice to:

Name:

Address:

Signed: Date:

*[Landlord] *[on behalf of the landlord] (**delete whichever is inapplicable*)

IMPORTANT NOTE FOR THE TENANT

If you have any doubts about the validity of this notice, get advice immediately from a solicitor or a surveyor.

NOTES

The sections and Schedule mentioned below are sections of, and a Schedule to, the Landlord and Tenant Act 1954, as amended, (most recently by the Regulatory Reform (Business Tenancies) (England and Wales) Order 2003).

Purpose of this notice

You were earlier given a notice bringing your tenancy to an end, but there has now been a change of landlord. This new notice is given to you by your new landlord and withdraws the earlier notice, which now has no effect. However, the new landlord can, if he or she wishes, give you a fresh notice with the intention of bringing your tenancy to an end (section 44 and paragraph 6 of Schedule 6)

Validity of this notice

The landlord who has given you this notice may not be the landlord to whom you pay your rent (sections 44 and 67). This does not necessarily mean that the notice is invalid.

If you have any doubts about whether this notice is valid, get advice immediately from a solicitor or a surveyor. If this notice is *not* valid, the original notice will have effect. Your tenancy will end on the date given in that notice (stated in paragraph 4 of this notice).

Further information

An explanation of the main points to consider when renewing or ending a business tenancy, "Renewing and Ending Business Leases: a Guide for Tenants and Landlords", can be found at www.odpm.gov.uk. Printed copies of the explanation, but not of this form, are available from 1st June 2004 from Free Literature, PO Box 236, Wetherby, West Yorkshire, LS23 7NB (0870 1226 236).

[3430]

FORM 7

LANDLORD'S NOTICE ENDING A BUSINESS TENANCY (WITH REASONS FOR REFUSING A NEW TENANCY) WHERE THE LEASEHOLD REFORM ACT 1967 MAY APPLY

Section 25 of the Landlord and Tenant Act 1954 and paragraph 10 of Schedule 3 to the Leasehold Reform Act 1967

IMPORTANT NOTE FOR THE LANDLORD: Use this form where you wish to oppose the grant of a new tenancy, and the tenant may be entitled to acquire the freehold or an extended lease. Complete this form and send it to the tenant. If you are opposed to the grant of a new tenancy, and the tenant is not entitled to acquire the freehold or an extended lease, use form 2 in Schedule 2 to the Landlord and Tenant Act 1954, Part 2 (Notices) Regulations 2004 instead of this form.

To: (*insert name and address of tenant*)

From: (*insert name and address of landlord*)

1 This notice relates to the following property: (*insert address or description of property*)

2 I am giving you notice under section 25 of the Landlord and Tenant Act 1954 to end your tenancy on (*insert date*).

3 I am opposed to the grant of a new tenancy.

4 You may ask the court to order the grant of a new tenancy. If you do, I will oppose your application on the ground(s) mentioned in paragraph(s)* of section 30(1) of that Act. I draw your attention to the Table in the Notes below, which sets out all the grounds of opposition.

* (*insert letter(s) of the paragraph(s) relied on*)

5 If you wish to ask the court for a new tenancy you must do so by the date in paragraph 2 unless, before that date, we agree in writing to a later date

6 I can ask the court to order the ending of your tenancy without granting you a new tenancy. I may have to pay you compensation if I have relied only on one or more of the grounds mentioned in paragraph (e), (f) and (g) of section 30(1). If I ask the court to end your tenancy, you can challenge my application.

7 If you have a right under Part 1 of the Leasehold Reform Act 1967 to acquire the freehold or an extended lease of property comprised in the tenancy, notice of your desire to have the freehold or an extended lease cannot be given more than two months after the service of this notice. If you have that right, and give notice of your desire to have the freehold or an extended lease within those two months, this notice will not operate, and I may take no further proceedings under Part 2 of the Landlord and Tenant Act 1954.

*8 If you give notice of your desire to have the freehold or an extended lease, I will be entitled to apply to the court under section 17/section 18** of the Leasehold Reform Act 1967, and propose to do so. If I am successful I may have to pay you compensation. (***delete the reference to section 17 or section 18, as the circumstances require*)

OR

PART II STATUTORY INSTRUMENTS

*8 If you give notice of your desire to have the freehold or an extended lease, I will be entitled to apply to the court under section 17/section 18** of the Leasehold Reform Act 1967, but do not propose to do so. (***delete the reference to section 17 or section 18, as the circumstances require*)

OR

*8 If you give notice of your desire to have the freehold or an extended lease, I will not be entitled to apply to the court under section 17 or section 18 of the Leasehold Reform Act 1967.

**DELETE TWO versions of this paragraph, as the circumstances require*

*9 I know or believe that the following persons have an interest superior to your tenancy or to be the agent concerned with the property on behalf of someone who has such an interest (*insert names and addresses*):

**delete if inapplicable*

10 Please send all correspondence about this notice to:

Name:

Address:

Signed: Date:

*[Landlord] *[On behalf of the landlord] *[Mortgagee] *[On behalf of the mortgagee]

(**delete if inapplicable*)

IMPORTANT NOTE FOR THE TENANT

This Notice is intended to bring your tenancy to an end on the date specified in paragraph 2.

Your landlord is not prepared to offer you a new tenancy. You will not get a new tenancy unless you successfully challenge in court the grounds on which your landlord opposes the grant of a new tenancy.

If you want to continue to occupy your property you must act quickly. The notes below should help you to decide what action you now need to take. If you want to challenge your landlord's refusal to renew your tenancy, get advice immediately from a solicitor or a surveyor.

NOTES

Unless otherwise stated, the sections mentioned below are sections of the Landlord and Tenant Act 1954, as amended, (most recently by the Regulatory Reform (Business Tenancies) (England and Wales) Order 2003)

Ending of your tenancy

This notice is intended to bring your tenancy to an end on the date given in paragraph 2. Section 25 contains rules about the date that the landlord can put in paragraph 2 of this notice.

Your landlord is not prepared to offer you a new tenancy. If you want a new tenancy you will need to apply to the court for a new tenancy and successfully challenge the landlord's opposition (see the section below headed "*Landlord's opposition to new tenancy*"). If you wish to apply to the court you must do so before the date given in paragraph 2 of this notice, unless you and your landlord have agreed in writing, before that date, to extend the deadline (sections 29A and 29B).

If you apply to the court your tenancy will continue after the date given in paragraph 2 of this notice while your application is being considered (section 24). You may not apply to the court if your landlord has already done so (section 24(2A) and (2B)).

You may only stay in the property after the date given in paragraph 2 (or such later date as you and the landlord may have agreed in writing) if before that date you have asked the court to order the grant of a new tenancy or the landlord has asked the court to order the ending of your tenancy without granting you a new one.

If you are in any doubt about what action you should take, get advice immediately from a solicitor or a surveyor.

Landlord's opposition to new tenancy

If you apply to the court for a new tenancy, the landlord can only oppose your application on one or more of the grounds set out in section 30(1). If you match the letter(s) specified in paragraph 4 of the notice with those in the first column in the Table below, you can see from the second column the ground(s) on which the landlord relies.

Paragraph of section 30(1)	*Grounds*
(a)	Where under the current tenancy the tenant has any obligations as respects the repair and maintenance of the holding, that the tenant ought not to be granted a new tenancy in view of the state of repair of the holding, being a state resulting from the tenant's failure to comply with the said obligations.
(b)	That the tenant ought not to be granted a new tenancy in view of his persistent delay in paying rent which has become due.
(c)	That the tenant ought not to be granted a new tenancy in view of other substantial breaches by him of his obligations under the current tenancy, or for any other reason connected with the tenant's use or management of the holding.
(d)	That the landlord has offered and is willing to provide or secure the provision of alternative accommodation for the tenant, that the terms on which the alternative accommodation is available are reasonable having regard to the terms of the current tenancy and to all other relevant circumstances, and that the accommodation and the time at which it will be available are suitable for the tenant's requirements (including the requirement to preserve goodwill) having regard to the nature and class of his business and to the situation and extent of, and facilities afforded by, the holding.
(e)	Where the current tenancy was created by the sub-letting of part only of the property comprised in a superior tenancy and the landlord is the owner of an interest in reversion expectant on the termination of that superior tenancy, that the aggregate of the rents reasonably obtainable on separate lettings of the holding and the remainder of that property would be substantially less than the rent reasonably obtainable on a letting of that property as a whole, that on the termination of the current tenancy the landlord requires possession of the holding for the purposes of letting or otherwise disposing of the said property as a whole, and that in view thereof the tenant ought not to be granted a new tenancy.
(f)	That on the termination of the current tenancy the landlord intends to demolish or reconstruct the premises comprised in the holding or a substantial part of those premises or to carry out substantial work of construction on the holding or part thereof and that he could not reasonably do so without obtaining possession of the holding.
(g)	On the termination of the current tenancy the landlord intends to occupy the holding for the purposes, or partly for the purposes, of a business to be carried on by him therein, or as his residence.

In this Table "the holding" means the property that is the subject of the tenancy.

In ground (e), "the landlord is the owner an interest in reversion expectant on the termination of that superior tenancy" means that the landlord has an interest in the property that will entitle him or her, when your immediate landlord's tenancy comes to an end, to exercise certain rights and obligations in relation to the property that are currently exercisable by your immediate landlord.

If the landlord relies on ground (f), the court can sometimes still grant a new tenancy if certain conditions set out in section 31A are met.

If the landlord relies on ground (g), please note that "the landlord" may have an extended meaning. Where a landlord has a controlling interest in a company then either the landlord or the company can rely on ground (g). Where the landlord is a company and a person has a controlling interest in that company then either of them can rely on ground (g) (section 30(1A) and (1B)). A person has a "controlling interest" in a company if, had he been a company, the other company would have been its subsidiary (section 46(2)).

The landlord must normally have been the landlord for at least five years before he or she can rely on ground (g).

Rights under the Leasehold Reform Act 1967

If the property comprised in your tenancy is a house, as defined in section 2 of the Leasehold Reform Act 1967 ("the 1967 Act"), you may have the right to buy the freehold of the property or an

PART II STATUTORY INSTRUMENTS

extended lease. If the house is for the time being let under two or more tenancies, you will not have that right if your tenancy is subject to a sub-tenancy and the sub-tenant is himself or herself entitled to that right.

You will have that right if all the following conditions are met:

(i) your lease was originally granted for a term of more than 35 years, or was preceded by such a lease which was granted or assigned to you; and

(ii) your lease is of the whole house; and

(iii) your lease is at a low rent. If your tenancy was entered into before 1 April 1990 (or later if you contracted before that date to enter into the tenancy) "low rent" means that your present annual rent is less than two-thirds of the rateable value of your house as assessed either on 23 March 1965, or on the first day of the term in the case of a lease granted to commence after 23 March 1965; and the property had a rateable value other than nil when the tenancy began or at any time before 1 April 1990. If your tenancy was granted on or after 1 April 1990, "low rent" means that the present annual rent is not more than £1,000 in London or £250 elsewhere; and

(iv) you have been occupying the house (or any part of it) as your only or main residence (whether or not it has been occupied for other purposes) either for the whole of the last two years, or for a total of two years in the last ten years; and

(v) the rateable value of your house was at one time within certain limits.

Claiming your rights under the 1967 Act

If you have a right to buy the freehold or an extended lease and wish to exercise it you must serve the appropriate notice on the landlord. A special form is prescribed for this purpose; it is Form 1 as set out in the Schedule to the Leasehold Reform (Notices) (Amendment) (England) Regulations 2002 (SI 2002/1715) or, if the property is in Wales, the Leasehold Reform (Notices) (Amendment) (Wales) Regulations 2002 (SI 2002/3187) (W 303). Subject to the two exceptions mentioned below, you must serve the notice claiming to buy the freehold or an extended lease within two months after the date of service of this notice. The first exception is where, within that two-month period, you apply to the court to order the grant of a new tenancy. In that case your claim to buy the freehold or an extended lease must be made when you make the application to the court. The second exception is where the landlord agrees in writing to your claim being made after the date on which it should have been made.

There are special rules about the service of notices. If there has been any delay in your seeing this notice, you may need to act very quickly.

If you are in any doubt about your rights under the 1967 Act or what action you should take, get advice immediately from a solicitor or a surveyor.

Landlord's opposition to claims under the 1967 Act

If your landlord acquired his or her interest in the house not later than 18 February 1966 he or she can object to your claim to buy the freehold or an extended lease on the grounds that he or she needs to occupy the house or that the house is needed for occupation by a member of his or her family. This objection will be under section 18 of the 1967 Act.

If you claim an extended lease, your landlord can object under section 17 of the 1967 Act on the grounds that he or she wishes to redevelop the property.

You will be able to tell from paragraph 8 of this notice whether your landlord intends to apply to the court and, if so, whether for the purposes of occupation or redevelopment of the house.

Compensation

If you cannot get a new tenancy solely because one or more of grounds (e), (f) and (g) in section 30(1) applies, you may be entitled to compensation under section 37. If your landlord has opposed your application on any of the other grounds as well as (e), (f) or (g) you can only get compensation if the court's refusal to grant a new tenancy is based solely on one or more of grounds (e), (f) and (g). In other words, you cannot get compensation under section 37 if the court has refused your tenancy on other grounds, even if one or more of grounds (e), (f) and (g) also applies.

If your landlord is an authority possessing compulsory purchase powers (such as a local authority) you may be entitled to a disturbance payment under Part 3 of the Land Compensation Act 1973.

If you have a right under the 1967 Act to buy the freehold or an extended lease but the landlord is able to obtain pos-session of the premises, compensation is payable under section 17(2) or section 18(4) of the 1967 Act. Your solicitor or surveyor will be able to advise you about this.

Negotiations with your landlord

If you try to buy the property by agreement or negotiate an extended lease with the landlord, remember:

- that your present tenancy will not be extended under the 1954 Act after the date in paragraph 2 of this notice unless you agree in writing to extend the deadline for applying to the court under the 1954 Act or you (or the landlord) has applied to the court before that date (sections 29, 29A and 29B), and

- that you may lose your right to serve a notice claiming to buy the freehold or an extended lease under the 1967 Act if you do not observe the two-month time limit referred to in the note headed *Claiming your rights under the 1967 Act*.

Validity of this notice

The landlord who has given you this notice may not be the landlord to whom you pay your rent (sections 44 and 67). This does not necessarily mean that the notice is invalid.

If you have any doubts about whether this notice is valid, get advice immediately from a solicitor or a surveyor

Further information

An explanation of the main points to consider when renewing or ending a business tenancy, "Renewing and Ending Business Leases: a Guide for Tenants and Landlords", can be found at www.odpm.gov.uk. Printed copies of the explanation, but not of this form, are available from 1st June 2004 from Free Literature, PO Box 236, Wetherby, West Yorkshire, LS23 7NB (0870 1226 236).

[3431]

(*Forms 8–17 outside the scope of this work.*)

COMMONHOLD REGULATIONS 2004

(SI 2004/1829)

NOTES

Made: 14 July 2004.

Authority: Commonhold and Leasehold Reform Act 2002, ss 3, 9(2), 11(3), 13, 17(1), 19(1), 21(2), 24(6), 31(2), 32(1), 37(1), 45(2), 51(3), 57(3), 58(5), Sch 3, paras 2, 16.

Commencement: 27 September 2004.

PART I GENERAL

1 Citation, commencement and interpretation

(1) These Regulations may be cited as the Commonhold Regulations 2004 and shall come into force on the day on which section 2 of the Act comes into force.

(2) In these Regulations a section referred to by number alone means the section so numbered in the Act and a Schedule referred to by number alone means the Schedule so numbered in these Regulations.

(3) In these Regulations—

(a) "the Act" means the Commonhold and Leasehold Reform Act 2002; and

(b) "the Rules" means the Commonhold (Land Registration) Rules 2004 and a Form referred to by letters alone or by letters and numbers means the Form so designated in Schedule 1 to the Rules.

[3432]

NOTES

Commencement: 27 September 2004.

2 Joint unit-holders

(1) In the application of the following provisions to a commonhold unit with joint unit-holders a reference to a unit-holder is a reference to the joint unit-holders together—

(a) regulations 10(2), 18(2)(a) and 18(3); and

(b) paragraphs 4.8.5 to 4.8.9 in Schedule 3.

(2) In the application of the following provisions to a commonhold unit with joint unit-holders a reference to a unit-holder includes a reference to each joint unit-holder and to the joint unit-holders together—

(a) regulations 11(1) and 18(2)(b);

(b) articles 4(d) and 75 in Schedule 2; and

(c) all provisions in Schedule 3 except paragraphs 4.8.5 to 4.8.9.

(3) In section 13(2)—

(a) omit paragraphs (a), (c), (g) and (h);

(b) in paragraph (b) omit "and (3)"; and

(c) in paragraph (f) after "section 35(1)(b)," insert "and".

(4) In section 13(3)—
(a) after paragraph (a) insert—
"(aa) section 14(3),
(ab) section 15(3),";
(b) after paragraph (b) insert—
"(ba) section 19(2) and (3),"; and
(c) after paragraph (f) insert—
"(fa) section 38(1),
(fb) section 39(2),".

[3433]

NOTES

Commencement: 27 September 2004.

PART II
REGISTRATION

3 Consents required prior to the creation of a commonhold additional to those required by section 3(1)(a) to (c)

(1) An application under section 2 may not be made in respect of a freehold estate in land without the consent of anyone who is—
(a) the estate owner of any unregistered freehold estate in the whole or part of the land;
(b) the estate owner of any unregistered leasehold estate in the whole or part of the land granted for a term of more than 21 years;
(c) the owner of any mortgage, charge or lien for securing money or money's worth over the whole or part of any unregistered land included in the application; or
(d) subject to paragraph (2), the holder of a lease granted for a term of not more than 21 years which will be extinguished by virtue of section 7(3)(d) or 9(3)(f).

(2) An application under section 2 may be made without the consent of a person who would otherwise be required to consent by virtue of paragraph (1)(d) if—
(a) the person is entitled to the grant of a term of years absolute—
(i) of the same premises as are comprised in the extinguished lease;
(ii) on the same terms as the extinguished lease, except to the extent necessary to comply with the Act and these Regulations and excluding any terms that are spent;
(iii) at the same rent as the rent payable under, and including the same provisions for rent review as were included in, the extinguished lease as at the date on which it will be extinguished;
(iv) for a term equivalent to the unexpired term of the lease which will be extinguished; and
(v) to take effect immediately after the lease is extinguished by virtue of section 7(3)(d) or 9(3)(f); and
(b) before the application under section 2 is made, the person's entitlement to the grant of a term of years absolute has been protected by a notice in the land register to the freehold title(s) for the land in the application or, in the case of unregistered land, by an entry in the land charges register in the name of the estate owner of the freehold title.

[3434]

NOTES

Commencement: 27 September 2004.

4 Details of consent

(1) Consent to an application under—
(a) section 2 must be given in Form CON 1; and
(b) section 8(4) must be given in Form CON 2.

(2) Subject to paragraphs (3), (4) and (7), consent is binding on a person who gives consent or who is deemed to have given consent.

(3) Consent may be given subject to conditions.

(4) Subject to any condition imposing a shorter period, consent will lapse if no application is made within a period of 12 months beginning with the date on which consent was given.

(5) Consent is deemed to have been given by—
(a) the person making the application where that person's consent would otherwise be required in accordance with section 3, but has not been expressly given; and

(b) a successor in title to a person who has given consent or who is deemed to have given consent.

(6) Consent given for the purpose of one application has effect for the purpose of another application ("the new application") only where the new application is submitted—

(a) in place of a previous application which has been withdrawn by the applicant, or rejected or cancelled by the Registrar; and

(b) within a period of 12 months beginning with the date on which the consent was given.

(7) Consent may be withdrawn at any time before the date on which any application is submitted to the Registrar.

(8) In this regulation, "consent" means consent for the purposes of section 3.

[3435]

NOTES

Commencement: 27 September 2004.

5 Dispensing with a requirement for consent

The court may dispense with the requirement for consent to an application under section 2 if a person whose consent is required—

(a) cannot be identified after all reasonable efforts have been made to ascertain his identity;

(b) has been identified but cannot be traced after all reasonable efforts have been made to trace him; or

(c) has been sent the request for consent and all reasonable efforts have been made to obtain a response but he has not responded.

[3436]

NOTES

Commencement: 27 September 2004.

6 Statement under section 9(1)(b): Registration with unit-holders

A statement under section 9(1)(b) which accompanies an application under section 2 must, in relation to each commonhold unit, state—

(a) the full name of the proposed initial unit-holder or if there are proposed joint unit-holders the full name of each of them;

(b) the address for service of the proposed unit-holder or if there are proposed joint unit-holders the address for service of each of them;

(c) the unit number of the commonhold unit; and

(d) the postal address of the commonhold unit (if available).

[3437]

NOTES

Commencement: 27 September 2004.

7 Multiple site commonholds

For the purposes of an application under section 2 made jointly by two or more persons, each of whom is the registered freeholder of part of the land to which the application relates ("a part site") section 11 is modified so that, in addition to complying with the requirements in section 11(3), in defining the extent of a commonhold unit, the commonhold community statement must provide for the extent of each commonhold unit to be situated wholly upon one part site, and not situated partly on one part site and partly on one or more other part sites.

[3438]

NOTES

Commencement: 27 September 2004.

PART III
COMMONHOLD UNIT

8 Requirements of a plan defining the extent of a commonhold unit

A plan referred to in a commonhold community statement for the purposes of defining the extent of a commonhold unit must delineate the boundaries of the commonhold unit with any adjoining property.

[3439]

NOTES

Commencement: 27 September 2004.

9 Definition of a commonhold unit

(1) In defining the extent of a commonhold unit a commonhold community statement—

(a) may exclude, from the definition, the structure and exterior of a self-contained building, or of a self-contained part of a building, which only contains one commonhold unit or part of one commonhold unit; and

(b) must exclude, from the definition, the structure and exterior of a self-contained building, or of a self-contained part of a building, in any other case.

(2) In this regulation—

"self-contained building" means a building which is structurally detached;

"self-contained part of a building" means a part of a building—

(a) which constitutes a vertical division of the building;

(b) the structure of which is such that it could be redeveloped independently of the rest of the building; and

(c) in relation to which the relevant services provided for occupiers are provided independently of the relevant services provided for the occupiers of the rest of the building, or could be so provided without involving the carrying out of works likely to result in a significant interruption in the provision of any relevant services for occupiers of the rest of the building;

"relevant services" are services provided by the means of pipes, cables or other fixed installations; and

"structure and exterior" includes the relevant services in or to the building but does not include those which are within and exclusively to one commonhold unit.

[3440]

NOTES

Commencement: 27 September 2004.

10 Requirement to notify Registrar

(1) This regulation applies to an amendment of a commonhold community statement which redefines the extent of a commonhold unit over which there is a registered charge.

(2) The unit-holder of a commonhold unit over which there is a registered charge must give notice of the amendment to the Registrar in Form COE.

(3) On receipt of such notification the Registrar must alter the register to reflect the application of section 24(4) or (5).

[3441]

NOTES

Commencement: 27 September 2004.

11 Leasing of a residential commonhold unit

(1) A term of years absolute in a residential commonhold unit or part only of a residential commonhold unit must not—

(a) be granted for a premium;

(b) subject to paragraph (2), be granted for a term longer than 7 years;

(c) be granted under an option or agreement if—

(i) the person to take the new term of years absolute has an existing terms of years absolute of the premises to be let;

(ii) the new term when added to the existing term will be more than 7 years; and

(iii) the option or agreement was entered into before or at the same time as the existing term of years absolute;

(d) contain an option or agreement to renew the term of years absolute which confers on the lessee or on the lessor an option or agreement for renewal for a further term which, together with the original term, amounts to more than 7 years;

(e) contain an option or agreement to extend the term beyond 7 years; or

(f) contain a provision requiring the lessee to make payments to the commonhold association in discharge of payments which are due, in accordance with the commonhold community statement, to be made by the unit-holder.

(2) A term of years absolute in a residential commonhold unit or part only of a residential commonhold unit may be granted for a term of not more than 21 years to the holder of a lease which has been extinguished by virtue of section 7(3)(d) or 9(3)(f) if the term of years absolute—

(a) is granted of the same premises as are comprised in the extinguished lease;

(b) is granted on the same terms as the extinguished lease, except to the extent necessary to comply with the Act and these Regulations and excluding any terms that are spent;

(c) is granted at the same rent as the rent payable under, and including the same provisions for rent review as were included in, the extinguished lease as at the date on which it was extinguished;

(d) is granted for a term equivalent to the unexpired term of the lease immediately before it was extinguished or, if the unexpired term of the lease immediately before it was extinguished is more than 21 years, for a term of 21 years;

(e) takes effect immediately after the lease was extinguished; and

(f) does not include any option or agreement which-

(i) may create a term or an extension to a term which, together with the term of the years absolute, would amount to more than 21 years; or

(ii) may result in the grant of a term of years absolute containing an option or agreement to extend the term.

[3442]

NOTES

Commencement: 27 September 2004.

PART IV
COMMONHOLD ASSOCIATION

12 The name of the commonhold association

(1) The name by which a commonhold association is registered under the Companies Act 1985 must end with "commonhold association limited" or, if the memorandum of association states that the commonhold association's registered office is to be situated in Wales, those words or the Welsh equivalent ("Cymdeithas Cydradd-Ddaliad Cyfyngedig").

(2) The name by which a company other than a commonhold association is registered may not end with "commonhold association limited" or the Welsh equivalent "Cymdeithas Cydradd-Ddaliad Cyfyngedig".

(3) In this regulation references to the words "limited" and "cyfyngedig" include the abbreviations "ltd" and "cyf".

[3443]

NOTES

Commencement: 27 September 2004.

13 Memorandum of association

(1) The memorandum of association of a commonhold association must be in the form in Schedule 1 (memorandum of association) or a form to the same effect.

(2) The memorandum of association of a commonhold association must contain all the provisions contained in the form in Schedule 1 and each provision in that Schedule will have effect for a commonhold association whether or not it is adopted under paragraph 2(2) of Schedule 3 to the Act.

(3) In its memorandum of association, a commonhold association must—

(a) include the name of the commonhold association on the front page and in paragraph 1;

(b) omit "England and Wales" or "Wales" from paragraph 2; and

(c) include the name of the commonhold in paragraph 3.

(4) A commonhold association may include additional provisions in its memorandum of association immediately after the provision which appears as paragraph 5 in Schedule 1 where the additional provisions are preceded by a heading which must include "additional provision specific to this commonhold association" and each new provision must be given a number.

[3444]

NOTES

Commencement: 27 September 2004.

14 Articles of association

(1) The articles of association of a commonhold association must be in the form in Schedule 2 (articles of association) or a form to the same effect.

(2) Subject to the following paragraphs, the articles of association of a commonhold association must contain all the provisions in the form in Schedule 2 and each provision in that Schedule will have effect for a commonhold association whether or not it is adopted under paragraph 2(2) of Schedule 3 to the Act.

(3) In its articles of association a commonhold must include the name of the commonhold association on the front page.

(4) In its articles of association a commonhold association may substitute—

(a) any time period for the time periods in articles 7, 18 and 48(f) except that the time period may not be reduced below the time periods mentioned in those articles;

(b) any number of meetings for the number of meetings in article 48(f) except that the number may not be reduced below three;

(c) any figure for the figures in article 13 except that the figure may not be reduced below the figures mentioned in that article and different provision may be made for different purposes; and

(d) a time or date for "at any time" in article 36.

(5) A commonhold association may omit "Failing that it may be delivered at the meeting to the chairman, secretary or to any director." from article 36 of its articles of association.

(6) A commonhold association may include additional provisions in its articles of association where each additional provision is immediately preceded by a heading which must include "additional provision specific to this commonhold association" and is identified with the numeral of the immediately preceding article followed by a capital letter, such letters to be allocated in alphabetical order in respect of each number.

(7) Where the articles of association of a commonhold association contain provisions for the appointment of alternate directors, article 38 is to have effect for a commonhold association with " (other than alternate directors)" inserted after "the number of directors".

(8) Where the commonhold community statement gives the developer the right to appoint and remove directors the following provisions have effect for a commonhold association whether or not they are adopted under paragraph 2(2) of Schedule 3 to the Act—

(a) during the transitional period the developer may appoint up to two directors in addition to any directors appointed by the subscribers, and may remove or replace any director so appointed;

(b) after the end of the transitional period and for so long as the developer is the unit-holder of more than one quarter of the total number of commonhold units in the commonhold, he may appoint up to one quarter of the directors of the commonhold association, and may remove or replace any director so appointed;

(c) a director appointed by the developer pursuant to paragraph (a) or (b) is known as a "developer's director";

(d) any appointment or removal of a developer's director made pursuant to paragraph (a) or (b) must be by notice in writing signed by or on behalf of the developer and will take effect immediately it is received at the office of the commonhold association or by the secretary, or as and from the date specified in the notice (if later);

(e) if at any time the commonhold association resolves to specify or reduce the maximum number of directors, and as a consequence the number of developer's directors exceeds the number permitted under paragraph (b), the developer must immediately reduce the number of developer's directors accordingly and where such reduction has not been effected by the start of the next directors' meeting, the longest in office of the developer's directors must cease to hold office immediately so as to achieve the required reduction in numbers;

(f) if the developer ceases to be the unit-holder of more than one quarter of the total number of units in the commonhold, he may no longer appoint, replace or remove a director and any developer's directors previously appointed by him under this article will cease to hold office immediately;

(g) a developer's director who is removed from office or who ceases to hold office under this article will not have any claim against the commonhold association in respect of such removal from, or cessation to hold, office;

(h) at any time at which the developer is entitled to exercise the power to appoint and remove developer's directors, the developer is not entitled to vote upon a resolution fixing the number of directors of the commonhold association, or upon a resolution for the appointment or removal from office of any director not appointed by him, or upon any resolution concerning the remuneration of any director not appointed by him;

(i) a developer's director may provide information to the developer that he receives by virtue of his being a director; and

(j) the provisions in articles 40, 41 and 54 do not apply to a developer's director.

(9) Where the provisions in paragraph (8) have effect for a commonhold association—

(a) articles 45 and 46 are to have effect for a commonhold association but with "(other than a vacancy in respect of a developer's director)" inserted after "fill a vacancy"; and

(b) article 61 is to have effect for a commonhold association but with "At least one of the persons present at the meeting must be a director other than a developer's director." inserted at the end.

(10) In this regulation an article referred to by number alone means the article so numbered in Schedule 2.

[3445]

NOTES

Commencement: 27 September 2004.

15 Commonhold community statement

(1) The commonhold community statement must be in the form in Schedule 3 (commonhold community statement) or a form to the same effect.

(2) The commonhold community statement must contain all the provisions contained in the form in Schedule 3 and will be treated as including those provisions.

(3) The commonhold community statement must include the name of the commonhold on the front page and signature page and must include the information relevant to the commonhold in the paragraphs in the Annexes.

(4) The commonhold community statement must be signed at the end in the following form—

(a) on application for registration under section 2—

"Signed [by] [on behalf of] the applicant: ....
Name: (please print) ....
Title: .... "; or

(b) where an amended commonhold community statement is registered in accordance with section 33—

"Signed [by] [on behalf of] [the commonhold association] [the developer]:
....
Name: (please print) ....
Title: .... "

(5) The commonhold community statement must include information relevant to the commonhold in—

(a) paragraph 2 of Annex 3 if the directors of the commonhold association have established funds to finance the repair and maintenance of the common parts or commonhold units; and

(b) paragraph 5 of Annex 4 if there are other risks insured in addition to fire.

(6) The commonhold community statement is treated as including "0 per cent" in paragraph 1 of Annex 4 unless different provision is made in its place.

(7) Where, by virtue of regulation 9(1)(b), in defining the extent of a commonhold unit, the commonhold community statement excludes the structure and exterior of a self-contained building, or of a self-contained part of a building, the commonhold community statement is treated as including provision which imposes a duty on the commonhold association to insure the whole of the self-contained building, or self-contained part of the building.

(8) Subject to paragraphs (9) to (12), the commonhold community statement may include further definitions and may include further numbered provisions relevant to the commonhold at the end of a Part or a Section or in an Annex.

(9) Where further definitions are included in the commonhold community statement each definition must be inserted in alphabetical order into paragraph 1.4.5 in the commonhold community statement.

(10) Where further provisions are included in the commonhold community statement which confer rights on the developer—

(a) the provisions must be inserted in an Annex headed "DEVELOPMENT RIGHTS", such Annex must be numbered and be the last Annex in the commonhold community statement and a reference to its heading must be included in the table of contents in the commonhold community statement;

(b) a paragraph containing "Annex [ ] specifies the rights of the developer which are designed to permit him to undertake development business or to facilitate his undertaking of development business." must be inserted in Section 1.3 in the commonhold community statement with the Annex number inserted in place of the brackets; and

(c) paragraph 4.8.14 in the commonhold community statement is treated as including "; or to remove any surrendered development rights" at the end.

(11) Where any other provisions are included in the commonhold community statement in a Part or Section—

(a) each additional provision must be inserted in numerical order continuing the numbers within the relevant Part or Section;

(b) each additional provision must be immediately preceded by a heading which must include "additional provision specific to this commonhold" in the relevant Part or Section; and

(c) a reference to the heading must be included in the table of contents in the commonhold community statement.

(12) Where any other provisions are included in the commonhold community statement in an Annex—

(a) a heading which must include "ADDITIONAL PROVISIONS SPECIFIC TO THIS COMMONHOLD" must be inserted at the end of Part 4 followed by a numbered paragraph which reads "Additional provisions are set out in Annex" followed by the number given to the Annex by the commonhold association;

(b) a paragraph must be inserted in Section 1.3 in the commonhold community statement giving the number of the Annex and details of its contents; and

(c) a reference to its heading must be included in the table of contents in the commonhold community statement.

(13) In this regulation "commonhold community statement" means the commonhold community statement of a commonhold and a reference to a Part, Section or Annex means a Part, Section or Annex in the commonhold community statement.

[3446]

NOTES

Commencement: 27 September 2004.

16 Forms

The Forms contained in Schedule 4 (forms) or forms to the same effect must be used in accordance with the commonhold community statement of a commonhold.

[3447]

NOTES

Commencement: 27 September 2004.

PART V
OPERATION OF A COMMONHOLD

17 Enforcement

Jurisdiction is conferred on the court to deal with the exercise or enforcement of a right conferred, or duty imposed, by or by virtue of—

(a) a commonhold community statement;

(b) these Regulations; or

(c) Part 1 of the Act.

[3448]

NOTES

Commencement: 27 September 2004.

18 Development Rights

(1) The rights (if any) conferred on the developer in a commonhold community statement are restricted or regulated in accordance with the following paragraphs.

(2) The developer must not exercise development rights in such manner as to interfere unreasonably with—

(a) the enjoyment by each unit-holder of the freehold estate in his unit; and

(b) the exercise by any unit-holder or tenant of his rights under the commonhold community statement.

(3) The developer may not remove land from the commonhold that has been transferred to a unit-holder unless the unit-holder consents in writing before the land is removed.

(4) Any damage to the common parts or a commonhold unit caused by the developer in the course of undertaking development business must be put right by the developer as soon as reasonably practicable taking into account the future works required to complete the development and the degree of interference caused by the damage.

(5) The developer must not exercise development rights if the works for which the development rights were conferred have been completed, save that any rights permitting or facilitating the undertaking of development business of the type referred to in paragraph 3 of Schedule 4 to the Act

may be exercised for such further period as the developer continues to undertake that type of development business in relation to the whole or, as the case may be, the relevant part, of the commonhold.

(6) In this regulation "developer" includes a person acting on his authority.

[3449]

NOTES
Commencement: 27 September 2004.

PART VI
TERMINATION

19 Termination

(1) The liquidator must, in accordance with section 45(2), apply to the court for an order determining—

(a) the terms and conditions on which a termination application may be made; and
(b) the terms of the termination statement to accompany a termination application

within the period of 3 months beginning with the date on which the liquidator was appointed.

(2) An application under section 51(1) must be accompanied by the certificate of incorporation of the successor commonhold association given in accordance with section 13 of the Companies Act 1985 and any altered certificates of incorporation issued under section 28 of that Act.

[3450]

NOTES
Commencement: 27 September 2004.

(*Schs 1–4 outside the scope of this work.*)

COMMONHOLD (LAND REGISTRATION) RULES 2004

(SI 2004/1830)

NOTES
Made: 14 July 2004.
Authority: Commonhold and Leasehold Reform Act 2002, s 65.
Commencement: 27 September 2004.

General

1 Citation and commencement

These rules may be cited as the Commonhold (Land Registration) Rules 2004 and shall come into force on the day that section 2 of the Act comes into force.

[3451]

NOTES
Commencement: 27 September 2004.

2 Interpretation

(1) In these rules—

"the Act" means Part 1 of the Commonhold and Leasehold Reform Act 2002,
"commonhold entries" means the entries referred to in paragraphs (a) to (c) of rule 28(1) and
"main rules" means the Land Registration Rules 2003.

(2) In these rules except where otherwise stated, a form referred to by letters or numbers means the form so designated in Schedule 1 to these rules.

[3452]

NOTES
Commencement: 27 September 2004.

3 Land registration rules

(1) Land registration rules within the meaning of the Land Registration Act 2002 have effect in relation to anything done by virtue of or for the purposes of the Act as they have effect in relation to anything done by virtue of or for the purposes of the Land Registration Act 2002 subject to paragraphs (2) and (3).

(2) Rules 3(3)(a), 3(4)(a), 126, 127 and 214 of the main rules shall not apply to any application made under the Act.

(3) In its application to the Act—

(a) subject to paragraph (2), rule 3 of the main rules (individual registers and more than one registered estate, division and amalgamation) shall apply as if the words "and are vested in the same proprietor" in paragraph (1) and the words "and are vested in the same proprietor" in paragraph (4) were omitted,

(b) rule 54 of the main rules (outline applications) shall apply as if paragraph (6) of that rule referred to the forms in Schedule 1 to these rules,

(c) rules 136 to 138 of the main rules (exempt information documents) shall apply as if a commonhold community statement and a memorandum and articles of association of a commonhold association were excluded from the definition of a "relevant document" in rule 136(7),

(d) for the purposes of rule 208 of the main rules (Welsh language forms) the forms in Schedule 1 to these rules shall be treated as if they were scheduled forms within the meaning of the main rules,

(e) rules 210 and 211 of the main rules (documents in a Schedule 1 form and electronically produced forms) shall apply to the forms in Schedule 1 to these rules as they apply to the forms in Schedule 1 to the main rules, and

(f) Parts 3 and 4 of Schedule 6 to the main rules (information to be included in the results of certain official searches) shall apply as if the words "relevant pending application" included any application made under the Act.

[3453]

NOTES

Commencement: 27 September 2004.

Applications

4 Lodging a copy document

(1) This rule applies to—

(a) the commonhold association's certificate of incorporation,
(b) any altered certificate of incorporation,
(c) the memorandum and articles of association of the commonhold association,
(d) any altered memorandum or articles of association of the commonhold association,
(e) a commonhold community statement,
(f) any amended commonhold community statement,
(g) an order of the court under the Act, and
(h) a termination statement.

(2) Where the Act or these rules requires an application to be accompanied by a document referred to in paragraph (1), a certified copy of that document may be submitted in place of the original.

(3) Where the original document is lodged a certified copy must accompany it.

[3454]

NOTES

Commencement: 27 September 2004.

5 Application for registration

(1) An application to register a freehold estate in land as a freehold estate in commonhold land must be made in Form CM1 accompanied, where appropriate, by the statement required by section 9(1)(b) of the Act.

(2) The statement required by section 9(1)(b) of the Act shall be in Form COV.

(3) Unless the Registrar otherwise directs, the application must be accompanied by a [statement of truth] made by the applicant that complies with rule 6.

[3455]

NOTES

Commencement: 27 September 2004.
Para (3): words "statement of truth" in square brackets substituted by SI 2008/1920, r 3.

6 [Statement of truth]

(1) The [statement of truth] referred to in rule 5(3) must comply with paragraphs (2) to (6).

(2) The [statement] must list the consents, or orders of court dispensing with consent, that have been obtained under or by virtue of section 3 of the Act.

(3) Where there is a restriction entered in any individual register affected by the application, the [statement] must confirm that either the restriction does not protect an interest in respect of which the consent of the holder is required or, if it does that the appropriate consent has been obtained.

(4) The [statement] must confirm that—

(a) no other consents are required under or by virtue of section 3 of the Act,
(b) no consent has lapsed or been withdrawn, and
(c) if a consent is subject to conditions, all conditions have been fully satisfied.

(5) Where the application involves the extinguishment under section 22 of the Act of a charge that is the subject of an entry in the register the [statement] must—

(a) identify the charge to be extinguished
(b) identify the title of the owner of the charge,
(c) give the name and address of the owner of the charge, and
(d) confirm that the consent of the owner of the charge has been obtained.

(6) The Registrar must accept the [statement of truth] as conclusive evidence that no additional consents are required under or by virtue of section 3 of the Act and must cancel any entry in the register relating to an interest that has been identified in the [statement of truth] to be extinguished.[3456]

NOTES

Commencement: 27 September 2004.
Provision heading: substituted by SI 2008/1920, r 4(1).
Para (1): words "statement of truth" in square brackets substituted by SI 2008/1920, r 4(1).
Paras (2)–(5): word "statement" in square brackets in each place it occurs substituted by SI 2008/1920, r 4(2).

7 Form of consent

The form of consent required under or by virtue of sections 3 and 41 of the Act is Form CON 1.

[3457]

NOTES

Commencement: 27 September 2004.

8 Rejection or cancellation of application

In addition to the Registrar's powers contained in rule 16 of the main rules, the Registrar may reject an application on delivery or he may cancel it at any time thereafter if plans submitted with it (whether as part of the commonhold community statement or otherwise) are insufficiently clear or accurate.

[3458]

NOTES

Commencement: 27 September 2004.

9 Title to interests

(1) Where a consent required under or by virtue of section 3 of the Act has been lodged relating to an interest which is unregistered or is the subject of only a notice, caution or restriction in the register, the applicant must also lodge sufficient evidence to satisfy the Registrar that the person whose consent has been lodged is the person who was entitled to that interest at the time the consent was given.

(2) For the purposes of paragraph (1), the Registrar may accept as sufficient evidence of entitlement a conveyancer's certificate that he is satisfied that the person whose consent has been lodged in relation to that interest is the person who was entitled to it at the time the consent was given and that he holds evidence of this.

[3459]

NOTES

Commencement: 27 September 2004.

10 Service of notice—extinguished leases

(1) Subject to paragraph (3), where, as the result of an application under section 2 of the Act, a lease the title to which is registered is extinguished under section 9(3)(f) of the Act, the Registrar must give notice of the closure of the leasehold title to the following—

(a) the registered proprietor of the leasehold title,
(b) the registered proprietor of any charge affecting the leasehold title, and
(c) the person entitled to the benefit of a notice, a restriction or a caution against dealings entered in the register of the leasehold title.

(2) Subject to paragraph (3), where, as the result of an application under section 2 of the Act, an unregistered lease which is noted in the register of the freehold title is extinguished under section 9(3)(f) of the Act, the Registrar must give notice of the completion of the application to the holder of the leasehold estate that has been extinguished.

(3) The Registrar is not obliged to give notice to a person referred to in paragraph (1) or (2) or in both if—

(a) that person consented under section 3 of the Act to the application, or

(b) that person's name and his address for service under rule 198 of the main rules are not set out in the relevant individual register.

[3460]

NOTES

Commencement: 27 September 2004.

11 Service of notice at end of transitional period—extinguished leases

(1) Subject to paragraph (3), where a lease the title to which is registered is extinguished under section 7(3)(d) of the Act and rule 29 (2) applies, the Registrar must give notice of the closure of the leasehold title to the following—

(a) the registered proprietor of the leasehold title,

(b) the registered proprietor of any charge affecting the leasehold title, and

(c) the person entitled to the benefit of a notice, a restriction or a caution against dealings entered in the register of the leasehold title.

(2) Subject to paragraph (3), where an unregistered lease which is noted in the register of the freehold title is extinguished under section 7(3)(d) and rule 29(2) applies, the Registrar must give notice of the completion of the application to the holder of the leasehold estate that has been extinguished.

(3) The Registrar is not obliged to give notice to a person referred to in paragraph (1) if—

(a) that person consented under section 3 of the Act to the application, or

(b) that person's name and his address for service under rule 198 of the main rules are not set out in the relevant individual register.

[3461]

NOTES

Commencement: 27 September 2004.

12 Court order

An application to give effect in the register to an order of the court under the Act, other than a succession order, must be made in Form AP1 of the main rules.

[3462]

NOTES

Commencement: 27 September 2004.

13 Registration of an amended commonhold community statement

(1) An application to register an amended commonhold community statement must be made in Form CM3.

(2) The application must be accompanied by a new version of the commonhold community statement incorporating the amendments.

(3) On completion of the application, the Registrar must enter a note of the amended commonhold community statement in the register of the title to the common parts in a manner that distinguishes it from previous versions of the commonhold community statement.

[3463]

NOTES

Commencement: 27 September 2004.

14 Cessation of commonhold during the transitional period

(1) An application for the freehold estate in land to cease to be registered as a freehold estate in commonhold land during the transitional period must be made in Form CM2.

(2) When satisfied that the application is in order, the Registrar must cancel to the necessary extent the commonhold entries made in the register under rule 28(1)(a) to (c).

(3) Unless the Registrar otherwise directs, the application must be accompanied by—

(a) a [statement of truth] made by the applicant that complies with rule 6 to the extent necessary, and

(b) all necessary consents in Form CON 2.

[3464]

NOTES

Commencement: 27 September 2004.
Para (3): in sub-para (a) words "statement of truth" in square brackets substituted by SI 2008/1920, r 5.

15 Transfer of part of a commonhold unit

(1) An application to register a transfer of the freehold estate in part only of a commonhold unit must be accompanied by an application in Form CM3 to register the commonhold community statement that has been amended in relation to the transfer.

(2) The Registrar may reject on delivery the application to register the transfer, or he may cancel it at any time thereafter, if it is not accompanied by an application to register the amended commonhold community statement.

[3465]

NOTES

Commencement: 27 September 2004.

16 Transfer of part of the common parts

(1) An application to register a transfer of the freehold estate in part of the common parts must be accompanied by an application in Form CM3 to register the commonhold community statement that has been amended in relation to the transfer.

(2) The Registrar may reject on delivery the application to register the transfer, or he may cancel it at any time thereafter, if it is not accompanied by an application to register the amended commonhold community statement.

[3466]

NOTES

Commencement: 27 September 2004.

17 Alteration of the extent of a commonhold unit

(1) An application to register an amended commonhold community statement in Form CM3 which would have the effect of altering the extent of a commonhold unit (other than by removing the whole of the unit) must be accompanied by an application to register any relevant transfer.

(2) Where there is a relevant transfer, the Registrar may reject on delivery the application to register the amended commonhold community statement, or he may cancel it at any time thereafter, if paragraph (1) is not complied with.

[3467]

NOTES

Commencement: 27 September 2004.

18 Alteration of the extent of the common parts

(1) An application to register an amended commonhold community statement in Form CM3 which would have the effect of altering the extent of the common parts (unless section 30(4) of the Act applies) must be accompanied by an application to register any relevant transfer.

(2) Where there is a relevant transfer, the Registrar may reject on delivery the application to register the amended commonhold community statement, or he may cancel it at any time thereafter, if paragraph (1) is not complied with.

[3468]

NOTES

Commencement: 27 September 2004.

19 Registration of an altered memorandum or articles of association

(1) An application to register an altered memorandum or articles of association must be made in Form CM3.

(2) The application must be accompanied by a new version of the memorandum or articles of association of the commonhold association incorporating the amendments.

PART II
STATUTORY INSTRUMENTS

(3) On completion of the application, the Registrar must enter a note of the altered memorandum or articles of association in the register of the title to the common parts in a manner that distinguishes them from previous versions of the memorandum or articles of association of the commonhold association.

[3469]

NOTES

Commencement: 27 September 2004.

20 Application to add land

(1) An application to add land within the meaning of section 41 of the Act must be made in Form CM4.

(2) Such an application must be accompanied by an application to register the amended commonhold community statement in Form CM3.

(3) The Registrar may reject on delivery the application to add land, or he may cancel it at any time thereafter, if it is not accompanied by an application to register the amended commonhold community statement.

(4) Unless the Registrar otherwise directs the application must be accompanied by a [statement of truth] by the applicant that complies with rule 6 to the extent necessary.

[3470]

NOTES

Commencement: 27 September 2004.

Para (4): words "statement of truth" in square brackets substituted by SI 2008/1920, r 6.

21 Termination application following a voluntary winding up

(1) A termination application must be—

(a) made in Form CM5, and

(b) accompanied by the order, appointment by the Secretary of State or resolution under which the liquidator was appointed and such other evidence as the Registrar may require.

(2) Where a termination application is made and the liquidator notifies the Registrar that he is content with the termination statement, or sends to the Registrar a copy of the court's determination of the terms of the termination statement, the Registrar must—

(a) enter the commonhold association as proprietor of the commonhold units, and

(b) cancel the commonhold entries on every registered title affected.

[3471]

NOTES

Commencement: 27 September 2004.

22 Application to terminate a commonhold registration following the winding-up of a commonhold association by the court

(1) An application to terminate a commonhold registration where the court has made a winding-up order in respect of a commonhold association and has not made a succession order must be made in Form CM5.

(2) When the Registrar has received notification under section 54(2)(c) to (f) of the Act, and is otherwise satisfied that the application is in order, he may cancel the commonhold entries on the registered titles affected.

[3472]

NOTES

Commencement: 27 September 2004.

23 Registration of a successor commonhold association

(1) Where a succession order is made, an application must be made to the Registrar to register the successor commonhold association in Form CM6.

(2) Unless the Registrar otherwise directs, the application must be accompanied by—

(a) the succession order,

(b) the memorandum and articles of association of the successor commonhold association, and

(c) the winding up order.

(3) When satisfied that the application is in order, the Registrar must—

(a) cancel the note of the memorandum and articles of association of the insolvent commonhold association in the property register of the registered title to the common parts,

(b) enter a note of the memorandum and articles of association of the successor commonhold association in the property register of the registered title to the common parts, and

(c) give effect to the terms of the succession order in the individual registers of the registered titles affected.

(4) Where a succession order includes provisions falling within section 52(4) of the Act, the successor commonhold association must make an application to give effect in the register to those provisions so far as necessary.

[3473]

NOTES

Commencement: 27 September 2004.

24 Application to register surrender of a development right

(1) An application to note the surrender of a right conferred by section 58(2) of the Act in the register must be accompanied by a notice in Form SR1.

(2) When satisfied as to the application, the Registrar must complete it by entering the notice surrendering the right in the property register of the registered title to the common parts.

[3474]

NOTES

Commencement: 27 September 2004.

25 Official copies

An application for official copies of the individual register and title plan of the common parts in relation to a commonhold must be made by inserting the following words in [panel 7] of Form OC1 in Schedule 1 of the main rules—

"official copy(ies) of the register and title plan of the common parts in a commonhold development."

[3475]

NOTES

Commencement: 27 September 2004.
Words "panel 7" in square brackets substituted by SI 2008/1920, r 7.

26 Searches of the index map

If a person who applies for a search of the index map requires the title numbers of the units in relation to a commonhold, he must insert the common parts title number followed by the words "common parts" in panel 2 of Form SIM in Schedule 1 of the main rules or supply a plan of the commonhold land showing sufficient detail to enable the land to be clearly identified on the Ordnance Survey map.

[3476]

NOTES

Commencement: 27 September 2004.

The Register

27 Restrictions

To give effect to the terms of the Act the Registrar must—

(a) enter a restriction in Form CA in Schedule 2 in the individual register of the common parts title, and

(b) enter a restriction in Form CB in Schedule 2 in the individual register of each unit title.

[3477]

NOTES

Commencement: 27 September 2004.

28 Completion of application for registration

(1) When satisfied that an application under section 2 of the Act is in order, the Registrar must complete it by entering in the individual register of the affected registered titles—

(a) a note that the freehold estate is registered as a freehold estate in commonhold land,

(b) a note of the memorandum and articles of association of the commonhold association and the commonhold community statement,
(c) where the application is not accompanied by Form COV, a note that the rights and duties conferred and imposed by the commonhold community statement will not come into force until the end of the transitional period, and
(d) where the application is not accompanied by Form COV, the applicant as proprietor of the registered title to each of the units and as proprietor of the registered title to the common parts.

(2) Where an application to register the freehold estate in land as the freehold estate in commonhold land is accompanied by Form COV, the Registrar must—
(a) cancel notice of any lease extinguished under section 9(3)(f) of the Act, and
(b) close the title if the lease is registered.

[3478]

NOTES
Commencement: 27 September 2004.

29 End of transitional period

(1) This rule applies where an application has been made under section 2 of the Act and was not accompanied by Form COV.

(2) Where the Registrar is aware that the transitional period has come to an end, he must—
(a) cancel the entries made in the register under rule 28(1)(c),
(b) cancel notice of any lease extinguished under section 7(3)(d) of the Act, and
(c) close the title to any such lease where the lease is registered.

[3479]

NOTES
Commencement: 27 September 2004.

30 Leases of commonhold units

When a term of years absolute is created in a commonhold unit and the lease is registered, the Registrar must enter a note in the property register of the leasehold title that it is a lease of a commonhold unit.

[3480]

NOTES
Commencement: 27 September 2004.

31 Changing size: charged unit

On an application to which rule 15 or rule 17 relates and where section 24(1) of the Act applies, on receipt of Form COE, the Registrar must give effect in the register to section 24(4) and (5) of the Act as appropriate.

[3481]

NOTES
Commencement: 27 September 2004.

32 Charges over common parts

Where a charge is extinguished, in whole or in part, under section 28(3) or section 28(4) of the Act, the Registrar must cancel or alter as appropriate any entry of the charge in the register to the extent that it is extinguished.

[3482]

NOTES
Commencement: 27 September 2004.

SCHEDULE 1
FORMS

FORM CM1
APPLICATION TO REGISTER A FREEHOLD ESTATE IN COMMONHOLD LAND

Application to register a freehold estate in commonhold land

Land Registry

If you need more room than is provided for in a panel, use continuation sheet CS and attach to this form.

1. **Administrative area and postcode** if known

2. **This application affects** *Place "X" in the appropriate box.*

   ☐ unregistered land for which Form FR1 accompanies this application

   ☐ the **whole** of the title number(s) ______________________

   ☐ **part** of the title number(s) ______________________

3. If you have already made this application by **outline application,** insert reference number: ☐

4. **If the application is for registration with unit-holders you must complete Form COV and lodge it with this application**

5. **Application and fee** *A fee calculator for all types of applications can be found on Land Registry's website at www1.landregistry.gov.uk/fees*

   Registration of commonhold Fee paid £

   Fee payment method: *Place "X" in the appropriate box.*
   I wish to pay the appropriate fee payable under the current Land Registration Fee Order:

   ☐ by cheque or postal order, amount £ __________ made payable to "Land Registry".

   ☐ by Direct Debit under an authorised agreement with Land Registry.

   FOR OFFICIAL USE ONLY
   Record of fee paid

   Particulars of under/over payment

   Fees debited £

   Reference number

6. **Documents lodged with this form** *Place "X" in the appropriate boxes. We shall retain any original document which is not accompanied by a certified copy.*

   ☐ Certified copy of certificate of incorporation of commonhold association

   ☐ Certified copy of any altered certificate of incorporation of commonhold association

   ☐ Certified copy of memorandum and articles of association of commonhold association

   ☐ Two certified copies of commonhold community statement ☐ Director's certificate

   ☐ Form(s) CON1/Court order(s) ☐ Statement of truth

   ☐ ☐

7. **The applicant is:** *Please provide the full name of the person applying to be registered as the proprietor of the commonhold.*

   The application has been lodged by:
   Land Registry Key No. (if appropriate)
   Name (if different from the applicant)
   Address/DX No.

   Reference
   E-mail
   Telephone No. Fax No.

   FOR OFFICIAL USE ONLY
   Codes
   Dealing

   Status
   RED

PART II
STATUTORY INSTRUMENTS

8. Where you would like us to deal with someone else *We shall deal only with the applicant, or the person lodging the application if different, unless you place "X" against one or more of the statements below and give the necessary details.*

☐ Send title information document to the person shown below

☐ Raise any requisitions or queries with the person shown below

☐ Return original documents lodged with this form (see italic text in panel 6) to the person shown below

If this applies only to certain documents, please specify.

Name
Address/DX No.

Reference
E-mail

Telephone No.	Fax No.

9. Full name(s) and address(es) for service of every applicant for entry on the register. The address(es) will be entered on the register and used for correspondence and the service of notices. *You may give up to three addresses for service one of which **must** be a postal address but does not have to be within the UK. The other addresses can be a combination of either a postal address, a box number at a UK document exchange or an electronic address. For a company include company's registered number, if any. For Scottish companies use an SC prefix and for limited liability partnerships use an OC prefix before the registered number, if any. For foreign companies give territory in which incorporated.*

10. Information in respect of any new charge
Do not give this information if a Land Registry MD reference is printed on the charge, unless the charge has been transferred.
Full name and address (including postcode) for service of notices and correspondence of the person to be registered as proprietor of each charge. *You may give up to three addresses for service. See panel 9 as to the details you should include.*

Unless otherwise arranged with Land Registry Head Office, we require a certified copy of the chargee's constitution (in English or Welsh) if it is a body corporate but is not a company registered in England and Wales or Scotland under the Companies Acts.

11. Name, address(es) and company registration number of the commonhold association *If it is not the applicant. See panel 9 as to the details you should include.*

12. Signature of applicant or their conveyancer ____________________ **Date** ____________

The completion of this panel on the form is voluntary. No individual property or person will be identified from the information given. The information will be used by Land Registry to improve its forecasting and may be supplied to the Ministry of Justice. *Place "X" in the appropriate box.*

The property the subject of this application is

☐ residential ☐ non-residential ☐ mixed

[3483]

NOTES

Commencement: 27 September 2004.
Substituted by SI 2008/1920, r 8, Schedule.

FORM CM2

APPLICATION FOR THE FREEHOLD ESTATE TO CEASE TO BE REGISTERED AS A FREEHOLD ESTATE IN COMMONHOLD LAND DURING THE TRANSITIONAL PERIOD

Application for the freehold estate to cease to be registered as a freehold estate in commonhold land during the transitional period

Land Registry

CM2

If you need more room than is provided for in a panel, use continuation sheet CS and attach to this form.

1. Administrative area and postcode if known

2. Title number(s)

3. Do you wish the land to be amalgamated into one title? *Place "X" in the appropriate box.*

☐ Yes

☐ No

4. If you have already made this application by **outline application,** insert reference number: ☐

5. Application and fee *A fee calculator for all types of applications can be found on Land Registry's website at www1.landregistry.gov.uk/fees*

Cessation of commonhold Fee paid £

Fee payment method: *Place "X" in the appropriate box.*
I wish to pay the appropriate fee payable under the current Land Registration Fee Order:

☐ by cheque or postal order, amount £ ____________ made payable to "Land Registry".

☐ by Direct Debit under an authorised agreement with Land Registry.

FOR OFFICIAL USE ONLY
Record of fee paid

Particulars of under/over payment

Fees debited £

Reference number

6. Documents lodged with this form *Place "X" in the appropriate boxes. We shall retain any original document which is not accompanied by a certified copy.*

☐ Form(s) CON2 ☐ Statement of truth

☐ ☐ ☐

7. The applicant is: *Please provide the full name of the person making the application.*

The application has been lodged by:
Land Registry Key No. (if appropriate)
Name (if different from the applicant)
Address/DX No.

Reference
E-mail

Telephone No.	Fax No.

FOR OFFICIAL USE ONLY
Codes
Dealing
CTB
Status
RED

8. Where you would like us to deal with someone else *We shall deal only with the applicant, or the person lodging the application if different, unless you place "X" against one or more of the statements below and give the necessary details.*

☐ Send title information document to the person shown below

☐ Raise any requisitions or queries with the person shown below

☐ Return original documents lodged with this form (see italic text in panel 6) to the person shown below
If this applies only to certain documents, please specify.

Name
Address/DX No.

Reference
E-mail

Telephone No.	Fax No.

9. The Transitional period referred to in section 8 of the Commonhold and Leasehold Reform Act 2002 has not come to an end.

Signature of applicant or their conveyancer ____________________ **Date** ____________

[3484]

NOTES

Commencement: 27 September 2004.
Substituted by SI 2008/1920, r 8, Schedule.

FORM CM3
APPLICATION FOR THE REGISTRATION OF AN AMENDED COMMONHOLD COMMUNITY STATEMENT AND/OR ALTERED MEMORANDUM AND ARTICLES OF ASSOCIATION

Application for the registration of an amended commonhold community statement and/or altered memorandum and articles of association

Land Registry

CM3

If you need more room than is provided for in a panel, use continuation sheet CS and attach to this form.

1. **Administrative area and postcode** if known

2. **Title number of common parts**

3. **Title number(s) of units** *if extent of unit is changed*

4. **Document(s) which has been amended/altered** *Place "X" in the appropriate box(es).*

☐ Commonhold community statement

☐ Memorandum and articles of association

5. If you have already made this application by **outline application,** insert reference number:

6. **Application and fee** *A fee calculator for all types of applications can be found on Land Registry's website at www.landregistry.gov.uk/fees.*

Amendment of commonhold community statement and/or alteration of memorandum and articles of association Fee paid £

Fee payment method: *Place "X" in the appropriate box.*
I wish to pay the appropriate fee payable under the current Land Registration Fee Order:

☐ by cheque or postal order, amount £______________ made payable to "Land Registry".

☐ by Direct Debit under an authorised agreement with Land Registry.

FOR OFFICIAL USE ONLY
Record of fee paid

Particulars of under/over payment

Fees debited £

Reference number

7. **Documents lodged with this form** *Place "X" in the appropriate boxes. We shall retain any original documents which is not accompanied by a certified copy.*

☐ Certified copy of memorandum and articles of association

☐ Two certified copies of commonhold community statement (see panel 10)

☐ Consents/Court orders ☐ Director's certificate

☐ Form COE ☐ ☐

8. **The applicant is:** *Please provide the full name of the person making the application.*

The application has been lodged by:
Land Registry Key No. (if appropriate)
Name (if different from the applicant)
Address/DX No.

Reference
E-mail

Telephone No. | Fax No.

FOR OFFICIAL USE ONLY
Codes
Dealing
ACS
Status
RED

PART II
STATUTORY INSTRUMENTS

9. Where you would like us to deal with someone else *We shall deal only with the applicant, or the person lodging the application if different, unless you place "X" against one or more of the statements below and give the necessary details.*

☐ Send title information document to the person shown below

☐ Raise any requisitions or queries with the person shown below

☐ Return original documents lodged with this form (see italic text in panel 7) to the person shown below
If this applies only to certain documents, please specify.

Name
Address/DX No.

Reference
E-mail

Telephone No	Fax No.

10. If the application is to amend the commonhold community statement, please summarise the amendments below

11. Signature of applicant or their conveyancer ________________ **Date** ________

[3485]

NOTES

Commencement: 27 September 2004.

FORM CM4
APPLICATION TO ADD LAND TO A COMMONHOLD REGISTRATION

Application to add land to a commonhold registration **Land Registry** **CM4**

If you need more room than is provided for in a panel, use continuation sheet CS and attach to this form.

1. Administrative area and postcode if known

2. Existing commonhold title number(s) to which land is to be added *Common parts and/or units as appropriate.*

3. Title number(s) of land to be added to commonhold

4. If you have already made this application by **outline application**, insert reference number:

5. Application and fee *A fee calculator for all types of applications can be found on Land Registry's website at www1.landregistry.gov.uk/fees*

Addition of land to commonhold	Fee paid £

Fee payment method: *Place "X" in the appropriate box.*
I wish to pay the appropriate fee payable under the current Land Registration Fee Order:

☐ by cheque or postal order, amount £______________ made payable to "Land Registry".

☐ by Direct Debit under an authorised agreement with Land Registry.

OFFICIAL USE ONLY
Record of fee paid

Particulars of under/over payment

Fees debited £

Reference number

6. Documents lodged with this form *Place "X" in the appropriate boxes. We shall retain any original document which is not accompanied by a certified copy.*

☐ Form(s) CON1/Court order ☐ Director's certificate ☐ Form COE
☐ Statement of truth ☐

7. The applicant is: *Please provide the full name of the person making the application.*

The application has been lodged by:
Land Registry Key No. (if appropriate)
Name (if different from the applicant)
Address/DX No.

Reference
E-mail

Telephone No.	Fax No.

FOR OFFICIAL USE ONLY
Codes
Dealing

Status
RED

8. Where you would like us to deal with someone else *We shall deal only with the applicant, or the person lodging the application if different, unless you place "X" against one or more of the statements below and give the necessary details.*

☐ Send title information document to the person shown below

☐ Raise any requisitions or queries with the person shown below

☐ Return original documents lodged with this form (see italic text in panel 6) to the person shown below
If this applies only to certain documents, please specify.

Name
Address/DX No.

Reference
E-mail

Telephone No.	Fax No.

9. A separate application in Form CM3 amending the commonhold community statement accompanies this application

Signature of applicant or their conveyancer ____________________ **Date** ____________

[3486]

NOTES

Commencement: 27 September 2004.
Substituted by SI 2008/1920, r 8, Schedule.

FORM CM5

APPLICATION FOR THE TERMINATION OF A COMMONHOLD REGISTRATION

Application for the termination of a commonhold registration

Land Registry **CM5**

If you need more room than is provided for in a panel, use continuation CS and attach to this form.

1. **Administrative area and postcode** if known

2. **Title number(s)**

3. If you have already made this application by **outline application,** insert reference number:

4. **Application and fee** *A fee calculator for all types of applications can be found on Land Registry's website at www.landregistry.gov.uk/fees.*

Termination of commonhold Fee paid £

Fee payment method: *Place "X" in the appropriate box.*
I wish to pay the appropriate fee payable under the current Land Registration Fee Order:

☐ by cheque or postal order, amount £ __________ made payable to "Land Registry".

☐ by Direct Debit under an authorised agreement with Land Registry.

FOR OFFICIAL USE ONLY
Record of fee paid

Particulars of under/over payment

Fees debited £

Reference number

5. **Documents lodged with this form when the termination is by way of voluntary winding up** *Place "X" in the appropriate boxes. We shall retain any orginal document which is not accompanied by a certified copy.*

☐ Termination statement ☐ Court order ☐ Evidence of liquidator's appointment

☐ ☐

6. **Documents lodged with this form when the termination is by way of winding up by the court (no succession order)** *Place "X" in the appropriate boxes. We shall retain any original document which is not accompanied by a certified copy.*

☐ Liquidator's notification that section 54 of the Commonhold and Leasehold Reform Act 2002 applies

☐ ☐

☐ ☐

7. **The application has been lodged by:**
Land Registry Key No. (if appropriate)
Name
Address/DX No.

Reference
E-mail

Telephone No. Fax No.

FOR OFFICIAL USE ONLY
Codes
Dealing
TRM
Status
RED

PART II STATUTORY INSTRUMENTS

8. Where you would like us to deal with someone else *We shall deal only with the applicant, or the person lodging the application if different, unless you place "X" against one or more of the statements below and give the necessary details.*

☐ Send title information document to the person shown below

☐ Raise any requisitions or queries with the person shown below

☐ Return original documents lodged with this form (see italic text in panels 5 and 6) to the person shown below
If this only applies to certain documents, please specify.

Name
Address/DX No.

Reference
E-mail

Telephone No.	Fax No.

9. Full name(s) and address(es) of every applicant *For a company include company's registered number, if any. For Scottish companies use an SC prefix and for limited liability partnerships use an OC prefix. For foreign companies give territory in which incorporated.*

10. Signature of applicant or their conveyancer ____________________ **Date** ____________

[3487]

NOTES
Commencement: 27 September 2004.

FORM CM6
APPLICATION FOR THE REGISTRATION OF A SUCCESSOR COMMONHOLD ASSOCIATION

Application for the registration of a successor commonhold association **Land Registry** **CM6**

If you need more room than is provided for in a panel, use continuation sheet CS and attach to this form.

1. **Administrative area and postcode** if known

2. **Title number(s)**

3. If you have already made this application by **outline application,** insert reference number:

4. **Documents lodged with this form** *Place "X" in the appropriate boxes. We shall retain any original document which is not accompanied by a certified copy.*

☐ Succession Order

☐ Certified copy of memorandum and articles of association of commonhold association

☐ Winding up order

5. **The applicant is:** *Please provide the full name of the person making the application.*

The application has been lodged by:
Land Registry Key No. (if appropriate)
Name (if different from the applicant)
Address/DX No.

Reference
E-mail

Telephone No. Fax No.

FOR OFFICIAL USE ONLY
Codes
Dealing
SCA
Status
RED

6. **Where you would like us to deal with someone else** *We shall deal only with the applicant, or the person lodging the application if different, unless you place "X" against one or more of the statements below and give the necessary details.*

☐ Send title information document to the person shown below

☐ Raise any requisitions or queries with the person shown below

☐ Return original documents lodged with this form (see italic text in panel 4) to the person shown below
If this applies only to certain documents, please specify.

Name
Address/DX No.

Reference
E-mail

Telephone No. Fax No.

7. Full name(s) and address(es) for service of notices and correspondence of every applicant for entry in the register *You may give up to three addresses for service **one** of which **must** be a postal address but does not have to be within the UK. The other addresses can be a combination of either a postal address, a box number at a UK document exchange or an electronic address. For a company include company's registered number, if any. For Scottish companies use an SC prefix and for limited liability partnerships use an OC prefix before the registered number, if any. For foreign companies give territory in which incorporated.*
8. Signature of applicant or their conveyancer __________________ **Date** __________

[3488]

NOTES

Commencement: 27 September 2004.

FORM COE
NOTIFICATION OF CHANGE OF EXTENT OF A COMMONHOLD UNIT OVER WHICH THERE IS A REGISTERED CHARGE

Notification of change of extent of a commonhold unit over which there is a registered charge

Land Registry **COE**

This form must be lodged with Form CM3 and where appropriate Form CM4.

1. Title number *A separate form should be used for each title affected.*

2. Property

3. Name of chargee

4. Date of charge(s)

5. I/We *[insert name of chargee]* ______________________ give notice that the extent of the above property has been redefined.

Place "X" in the appropriate box.

☐ Land has been removed from the property and, pursuant to section 24(4) of the Commonhold and Leasehold Reform Act 2002, the registered charge over the property has been extinguished to the extent that it relates to the land which has been removed.

or

☐ Land has been added to the property and, pursuant to section 24(5) of the Commonhold and Leasehold Reform Act 2002, the registered charge over the property has been extended so as to relate to the land which has been added.

The Registrar is requested to alter the register of the above property as necessary to reflect this amendment.

6. Signature of person giving the notification or their conveyancer ______________ **Date** ______________

[3489]

NOTES

Commencement: 27 September 2004.

PART II STATUTORY INSTRUMENTS

FORM CON1
CONSENT TO THE REGISTRATION OF LAND AS COMMONHOLD LAND

Consent to the registration of land as commonhold land

Land Registry

CON1

If you need more room than is provided for in a panel, use continuation sheet CS and attach to this form.

VERY IMPORTANT
This consent will bind you and any successors in title. Before signing this form you are strongly advised to seek legal advice.

1. Details of the freehold land the subject of the application to become commonhold ("the land")

Title number(s):

Property:

2. Details of the person giving consent and their interest in the land

Name of the consenter:

Address

Details of the interest:

3. Declaration *Place "X" in the appropriate box(es)*

☐ I understand that my charge will be extinguished as to the common parts on the vesting of those common parts in the commonhold association.

☐ I understand that my charge will be extinguished under section 22(4) of the Commonhold and Leasehold Reform Act 2002.

☐ I confirm that I have no interest which will be extinguished as a result of the application to register land as commonhold land.

☐ I understand that my interest will be extinguished under section 7(3)(d) or section 9(3)(f) of the Commonhold and Leasehold Reform Act 2002.

4. I, ______________________________ as [registered proprietor] [beneficial owner] [trustee/personal representative of the registered proprietor] *[Delete as appropriate]* **of the above interest, consent to the registration of the land as a freehold estate in commonhold land.**

5. Signature of person giving the consent or their conveyancer ______________________________ **Date** ____________________

NOTE: This consent is valid for a period of 12 months beginning with the date that the consent was given. It cannot be withdrawn once the commonhold application is lodged for registration.

[3490]

NOTES

Commencement: 27 September 2004.

FORM CON2

CONSENT TO AN APPLICATION FOR THE FREEHOLD ESTATE TO CEASE TO BE REGISTERED AS A FREEHOLD ESTATE IN COMMONHOLD LAND DURING THE TRANSITIONAL PERIOD

Consent to an application for the freehold estate to cease to be registered as a freehold estate in commonhold land during the transitional period

Land Registry

CON2

If you need more room than is provided for in a panel, use continuation sheet CS and attach to this form.

VERY IMPORTANT
This consent will bind you and any successors in title. Before signing this form you are strongly advised to seek legal advice.

1. Details of the freehold land the subject of the application to cease to be commonhold ("the land")

Title number(s):

Property:

2. Details of the consenter and their interest in the land

Name of the consenter:

Address:

Details of the interest:

3. I, ________________ as [registered proprietor] [beneficial owner] [trustee/personal representative of the registered proprietor] *[Delete as appropriate]* **of the above interest, consent to the application for the freehold estate to cease to be registered as a freehold estate in commonhold land.**

4. Signature of person giving the consent or their conveyancer ________________ Date ________

NOTE: This consent is valid for a period of 12 months beginning with the date that the consent was given. It cannot be withdrawn once the commonhold application is lodged for registration.

[3491]

NOTES

Commencement: 27 September 2004.

FORM COV
APPLICATION FOR REGISTRATION WITH UNIT-HOLDERS

Application for registration with unit-holders

Land Registry

Section 9 Statement

This form must be lodged with form CM1

1. Applicant
I/We, *[insert full name(s)]* ______________________ request that section 9 of the Commonhold and Leasehold Reform Act 2002 ("the Act") should apply to my/our application.

2. Signature of applicant or their conveyancer ______________________ **Date** ______________

List of commonhold units required by section 9(2)

NB1*: In the case of joint unit holders, if no nomination to be registered as a member of the commonhold association has been made under Schedule 3 Part 2 Paragraph 8(2) of the Act then the person whose name appears first in the proprietorship register, i.e. the first named person set out in the panels below, will be entitled to be entered in the register of members of the association under Schedule 3 Part 2 Paragraph 8(4) of the Act.*

NB2*: You may give up to three addresses for service* ***one*** *of which* ***must*** *be a postal address but does not have to be within the UK. The other addresses can be any combination of a postal address, a box number at a UK document exchange or an electronic address. For a company include the company's registered number if any. For Scottish companies, use an SC prefix. For limited liability partnerships, use an OC prefix before the registered number if any. For foreign companies give territory in which incorporated.*

UNITS	UNIT HOLDER(S)
Unit number: Postal address: Title number(s):	Full name(s) and address(es) for service for entry in the register *See NB1 and NB2.*
Unit number: Postal address: Title number(s):	Full name(s) and address(es) for service for entry in the register *See NB1 and NB2.*

Continue overleaf

UNITS	UNIT HOLDER(S)
Unit number: Postal address: Title number(s):	Full name(s) and address(es) for service for entry in the register *See NB1 and NB2 overleaf.*
Unit number: Postal address: Title number(s):	Full name(s) and address(es) for service for entry in the register *See NB1 and NB2 overleaf.*
Unit number: Postal address: Title number(s):	Full name(s) and address(es) for service for entry in the register *See NB1 and NB2 overleaf.*
Unit number: Postal address: Title number(s):	Full name(s) and address(es) for service for entry in the register *See NB1 and NB2 overleaf.*
Unit number: Postal address: Title number(s):	Full name(s) and address(es) for service for entry in the register *See NB1 and NB2 overleaf.*

If you need to add further unit details, provide these on a further copy or copies of this page and attach the page(s) to this form.

[3492]

NOTES

Commencement: 27 September 2004.

FORM SR1
NOTICE OF SURRENDER OF DEVELOPMENT RIGHT(S)

Notice of surrender of development right(s)

Land Registry

SR1

If you need more room than is provided for in a panel, use continuation sheet CS and attach to this form.

1. **Administrative area and postcode** if known

2. **Title number**

3. **Property**

4. We *[developer or their successor in title]* of *[address]*

notify the Registrar that: *Place "X" in the appropriate box and complete as applicable.*

☐ **the following development right(s) contained in** *[insert appropriate reference from the commonhold community statement]* of the commonhold community statement *[version no.]* dated *[enter date]* are surrendered: *Specify rights.*

☐ **all the development rights contained in** *[insert appropriate reference from the commonhold community statement]* of the commonhold community statement *[version no.]* dated *[enter date]* are surrendered

5. **Signature of person surrendering the right or their conveyancer** ______________ **Date** ______________

[3493]

NOTES

Commencement: 27 September 2004.

SCHEDULE 2
COMMONHOLD RESTRICTIONS

Rule 27

Form CA (Restriction in common parts title)

No charge by the proprietor of the registered estate is to be registered other than a legal mortgage which is accompanied by a certificate by a conveyancer or a director or secretary of the commonhold association that the creation of the mortgage was approved by a resolution complying with section 29(2) of the Commonhold and Leasehold Reform Act 2002.

Form CB (Restriction in unit title)

No disposition by the proprietor of the registered estate (other than a transfer or charge of the whole of the land in the title) is to be registered without a certificate by a conveyancer or a director or secretary of the commonhold association that the disposition is authorised by and made in accordance with the provisions of the Commonhold and Leasehold Reform Act 2002.

[3494]

NOTES

Commencement: 27 September 2004.

LANDLORD AND TENANT (NOTICE OF RENT) (ENGLAND) REGULATIONS 2004

(SI 2004/3096)

NOTES

Made: 22 November 2004.
Authority: Commonhold and Leasehold Reform Act 2002, s 166.
Commencement: 28 February 2005.

1 Citation, commencement, application and interpretation

(1) These Regulations may be cited as the Landlord and Tenant (Notice of Rent) (England) Regulations 2004 and shall come into force on 28th February 2005.

(2) These Regulations apply in relation to dwellings in England only.

(3) In these Regulations, "the 2002 Act" means the Commonhold and Leasehold Reform Act 2002.

[3495]

NOTES

Commencement: 28 February 2005.

2 Additional content and form of notice of rent due

(1) A notice under subsection (1) of section 166 of the 2002 Act (requirement to notify long leaseholders that rent is due) shall contain (in addition to the information specified in accordance with paragraphs (a) and (b) of subsection (2) of that section and, if applicable, paragraph (c) of that subsection)—

(a) the name of the leaseholder to whom the notice is given;
(b) the period to which the rent demanded is attributable;
(c) the name of the person to whom payment is to be made, and the address for payment;
(d) the name of the landlord by whom the notice is given and, if not specified pursuant to sub-paragraph (c) above, his address; and
(e) the information provided in the notes to the form set out in the Schedule to these Regulations.

(2) A notice under subsection (1) of section 166 of the 2002 Act shall be in the form set out in the Schedule to these Regulations.

[3496]

NOTES

Commencement: 28 February 2005.

SCHEDULE
FORM OF RENT DEMAND NOTICE

Regulation 2

COMMONHOLD AND LEASEHOLD REFORM ACT 2002, SECTION 166

NOTICE TO LONG LEASEHOLDERS OF RENT DUE

To (*insert name(s) of leaseholder(s)*):

.... **(note 1)**

This notice is given in respect of (*address of premises to which the long lease relates*)

....

It requires you to pay rent of £ .... on (*insert date*) .... **(note 2)**

This rent is payable in respect of the period (*state period*) ....

[In accordance with the terms of your lease the amount of £ .... is/was due on .... (*insert date on which rent due in accordance with the lease*).] **(note 3)**

Payment should be made to (*insert name of landlord(s) or, if payment to be made to an agent, name of agent*) at (*insert address*)

....

....

This notice is given by (*insert name of landlord(s) and, if not given above, address*)

NOTES FOR LEASEHOLDERS

Read this notice carefully. It sets out the amount of rent due from you and the date by which you must pay it. You are advised to seek help immediately, if you cannot pay, or dispute the amount. Those who can help you include a citizens' advice bureau, a housing advice centre, a law centre and a solicitor. Show this notice and a copy of your lease to whoever helps you.

The landlord may be able to claim additional sums from you if you do not pay by the date specified in this notice. You have the right to challenge the reasonableness of any additional sums at a leasehold valuation tribunal.

Section 167 of the Commonhold and Leasehold Reform Act 2002 and regulations made under it prevent your landlord from forfeiting your lease for non-payment of rent, service charges or administration charges (or a combination of them) if the amount owed is £350 or less, or none of the unpaid amount has been outstanding for more than three years.

NOTES FOR LANDLORDS

1 If you send this notice by post, address it to the leaseholder at the dwelling in respect of which the payment is due, unless he has notified you in writing of a different address in England and Wales at which he wishes to be given notices under section 166 of the Commonhold and Leasehold Reform Act 2002.

2 This date must not be *either* less than 30 days or more than 60 days after the day on which this notice is given *or* before that on which the leaseholder would have been liable to make the payment in accordance with the lease.

3 Include this statement only if the date for payment is not the same as the date determined in accordance with the lease.

[3497]–[3518]

NOTES

Commencement: 28 February 2005.

SMOKE-FREE (PREMISES AND ENFORCEMENT) REGULATIONS 2006

(SI 2006/3368)

NOTES

Made: 13 December 2006.
Authority: Health Act 2006, ss 2(5), 10(1), (2), 79(3).
Commencement: 1 July 2007.

1 Citation, commencement, application and interpretation

(1) These Regulations may be cited as the Smoke-free (Premises and Enforcement) Regulations 2006 and shall come into force on 1st July 2007.

(2) These Regulations apply in relation to England only.

(3) In these Regulations "the Act" means the Health Act 2006.

[3519]

NOTES

Commencement: 1 July 2007.

2 Enclosed and substantially enclosed premises

(1) For the purposes of section 2 of the Act, premises are enclosed if they—

(a) have a ceiling or roof; and

(b) except for doors, windows and passageways, are wholly enclosed either permanently or temporarily.

(2) For the purposes of section 2 of the Act, premises are substantially enclosed if they have a ceiling or roof but there is—

(a) an opening in the walls; or

(b) an aggregate area of openings in the walls,

which is less than half of the area of the walls, including other structures that serve the purpose of walls and constitute the perimeter of the premises.

(3) In determining the area of an opening or an aggregate area of openings for the purposes of paragraph (2), no account is to be taken of openings in which there are doors, windows or other fittings that can be opened or shut.

(4) In this regulation "roof" includes any fixed or moveable structure or device which is capable of covering all or part of the premises as a roof, including, for example, a canvas awning.

[3520]

NOTES

Commencement: 1 July 2007.

3 (*Outside the scope of this work.*)

LASTING POWERS OF ATTORNEY, ENDURING POWERS OF ATTORNEY AND PUBLIC GUARDIAN REGULATIONS 2007

(SI 2007/1253)

NOTES

Made: 16 April 2007.
Authority: Mental Capacity Act 2005, ss 13(6)(a), 58(3), 64(1), Schs 1, 4.
Commencement: 1 October 2007.

PART 1
PRELIMINARY

1 Citation and commencement

(1) These Regulations may be cited as the Lasting Powers of Attorney, Enduring Powers of Attorney and Public Guardian Regulations 2007.

(2) These Regulations shall come into force on 1 October 2007.

[3521]

NOTES

Commencement: 1 October 2007.

2 Interpretation

(1) In these Regulations—

"the Act" means the Mental Capacity Act 2005;

"court" means the Court of Protection;

"LPA certificate", in relation to an instrument made with a view to creating a lasting power of attorney, means the certificate which is required to be included in the instrument by virtue of paragraph 2(1)(e) of Schedule 1 to the Act;

"named person", in relation to an instrument made with a view to creating a lasting power of attorney, means a person who is named in the instrument as being a person to be notified of any application for the registration of the instrument;

"prescribed information", in relation to any instrument intended to create a lasting power of attorney, means the information contained in the form used for the instrument which appears under the heading "prescribed information".

[3522]

NOTES

Commencement: 1 October 2007.

3 Minimal differences from forms prescribed in these Regulations

(1) In these Regulations, any reference to a form—

(a) in the case of a form set out in Schedules 1 to 7 to these Regulations, is to be regarded as including a Welsh version of that form; and

(b) in the case of a form set out in Schedules 2 to 7 to these Regulations, is to be regarded as also including—

(i) a form to the same effect but which differs in an immaterial respect in form or mode of expression;

(ii) a form to the same effect but with such variations as the circumstances may require or the court or the Public Guardian may approve; or

(iii) a Welsh version of a form within (i) or (ii).

[3523]

NOTES

Commencement: 1 October 2007.

4 Computation of time

(1) This regulation shows how to calculate any period of time which is specified in these Regulations.

(2) A period of time expressed as a number of days must be computed as clear days.

(3) Where the specified period is 7 days or less, and would include a day which is not a business day, that day does not count.

(4) When the specified period for doing any act at the office of the Public Guardian ends on a day on which the office is closed, that act will be done in time if done on the next day on which the office is open.

(5) In this regulation—

"business day" means a day other than—

(a) a Saturday, Sunday, Christmas Day or Good Friday; or

(b) a bank holiday under the Banking and Financial Dealings Act 1971, in England and Wales; and

"clear days" means that in computing the number of days—

(a) the day on which the period begins, and

(b) if the end of the period is defined by reference to an event, the day on which that event occurs,

are not included.

[3524]

NOTES

Commencement: 1 October 2007.

PART 2
LASTING POWERS OF ATTORNEY

Instruments intended to create a lasting power of attorney

5 Forms for lasting powers of attorney

The forms set out in Parts 1 and 2 of Schedule 1 to these Regulations are the forms which, in the circumstances to which they apply, are to be used for instruments intended to create a lasting power of attorney.

[3525]

NOTES

Commencement: 1 October 2007.

6 Maximum number of named persons

The maximum number of named persons that the donor of a lasting power of attorney may specify in the instrument intended to create the power is 5.

[3526]

NOTES

Commencement: 1 October 2007.

7 Requirement for two LPA certificates where instrument has no named persons

Where an instrument intended to create a lasting power of attorney includes a statement by the donor that there are no persons whom he wishes to be notified of any application for the registration of the instrument—

(a) the instrument must include two LPA certificates; and
(b) each certificate must be completed and signed by a different person.

[3527]

NOTES

Commencement: 1 October 2007.

8 Persons who may provide an LPA certificate

(1) Subject to paragraph (3), the following persons may give an LPA certificate—

(a) a person chosen by the donor as being someone who has known him personally for the period of at least two years which ends immediately before the date on which that person signs the LPA certificate;
(b) a person chosen by the donor who, on account of his professional skills and expertise, reasonably considers that he is competent to make the judgments necessary to certify the matters set out in paragraph (2)(1)(e) of Schedule 1 to the Act.

(2) The following are examples of persons within paragraph (1)(b)—

(a) a registered health care professional;
(b) a barrister, solicitor or advocate called or admitted in any part of the United Kingdom;
(c) a registered social worker; or
(d) an independent mental capacity advocate.

(3) A person is disqualified from giving an LPA certificate in respect of any instrument intended to create a lasting power of attorney if that person is—

(a) a family member of the donor;
(b) a donee of that power;
(c) a donee of—
  (i) any other lasting power of attorney, or
  (ii) an enduring power of attorney,
  which has been executed by the donor (whether or not it has been revoked);
(d) a family member of a donee within sub-paragraph (b);
(e) a director or employee of a trust corporation acting as a donee within sub-paragraph (b);
(f) a business partner or employee of—
  (i) the donor, or
  (ii) a donee within sub-paragraph (b);
(g) an owner, director, manager or employee of any care home in which the donor is living when the instrument is executed; or
(h) a family member of a person within sub-paragraph (g).

(4) In this regulation—

"care home" has the meaning given in section 3 of the Care Standards Act 2000;

"registered health care professional" means a person who is a member of a profession regulated by a body mentioned in section 25(3) of the National Health Service Reform and Health Care Professions Act 2002; and

"registered social worker" means a person registered as a social worker in a register maintained by—

(a) the General Social Care Council;
(b) the Care Council for Wales;
(c) the Scottish Social Services Council; or
(d) the Northern Ireland Social Care Council.

[3528]

NOTES

Commencement: 1 October 2007.

9 Execution of instrument

(1) An instrument intended to create a lasting power of attorney must be executed in accordance with this regulation.

(2) The donor must read (or have read to him) all the prescribed information.

(3) As soon as reasonably practicable after the steps required by paragraph (2) have been taken, the donor must—

(a) complete the provisions of Part A of the instrument that apply to him (or direct another person to do so); and

(b) subject to paragraph (7), sign Part A of the instrument in the presence of a witness.

(4) As soon as reasonably practicable after the steps required by paragraph (3) have been taken—

(a) the person giving an LPA certificate, or

(b) if regulation 7 applies (two LPA certificates required), each of the persons giving a certificate,

must complete the LPA certificate at Part B of the instrument and sign it.

(5) As soon as reasonably practicable after the steps required by paragraph (4) have been taken—

(a) the donee, or

(b) if more than one, each of the donees,

must read (or have read to him) all the prescribed information.

(6) As soon as reasonably practicable after the steps required by paragraph (5) have been taken, the donee or, if more than one, each of them—

(a) must complete the provisions of Part C of the instrument that apply to him (or direct another person to do so); and

(b) subject to paragraph (7), must sign Part C of the instrument in the presence of a witness.

(7) If the instrument is to be signed by any person at the direction of the donor, or at the direction of any donee, the signature must be done in the presence of two witnesses.

(8) For the purposes of this regulation—

(a) the donor may not witness any signature required for the power;

(b) a donee may not witness any signature required for the power apart from that of another donee.

(9) A person witnessing a signature must—

(a) sign the instrument; and

(b) give his full name and address.

(10) Any reference in this regulation to a person signing an instrument (however expressed) includes his signing it by means of a mark made on the instrument at the appropriate place.

[3529]

NOTES

Commencement: 1 October 2007.

Registering the instrument

10 Notice to be given by a person about to apply for registration of lasting power of attorney

Schedule 2 to these Regulations sets out the form of notice ("LPA 001") which must be given by a donor or donee who is about to make an application for the registration of an instrument intended to create a lasting power of attorney.

[3530]

NOTES

Commencement: 1 October 2007.

11 Application for registration

(1) Schedule 3 to these Regulations sets out the form ("LPA 002") which must be used for making an application to the Public Guardian for the registration of an instrument intended to create a lasting power of attorney.

(2) Where the instrument to be registered which is sent with the application is neither—

(a) the original instrument intended to create the power, nor

(b) a certified copy of it,

the Public Guardian must not register the instrument unless the court directs him to do so.

(3) In paragraph (2) "a certified copy" means a photographic or other facsimile copy which is certified as an accurate copy by—

(a) the donor; or

(b) a solicitor or notary.

[3531]

NOTES

Commencement: 1 October 2007.

12 Period to elapse before registration in cases not involving objection or defect

The period at the end of which the Public Guardian must register an instrument in accordance with paragraph 5 of Schedule 1 to the Act is the period of 6 weeks beginning with—

(a) the date on which the Public Guardian gave the notice or notices under paragraph 7 or 8 of Schedule 1 to the Act of receipt of an application for registration; or

(b) if notices were given on more than one date, the latest of those dates.

[3532]

NOTES

Commencement: 1 October 2007.

13 Notice of receipt of application for registration

(1) Part 1 of Schedule 4 to these Regulations sets out the form of notice ("LPA 003A") which the Public Guardian must give to the donee (or donees) when the Public Guardian receives an application for the registration of a lasting power of attorney.

(2) Part 2 of Schedule 4 sets out the form of notice ("LPA 003B") which the Public Guardian must give to the donor when the Public Guardian receives such an application.

(3) Where it appears to the Public Guardian that there is good reason to do so, the Public Guardian must also provide (or arrange for the provision of) an explanation to the donor of—

(a) the notice referred to in paragraph (2) and what the effect of it is; and

(b) why it is being brought to his attention.

(4) Any information provided under paragraph (3) must be provided—

(a) to the donor personally; and

(b) in a way that is appropriate to the donor's circumstances (for example using simple language, visual aids or other appropriate means).

[3533]

NOTES

Commencement: 1 October 2007.

14 Objection to registration: notice to Public Guardian [to be given by the donee of the power or a named person]

(1) This regulation deals with any objection to the registration of an instrument as a lasting power of attorney which is to be made to the Public Guardian [by the donee of the power or a named person].

(2) Where [the donee of the power or a named person]—

(a) is entitled to receive notice under paragraph 6, 7 or 8 of Schedule 1 to the Act of an application for the registration of the instrument, and

(b) wishes to object to registration on a ground set out in paragraph 13(1) of Schedule 1 to the Act,

he must do so before the end of the period of 5 weeks beginning with the date on which the notice is given.

(3) A notice of objection must be given in writing, setting out—

(a) the name and address of the objector;

(b) … the name and address of the donor of the power;

(c) if known, the name and address of the donee (or donees); and

(d) the ground for making the objection.

(4) The Public Guardian must notify the objector as to whether he is satisfied that the ground of the objection is established.

(5) At any time after receiving the notice of objection and before giving the notice required by paragraph (4), the Public Guardian may require the objector to provide such further information, or produce such documents, as the Public Guardian reasonably considers necessary to enable him to determine whether the ground for making the objection is established.

(6) Where—

(a) the Public Guardian is satisfied that the ground of the objection is established, but

(b) by virtue of section 13(7) of the Act, the instrument is not revoked,

the notice under paragraph (4) must contain a statement to that effect.

(7) Nothing in this regulation prevents an objector from making a further objection under paragraph 13 of Schedule 1 to the Act where—

(a) the notice under paragraph (4) indicates that the Public Guardian is not satisfied that the particular ground of objection to which that notice relates is established; and

(b) the period specified in paragraph (2) has not expired.

[3534]

NOTES

Commencement: 1 October 2007.

Heading, para (1): words in square brackets inserted by SI 2007/2161, regs 2, 3(1), (2).

Para (2): words in square brackets substituted by SI 2007/2161, regs 2, 3(3).

Para (3): words omitted revoked by SI 2007/2161, regs 2, 3(4).

[14A Objection to registration: notice to Public Guardian to be given by the donor

(1) This regulation deals with any objection to the registration of an instrument as a lasting power of attorney which is to be made to the Public Guardian by the donor of the power.

(2) Where the donor of the power—

(a) is entitled to receive notice under paragraph 8 of Schedule 1 to the Act of an application for the registration of the instrument, and

(b) wishes to object to the registration,

he must do so before the end of the period of 5 weeks beginning with the date on which the notice is given.

(3) The donor of the power must give notice of his objection in writing to the Public Guardian, setting out—

(a) the name and address of the donor of the power;

(b) if known, the name and address of the donee (or donees); and

(c) the ground for making the objection.]

[3535]

NOTES

Commencement: 1 October 2007.

Inserted by SI 2007/2161, regs 2, 4.

15 Objection to registration: application to the court

(1) This regulation deals with any objection to the registration of an instrument as a lasting power of attorney which is to be made to the court.

(2) The grounds for making an application to the court are—

(a) that one or more of the requirements for the creation of a lasting power of attorney have not been met;

(b) that the power has been revoked, or has otherwise come to an end, on a ground other than the grounds set out in paragraph 13(1) of Schedule 1 to the Act;

(c) any of the grounds set out in paragraph (a) or (b) of section 22(3) of the Act.

(3) Where any person—

(a) is entitled to receive notice under paragraph 6, 7 or 8 of Schedule 1 to the Act of an application for the registration of the instrument, and

(b) wishes to object to registration on one or more of the grounds set out in paragraph (2),

he must make an application to the court before the end of the period of 5 weeks beginning with the date on which the notice is given.

(4) The notice of an application to the court, which a person making an objection to the court is required to give to the Public Guardian under paragraph 13(3)(b)(ii) of Schedule 1 to the Act, must be in writing.

[3536]

NOTES

Commencement: 1 October 2007.

16 Notifying applicants of non-registration of lasting power of attorney

Where the Public Guardian is prevented from registering an instrument as a lasting power of attorney by virtue of—

(a) paragraph 11(1) of Schedule 1 to the Act (instrument not made in accordance with Schedule),

(b) paragraph 12(2) of that Schedule (deputy already appointed),

(c) paragraph 13(2) of that Schedule (objection by donee or named person on grounds of bankruptcy, disclaimer, death etc),

(d) paragraph 14(2) of that Schedule (objection by donor), or

(e) regulation 11(2) of these Regulations (application for registration not accompanied by original instrument or certified copy),

he must notify the person (or persons) who applied for registration of that fact.

[3537]

NOTES

Commencement: 1 October 2007.

17 Notice to be given on registration of lasting power of attorney

(1) Where the Public Guardian registers an instrument as a lasting power of attorney, he must—

(a) retain a copy of the instrument; and

(b) return to the person (or persons) who applied for registration the original instrument, or the certified copy of it, which accompanied the application for registration.

(2) Schedule 5 to these Regulations sets out the form of notice ("LPA 004") which the Public Guardian must give to the donor and donee (or donees) when the Public Guardian registers an instrument.

(3) Where it appears to the Public Guardian that there is good reason to do so, the Public Guardian must also provide (or arrange for the provision of) an explanation to the donor of—

(a) the notice referred to in paragraph (2) and what the effect of it is; and

(b) why it is being brought to his attention.

(4) Any information provided under paragraph (3) must be provided—

(a) to the donor personally; and

(b) in a way that is appropriate to the donor's circumstances (for example using simple language, visual aids or other appropriate means).

(5) "Certified copy" is to be construed in accordance with regulation 11(3).

[3538]

NOTES

Commencement: 1 October 2007.

Post-registration

18 Changes to instrument registered as lasting power of attorney

(1) This regulation applies in any case where any of paragraphs 21 to 24 of Schedule 1 to the Act requires the Public Guardian to attach a note to an instrument registered as a lasting power of attorney.

(2) The Public Guardian must give a notice to the donor and the donee (or, if more than one, each of them) requiring him to deliver to the Public Guardian—

(a) the original of instrument which was sent to the Public Guardian for registration;

(b) any office copy of that registered instrument; and

(c) any certified copy of that registered instrument.

(3) On receipt of the document, the Public Guardian must—

(a) attach the required note; and

(b) return the document to the person from whom it was obtained.

[3539]

NOTES

Commencement: 1 October 2007.

19 Loss or destruction of instrument registered as lasting power of attorney

(1) This regulation applies where—

(a) a person is required by or under the Act to deliver up to the Public Guardian any of the following documents—

(i) an instrument registered as a lasting power of attorney;

(ii) an office copy of that registered instrument;

(iii) a certified copy of that registered instrument; and

(b) the document has been lost or destroyed.

(2) The person required to deliver up the document must provide to the Public Guardian in writing—

(a) if known, the date of the loss or destruction and the circumstances in which it occurred;

(b) otherwise, a statement of when he last had the document in his possession.

[3540]

NOTES

Commencement: 1 October 2007.

20 Disclaimer of appointment by a donee of lasting power of attorney

(1) Schedule 6 to these Regulations sets out the form ("LPA 005") which a donee of an instrument registered as a lasting power of attorney must use to disclaim his appointment as donee.

(2) The donee must send—

(a) the completed form to the donor; and

(b) a copy of it to—

(i) the Public Guardian; and

(ii) any other donee who, for the time being, is appointed under the power.

[3541]

NOTES

Commencement: 1 October 2007.

21 Revocation by donor of lasting power of attorney

(1) A donor who revokes a lasting power to attorney must—

(a) notify the Public Guardian that he has done so; and

(b) notify the donee (or, if more than one, each of them) of the revocation.

(2) Where the Public Guardian receives a notice under paragraph (1)(a), he must cancel the registration of the instrument creating the power if he is satisfied that the donor has taken such steps as are necessary in law to revoke it.

(3) The Public Guardian may require the donor to provide such further information, or produce such documents, as the Public Guardian reasonably considers necessary to enable him to determine whether the steps necessary for revocation have been taken.

(4) Where the Public Guardian cancels the registration of the instrument he must notify—

(a) the donor; and

(b) the donee or, if more than one, each of them.

[3542]

NOTES

Commencement: 1 October 2007.

22 Revocation of a lasting power of attorney on death of donor

(1) The Public Guardian must cancel the registration of an instrument as a lasting power of attorney if he is satisfied that the power has been revoked as a result of the donor's death.

(2) Where the Public Guardian cancels the registration of an instrument he must notify the donee or, if more than one, each of them.

[3543]

NOTES

Commencement: 1 October 2007.

PART 3
ENDURING POWERS OF ATTORNEY

23 Notice of intention to apply for registration of enduring power of attorney

(1) Schedule 7 to these Regulations sets out the form of notice ("EP1PG") which an attorney (or attorneys) under an enduring power of attorney must give of his intention to make an application for the registration of the instrument creating the power.

(2) In the case of the notice to be given to the donor, the attorney must also provide (or arrange for the provision of) an explanation to the donor of—

(a) the notice and what the effect of it is; and

(b) why it is being brought to his attention.

(3) The information provided under paragraph (2) must be provided—

(a) to the donor personally; and

(b) in a way that is appropriate to the donor's circumstances (for example using simple language, visual aids or other appropriate means).

[3544]

NOTES

Commencement: 1 October 2007.

24 Application for registration

(1) Schedule 8 to these Regulations sets out the form ("EP2PG") which must be used for making an application to the Public Guardian for the registration of an instrument creating an enduring power of attorney.

(2) Where the instrument to be registered which is sent with the application is neither—

(a) the original instrument creating the power, nor

(b) a certified copy of it,

the Public Guardian must not register the instrument unless the court directs him to do so.

(3) "Certified copy", in relation to an enduring power of attorney, means a copy certified in accordance with section 3 of the Powers of Attorney Act 1971.

[3545]

NOTES

Commencement: 1 October 2007.

25 Notice of objection to registration

(1) This regulation deals with any objection to the registration of an instrument creating an enduring power of attorney which is to be made to the Public Guardian under paragraph 13(4) of Schedule 4 to the Act.

(2) A notice of objection must be given in writing, setting out—

(a) the name and address of the objector;

(b) if different, the name and address of the donor of the power;

(c) if known, the name and address of the attorney (or attorneys); and

(d) the ground for making the objection.

[3546]

NOTES

Commencement: 1 October 2007.

26 Notifying applicants of non-registration of enduring power of attorney

Where the Public Guardian is prevented from registering an instrument creating an enduring power of attorney by virtue of—

(a) paragraph 13(2) of Schedule 4 to the Act (deputy already appointed),

(b) paragraph 13(5) of that Schedule (receipt by Public Guardian of valid notice of objection from person entitled to notice of application to register),

(c) paragraph 13(7) of that Schedule (Public Guardian required to undertake appropriate enquiries in certain circumstances), or

(d) regulation 24(2) of these Regulations (application for registration not accompanied by original instrument or certified copy),

he must notify the person (or persons) who applied for registration of that fact.

[3547]

NOTES

Commencement: 1 October 2007.

27 Registration of instrument creating an enduring power of attorney

(1) Where the Public Guardian registers an instrument creating an enduring power of attorney, he must—

(a) retain a copy of the instrument; and

(b) return to the person (or persons) who applied for registration the original instrument, or the certified copy of it, which accompanied the application.

(2) "Certified copy" has the same meaning as in regulation 24(3).

[3548]

NOTES

Commencement: 1 October 2007.

28 Objection or revocation not applying to all joint and several attorneys

In a case within paragraph 20(6) or (7) of Schedule 4 to the Act, the form of the entry to be made in the register in respect of an instrument creating the enduring power of attorney is a stamp bearing the following words (inserting the information indicated, as appropriate)—

"THE REGISTRATION OF THIS ENDURING POWER OF ATTORNEY IS QUALIFIED AND EXTENDS TO THE APPOINTMENT OF .... (insert name of attorney(s) not affected by ground(s) of objection or revocation) ONLY AS THE ATTORNEY(S) OF .... (insert name of donor)".

[3549]

NOTES

Commencement: 1 October 2007.

29 Loss or destruction of instrument registered as enduring power of attorney

(1) This regulation applies where—

(a) a person is required by or under the Act to deliver up to the Public Guardian any of the following documents—

(i) an instrument registered as an enduring power of attorney;

(ii) an office copy of that registered instrument; or

(iii) a certified copy of that registered instrument; and

(b) the document has been lost or destroyed.

(2) The person who is required to deliver up the document must provide to the Public Guardian in writing—

(a) if known, the date of the loss or destruction and the circumstances in which it occurred;

(b) otherwise, a statement of when he last had the document in his possession.

[3550]

NOTES

Commencement: 1 October 2007.

PART 4
FUNCTIONS OF THE PUBLIC GUARDIAN

30–45 (*Outside the scope of this work.*)

46 Power to require information from donees of lasting power of attorney

(1) This regulation applies where it appears to the Public Guardian that there are circumstances suggesting that the donee of a lasting power of attorney may—

(a) have behaved, or may be behaving, in a way that contravenes his authority or is not in the best interests of the donor of the power,

(b) be proposing to behave in a way that would contravene that authority or would not be in the donor's best interests, or

(c) have failed to comply with the requirements of an order made, or directions given, by the court.

(2) The Public Guardian may require the donee—

(a) to provide specified information or information of a specified description; or

(b) to produce specified documents or documents of a specified description.

(3) The information or documents must be provided or produced—

(a) before the end of such reasonable period as may be specified; and

(b) at such place as may be specified.

(4) The Public Guardian may require—

(a) any information provided to be verified in such manner, or

(b) any document produced to be authenticated in such manner,

as he may reasonably require.

(5) "Specified" means specified in a notice in writing given to the donee by the Public Guardian.

[3551]

NOTES

Commencement: 1 October 2007.

47 Power to require information from attorneys under enduring power of attorney

(1) This regulation applies where it appears to the Public Guardian that there are circumstances suggesting that, having regard to all the circumstances (and in particular the attorney's relationship to or connection with the donor) the attorney under a registered enduring power of attorney may be unsuitable to be the donor's attorney.

(2) The Public Guardian may require the attorney—

(a) to provide specified information or information of a specified description; or

(b) to produce specified documents or documents of a specified description.

(3) The information or documents must be provided or produced—

(a) before the end of such reasonable period as may be specified; and

(b) at such place as may be specified.

(4) The Public Guardian may require—

(a) any information provided to be verified in such manner, or

(b) any document produced to be authenticated in such manner,

as he may reasonably require.

(5) "Specified" means specified in a notice in writing given to the attorney by the Public Guardian.

[3552]

NOTES

Commencement: 1 October 2007.

48 Other functions in relation to enduring powers of attorney

The Public Guardian has the following functions—

(a) directing a Court of Protection Visitor—

(i) to visit an attorney under a registered enduring power of attorney, or

(ii) to visit the donor of a registered enduring power of attorney,

and to make a report to the Public Guardian on such matters as he may direct;

(b) dealing with representations (including complaints) about the way in which an attorney under a registered enduring power of attorney is exercising his powers.

[3553]

NOTES

Commencement: 1 October 2007.

SCHEDULE 1
FORM FOR INSTRUMENT INTENDED TO CREATE A LASTING POWER OF ATTORNEY
Regulation 5

PART 1
FORM FOR INSTRUMENT INTENDED TO CREATE A PROPERTY AND AFFAIRS LASTING POWER OF ATTORNEY

LPA PA 10.07

For official use only
Date of registration

Lasting Power of Attorney Property and Affairs

This is a Lasting Power of Attorney (LPA). It allows you (the donor) to choose someone (the attorney) to make decisions on your behalf. Your attorney(s) can only use the completed LPA after it has been registered with the Office of the Public Guardian (OPG).

Getting started

Before you complete this LPA you **must** read the prescribed information on the next three pages so that you understand the purpose and legal consequences of making an LPA. You should refer to the separate notes on how to complete this LPA when you are directed to because they will help you to complete it.

Things you will need to do to complete this LPA

- decide who to appoint as your attorney(s) in the LPA
- decide if you want to appoint a replacement attorney in case your attorney(s) cannot act for you
- decide whether you want anyone to be notified when an application is made to register your LPA and, if you do, who you want to be notified
- choose at least one independent person to provide a certificate at Part B of the LPA
- fill in part A of the LPA. Your certificate provider(s) will need to complete Part B. Your attorney(s) will need to complete Part C
- have a witness to your signature at the end of Part A of the LPA

What to do after completing this LPA

An LPA can only be used after it has been registered with the OPG, so you will need to think about when you want it to be registered. There is a fee to register an LPA. Further information about how to register an LPA and what happens following registration is available from the OPG.

Information for you, your attorney(s) and your certificate provider(s) is available from the OPG. If you have any questions about how to complete this LPA please contact the OPG.

Office of the Public Guardian
Archway Tower
London N19 5SZ
0845 330 2900
www.publicguardian.gov.uk

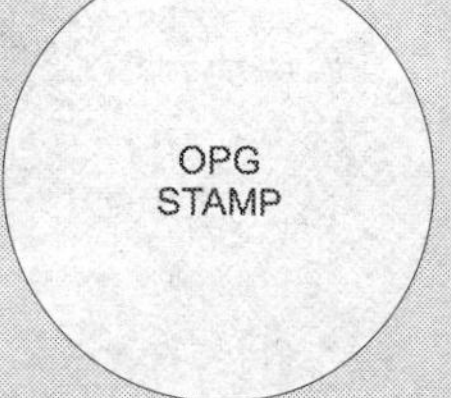

Important - This form **cannot** be used until it has been registered by the Office of the Public Guardian and stamped on **every** page.

PRESCRIBED INFORMATION

Lasting Power of Attorney — Property and Affairs

You must read this information carefully to understand the purpose and legal consequences of making an LPA. You must ask your attorney(s) and certificate provider(s) to read it too.

This form is a legal document known as a Lasting Power of Attorney (LPA). It allows you to authorise someone (the attorney(s)) to make decisions on your behalf about spending your money and managing your property and affairs. Your attorney(s) can only use the LPA after it is registered with the OPG.

If you want someone to make decisions about your personal welfare then you need a different form. You can get a Lasting Power of Attorney — Personal Welfare from the OPG and legal stationers.

Detailed information about why you might find an LPA useful is in the **'Guide for people who want to make a Property and Affairs LPA'.** You can get this from the OPG. You should read this guide before completing this LPA. You should ask your attorney(s) and certificate provider(s) to read it too.

Your attorney(s) cannot do whatever they like. They **must** follow the principles of the Mental Capacity Act 2005 which are:

- a person must be assumed to have capacity unless it is established that the person lacks capacity;
- a person is not to be treated as unable to make a decision unless all practicable steps to help the person to do so have been taken without success;
- a person is not to be treated as unable to make a decision merely because the person makes an unwise decision;
- an act done, or decision made, under the Mental Capacity Act for or on behalf of a person who lacks capacity must be done, or made, in the person's best interests; and
- before the act is done, or the decision is made, regard must be had to whether the purpose for which it is needed can be as effectively achieved in a way that is less restrictive of the person's rights and freedom of action.

Guidance about the principles is in the Mental Capacity Act 2005 Code of Practice. Your attorney(s) will have a duty to have regard to the Code. Copies of the Code can be obtained from Her Majesty's Stationary Office.

1. **CHOOSING YOUR ATTORNEY** Your attorney should be a person you know and trust who is at least 18 or a trust corporation. Your attorney must not be an undischarged or interim bankrupt. You can choose more than one attorney.

2. **CHOOSING MORE THAN ONE ATTORNEY** If you choose more than one attorney you must decide whether your attorneys should act together or together and independently (that is they can all act together but they can also act separately if they wish).
   You may appoint your attorneys together in respect of some matters and together and independently in respect of others. If you appoint more than one attorney and do not state whether they are appointed together or together and independently, when your LPA is registered they will be treated on the basis that they are appointed together. In this LPA, 'together' means jointly 'together and independently' means jointly and severally for the purposes of the Mental Capacity Act 2005.

Please do not detach these notes. They are part of the Lasting Power of Attorney.

PRESCRIBED INFORMATION

3. **CHOOSING A REPLACEMENT ATTORNEY** You can name a replacement(s) in case an attorney is unable to or no longer wishes to continue acting for you. Your attorney(s) can change their mind and may not want to act for you. If this is the case, they must tell you and the OPG.

4. **WHEN AN ATTORNEY CAN ACT** Once your LPA is registered your attorney(s) can act before you lack capacity and after you lack capacity. You may restrict your attorney(s) to act only when you lack capacity in your LPA. There is no one point at which you are treated as having lost capacity to manage your property and affairs. Your attorney(s) must help you to make as many of your own decisions as you can. When decisions have to be taken for you, your attorney(s) must always act in your best interests.

5. **DECISIONS YOUR ATTORNEY CAN MAKE FOR YOU** An attorney for property and affairs may make any decision that you could make about your property and affairs e.g. buy or sell property, manage investments or carry on a business and may access personal information. This is subject to the authority you give them and any decisions excluded by the Mental Capacity Act 2005. Some decisions will also involve personal welfare matters, such as a move to residential care. Your property and affairs attorney(s) will then need to consider your best interests with your attorney(s) for personal welfare (if you have one).

6. **RESTRICTING THE POWERS OF YOUR ATTORNEY(S) OR ADDING CONDITIONS** You can put legally binding restrictions and conditions on your attorney(s)' powers and the scope of their authority in the LPA. But these decisions may still need to be made and other people will have to decide for you. That could involve going to the Court of Protection and a decision being made in your best interests.

7. **GIVING GUIDANCE TO YOUR ATTORNEY** You can also give guidance to your attorney(s) in your LPA. This is not legally binding but should be taken into account when they are making decisions for you.

8. **PAYING ATTORNEYS** An attorney is entitled to be reimbursed for out-of-pocket expenses incurred in carrying out their duties. Professional attorneys, such as solicitors or accountants, charge for their services. You should discuss and record any decision you make about paying your attorney(s) in the LPA.

9. **NOTIFYING OTHER PEOPLE BEFORE REGISTRATION** You can name up to five people to be notified when an application to register your LPA is made. Anyone about to apply for registration of an LPA must notify these people. This gives you an important safeguard because if you lack capacity at the time of registration you will be relying on these people to raise any concerns they may have about the application to register. If you choose not to name anyone to be notified you will need to have two certificate providers under Part B of this form.

10. **CERTIFICATE TO CONFIRM UNDERSTANDING** Once you have filled in Part A of this form an independent person must fill in the certificate at Part B to confirm that, in their opinion, you are making the LPA of your own free and will, that you understand its purpose and the powers you are giving your attorney(s). This is an important safeguard and your LPA cannot be registered unless the certificate is completed.

Please do not detach these notes. They are part of the Lasting Power of Attorney.

PRESCRIBED INFORMATION

11. REGISTERING THE LPA *Your LPA cannot be used until it has been registered with the OPG.* Either you or your chosen attorney(s) can apply to register the LPA. If you register it immediately it can be used straightaway unless you have specified that it should only be used when you lack capacity. The form for registering the LPA is available from the OPG together with details of the registration fee.

12. REGISTER OF LPAs There is a register of LPAs kept by the OPG. It is possible to access the register of LPAs but access is controlled. On application to the OPG, and payment of a fee, people can find out basic information about your LPA. At the discretion of the OPG and according to the purpose for which they need it, they may be able to find out further information. There is additional guidance available from the OPG on the register.

13. CHANGING YOUR MIND You can cancel your LPA even after it is registered if you have the mental capacity to do so. You need to take formal steps to revoke the LPA. You must tell your attorney if you do and, if it is registered, you will need to ask the OPG to remove it from the register of LPAs.

FURTHER NOTICE FOR ATTORNEY(S)
You should read the **'Guide for people taking on the role of Property and Affairs attorney'** under an LPA before you agree to become an attorney and complete Part C of this LPA. The guide contains detailed information about what your role and responsibilities will be.

You must contact the OPG at once if the person you are acting for dies. If you are unable to continue acting you should take steps to disclaim the power and notify the OPG and the donor.

FURTHER NOTICE FOR CERTIFICATE PROVIDER(S)
You should read the separate **'Certificate Providers and witness guidance'** before you agree to become a certificate provider and complete Part B of this LPA. The guidance contains detailed information about your role and responsibilities. You may also like to read the guidance for property and affairs attorneys and donors. If you have any concerns about an LPA you are asked to certify please contact the OPG.

Please do not detach these notes. They are part of the Lasting Power of Attorney.

LPA PA 04.07

Lasting Power of Attorney Property and Affairs

Important
This LPA form cannot be used until it has been registered by the OPG and stamped on **every** page.

Before you complete this LPA form, you must read the prescribed information on pages 2, 3 and 4 and you should read the guidance produced by the OPG.

To help you complete the form, please refer to the Notes for completing an LPA — Property and Affairs.

PART A – Donor's statement

Your details

1. My name and date of birth are: See Note 1

☐ Mr. ☐ Mrs. ☐ Ms. ☐ Miss ☐ Other ____

First name

Middle name(s)

Last name

Date of birth D D M M Y Y Y Y

Any other names you are known by or have been known by in the past (e.g. maiden name) See Note 2

2. My contact details and e-mail are: See Note 3

Address

Postcode

Telephone no.

Mobile no.

E-mail address

The details of the attorney(s) you are appointing

3. I appoint the following attorney(s) in accordance with the provisions of the Mental Capacity Act 2005:

See Note 4

Attorney

☐ Mr. ☐ Mrs. ☐ Ms. ☐ Miss ☐ Other ________

See Note 5

First name(s)

Last name

Attorney

☐ Mr. ☐ Mrs. ☐ Ms. ☐ Miss ☐ Other ________

First name(s)

Last name

Appointment of a trust corporation as attorney

See Note 6

Company name

Note: (You do not have to appoint a trust corporation as one of your attorneys)

How your attorney(s) is to act for you

If you only have one attorney please cross through this page.

4. If you are appointing more than one attorney, how do you wish them to act?
   (If you do not choose an option your attorneys will be appointed together)

See Note 7

- ☐ together

See Note 8

- ☐ together and independently
- ☐ together in respect of some matters and together and independently in respect of others

If together in respect of some matters and together and independently in respect of others, details are as follows:

Replacement attorney(s)

5. I wish to appoint a replacement attorney: (You do not have to appoint a replacement attorney). See Note 9

☐ Yes ☐ No

If Yes, I appoint the following replacement attorney:

☐ Mr. ☐ Mrs. ☐ Ms. ☐ Miss ☐ Other ______ See Note 10

First name(s)

Last name

Restrictions on the appointment of a replacement attorney: (If you do not complete this section your first replacement will replace the first attorney who needs replacing). See Note 11

Placing restrictions and/or conditions on the attorney(s) you are appointing

You can use this section to specify that your LPA is only to be used when you lack capacity. If you decide to specify this, you should specify anything you want the attorney(s) to do to confirm that you lack capacity to make the decision in question.

You may also use this section to place restrictions on the ability of your attorney(s) to use your property and affairs to make gifts. Any restrictions and/or conditions you set out below **must** be followed by the attorney(s).

6. I wish to place restrictions and/or conditions on my attorney(s) in relation to my property and affairs: See Note 12

☐ Yes ☐ No

If Yes, the restrictions and conditions are as follows:

Guidance for your attorney(s) to consider

See Note 13

Your attorney(s) **should** consider the guidance set out below when making decisions in your best interests.

7. I wish my attorney(s) to consider the following guidance:

8. I have agreed to pay my attorney(s) a fee to act as my attorney(s):

See Note 14

☐ Yes ☐ No

If Yes, the following is additional information about fees that I have agreed with my attorney(s):

Notifying others when an application to register your LPA is made See Note 15

9. I wish the following people, 'the named persons', to be notified when an application to register my LPA is made:

☐ Mr. ☐ Mrs. ☐ Ms. ☐ Miss ☐ Other ______

Full name

Address

Postcode

Telephone no.

E-mail address

☐ Mr. ☐ Mrs. ☐ Ms. ☐ Miss ☐ Other ______

Full name

Address

Postcode

Telephone no.

E-mail address

☐ Mr. ☐ Mrs. ☐ Ms. ☐ Miss ☐ Other ______

Full name

Address

Postcode

Telephone no.

E-mail address

☐ Mr. ☐ Mrs. ☐ Ms. ☐ Miss ☐ Other ________

Full name

Address

Postcode

Telephone no.

E-mail address

☐ Mr. ☐ Mrs. ☐ Ms. ☐ Miss ☐ Other ________

Full name

Address

Postcode

Telephone no.

E-mail address

If you do not include anyone here you **must** have two certificate providers at Part B.

10. I confirm that

☐ I have read the prescribed information on pages 2, 3 and 4 of this LPA.

or

☐ The prescribed information has been read to me by

See Note 16

11. I confirm that

☐ I intend to give my attorney(s) authority to make decisions on my behalf, including in circumstances when I lack capacity subject to any restrictions I have made.

See Note 17

12. I confirm that

☐ the persons named in paragraph 9 are to be notified when an application to register this LPA is made

or

☐ I do not want anyone to be notified when an application to register this LPA is made and I understand that I need **two** people to provide a separate certificate each at Part B of this LPA.

See Note 18

13. I confirm that

☐ I have chosen my certificate provider(s) myself.

See Note 19

14. Signed by me as a deed

See Note 20

15. Date signed (delivered as a deed) D D M M Y Y Y Y

If you are unable to sign the form, please refer to the notes for completion and turn to page 14 of this LPA.

In the presence of

16. Signature of witness

See Note 21

17. Full name of witness

18. Address of witness

Postcode

Important - This form **cannot** be used until it has been registered by the Office of the Public Guardian and stamped on **every** page.

If you are unable to sign or make a mark, then you must ask someone else to sign for you in your presence and the presence of two witnesses. Please refer to notes 22 and 23.

I am signing this LPA at the donor's direction and in the donor's presence: See Note 22

19. Signed as a deed

20. Date signed (delivered as a deed) D D M M Y Y Y Y

21. Full name

22. Address

Postcode

In the presence of

23. Signature of witness See Note 23

24. Full name of witness

25. Address of witness

Postcode

26. Signature of witness

27. Full name of witness

28. Address of witness

Postcode

PART B – Certificate provider's statement

See Note 24

Who can provide a certificate?

The donor can choose someone they have known personally over the last two years (Category A) or someone who, because of their relevant professional skills and expertise, considers themselves able to provide the certificate (Category B).

Note: Category B providers are entitled to charge a fee for providing this certificate.

Who cannot provide a certificate? See Note 25

A certificate provider must not be:

- a member of the donor's or attorney's family,
- a business partner or paid employee of the donor or attorney(s),
- an attorney appointed in this form or another LPA or any EPA made by the donor,
- the owner, director, manager, or an employee of a care home in which the donor lives or their family member or partner,
- a director or employee of a trust corporation appointed as an attorney in this LPA.

You, the certificate provider, **must** read Part A and B of this LPA, and the prescribed information on pages 2, 3 and 4. You should also read the separate **'Certificate provider and witness guidance'** produced by the OPG before completing the certificate. You must discuss the LPA with the donor without the attorney(s) present. See Note 26

☐ I confirm that I am acting independently of the person making this LPA (the donor) and the person(s) appointed under the LPA and in particular I am not a person listed in the above section 'Who cannot provide a certificate?'. See Note 27

☐ I am aged 18 or over. See Note 28

The certificate provider

Name and contact details of certificate provider

☐ Mr. ☐ Mrs. ☐ Ms. ☐ Miss ☐ Other ______ See Note 29

First name

Middle name(s)

Last name

Address

Postcode

Telephone no. See Note 30

Mobile no.

E-mail address

The OPG may need to contact you to verify the information you provide.

Category of certificate provider – choose from category A **or** B – do not complete both See Note 31

Category A – Knowledge certification See Note 32

☐ I have known the donor personally over the last two years.

How do you know them?

Category B - Skills certification See Note 33

I am:

☐ a registered healthcare professional (includes GP)

☐ a barrister, solicitor or advocate

☐ a registered social worker

☐ an Independent Mental Capacity Advocate (IMCA)

☐ none of the above but consider that I have the relevant professional skills and expertise to be a certificate provider.

My relevant professional skills and expertise are:

I confirm and understand

☐ I confirm that I have read Parts A and B of this LPA, and the prescribed information on pages 2, 3 and 4. See Note 34

☐ I confirm that I have discussed the contents of this LPA with the donor and that the attorney(s) was not present. See Note 35

☐ I understand that I should make efforts to discuss this LPA with the donor without anyone present; and See Note 36

☐ I have discussed this LPA with the donor without anyone else present

or

☐ I have discussed this LPA with the donor in the presence of:

because

☐ I confirm that I am completing this certificate straight after discussing this LPA with the donor. See Note 37

Core certification

I certify

I certify that in my opinion, at the time when the donor is making this LPA, that: See Note 38

- ☐ the donor understands the purpose of this LPA and the scope of the authority under it;
- ☐ no fraud or undue pressure is being used to induce the donor to create this LPA; and
- ☐ there is nothing else that would prevent this LPA being created.

Do not sign this certificate if you have any doubt about any of the above. You should bring any concerns you have to the attention of the OPG.

Signature of certificate provider

Date signed See Note 39

D	D	M	M	Y	Y	Y	Y

Full name of certificate provider

Additional certificate provider's statement

This additional certificate only needs to be completed if there are no notified persons listed in the LPA.

Who can provide a certificate?
The donor can choose someone they have known personally over the last two years (Category A) or someone who, because of their relevant professional skills and expertise, considers themselves able to provide the certificate (Category B).

Note: Category B providers are entitled to charge a fee for providing this certificate.

Who cannot provide a certificate? See Note 40
A certificate provider must not be:

- a member of the donor's or attorney's family;
- a business partner or paid employee of the donor or attorney(s);
- an attorney appointed in this form or another LPA or any EPA made by the donor;
- the owner, director, manager, or an employee of a care home in which the donor lives or their family member or partner;
- a director or employee of a trust corporation appointed as an attorney in this LPA.

You, the certificate provider, **must** read Part A and B of this LPA, and the prescribed information on pages 2, 3 and 4. You should also read the separate **'Certificate provider and witness guidance'** produced by the OPG before completing the certificate. You must discuss the LPA with the donor without the attorney(s) present.

☐ I confirm that I am acting independently of the person making this LPA (the donor) and the person(s) appointed under the LPA and in particular I am not a person listed in the above section 'Who cannot provide a certificate?'.

☐ I am aged 18 or over.

The certificate provider

Name and contact details of certificate provider

☐ Mr. ☐ Mrs. ☐ Ms. ☐ Miss ☐ Other ________

First name

Middle name(s)

Last name

Address

Postcode

Telephone no.

Mobile no.

E-mail address

The OPG may need to contact you to verify the information you provide.

Category of certificate provider – choose from category A **or** B – do not complete both

Category A – Knowledge certification

☐ I have known the donor personally over the last two years.

How do you know them?

Category B - Skills certification

I am:

☐ a registered healthcare professional (includes GP)

☐ a barrister, solicitor or advocate

☐ a registered social worker

☐ an Independent Mental Capacity Advocate (IMCA)

☐ none of the above but consider that I have the relevant professional skills and expertise to be a certificate provider.

My relevant professional skills and expertise are:

I confirm and understand

☐ I confirm that I have read Parts A and B of this LPA, and the prescribed information on pages 2, 3 and 4.

☐ I confirm that I have discussed the contents of this LPA with the donor and that the attorney(s) was not present.

☐ I understand that I should make efforts to discuss this LPA with the donor without anyone present; and

☐ I have discussed this LPA with the donor without anyone else present

or

☐ I have discussed this LPA with the donor in the presence of:

because

☐ I confirm that I am completing this certificate straight after discussing this LPA with the donor.

Core certification

I certify

I certify that in my opinion, at the time when the donor is making this LPA, that:

☐ the donor understands the purpose of this LPA and the scope of the authority under it;

☐ no fraud or undue pressure is being used to induce the donor to create this LPA; and

☐ there is nothing else that would prevent this LPA being created.

Do not sign this certificate if you have any doubt about any of the above. You should bring any concerns you have to the attention of the OPG.

Signature of additional certificate provider

Date signed

D	D	M	M	Y	Y	Y	Y

Full name of additional certificate provider

PART C – Attorney's statement (Every attorney must complete a copy of this Part)

See Note 41

29. My contact details and date of birth are:

Attorney

☐ Mr. ☐ Mrs. ☐ Ms. ☐ Miss ☐ Other

See Note 42

First name

Middle name(s)

Last name

Date of birth D D M M Y Y Y Y

Telephone no. Mobile

E-mail address

See Note 43

30. ☐ I have read the prescribed information on pages 2, 3 and 4 or have had the prescibed information read to me. See Note 44

31. ☐ I understand the duties imposed on me under this Lasting Power of Attorney including the obligation to act in accordance with the principles of the Mental Capacity Act 2005 and the duty to have regard to the Code of Practice issued under the Act. See Note 45

32. ☐ I am not an undischarged bankrupt or an interim bankrupt. See Note 46

33. ☐ I understand that I cannot act under this Lasting Power of Attorney until this form has been registered by the Public Guardian. See Note 47

34. Signed by me as a deed *(You must not sign until after the donor has signed at paragraph 14 and the certificate provider has signed the certificate)* See Note 48

35. Date signed (delivered as a deed) D D M M Y Y Y Y

In the presence of

36. Signature of witness See Note 49

37. Full name of witness

38. Address of witness

Postcode

Important - This form **cannot** be used until it has been registered by the Office of the Public Guardian and stamped on **every** page.

PART C – Attorney's statement (Every attorney must complete a copy of this Part)

See Note 41

29. My contact details and date of birth are:

Attorney

☐ Mr. ☐ Mrs. ☐ Ms. ☐ Miss ☐ Other

See Note 42

First name

Middle name(s)

Last name

Date of birth D D M M Y Y Y Y

Telephone no. Mobile

See Note 43

E-mail address

30. ☐ I have read the prescribed information on pages 2, 3 and 4 or have had the prescibed information read to me. See Note 44

31. ☐ I understand the duties imposed on me under this Lasting Power of Attorney including the obligation to act in accordance with the principles of the Mental Capacity Act 2005 and the duty to have regard to the Code of Practice issued under the Act. See Note 45

32. ☐ I am not an undischarged bankrupt or an interim bankrupt. See Note 46

33. ☐ I understand that I cannot act under this Lasting Power of Attorney until this form has been registered by the Public Guardian. See Note 47

34. Signed by me as a deed *(You must not sign until after the donor has signed at paragraph 14 and the certificate provider has signed the certificate)* See Note 48

35. Date signed (delivered as a deed) D D M M Y Y Y Y

In the presence of

36. Signature of witness See Note 49

37. Full name of witness

38. Address of witness

Postcode

Important - This form **cannot** be used until it has been registered by the Office of the Public Guardian and stamped on **every** page.

PART II STATUTORY INSTRUMENTS

PART C – Attorney's statement – Trust Corporation

See Note 50

(This section only needs to be completed where the donor has chosen a trust corporation to be an attorney)

49. Name and address of a trust corporation See Note 51

A trust corporation

Company name

Address

Postcode

Company Registration no.

Company seal (if applicable)

50. ☐ I have read the prescribed information on pages 2, 3 and 4 or had the prescribed information read to me. See Note 52

51. ☐ I understand the duties imposed on me under this Lasting Power of Attorney including the obligation to act in accordance with the principles of the Mental Capacity Act 2005 and the duty to have regard to the Code of Practice issued under the Act.

This should not be executed until after the donor has signed at paragraph 14 and the certificate provider has signed the certificate. See Note 53

Note: The statements above are made by the trust corporation not the individuals above.

PART C – Replacement Attorney's statement

See Note 54

(To be completed by a replacement attorney if appointed. Only complete this if you are a replacement attorney chosen at paragraph 5.)

52. My contact details and date of birth are:

Attorney

☐ Mr. ☐ Mrs. ☐ Ms. ☐ Miss ☐ Other

See Note 55

First name

Middle name(s)

Last name

Date of birth D D M M Y Y Y Y

Telephone no. Mobile

See Note 56

E-mail address

53. ☐ I have read the prescribed information on pages 2, 3 and 4 or had the prescribed information read to me. See Note 57

54. ☐ I understand that if an original attorney's appointment is terminated I will replace the original attorney if I am still eligible to act as an attorney. See Note 58

55. ☐ I understand that I do not have the authority to act under this LPA until such time as a relevant attorney's appointment is terminated. See Note 59

56. ☐ I understand the duties imposed on me under this Lasting Power of Attorney including the obligation to act in accordance with the principles of the Mental Capacity Act 2005 and the duty to have regard to the Code of Practice issued under the Act. See Note 60

57. ☐ I am not an undischarged bankrupt or an interim bankrupt. See Note 61

58. ☐ I understand that I cannot act under this Lasting Power of Attorney until this form has been registered by the Public Guardian. See Note 62

59. Signed by me as a deed *(You must not sign until after the donor has signed at paragraph 14 and the certificate provider has signed the certificate).* See Note 63

60. Date signed (delivered as a deed) D D M M Y Y Y Y

(Continued over the page)

In the presence of

61. Signature of witness

See Note 64

62. Full name of witness

63. Address of witness

Postcode

Important - This form **cannot** be used until it has been registered by the Office of the Public Guardian and stamped on **every** page.

[3554]

NOTES

Commencement: 1 October 2007.

PART 2
FORM FOR INSTRUMENT INTENDED TO CREATE A PERSONAL WELFARE LASTING POWER OF ATTORNEY

LPA PW 10.07

For official use only
Date of registration

Lasting Power of Attorney
Personal Welfare

This is a Lasting Power of Attorney (LPA). It allows you (the donor) to choose someone (the attorney) to make decisions on your behalf where you lack capacity to make those decisions yourself. Your attorney(s) can only use the completed LPA after it has been registered with the Office of the Public Guardian (OPG).

Getting started

Before you complete this LPA you **must** read the prescribed information on the next three pages so that you understand the purpose and legal consequences of making an LPA. You should refer to the separate notes on how to complete this LPA when you are directed to because they will help you to complete it.

Things you will need to do to complete this LPA

- decide who to appoint as your attorney(s) in the LPA
- decide if you want to appoint a replacement attorney in case your attorney(s) cannot act for you
- decide whether you want anyone to be notified when an application is made to register your LPA and, if you do, who you want to be notified
- choose at least one independent person to provide a certificate at Part B of the LPA
- fill in part A of the LPA. Your certificate provider(s) will need to complete Part B. Your attorney(s) will need to complete Part C
- have a witness to your signature at the end of Part A of the LPA

What to do after completing this LPA

An LPA can only be used after it has been registered with the OPG, so you will need to think about when you want it to be registered. There is a fee to register an LPA. Further information about how to register an LPA and what happens following registration is available from the OPG.

Information for you, your attorney(s) and your certificate provider(s) is available from the OPG. If you have any questions about how to complete this LPA please contact the OPG.

Office of the Public Guardian
Archway Tower
London N19 5SZ
0845 330 2900
www.publicguardian.gov.uk

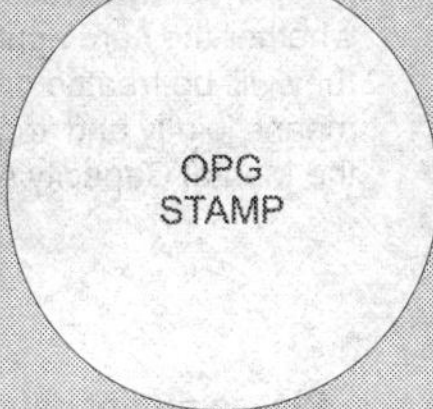

Important - This form **cannot** be used until it has been registered by the Office of the Public Guardian and stamped on **every** page.

PRESCRIBED INFORMATION

You must read this information carefully to understand the purpose and legal consequences of making an LPA. You must ask your attorney(s) and certificate provider(s) to read it too.

This form is a legal document known as a Lasting Power of Attorney (LPA). It allows you to authorise someone (the attorney(s)) to make decisions on your behalf about your personal welfare including your healthcare, if you lack capacity to make those decisions. Your attorney(s) can only use the LPA after it is registered with the OPG.

If you want someone to make decisions about your property and affairs then you need a different form. You can get a Lasting Power of Attorney — Property and Affairs from the OPG and legal stationers.

Detailed information about why you might find an LPA useful is in the **'Guide for people who want to make a personal welfare LPA'.** You can get this from the OPG. You should read this guide before completing this LPA. You should ask your attorney(s) and certificate provider(s) to read it too.

Your attorney(s) cannot do whatever they like. They **must** follow the principles of the Mental Capacity Act 2005 which are:

- a person must be assumed to have capacity unless it is established that the person lacks capacity;
- a person is not to be treated as unable to make a decision unless all practicable steps to help the person to do so have been taken without success;
- a person is not to be treated as unable to make a decision merely because the person makes an unwise decision;
- an act done, or decision made, under the Mental Capacity Act for or on behalf of a person who lacks capacity must be done, or made, in the person's best interests; and
- before the act is done, or the decision is made, regard must be had to whether the purpose for which it is needed can be as effectively achieved in a way that is less restrictive of the person's rights and freedom of action.

Guidance about the principles is in the Mental Capacity Act 2005 Code of Practice. Your attorney(s) will have a duty to have regard to the Code. Copies of the Code can be obtained from Her Majesty's Stationary Office.

1. **CHOOSING YOUR ATTORNEY** Your attorney should be a person you know and trust who is at least 18. You can choose more than one attorney.

2. **CHOOSING MORE THAN ONE ATTORNEY** If you choose more than one attorney you must decide whether your attorneys should act together or together and independently (that is they can all act together but they can also act separately if they wish).
   You may appoint your attorneys together in respect of some matters and together and independently in respect of others. If you appoint more than one attorney and do not state whether they are appointed together or together and independently, when your LPA is registered they will be treated on the basis that they are appointed together. In this LPA form, 'together' means jointly and 'together and independently' means jointly and severally for the purposes of the Mental Capacity Act 2005.

Please do not detach these notes. They are part of the Lasting Power of Attorney.

PRESCRIBED INFORMATION

3. **CHOOSING A REPLACEMENT ATTORNEY** You can name a replacement(s) in case an attorney is unable to or no longer wishes to continue acting for you. Your attorney(s) can change their mind and may not want to act for you. If this is the case, they must tell you and the OPG.

4. **WHEN AN ATTORNEY CAN ACT** An attorney for personal welfare can only act when you lack the capacity to make a particular decision yourself. There is no one point at which you are treated as having lost capacity to make decisions about your personal welfare. You may have capacity to make some decisions but not others; for example, you may be able to decide what to wear but not to consent to an operation. Your attorney(s) must help you to make as many of your own decisions as you can. When decisions have to be taken for you, your attorney(s) must always act in your best interests.

5. **DECISIONS YOUR ATTORNEY CAN MAKE FOR YOU** An attorney for personal welfare may make any decision that you could make about your welfare e.g. where you live and with whom, accessing your personal information like medical records, deciding what you wear, what you eat and how you spend your day. This is subject to the authority you give them and any decisions excluded by the Mental Capacity Act 2005. They will also be able to give and refuse consent to medical treatment according to your best interests. Your attorney(s) will only be able to make these decisions where you lack capacity to make them yourself. Some decisions will also involve property and affairs, such as a move to residential care. Your personal welfare attorney(s) will then need to consider your best interests with your attorney(s) for property and affairs (if you have one).

6. **LIFE-SUSTAINING TREATMENT** Your attorney(s) cannot make decisions about life-sustaining treatment for you unless you expressly state that in your LPA. Life-sustaining treatment means any treatment that a doctor considers necessary to sustain your life. Life-sustaining treatment is not a category of treatment. Whether or not a treatment is life-sustaining will depend on the circumstances of a particular situation. Some treatments will be life-sustaining in some situations but not in others; the important factor is if the treatment is needed to keep you alive. In the LPA you must specify whether you are giving your attorney(s) this power.

7. If you do not say that your attorney(s) can make decisions about life-sustaining treatment, the doctor in charge of your treatment will make the decision in your best interests. Where practicable and appropriate, your doctor will take into account the views of your attorney(s) and other people interested in your welfare as part of the best interests assessment. This is what happens in all cases where there is nobody authorised to take decisions on your behalf. However, if you have a separate valid and applicable advance decision, that should be followed by the doctor.

8. **RESTRICTING THE POWERS OF YOUR ATTORNEY(S) OR ADDING CONDITIONS** You can put legally binding restrictions and conditions on your attorney(s)' powers and the scope of their authority in the LPA. But these decisions may still need to be made and other people will have to decide for you. That could involve going back to your doctor or care worker or the Court of Protection and a decision being made in your best interests.

9. **GIVING GUIDANCE TO YOUR ATTORNEY** You can also give guidance to your attorney(s) in your LPA. This is not legally binding but should be taken into account when they are making decisions for you.

Please do not detach these notes. They are part of the Lasting Power of Attorney.

PRESCRIBED INFORMATION

10. PAYING ATTORNEYS An attorney is entitled to be reimbursed for out-of-pocket expenses incurred in carrying out their duties. Professional attorneys, such as solicitors or accountants, charge for their services. You should discuss and record any decision you make about paying your attorney(s) in the LPA.

11. NOTIFYING OTHER PEOPLE BEFORE REGISTRATION You can name up to five people to be notified when an application to register your LPA is made. Anyone about to apply for registration of an LPA must notify these people. This gives you an important safeguard because if you lack capacity at the time of registration you will be relying on these people to raise any concerns they may have about the application to register. If you choose not to name anyone to be notified you will need to have two certificate providers under Part B of this form.

12. CERTIFICATE TO CONFIRM UNDERSTANDING Once you have filled in Part A of this form an independent person must fill in the certificate at Part B to confirm that, in their opinion, you are making the LPA of your own free will, and that you understand its purpose and the powers you are giving your attorney(s). This is an important safeguard and your LPA cannot be registered unless the certificate is completed.

13. REGISTERING THE LPA *Your LPA cannot be used until it has been registered with the OPG.* Either you or your chosen attorney(s) can apply to register the LPA. If you register it immediately it is ready to be used when you lack capacity. The form for registering the LPA is available from the OPG together with details of the registration fee.

14. REGISTER OF LPAs There is a register of LPAs kept by the OPG. It is possible to access the register of LPAs but access is controlled. On application to the OPG, and payment of a fee, people can find out basic information about your LPA. At the discretion of the OPG and according to the purpose for which they need it, they may be able to find out further information. There is additional guidance available from the OPG on the register.

15. CHANGING YOUR MIND You can cancel your LPA even after it is registered if you have the mental capacity to do so. You need to take formal steps to revoke the LPA. You must tell your attorney if you do and, if it is registered, you will need to ask the OPG to remove it from the register of LPAs.

FURTHER NOTICE FOR ATTORNEY(S)

You should read the **'Guide for people taking on the role of Personal Welfare attorney'** under an LPA before you agree to become an attorney and complete Part C of this LPA. The guide contains detailed information about what your role and responsibilities will be.

You must contact the OPG at once if the person you are acting for dies. If you are unable to continue acting you should take steps to disclaim the power and notify the OPG and the donor.

FURTHER NOTICE FOR CERTIFICATE PROVIDER(S)

You should read the separate **'Certificate Providers and witness guidance'** before you agree to become a certificate provider and complete Part B of this LPA. The guidance contains detailed information about your role and responsibilities. You may also like to read the guidance for personal welfare attorneys and donors. If you have any concerns about an LPA you are asked to certify please contact the OPG.

Please do not detach these notes. They are part of the Lasting Power of Attorney.

LPA PW 04.07

Lasting Power of Attorney – Personal Welfare

Important
This LPA form cannot be used until it has been registered by the OPG and stamped on **every** page.

Before you complete this LPA form, you must read the prescribed information on pages 2, 3 and 4 and you should read the guidance produced by the OPG.

To help you complete the form, please refer to the Notes for completing an LPA – Personal Welfare.

PART A – Donor's statement

Your details

1. My name and date of birth are: See Note 1

☐ Mr. ☐ Mrs. ☐ Ms. ☐ Miss ☐ Other

First name

Middle name(s)

Last name

Date of birth D D M M Y Y Y Y

Any other names you are known by or have been known by in the past (e.g. maiden name) See Note 2

2. My contact details are: See Note 3

Address

Postcode

Telephone no.

Mobile no.

E-mail address

PART II STATUTORY INSTRUMENTS

The details of the attorney(s) you are appointing

3. I appoint the following attorney(s) in accordance with the provisions of the Mental Capacity Act 2005: See Note 4

Attorney

☐ Mr. ☐ Mrs. ☐ Ms. ☐ Miss ☐ Other See Note 5

First name(s)

Last name

Attorney

☐ Mr. ☐ Mrs. ☐ Ms. ☐ Miss ☐ Other

First name(s)

Last name

How your attorney(s) is to act for you

If you only have one attorney please cross through this part.

4. If you are appointing more than one attorney, how do you wish them to act? See Note 6
(If you do not choose an option your attorneys will be appointed together)

☐ together See Note 7

☐ together and independently

☐ together in respect of some matters and together and independently in respect of others

If together in respect of some matters and together and independently in respect of others, details are as follows:

Replacement attorney(s)

5. I wish to appoint a replacement attorney: (You do not have to appoint a replacement attorney). See Note 8

☐ Yes ☐ No

If Yes, I appoint the following replacement attorney:

☐ Mr. ☐ Mrs. ☐ Ms. ☐ Miss ☐ Other ______ See Note 9

First name(s) ______

Last name ______

Restrictions on the appointment of a replacement attorney: (If you do not complete this section your first replacement will replace the first attorney who needs replacing). See Note 10

Life-sustaining treatment

6. You **must** choose **one** of the two options below:

If you cannot sign or make a mark, please read the notes for completion.

See Note 11

Option A

I want to give my attorney(s) authority to give or refuse consent to life-sustaining treatment on my behalf

Your signature

Date signed D D M M Y Y Y Y

Option B

I **do not** want to give my attorney(s) authority to give or refuse consent to life-sustaining treatment on my behalf

Your signature

Date signed D D M M Y Y Y Y

In the presence of

See Note 12

Signature of witness

Full name of witness

Address of witness

Postcode

Placing restrictions and/or conditions on the attorney(s) you are appointing

Any restrictions and/or conditions you set out below **must** be followed by the attorney(s). For example, if you have given your attorney(s) powers with regard to life-sustaining treatment you can comment further here about any restrictions you want to add.

7. I wish to place restrictions and/or conditions on my attorney(s) in relation to my personal welfare: See Note 13

☐ Yes ☐ No

If Yes, the restrictions and conditions are as follows:

Guidance for your attorney(s) to consider

See Note 14

Your attorney(s) **should** consider the guidance set out below when making decisions in your best interests.

8. I wish my attorney(s) to consider the following guidance:

9. I have agreed to pay my attorney(s) a fee to act as my attorney(s):

See Note 15

☐ Yes ☐ No

If Yes, the following is additional information about fees that I have agreed with my attorney(s):

Notifying others when an application to register your LPA is made

See Note 16

10. I wish the following people, 'the named persons', to be notified when an application to register my LPA is made:

☐ Mr. ☐ Mrs. ☐ Ms. ☐ Miss ☐ Other

Full name

Address

Postcode

Telephone no.

E-mail address

☐ Mr. ☐ Mrs. ☐ Ms. ☐ Miss ☐ Other

Full name

Address

Postcode

Telephone no.

E-mail address

☐ Mr. ☐ Mrs. ☐ Ms. ☐ Miss ☐ Other

Full name

Address

Postcode

Telephone no.

E-mail address

☐ Mr. ☐ Mrs. ☐ Ms. ☐ Miss ☐ Other

Full name

Address

Postcode

Telephone no.

E-mail address

☐ Mr. ☐ Mrs. ☐ Ms. ☐ Miss ☐ Other

Full name

Address

Postcode

Telephone no.

E-mail address

If you do not include anyone here you **must** have two certificate providers at Part B.

11. I confirm that

☐ I have read the prescribed information on pages 2, 3 and 4 of this LPA

or

☐ the prescribed information has been read to me by

See Note 17

12. I confirm that

☐ I give my attorney(s) authority to make decisions on my behalf in circumstances when I lack capacity.

See Note 18

13. I confirm that

☐ I have chosen between Option A and option B with regard to life-sustaining treatment in paragraph 6 of this LPA.

See Note 19

14. I confirm that

☐ the person(s) named in paragraph 10 are to be notified when this LPA is registered

or

☐ I do not want anyone to be notified when an application to register this LPA is made and I understand that I need **two** people to provide a separate certificate each at Part B of this LPA.

See Note 20

15. I confirm that

☐ I have chosen my certificate provider(s) myself.

See Note 21

16. Signed by me as a deed

See Note 22

If you are unable to sign the form, please refer to the notes for completion and turn to page 14 of this LPA.

17. Date signed (delivered as a deed) D D M M Y Y Y Y

In the presence of

18. Signature of witness

See Note 23

19. Full name of witness

20. Address of witness

Postcode

Important - This form **cannot** be used until it has been registered by the Office of the Public Guardian and stamped on **every** page.

If you are unable to sign or make a mark, then you must ask someone else to sign for you in your presence and the presence of two witnesses. Please refer to notes 24 and 25.

I am signing this LPA at the donor's direction and in the donor's presence and I confirm that I have signed at paragraph 6 according to the donor's direction. See Note 24

21. Signed as a deed

22. Date signed (delivered as a deed) D D M M Y Y Y Y

23. Full name

24. Address

Postcode

In the presence of See Note 25

25. Signature of witness

26. Full name of witness

27. Address of witness

Postcode

28. Signature of witness

29. Full name of witness

30. Address of witness

Postcode

PART B - Certificate provider's statement

See Note 26

Who can provide a certificate?
The donor can choose someone they have known personally over the last two years (Category A) or someone who, because of their relevant professional skills and expertise, considers themselves able to provide the certificate (Category B).

Note: Category B providers are entitled to charge a fee for providing this certificate.

Who cannot provide a certificate? See Note 27
A certificate provider must not be:

- a member of the donor's or attorney's family;
- a business partner or paid employee of the donor or attorney(s);
- an attorney appointed in this form or another LPA or any EPA made by the donor;
- the owner, director, manager, or an employee of a care home in which the donor lives or their family member.

You, the certificate provider, **must** read Parts A and B of this LPA, and the prescribed information on pages 2, 3 and 4. You should also read the separate **'Certificate provider and witness guidance'** produced by the OPG before completing the certificate. You must discuss the LPA with the donor without the attorney(s) present. See Note 28

☐ I confirm that I am acting independently of the person making this LPA (the donor) and the person(s) appointed under the LPA and in particular I am not a person listed in the above section 'Who cannot provide a certificate?'. See Note 29

☐ I am aged 18 or over. See Note 30

The certificate provider

Name and contact details of the certificate provider

☐ Mr. ☐ Mrs. ☐ Ms. ☐ Miss ☐ Other ______ See Note 31

First name ______

Middle name(s) ______

Last name ______

Address ______

Postcode ______

Telephone no. ______ See Note 32

Mobile no. ______

E-mail address ______

The OPG may need to contact you to verify the information you provide.

PART II STATUTORY INSTRUMENTS

Category of certificate provider – choose from category A **or** B – do not complete both. See Note 33

Category A – Knowledge certification See Note 34

☐ I have known the donor personally over the last two years.

How do you know them?

Category B - Skills certification See Note 35

I am:

☐ a registered healthcare professional (includes GP)

☐ a barrister, solicitor or advocate

☐ a registered social worker

☐ an Independent Mental Capacity Advocate (IMCA)

☐ none of the above but consider that I have the relevant professional skills and expertise to be a certificate provider.

My relevant professional skills and expertise are:

I confirm and understand

☐ I confirm that I have read Parts A and B of this LPA and the prescribed information on pages 2, 3 and 4. See Note 36

☐ I confirm that I have discussed the contents of this LPA with the donor and that the attorney(s) was not present. See Note 37

☐ I understand that I should make efforts to discuss this LPA with the donor without anyone present; and See Note 38

☐ I have discussed this LPA with the donor without anyone else present

or

☐ I have discussed this LPA with the donor in the presence of:

because

☐ I confirm that I am completing this certificate straight after discussing this LPA with the donor. See Note 39

Core certification

I certify

See Note 40

I certify that in my opinion, at the time when the donor is making this LPA, that:

- ☐ the donor understands the purpose of this LPA and the scope of the authority under it;
- ☐ no fraud or undue pressure is being used to induce the donor to create this LPA; and
- ☐ there is nothing else that would prevent this LPA being created.

Do not sign this certificate if you have any doubt about any of the above. You should bring any concerns you have to the attention of the OPG.

Signature of certificate provider

Date signed D D M M Y Y Y Y

See Note 41

Full name of certificate provider

Additional certificate provider's statement

See Note 42

This additional certificate only needs to be completed if there are no notified persons listed in the LPA.

Who can provide a certificate?
The donor can choose someone they have known personally over the last two years (Category A) or someone who, because of their relevant professional skills and expertise, considers themselves able to provide the certificate (Category B).

Note: Category B providers are entitled to charge a fee for providing this certificate.

Who cannot provide a certificate?
A certificate provider must not be:

- a member of the donor's or attorney's family;
- a business partner or paid employee of the donor or attorney(s);
- an attorney appointed in this form or another LPA or any EPA made by the donor;
- the owner, director, manager, or an employee of a care home in which the donor lives or their family member.

You, the certificate provider, **must** read Part A and B of this LPA, and the prescribed information on pages 2, 3 and 4. You should also read the separate **'Certificate provider and witness guidance'** produced by the OPG before completing the certificate. You must discuss the LPA with the donor and without the attorney(s) present.

☐ I confirm that I am acting independently of the person making this LPA (the donor) and the person(s) appointed under the LPA and in particular I am not a person listed in the above section 'Who cannot provide a certificate?'.

☐ I am aged 18 or over.

The certificate provider

Name and contact details of certificate provider

☐ Mr. ☐ Mrs. ☐ Ms. ☐ Miss ☐ Other

First name

Middle name(s)

Last name

Address

Postcode

Telephone no.

Mobile no.

E-mail address

The OPG may need to contact you to verify the information you provide.

Category of certificate provider – choose from category A **or** B – do not complete both

Category A – Knowledge certification

☐ I have known the donor personally over the last two years.

How do you know them?

Category B - Skills certification

I am:

☐ a registered healthcare professional (includes GP)

☐ a barrister, solicitor or advocate

☐ a registered social worker

☐ an Independent Mental Capacity Advocate (IMCA)

☐ none of the above but consider that I have the relevant professional skills and expertise to be a certificate provider.

My relevant professional skills and expertise are:

I confirm and understand

☐ I confirm that I have read Parts A and B of this LPA and the prescribed information on pages 2, 3 and 4.

☐ I confirm that I have discussed the contents of this LPA with the donor and that the attorney(s) was not present.

☐ I understand that I should make efforts to discuss this LPA with the donor without anyone present; and

☐ I have discussed this LPA with the donor without anyone else present

or

☐ I have discussed this LPA with the donor in the presence of:

because

☐ I confirm that I am completing this certificate straight after discussing this LPA with the donor.

Core certification

I certify

I certify that in my opinion, at the time when the donor is making this LPA, that:

- [ ] the donor understands the purpose of this LPA and the scope of the authority under it;
- [ ] no fraud or undue pressure is being used to induce the donor to create this LPA; and
- [ ] there is nothing else that would prevent this LPA being created.

Do not sign this certificate if you have any doubt about any of the above. You should bring any concerns you have to the attention of the OPG.

Signature of certificate provider

Date signed

D D M M Y Y Y Y

Full name of certificate provider

PART C – Attorney's statement (Every attorney must complete a copy of this Part) See Note 43

31. My contact details and date of birth are:

Attorney

☐ Mr. ☐ Mrs. ☐ Ms. ☐ Miss ☐ Other ______ See Note 44

First name ______

Middle name(s) ______

Last name ______

Date of birth D D M M Y Y Y Y

Telephone no. ______ Mobile ______

E-mail address ______ See Note 45

32. ☐ I have read the prescribed information on pages 2, 3 and 4 or have had the prescribed information read to me. See Note 46

33. ☐ I understand the duties imposed on me under this Lasting Power of Attorney including the obligation to act in accordance with the principles of the Mental Capacity Act 2005 and the duty to have regard to the Code of Practice issued under that Act. See Note 47

34. ☐ I understand that I cannot act until this form has been registered by the Public Guardian. See Note 48

35. ☐ I understand that I cannot act under this Lasting Power of Attorney until the donor lacks capacity. See Note 49

36. Signed by me as a deed *(You must not sign until after the donor has signed at paragraph 16 and the certificate provider has signed the certificate)* See Note 50

______

37. Date signed (delivered as a deed) D D M M Y Y Y Y

In the presence of See Note 51

38. Signature of witness ______

39. Full name of witness ______

40. Address of witness ______

Postcode ______

Important - This form **cannot** be used until it has been registered by the Office of the Public Guardian and stamped on **every** page.

PART C – Attorney's statement (Every attorney must complete a copy of this Part)

See Note 43

31. My contact details and date of birth are:

Attorney

☐ Mr. ☐ Mrs. ☐ Ms. ☐ Miss ☐ Other

See Note 44

First name

Middle name(s)

Last name

Date of birth D D M M Y Y Y Y

Telephone no. Mobile

E-mail address

See Note 45

32. ☐ I have read the prescribed information on pages 2, 3 and 4 or have had the prescribed information read to me. See Note 46

33. ☐ I understand the duties imposed on me under this Lasting Power of Attorney including the obligation to act in accordance with the principles of the Mental Capacity Act 2005 and the duty to have regard to the Code of Practice issued under that Act. See Note 47

34. ☐ I understand that I cannot act until this form has been registered by the Public Guardian. See Note 48

35. ☐ I understand that I cannot act under this Lasting Power of Attorney until the donor lacks capacity. See Note 49

36. Signed by me as a deed *(You must not sign until after the donor has signed at paragraph 16 and the certificate provider has signed the certificate)* See Note 50

37. Date signed (delivered as a deed) D D M M Y Y Y Y

In the presence of

See Note 51

38. Signature of witness

39. Full name of witness

40. Address of witness

Postcode

Important - This form **cannot** be used until it has been registered by the Office of the Public Guardian and stamped on **every** page.

PART C – Replacement attorney's statement

See Note 52

(To be completed by a replacement attorney if appointed. Only complete this if you are a replacement attorney chosen at paragraph 5.)

41. My contact details and date of birth are:

Attorney

☐ Mr. ☐ Mrs. ☐ Ms. ☐ Miss ☐ Other

See Note 53

First name

Middle name(s)

Last name

Date of birth D D M M Y Y Y Y

Telephone no. Mobile

See Note 54

E-mail address

42. ☐ I have read the prescribed information on pages 2, 3 and 4 or have had the prescribed information read to me. See Note 55

43. ☐ I understand that if an original attorney's appointment is terminated I will replace the original attorney if I am still eligible to act as an attorney. See Note 56

44. ☐ I understand that I do not have the authority to act under this LPA until such time as a relevant attorney's appointment is terminated. See Note 57

45. ☐ I understand the duties imposed on me under this Lasting Power of Attorney including the obligation to act in accordance with the principles of the Mental Capacity Act 2005 and the duty to have regard to the Code of Practice issued under that Act. See Note 58

46. ☐ I understand that I cannot act under this Lasting Power of Attorney until this form has been registered by the Public Guardian. See Note 59

47. ☐ I understand that I cannot act until the donor lacks capacity. See Note 60

48. Signed by me as a deed *(You must not sign until after the donor has signed at paragraph 16 and the certificate provider has signed the certificate)* See Note 61

49. Date signed (delivered as a deed) D D M M Y Y Y Y

In the presence of

See Note 62

50. Signature of witness

51. Full name of witness

52. Address of witness

Postcode

Important - This form **cannot** be used until it has been registered by the Office of the Public Guardian and stamped on **every** page.

[3555]

NOTES

Commencement: 1 October 2007.

SCHEDULE 2
NOTICE OF INTENTION TO APPLY FOR REGISTRATION OF A LASTING POWER OF ATTORNEY: LPA 001

Regulation 10

LPA 001 10.07

Notice of intention to apply for registration of a Lasting Power of Attorney

This notice must be sent to everyone named by the donor in the Lasting Power of Attorney as a person who should be notified of an application to register. Relatives are not entitled to notice unless named in the Lasting Power of Attorney.

The application to register may be made by the donor or the attorney(s).

Where attorneys are appointed to act together they **all** must apply to register.

Details of the named person

Name

Address

Telephone no.

Postcode

To the named person - You have the right to object to the proposed registration of the Lasting Power of Attorney. You have **five weeks** from the day on which this notice is given to object. Details of how to object and the grounds for doing so are on the back page.

Details of the Lasting Power of Attorney (LPA)

Who is applying to register the LPA? ☐ the donor ☐ the attorney(s)

Which type of LPA is being registered? ☐ Property and Affairs ☐ Personal Welfare

(You must complete separate applications for each LPA you wish to register.)

On what date did the donor sign the LPA? D D M M Y Y Y Y

Details of the donor

Full name

Address

Telephone no.

Postcode

PART II
STATUTORY INSTRUMENTS

Details of the attorney(s)

Name of 1st attorney

Address

Telephone no.

Postcode

☐ solely ☐ together and independently

☐ together ☐ together in some matters and together and independently in others

Name of 2nd attorney

Address

Telephone no.

Postcode

☐ together ☐ together and independently

☐ together in some matters and together and independently in others

Name of 3rd attorney

Address

Telephone no.

Postcode

☐ together ☐ together and independently

☐ together in some matters and together and independently in others

Name of 4th attorney

Address

Telephone no.

Postcode

☐ together ☐ together and independently

☐ together in some matters and together and independently in others

Signature and date

This notice must be signed by all parties applying to register the lasting power of attorney.

Signed	Print name

Dated D D M M Y Y Y Y

How to object to the registering of a Lasting Power of Attorney (LPA)

You can ask the Office of the Public Guardian (OPG) to stop the LPA from being registered if one of the factual grounds at (A) below has occurred. You need to tell us by completing Form LPA7 which is available from the OPG and by providing evidence to accompany it. You must send us the completed LPA7 form **within five weeks** from the date this notice was given. Failure to tell us could result in the LPA being registered.

(A) Factual grounds – you can ask the Office of the Public Guardian to stop registration if

- The Donor is bankrupt or interim bankrupt (for property and affairs LPAs only)
- The Attorney is bankrupt or interim bankrupt (for property and affairs LPAs only)
- The Attorney is a trust corporation and is wound up or dissolved (for property and affairs LPAs only)
- The Donor is dead
- The Attorney is dead
- That there has been dissolution or annulment of a marriage or civil partnership between the Donor and Attorney (except if the LPA provided that such an event should not affect the instrument)
- The Attorney(s) lack the capacity to be an attorney under the LPA
- The Attorney(s) have disclaimed their appointment

Form LPA7 is available from the OPG on 0845 330 2900 or www.publicguardian.gov.uk

You have the right to object to the Court of Protection about the registration of the LPA, but only on the grounds mentioned at (B) below. To do this you must contact the Court and complete the application to object form they will send you. Using that form, you must set out your reasons for objecting. They must receive the objection within five weeks from the date this notice was given. You must also notify the OPG when you object to the Court by using the separate form LPA8 that the Court will send you. Failure to notify the OPG of an objection may result in registration of the LPA.

Note: If you are objecting to the appointment of a specific attorney, it will not prevent registration if other attorneys or a substitute attorney have been appointed.

(B) Prescribed grounds – you can only object to the Court of Protection against registration of the LPA on the following grounds:

- That the power purported to be created by the instrument* is not valid as a LPA. e.g. the person objecting does not believe the donor had capacity to make an LPA.
- That the power created by the instrument no longer exists e.g. the donor revoked it at a time when he/she had capacity to do so.
- That fraud or undue pressure was used to induce the donor to make the power.
- The attorney proposes to behave in a way that would contravene his authority or would not be in the donor's best interests.

Note: * The instrument means the LPA made by the donor.

The Court will only consider objections made if they are made on the above grounds. To obtain a Court objection form please contact the Court of Protection at Archway Tower, 2 Junction Road, London N19 5SZ or Telephone 0845 330 2900.

[3556]

NOTES

Commencement: 1 October 2007.

SCHEDULE 3

APPLICATION TO REGISTER A LASTING POWER OF ATTORNEY: LPA 002

Regulation 11

LPA002 Office of the Public Guardian

Application to register a Lasting Power of Attorney

Return your completed form to:
Office of the Public Guardian
Archway Tower
2 Junction Road
London N19 5SZ

Part 1 - The donor

Place a cross (**x**) against one option

Mr. ☐ Mrs. ☐ Ms. ☐ Miss ☐ Other ☐

If other, please specify

Last name

First name

Middle name

Address 1

Address 2

Address 3

Town/City

County

Postcode

Daytime Tel. no.

Date of birth

D D M M Y Y Y Y

If the exact date is unknown please state the year of birth

e-mail address

Please do not write below this line - For office use only

Part 2 - The persons making the application

Note: We need to know who is applying and how the attorney(s) have been appointed, please answer the questions in parts two and three carefully.

Place a cross (**x**) against one option

Is the donor applying to register the Lasting Power of Attorney? ☐ Yes

Is the attorney(s) applying to register the Lasting Power of Attorney? ☐ Yes

Part 3 - How have the attorney(s) been appointed?

The LPA states whether the attorney is to act soley, together or together and independently

Place a cross (**x**) against one option

There is only one attorney appointed ☐

There are attorneys appointed together and independently ☐

There are attorneys appointed together ☐

There are attorneys appointed together in some matters and together and independently in others ☐

Note: We need to know which, if any of the attorney(s) are making this application to register the LPA. You can tell us this by putting a cross in the box at the start of each attorney(s) details in section 4.

Part 4 - Attorney one

Place a cross (**x**) in this box if attorney one is applying to register ☐

Place a cross (**x**) against one option

Mr. ☐ Mrs. ☐ Ms. ☐ Miss ☐ Other ☐

If other, please specify

Last name

First name

Middle name

Company name *(if relevant)*

Address 1

Address 2

Address 3

Town/City

County

Postcode

DX number

Date of birth

D D M M Y Y Y Y

DX Exchange

Daytime Tel. no.

Occupation

e-mail address

Place a cross (**x**) against one option that best describes your relationship to the donor

Civil partner / Spouse ☐ Child ☐ Solicitor ☐ Other ☐ Other professional ☐

If 'Other' or 'Other professional', please specify

Part 4 - Attorney two

Place a cross (**x**) in this box if attorney two is applying to register ☐

Place a cross (**x**) against one option

Mr. ☐ Mrs. ☐ Ms. ☐ Miss ☐ Other ☐

If other, please specify

Last name

First name

Middle name

Company name *(if relevant)*

Address 1

Address 2

Address 3

Town/City

County

Postcode

DX number

Date of birth D D M M Y Y Y Y

DX Exchange

Daytime Tel. no.

Occupation

e-mail address

Place a cross (**x**) against one option that best describes your relationship to the donor

Civil partner / Spouse ☐ Child ☐ Solicitor ☐ Other ☐ Other professional ☐

If 'Other' or 'Other professional', please specify

4

Part 4 - Attorney three

Place a cross (**x**) in this box if attorney three is applying to register ☐

Place a cross (**x**) against one option

Mr. ☐ Mrs. ☐ Ms. ☐ Miss ☐ Other ☐

If other, please specify

Last name

First name

Middle name

Company name *(if relevant)*

Address 1

Address 2

Address 3

Town/City

County

Postcode

DX number

Date of birth D D M M Y Y Y Y

DX Exchange

Daytime Tel. no.

Occupation

e-mail address

Place a cross (**x**) against one option that best describes your relationship to the donor

Civil partner / Spouse ☐ Child ☐ Solicitor ☐ Other ☐ Other professional ☐

If 'Other' or 'Other professional', please specify

Part 4 - Attorney four

If there are additional attorneys, please provide the following details in the 'Additional information' section at the end of this form.

Place a cross (**x**) in this box if attorney four is applying to register ☐

Place a cross (**x**) against one option

Mr. ☐ Mrs. ☐ Ms. ☐ Miss ☐ Other ☐

If other, please specify

Last name

First name

Middle name

Company name *(if relevant)*

Address 1

Address 2

Address 3

Town/City

County

Postcode

DX number

Date of birth

D D M M Y Y Y Y

DX Exchange

Daytime Tel. no.

Occupation

e-mail address

Place a cross (**x**) against one option that best describes your relationship to the donor

Civil partner / Spouse ☐ Child ☐ Solicitor ☐ Other ☐ Other professional ☐

If 'Other' or 'Other professional', please specify

Part 5 - Notification of named persons

The donor or attorney(s) making the application must give notice to the named persons nominated by the donor in the section of the LPA marked 'Notifying others when an application to register your LPA is made'. The date on which the notice was given **must** be completed (which is the date it was posted or given to the named person). If the donor decided not to notify any named persons, please place a cross in the box provided.

The donor did not specify any named individuals in the LPA ☐

Place a cross (**x**) against one option

☐ I ☐ We

have given notice to register in the prescribed form (LP1) to the following person(s):

Date notice given ☐☐☐☐☐☐☐☐
D D M M Y Y Y Y

Last name

First name

Address 1

Address 2

Address 3

Town/City

County

Postcode

Part 5 - continued

Date notice given

D D M M Y Y Y Y

Last name

First name

Address 1

Address 2

Address 3

Town/City

County

Postcode

Date notice given

D D M M Y Y Y Y

Last name

First name

Address 1

Address 2

Address 3

Town/City

County

Postcode

Part 5 - continued

Date notice given

D D M M Y Y Y Y

Last name

First name

Address 1

Address 2

Address 3

Town/City

County

Postcode

Date notice given

D D M M Y Y Y Y

Last name

First name

Address 1

Address 2

Address 3

Town/City

County

Postcode

Part 6 - Fees

Guidelines on fee exemption and remission can be obtained from the Office of the Public Guardian.

Have you enclosed a cheque for the registration fee for this application? ☐ Yes ☐ No

Do you wish to apply for remission of the fee? ☐ Yes ☐ No

Do you wish to apply for exemption of the fee? ☐ Yes ☐ No

Do you wish to apply for postponement of the fee? ☐ Yes ☐ No

If you wish to apply for exemption, remission or postponement of all or part of the fee. You must complete the separate application form available from the Office of the Public Guardian.

Part 7 - Type of power

☐ I ☐ We

apply to register the LPA (the original of which accompanies this application) made by the donor under the provisions of the Mental Capacity Act 2005.

What type of Lasting Power of Attorney are you applying to register?

☐ Property and affairs **OR** ☐ Personal welfare

Date that the **donor** signed the Lasting Power of Attorney

D D M M Y Y Y Y

To your knowledge, has the donor made any other Enduring Powers of Attorney or Lasting Power of Attorney? ☐ Yes ☐ No

If Yes, please give details below including registration date if applicable

PART II STATUTORY INSTRUMENTS

Part 8 - Donor declaration

Note: This section should only be completed by the donor if they are applying for the registration of the Lasting Power of Attorney.

I apply to register the Lasting Power of Attorney (the original of which accompanies this application).

I certify that the above information is correct and that to the best of my knowledge and belief, I have completed the application in accordance with the provisions of the Mental Capacity Act 2005 and all statutory instruments made under it.

Signed

Date D D M M Y Y Y Y

Last name

First name

Part 9 - Attorney(s) declaration

Note: This section should only be completed by the attorney(s) if they are applying for the registration of the Lasting Power of Attorney.

☐ I ☐ We apply to register the Lasting Power of Attorney (the original of which accompanies this application).

☐ I ☐ We certify that the above information is correct to the best of my knowledge and belief.

☐ I ☐ We have completed the application within the provisions of the Mental Capacity Act 2005 and all statutory instruments made under it.

Signed

Date D D M M Y Y Y Y

Last name

First name

Signed

Date D D M M Y Y Y Y

Last name

First name

Part 9 - continued

Signed

Date

D D M M Y Y Y Y

Last name

First name

Signed

Date

D D M M Y Y Y Y

Last name

First name

Signed

Date

D D M M Y Y Y Y

Last name

First name

Part 10 - Declaration by a trust corporation

If you are a trust corporation making this application please complete this declaration.

I We

certify that the above information is correct and that to the best of my knowledge and belief, I have completed the application in accordance with the provisions of the Mental Capacity Act 2005 and all statutory instruments made under it.

Company name

Signature of authorised person(s)

Company seal (If applicable)

Last name

First name

Part 11 - Correspondence address

Place a cross (**x**) against one option

Mr. ☐ Mrs. ☐ Ms. ☐ Miss ☐ Other ☐

If other, please specify

Last name

First name

Middle name

Company name

Company reference

Address 1

Address 2

Address 3

Town/City

County

Postcode

DX number

DX Exchange

Daytime Tel. no.

e-mail address

Part 12 - Additional information

Please write down any additional information to support this application in the space below. If necessary attach additional sheets.

[3557]

NOTES

Commencement: 1 October 2007.

SCHEDULE 4

NOTICE OF RECEIPT OF AN APPLICATION TO REGISTER A LASTING POWER OF ATTORNEY: LPA 003A AND LPA 003B

Regulation 13

PART 1

NOTICE TO AN ATTORNEY OF RECEIPT OF AN APPLICATION TO REGISTER A LASTING POWER OF ATTORNEY

LPA 003A 10.07

Notice to an attorney of receipt of an application to register a Lasting Power of Attorney

Name of attorney

Take notice

An application to register a Lasting Power of Attorney (LPA) has been received by the Office of the Public Guardian.

We are sending you this notice because you are named as an attorney in the LPA and were not involved in the application to register.

You are hereby given notice of the proposed registration. **You have the right to object to the registration.** Details of how to do so are set out on page 2 of this notice. You have five weeks in which to object from the date this notice was given. (We will treat this notice as having been given two days after the date below.)

The names of the donor and the attorney(s) are set out below:

Donor's full name

The following attorney(s) have applied to register an LPA in the name of the above donor.

Attorney's full name

Attorney's full name

Attorney's full name

From
The Office of the Public Guardian
Archway Tower, 2 Junction Road
London N19 5SZ

Telephone 0845 330 2900

Dated

How to object to the registering of a Lasting Power of Attorney (LPA)

You can ask the Office of the Public Guardian (OPG) to stop the LPA from being registered if one of the factual grounds at (A) below has occurred. You need to tell us by completing Form LPA7 which is available from the OPG and by providing evidence to accompany it. You must send us the completed LPA7 form **within five weeks** from the date this notice was given. Failure to tell us could result in the LPA being registered.

(A) Factual grounds – you can ask the Office of the Public Guardian to stop registration if:

- The Donor is bankrupt or interim bankrupt (for property and affairs LPAs only)
- The Attorney is bankrupt or interim bankrupt (for property and affairs LPAs only)
- The Attorney is a trust corporation and is wound up or dissolved (for property and affairs LPAs only)
- The Donor is dead
- The Attorney is dead
- That there has been dissolution or annulment of a marriage or civil partnership between the Donor and Attorney (except if the LPA provided that such an event should not affect the instrument)
- The Attorney lacks the capacity to be an attorney under the LPA
- The Attorney disclaimed their appointment

Form LPA7 is available from the OPG on 0845 330 2900 or www.publicguardian.gov.uk

You have the right to object to the Court of Protection about the registration of the LPA, but only on the grounds mentioned at (B) below. To do this you must contact the Court and complete the application to object form they will send you. Using that form, you must set out your reasons for objecting. They must receive the objection within five weeks from the date this notice was given. You must also notify the OPG when you object to the Court by using the separate form LPA8 that the Court will send you. Failure to notify the OPG of an objection may result in registration of the LPA.

Note: If you are objecting to the appointment of a specific attorney, it will not prevent registration if other attorneys or substitute attorneys have been appointed.

(B) Prescribed grounds – you can only object to the Court of Protection against registration of the LPA on the following grounds:

- That the power purported to be created by the instrument* is not valid as a LPA. e.g. the person objecting does not believe the donor had capacity to make an LPA.
- That the power created by the instrument no longer exists e.g. the donor revoked it at a time when he/she had capacity to do so.
- That fraud or undue pressure was used to induce the donor to make the power.
- The attorney proposes to behave in a way that would contravene his authority or would not be in the donor's best interests.

Note: * The instrument means the LPA made by the donor.

The Court will only consider objections made if they are made on the above grounds. To obtain a Court objection form please contact the Court of Protection at Archway Tower, 2 Junction Road, London N19 5SZ or telephone 0845 330 2900.

[3558]

NOTES

Commencement: 1 October 2007.

PART 2
NOTICE TO DONOR OF RECEIPT OF AN APPLICATION TO REGISTER A LASTING POWER OF ATTORNEY

LPA 003B 10.07

Notice to donor of receipt of an application to register a Lasting Power of Attorney

Name of donor

Take notice

An application to register your Lasting Power of Attorney (LPA) has been received by the Office of the Public Guardian (OPG).

We are sending you this notice because your attorney(s) in the LPA has asked the OPG to register your LPA, so that it can be used.

You are hereby given notice of the proposed registration. **You have a right to object to the registration.** You have five weeks in which to object from the date this notice was given. (We will treat this notice as having been given two days after the date below). You can object by using form LPA6, which you can get from the OPG.

The names of your attorney(s) are set out below:

Attorney's full name

Attorney's full name

Attorney's full name

Attorney's full name

Dated

From
The Office of the Public Guardian
Archway Tower, 2 Junction Road
London N19 5SZ

Telephone 0845 330 2900

[3559]

NOTES
Commencement: 1 October 2007.

SCHEDULE 5
NOTICE OF REGISTRATION OF A LASTING POWER OF ATTORNEY: LPA 004

Regulation 17

LPA 004 10.07

Notice of registration of a Lasting Power of Attorney

This notice is to confirm registration of a Lasting Power of Attorney.

Case no.

The donor

The attorney(s)

The Lasting Power of Attorney was entered into the register on

Notification of registration of the LPA is given as required in Schedule 1 Part 2 Paragraph 15 of the Mental Capacity Act 2005.

[3560]

NOTES

Commencement: 1 October 2007.

SCHEDULE 6
DISCLAIMER BY DONEE OF A LASTING POWER OF ATTORNEY: LPA 005

Regulation 20

LPA 005 10.07

Disclaimer by a proposed or acting attorney under a Lasting Power of Attorney

Take notice that

☐ a proposed attorney

☐ an attorney acting under a Lasting Power of Attorney

has disclaimed appointment.

Details of attorney disclaiming appointment

Name

Address

Telephone no.

Postcode

Date of the Lasting Power of Attorney

On what date was the Lasting Power of Attorney made? D D M M Y Y Y Y

Signature and date

I disclaim my appointment as attorney under the Lasting Power of Attorney made by the donor.

Signed

Dated D D M M Y Y Y Y

Note: Where the LPA has been registered then a copy of this notice must be sent to the Office of the Public Guardian at: Archway Tower, 2 Junction Road, London N19 5SZ

Call OPG on 0845 330 2900 with any questions.

Details of the donor

Name	Address
Telephone no.	Postcode

Details of the other attorney(s)

Name	Address
Telephone no.	Postcode

Name	Address
Telephone no.	Postcode

Name	Address
Telephone no.	Postcode

[3561]

NOTES

Commencement: 1 October 2007.

SCHEDULE 7
NOTICE OF INTENTION TO APPLY FOR REGISTRATION OF AN ENDURING POWER OF ATTORNEY

Regulation 23

Form EP1PG

Mental Capacity Act 2005
Enduring Power of Attorney

Notice of intention to apply for registration of an Enduring Power of Attorney

To...

Of...

This form may be adapted for use by three or more attorneys

Give the name and address of the donor

TAKE NOTICE THAT

I ....

of ....

and I ....

of ....

The attorney(s) of ....

....

of ....

....

intend to apply to the Public Guardian for registration of the enduring power of attorney appointing me (us) attorney(s) and made by the donor on the ....

The grounds upon which you can object are limited and are shown at 2 overleaf

1. You have the right to object to the proposed registration on one or more of the grounds set out below. You must notify the Office of the Public Guardian of your objection within five weeks from the day this notice was given to you. You may make an application to the Court of Protection under rule 68 of the Court of Protection Rules 2007 for a decision on the matter. No fee is payable for such an application. If you do not make such an application, the Public Guardian will ask for the court's directions about registration.

Note: The instrument means the document used to make the enduring power of attorney made by the donor, which it is sought to register

2. The grounds on which you may object to the proposed registration are:

- That the power purported to be created by the instrument is not valid as an enduring power of attorney
- That the power created by the instrument no longer subsists
- That the application is premature because the donor is not yet becoming mentally incapable
- That fraud or undue pressure was used to induce the donor to make the power
- That the attorney is unsuitable to be the donor's attorney (having regard to all the circumstances and in particular the attorney's relationship to or connection with the donor).

The attorney(s) does not have to be a relative. Relatives are not entitled to know of the existence of the enduring power of attorney prior to being given this notice

Our staff will be able to assist with any questions you have regarding the objection (s). However, they cannot provide advice about your particular objection.

3. You can obtain the necessary forms to object by.

- Writing to us at the address on the foot of this form
- Calling us on 0845 330 2900
- Downloading the forms from our website at www.publicguardian.gov.uk

Note: Part 4 is addressed only to the donor

4. You are informed that while the enduring power of attorney remains registered, you will not be able to revoke it until the Court of Protection confirms the revocation.

Note: This notice should be signed by every one of the attorneys who are applying to register the enduring power of attorney

Note:
The attorney(s) must keep a record of the date on which notice was given to the donor and to relatives. This information will be required from the attorney(s) when an application to register the EPA is made

Signed: .... Dated: ....

Signed: .... Dated: ....

Please write to:
Customer Services
Archway Tower
2 Junction Road
London
N19 5SZ
www.publicguardian.gov.uk

[3562]

NOTES

Commencement: 1 October 2007.
Amended by SI 2007/2051, reg 12.

PART II STATUTORY INSTRUMENTS

SCHEDULE 8
APPLICATION TO REGISTER AN ENDURING POWER OF ATTORNEY

Regulation 24

Office of the Public Guardian
Mental Capacity Act 2005
Form EP2PG
Application for Registration of an Enduring Power of Attorney

IMPORTANT: Please complete the form in BLOCK CAPITA LS using a black ball-point pen. Place a clear cross 'X' mark inside square option boxes [x] - do not circle the option.

Part One - The Donor

Please state the full name and present address of the donor. State the donor's first name in 'Forename 1' and the donor's other forenames in full in 'Other Forenames'. Company Name should be completed with the name of the nursing/care home or hospital where applicable.

Mr ☐ Mrs ☐ Ms ☐ Miss ☐ Other ☐

Place a cross against one option [x]

If Other, please specify here:

Last Name:

Forename 1:

Other Forenames:

Company Name:

Address 1:

Address 2:

Address 3:

Town/City:

County:

Postcode:

Donor Date of Birth: D D M M Y Y Y Y

If the exact date is unknown please state the year of birth

Please do not write below this line - For Office Use Only

Produced in association with the Office of the Public Guardian

Part Two - Attorney One

Please state the full name and present address of the attorney. Professionals e,g, Solicitors or Accountants, should complete the Company Name field.

Mr ☐ Mrs ☐ Ms ☐ Miss ☐ Other ☐

Place a cross against one option ☒

If Other, please specify here:

Last Name:

Forename 1:

Other Forenames:

Company Name:

Address 1:

Address 2:

Address 3:

Town/City:

County:

Postcode:

DX No. (solicitors only):

DX Exchange (solicitors only):

Attorney Date of Birth: D D M M Y Y Y Y

Daytime Tel No.: (STD Code):

Email Address:

Occupation:

Relationship to donor:

Civil Partner / Spouse ☐ Child ☐ Other Relation ☐ No Relation ☐ Solicitor ☐ Other Professional ☐

Place a cross against one option ☒

If 'Other Relation' or 'Other Professional', specify relationship:

Part B of the Enduring Power of Attorney states whether the attorney is to act jointly, jointly and severally, or alone.

Appointment (*Place a cross against one option* ☒):

Jointly ☐

Jointly and Severally ☐

Alone ☐

Page 2 of 7

PART II STATUTORY INSTRUMENTS

Part Three - Attorney Two

Please state the full name and present address of the attorney. Professionals e.g. Solicitors or Accountants, should complete the Company Name field.

Mr ☐ Mrs ☐ Ms ☐ Miss ☐ Other ☐

Place a cross against one option ☒

If Other, please specify here:

Last Name:

Forename 1:

Other Forenames:

Company Name:

Address 1:

Address 2:

Address 3:

Town/City:

County:

Postcode:

DX No. (solicitors only):

DX Exchange (solicitors only):

Attorney Date of Birth: D D M M Y Y Y Y

Daytime Tel No.: (STD Code):

Email Address:

Occupation:

Relationship to donor:

Civil Partner / Spouse ☐ Child ☐ Other Relation ☐ No Relation ☐ Solicitor ☐ Other Professional ☐

Place a cross against one option ☒

If 'Other Relation' or 'Other Professional', specify relationship:

Part Four - Attorney Three

Please state the full name and present address of the attorney. Professionals e,g, Solicitors or Accountants, should complete the Company Name field.

Mr ☐ Mrs ☐ Ms ☐ Miss ☐ Other ☐

Place a cross against one option ☒

If Other, please specify here:

Last Name:

Forename 1:

Part Four Continued Overleaf

Part Four - Attorney Three cont'd

Other Forenames:

Company Name:

Address 1:

Address 2:

Address 3:

Town/City:

County:

Postcode: DX No. (solicitors only):

DX Exchange (solicitors only):

Attorney Date of Birth: D D M M Y Y Y Y Daytime Tel No.: (STD Code):

Email Address:

Occupation:

Relationship to donor:

Civil Partner / Spouse ☐ Child ☐ Other Relation ☐ No Relation ☐ Solicitor ☐ Other Professional ☐

Place a cross against one option ☒

If 'Other Relation' or 'Other Professional', specify relationship:

If there are additional attorneys, please complete the above details in the 'Additional Information' section (at the end of this form).

Part Five - The Enduring Power of Attorney

I (We) the attorney(s) apply to register the Enduring Power of Attorney made by the donor under the Enduring Powers of Attorney Act 1985, the original of which accompanies this application.

I (We) have reason to believe that the donor is or is becoming mentally incapable.

Date that the **Donor** signed the Enduring Power of Attorney. D D M M Y Y Y Y
You can find this in Part B of the Enduring Power of Attorney.

To your knowledge, has the Donor made any other Enduring Powers of Attorney?: Yes ☐ No ☐
Place a cross against one option ☒

If 'Yes', please give details below including registration date if applicable:

PART II STATUTORY INSTRUMENTS

Part Six - Notice of Application to Donor

Notice must be given personally to the donor. It should be made clear if someone other than the attorney(s) gives the notice. The date on which the notice was given MUST be completed.

I (We) have given notice of the application to register in the prescribed form (EP1PG) to the donor personally,

on this date: [ ][ ][ ][ ][ ][ ][ ][ ]

D D M M Y Y Y Y

If someone other than the attorney gives notice to the donor please complete the name and address details below. Please also complete the date above:

Full Name:

Address 1:

Address 2:

Address 3:

Town/City:

County: Postcode:

Part Seven - Notice of Application to Relatives

Please complete details of all relatives entitled to notice.

Please place a cross in the box ☒ if no relatives are entitled to notice: ☐

I (We) have given notice to register in the prescribed form (EP1PG) to the following relatives of the donor:

Full Name: Relationship to Donor:

Address: Date notice given:

D D M M Y Y Y Y

Full Name: Relationship to Donor:

Address: Date notice given:

D D M M Y Y Y Y

Full Name: Relationship to Donor:

Address: Date notice given:

D D M M Y Y Y Y

Full Name: Relationship to Donor:

Address: Date notice given:

D D M M Y Y Y Y

Full Name: Relationship to Donor:

Address: Date notice given:

D D M M Y Y Y Y

If there are additional relatives please complete the Relative Name, Relationship, Address and Date details in the 'Additional Information' section (at the end of this form).

Part Eight - Notice of Application to Co-Attorney(s)

Do not complete this section if it does not apply. If there are additional co-attorneys please complete the Attorney Name, Relationship, Address and Date details in the 'Additional Information' section (at the end of this form).

Are all the attorneys applying to register? Yes ☐ No ☐ *Place a cross against one option* ☒

If no, I (We) have given notice to my (our) co-attorney(s) as follows:

Full Name: ______ Relationship to Donor: ______

Address: ______

Date notice given: D D M M Y Y Y Y

Full Name: ______ Relationship to Donor: ______

Address: ______

Date notice given: D D M M Y Y Y Y

Part Nine - Fees

Guidelines on remission and postponement of fees can be obtained from the Office of the Public Guardian.

Have you enclosed a cheque for the registration fee for this application? Yes ☐ No ☐ *Place a cross against one option* ☒

Do you wish to apply for postponement, exemption or remission of the fee? Yes ☐ No ☐ *Place a cross against one option* ☒

If yes, please complete the application for exemption or remission form.

Part Ten - Declaration

Note: The application should be signed by all attorneys who are making the application. This must not pre-date the date(s) when the notices were given.

I (We) certify that the above information is correct and that to the best of my (our) knowledge and belief I (We) have complied with the provisions of the Mental Capacity Act 2005.

Signed: ______ Dated: D D M M Y Y Y Y

Signed: ______ Dated: D D M M Y Y Y Y

Signed: ______ Dated: D D M M Y Y Y Y

PART II STATUTORY INSTRUMENTS

Part Eleven - Correspondence Address

Solicitors please note: The address to which the correspondence should be sent **MUST** be entered here if this is different to the address of Attorney One. State the full name and present address. Insert the name of the Solicitor's Firm in the Company Name field, if appropriate, and the correspondence reference in the Company Reference field.

Mr ☐ Mrs ☐ Ms ☐ Miss ☐ Other ☐

Place a cross against one option ☒

If Other, please specify here:

Last Name:

Forename 1:

Other Forenames:

Company Name:

Company Reference:

Address 1:

Address 2:

Address 3:

Town/City:

County:

Postcode:

DX No. (solicitors only):

DX Exchange (solicitors only):

Daytime Tel No.:

(STD Code):

Email Address:

Part Twelve - Additional Information

Please write down any additional information to support this application in the space below. If necessary attach additional paper to the end of this form.

Page 7 of 7

[3563]

NOTES

Commencement: 1 October 2007.

EQUALITY ACT (SEXUAL ORIENTATION) REGULATIONS 2007

(SI 2007/1263)

NOTES

Made: 17 April 2007.
Authority: Equality Act 2006, s 81(1).
Commencement: 30 April 2007.

1 Citation, commencement and extent

(1) These Regulations may be cited as the Equality Act (Sexual Orientation) Regulations 2007 and shall come into force on 30th April 2007.

(2) These Regulations do not extend to Northern Ireland.

[3564]

NOTES

Commencement: 30 April 2007.

2 Interpretation

(1) References in these Regulations to discrimination are to any discrimination falling within regulation 3 (discrimination on grounds of sexual orientation) and related expressions shall be construed accordingly.

(2) In these Regulations—

"the Commission" means the Commission for Equality and Human Rights,

"criminal investigation" means an investigation into the commission of an alleged offence, and a decision whether to institute criminal proceedings,

"enactment" includes an enactment in or under an Act of the Scottish Parliament,

"fostering agency" means a fostering agency within the meaning of section 4(4) of the Care Standards Act 2000 and a person providing a fostering service within the meaning of section 2(14)(b) of the Regulation of Care (Scotland) Act 2001,

"the 2006 Act" means the Equality Act 2006,

"voluntary adoption agency" means an adoption society within the meaning of the Adoption and Children Act 2002 which is a voluntary organisation within the meaning of that Act, and a person, providing an adoption service within the meaning of section 2(11)(b) of the Regulation of Care (Scotland) Act 2001.

(3) In these Regulations—

(a) a reference to act or action includes a reference to deliberate omission,

(b) a reference to refusal includes a reference to deliberate omission, and

(c) a reference to providing a service, facility or benefit of any kind includes a reference to facilitating access to the service, facility or benefit.

[3565]

NOTES

Commencement: 30 April 2007.

3 Discrimination on grounds of sexual orientation

(1) For the purposes of these Regulations, a person ("A") discriminates against another ("B") if, on grounds of the sexual orientation of B or any other person except A, A treats B less favourably than he treats or would treat others (in cases where there is no material difference in the relevant circumstances).

(2) In paragraph (1) a reference to a person's sexual orientation includes a reference to a sexual orientation which he is thought to have.

(3) For the purposes of these Regulations, a person ("A") discriminates against another ("B") if A applies to B a provision, criterion or practice—

(a) which he applies or would apply equally to persons not of B's sexual orientation,

(b) which puts persons of B's sexual orientation at a disadvantage compared to some or all others (where there is no material difference in the relevant circumstances),

(c) which puts B at a disadvantage compared to some or all persons who are not of his sexual orientation (where there is no material difference in the relevant circumstances), and

(d) which A cannot reasonably justify by reference to matters other than B's sexual orientation.

(4) For the purposes of paragraphs (1) and (3), the fact that one of the persons (whether or not B) is a civil partner while the other is married shall not be treated as a material difference in the relevant circumstances.

(5) A person ("A") discriminates against another ("B") if A treats B less favourably than he treats or would treat another and does so by reason of the fact that, or by reason of A's knowledge or suspicion that, B—

(a) has brought or intended to bring, or intends to bring, proceedings under these Regulations,
(b) has given or intended to give, or intends to give, evidence in proceedings under these Regulations,
(c) has provided or intended to provide, or intends to provide, information in connection with proceedings under these Regulations,
(d) has done or intended to do, or intends to do, any other thing under or in connection with these Regulations, or
(e) has alleged or intended to allege, or intends to allege, that a person has contravened these Regulations.

(6) Paragraph (5) does not apply where A's treatment of B relates to B's—

(a) making or intending to make, not in good faith, a false allegation; or
(b) giving or intending to give, not in good faith, false information or evidence.

[3566]

NOTES
Commencement: 30 April 2007.

4 Goods, facilities and services

(1) It is unlawful for a person ("A") concerned with the provision to the public or a section of the public of goods, facilities or services to discriminate against a person ("B") who seeks to obtain or to use those goods, facilities or services—

(a) by refusing to provide B with goods, facilities or services,
(b) by refusing to provide B with goods, facilities or services of a quality which is the same as or similar to the quality of goods, facilities or services that A normally provides to—
  (i) the public, or
  (ii) a section of the public to which B belongs,
(c) by refusing to provide B with goods, facilities or services in a manner which is the same as or similar to that in which A normally provides goods, facilities or services to—
  (i) the public, or
  (ii) a section of the public to which B belongs, or
(d) by refusing to provide B with goods, facilities or services on terms which are the same as or similar to the terms on which A normally provides goods, facilities or services to—
  (i) the public, or
  (ii) a section of the public to which B belongs.

(2) Paragraph (1) applies, in particular, to—

(a) access to and use of a place which the public are permitted to enter,
(b) accommodation in a hotel, boarding house or similar establishment,
(c) facilities by way of banking or insurance or for grants, loans, credit or finance,
(d) facilities for entertainment, recreation or refreshment,
(e) facilities for transport or travel, and
(f) the services of a profession or trade.

(3) Paragraph (1) does not apply—

(a) in relation to the provision of goods, facilities or services by a person exercising a public function, or
(b) to discrimination in relation to the provision of goods, facilities or services, where such discrimination—
  (i) is unlawful by virtue of another provision of these regulations or by virtue of a provision of the Employment Equality (Sexual Orientation) Regulations 2003 ("the 2003 Regulations"), or
  (ii) would be unlawful by virtue of another provision of these Regulations or of the 2003 Regulations but for an express exception.

(4) For the purposes of paragraph (1) it is immaterial whether or not a person charges for the provision of goods, facilities or services.

[3567]

NOTES
Commencement: 30 April 2007.

5 Premises

(1) It is unlawful for a person to discriminate against another—

(a) in the terms on which he offers to dispose of premises to him,

(b) by refusing to dispose of premises to him, or

(c) in connection with a list of persons requiring premises.

(2) It is unlawful for a person managing premises to discriminate against an occupier—

(a) in the manner in which he provides access to a benefit or facility,

(b) by refusing access to a benefit or facility,

(c) by evicting him, or

(d) by subjecting him to any other detriment.

(3) It is unlawful for a person to discriminate against another by refusing permission for the disposal of premises to him.

(4) This regulation only applies to premises in Great Britain.

[3568]

NOTES

Commencement: 30 April 2007.

6 Exceptions to regulations 4 and 5

(1) Regulation 4 does not apply to anything done by a person as a participant in arrangements under which he (for reward or not) takes into his home, and treats as if they were members of his family, children, elderly persons, or persons requiring a special degree of care and attention.

(2) Regulation 5 does not apply to anything done in relation to the disposal or management of a part of any premises by a person ("the landlord") if—

(a) the landlord or a near relative of his resides, and intends to continue to reside, in another part of the premises,

(b) the premises include parts (other than storage areas and means of access) shared by residents of the premises, and

(c) the premises are not normally sufficient to accommodate—

(i) in the case of premises to be occupied by households, more than two households in addition to that of the landlord or his near relative, or

(ii) in the case of premises to be occupied by individuals, more than six individuals in addition to the landlord or his near relative.

(3) In paragraph (1) "near relative" means—

(a) spouse or civil partner,

(b) parent or grandparent,

(c) child or grandchild (whether or not legitimate)

(d) spouse or civil partner of a child or grandchild,

(e) brother or sister (whether of full blood or half blood), and

(f) any of the relationships listed in sub-paragraphs (b) to (e) that arises through marriage, civil partnership or adoption.

(4) Regulation 5(1) and (3) shall not apply to the disposal of premises by a person who—

(a) owns an estate or interest in the premises,

(b) occupies the whole of the premises,

(c) does not use the services of an estate agent for the purposes of the disposal, and

(d) does not arrange for the publication of an advertisement for the purposes of the disposal.

[3569]

NOTES

Commencement: 30 April 2007.

7–11 (*Outside the scope of this work.*)

12 Statutory requirements

Nothing in these Regulations shall make it unlawful to do anything which is necessary, or in so far as it is necessary, for the purpose of complying with—

(a) an Act of Parliament,

(b) an Act of the Scottish Parliament,

(c) legislation made or to be made—

(i) by a Minister of the Crown,

(ii) by Order in Council,

(iii) by the Scottish Ministers or a member of the Scottish Executive,

(iv) by the National Assembly for Wales, or

(v) by or by virtue of a Measure of the General Synod of the Church of England, or

(d) a condition or requirement imposed by a Minister of the Crown by virtue of anything listed in paragraphs (a) to (c).

[3570]

NOTES

Commencement: 30 April 2007.

13 (*Outside the scope of this work.*)

14 Organisations relating to religion or belief

(1) Subject to paragraphs (2) and (8) this regulation applies to an organisation the purpose of which is—

(a) to practise a religion or belief,
(b) to advance a religion or belief,
(c) to teach the practice or principles of a religion or belief,
(d) to enable persons of a religion or belief to receive any benefit, or to engage in any activity, within the framework of that religion or belief.

(2) This regulation does not apply—

(a) to an organisation whose sole or main purpose is commercial,
(b) in relation to regulation 7 (Educational establishments, local educational authorities, and education authorities).

(3) Nothing in these Regulations shall make it unlawful for an organisation to which this regulation applies, or for anyone acting on behalf of or under the auspices of an organisation to which this regulation applies—

(a) to restrict membership of the organisation,
(b) to restrict participation in activities undertaken by the organisation or on its behalf or under its auspices,
(c) to restrict the provision of goods, facilities or services in the course of activities undertaken by the organisation or on its behalf or under its auspices, or
(d) to restrict the use or disposal of premises owned or controlled by the organisation,

in respect of a person on the ground of his sexual orientation.

(4) Nothing in these Regulations shall make it unlawful for a minister—

(a) to restrict participation in activities carried on in the performance of his functions in connection with or in respect of an organisation to which this regulation relates, or
(b) to restrict the provision of goods, facilities or services in the course of activities carried on in the performance of his functions in connection with or in respect of an organisation to which this regulation relates,

in respect of a person on the ground of his sexual orientation.

(5) Paragraphs (3) and (4) permit a restriction only if imposed—

(a) if it is necessary to comply with the doctrine of the organisation; or
(b) so as to avoid conflicting with the strongly held religious convictions of a significant number of the religion's followers.

(6) In paragraph (4) the reference to a minister is a reference to a minister of religion, or other person, who—

(a) performs functions in connection with a religion or belief to which an organisation, to which this regulation applies, relates; and
(b) holds an office or appointment in, or is accredited, approved or recognised for purposes of, an organisation to which this regulation applies.

(7) For the purposes of paragraph (3)(d), "disposal" shall not include disposal of an interest in premises by way of sale where the interest being disposed of is the entirety of the organisation's interest in the premises, or the entirety of the interest in respect of which the organisation has power of disposal.

(8) This regulation does not apply where an organisation of the kind referred to in paragraph (1) or any person acting on its behalf or under its auspices—

(a) makes provision of a kind referred to in regulation 4, or
(b) exercises a function of a kind referred to in regulation 8,

on behalf of a public authority under the terms of a contract for provision of that kind between that authority and an organisation referred to in paragraph (1) or, if different, the person making that provision.

[3571]

NOTES

Commencement: 30 April 2007.

15–17 (*Outside the scope of this work.*)

18 Charities

(1) Nothing in these Regulations shall make it unlawful for a person to provide benefits only to persons of a particular sexual orientation, if—

(a) he acts in pursuance of a charitable instrument, and

(b) the restriction of benefits to persons of that sexual orientation is imposed by reason of or on the grounds of the provisions of the charitable instrument.

(2) Nothing in these Regulations shall make it unlawful for the Charity Commission for England and Wales or the holder of the office of the Scottish Charity Regulator to exercise a function in relation to a charity in a manner which appears to the Commission or to the holder to be expedient in the interests of the charity, having regard to the provisions of the charitable instrument.

(3) In this regulation—

"charitable instrument"—

(a) means an instrument establishing or governing a charity, and

(b) includes a charitable instrument made before these Regulations come into force; and

"charity"—

(a) in relation to England and Wales, has the meaning given by the Charities Act 2006,

(b) in relation to Scotland, means a body entered in the Scottish Charity Register.

[3572]

NOTES

Commencement: 30 April 2007.

19 Restriction of proceedings

(1) Except as provided by these Regulations, no proceedings, whether criminal or civil, may be brought against a person on the grounds that an act is unlawful by virtue of these Regulations.

(2) But paragraph (1) does not preclude—

(a) proceedings by the Commission under Part 1 of the 2006 Act,

(b) an application for judicial review,

(c) proceedings under the Immigration Acts,

(d) proceedings under the Special Immigration Appeals Commission Act 1997, or

(e) in Scotland, the exercise of the jurisdiction of the Court of Session to entertain an application for reduction or suspension of an order or determination or otherwise to consider the validity of an order or determination, or to require reasons for an order or determination to be stated.

[3573]

NOTES

Commencement: 30 April 2007.

20 Claims of unlawful action

(1) A claim that a person has done anything that is unlawful by virtue of these Regulations may be brought—

(a) in England and Wales, in a county court, by way of proceedings in tort, or

(b) in Scotland, in the sheriff court, by way of proceedings in reparation,

for breach of statutory duty.

(2) Proceedings in England and Wales alleging that a local education authority or the responsible body of an educational establishment listed in Schedule 3 has acted unlawfully by virtue of regulation 7 or 8 may not be brought unless the claimant has given written notice to the Secretary of State.

(3) Proceedings in Scotland alleging that an education authority or the responsible body of an educational establishment listed in Schedule 3 has acted unlawfully by virtue of regulation 7 or 8 may not be brought unless the pursuer has given written notice to the Scottish Ministers.

(4) In paragraph (1) the reference to a claim that a person has done an unlawful act includes a reference to a claim that a person is to be treated by virtue of these Regulations as having done an unlawful act.

(5) In proceedings under this regulation, if the claimant (or pursuer) proves facts from which the court could conclude, in the absence of a reasonable alternative explanation, that an act which is unlawful by virtue of these Regulations has been committed, the court shall assume that the act was unlawful unless the respondent (or defender) proves that it was not.

[3574]

NOTES

Commencement: 30 April 2007.

21 (*Outside the scope of this work.*)

22 Remedies for unlawful action

(1) In proceedings under regulation 20, the court (subject to paragraph (2))—

(a) (in addition to granting any remedy available to it in proceedings for tort) may grant any remedy that the High Court could grant in proceedings for judicial review,

(b) may award damages by way of compensation for injury to feelings (whether or not other damages are also awarded),

(c) may not award damages in proceedings in respect of an act that is unlawful by virtue of regulation 3(5) if the respondent proves that there was no intention to treat the claimant unfavourably on grounds of sexual orientation,

(2) In respect of a contravention of regulation 8, the court—

(a) shall not grant an injunction unless satisfied that it will not prejudice criminal proceedings or a criminal investigation, and

(b) shall grant any application to stay the proceedings under regulation 20 on the grounds of prejudice to criminal proceedings or to a criminal investigation, unless satisfied that the proceedings or investigation will not be prejudiced.

(3) In the application of this regulation to Scotland—

(a) a reference to the court shall be taken as a reference to the sheriff,

(b) a reference to the High Court shall be taken as a reference to the Court of Session,

(c) a reference to tort shall be taken as a reference to reparation,

(d) a reference to the claimant shall be taken as a reference to the pursuer,

(e) a reference to the respondent shall be taken as a reference to the defender,

(f) a reference to an injunction shall be taken as a reference to an interdict, and

(g) a reference to staying proceedings shall be taken as a reference to sisting proceedings.

[3575]

NOTES

Commencement: 30 April 2007.

23 Claims of unlawful action: timing

(1) Proceedings under regulation 20 may be brought only—

(a) within the period of six months beginning with the date of the act (or the last act) to which the proceedings relate, or

(b) with the permission of the court in which the proceedings are brought.

(2) In relation to immigration proceedings (as defined in regulation 21) the period specified in paragraph (1)(a) shall begin with the first date on which proceedings under regulation 20 may be brought.

[3576]

NOTES

Commencement: 30 April 2007.

24 Claims of unlawful action: information

(1) A claimant or a potential claimant may question a respondent or a potential respondent about the reasons for an action or about any matter that is or may be relevant and may do so—

(a) in the form set out in Part 1 of Schedule 2, or

(b) in a form to the like effect with such variation as the circumstances require.

(2) A respondent or potential respondent may reply (if he so wishes) to questions served under paragraph (1)—

(a) in the form set out in Part 2 of Schedule 2, or

(b) in a form to the like effect with such variation as the circumstances require.

(3) A claimant's or potential claimant's questions (whether or not put in a form mentioned in paragraph (1)), and a respondent or potential respondent's replies shall be admissible as evidence in proceedings in respect of the action or about any matter that is or may be relevant, to which the questions relate if (and only if) the questions are served—

(a) within the period of six months beginning with the date of the action (or last action) to which they relate, and

(b) in accordance with paragraph (4).

(4) A question may be served on a respondent or potential respondent and a reply may be served on a claimant or potential claimant—

(a) by delivering it to him,

(b) by sending it by post to him at his usual or last known residence or place of business,

(c) where the person to be served is acting by a solicitor, by delivering it at, or by sending it by post to, the solicitor's address for service,

(d) where the person to be served is a claimant or potential claimant, by delivering the reply, or sending it by post, to him at his address for reply as stated by him in the document containing the questions, or if no address is so stated, at his usual or last known residence, or

(e) where the person to be served is a body corporate or is a trade union or employers' association within the meaning of the Trade Union and Labour Relations (Consolidation) Act 1992, by delivering it to the secretary or clerk of the body, union or association at its registered or principal office, or by sending it by post to the secretary or clerk at that office.

(5) A court may draw an inference from—

(a) a failure to reply to a claimant's or potential claimant's questions within the period of eight weeks beginning with the date the questions were served, or

(b) an evasive or equivocal reply to such questions (whether or not put in a form mentioned in paragraph (1)).

(6) In this regulation—

(a) "claimant" means a person who has brought proceedings under these Regulations,

(b) "potential claimant" means a person who—

(i) thinks he may have been the subject of an act that is unlawful by virtue of these Regulations, and

(ii) wishes to consider whether to bring proceedings under these Regulations,

(c) "potential respondent" means a person questioned by a potential claimant for the purpose of considering whether to bring proceedings under these Regulations

(7) In the application of this regulation to Scotland—

(a) a reference to a claimant or potential claimant shall be taken as a reference to a pursuer or potential pursuer, and

(b) a reference to a respondent or potential respondent shall be taken as a reference to a defender or potential defender.

(8) Paragraph (5) does not apply in relation to a reply, or a failure to reply, to a question—

(a) if the respondent or potential respondent reasonably asserts that to have replied differently or at all might have prejudiced criminal proceedings or a criminal investigation,

(b) if the respondent or potential respondent reasonably asserts that to have replied differently or at all would have revealed the reason for not instituting or not continuing criminal proceedings, or

(c) if the respondent or potential respondent reasonably asserts that to have replied differently or at all would have frustrated the purpose of national security.

[3577]

NOTES

Commencement: 30 April 2007.

25 National security

(1) Rules of court may make provision for enabling a county court or sheriff court in which a claim is brought under regulation 20, where the court considers it expedient in the interests of national security—

(a) to exclude from all or part of the proceedings—

(i) the claimant,

(ii) the claimant's representatives, or

(iii) any assessors,

(b) to permit a claimant or representative who has been excluded to make a statement to the court before the commencement of the proceedings, or the part of the proceedings, from which he is excluded;

(c) to take steps to keep secret all or part of the reasons for the court's decision in the proceedings.

(2) The Attorney General or, in Scotland, the Advocate General for Scotland, may appoint a person to represent the interests of a claimant in, or in any part of, proceedings from which the claimant or his representatives are excluded by virtue of paragraph (1).

(3) A person may be appointed under paragraph (2) only—

(a) in relation to proceedings in England and Wales, if he has a general qualification (within the meaning of section 71 of the Courts and Legal Services Act 1990), or
(b) in relation to proceedings in Scotland, if he is—
  (i) an advocate, or
  (ii) qualified to practise as a solicitor in Scotland.

(4) A person appointed under paragraph (2) shall not be responsible to the person whose interests he is appointed to represent.

[3578]

NOTES

Commencement: 30 April 2007.

Regulations: the Act of Sederunt (Ordinary Cause, Summary Application, Summary Cause and Small Claim Rules) Amendment (Equality Act (Sexual Orientation) Regulations 2007) 2007, SSI 2007/339.

26 Validity and revision of contracts

(1) A term of a contract is void where—
(a) its inclusion renders the making of the contract unlawful by virtue of these Regulations,
(b) it is included in furtherance of an act which would be unlawful by virtue of these Regulations, or
(c) it provides for the doing of an act which would be unlawful by virtue of these Regulations.

(2) Paragraph (1) does not apply to a term whose inclusion constitutes, furthers or provides for unlawful discrimination against a party to the contract; but that term shall be unenforceable against that party.

(3) A term in a contract which purports to exclude or limit a provision of these Regulations is unenforceable by a person in whose favour the term would operate apart from this paragraph.

(4) Paragraph (3) does not apply to a contract settling a claim under regulation 20.

(5) On the application of a person interested in a contract to which paragraph (1) applies, a county court or sheriff court may make an order removing or modifying a term made unenforceable by that paragraph, but an order shall not be made unless all persons affected—
(a) have been given notice of the application (except where notice is dispensed with in accordance with rules of court), and
(b) have been afforded an opportunity to make representations to the court.

(6) An order under paragraph (5) may include provision in respect of a period before the making of the order.

[3579]

NOTES

Commencement: 30 April 2007.

27–34 (*Outside the scope of this work.*)

(*Sch 1 outside the scope of this work.*)

SCHEDULE 2
INFORMATION: FORMS

Regulation 24

PART 1
FORM OF QUESTIONS BY CLAIMANT OR POTENTIAL CLAIMANT

Regulation 24(1)(a)

To .... (name of person to be questioned) of .... (address)

1 (1) I ....(*name of questioner*) of .... (*address*) consider that you may have discriminated against me contrary to the Equality Act (Sexual Orientation) Regulations 2007.

(2) (*Give date, approximate time and a factual description of the treatment received and of the circumstances leading up to the treatment.*)

(3) I consider that this treatment may have been unlawful (because .... (*complete if you wish to give reasons, otherwise delete*)).

2 Do you agree that the statement in paragraph 1(2) above is an accurate description of what happened? If not, in what respect do you disagree or what is your version of what happened?

3 Do you accept that your treatment of me was unlawful discrimination?

If not—
(a) why not,

(b) for what reason did I receive the treatment accorded to me, and
(c) how far did considerations of sexual orientation affect your treatment of me?

4 (*Any other questions you wish to ask?*)

5 My address for any reply you may wish to give to the questions raised above is (that set out in paragraph 1(1) above) (the following address ....).

..............................(*signature of questioner*)

....................(*date*)

NB By virtue of regulation 24 of the Equality Act (Sexual Orientation) Regulations 2007 this questionnaire and any reply are (subject to the provisions of that regulation) admissible in proceedings under the Regulations. A court or tribunal may draw an inference from a failure to reply within eight weeks of service of this questionnaire or from an evasive or equivocal reply.

[3580]

NOTES

Commencement: 30 April 2007.

PART 2
FORM OF REPLY BY RESPONDENT OR POTENTIAL RESPONDENT

Regulation 24(2)(a)

To .... (*name of questioner*) of .... (*address*)

1 I .... (*name of person questioned*) of .... (*address*) hereby acknowledge receipt of the questionnaire signed by you and dated .... which was served on me on ....(*date*).

2 (I agree that the statement in paragraph 1(2) of the questionnaire is an accurate description of what happened.)

(I disagree with the statement in paragraph 1(2) of the questionnaire in that ....)

3 I accept/dispute that my treatment of you was unlawful discrimination by me against you.

(My reasons for so disputing are ....The reason why you received the treatment accorded to you and the answers to the other questions in paragraph 3 of your questionnaire are ....)

4 (*Replies to questions in paragraph 4 of the questionnaire.*)

(5 I have deleted (in whole or in part) the paragraph(s) numbered .... above, since I am unable/unwilling to reply to the relevant questions in the correspondingly numbered paragraph(s) of the questionnaire for the following reasons ....)

..............................(*signature of person questioned*)

..............................(*date*)

[3581]

NOTES

Commencement: 30 April 2007.

(*Sch 3 outside the scope of this work.*)

HOME INFORMATION PACK (NO 2) REGULATIONS 2007

(SI 2007/1667)

NOTES

Made: 8 June 2007.
Authority: Housing Act 2004, ss 161, 163, 164, 165, 250(2), Sch 8, paras 2, 11(b).
Commencement: 2 July 2007.

PART 1
CITATION, COMMENCEMENT AND INTERPRETATION

1 Citation and commencement

(1) These Regulations may be cited as the Home Information Pack (No 2) Regulations 2007.

(2) These Regulations shall come into force on 2nd July 2007.

[(3) Regulation 8(ca) and (cb) and Schedule 2A apply in relation to properties located or to be located in England.

(4) The remaining provisions of these Regulations apply in relation to properties located or to be located in England or Wales.]

[3582]

NOTES

Commencement: 2 July 2007.
Paras (3), (4): inserted by SI 2008/572, reg 3(a).

2 Interpretation—general provisions

(1) In these Regulations—

"the 2004 Act" means the Housing Act 2004;

"appropriate local land charges register" means the register described in section 4 of the Local Land Charges Act 1975;

"approved certification scheme" means a certification scheme approved by the Secretary of State under regulation 37 of these Regulations and from which such approval has not been withdrawn under regulation 39;

"the Chief Land Registrar" means the person appointed by the Lord Chancellor under section 99(3) of the Land Registration Act 2002;

"conservation area consent" means the consent described in section 74(1) of the Planning (Listed Buildings and Conservation Areas) Act 1990;

"developer" means a person who has built or converted, or is building or converting the property;

"edited information document" means, where the Chief Land Registrar has designated a document an exempt information document, the edited copy of that document lodged under rule 136(2)(b) or 138(4) of the Land Registration Rules 2003;

"energy performance certificate" means a certificate which complies with regulation 11(1) of the Energy Performance of Buildings (Certificates and Inspections) (England and Wales) Regulations 2007 or regulation 17E of the Building Regulations 2000;

"exempt information document" means the original and copies of a document so designated under rule 136(3) of the Land Registration Rules 2003;

["finished" in regulation 8(ca) and (cb) refers to the stage at which the construction of a property is sufficiently advanced so as to make a post-construction assessment (within the meaning of Schedule 2A) possible;]

"first point of marketing" means the time described in regulation 3;

"home condition report" means a document which complies with Schedule 9;

"home information pack" in relation to a property, means—

(a) where a duty arises under section 155(1) of the 2004 Act, the home information pack intended by the responsible person to be the one required by that provision; and

(b) where a duty arises under section 159(2) of that Act, the home information pack intended by the person to whom that section applies to be the one required by that provision;

"home information pack index" means the document required by regulation 8(a);

"home inspector" means a person who is a member of an approved certification scheme;

"individual register" means the register so named in rule 2 of the Land Registration Rules 2003, the contents and arrangement of which are described in rules 3 and 4 of those Rules;

["interim sustainability certificate" means the document required by regulation 8(cb)(i), which must comply with paragraph 3 of Schedule 2A;]

"lease" means a long lease except in regulation 8(i), regulation 26(b)(i), paragraph 3(l) of Schedule 4 and paragraph 3(a) of Schedule 5;

"listed building consent" means a consent under section 8(1), (2) or (3) of the Planning (Listed Buildings and Conservation Areas) Act 1990;

["new home" in [regulation 8(ca), (cb), (m) and (n) and Schedule 12] means—

(a) a property being designed;

(b) a property being constructed; or

(c) a property, the construction of which is finished, but has never been occupied;]

["nil-rated certificate" means the document required by regulation 8(ca)(ii) or (cb)(ii) which must comply with paragraph 4 of Schedule 2A;]

"occupant" includes a potential occupant;

"pack document" means a document (or part of a document) required or authorised by these Regulations to be included in the home information pack;

"planning permission" means a permission (granted or deemed to be granted) under Part 3 of the Town and Country Planning Act 1990;

"predicted energy assessment" means the document required by regulation 8(c);

"premises" includes buildings and land;

"property" means the residential property in respect of which a duty arises under section 155(1) or 159(2) of the 2004 Act;

["property information questionnaire" means the document required by regulation 8(m) or (n), as the case may be;]

"property interest" means the freehold interest (including a freehold estate in commonhold land) or the leasehold interest in the property that the seller is proposing to sell;

"recommendation report" has the meaning given by regulation 2(1) of the Energy Performance of Buildings (Certificates and Inspections) (England and Wales) Regulations 2007;

"records" includes documents, registers, files and archives, kept in any form;

"register of title" means the register kept by the Chief Land Registrar pursuant to section 1 of the Land Registration Act 2002;

"registered estate" means a legal estate the title to which is entered in the register of title, other than a charge the title to which is entered in that register;

"responsible person" also includes a person subject to a duty under section 159(2) of the 2004 Act;

"sale" includes the potential sale of a property interest;

"sale statement" means the document required by regulation 8(d);

"search" means an inspection or investigation (whether manual or electronic) of records;

"service charge" has the same meaning as in section 18 of the Landlord and Tenant Act 1985;

["sustainability certificate" means the document required by regulation 8(ca)(i) which must comply with paragraph 2 of Schedule 2A;]

"title plan" means the plan so named in rule 5(a) of the Land Registration Rules 2003; and

"year" means a period of 12 months.

(2) In these Regulations, any expression relating to commonhold land must be construed in accordance with—

(a) Part 1 of the Commonhold and Leasehold Reform Act 2002 if it is also used in that Act; or

(b) the Commonhold Regulations 2004 where those Regulations further define or elaborate upon an expression used in Part 1 of that Act,

and in relation to commonhold land, references to common parts are to those that relate to the property and the commonhold of which the property forms part.

(3) For the purposes of these Regulations—

(a) the property is physically complete if its building or its conversion for residential purposes has been completed; and

(b) where a question arises as to whether the property is physically complete, it must be considered physically complete if it—

(i) is wind and weather proof;

(ii) is safe and sanitary in relation to its occupants or visitors;

(iii) has facilities for the supply of space heating, hot and cold water and electricity; and

(iv) has washing and drainage facilities.

(4) In these Regulations, references to the amendment or revision of a document include its modification or variation.

(5) In these Regulations, references to a number of days, months or years are to a consecutive period of days or months.

[3583]

NOTES

Commencement: 2 July 2007.

Para (1): definitions "finished", "interim sustainability certificate", "nil-rated certificate", "sustainability certificate" inserted by SI 2008/572, reg 3(b); definition "new home" inserted by SI 2008/572, reg 3(b), and words in square brackets in that definition substituted by SI 2008/3107, regs 2, 8(a); definition "property information questionnaire" inserted by SI 2008/3107, regs 2, 8(b).

3 Interpretation—first point of marketing

(1) Subject to the provisions specified in paragraph (2), a reference in these Regulations to the "first point of marketing" is to the first time a duty arises under section 155(1) or 159(2) of the 2004 Act in relation to the sale of the property interest.

(2) The provisions referred to in paragraph (1) are—

(a) regulations 16(3), 17(3), 21(3), 22(3) and 23(3); and

(b) paragraphs (3), (4) and (5).

(3) No further first point of marketing shall arise where the property is taken off the market and then put back on the market before the end of the period of one year starting with the day on which the first point of marketing falls.

(4) Except in the circumstances described in paragraph (5), where the property is taken off the market and then put back on the market after the end of the period of one year starting with the day on which the first point of marketing falls—

(a) a further first point of marketing arises; and

(b) that first point of marketing is the time at which the property is put back on the market.

(5) No further first point of marketing shall arise where the property—

(a) is taken off the market for any period of time because the seller accepts an offer to buy the property; and

(b) is then put back on the market within 28 days of that offer being withdrawn or its acceptance repudiated.

[3584]

NOTES

Commencement: 2 July 2007.

PART 2
HOME INFORMATION PACK—GENERAL PROVISIONS

4 Required, authorised and excluded documents

(1) A home information pack—

(a) must include—

(i) the documents required under regulation 8 (including that regulation as modified by [regulations 10 and 10A]); and

(ii) the particular information so required to be included in a pack document; and

(b) may include—

(i) the documents authorised under regulation 9 (including that regulation as modified by [regulations 10 and 10A]); or

(ii) the particular information so authorised to be included in a pack document.

(2) A home information pack must not include any other documents or information contained in a document.

(3) A copy of a home information pack, or of a pack document provided to a potential buyer pursuant to section 156(1) of the 2004 Act must be separated and clearly distinguished by the responsible person from documents or information which are—

(a) provided to a potential buyer in close proximity to the pack or pack document; and

(b) neither required nor authorised by these Regulations to be included in the pack.

[3585]

NOTES

Commencement: 2 July 2007.

Para (1): in sub-para (a)(i), (b)(i) words in square brackets substituted by SI 2007/3301, reg 2(2)(a).

5 The home information pack

(1) Except where an official copy of a document is required or authorised by these Regulations to be included in the home information pack, the pack must be composed of original documents or true copies of them.

(2) For the purposes of these Regulations, a copy of a document containing a map, plan or drawing—

(a) which is in the seller's possession, under his control, or to which he has reasonable access; and

(b) in which colours are used to mark boundaries or other features,

is a true copy if those colours are reproduced with sufficient accuracy to enable them to be identified.

[3586]

NOTES

Commencement: 2 July 2007.

6 Copies of a home information pack

The copies of a home information pack or pack document provided or produced under section 156(1) or 167(1) of the 2004 Act must be—

(a) true copies of the home information pack or pack document; or

(b) where a pack document is an official copy, a true copy of it or another official copy.

[3587]

NOTES

Commencement: 2 July 2007.

7 Comprehension of documents

(1) Subject to paragraph (2), pack documents and true copies of documents made in accordance with regulation 6—

(a) must be legible; or

(b) in the case of maps, plans or drawings, must be clear.

(2) Paragraph (1) does not apply where, despite all reasonable efforts and enquiries by the responsible person—

(a) the only version of a pack document available is one which is illegible or unclear (either in whole or in part); and

(b) that document is to be included under any of the following provisions—

(i) regulation 8(f)(ii) (documents relied on to deduce unregistered title);

(ii) regulation 9(j) (documents referred to in the register of title);

(iii) regulation 8(g) or 9(k) (required or authorised commonhold information); or

(iv) regulation 8(h) or 9(l) (required or authorised leasehold information).

(3) Pack documents must be in—

(a) English, where the property is in England; or

(b) English, Welsh or a combination of English and Welsh, where the property (or part of the property) is in Wales.

[3588]

NOTES

Commencement: 2 July 2007.

PART II STATUTORY INSTRUMENTS

PART 3
CONTENTS OF HOME INFORMATION PACKS

8 Required pack documents

Subject to regulations 10, [10A,] 11, 12 and Parts 4 and 5, the home information pack must include the following—

(a) an index to the home information pack complying with Schedule 1 (the home information pack index);

(b) an energy performance certificate and its accompanying recommendation report for a property which is physically complete before or at the first point of marketing;

(c) a predicted energy assessment complying with Schedule 2 if the property is not physically complete before or at the first point of marketing;

[(ca) subject to regulation 34A, for a property finished before or at the first point of marketing, which is marketed as a new home—

(i) a sustainability certificate complying with paragraph 2 of Schedule 2A; or

(ii) a nil-rated certificate complying with paragraph 4 of that Schedule;

(cb) subject to regulation 34A, for a property not finished before or at the first point of marketing, which is marketed as a new home—

(i) an interim sustainability certificate complying with paragraph 3 of Schedule 2A; or

(ii) a nil-rated certificate complying with paragraph 4 of that Schedule;]

(d) a document complying with Schedule 3 (the sale statement);

(e) if the property interest is or includes the whole or part of a registered estate—

(i) an official copy of the individual register relating to that estate; and

(ii) an official copy of the title plan relating to that estate;

(f) if the property interest is or includes the whole or part of an estate, the title to which is not entered in the register of title—

(i) a certificate of an official search of the index map issued under rule 145(4) of the Land Registration Rules 2003 in relation to the parcel of land to which the property interest relates; and

(ii) such other documents on which the seller can reasonably be expected to rely in order to deduce title to that estate for the purposes of its sale;

(g) if the property interest is or includes the whole or part of a freehold estate in commonhold land—

(i) the documents described in paragraph 1 of Schedule 4; and

(ii) documents consisting of or containing information about the matters described in paragraph 2 of that Schedule;

(h) if the property interest is or includes the whole or part of a leasehold interest—

(i) the documents described in paragraph 1 of Schedule 5; …

(ii) … ;

(i) if the property interest is or includes the whole or part of an interest in dwelling-houses to which Part 5 of the 2004 Act applies by virtue of section 171(2) of that Act, such leases or licences—

(i) to which the dwelling-houses are subject or are expected to be subject at the time of, or following completion of the sale of the property interest; and

(ii) as have not been included in the pack under paragraph (h) of this regulation;

(j) a search report which relates to the property and which records the results of a search of all parts of the appropriate local land charges register—

(i) in the form of an official search certificate, in the case of an official search made pursuant to section 9 of the Local Land Charges Act 1975; or

(ii) in any other form but made in accordance with Parts 1 and 2 of Schedule 6, in the case of a personal search made pursuant to section 8 of that Act;

(k) a search report which—

(i) is made in accordance with Parts 1 and 2 of Schedule 6 and with Schedule 7; and

(ii) records the results of a search of records held by or derived from a local authority (local enquiries); …

(l) a search report which is made in accordance with Parts 1 and 2 of Schedule 6 and with Schedule 8 (drainage and water enquiries);

[(m) where the property is not a new home, a property information questionnaire complying with Schedule 11; and

(n) where the property is a new home, a property information questionnaire complying with Schedule 12].

[3589]

NOTES

Commencement: 2 July 2007.

Reference to '10A' in square brackets inserted by SI 2007/3301, reg 2(2)(b).

Paras (ca), (cb) inserted by SI 2008/572, reg 2(1); for transitional provision see reg 34A (as amended by SI 2008/572, reg 3(g)).

Para (h)(i): word omitted revoked by SI 2008/3107, regs 2, 3(a).

Para (h)(ii) revoked by SI 2008/3107, regs 2, 3(b).

Para (k)(ii): word omitted revoked by SI 2008/3107, regs 2, 9(a).

Paras (m), (n) inserted by SI 2008/3107, regs 2, 9(b).

9 Authorised pack documents

Subject to regulations 10, [10A,] 11, 12 and Parts 4 and 5, the home information pack may include documents consisting of or containing any of the following—

(a) a home condition report which complies with Schedule 9;

(b) documentary evidence of any safety, building, repair or maintenance work as has been carried out in relation to the property since the date of any home condition report included in the pack under paragraph (a);

(c) any warranty, policy or guarantee for defects in the design, building, or completion of the property, or its conversion for residential purposes;

(d) information about the design or standards to which a property has been or is being built;

(e) an accurate translation in any language of any pack document;

(f) an additional version of any pack document in another format, such as Braille or large print;

(g) a summary or explanation of any pack document, including legal advice on the content of the pack or any pack document;

(h) information identifying the property including a description, photograph, map, plan or drawing of the property;

(i) information about a pack document, about information contained within a pack document or about the home information pack, relating to—

(i) its source or supply; or

(ii) complaints or redress procedures arising from it;

(j) if the property interest is or includes the whole or part of a registered estate, official copies of any documents referred to in the individual register, including any edited information documents derived from such exempt information documents as are referred to in the register;

(k) if the property interest is or includes the whole or part of a freehold estate in commonhold land, information which—

(i) relates to one or more of the matters described in paragraph 3 of Schedule 4; and

(ii) would be of interest to potential buyers of the property interest;

(l) if the property interest is or includes the whole or part of a leasehold interest, information which—

(i) relates to one or more of the matters described in [paragraphs 1A to 3A] of Schedule 5; and

(ii) would be of interest to potential buyers of the property interest;

(m) one or more of the following search reports which must be made in accordance with Part 1 of Schedule 6 and may be made in accordance with Part 2 of that Schedule, which records the results of a search relating to the property and relating to any of the following matters—

(i) information held by or derived from a local authority, and dealing with matters supplementary to those contained in the search reports required by regulation 8(j) (search of the local land charges register) or 8(k) (local enquiries);

(ii) common land or town or village greens;

(iii) rights of access to, over or affecting the property interest;

(iv) ground stability, the effects of mining or extractions or the effects of natural subsidence;

(v) actual or potential environmental hazards, including the risks of flooding or contamination from radon gas or any other substance;

(vi) telecommunications services;

(vii) sewerage, drainage, water, gas or electrical services;

(viii) the potential or actual effects of transport services, including roads, waterways, trams and underground or over-ground railways; or

(ix) liabilities to repair or maintain buildings or land not within the property interest;

(n) where it would be of interest to potential buyers of the property interest, a document which—

(i) records the results of a search relating to other premises in the vicinity of the property; and

(ii) would otherwise be a report of the type required by regulation 8(j) (search of the local land charges register), 8(k) (local enquiries) or 8(l) (drainage and water enquiries) or authorised by paragraph (m) of this regulation, if references in those provisions and in Schedules 6, 7 and 8 to "property", "land" and "land on which the property is or will be situated" were references to those other premises;

(o) any documents referred to in a search report included in the pack under regulation 8(j) (search of the local land charges register), 8(k) (local enquiries), 8(l) (drainage and water enquiries) (subject to paragraph 2(4)(b) of Schedule 8) or paragraphs (m) or (n) of this regulation; and

(p) information which—

(i) relates to one or more of the matters described in Schedule 10; and

(ii) would be of interest to potential buyers of the property interest.

[3590]

NOTES

Commencement: 2 July 2007.

Reference to "10A," in square brackets inserted by SI 2007/3301, reg 2(2)(b).

Para (l)(i): words in square brackets substituted by SI 2008/3107, regs 2, 4.

10 Creation of interests

(1) [Subject to regulations 10A,] 12 and Parts 4 and 5, where the sale involves —

(a) the whole or part of a commonhold unit, which at the first point of marketing has not been registered by the Chief Land Registrar as a freehold estate in commonhold land; or

(b) a leasehold property interest, which at the first point of marketing has not yet been created,

regulations 8 and 9 apply as respects that freehold estate or leasehold interest, as modified by this regulation.

(2) Where paragraph (1)(a) applies—

(a) the sale statement must be completed as if the freehold estate had been registered by the Chief Land Registrar;

(b) regulations 8(e) (evidence of title for registered estates), 8(f) (evidence of title for unregistered estates) and 9(j) (documents referred to in the individual register) apply as if for "is or includes" in each paragraph, there were substituted "to be registered as a freehold estate in commonhold land arises from";

(c) paragraphs 1 and 2 of Schedule 4 (required commonhold information) do not apply;

(d) regulation 9(k) and paragraph 3 of Schedule 4 (authorised commonhold information) must be construed by reference to the information expected to be relevant to the interest to be registered as a freehold estate in commonhold land; and

(e) the home information pack must include documents consisting of or containing information which relates to the matters described in paragraph 4 of Schedule 4.

(3) Where paragraph (1)(b) applies—

(a) the sale statement must be completed as if the leasehold interest had been created;

(b) regulations 8(e) (evidence of title for registered estates), 8(f) (evidence of title for unregistered estates) and 9(j) (documents referred to in the individual register) apply as if for "is or includes" in each paragraph, there were substituted "is to be created from";

(c) paragraphs 1 and 2 of Schedule 5 (required leasehold information) do not apply;

(d) regulation 9(l) and paragraph 3 of Schedule 5 (authorised leasehold information) must be construed by reference to the information expected to be relevant to the interest to be created; and

(e) the home information pack must include documents consisting of or containing information which relates to the matters described in paragraph 4 of Schedule 5.

[3591]

NOTES

Commencement: 2 July 2007.

Para (1): words in square brackets substituted by SI 2007/3301, reg 2(2)(c).

[10A Leasehold information included during a temporary period

(1) This regulation applies where the first point of marketing falls before [1st January 2009] (except where a further first point of marketing arises under regulation 3(4) or Part 5).

(2) Subject to paragraph (3), the documents required for inclusion in a home information pack under regulations 8(h) and 10(3) shall be treated as if they are authorised for inclusion under regulation 9(l).

(3) This regulation does not apply to the document required under regulation 8(h) by virtue of paragraph 1(1)(a) of Schedule 5 (the lease).]

[3591A]

NOTES

Commencement: 14 December 2007.

Inserted by SI 2007/3301, reg 2(1).

Para (1): words in square brackets substituted by SI 2008/1266, reg 2(a).

11 Prohibitions relating to home condition reports

(1) A home condition report must not be included in the home information pack if it was not completed for the purposes of the sale by the seller of the property interest.

(2) No pack document may be described as a "home condition report" unless it complies with Schedule 9.

[3592]

NOTES

Commencement: 2 July 2007.

12 Exclusion of advertising information

(1) Information advertising or marketing goods or services must not be included in the home information pack or a pack document—

(a) by a responsible person;

(b) at his request; or

(c) with his permission.

(2) In paragraph (1), "information advertising or marketing goods or services" does not include information in a document required to be included under regulation 8 (including that regulation as modified by [regulations 10 and 10A]).

[3593]

NOTES

Commencement: 2 July 2007.

Para (2): words in square brackets substituted by SI 2007/3301, reg 2(2)(a).

PART 4
ASSEMBLY OF HOME INFORMATION PACKS

13 Order of pack documents

Subject to the provisions of this Part, a copy of a home information pack provided or produced under section 156(1) or 167(1) of the 2004 Act must be composed of pack documents in the following order—

(a) firstly, the document required by regulation 8(a) (home information pack index);

[(aa) secondly—

(i) the document required by regulation 8(m) (PIQ for a property that is not a new home); or

(ii) the document required by regulation 8(n) (PIQ for a property that is a new home);]

(b) [thirdly]—

(i) the documents required by regulation 8(b) (energy performance certificate and recommendation report); or

(ii) the document required by regulation 8(c) (predicted energy assessment); …

[(ba) [fourthly]—

(i) such of the documents as are required by regulation 8(ca) (sustainability of finished new homes); or

(ii) such of the documents as are required by regulation 8(cb) (sustainability of new homes not finished); then]

(c) the remaining pack documents (which may be included in any order).

[3594]

NOTES

Commencement: 2 July 2007.

Para (aa) inserted by SI 2008/3107, regs 2, 11(a).

Para (b): word in square brackets substituted by SI 2008/3107, regs 2, 11(b); words omitted revoked by SI 2008/572, reg 3(c).

Para (ba) inserted by SI 2008/572, reg 3(d); word in square brackets substituted by SI 2008/3107, regs 2, 11(c).

14 Time at which pack documents are to be included

(1) Subject to regulations 16, 20 and 34, the documents required to be included in the home information pack under the following provisions of regulation 8 (including that regulation as modified by [regulations 10 and 10A]) must be included before or at the first point of marketing—

(a) paragraph (a) (home information pack index);

(b) paragraph (b) (energy performance certificate and recommendation report);

(c) paragraph (c) (predicted energy assessment);

[(ca) paragraph (ca) (sustainability of finished new homes);

(cb) paragraph (cb) (sustainability of new homes not finished);]

(d) paragraph (d) (sale statement);

(e) paragraph (e) (evidence of title for registered estates); …

(f) paragraph (f)(i) (official search of the index map for unregistered estates).

[(g) paragraph (m) (property information questionnaire relating to a property that is not a new home); and

(h) paragraph (n) (property information questionnaire for a property that is a new home)].

(2) Subject to regulations 17, 20 and 34, the remaining documents required by regulation 8 to be included in the home information pack must be included before the end of the period of 28 days starting with the first point of marketing.

(3) The pack documents authorised by these Regulations to be included in the home information pack under regulation 9 (including that regulation as modified by [regulations 10 and 10A]) may be included at any time.

[(4) The pack documents required by these Regulations to be included in the home information pack under regulation 8(m) and (n) must be included where the first point of marketing is on or after 6th April 2009.]

[3595]

NOTES

Commencement: 2 July 2007.

Para (1): words in square brackets substituted by SI 2007/3301, reg 2(2)(a); sub-paras (ca), (cb) inserted by SI 2008/572, reg 3(e); in sub-para (e) word omitted revoked by SI 2009/34, regs 2, 3(a); sub-paras (g), (h) inserted by SI 2009/34, regs 2, 3(b).

Para (3): words in square brackets substituted by SI 2007/3301, reg 2(2)(a).

Para (4): inserted by SI 2008/3107, regs 2, 12.

15 Age of pack documents when first included

(1) The documents included under the following provisions of regulation 8 (including that regulation as modified by [regulations 10 and 10A]) must be dated no earlier than the date that falls three months before the first point of marketing—

(a) official copies included in the home information pack under—

(i) paragraph (e) (evidence of title for registered estates);

(ii) paragraph (g) (required commonhold information); and

(iii) paragraph (h) (required leasehold information);

(b) a certificate of an official search of the index map included in the pack under paragraph (f)(i) (evidence of title for unregistered estates);

(c) paragraph (j) (search of the local land charges register);

(d) paragraph (k) (local enquiries); and
(e) paragraph (l) (drainage and water enquiries).

(2) The documents included under the following provisions of regulation 8 must be dated no earlier than the date that falls [3 years] before the first point of marketing—
(a) paragraph (b) (energy performance certificate and recommendation report); and
(b) paragraph (c) (predicted energy assessment).

(3) All other pack documents must be such versions of the documents as can reasonably be assumed to be the most recent to the first point of marketing.

(4) Where—
(a) a pack document has been amended at any time before its inclusion in the home information pack; and
(b) the amendment is not incorporated in the document,

that amendment must be included in the pack.

[3596]

NOTES

Commencement: 2 July 2007.
Para (1): words in square brackets substituted by SI 2007/3301, reg 2(2)(a).
Para (2): words in square brackets substituted by SI 2008/2363, reg 5.

16 Energy information unobtainable before or at the first point of marketing

(1) This regulation applies—
(a) where the first point of marketing occurs on or after [6th April 2009];
(b) where regulation 20 does not apply; and
(c) in relation to the following pack documents required to be included in the home information pack before or at the first point of marketing by virtue of regulation 14(1)—
(i) energy performance certificate and recommendation report (regulation 8(b)); and
(ii) predicted energy assessment (regulation 8(c)).

(2) If, despite all reasonable efforts and enquiries by the responsible person, a pack document to which this regulation applies cannot be obtained by him before or at the first point of marketing, the home information pack complies with the requirements of these Regulations where—
(a) the first point of marketing falls no earlier than the end of the period of 14 days starting with the day a request for the document is delivered in accordance with this Part;
(b) the responsible person continues to use all reasonable efforts to obtain the document, and in particular, to obtain the document before the end of the period of 28 days starting with the first point of marketing;
(c) the document is included in the home information pack as soon as reasonably practicable; and
(d) proof of the request for the document is included in the pack.

(3) The time at which the document is included in the home information pack becomes the first point of marketing for that document—
(a) for the purposes of regulation 15(2); and
(b) until such time (if any) as a further first point of marketing arises under regulation 3(4) or Part 5.

[3597]

NOTES

Commencement: 2 July 2007.
Para (1): in sub-para (a) words in square brackets substituted by SI 2008/3107, regs 2, 5(i).

17 Documents required within 28 days of the first point of marketing

(1) This regulation applies—
(a) where regulation 20 does not apply; and
(b) in relation to the pack documents required to be included in the home information pack before the end of the period of 28 days starting with the first point of marketing by virtue of regulation 14(2).

(2) The home information pack complies with the requirements of these Regulations where, in respect of a pack document to which this regulation applies—
(a) the day a request for the document is delivered falls before the first point of marketing;
(b) the responsible person believes on reasonable grounds that the latest time a document is likely to be obtained by him is at the end of the period of 28 days starting with the first point of marketing, and uses all reasonable efforts to obtain the document before then;
(c) where it is reasonable to expect that the document can be obtained by the responsible person earlier than the time identified in paragraph (b), he uses all reasonable efforts to obtain the document before then;

(d) the responsible person continues to use such efforts if the document cannot be obtained by him in accordance with paragraphs (b) or (c);
(e) the responsible person records on the home information pack index the information required under paragraph 1(f) of Schedule 1;
(f) the document is included in the home information pack as soon as the responsible person obtains it; and
(g) proof of the request for the document is included in the pack.

(3) The time at which the document is included in the home information pack becomes the first point of marketing for that document—
(a) for the purposes of any provision of these Regulations that requires the age or currency of a pack document to be determined by reference to a period preceding the first point of marketing; and
(b) until such time (if any) as a further first point of marketing arises under regulation 3(4) or Part 5.

[3598]

NOTES
Commencement: 2 July 2007.

18 Requests for documents under this Part

(1) In this Part, references to a request for a document are to a request—
(a) which is properly addressed to a person who usually provides or is likely to provide the type of document requested; and
(b) which—
(i) is made in such form;
(ii) contains all such information; and
(iii) is accompanied by such payment or an undertaking to make such payment,
as is usually necessary to obtain a document of the type requested.

(2) In this Part, proof of a request for a document means a written statement of the following matters—
(a) which of the required documents has been requested;
(b) the date that a request for the document is delivered in accordance with regulation 19;
(c) the name of the person to whom the request has been addressed;
(d) the date the responsible person believes the document is likely to become available; and
(e) confirmation that the request complies with paragraph (1).

[3599]

NOTES
Commencement: 2 July 2007.

19 Delivery of documents under this Part

(1) Subject to paragraphs (2) and (3), the day a request for the document is delivered shall, for the purposes of this Part, be taken to be, depending on the method of delivery—
(a) the day the request is served personally on the intended recipient;
(b) the day it would be delivered to the intended recipient's address in the ordinary course of post or (if sooner), the day on which it is proved to have been so delivered;
(c) the day it is left at the intended recipient's address;
(d) the second day after it is left at the document exchange of the person making the request or (if sooner), the day on which it is proved to have been so delivered; or
(e) the day it is sent by fax or electronic communication to the intended recipient's address or (if later), the day on which it is proved to have been so delivered.

(2) Subject to paragraph (3), where a request for a document is delivered to the Chief Land Registrar, the day the request is delivered shall, for the purposes of this Part, be taken to be the day it is delivered in accordance with, or under, the Land Registration Act 2002—
(a) personally;
(b) by post, and is the day it would be delivered to the Chief Land Registrar in the ordinary course of post or (if sooner), the day on which it is proved to have been so delivered;
(c) by document exchange, and is the second day after it is left at the document exchange of the person making the request or (if sooner), the day on which it is proved to have been so delivered;
(d) orally; or
(e) by telephone, fax or other electronic method.

(3) For the purposes of this Part, where a request for a document—
(a) is made in parts, the day the request is delivered shall be taken to be the day the last part is delivered as described in paragraphs (1) and (2);

(b) is delivered more than once, the day the request is delivered shall be taken to be the first day on which a request is delivered as described in paragraphs (1) and (2); and

(c) is delivered using more than one method of delivery, the day the request is delivered shall be taken to be the day on which the first request is delivered as described in paragraphs (1) and (2).

(4) In paragraph (1)(a), "served personally"—

(a) in relation to an individual, means leaving it with that individual;

(b) in relation to a business, means leaving it with an employee or owner of the business; and

(c) in relation to any other body of persons corporate or unincorporate, means leaving it with an employee or member of that body.

(5) References to a recipient's address—

(a) in paragraphs (1)(b) and (c) are, if the intended recipient is an individual—

(i) to his usual or last known residence; or

(ii) if his usual or last known residence is the property, to that address and an address (if any) at which it can reasonably be assumed he will be contacted;

(b) in paragraphs (1)(b) and (c), are if the intended recipient is a business or other body, to any principal or last known place of business from which a document of the type requested is usually or likely to be provided; and

(c) in paragraph (1)(e), are to any electronic address, identification or number published or provided by the intended recipient for the purposes of supplying the document requested.

[3600]

NOTES

Commencement: 2 July 2007.

20 Required pack documents which are completely unobtainable

(1) The provisions of regulation 8 specified in paragraph (2) do not apply where, after making all reasonable efforts and enquiries, the responsible person believes on reasonable grounds that the document in question—

(a) no longer exists in any form; or

(b) cannot be obtained from or created by any person.

(2) The provisions are—

(a) paragraph (c) (predicted energy assessment);

(b) paragraph (f)(ii) (documents relied on to deduce unregistered title);

(c) paragraph (g) (required commonhold information);

(d) paragraph (h) (required leasehold information); or

(e) paragraph (i) (leases or licences for dwelling-houses to which section 171(2) of the 2004 Act applies).

[3601]

NOTES

Commencement: 2 July 2007.

PART 5

ACCURACY OF HOME INFORMATION PACKS

21 Updating of required pack documents

(1) This regulation applies to any document included in a home information pack under regulation 8 (including that regulation as modified by [regulations 10 and 10A]).

(2) Where the responsible person amends such a document or obtains or creates a further version of it, he must—

(a) include the amended document or the further version in the pack;

(b) amend accordingly such translations, additional versions, summaries or explanations as are included in the pack under regulation 9(e), 9(f) or 9(g) or include a further version of such translations, additional versions, summaries or explanations; and

(c) remove such documents as have been wholly superseded by a document included under sub-paragraphs (a) or (b).

(3) The time at which the responsible person amends a document or obtains or creates a further version of it under paragraph (2) becomes the first point of marketing for that document—

(a) for the purposes of any provision of these Regulations that requires the age or currency of a pack document to be determined by reference to a period preceding the first point of marketing; and

(b) until such time (if any) as a further first point of marketing arises under regulation 3(4), Part 4 or this Part.

[3602]

NOTES

Commencement: 2 July 2007.
Para (1): words in square brackets substituted by SI 2007/3301, reg 2(2)(a).

22 Updating of predicted energy assessment

(1) If the property is not physically complete before or at the first point of marketing, and becomes complete after that time, the responsible person must include in the home information pack the documents which would be required by regulation 8(b) (energy performance certificate and recommendation report).

(2) The documents required to be included in the pack under paragraph (1) must—

(a) be so included before the end of the period of 14 days starting with the day on which the property becomes physically complete; and

(b) replace any document already included in the pack in accordance with regulation 8(c) (predicted energy assessment).

(3) The time at which the responsible person includes a document under paragraph (2) becomes the first point of marketing for that document—

(a) for the purposes of regulation 15(2); and

(b) until such time (if any) as a further first point of marketing arises under regulation 3(4), Part 4 or this Part.

[3603]

NOTES

Commencement: 2 July 2007.

[22A Updating of sustainability information for new homes

(1) If the property is not finished before or at the first point of marketing, and becomes finished after that time, the responsible person must replace any interim sustainability certificate included in the pack with—

(a) a sustainability certificate if a post-construction assessment of the property has taken place; or

(b) a nil-rated certificate if no such assessment has taken place.

(2) The document required to be included in the pack—

(a) under paragraph (1)(a) must be so included before the end of the period of 21 days starting with the day on which the post-construction assessment takes place; or

(b) under paragraph (1)(b) must be so included before the end of the period of 7 days starting with the day on which the property is finished.

(3) The responsible person may at any time replace a nil-rated certificate—

(a) with a sustainability certificate, where the property is finished; or

(b) with an interim sustainability certificate, where the property is not finished.

(4) In this regulation, "finished" and "post-construction assessment" have the same meaning as in paragraph 1 of Schedule 2A.]

[3603A]

NOTES

Commencement: 31 March 2008.
Inserted by SI 2008/572, reg 3(f).

23 Updating of authorised pack documents

(1) This regulation applies to any document included in a home information pack under regulation 9 (including that regulation as modified by [regulations 10 and 10A]).

(2) A responsible person—

(a) may include an amended document or further version in the pack; and

(b) may remove such documents as have been wholly superseded by a document or version included under sub-paragraph (a).

(3) The time at which the responsible person includes the amended document or further version under paragraph (2)(a) becomes the first point of marketing for that document—

(a) for the purposes of any provision of these Regulations that requires the age or currency of a pack document to be determined by reference to a period preceding the first point of marketing; and

(b) until such time (if any) as a further first point of marketing arises under regulation 3(4), Part 4 or this Part.

[3604]

NOTES

Commencement: 2 July 2007.

Para (1): words in square brackets substituted by SI 2007/3301, reg 2(2)(a).

24 Seller's check of the home information pack

If he is not the seller, the responsible person must provide the seller with a copy of any of the pack documents which the seller has requested him to provide for the purposes of ensuring the accuracy of the home information pack.

[3605]

NOTES

Commencement: 2 July 2007.

PART 6
EXCEPTIONS

25 Meaning of "non-residential premises"

(1) In this Part, "non-residential premises" includes—

(a) premises where the most recent use of the premises is or was primarily non-residential; and

(b) any dwelling-house where—

(i) it is clear from the manner in which it is marketed that it is due to be converted for primarily non-residential use by the time its sale is completed; and

(ii) all the relevant planning permissions and listed building consents exist in relation to the conversion.

(2) For the purposes of this Part, where a question arises as to whether premises are—

(a) non-residential premises; or

(b) residential property by virtue of being ancillary land to a dwelling-house,

the premises may be treated as non-residential premises if the conditions in paragraph (3) are met.

(3) The conditions referred to in paragraph (2) are that—

(a) the total area of the land is 5 hectares or more; and

(b) the most recent use of the land is or was primarily for one or more of the following purposes—

(i) horticulture or cultivation;

(ii) the breeding or keeping of animals or livestock; or

(iii) as grazing land or woodlands.

[3606]

NOTES

Commencement: 2 July 2007.

26 Exclusion from meaning of "non-residential premises"

In this Part, "non-residential premises" do not include—

(a) premises due to be converted to a dwelling-house by the time the sale of the property interest is complete; or

(b) a dwelling-house or a building ancillary to a dwelling-house used for either or both of the following purposes—

(i) letting under a lease; or

(ii) home working.

[3607]

NOTES

Commencement: 2 July 2007.

27 Exception for seasonal and holiday accommodation

The duties under sections 155 to 159 of the 2004 Act do not apply in relation to a property where—

(a) the dwelling-house which is or forms part of the property is subject to a condition imposed under section 72(1)(a) of the Town and Country Planning Act 1990 regulating the use of the dwelling-house to either or both of the following—

(i) occupation for less than 11 months in any 12 month period; or

(ii) use only for holiday accommodation; and

(b) that regulation of the use of the dwelling-house is clear from the manner in which the property is marketed.

[3608]

NOTES

Commencement: 2 July 2007.

28 Exception for mixed sales

The duties under sections 155 to 159 of the 2004 Act do not apply in relation to a property where—

(a) it is to be sold with one or more non-residential premises;

(b) the dwelling-house which is or forms part of the property is ancillary to those non-residential premises;

(c) at the time at which the first point of marketing would have occurred (were sections 155 to 159 of the 2004 Act to apply but for this regulation), the seller does not intend to accept an offer to buy the property in isolation from any one of those non-residential premises; and

(d) the seller's intention not to accept such an offer is clear from the manner in which the property is marketed.

[3609]

NOTES

Commencement: 2 July 2007.

29 Exception for dual use of a dwelling-house

The duties under sections 155 to 159 of the 2004 Act do not apply in relation to a property where—

(a) the dwelling-house which is or forms part of the property was most recently used for both residential and non-residential purposes; and

(b) the manner in which it is marketed suggests that it is suitable for—

(i) non-residential use; or

(ii) both residential and non-residential use.

[3610]

NOTES

Commencement: 2 July 2007.

30 Exception for portfolios of properties

(1) Subject to paragraph (2), the duties under sections 155 to 159 of the 2004 Act do not apply in relation to a property where—

(a) the dwelling-house which is or forms part of the property is to be sold with one or more other dwelling-houses;

(b) the other dwelling-houses mentioned in sub-paragraph (a)—

(i) . . .

(ii) are not dwelling-houses to which Part 5 of the 2004 Act applies by virtue of section 171(2) of that Act;

(c) at the time at which the first point of marketing would have occurred (were sections 155 to 159 of the 2004 Act to apply but for this regulation), the seller does not intend to accept an offer to buy any one of those dwelling-houses in isolation from another; and

(d) the seller's intention not to accept such an offer is clear from the manner in which the dwelling-houses are marketed.

(2) Paragraph (1) does not apply where the other dwelling-houses mentioned in sub-paragraph (a) are ancillary to the dwelling-house.

[3611]

NOTES

Commencement: 2 July 2007.
Para (1): sub-para (b)(i) revoked by SI 2008/3107, regs 2, 6.

31 Exception for unsafe properties

The duties under sections 155 to 159 of the 2004 Act do not apply in relation to a property—

(a) which is unoccupied;

(b) whose condition poses a serious risk to the health or safety of its potential occupants or visitors; and

(c) where the manner in which the property is marketed suggests it is unsuitable for occupation in its condition.

[3612]

NOTES

Commencement: 2 July 2007.

32 Exception for properties to be demolished

(1) The duties under sections 155 to 159 of the 2004 Act do not apply in relation to a property where—

(a) it is clear from the manner in which the property is marketed that—

(i) the dwelling-house which is or forms part of the property is suitable for demolition; and

(ii) the resulting site is suitable for re-development;

(b) all the relevant planning permissions, listed building consents; and conservation area consents exist in relation to the demolition; and

(c) in relation to the re-development—

(i) either outline planning permission or planning permission exists, or both; and

(ii) where relevant, listed building consent exists.

(2) In paragraph (1)(c)(i), "outline planning permission" has the same meaning as in article 1(2) of the Town and Country Planning (General Development Procedure) Order 1995.

[3613]

NOTES

Commencement: 2 July 2007.

33 Exception—properties marketed before the commencement date

(1) In this regulation, "commencement date" means the date appointed by the Secretary of State for the coming into force of sections 155(1), 156(1) and 159(2) of the 2004 Act in relation to the property.

(2) This regulation applies in relation to a property where—

(a) the property is put on the market by or on behalf of the seller before the commencement date;

(b) action taken at any time during the period starting with 1st June 2006 and ending before the commencement date by or on behalf of the seller, made public the fact that the property was on the market;

(c) such action was taken with the intention of selling the property before the commencement date; and

(d) such action was sustained to a reasonable extent after it was put on the market, during the period starting with 1st June 2006 and ending before the commencement date.

(3) A person is not a responsible person in relation to a property to which this regulation applies, by virtue of action taken on or after the commencement date, by or on behalf of the seller, which makes public the fact that the property is on the market.

(4) The duties under sections 155 to 159 of the 2004 Act do not apply in relation to a property to which this regulation applies, which is put back on the market on or after the commencement date—

(a) after the seller had accepted an offer to buy the property; and

(b) within 28 days of that offer being withdrawn or its acceptance repudiated.

[3614]

NOTES

Commencement: 2 July 2007.

34 Exception—first day marketing during a temporary period

(1) In the circumstances set out in paragraph (2) and subject to paragraph (3), the duties under sections 155 to 159 of the 2004 Act do not apply in relation to a property until the responsible person has in his possession or under his control (where they would otherwise be required by regulation 8)—

(a) an energy performance certificate relevant to the property and its accompanying recommendation report; or

(b) a predicted energy assessment relevant to the property complying with Schedule 2.

(2) The circumstances referred to in paragraph (1) are that—

(a) the property is put on the market by or on behalf of the seller before [6th April 2009];

(b) requests for all the required documents are delivered before the property is put on the market; and

(c) those requests comply with regulation 18(1).

(3) The exception described in paragraph (1) does not apply unless the responsible person also satisfies the following conditions—

(a) that where it is reasonable to expect that the responsible person can obtain a required document before the property is put on the market, he uses all reasonable efforts to obtain the document before then;

(b) that where he believes on reasonable grounds that he is unlikely to obtain all the required documents by the end of the period of 28 days starting with the date on which the property is put on the market, he uses all reasonable efforts to obtain the documents before then;

(c) that where sub-paragraphs (a) and (b) do not apply or he cannot obtain all the required documents in accordance with those provisions, he continues to use all reasonable efforts to obtain them.

(4) In this regulation—

(a) "responsible person" means the person who would be the responsible person if the duties under sections 155 to 159 of the 2004 Act applied;

(b) "required documents" means the documents that would be required under regulation 8 if sections 155 to 159 of the 2004 Act applied; and

(c) the day a request for a document is delivered shall be construed in accordance with regulation 19.

(5) Once the duties under sections 155 to 159 of the 2004 Act apply, the point at which the property is put on the market is the first point of marketing for that document—

(a) for the purposes of regulation 17(1) and (2) (documents required within 28 days of first point of marketing);

(b) for the purposes of any provision of these Regulations that requires the age or currency of a pack document to be determined by reference to a period preceding the first point of marketing; and

(c) until such time (if any) as a further first point of marketing arises under regulation 3(4), Part 4 or Part 5.

[3615]

NOTES

Commencement: 2 July 2007.
Para (2): in sub-para (a) words in square brackets substituted by SI 2008/3107, regs 2, 5(ii).

[34A Exception—transitional measure relating to regulation 8(ca) and (cb)

Regulation 8(ca) and (cb) do not apply to properties in relation to which any of the following documents have been received by a local authority before 1st May 2008—

(a) a notice given under regulation 12(2A)(a) of the Building Regulations 2000 (building notices);

(b) documents deposited under regulation 12(2A)(b) of those Regulations (full plans); or

(c) a notice given under section 47(1)(a) of the Building Act 1984 (initial notices).]

[3615A]

NOTES

Commencement: 31 March 2008.
Inserted by SI 2008/572, reg 3(g).

PART 7
ENFORCEMENT

35 Amount of penalty charge

The amount of a penalty charge specified in a notice given to a person under section 168 of the 2004 Act (penalty charge notices) shall be £200.

[3616]

NOTES

Commencement: 2 July 2007.

36 Exclusion of penalty charge for content of pack documents

Section 168(1)(a) of the 2004 Act does not apply to a breach of a duty under section 155(1) or 159(2) of that Act to the extent that—

(a) the content of a pack document, other than the home information pack index and the sale statement, fails to comply with any requirement of these Regulations; and

(b) the responsible person believes on reasonable grounds that the document does comply with that requirement.

[3617]

NOTES

Commencement: 2 July 2007.

PART 8
APPROVED CERTIFICATION SCHEMES

37 Approval of certification schemes

The Secretary of State shall approve one or more certification schemes, but before doing so must be satisfied that the scheme contains appropriate provision—

(a) for ensuring that its members are fit and proper persons who are qualified (by their education, training and experience) to produce home condition reports;
(b) for ensuring that its members have in force suitable indemnity insurance;
(c) for facilitating the resolution of complaints against its members;
(d) for requiring home condition reports made by its members to be entered onto the register kept pursuant to Part 9;
(e) for the keeping of a public register of its members; and
(f) for requiring all members of all certification schemes as have been approved, to make home condition reports using a standard form for the type of dwelling-house which is or forms part of the property, which—
    (i) includes a statement of the procedures for the resolution of complaints against members;
    (ii) includes a statement of such procedures as are maintained by the scheme for rectifying inaccuracies in a particular home condition report; and
    (iii) includes a numerical scale for rating the conditions within the property.

[3618]

NOTES

Commencement: 2 July 2007.

38 Terms of approved certification schemes

An approved certification scheme must contain provision—

(a) for ensuring that its objects and activities are compatible with protecting, promoting and facilitating the reliability and trustworthiness of home condition reports and home inspectors, with particular reference to potential and actual buyers, sellers and mortgage lenders of residential properties;
(b) for ensuring that the scheme produces and publishes a code as regards the conduct required of its members;
(c) for the conduct of inspections of residential properties by its members; and
(d) for ensuring that its members complete home condition reports complying with Schedule 9 using the standard form described in regulation 37(f).

[3619]

NOTES

Commencement: 2 July 2007.

39 Withdrawal of approval from certification schemes

The Secretary of State may withdraw approval from one or more certification schemes—

(a) with immediate effect; or
(b) with written notice—
    (i) with effect from a date specified in the notice; or
    (ii) temporarily for a period specified in the notice.

[3620]

NOTES

Commencement: 2 July 2007.

PART 9
HOME CONDITION REPORT REGISTER

CHAPTER 1
INTERPRETATION

40 Interpretation of this Part

(1) In this Part—

"agent" includes a person who—

(a) provides advice to another in a professional capacity; or
(b) acts on behalf of another with their authority;

"automated valuation supplier" means a person who carries out valuations of properties for the purposes of their sale other than by means of a visual inspection of the property;

"keeper of the register" means the Secretary of State or persons keeping the register or any part of the register on behalf of the Secretary of State;

"primary disclosure" means one or more of the following disclosures—

(a) an inspection of the register or a home condition report entered onto the register;
(b) the taking or giving of electronic or paper copies of the register or a home condition report entered onto the register; or
(c) the giving of information contained in or derived from the register or a home condition report entered onto the register;

"report reference number" means the number assigned to a home condition report in accordance with regulation 41;

"request" includes an electronic or automated request;

"register" means the register of home condition reports described in section 165 of the 2004 Act and further described in this Part, and includes parts of the register;

"secondary disclosure" means a disclosure of a home condition report or its contents where that information has been obtained by virtue of a primary disclosure; and

"seller" does not include former sellers.

(2) In this Part, references to a home condition report include—

(a) part of a home condition report; and
(b) a summary or explanation of a home condition report.

(3) In this Part, references to the obtaining, keeping or storing of a document or information include the obtaining, keeping or storing of such a document or information in any form.

(4) In this Part, a disclosure includes—

(a) a primary or secondary disclosure; and
(b) leaving or storing information in a place where it may be visible to another person.

[3621]

NOTES

Commencement: 2 July 2007.

CHAPTER 2
ARRANGEMENTS FOR KEEPING THE REGISTER

41 Registration of home condition reports

Each home condition report entered onto the register—

(a) shall be registered under a report reference number; and
(b) shall not be altered once so registered.

[3622]

NOTES

Commencement: 2 July 2007.

42 Retention of home condition reports

(1) Subject to paragraph (2), a home condition report entered onto the register must be cancelled from the register in the event that a person operating an approved certification scheme informs the keeper of the register that there is an inaccuracy in the report.

(2) Except in the circumstances described in paragraph (1), a home condition report entered onto the register must be kept on the register for no less than 15 years from the date on which it is entered onto the register.

[3623]

NOTES

Commencement: 2 July 2007.

43 Restrictions on disclosure by the keeper of the register in pursuance of a seller's instructions

(1) This regulation applies to home condition reports prepared for the purposes of the sale of the property interest by the seller.

(2) A home inspector may inform the keeper of the register in writing, pursuant to the seller's instruction, that the seller does not wish the keeper to make a primary disclosure of a home condition report to which this regulation applies, to—

(a) all persons; or
(b) all mortgage lenders or automated valuation suppliers.

(3) Nothing in this Part authorises the primary disclosure of a home condition report in contravention of such an instruction.

[3624]

NOTES
Commencement: 2 July 2007.

44 Other registers

For the purposes of these Regulations and section 165 of the 2004 Act—
(a) any other archive of home condition reports, or information obtained from a home condition report, is derived from the register whether or not obtained directly from the keeper of the register; and
(b) the restrictions on disclosures or the permitted disclosures set out in Chapters 3 and 4 of this Part shall apply—
(i) to such archives derived from the register as they apply to the register; and
(ii) to the keeper of such an archive as they apply to the keeper of the register.

[3625]

NOTES
Commencement: 2 July 2007.

CHAPTER 3
DISCLOSURE—GENERAL PROVISIONS

45 Section 157 conditions

Nothing in this Part authorises a disclosure where the person who proposes to make the disclosure is aware that a condition exists under section 157(3) of the 2004 Act which prohibits the proposed disclosure.

[3626]

NOTES
Commencement: 2 July 2007.

46 Suspicion of unauthorised use

Nothing in this Part authorises a disclosure where the person who proposes to make a disclosure or requested to make a disclosure, believes that it is likely to result in a disclosure not authorised by this Part.

[3627]

NOTES
Commencement: 2 July 2007.

47 Commercial use by the keeper of the register

Nothing in this Part authorises the commercial use of the register by the keeper of the register, otherwise than in accordance with the provisions of this Part.

[3628]

NOTES
Commencement: 2 July 2007.

48 Responsibility for proving purposes of disclosure

Where this Part refers to the purposes of a disclosure, it shall be the responsibility of the person seeking the disclosure to prove those purposes to the satisfaction of the person from whom disclosure is sought.

[3629]

NOTES
Commencement: 2 July 2007.

49 Responsibility for proving agency

Where this Part authorises the disclosure to the agent of a person, it shall be the responsibility of the purported agent to prove the existence of an agency arrangement to the satisfaction of the person from whom the disclosure is sought.

[3630]

NOTES

Commencement: 2 July 2007.

50 Possession of report reference number

(1) Before a primary disclosure authorised by this Part is made, the keeper of the register may require the person seeking the disclosure to provide the relevant report reference number.

(2) The keeper of the register may presume that any person who is in possession of a report reference number is lawfully in possession of such a number, unless the contrary is proved.

[3631]

NOTES

Commencement: 2 July 2007.

CHAPTER 4
AUTHORISED DISCLOSURES

51 Internal processing of information

Any person may make a primary or secondary disclosure, where necessary for the purposes of processing information—

(a) within a body of persons corporate or unincorporate;
(b) between principal and agent;
(c) between an employer and employee; or
(d) in order to manage the register.

[3632]

NOTES

Commencement: 2 July 2007.

52 Sellers and their agents

(1) The keeper of the register may make a primary disclosure to a seller or his agent.

(2) Before making a disclosure in accordance with paragraph (1), the keeper of the register may require the person seeking that disclosure to prove that he is the seller or his agent.

(3) Where the home condition report to be disclosed was entered onto the register for the purposes of the sale of the property interest by that seller—

(a) a seller may make a secondary disclosure to any person; and
(b) the seller's agent may make a secondary disclosure to a person only if the seller has authorised the agent to make that disclosure.

[3633]

NOTES

Commencement: 2 July 2007.

53 Potential buyers and their advisers

(1) The keeper of the register may make a primary disclosure to an actual or potential buyer or his agent.

(2) Before making a disclosure in accordance with paragraph (1), the keeper of the register may require the person seeking that disclosure to prove one or more of the following matters—

(a) that he is an actual or potential buyer or his agent;
(b) that the request relates to a home condition report for a property the buyer is genuinely interested in buying; or
(c) that the request is made for the purposes of—
  (i) checking the authenticity of a home condition report; or
  (ii) checking whether any home condition reports not included in the home information pack have been completed for the purposes of the sale of the property interest by the seller.

[3634]

NOTES
Commencement: 2 July 2007.

54 Mortgage lenders or automated valuation suppliers

(1) The keeper of the register may make a primary disclosure to a mortgage lender, an automated valuation supplier or their agents.

(2) Before making a disclosure in accordance with paragraph (1), the keeper of the register may require the person seeking that disclosure to prove one or more of the following matters—

(a) that they are a mortgage lender, automated valuation supplier or their agent;
(b) that the request relates to a report for a property that the mortgage lender or automated valuation supplier has been asked to consider by or on behalf of an actual or potential buyer; or
(c) that the request is made for the purposes of—
  (i) checking the authenticity of that report;
  (ii) valuing the property; or
  (iii) appraising the suitability of the property as security for mortgage or loan.

[3635]

NOTES
Commencement: 2 July 2007.

55 Approved certification schemes or complaints against home inspectors

(1) The keeper of the register may make a primary disclosure to a person operating an approved certification scheme or a person dealing with complaints against home inspectors.

(2) Before making a disclosure in accordance with paragraph (1), the keeper of the register may require the person seeking that disclosure to prove one or more of the following matters—

(a) that they operate an approved certification scheme or deal with complaints against home inspectors;
(b) that the request is made for the purposes of—
  (i) any complaint or disciplinary procedure relating to a home inspector; or
  (ii) monitoring or assessing the work of home inspectors; or
(c) that any request made by a person operating an approved certification scheme is made for the purposes of replacing archives of home condition reports prepared by its members, which—
  (i) have been destroyed; and
  (ii) were kept (and will be kept) for monitoring or assessing the work of members of that scheme.

[3636]

NOTES
Commencement: 2 July 2007.

56 Enforcement officers

(1) The keeper of the register may make a primary disclosure to an authorised officer of an enforcement authority.

(2) Before making a disclosure in accordance with paragraph (1), the keeper of the register may require the person seeking that disclosure to prove one or more of the following matters—

(a) that he is an authorised officer of an enforcement authority;
(b) that the request is made for the purposes of the enforcement by enforcement authorities of—
  (i) the duties under sections 155 to 159 and 167(4) of the 2004 Act; or
  (ii) any duty imposed under section 172(1) of that Act.

[3637]

NOTES
Commencement: 2 July 2007.

57 Office of Fair Trading

(1) The keeper of the register may make a primary disclosure to the Office of Fair Trading.

(2) Before making a disclosure in accordance with paragraph (1) in response to a request, the keeper of the register may require the Office of Fair Trading to prove that the request is made for the purposes of the enforcement by the Office of Fair Trading of its functions under the Estate Agents Act 1979 or the 2004 Act.

[3638]

NOTES
Commencement: 2 July 2007.

58 Information from which no particular property is identifiable

Any person may make a primary or secondary disclosure where no particular property would be identifiable in doing so.

[3639]

NOTES
Commencement: 2 July 2007.

59 Disclosures for the purposes of the 2004 Act or these Regulations

Any person may make a primary or secondary disclosure for the purposes of—

(a) section 156(1), (2) and (11) of the 2004 Act; or
(b) regulations 5, 6, 9(a) and 24.

[3640]

NOTES
Commencement: 2 July 2007.

60 Prevention of crime

Any person may make a primary or secondary disclosure for the purposes of or to facilitate—

(a) the prevention or detection of crime; or
(b) the apprehension or prosecution of offenders.

[3641]

NOTES
Commencement: 2 July 2007.

61 Legal proceedings and court orders

Any person may make a primary or secondary disclosure for the purposes of—

(a) the establishment, exercise or defence of legal rights; or
(b) an order of a court.

[3642]

NOTES
Commencement: 2 July 2007.

CHAPTER 5
FEES

62 Fees

(1) The fee prescribed under section 165(3) of the 2004 Act is £1.15 (one pound and fifteen pence).

(2) No fee may be charged for a primary disclosure.

[3643]

NOTES
Commencement: 2 July 2007.

SCHEDULE 1
HOME INFORMATION PACK INDEX

regulation 8(a)

Required matters

1. A home information pack index must—
   (a) display prominently the title, "Home Information Pack Index";
   (b) contain the address or proposed address (which may include a plot number) of the property;
   (c) contain a list of all the documents included in the home information pack;
   (d) be revised whenever a document is included in or removed from the pack;
   (e) where regulation 16, 17 or 20 apply, indicate—
      (i) that a document otherwise required by these Regulations is missing from the pack;

PART II STATUTORY INSTRUMENTS

(ii) specify which document it is; and
(iii) the reason why it is missing; and
(f) where regulation 16 or regulation 17(2)(e) apply, indicate—
(i) such steps as are being taken to obtain the document;
(ii) the date by which the responsible person expects to obtain the document;
(iii) the reason for any delay which has occurred or is likely to occur to the date described in paragraph (ii); and
(iv) where paragraph (iii) applies, the further date by which the responsible person expects to obtain the document.

Authorised matters

2. A home information pack index may indicate where a particular pack document can be found in the home information pack.

[3644]

NOTES

Commencement: 2 July 2007.

SCHEDULE 2
PREDICTED ENERGY ASSESSMENT

regulation 8(c)

A predicted energy assessment must—
(a) display prominently the title "Predicted Energy Assessment";
(b) contain the following statement—

"This document is a Predicted Energy Assessment required to be included in a Home Information Pack for properties marketed when they are incomplete. It includes a predicted energy rating which might not represent the final energy rating of the property on completion. Once the property is completed, the Pack should be updated to include information about the energy performance of the completed property."

(c) contain the address or proposed address (which may include a plot number) of the property;
(d) be compiled otherwise than by a visual inspection of the property;
(e) contain the asset rating within the meaning given by regulation 2(1) of the Energy Performance of Buildings (Certificates and Inspections) (England and Wales) Regulations 2007 which is—
(i) predicted for the building;
(ii) based on its plans and specifications; and
(iii) expressed in a way approved by the Secretary of State under regulation 17A of the Building Regulations 2000; and
(f) contain an explanation of that rating.

[3645]

NOTES

Commencement: 2 July 2007.

[SCHEDULE 2A
SUSTAINABILITY INFORMATION FOR NEW HOMES

regulation 8(ca) and 8(cb

Interpretation

1. In this Schedule—

"assessment" means an assessment as to sustainability, made in accordance with the Code for Sustainable Homes, using the rating system set out in that Code;

"Code Assessor" means a person trained and certified as such, pursuant to the terms of a contract entered into on 12th December 2006 between the Secretary of State and Building Research Establishment Limited (together with affiliate companies);

"Code for Sustainable Homes" means the standards and processes for determining sustainability, set out in the document, "The Code for Sustainable Homes: Setting the Sustainability Standards for New Homes;"

"construction" and related words include any related demolition and any off-site activities relating to the construction or demolition;

"design stage assessment" means an assessment based on an inspection by a Code Assessor of the plans and specifications for the property;

"post-construction stage assessment" means an assessment based on a visit to the constructed property by a Code Assessor or to another representative property;

"sustainability" relates to the extent to which—

(a) the materials used in the property;
(b) other aspects of the design and construction of the property; and
(c) any services, fittings and equipment provided in, or in connection with the property,

further the sustainable design principles; and

"the sustainable design principles" are any of the following principles—

(a) ensuring the health, safety, welfare and convenience of persons in or about the property and of others who may be affected by the property or matters connected with it;
(b) furthering the efficient management of the property and of its construction;
(c) furthering energy efficiency;
(d) furthering the efficient use of water and minimising flood risk;
(e) furthering efficient waste management;
(f) furthering the protection or enhancement of the environment; and
(g) furthering the prevention or detection of crime.

Sustainability certificate

2.—(1) A sustainability certificate must—

(a) confirm that there has been a post-construction assessment of the property;
(b) contain a single star rating from a minimum of zero stars to a maximum of six stars, awarded by a Code Assessor as to the sustainability of the property under the Code for Sustainable Homes;
(c) contain an explanation of that rating;
(d) contain a certificate number;
(e) contain the date it is issued; and
(f) contain a percentage rating against categories relating to the sustainable design principles.

(2) A certificate prepared under this paragraph must be prepared by the Code Assessor based on his post-construction assessment of the property.

Interim sustainability certificate

3.—(1) An interim sustainability certificate must—

(a) confirm that there has been a design stage assessment of the designs for the property;
(b) contain a single star rating from a minimum of zero stars to a maximum of six stars, awarded by a Code Assessor as to the general sustainability of the plans and specifications for the property under the Code for Sustainable Homes;
(c) contain an explanation of that star rating;
(d) contain a certificate number;
(e) contain the date it is issued; and
(f) contain a percentage rating against categories relating to the sustainable design principles.

(2) A certificate prepared under this paragraph must be prepared by the Code Assessor based on a design stage assessment of the plans and specifications for the property.

Nil-rated certificate

4.—(1) A nil-rated certificate must be made in the form specified in the Code for Sustainable Homes, and must contain the matters specified in that form.

(2) A nil-rated certificate may be prepared by any person.]

[3645A]

NOTES

Commencement: 31 March 2008.
Inserted by SI 2008/572, reg 2(2).

SCHEDULE 3
SALE STATEMENT

regulation 8(d)

A sale statement must—

(a) display prominently the title "Sale Statement";
(b) contain the address or proposed address (which may include a plot number) of the property;
(c) state whether the property interest is—
  (i) a freehold estate other than a freehold estate in commonhold land;
  (ii) a freehold estate in commonhold land; or
  (iii) a leasehold interest;

PART II STATUTORY INSTRUMENTS

(d) state whether at the first point of marketing—
(i) the property interest is or includes the whole or part of a registered estate; or
(ii) the property interest is or includes the whole or part of an estate, the title to which is not entered in the register of title;
(e) contain the name of the seller, and state the capacity in which they are selling the property;
(f) state whether the property—
(i) is being sold entirely with vacant possession; or
(ii) is a property to which Part 5 of the 2004 Act applies by virtue of section 171(2) of that Act; and
(g) if it is a property to which Part 5 of the 2004 Act applies by virtue of section 171(2) of that Act, state the nature of any lack of vacant possession.

[3646]

NOTES
Commencement: 2 July 2007.

SCHEDULE 4
COMMONHOLD INFORMATION

regulation 8(g), 9(k) and 10(2)

Required commonhold documents

1.—(1) Subject to sub-paragraph (2), the documents referred to in regulation 8(g)(i) are—
(a) an official copy of such of the following documents as are kept by the Chief Land Registrar—
(i) the individual register and title plan relating to the common parts; and
(ii) the commonhold community statement referred to in that register;
(b) except where they are described in the commonhold community statement, such regulations or rules as are made for the purposes of managing the commonhold by—
(i) the commonhold association;
(ii) such managing agents as are appointed, or proposed for appointment by the commonhold association to manage the commonhold; or
(iii) such other persons as manage or are likely to manage the commonhold,
and their predecessors (if any); and
(c) the most recent requests for payment or financial contribution where made in respect of the property, relating to the 12 months preceding the first point of marketing, towards such of the following as are relevant to the property—
(i) commonhold assessment;
(ii) reserve funds;
(iii) insurance against damage for the common parts (if made separately to the requests relating to commonhold assessment included under sub-paragraph (i)); and
(iv) insurance for any person in respect of personal injury or death caused by or within the common parts (if made separately to the requests relating to commonhold assessment included under sub-paragraph (i)).

(2) Except for the documents specified in sub-paragraph (1)(a), the documents required by that sub-paragraph are only those which are in the seller's possession, under his control or to which he can reasonably be expected to have access, taking into account the enquiries that it would be reasonable to make of—
(a) the unit-holder (unless the seller is the unit-holder); and
(b) the persons described in sub-paragraph (1)(b) and their predecessors (if any).

Required commonhold information

2.—(1) Subject to sub-paragraph (2), the matters referred to in regulation 8(g)(ii) are—
(a) the names and addresses of—
(i) such managing agents as are appointed, or proposed for appointment by the commonhold association to manage the commonhold; and
(ii) such other persons as manage or are likely to manage the commonhold;
(b) such amendments as are proposed to the following—
(i) the commonhold community statement; and
(ii) the regulations or rules described in paragraph 1(1)(b); and
(c) a summary of such works as are being undertaken or proposed, affecting the property or the common parts.

(2) The information required by sub-paragraph (1) is only that which the seller can reasonably be expected to be aware of, taking into account the enquiries that it would be reasonable to make of—
(a) the unit-holder (unless the seller is the unit-holder); and

(b) the persons described in paragraph 1(1)(b) and their predecessors (if any).

Authorised commonhold information

3. The matters referred to in regulation 9(k) are—
   (a) the commonhold community statement;
   (b) the rights or obligations of the unit-holder under the commonhold community statement or otherwise, including whether the unit-holder has complied with such obligations;
   (c) the rights or obligations of the commonhold association under the commonhold community statement or otherwise, including whether it has complied with such obligations;
   (d) the commonhold association and any information that might affect the unit-holder's relationship with it;
   (e) any agent of the commonhold association or other manager of the property and any information that might affect the unit-holder's relationship with such persons;
   (f) the membership of the commonhold association;
   (g) the status or memorandum and articles of association of any company related to the management of the property or the commonhold;
   (h) any commonhold assessment payable for the property, including whether payments for such assessment are outstanding;
   (i) any reserve fund levy relating to the property or the commonhold, including whether payments for such levies are outstanding;
   (j) any planned or recent works relating to the property or the commonhold;
   (k) responsibility for insuring the property or the commonhold, including the terms of such insurance and whether payments relating to it are outstanding; and
   (l) any lease or licence relating to the property.

Creation of commonhold interests

4. The matters referred to in regulation 10(2)(e) are—
   (a) the terms of the commonhold community statement that will or is expected to apply in relation to the property interest once it has been registered as a freehold estate in commonhold land; and
   (b) estimates of the payment or financial contribution likely to be required of the unit-holder within 12 months of completion of the sale of the property interest towards—
      (i) commonhold assessment;
      (ii) reserve funds;
      (iii) insurance against damage for the common parts (if not to be included in contributions towards commonhold assessment); and
      (iv) insurance for any person in respect of personal injury or death caused by or within the common parts (if not to be included in contributions towards commonhold assessment).

[3647]

NOTES

Commencement: 2 July 2007.

SCHEDULE 5
LEASEHOLD INFORMATION

regulations 8(h), 9(l) and 10(3)

Required leasehold documents

1.—(1) Subject to sub-paragraph (2), the documents referred to in regulation 8(h)(i) are—
   (a) the lease in the form of—
      (i) an official copy;
      (ii) the original lease (or a copy of it in accordance with regulation 6); or
      (iii) an edited information document if, despite all reasonable efforts and enquiries by the responsible person, the lease can only be obtained by him in that form;
   (b)–(d) …

(2) …

[Authorised leasehold information

1A. The matters referred to in regulation 9(l) ("authorised leasehold information") are set out in paragraphs 2, 3 and 3A.]

…

2.—(1) [Authorised leasehold information includes]—
   (a) the names and addresses of—

PART II STATUTORY INSTRUMENTS

(i) the current lessor or proposed lessor;
(ii) such managing agents as are appointed or proposed for appointment by the lessor to manage the property; and
(iii) such other persons as manage or are likely to manage the property;

(b) such amendments as are proposed to the following—
(i) the lease; and
(ii) the regulations or rules described in paragraph 1(1)(b); and

(c) where section 20 of the Landlord and Tenant Act 1985 applies to any qualifying works or qualifying long term agreement in respect of the property, a summary of—
(i) such works or agreements in relation to which a relevant contribution (or any part of a relevant contribution) has not been paid by the first point of marketing;
(ii) the total or estimated total cost of such works or agreements;
(iii) the expected remaining relevant contribution of a lessee of the property;
(iv) the date or estimated date that such works or agreements will be concluded; and
(v) the date or estimated date that the remaining relevant contribution will be required of a lessee of the property.

(2) …

…

3. [Authorised leasehold information includes the following matters relating to interests, rights and obligations affecting the property,]—

(a) any lease of the property, [other than the lease which is a required document under paragraph 1,] including those that are superior or inferior to the property interest;
(b) any licence relating to the property;
(c) any freehold estate to which the lease relates including any proposals to buy a freehold interest relating to the property;
(d) the rights or obligations of the lessee under the lease or otherwise, including whether the lessee has complied with such obligations;
(e) the rights or obligations of the lessor under the lease or otherwise, including whether the lessor has complied with such obligations;
(f) the lessor of the property and any information that might affect the lessee's relationship with the lessor;
(g) any agent of the lessor or other manager of the property and any information that might affect the lessee's relationship with such persons;
(h) the membership or existence of any body of persons corporate or unincorporate which manages the property or building in which the property is situated;
(i) the status or memorandum and articles of association of any company related to the management of the property or building in which the property is situated;
(j) the rent payable for the property, including whether payments for such rent are outstanding;
(k) any service charges payable in respect of the property, including whether payments for such charges are outstanding;
(l) any reserve fund relating to the property for necessary works to it or the building in which the property is situated, including whether payments to such a fund are outstanding;
(m) any planned or recent works to the property or the building in which the property is situated; and
(n) any responsibility for insuring the property or the building in which the property is situated, including the terms of such insurance and whether payments relating to it are outstanding.

[3A. Authorised leasehold information also includes the following matters relating to the management of the property—

(a) such regulations or rules as are made for the purposes of managing the property by—
(i) the current lessor or proposed lessor;
(ii) such managing agents as are appointed or proposed for appointment by the lessor to manage the property; and
(iii) such other persons as manage or are likely to manage the property,

and their predecessors (if any);

(b) statements or summaries of service charges supplied in respect of the property under section 21 of the Landlord and Tenant Act 1985 or otherwise, and relating to the 36 months preceding the first point of marketing; and
(c) the most recent requests for payment or financial contribution where made in respect of the property, relating to the 12 months preceding the first point of marketing, towards such of the following as are relevant to the property—
(i) service charges;
(ii) ground rent;

(iii) insurance against damage for the building in which the property is situated (if made separately from the request relating to service charges included under sub-paragraph (i)); and

(iv) insurance for any person in respect of personal injury or death caused by or within the building in which the property is situated (if made separately from the request relating to service charges included under sub-paragraph (i)).]

Creation of leasehold interests

4. The matters referred to in regulation 10(3)(e) are—

(a) the terms of the lease that will or is expected to be granted in order to create the property interest; and

(b) estimates of the payment or financial contribution likely to be required of the lessee within 12 months of completion of the sale of the property interest towards—

(i) service charges;

(ii) ground rent;

(iii) insurance against damage for the building in which the property is situated (if not to be included in contributions towards service charges); and

(iv) insurance for any person in respect of personal injury or death caused by or within the building in which the property is situated (if not to be included in contributions towards service charges).

[3648]

NOTES

Commencement: 2 July 2007.

Para 1: sub-paras (1)(b)–(d), (2) revoked by SI 2008/3107, regs 2, 7(a).

Para 1A: inserted by SI 2008/3107, regs 2, 7(b).

Para 2: heading revoked by SI 2008/3107, regs 2, 7(b); in sub-para (1) words in square brackets substituted by SI 2008/3107, regs 2, 7(c); sub-para (2) revoked by SI 2008/3107, regs 2, 7(c).

Para 3: heading revoked by SI 2008/3107, regs 2, 7(c); in sub-para (1) words in square brackets substituted by SI 2008/3107, regs 2, 7(d).

Para 3A: inserted by SI 2008/3107, regs 2, 7(e).

SCHEDULE 6
GENERAL PROVISION ABOUT SEARCHES AND SEARCH REPORTS

regulations 8(j)(ii), 8(k) 8(l), 9(m) and 9(n)

PART 1
ALL SEARCH REPORTS (OTHER THAN OFFICIAL SEARCH CERTIFICATE OF THE LOCAL LAND CHARGES REGISTER)

General requirements

1. A search report must contain the following information—

(a) the address of the premises in respect of which the search is conducted;

(b) a statement of whether the following persons have any personal or business relationship with any person involved in the sale of the property (if such a relationship exists)—

(i) a person who conducted the search; and

(ii) a person who prepared the search report;

(c) such enquiries as formed the basis of the search and the information sought;

(d) subject to paragraph 3, the results of the search;

(e) the date on which the search was completed;

(f) a description of the records searched, and the name and address of the person who holds them;

(g) if the records searched are derived from other records, a description of those other records and the name and address of the person who holds them;

(h) a description of how relevant documents can be obtained (if they are not included in the home information pack under regulation 9(o) or otherwise);

(i) the names and addresses of the parties to the arrangements—

(i) under which the search was conducted; and

(ii) if different, under which the search report was prepared;

(j) the name of the persons liable in each of the following events—

(i) any negligent or incorrect entry in the records searched;

(ii) any negligent or incorrect interpretation of the records searched; and

(iii) any negligent or incorrect recording of that interpretation in the search report;

(k) a description of such complaints or redress procedures as exist in relation to the report; and

(l) the terms on which the report is made, including—

(i) the terms required by paragraphs 5, 6 and 7; and

(ii) the names of the persons who are liable to make the payments described in paragraphs 4(g), 4(h) 7(b) and 7(c).

Additional search information

2. A search report complying with this Part may contain or be accompanied by documents containing all or any of the following information—

(a) information which identifies the search or the search report;

(b) information which explains the results of the search, the search report or the enquiries or matters to which the results of the search relate; and

(c) information which identifies services or features local to the property, but not including any advertising or marketing information about them.

Unavailable search results

3. Subject to paragraph 4, the results of the search included in a search report under paragraph 1(d) must not fail to answer such enquiries as formed the basis of the search, nor fail to give the information originally sought, unless—

(a) a record from which the answer or result could be deduced is not held by or obtainable under any circumstances from—

(i) a local authority in the case of a search report required by regulation 8(j)(ii) (personal search of the local land charges register) or 8(k) (local enquiries), or authorised by regulation 9(m)(i) (supplementary local enquiries); or

(ii) any person in the case of any other search report, and

(b) a statement is also included in the search report indicating—

(i) that a particular result is not included; and

(ii) the reason under sub-paragraph (a) for failing to include the result.

[3649]

NOTES

Commencement: 2 July 2007.

PART 2
SPECIFIC REQUIRED SEARCH REPORTS

Access to local authority records

4. The results of the search included in the search report required by regulation 8(k) (local enquiries) may fail to answer the enquiries set out in Part 2 of Schedule 7, in the following circumstances—

(a) the first point of marketing falls before [6th April 2009] (except where a further first point of marketing arises under regulation 3(4) or Part 5);

(b) a record from which the answer or result could be deduced is held by a local authority;

(c) that local authority has a policy of not allowing other persons to inspect such records;

(d) a local authority is not requested to provide the search report;

(e) any enquiries not answered are the subject of a contract of insurance against the liabilities that if they had been answered, they would have affected—

(i) an actual buyer's decision to buy the property; or

(ii) the price an actual or potential buyer would be prepared to pay for it,

and result in financial loss;

(f) such a contract of insurance is effected by, and to be carried out by persons so authorised for the purposes of the Financial Services and Markets Act 2000;

(g) any liability for financial loss arising under paragraph (e) will be met by financial compensation to be paid by a person (other than the persons described in paragraph 6(a)(i) to (iii)) who is—

(i) a party to the contract of insurance; or

(ii) another person involved in the sale of the property; and

(h) such financial compensation is paid by a person mentioned in sub-paragraph (f) if any person mentioned in sub-paragraph (g) fails to pay it (or no longer exists and has no successor); and

(i) the search report—

(i) contains a description of the terms and effect of the insurance described in this paragraph; and

(ii) identifies which enquiries have not been answered and in respect of which the insurance has been obtained.

Terms for the preparation of required searches

5. Any person may prepare a report required by regulation 8(j)(ii) (personal search of the local land charges register), 8(k) (local enquiries) or 8(l) (drainage and water enquiries), but must do so on the following terms without exclusion or limitation—
   (a) that the search report will be prepared with reasonable care and skill; and
   (b) that a responsible person may copy or issue a copy of the report for the purposes of complying with any of the following provisions—
      (i) regulations 5, 6, 8(j)(ii), 8(k), 8(l) and 24; and
      (ii) section 156(1), (2) and (11) of the 2004 Act.

Third party contractual rights in relation to search reports

6. The person preparing a search report required by regulation 8(j)(ii) (personal search of the local land charges register), 8(k) (local enquiries) or 8(l) (drainage and water enquiries) must do so on terms enabling the provisions of the contract under which the report is prepared—
   (a) to be enforced in relation to the terms mentioned in paragraph 5, by—
      (i) the seller;
      (ii) a potential or actual buyer of the property interest; and
      (iii) a mortgage lender in respect of the property interest; and
   (b) to be enforced by such persons in their own right, whether or not they are a party to such a contract.

Insurance cover for third party contractual rights

7. The person preparing the search reports required by regulation 8(k) (local enquiries) or 8(l) (drainage and water enquiries) must do so on terms ensuring that—
   (a) any liability of any type arising under paragraph 6 is the subject of a contract of insurance against such risk effected by, and to be carried out by persons so authorised for the purposes of the Financial Services and Markets Act 2000;
   (b) any liability for financial loss arising under paragraph 6 will be met by financial compensation to be paid by a person (other than the persons described in paragraph 6(a)(i) to (iii)) who is—
      (i) a party to the contract of insurance; or
      (ii) another person involved in the sale of the property; and
   (c) such financial compensation is paid by a person mentioned in sub-paragraph (a), if any person mentioned in sub-paragraph (b) fails to pay it (or no longer exists and has no successor).

Permitted limit on liability for financial loss

8. The amount of the financial compensation referred to in paragraphs 4(g) and 7(b) may be limited to the amount the potential or actual buyer reasonably believed to be the value of the property interest—
   (a) at the time the search report was completed; and
   (b) for the purposes of residential use.

Inclusion of additional or more favourable terms for required search reports

9. A person may prepare the search reports required by regulation 8(j)(ii) (personal search of the local land charges register), 8(k) (local enquiries) or 8(l) (drainage and water enquiries) on any of the following terms—
   (a) terms additional to those described in paragraphs 5, 6 and 7 (without excluding or limiting them); and
   (b) terms more favourable to—
      (i) the seller;
      (ii) a potential or actual buyer of the property interest; or
      (iii) a mortgage lender in respect of the property interest,
   than those described in paragraphs 5, 6 and 7.

Less favourable terms

10. Any search report which contains terms less favourable to—
   (a) the seller;
   (b) a potential or actual buyer of the property interest; or
   (c) a mortgage lender in respect of the property interest,

than those required by this Part of this Schedule is not made in accordance with this Schedule.

Required searches by another name

11. This Schedule applies in relation to pack documents which contain the enquiries required (or enquiries to like effect) to be contained in a search report which would be included under regulation 8(j)(ii), 8(k) or 8(l), regardless of whether one or more of the following has occurred—

(a) they are included under regulation 9(m), Schedule 10 or another provision of these Regulations; or

(b) they are described as a local land charges search, local enquiries or drainage and water enquiries, or given similar descriptions.

[3650]

NOTES

Commencement: 2 July 2007.

Para 4: in sub-para (a) words in square brackets substituted by SI 2008/3107, regs 2, 5(iii).

SCHEDULE 7
LOCAL ENQUIRIES

regulation 8(k)

PART 1
GENERAL

Interpretation

1.—(1) In this Schedule—

"adoption" and "adopted" relate to an agreement made under section 38 of the Highways Act 1980;

"bond" means an indemnity or guarantee which is sought by a local authority as to the financial security of a developer;

"bond waiver" means an agreement that a local authority will not seek a bond from a developer;

"breach of condition notice" means a notice served under section 187A of the Town and Country Planning Act 1990;

"building preservation notice" means a notice served under section 3 of the Planning (Listed Buildings and Conservation Areas) Act 1990;

"building regulations approvals" means—

(a) plans passed under section 16 of the Building Act 1984; or

(b) a certificate given under regulation 21(6) of the Building Regulations 2000 (regularisation certificates);

"building regulations completion certificate" means a certificate given under regulation 17(1) of the Building Regulations 2000;

"building regulations" has the same meaning as in section 122 of the Building Act 1984;

"certificate of lawfulness of existing use or development" means a certificate issued under section 191(4) of the Town and Country Planning Act 1990;

"certificate of lawfulness of proposed use or development" means a certificate issued under section 191(2) of the Town and Country Planning Act 1990;

"competent person self-certification scheme" means a scheme under whose provisions building work which consists only of work of a type described in column 1 of the Table in Schedule 2A to the Building Regulations 2000 is carried out by a person who is described in the corresponding entry in column 2 of that Table;

"compulsory purchase order with a direction for minimum compensation" means an order confirmed or made under section 50(1) of the Planning (Listed Buildings and Conservation Areas) Act 1990;

"conservation area" means either or both of the following—

(a) an area designated under section 69 of the Planning (Listed Buildings and Conservation Areas) Act 1990; or

(b) an area so designated before 31st August 1974 by other means;

"contaminated land notice" means a notice given under section 78B(3) of the Environmental Protection Act 1990;

"cycle track" means a way constituting or comprised in a highway, being a way over which the public have the following, but no other, rights of way, that is to say, a right of way on pedal cycles (other than pedal cycles which are motor vehicles within the meaning of the Road Traffic Act 1988) with or without a right of way on foot;

"development plan" must be construed in accordance with section 38 of the Planning and Compulsory Purchase Act 2004;

"direction restricting permitted development" means a direction given under article 4 of the Town and Country Planning (General Permitted Development) Order 1995;

"drainage agreement" means an agreement made under section 22(2) of the Building Act 1984;

"enforcement notice" means a notice issued under section 172 of the Town and Country Planning Act 1990;

"footpath" means a highway over which the public have a right of way on foot only, not being a footway;

"footway" means a way comprised in a highway which also comprises a carriageway, being a way over which the public have a right of way on foot only;

"frontager" means the owner or occupier of premises that abut a road, footway or footpath;

"highway maintainable at public expense" means a highway which by virtue of section 36 of the Highways Act 1980, or any other enactment, is a highway which for the purposes of that Act, is a highway maintainable at the public expense;

"improvement" means the doing of any act under powers conferred by Part 5 of the Highways Act 1980 and includes the erection, maintenance, alteration and removal of traffic signs, and the freeing of a highway or road-ferry from tolls;

"land required for public purposes" means land to which paragraphs 5 and 6 of Schedule 13 to the Town and Country Planning Act 1990 relate;

"land to be acquired for road works" means land to be acquired by a public authority under any of sections 239 to 246 of the Highways Act 1980;

"listed building enforcement notice" means a notice issued under section 38 of the Planning (Listed Buildings and Conservation Areas) Act 1990;

"listed building repairs notice" means a notice served under section 48 of the Planning (Listed Buildings and Conservation Areas) Act 1990;

"mini-roundabout" means a roundabout consisting of a level or raised circular marking of a diameter of four metres or less;

"order requiring discontinuance of use or alteration or removal of buildings or works" means an order made under section 102 of the Town and Country Planning Act 1990;

"order revoking or modifying planning permission" means an order made under section 97 of the Town and Country Planning Act 1990;

"planning agreement" means an agreement made under section 106 of the Town and Country Planning Act 1990, as existing at any time before the enactment of the Planning and Compulsory Purchase Act 2004;

"planning contravention notice" means a notice served under section 171C of the Town and Country Planning Act 1990;

"planning contribution" means a contribution to be made pursuant to any regulations made under sections 46 to 48 of the Planning and Compulsory Purchase Act 2004;

"remediation notice" means a notice served under section 78E of the Environmental Protection Act 1990;

"railway" means a system of transport employing parallel rails which—

(a) provide support and guidance for vehicles carried on flanged wheels; and

(b) form a track which either is of a gauge of at least 350 millimetres or crosses a carriageway (whether or not on the same level),

but does not include a tramway;

"road hump" means an artificial hump in or on the surface of the highway which is designed to control the speed of vehicles, and references to a road hump include references to any other works (including signs or lighting) required in connection with such a hump;

"special road" means a highway, or a proposed highway, which is a special road in accordance with section 16 of the Highways Act 1980;

"stop notice" means a notice served under section 183 of the Town and Country Planning Act 1990;

"traffic calming works", in relation to a highway, means works affecting the movement of vehicular or other traffic for the purpose of—

(a) promoting safety (including avoiding or reducing, or reducing the likelihood of, danger connected with terrorism within the meaning of section 1 of the Terrorism Act 2000); or

(b) preserving or improving the environment through which the highway runs;

"tramway" means a system of transport used wholly or mainly for the carriage of passengers and employing parallel rails which—

(a) provide support and guidance for vehicles carried on flanged wheels; and

(b) are laid wholly or mainly along a street or in any other place to which the public has access (including a place to which the public has access only on making a payment);

"tree preservation order" means an order made under section 198 of the Town and Country Planning Act 1990; and

"trunk road" means a highway, or a proposed highway, which is a trunk road by virtue of section 10(1) or section 19 of the Highways Act 1980 or by virtue of an order or direction under section 10 of that Act or under any other enactment.

(2) In paragraph 8 "private sewer", "drain" and "disposal main" have the same meaning as in Schedule 9.

Enquiries

2.—(1) The search report required by regulation 8(k) must contain the enquiries set out in Part 2.

(2) Those enquiries must relate to the property.

(3) The enquiries in paragraphs 6 to 18 relate only to matters which are not entered on the appropriate local land charges register.

[3651]

NOTES

Commencement: 2 July 2007.

PART 2
ENQUIRIES

Planning and building decisions and pending applications

3. Which of the following relating to the property have been granted, issued or refused or (where applicable) are the subject of pending applications—

(a) a planning permission;
(b) a listed building consent;
(c) a conservation area consent;
(d) a certificate of lawfulness of existing use or development;
(e) a certificate of lawfulness of proposed use or development;
(f) building regulations approvals;
(g) a building regulations completion certificate; and
(h) any building regulations certificate or notice issued in respect of work carried out under a competent person self-certification scheme.

Planning designations and proposals

4. What designations of land use for the property or the area, and what specific proposals for the property, are contained in any existing or proposed development plan?

Roads

5. Which of the roads, footways and footpaths named in the application for this search are—

(a) highways maintainable at public expense;
(b) subject to adoption and supported by a bond or bond waiver;
(c) to be made up by a local authority who will reclaim the cost from the frontagers; or
(d) to be adopted by a local authority without reclaiming the cost from the frontagers?

Land required for public purposes

6. Is the property included in land required for public purposes?

Land to be acquired for road works

7. Is the property included in land to be acquired for road works?

Drainage agreements and consents

8. Do either of the following exist in relation to the property—

(a) an agreement to drain buildings in combination into an existing sewer by means of a private sewer; or
(b) an agreement or consent for—
  (i) a building; or
  (ii) extension to a building on the property,
  to be built over or in the vicinity of a drain, sewer or disposal main?

Nearby road schemes

9. Is the property (or will it be) within 200 metres of any of the following—

(a) the centre line of a new trunk road or special road specified in any order, draft order or scheme;
(b) the centre line of a proposed alteration or improvement to an existing road involving construction of a subway, underpass, flyover, footbridge, elevated road or dual carriageway;
(c) the outer limits of construction works for a proposed alteration or improvement to an existing road, involving—
  (i) construction of a roundabout (other than a mini-roundabout); or
  (ii) widening by construction of one or more additional traffic lanes;
(d) the outer limits of—

- (i) construction of a new road to be built by a local authority;
- (ii) an approved alteration or improvement to an existing road involving construction of a subway, underpass, flyover, footbridge, elevated road or dual carriageway; or
- (iii) construction of a roundabout (other than a mini-roundabout) or widening by construction of one or more additional traffic lanes;

(e) the centre line of the proposed route of a new road under proposals published for public consultation; or

(f) the outer limits of—

- (i) construction of a proposed alteration or improvement to an existing road involving construction of a subway, underpass, flyover, footbridge, elevated road or dual carriageway;
- (ii) construction of a roundabout (other than a mini-roundabout); or
- (iii) widening by construction of one or more additional traffic lanes, under proposals published for public consultation?

Nearby railway schemes

10. Is the property (or will it be) within 200 metres of the centre line of a proposed railway, tramway, light railway or monorail?

Traffic schemes

11. Has a local authority approved but not yet implemented any of the following for roads, footways and footpaths which abut the boundaries of the property—

- (a) permanent stopping up or diversion;
- (b) waiting or loading restrictions;
- (c) one way driving;
- (d) prohibition of driving;
- (e) pedestrianisation;
- (f) vehicle width or weight restriction;
- (g) traffic calming works including road humps;
- (h) residents parking controls;
- (i) minor road widening or improvement;
- (j) pedestrian crossings;
- (k) cycle tracks; or
- (l) bridge building?

Outstanding notices

12. Do any statutory notices which relate to the following matters subsist in relation to the property other than those revealed in a response to any other enquiry in this Schedule—

- (a) building works;
- (b) environment;
- (c) health and safety;
- (d) housing;
- (e) highways; or
- (f) public health?

Contravention of building regulations

13. Has a local authority authorised in relation to the property any proceedings for the contravention of any provision contained in building regulations?

Notices, orders, directions and proceedings under Planning Acts

14. Do any of the following subsist in relation to the property, or has a local authority decided to issue, serve, make or commence any of the following—

- (a) an enforcement notice;
- (b) a stop notice;
- (c) a listed building enforcement notice;
- (d) a breach of condition notice;
- (e) a planning contravention notice;
- (f) another notice relating to breach of planning control;
- (g) a listed building repairs notice;
- (h) in the case of a listed building deliberately allowed to fall into disrepair, a compulsory purchase order with a direction for minimum compensation;
- (i) a building preservation notice;
- (j) a direction restricting permitted development;
- (k) an order revoking or modifying planning permission;
- (l) an order requiring discontinuance of use or alteration or removal of buildings or works;
- (m) a tree preservation order; or
- (n) proceedings to enforce a planning agreement or planning contribution?

Conservation areas

15. Do the following apply in relation to the property—
 (a) the making of the area a conservation area before 31st August 1974; or
 (b) an unimplemented resolution to designate the area a conservation area?

Compulsory purchase

16. Has any enforceable order or decision been made to compulsorily purchase or acquire the property?

Contaminated land

17. Do any of the following apply (including any relating to land adjacent to or adjoining the property which has been identified as contaminated land because it is in such a condition that harm or pollution of controlled waters might be caused on the property)—
 (a) a contaminated land notice;
 (b) in relation to a register maintained under section 78R of the Environmental Protection Act 1990—
  (i) a decision to make an entry; or
  (ii) an entry; or
 (c) consultation with the owner or occupier of the property conducted under section 78G(3) of the Environmental Protection Act 1990 before the service of a remediation notice?

Radon gas

18. Do records indicate that the property is in a "Radon Affected Area" as identified by the Health Protection Agency?

[3652]

NOTES

Commencement: 2 July 2007.

SCHEDULE 8
DRAINAGE AND WATER ENQUIRIES

regulation 8(l)

PART 1
GENERAL

Interpretation

1.—(1) In this Schedule—

"the 1991 Act" means the Water Industry Act 1991;

"the 2000 Regulations" means the Water Supply (Water Quality) Regulations 2000;

"the 2001 Regulations" means the Water Supply (Water Quality) Regulations 2001;

"adoption agreement" means an agreement made or to be made under section 51A(1) or 104(1) of the 1991 Act;

"bond" means a surety granted by a developer who is a party to an adoption agreement;

"bond waiver" means an agreement with a developer for the provision of a form of financial security as a substitute for a bond;

"calendar year" means the twelve months ending with 31st December;

"discharge pipe" means a pipe from which discharges are made or are to be made under section 165(1) of the 1991 Act;

"disposal main" means (subject to section 219(2) of the 1991 Act) any outfall pipe or other pipe which—
 (a) is a pipe for the conveyance of effluent to or from any sewage disposal works, whether of a sewerage undertaker or of any other person; and
 (b) is not a public sewer;

"drain" means (subject to section 219(2) of the 1991 Act) a drain used for the drainage of one building or of any buildings or yards appurtenant to buildings within the same curtilage;

"effluent" means any liquid, including particles of matter and other substances in suspension in the liquid;

"financial year" means the twelve months ending with 31st March;

"lateral drain" means—
 (a) that part of a drain which runs from the curtilage of a building (or buildings or yards within the same curtilage) to the sewer with which the drain communicates or is to communicate; or
 (b) (if different and the context so requires) the part of a drain identified in a declaration of vesting made under section 102 of the 1991 Act or in an agreement made under section 104 of that Act;

"licensed water supplier" means a company which is the holder for the time being of a water supply licence under section 17A(1) of the 1991 Act;

"maintenance period" means the period so specified in an adoption agreement as a period of time—

(a) from the date of issue of a certificate by a sewerage undertaker to the effect that a developer has built (or substantially built) a private sewer or lateral drain to that undertaker's satisfaction; and

(b) until the date that private sewer or lateral drain is vested in the sewerage undertaker;

"map of waterworks" means the map made available under section 198(3) of the 1991 Act in relation to the information specified in subsection (1A);

"private sewer" means a pipe or pipes which drain foul or surface water, or both, from premises, and are not vested in a sewerage undertaker;

"public sewer" means, subject to section 106(1A) of the 1991 Act, a sewer for the time being vested in a sewerage undertaker in its capacity as such, whether vested in that undertaker—

(a) by virtue of a scheme under Schedule 2 to the Water Act 1989;

(b) by virtue of a scheme under Schedule 2 to the 1991 Act;

(c) under section 179 of the 1991 Act; or

(d) otherwise;

"public sewer map" means the map made available under section 199(5) of the 1991 Act;

"resource main" means (subject to section 219(2) of the 1991 Act) any pipe, not being a trunk main, which is or is to be used for the purpose of—

(a) conveying water from one source of supply to another, from a source of supply to a regulating reservoir or from a regulating reservoir to a source of supply; or

(b) giving or taking a supply of water in bulk;

"sewerage services" includes the collection and disposal of foul and surface water and any other services which are required to be provided by a sewerage undertaker for the purpose of carrying out its functions;

"sewerage undertaker" means the company appointed to be the sewerage undertaker under section 6(1) of the 1991 Act for the area in which the property is or will be situated;

"surface water" includes water from roofs and other impermeable surfaces within the curtilage of the property;

"water main" means (subject to section 219(2) of the 1991 Act) any pipe, not being a pipe for the time being vested in a person other than the water undertaker, which is used or to be used by a water undertaker or licensed water supplier for the purpose of making a general supply of water available to customers or potential customers of the undertaker or supplier, as distinct from for the purpose of providing a supply to particular customers;

"water meter" means any apparatus for measuring or showing the volume of water supplied to, or of effluent discharged from any premises;

"water supplier" means the company supplying water in the water supply zone, whether a water undertaker or licensed water supplier;

"water supply zones" in relation to a calendar year means the names and areas designated by a water undertaker within its area of supply that are to be its water supply zones for that year; and

"water undertaker" means the company appointed to be the water undertaker under section 6(1) of the 1991 Act for the area in which the property is or will be situated.

(2) In this Schedule, references to a pipe, including references to a main, a drain or a sewer, shall include references to a tunnel or conduit which serves or is to serve as the pipe in question and to any accessories for the pipe.

Enquiries and responses

2.—(1) The search report required by regulation 8(l) must contain—

(a) the enquiries (or requests) set out in sub-paragraph (1) of each paragraph of Part 2; and

(b) in relation to each such enquiry (or request), a response in the terms set out in sub-paragraph (2) of each such paragraph, which is the appropriate response as regards the property.

(2) Only one of the alternative responses in sub-paragraph (2) of each paragraphs 3 to 11 and 13 to 24 may be the appropriate response.

(3) Where the search report is made using a document which reproduces all of the enquiries (or requests) and responses set out in Part 2, such of those responses as are not appropriate must be deleted or struck out.

(4) Where a response set out in sub-paragraph (2) of a paragraph of Part 2—

(a) includes words highlighted in italics which request the giving of information about specified matters—

(i) the appropriate response or the search report must include the information to which those matters refer; and

(ii) where information is so included and the search report is made using a document which reproduces that response, the words in italics may be deleted or struck out; and

(b) refers to an additional document being included, that document must accompany the search report required by regulation 8(1).

[3653]

NOTES

Commencement: 2 July 2007.

PART 2
ENQUIRIES AND RESPONSES

Public sewer map

3.—(1) Where relevant, please include a copy of an extract from the public sewer map.

(2) A copy of an extract from the public sewer map is included in which the location of the property is identified;

(a) A copy of an extract of the public sewer map is included, showing the public sewers, disposal mains and lateral drains in the vicinity of the property; or

(b) No map is included, as there are no public sewers in the vicinity of the property.

Foul water

4.—(1) Does foul water from the property drain to a public sewer?

(2)

(a) Records indicate that foul water from the property drains to a public sewer;

(b) Records indicate that foul water from the property does not drain to a public sewer; or

(c) This enquiry appears to relate to a plot of land or a recently built property. It is recommended that drainage proposals are checked with the developer.

Surface water

5.—(1) Does surface water from the property drain to a public sewer?

(2)

(a) Records indicate that surface water from the property does drain to a public sewer;

(b) Records indicate that surface water from the property does not drain to a public sewer; or

(c) This enquiry appears to relate to a plot of land or a recently built property. It is recommended that drainage proposals are checked with the developer.

Public adoption of sewers and lateral drains

6.—(1) Are any sewers or lateral drains serving or which are proposed to serve the property the subject of an existing adoption agreement or an application for such an agreement?

(2)

(a) Records indicate that in relation to sewers and lateral drains serving the development of which the property forms part—

(i) an adoption agreement is currently in preparation;

(ii) an adoption agreement exists and the sewers and lateral drains are not yet vested in the sewerage undertaker, although the maintenance period has commenced;

(iii) an adoption agreement exists and the sewers and lateral drains are not yet vested in the sewerage undertaker and the maintenance period has not yet commenced;

(iv) an adoption agreement exists and is supported by a bond;

(v) an adoption agreement exists and is the subject of a bond waiver; or

(vi) an adoption agreement exists and is not supported by a bond or by a bond waiver; or

(b) Records confirm that sewers serving the development, of which the property forms part are not the subject of an existing adoption agreement or an application for such an agreement; or

(c) The property is part of an established development and is not subject to an adoption agreement.

Public sewers within the boundaries of the property

7.—(1) Does the public sewer map indicate any public sewer, disposal main or lateral drain within the boundaries of the property?

(2)

(a) The public sewer map included indicates that there is a public sewer, disposal main or lateral drain within the boundaries of the property;
(b) The public sewer map indicates that there are private sewers or lateral drains subject to an existing adoption agreement within the boundaries of the property; or
(c) The public sewer map indicates that there are no public sewers, disposal mains or lateral drains within the boundaries of the property. However, it has not always been a requirement for such public sewers, disposal mains or lateral drains to be recorded on the public sewer map. It is therefore possible for unidentified sewers, disposal mains or lateral drains to exist within the boundaries of the property.

Public sewers near to the property

8.—(1) Does the public sewer map indicate any public sewer within 30.48 metres (100 feet) of any buildings within the property?

(2)

(a) The public sewer map included indicates that there is a public sewer within 30.48 metres (100 feet) of a building within the property;
(b) The public sewer map indicates that there is a public sewer or lateral drain subject to an existing adoption agreement within 30.48 metres (100 feet) of a building within the property; or
(c) The public sewer map indicates that there are no public sewers within 30.48 metres (100 feet) of a building within the property. However, it has not always been a requirement for such public sewers to be recorded on the public sewer map. It is therefore possible for unidentified sewers or public sewers to exist within the boundaries of the property.

Building over a public sewer, disposal main or drain

9.—(1) Has a sewerage undertaker approved or been consulted about any plans to erect a building or extension on the property over or in the vicinity of a public sewer, disposal main or drain?

(2)

(a) Records indicate that a sewerage undertaker has approved or has been consulted about plans to erect a building or extension on the property over or in the vicinity of a public sewer, disposal main or drain;
(b) Records indicate that a sewerage undertaker has rejected plans to erect a building or extension on the property over or in the vicinity of a public sewer, disposal main or drain; or
(c) There are no records in relation to any approval or consultation about plans to erect a building or extension on the property over or in the vicinity of a public sewer, disposal main or drain. However, the sewerage undertaker might not be aware of a building or extension on the property over or in the vicinity of a public sewer, disposal main or drain.

Map of waterworks

10.—(1) Where relevant, please include a copy of an extract from the map of waterworks.

(2)

(a) A copy of an extract from the map of waterworks is included in which the location of the property is identified;
(b) A copy of an extract of the map of waterworks is included, showing water mains, resource mains or discharge pipes in the vicinity of the property; or
(c) No map is included, as there are no water mains, resource mains or discharge pipes in the vicinity of the property.

Adoption of water mains and service pipes

11.—(1) Is any water main or service pipe serving or which is proposed to serve the property the subject of an existing adoption agreement or an application for such an agreement?

(2)

(a) Records confirm that in relation to water mains and service pipes serving the development, of which the property forms part—
  (i) an adoption agreement is currently in preparation;
  (ii) an adoption agreement exists and the water mains or service pipes are not yet vested in the water undertaker;
  (iii) an adoption agreement exists and is supported by a bond; or
  (iv) an adoption agreement exists and is not supported by a bond; or
(b) Records confirm that water mains or service pipes serving the property are not the subject of an existing adoption agreement or an application for such an agreement.

Sewerage and water undertakers

12.—(1) Who are the sewerage and water undertakers for the area?

(2) *Give company name and address* is the sewerage undertaker for the area, and *give company name and address* is the water undertaker for the area.

Connection to mains water supply

13.—(1) Is the property connected to mains water supply?

(2)

(a) Records indicate that the property is connected to mains water supply;
(b) Records indicate that the property is not connected to mains water supply and water is therefore likely to be provided by virtue of a private supply; or
(c) This enquiry relates to a plot of land or a recently built property. It is recommended that the water supply proposals are checked with the developer.

Water mains, resource mains or discharge pipes

14.—(1) Are there any water mains, resource mains or discharge pipes within the boundaries of the property?

(2)

(a) The map of waterworks indicates that there are water mains, resource mains or discharge pipes within the boundaries of the property;
(b) The map of waterworks does not indicate any water mains, resource mains or discharge pipes within the boundaries of the property; or
(c) The map of waterworks indicates that there is a water main subject to an existing adoption agreement within the boundaries of the property.

Current basis for sewerage and water charges

15.—(1) What is the current basis for charging for sewerage and water services at the property?

(2)

(a) The charges are based on actual volumes of water measured through a water meter ("metered supply");
(b) The charges are based on the rateable value of the property of £ *give rateable value* and the charge for the current financial year is £ *give amount of charge*;
(c) The charges are made on a basis other than rateable value or metered supply. They are based on *give basis for charges* and are £ *give amount of charge* for each financial year.
(d) Records indicate that this enquiry relates to a plot of land or a recently built property.

Charges following change of occupation

16.—(1) Will the basis for charging for sewerage and water services at the property change as a consequence of a change of occupation?

(2)

(a) The basis for the charges will change and will be based on an unmeasured supply;
(b) The basis for the charges will change and will be based on a metered supply;
(c) The basis for the charges will change and will be based on *give basis for charges*;
(d) The basis for the charges will change and will be based on rateable value;
(e) There will be no change in the current charging arrangements as a consequence of a change of occupation; or
(f) Records indicate that this enquiry relates to a plot of land or a recently built property. It is recommended that the charging proposals are checked with the developer.

Surface water drainage charges

17.—(1) Is a surface water drainage charge payable?

(2)

(a) Records confirm that a surface water drainage charge is payable for the property at £ *give level of charge* for each financial year; or
(b) Records confirm that a surface water drainage charge is not payable for the property.

Water meters

18.—(1) Please include details of the location of any water meter serving the property.

(2)

(a) Records indicate that the property is not served by a water meter; or
(b) Records indicate that the property is served by a water meter, which is located—
 (i) within the dwelling-house which is or forms part of the property, and in particular is located at *give details of location*; or

(ii) is not within the dwelling-house which is or forms part of the property, and in particular is located at *give details of location*.

Sewerage bills

19.—(1) Who bills the property for sewerage services?

(2)

(a) The property is billed for sewerage services by give company name, billing address, enquiry telephone number and website address; or

(b) The property is not billed for sewerage services.

Water bills

20.—(1) Who bills the property for water services?

(2)

(a) The property is billed for water services by give company name, billing address, enquiry telephone number and website address; or

(b) The property is not billed for water services.

Risk of flooding due to overloaded public sewers

21.—(1) Is the dwelling-house which is or forms part of the property at risk of internal flooding due to overloaded public sewers?

(2)

(a) Records confirm that the property is at risk of internal flooding due to overloaded public sewers (following an actual flooding event or otherwise) and a report is included describing—

(i) this and the action proposed by the sewerage undertaker to remove the risk;

(ii) who will undertake this action and when; and

(iii) whether mitigation measures have been installed to reduce the risk of flooding to the property;

(b) An investigation is currently being carried out by the sewerage undertaker to determine if the property should be recorded on a register as being at risk of internal flooding due to overloaded public sewers, and a report is included describing—

(i) the action proposed by the water undertaker to remove the risk; and

(ii) who will undertake the action and when; or

(c) The property is not recorded as being at risk of internal flooding due to overloaded public sewers.

Risk of low water pressure or flow

22.—(1) Is the property at risk of receiving low water pressure or flow?

(2)

(a) Records confirm that the property is recorded on a register kept by the water undertaker as being at risk of receiving low water pressure or flow, and a report is included describing—

(i) the action proposed by the water undertaker to remove the risk; and

(ii) who will undertake the action and when;

(b) An investigation is currently being carried out by the water undertaker to determine if the property should be recorded on a register as being at risk of receiving low water pressure or flow, and a report is included describing—

(i) the action proposed by the water undertaker to remove the risk; and

(ii) who will undertake the action and when; or

(c) Records confirm that the property is not recorded on a register kept by the water undertaker as being at risk of receiving low water pressure or flow.

Water quality analysis

23.—(1) Please include details of a water quality analysis made by the water undertaker for the water supply zone in respect of the most recent calendar year.

(2)

(a) The analysis confirmed that all tests met the standards prescribed by the 2000 Regulations or the 2001 Regulations;

(b) The analysis confirmed that tests met the standards prescribed by the 2000 Regulations or the 2001 Regulations, except that *give number* tests of *give total number* tests failed to meet the standard for nitrate;

(c) The analysis confirmed that tests met the standards prescribed by the 2000 Regulations or the 2001 Regulations, except that *give number* tests of *give total number* tests failed to meet the standard for lead;

(d) The analysis confirmed that tests failed to meet the standards of the 2000 Regulations or the 2001 Regulations in relation to both nitrate and lead, and these are *give further details of such tests*; or

(e) The analysis records confirmed that tests failed to meet the standards of the 2000 Regulations or the 2001 Regulations in relation to another substance or substances, and these are *include further details*.

Authorised departures from water quality standards

24.—(1) Please include details of any departures—

(a) authorised by the Secretary of State under Part 6 of the 2000 Regulations from the provisions of Part 3 of those Regulations; or

(b) authorised by the [Welsh Ministers] under Part 6 of the 2001 Regulations from the provisions of Part 3 of those Regulations.

(2)

(a) There are no such authorised departures for the water supply zone; or

(b) [The Secretary of State has or the Welsh Ministers have] authorised a departure from the standards prescribed by the 2000 Regulations or the 2001 Regulations, in the water supply zone, and—

(i) the departure permits the water undertaker or water supplier to supply water that does not meet the standard for *give substance* whilst remedial action to restore normal water quality is taken;

(ii) the maximum permitted departure is up to *give number* micrograms per litre; and

(iii) the measures taken to restore normal water quality are due to be completed by *give approximate month and year*.

Sewage treatment works

25.—(1) Please state the distance from the property to the nearest boundary of the nearest sewage treatment works.

(2) The nearest sewage treatment works is *give distance in kilometres or miles* to the *give direction* of the property. The name of the nearest sewage treatment works is *give name*.

[3654]

NOTES

Commencement: 2 July 2007.

Para 24: in sub-paras (1)(b), (2)(b) words in square brackets substituted by SI 2007/3301, reg 4.

SCHEDULE 9
HOME CONDITION REPORT

regulation 9(a)

Home condition reports

1. A home condition report—

(a) must be made by a home inspector—

(i) following an inspection carried out by him in accordance with the provisions of the approved certification scheme of which he is a member and in which capacity the report is made; and

(ii) using the standard form for home condition report referred to in regulation 37(f).

(b) must be entered onto the register kept pursuant to Part 9.

Terms for the preparation of a home condition report

2. A home inspector must prepare a home condition report on the following terms without exclusion or limitation—

(a) that the report will be prepared with reasonable care and skill;

(b) that the home inspector will provide in the report an objective opinion about the condition of the property;

(c) that such an opinion will be based on his inspection;

(d) that the home inspector will identify in the report such conditions within the property as appear to—

(i) be defects that are serious or require urgent attention, or both;

(ii) give rise to a need for repair or replacement; or

(iii) give rise to further investigation;

(e) that a responsible person may copy or issue a copy of the report for the purposes of—

(i) regulations 5, 6, 9(a) and 24; and

(ii) section 156(1), (2) and (11) of the 2004 Act; and

(f) that any person may do one or more of the following for the purposes of a disclosure or other act authorised by Part 9—

(i) copy a report;
(ii) issue a copy of a report;
(iii) rent or lend a report;
(iv) communicate a report; or
(v) make an adaptation of a report or do any of the above in relation to an adaptation.

Third party contractual rights in relation to home condition reports

3. A home inspector must prepare a home condition report on terms enabling the provisions of the contract under which the report is prepared to be enforced in relation to the terms mentioned in paragraph 2, by the following persons in their own right (whether or not they are a party to such a contract)—

(a) the seller;
(b) a potential or actual buyer of the property interest; and
(c) a mortgage lender in respect of the property interest.

Inclusion of additional or more favourable terms for home condition reports

4. A home inspector may prepare a home condition report on any of the following—

(a) terms additional to those described in paragraphs 2 and 3 (but without excluding or limiting them); and
(b) terms more favourable to—
 (i) the seller;
 (ii) a potential or actual buyer of the property interest; or
 (iii) a mortgage lender in respect of the property interest,

than those described in paragraphs 2 and 3.

Less favourable terms

5. Any home condition report which contains terms less favourable to—

(a) the seller;
(b) a potential or actual buyer of the property interest; or
(c) a mortgage lender in respect of the property interest,

than those required by this Schedule is not made in accordance with this Schedule.

Completion of home condition reports by home inspectors

6. A home condition report must be completed by a home inspector so as to contain his record of the following information—

(a) his name;
(b) whether he has any personal or business relationship with any person involved in the sale of the property;
(c) the report reference number against which the report is registered under paragraph 1(b);
(d) the name of the approved certification scheme of which he is a member and in which capacity the report is made;
(e) such membership number or identification code as has been allocated to him by the scheme;
(f) the name and address of his employer, or if he is self-employed, the name under which he trades;
(g) the date of the inspection and the date on which the report is completed;
(h) the address of the property;
(i) the year in which the property was built or, if this cannot be ascertained by him, his estimate of the year in which it was built;
(j) the number of—
 (i) storeys or levels in the property; and
 (ii) rooms on each storey or level of the property;
(k) such provision as has been made for the parking of vehicles relating to occupants of or visitors to the property;
(l) such mains utility services as are connected to the property and the condition of their visible parts;
(m) if the property is or forms part of a flat or maisonette—
 (i) the number of storeys or levels of the building in which the flat or maisonette is situated;
 (ii) the number of flats and maisonettes in that building or, if this cannot be ascertained by him, his estimate of the number of flats and maisonettes;
 (iii) whether the building contains a lift;
 (iv) the general condition of such areas that lead to the property as are common to both it and any neighbouring premises; and
 (v) the general condition of the building in which the flat or maisonette is situated;
(n) risks to the health or safety of the property's occupants or visitors, so far as he can ascertain them;

(o) the condition of the outside parts of the property including such—
  (i) roof coverings;
  (ii) rainwater pipes and gutters;
  (iii) chimney stacks; and
  (iv) walls, doors and windows,
  as relate to the property;
(p) the condition of the inside parts of the property including—
  (i) roof structures accessible directly from the property;
  (ii) ceilings and floors;
  (iii) internal walls; and
  (iv) kitchen and bathroom fittings,
  and whether their appearance suggests that they have been materially affected by dampness;
(q) the general condition of such outbuildings as are part of the property;
(r) whether any parts of the property to which he would normally expect to have access were not accessible to him on the day of the inspection; and
(s) any other provision required by the approved certification scheme of which he is a member and in which capacity the report is made.

Conduct of inspections

7. Nothing in this Schedule shall be construed as requiring a home inspector to—
  (a) inspect such parts of the property as are not reasonably accessible on the day of the inspection; or
  (b) move furniture, fittings or personal items at the property during an inspection.

Prohibition on personal and security information

8. A home condition report must not contain any of the following—
  (a) information or data from which another living individual can be identified from the report other than the information required under paragraphs 6(a) (name of inspector), 6(f) (name of employer) or 6(h) (address of property);
  (b) any expression of opinion about a living individual; or
  (c) information about security features at the property and, in particular, burglar alarm systems, safes or locks.

[3655]

NOTES

Commencement: 2 July 2007.

SCHEDULE 10
ADDITIONAL RELEVANT INFORMATION

regulation 9(p)

The matters referred to in regulation 9(p)(ii) are—
  (a) energy performance, environmental impact or sustainability;
  (b) potential or actual environmental hazards that might affect the property or its occupants;
  (c) the price at which—
    (i) the property is available for sale; or
    (ii) was previously sold;
  (d) the length of time the property has been available for sale either generally or through a particular person;
  (e) location or address;
  (f) aspect, view, outlook or environment;
  (g) proximity and identity of local services, facilities or amenities;
  (h) Welsh speaking communities in the local area;
  (i) the use of the Welsh language;
  (j) the property's contents, fixtures or fittings;
  (k) history of the property, including age, ownership or use of the property or land on which it is or will be situated;
  (l) tenure or estate;
  (m) application of any statutory provision which restricts the use of land or which requires it to be preserved or maintained in a specified manner;
  (n) existence or nature of any restrictive covenants, or of any restrictions on resale, restrictions on use or pre-emption rights;
  (o) existence of any easements, servitudes or wayleaves;
  (p) any information held or provided by the Chief Land Registrar relating to the property;
  (q) equitable interests in the property;
  (r) rights of way or access to or over—
    (i) the property (not including any ancillary land); or

(ii) land outside the property;

(s) rights of way or access to or over any ancillary land to the property including—

(i) obligations to maintain such land; or

(ii) whether any payments for maintaining such land are outstanding;

(t) obligations to maintain the boundaries of the property;

(u) communications from any public authority or person with statutory functions, that affect or might affect the property, including whether any request made by them (under any enactment or otherwise) has been complied with;

(v) acquisition of any land by a public authority or person with statutory functions that affects or might affect the property;

(w) standards of safety, building, repair or maintenance to which the property, its contents or the building in which it is situated ought to comply, and whether such standards have been complied with;

(x) the property's suitability or potential suitability for occupancy by a disabled person;

(y) alterations or other works relating to the property and—

(i) the date or approximate date they occurred;

(ii) whether any necessary permissions for such alterations or works have been obtained; or

(iii) whether relevant consultations have been conducted;

(z) identity of a person by whom the property, its fixtures or components were designed, constructed, built, produced, treated, processed, repaired, reconditioned or tested;

(aa) measurements of the property;

(bb) use or occupation of the property or use or occupation of other premises which affects or might affect the property;

(cc) insurance policies, warranties, certificates or guarantees for the property or its contents;

(dd) utility services connected to the property;

(ee) taxes, levies or charges relating to the property; and

(ff) information of any type mentioned in this Schedule relating to neighbouring, adjoining or nearby land or premises.

[3656]

NOTES

Commencement: 2 July 2007.

[SCHEDULE 11
PROPERTY INFORMATION QUESTIONNAIRE

Regulation 8(m)

PART 1
GENERAL

1.—(1) The property information questionnaire ("PIQ") required by regulation 8(m) must contain—

(a) the title and statement in paragraph 2 of Part 2 of this Schedule;

(b) the information in paragraph 3 of Part 2;

(c) the questions in paragraph 3 of Part 2 in the manner prescribed by the paragraph; and

(d) the responses to the questions completed by the seller.

(2) Where the property interest is or includes the whole or part of a leasehold interest, the PIQ must also contain—

(a) the information and questions set out in Part 3 of this Schedule in the manner prescribed by that paragraph; and

(b) the responses to the questions completed by the seller.]

[3656A]

NOTES

Commencement: 6 April 2009.
Inserted by SI 2008/3107, regs 2, 10.

[PART 2
INFORMATION REQUIRED IN RESPECT OF ALL PROPERTIES

General information

2. The PIQ must contain the following at the start of the document—

(a) the title "Property Information Questionnaire" and below it "Part 1"; and

(b) the following statement—

"About this form—

This form should be completed by the seller. The seller may be the owner or owners; a representative with the necessary authority to sell the property for an owner who has died; a representative with the necessary authority to sell the property for a living owner (e.g. a power of attorney) or be selling in some other capacity. The form should be completed and read as though the questions were being answered by the owner.

If you are the seller, you should be aware that—

Answers given in this form should be truthful and accurate to the best of your knowledge. The questions have been designed to help the smooth sale of your home. Misleading or incorrect answers are likely to be exposed later in the conveyancing process and may endanger the sale.

Information included in this form does not replace official documents or legal information. You should be prepared to provide such documents on request in support of the answers given in this form.

If you hold any guarantees for work on your property, your buyer's conveyancer is likely to ask for evidence, which it is in your interests to make available as soon as possible.

If anything changes to affect the information given in this form prior to the sale of your home, you should inform your conveyancer or estate agent immediately.

If you are an estate agent, you should be aware that—

This form should be completed by the seller but it is your responsibility to ensure that it is included in the Home Information Pack.

The Property Misdescriptions Act 1991 does not apply where the form has been completed solely by the seller.

If you are the buyer, you should be aware that—

The information contained in this document should have been completed truthfully and accurately by the seller. However, the information only relates to the period during which the seller has owned the property (see question 1) and does not replace official documents or legal information and you should confirm any information with your conveyancer.

The seller must provide the information set out in Part 1 of this questionnaire.

Where the property being sold is a leasehold property, the seller must also complete Part 2 of this questionnaire.".

3. Part 1 of the PIQ must contain the following information—

(a) the postal address of the property;
(b) the name of the seller; and
(c) the date the PIQ was completed.

Questions

4. Part 1 of the PIQ must reproduce the following questions and statements in the order that they are set out—

"All properties

1. When was the property purchased?

Answer—this should be the month and year.

2. Is your property a listed building or contained in a listed building?

Answer—should be "yes", "no" or "don't know" as appropriate.

3. What council tax band is the property in? [Note: Buyers should be aware that improvements carried out by the seller may affect the property's council tax banding following a sale.]

Answer—should be A, B, C, D, E, F, G or H as appropriate.

4. What parking arrangements exist at your property?

Answer—should be "garage", "allocated parking space", "driveway", "on street", "resident permit", "metered parking", "shared parking" or specify other.

Other issues affecting the property

5. Has there been any damage to your property as a result of storm or fire since you have owned it?

Answer—should be "yes", "no" or "don't know" as appropriate.

(a) If "yes", please give details.

6. If you have answered "yes" to question 5, was the damage the subject of an insurance claim?

Answer—should be "yes", "no" or "don't know" as appropriate.

(a) If "yes", please state whether any of these claims are outstanding.

7. Are you aware of any flooding at your property since you have owned it or before?

Answer—should be "yes" or "no" as appropriate.

(a) If "yes", please give details.

8. Have you checked the freely available flood risk data at the Environment Agency's website (http://www.environment-agency.gov.uk/subjects/flood)?

Answer—should be "yes", "no" or "don't know" as appropriate.

(a) If "yes", please give details.
(b) If "no", the buyer is advised to check the Environment Agency website for an indication of flood risk in the area.

9. Has there been any treatment of or preventative work for dry rot, wet rot or damp in the property since you have owned the property?

Answer—should be "yes", "no" or "don't know" as appropriate.

(a) If "yes", please give details of any guarantees relating to the work and who holds the guarantees.

Utilities and services

10. Is there central heating in your property?

Answer—should be "yes", "no" or "don't know" as appropriate.

(a) If "yes", please give details of the type of central heating (examples: gas-fired, oil fired, solid fuel, liquid gas petroleum).

11. When was your central heating or other primary heating system last serviced?

Answer—should be details of year and whether a report is available or "not serviced" or "don't know" as appropriate.

12. When was the electrical wiring in your property last checked?

Answer—should be details of year and whether a report is available or "not checked" or "don't know" as appropriate.

13. Please indicate which services are connected to your property.

Answer—

Services	*Connected*
Electricity	
Gas	
Water mains or private water supply	
Drainage to public sewer (If not connected, please indicate whether there is a cesspool or septic tank.)	
Telephone	
Cable TV or satellite	
Broadband	

Changes to the property

14. Have you carried out any structural alterations, additions or extensions (e.g. provision of an extra bedroom or bathroom) to the property?

Answer—should be "yes", "no" or "don't know" as appropriate.

(a) If "yes", please give details of the nature of the work.
(b) Was building regulation approval obtained?

Answer—should be "yes", "no" or "don't know" as appropriate.

(c) Was planning permission obtained?

Answer—should be "yes", "no" or "don't know" as appropriate.

(d) Was listed building consent obtained?

Answer—should be "yes", "no" or "don't know" as appropriate.

If the response was "no" for any of (b) to (d), please state why not (e.g. "not required" or "work completed under approved person scheme").

15. Have you had replacement windows, doors, patio doors or double glazing installed in your property?

Answer—should be "yes", "no" or "don't know" as appropriate.
(a) If "yes", please give details of changes and guarantees, if held.

Access

16. Do you have right of access through any neighbouring homes, buildings or land?
Answer—should be "yes", "no" or "don't know" as appropriate.
(a) If "yes", please give details.

17. Does any other person have a right of access through your property?
Answer—should be "yes", "no" or "don't know" as appropriate.
(a) If "yes", please give details.

Leasehold properties

18. Is your property a leasehold property?

If "yes", please complete Part 2 of this questionnaire. If "no", there is no need to complete Part 2 of this questionnaire.".]

[3656B]

NOTES

Commencement: 6 April 2009.
Inserted by SI 2008/3107, regs 2, 10.

PART 3
INFORMATION REQUIRED IN RESPECT OF LEASEHOLD PROPERTIES

[5. Part 2 of the PIQ must reproduce the following questions and statements in the order that they are set out—

"PART 2

Only complete this part if the property is a leasehold property.

If the lease is a new one and has not yet been granted, please answer the questions based on the draft terms of the lease.

Before entering into a binding commitment, buyers should confirm any matter relating to the leasehold ownership by reading the lease and checking the position with their conveyancer.

Additional information for leasehold properties

19. What is the name of the person or organisation to whom you pay—
(a) ground rent; and
(b) service charges (if different from (a) above)?

20. How many years does your lease have left to run?

21. How much is your current annual ground rent?

22. How much is your current annual service charge?

23. How much is your current annual buildings insurance premium (if not included in the service charge)?

24. Are you aware of any proposed or ongoing major works to this property?
Answer—should be "yes", "no" or "don't know" as appropriate.
(a) If "yes", what type of works are they and what is the expected cost relating to this property (if known)?

25. Does the lease prevent you from—
(a) sub-letting?
Answer—should be "yes", "no" or "don't know" as appropriate.
(b) keeping pets?
Answer—should be "yes", "no" or "don't know" as appropriate.

26. Does the lease allow you to—
(a) use a car park or space?
Answer—should be "yes", "no" or "don't know" as appropriate.
(b) have access to a communal garden (where applicable)?
Answer—should be "yes", "no" or "don't know" as appropriate.

27. Leases often permit or prevent certain types of activity relating to the use of the property, those referred to in question (25) are examples. Are there any other conditions or restrictions in the lease which could significantly impact on a person's use of the property?
(a) If "yes", please specify.

Explanatory Notes to Numbered Items

19. The landlord will normally be the person to whom the ground rent is payable, although it is possible that an agent may be employed to collect this on the landlord's behalf. The person or the organisation to whom the service charge is payable may be your landlord or head landlord or a residents' management company – you should find the landlord's details on your latest service charge demand. It is also possible that an agent has been employed to collect service charges on their behalf.

20. The number of years is calculated by taking the original number of years the lease was granted for and deducting the number of years that have expired since the lease was first granted.

21. This information will be found in the lease.

22. This information should be found on the previous year's service charge demands.

24. Leaseholders should have been notified of this as part of the required consultation process where their contribution towards the work exceeds £250.

Please note: All leaseholders should have their own copy of the lease although sometimes this is held by the mortgage lender or the conveyancer who handled the purchase. A copy can normally be obtained from the Land Registry – www.landregisteronline.gov.uk. It is unlikely that the managing agent will be able to provide a copy of the lease.".]

[3656C]

NOTES

Commencement: 6 April 2009.
Inserted by SI 2008/3107, regs 2, 10.

[SCHEDULE 12
PROPERTY INFORMATION QUESTIONNAIRE (NEW HOMES)

PART 1
GENERAL

1.—(1) The property information questionnaire ("PIQ") required by regulation 8(n) must contain—

(a) the title and statement in paragraph 2 of Part 2 of this Schedule;
(b) the information in paragraph 3 of Part 2;
(c) the questions in paragraph 4 of Part 2 in the manner prescribed by the paragraph; and
(b) the responses to the questions completed by the seller.

(2) Where the property interest is or includes the whole or part of a leasehold interest, the PIQ must also contain—

(a) the information and questions set out in Part 3 of this Schedule in the manner prescribed by that part; and
(b) the responses to the questions completed by the seller.

[3656D]

NOTES

Commencement: 6 April 2009.
Inserted by SI 2008/3107, regs 2, 10.

PART 2
INFORMATION REQUIRED IN RESPECT OF ALL PROPERTIES

General information

2. The PIQ must contain the following at the start of the document—

(a) the title "Property Information Questionnaire" and below it "Part 1"; and
(b) the following statement—

"About this form—

This form should be completed by the seller. The seller may be the owner or owners; a representative with the necessary authority to sell the property for an owner who has died; a representative with the necessary authority to sell the property for a living owner (e.g. a power of attorney) or be selling in some other capacity. The form should be completed and read as though the questions were being answered by the owner.

If you are the seller, you should be aware that—

Answers given in this form should be truthful and accurate to the best of your knowledge. The questions have been designed to help the smooth sale of your home. Misleading or incorrect answers are likely to be exposed later in the conveyancing process and may endanger the sale.

Information included in this form does not replace official documents or legal information. You should be prepared to provide such documents on request in support of the answers given in this form.

If anything changes to affect the information given in this form prior to the sale of your home, you should inform your conveyancer or estate agent immediately.

If you are an estate agent, you should be aware that—

This form should be completed by the seller but it is your responsibility to ensure that it is included in the Home Information Pack.

The Property Misdescriptions Act 1991 does not apply where the form has been completed solely by the seller.

If you are the buyer, you should be aware that—

The information contained in this document should have been completed truthfully and accurately by the seller. However, the information does not replace official documents or legal information, you should confirm any information with your conveyancer.

The seller must provide the information set out in Part 1 of this questionnaire.

Where the property being sold is a leasehold property, the seller must also complete Part 2 of this questionnaire.".

3. Part 1 of the PIQ must contain the following information—

(a) the postal address or proposed address (which may include a plot number);
(b) the name of the seller; and
(c) the date the PIQ was completed.

Questions

4. Part 1 of the PIQ must reproduce the following questions and statements in the order that they are set out—

"All properties

1. Is the property a listed building or contained in a listed building?

Answer—should be "yes" or "no".

2. Has the property received building regulation approval?

Answer—should be "yes" or, "no". If "yes", please give details.

3. Has the property received a building regulation completion certificate?

Answer—should be "yes" or "no". If "no", please give details.

4. Is the property sold with a warranty?

Answer—should be "yes" or "no". If "yes", please give the name of the provider.

5. What parking arrangements exist or are planned for the property?

Answer—should be "garage", "allocated parking space", "driveway", "on street", "resident permit", "metered parking", "shared parking" or specify other.

Other matters affecting the property

6. Has there been any damage to the property as a result of storm or fire since you have owned it?

Answer—should be "yes" or "no" as appropriate. If "yes", please give details.

7. Are you aware of any flooding at the property since you have owned it or before?

Answer—should be "yes", "no" or "don't know" as appropriate. If "yes", please give details. (Note: The buyer is advised to check the Environment Agency website for an indication of flood risk in the area.)

8. Has there been or is there any preventative work planned for dry rot, wet rot or damp in the property?

Answer—should be "yes", "no" or "don't know" as appropriate. If "yes" please give details.

(a) If the answer to 8 was "yes", are there any guarantees relating to this work? If "yes", please give details.

Utilities and services

9. Is there or will there be central heating in the property?

Answer/response—should be "yes", "no" or "don't know" as appropriate. If "yes" please give details of the type of central heating.

10. Please indicate which services are or will be connected to the property.

Services	*Connected*	*To be connected*
Electricity		
Gas		
Water mains or private water supply		
Drainage to public sewer (If not connected, please indicate whether there will be a cesspool or septic tank)		
Telephone		
Cable TV or satellite		
Broadband		

Access

11. Is there a right of access through any neighbouring homes, buildings or land?

Answer—should be "yes", "no" or "don't know" as appropriate. If "yes" please give details.

12. Does any other person have a right of access through the property?

Answer—should be "yes", "no" or "don't know" as appropriate. If "yes" please give details.

Leasehold properties

13. Is the property a leasehold property?

If "yes", please complete Part 2 of this questionnaire. If "no", there is no need to complete Part 2 of this questionnaire.".]

[3656E]

NOTES

Commencement: 6 April 2009.
Inserted by SI 2008/3107, regs 2, 10.

PART 3
INFORMATION REQUIRED IN RESPECT OF LEASEHOLD PROPERTIES

5. Part 2 of the PIQ must reproduce the following questions and statements in the order that they are set out—

"PART 2

Only complete this part if the property is a leasehold property.

If the lease is a new one and has not yet been granted, please answer the questions based on the draft terms of the lease.

Before entering into a binding commitment, buyers should confirm any matter relating to the leasehold ownership by reading the lease, if one is available, and checking the position with their conveyancer.

Additional information for leasehold properties

14. Is there a lease for the property?

Answer/response—should be "yes" or "no".

(a) If "yes" please answer the remaining questions.
(b) If "no", please answer the remaining questions to the extent that the information is available.

15. What is the name of the person or organisation to whom the following will be paid?
(a) ground rent
(b) service charges (if different from (a) above)

16. What is the length of the lease?

17. How much is the proposed ground rent?

18. How much is the proposed annual service charge?

19. How much is the proposed annual buildings insurance premium (if not included in the annual service charge)?

20. Does the lease prevent—

(a) subletting?

Answer—should be "yes", "no" or "don't know" as appropriate. If "yes" please give details.

(b) keeping pets?

Answer—should be "yes", "no" or "don't know" as appropriate. If "yes" please give details.

21. Does the lease allow—

(a) the use of a car park or space?

Answer—should be "yes", "no" or "don't know" as appropriate. If "yes" please give details.

(b) access to a communal garden (where applicable)?

Answer—should be "yes", "no" or "don't know" as appropriate. If "yes" please give details.

22. Leases often permit or prevent certain types of activity relating to the use of the property, those referred to in question (20) are examples. Are there any other conditions or restrictions in the lease which could significantly impact on a person's use of the property? If "yes", please specify."]

[3656F]

NOTES

Commencement: 6 April 2009.

Inserted by SI 2008/3107, regs 2, 10.

RIGHTS OF WAY (HEARINGS AND INQUIRIES PROCEDURE) (ENGLAND) RULES 2007

(SI 2007/2008)

NOTES

Made: 6 July 2007.

Authority: Tribunals and Inquiries Act 1992, s 9.

Commencement: 1 October 2007.

PART 1
PRELIMINARY

1 Citation, commencement and extent

(1) These Rules may be cited as the Rights of Way (Hearings and Inquiries Procedure) (England) Rules 2007 and come into force on 1st October 2007.

(2) These Rules apply in relation to England only.

[3657]

NOTES

Commencement: 1 October 2007.

2 Interpretation

In these Rules—

"the 1980 Act" means the Highways Act 1980;

"the 1981 Act" means the Wildlife and Countryside Act 1981;

"the 1990 Act" means the Town and Country Planning Act 1990;

"the applicant" has the meaning given by rule 4(4)(b);

"the authority" means the authority who made the order in question;

"a decision by the Secretary of State as respects an order" does not include a transferred decision;

"inspector" means—

(a) a person appointed by the Secretary of State to make a transferred decision, or

(b) a person holding a hearing or inquiry and making a report to the Secretary of State in order for him to make a decision on whether or not to confirm the order in question;

"order", save where the context otherwise requires, means an order (other than an order made by the Secretary of State) to which the provisions of Schedule 6 to the 1980 Act (provisions as to making, confirmation, validity and date of operation of certain orders relating to footpaths, bridleways and restricted byways), Schedule 15 to the 1981 Act (procedure in connection with certain orders under Part III) or Schedule 14 to the 1990 Act (procedure for footpaths and bridleways orders) apply;

"proof of evidence" means a written statement of evidence;

"relevant documents" has the meaning given by rule 20(2);

"relevant person" has the meaning given by rule 4(4)(f);

"start date", in relation to any given hearing or inquiry, has the meaning given by rule 4(3)(a);

"statement of case " means a written statement containing full particulars of the case which a person proposes to put forward at a hearing or inquiry and includes—

- (a) copies of any supporting documents which that person intends to refer to or put in evidence, and
- (b) a list of those documents;

"subsequent material" means any material, consisting of any document, any oral representations or any evidence, which was not submitted to the Secretary of State or the inspector before the close of the hearing or inquiry, as the case may be, but is submitted thereafter, but does not include a report made under rule 11(2) or 23(2) in respect of the hearing or inquiry in question; and

"transferred decision" means a decision made by a person appointed by the Secretary of State pursuant to paragraph 2A of Schedule 6 to the 1980 Act (provisions as to making, confirmation, validity and date of operation of certain orders relating to footpaths, bridleways and restricted byways), paragraph 10 of Schedule 15 to the 1981 Act (procedure in connection with certain orders under Part III) or paragraph 4 of Schedule 14 to the 1990 Act (procedure for footpaths and bridleways orders).

[3658]

NOTES

Commencement: 1 October 2007.

3 Application of Rules

(1) Parts 1, 2, 3 and 6 apply to hearings afforded by the Secretary of State under—

- (a) paragraph 2(2) of Schedule 6 to the 1980 Act (provisions as to making, confirmation, validity and date of operation of certain orders relating to footpaths, bridleways and restricted byways);
- (b) paragraph 7(2) of Schedule 15 to the 1981 Act (procedure in connection with certain orders under Part III); or
- (c) paragraph 3(3) of Schedule 14 to the 1990 Act (procedure for footpaths and bridleways orders).

(2) Parts 1, 2, 4 and 6 apply to local inquiries caused by the Secretary of State to be held under the provisions mentioned in paragraph (1)(a) to (c).

(3) Parts 1, 5 and 6 apply to hearings afforded by the Secretary of State and to inquiries caused by him to be held under paragraph 2(3) of Schedule 6 to the 1980 Act (provisions as to making, confirmation, validity and date of operation of certain orders relating to footpaths, bridleways and restricted byways), paragraph 8(2) of Schedule 15 to the 1981 Act (procedure in connection with certain orders under Part III) or paragraph 3(6) of Schedule 14 to the 1990 Act (procedure for footpaths and bridleways orders).

(4) The Highways (Inquiries Procedure) Rules 1994 do not apply to any hearing or inquiry mentioned in paragraphs (1) to (3).

[3659]

NOTES

Commencement: 1 October 2007.

PART 2
INITIAL STAGES OF HEARING OR INQUIRY

4 Notice to be given by the Secretary of State

(1) The Secretary of State shall give a notice which complies with paragraph (3) to the persons mentioned in paragraph (4).

(2) The notice shall be given as soon as practicable after an order has been submitted to the Secretary of State for confirmation in accordance with—

- (a) regulation 4 (procedure for public path orders) of the Town and Country Planning (Public Path Orders) Regulations 1993;

(b) regulation 4 (procedure for orders) of the Public Path Orders Regulations 1993; or

(c) regulation 7 (making, submission and confirmation of modification and reclassification orders) of, and Schedule 4 (additional provisions in relation to the making, submission and confirmation of modification and reclassification orders) to, the Wildlife and Countryside (Definitive Maps and Statements) Regulations 1993.

(3) The notice under paragraph (1) shall—

(a) be dated, and such date shall be the "start date" for the purposes of these Rules;

(b) state whether the consideration of the order will take the form of a hearing or inquiry;

(c) state the date, time and place of the hearing or inquiry, as the case may be;

(d) give a brief description of—

(i) the land to which the order the subject of the hearing or inquiry relates; and

(ii) the effect of the order;

(e) state the address (including an e-mail address) to which communications about the hearing or inquiry are to be sent;

(f) state the time and place where the documents relating to the hearing or inquiry are to be made available by the authority under rule 29(1) (inspection and copying of documents);

(g) in the case of a hearing, explain the requirements of rule 6 (submission of statements of case for the hearing); and

(h) in the case of an inquiry, explain the requirements of rule 17 (submission of statements of case for the inquiry) and rule 20 (proofs of evidence).

(4) Subject to paragraph (5), the notice under paragraph (1) shall be given to—

(a) the authority;

(b) every person (in these Rules referred to as "the applicant") who applied for an order under—

(i) section 118ZA (application for a public path extinguishment order) or 119ZA (application for a public path diversion order) of the 1980 Act;

(ii) sections 118C (application by a proprietor of a school for a special extinguishment order) and 119C (application by a proprietor of a school for a special diversion order) of the 1980 Act; or

(iii) section 53(5) of the 1981 Act (which relates to applications for a definitive map modification order);

(c) in the case of an order to which the provisions of Schedule 6 to the 1980 Act (provisions as to making, confirmation, validity and date of operation of certain orders relating to footpaths, bridleways and restricted byways) apply, every person who was required to be given notice of that order by paragraph 1(3)(b)(i), (ii) and (iv) of that Schedule;

(d) in the case of an order to which the provisions of Schedule 15 to the 1981 Act (procedure in connection with certain orders under Part III) apply, every person who was required to be given notice of that order by paragraph 3(2)(b)(i), (ii) and (iv) of that Schedule;

(e) in the case of an order to which the provisions of Schedule 14 to the 1990 Act (procedure for footpaths and bridleways orders) apply, every person who was required to be given notice of that order by paragraph 1(2)(b)(i) to (iii) and (v) of that Schedule; and

(f) every person (in these Rules referred to as a "relevant person") who has duly made, and not withdrawn, any representation or objection referred to in paragraph 2(2) of Schedule 6 to the 1980 Act (provisions as to making, confirmation, validity and date of operation of certain orders relating to footpaths, bridleways and restricted byways), paragraph 7(1) of Schedule 15 to the 1981 Act (procedure in connection with certain orders under Part III), or paragraph 3(1) of Schedule 14 to the 1990 Act (procedure for footpaths and bridleways orders), as the case may be.

(5) Paragraph (4)(c), (d) and (e) (as the case may be) do not apply in the case of an order in respect of which the Secretary of State has given a direction to which this paragraph applies.

(6) Paragraph (5) applies to—

(a) a direction under paragraph 1(3C) of Schedule 6 to the 1980 Act (provisions as to making, confirmation, validity and date of operation of certain orders relating to footpaths, bridleways and restricted byways) that it shall not be necessary to comply with paragraph 1(3)(b)(i) of that Schedule;

(b) a direction under paragraph 3(4) of Schedule 15 to the 1981 Act (procedure in connection with certain orders under Part III) that it shall not be necessary to comply with paragraph 3(2)(b)(i) of that Schedule; and

(c) a direction under paragraph 1(6) of Schedule 14 to the 1990 Act (procedure for footpaths and bridleways orders) that it shall not be necessary to comply with paragraph 1(2)(b)(i) of that Schedule.

(7) Where the Secretary of State has given a direction referred to in paragraph (6), the authority shall give a notice complying with paragraph (3) addressed to "the owners and any occupiers" of the land in question, by affixing a copy or copies of the notice to some conspicuous object or objects on the land.

(8) The Secretary of State shall ensure that a copy of the notice given by him under paragraph (1) is available for inspection on a website maintained by him until the hearing or inquiry is completed and the decision is notified under Part 3 or Part 4 (as the case may be).

[3660]

NOTES
Commencement: 1 October 2007.

PART 3
HEARINGS

5 Date and notification of hearing

(1) The date fixed by the Secretary of State for a hearing shall be—
  (a) not later than twenty weeks after the start date; or
  (b) where he considers that a date within such twenty-week period would not be practicable, the earliest date which he considers to be practicable after the expiry of that twenty-week period.

(2) The Secretary of State may at any time change the date, time or place fixed for the hearing (whether or not, in the case of a change of date, the new date is within the period mentioned in paragraph (1)(a)) and shall give such notice of the change as appears to him to be reasonable to every person mentioned in rule 4(4).

(3) Not less than four weeks before the date fixed for the hearing, the authority—
  (a) shall cause a notice of the hearing to be displayed in a prominent position at each end of so much of any way or proposed way as is affected by the order and in such other places in the locality as the authority may consider appropriate;
  (b) shall publish a notice of the hearing in one or more newspapers circulating in the locality in which the land to which the order relates is situated; and
  (c) may publish notice of the hearing by any additional means they consider appropriate.

(4) Every notice referred to in paragraph (3) shall contain—
  (a) the date, time and place of the hearing;
  (b) a brief description of—
    (i) the land to which the order that is the subject of the hearing relates; and
    (ii) the effect of the order; and
  (c) details of where and when copies of the order and documents relating to the hearing may be inspected and copied.

[3661]

NOTES
Commencement: 1 October 2007.

6 Submission of statements of case for the hearing

(1) The authority shall ensure that, within eight weeks of the start date, the Secretary of State has received their statement of case.

(2) As soon as practicable after the receipt of the statement of case mentioned in paragraph (1), the Secretary of State shall send a copy of that statement (excluding copies of any supporting documents) to the applicant (if any), each relevant person and any other person who has submitted or subsequently submits a statement of case under paragraph (5).

(3) The applicant shall ensure that, within 12 weeks of the start date, the Secretary of State has—
  (a) received his statement of case; or
  (b) received notice that he intends to rely on the authority's statement of case as his own.

(4) The Secretary of State shall, as soon as practicable after receiving the applicant's statement of case or notice under paragraph (3)—
  (a) send a copy of that statement or notice to the authority; and
  (b) send a copy of that statement (excluding copies of any supporting documents) or notice to each relevant person and to any other person who has submitted or subsequently submits a statement of case under paragraph (5).

(5) Every relevant person and every other person who wishes to give evidence at the hearing shall ensure that, within 12 weeks of the start date, the Secretary of State has received his statement of case.

(6) The Secretary of State shall, as soon as practicable—
  (a) send a copy of each statement which he receives under paragraph (5) to the authority;
  (b) send a copy of each such statement (excluding copies of any supporting documents) to the applicant (if any); and

(c) send a copy of each such statement (excluding copies of any supporting documents) to every other person who has submitted or subsequently submits a statement of case under paragraph (5).

[3662]

NOTES

Commencement: 1 October 2007.

7 Provision of further information

(1) The Secretary of State may require such further information as he may specify from any person in respect of his statement of case mentioned in rule 6.

(2) Any information required under paragraph (1) shall be provided in writing within such period as the Secretary of State may reasonably require.

(3) The Secretary of State shall, as soon as practicable after receipt of the further information required under paragraph (1), send a copy to the authority and to every other person who has submitted or subsequently submits a statement of case or notice under rule 6.

[3663]

NOTES

Commencement: 1 October 2007.

8 Appearances at the hearing

(1) The persons entitled to appear at the hearing are—

(a) the authority;

(b) the applicant;

(c) every relevant person; and

(d) every other person who has submitted a statement of case as mentioned in rule 6(5).

(2) The Secretary of State may permit any other person to appear at the hearing, and such permission shall not be unreasonably withheld.

(3) Any person entitled or permitted to appear may appear in person or be represented by any other person.

[3664]

NOTES

Commencement: 1 October 2007.

9 Procedure at the hearing

(1) Except as otherwise provided in these Rules, the inspector shall determine the procedure at the hearing.

(2) The hearing shall take the form of a discussion led by the inspector, and cross-examination shall not be permitted unless the inspector considers that cross-examination is required to ensure a thorough examination of the main issues.

(3) Where the inspector considers that cross-examination is required under paragraph (2), he shall consider, after consulting every person who—

(a) is entitled or permitted to appear at the hearing, and

(b) is present at that hearing,

whether the hearing should be closed and an inquiry should be held instead.

(4) At the start of the hearing the inspector shall identify—

(a) what are in his opinion the main issues to be considered at the hearing; and

(b) any matters on which he requires further explanation from any person appearing at the hearing.

(5) Paragraph (4) shall not preclude the addition in the course of the hearing of other issues for consideration or preclude any person entitled or permitted to appear at the hearing from referring to other issues which he considers to be relevant to the hearing.

(6) Subject to paragraph (7), any person appearing at the hearing may give, or call another person to give, oral evidence, and may present, or call another person to present, any matter.

(7) The inspector may at any stage in the proceedings refuse to permit—

(a) the giving or production of evidence, or

(b) the presentation of any matter,

which he considers to be irrelevant or repetitious.

(8) Where under paragraph (7) the inspector refuses to permit the giving or production of evidence or the presentation of any matter, the person wishing to give or produce evidence or to

present any matter, or to call any other person to give or produce evidence or to present any matter, may submit to the inspector any evidence or other matter in writing before the close of the hearing.

(9) The inspector may—

(a) require any person present at a hearing who, in his opinion, is behaving in a disruptive manner to leave; and

(b) refuse to permit that person to return or permit him to return only on such conditions as he may specify.

(10) Any person mentioned in paragraph (9) may submit to the inspector any evidence or other matter in writing before the close of the hearing.

(11) The inspector may, at the hearing, allow any person to alter or add to his statement of case received by the Secretary of State under rule 6 so far as may be necessary for the purposes of the hearing.

(12) Where the inspector has allowed an alteration or addition under paragraph (11), he shall (if necessary by adjourning the hearing) give—

(a) every other person appearing at the hearing,

(b) every other person present at the hearing who was entitled to receive a copy of the statement of case in question under rule 6, and

(c) such other persons as he considers appropriate,

an adequate opportunity of considering the alteration or addition.

(13) The inspector may—

(a) proceed with the hearing in the absence of any person entitled or permitted to appear at it;

(b) take into account any written representations, evidence or any other document received by him from any person before the hearing opens or during the hearing, provided he discloses it at the hearing; and

(c) from time to time adjourn the hearing.

[3665]

NOTES

Commencement: 1 October 2007.

10 Site inspections and adjourning the hearing to the land

(1) The inspector may make an unaccompanied inspection of the land to which the order relates before or during the hearing without giving notice of his intention to the persons entitled or permitted to appear at the hearing.

(2) During the hearing or after its close, the inspector—

(a) may inspect the land to which the order relates in the company of the authority and any person entitled or permitted to appear at the hearing; and

(b) shall make such an inspection if so requested before or during the hearing by the authority or any person entitled or permitted to appear at the hearing.

(3) The inspector shall not be required to make more than one inspection under paragraph (2)(b).

(4) In all cases where the inspector intends to make an accompanied inspection under paragraph (2), he shall announce during the hearing the date and time at which he proposes to make it.

(5) The inspector shall not be bound to defer an inspection in the event that any person entitled or permitted to appear at the hearing is not present at the appointed time.

(6) Where it appears to the inspector that one or more matters would be more satisfactorily resolved by adjourning the hearing to the land to which the order relates, he may adjourn the hearing to that land and may conclude the hearing there, provided he is satisfied that—

(a) the hearing would proceed satisfactorily and that no person entitled or permitted to appear at the hearing would be placed at a disadvantage; and

(b) no person entitled or permitted to appear at the hearing has raised any reasonable objection to the hearing being continued on that land.

(7) Nothing in this rule—

(a) entitles or requires the inspector (or those accompanying him, where applicable) to access land in order to make an inspection or to continue a hearing where such access would be unlawful; or

(b) requires the inspector to access land to make an inspection where making such an inspection would not, in the inspector's opinion, be expedient for reasons of safety.

(8) For the purposes of paragraph (7)(a), access is lawful on any occasion if the inspector (and those accompanying him, where applicable) may access the land on that occasion without committing an offence or trespassing on the land.

[3666]

NOTES

Commencement: 1 October 2007.

11 Procedure after hearing—decisions by the Secretary of State

(1) This rule applies where a hearing has been held for the purposes of a decision by the Secretary of State as respects an order.

(2) After the close of the hearing, the inspector shall make a report in writing to the Secretary of State which shall include his conclusions and either his recommendations or his reasons for not making any recommendations.

(3) When making his decision the Secretary of State may disregard any subsequent material.

(4) Paragraph (5) applies where, after the close of the hearing, the Secretary of State—

(a) differs from the inspector on any matter of fact mentioned in, or appearing to him to be material to, a conclusion reached by the inspector, and is, for that reason, minded to disagree with a recommendation made by the inspector, or

(b) takes into consideration any subsequent material which he considers to be relevant to his decision.

(5) Where this paragraph applies, the Secretary of State shall not come to a decision without first—

(a) giving notice to the persons mentioned in paragraph (6)—

(i) that he is minded to disagree with a recommendation made by the inspector, and of the reasons for being so minded, or

(ii) of the subsequent material which he considers to be relevant to his decision; and

(b) affording the persons mentioned in paragraph (6) an opportunity to make written representations to him and to ask for the hearing to be re-opened.

(6) The persons referred to in paragraph (5) are every person who—

(a) was entitled to appear at the hearing, or

(b) appeared at the hearing with the Secretary of State's permission.

(7) Those persons making written representations or requesting that the hearing be re-opened under paragraph (5) shall ensure that such representations or requests are received by the Secretary of State within three weeks of the date of the Secretary of State's notice under that paragraph.

(8) The Secretary of State may, if he thinks fit, cause a hearing to be re-opened.

(9) Where a hearing is re-opened under paragraph (8)—

(a) the Secretary of State shall, not less than eight weeks before the date of the re-opened hearing, send to every person who was entitled to appear at the hearing, and every person who appeared at the hearing with the Secretary of State's permission, a written statement of the matters with respect to which further evidence or argument is invited; and

(b) paragraphs (2) to (4) of rule 5 shall apply as if the references to a hearing were references to a re-opened hearing.

[3667]

NOTES

Commencement: 1 October 2007.

12 Procedure after hearing—transferred decisions

(1) This rule applies where a hearing has been held for the purposes of a transferred decision.

(2) When making his decision the inspector may disregard any subsequent material.

(3) If, after the close of the hearing, the inspector takes into consideration any subsequent material which he considers to be relevant to his decision, he shall not come to a decision without first—

(a) giving notice of the subsequent material which he considers to be relevant to his decision to every person who was entitled to appear at the hearing and every person who appeared at the hearing with the Secretary of State's permission; and

(b) affording such persons an opportunity to make written representations to him and to ask for the hearing to be re-opened.

(4) Any person wishing to avail himself of the opportunity mentioned in paragraph (3)(b) shall ensure that such written representations or requests to re-open the hearing are received by the Secretary of State within three weeks of the date of the notification mentioned in paragraph (3)(a).

(5) The inspector may, if he thinks fit, cause a hearing to be re-opened.

(6) Where a hearing is re-opened under paragraph (5)—

(a) the inspector shall send to every person who was entitled to appear at the hearing, and every person who appeared at the hearing with the Secretary of State's permission, a written statement of the matters with respect to which further evidence or argument is invited; and

(b) paragraphs (2) to (4) of rule 5 shall apply as if the references to a hearing were references to a re-opened hearing.

[3668]

NOTES

Commencement: 1 October 2007.

13 Notification of decision—decisions by the Secretary of State

(1) This rule applies where a hearing has been held under these Rules for the purposes of a decision by the Secretary of State.

(2) The Secretary of State shall, as soon as practicable, give notice of his decision and his reasons for it, to—

(a) every person who was entitled to appear at the hearing under rule 8(1);

(b) every person who appeared at the hearing with the Secretary of State's permission; and

(c) every other person who was notified by the Secretary of State in accordance with rule 4(4)(c) to (f).

(3) Where a copy of the inspector's report is not sent with the notice of the decision given under paragraph (2), that notice shall include a statement of the inspector's conclusions and of any recommendations made by him.

(4) If a person entitled to be notified of the Secretary of State's decision has not received a copy of the report mentioned in paragraph (3), he shall be supplied with a copy of it on written application to the Secretary of State.

(5) As soon as practicable after giving notice of his decision under paragraph (2), the Secretary of State shall make a copy of that notice available for inspection for a period of three months on a website maintained by him.

(6) In this rule, "report" does not include any documents appended to the inspector's report, but any person who has received a copy of the report may apply in writing to the Secretary of State for an opportunity to inspect any such documents and the Secretary of State shall afford him that opportunity.

[3669]

NOTES

Commencement: 1 October 2007.

14 Notification of decision—transferred decisions

(1) This rule applies where a hearing has been held under these Rules for the purposes of a transferred decision.

(2) The inspector shall, as soon as practicable, give notice of his decision and his reasons for it, to—

(a) every person who was entitled to appear at the hearing under rule 8(1);

(b) every person who appeared at the hearing with the Secretary of State's permission; and

(c) every other person who was notified by the Secretary of State in accordance with rule 4(4)(c) to (f).

(3) Any person entitled to be notified of the inspector's decision under paragraph (2) may apply in writing to the Secretary of State for an opportunity of inspecting any documents referred to in that notification, and the Secretary of State shall afford him that opportunity.

(4) The Secretary of State shall ensure that, as soon as practicable after the notice has been given under paragraph (2), a copy of that notice is made available for inspection for a period of three months on a website maintained by him.

[3670]

NOTES

Commencement: 1 October 2007.

PART 4
INQUIRIES

15 Procedure where the Secretary of State causes a pre-inquiry meeting to be held

(1) The Secretary of State shall cause a pre-inquiry meeting to be held if such a meeting appears to him to be necessary.

(2) The Secretary of State shall give not less than 14 days' notice of a pre-inquiry meeting to every person to whom notice of the inquiry was given under rule 4(4).

(3) The inspector—

- (a) shall preside at the pre-inquiry meeting;
- (b) shall determine the matters to be discussed and the procedure to be followed;
- (c) may require any person present at the pre-inquiry meeting who, in his opinion, is behaving in a disruptive manner to leave; and
- (d) may refuse to permit that person to return or to attend any further pre-inquiry meeting or may permit him to return or attend only on such conditions as he may specify.

(4) Where a pre-inquiry meeting is held pursuant to paragraph (1), the Secretary of State may cause a further pre-inquiry meeting to be held and he shall arrange for such notice to be given of that further meeting as appears to him necessary.

(5) Paragraphs (3) and (6) shall apply to any pre-inquiry meeting held pursuant to paragraph (4).

(6) Where a pre-inquiry meeting is held, the inspector—

- (a) shall arrange a timetable for proceedings at the inquiry where it appears likely that the inquiry will last for eight days or more;
- (b) may, in respect of inquiries which appear likely to last for a shorter period, arrange a timetable for the proceedings.

(7) In this rule, "pre-inquiry meeting" means a meeting held before an inquiry to consider what may be done to ensure that the inquiry is conducted efficiently and expeditiously.

[3671]

NOTES

Commencement: 1 October 2007.

16 Date and notification of inquiry

(1) The date fixed by the Secretary of State for an inquiry shall be—

- (a) not later than twenty-six weeks after the start date; or
- (b) where he considers that a date within such twenty-six-week period would not be practicable, the earliest date which he considers to be practicable after the expiry of that twenty-six-week period.

(2) The Secretary of State may at any time change the date, time or place fixed for the inquiry (whether or not, in the case of a change of date, the new date is within the period mentioned in paragraph (1)(a)) and shall give such notice of the change as appears to him to be reasonable to every person mentioned in rule 4(4).

(3) Not less than four weeks before the date fixed for the inquiry, the authority—

- (a) shall cause a notice of the inquiry to be displayed in a prominent position at each end of so much of any way or proposed way as is affected by the order and in such other places in the locality as the authority may consider appropriate;
- (b) shall publish a notice of the inquiry in one or more newspapers circulating in the locality in which the land to which the order relates is situated; and
- (c) may publish notice of the inquiry by any additional means they consider appropriate.

(4) Every notice referred to in paragraph (3) shall contain—

- (a) the date, time and place of the inquiry;
- (b) a brief description of—
  - (i) the land to which the order that is the subject of the inquiry relates; and
  - (ii) the effect of the order; and
- (c) details of where and when copies of the order and documents relating to the inquiry may be inspected and copied.

[3672]

NOTES

Commencement: 1 October 2007.

17 Submission of statements of case for the inquiry

(1) The authority shall ensure that, within eight weeks of the start date, the Secretary of State has received their statement of case.

(2) As soon as practicable after the receipt of the statement of case mentioned in paragraph (1), the Secretary of State shall send a copy of that statement (excluding copies of any supporting documents) to the applicant (if any), each relevant person and any other person who has submitted or subsequently submits a statement of case under paragraph (5).

(3) The applicant shall ensure that, within 14 weeks of the start date, the Secretary of State has—

(a) received his statement of case, or
(b) received notice that he intends to rely on the authority's statement of case as his own.

(4) The Secretary of State shall, as soon as practicable after receiving the applicant's statement of case or notice under paragraph (3)—

(a) send a copy of that statement or notice to the authority; and
(b) send a copy of that statement (excluding copies of any supporting documents) to each relevant person and to any other person who has submitted or subsequently submits a statement of case under paragraph (5).

(5) Every relevant person and every other person who wishes to give evidence at the inquiry shall ensure that, within 14 weeks of the start date, the Secretary of State has received his statement of case.

(6) The Secretary of State shall, as soon as practicable—

(a) send a copy of each statement which he receives under paragraph (5) to the authority;
(b) send a copy of each such statement (excluding copies of any supporting documents) to the applicant (if any); and
(c) send a copy of each such statement (excluding copies of any supporting documents) to every other person who has submitted or subsequently submits a statement of case under paragraph (5).

[3673]

NOTES

Commencement: 1 October 2007.

18 Provision of further information

(1) The Secretary of State may require such further information as he may specify from any person in respect of his statement of case mentioned in rule 17.

(2) Any information required under paragraph (1) shall be provided in writing within such period as the Secretary of State may reasonably require.

(3) The Secretary of State shall, as soon as practicable after receipt of the further information required under paragraph (1), send a copy to the authority and to every other person who has submitted or subsequently submits a statement of case or notice under rule 17.

[3674]

NOTES

Commencement: 1 October 2007.

19 Appearances at the inquiry

(1) The persons entitled to appear at the inquiry are—

(a) the authority;
(b) the applicant;
(c) every relevant person; and
(d) every other person who has submitted a statement of case in respect of the inquiry as mentioned in rule 17(5).

(2) The Secretary of State may permit any other person to appear at the inquiry, and such permission shall not be unreasonably withheld.

(3) Any person entitled or permitted to appear may appear in person or be represented by any other person.

[3675]

NOTES

Commencement: 1 October 2007.

20 Proofs of evidence

(1) Any person entitled or permitted to appear at the inquiry under rule 19 who proposes to give, or to call another person to give, evidence at the inquiry by reading a proof of evidence shall send the proof of evidence in question (together with any summary required under paragraph (4)) to the Secretary of State.

(2) Where a proof of evidence (together with any summary required under paragraph (4)) (the "relevant documents") is sent to the Secretary of State under paragraph (1), the Secretary of State shall as soon as practicable send the relevant documents to the persons specified in paragraph (3).

(3) The persons referred to in paragraph (2) are—

(a) in the case of relevant documents received from the authority, the applicant, each relevant person and any other person who has submitted or subsequently submits a statement of case;

(b) in the case of relevant documents received from the applicant, the authority, each relevant person and any other person who has submitted or subsequently submits a statement of case;

(c) in the case of relevant documents received from a relevant person, the authority, the applicant, each other relevant person and any other person who has submitted or subsequently submits a statement of case;

(d) in the case of relevant documents received from any person other than the authority, the applicant or a relevant person, the authority, the applicant, each relevant person and any other person who has submitted or subsequently submits a statement of case.

(4) A written summary shall be required where the proof of evidence in question exceeds one thousand five hundred words.

(5) The person sending the relevant documents shall ensure that they are received by the Secretary of State no later than four weeks before the date fixed for the holding of the inquiry.

(6) Where a written summary is provided in accordance with paragraphs (1) and (4), only that summary shall be read at the inquiry, unless the inspector permits or requires otherwise.

[3676]

NOTES

Commencement: 1 October 2007.

21 Procedure at the inquiry

(1) Except as otherwise provided in these Rules, the inspector shall determine the procedure at the inquiry.

(2) At the start of the inquiry the inspector shall identify—

(a) what are in his opinion the main issues to be considered at the inquiry; and

(b) any matters on which he requires further explanation from any person appearing at the inquiry.

(3) Paragraph (2) shall not preclude the addition in the course of the inquiry of other issues for consideration or preclude any person entitled or permitted to appear at the inquiry from referring to other issues which he considers to be relevant to the inquiry.

(4) Unless in a particular case the inspector otherwise determines, the authority shall begin and any other persons appearing at the inquiry shall be heard in such order as the inspector shall determine.

(5) Subject to paragraph (7), a person appearing at an inquiry may give, or call another person to give, oral evidence, and may present, or call another person to present, any matter.

(6) Subject to paragraph (7), any person appearing at the inquiry may cross-examine any person giving evidence orally or in writing or presenting any matter at the inquiry.

(7) The inspector may at any stage in the proceedings refuse to permit—

(a) the giving or production of evidence,

(b) any cross-examination, or

(c) the presentation of any matter,

which he considers to be irrelevant or repetitious.

(8) Where under paragraph (7) the inspector refuses to permit the giving or production of evidence or the presentation of any matter, the person wishing to give or produce evidence or to present any matter, or to call any other person to give or produce evidence or to present any matter, may submit to the inspector any evidence or other matter in writing before the close of the inquiry.

(9) Where a person gives evidence at an inquiry by reading a summary of his proof of evidence, the proof of evidence shall be treated as tendered in evidence, unless the person required to provide the summary notifies the inspector that he wishes to rely on the contents of that summary alone.

(10) The inspector may—

(a) require any person present at an inquiry who, in his opinion, is behaving in a disruptive manner to leave; and

(b) refuse to permit that person to return or permit him to return only on such conditions as he may specify.

(11) Any person mentioned in paragraph (10) may submit to the inspector any evidence or other matter in writing before the close of the inquiry.

(12) The inspector may, at the inquiry, allow any person to alter or add to his statement of case received by the Secretary of State under rule 17 or his proof of evidence or summary received by the Secretary of State under rule 20 so far as may be necessary for the purposes of the inquiry.

(13) Where the inspector has allowed an alteration or addition under paragraph (12), he shall (if necessary by adjourning the inquiry) give the persons mentioned in paragraph (14) an adequate opportunity of considering the alteration or addition.

(14) The persons referred to in paragraph (13) are—

(a) in the case of an alteration or addition to a statement of case—

(i) every other person appearing at the inquiry;

(ii) every other person present at the inquiry who was entitled to receive a copy of the statement of case in question under rule 17; and

(iii) such other persons as the inspector considers appropriate; and

(b) in the case of an alteration or addition to a proof of evidence or summary—

(i) every other person appearing at the inquiry;

(ii) every other person present at the inquiry who was entitled to receive a copy of the relevant documents in question under rule 20; and

(iii) such other persons as he considers appropriate.

(15) The inspector may—

(a) proceed with the inquiry in the absence of any person entitled or permitted to appear at it;

(b) take into account any written representations, evidence or any other document received by him from any person before the inquiry opens or during the inquiry, provided he discloses it at the inquiry; and

(c) from time to time adjourn the inquiry.

[3677]

NOTES

Commencement: 1 October 2007.

22 Site inspections and adjourning the inquiry to the land

(1) The inspector may make an unaccompanied inspection of the land to which the order relates before or during the inquiry without giving notice of his intention to the persons entitled or permitted to appear at the inquiry.

(2) During the inquiry or after its close, the inspector—

(a) may inspect the land to which the order relates in the company of the authority and any person entitled or permitted to appear at the inquiry; and

(b) shall make such an inspection if so requested before or during the inquiry by the authority or any person entitled or permitted to appear at the inquiry.

(3) The inspector shall not be required to make more than one inspection under paragraph (2)(b).

(4) In all cases where the inspector intends to make an accompanied inspection under paragraph (2), he shall announce during the inquiry the date and time at which he proposes to make it.

(5) The inspector shall not be bound to defer an inspection in the event that any person entitled or permitted to appear at the inquiry is not present at the appointed time.

(6) Where it appears to the inspector that one or more matters would be more satisfactorily resolved by adjourning the inquiry to the land to which the order relates, he may adjourn the inquiry to that land and may conclude the inquiry there, provided he is satisfied that—

(a) the inquiry would proceed satisfactorily and that no person entitled or permitted to appear at the inquiry would be placed at a disadvantage; and

(b) no person entitled or permitted to appear at the inquiry has raised any reasonable objection to the inquiry being continued on that land.

(7) Nothing in this rule—

(a) entitles or requires the inspector (or those accompanying him, where applicable) to access land in order to make an inspection or to continue an inquiry where such access would be unlawful; or

(b) requires the inspector to access land to make an inspection where making such an inspection would not, in the inspector's opinion, be expedient for reasons of safety.

(8) For the purposes of paragraph (7)(a), access is lawful on any occasion if the inspector (and those accompanying him, where applicable) may access the land on that occasion without committing an offence or trespassing on the land.

[3678]

NOTES

Commencement: 1 October 2007.

23 Procedure after inquiry—decisions by the Secretary of State

(1) This rule applies where an inquiry has been held for the purposes of a decision by the Secretary of State as respects an order.

(2) After the close of the inquiry the inspector shall make a report in writing to the Secretary of State which shall include his conclusions and either his recommendations or his reasons for not making any recommendations.

(3) When making his decision the Secretary of State may disregard any subsequent material.

(4) Paragraph (5) applies where, after the close of the inquiry, the Secretary of State—

(a) differs from the inspector on any matter of fact mentioned in, or appearing to him to be material to, a conclusion reached by the inspector, and is, for that reason, minded to disagree with a recommendation made by the inspector, or

(b) takes into consideration any subsequent material which he considers to be relevant to his decision.

(5) Where this paragraph applies, the Secretary of State shall not come to a decision without first—

(a) giving notice to the persons mentioned in paragraph (6)—

(i) that he is minded to disagree with a recommendation made by the inspector, and of the reasons for being so minded, or

(ii) of the subsequent material which he considers to be relevant to his decision; and

(b) affording the persons mentioned in paragraph (6) an opportunity to make written representations to him and to ask for the inquiry to be re-opened.

(6) The persons referred to in paragraph (5) are every person who—

(a) was entitled to appear at the inquiry, or

(b) appeared at the inquiry with the Secretary of State's permission.

(7) Those persons making written representations or requesting that the inquiry be re-opened under paragraph (5) shall ensure that such representations or requests are received by the Secretary of State within three weeks of the date of the Secretary of State's notice under that paragraph.

(8) The Secretary of State may, if he thinks fit, cause an inquiry to be re-opened.

(9) Where an inquiry is re-opened under paragraph (8)—

(a) the Secretary of State shall, not less than eight weeks before the date of the re-opened inquiry, send to every person who was entitled to appear at the inquiry, and every person who appeared at the inquiry with the Secretary of State's permission, a written statement of the matters with respect to which further evidence or argument is invited; and

(b) paragraphs (2) to (4) of rule 16 shall apply as if the references to an inquiry were references to a re-opened inquiry.

[3679]

NOTES

Commencement: 1 October 2007.

24 Procedure after inquiry—transferred decisions

(1) This rule applies where an inquiry has been held for the purposes of a transferred decision.

(2) When making his decision the inspector may disregard any subsequent material.

(3) If, after the close of the inquiry, the inspector takes into consideration any subsequent material which he considers to be relevant to his decision, he shall not come to a decision without first—

(a) giving notice of the subsequent material which he considers to be relevant to his decision to every person who was entitled to appear at the inquiry and every person who appeared at the inquiry with the Secretary of State's permission; and

(b) affording such persons an opportunity to make written representations to him and to ask for the inquiry to be re-opened.

(4) Any person wishing to avail himself of the opportunity mentioned in paragraph (3)(b) shall ensure that such written representations or requests to re-open the inquiry are received by the Secretary of State within three weeks of the date of the notification mentioned in paragraph (3)(a).

(5) The inspector may, if he thinks fit, cause an inquiry to be re-opened.

(6) Where an inquiry is re-opened under paragraph (5)—

(a) the inspector shall send to every person who was entitled to appear at the inquiry, and every person who appeared at the inquiry with the Secretary of State's permission, a written statement of the matters with respect to which further evidence or argument is invited; and

(b) paragraphs (2) to (4) of rule 16 shall apply as if the references to an inquiry were references to a re-opened inquiry.

[3680]

NOTES

Commencement: 1 October 2007.

25 Notification of decision—decisions by the Secretary of State

(1) This rule applies where an inquiry has been held under these Rules for the purposes of a decision by the Secretary of State.

(2) The Secretary of State shall, as soon as practicable, give notice of his decision, and his reasons for it, to—

(a) every person who was entitled to appear at the inquiry under rule 19(1);

(b) every person who appeared at the inquiry with the Secretary of State's permission; and

(c) every other person who was notified by the Secretary of State in accordance with rule 4(4)(c) to (f).

(3) Where a copy of the inspector's report is not sent with the notice of the decision given under paragraph (2), that notice shall include a statement of the inspector's conclusions and of any recommendations made by him.

(4) If a person entitled to be notified of the Secretary of State's decision has not received a copy of the report mentioned in paragraph (3), he shall be supplied with a copy of it on written application to the Secretary of State.

(5) As soon as practicable after giving notice of his decision under paragraph (2), the Secretary of State shall make a copy of that notice available for inspection for a period of three months on a website maintained by him.

(6) In this rule, "report" does not include any documents appended to the inspector's report, but any person who has received a copy of the report may apply in writing to the Secretary of State for an opportunity to inspect any such documents and the Secretary of State shall afford him that opportunity.

[3681]

NOTES

Commencement: 1 October 2007.

26 Notification of decision—transferred decisions

(1) This rule applies where an inquiry has been held under these Rules for the purposes of a transferred decision.

(2) The inspector shall, as soon as practicable, give notice of his decision, and his reasons for it, to—

(a) every person who was entitled to appear at the inquiry under rule 19(1);

(b) every person who appeared at the inquiry with the Secretary of State's permission; and

(c) every other person who was notified by the Secretary of State in accordance with rule 4(4)(c) to (f).

(3) Any person entitled to be notified of the inspector's decision under paragraph (2) may apply in writing to the Secretary of State for an opportunity of inspecting any documents referred to in that notification and the Secretary of State shall afford him that opportunity.

(4) The Secretary of State shall ensure that, as soon as practicable after the notice has been given under paragraph (2), a copy of that notice is made available for inspection for a period of three months on a website maintained by him.

[3682]

NOTES

Commencement: 1 October 2007.

PART 5
MODIFICATION OF ORDERS

27 Modification of orders

(1) This rule applies where the Secretary of State has given notice of his proposal to modify an order under—

(a) paragraph 2(3)(a) of Schedule 6 to the 1980 Act (provisions as to making, confirmation, validity and date of operation of certain orders relating to footpaths, bridleways and restricted byways);

(b) paragraph 8(2)(a) of Schedule 15 to the 1981 Act (procedure in connection with certain orders under Part III); or

(c) paragraph 3(6)(a) of Schedule 14 to the 1990 Act (procedure for footpaths and bridleways orders).

(2) Where in accordance with the notice referred to in paragraph (1) any person has duly made and not withdrawn any representation or objection with respect to the proposal to modify the order, the Secretary of State shall give notice to—

(a) the persons referred to in rule 4(4); and

(b) any person who has duly made and not withdrawn any representation or objection with respect to the proposal to modify the order.

(3) Rule 4(3) shall apply to a notice given under paragraph (2) of this rule as it applies to a notice given under rule 4(1), but the notice given under paragraph (2) of this rule shall also describe the effect of the Secretary of State's proposal to modify the order.

(4) Rules 4(7) and 5 to 14 shall apply to hearings afforded by the Secretary of State in accordance with paragraph 2(3) of Schedule 6 to the 1980 Act (provisions as to making, confirmation, validity and date of operation of certain orders relating to footpaths, bridleways and restricted byways), paragraph 8(2) of Schedule 15 to the 1981 Act (procedure in connection with certain orders under Part III) or paragraph 3(6) of Schedule 14 to the 1990 Act (procedure for footpaths and bridleways orders), except that—

(a) in the application of rule 4(7), the notice given shall also describe the effect of the Secretary of State's proposal to modify the order; and

(b) in the application of rule 6, for the references in rule 6(3) and (5) to "12 weeks of the start date" there shall be substituted "eight weeks of the start date".

(5) Rules 4(7) and 15 to 26 shall apply to inquiries caused to be held by the Secretary of State in accordance with the provisions of the 1980 Act, the 1981 Act or the 1990 Act mentioned in paragraph (4), except that—

(a) in the application of rule 4(7), the notice given shall also describe the effect of the Secretary of State's proposal to modify the order; and

(b) in the application of rule 17, for the references in rule 17(3) and (5) to "14 weeks of the start date" there shall be substituted "eight weeks of the start date".

[3683]

NOTES

Commencement: 1 October 2007.

PART 6
GENERAL

28 Further time

The Secretary of State may, at any time in any particular case, allow further time for the taking of any step or the doing of any thing which is required or enabled to be taken or done by virtue of these Rules, and references in these Rules to a period within which any step or thing is required or enabled to be taken or done shall be construed accordingly.

[3684]

NOTES

Commencement: 1 October 2007.

29 Inspection and copying of documents

(1) The authority shall afford any person who so requests an opportunity to inspect and take copies of—

(a) the order as submitted to the Secretary of State for confirmation in accordance with the provisions listed in rule 4(2)(a) to (c);

(b) any representations or objections duly made and not withdrawn in respect of the order, as mentioned in rule 4(4)(f);

(c) the notice given by the Secretary of State pursuant to rule 4(1);

(d) any statement of case mentioned in rule 6 (as regards hearings) or rule 17 (as regards inquiries);
(e) any further information received as mentioned in rule 7(3) (as regards hearings) or rule 18(3) (as regards inquiries);
(f) any representations which have been made in consequence of rules 11(5) or 12(3) (as regards hearings), and rules 23(5) or 24(3) (as regards inquiries);
(g) any relevant documents; and
(h) any other document which is in the possession of the authority and which relates to the decision of the Secretary of State or the inspector's report in respect of the order.

(2) The inspector may—
(a) at any time, request from any person entitled or permitted to appear at the hearing or inquiry (as the case may be) copies of any document or information available to that person; and
(b) specify a reasonable time within which such copies should be received by him.

(3) Any person so requested shall ensure that the copies referred to in paragraph (2) are received by the inspector within the period specified pursuant to paragraph (2)(b).

[3685]

NOTES
Commencement: 1 October 2007.

30 Notices

Subject to rule 31, any notice required under these Rules shall be in writing.

[3686]

NOTES
Commencement: 1 October 2007.

31 Use of electronic communications

(1) Any requirement imposed under these Rules as to the giving or sending by one person to another of a notice or other document may be met by means of an electronic communication if—
(a) the use of such a communication results in the information contained in that notice or document being available to the other person in all material respects as it would appear in a notice or document given or sent in printed form; and
(b) the other person has consented to the information being made available to him by such means.

(2) Where, under paragraph (1), an electronic communication is used for the purposes of giving or sending a document, any requirement for the notice or document to be given or sent by a particular time shall be met in respect of an electronic communication only if the conditions mentioned in paragraph (1) are met by that time.

(3) For the purposes of paragraph (1)(a), "in all material respects" means in all respects material to an exact reproduction of the information that the notice or document would contain were it to be given or sent in printed form.

(4) In this rule, "electronic communication" has the meaning given in section 15(1) of the Electronic Communications Act 2000.

[3687]

NOTES
Commencement: 1 October 2007.

32 Transitional provision

These Rules shall not apply to any hearing or inquiry held in relation to an order submitted to the Secretary of State for confirmation before the date on which these Rules come into force.

[3688]

NOTES
Commencement: 1 October 2007.

LAND REGISTRATION FEE ORDER 2009

(SI 2009/845)

NOTES
Made: 1 April 2009.
Authority: Land Registration Act 2002, ss 102, 128(1).
Commencement: 6 July 2009.

PART 1
GENERAL

1 Citation, commencement and interpretation

(1) This Order may be cited as the Land Registration Fee Order 2009 and shall come into force on 6 July 2009.

(2) In this Order—

"account holder" means a person holding a credit account,
"the Act" means the Land Registration Act 2002,
"CLRA" means the Commonhold and Leasehold Reform Act 2002,
"charge" includes a sub-charge,
"common parts" has the same meaning as in the CLRA,
"a commonhold" has the same meaning as in the CLRA,
"commonhold association" has the same meaning as in the CLRA,
"commonhold community statement" has the same meaning as in the CLRA,
"commonhold land" has the same meaning as in the CLRA,
"commonhold unit" has the same meaning as in the CLRA,
"credit account" means an account authorised by the registrar under article 14(1),
"developer" has the same meaning as in the CLRA,
"large scale application" has the same meaning as in article 6(1)(b),
"monetary consideration" means a consideration in money or money's worth (other than a nominal consideration or a consideration consisting solely of a covenant to pay money owing under a mortgage),
"premium" means the amount or value of any monetary consideration given by the lessee as part of the same transaction in which a lease is granted by way of fine, premium or otherwise, but, where a registered leasehold estate of substantially the same land is surrendered on the grant of a new lease, the premium for the new lease shall not include the value of the surrendered lease,
"profit" means a profit a prendre in gross,
"remote terminal" means a remote terminal communicating with the registrar's computer system in accordance with a notice given under Schedule 2 to the rules,
"rent" means the largest amount of annual rent the lease reserves within the first five years of its term that can be quantified at the time an application to register the lease is made,
"the rules" means the Land Registration Rules 2003 and a rule referred to by number means the rule so numbered in the rules,
"Scale 1" means Scale 1 in Schedule 1,
"Scale 2" means Scale 2 in Schedule 2,
"scale fee" means a fee payable in accordance with a scale set out in Schedule 1 or 2 whether or not reduced in accordance with article 2(6),
"scale fee application" means an application which attracts a scale fee, or which would attract such a fee but for the operation of article 6,
"share" in relation to land, means an interest in that land under a trust of land,
"surrender" includes a surrender not made by deed,
"termination application" has the same meaning as in the CLRA,
"unit-holder" has the same meaning as in the CLRA,
"voluntary application" means an application for first registration (other than for the registration of title to a rentcharge, a franchise or a profit) which is not made wholly or in part pursuant to section 4 of the Act (when title must be registered).

(3) Expressions used in this Order have, unless the contrary intention appears, the meaning which they bear in the rules.

[3689]

NOTES
Commencement: 6 July 2009.

PART 2
SCALE FEES

2 Applications for first registration and applications for registration of a lease by an original lessee

(1) The fee for an application for first registration of an estate in land is payable under Scale 1 on the value of the estate in land comprised in the application assessed under article 7, unless the application is—

(a) for the registration of title to a lease by the original lessee or his personal representative, where paragraph (2) applies,
(b) a voluntary application, where either paragraph (6) or article 6(3) applies, or
(c) a large scale application, where article 6 applies.

(2) The fee for an application by the original lessee or his personal representative for the registration of title to a lease, or for the registration of the grant of a lease, is payable under Scale 1—

(a) on an amount equal to the sum of the premium and the rent, or
(b) where
  (i) there is no premium, and
  (ii) either there is no rent or the rent cannot be quantified at the time the application is made,

on the value of the lease assessed under article 7 subject to a minimum fee of £50,

unless either of the circumstances in paragraph (3) applies.

(3) Paragraph (2) shall not apply if the application is—

(a) a voluntary application, where paragraph (6) applies, or
(b) a large scale application, where article 6 applies.

(4) The fee for an application for the first registration of a rentcharge is £50.

(5) The fee for an application for the first registration of a franchise or a profit is payable under Scale 1 on the value of the franchise or the profit assessed under article 7.

(6) The fee for a voluntary application (other than a large scale application, where article 6(3) applies) is the fee which would otherwise be payable under paragraph (1) or (2) reduced by 25 per cent and, where the reduced fee would be a figure which includes pence, the fee must be adjusted to the nearest £10.

(7) In paragraph (2) "lease" means—

(a) a lease which grants an estate in land whether or not the grant is a registrable disposition, or
(b) a lease of a franchise, profit or manor the grant of which is a registrable disposition.

[3690]

NOTES
Commencement: 6 July 2009.

3 Transfers of registered estates for monetary consideration, etc

(1) Subject to paragraphs (2), (3) and (4), the fee for an application for the registration of—

(a) a transfer of a registered estate for monetary consideration,
(b) a transfer for the purpose of giving effect to a disposition for monetary consideration of a share in a registered estate, or
(c) a surrender of a registered leasehold estate for monetary consideration, other than a surrender to which paragraph (3) of Schedule 4 applies,

is payable under Scale 1 on the amount or value of the consideration.

(2) Paragraph (1) shall not apply if the application is—

(a) a large scale application, where article 6 applies, or
(b) for the registration of a transfer of a registered estate made pursuant to an order of the Court under the Matrimonial Causes Act 1973 or the Civil Partnership Act 2004, where article 4(1)(h) applies.

(3) Where a sale and sub-sale of a registered estate are made by separate deeds of transfer, a separate fee is payable for each deed of transfer.

(4) Where a single deed of transfer gives effect to a sale and a sub-sale of the same registered estate a single fee is assessed upon the greater of the monetary consideration given by the purchaser and the monetary consideration given by the sub-purchaser.

(5) The fee for an application to cancel an entry in the register of notice of an unregistered lease which has determined is payable under Scale 1 on the value of the lease immediately before its determination assessed under article 7.

[3691]

PART II
STATUTORY INSTRUMENTS

NOTES

Commencement: 6 July 2009.

4 Transfers of registered estates otherwise than for monetary consideration, etc

(1) Unless the application is a large scale application (where article 6 applies), the fee for an application for the registration of—

(a) a transfer of a registered estate otherwise than for monetary consideration (unless paragraph (2) applies),

(b) a surrender of a registered leasehold estate otherwise than for monetary consideration,

(c) a transfer of a registered estate by operation of law on death or bankruptcy, of an individual proprietor,

(d) an assent of a registered estate (including a vesting assent),

(e) an appropriation of a registered estate,

(f) a vesting order or declaration to which section 27(5) of the Act applies,

(g) an alteration of the register, or

(h) a transfer of a registered estate made pursuant to an order of the Court under the Matrimonial Causes Act 1973 or the Civil Partnership Act 2004,

is payable under Scale 2 on the value of the registered estate which is the subject of the application, assessed under article 7, but after deducting from it the amount secured on the registered estate by any charge subject to which the registration takes effect.

(2) Where a transfer of a registered estate otherwise than for monetary consideration is for the purpose of giving effect to the disposition of a share in a registered estate, the fee for an application for its registration is payable under Scale 2 on the value of that share.

[3692]

NOTES

Commencement: 6 July 2009.

5 Charges of registered estates or registered charges

(1) The fee for an application for the registration of a charge is payable under Scale 2 on the amount of the charge assessed under article 8 unless it is an application to which paragraph (2), (3) or (4) applies.

(2) No fee is payable for an application to register a charge lodged with or before the completion of either a scale fee application or an application to which paragraph (17) in Part 1 of Schedule 3 applies ("the primary application") that will result in the chargor being registered as proprietor of the registered estate included in the charge unless—

(a) the charge includes a registered estate which is not included in the primary application, where paragraph (4) applies, or

(b) the primary application is a voluntary application, in which case this paragraph shall apply only if the application to register the charge accompanies the primary application.

(3) No fee is to be paid for an application to register a charge made by a predecessor in title of the applicant that is lodged with or before completion of an application for first registration of the estate included in the charge.

(4) Where a charge also includes a registered estate which is not included in the primary application ("the additional property") any fee payable under Scale 2 is to be assessed on an amount calculated as follows:

(Value of the additional property / Value of all the property included in the charge) × Amount secured by the charge

(5) The fee for an application for the registration of—

(a) a transfer of a registered charge for monetary consideration, or

(b) a transfer for the purpose of giving effect to a disposition for monetary consideration of a share in a registered charge,

is payable under Scale 2 on the amount or value of the consideration.

(6) The fee for an application for the registration of the transfer of a registered charge otherwise than for monetary consideration is payable under Scale 2 on—

(a) the amount secured by the registered charge at the time of the transfer, or

(b) where the transfer relates to more than one charge, the aggregate of the amounts secured by the registered charges at the time of the transfer.

(7) The fee for an application for the registration of a transfer for the purpose of giving effect to a disposition otherwise than for monetary consideration of a share in a registered charge is payable under Scale 2 on—

(a) the proportionate part of the amount secured by the registered charge at the time of the transfer, or

(b) where the transfer relates to more than one charge, the proportionate part of the aggregate of the amounts secured by the registered charges at the time of the transfer.

(8) This article takes effect subject to article 6 (large scale applications).

[3693]

NOTES

Commencement: 6 July 2009.

6 Large scale applications, etc

(1) In this article—

(a) "land unit" means—

(i) the land registered under a single title number other than, in the case of an application to register a charge, any estate under any title number which is included in a primary application within the meaning of article 5(2), or

(ii) on a first registration application, a separate area of land not adjoining any other unregistered land affected by the same application.

(b) "large scale application" means a scale fee application which relates to 20 or more land units, other than an application to register a disposition by the developer affecting the whole or part of the freehold estate in land which has been registered as a freehold estate in commonhold land, or a low value application,

(c) "low value application" means a scale fee application, other than an application for first registration, where the value of the land or the amount of the charge to which it relates (as the case may be) does not exceed £30,000.

(2) Subject to paragraphs (3) and (4), the fee for a large scale application is the greater of—

(a) the scale fee, and

(b) a fee calculated on the following basis —

(i) where the application relates to not more than 500 land units, £12 for each land unit, or

(ii) where the application relates to more than 500 land units, £6,000 plus £6 for each land unit in excess of 500.

(3) If a large scale application is a voluntary application, the fee payable under paragraph (2) is reduced by 25 per cent and, where the reduced fee would be a figure which includes pence, the fee must be adjusted to the nearest £10.

(4) The maximum fee payable for a large scale application for first registration is £52,000 unless the application is a voluntary application in which case the maximum fee is £39,000.

[3694]

NOTES

Commencement: 6 July 2009.

PART 3

VALUATION

7 Valuation (first registration and registered estates)

(1) The value of the estate in land, franchise, profit, manor or share is the maximum amount for which it could be sold in the open market free from any charge—

(a) in the case of a surrender, at the date immediately before the surrender, and

(b) in any other case, at the date of the application.

(2) As evidence of the amount referred to in paragraph (1), the registrar may require a written statement signed by the applicant or his conveyancer or by any other person who, in the registrar's opinion, is competent to make the statement.

(3) Where an application for first registration is made on—

(a) the purchase of a leasehold estate by the reversioner,

(b) the purchase of a reversion by the leaseholder, or

(c) any other like occasion,

and an unregistered interest is determined, the value of the land is the combined value of the reversionary and determined interests assessed in accordance with paragraphs (1) and (2).

[3695]

NOTES

Commencement: 6 July 2009.

8 Valuation (charges)

(1) On an application for registration of a charge, the amount of the charge is—

(a) where the charge secures a fixed amount, that amount,
(b) where the charge secures further advances and the maximum amount that can be advanced or owed at any one time is limited, that amount,
(c) where the charge secures further advances and the total amount that can be advanced or owed at any one time is not limited, the value of the property charged,
(d) where the charge is by way of additional or substituted security or by way of guarantee, an amount equal to the lesser of—
  (i) the amount secured or guaranteed, and
  (ii) the value of the property charged, or
(e) where the charge secures an obligation or liability which is contingent upon the happening of a future event ("the obligation"), and is not a charge to which sub-paragraph (d) applies, an amount equal to—
  (i) the maximum amount or value of the obligation, or
  (ii) if that maximum amount is greater than the value of the property charged, or is not limited by the charge, or cannot be calculated at the time of the application, the value of the property charged.

(2) Where a charge of a kind referred to in paragraph (1)(a) or (1)(b) is secured on unregistered land or other property as well as on a registered estate or registered charge, the fee is payable on an amount calculated as follows—

(Value of the registered estate or registered charge / Value of all the property charged) × Amount of the charge

(3) Where one deed contains two or more charges made by the same chargor to secure the same debt, the deed is to be treated as a single charge, and the fee for registration of the charge is to be paid on the lesser of—
(a) the amount of the whole debt, and
(b) an amount equal to the value of the property charged.

(4) Where one deed contains two or more charges to secure the same debt not made by the same chargor, the deed is to be treated as a separate single charge by each of the chargors and a separate fee is to be paid for registration of the charge by each chargor on the lesser of—
(a) the amount of the whole debt, and
(b) an amount equal to the value of the property charged by that chargor.

(5) In this article "value of the property charged" means the value of the registered estate or the amount of the registered charge or charges affected by the application to register the charge, less the amount secured by any prior registered charges.

[3696]

NOTES
Commencement: 6 July 2009.

PART 4
FIXED FEES AND EXEMPTIONS

9 Fixed fees

(1) Subject to paragraph (2) and to article 10, the fees for the applications and services specified in Schedule 3 shall be those set out in that Schedule.

(2) Where an application is one specified in paragraphs (1), (2) or (10) in Part 1 of Schedule 3 affecting the whole or part of the freehold estate in land which has been registered as a freehold estate in commonhold land registered in the name of the developer under more than one title number, the fee is to be assessed as if the application affects only one title.

[3697]

NOTES
Commencement: 6 July 2009.

10 Exemptions

No fee is payable for any of the applications and services specified in Schedule 4.

[3698]

NOTES
Commencement: 6 July 2009.

PART 5
GENERAL AND ADMINISTRATIVE PROVISIONS

11 Cost of surveys, advertisements and special enquiries

The applicant is to meet the costs of any survey, advertisement or other special enquiry that the registrar requires to be made or published in dealing with an application.

[3699]

NOTES

Commencement: 6 July 2009.

12 Applications not otherwise referred to

The fee payable for an application in respect of which no other fee is payable under this Order shall be £50.

[3700]

NOTES

Commencement: 6 July 2009.

13 Method of payment

(1) Except where the registrar otherwise permits, every fee shall be paid by means of a cheque or postal order crossed and made payable to Land Registry.

(2) Where there is an agreement with the applicant, a fee may be paid by direct debit to such bank account of the land registry as the registrar may from time to time direct.

(3) Where the amount of the fee payable on an application is immediately quantifiable, the fee shall be payable on delivery of the application.

(4) Where the amount of the fee payable on an application is not immediately quantifiable, the applicant shall pay the sum of £50 towards the fee when the application is made and shall lodge at the same time an undertaking to pay on demand the balance of the fee due, if any.

(5) Where an outline application is made, the fee payable shall be the fee payable under paragraph (9) of Part 1 of Schedule 3 in addition to the fee otherwise payable under this Order.

[3701]

NOTES

Commencement: 6 July 2009.

14 Credit accounts

(1) Any person may, if authorised by the registrar, use a credit account in accordance with this article for the payment of fees for applications and services of such kind as the registrar shall from time to time direct.

(2) To enable the registrar to consider whether or not a person applying to use a credit account may be so authorised, that person shall supply the registrar with such information and evidence as the registrar may require to satisfy him of that person's fitness to hold a credit account and the ability of that person to pay any amounts which may become due from time to time under a credit account.

(3) To enable the registrar to consider from time to time whether or not an account holder may continue to be authorised to use a credit account, the account holder shall supply the registrar, when requested to do so, with such information and evidence as the registrar may require to satisfy him of the account holder's continuing fitness to hold a credit account and the continuing ability of the account holder to pay any amounts which may become due from time to time under the account holder's credit account.

(4) Where an account holder makes an application where credit facilities are available to him, he may make a request, in such manner as the registrar directs, for the appropriate fee to be debited to the account holder's credit account, but the registrar shall not be required to accept such a request where the amount due on the account exceeds the credit limit applicable to the credit account, or would exceed it if the request were to be accepted.

(5) Where an account holder makes an application where credit facilities are available to him, and the application is accompanied neither by a fee nor a request for the fee to be debited to his account, the registrar may debit the fee to his account.

(6) The registrar shall send a statement of account to each account holder at the end of each calendar month or such other interval as the registrar shall direct.

(7) The account holder must pay any sums due on his credit account before the date and in the manner specified by the registrar.

(8) The registrar may at any time terminate or suspend any or all authorisations given under paragraph (1).

(9) In this article "credit limit" in relation to a credit account authorised for use under paragraph (1) means the maximum amount (if any) which is to be due on the account at any time, as notified by the registrar to the account holder from time to time, by means of such communication as the registrar considers appropriate.

[3702]

NOTES

Commencement: 6 July 2009.

15 (*Revokes the Land Registration Fee Order 2006, SI 2006/1332.*)

SCHEDULE 1
SCALE 1

Articles 2 & 3

NOTE 1: Where the amount or value is a figure which includes pence, it must be rounded down to the nearest £1.

NOTE 2: The third column, which sets out the reduced fee payable where article 2(6) (voluntary registration: reduced fees) applies, is not part of the scale.

Amount or value	*Fee*	*Reduced fee where article 2(6) (voluntary registration: reduced fees) applies*
£	£	£
0–50,000	50	40
50,001–80,000	80	60
80,001–100,000	130	100
100,001–200,000	200	150
200,001–500,000	280	210
500,001–1,000,000	550	410
1,000,001 and over	920	690

[3703]

NOTES

Commencement: 6 July 2009.

SCHEDULE 2
SCALE 2

Articles 4 & 5

NOTE: Where the amount or value is a figure which includes pence, it must be rounded down to the nearest £1.

Amount or value	*Fee*
£	£
0–100,000	50
100,001–200,000	70
200,001–500,000	90
500,001–1,000,000	130
1,000,001 and over	260

[3704]

NOTES

Commencement: 6 July 2009.

SCHEDULE 3

Articles 9 & 13

PART 1
FIXED FEE APPLICATIONS

	Fee
(1) To register:	
(a) a standard form of restriction contained in Schedule 4 to the rules, or	
(b) a notice (other than a notice to which section 117(2)(b) of the Act applies), or	
(c) a new or additional beneficiary of a unilateral notice	
—total fee for up to three registered titles affected	£50
—additional fee for each subsequent registered title affected	£25
Provided that no such fee is payable if, in relation to each registered title affected, the application is accompanied by a scale fee application or another application which attracts a fee under this paragraph.	
(2) To register a restriction in a form not contained in Schedule 4 to the rules—for each registered title	£100
(3) To register a caution against first registration (other than a caution to which section 117(2)(a) of the Act applies)	£50
(4) To alter a cautions register—for each individual cautions register	£50
(5) To close or partly close a registered leasehold or a registered rentcharge title other than on surrender—for each registered title closed or partly closed	£50
Provided that no such fee is payable if the application is accompanied by a scale fee application.	
(6) To upgrade from one class of registered title to another	£50
Provided that no such fee is payable if the application for upgrading is accompanied by a scale fee application.	
(7) To cancel an entry in the register of notice of an unregistered rentcharge which has determined—for each registered title affected	£50
Provided that no such fee is payable if the application is accompanied by a scale fee application.	
(8) To enter or remove a record of a defect in title pursuant to section 64(1) of the Act	£50
Provided that no such fee is payable if the application is accompanied by a scale fee application.	
(9) An outline application made under rule 54:	
(a) where delivered from a remote terminal	£3
(b) where delivered by any other permitted means	£6
Such fee is payable in addition to any other fee which is payable in respect of the application.	
(10) For an order in respect of a restriction under section 41(2) of the Act—for each registered title affected	£50
(11) To register a person in adverse possession of a registered estate—for each registered title affected	£150
(12) For registration as a person entitled to be notified of an application for adverse possession—for each registered title affected	£50
(13) For the determination of the exact line of a boundary under rule 118—for each application	£100
(14) To register a freehold estate in land as a freehold estate in commonhold land which is not accompanied by a statement under section 9(1)(b) of the CLRA:	
(a) up to 20 commonhold units	£50

Fee

(b) for every 20 commonhold units, or up to 20 commonhold units, thereafter £15

(15) To add land to a commonhold:

(a) adding land to the common parts title £50

(b) adding land to a commonhold unit £50

(c) adding commonhold units

—up to 20 commonhold units £50

—for every 20 commonhold units, or up to 20 commonhold units, thereafter £15

(16) To apply for a freehold estate in land to cease to be registered as a freehold estate in commonhold land during the transitional period, as defined in the CLRA...... £50

(17) To register a freehold estate in land as a freehold estate in commonhold land, which is accompanied by a statement under section 9(1)(b) of the CLRA

—for each commonhold unit converted £50

(18) To register an amended commonhold community statement which changes the extent of the common parts or any commonhold unit:

(a) for the common parts £50

(b) for up to three commonhold units £50

(c) for each subsequent commonhold unit £25

Provided that no such fee shall be payable if, in relation to each registered title affected, the application is accompanied by a scale fee application or another application that attracts a fee under this Part.

(19) To register an amended commonhold community statement, which does not change the extent of a registered title within the commonhold £50

Provided that no such fee shall be payable if, in relation to each registered title affected, the application is accompanied by a scale fee application or another application that attracts a fee under this Part.

(20) To register an alteration to the Memorandum or Articles of Association of a commonhold association £50

(21) To make a termination application

—for each registered title affected £50

(22) To note the surrender of a development right under section 58 of the CLRA £50

[3705]

NOTES

Commencement: 6 July 2009.

PART 2
SERVICES—INSPECTION AND COPYING

NOTE: In this Part "lease" means a lease or a copy of a lease.

(1) Inspection, from a remote terminal:

(a) for each individual register £4

(b) for each title plan £4

(c) for any or all of the documents (other than leases) referred to in an individual register—for each registered title £6

(d) for each lease referred to in an individual register £12

(e) for the individual register and title plan of a commonhold common parts title—for each registered title £4

(f) for each individual caution register £4

(g) for each caution plan £4

(h) for any other document kept by the registrar which relates to an application to him—for each document £6

(2) Inspection (otherwise than under paragraph (1)):

(a) for each individual register £8

(b) for each title plan £8

(c) for any or all of the documents (other than leases) referred to in an individual register—for each registered title £12

(d) for each lease referred to in an individual register £24

(e) for the individual register and title plan of a commonhold common parts title—for each registered title £8

(f) for each individual caution register £8

(g) for each caution plan £8

(h) for any other document kept by the registrar which relates to an application to him—for each document £12

(3) Official copy in respect of a registered title:

(a) for each individual register

(i) where an official copy in electronic form is requested from a remote terminal £4

(ii) where an official copy in paper form is requested by any permitted means £8

(b) for each title plan

(i) where an official copy in electronic form is requested from a remote terminal £4

(ii) where an official copy in paper form is requested by any permitted means £8

(c) for each commonhold common parts individual register and title plan:

(i) where an official copy in electronic form is requested from a remote terminal £4

(ii) where an official copy in paper form is requested by any permitted means £8

(4) Official copy in respect of the cautions register

(a) for each individual caution register

(i) where an official copy in electronic form is requested from a remote terminal £4

(ii) where an official copy in paper form is requested by any permitted means £8

(b) for each caution plan ....

(i) where an official copy in electronic form is requested from a remote terminal £4

(ii) where an official copy in paper form is requested by any permitted means £8

(5) Official copy of any or all of the documents (other than a lease) referred to in an individual register—for each registered title

(a) where an official copy in electronic form is requested from a remote terminal £6

(b) where an official copy in paper form is requested by any permitted means ... £12

(6) Official copy of a lease referred to in an individual register–for each lease

(a) where an official copy in electronic form is requested from a remote terminal and a copy of the lease is held in electronic form by the registrar £12

(b) where an official copy in electronic form is requested from a remote terminal and a copy of the lease is not held in electronic form by the registrar... £24

(c) where an official copy in paper form is requested by any permitted means ... £24

(7) Official copy of any other document kept by the registrar which relates to an application to him—for each document

(a) where an official copy in electronic form is requested from a remote terminal and a copy of the document is held in electronic form by the registrar . £6

(b) where an official copy in electronic form is requested from a remote terminal and a copy of the document is not held in electronic form by the registrar........ £12

(c) where an official copy in paper form is requested by any permitted means ... £12

(8) Copy of an historical edition of a registered title (or of part of the edition where rule 144(4) applies)—for each title £10

[3706]

NOTES

Commencement: 6 July 2009.

PART 3
SERVICES—SEARCHES

(1) An official search of an individual register or of a pending first registration application made to the registrar from a remote terminal—for each title........ £4

(2) An official search of an individual register by a mortgagee for the purpose of section 56(3) of the Family Law Act 1996 made to the registrar from a remote terminal........ £4

(3) An official search of an individual register or of a pending first registration application other than as described in paragraphs (1) and (2)—for each title........ £8

(4) The issue of a certificate of inspection of a title plan........ £8

(5) An official search of the index map

(a) where no or not more than five registered titles are disclosed........ £5

(b) where more than five registered titles are disclosed

(i) for the first five titles........ £5

(ii) for every ten titles, or up to ten titles, thereafter........ £3

(6) Search of the index of proprietors' names—for each name........ £12

(7) An official search of the index of relating franchises and manors—for each administrative area

(a) where the application is made from a remote terminal........ £4

(b) where the application is made by any other permitted means........ £8

[3707]

NOTES

Commencement: 6 July 2009.

PART 4
SERVICES—OTHER INFORMATION

(1) Application for return of a document under rule 204........ £10

(2) Application that the registrar designate a document an exempt information document........ £26

[3708]

NOTES

Commencement: 6 July 2009.

SCHEDULE 4
EXEMPTIONS

Article 10

No fee is payable for:

(1) reflecting a change in the name, address or description of a registered proprietor or other person referred to in the register, or in the cautions register, or changing the description of a property,

(2) giving effect in the register to a change of proprietor where the registered estate or the registered charge, as the case may be, has become vested without further assurance (other than on the death or bankruptcy of a proprietor) in some person by the operation of any statute (other than the Act), statutory instrument or scheme taking effect under any statute or statutory instrument,

(3) registering the surrender of a registered leasehold estate where the surrender is consideration or part consideration for the grant of a new lease to the registered proprietor of substantially the same premises as were comprised in the surrendered lease and where a scale fee is paid for the registration of the new lease,

(4) registering a discharge of a registered charge,

(5) registering a home rights notice, or renewal of such a notice, or renewal of a home rights caution under the Family Law Act 1996,

(6) entering in the register the death of a joint proprietor,

(7) cancelling the registration of a notice, (other than a notice in respect of an unregistered lease or unregistered rentcharge), caution against first registration, caution against dealings, including a withdrawal of a deposit or intended deposit, inhibition, restriction, or note,

(8) the removal of the designation of a document as an exempt information document,

(9) approving an estate layout plan or any draft document with or without a plan,

(10) an order by the registrar (other than an order under section 41(2) of the Act),

(11) deregistering a manor,

(12) an entry in the register of a note of the dissolution of a corporation,

(13) registering a restriction in Form A in Schedule 4 to the rules,

(14) an application for day list information on any one occasion from a remote terminal,

(15) an application to lodge a caution against first registration or to make a register entry where in either case the application relates to rights in respect of the repair of a church chancel.

[3709]

NOTES

Commencement: 6 July 2009.

LAND REGISTRATION (PROPER OFFICE) ORDER 2009

(SI 2009/1393)

NOTES

Made: 9 June 2009.
Authority: Land Registration Act 2002, s 100(3).
Commencement: 1 October 2009.

1 Citation and commencement

This Order may be cited as the Land Registration (Proper Office) Order 2009 and shall come into force on 1 October 2009.

[3710]

NOTES

Commencement: 1 October 2009.

2 Applications to which this Order applies

(1) This Order applies to any application to the registrar except an application delivered to the registrar—

(a) in accordance with a written arrangement as to delivery made between the registrar and the applicant or between the registrar and the applicant's conveyancer, or

(b) under the provisions of any relevant notice given under Schedule 2 to the Land Registration Rules 2003.

(2) In this article "conveyancer" means—

(a) a solicitor,

(b) a licensed conveyancer within the meaning of section 11(2) of the Administration of Justice Act 1985,

(c) a fellow of the Institute of Legal Executives,

(d) a barrister,

(e) a duly certificated notary public, or

(f) a registered European lawyer within the meaning of the European Communities (Lawyer's Practice) Regulations 2000 who by virtue of regulations 6 and 12 of those Regulations is entitled to prepare for remuneration an instrument creating or transferring an interest in land in England and Wales.

[3711]

NOTES

Commencement: 1 October 2009.

3 Designation of the proper office

(1) The proper office for the receipt of an application to which this Order applies is any office of the land registry specified in column 1 of the Schedule which is opposite an administrative area shown in column 2 of the Schedule in which the land to which that application relates is wholly or partly situated.

(2) In the Schedule, reference to an office of the land registry does not include any sub-office of that office.

[3712]

NOTES

Commencement: 1 October 2009.

4 (*Revokes the Land Registration (Proper Office) Order 2008, SI 2008/3201.*)

SCHEDULE 1

Article 3

Column 1 **Proper office of the land registry**	**Column 2** **Administrative Area**
Land Registry, Birkenhead Office	Cheshire East Cheshire West and Chester Halton Hammersmith and Fulham Kensington and Chelsea Knowsley District Liverpool District Sefton District St Helens District Staffordshire City of Stoke-on-Trent Warrington Wirral District

Column 1 **Proper office of the land registry**	**Column 2** **Administrative Area**
Land Registry, Coventry Office	Birmingham District Coventry District Dudley District Sandwell District Solihull District Walsall District City of Wolverhampton District Worcestershire
Land Registry, Croydon Office	Bexley Bromley Camden Croydon Kingston upon Thames Merton Sutton City of Westminster
Land Registry, Durham Office	Cumbria Darlington County Durham Gateshead District Hartlepool Middlesbrough Newcastle upon Tyne District North Tyneside District North Yorkshire Northumberland Redcar and Cleveland South Tyneside District Stockton-on-Tees Sunderland District Surrey York
Land Registry, Fylde Office	Blackburn with Darwen Blackpool Bolton District Bury District Lancashire Manchester District Oldham District Rochdale District Salford District Stockport District Tameside District Trafford District Wigan District

Column 1 Proper office of the land registry	Column 2 Administrative Area
Land Registry, Gloucester Office	Bracknell Forest City of Bristol Gloucestershire Oxfordshire Reading Slough South Gloucestershire Warwickshire West Berkshire Windsor and Maidenhead Wokingham
Land Registry, Kingston Upon Hull Office	East Riding of Yorkshire City of Kingston upon Hull Lincolnshire Norfolk North East Lincolnshire North Lincolnshire Suffolk
Land Registry, Leicester Office	Buckinghamshire Leicester Leicestershire Milton Keynes Northamptonshire Rutland
Land Registry, Nottingham Office	Barnsley District Bradford District Calderdale District City of Derby Derbyshire Doncaster District Kirklees District Leeds District City of Nottingham Nottinghamshire Rotherham District Sheffield District Wakefield District
Land Registry, Peterborough Office	Bedford Cambridgeshire Central Bedfordshire Essex Luton City of Peterborough Southend-on-Sea Thurrock

Column 1 Proper office of the land registry	Column 2 Administrative Area
Land Registry, Plymouth Office	Bath & North East Somerset Cornwall Devon Isles of Scilly North Somerset City of Plymouth Sedgemoor Taunton Deane Torbay West Somerset
Land Registry, Portsmouth Office	City of Brighton & Hove East Hampshire East Sussex Havant Isle of Wight Portsmouth West Sussex
Land Registry, Stevenage Office	Barking and Dagenham Hackney Havering Hertfordshire The Inner Temple and the Middle Temple Islington City and County of The City of London Newham Redbridge Tower Hamlets Waltham Forest
Land Registry, Swansea Office Cofrestrfa Tir Swyddfa Abertawe	Barnet Brent Ealing Enfield Haringey Harrow Hillingdon Hounslow

Column 1 Proper office of the land registry	Column 2 Administrative Area
Land Registry, Telford Office	Greenwich County of Herefordshire Lambeth Lewisham Richmond upon Thames Shropshire Southwark Wandsworth County of The Wrekin (otherwise known as The Wrekin)
Land Registry, Tunbridge Wells Office	Kent Medway
Land Registry, Wales Office Cofrestrfa Tir Swyddfa Cymru	All counties and county boroughs in Wales
Land Registry, Weymouth Office	Basingstoke and Deane Bournemouth Dorset Eastleigh Fareham Gosport Hart Mendip New Forest Poole Rushmoor South Somerset Southampton Swindon Test Valley Wiltshire Winchester

[3713]

NOTES

Commencement: 1 October 2009.

Index